lonely planet

P9-DEF-277

Mexico

John Noble
Michele Matter
Nancy Keller
Daniel C Schechter
James Lyon
Scott Doggett

LONELY PLANET PUBLICATIONS
Melbourne • Oakland • London • Paris

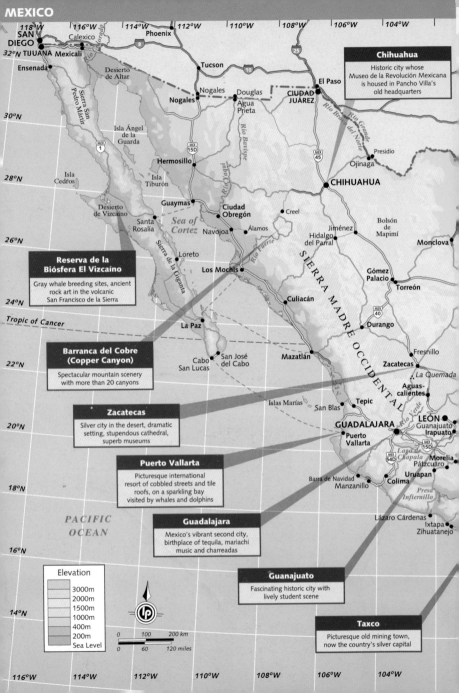

MEXICO

Chihuahua
Historic city whose Museo de la Revolución Mexicana is housed in Pancho Villa's old headquarters

Reserva de la Biósfera El Vizcaíno
Gray whale breeding sites, ancient rock art in the volcanic San Francisco de la Sierra

Barranca del Cobre (Copper Canyon)
Spectacular mountain scenery with more than 20 canyons

Zacatecas
Silver city in the desert, dramatic setting, stupendous cathedral, superb museums

Puerto Vallarta
Picturesque international resort of cobbled streets and tile roofs, on a sparkling bay visited by whales and dolphins

Guadalajara
Mexico's vibrant second city, birthplace of tequila, mariachi music and charreadas

Guanajuato
Fascinating historic city with lively student scene

Taxco
Picturesque old mining town, now the country's silver capital

Elevation
- 3000m
- 2000m
- 1500m
- 1000m
- 400m
- 200m
- Sea Level

0   100   200 km
0   60   120 miles

PACIFIC OCEAN

Sea of Cortez

SIERRA MADRE OCCIDENTAL

Tropic of Cancer

SAN DIEGO, TIJUANA, Ensenada, Mexicali, Calexico, Phoenix, Tucson, Nogales, Douglas, Agua Prieta, CIUDAD JUÁREZ, El Paso, Presidio, Ojinaga, CHIHUAHUA, Hermosillo, Guaymas, Ciudad Obregón, Navojoa, Álamos, Creel, Jiménez, Hidalgo del Parral, Bolsón de Mapimí, Monclova, Gómez Palacio, Torreón, Los Mochis, Culiacán, Durango, Fresnillo, Zacatecas, La Quemada, Aguascalientes, La Paz, Cabo San Lucas, San José del Cabo, Mazatlán, Islas Marías, San Blas, Tepic, GUADALAJARA, LEÓN, Guanajuato, Irapuato, Puerto Vallarta, Lago de Chapala, Morelia, Pátzcuaro, Uruapan, Barra de Navidad, Manzanillo, Colima, Presa Infiernillo, Lázaro Cárdenas, Ixtapa, Zihuatanejo, Santa Rosalía, Loreto, Isla Cedros, Isla Tiburón, Isla Ángel de la Guarda, Desierto de Vizcaíno, Desierto de Altar, Sierra San Pedro Mártir, Sierra de la Giganta

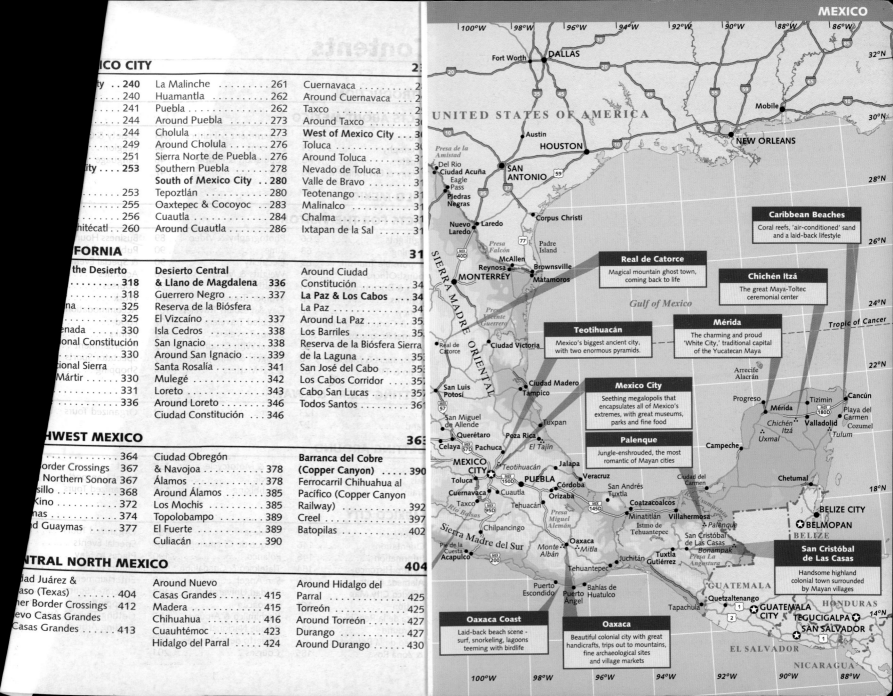

MEXICO

Caribbean Beaches
Coral reefs, 'air-conditioned' sand and a laid-back lifestyle

Real de Catorce
Magical mountain ghost town, coming back to life

Chichén Itzá
The great Maya-Toltec ceremonial center

Teotihuacán
Mexico's biggest ancient city, with two enormous pyramids.

Mérida
The charming and proud 'White City,' traditional capital of the Yucatecan Maya

Mexico City
Seething megalopolis that encapsulates all of Mexico's extremes, with great museums, parks and fine food

Palenque
Jungle-enshrouded, the most romantic of Mayan cities

San Cristóbal de Las Casas
Handsome highland colonial town surrounded by Mayan villages

Oaxaca Coast
Laid-back beach scene - surf, snorkeling, lagoons teeming with birdlife

Oaxaca
Beautiful colonial city with great handicrafts, trips out to mountains, fine archaeological sites and village markets

Mexico
7th edition – September 2000
First published – October 1982

Published by
Lonely Planet Publications Pty Ltd ABN 36 005 607 983
90 Maribyrnong St, Footscray, Victoria 3011, Australia

Lonely Planet Offices
Australia Locked Bag 1, Footscray, Victoria 3011
USA 150 Linden St, Oakland, CA 94607
UK 10a Spring Place, London NW5 3BH
France 1 rue du Dahomey, 75011 Paris

Photographs
Most of the images in this guide are available for licensing from
Lonely Planet Images.
email: lpi@lonelyplanet.com.au

Front cover photograph
Una casa en San Cristóbal de Las Casas (Dan Herrick)

ISBN 1 86450 089 1

text & maps © Lonely Planet 2000
photos © photographers as indicated 2000

Printed by The Bookmaker International Ltd
Printed in China

Although the authors
and Lonely Planet try
to make the informa-
tion as accurate as
possible, we accept
no responsibility for
any loss, injury or
inconvenience sus-
tained by anyone
using this book.

Contents

4   Contents

CHAPTERS

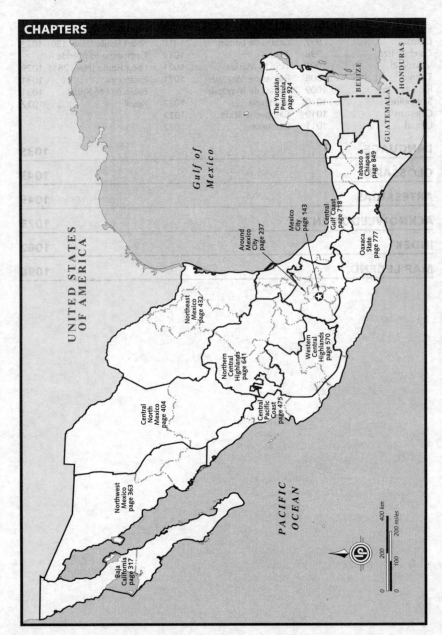

UNITED STATES OF AMERICA

Gulf of Mexico

PACIFIC OCEAN

BELIZE

HONDURAS

GUATEMALA

The Yucatán Peninsula
page 324

Tabasco & Chiapas
page 849

Mexico City page 143

Central Gulf Coast
page 718

Around Mexico City
page 237

Oaxaca State
page 777

Northeast Mexico
page 432

Western Central Highlands
page 570

Northern Central Highlands
page 641

Central North Mexico
page 404

Central Pacific Coast
page 475

Northwest Mexico
page 363

Baja California
page 317

400 km

200 miles

0   100   200

0   200   400

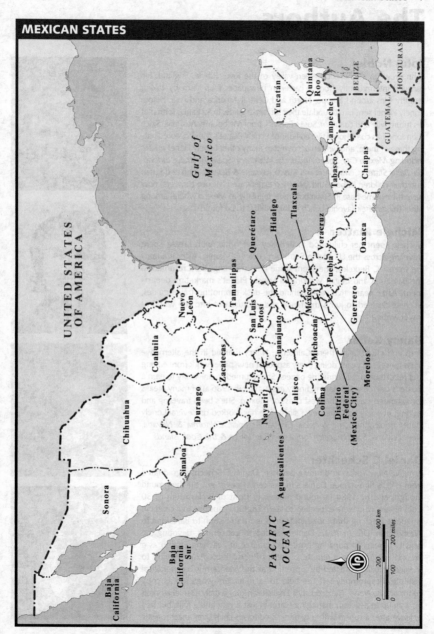

MEXICAN STATES

The Authors

John Noble

John grew up in the cool, green valley of the River Ribble, England. He escaped intermittently from a career in newspaper journalism by taking lengthy trips around Europe, North and Central America and Asia, before Lonely Planet sent him to update their *Sri Lanka* guide. In Sri Lanka John met his future wife and coauthor, Susan Forsyth, from Melbourne, Australia. Since then John has coauthored five editions of Lonely Planet's *Mexico*, coordinating three of them, and written or cowritten many other Lonely Planet guides including *Mexico City, Spain, Andalucía, Walking in Spain, Australia, Indonesia, Baltic States, Central Asia* and *Russia, Ukraine & Belarus*. John and Susan and their children Isabella and Jack (also experienced Mexico travelers) now have their home base in Spain but travel regularly to Mexico where, among other things, their favorite beach in the world is to be found.

Michele Matter

Michele spent her childhood in Berkeley, California, with breaks spent traveling across the US and to South America with family. After graduating from UC Berkeley, she spent some time traveling, then returned to the Bay Area and began working in Lonely Planet's marketing department. After nearly five years behind the desk promoting travel guides, Michele decided to jump the fence and venture out into the world of travel writing.

Nancy Keller

Born and raised in northern California, Nancy worked in the alternative press for several years, doing every aspect of newspaper work from editing and reporting to delivering the papers. She returned to university to earn a master's degree in journalism, finally graduating in 1986 after many breaks for extended stays on the west coast of Mexico. She's been traveling and writing, in many countries, ever since. She has worked on several Lonely Planet books, including *Mexico, Central America, California & Nevada, New Zealand, South Pacific, Tonga* and *Rarotonga & the Cook Islands*.

Daniel C Schechter

A native New Yorker and movie devotee, Daniel C Schechter graduated from NYU's film school. Daniel's movie career never got off the ground though, and by 1984 he found himself in front of a classroom of 30 Colombians who were expecting to learn English. Thus began a career in language teaching that took him from Bogotá to Lisbon to Barcelona to Washington, DC. In 1992, Daniel decided to get serious, devoting the next two years to pursuing a master's degree in Teaching English as a Second Language in a remote corner of Puerto Rico. After moving to Mexico, initially attracted by a position at the Monterrey Technological Institute, he promptly left the field for a minimum-wage job as copy editor at *The News*, Mexico City's English-language daily. Daniel worked his way up to assistant managing editor in just a year and a half, but had to leave after a run-in with a tyrannical editor-in-chief over anachronistic

editorial policies. Next came a less chaotic stint at *Business Mexico*, where as executive editor he had the luxury of approving the publication of his own stories on travel, culture and food. Currently Daniel and his wife, Myra, are seeking breathable air outside of Mexico City.

James Lyon

An Australian by birth, a skeptic by nature and a social scientist by training, James has worked on Lonely Planet guides to *Bali & Lombok*, *Mexico*, *Maldives*, *South America* and *USA*. He particularly enjoys Mexico for the depth of its history, the vibrancy of its culture and the beauty of its colonial towns. For this edition he covered the Central Gulf Coast, and the Northern Central and Western Central Highlands, climbing the odd volcano, taking as many back roads as possible, and learning to drive like a Mexican.

Scott Doggett

Scott is a graduate of UC Berkeley and the Mass Media Institute at Stanford University. His professional life began in 1983 as a photographer covering wars in Central America. His initial career was followed by reporting assignments for United Press International in Los Angeles, Pakistan and Afghanistan and, from 1989 through 1996, seven years as a staff editor for the *Los Angeles Times*. Today he is the author of Lonely Planet's guides to *Panama*, *Las Vegas* and *Yucatán*, and coauthor of Lonely Planet's guide to the *Dominican Republic and Haiti*. Scott has written guidebooks to Amsterdam and Los Angeles, and coauthored and coedited the anthology *Travelers' Tales: Brazil*. With his wife, Annette Haddad, Scott also cowrites a weekly business column for the *Los Angeles Times*.

FROM THE AUTHORS

John Noble Special thanks to Danny, Jim Lad, Michele, Nancy, Tom, Robert, Ben, Elaine, Don, Tracey, Monica, Margaret and Jacqueline for being great colleagues and fun to work with despite a few missed deadlines; to Friedrich Petry, a flawless research assistant on the Oaxaca coast; to Jorge and Guillermina for their hospitality in Oaxaca; to Jen Loy for valuable information on airfares; and to Don in Puerto Escondido, Juan and Kim in Oaxaca, Fernando in San Cristóbal, Romeo at Ejido Emiliano Zapata, Scott Doggett, and everyone at Ecogrupos de México, Mundo Joven and Viajes Educativos for varied information and help. Extra special thanks to Ron Mader, Danny Schechter, Myra Ingmanson and Anthony Wright for warm hospitality and copious information in La Capital. And gracias to Café Tacuba for your songs, which kept me afloat through many long hours of writing up.

Michele Matter Thanks to John Noble and to Tom Downs for their help and advice. Thanks to the staff of the tourist offices that I stopped in along the way for their willingness to answer my numerous questions. Many thanks to Kate Hoffman for getting me started toward Baja in the first place. Thanks also to Carolyn Miller and Eric Kettunen for their support and encouragement (and also to Aimee, Maria and Morgan). And many thanks to my family, especially to my mother, Ligia, and to my brother, Michael, for being great travel companions.

Nancy Keller First, greatest thanks and appreciation to John Noble and Tom Downs. Thanks also to fellow authors Tom Brosnahan and James Lyon for their encouragement, now as ever. Saludes, abrazos y gracias a mi familia adoptiva, la familia Osuna Morales, en Mazatlán, Sinaloa. Hola, Rosy! Hola, Mirla! Hola, Kina! Thanks and love also to Ernie and Sophie, also in Mazatlán.

I wholeheartedly thank the many people in Mexico who were helpful as I was working on the Northwest Mexico and Central Pacific Coast chapters. In Hermosillo, thanks to Adolfo Salido of the tourist office. In San Carlos, thanks to Heriberto Duarte Rosas of the tourist office. In Álamos, thanks to Teri Arnold of La Puerta Roja Inn; Jim and Nancy Swickard of Hacienda de los Santos, their daughter Jamie and granddaughter Mariah; Jennifer MacKay of Solipaso; Doña Celsa Duarte Lozoya of Restaurant Las Palmeras; Luz del Carmen Parra Vázquez of the tourist office; and Trini.

In Creel, muchas gracias a Margarita Quintero Estrada, Mercedes, Ivan and the staff at Margarita's; Arturo Gutierrez of Umarike Expediciones; Federico and Luis of Best Western Hotel; Sheamus O'Shea and family, and Bob Phelps. On the Copper Canyon railway, thanks to Dan the Caravan guide, and Pedro Palma of Tara Adventures, based in Chihuahua.

In Rincón de Guayabitos, thanks to Karen Hofstad, her son Mark and partner German, of Villas Buena Vida. In Chacala, thanks to Dra Laura del Valle of Mar de Jade. In Melaque, thanks to Evelia, Rafael, Rafael Jr and Livi of Hotel Bahía, to Suzanne Bernard ('Fleur de Soleil'), and as always, to Philomena Garcia and family.

Thanks also to Rich Zubaty and Margaret (Rico and Margarita) of Puerto Ángel. Last but certainly not least, special thanks for special helpfulness to Jerry Hoy, back home in Forestville – what a pal!

Daniel C Schechter I'd like to thank the following people for sharing their knowledge of Mexico and for demonstrating rare patience in responding to my often incoherent questions: Jossie Aguilar of the Chihuahua state tourist office, Mario Andrade, Pepe Dávila of the Cuatrociénegas Semarnap office, Gary Deaton and Olaf Carrera at American Chamber Mexico, Rita de Tepoztlán, Mario Flores at the Museo Arqueológico, Carlos Pellicer in Tepoztlán, Nancy Jasso of Infotur Monterrey, Lowry McAllen, and William Peña at Balneario Las Estacas. Thanks, too, to John Noble for his encouragement and sound judgment; and to Myra, my companion, editor, trip planner and occasional career counselor.

James Lyon Thanks to the staff of the many state and municipal tourist offices who were more than helpful, and especially to Desmond O'Shaughnessy Doyle in Guanajuato and Angélica González Morán in Guadalajara. Thanks to Danny and Myra for their hospitality in Mexico City. And as ever, thanks to my family, Pauline, Mike and Ben, for keeping the home fires burning.

This Book

This is the 7th edition of *Mexico*. Past authors include Doug Richmond, Dan Spitzer, Scott Wayne, Mark Balla, Wayne Bernhardson, Tom Brosnahan, Susan Forsyth, Mark Honan, as well as several authors of this edition who have covered Mexico before. John Noble has been the coordinating author for the past three editions. He wrote the intro chapters, Mexico City, Oaxaca State and Tabasco & Chiapas. Daniel C Schechter wrote Around Mexico City, Central North Mexico and Northeast Mexico. Michele Matter wrote Baja California. Nancy Keller wrote Northwest Mexico and Central Pacific Coast. James Lyon wrote Western Central Highlands, Northern Central Highlands and Central Gulf Coast. Scott Doggett wrote the Yucatán Peninsula.

FROM THE PUBLISHER

Nearly the entire Oaktown office chipped in to edit, map, illustrate and design *Mexico*. Lead editor Robert Reid stood on the shoulders of senior editor Tom 'Prom Clowns' Downs, and both were joined by a jolly saucy crew of editors (in order of appearance): Rebecca Northen, Suki Gear, China Williams, Ben Greensfelder, Don Root, Jacqueline Volin, Kevin 'Heavy Metal Poisoning' Anglin, Elaine Merrill, Rachel Bernstein, Erin Corrigan and David Zingarelli. Brigitte Barta and Kate Hoffman – like Luís Hernández's last-second goal for Mexico against Holland in the 1998 World Cup – came through in the clutch with some help too. Lead cartographer Monica Lepe earned her nickname 'Queen of Mexico Map Makers (QoMMM)' for her year-plus commitment to the book – and only Monica remained calm when the nearby 'taco truck' didn't show up for a week. Much of LP's cartography department helped her make the maps, including (also in order of appearance) Alex Guilbert, Tracey Croom, Matt DeMartini, Mary Hagemann, Colin Bishop, Eric 'the Red' Thomsen, Patrick Phelan, John 'S-P-E' Spelman, Annette Olson, Kat Smith, Sean Brandt and Andy 'Hammonds' Rebold. The illustrations were drawn by Hugh D'Andrade, Hayden 'Mr H' Foell, Beca Lafore, Hannah Reineck, Jennifer Steffey and Lisa Summers; Beca coordinated all the 'ills' – and like her favorite Loverboy song was loving every minute of it. Margaret Livingston oversaw the layout and design of the 1096 pages with guidance from Susan Rimerman; Margaret also inspired plans to make a movie of the process. Josh Schefers and Richard Wilson helped lay out the book, sometimes with aid of in-house iced coffee. The charmed and dangerous Jennifer Steffey selected photos and designed the glorious 'color wraps.' Simon Bracken designed the cover, and Ken DellaPenta indexed the book. Thanks to all the authors for making *Mexico* great and for keeping patient when packages didn't arrive on time. Now for some mezcal. Who wants the worm?

Foreword

ABOUT LONELY PLANET GUIDEBOOKS

The story begins with a classic travel adventure: Tony and Maureen Wheeler's 1972 journey across Europe and Asia to Australia. Useful information about the overland trail did not exist at that time, so Tony and Maureen published the first Lonely Planet guidebook to meet a growing need.

From a kitchen table, then from a tiny office in Melbourne (Australia), Lonely Planet has become the largest independent travel publisher in the world, an international company with offices in Melbourne, Oakland (USA), London (UK) and Paris (France).

Today Lonely Planet guidebooks cover the globe. There is an ever-growing list of books, and there's information in a variety of forms and media. Some things haven't changed. The main aim is still to help make it possible for adventurous travelers to get out there – to explore and better understand the world.

At Lonely Planet we believe travelers can make a positive contribution to the countries they visit – if they respect their host communities and spend their money wisely. Since 1986 a percentage of the income from each book has been donated to aid projects and human-rights campaigns.

Updates Lonely Planet thoroughly updates each guidebook as often as possible. This usually means there are around two years between editions, although for more unusual or more stable destinations the gap can be longer. Check the imprint page (following the color map at the beginning of the book) for publication dates.

Between editions, up-to-date information is available in two free newsletters – the paper *Planet Talk* and email *Comet* (to subscribe, contact any Lonely Planet office) – and on our website at www.lonelyplanet.com. The *Upgrades* section of the website covers a number of important and volatile destinations and is regularly updated by Lonely Planet authors. *Scoop* covers news and current affairs relevant to travelers. And, lastly, the *Thorn Tree* bulletin board and *Postcards* section of the site carry unverified, but fascinating, reports from travelers.

Correspondence The process of creating new editions begins with the letters, postcards and emails received from travelers. This correspondence often includes suggestions, criticisms and comments about the current editions. Interesting excerpts are immediately passed on via newsletters and the website, and everything goes to our authors to be verified when they're researching on the road. We're keen to get more feedback from organizations or individuals who represent communities visited by travelers.

Lonely Planet gathers information for everyone who's curious about the planet – and especially for those who explore it firsthand. Through guidebooks, phrasebooks, activity guides, maps, literature, newsletters, image library, TV series and website, we act as an information exchange for a worldwide community of travelers.

Research Authors aim to gather sufficient practical information to enable travelers to make informed choices and to make the mechanics of a journey run smoothly. They also research historical and cultural background to help enrich the travel experience and allow travelers to understand and respond appropriately to cultural and environmental issues.

Authors don't stay in every hotel because that would mean spending a couple of months in each medium-size city and, no, they don't eat at every restaurant because that would mean stretching belts beyond capacity. They do visit hotels and restaurants to check standards and prices, but feedback based on readers' direct experiences can be very helpful.

Many of our authors work undercover; others aren't so secretive. None of them accept freebies in exchange for positive write-ups. And none of our guidebooks contain any advertising.

Production Authors submit their raw manuscripts and maps to offices in Australia, the USA, the UK or France. Editors and cartographers – all experienced travelers themselves – then begin the process of assembling the pieces. When the book finally hits the shops, some things are already out of date, we start getting feedback from readers and the process begins again....

WARNING & REQUEST

Things change – prices go up, schedules change, good places go bad and bad places go bankrupt – nothing stays the same. So, if you find things better or worse, recently opened or long since closed, please tell us and help make the next edition even more accurate and useful. We genuinely value all the feedback we receive. Julie Young coordinates a well-traveled team that reads and acknowledges every letter, postcard and email and ensures that every morsel of information finds its way to the appropriate authors, editors and cartographers for verification.

Everyone who writes to us will find their name in the next edition of the appropriate guidebook. They will also receive the latest issue of *Planet Talk*, our quarterly printed newsletter, or *Comet*, our monthly email newsletter. Subscriptions to both newsletters are free. The very best contributions will be rewarded with a free guidebook.

Excerpts from your correspondence may appear in new editions of Lonely Planet guidebooks, the Lonely Planet website, *Planet Talk* or *Comet*, so please let us know if you *don't* want your letter published or your name acknowledged.

Send all correspondence to the Lonely Planet office closest to you:

Australia: Locked Bag 1, Footscray, Victoria 3011
USA: 150 Linden St, Oakland, CA 94607
UK: 10A Spring Place, London NW5 3BH
France: 1 rue du Dahomey, 75011 Paris

Or email us at: talk2us@lonelyplanet.com.au

For news, views and updates, see our website: www.lonelyplanet.com

HOW TO USE A LONELY PLANET GUIDEBOOK

The best way to use a Lonely Planet guidebook is any way you choose. At Lonely Planet, we believe the most memorable travel experiences are often those that are unexpected, and the finest discoveries are those you make yourself. Guidebooks are not intended to be used as if they provided a detailed set of infallible instructions!

Contents All Lonely Planet guidebooks follow the same format. The Facts about the Country chapters or sections give background information ranging from history to weather. Facts for the Visitor gives practical information on issues like visas and health. Getting There & Away gives a brief starting point for researching travel to and from the destination. Getting Around gives an overview of the transport options available when you arrive.

The peculiar demands of each destination determine how subsequent chapters are broken up, but some things remain constant. We always start with background, then proceed to sights, places to stay, places to eat, entertainment, getting there and away, and getting around information – in that order.

Heading Hierarchy Lonely Planet headings are used in a strict hierarchical structure that can be visualized as a set of Russian dolls. Each heading (and its following text) is encompassed by any preceding heading that is higher on the hierarchical ladder.

Although inclusion in a guidebook usually implies a recommendation, we cannot list every good place. Exclusion does not necessarily imply criticism. In fact, there are a number of reasons why we might exclude a place – sometimes it is simply inappropriate to encourage an influx of travelers.

Entry Points We do not assume guidebooks will be read from beginning to end, but that people will dip into them. The traditional entry points are the list of contents and the index. In addition, however, some books have a complete list of maps and an index map illustrating map coverage.

There may also be a color map that shows highlights. These highlights are dealt with in greater detail later in the book, along with planning questions. Each chapter covering a geographical region usually begins with a locator map and another list of highlights. Once you find something of interest in a list of highlights, turn to the index.

Maps Maps play a crucial role in Lonely Planet guidebooks and include a huge amount of information. A legend is printed on the back page. We seek to have complete consistency between maps and text, and to have every important place in the text captured on a map. Map key numbers usually start in the top left corner.

Introduction

To explore Mexico is to traverse vast deserts, journey around (or up) snow-capped volcanoes, walk along tropical beaches and hike through ancient ruins; and it is to walk the streets of teeming modern cities, timeless villages and chic resorts. Mexico is an experience that offers a multitude of cultures, cuisines, environments, handicrafts, art and history.

The country's diversity stems partly from topography. (The Spanish conquistador Hernán Cortés, when asked to describe Mexico, simply crumpled a piece of paper and set it on a table.) The country's endless mountain ranges have always allowed its peoples to pursue their destiny in some degree of isolation.

Great cultures and empires, among them the Olmec, the Maya and the Aztecs, flourished here centuries ago. Their direct descendants – over 50 distinct indigenous peoples, each with their own language – retain their distinct identities amid the country's *mestizo* (mixed-blood) majority, and maintain diverse ancient traditions despite the country's ongoing modernization. Such contrasts are common in Mexico: traditional sources of livelihood such as fishing, agriculture, handwoven textiles and handcrafted ceramics coexist with modern manufacturing, transportation and a big tourism industry. Everywhere, extremes of wealth and poverty rub shoulders.

Even as modern roads, airplanes and television have brought the various regions closer together and helped to forge a national consciousness, being Mexican continues to mean very different things to the distinct peoples of Mexico's many regions. If you're looking for the 'real' Mexico, don't expect just one conclusion.

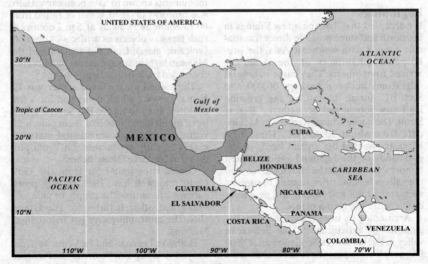

Facts about Mexico

HISTORY

There is nothing new about the 'New World,' as a look at Mexico's history reveals. The first people in this land may have arrived more than 20,000 years before Columbus reached the American continent. Their descendants built a succession of highly developed civilizations, which flourished from about 1200 BC to 1521 AD. Among these, the Maya and Aztec cultures are the best known. Traveling in Mexico, you'll also have the opportunity to explore the achievements of the mysterious Olmecs of the Gulf Coast, the Zapotecs of Oaxaca, the great imperial city of Teotihuacán (near Mexico City), the warlike Toltecs and others.

Historians traditionally divide Mexico's history before the Spanish conquest (the pre-Hispanic era) into four periods – Archaic, before 1500 BC; Preclassic or Formative, 1500 BC to 250 AD; Classic, 250 to 900 AD; and Postclassic, 900 to the fall of the Aztec empire in 1521. However you divide it, Mexico's history is a fascinating procession of peoples and cultures.

Beginnings

It's accepted that, barring a few Vikings in the north and some possible direct transpacific contact with southeast Asia, the pre-Hispanic inhabitants of the Americas arrived from Siberia. They came in several migrations between perhaps 60,000 and 8000 BC, during the last ice age, crossing land now submerged beneath the Bering Strait. The earliest human traces in Mexico date from about 20,000 BC. These first Mexicans hunted big animal herds in the grasslands of the highland valleys. When temperatures rose at the end of the Ice Age the valleys became drier, ceasing to support such animal life and forcing the people to derive more food from plants.

Archaeologists have traced the slow beginnings of agriculture in the Tehuacán valley in Puebla state, where, soon after 6500 BC, people were planting seeds of chili and a kind of squash. Between 5000 and 3500 BC they started to plant mutant forms of a tiny wild maize and to grind the maize into meal. After 3500 BC a much better variety of maize, and also beans, enabled the Tehuacán valley people to live semipermanently in villages and spend less time in seasonal hunting camps. Pottery appeared by 2300 BC.

The Olmecs

Mexico's ancestral civilization arose near the Gulf Coast, in the humid lowlands of southern Veracruz and neighboring Tabasco. These were the Olmecs, a name coined in the 1920s meaning 'People from the Region of Rubber.' Their civilization is famed for the awesome 'Olmec heads,' stone sculptures up to 3m high with grim, pug-nosed faces combining the features of human babies and jaguars – a mixture referred to as the 'were-jaguar' – and wearing curious helmets.

The first known great Olmec center, San Lorenzo, in Veracruz state, flourished from about 1200 to 900 BC. The basalt material for eight Olmec heads and many other stone monuments known to have been carved here was probably dragged, rolled or rafted from 60 to 80km away. Finds at San Lorenzo of such faraway objects as artifacts of obsidian (volcanic glass), from Guatemala and the Mexican highlands, suggest that San Lorenzo controlled trade over a large region.

The second great Olmec center was La Venta, Tabasco, which flourished for a few centuries up to about 600 BC. Several tombs were found here. In one of them jade, a favorite pre-Hispanic ornamental material, makes an early appearance. La Venta produced at least five Olmec heads.

Olmec sites found far from the Gulf Coast may well have been trading posts/ garrisons to ensure the supply of jade, obsidian and other luxuries for the Olmec elite. The most impressive is Chalcatzingo, Morelos.

Both San Lorenzo and La Venta were destroyed violently. But Olmec art and religion and quite possibly Olmec social organization strongly influenced later Mexican civilizations. Apart from the were-jaguar, Olmec gods included fire and maize deities and the feathered serpent, all of which persisted throughout the pre-Hispanic era.

Early Monte Albán

By 300 BC settled village life, based on agriculture and hunting, had developed throughout the southern half of Mexico. Monte Albán, the hilltop center of the Zapotecs of Oaxaca, was growing into a town of perhaps 10,000. Many carvings here have hieroglyphs or dates in a dot-and-bar system, which quite possibly means that the elite of Monte Albán invented writing and the written calendar in Mexico.

Izapa & the Early Maya

The temple center of Izapa, near the Pacific coast almost on Mexico's border with Guatemala, flourished from about 200 BC to 200 AD. Izapan culture is considered the link between the Olmecs and the next great civilization in southern Mexico, the Maya. Among Izapa's pyramids stood many tall stone slabs, called steles, fronted by round altars. The steles were carved with mythological scenes showing Olmec-derived gods, and the characteristic stele-altar pairing appears in early Maya sites. Izapa and the Maya also share the 'Long Count' calendar (see the Calendar section later in this chapter).

By the close of the Preclassic period, in 250 AD, the Maya in the Yucatán Peninsula and the Petén forest of Guatemala were already building stepped temple pyramids and using the corbeled vault – the characteristically Mayan version of an arch: two straight stone surfaces leaning toward one another, nearly meeting at the top and surmounted by a capstone.

Teotihuacán

The first great civilization in central Mexico emerged in a valley about 50km northeast of the center of modern Mexico City. Teotihuacán grew into a city of an estimated 125,000 people during its apogee between 250 and 600 AD, and it controlled what was probably the biggest pre-Hispanic Mexican empire. Teotihuacán had writing and books, the bar-and-dot number system and the 260-day sacred year (see the Calendar section later in this chapter).

The building of a magnificent planned city began about the time of Christ. The greatest of its buildings, the 70m-high, 220 sq meters Pirámide del Sol (Pyramid of the Sun), was constructed by 150 AD. Most of the rest of the city, including the almost-as-big Pirámide de la Luna (Pyramid of the Moon), was built between about 250 and 600 AD.

Empire Teotihuacán probably became an imperialistic state sometime after 400 AD. It may have controlled the southern two-thirds of Mexico, all of Guatemala and Belize, and bits of Honduras and El Salvador. But it was an empire probably geared toward tribute-gathering rather than full-scale occupation.

Cholula, near Puebla, with a pyramid even bigger than the Pirámide del Sol, was within Teotihuacán's cultural sphere. Teotihuacán may also have had hegemony over the Zapotecs of Oaxaca during the zenith of their capital, Monte Albán, which grew into a city of perhaps 25,000 between about 300 and 600 AD. In about 400 AD Teotihuacán invaders reached what's now Guatemala and they probably controlled some of the Maya in northern Guatemala.

Fall of Teotihuacán In the 7th century Teotihuacán was burned, plundered and abandoned. It is likely that the state had already been weakened by the rise of rival powers in central Mexico or by an environmental desiccation caused by the deforestation of the surrounding hillsides.

But Teotihuacán's influence on Mexico's later cultures was huge. Many of its gods, such as the feathered serpent Quetzalcóatl, an all-important symbol of fertility and life, itself inherited from the Olmecs, and Tláloc, the rain and water deity, were still being worshiped by the Aztecs a millennium later.

The Classic Maya

The Classic Maya region falls into three areas. The northern area is the Yucatán

Peninsula; the central area is the Petén forest of northern Guatemala and adjacent lowlands in Mexico (to the west) and Belize (to the east); the southern area consists of the highlands of Guatemala and Honduras and the Pacific coast of Guatemala. It was the northern and central areas – the lowlands – that produced pre-Hispanic America's most brilliant civilization, the Classic Maya, between about 250 and 900 AD. Many of the major Mayan ruins sites are outside Mexico, with Tikal in the Petén supreme in splendor.

Scholars used to think the Classic Maya were organized into about 20 independent, often warring city-states. But advances in the understanding of Maya writing have yielded a new theory that in the first part of the Classic period most of the city-states were grouped into two loose military alliances centered on Tikal and Calakmul, in Mexico's Campeche state. Tikal is believed to have conquered Calakmul in 695, but to have been unable to exert unified control over Calakmul's former subject states.

Cities A typical Mayan city functioned as the religious, political and market hub for the surrounding farming hamlets. Its ceremonial center focused on plazas surrounded by tall temple pyramids (usually the tombs of probably deified rulers) and lower buildings, so-called palaces, with warrens of small rooms. Steles and altars were carved with dates, histories and elaborate human and divine figures. Stone causeways called *sacbeob*, probably built for ceremonial use, led out from the plazas.

Classic Mayan centers in Mexico fall into four zones: Chiapas, in the central Mayan area, and Río Bec, Chenes and Puuc, all on the Yucatán Peninsula.

Chiapas – the chief Chiapas sites are Yaxchilán, its tributary Bonampak (where vivid battle murals were found in 1948), Palenque, which to many people is the most beautiful of all Mayan sites, and Toniná. Palenque rose to prominence under the 7th-century ruler Pakal, whose treasure-loaded tomb deep inside the fine Templo de las Inscripciones was discovered in 1952.

Río Bec & Chenes – these zones, noted for their lavishly carved buildings, are in a wild, little-investigated zone of the southern Yucatán Peninsula. The archaeological sites here, which include Calakmul, draw few visitors (see the Escárcega to Xpujil and Xpujil sections in the Yucatán Peninsula chapter).

Puuc – this zone was the focus of northern Classic Mayan culture. Its most important city was Uxmal, south of Mérida. Puuc ornamentation, which reached its peak on the Governor's Palace at Uxmal, featured intricate stone mosaics, part geometric but also incorporating faces of the hook-nosed sky-serpent/rain-god, Chac. The amazing Codz Poop (Palace of Masks) at Kabah, south of Uxmal, is covered with nearly 300 Chac faces. Chichén Itzá, east of Mérida, is another Puuc site, though it also owes much to a later era (see the Toltecs section later in this chapter).

Art Art was typically elegant but cluttered, and narrative in content. Fine carved steles showing historical and mythological events have survived, with those in the central area generally superior to those in the north and south. Mayan potters achieved marvelous multicolored effects on grave vessels, created to accompany the dead to the next world. Jade, the most precious substance, was carved into beads or thin plaques.

Calendar The Maya developed a complex, partly pictorial, partly phonetic writing system with 300 to 500 symbols, whose decipherment in the 1980s greatly advanced modern understanding of the culture.

The Maya refined a calendar used by other pre-Hispanic peoples into a tool for the exact recording of earthly and heavenly events. They could predict eclipses of the sun and the movements of the moon and Venus, and they measured time in three ways:

- in *tzolkins* (sacred or almanac years) composed of 13 periods of 20 days;
- in *haabs* ('vague' solar years) of 18 20-day 'months,' which were followed by a special five-day 'portentous' period called the *uayeb*; the last day of each 'month' was known as the 'seating' of the next month, in line with the Mayan belief that the future influences the present;
- in units of one, 20, 360, 7200 and 144,000 days.

All of Mexico's pre-Hispanic civilizations used the first two counts, whose interlocking

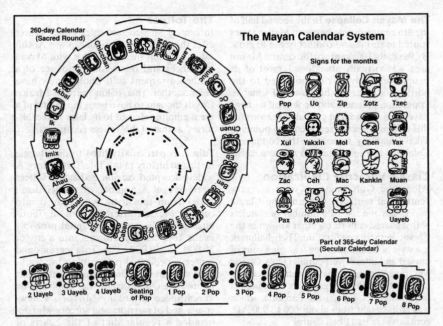

The Mayan Calendar System

260-day Calendar (Sacred Round)

Signs for the months

Pop	Uo	Zip	Zotz	Tzec
Xul	Yakkin	Mol	Chen	Yax
Zac	Ceh	Mac	Kankin	Muan
Pax	Kayab	Cumku	Uayeb	

Part of 365-day Calendar (Secular Calendar)

2 Uayeb 3 Uayeb 4 Uayeb Seating of Pop 1 Pop 2 Pop 3 Pop 4 Pop 5 Pop 6 Pop 7 Pop 8 Pop

enabled a date to be located precisely within a period of 52 years called a Calendar Round. But the Maya were the preeminent users of the third count, known as the Long Count, which was infinitely extendable. Their inscriptions enumerate the Long Count units elapsed from a starting point (Creation) that corresponds to August 13, 3114 BC. Numbers were written in a system of dots (counted as one) and bars (counted as five).

Religion Religion permeated every facet of Mayan life. The Maya believed in predestination and had a complex astrology. To win the gods' favors they also carried out elaborate rituals involving the alcoholic drink *balche*; bloodletting from ears, tongues or penises; and dances, feasts and sacrifices. The Classic Maya seem to have practiced human sacrifice on a small scale, the Postclassic on a larger scale. Beheading was probably the most common method. At Chichén Itzá, victims were thrown into a deep *cenote* (well) to bring rain.

The Maya inhabited a universe with a center and four directions (each with a color: east, red; north, white; west, black; south, yellow; the center, green), 13 layers of heavens, and nine layers of underworld to which the dead descended. The earth was the back of a giant reptile floating on a pond. (It's not *too* hard to imagine yourself as a flea on this creature's back as you look across a Mayan landscape!) The current world was just one of a succession of worlds destined to end in cataclysm and be succeeded by another. This cyclical nature of things enabled the future to be predicted by looking at the past.

Mayan gods included Itzamná, the fire deity and creator; Chac, the rain god; Yum Kaax, the maize and vegetation god; and Ah Puch, the death god. The feathered serpent, known to the Maya as Kukulcán, was introduced from central Mexico in the Postclassic period. Also worshiped were dead ancestors, particularly rulers, who were believed to be descended from the gods.

The Mayan Collapse In the second half of the 8th century, trade between Mayan states started to shrink and conflict began to grow. By the early 10th century the central Mayan area was virtually abandoned, most of its people probably having migrated to the northern area or the highlands of Chiapas. Population pressure and ecological damage have been considered probable reasons for this collapse. Recent research also points to Tikal's inability to control the conquered Calakmul territory after 695 AD as a cause.

Classic Veracruz Civilization

Along the Gulf Coast, in what are now central and northern Veracruz, the Classic period saw the rise of a number of statelets with a shared culture, together known as the Classic Veracruz civilization. Their hallmark is a style of abstract carving featuring pairs of curved and interwoven parallel lines. Classic Veracruz appears to have been particularly obsessed with the ball game; its most important center, El Tajín, near Papantla, which was at its height from about 600 to 900 AD, contains at least 11 ball courts.

The Ball Game

Probably all pre-Hispanic Mexican cultures played the ball game, which may have varied from place to place and era to era but had certain lasting features. Special H-shaped ball courts appear at archaeological sites all over Mexico. The game seems to have been played between two teams, and its essence was apparently to keep a rubber ball off the ground by flicking it with hips, thighs and possibly knees or elbows. The vertical or sloping walls around the courts were probably part of the playing area, not stands for spectators. The game had, at least sometimes, deep religious significance. It perhaps served as an oracle, with the result indicating which of two courses of action should be taken. Games could be followed by the sacrifice of one or more of the players – whether winners or losers, no one is sure.

✳ ✳ ✳ ✳ ✳ ✳ ✳ ✳ ✳ ✳ ✳

The Toltecs

In central Mexico one chief power center after the decline of Teotihuacán was Xochicalco, a hilltop site in Morelos with Mayan influences and impressive evidence of a feathered serpent cult. Cholula may have been another. Tula, 65km north of Mexico City, is thought to have been the capital of a great empire referred to by later Aztec 'histories' as that of the Toltecs (Artificers).

Tula It is particularly hard to disentangle myth and history in the Tula/Toltec story. A widely accepted version is that the Toltecs were one of a number of semicivilized tribes from the north who moved into central Mexico after the fall of Teotihuacán. Tula became their capital, probably in the 10th century, growing into a city of 30,000 to 40,000. The Tula ceremonial center is dedicated primarily to the feathered serpent god Quetzalcóatl, but annals relate that Quetzalcóatl was displaced by Tezcatlipoca (Smoking Mirror), a newcomer god of warriors and sorcery who demanded a regular diet of the hearts of sacrificed warriors. A king identified with Quetzalcóatl fled to the Gulf Coast and set sail eastward on a raft of snakes, promising one day to return.

Tula seems to have become the capital of a militaristic kingdom that dominated central Mexico, with warriors organized in orders dedicated to different animal-gods – the coyote, jaguar and eagle knights. Mass human sacrifice may have started at Tula.

The influence of Tula on contemporary and subsequent civilizations was enormous. It is seen at Paquimé in Chihuahua, at Gulf Coast sites such as Castillo de Teayo, and in western Mexico. Pottery from as far south as Costa Rica has been found at Tula, and there's even probable Tula influence in temple mounds and artifacts found in Tennessee and Illinois.

Tula was abandoned about the start of the 13th century, seemingly destroyed by Chichimecs, as the periodic hordes of barbarian raiders from the north came to be known. Many later Mexican peoples revered the Toltec era as a golden age.

Chichén Itzá Mayan scripts relate that toward the end of the 10th century much of the northern Yucatán Peninsula was conquered by one Kukulcán, who bears many similarities to Quetzalcóatl. The Mayan site of Chichén Itzá, in northern Yucatán, contains many Tula-like features, from flat beam-and-masonry roofs (contrasting with the Mayan corbeled roof) to gruesome chacmools – reclining human figures holding dishes for human hearts torn out in sacrifices. There's a resemblance that can hardly be coincidental between Tula's Pirámide B (Pyramid B) and Chichén Itzá's Temple of the Warriors. Many writers therefore believe Toltec exiles invaded Yucatán and created a new, even grander version of Tula at Chichén Itzá.

To confuse matters, however, there's a respectable body of opinion that believes the Tula-style features at Chichén Itzá actually *predated* Tula, implying that Chichén Itzá, not Tula, was the epicenter of whatever culture this was.

The Aztecs

Rise of the Aztecs The Aztecs' legends relate that they were the chosen people of their tribal god Huizilopochtli. Originally nomads from the north or west of Mexico who were led to the Valle de México (site of present-day Mexico City) by their priests, the Aztecs settled on islands in the lakes that then filled much of the valley.

The Aztec capital, Tenochtitlán, was founded on one of those islands in the first half of the 14th century. Around 1427 the Aztecs rebelled against Azcapotzalco, then the strongest statelet in the valley, and themselves became the most powerful people in the valley.

The Aztec Empire In the mid-15th century the Aztecs formed the Triple Alliance with two other valley states, Texcoco and Tlacopan, to wage war against Tlaxcala and Huejotzingo, east of the valley. The prisoners they took would form the diet of sacrificed warriors that their god Huizilopochtli demanded to keep the sun rising every day. For the dedication of Tenochtitlán's Templo

JOHN NEUBAUER

Lone sentinel, Chichén Itzá

Mayor (Great Temple) in 1487, the Aztec king Ahuizotl had 20,000 captives sacrificed.

The Triple Alliance brought most of central Mexico from the Gulf Coast to the Pacific (though not Tlaxcala) under its control. The total population of the empire's 38 provinces may have been about 5 million. The empire's purpose was to exact tribute of resources absent from the heartland. Jade, turquoise, cotton, paper, tobacco, rubber, lowland fruits and vegetables, cacao, precious feathers were needed for the glorification of the Aztec elite and to support the many nonproductive servants of its war-oriented state.

Ahuizotl's successor was Moctezuma II Xocoyotzin, a reflective character who believed – perhaps fatally – that the Spaniard Hernán Cortés, who arrived on the Gulf Coast in 1519, might be Quetzalcóatl, returned from the east to reclaim his throne (see The Spanish Conquest, later in this chapter).

Economy & Society By 1519 Tenochtitlán and the adjoining Aztec city of Tlatelolco probably had more than 200,000 inhabitants, and the Valle de México as a whole over a million. They were supported by a variety of intensive farming methods using only stone and wooden tools, including irrigation, terracing and swamp reclamation.

The basic unit of Aztec society was the *calpulli*, consisting of a few dozen to a few hundred extended families, owning land communally. The king held absolute power but delegated important roles such as priest or tax collector to members of the *pilli* (nobility). Military leaders were usually *tecuhtli*, elite professional soldiers. Another special group was the *pochteca*, militarized merchants who helped extend the empire, brought goods to the capital and organized large markets, which were held daily in big towns. At the bottom of society were pawns (paupers who could sell themselves for a specified period), serfs and slaves.

Culture & Religion Tenochtitlán-Tlatelolco had hundreds of temple complexes. The greatest, located on and around modern Mexico City's Zócalo, marked the center of the universe. Its main temple pyramid was dedicated to Huizilopochtli and the rain god, Tláloc.

Much of Aztec culture was drawn from earlier Mexican civilizations. They had writing, bark-paper books and the Calendar Round. They observed the heavens for astrological purposes. Celibate priests performed cycles of great ceremonies, typically including sacrifices and masked dances or processions enacting myths.

The Aztecs believed they lived in the 'fifth world,' whose four predecessors had each been destroyed by the death of the sun and of humanity. Aztec human sacrifices were designed to keep the sun alive. Like the Maya, the Aztecs saw the world as having four directiions, 13 heavens and nine hells. Those who died by drowning, leprosy, lightning, gout, dropsy or lung disease went to the paradisiac gardens of Tláloc, the god who had killed them; warriors who were sacrificed or died in battle, merchants killed while traveling far away, and women who died giving birth to their first child all went to heaven as companions of the sun; everyone else traveled for four years under the northern deserts, in the abode of the death god Mictlantecuhtli, before reaching the ninth hell, where they vanished altogether.

Other Postclassic Civilizations

On the eve of the Spanish conquest most Mexican civilizations shared deep similarities. Each was politically centralized and divided into classes, with many people occupied in specialist tasks, including professional priests. Agriculture was productive despite the lack of draft animals, metal tools and the wheel. Maize tortillas and *pozol* (maize gruel) were staple foods. Beans provided important protein, and a great variety of other crops were grown in different regions: squashes, tomatoes, chilies, avocados, peanuts, papayas, pineapples. Luxury foods for the elite included turkey, domesticated hairless dog, game, and chocolate drinks. War was widespread, often in connection with the need to take prisoners for sacrifice to a variety of gods.

Yucatán The 'Toltec' phase at Chichén Itzá lasted until about 1200. After that, the city of Mayapán dominated most of the Yucatán Peninsula until the 15th century, when rebellions broke out and the peninsula became a quarreling-ground of numerous city-states, with a culture much decayed from Classic Mayan glories.

Oaxaca After about 1200 the remaining Zapotec settlements, such as Mitla and Yagul, were increasingly dominated by the Mixtecs, famed metalsmiths and potters from the uplands around the Oaxaca-Puebla border. Mixtec and Zapotec cultures became entangled before much of their territory fell to the Aztecs in the 15th and 16th centuries.

Gulf Coast The Totonacs, a people who may have occupied El Tajín in its later years, established themselves in much of Veracruz state. To their north, the Huastecs, who inhabited another web of probably independent statelets, flourished from 800 to 1200. In the 15th century the Aztecs subdued most of these areas.

The West One civilized people who avoided conquest by the Aztecs were the Tarascos, who ruled modern Michoacán from their capital, Tzintzuntzan, about 200km west of Mexico City. They were skilled artisans and jewelers.

The Spanish Conquest

Ancient Mexican civilization, nearly 3000 years old, was shattered in the two short years from 1519 to 1521 by a tiny group of invaders who destroyed the Aztec empire, brought a new religion and reduced the native people to second-class citizens and slaves. So alien to each other were the newcomers and the indigenous people that each doubted whether the other was human (the Pope gave the Mexicans the benefit of the doubt in 1537).

From this traumatic encounter arose modern Mexico. Most Mexicans are *mestizo*, of mixed indigenous and European blood, and thus descendants of both cultures. But while Cuauhtémoc, the last Aztec emperor, is now an official hero, Cortés, the leader of the Spanish conquerors, is seen as a villain, and his indigenous allies as traitors.

Early Expeditions The Spaniards had been in the Caribbean since Columbus arrived in 1492, with their main bases on the islands of Hispaniola and Cuba. Realizing that they had not reached the East Indies, they began looking for a passage through the land mass to their west but were distracted by tales of gold, silver and a rich empire there.

Early expeditions from Cuba, led by Francisco Hernández de Córdoba in 1517 and Juan de Grijalva in 1518, were driven back from Mexico's Gulf Coast by hostile locals. In 1518 the governor of Cuba, Diego Velázquez, asked Hernán Cortés, a Spanish colonist on the island, to lead a new expedition westward. As Cortés gathered ships and men, Velázquez became uneasy about the costs and Cortés' loyalty and tried to cancel the expedition. Cortés ignored him and set sail on February 15, 1519, with 11 ships, 550 men and 16 horses.

Cortés' cunning and Machiavellian tactics are legendary, but the Aztecs played military

politics too. The story of their confrontation is one of the most bizarre in history.

Cortés & the Aztecs The Spaniards landed first at Cozumel, off the Yucatán Peninsula, then sailed around the coast to Tabasco, where they defeated some hostile locals and Cortés delivered the first of many lectures to Mexicans on the importance of Christianity and the greatness of King Carlos I of Spain. The locals gave him 20 maidens, among them Doña Marina (La Malinche), who became his interpreter, aide and lover.

The expedition next put in near the present city of Veracruz. In the Aztec capital of Tenochtitlán, tales of 'towers floating on water,' bearing fair-skinned beings, reached Moctezuma II, the Aztec god-king. Lightning struck a temple, a comet sailed through the night skies and a bird 'with a mirror in its head' was brought to Moctezuma, who saw warriors in it. According to the Aztec calendar, 1519 would see the legendary god-king Quetzalcóatl return from the east. Unsure if Cortés really was the god returning, Moctezuma sent messengers to attempt to discourage Cortés from traveling to Tenochtitlán.

Hernán Cortés

A Historical Who's Who

Ahuizotl (d. 1502) Aztec emperor from 1486 to 1502, who expanded the empire.

Allende, Ignacio (1779-1811) One of the instigators of the independence struggle in 1810.

Alvarado, Pedro de (1486-1541) One of the leading conquistadors who accompanied Cortés; later he conquered Guatemala and El Salvador.

Axayacatl Aztec emperor from 1469 to 1481, father of Moctezuma II Xocoyotzin.

Calles, Plutarco Elías (1877-1945) Mexican Revolution leader, and president from 1924 to 1928.

Cárdenas, Cuauhtémoc (b. 1933) Son of Lázaro Cárdenas. He ran for president as a left-of-center opposition candidate in 1988 and is thought to have been cheated out of victory by PRI fraud; elected Mexico City mayor in 1997; stood for presidency again in 1994 and 2000.

Cárdenas, Lázaro (1895-1970) A general and a statesman, he was considered a true president of the people, serving from 1934 to 1940. Cárdenas carried out major land reforms and expropriated foreign oil company operations.

Carlota Marie Charlotte Amélie (1840-1927) Daughter of King Leopold I of Belgium, she married Archduke Maximilian of Hapsburg and accompanied him to Mexico in 1864 to become empress. After her husband's execution in 1867 she lived on for 60 years, mentally unstable, a ward of the Vatican.

Carranza, Venustiano (1859-1920) Leader of the Constitutionalist side, opposed to Pancho Villa and Emiliano Zapata, in the revolution. President from 1917 to 1920, he was overthrown by an alliance led by Álvaro Obregón and assassinated, which effectively ended the revolution.

Cortés, Hernán (1485-1547) Spanish conquistador, sometimes known as Hernando or Fernando, who invaded Mexico and conquered the Aztecs. Much maligned today in Mexico, Cortés was the person chiefly responsible for introducing Hispanic civilization into Mexico.

Cuauhtémoc (c. 1495-1525) Last Aztec emperor, defeated and later executed by Cortés.

Cuitláhuac (d. 1520) Aztec emperor who succeeded Moctezuma II Xocoyotzin in 1520, but died the same year.

Díaz, Porfirio (1830-1915) Elected president in 1877 and reelected on numerous occasions on a slogan of 'order and progress,' he became a dictator who pursued public-works projects and encouraged foreign investment at the expense of the poor and of civil liberties. His policies precipitated the Mexican Revolution in 1910.

Díaz del Castillo, Bernal (1492-1581) Captain in Cortés' army and author of *History of the Conquest of New Spain*, an eyewitness account of the Spanish conquest of Mexico and Guatemala.

Echeverría, Luis (1922) A left-leaning president from 1970 to 1976, he aided agriculture and expanded rural social services, but his term was blighted by violent unrest and the beginnings of severe corruption.

Guerrero, Vicente (1782-1831) A leader in the later stages of the struggle for independence from Spain. Subsequently a liberal president but deposed by conservatives in 1829 and executed in 1831.

Hidalgo y Costilla, Miguel (1753-1811) Parish priest of Dolores who sparked the independence struggle in 1810 with his famous *grito*, or call for independence.

Huerta, Victoriano (1854-1916) Leader of Madero's forces against a 1913 counterrevolution, he switched sides to become president himself. One of Mexico's most disliked and ineffective leaders, he was forced to resign in 1914.

Iturbide, Agustín de (1783-1824) An officer in the royalist army against Guerrero, he switched sides to negotiate with the rebels and achieve independence from Spain (1821). Iturbide set himself up as Emperor Agustín I of Mexico, but his reign lasted less than a year (1822-23).

A Historical Who's Who

Juárez, Benito (1806-72) A Zapotec lawyer from Oaxaca, Juárez was prominent in the group of liberals who deposed Santa Anna and then passed laws against the church, which precipitated the three-year War of the Reform. Elected president in 1861, he was forced to flee because of the French takeover by Napoleon III and Emperor Maximilian. After the French left, Juárez resumed the presidency until his death.

Las Casas, Bartolomé de (1474-1566) Spanish missionary and a leading campaigner for indigenous peoples' rights; Bishop of Chiapas in the 1540s.

Madero, Francisco (1873-1913) A liberal politician, Madero began the Mexican Revolution, leading the first major opposition to Porfirio Díaz and forcing him to resign. But he proved unable to quell factional fighting, and his presidential term (1911-13) ended in front of a firing squad.

Malinche, La (Doña Marina) (c. 1501-50) Cortés' indigenous mistress and interpreter, she is considered to have had a major influence on Cortés' strategy in subduing the Aztecs.

Ferdinand Maximilian (1832-67) Hapsburg archduke sent by Napoleon III of France in 1864 to rule as emperor of Mexico. His rule was short-lived and he was forced to surrender to Juárez's forces, who executed him by firing squad in 1867.

Moctezuma I Ilhuicamina Aztec emperor from 1440 to 1469.

Moctezuma II Xocoyotzin (1466-1520) Aztec emperor from 1502 to 1520. An indecisive leader, he failed to fend off the Spanish invasion led by Cortés.

Morelos y Pavón, José María (1765-1815) A liberal priest like Hidalgo, he assumed leadership of the independence movement after Hidalgo's execution and proved a brilliant leader and strategist, but was captured and executed in 1815. His home city Valladolid was renamed Morelia in his honor.

Obregón, Álvaro (1880-1928) A revolutionary leader who supported Madero, then Carranza, but rebelled when Carranza tried to keep power illegally. Obregón's presidency (1920-24) saw revolutionary reforms, especially in education. He was assassinated in 1928.

Salinas de Gortari, Carlos (b. 1948) President from 1988 to 1994, Salinas revived the economy, but his final year in power was clouded by the Zapatista uprising in Chiapas and the assassination of his chosen successor, Luis Donaldo Colosio. Salinas' reputation disintegrated after he left power when he was blamed for the 1994-95 peso crash and suspected of links with drug mobs. He took up residence in Ireland.

Santa Anna, Antonio López de (1794-1876) Santa Anna unseated Iturbide in 1823 and headed 11 of the 50 governments in Mexico's first 35 years of independence, a period of chronic economic decline and corruption. He was a leading player in conflicts with the USA in which Mexico lost huge tracts of territory.

Villa, Francisco 'Pancho' (1878-1923) Bandit in Chihuahua and Durango who became a charismatic fighting leader in the revolution but fell out with Carranza. He was assassinated in 1923.

Zapata, Emiliano (1879-1919) A peasant leader from Morelos state, Zapata was the most radical of the revolution's leaders, fighting principally for the return of land to the peasants. He was at odds both with the conservative supporters of the old regime and their liberal opponents. After winning numerous battles (some in association with Pancho Villa), he was ambushed and killed in 1919 on Carranza's orders.

Zedillo Ponce de León, Ernesto (b. 1951) PRI president from 1994 to 2000, Zedillo steered Mexico out of the peso crisis and made serious efforts to democratize the country.

The Spaniards were well received at the Gulf Coast communities of Zempoala and Quiahuiztlán, which resented Aztec dominion. Cortés thus gained his first indigenous allies. He set up a coastal settlement called Villa Rica de la Vera Cruz and then apparently scuttled his ships to stop his men retreating. Leaving about 150 men at Villa Rica, Cortés set off for Tenochtitlán. On the way he won over the Tlaxcalan people, who became valuable allies.

After considerable vacillation, Moctezuma finally invited Cortés to meet him, denying responsibility for an ambush at Cholula that had resulted in the Spanish massacring many of that town's inhabitants. The Spaniards and 6000 indigenous allies thus approached the Aztecs' lake-island capital, a city bigger than any in Spain. Entering Tenochtitlán on November 8, 1519, along one of the causeways that linked it to the lakeshore, Cortés was met by Moctezuma, who was carried by nobles in a litter with a canopy of feathers and gold. The Spaniards were lodged – as befitted gods – in the palace of Axayacatl, Moctezuma's father.

Though entertained in luxury, the Spaniards were trapped. But Moctezuma continued to behave hesitantly, and the Spaniards took him hostage. Believing Cortés a god, Moctezuma told his people he went willingly, but hostility rose in the city, aggravated by the Spaniards' destruction of Aztec idols.

Fall of Tenochtitlán After the Spaniards had been in Tenochtitlán about six months, Moctezuma informed Cortés that another fleet had arrived on the Veracruz coast. It was led by Pánfilo de Narváez, sent by Diego Velázquez to arrest Cortés. Cortés left 140 Spaniards under the authority of Pedro de Alvarado in Tenochtitlán and sped to the coast with the others. They succeeded in routing Narváez's much bigger force, and most of the defeated men joined Cortés.

Meanwhile, things boiled over in Tenochtitlán. Apparently fearing an attack, the Spaniards struck first and killed about 200 Aztec nobles trapped in a square during a festival. Cortés and his enlarged force returned to the Aztec capital and were allowed to rejoin their comrades – only then to come under fierce attack. Trapped in Axayacatl's palace, Cortés persuaded Moctezuma to try to pacify his people. According to one version of the events, the king went up to the roof to address the crowds but was wounded by missiles and died soon afterward; other versions have it that the Spaniards killed him.

The Spaniards fled on the night of June 30, 1520, but several hundred of them, and thousands of their indigenous allies, were killed on this Noche Triste (Sad Night). The survivors retreated to Tlaxcala, where they prepared for another campaign by building boats in sections, which could be carried across the mountains for a waterborne assault on Tenochtitlán. When the 900 Spaniards reentered the Valle de México they were accompanied by some 100,000 native allies. For the first time, the odds were in their favor.

Moctezuma had been replaced by his nephew, Cuitláhuac, who then died of smallpox, brought to Mexico by one of Narváez's soldiers. He was succeeded by another nephew, the 18-year-old Cuauhtémoc. The attack started in May 1521. Cortés had to resort to razing Tenochtitlán building by building. By August 13, 1521, the resistance had ended. The captured Cuauhtémoc asked Cortés to kill him, but was kept alive till 1525 as a hostage, undergoing occasional foot-burning as the Spanish tried to make him reveal the whereabouts of treasure.

Colonial Era
Encomienda System The Spaniards renamed Tenochtitlán 'México' and rebuilt it as the capital of Nueva España (New Spain), as the new colony was called.

To reward his soldiers, Cortés granted them *encomiendas* – rights to the labor or tribute of groups of indigenous people. The settlers were also supposed to convert, protect and 'civilize' these people, but in reality the system often produced little more than slavery. In 1528, on a visit to Spain, Cortés himself received 22 towns as encomiendas and was given the title Marqués del Valle de Oaxaca by the Spanish crown, but he was denied the role of governor. He finally returned to Spain in 1540 and died there in 1547. The rest of the 16th century saw a long, eventually successful struggle by the Spanish crown to restrict the power of the conquistadors in the colony. By the 17th century the number of encomiendas had fallen drastically, and the system was abolished in the 18th century.

Nueva España By 1524 virtually all the Aztec empire, plus outlying regions such as Colima, the Huasteca area and the Isthmus of Tehuantepec, had been brought under at least loose control of the colony. In 1527 Spain set up Nueva España's first *audiencia*, a high court with government functions. Its leader, Nuño de Guzmán, was among the worst of Mexican history's long list of corrupt, violent leaders. After leading a bloody expedition to western Mexico, from Michoacán up to Sonora, he was eventually recalled to Spain.

The second audiencia (1530-35) brought some order to the colony. The king subsequently appointed Antonio de Mendoza as Nueva España's first viceroy – his personal representative to administer the colony. Mendoza, who ruled for 15 years, brought stability, limited the worst exploitation of the indigenous people, encouraged missionary efforts and ensured steady revenue to the Spanish crown.

Central America had been conquered in the 1520s by Spanish forces from Mexico and Panama, and in the 1540s the subjection of the Yucatán Peninsula, by two men both named Francisco de Montejo, was accomplished. In the north, Nueva España's territory ended at the 'Chichimec frontier' – a line running roughly between modern Tampico and Guadalajara, beyond which dwelt fierce seminomads.

Big finds of silver in Zacatecas in the mid-1540s, followed by further finds at Guanajuato, San Luis Potosí and Pachuca, spurred Spanish attempts to subdue the north. They did not succeed until the 1590s, when the Spanish offered the Chichimecs food and clothing in return for peace. By 1700 the viceroyalty of Nueva España, still ruled from Mexico City, would also officially include Spain's Caribbean islands and the Philippines. In practice, Central America, the Caribbean and the Philippines were governed separately.

The northern borders were slowly extended by missionaries and a few settlers, and by the early 19th century Nueva España included most of the modern US states of Texas, New Mexico, Arizona, California, Utah and Colorado, though control there was often tenuous.

Indigenous People & Missionaries
Despite the efforts of Viceroy Mendoza and Mexico City's first bishop, Juan de Zumárraga, the populations of the conquered peoples declined disastrously, mainly because of a series of plagues, many of them new diseases brought by the Spaniards. The population of Nueva España fell from an estimated 25 million at the conquest to little over a million by 1605.

The indigenous peoples' only real allies were some of the monks who started arriving in Nueva España in 1523 to convert them. Many of these monks were compassionate, brave men; the Franciscan and Dominican orders distinguished themselves by protecting the local people from the colonists' worst excesses (see 'A Different Sort of Liberator').

The monks' missionary work helped extend Spanish control over Mexico. By 1560 they had built more than 100 monasteries, some fortified, and had carried out millions of conversions. Under the second viceroy, Luis de Velasco, indigenous slavery was abolished in the 1550s, to be partly replaced by black slavery. Forced labor on encomiendas was also stopped, but a new system of about 45 days' forced labor a year (the *cuatequil*) was introduced for all indigenous people. That system too was widely abused by the Spaniards until abolished about half a century later.

A Different Sort of Liberator

The Spanish invaders of the Americas acquired a reputation – often deserved – for brutality toward the indigenous peoples: the notorious 'Black Legend' of the Spaniards' deliberate sadism. While the Black Legend allowed northern Europeans such as the British to claim a moral high ground to which they probably had no right, it had ample basis in fact.

Accounts by the subjugated Aztecs and others, and by the conquering Spanish themselves are full of descriptions of beheadings, amputations, burnings, brandings and various other tortures and punishments inflicted on the populace by the newcomers. In the invaders' footsteps followed representatives of the Catholic Church, enforcing 'Christian principles' among peoples they regarded as pagans. Since those early days, the official church has often been identified with brutal authority, but a strong counter-current of thought began in early colonial times and has survived to the present.

The outstanding figure was Bartolomé de Las Casas. Born in Seville in 1474, Las Casas joined a 1502 expedition against the indigenous people of Higuey, on the island of Hispaniola; he soon held encomiendas there and in Cuba. However, he experienced a conversion that convinced him of the evils of the system and devoted the rest of his life to the cause of justice for the indigenous peoples of Spanish America.

Renouncing his encomiendas, Las Casas returned to Spain to argue passionately for reform of the abuses he had observed in the Indies. His polemical *Very Brief Account of the Destruction of the Indies* persuaded King Carlos I to enact the New Laws of 1542, which included a major reform of the encomienda system. Though the New Laws went largely unenforced because they nearly caused a rebellion among encomienda holders, Las Casas continued to speak out against corrupt officials and *encomenderos* from his position as bishop of Chiapas, and then as Protector of the Indians at the Spanish court in Madrid, until his death in 1566.

Before the court, the audacious Dominican reported one cacique's statement that if Spaniards went to heaven, the native people would prefer hell. Las Casas went so far as to defend the practice of cannibalism, to advocate restitution for all the wealth that Spain had plundered from the Americas, and even to imply that the lands themselves should be returned to the indigenous people in the interests of good government:

'When we entered there … would we have found such great unions of peoples in their towns and cities if they had lacked the order of a good way of life, peace, concord and justice?'

Las Casas' advocacy undoubtedly mitigated some of the worst abuses against the indigenous Americans. In this sense, he was a role model for the Latin American activist clergy of recent decades, which, inspired by liberation theology, has worked to alleviate poverty and human-rights abuses despite great personal risk. Las Casas was the original liberation theologist.

Las Casas also left valuable observations of indigenous customs and history. His is a broad legacy with great modern relevance.

✸✸✸✸✸✸✸✸✸✸✸✸✸✸✸✸✸✸✸✸✸✸✸✸✸

The Criollos In colonial times a person's place in society was determined by skin color, parentage and birthplace. Spanish-born colonists – known as *peninsulares* or, derisively, *gachupines* – were a minuscule part of the population but were at the top of the tree and considered nobility in Nueva España, however humble their origins in Spain.

Next on the ladder were *criollos*, people born of Spanish parents in Nueva España. By the 18th century some criollos had acquired fortunes in mining, commerce, ranching or agriculture *(haciendas*, large landed estates, had begun to grow up as early as the 16th century). Not surprisingly, criollos sought political power commensurate with their wealth.

Below the criollos were the mestizos, and at the bottom of the pile were the indigenous people and African slaves. Though the poor were, by the 18th century, paid for their labor, they were paid very little. Many were *peones*, bonded laborers tied by debt to their employers. Indigenous people still had to pay tribute to the crown.

Aware of the threat to Nueva España from British and French expansion in North America, King Carlos III (1759-88) sought to bring the colony under firmer control and improve the flow of funds to the crown. He reformed the colonial administration and expelled the Jesuits, whom he suspected of disloyalty, from the entire Spanish empire. The Jesuits in Nueva España had played major roles in missionary work, education and administration, and two-thirds of them were criollos.

Continuing its attack on the powerful Catholic Church in Nueva España, the Spanish crown in 1804 decreed the transfer of many church assets to the royal coffers. The church had to call in many debts, which hit criollos hard and created widespread discontent.

The catalyst for rebellion came in 1808, when France's Napoleon Bonaparte occupied most of Spain and put his brother Joseph on the Spanish throne. Direct Spanish control over Nueva España evaporated. Rivalry between peninsulares and criollos in the colony intensified.

Independence

War of Independence In 1810 a criollo coterie based in Querétaro began planning a rebellion. News of the plans leaked to the authorities, so the group acted immediately. On September 16 one of its members, Miguel Hidalgo y Costilla, priest of the town of Dolores, summoned his parishioners and issued his now-famous call to rebellion, the Grito de Dolores, whose exact words have been lost to history but whose gist was:

My children, a new dispensation comes to us this day. Are you ready to receive it? Will you be free? Will you make the effort to recover from the hated Spaniards the lands stolen from your forefathers 300 years ago? We must act at once … Long live Our Lady of Guadalupe! Death to bad government!

A mob formed and marched quickly on San Miguel, Celaya and Guanajuato, massacring peninsulares in Guanajuato. Over the next month and a half the rebels captured Zacatecas, San Luis Potosí and Morelia. On October 30 their army, numbering about 80,000, defeated loyalist forces at Las Cruces outside Mexico City, but Hidalgo hesitated to attack the capital. The rebels occupied Guadalajara but then were pushed northward by their opponents, their numbers shrank, and in 1811 their leaders, including Hidalgo, were captured and executed.

José María Morelos y Pavón, a former student of Hidalgo and also a parish priest, assumed the rebel leadership, blockading Mexico City for several months. He convened a congress at Chilpancingo, which adopted guiding principles for the independence movement including universal male suffrage, popular sovereignty and abolition of slavery. Morelos was captured and executed in 1815, and his forces split into several guerrilla bands, the most successful of which was led by Vicente Guerrero in the state of Oaxaca.

Emperor Agustín I In 1821 the royalist general Agustín de Iturbide defected during an offensive against Guerrero and conspired with the rebels to declare independence from Spain. Iturbide and Guerrero worked out the Plan de Iguala, which established three guarantees – religious dominance by the Catholic Church, a constitutional monarchy and equal rights for criollos and peninsulares. The plan won over all influential sections of society, and the incoming Spanish viceroy in 1821 agreed to Mexican independence. Iturbide, who had command of the army, soon arranged his own nomination to the throne, which he ascended as Emperor Agustín I in 1822.

The Mexican Republic

Iturbide was deposed in 1823 by a rebel army led by another opportunistic soldier, Antonio López de Santa Anna. A new constitution in 1824 established a federal Mexican republic of 19 states and four territories. Guadalupe Victoria, a former independence fighter, became its first president. Mexico's southern boundary was the same as it is today, Central America having set up a separate federation in 1823. In the north, Mexico, like Nueva España, included much of what's now the southwestern USA.

Vicente Guerrero stood as a liberal candidate in the 1828 presidential elections and was defeated, but was eventually awarded the presidency after another Santa Anna-led revolt. Guerrero abolished slavery but was deposed and executed by his conservative vice president, Anastasio Bustamante. The struggle between liberals, who favored social reform, and conservatives, who opposed it, would be a constant theme in 19th-century Mexican politics.

Santa Anna Intervention in politics by ambitious military men was also becoming a habit. Santa Anna, a national hero after defeating a small Spanish invasion force at Tampico in 1829, overthrew Bustamante and was elected president in 1833. Thus began 22 years of chronic instability in which the presidency changed hands 36 times; 11 of those terms went to Santa Anna. Economic decline and corruption became entrenched, and Santa Anna quickly turned into a conservative. His main contributions to Mexico were manifestations of his megalomaniacal personality. Most memorably, he had his amputated, mummified leg (lost in an 1838 battle with the French) disinterred in 1842 and paraded through Mexico City.

Santa Anna is also remembered for helping to lose large chunks of Mexican territory to the USA. North American settlers in Texas, initially welcomed by the Mexican authorities, grew restless and declared Texas

independent in 1836. Santa Anna led an army north and wiped out the defenders of an old mission called the Alamo in San Antonio, but he was routed on the San Jacinto River a few weeks later.

In 1845 the US Congress voted to annex Texas, and US president Polk demanded further Mexican territory. That led, in 1846, to the Mexican-American War, in which US troops captured Mexico City. At the end of the war, by the Treaty of Guadalupe Hidalgo (1848), Mexico ceded Texas, California, Utah, Colorado, and most of New Mexico and Arizona to the USA. A Santa Anna government sold the remainder of New Mexico and Arizona to the USA in 1853 for US$10 million, in the Gadsden Purchase. This loss precipitated the liberal-led Revolution of Ayutla, which ousted Santa Anna for good in 1855.

Mexico almost lost the Yucatán Peninsula, too, in the so-called War of the Castes in the late 1840s, when the Maya people rose up against their criollo overlords and narrowly failed to drive them off the peninsula.

Juárez & the French Intervention The new liberal government ushered in the era known as the Reform, in which it set about dismantling the conservative state that had developed in Mexico. The key figure was Benito Juárez, a Zapotec from Oaxaca and a leading lawyer and politician. Laws requiring the church to sell much of its property helped precipitate the internal War of the Reform (1858-61) between the liberals, with their 'capital' at Veracruz, and conservatives, based in Mexico City. The liberals eventually won, and Juárez became president in 1861. But Mexico was a shambles and heavily in debt to Britain, France and Spain. These three countries sent a joint force to collect their debts, but France's Napoleon III decided to go further and take over Mexico, leading to yet another war.

Though the French were defeated at Puebla by General Ignacio Zaragoza on May 5, 1862, they took Puebla a year later and went on to capture Mexico City. In 1864 Napoleon invited the Austrian archduke, Maximilian of Hapsburg, to become emperor of Mexico. The French army drove Juárez and his government into the provinces.

Maximilian and Empress Carlota entered Mexico City on June 12, 1864, and moved into the Castillo de Chapultepec. But their reign was brief. In 1866, under pressure from the USA, Napoleon began to withdraw the troops who sustained Maximilian's rule. Maximilian refused to abandon his task but was defeated at Querétaro in 1867 by forces loyal to Juárez, and executed there by firing squad.

Juárez immediately set an agenda of economic and educational reform. For the first time, schooling was made mandatory. A railway was built between Mexico City and Veracruz. A rural police force, the *rurales*, was organized to secure the transport of cargo through Mexico.

The Porfiriato Juárez died in 1872. When his successor, Sebastián Lerdo de Tejada, stood for reelection in 1876, Porfirio Díaz, an ambitious liberal, launched a rebellion on the pretext that presidents should not serve more than one term of office. The following year Díaz, the sole candidate, won the presidential elections, and for the next 33 years he ran Mexico, brushing aside any 'no reelection' principles to serve six successive presidential terms from 1884. Díaz brought Mexico into the industrial age, launching public-works projects throughout the country, particularly in Mexico City. Telephone and telegraph lines were strung and the railway network spread.

Díaz kept Mexico free of the civil wars that had plagued it for over 60 years, but at a cost. Political opposition, free elections and a free press were banned. Many of Mexico's resources went into foreign ownership, peasants were cheated out of their land by new laws, workers suffered appalling conditions, and the country was kept quiet by a ruthless army and the now-feared rurales. Land and wealth became concentrated in the hands of a small minority. Some hacienda owners amassed truly vast landholdings – in Chihuahua Don Luis Terrazas, for instance, had at least 14,000 sq km – and commensurate

political power. Many rural workers were tied by debt to their bosses, just like their colonial forebears.

In the early 1900s a liberal opposition formed, but it was forced into exile in the USA. In 1906 the most important group of exiles issued a new liberal plan for Mexico from St Louis, Missouri. Their actions precipitated strikes throughout Mexico – some violently suppressed – that led, in late 1910, to the Mexican Revolution.

The Mexican Revolution

The revolution was a 10-year period of shifting allegiances between a spectrum of leaders, in which successive attempts to create stable governments were wrecked by new outbreaks of devastating fighting.

Madero & Zapata Francisco Madero, a wealthy liberal from Coahuila, campaigned for the presidency in 1910 and would probably have won if Díaz hadn't jailed him. On his release Madero drafted the Plan de San

Women of the revolution

Luis Potosí, which called for the nation to rise in revolution on November 20. The call was heard, and the revolution spread quickly across the country. When revolutionaries under the leadership of Francisco 'Pancho' Villa took Ciudad Juárez in May 1911, Díaz resigned. Madero was elected president in November 1911.

But Madero was unable to contain the factions fighting for power throughout the country. The basic divide that would dog the whole revolution was between liberal reformers like Madero and more radical leaders such as Emiliano Zapata from the state of Morelos, who was fighting for the transfer of hacienda land to the peasants with the cry *'Tierra y Libertad!'* ('Land and Freedom!'). Madero sent federal troops to disband Zapata's forces, and the Zapatista movement was born.

In November 1911 Zapata promulgated the Plan de Ayala, calling for restoration of all land to the peasants. Zapatistas won several battles against government troops in central Mexico. Other forces of varied political complexion took up local causes elsewhere. Soon all Mexico was plunged into military chaos.

Huerta In February 1913 two conservative leaders – Félix Díaz, nephew of Porfirio, and Bernardo Reyes – commenced a counter-revolution that brought 10 days of fierce fighting, the 'Decena Trágica,' to Mexico City. The fighting ended only after the US ambassador to Mexico, Henry Lane Wilson, negotiated for Madero's general, Victoriano Huerta, to switch to the rebel side and help depose Madero's government. Huerta himself became president; Madero and his vice president, José María Pino Suárez, were executed.

But Huerta only fomented greater strife. In March 1913 three revolutionary leaders in the north united against him under the Plan de Guadalupe: Venustiano Carranza, a Madero supporter, in Coahuila; Pancho Villa in Chihuahua; and Álvaro Obregón in Sonora. Zapata too was fighting against Huerta. Terror reigned in the countryside as Huerta's troops fought, pillaged and plun-

THE CENTER FOR AMERICAN HISTORY/UNIVERSITY OF TEXAS – AUSTIN

A sea of sombreros surrounds Carranza.

dered. Finally he was defeated and forced to resign in July 1914.

Constitutionalists vs Radicals Carranza called the victorious factions to a conference in Aguascalientes but failed to unify them, and war broke out again. This time Obregón and Carranza – the 'Constitutionalists,' with their capital at Veracruz – were pitted against the populist Villa and the radical Zapata. But Villa and Zapata, despite a famous meeting in Mexico City, never formed a serious alliance, and the fighting became increasingly anarchic. Villa never recovered from a defeat by Obregón in the battle of Celaya (1915). Carranza eventually emerged the victor, to form a government that was recognized by the USA. A new reformist constitution, still largely in force today, was enacted in 1917.

In Morelos the Zapatistas continued to demand reforms. Carranza had Zapata assassinated in 1919, but the following year Obregón turned against Carranza and, together with fellow Sonorans Adolfo de la Huerta and Plutarco Elías Calles, raised an army, chased Carranza out of office and had him assassinated.

The 10 years of violent civil war cost an estimated 1.5 to 2 million lives – roughly one in eight Mexicans – and shattered the economy.

From Revolution to WWII

Obregón & Calles As president from 1920 to 1924, Obregón turned to national reconstruction. More than 1000 rural schools were built, and some land was redistributed from big landowners to the peasants. Education minister José Vasconcelos commissioned top artists, such as Diego Rivera, David Alfaro Siqueiros and José Clemente Orozco, to decorate important public buildings with large, vivid murals on social and historical themes.

Plutarco Elías Calles, president from 1924 to 1928, built more schools and distributed more land. He also closed monasteries, convents and church schools, and prohibited religious processions. These measures precipitated the bloody Cristero Rebellion by Catholics, which lasted until 1929.

At the end of Calles' term, in 1928, Obregón was elected president again but was assassinated by a Cristero. Calles reorganized his supporters to found the Partido Nacional Revolucionario (PNR, National Revolutionary Party), precursor of today's PRI and the initiator of a long tradition of official acronyms.

Cárdenas Lázaro Cárdenas, former governor of Michoacán, won the presidency in 1934 with the PNR's support and stepped up the reform program. Cárdenas redistributed almost 200,000 sq km of land – nearly double the amount distributed since 1920 – mostly through the establishment of *ejidos* (peasant landholding cooperatives). Thus, most of Mexico's arable land had been redistributed, and nearly one-third of the population had received land. Cárdenas also set up the million-member Confederación de Trabajadores Mexicanos (CTM, Confederation of Mexican Workers, a labor union) and boldly expropriated foreign oil-

company operations in Mexico in 1938, forming Petróleos Mexicanos (Pemex, the Mexican Petroleum Company). After the oil expropriation foreign investors avoided Mexico, which slowed the economy.

Cárdenas reorganized the PNR into the Partido de la Revolución Mexicana (PRM), a coalition of representatives from agriculture, the military, labor and the people at large.

Following Cárdenas, the presidency of Manuel Ávila Camacho (1940-46) marked a transition toward more conservative government at the end of the first two postrevolutionary decades. Camacho sent Mexican troops to help the WWII Allies in the Pacific and supplied raw materials and labor to the USA. The war's curtailment of manufactured imports boosted Mexican industry and exports.

After WWII

As the Mexican economy expanded, new economic and political groups demanded influence in the ruling PRM. To recognize their inclusion, the party was renamed the Partido Revolucionario Institucional (PRI, or 'El Pree'). President Miguel Alemán (1946-52) continued development by building hydroelectric stations, irrigation projects and UNAM, the National Autonomous University of Mexico, and by extending the road system. Pemex grew dramatically and, with the rise of other industries, spawned some of Mexico's worst corruption.

Alemán's successor, Adolfo Ruiz Cortines (1952-58), began to confront a new problem: explosive population growth. In two decades Mexico's population had doubled, and many people began migrating to urban areas to search for work. Adolfo López Mateos (1958-64), one of Mexico's most popular post-WWII presidents, redistributed 120,000 sq km of land to small farmers, nationalized foreign utility concessions, implemented social welfare and rural education programs, and launched health campaigns. These programs were helped by strong economic growth, particularly in tourism and exports.

Unrest, Boom & Bust

President Gustavo Díaz Ordaz (1964-70) was a conservative with an agenda that emphasized business. Though he fostered education and tourism, and the economy grew by 6% a year during his term, he is better remembered for his repression of civil liberties. He sacked the president of the PRI, Carlos Madrazo, who had tried to democratize the party. University students in Mexico City were the first to express their outrage with the Díaz Ordaz administration. Discontent came to a head in the months preceding the 1968 Olympic Games in Mexico City, the first ever held in a developing nation. Single-party rule and restricted freedom of speech were among the objects of protest. More than half a million people rallied in Mexico City's Zócalo on August 27. On October 2, with the Olympics only a few days away, a rally was organized in Tlatelolco, Mexico City. The government sent in heavily armed troops and police. Several hundred people died in the ensuing massacre.

President Luis Echeverría (1970-76) sought to distribute wealth more equitably than in the past. He instituted government credit for the troubled agricultural sector, launched family-planning programs, and expanded rural clinics and the social security system. But unrest increased, and there was a guerrilla insurrection in Guerrero state, all fueled partly by the corruption that was now rife among government officials.

José López Portillo (1976-82) presided during the jump in world oil prices caused by the OPEC embargo of the early 1970s. He announced that Mexico's main problem now was how to manage its enormous prosperity: on the strength of the country's vast oil reserves, international institutions began lending Mexico billions of dollars. Then, just as suddenly, a world oil glut sent prices plunging. Mexico's worst recession for decades began.

Miguel de la Madrid (1982-88) was largely unsuccessful in coping with the problems he inherited. The population continued to grow at Malthusian rates; the economy made only weak progress, crushed by the huge debt burden from the oil boom years;

and the social pot continued to simmer. Things were not helped by the 1985 Mexico City earthquake, which killed at least 10,000 people, destroyed hundreds of buildings and caused more than US$4 billion in damage.

In a climate of economic helplessness and rampant corruption, dissent grew on both the left and the right and even within the PRI. There were sometimes violent protests over the PRI's now-routine electoral fraud and strong-arm tactics.

Salinas: Free Trade, Rebellion & Assassinations

Cuauhtémoc Cárdenas, son of the 1930s president Lázaro Cárdenas, walked out of the PRI to stand as a presidential candidate for the new center-left Frente Democrático Nacional (FDN, National Democratic Front) in 1988. It's widely believed that Cárdenas received more votes than the PRI candidate, Carlos Salinas de Gortari, but vote counting was interrupted by a mysterious computer failure. In the end Cárdenas was awarded 31% of the vote, while Salinas received 50.7% – still the lowest up to that point of any PRI candidate.

Harvard-educated Salinas (1988-94) set about transforming Mexico's state-dominated economy into one of private enterprise and free trade. The apex of his program was NAFTA, the North American Free Trade Agreement (see Policy in the Economy section later in this chapter), which came into effect on January 1, 1994. The same day a group of 2000 or so indigenous-peasant rebels calling themselves the Ejército Zapatista de Liberación Nacional (EZLN, Zapatista National Liberation Army) shocked Mexico by taking over San Cristóbal de Las Casas and three other towns in the country's southernmost state, Chiapas. They were fighting to end decades of evictions, discrimination and disappearances in their impoverished state, over which a wealthy minority had maintained a near-feudal grip since before the Mexican Revolution.

Though the EZLN was driven out of the towns within a few days (about 150 people were killed in the uprising), the uprising struck a chord nationally among all who felt that Salinas and NAFTA were merely widening the gap between rich and poor and who believed that the Mexican system prevented real social or political change. The rebels retreated under a truce to a base in the Chiapas jungle, and their leader, Subcomandante Marcos, became something of a folk hero.

In March 1994 Luis Donaldo Colosio, Salinas' chosen successor as PRI presidential candidate, was assassinated in Tijuana. Conspiracy theories abound about the killing – relations between Salinas and Colosio had deteriorated markedly – but by 1999 the only person who had been convicted was the one who pulled the trigger and was captured on the spot.

After the EZLN uprising Salinas pushed through electoral reforms against ballot-stuffing and double voting, and the 1994 presidential election was regarded as the cleanest yet – though on polling day at least a million voters still mysteriously found they were not on the electoral roll. The FDN's left-wing successor, the Partido de la Revolución Democrática (PRD, Democratic Revolution Party), claimed that thousands of its members had been murdered during Salinas' term.

Colosio's replacement as PRI candidate, 43-year-old Ernesto Zedillo, won the election with 50% of the vote. Before he took office in December, the PRI's secretary-general, José Francisco Ruiz Massieu, was assassinated in Mexico City.

Drugs Mexico had long been a marijuana and heroin producer, but a huge impetus to its drug gangs was given by a mid-1980s US crackdown on drug shipments from Colombia through the Caribbean to Florida. Drugs being transported from South America to the USA now went through Mexico instead. Three main Mexican cartels emerged: the Pacific or Tijuana cartel, headed by the Arellano Félix brothers; the (Ciudad) Juárez cartel, run by Amado Carrillo Fuentes; and the Matamoros-based Gulf cartel of Juan García Ábrego. These cartels bought up politicians, top antidrug officials and whole police forces.

Many Mexicans believe organized crime was actually controlled by the PRI, which offered protection in return for huge payoffs, and that President Salinas and his brother Raúl and other PRI high-ups were deeply involved in drug money. Raúl, arrested in 1995 after his brother left office, was sentenced in 1999 to 50 years in prison (reduced on appeal to 27½ years) for plotting the murder of Ruiz Massieu. While in jail awaiting this judgment, Raúl was also under investigation for drug trafficking and money laundering. Many believe the murders of Ruiz Massieu and of Luis Donaldo Colosio were both related to the drug trade. Carlos Salinas, meanwhile, was in self-imposed exile in Ireland (see the following section).

Zedillo

Peso Crash Within days of President Zedillo's taking office in late 1994, Mexico's currency, the peso, suddenly collapsed, bringing on a rapid and deep economic recession that hit everyone hard, and the poor hardest. It led to, among other things, a big increase in crime, intensified discontent with the PRI, and large-scale Mexican emigration to the US. It's estimated that by 1997 more than 2.5 million Mexicans a year were entering the USA illegally. Zedillo's policies pulled Mexico gradually out of recession. Despite a hiccup caused by international economic factors in 1998, by the end of his term in 2000, Mexicans' purchasing power was again approaching what it had been in 1994.

Reform Zedillo was an uncharismatic figure, but perceived as more honest than his predecessors. Early in his term he replaced en masse the notoriously partial supreme court, and it was under Zedillo's administration that Raúl Salinas was arrested and convicted of masterminding the 1994 murder of Ruiz Massieu. That an ex-president's brother would be arrested for anything was a surprise, for him to receive such a conviction was unheard of.

Carlos Salinas de Gortari, vilified for the economic crisis that Mexico had plunged into after he left office, went on a brief hunger strike in Monterrey following Raúl's arrest, demanding that Zedillo clear his (Carlos') name. When Zedillo failed to comply, Carlos fled first to the USA, then Canada, then the Caribbean. Eventually he resurfaced in Dublin, Ireland – a country that has no extradition treaty with Mexico.

Zedillo set his sights on genuine democratic reform and set up a new, independent electoral apparatus that achieved in 1997 Mexico's freest and fairest elections since 1911. Voting took place for the federal Chamber of Deputies – of which the PRI lost control for the first time. To ward off a feared split in the PRI between the traditionalist old guard and the reforming, technocratic new guard (such as himself), Zedillo also introduced a primary-election system for the selection of the party's candidate for the 2000 presidential election, replacing the traditional method by which each president personally chose his successor.

The PRI also refrained from its traditional strongarm, corrupt methods in many local elections. By 1999 ten of Mexico's 31 states had elected non-PRI governors and Mexico City had a non-PRI mayor. The party remained at its most unreconstructed and antediluvian in southern states such as Guerrero and Chiapas, both, hardly surprisingly, scenes of armed left-wing insurgency. When, for instance, Guerrero's famed Pacific resort Acapulco elected a PRD mayor in 1999, several prominent PRD figures and members of their families suddenly found themselves arrested, kidnapped, tortured and in one case killed.

Rebels In Chiapas Zedillo at first negotiated with the EZLN, but then in February 1995 he sent in the army to 'arrest' Subcomandante Marcos and other leaders. The rebels escaped deeper into the jungle. On-and-off negotiations eventually brought an agreement on indigenous rights in 1996 (see 'The Zapatistas' in the Tabasco & Chiapas chapter), but Zedillo balked at turning the agreement into law. The climate in Chiapas remained tense, with the army, and armed paramilitary groups often supported or or-

ganized by the state authorities, harassing Zapatista supporters. In 1997 pro-PRI paramilitaries massacred 45 people, mostly women and children, in a chapel in the village of Acteal, in the worst single incident of the conflict. By 1999 the army appeared to be trying to harass and intimidate Zapatista support out of existence while drawing an ever-tighter noose around the Zapatistas' jungle headquarters.

Another left-wing rebel movement, the Ejército Popular Revolucionario (EPR, People's Revolutionary Army), emerged in 1996 in two other impoverished southern states, Guerrero (where 17 peasant political activists had been killed by police in the 1995 Aguas Blancas massacre) and Oaxaca. After a wave of attacks against police and military posts in several states, in which some 20 people died, the EPR reverted to mainly propaganda and publicity activities.

Crime By 1997 most illegal drugs entering the USA were coming through Mexico – an annual flow of about 770 tons of cocaine, 7700 tons of marijuana, and 6 tons of heroin, plus growing quantities of methamphetamine (speed). The Mexican cartels were taking up to half the Colombian cocaine shipments themselves and rapidly developing their own production of heroin and speed. The drug gangs' profits amounted to US$15 billion or more a year.

Zedillo brought the armed forces into the fight against the drug mobs, but in 1997 his trusted top drug fighter, General Jesús Gutiérrez Rebollo, was himself arrested on charges of being in the pay of the Juárez mob. There were some successes. In 1996 Juan García Ábrego, of the Gulf cartel, was captured, deported to the USA and jailed for life in Houston. It was rumored that he had lost a crucial protector when Raúl Salinas was arrested in 1995. Amado Carrillo Fuentes of the Juárez mob was killed in 1997 in Mexico City by surgeons performing plastic surgery on him, but the Juárez mob and the Pacific (Tijuana) cartel emerged as the big two smuggling rings. Tijuana was the scene of literally hundreds of drug-related murders – including those of judges, witnesses, honest police and journalists – in the late 1990s. The increasing power and violence of criminal organizations was attributed by some to the weakening of the PRI's strong centralized hold over Mexican life in general and over organized crime in particular.

While some high-profile drug hoodlums were arrested or convicted, many others stayed free. The mobs were just too powerful and had too many highly placed friends to be easily defeated. In 1999 Mario Villanueva, the PRI state governor of Quintana Roo, on Mexico's Caribbean coast, disappeared eight days before his term of office (and immunity from prosecution) expired. Quintana Roo is the Mexican arrival point of a lot of the cocaine smuggled to the USA by the Juárez mob, and Villanueva was under investigation for drug trafficking.

A general rise in crime in the second half of the 1990s, especially in Mexico City, hurt the tourism industry and brought Mexico a lot of bad publicity.

GEOGRAPHY

Covering almost 2 million sq km, Mexico is big: it's nearly 3500km as the crow flies from Tijuana, in the northwest, to Cancún in the southeast, or about 4600km by road. To get from the US border at Ciudad Juárez to Mexico City, you must travel 1850km (about 24 hours by bus). From Mexico City to the Guatemalan border at Ciudad Cuauhtémoc is over 1200km.

Mexico curves from northwest to southeast, narrowing to the Isthmus of Tehuantepec in the south and then continuing northeast to the Yucatán Peninsula. To the west and south it's bordered by the Pacific Ocean. The Sea of Cortez (Golfo de California) lies between the mainland and Baja California, the world's longest peninsula – 1300km of mountains, deserts, plains and beaches. Mexico's east coast is bordered by the Gulf of Mexico all the way from the US border to the northeastern tip of the Yucatán Peninsula. The eastern Yucatán Peninsula faces the Caribbean Sea.

The country has a 3326km northern border with the US, the eastern half of which is formed by the Río Bravo del Norte

(Rio Grande, as it's called in the US). In the south and southeast are a 962km border with Guatemala and a 250km border with Belize.

Topography

Sierra Madre & Altiplano Central
Northern and central Mexico – as far south as Mexico City – have coastal plains on the east and west and two north-south mountain ranges, the Sierra Madre Oriental and Sierra Madre Occidental, framing a group of broad central plateaus known as the Altiplano Central.

On the west coast a relatively dry coastal plain stretches south from Mexicali, on the US border, almost to Tepic, in Nayarit state. Inland from this plain is the rugged Sierra Madre Occidental, crossed by only two main transport routes – the Barranca del Cobre (Copper Canyon) railway, from Chihuahua to Los Mochis, and the dramatic highway 40 from Durango to Mazatlán.

The Altiplano Central is divided into northern and central parts, themselves split by minor ranges, and varies in altitude from about 1000m in the north to more than 2000m in the center of the country. The northern plateau extends northward into Texas and New Mexico. The central plateau is mostly a series of rolling hills and broad valleys and includes some of the best farm and ranch land in Mexico.

The altiplano is delimited on the east by the Sierra Madre Oriental, which runs as far south as the state of Puebla and includes peaks as high as 3700m. The Gulf Coast plain, crossed by many rivers flowing down from the Sierra Madre, is an extension of a similar coastal plain in Texas. In northeastern Mexico the plain is wide and semimarshy near the coast, but as it nears the port of Veracruz it narrows.

Cordillera Neovolcánica
The Altiplano Central and the two Sierra Madres end where they meet the Cordillera Neovolcánica. This volcanic range running east-west across the middle of Mexico includes the active volcanoes Popocatépetl (5452m) and Volcán de Fuego de Colima (3960m), as

well as the nation's other highest peaks – Pico de Orizaba (5611m) and Iztaccíhuatl (5286m) – and its youngest volcano, Paricutín (2800m), which appeared only in 1943. Mexico City lies in the heart of the volcanic country, 70km northwest of Popocatépetl.

The South South of Cabo Corrientes (west of Guadalajara), the Pacific lowlands narrow to a thin strip. The main mountain range in the south of Mexico is the Sierra Madre del Sur, which stretches across the states of Guerrero and Oaxaca to the low Isthmus of Tehuantepec, the narrowest part of Mexico at just 220km wide. The north side of the isthmus is part of a wide, marshy plain, strewn with meandering rivers, which stretches from Veracruz to the Yucatán Peninsula.

In the southernmost state, Chiapas, the Pacific lowlands are backed by the Sierra Madre de Chiapas, behind which is the Río Grijalva basin and then the Chiapas highlands. East of these highlands is a tropical rain-forest area stretching into northern Guatemala. The jungle melts into a region of tropical savanna on the flat, low Yucatán Peninsula. The tip of the Yucatán is arid, almost desertlike.

CLIMATE

The tropic of Cancer cuts across Mexico north of Mazatlán and Tampico. South of the tropic it's hot and humid along the coastal plains on either side of the country and on the Yucatán Peninsula. Inland, at higher elevations, such as in Guadalajara or Mexico City, the climate is much more dry and temperate, and the mountain peaks are often capped with snow.

The hottest months, May to October, are also the wettest. The hottest and wettest periods of all fall between June and September for most of the country. Low-lying coastal areas are wetter and hotter than elevated inland ones, but there's considerable local variation: among coastal resorts, Acapulco receives twice as much rain as Mazatlán (nearly all of it, more than 170cm, between May and October); Acapulco and Cancún share similar temperatures, but Mazatlán and Cozumel are a few degrees cooler.

Mexico City's rainfall and temperatures are both on the low side for an inland Mexican city: Taxco and Pátzcuaro both get about twice as much rain as the capital and are a few degrees warmer; Oaxaca is also a few degrees warmer but similarly dry.

Northwestern Mexico and inland northern areas are drier than the rest of the country. In the east rainfall is particularly high on the eastern slopes of the Sierra Madre Oriental and on the northern side of the Isthmus of Tehuantepec. North winds can make inland northern Mexico decidedly chilly in winter, with temperatures sometimes down to freezing.

ECOLOGY & ENVIRONMENT

Bridging temperate and tropical regions and lying in the latitudes that contain most of the world's deserts, Mexico has an enormous range of natural environments. Its rugged, mountainous topography adds to the variety by creating countless microclimates, which support one of the most diverse arrays of plant and animal species on the planet. But many of Mexico's species are endangered. The human impact on the environment has been enormous, and the country has a litany of environmental problems as long as a rainforest liana – problems that threaten not only the fauna and flora but the people too.

Problems

Mexico's environmental crises are typical of a poor country with an exploding population struggling to develop. From early in the 20th century, urban industrial growth, intensive chemical-based agriculture, and the destruction of forests for logging and to permit grazing and development were seen as paths toward prosperity, and scant attention was paid to the environmental effects of these actions. A growth in environmental awareness since the 1970s has achieved only very limited changes.

The country's most infamous environmental problem is the pollution from traffic and industry, which chokes the air of

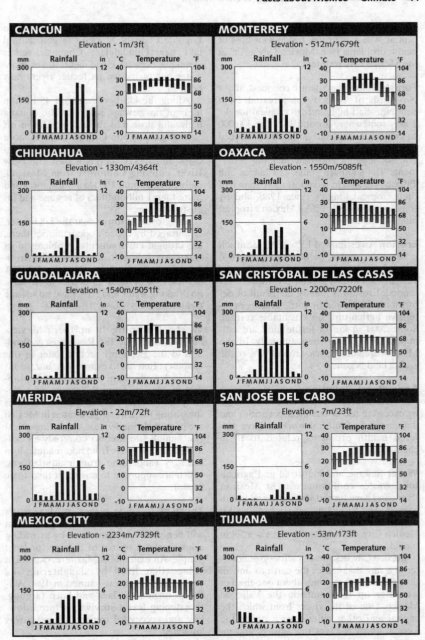

Mexico's ever-growing cities, above all the capital, where it brings residents a host of health problems (see 'Mexico City's Air' in the Mexico City chapter).

Forests Before the Spanish conquest, about two-thirds of Mexico was forested, from cool pine-clad highlands to tropical jungle. Today somewhere around 15% (or 300,000 sq km) is forested, and this is being reduced at a rate of about 5000 sq km a year for grazing, logging and new farming settlements. The southern states of Chiapas and Tabasco are said to have lost more than half their tropical jungles since 1980, and by some estimates only 2% of Mexico's tropical jungles remain.

Erosion An estimated 13% of Mexican soil is severely eroded (with more than 1000 tons of soil lost per square kilometer per year in such areas) and 66% is moderately eroded. Erosion is mainly the result of deforestation followed by cattle grazing or intensive agriculture on unsuitable terrain. Some 2000 sq km of fertile land are estimated to be desertified annually. In the Mixteca area of Oaxaca, around 80% of the arable land is gone.

Agricultural Pollution Some rural areas and watercourses have been contaminated by excessive use of chemical pesticides and defoliants. Agricultural workers have suffered health problems related to these chemicals.

Water Sewage and industrial and agricultural wastes contaminate most Mexican rivers, and have turned some into real health hazards. The Río Pánuco carries some 2000 tons of untreated sewage a day, mainly from Mexico City, which gets rid of it via a 50km tunnel.

Mexico City, despite extracting groundwater at a rate that causes the earth to sink all over the city, has to pump about one-third of its water up from outside the Valle de México. One of the rivers from which the capital and other cities take water is the Lerma, which receives raw sewage and industrial effluent from 95 towns on its way to Lago de Chapala, Mexico's biggest natural lake, near Guadalajara. Chapala itself is shrinking because Guadalajara takes more water out of it than its feeder rivers now bring in.

Along the US border, about 45 million liters of raw sewage enter the Río Tijuana daily and flow into the Pacific Ocean off San Diego. The Rio Grande receives more than 370 million liters of raw sewage, pesticides and heavy metals a day. The New River, entering California from Mexicali, daily carries about 100 toxic substances and more than 1 billion liters of sewage and industrial waste.

The growth of towns near the US border, encouraged by the job opportunities there, has brought environmental problems in its wake. According to the Border Environment Cooperation Commission, a NAFTA agency, 18% of Mexican border towns have no drinking water and 30% have no sewage treatment.

Waste Dumping In northern Mexico, *maquiladoras* (see the Resources & Products in the Economy section, later in this chapter) often fail to export their hazardous wastes, leaving them to be stored improperly in Mexico. Some US companies illegally dump toxic waste in Mexico. Facilities for storing toxic waste generated in Mexico are hopelessly inadequate, consisting of just one landfill site, able to take only an estimated 12% of waste from non-maquiladora industry (and none from maquiladoras, which are supposed to re-export their toxic waste).

Tourism In some places in Mexico it's hoped that ecologically sensitive tourism will benefit the environment by providing a less harmful source of income for local people. An example is Mazunte, Oaxaca, a village that lived by slaughtering sea turtles until that was banned in 1990. Villagers turned to slash-and-burn farming, threatening forest survival, before a low-key and successful tourism program was launched.

In other cases, despite official lip service paid to conservation, large-scale tourism developments look likely to wreck fragile ecosystems. Developments along the 'Maya Riviera' south of Cancún may very well kill off large sections of coral reef, mangrove swamp, turtle-nesting beaches and everything in between.

Environmental Movement

Environmental consciousness first grew in the 1970s, initially among the middle class and mainly in Mexico City. It's still strongest in the capital, where no one can fail to notice the air pollution. Nongovernmental action is carried out by a growing number of groups around the country, mainly small organizations working on local issues. Often they're led by members of the middle class, though there are rural community initiatives too.

Government is routinely criticized for lacking the will, as well as the money, to tackle environmental problems seriously. Since the mid-1980s the federal government has – in public at least – recognized the need for economic development to be environmentally sustainable. President Salinas tried to tackle Mexico City's air pollution problem, banned the hunting of sea turtles, which are endangered, and set up an important conservation and research agency, CONABIO, the National Commission for the Knowledge and Use of Biodiversity. President Zedillo in 1994 placed most government environmental agencies under the new Secretaría de Medio Ambiente, Recursos Naturales y Pesca (SEMARNAP, Department of Environment, Natural Resources & Fisheries). SEMARNAP's mandate is to foster environmental protection and the orderly use of natural resources, with an emphasis on sustainable development.

Flora & Fauna

For information on flora & fauna, national parks and literature about Mexico's environment, see the Wild Mexico special section.

GOVERNMENT & POLITICS

Mexico is a federal republic of 31 states and one federal district, with the states further divided into 2394 municipios (municipalities). A two-chamber federal congress, with a 128-member upper chamber, the Cámara de Senadores (Senate), and a 500-member lower chamber, the Cámara de Diputados (Chamber of Deputies), makes the laws. A directly elected president carries out the laws, and an independent judiciary decides disputes according to Napoleonic law. Women gained the vote in 1954, and an Equal Rights Amendment was added to the constitution in 1974. The legislatures and governors of Mexico's states are elected by their citizens, as are the ayuntamientos (town councils), which run municipios, and their presidents.

In practice Mexican political life was dominated from the 1920s to the late 1990s by one party, the Partido Revolucionario Institucional (PRI, Institutional Revolutionary Party), and its predecessors, with the national president ruling in the tradition of strong, centralized leadership going back to Moctezuma. Accusations of fraud, corruption, bribery, intimidation and violence have long accompanied at every level the all-conquering PRI's election tactics and style of governing. Though the Chamber of Deputies has, on paper, the power of the purse and weighty powers to oversee the executive, the president's will was rarely denied. And the fiscal and political power of the states was very much subordinate to the federal government.

No significant challenge from opposition parties arose till the 1980s. Carlos Salinas de Gortari, president from 1988 to 1994, signaled the tentative beginnings of democratization. Limited anticorruption measures were introduced for the election of his successor in 1994, and during his term governors representing the center-right Partido de Acción Nacional (PAN) were elected in three Mexican states (Baja California, Chihuahua and Guanajuato) – the first time ever that the PRI conceded any state governorship.

The first real cracks in the monolith of PRI dominance were opened by President Ernesto Zedillo (1994-2000). Responding to growing dissatisfaction with corruption and economic problems, to mounting clamor in

Mexico for real democratic change, and to pressure from other countries that came with NAFTA, Zedillo turned Mexico in the direction of a genuinely pluralist democracy – despite opposition from the PRI old guard with its vested interest in absence of change.

Zedillo freed from government control the body that organizes elections, the Instituto Federal Electoral (IFE), and let it spend hundreds of millions of dollars to build an electoral apparatus transparent enough to overcome fraud.

The first elections under this new setup, in 1997, were for all 500 seats in the Chamber of Deputies and a quarter of the Senate. The Mexico City mayor was chosen by popular vote at the same time, after decades of the capital's being run directly by the federal government. The PRI, unprecedentedly, lost overall control of the Chamber of Deputies, with the PAN and the center-left Partido de la Revolución Democrática (PRD) each winning about a quarter of the seats. The Mexico City mayoralty went to Cuauhtémoc Cárdenas, of the PRD, who had lost the 1988 presidential election to Salinas. The elections were not flawless, but they were hailed as the freest and fairest in Mexico since 1911.

Further state elections left 10 of Mexico's states as well as Mexico City under PAN or PRD governorship by the end of 1999. Despite their obvious differences these two opposition parties even talked about – though they did not succeed in – forming an alliance to unseat the PRI in the July 2000 elections for Zedillo's successor as president. For 2000 the three main parties all broke new ground by using a primary-election system to choose their presidential candidates. This was particularly historic in the case of the PRI, whose candidates had previously been picked by the *dedazo* (fingering) method – which simply meant that the outgoing president, himself forbidden by law from serving more than one *sexenio* (six-year term), chose a candidate to succeed him from within PRI ranks. Since the 1930s that candidate had invariably become president. The PRI presidential candidate for 2000 was chosen by a nationwide primary

election open to all registered voters, regardless of party affiliation. Approximately 10 million people voted, and Francisco Labastida, a former Interior Minister widely thought to be favored by Zedillo and the party modernizers, won by a wide margin.

The main opposition parties' candidates in the 2000 election, both chosen in primaries restricted to party members, were to be Vicente Fox, a former Coca-Cola executive and Guanajuato state governor, for the PAN, and Cuauhtémoc Cárdenas, who resigned as Mexico City mayor in 1999, for the PRD.

ECONOMY
Resources & Products

Mexico is one of Latin America's most industrialized nations. Manufacturing employs about 18% of the workforce and produces about a quarter of the gross national product and most of the country's exports. Motor vehicles, processed food, steel, chemicals, paper and textiles have joined more traditional products such as sugar, coffee, silver, lead, copper and zinc. Among Mexico's biggest national assets are its oil reserves, the eighth largest in the world, and its gas reserves. Concentrated mainly along the Gulf Coast and belonging to a government-owned monopoly, Pemex, these reserves yield about one-tenth of Mexico's export earnings and one-third of the government's revenues.

Half of Mexico's output is produced within 150km of Mexico City, though northern states such as Nuevo León and Baja California are increasingly important, aided by their proximity to that major export market, the USA, and by their many maquiladoras. Maquiladoras are factories (usually foreign-owned) that are allowed to import raw materials, parts and equipment duty-free for processing or assembly by inexpensive Mexican labor. Maquiladoras employ almost 1 million Mexicans.

Mining, Mexico's income source in colonial times, remains significant in the northern half of the country and accounts for about 3% of the national product. Mexico is still the world's largest silver producer.

About 30% of the workforce is in service industries. Tourism is one of the most important of these. Some 20 million foreign visitors a year, more than half of them cross-border day-trippers, bring in around US$8 billion of foreign exchange (petrochemical exports are of a similar order), and the domestic tourism business is three times as big. Agriculture occupies about 25% of Mexico's workers but produces only about 8% of the national product. Around 10% to 12% of Mexico is planted with maize, wheat, rice and beans, but the country still imports more grain than it exports. Small farming plots became prevalent after the redistribution of hacienda land to ejidos following the revolution. These plots are often farmed at subsistence level, their owners lacking the technology and capital to render them more productive. Larger-scale farming goes on primarily along the Gulf Coast (coffee and sugarcane), in the north and northwest (livestock, wheat and cotton), and in the Bajío area, north of Mexico City (wheat and vegetables).

Policy
NAFTA The oil boom of the 1970s encouraged Mexico to undertake ambitious spending projects, piling up a big burden of national debt that could not be paid when revenues slumped in the early 1980s oil bust. In response, particularly from 1988 to 1994 under President Salinas, debt was rescheduled, austerity measures were introduced, and government enterprises from banks and utilities to steel mills were sold off. Inflation was cut from well over 100% to less than 10% under Salinas. By the early 1990s Mexico was showing steady growth, and the peso had been stabilized.

The key to Salinas' plans was the North American Free Trade Agreement (NAFTA), which took effect on January 1, 1994. NAFTA (known to Mexicans as the TLC, Tratado de Libre Comercio) is gradually (over a 15-year period) eliminating restrictions on trade and investment between the US, Mexico and Canada. The hope was that NAFTA would bring Mexico increased employment and growing exports, as well as cheaper imports.

Opponents charge that the gap between rich and poor is being widened as new imports, for example, cheap maize produced by US agribusiness, damage uncompetitive sectors of the Mexican economy.

Peso Crisis The peso collapse of 1994-95 happened after Salinas left office but was a consequence of his policies. The foreign investment that had poured into Mexico in the early 1990s slowed to a trickle in 1994, owing to a number of factors including political alarms in Mexico, rising US interest rates, and fears that the peso was overvalued. After the government spent nearly all its foreign reserves in a futile attempt to support the peso, Salinas' successor Ernesto Zedillo had to let the peso float to find its own level. It fell far and fast, and Mexico had to be bailed out by a multibillion-dollar package of emergency credit from the US, Canada and international financial bodies.

The government raised taxes and interest rates, cut spending and announced new privatizations. More than 1.5 million people lost their jobs, prices and crime soared, production and standards of living fell, borrowers went broke. Inflation in 1995 was over 50%. More Mexicans looked to (usually illegal) migration to the USA as the only way out of poverty.

Recovery The government's austerity measures and its successful raising of new capital on private markets, coupled with big help for exports from NAFTA and the cheap peso, began to pull Mexico out of the slump surprisingly quickly. Foreign investment revived, and Mexico repaid most of its emergency debt ahead of schedule. By 1998 production was rising about 6% a year and inflation was down to around 15%.

The peso crisis and resulting recession, however, had slashed Mexicans' average spending power by 50%. One 1997 study concluded that more than one-fifth of the people in the Distrito Federal (which encompasses about half of Mexico City) were living in extreme poverty, on 'marginal levels of basic subsistence.' Yet the majority of Mexico's 20 to 25 million poorest people live in *rural* areas, which receive much less welfare spending than cities. The poorest states are Guerrero, Oaxaca, Chiapas, Veracruz, Puebla and Hidalgo.

A slump in oil prices in 1998 and the global economic crisis of 1997-98 caused a blip in Mexico's recovery. Even the long-standing government subsidy on tortillas was abolished on January 1, 1999, bringing the price of this staple food to nearly double what it was a year before. The 1999 budget was the most austere in nearly 20 years. But Mexico came through the crisis much better than other big Latin American economies such as Brazil's.

By late 1999 Mexico's economic outlook was brightening quickly. Inflation for the year looked likely to better the government's target of 13% and the crucial US market was growing steadily. Real incomes – allowing for inflation – were starting to rise again, and consumption and production were expected to grow in 2000.

But Mexicans still had less purchasing power than in 1994. The minimum wage is about US$3.50 a day. That is what many people in unskilled jobs are actually paid, and most workers earn under US$10 a day. Then there are the millions in the so-called informal economy: street hawkers, traffic signal fire-eaters, buskers, home workers, criminals – anybody whose work is not officially registered and who doesn't pay taxes. Perhaps one-third of Mexico's work force is 'informal.' Few of these people scrape together much more than the minimum wage. Meanwhile, Mexico's growing population adds more than a million people to the labor market every year.

POPULATION & PEOPLE

In 1997 Mexico's population was estimated at 93.7 million. In 1940 the population was counted at 20 million, in 1960 at 35 million, in 1970 at 49 million, in 1980 at 67 million and in 1990 at 81 million.

About two-thirds of Mexicans live in towns or cities of more than 5000 people, and one-third are aged under 15. The biggest cities are Mexico City (with perhaps 20 million people), Guadalajara (with a conurbation estimated at 5 million) and Monterrey (conurbation estimated at 3 million). Tijuana, Puebla and Ciudad Juárez all have populations close to 1 million. The most populous state is the state of México, which includes the rapidly growing outer areas of Mexico City and has more than 12 million people.

By official figures, the population is growing by about 1.4% a year, which is down from rates of more than 3% between 1950 and 1980 but still means an extra 1.3 million mouths to feed every year. Of even more concern is the growth of the cities, which attract thousands of newcomers from the poorer countryside every day.

Ethnic Groups

The major ethnic division is between mestizos and *indígenas* or *indios* (indigenous people). Mestizos are people of mixed ancestry – usually Spanish and indigenous, although African slaves and other Europeans were also significant elements. Indigenous people are descendants of Mexico's pre-Hispanic inhabitants who have retained their sense of distinct identity. Mestizos are the overwhelming majority, and together with the few people of supposed pure Spanish descent they hold most positions of power in Mexican society. (If you were to judge from Mexican TV soap operas, all Mexicans are of pure Spanish descent, but let's not worry about that for now.)

Researchers have listed at least 139 vanished indigenous languages. The 50 or so indigenous cultures that have survived, some now with only a few hundred people, have done so largely because of their rural isolation. Indigenous people in general remain second-class citizens, often restricted to the worst land or forced to migrate to city slums or the USA in search of work. Their main wealth is traditional and spiritual, their way of life imbued with communal customs and rituals bound up with nature. Indigenous traditions, religion, arts, crafts and costumes are fascinating; there is more information on them in the various regional chapters, in this chapter under Arts and Religion, and in the Artesanías special section at the end of the book.

Official figures count as indigenous only people who list themselves in censuses as speakers of indigenous languages. They number about 7 million, though people of predominantly indigenous ancestry may total as many as 25 million. The biggest indigenous group is the Nahua, descendants of the Aztecs. At least 1.7 million Nahuatl speakers are spread around central Mexico, chiefly in Puebla, Veracruz, Hidalgo, Guerrero and San Luis Potosí states. There are approximately 1 million Maya speakers on the Yucatán Peninsula; 500,000 Zapotecs, mainly in Oaxaca; 500,000 Mixtecs, mainly in Oaxaca, Guerrero and Puebla; 260,000 Totonacs, in Veracruz and Puebla; and 130,000 Purépecha in Michoacán – each group directly descended from a well-known pre-Hispanic people (Purépecha is the most common name for the descendants of the pre-Hispanic Tarascos).

Descendants of lesser-known pre-Hispanic peoples include the approximately 330,000 Otomí, mainly in Hidalgo and México states; 150,000 Mazahua, in México state; and 150,000 Huastecs in San Luis Potosí and northern Veracruz. The Tzotzils and Tzeltals of Chiapas are probably descendants of Maya who migrated to the highlands at the time of the Classic Maya downfall. Among less numerous indigenous peoples, the Huichol of Jalisco and Nayarit are renowned for the importance of the hallucinogenic drug peyote in their spiritual life, and the Mazatecs of northern Oaxaca for their use of hallucinogenic mushrooms.

ARTS
Painting & Sculpture

Mexicans have had a talent for painting – and an excitement about bright colors – since pre-Hispanic times. Today the many murals decorating Mexican walls and the wealth of modern and historic art in Mexico's many galleries are among the highlights of the country for many visitors. Mexican creativity is also expressed in myriad folk arts, which are very much a living tradition – see the Artesanías special section.

Pre-Hispanic Art Mexico's first civilization, the Olmecs of the Gulf Coast, produced some of the most remarkable pre-Hispanic stone sculptures, depicting deities, animals, and wonderfully lifelike human forms. Most awesome are the huge Olmec heads, which combine the features of human babies and jaguars. The earliest outstanding Mexican murals are found at Teotihuacán, where the colorful *Paradise of Tláloc* depicts in detail the delights awaiting those who died at the hands of the water god, Tláloc. The Teotihuacán mural style spread to other parts of Mexico, such as Monte Albán, in Oaxaca.

The Classic Maya of southeast Mexico, at their cultural height from about 250 to 800 AD, were perhaps ancient Mexico's most artistic people. They left countless beautiful stone sculptures of complicated design and meaning but possessing an easily appreciable delicacy of touch – a talent also expressed in their unique architecture. Subjects are typically rulers, deities and ceremonies. The Maya also created some marvelous multicolored murals and pottery, most famously the murals of Bonampak, in Chiapas. The art of the Aztecs (whose civilization lasted from about 1350 to 1521) reflects their harsh world-view, with many carvings of skulls and complicated symbolic representations of gods.

Other pre-Hispanic peoples with major artistic legacies include the Toltecs of central Mexico (10th to 13th centuries), who had a fearsome, militaristic style of carving; the Mixtecs of Oaxaca and Puebla (13th to 16th centuries), who were excellent goldsmiths and jewelers; and the Classic Veracruz civilization (about 400 to 900 AD), which left a wealth of pottery and stone carving.

Pre-Hispanic art can be found at archaeological sites and museums throughout Mexico. The Museo Nacional de Antropología, in Mexico City, provides an excellent overview, with fine reproductions as well as original works.

Colonial Period Mexican art during Spanish rule was heavily Spanish-influenced and chiefly religious in subject, though later in the period portraits grew in popularity under wealthy patrons. The influence of indigenous artisans is seen in the elaborate altarpieces and sculpted walls and ceilings, overflowing with tiny detail, in churches and monasteries, as well as in some fine frescoes, such as those at Actopan monastery in Hidalgo state. Miguel Cabrera (1695-1768), from Oaxaca, was probably the leading painter of the era – his scenes and figures have a sureness of touch lacking in others' more labored efforts. His work can be seen in churches and museums scattered all over Mexico.

Independent Mexico The landscapes of José María Velasco (1840-1912) capture the magical qualities of the country around Mexico City and areas farther afield, such as Oaxaca.

The years before the 1910 revolution saw the beginnings of socially conscious art and of a real break from European traditions. Slums, brothels and indigenous poverty began to appear on canvases. The cartoons and engravings of José Guadalupe Posada (1852-1913), with their characteristic *calavera* (skull) motif, satirized the injustices of the Porfiriato period and were aimed at a wider audience than most previous Mexican art. Gerardo Murillo (1875-1964), who took the name Doctor Atl (from a Nahuatl word meaning 'water'), displayed some scandalously orgiastic paintings at a 1910 show marking the centenary of the independence movement.

The Muralists Immediately following the Mexican Revolution, in the 1920s, education minister José Vasconcelos commissioned leading young artists to paint a series of murals on public buildings to spread a sense of Mexican history and culture and the need for social and technological change. The trio of great muralists were Diego Rivera (1885-1957), José Clemente Orozco (1883-1949) and David Alfaro Siqueiros (1896-1974).

Rivera's work carried a clear left-wing message, emphasizing past oppression of indigenous people and peasants. He had an intense interest in indigenous Mexico and tried hard to pull the country's indigenous and Spanish roots together into one national identity. His murals are colorful, crowded tableaus depicting historical people and events or symbolic scenes of Mexican life, with a simple, clear-cut moral message. They're realistic, if not always lifelike. To appreciate them you need a little knowledge of Mexican history and, preferably, an explanation of the details. Some of Rivera's greatest works can be seen in Mexico City (see 'Diego & Frida' in that chapter) and at the Palacio de Cortés, Cuernavaca.

Siqueiros, who fought on the Constitutionalist side in the revolution (while Rivera was in Europe), remained a political activist afterward, spending time in jail as a result and leading an attempt to kill Leon Trotsky in Mexico City in 1940. His murals lack Rivera's realism but convey a more clearly Marxist message through dramatic, symbolic depictions of concepts such as the oppressed and the people, and through grotesque caricatures of the oppressors. Some of his best works can be seen at the Palacio de Bellas Artes, Castillo de Chapultepec and Ciudad Universitaria, all in Mexico City.

Orozco was less of a propagandist, conveying emotion, character and atmosphere and focusing more on the universal human condition than on historical or political specifics. By the 1930s Orozco grew disillusioned with the revolution. Some of his most powerful works, such as those in the Palacio de Bellas Artes, depict oppressive scenes of degradation, violence or injustice but do not offer any simplistic political solution. His work is reckoned to have reached its peak in Guadalajara from 1936 to 1939, particularly in the 50-odd frescoes in the Instituto Cultural Cabañas.

Rivera, Siqueiros and Orozco were also great artists on a smaller scale. Some of their portraits, drawings and other works can be seen in places like the Museo de Arte Moderno and Museo de Arte Carrillo Gil in Mexico City and in Casa de Diego Rivera in Guanajuato.

The mural movement continued long after WWII. Rufino Tamayo (1899-1991) from Oaxaca, also represented in the Palacio de Bellas Artes, was relatively unconcerned with politics and history but was absorbed by abstract and mythological scenes and effects of color. Juan O'Gorman (1905-81), a Mexican of Irish ancestry, was even more realistic and detailed than Rivera. His mosaic on the Biblioteca Central at Mexico City's Ciudad Universitaria is probably his best-known work, but is atypical of his overall style.

Other 20th-Century Artists Frida Kahlo (1907-54), physically crippled by a road accident and mentally tormented in her tempestuous marriage to Diego Rivera, painted anguished, penetrating self-portraits and grotesque, surreal images that expressed her left-wing views and externalized her inner tumult. After several decades of being seen as an interesting oddball, Kahlo suddenly seemed to strike an international chord in the 1980s, almost overnight becoming hugely popular and as renowned as Rivera (see 'Diego & Frida,' in the Mexico City chapter). Frida fans will enjoy the Internet site The Original Frida Kahlo Home Page (www.cascade.net/kahlo).

After WWII, young Mexican artists reacted against the muralist movement, which they saw as too didactic and too obsessed with *Mexicanidad* (Mexicanness). They opened Mexico up to world trends such as abstract expressionism and op art. The Museo José Luis Cuevas, in Mexico City, was founded by and named after one of the leaders of this trend. Other interesting artists to look for include Zacatecans Francisco Goitia (1882-1960) and Pedro Coronel (1923-85), and Francisco Toledo (born 1940), from Oaxaca. Along with Mexico City, Oaxaca currently has one of the liveliest art scenes in the country, with contemporary Oaxacan painters such as Luis Zárate and Rodolfo Morales among its leading figures.

Architecture
Pre-Hispanic The ancient civilizations of Mexico produced some of the most spectacular, eye-pleasing architecture ever built. At sites such as Teotihuacán near Mexico City, Monte Albán in Oaxaca, and Chichén Itzá and Uxmal in Yucatán, you can still see fairly intact pre-Hispanic cities. Their spectacular ceremonial centers, used by the religious and political elite, were designed to impress, with great stone pyramids, palaces and ball courts. Pyramids usually functioned as the bases for small shrines on their summits. Mexico's three biggest pyramids are the Pirámide del Sol and Pirámide de la Luna, both at Teotihuacán, and the Great Pyramid of Cholula, near Puebla.

There are many differences in style between pre-Hispanic civilizations: while Teotihuacán, Monte Albán and Aztec buildings were relatively simple, designed to awe by their grand scale, Mayan architecture paid more attention to aesthetics, with intricately patterned façades, delicate 'combs' on temple roofs, and sinuous carvings. Buildings at Mayan sites such as Uxmal, Chichén Itzá, and Palenque are some of the most beautiful human creations in Mexico.

Colonial One of the first preoccupations of the Spanish was to replace pagan temples with Christian churches. A classic case is the Great Pyramid of Cholula, now topped by a small colonial church. Many of the fine mansions, churches, monasteries and plazas that today contribute so much to Mexico's beauty were created during the 300 years of Spanish rule. Most were in basically Spanish styles, but with unique local variations.

Gothic & Renaissance These styles dominated in Mexico in the 16th and early 17th centuries. Gothic, which originated in medieval Europe, is typified by soaring buttresses, pointed arches, clusters of round columns and ribbed ceiling vaults. The Renaissance style saw a return to the disciplined ancient Greek and Roman ideals of harmony and proportion: columns and shapes such as the square and circle predominated. The usual Renaissance style in Mexico was plateresque – from *platero* (silversmith), because its decoration resembled the elaborate ornamentation that went into silverwork. Plateresque was commonly used on the façades of buildings, particularly church doorways, which had round arches bordered by classical columns and stone sculpture. A later, more austere Renaissance style was called Herreresque, after the Spanish architect Juan de Herrera. Two of Mexico's outstanding Renaissance buildings are Mérida's cathedral and Casa de Montejo. Mexico City and Puebla cathedrals mingle Renaissance and baroque styles.

Gothic and Renaissance influences were combined in many of the fortified monasteries that were built as Spanish monks carried their missionary work to all corners of the country. Monasteries usually had a large church, a cloister where the monks lived and worked, a big atrium (churchyard) and often a *capilla abierta* (open chapel), from which priests could address large crowds of local people. Notable monasteries include Actopan and Acolman in central Mexico, and Yanhuitlán, Coixtlahuaca and Teposcolula, in Oaxaca.

The influence of the Muslims, who had ruled much of Spain until the 15th century, was also carried to Mexico. Examples of the Muslim-influenced Spanish Christian style, known as Mudéjar, can be seen in some beautifully carved wooden ceilings and in the *alfiz*, a rectangle framing a round arch. The 49 domes of the Capilla Real in Cholula almost resemble a mosque.

Baroque Baroque style, which reached Mexico in the early 17th century, was a reaction against strict Renaissance styles, combining classical influences with other elements and aiming at dramatic effect rather than pure proportion. Curves, color, contrasts of light and dark, and increasingly elaborate decoration were among its hallmarks. Painting and sculpture were integrated with architecture, most notably in ornate, often enormous altarpieces *(retablos)*.

Early, more restrained baroque buildings include the churches of Santiago Tlatelolco in Mexico City, San Felipe Neri in Oaxaca and San Francisco in San Luis Potosí. Among later baroque works are the marvelous façade of Zacatecas' cathedral and the churches of San Cristóbal in Puebla and La Soledad in Oaxaca.

Mexican baroque reached its final form, Churrigueresque, between 1730 and 1780.

Named after a Barcelona architect, José Benito Churriguera, this style was characterized by riotous surface ornamentation. Its hallmark is the *estípite* – a pilaster (a vertical pillar projecting only partly from a wall) in the form of a very narrow upside-down pyramid. The estípite helped give Churrigueresque its typical 'top-heavy' effect.

Outstanding Churrigueresque churches include the Sagrario Metropolitano in Mexico City; San Martín in Tepotzotlán; San Francisco, La Compañía and La Valenciana in Guanajuato; Santa Prisca and San Sebastián in Taxco; and the Ocotlán sanctuary at Tlaxcala.

Mexican indigenous artisans added profuse, detailed sculpture in stone and colored stucco to many baroque buildings. Among the most exuberant examples are the Capilla del Rosario in Santo Domingo church, Puebla, and the nearby village church of Tonantzintla. Arabic influence continued with the popularity of *azulejos* (colored tiles) on the outside of buildings, particularly in and around Puebla.

Neoclassical Neoclassical style was another return to Greek and Roman ideals. In Mexico it lasted from about 1780 to 1830. Outstanding examples include the Colegio de Minería in Mexico City, the Alhóndiga de Granaditas in Guanajuato and the second tiers of the Mexico City cathedral's towers. Eduardo Tresguerras and Spanish-born Manuel Tolsá were the most prominent neoclassical architects.

19th & 20th Centuries Independent Mexico saw revivals of Gothic and colonial styles. In the late 19th and early 20th centuries many buildings copied French or Italian styles. The Palacio de Bellas Artes in Mexico City is one of the finest buildings from this era.

After the revolution of 1910 to 1921, art deco appeared in buildings such as the Lotería Nacional and Frontón México in Mexico City, but more important was an attempt to return to pre-Hispanic roots in the search for a national identity. This trend was known as Toltecism, and many public buildings exhibit the heaviness of Aztec or Toltec monuments. It culminated in the 1950s with the UNAM campus in Mexico City, where many buildings are covered with colorful murals.

More modern architects have provided Mexico – especially Mexico City and Monterrey – with some eye-catching and adventurous buildings. Among these are the 1960s Museo Nacional de Antropología (Mexico City), with a large umbrella-like stone fountain in its central courtyard; the early 1990s Centro Bursátil, a skyward-pointing arrowhead of reflecting glass beside the capital's main boulevard, Paseo de la Reforma; Monterrey's Faro del Comercio, a tall orange concrete slab erected in the 1980s in the city's main plaza; and the Centro de Tecnología Avanzada para la Producción at Monterrey's Instituto Tecnológico, a building that appears to have been sliced in two, leaving the halves toppling away from each other.

Music

In Mexico live music may start up at any time on streets, plazas or even buses. The musicians play for a living and range from marimba (wooden xylophone) teams and mariachi bands (trumpeters, violinists, guitarists and a singer, all dressed in smart cowboy-like costumes) to ragged lone buskers with out-of-tune guitars and sandpaper voices. Mariachi music – perhaps the most 'typical' Mexican music of all – originated in the Guadalajara area but is played nationwide (see 'Mariachis' in the Western Central Highlands chapter). Marimbas are particularly popular in the southeast and on the Gulf Coast.

On a more organized level, Mexico has a thriving popular music business. Its outpourings can be heard live at fiestas, nightspots and concerts or bought from music shops or cheap bootleg-tape vendors. (Ask tape vendors to play cassettes before you buy them, as there are many defective or blank copies.)

Rock & Pop Mexican rock was pretty raw and basic until the mid-to-late 1980s, when a more sophisticated music began to emerge.

Sousaphone player, Easter parade, Tepoztlan

El Tri, still together after more than 30 years, head up the earlier generation with their still-energetic rock & roll. The changes of the '80s were spearheaded by mystical Def Leppard-type rockers Caifanes, a middle-class Mexico City group typical of the sort of Mexicans exposed earliest to North American and European music. Caifanes are still together under the name Jaguares. Foreign rock acts were not allowed to play live in Mexico until the late '80s. Their arrival greatly broadened rock's appeal and today Mexico, so close to the big US Spanish-speaking market, is arguably the most important hub of Spanish-language rock. Talented and versatile Mexico City bands such as Café Tacuba and Maldita Vecindad took *rock en español* to new heights and new audiences (well beyond Mexico) in the '90s, mixing a huge range of influences – from rock & roll, ska and punk to traditional Mexican *son*, bolero or mariachi. Four-piece Café Tacuba's exciting handling of so many styles – yet still with their own very strong musical identity – led the *New York Times* to compare their 1994 album *Re* with the Beatles' *White Album*. Their most recent production is the 1999 double album *Revés/ YoSoy*. Maná from Guadalajara are an unashamedly commercial band with British and Caribbean influences sounding strongly reminiscent of the Police. They have been around since the '80s and are still strong. Important late '90s arrivals were mostly from Monterrey, notably the politically minded hip-hop trio Control Machete; crude, rude rappers Molotov; and the twosome Plastilina Mosh (programmer Alejandro Rosso and vocalist/guitarist Jonas), a kind of Mexican Beastie Boys whose 1998 debut album *Aquamosh* was a huge success, selling over 1 million copies.

Meanwhile, romantic balladeer Luis Miguel (born in Veracruz in 1970) is probably the most widely known Mexican pop act. If you don't know his voice you will almost certainly have read about his love life. You probably also read about Gloria Trevi, characterized as the controversial 'Mexican Madonna' until she vanished in 1998 after Chihuahua authorities ordered the arrest of her and her manager Sergio Andrade Sánchez for alleged sexual abuse and kidnapping of minors. The story went that the school for young female talent run by Trevi was actually a harem for Andrade. In a saga that gripped Mexico and produced hundreds of false 'sightings' all over the world, the pair were on the run for over a year before being arrested in Rio de Janeiro in January 2000.

Mexican Regional Music The deepest-rooted Mexican folk music is *son* (literally, 'sound'), a broad term covering a range of country styles that grew out of the fusion of indigenous, Spanish and African musical cultures. Son is essentially guitars plus harp or violin, often played for a foot-stamping dance audience, with witty, often improvised lyrics. The independent label Discos Corasón is doing much to promote these most traditional of Mexican musical forms.

Particularly celebrated brands of son come from Jalisco *(sones jaliscenses* originally formed the repertoire of many mari-achi bands); Veracruz, whose *son jarocho*, performed preeminently by harpist La Negra Graciana, is particularly African-influenced; and the hot Río Balsas basin southwest of Mexico City with the elaborate violin passages of its *sones calentanos*. This last region has produced perhaps the greatest son musician of recent decades, violinist Juan Reynoso. Another area renowned for its son is the Huasteca, whose *son huasteco* trios feature a solo violinist and two guitarists singing falsetto between soaring violin passages. Keep an eye open for son festivals or performances by such groups as Camperos de Valles or Trio Tamazunchale if you're traveling in the Huasteca proper, Hidalgo state or northern Puebla.

More modern regional music is rooted in a strong rhythm from several guitars, with voice, accordion, violin or brass providing the melody. *Ranchera* is Mexico's urban 'country music.' Developed in the expanding towns and cities of the 20th century, it's mostly melodramatic, sentimental stuff with a nostalgia for rural roots: vocalist-and-combo music, maybe with a mariachi backing. Women such as Eugenia León and men such as Juan Gabriel and Alejandro Fernández are among the leading ranchera artists now that past generations of female stars such as Lola Beltrán, Lucha Reyes and Amalia Mendoza are gone.

Norteño is country ballad and dance music, originating in northern Mexico but enjoying countrywide popularity. Its roots are in *corrido* ballads dealing with latino/ anglo strife in the borderlands in the 19th century and themes from the Mexican Revolution. Today's ballads tend to deal with small-time crooks such as drug-runners or *coyotes* trying to survive amid big-time corruption and crime. Norteño *conjuntos* (groups) go for 10-gallon hats, and backing for the singer is guitar-based, with accordion, bass and drums. Los Tigres del Norte, the superstars of this genre, added saxophone and absorbed popular *cumbia* rhythms from Colombia.

Banda is a 1990s development of norteño, substituting large brass sections for guitars and accordion, playing a combination of

Latin and more traditional Mexican rhythms. Banda del Recodo from Mazatlán are the biggest name in banda. This music also gave birth to an energetic new dance, *la quebradita*.

Grupera, a feebler blend of ranchera, norteño and cumbia, is very popular, especially at fiestas deep in rural Mexico. Límite and Banda Machos are star exponents.

Música Tropical Though its origins lie in the Caribbean and South America, several brands of *música tropical* or *música afroantillana* have become integral parts of the Mexican musical scene. Two types of dance music – *danzón*, originally from Cuba, and cumbia, from Colombia – both took deeper root in Mexico than in their original homelands (see the Dance section, following). Banda groups play a lot of cumbia, and leading Mexican exponents have included Sonora Dinamita and (before they split in the mid-1990s) Los Bukis, whose *Me Volví a Acordar de Ti* was the biggest-selling Mexican recording ever.

Canto Nuevo This is the name usually given in Latin America to what's called *nueva canción* in Spain and *nueva trova* in Cuba – troubadour-type folk songs, often with a protest theme and poetic lyrics, typically performed by singer-songwriters *(cantautores)* with a solitary guitar. Fernando Delgadillo and Alberto Escobar are leading exponents, while others such as Betsy Pecanins and the highly versatile Eugenia León have moved on to other styles such as norteño, ranchera and – in Pecanins' case – blues.

Dance

Indigenous Dance Colorful traditional indigenous dances are an important part of many Mexican fiestas. Many bear traces of pre-Hispanic ritual. There are hundreds of them, some popular in many parts of the country, others danced only in a single town or village. Nearly all require special costumes, sometimes including masks. Among the most superb costumes are those of the Zapotec Danza de las Plumas (Feather Dance), from Oaxaca state, and the Nahua Danza de los Quetzales (Quetzal Dance),

from Puebla state, which feature enormous feathered headdresses or shields.

Some dances have evolved from old fertility rites. Others tell stories of Spanish or colonial origin. The Danza de las Plumas represents the Spanish conquest of Mexico. *Moros y Cristianos* is a fairly widespread dance that reenacts the victory of Christians over Muslims in 15th-century Spain. The costumes of Los Viejitos (The Old Men), which can be seen in Pátzcuaro, Michoacán, originated in mockery of the Spanish, whom the local Tarasco people thought aged very fast.

Some dances are these days performed outside their religious context as simple spectacles. The Ballet Folklórico in Mexico City brings together traditional dances from all over the country. Other folkloric dance performances can be seen in several cities and at festivals such as the Guelaguetza, in Oaxaca on the last two Mondays of July, and the Atlixcáyotl, in Atlixco, Puebla, on the last Sunday in September, which gather performers from wide areas.

Latin Dance Caribbean and South American dance and dance music – broadly described as *música afroantillana* or *música tropical* – have become highly popular in Mexico. Basically this is tropical-style ballroom dancing, to percussion-heavy, infectiously rhythmic music that often includes electric guitars or brass. Mexico City has a dozen or more clubs and large dance halls devoted to this scene; *aficionados* can go to a different hall each night of the week, often with big-name bands and performers from the Caribbean and South America. One of the more formal, old-fashioned varieties of Latin dance is danzón, originally from Cuba and associated particularly with the port city of Veracruz. For danzón, high heels and a dress are de rigueur for women, as is a Panama hat for men. Steps are small, movement is from the hips down, and danzón can be danced only to danzón music. Cumbia, originally from Colombia but now with its adopted home in Mexico City, has set steps too but is livelier, more flirtatious and less structured than danzón: you move the top half of your body too.

Musically it rests on thumping bass lines with an addition of brass, guitars, mandolins and sometimes marimbas. *Salsa* developed out of the meeting in New York in the 1950s of jazz with son, cha-cha and rumba brought by immigrants from Cuba and Puerto Rico. Musically it boils down to brass (with trumpet solos), piano, percussion, singer and chorus – the dance is a hot one with a lot of exciting turns. *Merengue*, mainly from Colombia and Venezuela, is a cumbia/salsa blend with a hopping step; the rhythm catches the shoulders, and the arms go up and down. The music is strong on maracas, and its musicians go for puffed-up sleeves.

Literature

Mexico's best-known novelist internationally is probably Carlos Fuentes (born 1928), and his most highly regarded novel is *Where the Air is Clear*, written in the 1950s. Like his *Death of Artemio Cruz*, it's an attack on the failure of the Mexican Revolution. Fuentes' *Aura* is a magical book with one of the most stunning endings of any novel. *The Old Gringo* is a novel-form version of the mysterious disappearance of San Francisco journalist Ambrose Bierce while covering Pancho Villa during the Mexican Revolution.

In Mexico, Juan Rulfo is generally regarded as the country's supreme novelist. His *Pedro Páramo* (1955), set before and during the revolution, has been described as 'Wuthering Heights set in Mexico and written by Kafka.' Among younger writers, Laura Esquivel achieved a big success with *Like Water for Chocolate* (1989), a passionate love story interwoven with both fantasy and recipes (!), set in rural Mexico at the time of the revolution.

Octavio Paz (1914-98), a poet, essayist and winner of the 1990 Nobel Prize in Literature, wrote perhaps the most probing examination of Mexico's myths and the Mexican character in *The Labyrinth of Solitude* (1950).

For information on fiction and books about Mexico by non-Mexican authors, see Books in the Facts for the Visitor chapter.

SOCIETY & CONDUCT

Despite strong currents of machismo and nationalism, Mexicans are in general friendly, humorous, and helpful to visitors – the more so if you address them in Spanish, however rudimentary.

Traditional Culture

Traditional culture is strong in Mexico. The Catholic religion – with its calendar of saints' days and major festivals such as Semana Santa (Holy Week), Día de los Muertos (Day of the Dead, November 2), Día de la Virgen de Guadalupe (December 12) and Christmas – is one deep-rooted source of tradition. These events lead people to gather for the same processions and rituals, dance the same dances in the same costumes and create the same kind of special festival handicrafts year after year in traditions that evolve only slowly and in some cases go back hundreds of years.

The roots of another vital thread of tradition go back to before the arrival of Catholicism with the Spanish. This is the cultures of Mexico's many surviving indigenous peoples. In many cases these peoples' entire ways of life – from their colorful traditional costumes and the many traditional crafts they produce to the agricultural calendar they follow and their whole communalist social organization – are governed by traditions that are still in varying degrees pre-Hispanic.

Many Mexican traditions interweave indigenous and Hispanic influences. El Día de los Muertos, for instance, is in Catholic terms All Souls' Day, yet the manner in which it's celebrated in Mexico has strong overtones of ancestor-worship. Churches are often built on the sites of pre-Hispanic temples.

The faith that so many Mexicans have in their traditional form of medicine – a mixture of charms, chants, herbs, candles, incense – is further evidence of the strength of pre-Hispanic tradition.

You'll find more information on aspects of Mexican traditional culture in sections of this book such as Music, Dance and Religion in this chapter, Public Holidays & Special

Events in Facts for the Visitor, and the Artesanías special section, as well as in regional chapters where local traditions are covered.

The Family & Machismo Traditional family ties remain very strong in Mexico. Despite tensions, family loyalty is strong. One gringo who lived in Mexico for several years commented that Mexicans never really reveal their true selves outside the family: 'However well you think you know someone, you eventually realize that everything they say or do is an act of one kind or another – but that doesn't stop them from being friendly, loyal or charming.' An invitation to a Mexican home is quite an honor for an outsider; as a guest you will probably be treated royally and will enter a part of real Mexico to which few outsiders are admitted.

Not unconnected with Mexican family dynamics is the phenomenon of machismo, an exaggerated masculinity aimed at impressing other males as well as women. Its manifestations range from aggressive driving and the carrying of weapons to heavy drinking.

The macho image may have roots in Mexico's often-violent past and seems to hinge on a curious network of family relationships. Since it's not uncommon for Mexican husbands to have mistresses, wives in response lavish affection on their sons, who end up idolizing their mothers and, unable to find similar perfection in a wife, take a mistress . . . The strong mother-son bond also means that it's crucial for a Mexican wife to get along with her mother-in-law. And while the virtue of daughters and sisters has to be protected at all costs, other women – including foreign tourists without male companions – may be seen as fair game by Mexican men.

The other side of the machismo coin is women who emphasize their femininity. Such stereotyping, however, is not universal and is under pressure from more modern influences. The women's movement has made some advances since it began in the 1970s as a small middle-class affair, but abortion, for instance, remains illegal in most cases.

Dos & Don'ts

Most tourists and travelers in Mexico are assumed to be citizens of the USA. Away from tourist destinations, your presence may bring any reaction from curiosity or wonder to fear or, very occasionally, brusqueness. But any negative response will usually evaporate as soon as you show that you're friendly.

Language difficulties may be the biggest barrier to friendly contact: some people are shy or will ignore you because they don't imagine a conversation is possible; just a few words of Spanish will often bring smiles and warmth, probably followed by questions. Then someone who speaks a few words of English will pluck up the courage to try them out.

Some indigenous peoples adopt a cool attitude toward visitors: they have learned to mistrust outsiders after five centuries of exploitation. They don't like being gawked at by tourists and can be very sensitive about cameras: if in doubt about whether it's OK to take a photo, always ask first.

In general, it's recommended that women dress conservatively in towns and in off-the-beaten-track places – avoid shorts, sleeveless tops, etc. Everyone should lean toward the more respectful end of the dress spectrum when visiting churches.

Nationalism

Most Mexicans are fiercely proud of their own country at the same time as they despair of it ever being governed well. Their independent-mindedness has roots in Mexico's 11-year war for independence from Spain in the early 19th century and subsequent struggles against USA and French invaders. Any threat of foreign economic domination – as many Mexicans fear will result from NAFTA – is deeply resented. The classic Mexican attitude toward the USA is a combination of the envy and resentment that a poor neighbor feels for a rich one. The word *gringo*, incidentally, isn't exactly a compliment, but it's not necessarily an insult either: the term can simply be – and often is – a simple, un-value-laden synonym for 'American,' 'citizen of the USA.'

Time

The fabled Mexican attitude toward time – *'mañana, mañana…'* – has probably become legendary simply from comparison with the USA. But it's true, especially outside the big cities, that the urgency Europeans and North Americans are used to is often lacking. Most Mexicans value *simpatía* (congeniality) over promptness. If something is really worth doing, it gets done. If not, it can wait. Life should not be a succession of pressures and deadlines. According to many Mexicans, life in the 'businesslike' cultures has been de-sympathized. You may come away from Mexico convinced that the Mexicans are right!

Treatment of Animals

As in most countries where humans may not have enough to eat, animals in Mexico are rarely mollycoddled in the way they often are in wealthier societies. In general Mexicans view animals in terms of their direct practical use – as food, as beasts of burden and in the case of some wild animals, despite some protective legislation, as sources of money (the money they or their hides or shells or feathers or eggs will fetch if sold). Mexicans may not be as sensitive to animal welfare as some other cultures but they don't in general wantonly mistreat animals. Bullfighting and cockfighting, it may be argued, are evidence to the contrary; but such is the weight of tradition, ritual and preparation surrounding these activities, especially bullfighting, that Mexicans could hardly be expected to regard them as anything other than sport or art.

RELIGION
Roman Catholicism

About 90% of Mexicans profess Catholicism. Though its grip over emerging generations today is perhaps marginally less strong than over their predecessors, Catholicism's dominance is remarkable considering the rocky history that the Catholic Church has had in Mexico, particularly in the last two centuries.

The church was present in Mexico from the very first days of the Spanish conquest. Until independence it remained the second most important institution after the crown's representatives and was really the only unifying force in Mexican society. Almost everyone belonged to the church because, spirituality aside, it was the principal provider of social services and education.

The Jesuits were among the foremost providers and administrators, establishing missions and settlements throughout Mexico. Their expulsion from the Spanish empire in the 18th century marked the beginning of stormy church-state relations in Mexico. In the 19th and 20th centuries (up to 1940), Mexico passed numerous measures restricting the church's power and influence. The bottom line was money and property, both of which the church was amassing faster than the generals and political bosses. The 1917 Mexican constitution prevented the church from owning property or running schools or newspapers, and banned clergy from voting, from wearing clerical garb and from speaking out on government policies and decisions. Church-state relations reached their nadir in the 1920s, when the Cristeros (Catholic rebels) burned government schools, murdered teachers and assassinated a president, while government troops killed priests and looted churches. Most of the anti-church provisions in the constitution ceased to be enforced during the second half of the 20th century, and in the early 1990s President Salinas had them removed from the constitution. In 1992 Mexico finally established diplomatic relations with the Vatican.

The Mexican Catholic Church is one of Latin America's more conservative. Only in the south of the country have its leaders gotten involved in political issues such as human rights and poverty. The most notable figure in this regard is Samuel Ruiz, long-time bishop of San Cristóbal de Las Casas, who retired in 1999.

The Mexican church's most binding symbol is *Nuestra Señora de Guadalupe*, the dark-skinned Virgin of Guadalupe, a manifestation of the Virgin Mary who appeared to an indigenous Mexican in 1531 on a hill near Mexico City. The Guadalupe

The Virgin of Guadalupe

Virgin became a crucial link between Catholic and indigenous spirituality, and as Mexico grew into a mestizo society she became the most potent symbol of Mexican Catholicism. Today she is the country's patron, her blue-cloaked image is ubiquitous, and her name is invoked in religious ceremonies, political speeches and literature.

Other Christians
Around 5% of Mexicans profess other varieties of Christianity. Some are members of the Methodist, Baptist, Presbyterian or Anglican churches set up by American missionaries in the 19th century. Others were converted by a new wave of North American missionaries – this time of evangelical leanings – entering Mexico in the 20th century. Among these are the Wycliff Bible Translators, also known as the Summer Institute of Linguistics. In recent decades Pentecostal evangelical churches such as the Assembly of God and Church of God have gained many converts, particularly among the rural and indigenous peoples of southeast Mexico, sometimes leading to strife with Catholics.

Indigenous Religion
The missionaries of the 16th and 17th centuries won the indigenous people over to Catholicism as much by grafting it on to pre-Hispanic religions as by deeper conversion. Often old gods were simply identified with Christian saints, and the old festivals continued to be celebrated, much as they had been in pre-Hispanic times, on the nearest saint's day. Acceptance of the new religion was greatly helped by the appearance of the Virgin of Guadalupe in 1531.

Today, despite modern inroads into indigenous life, indigenous Christianity is still fused with more ancient beliefs. In some remote regions Christianity is only a veneer at most. The Huichol people of Jalisco have two Christs, but neither is a major deity. Much more important is Nakawé, the fertility goddess. The hallucinogenic drug peyote is a crucial source of wisdom in the Huichol world. Elsewhere, among peoples such as the Tarahumara and many Tzotzil people in highland Chiapas, drunkenness is an almost sacred element at festival times.

Even among the more orthodox Christian indigenous peoples it is not uncommon for spring saints' festivals, or the pre-Lent carnival, to be accompanied by remnants of fertility rites. The famous Totonac voladores (see the 'Voladores' in the Central Gulf Coast chapter) enact one such ritual. The Guelaguetza dance festival, which draws thousands of visitors to Oaxaca every summer, has roots in pre-Hispanic maize-god rituals.

In the traditional indigenous world almost everything has a spiritual dimension – trees, rivers, plants, wind, rain, sun, animals and hills have their own gods or spirits. Even Coca-Cola is believed to have supernatural powers by the Tzotzil people of San Juan Chamula, Chiapas.

Witchcraft, magic and traditional medicine survive. Illness is sometimes seen as a 'loss of soul' resulting from the sufferer's wrongdoing or from the malign influence of someone with magical powers. A soul can be 'regained' if the appropriate ritual is performed by a *brujo* (witch doctor) or *curandero* (curer).

Judaism
Jews make up 0.1% of Mexico's population. Most of them live in the state of México and Mexico City, where there are several synagogues.

LANGUAGE
The predominant language of Mexico is Spanish. Mexican Spanish is unlike Castilian Spanish, the language of much of Spain, in two main respects: in Mexico the Castilian lisp has more or less disappeared and numerous indigenous words have been adopted.

Travelers in cities, towns and larger villages can almost always find someone who speaks at least some English. All the same, it is advantageous and courteous to know at least a few words and phrases of Spanish. Mexicans will generally respond much more positively if you attempt to speak to them in their own language.

About 50 indigenous languages are spoken as their mother tongue by 7 million or more people in Mexico, of whom about 15% don't speak Spanish.

For a guide to Spanish pronunciation and vocabulary, see the Language chapter.

WILD MEXICO

Mexico is one of the most biologically diverse countries on earth. It's home to 1041 bird species, 439 mammals, 989 amphibians and reptiles, and about 26,000 plants – in each case, about 10% of the total number of species on our planet, on just 1.4% of the earth's land. Just a dozen or so countries, all in the tropics, harbor two-thirds of the earth's plant and animal species, and Mexico is among them. Many Mexican species are endemic (found nowhere else), including more than half of its reptiles and amphibians, and 139 of its mammals. Over one-third of all the world's marine mammals have been found in the Sea of Cortez. The southern state of Chiapas alone has some 10,000 plant species, more than 600 birds (twice as many as the USA) and 1200 butterflies (more than twice as many as the USA and Canada combined).

You're not likely to bump into much of Mexico's terrestrial wildlife, however, unless you make the effort to visit remote areas. Probably the most concentrated selection of purely Mexican wildlife is to be found at the zoo in Tuxtla Gutiérrez, Chiapas, which is devoted mainly to endangered species among the wide variety of fauna in that state. Parque-Museo La Venta, in Villahermosa, Tabasco, also has a good range of local wildlife. But as interest in Mexican nature increases, the possibilities for visiting interesting natural areas themselves are growing. Fascinating and beautiful areas that were once impossible for the nonspecialist to access are opening up, and a growing number of 'ecoturismo' firms offer their services to help you visit them.

Ecotourism has been a buzz word in Mexico for a few years. Some cynical opportunists use it to describe mass-tourism activities that threaten to destroy the very nature they feed off. One thinks, for instance, of some of the goings-on along the so-called 'Maya Riviera' south of Cancún. By contrast, visitors who want to experience Mexico's natural wonders in a more harmonious and sensitive manner will find enthusiastic help available from a good number of smaller-scale operators and organizations – including some run by local communities themselves. If you use such local services, the income you provide may well be helping to conserve ecosystems that would otherwise be threatened by less sustainable modes of extracting a livelihood. (See the Organized Tours section in the Getting Around chapter.)

The Wild Mexico map shows a selection of the best sites for observing Mexican flora, fauna and geological features (you'll find more information on most of them in the regional chapters).

Vegetation Zones

Above: Most of the world's cactus species are found in Mexico.

Northern Mexico is dominated by two deserts – the Desierto Sonorense (Sonoran Desert), west of the Sierra Madre Occidental, and the Desierto Chihuahuense (Chihuahuan Desert), occupying much of the Altiplano Central. The deserts are sparsely vegetated with cacti, agaves, yucca, scrub and short grasses. West of Monclova in Coahuila state, the Cuatrociénegas valley is an oasis in the desert, renowned for its varied wildlife, which includes dozens of endemic species including several each of turtle and fish. Both deserts stretch north into the USA; the Desierto Sonorense also extends down into Baja California (although Baja has a surprising range of other habitats too, and because of its isolation, rather specialized flora and fauna). Most of the world's 1000 or so cactus species are found in Mexico.

The Sierra Madre Occidental and Oriental, the Cordillera Neovolcánica (running east-west across the middle of the country), and the Sierra Madre del Sur still have some big stretches of pine forest and (at lower elevations) oak forest, though human occupation has stripped away much of the forest around the valleys.

Between the Desierto Chihuahuense and the Sierra Madre Occidental and Oriental, as well as in the northeast, a lot of land has been turned over to irrigation or grazing, or has become wasteland, but there are still natural grasslands dotted with mesquite, a hardy bush of the bean family.

The natural vegetation of much of low-lying southeast Mexico – from southern Veracruz to eastern Chiapas and on to Quintana Roo – is evergreen tropical forest – rain forest in parts. The forest is dense and diverse, with ferns, epiphytes, palms, tropical hardwoods such as mahogany, and fruit trees such as the mamey and the *chicozapote* (sapodilla), which yields *chicle* (natural chewing gum). Again, human impact has destroyed much: the largest remaining tropical forest area is the Selva Lacandona (Lacandón Jungle) in eastern Chiapas, and it too is vanishing – perhaps Mexico's biggest ecological tragedy of all. The Yucatán Peninsula changes from rain forest in the south to dry thorny forest in the north.

On the drier, western side of mainland Mexico – the western slopes of the Sierra Madre Occidental, the western and southern portions of the Cordillera Neovolcánica, and in much of the southern states of Oaxaca and Chiapas – there's deciduous and semideciduous tropical forest, less varied than the eastern tropical forests. Much of this plant community has in fact been turned into ranches and cropland.

Here and there in the southern half of the country, mountaintop pine forest that's often covered in clouds turns into cloud forest, an unusual environment with lush, damp vegetation and epiphytes growing on tree branches. The Sierra Norte of Oaxaca and El Triunfo Biosphere Reserve in Chiapas preserve some of Mexico's outstanding cloud forests.

Along the dry Pacific coastal plain, from the southern end of the Desierto Sonorense to the state of Guerrero, as well as on the northern Gulf Coast plain and in the northern Yucatán Peninsula, the predominant vegetation is thorn forest, composed of thorny bushes and small trees, including many acacias. Some of this flora occurs naturally, some occurs on overgrazed grassland or abandoned slash-and-burn farmland.

Fauna

Land Mammals & Reptiles

In the north, domesticated grazing animals have pushed the larger wild beasts, such as the puma (mountain lion), wolf, deer and coyote, into isolated, often mountainous, pockets. Raccoons, armadillos, skunks, rabbits and snakes are

still fairly common, however. The last four are found in much of the rest of the country too. Vampire bats live in deep sinkholes known as *sótanos* in the northeast and emerge at night to drink the blood of cattle and horses. In large numbers they can weaken animals, but otherwise they're harmless except when they carry diseases such as rabies.

The remaining tropical forests of the south and east still harbor (in places) howler and spider monkeys, jaguars, ocelots, tapirs, anteaters, peccaries (a type of wild pig), deer and some mean tropical reptiles, including boa constrictors. The big cats are reduced to isolated pockets mainly in eastern Chiapas, though they also exist around Celestún in Yucatán. You may well hear howler monkeys (early in the morning) and see spider monkeys near the Maya ruins at Palenque.

In all warm parts of Mexico you'll come across two harmless though sometimes alarming reptiles: the iguana, a lizard that can grow a meter or so long and comes in many different colors, and the gecko, a tiny, usually green lizard that may shoot out from behind a curtain or cupboard when disturbed. Geckos might make you jump, but they're good news – they eat mosquitoes. Less welcome are scorpions, also common in warmer parts of the country.

Marine Life

Mexico's coasts – from Baja California to Chiapas and from the northeast to the Yucatán Peninsula – are among the world's chief breeding grounds for sea turtles – see 'Mexico's Turtles: Not Saved Yet' in the Oaxaca State chapter.

Dolphins can be seen off much of the Pacific coast, while some wetlands, mainly in the south of the country, harbor crocodiles or caimans.

Baja California is a famous site for whale-watching in the early months of the year, but it's also a breeding ground for other big sea creatures such as sea lions and elephant seals.

Underwater life is richest along the Yucatán Peninsula's Caribbean coast, where there are coral reefs.

Top: These iguana's eyes are smiling.

Right: Endangered sea turtle hatchling, Isla Mujeres Turtle Farm

WILD MEXICO

UNITED STATES OF AMERICA

Desierto Sonorense

Desierto Chihuahuense

Chihuahua

Sea of Cortez

PACIFIC OCEAN

Sierra Madre Occidental

Altiplano Central

Puerto Vallarta

Guadalajara

Tijuana

Alpine Forests
2 Parque Nacional Sierra San Pedro Mártir
18 Parque Nacional Cumbres de Monterrey
29 Parque Nacional Desierto de los Leones
30 Parque Nacional Iztaccíhuatl-Popocatépetl
47 Parque Nacional Cañón del Sumidero

Ancient Volcanic Landscape
11 Reserva de la Biósfera El Pinacate
    y Gran Desierto de Altar

Birds
1 Parque Nacional Constitución de 1857
13 Alamos
15 Creel
18 Parque Nacional Cumbres de Monterrey
22 Mexcaltitán
23 San Blas
25 Reserva de la Biósfera Sierra Gorda
26 Lagoons near Manzanillo
32 Celestún
33 Río Lagartos
34 Área de Protección de Flora y Fauna
    Yum Balam
35 Isla Contoy
41 Pie de la Cuesta
43 Parque Nacional Lagunas de Chacahua
44 Laguna de Manialtepec
51 Laguna Miramar
52 Reserva de la Biósfera Montes Azules
53 Reserva de la Biósfera El Triunfo
54 Reserva de la Biósfera La Encrucijada

Butterflies
28 Santuario de Mariposas El Rosario

Canyons
2 Parque Nacional Sierra
    Pedro Mártir
14 Parque Nacional Cascada
    de Basaseachi
16 Barranca del Cobre

Cloud Forests
19 Reserva de la Biósfera El Cielo
42 Sierra Norte
53 Reserva de la Biósfera El Triunfo

Desert Oasis
17 Área de Protección de Flora
    y Fauna Cuatrociénegas

Dolphins
10 Cabo San Lucas
24 Bahía de las Banderas
45 Puerto Escondido
46 Mazunte

Elephant Seals & Sea Lions
3 Islas San Benito
4 Isla Cedros

Mangroves
54 Reserva de la Biósfera
    La Encrucijada

0   100   200 km
0   60   120 miles

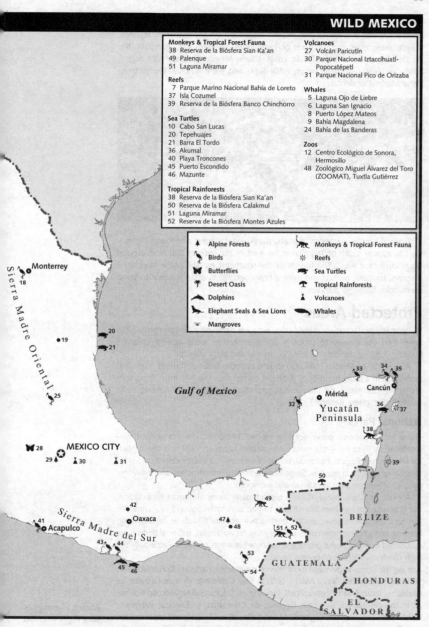

Monkeys & Tropical Forest Fauna
38 Reserva de la Biósfera Sian Ka'an
49 Palenque
51 Laguna Miramar

Reefs
 7 Parque Marino Nacional Bahía de Loreto
37 Isla Cozumel
39 Reserva de la Biósfera Banco Chinchorro

Sea Turtles
10 Cabo San Lucas
20 Tepehuajes
21 Barra El Tordo
36 Akumal
40 Playa Troncones
45 Puerto Escondido
46 Mazunte

Tropical Rainforests
38 Reserva de la Biósfera Sian Ka'an
50 Reserva de la Biósfera Calakmul
51 Laguna Miramar
52 Reserva de la Biósfera Montes Azules

Volcanoes
27 Volcán Paricutín
30 Parque Nacional Iztaccíhuatl-
    Popocatépetl
31 Parque Nacional Pico de Orizaba

Whales
 5 Laguna Ojo de Liebre
 6 Laguna San Ignacio
 8 Puerto López Mateos
 9 Bahía Magdalena
24 Bahía de las Banderas

Zoos
12 Centro Ecológico de Sonora,
    Hermosillo
48 Zoológico Miguel Álvarez del Toro
    (ZOOMAT), Tuxtla Gutiérrez

🐾 Alpine Forests
🐦 Birds
🦋 Butterflies
🌴 Desert Oasis
🐬 Dolphins
🦭 Elephant Seals & Sea Lions
〰 Mangroves

🐒 Monkeys & Tropical Forest Fauna
✳ Reefs
🐢 Sea Turtles
🌴 Tropical Rainforests
🌋 Volcanoes
🐋 Whales

Monterrey

Sierra Madre Oriental

Gulf of Mexico

Mérida

Cancún

Yucatán
Peninsula

MEXICO CITY

Oaxaca

Sierra Madre del Sur

Acapulco

BELIZE

GUATEMALA

HONDURAS

EL
SALVADOR

Birds

Coastal Mexico is a major bird habitat, especially on the estuaries, lagoons, islands, mangroves and wetlands of Tamaulipas, northern Veracruz state, the Yucatán Peninsula and the Pacific coast. Inland Mexico abounds with eagles, hawks and buzzards, while innumerable ducks and geese winter in the northern Sierra Madre Occidental.

Tropical species – trogons, parrots, parakeets, tanagers and many others – start to appear south of Tampico in the east of the country and from around Mazatlán in the west. The forests of the southeast are still home to colorful macaws, toucans, parrots and even a few quetzals. Yucatán is home to some spectacular flamingo colonies.

Protected Areas

Sadly, many protected areas in Mexico are so in name only. Governments have never had the money to properly police protected areas against unlawful hunting, logging, farming, grazing or animal and plant collection.

About 8% of Mexico (144,000 sq km) is under federal, state or municipal protection in a large number of different categories. The two most important protective categories are Parque Nacional (National Park) and Reserva de la Biósfera (Biosphere Reserve).

National Parks

There are 64 national parks, totaling around 14,000 sq km. Many are tiny – smaller than 10 sq km – and most were created between 1934 and 1940, often for their archaeological, historical, scenic or recreational value rather than for biological or ecological reasons. Some have no visitor infrastructure and draw few people, others are alive with weekend picnickers.

Mexico's national parks officially restrict many forms of human exploitation, but little attempt has ever been made to find alternative sources of income for the local people. Consequently, destructive activities such as tree-cutting, hunting and grazing have continued illegally. Nevertheless, national parks have succeeded in giving some protection to some big tracts of forest – especially the high coniferous forests of central Mexico.

Among the better-known and most interesting national parks are Constitución de 1857 and Sierra San Pedro Mártir, both in Baja California; Pico de Orizaba, La Malinche, Iztaccíhuatl-Popocatépetl, Nevado de Toluca and Nevado de Colima, all in the central volcanic belt; Lagunas de Chacahua, in Oaxaca; Palenque, Cañón del Sumidero and Lagos de Montebello, all in Chiapas; and Dzibilchaltún and Tulum, on the Yucatán Peninsula. Marine national parks, created in the

Above: Flamingoes take flight near Río Lagartos, Yucatán

1990s to protect aquatic ecosystems, include the Cozumel reefs and the west coast of Isla Mujeres, both off the Yucatán Peninsula, and the Bahía de Loreto in Baja California Sur.

Biosphere Reserves

Biosphere reserves came into being as a result of a 1970s initiative by UNESCO (United Nations Educational, Scientific & Cultural Organization), which recognized that it was impractical for developing countries to take productive areas out of economic use. Biosphere reserves encourage local people to take part in planning and developing sustainable economic activities outside the reserves' strictly protected zonas núcleo (core areas). Today there are 23 biosphere reserves in Mexico, covering 87,610 sq km. They focus on whole ecosystems with genuine biodiversity, ranging from deserts through dry and temperate forests to tropical forests and coastal areas. Sian Ka'an Biosphere Reserve on the Yucatán Peninsula, is a UNESCO World Heritage Site, and El Vizcaíno Biosphere Reserve in Baja California Sur includes whale sanctuaries that constitute another World Heritage Site.

Mexican biosphere reserves have had varied success. Sian Ka'an is one of the most successful: here some villagers have turned from slash-and-burn farming and cattle grazing to drip irrigation and multiple crops, thus conserving the forest and increasing food yields; lobster fishers have seen lobster numbers cease to fall after they accepted a two-month off-season for egg-laying and began returning pregnant females to the sea. Controlled tourism is seen as an important source of income in several biosphere reserves.

Biosphere reserves tend to be harder to access than national parks. Among the most visited or most interesting ones are El Vizcaíno and Sierra de la Laguna, in Baja California Sur; El Pinacate y Gran Desierto de Altar, in Sonora; El Cielo, in Tamaulipas; Montes Azules, La Encrucijada and El Triunfo, all in Chiapas; and Calakmul and Sian Ka'an, on the Yucatán Peninsula.

Information Sources

Some useful and fascinating books on Mexico's environment and plant and animal life – including practical ecotourism guidebooks – are mentioned in the Books section of the Facts for the Visitor chapter. The website Eco Travels in Latin America (www.planeta.com) brims with invaluable information and links for those wanting to experience Mexican flora and fauna firsthand. For readers of Spanish, the site of CONABIO, Mexico's national biodiversity commission (www.conabio.gob.mx), is another excellent resource.

Facts for the Visitor

HIGHLIGHTS

Reducing the marvels of Mexico to a finite 'best of' list is a tough task and any result is bound to be very subjective. Travel highlights are personal and much depends on the company you're in, the food you just ate and so on. And Mexico has so many marvels … but here goes:

Coasts

Baja California – fine beaches around the resorts of La Paz, San José del Cabo and Cabo San Lucas; diving at Mulegé and Cabo San Lucas; kayaking, diving, snorkeling at Loreto; surfing near San José del Cabo and Cabo San Lucas

Pacific Coast – Mazatlán, still-picturesque Puerto Vallarta and Acapulco are classic larger resorts with lots of fine beaches; San Blas, Chamela, Cuyutlán, Paraíso, Puerto Escondido, Mazunte, San Agustinillo, Zipolite, Puerto Ángel, Puerto Arista and Barra de Zacapulco are smaller (in some cases very small) places with good, sometimes untouched beaches and more local character; Bahías de Huatulco is an in-between case – an incipient mega-resort along a string of still beautiful bays; there's great surfing at San Blas and Puerto Escondido

Gulf Coast – Veracruz: revel in the tropical port atmosphere

Yucatán Peninsula – Cancún has beautiful white sand and azure Caribbean waters but unsympathetic mega-resort development; nearby Isla Mujeres is a lot more laid back and has good snorkeling and diving; Playa del Carmen offers good beaches, good snorkeling and diving, good food and groovy nightlife; at Cozumel island there's legendary diving; Tulum presents you with ancient Mayan ruins as well as several kilometers of palm-fringed white sand and cabañas; the Xcalak area is little developed, with pretty beaches and access to the large but little-explored coral atoll Banco Chinchorro

Archaeological Sites

In the north, head for Paquimé at Casas Grandes, Chihuahua, an adobe-built trading center of 900-1340 AD.

Near Mexico City don't miss Teotihuacán, with its giant Pyramids of the Sun and Moon. Elsewhere in central Mexico, the hilltop ruins at Xochicalco, Tula with its fearsome warrior statues, and Cacaxtla with its colorful battle frescoes are all well worth journeying to. El Tajín, near the Gulf Coast, was a classic Veracruz capital and has the very unusual Pyramid of the Niches.

In the southern state of Oaxaca, the large ancient Zapotec capital Monte Albán has a superb hilltop setting. Farther east, in Chiapas, you enter the Maya region: Palenque is a site of exquisite architecture surrounded by emerald rain forest, while the more remote Yaxchilán and Bonampak (the latter with famous murals) are in the midst of the Lacandón Jungle.

On the Yucatán Peninsula, don't miss the great, well-restored city of Chichén Itzá, which fuses Mayan and central Mexican styles, or Uxmal with its elaborate temples dedicated to the Mayan rain god Chac. With time at your disposal, you can travel the Puuc Route of four separate Maya sites near Uxmal, and seek out other important but more remote Maya sites in the Xpujil vicinity or deep in the jungle at Cobá.

Colonial Cities

Mexico is blessed with many charming, historic, Spanish-built towns full of centuries-old carved-stone architecture, plazas with splashing fountains and often lively modern cultural and entertainment scenes. Many of their fine old courtyarded mansions are now charming hotels. Outstanding colonial cities include Zacatecas, with its stupendous cathedral; San Miguel de Allende, home to many artists and expatriots; Guanajuato, a city in a ravine with a great student life; Puebla, with perhaps the greatest concentration of colonial buildings in the country; Taxco, the hillside 'silver town' of winding, cobbled streets; Cuernavaca, famed for its language schools; Oaxaca, remote yet cosmopolitan with beautifully clear southern light; San Cristóbal de Las Casas, a big travelers' center in the cool highlands of Chiapas; and

Mérida, the proud capital of Yucatán state with its narrow streets and shady parks.

Small Towns

South of Monterrey, don't miss Real de Catorce, a mountain silver-mining town that went 'ghost' but is now coming back to life. In northwest Mexico are Creel, surrounded by pine forests in the midst of the awesome Barranca del Cobre (Copper Canyon), and Álamos, with cobbled streets lined by Moorish-influenced buildings created by 16th-century Andalusian architects (a good spot for nature-lovers, too).

East of Mexico City, Cuetzalan sits in a mountainous but lush coffee-growing region and is famed for its Sunday market attended by indigenous Nahua people in traditional dress. North of the capital is Tequisquiapan, a charming little spa of clean, colonial streets and brilliant purple bougainvillea. Westward lies Pátzcuaro, a highland town with stately colonial architecture at the heart of indigenous Purépecha country, famous for its Day of the Dead celebrations; and south of the capital there's Tepoztlán, legendary birthplace of the ancient plumed serpent god Quetzalcóatl, in a valley beneath jagged cliffs and now an international new-age energy center.

Nature

Watch whales at Laguna Ojo de Liebre, Laguna San Ignacio or Puerto López Mateos in Baja California, or off Puerto Vallarta. Observe sea turtles near Puerto Vallarta, Zihuatanejo, Mazunte, or Tepehuajes or El Tordo in Tamaulipas.

Climb or just gaze at the dormant and not-so-dormant peaks of central Mexico's volcanic belt: Pico de Orizaba, La Malinche, Iztaccíhuatl, Popocatépetl, Nevado de Toluca and Paricutín.

See teeming birdlife on lagoons and estuaries near the Pacific coast, as at Mexcaltitán, San Blas, Puerto Vallarta, Manzanillo, Playa Azul, Zihuatanejo, the Lagunas de Chacahua and Manialtepec and the Reserva de la Biósfera La Encrucijada. On the Yucatán Peninsula bird-lovers should head for Celestún and Río Lagartos (both famous for flamingoes), Isla Contoy and San Felipe. Inland biosphere reserves famous for their birds include El Cielo in Tamaulipas (northeast Mexico) and the rare cloud forests of El Triunfo, Chiapas.

Swim amid the majesty of Mexico's northern deserts at the spring-fed pools of Cuatrociénegas. Visit pristine Laguna Miramar in the rain forests of Chiapas' Lacandón Jungle and seek out howler and spider monkeys, toucans, macaws and even jaguars.

Marvel at trees and earth turned orange by millions of monarch butterflies at El Rosario sanctuary in Michoacán.

Explore the spectacular Barranca del Cobre (Copper Canyon) area in the Sierra Madre Occidental in Mexico's northwest – actually 20 canyons, some over 2000m deep.

Also see the Wild Mexico special section in the Facts about Mexico chapter.

Museums

Mexico has some great museums. Our favorites include:

Museo Nacional de Antropología, Mexico City – the king of Mexican museums, full of stupendous relics of pre-Hispanic Mexico

Museo Nacional de Arte, Mexico City – check José María Velasco's landscapes

Papalote Museo del Niño, Mexico City – hands-on children's museum – real fun

Museo Frida Kahlo, Mexico City – home of the haunted artist

RICHARD I'ANSON

Maya Room, Museo Nacional de Antropología

Museo-Léon Trotsky, Mexico City – revolutionary's last refuge

Museo Dolores Olmedo Patiño, Mexico City – magnificent collection of Diego Rivera and Frida Kahlo art, amid beautiful gardens

Museo Amparo, Puebla – fine pre-Hispanic and colonial art and artifacts in modern presentation

Museo de Cuauhnáhuac, Cuernavaca – history and cultures of Mexico exhibited in former fortress of conquistador Hernán Cortés

Museo de los Seris, Kino Nuevo, Sonora – fascinating exhibits on the indigenous Seri people

Museo Histórico de la Revolución Mexicana, Chihuahua – Pancho Villa's old headquarters, now a museum of the Mexican Revolution

Museo de Historia Mexicana, Monterrey – creative, interactive survey of the whole of Mexican history – and rain forest ecology

Museo de las Aves, Saltillo – over 670 species of stuffed birds in convincing dioramas (Mexico ranks sixth in the world in avian diversity)

Instituto Cultural de Cabañas, Guadalajara – chapel with 50-odd masterpiece frescoes by 20th-century muralist José Clemente Orozco

Museo Pedro Coronel, Zacatecas – art from Asia, Africa, ancient Mexico, Rome, Greece and Egypt, and 20th-century Europe

Museo Rafael Coronel, Zacatecas – astonishing display of over 2000 masks used in Mexican traditional dances and rituals

Museo de las Mómias, Guanajuato – corpses disinterred from a public cemetery, a quintessential example of Mexico's obsession with death

Museo de Antropología de la Universidad Veracruzana, Jalapa – the world's best display of ancient Olmec artifacts

Museo de las Culturas de Oaxaca – extensive and beautifully conceived telling of Oaxaca's history, in a well-restored monastery

Parque-Museo La Venta, Villahermosa – excellent open-air combined Olmec archaeological museum and zoo of Tabasco wildlife

Museo Regional de Antropología, Mérida – history of Yucatán Peninsula in a grandiose early-20th-century palace

Museo de la Cultura Maya, Chetumal – bold modern museum covering all of Mayan culture

Grab Bag

Perhaps Mexico's most unforgettable journey is the Ferrocarril Chihuahua al Pacífico, otherwise known as the Copper Canyon

Railway, which traverses the awesome Barranca del Cobre (see Nature, above).

When it comes to big cities, you can't beat the Really Big Three – Mexico City, Guadalajara and Monterrey – for, well, big-city atmosphere . . . bustle, nightlife, the sense of things happening. Guadalajara, the 'most Mexican' city, a center of music, art and more, is, at heart, a colonial city. Monterrey, by contrast, is the most *norteamericano* city, with the raw energy of a brash industrial capital. And Mexico City? It's ancient, modern, beautiful, ugly, it's rich, poor, enormous. With nearly a quarter of the nation's people, it's the center of Mexico's culture, economy, politics . . . It's got everything – except clean air.

Finally, four highlights you'll encounter throughout Mexico:

Music – Mexico is rarely without music: marimbas on the plaza in Veracruz, buskers on the Mexico City metro, brass bands on bandstands everywhere, mariachis tootling on the street in Saltillo, up-and-coming rockers at Rockotitlán in Mexico City, a *son* trio in a Cuetzalan doorway, Plastilina Mosh. Tune in and turn on. And make sure you hear Café Tacuba.

Handicrafts – Mexicans love color and are endlessly inventive with their hands – see the Artesanías special section.

Fiestas – fireworks, parades, music, fun – there's something happening, somewhere, every day (see Public Holidays & Special Events, later in this chapter)

Mexicans – *¡simpáticos, hombre!*

PLANNING
When to Go

Any time is a good time to visit Mexico, though the coastal and lowland regions, particularly in the southern half of the country, are pretty hot from May to September and can get unpleasantly humid. The interior of the country has a more moderate climate than the coasts. In fact it's sometimes decidedly chilly in the north and the central highlands in winter (November to February).

July and August are peak holiday months for both Mexicans and foreigners. Other big holiday seasons are mid-December to early January (for both foreigners and Mexicans), and a week either side of Easter (for Mexicans). At these times the coastal resorts attract big tourist crowds, room prices go up in popular places and rooms and public transportation are heavily booked, so advance reservations are often advisable.

Maps

Nelles Verlag, Hallwag and Rand McNally all produce decent country maps of Mexico at scales of around 1:2,500,000 (1cm: 25km). The AAA's (American Automobile Association's) *Mexico* is also useful. For road atlases, see Maps in the Car & Motorcycle section in the Getting Around chapter. Some regional and a few city maps are available outside Mexico. For an Internet source, try the Adventurous Traveler Bookstore (www.adventuroustraveler.com).

City, town and regional maps of varying quality are often available free from local tourist offices in Mexico, and you can often find commercially published ones at bookstores or newsstands. INEGI (Instituto Nacional de Estadística, Geografía e Informática) publishes a large-scale series of 1:50,000 (1cm:500m) maps covering all of Mexico. INEGI has an office in every Mexican state capital where you can buy these maps, and at least three shops in Mexico City (also see the Maps section in the Mexico City chapter).

What to Bring

The clothing you bring should depend on how, when and where you want to travel, and how you would like to be perceived by Mexicans. You might want to conform to Mexican norms.

Mexicans tend to dress informally but conservatively. Even in the hot regions, men wear long trousers. A *guayabera* – a fancy shirt decorated with tucks and worn outside the belt – substitutes for a jacket and tie on more formal occasions. Many women wear stylish dresses, blouses or skirts.

The local people do not expect you to dress as they do, but you should know that, except in beach resorts, shorts and T-shirts are the marks of the tourist. In the hotter

regions, these plus light cotton trousers or skirts, trainers or sandals, and light blouses or shirts should see you through. Jeans are often uncomfortably heavy in warm, humid areas but are good for upland areas in the cooler months. Bring a light sweater or jacket – even on the coast you may want it for evening boat rides. A light rain jacket, preferably loose-fitting, is good to have from October to May and is a necessity from May to October. If you plan to party it up at night in cities or resorts, don't forget suitable clothing for that purpose.

In lowland areas such as the Pacific and Gulf Coasts, Yucatán and Tabasco, everyone should have a hat and sunblock. If your complexion is particularly fair or you burn easily, consider wearing long sleeves and long pants.

Basic toiletries such as shampoo, shaving cream, razors, soap and toothpaste are readily available throughout Mexico except in small or remote villages. You should bring your own contact lens solution, tampons, contraceptives and insect repellent – they are available in Mexico, but not always readily so.

Other recommended items are sunglasses, a flashlight (torch), a pocketknife, a traveler's alarm clock, a couple meters of cord, a small sewing kit, a money belt or pouch that you can wear under your clothes, a small padlock and a small Spanish dictionary. You can pick up a hat when you get to Mexico.

For carrying it all, a backpack is the most convenient if you'll be doing much traveling. You can make it reasonably theft-proof with small padlocks. A light daypack, too, is useful.

RESPONSIBLE TOURISM

A responsible tourist is, perhaps, one who treats the visited place as if it were home. Would you wander into your hometown church during a service and start taking flash photos? If the drains at your home were blocked, would you put toilet paper down them to clog them further?

Most places you're likely to go in Mexico welcome tourism as a money earner, but be sensitive with indigenous peoples who have some delicate traditions and unusual beliefs. Respect their ceremonies. Many have a deep dislike of being photographed – only snap them if you're sure (probably having asked them) that they won't mind.

As for Mexico's environment, well, a lot of it's a mess, but everyone has an obligation to help stop it getting worse. We'll assume that you've decided the planet can cope with you flying in an airplane to Mexico and riding buses once you're there. Once in Mexico, you can certainly do your bit by, for instance, not buying turtle, iguana or black coral products, and patronizing ecotourism projects that aim to preserve or restore the environments they visit. As the saying goes, take only photos, leave only footprints – but don't leave footprints on the coral. Many of the most ecologically conscious tourism enterprises in Mexico are community-run, and community initiatives enable you also to ensure that any profit made from your visit goes to the people you have visited. Another way you can do this is to buy crafts and commodities direct from producer cooperatives, producing villages or from the artisans themselves.

TOURIST OFFICES
Local Tourist Offices

Just about every place of interest to tourists has a national, state or city/town tourist office. They can be helpful with maps and brochures, and often some staff members speak English.

You can call the Mexico City office of the national tourism ministry SECTUR (☎ 5-250-01-23, 800-903-92-00) at any time – 24 hours a day, seven days a week – for information or help in English or Spanish.

Tourist Offices Abroad

In the USA and Canada you can call ☎ 800-446-3942 for Mexican tourist information. You can also contact a Mexican Government Tourism Office at the following locations:

Chicago
(☎ 312-606-9252) 300 North Michigan Ave, 4th Floor, 60601

Houston
(☎ 713-780-8395) 1400 West Office Drive, 77042

Los Angeles
(☎ 213-351-2076) 2401 W 6th St, 5th Floor, 90057

Miami
(☎ 305-718-4091) 1200 NW 78th Avenue No 208, 33126-1817

Montreal
(☎ 514-871-1052) 1 Place Ville Marie, Suite 1931, H3B 2C3

New York
(☎ 212-821-0304) 21 East 63rd St, 3rd Floor, 10021

Toronto
(☎ 416-925-2753) 2 Bloor St West, Suite 1502, M4W 3E2

Vancouver
(☎ 604-669-2845) 999 West Hastings St, Suite 1110

Look for the following Mexican Government Tourism Offices in Europe:

France
(☎ 01 42 61 51 80) 4 rue Notre Dame des Victoires, 75002 Paris

Germany
(☎ 069-253-509) Wiesenhuettenplatz 26, D60329 Frankfurt-am-Main

Italy
(☎ 06-487-2182) Via Barberini 3, 00187 Rome

Spain
(☎ 91-561-18-27) Calle Velázquez 126, Madrid 28006

UK
(☎ 020-7734-1058) 60-61 Trafalgar Square, 3rd floor, London WC2N 5DS

VISAS & DOCUMENTS

Visitors to Mexico should have a valid passport. Visitors of some nationalities have to obtain visas, but others (when visiting as tourists) require only the easily obtained Mexican government tourist card. Because the regulations sometimes change, it's wise to confirm them at a Mexican Government Tourism Office or Mexican embassy or consulate before you go. Several Mexican embassies and consulates, and foreign embassies in Mexico, have websites with useful information on tourist permits, visas, travel with minors and so on – see 'Embassies & Consulates' – but they don't all agree with each other, so you should back up any Internet findings with some phone calls. The Lonely Planet website (www.lonelyplanet.com) has links to updated visa information.

Travelers under 18 who are not accompanied by *both* parents need special documentation – see Under-18 Travelers.

Passport

Though it's not recommended, US tourists can enter Mexico without a passport if they have official photo identification, such as a driver's license, plus some proof of their citizenship, such as a birth certificate certified by the issuing agency or their original certificate of naturalization (not a copy). Citizens of other countries who are permanent residents in the USA have to take their passport and Permanent Resident Alien Card.

Canadian tourists may enter Mexico with official photo identification plus proof of citizenship, such as a birth certificate or notarized affidavit of it. Naturalized Canadian citizens, however, require a valid passport.

It is much better to have a passport, because officials are used to passports and may delay people who have other documents. This applies to officials you have to deal with on reentry to the USA or Canada as well as to Mexican officials: the only proof of citizenship recognized by US or Canadian immigration is a passport or (for non-naturalized citizens) a certified copy of your birth certificate. In Mexico you will often need your passport when you change money, as well.

Citizens of other countries need to show a passport valid for at least six months after they arrive in Mexico.

Dual Nationals Mexicans with dual nationality must carry proof of both their citizenships and must identify themselves as Mexican when entering or leaving Mexico. They are considered Mexican by the Mexican authorities but are not subject to compulsory military service.

Visas

Citizens of the USA, Canada, EU countries, Australia, New Zealand, Norway, Switzerland, Iceland, Israel, Japan, Argentina and Chile are among those who do not require visas to enter Mexico as tourists. But they must obtain a Mexican government tourist card – see Travel Permits. Countries whose nationals *do* have to obtain visas include South Africa, Brazil and most eastern European nations – check well ahead of travel with your local Mexican embassy or consulate.

Non-US citizens passing through the USA on the way to or from Mexico, or visiting Mexico from the USA, should check their US visa requirements.

Travel Permits

The Mexican tourist card – officially the Forma Migratoria para Turista (FMT) – is a small paper document that you must get stamped by Mexican immigration when you enter Mexico and must keep till you leave. The card is available free of charge at official border crossings, international airports and ports, and often from airlines, travel agencies, Mexican consulates and Mexican Government Tourism Offices. At the US-Mexico border you won't usually be given one automatically – you have to ask for it.

At many US-Mexico border crossings you don't *have* to get the card stamped at the border itself, as the Instituto Nacional de Migración (INM, National Immigration Institute) has control points on the highways into the interior where it's also possible to do it – but it's advisable to do it at the border itself, in case there are difficulties elsewhere.

One section of the card – to be filled in by the immigration officer – deals with the length of your stay in Mexico. You may be asked a couple of questions about how long you want to stay and what you'll be doing, but normally you will be given the maximum 180 days if you ask for it. It's always advisable to put down more days than you think you'll need, in case you are delayed or change your plans.

Look after your tourist card, as it will probably be checked when you leave the country.

Mexican Embassies & Consulates Abroad

Unless otherwise noted, details are for embassies or their consular sections.

Argentina
(☎ 01-4821-7172) Larrea 1230, 1117 Buenos Aires

Australia
(☎ 02-6273-3905) 14 Perth Ave, Yarralumla, Canberra, ACT 2600

Consulate: (☎ 02-9326-1311) Level 1, 135-153 New South Head Rd, Edgecliff, Sydney, NSW 2027

Austria
(☎ 01-310-7383) Turkenstrasse 15, 1090 Vienna

Belgium
(☎ 02-629-0711) Av Franklin Roosevelt 94, 1050 Brussels

Belize
(☎ 02-30-193/194) 20 North Park St, Fort George Area, Belize City

Brazil
(☎ 061-244-1011) SES Av das Nacoes Lote 18, 70412-900 Brasilia

Canada
(☎ 613-233-8988/6665) 45 O'Connor St, Suite 1500, Ottawa, ON K1P 1A4

Consulate: (☎ 514-288-2502) 2000 rue Mansfield, Suite 1015, Montreal, PQ H3A 2Z7

Consulate: (☎ 416-368-2875) Commerce Court West, 199 Bay St, Suite 4440, Toronto, ON M5L 1E9

Consulate: (☎ 604-684-1859) 810-1130 West Pender St, Vancouver, BC V6E 4A4

Costa Rica
(☎ 225-4430) Avenida 7a No 1371, San José

Denmark
(☎ 3961-0500) Strandvejen 64E, 2900 Hellerup, Copenhagen

El Salvador
(☎ 243-0445) Calle Circunvalación y Pasaje No 12, Colonia San Benito, San Salvador

France
(☎ 01 53 70 27 40) 9 rue de Longchamps, 75116 Paris

Consulate: (☎ 01 42 61 51 80) 4 rue Notre Dame des Victoires, 75002 Paris

Germany
(☎ 0228-914-8620) Adenauerallee 100, 53113 Bonn

Consulate: (☎ 030-324-9047) Kurfurstendamm 72, 10709 Berlin

Consulate: (☎ 069-299-8750) Hochstrasse 35-37, 60330 Frankfurt-am-Main

Guatemala
(☎ 333-7254) Edificio Centro Ejecutivo, 15ª Calle No 3-20, 7° Nivel, Zona 10, Guatemala City

Consulate: (☎ 331-8165) 13ª Calle No 7-30, Zona 9, Guatemala City

Consulate: (☎ 763-1312) 9a Avenida No 6-19, Zona 1, Quetzaltenango

Honduras
(☎ 32-0138) Avenida República de México 2402, Colonia Palmira, Tegucigalpa

Ireland
(☎ 01-260-0699) 43 Ailesbury Rd, Ballsbridge, Dublin 4

Israel
(☎ 03-544-6705) Grand Beach Hotel, 250 Hayarkon, 63113 Tel Aviv

Italy
(☎ 06-440-2309) Via Lazzaro Spallanzani 16, 00161 Rome

Consulate: (☎ 02-7602-0541) Via Cappuccini 4, 20122 Milan

Japan
(☎ 03-3580-8734) 2-15-1 Nagata-cho, Chiyoda-ku, Tokyo 100

Netherlands
(☎ 070-360-2900) Nassauplein 17, 2585 EB The Hague

New Zealand
(☎ 04-472-5555) 8th Floor, 111-115 Customhouse Quay, Wellington

Nicaragua
(☎ 0-278-1860) Carretera a Masaya Km 4.5, 25 varas arriba (next to Optica Matamoros), Altamira, Managua

Mexican Embassies & Consulates Abroad

Norway
(☎ 22 43 11 65)
Drammensveien 108B,
0244 Oslo

South Africa
(☎ 12-342-6190) Southern
Life Plaza, 1st Floor, CNR
Schoeman & Festival Streets,
Hatfield, 0083 Pretoria

Spain
(☎ 91-369-2814)
Carrera de San Jerónimo 46,
28014 Madrid

Consulate: (☎ 93-201-1822)
Avinguda Diagonal 626,
08021 Barcelona

Consulate: (☎ 95-456-3944)
Calle San Roque 6,
41001 Sevilla

Sweden
(☎ 08-661-2213) Grevgatan
3, 11453 Stockholm

Switzerland
(☎ 31-351-4060)
Bernestrasse 57, 3005 Bern

UK
(☎ 020-7235-6393)
8 Halkin St,
London SW1X 7DW

USA
(☎ 202-728-1694) 1911
Pennsylvania Ave NW,
Washington, DC 20006

Consulate: (☎ 202-736-
1000) 2827 16th St NW,
Washington, DC 20009

Mexican Consulates in the USA

There are consulates in many other US cities besides Washington, DC, particularly in the border states.

Arizona
Douglas (☎ 520-364-3107)
Nogales (☎ 520-287-2521)
Phoenix (☎ 602-242-7398)
Tucson (☎ 520-882-5595)

California
Calexico (☎ 760-357-3863)
Fresno (☎ 209-233-3065)
Los Angeles
 (☎ 213-351-6800)
Sacramento
 (☎ 916-441-2987)
San Bernardino
 (☎ 909-889-9837)
San Diego
 (☎ 619-231-9741)
San Francisco
 (☎ 415-392-6576)
San Jose (☎ 408-294-8334)

Colorado
Denver (☎ 303-331-1110)

Florida
Miami (☎ 305-716-4979)
Orlando (☎ 407-422-0514)

Georgia
Atlanta (☎ 404-266-2233)

Illinois
Chicago (☎ 312-855-1380)

Louisiana
New Orleans
 (☎ 504-522-3596)

Massachusetts
Boston (☎ 617-426-4942)

Michigan
Detroit (☎ 313-567-7709)

Missouri
St Louis (☎ 314-436-3426)

New Mexico
Albuquerque
 (☎ 505-247-2139)

New York
New York
 (☎ 212-217-6400)

Oregon
Portland (☎ 503-274-1442)

Pennsylvania
Philadelphia
 (☎ 215-922-4262)

Texas
Austin (☎ 512-478-9031)
Brownsville
 (☎ 956-542-5182)
Corpus Christi
 (☎ 361-882-3375)
Dallas (☎ 214-630-1604)
Del Rio (☎ 830-775-2352)
Eagle Pass (☎ 830-773-9255)
El Paso (☎ 915-533-3644)
Houston (☎ 713-271-6800)
Laredo (☎ 956-723-0990)
McAllen (☎ 956-686-4684)
Midland (☎ 915-687-2334)
San Antonio
 (☎ 210-227-9145)

Utah
Salt Lake City
 (☎ 801-521-8502)

Washington state
Seattle (☎ 206-448-6819)

Embassies & Consulates in Mexico

All embassies are in Mexico City. Many countries also have consulates in other cities around Mexico.

As a tourist, it's important to realize what your embassy can and can't do. Generally speaking, it won't be much help in emergencies if the trouble you're in is remotely your own fault. Remember that you are bound by the laws of the country you are in. Your embassy will not be sympathetic if you end up in jail after committing a crime locally, even if such actions are legal in your own country.

In genuine emergencies you might get some assistance, but only if other channels have been exhausted. For example, if you need to get home urgently, a free ticket home is exceedingly unlikely – the embassy would expect you to have insurance. If you have all your money and documents stolen, it might assist in getting a new passport, but a loan for onward travel is out of the question.

The following is a selective list of embassies in Mexico City. They often keep limited business hours – usually something like Monday to Friday from 9 or 10 am to 1 or 2 pm – and close on both Mexican and their own national holidays. But many provide 24-hour emergency telephone contact. If you're telephoning from outside Mexico City, dial the long-distance access code 01 before the number given below. If you're visiting your embassy, it's best to call ahead to check hours and confirm that the address you're heading for is the right one for the service you want. The addresses below include the *colonias* (neighborhoods) of Mexico City in which the embassies are located and any metro stations convenient to them.

Australia
Embassy: (☎ 5-531-52-25) Rubén Darío 55, Polanco; Australians needing out-of-hours assistance can call reverse-charges the Australian number ☎ 61-2-6261-1446; open 8.30 am to 2 pm Monday to Friday, 3 to 5 pm Monday to Thursday; Ⓜ Polanco or Auditorio
Consulate: Guadalajara (☎ 3-615-74-18) López Cotilla 2030

Belize
Embassy: (☎ 5-520-12-74) Bernardo de Gálvez 215, Lomas de Chapultepec

Canada
Embassy: (☎ 5-724-79-00, ☎ 800-706-29-00) Schiller 529, Polanco, 400m north of the Museo Nacional de Antropología; open 9 am to 1 pm and 2 to 5 pm Monday to Friday; Ⓜ Polanco

Consulates:
Acapulco (☎ 7-484-13-05, fax 7-484-13-06) Plaza Marbella, Local 23
Guadalajara (☎ 3-616-56-42) Hotel Fiesta Americana, Local 30, Aceves 225
Mazatlán (☎ 69-13-73-20) Hotel Playa Mazatlán, Zona Dorada
Oaxaca (☎ 9-513-37-77) Pino Suárez 700, Local 11B
Puerto Vallarta (☎ 3-222-53-98) Zaragoza 160, Plaza Principal
Tijuana (☎ 6-684-04-61) Gedovius 5-202

France
Embassy: (☎ 5-282-97-00) Lafontaine 32, Polanco; open 9 am to 1 pm Monday to Friday; Ⓜ Auditorio
Consulates:
Acapulco (☎ 7-469-12-08, fax 7-484-51-03) Hyatt Regency Hotel, La Costera 1

Guadalajara (☎ 3-616-55-16) López Mattes Nte 484
Mazatlán (☎ 69-85-12-28) Domínguez 1008, Colonia Centro
Mérida (☎ 9-925-2291, fax 925-7009) Calle 33B No 528
Veracruz (☎ 2-935-06-49)

Germany
Embassy: (☎ 5-283-22-00) Lord Byron 737, Polanco; open 9 am to noon Monday to Friday; Ⓜ Polanco
Consulates:
Acapulco (☎ 7-484-18-60, fax 7-484-38-10) Antón de Alaminos 26, Fraccionamiento Costa Azul
Guadalajara (☎ 3-613-96-23) Corona 202 at Madero
Mazatlán (☎ 69-81-20-77) Jacarandas 10, Colonia Loma Linda
Mérida (☎ 9-981-2976) Calle 7 No 217
Tampico-Ciudad Madero (☎ 1-212-98-17)

Embassies & Consulates in Mexico

Guatemala

Embassy: (☎ 5-540-75-20)
Avenida Explanada 1025,
Lomas de Chapultepec

Consulates:
Chetumal (☎ 9-832-8585)
Avenida Héroes de
Chapultepec 354
Comitán (☎ 9-632-04-91)
1ª Calle Sur Pte 26
Guadalajara (☎ 3-811-15-03)
Mango 1440
Tapachula (☎ 9-626-12-52)
2ª Oriente 33

Netherlands

Embassy: (☎ 5-258-99-21,
emergency ☎ 5-505-07-52)
Avenida Vasco de Quiroga
3000, 7° piso, Santa Fe; open
8.30 am to 4 pm Monday to
Friday

Consulates:
Acapulco (☎ 7-485-90-50
ext 3001) Hotel Costa Club
Acapulco, La Costera 123
Guadalajara (☎ 3-673-22-11)
Avenida Vallarta 5500,
Lomas Universidad
Mérida (☎ 9-924-3122, 9-
924-4147) Calle 64 No 418
Tampico-Ciudad Madero
(☎ 1-219-28-59)

New Zealand

Embassy: (☎ 5-281-54-86)
Lagrange 103, 10° piso, Los
Morales

UK

Embassy: (☎ 5-207-20-89)
Río Lerma 71, Colonia
Cuauhtémoc, north of the
Monumento a la Indepen-
dencia; open 8.30 am to
3.30 pm Monday to Friday;
consular section at rear (Río
Usumacinta 30) open 9 am
to 2 pm Monday to Friday;
Ⓜ Insurgentes

Consulates:
Acapulco (☎ 7-484-17-56,
fax 7-481-25-33) Casa
Consular, Centro de Conven-
ciones, La Costera 4455
Guadalajara (☎ 3-616-06-29)
Eulogio Parra 2539
Mérida (☎ 9-928-6152,
fax 9-928-3962)
Calle 53 No 489
Tampico-Ciudad Madero
(☎ 1-212-97-84)
Veracruz (☎ 2-931-12-85)

USA

Embassy: (☎ 5-209-91-00,
always attended) Paseo de la
Reforma 305 at Río Danubio,
Colonia Cuauhtémoc, not far
from the Monumento a la
Independencia; open 9 am to
5 pm Monday to Friday,
closed on Mexican and US
holidays; visa office (☎ 01-
900-849-3737) at side of
embassy on Río Danubio,
open 7 to 10 am Monday to
Friday except holidays;
Ⓜ Insurgentes

Consulates:
Acapulco (☎ 7-469-05-56,
fax 7-484-03-00)
Hotel Continental Plaza,
La Costera 121, Local 14
Ciudad Juárez (☎ 16-11-30-
00) López Mateos 924 Nte
Guadalajara (☎ 3-825-27-00)
Progreso 175
Matamoros (☎ 88-12-44-02)
Calle 1 No 2002
Mazatlán (☎ 69-16-58-89)
Loaiza 202, Zona Dorada
Mérida (☎ 9-925-5409,
fax 9-925-6219) Paseo de
Montejo 453
Monterrey (☎ 8-345-21-20)
Avenida Constitución 411 Pte
Nuevo Laredo (☎ 87-14-05-
12) Allende 3330
Oaxaca (☎ 9-514-30-54)
Alcalá 201
Puerto Vallarta (☎ 3-222-00-
69) Zaragoza 160,
Plaza Principal
San Luis Potosí (☎ 4-812-15-
28) Avenida Carranza 2076
San Miguel de Allende
(☎ 4-152-23-57)
Plaza Golondrinas
Tijuana (☎ 6-681-74-00)
Tapachula 96

Embassy & Consulate Websites

Many Mexican embassies and consulates and foreign embassies in Mexico City have websites. Links
to most of them can be found on http://mexico.web.com.mx/mx/embajadas.html. Two particularly
useful sites, with tourist information and data on Mexican visas and tourist permits, are those of the
Mexican embassy in Washington, DC (www.embassyofmexico.org) and the Mexican consulate in
New York (www.quicklink.com/mexico).

Tourist cards are not needed for visits shorter than 72 hours within the frontier zones along Mexico's northern and southern borders. The frontier zone is the territory between the border itself and the INM's control points on the highways leading into the Mexican interior (usually 20 to 30km from the border). A few extra zones are also exempt from the tourist card requirement for visits of less than 72 hours, including the Tijuana-Ensenada corridor in Baja California; San Felipe, Baja California; and the Sonoita-Puerto Peñasco corridor in Sonora.

A tourist card only permits you to engage in what are considered to be tourist activities (including sports, health, artistic and cultural activities). In recent years Mexico has expelled – especially from Chiapas – dozens of foreigners it considered to be pursuing activities not permitted by a tourist card. If the purpose of your visit is, for instance, journalistic or to do with human rights observation you will very likely need a visa.

The Tourist Fee Since 1999, foreign tourists (of any age) and business travelers visiting Mexico have been charged a fee of 150 pesos (about US$16 at the time of writing) called the Derecho para No Inmigrante (DNI, Nonimmigrant Fee). If you enter Mexico by air, the fee is included in the price of your air ticket.

If you enter by land you must pay the fee at a branch of any of 27 Mexican banks listed on the back of your tourist card, at any time before you reenter the frontier zone on your way out of Mexico (or before you check in at an airport to fly out of Mexico). It makes sense to get the job done as soon as possible, and at least some Mexican border posts have on-the-spot bank offices where you can do so.

When paying at a bank, you need to present your tourist card or business visitor card, which will be stamped to prove that you have paid. This will probably be checked when you leave the country.

Tourists only have to pay the fee once in any 180-day period. You are entitled to leave and reenter Mexico as many times as you like within 180 days without paying again. A similar multi-entry rule applies to business

travelers, but their limit is 30 days, after which they have to pay the fee again. If you are going to return within the stipulated period, retain your stamped tourist/business visitor's card when you leave Mexico.

The fee does not have to be paid by people visiting Mexico for less than 72 hours and who remain in seaports or within the frontier zone or certain nearby exempted areas: Tijuana-Ensenada, Sonoita-Puerto Peñasco, Ciudad Juárez-Paquimé, Piedras Negras-Santa Rosa, and Reynosa-China-Presa El Cuchillo.

Tourist Card Extensions & Lost Cards If the number of days given on your tourist card is for some reason less than the 180-day maximum, its validity may be extended one or more times, at no cost, up to the maximum. To get a card extended you have to apply to the INM, which has offices in many towns and cities. The procedure is free and usually accomplished in a few minutes; you'll need your passport, tourist card, photocopies of the important pages of these documents, and – at some offices – evidence of 'sufficient funds.' A major credit card is usually OK for the latter, or an amount in traveler's checks which could vary from US$100 to US$1000 depending on which office you are dealing with.

Most INM offices will not extend a card until a few days before it is due to expire – don't bother trying earlier.

If you lose your card or need further information, contact the SECTUR tourist office in Mexico City (☎ 5-250-01-23, 800-903-92-00) or your embassy or consulate. Your embassy or consulate may be able to give you a letter enabling you to leave Mexico without your card, or at least an official note to take to your local INM office, which will have to issue a duplicate.

Travel Insurance

A travel insurance policy to cover theft, loss (including plane tickets), delay or cancellation of flights, and medical problems is a good idea. It's also a good idea to buy insurance as early as possible. If you buy it the week before you fly, you may find, for example, that you're not covered for delays to your flight caused by strikes.

Mexican medical treatment is generally inexpensive for common diseases and minor treatment, but if you suffer some serious medical problem, you may want to find a private hospital or fly out for treatment. Travel insurance can cover the costs of that. Some US health insurance policies stay in effect (at least for a limited time) if you travel abroad, but it's worth checking exactly what you'll be covered for in Mexico. For people whose medical insurance or national health systems don't extend to Mexico – which includes most non-Americans – a travel policy is advisable.

You may prefer a policy that pays doctors or hospitals directly rather than requiring you to pay on the spot and claim later. If you have to claim later, make sure you keep all documentation. Some policies ask you to call back (reverse charges) to a center in your home country, where an immediate assessment of your problem is made.

Some policies offer lower and higher medical-expense options; the higher ones are chiefly for countries such as the USA, which have extremely high medical costs. There is a wide variety of policies available, so check the small print.

Some policies specifically exclude 'dangerous activities,' which can include scuba diving, motorcycling and even trekking. A locally acquired motorcycle license is not valid under some policies. Check that the policy covers ambulances or an emergency flight home.

Driver's License & Permits

If you're thinking of renting a vehicle in Mexico, take your driver's license and a major credit card with you. For more information on rentals, see the Getting Around chapter. For the paperwork involved in taking your own vehicle into Mexico, see the Getting There & Away chapter.

Hostel, Student, Youth & Teacher Cards

An HI (Hostelling International) card or a membership card of a national youth hostel association will save you paying for US$2

'welcome stamps' for your first six nights at hostels in the REMAJ group and may bring you a US$1 discount in AMAJ group hostels (see Accommodations, later in this chapter). Take your hostel card along if you have one, but it's not worthwhile to get one specially for a Mexico trip.

The ISIC student card, the GO25 card for any traveler aged 12 to 25, and the ITIC card for teachers can all help you obtain reduced-price air tickets to or from Mexico at student and youth-oriented travel agencies. In Mexico, notices at museums, archaeological sites and so on usually state that reduced entry prices for students are only for those with Mexican education system credentials, but in practice the ISIC card will sometimes get you a reduction. It may also get you discounts on some bus tickets and in a few hostel-type accommodations. The GO25 and ITIC are less recognized in Mexico, but still worth taking along.

All three cards can be obtained in Mexico. One outlet is the youth/student travel agency Mundo Joven, with offices in Mexico City, Cuernavaca, Guadalajara, León, Puebla, Monterrey and Querétaro (see Travel Agencies in the Mexico City chapter). You need proof of your student/teacher status for the ISIC/ITIC.

Under-18 Travelers

Every year numerous parents try to run away from the USA or Canada to Mexico with their children to escape the legal machinations of the children's other parent. To prevent this, minors (people under 18) entering Mexico without one or both of their parents may be – and often are – required to show a notarized consent form, signed by the absent parent or parents, giving permission for the young traveler to enter Mexico. A form for this purpose is available from Mexican consulates. In the case of divorced parents, a custody document may be acceptable instead. If one or both parents are dead, or the traveler has only one legal parent, a notarized statement saying so may be required.

These rules are aimed primarily at visitors from the USA and Canada but apparently apply to all nationalities. Procedures vary from country to country; contact a Mexican consulate to find out exactly what you need to do.

Photocopies

All important documents (passport data pages and visa pages, birth certificate, vehicle papers, credit or bank cards, insurance papers, air tickets, driver's license, traveler's check receipts or serial numbers, etc) should be photocopied before you leave home. Leave one copy with someone at home and keep another with you, separate from the originals. When you get to Mexico, add a photocopy of your tourist permit and, if you're driving, vehicle import papers.

CUSTOMS

Drivers entering Mexico (except Baja California or going as far as Puerto Peñasco in Sonora state or within the border zone elsewhere, which extends 20 to 30km into mainland Mexico) must have vehicle permits and should have Mexican insurance – see the Getting There & Away chapter.

Things that visitors are allowed to bring into Mexico duty-free include items for personal use, such as clothing, footwear and toiletries; medicine for personal use, with prescription in the case of psychotropic drugs (medicines that can alter perception or behavior); one still or video or movie camera; up to 12 rolls/reels of film or video-cassettes; one portable computer; and, if you're 18 or older, 3L of wine, beer or liquor and 400 cigarettes. These limits are not always applied very strictly.

The normal customs inspection routine when you enter Mexico is to complete a customs declaration form (which lists duty-free allowances), then choose between going through a goods-to-declare channel or a nothing-to-declare channel. Those declaring items have their belongings searched, and duty is collected. Those not declaring items have to pass a full-size traffic signal. The signal responds randomly: a green light lets you pass without inspection, a red light means your baggage will be searched.

MONEY

Currency

Mexico's currency is the peso. The peso is divided into 100 centavos. Coins come in denominations of five, 10, 20 and 50 centavos and one, two, five, 10, 20 and 50 pesos, and there are notes of 10, 20, 50, 100, 200 and 500 pesos.

The $ sign is used to refer to pesos in Mexico. The designations 'N$' and 'NP' (both for *nuevos pesos*) and 'MN' (*moneda nacional*) all refer to pesos. Prices quoted in US dollars will normally be written 'US$5,' '$5 Dlls' or '5 USD' to avoid misunderstanding.

Coins and notes minted between 1993 and 1995 bear the wording 'nuevos pesos' (new pesos), or the abbreviation N$. They are worth exactly the same as more recent coins and notes which simply say 'pesos' or $.

Since the peso's exchange value is unpredictable, prices in this book are given in US dollar equivalents.

Exchange Rates

The peso has been relatively stable since the currency crisis of 1994-95, when it lost 60% of its value in three months. Exchange rates as this book went to press were:

country	unit		N$
Australia	A$1	=	5.71 pesos
Belize	BZ$1	=	4.66 pesos
Canada	C$1	=	6.35 pesos
Euro	€1	=	9.00 pesos
France	FF1	=	1.37 pesos
Germany	DM1	=	4.60 pesos
Guatemala	Q1	=	1.21 pesos
Japan	¥10	=	8.81 pesos
New Zealand	NZ$1	=	4.56 pesos
UK	UK£1	=	14.65 pesos
USA	US$1	=	9.31 pesos

Exchanging Money

The easiest money in Mexico is a major international credit card or debit card. Cards such as Visa, American Express and Master-Card (Eurocard, Access) are accepted by virtually all airlines, car rental companies and travel agents in Mexico, and by many hotels, restaurants and shops.

You can use major credit cards and some bank cards, such as those on the Cirrus and Plus systems, to withdraw cash pesos from ATMs (bank cash machines, which are very common in Mexico) and over the counter at banks. ATMs are generally the easiest source of cash. Despite the handling fee that may be charged to your account, you win by using ATMs because you get a good exchange rate and avoid the commission you would pay when changing cash or traveler's checks.

Mexican banks call their ATMs by a variety of names – usually something like *caja permanente* or *cajero automático*. Each ATM displays the cards it will accept. If an ATM refuses to give you money, simply try another ATM nearby.

To guard against robbery when using ATMs, try to use them during working hours and choose ones that are securely inside a bank building, rather than ones open to the street or enclosed only by glass.

Traveler's Checks & Cash If you have a credit card or bank card, as a backup you should still take along some major-brand traveler's checks (best denominated in US dollars), or – less desirable for security reasons – cash US dollars. If you don't have a credit or bank card, use US-dollar traveler's checks. American Express is a good brand to have because it's recognized everywhere, which can prevent delays. American Express in Mexico City maintains a 24-hour hotline (☎ 5-326-27-00) for lost American Express traveler's checks and cards; you can call it collect from anywhere in Mexico.

You should be able to change non-US-dollar checks and currency (especially Canadian dollars) in main cities, but it can require some time-consuming hassles, and in smaller cities and towns you may get poor exchange rates or be unable to exchange at all.

Banks & Casas de Cambio You can exchange money in banks or at *casas de cambio* ('exchange houses,' often single-window kiosks). Banks go through a more time-consuming procedure than casas de cambio and usually have shorter exchange hours (typically 9 am to 3 or 4 pm Monday to Friday). Casas de cambio can easily be found in just about every large or medium-size town and in many smaller ones. They're quick and often open evenings or weekends, but some may not accept traveler's checks, which rarely happens in banks.

Exchange rates vary a little from one bank or casa de cambio to another. Different rates are also often posted for *efectivo* (cash) and *documento* (traveler's checks).

If you have trouble finding a place to change money, particularly on a weekend, you can always try a hotel – though the exchange rate won't be the best.

International Transfers Should you need money wired to you in Mexico, an easy and quick method is the Western Union 'Dinero en Minutos' (Money in Minutes) service. It's offered by the approximately 300 Elektra electronics stores around Mexico (most are open 9 am to 9 pm daily), by the *telégrafos* (telegraph) offices in many cities, and by some other shops – all are identified by black-and-yellow signs bearing the words Western Union and Dinero en Minutos. Your sender pays the money at their nearest Western Union branch, along with a fee, and gives the details on who is to receive it and where. When you pick it up, take along photo identification. Western Union has offices worldwide; information can be obtained at ☎ 5-721-30-80 or 5-546-73-61 in Mexico, ☎ 800-325-6000 in the USA, or at www.westernunion.com.

Security

Ideally, when you're out and about, carry only what you'll need that day. Leave the rest in the hotel's *caja fuerte* (safe). If there isn't a safe, you have to decide whether it's better to carry your funds with you or try to secrete them in your room. Baggage that you can lock up is an advantage here. It's also a good idea to divide your funds into several stashes kept in different places. See Dangers & Annoyances, later in this chapter, for more tips on safeguarding your money.

Costs

With a few exceptions such as Baja California, the city of Monterrey and along the Yucatán Peninsula's Caribbean coast (in all of which rooms can cost double what they do elsewhere), a single budget traveler in Mexico can expect to pay US$12 to US$25 a day for the basics of camping or staying in budget accommodations and eating two meals a day in restaurants. Add in other costs (snacks, purified water and soft drinks, entry to archaeological sites, long-distance buses, etc), and you'll spend more like US$20 to US$35 a day. If there are two or more of you sharing rooms, costs per person drop considerably. Double rooms are often only a dollar or two more than singles, and triples or quadruples only slightly dearer than doubles.

In the middle range you can live well in most of Mexico for US$30 to US$50 per person per day, even in the large cities and expensive resorts. In most places two people can easily find a clean, modern room with private bath and TV for US$25 to US$35 and have the rest to pay for food, admission fees, transport and incidentals.

At the top of the scale are a few hotels and resorts that charge upwards of US$200 for a room, and restaurants where you can pay US$50 per person, but you can also stay at very comfortable smaller hotels for US$40 to US$75 a double and eat extremely well for US$20 to US$40 per person per day.

These figures do not take account of extra expenses like internal airfares or car rentals (which you're more likely to need if you're on a quick trip – see the Getting Around chapter for more information), or of any shopping you do in Mexico – which you should certainly budget for!

Tipping & Bargaining

In general, workers in small, cheap restaurants don't expect much in the way of tips, while those in expensive resort establishments expect you to be lavish in your largesse. Tipping in the resorts frequented by foreigners (Acapulco, Cancún, Cozumel) is up to US levels of 15%; elsewhere 10% is usually plenty. If you stay a few days in one place, you should leave up to 10% of your room costs for the people who have kept your room clean (assuming they *have*). A porter in a mid-range hotel would be happy with US$1 for carrying two bags. Taxi drivers don't generally expect tips unless they provide some special service, but gas station attendants do (US$0.25 to US$0.50).

Though you can attempt to bargain down the price of some hotel rooms, especially in cheaper places and in the off-season, the rates are normally fairly firm. In markets bargaining is the rule, and you may pay much more than the going rate if you accept the first price quoted. You should also bargain with drivers of unmetered taxis.

Taxes

Mexico's Impuesto de Valor Agregado (Value-Added Tax), abbreviated IVA ('EE-bah'), is levied at 15%. By law the tax must be included in virtually any price quoted to you and should not be added afterward. Signs in shops and notices on restaurant menus often state *'IVA incluido.'* Occasionally they state instead that IVA must be added to the quoted prices.

Impuesto Sobre Hospedaje (ISH, 'ee-ESS-e-AHCH-e,' the Lodging Tax) is levied on the price of hotel rooms. Each Mexican state sets its own rate, but in most it's 2%.

Most budget accommodations include both IVA and ISH in quoted prices (though it's sometimes worth checking). In top-end hotels a price may often be given as, say, 'US$100 *más impuestos*' ('plus taxes'), in which case you must add about 17% to the figure. When in doubt, ask, *'¿Están incluidos los impuestos?'* ('Are taxes included?')

Prices in this book all, to the best of our knowledge, include IVA and ISH. See the Getting There & Away and Getting Around chapters for details of taxes on air travel. See Visas & Documents earlier in this chapter for details of the US$16 tourist fee, payable by all tourists.

POST & COMMUNICATIONS
Postal Rates

An airmail letter or postcard weighing up to 20g costs US$0.45 to the US or Canada, US$0.55 to Europe and US$0.60 to Australasia. Heavier items weighing between 20g and 50g cost US$0.75, US$0.85 and US$1 respectively.

Sending Mail

Almost every town in Mexico has an *oficina de correos* (post office) where you can buy stamps and send or receive mail. They're usually open Saturday mornings as well as long hours Monday to Friday.

Delivery times are elastic, and packages in particular sometimes go missing. If you're sending something by airmail, clearly mark it 'Vía Aérea.' Registered *(certificado* or *registrado)* service helps ensure delivery and costs just US$0.80 extra for international mail. An airmail letter from Mexico to the USA or Canada can take four to 14 days to arrive (but don't be surprised if it takes longer). Mail to Europe may take between one and three weeks, to Australasia a month or more.

If you're sending a package internationally from Mexico, be prepared to open it for customs inspection at the post office – take packing materials with you, or don't seal it till you get there.

Express Mail & Couriers The Mexpost express mail service, available at some post offices, supposedly takes three working days to anywhere in the world; it costs US$12 to send up to 500g to the US or Canada, or US$15.50 to Europe.

For assured and speedy delivery, you can use one of the expensive international courier services, such as United Parcel Service (UPS, ☎ 5-228-79-00, 800-902-92-00), Federal Express (☎ 800-900-11-00) or DHL (☎ 5-345-70-00). Packages weighing up to 500g cost about US$20 to the US or Canada or US$25 to Europe.

Receiving Mail

You can receive letters and packages care of a post office if they're addressed as follows (for example):

Jane SMITH (last name in capitals)
Lista de Correos
Acapulco
Guerrero 00000 (post code)
MEXICO

When the letter reaches the post office, the name of the addressee is placed on an alphabetical list, which is updated daily. If you can, check the list yourself – it's often pinned on the wall – because the letter may be listed under your first name instead of your last. To claim your mail, present your passport or other identification. There's no charge; the snag is that many post offices hold 'Lista' mail for only 10 days before returning it to the sender. If you think you're going to pick mail up more than 10 days after it has arrived, have it sent to (for example):

Jane SMITH (last name in capitals)
Poste Restante
Correo Central
Acapulco
Guerrero 00000 (post code)
MEXICO

Poste Restante may hold mail for up to a month, but there is no posted list of what has been received. Again, there's no charge for collection.

If you have an American Express card or American Express traveler's checks, you can have mail sent to you c/o any of the 50-plus American Express offices in Mexico (the Mexico City office holds mail for two months before returning it to the sender). Take along your card or a traveler's check to show when you collect the mail.

Inbound mail usually takes as long to arrive as outbound mail does, and international packages coming into Mexico may go missing, just like outbound ones.

Telephone

Local calls are cheap. International calls can be very expensive – but they needn't be if you call from the right place at the right time.

The Mexican telephone system is being opened up to competition but this makes little practical difference to travelers so far, except that you should beware of some public pay phones with exorbitant call charges.

There are three main types of places you can place a call from. The cheapest is usually a public pay phone. A bit more expensive is a *caseta de teléfono* or *caseta telefónica* – a call station, maybe in a shop or restaurant, where an on-the-spot operator connects the call for you and you take it in a booth. The third option is to call from your hotel, but hotels can – and do – charge what they like for this service. It's nearly always cheaper to go elsewhere.

Mexican Telephone Area Codes & Numbers

Mexican area codes and numbers were all being changed in 1999-2000. In each case the last one or two digits of the area code were lopped off and transferred to the start of the number. For example the area code for the town of Tlaxcala used to be 246, and all Tlaxcala numbers had five digits. Now the Tlaxcala area code is 2 and all numbers have seven digits, starting with 46. Mexico City used to have the area code 5 and all Mexico City numbers had seven digits. Now Mexico City has no area code and all its numbers have eight digits, starting with 5.

In practice the changes make no difference to what you dial on a long-distance call, but they do make a difference to what you dial on local calls.

These changes were being made gradually by groups of towns and cities through 1999 and 2000. In this book, for places where the change was made in 1999 we give the new area code (immediately beneath the city or town heading) and use the new numbers. Where the change was due to be made in 2000 we give the old telephone numbers – but readers will find a boxed note explaining the change in the introductory paragraphs on the city or town in question.

Telephone numbers given in this book's introductory chapters, or in city or town sections other than the city or town they are located in, are preceded by their area code. Phone numbers given in their own city or town sections are not.

Public Pay Phones These are common in towns and cities: you'll usually find some at airports, bus stations, and around the main square of any sizable town. Most work OK. Pay phones are operated by a number of different companies: the most common, and most reliable on costs, are those marked with the name of the country's biggest phone company, Telmex. Telmex pay phones work on *tarjetas telefónicas* or *tarjetas Ladatel* (phone cards), which come in denominations of 30, 50 or 100 pesos (about US$3, US$5 and US$10). These cards are sold at many kiosks and shops – look for the blue-and-yellow sign reading '*De Venta Aquí Ladatel.*' 'Ladatel' means *teléfono de larga distancia* (long distance telephone), but these phones work for both local and long-distance calls.

Especially in parts of Mexico frequented by US tourists, you may notice a variety of other pay phones that advertise that they accept credit cards or that you can make easy collect calls to the USA on them. While some of these phones are doubtless fair value, there are some on which very high rates – as high as US$23 for the first minute – have been charged. We suggest being very sure about what you'll pay before making a call on a non-Telmex phone.

Casetas Casetas de teléfono can be more expensive than Telmex pay phones, but not always so – and you don't need a phone card to use them, and they eliminate street noise. Many offer similar off-peak discounts – for instance 50% off domestic long-distance calls and 33% off international calls at night and for much of the weekend.

Casetas usually have a telephone symbol outside, or signs saying '*teléfono,*' 'Lada' or 'Larga Distancia.' In Baja California they are known as *cabinas*.

Prefixes, Codes & Costs When dialing a call yourself in Mexico, you need to know what *prefijo* (prefix) and *claves* (country or area codes) to include before the number. Mexican area codes and numbers were all being changed in 1999-2000 (see 'Mexican Telephone Area Codes & Numbers').

In the following table, the third column represents the approximate cost per minute of calls from Telmex payphones.

call to	prefix & codes	cost
City/Town You Are In	No Prefix or Code	US$0.05
Other City/Town in Mexico	01 + Area Code	US$0.40
Other Countries	00 + Country Code + Area Code	US$1.25 (USA or Canada), US$2.50 (Europe or Australasia)

So if you're in Mexico City and you want to call the Mexico City number 5-876-54-32, just dial 5-876-54-32. To call from Mexico City to the Oaxaca number 517-65-43, dial 01, then the Oaxaca area code 9, then 517-65-43. (If calling from one town to another with the same area code, you may still have to dial 01 and the area code.)

To call the New York City number 987-6543 from Mexico, dial ☎ 00, then the US country code 1, then the New York City area code 212, then 987-6543.

If you need to speak to a domestic operator, call ☎ 020; for an international operator, call ☎ 090. For Mexican directory information, call ☎ 040.

Mexican toll-free numbers – ☎ 800 followed by seven digits – always require the ☎ 01 prefix. You can call these numbers from Telmex pay phones without inserting a telephone card.

International Country Codes

Australia ☎ 61	Guatemala ☎ 502
Belize ☎ 501	Italy ☎ 39
Canada ☎ 1	New Zealand ☎ 64
Cuba ☎ 53	Spain ☎ 34
France ☎ 33	UK ☎ 44
Germany ☎ 49	USA ☎ 1

✿✿✿✿✿✿✿✿✿✿✿✿✿

Most US toll-free numbers are ☎ 800 or 888 followed by seven digits. Most US and Canada toll-free numbers can be called from either of the two countries. Some US and Canada toll-free numbers can also be reached from Mexico (dial ☎ 001 before the 800), but you will probably have to pay for the call.

North American Calling Cards If you have an AT&T, MCI or Sprint card, or a Canadian calling card, you can use them for calls from Mexico to the USA or Canada by dialing the access numbers below. You can check with your phone company before going to Mexico about costs and exactly what procedures you'll have to follow. Normally, after dialing the access number you either have to enter your calling card number or follow voice prompts or operator instructions:

AT&T	☎ 001-800-462-4240
MCI	☎ 001-800-674-7000
Sprint	☎ 001-800-877-8000
AT&T Canada	☎ 001-800-123-0201
Bell Canada	☎ 001-800-010-1990

Warning: If you get an operator who asks for your Visa or MasterCard number instead of your calling card number, or says the service is unavailable, hang up. There are various scams in which calls are rerouted to super-expensive credit-card phone services.

International Calling Cards There's a wide range of international calling cards. Lonely Planet's eKno Communication Card provides budget international calls, a range of messaging services, free email and travel information. You can join online at www.ekno.lonelyplanet.com or by phone from Mexico by dialing the eKno access number (☎ 001-800-514-0287).

Collect Calls A *llamada por cobrar* (collect call) can cost the receiving party much more than if *they* call *you*, so you may prefer to find a phone where you can receive an incoming call, then pay for a quick call to the other party to ask them to call you back.

If you do need to make a collect call, you can do so from pay phones without a card. Call an operator on ☎ 020 for domestic calls, or ☎ 090 for international calls, or use a Home Country Direct service (see below). Mexican international operators can usually speak English.

Some telephone casetas and hotels will make collect calls for you, but they usually charge for the service. We've also come across casetas and shops that proudly announce that you can place collect calls for free, but then charge exorbitant rates to the receiving party (for example, US$24 per minute to the US). So take care.

Home Country Direct sservice, by which you make an international collect call via an operator in the country you're calling, is available for several countries. You can get information on Home Direct services from your phone company before you leave for Mexico, and you can make the calls from pay phones without any card. For Home Direct calls to the USA through AT&T, MCI or Sprint, and to Canada via AT&T Canada or Bell Canada, dial the numbers given above under North American Calling Cards. Mexican international operators may be able to tell you access numbers for other countries. The Mexican term for Home Country Direct is *País Directo*.

Calling Mexico To call a number in Mexico from another country, dial your international access code, then the Mexico country code – ☎ 52 – then the area code and number.

Fax

Public fax service is offered in many Mexican towns by the public *telégrafos* (telegraph) office or offices of the company Telecomm. Also look for '*Fax Público*' signs on shops, businesses and telephone casetas, and in bus stations and airports. Typically you pay around US$1.50 to US$2 a page to the US or Canada, US$2.50 to Europe or Australasia.

Email & Internet Access

Many Mexican cities and towns have cybercafés or other public Internet services where you can surf the net, use web-based email

services such as Yahoo! Mail (www.yahoo .com) or Hotmail (www.hotmail.com), and sometimes send and receive email using the cybercafé's account. Typical charges for half an hour online range from US$1 to US$2. You'll find many such services mentioned under Information in city sections in this book. Websites with listings of Mexican cybercafés include www.netcafeguide.com, www.planeta.com and www.amcc.org.mx.

For those traveling with their own computers, CompuServe (www.compuserve .com) has nodes (access numbers) in eight Mexican cities and one node (☎ 800-720-00-00) that you can access from anywhere in the country.

America Online (www.aol.com) has 10 AOL Globalnet nodes around Mexico. Those in Cancún, Guadalajara, Mexico City, Monterrey and Querétaro are at 28,800 bps; the others are 9600 bps. There's a US$6 hourly surcharge on whatever monthly rate the AOL member is already paying.

Some Mexican hotel rooms have direct-dial phones and phone sockets that allow you to unplug the phone and insert a phone jack that runs directly to your computer. In others you're confronted with switchboard phone systems and/or room phones with a cord running directly into the wall, both of which make it impossible to go online from your room. In such cases you can ask to borrow reception's fax line for a couple of minutes – nine times out of 10 they'll comply, especially if you wait till nighttime, when the boss is away.

It's also possible to plug in your computer at some telephone casetas.

When traveling with a computer, remember that the voltage abroad may vary from that at home, risking damage to your equipment. The best investment is a universal AC adapter for your appliance. Your PC-card modem may or may not work outside your home country – the safest option is to buy a reputable 'global' modem before you leave home, or buy a local PC-card modem if you're spending an extended time in any one country. Telephone sockets can differ from country to country, so ensure that you have at least a US RJ-11 telephone adapter that works with your modem. You can almost always find an adapter that will convert from RJ-11 to the local variety. For more information on traveling with a portable computer, see www.teleadapt.com.

INTERNET RESOURCES
The World Wide Web is a rich resource for travelers. You can research your trip, hunt down bargain airfares, book hotels, check on weather conditions or chat with locals and other travelers about the best places to visit (or avoid!).

Lonely Planet
There are few better places to start your Web explorations than the Lonely Planet website (www.lonelyplanet.com). Here you'll find succinct summaries on traveling to most places on earth, postcards from other travelers, and the Thorn Tree bulletin board where you can ask questions before you go or dispense advice when you get back. You can also find travel news, updates to many of our most popular guidebooks, and the subWWWay section, which links you to the most useful travel resources elsewhere on the Web.

Mexico-Specific Sites
Dozens of fascinating Mexico-specific sites are there to be scrutinized as you prepare your trip, or to help you while you're there.

Mexico Online (www.mexonline.com) and Mexico Connect (http://mexconnect.com) both combine news, message/discussion centers and a wide variety of other content and links. Mexico Online is good for, among other things, travel, politics, Mexican soccer and baseball, culture and organizations (government and otherwise); turn to Mexico Connect for matters of food, practical information for living in Mexico, art and history.

The Mexico and Mundo Maya sections of Eco Travels in Latin America (www.planeta.com) are marvelous resources for anyone at all interested in Mexican travel or the Mexican environment. You'll find articles, lists and links covering birds, butterflies, books, language schools, cybercafés, pro-

tected areas, environmental organizations and a whole lot more on this constantly growing site, hosted by a dedicated Mexico City-based American, Ron Mader.

Mexico (http://mexico-travel.com), the official site of SECTUR, Mexico's Ministry of Tourism, contains a lot of interesting stuff but updating has been meager since the site was launched in 1996.

Mexico Channel (www.trace-sc.com) is a truly impressive collection of Mexico links in fields as diverse as politics, sports, music, airlines and Chiapas. Other excellent directory-type sites include México Web (http://mexico.web.com.mx) and Andanzas al Web Latino (http://lib.nmsu.edu/subject/bord/latino.html).

The Mexico City English-language newspaper *The News* has extracts from its current day's print issue at www.novedades.com.mx/the-news.htm.

Also see regional chapters for other recommended websites dealing with specific areas or aspects of Mexico.

BOOKS
You can buy books in English in most major centers in Mexico, but only Mexico City has an extensive choice. The Mexican-published titles mentioned here are widely available, but it's wise to obtain other books before going to Mexico. A few libraries in places such as Mexico City, San Miguel de Allende, Oaxaca and San Cristóbal de Las Casas have good collections of English-language books on Mexico.

Many books are published in different editions by different publishers in different countries. As a result, a book might be a hardcover rarity in one country while it's readily available in paperback in another. Fortunately, bookstores and libraries can search by title or author, so your local bookstore or library is the best place to find out about the availability of the following recommendations.

Lonely Planet
Lonely Planet has three guides covering specific parts of Mexico in detail: *Baja California*, *Yucatán* and *Mexico City*. *Guatemala,*

Belize & Yucatán – La Ruta Maya combines coverage of southeast Mexico and the two neighboring countries – the whole Maya cultural area – in one volume.

A handy companion for anyone traveling in Mexico is Lonely Planet's *Latin American Spanish phrasebook*, which contains practical, up-to-date words and expressions in Latin American Spanish.

Lonely Planet's *Read This First: Central & South America* offers more tips on preparing for a trip to Mexico.

Lonely Planet's *World Food Mexico* is an intimate, full-color guide to exploring Mexico and its cuisine. This book covers every food or drink situation the traveler could encounter and plots the evolution of Mexican cuisine. Its very useful language section includes a definitive culinary dictionary and useful phrases to help you on your eating adventure.

The *Lonely Planet Pisces Diving & Snorkeling Baja California*, by Walt Peterson, and *Lonely Planet Pisces Diving & Snorkeling Cozumel*, by George S Lewbel and Larry R Martin, are good guides for divers. The *Pisces Watersports Guide to Cancún*, by Susanne and Stuart Cummings, is worth seeking out; it includes Isla Mujeres, Playa del Carmen, Akumal, and Tulum. The *Pisces Guide to Caribbean Reef Ecology* by William S Alevizon, brims with bright color photos and introduces its subject with lively text.

Green Dreams: Travels in Central America by Stephen Benz, in the Lonely Planet Journeys series, is a witty account of 'green' tourism in southern Mexico and Central America.

Guidebooks

The People's Guide to Mexico by Carl Franz (motto: 'Wherever you go . . . there you are') has for a quarter of a century been an invaluable, amusing resource for anyone on an extended trip. It doesn't attempt hotel, transport, or sightseeing specifics but does provide a great all-round introduction to Mexico.

An excellent book for those keen to experience Mexico's natural wonders is Ron Mader's *Mexico – Adventures in Nature*, with practical information on visiting some

60 sites of natural interest all around Mexico, from a very ecologically aware perspective. *Backpacking in Mexico* by Tim Burford gives detailed hiking directions for about a dozen walks in diverse regions and points the reader to many more areas of archaeological interest. Both books provide plenty of useful and interesting background information. *Mexico's Volcanoes* by RJ Secor covers routes up the main peaks of Mexico's central volcanic belt.

Blue Guide Mexico by John Collis and David M Jones is a comprehensive, authoritative guide to the country's archaeology, architecture and art.

Several series of straightforward guides to single sites or regions are fairly widely available in Mexico, including the INAH-SALVAT *Official Guide* booklets on museums and archaeological sites, which cost US$4 to US$5. Also useful, and cheaper, is the *Easy Guide* series by Richard Bloomgarden.

A Guide to Ancient Maya Ruins and the harder-to-find *A Guide to Ancient Mexican Ruins*, both by C Bruce Hunter, between them provide maps and details on more than 40 sites.

Travel

Incidents of Travel in Central America, Chiapas & Yucatan and *Incidents of Travel in Yucatan*, by John L Stephens, are fascinating accounts of adventure and discovery by a 19th-century American, which provided the outside world's first serious look at many Mayan archaeological sites.

Graham Greene's *Lawless Roads* traces Greene's wanderings down eastern Mexico to Chiapas in the 1930s, a time of conflict between Catholics and the atheistic state. Greene found Mexican food to be 'all a hideous red and yellow, green and brown.'

Time Among the Maya: Travels in Belize, Guatemala & Mexico, by Ronald Wright, is a search for the Maya concept of time, yielding an insightful understanding of the peoples and cultures – ancient and modern – of southeast Mexico, Belize and Guatemala. The book also confronts the subject of violence against the Maya peoples.

History & Society

General Lesley Byrd Simpson's *Many Mexicos* is a classic collection of short essays ranging from pre-Columbian times to the present. *Sons of the Shaking Earth*, by Eric Wolf, is a wonderfully readable introduction to Mexican history and Mesoamerican ethnology. Michael C Meyer & William L Sherman's *The Course of Mexican History* is one of the best general accounts of Mexican history and society.

Ancient Mexico Two books by Michael D Coe – *The Maya* and *Mexico* – give a learned but concise and well-illustrated picture of all ancient Mexico's great cultures. Both have gone through several editions. Coe's *Breaking the Maya Code* tells the fascinating story of the decipherment of Mayan writing.

Nigel Davies' *Ancient Kingdoms of Mexico* is a succinct but scholarly study of the Olmec, Teotihuacán, Toltec and Aztec civilizations. Diagrams, illustrations, plans and maps complement the text.

Jacques Soustelle's *Daily Life of the Aztecs* (1962) is a classic on its subject. Also good is *The Aztecs*, by Richard F Townsend. *The Cities of Ancient Mexico*, by Jeremy A Sabloff, has fascinating descriptions of Mexico's ancient cities and what it was like to live in them.

Spanish Conquest William Henry Prescott's mammoth *History of the Conquest of Mexico* remains a classic, even though it was published in 1843 by an author who never went to Mexico. Only with Hugh Thomas' *Conquest: Montezuma, Cortes & The Fall of Old Mexico* – first published, in Britain in 1993, as *The Conquest of Mexico* – did the 20th century produce an equivalent tome. *History of the Conquest of New Spain*, by Bernal Díaz del Castillo, is an eyewitness account of the Spanish arrival by one of Cortés' lieutenants.

Modern Mexico Alan Riding's *Distant Neighbors*, published in the 1980s, remains a good introduction to modern Mexico and its love-hate relationship with the United States. In Britain it's called *Mexico, Inside the Volcano*. *The Mexicans*, by Patrick Oster, is a sort of microcosmic counterpart to Riding's book, focusing on the lives of 20 individual Mexicans.

Art, Architecture & Crafts

The Art of Mesoamerica, by Mary Ellen Miller in the Thames & Hudson World of Art series, is a good survey of pre-Hispanic art and architecture. On colonial architecture the most important book is George Kubler's *Mexican Architecture of the Sixteenth Century* (1948).

Good books on Mexico's 20th-century artists include Diego Rivera's autobiography *My Art, My Life*; Patrick Marnham's 1998 biography of Rivera, *Dreaming with his Eyes Open*; *The Fabulous Life of Diego Rivera*, by BD Wolfe; *Frida: A Biography of Frida Kahlo*, by Hayden Herrera; *Frida Kahlo*, by Malka Drucker; and *The Mexican Muralists*, by Alma M Reed.

Mexico City bookstores are full of beautifully illustrated coffee-table books in English on Mexican arts, archaeology and anthropology. One such is *Mask Arts of Mexico*, by Ruth D Lechuga and Chloe Sayer, a finely illustrated work by two experts in the field. Sayer has also written two fascinating books tracing the evolution of crafts from pre-Hispanic times to the present, with dozens of beautiful photos. *Arts & Crafts of Mexico* is a wide-ranging overview, while *Mexican Textiles*, originally published in Britain as *Mexican Costume*, is a comprehensive treatment of its absorbing topic, with a wealth of detail about Mexican life.

Flora, Fauna & Environment

Roland H Wauer's *Naturalist's Mexico* (1992) describes visits to dozens of areas of natural interest all around Mexico based on three decades of annual trips.

Tropical Mexico: The Ecotravellers' Wildlife Guide by Les Beletsky is a field guide to wildlife from Oaxaca to the Yucatán Peninsula, with color illustrations of more than 500 creatures. Dedicated birders should seek out the Spanish-language *Aves de México*, by Roger Tory Peterson and Edward L

Chalif, published by Mexico's Editorial Diana. The English-language version of this book, *A Field Guide to Mexican Birds*, omits pictures of birds that also appear in Peterson's guides to US birds. An alternative is *A Guide to the Birds of Mexico & Northern Central America*, by Steve NG Howell and Sophie Webb.

Joel Simon's *Endangered Mexico: An Environment on the Edge* examines Mexico's varied environmental crises, from dumping on the northern border to the destruction of the Lacandón jungle, with the benefit of a lot of excellent first-hand journalistic research – a compelling and frightening read about Mexico today. *Defending the Land of the Jaguar* by Lane Simonian is the absorbing story of Mexico's long, if weak, tradition of conservation.

See Guidebooks, earlier, for further books likely to appeal to nature lovers.

Fiction

Many foreign novelists have been inspired by Mexico. *The Power and the Glory*, by Graham Greene, dramatizes the state-church conflict that followed the Mexican Revolution. *Under the Volcano* (1938), by British dipsomaniac Malcolm Lowry, follows a British diplomat who drinks himself to death on the Day of the Dead in a fictionalized Cuernavaca. Sounds simplistic, but it delves into the Mexican psyche, as well as Lowry's own, at a time of deep conflict. DH Lawrence's *Mornings in Mexico* is a readable collection of short stories set in both Mexico and New Mexico.

B Traven is best known as the author of that classic 1935 adventure story of gold and greed in northwest Mexico, *The Treasure of the Sierra Madre* (made into an equally classic John Huston/Humphrey Bogart film in 1948). Traven wrote many other novels set in Mexico, chiefly the six of the 'Jungle' series – among them *The Rebellion of the Hanged*, *General from the Jungle* and *Trozas* – focusing on the oppression of indigenous Mexicans in Chiapas in the years leading up to the Mexican Revolution. The identity of Traven himself is one of literature's big mysteries.

Carlos Castaneda's *Don Juan* series, which reached serious cult status in the 1970s, tells of a North American's experiences with a peyote guru somewhere in northwestern Mexico.

The 1990s brought some fine new English-language novels set in Mexico. Cormac McCarthy's marvelous *All the Pretty Horses* is the laconic, tense, poetic tale of three young latter-day cowboys riding south of the border. *The Crossing* and *Cities of the Plain* completed his 'Border Trilogy'. James Maw's exciting *Year of the Jaguar* takes its youthful English protagonist in search of the father he has never met, from the US border to Chiapas – a book which catches the feel of Mexican travel superbly.

For information on Mexican literature, see the Arts section in the Facts about Mexico chapter.

Books Published in Mexico

Mexican publisher Minutiae Mexicana produces a range of interesting booklets, including *A Guide to Mexican Witchcraft*, *A Guide to Mexican Mammals & Reptiles*, *The Maya World*, *A Guide to Mexican Ceramics* and even *A Guide to Tequila, Mezcal & Pulque*. They're widely available at around US$5 each. A similar Mexican-produced paperback series with many titles in English is Panorama.

NEWSPAPERS & MAGAZINES
English Language

The long-established English-language daily paper *The News* is published in Mexico City and distributed throughout Mexico. It covers main items of Mexican and foreign news, has long stock exchange listings and occasional interesting Mexico features and will keep you in touch with Mexican as well as foreign sports.

Most cities that attract long-stay English-speakers – San Miguel de Allende, Guadalajara, Oaxaca, Puerto Vallarta and Puerto Escondido, for example – have a small English-language newspaper, magazine or newsletter.

You can find US papers and magazines, and sometimes Canadian and European ones, all at least a day old, on sale in the major cities and tourist towns.

Spanish Language

Mexico has a thriving local press, as well as national newspapers such as *La Crónica*, *Reforma*, *Excelsior*, *El Universal* and *Uno más Uno*. In theory the press is free. In practice it's subject to pressure from politicians and even drug barons. *La Jornada* is a good national daily with a nonestablishment viewpoint; it covers a lot of stories other papers don't.

México Desconocido (Unknown Mexico) is a colorful monthly magazine with intelligent coverage of many interesting places. Buy it at newsstands for US$2. (It has a good Internet site, partly in English, at www.mexicodesconocido.com.mx.) The bimonthly *Arqueología Mexicana* (Mexican Archaeology) is beautifully illustrated and full of fascinating features. You can often find back numbers or special issues of both magazines relating to sites or areas you are visiting.

RADIO & TV

Mexican TV is dominated by Televisa, the biggest TV company in the Spanish-speaking world, which runs four of the six main national channels – channels 2 ('El Canal de las Estrellas,' the Channel of the Stars), 4, 5 and 9. Its rival, TV Azteca, has two main channels – Azteca Siete (7) and Azteca Trece (13). Mexican airtime is devoted mainly to ads, low-budget *telenovelas* (soaps), soccer, game/chat/variety shows, movies and comedy. Nudity, graphic violence and offensive language are pretty much kept off the screen. Better than the commercial channels, but not available everywhere, are two cultural channels: Once TV (Eleven TV), run by Mexico City's Instituto Politécnico Nacional, and Canal 22, run by Conaculta, the National Culture & Arts Council.

Cable and satellite TV are widespread, and you'll find at least a few channels in many mid-range and top-end hotel rooms. The main cable providers are Multivisión and Cablevision: at our last check, both rivals offered the Cartoon Network, MTV

and the sports channel ESPN; Cablevision also had CNN in English, Fox Sports, and the r son channel (No 17), devoted to Mexican, Caribbean and Latin music.

Mexico has around 1000 AM and FM radio stations, most of them privately run (many by Televisa). They offer a variety of music, often that of the region where you're listening. In the evening you may be able to pick up US stations on the AM (medium wave) band.

PHOTOGRAPHY & VIDEO
Film & Equipment

Camera and film processing shops, pharmacies and hotels all sell film. Most types of film (with the general exception of Kodachrome slide film) are available in larger cities and resorts. A 36-exposure 100-ASA print film generally costs US$5 to US$6. Film being sold at lower prices may be outdated. If the date on the box is obscured by a price sticker, look under the sticker. Avoid film from sun-exposed shop windows.

If your camera breaks down, you'll be able to find a repair shop in most sizable towns, and prices will be agreeably low.

Videotapes on sale in Mexico (like the rest of the Americas and Japan) nearly all use the NTSC image registration system. This is incompatible with the PAL system common to most of Western Europe and Australia and the SECAM system used in France.

Technical Tips

Mexico is a photographer's paradise. You'll get better results if you take pictures in the morning or afternoon rather than at midday, when the bright sun bleaches out colors and contrast. Wide-angle and zoom lenses are useful, and it helps to have a polarizing filter to cut down the glare from reflections of sunlight on the ocean.

To avoid damage by airport X-ray machines, carry your film in a lead-lined pouch or have it hand-inspected.

Photographing People

Be sensitive about photographing people; if in doubt, ask first. Indigenous people in particular can be reluctant to be photographed. It's not a good idea to photograph soldiers.

TIME

Daylight saving time (*horario de verano*) runs from the first Sunday in April to the last Sunday in October. Most of the country observes Hora del Centro, the same as US Central Time – GMT minus six hours in winter, and GMT minus five hours during daylight saving. Five western states, Chihuahua, Nayarit, Sinaloa, Sonora and Baja California Sur, are on Hora de las Montañas, the same as US Mountain Time – GMT minus seven hours in winter, GMT minus six hours during daylight saving. Baja California (Norte) observes Hora del Pacífico, the same as US Pacific Time – GMT minus eight hours in winter, GMT minus seven hours during daylight saving. The northwestern state of Sonora is on Hora de las Montañas in winter but does not observe daylight saving, so is on Hora del Pacífico in summer – in other words, GMT minus seven hours all year.

A few remote country areas in other parts of the country also do not observe daylight saving, which can complicate things like bus schedules.

If you cross into Mexico from New Mexico or El Paso, Texas, or from Arizona between the first Sunday in April and the last Sunday in October, put your watch forward one hour. Otherwise, there's no time change crossing by land from the USA into Mexico.

ELECTRICITY

Electrical current in Mexico is the same as in the USA and Canada: 110V, 60 Hz. Though most plugs and sockets are the same as in the USA, Mexico actually has three different types of electrical socket: older ones with two equally sized flat slots, newer ones with two flat slots of differing sizes, and a few with a round hole for a grounding (earth) pin. If your plug doesn't fit the Mexican socket, the best thing to do is get an adapter or change the plug. Mexican electronics stores have a variety of adapters and extensions that should solve the problem.

WEIGHTS & MEASURES

Mexico uses the metric system. For conversion between metric and US or Imperial measures, see the table at the back of this book.

LAUNDRY

Sizable Mexican towns have *lavanderías* (laundries) where you can take in a load of washing and have it done for you the same or next day. A 3kg load costs between US$2.50 and US$5. At some laundries you can do your own washing, which reduces the cost.

TOILETS

Public toilets are virtually nonexistent, so take advantage of facilities in places such as hotels, restaurants, bus stations and museums, which usually cost a peso or two. If there's a bin beside the toilet, put paper, etc, in it – it's there because the drains can't cope otherwise.

HEALTH

Travel health depends on your predeparture preparations, your daily health care while traveling and how you handle any medical problem that does develop. While the potential dangers can seem quite frightening, in

ROBERT REID

Voltage meters in Pátzcuaro

reality few travelers experience anything more than upset stomachs.

Predeparture Planning

Immunizations Plan ahead for vaccinations: some of them require more than one injection, while some should not be given together. It's recommended that you seek medical advice at least six weeks before travel.

Record all vaccinations on an International Health Certificate which is available from your doctor or government health department.

Discuss your requirements with your doctor (there is often a greater risk of disease with children and in pregnancy), but vaccinations you should consider for this trip include the following:

Diphtheria, Tetanus & Measles Diphtheria can be a fatal throat infection and tetanus can be a fatal wound infection. Everyone should have these vaccinations. After an initial course of three injections, boosters are necessary every 10 years. You should be up-to-date with your measles immunity too.

Hepatitis A This is the most common travel-acquired illness after diarrhea and can put you out of action for weeks. Havrix 1440 is a vaccination that provides long-term immunity (possibly more than 10 years) after an initial injection and a booster at six to 12 months. Gamma globulin is not a vaccination but is a ready-made antibody collected from blood donations. It should be given close to departure because, depending on the dose, it only protects for two to six months.

Hepatitis B This disease is spread by blood or by sexual activity. Travelers who should consider a Hepatitis B vaccination include those who might be exposed to blood (for example health-care workers), have sexual contact with the local population, stay longer than six months, or be exposed through medical treatment (for instance by inadequately screened blood transfusions). It involves three injections, the quickest course being over three weeks with a booster at 12 months. The US Centers for Disease Control & Prevention recommend Hepatitis B vaccine for all infants and for children aged 11 or 12 years who did not receive it as infants.

Malaria Medication Antimalarial drugs do not prevent you from being infected, but they kill the malaria parasites during a stage in their

Medical Kit Check List

Following is a list of items you should consider including in your medical kit – consult your pharmacist for brands available in your country.

- ❏ **Aspirin or paracetamol** (acetaminophen in the USA) – for pain or fever
- ❏ **Antihistamine** – for allergies, eg, hay fever; to ease the itch from insect bites or stings; and to prevent motion sickness
- ❏ **Cold and flu tablets, throat lozenges and nasal decongestant**
- ❏ **Multivitamins** – especially useful for long trips, when dietary vitamin intake may be inadequate
- ❏ **Antibiotics** – consider including these if you're traveling well off the beaten track; see your doctor, as they must be prescribed, and carry the prescription with you
- ❏ **Loperamide or diphenoxylate** –'blockers' for diarrhea
- ❏ **Prochlorperazine or metaclopramide** – for nausea and vomiting
- ❏ **Rehydration mixture** – to prevent dehydration, which may occur, for example, during bouts of diarrhea; particularly important when traveling with children
- ❏ **Insect repellent, sunscreen, lip balm and eye drops**
- ❏ **Calamine lotion, sting relief spray or aloe vera** – to ease irritation from sunburn and insect bites or stings
- ❏ **Antifungal cream or powder** – for fungal skin infections and thrush
- ❏ **Antiseptic (such as povidone-iodine)** – for cuts and grazes
- ❏ **Bandages, Band-Aids (plasters) and other wound dressings**
- ❏ **Water purification tablets or iodine**
- ❏ **Scissors, tweezers and a thermometer** – note that mercury thermometers are prohibited by airlines

development and significantly reduce the risk of becoming very ill or dying. Expert advice on medication should be sought, as there are many factors to consider, including the area to be visited, the risk of exposure to malaria-carrying mosquitoes, the side effects of medication, your medical history and whether you are a child or an adult or pregnant. In Mexico at the time of writing there was malaria risk in some rural areas of Campeche, Chiapas, Guerrero, Michoacán, Nayarit, Oaxaca, Quintana Roo, Sinaloa and Tabasco states.

Rabies Vaccination should be considered if you are spending a month or longer in the country, especially if you will be cycling, handling animals, caving or traveling to remote areas; it should also be considered for children (who may not report a bite). Pretravel rabies vaccination involves three injections over 21 to 28 days. If someone who has been vaccinated is bitten or scratched by an animal, they will require two booster injections of vaccine; those not vaccinated require more.

Typhoid This is an important vaccination for those traveling to areas where hygiene is a problem. It is available as either an injection or oral capsules.

Yellow Fever Mexico requires travelers arriving from areas infected with *fiebre amarilla* (yellow fever) – which are all in Africa or tropical South America – to have had yellow fever vaccination and to carry a yellow fever certificate. Discuss this with your doctor if necessary.

Health Insurance Make sure you have adequate health insurance. See Travel Insurance under Visas & Documents earlier in this chapter for details.

Medical Information Services Useful travel health information is available from several public information services. In the USA the Centers for Disease Control & Prevention (CDC) has an international travelers' hot line (☎ 877-394-8747). In Canada there's Health Canada (☎ 613-957-8739). In the UK you can obtain a printed health brief for any country by calling MASTA (Medical Advisory Services for Travellers Abroad, ☎ 0906-8-224100). In Australia call the Australian Government Health Service or consult a clinic such as the Travellers Medical & Vaccination Centre (TMVC, ☎ 1300-658844), which has 19 clinics in Australia and New Zealand.

There are a number of excellent travel health sites on the Internet. From the

Lonely Planet website, there are links to the CDC, MASTA and TMVC (which offers online personal travel health reports).

Travel Health Guides If you plan to travel in remote areas for a long period of time, you might consider taking a more detailed health guide.

Healthy Travel Central & South America, Isabelle Young, Lonely Planet Publications, 2000. Includes guidelines on treating travel illnesses from Mexico.

Travelers' Health, Dr Richard Dawood, Oxford University Press and Random House, 1994. Comprehensive, easy to read, authoritative and highly recommended, though rather large to lug around.

Travel with Children, Maureen Wheeler, Lonely Planet Publications, 1995. Includes advice on travel health for younger children.

Other Preparations Make sure you're healthy before you start traveling. If you are going on a long trip, make sure your teeth are OK. If you wear glasses, take a spare pair and your prescription.

If you require a particular medication, take an adequate supply, as it may not be available locally. Take part of the packaging

Everyday Health

Normal body temperature is up to 37°C (98.6°F); more than 2°C (4°F) higher indicates a high fever. The normal adult pulse rate is 60 to 100 per minute (children 80 to 100, babies 100 to 140). As a general rule, the pulse increases about 20 beats per minute for each 1°C (2°F) rise in fever.

Respiration (breathing) rate is also an indicator of illness. Count the number of breaths per minute: between 12 and 20 is normal for adults and older children (up to 30 for younger children, 40 for babies). People with a high fever or serious respiratory illness breathe more quickly than normal. More than 40 shallow breaths a minute may indicate pneumonia.

❋ ❋ ❋ ❋ ❋ ❋ ❋ ❋ ❋ ❋ ❋ ❋

showing the generic name, rather than the brand, which will make getting replacements easier. To avoid any problems, it's a good idea to have a legible prescription or letter from your doctor to show that you use the medication legally.

Basic Rules

Food Vegetables and fruit should be washed with purified water or peeled where possible. Beware of ice cream that might have melted and refrozen: if there's any doubt, steer well clear. Shellfish such as mussels, oysters and clams should be avoided, as should undercooked meat, particularly in the form of mince. Steaming does not make shellfish safe for eating.

If a place looks clean and well run and the vendor looks clean and healthy, then the food is probably safe. The food in busy restaurants is cooked and eaten quite quickly with little standing around, and it is probably not reheated.

Water The number-one rule is *be careful of the water*, especially of ice. If you don't know for certain that the water is safe, assume the worst. Reputable brands of bottled water or soft drinks are generally fine, although in some places bottles may be refilled with tap water. Only use water from containers with a serrated seal – not tops or corks. Take care with fruit juice, particularly if water may have been added. Milk should be treated with suspicion, as it is often unpasteurized, though boiled milk is fine if it is kept hygienically. Tea or coffee should also be OK, since the water should have been boiled. Canned or bottled carbonated beverages, including carbonated water, are usually safe, as are beer, wine and liquor.

Many Mexican hotels have large bottles of purified water from which you can fill your water bottle or canteen. Inexpensive purified water *(agua purificada)* is available from supermarkets, grocery shops and liquor stores.

Water Purification The simplest way of purifying water is to boil it thoroughly. At high altitudes, water boils at a lower temperature,

Nutrition

If your food is poor or limited in availability, if you're traveling hard and fast and therefore missing meals, or if you simply lose your appetite, you can soon start to lose weight and place your health at risk.

Make sure your diet is well balanced. Cooked eggs, tofu, beans, lentils and nuts are all safe ways to get protein. Fruit you can peel (bananas, oranges or mandarins, for example) is usually safe and a good source of vitamins (melons can harbor bacteria in their flesh and are best avoided). Try to eat plenty of grains (including rice) and bread. Remember that although food is generally safer if it is cooked well, overcooked food loses much of its nutritional value. If your diet isn't well balanced or if your food intake is insufficient, it's a good idea to take vitamin and iron pills.

Make sure you drink enough in hot climates – don't rely on feeling thirsty to indicate when you should drink. Not needing to urinate or small amounts of very dark yellow urine are danger signs. Always carry a water bottle on long trips. Excessive sweating can lead to salt loss and therefore muscle cramping. Salt tablets are not a good idea as a preventative, but in places where salt is not used much, adding salt to food can help.

❋❋❋❋❋❋❋❋❋❋❋❋❋

so germs are less likely to be killed. Boil it longer in these environments.

For a long trip, consider purchasing a water filter. There are two main kinds of filter. Total filters remove all parasites, bacteria and viruses, and make water safe to drink. They are often expensive but can be more cost effective than buying bottled water. Simple filters (even such as a nylon mesh bag) remove dirt and larger foreign bodies from the water, so that chemical solutions work much more effectively; if water is dirty, chemical solutions may not work at all. When buying a filter, read the specifications so that you know exactly what it removes from the water and what it doesn't. Use of a simple filter will not remove all dangerous organisms, so if you cannot boil water, it should be treated chemically. Chlorine tablets (Puritabs, Steritabs or other brand names) will kill many pathogens, but not some parasites like giardia and amoebic cysts. Iodine is more effective in purifying water and is available in tablet form (such as Potable Aqua). Follow the directions carefully and remember that too much iodine can be harmful. The Spanish for 'water purification tablets/drops' is *pastillas/gotas para purificar agua.*

Medical Problems & Treatment

We know from our own experience that it is possible to take dozens of journeys in every region of Mexico, climbing volcanoes, trekking to pyramids in remote jungle, camping out, staying in cheap hotels and eating in all sorts of markets and restaurants without getting anything worse than occasional traveler's diarrhea. But some of us *have* experienced hepatitis, dysentery and giardiasis, and we have known people who caught dengue fever and typhoid, so we know that these things can happen.

If you come down with a serious illness, be careful to find a competent doctor, and don't be afraid to get second opinions. You may want to telephone your doctor at home as well. Self-diagnosis and treatment can be risky, so you should always seek medical help. Drug dosages given in this section are for emergency use only. Correct diagnosis is vital.

Antibiotics should ideally be administered only under medical supervision. Take only the recommended dose at the prescribed intervals and use the whole course, even if the illness seems to be cured earlier. Stop immediately if there are any serious reactions, and don't use the antibiotic at all if you are unsure that you have the correct one. If you are allergic to commonly prescribed antibiotics such as penicillin or sulpha drugs, carry this information when traveling.

An embassy, consulate or five-star hotel can usually recommend a good place to go for medical advice. Almost every Mexican town and city has a hospital and/or a clinic, as well as Cruz Roja (Red Cross) emergency

facilities. Most major hotels have a doctor available. Hospitals are generally inexpensive for common ailments (diarrhea, dysentery) and minor treatments (stitches, sprains). Clinics are often too overburdened with local problems to be of much help, but they are linked by radio to emergency services.

If you use these services, try to ascertain the competence of the staff treating you. In big cities and major tourist resorts you should be able to find an adequate hospital. Care in more remote areas is limited.

Most hospitals have to be paid at the time of service, and doctors usually require immediate cash payment. Some facilities may accept credit cards.

In some serious cases it may be best to fly elsewhere for treatment, difficult as that may be. Medical treatment in Mexico is not always what it should be.

Environmental Hazards

Altitude Sickness Lack of oxygen at high altitudes (over 2500m) affects most people to some extent. The effect may be mild or severe and occurs because less oxygen reaches the muscles and brain, requiring the heart and lungs to work harder. Symptoms of Acute Mountain Sickness (AMS) usually develop during the first 24 hours at altitude but may be delayed up to three weeks. Mild symptoms include headache, lethargy, dizziness, difficulty sleeping and loss of appetite. AMS may become more severe without warning and can be fatal. Severe symptoms include breathlessness, a dry, irritative cough (which may progress to the production of pink, frothy sputum), severe headache, lack of coordination and balance, confusion, irrational behavior, vomiting, drowsiness and unconsciousness. There is no hard-and-fast rule as to what is too high: AMS has been fatal at 3000m, although 3500m to 4500m is the usual range.

Treat mild symptoms by resting at the same altitude until recovery, usually a day or two. Paracetamol or aspirin can be taken for headaches. If symptoms persist or become worse, however, *descend immediately*; even 500m can help. Drug treatments should never be used to avoid descent or to enable further ascent.

The drugs acetazolamide (Diamox) and dexamethasone are recommended by some doctors for the prevention of AMS, but their use is controversial. They can reduce the symptoms, but they may also mask warning signs; severe and fatal AMS has occurred in people taking these drugs. In general, we do not recommend them for travelers.

To prevent acute mountain sickness:

- Ascend slowly – take frequent rest days, spending two to three nights at each rise of 1000m.
- It is always wise to sleep at a lower altitude than the greatest height reached during the day. Above 3000m, care should be taken not to increase the sleeping altitude by more than 300m per day.
- Drink extra fluids. Mountain air is dry and cold and moisture is lost as you breathe. Evaporation of sweat may occur unnoticed and result in dehydration.
- Eat light, high-carbohydrate meals for more energy.
- Avoid alcohol, as it may increase the risk of dehydration.
- Avoid sedatives.

Fungal Infections These occur more commonly in hot weather and are usually found on the scalp, between the toes or fingers, in the groin and on the body (ringworm). Moisture encourages them. You get ringworm (a fungal infection, not a worm) from infected animals or other people.

To prevent fungal infections, wear loose, comfortable clothes, avoid artificial fibers, wash frequently and dry carefully. If you get an infection, wash the infected area at least daily with a disinfectant or medicated soap and water, and rinse and dry well. Apply an antifungal cream or powder like tolnifate (Tinaderm). Try to expose the infected area to air or sunlight as much as possible, and wash towels and underwear in hot water, change them often and let them dry in the sun.

Heat Exhaustion Dehydration and salt deficiency can cause heat exhaustion. Take time to acclimatize to high temperatures, drink sufficient liquids and do not do anything too physically demanding.

Salt deficiency is characterized by fatigue, lethargy, headaches, giddiness and muscle cramps; salt tablets may help, but adding extra salt to your food is better.

Anhydrotic heat exhaustion, which is caused by an inability to sweat, is quite rare. It is more likely to strike people who have been in a hot climate for some time, rather than newcomers.

Heatstroke This serious, occasionally fatal, condition can occur if the body's heat-regulating mechanism breaks down and body temperature rises to dangerous levels. Long, continuous periods of exposure to high temperatures and insufficient fluids can leave you vulnerable to heatstroke.

Symptoms are feeling unwell, not sweating very much (or at all) and a high body temperature (39°C to 41°C or 102°F to 106°F). Where sweating has ceased, the skin becomes flushed and red. Severe, throbbing headaches and lack of coordination also occur, and the sufferer may be confused or aggressive. Eventually the victim becomes delirious or convulses. Hospitalization is essential, but in the interim get victims out of the sun, remove their clothing, cover them with a wet sheet or towel and then fan continually. Give fluids if they are conscious.

Hypothermia Too much cold can be just as dangerous as too much heat. If you are outdoors at high altitudes, particularly at night, be prepared.

Hypothermia occurs when the body loses heat faster than it can produce it and the core temperature of the body falls. It is surprisingly easy to progress from very cold to dangerously cold due to a combination of wind, wet clothing, fatigue and hunger, even if the air temperature is above freezing. It is best to dress in layers; silk, wool and some of the new artificial fibers are all good insulating materials. A hat is important, as a lot of heat is lost through the head. A strong, waterproof outer layer (and a 'space' blanket for emergencies) are essential. Carry basic supplies, including food containing simple sugars to generate heat quickly, and fluid to drink.

Symptoms of hypothermia are exhaustion, numbness (particularly in the toes and fingers), shivering, slurred speech, irrational or violent behavior, lethargy, stumbling, dizzy spells, muscle cramps and violent bursts of energy. Irrationality may take the form of sufferers claiming they are warm and trying to take off their clothes.

To treat mild hypothermia, first get victims out of the wind and/or rain and replace wet clothing with dry, warm clothing. Give them hot liquids – not alcohol – and some high-calorie, easily digestible food. Do not rub victims; instead, allow them slowly to warm themselves. This should be enough to treat the early stages of hypothermia. Early recognition and treatment of mild hypothermia are the only ways to prevent severe hypothermia, which is a critical condition.

Jet Lag This is experienced when you travel by air across more than three time zones. You may experience fatigue, disorientation, insomnia, anxiety, impaired concentration and loss of appetite. These effects will usually be gone within three days, but to minimize the impact of jet lag, try the following:

• Rest for a couple of days prior to departure.
• Try to select flight schedules that minimize sleep deprivation.
• Avoid excessive eating (which bloats the stomach) and alcohol (which causes dehydration) during the flight. Drink plenty of noncarbonated, nonalcoholic drinks such as fruit juice or water.
• Avoid smoking.
• Wear loose-fitting clothes and perhaps bring an eye mask and earplugs to help yourself sleep.
• Try to sleep at the appropriate time for the time zone you are traveling to.

Motion Sickness Eating lightly before and during a journey will reduce the chances of motion sickness. Try to find a place that minimizes movement – near the wing on aircraft, close to midships on boats, near the center on buses. Fresh air usually helps; reading and cigarette smoke don't. Commercial motion-sickness preparations, which can cause drowsiness, have to be taken before the trip commences. Ginger (available in capsule form) and peppermint (including mint-flavored sweets) are natural preventatives.

Prickly Heat This is an itchy rash caused by excessive perspiration trapped under the skin. It usually strikes people who have just arrived in a hot climate. Keeping cool, bathing often, drying the skin, using a mild talcum or prickly-heat powder, or resorting to air-con may help.

Sunburn In the tropics or deserts or at high altitude, you can get sunburned surprisingly quickly, even on cloudy days. Use a sunscreen, hat, and barrier cream for your nose and lips. Calamine lotion and aloe vera gel are good for mild sunburn. Protect your eyes with good-quality sunglasses, particularly if you will be near water, sand or snow.

Infectious Diseases

Diarrhea Simple things such as a change of water, food or climate can cause a mild bout of diarrhea, but a few rushed toilet trips with no other symptoms are not indicative of a major problem.

Dehydration is the main danger with any diarrhea, particularly in children or the elderly. Under all circumstances, *fluid replacement* (at least equal to the volume lost) is the most important thing to remember. Weak black tea with a little sugar, soda water, or soft drinks allowed to go flat and diluted 50% with clean water are all good. With severe diarrhea, a rehydrating solution is preferable to replace minerals and salts lost. Commercially available oral rehydration salts (ORS) are very useful; add them to boiled or bottled water. In an emergency, you can make a solution of six teaspoons of sugar and a half teaspoon of salt to a liter of boiled or bottled water. You need to drink at least the same volume of fluid that you are losing in bowel movements and vomiting. Urine is the best guide to the adequacy of replacement – if you have small amounts of concentrated urine, you need to drink more. Keep drinking small amounts often. Stick to a bland diet as you recover.

Lomotil or Imodium can be used to bring relief from the symptoms, although they do not cure the problem. Only use these drugs if you do not have access to toilets – if you *must* travel. For children under 12, Lomotil and Imodium are not recommended. Do not use these drugs if the person has a high fever or is severely dehydrated.

In certain situations, antibiotics may be required: diarrhea with blood or mucus (dysentery), any fever, watery diarrhea with fever and lethargy, persistent diarrhea that doesn't improve after 48 hours, and severe diarrhea. In these situations, gut-paralyzing drugs like Imodium or Lomotil should be avoided.

Seek urgent medical help if you suspect dysentery, as a stool test is necessary to diagnose which kind you have. Where this is not possible, the recommended drugs for bacterial dysentery (the most likely cause of severe diarrhea in travelers) are norfloxacin (400mg twice daily for three days) or ciprofloxacin (500mg twice daily for five days). These are not recommended for children or pregnant women. The drug of choice for children would be co-trimoxazole (Bactrim, Septrin or Resprim), with dosage dependent on weight. A five-day course is given. Ampicillin or amoxycillin may be given in pregnancy, but medical care is necessary.

Amoebic dysentery is characterized by a gradual onset of low-grade diarrhea, often with blood and mucus. Cramping abdominal pain and vomiting are less likely than in other types of diarrhea, and fever may not be present. It will persist until treated and can recur and cause other health problems.

Giardiasis – the parasite causing this intestinal disorder, another type of diarrhea, is present in contaminated water. Symptoms are stomach cramps, nausea, a bloated stomach, watery, foul-smelling diarrhea and frequent gas. Giardiasis can appear several weeks after you have been exposed to the parasite. Symptoms may disappear for a few days and then return; this can go on for several weeks. Tinidazole, known as Fasigyn, or metronidazole (Flagyl) are the recommended drugs. Treatment is a 2g single dose of Fasigyn or 250mg of Flagyl three times daily for five to 10 days.

Cholera is the worst of the watery diarrheas, and medical help should be sought. Outbreaks of cholera are generally widely reported, so avoid such problem areas. *Fluid replacement is the most vital treatment* – the risk of dehydration is severe, as you may lose up to 20L a day. If there is a delay in getting to a hospital, then begin taking tetracycline. The adult dose is 250mg four times daily. It is not recommended for children under nine years, nor for pregnant women. Tetracycline may help shorten the illness, but adequate fluids are required.

Hepatitis Hepatitis is a general term for inflammation of the liver. It is common worldwide. Symptoms are fever, chills, headache, fatigue, feelings of weakness, and aches and pains, followed by loss of appetite, nausea, vomiting, abdominal pain, dark urine, light-colored feces and jaundiced (yellow) skin. The whites of the eyes may turn yellow.

Hepatitis A is transmitted by contaminated food and drinking water. If you contract it, you should seek medical advice, but there is not much you can do apart from rest, drink lots of fluids, eat lightly and avoid fatty foods. People who have had hepatitis should avoid alcohol for some time after the illness, as the liver needs time to recover.

Hepatitis E is transmitted in the same way, and can be very serious in pregnant women.

Incidence of **Hepatitis B** is low in Mexico. It is spread through contact with infected blood, blood products or body fluids – for example, through sexual contact, unsterilized needles and blood transfusions, body-piercing, tattooing, having a shave, or contact with blood via small breaks in the skin. Symptoms of type B may be more severe and may lead to long-term problems. **Hepatitis D** is spread in the same way, but the risk is mainly from shared needles.

Hepatitis C can lead to chronic liver disease. The virus is spread by contact with blood, usually via contaminated transfusions or shared needles. Avoiding these is the only means of prevention.

HIV & AIDS HIV, the Human Immunodeficiency Virus, develops into AIDS, Acquired Immune Deficiency Syndrome, which is a fatal disease. Nearly 40,000 AIDS cases had been recorded in Mexico by 1999. Any exposure to blood, blood products or body fluids may put the individual at risk. The disease is often transmitted through sexual contact or dirty needles – vaccinations, acupuncture, tattooing and body piercing can be potentially as dangerous as intravenous drug use. HIV/AIDS can also be spread through infected blood transfusions; in developing countries such as Mexico it is possible that blood for a transfusion will not have been screened for HIV. Difficult or impossible though this may be, the only recourse of a traveler needing a blood transfusion may be to try to insist on the use of blood that has been properly tested for HIV.

If you do need an injection, ask to see the syringe unwrapped in front of you, or take a needle and syringe pack with you.

Be aware that fear of HIV infection should never preclude treatment for serious medical conditions.

Schistosomiasis Also known as bilharzia, this disease is carried in water by minute worms. The worm enters through the skin and attaches itself to the intestines or bladder. The first symptom may be a tingling and sometimes a light rash around the area where the worm entered. Weeks later, a high fever may develop. A general feeling of being unwell may be the first symptom, or there may be no symptoms. Once the disease is established, abdominal pain and blood in the urine are other signs. The infection often causes no symptoms until the disease is well established (several months to years after exposure), and damage to internal organs is irreversible.

Avoid swimming or bathing in fresh water where bilharzia is present. Even deep water can be infected. If you do get wet, dry off quickly and dry your clothes as well.

A blood test is the most reliable test, but it will not show positive until a number of weeks after exposure.

Sexually Transmitted Diseases Gonorrhea, herpes and syphilis are among these diseases; sores, blisters or rashes around the genitals, and discharges or pain when urinating, are common symptoms. In some STDs, such as wart virus and chlamydia, symptoms may be less marked or not observed at all, especially in women. Syphilis symptoms eventually disappear completely, but the disease continues and can cause severe problems in later years. While abstinence from sexual contact is the only 100% effective prevention of STDs, using condoms is also effective. Gonorrhea and syphilis are treated with antibiotics. Each STD requires specific antibiotics. There are no cures for herpes or HIV/AIDS.

Typhoid Typhoid fever is a dangerous gut infection caused by contaminated water and food. Medical help must be sought.

In its early stages, sufferers may feel they have a bad cold or flu on the way, as early symptoms are headache, body aches and a fever that rises a little each day until it is around 40°C (104°F) or more. The victim's pulse is often slow relative to the degree of fever present – unlike a normal fever, in which the pulse increases. There may also be vomiting, abdominal pain, diarrhea or constipation.

In the second week, the high fever and slow pulse continue and a few pink spots may appear on the body; trembling, delirium, weakness, weight loss and dehydration may occur. Complications such as pneumonia, perforated bowel or meningitis may occur.

The fever should be treated by keeping victims cool and giving them fluids to avoid dehydration. Ciprofloxacin (750mg twice a day for 10 days) is good for adults.

Chloramphenicol is recommended in many countries. The adult dosage is two 250mg capsules, four times a day. Children between eight and 12 years should have half the adult dose, and younger children one-third the adult dose.

Rabies This is a fatal viral infection. Many animals can be infected (such as dogs, cats, bats and monkeys), and it is their saliva that is infectious. Any bite, scratch or even lick from a warm-blooded, furry animal should be cleaned immediately and thoroughly. Scrub with soap and running water, and then apply alcohol or iodine solution. Medical help should be sought promptly to receive a course of injections to prevent the onset of symptoms and death.

Tetanus Tetanus occurs when a wound is infected by a germ that lives in soil and in the feces of horses and other animals. It enters the body via breaks in the skin. All wounds should be cleaned promptly and adequately and an antiseptic cream or solution applied. Use antibiotics if the wound becomes hot or throbs or pus is seen. The first symptom may be discomfort in swallowing, or stiffening of the jaw and neck; this is followed by painful convulsions of the jaw and whole body. The disease can be fatal.

Typhus This disease is spread by ticks, mites or lice. It begins with fever, chills, headache and muscle pains, followed a few days later by a body rash. Often a large, painful sore appears at the site of the bite, and nearby lymph nodes are swollen and painful. Typhus can be treated under medical supervision. Seek local advice on areas where ticks pose a danger and always check your skin (including hair) carefully for ticks after walking in a danger area such as a tropical forest. Strong insect repellent can help.

Insect-Borne Diseases

Protecting yourself against insect bites will help to prevent the following diseases. Travelers are especially advised to prevent mosquito bites at all times. In general mosquitoes in Mexico are most bothersome from dusk to dawn and during the rainy season (May to October in most

places). The main points to remember are as follows:

- Wear light-colored clothing.
- Wear long pants and long-sleeved shirts.
- Use mosquito repellents containing the compound DEET on exposed areas (note that prolonged overuse of DEET may be harmful, especially to children, but its use is considered preferable to being bitten by disease-transmitting mosquitoes).
- Avoid highly scented perfumes or aftershaves.
- Use a mosquito net impregnated with mosquito repellent (permethrin) – it may be worth taking your own.

Malaria This serious, potentially fatal disease is spread by mosquito bites. In endemic areas, it is extremely important to avoid mosquito bites and to take tablets to prevent malaria. Symptoms range from fever, chills and sweating, headache, diarrhea and abdominal pains to a vague feeling of ill-health. Seek medical help immediately if malaria is suspected. Without treatment, malaria can rapidly become more serious and can be fatal.

If medical care is unavailable, malaria tablets can be used for treatment. You need to use a different malaria tablet than the one you were taking when you contracted malaria. The treatment dosages are mefloquine (two 250mg tablets and another two six hours later) or fansidar (a single dose of three tablets). If you were previously taking mefloquine, alternatives are halofantrine (three doses of two 250mg tablets every six hours) or quinine sulphate (600mg every six hours). There is a greater risk of side effects with these dosages than in normal use.

Dengue Fever There is no preventative drug for this mosquito-spread disease, which can be fatal in children. A sudden onset of fever, headaches and severe joint and muscle pains are the first signs before a rash develops. Recovery may be prolonged.

Chagas' Disease In remote rural areas of Central and South America, this parasitic disease is transmitted by a bug that hides in the wall crevices and thatched roofs of mud huts and on palm fronds. It bites at night, and a hard, violet-colored swelling appears in about a week. Chagas' disease can be treated in its early stages, but untreated infections can lead to death some years later.

Filariasis This is a mosquito-transmitted parasitic infection found in many parts of Central and South America. Possible symptoms include fever, pain and swelling of the lymph glands, inflammation of lymph drainage areas, swelling of a limb or the scrotum, skin rashes and blindness. Treatment is available to eliminate the parasites from the body, but some of the damage already caused may not be reversible. Medical advice should be obtained promptly if infection is suspected.

Leishmaniasis This is a group of parasitic diseases transmitted by sandfly bites. Cutaneous leishmaniasis affects the skin tissue, causing ulceration and disfigurement, and visceral leishmaniasis affects the internal organs. Laboratory testing is required for diagnosis and correct treatment. Visceral leishmaniasis can be fatal for children under five and people with immune system deficiencies.

Avoiding sandfly bites is the best precaution, yet another reason to cover up and apply repellent. Bites are usually painless and itchy.

Cuts & Stratches

Wash any cut well and treat it with an antiseptic, such as povidone-iodine. When possible, avoid bandages and Band-Aids, which can keep wounds wet. Coral cuts are notoriously slow to heal, and if they are not thoroughly cleaned with an antiseptic, small pieces of coral can become embedded in the wound. Severe pain, throbbing, redness, fever or generally feeling unwell suggest infection and the prompt need for antibiotics, as coral cuts may result in serious infections.

Bites & Stings

Insects & Arachnids Bee and wasp stings are usually painful rather than dangerous.

But allergic people may experience severe breathing difficulties and require urgent medical care. Calamine lotion or Stingose spray will give relief, and ice packs will reduce pain and swelling.

Some spiders have dangerous bites, but antivenins are usually available.

Scorpion stings are notoriously painful, and in some parts of Central America can be fatal. Scorpions often shelter in shoes or clothing.

Jellyfish Local advice is the best way of avoiding contact with these sea creatures, which have stinging tentacles. Dousing in vinegar will deactivate any stingers that have not 'fired.' Calamine lotion, antihistamines and analgesics may reduce the reaction and relieve the pain.

Leeches Leeches may be present in damp rain forest conditions; they attach themselves to your skin to suck your blood. An insect repellent may keep them away. Salt or a lighted cigarette end will make them fall off. Do not pull them off, as the bite is then more likely to become infected. Clean and apply pressure if the point of attachment is bleeding.

Snakes To minimize your chances of being bitten, wear boots, socks and long trousers when walking through undergrowth where snakes may be present. Don't put your hands into holes and crevices, and be careful when collecting firewood.

Snake bites do not cause instantaneous death, and antivenins are usually available. Immediately wrap the bitten limb tightly, as you would for a sprained ankle, and then attach a splint to immobilize it. Keep the victim still and seek medical help, and take the dead snake along for identification if possible. Don't attempt to catch the snake if there is a possibility of being bitten again. Tourniquets and sucking out the poison are now comprehensively discredited.

Women's Health

Antibiotic use, synthetic underwear, sweating and contraceptive pills can lead to fungal vaginal infections in hot climates. Wearing loose-fitting clothes and cotton underwear will help prevent these infections.

Fungal infections, characterized by a rash, itch and discharge, can be treated with a vinegar or lemon-juice douche or with yogurt. Nystatin, miconazole or clotrimazole pessaries or vaginal cream are the usual treatments.

Sexually transmitted diseases are a major cause of vaginal problems. Symptoms include a smelly discharge, painful intercourse and sometimes a burning sensation when urinating. Sexual partners must also be treated. Medical attention should be sought. Remember that in addition to these diseases, HIV or hepatitis B can also be acquired from sexual contact. Besides abstinence, the best thing is to practice safe sex using condoms.

Pregnancy Some vaccinations normally used to prevent serious diseases are not advisable during pregnancy, making travel to some places inadvisable. In addition, some diseases, such as malaria, are much more serious for pregnant women (and may increase the risk of a stillborn child).

Most miscarriages occur during the first three months of pregnancy. Miscarriage is not uncommon, and it can occasionally lead to severe bleeding. The last three months should also be spent within reasonable distance of good medical care. A baby born as early as 24 weeks stands a chance of survival, but only in a good modern hospital. Pregnant women should avoid all unnecessary medication; vaccinations and malarial prophylactics should still be taken where needed. Additional care should be taken to prevent illness, and particular attention should be paid to diet and nutrition.

WOMEN TRAVELERS

In this land that invented machismo, women have to make some concessions to local custom – but don't let that put you off. In general, Mexicans are great believers in the difference (rather than the equality) between the sexes. Lone women must expect some catcalls and attempts to chat them up. Normally these men only want to talk to you, but it can get tiresome; the best way to

Don't touch.

discourage unwanted attention is to avoid eye contact (sunglasses help here) and, if possible, ignore the attention altogether. Otherwise use a cool but polite initial response and a consistent, firm 'No.' It is possible to turn uninvited attention into a worthwhile conversation by making clear that you *are* willing to talk, but no more.

Don't put yourself in peril by doing things Mexican women would not do, such as challenging a man's masculinity, drinking in a cantina, hitchhiking without a male companion, or going alone to isolated places.

Wearing a bra will spare you a lot of unwanted attention. A wedding ring and talk of your husband may help, too. Except in beach resorts, it's advisable to wear shorts only when at a swimming pool. You might even consider swimming in shorts and a T-shirt, as many Mexican women do.

GAY & LESBIAN TRAVELERS

Though it might ostensibly be one of the world's more heterosexual countries, Mexico is more broad-minded than visitors might expect. Gays and lesbians tend to keep a low profile but in general rarely attract open discrimination or violence. Gay and lesbian travelers will find active scenes in cities such as Mexico City, Puerto Vallarta, Acapulco, Guadalajara, Monterrey and Ciudad Juárez.

A good source of information on the Internet is The Gay Mexico Network (www.gaymexico.net). *Sergay* is a Spanish-language magazine, focused on Mexico City but with bar and disco listings for the whole country. You can find it on the Internet at www.sergay.com.mx.

The *Damron Women's Traveller*, with listings for lesbians, and *Damron Address Book*, for men, are both published annually by Damron Company of San Francisco, USA. *Men's Travel in Your Pocket, Women's Travel in Your Pocket* and *Gay Travel A to Z* (for men and women), all published by Ferrari Publications, and *Gay Mexico: The Men of Mexico,* by Eduardo David, are also useful. They can be obtained at any good bookstore, as well as on the Internet.

DISABLED TRAVELERS

Mexico doesn't yet make many concessions to the disabled, though some hotels and restaurants (mostly towards the top end of the market) and public buildings are starting to provide wheelchair access. Mobility is easiest in the major tourist resorts and the more expensive hotels. Public transportation is mainly hopeless; flying, taxi and car are easiest.

Mobility International USA (☎ 541-343-1284, www.miusa.org), PO Box 10767, Eugene, OR 97440 USA, runs exchange programs (including in Mexico) and publishes *A World of Options: A Guide to International Educational Exchange, Community Service & Travel for People with Disabilities*. In Europe, Mobility International (☎ 02-201 5608, mobint@arcadis.be) is at Boulevard Baudouin 18, Brussels B-1000, Belgium.

The Council on International Educational Exchange (see Courses, later in this chapter) can help disabled people interested in working, studying or volunteering outside their home countries.

Twin Peaks Press (☎ 360-694-2462, www .pacifier.com/~twinpeak), PO Box 129, Vancouver, WA 98666-0129 USA, publishes and sells many books for disabled travelers.

An excellent website for disabled travelers to check is www.access-able.com.

SENIOR TRAVELERS

The American Association of Retired Persons (AARP, ☎ 800-424-3410, www.aarp .org), 601 E St NW, Washington, DC 20049 USA, is an advocacy and service group for Americans 50 years and older and a good resource for travel bargains. Membership for one/three years is US$8/20.

Membership in the National Council of Senior Citizens (☎ 301-578-8800, www.aoa .dhhs.gov/AOA/dir/149.html), 8403 Colesville Road, Suite 1200, Silver Spring, MD 20910 USA, gives access to discount information and travel-related advice.

Grand Circle Travel (☎ 800-597-3644, www.gct.com), 347 Congress St, Boston, MA 02210 USA, offers escorted tours and travel information in a variety of formats.

TRAVEL WITH CHILDREN

Mexicans as a rule like children. Any child whose hair is less than jet black will get called *güera* (blond) if she's a girl, *güero* if he's a boy. Children are welcome at all kinds of hotels and in virtually every café and restaurant.

Most children are excited and stimulated by the colors, sights and sounds of Mexico, but younger children especially don't like traveling all the time – they're happier if they can settle into places and make friends. Try to give them time to get on with some of the activities they are used to back home.

Children are likely to be more affected than adults by heat or disrupted sleeping patterns. They need time to acclimatize and extra care to avoid sunburn. Take care to replace fluids if a child gets diarrhea (see the Health section).

Apart from the obvious attractions of beaches, coasts and swimming pools, in some places you can find excellent special attractions such as amusement parks, zoos, aquariums and boat rides. In Mexico City don't miss the marvelous hands-on children's museum, Papalote Museo del Niño. Archaeological sites can be fun if the kids are into climbing pyramids and exploring tunnels.

Diapers (nappies) are widely available, but you may not easily find creams, lotions, baby foods or familiar medicines outside larger cities and tourist towns. Bring what you need.

It's usually not hard to find an inexpensive baby-sitter if the grown-ups want to go out on their own; just ask at your hotel.

On flights to and within Mexico children under two generally travel for 10% of the adult fare, and those between two and 12 normally pay 67%. Children pay full fare on Mexican long-distance buses unless they're small enough to sit on your lap.

Lonely Planet's *Travel with Children*, by Maureen Wheeler, has lots of practical advice on the subject, as well as firsthand stories from many Lonely Planet authors, and others, who have done it.

DANGERS & ANNOYANCES

Mexico – especially its big cities and above all Mexico City – experienced a big increase in crime after the economic crisis of the mid-1990s. By the end of the decade the authorities were finally taking steps to counter this. Generally, with a few precautions you can minimize danger to your physical safety. But lone women, and even pairs of women, should always be very cautious about going to remote beach spots, and everyone should be very cautious about what taxis they take in Mexico City (see the Mexico City chapter). On the whole, though, it's your possessions that are more at risk, particularly possessions that you carry around with you – but again, a few sensible steps reduce the risk.

Official information can make Mexico sound more alarming than it really is, but for a variety of useful information on travel to Mexico, including potential risks, you can contact your country's foreign affairs department, by telephone or on the Internet: Australia (☎ 02-6261-3305, www.dfat.gov.au); Canada (☎ 613-944-6788, ☎ 800-267-6788, www.dfait-maeci.gc.ca); UK (☎ 020-7238-4503, www.fco.gov.uk); USA (☎ 202-647-5225, http://travel.state.gov). If you're already in Mexico, you can contact your embassy.

Theft & Robbery

Tourists are vulnerable as they are generally presumed to be wealthy (by Mexican standards) and to be carrying valuables. Pocket-picking and purse- or bag-snatching are risks in all large Mexican cities, particularly Mexico City. Crowded buses, bus stops, bus stations, airports, the Mexico City metro, markets, thronged streets and plazas and anywhere frequented by large numbers of tourists are all possible haunts of these thieves. Robbery or mugging is more likely in less crowded places such as empty pedestrian underpasses, remote beach spots and quiet streets after dark.

Violent crimes are rare in major coastal resorts, which tend to have a large and visible police presence.

Pickpockets often work in teams: one or two of them may grab your bag or camera (or your arm and leg), and while you're trying to get it free another will pick your pocket. Or one may 'drop' something as a crowd jostles onto a bus and as he or she 'looks for it,' a pocket will be picked or a bag slashed. The operative principle is to distract you and get you off balance. If your valuables are *underneath* your clothing, the chances of losing them are greatly reduced.

Robberies and muggings are less common than pocket-picking and purse-snatching, but they are more alarming and more serious, as resistance may be met with violence. Robbers may force you to remove your money belt or neck-strap pouch, watch, rings, etc. They may be armed. Usually they will not harm you: what they want is your money, fast. But there have been cases of robbers beating victims, or forcing them to drink large amounts of alcohol, to extract credit or bank card personal numbers. Sometimes the police themselves have been the criminals. Mexico City taxis, which have become notorious for robberies, sometimes violent, are especially dangerous if you take the wrong kind of cab (see the Mexico City chapter).

Precautions To avoid being robbed in cities, do not go where there are few other people. This includes empty streets or empty metro cars at night, little-used pedestrian underpasses and similarly lonely places.

On beaches and in the countryside, do not camp overnight in lonely places unless you can be absolutely sure they're safe.

You must protect yourself, or you can expect to lose a considerable amount. In Mexican cities adhere to the following precautions *without fail*.

- Unless you have immediate need of them, leave most of your cash, traveler's checks, passport, jewelry, air tickets, credit cards, watch, and perhaps your camera in a sealed, signed envelope in your hotel's safe. Virtually all hotels except the very cheapest provide safekeeping for guests' valuables.

- Leaving valuables in a locked suitcase in your hotel room is often safer than carrying them on the streets of most Mexican cities.

- Wear a money belt, shoulder wallet, or a pouch on a string around your neck, *underneath your clothing*, and place your remaining valuables in it. Visible round-the-waist money belts are an invitation to thieves. You can carry a small amount of ready money in a pocket.

- Walk with purpose and be alert to people around you.

- Don't keep money (cash or plastic), purses or bags in open view any longer than you have to. At ticket counters in bus stations and airports, keep your bag between your feet, particularly when you're busy with a ticket agent.

- Use ATMs only in secure locations, not those open to the street.

- Do not leave anything at all valuable-looking visible in a vehicle when you park it in a city.

Highway Robbery Bandits sometimes hold up buses, cars and other vehicles on intercity routes, especially at night, taking luggage or valuables. Sometimes buses are robbed by people who board as passengers. The best ways to avoid highway robbery are not to travel at night and to use toll highways as much as possible. Deluxe and 1st-class buses usually use toll highways, where they exist; 2nd-class buses don't. Roads with particularly bad reputations as we researched this edition included highways 15 and 15D in Sinaloa state, highway 134 between Ciudad Altamirano and Ixtapa/Zihuatanejo, highway 186 from Villahermosa to Chetumal, highway 200 along the Pacific coast, especially between Zihuatanejo and Puerto Escondido, and highway 147 from Tuxtepec to Palomares (Oaxaca state). Night buses between Palenque and Mérida have had a record of theft from passengers for years.

LEGAL MATTERS
Mexican Law

Mexican law is based on the Napoleonic code, presuming an accused person is guilty until proven innocent.

The minimum jail sentence for possession of more than a token amount of any narcotic, including marijuana and amphetamines, is 10 years. As in most other countries, the purchase of controlled medication requires a doctor's prescription.

It's against Mexican law to take any weapon or ammunition into the country (even unintentionally) without a permit from a Mexican embassy or consulate.

Road travelers should expect occasional police or military checkpoints. They are normally looking for drugs, weapons or illegal migrants. Drivers found with drugs or weapons on board may have their vehicle confiscated and may be detained for months while their cases are investigated.

See the Getting Around chapter for information on legal aspects of road accidents.

Help

If arrested, you have the right to notify your embassy or consulate. Consular officials can tell you your rights and provide lists of local lawyers. They can also monitor your case, make sure you are treated humanely, and notify your relatives or friends – but they can't get you out of jail. More Americans are in jail in Mexico than any other country except the USA – about 450 at any one time.

Most of Mexico's 31 states have a Protección al Turista (Tourist Protection) department, often found in the same building as the state tourist office (and contactable through tourist offices). Protección al Turista exists to help you with legal problems such as complaints or reporting crimes or lost articles. The national tourism ministry, SECTUR (☎ 5-250-01-23, 800-903-92-00), offers 24-hour telephone advice on tourist protection laws and where to obtain help.

If you are the victim of a crime, your embassy or consulate, or SECTUR, can give advice. In some cases, you may feel there is little to gain by going to the police, unless you need a statement to present to your insurance company. If you go to the police and your Spanish is poor, take a more fluent speaker. Also take your passport and tourist card, if you still have them. If you just want to report a theft for purposes of an insurance claim, say you want to *'poner una acta de un robo'* (make a record of a robbery). This should make it clear that you merely want a piece of paper and you should get it without too much trouble.

If Mexican police wrongfully accuse you of an infraction (as they have often been known to do in the hope of obtaining a bribe), you can ask for the officer's identification or to speak to a superior or to be shown documentation about the law you have supposedly broken. You can also note the officer's name, badge number, vehicle number and department (federal, state or municipal). Pay any traffic fines at a police station and get a receipt. Then make your complaint to Protección al Turista or to SECTUR.

Information

Useful warnings on Mexican law are found in the US State Department's *Tips for Travelers to Mexico* and in State Department consular information sheets, public announcements or travel warnings on Mexico. All are available on the Internet at http://travel.state.gov.

BUSINESS HOURS

Shops are generally open Monday to Saturday from 9 or 10 am to 7 pm. Some in hot regions and small towns may close for siesta from around 2 to 4 pm, then stay open till 9 pm. Some shops don't open Saturday afternoon. Shops in malls and tourist resorts often open Sunday, too.

Offices have similar Monday to Friday hours, with greater likelihood of the 2 to 4 pm lunch break. Those with tourist-related business might open for a few hours on Saturday.

Some Mexican churches – particularly those that contain valuable works of art – are locked when not in use. But most churches are in frequent use – be careful not to disturb services when you visit them.

Archaeological sites are usually open daily from 8 or 9 am to about 5 pm. This is unfortunate, because in many hot regions the hours before 8 am and after 5 pm, especially in summer, are cooler and much more pleasant, and there's plenty of golden light. If they have a closing day, it's usually Monday. Museums often close Monday, too. On Sunday nearly all archaeological sites and museums are free, and the major ones can get very crowded.

PUBLIC HOLIDAYS & SPECIAL EVENTS

Mexico's frequent fiestas are full-blooded, highly colorful affairs that often go on for several days and add much spice to life. There's a major national holiday or celebration almost every month, to which each town adds nearly as many local saints' days, fairs, arts festivals and so on.

Christmas-New Year and Semana Santa, the week leading up to Easter, are the chief Mexican holiday periods. If you're traveling at either time, try to book transport and accommodations in advance.

National Holidays

Banks, post offices, government offices and many shops throughout Mexico are closed on the following days:

January 1
  Año Nuevo – New Year's Day

February 5
  Día de la Constitución – Constitution Day

February 24
  Día de la Bandera – Day of the (national) Flag

March 21
  Día de Nacimiento de Benito Juárez – anniversary of Benito Juárez's birth

May 1
  Día del Trabajo – Labor Day

May 5
  Cinco de Mayo – anniversary of Mexico's 1862 victory over the French at Puebla, celebrated grandly in Puebla

September 16
  Día de la Independencia – commemoration of the start of Mexico's war for independence from Spain; the biggest celebrations are in Mexico City, the evening before.

October 12
Día de la Raza – commemorating Columbus' discovery of the New World and the founding of the Mexican (mestizo) people

November 20
Día de la Revolución – anniversary of the Mexican Revolution of 1910

December 25
Día de Navidad – Christmas Day; the Christmas feast traditionally takes place in the early hours of December 25, after midnight mass.

Other National Celebrations

Though not official holidays, some of these are among the most important festivals on the Mexican calendar. Many offices and businesses close.

January 6
Día de los Reyes Magos – Three Kings' Day (Epiphany); Mexican children traditionally receive gifts this day, rather than at Christmas (but some get two loads of presents!).

February 2
Día de la Candelaría – Candlemas; processions, bullfights, and dancing in many towns commemorate the presentation of Jesus in the temple 40 days after his birth.

Late February or early March
Carnaval – Carnival; taking place the week or so before Ash Wednesday (which falls 46 days before Easter Sunday), this is the big bash preceding the 40-day penance of Lent; it's celebrated most festively in Mazatlán, Veracruz and La Paz, with huge parades and masses of music, food, drink, dancing, fireworks and fun.

March or April
Semana Santa – Holy Week, starting on Palm Sunday (Domingo de Ramos); business closures are usually from Good Friday (Viernes Santo) to Easter Sunday (Domingo de Resurrección); particularly colorful celebrations are held in San Miguel de Allende, Taxco and Pátzcuaro; most of Mexico seems to be on the move at this time.

September 1
Informe Presidencial – the president's state of the nation address to the legislature

November 1
Día de Todos los Santos – All Saints' Day

November 2
Día de los Muertos – Day of the Dead, Mexico's most characteristic fiesta; the souls of the dead are believed to return to earth this day. Families build altars in their homes and visit graveyards to commune with their dead on the night of

November 1-2 and the day of November 2, taking garlands and gifts of, for example, the dead one's favorite foods. A happy atmosphere prevails. The souls of dead children, called *angelitos* because they are believed to have automatically become angels, are celebrated the previous day, All Saints' Day. Like many Mexican rituals, these events have pre-Hispanic roots. Those around Pátzcuaro are most famous, but every cemetery in the country comes alive this day.

December 12
Día de Nuestra Señora de Guadalupe – Day of Our Lady of Guadalupe, Mexico's national patron, the manifestation of the Virgin Mary who appeared to an indigenous Mexican, Juan Diego, in 1531; a week or more of celebrations throughout Mexico leads up to the big day, with children taken to church dressed as little Juan Diegos or indigenous girls; the biggest festivities are at the Basílica de Guadalupe in Mexico City.

December 16-24
Posadas – candlelit parades of children and adults, reenacting the journey of Mary and Joseph to Bethlehem, held for nine nights, more in small towns than big cities

Local Fiestas

Every city, town, *barrio* (neighborhood) and village has its own fiestas, often in honor of its patron saint(s). Street parades of holy images, special costumes, fireworks, dancing, lots of music, plenty of drinking – even bull-running through the streets in some places – are all part of the scene. There are festivals of arts, dance, music and handicrafts, and celebrations for harvests of avocados, grapes and even radishes. Trade and business fairs often serve as a focus for wider festivities.

ACTIVITIES

Opportunities for active tourism in Mexico are increasing all the time, thanks to the desire of more and more Mexicans and foreigners to do more with their free time than just lie on beaches, sightsee, eat and drink. This section is a very brief introduction to some of the things you can *do* in Mexico. You'll find details in this book's destination sections. This chapter's Books section mentions some useful guides for hikers, divers and nature lovers.

Two good sources on organizations involved in active tourism in Mexico are the

website Eco Travels in Latin America (www
.planeta.com) and the association known as
AMTAVE, a grouping of over 50 adventure
travel and ecotourism operators in Mexico
(see Organized Tours in the Getting Around
chapter for more on AMTAVE).

Hiking, Cycling & Horse Riding

Hiking trails in the Barranca del Cobre
(Copper Canyon) area and Baja California
are among the most popular and developed.
There's a variety of long and short day-hike
possibilities in many parts of the country,
though in coastal regions heat and humidity
are often a deterrent. Walking alone across
remote territory is not advised for safety
reasons.

In a growing number of places around
Mexico you'll find horses or bicycles – sometimes mountain bikes – to rent for excursions.
There are also some riding ranches for trail or
beach rides. There's certainly plenty of fine
mountain-biking country in areas such as
Baja California, Oaxaca, Puebla and Chihuahua. The sport is increasingly popular with
Mexicans; the Internet sites http://megalink
.net.mx/bike/dhill.htm and México en Bici-
cleta (www.meb.com.mx) are good sources.

Mountain & Rock Climbing

Popocatépetl, the famous volcano east of
Mexico City, was off-limits at the time of
writing because of a spell of volcanic activity
that began in 1994. For a guided mountain
trip – and a guide is certainly recommended
for the two other major peaks east of the
capital, Iztaccíhuatl and Pico de Orizaba
(Citlaltépetl) – you should book at least a
week ahead. For Iztaccíhuatl you're looking
at a minimum of US$150 for two people. La
Malinche and Nevado de Toluca are two
dormant or extinct volcanoes whose summits can be reached without any technical
stuff. The Internet site Explore!Mexico
(www.geocities.com/Yosemite/4343/bilk.html)
has links to much interesting material on
climbing.

Water Sports

Most imaginable water sports are practised
along Mexico's coasts. Most resorts offer
snorkel gear rentals and can arrange boat
and fishing trips. You can practice sea
kayaking around places like Loreto, Baja
California Sur, and Puerto Vallarta and
Zihuatanejo on the Pacific coast. Water-
skiing, parasailing, Jet Skis and 'banana'
riding are popular at many resorts. You
might want to check on the safety of the
equipment before taking off.

Inland are many *balnearios*, bathing
places with swimming pools, often centered
on hot springs in picturesque surroundings.

Snorkeling & Diving There are some won-
derful waters along both the Caribbean and
Pacific coasts, but good visibility is more pre-
dictable on the Caribbean. Fine Caribbean
diving spots include Isla Mujeres, Playa del
Carmen, Cozumel, Punta Allen, Banco
Chinchorro, Akumal, Puerto Morelos and
Paamul, with notable snorkeling too at the
first five of those places. On the Pacific coast,
Puerto Vallarta, Zihuatanejo, Acapulco and
Huatulco are among the best places for
diving and snorkeling. Mulegé and Cabo
San Lucas are outstanding diving spots in
Baja California.

Surfing & Windsurfing The Pacific coast
has some superb waves. Among the best are
the summer breaks at spots between San
José del Cabo and Cabo San Lucas (Baja
California); the 'world's longest wave,' on
Bahía de Matanchén (near San Blas); and
the 'Mexican Pipeline,' at Puerto Escondido.
Other fine surf spots include Ensenada,
Mazatlán, Barra de Navidad, Manzanillo,
Troncones Point (near Zihuatanejo) and
Playa Revolcadero (near Acapulco). Many
surf beaches are most easily reached with
your own vehicle.

Los Barriles is Baja California's windsurfing capital. Farther south, Puerto Vallarta
and Manzanillo can be good.

White-Water Rafting Veracruz state,
where rivers fall dramatically from the
Sierra Madre to the coastal plain, is the epicenter of this newly popular activity, called
descenso de ríos in Mexico. The Río Filo-
Bobos, with grade 2 rapids, is often used for

beginners' trips, as is the grade 2-3 Río Actopan.

Río Antigua and its tributary Río Pescados are more challenging, especially the upper reaches where the grade 4 Barranca Grande rapids are navigable in winter. Jalapa, a base for several rafting operators, is a convenient starting point. Other rivers in Chiapas (out of Palenque), Oaxaca and Morelos states will give you a good splash as well.

Use a reliable company with good equipment and experienced guides.

Fishing

There are opportunities for lake and reservoir fishing inland, and lagoon, river and sea fishing on and near the Gulf and Caribbean coasts, but it's sport fishing off the Pacific coast that Mexico is justly famous for. See destination sections in the Baja California and Central Pacific Coast chapters for more detail on what you can fish for – for example, marlin, swordfish, sailfish and tuna – and when. Fishing permits are required – contact a Mexican Government Tourism Office or a Mexican consulate for information.

Wildlife & Bird-Watching

Observing Mexico's varied and exotic fauna is an increasingly popular and increasingly practicable pastime: see the Wild Mexico special section in the Facts about Mexico chapter for an introduction to this activity, which is rapidly growing in popularity and practicability.

COURSES

Taking classes in Mexico can be a great way to meet people and get an inside angle on local life as well as study the language or culture. Mexican universities and colleges often offer tuition to complement courses you may be taking back home. For long-term study in Mexico you'll need a student visa – contact a Mexican consulate.

The International Study & Travel Center (ISTC, ☎ 612-626-4782), 48 Coffman Union, 300 Washington Ave SE, Minneapolis, MN 55455 USA, has a study abroad database on its website (www.istc.umn.edu) with numerous possibilities in Mexico. There are also helpful links on the Lonely Planet site (www.lonelyplanet.com).

Language Courses

There are Spanish language schools in many of Mexico's most attractive cities, among them Cuernavaca, Guadalajara, Guanajuato, Mérida, Mexico City, Morelia, Oaxaca, Puerto Vallarta, San Cristóbal de Las Casas, San Miguel de Allende and Taxco. Some are private, some affiliated to universities.

Course lengths range from a week to a year. In some places you can enroll on the spot and start any Monday. You may be offered accommodations with a local family as part of the deal. This will help your language skills as much as any formal tuition. In some schools, courses in art, crafts or in-depth study of Mexico are also available.

Costs per week, with accommodations and meals included, can range from as little as US$100 to over US$300, depending on the town and school.

There are useful language-school listings on the Eco Travels in Latin America website (www.planeta.com). Information is also available from the National Registration Center for Study Abroad (☎ 414-278-0631, www.nrcsa.com), PO Box 1393, Milwaukee, WI 53201 USA, and the Council on International Educational Exchange (CIEE, ☎ 888-268-6245, 212-822-2600, www.ciee.org), 205 East 42nd St, New York, NY 10017 USA.

The Institute of International Education (www.iie.org), 809 United Nations Plaza, New York, NY 10017 USA, publishes *Spanish Study in Mexico*, profiling 43 Spanish-language schools in Mexico, and *An International Student's Guide to Mexican Universities*.

Other Courses

Fans of Mexican food can learn from experts how to prepare the whole enchilada at several cookery schools around the country – see this book's Tlaxcala and Oaxaca sections for mentions of a couple. The Mexico City chapter has information on seminars on social issues at the city's Casa de los Amigos.

WORK

Mexicans themselves need jobs, and people who enter Mexico as tourists are not legally allowed to take employment. The many expats working in Mexico have usually been posted there by their companies with all the right papers.

English-speakers may find teaching jobs in language schools, *preparatorias* (high schools) or universities, or can offer personal tutoring. Mexico City is the best place to get English-teaching work; Guadalajara is also good. It's possible in other major cities. The pay is low, but you can live on it.

The News and cities' telephone yellow pages are sources of job opportunities. Ads in *The News* – mostly for work in Mexico City – quote pay rates of US$6 to US$10 an hour. Positions in high schools or universities are more likely to become available with the beginning of each new term – contact institutions that offer bilingual programs or classes in English; for universities, arrange an appointment with the director of the language department. Language schools tend to offer short courses, so teaching opportunities with them come up more often and your commitment is for a shorter time, but they may pay less than high schools and universities.

A foreigner working in Mexico normally needs a permit or government license, but a school will often pay a foreign teacher in the form of a *beca* (scholarship), and thus circumvent the law, or the school's administration will procure the appropriate papers.

It's helpful to know at least a little Spanish, even though some institutes insist that only English be spoken in class.

Teaching apart, you might find a little bar or restaurant work in tourist areas. It's likely to be part-time and short-term.

Volunteer Work

The website of the International Study & Travel Center (see Courses) has a volunteer work database with many possibilities in Mexico. The Council on International Educational Exchange (see Courses) also has information on volunteer programs in Mexico. *Volunteer Vacations*, by Bill McMillon (Chicago Review Press, 1999), lists lots of volunteer work organizations and information sources.

One World Workforce (☎ 800-451-9564, www.1ww.org), PO Box 20006, Boulder, CO 80308 USA, sends paying volunteers to work on environmental conservation projects in Mexico such as protecting sea turtle nests. Cost is around US$600 to US$700 for a week. Earthwatch (☎ 800-776-0188, www.earthwatch.org), 680 Mount Auburn St, Watertown, MA 02471 USA (also with offices in Britain and Australia), runs environmental projects in Mexico that you pay to take part in (usually US$1000-plus for one to two weeks).

Amigos de las Americas (☎ 800-231-7796, fax 713-782-9267), 5618 Star Lane, Houston, TX 77057 USA, sends paying volunteers to work on summer public health projects in Latin America. Volunteers receive prior training.

The Casa de los Amigos (see Places to Stay in the Mexico City chapter) has files on volunteer opportunities in Latin America and can place fluent Spanish-speaking volunteers on projects in Mexico City focusing on issues such as education, street children, AIDS, refugees or democratic struggle. Most openings are for full-time work of six months or longer.

ACCOMMODATIONS

Accommodations in Mexico range from hammocks, palm-thatched huts and campgrounds through hostels, *casas de huéspedes* (guesthouses) and budget hotels to world-class luxury resorts.

Almost any tourism-related Internet site can connect you to plenty of Mexican hotel websites and provide hotel information.

Reservations

It's advisable to reserve a room in advance at particularly popular places or if you plan to visit busy areas during the Christmas-New Year holidays, Semana Santa, or during July and August. You can request a reservation by telephone or fax, asking whether a deposit is required and how to send it, and requesting confirmation.

Camping

Most organized campgrounds are actually trailer parks, set up for RVs (camper vans) and trailers (caravans), but they accept tent campers at lower rates. Some are very basic, others quite luxurious. Expect to pay about US$3 to US$5 to pitch a tent, and US$8 to US$15 for two people to use the full facilities of a good campground. Some restaurants or guesthouses in small beach spots will let you pitch a tent on their land for a couple of dollars per person.

Campgrounds are most common on the Yucatán Peninsula, in Baja California and along the Pacific coast. We recommend *The People's Guide to RV Camping in Mexico*, by Carl Franz, or *Traveler's Guide to Mexican Camping* by Mike & Terri Church.

All Mexican beaches are considered public property. You can camp for nothing on most of them, but they can be risky places for your belongings.

Hammocks & Cabañas

These are mainly found in low-key beach spots in the south of the country.

You can rent a hammock and a place to hang it – usually under a palm roof outside a small casa de huéspedes or beach restaurant – for US$2 in some places, though it might be US$10 on the more expensive Caribbean coast. If you have your own hammock the cost comes down a bit. It's easy enough to buy hammocks in Mexico; Mérida specializes in them, and you'll find them on sale in many places in Oaxaca, Chiapas and the Yucatán Peninsula. Mosquito repellent is handy if you're sleeping in a hammock.

Cabañas are, basically, huts – usually with a palm-thatched roof. Some have dirt floors and nothing inside but a bed; others are deluxe, with electric light, mosquito nets, fans, fridge, bar and decor. Prices for simple cabañas range from US$5 to US$25, the most expensive ones being on the Caribbean – where you'll also find luxury cabañas costing US$100!

Hostels

For a long time most hostels in Mexico were *villas juveniles* or *albergues de juventud* attached to youth sports centers in university and resort cities. Though usually clean and cheap, these tend to be inconveniently located and full of Mexican youth groups. They usually have single-sex dormitories. Prepared meals are often available, but there's no guest kitchen. A bed usually costs about US$4.

In the past few years a growing number of hostels geared to independent budget travelers have opened up in cities and towns such as Mexico City, Cuernavaca, Oaxaca, San Miguel de Allende, San Cristóbal de Las Casas and Mérida. These hostels typically have small dormitories, a relaxed atmosphere, breakfast or café service and often a guest kitchen. A bunk or (in some) a bed can cost anywhere from US$4 to US$20.

Hostels offer an alternative to budget or medium-range hotels. For single travelers in particular, they can represent a good value for the money and good places to meet other travelers.

Some hostels are grouped in small chains affiliated to – though not full members of – Hostelling International (HI, the former International Youth Hostel Federation). One chain is REMAJ (Red Mexicana de Alojamiento para Jóvenes, Mexican Young People's Lodging Network). REMAJ (☎ 5-662-82-44, fax 5-663-15-56) is run by Mexico City-based youth/student travel agency Mundo Joven, Insurgentes Sur 1510D, México DF 03920. Capacity at REMAJ hostels ranges from 20 to over 200 people and prices per night are anywhere from US$6 to US$18. REMAJ's website is www.hostellingmexico.com; you can book for any hostel by email to hostellingmexico@remaj.com. To stay in a REMAJ hostel you need to have an HI membership card (or a membership card from your home-country youth hostel organization), or you must buy 'welcome stamps' for US$2 a night (in addition to the nightly hostel charge). After six nights the card on which you stick the welcome stamps becomes equivalent to an HI card.

The other chain is AMAJ (Asociación Mexicana de Albergues Juveniles, Mexican Youth Hostels Association, www.hostels

.com.mx). It's run by another Mexico City-based youth/student travel agency, Viajes Educativos (☎ 5-661-42-35, fax 5-661-42-35, tourjoven@infosel.net.mx), Local B10, Insurgentes Sur 421, Colonia Hipódromo Condesa, México DF 06170. You can reserve a place in any AMAJ hostel by emailing info@hostels.com.mx. Hostel cards are not required in AMAJ hostels, but they will get you a US$1 discount in some.

Casas de Huéspedes & Posadas

The cheapest and most congenial accommodations are often at a casa de huéspedes, a home converted into simple guest lodgings. Good casas de huéspedes are usually family-run, with a relaxed, friendly atmosphere. Rooms may or may not have a private bathroom. A double typically costs US$10 to US$15, though a few places are more comfy and more expensive. Some posadas (inns) are like casas de huéspedes; others are small hotels.

Hotels

Cuarto sencillo (literally, single room) usually means a room with one bed, which is often a cama matrimonial (double bed). One person can usually occupy such a room for a lower price than two people. A cuarto doble is usually a room with two beds, often both 'matrimonial.'

Cheap hotels exist in every Mexican town. There are many clean, friendly ones; there are also dark, dirty, smelly ones. You can get a decent double room with private shower and hot water in most of the country for under US$15, but in Baja California or on the Caribbean coast you may have to pay double that. Fortunately for small groups of travelers, many hotels have rooms for three, four or five people that cost little more than a double.

Mexico specializes in good middle-range hotels where two people can usually get a room with private bath, TV and perhaps air-con for US$20 to US$40. Often there's an elevator and a restaurant and bar. You can expect these places to be pleasant, respectable, safe and comfortable.

Among the most charming lodgings are the many old mansions, inns, even convents, turned into hotels. Some date from colonial times, others from the 19th century. Most are wonderfully atmospheric, with fountains gurgling in old stone courtyards. Some are a bit spartan (but relatively low in price), others have been modernized and can be posh and expensive. These are often the lodgings you will remember most fondly after your trip.

Mexico has plenty of large, modern hotels, particularly in the largest cities and resorts. They offer the expected levels of luxury at expectedly lofty prices. If you like to stay in luxury but also enjoy saving some money, choose a Mexican hotel, not one that's part of an international chain.

Apartments

In some places there are apartamentos with fully equipped kitchens designed for tourists. Some are very comfortable, and they can be a good value for three or four people. Tourist offices and ads in local papers (especially English-language papers) are good sources of information on apartments.

FOOD

Mexican cuisine is enormously varied, full of regional differences and subtle surprises. You'll eat well in Mexico, and the choice is wide in all sizable towns. In addition to the Mexican fare that we describe here, there's all sorts of international food too, even some good vegetarian restaurants. For inexpensive fresh fruit, vegetables, tortillas, cheese and bread, pop into the local market.

Staples

Mexicans eat three meals a day: desayuno (breakfast), comida (lunch) and cena (supper). Each includes one or more of three national staples: tortillas, frijoles and chiles.

Tortillas are thin round patties of pressed corn (maíz) or wheat-flour (harina) dough cooked on griddles. Both can be wrapped around or served under any type of food. Frijoles are beans, eaten boiled, fried or refried in soups, on tortillas, or with just about anything.

Chiles are spicy-hot chili peppers; they come in dozens of varieties and can be

BRUCE GEDDES

Towers of tortillas

consumed in hundreds of ways. Some types, such as the *habanero* and *serrano*, are always very hot, while others, such as the *poblano*, vary in spiciness according to when they were picked. If you are unsure about your tolerance for hot chilies, ask if they are *dulce* (sweet), *picante* (hot), or *muy picante* (very hot).

Street & Market Meals

The cheapest food in Mexico is served up by the thousands of street stands selling all manner of hot and cold food and drinks. At these places you can often get a taco or a glass of orange juice for less than US$0.25. Many are very popular and well patronized, but hygiene can be a risk. Deciding whether to use them is a matter of judgment; those with a lot of customers are likely to be the best and safest.

A grade up from street fare are the *comedores* found in many markets. They offer Mexico's cheapest sit-down meals – you sit on benches at long tables and the food is prepared in front of you. Usually comedores serve typical local fare, and – at the best ones – it's like home cooking. It's best to go at lunchtime, when ingredients are fresher, and pick a comedor that's busy – which usually means it's good.

Breakfast

The simplest breakfast is coffee or tea and *pan dulce* (sweet rolls), a basket of which is set on the table; you pay for the number consumed. Many restaurants offer combination breakfasts for about US$1.50 to US$3.50, typically composed of *jugo de fruta* (fruit juice), *café* (coffee), *bolillo* (bread roll) or *pan tostado* (toast) with *mantequilla* (butter) and *mermelada* (jam), and *huevos* (eggs), which are served in a variety of ways:

huevos pasados por agua – lightly boiled eggs (too lightly for many visitors' tastes)
huevos cocidos – harder-boiled eggs (specify the number of minutes if you're in doubt)
huevos estrellados – fried eggs
huevos fritos (con jamón/tocino) – fried eggs (with ham/bacon)
huevos mexicanos – eggs scrambled with tomatoes, chilies and onions (representing the red, green and white of the Mexican flag)
huevos motuleños – tortilla topped with slices of ham, fried eggs, cheese, peas and tomato sauce
huevos rancheros – fried eggs on tortillas, covered in salsa
huevos revueltos – scrambled eggs
huevos poches – poached eggs

Mexicans often eat meat for breakfast, but in many places frequented by travelers, granola, *ensalada de frutas* (fruit salad), *avena* (porridge) and even Corn Flakes are available.

Lunch

La comida, the main meal of the day, is usually served between 1 and 3 or 4 pm. Most restaurants offer not only à la carte fare but also special fixed-price menus called *comida corrida, cubierto* or *menú del día*. These menus constitute the best food bargains, because you get several courses (often with some choice) for much less than such a meal would cost à la carte. Prices may range from US$1.50 at a market comedor for a simple meal of soup, a meat dish, rice and coffee to US$10 or more for elaborate meals beginning with oyster stew and finishing with *profiteroles* – but typically you'll get four or five courses for US$2.50 to US$4.50. Drinks usually cost extra.

Dinner/Supper

La cena, the evening meal, is usually lighter than the comida. Fixed-price meals are rarely offered, so you can usually save money by eating your principal meal at lunchtime.

Snacks

Antojitos, or 'little whims' – nowadays called *especialidades mexicanas* or *platillos mexicanos* on some menus – are traditional Mexican snacks or light dishes. Some are actually small meals in themselves. They can be eaten at any time, on their own or as part of a larger meal. There are many, many varieties, some of which are peculiar to local areas, but here are some of the more common ones:

burrita – flour tortilla folded over a filling of ham and cheese, heated a little to make the cheese melt

burrito – any combination of beans, cheese, meat, chicken or seafood seasoned with salsa or chili and wrapped in a wheat-flour tortilla – especially popular in northern Mexico

chilaquiles – fried tortilla chips with sauce or scrambled eggs, often with grated cheese on top

chiles rellenos – chilies stuffed with cheese, meat or other foods, deep fried and baked in sauce

empanada – small pastry with savory or sweet filling

enchilada – ingredients similar to those used in burritos and tacos rolled up in a tortilla, dipped in sauce and then baked or partly fried; *enchiladas Suizas* (Swiss enchiladas) come smothered in a blanket of thick cream

enfrijolada – soft tortilla in a frijole sauce with cheese and onion on top

entomatada – soft tortilla in a tomato sauce with cheese and onion on top

gordita – fried maize dough filled with refried beans, topped with cream, cheese and lettuce

guacamole – mashed avocados mixed with onion, chili, lemon, tomato and other ingredients

quesadilla – flour tortilla topped or filled with cheese and occasionally other ingredients and then heated

queso fundido – melted cheese served with tortillas

sincronizada – a lightly grilled or fried flour-tortilla 'sandwich,' usually with a ham and cheese filling

sope – thick patty of corn dough lightly grilled then served with *salsa verde* or *salsa roja* (see Other Foods) and frijoles, onion and cheese

taco – the Número Uno Mexican snack: soft corn tortilla wrapped or folded around the same fillings as a burrito

tamal – corn dough stuffed with meat, beans, chilies or nothing at all, wrapped in corn husks or banana leaves and then steamed

torta – Mexican-style sandwich in a roll

tostada – crisp-fried, thin tortilla that may be eaten as a nibble while you're waiting for the rest of a meal or can be topped with meat or cheese, tomatoes, beans and lettuce

Soup

There are many *sopas* (soups) made from meats, vegetables and seafoods, including:

caldo – broth *(caldo tlalpeño* is a hearty chicken, vegetables and chili variety)

gazpacho – chilled vegetable soup spiced with hot chilies

menudo – tripe soup made with the spiced entrails of various four-legged beasts

pozole – rich, spicy stew of hominy (large maize kernels) with meat and vegetables

Note that *sopa de arroz* is not soup at all but rice pilaf.

Seafood

Seafood is good along the coasts and in the major cities, where customers abound. Be suspicious of seafood in out-of-the-way mountain towns, and take care with uncooked seafood.

Fish is often eaten as a *filete* (filet), *frito* (fried whole fish), or *al mojo de ajo* (fried in butter and garlic). *Ceviche*, the popular Mexican cocktail, is raw seafood (fish,

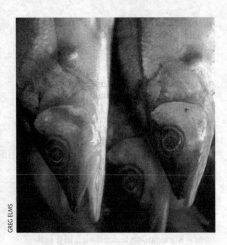

GREG ELMS

shrimp, etc) marinated in lime and mixed with onions, chilies, garlic and tomatoes. There are other seafood *cocteles* (cocktails) as well.

Fish

atún – tuna
corvina – bass
filete de pescado – fish filet
huachinango – red snapper
mojarra – perch
pescado – fish after it has been caught
pez – fish that's still alive in the water
pez espada – swordfish
robalo – sea bass
salmón (ahumada) – (smoked) salmon
tiburón – shark
trucha – trout

Other Seafood

abulón – abalone
almejas – clams
calamar – squid
camarones – shrimp
camarones gigantes – prawns
cangrejo – large crab
caracol – snail
jaiba – small crab
langosta – lobster
mariscos – shellfish
ostiones – oysters
pulpo – octopus

Meat & Poultry

Meat and poultry are often listed separately as *carnes* and *aves* on Mexican menus.

Meat

bistec, bisteck, bistec/bisteck de res – beef-steak
cabra – goat
cabrito – kid (young goat)
carne – meat, usually beef if not otherwise specified
carnero – mutton
carnitas – deep-fried pork
cerdo – pork
chicharrón – deep-fried pork rind; pigskin cracklings
chorizo – spicy pork sausage
cochinita – suckling pig
conejo – rabbit
cordero – lamb
hamburguesa – hamburger
hígado – liver
jamón – ham
puerco – pork
res – beef
salchicha – spicy pork sausage
ternera – veal
tocino – bacon
venado – deer (venison)

Poultry

faisán – pheasant; turkey
guajolote – turkey
pato – duck
pavo – turkey
pechuga – chicken breast
pollo – chicken

Cuts & Preparation

Meat, poultry and seafood are prepared and served in many ways, including the following:

adobado – marinated, seasoned and dried
ahumado – smoked
a la parrilla – grilled, perhaps over charcoal
a la plancha – 'planked': grilled on a hotplate
a la tampiqueña – 'Tampico style': sautéed, thinly sliced meat, officially also marinated in garlic, oil and oregano
a la veracruzana – 'Veracruz style': topped with tomato, olive and onion sauce

al carbón – charcoal-grilled
al horno – baked
al mojo de ajo – in garlic sauce
al pastor – 'shepherd-style': roasted on a
stake or spit
alambre – shish kebab, 'en brochette'
arrachera – skirt steak
asada – grilled
barbacoa – literally 'barbecued,' but meat is
usually covered and placed under hot
coals
bien cocido – well-done
birria – stew-cum-broth of kid or mutton
and chopped onion
cabeza – head
cecina – thin-sliced beef, soaked in lemon or
orange and salt, then grilled
chuleta – chop (such as a lamb chop)
cocido – boiled
coctel – appetizer (seafood, fruit, etc) in sauce
costillas – ribs
empanizado – breaded
filete – filet of fish or meat
frito – fried
lengua – tongue
lomo – loin
milanesa – breaded Italian-style
mixiotes – stew of sliced lamb
mole – sauce made from chilies and other ingredients, often served over chicken or
turkey
mole poblano – delicious Puebla-style mole,
with many ingredients, including hot
chilies and bitter chocolate
molleja – gizzard
patas – trotters (feet)
pibil – meat (usually suckling pig or chicken)
flavored with ingredients such as garlic,
pepper, chili, oregano and orange juice,
then baked (best the traditional way – in
a pit called a *pib*)
pierna – leg
poco cocido – rare

Vegetables

Legumbres (legumes) and *verduras* (vegetables) are usually mixed into salads, soups
and sauces or used as garnishes. But there
are still plenty of options for vegetarians,
and many Mexican towns have good vegetarian restaurants.

aguacate – avocado
betabel – beet
calabaza – squash or pumpkin
cebolla – onion
champiñones – mushrooms
chícharos – peas
col – cabbage
coliflor – cauliflower
ejotes – green beans
elote – corn on the cob; commonly served
from steaming bins on street carts
ensalada (verde) – (green) salad
espárragos – asparagus
espinaca – spinach
frijoles – beans, usually black
hongos – mushrooms
lechuga – lettuce
lentejas – lentils
nopales – green prickly-pear cactus ears
papas – potatoes
papas fritas – french fries (chips)
pepino – cucumber
rábano – radish
zanahoria – carrot

Fruit

chabacano – apricot
coco – coconut
durazno – peach
ensalada de frutas – plain mixed seasonal
fruits
fresa – strawberry or other berry
fruta – fruit
guanabana – green pearlike fruit
guayaba – guava (better yellow than pink)
higo – fig
jitomate – tomato (not to be confused with
tomate)
limón – lime or lemon
mamey – sweet, orange tropical fruit
mango – mango
manzana – apple
melón – melon
naranja – orange
papaya – papaya
pera – pear
piña – pineapple
plátano – banana
tomate or *tomatillo* – green tomato-like fruit
used to make salsa verde
toronja – grapefruit

tuna – nopal (prickly-pear) cactus fruit
uva – grape
zapote – sweet fruit of the chicle tree, best liquidized with, for example, orange juice or Kahlua

Desserts

Most *postres* (desserts) are small after-thoughts to a meal.

arroz con leche – rice pudding
crepa – crêpe; thin pancake
flan – custard; crème caramel
galletas – cookies/biscuits
gelatina – Jell-O (jelly)
helado – ice cream
nieve – sorbet
pastel – pastry or cake
pay – fruit pie

Other Foods

Other useful food words are:

aceite – oil
aceitunas – olives
arroz – rice

azúcar – sugar
bocadillo – sandwich, often in a long roll (see *sandwich* below)
catsup – ketchup; US-style spiced tomato sauce
chipotle – chilies dried, then fermented in vinegar; many Mexicans feel a meal is not complete without it
cilantro – fresh coriander leaf
crema – cream
entremeses – hors d'oeuvres
huitlacoche – a kind of mold that grows on maize, considered a delicacy since Aztec times
leche – milk
mantequilla – butter
margarina – margarine
paleta – flavored ice on a stick
pan (integral) – (whole-grain) bread
pimienta – pepper
queso – cheese
salsa roja/verde – red/green sauce made with chilies, onions, tomato, lemon or lime juice and spices
sal – salt
sandwich – toasted sandwich

Mexican ice cream: *muy delicioso*

GREG ELMS

At the Table

Note that *el menú* can mean either the menu or the special fixed-price meal of the day. If you want the menu, ask for *la carta*.

copa – wineglass
cuchara – spoon
cuchillo – knife
cuenta – check (bill)
mesero/a – waiter
plato – plate
propina – tip
servilleta – napkin
taza – cup
tenedor – fork
vaso – glass

DRINKS

As befits a country with such a warm climate, a huge variety of *bebidas* (drinks) are imbibed in Mexico. Don't drink any water, ice or drinks made with water unless you know the water has been purified or boiled (see the Health section, earlier in this chapter). You can buy bottles of inexpensive purified or mineral water everywhere.

Nonalcoholic Drinks

Tea & Coffee Ordinary Mexican *café*, grown mostly near Córdoba and Orizaba and in Chiapas, is flavorful but often served weak. Those addicted to stronger caffeine shots should ask for 'Nescafé' – unless they're lucky enough to be in one of the real coffeehouses that are now appearing. A few of these serve Mexican organic coffee, from Oaxaca or Chiapas. Tea, invariably in bags, is a profound disappointment to any real tea drinker.

café americano – black coffee
café con crema – coffee with cream, served separately
café con leche – coffee with hot milk, half-and-half
café negro – black coffee
espresso – espresso, brewed using steam pressure
Nescafé – any instant coffee *(agua para Nescafé* is a cup of boiled water presented with a jar of instant coffee)

GREG ELMS

té de manzanilla – chamomile tea
té negro – black tea, to which you can add *leche* (milk) if you wish

Fruit & Vegetable Drinks Pure fresh juices *(jugos)* are popular in Mexico and readily available from street-side stalls and juice bars. If you see the fruit being squeezed in front of you, as is often the case, it will almost certainly be safe to drink. Every fruit and a few of the squeezable vegetables are used.

Licuados are blends of fruit or juice with water and sugar. *Licuados con leche* use milk instead of water. The delicious combinations are practically limitless. In juice bars you can expect that purified water is used, but don't assume the same for street-side juice stalls.

Aguas de fruta (also called *aguas frescas* or *aguas preparadas)* are made by adding sugar and water to fruit juice or a syrup made from mashed grains or seeds. You'll often see them in big glass jars on the counters of juice stands.

Atole is a sweet, hot drink thickened with *masa* (corn dough) and flavored with chocolate, cinnamon or various fruits. It is often consumed at breakfast with tamales.

Soft Drinks *Refrescos* are bottled or canned soft drinks, and there are some interesting and tasty local varieties.

Many brands of *agua mineral* (mineral water) are derived from Mexican springs – Tehuacán and Garci Crespo are two of the best and can sometimes be obtained with refreshing flavors, as well as plain.

Alcoholic Drinks

Mexico produces a fascinating variety of alcoholic drinks made from grapes, grains and cacti. Foreign liquors are widely available, too.

Those for whom alcohol is a problem, not a pleasure, will find Alcoholics Anonymous schedules for Mexico (many meetings are in English), and other tips about staying off the bottle, on the Mexico Mike Internet site (www.mexicomike.com).

Drinking Places Everyone knows about Mexican cantinas, those pits of wild drinking and wilder displays of machismo. A friend was once in a cantina in Mexico City where it was hardly noticed when a man drew his pistol and fired several rounds into the ceiling. Cantinas are generally loud but not quite that loud.

In fact most Mexican drinking establishments are far less daunting than cantinas. Most travelers and a great number of Mexicans do any drinking they do in cafés, bars or lounges where anyone will feel at home. A relatively recent innovation is the 'pub' – usually a place with recorded rock or dance music and themed decor of some kind, geared to a young social crowd.

Cantinas are usually for men only – no women or children allowed. They don't usually have 'Cantina' signs outside, but can be identified by Wild West-type swinging half-doors, signs prohibiting minors, and a generally raucous atmosphere. Those who enter must be prepared to drink hard. They might be challenged by a local to go one-for-one at a bottle of tequila, mezcal or brandy. If you're not up to that, excuse yourself and beat a retreat.

Some of the nicer cantinas don't get upset about the presence of a woman if she is accompanied by a regular patron. Leave judgment of the situation up to a local, though.

Besides cantinas, Mexico has lots of bars, lounges, 'pubs' and cafés where all are welcome.

Mezcal, Tequila & Pulque Mezcal can be made from the sap of several species of the maguey plant, a spray of long, thick spikes sticking out of the ground. Tequila is a type of mezcal made only from the maguey *Agave tequilana weber*, grown in Jalisco and a few other states. The production method for both is similar (see 'Tequila' in the Western Central Highlands chapter), except that for mezcal the chopped up *piña* (core) of the plant is baked, whereas for tequila it's steamed. The final product is a clear liquid (sometimes artificially tinted) which is at its most potent as tequila. The longer the aging process, the smoother the drink and the higher the price. A repugnant *gusano* (worm) is added to each bottle of mezcal.

For foreigners not used to the potency of straight tequila, Mexican bartenders invented the margarita, a concoction of tequila, lime juice and liqueur served in a salt-rimmed glass. Sangrita is a sweet, non-alcoholic, tomato, citrus, chile and spice drink often downed as a tequila chaser.

Pulque is a cheap drink derived directly from the sap of the maguey, much less potent than tequila or mezcal. The foamy, milky, slightly sour liquid spoils quickly and cannot easily be bottled and shipped. Most pulque is produced around Mexico City and served in male-dominated, working-class *pulquerías*.

How to Drink Tequila Like a Pro

There's almost as much mystique about drinking tequila or mezcal as there is about the Japanese tea ceremony. Some insist that if you don't want to look silly you must:

1) lick the back of your hand and sprinkle salt on it
2) lick the salt
3) down the shot *(trago)* in one gulp
4) suck on a wedge of lime
5) lick more salt
6) if you're drinking mezcal, eat the worm when the bottle is finished

In fact, Mexicans may equally well suck a lime *before* downing the shot instead of after it. Nor is there any law whatsoever against savoring tequila or mezcal in a much more measured manner like, say, a glass of brandy. Some real tequila aficionados argue that a quality tequila is wasted if thrown back in one shot.

Beer Breweries were established in Mexico by German immigrants in the late 19th century. Mexico's several large brewing companies produce more than 25 brands of *cerveza* (beer), many of which are excellent. Each major company has a premium beer, such as Bohemia and Corona de Barril (usually served in bottles); several standard beers, such as Carta Blanca, Superior and Dos Equis ('Two Xs'); and 'popular' brands, such as Corona, Tecate and Modelo. All are blond lagers meant to be served chilled. Each of the large companies also produces an *oscura* (dark) beer, such as Negra Modelo or Dos Equis Oscura. There are some regional beers, too, brewed to similar tastes.

Wine Wine is far less popular than beer and tequila, and home-grown wines are usually the cheapest on any Mexican restaurant's wine list, but the country's few large wine growers, all around Ensenada in Baja California, produce some quite drinkable vintages.

Pedro Domecq, which also owns Sauza, one of the two big tequila firms, has the highest profile. Its Cabernet Sauvignon XA, costing US$15 to US$20 in restaurants, is probably the most popular Mexican red. Its Zinfandel XA is of similar quality. Domecq's Calafia and Los Reyes reds and whites cost little over half that.

The top three wineries in quality are generally considered to be Chateau Camou, Bodegas de Santo Tomás and Monte Xanic. The very best wines fetch US$60 a bottle in upmarket restaurants.

Other northern centers, such as Zacatecas and Parras (home of the Americas' oldest winery), produce less polished but still perfectly drinkable wines.

Wine mixed with fruit juice is the basis of the tasty *sangría*.

ENTERTAINMENT

Little beats a Mexican fiesta for entertainment, but if none is being celebrated, you have alternatives. People-watching from a café on a plaza is well up on the list. In the larger cities and resorts the range of entertainment is broad, with dance clubs, music bars (rock, jazz, salsa, mariachi, folk, etc – live or recorded) and other bars and lounges abounding. In the big cities you'll also find opera, classical concerts, and Spanish-language theater. Cinemas screen many foreign movies, always in their original language, with Spanish subtitles, unless they are children's films.

One thing specially worth making an effort to see is a performance of Mexican folk dance, always colorful and interesting (see Arts in the Facts about Mexico chapter). If you can't catch dance in its natural setting – at a fiesta – some good regular shows are put on in theaters and hotels. The most dazzlingly elaborate is Mexico City's Ballet Folklórico.

SPECTATOR SPORTS

Events such as soccer games, bullfights and *charreadas* (rodeos) can be fascinating; if the action doesn't enthrall you, the crowd probably will.

Soccer (Football)

Fútbol is the country's favorite sport. Mexico has an 18-team national Primera División, and some impressive stadiums. Mexico City's Estadio Azteca (Aztec Stadium) hosted the 1970 and 1986 World Cup finals.

The two most popular teams in the country are América, of Mexico City, nicknamed Las Águilas (the Eagles), and Guadalajara (Las Chivas, the Goats). They attract large followings wherever they play. Other leading clubs are UNAM (the Universidad Autónoma de Mexico, nicknamed Las Pumas), Cruz Azul, Atlante, Toros Neza and Necaxa, all from Mexico City; Universidad de Guadalajara, Universidad Autónoma de Guadalajara (Los Tecos), and Atlas, all from Guadalajara; Toluca, Celaya, Santos (of Torreón) and Monterrey.

The biggest games of the year are those between América and Guadalajara, known as 'Los Clásicos.' These teams attract crowds of 100,000 when they meet at the Estadio Azteca. Crowds at other games range from a few thousand to around 70,000. Games are spaced over the weekend from Friday to Sunday; details are printed in *The News* and the Spanish-language press. Attending a game is fun; rivalry between opposing fans is generally good-humored. Tickets can be bought at the gate and can cost from less than US$1 to US$10, depending on the quality of your seat.

Mexico's soccer calendar is divided into a *torneo de invierno* (winter season, August to December) and a *torneo de verano* (summer season, January to May), each ending in eight-team playoffs (La Liguilla) and eventually a two-leg final to decide the champion.

The website www.mexicansoccerlinks .com is good.

Baseball

Professional *béisbol* is fairly popular. The winner of the October-to-January Liga Mexicana del Pacífico, with teams from the northwest, represents Mexico in the February Serie del Caribe (the biggest event in Latin American baseball) against the champions of Venezuela, Puerto Rico and the Dominican Republic. Younger American players on the way up often play in the Pacific league. The Béisbol Liga Mexicana (www.lmb.com.mx), with 16 teams spread down the center and east of the country, plays from March to August. *Afición* newspaper has good baseball coverage.

Other Sports

A *charreada* is a rodeo, held particularly in the northern half of the country during fiestas and at regular venues often called *lienzos charros*.

The fast, exciting Basque game *pelota*, brought by the Spanish, is played in Mexico as *jai alai* ('HIGH-lie'). It's a bit like squash, played on a long court with a hard ball and with curved baskets attached to the arm. You can see it played by semiprofessionals in Mexico City and Tijuana, among other places.

As much showbiz as sport is *lucha libre*, wrestling. Participants give themselves names like Shocker, Los Karate Boy and Heavy Metal, then clown around in fancy dress.

SHOPPING

See the Artesanías special section for words and pictures on the wonderful range of *artesanías* (handicrafts), which are Mexico's outstanding buys. If you buy crafts in the villages where they are made or from individual vendors on the streets or small markets in towns – and not from shops or large centralized crafts markets – then a lot more of the profit will go to the (usually

The Fiesta Brava

To many gringo eyes the *corrida de toros* (bullfight) hardly seems to be sport or, for that matter, entertainment. Mexicans see it as both and more. It's as much a ritualistic dance as a fight, and readily lends itself to a variety of symbolic interpretations, mostly related to machismo. It's said that Mexicans arrive on time for only two events – funerals and bullfights.

The corrida de toros (literally, running of the bulls) or *fiesta brava* (wild festival) begins promptly at 4, 4.30 or 5 pm on a Sunday. To the sound of music, usually a Spanish *paso doble*, the matador, in his *traje de luces* (suit of lights), and the toreros (his assistants) give the traditional *paseíllo* (salute) to the fight authorities and the crowd. Then the first of the day's bulls (there are usually six in an afternoon) is released from its pen for the first of the ritual's three *suertes* (acts) or *tercios* (thirds).

The cape-waving toreros tire the bull by luring him around the ring. After a few minutes two *picadores*, on heavily padded horses, enter and jab long lances *(picas)* into the bull's shoulders to weaken him. Somehow this is often the most gruesome part of the whole process.

After the picadores leave the ring the *suerte de banderillas* begins, as the toreros attempt to stab three pairs of elongated darts into the bull's shoulders without getting impaled on his horns. After that the *suerte de muleta* is the climax, in which the matador has exactly 16 minutes to kill the bull. Starting with fancy cape work to tire the animal, the matador then exchanges his large cape for the smaller muleta and takes sword in hand, baiting the bull to charge before delivering the fatal *estocada* (lunge) with his sword. The matador must deliver the estocada into the neck from a position directly in front of the animal.

If the matador succeeds, and he usually does, the bull collapses and an assistant dashes into the ring to slice its jugular. If the applause from the crowd warrants, he will also cut off an ear or two and sometimes the tail for the matador. The dead bull is dragged from the ring to be butchered for sale.

A 'good' bullfight depends not only on the skill and courage of the matador but also the spirit of the bulls. Animals lacking heart for the fight bring shame on the ranch that bred them. Very occasionally, a bull that has fought outstandingly is *indultado* (spared) – an occasion for great celebration – and will then retire to stud.

The veteran Eloy Cavasos, from Monterrey, is often acclaimed as Mexico's best matador. Alfredo Lomeli and Eulalio 'Zotoluco' López are younger stars. Bullfights featuring star matadors from Spain such as Enrique Ponce, El Juli, José Tomás or El Cordobés have added spice. *The News* runs an informative weekly bullfighting column called Blood on the Sand.

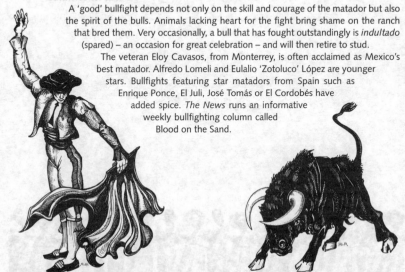

poor) people who make them, instead of to entrepreneurs.

For everyday purchases, wealthier urban Mexicans like to shop in glitzy modern malls, big super/hypermarkets and department stores. These are usually in residential districts where the travelers have little reason to go. In city centers you're more likely to find smaller, older shops and markets, which are probably more fun in any case!

Getting There & Away

AIR

Most visitors to Mexico arrive by air.

Airports & Airlines

About 30 Mexican cities receive direct flights from North America. Mexico City receives the most, followed by Guadalajara, Cancún, Monterrey and Acapulco. There are connections to many other places in Mexico, the majority of which go through Mexico City.

Airlines with the most service from the USA and Canada to Mexico include Air Canada, Alaska, America West, American, Canadian, Continental, Delta, Northwest, TWA, United and the two main Mexican airlines, Aeroméxico and Mexicana.

You can fly to Mexico without changing planes from at least 25 US and Canadian cities, and there are one-stop connecting flights from many others.

From Europe there are flights to Mexico City and Cancún. Only a few airlines fly nonstop, among them Aeroméxico, Air France, British Airways, Iberia, KLM Royal Dutch Airlines and Lufthansa Airlines. US airlines will require that you change planes in the USA, as may alliance partners such as KLM and Northwest.

From Havana, Cuba, you can fly into Mexico City by Mexicana and to Cancún and six other cities by Aerocaribe, a Mexicana subsidiary. The same two airlines and Guatemala's Aviateca fly Guatemala-Mexico routes including Flores-Palenque/Cancún/Chetumal, and Guatemala City-Mexico City/Cancún/Mérida. Aerocaribe also flies from Belize to Chetumal, Cancún and Mérida.

From other Central American countries, you generally have to fly into Mexico City unless you change planes in Guatemala. Airlines include Mexicana, Aviateca, TACA of El Salvador and Panama's Copa Airlines.

Flights from South America go to Mexico City except for a few to Cancún from major cities such as Buenos Aires, Lima, Rio de Janeiro and São Paulo. Carriers between South America and Mexico include Mexicana, Aeroméxico, Copa (from Lima and Quito), Varig (from Brazil) and Aerolíneas Argentinas.

See the Getting There & Away sections under individual cities for more on who flies where.

Buying Tickets

The cost of flying to Mexico depends on where you are flying from and to, what time of year you fly (you pay more around Christmas and New Year's and during the summer holidays), how long you're traveling (usually the longer the trip, the more expensive) and whether you have access to discount or advance-purchase fares or special offers.

Start shopping for airfares as soon as you can; the cheapest tickets often have to be bought months in advance, and popular flights sell out early. Airlines are a good source of information on routes, timetables and standard fares, but they don't usually sell the cheapest tickets. There are dozens of fares for any given route: consult travel agents and the Internet.

Some travel agencies specialize in officially or unofficially discounted air tickets. In the USA, the cheapest fares are available through 'consolidators.' In the UK, there are unbonded agencies known as bucket shops. Their tickets often cost less than advance-purchase fares.

Most discount ticket agencies are well established and honorable, but unscrupulous agents might take your money and disappear before issuing a ticket, or issue an invalid or unusable ticket. Check carefully before handing over the money, and confirm the reservation directly with the airline.

Charter flights can offer cheap deals too, and some agencies specialize in these. The dates of charter flights are fixed.

A Round-the-World ticket can be a real bargain, sometimes costing the same or less than an ordinary roundtrip ticket to Mexico.

Warning

The information in this chapter is particularly vulnerable to change: prices for international travel are volatile, routes are introduced and canceled, schedules change, special deals come and go, and rules and visa requirements are amended. Airlines and governments seem to take a perverse pleasure in making price structures and regulations as complicated as possible. You should check directly with the airline or a travel agent to make sure you understand how a fare (and any ticket you may buy) works. In addition, the travel industry is highly competitive and there are many hidden costs and benefits.

The upshot of this is that you should get opinions, quotes and advice from as many airlines and travel agents as possible before you part with your hard-earned cash. The details given in this chapter should be regarded as pointers and are not a substitute for your own careful, up-to-date research.

Prices start at about UK£900 from Britain or A$2100 from Australia, though they tend to be more expensive if you want to include Mexico.

Note that fares given in this book are a guide only; they are approximate and based on the rates advertised at research time. Quoted airfares do not imply a recommendation for the carrier.

Buying Tickets Online The Internet can be a useful source of cheap-fare quotes and even bookings. To buy a ticket on the Internet, you need to use a credit card.

Two sites to check for fares from North America are Travelocity (www.travelocity .com) and Expedia (http://expedia.msn .com). In North America or Britain, try Flifo (www.flifo.com). For flights from Britain, look at Cheap Tickets (www.cheaptickets .com) and Ebookers (www.ebookers.com). In Europe, try www.etn.nl. In Australia, try www.travel.com.au. The Lonely Planet website (www.lonelyplanet.com) has more links.

Most airlines also have their own website with online ticket sales, sometimes discounted for online customers. Internet users will find links to 500 or so such sites at http:// dir.yahoo.com/Business_and_Economy/ Companies/Travel/Airlines.

Travelers with Special Needs

If you have special needs of any sort – you're vegetarian, traveling in a wheelchair, taking the baby – let the airline know as soon as possible so they can make arrangements accordingly. Remind them when you reconfirm your booking (at least 72 hours before departure) and again when you check in at the airport. Don't trust a travel agent to do this for you.

Departure Tax

A departure tax equivalent to about US$17 is levied on international flights from Mexico. If you buy your ticket in Mexico, the tax is included in your ticket cost; if you buy it outside Mexico, the tax may or may not be included. The letters XD on your ticket show that the tax has been paid. If it hasn't, you must pay with cash during airport check-in.

The USA & Canada

Some good fares are offered by well-known student travel agencies with branches in major cities, including STA Travel (www.statravel.com), Council Travel (www.counciltravel.com) and, in Canada, Travel CUTS (www.travelcuts.com). You don't have to be a student to use these agencies.

Check with a travel agent or look in newspapers and magazines for cheap tickets through consolidators. (They're the ones listing tables of destinations and fares and toll-free numbers to call.)

The Sunday editions of the *San Francisco Chronicle-Examiner*, *New York Times* and *Los Angeles Times* usually advertise cheap flights to Mexico City. Free papers such as New York's *Village Voice* and the Bay Area's *Express* and *San Francisco Bay Guardian* are also good places to look.

Here are some typical examples of tickets, *roundtrip*, at one week's notice in the low season (full fare/discounted fare):

from	to Mexico City	to Cancún	to Acapulco
Chicago	US$450/ 360	US$500/ 375	US$540/ 410
Dallas/ Fort Worth	US$560/ 360	US$700/ 275	US$640/ 460
Los Angeles	US$450/ 370	US$540/ 430	US$500/ 360
Miami	US$530/ 390	US$510/ 350	US$470/ 460
New York	US$600/ 400	US$570/ 280	US$675/ 500
Toronto	C$970/ 720	C$880/ 660	C$1320/ 850

Another possibility is a package-tour flight. Check newspaper travel ads and call a package-tour agent, asking if you can buy 'air only' (just the roundtrip air transportation, not the hotel or other features). This is usually cheaper than buying a discounted roundtrip ticket.

Australia & New Zealand

There are no direct flights from Australia or New Zealand to Mexico. The cheapest way to get there is usually via the USA (normally Los Angeles). Other routes are via Japan or via South America with airlines such as Aerolíneas Argentinas. From Sydney/ Melbourne to Mexico City via Los Angeles, typical low/high-season roundtrip fares are around A$2000/2300. Check US visa requirements if you're traveling via the USA.

Both Flight Centre (☎ 02-9281-6466, www.flightcentre.com.au) and STA Travel (www.statravel.com) are major dealers in cheap airfares in both Australia and New Zealand, with offices in numerous cities. Also check the Internet and travel agents' ads in the yellow pages and newspapers.

Europe

Typically, a discounted or advance-purchase roundtrip fare from anywhere in western Europe to Mexico for up to six months costs between UK£350 and UK£450. Most likely, the earlier you buy, the cheaper the ticket will be. Fares also vary a little between high and low seasons.

With a normal roundtrip ticket, you can often change the date of the return leg, subject to seat availability, at little or no cost – it's worth checking before you buy the ticket. One-way and open-jaw tickets can be useful if you want to hop from one part of Mexico to another, or between Mexico and elsewhere in the Americas, without backtracking. With an open-jaw, you usually depart from, and return to, the same city in Europe.

Most ticket types are available at discount rates from cheap ticket agencies in Europe's bargain flight centers, such as London, Amsterdam and Paris.

If you're traveling via the USA, remember to check US visa requirements.

Ticket Agents in the UK For bargain tickets, try the Internet or the travel section in a good weekend newspaper, such as the *Sunday Times* or Saturday's *Independent*, or look in *Time Out* or other London magazines advertising cheap flights.

If a travel agent is registered with the ABTA (Association of British Travel Agents), as most are, ABTA will guarantee a refund or an alternative if the agent goes out of business after you have paid for your flight.

Reputable agencies offering good-value fares include the following (all have branches in other cities, too):

Journey Latin America (☎ 020-8747-3108, www .journeylatinamerica.co.uk), 12 & 13 Heathfield Terrace, Chiswick, London W4 4JE

STA Travel (☎ 020-7581-4132, www.statravel.com), 86 Old Brompton Rd, London SW7 3LQ

Trailfinders (☎ 020-7938-3939, www.trailfinder .com), 194 Kensington High St, London W8 7RG

usit CAMPUS (☎ 0870-240-1010, www .campustravel.co.uk), 52 Grosvenor Gardens, London SW1W 0AG

Ticket Agents Elsewhere in Europe International student/youth travel agencies with branches in many countries (and usually with good fares for everybody) include STA Travel (www.statravel.com), Council Travel (www.counciltravel.com),

Air Travel Glossary

Baggage Allowance This will be written on your ticket and usually includes one 20kg item to go in the hold, plus one item of hand luggage.

Bucket Shops These are unbonded travel agencies specializing in discounted airline tickets.

Cancellation Penalties If you have to cancel or change a discounted ticket, there are often heavy penalties involved; insurance can sometimes be taken out against these penalties. Some airlines impose penalties on regular tickets as well, particularly against 'no-show' passengers.

Check-In Airlines ask you to check in a certain time ahead of the flight departure (usually one to two hours on international flights). If you fail to check in on time and the flight is overbooked, the airline can cancel your booking and give your seat to somebody else.

Confirmation Having a ticket written out with the flight and date you want doesn't mean you have a seat until the agent has checked with the airline that your status is 'OK' or confirmed. Meanwhile you could just be 'on request.'

Consolidator This is the US equivalent of a bucket shop: a consolidator buys seats in bulk from airlines at considerable discounts and resells them to the public through travel agents or newspaper or magazine ads.

ITX An ITX, or 'independent inclusive tour excursion,' is often available on tickets to popular holiday destinations. Officially, it's a package deal combined with hotel accommodations, but many agents will sell you one of these for the flight only and give you phony hotel vouchers in the unlikely event that you're challenged at the airport.

Lost Tickets If you lose your airline ticket, an airline will usually treat it like a traveler's check and, after inquiries, issue you another one. Legally, however, an airline is entitled to treat it like cash: If you lose it, it's gone forever. Take good care of your tickets.

No-Shows These are passengers who fail to show up for their flight. Full-fare passengers who fail to turn up are sometimes entitled to travel on a later flight. The rest are penalized (see Cancellation Penalties).

On Request This is an unconfirmed booking for a flight.

Open-Jaw Tickets These are return tickets on which you fly to one place but return from another. If available, these can save you backtracking to your arrival point.

Overbooking Airlines hate to fly with empty seats, and because every flight has some passengers who fail to show up, airlines often book more passengers than they have seats. Usually excess passengers make up for the no-shows, but occasionally somebody gets bumped. Guess who it's most likely to be? The passengers who check in late.

Reconfirmation At least 72 hours prior to departure time of an onward or return flight, you must contact the airline and 'reconfirm' that you intend to be on the flight. If you don't do this, the airline can delete your name from the passenger list and you could lose your seat.

Restrictions Discounted tickets often have various restrictions on them – such as advance payment, minimum and maximum periods you must be away (for example, a minimum of two weeks or a maximum of one year) and penalties for changing the tickets.

Round-the-World Tickets RTW tickets give you a limited period (usually a year) in which to circumnavigate the globe. You can go anywhere the carrying airlines go, as long as you don't backtrack. The number of stopovers or total number of separate flights is decided before you set off, and they usually cost a bit more than a basic return flight.

Stand-By This is a discounted ticket on which you fly only if there is a seat free at the last moment. Stand-by fares are usually available only on domestic routes.

Travel Periods Ticket prices vary with the time of year. There is a low (off-peak) season and a high (peak) season, and often a low-shoulder season and a high-shoulder season as well. Usually the fare depends on your outward flight. If you depart in the high season and return in the low season, you pay the high-season fare.

Airline Toll-Free Numbers in Mexico

Many airlines have telephone numbers you can call toll free from anywhere in Mexico:

Aerolíneas Internacionales	☎ 800-990-91-00	Delta Air Lines	☎ 800-902-21-00
Aerolitoral	☎ 800-021-40-00	KLM Royal Dutch Airlines	☎ 800-900-08-00
Aeroméxico	☎ 800-021-40-00	Mexicana	☎ 800-366-54-00
America West	☎ 800-235-92-92		in Guadalajara;
American Airlines	☎ 800-904-60-00		☎ 800-502-20-00
Aviacsa/Aeroexo	☎ 800-006-22-00		in Mexico City
Aviateca	☎ 800-711-19-66	Northwest Airlines	☎ 800-900-08-00
Canadian Airlines	☎ 800-900-20-00	TAESA	☎ 800-904-63-00
Continental Airlines	☎ 800-900-50-00	United Airlines	☎ 800-003-07-77

usit CAMPUS (www.campustravel.co.uk) and Kilroy Travels (www.kilroytravels.com).

Other agencies specializing in cheap tickets and student/youth travel include the following:

France – Nouvelles Frontières (☎ 08-03-33-33-33, Minitel 3615 NF, www.nouvelles-frontieres.com) specializes in discount long-distance flights and has dozens of offices around France.

Germany – Alternativ Tours (☎ 030-8-81-20-89), Wilmersdorfer Strasse 94, Wilmersdorf, Berlin; and Atlas Reisewelt in many cities. Cheap flights are advertised in the Berlin magazines *Zitty* and *Tip*.

Ireland – usit NOW (☎ 01-679-8833, www.usitnow.ie), 19 Aston Quay, Dublin

Italy – CTS (☎ 06-462-04-31, www.cts.it), Via Genova 16, off Via Nazionale, Rome, has branches all over Italy.

Netherlands – NBBS Reizen (☎ 020-624-09-89), Rokin 66, Amsterdam; and Malibu Travel (☎ 020-626-32-20), Prinsengracht 230, Amsterdam

Scandinavia – Kilroy Travels, with branches in many cities, is a well-established cheap-flight agent, with especially good fares for people under 26 and students under 35.

Spain – Halcón Viajes (☎ 902-300-600), with over 500 branches around Spain, is reliable and has respectable fares; TIVE (☎ 91-347-77-88), Calle José Ortega y Gasset 71, Madrid (also in 40 other cities), has youth and student fares.

South America

Regular fares to/from Mexico City start at around US$500 for Caracas, US$550 for Lima, US$800 for São Paulo and US$900 for Buenos Aires. One-way and roundtrip fares are much the same. Asatej Group (www.asatej.org), with offices in nine Argentine cities and in Santiago de Chile and Montevideo, offers some good student/youth fares (for instance, Buenos Aires to Mexico for US$500 to US$600 roundtrip).

LAND
Border Crossings

There are about 40 official road crossing points on the US-Mexico border, including the following:

Arizona – Douglas/Agua Prieta, Nogales/Nogales, San Luis/San Luis Río Colorado and Naco/Naco (all open 24 hours); Sasabe/El Sásabe (open 8 am to 10 pm); Lukeville/Sonoita (open 8 am to midnight)

California – Calexico/Mexicali (two crossings, one open 24 hours); San Ysidro/Tijuana (open 24 hours); Otay Mesa/Mesa de Otay (near Tijuana airport; open 6 am to 10 pm); Tecate/Tecate (open 6 am to midnight)

New Mexico – Columbus/General Rodrigo M Quevedo (also called Palomas; open 24 hours)

Texas – Brownsville/Matamoros, McAllen/Reynosa, Laredo/Nuevo Laredo, Del Rio/Ciudad Acuña, Eagle Pass/Piedras Negras, Presidio/Ojinaga and El Paso/Ciudad Juárez (all open 24 hours)

There are 10 official border crossings between Guatemala and Mexico, and two between Belize and Mexico. The following are the most frequently used:

La Mesilla/Ciudad Cuauhtémoc on the Pan-American Highway (between Huehuetenango, Guatemala and San Cristóbal de Las Casas, Mexico)

Ciudad Tecún Umán/Ciudad Hidalgo and El Carmen/Talismán (both between Quetzaltenango, Guatemala and Tapachula, Mexico)

Santa Elena/Subteniente López (between Corozal, Belize and Chetumal, Mexico)

Drivers entering Mexico from the south must go through the same procedures as those entering from the USA (see Car & Motorcycle, later in this chapter). Some interior checkpoints of the Instituto Nacional de Migración (INM; National Immigration Institute) are a lot farther from the border than they are in the north – up to 70km.

Crossings to/from Guatemala's Petén region involving river transport are being used by a growing number of travelers (see the River section, later in this chapter).

More information on many of these crossings can be found in the regional chapters.

Bus

The USA Since 1997 buses have been permitted to travel between cities in the US and Mexican interiors. (Previously, they had to terminate at frontier towns.)

Bus companies providing cross-border service include Greyhound (☎ 800-231-2222 in the USA, www.greyhound.com), Autobuses Americanos (☎ 800-784-8333 in the USA), ADO Trailways (☎ 713-921-3838 in the USA) and El Expreso (☎ 713-650-6565 in the USA).

The greatest number of cross-border buses run to/from Texas. Greyhound mostly just goes to/from Mexican border cities such as Tijuana (US$15 from Los Angeles), Mexicali, Reynosa (US$25 from Houston), Nuevo Laredo and Matamoros (US$46 from Austin, Texas), though it also does a Los Angeles-Hermosillo run (US$60).

Autobuses Americanos and El Expreso link US cities such as Houston, Dallas, San Antonio, Albuquerque, Phoenix, Denver, Chicago and Miami with central and northern Mexican cities such as Ciudad Juárez, Chihuahua, Monterrey, Matehuala, San Luis Potosí, Zacatecas, San Miguel de Allende,

Guadalajara and Mexico City. ADO Trailways runs from Houston to Veracruz (US$67), Oaxaca and Tapachula near the Guatemalan border (US$96). The Crucero line runs buses from Hermosillo and Nogales in northwest Mexico to Tucson, Phoenix and Los Angeles in the USA.

Cross-border buses can suffer delays at the border, and it's usually no great inconvenience or greater expense to make your way to the border on one bus, cross it on foot, and then catch an onward bus on the other side. Greyhound serves many US border cities; to reach others, transfer to a smaller bus line.

Guatemala There are fairly frequent daytime buses between the main border points and Guatemalan towns such as Huehuetenango (2 hours, US$1 from La Mesilla) and Quetzaltenango (3½ hours, US$3.50 from La Mesilla; 2½ hours, US$1.75 from Ciudad Tecún Umán).

From Guatemala City, Transportes Fortaleza (☎ 230-3390), 19ª Calle 8-70, Zona 1, has hourly buses to Ciudad Tecún Umán (5 hours, US$5) from about 1.30 am to 6 pm. Transportes Galgos (☎ 253-4868), 7ª Avenida 19-44, Zona 1, runs a few daily buses to El Carmen (5 hours, US$6) and two daily to Tapachula, Mexico (6 to 7 hours, US$22). Transportes Velásquez, 20ª Calle & 2ª Avenida, Zona 1, runs hourly buses to La Mesilla (7 hours, US$4.50) from about 8 am to 4 pm. Two buses a day leave the Tapachula bus station for Guatemala City.

Information on the frequent bus service between the border and nearby Mexican towns is given in the Tabasco & Chiapas chapter.

A daily 1st-class bus by Servicio San Juan runs between Flores, Guatemala and Chetumal, Mexico (9 hours, US$35).

Belize Frequent buses run between Belize City and Chetumal (3 to 4 hours, US$5 to US$6). These and other buses link Chetumal with Orange Walk and Corozal in northern Belize. There's more information on border points and buses in the Yucatán Peninsula chapter.

Jars, jars, jars

Fruit stall in Mérida market

Nopales cactus paddles

Chicken stall humor

Tasty treats on banana leaves

Sonoran cactus

Rain forest near Cuetzalán

Cabo San Lucas' rugged Land's End

Cenote Dzitnup, an underground swimming hole near Valladolid, Yucatán

Train

Taking a train to the Mexican border may not be much cheaper than flying when you add in the cost of meals and other expenses. Trains tend to be a little slower, a little cheaper and less frequent than buses. Amtrak (☎ 800-872-7245, www.amtrak.com) serves four US cities from which access to Mexico is easy – cross from San Diego, California, to Tijuana; from El Paso, Texas, to Ciudad Juárez; from Del Rio, Texas, to Ciudad Acuña; and from San Antonio, Texas, take a bus to the border at Eagle Pass or Laredo.

South of the border, Mexican passenger train service is on the verge of collapse after decades of decline. At the time of writing, passenger train service had been withdrawn from all border cities and did not look likely to be reinstated in a hurry.

See the Getting Around chapter and Getting There & Away sections under individual cities for more on Mexican trains.

Car & Motorcycle

Driving into Mexico is not for everyone – you should know some Spanish and have basic mechanical aptitude, large reserves of patience and access to some extra cash for emergencies. You should also note warnings about risk areas for highway robbery (see Dangers & Annoyances in the Facts for the Visitor chapter) and avoid intercity driving at night.

Cars are most useful for travelers who:

- have plenty of time
- plan to go to remote places
- will be camping a lot
- have surfboards, diving equipment or other cumbersome luggage
- will be traveling with a group of four or more

Don't take a car if you:

- are on a tight schedule
- have a small budget
- plan to spend most of your time in urban areas
- will be traveling alone
- want a relaxing trip with minimum risks

Cars are fairly expensive to rent or buy in Mexico, so your best option is to take one in

from the USA. If that means buying it first, you may need a few weeks to find a good vehicle at a reasonable price. It may also take time at the end of your trip to sell the thing.

The best makes of car to take to Mexico are Volkswagen, Nissan/Datsun, Chrysler, General Motors or Ford, which have manufacturing or assembly plants in Mexico and dealers in most big Mexican towns. Big cars are unwieldy on narrow roads and use a lot of gasoline. A sedan with a trunk (boot) provides safer storage than a station wagon or hatchback. Volkswagen camper vans are economical, and parts and service are easy to find.

Take as many spare parts as you can manage and know what to do with (for example, spare fuel filters are very useful). Tires (including spare), shock absorbers and suspension should be in good condition. For security, have something to immobilize the steering wheel, such as 'the Club'; you should also consider getting a kill switch installed.

Motorcycling in Mexico is not for the faint-hearted. Roads and traffic can be rough, and parts and mechanics hard to come by. The only parts you'll find will be for Kawasaki, Honda and Suzuki bikes.

The rules for taking a vehicle into Mexico, described in the next sections, change from time to time. You can check with the American Automobile Association (AAA), a Mexican consulate or a Mexican Government Tourist Office, or call (in the USA) the Mexican tourist information number (☎ 800-446-3942). For more on driving and motorcycling in Mexico, see the Getting Around chapter.

Buying a Car in the USA The border states (particularly California and Texas) have many car lots, and every town has magazines and newspapers with ads from private sellers. Cars there are also likely to have aircon – very desirable in Mexico. To get an idea of used-car prices and trade-in values, consult the *Kelley Blue Book*, on the Internet (www.kbb.com) and at most libraries. About US$1500 to US$2500 should buy a car that will take you around Mexico and still be worth something at the end.

To avoid delay in getting your certificate of title or ownership for the vehicle – which you must take with you to Mexico – you can ask the state's department of motor vehicles for rush service on the transfer of ownership. Alternatively, ask for an official letter stating that you have bought the vehicle and applied for a transfer. If a lienholder's name (for example, a bank that has lent money for the vehicle) is shown on the certificate of title, you'll need a notarized letter giving their permission for you to take the vehicle into Mexico.

Motor Insurance It is very foolish to drive in Mexico without Mexican liability insurance. If you are involved in an accident, you can be jailed and have your vehicle impounded while responsibility is assessed – or, if you are to blame for an accident causing injury or death, until you guarantee restitution to the victims and payment of any fines. This could take weeks or months. A valid Mexican insurance policy is regarded as a guarantee that restitution will be paid, and it will also expedite release of the driver. Mexican law recognizes only Mexican *seguro* (car insurance), so a US or Canadian policy won't help.

Mexican insurance is sold in US border towns; as you approach the border from the USA you will see billboards advertising offices selling Mexican policies. At the busiest border crossings (to Tijuana, Mexicali, Nogales, Agua Prieta, Ciudad Juárez, Nuevo Laredo, Reynosa and Matamoros), there are insurance offices open 24 hours a day. Some deals are better than others.

Check the yellow pages in US border towns. Two organizations worth looking into, both of which offer lots of useful travel information, are Sanborn's (☎ 800-222-0158, www.sanbornsinsurance.com) and also the American Automobile Association (AAA, www.aaa.com). Short-term insurance is about US$6 a day for full coverage on a car worth US$5000; there are big discounts for longer periods.

Driver's License To drive a motor vehicle in Mexico, you need a valid driver's license

from your home country. Mexican police are familiar with US and Canadian licenses. Those from other countries may be scrutinized more closely, but they are still legal.

Vehicle Permit You will need a *permiso de importación temporal de vehículos* (temporary vehicle import permit) if you want to take a vehicle beyond Baja California, Puerto Peñasco in Sonora state or the border zone that extends 20 to 30km into Mexico along the rest of the US frontier and up to 70km from the Guatemalan and Belize frontiers.

Customs officials at the Baja California ports for ferries to the mainland and at INM posts in the US, Guatemalan and Belizean border zones will want to see the permit for your vehicle. You must get this at the *aduana* (customs) office at a border crossing or, in Baja, at the Pichilingue (La Paz) ferry terminal. (Permits are not available at Santa Rosalía, the other Baja ferry port.)

In addition to a passport or proof of US or Canadian citizenship, the person importing the vehicle will need originals and at least one photocopy of each of the following documents, which must all be in his/her own name (people at the office may make photocopies for a small fee):

• tourist card (go to *migración* before you go to the aduana)
• certificate of title for the vehicle
• current registration card or notice
• driver's license (see above)
• either a valid international credit card (such as Visa, MasterCard or American Express) issued by a non-Mexican bank or cash to pay a very large bond (see below)

If the vehicle is not fully paid for, you need a notarized letter from the lender authorizing its use in Mexico for a specified period. If the vehicle is leased or rented, bring the original contract (plus a copy), which must be in the name of the person importing the car, and a notarized letter from the rental firm authorizing the driver to take it into Mexico. Note that few US rental firms allow this.

Bonds for All?

In December 1999, Mexico briefly required all drivers of US-registered cars to pay a refundable deposit (bond) of up to US$800 by credit card or cash to obtain the vehicle permit. This regulation, intended to reduce illegal vehicle importations from the US by Mexicans, provoked such fierce opposition that it was abandoned almost immediately – but it is conceivable that something like it may be introduced in the future.

❀ ❀ ❀ ❀ ❀ ❀ ❀ ❀ ❀ ❀ ❀ ❀

One person cannot bring in two vehicles. If you have a motorcycle attached to your car, you'll need another adult traveling with you to obtain a permit for the motorcycle, and he/she will need to have all the right papers for it. If the motorcycle is registered in your name, you'll need a notarized affidavit authorizing the other person to take it into Mexico. A special permit is needed for vehicles weighing more than 3000kg (about 3.3 US tons).

At the border there will be a building with a parking area for vehicles awaiting permits. Go inside and find the right counter to present your papers. After some signing and stamping of papers, you sign a promise to take the car out of the country, the Banco del Ejército (also called Banjército; it's the army bank) charges a fee of US$12 to your credit card, and you go wait with your vehicle. Make sure you get back the originals of all documents. Eventually someone will come out and give you your vehicle permit and a sticker to be displayed on your windshield.

If you don't have an international credit card, you will have to deposit a cash bond with the Banco del Ejército or an authorized Mexican *afianzadora* (bonding company). The required bond amounts for medium or small cars range from about US$500 for vehicles over 15 years old to around US$6000 for a vehicle up to two years old. There may be taxes and very hefty processing fees to pay too. The bond should be refunded when

the vehicle finally leaves Mexico and the temporary import permit is canceled. If you plan to leave Mexico at a different border crossing, make sure the bonding company will give you a refund there. There are offices for Banco del Ejército and authorized Mexican bonding companies at or near all the major border points.

Your vehicle permit entitles you to take the vehicle in and out of Mexico for the period shown on your tourist card. If the car is still in Mexico after that time, the aduana may start charging fines to your credit card and the car can be confiscated. The permit allows the vehicle to be driven by the owner's spouse or adult children or by other people if the owner is in the vehicle.

When you leave Mexico for the last time, you must have the permit canceled by the Mexican authorities. An official may do this as you enter the border zone, usually 20 to 30km before the border itself. If not, you'll have to find the right official at the border crossing. If you leave Mexico without having the permit canceled, once the permit expires the authorities may assume you've left the vehicle in the country illegally and start charging fines to your credit card.

Only the owner may take the vehicle out of Mexico. If the vehicle is wrecked completely, you must obtain permission to leave it in the country from either the Registro Federal de Vehículos (Federal Registry of Vehicles) in Mexico City or a Hacienda (Treasury Dept) office in another Mexican city; your insurance company can assist you with this.

If you are visiting the state of Sonora only and are entering Mexico at Nogales and then heading south on highway 15, you do not have to pay the US$12 fee or a bond. All you need to show – at the Km 21 checkpoint south of Nogales – is your valid driver's license and proof of ownership or legal possession of the vehicle (such as registration, title, lease contract or notarized permission from leasing company or bank). If you are entering by another route, call ☎ 800-476-6672 for information on 'Sonora Only' permits.

RIVER

River routes across the jungle-straddled Mexico-Guatemala border are fun for the adventurously inclined. There are three main routes, all of which can be used to travel between the great Mayan ruins at Palenque, Mexico and the great Mayan ruins at Tikal, Guatemala.

The busiest and easiest route – which also enables you to visit the Mayan ruins at Yaxchilán and Bonampak, Mexico – is via a short boat ride on the Río Usumacinta between Frontera Corozal, Chiapas, Mexico and Bethel, Guatemala. The others (each with a river ride of four hours or so) are between Benemérito de las Américas, Chiapas and Sayaxché, Guatemala; and between La Palma, Tabasco, Mexico and El Naranjo, Guatemala. In each case, bus services reach the start and end of the river sections. There are additional details on all three of these river routes in the Tabasco & Chiapas chapter.

ORGANIZED TOURS

If you want just a short, easy holiday in Mexico, consider signing up for one of the many package deals offered by travel agents and in newspaper travel sections. Mexican government tourist offices can give you armfuls of brochures about these trips. Costs depend on where and when you go (peak time is usually December to February), but some packages give you flights and accommodations for little more than the cost of an individually bought airfare. For example, a seven-night off-season package trip from New York to Cancún or Acapulco can cost as little as US$500. Some packages also include a rental car and airport transportation in the price.

If you are looking for an adventure- or activity-focused group trip to Mexico, you'll find a wide selection, mainly from North America but also from Europe. Websites to check include Eco Travels in Latin America (www.planeta.com), Baja Travel Guide (www.bajatravel.com) and GORP (Great Outdoor Recreation Pages, www.gorp.com). Following is a partial list of tour operators with offerings to Mexico.

Adventure Center
(☎ 800-227-8747, www.adventure-center.com), 1311 63rd St, Suite 200, Emeryville, CA 94608 USA – ecologically minded adventure trips, including a trek in the mountains of Oaxaca

Adventure Specialists
(☎ 719-783-2519, 719-630-7687, www.gorp.com/adventur), Bear Basin Ranch, Westcliffe, CO 81252 USA – Barranca del Cobre (Copper Canyon) expeditions

Ceiba Adventures
(☎ 800-217-1060, www.primenet.com/~ceiba), PO Box 2274, Flagstaff, AZ 86003 USA – rain forest and archaeological river trips in the Mayan regions

Columbus Travel
(☎ 800-843-1060, www.canyontravel.com), 900 Ridge Creek, Bulverde, TX 78163 USA – Barranca del Cobre explorations for individuals and small groups (led by local guides)

Dragoman
(☎ 01728-861133, www.dragoman.co.uk), 97 Camp Green, Debenham, Stowmarket, Suffolk IP14 6LA, UK – longish (four to 27 weeks) camping or hotel-and-camping overland expeditions, combining Mexico with other countries in North, Central or South America

Explore Worldwide
(☎ 800-227-8747 in the USA, ☎ 01252-760000 in the UK, ☎ 02-9956-7766 in Australia, www.explore.co.uk) – small-group land trips with interesting itineraries

Field Guides
(☎ 800-728-4953, www.fieldguides.com), 9433 Bee Cave Rd, Building 1, Suite 150, Austin, TX 78733 USA – bird-watching trips to southern Mexico

Gecko Overland Trekking
(☎ 800-628-9161, www.geckooverland.com), PO Box 402456, Miami Beach, FL 33140-0456 USA – small-group van tours, camping most nights; most participants are in their 20s

Green Tortoise
(☎ 800-867-8647, www.greentortoise.com), 494 Broadway, San Francisco, CA 94133 USA – long-running 'alternative' bus company operating casual, young people's 'self-service adventure travel vacations'; you spend lots of nights on the bus (the seats convert to beds) and some camping. Some trips start from California, others from Guatemala.

Journey Latin America
(☎ 020-8747-3108, www.journeylatinamerica.co.uk), 12 & 13 Heathfield Terrace, Chiswick,

London W4 4JE, UK – small-group tours using local transport and budget hotels

Suntrek
(☎ 800-786-8735, www.suntrek.com), Sun Plaza, 77 West Third St, Santa Rosa, CA 95401 USA – small-group camping tours

The Touring Exchange
(☎ 604-872-1398 May to December in the USA, ☎ 112-3-48-85 December to April in Mexico,

www.bajatravel.com/tourex), Box 265, Port Townsend, WA 98368 USA – Pacific Coast bicycle tours and Baja California adventure trips

TrekAmerica
(☎ 800-221-0596 in the USA, ☎ 01295-256777 in the UK, www.trekamerica.com), PO Box 189, Rockaway, NJ 07866 USA – small-group camping expeditions; participants tend to be in their early 20s

Getting Around

The peak travel periods of Semana Santa (the week before Easter) and the Christmas-New Year holiday period of about 10 days are hectic and heavily booked throughout Mexico. Try to book transport in advance for those periods.

For some useful words and phrases when traveling, see the Language chapter at the back of this book.

AIR

All large and many smaller cities in Mexico have passenger airports. Aeroméxico and Mexicana are the country's two largest airlines. There are also numerous smaller ones, often flying routes between provincial cities that the big two don't bother with.

TAESA

The airline TAESA was suspended by the Mexican government in 1999 following a crash of one of its planes in central Mexico in which 18 people died. TAESA was told it must meet 69 conditions – including addressing problems of lack of financial resources, inadequate staffing and use of outdated manuals – before it could fly again.

If the airline does not resume operations, many of the TAESA routes mentioned in regional chapters of this book are likely to be taken over by other airlines.

✱✱✱✱✱✱✱✱✱✱✱✱

These airlines include Aero California (serving Mexico City and northern and western Mexico, including Baja California), Aerocaribe and Aerocozumel (Mexico City, the Gulf Coast, the south and southeast), Aerolíneas Internacionales (Mexico City, central and northern Mexico), Aerolitoral (central highlands, western and northern Mexico, Baja California), Aeromar (Mexico City, western Mexico, Monterrey),

Aviacsa (Mexico City, Guadalajara, Monterrey, Tijuana, Oaxaca, southeast Mexico) and TAESA (serving 18 cities around the country).

Most of these airlines will be included in travel agents' computerized reservation systems in Mexico and abroad, but you may find it impossible to get information on smaller airlines until you reach a city served by them.

Aerolitoral and Aeromar are feeder airlines for Aeroméxico and normally share its ticket offices and booking networks. A similar arrangement exists between Aerocaribe, Aerocozumel and Mexicana.

Fares

Depending on the fare you get, flying can be a good value for the money, especially considering the long bus trip that may be the alternative. Fares can vary considerably between airlines and may also depend on whether you fly at a busy or quiet time of day, week or year, and how far ahead you book and pay.

High season is generally July and August and from mid-December to about January 10. For the cheapest fares, you usually have to pay for the ticket a few days ahead, and you may have to fly late in the evening. Aeroméxico and Mexicana – theoretically competitors but both government controlled – work in tandem, with identical fare structures, but cheaper fares may be offered by other airlines. Roundtrip fares are often simply twice the price of one-way tickets, but some advance-payment cheaper deals exist.

There are two taxes on domestic flights: IVA, the consumer tax (15%), and TUA, an airport tax of about US$12.50. In Mexico, taxes are normally included in quoted fares and paid when you buy the ticket. If you bought the ticket outside Mexico, TUA is not included and you will have to pay it during check-in.

Here are some examples of the cheapest one-way, low-season, Aeroméxico/Mexicana fares from Mexico City, including taxes:

destination	fare
Acapulco	US$113
Cancún	US$235
Guadalajara	US$161
Mérida	US$128
Monterrey	US$141
Oaxaca	US$108
Puerto Vallarta	US$157
Tijuana	US$143
Zacatecas	US$115

Information on specific flights is given in the Getting There & Away sections under individual cities in this book. See the Getting There & Away chapter for airline toll-free numbers in Mexico.

BUS

Mexico has a good intercity road and bus network. Intercity buses are frequent and go almost everywhere, typically for US$3 or US$5 an hour (60 to 80km) on deluxe or 1st-class buses. For trips of up to three or four hours on busy routes, you can usually just go to the bus terminal, buy a ticket and head out without too much delay. For longer trips, or routes with infrequent service, book a ticket at least a day in advance, preferably two or three.

Immediate cash refunds of 80% to 100% are often available if you cancel your ticket more than three hours before the listed departure time. To check whether refunds apply, ask '¿Hay cancelaciones?'.

Most of Mexico's 90 or so long-distance bus companies in fact belong to one of three groups: Grupo Estrella Blanca, Grupo ADO and Grupo Flecha Amarilla. This makes little difference to the practicalities of travel, except that in bus stations Estrella Blanca companies may not have their own names up but may all be dealt with by one Estrella Blanca counter. No matter – you'll still find the bus you need without too much ado.

All deluxe and most 1st-class buses are air-conditioned, so bring a sweater or jacket. Most deluxe and 1st-class bus companies have computerized ticket systems that allow you to select your seat from an on-screen diagram. Try to avoid the back of the bus, which is where the toilets are and tends to give a bumpier ride. For a long journey, work out which side the sun will be on and sit on the other side. If the bus is not air-conditioned, it's a particularly good idea to get a window seat so you have some control over the window – other travelers may have different ideas from yours about what's too warm or too cool.

On deluxe and 1st-class buses, luggage is fairly safe if stowed in the luggage compartment below. Just keep your most valuable documents (passport, money, etc) in the cabin with you – and keep them closely protected. On 2nd-class buses you may want to keep everything with you – though some bus companies don't allow big baggage, such as backpacks, to be carried into the cabin. It's better not to allow your luggage to be hoisted onto the open luggage rack atop a 2nd-class bus unless you feel you can keep an eye on it (which is nearly impossible).

Food and drinks in bus stations are overpriced; try to bring your own. Drinks and snacks are provided on some deluxe services. The better buses have toilets, but you may want to carry some toilet paper.

In some outlying rural regions, passenger-carrying camiones (trucks) and camionetas (pickups) do the job of buses. Standing in the back of a lurching truck with a couple of dozen campesinos and their machetes, animals and harvested crops is at least an experience to remember. Fares are similar to a 2nd-class bus fare.

Highway robbery can happen in almost any part of Mexico. The danger is greatest at night, on isolated stretches of highway far from cities. See Dangers & Annoyances in Facts for the Visitor for more information.

Terminals & Schedules

Most cities and towns have a single, modern, main bus station where all long-distance buses arrive and depart. It's usually called the Central Camionera, Central de Autobuses, Terminal de Autobuses, Central de Camiones or simply El Central, and it is usually a long way from the center of town. Frequent local buses link bus stations with town centers. Note the crucial difference between the Central (bus station) and the Centro (city center).

If there is no single main terminal, bus companies will have their own terminals scattered around town.

Most bus lines have schedules posted at their ticket desks in the bus station, but the schedules aren't always comprehensive. If your destination isn't listed, ask – it may be en route to one that is. From big towns, many different bus companies may run on the same routes, so compare fares and classes of service.

Classes of Service

Long-distance buses range enormously in quality, from comfortable, nonstop, air-conditioned deluxe services to decaying, suspensionless ex-city buses grinding out their dying years on dirt roads to remote settlements. The differences among the

Bus Services

It is important to know the types of service offered:

Sin escalas Nonstop
Directo Very few stops
Semi-directo A few more stops than directo
Ordinario Stops wherever passengers want to get on or off; deluxe and 1st-class buses are never ordinario
Express Nonstop on short to medium-length trips; very few stops on long trips
Local Bus that starts its journey at the bus station you're in and usually leaves on time; preferable to de paso
De paso Bus that started its journey somewhere else but is stopping to let off and take on passengers. A de paso bus may be late and may or may not have seats available; unless the bus company has a computer booking system, you also may have to wait until it arrives before any tickets are sold. If the bus is full, you may have to wait for the next one.
Viaje redondo Roundtrip, available only on some journeys, most starting in Mexico City.

classes are not hard and fast, and terms such as *de lujo* (deluxe) and *primera clase* (1st class) can cover quite a wide range of comfort levels. Broadly, buses fall into three categories:

De lujo Deluxe services run mainly on the busy routes. Some bear names such as Plus, GL or Ejecutivo. The buses are swift, modern, comfortable and air-conditioned. They may cost just 10% or 20% more than 1st class, or double for the most luxurious lines, such as ETN, UNO and Turistar Ejecutivo, which offer reclining seats, plenty of legroom, few or no stops, snacks, hot and cold drinks, videos and toilets on board. Some people regard these latter super-deluxe buses as a class of their own – ejecutivo (executive). For simplicity, this book groups them with other deluxe services.

Primera (1ª) clase 1st-class buses have a comfortable *numerado* (numbered) seat for each passenger and often show videos. Their standards of comfort are perfectly adequate. They usually have air-conditioning and a toilet, they may show videos, and they stop infrequently. All sizable towns have 1st-class bus service. As with deluxe buses, you buy your ticket in the bus station before boarding.

Segunda (2ª) clase 2nd-class buses serve small towns and villages and offer cheaper, slower travel on some intercity routes. A few are almost as quick and comfortable as 1st-class buses; others are old, tatty, uncomfortable and liable to break down, and will stop anywhere for someone to get on or off. Except on some major runs, there's no apparent limit on capacity, which means if you board mid-route you might make the trip *parado* (standing) rather than *sentado* (seated). (Don't confuse parado with *parada*, bus stop.) If you board mid-route, you pay your fare to the conductor. Fares are about 10% or 20% lower than for 1st class.

TRAIN

Mexico's passenger train system, in decline for decades, almost ground to a complete halt in the late 1990s after the government decided to sell off as much of the rail network as possible. The private firms that bought railroads simply stopped running many passenger trains because they were so unprofitable. Whether passenger train service will ever recover is dubious.

Trains in Vain?

Closures of passenger train services continued after research for this book was finished. As we went to press, the only passenger lines that we were able to confirm as still operating were: Chihuahua-Los Mochis (the Copper Canyon Railway), Guadalajara-Tequila, Mérida-Izamal, Mexico City-Apizaco, Coatzacoalcos-Campeche, Coatzacoalcos-Tapachula and Frontera-Sierra Mojada. Information elsewhere in this book on train services should always be double-checked before you make travel plans.

✽✽✽✽✽✽✽✽✽✽✽✽

Of the few trains that still run, most do so only because the government hasn't yet sold off the railroads on which they run. These trains are still operated by the government railroad company, Ferrocarriles Nacionales de México (FNM, ☎ 5-547-10-84, ☎ 5-547-10-97). They are one-class only, offering a seat but no air-conditioning, food, drinks or sleeper cars. One exception is the comfortable, touristic Ferrocarril Chihuahua al Pacífico, known in English as the Copper Canyon Railway, now under private ownership, which still makes its spectacular daily journeys through the Sierra Madre Occidental between Chihuahua and Los Mochis (see the Northwest Mexico chapter for details).

Principal FNM services still running at the time of writing (with absolutely no guarantee that they would continue) were Mexico City-Querétaro-San Miguel de Allende-San Luis Potosí-Saltillo, three times weekly; Saltillo-Piedras Negras, three times weekly; Mexico City-Orizaba-Córdoba-Veracruz, two trains daily; Puebla-Oaxaca, daily; Aguascalientes-Torreón, daily; Ciudad Victoria-Tampico, three times weekly (and vice versa in all cases). There are also a few trains running across the Isthmus of Tehuantepec, Mexico's narrow southern waist, and on the Yucatán Peninsula, but these have long been inadvisable because of theft and robbery danger.

FNM trains are much cheaper than buses running the same routes (about one-third of the price of a 1st-class bus) and much slower (they take about twice as long even when on time).

For more information, see city Getting There & Away sections. The unofficial website www.ferrocarriles.com has updated passenger train schedules.

CAR & MOTORCYCLE

Driving in Mexico is not as easy as it is north of the border, but it is often easier and more convenient than the bus and is sometimes the only way to get to some of the most beautiful places or isolated towns and villages.

See Dangers & Annoyances in Facts for the Visitor for a warning about risks of highway robbery in some areas, and the Getting There & Away chapter for information about the requirements for bringing a vehicle into Mexico.

The Language chapter in the back of the book has some useful Spanish words and phrases for drivers. Two useful websites for drivers in Mexico are www.mexicomike.com and www.sanbornsinsurance.com.

Maps

Town and country roads are often poorly or idiosyncratically signposted. It pays to get the best road maps you can. The Mexican *Guía Roji Por Las Carreteras de México* road atlas is an excellent investment. In Mexico it costs US$6 from decent bookstores and some city newsstands. In the US or from Internet booksellers, you may come across it for around US$15. This atlas is updated annually and includes new highways, though minor roads may be overlooked or imperfect. You can also use the similar *Guía Verdi México Atlas de Carreteras*. The 'Travelogs' that Sanborn's insurance supplies free to its customers – sort of mile-by-mile companions for the driver – are very detailed and can be quite useful.

Road Rules

Drive on the right-hand side of the road.

Traffic laws and speed limits rarely seem to be enforced on the highways. Obey the laws strictly in the cities so you don't give the police an excuse to hit you with a 'fine' payable on the spot. Speed limits are usually 100km/hour on highways and 40km/hour or 30km/hour in towns and cities.

Anti-pollution rules in Mexico City prohibit every vehicle from driving there on one day each week. (See 'Driving Restrictions' in the Mexico City chapter.)

Accidents

Under Mexico's legal system, all drivers involved in a road accident are detained, and their vehicles impounded, while responsibility is assessed. For minor accidents, drivers will probably be released if they have insurance to cover any damage they may have caused. But the culpable driver's vehicle may remain impounded until damages are paid. If the accident causes injury or death, the responsible driver will be jailed until he or she guarantees restitution to the victims and payment of any fines. Determining responsibility *could* take weeks or even months. (Mexican drivers often *don't* stop after accidents.)

Your embassy can give you only limited help (see Legal Matters in the Facts for the Visitor chapter). Adequate insurance coverage is the only real protection.

Fuel & Service

All *gasolina* (gasoline) and diesel fuel in Mexico is sold by the government's monopoly, Pemex (Petróleos Mexicanos), for cash (no credit cards). Most towns, even small ones, have a Pemex station, and the stations are pretty common on most major roads. Nevertheless, in remote areas it's better to fill up when you can.

The gasoline on sale is all *sin plomo* (unleaded). There are two varieties: Magna Sin, equivalent to US regular unleaded, and Premium, equivalent to US super unleaded. At 1999 rates, Magna Sin cost about US$0.45 a liter (US$1.75 a US gallon), and Premium about US$0.50. Diesel fuel is also widely available at a little under US$0.40 a liter. Regular Mexican diesel has a higher sulfur content than US diesel, but there is a new 'Diesel Sin' with less sulfur than before. If

diesel drivers change their oil and filter about every 3500km, they should have no problems.

All stations have pump attendants (who expect tips), but they are not always trustworthy. When buying fuel, it's better to ask for a peso amount than to say *lleno* (full) – lleno usually finishes with fuel gushing down the side of your car. Check that the pump registers 0 pesos to start with, and be quick to check afterward that you have been given the amount you requested – the attendants often reset the pump immediately and start to serve another customer. Don't have the attendants do your gas, oil and water all at once, or you may not get what you paid for. Pressure gauges on air hoses are often absent, so carry and use your own.

Road Conditions

Mexican highways, even some toll highways, are not up to the standards of European or North American ones. Still, the main roads are serviceable and fairly fast when traffic is not heavy. A common problem is steep shoulders, so if your wheels go off the road surface the car tilts alarmingly. Sometimes there's a deep gutter, and if you go into it you may roll the car.

Driving at night is especially dangerous – unlit vehicles, rocks, pedestrians and animals on the roads are common. Hijacks and robberies do occur. It's not generally safe to pull over and sleep in your parked vehicle – you should plan to reach accommodations well before nightfall.

Especially on roads heading south from the US border, be prepared for fairly frequent drug and weapon searches by the army and police.

In towns and cities, you must be especially wary of *Alto* (Stop) signs, *topes* (speed bumps) and potholes. They are often not where you'd expect, and missing one can cost you in traffic fines or car damage. One-way streets are the rule in towns: Usually, alternating streets run in opposite directions, so if you cross one that's westbound only, the next one will probably go east.

Despite the half-witted exceptions you get in any country, Mexicans on the whole drive as cautiously and sensibly as people anywhere. The density of traffic on many roads, poor surfaces and the frequent hazards such as potholes, topes, dogs, livestock, bicycles and children all help keep speeds down.

Toll Roads Mexico has more than 6000km of *autopistas* (toll roads), usually four-lane. They are generally in much better condition and a lot quicker than the alternative free roads. They also have a reputation for being safer from highway robbery. Some are operated by the federal government, some by private concessions. *Cuotas* (tolls) vary from highway to highway: on average you pay about US$1 for every 10km to 20km.

Motorcycle Hazards Certain aspects of Mexican roads make them particularly hazardous for bikers:

• poor signage of road and lane closures (there may be nothing more than a rock placed 20m before where the work is being done)
• lack of hotels/motels on some stretches of highway
• lots of dogs on the roads
• debris and deep potholes
• vehicles without taillights; lack of highway lighting

Breakdown Assistance

The Mexican tourism ministry, SECTUR, maintains a network of *Ángeles Verdes* (Green Angels) – bilingual mechanics in green uniforms and green trucks who patrol major stretches of highway daily during daylight hours looking for motorists in trouble. They make minor repairs, replace small parts, provide fuel and oil, and arrange towing and other assistance by radio if necessary. Service is free; parts, gasoline and oil are provided at cost. If you are near a telephone when your car has problems, you can call their 24-hour hotline in Mexico City (☎ 5-250-82-21) or through the national 24-hour tourist assistance numbers in Mexico City (☎ 5-250-01-23, 800-903-92-00).

Most serious mechanical problems can be fixed efficiently and inexpensively by mechanics in towns and cities as long as the parts are available. Volkswagen, Ford, Nissan/Datsun, Chrysler and General Motors parts are the easiest to obtain; others may have to be ordered from the USA. For parts suppliers, consult the telephone directory's yellow pages under *Refacciones y Acesorios para Automóviles y Camiones*. For authorized dealer service, look under *Automóviles – Agencias*.

City Parking

It's not a good idea to park on the street overnight, and most cheap city hotels don't provide parking. Sometimes you can leave a car out front and the night porter will keep an eye on it. Usually you have to use a commercial *estacionamiento* (parking lot), which might cost US$4 or US$5 overnight and US$0.70 per hour during the day. Hotels with parking tend to be the more expensive ones.

If you're just overnighting and moving on in the morning, often you can find decent motels, with easy parking, on highways just outside cities.

Rental

Auto rental in Mexico is expensive by US or European standards, but it can be worthwhile if you want to visit several places in a short time and have three or four people to share the cost. It can also be useful for getting off the beaten track, where public transport is slow or scarce.

Cars can be rented in most of Mexico's cities and resorts, at airports and sometimes at bus and train stations. Most big hotels can arrange a car. Sometimes it's necessary to book a few days ahead.

Renters must have a valid driver's license (your license from home is OK), passport and major credit card, and are usually required to be at least 23 (sometimes 25) years old. Sometimes age 21 is acceptable, but you may have to pay more. You should get a signed rental agreement and read its small print.

In addition to the basic daily or weekly rental rate, you must pay for insurance, tax and fuel. Ask exactly what the insurance covers – sometimes it covers only 90% of the car's value in case of theft and doesn't cover 'partial theft,' such as wiper blades or tires.

Most agencies offer a choice between a per-kilometer deal or unlimited kilometers. The latter is usually preferable if you intend to do some hard driving. (If you don't, why are you renting a car?) Local firms are often cheaper than the big international ones. You usually can find a Volkswagen Beetle – often the cheapest car available – for around US$40 a day with unlimited kilometers and including insurance and tax, and often you can get a weekly rate equivalent to six single days. The extra charge for drop-off in another city, when available, is usually about US$0.30 per kilometer.

You can book cars in Mexico through the large international agencies in other countries. Doing this may get you lower rates. Here's contact information for some major firms operating in Mexico:

Avis
☎ 800-230-4898 in the USA
☎ 800-288-88-88 in Mexico
www.avis.com

Budget
☎ 800-472-3325 in the USA
☎ 800-700-17-00 in Mexico
www.drivebudget.com

Dollar
☎ 800-300-3665 in the USA
www.dollar.com

Europcar
☎ 800-003-95-00 in Mexico
www.europcar.com

Hertz
☎ 800-654-3001 in the USA
☎ 800-709-50-00 in Mexico
www.hertz.com

Thrifty
☎ 800-847-4389 in the USA
☎ 800-021-22-77 in Mexico
www.thrifty.com

See city sections in regional chapters for more information on car rental agencies.

BICYCLE

With the exception of Baja California, bicycling is not a common way to tour Mexico. The size of the country, reports of highway robbery, poor road surfaces and road hazards (see Road Conditions under Car & Motorcycle, above) are deterrents. However, this method of getting around Mexico is certainly not impossible if you're prepared for the challenges. You should be very fit, use the best equipment you can muster and be fully able to handle your own repairs. Take the mountainous topography and hot climate into account when planning your route.

A valuable help to anyone cycling in Mexico is *Bicycling Mexico* by Erica Weisbroth and Eric Ellman, published in 1990 but still applicable.

A few US and Canadian travel outfitters organize guided bike tours of parts of Mexico (see the Organized Tours section in the Getting There & Away chapter). It's also possible to rent bikes locally in some Mexican towns and cities for short excursions. (See Getting Around in individual city and town sections.)

HITCHHIKING

Hitchhiking is never entirely safe in any country in the world, and we don't recommend it. Travelers who decide to hitch should understand that they are taking a small but potentially serious risk. People who do choose to hitch will be safer if they travel in pairs and let someone know where they are planning to go. A woman traveling alone certainly should not hitchhike in Mexico, and even two women alone is not advisable.

However, some people do choose to hitchhike, and it's not an uncommon way of getting to some of the off-the-beaten-track archaeological sites and other places that tend to be poorly served by bus. Always be alert to possible dangers wherever you are.

If the driver is another tourist or a private motorist, you may get the ride for free. If it is a work or commercial vehicle, you should offer to pay.

BOAT

Vehicle and passenger ferries between Santa Rosalía and Guaymas, La Paz and Mazatlán and La Paz and Topolobampo connect Baja California with the Mexican mainland. Ferries also run to Isla Mujeres, Cozumel and Isla Holbox, off the Yucatán Peninsula. For details, see the relevant city and island sections. Information on the Baja ferries is also available on the website of the ferry company Sematur (www.ferrysematur.com.mx).

LOCAL TRANSPORT

Mexican street naming and numbering can be confusing. When asking directions, it's better to ask for a specific place, such as the Hotel Central or the Museo Regional, than for the street it's on. To achieve a degree of certainty, ask three people.

Bus

Generally known as *camiones*, local buses are the cheapest way to get around cities and to nearby villages. They run everywhere, frequently, and are cheap. Fares in cities are rarely more than US$0.40. Older buses are often noisy, dirty and crowded, but in some cities there are fleets of small, modern microbuses that tend to be more pleasant.

City buses halt only at specific *paradas* (bus stops), which may or may not be marked.

ROBERT REID

Colectivos, Combis & Peseros

Colectivos are minibuses that function as something between a taxi and a bus. (A *combi* is a VW minibus; *pesero* is a Mexico City word for colectivo.) They're cheaper than taxis, quicker and less crowded than buses. They run along set routes – sometimes displayed on the windshield – and will pick you up or drop you off on any corner along that route.

If you're not at the start of a colectivo's route, go to the curb and wave your hand when you see one. Tell the driver where you want to go; you normally pay at the end of the trip, and the fare usually depends on how far you go.

Metro

Mexico City, Guadalajara and Monterrey have metro (subway, underground railway) systems. Mexico City's in particular is a quick, cheap and useful way of getting around.

Taxi

Taxis are common in towns and cities. They're often surprisingly economical, and they're useful if you have a lot of baggage or need to get from point A to point B quickly. (But see the Mexico City Information section for a warning on that city's taxi crime epidemic.) In many cities, most taxis are Volkswagen Beetles. If a taxi has a meter, ask the driver if it's working (*'¿Funciona el taxímetro?'*). If it's not, or if the taxi doesn't have a meter, establish the price of the ride *before* getting in. (This usually involves a bit of haggling.)

Some airports and big bus stations have taxi *taquillas* (kiosks), where you buy a fixed-price ticket to your destination and then hand it to the driver instead of paying cash. This can save haggling and major rip-offs, but fares are usually higher than you could get on the street.

Boat

Here and there you may find yourself traveling by boat to an outlying beach or along a river or across a lake or lagoon. The craft are usually fast fiberglass outboard *lanchas* (launches). You may have to haggle a bit, but fares for such excursions are usually fixed.

ORGANIZED TOURS

Taking a guided tour can be an easy way to get a quick introduction to big cities such as Mexico City, Guadalajara or Monterrey. Tours are sometimes the most practical method of visiting remote natural attractions and other areas where public transportation isn't the greatest – places such as the Barranca del Cobre (Copper Canyon) or the Cuatrociénegas desert lagoons in the north; the Lagunas de Chacahua (Oaxaca); the Reserva de la Biósfera Sian Ka'an and some archaeological sites on the Yucatán Peninsula; and Laguna Miramar, the waterfalls near Palenque, or the Bonampak and Yaxchilán ruins (Chiapas). A knowledgeable and enthusiastic local guide can add much to your understanding and enjoyment of a place, especially if the focus of interest is, say, ecological (as above) or ethnological (such as the indigenous villages around San Cristóbal de Las Casas, Chiapas) and needs some explanation. A guide is a necessity in some protected areas where you are not allowed unaccompanied, such as the Sierra de San Francisco rock art sites in Baja California, or turtle-breeding beaches on the Tamaulipas coast, or the El Triunfo cloud forest in Chiapas.

Mexico's slowly growing number of community tourism initiatives have the benefit of channeling funds directly to local people and of bringing them into much closer contact with you, the visitor, than is usually possible. The village visits offered by the Museos Comunitarios del Estado de Oaxaca (Community Museums of Oaxaca State) are a fine example of such a program.

There are also enjoyable walking tours of historic towns such as Morelia, San Miguel de Allende and Alamos.

You'll find details on all these tours, and others, in the regional chapters. Most are best arranged locally (with some advance notice, in a few cases). AMTAVE (Asociación Mexicana de Turismo de Aventura y Ecoturismo) is a grouping of over 50 adventure travel and ecotourism operators from around Mexico. Its office (☎ 5-663-53-81, info@amtave.com) is at Avenida del Parque 22, Colonia Tlacopac, San Ángel, Mexico City, and its website is www.amtave.com. You can request a brochure. The postal address is AMTAVE, Insurgentes Sur 1971-251B, Colonia Guadalupe Inn, 01020 México DF, Mexico. Another good information source on organizations providing ecotourism and active tourism in Mexico is the website for Eco Travels in Latin America (www.planeta.com).

Mexico City

• pop 20 million (approx) • elev 2240m
☎ no area code

Mexico City is a place to love and loathe. Spread across more than 2000 sq km of a single valley high in Mexico's central uplands, it encapsulates the best and worst of Mexico the country. The result is a seething, cosmopolitan megalopolis that is by turns exhilarating and overpowering. One moment Mexico City is music, glamour and excitement; the next it's drabness, poverty, overcrowding and foul smells. This is a city of colonial palaces and sprawling slums; of ear-splitting traffic and peaceful plazas; of huge wealth and miserable poverty; of green parks and brown air.

Despite its problems, Mexico City is a magnet for Mexicans and visitors alike, because with nearly a quarter of the country's population, it far outstrips anywhere else in the country in economic, cultural and political importance. As one Mexican said to us, *'Lo que ocurre en México, ocurre en el DF'* – 'What happens in Mexico, happens in Mexico City.'

The city is known to Mexicans simply as México ('MEH-hee-ko'). If they want to distinguish it from Mexico the country, they call it either *la ciudad de México* or *el DF* ('el de EFF-eh'). The DF is the Distrito Federal (Federal District), in which in fact only half the city lies. The outlying parts of Mexico City lie in the state of México, which surrounds the Distrito Federal on three sides (the state of Morelos is on the fourth).

HISTORY

As early as 10,000 BC, humans and animals were attracted to the Lago de Texcoco, the lake that then covered much of the floor of the Valle de México. After 7500 BC the lake began to shrink, hunting became more difficult, and the inhabitants turned to agriculture. A loose federation of farming villages had evolved around Lago de Texcoco by approximately 200 BC. The biggest, Cuicuilco, was destroyed by a volcanic eruption about 100 AD.

Highlights

• The Museo Nacional de Antropología, a treasure house of Mexican archaeological marvels

• The Bosque de Chapultepec, a large inner-city woodland expanse with several good museums

• The old suburbs of Coyoacán and San Ángel, vibrant with weekend markets and full of colonial atmosphere and memories of Diego Rivera and Frida Kahlo

• The Zócalo, one of the world's biggest plazas, surrounded by the presidential palace, the city's cathedral and the remains of the most important Aztec temple

• Marvelous murals by 20th-century Mexican masters in the Palacio Nacional, Palacio de Bellas Artes, Museo Mural Diego Rivera and elsewhere

• A visit to the ancient waterways of Xochimilco and nearby Museo Dolores Olmedo Patiño, with its superb Rivera collection

• A meal out at one of Colonia Condesa's relaxed sidewalk bistros

• The spectacular show of the Ballet Folklórico de México in the beautiful Palacio de Bellas Artes

✳ ✳ ✳ ✳ ✳ ✳ ✳ ✳ ✳ ✳ ✳ ✳

After that the big influence in the area was Teotihuacán, 25km northeast of the lake. For centuries Teotihuacán was the capital of an empire stretching to Guatemala and beyond, but it fell in the 7th century. Among several city-states in the region in the following centuries, the Toltec empire, based at Tula, 65km north of modern Mexico City, was the most important. By the 13th century the Tula empire had collapsed, leaving a number of small statelets around the lake to compete for control of the Valle

Aztec Mexico City

The Aztecs, or Mexica ('meh-SHEE-kah'), a wandering Chichimec tribe from northern or western Mexico, settled first on the western shore of Lago de Texcoco, but other Valle de México inhabitants objected to Aztec habits such as wife-stealing and human sacrifice (to appease the Aztecs' guardian god, Huizilopochtli). In the early 14th century, fighting as mercenaries for Coxcox, ruler of Culhuacán, on the southern shore of the lake, the Aztecs defeated nearby Xochimilco and sent Coxcox 8000 human ears as proof of their victory. Coxcox granted them land and rashly allowed them to make his daughter an Aztec goddess. As described in *The Course of Mexican History*, by Michael Meyer & William Sherman:

> The princess was sacrificed and flayed. When her father attended the banquet in his honor, he was horrified to find that the entertainment included a dancer dressed in the skin of his daughter . . . Coxcox raised an army which scattered the barbarians.

Some time between 1325 and 1345 the Aztecs, wandering around the swampy fringes of the lake, finally founded their own city, Tenochtitlán, on an island near the lake's western shore. (Today the island site is the downtown area around the main square, the Zócalo.) The island was chosen, legend says, because there the Aztecs saw an eagle standing on a cactus, eating a snake – a sign, they believed, that they should stop their wanderings and build a city.

About 1370 the Aztecs began to serve as mercenaries for Azcapotzalco, on the western shore of the lake. When they rebelled against Azcapotzalco (about 1427), they became the greatest power in the Valle de México. Tenochtitlán rapidly became a sophisticated city-state whose empire would, by the early 16th century, stretch across most of central Mexico from the Pacific to the gulf and down into far southern Mexico. The Aztecs' sense of their own importance as the chosen people of the voracious Huizilopochtli grew too. In the mid-15th century they formed the Triple Alliance with the lakeshore states Texcoco and Tlacopan to conduct wars against Tlaxcala and Huejotzingo, which lay east of the valley. The purpose was to gain a steady supply of the prisoners needed to sate Huizilopochtli's vast hunger for sacrificial victims, so that the sun would continue to rise each day and floods and famines could be avoided. In four days in 1487, no less than 20,000 prisoners were sacrificed to dedicate Tenochtitlán's newly rebuilt main temple.

The Aztecs built a large city on a grid plan, with canals as thoroughfares. In the marshier parts they created raised gardens by piling up vegetation and mud and planting willows. These chinampas – versions of which can still be seen at Xochimilco in southern Mexico City – gave three or four harvests a year but were still not enough to feed the growing population. The Aztecs also needed to extract tribute from conquered tribes to supplement their resources – another reason for their imperial expansion in the 15th century. At the city's heart stood the main *teocalli* (sacred precinct), with its temple dedicated to Huizilopochtli and the water god, Tláloc. The remains of this temple, the Templo Mayor, can be seen today just off the Zócalo. Causeways linked the city to the lakeshore. This was the city that amazed the Spanish when they arrived in 1519, by which time its population was an estimated 200,000. That of the whole Valle de México was perhaps 1.5 million, making it already one of the world's biggest and densest urban areas.

de México. It was the Aztecs (see 'Aztec Mexico City') who emerged supreme.

Capital of Nueva España

Wrecked during and after the Spanish conquest (see History in the Facts about Mexico chapter), the Aztec capital Tenochtitlán was rebuilt as a Spanish city. The native population of the Valle de México shrank drastically – to fewer than 100,000 within a century of the conquest, by some estimates. But the city itself emerged by 1550 as the prosperous and elegant, if insanitary, capital of Nueva España. Broad, straight streets were laid out and buildings constructed to Spanish designs with local materials such as *tezontle*, a light-red volcanic rock that the Aztecs had used for their temples. Hospitals, schools, churches, palaces, parks and a university were built. But right up to the late 19th century the city suffered floods caused by the partial destruction in the 1520s of the Aztecs' canals. Lago de Texcoco often overflowed into the city, damaging streets and buildings, bringing disease and forcing the relocation of thousands of people.

Independence

On October 30, 1810, some 80,000 independence rebels had Mexico City at their mercy after defeating Spanish loyalist forces at Las Cruces, just west of the capital. But their leader Miguel Hidalgo decided against advancing on the city – a mistake that cost Mexico 11 more years of fighting before independence was achieved. By 1821 the city had a population of 160,000, which made it the biggest in the Americas.

Mexico City entered the modern age under the despotic Porfirio Díaz, who ruled Mexico for most of the period from 1877 to 1911 and attracted much foreign investment. Díaz ushered in a construction boom in the city and had railways built to the provinces and the USA. Some 150km of electric tramways threaded the streets, industry grew, and by 1910 the city had 471,000 inhabitants. A drainage canal and tunnel finally succeeded in drying up much of the Lago de Texcoco, allowing the city to expand farther.

The 20th Century

After Díaz fell in 1911, the Mexican Revolution brought war and hunger to the city's streets. In the 1920s the postrevolution minister of education, José Vasconcelos, commissioned talented young artists – among them Diego Rivera, David Alfaro Siqueiros and José Clemente Orozco – to decorate numerous public buildings with dramatic, large-scale murals conveying a new sense of Mexico's past and future.

After the Great Depression, a drive to industrialize attracted more and more money and people to the city. By 1940 the population reached 1.7 million. In the 1940s and '50s factories and skyscrapers rose almost as quickly as the population, which was increasing by 7% a year. The supply of housing, jobs and services could not keep pace with the influx of people; shantytowns appeared on the city's fringes; Mexico City was growing into the urban monster that we know today.

Despite continued economic growth into the 1960s, political and social reform lagged behind. Student-led discontent came to a head as Mexico City prepared for the 1968 Olympic Games. On October 2, 10 days before the games started, about 5000 to 10,000 people gathering in Tlatelolco, north of the city center, were encircled by troops and police. To this day, no one is certain how many people died in the ensuing massacre, but estimates have been put at several hundred.

Megalopolis

Mexico City continued to grow at a frightening rate in the 1970s, spreading beyond the Distrito Federal into the state of México and developing some of the world's worst traffic and pollution problems, only partly alleviated by the metro system (opened in 1969) and by attempts in the 1990s to limit traffic.

People have continued to pour into Mexico City despite the earthquake of September 19, 1985, which registered more than eight on the Richter scale, killed at least 10,000 (possibly 20,000) people, displaced thousands more and caused more than US$4 billion in damage.

Today an estimated 1100 newcomers arrive in the city daily, and its population is estimated at 20 million. Since 1940 Mexico City has multiplied in area more than 10 times, yet it's still one of the world's most crowded metropolitan areas. It is the industrial, retail, financial, communications and cultural center of the country; its industries generate more than one-third of Mexico's wealth, and its people consume 66% of Mexico's energy. Its cost of living is the highest in the nation.

Heavy subsidies are needed to keep the place from seizing up, and more than half the country's spending on social welfare is used here. Water extraction from the subsoil makes the city sink steadily – as much as 45cm a year in some fringe areas. Parts of the city center even sank 10m in the 20th century. Even so, one-third of the city's water has to be pumped in at great cost from outside the Valle de México. The challenges of supplying water to the city's growing population and disposing of waste water threaten to exceed even those of combating air pollution in the 21st century.

The poverty and overcrowding that always existed alongside the city's wealth were exacerbated by the recession of the mid-1990s. In 1996 it was estimated that more than one-fifth of the people in the Distrito Federal were living on marginal levels of basic subsistence, and another two-thirds were barely able to cover the expense of material necessities. And those figures did not include the outer parts of the city, where most of the newer shantytowns lie. Recovery since then has been very gradual. One effect of the crisis was a big rise in crime.

From 1928 to 1997 the Distrito Federal was ruled directly by the federal government. Since 1997 it has had political autonomy, and elected its own mayor for the first time that year. The winner, Cuauhtémoc Cárdenas of the left-of-center PRD party, headed an administration widely seen as honest and well-intentioned, and made the first serious efforts to combat police corruption, a major factor in the high crime levels. Cárdenas resigned in 1999 to campaign instead for the national presidency.

ORIENTATION

Mexico City's 350 *colonias* (neighborhoods) sprawl across the ancient bed of Lago de Texcoco and beyond. Though this vast urban expanse is daunting at first, the main areas of interest to visitors are fairly well defined and easy to traverse.

Centro Histórico

The historic heart of the city is the wide plaza known as El Zócalo, surrounded by the presidential palace, the city's cathedral and the excavated site of the Templo Mayor, the main temple of Aztec Tenochtitlán. The Zócalo and its surrounding neighborhoods are known as the Centro Histórico (Historic Center) and are full of notable old buildings and interesting museums. North, west and south of the Zócalo are many good, economical hotels and restaurants.

Alameda Central & Bellas Artes

Avenida Madero and Avenida Cinco de Mayo (or 5 de Mayo) link the Zócalo with the Alameda Central park, eight blocks to the west. On the east side of the Alameda stands the magnificent Palacio de Bellas Artes. The landmark Torre Latinoamericana (Latin American Tower) pierces the sky a block south of the Bellas Artes, beside one of the city's main north-south arterial roads, the Eje Central Lázaro Cárdenas.

Plaza de la República

Some 750m west of the Alameda, across Paseo de la Reforma, is the Plaza de la República, marked by the somber, domed art deco-style Monumento a la Revolución. This is a fairly quiet, mostly residential area with many budget and mid-range hotels.

Paseo de la Reforma

Mexico City's grandest boulevard, flanked by major hotels, embassies and banks, runs for many kilometers across the city's heart, connecting the Alameda to the Zona Rosa and the Bosque de Chapultepec.

Zona Rosa

The Zona Rosa (Pink Zone) is a glitzy shopping, eating, hotel and nightlife district

Shantytowns

Mexico City's notorious shantytowns are on its fringes, where most of the city's expansion is taking place. You may glimpse some as you enter or leave the city by road, though most of the main routes are lined by more established communities. Many of the oldest shantytowns – such as the vast Ciudad Nezahualcóyotl, east of the airport and home to well over a million people – are no longer really shantytowns, as they have succeeded in gaining services such as running water and electricity, and many of their inhabitants have earned enough money to build themselves relatively comfortable homes. Neza, as it's known, even has a soccer team, which reached the national championship final in 1997.

bound by Paseo de la Reforma to the north, Avenida Insurgentes to the east, and Avenida Chapultepec to the south.

Bosque de Chapultepec

The Wood of Chapultepec, known to gringos as Chapultepec Park, is to the west of the aforementioned districts. It's Mexico City's 'lungs,' a large expanse of greenery and lakes, and holds many major museums, including the renowned Museo Nacional de Antropología.

North of the Center

Five kilometers north of the center is the Terminal Norte, the largest of the city's four major bus terminals. Six kilometers north of the center is the Basílica de Guadalupe, Mexico's most revered shrine.

South of the Center

Avenida Insurgentes Sur connects Paseo de la Reforma to most points of interest in the south. Just west of Insurgentes, 1 to 2km south of the Zona Rosa, is Colonia Condesa, hub of the eating-out scene. Five to 10km farther south are the atmospheric former villages of San Ángel and Coyoacán and the

vast campus of UNAM, the National Autonomous University of Mexico. In the area to the southeast are the canals and gardens of Xochimilco.

The Eje System

Besides their regular names, many major streets in Mexico City are termed Eje (axis). The Eje system superimposes a grid of priority roads on this sprawling city's maze of smaller streets, making transport easier and quicker. The key north-south Eje Central Lázaro Cárdenas, running all the way from Coyoacán in the south to Tenayuca in the north, passes just east of the Alameda Central. Major north-south roads west of the Eje Central are termed Eje 1 Poniente (also called Guerrero, Rosales and Bucareli as it passes through the central area), Eje 2 Poniente (Avenida Florencia, Monterrey), etc. Major north-south roads to the east of the Eje Central are called Eje 1 Oriente (Alcocer, Anillo de Circunvalación), Eje 2 Oriente (Avenida Congreso de la Unión) and so on. The same goes for major east-west roads to the north and south of the Alameda Central and Zócalo: Rayón is Eje 1 Norte, Fray Servando Teresa de Mier is Eje 1 Sur.

Maps

Maps handed out by tourist offices in Mexico City are currently pretty basic. You can buy better maps of the city and country in many bookstores (including those in the Sanborns store chain and at top-end hotels) and at the shops of INEGI (see Planning in the Facts for the Visitor chapter). One convenient INEGI outlet is at Local (Office) CC23, Glorieta Insurgentes, just outside Insurgentes metro station. This shop stocks INEGI's own maps plus a variety of other maps of Mexico City, Mexico, Mexican states and other Mexican cities. It's open 8 am to 8 pm Monday to Friday, 8.30 am to 4 pm Saturday. There are other INEGI map shops at Local 61 in the airport and at Baja California 272, corner of Culiacán, near Chilpancingo metro station.

The *Guía Roji Ciudad de México* street atlas, costing US$8.50, has a comprehensive index and is updated annually.

Finding an Address

Some major streets, such as Avenida Insurgentes, keep the same name for many kilometers, but the names – and numbering – of many lesser streets switch every few blocks. Full addresses normally include the name of a colonia (neighborhood). Except for well-known city center districts, you may need help in finding a particular colonia. Often the easiest way to find an address is by asking where it is in relation to the nearest metro station.

INFORMATION
Tourist Offices

Mexico City has three tourist information offices in central areas, and others at the airport and the Terminal Norte bus station (see Getting There & Away). None of them has much giveaway material, but they willingly answer questions. Usually at least one member of staff in each office can speak English.

The tourist office of SECTUR, the national tourism ministry (☎ 5-250-01-23, 800-903-92-00), is located, inconveniently for most tourists, at Avenida Presidente Masaryk 172, on the corner of Hegel in the Polanco district, about 700m north of the Bosque de Chapultepec (Ⓜ Polanco). It has multilingual staff who willingly answer queries on the whole country and can provide computer printouts on some specific subjects.

SECTUR's two phone lines are staffed 24 hours, seven days a week, to provide tourist information and help with problems and emergencies. The office itself opens from 8 am to 6 pm Monday to Friday, 10 am to 3 pm Saturday.

The easier-to-reach Oficina de Turismo de la Ciudad de México (☎ 5-525-93-80), Amberes 54 at Londres, in the Zona Rosa (Ⓜ Insurgentes), provides information on Mexico City only. It's open 9 am to 8 pm daily.

The Cámara Nacional de Comercio de la Ciudad de México (Mexico City National Chamber of Commerce), Paseo de la Reforma 42 (Ⓜ Hidalgo or Juárez), has a tourist office (☎ 5-592-26-77 ext 1015), providing information on the city only. It's on the 4th floor and open 9 am to 2 pm and 3 to 6 pm Monday to Friday.

Tourist Card Extensions

The Instituto Nacional de Migración has offices at Avenida Chapultepec 284, Zona Rosa (☎ 5-626-72-00) and Homero 1832, Polanco (☎ 5-387-24-00). Both are open Monday to Friday, from 9 am to 1 pm. The Avenida Chapultepec office is just outside Insurgentes metro station. See Visas & Documents in the Facts for the Visitor chapter for information on extensions. It's advisable to phone the office first to ask what documents are needed.

Money

Exchange rates vary a bit among Mexico City's numerous money-changing outlets, so it's worth checking two or three before you part with your money. Most banks and casas de cambio (exchange offices) will change both cash and traveler's checks; some give a better rate for cash, others for traveler's checks. Some will change only US or Canadian dollars.

The greatest concentration of banks, ATMs and casas de cambio is on Paseo de la Reforma between the Monumento a Cristóbal Colón and the Monumento a la Independencia, but there are others all over the city, including at the airport, where some casas de cambio are open 24 hours.

Banks & ATMs Mexico City is chock-full of banks, most open 9 am to 5 pm Monday to Friday. Many have ATMs.

Casas de Cambio The city's dozens of casas de cambio have longer hours and quicker procedures than banks. Two downtown casas giving good rates are Cambios Exchange on Avenida Madero between Mata and Condesa (open 10 am to 7 pm daily), and Casa de Cambio Plus on Avenida Juárez facing the Alameda (open 9 am to 4 pm Monday to Friday).

The area around the Monumento a la Independencia on Paseo de la Reforma, near the Zona Rosa, is a fertile hunting ground for casas de cambio. One, Casa de Cambio

Tíber, Río Tíber 112 at Río Lerma, is open Monday to Friday 8.30 am to 5 pm, Saturday 8.30 am to 2 pm, and gives good rates. Money Exchange, Reforma at Lancaster, gives good rates for cash and American Express traveler's checks – open 9 am to 4 pm Monday to Friday.

In the Zona Rosa, Money Exchange, Liverpool 162, open 9 am to 8 pm Monday to Saturday, has reasonable rates for cash, but poor rates for traveler's checks. Londres, between Génova and Florencia, has many more casas de cambio.

American Express On the edge of the Zona Rosa, at Paseo de la Reforma 234, on the corner of Havre (**M** Insurgentes), is American Express (**☎** 5-207-72-82). It's open 9 am to 6 pm Monday to Friday, 9 am to 1 pm Saturday. You can change American Express traveler's checks here – at good rates, when we last checked. The office also has other financial and card services, a travel bureau and a mail pickup desk.

Wire Transfers The Western Union 'Dinero en Minutos' money wiring service (see Money in the Facts for the Visitor chapter) is available at several places, including:

Central de Telégrafos
Tacuba 8 (open 9 am to 10 pm Monday to Friday, 9 am to 8.30 pm Saturday, 9 am to 4.30 pm Sunday; **M** Allende)

Telecomm
Insurgentes 114, 1½ blocks north of Reforma (open 8 am to 8 pm Monday to Friday, 9 am to noon Saturday; nearest **M** Revolución)

Elektra Electronics Stores
(open 9 am to 9 pm daily)
Pino Suárez at El Salvador, three blocks south of the Zócalo (**M** Pino Suárez)
Balderas 62, two blocks south of the Alameda Central (**M** Juárez)
East side of Insurgentes Sur, two blocks south of Insurgentes metro

Post
The Correo Mayor, Mexico City's central post office, is a lovely early-20th-century building in Italian Renaissance style on Eje Central Lázaro Cárdenas at Tacuba, across

from the Palacio de Bellas Artes (**M** Bellas Artes). The stamp windows, open 9 am to 9 pm Monday to Friday, 9 am to 7 pm Saturday, and 9 am to noon Sunday, are marked 'estampillas.' The poste restante and lista de correos window, No 3, is open 8 am to 8 pm Monday to Friday, 9 am to 5 pm Saturday, 9 am to 1 pm Sunday. Have poste restante or lista de correos mail addressed this way:

Albert JONES (last name in capitals)
Poste Restante (or Lista de Correos)
Oficina Central de Correos
México 06002 DF
MEXICO

For other information, go to window No 16 or 49.

Other post offices in the city are typically open 8 am to 7 pm Monday to Friday and 9 am to 1 pm Saturday. Here are a few:

Zócalo
Inside Plaza de la Constitución 7 (the west side of the Zócalo)
Near Plaza de la República (**M** Revolución)
Corner of Ignacio Mariscal and Arriaga
Plaza Colón, Reforma at Ramírez, open 9 am to 7 pm Monday to Friday, 9 am to 5 pm Saturday
Zona Rosa (**M** Insurgentes or Sevilla)
Corner of Varsovia and Londres

If you carry an American Express card or American Express traveler's checks, you can use the American Express office (see Money) as your mailing address in Mexico City. Have mail addressed this way:

Lucy CHANG (last name in capitals)
Client Mail
American Express
Paseo de la Reforma 234
México 06600 DF
MEXICO

The office holds mail for about one month before returning it to the sender.

Telephone
See Post & Communications in the Facts for the Visitor chapter for information on telephones, rates and how to make calls.

There are thousands of pay phones on the streets of Mexico City. Shops selling phone cards are also plentiful, including at the airport – look for blue-and-yellow 'De Venta Aqui Ladatel' signs.

Fax
You can send faxes from the Central de Telégrafos, Tacuba 8 (Ⓜ Bellas Artes), 9 am to 10 pm Monday to Friday, 9 am to 8.30 pm Saturday, 9 am to 4.30 pm Sunday. One page to the USA or Canada costs about US$2. Many telephone *casetas*, shops and businesses – including at the airport and bus stations – offer fax service, look for 'fax' or *'fax público'* signs.

Email & Internet Access
Mexico City has many public Internet and email services. Prices in the following listings are for an hour online.

Centro Histórico
Centro de Estudios Superiores Lafoel (☎ 5-512-35-84) – Donceles 80; open 10 am to 8 pm Monday to Friday (US$4)

NETFM (☎ 5-510-96-73) – Plaza de la Computación y Electrónica, Eje Central Lázaro Cárdenas 54; open 10 am to 8 pm Monday to Saturday, noon to 5 pm Sunday (US$3.50)

Ultra Byte – on Uruguay east of Restaurante Danubio (US$3.25)

Plaza de la República Area
Sala Internet – Bucareli 8 in *El Universal* newspaper office; take photo ID to enter building; open 10 am to 3 pm and 4 to 7 pm Monday to Friday (free; maximum 1½ hours)

Zona Rosa
Café Internet – Hamburgo east of Florencia; open 10 am to 10 pm Monday to Saturday (US$3); food and drinks service

Java Chat – Génova 44K; open 9 am to 11 pm Monday to Friday, 10 am to 11 pm Saturday and Sunday (US$3.75); free coffee and soft drinks

Other Areas
Coffee Net (☎ 5-286-71-04) – Nuevo León 104B, Condesa; open 10 am to 10 pm daily except Sunday (US$3); pleasant environment, drinks available

Escape (☎ 5-550-76-84) – Avenida de la Paz 23, San Ángel

Internet Station – Arquímedes 130, Polanco

Internet Resources
One of the better visitor's introductions to the city on the Internet is Mexico City Virtual Guide (www.mexicocity.com.mx/mexcity.html), with a broad range of material on sights, hotels and restaurants (mainly top-end), a good reading list and interesting links. The Spanish-language version has more information than the English one. The Distrito Federal tourism department's site (www.mexicocity.gob.mx) has exhaustive listings of museums and galleries and what's on in them, and contact details for countless hotels, restaurants, travel agencies and transportation companies – but for the moment it's all in Spanish.

Tiempo Libre magazine's helpful website (www.tiempolibre.com.mx) has heaps of useful information, and not just about the current week's entertainment in Mexico City (which is what the magazine itself covers). It includes links to a number of museum websites and archives with the best collection of Mexico City restaurant reviews you'll find in a long time – all in Spanish, of course.

Some other sites are mentioned in relevant sections of this chapter.

Travel Agencies
A number of mid-range and top-end hotels have a travel agent's desk *(agencia de viajes)* on-site or can recommend travel agencies nearby.

Mundo Joven (☎ 5-661-32-33), at Insurgentes Sur 1510, Local D, and also at the Casa de Francia (☎ 5-525-04-07), Havre 15, Zona Rosa, specializes in cheap youth, student and teachers' travel tickets, and has worthwhile fares on domestic and one-way international flights from Mexico City. Mundo Joven can issue ISIC, ITIC and GO25 cards for US$12.50: for the first two you need a card or letter from your college showing that you are a full-time student or teacher. For a GO25 you just need your passport (and you have to be under 26). You can reach the Insurgentes head office on a 'San Ángel' minibus south from Insurgentes Ⓜ it's just south of Avenida Río Mixcoac.

Other youth/student travel agencies are Viajes Educativos (☎ 5-661-42-35), Local B10, Insurgentes Sur 421 (entrance on Aguascalientes just north of Chilpancingo metro), which can issue ISIC and HI cards and change dates on student and youth air tickets; and Cosmo Educación at Local 9, Avenida de la Paz 58, San Ángel (☎ 5-550-33-73) and at France 17A, Polanco (☎ 5-282-10-21).

The following travel agencies are also worth looking into for reasonably priced air tickets:

Tony Pérez
(☎ 5-533-11-48) Río Volga 1 at Río Danubio, behind the María Isabel-Sheraton Hotel

Viajes Universales
(☎/fax 5-512-71-20) Bucareli 12, 3rd floor

If you're looking for a guided adventure or ecotourism trip elsewhere in Mexico, a good place to start asking is Hostal Moneda, Moneda 8 just off the Zócalo (see Places to Stay – Mid-Range), where you can contact Ecogrupos de México (☎ 5-522-58-03, ☎/fax 5-522-58-21), an organization which offers a wide range of trips from white-water rafting in Veracruz state to whale-watching off Baja California.

Trips with Río y Montaña Expediciones (☎ 5-520-2041, www.rioymontana.com), Prado Norte 450, Lomas de Chapultepec, receive good reports. Rafting, climbing, mountain-biking and hiking are their stocks in trade.

Bookstores

Books in English and other non-Spanish languages can be found in bookstalls in top-end hotels, Sanborns stores and major museums, as well as most of the following recommended bookstores.

These are the most interesting downtown bookstores in the Centro Histórico and Alameda Central area:

American Bookstore
(☎ 5-512-03-06) Bolívar 23 – some novels and books on Mexico in English

Gandhi
Avenida Juárez 4 – good source of books about Mexico and Mexico City; novels in English, some Lonely Planet guides

Palacio de Bellas Artes
(☎ 5-521-92-51) – excellent arts bookstore with some English-language titles on Mexico

Pórtico de la Ciudad de México
Eje Central Lázaro Cárdenas 24 – excellent range of books in Spanish on Mexico, useful selection in English

In the Zona Rosa & Jardín del Arte, three stores are specially worth seeking out :

La Bouquinerie
Casa de Francia, Havre 15 – small French bookstore

Librería Británica
(☎ 5-705-24-74) Rosas Moreno 152 – best English-language stock in the city, including novels and books on Mexico

Tower Records
(☎ 5-525-48-29) Niza 19, Zona Rosa – city's best range of Lonely Planet guides

Two outstanding bookstores in San Ángel are:

Gandhi
(☎ 5-661-09-11) Avenida M A de Quevedo 128 to 132 – a Mexico City institution with a big range of books on most subjects, mostly in Spanish, a worthwhile music section and a popular upstairs café; open 9 am to 11 pm Monday to Friday, 10 am to 10 pm Saturday and Sunday

La Bouquinerie
(☎ 5-616-60-66) Camino al Desierto de los Leones 40 – Mexico's best French bookstore, open 10 am to 8 pm daily except Sunday

In Coyoacán, a good bookstore specializing in religion and philosophy titles in English and Spanish, and also selling Lonely Planet titles, is Nalandra Libros (☎ 5-554-75-22), Centenario 16.

Media

Mexico's English-language newspaper, *The News*, and the weekly *Tiempo Libre*, the city's Spanish-language what's-on magazine, are sold at many downtown and Zona Rosa newsstands, as well as by several of the bookstores mentioned above.

North American and European newspapers and magazines are sold at hotel newsstands and some of the above bookstores. La Casa de la Prensa, in the Zona Rosa at

Avenida Florencia 59 and Hamburgo 141 (Ⓜ Insurgentes), sells major British and American newspapers and magazines, plus a few French, Spanish and German ones. The Florencia branch is open 8 am to 10 pm Monday to Friday, 8 am to 4 pm Saturday and Sunday; the Hamburgo branch is open 8 am to 10 pm Monday to Saturday, 8 am to 9 pm Sunday.

Libraries

There are several useful foreign-run libraries in Mexico City:

Biblioteca Benjamín Franklin
(☎ 5-211-00-42; Ⓜ Cuauhtémoc) Londres 16, west of Berlín, run by the US embassy; wide range of books about Mexico, plus English-language periodicals. Users must be 20 or older. Open 3 to 7.30 pm Monday and Friday, 10 am to 3 pm Tuesday to Thursday

Canadian Embassy Library
(☎ 5-724-79-00; Ⓜ Polanco) Schiller 529, Polanco, in the embassy; many Canadian books and periodicals in English and French. Open 9 am to 12.30 pm Monday to Friday

Casa de Francia
(☎ 5-511-31-51; Ⓜ Insurgentes) Havre 15, Zona Rosa; good French library equipped with computers. Open 10 am to 8 pm Monday to Saturday

Consejo Británico (British Council)
(☎ 5-566-61-44; Ⓜ San Cosme) Antonio Caso 127; lots of books and magazines in English, plus aging British newspapers. Open 8.30 am to 7.30 pm Monday to Friday, 10 am to 1 pm Saturday

Instituto Goethe
(☎ 5-207-04-87; Ⓜ Insurgentes) Tonalá 43, Colonia Roma; German library. Open 9 am to 1 pm and 4 to 7.30 pm Tuesday to Thursday, and 10 am to 2 pm Saturday

Cultural Centers

The Consejo Británico and Instituto Goethe (see Libraries, above) and the Institut Français d'Amérique Latine (☎ 5-566-07-77) at Río Nazas 43 (Ⓜ San Cosme or Insurgentes) all put on films, exhibitions, concerts and other events from their home countries. The Casa de Francia (see Libraries) has a French bookstore and café and an exhibition hall.

Laundry

Three laundries, all charging US$2.50 to US$3 for you to wash and dry 3kg, or US$4 to US$5 for a 3kg service wash, are:

Lavandería Automática Édison – Édison 91 near Plaza de la República (Ⓜ Revolución); open 10 am to 7 pm Monday to Friday, 10 am to 6 pm Saturday

Lavandería Las Artes – Antonio Caso 82 near the Jardín del Arte; open 9 am to 7.30 pm Monday to Friday, 9 am to 8 pm Saturday

Lavandería Automática – Río Danubio 119B, not far north of the Zona Rosa; open 8.15 am to 6 pm Monday to Friday, 8.15 am to 5 pm Saturday

Medical Services

For recommendation of a doctor, dentist or hospital, you can call your embassy (see Embassies in the Facts for the Visitor chapter) or the 24-hour help line of the tourism ministry SECTUR (☎ 5-250-01-23). A private doctor's consultation generally costs between US$25 and US$40.

One of the best hospitals in all Mexico is the Hospital ABC (American British Cowdray Hospital, ☎ 5-230-80-00) at Calle Sur 136 No 116, just south of Avenida Observatorio in Colonia Las Américas, south of the Bosque de Chapultepec. There's an outpatient section and many of the staff speak English – but fees can be steep so adequate medical insurance is a big help. The nearest metro station is Observatorio, about 1km southeast.

For an ambulance, you can call the Cruz Roja (Red Cross, ☎ 5-557-57-57), or the general emergency numbers for ambulance, fire and police (☎ 060 and 080).

You can buy many medicines at pharmacies. Pharmacies in branches of the Sanborns store chain are among the best in the city.

Emergency

SECTUR (see Tourist Offices) is available by phone 24 hours a day to help tourists with problems and emergencies.

The Procuraduría General de Justicia del Distrito Federal (Federal District Attorney General) maintains mobile tourist assistance police units to go to the aid of visitors who are victims or witnesses of crime. Call ☎ 061 for help on the spot from these units.

The Procuraduría General de Justicia also has police offices to aid tourists with legal questions and problems. You can report crimes at these offices. One office (☎ 5-625-70-07, 5-625-81-53), at Avenida Florencia 20 in the Zona Rosa (Ⓜ Insurgentes), is always open, with English-speaking staff available. Another office can be found at the Terminal Sur de Autobuses.

Dangers & Annoyances
The recession of the mid-1990s brought a big increase in crime in Mexico City, with foreigners among the juicier and often easier targets for pickpockets, purse snatchers, thieves and armed robbers. Despite a reported decline in crime in 1999, levels

remain high and foreigners have been the victims of far too many violent incidents (including assaults *by* the police) for anyone to deny the risks. But there's no need to walk in fear whenever you step outside your hotel: a few precautions greatly reduce any dangers. (Please read Dangers & Annoyances in the Facts for the Visitor chapter for general hints applicable throughout Mexico.)

Mexico City's metro, buses and *peseros* (minibuses) are favorite haunts of pickpockets and thieves, particularly when they're crowded. Taxis are now even more notorious for robberies.

The riskiest time is after dark and, leaving taxis aside for a moment, the riskiest places are those where foreigners most often go. These include central metro stations and places such as the Bosque de Chapultepec,

---

Taxi Crime

In 1999 the US State Department warned: 'Robbery assaults on passengers in taxis are frequent and violent, with passengers subjected to beating, shootings and sexual assault.' Ask any foreigner living in Mexico City: if it hasn't happened to them, it has happened to someone they know. Many victims had hailed a cab on the street and were attacked or robbed by armed accomplices of the driver.

At the airport, use only the official yellow 'Transportación Terrestre' airport cabs (see Getting Around). Elsewhere in the city, you can telephone a radio taxi or a *sitio* (taxi stand): ask the dispatcher for the driver's name and the cab's license plate number. These cabs are more expensive than ordinary cruising street cabs, but the extra money buys you security. Radio taxi firms include Super Sitio 160 (☎ 5-271-91-46, 5-271-90-58), Taxi-Mex (☎ 5-538-14-40, 5-519-76-90), Taxi Radio Mex (☎ 5-584-05-71, 5-574-45-96), Sitio 101 (☎ 5-566-00-77, 5-566-72-66) and Servitaxis (☎ 5-516-60-20). Cab firms are listed under 'Sitios de Automóviles' in the telephone yellow pages. Hotels and restaurants will nearly always be able to call a reliable cab for you. The State Department specifically warned against taking taxis parked outside the Palacio de Bellas Artes, in front of nightclubs or restaurants, or cruising anywhere in the city.

If you *have to* hail a cab on the street – and it's much better never to do so – check that the cab has license plates and that the number on them matches the number painted on the bodywork. Also check the *carta de identificación,* an ID card which should be displayed visibly inside the cab, to see that the driver matches the photo. If a cab does not pass these tests, get another one. Sitio cabs have the letter S at the start of their license plate and an orange stripe along the bottom of the plate. Cruising *(libre)* taxis have the letter L and a green stripe.

Do not travel alone after dark, and do not carry ATM cards, credit cards or large amounts of cash. A fairly common practice among robbers is force hijack victims to tour the city and withdraw cash from ATMs.

If you become a robbery victim, give the perpetrator your valuables. They are not worth risking injury or death.

For more information on taxis, see this chapter's Getting Around section.

Mexico City's Air

Mexico City has some of the world's worst air. Severe pollution from traffic and industry is intensified by the mountains that ring the Valle de México and prevent air from dispersing, and by the city's altitude and consequent lack of oxygen. (Air at high altitudes contains less oxygen than air at sea level.)

Pollution is at its worst in the cooler months, especially November to February, when an unpleasant phenomenon called thermal inversion is most likely to occur: warm air passing over the Valle de México stops cool, polluted air near ground level from rising and dispersing. But at any time the pollution and altitude may make a visitor feel breathless and tired or may cause a sore throat, headache, runny nose or insomnia. People with serious lung, heart, asthmatic or respiratory problems are advised to consult a doctor before coming.

The major culprit is ozone, too much of which causes respiratory and eye problems in humans and corrodes rubber, paint and plastics. Leaks of unburned LPG (liquefied petroleum gas), used for cooking and heating, are a factor in ozone levels. But the primary problem is reckoned to be low-lead gasoline, introduced in 1986 to counter lead pollution, which until then was the city's worst atmospheric contaminant. The reaction between sunlight and combustion residues from low-lead gasoline produces a great deal of ozone. Mexico City's average ozone level is almost twice the maximum permitted in the USA and Japan.

In an attempt to reduce traffic pollution, since 1989 many cars in the city have been banned from the streets on one day each week by a program called Hoy No Circula (Don't Drive Today), and catalytic converters have been compulsory in all new cars in Mexico since the early 1990s. But ozone levels have remained high. Hoy No Circula unwittingly encouraged people to buy or rent extra cars to get around the once-a-week prohibition. Today there are around 4 million cars in the city – the number has doubled since 1980.

around the Museo Nacional de Antropología, the Zona Rosa and the area around the US embassy. Steer clear of empty streets after dark.

Using the metro only at less busy times enables you to find a less crowded car (at one end of the train), where thieves will find it harder to get close to you without being noticed (but avoid near-empty cars). During peak hours (roughly 7.30 to 10 am and 5 to 7 pm) all trains and buses in the central area are packed tight, which suits pickpockets. Hold on to any belongings tightly. Our advice is to avoid getting on or off trains at Hidalgo station, where pickpockets and bag snatchers wait for foreigners and follow them on to crowded trains. If you're on a train that's going through Hidalgo, use only the last cars, so that thieves waiting in the station are less likely to spot you.

Do not walk into a pedestrian underpass that is empty or nearly so; robbers may intercept you in the middle.

If you participate in any Mexican festivities (rallies or celebrations in the Zócalo, etc) be aware that half the pickpockets in the city will be there too.

Be aware of your surroundings and on your guard at the airport and bus stations, and be sure to keep your bag or pack between your feet when checking in.

Drivers should not drive alone at night. Thieves have stopped lone drivers at night, forced them to drink large quantities of alcohol and robbed them of ATM and credit cards.

Perhaps most important, don't risk injury by resisting robbers.

CENTRO HISTÓRICO

A good place to start your explorations of Mexico City is where the city began. The area known as the Centro Histórico focuses on the city's large main plaza, the Zócalo, and stretches for several blocks in each direction from there.

Mexico City's Air

The News publishes daily air quality reports and forecasts. Hourly reports (from 7 am to 8 pm) are posted on the Mexico City Air Quality Report Internet site (www.sima.com.mx) – this excellent site also explains in detail, in English and Spanish, how the pollution is measured. Ozone concentrations are worst around midday on sunny days.

Mexico City's air contamination is measured by the Índice Metropolitana de Calidad de Aire (IMECA, Metropolitan Air Quality Index). IMECA assesses five pollutants – ozone, sulfur dioxide, nitrogen dioxide, carbon monoxide and suspended particles. Readings below 100 are classed as 'satisfactory,' 101 to 200 is 'unsatisfactory,' 201 to 300 is 'bad,' and over 300 is 'very bad.' Ozone readings of more than 240 – which occur several times a year – or suspended particle levels of over 175 trigger phase one of the city's environmental contingency plan, which includes the Doble Hoy No Circula (Double Don't Drive Today) rule, which takes more vehicles off the streets. Three successive days of phase one trigger phase two, which immobilzes further vehicles, reduces industrial activity by 30% to 40%, and stops outdoor activities at schools. Phase three (rare) stops all industry and permits only emergency traffic.

The more exotic remedies suggested for the pollution crisis have included fleets of helicopters to sweep the smog away, and plodding a hole in the ring of mountains around the city, then using giant fans to blow the smog through it. More feasible, conceivably, is the idea of ionizing the air to create winds that would disperse pollution. Large ionizing antennae would alter the rate at which water vapor condenses, releasing heat and thus creating winds which would, it's hoped, blow pollution away. Tests of this proposal began in 1998 and 1999 in the Parque Ecológico de Xochimilco in the southeast section of the city: the scientists responsible claimed that it significantly lowered levels of ozone and other pollutants.

❀❀❀❀❀❀❀❀❀❀❀❀❀❀❀❀❀❀❀❀❀❀❀❀

The Centro Histórico is full of historic sites from the Aztec and colonial eras, and it contains some of the city's finest art and architecture and is home to a number of absorbing museums. It also bustles with modern-day street life. Sunday is a particularly good day to explore this innermost part of the inner city. Traffic and street crowds are thinner, a relaxed atmosphere prevails and museums are free.

A few years ago the Centro Histórico had become rather rundown, but since then it has been spruced up to better fit the image of the hub of a proud nation. Some streets have been pedestrianized, buildings have been refurbished, new museums have opened and many glossy eateries and shops and fashionable bars have appeared. The city authorities fight an ongoing battle with the operators of the many small sidewalk stalls in the Centro Histórico. Attempts to expel them – which make it easier to walk around and please shopkeepers – generally bring protests and riots and succeed only temporarily.

El Zócalo

The heart of Mexico City is the Plaza de la Constitución, more commonly known as El Zócalo (Ⓜ Zócalo).

The Spanish word *zócalo*, which means plinth or stone base, was adopted in 1843 when a tall monument to independence was constructed only as far as the base. The plinth is long gone, but the name remains – and has been adopted informally by a lot of other Mexican cities for their main plazas.

The center of Aztec Tenochtitlán, the ceremonial precinct known as the Teocalli, lay immediately north and northeast of the Zócalo. Today *conchero* dancers remind everyone of this heritage with daily get-togethers in the Zócalo to carry out a sort of pre-Hispanic aerobics, in feathered headdresses and shell *(concha)* anklets and bracelets, to the rhythm of booming drums.

In the 1520s Cortés paved the plaza with stones from the ruins of the Teocalli and other Aztec buildings. Until the early 20th century, the Zócalo was more often a maze of market stalls than an open plaza. With each side measuring more than 200m, it's one of the world's largest city squares.

The Zócalo is the home of the powers-that-be in Mexico City. On its east side is the Palacio Nacional (the presidential palace), on the north the Catedral Metropolitana, on the south the offices of the Distrito Federal government. The plaza is also a place for political protesters to make their points – it's often dotted with makeshift camps of strikers or campaigners.

Each day at 6 pm the huge Mexican flag flying in the middle of the Zócalo is ceremonially lowered by the Mexican army and carried into the Palacio Nacional.

Palacio Nacional

Home to the offices of the president of Mexico, the Federal Treasury and dramatic murals by Diego Rivera, the National Palace fills the entire east side of the Zócalo. Bring your passport if you want to see the murals, which are inside the palace.

The first palace on this spot was built of tezontle by Aztec emperor Moctezuma II in the early 16th century. Cortés destroyed the palace in 1521 and rebuilt it with a large courtyard so that he could entertain visitors with Nueva España's first recorded bullfights. In 1562 the crown bought the palace from Cortés' family to house the Spanish viceroys of Nueva España. It was destroyed during riots in 1692, rebuilt again and continued to be used as the viceregal residence until Mexican independence in the 1820s.

As you face the palace you see three portals. On the right (south) is the guarded entrance for the president and other officials. High above the center door hangs the **Campana de Dolores** (Bell of Dolores), rung in the town of Dolores Hidalgo by Padre Miguel Hidalgo in 1810 at the start of the Mexican War of Independence, and later moved to this place of honor.

Enter the palace through the center door. The colorful **Diego Rivera murals** around

the courtyard present Rivera's view of Mexican civilization from the arrival of Quetzalcóatl – the Aztec plumed serpent god whom some believed to be personified in Hernán Cortés – to the 1910 revolution. Painted between 1929 and 1935, the murals are open for public viewing 9 am to 5 pm daily (free). Detailed guide booklets in English to the murals are sold (together with a set of postcards) for US$3.50 at the foot of the stairs inside the entrance.

Catedral Metropolitana

Building of the Metropolitan Cathedral, on the north side of the Zócalo, began in 1573. Though its inside is disfigured by scaffolding as builders struggle to arrest its uneven descent into the soft ground below, the cathedral is still impressive. In Aztec times part of the cathedral site was occupied by a large *tzompantli* (rack for the skulls of sacrifice victims). Cortés reportedly found more than 136,000 skulls here and nearby.

Exterior With a three-naved basilica design of vaults on semicircular arches, the cathedral was built to resemble those of Toledo and Granada in Spain. Several parts have been added or replaced over the years. The grand portals facing the Zócalo, built in the 17th century in baroque style, have two levels of columns and marble panels with bas-reliefs. The central panel shows the Assumption of the Virgin Mary, to whom the cathedral is dedicated. The tall north portals facing Calle Guatemala, dating from 1615, are in pure Renaissance style.

The upper levels of the towers, with their unique bell-shaped tops, were added in the late 18th century, and the exterior was completed in 1813, when architect Manuel Tolsá added the clock tower, topped by statues of Faith, Hope and Charity, and a great central dome, all in neoclassical style, to create some unity and balance.

Interior A plumb line hung from the dome above the central nave graphically demonstrates the building's subsidence problem.

The cathedral's chief artistic treasure is the gilded 18th-century Altar de los Reyes

(Altar of the Three Kings), behind the main altar, a masterly exercise in controlled elaboration and a high point of the Churrigueresque style. The two side naves are lined by 14 richly decorated chapels. At the cathedral's southwest corner, the Capilla de los Santos Ángeles y Arcángeles (Chapel of the Holy Angels and Archangels) is another exquisite example of baroque sculpture and painting, with a huge main altarpiece and two smaller ones decorated by the 18th-century painter Juan Correa.

A lot of other art in the cathedral was damaged or destroyed in a 1967 fire. The intricately carved late-17th-century wooden choir stalls by Juan de Rojas and the huge, gilded Altar de Perdón (Altar of Pardon), all in the central nave, have been restored.

Sagrario Metropolitano Adjoining the east side of the cathedral is the 18th-century sacristy, built to house the archives and vestments of the archbishop. Its exterior is a superb example of the ultradecorative Churrigueresque style. It's not open to visitors.

Templo Mayor

The Teocalli of Aztec Tenochtitlán, demolished by the Spaniards in the 1520s, stood on the site of the cathedral and the blocks to its north and east. The decision to excavate the Teocalli's Templo Mayor (Main Temple), requiring the demolition of colonial buildings, wasn't made until 1978, after electricity workers by chance dug up an eight-ton stone-disc carving of the Aztec goddess Coyolxauhqui. The temple is thought to be on the exact spot where the Aztecs saw their symbolic eagle with a snake in its beak perching on a cactus – still the symbol of Mexico today. In Aztec belief this was, literally, the center of the universe.

The entrance to the temple site is just east of the cathedral, on pedestrianized Calle Seminario. The site (☎ 5-542-06-06) is open 9 am to 5 pm Tuesday to Sunday (US$2 including entrance to the Museo del Templo Mayor; free on Sunday).

A walkway around the site reveals the temple's multiple layers of construction. Explanatory material is all in Spanish. Like

many other sacred buildings in Tenochtitlán, the temple, first begun in 1375, was enlarged several times, with each rebuilding accompanied by the sacrifice of captured warriors. In 1487 these rituals were performed at a frenzied pace to rededicate the temple after one major reconstruction. Michael Meyer and William Sherman write in *The Course of Mexican History*:

In a ceremony lasting four days sacrificial victims taken during campaigns were formed in four columns, each stretching three miles. At least twenty thousand human hearts were torn out to please the god . . . . In the frenzy of this ghastly pageant, the priests were finally overcome by exhaustion.

What we see today are sections of several of the temple's different phases. Unfortunately hardly anything is left of the seventh and last version, built about 1502, which was seen by the Spanish conquistadors. A replica of the Coyolxauhqui stone lies near the west side of the site. At the center is a platform dating from about 1400; on its southern half, a sacrificial stone stands in front of a shrine to Huizilopochtli, the Aztec tribal god. On the northern half is a *chac-mool* figure before a shrine to the water god, Tláloc. By the time the Spanish arrived, a 40m-high double pyramid towered above this spot, with steep twin stairways climbing to shrines to the same two gods.

Other features of the site include a late-15th-century stone replica of a tzompantli, carved with 240 stone skulls, and the mid-15th-century Recinto de los Guerreros Águila (Sanctuary of the Eagle Warriors, an elite band of Aztec fighters), decorated with colored bas-reliefs of military processions.

Museo del Templo Mayor The excellent museum within the Templo Mayor site houses artifacts from the site and gives a good overview (in Spanish) of Aztec civilization, including their *chinampa* agriculture, their systems of government and trade, and their beliefs, wars and sacrifices. Pride of place is given to the great wheel-like stone of Coyolxauhqui (She of Bells on her Cheek). She is shown decapitated – the result of her murder by Huizilopochtli, her brother, who also killed his 400 brothers en route to becoming top god. Other outstanding exhibits include full-size terracotta eagle warriors.

Calle Moneda

As you walk back down Seminario toward the Zócalo from the Templo Mayor, Moneda is the first street on your left. Many of its buildings are made of tezontle. The streets off this east side of the Zócalo are a commercial area but lacking the glitz of the west side.

The **Museo de la Secretaría de Hacienda y Crédito Público** (Museum of the Secretariat of Finance & Public Credit, ☎ 5-228-12-45), Moneda 4, houses a good collection of Mexican art, ranging from works by the 18th-century master Juan Correa to 20th-century giants Diego Rivera and Rufino Tamayo and interesting contemporary artists. The setting, a colonial archbishop's palace with two lovely courtyards, adds to its attraction. It's open 10 am to 5 pm Tuesday to Sunday (US$0.80, free on Sunday).

The **Museo Nacional de las Culturas** (National Museum of Cultures, ☎ 5-512-74-52), Moneda 13, in a fine courtyarded building constructed in 1567 as the colonial mint, has exhibits showing the art, dress and handicrafts of several world cultures. Hours are 9.30 am to 5.45 pm Tuesday to Sunday (free).

A block farther east, then a few steps north to Academia 13, is a former convent housing the **Museo José Luis Cuevas** (☎ 5-542-89-59), founded by Cuevas, a leading modern Mexican artist. There are engravings by Picasso, drawings by Rembrandt, and work by Cuevas himself and other moderns. Hours are 10 am to 5.30 pm Tuesday to Sunday (US$0.50, free on Sunday).

Nacional Monte de Piedad

Facing the west side of the cathedral on the corner of Avenida Cinco de Mayo is Mexico's national pawnshop, founded in 1775 and now one of the world's largest secondhand shops. Housed in a large, dark building, it's open 8.30 am to 6 pm Monday to Friday, 8.30 am to 3 pm Saturday.

Plaza Santo Domingo

This plaza, two blocks north of the cathedral, is a less formal affair than the Zócalo.

Modern-day scribes, with typewriters and antique printing machines, work beneath the **Portal de Evangelistas**, along its west side.

The pink stone **Iglesia de Santo Domingo**, dating from 1736, is a beautiful baroque church, decorated on its east side with carved stone figures of Santo Domingo (St Dominic) and San Francisco (St Francis). Below the figures, the arms of both saints are symbolically entwined as if to convey a unity of purpose in their lives. The church's front, or southern, façade is equally beautiful, with 12 columns around the main entrance. Between the columns are statues of San Francisco and San Agustín (St Augustine), and in the center at the top is a bas-relief of the Assumption of the Virgin Mary.

On the corner of Brasil and Venezuela, opposite the church, is the 18th-century Palacio de la Escuela de Medicina, built as the headquarters of the Inquisition in Mexico. It houses the interesting **Museo de la Medicina Mexicana**, whose displays range from a model of a *baño de temazcal* – a kind of indigenous sauna, used for spiritual purification – to a reconstruction of a 19th-century pharmacy. It's open 10 am to 6 pm daily (free).

Murals

The **Secretaría de Educación Pública** is on Argentina 28, 3½ blocks north of the Zócalo. It's open 9 am to 5 or 6 pm Monday to Friday (free). Sometimes the attendants ask for ID, so it's best to take your passport. The two front courtyards are lined with 120 fresco panels on diverse subjects connected with the people of Mexico, done by Diego Rivera and assistants in the 1920s. On the ground floor you'll find themes of industry, agriculture and class struggle, and artisan and festival scenes; on the middle floor, murals covering science, work and coats of arms of the Mexican states. On the top floor, in the first courtyard are Mexican heroes such as Emiliano Zapata and the Aztec king Cuauhtémoc and panels on themes such as brotherhood, women and the arts; in the second courtyard are scenes of capitalist decadence and proletarian and agrarian revolution – Frida Kahlo can be spotted in one called *En El Arsenal*. The building's rear courtyard has a staircase adorned with *Patricios y Patricidas* by Siqueiros and others.

A block back toward the Zócalo, then half a block east at Justo Sierra 16, is the **Museo de San Ildefonso** (☎ 5-789-25-05), open 11 am to 6 pm daily except Monday (US$2, free on Tuesday). Built in the 16th century as the Jesuit college of San Ildefonso, it served from 1867 to 1978 as the Escuela Nacional Preparatoria, a prestigious teacher training college. From 1923 to 1933, Rivera, Orozco, Siqueiros and others were brought in to adorn it with murals. Most of the work in the main patio and on the grand staircase is by Orozco, inspired by the recently ended Mexican Revolution. Some interesting temporary exhibitions are held in the building. The amphitheater, off the lobby, holds a gigantic Creation mural by Rivera.

Museo Nacional de Arte
Several blocks west of the Zócalo, the National Museum of Art (☎ 5-512-32-24), at Tacuba 8 (Ⓜ Bellas Artes), contains exclusively Mexican work. In front stands a distinctive bronze equestrian statue of the Spanish king Carlos IV (who reigned from 1788 to 1808) by the sculptor and architect Manuel Tolsá. Called *El Caballito* (The Little Horse), it originally stood in the Zócalo but was moved here in 1852. A sign points out that the statue is preserved as a work of art (not, it's implied, out of respect for the Spanish king).

The museum – once the Communications Ministry – was built around 1900 in the style of an Italian Renaissance palace, with a grand marble staircase. The collections represent every style and school of Mexican art up to the early 20th century. The work of José María Velasco, depicting Mexico City and the countryside in the late 19th and early 20th centuries, is a highlight. Velasco's landscapes show the Lago de Texcoco still filling half the Valle de México, and Guadalupe and Chapultepec far outside the city in the 1870s.

The museum's hours are 10 am to 5.30 pm Tuesday to Sunday (US$2, free on Sunday).

Colegio de Minería
Opposite the Museo Nacional de Arte, at Tacuba 5, is the College of Mining, a neoclassical building designed by Manuel Tolsá and built between 1797 and 1813. Four meteorites found in Mexico are displayed in its entrance.

Casa de Azulejos
A block south of the Museo Nacional de Arte, between Avenida Cinco de Mayo and Avenida Madero, stands one of the city's gems. The Casa de Azulejos (House of Tiles) dates from 1596, when it was built for the Condes (Counts) del Valle de Orizaba. Although the superb tile work which has adorned the outside walls since the 18th century is Spanish and Moorish in style, most of the tiles were actually produced in China and shipped to Mexico on the Manila *naos* (Spanish galleons used up to the early 19th century).

The building now houses a Sanborns store and is a good place to buy a newspaper or have refreshments (see Places to Eat). The staircase climbing from the main restaurant has a 1925 mural by Orozco.

Torre Latinoamericana
The Latin American Tower, the landmark 1950s skyscraper on the corner of Avenida Madero and Eje Central Lázaro Cárdenas, has an observation deck and café on its 43rd and 44th floors, open 9.30 am to 10.30 pm every day (US$3). The views are spectacular, smog permitting. Tickets are sold at the street entrance on the Eje Central side of the building.

Palacio de Iturbide
A block east of the Casa de Azulejos, at Avenida Madero 17, rises the beautiful baroque façade of the Iturbide Palace. Built between 1779 and 1785 for colonial nobility, it was claimed in 1821 by General Agustín Iturbide, a hero of the Mexican struggle for independence from Spain. Responding favorably to a rent-a-crowd that gathered before the palace in 1822 beseeching him to be their emperor, Iturbide proclaimed himself Emperor Agustín I. But he abdicated

less than a year later, after General Santa Anna announced the birth of a republic.

The palace houses the Fomento Cultural Banamex (the cultural promotion section of Banamex bank), and some excellent art and crafts exhibitions are shown in the fine courtyard. Open hours are usually 10 am to 7 pm daily (free).

ALAMEDA CENTRAL & AROUND

A little less than 1km west of the Zócalo is the pretty Alameda Central, Mexico City's only sizable downtown park. In the blocks around the Alameda are some of the city's most interesting buildings and museums.

Bellas Artes metro station is at the northeast corner of the Alameda. You can also reach the Alameda from the Zócalo area on a 'M(etro) Chapultepec,' 'M(etro) Hidalgo' or 'M(etro) Auditorio' pesero heading west on Avenida Cinco de Mayo.

Alameda Central

This verdant park was once an Aztec marketplace. In early colonial times it became the site of *autos-da-fé*, in which heretics were sentenced and often burned or hanged. In 1592 Viceroy Luis de Velasco decided the growing city needed a pleasant area of pathways, fountains and trees. It took its name from the poplars *(álamos)* with which it was planted. By the late 19th century the park was dotted with European-style statuary, lit by gas lamps, and had a bandstand for free concerts. Today the Alameda is a popular, easily accessible refuge from the city streets. It's particularly busy on Sunday, when you may catch a rock or salsa band playing open-air.

Palacio de Bellas Artes

This splendid white marble concert hall and arts center, commissioned by President Porfirio Díaz, dominates the east end of the Alameda. Construction of the Palace of Fine Arts (☎ 5-521-92-51) began in 1904 under Italian architect Adamo Boari, who favored neoclassical and art nouveau styles. But the building's heavy marble shell began to sink into the spongy subsoil, and work was halted. Architect Federico Mariscal eventually finished the interior in the 1930s, with new designs reflecting the more modern art deco style.

Some of Mexico's finest murals dominate immense wall spaces on the second and third levels. On the second level are two large, striking early 1950s works by Rufino Tamayo: *México de Hoy* (Mexico Today) and *Nacimiento de la Nacionalidad* (Birth of Nationality), a symbolic depiction of the creation of the Mexican mestizo identity.

At the west end of the third level is Diego Rivera's famous *El Hombre, Contralor del Universo* (Man, Controller of the Universe), which was first commissioned for Rockefeller Center in New York. The Rockefeller family had the original destroyed because of its anticapitalist themes, but Rivera recreated it even more dramatically here in 1934. Capitalism, with accompanying death and war, is shown on the left; socialism, with health and peace, is on the right.

On the north side of the third level are David Alfaro Siqueiros' three-part *La Nueva Democracía* (New Democracy), painted in 1944-45, and Rivera's four-part *Carnaval de la Vida Mexicana* (Carnival of Mexican Life), from 1936. At the east end is José Clemente Orozco's eye-catching *La Katharsis* (Catharsis), from 1934-35: violence and degradation result from the conflict between 'natural' and 'social' poles of human nature, symbolized by naked and clothed figures, but a giant bonfire threatens to consume all in a spiritual rebirth.

The palace's theater has a beautiful stained-glass stage curtain depicting the highlands of Mexico, based on a design by Mexican painter Gerardo Murillo (also called Dr Atl). Tiffany Studios of New York assembled the curtain from almost a million pieces of colored glass. It's normally lit up for public viewing on Sunday mornings and just before performances.

You can view the murals and look around the *palacio* 10 am to 6 pm Tuesday to Sunday (US$2.50, free on Sunday). The palace also stages some top-class temporary art exhibitions and is home to the famous Ballet Folklórico (see Entertainment). A good bookstore and elegant café are on the premises too.

View of Mexico City's Centro Histórico and Zócalo

Aztec *conchero* dancers

Pilgrimage at Basílica de Guadalupe

Modern meets colonial in Mexico City's Zona Rosa

UNAM's Facultad de Medicína, Mexico City

Flags over the capital's Palacio Nacional

Monumento a la Independencia, Mexico City

Colonial façade, Mexico City

Mexico City Map Section

GREG ELMS

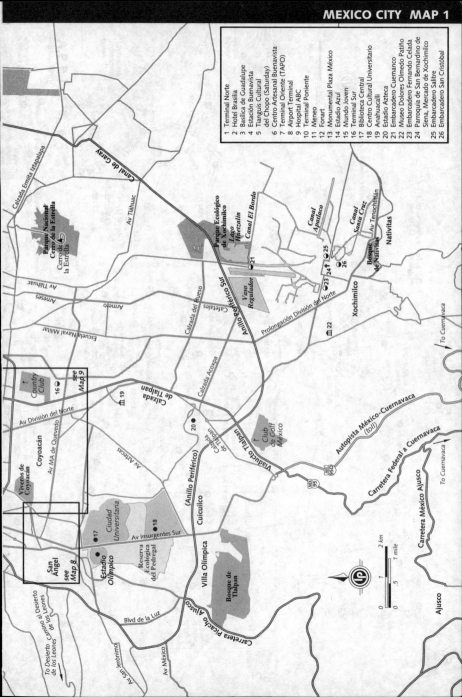

1 Terminal Norte
2 Hotel Brasilia
3 Basílica de Guadalupe
4 Estación Buenavista
5 Tianguis Cultural del Chopo (Saturday)
6 Centro Artesanal Buenavista
7 Terminal Oriente (TAPO)
8 Airport Terminal
9 Hospital ABC
10 Terminal Poniente
11 Meneo
12 Fonart
13 Monumental Plaza México
14 Estadio Azul
15 Mundo Joven
16 Terminal Sur
17 Biblioteca Central
18 Centro Cultural Universitario
19 Anahuacalli
20 Estadio Azteca
21 Embarcadero Cuemanco
22 Museo Dolores Olmedo Patiño
23 Embarcadero Fernando Celada
24 Parroquia de San Bernardino de Siena, Mercado de Xochimilco
25 Embarcadero Salitre
26 Embarcadero San Cristóbal

MAP 2 METRO

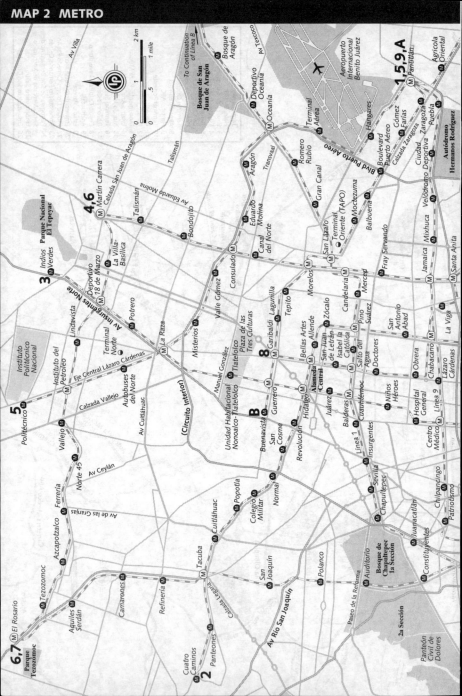

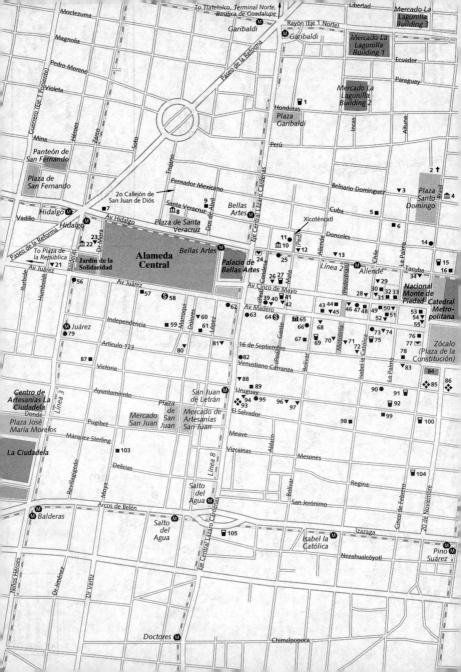

CENTRO HISTÓRICO & ALAMEDA CENTRAL

PLACES TO STAY
5 Pensión del Centro
6 Hotel Habana
7 Hotel de Cortés
9 Hotel Hidalgo
16 Hostel Catedral
17 Hotel Catedral
30 Hotel Juárez
32 Hotel Zamora
33 Hotel Washington
36 Hostal Moneda
43 Hotel Ritz
44 Hotel Buenos Aires
48 Hotel Gillow
49 Hotel Canadá
51 Hotel San Antonio
53 Holiday Inn Select
57 Hotel Bamer
59 Hotel Del Valle
61 Hotel Marlowe
67 Hotel Principal
76 Hotel Majestic
78 Gran Hotel Ciudad de México
87 Hotel Fleming
89 Hotel Capitol
98 Hotel Isabel
99 Hotel Montecarlo
101 Hotel Roble
103 Hotel San Diego

PLACES TO EAT
3 Hostería de Santo Domingo
12 Los Girasoles, Taco Inn
13 Café de Tacuba
18 Café del Centro
19 La Casa de las Sirenas
21 Sanborns
23 Café Trevi
26 Café El Popular

28 Café La Blanca
29 Tacos Beguis
31 Taquería Tlaquepaque
32 Café El Popular
34 Los Bisquets Bisquets Obregón
40 The Coffee Factory
42 Restaurante El Vegetariano
45 VIPS
46 Potzollcalli
49 Jugos Canadá
50 Pizza Hut
52 Restaurante El Vegetariano
54 Flash Taco
55 Shakey's Pizza y Pollo
60 Centro Naturista de México
68 Los Bisquets Bisquets Obregón
70 Comedor Vegetariano
71 La Casa del Pavo
72 Sanborns
74 VIPS
80 Hong King
81 Taquería Tlaquepaque
83 Super Soya
88 Churrería El Moro
94 Restaurante Danubio
96 Rincón Mexicano, Antojitos Tere
97 La Esquina del Pibe

OTHER
1 El Tenampa
2 Iglesia de Santo Domingo
4 Museo de la Medicina Mexicana
8 Museo Franz Mayer
10 Museo Nacional de Arte
11 Central de Telégrafos
14 Centro de Estudios Superiores Lafoel
15 Restaurante-Bar León
20 Museo de San Ildefonso

22 Museo Mural Diego Rivera
24 Main Post Office
25 Colegio de Minería
27 La Ópera Bar
35 Museo de la Secretaría de Hacienda y Credito Publico
37 Museo Nacional de las Culturas
38 Museo José Luis Cuevas
39 Casa de Azulejos
41 Bar Mata
47 Dulcería de Celaya
56 Mexicana
58 Casa de Cambio Plus
62 Gandhi
63 Torre Latinoamericana
64 Cambios Exchange
65 Palacio de Iturbide
66 American Bookstore
69 Salón Corona
73 Mixup
75 Opulencia
77 Post Office
79 Elektra
82 Pórtico de la Ciudad de México
84 Gobierno del Distrito Federal
85 El Palacio de Hierro
86 Liverpool
90 Turismo Zócalo
91 El Cirio
92 Pervert Lounge
93 NETFM, Plaza de la Computación y Electrónica
95 Ultra Byte
100 Altura
102 Elektra
104 La Llorona
105 Butterfly

Mexico City taxi cab

PLAZA DE LA REPÚBLICA, SAN RAFAEL & JUÁREZ

PLACES TO STAY
5 Hotel Texas
6 Casa de los Amigos
7 Hotel Édison
11 Hotel Ibiza
13 Hotel Oxford
14 Hotel Carlton
16 Hotel New York
19 Hotel Jena
21 Hotel Frimont
24 Palace Hotel
25 Hotel Corinto
28 Hotel Mayaland
29 Hotel Casa Blanca
31 Hotel Crowne Plaza
38 Hotel Mallorca
40 Hotel Compostela
41 Hotel Sevilla
45 Hotel Sevilla Palace
48 Fiesta Americana
51 Hotel María Cristina

PLACES TO EAT
2 Sanborns
3 El Tigre
4 Super Cocina Los Arcos
9 Potzollcalli
15 Restaurant Cahuich
17 Seafood Cocktail Stand
18 Restaurante Samy
26 VIPS
27 Tacos El Caminero
30 Sanborns
44 Sanborns
42 VIPS

OTHER
1 Antillanos
8 Lavandería Automática Édison
10 Post Office
12 Museo de San Carlos
20 Monumento a la Revolución & Museo Nacional de la Revolución
22 Torre Caballito
23 Consejo Británico

32 Cámara Nacional de Comercio de la Ciudad de México
33 TAESA
34 Iberia, Aerolíneas Argentinas
35 El Universal, Sala Internet
36 Viajes Universales
37 Librería Británica
39 Lavandería Las Artes
43 Telecomm
46 Post Office
47 Monumento a Cristóbal Colón
49 Aeroméxico, Aerolitoral
50 Institut Français de Amérique Latine
52 Monumento a Cuauhtémoc
53 Bar Milán
54 El Colmillo
55 Biblioteca Benjamin Franklin, Institute of International Education

Catedral Metropolitana.and Zócalo

Palacio de Bellas Artes

MAP 4 PLAZA DE LA REPÚBLICA, SAN RAFAEL & JUÁREZ

San Rafael

San Cosme

Herrera

Pimentel

Prieto

Covarrubias

Calzada Melchor Ocampo (Circuito Interior)

Ribera de San Cosme

Gómez Farías

Del Martínez

Río Usumacinta

Río Amoy

Lorenzana

Velázquez de León

Contreras

Barcelona

Altamirano

Av Insurgentes Centro

23

Av Parque Vía

Rosas Moreno

Schultz

Antonio Caso

39

38

Serapio Rendón

40 41

43

44

Sadi Carnot

42

Sullivan

Madrid

París

Río Éufrates

50

Jardín del Arte

Plaza

Villalongín

Río Elba

Río Nazas

Río Tigris

Río Danubio

Río Sena

Río Pánuco

Río Po

Río Lerma

51

Río Neva

Río Guadiana

Río Amazonas

Río Marne

Río Támesis

Paseo de la Reforma

52

Roma

Lucerna

Viena

Milán

53

Río Rhin

Río Papaloapan

Río Tíber

Río Volga

Hamburgo

Juárez

María Isabel
Sheraton Hotel

Génova

Copenhague

Niza

Av Insurgentes Centro

Londres

55

Berlín

Estocolmo

Amberes

Belgrado

Estrasburgo

Havre

Nápoles

Dinamarca

Liverpool

Marsella

Varsovia

Lancaster

Av Florencia

(pedestrian)

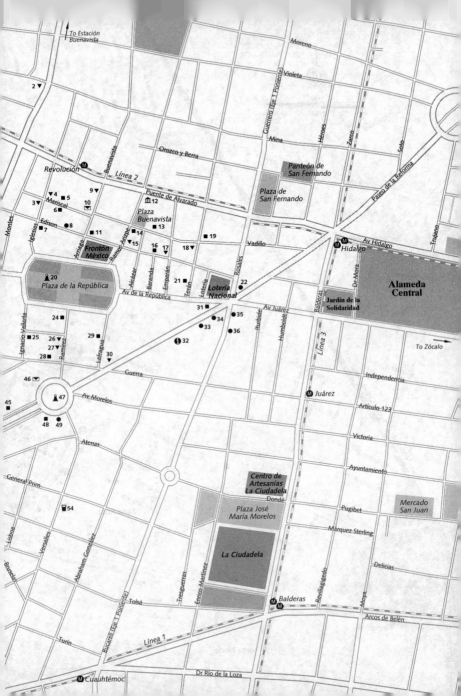

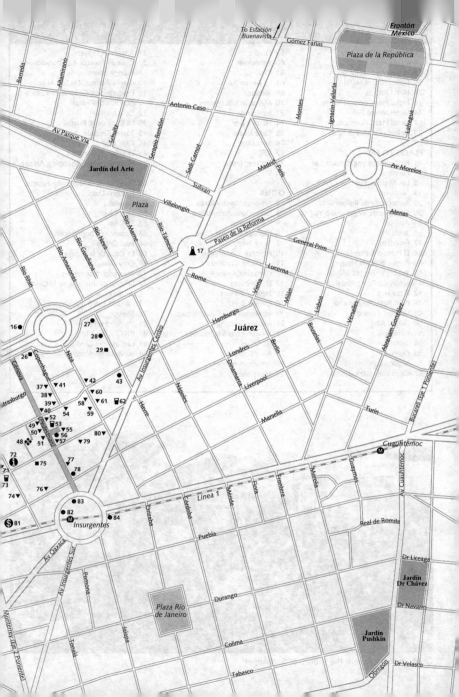

To Estación
Buenavista

Gómez Farías

**Frontón
México**

Plaza de la República

Antonio Caso

Av Parque Vía

Jardín del Arte

Schultz

Serapio Rendón

Sadi Carnot

Sullivan

Madrid

París

Montes

Ignacio Vallarta

Jalatlaco

Av Morelos

Plaza

Villalongín

Atenas

Río Marne

Río Tíber

Paseo de la Reforma

General Prim

🔔 17

Río Neva

Roma

Lucerna

Río Guadiana

Viena

Milán

Lisboa

Versalles

Abraham González

Río Amazonas

16 ●

27 ●

28 ●

29 ■

Av Insurgentes Centro

Hamburgo

Berlín

Juárez

Bucareli (Eje 1 Poniente)

Río Rhin

Copenhague

Niza

Londres

Dinamarca

Liverpool

Marsella

Turín

26 ■

Génova

Estrasburgo

37 ▼ 41 ▼
38 ▼
39 ▼
40 ▼

42 ▼ 43 ●
60 ▼
58 ▼ 61 ▼ 🚻 62
54   59

Nápoles

Havre

49 ▼ 52 ▼
50 ▼ 53 ▼
48 ▼ 51 ▼ 56 ▼ 55 ▼
        57 ▼

80 ▼
79 ▼

Cuauhtémoc Ⓜ

Guaymas

Av Cuauhtémoc

72 ▼
ⓘ
71 ▼
73 ▼
74 ▼

75 ■

77 ●
78 ●

76 ▼

Melchor

Frontera

Morelia

Real de Romita

Línea 1

Oaxaca

Córdoba

Flora

83 ●

82 ●
Ⓜ
Insurgentes

84 ●

Puebla

$ 81

Av Oaxaca

Av Insurgentes Sur

Pomona

Jalapa

Tonalá

Plaza Río
de Janeiro

Durango

Colima

Tabasco

Monterrey (Eje 1 Poniente)

Dr Liceaga

**Jardín
Dr Chávez**

Dr Navarro

**Jardín
Pushkin**

Dr Velasco

Obregón

ZONA ROSA

PLACES TO STAY
- 4 Casa González
- 9 Hotel Marquis Reforma
- 18 Four Seasons Hotel
- 26 Hotel Aristos
- 29 Hotel Internacional Havre
- 34 Hotel Marco Polo
- 67 Hotel Plaza Florencia
- 75 Calinda Geneve & Spa

PLACES TO EAT
- 1 Restaurante Vegetariano Las Fuentes
- 8 Les Moustaches
- 13 Sanborns
- 19 Anderson's de Reforma
- 20 Restaurante Vegetariano Yug
- 33 Auseba
- 35 Sushi Itto
- 37 Freedom
- 38 El Perro d'Enfrente
- 39 Angus Butcher House
- 40 Yuppie's Sports Café
- 41 Mesón del Perro Andaluz
- 42 Pizza Hut
- 46 Parri Pollo Restaurante
- 49 Dunkin' Donuts
- 50 Burger King
- 51 Konditori
- 54 Taco Inn
- 55 Comedor
- 57 McDonald's
- 58 Carrousel Internacional
- 59 Luaú
- 60 Sanborns
- 61 Chalet Suizo
- 65 La Beatricita
- 68 Ricocina
- 70 Mercado Insurgentes
- 71 Sanborns
- 74 Harry's Bar
- 75 Café Jardín
- 76 Sanborns
- 77 KFC
- 79 Coffee House
- 80 VIPS

OTHER
- 2 America West, Alitalia
- 3 Lavandería Automática
- 5 UK Embassy
- 6 Casa de Cambio Tíber
- 7 Tony Pérez
- 10 Aeroméxico, Aerolitoral
- 11 La Diana Cazadora
- 12 Canadian Airlines
- 14 US Embassy
- 15 Japan Air Lines
- 16 Centro Bursátil
- 17 Monumento a Cuauhtémoc
- 21 Money Exchange
- 22 Monumento a la Independencia (El Ángel)
- 23 Aero California
- 24 American Airlines
- 25 Mexicana
- 27 American Express
- 28 Casa de Francia, La Bouquinerie, Mundo Joven
- 30 Alaska Airlines, United Airlines
- 31 Procuraduría General de Justicia del Distrito Federal
- 32 Café Internet
- 36 La Casa de la Prensa
- 43 Tower Records
- 44 Gray Line
- 45 El Taller, El Almacén
- 47 Plaza del Ángel Shopping Arcade, Cabaré-Tito
- 48 Plaza La Rosa Shopping Arcade
- 52 Häagen-Dazs
- 53 Caramba
- 56 Java Chat
- 62 El Antro
- 63 Casanova Chapultepec
- 64 Post Office
- 66 La Casa de la Prensa
- 69 Grey Line
- 70 Mercado Insurgentes
- 72 Oficina de Turismo de la Ciudad de México
- 73 Cantina Las Bohemias
- 78 Mixup
- 81 Money Exchange
- 82 INEGI Map Shop
- 83 La Casa del Canto
- 84 Instituto Nacional de Migración

RICHARD I'ANSON

Outdoor restaurant in the suburb of San Ángel

Religious idols for sale, Mexico City

Monumento a la Revolución, Plaza de la República

MAP 8 CONDESA & ROMA

Zona Rosa

Roma Norte

Condesa

Parque España

Parque México

Bosque de Chapultepec 1a Sección

Paseo de la Reforma

Av Colegio Militar

(Pedestrian)

Línea 1

Av Chapultepec

Sevilla

Chapultepec

Vasconcelos (Circuito Interior)

Durango

Colima

Obregón

Calzada de Cerro

Melgar

Escutia (Eje 2 Sur)

Veracruz

Barrera

Solá

Alumnos

Montes de Oca

Vicente Suárez

Juana-catlán

Márquez

Reyes

Campeche

Ensenada

Saltillo

Franklin

Patriotismo

Baja California

Chilpancingo

To San Ángel

Hamburgo

Toledo

Sevilla

Londres

Medellín

Burdeos

Tokio

Tampico

Acapulco

Guadalajara

Cozumel

Salamanca

Ocotlán

Puebla

Sinaloa

Oaxaca

Av Sonora

Nuevo León

Parral

Laredo

Cadereyta

Tamaulipas

Michoacán

Av México

Amsterdam

Celaya

Popocatépetl

Casahuatipa

Av Sonora

Culiacán

Iztaccíhuatl

Chilpancingo

Av Mazatlán

Yautepec

Cuautla

Cuernavaca

Jojutla

Amatlán

Aldico

Parral

Tenancingo

Montes de Oca

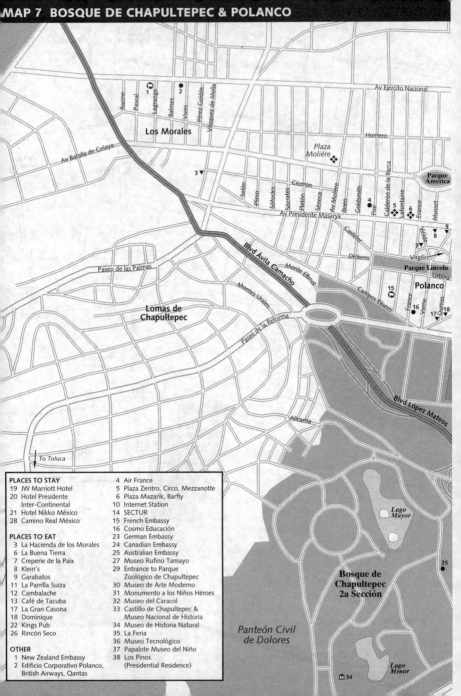

MAP 7 BOSQUE DE CHAPULTEPEC & POLANCO

Av Ejército Nacional

Los Morales

Racine
Pascal
Lagrange
Balmes
Vives
Pérez Galdós
Vázquez de Mella

Homero

Plaza
Moliére

Av Batalla de Celaya

Solón
Plinio
Sófocles
Sócrates
Platón
Cicerón
Séneca
Av Moliére
Ibsen
Goldsmith
Poe
Calderón de la Barca
Lafontaine
France
Musset

Parque
América

Av Presidente Masaryk

Castelar

Blvd Ávila Camacho

Monte Elbruz

Dickens

Virgilio

Parque Lincoln

Paseo de las Palmas

Urbina

Polanco

Montes Urales

Campos Elíseos

France
Verne
Lomas

Lomas de
Chapultepec

Paseo de la Reforma

Blvd López Mateos

Alicama

Lago
Mayor

To Toluca

Bosque de
Chapultepec
2a Sección

Panteón Civil
de Dolores

Lago
Menor

PLACES TO STAY
19 JW Marriott Hotel
20 Hotel Presidente
   Inter-Continental
21 Hotel Nikko México
28 Camino Real México

PLACES TO EAT
3 La Hacienda de los Morales
6 La Buena Tierra
7 Creperie de la Paix
8 Klein's
9 Garabatos
11 La Parrilla Suiza
12 Cambalache
13 Café de Tacuba
17 La Gran Casona
18 Dominique
22 Kings Pub
26 Rincón Seco

OTHER
1 New Zealand Embassy
2 Edificio Corporativo Polanco,
  British Airways, Qantas

4 Air France
5 Plaza Zentro, Circo, Mezzanotte
6 Plaza Mazarik, Barfly
10 Internet Station
14 SECTUR
15 French Embassy
16 Cosmo Educación
23 German Embassy
24 Canadian Embassy
25 Australian Embassy
27 Museo Rufino Tamayo
29 Entrance to Parque
   Zoológico de Chapultepec
30 Museo de Arte Moderno
31 Monumento a los Niños Héroes
32 Museo del Caracol
33 Castillo de Chapultepec &
   Museo Nacional de Historia
34 Museo de Historia Natural
35 La Feria
36 Museo Tecnológico
37 Papalote Museo del Niño
38 Los Pinos
   (Presidential Residence)

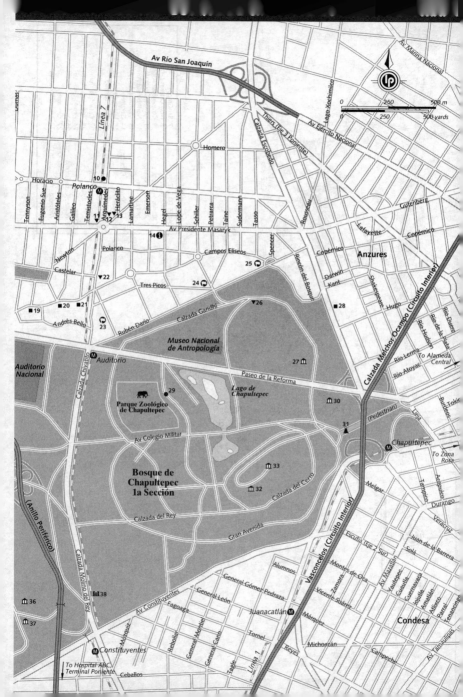

Av Río San Joaquín

Av Marina Nacional

Linea 7

Av Ejército Nacional

Lago Xochimilco

Thiers (Eje 3 Poniente)

Calzada Escobedo

Rousseau

Homera

Gutenberg

Horacio

Polanco

10

Tennyson

Eugenio Sue

Aristóteles

Galileo

Temístocles

Arquímedes

Heráclito

Lamartine

Emerson

Hegel

Lope de Vega

Schiller

Petrarca

Taine

Sudermann

Tasso

Spencer

Rincón del Bosque

Lafayette

Copérnico

Copérnico

Anzures

Darwin

Kant

Shakespeare

Hugo

15

12

13

Av Presidente Masaryk

14

Polanco

Campos Eliseos

25

Newton

Castelar

Tres Picos

24

26

28

Río Duero

Río de la Plata

Río Hudson

Río Lerma

Río Atoyac

Calzada Melchor Ocampo (Circuito Interior)

To Alameda Central

19

20

21

Andrés Bello

Ruben Darío

23

22

Calzada Gandhi

Museo Nacional
de Antropología

27

Auditorio
Nacional

Calzada Chivatito

Auditorio

29

Parque Zoológico
de Chapultepec

Lago de
Chapultepec

Paseo de la Reforma

30

Burdeos

Tokio

31

(Pedestrian)

Chapultepec

To Zona
Rosa

Melgar

Acapulco

Tampico

Durango

Veracruz

Av Colegio Militar

Bosque de
Chapultepec
1a Sección

33

32

Calzada del Cerro

Calzada del Rey

Gran Avenida

Escutia (Eje 2 Sur)

Vasconcelos (Circuito Interior)

Juan de la Barrera

Solá

Zamora

Montes de Oca

Vicente Suárez

Yautepec

Mazatlán

Cuernavaca

Cuautla

Tlaxcala

Atlixco

Amatlán

Pachuca

Tamaulipas

Tenancingo

Condesa

(Anillo Periférico)

Calzada Molino del Rey

36

38

37

Alumnos

General Gómez Pedraza

General León

Juanacatlán

Márquez

General Cano

General Mothiel

Reboull

Fagoaga

Tornel

Michoacán

Campeche

Av Yucatán

Mazatlán

Constituyentes

To Hospital ABC,
Terminal Poniente

Ceballos

Tagle

Linea 1

Reyes

0   250   500 m

0   250   500 yards

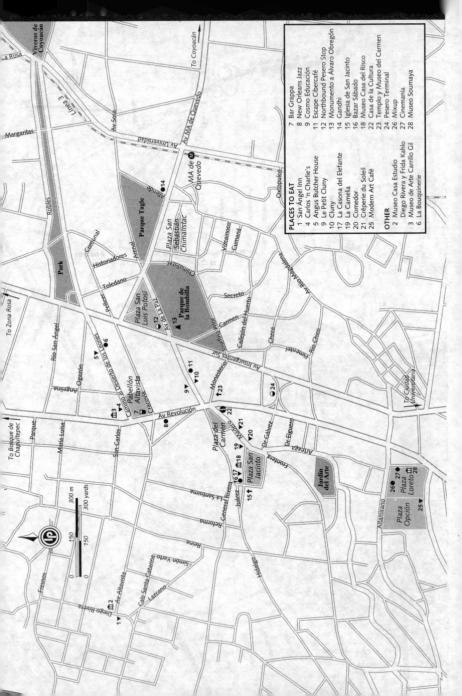

PLACES TO EAT
1 San Ángel Inn
4 Carlos 'n Charlie's
5 Angus Butcher House
10 Cluny
10 Le Petit Cluny
17 La Casona del Elefante
19 La Camelia
20 Comedor
21 Crêperie du Soleil
25 Modern Art Café

7 Bar Grappa
8 New Orleans Jazz
9 Cosmo Educación
11 Escape Cibercafé
12 Northbound Pesero Stop
13 Monumento a Álvaro Obregón
14 Gandhi
15 Iglesia de San Jacinto
16 Bazar Sábado
18 Museo Casa del Risco
22 Casa de la Cultura
23 Templo y Museo del Carmen
24 Pesero Terminal
26 Mixup
27 Cinemanía
28 Museo Soumaya

OTHER
2 Museo Casa Estudio Diego Rivera y Frida Kahlo
3 Museo de Arte Carrillo Gil
6 La Bouquinerie

Mexico City skyline

Reloj Calendario Azteca, Mexico City

MAP 9 COYOACÁN

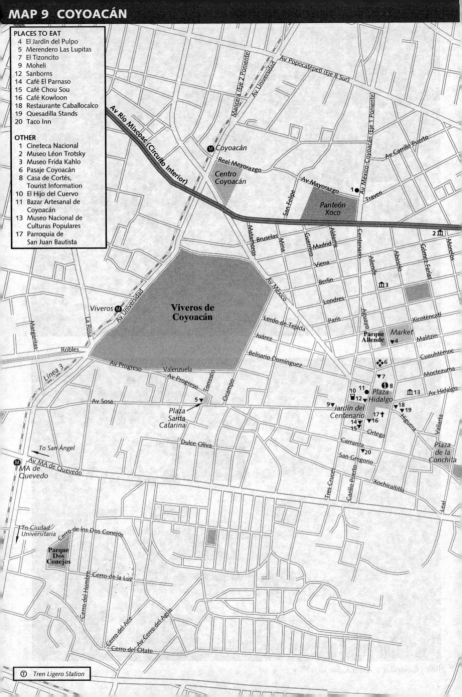

PLACES TO EAT
4 El Jardín del Pulpo
5 Merendero Las Lupitas
7 El Tizoncito
9 Moheli
12 Sanborns
14 Café El Parnaso
15 Café Chou Sou
16 Café Kowloon
18 Restaurante Caballocalco
19 Quesadilla Stands
20 Taco Inn

OTHER
1 Cineteca Nacional
2 Museo Léon Trotsky
3 Museo Frida Kahlo
6 Pasaje Coyoacán
8 Casa de Cortés,
   Tourist Information
10 El Hijo del Cuervo
11 Bazar Artesanal de
   Coyoacán
13 Museo Nacional de
   Culturas Populares
17 Parroquia de
   San Juan Bautista

① Tren Ligero Station

To Alameda
Central, Zócalo

Municipio Libre

Calzada de Tlalpan

Av General Emiliano Zapata

Av División del Norte

Av General Emiliano Zapata

Panamá | Eje Central Lázaro Cárdenas

Oriente 172

Av Repúblicas

Av Popocatepetl

Ermita

Av Presidente Calles

Calzada Ermita Iztapalapa

Ajusco

Av Río Churubusco (Circuito Interior)

San Pedro

Pirividad Corina

Corina

Centro Nacional
de las Artes

Ex-Convento de
Churubusco
(Museo Nacional de
las Intervenciones)

20 de Agosto

Calzada General Anaya

Av del Convento

Ciclistas
General
Anaya

García Torres

Country
Club

Mártires Irlandeses

Irlanda

Línea 2

Canadá

Jardín
Frida
Kahlo

Pallares y Portillo

Cerro de Jesús

Tepalcatitla

Av América

Av Inglaterra

Av MA de Quevedo

Av Canal de Miramontes

Pacífico

Av División del Norte

Tasqueña

Terminal Sur
Bus Station

Monserrat

Las
Torres

Av Tasqueña

Calzada de Tlalpan

To Anahuacalli

To Estadio
Azteca

Ciudad
Jardín

Museo Franz Mayer

The Franz Mayer Museum (☎ 5-518-22-65), a sumptuous collection of mainly Mexican art and crafts, is housed in the lovely 16th-century Hospital de San Juan de Dios, at Avenida Hidalgo 45, on little Plaza de Santa Veracruz, opposite the north side of the Alameda. This oasis of calm and beauty is the fruit of the efforts of Franz Mayer, who was born in Mannheim, Germany, in 1882, moved to Mexico, became a citizen, earned the name Don Pancho, and amassed a collection of Mexican silver, textiles, ceramics and furniture masterpieces.

The museum is open 10 am to 5 pm Tuesday to Sunday (US$1.50, free on Tuesday). The way into the main part of the museum is to the right as you enter. To the left is a gorgeous colonial garden courtyard. The suite of rooms on the courtyard's west side is done in antique furnishings and is very fine, especially the lovely chapel. On the north side is the delightful Cafetería del Claustro (see Places to Eat).

Museo Mural Diego Rivera

Among Diego Rivera's most famous murals is *Sueño de una Tarde Dominical en la Alameda* (Dream of a Sunday Afternoon in the Alameda), 15m long by 4m high, painted in 1947. The artist imagines many of the figures who walked in the city from colonial times onward, among them Cortés, Juárez, Santa Anna, Emperor Maximilian, Porfirio Díaz, and Francisco Madero and his nemesis, General Victoriano Huerta. All are grouped around a skeleton dressed in prerevolutionary women's garb. Rivera himself (as a pug-faced child), and his artist wife Frida Kahlo are depicted next to the skeleton.

The museum (☎ 5-510-23-29) housing this work is just west of the Alameda, fronting the Jardín de la Solidaridad. It was built in 1986 specifically for this mural – which had stood in the Hotel del Prado, nearby on Avenida Juárez, until the hotel was wrecked in the 1985 earthquake.

Charts in English and Spanish identify all the characters. There are also photos and other material on Rivera's life and work.

The museum is open 10 am to 6 pm Tuesday to Sunday (US$1).

PLAZA DE LA REPÚBLICA & AROUND

This plaza, 600m west of the Alameda Central, is dominated by the huge, domed Monumento a la Revolución. Revolución metro station is nearby.

Monumento a la Revolución

The Revolution Monument, begun in the 1900s under Porfirio Díaz, was originally meant to be not a monument at all, but a meeting chamber for senators and deputies. But construction (not to mention Díaz's presidency) was interrupted by the revolution. The structure was modified and given a new role in the 1930s: the tombs of the revolutionary and postrevolutionary heroes Pancho Villa, Francisco Madero, Venustiano Carranza, Plutarco Elías Calles and Lázaro Cárdenas are inside its wide pillars (not open to the public).

The interesting little Museo Nacional de la Revolución (☎ 5-546-21-15), with exhibits on the revolution and preceding decades, is entered from the northeast quarter of the garden around the monument. Hours are 9 am to 5 pm Tuesday to Saturday, 9 am to 3 pm Sunday (US$0.50, free on Sunday).

Frontón México

On the north side of Plaza de la República is the Frontón México, Mexico City's grand art deco arena for the sport of jai alai. See Spectator Sports later in this chapter for more on the Frontón.

Museo de San Carlos

The Museum of San Carlos (☎ 5-566-85-22), Puente de Alvarado 50, at Ramos Arizpe, has a nice collection of European art. It's housed in the former mansion of the Conde (Count) de Buenavista, designed by Manuel Tolsá in the late 18th century. Later home to Alamo victor Santa Anna, the mansion subsequently served as a cigar factory, lottery headquarters and school before being reborn as an art museum in 1968.

It's a Lottery!

The tall art deco tower on the west side of Paseo de la Reforma opposite Avenida Juárez (Ⓜ Hidalgo) is the headquarters of a Mexican passion: the Lotería Nacional (National Lottery).

Lottery tickets are sold all over Mexico by street vendors and at kiosks. Each is for a particular draw *(sorteo)* on a specific date, with prizes ranging from around US$600 to more than US$3 million. You can witness a draw by walking into the Lotería Nacional building almost any Monday, Tuesday or Friday after 7.30 pm (free). Take a seat in the cozy auditorium upstairs, and at exactly 8 pm the ceremony begins. Cylindrical cages spew out numbered wooden balls, which are plucked out by uniformed pages who announce the winning numbers and the amounts they have won.

Lottery tickets normally cost US$0.60, US$1 or US$1.50. Anyone can buy them. Having one at least enables you to fantasize for a day or two about what you would do with US$3 million. Retire to Mexico? Travel the world till you die? Give it to charity? Buy a lifetime supply of Bohemia lager? Winning numbers are posted at ticket sales points. Since the system is a bit complicated, get a ticket seller or some other initiate to check your ticket against the list of winners. Each draw usually has several series of tickets, each of which gets a share of the many prizes.

Mexicans resort to all sorts of calculations, hunches and superstitions to decide which numbers may be lucky. Spice is added by regular *zodiaco* draws, in which each ticket bears a sign of the zodiac as well as a number.

Four times a year, such as at Christmas, there are *sorteos especiales*, with tickets costing up to five times as much as usual, and prizes similarly higher. Other draws may be suspended for a couple of weeks beforehand to ensure good sales for the big one.

Profits from the lottery go to government charity projects.

GREG ELMS

The museum's permanent collection includes works by Goya, Rubens, Van Dyck, Zurbarán and Ingres. Good temporary exhibitions are also staged. Hours are 10 am to 6 pm Wednesday to Monday (US$2, free on Sunday).

PASEO DE LA REFORMA & ZONA ROSA

Paseo de la Reforma, Mexico City's main boulevard and one of its status addresses, runs southwest across the city from the Alameda Central and through the Bosque de Chapultepec. It's said that Emperor Maximilian of Hapsburg laid out the boulevard to connect his castle on Chapultepec Hill with the older section of the city. He could look along it from his bedroom and ride along it to work in the Palacio Nacional, on the Zócalo.

You'll almost certainly pass along Reforma at some time, or call at one of the nearby banks, shops, hotels, restaurants or embassies. The Zona Rosa, a restaurant, hotel, shopping and entertainment district, lies on the south side of Reforma roughly 2km from the Alameda Central.

Reforma is dotted with striking architecture and sculpture.

A couple of blocks west of the Alameda Central on Reforma, in front of the Torre Caballito office building, is *El Caballito*, a huge golden-yellow creation by the sculptor Sebastián, representing a horse's head, in memory of the other *El Caballito*, today in front of the Museo Nacional de Arte, which once stood here. A few blocks southwest on Reforma is the **Glorieta Cristóbal Colón**, a traffic circle with a statue of Christopher Columbus at its center, created by French sculptor Charles Cordier in 1877.

Reforma's busy intersection with Avenida Insurgentes is marked by the **Monumento a Cuauhtémoc**, the last Aztec emperor. Two blocks northwest of this intersection is the **Jardín del Arte**, a sliver of shady park that becomes an interesting open-air artists' bazaar from 10 am to 4 pm on Sunday.

The most striking modern building on Reforma is the **Centro Bursátil**, Mexico City's stock exchange, an arrow of reflecting glass at Reforma 255, about 600m southwest of Insurgentes.

The glossy, in places sleazy **Zona Rosa** is an integral piece of the Mexico City jigsaw, and people-watching from its sidewalk cafés reveals plenty of variety among the passing parade of pedestrians. For details of how to spend money here, see Places to Stay, Places to Eat, Entertainment and Shopping.

On Reforma on the northwest flank of the Zona Rosa stands the symbol of Mexico City, the **Monumento a la Independencia**, a gilded statue of Victory on a tall pedestal, called by locals simply El Ángel (The Angel). The statue, by sculptor Antonio Rivas Mercado, was inaugurated in 1910. The female sculptures around the base portray Law, Justice, War and Peace; the male ones are Mexican independence heroes such as Miguel Hidalgo, Vicente Guerrero and José María Morelos. Inside the monument are the skulls of Hidalgo, Ignacio Allende, Juan Aldama and Mariano Jiménez (retrieved from their 1811-21 stint hanging outside the Alhóndiga de Granaditas in Guanajuato), and caskets containing the ashes or remains of Morelos, Guerrero and others. The Monumento a la Independencia is open 9 am to 6 pm daily (free).

A few blocks farther west, at Reforma's intersection with Sevilla, is **La Diana Cazadora** (Diana the Huntress), a 1942 bronze statue of a female archer by Juan Fernando Olaguíbel. Southwest from here, Reforma crosses the Bosque de Chapulte-

pec and then becomes the main road to Toluca.

Getting There & Away

Hidalgo metro station (see Dangers & Annoyances) is on Reforma at the Alameda Central; Insurgentes station is at the southern tip of the Zona Rosa, 500m south of Reforma; Chapultepec station is just south of Reforma at the east end of the Bosque de Chapultepec.

From the Zócalo area, westbound 'M(etro) Chapultepec' and 'M(etro) Auditorio' peseros on Avenida Cinco de Mayo go along Reforma to the Bosque de Chapultepec. If you get fed up with waiting for them, you can take the metro or walk to Reforma and catch another pesero there. Any 'M(etro) Auditorio,' 'Reforma Km 13' or 'Km 15.5 por Reforma' pesero or bus heading southwest on Reforma will continue along Reforma through the Bosque de Chapultepec.

In the opposite direction, the 'Zócalo' peseros heading east on Reforma will transport you to the Zócalo. 'M(etro) Hidalgo,' 'M(etro) La Villa' and 'M(etro) Indios Verdes' buses and peseros all head northeast up Reforma to the Alameda Central or beyond.

CONDESA

Condesa is a trendy but relaxed neighborhood south of the Zona Rosa. It has a couple of pleasant parks, some attractive 1930s and '40s neocolonial architecture, and a huge number of good, informal restaurants and coffee bars.

A focus is the peaceful, beautifully kept **Parque México**, full of trees, well-maintained paths, benches with cute little roofs, and signs exhorting everyone to demonstrate their eco-consciousness and treat their *parque* nicely. **Parque España**, two blocks northwest, has a children's fun fair. Parque México is a 500m walk north from Chilpancingo metro station (or a 1km walk south from Sevilla station) – or you can get a pesero south on Avenida Insurgentes from Insurgentes metro station to the intersection with Avenida Michoacán (there's a Woolworth store on the corner), and walk two blocks west.

The main cluster of Condesa bistro-type eateries (see Places to Eat) is about 500m west of Parque México, with Patriotismo and Juanacatlán metro stations also within walking distance.

BOSQUE DE CHAPULTEPEC

According to legend, one of the last kings of the Toltecs took refuge in the Chapultepec woods after fleeing from Tula. Later, the hill in the park served as a refuge for the wandering Aztecs before eventually becoming a summer residence for Aztec nobles. Chapultepec means Hill of Grasshoppers in the Aztec language, Náhuatl. In the 15th century – when Chapultepec was still separated from Tenochtitlán, the site of modern central Mexico City, by the waters of Lago de Texcoco – Nezahualcóyotl, ruler of nearby Texcoco, gave permission for the area to be made a forest reserve.

The Bosque de Chapultepec has remained Mexico City's largest park to this day. It now covers more than 4 sq km and has lakes, a zoo and several excellent museums. It has also remained an abode of Mexico's high and mighty. It contains both the current presidential residence, Los Pinos, and a former imperial and presidential palace, the Castillo de Chapultepec.

The Bosque de Chapultepec attracts thousands of visitors daily, particularly on Sunday, when vendors line its main paths and throngs of families come to picnic, relax and crowd into the museums. The park is divided into two main sections by two big roads – Calzada Molino del Rey and Boulevard López Mateos – which run north-south across the middle. Most of the major attractions are in or near the eastern, or first, section (*1ª sección*), which is open 5 am to 4.30 pm daily except Monday. Most of the museums in the park offer free admission on Sunday and holidays.

Monumento a los Niños Héroes

The six columns of the Monument to the Boy Heroes, near Chapultepec metro, mark the main entrance to the park. They commemorate six brave cadets at the national military academy, which used to be housed in the Castillo de Chapultepec. On September 13, 1847, when invading American troops reached Mexico City, the six cadets, having defended their school as long as they could, wrapped themselves in Mexican flags and leapt to their deaths rather than surrender.

Castillo de Chapultepec

Part of the castle on Chapultepec Hill was built in 1785 as a residence for the viceroys of Nueva España. The building was converted into a military academy in 1843. When Emperor Maximilian and Empress Carlota arrived in 1864, they refurbished it as their main residence. After their fall, the castle became home to Mexico's presidents, until 1940 when President Lázaro Cárdenas converted it into the **Museo Nacional de Historia** (National History Museum, ☎ 5-286-07-00).

Two floors of exhibits chronicle the rise and fall of colonial Nueva España, the establishment of independent Mexico, the dictatorship of Porfirio Díaz and the Mexican Revolution. Several of the 1st floor rooms are decorated with impressive murals on historical themes by famous Mexican artists. These include Juan O'Gorman's *Retablo de la Independencia* (Thanksgiving Panel for Independence), room 5; José Clemente Orozco's *La Reforma y la Caída del Imperio* (The Reform and Fall of the Empire), room 7; and David Alfaro Siqueiros' *Del Porfirismo a la Revolución* (From Porfirism to the Revolution), room 13. The rooms where Maximilian and Carlota lived, at the east end of the castle, are furnished in period style, including Carlota's marble bath. Above them are Porfirio Díaz's sumptuous rooms, flanking a patio with expansive views.

The museum is open 9 am to 5 pm Tuesday to Sunday (last tickets are sold at 4 pm). Recently, entry was free as half the castle was closed for maintenance work. Admission was previously US$1.90. To reach the castle, walk up the road that curves up the right-hand side of the hill behind the Monumento a los Niños Héroes. Alternatively, a little road-train runs up this road every

10 minutes or so while the castle is open, for US$0.30 roundtrip.

Museo del Caracol

From the Castillo de Chapultepec, the Museo del Caracol (☎ 5-553-62-85) is just a short distance back down the approach road. Shaped somewhat like a snail shell (*caracol*), this is officially a 'Galería de Historia' on the subject of the Mexican people's struggle for liberty. Displays cover social and political life from colonial days, the divisions of Nueva España in the 18th century, Miguel Hidalgo's leadership in the struggle for independence, and Francisco Madero's leadership in the revolution. The self-guided tour ends in a circular hall that contains only one item – the 1917 Constitution of Mexico. Hours are 9 am to 5 pm Tuesday to Sunday (US$1).

Museo de Arte Moderno

The two rounded buildings of the Museum of Modern Art (☎ 5-211-83-31) stand in their own sculpture garden just northwest of the Monumento a los Niños Héroes. The entrance faces Paseo de la Reforma. The museum's permanent collection is of work by Mexico's most famous 20th-century artists, including Dr Atl, Rivera, Siqueiros, Orozco, Kahlo, Tamayo and O'Gorman. Some of these artists' more intimate work, such as portraits, is shown here. There are also always temporary exhibitions by prominent Mexican and foreign artists. Hours are 10 am to 6 pm Tuesday to Sunday (US$1.50).

Parque Zoológico de Chapultepec

The first zoo in Chapultepec – and the Americas – is said to have been established by King Nezahualcóyotl well before the Spanish arrived. Cortés added a bird sanctuary. In 1975 a gift from China brought pandas. Rebuilt in the mid-1990s for US$30 million, the Chapultepec Zoo (☎ 5-553-62-29) is a mainly open-air place with a wide range of the world's creatures in relatively large enclosures. Something went badly wrong in 1998, when almost 400 of its 1800 animals died in nine months. It was hoped a new director appointed in 1999 would improve matters. The zoo is open 9 am to 4 pm Tuesday to Sunday (free). There's an inexpensive snack area inside.

Museo Nacional de Antropología

The National Museum of Anthropology (☎ 5-553-63-81), one of the finest museums of its kind in the world, stands in an extension of the Bosque de Chapultepec, on the north side of Paseo de la Reforma. It is open 9 am to 7 pm Tuesday to Sunday (US$2.50, extra for cameras).

The museum is fascinating and very large, with more than most people can absorb (without brain strain) in a single visit. A good plan is to concentrate on the regions of Mexico that you plan to visit or have visited, with a quick look at some of the other eye-catching exhibits. Labeling is in Spanish, but some of the spectacular exhibits need little explanation.

In a clearing about 100m in front of the museum's entrance, indigenous Totonac people perform their spectacular *voladores* rite – 'flying' from a 20m-high pole – several times a day, collecting money from onlookers afterward (see 'Voladores' in the Central Gulf Coast chapter).

The spacious museum building, constructed in the 1960s, is the work of Mexican architect Pedro Ramírez Vásquez. Its long, rectangular courtyard is surrounded on three sides by the museum's two-story display halls. An immense umbrella-like stone fountain rises up from the center of the courtyard.

The ground-floor halls are dedicated to pre-Hispanic Mexico. The upper level covers the way modern Mexico's indigenous peoples, the descendants of those pre-Hispanic civilizations, live today. With a few exceptions, each ethnological section upstairs covers the same territory as the archaeological exhibit below it, so you can see the great Mayan city of Palenque as it was in the 7th century, then go upstairs and see how Mayan people live today. Here's a brief guide to the ground-floor halls, counterclockwise around the courtyard:

Introducción a la Antropología
An introduction to anthropology, ethnology, and pre-Hispanic culture in general.

Sala Orígenes
The Origins Room shows evidence of the first people in the Americas, explaining their arrival from Asia and the beginnings of agriculture, and displays early findings from central Mexico.

Sala Preclásica
The preclassic period lasted from about 1500 BC to 250 AD. These exhibits highlight the transition from a nomadic hunting life to a more settled farming life around 1000 BC.

Sala Teotihuacana
Models and objects in here are from the wondrous city of Teotihuacán, near Mexico City, the Americas' first great and powerful state; the exhibit includes a full-size color model of part of the Templo de Quetzalcóatl.

Sala Tolteca
This room covers cultures of central Mexico between about 650 and 1250 AD and is named for one of the most important of these, the Toltecs; exhibits include a huge stone statue of Quetzalcóatl from Tula.

Sala Mexica
At the west end of the courtyard is the hall devoted to the Mexica, or Aztecs. Come here to see the famous sun, or 'calendar,' stone, with the face of the sun god Tonatiuh at the center of a web of symbols representing the five worlds, the four directions, the 20 days and more; the statue of Coatlicue ('She of the Skirt of Snakes'), the mother of the Aztec gods, found – like the sun stone – beneath the Zócalo in 1790; a replica of a carved stone tzompantli; an 'aerial view' painting of Tenochtitlán; and other graphic evidence of this awesome culture.

Sala Oaxaca
In the southern state of Oaxaca, cultural heights were scaled by the Zapotec and Mixtec peoples. Two tombs from the hilltop site of Monte Albán are reproduced full-size.

Sala Golfo de México
Important ancient civilizations along the Gulf of Mexico included the Olmec, Classic Veracruz, Totonac and Huastec. There are very fine stone carvings here, including two magnificent Olmec heads.

Sala Maya
The Maya Room has wonderful exhibits not only from southeast Mexico, but from Guatemala, Belize and Honduras too. The full-scale model of the tomb of King Pakal, discovered deep in the Templo de los Inscripciones at Palenque, is breathtaking. On the outside patio are replicas of the famous wall paintings of Bonampak and of Edificio II at Hochob, in Campeche, constructed as a giant mask of the rain god, Chac.

Sala Norte
The North Room covers the Casas Grandes (Paquimé) site and other cultures from dry northern Mexico. Similarities can be seen with indigenous cultures of the American southwest.

Sala Occidente
Exhibits here are on cultures of western Mexico – Nayarit, Jalisco, Michoacán, Colima and Guerrero states.

Museo Rufino Tamayo

The Tamayo Museum (☎ 5-286-65-99), a multilevel concrete and glass structure about 250m east of the Museo Nacional de Antropología, was built to house the fine collection of international modern art donated by Rufino Tamayo and his wife, Olga, to the people of Mexico. More than 150 artists, including Picasso, Warhol and Tamayo himself, are represented in the permanent collection, but you may find that their works have all been put away to make room for temporary exhibitions. The museum is open 10 am to 5.45 pm Tuesday to Sunday (US$1.50).

Segunda (2ª) Sección

The second section of the Bosque de Chapultepec lies west of Boulevard López Mateos. The nearest metro station is Constituyentes, near its southern perimeter.

One highlight is **La Feria** (☎ 5-230-21-12), a large amusement park with some hair-raising rides, open Tuesday to Friday 11 am to 7 pm, Saturday and Sunday 10 am to 9 pm. A US$7.50 ticket includes most rides; a US$1.50 children's ticket is good for 22 rides or games. Another is **Papalote Museo del Niño** (☎ 5-160-60-60), a hands-on children's museum that is a sure-fire hit if you have children in tow. Activities range from a tunnel slide and a conventional playground to giant-soap-bubble making and all manner of technical/scientific gadget-games. Everything is attended by young, child-friendly supervisors, and you can be sure that your kids will not want to leave. The hours during school terms are 9 am to 1 pm and 2 to 6 pm

Monday to Friday, and 10 am to 2 pm and 3 to 7 pm Saturday, Sunday and holidays. During school vacations the weekend hours apply every day. Papalote is also open 7.30 to 11.30 pm Thursday to Saturday. Each four-hour session costs US$3 for children aged two to 11 and the over-60s, and US$4 for others.

Also in Chapultepec's Segunda Sección visitors will find two lakes and the **Museo Tecnológico** (☎ 5-516-09-64) and **Museo de Historia Natural** (☎ 5-515-22-22).

Getting There & Away

Chapultepec metro station is at the east end of the Bosque de Chapultepec, near the Monumento a los Niños Héroes and Castillo de Chapultepec. Auditorio metro station is on the north side of the park, 500m west of the Museo Nacional de Antropología.

You can also reach the park from the Zócalo area on a 'M(etro) Chapultepec' or 'M(etro) Auditorio' pesero westbound on Avenida Cinco de Mayo. From anywhere on Paseo de la Reforma west of the Alameda Central, peseros and buses saying 'M(etro) Chapultepec,' 'M(etro) Auditorio,' 'Km 15.5 por Reforma' or 'Reforma Km 13' will reach Chapultepec metro station, and all except 'M(etro) Chapultepec' vehicles will cross the first section of the park on Paseo de la Reforma: you can get off right outside the Museo Nacional de Antropología (watch out for pickpockets).

Returning downtown, 'Zócalo' peseros heading east on Paseo de la Reforma will take you to the Zócalo. Any 'M(etro) Hidalgo,' 'M(etro) Garibaldi,' 'M(etro) Villa,' 'M(etro) La Villa' and 'M(etro) Indios Verdes' pesero or bus, from Chapultepec metro station or heading east on Reforma, will go along Reforma at least as far as Hidalgo metro station.

POLANCO

In this affluent residential quarter north of the Bosque de Chapultepec, the streets are named after writers and scientists, and the spring blossoms are even more of a treat than elsewhere in the city. Polanco contains lots of restaurants, several art galleries and embassies, some expensive hotels and shops, and the SECTUR tourist office (see Information). Much of the architecture is in the appealing neocolonial style of the 1930s and '40s, with prettily carved stone doorways and window surrounds. You could visit this part of the city before or after the nearby Museo Nacional de Antropología.

TLATELOLCO & GUADALUPE
Tlatelolco – Plaza de las Tres Culturas

About 2km north of the Alameda Central up the Eje Central is the Plaza de las Tres Culturas (Plaza of the Three Cultures), so called because it symbolizes the fusion of pre-Hispanic and Spanish roots into the Mexican mestizo identity. The Aztec pyramids of Tlatelolco, the 17th-century Spanish Templo de Santiago, and the modern Secretaría de Relaciones Exteriores (Foreign Ministry) building, on the plaza's south side, represent the three cultures.

Tlatelolco was founded by Aztecs in the 14th century as a separate dynasty from Tenochtitlán, on a separate island in Lago de Texcoco. In pre-Hispanic times it was the scene of the largest market in the Valle de México. Cortés defeated Tlatelolco's Aztec defenders, led by Cuauhtémoc, here in 1521. An inscription about that battle in the plaza today translates: 'This was neither victory nor defeat. It was the sad birth of the mestizo people that is Mexico today.'

Tlatelolco is also a symbol of more modern troubles. On October 2, 1968, 300 to 400 student protesters were massacred by government troops on the eve of the Mexico City Olympic Games. And in 1985, the area suffered some of the worst damage and casualties in the Mexico City earthquake when apartment blocks collapsed, killing hundreds of people.

The plaza is a calm oasis amid the city, but haunted by echoes of its somber history. You can view the remains of Tlatelolco's main pyramid-temple and other Aztec buildings from a walkway around them. The Spanish, recognizing the religious significance of the place, built a monastery here and then, in 1609, the Templo de Santiago. Just inside the main (west) doors of this church is the baptismal font of Juan Diego (see the Basílica de Guadalupe section, following). Outside the north wall of the church stands a monument to the victims of the 1968 massacre, erected in 1993. The full truth about the massacre has never come out: the traces were hastily cleaned away, and Mexican schoolbooks still do not refer to it.

Northbound 'Eje Central, Central Camionera, Tenayuca' peseros and buses pass right by the Plaza de las Tres Culturas. You can catch them on the Eje Central at Donceles, one block north of the Palacio de Bellas Artes. Alternatively, take the metro to Tlatelolco station, exit on to the busy Manuel González, and turn right. Walk to the first major intersection (Eje Central Lázaro Cárdenas), turn right, and you'll soon see the plaza on the far (east) side of the road – 900m from the metro station.

Basílica de Guadalupe

On December 9, 1531, the story goes, a Mexican indigenous Christian convert named Juan Diego, standing on the Cerro del Tepeyac (Tepeyac Hill), site of an old Aztec shrine, saw a vision of a beautiful lady in a blue mantle trimmed with gold. He told the local priest that he had seen the Virgin Mary, but the priest didn't believe him. Juan returned to the hill, saw the vision again, and an image of the lady was miraculously emblazoned on his cloak. Eventually the church accepted his story, and a cult grew up around the place.

Over the following centuries Nuestra Señora de Guadalupe (Our Lady of Guadalupe), as this Virgin became known – after a Spanish manifestation of the Virgin whose cult was particularly popular in early colonial times – came to receive credit for all manner of miracles, hugely aiding the acceptance of Catholicism by Mexicans. In 1737, after she had extinguished a typhoid outbreak in Mexico City, she was officially declared the Patrona Principal (Principal Patron) of Nueva España. Today her image is seen throughout the country, and her shrines around the Cerro del Tepeyac are the most revered in Mexico, attracting thousands of pilgrims daily from all over the country – and hundreds of thousands on the days leading up to her feast day, December 12. See Special Events for more on these festivities.

Some pilgrims travel the last meters to the modern **Basílica de Nuestra Señora de Guadalupe**, at the foot of the Cerro del Tepeyac, on their knees. By the 1970s the old yellow-domed basilica here, built around 1700, was being swamped by the number of worshippers and was leaning alarmingly as it slowly sank into the soft earth beneath it. So the new basilica was built next door. Designed by Pedro Ramírez Vásquez, architect of the Museo Nacional de Antropología, it's a vast, rounded, open-plan structure with the capacity to hold thousands of worshippers. The sound of so many people singing together is quite thrilling. The image of the Virgin hangs above the main altar, with moving walkways beneath it to bring visitors as close as possible.

The rear of the **Antigua Basílica** (Old Basilica) is now the **Museo de la Basílica de Guadalupe** (☎ 5-577-60-22), with a fine collection of *retablos* and colonial religious art. It's open 10 am to 6 pm Tuesday to Sunday (US$0.30).

Stairs behind the Antigua Basílica climb about 100m to the hilltop **Capilla del Cerrito** (Hill Chapel), on the spot where Juan Diego saw his vision. From here, stairs lead down the east side of the hill to the **Jardín del Tepeyac** (Tepeyac Garden), from which a path leads back to the main plaza, reentering it beside the 17th-century **Capilla de Indios** (Chapel of Indians). This is next to the spot where, according to tradition, Juan Diego lived from 1531 until his death in 1548.

An easy way to reach the Basílica de Guadalupe is to take the metro to La Villa-Basílica station, then follow the crowds two blocks north along Calzada de Guadalupe. You can reach the same metro station on any 'M(etro) La Villa' pesero or bus northeast on Paseo de la Reforma. A 'M(etro) Hidalgo' or 'M(etro) Chapultepec' pesero or bus south down Calzada de los Misterios, a block west of Calzada de Guadalupe, will return you to downtown.

SAN ÁNGEL

Sixty years ago San Ángel ('san AHN-hell'), 8.5km south of the Bosque de Chapultepec, was a village separated from Mexico City by open fields. Today it's one of the city's most charming suburbs, with many quiet cobbled streets lined by both old colonial houses and expensive modern ones, and a variety of other things to see and do. The museums are closed on Monday.

Avenida Insurgentes Sur runs north-south through eastern San Ángel. Tourist information is available at the Casa de la Cultura (☎ 5-616-12-54) at the corner of Avenida Revolución and Madero, 9 am to 8 pm daily.

Plaza San Jacinto & Bazar Sábado

Every Saturday the Bazar Sábado (see Shopping) brings a festive atmosphere, masses of color and crowds of people to San Ángel's pretty little Plaza San Jacinto.

The 16th-century Iglesia de San Jacinto, off the west side of the plaza, is entered from a peaceful garden where you can take refuge from the crowded market areas. The Museo Casa del Risco, Plaza San Jacinto 15, in an 18th-century mansion with two pretty courtyards, has a hall for temporary exhibitions on the 1st floor and, upstairs, a permanent exhibition of 14th- to 19th-century European art and 17th- to 19th-century Mexican art. It's open 10 am to 5 pm daily except Monday (free).

Museo Casa Estudio Diego Rivera y Frida Kahlo

One kilometer northwest of Plaza San Jacinto, at Calle Diego Rivera 2, on the corner of Altavista, is the Diego Rivera & Frida Kahlo Studio Museum (☎ 5-550-11-89). The famous artist couple (see 'Diego & Frida') lived in this 1930s avante garde abode – with a separate house for each of them – from 1934 to 1940, when they divorced. Rivera stayed on until his death in 1957.

The museum has only a few examples of Rivera's art and none of Kahlo's, but has a lot of memorabilia. Rivera's house (the pink one) has an upstairs studio. The museum is open 10 am to 6 pm daily except Monday (US$1, free Sunday).

Across the street is the San Ángel Inn restaurant, in the 18th-century Ex-Hacienda de Goicoechea, once the home of the marquises of Selva Nevada and the counts of Pinillos. If your budget won't run to a meal here (see Places to Eat), you can still have a stroll in the gardens and perhaps a drink in the cocktail bar.

Museo de Arte Carrillo Gil

The Carrillo Gil Art Museum (☎ 5-550-62-89), Avenida Revolución 1608, has a permanent collection by first-rank Mexican artists, with numerous works by Rivera, Siqueiros and Orozco (including some of Orozco's grotesque, satirical early drawings and watercolors). Temporary exhibits are excellent too. Hours are 10 am to 6 pm Tuesday to Sunday (US$1, free on Sunday). There's a pleasant bookstore-café in the basement.

Templo y Museo del Carmen

The cool, peaceful, tile-domed 17th-century Templo del Carmen is at Avenida Revolución 4. The museum (☎ 5-550-48-96), in the former monastic quarters to one side of the church, is mainly devoted to colonial-era furniture and religious art – but its big tourist attraction is the mummified bodies in the crypt, which are thought to be 18th-century monks, nuns and gentry. You can also walk out into the pretty garden, once much bigger, from which cuttings and seeds were sent all over colonial Mexico. The museum is open 10 am to 5 pm Tuesday to Sunday (US$1.75, free on Sunday).

Parque de la Bombilla

This pleasant park lies just east of Avenida Insurgentes. The Monumento a Álvaro Obregón marks the spot where the Mexican president was assassinated during a banquet in 1928. Obregón's killer was a young Christian fanatic, José de León Toral, who was involved in the Cristero rebellion against the government's anti-Church policies.

Plaza Loreto

Plaza Loreto, a 600m walk south of Plaza San Jacinto, is Mexico City's most attractive mall, converted from an old paper factory a few years ago. Several patios and courtyards are set between the brick buildings, and it's more than just a place to shop. Visitors to the mall will find a mini-amphitheater for performances, two multiscreen cinemas (one of them, Cinemanía, endowed with nice little lobby bar), a variety of eateries and the excellent **Museo Soumaya** (☎ 5-616-37-31). The museum houses one of the world's three major collections – 70 pieces – of the sculpture of Frenchman Auguste Rodin (1840-1917), plus work by Degas, Matisse, Renoir, Tamayo and other renowned artists. The Soumaya is open from 10.30 am to 6.30 pm Thursday to Monday, and from 10.30 am to 8.30 pm Wednesday (US$1, free on Monday).

Getting There & Away

'San Ángel' peseros and buses run south on Insurgentes from at least as far north as Estación Buenavista. Most terminate on Dr Gálvez between Insurgentes and Avenida Revolución.

Alternatively, take the metro to Viveros or M A de Quevedo station, then walk (20 to 30 minutes) or board a 'San Ángel' pesero or bus at either place.

Returning north to the city center, 'M(etro) Indios Verdes' and 'M(etro) La Raza' buses and peseros run all the way up Insurgentes to the northern part of the city; 'M(etro) Insurgentes' vehicles go to Insurgentes metro station. A good place to catch any of these is the corner of Insurgentes and Avenida La Paz.

Returning from central San Ángel to the metro stations, 'M(etro) Viveros' peseros head east on Avenida Robles, and 'M(etro) Tasqueña' peseros and buses east on Avenida MA de Quevedo go to MA de Quevedo metro station.

To Coyoacán, a 'M(etro) Tasqueña' pesero or bus will take you to the corner of Carrillo Puerto (2.5km), from which you can walk the five blocks north to the Jardín del Centenario.

CIUDAD UNIVERSITARIA

The University City, on the east side of Avenida Insurgentes 2km south of San Ángel, is the main campus of Latin America's biggest university, the Universidad Nacional Autónoma de México (UNAM), and one of the nation's modern architectural showpieces.

The university was founded in the 1550s but was suppressed from 1833 to 1910. Most of the Ciudad Universitaria was built between 1950 and 1953 by a team of 150 young architects and technicians headed by José García Villagrán, Mario Pani and Enrique del Moral. It's a monument both to national pride, with its buildings covered in optimistic murals linking Mexican and global themes, and to an idealistic education system in which almost anyone is entitled to university tuition. In recent years, however, UNAM has struggled to compete academically with increasingly prestigious private universities.

UNAM has some 270,000 students and 30,000 teachers. It has often been a center of political dissent, most notably in the lead-up to the 1968 Mexico City Olympics.

In 1999-2000 the university was closed by a student strike for 9½ months. Initially protesting a proposed rise in tuition fees (from a token US$0.02 a semester to an average US$65), the strikers quickly developed wider demands such as a far-reaching reorganization of the university. The strike also became a broader protest against the Zedillo government's international free-market economic policies. But leadership of the strike passed increasingly into the hands of radicals, and support for it waned. Eventually police retook the occupied UNAM campus. It was a testament to the scars left on Mexico's psyche by the 1968 Tlatelolco massacre that they carried no firearms and no one was injured.

The strike did further damage to UNAM's battered academic reputation. During the strike many of UNAM's best students abandoned it to study elsewhere. Ironically, the proposed tuition hike would have helped improve facilities at UNAM.

Most of the faculty buildings are scattered over an area about 1km square at the north end of the campus. As you enter from Insurgentes, it's easy to spot the **Biblioteca Central** (Central Library) – 10 stories high, almost windowless, and covered on every side with mosaics by Juan O'Gorman. The south wall, with two prominent circles toward the top, covers colonial times. The theme of the north wall is Aztec culture. The east wall shows the creation of modern Mexico. The west wall is harder to interpret but may be dedicated to Latin American culture as a whole.

La Rectoría, the Rectorate administration building, southwest of the library, at the top (west) end of the wide, grassy Jardín Central, has a vivid 3-D Siqueiros mosaic on its south wall, showing students urged on by the people.

The building south of the Rectorate contains the university's modern art museum, the **Museo Universitario de Ciencias y Artes**.

The **Auditorio Alfonso Caso**, at the bottom (east) end of the Jardín Central, bears a mural by José Chávez Morado showing the conquest of energy, with humanity progressing from the shadow of a primitive jaguar god into an ethereal future. A little farther east, on the west wall of the **Facultad de Medicina**, a mosaic by Francisco Eppens interprets the theme of life and death. The central mask has a Spanish profile on the left and a Mexican indigenous one on the right, together making up a mestizo face in the middle. A maize cob and symbols of Aztec and Mayan gods represent forces of life and death.

The **Estadio Olímpico** (Olympic Stadium), on the west side of Insurgentes opposite this northern part of the campus, is designed to resemble a volcano cone and holds up to 80,000 people. There's a Rivera mosaic over its main entrance.

A second main section of the campus, about 2km farther south, contains the **Centro Cultural Universitario**, with concert halls, theaters and cinemas, the **Unidad Bibliográfica**, housing part of Mexico's National Library, and the **Espacio Escultórico** (Sculptural Space), focused on a striking work by Mathias Goeritz, which consists of concrete

shapes about a round platform, set on a bare lava bed.

There are student cafés, open to everyone when school is in session, in the Facultad de Economía and the Unidad Posgrado, both off the east end of the Jardín Central, and in the Centro Cultural Universitario.

Getting There & Away

Any pesero or bus marked 'Villa Olímpica,' 'Perisur' or 'Cuicuilco' traveling south on Insurgentes from Paseo de la Reforma or San Ángel will take you to the Ciudad Universitaria. If none shows up, take one marked 'San Ángel' and change at San Ángel.

For the northern part of the campus, get off at the first yellow footbridge crossing Insurgentes, a little more than 1km from San Ángel, just before the Estadio Olímpico. For the southern part of the campus, get off at the second yellow footbridge *after* the Estadio Olímpico.

Returning to the north, the 'San Ángel,' 'M(etro) Insurgentes,' 'M(etro) La Raza' and 'M(etro) Indios Verdes' buses or peseros go along Insurgentes as far as their respective destinations.

Copilco metro station is near the northeast edge of the campus, 1km east of the Biblioteca Central.

COYOACÁN

About 10km south of downtown Mexico City, Coyoacán ('Place of Coyotes' in the Aztec language, Náhuatl) was Cortés' base after the fall of Tenochtitlán. It remained a small town outside Mexico City until urban sprawl reached it 50 years ago. Close to the university and once home to Leon Trotsky and Frida Kahlo (whose houses are now fascinating museums), it still has its own identity, with narrow colonial-era streets, plazas, cafés and a lively atmosphere. Especially on Saturdays and Sundays, assorted musicians, mimes and craft markets (see Shopping) draw large but relaxed crowds from all walks of life to Coyoacán's central plazas.

There's a helpful tourist information office (☎ 5-659-22-56 ext 181), open 9 am to 8 pm daily, in the Casa de Cortés at Plaza Hidalgo 1.

Viveros

A pleasant way of approaching Coyoacán is via the Viveros de Coyoacán (Coyoacán Nurseries), a swath of greenery, popular with joggers, about 1km west of Coyoacán's central plazas. You can stroll here any day between 6 am and 6 pm. From Viveros metro station, walk south along Avenida Universidad, then take the first street on the left, Valenzuela, to enter the Viveros.

A block south of the Viveros, along Ocampo, is the pretty, little **Plaza Santa Catarina**. The 700m walk east from here along Avenida Sosa to Coyoacán's central plazas takes you past some fine 16th- and 17th-century houses.

Plaza Hidalgo & Jardín del Centenario

The focuses of Coyoacán life, and scenes of most of the weekend fun, are its twin central plazas – the eastern Plaza Hidalgo, with a statue of Miguel Hidalgo, and the western Jardín del Centenario, with a coyote fountain.

The Coyoacán tourist office is housed in the former Coyoacán town hall, also called the **Casa de Cortés**, on the north side of Plaza Hidalgo. It's said that on this spot the Spanish tortured the defeated Aztec emperor Cuauhtémoc to try to make him reveal the whereabouts of treasure. The building was the headquarters of the Marquesado del Valle de Oaxaca, the Cortés family's lands in Mexico, which included Coyoacán.

The 16th-century **Parroquia de San Juan Bautista**, Coyoacán's church, and its adjacent ex-monastery stand by the southern part of Plaza Hidalgo. Half a block east of Plaza Hidalgo, at Avenida Hidalgo 289, is the **Museo Nacional de Culturas Populares** (☎ 5-554-89-68), which has exhibitions on popular cultural forms such as *lucha libre* (wrestling), *nacimientos* (nativity models) and circuses. It's open 10 am to 6 pm Tuesday to Sunday (usually free).

Museo Frida Kahlo

The 'Blue House,' at Londres 247, six blocks north of Plaza Hidalgo, was the long-time home of artist Frida Kahlo (see 'Diego & Frida').

Kahlo and her husband, Diego Rivera, were part of a glamorous but far from harmonious leftist intellectual circle (which included, in the 1930s, Leon Trotsky), and the house is littered with mementos of the couple. As well as some of their own and other artists' work, it contains pre-Hispanic objects and Mexican crafts collected by them.

The Kahlo art on display consists mostly of lesser works, but it still expresses the anguish of her existence: one painting, *El Marxismo Dará la Salud* (Marxism Will Give Health), shows her casting away her crutches. In the upstairs studio an unfinished portrait of Stalin, who became a Kahlo hero when she and Rivera fell out with Trotsky (after she'd had an affair with Trotsky), stands before a poignantly positioned wheelchair. The folk art collection includes Mexican regional costumes worn by Kahlo, and Rivera's collection of small retablo paintings done by Mexicans to give thanks for miracles.

The house and its garden (☎ 5-554-59-99) are open 10 am to 5.45 pm Tuesday to Sunday (US$2). Guided tours in English are given every half hour from 3 to 4.30 pm on Saturday and 11 am to 3.30 pm on Sunday.

Museo Léon Trotsky

Having come second to Stalin in the power struggle in the Soviet Union, Trotsky was expelled from that country in 1929 and condemned to death *in absentia*. In 1937 Trotsky found refuge in Mexico, thanks to the support of Diego Rivera and Frida Kahlo. At first

Police hold the ice ax used to kill Trotsky.

Trotsky and his wife, Natalia, lived in Frida Kahlo's Blue House, but after falling out with Kahlo and Rivera in 1939 they moved a few streets away, to this house at Viena 45.

The house has been left much as it was on the day in 1940 when a Stalin agent finally caught up with Trotsky and killed him here. High walls and watchtowers – once occupied by armed guards – surround the house and its small garden. These defenses were built after a first attempt on Trotsky's life, on May 24, 1940, when attackers led by the Mexican artist Siqueiros pumped bullets into the house. Trotsky and Natalia survived by hiding under their bedroom furniture. The bullet holes remain.

The final, fatal attack took place in Trotsky's study. The assassin had several identities but is usually known as Ramón Mercader, a Catalan. He had managed to become the lover of Trotsky's secretary and gain the confidence of the household. On August 20, 1940, Mercader went to Trotsky at his desk and asked him to look at a docu-

Diego & Frida

Diego Rivera, born in Guanajuato in 1886, first met Frida Kahlo, 21 years his junior, when he was working on a mural at Mexico City's prestigious Escuela Nacional Preparatoria (National Preparatory School), where she was a student in the early 1920s. Rivera was already at the forefront of Mexican art and a socialist; his commission at the Escuela Nacional Preparatoria was the first of many semi-propagandistic murals on public buildings that he was to execute over three decades. He was also already an inveterate womanizer: he had fathered children by two Russian women in Europe and in 1922 married Lupe Marín in Mexico. She bore him two more children before their marriage broke up in 1928.

Kahlo, born in Coyoacán in 1907, had contracted polio at the age of six, which left her right leg permanently thinner than her left. At school she was a tomboyish character. In 1925 she was horribly injured in a bus accident that left her with multiple fractures in her back and right leg, plus broken ribs, collarbone and pelvis. She made a miraculous recovery but suffered much pain thereafter and underwent many operations to try to alleviate it. It was during convalescence from her accident that she began painting. Pain – physical and emotional – was to be a dominating theme of her art.

Kahlo and Rivera both moved in left-wing artistic circles and met again in 1928. They married the following year. The liaison, which has been described as a union between an elephant and a dove (he was big and fat, she short and thin), was always a passionate love-hate affair. Rivera wrote: 'If I ever loved a woman, the more I loved her, the more I wanted to hurt her. Frida was only the most obvious victim of this disgusting trait.' Both had many extramarital affairs.

Kahlo's beauty, bisexuality and unconventional behavior – she drank tequila, told dirty jokes and held wild parties – fascinated many people. In 1934 the pair, after a spell in the USA, moved into a new home built by Juan O'Gorman in San Ángel; the place had separate houses for each of them, linked by an aerial walkway. In 1937 exiled Russian revolutionary Leon Trotsky arrived in Mexico with his wife, Natalia. The Trotskys moved into the 'Blue House' in Coyoacán, where Kahlo had been born, a few kilometers from San Ángel. Kahlo and Trotsky wound up having an affair. In 1939 Rivera quarreled with Trotsky, and the Trotskys moved to a different house in Coyoacán.

The following year Rivera and Kahlo divorced, and Rivera went to San Francisco. Soon afterward, Trotsky was assassinated at his Coyoacán home. Kahlo and Rivera remarried but she moved into the Blue House and he stayed at San Ángel – a state of affairs that endured for the rest of their lives, though their relationship endured too. Kahlo remained Rivera's most trusted critic, Rivera was Kahlo's biggest fan.

ment. Mercader then pulled an ice ax from under his coat and smashed the pick end of it into Trotsky's skull. Trotsky died the next day; Mercader was arrested and spent 20 years in prison. Books and magazines on Trotsky's desk and in bookcases give an intriguing glimpse of the revolutionary's preoccupations.

Other memorabilia and biographical notes are displayed in outbuildings. The garden contains a tomb holding the Trotskys' ashes.

To enter the house (☎ 5-554-06-87), go to its northern entrance, at Avenida Río Churubusco 410, near the corner of Morelos. Hours are 10 am to 5 pm Tuesday to Sunday (US$1, half-price for ISIC cardholders).

Ex-Convento de Churubusco

The 17th-century former Monastery of Churubusco, scene of one of Mexico's heroic military defeats, stands less than 1.5km east of the Trotsky Museum, on Calle 20 de Agosto, east of Avenida División del Norte.

Diego & Frida

Kahlo had only one exhibition in Mexico in her lifetime, in 1953. She arrived at the opening on a stretcher. Rivera said of the exhibition, 'Anyone who attended it could not but marvel at her great talent.' She died, at the Blue House, in 1954. The final words in her diary were, 'I hope the leaving is joyful and I hope never to return.' Rivera called the day of her death 'the most tragic day of my life . . . Too late I realized that the most wonderful part of my life had been my love for Frida.'

In 1955 Rivera married Emma Hurtado, his dealer. He died in 1957.

Kahlo & Rivera Sites in Mexico City

There's much more of his work than hers on view – partly because he was a more prolific, public and versatile artist, partly because some of her best work is in private collections or other countries.

Anahuacalli – fortresslike museum designed by Rivera to house his pre-Hispanic art collection (see the Coyoacán section in this chapter)

Museo Casa Estudio Diego Rivera y Frida Kahlo – their double house (San Ángel)

Museo de Arte Moderno – includes works by Kahlo and Rivera (Bosque de Chapultepec)

Museo de San Ildefonso – the former Escuela Nacional Preparatoria (Centro Histórico)

Museo Dolores Olmedo Patiño – 137 Rivera works and a room of Kahlos in the excellent collection of a Rivera associate (Xochimilco & Around)

Museo Frida Kahlo – the 'Blue House' (Coyoacán)

Museo Mural Diego Rivera – Rivera's mural *Sueño de una Tarde Dominical en la Alameda* (Alameda Central & Around)

Palacio de Bellas Artes – 1930s Rivera murals (Alameda Central & Around)

Palacio Nacional – Rivera's mural history of Mexican civilization (Centro Histórico)

Secretaría de Educación Pública – 120 fresco panels painted by Rivera and helpers in the 1920s (Centro Histórico)

On August 20, 1847, an American army was advancing on Mexico City from Veracruz. Mexicans who defended this old monastery fought until they ran out of ammunition and were finally beaten only after hand-to-hand fighting. General Pedro Anaya, asked by US general David Twiggs to surrender his ammunition, is said to have answered, 'If there was any, you wouldn't be here.' Cannon and memorials outside the monastery recall these events.

Most of the monastery is now occupied by the interesting **Museo Nacional de las Intervenciones** (National Interventions Museum, ☎ 5-604-06-99), open 9 am to 6 pm Tuesday to Sunday (US$1.50). Displays include an American map showing operations in 1847 (note how far outside the city Churubusco was then), and material on the French occupation in the 1860s and the plot by US ambassador Henry Lane Wilson to bring down the Madero government in 1913. Parts of the peaceful old monastery gardens are also open.

You can reach Churubusco on an eastbound 'M(etro) Gral Anaya' pesero or bus – catch it on Xicoténcatl at Allende, a few blocks north of Coyoacán's Plaza Hidalgo. Alternatively, it's a 500m walk from the General Anaya metro station.

Anahuacalli

This dramatic museum (☎ 5-617-37-97), at Calle del Museo 150, 3.5km south of central Coyoacán, was designed by Diego Rivera to house his own collection of pre-Hispanic art. It also contains one of his studios and some of his work.

The fortresslike building is made of dark volcanic stone and incorporates many pre-Hispanic stylistic features. Its name means House of Anáhuac (Anáhuac was the Aztec name for the Valle de México). If the air is clear, there's a great view over the city from the roof.

The archaeological exhibits are mostly of pottery and stone figures, chosen primarily for their artistic qualities. Among Rivera's own art, the most interesting pieces are studies for major murals such as *El Hombre, Contralor del Universo*, which is in the Palacio de Bellas Artes. The Anahuacalli is open 10 am to 6 pm daily except Monday (US$1).

From Coyoacán, catch a 'Villa Coapa' pesero south on Tres Cruces. This will eventually travel south on Avenida División del Norte. Three kilometers from Coyoacán, get off at Calle del Museo (there are traffic lights and a church at the intersection), and walk 600m southwest along Calle del Museo, curving to the left at first, then going slightly uphill. Returning northward, take a 'M(etro) División del Norte' pesero or bus along Avenida División del Norte.

Getting There & Away

The nearest metro stations to Coyoacán are Viveros, Coyoacán and General Anaya, all 1.5 to 2km away. If you don't fancy a walk, from Viveros station walk south to Valenzuela and catch an eastbound 'M(etro) Gral Anaya' pesero to Allende; or from Coyoacán station take a 'Coyoacán' pesero southeast on Avenida México. From General Anaya station too, many peseros and buses go to central Coyoacán.

To return to these metro stations from central Coyoacán, there are 'M(etro) Viveros' peseros going west on Malitzin from Allende, 'M(etro) Coyoacán' peseros north on Aguayo, and 'M(etro) Gral Anaya' peseros east on Xicoténcatl from Allende.

To reach San Ángel from Coyoacán, there are 'San Ángel' peseros and buses heading west on Malitzin from Allende, or west on Avenida MA de Quevedo, five blocks south of Plaza Hidalgo. To reach the Ciudad Universitaria, take a 'M(etro) Copilco' pesero west on Malitzin, from Allende.

XOCHIMILCO & AROUND

About 20km south of downtown Mexico City, the urban sprawl is strung with a network of canals lined by gardens and houses with patches of waterside lawn. These are the so-called 'floating gardens' of Xochimilco ('so-chi-MEEL-co'), remnants of the chinampas where the Aztecs grew much of their food. A gondola trip along the canals is an enjoyable, if not often tranquil, experience. Nearby are the enjoyable Parque Ecológico de Xochimilco and one of the city's best art museums, the Museo Dolores Olmedo Patiño.

Museo Dolores Olmedo Patiño

The Olmedo Patiño museum (☎ 5-555-08-91) at Avenida México 5843, a little over 2km west of Xochimilco, has perhaps the biggest and most important Diego Rivera collection of all. It's a fascinating place, set in a peaceful 16th-century hacienda with large gardens.

Dolores Olmedo Patiño, who still lives in part of the mansion, was a rich socialite and a patron of Diego Rivera, amassing a large collection of his art. The museum's 137 Rivera works – oils, watercolors, drawings and lithographs drawn from many periods of his life – are displayed with a fine collection of memorabilia and pre-Hispanic pottery figures and metalwork. There's also a room of Frida Kahlo paintings. Elsewhere in the museum you'll find Emperor Maximilian's 365-piece silverware set, and a colorful collection of Mexican folk art.

The museum is open 10 am to 6 pm daily except Monday (US$1). To get there take the metro to Tasqueña, then the Tren Ligero (streetcar, US$0.20) from Tasqueña metro station to La Noria. Leaving La Noria station, turn left at the top of the steps, walk down to the street and continue ahead to an intersection with a footbridge over it. Here turn sharp left, almost doubling back on your path, on to Antiguo Camino Xochimilco. The museum is 300m down this street. Altogether the trip is about one hour from the city center.

Xochimilco

Xochimilco means 'Place where Flowers Grow' in Náhuatl. Pre-Hispanic inhabitants piled up vegetation and lake mud in the shallow waters of Lago de Xochimilco, a southern offshoot of Lago de Texcoco, to make fertile gardens called chinampas, which became an economic base of the Aztec empire. As the chinampas proliferated, much of the lake was transformed into a series of canals. About 180km of these

canals remain today. Partly thanks to a recent environmental recovery program, Xochimilco's canals remain one of Mexico City's favorite destinations for a bit of fun and relaxation.

Xochimilco also boasts its own tourist information office (☎ 5-676-08-10) at Pino 36, just off the central plaza, open 9 am to 9 pm daily (to 8 pm Sundays), a bustling daily market (the Mercado de Xochimilco) occupying the two blocks south of the plaza and the Parroquia de San Bernardino de Siena on the east side of the plaza. This 16th-century church, with an elaborate, gold-painted retablo, and its pretty gardens are open from 7 am to 1 pm and 4.30 to 8 pm daily.

Most people board their *trajinera* (gondola) at one of the *embarcaderos* (boat landings) near the center of Xochimilco such as Salitre or San Cristóbal, both 400m east of the plaza, or Fernando Celada, 400m west on Guadalupe Ramírez. Hundreds of colorful trajineras, each punted by one man with a pole, wait to cruise the canals with parties of merrymakers or tourists.

On weekends, especially Sundays, a fiesta atmosphere takes over as the town and waterways of Xochimilco become jammed with people arranging boats, cruising the canals or trying to talk you into buying something. For a more relaxed atmosphere, come on a weekday.

Official prices for the boats are posted at the embarcaderos and you needn't pay more. At most of the embarcaderos a four-person boat (yellow roof) is US$5 an hour; an eight-person boat (red), US$6; a 12-person boat (blue), US$8; and a 16-person boat (green), US$10. On Saturdays, Sundays and holidays, 60-person *lanchas* (motor boats) charging US$0.50 a person depart from the Salitre and Caltongo embarcaderos.

Fixed prices for boat-borne food, drink and even mariachi and marimba music are also posted at the embarcaderos! You can get a taste of Xochimilco in one hour, but it's worth going for longer; you can see more and get a proper chance to relax.

To reach Xochimilco, take the metro to Tasqueña station, then take the Tren Ligero (streetcar, US$0.20), which starts there, to its last stop, Embarcadero. From Embarcadero station, walk to the left (north) along Avenida Morelos to the market, plaza and church. Five of the eight embarcaderos are within 500m of the plaza.

Alternatively, 'Xochimilco' buses and peseros run from outside Tasqueña metro station. It's about 45 minutes from Tasqueña to Xochimilco either way. The last Tren Ligero back to Tasqueña leaves Embarcadero station about 11 pm.

Parque Ecológico de Xochimilco

About 3km north of downtown Xochimilco, this 2 sq km park (☎ 5-673-80-61) contains lakes, an incipient botanical garden and a truly surprising number and variety of water birds. It's enjoyable to walk round the pathways – despite the lack of shade – but you can also move around by bicycle (US$0.70 for 30 minutes), pedal boat or trajinera. There's a visitor center with displays on the plants and birds. In summer the Parque Ecológico de Xochimilco is open 9 am to 7 pm Tuesday to Sunday, in winter 10 am to 6 pm the same days (US$1.50).

Just west of the park – a 2km walk from the entrance – is the Embarcadero Cuemanco, the best place to take a trajinera if you want to see the genuine chinampas of northern Xochimilco.

To reach Parque Ecológico de Xochimilco, take a 'Tlahuac' pesero northbound on Calzada de Tlalpan outside General Anaya metro station. You reach the park entrance – beside a blue footbridge with blue-and-red spiral towers near each end – after 20 to 30 minutes.

PARQUE NACIONAL DESIERTO DE LOS LEONES

This 20 sq km national park of cool, fragrant, pine, fir and oak forests echoing to the sound of birdsong, some 23km southwest of downtown Mexico City, is a fine place to head for when the carbon monoxide and concrete get too much. It's 800m higher than the city center, in the hills on the rim of the Valle de México. The park's name, literally meaning Desert of the Lions, comes from the Ex-

Convento del Desierto de Santa Fe, the 17th-century former Carmelite monastery in the park – the Carmelites called their isolated monasteries 'deserts' to commemorate Elijah, who lived as a recluse in the desert near Mt Carmel. 'Leones' probably stems from José Manuel de León who at one stage administered the monastery's finances.

The monastery was built in 1606-11, wrecked by an earthquake in 1711, and rebuilt in 1722-23. In 1801 the monks left in order to escape the too wet, too cool climate and their too frequent visitors.

Today the Ex-Convento, restored with exhibition halls and a medium-to-expensive restaurant, is open 10 am to 5 pm – officially just Tuesday to Sunday but you may also find it open on Mondays. There are pretty patios within, and lovely gardens around the buildings. The rest of the park has extensive walking trails and is very popular with weekend picnickers. Sometimes robberies are reported in the park, so take care of your things and don't wander off the main paths.

One good walk is from the spot known as Cruz Blanca at 3130m up to the chapel-crowned Cerro San Miguel at about 3800m. The route – 1½ to two hours one-way – follows part of the Barda de la Excomunión, the perimeter wall of the old monastery's property. To reach Cruz Blanca, turn right up a side road, immediately before a barrier where a US$1 charge on vehicles is levied, halfway from highway 15 to the Ex-Convento. It's about 4km from here up to Cruz Blanca, where you should find a *vigilante* (forest warden) who can direct you to Cerro San Miguel.

The national park is open 6 am to 5 pm daily.

Getting There & Away

On Saturday and Sunday there are peseros to the Ex-Convento from near Tacubaya metro station. Take the 'Av Jalisco Calle Manuel Dublan' exit from the station's line 9 platforms, cross the street outside and walk through to far end of the market.

Any day, you can take one of Flecha Roja's frequent 'Toluca Intermedio' buses from the Terminal Poniente bus station to La

Venta, which is on highway 15, to Toluca (US$0.70). The ride takes about 20 minutes. Tell the driver you are going to the Desierto de los Leones and you should be dropped at a yellow footbridge over a tangle of merging highways just short of a toll station *(caseta de cobro)*. Cross the footbridge, and toward its far end you'll see, on your right, the Desierto de los Leones signposted up a side road to the south. On Saturday and Sunday, peseros or taxis may wait here to take people up the 4km paved road to the Ex-Convento. Other days you'll probably have to walk, but traffic will be light and it's a pleasant stroll, gently rising nearly all the way.

COURSES

The Centro de Enseñanza Para Extranjeros (Foreigners' Teaching Center) at UNAM, though not functioning at the time of writing because of the UNAM students' strike, normally offers six-week intensive courses in Spanish language and Latin American culture five times a year. Beginners and others will find courses that cater to them. Though classes can be quite large, the courses have received good reports. For US$265 (US$375 for summer courses), you get three or more hours in the classroom five days a week. UNAM also runs courses on Latin American culture, history and society. For information contact CEPE (☎ 5-622-24-70, fax 5-616-26-72, cepe@servidor .unam.mx), Avenida Universidad 3002, Ciudad Universitaria, 04510 México DF, México, or visit the UNAM Internet site at http://serpiente.dgsca.unam.mx.

The United States International University (☎ 5-264-21-87, fax 5-264-21-88, www .usiumexico.edu), a small, private university with well-qualified staff, offers a one-week 15-hour Spanish course, focusing on survival Spanish and Mexican Spanish, for US$85, starting every Monday. It also does a five-week intensive Spanish language summer course with cultural components for US$1400, including accommodation and two meals daily. For information, call, fax or write (USIU-Mexico, Álvaro Obregón 110, Colonia Roma, México DF 06700, Mexico). This university also puts on a variety of

other events and activities, such as guided cultural tours and open lectures and seminars, many of which can be joined on a one-time basis. It's worth popping by to see what's coming up if you're in the city for more than a few days.

The Institute of International Education (see Courses in the Facts for the Visitor chapter) has an office (☎ 5-211-00-42) at Londres 16 in Colonia Juárez, east of the Zona Rosa.

The Casa de los Amigos (see Places to Stay) holds several open seminars a year – usually four to seven days – on social issues such as the Mexico City environment, urban popular movements, and women, children and health in Mexico. They include visits to local service organizations and work on community projects. The fee of around US$50 a day includes lodging and most meals. Participants don't need to speak Spanish.

ORGANIZED TOURS

Many travel agencies, including those in most top-end and mid-range hotels, can book you on bus tours within and outside the city, with English-language guides. A half-day whirl around the Zócalo area and the Museo Nacional de Antropología costs around US$25. Full-day city tours are in the region of US$40. The international tour company Gray Line (☎ 5-514-30-80), Hamburgo 182B in the Zona Rosa, is one well established agency offering such tours. A local alternative (no relation) is Grey Line (☎ 5-208-11-63), Londres 166, Zona Rosa.

See the earlier Travel Agencies section for information on Mexico City organizations providing adventure trips or ecotourism outside the city.

SPECIAL EVENTS

Every major Mexican festival described in the Facts for the Visitor chapter is celebrated in Mexico City. Unique local events, or those with a special flavor in the capital, are described below.

Festival del Centro Histórico

This excellent three-week program of classical and popular music, dance, exhibitions and other cultural events, with top-class Mexican and international performers, takes place in numerous picturesque and historic plazas, palaces, theaters and archaeological sites in the Centro Histórico and Alameda area; check the website at www.festival .org.mx.

Semana Santa

The most evocative events of Holy Week are in the humble Iztapalapa district, about 9km southeast of the Zócalo (Ⓜ Iztapalapa), where more than 150 locals act out realistic scenes from the Passion and death of Christ. Palm Sunday sees the triumphal entry into Jerusalem. On Holy Thursday the betrayal by Judas and the Last Supper are played out in Iztapalapa's plaza, and Christ's address in Gethsemane is enacted on Cerro de la Estrella, the hill rising to the south. The most emotive scenes begin at noon on Good Friday, in the plaza. Christ is sentenced, beaten, and has a crown of real thorns placed on his head, then carries his 90kg cross 4km up Cerro de la Estrella, where he is tied to the cross and 'crucified.' Afterward he is carried down the hill and taken to the hospital.

Día de la Independencia

On the evening of September 15 thousands gather in the Zócalo to hear the president of Mexico recite a version of the Grito de Dolores (Cry of Dolores), Miguel Hidalgo's famous rallying call to rebellion against the Spanish in 1810, from the central balcony of the National Palace at 11 pm. The president then rings the ceremonial Campana de Dolores (Bell of Dolores), and there's lots of cheering, fireworks and throwing of confetti, usually in the faces of other merrymakers. Leave your valuables in the hotel safe!

Día de Nuestra Señora de Guadalupe

At the Basílica de Guadalupe in the northern part of the city, December 12, the Day of Our Lady of Guadalupe, caps 10 days of festivities honoring Mexico's religious patron, the Virgin of Guadalupe. From December 3, ever-growing crowds flood toward the basil-

ica and its broad plaza. On December 11 and 12 groups of indigenous dancers and musicians from all over Mexico perform on the plaza in uninterrupted succession for two days. The numbers of pilgrims reach the millions by December 12, when religious services go on in the basilica almost round the clock.

Christmas & Día de los Reyes Magos

For the couple of weeks before Christmas the Alameda Central is ringed with brightly lit fairy-tale castles and polar grottoes, where families flock in and children pose for photos with Mexican Santa Clauses and their reindeer. Between Christmas and January 6 – the Day of the Three Kings (Reyes Magos) – Santa Claus is replaced by the Three Kings, who are equally popular and look, if anything, even more ill at ease than the Santas.

PLACES TO STAY

Mexico City has a full range of accommodations, from basic but centrally located places (charging anywhere up to US$17.50 for a typical double room) through comfortable mid-range hotels (US$17.50 to US$50 a double) to a wide range of top-end hotels costing from US$50 up to the sky. In general, the best cheap and moderately priced rooms are in the areas west of the Zócalo, near the Alameda Central and near the Plaza de la República; luxury hotels are mostly in the Zona Rosa, along Paseo de la Reforma, and in the Polanco district.

Accommodations are described here in rough order of preference for each area. Where two prices are given for double rooms, the lower is for two people in one bed, the higher for twin beds. Remember that many hotels have rooms for three or four people, costing not very much more than a double.

Places to Stay – Budget

Rooms in these hotels have private baths unless otherwise mentioned. Many also have TV and carafes or bottles of purified water. Hot water supplies are erratic in some.

Centro Histórico Most of the suitable places in the Centro Histórico are on Avenida Cinco de Mayo and the streets to its north and south.

Hostels The *Pensión del Centro* (☎ 5-512-08-32, *Cuba 74, apartment 203*), at the corner of Chile (Ⓜ Allende), is a small (14-bunk), clean, friendly, backpacker hostel. The cost, including self-service breakfast, is US$8 the first night and US$6.50 thereafter (US$7 and US$6 respectively with an ISIC or GO25 card). There's a guest kitchen, and you can use the Internet for US$3 a half hour. It's one of the HI-affiliated AMAJ group. Dormitory accommodations at *Hostal Moneda* (see Places to Stay – Mid-Range) also fall into the budget category.

Hotels The *Hotel Isabel* (☎ 5-518-12-13, *Isabel la Católica 63*), at El Salvador (Ⓜ Isabel la Católica), is popular with budget travelers because of its convenient location, comfy if old-fashioned rooms, and decent, moderately priced restaurant. All rooms have TV and some are very large; those overlooking the street are noisy but brighter. Singles/doubles cost US$13/15, or US$8/9 on the upper floors with shared bathroom and good views from some rooms.

Hotel Juárez (☎ 5-512-69-29, *1ª Cerrada de Cinco de Mayo 17*) has 39 rooms on a quiet side street off Avenida Cinco de Mayo only 1½ blocks from the Zócalo (Ⓜ Zócalo or Allende). It's simple but clean and presentable, with 24-hour hot water and low prices of US$8 a single, US$8.50 or US$9 a double. Rooms have TV, but only a few have windows. Those fronting the street can be noisy. If you're there by 2 pm you should get a room.

Hotel Habana (☎ 5-518-15-89, *Cuba 77*) is an excellent value. Its 40 clean, decent-sized rooms, painted a variety of pastel shades and with TV and good tiled bathrooms, cost US$11 a single, US$11 or US$16 a double (Ⓜ Allende).

Hotel San Antonio (☎ 5-512-99-06, *2ª Cerrada de Cinco de Mayo 29*) is just south of the Hotel Juárez across Avenida Cinco de Mayo, on the corresponding side street

(Ⓜ Zócalo or Allende). All the 40 small, clean rooms (US$9 single or double) have TV, and it's quiet and convenient. Rooms on the street side are brighter.

Hotel Zamora (☎ 5-512-82-45, *Avenida Cinco de Mayo 50*), between La Palma and Isabel la Católica (Ⓜ Allende or Zócalo), has absolutely no frills, but it's clean, friendly and cheap, with hot showers and a safe. Singles and one-bed doubles are US$6.50 with shared bathrooms, US$9 with private bath; two-bed doubles are US$10 and US$13.50 respectively.

Hotel Principal (☎ 5-521-13-33, *Bolívar 29*), between Avenida Madero and 16 de Septiembre (Ⓜ Allende or Zócalo), is a friendly place with most rooms opening on to a plant-draped central hall. Singles/doubles with shared bathrooms are US$6/7. With private bathroom, TV and safe it's US$12 a single, and US$14 or US$16 for doubles. The twin rooms are quite large.

Hotel Washington (☎ 5-512-35-02, *Avenida Cinco de Mayo 54*), at La Palma near Hotel Juárez (Ⓜ Allende or Zócalo), has small but adequate rooms with TV. Singles are US$12, doubles US$13 or US$15.

Hotel Roble (☎ 5-522-78-30, *Uruguay 109*) is two blocks south of the Zócalo (Ⓜ Zócalo or Pino Suárez). It's at the top end of the budget range, with good rooms at US$15 a single or US$17 or US$19.50 a double. A bright, busy restaurant adjoins.

Hotel Buenos Aires (☎ 5-518-21-04, *Motolinía 21*) has good prices: rooms with shared bathrooms are US$7, singles/doubles with private bath and TV are US$8/9 (US$10 for twin-bed doubles). Rooms are plain but clean, and management is friendly (Ⓜ Allende).

DH Lawrence once stayed at *Hotel Montecarlo* (☎ 5-518-14-18, *Uruguay 69*). Though renovated and clean, it's rather dark and echoing. But its closeness to the Zócalo (Ⓜ Zócalo) and its prices of US$8/9 with shared bathrooms, US$10/11 with private bath, make it worth considering.

South of the Alameda Central This is a convenient, if drab, area.

Hotel Del Valle (☎ 5-521-80-67, *Independencia 35*), just a block from the Alameda

(Ⓜ San Juan de Letrán or Juárez), is a friendly sort of place whose medium-sized, slightly worn rooms have TV and are reasonably priced at US$10 for singles, US$10 or US$12 for doubles.

Hotel San Diego (☎ 5-521-60-10, *Moya 98*), 5½ blocks from the Alameda (Ⓜ Salto del Agua), is a bit far from the action, but offers good value. The 87 spacious, modern rooms boast satellite TV, tiled bathrooms, and prices of US$10 or US$11 a single, US$14 a double. There's a good restaurant, a bar and a garage.

Hotel Fornos (☎ 5-521-95-94, *Revillagigedo 92*), 700m from the Alameda (Ⓜ Balderas), has pleasant, smallish rooms. One or two people in a double bed pay US$11 or US$12; a twin room is US$19 (US$23 with jacuzzi). The hotel has a parking lot and restaurant.

Near Plaza de la República This area, about 1km west of the Alameda, is slightly less convenient, but prices are good and the neighborhood is mainly quiet and residential. The metro station is Revolución.

The small *Hotel Ibiza* (☎ 5-566-81-55, *Arriaga 22*), at Édison, is a good value. Nice, clean little singles/doubles, with bright bedspreads and TV, are US$8/10.

For a bit more comfort, *Hotel Édison* (☎ 5-566-09-33, *Édison 106*) has 45 pleasant, clean rooms around a small, plant-filled courtyard. They cost US$15 for singles, US$17 or US$19 for doubles. There's a garage, and a bakery is just across the street.

Hotel Frimont (☎ 5-705-41-69, *Terán 35*) is a good value with 100 clean, carpeted, decent-sized rooms costing US$15.50 a single, US$17 or US$19.50 a double, and an inexpensive restaurant.

Hotel Texas (☎ 5-705-57-82, *Mariscal 129*) has helpful staff and 60 cozy, clean rooms with free bottled water. Singles are US$15, doubles US$17.50 or US$19.50, and there's a garage.

Hotel Carlton (☎ 5-566-29-11, *Mariscal 32B*), at Ramos Arizpe, an old budget favorite, has started a long-due refurbishment. The rooms are carpeted, have TV, and are vaguely cozy, for US$10/11 a single/double

modernized, or US$9/10 unmodernized. There's an economical restaurant (four-course *comida* US$1.75). A few prostitutes look for work in Plaza Buenavista, the quiet little square in front of the hotel.

Hotel Oxford (☎ 5-566-05-00, *Mariscal 67*), also on Plaza Buenavista, is still waiting for refurbishment – the carpets don't appear to have been washed for a decade – but it has large singles and doubles with TV for US$7 to US$10. Upper rooms overlook the plaza.

The Quaker center *Casa de los Amigos* (☎ 5-705-05-21, *Mariscal 132, amigos@laneta .apc.org*) offers lodging to people interested in participating in its community or in becoming involved with other social concerns, such as doing research or community service in Mexico (see Work in the Facts for the Visitor chapter and Courses in this chapter). There's a four-night minimum stay for first-timers, and the Casa requires the completion of a questionnaire before accepting bookings. The questionnaire and bookings can be done by email. It's a good place for meeting people with an informed interest in Mexico and Central America. There's a guest kitchen and a US$1.50 breakfast is served Monday to Friday. There's room for 40 people in single-sex dormitories and private rooms. The suggested donation for a dorm bed is US$7; for a room with shared bath, US$7 or US$7.50 a single and US$11.50 a double; and for a double with private bath, US$13.50. Alcohol and smoking are banned in the building.

Condesa The *Home Hostel* (☎ 5-511-26-98, *Tabasco 303*) is a pleasant, small hostel on a quiet, leafy street in the groovy Condesa district, south of the Zona Rosa. It accommodates 20 people at US$8 each in four separate-sex bunk rooms. There's a kitchen and TV/sitting room. Home Hostel is part of the HI-affiliated REMAJ hostel group. It's 700m southwest of Insurgentes metro.

Places to Stay – Mid-Range
Hotels in this range provide comfortable and attractive, if sometimes small, rooms in modern or colonial buildings. All rooms

have private bath (usually with shower, sometimes with tub) and color TV.

Centro Histórico A couple of superior hostels are now challenging the mid-range hotels in this area.

Hostels A stone's throw from the Zócalo, the *Hostel Moneda* (☎ 5-522-58-03, ☎/fax 5-552-58-21, Moneda 8), a member of the HI-affiliated hostel group AMAJ, opened early in 2000 (Ⓜ Zócalo). It has 94 beds in double and triple rooms and six-person dormitories, all with private bath, at US$8 to US$12 per person including breakfast.

A kitchen, roof garden, a 'downtown backpackers' café,' areas for TV, Internet and laundry, and recycling and energy-conserving technologies are all part of the project. The hostel plans to offer an airport shuttle service, a range of English-language city tours (including bicycle tours and nightlife tours) and ecotourism ventures outside the city. For more information or online bookings, go to www.hostalmoneda.com.mx.

Almost as close to the Zócalo is the 209-bunk *Hostel Catedral* (☎ 5-662-82-44, fax 5-663-15-56, Guatemala 4), which also opened in early 2000 and charges US$19 for hostel card holders. Rooms hold from three to 10 people. The hostel, open 24 hours, is the flagship of the HI-affiliated hostel group REMAJ, and incorporates a restaurant, guest kitchen, Internet center, laundry, pool table and travel agency (Ⓜ Zócalo).

Hotels The *Hotel Canadá* (☎ 5-518-21-06, Avenida Cinco de Mayo 47), east of Isabel la Católica (Ⓜ Allende), is bright, modern and tidy, and the location is excellent, though the 100 rooms are mostly modestly sized and exterior ones get some street noise. They cost US$20 or US$22 a single, US$22 or US$24 a double, and all have safes and bottled drinking water.

Hotel Catedral (☎ 5-518-52-32, Donceles 95), just a block north of the Catedral Metropolitana, is shiny and bright, with a reasonable restaurant off the bright lobby. The 120 rooms are well kept and pleasant at US$24.50 a single, US$30 or US$35 a

double. There's a roof terrace with good views (Ⓜ Zócalo).

Hotel Gillow (☎ 5-518-14-40, Isabel la Católica 17), at the corner of Avenida Cinco de Mayo (Ⓜ Allende), has a pleasant leafy lobby and cheerful rooms. Singles are US$25, doubles US$29 or US$35. There's a moderately priced restaurant too.

Hotel Capitol (☎ 5-512-04-60, Uruguay 12) is close to the Torre Latinoamericana (Ⓜ San Juan de Letrán). Rooms, mostly around a central hall with a fountain, are modern and pleasant, and cost US$21.50 a single, US$27 to US$32 a double (the most expensive are suites with jacuzzi).

Near the Alameda Central The *Hotel Bamer* (☎ 5-521-90-60, Avenida Juárez 52) faces the Alameda, and many of the 111 comfortable, air-conditioned, mostly very large rooms have fantastic views of the park. Singles/doubles cost US$33/38. There are some smaller rooms at the sides, without Alameda views or bathtub (but with shower), for US$23 single or double. The ground-floor cafeteria serves good, reasonably priced breakfasts and lunches (Ⓜ Bellas Artes).

Hotel Fleming (☎ 5-510-45-30, Revillagigedo 35), 2½ blocks south of the Alameda (Ⓜ Juárez), has 100 comfortable rooms with large tiled bathrooms; some on the higher floors have great views. Singles are US$24, doubles US$27 or US$30. There's a nice restaurant and parking.

Hotel Marlowe (☎ 5-521-95-40, Independencia 17) is one short block south of the Alameda. It's bright and comfortable, and the 120 rooms are pleasant, tasteful and quite big. Singles are US$23, doubles US$27 or US$29 (Ⓜ San Juan de Letrán).

One block north of the Alameda, *Hotel Hidalgo* (☎ 5-521-87-71, Santa Veracruz 37) is on a fairly grungy street, but the 100 rooms are modern and excellent. It has a restaurant and garage. Singles/doubles are US$17/20 (Ⓜ Bellas Artes).

Near Plaza de la República The nearest metro station here is Revolución.

Hotel Mayaland (☎ 5-566-60-66, Antonio Caso 23) is a good value. The 100 rooms are small but clean and pleasing, with air-con, drinking water and about 100 channels on TV. They cost US$26 for singles, US$28 or US$33 for doubles. There's a decent little restaurant and parking.

The 200-room *Palace Hotel* (☎ 5-566-24-00, Ramírez 7) has a bustling lobby and comfortable rooms, some recently remodernized, at US$24 or US$30 for singles, US$27 or US$34 for doubles. Some hold up to six people, and the hotel has a restaurant, bar and garage. The similarly-priced *Hotel Corinto* (☎ 5-566-65-55, Ignacio Vallarta 24) is sleek and polished with a good restaurant, bar, helpful staff, and even a small rooftop pool. The 155 rooms, though small, are comfortable, quiet and air-conditioned.

Back north of Plaza de la República, the 45-room *Hotel New York* (☎ 5-566-97-00, Édison 45), recently upgraded, has bright, comfy rooms of a reasonable size for US$25 single, US$33 or US$42 a double, and a nice little restaurant. *Hotel Jena* (☎ 5-566-02-77, Terán 12), at Mariscal, is a modern, gleaming building with a posh feel. Its 120-plus rooms are ultra-clean and among the most luxurious in the middle range. Singles are US$35, doubles US$38 or US$41. There's a piano bar and a slightly pricey restaurant.

Near the Jardín del Arte The Jardín del Arte is a small park about 1km north of the Zona Rosa, close to the Reforma/Insurgentes intersection. Three decent midsize hotels, all with parking, are on Serapio Rendón within a block of the park. Buses and peseros pass nearby on Insurgentes and Reforma.

Hotel Mallorca (☎ 5-566-48-33, Serapio Rendón 119) has clean, pleasant, carpeted rooms with singles at US$19 and doubles from US$21. It's popular with Mexican couples and families. The 'doble chico' and 'doble grande' doubles (US$23 and US$25) are large.

Hotel Sevilla (☎ 5-566-18-66, Serapio Rendón 124) has a sección tradicional with decent enough rooms costing from US$19 to US$25 single or double, and a nicer sección nueva, with some rooms overlooking the park, for US$36 to US$46 single or double. Rooms are mostly moderately sized. The

hotel also has a shop, travel agency and restaurant.

Hotel Compostela (☎ 5-566-07-33, Sullivan 35), at Serapio Rendón, has smallish but pleasant rooms at US$15 for singles, US$17.50 or US$19 for doubles.

Near the Zona Rosa Accommodations right in the posh Zona Rosa are expensive, but there are a couple of excellent good mid-range places nearby – both very popular, so it's highly advisable to book ahead. The nearest metro station to both is Insurgentes (800m south).

Casa González (☎ 5-514-33-02, fax 5-511-07-02, Río Sena 69) is a 500m walk north from the heart of the Zona Rosa, in a quieter neighborhood. Two beautiful houses set in small plots of lawn have been converted into a lovely guesthouse. It's an exceptional place run by a charming family, perfect for those staying more than one or two nights, and a good value at US$25 to US$35 a single and US$29 to US$35 a double (plus one double at US$57.50 and a family room at US$57.50 for four or US$69 for five). Good home-cooked meals are available in the pretty dining room. They may have parking. No sign marks the houses: ring the bell to enter.

Hotel María Cristina (☎ 5-703-12-12, fax 5-592-34-47, Río Lerma 31), 600m north of the center of the Zona Rosa, is a colonial-style gem. It has 150 comfy rooms, small manicured lawns, baronial public rooms, and a patio with a fountain. There's a fine medium-priced restaurant, a bar and parking. Singles/doubles are US$43/47, suites US$54 and up.

Near Terminal Norte The *Hotel Brasilia* (☎ 5-587-85-77, Avenida de los Cien Metros 4823) is a five- to eight-minute walk south of the northern bus terminal (Ⓜ Autobuses del Norte). It has 200 decent rooms from US$16 to US$24, single or double. There's a restaurant and bar.

Places to Stay – Top End
Top-end accommodations here range from comfortable medium-size tourist-oriented

hotels, some with rooms for well under US$100, to modern luxury high-rises geared toward international business travelers, where the cheapest rooms are more than US$300. For the hotels in the Best Western group you can call ☎ 800-528-1234 in the USA or Canada for reservations.

Centro Histórico The *Holiday Inn Select* (☎ 5-521-21-21, 800-009-99-00, Cinco de Mayo 61) is a 110-room recent addition, with a prime site just across the street from the Catedral Metropolitana. The rooms – modern, pleasant and comfortable without being huge – cost US$82 single or double. The rooftop restaurant has marvelous views (Ⓜ Zócalo).

The 124-room *Gran Hotel Ciudad de México* (☎ 5-510-40-40, 16 de Septiembre 82), just off the Zócalo (Ⓜ Zócalo), is a feast of century-old Mexican art nouveau. Sit on one of the plush settees in the spacious lobby, listen to the songbirds in the large cages, and watch the open ironwork elevator glide toward the brilliant canopy of art nouveau stained glass high above you. The large, comfortable standard rooms cost US$101 single or double. Buffet breakfasts are a specialty of the hotel's restaurants.

Hotel Ritz (☎ 5-518-13-40, Avenida Madero 30), 3½ blocks west of the Zócalo (Ⓜ Allende), caters to business travelers and North American tour groups, offering 120 comfortable rooms with mini-bars at US$71 a single or double. There's a restaurant and a good little bar with live piano music. It's a Best Western hotel.

The long-established *Hotel Majestic* (☎ 5-521-86-00, Avenida Madero 73), on the west side of the Zócalo (Ⓜ Zócalo), has lots of colorful tiles in the lobby, and a few rooms (the more expensive ones) overlooking the vast plaza. Avoid the rooms facing Madero (too noisy) and around the inner glass-floored courtyard (unless you don't mind people looking through your windows). Rates are US$100 a room and US$176 or US$235 a suite, single or double. The 7th-floor café-restaurant has a good Zócalo view. This is another Best Western hotel.

Alameda Central The *Hotel de Cortés* (☎ 5-518-21-81, Avenida Hidalgo 85), facing the north side of the Alameda Central (Ⓜ Hidalgo), has a somewhat forbidding façade of dark tezontle stone, but inside is a charming small colonial hotel. Originally built in 1780 as a monks' hospice, it now has modern, comfortable rooms with small windows that look out on the courtyard. Noise can be a problem, though. Singles/doubles are US$82/94; suites cost from US$153. There's a nightly marimba and traditional dance show in the courtyard restaurant. It's yet another Best Western hotel.

Near Plaza de la República Several mainly business-oriented hotels on and near Paseo de la Reforma provide a convenient location between the Alameda and Zona Rosa. They include:

Fiesta Americana (☎ 5-705-15-15, Reforma 80) – a 26-story, 610-unit slab with stylish rooms that cost US$151/166 singles/doubles (closest to Ⓜ Revolución)

Hotel Casa Blanca (☎ 5-705-13-00, Lafragua 7) – just north of Reforma, with 300 comfy rooms at US$67/82 (Ⓜ Revolución)

Hotel Crowne Plaza (☎ 5-128-50-00, Reforma 1) – a smooth 490-room luxury hotel; standard rooms US$217 (Ⓜ Hidalgo)

Hotel Sevilla Palace (☎ 5-566-88-77, Reforma 105) – helpful service and good, modern rooms at US$115 single or double (nearest Ⓜ Revolución)

Zona Rosa & Around The nearest metro station here is Insurgentes, unless stated otherwise.

Hotel Internacional Havre (☎ 5-211-00-82, Havre 21) has just 48 big, comfy rooms with nice furniture and TV, and fine views from the top floors. Singles/doubles are US$71/78. Management is helpful, and there's free guarded parking and an on-site restaurant.

Hotel Plaza Florencia (☎ 5-211-00-64, Avenida Florencia 61) is pleasant and modern, with 142 tasteful – though not huge – rooms all with one or two double beds, air-con, mini-bar and cable TV. Standard rooms are US$130 for one to four people, better ones go up to US$160. There's a restaurant.

The *Calinda Geneve & Spa* (☎ 5-211-00-71, 800-900-00-00, Londres 130), west of Génova, is older than most Zona Rosa hotels, but well kept, with a formal colonial lobby from which you can walk into a glass-canopied Sanborns restaurant or, at the other end, the popular Café Jardín (see Places to Eat). The 320 rooms, with a bit of period style, air-con, mini-bar and cable TV, cost US$115 a single or double. As the name advertises, there's also a spa.

The 326-room *Hotel Aristos* (☎ 5-211-01-12, Reforma 276) is on the corner of the popular restaurant street Copenhague. Rooms are not huge but comfortable and pleasant enough. The hotel sports a bar with mariachis, and two nightclubs. The regular room price is US$117 single or double, but promotions often cut that by more than half.

Hotel Marquis Reforma (☎ 5-211-36-00, Paseo de la Reforma 465), at Río de la Plata (Ⓜ Sevilla), opened in 1991 with design and decor that draw from the city's rich art deco heritage and update it for the 21st century. It has lots of colored marble, well-trained multilingual staff, and facilities such as an outdoor spa with whirlpool baths. The 98 deluxe rooms cost US$293 and the 110 lavish suites are from US$387.

María Isabel-Sheraton Hotel (☎ 5-207-39-33, 800-325-3535 in the USA, Paseo de la Reforma 325), at the Monumento a la Independencia (El Ángel), is older (1962), but as attractive and solidly comfortable as ever with spacious public rooms, excellent food and drink, nightly mariachi entertainment, and all the services of a top-class hotel, including pool, fitness and medical centers and two lighted tennis courts. The 755 reasonably sized rooms and suites offer all the comforts. Standard rooms cost US$234 single or double.

Other Zona Rosa hotels include:

Hotel Marco Polo (☎ 5-511-18-39, Amberes 27, marcopolo@data.net.mx) – this trendy lodging attracts foreign customers from the art and business worlds; 60 stylishly modern rooms at US$164/188 a single/double

Four Seasons Hotel (☎ 5-230-18-18, Reforma 500) – refined, modern, business-oriented hotel with most of its 240 spacious rooms overlooking a handsome garden-courtyard; singles/doubles start at US$280/315 (Ⓜ Sevilla)

Colonia Roma An elegant small hotel in a modernized early-20th-century mansion, *La Casona* (☎ 5-286-30-01, at Durango 280, casona@data.net.mx) has tasteful rooms for US$144 single or double, including continental breakfast. There's also a reasonably priced little restaurant on site. Book ahead (Ⓜ Sevilla).

Polanco The Polanco area, just north of Bosque de Chapultepec, has some of the city's best business hotels – including three high-rises in a row along Campos Elíseos. Metro is Auditorio, unless otherwise stated:

Camino Real México (☎ 5-203-21-21, Calzada General Escobedo 700) – bold, modern architecture, 713 rooms from US$244 single or double, but US$117 including breakfast Friday and Saturday (Ⓜ Chapultepec)

Hotel Nikko México (☎ 5-280-11-11, 800-908-88-00, Campos Elíseos 204) – 745-room high-rise blending modern luxury with excellent service in a dramatically designed building; standard rooms are US$328 single or double but discounts may be available Friday to Sunday nights

Hotel Presidente Inter-Continental (☎ 5-327-77-00, 800-904-44-00, Campos Elíseos 218) – six quality restaurants and 659 spacious, modern rooms from US$375

JW Marriott Hotel (☎ 5-282-88-88, Andrés Bello 29) – 312 rooms and suites costing from US$280 single or double (from US$210 including breakfast on Friday and Saturday nights)

PLACES TO EAT

This cosmopolitan capital has eateries for all tastes and budgets, with plenty of European, North American, Middle Eastern, Asian and Argentine restaurants as well as Mexican ones. Some of the best places are cheap; some of the more expensive ones are well worth the extra money. In the few restaurants we describe as formal, men should wear a jacket and tie, and women something commensurate. Phone numbers are given for places where it's worth reserving a table.

The city's cheapest food is at its thousands of street stands – see Food in the Facts for the Visitor chapter for a word on these.

Chain Restaurants

The city is liberally provided with modern chain restaurants whose predictable food is a sound fallback if you fancy somewhere easy and reliable, if not often inspired, to eat. Numerous branches of *VIPS* and *Sanborns*, with Mexican and international food, are found in affluent and touristed parts of the city such as the Zona Rosa, the Alameda area and Paseo de la Reforma. At both places salads, *antojitos* and toasted sandwiches cost around US$2.50 to US$4.50, with most main dishes from US$4 to US$6. You'll find several branches of these major chains shown on our maps. Less widespread chains include the cheery *Taco Inn* (serving tacos), *Sushi Itto* (Japanese food), *Potzollcalli* (Mexican food) and the wide-ranging *Los Bisquets Bisquets Obregón* and *El Portón*. International chains such as *Pizza Hut*, *McDonald's* and *KFC* are here too.

Centro Histórico

For places to eat overlooking the zócalo, see 'Square Meals: Eating around the Zócalo.'

Budget The *Café El Popular* (*Avenida Cinco de Mayo 52*), 1½ blocks west of the Zócalo, is a good, cheap neighborhood place with tightly packed tables, open 24 hours a day. They serve good breakfasts (fruit, eggs, *frijoles*, roll and coffee for US$2), and all

Diners at the ubiquitous VIPS

JOHN NEUBAUER

sorts of other food, such as a quarter chicken with mole or *carne asada a la tampiqueña* (both around US$2.50). Good, strong *café con leche* is US$0.70. A second branch of *Café El Popular* (*Avenida Cinco de Mayo 10*) has the same menu, more space and bright yellow plastic furnishings.

Café La Blanca (*Avenida Cinco de Mayo 40*), west of Isabel la Católica, is big, always busy, and good for people-watching over a café con leche (US$1). You can have their three-course lunch for US$3.75.

A good place to start the day is *Los Bisquets Bisquets Obregón* (*Madero 29* and *Tacuba 85*), serving combination breakfasts which include coffee, juice, roll and *pan dulce* as well as a main egg or meat dish, for US$3.50 to US$4.50. At lunchtime a two-course comida with a drink costs the same. Hours are 7.30 am to 10.30 am daily.

At *La Casa del Pavo* (*Motolinía 40A*), chefs in white aprons slice roast turkeys all day long and serve them up at low prices. The four-course *comida corrida* offers good value at US$2.50, and there are turkey tacos and turkey tortas too.

Taco Inn on Plaza Tolsá, outside the Museo Nacional de Arte, offers more than 30 good taco choices from US$1.30 to US$3.25 a serving. For something filling, the *Hawaiiano Inn* (four tacos with beef, pineapple, cheese and ham) at US$2.75 is good. There's a three-taco *vegetariano* option for US$2.

Taquería Tlaquepaque (*Isabel la Católica 16*) is a good answer to late-night hunger. Three tasty tacos cost between US$0.50 and US$2.50 depending on what's in them. It's open 7 am to 3 am Monday to Saturday, to 1 am Sunday night. *Tacos Beguis* (*Isabel la Católica 8*), just up the street, is another decent *taquería*: most varieties are US$0.40.

Potzollcalli, on Cinco de Mayo just east of Motolinía, is one in a chain of clean, bright and good Mexican restaurants, with specialties like *taquiza mixta* (five types of taco with rice) and chicken or meat grills all around US$5.

Rincón Mexicano (*Uruguay 27*) and *Antojitos Tere* (*Uruguay 29*), both west of Bolívar, are tiny hole-in-the-wall eateries with home cooking and very low prices. A set lunch at either costs just US$1.50. They're open till 6 pm daily except Sunday.

The Hotel Isabel's *Restaurant Isabel (Isabel la Católica 63)* does breakfasts for US$2.25 to US$3.50, decent-value two-course dinners for US$3.25 to US$4.50, and a wide range of reasonably priced á la carte fare.

Vegetarian & Juice Bars Don't be put off by the unimpressive stairway entrance to *Restaurante El Vegetariano (Avenida Madero 56)*: upstairs are three busy, high-ceilinged rooms where a pianist plunks out old favorites as you dine. The food is tasty, filling and an excellent value: three- or four-course lunches go for US$3 or US$3.25. It's open 8.30 am to 6.30 pm daily except Sunday. There's a more modern, street-level branch nearby *(Mata 13)*.

Comedor Vegetariano (Motolinía 31) serves up a good US$2.50 comida from 1 to 5 pm daily.

Jugos Canadá (2ª Cerrada de Cinco de Mayo), on Avenida Cinco de Mayo next door to the Hotel Canadá, is good to pop into for a refreshing pure fruit juice, *licuado* or fruit salad. A *cóctel biónico* of five fruit juices, condensed milk, granola and cocoa, is yours for US$1.25.

Super Soya (16 de Septiembre 79), opposite the Gran Hotel Ciudad de México, is in a similar vein, with an array of gaudy signs listing all the juices, licuados, fruit salads, tortas and tacos it can manage. You could wash down a couple of vegetarian tacos (US$0.50 each) with a 'Dracula' – mixed beetroot, pineapple, celery and orange juice (US$1). It's open 9 am to 9.30 pm Monday to Saturday, 11 am to 8 pm Sunday.

Coffee One quick caffeine stop is *The Coffee Factory*, on Madero just east of Sanborns Casa de Azulejos, open daily. Espresso costs US$1, cappuccino US$1.75. Prices are about half that at tiny *Café del Centro* almost opposite the Hotel Catedral on Donceles; it has good cakes, muffins and burritos too.

Mid-Range & Top End *Café de Tacuba (☎ 5-518-49-50, Tacuba 28)*, just west of Allende metro station, is a gem of old-time

Mexico City, opened in 1912. Colored tiles, stained glass, brass lamps and oil paintings set the mood. The cuisine is traditional Mexican and delicious. There's a five-course lunch for US$8 (plus drinks). À la carte main dishes are US$4.50 to US$8.75. It's open 8 am to 11.30 pm daily.

The restaurants in *Sanborns Casa de Azulejos (Avenida Madero 4)* are worth a visit just to see the 16th-century tile-bedecked building housing them (see Things to See & Do). The main restaurant is in a covered courtyard around a Moorish fountain, with odd murals of mythical landscapes. The food is Mexican and good, if not exceptional, at about US$2.50 to US$4.50 for *platillos mexicanos* and US$5 to US$6 per main dish. The ground-floor lunch-counter section in the northwest corner of the building, and another restaurant above it, have similar prices but less atmosphere. All eating areas are open from 7 am to 1 am.

Pizza Hut, on La Palma just south of Avenida Cinco de Mayo, charges US$5.50 to US$8 for its pizzas.

La Esquina del Pibe (Bolívar 51), at Uruguay, is a busy Argentine grill house, one of the more economical of this popular type of establishment. There's a set lunch for US$5.25, and à la carte grills for US$6 to US$10.50. Four people can get a combined mixed grill for US$18.50 or US$30. It's open 1 to 11 pm daily (to 8 pm on Sunday).

Restaurante Danubio (☎ 5-512-09-76, Uruguay 3) has been here, specializing in seafood, since the 1930s, and still does it well. It serves a huge and excellent six-course set-price lunch – including fish *and* meat courses – for US$7.50. À la carte fish main courses are mostly around US$6 to US$8.50. Lobster *(langosta)* and crayfish *(langostinos)* are the specialties, but prices for them are stratospheric. The Danubio is open 1 to 10 pm daily, but you'll be lucky to get a table for Sunday lunch.

Hostería de Santo Domingo (Belisario Domínguez 72), six blocks northwest of the Zócalo, is small but intense and atmospheric. Handicrafts crowd the walls and ceiling, good and unusual regional cooking fills the menu and the customers. A typical

Square Meals: Eating Around the Zócalo

Two average eateries at the northwest corner of the Zócalo have sidewalk tables that are good for watching the city in action. *Shakey's Pizza y Pollo* does pizzas (US$4.25 to US$8.75 for the smallest size), chicken nuggets and so on. *Flash Taco* offers Mexican and Tex-Mex staples (two tacos US$0.90 to US$2.75, fajitas US$3.75).

For a truly marvelous view, head up to the *Restaurante El Campanario/Cafetería El Invernadero* (5 de Mayo 61) on the roof of the Holiday Inn Select hotel, almost within touching distance of the Catedral Metropolitana's bells and with a magnificent panorama over the Zócalo and much of the rest of the city. They serve a buffet breakfast for US$6.50. Later in the day, most main dishes are US$5 to US$7. You can also enjoy the view just for the price of a drink.

Restaurante Terraza (Avenida Madero 73) overlooks the Zócalo from the 7th floor of the Hotel Majestic. The daily buffet breakfast is US$7, and Monday to Friday there's a set lunch for US$5.50 (Saturday and Sunday it's buffet lunch for US$10.50). You can have something lighter or à la carte if you wish.

Cafetería Mirador (16 de Septiembre 82), on the top floor of the Gran Hotel Ciudad de México, has a small terrace with a great view over the Zócalo. Buffet breakfast is US$6.

La Casa de las Sirenas (Guatemala 32), in a 17th-century house just behind the cathedral, serves up excellent alta cocina Mexicana on its terrace, which has views of the Zócalo, Palacio Nacional and Templo Mayor. Soups and salads are good here. Meat, seafood and poultry main dishes are mostly US$7.50 to US$11, and you could finish off with a crêpe for US$5. To drink – well, the Sirenas offers over 250 varieties of tequila, costing from US$2 to US$13.50 a shot, in the restaurant or in the Salones Tequila on the lower floors. Hours are 8 am to 11 pm Monday to Saturday, 8 am to 7 pm Sunday.

---

three-course à la carte meal costs about US$12. It's open 9 am to 10.30 pm Monday to Saturday, 9 am to 9 pm Sunday. A pianist or a trio plays from 3 pm.

Los Girasoles (☎ 5-510-06-30, *Plaza Tolsá*), beside the Museo Nacional de Arte, is one of the best of a recent wave of restaurants specializing in *alta cocina Mexicana* (Mexican *haute cuisine*). Recipes are either traditional or innovative but all with a very Mexican flavor. You might start with *crema de tres quesos* (three-cheese soup) and follow up with *Sábados 1 a 3* (Sonoran ranch-style beef medallions with *chipotle*). Starters and soups are mostly US$3.50 to US$6.50, main courses US$6 to US$9.50. Los Girasoles is open 1.30 pm to midnight Monday to Saturday, 1.30 to 4 pm Sunday. There are pleasant outside tables as well as indoor seating.

Alameda Central & Around
Budget One of the prettiest, most peaceful restaurants in the city is the *Cafetería del*

Claustro, or Cloister Café (*Avenida Hidalgo 45*), in the Museo Franz Mayer opposite the north side of the Alameda. The museum and café are open 10 am to 5 pm Tuesday to Sunday: if you only want to visit the café you need a US$0.50 ticket for the cloister. Marble-top tables are set in the lovely courtyard, with taped baroque music setting the mood. The good, self-service food includes sandwiches, salads, quiche and excellent cakes for US$1 to US$1.50.

Café Trevi on Dr Mora, facing the west side of the Alameda, is a good Italian and Mexican restaurant, open 8 am to 11.30 pm daily. It serves breakfasts till noon for US$1.70 to US$2.50, and its six-course set-price daily meal is just US$2.50. Pasta dishes and one-person pizzas range from US$1.75 to US$4.

One block south of the southeast corner of the Alameda, there's a cluster of bright, inexpensive eateries around the intersection of Independencia and López. Pick of the bunch is the clean, bustling *Taquería Tla-quepaque (Independencia 4)*, where bow-tied waiters serve up dozens of types of taco, priced at US$0.90 to US$3.25 for three. The *chuletas, nopales y queso* variety (chopped pork, cactus tips and cheese), at the top of the range, is delicious.

For a taste of lingering Spanish influence in Mexico, you can't beat a helping of *churros y chocolate*. Churros are long, thin, deep-fried doughnuts, just made to be dipped in a cup of thick hot chocolate. A fine spot for this experience is *Churrería El Moro (San Juan de Letrán 42)*, on the Eje Central 2½ blocks south of the Torre Latino-americana, where chocolate with four churros sets you back US$2. It's always open, and often busy in the wee hours with people winding down after a night on the town.

Vegetarian The *Centro Naturista de México (Dolores 10B)*, half a block south of the Alameda, is a health food shop with a vegetarian restaurant serving lunches of soup, two main courses, salad, dessert, bread, water, tortillas and dessert for US$2, or an all-you-can-eat buffet for US$2.50, from 12.30 to 7 pm daily.

Markets The best and freshest produce in the city is generally agreed to be at *Mercado San Juan*, on Pugibet west of Plaza de San Juan, 500m south of the Alameda, open 8 am to 5 pm daily (to 4 pm Sunday and holidays). Here you'll find rarities such as tofu, and *chapulines* (grasshoppers) from Oaxaca, as well as good fruit, vegetables, cheese, meat and fish.

Mid-Range The Palacio de Bellas Artes' elegant *Café del Palacio* serves salads for US$4 to US$5.50 and tempting *emparedados* (sandwiches), including smoked salmon, smoked turkey and cream cheese varieties, for US$4 to US$7.

Mexico City has a small Chinatown centered on Dolores south of the Alameda. One of the best restaurants here is the small *Hong King (Dolores 25)*, with set meals from US$4.50 to US$9 per person (minimum two people) and menus in Chinese,

Spanish and English. Most à la carte dishes cost between US3.25 and US$6, though some vegetarian offerings are under US$3. It's open 12.30 pm to 11 pm every day.

Plaza de la República & Around

There are several small, homey, neighborhood restaurants here. *Restaurant Cahuich (Ramos Arizpe 30)*, at Édison, is a good, clean little place where a breakfast of juice, eggs and coffee, or a comida corrida, will set you back about US$2.50. There's well-priced à la carte fare too, and it's open 8 am to 1 am daily. *Restaurante Samy (Mariscal 42)* is also clean and pleasant, offering fixed-price breakfasts for US$1 to US$2, and a four-course comida corrida for US$2.25.

At *Super Cocina Los Arcos (Iglesias 26)*, at Mariscal, US$1.50 to US$2.50 could buy you breakfast, or three tacos, or *bistec* prepared in one of several ways, or plenty of other staples. Across the corner, *El Tigre* serves tasty hot tortas with fillings of ham, egg, cheese and so on for about US$0.90 to US$1.50, plus tacos, *sincronizadas*, juices and licuados.

Potzollcalli, on Arriaga just south of Puente de Alvarado, has the same menu and prices as the Cinco de Mayo branch (see Centro Histórico).

A great place for a quick lunch is the *seafood cocktail stand* on Emparán just north of Édison. It has stood here daily (except Sunday) since at least the mid-1980s and includes many besuited office workers among its regular customers. A *mediano* (medium-size) prawn or crab cocktail at US$2.50 is filling, and there are even bigger ones at US$4.50.

About 100m south of Plaza de la República on Ramírez, next to a branch of VIPS, *Tacos El Caminero* is a busy, slightly upscale taquería doling out three good tacos for US$2.25, or six for US$3.75. It stays open till 1 am (11 pm on Sunday).

Zona Rosa

The Zona Rosa is packed with places to eat and drink. Some streets are closed to traffic, making the sidewalk cafés more pleasant.

Budget Some of the cheapest meals are at the *Mercado Insurgentes* on Londres. One corner of this crafts market is given over to typical Mexican market *comedores*, serving up hot lunches daily to customers who sit on benches in front of the cooks and their stoves. You'll find many of the same typical Mexican dishes here as you would in restaurants, at much lower prices – around US$1.75 for a comida corrida. Pick one that's busy.

A bit farther west along Londres are some of the area's most economical restaurants, the best of them packed at lunchtime. *Ricocina (Londres 168)* does a three-course comida including drinks for US$3 to US$3.50, and breakfasts such as juice, coffee and eggs/hot cakes/French toast for US$2.25. The four-course, US$3 comida offered at *La Beatricita (Londres 190D)* includes drinks.

Another decent cheap comida is served at the nameless little comedor beside Java Chat cybercafé in an alley off Génova. Three courses here cost only US$1.50.

An excellent choice for good, quick tacos is *Taco Inn (Hamburgo 96)*, opposite Copenhague near the hub of the Zona Rosa, part of the same chain as the Taco Inn on Plaza Tolsá (see Centro Histórico, earlier).

Junk food junkies will be in heaven on Génova between Hamburgo and Liverpool, where *Dunkin' Donuts, Burger King, McDonald's* and *KFC* all congregate. On the corner of Génova and Hamburgo is delicious *Häagen-Dazs* ice cream.

Mid-Range The perennially popular *Konditori (Génova 61)* serves a mixture of Italian, Scandinavian and Mexican fare in its elegant small dining rooms and spacious sidewalk café, which is a good spot for people-watching on the Zona Rosa's busiest pedestrian street. Pasta or good pancake dishes cost around US$4, meat or fish US$5.50 to US$7, and there are good cakes and pastries. It's open 8 am to 11.30 pm daily.

Parri Pollo Restaurante (Hamburgo 154) is a busy, barn-like place serving grilled beef, pork and chicken in various ways, from tacos to steaks or whole birds. Staff tend the grill and scurry to and fro. You can eat three tacos for US$2, but you're more likely to spend US$5.50 or more on a main course and a drink. It's open 8 or 9 am to midnight or later, daily.

If Japanese food is your fancy, try *Sushi Itto (Hamburgo 141)*, a no-fuss little chain eatery with moderately priced sushi and sashimi, and combination meals from US$7 to US$10.

The pleasant, modern *Café Jardín (Londres 130)*, attached to the Calinda Geneve & Spa hotel, does a reasonable-value US$6 buffet lunch as well as à la carte fare from burgers or enchiladas to meat or fish, all around US$4 to US$6.

One of the Zona Rosa's busiest restaurant streets is Copenhague, a single block lined with bustling mid-range and upscale eateries. *Freedom (Copenhague 25)* is both a lively bar (see Entertainment) and a good Tex-Mex/US restaurant doing barbecued ribs, nachos, pasta, burgers, salads and the like. Most main dishes are between US$5 and US$8. Also good and popular are the *Mesón del Perro Andaluz (☎ 5-514-74-80, Copenhague 26)*, serving meat and seafood – with some Spanish dishes as its name suggests – and *El Perro d'Enfrente (☎ 5-511-89-37)* with Italian food. Main dishes in both are mostly between US$5 and US$7.50.

Yuppie's Sports Café (Génova 34), at Hamburgo, is a sort of American-style lounge/café/bar where (if you can cope with the place's name *and* being searched on the door) you can eat around a low table in big, comfy easy chairs, or sit at the bar. There are lots of TVs and baseball photos. Salads, burgers and pizzas are US$3.50 to US$5, steaks from US$9.50.

The *Carrousel Internacional (Niza 33)* is a lively bar/restaurant with mariachis singing energetically most of the time. Come for spaghetti or a salad (around US$4) or a grill or fish (US$6 to US$8), or a drink, and enjoy the music. It's open 11.30 am to midnight daily.

Chalet Suizo (Niza 37) has dependably good food well served in mock Swiss rusticity. They have fondues and a range of meat dishes, including duck in orange sauce, between US$5.50 and US$9 per person. It's open noon to midnight daily.

Across the street, **Luaú** (Niza 38) is a Chinese-Polynesian fantasy with fountains and miniature gardens. The best deals are the set-price Cantonese meals at US$5.50 to US$14 per person. Hours are noon to 11 pm daily (to midnight Friday and Saturday, to 10 pm Sunday).

Vegetarian The good **Restaurante Vegetariano Yug** (Varsovia 3), just south of Reforma, does a lunch buffet for US$4 from 1 to 5 pm daily, and daily four-course comidas corridas with good wholewheat bread for a little less. There's à la carte fare too. The clientele are mostly local office workers.

A couple of blocks north of the Zona Rosa, the big, leafy and attractive **Restaurante Vegetariano Las Fuentes** (Río Pánuco 127) serves tasty food in large portions. Full meals of soup, salad bar, main course and a drink cost US$7.25; big breakfasts are US$4.25. It's open 8 am to 6 pm daily.

Coffee The **Auseba** (Hamburgo 159B) has glass cases filled with enticing cakes and other sweet offerings, and large windows for watching Hamburgo go by. Most cakes and pastries are around US$2 each, but you can get a *pan danés* (Danish pastry) for US$0.70. Tea and coffee are between US$1.25 and US$1.75.

Handy for good coffee and cakes is the **Coffee House** (Londres 106), just east of Génova. They have espresso for US$0.90 and slices of good cheesecake from US$2.

Top End The **Angus Butcher House** (☎ 5-207-68-80, Copenhague 31), on the corner of Hamburgo, serves fine steaks, for which you can pay anywhere from US$9 to US$27, and it's always thronged. There's a good outdoor area under an awning as well as indoor tables. It's open daily from 1 pm to 1 am.

Harry's Bar (Liverpool 155) – the entrance is on Amberes – is a bright grill/steakhouse-style place popular with gringos and Mexicans. TV screens show sports most of the time. Steaks, chicken and seafood are mostly US$7 or US$8. It's open daily except

Sunday. In the same chain and also popular is **Anderson's de Reforma** (Reforma 382), at Oxford, open daily. The many varieties of steak and seafood go for US$8 and up. Both places make a cover charge of US$1.25.

One of the city's best sophisticated and formal restaurants lies 1½ blocks from the Zona Rosa, just north of Reforma. This is the French **Les Moustaches** (☎ 5-533-33-90, Río Sena 88), where starters cost from US$4.50 up to *pâté de foie gras* at around US$17, and main courses – chicken, duck, meat or fish – are from US$8.50 to about US$17. For dessert, there are tempting crêpes and soufflés around US$5. Many tables are in an elegant greenery-filled patio. Les Moustaches is open 1 pm to midnight Monday to Saturday.

Condesa

This relaxed, fashionable and agreeable neighborhood 1 to 2km south of the Zona Rosa has suddenly, since the mid-1990s, become the hub of the Mexico City eating-out scene. Its leafy streets have sprouted dozens of informal, mid-range, bistro-style restaurants and good cafés, many with sidewalk tables. Cuisines from all over the globe are represented here.

Condesa's culinary heart is the intersection of Avenida Michoacán, Vicente Suárez and Atlixco, 500m west of Parque México. One long-established place here is **Fonda Garufa** (Avenida Michoacán 91), serving up a big range of good pasta, vegetarian brochettes and salads for US$3 to US$4.50, plus seafood and other grills. It's open 1 pm to midnight daily (to 1 am Thursday to Saturday, to 11 pm Sunday).

Mama Rosa's (Atlixco 105) and **Café La Gloria** (Vicente Suárez 41), on the same intersection, are in a similar vein. The hugely popular Mama Rosa's serves almost everything from chicken, wood-oven pizzas and meat dishes – all around US$6 to US$8.50 – to pasta, salads and seafood. Go by about 8 pm to ensure a table for dinner. La Gloria cooks up French, Italian, Japanese and other fare, with pasta and salads around US$4, and chicken/fish/meat for US$5.50 to US$8.50. **Creperie de la Paix**, also here, is very popular for its variety of sweet and savory crêpes from US$2.50 to US$4. The busy *La Buena Tierra* *(Atlixco 94)* characterizes its food as *'gastronómica natural'*. Specialties include whole wheat *focaccia* and pita-bread tacos (US$2.50 to US$4.50). For a starter (US$2 to US$4), try smoked marlin or *arroz Buena Tierra* (whole grain rice with vegetables, fruit and curry). Pasta, fish and chicken main dishes cost from US$3.50 to US$7. There are big juice concoctions too.

El Zorzal (☎ 5-553-51-81), on Vicente Suárez just east of Avenida Michoacán, serves up classic Argentine steaks and is immensely popular – you'll spend US$10 to US$15 on a full meal with a drinks. *Café La Selva* *(Vicente Suárez 38)* on the same block serves good organic coffee from Chiapas, produced by a group of small-scale indigenous coffee growers.

Just east of Avenida Tamaulipas, the Algerian *Le Cous-Coussier* *(Avenida Michoacán 74)* specializes (of course) in good couscous, at US$5 to US$6. *El Tizoncito* *(Avenida Tamaulipas 122 at Campeche)* serves up excellent *tacos al pastor* till 3.30 am for around US$0.80 each, with fillings such as fish, prawn and chicken. Half a block north on Tamaulipas is the Japanese deli *Sushi Shalala*.

Farther north, *Il Principio* *(Montes de Oca 17 at Avenida Tamaulipas)* is good for Mediterranean food, from lentil soup with banana at US$2.25 to risotto for around US$7. It's open from 1.30 pm to 12.30 or 1.30 am daily.

Amar Kemel *(Montes de Oca 43)* serves generous quantities of excellent Middle Eastern food: falafel, kofta kebabs, tabuli and hummus are all priced between US$3 and US$5, and there are soups, salads, pita bread tacos, and dishes based on *kepe* (ground beef), rice, fish and chicken. For a selection of varied starters with pita bread, ask for the *messe*. Hours are 1.30 to 11 pm Monday to Wednesday, 1.30 pm to midnight Thursday to Saturday, 1.30 to 8 pm Sunday.

Tierra Gaucha *(Montes de Oca 18)* is a little less expensive than other Condesa Argentine steak houses – US$6 to US$9 for steaks and other meats.

Chapultepec & Polanco
Budget & Mid-Range There's a reasonable restaurant inside the *Museo Nacional de Antropología*, open the museum's hours. Mexican and international main dishes are mostly between US$4 and US$7. *Rincón Seco*, also called *Café Capuchino*, 200m north of the museum entrance, is a basic, open-air eatery with tortas at US$1, or meat, salad and fries for US$2.50.

For meat eaters, a good economical choice in Polanco is *La Parrilla Suiza*, on the traffic circle at Avenida Presidente Masaryk and Arquímedes, 600m northwest of the Museo Nacional de Antropología. It gets packed at lunchtime, when it serves a comida for US$2.50. Mixed grills go for US$6, taco serves US$1.50 to US$2.50. It's open noon to midnight or later, daily.

Café de Tacuba *(Newton 88)*, northeast of Arquímedes, is a pleasant little place with colored windows, a beamed ceiling and a bit of character, serving Mexican and international fare. Set-price lunches cost US$4 or US$7, and it serves good breakfasts too.

For other moderately priced fare in Polanco, head for Avenida Presidente Masaryk, between Dumas and France, where a string of sidewalk cafés lines the south side of the street. Among them are *Klein's* *(Masaryk 360B)*, serving breakfasts, antojitos and hot and cold tortas from US$2, and meat or chicken dishes for US$5 to US$7, and the busy *Garabatos* *(Masaryk 350)*, with deli sandwiches for US$5 to US$7 and a US$4.50 *menú del día* Monday to Friday.

Not far away, on France, is a busy branch of Condesa's popular *La Buena Tierra*, open 7 am to 11 pm daily. Another successful Condesa restaurant with a Polanco branch is *Creperie de la Paix* *(France 79)*.

The *Kings Pub* *(Arquímedes 31)* does good steaks for US$8-plus, and pasta and salads for around US$4, in surroundings vaguely reminiscent of an old-fashioned English pub.

Top End *Cambalache* (☎ 5-280-20-80, *Arquímedes 85)*, just north of Avenida Presidente Masaryk, is a cozy Argentine steak house, serving up great steaks from US$10.50

to US$12.50, chicken from US$8.50 and pasta around US$5.50. There's an ample wine list. Hours are 1 pm to 1 am daily.

Dominique on Campos Elíseos offers tempting French Caribbean food, full of tropical fruits and vegetables, fish and juicy meat, with a spicy oriental and/or classical French touch. Most main dishes cost US$7 to US$12. The formal *La Gran Casona* (☎ 5-280-78-33, *Dumas 4*) offers tip-top Mexican cuisine in an elegant setting. Starters are around US$5 to US$10, main dishes US$10 to US$15. It's open noon to midnight daily.

La Hacienda de los Morales (☎ 5-281-45-54, *Vázquez de Mella 525*) is about 1.5km northwest of the middle of Polanco, south of Avenida Ejército Nacional. It's easiest to go by taxi. Once a colonial country hacienda, it's now surrounded by the city, which makes the spacious rooms and pretty gardens all the more appealing. Excellent Mexican and international dishes – with some particularly good fish choices – are served in numerous dining rooms by the experienced staff. A three-course meal with drinks will cost around US$25 to US$40. Reservations are advisable, and dress is formal for dinner (though not for lunch). It's open 1 pm to 1 am daily.

Polanco's luxury hotels contain some of the city's best restaurants – among them three French highlights, all open Monday to Saturday: *Maxim's de Paris* (☎ 5-327-77-00, *Hotel Presidente Inter-Continental, Campos Elíseos 218*), with a dinner-dance Friday and Saturday nights; *Les Célébrités* (☎ 5-280-11-11, *Hotel Nikko México, Campos Elíseos 204*); and *Fouquet's de Paris* (☎ 5-203-21-21, *Camino Real México, Calzada General Escobedo 700*). All are formal, with reservations recommended, and a full dinner at any of them runs US$30 to US$50 (maybe more at Maxim's).

San Ángel
Budget & Mid-Range The nameless little comedor on the east side of Plaza San Jacinto next to Restaurante La Vuelta offers a good comida corrida for US$2, and on Saturday and Sunday great *caldo de camarón* (prawn soup) for US$2.50 or US$3.75. *La Casona del Elefante* (*Plaza San Jacinto 9*) is

an Indian restaurant with a few pleasant outdoor tables, and not a bad value with a vegetarian *thali* plate for US$4, or chicken curry for US$3.50.

Crêperie du Soleil, on Madero near Plaza del Carmen, does tempting *crepas* (sweet US$1 to US$2, savory US$2.50 to US$3.50), tortas and coffee.

The famous bookstore *Gandhi* (*Avenida MA de Quevedo 128 to 132*), 400m east of Parque de la Bombilla (Ⓜ MA de Quevedo), has a welcome café where customers linger over coffee, snacks, books, newspapers and chess – open 9 am to 11 pm Monday to Friday, 10 am to 10 pm Saturday and Sunday.

Avenida de la Paz between Revolución and Insurgentes is thick with places to eat. *Cluny* (*Avenida de la Paz 57*) serves up a scrumptious variety of crepas (savory US$5 to US$6, sweet around US$4) – open 1 pm to midnight daily (to 11 pm Sunday) – but you'll often have to wait for a table in the evening. Across the street, *Le Petit Cluny* (*Avenida de la Paz 58*) is probably San Ángel's best and most popular Italian restaurant. Quality pizza and pasta costs around US$6 or US$7 – open 8 am to midnight Tuesday to Saturday, 8 am to 10.30 pm Sunday.

The winner by a mile of our prize for Mexico City's best-decorated restaurant is the *Modern Art Café* in Plaza Opción, the mall neighboring Plaza Loreto in southern San Ángel. This is an art gallery *and* restaurant, with its walls covered in bright contemporary paintings and its floor dotted with quirky modern sculpture. Even the chairs you sit on and the plates you eat off are works of art. Nearly all of it's for sale. The food is brick-oven pizzas, pasta, burgers, salads, meat, in the US$5 to US$9 range, and there's a bar too. It's all open Sunday to Thursday 1 pm to midnight, Friday and Saturday 1 pm to 3 or 4 am.

Top End The liveliest place on Plaza San Jacinto is *La Camelia*, with people waiting in line to enjoy its seafood (US$7 to US$13) and trendy atmosphere.

Carnivores could do much worse than head for Camino al Desierto de los Leones between Revoluciòn and Insurgentes, where you'll the popular find *Carlos 'n Charlie's* serving meat and fish dishes for around US$8, and the *Angus Butcher House* with fine steaks from US$9 to US$27.

To dine in style, head for the *San Ángel Inn* (☎ 5-616-14-02, *Diego Rivera 50*), a 15-minute walk northwest of Plaza San Jacinto. This is an ex-hacienda with a lovely flowery courtyard and gardens, transformed into a restaurant serving delicious Mexican and European cuisine. Ordering carefully, you can eat two courses for US$9, but you could easily spend US$25 or more on a full meal. It's open 1 pm to 1 am daily.

Coyoacán

For inexpensive Mexican fare, leave Plaza Hidalgo along Higuera. The municipal building on the left is filled with stands charging US$0.60 apiece for quesadillas with various tasty fillings. Or go half a block north from the plaza to the cheerful *El Tizoncito* (*Aguayo 3*), which serves up many varieties of taco, including shrimp, fish and *nopalqueso* (cactus tips and cheese), at US$0.60 to US$1 each. South of the plaza, there's a *Taco Inn* (see Centro Histórico, earlier) at Carrillo Puerto and Carranza.

A good spot for breakfast, snacks or coffee is *Moheli*, a café-cum-gallery on Sosa a few steps from the Jardín del Centenario. Yogurt, fruit, granola and honey will cost you US$2, a Greek salad US$3, or a bagel with salami US$2.50.

The bright *Café Kowloon* (*Jardín del Centenario 6*) and *Café Chou Sou*, just south on Carrillo Puerto, both serve Chinese set lunches for US$2.75 to US$4.

Among the many pleasant cafés around the Jardín del Centenario is fashionable *Café El Parnaso*, with a bookstore in the back. Good burritos and croissants with ham and cheese, *pan árabe* (pita bread) tacos and set breakfasts all cost between US$2.50 and US$3.50. *Restaurante Caballocalco* (*Higuera 2*), facing the east side of Plaza Hidalgo, is relaxed and not too expensive, with good soups from US$2.25 to US$3.25, and meat and seafood for US$4 to US$10.

The excellent *El Jardín del Pulpo* (The Octopus's Garden), on the corner of Coyoa-

cán's main market, on Allende 2½ blocks north of Plaza Hidalgo, serves fish platters at US$6.50 to US$7 and seafood cocktails or *caldos* (broths) at US$3 to US$5. Everyone sits on benches at long tables.

Merendero Las Lupitas lies 700m west of the Jardín del Centenario, on Plaza Santa Catarina, conveniently close to the Viveros de Coyoacán. This friendly, colorful little place serves a variety of typical Mexican dishes with the flavor of home cooking for all three meals: snacks and antojitos are about US$3 to US$5, main courses US$4 to US$8.

ENTERTAINMENT

There's a vast choice of entertainment in Mexico City, as a glance through *Tiempo Libre*, the city's pretty comprehensive what's-on magazine, will show. *Tiempo Libre*, published every Thursday, is sold at newsstands (US$0.70) and appears on the Internet at www.tiempolibre.com.mx. Even with limited Spanish, it's not too hard to decipher what's going on, from music and movies to exhibitions and lots of entertainment for children. *The News* and Mexican newspapers also carry some what's-on information.

Major gigs by Mexican and visiting rock and pop performers often take place at the *Auditorio Nacional* (☎ 5-280-92-50, *Paseo de la Reforma 50, Bosque de Chapultepec*). The ticket agency Ticketmaster (☎ 5-325-90-00) sells tickets for many of these and other big events, and lists them in its free monthly leaflet, *La Guía de Entretenimiento*. Ticketmaster sales outlets include:

Auditorio Nacional
Paseo de la Reforma 50, Bosque de Chapultepec

El Palacio de Hierro
Durango 230, Colonia Roma

Mixup music store
Avenida Madero 51, Centro Histórico
Génova 76, Zona Rosa
Plaza Loreto, San Ángel

Dance, Classical Music & Theater

The *Palacio de Bellas Artes* (☎ 5-512-25-93), beside the Alameda Central, is home to the Orquesta Sinfónica Nacional (National

Symphony Orchestra) and is a big venue for classical music in general, but its most famous show is the Ballet Folklórico de México, a two-hour festive blur of costumes, music and dance from all over Mexico. This famous company has been performing such shows since the 1950s and they are as spectacular and professional as ever. Tickets are not cheap, however, at US$12 to US$29. Performances are normally at 8.30 pm on Wednesday, and 9.30 am and 8.30 pm on Sunday. Tickets are usually available on the day of the show or the day before at the *taquillas* (ticket windows) in the Bellas Artes lobby, open 11 am to 7 pm Monday to Saturday, 9 am to 7 pm Sunday. You can also get them from Ticketmaster.

The city also offers a big choice of other classical concerts, ballet and contemporary dance, as well as Spanish-language theater. Check *Tiempo Libre*.

Cinemas

Foreign movies (except for children's and educational films) are always shown in their original language, with Spanish subtitles. Cinema tickets are usually around US$2, half-price in most cinemas on Wednesdays. Classic and art-house films are shown at the *Cineteca Nacional* (☎ 5-688-32-72, *Avenida México-Coyoacán 389*), 700m east of the Coyoacán metro station; *Cinemanía* (☎ 5-616-48-36, *Plaza Loreto*), San Ángel; the *Centro Cultural Universitario* (☎ 5-665-25-80, *Avenida Insurgentes Sur 3000*) in the Ciudad Universitaria, and elsewhere. *The News* has partial cinema listings on Friday and Sunday.

Mariachis

Plaza Garibaldi, five blocks north of the Palacio de Bellas Artes (Ⓜ Bellas Artes or Garibaldi), is where the city's mariachi bands gather in the evenings. Outfitted in their fancy costumes, they tootle their trumpets, tune their guitars and stand around with a drink until approached by someone who'll pay for a song (about US$5) or whisk them away to entertain at a party. You can wander and listen to the mariachis in the plaza for free, and stay on in one of the bars

or clubs around the plaza, some of which have live Latin dance music as a change from the mariachis. The bars usually have no entry fee and typically charge around US$2 for a shot of tequila or US$20 for a bottle – ask prices *before* you order drinks in these places. *El Tenampa* bar, on the north side of the plaza, has in-house mariachis and is daubed with murals of Mexican film stars. For food, there are taquerías in the northeast corner of the plaza.

The place gets going by about 8 pm and stays busy till around midnight.

Nightlife

The 'Espectáculos Nocturnos,' 'Espectáculos Populares' and 'Bares y Cantinas' sections in *Tiempo Libre* have fairly good information on live music events, bars/clubs, dance halls, cabaret, jazz and more.

Centro Histórico Youthful bars and dance clubs in marvelous old palacios and mansions are the chief nocturnal draw downtown. Friday and Saturday nights, from about 10 pm, are the happening times. Places veer rapidly in and out of mode. If you seek out some of the following, crowds on the street will guide you to others.

Altura (☎ 5-510-98-55, *Uruguay 87*), at Cinco de Febrero – rooftop dancing Wednesday to Sunday from 9 pm atop a dramatically lit, medieval palacelike building; men pay around US$6, women free (Ⓜ Zócalo)

Bar Mata (☎ 5-518-02-37, *Mata 11, 4th floor*), at Avenida Cinco de Mayo – one of the original Centro clubs, with a casual atmosphere, good music and a roof terrace with great views; most drinks around US$2.75; open 8 pm to 2 am Wednesday to Saturday, no cover charge (Ⓜ Bellas Artes)

El Cirio (*Carranza 73*), in the 18th-century Antiguo Palacio de los Condes de Xala – latest rage as we researched this edition; clean casual is the look (Ⓜ Zócalo)

La Llorona (☎ 5-709-84-20, *Mesones 87*), at Cinco de Febrero – the most popular Centro club at the time of writing; young, not very hip-looking crowd, men wearing collars; beautiful colonial mansion but bouncers like to keep crowds waiting outside; open Thursday to Saturday from 9.30 pm, entry US$13 (Ⓜ Pino Suárez)

Opulencia (☎ 5-512-04-17, *Isabel la Católica 26*), at Madero – a good street-corner upstairs location with big windows, lilac lighting and a young, average-Joe sort of crowd; open from 10 pm Friday and Saturday only; men pay US$17, women free, drinks free (Ⓜ Allende)

Pervert Lounge (☎ 5-518-09-76, *Uruguay 70*) – a different, more offbeat crowd, house, trip-hop, acid jazz; open Wednesday to Saturday from 11 pm, entry US$6 (Ⓜ Allende)

A very different type of club, neither flashy nor trendy but a lot of fun, is the little *Restaurante-Bar León* (☎ 5-510-30-93, *Brasil 5*). Live salsa, merengue and rumba rhythms drive customers to the tightly packed dance floor 9 pm to 3 am Wednesday to Saturday – cover charge is US$3.50 (women free on Thursday); drinks are US$2 and up. The nearest metro stations are Allende and Zócalo.

La Ópera Bar (☎ 5-512-89-59, *Avenida Cinco de Mayo 14*), a block east of the Palacio de Bellas Artes (Ⓜ Allende), is an ornate early-20th-century watering hole that opened its doors to women in the 1970s. Booths of dark wood and a massive bar are all original, and there's a hole in the ceiling said to have been made by a bullet from Pancho Villa. Drinks cost US$1.75 and up, lots of food is served at middling prices, and musicians serenade. It's a fun place to spend a couple of hours – open 1 pm to midnight Monday to Saturday, 1 to 6 pm Sunday.

Beer lovers should make for the no-frills *Salón Corona* (*Bolívar 24*). Amiable staff serve up *tarros* (mugs) of light or dark *cerveza de barril* (draft beer) and bottles of almost every known Mexican beer for US$1.25 each. You can accompany your ale with all sorts of tacos for US$0.60 to US$0.80 each, or a bowl of *caldo de camarones* (shrimp soup, US$0.90). The Corona, going since 1928, is open 8 am to 11.30 pm daily.

East & South of the Zona Rosa Bars come and bars go, but the hub of a fun scene of younger (20 to 40) expats, associated Mexicans and some travelers recently has been a couple of cool bars a few blocks east of the Zona Rosa. There's no cover at either.

El Colmillo (☎ 5-592-61-14, *Versalles 52*), a groovy hangout run by a pair of British clubbers, is open from 9 or 10 pm to 4 am Wednesday to Saturday. Downstairs there's loud dance music, a dance floor and a bar/lounge area; upstairs there's jazz Thursday to Saturday. Cover is US$4.50 for one or the other, US$6.50 for both. A beer is US$2, cocktails from US$4.50. The door doesn't keep people waiting long.

Bar Milán (☎ 5-592-00-31, *Milán 18*), owned by well-known Mexican actor Demian Bichir, is really a fairly straightforward music bar, open 9 pm to 2 am nightly except Monday. But it plays great, varied music and gets packed by about midnight on Friday and Saturday. A beer is US$2, cocktails from US$2, tequila from US$2.75.

The spot for live Cuban *son*, very popular with Mexico City's expat community, is *Mama Rumba* (☎ 5-564-69-20, *Querétaro 230*), in Colonia Roma, 1km south of the Zona Rosa. The music starts around 11 pm nightly except Monday, and it's funkiest from Thursday to Saturday. Cover is US$3.50 to US$4 (women free Tuesday). The bar is small and tightly packed, but you can't miss its bright neon lights as you approach.

Zona Rosa The glitzy Zona Rosa (Ⓜ Insurgentes) peaks from about 11 pm to 2 or 3 am on Friday and Saturday. At times the Zona can seem pretty sleazy with so many dark suited doorway-blockers with greased-back hair and so many touts trying to talk passersby into 'table dances' and 'ladies' bars, no koh-vair-r-r-r-r-r.' (Ladies bars' are striptease joints; table dance clubs have women who for a fee will dance with, and sit on the knees of, male customers.) But there are plenty of fun places too. They change by the year. Those mentioned here are some of those most worth heading for.

Cantina Las Bohemias, on Londres west of Amberes, is a bright, jolly place popular with women as well as men (it's not a *real* cantina). A beer is US$1 to US$1.50, spirits from US$1.25. *Freedom* (*Copenhague 25*) gets busy in the evening with a youngish after-work crowd. It has at least three bars on two levels, plays loud dance music, and is fun. A beer is US$2. There's just about room to dance upstairs, and good food downstairs. Another popular but more expensive bar-cum-restaurant is *Yuppie's Sports Bar* *(Génova 34)*, at Hamburgo.

For live music, the *Carrousel Internacional* restaurant/bar *(Niza 33)*, at Hamburgo, has mariachis singing energetically most of the time (see Places to Eat), and a loud and lively disco section next door (cover US$5).

Live, very raw heavy rock can be experienced 6 pm to midnight nightly at *La Casa del Canto (Glorieta Insurgentes CC-04)*, near the exit of Insurgentes metro station. It's a small, very basic place which allows the decibels full effect (cover US$1.25).

A popular dance club, *Caramba (☎ 5-553-55-31, Génova 44)* attracts a youngish, mainly Mexican crowd with its varied music – open 9 pm to 4 am Thursday to Saturday (men pay US$15, women free till 10.30 pm, US$10 after 10.30 pm; drinks free). There are several more clubs around the Zona Rosa, especially on Niza and Avenida Florencia.

Polanco This well-heeled neighborhood north of the Bosque de Chapultepec gets quite lively after dark. *Barfly (☎ 5-282-26-56)* in Plaza Mazarik, on Avenida Presidente Masaryk between France and Lafontaine, jumps to live Cuban sounds from 11.30 pm Tuesday to Saturday (cover US$6). Upstairs in neighboring Plaza Zentro, *Circo (☎ 5-282-27-29, Avenida Presidente Masaryk 407)* is a popular bar with live music, usually rock-oriented, after 11 pm Wednesday to Sunday (cover US$3.50), and the thriving Italian restaurant *Mezzanotte (☎ 5-282-01-30)* jumps with a New-York-club-style dance floor Thursday to Saturday nights.

Insurgentes Sur & San Ángel Mexico City has produced some great rock bands but is short on good venues. All the more reason, therefore, to be grateful for *Rocko-titlán (☎ 5-687-78-93, Insurgentes Sur 953)*, on Plaza Baja California, a time-honored stage for homegrown Mexican rock music. The graffiti-daubed, cavelike space presents live bands – usually up-and-coming outfits –

nightly except Monday, usually at 10 pm. Entry is US$2 to US$10 depending who's on (and a beer is US$1.50). If you like this kind of thing, it's fun. You can drop by to pick up a schedule. About the easiest way to get there is by a 'San Ángel' pesero southbound on Insurgentes from Insurgentes metro station for 4.5km.

In San Ángel itself, the Indian restaurant *La Casona del Elefante (☎ 5-616-22-08, Plaza San Jacinto 9)* puts on live jazz from 10 pm to 1 am Friday and Saturday (no cover). In the evenings *La Camelia* restaurant on Plaza San Jacinto becomes a lively, almost rowdy music bar for an 18-35 crowd, with beer at US$2 and cocktails and tequila from US$3.50. *New Orleans Jazz (☎ 5-550-19-08, Avenida Revolución 1655)* serves up good, varied jazz from 8 or 9 pm Tuesday to Saturday. It's a restaurant too (spaghetti, crêpes, chicken – all US$3.50 to US$5). There's a cover charge of US$2.50 to US$5.

Bar Grappa (☎ 5-616-45-04), upstairs in Pabellón Altavista mall at Avenida Revolución and Camino al Desierto de los Leones, San Ángel, is a fun place with a youngish, chic-ish crowd. The space, not designed for quiet, intimate conversation, is long and dark, with a large video screen and loud mixed music. It is open from 9.30 pm Thursday to Saturday (men US$7, women free).

Coyoacán For free entertainment, you can't beat the musicians, comedians and mimes who turn Coyoacán's central plazas into a big open-air party most evenings, and all day Saturday and Sunday. There are also good cafés and bars around the plaza, where you can take in the atmosphere. *El Hijo del Cuervo (☎ 5-659-51-96, Jardín del Centenario 17)*, with a youngish crowd of Mexicans and foreigners, plays a mixture of recorded Mexican and gringo rock, and stages occasional live music or theater. It gets busy most evenings (open 1 pm to midnight Tuesday to Sunday, 5 pm to midnight Monday). A beer is US$1.75, tequila from US$2.25.

Dance Halls The city's many Latin dance aficionados have a whole circuit of large *salones de baile*, some capable of holding thousands of people. You need to dress smart and know how to dance salsa, merengue, cumbia or danzón to really enjoy these places, and it's best to go in a group, or at least with someone to dance with. A good one is *Antillanos* (☎ 5-592-04-39, *Pimentel 78, Colonia San Rafael*), 1.5km north of the Zona Rosa (Ⓜ San Cosme). Top bands from Mexico, Cuba, Puerto Rico or Colombia grind out infectious rhythms Tuesday to Saturday from 9 pm to 3 am. Entry is US$5. Tequila, rum and whisky are served by the bottle at around US$20.

Meneo (☎ 5-523-94-48, *Nueva York 315*) just west of Insurgentes Sur, has salsa and merengue bands from 9 pm to 3 am Thursday to Saturday. Entry costs around US$8 and men must wear a jacket; to get there, take a 'San Ángel' pesero 5km south from Insurgentes metro station.

Gay & Lesbian Venues The Zona Rosa is the focus of the gay scene. One of the longest-established spots is the relaxed bar *El Almacén* (☎ 5-207-07-27, *Avenida Florencia 37A*), open daily from 4.30 pm and welcoming lesbians as well as gay men. Downstairs is the pounding men-only disco-bar *El Taller* (☎ 5-533-49-84), open 9 pm to 4 am daily except Monday (US$3 cover Thursday to Saturday), with a darkroom.

A fashionable disco, mainly for men, is *El Antro* (☎ 5-511-16-13, *Londres 77*), open Wednesday to Sunday nights with a piano bar, video lounge, darkroom, big dance floor and a variety of good shows and strippers (cover US$3 to US$5).

Cabaré-Tito (☎ 5-514-94-55, *Local 20A Interior, Plaza del Ángel, Londres 161*) is an innovative gay bar/disco/theater often featuring cabaret, drama or discussion sessions. The venue is open from 1 pm daily and attracts a wide range of people including some heterosexuals.

Butterfly (☎ 5-761-18-81, *Izazaga 5*) is a big, hi-tech gay dance club with great music, a few steps east of Eje Central Lázaro Cárdenas (Ⓜ Salto del Agua). It is open from 9 pm to 4 am nightly. The US$3.50 cover includes two drinks.

Enigma (☎ 5-207-73-67, *Morelia 111, Colonia Roma*), 700m south of Cuauhtémoc metro, is a mainly lesbian disco-bar with regular transvestite shows. It's open from 9 pm to 3.30 am Monday to Saturday, from 6 pm to 2 am Sunday. Entry ranges from free to US$3.50.

Sergay magazine, available free in some of the above clubs and bars, has useful information on the Mexico City gay scene. It's on the Internet at www.sergay.com.mx. Also check *Don Pato's Gay Mexico City* (www.donpato.com/bars.html). *Tiempo Libre* has long gay listings on its website.

SPECTATOR SPORTS
Soccer (Football)

The capital stages two or three matches in the national Primera División almost every weekend from August to May. *The News* carries details on upcoming games. The Mexico City team América, nicknamed Las Águilas (the Eagles), is the most popular in the country. Las Pumas, of UNAM, come second in popularity in the capital, with Cruz Azul (known as Los Cementeros) third.

The biggest crowds flock to games between any pairing of América, Las Pumas, Cruz Azul and Guadalajara (Las Chivas), which is the biggest club outside the capital. The biggest match of all is 'El Clásico,' between América and Guadalajara, which fills the awesome Estadio Azteca with 100,000 flag-waving fans – an occasion surprising for the friendliness of the rivalry between the two bands of fans. This is about the only game of the year in the capital where you should get a ticket in advance.

Most big matches are played at the Estadio Azteca (☎ 5-617-80-80, *Calzada de Tlalpan 3465*). When games are on, peseros run to the stadium from Tasqueña metro station; you can also get there by the Tren Ligero (streetcar) from Tasqueña metro station to Estadio Azteca station. The Pumas' home is the Estadio Olímpico at the Ciudad Universitaria, and Cruz Azul's is the Estadio Azul at Indiana 260, next door to the Monumental Plaza México bullring (see Bullfights). Tickets for games are usually available at the gate right up to kickoff;

prices range from less than US$1 to about US$10.

Baseball

Mexico City has two teams in the Liga Mexicana de Béisbol, the Diablos Rojos (officially Club México) and the Tigres. Both play at the Parque del Seguro Social (Avenida Cuauhtémoc 462), a block south of Centro Médico metro station. The season runs from March to August and crowds approach 10,000 when the two local teams play each other. Games usually start at 6.30 pm. Ticketmaster (see Entertainment) sells tickets for games and lists dates in its *La Guía de Entretenimiento*. *Afición* sports paper also details upcoming games.

Bullfights

The Monumental Plaza México (☎ 5-563-39-61, Rodin 241), a deep concrete bowl holding 48,000 spectators, is one of the largest bullrings in the world. It's a few blocks west of Avenida Insurgentes Sur, 5.5km south of Paseo de la Reforma and a 10-minute walk from San Antonio metro station. 'Plaza México' peseros run along Insurgentes Sur on bullfight afternoons.

If you're not put off by its very concept, a *corrida de toros* (bullfight) is quite a spectacle, from the milling throngs and hawkers outside the arena to the pageantry and drama in the ring itself and the crowd response it provokes. Six bulls are usually fought in an afternoon, two each by three matadors.

The spectacle of the *corrida de toros*

From October or November to March or April, professional fights are held at the Monumental most Sundays, starting at 4 pm. From June to October, junior matadors fight young bulls. *The News* runs a weekly bullfighting column, 'Blood on the Sand,' which will tell you what's in store.

The taquillas (ticket windows) by the bullring's main entrance on Rodin have printed lists of ticket prices. The cheapest seats, less than US$2, are in the Sol General section – the top tiers of seating on the sunny side of the arena. These are OK if the weather's not too hot – and many of them fall into shade as the afternoon goes on, in any case. The Sombra General – the top tiers on the shady side – costs slightly more. The best seats are in the Barreras, the seven rows nearest the arena, and normally cost US$15 to US$25. Between the Barreras and the General sections are first the Primer (1er) Tendido, then the Segundo (2o) Tendido.

Except for the biggest corridas, tickets are available right up to the time the third bull is killed, though the best seats may sell out early. You can buy advance tickets from 9.30 am to 1 pm and 3.30 to 7 pm Thursday to Saturday, and from 9.30 am onward Sunday. Most major hotels and many travel agencies also sell tickets at a mark-up.

For more on bullfights, see 'The Fiesta Brava' in the Facts for the Visitor chapter.

Jai Alai

This old Basque game, reminiscent of squash, is fast and elegant when played by experts, and some of the best is played at the Frontón México (☎ 5-546-32-40) at Plaza de la República (Ⓜ Revolución). At this writing the Frontón had been closed for over two years by a strike of its workers. When it's in action, the attraction for spectators is not just the game but the chance to bet on it. Before the strike, games were played nightly except Monday almost all year, starting at 7 pm (5 pm on Sunday). Admission around US$5. It's something of an upperclass sport: officially, formal dress is required (jacket and tie for men), but in practice visitors may get away with less.

SHOPPING
Shops

The well-heeled of Mexico City do a lot of their shopping in department stores and modern malls. The malls are full of designer clothing and shoe stores, toy shops, jewelers, cosmeticians, sometimes a music store. Among the more interesting of them, for their design or for the shops themselves, are Plaza Loreto, between Altamirano and Río de la Magdalena in San Ángel; Pabellón Altavista at Avenida Revolución and Camino al Desierto de los Leones, San Ángel; Perisur at Periférico Sur 4690, near the intersection with Avenida Insurgentes Sur, with several large department stores; and Plaza Molière at Molière and Horacio in Polanco.

One of the biggest and best handicrafts stores in the city is the government-run Fonart, out at Patriotismo 691 between the Bosque de Chapultepec and San Ángel (600m north of Mixcoac metro station). The store holds beautiful wares from around the country ranging from Olinalá lacquered boxes and Oaxacan *alebrijes* to blankets from Teotitlán del Valle, all sorts of attractive pottery and a big variety of glassware. Prices are fixed and fair. Fonart is open 9 am to 8 pm Monday to Saturday, 10 am to 7 pm Sunday. Three good areas of the city for smaller stores are the Centro Histórico, the Zona Rosa and Polanco.

Centro Histórico The streets south, west and north of the Zócalo are full of shops specializing in everyday goods, from shoes or screws to fireworks or cakes. You'll find clusters of similar shops all together on the same street or block – for example photography and camera repair shops around the intersection of Brasil and Donceles, sports gear and backpacks on Carranza west of Bolívar, bridal gowns on Chile north of Tacuba, shoe shops on 16 de Septiembre, Pino Suárez and 20 de Noviembre, stationery on El Salvador between Cinco de Febrero and Bolívar. About 50 computer stores huddle in the Plaza de la Computación y Electrónica on Eje Central Lázaro Cárdenas, south of Uruguay.

There are also two large department stores, both open daily, within a block south of the Zócalo: El Palacio de Hierro on Cinco de Febrero, and Liverpool at Venustiano Carranza 92.

For delicate Mexican sweets such as candied fruits, sugared almonds and crystallized strawberries, as well as honey and fruit jams, go to Dulcería de Celaya, Avenida Cinco de Mayo 39, west of Isabel la Católica. These treats cost US$0.25 or more apiece, but anyone can afford at least one or two. The *dulcería* is open every day from 10.30 am to 7 pm.

Zona Rosa This is a good area for boutiques and art and antique shops. Plaza La Rosa, an arcade between Hamburgo and Londres just west of Génova, is a good place to start if you're after clothes. Plaza del Ángel, another arcade between Hamburgo and Londres, this time just west of Amberes, has many classy antique and art shops.

Tower Records at Niza 19 and Mixup at Génova 76 are two of the biggest music stores in the city. The steps leading up from the plaza around Insurgentes metro station to Génova are lined by stalls selling bootleg cassette tapes at US$2 or so each.

Polanco Designer clothing houses are strung along Avenida Presidente Masaryk in the blocks west of France. The futuristic-looking Plaza Molière mall at Molière and Horacio includes a branch of El Palacio de Hierro department store, dealing mainly in clothes, toys and cosmetics.

Markets

There are numerous interesting markets around the city where you can buy all sorts of Mexican handicrafts, souvenirs and everyday goods.

Mercado Insurgentes This stretches from Londres to Liverpool, just west of Amberes in the Zona Rosa (Ⓜ Insurgentes). It's packed with Mexican crafts – silver, textiles, pottery, leather, carved wood figures – and is open 9 am to 7.30 pm Monday to Saturday, 10 am to 4 pm Sunday. You need to bargain a bit to get sensible prices.

La Ciudadela & San Juan About 600m south of the Alameda, on Balderas at Dondé (Ⓜ Balderas), the Centro de Artesanías La Ciudadela is full of crafts at prices that are fair even before you try to bargain. You'll find brightly dyed sarapes, pretty lacquerware boxes and trays, masks, silver jewelry, pottery, Huichol bead masks, guitars, maracas – and baskets of every shape and size, some large enough to hide in. It's open daily.

The Mercado de Artesanías San Juan, four blocks east at Dolores and Ayuntamiento (Ⓜ San Juan de Letrán), has a similar range of goods and prices that are, if anything, a little cheaper. It's open 9 am to 7 pm Monday to Sunday, 9 am to 4 pm Sunday.

La Lagunilla & Tepito Two of the city's biggest markets, both open daily, merge into each other along Rayón and Héroe de Granaditas, 1km north of the Zócalo. Both deal mainly in everyday wares, and they're lively, crowded places. Garibaldi metro station is just west of La Lagunilla. Lagunilla metro station serves both markets.

La Lagunilla is centered on three large buildings. Building No 1 is full of clothes and fabrics, No 2 is for furniture, and No 3 is devoted to *comestibles* (food). Tepito takes over where La Lagunilla ends and stretches several hundred meters east along Rayón and Héroe de Granaditas and deep into most of the side streets. Much of what's sold here is said to be *fayuca* (contraband), and the market has a reputation for pickpockets and thieves – so take care. It's composed mainly of street-side stalls and focuses on clothes (new and second-hand), antiques and leisure goods such as videotapes, CD players, TVs, Rollerblades and toys – which gives it a particularly fun atmosphere. The only large building, at Héroe de Granaditas and Aztecas, is packed with every kind of shoe and boot you could imagine.

Centro Artesanal Buenavista Just east of the Buenavista train station, at Aldama 187, this large handicrafts 'market' is actually a huge fixed-price store. Much adver-

tised and often visited by tour groups, it has a vast assortment of stuff. Some of it is quality – but bargains can be scarce. It's open 9 am to 6 pm daily.

Tianguis Cultural del Chopo This unusual little market, held from about 10 am to 4 pm every Saturday on Hidalgo just north of the Centro Artesanal Buenavista, is devoted mainly to punk and death metal music and fashions, but some stalls specialize in other musical genres such as rock, Cuban music and Mexican regional sounds.

La Merced & Sonora The Mercado La Merced, 1km southeast of the Zócalo, occupies four whole blocks dedicated to the buying and selling of Mexicans' daily needs, which makes for an interesting wander. A couple of blocks south, on the south side of Fray Servando Teresa de Mier, is Mercado Sonora, which has four diverse specialties: toys, caged birds, herbs and folk medicine. Merced metro station is in the middle of La Merced market.

Bazar Sábado The 'Saturday Bazaar,' at Plaza San Jacinto 11 in the southern suburb San Ángel, is a showcase for some of Mexico's very best handcrafted jewelry, woodwork, ceramics and textiles. Prices are high but so is quality. It's held from 10 am to 7 pm every Saturday. At the same time, artists and artisans display work in Plaza San Jacinto itself, in surrounding streets and in nearby Plaza del Carmen. There are some interesting boutiques and antique shops between the two plazas too.

Coyoacán On Saturday and Sunday a colorful jewelry and craft market spreads over much of Coyoacán's central Jardín del Centenario. Hippie jewelry, Mexican indigenous crafts, leatherwork and tie-dye clothes are among the stocks-in-trade. The Bazar Artesanal de Coyoacán, on the west side of the adjoining Plaza Hidalgo (open Saturday and Sunday only), and Pasaje Coyoacán, 1½ blocks farther north, at Aguayo and Cuauhtémoc (open daily except Monday), have more crafts.

GETTING THERE & AWAY
Air
For information on international and domestic flights and departure taxes, see the Getting There & Away and Getting Around chapters, respectively.

Airport Aeropuerto Internacional Benito Juárez (☎ 5-571-36-00), 6km east of the Zócalo, is Mexico City's only passenger airport (Ⓜ Terminal Aérea).

The single terminal is divided into six *salas* (halls):

Sala A – domestic arrivals

Sala B – check-in for Aeroméxico, Mexicana and Aero California, Aeromar and some other domestic flights; Hotel Marriott

Sala C – check-in for Aviacsa and Aerolíneas Internacionales

Sala D – check-in for TAESA and some other domestic flights

Sala E – international arrivals

Sala F – international flights check-in; Hilton Hotel

The terminal has hosts of shops and facilities, including some good bookstores. You can change money at many bank branches and casas de cambio: Tamize in Sala E is one casa de cambio that stays open 24 hours. You can also obtain pesos from numerous ATMs.

There are plenty of pay phones and telephone casetas (call stations), plus shops selling cards for the pay phones. In Salas A and E are car rental agencies and luggage lockers, open 24 hours (US$3 for up to 24 hours). Sala A has a tourist information office (☎ 5-762-67-73) open 9 am to 8.30 pm daily (it will book hotel rooms for you), and post and telegraph offices.

The airport is a bad place to buy film. You'll almost certainly find a better range and prices at your destination. Direct buses to Cuernavaca, Querétaro, Celaya, Pachuca, Toluca and Puebla depart from outside Sala D. Most go roughly hourly from about 7 am to 9 pm.

Airlines If you already have an onward air ticket from Mexico City, you're all set. If not, a visit to a couple of the city's many travel agencies (see this chapter's Information

section) is a good way of finding a suitable ticket. Here's where to find the offices of major domestic and international airlines:

Aero California
(☎ 5-207-13-92) Paseo de la Reforma 332

Aerocaribe
(☎ 5-448-30-00) Xola 535, Piso 28, Colonia del Valle, or through Mexicana

Aeroexo
(☎ 5-716-90-04) Airport

Aerolíneas Argentinas
(☎ 5-130-30-30) Paseo de la Reforma 24

Aerolíneas Internacionales
(☎ 5-543-12-23) Beistegui 815, Colonia Del Valle

Aerolitoral
Same as Aeroméxico

Aeromar
(☎ 5-627-02-07) Airport

Aeroméxico
(☎ 5-133-40-00) 14 offices around the city, including Paseo de la Reforma 80 and Paseo de la Reforma 445

Air France
(☎ 5-627-60-60) Poe 90, Polanco

Alaska Airlines
(☎ 5-208-38-12) Hamburgo 213, 10th floor, Zona Rosa

Alitalia
(☎ 5-533-55-90) Río Tiber 103, 6th floor, Colonia Cuauhtémoc

Allegro
(☎ 5-564-15-32) Baja California 128, Colonia Roma Sur

America West
(☎ 5-514-01-94) Río Tíber 103, 6th floor, Colonia Cuauhtémoc

American Airlines
(☎ 5-209-14-00) Paseo de la Reforma 300

Aviacsa
(☎ 5-716-90-04) Airport

Aviateca
(☎ 5-211-66-04) Paseo de la Reforma 509, Lomas de Chapultepec

British Airways
(☎ 5-387-03-00) Balmes 8, Colonia Los Morales

Canadian Airlines
(☎ 5-208-18-83) Paseo de la Reforma 385, 14th floor

Continental Airlines
(☎ 5-283-55-00) Andrés Bello 45, Polanco

MEXICO CITY

Cubana
(☎ 5-250-63-55) Temístocles 246, Polanco

Delta Airlines
(☎ 5-279-09-09) Horacio 1855, Polanco

Iberia
(☎ 5-130-30-30) Paseo de la Reforma 24

Japan Air Lines
(☎ 5-533-55-15) Paseo de la Reforma 295

KLM
(☎ 5-202-44-44) Paseo de las Palmas 735, 7th floor, Lomas de Chapultepec

LACSA
(☎ 5-211-66-04) Paseo de la Reforma 509, Lomas de Chapultepec

Lufthansa
(☎ 5-230-00-00) Paseo de las Palmas 239, Lomas de Chapultepec

Mexicana
(☎ 5-448-09-90) 19 offices around the city, including Avenida Juárez 82 at Balderas and Paseo de la Reforma 312 at Amberes

Northwest Airlines
(☎ 5-202-44-44) Paseo de las Palmas 735, 7th floor, Lomas de Chapultepec

Qantas
(☎ 5-387-03-00) Balmes 8, Colonia Los Morales

TAESA
(☎ 5-227-07-00) Paseo de la Reforma 30

United Airlines
(☎ 5-627-02-22) Hamburgo 213, Zona Rosa

Bus

Mexico City has four main long-distance bus terminals, basically serving the four points of the compass: Terminal Norte (north), Terminal Oriente (called TAPO, east), Terminal Sur (south) and Terminal Poniente (west). All terminals have baggage checkrooms or lockers; toilets; newsstands; pay phones or casetas where you can make long-distance calls; post and fax offices; and cafeterias. There are also a few buses to nearby cities from Mexico City airport. Review the following for helpful tips on long-distance bus travel.

For trips up to five hours, just go to the bus station, buy your ticket and go. For longer trips, many buses leave in the evening or at night, and service may be limited, so buy your ticket in advance. Turismo Zócalo (☎ 5-510-92-19), Carranza 67 in the Centro Histórico, sells tickets for the deluxe ETN,

UNO and ADO GL services, which could save you an extra trip out to one of the bus stations. If you speak some Spanish, you can telephone bus companies to ask about schedules – they're listed in the phone directory's yellow pages under 'Camiones y Automóviles Foráneos para Pasajeros.'

Most destinations are served by just one of the four terminals, but for a few major destinations you have a choice of terminal. Some companies require you to check in luggage at their counter at least 30 minutes prior to departure.

Destinations See the 'Buses from Mexico City' table for a list of main daily services to a selection of destinations from Mexico City. More information can be found in other town and city sections of this book. It's all subject to change, of course!

Terminal Norte The Terminal Central Autobuses del Norte (☎ 5-587-52-00), Avenida de los Cien Metros 4907, is about 5km north of the Zócalo (Ⓜ Autobuses del Norte). It's the largest of the four terminals, and its name has many variations, including Autobuses del Norte, Central del Norte, Central Camionera del Norte, or just CN. It serves places north of Mexico City, plus Guadalajara, Puerto Vallarta, Colima and Manzanillo to the west, and Pachuca, Papantla and Tuxpan to the northeast.

More than 30 different bus companies offer services from this terminal. In the main, deluxe and 1st-class ticket counters are located in the southern half of the building (to the right as you enter from the street), and 2nd-class counters are in the northern half.

There are luggage checkrooms (guarda equipaje or guarderías) at the south end of the terminal (always open) as well as in the central passage. Both charge US$1 or US$2 per item per 24 hours, depending on size. Don't leave valuables in your bags.

Near the middle of the main concourse are a Distrito Federal tourist information module (☎ 5-587-15-52), open 9 am to 4 pm Monday to Friday, a Banorte ATM and a casa de cambio with poor rates.

Buses from Mexico City

Destination	Distance (km)	Journey (hours)	Terminal in Mexico City	Class	Bus Company	No of Daily Departures	Price (US$)
Acapulco	400	5 to 6	Sur	deluxe	Estrella de Oro	5	31
				deluxe	Turistar Ejecutivo	3	31
				1st	Futura	5	19
				1st	Estrella de Oro	21	20
				2nd	Futura	21	21
			Norte	1st	Estrella Blanca	9	22
Bahías de Huatulco	840 via Salina Cruz	14	Sur	1st	Cristóbal Colón	1	33
			Oriente	1st	Cristóbal Colón	1	33
	900 via Cuajinicuilapa	15	Sur	1st	Flecha Roja	1	35
Campeche	1360	20	Oriente	deluxe	ADO	1	57
				1st	ADO	3	49
Cancún	1772	20	Oriente	deluxe	ADO	1	75
				1st	ADO	3	63
Chetumal	1450	24	Oriente	1st	ADO	2	52
Chihuahua	1470	21	Norte	1st	Transportes Chihuahuaenses	19	76
				1st	Ómnibus de México	9	76
Ciudad Juárez	1840	24	Norte	1st	Futura/Elite	18	96
				1st	Ómnibus de México	9	96
Cuernavaca	90	1¼	Sur	1st	Pullman de Morelos	frequent	4
			Airport	1st	Pullman de Morelos	16	7
Guadalajara	535	7 to 8	Norte	deluxe	ETN	23	40
				1st	Primera Plus	27	30
				1st	Futura/Elite	19	28
				2nd	Flecha Amarilla	22	25
			Poniente	deluxe	ETN	5	40
Guanajuato	380	4½	Norte	deluxe	ETN	8	27
				1st	Primera Plus	10	22
				2nd	Flecha Amarilla	4	15.50
Jalapa	315	5	Oriente	deluxe	UNO	6	24
				deluxe	ADO	8	16
				1st	ADO	21	14
				2nd	AU	19	11
			Norte	1st	ADO	2	12
Matamoros	970	15	Norte	1st	Futura/Elite	5	51
Mazatlán	1041	17	Norte	1st	Futura/Elite	24	61
				1st	Transportes del Pacífico	16	61
				2nd	Transportes del Pacífico	3	53

Buses from Mexico City

Destination	Distance (km)	Journey (hours)	Terminal in Mexico City	Class	Bus Company	No of Daily Departures	Price (US$)
Mérida	1550	20	Oriente	deluxe	ADO	2	61
				1st	ADO	3	52
Mexicali	2667	40	Norte	1st	Futura/Elite	16	114
				1st	Transportes del Pacífico	12	114
				2nd	Transportes Norte de Sonora	9	99
Monterrey	934	11 or 12	Norte	deluxe	Estrella Blanca	10	65
				1st	Futura/Elite	18	49
Morelia	304	4	Poniente	deluxe	ETN	28	22
				1st	Pegasso Plus	35	16
				2nd	Herradura de Plata	11	16
				2nd	Vía Plus/2000	13	15
				2nd	México Toluca	13	13
				2nd	Zinacantepec y Ramales Flecha Amarilla	11	13
			Norte	1st	Primera Plus	19	17
				2nd	Flecha Amarilla	59	14
Nogales	2227	33	Norte	1st	Futura/Elite	5	113
				1st	Transportes del Pacífico	4	114
Nuevo Laredo	1158	15	Norte	deluxe	Estrella Blanca	5	84
				1st	Estrella Blanca	11	62
Oaxaca	442	6½	Oriente	deluxe	UNO	6	33
				deluxe	Cristóbal Colón	5	23
				1st	ADO	6	20
				1st	Cristóbal Colón	4	20
				2nd	AU	13	16 or 18*
			Norte	1st	ADO	6	20
			Sur	deluxe	Cristóbal Colón	1	23
				1st	Cristóbal Colón	3	20
Palenque	1010	16	Oriente	1st	ADO	2	39
Papantla	290	5	Norte	1st	ADO	5	11
Pátzcuaro	370	5	Poniente	1st	Pegasso Plus	10	16
				2nd	Flecha Amarilla	5	14.50
			Norte	1st	Primera Plus	2	16
				2nd	Herradura de Plata	6	15.50

*Cheaper fare is for longer nine-hour route

Buses from Mexico City

Destination	Distance (km)	Journey (hours)	Terminal in Mexico City	Class	Bus Company	No of Daily Departures	Price (US$)
Puebla	130	2	Oriente	deluxe	Estrella Roja	24	6.50
				deluxe	Pullman Plus		
				1st	Primera Más	53	5.50
				1st	ADO	frequent	6
				2nd	Estrella Roja	84	5
				2nd	AU	102	5
			Norte	1st	ADO	55	6
			Sur	1st	Cristóbal Colón	16	6
			Airport	2nd	Estrella Roja	42	8.50
Puerto Escondido	790 via Cuajinicuilapa	13	Sur	1st	Flecha Roja	1	32
	750 via Miahuatlán	13½	Sur	1st	Cristóbal Colón	1	32
Puerto Vallarta	880	12 to 13	Norte	1st	Futura/Elite	4	61
Querétaro	215	2½ to 3	Norte	deluxe	ETN	37	16
				1st	Primera Plus	48	13
				1st	Futura/Elite	48	12
				1st	Ómnibus de México	38	12
				2nd	Flecha Amarilla	82	10
			Airport	1st	Aero Plus	14	16
San Cristóbal de Las Casas	1065	19	Oriente	deluxe	UNO	1	67
				deluxe	Cristóbal Colón	1	48
				1st	Cristóbal Colón	3	43
				2nd	Cristóbal Colón	2	37
San Luis Potosí	417	5 to 6	Norte	deluxe	ETN	16	30
				1st	Primera Plus	6	25
				1st	Futura/Elite	24	22
				1st	Ómnibus de México	15	22
				2nd	Flecha Amarilla	19	20
San Miguel de Allende	280	3½ to 4	Norte	deluxe	ETN	4	22
				1st	Primera Plus	3	16
				1st	Pegasso Plus	2	16
				2nd	Flecha Amarilla	30	14
				2nd	Herradura de Plata	29	14
Tapachula	1110	19	Oriente	deluxe	Cristóbal Colón	2	51
				1st	Cristóbal Colón	4	44
Taxco	170	3	Sur	1st	Cuernavaca	10	8
				1st	Estrella de Oro	6	7.75

Buses from Mexico City

Destination	Distance (km)	Journey (hours)	Terminal in Mexico City	Class	Bus Company	No of Daily Departures	Price (US$)
Teotihuacán	50	1	Norte	2nd	Autobuses México-San Juan Teotihuacan	33**	1.50
Tepoztlán	80	1	Sur	1st	Pullman de Morelos	16	3.75
Tijuana	2837	42	Norte	1st	Futura/Elite	16	116
				1st	Transportes del Pacífico	12	116
Toluca	64	1	Poniente	deluxe	ETN	40	4
				1st	TMT	200	2.75
				2nd	Flecha Roja	165	2.50
			Airport	1st	TMT	19	3
Tula	65	1¼	Norte	1st	Ovni	21	3.50
				2nd	AVM	72	2.75
Tuxtla Gutiérrez	980	17	Oriente	deluxe	UNO	1	63
				deluxe	Cristóbal Colón	2	47
				1st	Cristóbal Colón	4	40
				2nd	Cristóbal Colón	2	35
Uruapan	430	6	Poniente	deluxe	ETN	7	27
				1st	Vía Plus/2000	13	19 or 20
				1st	Flecha Amarilla	5	18
			Norte	1st	Primera Plus	6	19
				2nd	Flecha Amarilla	3	17
Veracruz	430	5	Oriente	deluxe	UNO	6	33
				deluxe	ADO	15	24
				1st	ADO	17	20
				2nd	AU	18	17
			Norte	1st	ADO	5	20
Villahermosa	780	11	Oriente	deluxe	UNO	3	56
				deluxe	ADO	6	40
				1st	ADO	17	34
				2nd	AU	3	31
			Norte	deluxe	ADO	1	56
				1st	ADO	3	34
Zacatecas	600	6 to 8	Norte	1st	Ómnibus de México	15	35
Zihuatanejo	640	9	Sur	deluxe	Estrella de Oro	1	41
				1st	Estrella de Oro	3	27 to 31
				1st	Futura	3	33
			Poniente	2nd	México Toluca Zinacantepec y Ramales	4	16

**7 am to 3 pm; make sure your bus is heading for 'Los Pirámides'

Terminal Oriente (TAPO) The Terminal de Autobuses de Pasajeros de Oriente (☎ 5-762-59-77), usually known by its acronym TAPO, is at Calzada Ignacio Zaragoza 200, at the intersection with Avenida Eduardo Molina, about 2km east of the Zócalo (Ⓜ San Lázaro). This is the terminal for buses serving places east and southeast of Mexico City, including Puebla, central and southern Veracruz, Yucatán, Oaxaca and Chiapas.

There's a Banamex ATM, giving cash on Visa, Cirrus, MasterCard and Plus System cards, in the passage between the metro and the terminal's circular main hall. Luggage lockers are underneath the ticket hall of the Estrella Roja bus company.

Terminal Sur Terminal Central de Autobuses del Sur (☎ 5-689-97-95), at Avenida Tasqueña 1320, 10km south of the Zócalo (Ⓜ Tasqueña), operates buses to Tepoztlán, Cuernavaca, Taxco, Acapulco and other destinations. There are no money-changing facilities here.

Terminal Poniente The Terminal Poniente de Autobuses (☎ 5-271-45-19), on Avenida Sur 122 at Avenida Río de Tacubaya, is south of the Bosque de Chapultepec, 8km southwest of the Zócalo (Ⓜ Observatorio). This is the place for frequent shuttle services to nearby Toluca and for most buses to the state of Michoacán.

Airport Inter-city buses serving the airport leave and arrive outside the airport's Sala (Hall) D. Most leave hourly from about 7 am to 9 pm.

Train

The city's central station is the Terminal de Ferrocarriles Nacionales de México (FNM), better known as Estación Buenavista (Buenavista Station). It's a cavernous building at Insurgentes Norte and Mosqueta (Eje 1 Norte), 1.2km north of Plaza de la República.

Owing to the closure of most Mexican passenger train services (see the Getting Around chapter), only three trains were running to/from Mexico City at the time of research and their future was doubtful.

Tickets for morning trains are sold from 2 pm the day before. Tickets for night trains are sold from 9 am the same day. The station has an information desk (☎ 5-547-10-84, 5-547-10-97), open 8 am to 8 pm daily. Spanish is usually spoken here, but someone in the nearby public relations office will probably speak English; you'll be transferred to them if you need help on the phone. Downstairs from the main hall is a luggage checkroom, open 7.30 am to 9.30 pm daily (US$0.80 per item per day). Make calls from card phones upstairs, or from the telephone caseta in the main hall (which also has fax service).

Schedules and fares are subject to change; please confirm them in advance.

San Miguel de Allende & Saltillo Train No 1 leaves Mexico City for Saltillo on Monday, Wednesday and Friday. Train No 2 leaves Saltillo for Mexico City on Wednesday, Friday and Sunday. The one-way fare from Mexico City to Saltillo is US$18.50. Service beyond Saltillo to Monterrey and Nuevo Laredo was indefinitely suspended at the time of writing.

Train 1

departs	
Mexico City	9 am
Querétaro	12.55 pm
San Miguel de Allende	2.35 pm
San Luis Potosí	5.10 pm
arrives	
Saltillo	11.50 pm

Train 2

departs	
Saltillo	2.30 am
San Luis Potosí	10.05 am
San Miguel de Allende	1.09 pm
Querétaro	2.42 pm
arrives	
Mexico City	7 pm

Veracruz Two daily trains run from Mexico City to Veracruz via Orizaba, Fortín de las Flores and Córdoba, and vice versa. Train No 51 departs Mexico City at 8.45 am, reaching Veracruz at 7.20 pm; No 53 leaves at 8.15 pm, arriving at 5.50 am. Train No 52 leaves Veracruz at 8.20 am, reaching Mexico City at 7.10 pm, and No 54 leaves Veracruz at 10 pm, arriving at 7.40 am. One-way fares from Mexico City are US$5.25 to Córdoba and US$6.50 to Veracruz.

Car & Motorcycle

Touring Mexico City by car is strongly discouraged, unless you are familiar with the streets and have a healthy reserve of stamina and patience. You may, however, want to rent a car here for travel outside the city. If you're traveling through Mexico by car, find a hotel that has off-street parking (many do). For safety reasons, avoid driving alone at night in the city.

One hazard you will hopefully now be spared is the bogus traffic fine or bribe, extracted by traffic cops as a routine means of increasing their miserly salaries. In 1999, the city police chief Alejandro Gertz banned male traffic police from levying fines for motoring infractions in the Distrito Federal. Only the city's 64 female traffic officers were allowed to continue doing so. The anti-corruption measure was based on the theory that since women are not often the main household breadwinners, they will feel less pressure to supplement their earnings illegally.

Rental Many car rental companies, including the big international names, have offices at the airport and in or near the Zona Rosa; ask at any of the large hotels there. Most hotels can put you in touch with a car rental

Mexico City's gridlock

JOHN NEUBAUER

Driving Restrictions

As part of its efforts to combat pollution, Mexico City operates an Hoy No Circula (Don't Drive Today) program banning many vehicles, wherever they are registered, from being driven in the city between 5 am and 10 pm on one day each week. The major exceptions are cars of 1993 model or newer (supposedly less polluting), which have a *calcomanía de verificación* (verification hologram sticker) numbered 0. This sticker, obtained under the city's notoriously corrupt vehicle pollution assessment system, exempts the vehicle from the Hoy No Circula provisions.

For other vehicles (including foreign-registered ones), the last digit of the registration number determines the day when they cannot circulate. Any car may operate on Saturday and Sunday:

day	prohibited last digits
Monday	5, 6
Tuesday	7, 8
Wednesday	3, 4
Thursday	1, 2
Friday	9, 0
Saturday	–
Sunday	–

Several times a year, when ozone readings in the city top 240 IMECA points (see 'Mexico City's Air'), the city's environmental contingency plan comes into action, with a Doble Hoy No Circula (Double Don't Drive Today) rule. This rule affects vehicles with verification hologram No 2 (older, more polluting vehicles). Those with plates ending in an even digit are banned on the first day, and those ending in an odd digit are banned the next. If the contingency lasts into a third day, all hologram No 2 vehicles are banned.

Cars with hologram No 1 (intermediate polluters) follow the simple Hoy No Circula restrictions all the time, even during contingency phases one and two. Further information on the driving restriction program is available at ☎ 5-526-95-63 or online at www.sima.com.mx.

agent (who may be the hotel owner's brother-in-law). Prices vary quite a lot between agencies. The seemingly better deals offered by some small ones should be compared carefully with a larger international chain before you take the plunge. One local firm offering good rates is Casanova Chapultepec (☎ 5-514-04-49), at Avenida Chapultepec 442 on the fringe of the Zona Rosa, with VW sedans for US$30 a day, including tax, insurance and unlimited mileage (minimum two days, book one day ahead).

For more on car rentals, see the Getting Around chapter.

Ángeles Verdes The Green Angels (see the Breakdown Assistance section in the Getting Around chapter) can be contacted in Mexico City at ☎ 5-250-82-21.

GETTING AROUND

Crime levels make some precautions advisable on all transport (including taxis) – please read the Dangers & Annoyances section earlier in this chapter.

Mexico City has a good, cheap, easy-to-use metro (underground railway). Peseros (minibuses), buses and/or trolley buses ply all main routes and are also cheap and useful. Taxis are plentiful but some are potentially hazardous (see Dangers & Annoyances).

Obvious though it may sound, always look both ways when you cross a street. Some one-way streets have bus lanes running counter to the flow of the rest of the traffic, and traffic on some divided streets runs in the same direction on both sides.

To/From the Airport

Unless you are renting a car, use a taxi or the metro to travel to and from the airport. No bus or pesero runs directly between the airport and city center.

Metro Officially, you're not supposed to travel on the metro with anything larger than a shoulder bag – and at busy times the crowds make it inadvisable in any case. However, this rule is often not enforced at quieter times, especially before 7 am, after 9 pm and on Sunday.

Commuters ride the rails in style.

The airport metro station is Terminal Aérea, on *Línea* (Line) 5. It's 200m from the airport terminal building: leave the terminal by the exit at the end of Sala A (the domestic flight arrivals area) and continue walking in the same direction until you see the metro logo, a stylized 'M,' and the steps down to the station. One ticket costs US$0.15. To get to the hotel areas in the city center, follow signs for 'Dirección Pantitlán'; at Pantitlán station you have to change trains: follow signs for 'Dirección Tacubaya' (Línea 9). Change trains again at Chabacano, where you follow signs for 'Dirección Cuatro Caminos' (Línea 2), which takes you to the Zócalo, Allende, Bellas Artes, Hidalgo and Revolución stations (but note the warning about Hidalgo in Dangers & Annoyances).

Taxi Comfortable 'Transportación Terrestre' taxis from the airport give good service and are controlled by a fixed-price ticket system.

Kiosks in the terminal sell Transportación Terrestre tickets: one is in the international baggage collection area, one is in Sala E (the international flight arrivals area), and the other is in Sala A (domestic arrivals). Maps on display near the kiosks divide the city into *zonas* (zones), which determine the fare from the airport. You can choose between *ordinario* and more expensive *ejecutivo* cabs. The Zócalo is in zona 2 (US$6.50 ordinario), the Alameda Central is in zona 3 (US$8) and the Zona Rosa is in zona 4 (US$9.50). One ticket is valid for up to four people and luggage that will fit in the trunk of the cab. If you simply mention a landmark such as 'Zócalo' or 'Plaza de la República' to the ticket clerk, you should receive a ticket for the correct zone – but it's advisable to check the map, and count your change, as rip-offs are not unknown. Walk to the taxi stand (taxi rank), and hand the ticket to the driver after getting into the car. (Porters may want to take your ticket and your luggage the few steps to the taxi, and will then importune you for a tip.) At the end of a trip the driver is not supposed to expect a tip.

To/From the Bus Terminals

The metro is the fastest and cheapest way to any bus terminal, but the prohibition against luggage bigger than a shoulder bag may keep you from using it. Each terminal is also reachable by bus, pesero and/or trolley bus. They also operate ticket-taxi systems; these *taxis autorizados* are cheaper than those from the airport.

Terminal Norte The metro station (on Línea 5) outside the front door is named Autobuses del Norte, but on some maps it's marked Central Autobuses del Norte, or Autobuses Norte, or just 'TAN' (for 'Terminal de Autobuses del Norte'). Traveling from the Terminal Norte to the center, follow signs for 'Dirección Pantitlán,' then change at La Raza, or at Consulado then Candelaria. At La Raza you must walk for seven or eight minutes.

The terminal's Taxi Autorizado kiosk is in the central passageway: a cab for one to four people to the Plaza de la República, Alameda, Zócalo or Terminal Oriente (TAPO),

all in zona 3, costs US$3.50 (add US$1 to fares between 10 pm and 6 am).

You can also reach the center by trolley bus, pesero or bus. Trolley buses marked 'Eje Central,' 'Tasqueña,' 'Terminal Sur' or 'Central Camionera del Sur' waiting in front of the terminal head south along Eje Central Lázaro Cárdenas, going within one block of the Alameda Central and six blocks from the Zócalo, and terminate at the Terminal Sur (Southern Bus Station) at Tasqueña, some 15km from the Terminal Norte. Fare is US$0.15. For peseros or buses going downtown, cross under the road through the underpass. Vehicles heading for central areas include those marked 'M(etro) Insurgentes,' 'M(etro) Revolución,' 'M(etro) Hidalgo' or 'M(etro) Bellas Artes.'

To reach the Terminal Norte from central areas, there are peseros, trolley buses and buses heading north on Eje Central at Donceles, one block north of the Palacio de Bellas Artes. They're marked with some variation of the terminal's name such as 'Central Camionera Norte,' 'Central Norte,' 'Terminal Norte' or 'Central Camionera.' On Avenida Insurgentes, anywhere north of Insurgentes metro station, take a northbound 'Central Camionera' or 'Central Norte' bus or pesero.

Terminal Oriente (TAPO) This terminal is next door to San Lázaro metro station. For peseros or city buses from TAPO, follow the signs to Calle Eduardo Molina: the bus stop is on the road outside. Peseros marked 'Zócalo' or 'Alameda' run to the city center, passing a few blocks north of the Zócalo.

The taxi autorizado fare to the Zócalo (zona 1) is US$2.25; to the Alameda or Plaza de la República (zona 2), US$2.50. Add US$1 between 10.30 pm and 6.30 am.

To get to TAPO from central parts of the city, you can take a 'M(etro) San Lázaro' pesero on Arriaga at Mariscal, near Plaza de la República, or heading east on Donceles north of the Zócalo.

Terminal Sur Tasqueña metro station is a two-minute walk through a crowded hawkers' market from the Terminal Sur.

A taxi autorizado from Terminal Sur costs US$4.50 to the Zona Rosa, Alameda or Zócalo (zona 4), and US$5.25 to the streets north of Plaza de la República (zona 5). Add US$1 between 10 pm and 6 am.

'Eje Central' and 'Central Camionera Norte' trolley buses run north from Terminal Sur along Eje Central Lázaro Cárdenas to the Palacio de Bellas Artes in the city center, then on to the Terminal Norte. Walk to the left from Terminal Sur's main exit, and you'll find the trolley buses waiting on the far side of the main road.

Heading south from the city center to Terminal Sur, trolley buses are marked with some combination of 'Eje Central,' 'Tasqueña/Taxqueña,' 'Autobuses Sur,' 'Terminal Sur' or 'Central Camionera del Sur.' You can pick them up one block north of the Palacio de Bellas Artes, on the Eje Central at Santa Veracruz. From San Ángel or Coyoacán, you can take a 'M(etro) Tasqueña' pesero or bus east on Avenida Miguel Ángel de Quevedo.

Terminal Poniente Observatorio metro station is a couple of minutes' walk from the terminal. A taxi ticket to the Zona Rosa costs US$3.50, to the Zócalo US$4.25.

To/From the Train Station
Buenavista metro station is just outside the Estación Buenavista train station.

Many peseros and buses run along Avenida Insurgentes right past Estación Buenavista. To catch them, turn to the right outside the station and cross to the far side of Insurgentes. Ones marked 'M(etro) Insurgentes' run as far as the intersection with Avenida Chapultepec, 1km south of Paseo de la Reforma; ones marked 'San Ángel' continue to the southern suburb of that name.

To reach Estación Buenavista from central areas of the city, there are many buses and peseros going north on Avenida Insurgentes. Any saying 'Buenavista,' 'Central Camionera,' 'Central Norte,' 'M(etro) La Raza' or 'M(etro) Indios Verdes' will do. As you head north on Insurgentes, look for a large Suburbia store on the right and get off at the next stop. The station is topped with the words 'Ferrocarriles Nacionales de México.'

Pesero, Bus & Trolley Bus
About 2.5 million people use Mexico City's thousands of peseros (also called *micros* or *minibuses*) and buses daily. They run from about 5 am to midnight and are most crowded during the rush hours – roughly 7.30 to 10 am and 5 to 7 pm. During other hours, the routes of most use to travelers are not too crowded.

Peseros are usually gray and green minibuses, but occasionally, in the outer suburbs, they're Volkswagen *combi*-type vehicles. They run along fixed routes, often starting or ending at metro stations, and will stop to pick up or drop off at virtually any street corner. Route information is displayed on the front of vehicles, often painted in random order on the windshield. Fares are US$0.20 for trips of up to 5km, US$0.25 for 5km to 12km, and US$0.35 for more than 12km. Add 20% between 10 pm and 6 am.

Municipally operated full-size buses are gradually replacing peseros, which are privately owned, on many routes. Buses, and the few trolley bus services, are more limited in their stops than peseros; fares are US$0.20 or so. There are a few express buses, which stop only every kilometer or so.

Information on services to specific places around the city is given in the relevant sections of this chapter.

Metro
The metro system offers the quickest and most crowded way to get around Mexico City. The fare is US$0.15 a ride, including transfers.

About 4.7 million people ride the metro on an average weekday, making it the world's third-busiest underground railway, after Moscow's and Tokyo's. It has 162 stations and 191km of track on 11 lines (líneas). An extension of the newest line, Línea B, was due to open in 2000.

The stations are generally clean and well organized but often crowded, sometimes fearfully so. Cars at the ends of trains are usually the least crowded. The platforms can become dangerously packed with passengers during the morning and evening rush hours (roughly 7.30 to 10 am and 5 to 7 pm). At these times some trains have cars reserved for women and children, boarded through special 'Solo Mujeres y Niños' lanes. Generally speaking, the best times to ride the metro are late morning, in the evening and Sunday.

From Monday to Friday, trains start at 5 am and end their final runs at 1 am; on Saturday the times are 6 am and 2 am; on Sunday, 7 am and 1 am.

With such crowded conditions, it's not surprising that pickpocketing is rife and that luggage bigger than a shoulder bag is not allowed. Be careful with belongings. Hidalgo station is particularly notorious for thefts.

The metro is easy to use. Signs in stations reading 'Dirección Pantitlán,' 'Dirección Universidad' and so on name the stations at the end of the metro lines. Check a map for the *dirección* you want. Buy a *boleto* (ticket) – or several at once – at the booth, feed it into the turnstile, and you're on your way.

When changing trains, look for 'Correspondencia' (Transfer) signs.

Taxi

Please read first the section on Taxi Crime under Dangers & Annoyances in this chapter's Information section.

Mexico City has several classes of taxi. Cheapest are the regular cruising street cabs – mostly Volkswagen Beetles, but also small Nissans and other Japanese models. They have license plate numbers beginning with the letter L (for *libre*, free) and a green stripe along the bottom of the license plate. Larger and more expensive, but safer, are radio taxis, Transportación Terrestre cabs from the airport, and *sitio* (taxi stand) cars, which have license plates beginning with S and bearing an orange stripe.

In cruising cabs, fares are computed by digital meter *(taxímetro)*. At this writing, they should start with 5 pesos (US$0.50) on the meter. The total cost of a 3 or 4km ride in moderate traffic – from the Zócalo to the Zona Rosa, for instance – should be about US$1.50. Between 10 pm and 6 am, 20% is added to fares.

A radio or sitio cab costs three or four times as much, but it can't be emphasized enough that the extra cost brings a degree of security you could never have in a cruising cab.

You need not tip taxi drivers unless they have provided some special service.

Around Mexico City

Some of the best things to see and do in Mexico are within a day's travel of the capital. Many of them, such as the ancient city of Teotihuacán or the quaint town of Tepoztlán, can easily be visited as day trips. Other destinations, such as the colonial cities of Puebla and Taxco, are a bit farther away and have so many attractions that you should plan to spend at least one night.

Alternatively, you can stop at most of the places covered in this chapter on your way between the capital and other parts of Mexico. This chapter is divided into four sections – north, east, south and west of Mexico City – and each covers at least one major route to/from the capital. Another option is a circular tour around the capital, which would make a fascinating trip. The roads going around the Distrito Federal generally are not quite as good as those going to and from it, but it is still quite feasible to take this option, either in your own vehicle or on the local buses.

Geographically, the whole area is elevated. South of Mexico City, the Cordillera Neovolcánica, with Mexico's highest volcanoes, runs from Pico de Orizaba in the east to Nevado de Toluca in the west (and continues as far west as Colima). North of this range is the Altiplano Central (Central Plateau). The altitude makes for a very pleasant climate, cooler and less humid than the lowlands, with rain falling in brief summer downpours. It also makes for a variety of landscapes, from dramatic gorges to fertile plains, fragrant pine forests and snow-capped peaks. Geologically, it remains an active area, with some still-smoking volcanoes and natural hot springs.

Historically, the area was home to a succession of important indigenous civilizations (notably Teotihuacán, Toltec and Aztec), and a crossroads of trade and cultural exchange. By the late 15th century, all but one of the small states of central Mexico were under the domination of the Aztec empire. Remnants of pre-Hispanic

Highlights

- Teotihuacán – Mexico's biggest ancient city and the site of two enormous, spectacular pyramids
- Volcanoes – the towering volcanoes of Popocatépetl, a smoking behemoth ringed by tranquil villages, and Iztaccíhuatl, a snowcapped challenge for mountaineers
- Cacaxtla ruins – with their vividly colored frescoes of warriors in battle
- Puebla – charming city which faithfully preserves the Spanish imprint
- Taxco – Mexico's picturesque silver capital, a gorgeous colonial antique

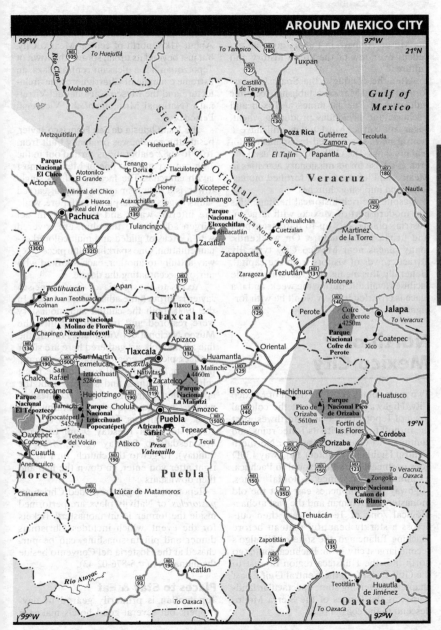

history can be seen at many archaeological sites, and in museums rich with artifacts; the Museo Amparo in Puebla gives an excellent overview of the area's history and culture.

After the conquest, the Spanish transformed central Mexico, establishing ceramic industries at Puebla, mines at Taxco and Pachuca, and haciendas producing wheat, sugar and cattle. Most towns still have a central plaza surrounded by Spanish colonial buildings. The Catholic church used the area as a base for its missionary activities in Mexico, and left a series of fortified monasteries and imposing churches.

Despite the rich historical heritage, this is a modern part of Mexico, with large industrial plants and up-to-date transport and urban infrastructure. On weekends, many places near Mexico City typically attract crowds of visitors from the capital. Generally, this means that there are ample facilities available during the week, and if a place is crowded it likely won't be with foreigners.

North of Mexico City

Two main routes go to the north of Mexico City. Highway 57D goes past the colonial town of Tepotzotlán, swings northwest past the turnoff for Tula with its Toltec ruins, and continues to Querétaro (see the Northern Central Highlands chapter). Highway 130D goes northeast from the capital to Pachuca, a mining town since colonial times. Highway 132D branches east past the old monastery at Acolman and the vast archaeological zone of Teotihuacán, then cuts across a starkly beautiful plateau before reaching Tulancingo, the state of Hidalgo's second largest city. From Pachuca, routes go north into the Huasteca region or east to the Gulf Coast (see the Central Gulf Coast chapter), traversing some spectacular landscapes as the fringes of the Sierra Madre descend to the coastal plain.

TEPOTZOTLÁN
• pop 34,200   • elev 2300m   ☎ no area code

About 41km north of central Mexico City, but just beyond its urban sprawl, the town of Tepotzotlán has a pleasant central plaza, an extreme example of Churrigueresque architecture and the Museo Nacional del Virreinato (National Museum of the Viceregal Period).

The Jesuit **Iglesia de San Francisco Javier**, beside the *zócalo*, was originally built from 1670 to 1682; elaborations carried out in the 18th century made it one of Mexico's most lavish churches. The façade, with its single tower, is a phantasmagoric array of carved saints, angels, people, plants and more, while the interior walls, and the Camarín del Virgen adjacent to the altar, are covered with a circus of gilded and multicolored ornamentation. One sparkling altarpiece gives way artfully to another, each adorned with mirrors accentuating the dazzle.

Access to the Iglesia de San Francisco Javier is through the adjacent monastery. In the 1960s both the church and monastery were restored and transformed into the **Museo Nacional del Virreinato**. Among the fine art and folk art gathered here are silver chalices, pictures created from inlaid wood, porcelain, furniture and some of the finest religious paintings and statues from the epoch. Don't miss the Capilla Doméstica, whose Churrigueresque main altarpiece is thick with mirrors. The museum is open 10 am to 5 pm Tuesday, 9 am to 6 pm Wednesday to Sunday (US$2, free on Sunday). To get to the church, turn to the right after you enter, go down the hall and then downstairs.

Tepotzotlán's highly regarded Christmas *pastorelas*, or Nativity plays, are performed inside the former Jesuit monastery. Tickets for the event, which includes Christmas dinner and piñata smashing, can be purchased at the Hostería del Convento beside the monastery (☎ 5-876-02-43).

Places to Stay & Eat
Tepotzotlán is primarily geared to daytrippers, but several good hotels make an

overnight stay possible. On the west side of the zócalo, *Hotel Posada San José* (☎ 5-876-05-20) is one of the best deals around; it has lovely colonial-style rooms for under US$16. About 500m from the zócalo on the way to the *autopista* is *Hotel Posada del Virrey* (☎ 5-876-18-64, *Insurgentes 13*) – the entrance is on Colón. The hotel has clean, colorful singles/doubles with TVs on two arcaded levels (US$21/32); some rooms are equipped with Jacuzzi.

Three popular restaurants are clustered under the arcades on the north side of the zócalo: *Los Virreyes*, *Montecarlo* and *Casa Mago*, all serving Mexican traditional favorites. They're a bit pricey – expect to shell out US$2.50 for soup, US$4 for salad, and US$4 or more for beef or chicken main courses – but you're paying for the festive ambiance, heightened by roving *ranchero* bands, which play Mexican-style country music. Adjacent to the Hotel Posada San José, *Restaurant-Bar Pepe* is similarly priced but smaller and more intimate than its counterparts across the zócalo. Occupying a pretty courtyard beside the monastery museum (and open during the same hours), *La Hostería del Convento* serves soups for US$2 and original main courses for US$5 to US$6.50.

Cheaper fare is available at the market behind the Palacio Municipal, where stalls serve fine *pozole*, quesadillas, fresh fruit juices and chicken soup.

Getting There & Away

Tepotzotlán is 1.5km west of the Caseta Tepotzotlán, the first tollbooth on highway 57D from Mexico City to Querétaro.

From Mexico City's Terminal Norte station, Autotransportes Valle de Mezquital (AVM) buses en route to Tula stop at the tollbooth every 15 minutes. From there, take a local bus (US$0.30) or taxi (US$1.50), or walk along Avenida Insurgentes. You can also take a colectivo or bus to Tepotzotlán from Cuatro Caminos metro station in Mexico City (US$0.90). Returning buses, marked 'Toreo,' depart from opposite the Posada San José.

TULA

• pop 26,000 • elev 2060m ☎ 7

The probable capital of the ancient Toltec civilization stood 65km north of what is now Mexico City. Though less spectacular than Teotihuacán, Tula is still an absorbing site, best known for its fearsome 4.5m-high stone warrior figures. The modern town has a refinery and cement works on its outskirts, but the center is pleasant enough.

History

Tula was an important city from about 900 to 1150 AD, reaching a peak population of about 35,000. The Aztec annals tell of a king called Topiltzin – fair-skinned, long-haired and black-bearded – who founded a city in the 10th century as the capital of his Toltec people. There's debate about whether Tula was this capital, though.

The Toltecs were mighty empire-builders to whom the Aztecs themselves looked back with awe, claiming them as royal ancestors. Topiltzin was supposedly a priest-king dedicated to the peaceful worship (which included sacrifices of animals only) of the feathered serpent god Quetzalcóatl. Tula is known to have housed followers of the less likable Tezcatlipoca (Smoking Mirror), god of warriors, witchcraft, life and death; worshiping Tezcatlipoca required human sacrifices. The story goes that Tezcatlipoca appeared in various guises in order to provoke Topiltzin. As a naked chili-seller, he aroused the lust of Topiltzin's daughter and eventually married her; as an old man, he persuaded the sober Topiltzin to get drunk.

Eventually, the humiliated leader left for the Gulf Coast, where he set sail eastward on a raft of snakes, promising one day to return and reclaim his throne. (This caused the Aztec emperor Moctezuma much consternation when Hernán Cortés arrived on the Gulf Coast in 1519.) The conventional wisdom is that Topiltzin set up a new Toltec state at Chichén Itzá in Yucatán, while the Tula Toltecs built a brutal, militaristic empire that dominated central Mexico. (See Chichén Itzá in the History section of Facts about Mexico for a rival theory.)

Tula was evidently a place of some splendor – legends speak of palaces of gold, turquoise, jade and quetzal feathers, of enormous cobs of maize and colored cotton that grew naturally. Possibly its treasures were looted by the Aztecs or Chichimecs.

In the mid-12th century, the ruler Huémac apparently moved the Toltec capital to Chapultepec after factional fighting at Tula, then he committed suicide. Tula was abandoned about the beginning of the 13th century, seemingly after violent Chichimec destruction.

Orientation & Information
The archaeological zone is 2km north of the town center (see Getting Around for directions). The main street is Zaragoza, which runs from the outskirts of town to the zócalo. There are a couple of banks on Juárez, a block-long pedestrian street off the zócalo. Pay phones abound.

Town Center
The fortress-like church on Zaragoza was part of the 16th-century fortified monastery of San José. Inside, its vault ribs are picked out in gold. On the library wall in the zócalo is a mural of Tula's history.

Zona Arqueológica
The old settlement of Tula covered nearly 17 sq km and stretched to the far side of the modern town, but the present focus is the ruins of the main ceremonial center, perched on a hilltop with good views over rolling countryside.

Tula's ruins are open 9.30 am to 5 pm daily (US$2, free on Sunday). Half a kilometer from the entrance, there's a museum displaying pottery and several large sculptures taken from the site. Another 700m, you will reach the center of the ancient city. At the site, there are explanatory signs in English, Spanish and Nahuatl.

Juego de Pelota No 1 This I-shaped ball court, a copy of an earlier one at Xochicalco, is the first large structure you'll reach from the museum. Researchers believe its walls were once decorated with sculpted panels that were removed under Aztec rule.

Coatepantli Near the north side of Pirámide B stands the Coatepantli (Serpent Wall), 40m long, 2.25m high, and carved with rows of geometric patterns and a row of snakes devouring human skeletons. Traces remain of the original bright colors with which most Tula structures were painted.

Pirámide B Also known as the temple of Quetzalcóatl or Tlahuizcalpantecuhtli (Morning Star), Pirámide B can be scaled via steps on its south side. At the top of the stairway stand the remains of two columnar roof supports that once depicted feathered serpents with their heads on the ground and their tails in the air.

The four basalt warrior-telamones at the top and the pillars behind, supported the roof of a temple. Wearing headdresses, butterfly-shaped breastplates, and short skirts held in place by sun disks, the warriors hold spear-throwers in their right hands, knives and incense bags in their left hands. The telamon on the left side is a replica of the original, now in the Museo Nacional de Antropología (for more information about the museum, see its entry under Bosque de Chapultepec section in the Mexico City chapter). The columns behind the telamones depict crocodile heads (which symbolize the Earth), warriors, symbols of warrior orders, weapons and the head of Quetzalcóatl.

On the north wall of the pyramid, protected by scaffolding, are some of the carvings that once surrounded all four sides of the structure. These show the symbols of the warrior orders: jaguars, coyotes, eagles eating hearts, and what may be a human head in the mouth of Quetzalcóatl.

Gran Vestíbulo Now roofless, the Great Vestibule extends along the front of the pyramid, facing the plaza. The stone bench carved with warriors originally ran the length of the hall, possibly to seat priests and nobles observing ceremonies in the plaza.

Palacio Quemado The Burnt Palace you will see immediately to the west of Pirámide B is really a series of halls and court-

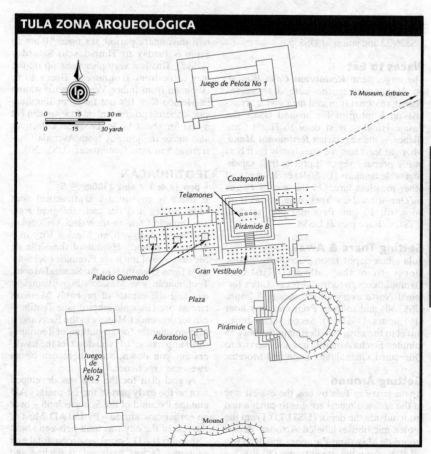

TULA ZONA ARQUEOLÓGICA

Juego de Pelota No 1

To Museum, Entrance

0   15   30 m
0   15   30 yards

Coatepantli

Telamones

Pirámide B

Gran Vestíbulo

Palacio Quemado

Plaza

Pirámide C

Adoratorio

Juego de Pelota No 2

Mound

yards with more low benches and relief carvings, one showing a procession of nobles. It was probably used for meetings or ceremonies.

Plaza The plaza in front of Pirámide B would have been the scene of religious and military displays. At its center is the *adoratorio*, a ceremonial platform. **Pirámide C**, on the east side of the plaza, is Tula's biggest structure but is largely unexcavated. To the west is **Juego de Pelota No 2**, the largest ball court in central Mexico at more than 100m in length.

Places to Stay

The best budget place in Tula is *Hotel Casa Blanca* (☎ 732-11-86) on Pasaje Hidalgo, a narrow street that starts beside the Singer store on Hidalgo. At rates of US$7.50/10.50 (US$2 more with TV), its sparkling clean, bright and quiet singles/doubles are a great deal. Parking access is via Zaragoza.

The modern *Hotel Lizbeth* (☎ 732-00-45, Ocampo 200), just 1½ blocks from the bus station (turn to the right at the station entrance), has clean, comfortable rooms with TVs for US$21/24. Tula's top hotel is the ultra-modern *Hotel Sharon* (☎ 732-09-76,

Callejón de la Cruz 1), at the turnoff to the archaeological site. Singles/doubles start at US$26/32 and suites at US$55.

Places to Eat

The large, clean *Restaurant Casa Blanca*, on Hidalgo near the cathedral, serves decent, reasonably priced meals with breakfasts and antojitos for around US$2. On Pasaje Hidalgo, next door to Hotel Casa Blanca, is the vegetarian *Restaurant Maná*, where at least half a dozen family members busily prepare veggie burgers, fruit salads, vegetable *licuados* (US$0.90 each item) and other meatless fare. On the zócalo, *Pizzas In/Out* offers 'New York-style' pizzas from noon till 10 pm. Personal pies start at US$4.50, large pies at US$8.

Getting There & Away

Tula's bus depot is on Xicoténcatl, three blocks from the cathedral. First-class Ovnibus buses go to/from Mexico City's Terminal Norte every 40 minutes (1¼ hours, US$3.50) and to/from Pachuca every hour (1¾ hours, US$3.50). Second-class buses travel to the same two destinations every 15 minutes. Flecha Amarilla has daily service to Querétaro, Guanajuato, León and Morelia.

Getting Around

If you arrive in Tula by bus, the easiest way to the archaeological zone is to catch a taxi from outside the depot (US$1.75). From the center, microbuses labeled 'Actopan' depart from 5 de Mayo and Zaragoza and drop you off 100m from the site entrance ($0.30).

ACOLMAN

• pop 3,840 • elev 2250m

Thirty-two km north of Mexico City, just beside highway 132D (the toll road to Teotihuacán), you'll see what look like battlements surrounding the **Ex-Convento de San Agustín Acolman**. The historic building, with its massive thick walls, colonnaded courtyards and carved stonework, is the site of many frescos. The adjacent church of San Agustín, built between 1539 and 1560, has a spacious Gothic interior and one of the earliest examples of a plateresque façade. The

old monastery now houses a museum with artifacts and paintings from the early Christian missionary period; it's open 10 am to 5 pm Saturday to Thursday to Saturday (US$2). This is a very pleasant stop on the way to or from Teotihuacán. Buses go to Acolman from Indios Verdes metro station in Mexico City. It's not far from Teotihuacán; if there's no convenient bus you can get a taxi for about US$4. Frequent colectivos also make the journey from Avenida Guerrero in San Juan Teotihuacán (US$0.50).

TEOTIHUACÁN

• pop 18,460 • elev 2300m ☎ 5

If there is any must-see attraction near Mexico City, it is the archaeological zone Teotihuacán ('teh-oh-tih-wah-KAN'), 50km northeast of downtown Mexico City in a mountain-ringed offshoot of the Valle de México. Site of the huge Piramides del Sol y de la Luna (Pyramids of the Sun and Moon), Teotihuacán was Mexico's biggest ancient city and the capital of probably Mexico's largest pre-Hispanic empire (see Teotihuacán section under History in the Facts about Mexico chapter for an outline of Teotihuacán's importance). If you don't let the hawkers get you down, a day here can be an awesome experience.

A grid plan for the city was developed around the early part of the 1st-century AD and the Pyramid of the Sun was built – over an earlier cave shrine – by 150 AD. Most of the rest of the city was built between about 250 and 600 AD. Social, environmental and economic factors hastened its decline and eventual collapse in the 7th-century AD.

The city was divided into quarters by two great avenues that met near the so-called La Ciudadela (the Citadel). One, running roughly north-south, is the famous Calzada de los Muertos (Avenue of the Dead) – so called because the later Aztecs believed the great buildings lining it were vast tombs, built by giants for Teotihuacán's first rulers. The major buildings are typified by a *talud-tablero* style, in which the rising portions of stepped, pyramid-like buildings consist of both sloping (talud) and upright (tablero) sections. They were often covered in lime

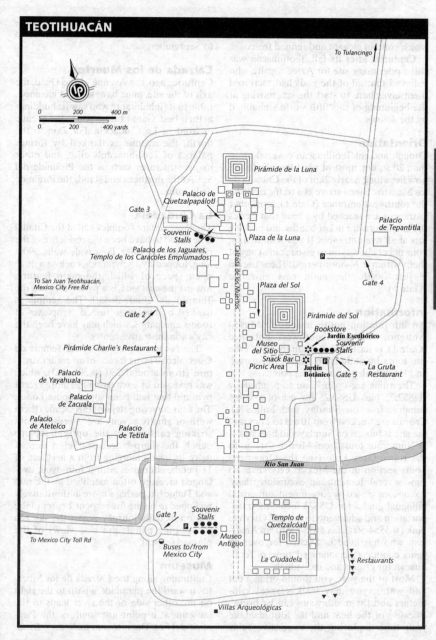

TEOTIHUACÁN

0   200   400 m
0   200   400 yards

To Tulancingo

Pirámide de la Luna

Palacio de
Quetzalpapálotl

Gate 3

Souvenir
Stalls

Palacio de los Jaguares,
Templo de los Caracoles Emplumados

Plaza de la Luna

Palacio
de Tepantitla

Gate 4

To San Juan Teotihuacán,
Mexico City Free Rd

Plaza del Sol

Gate 2

Pirámide del Sol

Pirámide Charlie's Restaurant

Palacio
de Yayahuala

Palacio
de Zacuala

Palacio de Atetelco

Palacio
de Tetitla

Bookstore

Jardín Escultórico

Souvenir
Stalls

Museo
del Sitio

Snack Bar

Picnic Area

Jardín
Botánico   Gate 5

La Gruta
Restaurant

Río San Juan

Gate 1

Souvenir
Stalls

Museo
Antiguo

To Mexico City Toll Rd

Buses to/from
Mexico City

Templo de
Quetzalcóatl

La Ciudadela

Restaurants

Villas Arqueológicas

AROUND MEXICO CITY

and colorfully painted. Most of the city was made up of residential compounds, some of which contain elegant and refined frescos.

Centuries after its fall, Teotihuacán was still a pilgrimage site for Aztec royalty, who believed that all of the gods had sacrificed themselves here to start the sun moving at the beginning of the 'fifth world,' inhabited by the Aztecs.

Orientation

Though ancient Teotihuacán covered more than 20 sq km, most of what there is to see now lies along nearly 2km of the Calzada de los Muertos. Buses arrive at a traffic circle by the southwest entrance (Gate 1); four other entrances are reached by a road that circles the site. There are ticket booths and parking lots at all five entrances. If you wish to exit, your ticket allows you to go back in at any of them within a 24-hour period. The museum is just inside the main east entrance (Gate 5).

Information

An information booth inside the Museo Antiguo, near the southwest entrance (Gate 1), is staffed from 9 am to 4 pm. Free site tours by authorized guides, in Spanish and English, depart from this point.

The ruins are open 7 am to 6 pm daily (US$2.75 plus US$3.25 for use of a video camera, free on Sunday and holidays). Crowds are thickest from 10 am to 2 pm, and the site is busiest on Sunday and holidays.

Numerous tours from Mexico City go to the ruins. Grey Line (see the Organized Tours section in the Mexico City chapter) runs several Teotihuacán excursions daily. Excursions are led by government-authorized bilingual guides for US$23 including transportation and admission to the site. Gwynne Fink (☎ 5554-5602, fax 5658-5350), an American who has lived in Mexico for over 40 years, conducts 'personalized' tours of Teotihuacán for groups and individuals.

Most of the year, you should bring a hat and water; you may walk several kilometers and the midday sun can be brutal. Because of the heat and the altitude, take your time exploring the expansive ruins

and climbing the steep pyramids. Afternoon rain showers are common from June to September.

Calzada de los Muertos

Centuries ago, the Avenue of the Dead, the axis of the site, must have seemed incomparable to its inhabitants, who saw its buildings at their best. Gate 1 brings you to the avenue in front of La Ciudadela. For 2km to the north, the avenue is flanked by former palaces of Teotihuacán's elite, and other major structures such as the Pirámide del Sol. At the northern end stands the Pirámide de la Luna.

La Ciudadela

The large square complex called the Citadel is believed to have been the residence of the city's supreme ruler. Four wide walls, 390m long, topped by 15 pyramids, enclose a huge open space of which the main feature, toward the east side, is a pyramid called the Templo de Quetzalcóatl. The temple is flanked by two large ruined complexes of rooms and patios, which may have been the city's administrative center.

The fascinating feature of the **Templo de Quetzalcóatl** is the façade of an earlier structure (from around 250 to 300 AD), which was revealed by excavating the more recent pyramid that had been superimposed on it. The four surviving steps of this façade (there were originally seven) are encrusted with striking carvings. In the upright tablero panels the sharp-fanged feathered serpent deity, its head emerging from a necklace of 11 petals, alternates with a four-eyed, two-fanged creature often identified as the rain god Tláloc but perhaps more authoritatively reckoned to be the fire serpent, bearer of the sun on its daily journey across the sky. On the sloping panels are side views of the plumed serpent.

Museum

Continuing along the Calzada de los Muertos toward the pyramids, a path to the right on the other side of the river leads to the museum at a point just south of the Pirámide del Sol. The museum makes a refreshing stop midway through the site. Around the building, there's a lovely sculpture garden with Teotihuacán artifacts, a botanical garden, public toilets, a snack bar and picnic tables, and a bookstore.

The museum (free admission with site ticket) is thematically divided with explanations in Spanish, English and Nahuatl. There are excellent displays of artifacts, fresco panels, and an impressive large-scale model of the city set under a plexiglas walkway, from which the real Pirámide del Sol can be viewed through a wall-size window.

Pirámide del Sol
The world's third-largest pyramid (surpassed in size only by the pyramid of Cholula and Egypt's Cheops) stands on the east side of the Calzada de los Muertos. It has a base of 222 sq m and is now just over 70m high. The pyramid was built around 100 AD, from 3 million tons of stone, brick and rubble without the use of metal tools, pack animals or the wheel.

The Aztec belief that the structure was dedicated to the sun god was validated in 1971, when archaeologists uncovered a 100m-long underground tunnel leading from near the pyramid's west side to a cave directly beneath its center. Here they found religious artifacts. It is thought that the sun was worshiped here before the pyramid was built and that the city's ancient inhabitants traced the very origins of life to this grotto.

At Teotihuacán's height, the pyramid's plaster was painted bright red, which must have been a radiant sight at sunset. Climb the pyramid's 248 steps for an overview of the entire ancient city.

Pirámide de la Luna
The Pyramid of the Moon, at the north end of Calzada de los Muertos, is not as big as the Pirámide del Sol, but it is more gracefully proportioned. Its summit is virtually at the same height, because it is built on higher ground. It was completed about 300 AD.

The Plaza de la Luna, in front of the pyramid, is a handsome arrangement of some 12 temple platforms. Some experts attribute astronomical symbolism to the total 13 (made by the 12 platforms plus the pyramid), a key number in the day-counting system of the Mesoamerican ritual calendar. The altar in the plaza's center is thought to have been the site of religious dancing.

Palacio de Quetzalpapálotl
Off the southwest corner of the Plaza de la Luna is the Palace of the Quetzal Butterfly, where it is thought a high priest lived. A flight of steps leads up to a roofed portico with an abstract mural and, just off that, a well-restored patio whose thick columns are carved with images of the quetzal bird or a hybrid quetzal butterfly.

The **Palacio de los Jaguares** and **Templo de los Caracoles Emplumados** lie behind and below the Palacio de Quetzalpapálotl. On the lower walls of several of the chambers off the patio of the Jaguar Palace are parts of murals showing the jaguar god in feathered headdresses, blowing conch shells and apparently praying to the rain god Tláloc.

The Temple of the Plumed Conch Shells, entered from the Jaguar Palace patio, is a now-subterranean structure of the 2nd- or 3rd- century AD. Carvings on what was its façade show large shells – possibly used as musical instruments – decorated with feathers and four-petal flowers. The base on which the façade stands has a green, blue, red and yellow mural of birds with water streaming from their beaks.

Palacio de Tepantitla
Teotihuacán's most famous fresco, the worn **Paradise of Tláloc**, is in the Tepantitla Palace, a priest's residence about 500m northeast of the Pirámide del Sol. The mural flanks a doorway in a covered patio in the northeast corner of the building. The rain god Tláloc, attended by priests, is shown on both sides. Below, on the right of the door, appears his paradise, a garden-like place with people, animals and fish swimming in a mountain-fed river. Left of the door, tiny human figures are engaged in a unique ball game. Frescos in other rooms show priests with feather headdresses.

Palacio de Tetitla & Palacio de Atetelco

Another group of palaces lies west of the site's main area, several hundred meters from Gate 1. Their many murals, discovered in the 1940s, are often well-preserved or restored and perfectly intelligible. Inside the sprawling Tetitla Palace, no fewer than 120 walls have murals, with Tláloc, jaguars, serpents and eagles among the easiest figures to make out. Some 400m west is the Atetelco Palace, whose vivid jaguar or coyote murals – a mixture of originals and restorations – are in the so-called Patio Blanco in the northwest corner. Processions of these creatures in shades of red perhaps symbolize warrior orders.

About 100m farther north lie Zacuala and Yayahuala, a pair of enormous walled compounds that probably served as living quarters for large groups of families. Separated by the original alleyways, the two structures are comprised of numerous rooms and patios but few entranceways, perhaps to discourage unwanted guests.

Places to Stay

If there's one place to splurge on lodging in Mexico, this is it. The Club Med-run *Villas Arqueológicas* (☎ 956-09-09), immediately south of the ancient city, has charming air-con singles/doubles for US$39/49 Monday to Thursday, US$50/58 Friday to Sunday. It also has a pool, tennis court, billiards table and French-Mexican restaurant.

The town of San Juan Teotihuacán, 3km west of the Pirámide del Sol, features several less costly options for spending the night. One of them is *Hotel Piramides Plaza* (☎ 956-01-67, *Guerrero 12*), a couple of blocks from the central plaza, offering clean, basic rooms with baths for US$9.50/12.50. You can camp at *Trailer Park Teotihuacán* (☎ 956-03-13, *López Mateos 17*), on a peaceful street behind a 16th-century Jesuit church. The park, which has baths with hot showers, charges US$2.75 per person for setting up a tent and US$5.25 plus US$1 per person for hooking up a trailer. At the east end of town closer to the pyramids, *Hotel Posada Sol y Luna* (☎ 956-23-68, *Jiménez*

Cantú 13) is a superior value, with luxurious singles/doubles that are available for US$17/20.

Places to Eat

Except for some dusty eateries along the ring road on the southeast side of the archaeological site, meals are pricey in the vicinity of the ruins. The most convenient place is on the 3rd floor of the Museo Antiguo, where there's a restaurant with views of La Ciudadela. On the ring road south of Gate 2, *Pirámide Charlie's* serves savory but costly meals (soup for US$2.75, chicken dishes starting at US$7.75, beef and seafood dishes for about US$10).

A very unusual place to dine is *La Gruta* (the Cave), 75m east of Gate 5. Meals have been served in this cool, wide-mouthed natural cave for a century; Porfirio Díaz (Mexican president for 33 years prior to the Mexican Revolution) ate here in 1906. The food's quite good and fairly priced – soups and salads are around US$3 and meat and fish dishes are about US$7. Among the highlights on the menu are nopal salad with tamarind dressing and chicken breast stuffed with squash blossoms and *xoconostle*, a tart cactus fruit.

Getting There & Away

Autobuses México-San Juan Teotihuacán runs 2nd-class buses from Mexico City's Terminal Norte to the ruins every 15 minutes during the day (one hour, US$1.50). The ticket office is at the north end of the terminal. Make sure your bus is going to 'Los Pirámides' as opposed to the nearby town of San Juan Teotihuacán.

Buses arrive and depart from the traffic circle near Gate 1, also making stops at Gates 2 and 3. Return buses are more frequent after 1 pm. The last bus back to the capital from the traffic circle leaves about 6.30 pm. Some terminate at the Indios Verdes metro station in the north of Mexico City, but most continue to Terminal Norte.

Getting Around

To get to the pyramids from San Juan Teotihuacán, take any combi labeled 'San Martín' departing from Avenida Hidalgo beside the central plaza (US$0.30). Combis returning to San Juan make stops at Gates 1, 2 and 3.

PACHUCA

- pop 210,000 • elev 2426m ☎ 7

Pachuca, capital of the state of Hidalgo, lies 90km northeast of Mexico City. It has grown rapidly in the last few years and brightly painted houses climb the dry hillsides around the town. Pachuca has a few interesting sights, and it is a good departure point for trips north and east into the dramatic Sierra Madre Oriental.

Silver was found in the area as early as 1534, and the mines of Real del Monte, 9km northeast, still produce substantial amounts of the metal. Pachuca was also the gateway by which soccer entered Mexico, brought by miners from Cornwall, England, in the 19th century. Further evidence of the Cornish influence, the meat pies known as pasties (pastes) are sold in bakeries and restaurants around town.

Orientation

The rectangular **Reloj Monumental** (Clock Tower), built between 1904 and 1910 to commemorate the independence centennial, stands at the north end of Pachuca's Plaza de la Independencia (zócalo), flanked by Avenida Matamoros on the east and Avenida Allende on the west. Guerrero runs parallel to Allende, about 100m to the west. To the south, by about 700m, both Guerrero and Matamoros reach the modern Plaza Juárez.

Information

There's a tourist module (☎ 715-14-11) in the base of the clock tower, theoretically open 9 am to 3 pm Monday to Friday and 10 am to 6 pm Saturday to Sunday, but in reality the desk is often not occupied. When it is, staff seem surprised, then indignant, to receive requests for information. Tiny maps are given out, while large but inaccurate maps are sold for US$0.30.

There are banks (with ATMs) on Plaza de la Independencia. The post office is on the corner of Juárez and Iglesias. Internet access

is available for US$2 per hour at Coffee Net (Segura 601), a block west of the post office; it is open 10 am to 3 pm, and 5 to 8 pm daily.

Lookout Points

For a jaw-dropping view of the city, catch a 'Mirador' combi (US$0.30) from Plaza de la Constitución a few blocks northeast of the zócalo to an observation point on the road to Real del Monte. Even more extraordinary views can be had from the Cristo Rey monument on the Cerro de Santa Apolonia north of town.

Centro Cultural Hidalgo

The ex-monastery of San Francisco has become the Centro Cultural Hidalgo, which embodies two museums and a gallery, theater, library and several lovely plazas. Located four blocks east of Plaza Juárez, the center is open 10 am to 6 pm Tuesday to Sunday (free).

Museo Nacional de la Fotografía displays early photographic technology and selections from the 1.5 million photos in the archives of the Instituto Nacional de Antropología e Historia (INAH). The photos – some by Europeans and Americans, many more by pioneer Mexican photojournalist Agustín Victor Casasola – provide fascinating glimpses of Mexico from 1873 to the present.

CHARLOTTE HINDLE

AROUND MEXICO CITY

Museo de Minería

This museum provides an interesting overview of the mining industry that has shaped the region. Well-displayed photos show conditions in the mines from early years to the present. Also on display are helmets and headlamps, old mining maps and shrines taken from mines. Located at Mina 110, half a block east of Matamoros, it's open 10 am to 2 pm and 3 to 6 pm Tuesday to Sunday (US$0.50, free for miners and ex-miners). Guided tours (in Spanish) with a video program are given.

Places to Stay

Hotel Grenfell (☎ 715-05-15) occupies an imposing building on the west side of the zócalo but is much less impressive inside. Sizable but bare singles/doubles cost US$6.50/7.50 with private bath, US$4.25/5.25 with shared bath.

A better value is *Hotel de los Baños* (☎ 713-07-00, Matamoros 205), half a block southeast of the zócalo, with a skylight over a handsomely enclosed courtyard. Rooms vary in price and quality but all have TVs, phones and clean baths. Particularly nice are rooms 26 and 28; these are large and elegantly furnished and have balconies. Singles are a bargain at US$9.50; doubles range from US$12 to US$17. Parking in a nearby garage is an additional US$2.75.

Another good choice is the colonial-style *Hotel Noriega* (☎ 715-15-55, Matamoros 305), one block south of Hotel de los Baños. There's a leaf-covered courtyard, stately staircase and decent restaurant. Singles/doubles with private baths cost US$9.50/10.50, US$1 more for TV. Have a look at a few rooms, though, before checking in – some are tiny and claustrophobic, while others like rooms 39 and 42 are large and airy. Parking is available behind the hotel.

The modern *Hotel Emily* (☎ 715-08-68), on the south side of the zócalo, has large comfortable rooms, some facing a back patio, others with balconies on the plaza, for US$21/25. Room 306 offers a lovely vista of the clock tower backed by hillsides crammed with houses. There's a parking garage underneath the hotel. *Hotel Ciro's* (☎ 715-40-83), which is owned by members of the same family, stands on the opposite side of the plaza like a mirror image of the Emily, with similar prices and quality.

Places to Eat

Pasties are available all over town, including the bus station. Baked in pizza ovens, they contain a variety of fillings probably never imagined by those Cornish miners, such as *mole verde*, beans, pineapple and rice pudding. *Pastes Kiko's* in the arcade opposite the Juárez monument and the nearby *Pastes San Juan* are especially popular.

Restaurant Blanca, on the southwest corner of the zócalo, serves 'authentic' pasties, filled with potatoes, leeks, parsley, ground beef and black pepper (as in the original recipe). Decorated with stained glass panels of mining scenes, the cavernous dining hall also offers set breakfasts (US$2.50 to US$3.50), salads (US$2) and antojitos (US$2.25). Next door to the Hotel de los Baños is the attractive *Restaurant-Bar Cabales*, which features a fine bar ringed with swiveling stools and good, reasonably priced food (the five-course meal of the day runs US$3.25).

Café Reencuentro, under the arcade on Plaza Juárez, is a great hangout. This intimate coffeehouse, run by two women (one German, one American/Mexican), features live blues and folk music from 8 to 11 pm nightly, performed on a circular stage in the center of the room. Aside from the music, the café's popularity could also be due to its homemade German/Austrian cakes, pies and strudels (US$1.75) or its yummy baguettes and quiches (US$2), best enjoyed with a cup of Turkish or Viennese coffee.

Getting There & Away

First-class buses leave Mexico City's Terminal Norte for Pachuca every 15 minutes (US$3.25). From Pachuca, there is 1st-class service daily to the following: Mexico City, every 15 minutes (1¼ hours, US$3.25); Poza Rica, 4 buses (4½ hours, US$8); Tampico, 2 buses (8½ hours, US$20). Buses serving destinations closer to Pachuca are nearly all 2nd-class; these frequently go to/from Tula,

Tulancingo and Tamazunchale, while several go daily to/from Huejutla and Querétaro.

Getting Around

The bus station is several kilometers southwest of downtown, beside the road to Mexico City. Green-striped colectivos marked 'El Centro' take you to Plaza Constitución (US$0.30), a short walk from the zócalo; in the reverse direction, you can hop on along Allende. The trip by taxi costs US$1.75.

AROUND PACHUCA

Three scenic roads ascend into the forested, sometimes foggy Sierra Madre. Highway 105 goes north to Huejutla and Tampico. Highway 85 – the Pan-American Highway – goes via Actopan and Ixmiquilpan to Tamazunchale and Ciudad Valles in the Huasteca (see the Central Gulf Coast chapter). Highway 130 goes east to Tulancingo and Poza Rica.

Parque Nacional El Chico
☎ 7

Nine km north of Pachuca, a road branches northwest (left) off highway 105 and winds 20km or so to the picturesque old mining town of **Mineral del Chico**, located in Parque Nacional El Chico. The park has spectacular rock formations popular with climbers, pine forests with lovely walks, and rivers and dams for fishing.

Río y Montaña Expediciones in Mexico City (☎ 5-520-20-41) organizes three-day expeditions, including training in rock climbing, to El Chico for groups of six or more persons. The company supplies all climbing and camping equipment, but you must arrange your own transportation to the park. For further information, consult their website, www.rioymontana.com.

Places to Stay & Eat Five km from highway 105 (on the road toward Mineral del Chico) is a right turn that leads 1.2km by dirt road to *La Cabaña del Lobo* (☎ 5-776-22-22 *in Mexico City*), which is in a remote valley ringed by pine-covered mountains. The hotel features a row of cozy single/

double rooms with clean baths and hot water (US$17/21) overlooking a campfire/playground area, and a restaurant, which serves regional favorites. Nearby are trails to lakes and waterfalls. Three rooms have fireplaces – it can be chilly up here.

There are several *campgrounds* with rudimentary facilities between Km 7 and 10 of the road to Mineral del Chico, all charging US$1 per tent plus US$0.15 per person.

In Mineral del Chico, there are a couple of fine hotels. These places fill up fast on weekends, but are empty during the week. *Hospedaje El Chico* (☎ 715-47-41), on the plaza, is sparkling clean and comfortable. Singles/doubles cost US$13/17, less without carpeting. Just up the street, *La Posada del Amanacer* (☎ 715-01-90) is an adobe structure with 11 rooms, all with fireplaces, on two levels beside a lovely patio. Rooms with two single beds cost US$20, those with one double bed are US$25. Its restaurant is open weekends only.

Getting There & Away From Pachuca, Flecha Roja runs four 2nd-class buses daily to Mineral del Chico (one hour, US$1). Colectivos depart from Calle Galeana (west of the market, through an arch labeled 'Barrio el Arbolito') every half hour (US$0.70).

Highway 105

Two km past the park turnoff for Parque Nacional El Chico, **Real del Monte** (also known as Mineral del Monte) was the scene of a miners' strike in 1776 – commemorated as the first strike in the Americas. Most of the town was settled in the 19th century, after a British company took over the mines. The field opposite the Dolores mine was the first in the country where soccer was played. Cornish-style cottages line many of the steep cobbled streets, and there is an English cemetery nearby. Flecha Roja buses leave from the Pachuca station every half hour for Real del Monte (½ hour, US$0.50).

Eleven km north of Real del Monte is a turnoff east to **Huasca** (or Huasca de Ocampo), which has a 17th-century church, *balnearios* and a variety of local crafts. Some old haciendas have been converted into attractive hotels. Nearby is a canyon with imposing basalt columns and a waterfall.

At **Atotonilco el Grande**, 34km from Pachuca, there's a 16th-century fortress-monastery, and a balneario beside some hot springs. Market day is Thursday. The highway then descends to Metzquititlán, in the fertile Río Tulancingo valley (see Tampico & the Huasteca in the Central Gulf Coast chapter for information about other places along this route).

Actopan
• pop 24,100 • elev 2400m ☎ 7

Actopan, 37km northwest of Pachuca on highway 85, has one of the finest of Hidalgo's many 16th-century fortress-monasteries. Founded in 1548, **Convento de San Nicolás de Tolentino** is in an excellent state of preservation. Its church has a lovely plateresque façade and a single tower showing Moorish influence. Mexico's best 16th-century frescos are in the cloister: hermits are depicted in the Sala De Profundis; and saints, Augustinian monks and a meeting between Fray Martín de Acevedo (an important early monk at Actopan) and two indigenous nobles (Juan Inica Actopa and Pedro Ixcuincuitlapilco) are shown on the stairs. To the left of the church, a vaulted *capilla abierta* is also adorned with frescos.

Wednesday is **market day** in Actopan, and has been for at least 400 years. Local handicrafts are sold, along with regional dishes such as barbecued lamb.

PAI (Pachuca-Actopan-Ixmiquilpan) runs 1st-class buses every 12 minutes from Pachuca to Actopan (20 minutes, US$1.50). There is frequent 2nd-class service from Mexico City.

Ixmiquilpan
• pop 29,100 • elev 1700m ☎ changing

Ixmiquilpan, 75km from Pachuca on highway 85 (1½ hours by frequent buses), is a former capital of the Otomí people, ancient inhabitants of Hidalgo. The arid Mezquital valley in which the town stands remains an Otomí enclave; about half of Mexico's 350,000 Otomí live in Hidalgo. Traditional Otomí women's dress is a *quechquémitl* (an embroidered shoulder cape) worn over an embroidered cloth blouse. The Mezquital valley Otomí make Mexico's finest *ayates*, cloths woven from *ixtle*, the fiber of the maguey cactus. The Otomí also use maguey to make food, soap and needles.

The busy Monday **market** is the best place to find Otomí crafts such as miniature musical instruments made of juniper wood with pearl or shell inlay, colorful drawstring bags or embroidered textiles. During the rest of the week, you can go to the nearby community of El Nith (east of Ixmiquilpan) to find such items and visit the workshops where they're made. Combis depart from Jesús del Rosal near the market; taxis make the trip for US$2.

Ixmiquilpan's monastery was founded by Augustinians in the mid-1500s. The nave of its **church**, crowned by a huge Gothic vault, is unusual for a band of frescos depicting indigenous warriors in combat. Uncovered in recent decades, the murals show a clash between soldiers in Aztec military garb and scantily clad warriors using obsidian swords. Experts speculate the murals were painted by Mexica artists as propaganda against Chichimec invaders.

Feria del Jitomate (Tomato Fair) is celebrated throughout August with bullfights and dancing.

Places to Stay & Eat The town's best value is *Hotel Plaza Isabel* (☎ 3-13-96) on Juárez behind the Presidencia Municipal building. Clean wood-paneled single/double rooms, most facing the hotel's interior, cost US$10.50/16. On the edge of town, near the highway, is the modern, comfortable *Hotel del Valle Inn* (☎ 3-24-53, Cardonal 50), offering 28 standard-size peach-painted

On October 1, 2000, the telephone area code is due to change to ☎ 7 from 772, with the digits 72 added to the start of every local number (for example, the number 7-65-43 will become 727-65-43).

rooms, with firm mattresses, ceiling fans, and TVs for US$16/26. There is a tiny, circular swimming pool behind the hotel and a good restaurant.

For cheap and filling local fare, check out Ixmiquilpan's *market* where miles of stalls display large clay pots of items like chicken in mole verde and chiles rellenos. *Fonda El Herradero (Juárez 9)*, behind the Presidencia building, offers toothsome home cooking in an elegant colonial setting. Service is superb and prices are very reasonable with a *comida corrida* for under US$2.50. Cold, fresh fruit juices are served from huge pitchers. It's open 11 am to 7 pm.

Highway 130

Just 46km east of Pachuca is **Tulancingo** (population 87,000, altitude 2140m), which was briefly the Toltec capital before Tula. There's a Toltec pyramid at the foot of a cliff at **Huapalcalco**, 3km north. Market day is Thursday.

The Otomí village of **Tenango de Doria** is a rugged 40k north of Tulancingo by sometimes impassable roads. The residents make cotton fabric colorfully embroidered with animals and plants. In **Huehuetla**, 50km north of Tulancingo, there is one of the few communities of the tiny Tepehua indigenous group who embroider floral and geometric patterns on their quechquémitls and *enredos* (wraparound skirts).

Beyond Tulancingo, highway 130 descends toward Huauchinango in the state of Puebla (see the Northern Veracruz section in the Central Gulf Coast chapter).

East of Mexico City

Toll highway 150D goes east to Puebla across a high, dry region studded with volcanic peaks, including Popocatépetl, Iztaccíhuatl and La Malinche. The mountains offer scope for anything from pleasant alpine strolls to demanding technical climbs – though Popocatépetl is off limits because of recent volcanic activity. Just north of the highway, the tiny state of Tlaxcala (population 912,000) features a charming capital,

and relics from a rich pre-Hispanic and colonial history.

Puebla itself is one of Mexico's best preserved colonial cities, a pivot of its history, and a lively modern metropolis with a lot to see and do. Nevertheless, the state of Puebla is predominantly rural, with about half a million indigenous people. The indigenous presence helps give Puebla a rich handicraft output, including pottery, carved onyx and fine handwoven and embroidered textiles.

You can continue east from Puebla on highway 150D, past Pico de Orizaba (Mexico's highest mountain), and descend from the highlands to the coast of Veracruz state (see the Central Gulf Coast chapter). Alternatives are to swing north on highway 140 toward the remote Sierra Norte de Puebla, or descend to the Gulf Coast via Jalapa. South and east of Puebla, there's a choice of scenic routes through the mountains to the state and city of Oaxaca.

POPOCATÉPETL & IZTACCÍHUATL

Mexico's second and third highest mountains, Popocatépetl ('po-po-ka-TEH-pet-l') and Iztaccíhuatl ('iss-ta-SEE-wat-l'), form the eastern rim of the Valle de México, 72km southeast of Mexico City and 43km west of Puebla. While the craterless Iztaccíhuatl remains dormant, Popocatépetl in recent years has spouted plumes of gas and ash, forced the evacuation of 25,000 people, and spurred experts to issue warnings to the 30 million people who live within striking distance of the volcano. At the time of writing, leading vulcanologists were continuing to watch Popocatépetl with concern.

After explosions under the 5452m volcano Popocatépetl – which is Nahuatl for 'Smoking Mountain' – sent 5000 tons of hot ash into the sky, soldiers on December 22, 1994, evacuated 16 nearby villages. Popo, as the volcano is called locally, has been occasionally spewing ash since then, and in June 1997, after a large explosion, ash mixed with rain fell over Mexico City.

The federal agency Cenapred (National Disaster Prevention Center) keeps an eye on volcanic activity via variations in gas

AROUND MEXICO CITY

POPOCATÉPETL & IZTACCÍHUATL

To San Rafael
La Cabeza 5100m
Shelter (Ayoloco)
El Pecho 5286m
Las Rodillas 5100m
Shelter (República de Chile)
Los Pies 4700m
Río Alseseca
La Joya Parking Lot
Río Apoi
Altzomoni Lodge
TV & Microwave Station
PARQUE NACIONAL IZTACCÍHUATL-POPOCATÉPETL
Paso de Cortés 3650m
Cortez Monument, Visitor's Center
To Cholula
CLOSED TO THE PUBLIC DUE TO VOLCANIC ACTIVITY
To Amecameca, Mexico City
Tlamacas 3950m
Popocatépetl 5452m
Crater Rim
POPOCATÉPETL

emissions and seismic intensity, and provides information to the public through its website (www.cenapred.unam.mx).

Historically, Popo has been relatively kind. It has had 14 eruptive periods since the Spanish arrived in 1519, but none have caused a major loss of life or property. It's been over a thousand years since Popo delivered a really big blast, but experts don't discount the possibility of one now and it is for this reason that Mexican authorities are not allowing anyone on the mountain except scientists monitoring its activity.

Iztaccíhuatl (White Woman), 20km from Popo summit to summit, remains open to climbers and is perhaps all the more fetching because of her neighbor's unpredictable outbursts. Legend has it that Popo was a warrior who was in love with Izta, the emperor's daughter. As the story goes, Izta died of grief while Popo was away at war. Upon his return, he created the two mountains, laid her body on one and stood holding her funeral torch on the other. With some imagination, Izta does resemble a woman lying on her back. From the Mexico City side, you can, if the sky's clear, make out four peaks from left to right known as La Cabeza (the Head), El Pecho (the Breast), Las Rodillas (the Knees) and Los Pies (the Feet).

Amecameca
• pop 28,200 • elev 2480m ☎ 5

From the Mexico City side, the town of Amecameca, 60km by road from the city, is the key staging post for an Izta climb. But with a pair of volcanoes as a backdrop for the town's everyday activities and a few 16th-century churches, it makes an interesting destination in itself. There are ATMs around the plaza and a post office in the city hall. The best way to get around town is by bicycle-taxi (US$0.30).

San Carlos hotel on the southeast corner of the plaza has 30 clean, comfortable singles/doubles for US$5.25/8.50, US$5 more with TV. *Pepe's* on the south of the plaza has a pretty good comida corrida for US$2.50, as well as rabbit stew (US$2). A lively market is held on weekends in front of the church.

The Santuario del Sacromonte, 90m above Amecameca to the west, is an important pilgrimage site built over a cave that was the retreat of the Dominican friar Martín de Valencia in the early 16th century. It makes a delightful walk with awesome views of the town spread out beneath the volcanoes. Go through the arch on the southwest side of the plaza and walk down Avenida Fray Martín till the end. From there, follow the stations of the cross uphill to the sanctuary.

From Mexico City's Terminal Oriente (TAPO), the 2nd-class Volcanes bus line runs every 15 minutes to/from Amecameca (1¼ hours, US$1.50) and Cuautla. From Amecameca bus station, turn right and walk two blocks to the plaza.

Hiking

Izta's highest peak is El Pecho at 5286m, and all routes to it require a night on the mountain. Between the starting point at La Joya parking lot and Las Rodillas, there is a shelter hut that could be used during an ascent of El Pecho. On average, it takes five hours to reach the hut from La Joya, another six hours from the hut to El Pecho, and six hours back to the base. Before making the ascent, climbers should register at the La Joya visitor's center by writing down their names (and should cross them out when they've returned).

If you'd rather not climb Izta but would still like to spend a day enjoying the mountain scenery, Paso de Cortés has plenty of lower-altitude trails through pine forests and grassy meadows; some offer breathtaking glimpses of the nearby peaks. Trails begin at La Joya. Taxis departing from the southeast side of Amecameca's zócalo will take you to La Joya (40 minutes), wait for three hours, then take you back for US$20.

A longer stay at the Paso de Cortés is possible at *Altzomoni Lodge*, which provides basic accommodations for US$2 per night. The lodge is by a TV and microwave station roughly halfway between the visitor's center at the Paso and La Joya. Bring bedding and drinking water. Still more basic accommodations can be found at Paso de

Cortés. The visitor's center contains 25 beds with blankets and a bathroom but no electricity.

Other trails depart from the village of San Rafael, on the road east of Tlalmanalco.

Climate & Conditions It can be windy and well-below freezing on the upper slopes of Izta any time of year and it is nearly always below freezing near the summit at night. Ice and snow are fixtures here; the average snow line is 4200m. The best months for ascents are October to February, when there is hard snow for crampons. The rainy season, April to September, brings with it the threat of whiteouts, thunderstorms and avalanches.

Anyone can be affected by altitude problems, including life-threatening altitude sickness. Even the Paso de Cortés (3650m), the turnoff for Izta, is at a level where you should know the symptoms (see Altitude Sickness in the Health section of the Facts for the Visitor chapter).

Guides Iztaccíhuatl should be attempted by experienced climbers *only*, and because of hidden crevices on the ice-covered upper slopes, a guide is highly recommended.

Mexico City-based guide Mario Andrade has led many Izta ascents. His fee for leading climbers up Izta is US$140 per person; the cost includes transportation from Mexico City to Izta and back, lodging and national park entry fees, and the use of rope. Contact Andrade, who speaks Spanish and English, at his Mexico City home (☎ 5-875-01-05). His mailing address is PO Box M-10380, México DF, Mexico. In Amecameca, José Luis Ariza, a member of the rescue squad Búsqueda y Salvamento, leads climbers up Izta's peak year round and charges US$100 for one person, US$50 for each additional person. Ariza, who has scaled peaks throughout Latin America, can be reached at his home in Amecameca (☎ 5-978-13-35).

TEXCOCO
• pop 19,700 • elev 2778m

Some of Diego Rivera's finest mural work can be found at the agriculture school of the **Universidad Autónoma de Chapingo** just outside Texcoco, 67km from Mexico City via highway 136. In the chapel of the former hacienda, now part of the university's administration building, sensual murals intertwine images of the Mexican struggle for agrarian reform and the Earth's fertility cycles. One of the 24 panels covering the chapel's walls and ceiling depicts buried martyrs of reform symbolically fertilizing the land and thus the future. The chapel is open 9 am to 3 pm Monday to Friday and 10 am to 2 pm Saturday to Sunday. Take a local bus from metro Zaragoza, or a direct bus from TAPO, to downtown Texcoco where there are 'Chapingo' combis.

Also worth visiting in this area are the **Parque Nacional Molino de Flores Nezahualcóyotl**, 3km east of Texcoco, and the archaeological site of **Baños de Nezahualcóyotl**, 5km farther. Established in 1585 as the first wheat mill in the region, the Molino later served as a *pulque* hacienda before being expropriated by the government in 1937. Today many of the original buildings are in ruins, but some have been partly restored and opened to the public. Works of local artists are exhibited in the *tinacal* where pulque was processed. A walk past the main building will take you to an unusual little church built into the side of a gorge, accessible on one side by a hanging bridge. To get to the park, take a 'Molino de Flores' combi from downtown Texcoco.

The little known, but interesting archaeological site Baños de Nezahualcóyotl contains the remains of temples, a palace, fountains, spring-fed aqueducts, and baths built by the Texcocan poet-king, Nezahualcóyotl. He was perhaps the only Mesoamerican ruler to observe a type of monotheistic religion, worshiping an abstract god with feminine and masculine qualities. The site is on a hilltop with a view as far as Xochimilco (when the pollution isn't bad). To get there, take a 'Tlamincas' combi from downtown Texcoco, or from the right fork just outside the national park's entrance, and get off at the sign pointing to the site. From there, it's a kilometer walk to the summit.

TLAXCALA
• pop 63,300 • elev 2252m ☎ 2

About 120km east of Mexico City and 30km north of Puebla, this quiet colonial town is the capital of Tlaxcala state, Mexico's smallest. It makes a pleasant day trip from either city.

History
In the last centuries before the Spanish conquest, numerous small warrior kingdoms *(señoríos)* arose in the Tlaxcala area. Some of them formed a loose federation that managed to stay independent of the Aztec empire as it spread from the Valle de México in the 15th century. The most important kingdom seems to have been Tizatlán, now on the edge of Tlaxcala city.

When the Spanish arrived in 1519 the Tlaxcalans fought fiercely at first, but then became Cortés' staunchest allies against the Aztecs (with the exception of one chief, Xicoténcatl the Younger, who tried at least twice to rouse his people against the Spanish and is now a Mexican hero). The Spanish rewarded the Tlaxcalans with privileges and used them to help pacify and settle Chichimec areas to the north. In 1527 Tlaxcala became the seat of the first bishopric in Nueva España, but a plague in the 1540s decimated the population and the town never played an important role again.

More recently, Tlaxcala made headlines when Bill and Hillary Rodham Clinton stopped over during a diplomatic visit in May of 1997. Many Tlaxcalans are still not sure why the US president and first lady chose their town.

Orientation
Two central plazas meet on the corner of Independencia and Muñoz. The northern one, surrounded by colonial buildings, is the zócalo, called Plaza de la Constitución. The other, Plaza Xicohténcatl, has a crafts market on weekends. Tlaxcala's bus station is 1km southwest of the plazas.

Information
The Tlaxcala state tourist office (☎ 462-00-27), on the corner of Juárez and Lardizabal,

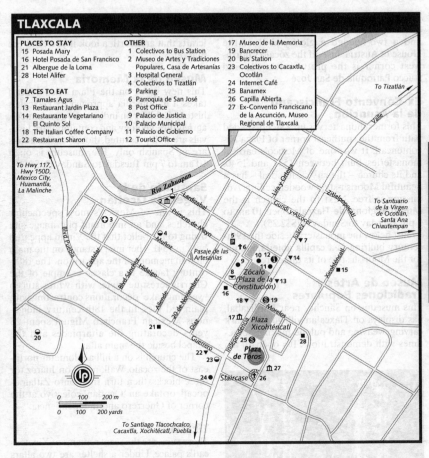

TLAXCALA

PLACES TO STAY
15 Posada Mary
16 Hotel Posada de San Francisco
21 Albergue de la Loma
28 Hotel Alifer

PLACES TO EAT
7 Tamales Agus
13 Restaurant Jardín Plaza
14 Restaurante Vegetariano El Quinto Sol
18 The Italian Coffee Company
22 Restaurant Sharon

OTHER
1 Colectivos to Bus Station
2 Museo de Artes y Tradiciones Populares, Casa de Artesanías
3 Hospital General
4 Colectivos to Tizatlán
5 Parking
6 Parroquia de San José
8 Post Office
9 Palacio de Justicia
10 Palacio Municipal
11 Palacio de Gobierno
12 Tourist Office
17 Museo de la Memoria
19 Bancrecer
20 Bus Station
23 Colectivos to Cacaxtla, Ocotlán
24 Internet Café
25 Banamex
26 Capilla Abierta
27 Ex-Convento Franciscano de la Ascunción, Museo Regional de Tlaxcala

To Tizatlán
To Santuario de la Virgen de Ocotlán, Santa Ana Chiautempan
To Hwy 117, Hwy 150D, Mexico City, Huamantla, La Malinche
Río Zahuapan
Lardizabal
Primero de Mayo
Muñoz
Blvd Puebla
Castelar
Blvd Sánchez Hidalgo
Allende
20 de Noviembre
Díaz
Guerrero
Independencia
Lira y Ortega
Gundi y Alcocer
Zitlalpopocatl
Xicohténcatl
Morelos
Valle
Pasaje de las Artesanías
Zócalo (Plaza de la Constitución)
Plaza Xicohténcatl
Plaza de Toros
Staircase

0   100   200 m
0   100   200 yards

To Santiago Tlacochcalco, Cacaxtla, Xochitécatl, Puebla

AROUND MEXICO CITY

is open 9 am to 7 pm Monday to Friday and 10 am to 6 pm Saturday and Sunday. Its accommodating staff speak some English. The office runs tours of the city and most of the outlying areas on Saturday, with departures scheduled from the Hotel Posada de San Francisco at 10.15 am (US$1.75, including transport).

The post office is on the west side of the zócalo; Bancrecer (with ATM) has a branch on the southeast corner. There is an Internet café on Independencia just south of Guerrero, open 9 am to 8 pm daily.

Zócalo

The spacious, shady zócalo is one of the best looking in Mexico. Most of its north side is taken up by the 16th-century **Palacio Municipal**, a former grain storehouse, and the **Palacio de Gobierno**; inside the latter, there are more than 450 sq meters of vivid murals of Tlaxcala's history by Desiderio Hernández Xochitiotzin. The 16th-century building on the northwest side of the zócalo, adjacent to the post office, is the **Palacio de Justicia**, the former Capilla Real de Indios, constructed for the use of indigenous nobles.

The handsome mortar bas-reliefs around its doorway depict the seal of Castilla y León and a two-headed eagle, symbol of the House of Austria. Just off the zócalo's north-west corner is the pretty brick, tile and stucco **Parroquia de San José**.

Ex-Convento Franciscano de la Asunción

This former monastery is up a steep, shaded path from the southeast corner of Plaza Xicohténcatl. It was one of Mexico's earliest monasteries, built between 1537 and 1540, and its church – the city's cathedral – has a beautiful Moorish-style wooden ceiling. Admission is free. Next to the church is the **Museo Regional de Tlaxcala**, open 10 am to 5 pm Tuesday to Sunday (US$2.25).

Just below the monastery, beside the 19th-century bullring, is a **capilla abierta**, unique for the Moorish style of its three arches.

Museo de Artes y Tradiciones Populares

This museum, on Sánchez near Lardizabal, has displays on Tlaxcalan village life, mask carving, weaving and pulque-making, sometimes with demonstrations. It's open 10 am

JOHN NEUBAUER

Santuario de la Virgen de Ocotlán

to 6 pm daily except Monday (US$0.70). Next door, the Casa de Artesanías has handicrafts that are worth a look if you're in the market.

Museo de la Memoria

This new space on the Plaza Xicohténcatl takes a multimedia approach to Tlaxcala's history. Exhibits on indigenous government, agriculture, geology and contemporary festivals are well-presented, though explanations are in Spanish only. The museum is open 10 am to 7 pm Tuesday to Sunday (US$1).

Santuario de la Virgen de Ocotlán

This is one of Mexico's most spectacular churches, and an important pilgrimage site owing to the belief that the Virgin appeared here in 1541 – her image stands on the main altar in memory of the apparition. The 18th-century façade is a classic example of the Churrigueresque style, with white stucco 'wedding cake' decorations contrasting with plain red tiles. In the 18th century, indigenous Mexican Francisco Miguel spent 25 years decorating the altarpieces and the chapel beside the main altar.

The church is on a hill a kilometer northeast of the zócalo. Walk north on Juárez for three blocks, then turn right onto Zitlalpopocatl, or take an 'Ocotlán' colectivo at the corner of Guerrero and Independencia.

Tizatlán

These ruins are the scant remains of Xicoténcatl's palace. Under a shelter are two altars with some faded frescos showing gods such as Tezcatlipoca (Smoking Mirror), Tlahuizcalpantecuhtli (Morning Star) and Mictlantecuhtli (Underworld). The Templo San Esteban, next to the ruins, has a 16th-century Franciscan capilla abierta and frescos showing angels playing medieval instruments. The site is on a small hill 4km north of the town center; take a 'Tizatlán Iglesia' colectivo from the corner of Sánchez and Muñoz.

Courses

Estela Silva's Mexican Home Cooking program (☎ 468-09-78, fax 46-2-49-98, mexicanhomecooking@yahoo.com) offers visitors hands-on instruction in the preparation of classic Mexican dishes. A basic five-day course that focuses on Puebla cuisine is set in the Talavera-tiled kitchen of Silva's hacienda-style home, which is in the small village of Santiago Tlacochcalco, a few kilometers south of Tlaxcala. The cost of the program, including lodging (she has three double rooms with private baths and fireplaces) and three meals daily for a week, is US$850. The postal address is Apdo 64, Tlaxcala, Tlax, Mexico 90000.

Special Events

On the third Monday in May, the figure of the Virgin of Ocotlán is carried from its hilltop residence to other churches, attracting crowds of believers and onlookers. Throughout the month, processions commemorating the miracle attract pilgrims from around the republic and as far away as Canada.

The neighboring town of Santa Ana Chiautempan hosts the Feria Nacional del Sarape (National Sarape Fair) for two weeks on either side of July 26 to correspond with the celebration of its patron saint's day.

Places to Stay

The cheapest option in Tlaxcala is the friendly, if basic, *Posada Mary* (☎ 462-96-55, *Xicohténcatl 19*), a concrete shell enclosing a parking lot, with rooms for US$4.50.

The modern *Albergue de la Loma* (☎ 462-04-24, *Guerrero 58*), at the top of 61 steps, has big, clean singles/doubles with tiled bathrooms for US$15/16, some offering views of the city. The central *Hotel Alifer* (☎ 462-56-78, alifer@tlax.net.mx, *Morelos 11*) has clean rooms, with TVs and phones, around a paved parking lot for US$16/24. The hillside hotel is less than two blocks from the zócalo, but the last 50m stretch is a steep climb.

Hotel Posada San Francisco (☎ 462-60-22, *info@posadasnfrancisco.com*), on the south side of the zócalo in a restored 19th-century mansion, has a couple of restaurants, tennis courts and an inviting pool; prices start at US$56/64.

Places to Eat

For breakfast and healthy snacks and meals, try the popular *Restaurant Vegetariano El Quinto Sol* on Juárez; it features fresh salads, veggie burgers and a large variety of juices. Fixed-price meals (for US$2.75) are a good value. A little farther up Juárez, the tiny *Tamales Agus* serves traditional mole and salsa verde tamales along with assorted *atole* drinks.

There's a row of places under the arcades on the east side of the zócalo. *Restaurant Jardín Plaza* is the best of the bunch, with regional food served in a pleasant indoor-outdoor setting. On the south side, *The Italian Coffee Company*, a Mexican franchise, offers top-notch espresso, cappuccino and other coffee drinks, as well as a variety of gourmet teas.

For scrumptious tacos, try the clean, unpretentious *Restaurant Sharon* (*Guerrero 14*), near Independencia. It is open 1 to 7 pm daily except Saturday and an order of three beef or pork tacos costs US$2.50.

Shopping

Embroidered capes and *huipiles* from Santa Ana Chiautempan, carved canes from Tizatlán, amaranth candies from San Miguel del Milagro and other local handicrafts are sold every day along the Pasaje de Artesanías, which forms an arc northeast of the Muñoz-Allende intersection.

Getting There & Away

The bus station is west of the zócalo. Flecha Azul 2nd-class buses travel to and from Puebla every eight minutes for US$1. To/from Mexico City's Terminal Oriente (TAPO) Autobuses Tlaxcala-Apizaco-Huamantla (ATAH) operates its 1st-class 'expresso' buses every 20 minutes (two hours, US$5.75) and 'ordinario' buses every half-hour (three hours, US$4.75).

Getting Around

Buses and colectivos in Tlaxcala cost US$0.30. Most colectivos at the bus station go to the town center. From the center to the bus station, catch a blue-and-white colectivo along the east side of Boulevard Sánchez.

There is a 24-hour parking lot underneath the plaza that's located behind the Parroquia de San José.

CACAXTLA & XOCHITÉCATL

The hilltop ruins at Cacaxtla ('ca-CASHT-la') feature vividly colored and well-preserved frescos showing, among many other scenes, nearly life-size jaguar and eagle warriors engaged in battle. The ruins were discovered in September 1975 when a group of men from the nearby village of San Miguel del Milagro, in search of a reputedly valuable cache of relics, dug a tunnel and came across a mural.

The much older ruins at Xochitécatl ('so-chi-TEH-catl'), 2km away, include an exceptionally wide pyramid as well as a circular pyramid. A German archaeologist led the first systematic exploration of the site in 1969, but it wasn't until 1994 that the pyramids were uncovered and opened to the public. The two archaeological sites, 32km northwest of Puebla and 20km southwest of Tlaxcala, are among Mexico's most interesting.

Though both sites can be toured on one's own, explanatory signs tend to be either sketchy or overly technical. One alternative is to join a Sunday tour conducted by the Tlaxcala tourist office, departing from the Hotel Posada de San Francisco in Tlaxcala at 10.15 am and returning at 2.30 pm. The fee of US$1.50 includes transport and entry to both sites and explanations by authorized guides. It is also possible to hire a guide at the site between Thursday and Sunday.

History

Cacaxtla was the capital of a group of Olmeca-Xicallanca or Putún Maya, who first came to central Mexico as early as 400 AD. After the decline of Cholula (which they may have helped bring about) around 600 AD, they became the chief power in southern Tlaxcala and the Puebla valley. Cacaxtla peaked from 650 to 900 AD before being abandoned by the year 1000 AD in the face of possibly Chichimec newcomers.

Two kilometers west of Cacaxtla, atop a higher hill, the ruins of Xochitécatl predate Christ by a millennium. Just who first occupied the area is a matter of dispute, but experts agree that whereas Cacaxtla primarily served as living quarters for the ruling class, Xochitécatl was chiefly used for gory ceremonies to honor Quecholli, the fertility god. That isn't to say Cacaxtla didn't hold similar ceremonies; the skeletal remains of more than 200 mutilated children found there attest to Cacaxtla's bloody past.

Cacaxtla

From the parking lot, which is opposite the entrance to the site, it's a 200m walk to the Cacaxtla ticket office, museum, shop and restaurant. The site is open 10 am to 5.30 pm daily (US$2.75, free on Sunday and holidays). Save your ticket, as it will get you into the Xochitécatl ruins as well, and vice versa.

From the ticket office, it's another 300m to the main attraction – a natural platform 200m long and 25m high called the Gran Basamento (Great Base), which is now under a huge metal roof. Here stood Cacaxtla's main religious and civil buildings and the residences of its ruling priestly classes. At the top of the entry stairs is an open space called the Plaza Norte. From here, you will follow a clockwise path around the ruins until you reach the **murals**.

Archaeologists have yet to determine the identity of the muralists. Many of the symbols found in the murals are clearly from the Mexican highlands. Yet a Mayan influence, from Yucatán, appears in all of them. The combined appearance of Mayan style and Mexican-highlands' symbols in a mural is unique to Cacaxtla and the subject of much speculation.

Before reaching the first mural you come to a small patio whose main feature is an altar fronted by a small square pit in which numerous human remains were discovered. Just beyond the altar, along the west edge of the complex, you come upon the Templo de Venus, which contains two anthropomorphic figures in blue – a man and a woman – wearing short jaguar skins. The name of the temple is attributed to the appearance of numerous half stars around the female figure, which are associated with the planet Venus.

On the opposite side of the path toward the Plaza Norte, the Templo Rojo (named for the amount of red paint used), contains four murals, only one of which is currently visible. Its weird imagery is dominated by a row of maize crops whose husks contain human heads.

Facing the north side of the Plaza Norte is the long Mural de la Batalla (Battle Mural), dating from before 700 AD. It shows two groups of warriors, one wearing jaguar skins and the other bird feathers, engaged in ferocious battle. The Olmeca-Xicallanca (the jaguar-warriors with round shields) are clearly repelling invading Huastecs (the bird-warriors adorned with jade ornaments and deformed skulls).

At the end of the Mural de la Batalla, turn left and climb some steps to see the second main group of murals, to your right behind a fence. The two major murals from about 750 AD show a figure in jaguar costume and a black-painted figure in bird costume (who may be the Olmeca-Xicallanca priest-governor) standing upon a plumed serpent.

Xochitécatl

To enter the Xochitécatl site, show your ticket from Cacaxtla to a guard at the entrance of the parking lot, or buy a ticket from him. From there, follow a path around to the circular Pirámide de la Espiral, atop which there's a cross put there by people from a neighboring village long before they knew the hill contained a pyramid. The path then leads to three other pyramids – the lowest in stature is (Basamento de los Volcanes), the next is the mid-size (Pirámide de la Serpiente), and the last is the quite large (Pirámide de las Flores). The site is open 10 am to 5.30 pm daily (US$2.75, free on Sunday and holidays or with your Cacaxtla ticket).

Pirámide de la Espiral Because of its outline and the materials used, archaeologists believe this circular pyramid was built between 1000 and 800 BC. Its form and location atop a high hill suggest it may have been used as an astronomical observation post or as a temple to Ehecatl, the wind god.

Basamento de los Volcanes Only the base of this pyramid remains, and it is made of materials from two periods. Cut square stones were placed over the original stones, visible in some areas, and then stuccoed over. The colored stones used to build Tlaxcala's municipal palace appear to have come from this site.

Pirámide de la Serpiente This structure gets its name from a large piece of carved stone with the head of a snake at one end. Its most interesting feature is the huge pot found at its center, carved from a single boulder that was hauled from another region. Scientists surmise it was used to hold water.

Pirámide de las Flores Experts speculate that rituals honoring the fertility god were held at this pyramid, within which were found several sculptures and the remains of 30 sacrificed infants. Near the pyramid's base – the fourth widest in Latin America – is a pool carved from a massive rock, where the infants were believed to have been washed before being killed.

Getting There & Away

The Cacaxtla site is 1.5km uphill from a back road between San Martín Texmelucan (near highway 150) and highway 119, which is the secondary road between Puebla and Tlaxcala. By car, turn west off highway 119 just south of Tlaxcala. A sign 1.5km west of the village of Nativitas points to Cacaxtla and to the nearby village of San Miguel del Milagro.

By public transport from Tlaxcala, take a 'San Miguel del Milagro' colectivo from the corner of Independencia and Guerrero; it will drop you off about 500m from Cacaxtla. Alternatively, a 'Nativitas-Texoloc-Tlaxcala' colectivo, which departs from the same corner, goes to the town of Nativitas, 3km from Cacaxtla; from there, catch a 'Zona Arqueológica' colectivo directly to the site. From Cacaxtla to Xochitécatl, take a taxi (US$3), or hike the 2km.

LA MALINCHE

This dormant 4460m volcano, named after Cortés' indigenous interpreter and lover, is

43km southeast of Tlaxcala and 73km northeast of Puebla. Its long, sweeping slopes dominate the skyline north of Puebla.

The main route to the summit is from highway 136; turn south at the sign 'Centro Vacacional Malintzi.' Before you reach the center, you must register at the entrance to Parque Nacional La Malintzi, which is open 9 am to 5 pm daily.

Centro Vacacional Malintzi (☎ 2-462-40-98, fax 2-461-07-00) is a state-run resort with woodsy grounds and fine views of the peak. Cabins with fireplaces, kitchens and basic accommodations for up to six people are US$28, slightly higher during holiday seasons. You may also camp for US$2. Those not staying at the center can leave their car in its parking lot for US$1.25.

Above the center, the road becomes impassable by car. Then it's a kilometer by footpath, through trees initially, on to a ridge leading to the top – an arduous hike of about five hours. Hikers should take precautions against altitude sickness (see Health in Facts for the Visitor). La Malinche is snow-capped only a few weeks each year.

There are three buses a day that go to the Centro Vacacional Malintzi (US$1) from downtown Apizaco, at Avenida Hidalgo and Aquiles Serdán, in front of the Elektra store. Apizaco can be reached via frequent buses from Tlaxcala.

HUAMANTLA
• **pop 36,000** • **elev 2500m** ☎ 2

This town dates from 1534 and is a national historic monument. Two of the most notable buildings are the 16th-century **Ex-Convento de San Francisco** and the 17th-century baroque **Iglesia de San Luis Obispo**.

During the first three weeks of August, Huamantla celebrates its *feria*. A day before the feast of the Assumption (August 15), inhabitants cover the town's streets with beautiful carpets made of flowers and colored sawdust. The Saturday following this event, there is a 'running of the bulls,' similar to that in Pamplona, Spain – but much more dangerous, because there is nothing to hide behind and the bulls charge from two directions.

Worthy hotels in the area include *Hotel Mesón del Portal* (☎ 472-26-26, Parque Juárez 9), which charges US$11/13 for singles/doubles, and *Hotel Cuamanco* (☎ 472-22-09), on Highway 136 east of town, which charges US$13/19. Rates are higher during Huamantla's feria, for which rooms are booked well in advance.

PUEBLA
• **pop 1.2 million** • **elev 2162m** ☎ 2

Few Mexican cities preserve the Spanish imprint as faithfully as Puebla. There are more than 70 churches and, in the central area alone, a thousand other colonial buildings – many adorned with the hand-painted tiles for which the city is famous. Located on the Veracruz-Mexico City road, and set in a broad valley with Popocatépetl and Iztaccíhuatl rising to the west, Puebla has always played a main role in national affairs.

Strongly Catholic, *criollo* and conservative, its people *(poblanos)* maintained Spanish affinities longer than most in Mexico. In the 19th century, their patriotism was regarded as suspect and today Puebla's Spanish-descended families have a reputation among other Mexicans for snobbishness. Nevertheless, it's a lively city with much to see and do. The historic center, where a great deal of conservation and restoration has taken place, has a prosperous modern dimension too, with its share of fancy boutiques. Cerro de Guadalupe is a peaceful retreat from city noises, as well as the site of a celebrated Mexican military victory and a clutch of museums. On the negative side, some areas of Puebla are squalid, polluted and unsafe to walk at night.

History
Founded by Spanish settlers in 1531 as Ciudad de los Ángeles with the aim of surpassing the nearby pre-Hispanic religious center of Cholula, the city became Puebla de los Ángeles eight years later and quickly grew into an important Catholic center. Fine pottery had always been made from the local clay, and after the colonists introduced new materials and techniques, Puebla pottery became an art and an industry. By

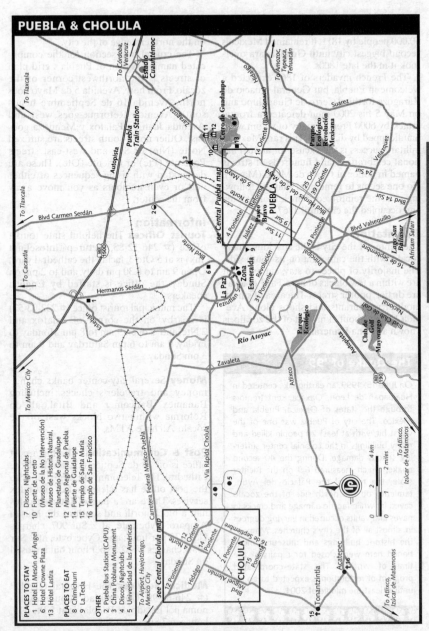

PUEBLA & CHOLULA

AROUND MEXICO CITY

PLACES TO STAY
1 Hotel El Mesón del Ángel
6 Hotel Crowne Plaza
13 Hotel Lastra

PLACES TO EAT
8 Chimichurri
9 La Tecla

OTHER
2 Puebla Bus Station (CAPU)
3 China Poblana Monument
4 Discos, Nightclubs
5 Universidad de las Américas
7 Discos, Nightclubs
10 Fuerte de Loreto
11 Museo de la No Intervención
   (Museo de Historia Natural)
12 Planetario de Guadalupe
14 Fuerte de Guadalupe
15 Templo de Santa María
16 Templo de San Francisco

the late 18th century, the city was also an important textile and glass producer. With 50,000 people by 1811, it remained Mexico's second-biggest city until Guadalajara overtook it in the late 1800s.

The French invaders of 1862 expected a welcome in Puebla, but General Ignacio de Zaragoza fortified Cerro de Guadalupe and on May 5 his 2000 men defeated a frontal attack by 6000 French, many of whom were handicapped by diarrhea. This rare Mexican military success is the excuse for annual national celebrations and hundreds of streets named in honor of Cinco de Mayo (May 5). No one seems to remember that the following year the reinforced French took Puebla and occupied the city until 1867.

Orientation

The center of the city is the spacious, shady zócalo, with the cathedral on its south side. The majority of places to stay, eat and visit are within a few blocks of here. Farther away are dirtier, poorer streets. The area of smart, modern restaurants and shops along Avenida Juárez, about 2km west of the zócalo, is known as Zona Esmeralda.

The Quake of '99

On June 15, 1999, an earthquake centered in Huajuapan de León, Oaxaca, sent tremors through the states of Oaxaca, Puebla and México. The city of Puebla was one of the worst hit, with at least 20 people killed and many buildings in the colonial center suffering serious damage. During the 40-second quake, which measured 6.9 on the Richter scale, the roof of the Palacio del Ayuntamiento on the north side of the zócalo caved in, while façade damage and cracks in naves and vaults occurred in varying degrees in almost all of the city's churches. Many of the historic buildings and museums mentioned here were closed for repairs at the time of writing. The state-coordinated program of restoration is expected to go on until at least the middle of 2001.

✺✺✺✺✺✺✺✺✺✺✺✺✺✺

Buses arrive at a modern bus station, the Central de Autobuses de Puebla (CAPU), on the northern edge of the city.

The crucial intersection for the complicated naming system of Puebla's grid plan of streets is the northwest corner of the zócalo. From here, Avenida 5 de Mayo goes north, Avenida 16 de Septiembre heads south, Avenida Reforma goes west and Avenida Juan de Palafox y Mendoza goes east. Other north-south streets are suffixed Norte (Nte) or Sur, and west-east streets Poniente (Pte) or Oriente (Ote). These are designated with rising sequences of either odd or even numbers as you move away from the center.

Information

Tourist Offices The helpful state tourist office (☎ 246-12-85, securep@infosel.net.mx) is at 5 Ote 3, facing the cathedral yard. Open 9 am to 8.30 pm daily, and to 2 pm on Sunday, the office is staffed by English speakers.

The municipal tourist office (☎ 232-03-57) is nearby, on the corner of Palafox and 2 Nte, and is open 9 am to 8 pm Monday to Friday, 9 am to 6 pm Saturday and 9 am to 3 pm Sunday.

Money Several city-center banks change money and traveler's checks including Banamex, Bancomer and Bital, all on Reforma within two blocks west of the zócalo. All have ATMs.

Post & Communications The main post office is on 16 de Septiembre, south of the cathedral. The Telecomm office next door to the post office has telegram, fax and telex services. There are a pair of Internet cafés half a block north and south of the Museo Amparo: Cybercafé, at 2 Sur 907, charges US$1.75 per hour; and Cyberbyte, at 2 Sur 505B, charges US$2.25 per hour but is closed on Sunday.

Medical Services The Hospital UPAEP (☎ 246-60-99; Universidad Popular Autónoma del Estado de Puebla) is at 5 Pte 715, between 7 Sur and 9 Sur.

AROUND MEXICO CITY

CENTRAL PUEBLA

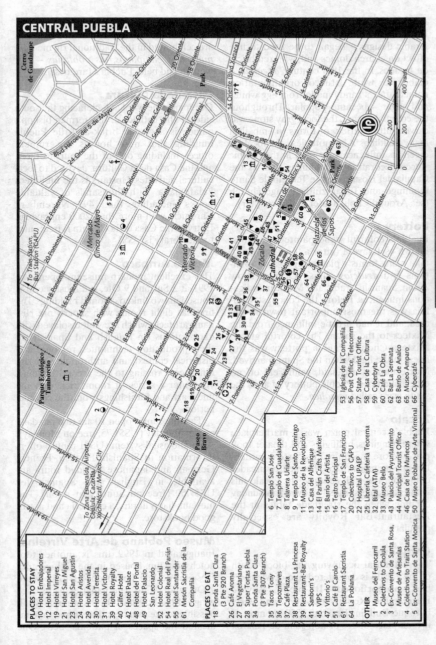

PLACES TO STAY
10 Hotel Embajadores
12 Hotel Imperial
19 Hotel Virreyes
21 Hotel San Miguel
23 Hotel San Agustín
24 Hotel Aristos
29 Hotel Avenida
30 Hotel Teresita
31 Hotel Victoria
39 Hotel Royalty
40 Gilfer Hotel
42 Hotel Palace
48 Hotel del Portal
49 Hotel Palacio
    San Leonardo
52 Hotel Colonial
54 Hotel Real del Parián
55 Hotel Santander
61 Mesón Sacristía de la
    Compañia

PLACES TO EAT
18 Fonda Santa Clara
    (3 Pte 920 Branch)
26 Café Aroma
27 El Vegetariano
28 Super Tortas Puebla
34 Fonda Santa Clara
    (3 Pte 307 Branch)
35 Tacos Tomy
36 Tepoznieves
37 Café Plaza
38 Restaurant La Princesa
39 Restaurant-Bar Royalty
41 Sanborn's
45 VIPS
47 Vittorio's
51 Café El Carolo
61 Restaurant Sacristía
64 La Poblana

OTHER
1 Museo del Ferrocarril
2 Colectivos to Cholula
3 Ex-Convento de Santa Rosa,
    Museo de Artesanías
4 Colectivos to Train Station
5 Ex-Convento de Santa Monica

6 Templo San José
7 Templo de Guadalupe
8 Talavera Uriarte
9 Templo de Santo Domingo
11 Museo de la Revolución
13 Casa del Alfeñique
14 El Parián Crafts Market
15 Barrio del Artista
16 Teatro Principal
17 Templo de San Francisco
20 Colectivos to CAPU
22 Hospital UPAEP
25 Librería Cafetería Teorema
32 Bital (ATM)
33 Museo Bello
43 Palacio del Ayuntamiento
44 Municipal Tourist Office
46 Casa de los Muñecos
50 Museo Poblano de Arte Virreinal

53 Iglesia de la Compañia
56 Post Office, Telecomm
57 State Tourist Office
58 Casa de la Cultura
59 Cyberbyte
60 Café La Obra
63 Bar La Serenata
63 Barrio de Analco
65 Museo Amparo
66 Cybercafé

Architecture

In the 17th century, local tiles – some in Arabic designs – began to be used to fine effect on church domes and, with red brick, on façades. In the 18th century, *alfeñique* – elaborate white stucco ornamentation named after a candy made from egg whites and sugar – became popular. Throughout the colonial period, the local gray stone was carved into a variety of forms to embellish many buildings. Also notable is the local indigenous influence, best seen in the prolific stucco decoration of buildings such as the Capilla del Rosario in the Templo de Santo Domingo and Tonantzintla village church (see Around Cholula later in this chapter).

Pottery

Puebla's colorful hand-painted ceramics, known as Talavera (after a town in Spain), take many forms – plates, cups, vases, fountains and *azulejos* (tiles). Designs show Asian, Spanish-Arabic and Mexican indigenous influences. Before the conquest, Cholula was the most important town in the area, and it had artistic influence from the Mixtecs to the south. The colorful glazed Mixteca-Cholula-Puebla pottery was the finest in the land when the Spanish arrived; Moctezuma, it was said, would eat off no other. The finest Puebla pottery of all is the white ware called *majolica*.

Zócalo

Puebla's central plaza was a marketplace where hangings, bullfights and theater took place before it acquired its current garden-like appearance in 1854. The nearby arcades date from the 16th century. The zócalo fills with entertainers (mostly clowns) on Sunday evening when the streetside tables at the Restaurant-Bar Royalty are especially popular.

Cathedral

The cathedral occupying the block south of the zócalo is considered one of Mexico's best proportioned. It blends severe Herreresque-Renaissance style and early baroque. Building began in 1550 but most of it took place under bishop Juan de Palafox in the 1640s. At 69m, the towers are the highest in the country. The cathedral's bells are celebrated in the traditional rhyme *Para mujeres y campanas, las poblanas* – 'For women and bells, Puebla's (are best).'

Casa de la Cultura

Occupying the whole block facing the south side of the cathedral, the former bishop's palace is a classic brick-and-tile Puebla building that now houses government offices, including one of the tourist offices, and the Casa de la Cultura, devoted to local cultural activities. Upstairs is the **Biblioteca Palafoxiana**, with thousands of valuable books, including the 1493 Nuremberg Chronicle with more than 2000 engravings. Entry to the Casa de la Cultura is free; entry to the library is US$1.

Museo Amparo

This excellent modern museum, opened in 1991 at 2 Sur and 9 Ote, is a must-see. It is housed in two linked colonial buildings. The first has eight rooms with superb pre-Hispanic artifacts, which are well-displayed with explanations (in English and Spanish) of their production techniques, regional and historical context and anthropological significance. Crossing to the second building, you enter a series of rooms rich with the finest art and furnishings from the colonial period.

The museum is open 10 am to 6 pm daily except Tuesday (US$1.75, free on Monday). An audiovisual system (US$1 rental) offers information in Spanish, English, French, German and Japanese. Guided tours are available in English and Spanish for US$7.50 (free on Sunday at noon). The museum has a library, a cafeteria and a very good bookstore.

Museo Poblano de Arte Virreinal

Inaugurated in 1999, this is another top-notch museum, housed in the 17th-century Hospital de San Pedro on 4 Nte between 4 Ote and 2 Ote. The galleries were once wings of the hospital. On the walls, it is still possible to see numbers that at one time indicated the spaces of patients' beds. One

AROUND MEXICO CITY

Museum Hours

Nearly all of Puebla's many museums are open 10 am to 5 pm daily except Monday. Admission prices vary; most are free on Sunday. The main exception to these rules is the Museo Amparo, which is open 10 am to 6 pm daily except Tuesday (free on Monday).

❊❊❊❊❊❊❊❊❊❊❊❊

gallery displays temporary exhibits on the art of the viceregal period (16th to 19th century) in Mexico, while another houses a fascinating permanent exhibit on the hospital's history, including a fine model of the building. The museum features a library and an excellent bookstore, with many art and architecture books in English. Entry is US$1.75.

Museo Bello

This house at 3 Pte 302 is filled with the diverse art and crafts collection of 19th-century industrialist José Luis Bello and his son Mariano. There is exquisite French, English, Japanese and Chinese porcelain, and a large collection of Puebla Talavera. Admission is US$1.25 (free on Sunday). Tours are available in Spanish and English.

Casa de los Muñecos

The tiles on the House of Puppets on 2 Nte, near the zócalo's northeast corner, caricature the city fathers who took the house's owner to court because his home was taller than theirs. Inside is the Museo Universitario (US$0.50, closed at the time of writing due to earthquake damage), which tells the story of education in Puebla.

Iglesia de la Compañía

This Jesuit church with a 1767 Churrigueresque façade, on the corner of Palafox and 4 Sur, is also called Espíritu Santo. Beneath the altar is a tomb said to be that of a 17th-century Asian princess who was sold into slavery in Mexico and later freed. She supposedly originated the colorful China Poblana costume – a shawl, frilled blouse, embroidered skirt and gold and silver adornments. This costume became a kind of 'peasant chic' in the 19th century. But *china* also meant maidservant and the style may have come from Spanish peasant costumes.

One of the building's towers fractured and a cupola collapsed during the June 1999 earthquake. Next door, the 16th-century Edificio Carolino, now the main building of Puebla University, was also severely damaged by the quake.

Casa del Alfeñique

This house, on the corner of 6 Nte and 4 Ote, is an outstanding example of the 18th-century decorative style alfeñique. Inside is the Museo del Estado with 18th- and 19th-century Puebla paraphernalia such as China Poblana gear, carriages and furniture. The entry fee is US$1.50.

Teatro Principal & Barrio del Artista

The theater on 6 Nte between 6 and 8 Ote dates from 1759, making it one of the oldest in the Americas – sort of. It went up in flames in 1902 and was rebuilt in the 1930s. You can go inside between 10 am and 5 pm, if it's not in use. Nearby, the pedestrian-only 8 Nte, between 4 and 6 Ote, is the Barrio del Artista, which has open studios where you can meet artists and buy their work.

Templo de San Francisco

The north doorway of San Francisco, just east of Boulevard Héroes del 5 de Mayo on 14 Ote (Xonaca), is a good example of 16th-century plateresque; the tower and fine brick-and-tile façade were added in the 18th century. Structural damage occurred in the June 1999 quake. In a glass case in the church's north chapel is the body of San Sebastián de Aparicio, a Spaniard who came to Mexico in 1533 and planned many of the country's roads before becoming a monk. His body attracts a stream of worshipers.

Museo de la Revolución

This house at 6 Ote 206 was the scene of the first battle of the 1910 revolution. Betrayed only two days before a planned uprising against Porfirio Díaz's dictatorship, the Serdán family (Aquiles, Máximo, Carmen and Natalia) and 17 others fought 500 soldiers until only Aquiles, their leader, and Carmen were left alive. Aquiles, hidden under the floorboards, might have survived if the damp hadn't provoked a cough that gave him away. The house retains its bullet holes and other memorabilia, including a room dedicated to women of the revolution. Entry is US$1.50.

Templo de Santo Domingo

Santo Domingo, 2½ blocks north of the zócalo on Avenida 5 de Mayo, is a fine church, but its Capilla del Rosario (Rosary Chapel), south of the main altar, is a real gem. Built between 1650 and 1690, it has a sumptuous baroque proliferation of gilded plaster and carved stone with angels and cherubim popping out from behind every leaf. See if you can spot the heavenly orchestra.

Ex-Convento de Santa Rosa & Museo de Artesanías

This 17th-century ex-nunnery houses an extensive collection of Puebla state handicrafts. You must take an English or Spanish tour with a guide, who may try to rush you through the fine displays of traditional indigenous costumes, pottery, onyx, glass and metal work. *Mole poblano* is said to have been created in the kitchen of the ex-convent (see 'Puebla Originals,' later in this section). Enter from 14 Pte between 3 and 5 Nte (US$1.50).

Museo del Ferrocarril

A dozen vintage locomotives from the majestic to the quaint repose outside the old station, facing the junction of 11 Nte and 12 Pte. Admission is free.

Cerro de Guadalupe

The hilltop park, 2km northeast of the zócalo, contains the historic forts of Loreto and Guadalupe and the Centro Cívico 5 de Mayo, a group of museums and exhibitions. Good views, relatively fresh air and eucalyptus woods add to the appeal. Take a No 72 bus (US$0.30) up Avenida 5 de Mayo.

Fuerte de Loreto, at the west end of the hilltop, was one of the Mexican defense points on May 5, 1862, during the victory over the invading French. Today, it houses **Museo de la No Intervención** (US$2), which has displays of uniforms and documents relating to the French occupation of Mexico.

A short walk east of the fort, beyond the domed auditorium, are the **Museo Regional de Puebla** (US$2.25), which traces human history in the state, **Museo de Historia Natural** (US$1.25) and the pyramid-shaped **Planetario de Puebla** (US$2.50). At the east end of the hilltop is **Fuerte de Guadalupe** (US$2), which also played a part in the battle of May 5, 1862.

Places to Stay

Despite Puebla's abundance of hotels, which are easily recognizable by the big red 'H' signs over their doors, decent budget options tend to fill up fast with most places catering toward a higher-end market. Reasonably priced hotels are most densely clustered along the streets west of the cathedral.

Budget The *Hotel Avenida* (☎ 232-21-04, 5 Pte 336), 1½ blocks west of the cathedral, offers singles/doubles facing a courtyard for US$6.50/10 with private baths or US$4.25/7.50 without. It's about as clean as a hotel can be with flaking plaster and missing tiles. Around the block, *Hotel Victoria* (☎ 232-89-92, 3 Pte 306) is gloomy and faded, but friendly enough and clean. Rooms with private baths are US$7.50/13. A few blocks west, *Hotel Virreyes* (☎ 242-49-68, 3 Pte 912) has large, clean, wood-beamed rooms along two wide balconies above a courtyard parking lot. It's a bit rundown, but not bad for US$11/14 with private bath, US$6.50/8.50 without.

North of the center, clean but worn rooms at *Hotel Embajadores* (☎ 232-26-37), on the 5 de Mayo pedestrian plaza between 6 and 8 Ote, are US$8.50/13 with private bath. Just south of the Parián crafts market is the friendly *Hotel Real del Parián* (☎ 246-19-68, 2 Ote 601). At US$8.50/12.50, its freshly painted rooms are a good deal. If possible, choose a room with a balcony; interior rooms are stuffier.

Mid-Range The *Hotel Teresita* (☎ 232-70-72, 3 Pte 309), 1½ blocks west of the zócalo, offers carpeted single/double rooms with tiled baths and good beds for US$12/19, slightly more with windows facing the street. On the next block, *Hotel San Agustín* (☎ 232-50-89, 3 Pte 531) has small, rather stuffy rooms, each named after a town in the Puebla state, with tiny TVs and unreliable fluorescent lighting. The US$15/19 price includes a space in the Hotel Virreyes parking lot and breakfast. Just up the street, *Hotel San Miguel* (☎ 242-48-60, 3 Pte 721) has clean, respectably sized rooms with private baths and TVs for US$20/26. Parking is unavailable, but you're entitled to a discount at a garage on the next block.

Hotel Imperial (☎ 242-49-80, 4 Ote 212) caters to its guests' every need, offering laundry service, voice mail, fax and photocopy services, parking, gym with exercise equipment, restaurant with pool table and *golfito* – a two-hole miniature golf course in the back patio. With 65 comfortable rooms, the Imperial charges a basic rate of US$20/29, or US$22/36 for more stylish rooms in the new 'executive' wing.

Some of the pricier, mid-range places have lots of charm. *Hotel Colonial* (☎ 246-41-99, 4 Sur 105), on the corner of 3 Ote facing the university, has 70 lovely rooms. Most rooms are big and tiled, and have TVs and phones. Upstairs exterior rooms are best. Once part of a Jesuit monastery, it maintains a hearty colonial atmosphere despite modernization. At US$29/36, the Colonial may be the best value in Puebla. It's often full, so reserve ahead.

The 45-room *Hotel Royalty* (☎ 242-47-40, Portal Hidalgo 8) is another friendly, well-kept colonial-style place, located on the zócalo. The smallish rooms are comfortable and colorful, with carpet and TVs, for a reasonable US$31/40.

Hotel Palace (☎ 232-24-30, 2 Ote 13) is yet another pleasant and centrally located mid-range place. It asks US$27 for a single, or US$38 for two beds. Next door, the more

modern but similarly priced *Gilfer Hotel* (☎ 246-06-11, 2 Ote 11) has 92 comfortable singles/doubles with TVs, phones and a safe for US$29/36. The outwardly colonial *Hotel del Portal* (☎ 246-02-11, Palafox y Mendoza 205), half a block from the zócalo, has a modern interior. Rooms with balconies (US$36/46) go for more than those on the inside (US$29/38).

The attractively remodeled *Hotel Santander* (☎ 246-31-75, 5 Pte 111), just west of the cathedral, offers rooms with wood-beamed ceilings, fine colonial-style furniture and tiled baths for US$32/40.

Top End The *Hotel Aristos* (☎ 232-05-65, Reforma 533) is a big fancy place at the corner of 7 Sur. Its 120 air-conditioned singles and doubles are not that spacious for US$65, but the rate drops to a very reasonable US$30 on weekends. The central *Hotel Palacio San Leonardo* (☎ 246-05-55, 2 Ote 211) has an elegant lobby with a colored glass ceiling and a rooftop pool but charges way too much for its rooms – US$81.

Honeymooners, or those ready for a splurge, may consider a stay at the *Mesón Sacristía de la Compañía* (☎ 242-35-54, sacristia@mail.g-networks.net, 6 Sur 304). This 18th-century building is in the heart of the Barrio de los Sapos and combines modern comfort with colonial splendor – at a price. Rooms for one or two people cost US$96 and two fabulous suites with canopied, king-size beds are US$133.

The 51-room *Hotel Lastra* (☎ 235-97-55, Calzada de los Fuertes 2633), 2km northeast of the zócalo on the Cerro de Guadalupe, offers a peaceful location, good views, easy parking and a pleasant garden. Singles and doubles, in various shapes and sizes, go for US$56/60 Monday to Thursday, or US$46/49 Friday to Sunday.

There are a few top hotels outside the city center, but you miss out on the charm of central Puebla. The best of these is the 190-room *Hotel El Mesón del Angel* (☎ 223-83-67, Hermanos Serdán 807), 6km northwest of the center just off the Mexico City highway. The basic rate is US$140. Room rates at the 214-room *Hotel Crowne Plaza*

(☎ 248-60-55), 3km nearer the center at Hermanos Serdán 141, start at US$170.

Places to Eat

Near the Zócalo The zócalo's culinary highlight is *Vittorio's*, on the east side at Portal Morelos (2 Sur 106). This Italian-run restaurant bills itself 'La Casa de la Pizza Increíble' in memory of a 20-sq-meter monster pizza baked back in 1981. The pizzas are still good, but not cheap at US$3 to US$6 for an individual, and US$8 to US$15 for a grande (which feeds three or four people).

The large dining hall at *Restaurant La Princesa (Portal Juárez 101)*, on the zócalo's west side, is packed at lunchtime for its five-course *cubiertos* (US$4.25). A huge jug of fresh fruit drink (melon, papaya, mango) costs US$2.50.

Other places around the zócalo have lots of atmosphere, but tend to be expensive. On the north side, the smart *Restaurant-Bar Royalty* has outdoor tables where you can watch the world go by for the price of a cappuccino (US$1.75). Fish and meat dishes run to US$10.

There's a *Sanborns (2 Ote 6)*, and a *VIPS* café and bookstore in a beautiful 19th-century, cast-iron building on the corner of 2 Ote and 2 Nte. *Café El Carolo*, on Palafox y Mendoza, half a block east of the zócalo, serves fruit salad, yogurt and other healthy stuff cheap, and a comida corrida for only US$2.

Zona Esmeralda The upscale stretch of Juárez between Paseo Bravo and the La Paz area has lots of slick international-style restaurants. Near 21 Sur, *La Tecla (Juárez 1909)* is open till 2 am every night, offering an enticing array of 'nouveau Mexican' cuisine in a stylish setting. Try the 'filete tecla' (US$4.50), a tender steak served over a *huitlacoche*/white sauce and graced with Roquefort cheese. At 27 Sur, *Chimichurri* is a popular Argentinian restaurant that serves steaks for US$8.50 to US$20 and pastas for US$3.75.

Poblano Specialties A super place to try poblano food is *Fonda Santa Clara*, which has two branches, both on 3 Pte. The one at No 307 is nearer to the zócalo and usually busier, but the food at No 920 is equally good and the atmosphere more festive. Santa Clara's delicious chicken mole costs US$7.50 and enchiladas US$5. Also quite tasty is the *mixiotes* – a stew of sliced mutton tied in a maguey-leaf bundle – served with guacamole (US$7.50).

Another good option for traditional poblano cuisine is *Restaurant Sacristía (6 Sur 304)* in the delightful patio of a colonial mansion on the Callejón de los Sapos. Try the *mole Sacristía*, made from roasted *chipotle* chilies. An average three-course meal here will cost about US$10.

Puebla Originals

Mole poblano, found on almost every menu in Puebla and imitated throughout Mexico, is a spicy chocolate sauce usually served over turkey (*pavo* or *guajolote*) or chicken – a real taste sensation if well prepared. Supposedly invented by Sor (Sister) Andrea de la Asunción of the Convento de Santa Rosa for a visit by the viceroy, it traditionally contains fresh chile, *chipotle* (smoked jalapeño), pepper, peanuts, almonds, cinnamon, aniseed, tomato, onion, garlic and, of course, chocolate.

A seasonal Puebla dish, available in July, August and September, is *chiles en nogada*, said to have been created in 1821 to honor Agustín de Iturbide, the first ruler of independent Mexico. Its colors are those of the national flag: large green chilies stuffed with meat and dried fruit are covered with a creamy white walnut sauce and sprinkled with red pomegranate seeds.

In April and May, you can try *gusanos de maguey* and in March *escamoles* – respectively maguey worms and ant larvae.

A substantial *poblano* snack is *cemitas*, sesame rolls filled with chiles rellenos, white cheese or ham and seasoned with the essential herb *pápalo* . . . sort of a super *torta*. *Camotes* are sticks of fruit-flavored jelly made of sweet potatoes and various fruits.

✽ ✽ ✽ ✽ ✽ ✽ ✽ ✽ ✽ ✽ ✽ ✽ ✽

La Poblana (7 Ote 17), around the corner from the Museo Amparo, fixes authentic Puebla *cemitas* (see 'Puebla Originals') for about US$1. The food court at the Mercado Victoria is an inexpensive place to sample Puebla specialties like mole and *chalupas*.

Vegetarian *El Vegetariano* (3 Pte 525), open from 7.30 am to 9.30 pm, has a long menu of meatless dishes such as chiles rellenos, nopales rellenos (stuffed cactus paddles) and *enchiladas suizas*, all of which come with salad, soup and a drink for around US$3.50, or à la carte for about US$2.50.

Cheap Eats & Snacks A *pan árabe* taco (with pita bread instead of tortillas) costs around US$0.75 at *Tacos Tony*, on 3 Pte a block west of the zócalo, where a trio of enormous cones of seasoned pork are kept grilling till 9.30 pm. The Talavera-tiled tabletops of *Super Tortas Puebla*, on 3 Pte between 5 Sur and 3 Sur, are set with dishes of marinated chilies, carrots and onions to spice up your sandwich.

Tepoznieves, on 3 Pte at 3 Sur, is Puebla's top traditional Mexican ice cream restaurant – hibiscus and tequila are among its long list of exotic flavors.

Café Aroma (3 Pte 520), across the street from El Vegetariano, is the place to go for good coffee. Open from 9 am to 8.45 pm, it has only six tables and they're usually occupied. A dose of espresso will cost you US$0.75. *Café Plaza*, on 3 Pte just off the zócalo, also brews a mean cup of java from a fresh-ground blend of Coatepec, Sierra de Puebla and Chiapas beans; the same blend is sold by the sack.

Entertainment
The *Librería Cafetería Teorema*, on the corner of Reforma and 7 Nte, is a bookstore-cum-café that fills up in the evenings with an arty/student crowd. There's live music most nights from 9.30 pm to 1 am (cover charge averages US$2).

At night, mariachis lurk around the Callejón de los Sapos, between Avenidas 5 and 7 Ote, just east of 4 Sur, but they are being crowded out by the bars on the nearby Plazuela de los Sapos, many of which become live music venues after dark. Some of these student hangouts charge a US$1 cover. *La Batalla* favors folk music, while *La Boveda* and *La Serenata*, a large hall with a good sound system, stage rock 'n' roll bands.

In the Zona Esmeralda, there are a number of trendy discos and *antros* (music bars), on Juárez just east of the La Paz neighborhood. Among the current hot spots are *Corcores*, the disco *Tasaja*, *Portos Tropical* for salsa and merengue, and the cutting-edge *Bar y Tono*; an average US$2 to US$3 cover is charged in these places.

On Sunday afternoon, *Café La Obra*, on 3 Ote near the Callejón de los Sapos, serves up live jazz and blues. Check with the tourist offices and the Casa de la Cultura for the word on cultural events.

Shopping
Quite a few shops along 18 Pte, west of the Ex-Convento de Santa Mónica, display and sell the pretty Puebla ceramics. The big pieces are expensive and difficult for a traveler to carry, but you could buy a small hand-painted Talavera tile for US$2 or US$3, or a plate for around US$10. Few of these places make pottery on site, but Talavera Uriarte still does, with a factory and showroom at 4 Pte 911. Factory tours are given throughout the day until 1 pm Monday to Friday.

Indigenous textiles and pottery can be found at the state-run handicraft shop on the 7 Ote side of the Casa de la Cultura, as well as at the Centro Artesanal Segusino on the upper level of the Mercado Victoria.

El Parián crafts market, between 6 and 8 Nte and Avenidas 2 and 4 Ote, has local Talavera, onyx and trees of life, as well as the sorts of leather, jewelry and textiles that you find in other cities. Much of the work is shoddy souvenirs, but there is some good stuff and prices are generally reasonable. Antique shops dominate the Callejón de los Sapos, and on Sunday, the Plazuela de los Sapos is the site of a lively outdoor antiques market. It's great for browsing, with a wonderful variety of old books, furniture, bric-a-brac and junk. Also on Sunday, there is a major market in the Barrio de Analco on the east side of the Boulevard Héroes del 5 de Mayo, where flowers, sweets, paintings and other items are sold.

Along 6 Ote east of 5 de Mayo, a number of shops sell traditional Puebla sweets such as *camotes* (candied sweet potato sticks) and *jamoncillos* (bars of pumpkin seed paste).

Getting There & Away

Air Aeropuerto Hermanos Serdán, 22km west of Puebla on the Cholula-Huejotzingo road, has flights to/from Guadalajara and Tijuana by Aero California, and to/from León and Mexico City by Aeromar.

Bus Puebla's bus station, Central de Autobuses de Puebla (CAPU), is 4km north of the zócalo and 1.5km off the autopista, by the corner of Boulevards Norte and Carmen Serdán. It has a left-luggage facility, phone office, Banca Serfin branch (with ATM), restaurant and various shops.

Buses to/from Puebla use Mexico City's Terminal Oriente (TAPO). The 130km trip takes about two hours. Three bus lines have frequent services: ADO, a 1st-class service, has direct buses leaving every 20 minutes (US$6); AU, a 2nd-class service, has direct buses leaving every 12 minutes (US$5); Estrella Roja has 1st-class buses leaving every 20 minutes (US$6) and frequent 2nd-class buses (US$5). Estrella Roja also runs buses to the Mexico City airport hourly from 3 am to 8 pm, for US$8.50.

There is daily bus service from Puebla to just about everywhere in the south and east of Mexico, including:

Acapulco – 510km, 7 hours; 12 am 1 deluxe (US$38), 5 1st-class (US$27)

Cuernavaca – 175km, 3 hours; 4 deluxe (US$8), hourly 1st-class (US$6.50)

Jalapa – 185km, 3 hours; 8 1st-class (US$7), frequent 2nd-class (US$6.50)

Oaxaca – 320km, 4½ hours; 1 UNO deluxe (US$26), 2 ADO GL deluxe (US$18), 7 1st-class (US$16), 5 2nd-class directos (US$15)

Tampico – 730km, 11 hours; 1 deluxe (US$27), 7 1st-class (US$21)

Tuxtla Gutiérrez – 870km, 13 hours; 1 UNO deluxe (US$63), 2 Maya de Oro deluxe (US$44), 3 1st-class (US$37)

Veracruz – 300km, 3½ hours; 5 ADO GL deluxe (US$15), 10 1st-class (US$13), hourly 2nd-class (US$11.50), takes an hour longer

Villahermosa – 690km, 9 hours; 1 UNO deluxe (US$50), 1 ADO GL deluxe (US$35), 3 1st-class (US$30)

Frequent colectivos to Cholula leave from the corner of 6 Pte and 13 Nte in Puebla. They cost US$0.50 and take 20 minutes.

Train The only train service available serves Oaxaca, a scenic and leisurely journey. The train is scheduled to leave Puebla at 6.40 am and reach Oaxaca 12 hours later, passing through the dramatic Sierra Madre de Oaxaca in daylight. The Puebla-Oaxaca fare is US$7, 2nd-class only. Tickets are sold on the morning of departure.

The station is in the north of Puebla, 200m north of the corner of 9 Nte and 80 Pte. 'Estación Nueva' colectivos take 20 minutes to reach the station from 14 Pte at 3 Nte in the city center. In the reverse direction, board the colectivo about 200m straight ahead from the station entrance and get off at Paseo Bravo. A taxi between the train station and the zócalo costs about US$3.

Car & Motorcycle Puebla is 123km from Mexico City by a fast autopista, highway 150D (tolls total about US$8.50). East of Puebla, 150D continues to Córdoba (negotiating a cloudy, winding 22km descent from the 2385m Cumbres de Maltrata en route) and Veracruz.

Getting Around

Most hotels and places of interest are within walking distance of the zócalo. From the bus station, you can take a taxi (US$2 ticket from the kiosk, US$2.50 after 10 pm); or exit the station at the 'Autobuses Urbanos' sign, and go up a ramp leading to the bridge over Boulevard Norte. On the other side of the bridge over Boulevard Norte, walk west (toward VIPS) and stop in front of the Chedraui supermarket. From there, you can catch a No 40 combi to Avenida 16 de Septiembre, four blocks south of the zócalo. The ride takes 15 to 20 minutes.

From the city center to the bus station, get any 'CAPU' colectivo from 9 Sur/Norte and Reforma, four blocks west of the zócalo. All city buses and colectivos cost US$0.30.

AROUND PUEBLA
Africam Safari
One of the best places in Mexico to see wildlife is this safari park 16km southeast of Puebla, on the road to Presa Valsequillo. The over 3000 animals – among them rhinoceros, bears and tigers – are in spacious 'natural' settings, and you can view them up close from within your car, a taxi or an Africam bus. It's best to arrive at the park in the morning, when the animals are most active. The park is open 10 am to 5 pm every day of the year. Entry fees are a bargain at US$5, US$4.50 for children. Phone Africam for further details (☎ 235-87-13). Estrella Roja runs daily buses from CAPU to Africam and back, including admission and a tour of the park, for US$7, US$6 for children.

CHOLULA
• pop 24,100 • elev 2170m ☎ 2
Ten km west of Puebla stands the largest pyramid ever built, Pirámide Tepanapa – the Great Pyramid of Cholula. By the 4th century AD, it measured 450m along each side of the base and 65m high, making it larger in volume than Egypt's Pyramid of Cheops. But overgrown and topped by a church, it's difficult even to recognize the huge grassy mound as a pyramid. The town of Cholula is fairly unimpressive, but the University of the Americas, with many foreign students, adds a cosmopolitan touch, and there's a hearty nightlife. The nearby villages of Tonantzintla and Acatepec have splendid churches.

A 1999 earthquake measuring 6.9 took its toll on some of Cholula's historic buildings, including the pyramid-top Santuario de Nuestra Señora de los Remedios.

History
Between 1 and 600 AD, Cholula grew into one of central Mexico's largest cities, and an important religious center, while powerful Teotihuacán flourished 100km to the northwest. The Great Pyramid was built over several times. Around 600 AD, Cholula fell to the Olmeca-Xicallanca, who built nearby Cacaxtla. Sometime between 900 and 1300 AD, Toltecs and/or Chichimecs took over. Later it fell under Aztec dominance. There was also artistic influence from the Mixtecs to the south.

By 1519, Cholula's population had reached 100,000, and the Great Pyramid was already overgrown. Cortés, having made friends with the nearby Tlaxcalans, traveled here at Moctezuma's request. Aztec warriors set an ambush but unfortunately for them, the Tlaxcalans tipped off Cortés about the plot and the Spanish struck first. Within one day, they killed 6000 Cholulans before the city was looted by the Tlaxcalans. Cortés vowed to build a church here for each day of the year, or one on top of every pagan temple, depending on which legend you prefer. Today there are 39 – far from 365 but still a lot for a small town.

The Spanish developed nearby Puebla to overshadow the old pagan center and Cholula never regained its importance, especially after a severe plague in the 1540s decimated the indigenous population.

Orientation & Information
Arriving buses and colectivos drop you off two or three blocks north of the zócalo. Two long blocks to the east, the pyramid with its domed church on top is a clear landmark. The helpful tourist office (☎ 247-31-16), open from 10 am to 8 pm, is at 4 Pte 103A, half a block northwest of the zócalo. No English is spoken but maps are available. Bancomer, Bital and Banamex, on the south side of the zócalo, change money and have ATMs. Casa de Cambio Azteca is half a block south on 2 Sur; the post office is three blocks west at 7 Sur 505. The Internet café La Gioconda (3 Ote 203), a block south of the zócalo, charges US$3.25 per hour for access; it's open 8 am to 8.30 pm. The IMSS (Social Security Institute) Hospital is on 4 Nte between 10 and 12 Ote.

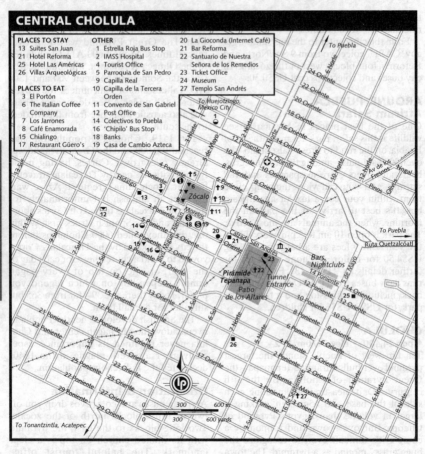

CENTRAL CHOLULA

PLACES TO STAY
13 Suites San Juan
21 Hotel Reforma
25 Hotel Las Américas
26 Villas Arqueológicas

PLACES TO EAT
3 El Portón
6 The Italian Coffee Company
7 Los Jarrones
8 Café Enamorada
15 Chialingo
17 Restaurant Güero's

OTHER
1 Estrella Roja Bus Stop
2 IMSS Hospital
4 Tourist Office
5 Parroquia de San Pedro
9 Capilla Real
10 Capilla de la Tercera Orden
11 Convento de San Gabriel
12 Post Office
14 Colectivos to Puebla
16 'Chipilo' Bus Stop
18 Banks
19 Casa de Cambio Azteca

20 La Gioconda (Internet Café)
21 Bar Reforma
22 Santuario de Nuestra Señora de los Remedios
23 Ticket Office
24 Museum
27 Templo San Andrés

Zona Arqueológica

Pirámide Tepanapa, probably originally dedicated to Quetzalcóatl, is topped by the church of **Nuestra Señora de los Remedios**. It's a classic symbol of conquest, but possibly an inadvertent one as the church may have been built before the Spanish knew the mound contained a pagan temple. Perhaps furthering the symbolic overtones, the June 1999 earthquake sent deep fractures through the church structure, but the pyramid suffered no damage. You can climb to the church, which was being reconstructed at the time of writing, by a path from the pyramid's northwest corner (no charge).

The Zona Arqueológica comprises the excavated areas around the pyramid and the tunnels underneath. Enter via the tunnel on the north side, open 10 am to 6 pm daily (US$2 plus US$3.25 for a video camera, free on Sunday and holidays). The small **museum**, across the road from the ticket office and down some steps, has the best introduction to the site – a large cutaway model of the pyramid mound showing the various superimposed structures. Admission is included with your site ticket.

Several pyramids were built on top of each other in various reconstructions. Over 8km of **tunnels** have been dug beneath the pyramid by archaeologists to penetrate each stage. From the tourist access tunnel, a few hundred meters long, you can see earlier layers of the building. Guides at the tunnel entrance charge US$4.25 for a one-hour tour; a few speak English. You don't need a guide to follow the tunnel through to the structures on the south and west sides of the pyramid, but they can be useful in pointing out and explaining various features as nothing is labeled.

The access tunnel emerges on the east side of the pyramid, from where you can take a path around to the **Patio de los Altares**, or Great Plaza, on the south side. This was the main approach to the pyramid and it is ringed by platforms and unique diagonal stairways. Three large stone slabs on its east, north and west sides are carved in the Veracruz interlocking-scroll design. At its south end is an Aztec-style altar in a pit dating from shortly before the Spanish conquest. On the west side of the mound is a reconstructed section of the latest pyramid, with two earlier layers exposed to view.

Zócalo
The **Ex-Convento de San Gabriel**, along the east side of Cholula's wide zócalo, also known as the Plaza de la Concordia, includes three fine churches. On the left, as you face the ex-convent, is the Arabic-style **Capilla Real**, which dates from 1540 and has 49 domes (almost half of which were damaged during the 1999 earthquake). In the middle is the 19th-century **Capilla de la Tercera Orden**, and on the right is the **Templo de San Gabriel**, founded in 1530 on the site of a pyramid. Due to significant earthquake damage, entry to the ex-convent was prohibited at the time of writing.

Special Events
Of the many festivals, one of the most important is the Festival de la Virgen de los Remedios, which is celebrated in the first week of September with daily traditional dances on the Great Pyramid. In the weeks that follow, Cholula's regional feria is held. On both the spring and fall equinoxes, the Quetzalcóatl ritual is reenacted with poetry, sacrificial dances, fabulous fireworks displays and music performed on pre-Hispanic instruments. The festivities take place in the Centro Ceremonial de Danzas by the fairgrounds. The bells of Cholula's numerous churches chime in concert on the Saturday in October that falls closest to a full moon.

Places to Stay
Cholula is an easy day trip from Puebla but there are accommodations if you'd rather stay. The best value in town is *Hotel Reforma* (☎ 247-01-49, *4 Sur 101*) at the corner of Morelos and 4 Sur, midway between the zócalo and the pyramid. All 13 rooms are nice, but size and features vary (all have private baths with hot water); the hotel charges US$8.50 for one person, US$9 to US$14 for two.

In the same price range, *Hotel Las Américas* (☎ 247-09-91, *14 Ote 6*), three blocks east of the pyramid, offers well-worn singles/doubles with TVs and private baths for US$7.50/13. There's a restaurant, pleasant courtyard garden and pool (which is filled only during the summer).

Suites San Juan (☎ 247-02-28, *5 Sur 103*), half a block from the market, has large clean rooms with enormous beds and TVs for US$18/21; windows face a noisy street. The parking lot is open to the public during the day.

The nicest place in town is the 50-room *Villas Arqueológicas* (☎ 247-19-66, *2 Pte 601*), south of the pyramid and across a few fields of flowers. A Club-Med property, it has lush gardens, a pool, French restaurant, and rooms at US$53/80.

Places to Eat
Café Enamorada, at the southern corner of the Portal Guerrero on the zócalo, is about the most popular place in town. It has live music most nights and serves sandwiches for US$1.50 to US$3 and tostadas, quesadillas and tacos for about US$2.50.

Underneath the plaza's attractive arcade, *Los Jarrones* serves set breakfasts at very fair prices; you can get a plate of waffles, dish of mixed fruit with yogurt and two cups of good coffee for under US$3. At the northern end of the arcade, *The Italian Coffee Company* is a Starbuck's-style establishment.

Restaurant Güero's (Hidalgo 101), across from the zócalo, is a cheerful hangout, decorated with antique photos of Cholula. Among the hearty Mexican favorites on the menu are *pozole*, *cemitas* and quesadillas served with a delicious *salsa roja* (US$1.50 for an order of three).

El Portón, on Hidalgo at 3 Sur, one block west of the zócalo, is popular for its daily set menu, which typically includes a choice of three soups, an entree (chicken, beef or vegetables) and dessert – all for under US$3. A few short blocks away, *Chialingo*, at 7 Pte and 3 Sur, is a much finer place, overlooking a lovely courtyard. Salads are around US$2.50, chicken US$4 and seafood US$8.50.

Entertainment
Southeast of the zócalo, *Bar Reforma*, on Morelos next to the Hotel Reforma, is Cholula's oldest drinking spot and serves freshly prepared sangrias and snacks.

Discos and *antros* (music bars), including *Rocka*, *The University Star* and *La Adelita*, are clustered near the university exit of the 'Recta,' as the highway to Puebla is known. Closer to the center on 14 Pte east of the pyramid, *Le Chat*, *Keops* and *El Caverno*, among others, come alive after about 10 pm Thursday to Saturday.

Getting There & Away
Frequent colectivos to Puebla leave from the corner of 5 Pte and 3 Sur. They cost US$0.50 and take 20 minutes. Estrella Roja has frequent buses between Mexico City's Terminal Oriente (TAPO) and Puebla that stop in Cholula on 12 Pte (US$3).

AROUND CHOLULA
Tonantzintla & Acatepec
The interior of the small **Templo de Santa María** in Tonantzintla is among the most exuberant in Mexico. Under the dome, the surface is covered with colorful stucco saints,

devils, flowers, fruit, birds and more – a great example of indigenous artisanship applied to Christian themes. Tonantzintla celebrates the Festival of the Assumption on August 15 with a procession and traditional dances.

The **Templo de San Francisco** in Acatepec, 1.5km southeast of Tonantzintla, dates from about 1730. The brilliant exterior is beautifully decorated with blue, green and yellow Talavera tiles set in red brick on an ornate Churrigueresque façade.

Both of these small churches are open 10 am to 1 pm and 3 to 5 pm daily.

Getting There & Away Autobuses Puebla-Cholula runs 'Chipilo' buses from Puebla bus station to Tonantzintla and Acatepec. In Cholula, you can pick them up on the corner of 7 Pte and Miguel Alemán. Between the two villages you can wait for the next bus or walk.

Huejotzingo
• pop 19,300 • elev 2280m ☎ 2

Huejotzingo ('weh-hot-SIN-goh'), 14km northwest of Cholula on highway 190, is known for its cider and sarapes. The fine 16th-century plateresque-style monastery has been restored as a museum, with exhibits on the Spanish missions and monastic life (open 10 am to 4.30 pm Tuesday to Sunday; US$2, free on Sunday). The fortified church is stark but imposing, with Gothic ribbing on its ceiling. There are old frescos and excellent carved stonework. On Shrove Tuesday, masked Carnaval dancers re-enact a battle between French and Mexicans. Estrella Roja buses service Huejotzingo from Puebla, Cholula and Mexico City.

SIERRA NORTE DE PUEBLA
These mountains covering much of remote northern Puebla state rise to over 2500m before falling away to the Gulf coastal plain. Despite deforestation, it's beautiful territory with pine forests and, at lower altitudes, semitropical vegetation. Sierra Norte handicrafts – among them *rebozos*, quechquémitls and baskets – are sold in markets at Cuetzalan, Zacapoaxtla, Teziutlán, Tlatlauquitepec and elsewhere.

The Nahua

Puebla state has about 400,000 of Mexico's most numerous indigenous people, the Nahua – more than any other state. Another 200,000 Nahua live in western parts of Veracruz state adjoining Puebla. The Nahua language (Nahuatl) was spoken by the Aztecs and, like the Aztecs, the Nahua were probably of Chichimec origin. Traditional Nahua women's dress consists of a black wool enredo (waist sash) and embroidered blouse and quechquémitl (shoulder cape). The Nahua are Christian but often also believe in a pantheon of supernatural beings, including *tonos* (people's animal 'doubles') and witches who can become blood-sucking birds and cause illness.

❋ ❋ ❋ ❋ ❋ ❋ ❋ ❋ ❋ ❋ ❋ ❋ ❋

The area has a large indigenous population, mostly Nahua and Totonac (see 'The Nahua' or 'The Totonacs' in the Central Gulf Coast chapter).

Cuetzalan
• **pop 4950** • **elev 1000m** ☎ **changing**
The colonial town of Cuetzalan, in the center of a lush coffee-growing region, is famed for a Sunday market that fills its zócalo and attracts scores of indigenous people in traditional dress.

Orientation & Information The main road into town from the south passes a tiny bus depot before ending 100m later at the zócalo. The center is on a hillside; from the zócalo most hotels and restaurants are uphill. Children will offer to guide you around for a small fee; most are friendly and

On September 1, 2000, the telephone area code is due to change to ☎ 2 from 233, with the digits 33 added to the start of every local number (for example, the number 7-65-43 will become 337-65-43).

helpful. There's a tourist office (☎ 1-00-04) on Hidalgo west of the zócalo (two doors down from a door with the large blue letters 'SEP' above it). It's open 9 am to 4 pm Wednesday to Sunday. No English is spoken but maps of the town are available. Banamex on Alvarado has an ATM.

Things to See & Do Two towers rise above Cuetzalan: the tall gothic spire of the zócalo's **Parroquia de San Francisco** and the tower of **Santuario de Guadalupe** to the west, with unusual decorative rows of clay vases. There's a **regional museum** on the zócalo opposite the Posada Jackeline.

Four and 5km northeast of town are two lovely waterfalls called **Las Brisas**. To reach them, catch one of the colectivos behind the Parroquia de San Francisco heading for the village of San Andrés. Or simply walk along the dirt road that begins just west of the bus depot, keeping to the right when it forks, until you come to San Andrés and its church with a striking green-tile dome. There, at least one child will offer to take you to the falls for US$2. You should accept the offer, as there are many trails in the forest and no signs to the falls. Bring bathing gear as the natural pools under the falls are enticing. Some of the area's 32km network of caves can be explored at **Atepolihui**, accessible from the village of San Miguel a half-hour walk from the end of Hidalgo.

Special Events For several lively days around October 4, Cuetzalan celebrates both the festival of San Francisco de Assisi and the Feria del Café y del Huipil. A traditional dance festival in mid-July attracts groups from all over the area.

Places to Stay The best value in town is *Posada Jackeline* (☎ 1-03-54, 2 de Abril 2) on the uphill side of the zócalo. Large, clean rooms with plenty of hot water cost US$5.25 per person.

Hotel Posada Cuetzalan (☎ 1-01-54, *Zaragoza 12*), 100m from the zócalo, has 40 rooms with white walls, lots of lightly stained wood and TVs. Singles/doubles cost

US$20/27. There's a swimming pool and two lovely, interior courtyards, too.

Best in town is the Casa de la Piedra (☎ *1-00-30, García 11*), two blocks below the zócalo. This old stone house has been superbly renovated in *rústico* style with fine wood floors and large picture windows. Two-level suites (US$34) accommodate up to four people and offer views of the valley; downstairs rooms have double beds (US$21). Secure parking is available.

Several places near Cuetzalan are designed for maximum appreciation of the area's beautiful landscapes. Just outside Cuetzalan on the Puebla road, the recently opened **Taselotzin** (☎ *1-04-80, fonmicro@fonaes.gob.mx*), which is run by local Nahua craftswomen, has singles/doubles in five cozy cabins (US$12/19), as well as dormitory-style lodging at US$5.25 per person, amid peaceful gardens. The restaurant serves pre-Hispanic dishes of the region, such as *quelites* (wild greens) and *acamayas* (river shrimp).

Five kilometers south of Cuetzalan, **Hotel Campestre Grutas Cuetzalan** (☎ *2-243-02-66 in Puebla*) has clean, cedar-panel rooms in bungalows for US$17/3O, and caves on the premises.

Places to Eat The *Restaurant Yoloxochitl*, opposite Posada Jackeline, has lots of charm, a lovely view and OK food. Salads and antojitos go for US$1.50, meat dishes are US$2. In season, mushrooms are served pickled, in *chipotle* sauce, and in a cocktail. One of several restaurants along Hidalgo, **La Terraza** offers top-flight views of Cuetzalan along with an assortment of seafood, salads and pastas (US$3.50).

Bar El Calate, on the east side of the zócalo, is a great place to try regional alcoholic drinks made from coffee, limes and berries, and *yolizpán*, a liqueur made from local herbs.

Restaurant Los Jarritos (*Plazuela López Mateos 7*), under the same ownership as Casa de Piedra, hosts Saturday night peñas, featuring regional dishes and drinks, folk music, quetzal dancers, local *huapango*

bands and *voladores* (literally 'flyers,' the Totonac ritual in which men, suspended by their ankles, whirl around a tall pole). Book early.

Getting There & Away ADO 1st-class buses (3¾ hours, US$7.50) leave Puebla for Cuetzalan at 4.15 pm daily, and Cuetzalan for Puebla at 4.30 pm daily. Second-class Vía buses (US$6.50) make the same run hourly. On weekends, ADO runs an additional 8.30 am bus from Puebla and a 6.30 pm departure from Cuetzalan. Get your return tickets early. Autotransportes Mexico-Texcoco runs five 1st-class buses daily (5½ hours, US$11) to/from Mexico City's Terminal Oriente (TAPO).

Yohualichán

About 8 km from Cuetzalan by cobblestone road, this pre-Hispanic site has niche pyramids similar to El Tajín. The site, adjacent to Yohualichán town plaza, is open 10 am to 5 pm Wednesday to Sunday (US$1.25, free on Sunday). To get there, catch any colectivo taking the road out of Cuetzalan from the end of Hidalgo (US$0.30), and get off when it stops beside the blue sign with a pyramid image on it. It's a half-hour walk from this turnoff.

SOUTHERN PUEBLA

The main route from Puebla to Oaxaca is a modern toll highway that turns south off 150D, 83km east of Puebla. Two older roads go through southern Puebla state toward Oaxaca.

Highway 150

Heading east from Puebla, this road parallels the 150D autopista, but it's a lot slower and more congested. Second-class buses stop at the towns en route. **Amozoc**, 17km from Puebla, produces pottery and many of the fancy silver decorations worn by *charros* (Mexican cowboys). **Tepeaca**, 38km from Puebla, has a big Friday market, mainly for everyday goods, and a 16th-century Franciscan monastery. The village of **Tecali**, 11km southwest of Tepeaca, is a center for the carving of onyx from the nearby quarries.

Tehuacán

• pop 172,500 • elev 1640m ☎ 2

Modern Tehuacán, on highway 150, 122km southeast of Puebla, is a pretty town with a fine zócalo. It's famed for its mineral water (the town's name is the water's generic term), which is sold in bottles all over Mexico; tours of the impressive **Peñafiel** plant, located 100m north of the Casas Cantarranas hotel (see Places to Stay, later in this section), are offered from 9 am to 12 pm and 4 pm to 6 pm daily except Friday. Just up the road, competitor Garci-Crespo offers informative tours of its facilities Monday to Saturday, including a visit to its underground springs.

The high, dry Tehuacán valley was the site of some of the earliest agriculture in Mexico. By 7000 to 5000 BC, people were planting avocados, chilies, cotton and maize. Pottery, the sign of a truly settled existence, appeared about 2000 BC. The **Museo del Valle de Tehuacán**, inside the Ex-Convento del Carmen three blocks northwest of the zócalo, explains some of the archaeological discoveries, and exhibits tiny preserved cobs of maize that were among the first to be cultivated. It's open 10 am to 6 pm daily except Monday (US$1).

Orientation & Information The main road into town coming from Puebla, Avenida Independencia, passes by the ADO bus station before reaching the north side of Parque Juárez – the zócalo. The main north-south road is Avenida Reforma. The city's most popular restaurants are located around the zócalo, as is the Palacio Municipal, which has a tourist office (☎ 383-15-14, ext 36) in the southwest corner; English is spoken and maps are available. The office is open 8 am to 8 pm Monday to Friday, 10 am to 7 pm Saturday and 11 am to 6 pm Sunday.

Special Events October 15 starts the two-week festival La Matanza, in which goats are slaughtered en masse. *Mole de cadera* is the regional specialty resulting from the carnage (available year-round at *Pizzeria Danny Richard*, across the street from the Museo del Valle de Tehuacán).

Places to Stay For economy lodging, *Hotel Monroy* (☎ 382-04-91, Reforma 7) offers basic but clean and spacious singles/doubles for US$12/15. *Bogh Suites Hotel* (☎ 382-34-74) on the northwest side of the zócalo has small but attractive rooms with TVs, phones and fans for a reasonable US$26/30. Parking at a lot across the street is included in the price.

Hotel México (☎ 382-24-19) at the corner of Reforma Nte and Independencia Pte is central but quite tranquil with large, comfortable rooms (US$30/33), several courtyards, a restaurant and swimming pool. The resort *Casas Cantarranas* (☎ 383-49-22, hotelcc@acnet.net, Avenida José Garci-Crespo 2215) features a large, blue-tile pool, spacious gardens and 45 fine rooms (US$43/49).

Getting There & Away ADO, at Independencia 119, has 1st-class buses running every half hour to/from Puebla (two hours, US$5), hourly service to/from Mexico City (four hours, US$10), four buses a day to Veracruz (four hours, US$9.50), and frequent direct service to Oaxaca (three hours, US$12). AU offers 2nd-class service.

Around Tehuacán

Twenty km southwest of Tehuacán, **Jardín Botánico de Cactáceas** displays some 250 species of cactus along well-maintained trails. Open 10 am to 6 pm daily, the cactus garden is 3km before Zapotitlán de Salinas, on highway 125 to Huajuapan de León. To get there, catch a green-and-white bus along 1 Sur, south of the cathedral.

Highway 190

This road swings southwest from Puebla to **Atlixco**, 31km away, a town known for its mineral springs, avocados and near-perfect climate. Another 36km brings you to **Izúcar de Matamoros**, which also has therapeutic balnearios but is best known for ceramic handicrafts.

South of Mexico City

Heading south from Mexico City, highway 95 and highway 95D (the toll road) climb to more than 3000m from the Valle de México into refreshing pine forests, then descend to Cuernavaca, capital of Morelos state and longtime popular retreat from Mexico City. On the way, highway 115D branches southeast to Tepoztlán, nestled beneath high cliffs, and to balnearios at Oaxtepec and Cuautla.

Morelos is one of Mexico's smallest and most densely populated states. Valleys at different elevations have a variety of microclimates, and many fruits, vegetables and grains have been cultivated since pre-Hispanic times. Archaeological sites at Cuernavaca, Tepoztlán and Xochicalco show signs of the agricultural Tlahuica civilization and the Aztecs who subjugated them. In the colonial era, most of the state was controlled by a few families, including descendants of Cortés. Their palaces and haciendas can still be seen, along with churches and monasteries from as early as the 16th century. Unsurprisingly, the *campesinos* of Morelos became fervent supporters of the Mexican Revolution, and local lad Emiliano Zapata is the state's hero.

South of Cuernavaca, spurs of highway 95D go to the remarkable silver town of Taxco and to the industrial city of Iguala, both in mountainous Guerrero state. The Iguala branch continues south as highway 95 (no autopista pretensions) to Chilpancingo and Acapulco (see the Central Pacific Coast chapter). The main 95D takes a more direct route to Chilpancingo. On this expensive superhighway, you can drive the 400km between Mexico City and Acapulco in three hours – the frequent tolls can total more than US$35. The alternative sections of free road are consequently heavily used, slow and dangerous. Driving at night in Guerrero is inadvisable because cars are sometimes stopped and robbed. The route from Iguala to Ixtapa via highways 51 and 134 is said to be particularly risky.

TEPOZTLÁN
- **pop 14,000** • **elev 1701m** ☎ 7

Eighty km from Mexico City, Tepoztlán (Place of Copper) sits in a valley surrounded by high, jagged cliffs. It's the legendary birthplace, more than 1200 years ago, of Quetzalcóatl, the omnipotent serpent god of the Aztecs. The town retains indigenous traditions, with many older people still speaking Nahuatl, and younger people now learning it in secondary school. Now something of an international hippie venue, Tepoztlán attracts writers, artists and astrologers, who claim the place has a creative energy, as well as many more conventional weekend visitors from Mexico City. Developers hoping to profit from the destination's popularity planned an enormous golf club complex a few years ago, but locals who feared their water supplies would be threatened organized against it successfully. Traces of the conflict are still visible in the form of widespread graffiti.

Orientation & Information
Everything here is easily accessible by walking, except the Pirámide de Tepozteco on the cliff-top to the north. Street names change in the center of town; for example, Avenida 5 de Mayo becomes Avenida Tepozteco north of the plaza.

Post and telegraph offices are on the north side of the main plaza. Long-distance and local telephone calls can be made from pay phones around town.

Ex-Convento Dominico de la Natividad
This monastery and the attached church were built by Dominican priests between 1560 and 1588 and are the chief feature of the town. The plateresque church façade has Dominican seals interspersed with indigenous symbols, floral designs and various figures including the sun, moon and stars, animals, angels and the Virgin Mary.

The arched entryway to the monastery is an elaborate mural of pre-Hispanic history and symbolism composed of 60 varieties of seeds. Every year on September 8, local artists create a new mural.

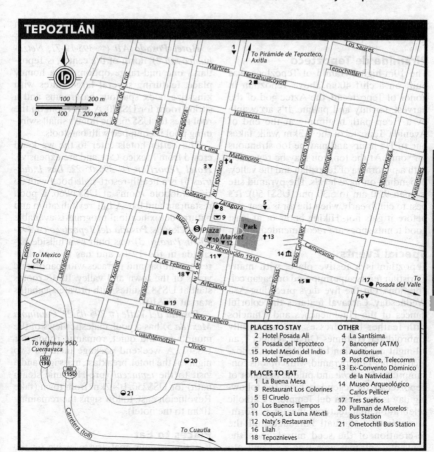

TEPOZTLÁN

PLACES TO STAY	**OTHER**
2 Hotel Posada Ali	4 La Santísima
6 Posada del Tepozteco	7 Bancomer (ATM)
15 Hotel Mesón del Indio	8 Auditorio
19 Hotel Tepoztlán	9 Post Office, Telecomm
	13 Ex-Convento Dominico
PLACES TO EAT	de la Natividad
1 La Buena Mesa	14 Museo Arqueológico
3 Restaurant Los Colorines	Carlos Pellicer
5 El Ciruelo	17 Tres Sueños
10 Los Buenos Tiempos	20 Pullman de Morelos
11 Coquis, La Luna Mextli	Bus Station
12 Naty's Restaurant	21 Ometochtli Bus Station
16 Lilah	
18 Tepoznieves	

The 400-year old monastery section is undergoing a major restoration. Some 4500 sq m of murals from the 16th and 17th centuries have been meticulously restored. The cells of the west wing house a museum covering the region's natural history, economy, social organization and religion. The monastery is open 10 am to 5 pm Tuesday through Sunday (free).

Museo Arqueológico Carlos Pellicer

This museum at Pablo González 2 (behind the Dominican church) has a small but in-

teresting collection of pieces from many parts of Mexico, donated to the people of Tepoztlán by the Tabascan poet Carlos Pellicer Cámara. The objects on display here are lively and vibrant, with an emphasis on human figures but also include some animals. The stone fragments depicting a pair of rabbits – the symbol for Ometochtli, one of the 400 gods of pulque – were discovered at the Tepozteco pyramid site.

The museum is open 10 am to 6 pm Tuesday through Sunday (US$0.50). Though there is no tourist office in Tepoztlán, the museum's knowledgeable staff can answer most of your questions.

Pirámide de Tepozteco

The 10m-high Pyramid of Tepozteco was built on a cliff 400m above Tepoztlán in honor of Tepoztécatl, the Aztec god of the harvest, fertility and pulque. It's accessible by a steep path beginning at the end of Avenida Tepozteco; the 1.3km walk takes one to 1½ hours and may be too strenuous for some. At the top, you may be rewarded with a panorama of Tepoztlán and the valley, depending on haze levels. The pyramid site is open 9.30 am to 5.30 pm (US$1.50). It's best to climb early, when the air is clear and before it gets hot. Hiking boots or at least good tennis shoes are recommended.

Special Events

Tepoztlán is a festive place, with many Christian feasts superimposed on pagan celebrations. On the five days preceding Ash Wednesday, **Carnaval** features the colorful dances of the Huehuenches and Chinelos with feather headdresses and beautifully embroidered costumes. On September 7, an all-night celebration takes place on Tepozteco hill near the pyramid, with copious consumption of *ponche* and pulque in honor of Tepoztécatl, the legendary king. The following day is the **Fiesta del Templo**, a Catholic celebration that features theater performances in the Nahuatl language and the re-creation of the seed mural upon the convent's entrance arch (see Ex-Convento Dominico de la Natividad earlier in this section). The holiday was first intended to coincide with, and perhaps supplant, the pagan Tepoztécatl festival, but the pulque drinkers get a jump on it by starting the night before.

Places to Stay

It can be difficult to find decent inexpensive accommodations here on weekends. About the cheapest place in town is *Hotel Mesón del Indio* (☎ 395-02-38, *Revolución 44*); its sign is barely larger than a loaf of bread. A friendly place with eight small moldy rooms beside a garden, each with private bath and hot water,

it costs US$12/13 for singles/doubles. Screen doors provide ample ventilation.

Hotel Posada Ali (☎ 395-19-71, *Netzahualcóyotl 2*), north of the center, is Tepoztlán's one mid-range option. It's a homey place, featuring several large suites with king-size beds, spacious bathrooms and a sitting room for US$40. A tiny room on the roof goes for US$26. The hotel's small swimming pool is equipped with barstools.

The better hotels cater to the weekend crowd from Mexico City, and are expensive. *Hotel Tepoztlán* (☎ 395-05-22, *Las Industrias 6*) is a health-resort-style hotel with 36 single/double rooms at US$49/66, a pool, restaurant and bar. A full 'revitalization and natural detoxification' program is available on weekends. *Posada del Tepozteco* (☎ 395-00-10, *Paraíso 3*) was built as a hillside hacienda in the 1930s and has two pools, a restaurant/bar and terraces with panoramic views of the town and valley. Its 18 rooms start at US$82, suites with private spa baths start at US$104.

Posada del Valle (☎ 395-05-21, *Camino a Mextitla 5*) has a pool, majestic views of the mountains, and quiet, romantic rooms for US$61. A weekend package includes two nights at the hotel, breakfast, massages and a visit to the *temazcal* (pre-Hispanic steam bath) for US$250. It's 2km from town (take Revolución east, follow signs the remaining 100m to the hotel).

Places to Eat

If eating is your goal, try to arrive on the weekend. During the week most of the finer restaurants are closed.

Avenida Revolución has a varied string of restaurants, including *Naty's Restaurant* at No 7, an inexpensive place to have breakfast and watch the action in the market. Fancier and more expensive places like *Coquis* at No 10 and *La Luna Mextli* at No 16 are combination restaurant, bar and art gallery.

Lilah, at the bottom of Revolución where the asphalt begins, offers delicious originals fusing elements from various cuisines. Wonderful salads, for around US$4, consist of organic ingredients from the restaurant's garden. There are also veggie burgers

(US$4), veggie lasagna (US$5.50), cappuccino and herbal teas.

For good traditional Mexican food, try **Restaurant Los Colorines** at Tepozteco 13. A popular restaurant with vibrant decor, it offers a variety of dishes from US$2 to US$5, and a large selection of tequilas served in tiny clay mugs. **El Ciruelo** at Zaragoza 17 is an elegant restaurant/bar that hosts live jazz on Friday and Saturday night. Open for lunch on Monday to Friday from 1 to 6 pm, it serves pizzas for US$5 to US$9, salads for US$3.50 to US$6 and main courses for US$6. Try the steak in tequila sauce.

Moving along Tepozteco toward the pyramid, **La Buena Mesa** serves pastas (US$4.50) and local favorites in a peaceful setting, with two terraces offering views of the cliffs, copious plants and trees, and hummingbirds. Closer to the archaeological site, **Axitla**, open Wednesday to Sunday, has an even more jungly setting. It offers abundant portions of fine Mexican and international food; a meal here will cost you US$8 to US$10.

An obligatory stop in Tepoztlán is the ice cream emporium **Tepoznieves**, scooping up 70 flavors, including cactus and pineapple/chili. **Los Buenos Tiempos** is a cool stall at the edge of the market on Revolución, serving perhaps Tepoztlán's finest coffee, espresso, cappuccino and homemade strudels starting at 8.30 am.

Shopping

On weekends, Tepoztlán's market stalls sell a melange of handicrafts, including sarapes, embroidery, weavings, carvings, baskets and pottery. Shops in the adjacent streets also have interesting wares (some from Bali and India) at upscale prices. A local craft product is miniature houses and villages carved from the cork-like spines of the local *pochote* tree. The shop Tres Sueños, on Revolución across from Lilah, sells work by local artists and craftspeople, as well as second-hand clothing, jewelry and books in English, French, German and Spanish.

Getting There & Away

Pullman de Morelos has hourly 1st-class service to/from Mexico City (Terminal Sur) till 8 pm (one hour, US$3.75), with buses departing from, and arriving at, Avenida 5 de Mayo 35, at the southern entrance to town. Frequent buses to Oaxtepec (15 minutes, US$0.75) and Cuautla (25 minutes, US$0.85) depart from the *caseta* (tollbooth) on the autopista outside town. Pullman de Morelos runs free combis between the 5 de Mayo terminal and the gas station near the autopista entrance; from there, walk down the left (exit) ramp to the caseta.

Ometochtli buses leave for Cuernavaca every 15 minutes from 5 am to 9 pm (23km, 30 minutes, US$1). The terminal is located on the road south of town on the way to the autopista.

If you're driving north from Cuernavaca on highway 95D, don't get off at the 'Tepoztlán' exit, which will put you on the slow federal highway. Take the exit marked 'Cuautla/Oaxtepec.'

OAXTEPEC & COCOYOC

Oaxtepec • pop 6000 • elev 1400m ☎ 7
Cocoyoc • pop 8600 • elev 1300m ☎ 7

The 200,000 sq m **Centro Vacacional Oaxtepec** ('wahs-teh-PEC') is a balneario with numerous pools and sulfur springs. The giant park was divided into two areas in 1999: a privately run aquatic amusement park with a wave pool and giant slides (admission US$3.25, half for children); and a recreational center – operated by the Mexican Social Security Institute (IMSS) though open to the general public – with pools, a stadium, restaurants and a cable car (admission US$4.25). Both parks are open daily 8 am to 6 pm.

For overnight stays, the **IMSS facility** has campgrounds (US$6.50 per adult) and four-person rooms (US$24 per room). With reservations, there's a 50% discount on admission to the Parque Acuático (☎ 356-01-01, ☎ 5-211-00-18 in Mexico City).

Hacienda Cocoyoc (☎ 356-22-11), 4km southwest of Oaxtepec on highway 113, was built in the 1600s, later becoming an important sugar refinery until Zapata declared war on all sugar plantations during the revolution. Today the hacienda is a refreshing resort hotel and spa with pools, restaurants, horseback riding and a nine-hole golf course. Rooms start at US$66; a suite with private pool costs up to US$160.

Getting There & Away

Oaxtepec is just north of highway 115D, 100km south of Mexico City. Cocoyoc is about 3km south of the same turnoff. Frequent 1st-class buses go from the capital's Terminal Sur to the Oaxtepec bus station beside the entrance to the springs complex (1½ hours, US$4). There are also buses to/from Tepoztlán, Cuernavaca, Cuautla and Puebla. Entrances to both parks are accessible from the Oaxtepec station; taxis and combis to Cocoyoc depart from there as well.

CUAUTLA

• **pop 128,800** • **elev 1290m** ☎ **7**

The balnearios at Cuautla ('KWOUT-la') and its pleasant year-round climate have been attractions since the time of Mocte-

zuma, who reputedly enjoyed soaking in the sun and sulfur springs. These days, however, the city is uninspiring and spread out, though the center is pleasant enough.

José María Morelos y Pavón, one of Mexico's first leaders in the independence struggle, used Cuautla as a base, but the royalist army besieged the city from February 19 to May 2, 1812. Morelos and his army were forced to evacuate when their food gave out. A century later, Cuautla was a center of support for the revolutionary army of Emiliano Zapata. Now, every April 10, the Agrarian Reform Minister lays a wreath at Zapata's monument in Cuautla, quoting the revolutionary's principles of land reform.

Orientation

Cuautla spreads north to south roughly parallel to the Río Cuautla. The main avenue into town, Avenida Insurgentes, joins the town's two main plazas – the Plaza Fuerte

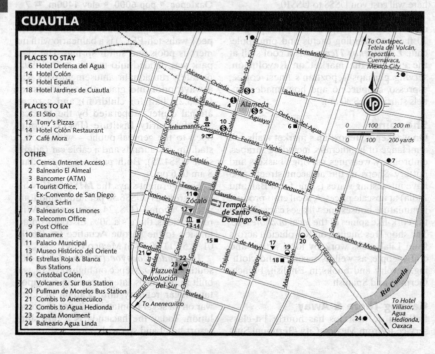

CUAUTLA

PLACES TO STAY
6 Hotel Defensa del Agua
14 Hotel Colón
15 Hotel España
18 Hotel Jardines de Cuautla

PLACES TO EAT
6 El Sitio
12 Tony's Pizzas
14 Hotel Colón Restaurant
17 Café Mora

OTHER
1 Cemsa (Internet Access)
2 Balneario El Almeal
3 Bancomer (ATM)
4 Tourist Office,
   Ex-Convento de San Diego
5 Banca Serfin
7 Balneario Los Limones
8 Telecomm Office
9 Post Office
10 Banamex
11 Palacio Municipal
13 Museo Histórico del Oriente
16 Estrellas Roja & Blanca
   Bus Stations
19 Cristóbal Colón,
   Volcanes & Sur Bus Station
20 Pullman de Morelos Bus Station
21 Combis to Anenecuilco
22 Combis to Agua Hedionda
23 Zapata Monument
24 Balneario Agua Linda

To Oaxtepec, Tetela del Volcán, Tepoztlán, Cuernavaca, Mexico City

Templo de Santo Domingo

Plazuela Revolución del Sur

To Anenecuilco

Río Cuautla

To Hotel Villasor, Agua Hedionda, Oaxaca

de Galeana, more commonly known as the Alameda, and the zócalo – and changes its name along the way to Batalla 19 de Febrero, then to Galeana, Los Bravos, Guerrero and Ordiera.

The zócalo has arcades with restaurants on the northern side, a church on the east, the Palacio Municipal on the west and the Hotel Colón on the south. Bus lines have separate terminals in the blocks east of the plaza.

Information

The tourist office (☎ 352-52-21) is three blocks north of the plaza, on the platform of the old train station, housed in the 16th-century Ex-Convento de San Diego. Open 9 am to 8 pm daily, the office is a font of information, well-stocked with literature on convents, balnearios, handicrafts and history, as well as a good map of Cuautla – very necessary since streets change names each block. The staff speak Spanish only.

Several banks can be found throughout the town (see Cuautla map for locations). A few blocks north of the tourist office at Batalla 19 de Febrero 107, Cemsa provides Internet access 9 am to 8 pm daily for US$3.25 per hour. Hospital General is on Avenida Reforma in the north of town near the Autopista México (☎ 353-6193).

Things to See & Do

Mexico's only steam-powered train departs from the old railroad station where in August 1911 presidential candidate Francisco Madero embraced Emiliano Zapata. The train does a circuit of Cuautla (US$0.50) on Saturday and Sunday after 5 pm.

The former residence of José María Morelos, on the southwest side of the plaza, houses the excellent **Museo Histórico del Oriente**, open 10 am to 5 pm Tuesday to Sunday (US$1.75). Each room covers a different historical period with well-lit displays of pre-Hispanic pottery, good maps and early photos of Cuautla and Zapata.

Plaza Revolución del Sur is one of Cuautla's loveliest plazas and in its center is with an imposing **Zapata monument** in its center, underneath which lie the rebel's remains.

Emiliano Zapata

Balnearios

The best-known balneario in Cuautla is **Agua Hedionda** (Stinky Water) on the east side of the river. Waterfalls replenish two lake-sized pools with the spring's cool sulfur-scented waters. The complex is open 7 am to 6 pm daily (US$2 for adults, half for kids). To get there, take an 'Agua Hedionda' combi (US$0.50) from Plaza Revolución del Sur.

Other balnearios you may want to visit in town include **El Almeal**, **Agua Linda** and **Los Limones**.

Places to Stay

Cheap hotels include *Hotel Colón* (☎ 352-29-90, *Guerrero 48*), on the main plaza, where OK singles/doubles with private baths cost US$8.50/10.50, US$1 more with TV. *Hotel España* (☎ 352-21-86, 2 de Mayo 22), half a block east, has parking and 27 spacious rooms with private baths and hot water at a bargain US$9.50 per room. *Hotel Jardines de Cuautla* (☎ 352-00-88, 2 de Mayo 94), opposite the Cristóbal Colón bus terminal, has clean, modern singles/doubles for US$13/19, parking, a garden and two tiny swimming pools. Unfortunately, quite a bit of noise intrudes from the busy streets below.

Two blocks east of the Alameda, *Hotel Defensa del Agua* (☎ 352-16-79, Defensa del Agua 34) surrounds a small garden/parking area with two small pools. Its pleasant colonial-style rooms, named after Cuautla war heroes, are a good deal at US$13/23, but avoid rooms with windows on the street.

If your only reason for visiting Cuautla is the Agua Hedionda park, *Hotel Villasor* (☎ 352-65-21, *villasor@clubinter.net*), a stone's throw from the balneario, is the place to stay. Comfortable rooms with TVs, fans and phones go for US$28, US$3 more on Friday and Saturday night.

Places to Eat
Cuautla's culinary highlights are few. There are a handful of adequate places around the plaza, such as *Tony's Pizzas* serving pizzas for US$3.75 to US$8. The restaurant at *Hotel Colón* is one of the only downtown restaurants open after 9 pm. The Alameda has several popular cafés with outdoor seating; it serves sandwiches, cappuccino, ice cream and milkshakes.

Inside Hotel Defensa del Agua, *El Sitio* is an elegant alternative, with salads for US$3.25, meat dishes around US$4.75 and seafood dishes around US$7. Its set lunch (US$4) features exotic local options. Across the street from Hotel Jardines de Cuautla is Café Mora, which serves Cuautla's finest espresso for just US$0.50 a cup.

Getting There & Away
Cristóbal Colón, a 1st-class line, and Sur and Volcanes, both 2nd-class, share a bus station at the eastern end of 2 de Mayo. Pullman de Morelos is across the street at Maximo Bravo 53D, with 1st-class service to Tepoztlán and Oaxtepec every 10 minutes until 9.15 pm. A block west is the Estrella Roja (2nd-class) and Estrella Blanca (EB) bus station; an elevated restaurant separates the two lines. The most useful services include:

Cuernavaca – 42km, 1¼ hours; every 15 minutes by Estrella Roja, 5 am to 7 pm (US$1.75)
Mexico City (TAPO) – 70km, 2½ hours via Amecameca; every 20 minutes by Volcanes (US$2.75)
Mexico City (Terminal Sur) – 70km, 1¾ hours; frequent Colón and Pullman de Morelos (US$4.25)

Oaxaca – 410km, 7 hours; 1 Colón (US$12.50), 2 Sur
Puebla – 125km, 2 hours; hourly Estrella Roja (US$2.50)

AROUND CUAUTLA
The road south of Cuautla leads through some significant territory of the revolutionary period, where General Emiliano Zapata was born, fought and met his death at the hands of treacherous federalists. North of Cuautla, off highway 115 to Amecameca, a road heads east along the southern slopes of the active volcano Popocatépetl, passing an extraordinary series of small towns with magnificent monasteries (see Popocatépetl & Iztaccíhuatl in the East of Mexico City section, earlier in this chapter). Here you will get a good glimpse of how traditional ways of life go on apparently undisturbed by their proximity to the smoking behemoth.

Ruta de Zapata
In **Anenecuilco**, about 10km south of Cuautla, what's left of the adobe cottage where Zapata was born on August 8, 1879, is now a museum featuring photographs of the rebel leader. Outside is a mural by Roberto Rodríguez which depicts Zapata exploding with the force of a volcano into the center of Mexican history, sundering the chains that bound his countrymen. The museum is open 8 am to 8 pm daily.

Directly south around 20km is the **Ex-Hacienda de San Juan Chinameca**, where in 1919 Zapata was lured into a fatal trap by Colonel Jesús Guajardo following orders of President Venustiano Carranza, who was eager to get rid of the rebel leader and consolidate the post-revolutionary government. Pretending to defect to the revolutionary forces, Guajardo set up a meeting with Zapata, who arrived at Chinameca accompanied by a guerrilla escort. Guajardo's men gunned down the general before he crossed the threshold of the abandoned hacienda.

The hacienda, with a small museum (hours vary), is on the left at the end of the town's main street, where there's a statue of Zapata astride a rearing horse. The museum caretaker, who was a young child when

Zapata was shot here, will tell you the story of that day and show you the bullet holes in the wall.

From Chinameca, highway 9 heads northwest 20km to Tlaltizapán, site of the **Museo de la Revolución del Sur** (open 9 am to 5 pm Tuesday to Sunday, donation requested) in what were the revolutionary forces' main barracks. It contains relics of General Zapata, including the bed where he slept, his rifle (the trigger retains his fingerprints) and the hat and clothing he was wearing at the time of his death (they are riddled with bullet holes and stained with blood).

Those with a passion for all things Zapata might like to check out the Emiliano Zapata website (www.zapatistas.org), which includes a 'Follow Zapata Through Morelos' section.'

From Cuautla, the yellow 'Chinameca' combis traveling to Anenecuilco and Chinameca (US$0.30) leave from Garduño and Matamoros every 10 minutes.

Tetela del Volcán
• pop 7870 • elev 2220 ☎ 7

This village 22km east of highway 115 is one of several built around Augustinian monasteries on Popo's southern slopes. From the outside of Tetela's 16th-century **Ex-Convento de San Juan Bautista**, there are majestic views of the monastery crowned by the volcano. Like other villages in Popo's vicinity, Tetela has a notable military presence standing by should an evacuation be necessary. There's a civil protection headquarters off the plaza, keeping residents posted on the latest volcanic activity.

Fine accommodations are part of the reason for staying here. *Albergue Suizo* (☎ 357-00-56) is approached by the first left after you go through Tetela's entryway arches. The tall brick structure, whose roof does vaguely resemble that of a Swiss chalet, has large rooms with a view (though not of Popo), and spacious baths with copious hot water for US$8/10.50. Popo can be glimpsed through a wall of windows around the top-level dining room.

About a 15-minute drive east of Tetela, on the way to Hueyapan, is the pristine Rio Amatzinac. You can hike along an old cobblestone road and over stone bridges spanning the river.

From Cuautla, microbuses to Tetela depart from near the Estrella Roja station (40 minutes).

CUERNAVACA
• pop 311,100 • elev 1480m ☎ 7

With a mild climate, once described as 'eternal spring,' Cuernavaca ('kwehr-nah-VAH-kah') has been a retreat from Mexico City since colonial times. It attracts the wealthy and fashionable from Mexico and abroad, many of whom have stayed on to become temporary or semipermanent residents. A number of their residences have become attractions in themselves, now housing museums, galleries, expensive restaurants and hotels. As the local population grows and more and more visitors come, especially on weekends, Cuernavaca is unfortunately losing some of its charm and acquiring the problems that people from the capital try to escape – crowds, traffic, smog and crime.

Much of the city's elegance is hidden behind high walls and in colonial courtyards, and is largely inaccessible to the casual visitor on a tight budget. A stroll through the lively zócalo costs nothing, but try to allow a few extra pesos to enjoy the food and ambiance at some of the better restaurants. Cuernavaca is also worth visiting to see the famed Palacio de Cortés, and the nearby pre-Hispanic sites and balnearios. A lot of visitors stay longer to enroll in one of the many Spanish-language schools.

History
The people settling in the valleys of modern Morelos around 1220 developed a highly productive agricultural society based at Cuauhnáhuac (Place at the Edge of the Forest). The Mexica (Aztecs), who dominated the Valle de México, called them 'Tlahuica,' which means 'people who work the land.' In 1379, a Mexica warlord conquered Cuauhnáhuac, subdued the Tlahuica and required them to pay an annual tribute that included 8000 sets of clothing, 16,000 pieces of

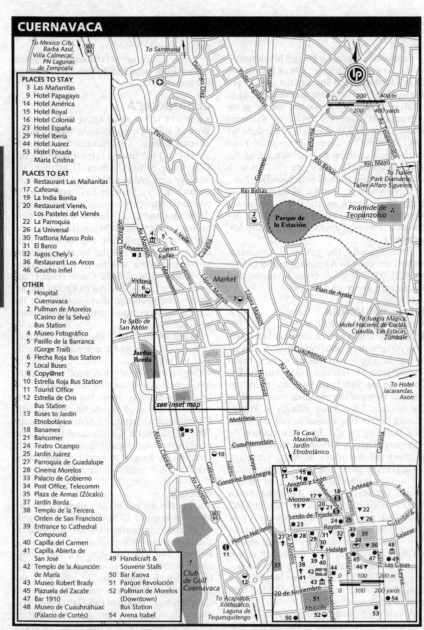

CUERNAVACA

To Mexico City,
Barba Azul,
Villa Calmecac,
PN Lagunas
de Zempoala

MEX 95

To Sammaná

To Trailer
Park Diamante,
Taller Alfaro Siqueiros

Río Mayo

Río Balsas

Río Balsas

Parque de
la Estación

Pirámide de
Teopanzolco

Market

Plan de Ayala

Cuauhtémoc

Av Atlacomulco

To Jungla Mágica,
Hotel Hácienda de Cortés,
Cuautla, Las Estacas,
Zúmbale

To Hotel
Jacarandas,
Axon

To Salto de
San Antón

Jardín
Borda

see inset map

Motolinia

Cuauhtemotzin

González Bocanegra

To Casa
Maximiliano,
Jardín
Etnobotánico

MEX 95

Himno Nacional

Club
de Golf
Cuernavaca

To Acapulco,
Xochicalco,
Laguna de
Tequesquitengo

PLACES TO STAY
3   Las Mañanitas
9   Hotel Papagayo
14 Hotel América
15 Hotel Royal
16 Hotel Colonial
23 Hotel España
29 Hotel Iberia
44 Hotel Juárez
53 Hotel Posada
    María Cristina

PLACES TO EAT
3   Restaurant Las Mañanitas
17 Cafeona
19 La India Bonita
20 Restaurant Vienés,
    Los Pasteles del Vienés
22 La Parroquia
26 La Universal
30 Trattoria Marco Polo
31 El Barco
32 Jugos Chely's
36 Restaurant Los Arcos
46 Gaucho Infiel

OTHER
1   Hospital
    Cuernavaca
2   Pullman de Morelos
    (Casino de la Selva)
    Bus Station
4   Museo Fotográfico
5   Pasillo de la Barranca
    (Gorge Trail)
6   Flecha Roja Bus Station
7   Local Buses
8   Copy@net
10 Estrella Roja Bus Station
11 Tourist Office
12 Estrella de Oro
    Bus Station
13 Buses to Jardín
    Etnobotánico
18 Banamex
21 Bancomer
24 Teatro Ocampo
25 Jardín Juárez
27 Parroquia de Guadalupe
28 Cinema Morelos
33 Palacio de Gobierno
34 Post Office, Telecomm
35 Plaza de Armas (Zócalo)
37 Jardín Borda
38 Templo de la Tercera
    Orden de San Francisco
39 Entrance to Cathedral
    Compound
40 Capilla del Carmen
41 Capilla Abierta de
    San José
42 Templo de la Asunción
    de María
43 Museo Robert Brady
47 Bar 1910
48 Museo de Cuauhnáhuac
    (Palacio de Cortés)

49 Handicraft &
    Souvenir Stalls
50 Bar Kaova
51 Parque Revolución
52 Pullman de Morelos
    (Downtown)
    Bus Station
54 Arena Isabel

Inset map

13
14
15
16
Aragón y León
Morrow
17
19
20
21
Lerdo de Tejada
23
24
25
Rayón
27
28
29
31
30
32
33
34
35
36
38
39
40
42
44
41
43
20 de Noviembre
Abasolo
50
52
53
54

Av Morelos
Juárez
Galeana
Hidalgo
Matamoros
Guerrero
Arteaga
E Zarco
Gutenberg
Salazar
Las Casas
La Cureña

Gondolas on the Aztec canals of Xochimilco, Mexico City

Art for sale at San Angel's Bazar Sábado, Mexico City

Need a ride? Mexico City's infamous VW taxis

Ruins atop a Xochitécatl pyramid, near Mexico City

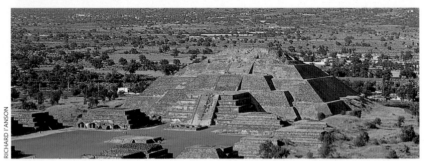

Teotihuacán's Pirámide de la Luna - 1700 years old and counting

Stone warrior, Tula

Spanish church on a pagan temple in Cholula

amate bark paper and 20,000 bushels of maize. The tributes payable by the subject states were set out in a register the Spanish later called *Códice Mendocino* in which Cuauhnáhuac was represented by a three-branched tree; this symbol now appears on the city's coat of arms.

The successor to the Mexican lord married the daughter of the Cuauhnáhuac leader, and from this marriage was born Moctezuma I Ilhuicamina, the great 15th-century Aztec king who was a predecessor of the Moctezuma II Xocoyotzin encountered by Cortés. The Tlahuica prospered under the Aztec empire, themselves dominating small states to the south and trading extensively with other regions. Their city was also a center for religious ceremonies and learning, and archaeological remains show they had a considerable knowledge of astronomy.

When the Spanish arrived, the Tlahuica were fiercely loyal to the Aztec empire, savagely resisting the advance of the conquistadors. In April 1521, they were finally overcome, and Cortés torched the city. Destroying the city pyramid, Cortés used the stones to build a fortress-palace on the pyramid's base. He also had built from the rubble the Catedral de la Asunción, another fortress-like structure in a walled compound; in the 1520s, there was not much reason to trust in the benign favor of the new Catholic 'converts.' Soon the city became known as Cuernavaca, a more pronounceable (to the Spanish) version of its original name.

In 1529, Cortés received his somewhat belated reward from the Spanish crown when he was named Marqués del Valle de Oaxaca, with an estate that covered 22 towns, including Cuernavaca, and a charge of 23,000 indigenous Mexicans. He introduced sugarcane and other crops, and new farming methods, which resulted in Cuernavaca becoming an agricultural center for the Spanish, as it had been for the Aztecs. Cortés made Cuernavaca his home for the rest of his stay in Mexico, and his descendants dominated the area for nearly 300 years.

With its pleasant climate, rural surroundings and colonial elite, Cuernavaca became a refuge and a retreat for the rich and powerful. One of these was José de la Borda, the 18th-century Taxco silver magnate. His lavish home and garden were later a retreat for Emperor Maximilian and Empress Carlota. Cuernavaca also attracted artists and writers, and achieved literary fame as the setting for Malcolm Lowry's 1947 novel *Under the Volcano*. The very rich of Mexico City are now just as likely to go to Acapulco or Dallas for the weekend, but many still have magnificent properties in the suburbs of Cuernavaca.

Orientation

The zócalo, also called the Plaza de Armas, is the heart of the city and the best place to begin a tour of Cuernavaca. Most of the budget hotels and important sites are nearby. The various bus lines use different terminals, most within walking distance of the zócalo.

Highway 95D, the toll road, skirts the east side of Cuernavaca. If you're coming from the north, take the Cuernavaca exit and cross to highway 95 (where you'll see a statue of Zapata on horseback). Highway 95 becomes Boulevard Zapata as you go south into town, then Avenida Morelos; south of Avenida Matamoros, Morelos is one-way, northbound only. To reach the center, veer left and go down Matamoros.

Information

Tourist Offices The state tourist office (☎ 314-38-72), inconveniently located at Morelos Sur 187, is understaffed and not very well-informed. No maps are available. It's supposedly open 8 am to 6 pm Monday to Friday and 10 am to 4 pm Saturday to Sunday, but phone ahead to be sure

Post & Communications The post office, on the south side of the Plaza de Armas, is open 8 am to 7 pm Monday to Friday, and 9 am to 1 pm Saturday. Next door a Telecomm office offers fax and telegram services.

Excellent Internet service is provided by Copy@net at Morelos 178 at Motolinía (US$3.75 per hour). The air-conditioned space is open Monday to Saturday from 8 am to 9 pm.

If you would rather surf the Web on a Mac, check out Axon (Cuauhtémoc 129B) with Internet access on six Macintosh computers, including two iMacs, for US$4.25 per hour. It's open 9.30 am to 9 pm Monday to Friday and 10 am to 8 pm Saturday.

Medical Services Hospital Cuernavaca is at Cuauhtémoc 305 at the corner of 5 de Mayo in the Colonia Lomas de la Selva (☎ 311-24-82).

Plaza de Armas & Jardín Juárez

The Plaza de Armas, Cuernavaca's zócalo, is flanked on the east by the Palacio de Cortés, on the west by the Palacio de Gobierno and on the northeast and south by a number of restaurants.

Adjoining the plaza's northwest corner is the smaller Jardín Juárez with a central gazebo designed by tower specialist Gustave Eiffel. It's the only main plaza in Mexico *without* a church, chapel, convent or cathedral overlooking it. Roving vendors sell balloons, ice cream and corn on the cob under the trees, which fill up with legions of cacophonous grackles at dusk.

Palacio de Cortés

Cortés' imposing medieval-style fortress stands at the southeastern end of the Plaza de Armas. Construction of this two-story stone palace was accomplished between 1522 and 1532, and was done on the base of the pyramid that Cortés destroyed, still visible from various points on the ground floor. Cortés resided here until he returned to Spain in 1540. The palace remained with Cortés' family for most of the next century, but by the 18th century it was being used as a prison, and during the Porfirio Díaz era it became government offices.

Today the palace houses the **Museo de Cuauhnáhuac**, with two floors of exhibits highlighting the history and cultures of Mexico. On the ground floor, exhibits focus on pre-Hispanic cultures, including the local Tlahuica and their relationship with the Aztec empire.

Upstairs, exhibits cover events from the Spanish conquest to the present. On the balcony is a fascinating mural by Diego Rivera, commissioned in the mid-1920s as a gift to the people of Cuernavaca by Dwight Morrow, the US ambassador to Mexico. From right to left, scenes from the conquest up to the 1910 revolution emphasize the cruelty, oppression and violence that have characterized Mexican history.

The museum is open 10 am to 5 pm Tuesday to Sunday (US$2, free on Sunday).

Jardín Borda

These gardens were built in 1783 for Manuel de la Borda, as an addition to the stately residence built by his father, José de la Borda, the Taxco silver magnate. From 1866, the house was the summer residence of Emperor Maximilian and Empress Carlota, who entertained their courtiers in the gardens.

From the entrance on Morelos, you can tour the house and gardens to get an idea of how Mexico's aristocracy lived. In typical colonial style, the buildings are arranged around courtyards. In one wing, the **Museo de Sitio** has exhibits on daily life during the empire period, and original documents with the signatures of Morelos, Juárez and Maximilian.

Several romantic paintings on the walls of the Sala Manuel M Ponce, a recital hall near the entrance, show scenes of the garden in Maximilian's time. One of the most famous paintings depicts Maximilian in the garden with La India Bonita, the 'pretty Indian' who was to become his lover.

The gardens are formally laid out on a series of terraces, with paths, steps and fountains, and they originally featured a botanical collection with hundreds of varieties of fruit trees and ornamental plants. The vegetation is still exuberant, with large trees and semitropical shrubs, though there is no longer a wide range of species, and the pretty pond you see in the painting now looks more like a dirty concrete swimming pool. Also, because of a water shortage in the city, the fountains have been turned off, which greatly diminishes the aesthetic appeal of the gardens. You can hire a little boat and go rowing for US$2 an hour. The house and garden are open 10 am to 5.30 pm Tuesday through Sunday (US$1, free on Sunday). A café near the entrance serves cake and empanadas.

Beside the house is the Parroquia de Guadalupe, also built by José de la Borda, and dedicated in December 1784.

Recinto de la Catedral
Cuernavaca's cathedral stands in a large high-walled compound (recinto) on the corner of Morelos and Hidalgo (the entrance gate is on Hidalgo). Like the Palacio de Cortés, the cathedral was built on a grand scale and in a fortress-like style, as a defense against the natives and to impress and intimidate them. Franciscans started work under Cortés in 1526, using indigenous labor and stones from the rubble of Cuauhnáhuac; it was one of the earliest Christian missions in Mexico. The first part to be built was **Capilla Abierta de San José**, the open chapel on the west side of the cathedral.

The cathedral itself, **Templo de la Asunción de María**, is plain and solid, with an unembellished façade. The side door, which faces north to the compound's entrance, shows a mixture of indigenous and European features – the skull and crossbones above it is a symbol of the Franciscan order. Inside are frescos discovered early in the 20th century. They are said to show the persecution of Christian missionaries in Japan, though it's difficult to decipher them. Cuernavaca was a center for Franciscan missionary activities in Asia, and the frescos were supposedly painted in the 17th century by a Japanese convert to Christianity.

The cathedral compound also holds two smaller churches, one on either side of the Hidalgo entrance. On the right as you enter is the **Templo de la Tercera Orden de San Francisco**, which was commenced in 1723; its exterior was carved in 18th-century baroque style by indigenous artisans, and its interior with ornate, gilded decorations. Left as you enter is the 19th-century **Capilla del Carmen**, where believers seek cures for illness. Mass in English is given here at 9.30 am on Sunday.

Museo Robert Brady
Robert Brady (1928-86), an American artist and collector, lived in Cuernavaca for 24 years. His home, the Casa de la Torre, was originally part of the monastery within the Recinto de la Catedral. Brady had it extensively renovated and decorated with paintings, carvings, textiles, antiques and decorative and folk arts he'd acquired in his travels around the world. There are several paintings by well-known Mexican artists, including Tamayo, Kahlo and Covarrubias, but the main attraction is the sheer size and diversity of the collection, and the way it is arranged with delightful combinations and contrasts of styles, periods and places.

A short walk from the zócalo, at Netzahualcóyotl 4, the museum is open 10 am to 6 pm Tuesday to Sunday (US$2).

Salto de San Antón
Less than 1km west of the Jardín Borda is the salto, a 36m waterfall surrounded by lush vegetation. A walkway is built into the cliff face so you can go right behind the falls, where there are a few picnic tables. The village of San Antón, above the falls, is a traditional center for pottery. The Ruta 4 bus, marked 'Salto,' goes from the corner of Abasolo and Morelos directly to the entrance. The salto is open 10 am to 6 pm Tuesday to Sunday (US$0.50).

Casa Maximiliano
In Cuernavaca's suburbs, 1.5km southeast of the center, this 1866 house was once a rural retreat for the Emperor Maximilian, where he would meet his indigenous lover. It was called La Casa del Olvido (the House of Forgetfulness), because Maximilian 'forgot' to include a room for his wife there. He did remember to include a small house in the back for his lover; it is now the **Museo de Medicina Tradicional**, a museum of traditional herbal medicine. Around the museum, the **Jardín Etnobotánico** has a collection of 455 herbs and medicinal plants from around the world, all labeled with their botanical names. The museum and garden are open 9 am to 5 pm daily (free). Catch a Ruta 6 'Jardines' bus from the corner of Morelos and Degollado.

Pirámide de Teopanzolco

This small archaeological site is on Río Balsas in the Colonia Vista Hermosa. There are actually two pyramids, one inside the other. You can climb upon the outer base and see the older pyramid within, with a double staircase leading up to the remains of a pair of temples. The older pyramid was built over 800 years ago by the Tlahuicas; the outside one was under construction by the Aztecs when Cortés arrived and was never completed. The name Teopanzolco means 'Place of the Ancient Temple,' and may relate to an ancient construction to the west of the current pyramid, where artifacts dating from around 7000 BC have been

Language Courses

Many foreigners come to Cuernavaca to study Spanish. The best schools offer small-group or individual instruction, at all levels, with four to five hours per day of intensive instruction plus a couple of hours' conversation practice. Classes begin each Monday, and most schools recommend a minimum enrollment of four weeks, though you can study for as many weeks as you want.

Tuition fees vary from US$140 to US$200 per week, usually payable in advance. You may get a discount outside the peak months of January, February, July and August; some schools offer discounts if you stay more than four weeks. Most schools also charge a nonrefundable one-time enrollment fee of US$75 to US$100.

The schools can arrange for students to live with a Mexican family to experience 'total immersion' in the language. The host families charge about US$18 per day with shared room and bath, or about US$25 per day with private room and bath; price includes three meals daily. The schools can often help with hotels too. For free brochures, write or call:

CALE – Center of Art and Languages
(☎ 313-06-03, fax 313-73-52) Nueva Tabachin 22B bis, Colonia Tlaltenango, CP 62170 Cuernavaca, Morelos, Mexico, www.gl.com.mx/cale; former students cite CALE's personalized approach to learning as its best asset

Cemanahuac Educational Community
(☎ 318-64-19, fax 312-54-18) Apdo Postal 5-21, CP 62051 Cuernavaca, Morelos, Mexico, www .cemanahuac.com; emphasis is placed on language acquisition and cultural awareness

Center for Bilingual Multicultural Studies
(☎ 317-10-87, fax 317-05-33, ☎ 800-932-2068 in the USA) Apdo Postal 1520, CP 62000 Cuernavaca, Morelos, Mexico, www.bilingual-center.com; the center is accredited by the Universidad Autónoma del Estado de Morelos and affiliated with more than 100 foreign universities

Cetlalic Alternative Language School
(☎/fax 313-26-37) Apdo Postal 1-201, CP 62000 Cuernavaca, Morelos, Mexico, cetlalic@ mail.giga.com, www.giga.com/~cetlalic; emphasis is placed on language learning, cultural awareness and social responsibility

Cuauhnáhuac Instituto Colectivo de Lengua y Cultura
(☎ 312-36-73, fax 318-26-93) Apdo Postal 5-26, CP 62051 Cuernavaca, Morelos, Mexico, inform@cuauhnahuac.edu.mx; the school helps students earn university language credits and members of the business and medical communities develop language interests

Encuentros Comunicación y Cultura
(☎/fax 312-50-88) Apdo Postal 2-71, CP 62158, Cuernavaca, Morelos, Mexico, http://cuernavaca .infosel.com.mx/encuentros/spanish.htm; the program focuses on professionals and travellers needing to learn Spanish

❋ ❋

found as well as others with an Olmec influence.

Several other smaller platform structures surround the double pyramid. Near the rectangular platform to the west a tomb was discovered, containing the remains of 92 men, women and children mixed with ceramic pieces. They are believed to be products of human sacrifice in which decapitation and dismemberment were practiced.

The site is open 9 am to 6 pm daily (US$1.75, free on Sunday). No buses go directly to the entrance. Catch a Ruta 4 'Barona' bus at Degollado and Guerrero, get off at Río Balsas, turn right and walk four blocks; or take a taxi to the site.

Language Courses

Experiencia – Centro de Intercambio Bilingüe y Cultural
(☎ 312-65-79, fax 318-52-09) Apdo Postal 596, CP 62050 Cuernavaca, Morelos, Mexico, experiencia@infosel.net.mx; the *intercambio* program offers two-hour, twice weekly conversational exchanges between Mexican and international students

IDEAL Latinoamerica
(☎ 311-75-51, fax 311-59-10) Apdo Postal 2-65, CP 62158 Cuernavaca, Morelos, Mexico, www
.ideal-l.com; the program immerses the student in the Spanish language and Mexican culture, while respecting the individual's pace and style of learning

IDEL – Instituto de Idiomas y Culturas Latinoamericanas
(☎/fax 313-01-57) Apdo Postal 1271-1, CP 62001 Cuernavaca, Morelos, Mexico, moises@
www.intersur.com; IDEL complements language study with excursions to places of historical interest in and around Cuernavaca, video presentations, cultural events and parties

Instituto de Idioma y Cultura en Cuernavaca
(☎ 317-04-55, fax 317-57-10) Apdo Postal 2-42, CP 62158 Cuernavaca, Morelos, Mexico, www
.webs21.com/icc; a different teacher each week gives students exposure to different voices and personalities

Praktilingua
☎/fax 318-02-67. Apdo Postal 5-124, CP 62051 Cuernavaca, Morelos, Mexico, prakti@intersur
.com; recommended by former students for its individual attention and friendly atmosphere

Prolingua Instituto Español Xochicalco
(☎/fax 318-42-86) Apdo Postal 1-888, CP 62000 Cuernavaca, Morelos, Mexico, www.axon.com
.mx/prolingua; the program helps develop conversational fluency while building awareness of Mexican culture, history and traditions through lectures

Spanish Language Institute
(☎ 311-00-63, fax 317-52-94) Apdo Postal 2-3, CP 62191 Cuernavaca, Morelos, Mexico, sli@
infosel.net.mx; cultural courses include Mexican customs and Latin American literature

Universal Centro de Lingua y Comunicación
(☎ 318-29-04, fax 318-29-10) Apdo Postal 1-1826, Cuernavaca, Morelos, Mexico 62000, www
.universal-spanish.com; Universal mixes language study with visits to local communities and visits from local politicians, community leaders and scholars

Universidad Autónoma del Estado de Morelos
(☎ 316-16-26, fax 322-35-13) Río Pánuco 20, Colonia Lomas del Mirador, CP 62350 Cuernavaca, Morelos, Mexico, www2.uaem.mx/clahpe; the university's Centro de Lengua, Arte e Historia para Extranjeros uses a communicative approach augmented by authentic audio, video and print source materials

Other Things to See & Do

The great Mexican muralist David Alfaro Siqueiros had his workshop *(taller)* in Cuernavaca from 1964 until his death in 1974. The **Taller Alfaro Siqueiros**, at Venus 52 in Fraccionamiento Jardines de Cuernavaca, is open 10 am to 5 pm Tuesday through Sunday (US$0.50). On display are four murals left unfinished at the artist's death, a photographic display of his major works, and other mementos of his life.

If you are interested in history, the **Museo Fotográfico de Cuernavaca** has a few early photographs and maps of the city. Open 9 am to 3 pm Monday to Friday and 10 am to 2 pm Saturday and Sunday, it's in a cute little 1897 building called the Castellito, at Güemes 1, 1km north of the zócalo. By the fountain at the base of Güueëmes is the entrance to the **Pasillo de la Barranca**, a trail that follows a deep gorge bursting with flowers and butterflies, well below the roar of traffic. There are a few waterfalls and no trash along the half-kilometer trail, which emerges by the arches at Guerrero and Gómez Farías.

Jungla Mágica (☎ 315-87-76), at Bajada de Chapultepec 27, is a children's park with a jungle theme and a popular bird show, as well as boating and picnicking facilities where you can swim with dolphins.

The park is open Thursday to Sunday from 10 am to 6 pm (US$2 for adults, US$1.50 for kids). To get there, take a Ruta 17 bus and tell the driver you're going to 'La Luna,' which is a roundabout; walk two blocks along Chapultepec and you'll come to the entrance of the park.

Special Events

These are among the festivals and special events you can see in Cuernavaca:

Carnaval – in the five days before Ash Wednesday, this colorful celebration features street performances by the Chinelo dancers of Tepoztlán, parades, art exhibits and more; late February or early March

Feria de la Primavera – the Spring Fair includes cultural and artistic events, concerts and a beautiful exhibit of the city's spring flowers; March 21 to April 10

San Isidro Labrador – in honor of the saint, local farmers adorn their mules and oxen with flowers and bring them to town for a blessing; May 15

Places to Stay

Accommodations in Cuernavaca don't offer great value for the money. The cheap places tend to be depressingly basic, the mid-range ones are lacking in charm and the top-end hotels are wonderful but very expensive. On weekends and holidays, the town fills up with visitors from the capital, so phone ahead or try to secure your room early in the day.

Budget The cheapest places are on Aragón y León between Morelos and Matamoros – a section of street worked by a handful of hookers. The improved version of *Hotel América (☎ 318-61-27, Aragón y León 14)* is the best of these – basic but very clean. Singles/doubles with private baths and hot water are US$10.50/15; there's a room on the roof with a separate bathroom for US$8.

Around the corner, *Hotel Royal (☎ 318-64-80, Matamoros 11)* features clean rooms with hot water for US$11.50/14, or with TVs for US$3.75 more. It also has a central parking lot.

A hostel affiliated with Hostelling International (HI), *Villa Calmecac (☎ 313-21-46, Zacatecas 114, Colonia Buenavista, meliton@mail.giga.com)* is very pleasant though quite a distance from the center. Made of adobe-wood construction, the building is equipped with rainwater-collection and sewage-recycling devices and surrounded by organic gardens of local plants. The hostel charges US$10.50 per person (US$12.75 with an all-natural buffet breakfast) for a bunk bed in one of its eight rustic-style rooms, or 10% less with an HI card. There are two sparkling clean baths, each with three shower stalls and toilets. Villa Calmecac is located 800m west of the Mexico City autopista. From the center, it's a 20-minute ride on a Ruta 1, 2 or 3 bus from Morelos and Degollado. Zacatecas is two blocks past the Zapata monument on the left. Visitors must check in before 9 pm.

Trailer Park Diamante (☎ 316-07-61), on Mesalina in Colonia Las Delicias, offers hookups for US$10.50 per night. It's fairly peaceful, except for the drone from the nearby autopista, and there are a couple of pools. To get there, drive up Río Frío, which becomes Diana; after the Oxxo convenience store, turn right on Mesalina and go downhill about 200m.

Mid-Range Up the street and price scale from the Hotel América, *Hotel Colonial* (☎ 318-14-64, Aragón y León 19) charges US$12.50/20 for pleasant single/double rooms, some facing a cute garden, with private baths.

Centrally located next to the cathedral, *Hotel Juárez* (☎ 314-02-19, Netzahualcóyotl 19) offers 13 simple but spacious and airy rooms with 24-hour hot water for US$16/18, as well as a swimming pool encircled by a lawn. The *Hotel Iberia* (☎ 312-60-40, Rayón 7) has long been patronized by travelers and foreign students. At US$16.50/18.50, its small, basic rooms set around a tiled parking lot are a tad pricey, but it is only a short walk to the zócalo. The colonial *Hotel España* (☎ 318-67-44, Morelos 190) is nicer than the Iberia because it has toilet seats, shower curtains and better ventilation, but in other cities its fairly worn rooms (US$14/18, US$2 extra for color TV) would cost less. The downstairs restaurant specializes in Spanish cuisine.

Hotel Papagayo (☎ 314-17-11, Motolinía 13) is the most attractive place in this price range, with 77 modern rooms, two swimming pools, a playground (bordered by poinsettias and mango trees) and plenty of parking. The rate of US$18/27 includes breakfast at the central restaurant served with complimentary lounge music on weekends.

Top End *Las Mañanitas* (☎ 314-14-66, mananita@intersur.com, Linares 107) is one of the finest hotels in Mexico. Prices run from US$125 for standard rooms up to US$274 for gorgeous garden suites. Renowned for its large private garden where peacocks stroll around while guests enjoy the pool, this hotel has been included in several listings of the world's best hotels. Its restaurant is also justly famous.

Hotel Posada María Cristina (☎ 318-57-67, Juárez 300) is one of Cuernavaca's long-time favorites, with tastefully appointed rooms in a nicely restored colonial building, two restaurants, lovely hillside gardens and an inviting pool. Rooms start at US$67 (US$84 on Saturday), and private cabañas are available for US$110 (US$137 on Saturday).

East of the center in the Colonia Chapultepec, *Hotel Jacarandas* (☎ 315-77-77, Cuauhtémoc 133) is set on rambling grounds graced with lots of trees and gardens and three pools at varying temperatures. Standard rooms are US$71; suites with terraces start at US$93. From the hotel, there are buses along Cuauhtémoc to the center.

Built in the 17th century by Martín Cortés, who succeeded Hernán Cortés as Marqués del Valle de Oaxaca, Hacienda de San Antonio Atlacomulco was renovated in 1980 to become *Hotel Hacienda de Cortés* (☎ 316-08-67, Plaza Kennedy 90). The hotel's 18 luxurious suites, each with its own terrace and garden, start at US$97. There's a swimming pool built around old stone columns. Located about 4km southeast of the center, in Atlacomulco, it's worth visiting even if you're not staying at the hotel, just to stroll the lovely grounds and have lunch underneath the magnificent colonial arches of the restaurant.

Places to Eat
Budget For a simple healthy snack of yogurt with fruit, *escamochas* (a kind of fruit salad), corn on the cob or ice cream, you could patronize one of the booths at the *Jardín Juárez gazebo*, then eat your treat on one of the park's many benches.

Heading south down Galeana from Jardín Juárez, *Jugos Chely's* has fresh fruit juice combos (US$1.25), such as zanayogui (carrot and orange), toronjil (grapefruit, pineapple and parsley) and mexicano (nopal, orange and lime), as well as burgers and quesadillas. Along this noisy street, there are several other small greasy joints that all hang out numerous signs shouting their offerings – these places are best avoided.

The popular *El Barco (Rayón 5)* near Comonfort serves Guerrero-style *pozole* from a clean, tiled kitchen with plenty of clay pottery. Small or large bowls (US$2/2.50) of pozole verde or rojo (shredded pork and hominy in delicious broth) are served with oregano, chili, chopped onions and limes. Specify '*maciza*' unless you want your pozole to include bits of fat. El Barco also serves pitchers of ice-cold *agua de jamaica* and various tequilas.

Cafeona, on Morrow just west of Matamoros, is a little corner of Chiapas in Cuernavaca. It's a cool hangout, decorated with Chiapan crafts and serving organic coffee from the southern state, as well as raspberry pies, tamales and fruit salads with granola (US$1.75 each).

Mid-Range On the east side of Jardín Juárez, *La Parroquia*, which is open 7.30 am to midnight, is one of Cuernavaca's favorite restaurants. It has a good view of the plaza, but you pay for the location – main meal dishes, for example, cost around US$7. Nearby, *La Universal*, which is open 9 am to midnight, occupies a strategic position on the corner of the two plazas, with tables under an awning facing the Plaza de Armas. It's a popular place to be seen, but the food is just average and seems overpriced – the comida corrida costs US$6.50.

On the south side of the Plaza de Armas, *Restaurant Los Arcos* is a popular meeting place among the international student crowd, and it is open till midnight. Have a seat under the umbrellas of its outdoor tables, sip a coffee or a soda and watch the action on the plaza. The varied bilingual menu has something for everyone and is not too expensive.

The Plazuela del Zacate at Galeana and Hidalgo has a number of upscale snacking options (with outdoor seating), such as *El Encierro*, which serves tasty sandwiches and hot dogs (US$1.75 to US$3.75). Just east of there, the plaza funnels into Las Casas, which is where you'll find *Gaucho Infiel*, a good Argentine steak place with a charcoal grill. Steaks go for US$5 to US$7.50, and *parrillada* (an assortment of meats and sausages that typically feeds two) for US$10.50.

La India Bonita (Morrow 106), northwest of Jardín Juárez, is a lovely courtyard restaurant with tasty, traditional Mexican food. The house specialties are: chicken in mole sauce (US$7), charcoal-grilled filet mignon (US$8.75), huitlacoche crepes (US$5.50) and a special Mexican platter with seven different selections (US$8). Hours are 8.30 am till 7.30 pm Tuesday to Saturday and 8.30 am till 6.30 pm Sunday.

Restaurant Vienés (Lerdo de Tejada 4) offers middle-European dishes, such as knackwurst with sauerkraut and German fried potatoes, for an average of US$8 per main course. A set lunch goes for US$8.50. It's open 1 to 10 pm daily. The same owners run *Los Pasteles del Vienés*, next door, which serves the best cakes, cookies, cream puffs and chocolate-rum truffles you've tasted since the last time you were in Vienna. Their superb coffee comes with free refills. *Trattoria Marco Polo (Hidalgo 30)*, open till 11 pm, makes excellent pizzas, with single-serving pies for about US$2.75 and large pies for US$6. There's a lovely view of the cathedral compound from the balcony tables.

Top End If you can afford an indulgence, try *Restaurant Las Mañanitas* (☎ *314-14-66, Linares 107*) at the hotel of the same name. One of Mexico's best and most famous restaurants, it has tables inside the mansion or on the garden terrace where you can see peacocks and flamingos strolling through an emerald-green garden and swans gliding around a pond. The menu, which waiters will show you on a large blackboard, features meals from around the world. You should bring at least US$20 in cash per person, unless you have an American Express card. If you'd rather not spend all that cash, you may have a drink in the garden. Las Mañanitas is open 1 to 5 pm and 7 to 10.30 pm daily; reservations are recommended.

Entertainment

Hanging around the central plazas is always a popular activity in Cuernavaca, especially on Sunday and Thursday from 6 pm on, when open-air concerts are often held.

Cinema Morelos, on the corner of Morelos and Rayón, is the state theater of Morelos, hosting a variety of cultural offerings, including quality film series, plays and dance performances. *Teatro Ocampo* on the west side of Jardín Juárez stages contemporary plays; a calendar of cultural events is posted at its entrance. Less highbrow entertainment is available at the *Arena Isabel*, in the form of *lucha libre* (wrestling). Look for posters around town for lineups.

Plazuela del Zacate and adjacent Las Casas come alive in the evening with many bars featuring live music. *Bar Eclipse* has performers on two levels, folk on the bottom and rock on top. The intimate *El Romántico*, as the name implies, is a venue for ballad singers.

The better discos charge a cover of at least US$5; women are usually admitted free Friday and Saturday nights. Some discos enforce dress codes and the trendier places post style police at the door. *Barba Azul* (*Prado 10*) in Colonia San Jeronimo, and *Kaova*, near the corner of Abasolo and Morelos, are two of the most popular places. The revolutionary-themed *1910* (☎ 315-04-77) on Juárez is so popular you need to make a reservation well in advance to get in. For live salsa dance music, try the very cool *Zúmbale* (*Bajada de Chapultepec 13*), near Glorieta La Luna (US$10 cover), or the glitzy *Sammaná* (☎ 313-47-27, *Domingo Diéz 1522*), across the street from Carlos & Charlie's. It's open Wednesday to Saturday nights. Since public transport is sparse during these hours, taxi is the best way to get to the clubs. The fare to Zúmbale or Sammaná should be US$2 or US$3 from the center.

Shopping

Cuernavaca has no distinctive handicrafts, but if you want an onyx ashtray, a leather belt or some second-rate silver, try the stalls just south of the Palacio de Cortés. Assorted ceramic figurines of campesina women, animals and miniature buildings are sold on 3 de Mayo, south of the center, at prices far lower than what you'd find elsewhere.

Getting There & Away

Bus Quite a few bus companies serve Cuernavaca. There are five separate long-distance terminals, operated by the main lines:

Pullman de Morelos (PDM) – There are two stations; one on the corner of Abasolo and Netzahualcóyotl, and the other at Casino de la Selva, northeast of the center.

Estrella de Oro (EDO) – Avenida Morelos Sur 900

Estrella Roja (ER) – On the corner of Galeana and Cuauhtemotzin

Flecha Roja (FR) – Avenida Morelos 503, between Arista and Victoria

To get to the Estrella de Oro terminal, which is 1.5km south of the center, take a Ruta 20 bus down Galeana; in the other direction, catch any bus up Morelos. Ruta 17 buses up Morelos stop within one block of the Pullman de Morelos terminal at Casino de la Selva. The rest of the terminals are within walking distance of the zócalo. Many local buses and those to nearby towns go from the southern corner of the city market.

Daily 1st-class buses from Cuernavaca include:

Acapulco – 315km, 4 hours; 7 EDO (US$18, deluxe US$25), 7 FR (US$16.50, deluxe US$18)

Chilpancingo – 180km, 2 hours; 6 EDO (US$9.50), 7 FR (US$9)

Cuautla – 42km, 1¼ hours; 65 ER (US$1.75)

Grutas de Cacahuamilpa – 80km, 2½ hours; 6 FR (US$1.75)

Guadalajara – 635km, 9 hours; 2 FR (US$33)

Mexico City (Terminal Sur) – 89km, 1¼ hours; PDM deluxe from downtown terminal every 15 minutes (US$4), PDM 'ejecutivo' from Casino de la Selva every 25 minutes (US$4.75), 33 FR (US$4)

Mexico City Airport – 100km, 1¾ hours; PDM hourly from Casino de la Selva (US$7, tickets may be purchased at PDM downtown terminal)

Oaxtepec – 25km, 1 hour; ER every 15 minutes (US$1.50)

Puebla – 175km, 3¾ hours; 16 ER (US$6.50)

Taxco – 80km, 1½ hours; 14 FR (US$3.50), 3 EDO (US$3.75)

Tepoztlán – 23km, 30 minutes; every 15 minutes till 10 pm from the local bus terminal at the city market (US$1)

Toluca – 153km, 2½ hours; 30 FR (US$3.25)
Zihuatanejo – 450km, 7 hours; 2 EDO (US$25)

Car & Motorcycle Cuernavaca is 89km south of Mexico City, a 1½ hour drive on highway 95 and a one-hour trip on the toll highway 95D (US$5.25). Both roads continue south to Acapulco; highway 95 goes through Taxco, and highway 95D is more direct and much faster (US$30).

Getting Around

You can walk to most places of interest in central Cuernavaca. The local buses (US$0.30) have their destinations marked on their windshields. Taxis will go to most places in town for under US$2. Radio taxi services include Citlalli (☎ 317-75-26) and Independéncia (☎ 313-14-14).

AROUND CUERNAVACA

Many places can be visited on day trips from Cuernavaca, on the way north to Mexico City or south to Taxco.

Xochicalco

Atop a desolate plateau 15km southwest of Cuernavaca as the crow flies but about 38km by road is the ancient ceremonial center of Xochicalco ('so-chee-CAL-co'), one of the most important archaeological sites in central Mexico. In Nahuatl, the language of the Aztecs, Xochicalco means 'Place of the House of Flowers.'

Today it is a collection of white stone ruins covering approximately 10 sq km, many yet to be excavated. They represent the various cultures – Toltec, Olmec, Zapotec, Mixtec and Aztec – for which Xochicalco was a commercial, cultural or religious center. When Teotihuacán began to weaken around 650 to 700 AD, Xochicalco began to rise in importance, achieving its maximum splendor between 650 and 850 AD with far-reaching commercial and cultural relations. Around the year 650, a congress of spiritual leaders met in Xochicalco, representing the Zapotec, Mayan and Gulf Coast peoples, to correlate their respective calendars.

The most famous monument here is the Pirámide de Quetzalcóatl (Pyramid of the Plumed Serpent). Archaeologists have surmised from its well-preserved bas-reliefs that astronomer-priests met here at the beginning and end of each 52-year cycle of the pre-Hispanic calendar. Xochicalco remained an important center until around 1200, when its excessive growth caused a fall similar to that of Teotihuacán. Signs at the site are in English and Spanish, but information appearing beside displays at an impressive museum 200m from the ruins is in Spanish only.

Getting There & Away Flecha Roja and Pullman de Morelos run hourly buses to within 4km of the site, from where you can walk (uphill) or catch a taxi (US$2). The site is open 10 am to 5 pm every day (US$2.75, free on Sunday).

Las Estacas

Set amid botanical gardens with plenty of flowers, Las Estacas is designed for relaxation in nature. At this balneario near the town of Tlaltizapán, you can swim in numerous pools or in a cool, clear river, replenished by underground springs at the rate of 7500 liters per second. There's scuba diving equipment for rent and diving classes are offered. It's open 8 am to 6 pm daily (US$7.50 for adults, US$3.75 for kids four to 10); try to arrive Monday to Friday if you're seeking tranquility.

Las Estacas' brand-new HI-affiliated hostel, *Fuerte Bambú* resembles a jungle village and features a row of cool, well-ventilated adobe/reed houses, referred to as *villas ecológicas*. There are three bunk beds in each of the houses (US$16 for adults, US$13 for children). Spacious bathhouses are adjacent to the villas. Other accommodations include a 14-room hotel (US$54/63) and a cluster of four-person, palm-thatched huts (US$19), or you can camp. The fee for any of these options includes park admission. Reservations (☎ 7-345-00-77, ☎ 5-563-24-28 in Mexico City, estacas@mpsnet.com .mx) for the hostel, hotel, huts or camping are encouraged.

Getting There & Away Combis from Jojutla (50 minutes south of Cuernavaca by frequent Pullman de Morelos buses) go directly to the park entrance (US$0.75). By car, By car, take the Cuautla exit off the Mexico City-Acapulco autopista, then take highway 138 east to Yautepec. From there head, south on route 2 toward Tlaltizapán and follow signs to Las Estacas.

Parque Nacional Lagunas de Zempoala

Only 25km northwest of Cuernavaca, by winding roads, is a group of seven lakes high in the hills. Some of them are stocked with fish for anglers, and the surrounding forest offers some pleasant walks and camping. Departing every half hour from Cuernavaca, Flecha Roja buses to Toluca make a stop at the park (US$2.30). The journey takes an hour.

Laguna de Tequesquitengo

This lake, 37km south of Cuernavaca, is a popular location for water sports, particularly water-skiing. There are hotels, restaurants and other facilities around the lakeshore.

In the area, there are several of the state of Morelos' famous balnearios – often natural springs that have been used as bathing and therapeutic places for hundreds of years – including **El Rollo** in Tlaquiltenango, which is geared for family fun with several large slides.

Two km north of the lake is the sublime *Hotel Hacienda Vista Hermosa* (☎ 7-345-53-61, *tourbymexico@infosel.net.mx*), which in the 16th century served as a cane-alcohol refinery. Accommodations are in 105 rooms and suites, some retaining their original colonial-era furniture, amid 80,000 sq m of lush gardens and palm-lined pathways. A standard double room costs US$132 with meals in the majestic dining room, or US$70 without meals. There's a sprawling swimming pool built around the old aqueduct. You may use the facilities without staying at the hotel for US$27 per day for adults, US$16 for children under 12; the fee includes lunch and the use of dressing rooms.

Pullman de Morelos runs five or more buses daily from Cuernavaca to the town of Tequesquitengo, on the southeast edge of the lake (1½ hours, US$1.75).

TAXCO

● **pop 95,100** ● **elev 1800m** ☎ 7

The old silver-mining town of Taxco ('TASS-co'), 160km southwest of Mexico City, is a gorgeous colonial antique, and one of the most picturesque and pleasant places in Mexico. Clinging to a steep hillside, its narrow, cobblestone streets twist and turn between well-worn buildings, open unexpectedly onto pretty plazas and reveal delightful vistas at every corner. Unlike many Mexican towns from the colonial era, it has not surrounded itself with industrial suburbs, and even the traffic in Taxco has a certain charm. Rather than the daily tides of commuting cars, a fleet of VW taxis and combis scurry through the labyrinth like ants on an anthill. And few streetscapes are defaced with rows of parked cars, because there's simply no room for them.

The federal government has declared the city a national historical monument, and local laws preserve Taxco's colonial-style architecture and heritage. Old buildings are preserved and restored wherever possible, and any new buildings must conform to the old in scale, style and materials – have a look at the colonial Pemex station.

Though Taxco's silver mines are almost exhausted, handmade silver jewelry is one of the town's main industries. There are hundreds of silver shops, and visiting them is an excellent reason to wander the streets. Taxco's hotels and restaurants tend to be priced higher than elsewhere in Mexico, but they are generally so appealing that they are a good value anyway.

Orientation

Taxco's twisting streets may make you feel like a mouse in a maze, and even maps of the town look confusing at first, but you'll learn your way around – in any case it's a nice place to get lost. Plaza Borda, also called the zócalo, is the heart of the town, and its church, Santa Prisca, is a good landmark.

Highway 95 becomes Avenida de los Plateros beyond the remains of the old

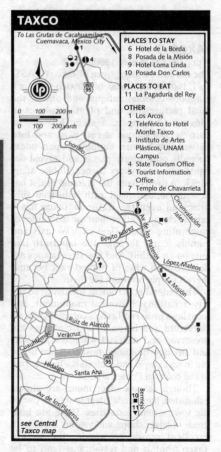

TAXCO

To Las Grutas de Cacahuamilpa,
Cuernavaca, Mexico City

0   100   200 m
0   100   200 yards

Chorrillo

Circunvalación Tales

Benito Juárez

López Mateos

La Misión

Ruiz de Alarcón

Veracruz

Cuauhtémoc

Hidalgo

Santa Ana

Av de los Plateros

Bermeja

see Central
Taxco map

PLACES TO STAY
6 Hotel de la Borda
8 Posada de la Misión
9 Hotel Loma Linda
10 Posada Don Carlos

PLACES TO EAT
11 La Pagaduría del Rey

OTHER
1 Los Arcos
2 Teleférico to Hotel
   Monte Taxco
3 Instituto de Artes
   Plásticos, UNAM
   Campus
4 State Tourism Office
5 Tourist Information
   Office
7 Templo de Chavarrieta

aqueduct (Los Arcos) at the north end of
town, then winds its way around the eastern
side of central Taxco. Both bus stations are
on Plateros. La Garita branches west from
Plateros opposite the Pemex station, and
becomes the main thoroughfare through the
middle of town. It follows a convoluted
route, more or less southwest (one-way
only), to the Plaza Borda, changing its name
to Juárez on the way. Past the plaza, this
main artery becomes Cuauhtémoc, and goes
down to the Plazuela de San Juan. Most of
the essentials are along this La Garita-
Juárez-Cuauhtémoc route, or pretty close to

it. Several side roads go east back to Plateros, which is two-way and therefore the
only way a vehicle can get back to the north
end of town. The basic combi route is a
counterclockwise loop going north on
Plateros and south through the center of
town.

Information

Tourist Offices The Secretaría de Fomento
Turístico (☎ 622-66-16) has an office in the
Centro de Convenciones de Taxco, on
Plateros at the north end of town, where the
old aqueduct crosses the highway. Helpful
English-speaking staff arrange guided tours
of Taxco (US$32 for groups up to ten). The
office is open 9.30 am to 7 pm Monday to
Saturday and 10 am to 5 pm Sunday. A non-
government Tourist Information Office
(☎ 622-07-98), 1km farther south along
Avenida de los Plateros, functions primarily
to arrange city tours, but its knowledgeable
English (and French and German) speaking
staff can answer most questions. The Flecha
Roja bus station also has a tourist information booth.

Money There are several banks with ATMs
around the town's main plazas.

Post & Communications The post office,
which is open 8 am to 4 pm Monday to
Friday and 9 am to 1 pm Saturday, is at
Plateros 382, at the south end of town. The
Telecomm office (telegram, telegraph and
fax), on the south side of Plazuela de Bernal,
is open 9 am to 3 pm Monday to Saturday.
There are card phones near Plaza Borda and
in hotel lobbies; cards are sold at hotels,
banks and stores.

The hip but overpriced Café Internet
Azul (Hidalgo 7-1) is open till 11 pm daily.
Inset into the tops of high conical steel
tables, its four monitors are difficult to see
clearly. It charges US$0.10 per minute (25-
minutes minimum). But watch out – if you
use 26 minutes, you'll be charged for another
25-minute block of time. Less stylish but a
little cheaper (US$2 per half hour) is
Arroba, which is in Plaza Taxco and is open
10 am to 8.30 pm daily.

Templo de Santa Prisca

On Plaza Borda, this church of rose-colored stone is a treasure of baroque architecture; its façade is decorated in the Churrigueresque style with elaborately sculpted figures. Over the doorway, the oval bas-relief depicts Christ's baptism. Inside, the intricately sculpted altarpieces covered with gold are equally fine examples of Churrigueresque art.

The local Catholic hierarchy allowed Don José de la Borda to donate this church to Taxco on the condition that he mortgage his personal mansion and other assets to guarantee its completion. It was designed by

Spanish architects Diego Durán and Juan Caballero and constructed between 1751 and 1758, and it almost bankrupted Borda.

Museo Guillermo Spratling

This three-story museum of archaeology and history is at Delgado 1, directly behind the Templo de Santa Prisca. Pre-Hispanic art exhibits on the two upper floors include jade statuettes, Olmec ceramics and other interesting pieces, mostly from the private collection of William Spratling. Admission is US$2. It is open 10 am to 5 pm Tuesday through Sunday.

CENTRAL TAXCO

To Las Grutas de Cacahuamilpa,
Cuernavaca, Mexico City

To Hotel Victoria

To La Ventana de Taxco, Taxco El Viejo, Acapulco

To La Pagaduría del Rey, Posada Don Carlos

To La Ixcateopan

0   50   100 m
0   50   100 yards

PLACES TO STAY
4   Hotel Posada San Javier
6   Hotel Agua Escondida
12 Hotel Posada de los Castillo
13 Hotel Los Arcos
20 Hotel Casa Grande
23 Hotel Meléndez
24 Casa de Huéspedes Arellano
28 Hotel Posada Santa Anita
31 Hotel Santa Prisca

PLACES TO EAT
10 Del Angel Inn, La Casona
15 Freddie's Café
16 Restaurant/Bar Paco
20 La Concha Nostra
21 Bora Bora Pizza
29 Hostería Bar El Adobe
30 La Hamburguesa
32 Restaurant Santa Fe

OTHER
1   Ex-Convento de San Bernardino
2   Bank
3   Palacio Municipal
4   Parking
7   Telecomm Office
8   Casa Borda (Museo de Arte Popular de Guerrero)
9   Museo de la Platería
    Patio de las Artesanías
11 Joyería Elena de los Ballesteros
12 Emilia Castillo
14 Museo de Arte Virreinal (Casa Humboldt)
15 Arroba
17 Bar Berta
18 Museo Guillermo Spratling
19 Templo de Santa Veracruz
22 Bancomer
25 Mercado de Artesanías Plata
26 Combis to Las Grutas de Cacahuamilpa
27 Flecha Roja & Turistar Bus Station
33 Café Internet Azul
34 Capilla de La Santísima Trinidad
35 Capilla de San Nicolas
36 Estrella de Oro Bus Station
37 Post Office
38 Capilla de San Miguel
39 IMSS Hospital
40 Combis to Ixcateopan

Museo de Arte Virreinal

On Ruiz de Alarcón, a couple of blocks down the hill from the Plazuela de Bernal, is one of the oldest colonial homes in Taxco. It is commonly known as **Casa Humboldt**, though the German explorer and naturalist Friedrich Heinrich Alexander von Humboldt stayed here for only one night in 1803. The restored building now houses a museum of colonial religious art, with a small but well-displayed collection, labeled in English and Spanish (US$1). An interesting exhibit describes some of the restoration work on the Templo de Santa Prisca, during which some fabulous material was found in the basement. It is open 10 am to 5 pm Tuesday through Sunday.

Casa Borda (Museo de Arte Popular de Guerrero)

Built by José de la Borda in 1759, the Casa Borda now serves as a cultural center exhibiting sculpture, painting, and photos by artists from Taxco and elsewhere (free). The building, though, is the main attraction. Due to the unevenness of the terrain, the entrance off the Plaza Borda is on the ground floor, but the rear window looks out on a precipitous four-story drop. A bookstore inside sells the only decent map of Taxco. It is open 10 am to 5 pm Tuesday through Sunday.

Museo de la Platería

The small museum of silverwork exhibits some superb examples of the silversmith's art and outlines (in Spanish) its development in Taxco (US$1). Included are some classic designs by William Spratling, and prize-winning pieces from national and international competitions. Notice the very colorful, sculptural combinations of silver with semiprecious minerals such as jade, lapis lazuli, turquoise, malachite, agate and obsidian – a feature of much of the silverwork for sale in the town, and a link with pre-Hispanic stone-carving traditions.

To get to the museum, enter the Patio de las Artesanías building on the corner of Plaza Borda, on your left as you face Santa Prisca, turn left and go to the end of the hall

and down the stairs. It is open 10 am to 5 pm Tuesday through Sunday.

Teleférico & Monte Taxco

From the northern end of Taxco, near Los Arcos, a Swiss-made cable car ascends 173m to the luxurious Hotel Monte Taxco (see Places to Stay), affording fantastic views of Taxco and the surrounding mountains. The cable car runs 8 am to 7 pm daily (US$2.75 round-trip, half for children). To find it, walk uphill from Los Arcos and turn right into the gate of the Instituto de Artes Plásticos; you can see the terminal from the gate.

Special Events

Try to time your visit to Taxco during one of its annual festivals, but be sure to reserve a hotel room in advance. During Semana Santa, in particular, visitors pour into the city to see the processions and events.

Fiestas de Santa Prisca & San Sebastián – the festivals of Taxco's two patron saints are celebrated on January 18 (Santa Prisca) and January 20 (San Sebastián), when people parade by the entrance of the Templo de Santa Prisca with their pets and farm animals in tow for an annual blessing.

Jueves Santo – on the Thursday before Easter, the institution of the Eucharist is commemorated with beautiful presentations and street processions of hooded penitents, some of whom flagellate themselves with thorns as the procession winds through town.

Jornadas Alarconianas – in memory of Taxco-born playwright Juan Ruiz de Alarcón, a cultural festival takes place in the summertime (check with the tourist office for exact dates). Taxco's convention center, plazas and churches all host concerts and dance performances by internationally renowned performing artists. Other concerts take place inside the Grutas de Cacahuamilpa.

El Día del Jumil – this unusual festival is celebrated on the first Monday after the Day of the Dead at the start of November (see 'El Día del Jumil').

Feria de la Plata – the weeklong national silver fair is held during the last week in November or the first week in December (check with the tourist office for exact dates). Silverwork competitions are held in various categories (statuary, jewelry, etc) and some of Mexico's best silverwork is on display. Other festivities include organ recitals in Santa Prisca, rodeos, burro races, concerts and dances.

Reversals of Fortune

Taxco was called Tlachco (literally, 'place where ball is played') by the Aztecs, who dominated the region from 1440 until the Spanish arrived. In 1529, the colonial city was founded by Captain Rodrigo de Castañeda, acting under a mandate from Hernán Cortés. Among the town's first Spanish residents were three miners – Juan de Cabra, Juan Salcedo and Diego de Nava – and the carpenter Pedro Muriel. In 1531, they established the first Spanish mine on the North American continent.

The Spaniards came searching for tin, which they found in small quantities, but by 1534 they had discovered tremendous lodes of silver. That year the Hacienda El Chorrillo was built, complete with water wheel, smelter and aqueduct – the remains of which form the old arches (Los Arcos) over the highway at the northern end of present-day Taxco. The hacienda has gone through several metamorphoses and now houses the national university's art school and Spanish-language institute.

The prospectors quickly emptied the first veins of silver from the hacienda and left Taxco. Further quantities of silver were not discovered until two centuries later, in 1743. Don José de la Borda, who had arrived in 1716 from France at the age of 16 to work with his miner brother, accidentally uncovered one of the area's richest veins. According to a Taxco legend, Borda was riding near where the Templo de Santa Prisca now stands when his horse stumbled, dislodged a stone and exposed the silver.

Borda went on to make three fortunes, and lose two. He introduced new techniques of draining and repairing mines, and he reportedly treated his indigenous workers much better than those working in other colonial mines. The Templo de Santa Prisca was the devout Borda's gift to Taxco. He is remembered for the saying *'Dios da a Borda, Borda da a Dios'* ('God gives to Borda, Borda gives to God').

His success attracted many more prospectors and miners, and new veins of silver were found, and emptied. With most of the silver gone, Taxco became a quiet town with a dwindling population and economy. In 1929, an American professor and architect named William (Guillermo) Spratling arrived and, at the suggestion of then US Ambassador Dwight Morrow, set up a small silver workshop as a way to rejuvenate the town. (Another version has it that Spratling was writing a book in Taxco and resorted to the silver business because his publisher went broke. A third has it that Spratling had a notion – and acted on it – to design and create jewelry that synthesized pre-Columbian motifs with Art Deco modernism.) The workshop became a factory and Spratling's apprentices began establishing their own shops. Today there are more than 300 silver shops in Taxco.

AROUND MEXICO CITY

❋❋❋❋❋❋❋❋❋❋❋❋❋❋❋❋❋❋❋❋❋❋❋❋

Las Posadas – from December 16 to 24, nightly candlelit processions pass through the streets of Taxco singing from door to door. Children are dressed up to resemble various Biblical characters, and at the end of the processions, they attack piñatas.

Courses

The Centro de Enseñanza Para Extranjeros (CEPE; ☎ 622-01-24, marta@servidor.unam .mx), a branch of the national university, offers six-week Spanish language courses in the Ex-Hacienda El Chorrillo, just south of the Arcos entrance. Advanced students may take additional courses in Mexican art history, geography, literature and Chicano Studies. The basic cost of US$325 covers one language course and two culture/history courses. CEPE arranges lodging with families in Taxco. For details, write to Apdo Postal No 70, 40220 Taxco, Gro, Mexico.

Places to Stay

Budget Occupying the upper level of the former mining court building, *Hotel Casa Grande* (☎ 622-09-69, *Plazuela de San Juan 7*) has 12 clean, basic rooms around an inner courtyard. Rooftop rooms are the airiest but can be noisy. Singles/doubles are US$8.50/16 with private bath or US$6.50/9.50 for use of a tiny, dirty shared bath. Laundry facilities are available.

The central *Casa de Huéspedes Arellano* (☎ 622-02-15, Los Pajaritos 23) offers 10 simple but clean rooms for US$13/19 or US$8.50/13 with shared bath. It's a family-run place with terraces for sitting and a place on the roof for washing clothes. To find it, walk down the alley on the south side of Santa Prisca until you reach a staircase going down to your right. Follow it past the stalls to a flight of stairs to your left; the Casa de Huéspedes is 30 steps down, on the left.

Mid-Range One of the most attractive places to stay in Taxco at any price is *Hotel Posada San Javier* (☎ 622-31-77, Ex-Rastro 6), a block down the hill from the Palacio Municipal. Though centrally located, it's peaceful, with a private parking area and a lovely, large enclosed garden around a big swimming pool. Its comfortable, high-ceilinged single/double rooms, many with private terraces, start at US$21/25; junior suites at US$25/28.

Hotel Los Arcos (☎ 622-18-36, Ruiz de Alarcón 4) has 26 clean, spacious rooms at US$16/21. The former 17th-century monastery retains a wonderful courtyard, lounging areas, a spectacular rooftop terrace and lots of character. Across the road, *Hotel Posada de los Castillo* (☎ 622-13-96, Juan Ruiz de Alarcón 7), owned by a renowned family of silver workers, is another place with colonial charm and reasonable prices – US$16/19. The hotel's patio contains a shop displaying Emilia Castillo's unique silver designs.

Hotel Meléndez (☎ 622-00-06, Cuauhtémoc 6) is an older place with pleasant terrace sitting areas, a nice off-street restaurant and a good location between the Plazuela de San Juan and Plaza Borda. Its 33 newly furnished rooms are US$23/29. Right on the zócalo, *Hotel Agua Escondida* (☎ 622-07-26, Plaza Borda 4) has large and small swimming pools on a high terrace and a basement garage. The comfy, airy rooms cost US$31/38.

On the south side of the Plazuela de San Juan, the elegant *Hotel Santa Prisca* (☎ 622-09-80, Cena Obscuras 1) features a quiet interior patio and a pleasant restaurant. Rooms (most with private terraces) are US$20/31 or US$23/36 with breakfast; suites are available for US$37. The parking lot is reached through a tunnel at the hotel's uphill end.

Near the Flecha Roja bus station, *Hotel Posada Santa Anita* (☎ 622-07-52, Avenida de los Plateros 52) has small, quiet rooms for US$10.50/19. A kilometer north of the Santa Anita at a bend in the highway, *Hotel Loma Linda* (☎ 622-02-06, rpopoca@taxco.net, Plateros 52) is perched on the ledge of a vast chasm. There's a restaurant, swimming pool and motel-style parking. Singles/doubles are US$21/26.

Top End The sprawling *Hotel Victoria* (☎ 622-00-04, Carlos J Nibbi 14), on a street named after the American who ran the place in the 1950s, dominates Taxco's southern hills. Under the same ownership as the Hotel Borda, the Victoria is similarly overpriced, with rooms starting at US$42, but it has more character. It feels like a colonial village wrapped around a bend in the mountainside complete with cobblestone streets and little overgrown nooks.

Taxco's other top-end hotels are outside of the center. The four-star *Hotel de la Borda* (☎ 622-00-25, Cerro del Pedregal 2) is a sprawling, mission-style complex perched on a hill, with a pool and a large dining room. The hotel's spacious rooms, some with panoramic city views, are less elegant than you'd expect for US$47. *Posada Don Carlos* (☎ 622-00-75, Calle del Consuelo 8), which has eight tastefully appointed rooms, six with balconies offering superb views of Taxco, for US$42/47. There's a small swimming pool on a terrace facing town. The hill to the Don Carlos is a tough climb – take a taxi for US$1.

A more expensive but far superior option to the other top-end hotels is the luxurious *Posada de la Misión* (☎ 622-00-63, Cerro de la Misión). Its 120 large single/double rooms, featuring private terraces with fine views of

Taxco, are US$67/74, including breakfast; prices are higher on weekends. Overlooking the large pool is a mosaic mural of the Aztec emperor Cuauhtémoc designed by Juan O'Gorman.

Way up on top of the mountain that it's named after, the five-star *Hotel Monte Taxco* (☎ 622-13-00) is considered the most fabulous place to stay in Taxco, but magnificent views can be had elsewhere for far less. It can be reached by car, taxi or cable car. Rates of US$92 for standard rooms (more on weekends), or US$150 for suites, include use of the swimming pool but not of the hotel's tennis courts, underequipped gym or steam baths. There are also restaurants, bars, a disco and a state-run handicrafts shop.

Places to Eat

Restaurant Santa Fe (*Hidalgo 2*), a few doors downhill from the Plazuela de San Juan, is often recommended by locals, and it

---

El Día del Jumil

Jumiles are small beetles (about 1cm long), which migrate annually to the Cerro de Huixteco (hill behind Taxco) to reproduce. They begin to arrive around September; the last ones are gone by about January or February. During this time, the jumiles are a great delicacy for the people of Taxco, who eat them alone or mixed in salsa with tomatoes, garlic, onion and chilies, or even *alive*, rolled into tortillas. (You can buy live jumiles in the market during this time; the Restaurant Santa Fe serves *salsa de jumil* prepared in the traditional way.)

Traditionally, the entire population of the town climbs the Cerro de Huixteco on Día del Jumil (the first Monday after the Day of the Dead, usually the first week of November) to collect jumiles, bring picnic baskets and share food and fellowship. Many families come early and camp on the hill over the preceding weekend. The celebration is said to represent the jumiles giving energy and life to the people of Taxco for another year.

✽ ✽ ✽ ✽ ✽ ✽ ✽ ✽ ✽ ✽ ✽ ✽ ✽

---

does indeed serve good food at fair prices, though service can be brusque. Set breakfasts cost US$4.50 or less, and the US$4 comida corrida includes four courses.

Overlooking Plaza Borda through large picture windows, the *Restaurant/Bar Paco* is great for people-watching. The food is good too, but you pay for the view – meat dishes start at US$8.50 and chicken at US$6. Try the delicious enchiladas with mole (US$4.75). The Paco is open from 1 to 10 pm daily; Thursday to Saturday evenings, it hosts 'romantic' music performers.

Bora Bora Pizza, appropriately located at Delicias 4, just off Cuauhtémoc near the Plaza Borda, is open 1 pm to midnight. The restaurant serves the best pizza in Taxco (though some have complained of service that is less than cordial). Prices range from US$2.50 for a small up to US$9 for a maxi.

Del Angel Inn (*Muñoz 3*), on the left side of the Santa Prisca, has a spectacular roof terrace with bar. It's definitely tourist-oriented but the food isn't bad. For US$6.50, a set lunch includes fresh bread with herbed butter, soup, a main course and dessert. Salads and pastas go for around US$4, Mexican dishes from US$5 to US$10. Next door, *La Casona* has similar fare for a little cheaper, as well as an excellent balcony with a view down the hillside of Taxco.

Hostería Bar El Adobe (*Plazuela de San Juan 13*) has a less captivating view but a lovely interior. Regional specialties include garlic soup with shrimp (US$2.50) and Taxco-style *cecina* (salted strip steak) served with sliced *chiles poblanos* and guacamole (US$5.25).

For late-night snacks, try *La Hamburguesa*, on the west side of Plazuela San Juan; it has burger/fries combos starting at US$2 and excellent enchiladas. Across the plaza, *La Concha Nostra* is a laid-back bar/restaurant, atop the Casa Grande, that serves pizzas (minis start at US$1.75, grandes US$5), salads (US$1.75) and various snacks until well after midnight. From the balcony, you can watch the action on Plazuela San Juan.

The top two restaurants in Taxco are on hills facing the city center and are best reached by taxi. *La Ventana de Taxco*, south of town, specializes in Italian food; its Piccata Lombarda (veal sautéed in a lemon, butter and parsley sauce) is superb; expect to spend about US$25 for dinner. *La Pagaduría del Rey*, in the Barrio Bermeja outside of the center of town, is equally fancy but less expensive, with salads and pastas from US$3.75 and Mexican dishes for around US$6. It's a great place simply to sip a drink and admire the view.

Another fine place for a drink is *Bar Berta*, just off the Plaza Borda at the beginning of Cuauhtémoc. With simple green tables on two levels and bullfight posters on the walls, it's the sort of place Hemingway would have felt at home in. Try the house specialty, a Berta, which is tequila, honey, lime and mineral water.

Coffee aficionados will appreciate *Freddie's Café* at the rear of the Fonart crafts shop in the Plaza Taxco shopping center next door to the Casa Humboldt. In addition to the cappuccino and espresso, Freddie's serves good grilled cheese sandwiches (US$1.50). Seating is on a long balcony with a view of Monte Taxco.

Shopping

Silver With more than 300 shops selling silverwork, the selection is mind-boggling. Look at some of the best places first, to see what's available, then try to focus on the things you're really interested in, and shop around for those. If you are careful and willing to bargain a bit, you can buy wonderful pieces at reasonable prices.

Most shops are both *menudeo* and *mayoreo* (retail and wholesale); to get the wholesale price you will have to buy maybe 10 pieces of a kind.

The price of a piece is principally determined by its weight; the creative work serves mainly to make it salable, though items with exceptional artisanship can command a premium. If you're serious about buying silver, find out the current peso-per-gram rate and weigh any piece before you agree on a price. All the silver shops have scales, mostly electronic devices that should be accurate. If a piece costs less than the going price per gram, it's not real silver. Don't buy anything

that doesn't have the Mexican government '.925' stamp, which certifies that the piece is 92.5% sterling silver (most pieces also bear a set of initials identifying the workshop where they were made). If a piece is too small or delicate to stamp, a reputable shop will supply a certificate as to its purity. Anyone who is discovered selling forged .925 pieces is sent to prison.

The shops in and around the Plaza Borda tend to have higher prices than those farther from the center, but they also tend to have more interesting work. The shops on Avenida Plateros are often branches of downtown businesses, set up for the tourist buses that can't make it through the narrow streets.

Several shops are in the Patio de las Artesanías building on the Plaza Borda. Pineda's, on the corner of Muñoz and the plaza, is a famous shop; a couple of doors down Muñoz at No 4, the Joyería Elena de los Ballesteros is another. The tableware on display in the showroom of Emilia Castillo, at Juan Ruiz de Alarcón 7, is a unique blend of porcelain and silver. For quantity rather than quality, see the stalls in the Mercado de Artesanías Plata, open till 7 pm, with vast quantities of rings, chains and pendants. The work is not as well-displayed here, but you can often spot something special.

Other Crafts It's easy to overlook them among the silver, but there are other things to buy in Taxco. Finely painted wood and papier-mâché trays, platters and boxes are sold along the Calle del Arco, on the south side of Santa Prisca, as well as bark paintings and wood carvings. Quite a few shops sell semiprecious stones, fossils and mineral crystals, and some have a good selection of masks, puppets and semi-antique carvings.

Getting There & Away

Taxco has two long-distance bus terminals, both on Avenida Plateros. First-class Flecha Roja and Futura buses and deluxe Turistar buses, as well as several 2nd-class bus lines, use the terminal at Avenida de los Plateros 104. Estrella de Oro (1st-class) terminal is at the south end of town. Combis pass both terminals every few minutes and will take you up the hill to the Plaza Borda for US$0.30 (see Getting Around). Book early for buses out of Taxco as it can be hard to get a seat.

Daily long-distance departures (directos unless otherwise stated) include:

Acapulco – 266km, 4½ hours; 5 Estrella de Oro (US$12), 4 Turistar (US$11.50)

Chilpancingo – 130km, 3 hours; 5 Estrella de Oro, 4 Turistar (US$5.75)

Cuernavaca – 80km, 1½ hours; 3 Estrella de Oro (US$3.75), Flecha Roja hourly until 7 pm (US$3.50)

Iguala – 35km, 1 hour; every 20 minutes by various 2nd-class operators (US$1.25)

Ixtapan de la Sal – 68km, 2 hours; 3 Turistar (US$2.75), 12 Tres Estrellas departing from Flecha Roja terminal (US$3)

Mexico City (Terminal Sur) – 170km, 3 hours; 6 Estrella de Oro (US$7.75), Futura hourly (1st-class US$7.75, deluxe US$8.50)

Toluca – 145km, 3 hours; 3 Turistar (US$6), 12 Tres Estrellas departing from Flecha Roja terminal (US$5.75)

Getting Around

Apart from walking, combis and taxis are the most popular ways of getting around the steep, winding streets of Taxco. Combis (white Volkswagen minibuses) are frequent and cheap (US$0.30) and operate from 7 am to 8 pm. The 'Zócalo' combi departs from Plaza Borda, goes down Cuauhtémoc to the Plazuela de San Juan, then heads down the hill on Hidalgo. It turns right at Morelos, left at Avenida Plateros and goes northwards until La Garita, where it turns left and goes back to the zócalo. The 'Arcos/Zócalo' combi follows basically the same route except that it continues past La Garita to Los Arcos, where it does a U-turn and heads back to La Garita. Combis marked 'PM' for 'Pedro Martín' go to the south end of town, past the Estrella de Oro bus station. Taxis cost US$1 to US$1.50 for trips around town.

A large parking garage is at the Plaza Taxco shopping center, charging US$0.50 an hour. Access is off Plateros via Estacadas. An elevator takes you up to the shopping center, on Ruiz de Alarcón next door to the Casa Humboldt.

AROUND TAXCO
Taxco El Viejo

The original site of Taxco was 11km south at Taxco El Viejo, where the indigenous Tlahuica mined tin and silver deposits which were later heavily exploited by the Spaniards. The principal attraction of the area today is a pair of ranches north and south of Taxco El Viejo where silver is crafted in peaceful settings.

Ex-Hacienda San Juan Bautista Just south of Taxco El Viejo, the Ex-Hacienda San Juan Bautista is one of seven silver refining facilities established around Taxco and Taxco El Viejo during the region's first silver boom. The old hacienda, which today houses the School of Earth Sciences of the Universidad Autónoma de Guerrero, is worth exploring for its lovely, poinsettia-lined patios and remnants of its former use.

Enter through an archway on the left side of the highway, then turn left and uphill past some new school buildings. An architectural innovation of the facility was the intra-wall conduits for transporting water from the main aqueduct to the tanks in the patios, where mercury was added to extract silver (a process that polluted extensive groundwater sources). The building also contains the university's mineralogy museum, open Monday to Friday (free).

Rancho Spratling Although William Spratling died in 1967, his former workshop continues to produce some of the finest silver in Mexico and employs the same handcrafted methods and classic designs that have made Spratling pieces collectibles. The former Spratling ranch, located just south of the Ex-Hacienda San Juan Bautista, has been pridefully maintained, and a new generation of artisans adhere to Spratling's standards under the guidance of maestro Don Tomás, one of Spratling's principal workers for many years.

Visitors are encouraged to enter the workshop and see how fine silver is crafted.

Also on the premises is a showroom displaying work designed by Spratling; a second room features new designs by Don Tomás' apprentices. Hours are 9 am to 1 pm and 2 to 5 pm Monday through Saturday (free).

Rancho Cascada Los Castillo The metal workshops of the Castillo family are located on the lovely grounds of the Rancho Cascada Los Castillo, off the highway north of Taxco El Viejo. On the way to the workshops, through rambling gardens, is a museum in a circular hut displaying the antiquities collection of Antonio Castillo, a master craftsman and contemporary of Spratling's. Inside the workshops, which are housed in a series of low buildings, craftspeople create silver, copper, tin and *alpaca* (nickel silver) objects. Visiting hours are 9 am to 6 pm Monday to Friday and 9 am to 1 pm Saturday.

Getting There & Away Taxco El Viejo is 25 minutes south of Taxco on highway 95. From Taxco, catch any of the frequent 2nd-class buses heading for Iguala at the Flecha Roja terminal. Ask the driver to let you off at either of the *ranchos* or the ex-hacienda, as all have entrances along the highway. To visit all three destinations, you could get off at the Rancho Spratling, walk back up the highway to the Ex-Hacienda San Juan Bautista (half a kilometer), then catch a bus back toward Taxco and get off at the Rancho Cascada Los Castillo. From there, take any bus or combi heading north to return to Taxco.

Ixcateopan

The village of Ixcateopan, southwest of Taxco, was the birthplace of Cuauhtémoc, the final Aztec emperor, who was defeated and later executed by Cortés. The emperor's remains were returned to his native village and entombed in the church on the town plaza, also the site of the historical **Museo de la Mexicanidad**. Marble is quarried nearby and, being the most common stone in the area, was often used in construction – Ixcateopan is one of the few towns in the world with marble streets.

Getting There & Away A combi marked 'Ixcateopan' departs Taxco, from about 100m south of the Seguro Social building, approximately every half hour from 7 am to 5 pm (1½ hours, US$1.50).

Las Grutas de Cacahuamilpa

The caverns of Cacahuamilpa are a beautiful natural wonder of stalactites, stalagmites and twisted rock formations, with huge chambers up to 82m high. Thirty km northeast of Taxco, they are protected as a national park and well-worth visiting.

You must tour the caves with a group and a guide, through 2km of an illuminated walkway. Many of the formations are named for some fanciful resemblance – 'the elephant,' 'the champagne bottle,' 'Dante's head,' 'the tortillas' and so on – and the lighting is used to enhance these resemblances. Much of the guide's commentary focuses on these, but the geological information is minimal. After the tour, you can return to the entrance at your own pace. The entire tour takes two hours.

From the cave entrance, a path goes down the steep valley to Río Dos Bocas, where two rivers emerge from the caves. The pretty walk down and back takes 30 minutes.

Cave tours, in Spanish, depart from the visitor's center every hour on the hour from 10 am to 5 pm (US$1.50). An English-speaking guide *might* be available for large groups of foreigners. There are restaurants, snacks and souvenir shops at the visitor's center.

Getting There & Away From Taxco, blue-striped combis depart every two hours from opposite the Flecha Roja bus terminal and go right to the visitor's center at the caves (one hour, US$1.25). Alternatively, you can take any bus heading for Toluca or Ixtapan de la Sal, get off at the 'Grutas' crossroads and walk 1km down the road to the entrance, on your right. The last combis leave the site at 5 pm on Monday to Friday and 6 pm on Saturday to Sunday; after this you might be able to catch a bus to Taxco at the crossroads.

West of Mexico City

The main road west from the capital, highway 15D, goes to Toluca, which has a pleasant center, an interesting museum and several art galleries. There are ruins nearby, and some of the surrounding villages are known for their handicrafts. The countryside to the east, south and west of Toluca is scenic, with pine forests, rivers and a huge volcano. Valle de Bravo is a lakeside resort and colonial gem 70km west of Toluca. Two highways head south from Toluca: highway 55 passes handicraft centers, impressive pyramids and spas at Ixtapan de la Sal and Tonatico, then continues on to Taxco; toll highway 55D is the fast route to Ixtapan de la Sal.

TOLUCA

• **pop 368,400** • **elev 2660m** ☎ **7**

Toluca, 64km west of Mexico City, is 400m higher than the capital and the extra altitude is noticeable. The eastern outskirts are an industrial area, but the colonial-era city center has attractive plazas and lively arcades. Its cultural sites include a good number of museums and art galleries.

Toluca was an indigenous settlement from at least the 13th century; the Spanish founded the city in the 16th century after defeating the Aztecs and Matlazincas who lived in the valley. It became part of the Marquesado del Valle de Oaxaca, Hernán Cortés' personal estates in Mexico. Since 1830, it has been capital of the state of México, which surrounds the Distrito Federal on three sides like an upside-down U.

Orientation

The main road from Mexico City becomes Paseo Tollocan, a dual carriageway, as it approaches Toluca. On reaching the east side of the city proper, Paseo Tollocan bears southwest and becomes a ring road around the south side of the city center. The bus station and the large Mercado Juárez are 2km southeast of the city center, just off Paseo Tollocan.

The vast Plaza de los Mártires, with the Palacio de Gobierno and the cathedral, is the center of town, but most of the life is in the block to the south, a pedestrian precinct that is surrounded by arched colonnades on its east, south and west sides. These arcades are lined with shops and restaurants and thronged with people most of the day. The pleasant Parque Alameda is three blocks to the west along Hidalgo.

Information

Tourist Offices The state tourist office (☎ 212-60-48) is 2km from the center in the Edificio de Servicios Administrativos, office 110, at the corner of Urawa and Paseo Tollocan. Good maps of Toluca and the state of México are available, and English is spoken. It's closed on weekends.

Money There are many banks with ATMs near the Portal Madero; Banca Serfin at Matamoros will change money or traveler's checks. There's a Centro de Cambio next to the VIPS restaurant on Juárez.

Post & Communications The main post office is on the corner of Hidalgo and Sor Juana Inés de la Cruz, 500m east of Portal Madero. There are pay phones all around the arcade, and a phone office, at the north end of the underground parking lot west of the cathedral, open 7 am to 8.45 pm daily for long-distance phone calls and faxes.

Ciber Mundo, in the Gran Plaza Toluca shopping mall, provides Internet access 9 am to 9.30 pm daily and charges US$3.25 an hour. Damascus Café at Hidalgo Pte 412-4, half a block west of the arcade, charges US$2.75 per hour for Internet access, and also reads Tarot cards and the I Ching. It's open 11 am to 8.30 pm Monday to Saturday.

Medical Services The hospital, Sanatorio Toluca (☎ 217-78-00), is at Peñaloza 233, a little west of the center southwest along Paseo Tollocan.

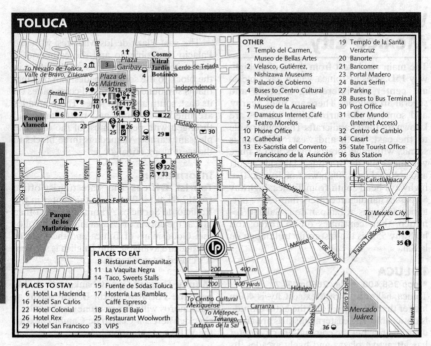

TOLUCA

OTHER
1 Templo del Carmen, Museo de Bellas Artes
2 Velasco, Gutiérrez, Nishizawa Museums
3 Palacio de Gobierno
4 Buses to Centro Cultural Mexiquense
5 Museo de la Acuarela
7 Damascus Internet Café
9 Teatro Morelos
10 Phone Office
12 Cathedral
13 Ex-Sacristía del Convento Franciscano de la Asunción
19 Templo de la Santa Veracruz
20 Banorte
21 Bancomer
23 Portal Madero
24 Banca Serfin
27 Parking
28 Buses to Bus Terminal
30 Post Office
31 Ciber Mundo (Internet Access)
32 Centro de Cambio
34 Casart
35 State Tourist Office
36 Bus Station

PLACES TO EAT
8 Restaurant Campanitas
11 La Vaquita Negra
14 Taco, Sweets Stalls
15 Fuente de Sodas Toluca
17 Hostería Las Ramblas, Caffé Espresso
18 Jugos El Bajío
25 Restaurant Woolworth
33 VIPS

PLACES TO STAY
6 Hotel La Hacienda
16 Hotel San Carlos
22 Hotel Colonial
26 Hotel Rex
29 Hotel San Francisco

City Center

The 19th-century **Portal Madero**, running 250m along Avenida Hidalgo, is lively and bustling, as is the arcade along the pedestrian street to the east. A block north, the big, open expanse of the **Plaza de los Mártires** is surrounded by fine old government buildings; the 19th-century **cathedral** and the 18th-century **Templo de la Santa Veracruz** are on its south side. The octagonal-shaped building in the plaza beside the cathedral was once the sacristy of the Convento Franciscano de la Asunción, which stood here until the 19th century. Today it is used as a meeting hall for city functions.

Immediately northeast of the Plaza de los Mártires is the fountained **Plaza Garibay**, at the east end of which stands the unique **Cosmo Vitral Jardín Botánico** (Cosmic Stained-Glass Window Botanical Garden). Built in 1909 as a market, and until 1975 the site of the weekly *tianguis* (regional market),

this now houses 3500 sq m of lovely gardens, lit through 48 stained-glass panels by the Tolucan artist Leopoldo Flores. It's open 9 am to 5 pm Tuesday to Sunday (US$0.50). On the north side of Plaza Garibay is the 18th-century **Templo del Carmen**.

Mercado Juárez & Casart

The Juárez Market, on Fabela behind the bus station, is open daily. On Friday, villagers from all around swarm in to buy and sell fruit, flowers, pots, clothes and plastic goods. The market is huge, colorful and chaotic, but it's not a great place to buy local handicrafts.

You can see quality arts and crafts of the region in more peaceful surroundings at Casart (Casa de Artesanía), the state crafts store on Paseo Tollocan. It is open 10 am to 6.45 pm daily. There's a big range, and the crafts sold at the store are often the top-end pieces from the villages where the crafts are made. Prices are fixed and higher than you can get with some haggling in the markets, but you can gauge prices and quality here before going elsewhere to buy.

You can watch craftspeople, such as basket weavers from San Pedro Actopan, at work in the store. Honey cookies from Sultepec and Tejupilco are baked on the premises.

Centro Cultural Mexiquense

The impressive State of México Cultural Center, 4.5km west of the city center, comprises three very good museums and a library. The **Museo de Culturas Populares** has superb examples of the traditional arts and crafts of México state, with some astounding trees of life, whimsical Day of the Dead figures and a fine display of charro equipment – saddles, sombreros, swords, pistols, ropes and spurs. The **Museo de Antropología e História** features top-notch exhibits on the history of the state from prehistoric times to the 20th century, with a good collection of pre-Hispanic artifacts. The **Museo de Arte Moderno** traces the development of Mexican art from the late 19th-century Academia de San Carlos to the Nueva Plástica, and includes paintings by Tamayo, Orozco and many others. The museums are open 10 am to 6 pm daily (US$0.75, free on Sunday). 'Centro Cultural' buses go along Lerdo de Tejada, passing Plaza Garibay.

Other Museums

The ex-convent buildings adjacent to Plaza Garibay house Toluca's **Museo de Bellas Artes**, which has paintings from the colonial period to the early 20th century (US$0.25). On Bravo, opposite the Palacio de Gobierno, are museums devoted to the work of José María Velasco, Felipe Gutiérrez and Luis Nishizawa. The latter was an artist of Mexican-Japanese parentage whose work shows influences from both cultures. The **Museo de la Acuarela**, on Pedro Ascencio, displays a fine collection of watercolors by Mexican and American artists, including a wonderful series of cathedral façades by Vicente Mendiola. All of these museums are open 10 am to 6 pm Tuesday to Sunday.

Places to Stay

Rooms at **Hotel Rex** (☎ 215-93-00, Matamoros Sur 101), some facing the arcade, are basic but acceptable. Rooms with private baths and TVs cost US$12 for one or two people. Across the street, the friendly **Hotel San Carlos** (☎ 214-43-36, Portal Madero 210) is upgrading and raising prices, but old rooms remain a good deal at US$9.50/15 for singles/doubles; remodeled rooms with new furniture and carpet are US$17/28. Neither hotel has parking but a lot on Matamoros charges US$3.25 for the night.

Hotel La Hacienda (☎ 214-35-33, Hidalgo Poniente 508), half a block east of the Alameda, charges US$16/27 for quiet, decent rooms with colonial touches like wood-beam ceilings. There's also a garage. For true colonial ambiance, try **Hotel Colonial** (☎ 215-97-00, Hidalgo Oriente 103), just east of Juárez. It has well-maintained, stylish rooms around an interior courtyard for US$21/27. Guests can use a parking lot on Juárez, the next left turn off of Hidalgo.

Hotel San Francisco (☎ 213-44-15, Rayón Sur 104), around the corner from the Gran Plaza Toluca, has pretensions to luxury, including a glass-walled elevator shaft for viewing the slick skylit atrium restaurant. Modern rooms are US$37/45. There's plenty of parking.

Places to Eat

Toluqueños like to snack, and you can join them in the arcades around the Plaza Fray Andrés de Castro, beside the cathedral. Stalls selling authentic *tacos de obispo*, a sausage from Tenancingo, are easily found because there are crowds of people flocking around them. The contents of these arm-width sausages – barbecued chopped beef spiced with epazote, nuts, raisins, almonds and marrow – are stuffed into tortillas and sold in large quantities for US$0.30 apiece. Other stalls sell *jamoncillos* and *mostachones* (sweets made of burned milk) and candied fruit accompanied by lots of bees. Nearby, **Jugos El Bajío** offers *tortas*, fresh fruit juices and fruit cocktails; around the corner, **Fuente de Sodas Toluca** is exactly the same in design and menu.

On the northwest corner of the arcade, **La Vaquita Negra**, the place with green and red sausages hanging over the counter, serves first-rate tortas for US$0.75 to US$1.25. You can garnish the tortas with pickled peppers and onions, which are also sold in jars. It's open till 8.30 pm.

Hostería Las Ramblas *(Portal 20 de Noviembre 105)*, on the pedestrian mall, is one of Toluca's best and most atmospheric places, with a daily set lunch for US$4. It serves a variety of tasty antojitos, including *sopes*, mole verde and *sesos* (brains) *a la mexicana* for under US$3 each. Two doors down is **Caffé Espresso**, a relaxing hangout serving espresso (US$1) and hot and cold cappuccinos (US$1.25).

Restaurant Woolworth, opposite the Hotel San Carlos, offers large set breakfasts for about US$3 with unlimited free coffee refills. There's a terribly popular **VIPS** inside the Grand Plaza shopping mall, serving bland fare at inflated prices: burgers US$4, Mexican specialties US$2.50 to US$5 and entrees starting at US$4.50.

Restaurant Campanitas, across the street from the Teatro Morelos, prepares 'nouveau' Mexican dishes – original creations consisting largely of Mexican ingredients. Expect to pay US$2 to US$3 for pastas and salads and US$4 to US$5 for seafood. Daily specials are variations on mutton, quail and, when in season, the delicacy *escamoles* (ant larvae).

Getting There & Away

In Mexico City, Toluca buses use the Terminal Poniente (at Metro Observatorio). The 1st-class TMT line runs buses between the two cities every five minutes from 5.30 am to 10 pm; the trip takes an hour (US$2.75).

Toluca's bus station is at Berriozábal 101, 2km southeast of the center. Ticket offices for many destinations are at the gate entrances, or right on the platforms. There are frequent departures to Querétaro (gate 2), Morelia (gate 5), Valle de Bravo (gate 6), Chalma and Malinalco (gate 9), Metepec (platform 10) and Cuernavaca, Taxco and Ixtpapan de la Sal (platform 12).

Getting Around

'Centro' buses go from outside the bus station to the town center; 'Terminal' buses go from Juárez (south of Lerdo de Tejada) in the center to the bus station (US$0.30). Taxis from the bus station or market to the city center cost about US$1.50 – make sure the meter is running.

AROUND TOLUCA
Calixtlahuaca

This Aztec site is 2km west of highway 55, 8km north of Toluca. It's partly excavated and restored. The site has some unusual features such as a circular pyramid that supported a temple to Quetzalcóatl and Calmecac, believed to have been a school for the children of priests and nobles. Entry is US$1.50 (closed on Monday, free on Sunday). A bus goes to within a short walk of the site.

Metepec

• **pop 147,400** • **elev 2610m** ☎ 7

Virtually a suburb of Toluca, 7km to the south on highway 55, Metepec is the center for producing elaborate and symbolic pottery *árboles de vida* (trees of life) and Metepec suns (earthenware discs brightly painted with sun and moon faces). A number of shops along the so-called Corredor Artesanal, on Comonfort south of Paseo San Isidro, sell árboles de vida. Prices range from US$7 for a miniature árbol de la vida up to US$50 for a meter-high tree. Just north of Paseo San Isidro is the Corral Artesanal, a series of small shops along an arcade selling local crafts, and a restaurant.

The potters' workshops *(alfarerías)* are spread out all over town; the triangular tourism module in front of the Cerro del Calvario has a map locating them. The workshop of Beto Hernández at Altamirano 58 between Allende and Ascencio is itself a work of art with fountains, altars, and designs embedded in the cobblestone walkway, and a sort of chapel built around the lavishly decorated kiln. Within the various display rooms are some pretty amazing trees, many unpainted, at reasonably prices. The most elaborate and expensive trees are in the front gallery. A few doors down at Altamirano 212 the workshop of Adrián Luis González is equally remarkable; the floor of the upstairs gallery is adorned with butterflies and suns made by González. A fascinating genealogical tree shows members of the González family (Adrián himself is near the top) with their accoutrements. The tree demonstrates the process of its own creation, with subsequent levels at different stages of production – from unbaked clay at the bottom to a gold-paint finish at the top.

A pleasant hike with great views can be made to the top of Cerro del Calvario, a hill decorated with a huge pottery mural.

Frequent 2nd-class buses reach Metepec from the Toluca bus station.

NEVADO DE TOLUCA

The extinct volcano Nevado de Toluca (or Xinantécatl), 4690m high, lies across the horizon south of Toluca. A road runs 48km up to its crater, with the two lakes, El Sol and La Luna. The earlier you reach the summit, the better the chance of clear views. The summit area is snowy (nevado) from November to March, and sometimes OK for cross-country skiing, but the park is closed during the heaviest snows.

Buses on highway 134, the Toluca-Tejupilco road, will stop at the turnoff for highway 10 to Sultepec, which passes the park entrance 8km to the south. On weekends, it should be possible to hitch a ride the 27km from the junction of highways 134 and 10 to the crater. Taxis leaving from the corner of Aquiles Serdán and 5 de Febrero in Toluca will take you to the top for US$26, or there and back (including some time for you to look around) for US$50.

From the park entrance, a road winds 3.5km up to the main gate at an area called Parque de los Venados, where a US$0.50 entrance fee is charged. From there, it's a 17km drive along an unsurfaced road up to the crater. Six km from the crater, there's a boom gate, a shelter and a café. From that point, the crater can also be reached by a 1.5km hike via the Paso del Quetzal, a very scenic walking track.

Places to Stay & Eat

You can stay at **Posada Familiar** in the Parque de los Venados, **Albergue Ejidal**, 2km farther up, or a **state-run shelter** 6km from the crater. Camping is permitted by the first two. Posada Familiar has 13 rooms (US$6.50 per room) with shared baths and hot showers. There's a kitchen without utensils, and a common area with a fireplace. It's closed on Wednesday. Albergue Ejidal has 64 bunk beds (sleeping bag required) at US$3.25 per person, hot water, and a large dining area with a huge fireplace. Before you go up, ask the attendant in the Parque de los Venados to open Albergue Ejidal for you. The state-run shelter near the summit (at 4050m) has foam mattresses and blankets but no bathrooms.

On weekends, food is served at stalls in the Parque de los Venados and at the summit café. During the week, bring your own food and water.

VALLE DE BRAVO
● pop 21,500 ● elev 1800m ☎ changing
About 70km west of Toluca, this was a quiet colonial-era village in the hills until the 1940s, when it became a base for construction of a dam and hydroelectric station. The new lake gave the town a waterside location and it was soon a popular weekend and holiday spot for the wealthy. Nevertheless, this vibrant country community still retains its colonial charm.

Sailing on the lake is the main activity in Valle de Bravo – hour-long cruises by colectiva boat cost US$2.25 per person. Water-skiing, horse riding and hanggliding are also popular.

You can walk and camp in the hills around town, which attract monarch butterflies from December to March. A climb up the rock promontory La Peña, northwest of

In 2000, the telephone area code is due to change to ☎ 7 from 726, with the digits 26 added to the start of every local number (for example, the number 7-65-43 will become 267-65-43).

AROUND MEXICO CITY

the center, will give you a view of the whole lake.

Places to Stay & Eat

The town's budget hotels are a cut above those found elsewhere. *Hotel Mary* has simple clean singles/doubles (US$13/19) around a pretty courtyard. *Hotel Blanquita*, in the same building on the plaza, is OK too, with rooms for US$8.50 during the week, US$14 on weekends. The reception desk is in the mom & pop store in front.

Posada Casa Vieja (☎ 2-03-38, Juárez 101) offers a very good value, charging US$13/19 for pleasant rooms facing an idyllic patio with a fountain and lots of chirping birds. There's parking in the courtyard, but the entranceway is a tight squeeze.

Centro Vacacional ISSEMYM (☎ 2-00-04, Independencia 404), just above the market, is a holiday center for state workers but it accepts other guests. Featuring several pools and other recreational facilities, it's a good deal at US$25 for single or double rooms (US$29 with three meals).

Hotel Villa Enigma (☎ 2-44-74, Santa María 121) is a totally original concept, and quite luxurious for the price. Singles/doubles are US$37/58. Its suites are on three levels, with kitchen, bedroom and living room (in ascending order) connected by a spiral staircase. The rooftop bar opens at 11 pm.

There are scores of restaurants and cafés but the fancier places only open on weekends. *Bertolli's*, a stylish bar/restaurant on Salitre on the way to the piers, bakes pizzas in a brick oven, charging US$9 for a medium pie and US$12 for a large. Farther down Salitre is *Los Veleros*, an elegant adobe brick building with dining on a balcony overlooking a large garden. The restaurant charges US$7 to US$10 for seafood main courses. For ambiance, have a drink and/or a light meal at the floating lakefront restaurant-bars *La Balsa Avándaro* and *Los Pericos* (open 10 am to 6 pm Wednesday to Monday).

Getting There & Away

The bus terminal is on 16 de Septiembre. Autobuses Zinacantepec runs hourly 2nd-class directos until 5.30 pm to Mexico City's Terminal Poniente, all of which make a stop near Toluca's terminal (three hours, US$5.75). There is also frequent service to Zitácuaro (US$3). If you're driving between Toluca and Valle de Bravo, the southern route via highway 134 is quicker and more scenic.

TEOTENANGO

Tenango de Arista, 25km south of Toluca on highway 55, is overlooked from the west by the large, well-restored hilltop ruins of Teotenango, a Matlazinca ceremonial center dating from the 9th century. The site is quite extensive – several pyramids, plazas and a ball court – and has great views. **Museo del Estado**, near the entrance, has Teotenango pottery and sculpture, as well as a section devoted to the prehistory of the region. The ruins and museum are open 9 am to 5 pm daily except Monday (US$0.70, free on Wednesday).

From Toluca bus station, buses run every 10 minutes to the center of Tenango, from which you can walk to the site in 20 to 30 minutes or take a taxi (US$0.50).

Driving from Toluca on highway 55, pass the toll highway and turn right into Teotenango; signs show you where to make a right turn on to a road that passes north of the hill.

MALINALCO

• pop 6520 • elev 1740m ☎ changing

One of the few reasonably well-preserved Aztec temples stands above beautiful but little-visited Malinalco, 20km east of Tenancingo. The site is 1km west of the town center, approached by a well-maintained footpath with signs about the area in Spanish, English and Nahuatl. The views over the valley from the summit have inspired legions of painters.

In 2000, the telephone area code is due to change to ☎ 7 from 714, with the digits 14 added to the start of every local number (for example, the number 7-65-43 will become 147-65-43).

The Aztecs conquered this area in 1476 and were still building a ritual center here when they were themselves conquered by the Spanish. The Temple of Eagle and Jaguar Warriors, where sons of Aztec nobles were initiated into warrior orders, survived because it is hewn from the mountainside itself. Its entrance is carved in the form of a fanged serpent. The site is open 10 am to 5.30 pm daily except Monday (US$2, free on Sunday).

Malinalco also has a fine 16th-century Augustinian convent, fronted by a tranquil tree-lined yard. Floral and herbal frescos adorn its cloister. The tourist office (☎ 7-01-11, ext 21), next door to the Palacio Municipal, hands out maps of the town. It's open 9 am to 3 pm daily. There's an ATM on Hidalgo, on the north side of the convent.

Places to Stay

Like other destinations near Mexico City, Malinalco is geared toward weekend visitors, which means you'll have no trouble finding a room Sunday to Thursday nights but your dining options may be limited. Conversely, weekend hotel reservations are recommended. *Villa Hotel* (☎ 7-00-01, *Guerrero 101*), on the south side of the plaza, is a friendly place with 10 rooms, six basic ones with cliff views sharing a single bath at US$5.25 per person, and four elegant ones facing the plaza (US$25 for one or two persons). Part of the Villa's charm is the brick bread oven in the central courtyard. *Posada Familiar María Dolores* (☎ 7-03-54, *Juárez Nte 113*), half a block south of the plaza by the street market, has clean, cozy singles/doubles (US$9.50/16) and pretty gardens.

Hotel Marmil (☎ 7-09-16, *Progreso 606*), the ocher building near the northern entrance into town, is Malinalco's best place to stay. Standard rooms with large comfy beds (US$14/21) have balconies facing a lush patio; double rooms in the new rear wing are US$19. Just north of the Marmil in a woodsy area, *Hotel Las Cabañas* (☎ 7-01-01, *Progreso 1*) has a swimming pool and 20 country cabins, each with two bedrooms, a fireplace and a kitchen with refrigerator and gas stove, at US$13 per person.

Places to Eat

Malinalco has many good restaurants that serve a wide variety of cuisines, but only a few are open during the week. One of these is the elegant *Las Palomas* (*Guerrero 104*), which has a tiled country kitchen at the front, citrus and mango trees on the patio and a *palapa* bar. Its reasonably priced menu consists of all-natural Mexican originals. Healthy breakfasts are US$1.50 to US$3, salads US$3, meat dishes US$6.50 and trout dishes US$5.25.

On the plaza, *Los Placeres* is an excellent choice, with a laid-back atmosphere, good music and great views of the cliffs in back. Its varied menu features hearty breakfasts with good coffee and tea, bagels with cheese or salmon (US$4), original salads (US$2.75), crepes (US$3.75) and exotic specials. Unfortunately, it's only open Friday to Sunday. Behind the arches, *El Portal* is another weekend place; it is an Italian-run restaurant that serves good pastas and salads.

Les Chefs, at Morelos 107 behind the convent, is a double restaurant: one serves pizzas (US$4.25 to US$6.50), the other serves French cuisine with a strong Mexican flavor. The French chef has at least seven delicious ways of making trout (US$4.50). Across the street, *Beto's* bar serves seafood, including shark *empanadas* (US$0.75), terrific shrimp cocktails (US$2.75), and Malinalco-style mackerel wrapped in banana leaf and stewed with onion, tomato, epazote and fiery chile verde. Beto's kitchen is open 12 to 8 pm daily.

Getting There & Away

You can reach Malinalco by bus from Tenancingo or from the Toluca bus station. From Mexico City's Terminal Poniente, there are two direct buses at 5.10 pm and 5.50 pm; alternatively, take one of many buses to Jajalpa (en route to Tenancingo), then get a local bus. By car from Mexico City, turn south at La Marquesa and follow the signs to Malinalco.

Direct buses back to Mexico City depart at 5.10 pm daily. There is frequent colectivo service to Tenango, from where you can catch a Toluca or Mexico City bus.

AROUND MEXICO CITY

CHALMA

One of Mexico's most important shrines is in the village of Chalma, 12km east of Malinalco. In 1533, an image of Christ, El Señor de Chalma, miraculously appeared in a cave to replace one of the local gods, Oxtéotl, and proceeded to stamp out dangerous beasts and do other wondrous things. The Señor now resides in Chalma's 17th-century church. The biggest of many annual pilgrimages here is for Pentecost (May 3) when thousands of people camp, hold a market and perform traditional dances.

Tres Estrellas del Centro runs hourly 2nd-class buses from Toluca to Chalma (US$2). A number of companies run 2nd-class buses from Mexico City's Terminal Poniente. There is frequent bus service from Malinalco.

IXTAPAN DE LA SAL

• pop 13,700 • elev 1880m ☎ 7

The spa town of Ixtapan features a kind of giant curative water park, the **Balneario, Spa y Parque Acuático Ixtapan**, combining thermal water pools with waterfalls, lakes, water slides, a wave pool and a miniature railway. It's unashamedly a tourist town, but it's worth a stop if you want to take the waters or give your kids a fun day. The spa section is open 7 am to 7 pm, while the aquatic park is open 10 am to 6 pm daily; admission is US$7.50 for adults, half that for kids.

Hotels are clustered along Juárez south of the aquatic park, with a good range of lodging. The one resort in town, *Hotel Ixtapan* (☎ 143-00-21, ixtapan@spamexico

.com), adjacent to the park, has rooms with all the modern conveniences for US$180 including meals (tennis and golf fees are extra).

About 5km farther on highway 55 is **Tonatico** with its own mineral bath/fun park complex, though it's about a tenth of the size (and a third of the price) of Ixtapan de la Sal's and consequently more relaxed. Pleasant rooms at the on-site *Hotel Balneario Municipal* (☎ 141-06-04), featuring ceiling fans and clean bathrooms, are only US$6.50 per person, US$2 more on weekends. At the south end of town is a spectacular waterfall (El Salto) and camping nearby at *Rancho La Piedra*, which has a thatched-roof restaurant serving delicious regional specialties and fresh trout.

Getting There & Away

From the new bus terminal on highway 55 between Ixtapan and Tonatico, Tres Estrellas del Centro runs frequent buses to Toluca, Taxco and Cuernavaca, each for US$3. There is also hourly service to Mexico City via autopista until 6 pm daily (US$5.25). Buses to/from the terminal go up and down Juárez in Ixtapan (US$0.20); taxis charge US$1.75.

Going north to Toluca, toll highway 55D parallels part of highway 55, bypassing Tenango and Tenancingo. Going south to Taxco, you could pass on the Grutas de la Estrella, but the Grutas de Cacahuamilpa are a must (see Around Taxco in the South of Mexico City section, earlier in this chapter).

Baja California

Baja California's native peoples left memorable murals in caves and on canyon walls, but permanent European settlement failed to reach the world's longest peninsula until the Jesuit missions of the 17th and 18th centuries, which collapsed as indigenous people fell prey to European diseases.

Mainland ranchers, miners and fishermen settled when foreigners built port facilities and acquired huge land grants in the 19th century. During US prohibition, Baja became a popular south-of-the-border destination for gamblers, drinkers and other 'sinners.' It still attracts more than 50 million visitors annually for duty-free shopping, sumptuous seafood and activities such as horseback riding, diving, snorkeling, windsurfing, clamming, whale-watching, fishing, sailing, kayaking, cycling, surfing and hiking.

Travelers to Baja California will find that prices are not nearly as cheap as elsewhere in Mexico – food and accommodations in Baja can sometimes cost double what they do in the rest of the country. The cost of food can range from US$2 for a taco at a

Highlights

- Tijuana – World's most-visited border town; historically notorious for low-life partying but now an impressive locus of commerce, education and cultural activities

- Reserva de la Biósfera El Vizcaíno – Biosphere reserve; includes major gray whale breeding sites at Laguna Ojo de Liebre and Laguna San Ignacio and pre-Hispanic rock art in the dissected volcanic plateau of San Francisco de la Sierra, a UNESCO World Heritage Site

- Loreto – First capital of the Californias; notable for two restored missions, its own and nearby San Francisco Javier; also known for kayaking on the Sea of Cortez and mountain biking in the Sierra de la Giganta

- La Paz – The capital of Baja California Sur, providing beautiful beaches, a palm-lined *malecón*, a handful of colonial buildings and spectacular sunsets over the bay

- Los Cabos – An uneasy mixture of nightclubs and time-shares (Cabo San Lucas and vicinity), suitably unpretentious tropical retreats (San José del Cabo and the eastern cape), artists' colonies (Todos Santos) and biological wonders (Sierra de la Laguna, probably the best hiking and backpacking area on the peninsula)

BAJA CALIFORNIA

stand to US$25 for a lobster at a restaurant, but a good, moderately priced meal tends to cost around US$8.

La Frontera & the Desierto del Colorado

La Frontera, the northernmost part of the state of Baja California, corresponds roughly to the colonial Dominican mission frontier. Many view its cities and beaches as hedonistic enclaves, but Tijuana and Mexicali are major manufacturing centers, and Mexicali's Río Colorado hinterland is a key agricultural zone. The region attracts many undocumented border crossers, both experienced migrants who traditionally spend the harvest season north of the border and desperate novices who have no idea what to expect there.

TIJUANA
• pop 966,100 • elev 100m ☎ 6

Tijuana ('tee-WHA-nah'), immediately south of the US border, has never completely overcome its 'sin city' image, but its universities, office buildings, housing developments, shopping malls and industries mark it as a fast-growing city of increasing sophistication. Most of 'La Revo' (Avenida Revolución) appeals to a younger crowd from the US who take advantage of Mexico's permissive drinking laws (18-year-olds may frequent bars!) to party until dawn.

At the end of WWI Tijuana had fewer than 1000 inhabitants but soon drew US tourists for gambling, greyhound racing, boxing and cockfights. Mexican president Lázaro Cárdenas outlawed casinos and prostitution in the 1930s, but the US depression probably had a greater negative impact on the economy. Jobless Mexican returnees increased Tijuana's population to about 16,500 by 1940.

During WWII and through the 1950s, the US government's temporary *bracero* program allowed Mexicans to alleviate labor shortages north of the border. These workers replaced Americans who were stationed overseas in the military and caused Tijuana's population to increase to 180,000 by 1960. In each succeeding decade those numbers have probably doubled, and the present population may exceed the official census figure by at least half.

Growth has brought severe social and environmental problems – impoverished migrants still inhabit hillside dwellings of scrap wood and cardboard. They lack clean drinking water and trash collection, and worn tires are implanted in the hillsides to keep the soil from washing away during storms.

Another one of the problems facing Tijuana in the past few years has been an outbreak of drug-related crimes. Considered the headquarters of the Pacific (or 'Tijuana') cartel headed by the Arellano Félix brothers, Tijuana has had its share of well-publicized crimes that have put it in the spotlight. It is still a safe place to travel, but exercise caution when traveling at night or in isolated areas.

Orientation
Tijuana is south of the US border post of San Ysidro, California. Its central grid consists of north-south *avenidas* and east-west *calles* (most of the latter are referred to by their numbers more frequently than their names). South of Calle 1ª, Avenida Revolución (La Revo) is the main commercial center.

East of the Frontón Palacio Jai Alai, which is La Revo's major landmark, Tijuana's 'new' Zona Río commercial center straddles the river. Mesa de Otay, to the northeast, is another border crossing and contains the airport, *maquiladoras* (assembly-plant operations, usually foreign-owned), residential neighborhoods and shopping areas. The city is changing to a new numbering system, and though some businesses still use their old addresses, the transition is going relatively smoothly.

Information
Tourist Offices The Secture (Secretaría de Turismo del Estado) office (☎ 688-05-55), at the corner of Avenida Revolución and Calle 1ª, is open 8 am to 5 pm Monday through

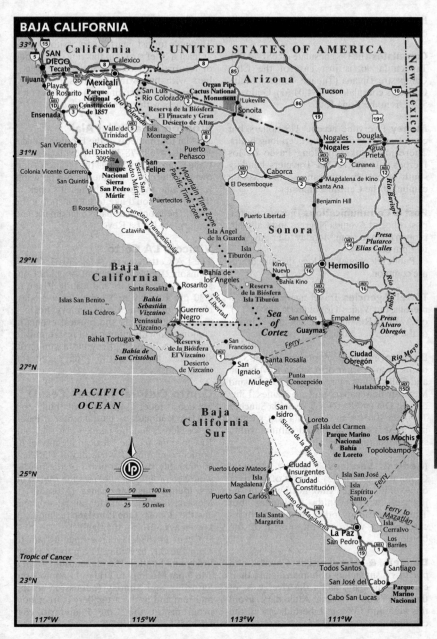

BAJA CALIFORNIA

California UNITED STATES OF AMERICA

New Mexico

33°N

SAN DIEGO
Tecate Calexico
Tijuana
Playas de Rosarito Mexicali
Ensenada Parque Nacional Constitución de 1857

San Luis Río Colorado
Organ Pipe Cactus National Monument
Lukeville
Reserva de la Biósfera El Pinacate y Gran Desierto de Altar
Sonoita

Arizona

Tucson

New Mexico

Valle de Trinidad
Isla Montague

Nogales Douglas
Nogales Agua Prieta
Cananea
Caborca
El Desemboque Santa Ana
Magdalena de Kino
Benjamin Hill

San Vicente
Picacho del Diablo 3095m
Parque Nacional Sierra San Pedro Mártir

31°N

Colonia Vicente Guerrero
San Quintín

El Rosario

Cataviña

San Felipe

Puertecitos

Puerto Peñasco

Sonora

Puerto Libertad

Presa Plutarco Elías Calles

29°N

Baja California

Santa Rosalíita

Islas San Benito
Isla Cedros

Bahía Tortugas

Rosarito

Bahía de los Ángeles

Isla Ángel de la Guarda

Isla Tiburón

Kino Nuevo
Bahía Kino

Reserva de la Biósfera Isla Tiburón

Hermosillo

Bahía Sebastián Vizcaíno
Península Vizcaíno

Guerrero Negro

Sea of Cortez

San Carlos Empalme
Guaymas

Presa Álvaro Obregón

Río Yaqui

27°N

PACIFIC OCEAN

Bahía de San Cristóbal

Reserva de la Biósfera El Vizcaíno
Desierto de Vizcaíno

San Francisco
San Ignacio
Mulegé

Santa Rosalía

Punta Concepción

Ciudad Obregón

Río Mayo

Huatabampo

Baja California Sur

San Isidro

Loreto
Isla del Carmen
Parque Marino Nacional Bahía de Loreto

Los Mochis
Topolobampo

25°N

Puerto López Mateos
Isla Magdalena
Puerto San Carlos

Ciudad Insurgentes
Ciudad Constitución

Isla San José
Isla Espíritu Santo

Ferry to Mazatlán

0   50   100 km
0   25   50 miles

Isla Santa Margarita

Llano de Magdalena

La Paz
San Pedro

Isla Cerralvo
Los Barriles

Tropic of Cancer

23°N

Todos Santos

San José del Cabo
Cabo San Lucas

Santiago

Parque Marino Nacional

117°W   115°W   113°W   111°W

BAJA CALIFORNIA

Friday, 10 am to 5 pm Saturday and Sunday, and has a friendly, English-speaking staff.

Consulates The US consulate (☎ 681-74-00), Tapachula 96, is just east of the Club Campestre Tijuana (Tijuana Country Club). Canada's consulate (☎ 684-04-61), Gedovius 5-202, is in the Zona Río.

Money Everyone accepts US dollars, but countless *casas de cambio* keep long hours. There are banks all along Paseo de los Héroes, all with ATMs. Travelers heading south or east by bus can use the casa de cambio at the Central Camionera.

Post & Communications Tijuana's central post office, at Avenida Negrete and Calle 11ª, is open 8 am to 4 pm Monday to Friday, 9 am to 1 pm Saturday.

Public telephones and long-distance offices are common.

Travel Agencies Travel agencies are numerous, but Viajes Honold's (☎ 688-11-11), on Avenida Revolución near Calle 2ª, is one of the longest established.

Bookstores The book department in Sanborns, at the corner of Avenida Revolución and Calle 8ª, has a large selection of US and Mexican newspapers and magazines. Librería El Día (☎ 684-09-86), Avenida Sánchez Taboada 10050A in the Zona Río, specializes in Mexican history and culture, with a small selection in English.

Medical Services Tijuana's Hospital General (☎ 684-09-22) is north of the river on Avenida Padre Kino, northwest of the junction with Avenida Rodríguez, but Tijuana has many other medical facilities catering to visitors from north of the border.

Dangers & Annoyances Coyotes and *polleros* – smugglers of humans – and their clients congregate along the river west of the San Ysidro crossing. After dark, avoid this area and Colonia Libertad, east of the crossing.

La Revo

South of Calle 1ª, Avenida Revolución is Tijuana's tourist heart. Every visitor braves at least a brief stroll up this raucous avenue of futuristic discos, fine restaurants, seedy bars with bellowing hawkers, brash taxi drivers, tacky souvenir shops and street photographers with zebra-striped *burros*.

Frontón Palacio Jai Alai

Jai Alai tournaments at the Frontón Palacio Jai Alai (☎ 685-78-33), at Revolución and Calle 8ª, are on hold while the Fronton's new owner determines whether or not he wants to continue the games, though it's open to the public if you'd like to take a shot at the sport. The Frontón remains a landmark, and centerpiece for La Revo.

Vinícola LA Cetto

The LA Cetto winery (☎ 685-30-31, Cañón Johnson 2108), southwest of Avenida Constitución, offers tours and tasting 10 am to 5.30 pm Tuesday to Sunday, for a modest charge. In summer, the winery hosts a number of festivals and musical events in conjunction with a number of restaurants in town. It's a little bit pricey, but a wonderful showcase for both the winery and the restaurants.

Centro Cultural Tijuana (Cecut)

Mexico's federal government built this modern landmark, a cultural center at Paseo de los Héroes and Independencia in the Zona Río, to reinforce the Mexican identity of its border populations. It is a facility of which any comparably sized city north of the border would be proud. Cecut houses the **Museo de las Identidades Mexicanas** (Museum of Mexican Identities), an art gallery, a theater and the globular **Cine Planetario** (colloquially known as La Bola – 'the Ball').

Cecut (☎ 684-11-11) is open 10 am to 8 pm Tuesday to Friday, 11 am to 9 pm Saturday and Sunday. The planetarium is open 2 to 9 pm Monday to Friday, 11 am to 9 pm Saturday and Sunday (admission to the museum and to the art gallery is free; most programs at the Cine Planetario cost US$4.50).

Tarahumaras outside Creel

Chihuahua storefront

All aboard the Copper Canyon Railway!

View of the Barranca del Cobre (Copper Canyon)

Mazatlán's fluorescent Carnaval

Mex to the X: La Quebrada cliff diver, Acapulco

No red card for fouls in pre-hispanic ball game

Places to Stay

Budget Perhaps downtown's best budget hotel is *Hotel Lafayette (☎ 685-39-40, Revolución 926)*, above Café La Especial, but it's often full, especially on weekends. Singles/doubles are US$20/26. Centrally located *Hotel Arreola (☎ 685-90-81, Revolución 10800)* has carpeted rooms with TV and telephone for US$21/27. *Motel Plaza Hermosa (☎ 685-33-53, Constitución 1821)* is a good value at US$25/32, with secure parking.

Mid-Range *Hotel Nelson (☎ 685-43-03, Revolución 721)* is a long-time favorite for its central location and tidy, carpeted rooms. Rooms with color TV, a view and the less-than-soothing sounds of La Revo cost from US$42/47.

Bullfight posters and photographs adorn the walls of *Hotel Caesar (☎ 688-16-06, Revolución 1079)*, where rates are US$30/40; its restaurant claims to have created the Caesar salad. Rooms at the newer and excellent *Hotel La Villa de Zaragoza (☎ 685-18-32)*, on Avenida Madero directly behind the Frontón, include TV, telephone, heat and aircon for around US$33/40. This is a nice place to stay, especially if you want to get a little bit away from the noise of La Revo.

Top End *Motel León (☎ 685-63-20, Calle 7ª No 1939)* is conveniently central and offers telephone, room service and parking for US$40/45.

Modern, efficient *Hotel Real del Río (☎ 634-31-00, fax 634-30-53, Velasco 1409)*, in the Zona Río, charges US$71/78. The 23-story *Grand Hotel Tijuana (☎ 681-70-00, Agua Caliente 4500)* houses a shopping mall, offices, restaurants, a pool and convention facilities, and it has golf course access. Rooms are US$102, but if you have an AAA card ask for discounts.

Places to Eat

On the east side of Avenida Revolución, at the foot of the stairs near the corner of Calle 3ª, *Café La Especial* has decent Mexican food at reasonable prices and is far quieter than the average eatery in La Revo. Also on the east side of Avenida Constitución, between Calle 1ª and Calle 2ª, *Los Norteños* is a popular juice bar and taco stand.

One of Tijuana's best values is the diner-style *Tortas Ricardo (Avenida Madero 1410)*, a bright and cheerful place. Breakfasts are excellent, the tortas are among the best in town, and it's open 24 hours. *Tía Juana Tilly's*, a popular gringo hangout, is next to the Frontón Palacio Jai Alai, while *Tilly's Fifth Avenue* is at Revolución and Calle 5ª. Both serve the standard Mexican entrees, plus steak and seafood. At Revolución and Calle 8ª, *Sanborns* has both a bar and a restaurant. For generous portions of reasonably priced pizza and pasta, try *Vittorio's (Revolución 1269)*.

Several restaurants in the Plaza Fiesta mall, at Paseo de los Héroes and Independencia, are worth a try. *Sótano Suizo* has a nice atmosphere and moderate prices. Try *Taberna Española* for Spanish tapas. Nearby *Molcajete's (Paseo de los Héroes 9311)* has good food, and is open till 2 am. At Sánchez Taboada and Calle 9ª, *Buenos Aires* offers Argentine dishes centered on beef and pasta.

Entertainment

Rowdy Avenida Revolución is the place for 'upside-down margaritas,' and ear-splitting live and recorded music at places such as the *Hard Rock Café* and many others. For a sense of the nightlife away from the craziness of La Revo, try *Ahjijo* or *Mi Barra*, both in the Plaza Fiesta mall in the Zona Río, which are frequented by the young crowd of Tijuana.

Equally or more interesting are *banda/norteña* venues like *Las Pulgas (Revolución 1501)*, and the *Jalapeño Club (Revolución 17140)*. Most fancier discos are in the Zona Río, such as the kitschy *Baby Rock (Avenida Diego Rivera 1482)*.

Spectator Sports

From May to September, Sunday bullfights take place at two bullrings: El Toreo de Tijuana, on Boulevard Agua Caliente northwest of Club Campestre Tijuana, and the oceanfront Plaza de Toros Monumental. Call ☎ 685-22-10 or ☎ 685-15-72 for reservations at either bullring (☎ 619-232-5049 in San Diego). Tickets cost US$19 to US$45.

BAJA CALIFORNIA

TIJUANA

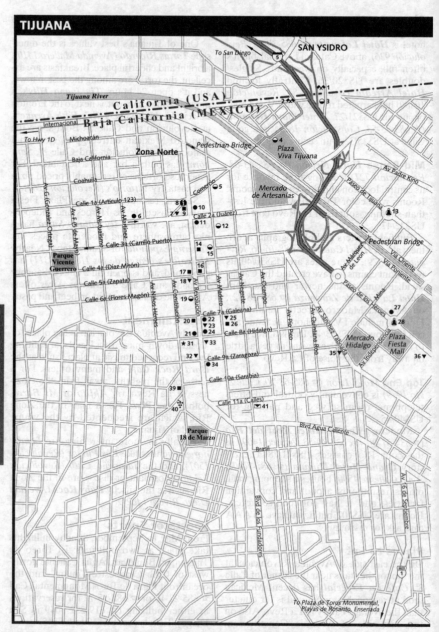

To San Diego
SAN YSIDRO

Tijuana River
California (USA)
Baja California (MEXICO)
Internacional

To Hwy 1D
Michoacán
Baja California
Zona Norte
Coahuila
Calle 1a (Artículo 123)

Av G (González Ortega)
Av F E (5 de Mayo)
Av Mutualismo
Av Martínez

Pedestrian Bridge
Plaza
Viva Tijuana

Av Padre Kino
Paseo de Tijuana
Paseo de Tijuana

Comercio
Mercado
de Artesanías

Calle 2a (Juárez)
Calle 3a (Carrillo Puerto)

Parque
Vicente
Guerrero

Calle 4a (Díaz Mirón)
Calle 5a (Zapata)
Calle 6a (Flores Magón)

Av Niños Héroes
Av Constitución
Av Revolución
Av Madero
Av Negrete
Av Ocampo

Pedestrian Bridge
Via Oriente
Via Poniente

Av Mutualismo
de León

Paseo de los Héroes
Mina

Calle 7a (Galeana)
Calle 8a (Hidalgo)
Calle 9a (Zaragoza)
Calle 10a (Sarabia)
Calle 11a (Calles)

Av Pío Pico
Av Quintana Roo
Av Sánchez Taboada
Av Independencia

Mercado
Hidalgo
Plaza
Fiesta
Mall

Parque
18 de Marzo

Brasil

Blvd Agua Caliente

Blvd de los Fundadores

Av 16 de Septiembre

MEX 1

To Plaza de Toros Monumental,
Playas de Rosarito, Ensenada

- 1
- 2
- 3
- 4
- 5
- 6
- 7
- 8
- 9
- 10
- 11
- 12
- 13
- 14
- 15
- 16
- 17
- 18
- 19
- 20
- 21
- 22
- 23
- 24
- 25
- 26
- 27
- 28
- 31
- 32
- 33
- 34
- 35
- 36
- 39
- 40
- 41

TIJUANA

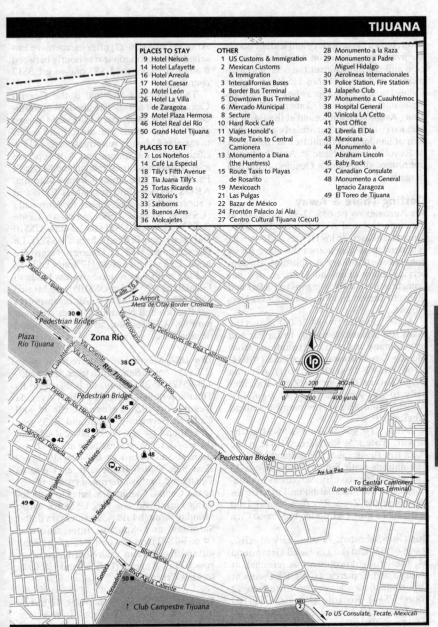

PLACES TO STAY
9 Hotel Nelson
14 Hotel Lafayette
16 Hotel Arreola
17 Hotel Caesar
20 Motel León
26 Hotel La Villa
de Zaragoza
39 Motel Plaza Hermosa
46 Hotel Real del Río
50 Grand Hotel Tijuana

PLACES TO EAT
7 Los Norteños
14 Café La Especial
18 Tilly's Fifth Avenue
23 Tía Juana Tilly's
25 Tortas Ricardo
32 Vittorio's
33 Sanborns
35 Buenos Aires
36 Molcajetes

OTHER
1 US Customs & Immigration
2 Mexican Customs
& Immigration
3 Intercalifornias Buses
4 Border Bus Terminal
5 Downtown Bus Terminal
6 Mercado Municipal
8 Secture
10 Hard Rock Café
11 Viajes Honold's
12 Route Taxis to Central
Camionera
13 Monumento a Diana
(the Huntress)
15 Route Taxis to Playas
de Rosarito
19 Mexicoach
21 Las Pulgas
22 Bazar de México
24 Frontón Palacio Jai Alai
27 Centro Cultural Tijuana (Cecut)

28 Monumento a la Raza
29 Monumento a Padre
Miguel Hidalgo
30 Aerolíneas Internacionales
31 Police Station, Fire Station
34 Jalapeño Club
37 Monumento a Cuauhtémoc
38 Hospital General
40 Vinícola LA Cetto
41 Post Office
42 Librería El Día
43 Mexicana
44 Monumento a
Abraham Lincoln
45 Baby Rock
47 Canadian Consulate
48 Monumento a General
Ignacio Zaragoza
49 El Toreo de Tijuana

BAJA CALIFORNIA

Shopping

Jewelry, wrought-iron furniture, baskets, silver, blown glass, pottery and leather goods are available in stores on Avenidas Revolución and Constitución; at the Mercado Municipal on Avenida Niños Héroes between Calles 1ª and 2ª; at the sprawling Mercado de Artesanías, just south of Comercio (Calle 1ª) along Avenida Ocampo; and at the Bazar de México (which has a particularly good selection of handcrafted furniture), at the corner of Revolución and Calle 7ª. Auto body and upholstery shops along Ocampo offer real bargains.

Getting There & Away

Air Aeroméxico (☎ 685-22-30, 683-27-00 at the airport), Local A 12-1 in the Plaza Río Tijuana, at Paseo de los Héroes and Avenida Independencia, also houses the office for its commuter subsidiary Aerolitoral. Besides serving many mainland Mexican destinations, they have daily nonstops to La Paz and flights to Tucson and Phoenix, both via Hermosillo.

Aero California (☎ 684-21-00), also in the Plaza Río Tijuana, flies daily to La Paz and serves many mainland destinations from Mexico City northward. Mexicana (☎ 634-65-66, 682-41-83 at the airport), Avenida Diego Rivera 1511, in the Zona Río, flies daily to Los Angeles (but not *from* Los Angeles) and also serves many mainland Mexican cities.

TAESA (☎ 684-84-84, 683-55-94 at the airport), Paseo de los Héroes 1011, in the Plaza Río Tijuana, flies to mainland Mexican destinations, with Sunday connections to Chicago via Mexico City. Aerolíneas Internacionales, in the Plaza Jardín on Paseo de los Héroes in the Zona Río, flies to mainland destinations from Hermosillo to Mexico City.

Bus Only Suburbaja (a subsidiary of ABC, ☎ 688-07-52) and the US-based Greyhound use the handy downtown bus terminal, at Madero and Comercio (Calle 1ª). Frequent Suburbaja buses leave for Ensenada (2 hours, US$4), Rosarito (1 hour, US$0.65) and Tecate (1½ hours, US$3); these are all local buses that make many stops.

From Plaza Viva Tijuana near the border, ABC (☎ 683-56-81) and Autotransportes Aragón (☎ 683-56-22) offer inexpensive Ensenada buses. Aragón leaves hourly between 6 am and 10 pm for US$7 one-way, US$12 roundtrip.

The main bus terminal is the Central Camionera (☎ 621-29-82), about 5km southeast of downtown, where Elite and Crucero offer 1st-class buses with air-con and toilets to mainland Mexico. Autotransportes del Pacífico, Norte de Sonora and ABC operate mostly 2nd-class buses to mainland Mexico's Pacific Coast and around Baja California. ABC's Servicio Plus resembles Elite and Crucero. ABC has buses to Ensenada (US$8.50 1st-class, US$7 2nd-class), Tecate (US$3), Mexicali (US$11.50 1st-class, US$10 2nd-class), San Felipe (6 hours, US$22), La Paz (22 hours, US$70), Guerrero Negro (13 hours, US$34) and Loreto (17 hours, US$57).

Elite and Crucero have express buses to Guadalajara (35 hours, US$105) and Mexico City (42 hours, US$123). Autotransportes del Pacífico and Norte de Sonora are comparable. All lines stop at major mainland destinations.

The USA Mexicoach runs frequent buses (US$1) from its San Ysidro terminal (☎ 619-428-9517), 4570 Camino de la Plaza, to its Tijuana terminal (☎ 685-14-70) at Avenida Revolución 1025, between Calle 6ª and Calle 7ª. Between 5.45 am and 10.35 pm, Greyhound (☎ 686-06-95, 800-231-2222 in the USA), 120 West Broadway in San Diego, stops at San Ysidro (☎ 619-428-1194), 799 East San Ysidro Boulevard, en route to Tijuana's downtown terminal (☎ 686-06-95) or the Central Camionera. Fares to both locations are US$5 one-way, US$8 roundtrip Monday through Friday; and an extra dollar Saturday and Sunday. Intercalifornias (☎ 683-62-81), on the east side of the road just south of the San Ysidro border crossing, goes to Los Angeles (US$18) and US California's Central Valley.

Trolley San Diego's popular light-rail trolley (☎ 619-233-3004) runs from downtown San Diego to San Ysidro every 15 minutes from about 5 am to midnight (US$1.75). From San Diego's Lindbergh Field airport, city bus No 2 goes directly to the Plaza America trolley stop in downtown San Diego, across from the Amtrak depot.

Car & Motorcycle The San Ysidro border crossing, a 10-minute walk from downtown Tijuana, is open 24 hours, but motorists may find the Otay Mesa crossing (open 6 am to 10 pm) much less congested. For rentals, agencies in San Diego are the cheapest option. Keep in mind that most car rental agencies in San Diego only allow rentals as far as Ensenada. California Baja Rent-A-Car (☎ 619-470-7368) in Spring Valley, California, is a good option if you plan to continue driving beyond Ensenada.

Getting Around
To/From the Airport Sharing can reduce the cost of a taxi (about US$10 if hailed on the street) to busy Aeropuerto Internacional Abelardo L Rodríguez (☎ 683-24-18) in Mesa de Otay, east of downtown. Alternatively, take any 'Aeropuerto' bus from the street just south of the San Ysidro border taxi stand (about US$0.30); from downtown, catch it on Calle 5ª between Avenidas Constitución and Niños Héroes.

Bus & Taxi For about US$0.30, local buses go everywhere, but slightly pricier route taxis are much quicker. To get to the Central Camionera take any 'Buena Vista,' 'Centro' or 'Central Camionera' bus from Calle 2ª, east of Constitución. For a quicker and more convenient option, take a gold-and-white 'Mesa de Otay' route taxi from Avenida Madero between Calles 2ª and 3ª (US$0.50).

Tijuana taxis lack meters, but most rides cost about US$5 or less. However, beware of the occasional unscrupulous taxi driver.

AROUND TIJUANA
Playas de Rosarito
• pop 9040
South of Tijuana, the valley of Rosarito marks the original boundary between mainland California and Baja California. Recently declared a separate municipality, the

town of Playas de Rosarito (21km from Tijuana) dates from 1885, but the Hotel Rosarito (now the landmark Rosarito Beach Hotel) and its long, sandy beach pioneered local tourism in the late 1920s. The town's main street – the noisy commercial strip of Boulevard Juárez (a segment of the Carretera Transpeninsular, highway 1) – has many good restaurants and moderately priced accommodations.

The amphitheater at the beachfront **Parque Municipal Abelardo L Rodríguez** contains Juan Zuñiga Padilla's impressive 1987 mural *Tierra y Libertad* (Land and Liberty).

From downtown Tijuana, route taxis for Playas de Rosarito leave from Avenida Madero between Calles 3ª and 4ª in downtown Tijuana (US$1).

Tecate
• pop 10,900 • elev 500m
About 55km east of Tijuana by highway 2, the east-west route linking Tijuana and Mexicali, Tecate resembles more of a mainland Mexican village than a border town but hosts several popular tourist events, such as bicycle races. Its landmark brewery, open for tours by reservation only, produces two of Mexico's best-known beers, Tecate and Carta Blanca, but maquiladoras drive the local economy. The border crossing, open 6 am to midnight daily, is less congested than either Tijuana or Mesa de Otay.

ENSENADA
• pop 193,600 ☎6
In the last few years, Ensenada has gone through a major renovation. Both the waterfront *malecón* and sidewalks along Avenida López Mateos (Calle 1ª) from Avenida Castillo to Avenida Macheros have been widened to accommodate outside patios for restaurants and shops. And even though you still have a mix of Americans strolling the streets with shopping lists of pharmaceuticals (which are generally much cheaper in Ensenada than in the US), the town has a very quaint feel to it. Outdoor activities such as fishing and surfing are popular, and Ensenada is the locus of Baja's wine industry. US

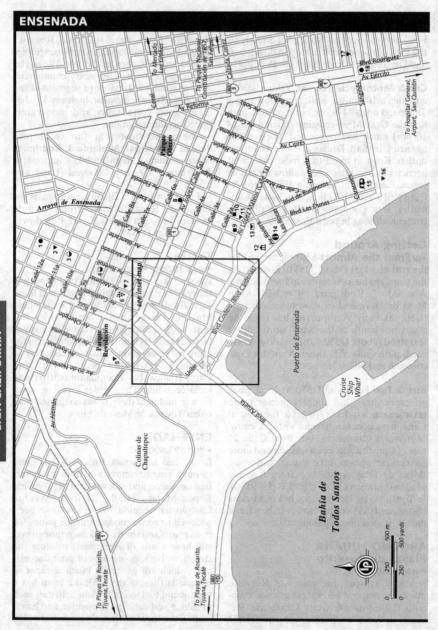

ENSENADA

ENSENADA

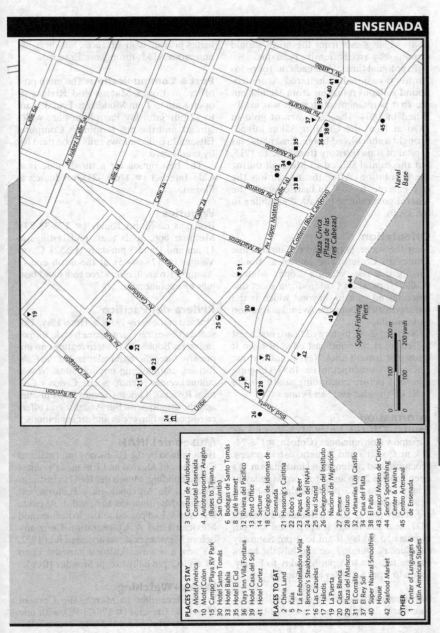

Plaza Cívica
(Plaza de las
Tres Cabezas)

Naval
Base

Sport-Fishing
Piers

0   100   200 m
0   100   200 yards

BAJA CALIFORNIA

PLACES TO STAY
9   Motel América
10 Motel Colon
15 Campo Playa RV Park
30 Hotel Santo Tomás
33 Hotel Bahía
35 Hotel El Cid
36 Days Inn Villa Fontana
39 Hotel Casa del Sol
41 Hotel Cortez

PLACES TO EAT
2   China Land
5   Kaia
8   La Embotelladora Vieja
11 Bronco's Steakhouse
16 Las Cazuelas
17 Haliotis
19 La Puerta
20 Casa Blanca
29 Plaza del Marisco
31 El Corralito
37 El Rey Sol
40 Super Natural Smoothies
    House
42 Seafood Market

OTHER
1   Center of Languages &
    Latin American Studies

3   Central de Autobuses,
    Computel Ensenada
4   Autotransportes Aragón
    (Buses to Tijuana,
    San Quintín)
6   Bodegas de Santo Tomás
12 Riviera del Pacífico
13 Post Office
14 Secture
18 Colegio de Idiomas de
    Ensenada
21 Hussong's Cantina
22 Lobo's
23 Papas & Beer
24 Museo del INAH
25 Taxi Stand
26 Delegación del Instituto
    Nacional de Migración
27 Pemex
28 Cotuco
32 Artesanías Los Castillo
34 Casa del Plata
38 El Patio
43 Caracol Museo de Ciencias
44 Serio's Sportfishing
    Center & Marina
45 Centro Artesanal
    de Ensenada

visitors sometimes make the city a reluctant host for spontaneous Fourth of July celebrations, when guests from the north should scrupulously avoid offensive behavior.

In colonial times, Ensenada de Todos los Santos occasionally sheltered Acapulco-bound galleons returning from Manila, but the first permanent settlement was established in 1804. The discovery of gold in 1870 at Real del Castillo, 35km inland, brought a short-lived boom. Ensenada was capital of Baja territory from 1882 to 1915, but the capital shifted to Mexicali during the revolution. After the revolution the city catered to 'sin' industries until the federal government outlawed gambling in the 1930s.

Orientation

Near the water, hotels and restaurants line Boulevard Costero, also known as Boulevard Cárdenas. Avenida López Mateos (Calle 1ª) parallels Costero for a short distance inland (north), beyond which is the tourist district – between Avenidas Ryerson and Castillo.

North of town, highway 3 heads northeast to Tecate; at the southeast edge of town it leads east toward Ojos Negros and Parque Nacional Constitución de 1857 (Laguna Hanson) before continuing south to the Valle de Trinidad and San Felipe.

Information

Tourist Offices Ensenada's Comité de Turismo y Convenciones (Cotuco; ☎ 178-24-11), at Costero and Azueta, carries maps, brochures and current hotel information. It's open 9 am to 2 pm and 3 to 7 pm Monday to Friday, 10 am to 3 pm Saturday, 11 am to 3 pm Sunday.

Secture (☎ 172-30-22), Boulevard Costero 1477, near Las Rocas, is open 9 am to 7 pm Monday to Friday, 9 am to 3 pm Saturday and Sunday. During June and July, the hours change to 8 am to 5 pm Monday to Friday, 10 am to 3 pm Saturday and Sunday.

Immigration The Delegación del Instituto Nacional de Migración (☎ 174-01-64), Azueta 101, is open 8 am to 3 pm daily.

Money Most banks and casas de cambio are on Avenidas Ruiz and Juárez. Only banks provide cash advances, but there are numerous ATMs throughout Ensenada.

Post & Communications The main post office, at López Mateos and Riviera, is open 8 am to 7 pm Monday to Friday, 8 am to 12 pm Saturday. Pay phones are widespread, and the bus terminal's Computel Ensenada office allows calls to be paid for by credit card.

The best option for getting online is at Café Internet (☎ 176-13-31), on Juárez at Floresta.

Wineries

Bodegas de Santo Tomás (☎ 178-33-33), Miramar 666, holds tours and tastings at 11 am and 1 and 3 pm daily (US$2). Cavas Valmar (☎ 178-64-05), at the north end of Avenida Riveroll, offers free tours and tastings by appointment.

Riviera del Pacífico

Opened in the early 1930s as Hotel Playa Ensenada, this extravagant, Spanish-style, former casino on Boulevard Costero features an impressive three-dimensional mural of the Californias, emphasizing mission sites. Now a cultural center (Centro Social, Cívico y Cultural Riviera), it houses a renovated museum and the atmospheric Bar Andaluz and offers retrospective film cycles and art exhibitions.

Museo del INAH

Built in 1886 by the US-owned International Company of Mexico and Ensenada's oldest public building, Museo del INAH (Instituto Nacional de Antropología y Historia, ex-Aduana Marítima de Ensenada), Avenida Ryerson 1, had passed to the British-owned Mexican Land & Colonization Company before Mexican customs acquired it in 1922. It's now a historical/cultural museum, open 10 am to 5 pm daily except Monday (free).

Whale-Watching

From December to March, the Caracol Museo de Ciencias (☎ 178-71-92), with one office at Obregón 1463 and one on the

BAJA CALIFORNIA

sport-fishing piers, arranges offshore whale-watching cruises.

Fishing

Ensenada is known for its sport fishing. There are many charter companies to be found along the newly renovated malecón. One option is Serio's Sportfishing Center & Marina (☎ 178-21-85).

Language Courses

The Colegio de Idiomas de Ensenada (☎ 176-01-09), Boulevard Rodríguez 377, offers intensive Spanish instruction, as does the Center of Languages and Latin American Studies (☎ 178-76-00), Riveroll 1287.

Special Events

The events listed below constitute a tiny sample of the 70-plus sporting, tourist and cultural happenings that take place each year. Dates change, so contact tourist offices for details.

Carnaval – Mardi Gras; sometime between mid-February and early March

Baja 500 – off-road car race; June

Fiesta de la Vendimia – wine harvest; mid-August

Fiestas Patrias – Mexican independence days; mid-September

Desfile Navideño Club Amigos de Ensenada – Christmas parade; mid-December

Places to Stay

Budget For camping, *Campo Playa RV Park* (☎ 176-29-18), at Las Dunas and Sanginés, has shady sites for RVs (US$13 to US$20 depending on the vehicle's size), but there's loud music nearby on weekends.

Motel América (☎ 176-13-33), at López Mateos and Espinoza, has simple rooms with kitchenettes for US$20/25 single/double. *Motel Colon* (☎ 176-19-10, Guadalupe 174) offers off-street parking. All the rooms are comfortable and have TV and fans. The older rooms are a good deal at US$20, and they include kitchenettes.

Mid-Range Renovated *Days Inn Villa Fontana* (☎ 178-34-34, López Mateos 1050), between Blancarte and Alvarado, has com-

fortable rooms with view, air-con, cable TV and Jacuzzi from US$46 (US$60 on Friday and Saturday). It also has a swimming pool.

Popular *Hotel Bahía* (☎ 178-21-03) covers a block on López Mateos and Costero, between Riveroll and Alvarado. Carpeted rooms with balconies cost US$39/59.

Hotel Cortez (☎ 178-23-07, López Mateos 1089) offers similar amenities. Singles and doubles with air-con, TV, pool access and gym cost US$46; it often fills up early.

Top End *Hotel Casa del Sol* (☎ 178-15-70, López Mateos 1001), has rooms with air-con, TV and pool access for US$53/58. Conveniently central *Hotel Santo Tomás* (☎ 174-03-01, fax 178-15-04, ☎ 800-303-2684 in the USA, Costero 609), between Miramar and Macheros, charges around US$60 on weekdays. Across from the Villa Fontana, *Hotel El Cid* (☎ 178-24-01, fax 78-36-71, López Mateos 993) offers rooms from US$65/90. It has a swimming pool, an outstanding restaurant and a disco.

Places to Eat

At the seafood market on the malecón sidewalk running parallel to Boulevard Costero near the sport-fishing piers, try the deep-fried fish or shrimp tacos. *Plaza del Marisco*, on Costero across from the Pemex station, is a similar cluster of seafood taco stands of good quality.

Modest *El Corralito* (López Mateos 627) is a good breakfast spot, as is *Casa Blanca* (Ruiz 254), which also offers decent fixed-price lunches for about US$2.

Las Cazuelas, at Sanginés near the corner of Costero, has a pricey seafood menu, but *antojitos* are more reasonable. *Haliotis* (Delante 179), east of Avenida Ejercito, is a good option for seafood – the restaurant's name means abalone. *China Land* (Riveroll 1149) is one of Ensenada's most popular Chinese restaurants.

Most meals are expensive at the venerable Franco-Mexican institution *El Rey Sol* (☎ 178-17-33), at López and Blancarte, but selective diners can find good values. Cavernous *La Embotelladora Vieja* (☎ 174-08-07), at Miramar and Calle 7ª, is modernized for upscale dining with huge wine casks and other features intact. It has good food, particularly lobster; it's closed on Tuesdays. If you crave steak, try **Bronco's Steakhouse** (*López Mateos 1525*).

One of the newer restaurants in town is **La Puerta**, on Calle 4ª between Obregón and Ruiz, which serves traditional Mexican dishes; one specialty is the cactus turnover. **Kaia** (*Moctezuma 479*), a cozy, romantic place tucked away from the street, is a little pricey. **Super Natural Smoothies House**, on López Mateos next to the Hotel Cortez, offers excellent smoothies and moderately priced sandwiches.

Entertainment
Historic **Hussong's Cantina** (*Ruiz 113*) is the oldest cantina in the Californias. **Papas & Beer** (☎ 174-01-45), at López Mateos and Ruiz, is a popular restaurant and nightclub. **El Patio**, on López Mateos at Blancarte, is another popular nightspot, as is **Lobo's**, at the corner of Ruiz and Calle 2ª.

Shopping
Galería de Pérez Meillon in Local 39 at the Centro Artesanal de Ensenada, Costero 1094, sells pottery and other crafts from Baja California's Paipai, Kumiai and Cucapah peoples, as well as from Chihuahua state's Tarahumara people. Taxco silver is available at Artesanías Los Castillo (☎ 178-29-61), López Mateos 815, and next door at Casa de Plata.

Getting There & Away
Air Aerocedros (☎ 177-35-34), at Aeropuerto El Ciprés, south of town, flies to Guerrero Negro and Isla Cedros (see the Desierto Central & Llano de Magdalena section, later in this chapter).

Bus Ensenada's Central de Autobuses (☎ 178-66-80) is at Riveroll 1075. Elite (☎ 178-67-70) and Norte de Sonora (☎ 178-66-77) serve mainland Mexican destinations as far as Guadalajara (US$101, 35 hours) and Mexico City (US$116, 45 hours). Norte de Sonora's 2nd-class fares are about 15% cheaper.

ABC (☎ 178-66-80) serves La Paz (23 hours, US$65), San Felipe (3 hours, US$17), Guerrero Negro (10 hours, US$28), Tecate (1½ hours, US$8) and Tijuana (1½ hours, US$8). If going to Tijuana, make sure to specify whether you want to go to the main terminal, or to the border ('La Línea').

Autotransportes Aragón (☎ 178-85-21), Riveroll 861, goes hourly to Tijuana (US$7), from 5 am to 11pm.

AROUND ENSENADA
North of Ensenada on highway 3, some Dominican mission ruins remain at the village of **Guadalupe** (population 1220). Early 20th-century Russian immigrants settled here; their history is now documented by the Museo Comunitario de Guadalupe. The Fiesta de la Vendimia (Wine Harvest Festival) takes place in August; the Domecq and Cetto wineries are open for tours.

PARQUE NACIONAL CONSTITUCIÓN DE 1857
From Ojos Negros, east of Ensenada at Km 39 on highway 3, a 43km dirt road climbs to the Sierra de Juárez and Parque Nacional Constitución de 1857, highlight of which is the marshy, pine-sheltered **Laguna Hanson** (also known as Laguna Juárez). At 1200m, the lake abounds with migratory birds in autumn.

Camping is pleasant, but livestock have contaminated the water, so bring your own water. Firewood is scarce along the lake but abundant in the hills. Only pit toilets are available. Nearby granite outcrops offer stupendous views but tiring ascents through dense brush and massive rock falls – beware of ticks and rattlesnakes. Technical climbers will find short but challenging routes.

The park is also accessible by a steeper road east of Km 55.2, 16km southeast of the Ojos Negros junction.

PARQUE NACIONAL SIERRA SAN PEDRO MÁRTIR
In the Sierra San Pedro Mártir, east of San Telmo and west of San Felipe, Baja's most notable national park comprises 630 sq km of coniferous forests, granite peaks exceed-

ing 3000m and deep canyons cutting into its steep eastern scarp. The elusive desert bighorn sheep inhabits some remote areas of the park. Snow falls in winter, and the area also gets summer thunderstorms.

Camping areas and hiking trails are numerous, but maintenance is limited; carry a compass and a topographic map, along with cold- and wet-weather supplies, canteens and water purification tablets. Below 1800m, beware of rattlesnakes.

The **Observatorio Astronómico Nacional**, Mexico's national observatory, is 2km from the parking area at the end of the San Telmo road. It's open 11 am to 1 pm, Saturday only.

Picacho del Diablo

Few climbers who attempt Picacho del Diablo (Devil's Peak), the peninsula's highest point, reach the 3095m summit, because finding routes is so difficult. *The Baja Adventure Book*, by Walt Peterson, includes a good map and describes possible routes.

Getting There & Away

From San Telmo de Abajo, south of Km 140 on the Transpeninsular (highway 1), and about 52km south of San Vicente, a graded dirt road climbs through San Telmo to the park entrance, about 80km east. The road is passable to most passenger vehicles, but you do have to cross a river along the way, and snowmelt can raise it to hazardous levels.

MEXICALI
- **pop 505,000 ☎ 6**

European settlement came late to the Río Colorado lowlands, but the Mexicali area grew rapidly – in more than one sense – as irrigation allowed early-20th-century farmers to take advantage of rich alluvial lowlands and a long, productive agricultural season. Many visitors pass through Mexicali en route to San Felipe or mainland Mexico; the state capital does not pander to tourists, but the Centro Cívico-Comercial (Civic and Commercial Center) features government offices, a medical school, the Plaza de Toros Calafia bullring, cinemas, a bus station, hospitals and restaurants.

Orientation

Mexicali straddles the Río Nuevo, opposite Calexico, California. Most of the historic center's main streets parallel the border. Avenida Madero passes through the central business district of modest restaurants, shops, bars and budget hotels. The broad diagonal Calzada López Mateos heads southeast through newer industrial and commercial areas and becomes highway 2 (to Sonora). Many of Mexicali's hotels and restaurants are in the Zona Hotelera, which runs along Calzadas Sierra and Juárez (which becomes highway 5 to San Felipe).

Information

Tourist Offices Secture (☎ 566-11-16, 566-12-77) is open 8 am to 5 pm Monday to Friday, 10 am to 3 pm Saturday, and is located at Calzadas Montejano and Juárez in the Zona Hotelera. The private Comité de Turismo y Convenciones (Cotuco, ☎ 557-23-76), at Calzada López Mateos and Camelias, is opposite the Teatro del Estado, about 3km southeast of the border. It's open 8 am to 5 pm Monday to Friday.

Money Casas de cambio are abundant and keep long hours, while banks offer exchange services weekday mornings only. Most banks in Mexicali and Calexico have ATMs.

Post & Communications The post office, on Avenida Madero near Morelos, is open 8 am to 6.30 pm Monday to Friday, 8 am to 3 pm Saturday, 9 am to 1 pm Sunday. Both pay phones and *cabinas* (call offices; mostly in pharmacies but also in other small businesses) are common.

Bookstores Librería Universitaria, near the Universidad Autónoma on Calzada Juárez, has a good selection of books on Mexican history, archaeology, anthropology and literature. It also carries the Guías Urbanas series of Mexican city maps.

Medical Services The Hospital Civil (☎ 556-11-28), at Calle del Hospital and Avenida Libertad, is near the Centro Cívico-Comercial. Closer to the border are many

BAJA CALIFORNIA

MEXICALI

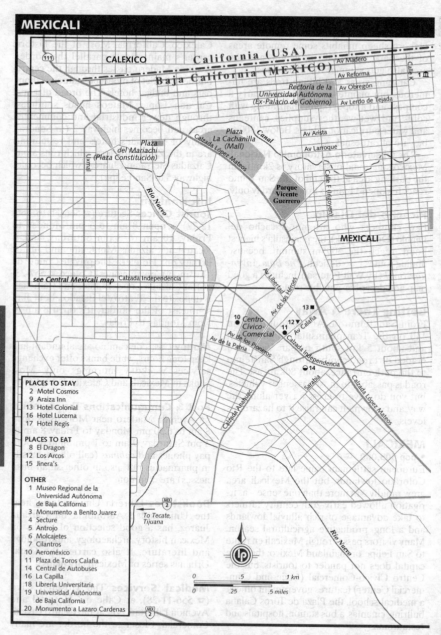

PLACES TO STAY
2　Motel Cosmos
9　Araiza Inn
13　Hotel Colonial
16　Hotel Lucerna
17　Hotel Regis

PLACES TO EAT
8　El Dragon
12　Los Arcos
15　Jinera's

OTHER
1　Museo Regional de la
　　Universidad Autónoma
　　de Baja California
3　Monumento a Benito Juarez
4　Secture
5　Antrojo
6　Molcajetes
7　Cilantros
10　Aeroméxico
11　Plaza de Toros Calafia
14　Central de Autobuses
16　La Capilla
18　Librería Universitaria
19　Universidad Autónoma
　　de Baja California
20　Monumento a Lazaro Cardenas

CALEXICO
California (USA)
Baja California (MEXICO)

Av Madero
Av Reforma
Av Obregón
Av Lerdo de Tejada

Rectoría de la
Universidad Autónoma
(Ex-Palacio de Gobierno)

Plaza
del Mariachi
(Plaza Constitución)

Plaza
La Cachanilla
(Mall)

Calzada López Mateos

Canal

Av Arista
Av Larroque

Parque
Vicente
Guerrero

Río Nuevo

Uxmal

Calle F (Ingoyen)

Calle K

MEXICALI

see Central Mexicali map　Calzada Independencia

Av Libertad

Av de los Héroes

Centro
Cívico-
Comercial

Av de los Pioneros
Av de la Patria

Av Calafia

Calzada Independencia

Calzada Ahtahuac

Sarabia

Calzada López Mateos

To Tecate,
Tijuana

MEX 2

Río Nuevo

MEX 2

0　　　.5　　　1 km
0　.25　.5 miles

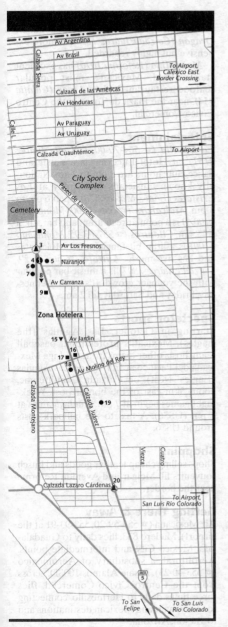

clinics, laboratories and hospitals. Locally trained dentists offer quality work at very good prices.

Things to See & Do

The country's largest Chinatown, **La Chinesca**, is south of Calzada López Mateos, centered around Avenida Juárez and Altamirano; the nearby Plaza del Mariachi is a good place to hear banda groups rehearse in the late afternoon.

Most of Mexicali's historic buildings are northeast of López Mateos. The **Catedral de la Virgen de Guadalupe**, at Reforma and Morelos, is the city's major religious landmark. Now the rectory of the Universidad Autónoma, the former **Palacio de Gobierno** (built between 1919 and 1922) interrupts Avenida Obregón just east of Calle E. To the north, at Reforma and Calle F, the ex-headquarters of the **Colorado River Land Company** dates from 1924. At Zaragoza and Calle E, two blocks southwest of the rectory, the former brewery **Cervecería Mexicali** (opened in 1923) now sits vacant.

The modest eight-room **Museo Regional de la Universidad Autónoma de Baja California** (☎ 552-57-15), at Reforma and Calle L, features exhibits on geology, paleontology, human evolution, colonial history and photography. It's open 9 am to 3 pm Monday to Friday, 9 am to 6 pm Saturday and Sunday (free).

The ultramodern **Teatro del Estado** (State Theater, ☎ 554-64-18), on López Mateos just north of Compresora, seats 1100. The Instituto de Cultura de Baja California presents film cycles at the Teatro del Estado's Café Literario.

Special Events

From mid-October to early November, the **Fiesta del Sol** (Festival of the Sun) commemorates the city's founding in 1903. Events include concerts, art exhibits, a crafts exposition, theatrical performances and parades. It also features local industrial and agricultural products.

Places to Stay

Budget Central Mexicali's best budget option is family-oriented *Hotel México*

(☎ 554-06-69, *Lerdo de Tejada 476*), between Altamirano and Morelos, with singles/doubles at US$23/27; air-con, TV, private bath and parking are available.

Mid-Range The respectable *Hotel Plaza* (☎ 552-97-57, *Madero 366*) charges US$31/39. *Hotel Casa Grande* (☎ 553-57-71, *Colón 612*) has air-con, TV and a swimming pool for US$32/36. Convenient to the border, the landmark *Hotel del Norte* (☎ 552-81-01, *Melgar 205*) has 52 rooms, some with color TV and air-con, for US$34/42 including breakfast.

In the Zona Hotelera, *Hotel Regis* (☎ 566-34-35, *Calzada Juárez 2150*), with air-con, TV, phone and off-street parking for US$34/47, is a good deal. Popular *Motel Cosmos* (☎ 568-11-55, *Sierra 1493*) offers TV, phone, air-con and parking for US$48/54; make reservations because it fills up early.

Top End Highly regarded *Hotel Colonial* (☎ 556-53-12, *López Mateos 1048*) charges US$92, single or double.

In the Zona Hotelera, popular *Hotel Lucerna* (☎ 564-70-00, *Calzada Juárez 2151*), about 5km from downtown, has rooms for US$106/117. *Araiza Inn* (☎ 566-13-00, *Juárez 2220*) is a deluxe hotel with rooms for US$89/95.

Places to Eat
One good, inexpensive breakfast choice is *Petunia 2* (*Avenida Madero 436*), between Altamirano and Morelos. Part of Hotel del Norte, *Restaurant del Norte* is a coffee shop offering mediocre but cheap specials. *El Sarape* (*Bravo 140*) is a raucous spot with live music.

For excellent Mexican food, try *Jinera's* (*Calzada Juárez 1342*), in the Zona Hotelera. A bit pricier, *La Villa del Seri*, (☎ 553-55-03), at Reforma and Calle D, specializes in Sonoran beef but also has excellent seafood and antojitos. *Cenaduría Selecta* (*Arista 1510*), at Calle G, is an institution, specializing in antojitos.

Opened in 1928, the inexpensive *Alley 19* (*Avenida Juárez 8*), near Azueta, is Mexicali's oldest continuously operating Chinese restaurant. Housed in a huge pagoda, *El Dragón* (*Calzada Juárez 1830*) is more expensive but highly regarded.

Mandolino (*Reforma 1070*) has excellent Italian food. Mexicali's most popular seafood restaurant is *Los Arcos* (*Calafia 454*), near the Plaza de Toros in the Centro Cívico-Comercial.

Entertainment
La Capilla (☎ 564-70-00, *Calzada Juárez 2151*), at Hotel Lucerna, is a music and dance club; hours are 8 pm to 2 am. Nationally known musicians often play at *Los Cristales* (*López Mateos 570*), open 6 pm to 3 am. *Molcajetes* (☎ 556-07-00, *Montejano 1100A*) is a popular restaurant and bar, open till 2 am. *Cilantros* (☎ 557-03-95, *Montejano 1100*) is a little bit fancier than Molcajetes and has live music. *Antrojo* (☎ 568-21-29, *Calzada Juárez 1807*) is a music bar popular with the younger crowd. It's open Wednesday, Friday and Saturday till 2 am.

Spectator Sports
Starting in October, Las Águilas (the Eagles), Mexicali's professional baseball team, hosts other teams from the Liga Mexicana del Pacífico at El Nido de Las Águilas (Eagles' Nest), on Calzada Cuauhtémoc, about 5km east of the border post. Weeknight games begin at 7 pm, Sunday games at 1 pm (US$6). A taxi to the ballpark costs around US$6.

Shopping
Shops selling cheap leather goods and kitsch souvenirs fill Melgar and Avenida Reforma near the border.

Getting There & Away
Air Mexicana (☎ 553-59-20, 552-93-91 at the airport), Madero 833, flies daily to Guadalajara, Mexico City and intermediate points. Aerolitoral, a subsidiary of Aeroméxico (☎ 553-40-23), Pasaje Alamos 1008D, across from the Centro Cívico-Comercial, flies three times daily to Hermosillo, connecting to many mainland Mexican destinations and to Tucson, Arizona.

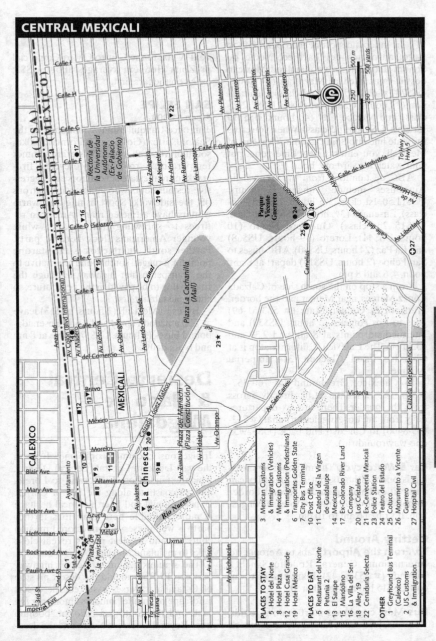

CENTRAL MEXICALI

PLACES TO STAY
5 Hotel del Norte
8 Hotel Plaza
12 Hotel Casa Grande
19 Hotel México

PLACES TO EAT
9 Restaurant del Norte
9 Petunia 2
13 El Sarape
15 Mandolino
16 La Villa del Seri
18 Alley 19
22 Cenaduría Selecta

OTHER
1 Greyhound Bus Terminal
  (Calexico)
2 US Customs
  & Immigration
3 Mexican Customs
  & Immigration (Vehicles)
4 Mexican Customs
  & Immigration (Pedestrians)
6 Transportes Golden State
7 City Bus Terminal
10 Post Office
11 Catedral de la Virgen
   de Guadalupe
14 Mexicana
17 Ex-Colorado River Land
   Company
20 Los Cristales
21 Ex-Cervecería Mexicali
23 Police Station
24 Teatro del Estado
25 Cotuco
26 Monumento a Vicente
   Guerrero
27 Hospital Civil

Bus Long-distance bus companies leave from the Central de Autobuses (☎ 557-24-51), on Independencia near López Mateos. Autotransportes del Pacífico, Norte de Sonora and Elite serve mainland Mexican destinations such as Mazatlán (24 hours, US$78 1st-class, US$65 2nd-class), Guadalajara (33 hours, US$97 1st-class, US$87 2nd-class) and Mexico City (40 hours, US$119 1st-class, US$106 2nd-class). When you cross the state line into Sonora, some 70km east of Mexicali, you enter a new time zone; put your watch forward one hour.

ABC destinations from the Central de Autobuses include Tijuana (2 hours, US$11.50 1st-class; 2½ hours, US$10 2nd-class), Ensenada (3½ hours, US$17 1st-class, US$15 2nd-class), Guerrero Negro (10 hours, US$44), Loreto (19 hours, US$68) and La Paz (24 hours, US$80). ABC buses to San Felipe (2 hours, US$13) depart at 8 am, noon, 4, 6 and 8 pm.

From a stop on the south side of Calzada López Mateos, near Melgar and the border, Transportes Golden State (☎ 553-61-69) goes to Los Angeles (5 hours, US$30) and intermediate points at 8 am and 2.30 and 10.30 pm. The Calexico, California, stop is at Church's Fried Chicken, 344 Imperial Avenue.

In Calexico, Greyhound (☎ 760-357-1895), 121 East First St, is directly across from the border. There are six departures daily from the Los Angeles terminal (☎ 213-629-8400) to Calexico and back (US$29/51 one-way/roundtrip).

Car & Motorcycle The main border crossing is open 24 hours, but US and Mexican authorities have opened a second border complex east of downtown to ease congestion. It's open 6 am to 10 pm.

Getting Around

To/From the Airport Cabs to Aeropuerto Internacional General Rodolfo Sánchez Taboada (☎ 553-67-42), 12km east of town, cost US$15 but may be shared.

Bus Most city buses start from Avenida Reforma, just west of López Mateos; check the placard for the destination. Local fares are about US$0.30.

Taxi A taxi to the Centro Cívico-Comercial or Zona Hotelera averages about US$5; agree on the fare first.

SAN FELIPE
* pop 11,300

This once-tranquil fishing community on the Sea of Cortez (Golfo de California), 200km south of Mexicali, suffers blistering summer temperatures, roaring motorcycles, firecrackers, real-estate speculators and aggressive restaurateurs who almost yank patrons off the sidewalk. Sport fishing and warm winters have attracted many American retirees to sprawling trailer parks, while younger Americans flock here to party. Farther south, **Puertecitos** is the starting point for a rugged southbound alternative to the Transpeninsular highway, although the road is due to be paved in the near future, so check passability first.

Buses to Mexicali (2 hours, US$13) leave at 7.30 am, noon and 4 and 8 pm; Ensenada-bound buses (3 hours, US$17) leave at 8 am and 6 pm daily.

Desierto Central & Llano de Magdalena

Indigenous Cochimí people once foraged the vast Desierto Central (Central Desert), which extends from El Rosario to Loreto, and its coastline along the Sea of Cortez. Baja's colonial and later historical heritage is more palpable here than it is farther north – well-preserved or restored mission churches and modest plazas reveal close links to mainland Mexico.

The sinuous 125km stretch of highway between El Rosario and the desert pit stop of Cataviña traverses a surrealistic desert landscape of granite boulders among *cardón* cacti and the contorted *cirio*, or 'boojum tree.' Beyond Guerrero Negro and the desolate Desierto de Vizcaíno, the oasis of San Ignacio augurs the semitropical Gulf Coast between Mulegé and Cabo San Lucas. Paralleling the gulf, the Sierra de la Giganta divides the region into an eastern subtropical zone and a western zone of elevated plateaus and dry lowlands. South of Loreto, the Transpeninsular highway turns west to the Llano de Magdalena (Magdalena Plain), a rich farming zone, which also offers fishing, whale-watching, surfing and windsurfing.

South of the 28th parallel, the border between the states of Baja California and Baja California Sur, the hour changes; Pacific time (to the north) is an hour behind Mountain time (to the south).

GUERRERO NEGRO
* **pop 10,200** ☎ **1**

The town of Guerrero Negro is renowned for Laguna Ojo de Liebre (known in English as Scammon's Lagoon), which annually becomes the mating and breeding ground of California gray whales. Each year, the whales migrate 9660km (6000 miles) from the Bering Sea to the lagoon, where they stay from early January through March. The lagoon is south of the town's evaporative saltworks (the largest of its kind in the world), about 24km from the junction of highway 1.

The town comprises two distinct sectors: a disorderly strip along Boulevard Zapata, west of the Transpeninsular, and an orderly company town farther west run by Exportadora de Sal (ESSA). Nearly all accommodations, restaurants and other services are along Boulevard Zapata.

There's a Banamex with an ATM at the far end of the commercial district on Boulevard Zapata, just at the start of the company town.

Places to Stay

The whale-watching season can strain local accommodations; reservations are advisable from January to March.

Malarrimo Trailer Park (☎ 157-01-00), at the eastern entrance to town, charges US$5 (tents) and US$10 (RVs). Hot water is plentiful and toilets are clean, but check electri-

cal outlets. *Cabañas Don Miguelito*, part of the Malarrimo complex, has pleasant single/double rooms for US$22/29. *Motel Las Ballenas* (☎ 157-01-16) has hot water and color TV in every room, for US$15/17. It's just north of *Hotel El Morro* (☎ 157-04-14), on the north side of Boulevard Zapata, which has comfortable but basic rooms for US$22/30.

Places to Eat

Guerrero Negro's many taco stands keep erratic hours. *Cocina Económica Letty*, a good breakfast choice on the south side of Boulevard Zapata, has moderately priced antojitos and seafood. Specializing in seafood, both as antojitos and as sophisticated international dishes, *Malarrimo* (see Places to Stay, above) is not cheap, but portions are generous.

Getting There & Away

Air The Aeroméxico subsidiary Aerolitoral (☎ 157-17-33), on the north side of Boulevard Zapata near the Pemex station, flies Monday, Wednesday and Friday to Hermosillo (US$216), connecting to mainland Mexican cities and Phoenix, Arizona. It leaves from the new airfield 2km north of the state border, just west of the Transpeninsular highway.

Aerocedros (☎ 157-16-26), on the south side of Boulevard Zapata, flies to Isla Cedros (US$53) and Ensenada (US$160).

Bus The bus station is on the south side of Boulevard Zapata. Northbound services include Ensenada (10 hours, US$28) and Tijuana (13 hours, US$34); southbound services include Mulegé (4 hours, US$15), Loreto (6 hours, US$23) and La Paz (11 hours, US$38).

RESERVA DE LA BIÓSFERA EL VIZCAÍNO

Sprawling from Laguna San Ignacio, Guerrero Negro and Isla Cedros across to the Sea of Cortez, this 25,000-sq-km reserve is Latin America's largest single protected area and includes the major gray whale calving areas of Laguna San Ignacio and

Laguna Ojo de Liebre. Guerrero Negro travel agencies arrange whale-watching trips for about US$40.

A bit farther south, *pangueros* (boatmen) from Ejido Benito Juárez take visitors for whale-watching excursions on Laguna Ojo de Liebre's shallow waters for about US$15 (US$10 for children).

About 8km south of Guerrero Negro, an excellent graded road leads 25km west to Ojo de Liebre, where the US$3 parking fee includes the right to camp; the *ejido* (communal landholding) runs a simple but very good restaurant.

Whales are not usually present until after January 1.

ISLA CEDROS
• **pop 1470**

Isla Cedros is not a touristy destination – it has few services, and you can't even get a margarita – but this mountainous northward extension of Península Vizcaíno supports unusual flora, marine mammals such as elephant seals and sea lions, and the endangered Cedros mule deer. The hiking is good here, but water is scarce.

Most of the island's inhabitants live in the port of Cedros on the eastern shore, but a fair number live at Punta Morro Redondo, the transshipment point for salt barged over from Guerrero Negro.

Places to Stay & Eat
Manuel Aguilar maintains a basic guesthouse, with rooms for US$10. *La Paceñita* has good, reasonably priced antojitos, fish and shrimp.

Getting There & Away
Aerocedros (☎ 157-16-26 in Guerrero Negro) flies Tuesday and Friday to and from Guerrero Negro (US$53) and Ensenada (US$110). Flights leave Ensenada at 9.30 am and stop in Guerrero Negro before arriving at Isla Cedros. Flights return to Ensenada by the same route, leaving the island at 12.30 pm.

Taxis charge about US$5 per person from Cedros port to the airfield at Punta Morro Redondo, 8km south of town.

SAN IGNACIO
• **pop 760** • **elev 200m** ☎ changing

Jesuits located Misión San Ignacio de Kadakaamán in this soothing oasis in 1728, planting dense groves of date palms and citrus trees, but it was Dominicans who supervised construction of the striking church (finished in 1786) that still dominates the cool, laurel-shaded plaza. With lava-block walls nearly 1.2m thick and surrounded by bougainvillea, this is one of Baja's most beautiful churches.

The lush village of San Ignacio proper is about 1.6km south of the Transpeninsular and is a welcome sight after the scrub brush and dense cacti of the Desierto de Vizcaíno. Most services are around the plaza, including public telephones, but there is no bank.

In June 2000, the telephone area code was due to change to ☎ 1 from 115, with the digits 15 added to the start of every local number (for example, the number 7-65-43 would become 157-65-43).

Places to Stay & Eat
Just south of Hotel La Pinta, on the west side of the road into town, palm-shaded *El Padrino RV Park* (☎ 4-00-89) has around 50 sites, 16 with full hookups. Fees are US$7 for camping, US$10 for large RVs. *Rice & Beans RV Park* (☎ 4-02-83), on the road to San Lino, just off the Transpeninsular west of town, charges US$10 for full hookup.

Motel La Posada (☎ 4-03-13, *Carranza 22*), southeast of the plaza, has spartan doubles with hot showers for about US$20. It's a bit difficult to find: take Avenida Hidalgo east from the plaza, turn right at Callejón Ciprés, then turn left onto Venustiano Carranza. The pseudocolonial *Hotel La Pinta* (☎/fax 4-03-00), on the main road just before entering San Ignacio, appeals to more affluent travelers, with singles and doubles at US$65.

Specializing in local beef, Hotel La Pinta's restaurant serves typical antojitos at upscale prices. *Tota*, a block west of Motel La

Posada, serves good, reasonably priced anto-jitos and seafood dishes. *Flojos*, at El Padrino RV Park, prepares good, fresh seafood; its lobster is cheaper than Tota's. The *restaurant* at Rice & Beans RV Park serves excellent shrimp burritos.

Getting There & Away

At least five buses daily in each direction pick up passengers at the San Lino junction, just outside of town on the Transpeninsular.

AROUND SAN IGNACIO
San Francisco de la Sierra

From Km 118 on the Transpeninsular, 43km northwest of San Ignacio, a graded but poorly consolidated road climbs east to San Francisco de la Sierra, gateway to the Desierto Central's most spectacular pre-Columbian rock art. **Cueva del Ratón**, about 2.5km before San Francisco, is the most accessible site, but independent visitors *must* obtain permission from the Instituto Nacional de Antropología y Historia (INAH) office in San Ignacio to visit it, and a local guide must open the locked gate. The INAH office (☎ 4-02-22) is open 8 am to 3 pm Monday through Saturday. For US$25 per group, Oscar Fischer, at Motel La Posada in San Ignacio, arranges day trips to Cueva del Ratón, which has representations of *monos* (human figures), *borregos* (bighorn sheep) and deer.

In the dramatic Cañón San Pablo, **Cueva Pintada**, **Cueva de las Flechas** and other sites are better preserved. Cueva Pintada's rock overhang is the most impressive. The

The Rock Art of the Desierto Central

When Jesuit missionaries inquired as to who created the giant rock paintings of San Francisco de la Sierra and about the meaning of those paintings, the Cochimí people responded with a bewilderment that was, in all likelihood, utterly feigned. The Cochimí claimed ignorance of both symbols and techniques, but it was not unusual, when missionaries came calling, to deny knowledge of the profound religious beliefs which those missionaries wanted to eradicate.

At sites such as Cueva Pintada, Cochimí painters and their predecessors decorated high rock overhangs with vivid red and black representations of human figures, bighorn sheep, pumas and deer, as well as of more abstract designs. It is speculated that the painters built scaffolds of palm logs to reach the ceilings. Postcontact motifs include Christian crosses, but these are few and small in contrast to the dazzling pre-Hispanic figures surrounding them.

Cueva de las Flechas, across Cañón San Pablo, has similar paintings, but the uncommon feature of arrows through some of the figures is the subject of serious speculation. One interpretation is that these paintings depict a period of warfare. Similar opinions suggest that they record a raid or an instance of trespass on tribal territory or perhaps constitute a warning against such trespass. One researcher, however, has hypothesized that the arrows represent a shaman's metaphor for death in the course of a vision quest; if that is the case, it is no wonder that the Cochimí would claim ignorance of the paintings and their significance in the face of a missionary presence unrelentingly hostile to such beliefs.

Such speculation is impossible to prove since the Cochimí no longer exist, but in the mid-1990s the Instituto Nacional de Antropología y Historia (INAH) undertook the largest systematic archaeological survey of a hunter-gatherer people yet attempted in Mexico. Results revealed that, besides well-known features such as rock art sites and grinding stones, the Cochimí left evidence of permanent dwellings. In recognition of its cultural importance, San Francisco de la Sierra has been declared a UNESCO World Heritage Site. It is also part of the Reserva de la Biosfera El Vizcaíno.

The sierra is an INAH-protected archaeological zone, which means that foreigners need entry permits to conduct research – not everyone has been scrupulous in that regard. INAH has instituted regulations for tourists and imposes a modest admission fee to guarantee basic infrastructure.

No Salt Por Favor

Despite having survived and recovered from the brutality of commercial whaling, the California gray whale faces contemporary challenges in Baja California. Recently it was an innocent bystander in a tug-of-war between Mexican government agencies with dramatically different visions of Laguna San Ignacio.

The point of contention was a 520-sq-km saltworks, which Exportadora de Sal (ESSA) wanted to establish at the 470-sq-km lagoon. (Those statistics deceptively understate the scale of the project, since ancillary works would have directly affected 2100 sq km and indirectly impacted up to 15,000 sq km of El Vizcaíno Biosphere Reserve.) ESSA, a Guerrero Negro-based and state-owned enterprise with a large minority holding (49%) by the Japanese multinational Mitsubishi Corporation, proposed a 1.6km canal to pump water continuously from Laguna San Ignacio to a 300-sq-km system of dikes and ponds. A 25km conveyor belt would have shifted the salt to a 2km pier near Punta Abreojos, northwest of the lagoon. Projected production was 7 million tons of salt yearly, a figure that would have made ESSA the world's largest salt producer.

Mexico's powerful Secretaría de Comercio y Fomento Industrial (SECOFI, Secretariat of Commerce and Industrial Development) backed the project, but the resolute Instituto Nacional de Ecología (INE, National Ecology Institute) vigorously objected to the project's potential impact on the gray whale, the endangered peninsular pronghorn antelope and the mangrove wetlands that serve as incubators for fish and shellfish. The impact on the whales, though, was the biggest, literally and figuratively, and most controversial issue.

One problem is that nobody really knows how much disruption the whales can tolerate during courtship and during the birth and raising of their young. ESSA claims that whale numbers have doubled in its three decades of operations at Laguna Ojo de Liebre, but conservationists are skeptical of the company's data. In addi-

tion, less than half of the narrower and shallower Laguna San Ignacio is suitable for whales. It might also suffer more from turbulence caused by pumping, which could reduce salinity and temperature in areas frequented by newborn calves. While gray whales have adapted to some human activities at Ojo de Liebre, studies have shown that noises such as oil drilling seriously disturb the big creatures.

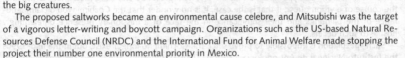

The proposed saltworks became an environmental cause celebre, and Mitsubishi was the target of a vigorous letter-writing and boycott campaign. Organizations such as the US-based Natural Resources Defense Council (NRDC) and the International Fund for Animal Welfare made stopping the project their number one environmental priority in Mexico.

In March 2000, environmentalists won a major victory when President Ernesto Zedillo unexpectedly announced that the Mexican government was canceling plans for the project. Though the government and Mitsubishi claimed that an environmental impact study had found that the plant would not harm the whales, they announced that the proposal was being halted to preserve the entire Vizcaíno Biosphere Reserve. Speaking at a meeting on national environmental policy, President Zedillo said, 'We're dealing with a unique place in the world both for the species that inhabit it and for its natural beauty, which we should preserve.'

awesome mule-back descent of Cañón San Pablo requires at least two days, preferably three. Visitors must refrain from touching the paintings, smoking at sites and employing flash photography (400 ASA film suffices even in dim light).

Entrance to Cueva del Ratón requires a modest tip to the guide. Visitors to Cañón San Pablo must hire a guide with mule through INAH for US$12 per day, plus a mule for each person for US$7 per day and additional pack animals for supplies (US$6 per day each). You must also feed the guide. The best season for visiting is early spring, when the days are fairly long but temperatures are not yet unpleasantly hot. Backpacking is permitted, but you must still hire a guide and mule.

Laguna San Ignacio
Along with Laguna Ojo de Liebre and Bahía Magdalena, Laguna San Ignacio is one of the Pacific coast's major winter whale-watching sites, with three-hour excursions costing around US$30 per person. Kuyima (☎ 4-00-70), a cooperative based at the east end of the plaza in San Ignacio, can arrange transport and accommodations, but most vehicles can make the 61km drive to La Fridera in about two hours.

In other seasons the area offers outstanding bird-watching in the stunted mangroves and at Islas El Pelícano, where ospreys and cormorants nest (landing on the island is prohibited). Laguna San Ignacio has attracted controversy because ESSA plans to develop an even larger saltworks here than at Guerrero Negro. (See 'No Salt, Por Favor.')

SANTA ROSALÍA
- pop 10,500 ☎ changing

Imported timber frames the clapboard houses lining the main streets of Santa Rosalía, a copper town built on the Sea of Cortez coast by the French-owned Compañía del Boleo in the 1880s. The French also assembled a prefabricated church here that was designed by Alexandre Gustave Eiffel (the same!) for Paris' 1889 World's Fair. And they bequeathed a bakery that sells Baja's best baguettes.

In June 2000, the telephone area code was due to change to ☎ 1 from 115, with the digits 15 added to the start of every local number (for example, the number 7-65-43 would become 157-65-43).

Orientation & Information
Central Santa Rosalía nestles in the canyon of its namesake arroyo, west of the Transpeninsular, but French administrators built their houses on the northern Mesa Francia, now home to municipal authorities and the historic Hotel Francés. Santa Rosalía's narrow *avenidas* run east-west, while its short *calles* run north-south; one-way traffic is the rule. Plaza Benito Juárez, four blocks west of the highway, is the town center.

Travelers bound for Mulegé, which has no banks, should change US cash or traveler's checks here, where Banamex also has an ATM.

The post office is at Avenida Constitución and Calle 2. Hotel del Real, on the exit road from town, has long-distance cabinas.

Iglesia Santa Bárbara
Designed and erected in Paris, disassembled and stored in Brussels, intended for West Africa, Gustave Eiffel's prefab church was finally shipped here when a Compañía del Boleo director chanced upon it 1895. It was reassembled by 1897. It has attractive stained-glass windows.

Places to Stay & Eat
Just south of town at the Km 192 of the Transpeninsular, *Las Palmas RV Park* (☎ 2-01-09) has grassy sites with hot showers and clean toilets and laundry for US$7 (tents), US$10 (RVs). The family-run *Motel San Victor* (☎ 2-01-16, Avenida Progreso 32) has a dozen tidy rooms with ceiling fans, air-con and tiled baths for US$10 single or double. Historic *Hotel Francés* (☎ 2-20-52), on Mesa Francia, offers an atmospheric bar, views of the rusting copper works, air-con and a small swimming pool; singles/doubles are US$27/32.

Just up the hill is *Hotel El Morro* (☎ 2-04-14), 1.5km south of town. With a small pool, balconies overlooking the water and air-con in each room, these are Santa Rosalía's most upscale accommodations at US$30/35.

Taco stands are numerous along Avenida Obregón, while *Cenaduría Gaby*, on Calle 5 just north of Obregón, serves reasonably priced antojitos. South of downtown, the waterfront *Restaurant Selene* serves sumptuous though pricey seafood.

Panadería El Boleo, on Obregón between Calles 3 and 4, is an obligatory stop for Mexican and French-style baked goods. Baguettes usually sell out early.

Getting There & Away

Bus At least six buses daily in each direction stop at the terminal, which is south of town on the west side of the Transpeninsular, about 250m south of the ferry terminal. Northbound destinations include San Ignacio (1½ hours, US$4.50), Guerrero Negro (3 hours, US$11), Ensenada (12 hours, US$36.50) and Tijuana (14 hours, US$42); southbound fares include Mulegé (1½ hours, US$4), Loreto (3 hours, US$10), Ciudad Constitución (5 hours, US$16) and La Paz (8 hours, US$23).

Boat Sematur passenger/auto ferries sail to Guaymas on Tuesday and Friday at 11 pm, arriving at 8 am; the return ferry to Santa Rosalía sails at 9 am Tuesday and Friday, arriving at 3 pm. Strong winter winds may cause delays.

Ticket windows at the terminal (☎ 2-00-13), on the highway, are open 8 am to 1 pm and 3 to 6 pm Tuesday and Friday, 6 to 7.30 am Sunday and Wednesday, 8 am to 3 pm Thursday and Saturday. See the accompanying chart for vehicle fares. Make reservations at least three days in advance and, even if you have reservations, arrive early at the ticket office. Passenger fares are US$15. Vehicle rates vary with vehicle length:

vehicle	length	rate
Car	Up to 5m	US$169
	5.01 to 6.5m	US$219
Car with Trailer	Up to 9m	US$304
	9.01m to 17m	US$572
Motorcycle		US$43

Before shipping any vehicle to the mainland, officials require a vehicle permit (see the Car & Motorcycle section of the Getting There & Away chapter for details on bringing a car into Mexico). Vehicle permits are no longer obtainable in Santa Rosalía, so get them in Tijuana, Ensenada, Mexicali or La Paz.

MULEGÉ

• pop 3170 ☎ changing

Beyond Santa Rosalía, the Transpeninsular hugs the eastern scarp of the Sierra de la Giganta before winding through the Sierra Azteca and dropping into the subtropical oasis of Mulegé, a popular divers' destination. The village of Mulegé straddles the palm-lined Arroyo de Santa Rosalía (Río Mulegé), 3km inland from the gulf.

Information

Most services, including the post office, are on or near Jardín Corona, the town plaza. Mulegé has no bank, but merchants change cash dollars or accept them for payment. There are a number of pay phones located on the plaza.

In June 2000, the telephone area code was due to change to ☎ 1 from 115, with the digits 15 added to the start of every local number (for example, the number 7-65-43 would become 157-65-43).

Things to See & Do

Across the highway, near the south bank of the arroyo, the hilltop **Misión Santa Rosalía de Mulegé** was founded in 1705, completed in 1766, and abandoned in 1828. A short path climbs to a scenic overlook of the palm-lined arroyo.

Desperately needing major restoration, the former territorial prison is now the **Museo Mulegé**, overlooking the town. Its eclectic artifacts include cotton gins, antique diving equipment and firearms. Hours are 9 am to 2 pm (free).

Diving

Cortez Divers (formerly Mulegé Divers, ☎ 3-05-00) at Moctezuma 75A, owned by a

Swiss couple, offers diving instruction and excursions, snorkel equipment rental and bike rental. It's open 10 am to 1 pm and 4 to 7 pm, Monday to Saturday.

Places to Stay

Friendly **Huerta Saucedo RV Park** (☎ 3-03-00), south of town on the gulf side of the highway, rents 35 RV spaces for about US$15 to US$18 (US$4 for tent camping). Also available are cabins on the river ranging from US$65 to US$110; canoe and paddleboat rentals are available as well.

The **Canett Casa de Huéspedes** (☎ 3-02-72), on Madero east of Jardín Corona, isn't bad for US$7, but the church bells next door start ringing at 6 am. **Casa de Huéspedes Manuelita** (☎ 3-01-75), on Moctezuma, is comparable.

Poet Alán Gorosave once inhabited shady **Hotel Las Casitas** (☎ 3-00-19, Madero 50) near Martínez, where all singles/doubles have hot showers and air-con for US$20/23. **Hotel Hacienda** (☎ 3-00-21, Madero 3), an ongoing construction project, has rooms with twin beds, fridge, air-con and hot shower for US$35, and there's a small pool.

Places to Eat

Asadero Ramon (formerly Dany's), at Madero and Romerio Rubio, offers the closest the humble taco will ever get to haute cuisine, with various fillings and a cornucopia of tasty condiments at reasonable prices. Try **Las Casitas**, in its namesake hotel, for antojitos and a few seafood dishes, or **Los Equipales**, on Moctezuma just west of Zaragoza, for outstanding meals that are a good value for the money. **El Candil**, on Zaragoza near the plaza, has filling meat and seafood dishes at moderate prices; its bar is a popular meeting place.

Getting There & Away

Half a dozen buses pass daily in each direction at the Y-junction ('La Y Griega') on the Transpeninsular at the western edge of town.

LORETO
• pop 8300 ☎ changing

In 1697 Jesuit Juan María Salvatierra established the Californias' first permanent Euro-
pean settlement at this modest port of cobbled streets some 135km south of Mulegé, between the Transpeninsular and the gulf. Though aggressive tourist development in nearby Nopoló has threatened to siphon off Loreto's water or turn it into Cabo San Lucas Norte, local pressure recently forced Mexico's federal government to establish Parque Marino Nacional Bahía de Loreto, protecting 2065 sq km of shoreline, ocean and offshore islands. Fishing, diving, snorkeling and kayaking are popular in this area.

In June 2000, the telephone area code was due to change to ☎ 1 from 113, with the digits 13 added to the start of every local number (for example, the number 7-65-43 would become 137-65-43).

Orientation

Loreto has an irregular street plan. Most hotels and services are near the landmark mission church on Salvatierra, while the attractive malecón (waterfront boulevard) is ideal for evening strolls. The Plaza Cívica is just north of Salvatierra, between Madero and Davis.

Information

Tourist Offices Loreto's Departamento de Turismo Municipal (☎ 5-05-73), on the west side of the Plaza Cívica, is open 8.30 am to 3 pm Monday to Friday. Helpful English-speaking staff is usually on duty, and it has a good selection of brochures and flyers.

Money Bancomer, at Salvatierra and Madero, has an ATM and changes US cash and traveler's checks Monday to Friday mornings but sometimes runs short of cash.

Post & Communications The post office is on Deportiva, north of Salvatierra; it's open 8 am to 3 pm. Several businesses along Salvatierra have long-distance cabinas, but they charge for international collect calls.

The Internet Café (☎ 5-08-02), on Salvatierra between Ayuntamiento and Independencia, is on the 2nd floor of La Giganta real

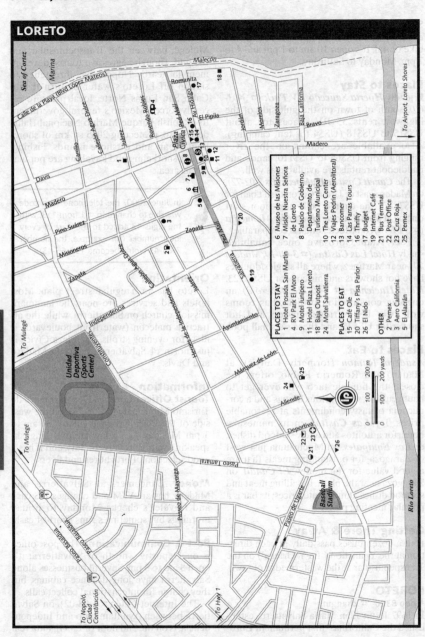

LORETO

PLACES TO STAY
1 Hotel Posada San Martín
4 RV Park El Moro
9 Motel Junípero
11 Hotel Plaza Loreto
24 Motel Salvatierra

PLACES TO EAT
15 Café Ole
20 Tiffany's Pisa Parlor
26 El Nido

OTHER
2 Pemex
3 Aero California
5 El Alacrán
6 Museo de las Misiones
7 Misión Nuestra Señora de Loreto
8 Palacio de Gobierno, Departamento de Turismo Municipal
10 The Loreto Center
12 Viajes Pedrín (Aerolitoral)
13 Bancomer
14 Las Parras Tours
16 Thrifty
17 Budget
18 Baja Outpost
19 Internet Café
21 Bus Terminal
22 Post Office
23 Cruz Roja
25 Pemex

estate agency. Computers are available at US$3 for each half hour.

Things to See & Do

Above the entrance to **Misión Nuestra Señora de Loreto**, the inscription 'Cabeza y Madre de Las Misiones de Baja y Alta California' (Head and Mother of the Missions of Lower and Upper California) aptly describes the mission's role in the history of the Californias.

Alongside the church, INAH's revamped **Museo de las Misiones** (☎ 5-04-41) chronicles the settlement of Baja California, paying more attention to the indigenous heritage than it once did. It's open 9 am to 1 pm and 1.45 to 6 pm Tuesday to Friday (US$1.75).

Activities

Loreto is an ideal location for all types of outdoor activities, and a number of outfitters cover the range from kayaking and diving along the reefs around Isla del Carmen to horseback riding, hiking and mountain biking in the Sierra de la Giganta.

Las Parras Tours (☎ 5-10-10, Madero 16) offers diving, as well as kayaking, biking and hiking trips to Misión San Francisco Javier. Baja Outpost (☎ 5-12-29), on Lopez Mateos between Jordán and Hidalgo, a well-run outfitter, offers diving, snorkeling, whale-watching and kayaking expeditions. The Loreto Center (☎ 5-07-98), on Hidalgo and Pino Suárez, offers diving, hiking, fishing and whale-watching expeditions (plus a child-care center).

Places to Stay

Half a block from the beach, friendly *RV Park El Moro (☎ 5-05-42, Rosendo Robles 8)* has 12 sites with full hookups for US$8 to US$10, depending on vehicle size. It has clean baths and hot showers as well. Clean and comfortable single/double rooms run US$30/40.

Basic *Hotel Posada San Martín (☎ 5-07-92)*, at Juárez and Davis, charges from US$12 to US$40 depending on the room, but it is often full. *Motel Salvatierra (☎ 5-00-21, Salvatierra 123)* has clean but worn

rooms with air-con and hot showers for US$18/20. The central and very attractive *Hotel Plaza Loreto (☎ 5-02-80, Hidalgo 2)* charges US$45/55. Across the street, *Motel Junípero (☎ 5-01-22)* has pleasant rooms for US$30/35. *Baja Outpost (☎ 5-11-34)*, on the waterfront between Jordán and Hidalgo, offers beautiful rooms for US$56.

Places to Eat

Inexpensive *Café Olé (Madero 14)*, serves good breakfasts and antojitos. *Tiffany's Pisa Parlor*, on Hidalgo just off of Independencia, serves excellent pizza and apple pie. *El Nido*, across from the bus station on Salvatierra, is the local branch of the Baja steakhouse chain.

Shopping

For varied handicrafts, try El Alacrán, at Salvatierra and Misioneros.

Getting There & Away

Air Aero California (☎ 5-05-00), on Juárez between Misioneros and Zapata, flies daily to Los Angeles. Aerolitoral, represented by Viajes Pedrín (☎ 5-02-04), on the south side of Hidalgo at Madero, flies daily to and from La Paz and to Los Angeles.

Bus Loreto's bus station (☎ 5-07-67) is near the convergence of Salvatierra, Paseo de Ugarte and Paseo Tamaral. Northbound buses leave at 2 pm (Santa Rosalía, US$10), 3 pm (Tijuana, US$57), 5 pm (Santa Rosalía), 9 pm (Mexicali, US$68), 11 pm (Guerrero Negro, US$23) and 1 am (Tijuana). Southbound buses for La Paz (US$16) and intermediate stops leave at midnight, 8 am and 1, 2 and 11 pm.

Car Both Thrifty and Budget car rental agencies are located on Hidalgo, east of Madero.

Getting Around

To/From the Airport Taxis to Aeropuerto Internacional de Loreto (☎ 5-04-99), reached by a lateral off the highway south of the Río Loreto, cost US$7 for one person, US$2 for each additional passenger.

AROUND LORETO

About 2km south of Loreto on the Transpeninsular is the junction for the spectacular 35km mountain road to beautifully preserved **Misión San Francisco Javier de Viggé-Biaundó**. Every December 3, pilgrims celebrate the saint's fiesta at this mission founded in 1699. *Restaurant Palapa San Javier* serves simple meals, cold sodas and beer and offers simple accommodations.

CIUDAD CONSTITUCIÓN

• pop 35,500 • elev 50m ☎ changing

Conveniently close to whale-watching sites, inland Ciudad Constitución, 215km northwest of La Paz, has grown dramatically with the development of commercial agriculture. Most services are within a block or two of the north-south Transpeninsular, commonly known as Boulevard Olachea.

The post office is on Galeana, west of Olachea; for phone service, try the cabinas on the east side of Olachea between Matamoros and Mina. For information on **whale-watching**, see the Around Ciudad Constitución section.

> In June 2000, the telephone area code was due to change to ☎ 1 from 113, with the digits 13 added to the start of every local number (for example, the number 7-65-43 would become 137-65-43).

Places to Stay

At the north end of town, near the junction of the highway to Puerto López Mateos, Austrian-run *Manfred's RV Trailer Park* (☎ 2-11-03) has spacious, shady, pull-through sites for US$12 for one person, US$14 for two. It gives a break to cyclists and motorcyclists (US$6 per site) and car campers (US$9 per site).

Hotel Casino (☎ 2-14-15), on Guadalupe Victoria east of Hotel Maribel, has singles/doubles for US$16/18. *Hotel Conchita* (☎ 2-02-66, Olachea 180) has basic rooms for US$11/16 with TV. *Hotel Maribel* (☎ 2-01-55, Guadalupe Victoria 156), near Olachea, is more expensive, at US$30/35, but the rooms are just as spartan.

Places to Eat

Constitución's many taco stands and the *Mercado Central*, on Olachea at Morelos have the cheapest eats. *Super Pollo*, at the north end of Olachea, specializes in grilled chicken. Next door, *Estrella del Mar* and *Rincón Jarocho*, on the east side of Olachea, are seafood restaurants. Another seafood choice is *Mariscos El Delfín*, at Olachea and Zapata.

Getting There & Away

Long-distance buses stop at the terminal (☎ 2-03-76) at Juárez and Zapata, one block east of Olachea. You can also catch buses to nearby Puerto San Carlos (US$3) and Puerto López Mateos (US$3.50) from this terminal.

AROUND CIUDAD CONSTITUCIÓN
Puerto López Mateos

• pop 2390

Shielded from the open Pacific by the offshore barrier of Isla Magdalena, Puerto Adolfo López Mateos is one of Baja's best whale-watching sites. Whales are visible from the shore near Playa El Faro. Three-hour panga (skiff) excursions cost about US$50 per hour for up to six people are easy to arrange.

Places to Stay & Eat Free *camping*, with pit toilets only (bring water), is possible at tidy Playa Soledad, which is near Playa El Faro.

The only other accommodations in Puerto López Mateos are at the small and simple but tidy Posada Ballena López, for US$10/15 singles/doubles.

Besides a couple of so-so taco stands, López Mateos has several decent restaurants. *Restaurant California*, across from the church, is good, as is *Cabaña Brisa*.

Getting There & Away Puerto López Mateos is 34km west of Ciudad Insurgentes by a good paved road. Autotransportes Águila provides twice-daily buses from Ciudad Constitución (US$2) at 11.30 am and 7 pm; return service to Constitución leaves at 6.30 am and 12.30 pm.

Puerto San Carlos
- pop 3640 ☎ changing

On Bahía Magdalena, 56km west of Ciudad Constitución, Puerto San Carlos is a deepwater port from which Llano de Magdalena produce is shipped. From January through March, pangueros take up to five or six passengers for whale-watching excursions for US$40 per hour.

> In June 2000, the telephone area code was due to change to ☎ 1 from 113, with the digits 13 added to the start of every local number (for example, the number 7-65-43 would become 137-65-43).

Places to Stay & Eat Accommodations can be tougher to find during whale-watching season, but free *camping* is possible north of town on the shabby public beach. *Motel Las Brisas* (☎ 6-01-52), on Madero, has basic but clean singles/doubles from US$14/17 and *Hotel Palmar* (☎ 6-00-35), on Puerto Morelos, charges US$18/24. *Hotel Alcatraz* (☎ 6-00-17) has rooms with TV for US$50/70; its *Restaurant Bar El Patio* is the town's best eatery.

Mariscos Los Arcos on Puerto La Paz has tremendous shrimp tacos and seafood soup.

Getting There & Away From a small house on Calle Puerto Morelos, Autotransportes Águilar runs buses at 7.30 am daily to Ciudad Constitución (US$3) and La Paz (US$11). This is the only public transportation from Puerto San Carlos.

La Paz & Los Cabos

The southernmost part of the peninsula contains the city of La Paz and areas to its south including the popular resorts of Los Cabos. Los Cabos refers to the towns of San José del Cabo and Cabo San Lucas, as well as to the Corridor (the strip of beaches and luxury resorts that lines the coastline between the two towns). This is the costliest and most tourist-oriented part of the peninsula.

LA PAZ
- pop 154,300 ☎ 1

Hernán Cortés established Baja's first European outpost near La Paz, but permanent settlement waited until 1811. US troops occupied the city during the Mexican-American War (1846-48). In 1853 the quixotic American adventurer William Walker proclaimed a 'Republic of Lower California,' but he soon left under Mexican pressure.

After Walker's fiasco La Paz settled down. It had a rich pearl industry but that pretty nearly disappeared during the revolution of 1910-20. Today the capital of Baja California Sur is a peaceful place with beautiful beaches, a palm-lined malecón, a handful of colonial buildings and spectacular sunsets over the bay. It is also a popular winter resort, and its port of Pichilingue receives ferries from the mainland ports of Topolobampo and Mazatlán.

Orientation
Approaching La Paz from the southwest, the Transpeninsular becomes Abasolo as it runs parallel to the bay. Four blocks east of 5 de Febrero, Abasolo becomes Paseo Obregón, leading along the palm-lined malecón toward Península Pichilingue.

La Paz's grid makes basic orientation easy, but the center's crooked streets and alleys change names almost every block. The city's heart is Jardín Velasco (Plaza Constitución), three blocks southeast of the tourist pier.

Information
Tourist Offices The well-organized staff at the Coordinación Estatal de Turismo (☎ 124-01-99), on the waterfront at Paseo Obregón and 16 de Septiembre, distribute a variety of leaflets and keep a current list of hotel rates. The tourist office is open 9 am to 11 pm Monday to Friday, 9 am to 1 pm Saturday.

Immigration Servicios Migratorios (☎ 125-34-93), at Paseo Obregón 2140 in the Edificio Milhe between Allende and Juárez, is open 9 am to 5 pm Monday to Friday.

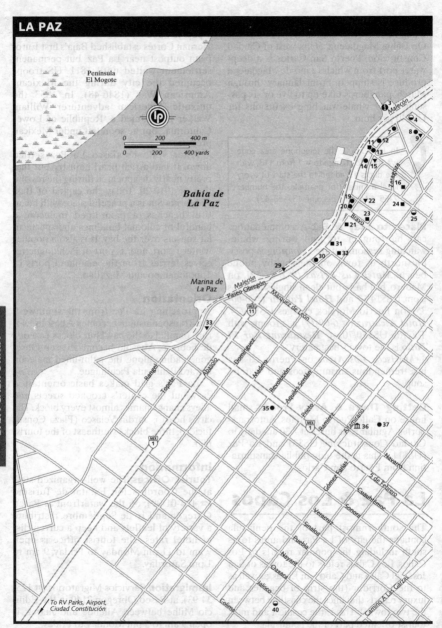

LA PAZ

Península
El Mogote

0   200   400 m
0   200   400 yards

Bahía de
La Paz

Marina de
La Paz

Malecón
Paseo Obregón

Márquez de León

Rangel

Topete

Abasolo

Domínguez

Madero

Revolución

Aquiles Serdán

Prieto

Ramírez

Altamirano

Navarro

Gómez Farías

5 de Febrero

Cuauhtémoc

Veracruz

Sonora

Sinaloa

Puebla

Nayarit

Oaxaca

Jalisco

Colima

Camino A Las Garzas

Zaragoza

Bravo

Malecón

To RV Parks, Airport,
Ciudad Constitución

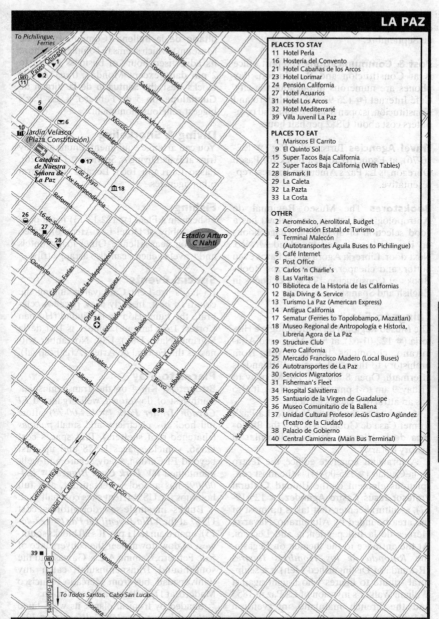

LA PAZ

PLACES TO STAY
11 Hotel Perla
16 Hostería del Convento
21 Hotel Cabañas de los Arcos
23 Hotel Lorimar
24 Pensión California
27 Hotel Acuarios
31 Hotel Los Arcos
32 Hotel Mediterrané
39 Villa Juvenil La Paz

PLACES TO EAT
1 Mariscos El Carrito
9 El Quinto Sol
15 Super Tacos Baja California
22 Super Tacos Baja California (With Tables)
28 Bismark II
29 La Caleta
32 La Pazta
33 La Costa

OTHER
2 Aeroméxico, Aerolitoral, Budget
3 Coordinación Estatal de Turismo
4 Terminal Malecón
   (Autotransportes Águila Buses to Pichilingue)
5 Café Internet
6 Post Office
7 Carlos 'n Charlie's
8 Las Varitas
10 Biblioteca de la Historia de las Californias
12 Baja Diving & Service
13 Turismo La Paz (American Express)
14 Antigua California
17 Sematur (Ferries to Topolobampo, Mazatlan)
18 Museo Regional de Antropología e Historia,
    Librería Agora de La Paz
19 Structure Club
20 Aero California
25 Mercado Francisco Madero (Local Buses)
26 Autotransportes de La Paz
30 Servicios Migratorios
31 Fisherman's Fleet
34 Hospital Salvatierra
35 Santuario de la Virgen de Guadalupe
36 Museo Comunitario de la Ballena
37 Unidad Cultural Profesor Jesús Castro Agúndez
    (Teatro de la Ciudad)
38 Palacio de Gobierno
40 Central Camionera (Main Bus Terminal)

BAJA CALIFORNIA

Money Most banks (many with ATMs) and casas de cambio are located on or around 16 de Septiembre.

Post & Communications The post office is at Constitución and Revolución. Pay phones are numerous throughout the city. Café Internet (☎ 125-93-80), at Madero and Constitución, is open 8 am to 8 pm, and computers cost about US$2 per half hour.

Travel Agencies Turismo La Paz (☎ 122-76-76), at Esquerro 1679, a block off Paseo Obregón, is La Paz's American Express representative.

Bookstores The Museo Regional de Antropología e Historia (see below) has a good selection of Spanish-language books on Baja California and mainland Mexico. Next door, Librería Agora de La Paz is even better, and cheaper. Libros Libros Books Books, at Constitución 195, stocks books in English and Spanish.

Things to See & Do
The **Museo Regional de Antropología e Historia** (☎ 122-01-62), at 5 de Mayo and Altamirano, chronicles the peninsula from prehistory to the revolution of 1910 and its aftermath. Open 8 am to 6 pm Monday to Friday, 9 am to 1 pm Saturday (free), it also has an attractive cactus garden.

Across from the Jardín Velasco, La Paz's former Casa de Gobierno is now the **Biblioteca de la Historia de las Californias**, a history library.

A sprawling concrete edifice, the Teatro de la Ciudad (☎ 125-00-04) is the most conspicuous element of the **Unidad Cultural Profesor Jesús Castro Agúndez** (☎ 125-19-17), a cultural center that takes up most of the area bounded by Altamirano, Navarro, Héroes de la Independencia and Legaspi. At the entrance to the theater, on Legaspi, the *Rotonda de los Hombres Ilustres* (Rotunda of Distinguished Men) is a sculptural tribute to figures who fought against William Walker's invasion of La Paz in 1853 and the French mainland intervention of 1862.

At the periphery of the grounds at Navarro and Altamirano, is the **Museo Comunitario de la Ballena** (Community Whale Museum), which seems to completely ignore its advertised hours of business (9 am to 2 pm daily except Monday; free). A few blocks west, the **Santuario de la Virgen de Guadalupe**, on 5 de Febrero, is La Paz's biggest religious monument.

Diving & Snorkeling
You can arrange equipment rentals and day trips at Baja Diving & Service (☎ 122-18-26), Paseo Obregón 1663, Local 2, or several other agencies.

Fishing
Fisherman's Fleet (☎ 122-13-13) has a desk in the lobby of Hotel Los Arcos, on Paseo Obregón near Allende. Other major hotels and travel agencies can also arrange trips.

Special Events
La Paz's pre-Lent Carnaval is among the country's best. In early May, paceños celebrate the Fundación de la Ciudad (Hernán Cortés' 1535 landing). June 1 is Día de la Marina (Navy Day). Late November witnesses the Festival de Artes (Arts Festival).

Places to Stay
Budget At Km 4 on the Transpeninsular, southwest of downtown, well-organized *El Cardón Trailer Park* (☎ 124-00-78) offers full hookups, electricity and small *palapas* (thatched-roof shelters). Tent spaces cost US$6, vehicle spaces US$8 and up. Just beyond El Cardón, shady, secure and well-maintained *RV Park Casa Blanca* (☎ 124-00-09) has a pool, a restaurant, and full hookups for US$14; tent sites cost half that.

Bunks in single-sex dormitories cost US$7 at the *Villa Juvenil La Paz* (☎ 122-46-15), open 6 am to 11 pm. It's 20 blocks southwest of downtown, near the convergence of 5 de Febrero, Camino A Las Garzas and the southbound Transpeninsular; catch any 'Universidad' bus from Mercado Francisco Madero, at Degollado and Revolución.

Shaded by tropical plants, its walls lined with quirky art, *Pensión California* (☎ 122-

28-96, *Degollado 209* has singles/doubles for US$10/13 with ceiling fans and showers. Rooms are basic and slightly dark and dingy. The clean *Hostería del Convento* (☎ 122-35-08, *Madero 85*) offers simple rooms for US$8/12.

Mid-Range *Hotel Lorimar* (☎ 125-38-22, *Bravo 110*), with an attractive patio, is a popular choice. Its rooms are US$20/24, with air-con and tiled showers with hot water. The place has a comfortable, homey feel to it (but beware the pet parrot that wanders in and out of the bedrooms).

Rates at *Hotel Acuarios* (☎ 122-92-66, *Ramírez 1665*) are US$34/38 with air-con, TV and telephone. At *Hotel Mediterrané* (☎ 125-11-95, *Allende 36B*), rooms cost US$45/65, which includes free use of the kayaks; bikes are also available for rent.

Top End Historic *Hotel Perla* (☎ 122-07-77, *Paseo Obregón 1570*) has a swimming pool, restaurant, bar and nightclub – but the rooms are on the small side. All rooms have air-con, TV and private bath for around US$72.

Ask for a bay view at *Hotel Los Arcos* (☎ 122-27-44, *Paseo Obregón 498*), near Allende. It has two swimming pools, a sauna, a restaurant and a coffee shop. Rooms cost about US$84, with air-con, telephone, color TV and shower. At nearby *Hotel Cabañas de los Arcos*, at Rosales and Mutualismo, rooms set around a lush garden have fireplaces, thatched roofs, tiled floors, TV, air-con and minibars. Prices range from US$75 for a standard room to US$84 for a cabaña. If you feel like splurging, this is the way to go.

Places to Eat
Super Tacos Baja California, at Arreola and Mutualismo, is more expensive than most taco stands, but its quality fish and shrimp, plus exceptional condiments, justify the extra peso. There's a second stand at Ocampo and Mutualismo with tables. *Mariscos El Carrito*, at Paseo Obregón and Morelos, is a shady stand with an enclosed area with tables for taco-lovers weary of standing.

El Quinto Sol, at Independencia and Domínguez, has tasty vegetarian meals and large breakfast servings of yogurt (plain, with fruit or with muesli). *Licuados*, fresh breads and pastries are other specialties.

Popular *La Caleta*, on the malecón at Pineda, serves reasonably priced meals and is an ideal spot to drink a margarita on a deck overlooking the bay. *La Pazta (Allende 36B)*, in the Hotel Mediterrané, has moderately priced Italian specials. *Bismark II*, at Degollado and Altamirano, offers generous seafood platters. *La Costa*, at Topete and Navarro, offers some of the best seafood in Baja: it's the place to go for lobster.

Entertainment
Las Varitas (*Independencia 111*), near Domínguez, has live music and dancing (with cover charge). One of the main dance clubs is the *Structure Club*, at Paseo Obregón and Ocampo. *Carlos 'n Charlie's*, at Paseo Obregón and 16 de Septiembre, is another popular nightspot – lines are always long. Keep in mind that women walking alone at night are bound to get heckled – cabs are sometimes the best way to get from hotel to bar.

Shopping
Antigua California, on Paseo Obregón, features a wide selection of crafts from throughout the country.

Getting There & Away
Air Aeroméxico (☎ 122-00-91), at Paseo Obregón between Hidalgo and Morelos, has daily flights between La Paz and Los Angeles, Tijuana, Tucson and mainland Mexican cities. Its subsidiary Aerolitoral, at the same address and phone number, flies daily to Loreto.

Aero California (☎ 125-10-23) has offices at the airport and at Paseo Obregón 550, near the corner of Bravo; it operates daily nonstops between La Paz and Los Angeles, one daily nonstop to Tijuana, and daily flights to Tucson via Hermosillo. It also flies to mainland Mexican destinations, including Los Mochis (for the Copper Canyon Railway), Mazatlán and Mexico City.

Bus ABC (☎ 122-30-63) and Autotransportes Águila (☎ 122-42-70) use the Central

BAJA CALIFORNIA

Camionera at Jalisco and Héroes de la Independencia. Northbound ABC buses go to Ciudad Constitución (2 hours, US$8), Loreto (5 hours, US$7), Mulegé (6 hours, US$21), San Ignacio (9 hours, US$30), Guerrero Negro (11 hours, US$38), Ensenada (18 hours, US$63) and Tijuana (22 hours, US$70).

Frequent southbound ABC buses serve San José del Cabo (3 hours, US$10) and intermediate points via the Transpeninsular. Autotransportes Águila takes highway 19 to Todos Santos (US$3) and Cabo San Lucas (US$6) at least five times daily.

Buses by Autotransportes de La Paz (☎ 122-21-57) leave from Prieto and Degollado for Todos Santos (US$3.50), Cabo San Lucas (US$8) and San José del Cabo eight times daily, from 6.45 am until 7.45 pm.

Car Rental rates start around US$45 per day with 300km free; taxes and insurance are extra. Budget (☎ 122-76-55) is on Paseo Obregón between Morelos and Hidalgo. There are a number of other agencies along Paseo Obregón.

Boat Ferries to Mazatlán and Topolobampo leave from Pichilingue, 23km north of La Paz, but the Sematur office (☎ 125-23-46) is at Prieto and 5 de Mayo in La Paz. Before shipping any vehicle to the mainland, officials require a vehicle permit (see the Car & Motorcycle section of the Getting There & Away chapter). Vehicle permits are obtainable at Pichilingue 8 am to 3 pm Monday to Friday, 9 am to 1 pm Saturday and Sunday, but it's probably safer to get one in Tijuana, Mexicali or Ensenada. Confirm tickets by 2 pm the day before departure; at 3 pm that day, unconfirmed cabins are sold on a first-come, first-served basis.

Weather permitting (high winds often delay winter sailings), the ferry to Mazatlán departs at 3 pm daily except Saturday, arriving at 8 am the following day; the return schedule is identical. Approximate passenger fares are US$22 in *salón* (numbered seats), US$44 in *turista* (two- to four-bunk cabins with shared bath), US$67 in *cabina* (two bunks with private bath), and US$89 in *especial* (suite).

The Topolobampo ferry sails at 10 pm daily, arriving at 8 am; the return schedule is identical. Passenger fares are US$15.

Vehicle rates vary with vehicle length:

vehicle	length	rate to Mazatlán	rate to Topolo-bampo
Car	Up to 5m	US$240	US$147
	5.01 to 6.5m	US$312	US$191
Car & Trailer	Up to 9m	US$433	US$264
	9.01 to 17m	US$812	US$497
Motorcycle		US$48	US$33

Between November and March, the Marina de La Paz, southwest of central La Paz, can be a good place to hitch a lift on a yacht to mainland Mexico.

Getting Around

To/From the Airport The government-regulated Transporte Terrestre minivan service (☎ 125-32-74, 125-62-29) charges US$7 per person to or from the airport. Private taxis cost approximately US$20, but they may be shared.

To/From the Ferry Port From the downtown bus terminal (☎ 122-78-98), at Paseo Obregón and Independencia, Autotransportes Águila goes to the Pichilingue ferry terminal (US$1) hourly between 7 am and 5.30 pm.

Bus Most local buses leave from Mercado Francisco Madero, at the corner of Degollado and Revolución.

AROUND LA PAZ
Beaches

On Península Pichilingue, the beaches nearest to La Paz are **Playa Palmira** (with the Hotel Palmira and a marina) and **Playa Coromuel** and **Playa Caimancito** (both with restaurant-bars, toilets and palapas). **Playa Tesoro**, the next beach north, also has a restaurant.

Camping is possible at **Playa Pichilingue**, 100m north of the ferry terminal, and it has a restaurant and bar, toilets and shade. The road is paved to **Playa Balandra** and **Playa**

Tecolote (where kayak and windsurfer rentals are available). Tecolote also has a restaurant. Balandra is problematic for camping because of insects in the mangroves, but it's one of the more beautiful beaches, with an enclosed cove. **Playa Coyote**, on the gulf, is more isolated. Particularly stealthy thieves break into campers' vehicles in all these areas, especially the more remote ones.

LOS BARRILES
• pop 590   ☎ 1

South of La Paz, the Transpeninsular brushes the gulf at Los Barriles, Baja's windsurfing capital. Brisk westerlies, averaging 20 to 25 knots, descend the 1800m cordillera. Keep in mind that from April to August the winds really die down, and windsurfing is pretty much impossible.

Several fairly good dirt roads follow the coast south. Beyond Cabo Pulmo and Bahía Los Frailes, they are rough but passable for vehicles with good clearance and a short wheelbase. However, south of the junction with the road going to the village of Palo Escopeta and Los Cabos international airport, the road is impassable for RVs and difficult for most other vehicles, rendered so by the rains of November 1993. Pedestrians, mountain bikers, burros and mules will do just fine.

Places to Stay & Eat
Crowded *Martín Verdugo's Beach Resort* (☎ 121-00-54) charges US$10 for a small vehicle or US$12 for a larger one, with hot showers, full hookups, laundry and a sizable paperback book exchange. Camping costs US$5. Rooms are also available ranging from US$43 to US$51.

Other than camping, Los Barriles lacks inexpensive accommodations. *Hotel Playa del Sol* (☎ 121-02-12) offers clean, comfortable singles/doubles for around US$70/110, including meals. Rates are comparable at *Hotel Palmas de Cortez* (☎ 121-00-50).

Popular with gringos, *Tío Pablo* has a good pizza menu and massive portions of Mexican specialties like chicken fajitas, but the margaritas are weak. Despite the raucous decor and satellite TV, it's fairly sedate.

RESERVA DE LA BIÓSFERA SIERRA DE LA LAGUNA
Even travelers who deplore the ugly coastal development around Los Cabos will enjoy the Sierra de La Laguna, an ecological treasure between La Paz and Los Cabos. Several foothill villages provide access to these unique interior mountains.

Tranquil **Santiago**, 10km south of the junction for La Rivera and 2.5km west of the Transpeninsular, once witnessed a bloody Pericú indigenous revolt against the Jesuits. Its modest *Hotel Palomar* (☎ 1-122-21-90) has basic rooms amid pleasant grounds for about US$20, with tent sites going for US$5. There is a bar and restaurant as well, but the seafood is a little pricey.

Cañón San Dionisio, about 25km west of Santiago, is the northernmost of three major east-west walking routes across the sierra; the others are **Cañón San Bernardo**, west of Miraflores, and **Cañón San Pedro**, west of Caduaño, which is about 10km south of Santiago. San Dionisio offers scenic hiking in an ecologically unique area where cacti, palms, oaks, aspens and pines grow side by side. The trail requires scrambling over large granite boulders; if rainfall has been sufficient, there are pools suitable for swimming.

The best guide for hiking these routes is Walt Peterson's *Baja Adventure Book*.

SAN JOSÉ DEL CABO
• pop 21,700   ☎ changing

San José del Cabo is still a quaint town of narrow streets, Spanish-style buildings and shady plazas, despite its growth as a major tourist resort. Grandiose plans for a yacht marina at the outlet of the ecologically sensitive Arroyo San José fizzled because of local opposition and, having maintained its open space, San José remains one of the most pleasant destinations in Baja.

The Fiesta de San José, on March 19, celebrates the town's patron saint.

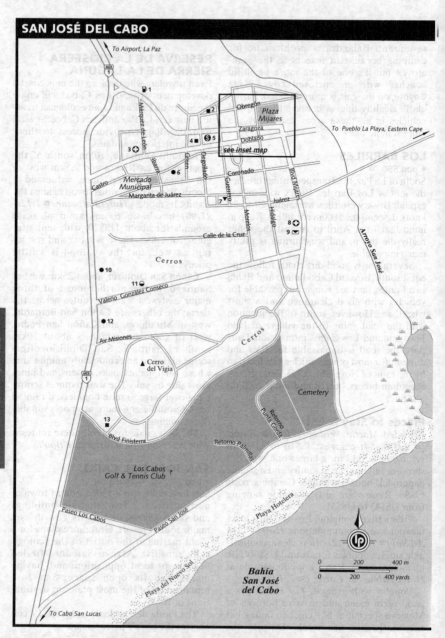

SAN JOSÉ DEL CABO

To Airport, La Paz

MEX 1

Obregón

Plaza Mijares

Zaragoza

Doblado

see inset map

To Pueblo La Playa, Eastern Cape

Marqués de León

Ibarra

Green

Degollado

Coronado

Guerrero

Blvd Mijares

Juárez

Morelos

Hidalgo

Arroyo San José

Castro

Mercado Municipal

Margarita de Juárez

Calle de la Cruz

Cerros

San Bernardo

Valerio González Conseco

Av Misiones

Cerros

Cerro del Vigía

Cemetery

Retorno Punta Coda

Blvd Finisterra

Retorno Palmillas

Los Cabos Golf & Tennis Club

Playa Hotelera

Paseo Los Cabos

Paseo San José

Bahía San José del Cabo

Playa del Nuevo Sol

To Cabo San Lucas

0   200   400 m
0   200   400 yards

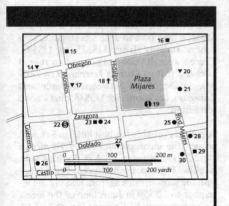

PLACES TO STAY
2 San José Inn
4 Posada Terranova
13 Howard Johnson Plaza
    Suite Resort
15 El Encanto Inn
16 Posada Señor Mañana
23 Hotel Ceci
29 Hotel Tropicana

PLACES TO EAT
7 El Paraje (The Tree House)
14 Fandango's
17 Jazmín's
20 Damiana
27 Morgan's Restaurant & Inn

OTHER
1 Pemex
3 Hospital Municipal
5 Banca Serfin
6 Deportiva Piscis
8 Cruz Roja
9 Post Office
10 Dollar
11 Bus Terminal
12 Thrifty
18 Iglesia San José
19 Dirección General de
    Turismo Municipal
21 Copal
22 Bancomer
24 Antigua Los Cabos
25 Palacio Municipal
26 Killer Hook Surf Shop
28 Thrifty
30 La Mina

Orientation

San José del Cabo consists of San José proper, about 1.5km inland, and a *zona hotelera* of tacky beachfront hotels, condos and time-shares. Linking the two areas, just south of shady Plaza Mijares, Boulevard Mijares is a *gringolandia* of restaurants and souvenir shops.

Information

Tourist Offices The English-speaking staff at the Dirección General de Turismo Municipal (☎ 2-29-60), in the Plaza Mijares, are very helpful. Hours are 8 am to 3 pm Monday to Friday.

Money The casa de cambio at Aeropuerto Internacional Los Cabos offers very poor rates, so avoid changing money until you get to town, where several casas de cambio keep long hours.

Banks pay better rates but keep shorter hours. Bancomer, at the corner of Zaragoza and Morelos, and Banca Serfin, which is at Zaragoza and Degollado, both cash traveler's checks and have ATMs; Bancomer has longer lines, but Serfin will not cash more than US$200.

Post & Communications The post office is on Mijares, north of Valerio González Conseco. Pay phones are numerous throughout the city.

In December 2000, the telephone area code is due to change to ☎ 1 from 114, with the digits 14 added to the start of every local number (for example, the number 7-65-43 will become 147-65-43).

Things to See & Do

The colonial-style **Iglesia San José** faces the shady Plaza Mijares, a nice place to relax and have an *helado*.

Between raids on Spanish galleons, 18th-century pirates took refuge at the freshwater **Arroyo San José**, now a protected wildlife area replenished by a subterranean spring.

BAJA CALIFORNIA

Among the common bird species to be found are coots, pelicans, herons, egrets and plovers.

San José's museum Los Cabos Centro Cultural is now closed.

Beaches
The beaches at the south end of Boulevard Mijares (known as Playa Hotelera) have a dangerous current so are not good for swimming. The best beaches for swimming are along the road to Cabo San Lucas. Playa Santa Maria at Km 13 is one of the nicest beaches in Los Cabos.

Fishing
In San José proper, Deportiva Piscis (☎ 2-03-32), on Castro near Ibarra, arranges fishing excursions and sells and rents tackle. Fishermen at **Pueblo La Playa**, a small fishing community about 2.5km east of the junction of Juárez and Mijares, arrange similar trips; ask them in the late afternoon as they cut up the day's catch on the beach.

Surfing
The best source of surfing information is Killer Hook Surf Shop (☎ 2-24-30), on Guerrero between Castro and Doblado, which also rents fishing gear and mountain bikes.

Places to Stay
Budget & Mid-Range Free *camping* is possible at Pueblo La Playa, east of the center. The best paying site, also at Pueblo La Playa, is Swedish-run *El Delfín RV Park* (☎ 2-11-99), which is too small for RVs but excellent for tents (US$9). It also has cozy twin-bedded cabañas for US$26/32 singles/doubles.

Though urgently in need of a plasterer and a painter, the friendly *San José Inn* (☎ 2-24-64), on Obregón between Degollado and Guerrero, has spacious singles/doubles with private baths, ceiling fans and hot water for US$12/14. The dorm room/hostel rate is no longer available, but if you are willing to share a room you can pay US$5. *Hotel Ceci* (☎ 2-00-51, *Zaragoza 22*), has 20 rooms with private showers and air-con, but the rooms are pretty basic and cost US$14 a person.

Woodsy, casual *Posada Señor Mañana* (☎ 2-04-62, *Obregón 1*), just north of Plaza Mijares, may be San José's best value, with rooms ranging from US$25 to US$38. There's a small pool and access to a shared kitchen. Inviting *Posada Terranova* (☎ 2-05-34), on Degollado between Doblado and Zaragoza, has rooms for US$48, plus a good restaurant.

Top End Probably the best hotel in San José proper, the inconspicuous *Hotel Tropicana* (☎ 2-23-11, *Mijares 30*) has doubles with satellite TV, a patio and pool. Prices vary with the season, ranging from US$112 in December to US$59 in June. One of the nicest places in town is *El Encanto Inn* (☎ 2-03-88, *Morelos 133*). It's a charming inn, with a beautifully landscaped garden, and thoughtfully decorated rooms. Rooms range from US$50 to US$75.

At the *Howard Johnson Plaza Suite Resort* (☎ 2-09-09), on Finisterra overlooking Los Cabos Golf & Tennis Club, rates start at US$90.

Places to Eat
The very clean Mercado Municipal, on Ibarra between Coronado and Castro, has numerous stalls offering simple and inexpensive but good and filling meals.

Jazmín's, on Morelos between Obregón and Zaragoza, offers a wide variety of tasty breakfasts, plus lunches and dinners at mid-range prices, with excellent but unobtrusive service and, incongruously, a paperback book exchange. *Morgan's Restaurant & Inn*, on the corner of Doblado and Hidalgo, serves excellent food at reasonable prices.

In a restored 18th-century house on Plaza Mijares, *Damiana* is a romantic seafood restaurant. *El Paraje* (also known as *The Tree House*), in an attractive adobe structure with a palapa roof at the corner of Guerrero and Margarita de Juárez, serves outstanding fish, fowl, meat and antojitos; it provides outside seating for warm nights or to flee the live entertainment inside of local Neil Diamond wannabes. At the corner of Alvaro and Morelos, *Fandango's* is a good option for dinner. For a treat, try the key lime pie.

Entertainment
Noisy nightlife doesn't dominate San José the way it does Cabo San Lucas. *La Playita*, part of its namesake hotel in Pueblo La Playa, offers live jazz several nights a week.

Shopping
Antigua Los Cabos, in a mission-style building in Plaza Florentina on Zaragoza between Morelos and Hidalgo, offers a nicely displayed selection of handcrafted household items such as sturdy glassware, plates, mugs and wall hangings. Copal, on the west side of Plaza Mijares, has an interesting assortment of crafts, especially masks.

La Mina, on Mijares, sells gold and silver jewelry in an imaginative setting.

Getting There & Away
Air All airlines have their offices at Los Cabos airport, which serves both San José and Cabo San Lucas.

Mexicana (☎ 2-06-06) flies daily to Los Angeles and Mexico City, less frequently to Denver, Colorado.

Alaska Airlines (☎ 2-10-15) flies daily to San Diego, San Francisco and Phoenix, less frequently to Los Angeles and San José, California (USA). Aero California (☎ 2-09-43, fax 2-09-42) flies at least daily to Los Angeles, Phoenix and Denver.

Continental Airlines (☎ 2-38-40) flies daily between Houston and Los Cabos, while America West (☎ 2-28-80) serves Phoenix daily. Aeroméxico (☎ 2-03-41) flies daily to San Diego and many mainland Mexican destinations, with international connections via Mexico City.

Bus Frequent buses leave for Cabo San Lucas (30 minutes, US$1) and La Paz (3 hours, US$8) from the terminal (☎ 2-11-00), on Valerio González Conseco, east of the Transpeninsular.

Car Dollar (☎ 2-01-00, 2-06-71 at the airport) is on the Transpeninsular just north of the intersection with Valerio González Conseco. Thrifty (☎ 2-16-71) is a block south on the Transpeninsular, with another office (☎ 2-41-51) at the corner of Doblado and Mijares.

Getting Around
To/From the Airport The official, government-run company Aeroterrestre (☎ 2-05-55) runs bright yellow taxis and minibuses to Aeropuerto Internacional Los Cabos, 10km north of San José, for about US$12. Local buses from the terminal on Valerio González Conseco to the airport junction cost less than US$1, but taking one means a half-hour walk to the air terminal.

LOS CABOS CORRIDOR
West of San José, all the way to Cabo San Lucas, a string of luxury resorts lines the once scenic coastline. Around Km 27, near *Hotel Palmilla*, are choice surfing beaches at **Punta Mirador** and at **Km 28** of the Transpeninsular. The reefs off Playa Chileno are excellent for diving, and experienced surfers claim that summer reef and point breaks at Km 28 (popularly known as Zipper's) match Hawaii's best.

CABO SAN LUCAS
• pop 28,500 ☎ changing

In the last 15 years or so Cabo San Lucas has become a mecca for both the fishing and golfing crowd and for younger Americans who treat Cabo as the quintessential party town, ideal for a weekend getaway or bachelor party. On many levels the town seems to have the feel of an endless playground. It has an amazing array of activities to offer, from beautiful beaches and water sports such as diving and kayaking to an endless string of bars and nightclubs that provide a continuous party.

Many residents seem a bit perplexed by the explosion of development in the last decade, and partially resent the time-share sellers who have metamorphosed a placid fishing village into a jumble of exorbitantly priced hotels and rowdy bars. But overall, Cabo has the feel of a place that will provide a good time, in a very laid-back atmosphere.

Orientation
Northwest of Cárdenas, central Cabo has a fairly regular grid, while southeast of Cárdenas, Boulevard Marina curves along the Harbor Cabo San Lucas toward Land's End

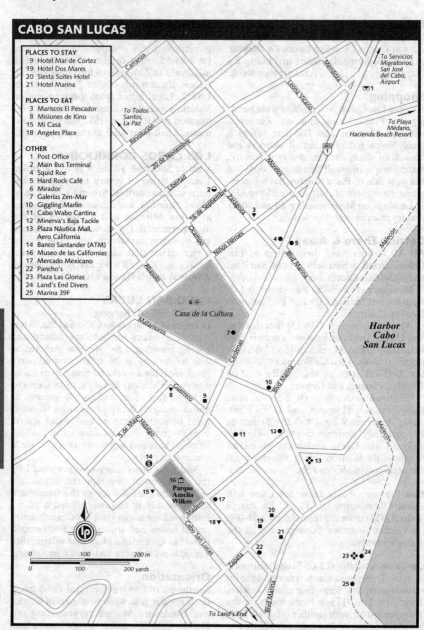

CABO SAN LUCAS

PLACES TO STAY
9 Hotel Mar de Cortez
19 Hotel Dos Mares
20 Siesta Suites Hotel
21 Hotel Marina

PLACES TO EAT
3 Mariscos El Pescador
8 Misiones de Kino
15 Mi Casa
18 Angeles Place

OTHER
1 Post Office
2 Main Bus Terminal
4 Squid Roe
5 Hard Rock Café
6 Mirador
7 Galerías Zen-Mar
10 Giggling Marlin
11 Cabo Wabo Cantina
12 Minerva's Baja Tackle
13 Plaza Náutica Mall,
    Aero California
14 Banco Santander (ATM)
16 Museo de las Californias
17 Mercado Mexicano
22 Pancho's
23 Plaza Las Glorias
24 Land's End Divers
25 Marina 39F

To Todos
Santos,
La Paz

To Servicios
Migratorios,
San José
del Cabo,
Airport

To Playa
Médano,
Hacienda Beach Resort

Casa de la Cultura

Harbor
Cabo
San Lucas

Parque
Amelia
Wilkes

Malecón

To Land's End

0   100   200 m
0   100   200 yards

(or 'Finisterra'), the tip of the peninsula where the Pacific Ocean and the Sea of Cortez meet. Few places have street addresses, so you will need to refer to the map to locate them.

In December 2000, the telephone area code is due to change to ☎ 1 from 114, with the digits 14 added to the start of every local number (for example, the number 7-65-43 will become 147-65-43).

Information

Immigration Servicios Migratorios (☎ 3-01-35), at Cárdenas and Gómez Farías northwest of downtown, is open 9 am to 2 pm.

Money Several downtown banks cash traveler's checks and have ATMs, including Banco Santander at Cárdenas and Cabo San Lucas.

Post & Communications The post office is on the south side of Cárdenas, near 16 de Noviembre, northeast of downtown. Long-distance cabinas have sprung up in many shops and pharmacies, and pay phones are abundant.

Dr Z's Internet Café and Bar (☎ 3-42-40) is on Cárdenas at Paseo del Pescador, northeast of downtown.

Dangers & Annoyances Beware timeshare sellers on Boulevard Marina; they distribute town maps and happily provide information (along with their sales pitch).

Beaches

For sunbathing and calm waters **Playa Médano**, in front of the Hacienda Beach Resort, on the Bahía de Cabo San Lucas, is ideal. **Playa Solmar**, on the Pacific, has a reputation for unpredictable, dangerous breakers. Nearly unspoiled **Playa del Amor**, near Land's End, is accessible by boat or a class-three scramble over the rocks (at least at high tide) from Hotel Solmar.

Diving

Among the best diving areas are Roca Pelícano, the sea lion colony off Land's End, and the reef off Playa Chileno, at Bahía Chileno east of town.

At most shops, two-tank dives cost around US$70, introductory courses around US$90 and full-certification courses from US$350 to US$400. Rental equipment is readily available at shops. Land's End Divers (☎ 3-22-00) is located on the marina at the Plaza Las Glorias. Cabo Acuadeportes (☎ 3-01-17), in front of the Hacienda Beach Resort, is the largest water-sports outfitter. In addition to diving excursions, they also offer snorkel, canoe and kayak trips, as well as windsurfing, sailing and waterskiing.

Fishing

Minerva's Baja Tackle (☎ 3-12-82), at Madero and Marina, charters fishing boats and rents gear. Panga (small boat with outboard motor) rates start around US$30 per hour, with a six-hour minimum for three people; Sportfisher 31- and 33-footers can take five or six for US$465 and US$500 per hour.

The Solmar Sportfishing Fleet (☎ 3-35-35) operates out of the Hotel Solmar. Rates range from US$260 for a 26-foot boat to US$650 for a 42-footer; Pangas rent at US$30 per hour with a 6-hour minimum.

Boat Trips

Trips to El Arco (the natural arch at Land's End), the sea lion colony and Playa del Amor on the *Kaleidoscope* (☎ 8-73-18) cost about US$40. Dos Mares (☎ 3-32-66) sails glass-bottomed boats at 10 and 11 am and 12 noon for three-hour trips to Playa del Amor (US$6).

From the Plaza Las Glorias dock, *Pez Gato I* and *Pez Gato II* (☎ 3-37-97) offer two-hour sunset sailings on catamarans, and segregate their clientele into 'booze cruises' and 'romantic cruises'; prices are US$35 for adults, US$18 for children. The semisubmersible *Nautilus VII* offers similarly priced one-hour tours to view whales, dolphins and sea turtles; make reservations

(☎ 3-30-33) at Marina 39F or by calling Baja Tourist & Travel Services (☎ 3-19-34). Sunset dinner cruises are available on the *Sun Rider* (☎ 3-22-52) for US$40 for adults. The boats leave at 5.30 pm from the Plaza Las Glorias dock.

Special Events

Cabo San Lucas is a popular staging ground for fishing tournaments in October and November. The main events are the Gold Cup, Bisbee's Black and Blue Marlin Jackpot, and the Cabo Tuna Jackpot. One local celebration is Día de San Lucas, honoring the town's patron saint, on October 18.

Places to Stay

Budget & Mid-Range Except for camping and RV parks, even mid-range accommodations are scarce. Many visitors may prefer to stay in San José del Cabo, which is cheaper and close enough for day trips.

Tents and RVs are welcome at *Surf Camp Club Cabo* (☎ 3-33-48), down a narrow dirt road east of Cabo San Lucas, toward San José del Cabo (look for the sign). A site costs US$10; a cabaña and two kitchenette apartments are available for US$39, single or double. About 3km east of Cabo on the Transpeninsular, spacious but shadeless *Cabo Cielo* (☎ 3-07-21) has full hookups, spotless baths and excellent hot showers for US$10.

In town, *Hotel Marina* (☎ 3-24-84), on Boulevard Marina near Guerrero, has modest poolside singles/doubles with air-con for US$45/60. The comparable *Hotel Dos Mares* (☎ 3-03-30), on Zapata between Hidalgo and Guerrero, charges US$39/45.

Pseudocolonial *Hotel Mar de Cortez* (☎ 3-00-32), at Cárdenas and Guerrero, has a pool and an outdoor restaurant-bar. Newer air-conditioned rooms cost US$48/53 in high season, but older rooms are a good value for US$36/41. Off-season rates (June to October) are about 25% lower.

Siesta Suites Hotel (☎/fax 3-27-73), on Zapata between Hidalgo and Guerrero, has kitchenette apartments for US$50 a double, plus US$10 for each additional person.

Top End The *Hacienda Beach Resort* (☎ 3-01-22), on Paseo de la Marina near Playa Médano, has fountains, tropical gardens, tennis and paddle-tennis courts, a swimming pool and a putting green. Garden patio rooms start around US$150, but beach cabañas cost US$236.

All rooms face the Pacific at *Hotel Solmar* (☎ 3-35-35), a secluded beachfront resort near Land's End that has tennis courts, a pool and horseback riding. Singles and doubles start at US$150 in low season (June to October) and US$165 in the high season (November to May).

Places to Eat

Try *Angeles Place*, on Hidalgo and Madero, for an excellent, inexpensive breakfast. For fine and reasonably priced seafood, try the modest but friendly *Mariscos El Pescador*, at the corner of Zaragoza and Niños Héroes. The new *Misiones de Kino*, at Guerrero and 5 de Mayo, serves excellent seafood at reasonable prices.

Near the eastern entrance to town, on Paseo del Pescador just south of Cárdenas and across from the Pemex station, popular *La Golondrina* is expensive but offers large portions. *Faro Viejo Trailer Park Restaurant*, on Mijares between Matamores and Abasolo, northwest of the center, lures the wealthy from their beachfront hotels for barbecued ribs, steaks and seafood.

Mi Casa, on Cabo San Lucas across from Parque Amelia Wilkes, has a pleasant, homey environment and excellent seafood. For pizza and pasta try *Romeo y Julieta*, west of the point where Boulevard Marina turns east toward Land's End.

Entertainment

One of the seemingly required activities for the young Cabo tourist is drinking a margarita on the beach. Two popular destinations for beach party-goers and people-watchers are *The Office* and *Billygan's Island*, both at Playa Médano. Another seemingly required stop on the Cabo drinking tour is the *Giggling Marlin*, at Matamoros and Boulevard Marina in the center.

Gold records and rock photos line the walls of **Cabo Wabo Cantina**, on Guerrero between Madero and Cárdenas, which features live music from late at night to early in the morning. Barhoppers will reportedly find Mexico's largest selection of tequilas at **Pancho's**, on Hidalgo between Zapata and Marina. The **Hard Rock Café** is on Cárdenas near Boulevard Marina. For a late-night dance club, try **Squid Roe**, at the corner of Cárdenas and Zaragoza, which stays open till 3 am.

Shopping

Cabo's most comprehensive shopping area is the sprawling Mercado Mexicano at Madero and Hidalgo, containing dozens of stalls with crafts from all around the country. Galerías Zen-Mar (☎ 3-06-61), on Cárdenas between Matamoros and Ocampo, offers Zapotec weavings, bracelets and masks, as well as traditional crafts from other mainland indigenous peoples.

Getting There & Away

Air The closest airport is Los Cabos, north of San José del Cabo; for flight information, see the San José del Cabo Getting There & Away section. Aero California's main office (☎ 3-37-00, fax 3-39-27) has moved to the Plaza Náutica mall, on Boulevard Marina near Madero.

Bus From the main terminal (☎ 3-04-00), at Zaragoza and 16 de Septiembre, buses leave for San José del Cabo (30 minutes, US$1) and La Paz (3½ hours, US$9). Autotransportes de La Paz has a separate terminal at the junction of highway 19 and the Cabo bypass, north of downtown, as does Enlaces Terrestres. These buses go to La Paz only.

Car Numerous rental agencies have booths along Boulevard Marina and elsewhere in town.

Getting Around

To/From the Airport The government-regulated airport minibus (☎ 3-12-20), costing US$11 per person, leaves Plaza Las Glorias at 9.30 and 11 am and 12.30, 3.30 and 4.30 pm. For US$20, shared taxis (☎ 3-01-04) can be a cheaper alternative for large groups.

Taxi Cabs are plentiful but not cheap; fares within town average about US$3 to US$5.

TODOS SANTOS
● pop 3770 ☎ 1

Founded in 1723 but nearly destroyed by the Pericú rebellion in 1734, Misión Santa Rosa de Todos los Santos limped along until its abandonment in 1840. In the late 19th century Todos Santos became a prosperous sugar town with several brick *trapiches* (mills), but depleted aquifers have nearly eliminated this thirsty industry. In recent years Todos Santos has seen a North American invasion, including artists from Santa Fe and Taos, New Mexico, and organic farmers whose produce gets premium prices north of the border.

Orientation

Todos Santos has a regular grid, but residents rely more on landmarks than street names for directions. The plaza is surrounded by Márquez de León, Legaspi, Avenida Hidalgo and Centenario.

Information

Tourist Offices Todos Santos' de facto tourist office is El Tecolote (☎ 145-02-95), at the corner of Juárez and Avenida Hidalgo among a cluster of shops. This English-language bookstore distributes a very detailed (some might say cluttered) town map and a sketch map of nearby beach areas.

Money Change cash weekday mornings only at BanCrecer, at the corner of Juárez and Obregón, which has an ATM. For traveler's checks, try Baja Money Exchange, at Heróico Colegio Militar and Hidalgo.

Post & Communications The post office is on Heróico Colegio Militar between Hidalgo and Márquez de León. The Message Center (☎ 145-00-33, fax 145-02-88), adjacent to El Tecolote at Juárez and Hidalgo, provides phone, fax and message services.

It's open 8.30 am to 6 pm Monday through Friday, 8.30 am to 2 pm Saturday.

Things to See & Do

Scattered around town are several former trapiches, including **Molino El Progreso**, at what was formerly El Molino restaurant, and **Molino de los Santana**, on Juárez opposite the hospital. The restored **Teatro Cine General Manuel Márquez de León** is on Legaspi, facing the plaza.

Nationalist and revolutionary murals at the **Centro Cultural Todosanteño**, a former schoolhouse on Juárez near Topete, date from 1933. The subjects range from indigenous people, Spanish conquistadors and Emiliano Zapata to athletics and 'emancipation of the rural spirit.'

Special Events

Todos Santos' two-day Festival de Artes (Arts Festival) is held in late January. At other times it's possible to visit local artists in their home studios. A tour of historic homes takes place in late February.

Places to Stay

Hotel Miramar (☎ 145-03-41), at the corner of Verduzco and Pedrajo southwest of the town center, charges US$13/19 for singles/doubles. Remodeled **Motel Guluarte** (☎ 145-00-06), at Juárez and Morelos, now has a swimming pool; rooms cost about US$16/25.

Distinctive **Hotel California** (☎ 145-00-02), on Juárez between Márquez de León and Morelos, has clean rooms for about US$40/45.

Hostería Las Casitas (☎ 145-02-55), a Canadian-run B&B on Rangel between Obregón and Hidalgo, charges US$45 to US$65 per double with a superb breakfast and also offers inexpensive tent sites.

Places to Eat

Taco stands along Heróico Colegio Militar between Márquez de León and Degollado offer fish, chicken, shrimp or beef at bargain prices. Family-run **Casa de Margarita**, on Pedrajo between Progreso and Villarino, has gained a devoted following for fine, reasonably priced antojitos and seafood; it has also taken over the Sunday champagne brunch from the now defunct El Molino Trailer Park restaurant.

The coffee-conscious can consume cappuccinos with savory pastries or enticing fruit salads at **Caffé Todos Santos**, on Centenario between Topete and Obregón

Moderately priced **Las Fuentes**, in a bougainvillea-shaded patio with three refreshing fountains on Degollado at Heróico Colegio Militar, has antojitos (try the chicken with mole sauce) and seafood specialties. Prices are high at **Café Santa Fe** (Centenario 4), which attracts patrons from La Paz and Cabo San Lucas to its plaza location for Italian dining, but it's worth the splurge.

Shopping

Galería de Todos Santos, at Topete and Legaspi, features imaginative artwork by Mexican and North American artists. Galería Santa Fe, alongside its namesake restaurant on the south side of the plaza, is well worth a visit, as is the Stewart Gallery, located on Obregón between Legaspí and Centenario.

Getting There & Away

At least six buses go daily to La Paz (1½ hours, US$3) and to Cabo San Lucas (1½ hours, US$3) from the bus station at Heróico Colegio Militar and Zaragoza.

Northwest Mexico

This chapter covers portions of the north-western states of Sonora and Sinaloa, including the Ferrocarril Chihuahua al Pacífico, the railway that runs from Los Mochis on the Sea of Cortez, through the spectacular Barranca del Cobre (Copper Canyon) in the Sierra Madre Occidental, to the interior of northern Mexico.

Not to be missed, the Copper Canyon, justifiably known as the 'Grand Canyon of Mexico,' is four times bigger than its American counterpart (it's actually made up of not one canyon but 20) and just as breathtaking. Many travelers begin their journey through the canyon at Los Mochis, which is easily reached by ferry from La Paz in Baja California.

Alternatively, travelers coming from the USA work their way south through Sonora, a large state known for its beef and agriculture (principally wheat and cotton) and covered by the great Desierto Sonorense (Sonoran Desert).

Highway 15, Mexico's principal Pacific coast highway, begins at the border town of Nogales, Sonora, opposite Nogales, Arizona, about 1½ hours south of Tucson. This is one of the most convenient border crossings between western Mexico and the USA. From Nogales, highway 15/15D heads south through the Desierto Sonorense for about four hours to Hermosillo and then cuts over to the coast at Guaymas, about 1½ hours south of Hermosillo. From Guaymas the highway parallels the beautiful Pacific coast for about 1000km, finally turning inland at Tepic (see the Central Pacific Coast chapter) and heading on to Guadalajara and Mexico City. There are regular toll booths along highway 15 (including two between Nogales and Hermosillo, each charging US$8 per car).

It can be dangerous to travel on Sinaloense highways after dark (for more information see the Dangers & Annoyances section of the Facts for the Visitor chapter).

- Hermosillo's Centro Ecológico de Sonora – displaying diversity of Sonoran Desert's flora and fauna with cacti galore and over 300 plant species

- Museo de los Seris in Bahía Kino – with fantastic exhibits on the Seri, a traditionally nomadic indigenous culture

- Álamos – a tranquil town in the foothills of Sierra Madre, with well-restored colonial mansions, cobblestone streets and the Mexican jumping bean

- Barranca del Cobre (Copper Canyon) – traveling through deep gorges and at dizzying heights on one of the world's most scenic train trips

NORTHWEST MEXICO

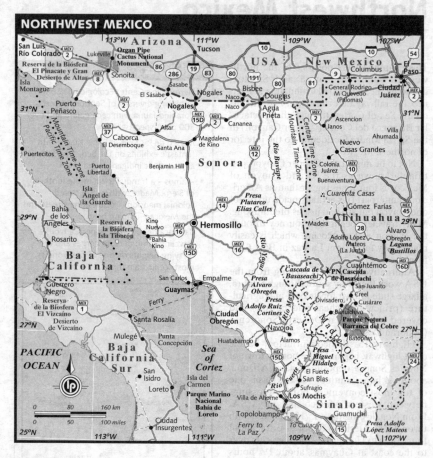

NOGALES

• pop 131,600 • elev 1170m ☎ 6

Like its border-city cousins Tijuana, Ciudad
Juárez, Nuevo Laredo and Matamoros,
Nogales is a major transit point for goods
and people traveling between the USA and
Mexico. On the northern side of the border
in Arizona is its smaller US counterpart, also
named Nogales. (The name means 'walnuts,'
a reference to the many walnut trees that
once flourished here.)

Nogales presents an easier introduction
to Mexico than do the larger border cities.
Nogales has everything they have – curio
shops overflowing with Mexican handicrafts,
trinkets and souvenirs, Mexican restaurants,
cheap bars and plenty of liquor stores and
pharmacies – but all on a much smaller
scale.

On the Arizona side, the small **Pimería
Alta Historical Society Museum** (☎ 520-287-
4621), 136 N Grand Ave, at the intersection
with Crawford, one block from the border
crossing, has interesting exhibits on the
history of Nogales. Opening hours are 10 am
to 4 pm Friday and Saturday.

Orientation

The commercial section of Nogales is only a few blocks wide, being hemmed in on either side by hills. The main commercial street is Obregón, two blocks west of the border crossing, which eventually runs south into Mexico's highway 15. Almost everything is within walking distance of the border crossing.

Information

Tourist Offices The Secretaría de Fomento al Turismo (☎ 312-06-66) occupies a tiny building beside the large white building on the west side of the big white arches at the border crossing. It is open 8.30 am to 6 pm daily.

Immigration If you are heading farther south into Mexico, pick up a Mexican tourist permit at the immigration office in the large, modern white building at the border crossing, on the west side of the big white arches. The office is open 24 hours a day. No one will tell you to get this tourist permit, and if you're staying within 21km of the border you don't need it. If you're heading farther south, however, you must have it.

The tourist permit is also available at the vehicle checkpoint, 21km south of the border, and if you're driving, it may be more convenient to get it there. Buses don't stop there, and if you're traveling by bus, be sure to pick up your permit at the immigration office. See the Facts for the Visitor chapter for more information on crossing the border between Mexico and the USA.

Money There are plenty of *casas de cambio*, where you can change US dollars to pesos or vice versa, on both sides of the border crossing (no commission is charged). On the Mexican side, dollars and pesos are used interchangeably.

Post & Communications On the Mexican side, the post office is on the corner of Juárez and Campillo, and is open 8 am to 7 pm Monday to Friday and 8 am to noon Saturday. The Telecomm office, with telegram, telex and fax, is next door. Telephone *casetas* for long-distance calls are everywhere in the

small Nogales shopping district. On the US side, the post office is at 300 N Morley Ave, three blocks north of the border crossing.

Places to Stay

Hotel San Carlos (☎ 312-13-46, Juárez 22) is very clean and has a helpful staff; rooms have bathroom, air-con, TV and phone. There is also parking. Singles/doubles cost US$21/25. *Hotel Regis* (☎ 312-51-81, Juárez 34) has a similar standard; rooms cost US$26/28. *Hotel Granada* (☎ 312-29-11), at López Mateos between Díaz and González

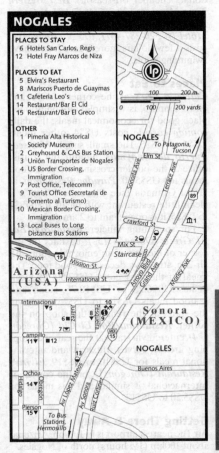

NOGALES

PLACES TO STAY
6 Hotels San Carlos, Regis
12 Hotel Fray Marcos de Niza

PLACES TO EAT
5 Elvira's Restaurant
8 Mariscos Puerto de Guaymas
11 Cafetería Leo's
14 Restaurant/Bar El Cid
15 Restaurant/Bar El Greco

OTHER
1 Pimería Alta Historical Society Museum
2 Greyhound & CAS Bus Station
3 Unión Transportes de Nogales
4 US Border Crossing, Immigration
7 Post Office, Telecomm
9 Tourist Office (Secretaría de Fomento al Turismo)
10 Mexican Border Crossing, Immigration
13 Local Buses to Long Distance Bus Stations

beside the highway, seven blocks south of the border crossing, has rooms for US$33. *Hotel Fray Marcos de Niza (☎ 312-16-51, Campillo 91)* is the fancy hotel on the Mexican side and charges US$40/45.

Sometimes when all the hotels on the Mexican side of Nogales are full, you can find rooms on the US side of the border. *Mi Casa RV Park (☎ 520-281-1150)*, 5km north of town at exit 8, highway 89, has spaces for US$21.50, with weekly and monthly discounts. *Motel 6 (☎ 520-281-2951, 141 W Mariposa Rd)* charges US$40/46 (several dollars cheaper off-season). *Best Western Time Motel (☎ 520-287-4627, 921 N Grand Ave)* is similarly priced. *Best Western Siesta Motel (☎ 520-287-4671, 673 N Grand Ave)* costs a few dollars more. These hotels have swimming pools.

Places to Eat

Cafeteria Leo's, at the corner of Obregón and Campillo, is a simple, air-conditioned place good for economical meals; the daily *comida corrida* costs US$4, other meals US$3 to US$5. The small, simple *Mariscos Puerto de Guaymas*, behind the tourist office at the border crossing, offers seafood meals for US$5.50. *Parador Restaurant*, at Hotel Granada (see Places to Stay), is a clean little restaurant with meals for US$2 to US$5; it is open 6 am to 2 am daily.

For something fancier, *Restaurant/Bar El Greco (Obregón 152)*, upstairs on the corner of Pierson, is an enjoyable spot with air-con, attractive decor and good food. The 'meal of the day' costs US$7.50; Mexican dishes US$6.25 to US$10.75, steak and seafood meals US$10 to US$25; enter via the stairs at the rear of the shop on the corner. *Restaurant/Bar El Cid (Obregón 124)*, entered via stairs at the rear of a shopping arcade, serves Mexican and international meals for US$10 to US$19. *Elvira's Restaurant (Obregón 1)*, on the corner of Internacional, is similar and has meals for US$5.50 to US$13.

Getting There & Away

Air The nearest airport is in Tucson, Arizona, about 100km (1½ hours) north of Nogales.

Bus

Mexico The main bus station is on highway 15, about 8km south of the city center. Elite, Transportes Norte de Sonora and Transportes del Pacífico have 1st-class air-conditioned buses that head south along highway 15 to Guadalajara and on to Mexico City. Crucero buses travel across the border from here to the Greyhound station on the Arizona side and to Tucson, Phoenix and Los Angeles (USA).

Tufesa has its own station, on the highway about 400m outside of Nogales, and has hourly buses 24 hours a day that go south as far as Culiacán. Transportes Baldomero Corral, at Km 4.5 on the highway, serves only the state of Sonora, with a bus departing every two hours, 7 am to 10.30 pm; stops include Hermosillo (3½ hours, US$11) and Álamos (nine hours, US$25).

Buses departing from the main bus station include:

Chihuahua – 962km, 12 hours; 1 1st-class (US$47), 6 2nd-class (US$42)

Guadalajara – 1692km, 25 hours; 34 buses (US$90 to US$103)

Guaymas – 416km, 5 hours; 42 buses (US$14.50 to US$19.50)

Hermosillo – 282km, 3½ hours; 59 buses (US$11 to US$13)

Los Mochis – 765km, 10 hours; 34 buses (US$30 to US$35)

Mazatlán – 1186km, 16 hours; 34 buses (US$63 to US$72)

Mexico City (Terminal Norte) – 2227km, 33 hours; 13 buses (US$115 to US$134)

Puerto Peñasco – 465km, 6 hours; 1 bus (US$23)

Tepic – 1476km, 21 hours; 34 buses (US$77 to US$88)

The USA From Tucson's Greyhound station (2 S 4th Ave), the CAS bus arrives at the Nogales, Arizona Greyhound station (35 N Terrace Ave), a block from the border crossing. The 1½-hour ride costs US$7. The Greyhound station also has three daily direct buses to Phoenix (3½ hours, US$22) and Los Angeles (10 hours, US$77), and four to Hermosillo (three hours, US$11) and Ciudad Obregón (six hours, US$21).

Opposite the Greyhound station, Unión Transportes de Nogales, 42 N Terrace Ave, has shuttle vans that take you to your door if you live in Tucson (one hour, US$8) or Phoenix (three hours, US$30). Buses operate from 5 am to 8 pm and depart whenever five people are on hand for the trip.

Crucero, in conjunction with Greyhound, runs an hourly bus, 4 am to 10 pm, between the main bus station on the Mexican side and the Greyhound bus station on the US side (US$3). Crucero on the US side has buses to Hermosillo and Ciudad Obregón (Mexico).

Car & Motorcycle Approaching Nogales from Tucson, the left lanes go to central Nogales. The right lanes, which go to a vehicular border crossing outside the city (favored by trucks), are the quickest way to enter Mexico, but the crossing is only open from 6 am to 10 pm. Outside these hours, you'll have to come through the city, where the border crossing is open 24 hours a day. As you approach Nogales, you'll see plenty of signs for Mexican auto insurance, which you'll need if you're bringing a vehicle into Mexico.

Temporary vehicle import procedures are dealt with at the Aguazarca inspection site at the 21km point on the highway south of Nogales. See the Car & Motorcycle section in the Getting There & Away chapter for more on bringing a vehicle into Mexico and on simplified procedures for those who are only visiting Sonora.

On the Arizona side of Nogales, Cropper Auto/Enterprise Rent-A-Car (☎ 520-281-2438, 800-325-8007, 1831 N Grand Ave) allows you to take its rental vehicles to Mexico. You can pick up the vehicle in either Nogales or Tucson (including the Tucson airport), and must return it where you got it. Hertz (☎ 520-287-2012, 800-654-3131, 1012 N Grand Ave) also rents vehicles for trips into Mexico, but its prices are higher and you must pick up and drop off the vehicle in Nogales (not Tucson).

On the Arizona side of Nogales, several attended lots near the border crossing offer parking for US$4 per day.

Getting Around

For the bus station, city buses marked 'Central' or 'Central Camionera' depart frequently from a corner on López Mateos, two blocks south of the border crossing (US$0.30). Everything else you'll need in Nogales is within easy walking distance of the border crossing. Taxis wait on either side of the border crossing, but are not allowed to cross it.

OTHER BORDER CROSSINGS

The Nogales border crossing is the quickest and easiest route in this region. Other 24-hour border crossings between Sonora and Arizona include **San Luis Río Colorado**, west of Nogales on the banks of the Río Colorado (Colorado River), 42km southwest of Yuma, Arizona, and **Agua Prieta**, about 130km east of Nogales opposite Douglas, Arizona. **Sonoita**, opposite Lukeville, Arizona and immediately south of the picturesque Organ Pipe Cactus National Monument, has a border crossing open 8 am to midnight daily. All these crossings are on Mexican highway 2, with frequent bus services from the Mexican side to places deeper into Mexico (though possibly not on the US side between San Luis Río Colorado and Yuma).

El Sásabe, opposite Sasabe, Arizona, about 60km west of Nogales, is in the middle of nowhere, with no bus connections on either side of the border and nowhere to get your Mexican car insurance if you're driving south. The crossing is open 8 am to 10 pm daily, but you're probably better off crossing somewhere else. About 90km east of Nogales, **Naco**, opposite Naco, Arizona, a few kilometers south of Bisbee, Arizona, has a 24-hour crossing.

AROUND NORTHERN SONORA

On the northeast coast of the Sea of Cortez (Golfo de California), **Puerto Peñasco** (population 60,000; ☎ 6) is a popular destination for travelers with trailers and RVs, making tourism an even more profitable industry than the shrimping and fishing for which this small town is also known. About a 1½-hour drive south of the Sonoita border crossing, this is southern Arizona's nearest beach.

Growing rapidly, Puerto Peñasco has many good hotels, motels, trailer parks and restaurants, and a marina. Fishing, surfing, scuba diving, kayaking and yacht cruises are popular activities. English is widely spoken and local businesses are as keen to take US dollars as pesos.

Puerto Peñasco's tourist office, the Secretaría de Fomento al Turismo (☎ 383-50-10, 383-61-22, Boulevard Benito Juárez 132B) can help with activities and accommodations; it is open 9 am to 4 pm Monday to Saturday. In the USA, Rocky Point Reservations (☎ 602-439-9004, 800-850-8122) also arranges stays in Puerto Peñasco. Recommended hotels include *Hotel Plaza Las Glorias*, *Playa Bonita*, *Viña del Mar*, *Costa Brava* and *Posada de León*.

Northwest of Puerto Peñasco is **Reserva de la Biósfera El Pinacate y Gran Desierto de Altar**, a reserve containing several extinct volcanic craters, a large lava flow, cinder cones, a cinder mine and vast sand dunes. Visitors must register at the entrance, reached by going down a 10km gravel road heading south from a turnoff about 10km east of Los Vidrios, which is on highway 2, due north of Puerto Peñasco. Until 1993, part of the reserve formed the Parque Nacional El Pinacate, a title still sometimes used.

The small town of **Cananea**, on highway 2 about halfway between Santa Ana and Agua Prieta, is a mining town that is not of much note today, but it is significant in Mexican history because the miners' revolt that broke out here on June 1, 1906, near the end of the rule of Porfirio Díaz, helped to precipitate the Mexican Revolution. Displays in the small town museum tell the story of the strike.

HERMOSILLO
● pop 504,000 ● elev 238m ☎ 6

On highway 15 about 280km south of Nogales, Hermosillo ('ehrr-mo-SEE-yo') was founded in 1700 by Juan Bautista Escalante for the resettlement of indigenous Pima and is now the large, bustling, multi-industry capital of the Sonora state. Like many cities in Mexico, Hermosillo industri-

alized quickly. In the early 1980s, it was little more than an agricultural and administrative center of 45,000 people. Many travelers pass through Hermosillo heading north or south. Smack in the middle of the great Desierto Sonorense, Hermosillo gets very hot in summer; the rest of the year it's quite pleasant.

Orientation
Highway 15 enters Hermosillo from the northeast and becomes Boulevard Francisco Eusebio Kino, a wide street lined with orange and laurel trees. Boulevard Kino continues west through the city, curves southwest and becomes Rodríguez, then Rosales as it passes through the city center, then Agustín de Vildosola before becoming highway 15 again south of the city. The major business and administrative sections of Hermosillo lie on either side of Boulevard Rosales and along Boulevard Encinas, which transects the center from northwest to southeast. The Periférico, once a beltway around Hermosillo, has become practically an inner loop due to the city's rapid expansion.

Information
Tourist Offices The Secretaría de Fomento al Turismo (☎ 217-00-76, 217-00-44, 800-716-25-55 in Mexico, ☎ 800-476-6672 in the USA, www.sonora.gob.mx/turismo) is on the 3rd floor of the south wing of the giant Centro de Gobierno building, which straddles Comonfort just south of Paseo Canal, on the south side of the city center. It's open 8 am to 5 pm Monday to Friday.

Another tourist information office, on highway 15 at the checkpoint about 15km north of Hermosillo, is open 8 am to 8 pm daily. Both have information on all Sonora and links with the Arizona tourist office in Phoenix.

Money Banks and casas de cambio are scattered along Hermosillo's Boulevards Rosales and Encinas. The American Express agent, Hermex Travel (☎ 213-44-15), is on the corner of Boulevard Rosales and Monterrey.

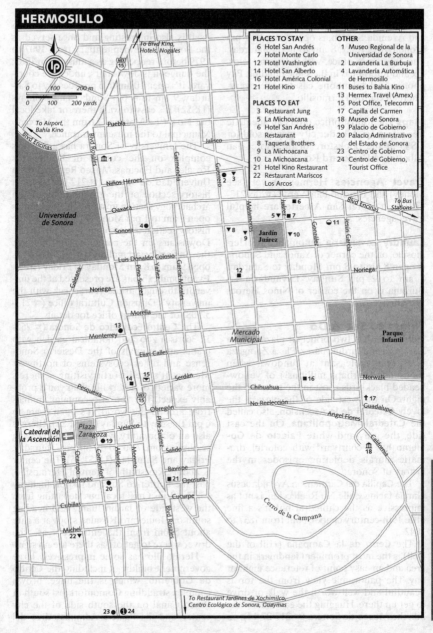

HERMOSILLO

To Blvd King,
Hotels, Nogales

0   100   200 m
0   100   200 yards

To Airport,
Bahía Kino

Blvd Encinas

Blvd Rosales

Puebla

Jalisco

Garmendia

Guerrero

Niños Héroes

Oaxaca

Matamoros

Sonora

Juárez

González

Luis Donaldo Colosio

Pino Suárez

Yáñez

García Morales

Morella

Monterrey

Elías Calles

Serdán

Chihuahua

No Reelección

Obregón

Velazco

Pino Suárez

Salido

Bavispe

Oposura

Cucurpe

Braun

Ocampo

Confort

Allende

Moreno

Tehuántepec

Cubillas

Michel

Pesqueira

Catedral de
la Ascensión

Plaza
Zaragoza

Universidad
de Sonora

Jardín
Juárez

Mercado
Municipal

Parque
Infantil

Norwalk

Guadalupe

Angel Flores

California

Cerro de la Campana

Blvd Encinas

To Bus
Stations

Jesús García

Noriega

Galeana

Noriega

Blvd Rosales

To Restaurant Jardines de Xochimilco,
Centro Ecológico de Sonora, Guaymas

23 ●   ❶ 24

PLACES TO STAY
6 Hotel San Andrés
7 Hotel Monte Carlo
12 Hotel Washington
14 Hotel San Alberto
16 Hotel América Colonial
21 Hotel Kino

PLACES TO EAT
3 Restaurant Jung
5 La Michoacana
6 Hotel San Andrés
    Restaurant
8 Taquería Brothers
9 La Michoacana
10 La Michoacana
21 Hotel Kino Restaurant
22 Restaurant Mariscos
    Los Arcos

OTHER
1 Museo Regional de la
    Universidad de Sonora
2 Lavandería La Burbuja
4 Lavandería Automática
    de Hermosillo
11 Buses to Bahía Kino
13 Hermex Travel (Amex)
15 Post Office, Telecomm
17 Capilla del Carmen
18 Museo de Sonora
19 Palacio de Gobierno
20 Palacio Administrativo
    del Estado de Sonora
23 Centro de Gobierno
24 Centro de Gobierno,
    Tourist Office

Post & Communications The main post office, on the corner of Boulevard Rosales and Avenida Serdán, is open 8 am to 7 pm Monday to Friday, 8 am to noon Saturday. The Telecomm office, with telegram, telex, fax and Internet, is in the same building. Pay phones and telephone casetas are everywhere in central Hermosillo.

Maps The tourist office offers an adequate free city map. A better city map is sold for US$3 at the bookstore of the Hotel San Alberto, on Boulevard Rosales.

Travel Agencies Hermex Travel (see Money) and Turismo Palo Verde (☎/fax 213-47-01), at Hotel San Alberto, are helpful travel agencies.

Laundry Lavandería Automática de Hermosillo, on the corner of Yañez and Sonora, is open 8 am to 8 pm Monday to Saturday, 8 am to 2 pm Sunday. Lavandería La Burbuja is on the corner of Niños Héroes and Guerrero.

Things to See & Do

Hermosillo has two principal plazas: Plaza Zaragoza and Jardín Juárez. Plaza Zaragoza is especially pleasant at sundown when thousands (perhaps millions!) of yellow-headed blackbirds roost in the trees for the night. On the west side of the plaza is the lovely **Catedral de la Ascensión**, also called the **Catedral Metropolitana**. On the east side, the gray-and-white **Palacio de Gobierno** has a courtyard with colorful, dramatic murals depicting episodes in the history of Sonora.

The **Capilla del Carmen**, on Avenida Jesús García facing Calle No Reelección, is not as impressive as the cathedral but it's a fine little 19th-century chapel, built from 1837 to 1842.

The **Cerro de la Campana** (Hill of the Bell) is the most prominent landmark in the area and an easy point of reference night or day. The panoramic view from the top is beautiful and well-worth the walk or drive to get up there. Hugging the east side of the hill, the **Museo de Sonora** (☎ 217-27-14), on

Jesús García, has fine exhibits on the history and anthropology of Sonora. The building itself is also interesting and once served as the Sonora state penitentiary from 1907 to 1979 before reopening as a museum in 1985; the dungeon is downstairs, under the courtyard. It's open 10 am to 5 pm Tuesday to Saturday, 9 am to 4 pm Sunday and holidays (US$2). It's easy to walk there, or take local bus No 8 ('La Matanza') from the Mercado Municipal to the museum entrance.

The University of Sonora has a fine arts complex on the corner of Boulevards Rosales and Encinas. **Museo Regional de la Universidad de Sonora** (☎ 212-06-09) has a history section on the ground floor and an archaeology section upstairs. The museum is open 9 am to 1 pm Monday to Saturday; the history section is also open 4 to 6 pm (free). Downstairs on the corner of the building, the **university art gallery** (☎ 213-42-67) is open 9 am to 8 pm Monday to Friday (free). Events and exhibits are presented at the university throughout the year; check with the university's Difusión Cultural office (☎ 213-52-08) or the tourist office for details.

The **Centro Ecológico de Sonora** (☎ 250-12-36) is a zoo and botanical garden with plants and animals of the Desierto Sonorense and other ecosystems of northwest Mexico. It's well-worth visiting – there's more variety of desert life than you'd probably expect. The zoo also contains animals from around the world. It's open 8 am to 6 pm Tuesday to Sunday (US$1.25). There is also an observatory, with telescope viewing sessions from 7.30 to 10.30 pm Thursday, Friday and Saturday (US$1.25). The center is about 5km south of central Hermosillo, past the Periférico Sur and just off highway 15. The 'Luis Orcí' local bus, departing from the west side of Jardín Juárez and heading south on Boulevard Rosales, stops at a gate about 500m from the entrance – ask the driver where to get off, as there are no signs.

Hermosillo has some impressively large government buildings, including the **Centro de Gobierno**, which is the huge, brown complex straddling Comonfort just south of Paseo Canal on the south side of the city center; and the **Palacio Administrativo del**

Estado de Sonora (see its courtyard) on Tehuantepec between Comonfort and Allende.

Hermosillo boasts a couple of enjoyable recreation parks with miniature golf, boats, bathing pools and other activities for children and adults. **Mundo Divertido** (☎ 260-35-05, Colosio 653) is open noon to 9 pm every day except Tuesday. **La Sauceda** (☎ 212-05-09) on Boulevard Serna, east of Cerro de la Campana, is open 9 am to 6 pm Tuesday to Sunday.

Special Events
The city's major annual event, the Exposición Ganadera (the Sonora state fair) is held in the Unión Gándara each year for 10 days near the end of April. La Vendimia, or Fiesta de la Uva (Festival of the Grape), is held on a weekend in late June.

Places to Stay
If you spend a night here in summer, you must have a room with air-con that works. Check the room before you accept it.

Budget *Hotel Washington* (☎ 213-11-83, *Noriega 68 Pte*), between Guerrero and Matamoros, has clean, simple air-conditioned rooms for US$13. *Hotel Monte Carlo* (☎ 212-33-54), on the corner of Juárez and Sonora, at the northeast corner of Jardín Juárez, is a reasonably priced older hotel with clean air-conditioned rooms with TV for US$16.50 to US$21. *Hotel América Colonial* (☎ 212-24-48, *Juárez 171 Sur*), between Avenida Serdán and Chihuahua, is a basic hotel with dark, bare rooms, but most do have TV and (noisy) air-con; singles/doubles/triples cost US$14/16/20.

Mid-Range *Hotel Kino* (☎ 213-31-31, *Pino Suárez 151 Sur*), conveniently situated near Boulevard Rosales, has a small indoor swimming pool, parking, a pleasant restaurant, and cool air-con throughout; rates are US$24/32 (for standard rooms) and US$38/44 (for suites). *Hotel San Alberto* (☎ 213-18-40), at Boulevard Rosales and Avenida Serdán, has a swimming pool, parking, bar, travel agency, bookstore,

restaurant annex and 80 air-conditioned rooms; rates are US$29/33/41/44. *Hotel San Andrés* (☎ 217-30-99, *Oaxaca 14*), near Juárez, a block from Jardín Juárez, has parking, a restaurant and 80 refurbished air-conditioned rooms around a pleasant courtyard; rooms with one bed cost US$37, with two beds cost US$39 to US$42.

Top End Many of Hermosillo's better hotels and motels are strung along Boulevard Kino in the northeast corner of the city. These include *Fiesta Americana* (☎ 250-60-00, *Boulevard Kino 369*) and *Araiza Inn* (☎ 210-27-17, *Boulevard Kino 353*) as well as *Señorial*, *Bugambilia*, *Gándara*, *Holiday Inn* and others.

Places to Eat
Some of the cheapest food in Hermosillo can be bought from the hot-dog carts on many street corners. The hot dogs, for US$0.60, are surprisingly good, especially when piled high with guacamole, refried beans, chilies, relish and/or mustard. Another street-cart treat is the *pico de gallo* – chunks of orange, apple, pineapple, cucumber, jicama, watermelon and coconut – refreshing on a hot day.

For a cool fruit salad, yogurt with fruit, ice cream, fruit or vegetable juice or other cold drinks, check out the many branches of *La Michoacana*. The three bordering Jardín Juárez, open till 9 pm, are convenient for getting snacks to take out on the plaza.

There are cheap food stalls in *Mercado Municipal*, on Matamoros between Avenidas Elias Calles and Monterrey. *Taquería Brothers*, on the corner of Sonora and Guerrero, is a simple stall serving great tacos and quesadillas.

Restaurant Jung (*Niños Héroes 75D*), near Boulevard Encinas, is a clean, cheerful air-conditioned vegetarian restaurant and health food store with a vast, reasonably priced menu plus buffets at breakfast, lunch and dinner. The breakfast buffet, served from 7.30 am, costs US$4 for the yogurt, fruit and cereal side, US$4 for the hot breakfast side, or US$5.50 for both. The *buffet de comidas*, served from 12.30 pm, costs US$6;

the *'buffet comida feliz'* from 5 to 7 pm costs US$4.50.

The simple air-conditioned restaurant at **Hotel Kino** (see Places to Stay) has reasonable meals, with breakfast and dinner for US$3.50 and a comida corrida for US$4.50. **Hotel San Andrés** also has a restaurant.

The pleasant air-conditioned **Restaurant Mariscos Los Arcos** *(Michel 43)*, on the corner of Ocampo, is famous for its seafood. Meals range from US$6 to US$10.50, with most around US$9.

Hermosillo's best-known restaurant is **Jardines de Xochimilco** (☎ 250-40-89), a pleasant place that serves the beef for which Sonora is famous and has mariachi bands. The dinner special for two (US$20) is a memorable feast. It's at Obregón 51 in Villa de los Seris, an old part of town just south of the center. Come in a taxi at night, as the neighborhood is not the best; anyone can direct you in the daytime. It's open 11 am to 9 pm daily; reservations are advised in the evening.

Shopping

If you always wanted to buy a pair of cowboy boots and a 10-gallon hat, you'll probably find what you want in Hermosillo. The city has one of the best selections of cowboy gear in Mexico. Ironwood carvings made by the Seri people are another distinctive product of the region and are sold in front of the post office and at other places around town.

Getting There & Away

Air The airport, about 10km from central Hermosillo on the road to Bahía Kino, is serviced by Aero California, Aerolitoral, Aeroméxico, America West, Mexicana and TAESA. Daily direct flights, all with connections to other centers, go to Chihuahua, Ciudad Juárez, Ciudad Obregón, Culiacán, Guadalajara, Guaymas/San Carlos, Guerrero Negro, La Paz, Los Angeles, Los Mochis, Mexicali, Mexico City, Monterrey, Phoenix, Tijuana and Tucson.

Bus The Central de Autobuses on Boulevard Encinas is about 2km southeast of the city center and has services by Crucero, Elite, Estrella Blanca (EB), Transportes del Pacífico (TP), Transportes Norte de Sonora (TNS) and others. Other companies have separate terminals nearby – Transportes Baldomero Corral (TBC) is next door. Across the street is Tufesa, and about a block west of Boulevard Encinas is Estrellas del Pacífico (EP). Services to many destinations depart round the clock. Daily 1st-class departures include:

Guadalajara – 1410km, 23 hours; 96 buses from the Central de Autobuses (US$75 to US$88); via Los Mochis, Mazatlán and Tepic

Guaymas – 134km, 1¾ hours; 48 Tufesa, 24 TNS, 20 TBC, 13 TP, 13 EP (US$4.75 to US$5.25)

Los Angeles (California) – 15 hours; 3 Crucero (US$66)

Mexico City (Terminal Norte) – 1945km, 30 to 33 hours; at least 60 buses from the Central de Autobuses (US$110 to US$127)

Nogales – 282km, 4 hours; frequent buses by most companies (US$11 to US$13)

Phoenix (Arizona) – 565km, 8 hours; 5 Crucero (US$32)

Tijuana – 892km, 13 hours; 24 TNS, 24 EB, 13 TP, 13 EP (US$44)

Tucson (Arizona) – 385km, 5½ hours; 5 Crucero, 3 TBC (US$20)

Second-class buses to Bahía Kino depart from the AMH & TCH bus terminal in central Hermosillo, on Sonora between González and Jesús García, 1½ blocks east of Jardín Juárez. They depart at 5.40, 6.30, 7.30, 8.30, 9.30 and 11.30 am and 12.30, 1.30, 3.30 and 5.30 pm; the dusty, bumpy two-hour trip costs US$4.25.

Getting Around

Local buses operate daily, 5.30 am to 10 pm (US$0.30). To get to the Central de Autobuses, take any 'Central,' 'Central Camionera' or 'Ruta 1' bus from Juárez on the east side of Jardín Juárez.

BAHÍA KINO

• pop 4040 ☎ changing

Named for Father Eusebio Kino, a Jesuit missionary who established a small mission here for the indigenous Seri people in the

On November 1, 2000, the telephone area code is due to change to ☎ 6 from 624, with the digits 24 added to the start of every local number (for example, the number 2-02-16 will become 242-02-16).

late 17th century, the bayfront town of Kino, 110km west of Hermosillo, is divided into old and new parts that are as different as night and day.

Kino Viejo, the old quarter on your left as you drive into Kino, is a dusty, run-down fishing village. Kino Nuevo, on your right, is basically a single beachfront road stretching about 8km north along the beach, lined with the holiday homes and retreats of wealthy gringos and Mexicans. It's a fine beach with soft sand and safe swimming. From around November to March the 'snowbirds' drift down in their trailers from colder climes. The rest of the time it's not crowded – but it's always a popular day outing for families

from Hermosillo escaping the city. The beach has many *palapas* providing welcome shade.

The **Museo de los Seris**, about halfway along the beachfront road in Kino Nuevo, has fascinating exhibits about the Seri, the traditionally nomadic indigenous people of this area. It's open 8 am to 3 pm Monday to Friday (free); there's a Seri *artesanías* shop next door. Seri ironwood carvings are sold in both Kino Nuevo and Viejo.

Places to Stay & Eat

Kino Nuevo Most people come to Kino for the day from Hermosillo, but there are several places to stay. Prices tend to be considerably higher than in Hermosillo. There are plenty of palapas all along the beach – you could easily string up a hammock and camp out under one of these for free.

At the far north end of Kino Nuevo, opposite the beach at the end of the bus line, the clean, attractive and well-equipped *Kino Bay RV Park* (☎ 2-02-16) has 180 tent or trailer spaces with full hookups (US$18) and

The Seris

The Seris are the least numerous indigenous people in Sonora, but one of the most recognized due to their distinctive handicrafts. Traditionally a nomadic people living by hunting, gathering and fishing – not agriculture, as was prevalent among many other indigenous groups in Mexico – the Seris roamed along the Sea of Cortez from roughly El Desemboque in the north to Bahía Kino in the south, and inland to Hermosillo.

The Seris are one of the few indigenous peoples who do not work for outsiders, preferring to live by fishing, hunting and handicrafts. Their most famous handicrafts are their ironwood carvings of animals, humans and other figures. Other important traditional handicrafts, including pottery and basketry, are no longer as important. The Seris were once one of the very few peoples in the world who were nomadic and also made pottery.

Though the Seris are no longer strictly nomadic, they still often move from place to place in groups; sometimes you can see them camped at Bahía Kino, or traveling up and down the coast. You will also see Seris in Hermosillo, where some sell ironwood carvings outside the post office. Many, though, live far from modern civilization in the large, protected Isla Tiburón (which belongs to the Seri) or in other inconspicuous places along the Sonora coast, and they still maintain many of their old traditions reflecting the rhythms of living between the desert and the sea.

A visit to the Museo de los Seris in Kino Nuevo is a rewarding experience. It has illuminating exhibits on aspects of Seri culture ranging from their distinctive clothing, traditional houses with frames of ocotillo cactus, musical instruments and handicrafts, to their nomadic social structure and nature-based religion.

❈❈❈❈❈❈❈❈❈❈❈❈❈❈❈❈❈❈❈❈❈❈❈❈❈❈❈

six air-conditioned motel rooms (US$50). The beachfront *Parador Bellavista (☎ 2-01-39)* has camping spaces (tents US$12, trailers US$18) and two air-conditioned rooms with kitchenette (US$30). *Posada Santa Gemma (☎ 2-00-26)*, also on the beach, offers tent and trailer spaces without hookups (US$17) and bungalows (US$130); prices seem to be negotiable. The beachfront *Restaurant & Hotel Saro (☎/fax 2-00-07)* has air-conditioned rooms with fridge and TV for US$45. Kino's luxury hotel, *Hotel Posada del Mar (☎/fax 2-01-55)*, has singles/doubles starting at US$33/39. All of these places offer both weekly and monthly discounts.

Various places to eat – all specializing in fresh seafood, of course – are along the beachfront road and in some of the hotels. *Restaurant La Palapa*, *Pargo Rojo* and *Taco Bar* are recommended.

Kino Viejo *Islandia Marina (☎/fax 2-00-81)*, on the beach, is a trailer park with tent spaces for US$6/10 without/with electricity, trailer spaces for US$15 with all hookups, plus eight free-standing self-contained bungalows. Beachfront bungalows cost US$33, others US$28; bring your own bed linen and dishes. A block away, the pricey, air-con *Restaurant Marlin* and *Roberto's* are popular restaurants. Other small open-air eateries, serving fresh barbecued fish or tacos, are dotted around Kino Viejo.

Getting There & Away

Bus Buses from Kino to Hermosillo run roughly every hour on the half hour, with the last bus departing from Kino Nuevo at 5.30 pm and Kino Viejo at 6 pm. If you come at a busy time (on a Sunday, for example, when lots of families are there) and you want to get the last bus of the day, catch it at the first stop, on the north end of Kino Nuevo, while there is still space.

Car & Motorcycle If you're driving, you can make the trip from Hermosillo to Bahía Kino in about an hour's drive. From central Hermosillo, head northwest out of town on Boulevard Encinas and just keep going.

GUAYMAS
- **pop 91,000** ☎ 6

Founded in 1769 by the Spaniards at the site of Yaqui and Guaymas indigenous villages on the shores of a sparkling blue bay, Guaymas is Sonora's main port. Fishing and commerce are its main economic activities. A ferry connects Guaymas with Santa Rosalía, Baja California. The tourist resort town of San Carlos is 20km northwest of Guaymas.

You can enjoy the view of the fishing boats, town and surrounding hills from El Pescador statue in the Plaza del Pescador. The town's other notable features include the Plaza de los Tres Presidentes, which commemorates the three Mexican presidents hailing from Guaymas, the 19th-century Iglesia de San Fernando and its Plaza 13 de Julio, the Palacio Municipal (built in 1899) and the old jail (1900).

Orientation & Information

Highway 15 becomes Boulevard García López as it passes along the northern edge of Guaymas. Central Guaymas and the port area are along Avenida Serdán, the town's main drag, running parallel to and just south of García López; everything you'll need is on or near Avenida Serdán. García López and Avenida Serdán intersect a few blocks west of the Guaymas map's extents.

The tourist office, the Delegación de Fomento al Turismo (☎/fax 224-41-14), at the corner of Avenida 6 and Calle 19, is open 9 am to 4 pm Monday to Friday. They're planning to build a new office in the seafront park near El Pescador statue.

The post office, Avenida 10 between Calles 19 and 20, is open 8 am to 7 pm Monday to Friday and 8 am to noon Saturday. Telecomm, with telegram, telex and fax, is next door. Two pharmacies on Avenida Serdán have telephone/fax casetas: Farmacia San Martín, between Calles 21 and 22 (open 8 am to midnight daily), and Farmacia León, on the corner of Calle 19.

Several banks on Avenida Serdán have ATMs, including BanCrecer at Calle 15, Bancomer at Calle 18, and Banamex at Calle 20.

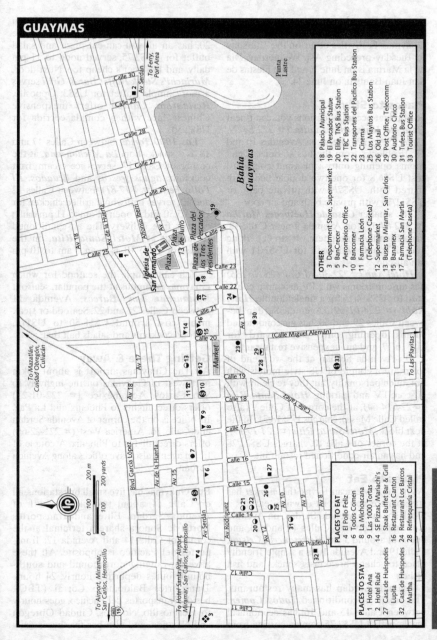

GUAYMAS

Calle 30
Av Serdán
To Ferry,
Port Area
Punta
Lastre
Calle 29
Calle 28
Calle 27
Calle 26
Bahía
Guaymas
Calle 25
Calle 24
Iglesia de
San Fernando
Alfonso Iberri
Av 15
Av de la Huerta
Av 18
Plaza
Plaza
13 de Julio
Plaza del
Pescador
Plaza de
los Tres
Presidentes
Calle 23
Calle 22
Calle 21
To Mazatlán,
Cuidad Obregón,
Culiacán
(Calle Miguel Alemán)
Calle 20
Av 17
Av 18
Market
Calle 19
Calle 18
Calle Yáñez
To Las Playitas
Blvd García López
Av de la Huerta
Av 15
Calle 17
Calle 16
Calle 15
Av 10
Av 9
Av 8
0   100   200 m
0   100   200 yards
Av Serdán
Av Rodríguez
Av 12
Calle 14
Calle 13
Av 13
(Calle Pradeau)
Calle 12
To Hotel Santa Rita, Airport,
Miramar, San Carlos, Hermosillo
To Airport, Miramar,
San Carlos, Hermosillo

PLACES TO STAY
1   Hotel Ana
2   Hotel Rubi
27 Casa de Huéspedes
    Lupita
32 Casa de Huéspedes
    Martha

PLACES TO EAT
4   El Pollo Feliz
6   Todos Comen
8   La Michoacana
9   Las 1000 Tortas
14 SE Pizzas, Mariachi's
16 Steak Buffet Bar & Grill
24 Restaurant Canton
28 Restaurant Los Barcos
    Refresquería Cristal

OTHER
3   Department Store, Supermarket
5   BanCrecer
7   Aeroméxico Office
10 Bancomer
11 Farmacia León
    (Telephone Caseta)
12 Supermarket
13 Buses to Miramar, San Carlos
15 Banamex
17 Farmacia San Martín
    (Telephone Caseta)
18 Palacio Municipal
19 El Pescador Statue
20 Elite, TNS Bus Station
21 TBC Bus Station
22 Transportes del Pacífico Bus Station
23 Cinema
25 Los Mayitos Bus Station
26 Old Jail
29 Post Office, Telecomm
30 Auditorio Cívico
31 Tufesa Bus Station
33 Tourist Office

Special Events

Carnaval is celebrated in a big way in Guaymas. Festivities occur on the Thursday to Tuesday preceding Ash Wednesday. Día de la Marina is on June 1, and the Fiestas de San Juan Bautista on June 24.

Places to Stay

For budget accommodations you can't beat *Casa de Huéspedes Lupita* (☎ 222-84-09, *Calle 15 No 125*) between Avenidas 10 and 12, 1½ blocks from the bus stations. Clean rooms opening onto a pleasant courtyard cost US$6/8 for one/two double beds with shared bath, US$7/9 with private bath, or US$11/16 with private bath and air-con.

The smaller *Casa de Huéspedes Martha* (☎ 222-83-32), on Avenida 9 near Calle 13, has a friendly atmosphere, off-street parking and 12 rooms with bath for US$7/11 with fan/air-con.

Hotel Ana (☎ 222-30-48, *Calle 25 No 135*) has air-con rooms with TV around a courtyard for US$14/16 for a single/double. *Hotel Rubí* (☎ 224-01-69), Avenida Serdán between Calles 29 and 30, has air-conditioned rooms opening onto a courtyard for US$16/17, and an inexpensive restaurant.

On Avenida Serdán at the west end of town are a couple of US-style motels with not much personality, but they're clean, with air-con, TV and parking. *Hotel Santa Rita* (☎ 224-14-64), at the corner of Calle 9 (also called Calle Mesa), charges US$18/21. In the next block, *Motel Santa Rita* (☎ 224-19-19), at the corner of Calle 10, charges US$22/28 and has an air-conditioned restaurant.

Places to Eat

As in most Mexican towns, the *market* has stalls where you can sit down to eat; it's a block south of Avenida Serdán, on Avenida Rodríguez between Calles 19 and 20, and opens at around 5 am. *Refresquería Cristal*, Calle 19 and Avenida 10, is a simple, friendly place for cheap breakfasts, snacks and fish dishes.

Avenida Serdán has many restaurants. The small air-conditioned *Todos Comen*, between Calles 15 and 16, has economical meals, with a US$2.75 comida corrida from noon to 3 pm daily; the restaurant is open 7 am to midnight daily. *SE Pizzas*, near Calle 20, has an all-you-can-eat pizza and salad buffet for US$2.75, served noon to 11 pm daily, and the beer's cheap too. Next door, *Mariachi's Steak Buffet Bar & Grill* serves a more ample buffet for US$3. Opposite, *Restaurant Canton* offers inexpensive Chinese fare with a comida corrida for US$2.50.

Las 1000 Tortas, between Calles 17 and 18, is a snack shop. *La Michoacana*, at the corner of Calle 17, serves ice cream, fruit cocktails, *aguas frescas* and *licuados*. *El Pollo Feliz* (☎ 4-17-81), between Calles 12 and 13, serves half/whole grilled chicken for US$3/5.50 and is open 11 am to 11 pm daily; call for free delivery. The air-conditioned restaurant at *Motel Santa Rita*, on the corner of Calle 10, is open 7 am to 10 pm daily.

You can sample the seafood for which Guaymas is famous at the popular, seafront *Restaurant Los Barcos*, Avenida 11 between Calles 21 and 22. Seafood or steak meals cost around US$8.50 to US$11, seafood cocktails and salads half that.

Getting There & Away

Air The Guaymas airport is about 10km northwest of Guaymas on the highway to San Carlos. Aeroméxico (☎ 222-01-23) offers direct flights to Phoenix and La Paz. Its office is on the corner of Avenida Serdán and Calle 16. America West (☎ 221-22-66) offers direct flights to Phoenix. A couple of travel agents also have offices along Avenida Serdán.

Bus Guaymas has five small bus stations, all on Calle 14, about two blocks south of Avenida Serdán. Elite and Transportes Norte de Sonora share a terminal at the corner of Calle 14 and Avenida 12; Transportes del Pacífico is opposite. All these have far-ranging northbound and southbound routes departing hourly, 24 hours. Transportes Baldomero Corral (TBC), beside Transportes del Pacífico, goes hourly to Hermosillo, Nogales, Ciudad Obregón and Navojoa, and also has five buses daily

(1.45 to 8.45 pm) direct to Álamos. Los Mayitos, between Avenidas 10 and 12, operates hourly buses north to Hermosillo and south to Navojoa, 6 am to 9 pm. Tufesa, at the corner of Avenida 10, has hourly buses heading south to Culiacán, and buses every half-hour heading north to Hermosillo and Nogales, 24 hours. All run 1st-class buses, though Pacífico also has 2nd-class buses. Distances, trip times and fares include:

Álamos – 247km, 4 hours; TBC only, US$9

Guadalajara – 1276km, 20 hours; US$71 to US$83

Hermosillo – 134km, 1¾ hours; US$3 to US$5.25

Los Mochis – 349km, 5 hours; US$14 to US$16

Mazatlán – 770km, 11 hours; US$34 to US$38

Mexico City (Terminal Norte) – 1811km, 28 hours; US$105 to US$121

Navojoa – 194km, 3 hours; US$7.25 to US$9

Nogales – 416km, 5 hours; US$16 to US$19

Tepic – 1060km, 16 hours; US$54 to US$62

Tijuana – 1026km, 15 hours; US$48 to US$58

Boat Ferries connect Guaymas with Santa Rosalía, Baja California. The ferry (transbordador) terminal (☎ 222-23-24) is on Avenida Serdán at the east end of town. Sailing days are Tuesday and Friday and ferries depart at 9 am.

Vehicle reservations are accepted by telephone a week in advance. Passenger tickets are sold at the ferry office on the morning of departure, or a few days before. Make reservations at least three days in advance and, even if you have reservations, arrive early at the ticket office. The office is open 6 am Tuesday and Friday, 8 am to 3 pm Monday and Wednesday and 8 to 11 am Saturday. Passenger fares are US$15. See the Santa Rosalía section in the Baja California chapter for vehicle fares.

Getting Around

To get to the airport, catch a bus from Avenida Serdán heading to Itson or San José, or take a taxi (US$6). Local buses run along Avenida Serdán frequently between 6 am to 9 pm daily (US$0.30). Several eastbound buses stop at the ferry terminal; ask for 'transbordador.'

AROUND GUAYMAS

The closest beach is **Miramar**, on the Bahía de Bacochibampo about 5km west of Guaymas. It's not a big tourist destination like San Carlos, but it does have an interesting industry – pearl farming.

The sprawling 150-room beachfront *Hotel Playa de Cortés* (☎/fax 6-221-01-35) has rooms for US$64 to US$170, plus a 90-space trailer park with full hookups and access to all hotel facilities for US$17 per space. 'Miramar' buses head west on Avenida Serdán (starting from between Calles 19 and 20) every 30 minutes, between 6.30 am and 8 pm (US$0.30).

San Carlos

• pop 1080 ☎ 6

On Bahía San Carlos, about 20km northwest of Guaymas, San Carlos is a beautiful desert-and-bay landscape. Twin-peaked Cerro Tetakawi is the symbol of the town. From around October to April, the town is full of *norteamericanos* and their trailers; the rest of the year it's quiet, except for a flurry of Mexican tourists in July and August.

San Carlos has two marinas: Marina San Carlos, which is in the heart of town; and the newer Marina Real at Algodones, which is in the northernmost sector of town. San Carlos is bursting with outdoor activities, such as snorkeling, diving, sailing, fishing, kayaking, mountain biking, motorcycling, horseback riding and golfing. There are also local tours, bay cruises, gyms and an Internet café. The view from the *mirador* (lookout) is spectacular, especially at sunset. Cañon de Nacapule, with lush green vegetation, is good for a 2½-hour circuit hike. The tourist offices can provide details on all activities.

San Carlos has two helpful bilingual tourist offices, both in the Edificio Hacienda Plaza on Boulevard Manlio Beltrones, the main road into San Carlos. The Delegación de Turismo (☎ 226-02-02, hdtours@prodigy.net.mx) and the Oficina de Turismo y Convenciones (Fondo Mixto; ☎/fax 226-13-14, ☎ 888-800-3866 in the USA, scl123@prodigy.net.mx) are both open 9 am to 5 pm Monday to Friday, 9 am to 2 pm Saturday.

Special Events Annual events include Carnaval, which is held the week following the Carnaval in Guaymas; a skydiving competition in March; women's fishing tournament in May; international fishing tournament in July; Labor Day fishing tournament in September; sailboat competition in October; and golf tournaments throughout the year.

Places to Stay & Eat *Teta Kawi Trailer Park*, operated by the Best Western Hotel Hacienda Teta Kawi (☎ 226-02-20) on Boulevard Manlio Beltrones, has camper/RV spaces for US$10/20. Campers can use all the hotel's facilities; rooms cost US$63 to US$84. *El Mirador RV Park* (☎/fax 227-02-13), overlooking Marina Real, has great views, many amenities, and 90 spaces; rates are US$22.

San Carlos' most economical hotel, *Posada del Desierto* (☎/fax 226-04-67), overlooking Marina San Carlos, has seven basic air-conditioned studio apartments with kitchen for US$34; cheaper weekly and monthly rates are available. *Motel Creston* (☎ 226-00-20), on Boulevard Manlio Beltrones, has a swimming pool and air-conditioned rooms for US$37. *Hotel Fiesta* (☎ 226-02-29), also on Boulevard Manlio Beltrones, is a popular hotel with swimming pool, restaurant and bar, and has beachfront rooms for US$38/47 a single/double.

At *Los Jitos Hotel & Spa* (☎ 226-14-13, *Carretera San Carlos Km 11*), weekday rates are US$38/51 and US$64 for suites; weekend rates are US$51/64 and US$76 for suites. It also operates *Loma Bonita Condohotel & Vacation Club*, which has condos for US$83/101 on weekdays/weekends. Both offer cheaper two-night and three-night packages.

The luxurious *San Carlos Plaza Hotel, Resort & Convention Center* (☎ 227-00-77/99, *Mar Bermejo Norte No 4, Algodones*) has standard rooms for US$142 to US$165 and suites for US$165 to US$735.

Twenty kilometers north of San Carlos and accessible only by boat, *Cañon Las Barajitas* (☎ 226-14-13) is an 800-hectare beachfront resort. Daily rates of US$80 per person (four persons minimum) also include transport, activities and three meals daily.

Good restaurants in San Carlos include the *San Carlos Grill*, which serves a variety of seafood and Mexican dishes; the international fare of *Piccolo's*; and *El Bronco*, a steakhouse serving famous Sonoran beef.

Getting There & Around Buses to San Carlos from Guaymas run west along Avenida Serdán (starting from between Calles 19 and 20) every 10 minutes, between 5.30 am and 11 pm (US$0.75). San Carlos also has a local bus, serving all its various sectors, 7 am to 8 pm (US$0.30).

CIUDAD OBREGÓN & NAVOJOA

Heading southeast from Guaymas, highway 15D passes through Ciudad Obregón (population 244,000). The town is 125km from Guaymas and is a modern agricultural center with nothing of interest to the tourist. Navojoa (population 94,800), 194km from Guaymas, is a similarly mundane place. From Navojoa a side road leaves the highway and heads east for 53km into the foothills of the Sierra Madre Occidental to the picturesque town of Álamos.

Navojoa has five bus stations within six blocks. Transportes del Pacífico, Transportes Norte de Sonora and Elite each have hourly buses, 24 hours a day, going north and south on highway 15D. Second-class buses to Álamos depart from the Transportes Baldomero Corral (TBC) station on the corner of Guerrero and No Reelección every half hour, between 6.30 am and 7 pm, and at 8 and 10 pm and midnight (one hour, US$1.50). TBC also has hourly buses north to Hermosillo (five hours, US$13.50), 11 daily buses to Nogales (eight hours, US$23.50) and three daily buses to Tucson (11 hours, US$33). The same buses to Álamos also depart from the Autobuses Los Mayitos station on the corner of Guerrero and Rincón; Los Mayitos goes north to Hermosillo hourly, between 6 am and 6 pm.

ÁLAMOS

• pop 7620 • elev 432m ☎ changing
This small, quiet town in the foothills of the Sierra Madre Occidental, 53km east of

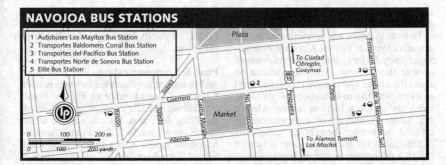

NAVOJOA BUS STATIONS

1 Autobuses Los Mayitos Bus Station
2 Transportes Baldomero Corral Bus Station
3 Transportes del Pacífico Bus Station
4 Transportes Norte de Sonora Bus Station
5 Elite Bus Station

Plaza

To Ciudad
Obregón,
Guaymas

Market

To Álamos Turnoff,
Los Mochis

Navojoa, has been declared a national historic monument. Its beautifully restored Spanish colonial architecture has a Moorish influence, brought by 17th-century architects from Andalusia in southern Spain. The façades of colonial mansions line narrow cobblestone streets, concealing courtyards lush with bougainvillea. Several of the old mansions have been converted to hotels and restaurants. The whole town has a distinctly peaceful, timeless feel. Sunday evenings are often spent strolling and people-watching on the Plaza de Armas – a lovely old tradition, enjoyed by locals and visitors alike.

Álamos is on the border of two large ecosystems – the great Desierto Sonorense to the north and the lush tropical jungles of Sinaloa to the south. Nature-lovers are attracted the area's 450 species of birds and animals (including some endangered and endemic species) and over 1000 species of plants. Horseback riding, hunting, fishing, hiking and swimming as well as dining in opulent colonial mansions are popular activities.

From mid-October to mid-April, when the air is cool and fresh, norteamericanos arrive to take up residence in their winter homes and the town begins to hum with foreign visitors. A fresh wave of visitors come in November through February for the quail and dove hunting season. Mexican tourists come in the scorching hot summer months of July and August, when school is out. At other times you may find scarcely another visitor.

History
In 1540, this was the campsite of Francisco Vázquez de Coronado, future governor of Nueva Galicia (the colonial name for much of western Mexico), during his wars against the indigenous Mayo and Yaqui (the Yaqui resisted all invaders until 1928). If he had known about the vast amounts of gold and silver that prospectors would later find, he would have stayed.

In 1683, silver was discovered at Promontorios, near Álamos, and the Europa mine was opened. Other mines soon followed and Álamos became a boom town of more than 30,000, one of Mexico's principal 18th-century mining centers. Mansions, haciendas, a cathedral, tanneries, metalworks, blacksmiths' shops and later a mint were built. El Camino Real (the King's Highway), a well-trodden Spanish mule trail through the foothills, connected Álamos with Culiacán and El Fuerte to the south.

After independence, Álamos became the capital of the newly formed province of Occidente, a vast area including all of the present states of Sonora and Sinaloa. Don José María Almada, owner of the richest silver mine in Álamos, was appointed as governor.

During the turmoil of the 19 th century and up to the Mexican Revolution, Álamos was attacked repeatedly, both by rebels seeking its vast silver wealth and by the fiercely independent Yaqui. The years of the revolution took a great toll on the town. By the 1920s, most of the population had left and many of the once-beautiful haciendas had fallen into disrepair. Álamos became practically a ghost town.

In 1948, Álamos was re-awakened by the arrival of William Levant Alcorn, a Pennsylvania dairy farmer who moved to Álamos, bought the 15-room Almada mansion on Plaza de Armas and restored it as the Hotel Los Portales. Alcorn brought publicity to the town and made a fortune selling Álamos real estate. A number of norteamericanos crossed the border, bought the crumbling old mansions for good prices and set about the task of lovingly restoring them to their former glory. Many of these people still live in Álamos today. Alcorn is also alive and well; you may find him sitting on the verandah of his hotel recounting intriguing stories of Álamos.

Orientation

The paved road from Navojoa enters Álamos from the west and leads to the green, shady Plaza Alameda, with outdoor cafés at either end where you can get a drink and sit and watch the world go by. The market is at the east end of Plaza Alameda; the other main square, Plaza de Armas, is two blocks south of the market.

The Arroyo La Aduana (Customs House Stream, which is usually dry) runs along the town's northern edge; the Arroyo Agua Escondida (Hidden Waters Stream, also usually dry) runs along the southern edge. Both converge at the east end of town with the Arroyo La Barranca (Ravine Stream), which runs from the northwest.

Information

Tourist Offices The Delegación de Turismo (☎ 8-04-50, Calle Juárez 6), under the Hotel Los Portales on the west side of Plaza de Armas, is open 9 am to 3 pm and 5 to 8 pm Monday to Friday.

In 2000, the telephone area code is due to change to ☎ 6 from 642, with the digits 42 added to the start of every local number (for example, the number 8-04-50 will become 428-04-50).

Money BanCrecer, Madero 37, is open for changing money 8.30 am to 3 pm Monday to Friday, 10 am to 2 pm Saturday. It has an ATM too.

Post & Communications The post office on Madero, at the entrance to town, is open 8 am to 3 pm Monday to Friday. Polo's Restaurant on Calle Zaragoza, one block off the Plaza de Armas, has a telephone caseta that is open 7 am to 9.30 pm daily. Another telephone caseta is in a shop on the south side of Plaza Alameda.

Bookstores Books about Álamos, and a variety of books in English, are available at El Nicho artesanías shop behind the cathedral, and at the gift shop of the Hotel Casa de los Tesoros. *A Brief History of Álamos* is an excellent source of information on the town. *The Stately Homes of Álamos* by Leila Gillette tells stories of many of the town's old homes.

Laundry The laundry is at the Dolisa Motel & Trailer Park, on Madero at the entrance to town.

Medical Services Don Fernando, who is a pharmacist at the Botica Económica pharmacy on the south side of Plaza Alameda, is highly praised and oft recommended by Álamos' expat community.

Things to See & Do

The **cathedral** is the tallest building in Álamos and also one of its oldest – construction lasted from 1786 to 1804 on the site of an early 17th-century adobe Jesuit mission. Legend relates that every family in Álamos contributed to the construction of the church. The high-ranking Spanish ladies of the town contributed plates from their finest sets of china to be placed at the base of the pilasters in the church tower. There is also a three-tiered belfry. Inside, the altar rail, lamps, censers and candelabra were fashioned from silver, but were all ordered to be melted down in 1866 by General Ángel Martínez after he booted out French imperialist troops from Álamos. Subterranean

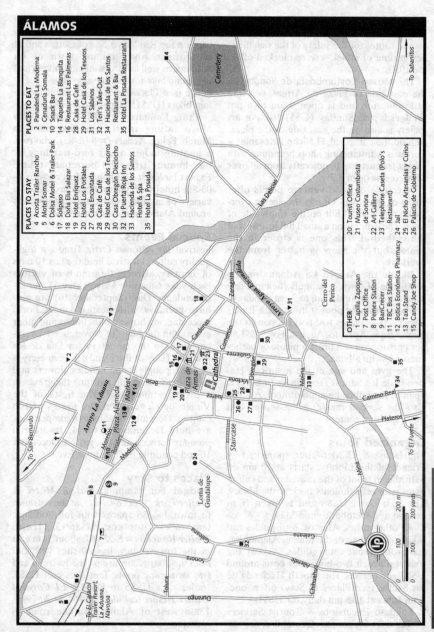

ÁLAMOS

PLACES TO STAY
4 Acosta Trailer Rancho
5 Motel Somar
6 Dolisa Motel & Trailer Park
17 Solipaso
18 Doña Elia Salazar
19 Hotel Enríquez
20 Hotel Los Portales
27 Casa Encantada
28 Casa de Café
29 Hotel Casa de los Tesoros
30 Casa Obregón Dieciocho
32 La Puerta Roja Inn
33 Hacienda de los Santos
   Hotel & Spa
35 Hotel La Posada

PLACES TO EAT
2 Panadería La Moderna
3 Cenaduría Somala
10 Snack Bar
14 Taquería La Blanquita
16 Restaurant Las Palmeras
28 Casa de Café
29 Hotel Casa de los Tesoros
31 Los Sabinos
32 Teri's Take-Out
34 Hacienda de los Santos
   Restaurant & Bar
35 Hotel La Posada Restaurant

OTHER
1 Capilla Zapopan
7 Post Office
9 Pemex Station
11 TBC Bus Station
12 Botica Económica Pharmacy
13 Taxi Stand
15 Candy Joe Shop
20 Tourist Office
21 Museo Costumbrista
   de Sonora
23 Art Gallery
23 Telephone Caseta (Polo's
   Restaurant)
24 Jail
25 El Nicho Artesanías y Curios
26 Palacio de Gobierno

NORTHWEST MEXICO

passageways between the church and several of the mansions – probably built as escape routes for the safety of the rich families in time of attack – were blocked off in the 1950s.

The **Museo Costumbrista de Sonora**, on the east side of Plaza de Armas, is a fine little museum and is open 9 am to 6 pm Wednesday to Sunday (US$1.10). An **art gallery** is also on the east side of the plaza. Behind the cathedral, **El Nicho Artesanías y Curios** is a fascinating shop brimming with curios, folk art and handicrafts from all over Mexico; it is open daily.

A couple of good **vantage points** offer views of the town. One is the scenic overlook atop a small hill on the south side of town. The other is on a small hill just west of the cathedral. This one is closer to the center, but the view is better from the overlook.

Beside the Arroyo La Aduana on the north side of town, a **tianguis** (flea market) is held from around 6 am to 2 pm Sunday.

The **swimming pool** at the Acosta Trailer Rancho (see Places to Stay) is open to the public from April to August. For US$1.50 per person, you can bring a picnic or barbecue, and swim all day.

The **gym** and **spa** at the luxurious Hacienda de los Santos (see Places to Stay) is open to the public by appointment. Álamos also has several masseurs/masseuses, and three spiritual centers.

Organized Tours

The Home & Garden Tour, sponsored by Friends of the Library, starts at 10 am on Saturday in front of the museum and culminates with refreshments back at the library. The tour costs US$8 and is given from around mid-October to mid-May.

At other times, Álamos' tour guides can take you to some of the homes. Álamos has six professional tour guides. Ask at the tourist office; a two-hour tour costs around US$7 per person. The superb Hacienda de los Santos (see Places to Stay) offers one-hour tours at 1.15 pm daily, for US$1.

Solipaso Excursions & Tourist Services (☎/fax 8-04-66, solipaso@compuserve.com, Cardenas 15), which is run by Jennifer and David MacKay, offers nature tours including trips on the Río Mayo, Sea of Cortez and of the former silver mining town of La Aduana, as well as bird-watching, hiking and mountain bike tours. They also have a guesthouse (see Places to Stay) and rent mountain bikes (US$15/70 per day/week).

Craig Leonard (☎ 8-01-42) offers Río Mayo rafting trips from December to March. Felipe Acosta (☎ 8-01-82), who runs a hunting lodge, offers bird-watching or bird-hunting trips and horseback riding. Expert biologist Stephanie Meyer (☎/fax 8-03-88, hotelrio@cybernet.com.mx) leads a variety of interpretive natural history tours around Álamos and southern Sonora.

Special Events

Festival Dr Alfonso Ortíz Tirado, a high-quality cultural festival held the last 10 days of January, attracts thousands of visitors each year. Cinco de Mayo (May 5) and Independence Day (September 16) are also huge holidays, with fiestas, dances, horse races, dancing horse competitions and other events. On the night of November 1, everyone goes to the cemetery for Día de los Muertos (Day of the Dead); the cemetery is cleaned, people bring candles, flowers and food, and walk around visiting the graves in a festive atmosphere. The fiesta of the Virgen de Concepción, the town's patron saint, is December 8. Singing competitions are held December 4 to 14. Traditional *posadas* (processions) begin on December 16 and continue to Christmas Eve.

Places to Stay

Budget For camping, **Dolisa Motel & Trailer Park** (☎/fax 8-01-31), at the entrance to town, has 36 spaces with full hookups; tent/trailer sites cost US$6/13. **Acosta Trailer Rancho** (☎ 8-02-46), about 1km east of the town center, has 20 sites with full hookups, barbecue areas, shady trees and two swimming pools. Tent sites cost US$5, trailer sites US$5 to US$12. **El Caracol Trailer Resort** (cellular ☎ 0164-84-20-79) is 13km west of Álamos on the road to Navojoa.

Hotel Enríquez (☎ 8-03-10), on the west side of Plaza de Armas, is a 250-year-old building with a central courtyard; basic singles/doubles cost US$8/13 with shared bath, US$11/17 with private bath. At the entrance to town, *Motel Somar* (☎ 8-01-95, *Madero 110)* has reasonably sized rooms with bath for US$13/15 to US$19/20 (higher priced rooms have air-con and TV).

Doña Elia Salazar (☎ 8-01-44, *Rosales 67)* is a private home that rents rooms for US$11 per person. The tourist office keeps a

---

Mexican Jumping Beans

Mexican jumping beans, or *brincadores*, are not really beans, and it's not really the 'beans' themselves that jump – it's the larvae of a small moth, the *Carpocapsa saltitans*. The moth lays its eggs on the flower of a shrub called the *Sebastiana palmieri* or *Sebastiana pavoniana*, of the spurge family. When the egg hatches, the caterpillar burrows into the plant's developing seed pod, which continues to grow and closes up leaving no sign that a caterpillar is inside. The larva eats the seed in the pod and builds itself a tiny web. By yanking the web, the caterpillar makes the pod 'jump.'

The brincadores only jump at certain times of the year, and they can only be found in one small part of the world – an area of about 650 sq km in southern Sonora and northern Sinaloa. Álamos is known as the 'jumping bean capital,' and the beans play a significant role in the economy of the town.

Twenty days after the first rain of the season, sometime in June, the seed pods with the caterpillars inside start jumping. People from Álamos and other small towns in the region take to the hills to gather the beans, locating them by the sound of rustling leaves. The hotter the weather, the more the jumping beans jump. They keep on jumping for about three to six months; the larva then spins a cocoon inside the seed, mutates and eventually emerges as a moth.

If you're in Álamos at the right time of year, you can go into the hills and find some brincadores yourself, or simply buy them from vendors in front of the cathedral. Trini, a popular tour guide and owner of the Candy Joe store on the north side of the Plaza de Armas, has been dubbed the 'jumping bean king.' He sells brincadores (about 40) in a small bag for US$2, or by the liter (about 1200) for US$40. He can send them internationally; write (in English or Spanish) to José Trinidad Hurtado S, Apartado Postal 9, Álamos, Sonora 85760, Mexico, or fax him at 52-642-8-00-22. The brincadores are sent out around July to September (minimum order 1L). If you get some jumping beans and they don't jump very much, close your hand around them to warm them up.

Interestingly, though Mexican jumping beans are sold as a curiosity in other parts of the world including the USA, Europe and Asia, they are almost never sold in other parts of Mexico.

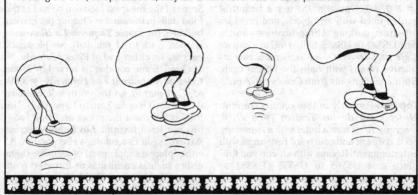

Álamos architecture

list of other *casas particulares* that also rent rooms.

Mid-Range *Dolisa Motel & Trailer Park* (see Budget) has pleasant rooms with air-con (some have fireplaces) for US$24/26 with one/two double beds, plus five attractive new rooms for US$37 and a suite with kitchen for US$45. *Acosta Trailer Rancho* (see Budget) has a hunting lodge and charges US$48 for rooms.

All other places in this category are restored Spanish colonial buildings. Least impressive (but still a fine place), *Hotel Los Portales* (☎ 8-02-01), on the west side of Plaza de Armas, is the restored mansion of the Almada family; singles/doubles cost US$29/40.

Some of Álamos' residents have turned their colonial-era homes into B&Bs, which provide a more personal environment. Roberto Bloor's *Casa Obregón Dieciocho* (☎ 8-07-90, Obregón 18) has a beautiful garden filled with art objects, and provides off-street parking. Three luxurious suites cost US$47 to US$55. Sally Hoff at *Casa de Café* (☎ 8-00-88, Obregón 3) rents two attractive rooms with bath for US$50 each. Both are open only from October to April.

Top End Formerly an 18th-century convent, *Hotel Casa de los Tesoros* (☎ 8-00-10, Obregón 10) is now a hotel with a swimming pool, cozy bar and courtyard restaurant with entertainment. Rooms with air-con and fireplace cost US$65 to US$75 (US$81 to US$104 from mid-October to mid-May, breakfast included). Los Tesoros also oper-

ates the similarly priced and luxurious *Casa Encantada (Juárez 20)*, a 10-room mansion with a beautiful courtyard and tiny swimming pool.

South of town, across the Arroyo Agua Escondida, *Hotel La Posada* (☎/fax 8-00-45, Calle 2 de Abril, Prolongación Sur, Barrio El Perico) is a restored former hospital. It has a restaurant, bar and some rooms with private kitchens and sleeping lofts; all have air-con and fireplace and cost US$65 to US$75.

Teri Arnold's *La Puerta Roja Inn* (☎/fax 8-01-42, Galeana 46) is less central but has a small swimming pool. She rents two charming rooms, plus a studio *casita* (small house) with kitchen out back, each for US$60, breakfast included; ask about weekly rates for the casita.

Jennifer and David MacKay of Solipaso (☎/fax 8-04-66, Cardenas 15) have a *guesthouse* just off Plaza de Armas. Rooms with bath cost US$65 (weekly US$400); the 'dungeon' room costs US$35 (weekly US$215). They also offer mountain bike rental and nature excursions (see Organized Tours).

For the utmost in beauty and luxury, *Hacienda de los Santos Hotel & Spa* (☎ 8-02-17, Molina 8) has three swimming pools, a gym, spa treatments, restaurant, bar and beautiful courtyards (also see Organized Tours, above). Rooms cost US$160 to US$287; off-premises rooms cost US$137.

Places to Eat

Some of the cheapest food can be had at the food stalls in the *market*. Outside the market building, the simple *Taquería La Blanquita* is open 7 am to 11 pm daily. Simple snack bars are on either end of Plaza Alameda.

Good 'home cooking' is served by Doña Celsa at *Restaurant Las Palmeras* (☎ 8-00-65, Cardenas 9), on the north side of Plaza de Armas; it is open 7 am to 10 pm daily. The food is tasty and the prices are good too – this is a town favorite. *Los Sabinos*, across Arroyo Agua Escondida, is also popular. At either place a simple meal of *antojitos* (light dishes such as enchiladas or tostadas) costs around US$2.25 to US$3.50, or a larger meat or seafood meal costs US$3.50 to

US$6.50. The little *Cenaduría Somala*, across Arroyo La Aduana north of town, is open daily until around 10 or 11 pm and is popular with locals.

Sally Hoff at *Casa de Café* (see Places to Stay) serves good coffee and pastries 8 am to noon daily from October to April.

The restaurant and bars at Álamos' beautifully restored colonial hotels provide an elegant atmosphere for a fine meal. The restaurant/bar at the *Hacienda de los Santos* serves breakfast, lunch, dinner and Sunday brunch, and a trio provides music every evening. At *Hotel Casa de los Tesoros*, you can dine in the air-conditioned restaurant, on the courtyard, or in the cozy bar. Indigenous dances are performed Saturday nights in winter; there's live dinner music all other evenings in winter, but only on Saturday in summer. *Hotel La Posada* (see Places to Stay) has a good restaurant too.

Panadería La Moderna, on Macías across the Arroyo La Aduana on the north edge of town, is Álamos' favorite bakery. The best time to come is around 1 pm, when the baked goods emerge from the outdoor oven.

Teri's Take-Out, operated by Teri Arnold at the La Puerta Roja Inn (see Places to Stay), offers reasonably priced gourmet take-out foods, serves luncheon and dinner parties in her dining room by appointment and does catering.

Getting There & Away

Access to Álamos is via a paved road 53km into the foothills from Navojoa. Transportes Baldomero Corral and other companies have frequent service to Álamos (see the preceding Ciudad Obregón & Navojoa section for bus information).

Álamos' Transportes Baldomero Corral bus station is on the north side of Plaza Alameda. Buses depart for Navojoa at 4 and 5 am, half-hourly from 6 am to 4.30 pm, and at 5.30, 6.30 and 9.15 pm (one hour, US$1.50). A direct bus to Tucson departs nightly at 9.15 pm (12 hours, US$34.50).

There's a taxi stand on the east end of Plaza Alameda, opposite the market.

AROUND ÁLAMOS

El Chalatón, a park about 2km southwest of town, is popular for swimming in summer. About 10km east of town, **Arroyo de Cuchujaqui** has a delightful swimming hole, and is enjoyable for fishing, camping and birdwatching. **Presa El Mocuzari** is also good for swimming, camping and fishing, with abundant largemouth bass, bluegill and catfish. Take the turnoff on the Navojoa-Álamos road, about 20km west of Álamos; the reservoir is about 12km from the turnoff.

Several small historic villages near Álamos make interesting day excursions. Check out **Minas Nuevas**, about 9km from Álamos on the Navojoa-Álamos road; the bus to Navojoa will drop you off there for US$0.30. Other historic villages near Álamos include **La Aduana** and **Promontorios**. You can visit all these places on your own, or the tourist office can arrange a guide to take you.

In La Aduana, on the plaza in front of the church, Samuel and Donna Beardsley operate *Casa La Aduana Gourmet Restaurant & Inn* (☎ 64-82-25-25). Open noon to 8 pm daily, the restaurant specializes in international gourmet meals; allow about two hours for a four-course meal (US$15 to US$20). Guest rooms cost US$50, suites US$80.

LOS MOCHIS

• pop 188,300 ☎ changing

Los Mochis (Place of Turtles) is a modern city with not a very long history. It was founded in 1903 by American Benjamin Johnston, who established sugarcane plantations and a sugar factory here.

Many travelers pass through Los Mochis, as it's the western terminus of the famous Ferrocarril Chihuahua al Pacífico (Chihuahua-Pacific Railway), which passes through the Barranca del Cobre (Copper Canyon). Topolobampo, 24km southwest of Los Mochis, is the mainland terminus of a ferry to/from La Paz, Baja California. Los Mochis is unremarkable otherwise, but it does have everything travelers may need.

Plazuela 27 de Septiembre, a pleasant plaza with flowers and a gazebo, is in front of the Parroquia del Sagrado Corazón de Jesús, on the corner of Obregón and Mina. With its white tower the church looks old on the outside, but inside it looks quite new. Parque Sinaloa y Jardín Botánico, a large park and botanical garden, is behind and to the left of the big Plaza Ley Fiesta Las Palmas shopping center at the intersection of Boulevards Castro and Rosales. A small museum, the Museo Regional del Valle del Fuerte, is at Rosales and Obregón.

Orientation

The streets are laid out on a grid. The main street through the city, running southwest from highway 15D directly into the center of town, changes names from Calzada López Mateos to Leyva as it enters the center. Boulevard Castro is another major artery. Some blocks in the center are split by smaller streets (not shown on the Los Mochis map) running parallel to the main streets.

Information

Tourist Offices The helpful Coordinación General de Turismo (☎/fax 15-10-90, turismo@red2000.com.mx), on the ground floor of the large government building on Allende at Ordoñez, is open 9 am to 3 pm Monday to Friday.

Money Banks are dotted around the center. Many have ATMs, including Bancomer, at Leyva and Juárez. Casas de cambio, which have longer opening hours, include two branches of Servicio de Cambio. The American Express agent is Viajes Araceli (☎ 12-20-84, Obregón 471A Pte), between Leyva and Flores.

Post & Communications The post office, on Ordoñez between Zaragoza and Prieto, is

On December 1, 2000, the telephone area code is due to change to ☎ 6 from 68, with the digit 8 added to the start of every local number (for example, the number 15-10-90 will become 815-10-90).

open 8 am to 6 pm Monday to Friday and 9 am to 1 pm Saturday.

There's a telephone/fax caseta on Leyva between Obregón and Hidalgo; another is on Allende near Hidalgo. Both offer discounts after 8 pm. Pay phones are plentiful around the center.

The Internet Club, 737 Degollado Sur, offers Internet and computer services 8.30 am to 10 pm Monday to Saturday and 10 am to 2 pm Sunday. Hugo's Internet Cafe, Leyva 537 Sur, has similar opening hours.

Laundry Lavamatic 2000, Allende 228 Sur between Juárez and Independencia, is open 7.30 am to 7 pm Monday to Saturday and 7.30 am to 1 pm Sunday. Lavarama, Juárez 27, opens similar hours.

Places to Stay

Budget You can camp at *Los Mochis-Copper Canyon RV Park* (☎ 12-68-17) on Calzada López Mateos 1km west of highway 15D. It has 140 spaces with full hookups for US$18. You can reserve and pay at the RV office (☎ 12-00-21), on the ground floor of the Hotel Santa Anita, at Leyva and Hidalgo; the entrance is around the corner from the hotel entrance.

Hotel Los Arcos (☎ 12-32-53), Allende near Obregón, has singles/doubles with shared bath for US$8/13. If rats in your hotel room, loud music all night from the bar next door and prostitutes in the lobby don't bother you, this may be your spot.

Otherwise, *Hotel Hidalgo* (☎/fax 18-34-53, Hidalgo 260 Pte, 2nd floor), between Zaragoza and Prieto, has small, basic rooms with private bath, air-con and TV for US$14/17/19, plus more economical rooms with private bath and ceiling fan for US$11.

Mid-Range The following are all clean, with private bath, air-con and cable TV in the rooms.

Hotel Fenix (☎ 12-26-23/25, Flores 365 Sur), between Independencia and Hidalgo, has been remodeled and is more attractive than most in its price range; rates are US$18/22/25, and it has a small restaurant. *Hotel Beltran* (☎ 12-06-88, Hidalgo 281 Pte),

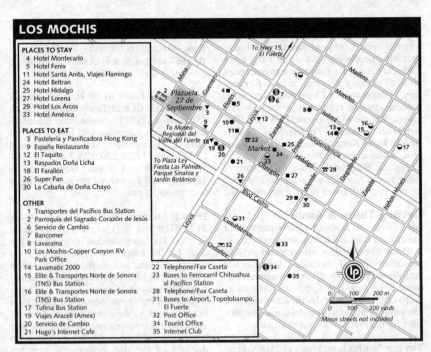

LOS MOCHIS

PLACES TO STAY
4 Hotel Montecarlo
5 Hotel Fenix
11 Hotel Santa Anita, Viajes Flamingo
24 Hotel Beltran
25 Hotel Hidalgo
27 Hotel Lorena
29 Hotel Los Arcos
33 Hotel América

PLACES TO EAT
3 Pastelería y Panificadora Hong Kong
9 España Restaurante
12 El Taquito
13 Raspados Doña Licha
18 El Farallón
26 Super Pan
30 La Cabaña de Doña Chayo

OTHER
1 Transportes del Pacífico Bus Station
2 Parroquia del Sagrado Corazón de Jesús
6 Servicio de Cambio
7 Bancomer
8 Lavarama
10 Los Mochis-Copper Canyon RV Park Office
14 Lavamatic 2000
15 Elite & Transportes Norte de Sonora (TNS) Bus Station
16 Elite & Transportes Norte de Sonora (TNS) Bus Station
17 Tufesa Bus Station
19 Viajes Araceli (Amex)
20 Servicio de Cambio
21 Hugo's Internet Cafe
22 Telephone/Fax Caseta
23 Buses to Ferrocarril Chihuahua al Pacífico Station
28 Telephone/Fax Caseta
31 Buses to Airport, Topolobampo, El Fuerte
32 Post Office
34 Tourist Office
35 Internet Club

on the corner of Zaragoza, has rooms for US$21/25/28.

Hotel Montecarlo (☎ 12-18-18, Flores 322 Sur), at the corner of Independencia, has rooms around a sunny courtyard with a bar at one end and a little restaurant at the other; rooms cost US$18/19/24. *Hotel Lorena* (☎ 12-02-39, Obregón 186 Pte), on the corner of Prieto, charges US$18/22/26 for rooms with one/two/three double beds, has an upstairs restaurant and makes box lunches for the train ride. *Hotel América* (☎ 12-13-55/56, Allende 655 Sur), between Castro and Cuauhtémoc, has rooms for US$22/26/29, and a little restaurant; rooms facing the rear are quieter. All three have enclosed parking where you can leave a vehicle while you visit the Copper Canyon.

Top End *Hotel Santa Anita* (☎ 18-70-46/31), on the corner of Leyva and Hidalgo, has an English-speaking staff, air-con,

restaurant, bar, travel agent, parking and singles/doubles for US$95/100 and suites for US$110. A bus for hotel guests only (US$5.50 per person) departs daily at 5.15 am for the Ferrocarril Chihuahua al Pacífico; you can park a vehicle here while you visit the canyon.

Places to Eat
Los Mochis has plenty of places for an inexpensive taco or quesadilla. The air-conditioned *La Cabaña de Doña Chayo* (Obregón 99 Pte), on the corner of Allende, has been serving tasty quesadillas and hand-made corn and flour tortillas filled with *carne asada* (grilled beef) and *machaca* (spiced shredded dried beef, US$1) since 1963; it is open 9 am to 1 am daily. The economical *El Taquito*, on Leyva between Hidalgo and Independencia, with air-con, plastic booths and a varied bilingual menu, is open 24 hours a day. Many hotels in Los Mochis also have restaurants.

NORTHWEST MEXICO

For slightly more upmarket dining, try *España Restaurante*, *(Obregón 525 Pte)*, which is open 7 am to 11 pm daily. Its house specialty, *paella especial de la casa*, costs US$6.50 per person (minimum two people); allow 45 minutes' preparation time. *El Farallón*, at the corner of Flores and Obregón, is a good seafood restaurant, with powerful air-con and meals for around US$7 to US$9.

Bakeries include *Pastelería y Panificadora Hong Kong* *(Hidalgo 569)* and *Super Pan*, on the corner of Boulevard Castro and Zaragoza. *Raspados Doña Licha*, corner Allende and Juárez, serves *raspados* (shaved ice covered with sweet fruit syrup) for US$1.

Getting There & Away
Air The airport is about 12km southwest of the city, on the road to Topolobampo.

Daily direct flights (all with connections to other cities) include Aeroméxico/Aerolitoral (☎ 15-25-70) to Chihuahua, Hermosillo, La Paz, Los Cabos and Mazatlán. Aero California (☎ 18-16-16) flies to Ciudad Obregón, Culiacán, Guadalajara, Hermosillo, La Paz, Mexico City and Tijuana.

Bus Los Mochis is on highway 15D; several major bus lines offer hourly buses heading north and south, 24 hours a day. Each 1st-class bus line has its own terminal. Elite and Transportes Norte de Sonora share two terminals on Degollado between Juárez and Morelos. Transportes del Pacífico is on Morelos between Zaragoza and Leyva. All serve the same places.

Tufesa is on Zapata between Juárez and Morelos. It only goes north (except to Culiacán in the south) and has fewer buses. Transportes Norte de Sinaloa, on the corner of Zaragoza and Ordoñez, has 2nd-class buses going south to Culiacán and north to Navojoa and Ciudad Obregón.

Distances, times and fares include:

Guadalajara – 927km, 13 hours; US$53 to US$61
Guaymas – 349km, 5 hours; US$14 to US$16
Hermosillo – 483km, 7 hours; US$19 to US$22
Mazatlán – 421km, 6 hours; US$20 to US$22
Mexico City (Terminal Norte) – 1462km, 23 hours; US$86 to US$99
Navojoa – 155km, 2 hours; US$6.50 to US$7
Nogales – 765km, 10 hours; US$30 to US$35
Tepic – 711km, 12 hours; US$40 to US$46
Tijuana – 1375km, 20 hours; US$69 to US$79

Second-class buses to El Fuerte (78km, 2 hours, US$3.50) and Topolobampo (24km, 45 minutes, US$0.75) leave from Cuauhtémoc between Zaragoza and Prieto. Departures to El Fuerte are at 7.30, 9, 10.30 and 11.30 am and 12.30, 2.30, 3.25, 3.45, 4.30, 4.45, 5.30, 6, 7.30 and 8 pm. Departures to Topolobampo are every 15 minutes between 5.45 am and 8 pm.

Train The train station in Los Mochis (☎/fax 24-11-51, ☎ 24-11-67) is east of the center on Serrano. The ticket window is open 5 to 7 am daily for the morning's departures. Tickets are also sold inside the office, which is open 9 am to 6 pm Monday to Friday and 9 am to 1 pm Saturday and Sunday.

You can buy *primera express* (1st class) tickets up to 30 days in advance of travel. Tickets for *clase económica* (economy class) trains are sold an hour before the train departs, or the day before. For primera express tickets, you can also make telephone reservations through Viajes Flamingo travel agency (☎ 12-16-13, hotelsbal@tsi.com.mx, www.tsi.com.mx/coppercanyon/index2.htm) at Hotel Santa Anita for the same price as at the train station (5% service charge for credit cards).

The primera express train leaves Los Mochis at 6.00 am, clase económica at 7.00 am. See Getting There & Away in the Barranca del Cobre (Copper Canyon) section, later in this chapter, for fares and detailed schedules.

Boat Ferries go from nearby Topolobampo to La Paz, Baja California. Tickets are sold at the ferry terminal in Topolobampo (see the Topolobampo section, later in this chapter, for more information).

Getting Around
Nearly everything in Los Mochis is within walking distance of the center.

Buses to the airport depart from Cuauhtémoc between Zaragoza and Prieto at 6.30, 8 and 11 am and 1.45 and 6 pm (12km, 45 minutes, US$1). A taxi to the airport costs US$13.

'Estación' buses to the train station (20 minutes, US$0.30) depart every five minutes, between 5.30 am and 8 pm, from Zaragoza between Hidalgo and Obregón. You can take the bus to get to the station for the clase económica train, which departs at 7 am, but it is probably safer to fork out US$6 for a taxi to get to the station in plenty of time for the 6 am primera express departure. Taxis might be your best transport option if arriving in Los Mochis by train.

TOPOLOBAMPO
• pop 6930 ☎ changing

Topolobampo, 24km south of Los Mochis, is the terminus for a ferry route to/from La Paz, Baja California.

Topolobampo has no hotels, but Mexicans love to come here to eat fresh seafood (both in town and at Playa El Maviri), go to the beach and enjoy the town's natural surroundings. A five-minute bus ride from Topolobampo is Playa El Maviri, a popular beach with plenty of seafood restaurants. Everyone recommends the *pescado zarandeado* (charcoal-grilled fish wrapped in foil). On the way to Playa El Maviri, you pass Cueva de los Murciélagos (Cave of Bats); you cannot enter this protected area, but it's beautiful to see the bats emerging at sunset and returning at sunrise.

Inexpensive *lanchas* (small motorized boats) will take you from either Topolobampo or Playa El Maviri to some beautiful natural spots that attract large populations of the animals they are named for. Isla de Pájaros (Island of Birds) is home to hun-

On December 1, 2000, the telephone area code is due to change to ☎ 6 from 686, with the digits 86 added to the start of every local number (for example, the number 2-01-41 will become 862-01-41).

dreds of birds, and Santuario de Delfines is a dolphin sanctuary. Other spots include Playa Las Copas, Isla Santa María with dunes where you can camp and Isla El Farallón with seals and sea lions, or you can also visit El Delfín 'El Pechocho,' a friendly dolphin who likes to swim with people.

Ferry tickets are sold at the Topolobampo ferry terminal (☎/fax 2-01-41), which is open 8 am to 9.30 pm daily. Passenger tickets are sold up to five days in advance; you can also buy your ticket on the day of departure, but there may be no space left, so it's best to get it earlier. The Topolobampo ferry sails at 10 pm daily, arriving in La Paz at 8 am; the return schedule is identical. Passenger fares are US$15. See Getting There & Away in the La Paz section of the Baja California chapter for vehicle fares.

EL FUERTE
• pop 10,900 • elev 180m ☎ changing

Founded in 1564 by the Spanish conqueror Francisco de Ibarra, El Fuerte (the Fort) is a picturesque little Spanish colonial town notable for its colonial ambiance and Spanish architecture. The large Palacio Municipal, plaza, church, museum and Hotel Posada del Hidalgo are its most notable features.

El Fuerte was an important Spanish settlement throughout the colonial period. For more than three centuries, it was a major farming and commercial center and trading post on El Camino Real, the Spanish mule trail between Guadalajara to the southeast, the mines of Álamos to the north and the Sierra Madre Occidental to the northeast. In 1824, El Fuerte became the capital of the state of Sinaloa, a title it retained for several years.

You can get a great view of the town, Río Fuerte and surrounding area by climbing the mirador (lookout) hill, behind the Posada del Hidalgo, just off the plaza. At the top, there's a replica of the original fort that El Fuerte is named for (which no longer exists). Excursions around El Fuerte include a three-hour round-trip (on your own or with a guide) to a set of petroglyphs; El Fuerte's two reservoirs (Domínguez and Hidalgo) are excellent for fishing.

On June 1, 2000, the telephone area code is due to change to ☎ 6 from 689, with the digits 89 added to the start of every local number (for example, the number 3-02-42 will become 893-02-42).

Bancomer, at the corner of Constitución and Juárez, one block off the plaza, is open 8.30 am to 2.30 pm Monday to Friday and has an ATM.

Places to Stay & Eat

The rich silver-mining Almada family of Álamos had strong connections in El Fuerte. In 1890, Rafael Almada built an opulent mansion that is now the **Hotel Posada del Hidalgo** (☎ 3-02-42) in the center of El Fuerte behind the church. It has beautiful interior gardens, swimming pool, restaurant/bar and 52 rooms; singles/doubles/triples cost US$95/100/110. Reservations are made at Hotel Santa Anita in Los Mochis.

Hotel San Francisco (☎ 3-00-55, Obregón 201), 2½ blocks from the plaza, has attractive rooms encircling a clean, colorful courtyard full of flowers, birds and a fountain. Rates are US$33/44/50. At the top of the mirador, **Hotel Río Vista** (☎ 3-04-13) is an imaginatively decorated hotel with seven rooms with bath for US$39.

Restaurant El Supremo, on the corner of Rosales and Constitución, one block off the plaza, is clean, pleasant and economical. **El Mesón del General Bar & Grill** (Juárez 202) is a fancier restaurant that specializes in seafood; its tables are set around an attractive, colorful courtyard. **El Rincón Chino**, at the rear of the same courtyard, serves tasty Chinese food. There's also a restaurant at **Hotel Posada del Hidalgo**.

Langostino (crayfish) and filete de lobina (filet of bass) are El Fuerte specialties.

Getting There & Away

In El Fuerte, buses to Los Mochis (78km, two hours, US$3.50) depart every 15 minutes between 5.30 am and 7 pm, from the corner of Juárez and 16 de Septiembre.

There's also a bus to El Carrizal, on highway 15D north of Los Mochis, allowing you to bypass Los Mochis if you're heading north; it departs from this corner daily at 10 am, noon and 4 pm (1½ hours, US$2.75). If you're driving to/from the north, take the El Carrizal-El Fuerte shortcut to save lots of time.

El Fuerte makes a good alternative to Los Mochis as a starting or ending point for a trip on the Ferrocarril Chihuahua al Pacífico. The train station is a few kilometers east of town. The eastbound primera express train departs El Fuerte at 7.26 am; clase económica leaves at 8.40 am. Westbound primera express leave at 6.16 pm and clase económica at 8.45 pm. Train tickets are sold on board. You can take a taxi to the station for about US$5.50.

See the Los Mochis section for details on getting to El Fuerte by bus, and Getting There & Away in Barranca del Cobre section for additional details about the Ferrocarril Chihuahua al Pacífico.

CULIACÁN
• pop 505,500 ☎ 67

Capital of the state of Sinaloa, Culiacán is equidistant from Los Mochis and Mazatlán – about 210km (a three-hour drive) from either place. Primarily a commercial, administrative and agricultural center, the city has little to attract tourists but is a good point to break up the journey. If you do spend time in Culiacán, you could check out the 17th-century cathedral, Palacio Municipal, Museo Regional de Sinaloa in the Centro Cívico Constitución, and malecón walkway along the Río Tamazula and Río Humaya.

Barranca del Cobre (Copper Canyon)

The Barranca del Cobre (Copper Canyon) is a natural wonder that actually refers to not one but 20 canyons carved out of the Sierra Tarahumara by over six different rivers. Together, these canyons are four times larger than Arizona's Grand Canyon.

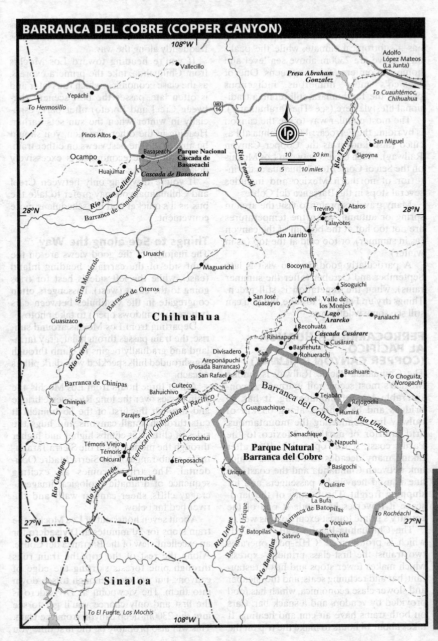

BARRANCA DEL COBRE (COPPER CANYON)

At an altitude of only 500m, the canyon's deepest point (Barranca de Urique, 1879m) has a subtropical climate, while the peaks high above are 2300m above sea level and home to conifers and evergreens. One of Mexico's most numerous indigenous peoples, the Tarahumara, still retain a traditional lifestyle here (see 'The Tarahumara').

The most popular way to see the canyon is by riding the Ferrocarril Chihuahua al Pacífico (also known as the Copper Canyon Railway), which travels between Los Mochis on the Sea of Cortez to Chihuahua in the interior of northern Mexico and includes several stops in the Barranca del Cobre.

Many travelers prefer to visit the area in spring or autumn, when the temperatures are not too hot at the bottom of the canyon (as in summer), or too cold at the top (as in winter).

A particularly good time to visit is late September and October (after the summer rains), when the vegetation is still green. Things dry up February to June, but you can still see some wildflowers.

FERROCARRIL CHIHUAHUA AL PACÍFICO (COPPER CANYON RAILWAY)

The Chihuahua-Pacific Railway is among Mexico's most scenic rail journeys. A considerable feat of engineering, it has 39 bridges and 86 tunnels along 655km of railway line connecting the mountainous, arid interior of northern Mexico to the Pacific coast. It was opened in 1961 after taking many decades to build. The major link between Chihuahua and the coast, the line is used heavily by passengers and for shipping freight. The beauty of the landscape it traverses has made it one of the country's prime tourist excursions as well.

The Chihuahua-Pacific Railway (CHP, which is pronounced 'CHE-pe') operates two trains: the first-class primera express, which makes fewer stops and has a restaurant, bar and reclining seats; and the cheaper and slower clase económica, which has food provided by vendors and a snack bar. Cars on both trains have air-con and heating. It takes about 14 hours to make the trip on the primera express, and at least two hours longer on the clase económica, which stops frequently along the way.

If you're heading toward Los Mochis from Chihuahua, take the primera express, as the clase económica, which runs later and is often late, passes the best scenery (between Creel and Loreto) after dark, especially in winter when the sun sets earlier. Heading in the other direction, you should be able to see the best views on either train, unless the clase económica is excessively delayed.

If you're traveling only between Creel and Chihuahua, you may prefer to take the bus, as it's quicker and the schedule is more convenient.

Things to See along the Way

The majority of the good views are on the right side of the carriage heading inland (east), while the left side is best for trips going to the coast (west). Passengers often congregate in the vestibules between cars (where the windows open) to take photos.

Departing from Los Mochis around sunrise, the train passes through flat, gray farmland and gradually begins to climb through fog-shrouded hills speckled with dark pillars of cacti.

About three hours from Los Mochis, the train passes over the long Río Fuerte bridge and through the first of the 86 tunnels. It cuts through small canyons and hugs the sides of cliffs as it climbs higher and higher through the mountains of the Sierra Tarahumara, a sub-range of the Sierra Madre Occidental. The trip becomes an exciting sequence of dramatic geological images – craggy cliffs, sheer canyon walls and the river bed far below.

About seven hours out of Los Mochis, the train stops for 20 minutes at **Divisadero** for an excellent view of the Barranca del Cobre. Along the rest of the trip, the train runs through pine forests skirting the edge of canyons, but not close enough to see down into them. The viewpoint at Divisadero is the first and only chance you'll get to see into the 2300m-deep canyon from the train. This will also probably be the first time you will see some of the Tarahumara people who inhabit the canyon. The Tarahumara come to the train station to display and sell their handicrafts to visitors. Hotels in Divisadero organize short trips into the canyon, but you can arrange a far better deal yourself with one of the Tarahumara who meet the train to sell handicrafts and food. If you hire a guide, you must have your own food for the trip; there are two restaurants and some snack stalls, but no stores in Divisadero. Your guide will lead you 1000m to the Río Urique. Carry enough water for the descent and be prepared for a change in climate from cool – Divisadero is 2240m high – to warm and humid near the river. Autumn is the best time to come; flash floods and suffocatingly high temperatures are a problem in summer. You could also spend two hours here if you switch from a primera express to clase económica train, which is roughly two hours behind. Store your bags with a hotel in the meantime (see Places to Stay, below).

On an eastbound train, **Creel**, approximately eight hours into the journey, probably makes the best base in the Barranca del Cobre region to break the journey and

explore the canyon. It's only a small town but it has several economical places to stay, and plenty of tours and things to do (see the Creel section, later in this chapter, for more information).

In between Los Mochis and Creel, there are several other overnight stops that allow you 24 hours before the train passes by again – time enough to explore. **El Fuerte** (altitude 180m), an attractive colonial town 90km from Los Mochis, can serve as an alternative starting point for the train trip (see the El Fuerte section, earlier in this chapter, for more information). **Cerocahui** (altitude 1600m) is a picturesque village in a valley with apple and peach orchards and pine and madrone trees. It is about 16km (35 minutes) from the Bahuichivo train stop. **Urique** (altitude 550m), a village at the bottom of the impressive Barranca de Urique, is also accessed from the Bahuichivo train stop and is a good base for all kinds of canyon hikes lasting anywhere from one to several days. The three- to four-day hike between Batopilas and Urique is becoming a popular trek (see Organized Tours in the Creel section, later in this chapter, for more information).

The Tarahumara

More than 50,000 indigenous Tarahumara live in the Sierra Tarahumara's numerous canyons, including the famous Barranca del Cobre (Copper Canyon). Isolated within this formidable topography, the Tarahumara retain many of their traditions; many still live in caves and log cabins (some of these dwellings can be seen near Creel) and they subsist on very basic agriculture of maize and beans.

The Tarahumara are famous for running long distances. Running is so significant to the Tarahumara that in their own language they call themselves Rarámuri – 'those who run fast.' Traditionally, the Tarahumara hunted by chasing down and exhausting deer, then driving them over cliffs to be impaled on wooden sticks. Today, they run grueling footraces of 160km (or more), without stopping, through rough canyons, kicking a small wooden ball ahead of them.

A tradition of quite a different sort is the *tesquinada*, a raucous gathering in which they consume copious amounts of *tesquino*, a potent maize beer.

Catholic missionaries have made some progress improving living conditions for the Tarahumara, but they haven't been entirely successful in converting them to Catholicism. Many of the Tarahumara attend church services, but continue to worship their ancestral gods, particularly Raiénari, the sun god and protector of men, and Mechá, the moon god and protector of women. Sorcerers are as important as Catholic priests and are the only members of the Tarahumara permitted to consume peyote, a hallucinogen derived from a small cactus. They often take peyote in order to perform a bizarre dance to cure the sick.

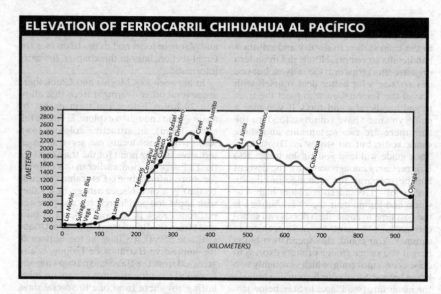

ELEVATION OF FERROCARRIL CHIHUAHUA AL PACÍFICO

About 5km southwest of Divisadero, **Posada Barrancas** station is next to **Areponápuchi** (altitude 2220m), the only village on the train line that is right on the rim of the canyon. Often referred to as Arepo, this village has magnificent views of the canyon, several places to stay and is a good point for going into the canyon by foot, car or horseback.

See Places to Stay, immediately following this section, for information about accommodations and organizing trips into the canyon at these stopover towns.

The last stretch of the train trip goes through **Cuauhtémoc**, the center of northern Mexico's Mennonite population, and **Chihuahua**, the capital of the state of Chihuahua (see the Central North Mexico chapter for more information).

Places to Stay

Cerocahui Five kilometers north of Cerocahui village, you can camp at **Rancho del Oro** campground on the banks of the Arroyo del Ranchito, a tranquil spot with a pleasant beach, good bird-watching (over 100 species have been spotted here), burial caves and archaeological sites a short walk

away. Tents can be rented if you don't have your own. Hot showers are available at the nearby **Hotel Paraíso del Oso**, which can also provide meals and other services. The campground is 12km from the Bahuichivo train station; there's a bus service.

Enrique ('Kike') Mancinas and his wife operate a small **hotel** behind the church that is clean and popular with backpackers; the six rooms with bath cost around US$17 each, and they take guests on trips.

Hotel Misión, opposite the Misión de Cerocahui church founded in 1690 by the Jesuit Padre Juan María de Salvatierra, has 38 comfortable rooms at US$140/190/220 a single/double/triple, including three meals daily. A variety of short and long excursions depart from the hotel by foot, vehicle and horseback. Reservations are made at the Hotel Santa Anita in Los Mochis (see that section, Places to Stay, Top End, earlier in this chapter). A hotel bus provides free transport to/from the Bahuichivo train station.

The luxurious new **Margarita's Cerocahui Wilderness Lodge** (☎/fax *1-456-02-45*), on a cliff about a 25-minute drive from Cerocahui, offers spectacular views. Room rates of US$160 for one or two people include all meals, plus transport to/from the Bahuichivo train station. Tours into the canyons are organized.

Urique Urique has several small hotels. *Hotel Cañon de Urique*, which has simple rooms with bath for US$6 each, is most often recommended by travelers. Kit, an American man, also rents *rooms*, and has a camping area. You can camp at *La Playita* beside the Río Urique; ask permission at the Presidencia Municipal. There are no private telephones in Urique, but you can contact these places by calling the town caseta (☎ 1-456-06-13).

To reach Urique, get off the train at the Bahuichivo train station and catch the 'Urique' bus; the ride takes four hours.

Posada Barrancas *Lucy González* (☎ 1-578-3007) also rents rooms in Arepo, with TV, carpet and private hot bath, for US$28 per day. *Loly Mancinas* rents rooms for about the same price. Both women sell food at the Divisadero train station; if you get off there, they'll make sure you get a ride to Arepo.

For friendly accommodations on a farm five minutes from the station, check out *Cabañas Díaz* (☎ 1-578-30-08). Pleasant cabanas cost US$28 for one to three people with shared hot bath, US$33 for one or two people with private bath and fireplace, or US$39 for three to four people with private bath and fireplace. They also have a large room with 10 bunk beds for US$110. They're known for their hospitality, delicious meals (US$4.50 per meal) and the tranquil, relaxing atmosphere. They'll organize any kind of canyon trip you would like, be it a hike to the rim of the canyon, halfway down or all the way down to the Río Urique. Van, horse and burro tours are all available. Someone from the Díaz family always comes to meet the train.

The *Mansión Tarahumara* (☎ 1-415-47-21 in Chihuahua), near the train station, is also known as El Castillo because it looks like a medieval stone castle. Singles/doubles cost US$121/172, meals and one walking tour included.

Perched on the rim of the canyon, *Hotel Posada Mirador* has 45 luxury rooms and suites – both with private terraces and magnificent views – and for US$155/200/235 a single/double/triple, including three meals daily. Right at the train stop and just a five-minute walk from the viewpoint, the *Hotel Rancho Posada* has 36 rooms for US$140/190/220, with three meals daily served at the Hotel Posada Mirador's spectacular dining room. Reservations for both are made at the Hotel Santa Anita in Los Mochis.

Divisadero At the train stop, the *Hotel Divisadero Barrancas* (☎ 1-415-11-99 in Chihuahua) has 48 rooms, all with that magnificent view. Singles/doubles cost US$121/181, with a surcharge at peak times; the price includes two walking tours and three meals daily. The restaurant/bar, with spectacular view, is open to the public. There are many snack stands at the train station, but no market. The Hotel Divisadero Barrancas will arrange guided tours into the canyon.

About a 25-minute walk along the rim to the southwest (take the dirt road, not the paved road, heading toward Arepo) is the *Rancho de Lencho Casa de Huéspedes*, run by the Mancinas family. They provide beds for US$5.50 per person and meals for US$3.50. Someone from the family is often at the Divisadero train station; the ranch is about equidistant (about 2.5km) from the Divisadero and Posada Barrancas train stations.

Getting There & Away

Train Primera express train tickets can be purchased in advance (up to 30 days in advance from the train stations in Chihuahua or Los Mochis, or from travel agencies. Clase económica train (and primera express, if still available) tickets can be purchased at the train station's ticket window an hour before each train's departure.

At the train station in Chihuahua (☎ 1-410-37-51), tickets can be bought at the ticket window, which is open 5 to 7 am daily, or at the train station's office, which is open 9 am to 5.30 pm Monday to Friday and 9 am to noon Saturday and Sunday.

Railway Schedule – Ferrocarril Chihuahua al Pacífico

Both the primera express and clase económica trains run every day. Trains tend to run late and the times given below are only an ideal schedule. The clase económica train, which makes more stops, is virtually never on time, often arriving at the end of the line around 1 am. There is no time change between Los Mochis and Chihuahua.

This schedule is only a guideline for departure times and fares. Check with a travel agent or the train stations in the originating cities for official schedules.

Copper Canyon Railway – Los Mochis to Chihuahua

Station	Primera Express Train No 73		Clase Económica Train No 75	
	Departs	Fare from Los Mochis	Departs	Fare from Los Mochis
Los Mochis	6.00 am	–	7.00 am	–
Sufragio	–	–	7.55 am	US$8.50
El Fuerte	7.26 am	US$17.25	8.40 am	US$8.50
Loreto	–	–	9.35 am	US$9.25
Témoris	–	–	11.40 am	US$15.00
Bahuichivo	11.12 am	US$36.25	12.50 pm	US$18.25
Cuiteco	–	–	1.05 pm	US$18.25
San Rafael	12.05 pm	US$40.75	2.00 pm	US$20.25
Posada Barrancas	12.25 pm	US$42.50	2.10 pm	US$20.75
Divisadero	12.35 pm	US$42.75	2.45 pm	US$21.00
Creel	2.14 pm	US$51.00	4.10 pm	US$25.25
San Juanito	–	–	4.55 pm	US$27.25
La Junta	–	–	6.35 pm	US$33.25
Cuauhtémoc	5.25 pm	US$74.50	7.50 pm	US$36.75
Chihuahua	7.50 pm	US$93.50	10.25 pm	US$46.00

Copper Canyon Railway – Chihuahua to Los Mochis

Station	Primera Express Train No 74		Clase Económica Train No 76	
	Departs	Fare from Chihuahua	Departs	Fare from Chihuahua
Chihuahua	6.00 am	–	7.00 am	–
Cuauhtémoc	8.15 am	US$19.00	9.25 am	US$9.50
La Junta	–	–	10.25 am	US$13.00
San Juanito	–	–	12.15 pm	US$18.75
Creel	11.26 am	US$42.50	1.00 pm	US$21.00
Divisadero	12.45 pm	US$51.00	2.30 pm	US$25.00
Posada Barrancas	1.20 pm	US$51.75	3.05 pm	US$25.25
San Rafael	1.30 pm	US$53.00	3.15 pm	US$26.00
Cuiteco	–	–	4.15 pm	US$27.75
Bahuichivo	2.32 pm	US$57.50	4.25 pm	US$28.25
Témoris	–	–	5.35 pm	US$31.00
Loreto	–	–	7.55 pm	US$37.00
El Fuerte	6.16 pm	US$82.00	8.45 pm	US$40.50
Sufragio	–	–	9.25 pm	US$43.25
Los Mochis	7.50 pm	US$93.50	10.25 pm	US$46.00

At the train station in Los Mochis (☎/fax 68-24-11-51, ☎ 68-24-11-67), the ticket window is also open 5 to 7 am daily for the morning's departures. Tickets are also sold inside the office, which is open 9 am to 6 pm Monday to Friday and 9 am to 1 pm Saturday to Sunday.

The Viajes Flamingo travel agency (☎ 68-12-16-13, hotelsbal@tsi.com.mx, www.tsi.com.mx/coppercanyon/index2.htm) at the Hotel Santa Anita in Los Mochis sells primera express tickets for the same price as train stations do, but it applies a 5% charge for credit cards.

Primera express tickets can be purchased in advance in the USA from Mexico by Train (☎/fax 956-725-3659, ☎ 800-321-1699, PO Box 2782, Laredo, TX 78044 USA). The cost is slightly higher if you do this (US$95 one-way, US$190 return), but you are assured of getting a seat. Mexico by Train will mail tickets, or arrange for you to pick them up at a hotel desk in Chihuahua or Los Mochis, or at the Chihuahua or Los Mochis train stations.

You can usually be pretty sure of getting a ticket a day or two in advance, though you should allow longer than this for travel during Semana Santa, July or August or at Christmas. For a same-day primera express ticket, go to the ticket office before 5 am.

Bus Buses operate twice daily between San Rafael and Creel, via Arepo and Divisadero (see Getting There & Away in the Creel section for more information).

CREEL
● pop 3900 ● elev 2338 ☎ 1

Creel, a pleasant small town surrounded by pine forests and interesting rock formations, is many travelers' favorite stop on the Ferrocarril Chihuahua al Pacífico (also known as the Copper Canyon Railway). You can stock up on maps and staples and catch a bus to Batopilas, a village 140km away deep in the heart of the Tarahumara canyon country. Creel is also a regional center for the Tarahumara people. You will see many Tarahumara in traditional dress and numerous shops selling Tarahumara handicrafts.

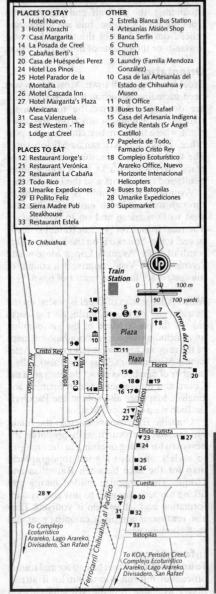

CREEL

PLACES TO STAY
1　Hotel Nuevo
3　Hotel Korachi
7　Casa Margarita
14　La Posada de Creel
19　Cabañas Berti's
23　Casa de Huéspedes Perez
24　Hotel Los Pinos
25　Hotel Parador de la Montaña
26　Motel Cascada Inn
27　Hotel Margarita's Plaza Mexicana
31　Casa Valenzuela
32　Best Western - The Lodge at Creel

PLACES TO EAT
12　Restaurant Jorge's
21　Restaurant Verónica
22　Restaurant La Cabaña
23　Todo Rico
28　Umarike Expediciones
29　El Pollito Feliz
32　Sierra Madre Pub Steakhouse
33　Restaurant Estela

OTHER
2　Estrella Blanca Bus Station
4　Artesanías Misión Shop
5　Banca Serfín
6　Church
8　Church
9　Laundry (Familia Mendoza González)
10　Casa de las Artesanías del Estado de Chihuahua y Museo
11　Post Office
13　Buses to San Rafael
15　Casa del Artesanía Indígena
16　Bicycle Rentals (Sr Ángel Castillo)
17　Papelería de Todo, Farmacio Cristo Rey
18　Complejo Ecoturístico Arareko Office, Nuevo Horizonte Intenacional Helicopters
24　Buses to Batopilas
28　Umarike Expediciones
30　Supermarket

To Chihuahua

Train Station

0　　50　　100 m
0　　50　　100 yards

Cristo Rey

Av Gran Visión
Av Raralipa
Villa
Av Ferrocarril
Arroyo del Creel

Plaza

Plaza

Flores

López Mateos

Elfido Batista

Cuesta

Batopilas

To Complejo Ecoturístico Arareko, Lago Arareko, Divisadero, San Rafael

Ferrocarril Chihuahua al Pacífico

To KOA, Pensión Creel, Complejo Ecoturístico Arareko, Lago Arareko, Divisadero, San Rafael

NORTHWEST MEXICO

Its high elevation means Creel can be very cold, even snowy, especially in winter. In summer, the cool air and piney aroma from the town's lumber mill are a welcome relief from the heat of the tropical coastal lowlands or the deserts of northern Mexico.

Orientation

Creel is a very small town. Most things you need, including many hotels and restaurants, are on López Mateos, the town's main street, which leads south from the town plaza, where there are two churches, the post office, bank, and Artesanías Misíon shop. The train station is one block north of the plaza. Across the tracks are a couple more hotels and restaurants, and the bus station.

Avenida Gran Visión is the highway through town; it heads east to Chihuahua, west to Divisadero and on to San Rafael. The road from Creel to San Rafael is newly paved. Lago Arareko is on the highway, 7km south of town. Avenida López Mateos and Avenida Gran Visión intersect a couple of kilometers south of the center of town.

Maps A large map of Creel is posted on the outside wall of Banca Serfin, on the north side of the plaza. Maps of the surrounding area, including a series of topographical maps of the canyons, are sold next door at the Artesanías Misíon shop. This shop also sells a number of fine books about the Barranca del Cobre and the Tarahumara, in Spanish and English. Maps are also sold at the Papelería de Todo shop on López Mateos.

Umarike Expediciones, across the tracks on Avenida Ferrocarril, sells probably the best map for hiking or biking in the area (it's to scale!), and also a good topographical map for the hike between Batopilas and Urique. They organize guided hiking and biking tours, or are glad to just give you information and let you do it yourself. They also rent mountain bikes, camping gear and rock climbing gear.

Information

Tourist Offices Creel has no formal tourist office, but information about local attractions is available from the Artesanías Misíon shop on the north side of the plaza (English and Spanish are spoken), from the tour operators and from most of the places to stay.

Money Banca Serfin on the plaza changes money; it's open 9 am to 3 pm Monday to Friday, and has an ATM. The supermarket on López Mateos changes US dollars and travelers' checks.

Post & Communications The post office on the plaza is open 9 am to 3 pm Monday to Friday. Pay phones are plentiful on López Mateos. The Papelería de Todo shop on López Mateos has a telephone caseta. Public email, Internet and fax are available at Umarike Expediciones on Avenida Ferrocarril, and at the Best Western – The Lodge at Creel, on López Mateos 61.

Laundry The public laundry at the Best Western – The Lodge at Creel, is open 9 am to 6 pm Monday to Saturday. A cheaper laundry is in the large two-story blue house on Villa, across the tracks from the plaza; there's no sign except for the family name, Familia Mendoza González. It's open 9 am to 7 pm Monday to Saturday. Another public laundry is at the KOA campground, south of town.

Museum

The Casa de las Artesanías del Estado de Chihuahua y Museo overlooks the plaza and contains excellent exhibits on Tarahumara culture and crafts. Don't miss this interesting museum. It's open 9 am to 1 pm and 2 to 6 pm Tuesday to Saturday, 9 am to 1 pm Sunday (admission US$0.50).

Complejo Ecoturístico Arareko

An excellent local hike (or drive) is to the Complejo Ecoturístico Arareko, a Tarahumara *ejido* (landholding cooperative) with over 200 sq km of pine forest with waterfalls, hot springs, caves (inhabited by the Tarahumara) and other rock formations. There are also deep canyons, farmlands, villages and **Lago Arareko** (see below).

The ejido offers camping and lodging near the lake (see Camping & Cabins in

Places to Stay, later in this section). You can also rent bikes or boats for excursions on the lake at Complejo Ecoturístico Arareko's office in Creel on López Mateos.

To get to the ejido from Creel, head south on López Mateos and veer left, passing the town cemetery on your left. About 1.5km south of town there's a gate where an entrance fee is charged (US$1.75) and you're given a map and printed information about the ejido. Continue straight ahead; caves and farmlands will appear on both sides of the road before you eventually arrive at the small Tarahumara village of San Ignacio, where there's a 400-year-old mission church.

Visitors often get lost trying to reach the lake from this point (the map isn't the best). Here's how to do it: from San Ignacio, continue straight ahead past the church, taking the trail up the hill. At the top of the hill, take the trail straight ahead through the next valley, and you'll come to the lake. If you do get lost, just remember that the highway is running parallel to you, on your right (west); it's an easy hitch back to Creel.

Organized Tours

Most of Creel's hotels offer tours of the surrounding area, with trips to canyons, rivers, hot springs, waterfalls and other places. Tarahumara Tours (☎ 456-00-65, www .umarike.com.mx/coppercanyon/taratours .htm), with an office on the plaza, offers all the same tours, sometimes at better prices than the hotels. There's also Umarike Expediciones (☎ 456-02-48, www.umarike.com .mx), on Avenida Ferrocarril, which offers guided hiking and mountain bike tours, rock climbing excursions and instruction, rents mountain bikes, rock climbing and camping gear and offers maps and information for do-it-yourself trips.

Tara Adventures (☎/fax 1-417-38-04, www.umarike.com.mx/coppercanyon/tara_ adventures.htm), Privada de José Martí No 5716, Colonia Granjas, Chihuahua, Chihuahua CP 31160, operated by popular bilingual naturalist and guide Pedro Palma Gutiérrez, has an excellent reputation for Copper Canyon adventures. (Tours can originate in Chihuahua, Creel or any place you like.)

All tours require a minimum number of people. The easiest place to get a group together is often at Casa Margarita, but any hotel will organize a tour if there are enough people wanting to go, usually four or five. Most hotels don't require that you be a guest in order to go on a tour. Expect to pay about US$11/25 per person for a half/full-day tour, but shop around – the pricier hotels tend to have more expensive tours. If you have your own transport you can do many of these excursions on your own. If you take any tour from Casa Margarita, they include a hot breakfast and box lunch. One or more destinations may be combined on the same tour.

You could also hire your own guide. Expect to pay around US$25 per person, per day. Inquire at the office of the Complejo Ecoturístico Arareko on López Mateos, the Tarahumara Tours' guides on the plaza, Umarike Expediciones, or ask around at the hotels.

One or more destinations may be combined on the same tour. Popular trips include:

Lago Arareko About 7km from Creel, this lake is an easy hike or drive south along the road to Cusárare; hitchhiking is also relatively easy. A few caves inhabited by Tarahumara can be seen along the way. The lake is surrounded by boulders and pine forests; there's also an old log cabin which was used as a set for the filming of the Mexican movie *El Refugio del Lobo* (Refuge of the Wolf).

Valle de los Monjes The vertical rock formations found in this valley gave rise to its traditional Tarahumara name of Bisabírachi, meaning the Valley of the Erect Penises. The erect penis was a powerful symbol of life and fertility in their culture. The valley, also sometimes called the Valley of the Gods, is 9km from Creel and is considered a day trip by horse. Tour operators can either rent horses or tell you where to get them.

Cascada Cusárare The 30m-high Cusárare waterfall is 22km south of Creel, near the Tarahumara village of Cusárare. The four to five-hour tour involves going 22km by car, stopping at Lago Arareko on the way, then 2.5km by foot to the waterfall. To do it yourself, if you're coming from Creel, don't take the first turnoff you see on your right where large signs point to the waterfall – this entrance leaves you with a longer, less interesting hike to reach the falls. Continue on for about another 5km, passing the sign to Cusárare village pointing off to your left, until you reach a small, inconspicuous sign pointing to your right saying 'Cascada Cusárare – Cusárare Waterfall.' Turn here, follow the road until you reach the small shop and a hotel (the expensive **Copper Canyon Lodge**, ☎ 248-340-7230, 800-776-3942 in the USA), and park there. You could camp here too, beside the river. The waterfall is about a 40-minute walk along the river, on an easy-to-follow trail (entrance US$0.75).

Recohuata Hot Springs This seven-hour trip begins with a 1½-hour truck ride and then a hike down 607m into the canyon to the hot springs (entrance US$1.75).

Cascada de Basaseachi Basaseachi Falls, 140km northwest of Creel, is a dramatic 246m-high waterfall (the highest in Mexico), especially spectacular in the rainy season. It takes all day to visit the falls – a bumpy three-hour drive, then about two hours walking down, half an hour at the waterfall, three hours walking up again, and a bumpy three-hour return ride. If you're up for it, it's worth it. If you're not up for the walk down into the canyon, you can still enjoy views of the falls and the canyon, from up on the rim. A new hotel, **Rancho San Lorenzo**, has several large cabins and an attractive camping area a five-minute walk from the falls.

Río Urique The seven-hour tour to this river, at the bottom of the Barranca de Urique, passes several indigenous villages.

Río Oteros The Río Oteros walk is considered a day hike, right off the beaten track; ask before you go.

Campos Menonitas An eight-hour excursion to the Mennonite country includes a visit to a Mennonite cheese factory and lunch at a Mennonite home, sampling their local products (see the Cuauhtémoc section in the Central North Mexico chapter for more on the Mennonites).

La Bufa This nine-hour tour takes you 105km from Creel through five spectacular canyons to La Bufa, a canyon 1750m deep with a cool river at the bottom.

Batopilas Batopilas is two hours farther along the same road to La Bufa and is offered as a two-day excursion from Creel. If you don't have two days to spare to visit Batopilas, the tour to La Bufa lets you experience some of that spectacular scenery in one day, with plenty of stops along the way. See the Batopilas section, later in this chapter, for more information.

Places to Stay

Camping & Cabins *Complejo Ecoturístico Arareko* (☎/fax 456-01-26) has a campground on the northeast shore of Lago Arareko, 7km south of town. Campsites with barbecue pits, picnic areas, water and bathrooms, but no electricity, cost US$1.75 per person, plus the US$1.75 entrance fee to the ejido. It also operates two lodges: *Albergue de Batosárachi* and *Cabaña de Segórachi*. Albergue de Batosárachi, 1km south of Lago Arareko, has three rustic cabins with bunk beds or individual rooms, and hot showers; you can cook in the communal kitchen or arrange to have meals prepared. It costs US$8 per person, and can accommodate 70 people. Cabaña de Segórachi, on the south shore of Lago Arareko, is more luxurious, with the use of a rowboat and other amenities included; it costs US$28 per person, and holds 15 people. They'll pick up lodge guests at the train or bus station.

There's a new, well-equipped *KOA Kampground* (☎ 456-06-65) on the south side of Creel, about a 15-minute walk from the center of town; head south on López Mateos and just keep going. Tent sites cost US$10, RV sites US$18/22/26 with no/partial/full hookups, and Kamping Kabins cost US$50/65 for four/six people. There's also a large dorm room with bunk beds; bunks cost US$7 (US$9.50 with breakfast). Cheaper weekly and monthly rates are available. Facilities include a communal kitchen and baths, restaurant, bar, small shop, laundry and tours. Vehicle storage costs US$5 per day.

Guesthouses & Hotels Creel's most popular place to stay is *Casa Margarita* (☎ 456-00-45, López Mateos 11), on the northeast corner of the plaza between the two churches, with a variety of accommodations and prices. A bed in the cramped dorm room costs US$5.50 (US$4.50 for a mattress on the floor), or US$9 for a more luxurious dorm. Pleasant rooms with private bath cost US$22 for one or two people. All of these prices include both breakfast and dinner. Casa Margarita is a great place to meet other travelers, as everyone gathers at the table to eat together – often in shifts, since the place is so popular.

The same family runs the comfortable **Hotel Margarita's Plaza Mexicana** (☎/fax 456-02-45, Elfido Batista s/n), a block from López Mateos. It has a restaurant, bar and 26 spacious rooms around a pleasant courtyard; singles/doubles cost US$42/48, including breakfast and a three-course dinner. Non-guests can come for the set dinner (US$5.50, call ahead).

Casa de Huéspedes Perez (☎ 456-00-47, Flores 257) has a communal kitchen and friendly family atmosphere; simple rooms with one to five beds and private bath cost US$5.50 per person. Another simple place, **Casa Valenzuela** (☎ 456-01-04, López Mateos 68) has basic rooms with shared or private bath for US$6 per person.

Cabañas Berti's (☎ 456-00-86, López Mateos 31) has singles/doubles with private bath and either heater or fireplace for US$11/17 or US$20 with TV. **Hotel Los Pinos** (☎ 456-00-44, López Mateos 39) has tidy, new-looking rooms with bath and heater for US$16/18 with one/two beds, plus off-street parking.

Pensión Creel is linked with the Best Western – The Lodge at Creel, which makes reservations and provides free transport. It's a 15-minute walk south of the plaza, down López Mateos, just south of KOA. Its 11 rooms (some with bunk beds) surround a stone courtyard, and there's a communal kitchen and sitting room. Rooms cost US$9/11 per person without/ with breakfast.

Across the tracks from the plaza, **La Posada de Creel** (☎/fax 456-01-42) has rooms with shared bath for US$6.50 per person, or with private bath for US$17 a single/double. Also across the tracks, **Hotel Korachi** (☎ 456-02-07) has simple rooms with bath at US$13/18/22/24 for one to four people, plus attractive cabana-style rooms with woodstoves for US$24/28/33/39, with private parking. In the countryside, 2km from Creel, are their seven rustic country houses, each can hold up to eight people. Next door, **Hotel Nuevo** (☎ 456-00-22) offers large, luxurious, log-and-stone cabana-style

rooms for US$51, plus ordinary singles/ doubles for US$23/39.

Motel Cascada Inn (☎ 456-02-53, López Mateos 49) has a covered swimming pool, parking, steakhouse and bar. Its 32 rooms (US$64) each have private bath, cable TV and two double beds – one soft and one hard. **Hotel Parador de la Montaña** (☎ 456-00-75, López Mateos 44) is larger and similarly priced.

The attractive **Best Western – The Lodge at Creel** (☎ 456-00-71, López Mateos 61) offers spacious, comfortable, self-contained wooden cabins, each with gas woodstove, two double beds and cable TV, for US$64/85 including continental breakfast. The honeymoon suite, with private Jacuzzi, costs US$120.

Places to Eat

Plenty of restaurants are on López Mateos, in the few blocks south of the plaza. Most are open daily from around 7.30 am to 10 pm and serve a lunchtime comida corrida for US$2.75 to US$3.25. The pleasant **Restaurant Verónica** is often recommended by locals, as are **Restaurant La Cabaña**, which specializes in steak, seafood and Mexican dishes; the smaller **Restaurant Estela**; and **Todo Rico. El Pollito Feliz** specializes in roasted chicken, Sinaloense style; a half/whole chicken, served with tortillas, costs US$3/5.50. Across the tracks, **Restaurant Jorge's** on Calle Cristo Rey is a tiny place with good food.

For more upmarket dining, **Sierra Madre Pub Steakhouse** in the Best Western – The Lodge at Creel is attractive, with good food and a pleasant bar. Breakfast costs around US$3.50 to US$4; a full-on dinner including soup, salad, main course and dessert might run around US$13 to US$15. Bottles of wine range from US$3 to US$38. It also serves pizza.

Shopping

Many shops in Creel sell Tarahumara handicrafts, including baskets, colorful dolls, wood carvings, violins, flutes, archery sets, pottery, clothing and more. Prices are very reasonable. The best place to buy them is at the Artesanías Misión shop on the north side of the plaza. All of the store's earnings go to support the Catholic mission hospital, which provides free medical care for the Tarahumara.

Getting There & Around
Air Nuevo Horizonte Internacional (☎ 456-01-11), López Mateos 32, offers helicopter tours around the canyons and other helicopter services.

Bus Travel between Creel and Chihuahua may be more convenient via bus rather than train, as the trip is shorter and the schedule more flexible. The Estrella Blanca bus station, across the tracks from the plaza, has seven daily buses to Chihuahua (256km, 4½ hours, US$14.50), passing through San Juanito (30km, 45 minutes, US$2.50), La Junta (102km, 2½ hours, US$7) and Cuauhtémoc (170km, three hours, US$9.50) on the way. A bus to Ciudad Juárez (9 hours, US$34.50) departs daily at 8.15 am.

Estrella Blanca also has a daily bus to San Rafael (55km, 1½ hours, US$3.50) via Divisadero (45km, one hour, US$2.50) and Posada Barrancas (Areponápuchi; 49km, 1¼ hours, US$2.75). It departs Creel daily at noon, and departs San Rafael for the return trip at 4 pm. Another bus also goes to San Rafael, via Divisadero and Posada Barrancas, from a stop on Villa, on the west side of the tracks, at 4 pm daily. The return trip departs San Rafael at 7.30 am the next morning.

A bus to Batopilas (140km, five hours, US$13.50) leaves from outside the Hotel Los Pinos on López Mateos, two blocks south of the plaza. The bus leaves Creel at 7.30 am Tuesday, Thursday and Saturday, and at 9.30 am Monday, Wednesday and Friday. The road between Creel and Batopilas is paved initially, but the second half is bumpy and rough.

Train Creel's train station is half a block from the main plaza. The westbound primera express train departs Creel 11.26 am and clase económica at 1.00 pm; the eastbound trains depart at 2.14 and 4.10 pm. See Getting There & Away in the Barranca del Cobre (Copper Canyon) section for schedules and ticket information.

Car & Motorcycle Now there's a paved road all the way from Creel to Divisadero and on to San Rafael. From San Rafael, if you have a sturdy 4WD vehicle, you could go to El Fuerte in the dry season (March to May is the best time) via Bahuichivo, Mesa de Arturo, La Reforma and Choix, crossing the Colosio reservoir in a two-vehicle ferry. Or you could go from San Rafael to Álamos via Bahuichivo, Témoris and Chinipas, crossing the Río Chinipas. Both of these roads are very rough; assaults have also occurred on these roads, making them dangerous (for more information, see the Dangers & Annoyances section in the Facts for the Visitor chapter).

Bicycle Umarike Expediciones, on Ferrocarril, rents mountain bikes for US$7/10 a half/full day, or US$9/14 with front shocks; prices include map, helmet and tool kit. Señor Ángel Castillo also rents mountain bikes, for the same prices; look for him at his small shop beside the railway tracks, roughly opposite the Hotel La Posada de Creel (the shop has no sign; the building is painted orange), or ask for him at Restaurant Verónica on López Mateos. The Complejo Ecoturístico Arareko office on López Mateos rents mountain bikes for US$2.25/22 per hour/day.

BATOPILAS
• pop 840 • elev 495m ☎ 1
Batopilas, a serene 19th-century silver-mining village 140km south of Creel, is deep in the heart of the canyon country. The journey from Creel to Batopilas is a thrilling ride from an altitude of 2338m at Creel to 495m at Batopilas, with dramatic descents and ascents through several canyons, climates and vegetative zones. Batopilas' climate is distinctly warmer and more tropical than Creel's. You are now surrounded by stands of mangoes, bananas and other tropical fruit trees rather than Creel's cool-loving pine forests.

Batopilas is a great starting point for many short and long treks; any hotel can help arrange canyon trips. An interesting

8km walk is to the Catedral Perdida (Lost Cathedral) at **Satevó**. No one knows why such an elaborate cathedral was built in a hauntingly beautiful but uninhabited canyon where there has never been a sizeable settlement. It was built so long ago that its origins are lost in the distant past.

Places to Stay & Eat

Batopilas has several small hotels and guesthouses. All of the following are clean, and the rooms come with fan and private bath. Opposite the church, *Hotel Mary*, a favorite with travelers, has simple rooms for about US$6.50 per person, and a good little restaurant. *Real de Minas* has rooms around a lovely courtyard for about US$42 per room; it's an attractive hotel, and a good value. *Juanita's* is similarly priced. *Hotel Batopilas* is cheaper, but not as well kept. All of these are in town near the church. These hotels do not have private phones, but you could contact them by calling the town caseta (☎ 456-06-24).

Riverside Lodge (☎ 248-340-7230, 800-776-3942 in the USA) is a luxurious hotel 'for the rich and famous' and is much more expensive; most of its business is in all-inclusive excursions from the USA. A new hotel, *Hacienda Río Batopilas*, operated by Margarita Quintero of Creel, is scheduled to open by the time this book is published; check with Hotel Margarita's Plaza Mexicana in Creel for current information.

Doña Mica's restaurant, near the plaza, is a good place to eat; let her know an hour ahead of time, if you want to eat there. *El Quinto Patio*, at the rear of Hotel Mary, is also good. *Restaurant Clarita*, on the main street, serves basic meals very cheaply, and Clarita offers the cheapest accommodations in town. *Restaurant Carolina's*, a 15-minute walk from the plaza, is not central, but it serves good food.

At La Bufa, on the way to Batopilas, an American named *Bush* rents rooms at his home and has a camping area. Any Creel-Batopilas bus will drop you off at La Bufa.

Getting There & Away

The bus to Creel (140km, five hours, US$13.50) departs from the plaza in Batopilas at 5 am daily. On Tuesday, Thursday and Saturday the return bus goes all the way from Batopilas to Chihuahua (396km, nine hours, US$29).

Central North Mexico

This chapter includes the entire state of Durango, much of the state of Chihuahua and a tiny part of the state of Coahuila. It covers a long-used travel route between the USA and central Mexico, along the high plains parallel to the Sierra Madre Occidental, across flat or undulating country with occasional rocky ranges jutting from the plains. Remote desert landscapes are the rule, but the arid, sparsely populated region is intersected by rivers flowing intermittently from the sierra. The irrigated areas are verdant oases where fruit, cotton and other crops are grown and where most of the towns have been established.

Most travelers hurry through the Central North area on their way to better-known attractions, but the region holds plenty of interest. History and archaeology buffs in particular will enjoy exploring the ruins at Paquimé and Cuarenta Casas – remnants of once-flourishing settlements of Mexico's northern indigenous peoples. And though most of the region's towns, with the notable exception of Durango, tend to be rough and rundown, some colonial gems are hidden amid the modern urban detritus.

Chihuahua state is in the Hora de las Montañas (Mountain Time) time zone, one hour behind Durango and Coahuila. The time in Chihuahua is the same as in the neighboring Mexican states of Sonora and Sinaloa to the west and the US state of New Mexico (and far west Texas around El Paso) to the north.

CIUDAD JUÁREZ & EL PASO (TEXAS)

Juárez: • pop 995,800 • elev 1145m
☎ changing
El Paso: • pop 583,000 • elev 1165m
☎ 915

Ciudad Juárez is a grimy, noisy, booming border town, inextricably linked with El Paso, its American neighbor just across the Rio Grande. The cities lie on a travel route that was being used long before the

Highlights

- Paquimé ruins – a restored complex of adobe structures marking the former site of a major indigenous trading settlement
- Chihuahua's Museo de la Revolución Mexicana – housed in Pancho Villa's former headquarters
- Durango – lively Plaza de Armas and movie locations of many classic Westerns
- Hidalgo del Parral – vivacious town with narrow streets and 19th-century mansions
- Around Madera – a forested region with pre-Hispanic cliffside dwellings
- Mina Ojuela – ghost mining town on a hilltop north of Torreón

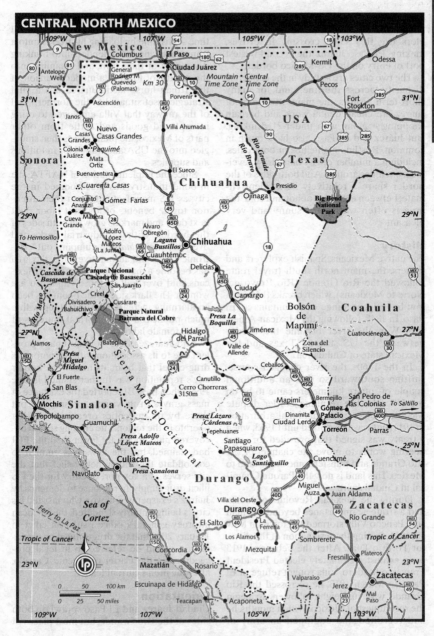

CENTRAL NORTH MEXICO

109°W New Mexico 107°W 105°W 103°W

9 Columbus 54
80 El Paso 180 62 Kermit 18 Odessa
Antelope 81 General 285
Wells Rodrigo M Ciudad Juárez Mountain Central
Quevedo Km 30 10 Time Zone Time Zone Pecos
(Palomas) Porvenir 54 10 Fort 385
31°N Ascención 45 Stockton 31°N
Janos 10 Villa Ahumada 90 385
Nuevo USA 67 285
Casas Casas Grandes Texas
Grandes El Sueco 67
Colonia Paquimé Rio Bravo 385
Sonora Juárez Mata Chihuahua Presidio
Ortiz Ojinaga Big Bend
Buenaventura 15 National
Cuarenta Casas Park
29°N Conjunto Gómez Farías 45 29°N
Anasazi 45D
Cueva Madera 28 Álvaro
Grande Adolfo Obregón
To Hermosillo López Laguna 18
16 Mateos Bustillos Chihuahua
(La Junta) 65 Cuauhtémoc 53
Cascada de Parque Nacional 16D Delicias
Basaseachi Cascada de Basaseachi 45D
San Juanito Ciudad Coahuila
Creel 24 Camargo Bolsón
27°N Divisadero Cusárare Presa La de 27°N
Bahuichivo Parque Natural Boquilla Mapimí
Barranca del Cobre Hidalgo Jiménez Cuatrociénegas
Álamos Batopilas del Parral Zona del 30
Presa 45 Valle de Silencio
Miguel Allende
Hidalgo 24 Ceballos 49
El Fuerte 45D
San Blas Canutillo Mapimí Bermejillo San Pedro de
Los Cerro Chorreras 45 Dinamita Gómez las Colonias To Saltillo
Mochis 3150m Palacio 40D
Topolobampo Presa Lázaro Ciudad Lerdo Torreón Parras
Guamuchil Cárdenas Santiago Tepehuanes 25°N
25°N Presa Adolfo Papasquiaro Lago Cuencamé
López Mateos Santiaguillo 40
Culiacán Durango Miguel
Navolato Presa Sanalona Villa del Oeste Auza Juan Aldama Zacatecas
Durango 40D 49
Sea of 40 La Río Grande 54
Cortez El Salto Ferreria 45
Los Álamos Sombrerete Plateros
Ferry to La Paz 15D Mezquital Fresnillo
Tropic of Cancer Tropic of Cancer
23°N Concordia 40 Valparaiso Zacatecas 23°N
Mazatlán Rosario 49
0 50 100 km Escuinapa de Hidalgo Jerez
0 25 50 miles Teacapan Acaponeta Mal 23
109°W 107°W 105°W Paso 103°W

conquistador Cabeza de Vaca found El Paso del Norte in the 16th century. Modern travelers use this same crossing in droves, making El Paso/Juárez the second-busiest port of entry on the US-Mexico border.

The two cities are a study in the economic disparity 'across the line,' and for many short-term visitors, the main attractions of Juárez are cheap dental work and bargain shopping – along with under-21 drinking. But Juárez and El Paso also have much in common. Bustling nightclubs in both cities, including a number of gay bars, draw revelers from miles around. And both sides of the border share a relatively benevolent climate; between extremes of hot and cold, the area is often warm, dry, sunny and very pleasant.

History

For native Mexicans, Spanish explorers and traders, the main north-south travel route followed the Rio Grande (Río Bravo del Norte to Mexicans), which breaks through a low but rugged range of mountains at El Paso. In 1848, following the Mexican-American War, the river became the border between the US state of Texas and the Mexican state of Chihuahua.

In the 1860s, the river changed course, shifting southward so that an additional couple of square kilometers came to be on the US side. The resulting border dispute was the subject of international arbitration in 1911, but wasn't resolved until 1963, when a treaty was signed that provided for engineering works to move the channel of the Rio Grande and transfer some of the land to Mexico. This land is now the Parque Chamizal in Ciudad Juárez.

During the Mexican Revolution, Juárez had a strategic importance beyond its small size. Pancho Villa stormed the town on May 10, 1911, forcing the resignation of the dictator Porfirio Díaz. After the February 1913 coup against legitimately elected President Francisco Madero, Villa sought refuge in El Paso. In March 1913, he recrossed the Rio Grande with just eight followers to begin the reconquest of Mexico. Within months, he had recruited and equipped an army of

thousands, La División del Norte, and in November he conquered Juárez for a second time – this time by loading his troops onto a train, deceiving the defenders into thinking it was one of their own, and steaming into the middle of town in a modern version of the Trojan horse tactic. Juárez was a vital strategic asset situated at the northern end of the railway that Villa employed to bring in captured goods and cattle from other parts of Mexico; the plunder was then smuggled into the USA and traded for munitions and supplies.

Since the implementation of NAFTA, the in-bond industry has mushroomed in the city, as US manufacturers turn their attention to the benefits of low-cost labor right next door and markets grow on both sides of the border. With 13 industrial parks and over 360 *maquiladoras* pumping out electronic goods and automotive parts, the area has become a magnet for job-seeking Mexicans, and over half of those employed are women. The dark side of the boom has been an alarming increase in crime, along with a much-publicized rash of brutal murders of young female laborers.

And Juárez suffers from an image problem due to its association with the notorious drug cartel that bears its name. The border city's reputation was further stained in late 1999, when the FBI reported the existence of mass graves in its vicinity, presumably put there by the narcotics organizations that operate in the region. The ensuing search uncovered nine bodies, far fewer than the FBI had claimed, but the news was enough to consolidate the widely held belief that the city serves as a key port of entry for the US illicit drug supply. In response to demands by Juárez's exasperated mayor, who insisted his city is being unfairly slandered, the Mexican attorney general's office issued an edict in January 2000 that the drug-smuggling organization would be referred to in legal proceedings as the Cartel of Vicente Carrillo, after the mob's current leader.

Orientation

Ciudad Juárez and El Paso sprawl on both sides of the Rio Grande, but most places of interest to travelers are concentrated in the central areas of the two cities, along the streets connected by the bridges: Santa Fe St/Avenida Juárez, and Stanton St/Avenida Lerdo. You can walk across either bridge, but by car you must take Stanton St going south and Avenida Juárez going north – the vehicle toll is US$1.50 in either direction. Juárez, lined with shops, restaurants, bars and seedy hotels, is the main tourist street in Ciudad Juárez and leads to the center of town. Avenida 16 de Septiembre heads east from Lerdo and becomes Paseo Triunfo de la República, the main drag, with many motels, restaurants and shopping centers.

About 4km east of the Santa Fe St/Avenida Juárez bridge, the toll-free Bridge of the Americas (Cordova Bridge) leads to a bypass road and the main highway south to Chihuahua. Even farther east, the Zaragoza toll bridge entirely avoids both El Paso and Juárez.

Information

Tourist Offices The Ciudad Juárez tourist office (☎ 11-31-74), at the southern end of the Bridge of the Americas, may be useful to those driving into town. Open 9 am to 9 pm daily, the bilingual office stocks a variety of informative brochures. More conveniently located on Villa just north of Guerrero is a tourist information module in the Garita de Metales, a small brick building that once served as a control point for metals exports. Open 11 am to 4 pm Monday to Thursday, 9 am to 4 pm Friday, it offers many of the same materials as the main office.

The El Paso Tourist Information Center (☎ 544-0062), in the little round pavilion at the intersection of Santa Fe and Main, is open 8 am to 5 pm daily.

Immigration If you don't intend to venture beyond Ciudad Juárez and you're staying less than 72 hours, you won't need a tourist card. Those moving deeper into Mexico must have a card and can get one from a Mexican immigration office (found at the ends of the Stanton St and Bridge of the Americas bridges).

Consulates The Mexican consulate in El Paso (☎ 533-3644), at 910 San Antonio Ave, is open 9 am to noon Monday to Friday. In Juárez, the US consulate (☎ 11-30-00) is at López Mateos 924 Nte.

Money Businesses in Ciudad Juárez generally accept US currency. Banks are clustered along 16 de Septiembre, with most open 9 am to 5 pm Monday to Friday. Of the numerous currency exchange booths along Juárez, only Comisiones San Luis, at the corner of 16 de Septiembre, changes traveler's checks. The *casa de cambio* at the bus station does too.

If you are in El Paso outside of banking hours, go to Valuta at the corner of Paisano and Mesa; it's open 24 hours and changes cash and traveler's checks.

Post & Communications The Ciudad Juárez post office, at the corner of Lerdo and Peña, is open 8 am to 8 pm Monday to Friday, 8 am to noon Saturday. El Paso's post office, at Mills and Stanton, is open 8.30 am to 5 pm Monday to Friday, 8.30 am to noon Saturday.

The El Paso Community College library (☎ 831-4019), 100 W Rio Grande Ave, offers free Internet access; terminals are available 5 to 8 pm Monday to Thursday, 9 am to 2.30 pm Saturday and 1 to 4.30 pm Sunday. You must provide a picture ID.

Things to See & Do

Charming and beautiful are not adjectives one often associates with Ciudad Juárez, but the city is no cultural desert, and a couple of the old buildings near the Plaza de Armas are of some interest.

The stone-sided **Misión de Nuestra Señora de Guadalupe** was built in the mid-1600s, and its hand-carved roof beams and

On December 1, 2000, the telephone area code for Ciudad Juárez is due to change to ☎ 1 from 16, with the digit 6 added to the start of every local number (for example, the number 11-50-00 will become 611-50-00).

CENTRAL NORTH

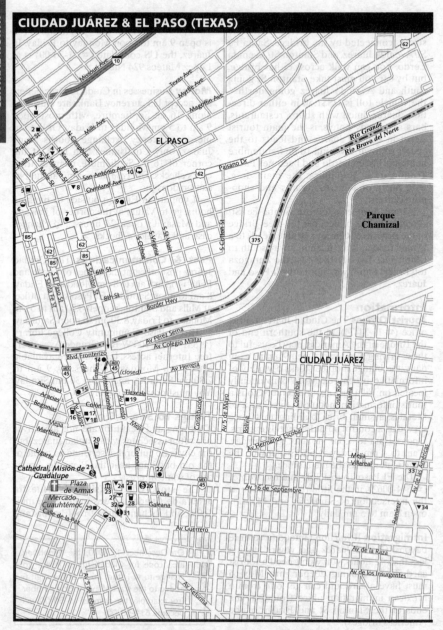

CIUDAD JUÁREZ & EL PASO (TEXAS)

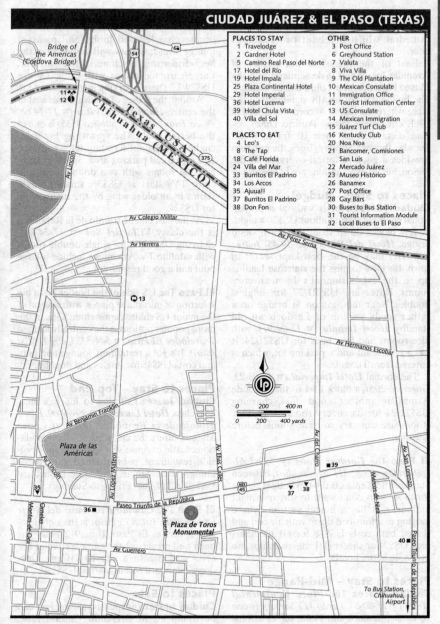

CIUDAD JUÁREZ & EL PASO (TEXAS)

PLACES TO STAY
1 Travelodge
2 Gardner Hotel
5 Camino Real Paso del Norte
17 Hotel del Río
19 Hotel Impala
25 Plaza Continental Hotel
29 Hotel Imperial
36 Hotel Lucerna
39 Hotel Chula Vista
40 Villa del Sol

PLACES TO EAT
4 Leo's
8 The Tap
18 Café Florida
24 Villa del Mar
33 Burritos El Padrino
35 Los Arcos
35 Ajuua!!
37 Burritos El Padrino
38 Don Fon

OTHER
3 Post Office
6 Greyhound Station
7 Valuta
8 Viva Villa
9 The Old Plantation
10 Mexican Consulate
11 Immigration Office
12 Tourist Information Center
13 US Consulate
14 Mexican Immigration
15 Juárez Turf Club
16 Kentucky Club
20 Noa Noa
21 Bancomer, Comisiones
    San Luis
22 Mercado Juárez
23 Museo Histórico
26 Banamex
27 Post Office
28 Gay Bars
30 Buses to Bus Station
31 Tourist Information Module
32 Local Buses to El Paso

Bridge of
the Americas
(Cordova Bridge)

Texas (USA)
Chihuahua (MEXICO)

Av Lincoln

Av Colegio Militar

Av Herrera

Av Pérez Serna

Av Hermanos Escobar

Av Benjamin Franklin

Plaza de las
Américas

Av Lincoln

Av López Mateos

Av Elías Calles

Plaza de Toros
Monumental

Av Huerta

Av Guerrero

Paseo Triunfo de la República

Ornelas

Montes de Oca

Paseo Triunfo de la República

Av del Charro

Av San Lorenzo

Marcos de Niza

Paseo Triunfo de la República

0   200   400 m
0   200   400 yards

To Bus Station,
Chihuahua,
Airport

choir mezzanine are impressive. The mission is on the west side of the plaza next to the cathedral, which was built two centuries later.

East of the plaza, at the corner of Avenidas Juárez and 16 de Septiembre, is the **Museo Histórico**, in the old customs building. The building is historically significant as the place where the Juárez Accord was signed in 1911, effectively ending Porfirio Díaz's 35-year dictatorship. Open 10 am to 6 pm Tuesday through Sunday (free), the museum provides a good historical overview of the region, but all explanations are in Spanish.

Places to Stay – Budget

Ciudad Juárez Hotels without a professional clientele start at about US$20 a night. A few blocks down from the northbound bridge, *Hotel del Río* (☎ *12-59-45, Juárez 488 Nte*) may be the best-kept secret in town. It's easy to miss the staircase leading up to the establishment's 18 neat, cozy rooms. Rates are US$21/27 for singles/doubles. Near the Stanton St bridge on a rather seedy section of Lerdo is an old standby, *Hotel Impala* (☎ *15-04-91*), with nice rooms and firm beds for US$21/24. It has a restaurant and a parking lot, which is entered from Tlaxcala.

The cordial *Hotel Imperial* (☎ *15-03-23, Guerrero 206*), a block east of the Plaza de Armas, is another good deal, charging US$21/24 for its cheery rooms with TVs. Room size can vary so have a look before deciding.

El Paso The *Gardner Hotel* (☎ *532-3661, epihostl@whc.net, 311 E Franklin*), between Stanton and Kansas, is the top budget choice for those who don't want to stay overnight in Juárez. It has a hostel section, where lodging in a four-bed dorm with air-con and shared bath costs US$16 for HI members plus US$2 for sheets (HI memberships are available at the hotel).

Places to Stay – Mid-Range

Ciudad Juárez The *Plaza Continental Hotel* (☎ *15-00-84, Lerdo 112 Sur*), between 16 de Septiembre and Peña, offers affordable luxury in the center of town. Some travelers will be charmed by the hotel's ornate chandeliered lobby and pleasant lounge areas; others will appreciate the beer-dispensing machine in the corridor. Large carpeted rooms with cable TV are US$29/33. There's parking in an adjacent lot.

Among the scores of roadside inns east of the center, *Hotel Chula Vista* (☎ *17-14-68, Paseo Triunfo de la República 3555*) is one of the better deals. The sprawling hotel includes a small pool, a restaurant, a bar/disco and a guarded parking area. Spacious comfortable rooms with two double beds and color TVs start at US$36; smaller single rooms in an older wing by the highway go for US$24.

At the east end of Triunfo de la República is the classy *Villa del Sol* (☎ *17-24-24*), charging US$52/58 for single/double rooms with satellite TV. Amenities include a large pool and a good restaurant.

El Paso The US side of the border has a big selection of mid-range places, with several of the major US chains represented. One of the more popular options is the centrally located *Travelodge El Paso* (☎ *544-3333, 409 E Missouri*). It's got a restaurant, lounge and pool and costs US$45 for singles and doubles.

Places to Stay – Top End

Ciudad Juárez Catering to Juárez's business class, *Hotel Lucerna* (☎ *29-99-00, Paseo Triunfo de la República 3976*), at López Mateos, offers the city's finest accommodations. Little expense was spared on its poolside restaurant, palm-studded gardens or lounge areas. Single or double rooms are US$103 (20% less Friday to Sunday).

El Paso The *Camino Real Paso del Norte* (☎ *534-3000, 101 S El Paso*) is the only five-star option in El Paso. The 1912 hotel has been well preserved; the vintage circular bar rests underneath a superb Tiffany glass dome. Standard rooms start at US$130.

Places to Eat

Ciudad Juárez Inexpensive, filling fare can be found at the *Mercado Cuauhtémoc*, beside the Plaza de Armas. A number of stalls on the lower level serve tacos, *tortas*, soups, *antojitos* and seafood.

Juárez is famous for its burritos, and some of the most authentic can be found at **Burritos El Padrino**, with branches on Mejía at Américas and on Paseo Triunfo de la República near the Hotel Chula Vista. At US$1 apiece, these mega-burritos are filled with beans, *mole*, shredded beef in *salsa verde* and so on.

Ciudad Juárez boasts some excellent steak and seafood restaurants. For smoked marlin tacos (US$1.75) and fresh fish fillets (starting at US$7), **Los Arcos**, at the corner of Américas and Paseo Triunfo de la República, is a fine catch. **Villa del Mar**, on Villa just off 16 de Septiembre, is clean, cheap and busy; try the *pescado entero normandi* (US$5) if black bass stuffed with shrimp and oysters and smothered in white salsa sounds good to you. Carnivores can take delight in **Café Florida**, at the corner of Mejía and Juárez, which serves choice cuts of beef from US$12.

Of several Chinese restaurants in town, the most authentic is probably **Don Fon**, on Paseo Triunfo de la República just west of Charro. Main courses run US$6 to US$10, and the restaurant features live lounge music nightly.

Ajuua!! (Ornelas 162 Nte), a large restaurant-bar popular with Texans, offers the full Mexican experience. Decorated to resemble a *pueblito mexicano*, complete with mariachis, the restaurant serves all the classics, including *chiles en nogada* (chilies stuffed with ground meat and fruit mixture) and *enmoladas* (tortillas drenched in mole sauce). Main courses go for US$6.50 to US$10.

El Paso Most of downtown El Paso shuts down by 6 pm. An exception is **The Tap** (408 E San Antonio), open until 2 am daily. Though it looks more like a bar than a restaurant, the Tap prepares tasty Mexican dishes ranging from US$4.25 to US$5.75. **Leo's**, on Mills just east of Stanton, offers good Tex-Mex fare in a cool, pleasant setting. Filling lunch specials are US$4.25. It's open only until 3 pm Monday to Friday.

Entertainment

Ciudad Juárez The bars and discos extending from the bridge down Juárez tend to be grimy and depressing – the venerable **Kentucky Club** being the greatest exception. The Kentucky's polished wood bar is a fine place to sip a margarita – legend has it the cocktail made its first appearance here. Farther down Juárez is **Noa Noa**, named after a hit song by bar owner Juan Gabriel and featuring a pool table and good *norteño* bands. The city's gay bars are concentrated near the corner of Peña and Lerdo, with the **Ritz** and **Club Olímpico** among the more popular spots.

El Paso Though generally somnolent, the downtown area has its pockets of nightlife. The most popular watering hole is **The Old Plantation**, at 301 S Ochoa. Although predominantly gay, the multilevel bar/disco has become a hit with straights too. **Club 101**, on San Francisco a block from the Amtrak station, is packed with swaying bodies on weekends. The Mexican cantina-style **Viva Villa**, on San Antonio east of Stanton, offers a list of 85 wines, most sold by the bottle, plus microbrewed beers on tap and handcrafted cigars.

Spectator Sports

Juárez's bullfighting season takes place from April through August. Events typically begin at 6 pm Sunday at the Plaza de Toros Monumental (☎ 13-16-56) on Paseo Triunfo de la República. Off-track betting is available at the Juárez Turf Club, which is a block from the Juárez bridge.

Shopping

The old Mercado Juárez, east of the town's center on Avenida 16 de Septiembre, has a large collection of souvenir stalls to overwhelm you with tacky shopping possibilities. More interesting is the Mercado Cuauhtémoc, on Mariscal beside the Plaza de Armas. Aimed primarily at locals, the big lively market has sections for herbs, piñatas, religious icons and flowers. The upper level of the building is given over to the standard tourist dross.

Getting There & Away

Air The Juárez airport (Aeropuerto Internacional Abraham González) is just east of highway 45D, about 18km south of the center of town. Direct flights are available to/from Mexico City, Chihuahua, Guadalajara, Mazatlán and Tijuana. Flights to other major cities go via Chihuahua or Mexico City. The main Mexican carriers are AeroMexico (☎ 800-021-40-00), Aero California (☎ 18-33-99) and TAESA (☎ 800-904-63-00).

Bus The Juárez bus station (Central de Autobuses) is on Teófilo Borunda, a long way from town. For information on getting there, see Getting Around. Main destinations, with daily departures, are:

Chihuahua – 373km, 5 hours; 3 deluxe (US$26), frequent 1st-class (US$19)

Mexico City (Terminal Norte) – 1840km, 24 hours; 16 1st-class (US$96)

Nuevo Casas Grandes – 315km, 4 hours; hourly 1st-class (US$12)

Frequent 1st-class buses also go to Durango, Monterrey, San Luis Potosí and Zacatecas. Autobuses Americanos buses going direct to US cities (for example, Albuquerque, Dallas and Denver) are generally cheaper than Greyhound from El Paso.

The El Paso Greyhound station (☎ 532-2365) has its main entrance on Santa Fe between Overland and San Antonio. Several buses a day travel to Los Angeles (15 hours, US$45), Chicago (34 hours, US$89), New York (48 hours, US$95), Miami (35 hours, US$99) and other major US cities.

Train El Paso's Amtrak station (☎ 545-2247) is at 700 San Francisco, three blocks west of the Civic Center Plaza. Trains run three times a week to Los Angeles (15 hours, US$179), Miami (48 hours, US$239), Chicago (48 hours, US$213) and New York (60 hours, US$291).

Mexican train service out of Ciudad Juárez has been suspended indefinitely.

Car & Motorcycle If you're driving into the Mexican interior, you must obtain a vehicle permit (see the Getting There & Away chapter). The only place to do so in the Ciudad Juárez area (even if you're heading in another direction) is at the major customs checkpoint at Km 30 on highway 45D south.

Beyond the checkpoint, the highway to Chihuahua is in good condition but it comes with a US$9 toll. Highway 2 to Nuevo Casas Grandes branches west at a traffic circle 25km south of town.

For liability and vehicle insurance while in Mexico, try these companies in El Paso: Sanborn's (☎ 779-3538), 440 Raynolds St; or AAA (☎ 778-9521), 1201 Airway Blvd.

Getting Around

Local buses to the Juárez bus station leave from Guerrero just west of Villa (in front of the Hotel Aremar). Catch a blue-striped 'C Camionera' bus or a green-top 'Permisionarios Unidos' bus (US$0.30); it's a 25-minute trip. From the bus station to the town center, turn left and go out to the highway; any bus labeled 'Centro' will drop you near the cathedral. Inside the bus station, a booth sells tickets for authorized taxis into town (US$6.50).

You can bypass central Juárez altogether if you take one of the hourly direct buses between the El Paso and Juárez bus stations (one hour, US$5).

Autobuses Twin Cities runs a shuttle service between the Juárez and El Paso downtown areas. Blue vans depart from the corner of Villa and Galeana every 10 minutes and head for San Antonio St in El Paso (US$0.20).

OTHER BORDER CROSSINGS

Though El Paso-Juárez is the most important and frequently used port of entry between central north Mexico and the USA, there are some alternative crossing points.

Columbus (New Mexico)-General Rodrigo M Quevedo

The small border town of General Rodrigo M Quevedo (also called Palomas) is about 150km west of Juárez, and the crossing is open 24 hours a day. Motorists can obtain a vehicle permit in one of the trailers beside the border checkpoint. There's a motel and an inexpensive hotel, as well as 2nd-class bus connections to Ciudad Juárez and Nuevo Casas Grandes.

Columbus has a campground and a motel, but no public transport connections into the USA. It's known as the site of the only foreign invasion of the continental USA – Pancho Villa sacked the town in 1916 (see 'Pancho Villa: Bandit-Turned-Revolutionary' in this chapter). A museum in Columbus has some exhibits about the attack.

Presidio (Texas)-Ojinaga

This little-used border crossing is 209km northeast of Chihuahua. A few buses run between Chihuahua and Ojinaga daily. From Presidio, Greyhound offers daily service to San Antonio, Houston and Dallas; there's no depot, just a bus stop on the corner of O'Riley and Anderson. Both Presidio and Ojinaga have some cheap places to stay and eat.

NUEVO CASAS GRANDES & CASAS GRANDES

Nuevo Casas Grandes: • pop 49,700
• elev 1463m ☎ changing
Casas Grandes: • pop 3430 • elev 1463m
☎ changing

Nuevo Casas Grandes is a four-hour bus trip southwest of Ciudad Juárez, and you could make it here for a quiet first night in Mexico. It's a peaceful, prosperous country town serving the surrounding farmlands. The substantial brick houses around town, which look like they should be in the US Midwest, were built by Mormon settlers in the late 19th century. The main reason to visit is to see the ruins of Paquimé, adjacent to the nearby village of Casas Grandes.

Orientation & Information

Most of the facilities useful to visitors are within a few blocks of 5 de Mayo and Constitución (the street with railway tracks down the middle). Available services include banks (ATMs at Banamex and Bancomer), a casa de cambio next to the Hotel California and a post office.

On December 1, 2000, the telephone area code for Nuevo Casas Grandes and Casas Grandes is due to change to ☎ 1 from 169, with the digits 69 added to the start of every local number (for example, the number 4-06-55 will become 694-06-55).

Paquimé Ruins

The name 'Casas Grandes' (Big Houses) comes from the Paquimé Ruins – the crumbling adobe remnants of what was the major trading settlement in northern Mexico between 900 and 1340 AD. Partially excavated and restored, the networks of eroded walls now resemble roofless mazes.

The Paquimé people had a flourishing civilization with significant ties to the pre-conquest cultures of Arizona and New Mexico. The structures here are similar to Pueblo houses of the US Southwest, with distinctive T-shaped door openings; archaeologists speculate the openings could be closed off against winter cold while still allowing smoke from cooking fires to escape. Timber beams set into the walls supported roofs and upper floors, some of which have been reconstructed. The largest dwellings had up to three levels.

The Paquimé irrigated the land to grow maize crops, and they built adobe cages to breed *guacamayas* (macaws), whose feathers were valued for ceremonial uses. As the city grew, it was influenced through trade with southern civilizations, particularly the Toltecs. Paquimé acquired some Toltec features, such as a ball court, of which there are remnants. At its peak, the local population is estimated to have been around 10,000.

Despite fortifications, Paquimé was invaded, perhaps by Apaches, in 1340. The city was sacked, burned and abandoned, and its great structures were left alone for more than 600 years. The site was partially excavated in the late 1950s, and subsequent exposure to the elements led to erosion of the walls. Today the walls have been dutifully restored, and some of the unique interior water systems and hidden cisterns have been rebuilt.

The Paquimé were great potters and produced earthenware with striking red, brown or black geometric designs over a cream background. Other pieces were made from black clay. Fine examples can be seen in the impressive **Museo de las Culturas del Norte** near the ruins, which also displays large-scale models of the Paquimé complex and other key northern trade centers. A fee of US$2.75 admits you to the museum and the ruins, both open 10 am to 5 pm Tuesday to Sunday.

The museum gift shop sells locally made pottery in the Paquimé style, but better quality items are sold at lower prices in a shop near the site entrance.

To reach the ruins, take a 'Casas Grandes/ Col Juárez' bus from Constitución in the center of Nuevo Casas Grandes; they run every half hour during the day. The 8km journey takes about 15 minutes (US$0.45). You will be let off at the picturesque main plaza of Casas Grandes, and from there signs direct you to the ruins, a 15-minute walk.

Places to Stay

In Nuevo Casas Grandes, most budget travelers stay at the dingy *Hotel Juárez* (☎ 4-02-33, *Obregón 110*), just south of 5 de Mayo and close to the bus station. It costs US$6.50/7.50 for singles/doubles. There's no heating or aircon, but for one or two nights it's tolerable.

The hospitable *Hotel California* (☎ 4-11-10, *Constitución 209*) offers sparkling clean, air-conditioned rooms with private bath for US$22/26. *Motel Piñón* (☎ 4-06-55), on Juárez as you enter town from the north, features well-designed air-conditioned rooms, cleverly incorporating Paquimé motifs into the decor, for US$26/32. It also has a swimming pool (summer only) and offers guide services to the ruins.

Top honors go to *Hotel Hacienda* (☎ 4-10-46, *Juárez 2603*), 1.5km north of town on highway 10, with a garden courtyard, swimming pool and restaurant. Comfortable air-conditioned rooms cost US$47/53.

Places to Eat

Nuevo Casas Grandes has several good, reasonably priced restaurants. *Constantino*, on Juárez just north of the main plaza, serves excellent steaks (US$7) and sandwiches (US$1.75). In addition to its pizzas (US$2.50 to US$8.50), the clean and popular *Dinno's Pizza*, at the corner of 5 de Mayo and Obregón, offers Chinese food including Szechuan-style dishes.

Nuevo Casas Grandes' classiest choice – though not a terribly expensive one – is *Restaurant Malmedy*, in the old Mormon community of Colonia Dublán at the north end of town. The chef prepares dishes from

Paquimé ruins

SCOTT DOGGETT

his native Belgium, such as shrimp *beignets*, in addition to original versions of Mexican favorites. Main courses range from US$4.50 to US$6.50, and portions are huge.

Getting There & Away
Daily buses run to/from Ciudad Juárez (315km, 4½ hours, US$11.75), to/from Chihuahua (352km, 5½ hours, US$15) and to/from Madera (242km, six hours, US$15). Other buses go daily to La Junta, Cuauhtémoc, Monterrey and Zacatecas.

Driving south to Madera, turn right onto highway 28 at Buenaventura. This road climbs through scenic mountains dotted with oaks and short stubby cactuses on its way to Zaragoza and Gómez Farías. It's best driven in the daylight.

AROUND NUEVO CASAS GRANDES
Trips in the areas west and south of Nuevo Casas Grandes take in some interesting little towns, cool forests and several archaeological sites. Most can be reached by bus, but to see the ancient rock carvings in the rugged **Arroyo de los Monos**, 35km to the south, you will need a vehicle with good clearance.

A good day trip could include the Mormon village of **Colonia Juárez** and the **Hacienda de San Diego** (a 1902 mansion owned by the Terrazas family, who had control of most of pre-revolutionary Chihuahua state). The mountain-flanked community of **Mata Ortiz** is 30km south of Nuevo Casas Grandes via unpaved roads. Mata Ortiz is a center for the production of pottery using materials, techniques and decorative styles like those of the ancient Paquimé culture. Juan Quezada, credited with reviving the Paquimé pottery tradition, is the most famous of the village's 300 potters, the best of whom can command US$1000 per piece. There are two hotels in Mata Ortiz: the *Posada de las Ollas*, with single/double rooms for US$39/59 including breakfast, and the similarly priced *Hotel del Adobe*. It may be possible to find cheaper accommodations in private homes. To reserve ahead for any of these arrangements, phone ☎ 169-5-02-45.

One bus a day makes the journey from Nuevo Casas Grandes to Mata Ortiz (1½ hours, US$3.25), departing at 4 pm from the market and returning the following morning at 8 am.

MADERA
• pop 14,000 • elev 2092m ☎ 1

In the sierra south of Nuevo Casas Grandes, Madera retains some forest despite a hearty timber industry. The surrounding area has several archaeological sites, as well as natural attractions.

About 66km west of Madera, **Cueva Grande** sits behind a waterfall during the rainy season; inside the cave are some ancient adobe buildings in the architectural style of the Mogollon culture, closely associated with Paquimé. More of these cliff dwellings can be seen at **Conjunto Anasazi**, about 35km west of Madera; a strenuous 4km ascent is required. In the same area are the **Puente Colgante** (Suspension Bridge) over the Río Huápoca, and some **thermal springs**.

The unpaved road to Cueva Grande should be attempted with a 4WD vehicle only. Motel Real del Bosque's guided van excursions take in the Conjunto Anasazi, Cueva Grande and other points west for US$16 per person (minimum of five participants). English-speaking taxi driver Salvador Chacón (☎ 572-09-38) will drive you to the Conjunto Anasazi and act as a guide for US$40. You can find him at the taxi stand opposite the bus station.

Cuarenta Casas
The existence of cliff dwellings at Cuarenta Casas (Forty Houses) was known to the Spaniards as early as the 16th century, when explorer Álvar Núñez Cabeza de Vaca wrote in his chronicles, ' . . . and here by the side of the mountain we forged our way inland more than 50 leagues and found 40 houses.' The number may have been exaggerated: About a dozen adobe apartments are carved into the west cliffside of a dramatic canyon at La Cueva de las Ventanas (Cave of the Windows). Last occupied in the 13th century, Cuarenta Casas is believed to

have been an outlying settlement of Paquimé, perhaps a garrison for defense of commercial routes to the Pacific coast. Though not as well preserved as the dwellings at Casas Grandes, the site's extraordinary natural setting makes it well worth a visit.

Cuarenta Casas is 43km north of Madera via a good paved road through pine forest. From the turnoff, a dirt road leads 1.5km to the site entrance, where a trail descends into the Arroyo del Garabato and climbs the western slopes to the cave. Signs in English, Spanish and Tarahumara provide historical background along the way. The 1.5km hike isn't easy and takes about 40 minutes in each direction. Expect freezing temperatures in winter. The site is open 9 am to 3 pm daily (free) – you must be off the premises by 4 pm.

From Madera, an 11.30 am bus goes by Cuarenta Casas en route to the town of Largo. In the reverse direction, it stops at the site at around 4 pm, allowing just enough time to make a day trip from Madera.

Places to Stay & Eat
For budget lodging, try **Motel Mara's**, on Calle 5 at Juárez, with battered but clean singles/doubles for US$7.50/10.50, or the more comfortable **Hotel María** (☎ 572-03-23), Calle 5 at 5 de Mayo, for US$13.50/18.50.

Large wood-paneled rooms with heaters are US$19/21 at **Parador de la Sierra** (☎ 572-02-77), on Calle 3 at Independencia. Rooms face a secluded courtyard but the next-door disco can make sleep difficult. The nicest place in town is **Motel Real del Bosque** (☎ 572-05-38), on the highway coming in from Chihuahua, with spacious singles and doubles for US$37. The motel conducts tours of the ruins and natural attractions in the area (see above).

Madera's lumberjacks support a number of cheap, simple restaurants in town, especially along Calle 5 around the bus station. Though there are no real standouts, **Restaurant Anasazi** is recommended for its home-cooked meals.

Getting There & Away
Second-class buses run hourly to/from Cuauhtémoc (US$9) and Chihuahua (US$14),

and three times per day to/from Nuevo Casas Grandes and Ciudad Juárez. The winding yet scenic cliff road linking Madera and Nuevo Casas Grandes should not be driven at night.

CHIHUAHUA
● pop 613,700 ● elev 1455m ☎ 1
Chihuahua is the prosperous capital city of the state of Chihuahua (Mexico's largest state). Some fine colonial buildings dot the city's center, while newer suburbs and industries sprawl around the edges. Most travelers stay here as an overnight stop on a journey to the north or south, or at the start or finish of a Copper Canyon Railway trip.

Chihuahua's main attraction is Pancho Villa's old house, Quinta Luz, and the museum of the Mexican Revolution that now occupies it. Among the city's other sights of interest is the market, visited early morning by Mennonites and colorfully attired Tarahumaras. Around town you'll see lots of men wearing cowboy hats and boots – a reminder that this is cattle country, as it has been since the days of the great haciendas.

History
Chihuahua, in the indigenous Nahua language, means 'dry and sandy zone.' The first Spanish settlers were miners seeking silver. Franciscan and Jesuit missionaries Christianized the agrarian people of the area, but brutal treatment by the Spaniards induced even the most tranquil tribes to rebel.

The city of Chihuahua gradually grew in size and became both an administration center for the surrounding territory and a commercial center for cattle and mining interests. In the War of Independence, rebel leader Miguel Hidalgo fled here, only to be betrayed, imprisoned by the Spaniards and shot. President Benito Juárez made Chihuahua his headquarters for a while when forced to flee northward by the French troops of Emperor Maximilian. The city also served as a major garrison for cavalry guarding vulnerable settlements from the incessant raids of the Apaches, until the tribe was

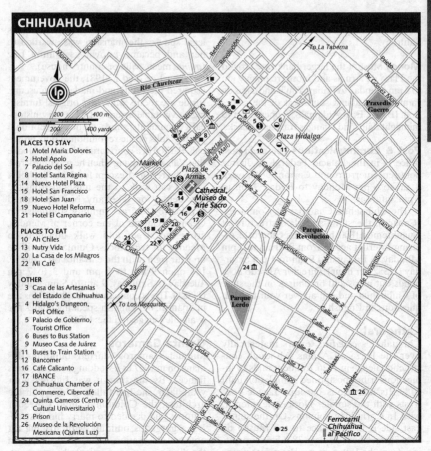

CHIHUAHUA

PLACES TO STAY
1 Motel María Dolores
2 Hotel Apolo
7 Palacio del Sol
8 Hotel Santa Regina
14 Nuevo Hotel Plaza
15 Hotel San Francisco
18 Hotel San Juan
19 Nuevo Hotel Reforma
21 Hotel El Campanario

PLACES TO EAT
10 Ah Chiles
13 Nutry Vida
20 La Casa de los Milagros
22 Mi Café

OTHER
3 Casa de las Artesanías
  del Estado de Chihuahua
4 Hidalgo's Dungeon,
  Post Office
5 Palacio de Gobierno,
  Tourist Office
6 Buses to Bus Station
9 Museo Casa de Juárez
11 Buses to Train Station
12 Bancomer
16 Café Calicanto
17 IBANCE
23 Chihuahua Chamber of
  Commerce, Cibercafé
24 Quinta Gameros (Centro
  Cultural Universitario)
25 Prison
26 Museo de la Revolución
  Mexicana (Quinta Luz)

subdued by the legendary 'Indian' fighter,
Colonel Joaquín Terrazas.

The Porfirio Díaz regime brought railways to Chihuahua and helped consolidate
the wealth of the huge cattle fiefdoms – the
land held by one cattle-owning family
equaled the size of Belgium.

After Pancho Villa's forces took Chihuahua in 1913 during the Mexican Revolution,
Villa established his headquarters here. He
had schools built and arranged other civic
works, contributing to his status as a local
hero. A statue of Villa graces the intersection of Universidad and División del Norte.

Orientation
Most areas of interest in Chihuahua are
within a dozen blocks of the central Plaza de
Armas – sometimes meaning a long walk or
a taxi ride. East-west streets northeast of Independencia ascend by odd numbers, for
example, Calle 3, 5, etc, while those to the
southwest ascend by even numbers.

Information
Tourist Offices On the ground floor of the
Palacio de Gobierno, near the entrance on
Aldama, the state tourist office (☎ 429-33-00
ext 1060) has an extraordinarily helpful,

English-speaking staff. It's open 9 am to 6.30 pm Monday to Friday and 9 am to 5 pm Saturday.

Money Most of the larger banks are around the Plaza de Armas and most are open 9 am to 5 pm Monday to Friday. You'll find casas de cambio on Aldama southwest of the cathedral; IBANCE, at Aldama 8, is open 8 am to midnight daily and changes traveler's checks.

Post & Communications The main post office is in the Palacio Federal on Juárez between Guerrero and Carranza. It's open 8 am to 6 pm Monday to Friday, 9 am to 1 pm Saturday.

The Chihuahua Chamber of Commerce (Canaco), the stone-and-glass structure at Cuauhtémoc 1800, houses the Cibercafé, offering Internet access from 8.30 am to 7 pm Monday to Friday and 9 am to 1 pm Saturday (US$2 per hour). Director Alfredo Sosa hands out maps and brochures on the state of Chihuahua and can answer your tourism questions, in English.

Cathedral

Chihuahua's *catedral* towers majestically over the Plaza de Armas. Although construction began in 1726, frequent raids by indigenous tribes postponed completion until 1789. Its marvelous baroque façade contrasts with the simpler Doric-style interior, with 16 Corinthian columns. On the southeast side is the entrance to the **Museo de Arte Sacro**, which displays 38 religious paintings from the 18th century. The painters represented were among the founders of Mexico City's first art schools, notably the Academia de San Carlos. The museum is open 10 am to 2 pm and 4 to 6 pm Monday to Friday (US$1).

Museo de la Revolución Mexicana (Quinta Luz)

Housed in the mansion and former headquarters of Pancho Villa, the Museum of the Mexican Revolution is a must-see for history buffs. After his assassination in 1923, a number of Villa's 'wives' (a list of whom is at the ticket counter) filed claim for his estate.

Government investigations determined that Luz Corral de Villa was the generalísimo's legal spouse; the mansion was awarded to her and became known as Quinta Luz (*quinta* means villa or country house).

When Luz died in 1981, the government acquired the estate and made it a museum. Inside are rooms with their original furnishings, a veritable arsenal of weaponry, historical documents and some exceptional photographs of the revolution and its principals. Parked in a courtyard is the black Dodge that Villa was driving when he was murdered. It's been restored, except for the bullet holes.

You can walk to the museum from the city center or take any bus designated 'Avaloz' or 'Juárez' running southeast on Ocampo. Get off at the corner of Méndez, cross the street and walk downhill on Méndez for two blocks. Quinta Luz will be on your right, with the entrance on Calle 10. It's open 9 am to 1 pm and 3 to 7 pm Tuesday to Saturday, 9 am to 5 pm Sunday (US$1). The accompanying explanations are in Spanish, but English-speaking guides are available (suggested fee: US$3).

Quinta Gameros

Manuel Gameros started building this mansion in 1907 as a wedding present for his fiancée. By the time it was finished four years later, she had fallen in love with the architect, the Colombian Julio Corredor Latorre, and decided to marry him instead. It's a gorgeous building with striking art nouveau decoration – the woodcarvings in the dining room are particularly exuberant. The upstairs rooms serve as galleries for the **Centro Cultural Universitario**, Universidad de Chihuahua's art collection. Quinta Gameros, at Bolívar and Calle 4, is open 11 am to 2 pm and 4 to 7 pm Tuesday through Sunday (US$1.50).

Palacio de Gobierno

This handsome, 19th-century building is on Aldama facing Plaza Hidalgo. Colonnades of arches surround the classic courtyard, and murals showing the history of Chihuahua cover the walls; the tourist office, in the same building, has a leaflet to help you follow

THE CENTER FOR AMERICAN HISTORY/UNIVERSITY OF TEXAS - AUSTIN

¡Viva la Revolución!

them. On one side of the courtyard is a small room with an eternal flame – actually a red lightbulb – marking the place where Hidalgo was shot.

Hidalgo's Dungeon

The cell in which Hidalgo was held prior to his execution is beneath the post office in the Palacio Federal (a later construction). The entrance is on Juárez – look for the cracked eagle's head inscribed 'Libertad.' The cell contains Hidalgo's crucifix, pistol and other personal effects, and a plaque recalls the verses the revolutionary priest dedicated to his captors in his final hours. Despite modern lighting, a real dungeon ambiance remains. It's open 9 am to 7 pm Tuesday to Sunday (US$0.10).

Museo Casa de Juárez

The home and office of Benito Juárez during the period of French occupation now holds this museum, at Juárez and Calle 5, which exhibits documents and artifacts related to the great reformer. It's open 9 am to 3 pm and 4 to 6 pm daily (US$1).

Places to Stay

Budget Calle Victoria, southwest of Ocampo, is a budget traveler's haven with a pair of low-priced favorites: *Hotel San Juan* (☎ 410-00-35) and *Nuevo Hotel Reforma*

(☎ 410-03-47). The Reforma is definitely the superior option with fairly clean, spacious single/double rooms, overhead fans and private bath for US$11/12. Choose a rear rooftop room for a peaceful night's sleep. The San Juan has more character – its patio entrance is attractively tiled – and offers parking, but the slightly lower price tag of US$8/9.25 means shabby rooms with sagging mattresses.

Chihuahua's least expensive option is *Nuevo Hotel Plaza* (☎ 415-58-34, Calle 4 No 206), directly behind the cathedral. Rooms are quite decent for the price of US$6.50/8, with central air-con and ample hot water, and the cheerful staff will make you feel right at home.

Motel María Dolores (☎ 410-47-70, Niños Héroes 917), at the corner of Calle 9, is a hospitable place and a very good deal, with modern air-conditioned rooms for US$12/17. No wonder it fills up fast.

Mid-Range Opposite the post office is Chihuahua's oldest inn, the *Hotel Apolo* (☎ 416-11-00, hapolo@chih1.telmex.net.mx, Juárez 907), with a Greco-Roman lobby and adequate rooms for US$26/29 singles/doubles. The singles face noisy Avenida Carranza. A block from the plaza, *Hotel Santa Regina* (☎ 415-38-89, Calle 3 No 102) offers a parking garage and an overpriced restaurant. US$29/34 gets you acceptable but worn rooms with marginally effective air-con. For the same price, *Hotel El Campanario* (☎ 415-45-45), on Díaz Ordaz between Libertad and Victoria, is a much better choice, with large comfortable rooms, bathtub included.

Visitors driving to Chihuahua will find a number of motels on the main roads into town. Along the approach from Ciudad Juárez, *Hotel Marrod* (☎ 419-03-23) offers air-conditioned rooms with breakfast for US$36/38.

Top End *Hotel San Francisco* (☎ 416-77-70), on Victoria right behind the cathedral, charges US$67/73 single/double for luxurious rooms with satellite TV and voice-mail service. A fine restaurant and cocktail lounge are on the premises. The high-rise,

Pancho Villa: Bandit-Turned-Revolutionary

Although best known as a hero of the Mexican Revolution, for much of his adult life Francisco 'Pancho' Villa was a murderous thief more given to robbing and womanizing than to any noble cause. Born Doroteo Arango on June 5, 1878, in the village of La Coyotada in rural Durango, the future revolutionary legend lived the rather unremarkable childhood of a typical peasant boy who later found work on a farm. That peaceful life took an abrupt turn on September 22, 1894, when 16-year-old Doroteo took the law into his own hands.

Accounts of what happened that day vary, but the popular version involves an alleged affront to the honor of his 12-year-old sister, Martina. According to this account, Doroteo was returning from work in the fields when he came upon the landowner attempting to abduct Martina. Doroteo ran to a cousin's house, took a pistol down from a wall, then ran down the landowner and shot him. Fearing reprisal, Doroteo took to the hills and abandoned his baptismal name, calling himself Francisco Villa. 'Pancho,' as his associates called him, spent the next 16 years as a bandit and cattle thief, variously riding with three vicious gangs.

Although the life of Pancho Villa the Revolutionary is well documented, his years as a bandit are obscured by contradictory claims, half-truths and outright lies. According to one story, Villa was once captured by three bounty hunters and would have been executed had he not killed a guard and escaped from prison. Another tale has Villa taking his new name from a *bandido* who was slain in a shoot-out – an action Villa supposedly took to demonstrate his authority over the dead man's gang. The tales abound, but one thing is certain: although an outlaw and ever the bully, Villa detested alcohol, and the sight of excessive drinking made his blood boil. In his *Memorias*, Villa gleefully recalled how he once stole a magnificent horse from a man who was preoccupied with getting drunk in a cantina.

Long after his outlaw years, Pancho Villa became uncharacteristically mum whenever the subject of his criminal past came up. When he did admit to banditry, he described his deeds in the loftiest terms, often referring to himself as the Mexican Robin Hood. But unlike the legendary English outlaw famed for robbing the rich and giving to the poor, Villa and the gangs he rode with killed many innocent people. For instance, José Solís, who rode with Villa as part of the Ignacio Parra gang, once killed an old man because he wouldn't sell him some bread.

By 1909, at age 31, Villa had bought a house in Chihuahua and was running a peaceful, if not entirely legitimate, business trading in horses and meat from dubious sources. That spring, Chihuahua's revolutionary governor Abraham González began recruiting men to break dictator Porfirio Díaz's grip on Mexico, and among the people he lobbied was Villa. González knew about Villa's past, but he also knew that he needed men like Villa – natural leaders who knew how to fight – if he ever hoped to depose Díaz. Thus, González encouraged Villa to return to marauding, but this time for a noble cause: agrarian reform. The idea appealed to Villa, and a year later he joined the revolution.

Villa had no trouble finding men to fight beside him against federal troops. There was much poverty, and rich Mexicans and Americans seemed to own all the land in Mexico. Villa's knowledge of the sierra and bandit tactics greatly aided him in battle; federal troops, who had been taught only to march in perfect step and fire in volleys, knew nothing about how to deal with these mobs of men who, armed with hand bombs and rifles, attacked one minute then disappeared the next. Villa's guerrilla tactics – lightning strikes, ambushes and night attacks – confounded them. When rebels under Villa's leadership took Ciudad Juárez in May 1911, Díaz resigned. Francisco Madero, a wealthy liberal from the state of Coahuila, was elected president in November 1911.

But Madero was unable to contain the various factions fighting for control throughout the country, and in early 1913 he was toppled from power by one of his own commanders, General

Pancho Villa: Bandit-Turned-Revolutionary

Victoriano Huerta, and executed. Pancho Villa fled across the US border to El Paso, but within a couple of months he was back in Mexico, one of four revolutionary leaders opposed to Huerta. Villa quickly raised an army of thousands, the División del Norte, and by the end of 1913 he had taken Ciudad Juárez (again) and Chihuahua. His victory at Zacatecas the following year is reckoned to be one of his most brilliant. Huerta was finally defeated and forced to resign in July 1914. With his defeat, the four revolutionary forces split into two camps, with the liberal Venustiano Carranza and Álvaro Obregón on one side and the more radical Villa and Emiliano Zapata on the other, though the latter pair never formed a serious alliance. Villa was defeated by Obregón in the big battle of Celaya (1915) and never recovered militarily.

But before their fighting days were over, Villa's soldiers would go down in history as the only force ever to invade the United States (Hawaii was not yet a state when the Japanese attacked Pearl Harbor 25 years later). Angered by troop support provided to Obregón by the US government in the battle of Celaya, and by the refusal of American merchants to sell them contraband despite cash advances for goods, in 1916 the Villistas ravaged the town of Columbus, New Mexico, and killed 18 Americans. The attack resulted in the US sending 12,000 soldiers into Mexico to pursue the invaders, but the slow-moving columns never did catch Villa's men.

In July 1920, after 10 years of revolutionary fighting, Villa signed a peace treaty with Adolfo de la Huerta, who had been chosen provisional president two months earlier. Villa pledged to lay down his arms and retire to a hacienda called Canutillo, 80km south of Hidalgo del Parral, for which the Huerta government paid 636,000 pesos. In addition, Villa was given 35,926 pesos to cover wages owed to his troops. He also received money to buy farm tools, pay a security guard and help the widows and orphans of the División del Norte.

For the next three years, Villa led a relatively quiet life. He bought a hotel in Parral and regularly attended cockfights. He installed one of his many 'wives,' Soledad Seañez, in a Parral apartment, and kept another at Canutillo. Then, one day while he was leaving Parral in his big Dodge touring car, a volley of shots rang out from a two-story house. Five of the seven passengers in the car were killed, including the legendary revolutionary. An eight-man assassin team fired the fatal shots, but just who ordered the killings remains a mystery.

THE CENTER FOR AMERICAN HISTORY/UNIVERSITY OF TEXAS - AUSTIN

deluxe **Palacio del Sol** (☎ 416-60-00, *palacio@infosel.net.mx, Independencia 116)*, on the corner of Niños Héroes, is also quite central and costs US$112/118 (30% less Friday to Sunday).

Places to Eat

Nuevo Hotel Reforma serves good, cheap food in its restaurant, with filling breakfasts for US$2 to US$3.50. Just up the street, *Mi Café (Victoria 807)* is another popular breakfast place, serving fresh juices and fruit salads besides the usual egg platters. Stellar service and stylish presentation make *La Casa de los Milagros (Victoria 812)* a fine choice for lunch or dinner. Housed in a beautiful old mansion, the restaurant takes on a special candlelit ambiance in the evenings. The menu features original salads (US$2.75), hearty sandwiches (US$2.25), and wonderful quesadillas (US$2.25).

Ah Chiles, on Aldama near Guerrero, offers a variety of tacos – sold by the eighth and quarter kilo (US$2/3.75) – and *montados*, which are similar to burritos but folded instead of rolled.

In a region famed for its beef, *Los Mezquites (Cuauhtémoc 2009)*, a few blocks southwest of Díaz Ordaz, takes pride in its quality cuts, which are broiled over mesquite charcoal. Prices are reasonable, with a 125g *arrachera* (skirt steak) for US$8 and a 250g T-bone for US$9. Attached is *La Carpa*, an open-air outlet serving choice sirloin tacos under the glow of nonstop sports TV.

Stock up for the train journey at *Nutry Vida (Aldama 117)*, near Calle 3. The natural-foods market sells a variety of whole wheat breads and pastries, veggie sandwiches and homemade yogurts.

Entertainment

The bar inside *Hotel San Juan* has lots of character and entertainment in the form of *norteño* troubadours. A block away, *Café Calicanto (Aldama 411)* provides pleasant outdoor seating in a tree-lined patio and live folk music and jazz nightly, accompanied by tasty regional snacks.

Chihuahua's nightlife percolates in the section of Juárez just above Colón. *La*

Taberna, behind Restaurant La Olla, is a lot of fun. A multilevel bar/restaurant/game room complex, linked by giant brewery vats, it features a neon-lit rooftop terrace with live rock and draft beer by the pitcher.

Shopping

Paquimé pottery, Urique baskets and Tarahumara clothing are reasonably priced at Casa de las Artesanías del Estado de Chihuahua, at Juárez 705 across from the post office. The state-run store purchases its crafts directly from the producers.

Getting There & Away

Air Chihuahua's airport has six flights a day to Mexico City and daily flights to Los Angeles and to major cities in northern Mexico.

Bus The bus station contains restaurants, a luggage storage facility and a telephone *caseta*. Chihuahua is a major center for buses in every direction. The ones most likely to interest travelers are:

Ciudad Juárez – 373km, 5 hours; frequent 1st-class (US$19)

Creel – 256km, 5 hours; hourly 2nd-class (US$14)

Cuauhtémoc – 103km, 1½ hours; 1st-class every half hour (US$5)

Durango – 667km, 9 hours; frequent 1st-class (US$31)

Hidalgo del Parral – 220km, 3 hours; frequent 1st-class (US$11), 4 2nd-class (US$7)

Madera – 276km, 3 hrs; hourly 2nd-class (US$14)

Mexico City (Terminal Norte) – 1468km, 18-22 hours; frequent 1st-class (US$76)

Nuevo Casas Grandes – 352km, 4½ hours; 6 1st-class, 12 2nd-class (US$15)

Zacatecas – 849km, 12 hours; frequent 1st-class (US$43)

Other buses go to Mazatlán, Ojinaga, Monterrey, Saltillo, San Luis Potosí, Torreón and Tijuana. Omnibus Americanos departs daily for Phoenix, Los Angeles, Albuquerque and Denver.

Train Chihuahua is the northeastern terminus of the Chihuahua al Pacífico line for

Barranca del Cobre (Copper Canyon) trains. The station is near the intersection of Méndez and Calle 24. Tickets are sold 5 to 7 am daily and 9 am to 5.30 pm Monday to Friday, 9 am to noon Saturday and Sunday.

The air-conditioned *primera express*, No 74, departs daily at 6 am for the 14-hour run through the canyon country to Los Mochis. Train No 73 from the coast arrives in Chihuahua at 7.50 pm. Fare is US$93.50 each way. The *clase económica* train, No 76, leaves Chihuahua daily at 7 am and takes at least two hours longer. Though not as luxurious as the 1st-class train, it's quite comfortable and air-conditioned. This train in turn has two fare categories: *turista* for US$46 and *subsidio* for much less but available only to locals with identification. For more information on the trains and stops along the way, see the Barranca del Cobre (Copper Canyon) section in the Northwest Mexico chapter.

Getting Around

From the airport, *colectivo* taxis shuttle travelers to the bus station (US$4.75).

The bus station is a half-hour ride east of town along Avenida Pacheco. To get there, catch a 'Circunvalación 2 Sur' bus on Carranza across the street from Plaza Hidalgo (US$0.30). From the bus stop in front of the station, the 'Circunvalación Maquilas' bus goes back to the center.

For the Chihuahua al Pacífico station, take a 'Cerro de la Cruz' bus on Carranza at Plaza Hidalgo, get off at the prison – it looks like a medieval castle – then walk behind the prison to the station.

A taxi stand on Victoria near the cathedral charges standard rates to the train station (US$2), bus station (US$4.25) and airport (US$8.50).

CUAUHTÉMOC
• **pop 80,400** • **elev 2010m** ☎ **1**

West of Chihuahua, Cuauhtémoc is a center for the Mennonite population of northern Mexico. From the town's west end, highway 65 runs north through the principal Mennonite zone, with entrances to the numbered *campos* (villages) along the way (see

The Mennonites

Founded by the Dutchman Menno Simonis in the 16th century, the Mennonite sect maintains a code of beliefs that from the start put it at odds with several governments of the world: Members take no oaths of loyalty other than to God, and they eschew military service. Persecuted for their beliefs, the Mennonites moved from Germany to Russia to Canada, and thousands settled in the tolerant, post-revolutionary Mexico of the 1920s.

In villages around Cuauhtémoc, you might encounter Mennonite men in baggy overalls and straw hats, and women in American Gothic dresses and black bonnets speaking their own dialect of old German. As much as their clothing, their northern European physical features set them apart – they seem to tower over their Mexican neighbors. Traditionally, they lead a spartan existence, speak little Spanish, and marry only among themselves, though their refusal to use machinery has been long forgotten – horse-and-buggy transport has been replaced by tractors and pickup trucks.

The Mennonite villages, called *campos* and numbered instead of named, are clustered along route 65, a four-lane highway heading straight north from Cuauhtémoc's western approach. Wide unpaved roads crisscross the campos through vast cornfields interrupted by the occasional farm building and suburban-type dwellings. It feels more like Iowa than Mexico. The Mennonites' best-known product is their cheese *(queso menonito)*, which is sold in many shops.

❋ ❋ ❋ ❋ ❋ ❋ ❋ ❋ ❋ ❋ ❋ ❋

'The Mennonites' in this chapter). The travel agency Cumbres Friessen (☎ 582-54-57), at Calle 3 No 466 in Cuauhtémoc, conducts tours (US$10 per person), in English, that include visits to a local cheesemaker and traditional Mennonite homes and schools.

Several Mennonite-run establishments along highway 65 offer accommodations. ***Loewen's RV Park*** (☎ 582-65-23), at Km 14 on the east side of the highway, has 40 hookups for US$11.50, along with bathrooms and laundry facilities. Closer to Cuauhtémoc, *Gasthaus Motel 12 (☎ 581-43-33)*, at Km 12 amid cornfields, has simple, spotless singles/doubles for US$16/17, or US$21 with kitchenette. You can sample home-cooked Mennonite dishes like *kilge* (noodles with lots of cream and smoked ham) for around US$3.50 at *Restaurant El Duff*, at Km 11.

In Cuauhtémoc, try the *Hotel San Francisco (☎ 582-31-52, Calle 3 No 132)*, near Morelos, with singles/doubles for US$8.50/12; or the very comfortable *Motel Tarahumara Inn (☎ 581-19-19)*, on the corner of Calle 5 and Allende, charging US$44 per single or double.

Cuauhtémoc is 1½ hours by bus or 3½ hours by train from Chihuahua. By car, one can head west via La Junta to the spectacular Cascada de Basaseachi waterfalls (see the Creel section in the Northwest Mexico chapter).

HIDALGO DEL PARRAL
• pop 96,300 • elev 1652m ☎ 1

Founded as a mining settlement in 1631, the town took the 'Hidalgo' tag later but is still commonly called just 'Parral.' Throughout the 17th century, enslaved natives mined the rich veins of silver, copper and lead from La Negrita mine, whose installations still loom above town but are no longer in use. A second silver boom took place in the late 19th century, and stone palaces dating from that period stand as evidence of the city's earlier prominence. One of these, the Casa Griensen, was the home of Elisa Griensen, who according to local legend chased out the US punitive expedition sent after Pancho Villa in retaliation for his raid on Columbus, New Mexico.

Parral is now most famous as the place where Pancho Villa was murdered on July 20, 1923 (see 'Pancho Villa: Bandit-Turned-Revolutionary' in this chapter). A hero to the *campesinos* of the state of Chihuahua, Villa was buried in Parral, with 30,000 attending his funeral. (The story has a sordid postscript: shortly after the general's burial, his corpse was beheaded by unknown

raiders.) In 1976, Villa's body was moved to Mexico City. The building from which Villa was shot, on Avenida Juárez at the west end of town, is now a library with a small collection of photos, guns and memorabilia upstairs. Outside to the right of the entrance, a star marks the spot where Villa hit the ground.

Parral is a pleasant if scruffy town, as well as the most interesting place to break a journey between Chihuahua and Durango. You'll be surprised by the remarkable courtesy of its drivers, who customarily halt for pedestrians!

Orientation

With its narrow, winding one-way streets, Parral can be confusing at first. Two main squares, Plaza Principal and Plaza Guillermo Baca, are roughly in a line along the north side of the river, linked by busy Avenida Herrera. The bus station at the east end of town is connected to the center of town by Avenida Independencia, which ends at the Hidalgo monument. From there, turn left and go over the bridge to Plaza Principal.

Information

The Cámara Nacional de Comercio (☎ 522-00-18), at Colegio 28 across from Hotel Acosta, functions as a tourist office, distributing maps and brochures. It's open 9 am to 1 pm and 3 to 7 pm Monday to Friday, 9 am to 1 pm Saturday.

Infosel at Herrera 26 – enter through the Iris sewing shop – provides fast Internet connections from 9.30 am to 1 pm and 4 to 7.30 pm Monday to Saturday.

Special Events

Pancho Villa is honored during the Jornadas Villistas in the latter half of July, featuring a series of cultural events plus parades and fireworks. The general's 1923 assassination is reenacted on July 20 with guns blazing from the Avenida Juárez library, and the following day a cavalcade of some 300 riders descends on Parral on horseback after a six-day journey from the north, recalling Villa's famous marathons.

Places to Stay & Eat

Hotel Acosta (☎ 522-02-21, *Barbachano 3*), near Plaza Principal, is the best value in town at US$13/16 for a single/double; ask for a 3rd-floor room and be sure to check out the view from the roof. The cheapest decent place is *Hotel Fuentes* (☎ 522-00-16, *coadriana@infosel.net.mx, Herrera 79*), recognizable by its pink stone façade opposite the cathedral. Rooms at this cheerful establishment vary in size, but all are clean and cost just US$8.50/10.50. English is spoken. Near the bus station, *Hotel Los Arcos* (☎ 523-05-97) is an excellent mid-range option, featuring nifty rooms around an elegant courtyard or along an outer terrace for US$23/28. Around the corner and up the scale is *Motel El Camino Real* (☎ 523-02-02), with a covered swimming pool. Comfortable rooms cost US$43 for one or two occupants.

Parral isn't exactly a culinary capital, but you won't go hungry. *Restaurant Turista*, at the hotel of the same name on Plaza Independencia, whips up a fine traditional Mexican breakfast for under US$3. Off the Plaza Principal, *El Gavilán Pollero* does charcoal-grilled chickens. A *medio pollo*, served with trimmings, is US$2.50. Next door, *La Michoacana* offers gourmet *paletas* (fruit ices on a stick).

Decorated with Tarahumara paraphernalia, *J Quissime Bar & Grill*, opposite Motel El Camino Real, is perhaps Parral's most atmospheric restaurant and one of the few places open after 10 pm. While the food is nothing to get excited about, nor is it that expensive, with Mexican dishes from US$3.50, steaks or black bass for US$6.50.

Getting There & Away

The bus station on the southeast outskirts of town is most easily reached by taxi (US$2). Regular 1st-class buses run to Chihuahua (three hours, US$11) and Durango (six hours, US$19), and six 2nd-class buses head to Valle de Allende (30 minutes, US$0.75).

AROUND HIDALGO DEL PARRAL

The road east to Jiménez goes through dry, undulating country, but just south of this road, the village of **Valle de Allende** is lush with trees and surrounded by green farmland. The stream through the valley is fed by mineral springs that start near **Ojo de Talamantes**, a few kilometers west, where there's a small bathing area.

Canutillo, 80km south of Parral on the road to Durango, is where Pancho Villa spent the last three years of his life (see 'Pancho Villa: Bandit-Turned-Revolutionary' in this chapter). His former hacienda, attached to a 200-year-old church, is now a museum. The two front rooms contain photographs of Villa, along with displays of his guns and other personal artifacts. Unfortunately, the roofs of the remaining rooms long ago collapsed, and the floors have given way to weeds.

TORREÓN

* **pop 481,500** • **elev 1150m** ☎ **changing**

Torreón, in the state of Coahuila, is part of a large metropolitan area that includes the contiguous cities of Gómez Palacio and Ciudad Lerdo, both in Durango. Established in 1887 as a railway town, Torreón continues to be a center for transport, as well as for mining, smelting and other industries. Some of the surrounding land has been irrigated for wheat and cotton. The whole district is known as La Laguna.

The 1910 battle for Torreón was Pancho Villa's first big victory in the Mexican Revolution, giving him control of the railways that radiate from the city. Villa waged three more battles for Torreón over the next few years, during which his troops in their revolutionary zeal slaughtered some 200 Chinese immigrants.

The city boasts an attractive central plaza and a couple of decent museums, and it makes a good base for exploring the surrounding desert region. Nevertheless, few tourists make it to Torreón. For a panoramic view, take a taxi up to the **Cerro del Cristo de las Noas** lookout. The Christ statue, flanked by TV antennas, is the second-tallest in the Americas.

Orientation

Torreón fans out east of the Río Nazas, with the central grid lying at the west end of town and the Plaza de Armas at the west end of the grid. Avenidas Juárez and Morelos extend east from the plaza, past the main government plaza and, east of Colón, several large shaded parks. The Torreón bus station is 6km east of the center on Juárez.

Information

The modern Protursa tourist office (☎ 32-22-44, promoto5@coah1.telmex.net.mx), 5km east of the center at Paseo de la Rosita 308D, hands out maps and guides of Torreón and the region. Some staff members speak English. It's open 9 am to 2 pm and 4 to 7 pm Monday to Friday, 9 am to 2 pm Saturday. The Cybernet Café, an Internet snack bar at Juárez 240 Pte, is open 9.30 am to 9.30 pm daily. It charges US$2 per hour for access.

On December 1, 2000, the telephone area code is due to change to ☎ 1 from 17, with the digit 7 added to the start of every local number (for example, the number 11-50-00 will become 711-50-00).

Museo Regional de la Laguna

This museum has a small but interesting collection of pre-Hispanic artifacts from the region and other parts of Mexico. It's in the Bosque Venustiano Carranza park, a couple of kilometers east of Torreón's main plaza, and is open 10 am to 5 pm daily (US$1.75).

Museo de la Revolución

Pancho Villa's Torreón escapades are documented in this tiny museum on Múzquiz beside the bridge to Gómez Palacio. Built in the 19th century to regulate the irrigation canal for a cotton plantation, the building now houses an unruly collection of photos, cannonballs, swords, posters and other memorabilia pertaining to the revolution. It's open 10 am to 4 pm Tuesday to Sunday.

Special Events

Starting in late August, the monthlong **Feria del Algodón** (cotton fair) has a little of everything: *charro* singers, games, rides, a circus, regional food specialties, prize livestock and –

the best reason to attend – an enormous beer garden with room for thousands.

Places to Stay & Eat

Hotel Galicia (☎ 16-18-19), on the east side of Torreón's main plaza, is the cheapest place to stay at US$9.25 for a single or double. It's a study in faded elegance, with tiled halls, stained glass and battered furniture. A major step up in price and quality is *Hotel del Paseo* (☎ 16-03-03, Morelos 574), which offers pleasant singles/doubles with firm beds for US$16/19. Still pricier and better is *Hotel Calvete* (☎ 16-15-30), the big white block on the corner of Juárez and Corona, featuring spacious air-conditioned rooms with large balconies starting at US$29/33. It has a restaurant downstairs and parking across the street.

Vegetarians and others will enjoy *Restaurant Del Granero* (Morelos 414 Pte), between Corona and Vicario, serving excellent whole-wheat *gorditas* (round corn cakes) and burritos (US$0.50) with tasty meatless fillings. Next door is a bakery doing whole-wheat versions of standard Mexican pastries. At the other end of the carnivorous spectrum is *Restaurant Principal*, specializing in *cabrito al pastor* (goat roasted on a stake) and *agujas norteñas* (barbecued goat short ribs). It's on Matamoros between Galeana and Jiménez, opposite the Teatro Martínez. For Spanish and Mexican cuisine in a relaxed pub-style setting, try the *Casa Alameda*, on Guerra across the street from the Alameda park. Snacks cost about US$3 and main courses range from US$4 to US$6.

Getting There & Away

There are bus stations in both Torreón and Gómez Palacio, and long-distance buses will stop at both or transfer you from one to the other without charge. Buses depart regularly for Chihuahua (six hours, US$23), Durango (3½ hours, US$13), Mexico City (14 hours, US$53), Saltillo (three hours, US$14) and Zacatecas (six hours, US$20). Taxis are the best way to get from the bus station to downtown (about US$2).

The train station is at the south end of Galeana. Train No 14 to Aguascalientes departs at 9 am Monday, Thursday and Saturday – the journey takes around 11 hours, stopping in Zacatecas along the way. The fare to Aguascalientes is US$6; tickets are purchased on board.

The tolls on the highway to Durango total nearly US$9. To Saltillo, highway 40D costs almost twice that; most vehicles take the slightly slower free road.

AROUND TORREÓN

The deserts north of La Laguna are starkly beautiful, with strange geological formations around **Dinamita** and many semiprecious stones for gem hunters. Farther north, the village of **Mapimí** was once the center of an incredibly productive mining area and serviced the nearby Ojuela mine between periodic raids by Cocoyomes and Tobosos. Benito Juárez passed through Mapimí in the mid-19th century during his flight from French forces. The house where he stayed, near the northwest corner of the Mapimí plaza, is now a small history museum (closed Wednesday) displaying some very good sepia photos of Ojuela in its heyday.

At the end of the 19th century, the Ojuela mine supported an adjacent town of the same name with a population of over 3000. Today a cluster of abandoned buildings cling to a hillside as a silent reminder of Ojuela town's bonanza years. A spectacular 300m-long suspension bridge, the **Puente de Ojuela**, was built over a 100m-deep gorge to carry ore trains from the mine. You can walk across the bridge, recently fortified with 5cm steel cables, to the mine entrance. A site guide (suggested fee: US$5) will accompany you through the 800m tunnel, and you'll emerge at a point that affords good views of the Bermejillo Valley.

To reach Mapimí from Torreón, go 40km north on highway 49 to Bermejillo, then 35km west on highway 30. It's easiest to get there with your own transport, but the Protursa tourist office in Torreón arranges tours. From Torreón's bus station, Autobuses de la Laguna 2nd-class buses depart every half hour for Mapimí (US$2.50). To visit Puente de Ojuela, get off 3km before Mapimí, at a shop selling rocks and minerals. From there,

a narrow road winds 7km up to the bridge. It's an hour walk, but you may be able to hitch a ride. Four kilometers from the turnoff, the road narrows further as the surface becomes cobblestoned and more suitable for hiking than driving. There's a US$2 entry fee for vehicles.

At Ceballos, 130km north of Torreón, a rough road goes east 40km to the **Zona del Silencio**, so called because conditions in the area are said to prevent propagation of radio waves. Peppered with meteorites, the Zona is also believed to be a UFO landing site. The mysterious overtones associated with the region amplified after a NASA test rocket crashed there during the 1970s. The ensuing search by US teams was of course veiled in secrecy, giving rise to all manner of suspicions.

The Zona del Silencio is in the **Reserva de la Biósfera Bolsón de Mapimí**, a desert biosphere reserve dedicated to the study of arid-region plants and animals, including a very rare tortoise. This is a remote area with rough roads.

DURANGO

• **pop 397,700** • **elev 1912m** ☎ **1**

Don't be too put off by the modernization on the outskirts of the city – proceed directly to Durango's delightful Plaza de Armas, where you'll discover fine colonial architecture. The city was founded in 1563 by conquistador Don Francisco de Ibarra and named after the Spanish city of his birth. Just north of town, Cerro del Mercado is one of the world's richest iron ore deposits and was the basis of Durango's early importance, along with gold and silver from the Sierra Madre.

Other industries of the area include farming, grazing, timber and paper. Durango is also in the movie business, with several locations outside the city, especially for Westerns. Many of the restaurants have movie or cowboy decor, and lots of shops sell cowboy boots, belts and hats. It's a fun town, and very friendly.

Orientation

Durango is a good town to walk around in, and most of the interesting places to see and stay are within a few blocks of the two main squares, the Plaza de Armas and the Plaza IV Centenario. For some greenery, go to the extensive Parque Guadiana on the west side of town.

Information

Tourist Offices The state tourist office (☎ 811-11-07, turismor@dgo1.telmex.net.mx), which doubles as the state film board, is at Florida 100. The staff, some of whom speak English, are helpful and have a variety of printed materials. The office is open 8 am to 3.30 pm and 4.30 to 8 pm Monday to Friday.

Money Several banks (with ATMs) are on the west side of the Plaza de Armas. For currency exchange, try Bancomer, open 9 am to 5 pm Monday to Friday, 9 am to 2 pm Saturday. A casa de cambio next to the Hotel Roma has quicker service but lower rates.

Post & Communications The post office is on 20 de Noviembre at Roncal, about 1.5km east of the Plaza de Armas. Hours are 9 am to 6 pm Monday to Friday, 9 am to 1 pm Saturday.

Email services include Coffee Tec.net, at 5 de Febrero and Boulevard Dolores del Río,

DURANGO

PLACES TO STAY
3 Hotel Buenos Aires
5 Hotel Posada San Jorge
6 Hotel Posada Santa Elena
9 Hotel Plaza Catedral
10 Hotel Gobernador
13 Hotel Casablanca
17 Hotel Roma
20 Hotel Ana Isabel

PLACES TO EAT
1 Cremería Wallander
2 Los Cuatro Vientos
4 Gorditas Gabino
5 Restaurant Bar 1800
8 Los Farolitos
12 Eli-Bano

OTHER
7 Teatro Ricardo Castro
11 State Tourist Office
14 Teatro Victoria
15 Museo de Arqueología de Durango Ganot-Peschard
16 Palacio de Gobierno
18 Bancomer
19 Buses to Bus Station
21 Coffee Tec.net
22 Quick Access Internet
23 Universidad Juárez
24 Casa del Conde de Suchil

and Quick Access Internet, at 5 de Febrero 911A Pte. Both charge US$1.75 an hour and are open Monday to Saturday.

Walking Tour

The Plaza de Armas is attractive, especially on Sunday when musicians perform on the bandstand and locals promenade. Below the bandstand is the university-sponsored handicrafts shop. Facing the plaza's north side is the **Catedral Basílica Menor**, with its imposing baroque façade, constructed from 1695 to 1750. Walk west on 20 de Noviembre and on your right you will see the elegant **Teatro Ricardo Castro**, which has served as a cinema and boxing arena in its century of existence.

Turn south on Martínez, past the **Teatro Victoria**, to the Plaza IV Centenario. On its north side is the **Palacio de Gobierno**, built on the estate of a Spanish mine owner and expropriated by the government after the War of Independence. Inside are colorful murals depicting the history of the state. On the plaza's east side is the **Universidad Juárez**, originally a Jesuit monastery. From there, walk east on 5 de Febrero to the **Casa del Conde de Suchil**, the 18th-century home of the Spanish governor of Durango, now the Banamex building. Two blocks farther east is the **Mercado Gómez Palacio**, a good place for a snack and a rest.

Museo de Arqueología de Durango Ganot-Peschard

Opened in 1998, the museum innovatively presents the archaeological record of the region's indigenous cultures, from prehistoric times to the Spanish conquest. Highlights include a photographic exhibit on rock paintings and an interesting section demonstrating the archaeological method. All descriptions are in Spanish. The museum, at Zaragoza 315 Sur between 5 de Febrero and 20 de Noviembre, is open 10 am to 6 pm Tuesday to Friday and 11 am to 7 pm Saturday and Sunday (US$0.50, free Tuesday).

Places to Stay

Budget Durango's cheapest digs can be found at the *Villa Deportiva Juvenil*

(☎ 818-70-71). This youth hostel, on Colegio Militar 400m south of the bus station, offers clean dorm beds for US$3.25 a night – plus a US$2 deposit.

In the center of town, *Hotel Buenos Aires* (☎ 812-31-28, *Constitución 126 Nte*) has tidy little rooms, some with bathrooms and hot water, and a rather complicated pricing system. Singles with black-and-white TV and no bathroom are US$7.50; doubles with color TV and bathroom are US$12.75. Other configurations are available; the chart by the reception desk sets it all down for you.

Hotel Ana Isabel (☎ 813-45-00, *5 de Febrero 219 Ote*), a stone's throw east of León de la Peña, has lovely rooms, some with balconies over a courtyard, for US$12.75/16. On the north side of the cathedral, *Hotel Plaza Catedral* (☎ 813-26-60, *Constitución 216 Sur*) occupies an attractive colonial building, but rooms are stuffy and have unfortunate carpeting. Singles/doubles are US$16/19.

Mid-Range *Hotel Roma* (☎ 812-01-22, *20 de Noviembre 705 Pte*) is in a large century-old building kitty-corner from the Teatro Ricardo Castro. Rates are US$18.50/23 single/double, including breakfast, for rooms that are small but in better shape than those at the Plaza Catedral. Room 218, a *media suite*, is the best deal, including two double beds, two balconies and an enormous bathroom with tub for US$26. Friendly and quiet, *Hotel Posada Santa Elena* (☎ 811-94-71, *Negrete 1007 Pte*) is a find. The small inn features 10 tastefully furnished rooms for US$27/33.

A block west of the Roma is *Hotel Casablanca* (☎ 811-35-99, *casabca@infosel .net.mx, 20 de Noviembre 811 Pte*), with large well-appointed rooms for US$36/41. If you're going to stay here it's worth shelling out an additional US$5 for an *habitación panorámica*, featuring king-size bed, marble tub and jaw-dropping views. One of Durango's finest hotels, *Hotel Posada San Jorge* (☎ 813-32-57, *Constitución 102 Sur*) is in a handsome 19th-century building. Its colonial-style rooms and junior suites, the latter with sofas and walk-in closets, are well worth the US$41/47 price tag.

Top End *Hotel Gobernador* (☎ 813-19-19, *20 de Noviembre 257 Ote*), 1km east of the Plaza de Armas, is the best hotel in town and features a swimming pool and an elegant restaurant. Air-conditioned singles or doubles, including phones, TV and the works, are US$75 and up.

Places to Eat

Durango boasts plenty of good restaurants, and those craving variety will find a range of ethnic establishments.

Fill up on scrumptious tacos for US$0.50 apiece at *Los Farolitos*, a popular spot on Martínez just north of 20 de Noviembre. Another good snacking option is *Gorditas Gabino* (*Constitución 100A Nte*), at the corner of Serdán, serving up *gorditas* stuffed with avocados, shredded beef in *salsa verde* and other tasty things for US$0.40 each. Fresh-squeezed juices and *licuados* are available too.

Just up the street, the very popular *Los Cuatro Vientos* (*Constitución 154 Nte*) offers quality seafood in an unpretentious setting. A hearty bowl of shrimp soup goes for US$2.75, octopus salad for US$4.25, and fresh fish fillets for around US$3. Service is rapid and portions are plentiful.

Fans of Middle Eastern cuisine should head for *Eli-Bano* (*Hidalgo 310 Sur*), where appetizers like hummus, tabbouleh and stuffed grape leaves are under US$3.

Restaurant Bar 1800, in the elegant courtyard of the Hotel Posada San Jorge, serves outstanding Mexican food, with main courses from US$6 to US$10.

A good place to stock up for a picnic or bus journey is the *Cremería Wallander* (*Independencia 128 Nte*), offering locally made yogurt, honey and granola. This bakery/gourmet deli prepares extraordinary *tortas* with special German cold cuts and Mennonite cheese on fresh-baked seeded rolls (US$2 to US$3.50).

Getting There & Away

Good bus connections are available from Durango to many of the places that travelers want to go. Daily departures include:

Chihuahua – 667km, 9 hours; 7 1st-class (US$31)

Hidalgo del Parral – 396km, 6 hours; 7 1st-class (US$19)

Mazatlán – 322km, 7 hours; 1 deluxe (US$21.50), 3 1st-class (US$18), 5 2nd-class (US$15)

Mexico City (Terminal Norte) – 920km, 12 hours; 1 deluxe (US$64), 11 1st-class (US$47.50)

Torreón – 247km, 3½ hours; 4 deluxe (US$18), frequent 1st-class (US$13), 7 2nd-class (US$12)

Zacatecas – 290km, 4 hours; frequent 1st-class (US$15), 7 2nd-class (US$12)

Getting Around

The bus station is on the east side of town; white Ruta 2 buses departing from the far side of the parking lot will get you to the Plaza de Armas for US$0.20. Taxis, which are metered, charge about US$1.75 to the center.

To reach the bus station from downtown, catch a blue-striped 'Camionera' bus from 20 de Noviembre beside the plaza. Get off at the intersection of Colegio Militar (a major thoroughfare), then go left toward the Villa monument and take the overpass across Pescador.

AROUND DURANGO
Movie Locations

The clear light and stark countryside have made Durango a popular location for Hollywood movies. Around 120 films have been shot in the area – mostly Westerns, including John Wayne vehicles and films by directors John Huston and Sam Peckinpah. Movie fans will enjoy visiting the sets, which appear to be undergoing a renaissance; a number of Mexican TV series and US productions are planned. Be sure to check with the tourist office before going out to the sets, as they may be off limits during production.

Villa del Oeste is 12km north of Durango just off highway 45. After its use in a number of Westerns, the main street, known locally as Calle Howard, was left undisturbed. When not in production, it's open to visitors 9 am to 7 pm (US$2). To get there, take a 2nd-class bus for Chupaderos from the bus station (US$2; every half hour) and tell the driver to drop you at Villa del Oeste. To get back to Durango, just flag down any passing bus headed toward the city.

Southwest of Durango is **Los Álamos**, a '1940s town' where *Fat Man and Little Boy* was filmed in 1989; the movie, about the making of the first A-bomb, starred Paul Newman. To get there, take Boulevard Arrieta south of town and stay on it for about 30km, past dramatic mesas and a steep river gorge. Watch for a rusty sign on the right announcing the turnoff for the set. From there it's another 1.5km over a rough road. Buses are not an option.

Museo de Arte Guillermo Ceniceros

Originally the site of a British-built ironworks, the Ferrería de los Flores was in 1998 converted into a museum to display the art of Durango native Guillermo Ceniceros. Profoundly influenced by his teacher, the formidable muralist David Alfaro Siqueiros, Ceniceros developed his own method of visual expression. Mysterious landscapes and feminine figures are his preferred subjects. Open 10 am to 6 pm Tuesday to Friday, 11 am to 6 pm Saturday and Sunday, the museum is in the town of La Ferrería, 4km southwest of Durango on the way to Los Álamos. Regular 'Ferrería' buses depart from the Plazuela Baca Ortiz in the center of town.

En Route to Mazatlán

The road west from Durango to Mazatlán, on the coast (see the Central Pacific Coast chapter), is particularly scenic, with a number of natural attractions on the way. In the area around **El Salto**, you can trek to waterfalls, canyons and forests. The spectacular stretch of road about 160km from Durango is called **El Espinazo del Diablo** (the Devil's Backbone). You enter a new time zone when you cross the Durango-Sinaloa state border; Sinaloa is one hour behind Durango.

Northeast Mexico

This chapter covers the state of Nuevo León and most of the states of Tamaulipas and Coahuila – together, a huge area stretching nearly 1000km from north to south and 500km from east to west. Many travelers enter Mexico at one of the region's five main border crossings from the USA, and take one of the several routes heading south to the Bajío region, central Mexico or the Gulf Coast. Most of them pass through this area as quickly as they can to get to what is seen as the 'real' Mexico. This is not surprising, as northeast Mexico does not have impressive pre-Hispanic ruins, charming colonial towns, or pretty palm-fringed beaches. What it does have is a geography unlike anywhere else in Mexico, and a unique emerging culture.

Geographically, the deserts of northeast Mexico are the southern extension of the Great Plains of the USA and Canada, impressive for their stark, rugged beauty and sheer expanse. The Rio Grande, called the Río Bravo del Norte in Mexico, is vital for irrigation in this arid region, and has been developed as a resource by joint Mexican-US projects. In fact, it may have been over-developed, and attention is now being paid to environmental quality along the river. The coastal areas have remote beaches, lagoons and wetlands, home to diverse marine life and a winter stopover for many migratory birds. Inland, numerous winding roads climb to the eastern and northern edges of the Sierra Madre Oriental, offering spectacular scenery and a refreshing highland climate.

Culturally, northeast Mexico and the south-central USA comprise a frontier of epic proportions. It was here that the two great colonizing movements, Spanish from the south and Anglo-Saxon from the north, confronted each other and displaced the indigenous peoples. The war between Mexico and the USA (1846-48) was probably inevitable, and though it established the Rio Grande as the political border between the two countries, the cultural and economic

Highlights

- Monterrey – the prosperous state capital, home to some of Mexico's finest modern architecture

- Area de Protección de la Flora y Fauna Cuatrociénegas – an isolated protected area in the Desierto Chihuahuense (Chihuahuan Desert), with hundreds of crystalline pools, amazing white gypsum sand dunes and numerous endemic species

- Saltillo – the high-sierra capital of Coahuila, with its pleasant climate and some lovely colonial buildings

- Parras – a tranquil town and desert oasis in Coahuila – and home to the Americas' oldest winery, Casa Madero

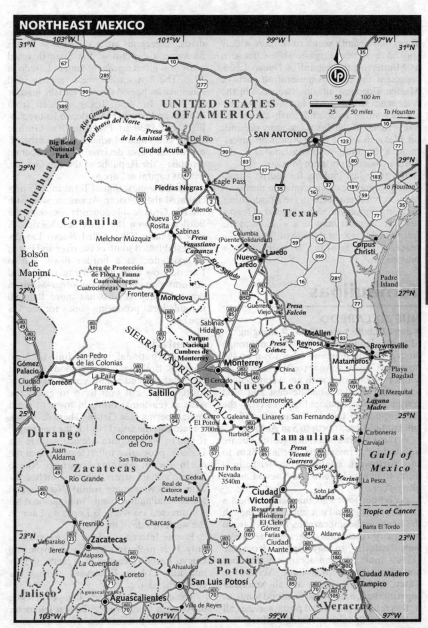

NORTHEAST MEXICO

boundaries remain much less distinct. There is so much Mexican influence in southern Texas that Spanish seems to be more widely spoken there than English, while cities such as Monterrey, the capital of Nuevo León, represent the most Americanized parts of Mexico. Economically, the two sides of the river seem worlds apart, but money and resources surge back and forth across the line – much of the Texas economy depends on Mexican labor, while American investment is booming in *maquiladoras* in the border towns of northern Mexico.

If you're just looking for tourist attractions you may be disappointed in northeast Mexico, but if you want to see a fascinating, evolving region you should spend at least a few days here. It may be a window to the future of Mexico in the age of NAFTA – a place where Tex-Mex is more than a burrito.

Tamaulipas

NUEVO LAREDO
• pop 273,800 • elev 438m ☎ changing
More foreign tourists enter Mexico through Nuevo Laredo than any other town on the northeast border. An excellent road runs south to Monterrey, with good connections to central Mexico and the east and west coasts. Two international bridges cross the Rio Grande to Laredo, Texas, from where Interstate 35 goes north to San Antonio.

A third international bridge, the Puente Solidaridad, crosses the border 38km to the northwest, enabling motorists in a hurry to bypass Laredo and Nuevo Laredo altogether.

As border towns go, this pair is almost a classic example, and not unpleasant, though the heat can be unbearable. Nuevo Laredo has many restaurants, bars and souvenir shops catering to day-trippers from the USA – most of them accept US currency and quote prices in dollars. 'Across the water,' in Laredo, there are all-American supermarkets, motels and fast-food joints, as well as reliable phone and postal services, all staffed with Spanish-speaking workers.

History
The area was sparsely populated with nomadic indigenous groups until Don Tomás Sánchez, a captain of the Spanish royal army, was given a grant of land at Laredo in 1775. The first settlers were ranchers, and missionaries passed through into the interior of Texas. In 1836, Texas seceded from Mexico and became an independent republic. From 1839 to 1841, the Rio Grande valley, and much of what is now northeastern Mexico, also declared itself a separate republic – the Republic of the Rio Grande, with its capital at Laredo.

The US annexation of Texas in 1845 precipitated the Mexican-American War, with the Rio Grande subsequently becoming the border between the USA and Mexico. A new Mexican town, called Nuevo Laredo, was established south of the river and began its existence as a border town. Nuevo Laredo now collects more in tariffs and customs revenue than any other Mexican port of entry. It also has more than 60 maquiladoras producing goods for the US market.

Orientation
Two international bridges link the two Laredos. Both have immigration offices at the southern end where you can get your tourist card, but you have to go to the *aduana* (customs) office in town to get a vehicle permit (see Getting There & Away). Puente Internacional No 1 is the one to use if you're walking into Mexico – there's a US$0.35 pedestrian toll. It leaves you at the north end of Avenida Guerrero, Nuevo Laredo's main street, which stretches for 2km (one way going south). Northbound traffic heading for Puente Internacional No 1 is directed via Avenida López de Lara on the western side of the city.

Puente Internacional No 2 is for vehicles only. It is preferred by drivers bypassing Nuevo Laredo's center, as it feeds directly into Luis Colosio Boulevard, skirting the city to the east.

The city center spreads along either side of Avenida Guerrero for the first kilometer from Puente Internacional No 1. The main

NUEVO LAREDO

PLACES TO STAY
8 Hotel Regis
11 Motel Romanos
13 Hotel Mesón Del Rey
17 Gran Hotel Rendón
18 Hotel Reforma
20 Hotel Alameda
21 Hotel La Finca
24 Motel Del Centro

PLACES TO EAT
6 El Dorado Bar & Grill
9 Restaurant La Principal
10 Café El Quinto Patio
12 Marco Pollo

OTHER
1 US Immigration
2 US Immigration
3 Mexican Immigration
4 Mexican Immigration
5 Parking
7 Buses to Central Bus Station
14 Local Buses
15 Palacio de Gobierno
16 Post Office
19 Banca Serfin
22 Banamex
23 Customs & Immigration Offices
25 Tourist Office

NORTHEAST MEXICO

---

plaza is seven blocks from the bridge, with a kiosk in the middle, the Palacio de Gobierno on the east side, and a few hotels and restaurants around it.

Nuevo Laredo's Central Camionera (Central Bus Station), the arrival and departure point for long-distance buses, is on the southern edge of town.

Information
Tourist Offices A tourist office (☎ 12-73-97) is at the corner of Herrera and Juárez, open 8 am to 8 pm Monday to Saturday, 10 am to 3 pm Sunday. Its friendly staff, two

of whom speak English, distribute maps and brochures.

Consulates A US consulate (☎ 14-05-12) at Allende 3330, near the corner of Nayarit on

On October 1, 2000, the telephone area code is due to change to ☎ 8 from 87, with the digit 7 added to the start of every local number (for example the number 12-23-91 will become 712-23-91).

the south side of town, is open 8 am to 5 pm Monday to Friday, but US citizens can call a Laredo number (☎ 210-727-9661) for after-hours emergency assistance. The consulate issues US visas on a case-by-case basis; applicants line up between 8 am and 2 pm for an interview.

Money Most *casas de cambio* will not change traveler's checks but most businesses will accept them with a purchase, and the main Mexican banks should change them. Businesses also accept cash dollars, but the exchange rate can be low.

Post & Communications The post office is on Camargo, behind the government offices on the side of the plaza. It's open 8 am to 6 pm Monday to Friday, 9 am to 12.30 pm Saturday. Two kinds of pay phones stand around the plaza and the center: Ladatel card-operated phones, and special coin-operated phones for calls across the border.

Talamas, a record store on Avenida Guerrero north of Washington, offers Internet access on its upper level, for a rather steep US$5.25 per hour. It's open 9 am to 11 pm Monday to Saturday, 11 am to 10 pm Sunday.

Special Events

Nuevo Laredo holds an agricultural, livestock, industrial and cultural fair the second and third weeks of September. The foundation of Nuevo Laredo (after it was severed from its northern section in 1848) is celebrated from June 13 to 15, with music, baseball games and bullfights.

Places to Stay

All of the hotels listed here have air-con, a necessity during Nuevo Laredo's blistering summers. There are also nicer, pricier places on highway 85 heading south.

Hotel La Finca (☎ 12-88-83, Avenida Reynosa 811), south of González, is the least expensive decent place in town, with clean, comfortable rooms at US$19 to US$21 (depending on the size of the room) for one person, and US$24 for two. Almost as good,

the *Motel Romanos* (☎ 12-23-91, Dr Mier 2420), the building with the Romanesque façade three blocks east of the plaza, charges US$18/27 singles/doubles for rooms with TV. *Gran Hotel Rendón* (☎ 12-00-66), at the corner of González and Avenida Juárez, is built around an attractive skylit courtyard. Simple, tidy rooms cost US$19/24; parking is available.

There are no standouts among the midrange hotels, but as the quality of rooms within each hotel varies, ask to see at least two rooms before registering. *Hotel Reforma* (☎ 12-62-50, Avenida Guerrero 822), a half block north of Canales, has bright, clean rooms with color TV and phone and firm mattresses for US$24/34. *Hotel Alameda* (☎ 12-50-50, González 2715), on the south side of the plaza, has similar rooms though saggier beds for slightly less at US$22/32. Another clean, central place is the *Hotel Regis* (☎ 12-90-35, Pino Suárez 3013) with rooms for US$28/31.

Hotel Mesón Del Rey (☎ 12-63-60, Avenida Guerrero 718) on the main plaza features spacious, quiet rooms and chilly central air-con – a good value for US$31/35. The entrance to the hotel's parking lot is on González. *Motel Del Centro* (☎ 12-13-10, Héroes de Nacataz 3330), at Avenida Allende, is a little oasis in the town center. Palm trees adorn the parking lot and one wing wraps around a swimming pool. Its large, comfortable rooms cost US$26/47, or US$30 with a king-size bed.

Places to Eat

There are lots of eating possibilities, though the places on Avenida Guerrero just south of the bridge can be overpriced tourist joints. *El Dorado Bar & Grill* at the corner of Belden and Ocampo, five blocks south of the bridge, has been a haunt for South Texans since opening in 1922 as the casino/restaurant 'El Caballo Blanco.' It still harbors a significant gringo presence, attracted by its 'Old West' atmosphere, Cajun cuisine and special cocktails – notably the New Orleans 'gin fizz' (US$4.50). In addition to soft-shell crabs (US$15) and frog's legs (US$12), the El Dorado offers a variety of border favorites such as *cabrito* (roasted young goat, US$12).

For authentic *norteño* fare, check out **Restaurant La Principal** *(Avenida Guerrero 624)*, half a block north of the plaza; look for the goats roasting over coals in the window. The popular restaurant offers all the cabrito variations – a substantial order of *pierna* costs US$10.50 and comes with salsa, salad, tortillas and beans. Charcoal-grilled chicken is the main attraction at the pleasant **Marco Pollo**, at the corner of Dr Mier and Matamoros, with overhead fans and tiled tables. A whole chicken, served with salsa and tortillas, costs US$6.50; half a chicken US$3.25.

The north side of the plaza has a couple of small cafés: **Café El Quinto Patio** is the better option. A popular hangout for cowboys and other local characters, the air-conditioned café serves pretty good enchiladas and *lonches* (rolls stuffed with avocado, ground beef or eggs). Nothing on the menu is more than US$3.

Two other places very popular with locals lie a kilometer or so down Avenida Guerrero from the international bridge. **El Rancho** *(Avenida Guerrero 2134)*, between Venezuela and Lincoln, is a taco-and-beer hall frequented by families, with a wide variety of tacos and regional dishes. The **Río Mar** *(Avenida Guerrero 2403)* is packed at night with people gobbling mouth-watering seafood dishes starting at US$5.

Spectator Sports
Two or three bullfights each month are held at the Plaza de Toros Lauro Luis Longoria (☎ 12-71-92, 888-240-8460 in the USA, Avenida Monterrey 4101), near Anáhuac. Admission ranges from US$6 to US$8; call for dates and times.

Shopping
It's worth browsing around some of the shops and markets for the odd souvenir. There's a crafts market on the east side of Avenida Guerrero half a block north of the main plaza, and the Mercado Monclovio Herrera on the west side of Avenida Guerrero, between Hidalgo and Belden. You'll find an assortment of T-shirts, silver, rugs, liquor, hats, leather and pottery. Lots of individual shops along this northern section of Avenida Guerrero deal in overpriced junk, but some quality work is available.

Getting There & Away
Air Nuevo Laredo airport is off the Monterrey road, 14km south of town. Mexicana, with an office (☎ 19-28-16) at the corner of Paseo Colón and Obregón, has direct flights to/from Mexico City and Guadalajara.

Bus Nuevo Laredo's bus station is 3km south of the international bridge, on Anáhuac. There's a left-luggage service at La Silla sweet shop. First- and 2nd-class buses serve every city in northern Mexico. The main 1st-class companies are Futura, Ómnibus de México and Sendor. Daily service from Nuevo Laredo includes:

Ciudad Victoria – 510km, 7 hours; 1 deluxe (US$40), 4 1st-class (US$26)

Mexico City (Terminal Norte) – 1158km, 15 hours; 3 deluxe (US$84), 11 1st-class (US$62)

Monclova – 248km, 4½ hrs; 6 2nd-class (US$11.50)

Monterrey – 224km, 3 hours; 8 deluxe (US$17), 1st-class every half hour (US$13), frequent 2nd-class (US$10)

Reynosa – 251km, 4 hours; 8 1st-class (US$12.50)

Saltillo – 310km, 4½ hours; hourly 1st-class (US$21)

San Luis Potosí – 740km, 10 hours; 4 deluxe (US$49), hourly 1st-class (US$37), 9 2nd-class (US$31)

Zacatecas – 683km, 8 hours; 5 1st-class (US$36), 2 2nd-class (US$31)

Buses also go to Aguascalientes, Durango, Guadalajara and Querétaro, and to major cities in Texas.

There are also direct buses to cities in Mexico from the Greyhound terminal across the border in Laredo, Texas, but these are more expensive than services from Nuevo Laredo. You can sometimes use these buses to go between Laredo and Nuevo Laredo bus stations, but you have to ask the driver – it's less hassle and often quicker just to walk over the international bridge.

Car & Motorcycle For a vehicle permit you must go to the customs office. From Puente Internacional No 1, turn right onto Boulevard Internacional and follow the 'vehicle permit' signs. After about 10 blocks, bear left onto Avenida López de Lara, moving into the left lane. Just past the train station on your left is a low white wall labeled 'Importación Temporal de Vehículos Extranjeros'; swing around to the other side of the boulevard at the traffic circle, pull in at the entrance and park. The low building left of the parking lot entrance houses an immigration office and customs bureau. The office is always open and should issue a permit without hassle if your papers are in order (see the Getting There & Away chapter). To avoid a fine, don't forget to cancel the permit when you leave the country.

The route south via Monterrey is the most direct to central Mexico, the Pacific Coast and the Gulf Coast. An excellent toll road, highway 85D, is fast but expensive (tolls total US$14 to Monterrey). The alternative free road (highway 85) is longer, rougher and slower. Highway 2 is a rural road following the Rio Grande to Reynosa and Matamoros. To the USA, the bridge toll is US$1.60.

Getting Around
Frequent city buses (US$0.40) make getting around Nuevo Laredo simple enough. Many buses go down Avenida Guerrero from the plaza; 'Carretera – Central' buses, with an aquamarine stripe, go to the bus station. To get from Puente Internacional No 1 to the nearest bus stop, go two blocks on Boulevard Internacional to Avenida Juárez, then left four blocks to Pino Suárez. Buses labeled 'Mirador' leave from that corner to the bus station. From the bus station, local buses go back into town.

A taxi to the bridge from the bus station will cost about US$4.25, about US$1 more in the reverse direction.

There's a secure parking garage four blocks south of the bridge on Victoria west of Avenida Guerrero (US$1 per hour).

REYNOSA
• pop 320,500 • elev 90m ☎ changing
Reynosa was founded in 1749 as Villa de Nuestra Señora de Guadalupe de Reynosa, 20km from its present location: flooding forced the move in 1802. Reynosa was one of the first towns to rise up in the independence movement of 1810, but little of historical interest remains.

Today, Reynosa is one of northeast Mexico's most important industrial towns, with oil refineries, petrochemical plants, cotton mills, distilleries and maquiladoras. Pipelines from here carry natural gas to Monterrey and into the USA. It's also the center of a big cattle-raising, cotton, sugarcane and maize-growing area.

As a commercial border crossing, Reynosa is busier than Matamoros but less important than Nuevo Laredo. It has good road connections into Mexico and Texas, but most travelers will probably find one of the other crossings more direct and convenient. Across the Rio Grande is the town of McAllen.

The tourist trade is geared to short-term Texan visitors, with restaurants, nightclubs, bars and bawdier diversions. Some handicrafts are available in the tourist markets, but the quality is generally low, while the prices are not.

Orientation
Reynosa's central streets are laid out on a grid pattern, between the Rio Grande and the Canal Anzalduas. The main plaza is on a rise a few blocks southwest of the international bridge, with the town hall, banks, hotels and a modern church, the Parroquia de Guadalupe.

South of the plaza, on Hidalgo, is a pedestrian mall lined with shops and cafés, extending to Colón at the southern edge of the grid. Between the bridge and the center lies the Zona Rosa, with restaurants, bars and nightclubs.

If you're driving in from Mexico, follow the signs to the Puente Internacional. Avoid the maze of streets in the industrial zone south of the canal.

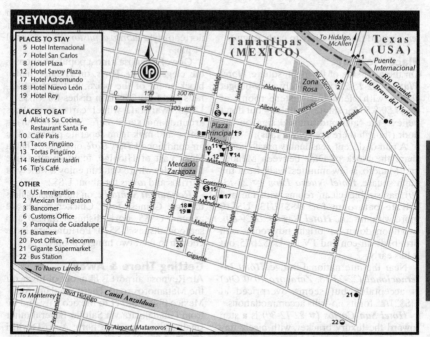

REYNOSA

PLACES TO STAY
5 Hotel Internacional
7 Hotel San Carlos
8 Hotel Plaza
12 Hotel Savoy Plaza
17 Hotel Astromundo
18 Hotel Nuevo León
19 Hotel Rey

PLACES TO EAT
4 Alicia's Su Cocina, Restaurant Santa Fe
10 Café Paris
11 Tacos Pingüino
13 Tortas Pingüino
14 Restaurant Jardín
16 Tip's Café

OTHER
1 US Immigration
2 Mexican Immigration
3 Bancomer
6 Customs Office
9 Parroquia de Guadalupe
15 Banamex
20 Post Office, Telecomm
21 Gigante Supermarket
22 Bus Station

NORTHEAST MEXICO

Information

Immigration US and Mexican immigration bureaus are at their respective ends of the bridge, and there's another Mexican post in the Reynosa bus station. Get a tourist card stamped at either post if you're proceeding beyond Reynosa deeper into Mexico.

Money You can change traveler's checks at Banamex, on Guerrero between Hidalgo and Juárez. The main banks have ATMs, some dispensing US dollars as well as pesos, and there are several casas de cambio along Zaragoza near the bridge.

On December 1, 2000, the telephone area code is due to change to ☎ 8 from 89, with the digit 9 added to the start of every local number (for example the number 22-13-10 will become 922-13-10).

Post & Communications The post office, adjacent to a Telecomm office on the corner of Díaz and Colón, is open 9 am to 4 pm Monday to Friday, 9 am to 1 pm Saturday.

Things to See & Do

Take a stroll around the main square and down Hidalgo, the pedestrian shopping strip, to the touristy crafts market, Mercado Zaragoza. The Zona Rosa has a slew of restaurants, bars and nightclubs, but comes to life only on the nights when the young Texas crowd comes in. Much sleazier entertainment – exotic dancing and prostitution – is the rule at 'boys' town,' a few kilometers west, just beyond where Aldama becomes a dirt road.

Special Events

The festival of Nuestra Señora de Guadalupe, on December 12, is the town's major event. Pilgrims start processions a week before and there are afternoon dance performances in front of the church. Reynosa's *feria* is held from late July to early August.

Places to Stay

On the west side of the main square, *Hotel Plaza* (☎ 22-15-75) is definitely a low-budget choice with clean but austere rooms at US$7.50/8.50 for singles/doubles – but don't believe the 'air-conditioning' sign on the door (though there are ceiling fans).

A pair of decent, reasonably priced hotels share the block of Díaz between Méndez and Madero, a few minutes' walk from the main square. *Hotel Nuevo León* (☎ 22-13-10) has sizable, clean rooms with fan and private bathroom for US$12/13, US$10 more with air-con. *Hotel Rey* (☎ 22-29-80), two doors down, has bright, tidy rooms with firm beds, air-con and TV for US$21/25, but it fills early.

Near the international bridge, *Hotel Internacional* (22-23-18, Zaragoza 1050 Ote) is acceptable but seems overpriced at US$21/25 for its no-frills accommodations.

Hotel San Carlos (☎ 22-12-80) is a step toward the luxury bracket, with nicely furnished, air-conditioned rooms, some overlooking the plaza, for US$33/37. There's a good restaurant and a parking garage. Half a block south of the Parroquia de Guadalupe, the pleasant *Hotel Savoy Plaza* (☎ 22-00-67, Juárez 860 Nte) has air-conditioned rooms at US$42 for one or two guests.

The top downtown place is the *Hotel Astromundo* (☎ 22-56-25, Juárez 675 Nte) between Guerrero and Méndez, featuring clean, spacious rooms with spotless bathrooms, cable TV, parking and a restaurant. Singles/doubles are US$44/49.

Places to Eat

Reynosa boasts quite a few centrally located places to eat, many offering hearty, inexpensive fare. On the north side of the plaza, *Alicia's Su Cocina* serves up huge portions of enchiladas, *sopes*, burritos, *gorditas* and other Mexican classics for under US$3. Other tasty snacks can be found at *Tacos Pingüino*, on the opposite side of the plaza, and *Tortas Pingüino* just around the corner

on Juárez, both open until 9.30 pm. Also on Juárez, the *Restaurant Jardín* is *the* place for norteño-style *cabrito al pastor*; it's open until 11 pm.

One of Reynosa's most popular options is the elegant *Café Paris*, on Hidalgo half a block south of the plaza, featuring breakfasts and tasty Mexican dishes for US$2 to US$3. Waitstaff wheel carts of pastries around and serve *café lechero*, pouring coffee and milk from separate pitchers. The air-conditioned *Tip's Café*, on Méndez half a block east of Hidalgo, features attractive tiled tables where you can enjoy a variety of burritos and *tortas* for about US$2.

Restaurant Santa Fe, on the plaza, claims to serve Chinese food. Chicken dishes are around US$5, pork dishes US$7.50 and seafood dishes US$10. Portions are large enough to feed two hungry people.

Getting There & Away

Air Reynosa airport is 8km out of town, off the Matamoros road. There are daily Aero-Mexico flights direct to Mexico City, and to/from Guadalajara via Saltillo. Several other small airlines operate here: Aero Davinci (☎ 58-04-85) flies to/from Poza Rica, Villahermosa and Ciudad del Carmen, and Aerolíneas Internacionales (☎ 26-73-00) to/from Aguascalientes and Tijuana.

Bus The Central de Autobuses is on the southeastern corner of the central grid, opposite the parking lot of the Gigante supermarket. Buses run to almost anywhere you'd want to go in Mexico. First-class lines include Transportes del Norte, ADO, Ómnibus de México, Transpais, Futura and Transportes Frontera. Daily service from Reynosa includes:

Aguascalientes – 808km, 12 hours; 12 1st-class (US$40)

Ciudad Victoria – 330km, 4½ hours; hourly 1st-class (US$14)

Guadalajara – 990km, 16 hours; 9 1st-class (US$51)

Matamoros – 104km, 2 hours; 9 1st-class (US$5), hourly 2nd-class (US$4.50)

Mexico City (Terminal Norte) – 970km, 15 hours; 5 1st-class (US$51)

Monterrey – 220km, 3 hours; frequent 1st-class (US$12)

Saltillo – 305km, 5 hours; frequent 1st-class (US$16)

San Luis Potosí – 737km, 10 hours; frequent 1st-class (US$32)

Tampico – 580km, 7 hours; frequent 1st-class (US$22)

Torreón – 536km, 9 hours; 11 1st-class (US$28)

Zacatecas – 678km, 10 hours; frequent 1st-class (US$37)

First-class buses also serve Chihuahua, Ciudad Juárez, Durango, Puebla, Querétaro, Veracruz and Villahermosa, with 2nd-class buses serving mainly local destinations. Greyhound runs direct buses to Houston daily (US$25) and to Chicago twice a week (US$79).

McAllen, Texas The nearest Texas transport center, McAllen, is 9km from the border. Valley Transit Company (☎ 956-686-5479 in McAllen) runs buses between the McAllen and Reynosa bus stations every 30 minutes between 6 am and 10 pm (US$2.50).

In Reynosa tickets can be purchased at the Greyhound desk at the Central de Autobuses.

Coming from McAllen, if you don't want to go all the way to the Reynosa bus station, get off at the Greyhound office on the US side and walk over the bridge into Reynosa.

Car & Motorcycle East of the bridge, there's an aduana office that can issue car permits. To get there, turn left up Avenida Alemán after clearing immigration, and follow the yellow arrows. Take the first left after the Matamoros turnoff; the entrance is at the end of the street.

Going west to Monterrey (220km), the toll highway 40D is excellent and patrolled by Green Angels; the tolls total US$14. (The less direct, toll-free highway 40 follows roughly the same route.) Highways 97 and 180 south to Tampico are two-lane, surfaced roads, but not too busy. Highway 101 branches off highway 180 to Ciudad Victoria and the scenic climb to San Luis Potosí. If you want to follow the Rio Grande up-

stream to Nuevo Laredo, highway 2 is not in bad shape, but it's quicker to travel on the US side. Side roads off highway 2 reach a number of obscure border crossings and the Presa Falcón (Falcon Reservoir), as well as Guerrero Viejo, a town that was submerged after the dam's construction in 1953, and moved to its current site at Nuevo Ciudad Guerrero, 33km to the southeast. It's a smooth 40-minute drive east to Matamoros via new toll highway 2D, which begins just past Reynosa airport (US$3.25).

Getting Around
Battered yellow microbuses rattle around Reynosa, providing cheap but jarring transport. From the international bridge to the bus station, catch one of the Valley Transit Company coaches coming from McAllen with 'Reynosa' on the front (US$2.50).

To get from the bus station to the town center, turn left after exiting the station and go half a block, then cross the Gigante parking lot to the bus stop on Colón. Take one of the buses labeled 'Olmo' (US$0.40).

Taxis between the bus station and the bridge should not cost more than US$4. Expect to pay around US$13 for a taxi to/ from the airport.

MATAMOROS
• **pop 323,800** ☎ **changing**
First settled during the Spanish colonization of Tamaulipas in 1686 as Los Esteros Hermosas (The Beautiful Estuaries), this city was renamed in 1793 after Padre Mariano Matamoros. In 1846, Matamoros was the first Mexican city to be taken by US forces in the Mexican-American War; Zachary Taylor then used it as a base for his attack on Monterrey. During the US Civil War, when sea routes to the Confederacy were blockaded, Matamoros transshipped cotton out of Confederate Texas, and supplies and war material into it.

Today, Matamoros is no historical monument. South of the central area is a broad circle of newer industrial zones, and, apart from its maquiladoras, Matamoros is a commercial center for a large agricultural hinterland – tanneries, cotton mills and distilleries

NORTHEAST MEXICO

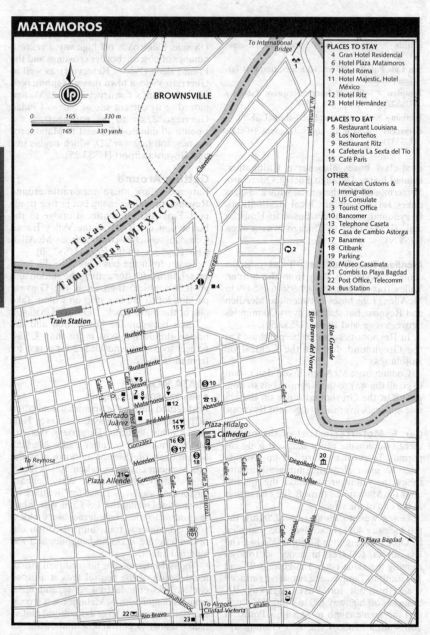

MATAMOROS

BROWNSVILLE

0   165   330 m
0   165   330 yards

Texas (USA)

Tamaulipas (MEXICO)

To International Bridge

Train Station

Hidalgo

Iturbide

Herrera

Bustamente

Bravo

Matamoros

Mercado Juárez

González

Morelos

Guerrero

Plaza Allende

Cuauhtémoc

To Reynosa

Plaza Hidalgo
Cathedral

Prieto

Degollado

Lauro Villar

Panama

Guatemala

To Playa Bagdad

To Airport
Ciudad Victoria

Canales

Rio Bravo

MEX 101

Ped Mall

Abasolo

Av Tamaulipas

Claveles

Obregón

Rio Bravo del Norte

Rio Grande

Calle 2
Calle 3
Calle 4
Calle 5 (Carranza)
Calle 6
Calle 8
Calle 1
Calle 9
Calle 11
Calle 13

PLACES TO STAY
4 Gran Hotel Residencial
6 Hotel Plaza Matamoros
7 Hotel Roma
11 Hotel Majestic, Hotel México
12 Hotel Ritz
23 Hotel Hernández

PLACES TO EAT
5 Restaurant Louisiana
8 Los Norteños
9 Restaurant Ritz
14 Cafetería La Sexta del Tío
15 Café Paris

OTHER
1 Mexican Customs & Immigration
2 US Consulate
3 Tourist Office
10 Bancomer
13 Telephone Caseta
16 Casa de Cambio Astorga
17 Banamex
18 Citibank
19 Parking
20 Museo Casamata
21 Combis to Playa Bagdad
22 Post Office, Telecomm
24 Bus Station

are among its main industries. But, there is more evidence of the past here than in most border towns, and the town center, with its church and plaza, looks typically Mexican.

Orientation
Matamoros lies across the Rio Grande from Brownsville, Texas. The river is spanned by a bridge with border controls at each end. The Rio Grande is a disappointing trickle in this area, as most of its water has been siphoned off upstream for irrigation.

From the southern end of the bridge, Obregón winds around toward the town's central grid, 1.5km to the southwest. The cheap lodging is around Abasolo, a pedestrian street a block north of Plaza Hidalgo. Nearby are two markets with tourist-oriented crafts.

Information
Tourist Offices An informal 'tourist bureau' is in a green and white shack on Obregón across from the Gran Hotel Residencial. Someone's usually there 9 am to 1 pm and 3 to 7 pm daily. English is spoken but actual information may be hard to obtain. If you need maps, brochures and printed giveaways, try the Brownsville Chamber of Commerce (☎ 956-542-4341, brnsvl@hiline.net), at 1600 E Elizabeth St, about 300m east of the bridge, open 8 am to 5 pm Monday to Friday.

Immigration The Mexican border post waves most pedestrians through on the assumption that they're there just for a day's shopping or eating, but some cars will get the red light to be checked. If you're planning to proceed farther south into Mexico,

On November 1, 2000, the telephone area code is due to change to ☎ 8 from 88, with the second digit 8 of the old code transferred to the start of every local number (for example the number 13-35-58 will become 813-35-58; if calling long distance, the number is 8-813-35-58).

go to the immigration office and ask for a tourist card and have it stamped before you leave Matamoros.

Consulates The US consulate (☎ 12-44-02), at Calle 1 No 2002, is open 8 to 10 am and 1 to 4 pm Monday to Friday; it does not issue visas.

Money Several banks on Plaza Hidalgo have ATMs; Citibank's machine dispenses dollars and pesos. Banamex on Calle 7 and Bancomer on Calle 6 will change cash or traveler's checks. Often you get a better rate for cash in the exchange houses around the central area, but few change traveler's checks; Casa de Cambio Astorga, on González just west of the plaza, is an exception.

In Brownsville, there are exchange houses on International Boulevard, the road running straight north from the international bridge. Some are open 24 hours a day.

Post & Communications A post office and a Telecomm office with fax service are 1km south of the center at Calle 11 and Río Bravo, both open 8 am to 6 pm Monday to Friday, 9 am to 1 pm Saturday. A telephone caseta, open 7 am to 10 pm daily, is on Calle 6 two blocks north of the plaza.

Museo Casamata
This fort, on the corner of Guatemala and Degollado, dates from 1845. One of a series of walls and fortifications built in the 19th century to defend the city, it was the scene of fighting in the Mexican-American War. It now contains memorabilia of the Mexican Revolution, early photos of Matamoros and some ill-assorted miscellany. Explanations are in Spanish only. The museum is open 8 am to 8 pm Monday to Saturday, 8 am to 3 pm Sunday (free).

Playa Bagdad
Matamoros' beach was formerly known as Playa Lauro Villar but it has adopted the name of Bagdad, from a town at the mouth of the Rio Grande that prospered during the US Civil War but later succumbed to floods, hurricanes and military attacks. It's 37km

east of Matamoros on highway 2, with a wide stretch of clean sand and a few beach-side seafood restaurants. Some mid-range motels are along the road approaching the beach. Blue combis to Playa Bagdad leave hourly from Calle 10 on the west side of Plaza Allende (1½ hours, US$2).

Special Events

From late June to early July, Expo Fiesta Matamoros features an amusement park, handicrafts displays and popular entertainers. In October the International Autumn Festival is the occasion for a variety of cultural events, from chamber music concerts to traditional dance displays.

Places to Stay

There are a couple of basic options around Abasolo near the center of town for less than US$20 a double. Mid-range lodging, with air-con and parking, starts at around US$40, and there's not much in between.

One option on the cheaper side, the *Hotel Majestic* (☎ 13-36-80, Abasolo 131), between Calles 8 and 9, is a family-run place that charges US$9.50/14 for beat-up singles/doubles with sagging beds and private bathrooms. There's no air-con but, while it doesn't live up to its name, it's fairly clean and the management is friendly. Nearby, the *Hotel México* (☎ 12-08-56) is similar to the Majestic but tidier. At US$13/17, rooms have ceiling fans and narrow bathrooms; top-level rooms are cooler with a pretty good view of the Hotel Ritz from the balcony.

Five short blocks from the bus station, twice that to the main plaza, the *Hotel Hernández* (☎ 13-35-58, Calle 6 No 105) is a four-story building set around a narrow courtyard with a few palm trees. Rooms are pretty drab, with single beds and fluorescent lighting, and go for US$25/31 with air-con and TV, US$16/21 without. There's parking across the street.

The *Hotel Roma* (☎ 16-05-73, 800-112-43-76, Calle 9 No 1420), between Matamoros and Bravo, charges US$35/40 for small modern rooms, some windowless, with cable TV, telephone and central air-con.

More expensive and luxurious, the *Hotel Ritz* (☎ 12-11-90, Matamoros 612) at Calle 7, offers a gym, fax and laundry services, a sports bar and a car rental agency. Small but lovely rooms with Talavera-tiled furniture are US$54/66.

Still pricier, the *Hotel Plaza Matamoros* (☎ 16-16-96), on the corner of Calle 9 and Bravo, has a handsome restaurant/atrium and fine spacious rooms with plush carpeting for US$63/72; US$53 per room on weekends. Matamoros' top hotel is the *Gran Hotel Residencial* (☎ 13-94-40, Obregón 249), 1.2km south of the international bridge. Its 120 air-conditioned rooms with terraces surround pleasant gardens and a few swimming pools. Rates are US$79/83.

Places to Eat

Half a block from Plaza Hidalgo, the no-nonsense *Cafetería La Sexta del Tío (Calle 6 No 171)* is good for breakfast. Join the locals at the counter for a cup of coffee and a plate of eggs (US$1.50) – try the *huevos guayín*, kind of an omelet stuffed with refried beans and laced with tomato sauce. Closer to the plaza, the *Café Paris* is a large operation with many booths, usually packed in the morning. Assorted pastries are brought around on carts; coffee and hot milk are poured from separate pitchers for *café lechero*. Breakfast specials start at US$1.75, Mexican *antojitos* around US$2. In the same price range is the *Restaurant Ritz* opposite the Hotel Ritz, open until 11 pm. It's a cozy place with big booths and an American-style menu. Main dishes include grilled chicken (US$3.25) and filet mignon (US$5.25), and there's a breakfast buffet for US$3.25.

The elegant *Restaurant Louisiana*, on Bravo between Calles 8 and 9, offers entrées from US$4.50 to US$9, including rib-eye steak with mushrooms (US$9), quail (US$8.50) and shish kebab (US$7.50). Except for the frog's legs, however, there's no Cajun food on the menu.

For authentic northern-Mexican cuisine, head for *Los Norteños (Matamoros 109)* between Calles 8 and 9. A cantina-style restaurant with a bar, simple tables and attentive waitstaff, it offers cabrito al pastor, served with salad, tortillas and *frijoles charros* (cowboy beans), for US$6.50.

Shopping

The 'new market,' or Mercado Juárez, occupies the block bordered by Calles 9 and 10, Abasolo and Matamoros. A lot of the stuff is second-rate but there's plenty of variety. Prices are 20% to 30% higher than the cheapest markets farther south, but you can bargain them down a bit.

Getting There & Away

Air Matamoros has an airport 17km out of town on the road to Ciudad Victoria. Aero-Mexico (☎ 12-24-60) has daily flights to/from Mexico City and Reynosa, while Aero California (☎ 12-22-00) flies to Mexico City and Ciudad Victoria.

Bus Both 1st- and 2nd-class buses run from the bus station on Canales, near the corner of Guatemala. The station has a 24-hour restaurant, a post office, a left-luggage service and a telephone caseta (which also sells city maps).

A number of big companies provide 1st-class service to/from Matamoros, including ADO, Transportes del Norte, Ómnibus de México and Transportes Frontera; Turistar offers deluxe service. Smaller 2nd-class lines go to local destinations. Daily service from Matamoros includes:

Ciudad Victoria – 320km, 4½ hours; frequent 1st-class (US$14)

Mexico City (Terminal Norte) – 1010km, 15 hours; 1 deluxe (US$66), 5 1st-class (US$51), 2 2nd-class (US$44)

Monterrey – 324km, 5 hours; frequent 1st-class (US$17)

Reynosa – 102km, 2 hours; hourly 1st-class (US$4.75)

Saltillo – 410km, 7 hours; hourly 1st-class (US$21)

Tampico – 570km, 6½ hours; frequent 1st-class (US$21)

Torreón – 640km, 9 hours; 10 1st-class (US$32)

Buses go to many other destinations including Chihuahua, Durango, Guadalajara, San Luis Potosí, Tijuana, Veracruz and Zacate-cas. Greyhound (☎ 16-37-57, 800-550-6210 in the USA) runs daily buses to Houston and Atlanta, and El Expreso Bus Company (☎ 11-52-88) has daily departures to points throughout the southeast US.

Brownsville, Texas You can get buses from the Brownsville bus station direct to several cities inside Mexico, but they cost more than from Matamoros, and they may take up to two hours to get over the international bridge, and through customs and immigration. It's quicker to walk across the bridge and take local transport to the Matamoros bus station.

The Brownsville bus station (☎ 956-546-7171) is at 1165 Saint Charles on the corner of 12th St. Facing the USA from the north end of the international bridge, go left (west) on Elizabeth, then two blocks south on 12th. There are buses to all the major cities in Texas, and connections to other US cities.

Car & Motorcycle Driving across the bridge to/from Brownsville costs US$1.60. At the Mexican end there is a turnoff immediately before the aduana building; pull in there to obtain your temporary vehicle permit. To cancel your permit on the way out, turn left through the opening in the median before you reach the toll booth, then park in the lane beside the aduana building.

The main routes on into Mexico are highway 180 south to Tampico and highway 101 southwest to Ciudad Victoria and into the Bajío region (see South of Matamoros, below, for more information on highways 180 and 101). These are both two-lane roads, not very busy, in fair condition and free of tolls. Officials at various checkpoints will want to see your tourist card and vehicle permit, and may check your vehicle for drugs or firearms. You can also go west to Monterrey via Reynosa.

Getting Around

Matamoros is served by small buses called maxi-taxis, which charge US$0.50 to anywhere in town; you can stop them on any street corner. Ruta 2 maxi-taxis pass by the

NORTHEAST MEXICO

bus station and go to the center of town. From the international bridge, regular taxis are on the right side of Obregón, maxi-taxis on the left beyond the taco stalls. Ruta 3 maxi-taxis go to the bus station. Alternatively, you could catch a free city tour bus from in front of the García crafts shop on Obregón near the bridge. Every half hour between 9 am and 6 pm, the service shuttles visitors from the bridge to Mercado Juárez and back.

Taxis from the bus station to the bridge or center of town cost about US$3, while those in the reverse direction are about twice as much.

SOUTH OF MATAMOROS

For its first 183km, the 500km highway 180 to Tampico is the same road as highway 101 to Ciudad Victoria. Most of the highway runs 30 to 40km inland, crossing unspectacular lowlands where sugarcane is the chief crop, though there are some more scenic stretches where the outliers of the Sierra Madre Oriental come close to the coast. Budget and mid-range hotels are found in San Fernando (137km from Matamoros), Soto La Marina (267km) and Aldama (379km). Side roads go east to the coast, most of which consists of lagoons separated from the Gulf by narrow sand spits. The longest is the Laguna Madre, extending some 230km along the northern Tamaulipas coast. (The lagoon dried up in the mid-20th century, forcing many to leave the area. When a 1967 hurricane replenished it, the area was resettled by *veracruzanos*.) The lagoons, sand dunes and coastal wetlands support a unique ecosystem, with many bird species and excellent fishing.

About 20km south of Matamoros, just past the airport, a side road crosses marshland for 60km before reaching **El Mezquital**, a small fishing village with a lighthouse and beach, on the long thin spit of land that divides the Laguna Madre from the Gulf. From San Fernando, 120km farther south, a road leads to **Carboneras**, another small fishing village facing the lagoon. There's not much here, but you might be able to get a boat out to the lagoon barrier island, where porpoises can sometimes be seen. Food and

gas are available, but there are no rooms for rent in either village.

From Soto La Marina, about 130km south of San Fernando, a road heads east for 50km, paralleling the Río Soto La Marina, to La Pesca (see below). Farther south, a 45km road runs east from Aldama, through the eastern fringes of the Sierra de Tamaulipas, to **Barra El Tordo**, another fishing village with a beach and good sport fishing. Facilities include four hotels (two budget, two mid-range), two restaurants and a campground.

La Pesca
• pop 1226

Despite resort development plans, La Pesca still has the ramshackle feel of an ordinary fishing village. There's a long, wide beach 6km east – Playa La Pesca – with shady *palapas* and seaside restaurants. The Río Soto La Marina and the Laguna Morales have abundant rainbow trout, kingfish, sea bass, porgy and sole. Most of the hotels can arrange boat rentals with fishing guides for around US$65 a day. A fishing tournament for sea bass takes place in November. Other activities include hunting, as well as surfing on the beaches that face the Gulf of Mexico.

There are five riverside hotels along the approach to La Pesca and one on the way out to the beach, all featuring piers with night-lights for fishing and grills for cooking your catch. Designed for family weekends, most places charge around US$35 for a two- or three-bed room, but will reduce rates for solo travelers during the week. The nondescript village has a few grocery stores and several taco stalls, and there is a restaurant at the Hotel Atlantida, on the first street on the right.

Ruta Puerto La Pesca runs nine buses a day between Ciudad Victoria's bus terminal and Playa La Pesca (3½ hours, US$7). You also can catch one of these buses from Soto La Marina's central plaza, an hour from La Pesca (US$2.25).

Turtle Reserves

The Kemp's ridley, currently classified as the world's most endangered sea turtle, digs its nests on the beaches from Tampico north to

La Pesca from March to July (see 'Mexico's Turtles: Not Saved Yet' in the Oaxaca State chapter). Working in tandem with the US Fish and Wildlife Service, government-administered turtle protection centers along this stretch of coast have had considerable success in reversing the decline of the Kemp's ridley. The centers collect the turtles' eggs and store them in corrals, keeping them out of reach of poachers. Researchers estimate that 75 percent of the eggs collected hatch successfully. Hatchlings are then released into the Gulf from June until September.

The Tamaulipas state environmental authority has recently opened one such center at La Pesca, the northern limit of the turtles' nesting grounds, to educate visitors about protection efforts. The center, 800m north of the main beach, offers a firsthand glimpse of the process during the months of peak activity. Visitors may even have a chance to help crews release the hatchlings.

CIUDAD VICTORIA
• pop 230,300 • elev 333m ☎ 1

About 40km north of the Tropic of Cancer, the capital of Tamaulipas state is a clean and pleasant city. It's around 310km south of Matamoros and Reynosa, well served by buses in every direction, and a good spot to break a journey between central Mexico and the Texas border. With the Sierra Madre forming an impressive backdrop to the city, there's just enough altitude to moderate the steamy heat of the coastal plains or the Rio Grande valley.

Orientation

Three highways converge at Ciudad Victoria, and a ring road allows through traffic to move between them without entering the city itself. The center is laid out in a grid pattern with one-way streets and a few pedestrian precincts. The north-south streets have both numbers (Calle 7, Calle 8, etc) and names (Díaz, Tijerina, respectively, etc).

Information

The tourist office (☎ 312-11-95) is on the south side of town on the corner of Rosales and 5 de Mayo. It's open 9 am to 3.30 pm and 6.30 to 9 pm daily. The staff are friendly but speak little English. Pick up a free copy of *Victoria* magazine, a city guide with maps.

The main post office is on Morelos northeast of the plaza. Internet access is available for US$2 per hour at Centro de Copiado Laser a Color, at Calle 8 No 224 between Juárez and Boulevard Balboa. It's open 7 am to 10 pm daily; reservations are necessary as there's only one computer. There is also a post office and a telecommunications center at the bus station (see Getting There & Away).

Things to See & Do

Ciudad Victoria has no compelling tourist attractions, but there is the **Museo de Antropología e Historia**, on Matamoros, one block north of Plaza Hidalgo, run by the University of Tamaulipas. It's a grab bag of mammoth bones, indigenous artifacts, colonial memorabilia, revolutionary photos, and one vintage carriage. It's open 9 am to 7 pm Monday to Friday.

Ciudad Victoria also has some interesting public buildings, such as the **Palacio de Gobierno del Estado**, on Juárez between Calles 15 and 16, and the **Teatro Juárez**, facing the north side of the Plaza Hidalgo, both with large murals. The Paseo Méndez, beside the tourist office, has plenty of greenery, and there are a couple of public pools in the Unidad Deportiva 'Ruiz Cortines,' open 4 to 9 pm Tuesday to Friday, 8 am to 6 pm Saturday and Sunday. There is an entrance on Calle 19 (Mier y Terán) between Berriozabal and Carrera Torres.

About 40km northeast of Ciudad Victoria, **Presa Vicente Guerrero** is a huge reservoir that attracts Mexicans and US citizens for bass fishing.

Places to Stay

The *Hostal De Escandón* (☎ 312-90-04, Tijerina 143), between Hidalgo and Juárez, is the best budget deal in town, with dormitory-style lodging on three levels around an inexpensive dining hall. Rooms are very clean and secure, with color TV, phones and fans. Rates are per person, depending on the

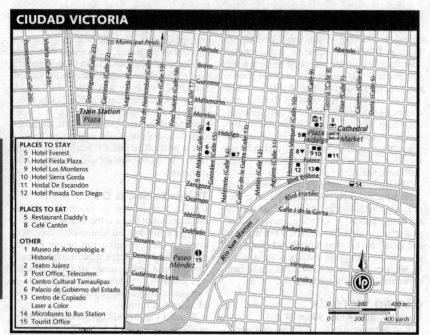

CIUDAD VICTORIA

PLACES TO STAY
5 Hotel Everest
7 Hotel Fiesta Plaza
9 Hotel Los Monteros
10 Hotel Sierra Gorda
11 Hostal De Escandón
12 Hotel Posada Don Diego

PLACES TO EAT
5 Restaurant Daddy's
8 Café Cantón

OTHER
1 Museo de Antropología e Historia
2 Teatro Juárez
3 Post Office, Telecomm
4 Centro Cultural Tamaulipas
6 Palacio de Gobierno del Estado
13 Centro de Copiado Laser a Color
14 Microbuses to Bus Station
15 Tourist Office

number of people in the room: US$9.50 with four occupants, US$10 with three, US$12 with two and US$16 for your own room. The place tends to be full, though, with groups of students or teachers.

Next best in the budget category is the **Hotel Los Monteros** (☎ 312-03-00), on Plaza Hidalgo. This busy hotel boasts a fine colonnaded courtyard with garden. Rooms (from US$14 for a single or double) are spacious and clean though kind of drab, and the beds are too soft for comfort. Another decent inexpensive option is the **Hotel Posada Don Diego** (☎ 312-12-79, Juárez 814 Ote) between Hermanos Vázquez and Colón, with singles/doubles at US$14/17 with TVs and narrow private bathrooms; add US$3 for air-con.

A big improvement is the **Hotel Fiesta Plaza** (☎ 312-78-77, Juárez 401), a block east of the Palacio de Gobierno. It's a welcoming place with small, comfortable air-conditioned rooms with phones and cable TV for US$26/29.

The **Hotel Sierra Gorda** (☎ 312-20-10), on the south side of Plaza Hidalgo, has a lot of style, but the rooms seem small for the price of US$37/42. The **Hotel Everest** (☎ 312-40-50), the tall structure on the west side of the plaza, charges US$60 per standard room; those in front have balconies with excellent plaza views. The hotel features an indoor pool and a parking garage.

Places to Eat

In the Hotel Everest, **Restaurant Daddy's** looks like a 1960s American coffee shop with booths, plastic decor and perky waitresses. It has some pretty good desserts and average meals for about US$5 with beverage. But the humble **Café Cantón** (Colón 114 Sur), on the next block, has much better coffee and stick-to-your-ribs breakfasts for under US$3 – perhaps that's why it's packed in the morning. Try the excellent huevos machacados, a norteño classic.

Outside the city center but well worth the trip is *Gorditas Doña Tota* on Berriozabal between Calles 5 and 6, nine blocks north of Plaza Hidalgo. The gorditas are about US$0.50 a piece.

Shopping

Ciudad Victoria is a good place to find garments made of Tamaulipas leather, distinctive for their hand-embroidered patterns. Try Heberli Piel, in the Centro Cultural Tamaulipas opposite the Palacio de Gobierno del Estado.

Getting There & Away

Air Aeropuerto Nacional General Pedro J Méndez is east of town off the Soto La Marina road. There are flights to Matamoros and Mexico City with Aero California (☎ 315-18-53) and to Mexico City with Aeromar (☎ 316-91-91).

Bus The bus station, on the east side of town near the ring road, has a left-luggage service. There is frequent 1st-class service to the following destinations:

Ciudad Mante – 141 km, 2½ hrs; (US$6)
Matamoros – 306km, 4¼ hours; (US$14)
Mexico City (Terminal Norte) – 702km, 10 hours; (US$39)
Monterrey – 285km, 3¾ hours; (US$14)
San Luis Potosí – 350km, 5½ hours; (US$19)
Tampico – 245km, 4 hours; (US$10.50)

Train From the old train station on the west side of town, the slow 2nd-class train No 172 departs for Tampico at 2.40 pm Tuesday, Thursday and Saturday, arriving about five hours later (US$4.50).

Car & Motorcycle From Ciudad Victoria, you can go southeast to Tampico for the Huasteca region or the Gulf Coast, or take one of the steep roads heading west ascending the Sierra Madre Oriental. For San Luis Potosí, take highway 101 southwest – an incredibly scenic route. For Mexico City, highway 85 south, via Ciudad Mante and Ciudad Valles, is the most direct.

Getting Around

From the bus station to the center of town, take a Ruta 25 bus, which goes down Bravo, three blocks north of Plaza Hidalgo (US$0.35). In the other direction, microbuses labeled 'Palmas' depart from Boulevard Balboa at the bridge over the Río San Marcos. Taxis charge around US$2.50 for the same trip.

SOUTH OF CIUDAD VICTORIA
Ciudad Mante
• pop 81,100 • elev 190m

Ciudad Mante is a center for processing the sugarcane and cotton grown in the area. You can cool off at the *balnearios* La Aguja and El Nacimiento, outside town. It's a quiet, clean place to stop for a night, with some cheap to mid-range hotels, motels and restaurants.

Reserva de la Biósfera El Cielo

A reserve of 1440 sq km, El Cielo covers a range of altitudes on the slopes of the Sierra, and is a transition zone between tropical, semi-desert and temperate ecosystems. Declared an international biosphere reserve by the UN in 1987, it marks the northern limit for quite a number of tropical species of plant and animal. Forty varieties of orchids can be found in the reserve, mostly within the cloud forest zone between 800 and 1400m. The reserve is also habitat to half the bird species in Mexico and 40 kinds of bats.

Though currently you don't need a permit to enter the reserve, the Tamaulipas Secretaría de Desarrollo Urbano y Ecología (☎ 1-312-60-18) in Ciudad Victoria recommends you register with them beforehand. The office, on the ninth floor of the Torre del Gobierno (the tall glass tower at the southeast end of town), is open 9 am to 3.30 pm and 6.30 to 8.30 pm Monday to Friday. They can tell you about conditions in the reserve and give you the phone numbers of local guides. The Casa de Piedra (see Places to Stay) can also arrange guides and transport to the reserve and has a shop with food and hiking supplies.

Several trails take off from the village of Gómez Farías, which is within the reserve,

11km up a side road off highway 85, about 100km south of Ciudad Victoria and 40km north of Ciudad Mante. One strenuous trail climbs 5km to the village of Alta Cima, the starting point for hikes into the cloud forest. Guides can be hired in Gómez Farías and Alta Cima.

Places to Stay There are two lodging options in Gómez Farías. The basic *Cabañas Campestre* has seven rooms at US$10 per person. The *Casa de Piedra* (☎ 1-316-69-41 *in Ciudad Victoria, fameco@prodigy.net.mx)* offers four rooms with two to four beds, fan and private bath. The price of US$26 for one person, US$32 for two, includes breakfast and possibly a ride from the highway turnoff (phone ☎ 1-232-43-89 beforehand).

Alternatively, you could stay at the *Canindo Research Station* within the cloud forest. Cabins there can accommodate 36 people at US$10 per person; make arrangements through the Secretaría de Desarrollo Urbano y Ecología (☎ 1-312-60-18) in Ciudad Victoria.

Getting There & Away From Ciudad Mante, buses go directly to Gómez Farías, or you can get there from Ciudad Victoria by taking a Ciudad Mante bus and getting off at Sabinas, then catching a local bus. You may be able to find someone in Gómez Farías to take you into the cloud forest by 4WD vehicle; it costs about US$140 for up to 10 passengers.

Nuevo León

It was the search for silver (not found) and slaves, and missionaries' desire to proselytize, that first brought the Spanish to this sparsely inhabited region. In 1579, Luis de Carvajal was commissioned to found Nuevo León. He set up abortive settlements in Monterrey and Monclova, and it was not until 1596 and 1644 respectively that the Spanish established themselves permanently at those sites, with the help of native Mexicans from Tlaxcala and other areas to the south. In the late 17th century,

Nuevo León and Coahuila were the starting points for Spanish expansion into Texas.

Slowly, ranching became viable around the small new towns, despite raids by hostile Chichimecs from the north that continued into the 18th century. Nuevo León had an estimated 1.5 million sheep by 1710.

As the 19th century progressed and the railways arrived, ranching continued to expand and industry developed, especially in Monterrey. By 1900, Nuevo León had 328,000 inhabitants.

MONTERREY
• pop 1,089,100 • elev 538m ☎ changing

Monterrey, capital of Nuevo León, is Mexico's second-biggest industrial center and third-biggest city (its metropolitan area has close to 3 million residents). It's perhaps the most Americanized city in Mexico, and parts of it, with leafy suburbs, 7-Eleven convenience stores and giant air-conditioned malls, look just like suburbs in Texas or California. Industry and commerce drive Monterrey, and its pursuit of profit also seems more American than Mexican.

The city's historic center was ambitiously made over in the mid-1980s, with a series of linked plazas and gardens, a pedestrian precinct on the west side and a historical zone on the east. Jagged mountains, including the distinctive saddle-shaped Cerro de la Silla (1288m), make a dramatic backdrop for the city, and provide opportunities for some worthwhile side trips; the surrounding countryside offers caves, canyons, lakes and waterfalls.

Most travelers bypass Monterrey in their haste to get to other parts of Mexico, but the city truly is a fascinating mixture of old and new, industry and style, tradition and efficiency. There's a lot to see here, particularly if you like modern art and architecture. For budget travelers, Monterrey's disadvantage is that lodging is expensive and the cheaper places are mainly in a seedy area outside the city center. The smog and the weather can be bad, too, but you are just as likely to find fresh breezes, blue skies and clear, dry desert air.

NORTHEAST MEXICO

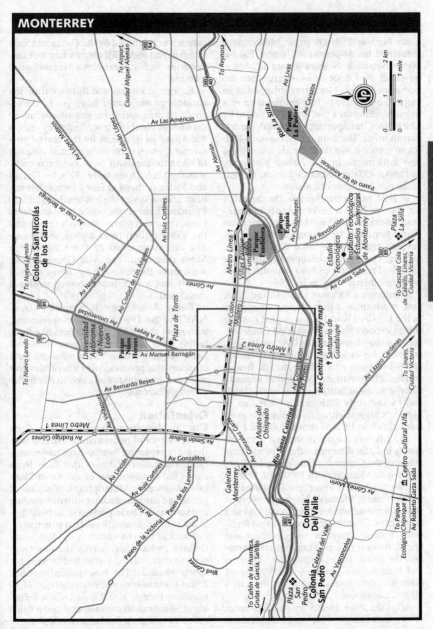

MONTERREY

To Airport,
Ciudad Miguel Alemán

To Reynosa

Av Las Américas

Av Galván López

Parque
La Pastora

Río La Silla

Av Livas

Av Cavazos

Colonia San Nicolás
de los Garza

Av Díaz de Berriga

Av Ruiz Cortines

Av Alemán

Paseo de las Américas

To Nuevo Laredo

Av Nogalar Sur

Av Ciudad de Los Ángeles

Av Gómez

Metro Línea 1

Villas Parque
Fundidora

Parque
Fundidora

Parque
España

Av Chapultepec

Av Revolución

Instituto Tecnológico
y Estudios Superiores
de Monterrey

Plaza
La Silla

To Nuevo Laredo

Universidad
Autónoma
de Nuevo León

Av Universidad

Av A Reyes

Plaza
de Toros

Av Manuel Barragán

Av Colón

Av Madero

Estadio
Tecnológico

Av Garza Sada

To Cascada Cola
de Caballo, Linares,
Ciudad Victoria

Parque
Niños
Héroes

Metro Línea 2

Santuario de
Guadalupe

see Central Monterrey map

Av Lázaro Cárdenas

To Linares,
Ciudad Victoria

Av Bernardo Reyes

Av Velázquez

Metro Línea 1

To Rodrigo Gómez

Av Simón Bolívar

Museo del
Obispado

Av Constitución

Av Pino

Av Lincoln

Av Gonzalitos

Río Santa Catarina

Av Gómez Morín

Av Ruiz Cortines

Galerías
Monterrey

Centro Cultural Alfa

To Parque
Chipinque

Av Roberto Garza Sada

Av Frías

Paseo de los Leones

Paseo de la Victoria

Blvd Gómez

Colonia
Del Valle

To Cañón de la Huasteca,
Grutas de García, Saltillo

Plaza
San
Pedro

Colonia
San Pedro

Calzada del Valle

Av Vasconcelos

To Ecológico Chipinque

History

After several unsuccessful attempts to found a city here, in 1596 Diego de Montemayor christened his 34-person settlement Ciudad Metropolitana de Nuestra Señora de Monterrey, after the Conde de Monterrey, then the viceroy of Mexico. Monterrey struggled as an outpost, but it slowly became the core of a sheep-ranching area that was often raided by Chichimecs. Its importance grew with the colonization of Tamaulipas in the mid-18th century, since it was on the trade route to the new settlements. In 1777, when Monterrey had about 4000 inhabitants, it became the seat of the new bishopric of Linares.

In 1824, Monterrey became the capital of the state of Nuevo León in newly independent Mexico. In the Mexican-American War, Monterrey was occupied by Zachary Taylor's troops after three days of fierce fighting. The city was occupied again in the 1860s by French troops, who were driven out by Benito Juárez's forces in 1866.

Monterrey's location close to the USA gave it advantages in trade and smuggling: In the US Civil War it was a staging post for cotton exports by the blockaded Confederates. Railway lines came in 1882, and tax exemptions for industry during the Porfiriato (1876-1910) attracted Mexican, US, British and French investment. Monterrey began to emerge as an industrial center in the 1860s and by the early 20th century was one of Mexico's biggest cities; its population grew from 27,000 in 1853 to about 80,000 in 1910.

The city was the site of the first heavy industry in Latin America – the iron and steel works of the Compañía Fundidora de Fierro y Acero de Monterrey. In 1890, José Schneider founded the Cervecería Cuauhtémoc, which became Mexico's biggest brewery as well as a manufacturer of glass, cartons and bottle caps. Other industries produced furniture, clothes, cigarettes, soap, cement and bricks. Two intermarried families, the Garzas and the Sadas, came to dominate business and built a huge empire – the Monterrey Group – that owned many of the city's biggest companies.

After the 1940s, electricity enabled scores of new industries to develop. Little planning went into the city's growth, and the environment was generally ignored. However, education was promoted by the Garza and Sada families, and today Monterrey has four universities and a prestigious technological institute.

Economic success and distance from the national power center have given Monterrey's citizens, called *regiomontanos*, an independent point of view. Monterrey resents 'meddling' in its affairs by the central government, which in turn often accuses the city of being too capitalist or, worse, too friendly with the USA. In the early 1970s, the Garzas and Sadas, perhaps in fear of wholesale nationalization under the left-leaning Mexican President Echeverría, broke the Monterrey Group into two parts – the Alfa Group and the VISA Group (now known as Femsa). The economic crisis of the 1980s struck Monterrey hard. The Alfa Group almost went broke, the city government ran short of money, and a government-owned steel mill was closed.

Today Monterrey is profiting from NAFTA, the 1994 free-trade agreement, with more than 450 US and Canadian firms basing their regional operations in Nuevo León's capital. It remains the pillar of a state economy that produces over 9% of Mexico's manufactured goods and close to 6% of the country's exports.

Orientation

Central Monterrey focuses on the `Zona Rosa, an area of pedestrianized streets with the more expensive hotels, shops and restaurants. The eastern edge of the Zona Rosa meets the southern end of the Gran Plaza (also known as Macroplaza), a series of plazas and gardens studded with monuments and surrounded by imposing public buildings, many of them strikingly modern structures.

South of the city center is the Río Santa Catarina, which cuts across the city from west to east – the dry riverbed is used for sports grounds. The bus station is about 2.5km northwest of the city center; most of the cheap lodging is in this part of town. Frequent buses run all over the city, and a light-rail subway system has been developed.

Streets in the center are on a grid pattern. The corner of Juárez and Aramberri, roughly halfway between the Zona Rosa and the bus station, is the center of town with regard to addresses. North of Aramberri, north-south streets have the suffix 'Norte' or 'Nte'; south of Aramberri, 'Sur.' West of Juárez, east-west streets have the suffix 'Poniente' or 'Pte'; east of Juárez, 'Oriente' or 'Ote.' Numbers get higher as they move away from the intersection.

Information

Tourist Offices Monterrey has a modern tourist office called Infotur (☎ 345-09-02, 800-832-22-00, 800-235-2438 in the USA), at Hidalgo 441 Ote, next door to the Hotel Colonial. The staff speak fluent English, are knowledgeable about Monterrey and the state of Nuevo León and have lots of leaflets and maps. They can also tell you about upcoming cultural events and entertainment in the city. The office is open 10 am to 5 pm Tuesday to Sunday.

Monterrey's official website (www.monterrey-mexico.com) has a great deal of useful information for visitors, including links to many museums and hotels.

Consulates The US consulate (☎ 345-21-20) is at Avenida Constitución 411 Pte. The UK, Canada, France, Germany, Spain and the Netherlands also have consulates in Monterrey; Infotur has their addresses.

Money Numerous city-center banks will change cash, though some do not handle traveler's checks. Most banks are open 9 am to 5 pm Monday to Friday and almost all have ATMs. Exchange houses are clustered along Ocampo between E Carranza and Escobedo.

Post & Communications The central post office is on Washington between Zaragoza and Zuazua, just north of the Gran Plaza. It's open 9 am to 7 pm Monday to Friday, 9 am to 1 pm Saturday.

La Tumba at Padre Mier 827 in the Barrio Antiguo offers computers connected to the Internet 1 to 9 pm Monday to Saturday

Beginning December 1, 2000, there will be no area code. The old code ☎ 8 will be added to the start of every local number (for example, the number 345-21-20 will become 8-345-21-20; if calling long distance, the number will be the same as the local number).

(US$3.25 per hour). In the Pasaje Tec, across from the entrance to the Instituto Tecnológico de Monterrey, is the Internet café Me Vuelvo a Morir, open 9 am to 9 pm Monday to Friday, 10 am to 9 pm Saturday (US$2.75 per hour).

Gran Plaza

A city block wide and a kilometer long, this great swath of urban open space is a controversial piece of redevelopment. Carved out in the 1980s by the demolition of several entire city blocks, many regard it as a grandiose monument to Monterrey's ambition. The once desolate space has been softened by greenery and offers well-planned vistas of the surrounding mountains. Enclosed by the best of the city's old and new architecture, the area provides respite from the urban bustle and helps manage traffic problems with underpasses and extensive underground parking lots.

Though the overall size of the Gran Plaza could have been overwhelming, it actually comprises a series of smaller spaces, interspersed with buildings, monuments, sculptures, fountains, trees and gardens – there are no vast expanses of unrelieved pavement. At the very southern end, nearest the Río Santa Catarina, the **Monumento Homenaje al Sol** is a tall sculpture on a traffic island that faces the **Palacio Municipal**, a modern building raised up on concrete legs.

The monument occupies the south side of **Plaza Zaragoza**, which itself comprises the southern third of the Gran Plaza. The semi-formal space is often busy with people walking through, having lunch or listening to music from the covered bandstand. Facing the southeast corner of Plaza Zaragoza is the **Museo de Arte Contemporáneo**

CENTRAL MONTERREY

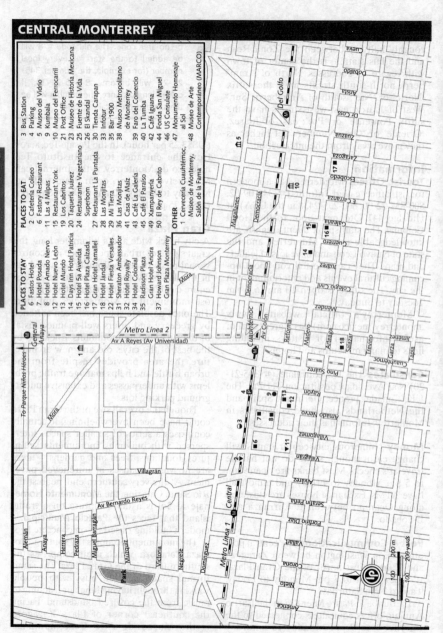

PLACES TO STAY
6   Fastos Hotel
7   Hotel Posada
8   Hotel Amado Nervo
12 Hotel Nuevo León
13 Hotel Mundo
14 Days Inn Hotel Patricia
15 Hotel 5a Avenida
16 Hotel Plaza Calzada
17 Gran Hotel Yamallel
18 Hotel Jandal
22 Hotel Fiesta Versalles
31 Sheraton Ambassador
32 Hotel Royalty
34 Hotel Colonial
35 Radisson Plaza
36 Gran Hotel Ancira
37 Howard Johnson
    Gran Plaza Monterrey

PLACES TO EAT
2   Cafetería Coliseo
6   Fastory Restaurant
11 Las 4 Milpas
15 Restaurant York
19 Los Cabritos
20 Taquería Juárez
24 Restaurante Vegetariano
    Superbom
27 Restaurant La Puntada
28 Las Monjitas
29 Mi Tierra
36 Las Monjitas
41 Casa de Maíz
43 Café La Galería
45 Café El Paraíso
49 Xampanyería
50 El Rey de Cabrito

OTHER
1   Cervecería Cuauhtémoc,
    Museo de Monterrey,
    Salón de la Fama
3   Bus Station
4   Parking
5   Museo del Vidrio
9   Kumbala
10 Museo del Ferrocarril
21 Post Office
23 Museo de Historia Mexicana
25 Fuente de la Vida
26 El Skandal
30 Tienda Carapan
33 Infotur
35 Bar 1900
38 Museo Metropolitano
    de Monterrey
39 Faro del Comercio
40 La Tumba
42 Café Iguana
44 Fonda San Miguel
46 US Consulate
47 Monumento Homenaje
    al Sol
48 Museo de Arte
    Contemporáneo (MARCO)

CENTRAL MONTERREY

(MARCO), with its gigantic black dove sculpture by Mexico's Juan Soriano. MARCO has major exhibitions of work by Mexican and international artists. It's open 11 am to 7 pm Tuesday and Thursday to Saturday, 11 am to 9 pm Wednesday and Sunday (US$2, free on Wednesday).

Just north of MARCO is the baroque-façaded **cathedral** (called 'Catedral'), built between 1635 and 1770 – the south bell tower was not completed until 1899. Facing the cathedral, across the plaza, is the 19th-century Palacio Municipal, which now houses the **Museo Metropolitano de Monterrey**. This museum has several upstairs galleries featuring the work of contemporary painters and sculptors. It's open 8 am to 8 pm daily (free). North of the museum, new and old buildings flank the east end of **Calle Morelos**, a bustling pedestrian mall.

The centerpiece of Plaza Zaragoza is the stunning **Faro del Comercio** (Beacon of Commerce), a tall, flat, orange concrete slab designed by the architect Luis Barragán in the love-it-or-hate-it-but-you-can't-ignore-it style. If you're lucky you'll see green laser beams from the top sweep over the city at night.

Across Padre Mier is the **Fuente de la Vida** (Fountain of Life) with Neptune riding a chariot. North of this, the modern **Teatro de la Ciudad** and **Congreso del Estado** buildings face each other from the east and west sides of the plaza. Farther north again, the **Biblioteca Central** (State Library) and the **Palacio de Justicia** (Courthouse) stand on either side of the **Parque Hundido** (Sunken Garden), a favorite spot for couples.

North again and down some steps, you come to the **Explanada de los Héroes** (Esplanade of the Heroes), also called the Plaza Cinco de Mayo, with statues of national heroes in each corner. It's the most formal and traditional of the spaces in the Gran Plaza and looks like a standard Plaza de Armas with the 1908 neoclassical **Palacio de Gobierno** on its north side. From the steps of the building you can look back down the length of the Gran Plaza to the south side of the river and up the hills beyond. Behind the Palacio de Gobierno, a small park faces the 1930s **post office** and federal government building, providing yet another architectural contrast.

Just east of the Explanada de los Héroes is yet another wide open space, the **Plaza 400 Años**. Graced with fountains and pools, it serves as a grand entryway to the **Museo de Historia Mexicana**, a 1994 addition to the Gran Plaza. The museum presents an exhaustive chronological survey of Mexican history, dividing its vast subject matter into four periods – Ancient Mexico, the Colonial Era, the 19th Century and Modern Mexico – plus a fifth area on rainforest ecology. Creatively designed and displayed, it appeals to kids and adults, with interactive exhibits on the Maya calendar and pre-Hispanic math, a number of touch-screen computer terminals, and excellent models of all the major pre-Conquest cities. There are superb examples of sacred art of the colonial period. The museum is open 11 am to 7 pm Tuesday to Thursday, 11 am to 8 pm Friday to Sunday (free Tuesday, US$1 Wednesday to Saturday, US$0.50 Sunday). All explanations are in Spanish only but English tours can be arranged by phoning ☎ 345-98-98.

Bordering the Plaza 400 Años to the south is the Paseo Santa Lucia, a canal-side promenade with restaurants that is popular with weekend strollers.

Zona Rosa

This is the area of top hotels, restaurants and shops just west of Plaza Zaragoza. It's bounded roughly by Morelos to the north, Zaragoza to the east, Hidalgo to the south, and E Carranza to the west. Two of the streets are pedestrian-only and it's usually a bustling place where it's a pleasure to walk around, window-shop or find somewhere to eat or drink.

Barrio Antiguo

This is the old neighborhood, east of the Gran Plaza, and it's one of the few parts of Monterrey where you can admire traditional architecture. In recent years it has become a rather trendy area of art galleries, antique shops and cafés. Friday and Saturday nights, streets are closed to traffic and it becomes a major party zone.

Alameda

Occupying eight city blocks a kilometer northwest of the city center, this lovely park offers fountains, paths and tall shade trees in pleasant contrast to the surrounding chaos. It's a venue for occasional Sunday morning children's concerts.

Cervecería Cuauhtémoc

This complex, at Avenida Alfonso Reyes 2202 (also called Avenida Universidad), is in the gardens of the old Cuauhtémoc brewery. Brought to you by the maker of Bohemia, Carta Blanca and Tecate beer, it now features an art gallery, a baseball hall of fame, brewery tours and . . . free beer!

The art gallery, the **Museo de Monterrey**, in a converted industrial building, displays items from its permanent collection of some 1500 works of Latin American art. The fourth floor of the museum now houses the Mediateca, an arts research center, consisting of a library with a well-organized collection of art books and periodicals, and a computer facility for viewing CD-ROMs and browsing Internet links to art museums around the world. The museum is open 11 am to 8 pm Tuesday to Sunday (free).

The **Salon de la Fama** (Hall of Fame) has photos, memorabilia, and facts and figures on Mexican baseball. It features many Mexican players who made the big leagues in the USA, and some Americans whose careers made more headway south of the border. It's open 9.30 am to 5.30 pm Tuesday to Friday, 10.30 am to 6 pm Saturday and Sunday (free).

Brewery tours are given hourly from 9.30 am to 4.30 pm Monday to Friday, 9.30 am to 1.30 pm Saturday (free). Tours in English are given in the morning by prior reservation (☎ 328-53-55). There is a very pleasant little garden facing the art gallery, a nice place to sit even if you don't partake of the free mug of Carta Blanca. There's also a café on the museum's ground level in a lovely space enclosed by the original brick factory walls and crowned by a skylight. Gourmet lunches are US$5.25 including beer. The complex is a kilometer north of the bus station.

Monterrey's Faro del Comercio and cathedral

Museo del Ferrocarril

The railroad museum, on Avenida Colón a few blocks west of Del Golfo metro station, is housed in the old Estación del Golfo, which operated as a station between the 1890s and 1930, linking northern Mexico with the Gulf port of Tampico. Train buffs will enjoy the displays of old signals and timetables, equipment for laying track and old photos of railroad workmen. All explanations are in Spanish. The east side of the building functions as the Casa de la Cultura with temporary art exhibits, children's workshops, concerts and film series. The museum is open 1 to 6 pm Monday, 10 am to 6 pm Tuesday to Saturday (free).

NORTHEAST MEXICO

SCOTT DOGGETT

Museo del Vidrio

This museum, at the corner of Zaragoza and Magallanes two blocks north of Avenida Colón, on the grounds of the Vitro factory and corporate offices, focuses on the history, manufacture and artistic use of glass in Mexico. Among the interesting exhibits are a set of 18th-century *pulque* glasses and a reproduction of a 19th-century stained-glass workshop. Another gallery for temporary exhibits of glass art is in a restored warehouse opposite the plant where beer and Coke bottles are made; samples of fine glasswork are sold in the gallery shop. It's open 9 am to 6 pm Friday to Wednesday (free). Call ahead to schedule a tour in English (☎ 329-10-00 ext 1136).

Parque Niños Héroes

A botanical garden, an aviary, a lake and several museums are among the recreational and cultural facilities in this large park. Most impressive is the permanent collection of painting and sculpture at **Pinacoteca de Nuevo León**, showing the outstanding work of the state's artists since colonial times. These galleries are open 10 am to 6 pm Tuesday to Sunday.

Kids will enjoy the **Museo de la Fauna y Ciencias Naturales**, featuring life-sized dioramas of stuffed wildlife in its 'natural' habitats, from Saharan Africa to the Arctic. It's open 10 am to 6.30 pm Tuesday to Sunday (US$0.50). There's a US$0.30 entry fee to the park itself; enter from Avenida Alfonso Reyes about 5km north of the city center.

Museo del Obispado

The former bishop's *obispado* (palace), on a hill 2.5km west of the Zona Rosa along Matamoros, gives fine views of the city and surrounding mountains, smog permitting. Initiated in 1787 on the orders of the bishop of Linares (who did not live to see its completion three years later), the building has an admirable Churrigueresque façade. It served as a fort during the US attack on Monterrey in 1846, and weathered the French intervention of the 1860s. Now it's a small historical museum with various colonial and revolutionary relics. It's open 10 am to 5 pm Tuesday to Sunday (US$1).

Instituto Tecnológico y de Estudios Superiores de Monterrey (ITESM)

The 'Tec,' in the southeast of the city on Avenida Garza Sada, is one of Mexico's best-regarded higher-education institutes. Founded in 1943 by a group of regiomontano industrialists, the Monterrey campus was the first of what was to become a nationwide university system. It has some surprising architecture, such as the Centro de Tecnología Avanzada para la Producción, which appears to have been sliced apart, leaving the two halves toppling away from each other. The Tec stadium, with a capacity for 30,000 spectators, hosts the Monterrey soccer club, one of the city's two top-flight teams (see Spectator Sports). Campus tours are given at 10 am and 4 pm Monday to Friday, departing from the Rectoría building (the one with the mural) near the entrance (☎ 328-40-80). English tours can be arranged with at least three days notice.

Colonia del Valle

Colonia del Valle, 6km southwest of the city center, is one of Monterrey's most exclusive suburbs, with big houses on lovely tree-lined streets. A mall and other areas of classy shops and restaurants are in the streets off Calzada del Valle. The wealthiest people live several kilometers farther south, high up on the slopes of the Meseta de Chipinque (see below).

Parque Ecológico Chipinque

Several kilometers up the hill from Colonia del Valle, this park is the most accessible section of the Parque Nacional Cumbres de Monterrey, offering city dwellers ample opportunities for hiking, mountain biking and bird watching. Trails are well maintained, and it doesn't take long to get into some pretty dense pine and oak forest, though much of the area was destroyed in an April 1998 blaze. From the entrance, a 7km drive brings you to the Meseta de Chipinque where there's a luxury hotel and access to the park's highest peak, Copete de las Águilas (2200m). Trail maps and snacks are available at the visitor's center, near the park entrance.

The park is open 6 am to 9.30 pm daily. Admission is US$0.50 for pedestrians, US$1 for cyclists (required to display an identification badge, which can be purchased at the entrance). Parking at the visitor's center is US$1.25; to drive up to the *meseta*, there's a charge of US$3.75 per car.

To get to Chipinque, take Avenida Constitución west (keep right), and turn south at Avenida Morín. By public transport, take a ruta 130 bus (from Ramón and Juárez) to 'Los Tubos,' and catch a taxi from there.

Centro Cultural Alfa

This cultural complex (☎ 347-11-28), Roberto Garza Sada 1000, in Colonia del Valle off Gómez Morín, is sponsored by the Alfa industrial group. It's well worth the trip. The main building, which looks like a water tank tipping over, has floors devoted to computers, astronomy, physics, Mexican antiquities and temporary exhibitions. The scientific displays have lots of educational hands-on exhibits, and everything is well lit and carefully labeled (in Spanish only). In the center of the building is the planetarium and an Omnimax cinema.

Outside is the Jardín Prehispánico, with replicas of some of the great Mexican archaeological finds. **El Universo**, a superb glass mural, was created by Rufino Tamayo for the headquarters of the Alfa group, but was considered so beautiful that a special building was constructed to display it to a wider audience. It's in the Pabellón building, which resembles a covered wagon.

The complex is open 3 to 9 pm Tuesday to Friday, 2 to 9 pm Saturday and noon to 9 pm Sunday (adults US$4.75, children US$3.75). Special buses go every hour from the Alameda, at the intersection of Washington and Villagrán (every half hour on Sunday); the last bus departs from the planetarium at 9 pm.

Organized Tours

Gray Line Tours (☎ 369-64-72) runs sightseeing excursions in English and Spanish. A basic morning city tour covers the Gran Plaza, Cervecería Cuauhtémoc and Museo del Vidrio (US$12). Tours outside the city include Centro Cultural Alfa, Grutas de García and Cascada Cola de Caballo (US$15 each). See Around Monterrey, later in this chapter, for more information on the latter two sites.

More economical, Troley Tours operates several pseudo trolley cars that make a loop around downtown every half hour with commentary in Spanish. These run 4 to 9 pm Tuesday to Sunday (US$0.50). You can hop on at Howard Johnson Gran Plaza Monterrey (see Places to Stay, below) or the Museo de Historia Mexicana at the Gran Plaza.

Special Events

Aniversario de Independencia – Monterrey's biggest celebrations are held on September 16, Mexico's independence day, with fireworks, free tequila and a big parade

Expo Monterrey – the annual trade and cultural fair happens in September, in the Parque Niños Héroes

Festival Cultural del Barrio Antiguo – in late November, this series of concerts, art expositions and literary conferences takes place in clubs and museums throughout Monterrey's old quarter

Nuestra Señora de Guadalupe – celebrations of the December 12 event begin as early as the last week of November. In the days leading up to the 12th, thousands of pilgrims head for the Santuario de Guadalupe, the pyramid-shaped structure south of the river. The festival is also celebrated in a big way in Abasolo, a village off the Monclova road.

Places to Stay

If you're willing to spend upward of US$50 a double, you'll find a wide range of decent hotels in Monterrey. Below that, quality is less consistent. Nearly all of the cheaper hotels, and some of the mid-range ones, are within a few blocks of the bus station, while the top-end places are in the Zona Rosa.

Places to Stay – Budget

Budget hotels in Monterrey fill up fast, especially on weekends. There is often a significant price increase for air-con. A room away from the noisy street is a plus.

NORTHEAST MEXICO

NORTHEAST MEXICO

Some of the best budget accommodations can be found on Amado Nervo, in the two blocks running south of the enormous bus station. The first place you come to is *Hotel Posada* (☎ 372-39-08, *Amado Nervo 1138*), which has neat single/double rooms with fans, TV and plenty of hot water for US$18/21, US$4 more with air-con. Several rooms on the upper floors have sweeping views, but front rooms can be terribly noisy.

On the next corner, *Hotel Amado Nervo* (☎ 375-46-32, *Amado Nervo 1110*) has some good rooms with TV from US$14/20, more for remodeled units. Only double rooms have air-con. Around the corner, *Hotel Mundo* (☎ 374-68-50, *Reforma 736 Pte*) is the best value around if you can stand the area. It may not be much to look at from the outside but its rooms are spacious, well maintained and quite comfortable. Rates are US$18 for one or two people, US$24 with air-con. The only drawback is there's no hotel parking lot.

Not as nice as the Mundo but all right all the same is *Hotel Nuevo León* (☎ 374-19-00, *Amado Nervo 1007*). Large enough to include lounge furniture, its rooms are in good shape at US$10.50/16, US$21/29 with air-con and TV. The hotel features an elevator and a parking garage.

Monterrey's cheapest accommodations are at *Villas Parque Fundidora* (☎ 355-73-70, *Madero 3500 Ote*), a youth hostel designed for large student groups but open to individual travelers. East of the center beside the rusting smokestacks of the old foundry (closed in 1986), the squat, white building features several air-conditioned dormitory rooms, the largest of which has 36 bunk beds (and one TV). A pair of large, clean communal bathrooms serves up to 65 guests. The price of US$7.25 per person includes breakfast. You must call ahead during office hours to reserve: 8.30 am to 2 pm and 4 to 7 pm Monday to Friday, 9 am to 1 pm Saturday. To get there, take a Ruta 2 bus up Madero, and tell the driver to let you off at 'Parque Acero.'

Places to Stay – Mid-Range

The mid-range in Monterrey starts at around US$35 for a double, though the places below US$40 are not discernibly better than their low-budget counterparts.

Bus Station Area Rooms at *Hotel Jandal* (☎ 372-31-72, *Cuauhtémoc 825 Nte*), on the corner of Salazar, were probably luxurious at one time but the stained carpets and cigarette burns show they haven't been kept up. Prices have, though, at US$36 for one or two people. *Hotel 5a Avenida* – called *quinta* Avenida – (☎ 375-65-65, *Madero 243 Ote*), at Galeana, is even shabbier but less costly, with singles/doubles from US$31/32. Downstairs is Restaurant York, offering a buffet breakfast.

For a few dollars more, *Days Inn Hotel Patricia* (☎ 375-07-50, *Madero 123 Ote*), between Juárez and Guerrero, is a quantum leap in comfort. The hotel has a lobby-restaurant, and modern, air-conditioned rooms for US$39/42. Similar in style but more expensive is *Hotel Plaza Calzada* (☎ 375-77-00, *Madero 250 Ote*), across the street from the 5a Avenida. It, too, has a lobby-restaurant, as well as fax and laundry services. Standard rooms with plush carpeting, big comfortable beds and variable air-con cost US$48/54. The parking lot entrance is on Galeana. A few blocks east along Madero is the towering *Gran Hotel Yamallel* (☎ 375-35-00, *Zaragoza 912 Nte*). Modern in style, it offers a parking garage, a restaurant, satellite TV and a view over the city from the upper floors. But both singles and doubles are rather small and worn for US$40 (less on weekends).

The *Fastos Hotel* (☎ 372-32-50, *Avenida Colón 956 Pte*), opposite the bus station via the overpass, is classy and comfortable, in contrast to the surrounding area. Elegant, air-conditioned rooms, each featuring a pair of large, firm beds, cost US$51.

City Center Eight blocks west of the Gran Plaza and just south of the Alameda, the friendly *Hotel Fiesta Versalles* (☎ 340-22-81, *Ramón 360 Pte*) may be the best value in central Monterrey. At US$47 (single or double), its air-conditioned rooms are spacious and attractively furnished. There's a café and a travel agency downstairs, and a parking lot across the street. Even more central, **Hotel Colonial** (☎ 343-67-91, Hidalgo 475 Ote), in the Zona Rosa, is a tempting splurge, but its rooms are not as large or fancy as you'd expect for US$59.

Places to Stay – Top End

Downtown Monterrey has plenty of places for over US$60. They mostly cater to business travelers and may give discounts on weekends. At all of them you can expect restaurants and bars, and carpeted rooms with air-con, heater, TV and phone. Prices listed in this section are the same for singles or doubles.

Hotel Royalty (☎ 340-28-00, Hidalgo 402 Ote), at E Carranza, offers large, comfortable rooms, some with views of the Gran Plaza, for US$69. A 'gentleman's spa' on the lower level features masseurs, a workout room and a barber shop. Across the street is the **Sheraton Ambassador** (☎ 380-70-00, Hidalgo 310 Ote), one of Monterrey's premier luxury hotels, with 239 rooms and suites from US$186 (US$129 Friday and Saturday).

Howard Johnson Gran Plaza Monterrey (☎ 380-60-00, 800-832-40-00, Morelos 574 Ote), fronting the Plaza Zaragoza, is one of the more popular top-end places. Formerly the Hotel Monterrey, it's been remodeled as a business hotel with an office center and non-smoking floors. Its 198 rooms, many with views of the Gran Plaza, cost US$107 with all the modern conveniences, including a direct line to Domino's pizza and a microwave oven for heating up your order.

For atmosphere, nothing rivals the **Radisson Plaza Gran Hotel Ancira** (☎ 150-70-00, 800-830-60-00, Ocampo 443 Ote), on the corner of Escobedo and Plaza Hidalgo. It's been around since 1912, and it's said that Pancho Villa once rode into the lobby, which now has shops, a piano player, a restaurant and hovering waitstaff. Big rooms and plenty of old-fashioned elegance go for US$219 (US$100 less on Friday and Saturday).

Places to Eat

Bus Station Area The all-night **Fastory Restaurant**, in the Fastos Hotel on Avenida Colón, offers Mexican food and coffee shop standards in a bland but reassuring setting. Spaghetti bolognese (no trimmings) costs US$3, enchiladas US$3.75 and breakfasts up to US$5. Across Avenida Colón is the more reasonably priced and personable **Cafetería Coliseo**, also open 24 hours, with fresh juices and *licuados* (fruit drinks), sandwiches, and a variety of homemade *guisados* (stews).

City Center Every block of the Zona Rosa seems to have at least one restaurant or café. The ever-popular **Restaurant La Puntada** (Hidalgo 123 Ote) has a long menu of Mexican items with nothing above US$3 (including the T-bone steak!). Everything is done with exemplary style and attention to quality, and portions are ample. La Puntada is closed Sunday. **Mi Tierra**, on Morelos a half-block west of E Carranza, serves up tasty tacos and quesadillas (five for US$3). For good international fare in a bizarre setting, try **Las Monjitas** on Escobedo just above Plaza Hidalgo, where the waitresses are dressed as nuns. Generous entrees go for US$4 to US$5. There's another branch at the corner of Morelos and Galeana.

Vegetarians will find a haven at **Restaurante Vegetariano Superbom**, upstairs at the corner of Padre Mier and Galeana. Open 8 am to 5 pm Sunday to Friday, it does an excellent buffet lunch for US$4.25.

A few blocks north of the center, **Taquería Juárez** (Galeana 123 Nte), at Aramberri, is a veritable *antojito* factory where you can watch your *flautas*, tacos and enchiladas being prepared by at least 10 white-capped women behind a long window. An order of five items, combined according to your preference, is served with guacamole and salad for US$1.75. It's closed Wednesday.

Barrio Antiguo In the old quarter, **Café El Paraíso** and **Café La Galería**, both on Morelos, offer art, atmosphere and espresso. **Casa de Maíz** (Abasolo 870), between Montemayor and Dr Coss, prepares a variety of corn-based snacks from southern Mexico, including *memelas*, *tlacoyos* and *molotes*, for less than US$4 each. All are creatively presented and served in healthy portions. Be

Norteño Cuisine

Blending Spanish and indigenous influences in ingredients and cooking methods, Mexico's cuisine ranks high on the lists of food lovers worldwide. But in the north, where the pre-Hispanic societies were more nomadic than their agriculturally based Aztec and Mayan counterparts to the south, dishes are less complex, still reflecting the habits of a post-conquest people in a dry, sparsely populated region.

Goat dishes rule in Monterrey and throughout northeast Mexico, owing to the animal's ability to thrive in this arid desert area. Restaurants throughout northeast Mexico with names like La Principal and Los Pastores use their windows to display *cabrito* – whole young goats split open, flattened on racks and roasted over coals for several hours.

Every part of the animal is eaten. You can order leg (*pierna*), breast (*pecho*), shoulder (*paleta*) or *riñonada*, a section of the lower back that is considered the best – crisp on the outside, tender and juicy as spring lamb on the inside. Even the head (*cabeza*) is relished, particularly for the tongue, though some may be unnerved by the sight of a baby goat's head sitting on a plate next to a pile of salad. Other goat variations include *machitos*, goat liver wrapped in tripe, and *fritada*, a sort of goat's blood broth – thick like gravy and not for everyone.

Steak, too, is good and very reasonable in Monterrey – a big, tender T-bone can cost as little as US$5. Beef is also eaten as *fajitas*, grilled strips of marinated skirt steak, served with flour tortillas and salsas and often sold by the kilo. *Carne machacado* is another northern specialty, a kind of beef jerky, salted, dried and pounded (*machacado*) until thin enough to shred. It is customarily scrambled with eggs, tomatoes and chilies.

Vegetarians shouldn't completely lose hope in Monterrey, however – the thick corn cakes known as *gorditas* may be stuffed with a variety of meatless fillings, such as *nopales* (chopped cactus paddles), beans and white cheese. And *glorias* from Linares are wonderful – delicious sweets made with burned milk, sugar and ground pecans.

Perhaps the premier place in Monterrey to sample cabrito is *El Rey de Cabrito* (Avenida Constitución 817 Ote), a vast dining hall at the southern edge of the Barrio Antiguo near MARCO. Your cabrito (US$9) arrives at the table still sizzling on a bed of onions, with a large salad and tortillas. Similar but less expensive restaurants specializing in cabrito include *Las 4 Milpas* (Madero 911), at Villagrán near the bus station, and *Los Cabritos* (Aramberri 1010 Pte) near the Alameda.

---

sure to order a pitcher of refreshing *agua de fruta*. **Xampanyería (Dr Coss 1219)**, across the street from MARCO, is a stylish Spanish *tapas* bar, with a courtyard dining room, comfortable lounge areas and Flamenco dancers. The varied menu, ranging from US$2.75 to US$6, includes meat and vegetable options. Catering to the late-night crowd, Xampanyería is open until 2 am Tuesday to Saturday nights.

Entertainment

Monterrey has numerous cinemas and an active cultural life including concerts, theater and art exhibitions. The tourist office can tell you what's on, and posters listing events are placed in strategic spots around town.

Monterrey's affluent younger set supports an active nightlife. On weekend nights, the Barrio Antiguo is very much the center of action – join the club-hopping crowds along Padre Mier east of Dr Coss. To name but a few of the nightspots, the excellent coffeehouse **La Tumba** (Padre Mier 827 Ote) has continuous live folk music until late (US$4 cover); **Fonda San Miguel** (☎ 342-09-20, Morelos 924 Ote) is a throbbing club with a big stage, a good sound system and rock by popular bands Thursday to Saturday nights (US$5 cover); and **Café Iguana** (Montemayor 927 Sur), more a space than a room, features comfortable lounging areas inside and out, modern/ancient art and cutting-edge DJs.

Sedate in comparison, the Zona Rosa has **Bar 1900**, an elegant after-hours cabaret inside the Gran Hotel Ancira. For salsa and merengue dancing, check out **El Skandal** (☎ 342-85-23, Ocampo 436 Pte) near the Mercado Colón, with live music until dawn.

In the expensive southwestern suburbs there are more places, such as **Barroco** (☎ 378-12-77) and **Nuvo** (☎ 335-95-26) in the club district known as Centrito Valle in Colonia del Valle, and **San Pedro Antiguo** (☎ 338-01-02, Juárez 326) in Colonia San Pedro. For these places you should be elegantly dressed, bring plenty of cash for drinks and taxis, and not arrive before 10 or 11 pm.

Much less formal entertainment can be found at **Kumbala**, a 'ladies' bar' (for men and women) at the corner of Reforma and Rayón near the bus station, featuring hot norteño music nightly. It's not the trendiest place, but Tuesday night beers are two for US$1.

North of town in Colonia San Nicolás de los Garza, an unusual type of nightclub, **Far West Rodeo** (☎ 351-30-30), presents Western-style rodeos with musical accompaniment Thursday to Sunday evenings (US$4 cover).

Spectator Sports

During bullfight season, March to August, *corridas* are held 5 pm Sunday at the Plaza de Toros Lorenzo Garza (☎ 374-05-05), Alfonso Reyes 2401 Nte, in Colonia del Prado. The professional soccer season is from August to May. Games are played Saturday at 5 pm at either the Estadio Tecnológico (☎ 328-40-57), at the Instituto Tecnológico de Monterrey, home of the Monterrey club (nicknamed the Pandilla Rayada, 'Striped Gang'), or the Estadio Universitario (☎ 376-05-24), home of the Tigres (Universidad de Nuevo León).

Monterrey's Sultanes baseball team plays from March to August at the Estadio de Béisbol Monterrey (☎ 351-80-22), in the Parque Niños Héroes near the university.

Check the newspaper *El Norte* for further details. There are occasional *charreadas* in which *charros* (cowboys) appear in all their finery to demonstrate their skills. Contact Infotur (see Tourist Offices, earlier in this section) for the current venues.

Shopping

Interesting shops with quality handicrafts from different parts of Mexico are Tienda Carápan, at Hidalgo 305 Ote, across the street from the Sheraton Ambassador, and Tikal, at Río Missouri 316 Pte in Colonia del Valle. There are no bargains, but some items are reasonably priced given their quality.

The two main downtown markets, Mercado Colón and Mercado Juárez, are big, bustling places selling everyday items. The wealthier regiomontanos prefer to shop at one of the big air-conditioned malls such as Plaza la Silla, south of town on Avenida Garza Sada; Plaza San Pedro, southwest in the suburb of San Pedro; or Galerías Monterrey, in the west of town at Avenida Insurgentes 2500.

Getting There & Away

Air There are direct flights, usually at least daily, to all major cities in Mexico and connections to just about anywhere else. Direct flights also go to Dallas, Houston, Los Angeles and San Antonio. Connections to other international destinations are best made through Houston. Airlines serving Monterrey are listed below, along with their nonstop destinations.

Aero California (☎ 345-97-00), Ocampo 145 Nte – Dallas, Guadalajara, Hermosillo, Mexico City

AeroMexico (☎ 343-55-60), Cuauhtémoc 818 Sur – Guadalajara, Houston, Mazatlán, Mexico City, Monclova, Puebla, Puerto Vallarta, Querétaro, San Antonio, Tijuana, Torreón and others

Aviacsa (☎ 369-07-79), Humberto Lobo 660, Colonia Del Valle – Cancún, Guadalajara, Houston, Las Vegas, Mexico City, Tijuana

Mexicana (☎ 356-66-11), Hidalgo 922 Pte – Cancún, Guadalajara, Mérida, Mexico City, Puebla, Tijuana, Veracruz, Villahermosa and others

TAESA (☎ 344-69-85), Hidalgo 480 Pte – Mérida, Mexico City

Bus Monterrey's huge bus station (Central de Autobuses) occupies three blocks along Avenida Colón between Villagrán and Rayón. It's a small city unto itself, with ticket desks strung out along its whole length, restaurants, pay phones, an exchange house and a 24-hour left-luggage service (US$0.25 an hour). The platform for local bus lines is accessed via a tunnel from Gate 5. First-class lines include Sendor (☎ 331-22-11), Ómnibus de México (☎ 374-07-16), and Futura (☎ 318-37-40); deluxe service is provided by Turistar (☎ 318-37-37). Autobuses Americanos is the line for Texas destinations. Daily service from Monterrey includes:

Aguascalientes – 588km, 8 hours; 2 deluxe (US$38), frequent 1st-class (US$29)

Chihuahua – 783km, 12 hours; 2 deluxe (US$51), 15 1st-class (US$42)

Ciudad Victoria – 285km, 4¼ hours; hourly 1st-class (US$14), frequent 2nd-class (US$12)

Durango – 573km, 10 hours; 3 deluxe (US$43), 11 1st-class (US$32), 2 2nd-class (US$29)

Guadalajara – 778km, 12 hours; 2 deluxe (US$55), 6 1st-class (US$41)

Matamoros – 324km, 4½ hours; frequent 1st-class (US$17)

Mexico City (Terminal Norte) – 934km, 11 hours; 6 deluxe (US$65), 11 1st-class (US$49)

Nuevo Laredo – 224km, 2½ hours; 4 deluxe (US$17), frequent 1st-class (US$13) and 2nd-class (US$10)

Reynosa – 220km, 3 hours; 1 deluxe (US$16), frequent 1st-class (US$12)

Saltillo – 85km, 1¾ hours; 2 deluxe (US$5.75), frequent 1st- and 2nd-class (US$4.25)

San Luis Potosí – 517km, 7 hours; 1 deluxe (US$32), 14 1st-class (US$24), frequent 2nd-class (US$21)

Tampico – 530km, 7¼ hours; 1 deluxe (US$37), frequent 1st-class (US$25)

Torreón – 316km, 4 hours; 4 deluxe (US$25), frequent 1st-class (US$19)

Zacatecas – 458km, 7 hours; 4 1st-class (US$22), frequent 2nd-class (US$19)

First-class buses also serve Acapulco, Ciudad Juárez, Mazatlán, Puebla and Querétaro, as well as US destinations including Laredo, San Antonio, Dallas and Houston.

Train Passenger train service to/from Monterrey has been suspended indefinitely.

Car There is enough to see within a day's drive of Monterrey to make car rental worth considering. Big companies such as Avis (☎ 344-65-80), Hertz (☎ 369-08-22) and Budget (☎ 369-08-19) have branches at the airport and in town as well. You may get a cheaper deal with one of the smaller local outfits like Alal (☎ 344-70-02) at Hidalgo 426 Ote, Execu-rent (☎ 343-65-55) at Escobedo 1013 Sur, or Sultana Internacional (☎ 344-63-63) at Escobedo 1011 Sur.

Getting Around
To/From the Airport Monterrey airport is off the road to Ciudad Alemán (highway 54), about 15km northeast of the city center. A taxi costs about US$13 from one of the downtown hotels, or via radio taxi service (☎ 333-51-64, 352-25-11). From the airport you can purchase a ticket for an authorized taxi at a booth in the arrivals area.

Metro Monterrey's Metro is a sensible alternative for getting around town. Its very simple plan consists of two lines: The elevated Línea 1 runs east to west in the north of the city, primarily going to outlying residential areas, and the underground Línea 2 runs north to south from near the Cuauhtémoc brewery (General Anaya station), past the bus station (Cuauhtémoc), and down to the Zona Rosa (Padre Mier) and the Gran Plaza (Zaragoza). The two lines cross at the intersection of Avenida Colón and Cuauhtémoc, where the giant overhead Cuauhtémoc Metro station is located.

The fare is US$0.30; tickets are dispensed from machines at the station entrances and can be purchased for multiple trips. Put in US$0.40 for both a Metro ticket and bus transfer token (single trip only). The Metro runs from 5 am to midnight daily. There are ATMs at many station entrances.

Bus Frequent buses (US$0.35) go to most everywhere in Monterrey, but often by circuitous routes. The following routes might be useful:

Bus station to center – No 18, from the corner of Amado Nervo and Reforma, goes down Juárez to the edge of the Zona Rosa – get off at Padre Mier, Hidalgo or Ocampo. For the Gran Plaza, the best place to get off is the corner of Juárez and 15 de Mayo.

Center to bus station – No 1 (blue) can be picked up on Juárez at Padre Mier. It takes you to Avenida Colón, within two blocks of the bus station.

Center to the Museo del Obispado – No 4 (red & black) goes west along Padre Mier. For the Obispado, get off when the bus turns left at Degollado, walk up the hill and turn left, then take the first right (a 10-minute walk).

Center to Del Valle/San Pedro – Ruta 131 (orange) from the corner of Juárez and Hidalgo goes to the big traffic circle in Colonia Del Valle, then heads west along Avenida Vasconcelos.

Center to Instituto Tecnológico – Take No 1 ('San Nicolás-Tecnológico') from the corner of Hidalgo and Pino Suárez.

Car There are large parking lots underneath the Gran Plaza, charging only US$2 for the whole night. Another lot, just east of the bus station off Avenida Colón, is US$7 for 24 hours.

AROUND MONTERREY

A number of sights near Monterrey are easily accessible in your own vehicle, and somewhat less accessible by bus.

Grutas de García

An illuminated, 2.5km route leads through 16 chambers in this cave system high in the Sierra El Fraile, reached by a 700m funicular railway ascent. The caves were formed about 50 million years ago and discovered by the parish priest in 1843. There are lots of stalactites and stalagmites, as well as petrified seashells.

This is a popular weekend outing, but the caves are open 10 am to 5 pm daily (US$3.25, including the funicular ride). On Saturday and Sunday mornings, Transportes Villa de García runs buses directly to the caves from local platforms 17-19 in the Monterrey bus station, returning in the afternoon. On other days the same line runs buses every 10 minutes to Villa de García, 9km from the caves (US$0.50); taxis go the rest of the way.

Alternatively, you could take a Gray Line tour (see Organized Tours in the Monterrey section). Driving from Monterrey, take highway 40 toward Saltillo. After 22km a sign points the way to the caves; turn right and go another 18km to the base of the funicular.

Cañón de la Huasteca

On the western edge of Monterrey, 16km from the center, this canyon is 300m deep and has some dramatic rock formations as well as cliffside drawings, evidence of its prehistoric inhabitants. There is a town at one end of it and a playground in the middle, somewhat reducing its attraction as a wilderness area. It's open 9 am to 6 pm daily (US$0.75 for a vehicle, US$0.10 per person). Reach the mouth of the canyon by taking a Ruta 206 bus, labeled 'Aurora,' from the corner of Ramón and Cuauhtémoc in Monterrey.

Cascada Cola de Caballo

'Horsetail Falls' is 6km up a rough road from El Cercado, a village 35km south of Monterrey by highway 85. The site has its share of hawkers and food stalls, but it's quite pretty and attracts a lot of picnickers. Horses and donkeys can be hired for the last kilometer to the falls (US$3.50). Farther up the valley, vegetation flourishes on the slopes of the sierra. Cola de Caballo can be visited 9 am to 7 pm daily (US$1.75). Autobuses Amarillos runs frequent buses to El Cercado from the Monterrey bus station (US$1.50); you'll have to catch a local bus from there to the falls. See Organized Tours in the Monterrey section for information on a sightseeing excursion.

The route to El Cercado passes close to the **Presa Rodrigo Gómez**, known as La Boca – an artificial lake where regiomontanos go swimming, sailing and waterskiing.

If you have your own vehicle, you can drive 33km up a rough road from El Cercado to the **Laguna de Sánchez**, a mountain lake surrounded by pine forests.

SOUTH OF MONTERREY

The excellent highway 40 (the main route toward Mexico City) goes southwest from Monterrey to Saltillo (85km), alongside the towering cliffs of the Sierra San José de los Nuncios.

Going southeast on highway 85 toward Ciudad Victoria, you follow the edge of the Sierra Madre Oriental through Mexico's most important citrus-growing area, centered on the towns of Allende, Montemorelos and Linares.

South of Montemorelos, the **Bioparque Estrella** has a large variety of large animals from Africa, Asia and the Americas, easily observed from the park's palapa-mobiles. The park is open 9 am to 7 pm Friday to Sunday, Tuesday to Sunday in July and August (US$4.75). To get there, take the turnoff for Rayones to the park entrance; turn left just past the 9km sign.

Sierra Madre Oriental

From Linares, scenic highway 58 heads west up into the Sierra Madre Oriental to the town of **Iturbide** (64km). Cut into the cliff beside the road is Los Altares, a giant bas-relief by Nuevo León sculptor Federico Cantú; it's dedicated to road builders. Beyond Iturbide, an 8km northward detour climbs another 1000m to **Galeana**, high on a wheat-producing plateau. The birthplace of the 1860s Republican general Mariano Escobedo, Galeana has a few hotels and one of the only *cenotes* outside of Yucatán, the Pozo del Gavilán. Nine kilometers north (turn right at the Río San Lucas junction) is a 15m-high natural bridge, the **Puente de Dios**, over which a local road passes. The best view is from the flat area to the left just before the bridge. The 3700m **Cerro El Potosí**, one of the state's highest peaks, is 35km west of Galeana. It's superb up on the sierra, with clear air, sparkling streams and unspoiled landscapes.

Highway 58 continues west down to the Altiplano Central, where it meets highway 57 between Saltillo and Matehuala.

Coahuila

The state of Coahuila is large, mostly desert and sparsely populated. The border crossings into Coahuila from Texas are less fre-

quently used than those farther southeast in Tamaulipas, because the road connections into Mexico and the USA are not as convenient for most travelers. Yet the remoteness and the harsh, arid landscapes will appeal to some and the state capital, Saltillo, is definitely worth a visit. For information about the west of the state, including the city of Torreón and the Zona del Silencio, see the Central North Mexico chapter.

History

The Spanish came to Coahuila in search of silver, slaves and souls. The region was explored by the Spanish as early as 1535 and the state capital of Saltillo was founded 42 years after, but incessant attacks by indigenous Chichimecs and, later, Apaches discouraged widespread settlement until the early 19th century. In 1800, Coahuila still had fewer than 7000 people. A few big landowners came to dominate the area. In southeast Coahuila, one holding of 890 sq km was bought from the crown for US$33 in 1731, and grew to 58,700 sq km by 1771, becoming the Marquesado de Aguayo, protected by a private cavalry. The population remained sparse, though; in 1800, Coahuila still had fewer than 7000 people.

After 1821, in the early years of independence, Coahuila and Texas were one state of the new Mexican republic, but Texas was lost after the Mexican-American War. As the 19th century progressed, ranching grew in importance, helped by the arrival of railways. By 1900, Coahuila had 297,000 inhabitants. In the 20th century, a steel foundry was established in Monclova, giving Coahuila a major industrial center.

BORDER CROSSINGS
Ciudad Acuña

• pop 79,200 • elev 1250m ☎ 8

Ciudad Acuña, across from the US town of Del Rio, is a fairly busy border crossing, open 24 hours a day. About 20km upriver, the **Presa de la Amistad** (Friendship Reservoir) is a joint Mexican-US water management project, offering good fishing and boating facilities. In October, the Fiesta de la Amistad is celebrated by both towns in a cross-border display of friendship. From Ciudad Acuña to Saltillo it's an eight-hour bus ride on good two-lane roads.

Piedras Negras
• **pop 114,400** • **elev 1450m** ☎ **8**

The border crossing between Piedras Negras and the US town of Eagle Pass is a major commercial route. Piedras Negras attracts quite a few short-term visitors from Texas. There's a crafts shop in the old San Bernardino mission that features work from all over Mexico, and the *casa de cultura* has occasional displays of Mexican art, music and dance.

Legend has it that Piedras Negras is the birthplace of the nacho – said to have been invented by Don Ignacio (Nacho) Anaya, a bar owner, to satisfy the snacking needs of his patrons from both sides of the border – and the town holds its International Nacho Festival in early October.

Highway 57 goes southeast to Allende, Sabinas and Monclova and continues to Saltillo, about eight hours away by bus. At the time of writing, trains connected the city with Saltillo.

MONCLOVA
• **pop 188,900** • **elev 1200m** ☎ **changing**

Not an attractive city, Monclova nevertheless offers a convenient stopover for those on their way to the Cuatrociénegas protected area. The city's Altos Hornos iron and steel works (AHMSA), founded in 1942, is one of the largest in Mexico.

Orientation & Information
The Monclova tourist office (☎ 634-43-00), on Madero opposite the fire station, just west of Boulevard Pape, is open 9 am to 1 pm and 2 to 6 pm Monday to Friday. Its helpful, English-speaking staff can give you excellent maps of Monclova and Coahuila's main destinations.

Things to See & Do
Monclova has a few fine 18th-century buildings, notably the Parroquia de Santiago on the Plaza Principal. The Museo Harold R Pape, the incongruous cylindrical structure

On December 1, 2000, the telephone area code is due to change to ☎ 8 from 86, with the digit 6 added to the start of every local number (for example, the number 33-09-10 will become 633-09-10).

beside the Boulevard Harold R Pape, functions primarily as a monument to the American industrialist who built up AHMSA, but also houses a small collection of pre-Hispanic objects, exhibits on the steel industry and works of modern art. It's open 10 am to 1 pm and 3 to 7 pm Tuesday to Sunday (free).

Getting There & Away
The main bus terminal is on Carranza, two blocks west of the plaza, with 1st- and 2nd-class service to/from Ciudad Acuña, Piedras Negras, Saltillo, Monterrey, Torreón and Mexico City. Second-class buses to Cuatrociénegas depart every two hours (1½ hours, US$3.50). There are several decent, inexpensive hotels on Privada Cuauhtémoc beside the station.

Highway 57 runs south to Saltillo, about 190km away, three hours by bus; 25km south of Monclova, highway 53 branches southeast to Monterrey (there are no fuel stations on this highway). Highway 30 heads west for 82km to Cuatrociénegas, then southwest to Torreón.

CUATROCIÉNEGAS
• **pop 9190** • **elev 750m** ☎ **changing**

In this valley in the middle of the Desierto Chihuahuense (Chihuahuan Desert), a network of underground springs forms rivers and numerous crystalline pools, creating the

In February 2000, the telephone area code was due to change to ☎ 8 from 869, with the digits 6 and 9 added to the start of every local number (for example, the number 6-02-99 would become 696-02-99).

conditions for a desert habitat of extraordinary biological diversity. The Galapagos-like isolation of the area also contributes to the existence of dozens of endemic species, including several kinds of turtles and eight kinds of fish. Because of the fragility of the ecosystem, in 1994 federal authorities created the Area de Protección de Flora y Fauna Cuatrociénegas, an 843 sq km protected area, but some of the pools have been set aside as recreational spots, ideal for swimming and snorkeling. Within the clear blue waters of these desert aquariums, you can observe a wide variety of small fish, as well as organisms called *estromatolitos*, formed by calcified algae colonies, which biologists believe are akin to the planet's first oxygen-producing forms of life.

Equally impressive is the area called Las Arenales, where glistening white sand dunes, formed by the crystallization of gypsum in the nearby Laguna Churince, create an eerily beautiful effect against a backdrop of six mountain ranges ringing the valley. The nearby town of Cuatrociénegas has several points of historical interest as well as a few hotels and restaurants, making it a good base for exploration of the reserve.

Visiting the Reserve

Access to the reserve is south of town along highway 30. Though it's possible to explore on your own, the desert tracks are minimally labeled. A good alternative is to arrange a tour through the Semarnap office (☎ 6-02-99, apffccienegas@infosel.net.mx), at Carranza 107 in town, half a block north of the plaza. Authorized guides will escort you through the reserve, but you'll need your own vehicle. The fee for a four-hour tour is US$9 to US$20, depending on the size of your group.

A visitor's center at Poza Las Tortugas, 7km south of town, is open 9 am to 6 pm daily, with maps and illustrated explanations, in Spanish, of the relevant natural phenomena. There are over 170 cerulean pools, or *pozas*, some up to 13m deep. **Poza La Becerra** (16km) is set up as a recreational facility with a diving pier, bathrooms and showers (US$1.50 admission). Swimming amid the

desert landscape is a marvelous experience. Though the water temperature can get as high as 32°C (90°F) in summer, cooler water spouts up from spring sources. Wearing suntan lotion is prohibited when swimming in the pozas.

You can also swim at the peaceful **Río Los Mezquites**, cooler than the pozas, with some shady palapas and picnic areas along the banks. Access to the river is 6.5km south of town: Turn left at the blue swimmer sign and go another 1.5km on an unpaved track. The entrance to Las Arenales is left of the Poza La Becerra; it's about a 4.5km drive out. Reaching heights of 13m, the white dunes are spotted with low desert brush, and you'll come across evidence of coyotes, rabbits, roadrunners and scorpions. Summer temperatures can be extreme, so bring plenty of water and avoid midday excursions.

Places to Stay & Eat

You may set up a tent within the protected area at Río Los Mezquites or Poza La Becerra. There are two decent hotels in Cuatrociénegas town. Located along the approach from Monclova, the *Motel Santa Fe* (☎ 6-04-25) is a good deal at US$18.50/23 for large, comfortable, single/double rooms, if you don't mind the racket made by the aircon unit. The central *Hotel Plaza* (☎ 6-00-66, Hidalgo 202), just east of the plaza, has beautiful colonial-style rooms for US$27/35. For breakfast, lunch and dinner, stop in at *El Doc (Zaragoza 103)*, on the east side of the plaza – it's about the only game in town.

Getting There & Away

The bus terminal occupies the south side of the plaza. There's frequent 2nd-class service to/from both Monclova (one hour, US$3.50) and Torreón (3½ hours, US$11). Five buses a day journey to each of the nearest border crossings at Ciudad Acuña and Piedras Negras.

SALTILLO

● pop 510,100 ● elev 1599m ☎ 8

Set high in the arid Sierra Madre Oriental, Saltillo was founded in 1577 and is the oldest city in the northeast. A pleasant place to

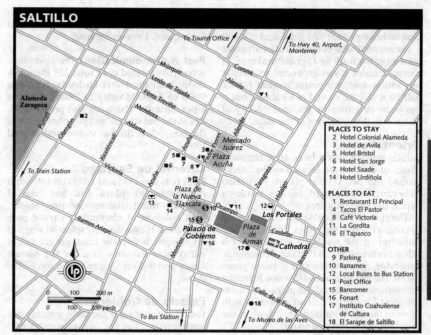

SALTILLO

To Tourist Office

To Hwy 40, Airport,
Monterrey

PLACES TO STAY
2 Hotel Colonial Alameda
3 Hotel de Avila
5 Hotel Bristol
6 Hotel San Jorge
7 Hotel Saade
14 Hotel Urdiñola

PLACES TO EAT
1 Restaurant El Principal
5 Tacos El Pastor
8 Café Victoria
11 La Gordita
16 El Tapanco

OTHER
9 Parking
10 Banamex
12 Local Buses to Bus Station
13 Post Office
15 Bancomer
16 Fonart
17 Instituto Coahuilense
de Cultura
18 El Sarape de Saltillo

Mercado
Juárez
Plaza
Acuña

Plaza de
la Nueva
Tlaxcala

Los Portales

Palacio de
Gobierno

Plaza
de
Armas

Cathedral

To Train Station

To Bus Station

To Museo de las Aves

NORTHEAST MEXICO

break a journey, it's on the main routes between the northeast border and central Mexico.

In the late-17th century, Saltillo was capital of an area that included Coahuila, Nuevo León, Tamaulipas, Texas and 'all the land to the north which reaches toward the pole.' These days it has a quiet central area with a small-town feel and some lovely colonial buildings, making it a popular destination though there are extensive new suburbs and major industries on the city's outskirts.

History
The first mission was established in 1591 as a center for the education and religious conversion of the local indigenous populations. Native Tlaxcalans were brought to help the Spanish stabilize the area, and they set up a colony beside the Spanish one at Saltillo. The Tlaxcalans' skill on the treadle-loom and the abundance of wool in the area led to

the development of a unique type of sarape, for which Saltillo became famous in the 18th and 19th centuries.

Capital of the state of Coahuila & Texas after Mexican independence, the city was occupied by US troops under Zachary Taylor in 1846 during the Mexican-American War. At Buenavista, south of Saltillo, the 20,000-strong army of General Santa Anna was repulsed by Taylor's force, a quarter the size, in the decisive battle for control of the northeast during that war.

President Benito Juárez came to Saltillo during his flight from the invading French forces in 1864, and the city was occupied again by foreign troops before being freed in 1866. During the Porfiriato, agriculture and ranching prospered in the area, and the coming of the railway helped trade and the first industries in the city, but Monterrey was by this time quickly overtaking Saltillo in size and importance.

Saltillo's industrial development started with the processing of local primary products, including wheat and wool, and it is still a commercial and communications center for a large livestock and agricultural area. In recent decades it has expanded to include big automobile and petrochemical plants. Saltillo is still the capital of Coahuila, but it has been outgrown by the modern city of Torreón in the southwest of the state.

Orientation

Saltillo spreads over a large area, but most places of interest are located in the blocks around the two central plazas. Periférico Echeverría, a ring road, enables traffic to bypass the inner-city area.

The austere Plaza de Armas is surrounded by fine colonial buildings, including the cathedral on the southeast side. The north side is bordered by Los Portales, a colonnade harboring a few cafés and a video-game parlor. The junction of Hidalgo and Juárez, at the southeast corner of the plaza, is a dividing point for Saltillo's street addresses, with those to the south suffixed 'Sur,' those to the east 'Ote' (Oriente), and so on.

Two blocks away is Plaza Acuña, with the market building on its north side. It's smaller, less formal and usually more lively than the Plaza de Armas. The Alameda Zaragoza is a large, shady public park, reached by going west down Victoria from behind the Palacio de Gobierno.

The bus station is on the south side of town, on Periférico Echeverría Sur – a 10-minute bus ride from the center.

Information

Tourist Offices In the old train station on the corner of Boulevard Coss and Acuña, about 1.5km north of downtown, the Protursa office (☎ 412-51-22, protursa@coah1 .telmex.net.mx) has a friendly English-speaking staff and abundant handouts including multiple-map guides to every region in the state. It's open 10 am to 7 pm Monday to Saturday, 10 am to 6 pm Sunday.

Money You can change cash and traveler's checks at the banks near the Plaza de Armas

(all have ATMs). There are casas de cambio on Victoria, open until 6 pm Monday to Friday, until 1 pm on Saturday.

Post & Communications The post office is centrally located at Victoria 223 Pte, a few doors from the Hotel Urdiñola. It's open 9 am to 4 pm Monday to Friday, 9 am to 1 pm Saturday. There are also postal facilities at the bus station, and pay phones are at the post office, the bus station and around town.

Catedral de Santiago

Built between 1745 and 1800, this cathedral dominates the plaza and has one of Mexico's finest Churrigueresque façades, with columns of elaborately carved pale gray stone. It's particularly splendid when lit up at night. Inside, the transepts are full of gilt ornamentation – look for the human figure perched on a ledge at the top of the dome.

Palacio de Gobierno

Facing the plaza are the state government headquarters. You are free to wander into this elegant 19th-century building. A mural in its second-floor passageway traces Coahuila's history and depicts its historical figures, most prominently Venustiano Carranza, who as governor of the state during the Revolution launched a revolt against the provisional president Huerta.

Plaza de la Nueva Tlaxcala

Behind the Palacio is this plaza, built in 1991 to commemorate the fourth centennial of Saltillo's foundation. A sculpted scene on its southern end alludes to the colonization of Coahuila. Allende, the plaza's east side, once divided the two sections of the old town – to the east was the section occupied by the Spaniards, to the west the area where the Tlaxcalans lived.

Instituto Coahuilense de Cultura

This gallery, on the south side of the plaza, exhibits painting, sculpture and crafts by artists from Coahuila and elsewhere. It's open 9 am to 6 pm Tuesday to Sunday (free).

NORTHEAST MEXICO

Alameda Zaragoza

This park, full of shady trees and pathways, has a playground and is a favorite spot for young couples. A pond at the southern end has an island shaped like Mexico.

Museo de las Aves

Definitely worth a visit, this museum, between Hidalgo and Allende, a few blocks south of the plaza, is devoted to the birds of Mexico, which ranks sixth in the world in avian diversity. Most of the exhibits are birds stuffed and mounted in convincing dioramas of their natural habitat. There are special sections on nesting, territoriality, birdsongs, navigation and endangered species. Over 670 bird species are displayed, along with bird skeletons, fossils and eggs. It's open 10 am to 6 pm Tuesday to Saturday, 11 am to 6 pm Sunday (US$0.50 adults, US$0.20 kids, free on Saturday).

Special Events

The Aniversario de Saltillo, to commemorate the city's foundation, is celebrated with a nine-day cultural festival in late July, followed by the annual fair.

For the Día del Santo Cristo de la Capilla celebration, in the week leading up to August 6, dance groups from around Coahuila perform on the esplanade in front of the cathedral, in honor of Saltillo's patron saint. The date commemorates the arrival of a statue of the crucified Christ brought over from Spain in 1608 and now housed in the Capilla del Santo Cristo within the cathedral.

Places to Stay

Budget The *Hotel De Avila* (☎ 412-59-16, *Padre Flores 211*) is in a good location at the northwest corner of Plaza Acuña (another sign calls it Hotel Jardín). Rooms are basic but not too bad, and the price is right with singles/doubles for US$8.50/9.50, US$1 more with TV. Somewhat better is the *Hotel Bristol* (☎ 410-43-37, *Aldama 405 Pte*), entered through a clothing store between Acuña and Padre Flores. Rooms for US$9/13 are a little shabby but clean, and there's a pleasant sunlit court with sofas. Another adequate budget option, across the

road from the bus station, the *Hotel Siesta* (☎ 417-07-24) charges US$14/19 for rooms with fans and TVs.

Mid-Range Beside the Siesta stands the *Hotel Saltillo* (☎ 417-22-00), beckoning visitors with its neon lights. It's a friendly place featuring standard rooms with color TV and phone for US$21, single or double. The hotel's 24-hour restaurant specializes in seafood.

On the same block as the Hotel Bristol and only marginally more comfortable is the *Hotel Saade* (☎ 412-91-20, *Aldama 397 Pte*). Prices range from $20/23 up to US$25/30 for rooms with TV and phone; worn carpeting and fluorescent lighting are the norm. Parking is available.

A place that offers lots of character and good value is the *Hotel Urdiñola* (☎ 414-09-40, *Victoria 251 Pte*). There's a sparkling white lobby with a wide stairway sweeping up to a stained-glass window. Large, airy rooms facing a long courtyard with pleasant gardens are US$29 for one person, US$32 for two. The hotel also has a decent inexpensive restaurant, helpful staff and parking just up the street.

The new *Hotel Colonial Alameda* (*410-00-88, Obregón 222*), a block east of the Alameda, is an excellent choice, achieving a winning combination of luxury and hospitality at US$42 per room. The Spanish colonial-style building features 21 large tasteful rooms, each containing a pair of huge beds. Not so impressive but still quite good is the *Hotel San Jorge* (☎ 412-22-22, *Acuña 240 Nte*), a modern well-maintained establishment with a restaurant, a small rooftop swimming pool and comfortable singles/doubles for US$43/47.

Top End There are several four- and five-star hotels, aimed at business-class travelers, along the highways heading north and east from Saltillo. The *Best Western Eurotel Plaza* (☎ 415-10-00, *V Carranza 4100*), on highway 40 to Monterrey just south of the Carranza monument, charges US$86 a room. Even classier is the *Camino Real Saltillo* (☎ 430-00-00) on highway 57 to San

Luis Potosí, at US$149 per room, discounted on Saturday and Sunday.

Places to Eat

Pan de Pulque, a local sweet bread made with the maguey beverage, is available at *Pan Mena (Madero 1350)*, west of the Alameda.

There are a number of snack places and cafés in Saltillo's center. On the southwest corner of Plaza Acuña, the busy *Tacos El Pastor* prepares tasty tacos *al pastor* (grilled spiced pork carved off a meter-high cone) and tacos *de lengua* (beef tongue) – an order of four is US$2. Across Aldama, *Café Victoria (Padre Flores 221)* is a popular hangout with a lunch counter, serving *café con leche*, sandwiches and set lunches for US$3. *La Gordita*, just north of the Palacio de Gobierno, produces fresh gorditas filled with hearty ingredients, but only until 12.30 pm.

Norteño-style cabrito is the specialty at *Restaurant El Principal (Allende 702 Nte)*, four blocks down the hill from Plaza Acuña, with assorted goat parts for US$3.75 to US$9 and steaks from US$7.50. Try *El Tapanco (Allende 225 Sur)*, for fine cuisine in splendid surroundings; you can dine alfresco on the back patio. The menu features a tempting array of salads, pastas and crepes for US$3.75 to US$4.25 – the *huitlacoche* crepes are superb. Main courses start at around US$8.50.

Shopping

Saltillo used to be so famous for its sarapes that a certain type was known as a 'Saltillo' even if it was made elsewhere in Mexico. The technique involves leaving out color fixatives in the dyeing process so that the different bands of color 'weep' or blend into each other. The finest sarapes have silk or gold and silver threads woven into them. These days the local workshops have stopped making classic all-wool sarapes and seem to be obsessed with jarring combinations of bright colors. But you can still get ponchos and blankets in more 'natural' colors, some of which are pure wool.

You can see these and other handicrafts at El Sarape de Saltillo on Hidalgo, a couple of blocks up the hill from the cathedral.

Wool is dyed and woven on treadle looms inside the shop. The Mercado Juárez, next to Plaza Acuña, also has a selection of sarapes, as well as hats, saddles and souvenirs. There is a branch of Fonart, the government-run crafts shop, on Allende just south of Juárez, with a variety of pottery, textiles and jewelry from around Mexico.

Getting There & Away

Air Mexicana (☎ 415-03-43), with an office in the Europlaza Mall at V Carranza 4120, has flights between Mexico City and Saltillo. Continental Airlines (☎ 488-31-14) flies to/from Houston.

Bus Saltillo's modern bus station is on the ring road at Libertad. First-class lines have ticket desks to the right end of the hall as you enter; 2nd-class is to the left.

Lots of buses serve Saltillo but few start their journeys here. This means that on some buses, 2nd-class ones in particular, you often can't buy a ticket until the bus has arrived and they know how much room there is for new passengers. You'd be better off taking a 1st-class bus. The 1st-class lines include Transportes del Norte and Ómnibus de México, while Transportes Frontera and Línea Verde are 2nd-class; Turistar is the deluxe bus line. Daily departures include the following:

Aguascalientes – 503km, 7 hours; 13 1st-class (US$25), 8 2nd-class (US$21)

Durango – 488km, 8 hours; 5 1st-class (US$28)

Guadalajara – 693km, 10 hours; 11 1st-class (US$37)

Matamoros – 410km, 7 hours; 13 1st-class (US$21)

Mexico City (Terminal Norte) – 870km, 10 hours; 2 deluxe (US$59), 11 1st-class (US$44), 2 2nd-class (US$38)

Monterrey – 85km, 1½ hours; 2 deluxe (US$5.75), frequent 1st-class (US$4.25)

Nuevo Laredo – 310km, 4 hours; 8 1st-class (US$21), 7 2nd-class (US$16.50)

Parras – 160km, 2½ hours; 8 2nd-class (US$5.25)

San Luis Potosí – 455km, 5 hours; 9 1st-class (US$19), frequent 2nd-class (US$17.50)

Torreón – 231km, 3 hours; frequent 1st-class (US$16) and 2nd-class (US$14.50)

Zacatecas – 373km, 5 hours; 7 1st-class (US$18.50), 6 2nd-class (US$16)

Buses also go to Chihuahua, Ciudad Acuña, Ciudad Juárez, Mazatlán, Monclova, Morelia, Piedras Negras, Reynosa, Querétaro and Tijuana. Autobuses Americanos has service to Chicago, Dallas, Houston and San Antonio.

Train At the time of writing, Saltillo's train station (☎ 414-95-84), on E Carranza, still offered passenger service to Mexico City and Piedras Negras, but seemed likely to discontinue the service.

Car & Motorcycle Saltillo is a junction of major roads. Highway 40 going northeast to Monterrey is a good four-lane road, with no tolls until you reach the Monterrey bypass. Going west to Torreón (277km), highway 40D splits off highway 40 after 30km, becoming an overpriced toll road (US$16). Highway 40 is free and perfectly all right.

Highway 57 goes north to Monclova (192km), penetrating the dramatic Sierra San Marcos y Pinos at Cima de la Muralla (a butterfly migration zone in the summer months), and onward to Piedras Negras (441km). Going south to Mexico City (852km), highway 57 climbs to over 2000m, then descends gradually along the Altiplano Central to Matehuala (260km) and San Luis Potosí (455km), through barren but often scenic country. To the southwest, highway 54 crosses high, dry plains toward Zacatecas (363km) and Guadalajara (680km).

Getting Around
The airport is 15km northeast of town on highway 40; catch a 'Ramos Arizpe' bus along Xicoténcatl (US$0.35) or a taxi. To reach the city center from the bus station, take minibus No 9 (US$0.30), which departs from Libertad, the first street on the right as you leave the station. To reach the bus station from the center, catch a No 9 on the corner of Aldama and Hidalgo. Taxis between the center and the bus station cost US$2.

PARRAS
• pop 24,000 • elev 1580m ☎ 8

Parras, 160km west of Saltillo off the Torreón road, is an oasis in the Coahuilan Desert. Underground streams from the sierra come to the surface here as springs, used to irrigate the grapevines for which the area is famous and giving the town its full name – Parras de la Fuente.

Parras was the birthplace of Francisco Madero, an important leader in the Mexican Revolution. An obelisk on Calle Arizpe honors him.

Information
The Parras tourist office (☎ 422-02-59) is on the roadside 2km north of town. Open 10 am to 2 pm and 4 to 7 pm Monday to Saturday, it has a helpful staff and plenty of useful maps and brochures.

Things to See & Do
The first winery in the Americas was established at Parras in 1597, a year before the town itself was founded. The winery, now called **Casa Madero**, is about 4km north of town in San Lorenzo on the road going to the main highway. Tours are conducted, in Spanish, 9 am to 5 pm daily; you can buy quality wine and brandy on site.

The town has an old aqueduct, some colonial buildings, and three *estanques* (large pools where water from the springs is stored) that are great for swimming. The **Iglesia del Santo Madero**, on the southern edge of town, sits on the plug of an extinct volcano. Expansive views reward those who make the steep climb.

An important manufacturer of *mezclilla* (denim), Parras is a good place to buy jeans. Its fig, date and nut orchards provide the basis for delectable fudgy sweets, on sale around town.

Special Events
The grape fair, the Feria de la Uva, goes on for most of the month of August, featuring parades, fireworks, horse races, religious celebrations on the Día de la Asunción (August 15), and traditional dances by descendants of early Tlaxcalan settlers.

Places to Stay

The best value for the money by far is the *Hotel Posada Santa Isabel* (☎ 422-05-72, *Madero 514*), with a swimming pool, restaurant and spacious, air-conditioned singles/doubles around a pretty courtyard for US$21/26.

Parras' cheapest option, the *Hotel Parras* (☎ 422-04-44, *Arizpe 105*) at Reforma, may also be the friendliest. The hotel's clean, basic rooms face an unruly interior garden – room No 6 is the airiest. Rates are US$7.50 for one or two people. Another reasonably priced place is the *Hotel La Siesta* (☎ 422-03-74, *Acuña 9*), around the corner from the bus station, with small, homey rooms for US$10.50/17.50.

A few kilometers north of town is the resort *Rincón del Montero* (☎ 422-05-40) with golf, tennis, swimming and horseback riding. Rooms or cabins start at US$62; RV hookups are available for US$21. Approaching from the north, turn left off the main road just below the tourist information module.

Places to Eat

On Cayuso opposite the parish church, *Restaurant Rincón del Recuerdo* has a welcoming feeling and good food, with main courses for US$3 to US$5. The restaurants *El Tiburón* and *Chávez*, on Reforma just north of Madero, serve decent, inexpensive seafood and tortas, respectively.

Getting There & Away

Only 2nd-class buses serve Parras; there are nine daily to/from Saltillo (2½ hours, US$5.25) and five to/from Torreón (2½ hours, US$7.50). A 1st-class bus might drop you at La Paila, from where you can find local transport. Parras is easy to reach by car; at La Paila, about halfway between Saltillo and Torreón, turn off the highway and go 27km south.

Central Pacific Coast

Stretching from Mazatlán to Acapulco, the central Pacific coast contains some of Mexico's principal beach resorts – Mazatlán, Puerto Vallarta, Zihuatanejo-Ixtapa and Acapulco – and some lesser-known but beautiful spots.

Coastal highways make travel easy up and down the coast, with frequent buses and easy driving, while several other highways connect the coast to the mountainous interior of the country. Due to the high volume of tourists, both national and international, air services to this region are also frequent and convenient.

MAZATLÁN
• pop 302,800 ☎ changing

Situated just 13km south of the Tropic of Cancer, Mazatlán is Mexico's principal Pacific coast fishing, shrimp and commercial port, as well as one of its prime Pacific resorts. Affectionately known as the 'Pearl of the Pacific,' Mazatlán is famous for its beaches and its sport fishing, with more than 7000 billfish (sailfish and marlin) tagged and released each year. Mazatlán is the shrimp capital of the world. It's home to Latin America's largest fleet of commercial shrimp vessels, with more than 600 shrimp boats, and nearly 40,000 tons of shrimp are processed here annually.

Another of Mazatlán's distinctions is that El Faro, high on a peak at the south end of the city, is the second-highest lighthouse in the world, after Gibraltar; you can climb up to it for a magnificent 360-degree view of the city and coast. The sunset is especially beautiful in Mazatlán, as the sun sets behind three offshore islands which gradually change color and fade into silhouettes, finally disappearing into the starry night.

In pre-Hispanic times Mazatlán (which means 'place of deer' in Náhuatl) was populated by Totorames, who lived by hunting, gathering, fishing and agriculture. Though a group of 25 Spaniards led by Nuño de Guzmán officially founded a settlement here

on Easter Sunday in 1531, almost three centuries elapsed before a permanent colony was established, in the early 1820s. During this time the Spanish referred to the area as

Highlights

• International beach resorts – particularly Acapulco and Puerto Vallarta
• Small beach resorts with local character – Playa Azul, San Blas, Cuyutlán and El Paraíso
• Delicious seafood all along the coast
• La Quebrada cliff divers in Acapulco
• Huichol crafts in Nayarit state
• Bird-watching in San Blas and Mexcaltitán

'Islas de Mazatlán' due to its many estuaries and lagoons, punctuated by hills.

Orientation

Mazatlán has both 'old' and 'new' sections. Old Mazatlán (the center) is concentrated on a wide peninsula at the southern end of the city, bound on the west by the Pacific Ocean and on the east by the Bahía Dársena. At the south end of the peninsula are El Faro (the lighthouse), Mazatlán's sport fishing fleet, the terminal for ferries to La Paz, and Isla de la Piedra, which is not really an island but a long peninsula with a popular beach. On the east side are the shrimp, fishing and commercial docks. The center of the 'old' city is the cathedral, on the Plaza Principal.

A beachside boulevard (which changes names frequently) runs along the Pacific side of the peninsula past Playa Olas Altas – Mazatlán's first tourist beach back in the 1950s – around some rocky outcrops, and north around the wide arc of Playa Norte to the Zona Dorada (Golden Zone), which begins at the traffic circle at Punta Camarón and heads a few blocks north. The Zona Dorada and the large hotels stretching along the beaches to the north comprise the major tourist zone.

Information

Tourist Offices The Coordinación General de Turismo (☎ 16-51-60/65, tursina@prodigy .net.mx, www.sinaloa.gob.mx) is on the 4th floor of the Banrural building (which, confusingly, is marked 'Banco Nacional de Comercio Exteriores') on Avenida Camarón Sábalo. The office offers helpful information, but it's inconveniently north of the Zona Dorada. It's open 9 am to 5 pm Monday to Friday and open for telephone inquiries 9 am to 8 pm Monday to Friday, 9 am to 1 pm Saturday.

Free bilingual tourist newspapers – *Pacific Pear*, *The Sun* and *Mazatlán Interactive* – are at the tourist office and at many hotels and tourist-oriented businesses. *Viejo Mazatlán* is an interesting free bilingual paper about the history and culture of Mazatlán.

In November 2000, the telephone area code is due to change to ☎ 6 from 69, with the digit 9 added to the start of every local number (for example, the number 16-51-60 will become 916-51-60).

Consulates See 'Embassies & Consulates in Mexico' in the Facts for the Visitor chapter for a listing of the Canada, France, Germany and USA consulates in Mazatlán. Other countries (including Brazil, Italy and the Netherlands) have consulates here too; the tourist office has a complete list.

Money Banks, most with ATMs and *casas de cambio*, are plentiful in both old and new Mazatlán. There are Bancomer and Banamex offices near the Plaza Principal. American Express (☎ 13-06-00) is in the Centro Comercial Balboa shopping center. Avenida Camarón Sábalo is in the Zona Dorada; it's open 9 am to 6 pm Monday to Friday, 9 am to 1 pm Saturday.

Post & Communications The main post office, on Juárez on the east side of Plaza Principal, is open 8 am to 7 pm Monday to Friday, 9 am to 1 pm Saturday. Next door, Telecomm has telegraph, telex, fax and Internet services and coin telephones; it's open 8 am to 7.30 pm Monday to Friday, 8 am to noon Saturday and Sunday. Miscelanea Hermes, at Serdán 1510, a block east of the cathedral, offers telephone, fax and Internet services, as does Computel next door, and Tel-Internet, Flores 912, near the post office. In the Zona Dorada, there's Netscape Cafe Internet on Camarón Sábalo. The main bus station has a post office, Telecomm office and telephone/fax office. Pay phones are plentiful around the city.

Emergency The emergency telephone number is ☎ 060.

Old Mazatlán

The heart of Old Mazatlán is the large 19th-century **cathedral** at Juárez and 21 de Marzo,

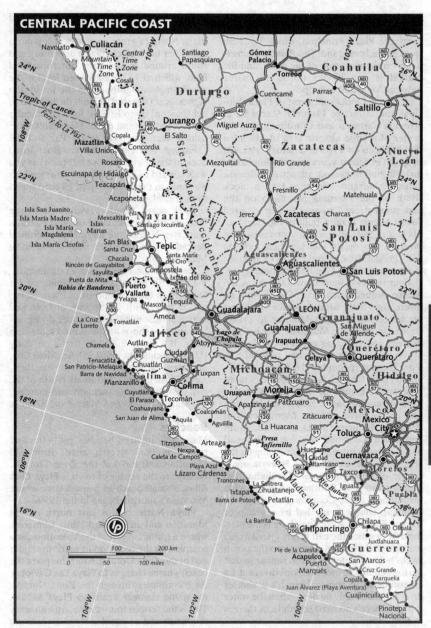

CENTRAL PACIFIC COAST

with its high, yellow twin towers and beautiful statues inside. Built from 1875 to 1890, it faces the **Plaza Principal**, which has lush trees and a bandstand. The **Palacio Municipal** is on the west side of the plaza, and the **market** is two blocks north on Juárez between Valle and Ocampo.

A couple blocks southwest of Plaza Principal, the attractive **Plazuela Machado**, at Avenida Carnaval and Constitución, is the center of a large historic area of Mazatlán that has been undergoing a massive renewal program in recent years. It's surrounded by historic buildings and attractive sidewalk cafés, restaurants and bars. Half a block south of the Plazuela Machado on the pedestrian street Carnaval, the three-tiered **Teatro Angela Peralta**, built in 1860 (and reopened in 1992 after a five-year restoration project), is open for viewing 9 am to 6 pm daily (US$0.50). Cultural events of all kinds are presented here (see Entertainment).

Four blocks toward Playa Olas Altas, the **Museo Arqueológico**, Sixto Osuna 76, is an interesting little archaeological museum open 9.30 am to 4 pm Monday to Friday (free). Opposite, the **Museo de Arte** has permanent and changing exhibits of Mexican artists and is open 10 am to 2 pm and 5 to 8 pm Tuesday to Sunday (US$1).

On Paseo Olas Altas are a couple of monuments: the **Escudo de Sinaloa y Mazatlán** (Sinaloa and Mazatlán Shield) at the south end of the cove and the **Monumento al Venado** (Monument to Deer) at the north end, which is a tribute to the city's Náhuatl name. Around the rocky outcropping on the seaside of the **Cerro de la Nevería** are a couple of other monuments, including the **Monumento a la Continuidad de la Vida** (Monument to the Continuity of Life), with a human couple being led by a group of leaping dolphins. Also along here is the platform from which the **cliff divers** *(clavadistas)* leap into a chasm and plunge into the ocean swells below. While this feat is similar to that performed by the more famous divers at La Quebrada in Acapulco, here it's a shorter dive, and it can only be done when the water is high – there's no fixed schedule, as there is in Acapulco.

From Paseo Olas Altas the seafront road goes north around the rocky outcrops to Playa Norte (a great area to watch pelican and other birds catching fish at sunset), and south around more rocky outcrops to **El Faro**, which at 157m above sea level is the second-highest lighthouse in the world (the highest is at Gibraltar). Climb the hill (Cerro del Crestón) up to El Faro for a spectacular view of the city and coast. Mazatlán's sport fishing fleet, the ferry to La Paz and the *Costalegre* and *Yate Fiesta* (see Boat Trips) dock in the marina to your left (east) as you walk toward El Faro on the causeway, which was built in the 1930s to join El Faro island to the mainland.

Back north, beside Playa Norte at the junction of Avenida del Mar and Avenida Gutiérrez Nájera, the large **Monumento al Pescador** is another well-known symbol of Mazatlán.

Between the center and Zona Dorada, the **Acuario Mazatlán**, on Avenida de los Deportes a block inland from Playa Norte, has 52 tanks with 250 species of fresh and saltwater fish and other creatures; diving, sea lion and bird shows are presented four times daily. It's open 9.30 am to 6 pm daily (US$4.50, children US$2.25). **Sea Shell City**, on Loaiza in the Zona Dorada, has thousands of shells large and small. North of the city, past the marina (actually two marinas: the Marina El Cid and Marina del Sábalo).

Beaches

Mazatlán's 16km of beaches get better and better as they stretch north from old Mazatlán and beyond the Zona Dorada. Nearest to the center of town is **Playa Olas Altas**, a small beach in a small cove where Mazatlán's tourism began in the 1950s.

Playa Norte begins just north of old Mazatlán and arcs toward Punta Camarón, where a traffic circle and the Valentino disco complex on the rocky point mark the south end of the Zona Dorada. After this point the beach's name changes to **Playa Las Gaviotas**. As it continues through the Zona Dorada, the name changes again, to **Playa Sábalo**. This is the serious tourist zone, with an army of tourists and an equal army of *ambulantes*

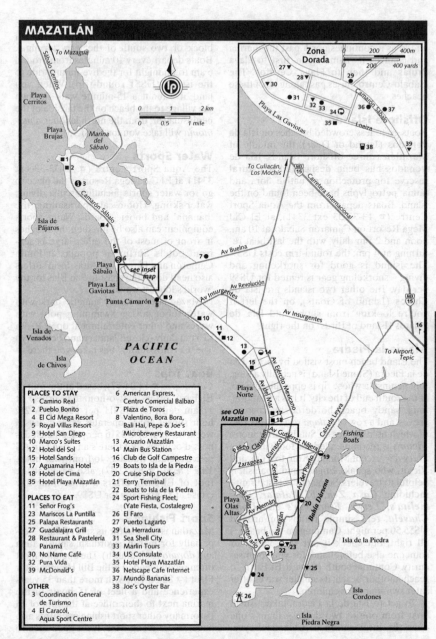

MAZATLÁN

To Mazagua
Sábalo Cerritos

Playa
Cerritos

Playa
Brujas

Marina
del
Sábalo

0   1   2 km
0   0.5   1 mile

Isla de
Pájaros

Camarón Sábalo

Playa
Sábalo

see inset
map

Playa Las Gaviotas

Punta Camarón

Isla
de Venados

Isla
de Chivos

PACIFIC
OCEAN

Zona Dorada

0   200   400m
0   200   400 yards

Playa Las Gaviotas

Camarón Sábalo

Loaiza

To Culiacán,
Los Mochis

Carretera Internacional

Av Buelna

Av Revolución

Av Insurgentes

Av Insurgentes

To Airport,
Tepic

Playa
Norte

Av del Mar

Av Ejército Mexicano

see Old
Mazatlán map

Calzada Leyva

Fishing
Boats

Av Gutiérrez Nájera

Paseo Clausen

Carrasco

Serdán

Zaragoza

Olas Altas

Av del Puerto

Bahía Dársena

Isla de la Piedra

Av Alemán

Barragán

Centenario

Playa
Olas
Altas

Isla
Cordones

Isla
Piedra Negra

PLACES TO STAY
1 Camino Real
2 Pueblo Bonito
4 El Cid Mega Resort
5 Royal Villas Resort
9 Hotel San Diego
10 Marco's Suites
12 Hotel del Sol
15 Hotel Sands
17 Aguamarina Hotel
18 Hotel de Cima
35 Hotel Playa Mazatlán

PLACES TO EAT
11 Señor Frog's
23 Mariscos La Puntilla
25 Palapa Restaurants
28 Guadalajara Grill
28 Restaurant & Pastelería
    Panamá
30 No Name Café
32 Pura Vida
39 McDonald's

OTHER
3 Coordinación General
   de Turismo
4 El Caracól,
   Aqua Sport Centre

6 American Express,
   Centro Comercial Balboa
7 Plaza de Toros
8 Valentino, Bora Bora,
   Bali Hai, Pepe & Joe's
   Microbrewery Restaurant
13 Acuario Mazatlán
14 Main Bus Station
16 Club de Golf Campestre
19 Boats to Isla de la Piedra
20 Cruise Ship Docks
21 Ferry Terminal
22 Boats to Isla de la Piedra
24 Sport Fishing Fleet,
    (Yate Fiesta, Costalegre)
26 El Faro
27 Puerto Lagarto
29 La Herradura
31 Sea Shell City
33 Marlin Tours
34 US Consulate
35 Hotel Playa Mazatlán
37 Mundo Bananas
38 Joe's Oyster Bar

(peddlers) selling everything from jewelry to hammocks. The beach becomes less populated as it continues north past the marina and changes its name again, first to **Playa Brujas** and then to **Playa Cerritos**. The 'Sábalo-Centro' buses pass along all of these beaches.

Offshore Islands

Boats go to less crowded beaches on **Isla de Venados** (Island of Deer), the middle of Mazatlán's three offshore islands. Isla de Venados has been designated a natural reserve for protection of native flora and fauna; petroglyphs have been found on the island. Boats depart from the Aqua Sport Centre (☎ 13-33-33 ext 3341), at El Cid Mega Resort on Camarón Sábalo, at 10 am, noon and 2 pm daily, with the last boat returning at 4 pm; the round-trip costs US$9. The island is good for snorkeling and diving – snorkeling gear is rented for US$9 per day. The other two islands are **Isla de Chivos** (Island of Goats), on the left if you're looking from shore, and **Isla de Pájaros** (Island of Birds) on the right.

Isla de la Piedra

The island beach most visited by locals, Isla de la Piedra (Stone Island) is actually a long, thin peninsula whose tip is opposite El Faro, at the south end of the city. It has a beautiful, long, sandy beach bordered by coconut groves, and a row of *palapa* restaurants, two of which hold dances on Sunday afternoons. *Victor's* is recommended for food; it's open every day except Monday, 8 am to 8 pm, and Victor, who speaks English and Spanish, is helpful to travelers. Some of the restaurants, including **Casa Zen**, **El Palmar**, **Carmelita's**, **Lety's**, **Florencio's** and **Doña Chavela**, rent simple rooms for around US$5.50 per night. Camping on the beach is all right, but check it out with Victor or someone else beforehand, for your own security. Continue south (toward El Faro) to reach another beach; its smaller waves offer safer swimming for children.

To get to Isla de la Piedra, take a small boat from one of two docks – there's one near the intersection of Calzada Leyva,

Avenida del Puerto, Avenida Zaragoza and Calzada Gutiérrez Nájera, and another a block or two south of the ferry terminal. Boats depart every 10 minutes from around 6 am to midnight for the five-minute ride to the island (US$1 round-trip). When you land, it's about a 15-minute walk through the village to the beach on the far side of the peninsula (or, from the north landing, a *pulmonía* will take you for US$1.75).

Water Sports

The Aqua Sport Centre (☎ 13-33-33 ext 3341), at El Cid Mega Resort, is the place to go for water sports, including scuba diving, water-skiing, Hobie cats, parasailing, the 'banana' and boogie boards. Water sports equipment can also be hired on the beaches in front of most of the other large beachfront hotels. Surfing is popular at Punta Camarón and Playa Olas Altas; local surfers also head down the coast to San Blas for the 'world's longest wave.'

Mazagua is a family aquatic park with water toboggans, a swimming pool with waves and other entertainment open 10 am to 6 pm daily (closed January and February.) The 'Cerritos-Juárez' bus takes you there.

Boat Trips

Costalegre (☎ 14-24-77), based at the foot of El Faro, offers a two-hour bay cruise at 11 am daily, for US$11 per person. A 2½ hour sunset cruise operates several days a week; the cost of US$16 per person includes hors d'oeuvres, and there's an open bar. All prices include transfers to/from your hotel. *Yate Fiesta* (☎ 85-22-37), also based at the foot of El Faro, offers a three-hour bay cruise at 11 am daily for US$9.

Sport Fishing

Mazatlán is famous for its sport fishing – especially for marlin, swordfish, sailfish, tuna and *dorado* (dolphinfish). The operator most often recommended is the Bill Heimpel Star Fleet (☎ 82-38-78), with more than 35 years experience and a fleet of 15 boats in the marina next to their office at the foot of El Faro; many other sport fishing operators also have offices along here. It's a good idea to

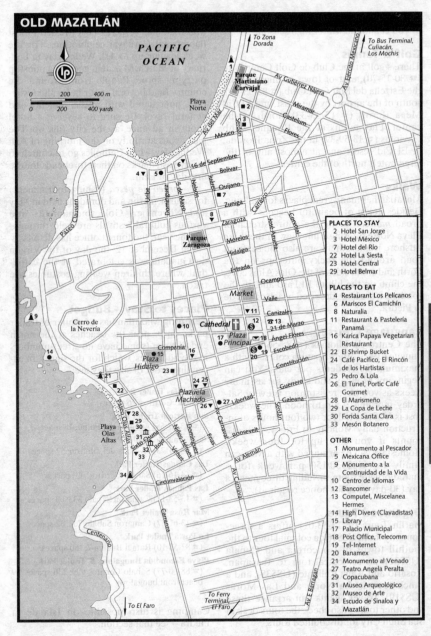

OLD MAZATLÁN

PACIFIC OCEAN

To Zona Dorada

To Bus Terminal, Culiacán, Los Mochis

Parque Martiniano Carvajal

Playa Norte

Parque Zaragoza

Market

Cerro de la Nevería

Cathedral

Plaza Principal

Plaza Hidalgo

Plazuela Machado

Playa Olas Altas

To El Faro

To Ferry Terminal, El Faro

PLACES TO STAY
2 Hotel San Jorge
3 Hotel México
7 Hotel del Río
22 Hotel La Siesta
23 Hotel Central
29 Hotel Belmar

PLACES TO EAT
4 Restaurant Los Pelicanos
6 Mariscos El Camichín
8 Naturalia
11 Restaurant & Pastelería Panamá
16 Karica Papaya Vegetarian Restaurant
22 El Shrimp Bucket
24 Café Pacifico, El Rincón de los Hartistas
25 Pedro & Lola
26 El Tunel, Portic Café Gourmet
28 El Marismeño
29 La Copa de Leche
30 Fonda Santa Clara
33 Mesón Botanero

OTHER
1 Monumento al Pescador
5 Mexicana Office
9 Monumento a la Continuidad de la Vida
10 Centro de Idiomas
12 Bancomer
13 Computel, Miscelanea Hermes
14 High Divers (Clavadistas)
15 Library
17 Palacio Municipal
18 Post Office, Telecomm
19 Tel-Internet
20 Banamex
21 Monumento al Venado
27 Teatro Angela Peralta
29 Copacubana
31 Museo Arqueológico
32 Museo de Arte
34 Escudo de Sinaloa y Mazatlán

CENTRAL PACIFIC COAST

make fishing reservations as far in advance as you can in the winter high season.

Golf & Tennis

There's golf at the Club de Golf Campestre (☎ 80-15-70), east of town on highway 15, the Estrella del Mar Golf Club (☎ 82-33-00), south of the airport by the coast, and El Cid Mega Resort (☎ 13-33-33), north of the center. Play tennis at the Racquet Club Gaviotas (☎ 13-59-39) in the Zona Dorada, at El Cid resort and at almost any of the large hotels north of the center.

Walks

Mazatlán has many great places for walking. Besides 16km of beautiful beaches, with a broad *malecón* along the entire stretch of Playa Norte offering a fine view of the three offshore islands, there are also the seafront road around the rocky outcrops on the north and south sides of the Olas Altas cove, the climb up the hill to El Faro and, to the southeast, the long, deserted beach of Isla de la Piedra.

Language Courses

The Centro de Idiomas (☎ 85-56-06), Domínguez 1908, offers Spanish courses with a maximum six students per class. You can begin any Monday and study for as many weeks as you like; registration is every Saturday morning, 9 am to noon. The weekly cost is US$120/150 for two/four hours of instruction daily Monday to Friday, with discounts if you sign up for four weeks. Homestays can be arranged with a Mexican family for US$130/150 per week for a shared/private room, including three meals a day (30-day advance notice required).

Organized Tours

Marlin Tours (☎ 13-53-01) offers a three-hour city tour (US$16); a colonial tour to the foothill towns of Concordia and Copala (US$31); an ecological tour to Teacapan, Rosario and Agua Caliente (US$35); and a ranch tour to La Noria and Las Moras (US$19). Travel agents can arrange these and other tours. Also check the tours desk in Sea Shell City for discounted tours.

Special Events

Mazatlán and Veracruz host Mexico's most flamboyant Carnaval celebrations. For the week leading up to Ash Wednesday in February or March, Mazatlán goes on a nonstop partying spree. People from around the country (and beyond) pour in for the festivities, punctuated with music, dancing and general revel. Be sure to reserve a hotel room in advance, as the city fills up. The party ends abruptly on the morning of Ash Wednesday, when Catholics go to church to receive ash marks on their foreheads for the first day of Lent.

A *torneo de pesca* (fishing tournament) for sailfish, marlin and dorado is held in May and November. Golf tournaments and various cultural festivals are held throughout the year; the tourist office has details.

On December 12, the day of the Virgen de Guadalupe is celebrated at the cathedral, where children wearing costumes are taken.

Places to Stay – Budget

Camping Mazatlán has a number of trailer parks on or near the beaches at the north end of town (some have no street numbers in the addresses; watch for the signs). In ascending order of size they are:

Maravillas Trailer Park
  Sábalo Cerritos; 26 spaces

San Bartolo Trailer Park
  (☎ 13-57-55) Avenida del Pulpo; 48 spaces

San Fernando Trailer Park
  (☎ 14-01-73) Avenida del Tiburón; 57 spaces

Las Canoas Trailer Park
  (☎ 14-16-16) Sábalo Cerritos; 60 spaces

Las Palmas Trailer Park
  (☎ 13-53-11) Camarón Sábalo 333; 68 spaces

Mar Rosa Trailer Park
  (☎ 13-61-87) Camarón Sábalo 702; 82 spaces

La Posta Trailer Park
  (☎ 83-53-10) Rafael Buelna 7; 180 spaces

Playa Escondida Bungalows & Trailer Park
  (☎ 88-00-77) Sábalo Cerritos 999; 236 spaces, 19 beachfront bungalows

Camping is also possible on Isla de la Piedra – see that section.

Hotels The *Hotel del Río* (☎ 82-46-54, *Juárez 2410*) is clean and friendly, and a very good deal; singles/doubles are US$7.75/9.75. *Hotel México* (☎ 81-38-06, *México 201*), a block from the beach, is very basic, but clean; rooms are US$6.50/11 with one/two beds. *Hotel San Jorge* (☎ 81-36-95), on Serdán at the corner of Gastelum, also a block from the beach, is old but clean, with singles/doubles for US$14.50/18.

Hotel Central (☎ 82-18-66, *Domínguez 2*), four blocks from Playa Olas Altas and four blocks from the cathedral, has well-kept rooms with air-con and TV for US$18.50/22.

The hotels on Playa Olas Altas are some of the most charming in town – old but re-furbished, well-maintained and full of char-acter. *Hotel Belmar* (☎ 85-11-11/12, *Olas Altas 166*), a formerly grand hotel but now somewhat faded, is a good deal, with a swimming pool, bar, parking and 150 rooms, 60 with private balconies overlooking the beach, some with TV and air-con. Rooms runs US$18/22 with pool view, or US$20/24 with sea view. *Hotel La Siesta* (☎ 81-26-40, *Olas Altas 11*), above El Shrimp Bucket restaurant, has a courtyard full of tropical plants and the Bucket's tables. The 51 rooms are large and clean, with air-con and TV, and some with sea-view balconies; rooms run US$29/34, or US$33/38 with sea view.

Between Old Mazatlán and the Zona Dorada, *Marco's Suites* (☎ 83-59-98, *Ave-nida del Mar 1234*) has a swimming pool, parking and rooms with kitchen and air-con at US$25/35 for two/four people; the Ice-landic owners keep it very clean and give re-ductions for longer stays.

At the south end of the Zona Dorada, *Hotel San Diego* (☎ 83-57-03), at Avenida del Mar and Buelna, on the traffic circle near the Valentino disco, has rooms with air-con and TV for US$18 to US$31.

Places to Stay – Mid-Range
There are some decent mid-range choices on Avenida del Mar, opposite Playa Norte, with frequent buses heading north and south. *Hotel del Sol* (☎ 85-11-03, *Avenida del Mar 800*), near the aquarium, is good value, with swimming pool, parking and air-conditioned rooms for US$31, or US$44 with kitchen and cable TV. *Hotel Sands* (☎ 82-00-00, *Avenida del Mar 1910*) has a swimming pool, restaurant/bar, parking and rooms (some with sea view) with balcony, air-con, fan, satellite color TV and refrigera-tor for US$34/38 with one/two beds. *Hotel de Cima* (☎ 85-18-55, *Avenida del Mar 48*) has a restaurant, bar, parking, swimming pool and air-conditioned rooms with TV for just US$44.

Places to Stay – Top End
Air/hotel packages may make room rates cheaper; travel agents should have informa-tion on all of Mazatlán's big luxury hotels.

Aguamarina Hotel (☎ 81-70-80, *Avenida del Mar 110*) has a pool, restaurant/bar, parking, travel agency and air-conditioned rooms with cable TV and phone for US$64 to US$75.

Mazatlán has many luxurious top-end hotels on the beaches north of town. Most imposing is the 1100-room *El Cid Mega Resort* (☎ 13-33-33), on Camarón Sábalo; rates start at US$93 per night. Other good choices are the *Pueblo Bonito* (☎ 14-37-00, *Camarón Sábalo 2121*), with rooms for US$140; the *Camino Real* (☎ 13-11-11), on Punta del Sábalo, with rooms for US$152/176 with marina/sea view; and the *Royal Villas Resort* (☎ 800-696-7000, 800-898-3564 in the USA, Camarón Sábalo 500), with rooms for US$182.

Places to Eat
Old Mazatlán The *Restaurant & Pastelería Panamá* (*Juárez 1702*), diagonally opposite the rear of the cathedral, is a popular air-conditioned restaurant, café and bakery, open 7 am to 10 pm daily, with a wide variety on the menu and luscious desserts. Several other branches are around town, including one on Camarón Sábalo in the Zona Dorada.

Mazatlán is famous for fresh seafood. The shrimp here is fantastic. Also don't miss trying *pescado zarandeado*, a delicious type of charcoal-broiled fish; a whole kilo, feeding two people well, usually costs around US$9 at the following restaurants, while shrimp is around US$4.50 to US$9 per dish. The popular open-air *Mariscos La Puntilla*, on a small point on the south end of the city with a view across the water to Isla de la Piedra, is a most enjoyable place to enjoy Mazatlán fresh seafood; it's open 10 am to 6 pm daily.

On Playa Norte, *Mariscos El Camichín (Paseo Claussen 97)* is a popular open-air patio restaurant with a jolly crowd eating delicious seafood under a cool palapa roof; it's open 11 am to 10 pm daily, with live music from 2 pm on. *Restaurant Los Pelícanos*, on the corner of Paseo Claussen and Uribe, is a small open-air thatched-roof place with some of the cheapest and tastiest seafood in Mazatlán. It has a great view of the entire arc of Playa Norte, and catches any sea breezes coming by; it's open 10 am to 6 pm Tuesday to Sunday.

Karica Papaya Vegetarian Restaurant (Ángel Flores 601) is great for vegetarians, with breakfast or lunch for US$4 and a whole-grain bakery next door; it's open 8.30 am to 5 pm daily. *Naturalia (Zaragoza 807)* is a whole-grain bakery and health food store, open 8 am to 8 pm Monday to Saturday.

Plazuela Machado is a peaceful place to enjoy a meal, snack or drink, especially in the evening when the plaza is softly lit and the sidewalk tables offer a romantic atmosphere. *Pedro & Lola* and *Café Pacífico* are two popular spots, and there are others. Next door to Café Pacífico, *El Rincón de los Hartistas* is a popular gathering spot for artists and cultural types in the evening (due in part to Mirla, the friendly proprietress). *El Tunel*, opposite the Teatro Angela Peralta, is good for inexpensive Mexican food, or try a *raspado* (flavored shaved ice covered in fruit syrup); it opens around 6 pm (closed Wednesday). Next door, the tiny *Portic Café Gourmet* is famous for baked goods and cappuccino.

Olas Altas also has several good restaurants. Below Hotel La Siesta, *El Shrimp Bucket (Olas Altas 11)* is one of Mazatlán's best known restaurants. Opened in 1963, it was the first in what has become an international chain of Carlos Anderson restaurants. It has air-con, with tables inside and out in the hotel's tropical courtyard, and is open

6 am to 11 pm daily, with live music every day except Monday. *La Copa de Leche* and *Fonda Santa Clara* are popular open-air restaurant/bars with sidewalk and interior tables, both open 7 am to 11 pm daily. *El Marismeño* is another possibility for seafood. More casual and less expensive, the open-air *Mesón Botanero (Olas Altas 25)* is an enjoyable seafood restaurant and watering hole popular with both locals and expats, especially at sunset and in the evening; the most expensive thing on the menu is the shrimp for US$4.50. It's open 11 am to 11 pm daily, till 1 am on Saturday and Sunday.

Zona Dorada & Around Mazatlán's Zona Dorada is packed with restaurants catering to the tourist trade. *No Name Café (Loaiza 417)* boasts 'the best damn ribs you'll ever eat' (US$10) and other delicious food in a pleasant ambiance with an air-conditioned sports bar and a tropical patio; it's open 8 am to 1 am daily. *Pura Vida* is a 100% organic, natural foods garden restaurant and juice bar. *Guadalajara Grill*, on Camarón Sábalo, is another Carlos Anderson restaurant. Homesick gringos (or their children) might like to know there's a *McDonald's* by the traffic circle at the south end of the Zona Dorada.

Between the Zona Dorada and the center, *Señor Frog's*, on Avenida del Mar, is a Mazatlán landmark that's almost always packed with Americans. Part of the Carlos Anderson chain, it advertises 'lousy food and warm beer,' but actually the food is good (just overpriced) and the beer only warm when they can't cool the bottles fast enough to keep up with demand. It's air-conditioned and open every day from noon until 1 am or later (food finishes at midnight).

Entertainment
Cultural Events Events of all kinds – concerts, opera (Mazatlán has its own opera company), theater and more – are presented at the historic Teatro Angela Peralta near Plazuela Machado; a kiosk on the walkway in front of the theater announces current and upcoming cultural events here and at other venues around the city. Also at the

theater, the Cine Club sponsors quality films at 6 pm every Saturday (admission is free).

If you get a chance, try to hear a rousing traditional *banda sinaloense* – a loud, boisterous multipiece brass band unique to the state of Sinaloa and particularly Mazatlán.

Bars & Discos Mazatlán has several discos, most in the Zona Dorada. Best known and most obvious is *Valentino*, in the very out-of-place, white-washed fairytale castle on the rocky outcropping at the traffic circle at the south end of the Zona Dorada. In the same complex are *Bora Bora*, a popular beachfront bar with a sand volleyball court, swimming pool and beachside dance floor; *Bali Hai*, a lively sports bar with big-screen videos; and *Pepe & Joe's Microbrewery Restaurant*.

About 500m north, *Joe's Oyster Bar*, at the Hotel Los Sábalos, is a pleasant beachfront bar with a fine view of the offshore islands. *Mundo Bananas*, on Camarón Sábalo, is a popular disco. The restaurant/bar *La Herradura*, also on Camarón Sábalo, popular with locals, is great for Mexican music, and sometimes a rousing banda sinaloense. Farther north, *El Caracól*, at El Cid Mega Resort on Camarón Sábalo, is another popular disco. The beachside restaurant/bar at the *Hotel Playa Mazatlán* is popular with the 30s-and-up age group for dancing under the stars from 7 pm to midnight every night. *Puerto Lagarto*, next to Guadalajara Grill on Camarón Sábalo, is another popular dining and dancing spot, as is *Señor Frog's* on Avenida del Mar (see Places to Eat).

Copacubana, on Olas Altas, has live music for dancing on weekends. On Sunday afternoon there's live music and dancing at a couple of palapas on the beach at Isla de la Piedra (see Boat Trips), patronized mostly by hard-drinking locals.

Fiesta Mexicana A Fiesta Mexicana, with a Mexican buffet, open bar, folkloric floor show and live music for dancing, is held 7 to 10.30 pm Tuesday, Thursday and Saturday at the Hotel Playa Mazatlán (☎ 13-53-20), Loaiza 202 in the Zona Dorada; call for reservations or reserve through travel agents. The cost is US$23. There's a similar fiesta at El Cid Mega Resort (☎ 13-33-33) on Wednesday; El Cid also offers other entertainment throughout the week.

Cinemas Mazatlán has several cinemas; check the local daily newspapers *El Sol del Pacífico* and *El Noroeste* for movie listings and other events. Films are often shown in English with Spanish subtitles.

Spectator Sports

The Plaza de Toros, on Avenida Buelna, inland from the Zona Dorada traffic circle, hosts bullfights 4 pm Sundays from Christmas to Easter; the 'Sábalo-Cocos' bus will drop you there. Tickets are sold at travel agencies, at major hotels, at the Bora Bora shop beside the Valentino disco, and at the Salon Bacanora (☎ 86-91-55) beside the Plaza de Toros.

Charreadas (rodeos) are held at the Lienzo *charro* ring (☎ 86-35-10) in Colonia Juárez.

Getting There & Away

Air The Mazatlán international airport is 20km south of the city. Airlines serving this airport, and their direct flights (all with connections to other places), include:

Aero California
(☎ 13-20-42) El Cid Mega Resort, Camarón Sábalo, Local 30 & 31; flies to Guadalajara, La Paz, Los Angeles, Mexico City

Aeroméxico
(☎ 82-34-44, 800-021-4000) Camarón Sábalo 310, Local 1 & 2, Zona Dorada; flies to Acapulco, Ciudad Juárez, Durango, Guadalajara, La Paz, Los Mochis, Mexico City, Monterrey, Tijuana, Torreón

Alaska Airlines
(☎ 85-27-30, 800-252-7522) Mazatlán airport; flies to Los Angeles, San Francisco

America West
(☎ 81-11-84, 800-235-9292) Mazatlán airport; flies to Phoenix

Mexicana
(☎ 82-77-22, 800-366-5400) Paseo Claussen 101B; flies to Denver, Guadalajara, La Paz, Los Cabos, Mexico City, Monterrey, Puerto Vallarta, Torreón

Bus The main bus station (Central de Autobuses) is just off Avenida Ejército Mexicano on Avenida de los Deportes, about three blocks inland from the beach, and ringed by inexpensive hotels. First- and 2nd-class bus lines operate from separate halls in the main terminal; buses to small towns nearby (such as Concordia, Copala and Rosario) operate from a smaller terminal, which is behind the main terminal.

Daily buses from the 1st-class hall go north and south along the coast on highway 15/15D – each company has hourly buses going north and south, 24 hours a day. Buses also travel inland over the mountains (and across a time zone boundary) to Durango; Elite has buses to Durango hourly, 24 hours. Bus companies include Elite, Transportes Norte de Sonora (TNS), Estrella Blanca and Transportes del Pacífico. Services include:

Durango – 321km, 7 hours (US$19 to US$22)

Guadalajara – 506km, 8 hours (US$27 to US$44)

Mexico City (Terminal Norte) – 1041km, 17 hours (US$61 to US$80)

Puerto Vallarta – 459km, 8 hours; 3 daily by Elite (US$28), or take a bus to Tepic, from where buses depart frequently for Puerto Vallarta

Tepic – 290km, 4½ to 5 hours (US$15 to US$17)

Tijuana – 1796km, 25 hours (US$86 to US$99)

Buses from the 2nd-class hall go to all the places listed above. There is also a four-hour trip to Santiago Ixcuintla at 6 am (235km, US$9.50). Five buses to Santiago Ixcuintla (6.15, 7.15 and 11.15 am, 1.45 and 4.15 pm; US$9.50) depart from Transporte Rápido del Sur's separate terminal on Avenida Ejército Mexicano by the main terminal.

To get to San Blas (290km), take a Tepic-bound bus to 'Crucero San Blas,' then wait for one of the hourly buses coming from Tepic.

Car Mazatlán's car rental agencies include Aga (☎ 81-35-80), Budget (☎ 13-20-00), Hertz (☎ 13-60-60), National (☎ 13-60-00), Price (☎ 86-66-16) and Quality (☎ 16-53-77). As always, it pays to shop around for the best rates.

Boat Ferries operate between Mazatlán and La Paz, Baja California Sur. The *transbor-*

dador (ferry) terminal (☎ 81-70-20/21) is at the south end of town; the office is open 8 am to 2 pm daily. Tickets are sold the morning of departure, or two days in advance. See the La Paz section in the Baja California chapter for schedule and fare details.

Getting Around

To/From the Airport *Colectivo* vans and a bus operate from the airport to town, but not from town to the airport. Taxis are more expensive.

Bus Local buses operate every day from around 5.30 am to 10.30 pm; fare is US$0.30. A good network of frequent buses provides convenient service to anywhere around the city you'd want to go. Useful routes include:

Sábalo-Centro – travels from the market in the center to the beach via Juárez, then north on Avenida del Mar to the Zona Dorada and farther north on Avenida Camarón Sábalo

Playa Sur – travels south along Avenida Ejército Mexicano near the bus station and through the city center, passing the market, then to the ferry terminal and El Faro

To get into the center of Mazatlán from the bus terminal, go to Avenida Ejército Mexicano and catch any bus going south (to your right if the bus terminal is behind you). Alternatively, you can walk 500m from the bus station to the beach and take a 'Sábalo-Centro' bus heading south (left) to the center.

Motorcycle Various companies in the Zona Dorada rent small motorcycles for getting around town – you'll see the bikes lined up beside the road. You need a driver's license to hire one; any type of license will do.

Pulmonías & Taxis Mazatlán has a special type of taxi called a pulmonía (pneumonia), a small open-air vehicle similar to a golf cart. There are also green-and-white taxis marked 'eco-taxi'; like pulmonías they tend to be slightly cheaper than normal taxis. Both types are plentiful around town. Be sure to agree on the price for the ride before you climb in; it never hurts to bargain.

AROUND MAZATLÁN

Several small, picturesque colonial towns in the Sierra Madre foothills make pleasant day trips from Mazatlán. **Concordia**, founded in 1565, has an 18th-century church with a baroque façade and elaborately decorated columns, and hot mineral springs nearby; the village is known for its manufacture of high-quality pottery and hand-carved furniture. It's about a 45-minute drive east of Mazatlán; head southeast on highway 15 for 20km to Villa Unión, turn inland on highway 40 (the highway to Durango) and go another 20km. **Copala**, 40km past Concordia on highway 40, and also founded in 1565, was one of Mexico's first mining towns. It still has its colonial church (1748), colonial houses and cobblestone streets.

Rosario, 76km southeast of Mazatlán on highway 15, is another colonial mining town, founded in 1655. Its most famous feature is the gold-leaf altar in its church Nuestra Señora del Rosario. **Cosalá**, a beautiful colonial mining village in the mountains north of Mazatlán, was founded in 1550 and has a 17th-century church, a historical and mining museum in a colonial mansion on the plaza, and two simple but clean hotels. Attractions nearby include **Vado Hondo**, a *balneario* (bathing resort) with a large natural swimming pool and three waterfalls, 15km from town; **La Gruta México**, a large cave 18km from town; and the **Presa El Comedero** reservoir, 20km from town, with hired rowboats for fishing. To get to Cosalá, go north on highway 15 for 113km to the turnoff (opposite the turnoff for La Cruz de Alota on the coast) and then go about 45km up into the mountains.

Buses to all these places depart from the small bus terminal at the rear of the main bus station in Mazatlán. Alternatively, there are tours (see Organized Tours in the Mazatlán section).

SANTIAGO IXCUINTLA

• pop 18,200 ☎ changing

Santiago Ixcuintla is mainly of interest as the jumping-off point for Mexcaltitán. It's not a tourist town, but it does have the **Centro Huichol** (☎ 5-11-71), at Calle 20 de Noviembre 452 Pte, a handicrafts center where in-

In November 2000, the telephone area code is due to change to ☎ 3 from 323, with the digits 23 added to the start of every local number (for example, the number 5-08-50 will become 235-08-50).

digenous Huichols make their distinctive arts and crafts; it's on the outskirts of town toward Mexcaltitán. You can stop here to see them at work or buy their products – prices are good. About 60 Huichols work here from October to June, but in summer most go to the mountains to plant crops. The center is open 10 am to 7 pm Monday to Saturday. A block from the bus station on the road to the church are some striking mosaic **murals**.

A couple of hotels are near the market. *Hotel Casino* (☎/fax 5-08-50, Ocampo 40) is pleasant, with parking and a restaurant/bar open 7 am to 10.30 pm daily. Singles/doubles are US$11/13.50 with fan and US$15/18 with air-con.

Getting There & Away

Turn off highway 15 63km northwest of Tepic; Santiago Ixcuintla is about 7km west of the turnoff. Buses to Santiago leave frequently from Tepic and Mazatlán. Santiago Ixcuintla has two 2nd-class bus stations, Transportes Norte de Sonora (TNS) and Transportes del Pacífico, half a block apart. Daily services from these stations include:

Guadalajara – 287km, 4½ hours; 5 buses by TNS (US$16.25), 1 bus by Transportes del Pacífico (US$16)

La Batanga – 37km, 1 hour; 4 buses by Transportes del Pacífico (US$1.50)

Mazatlán – 235km, 4½ hours; 3 buses by Transportes del Pacífico (US$11)

San Blas – 62km, 1¼ hours; 3 buses by TNS (US$3.75), 1 bus by Transportes del Pacífico (US$3)

Tepic – 70km, 1¼ hours; every half-hour, 5.30 am to 8 pm, by TNS (US$3.75)

Combis to La Batanga (the departure point for boats to Mexcaltitán) depart from the market (US$1.75); a taxi to La Batanga costs US$13.

MEXCALTITÁN
- **pop 1070 ☎ changing**

A small, ancient island village, Mexcaltitán is far from the tourist trail but a fascinating place to visit. Tourism has scarcely touched the island, though it does have a few facilities and a captivating small museum. To get there you must take a *lancha* (motorized wooden boat) through a large mangrove lagoon full of fish, shrimp and many aquatic birds.

Mexcaltitán is sometimes called the 'Venice of Mexico,' because the streets occasionally become flooded when the water level of the lagoon rises after heavy rains near the end of the rainy season, around September to November. At that time water flows through the dirt streets (between high cement sidewalks), and all travel is done in canoes. If the water level rises very high, families may sleep in canoes tied to the posts in their houses!

Be sure to bring plenty of insect repellent with you, as the lagoon is a breeding ground for mosquitoes.

History
Mexcaltitán has a long, enthralling history. It is believed that this small island – originally called Aztlán (meaning 'place of egrets') – was the homeland of the Aztec people, and that from here (around 1116) they departed on a generations-long pilgrimage, which eventually ended at Tenochtitlán (modern Mexico City) around 1325.

Orientation & Information
The island is a small oval, about 350m from east to west, 400m from north to south, and about 1km around the perimeter. At the center of the island is a plaza with a gazebo in the center, a church on the east side, and

In November 2000, the telephone area code is due to change to ☎ 3 from 323, with the digits 23 added to the start of every local number (for example, the number 2-02-11 will become 232-02-11).

the museum on the north side. The hotel is a block behind the museum.

All the telephones on the island go through one operator, who has a switchboard in the sitting room of her house. From outside the island, phone the switchboard (☎ 2-02-11) and ask for the extension you want.

Things to See & Do
The **Museo Aztlán del Origen**, on the north side of the plaza, is small but enchanting. Among the exhibits are many interesting ancient objects and a fascinating long scroll, the Codice Ruturini, telling the story of the peregrinations of the Aztec people, with notes in Spanish. The museum is open 10 am to 2 pm and 4 to 6 pm, Tuesday to Saturday (US$0.50).

You can arrange for **boat trips** on the lagoon for bird-watching, fishing and sightseeing – every family has one or more boats. There's a **billiards hall** beside the church.

Special Events
Semana Santa is celebrated in a big way. On Good Friday (in March or April) a statue of Christ is put on a cross in the church, then taken down and carried through the streets.

The Fiesta de San Pedro Apóstol, the patron saint of fishermen, is celebrated on June 29 with statues of St Peter and St Paul taken out into the lagoon in decorated lanchas for the blessing of the waters. Festivities start around June 20, leading up to the big day.

On the Día de Independencia, September 16, Miguel Hidalgo's Cry of Independence is reenacted at the church on the plaza, with fiestas and celebrations.

Places to Stay & Eat
Mexcaltitán has one hotel and a few restaurants. *Hotel Ruta Azteca* (☎ 2-02-11 ext 128, Venecia 5) is a simple hotel with rooms with one bed for US$11 or US$16.50, with two/three/four beds for US$16.50/22/27; the rooms with four beds have air-con.

The attractive *Restaurant Alberca*, by the water and accessible by a rickety wooden walkway, has a great view of the lagoon and catches any breezes coming by. It's open

9 am to 8 pm daily and specializes in shrimp dishes (US$4.50). *Mariscos Kika*, on an island opposite Mexcaltitán, is a pleasant restaurant with a children's playground, a view back toward Mexcaltitán, and seafood dishes for US$2.75 to US$4.50.

Getting There & Away

From Santiago Ixcuintla, take a bus, taxi or colectivo to La Batanga, a small wharf from where lanchas depart for Mexcaltitán. Colectivo lanchas between La Batanga and Mexcaltitán are coordinated with the Santiago Ixcuintla bus arrivals and departures. Lanchas depart La Batanga at 6, 8 and 11 am, and 1, 4 and 6 pm. The boat journey takes 15 minutes and costs US$0.65 per person. If you miss the colectivo lancha you can hire a private lancha for US$4.50; lanchas are available from around 8 am to 6 pm.

It's possible to reach Mexcaltitán from Tuxpan instead, but this route is more isolated and dangerous.

SAN BLAS

• pop 8710 ☎ changing

The small fishing village of San Blas, 70km northwest of Tepic, was an important Spanish port from the late 16th to the 19th century. The Spanish built a fortress here to protect their *naos* (trading galleons) from marauding British and French pirates. Today's visitors come to enjoy nature – isolated beaches, abundant exotic birds (250 species counted so far), a thick tropical jungle, estuaries and a navigable river.

San Blas has the amenities of a small beach resort town, such as hotels and restaurants, yet it retains the character of a typical Mexican village. One suspects that the real reason the village hasn't been de-

veloped as a major resort is the proliferation of *jejenes* (sandflies), tiny gnatlike insects with huge appetites for human flesh; their bites will leave you with an indomitable itch. Abundant mosquitoes compete with the jejenes for your last drop of blood. During daylight hours they're not too active, but around sunset they appear from nowhere to attack. Be sure to bring plenty of insect repellent and to accept a hotel room only if it has good window screens with no holes or tears.

Orientation

San Blas sits on a tongue of land bound on the west and southwest by El Pozo estuary, on the east by San Cristóbal estuary, and on the south by Playa El Borrego and the Pacific Ocean. A 36km paved road connects San Blas with highway 15. A coast road heads out around Bahía Matanchén to Santa Cruz village and on to Puerto Vallarta.

Just west of the bridge over the San Cristóbal estuary, the road passes the Cerro de la Contaduría and the ruins of the old Spanish fortress. At the Pemex station, the road splits into three branches, with the center one, Juárez, becoming the main street of San Blas and leading to the village's small zócalo. Calle Batallón de San Blas runs along the western side of the zócalo and leads south to the beach; this could be considered the village's other main street. Everything in town is within walking distance.

Information

Tourist Offices The small Secretaría de Turismo, Calle Mercado 29, offers free maps and information about San Blas, the state of Nayarit, and the Puerto Vallarta area, plus an English book exchange. It's open 9 am to 1 pm and 5 to 8 pm Monday to Saturday (plus Sunday in high season). At the time of writing, the office was planning on moving soon, and getting a telephone.

Money The Banamex bank on Juárez, about a block east of the zócalo, is open 8 am to 2 pm, Monday to Friday. It has an ATM. Opposite, the Agencia de Cambio is open 8 am to 2 pm, Monday to Saturday.

In November 2000, the telephone area code is due to change to ☎ 3 from 328, with the digits 28 added to the start of every local number (for example, the number 5-01-23 will become 285-01-23).

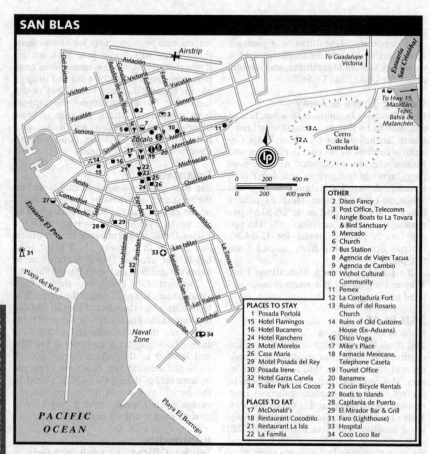

SAN BLAS

PLACES TO STAY
1 Posada Portolá
15 Hotel Flamingos
16 Hotel Bucanero
24 Hotel Ranchero
25 Motel Morelos
26 Casa María
29 Motel Posada del Rey
30 Posada Irene
32 Hotel Garza Canela
34 Trailer Park Los Cocos

PLACES TO EAT
17 McDonald's
18 Restaurant Cocodrilo
21 Restaurant La Isla
22 La Familia

OTHER
2 Disco Fancy
3 Post Office, Telecomm
4 Jungle Boats to La Tovara
    & Bird Sanctuary
5 Mercado
6 Church
7 Bus Station
8 Agencia de Viajes Tacua
9 Agencia de Cambio
10 Wichol Cultural
    Community
11 Pemex
12 La Contaduría Fort
13 Ruins of del Rosario
    Church
14 Ruins of Old Customs
    House (Ex-Aduana)
16 Disco Voga
17 Mike's Place
18 Farmacia Mexicana,
    Telephone Caseta
19 Tourist Office
20 Banamex
23 Cocún Bicycle Rentals
27 Boats to Islands
28 Capitanía de Puerto
29 El Mirador Bar & Grill
31 Faro (Lighthouse)
33 Hospital
34 Coco Loco Bar

Post & Communications The post office, on
Sonora at Echeverría, is open 8 am to 2 pm
Monday to Saturday. Next door, Telecomm,
with telegraph, telex and fax, is open 8 am to
2 pm, Monday to Friday. A telephone caseta
with fax at the south end of the zócalo, opposite the church, is open 8 am to 10 pm daily.
Several public telephones are on the zócalo.

Travel Agencies Agencia de Viajes Tacua
has two branches: one at Sinaloa 20, just off
the zócalo, and another in the Farmacia
Mexicana, on the south side of the zócalo,
opposite the church.

Things to See & Do
Climb the **Cerro de la Contaduría** to see the
ruins of the 18th-century Spanish fortress
and church (US$0.50); there's a fine view
from the top.

The **Wichol Cultural Community** (wichol@
huicholartphil.org.mx; www.huicholartphil
.org.mx), Juárez 64B, is a nonprofit Huichol
collective dedicated to spreading Huichol
art and culture. You can stop by to see art
being made, buy at good prices, and/or learn
about Huichol culture.

San Blas' main attractions are its natural
wonders – the surrounding beaches and

jungles. The nearest beach is **Playa El Borrego**, at the end of Teniente Azueta.

The best beaches are southeast of the village around Bahía de Matanchén, starting with **Playa Las Islitas**, 7km from San Blas. A paved road that bears south from the road to highway 15 passes the dirt road to Playa Las Islitas and continues past the Oceanography School and through the village of Aticama, 8km along the beach from Playa Las Islitas. Between Playa Las Islitas and Aticama the beach is wonderfully isolated; it's very popular with surfers, who claim that the world's longest wave sweeps ashore here. Farther on, **Playa Los Cocos** and **Playa Miramar**, also popular for surfing, have palapas under which you can lounge and drink fresh coconut milk.

Boat Trips

A boat trip through the jungle to the freshwater spring of **La Tovara** is one of the highlights of a visit to San Blas. Small boats (maximum 10 to 12 passengers) depart from the embarcadero (jetty) to your left as you cross the bridge into town. Boats go up the San Cristóbal estuary to the spring, passing thick jungle vegetation and mangroves; you'll see exotic birds, turtles and perhaps a few crocodiles. Bring your swimsuit to swim at La Tovara; there's a restaurant there too. The price is fixed at US$20 for one to four people, US$5 each extra person; the trip takes three hours. A shorter boat trip to La Tovara can be made from Matanchén village farther up the river; this takes two hours and costs US$18 for one to four people, US$4.50 each extra person. For an extra US$10 or so an excursion to visit the **Cocodrilario** (crocodile farm) can be added to either trip.

A five-hour bird-watching trip up the Estuario San Cristóbal to the **Santuario de Aves** (Bird Sanctuary), leaving from the same embarcadero by the bridge, costs US$49 for one to four people, US$16.50 each extra person.

Other boat trips depart from a landing on Estuario El Pozo. They include a trip to **Piedra Blanca** to visit the statue of the Virgin; to **Estero Casa Blanca** to gather clams; to **Isla del Rey** just across from San Blas; and to **Playa del Rey**, a 20km beach on the other side of Isla del Rey. Unfortunately, it's not advisable for a woman to go to Playa del Rey alone.

You can make an interesting trip farther afield to **Isla Isabel**, also called Isla María Isabelita, four hours northwest of San Blas by boat. The island is a bird-watcher's paradise, with colonies of many species, and there's a volcanic crater lake on the island. Isla Isabel is only about 1.5km long and 1km wide, with no facilities, so you must be prepared for self-sufficient camping. Permission is required to visit the island; the boat pilots can arrange it.

Special Events

Every year on January 31 the anniversary of the death of Father José María Mercado is commemorated with a parade, a demonstration march by Mexican marines and fireworks in the zócalo. Mercado lived in San Blas in the early 19th century and helped Miguel Hidalgo with the independence movement by sending him a set of old Spanish cannons from the village.

On February 3, festivities for San Blas, the town's patron saint, are an extension of those begun on January 31, with dance and musical presentations. Carnaval is celebrated the weekend before Ash Wednesday. The Virgen de Fátima is honored on May 13. The Día de la Marina is celebrated on June 1 with burro races on the beach, sporting events, dances and partying. Surfing competitions take place in summer; contact the tourist office for dates. A party called the Convivencia de la Fraternidad is put on by the tourist office on December 27 for all the foreign visitors in town.

Places to Stay

Considering its small size, San Blas has a fair selection of places to stay. Look at any room before you accept it and be sure that the window screens are without holes or tears.

Camping The *Trailer Park Los Cocos* (☎ 5-00-55) near Playa El Borrego, almost at the end of Calle Batallón de San Blas in a grassy area with lots of trees, charges US$9/11 for two people in tents/trailers (with hookups). Beware of the mosquitoes swarming at sunset. On Playa Los Cocos, about a 15-minute drive from town, the attractive beachfront *Playa Amor* trailer park has a fine view of the sunset and coast, no mosquitoes, and some palapa restaurants nearby; its tent/RV spaces (with hookups) are US$6.50/11. At the *Hotel Ranchero* (see Hotels) you can pitch a tent on the roof for US$2.75 per person.

Hotels The *Posada Irene* (☎ 5-03-99, Batallón de San Blas 122) has simple singles/doubles with private bath for US$8/9. *Hotel Ranchero* (Batallón de San Blas 102), at the corner of Michoacán, is a friendly place with eight rooms for US$11/13 with shared/private bath. Opposite, *Motel Morelos* (Batallón de San Blas 108) charges US$11/13 for simple singles/doubles with private bath. Behind this, *Casa María* (Canalizo 67) has singles/doubles with private bath for US$13.50/16.50. All of these places are simple, clean, family-run guest-houses with rooms around a central courtyard and friendly, homey ambiance where guests are treated like family. You can wash your clothes and cook at all of them.

Posada Portolá (☎ 5-03-86, Paredes 118) has eight spacious bungalows with simple kitchens for US$16.50 for two people (they hold up to four or five people), and a small single room with bath for US$4.50.

Hotel Bucanero (☎ 5-01-01, Juárez 75), about 1½ blocks from the zócalo, is old but full of character. A large stuffed crocodile greets you at the door; rooms are set around a spacious courtyard, with a big garden swimming pool off to one side. The 30 rooms, with one to six beds, cost US$22/26 for singles/doubles.

Motel Posada del Rey (☎ 5-01-23, Campeche and Callejón del Rey) is an attractive, clean, modern place with family ambiance, a small swimming pool and a third-floor ocean-view bar and grill. Singles/doubles with fan and air-con are US$22/27.

Hotel Flamingos (☎/fax 5-04-85, Juárez 105) occupies a beautifully restored historic building. Luxurious rooms are set around a lovely courtyard; a large garden (where a swimming pool is planned) is off to one side. Rooms with one bed are US$49 (US$61 mid-December to February); larger, more luxurious rooms with two or more beds are US$61 (US$77 in high season).

Hotel Garza Canela (☎ 5-01-12, Paredes 106 Sur) has a large garden, a swimming pool, an air-conditioned restaurant/bar, and 42 large rooms with air-con and satellite TV. Singles/doubles are US$50/63 (US$62/78 December 15 to May 1); they also have more expensive suites with kitchens.

Places to Eat

McDonald's (Juárez 36), half a block south-west of the zócalo, is a favorite among travelers for its good food at good prices (it's no relation to the burger chain). Filling meals are US$2.50 to US$7; open 7 am to 10 pm daily. Another favorite is the *Restaurant La Isla*, at the corner of Paredes and Mercado, a seafood restaurant with good food, reasonable prices and nautical decor featuring millions of shells; open Tuesday to Sunday, 2 to 9 pm. The restaurant/video bar *La Familia* (Batallón de San Blas 62) is another pleasant family restaurant with moderate prices, open 8 am to 10 pm daily. On the zócalo, the pleasant *Restaurant Cocodrilo* attracts lots of gringos in the evening; it's open 5.30 to 10.30 pm daily.

There's a good selection of places to eat on the beaches, too, with seafood the specialty (of course). *El Caballito* on Playa El Borrego, operated by the same family that runs Restaurant La Isla, offers the same good food at good prices, with pleasant ambiance.

Entertainment

Considering its small size, San Blas has quite an array of places to go to in the evening. For dancing there's *Disco Voga* in the Hotel Bucanero; *Mike's Place* over the McDonald's restaurant; and *Disco Fancy* (Canalizo 150). Pleasant bars include the 3rd-floor ocean-view *El Mirador Bar & Grill* at Motel Posada del Rey, and *Coco Loco* beside Trailer Park Los Cocos near Playa El Borrego. *Restaurant Cocodrilo* on the zócalo has a fine bar in the rear.

Getting There & Away

The bus station is on the corner of Sinaloa and Canalizo, at the northeast corner of the zócalo. Buses depart for Tepic (1½ hours, US$3.75; hourly, 6 am to 7 pm), Puerto Vallarta (3 hours, US$9.50; 7 and 10 am), Guadalajara (5 hours, US$16.50; 7 am) and Mazatlán (4 hours, US$16.50; 5 pm).

To Santa Cruz, the village at the far end of Bahía de Matanchén, buses depart from the bus station hourly, 6 am to 5 pm; there are also small buses departing from the corner of Sinaloa and Paredes at 8.20 and 10.30 am, 12.30 and 2.30 pm. The buses serve all the villages and beaches on Bahía de Matanchén, including Matanchén, Playa Las Islitas, Aticama, Playa Los Cocos and Playa Miramar. You can also take a taxi.

Getting Around

Bicycles can be rented from Motel Morelos and from Cocún, on opposite corners of Batallón de San Blas and Michoacán.

TEPIC

• pop 254,600 • elev 900m ☎ changing

Tepic is the bustling capital of the small state of Nayarit. It's the crossroads for highways 15/15D and 200, the two Pacific Coast highways; from here highway 15/15D turns inland toward Guadalajara and Mexico City. Local time is one hour behind Puerto Vallarta and Guadalajara in the neighboring state of Jalisco.

Many travelers pass through the outskirts of Tepic without stopping off. But it doesn't take long to visit the city, and there are a few things of interest, including a large neo-Gothic cathedral and several good museums. Indigenous Huichols, who live in the mountains of Nayarit, are often seen here, wearing their colorful traditional clothing. Huichol artwork (reasonably priced) is sold in front of the palacio municipal (city hall) opposite the cathedral and in shops, and is displayed in museums. Tepic's climate is noticeably cooler than on the coast.

Orientation

Plaza Principal, with the large cathedral at the east end, is the heart of the city. Running south from the cathedral, Avenida México is the city's main street. Six blocks south of Plaza Principal is another plaza, Plaza Constituyentes. Along Avenida México between these two plazas are banks, restaurants, the state museum and other places of interest. The bus station is on the southeastern side of the city. Peripheral roads allow traffic to pass through Tepic without entering the city center.

Information

Tourist Offices The Secretaría de Turismo (☎ 14-80-71), at the Ex-Convento de la Cruz at the foot of Avenida México, is open 8 am to 8 pm Monday to Saturday, 9 am to 3 pm Sunday. The Dirección de Turismo (☎ 16-56-61, 12-08-84), just off the Plaza Principal at the corner of Puebla Nte and Amado Nervo Pte, is open 9 am to 8 pm Monday to Friday, 9 am to 2 pm and 4 to 8 pm Saturday and Sunday, with free maps and information on Tepic and the state of Nayarit. If you're interested in the area and you can read Spanish, ask for the paperback *Estado de Nayarit Guía Turística*, a guidebook about Nayarit (US$4.50).

Money Banks and casas de cambio line Avenida México Nte between the two plazas.

Post & Communications The post office, on Durango between Allende and Morelos, is open 8 am to 5 pm Monday to Friday, Saturday 8.30 am to noon. Telecomm, with telegram, telex and fax, Avenida México 50 Nte on the corner of Morelos, is open 8 am to 6 pm Monday to Friday, 8 am to 4 pm Saturday. Post and Telecomm offices, and pay phones, are also found in the bus station.

The Cafetería La Parroquia (see Places to Eat) has an Internet cafe called the

In October 2000, the telephone area code is due to change to ☎ 3 from 32, with the digit 2 added to the start of every local number (for example, the number 14-80-71 will become 214-80-71).

Cibercafe La Parroquia. Cybercafé 3W, Hidalgo 61 Ote, is a pleasant bar with an Internet cafe, open 3 pm to midnight Sunday to Thursday, and 3 pm to 2 am Friday and Saturday.

Things to See & Do

The large **cathedral** on Plaza Principal was dedicated in 1750; the towers were completed in 1885. Opposite the church is the **palacio municipal** (city hall), where colorfully dressed Huichols sell handicrafts under the arches.

The 18th-century **Templo y Ex-Convento de la Cruz de Zacate** is at the end of Avenida México on the corner of Calzada del Ejército, about 2km south of the cathedral. It was here in 1767 that Father Junípero Serra organized his expedition that established the chain of Spanish missions in the Californias; you can visit the room where he stayed. In the ground outside the adjacent church there is a cross made up of age-old plants,

growing from the ground, which is said to have appeared miraculously and to have lived on untended.

There are colorful, impressive **murals** inside the Palacio de Gobierno and in the Cámara de Diputados on Avenida México. In the southwest section of the city is the large **Parque Paseo de la Loma**.

Cultural events are held at the **Fundación Alica de Nayarit**, Veracruz 256 Nte, half a block north of Plaza Principal; stop by anytime to see a schedule of events and view antique furnishings and other exhibits. Its opening hours are 9 am to 2 pm and 4 to 7 pm Monday to Friday, and from 9 am to 1 pm Saturday.

All of Tepic's museums have free admission. The **Museo Regional de Nayarit**, Avenida México 91, with a variety of interesting exhibits, is worth a visit; it's open 9 am to 2 pm and 4 to 8 pm Monday to Friday, 9 am to noon Saturday. The **Casa y Museo Amado Nervo**, Zacatecas 284 Nte, celebrates

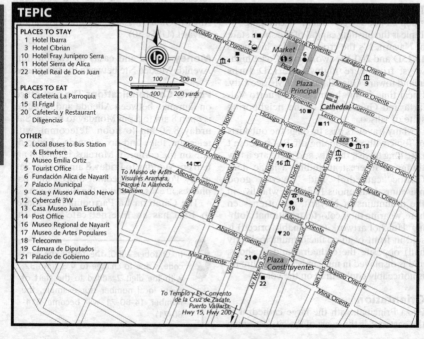

TEPIC

PLACES TO STAY
1 Hotel Ibarra
3 Hotel Cibrian
10 Hotel Fray Junípero Serra
11 Hotel Sierra de Alica
22 Hotel Real de Don Juan

PLACES TO EAT
8 Cafetería La Parroquia
15 El Frigal
20 Cafetería y Restaurant Diligencias

OTHER
2 Local Buses to Bus Station & Elsewhere
4 Museo Emilia Ortiz
5 Tourist Office
6 Fundación Alica de Nayarit
7 Palacio Municipal
9 Casa y Museo Amado Nervo
12 Cybercafé 3W
13 Casa Museo Juan Escutia
14 Post Office
16 Museo Regional de Nayarit
17 Museo de Artes Populares
18 Telecomm
19 Cámara de Diputados
21 Palacio de Gobierno

the life of the poet Amado Nervo, who was born in this house in 1870. It's open 10 am to 3 pm and 5 to 8 pm Tuesday to Saturday, 10 am to 5 pm Sunday.

Casa Museo Juan Escutia, Hidalgo 71 Ote, was the home of Juan Escutia, one of Mexico's illustrious 'Niños Héroes,' who died in 1847 at age 17 defending Mexico City's Castillo de Chapultepec from US forces. It's open 9 am to 2 pm and 4 to 6.30 pm Tuesday to Saturday, 10 am to 5 pm Sunday. Opposite, **Museo de Artes Populares**, Hidalgo 60 Ote, is also called the **Casa de los Cuatro Pueblos**. Contemporary popular arts of Nayarit's Huichol, Cora, Nahuatl and Tepehuano peoples are displayed and sold here, including clothing, yarn art, weaving, musical instruments, ceramics, and beadwork and more. It's open 9 am to 2 pm and 4 to 7 pm Monday to Friday, 9 am to 2 pm Saturday and Sunday.

Museo de Artes Visuales Aramara, Allende 329 Pte, is another museum of visual arts, open 9 am to 2 pm and 4 to 7 pm Monday to Saturday, 10 am to 3 pm Sunday. **Museo Emilia Ortiz**, Lerdo de Tejada 192 Pte, honors the painter Emilia Ortiz and her work; it's open from 9 am to 7 pm, Monday to Saturday.

Special Events
The Feria de la Mexicanidad, held mid-November to early December, celebrates Mexican culture with many events.

Places to Stay
Camping About 5km south of town, *Trailer Park Los Pinos* (☎ 13-12-32, *No 150 on the Tepic-Jalisco road)* offers 18 bungalows (all with kitchen) and 27 trailer spaces with full hookups.

Hotels The *Hotel Cibrian* (☎ 12-86-98/99, *Nervo 163 Pte)* is a good, clean hotel, charging US$12.50/15 a single/double. *Hotel Ibarra* (☎/fax 12-36-34, *Durango 297 Nte)* has singles/doubles for US$17/18.50. Both are fine places to stay, with clean, bright rooms, restaurants and enclosed parking.

In the block south of the cathedral, *Hotel Sierra de Alica* (☎ 12-03-25, *Avenida México*

180 Nte) has rooms for US$23/31. Right on the Plaza Principal, *Hotel Fray Junípero Serra* (☎ 12-25-25) is luxurious but more expensive, with rooms for US$41/45. Overlooking Plaza Constituyentes, *Hotel Real de Don Juan* (☎/fax 16-18-80/88, *Avenida México 105 Sur)* is an older-style hotel with character; rooms with one/two beds are US$47/52.

Two cheaper hotels are behind the bus station; neither is luxurious, but both are clean and acceptable, and all rooms have private bath. *Hotel Tepic* (☎ 14-76-15, *Dr Martinez 438)* has 85 small, clean singles/doubles for US$6.50/8; add US$1.75 for TV. Next door, *Hotel Nayar* (☎ 13-23-22, *Dr Martinez 430)* has 47 large rooms, at the same prices. Frequent local buses provide easy transport to the city center.

Places to Eat
A popular gathering spot with good food at good prices is the *Cafetería y Restaurant Diligencias* (*Avenida México 29 Sur)*, open 7 am to 10 pm Monday to Saturday, 5 to 10 pm Sunday. On the north side of Plaza Principal, *Cafetería La Parroquia*, upstairs under the arches, is pleasant for drinks and inexpensive light meals; open 8 am to 9.30 pm Monday to Saturday, 3 to 9.30 pm Sunday. Both places make excellent cappuccino. *El Frigal* (*Veracruz 112)*, at the corner of Zapata, an inexpensive courtyard vegetarian restaurant, is open 8.30 am to 9 pm daily. Several cheap places to eat are in or near the bus station.

Getting There & Away
Air Tepic's airport is in Pantanal, a 25-minute drive from Tepic, going toward Guadalajara. Aero California and Aeroméxico offer direct flights to Mexico City and Tijuana, with connections to other centers; Aeroméxico also has direct flights to Morelia.

Bus The bus station is on the southeastern outskirts of town; local buses marked 'Central' and 'Centro' make frequent connections between the bus station and the city center. The bus station has a cafeteria, left-luggage office, shops, post office, tourist information, telephone caseta and a Telecomm office with fax, telegram and telex. The main bus companies are Elite, Futura, Estrella Blanca and Ómnibus de México (all 1st-class), Transportes del Pacífico (1st- and 2nd-class) and TNS (2nd-class). Buses include:

Guadalajara – 216km, 3 hours; hourly or half-hourly, 24 hours, 1st-class (US$15.50) and 2nd-class (US$14)

Ixtlán del Río – 88km, 1½ hours; take Guadalajara buses which are not 'por autopista' (US$3.75 to US$5)

Mazatlán – 290km, 4½ to 5 hours; hourly, 24 hours, 1st-class (US$16.50) and 2nd-class (US$14.50)

Mexico City (Terminal Norte) – 751km, 10-12 hours; hourly, 24 hours, 1st-class (US$49) and 2nd-class (US$44)

Puerto Vallarta – 169km, 3½ hours, half-hourly, 3 am to 10 pm, by Transportes del Pacífico 2nd class (US$11); 9.30 pm and 2 am, by Elite (US$12)

San Blas – 70km, 1¼ hours; hourly, 5 am to 7 pm, by TNS (US$3.75)

Santiago Ixcuintla – 70km, 1¼ hours; hourly, 5.30 am to 8 pm, by TNS (US$3.75)

Getting Around
Local buses operate from around 6 am to 9 pm (US$0.20). Combis operate along Avenida México, from 6 am to midnight (US$0.20). There are also plenty of taxis.

AROUND TEPIC
Laguna Santa María del Oro
This idyllic lake surrounded by steep, forested mountains is in a volcanic crater 2km around and thought to be 100m to 200m deep, at an altitude of 730m. The clear, clean water takes on colors ranging from turquoise to slate. You can take some very pleasant walks around the lake and in the surrounding mountains, seeing numerous birds (250 species counted so far) and butterflies along the way. You can also climb to an abandoned gold mine, bicycle, swim, row on the lake, kayak and fish for black bass and perch. A few small restaurants serve fresh lake fish.

The attractive, peaceful **Koala Bungalows & RV Park** (☎ 3-214-05-09; koala45@ latinmail.com) has several sizes of well-maintained bungalows (US$22 to US$55, with cheaper monthly rates), camping spaces for trailers and tents (US$8 with full hookups, US$2.75 per person without hookups) and a restaurant. It's owned and operated by friendly Englishman Chris French, who's an excellent source of information about the lake.

To get to the lake, take the Santa María del Oro turnoff about 40km from Tepic along the Guadalajara road; from the turnoff it's about 10km to the village, then another 8km from the village to the lake. Buses to the lake depart from in front of the bus station in Tepic three times daily (50km, 1½ hours, US$2). Alternatively, buses to the village depart from the bus station in Tepic every half-hour; from there you can take another bus (or a taxi) to the lake.

Volcán Ceboruco
This extinct volcano, with a number of old craters, interesting plants and volcanic forms, has several short, interesting walks at the top. The 15km cobblestoned road up the volcano passes lava fields and fumaroles (steam vents), with plenty of vegetation growing on the slopes. The road begins at the village of Jala, 7km off the highway from Tepic to Guadalajara; the turnoff is 76km from Tepic, 12km before you reach Ixtlán del Río.

Ixtlán del Río
The small town of Ixtlán del Río, 1½ hours (88km) from Tepic on the road to Guadalajara, is unremarkable in itself, but Carlos Castaneda fans will remember that this is where Don Juan took Carlos in the book *Journey to Ixtlán*. You may see an occasional soul paying pilgrimage to the place, watching the plaza for crows. Outside Ixtlán is an archaeological site, **Los Toriles**, with an impressive round stone temple, the Templo a Quetzalcóatl. Any bus between Tepic and Guadalajara will drop you at Ixtlán.

Cerro de San Juan
About 10km southwest of town is the Cerro de San Juan ecological reserve, a good place for bird-watching.

Mirador del Águila

This lookout point on highway 15, about 11km northwest of Tepic, offers a wide view over a lush jungle canyon; bird-watching is best in the early morning and late afternoon.

CHACALA

The tiny coastal fishing village of Chacala, about 30km north of Rincón de Guayabitos and about 10km seaward from the turnoff on highway 200, occupies an amazingly beautiful little cove, with a lovely 1km beach bordered by lush green slopes. It has several palapa seafood restaurants right on the beach, a couple of camping grounds, and a few yachts anchored in the cove. Still, the outside world probably wouldn't have heard of little Chacala if it weren't for Mar de Jade.

Mar de Jade

On the beach at the south end of the cove, Mar de Jade has grown from the vision of a magnificent woman, Dr Laura del Valle, who lives there and operates a rural medical clinic in the nearby farming community of Las Varas.

It would take pages to fully describe all the interesting things happening at Mar de Jade. An ecological resort and retreat center, it attracts groups ranging from meditation, yoga and arts retreats to medical conferences. Immersion Spanish courses are offered throughout the year (classes begin on Mondays; minimum duration one week, with several three-week programs). University credit for rural medicine is available for volunteers in the medical clinic (Dr Laura is an Associate Professor of Family and Community Medicine at the School of Medicine, University of California, San Francisco). Other projects include organic gardening, house building, an open community kitchen and a community library. A one- to three-week 'spa intensive,' focusing on improving the health, is held several times each year.

Every summer, Mar de Jade offers a family camp. There's also a teenage summer camp (ages 12 to 18) incorporating immersion Spanish, intercultural exchange, ocean sports, games, theater, arts and crafts, Huichol art, Mexican cooking, dancing and music.

However, you don't have to participate in any of these things in order to visit Mar de Jade. Even garden-variety tourists are welcome to come and enjoy.

Room rates include healthy buffet-style meals served three times daily in the open-air dining room overlooking the ocean. Also included are exercise and hiking programs, dance classes, evening events, and use of all facilities.

Accommodations are in the big house by the beach, which is like a big communal home, and in secluded cabins spread around the grounds. Rooms are US$100/150 single/double, or US$60 for shared occupancy; suites are US$120/180 single/double. A private apartment is US$110 per person (minimum three adults). Children seven to 12 are US$25 (six and under free). Prices are 10% less from mid-April to mid-June and from mid-August to December 1. A 20% discount is given for three-week programs. You can also get a 20% discount on all rates by doing several hours a day of volunteer work around Mar de Jade.

Contact information for Mar de Jade is: www.mardejade.com; info@mardejade.com; ☎/fax in Puerto Vallarta 3-222-11-71; ☎ in Chacala 3-294-11-63.

Getting There & Away

To get to Chacala, you can get off the Puerto Vallarta-Tepic bus at Las Varas, 9km north on highway 200, and taxi from there (15 minutes).

RINCÓN DE GUAYABITOS

● pop 3000 ☎ changing

On the coast about 60km north of Puerto Vallarta, Rincón de Guayabitos is a low-key little beach resort town that makes a pleasant alternative to PV. Most of the tourists who come here are Mexican; it's extremely busy during the Mexican vacation times of Semana Santa, Christmas and the July and August school holidays. If you come at these times, reserve rooms in advance and be prepared for crowds and higher hotel prices. At other times, you can have the beautiful beach practically all to yourself, and relax, relax, relax. It's close enough to Vallarta that you can visit the city without having to stay there.

Guayabitos' activities include relaxing, walking on the beach, swimming, sport fishing, water sports, hiking up to the cross on the hill for the fine view, horseback riding, exploring other little beach towns nearby, and whale- watching November to March. You can take a boat out to the restaurant on Isla Islote offshore, and rent snorkel gear there. On the main street is a round, modern church with beautiful stained-glass windows.

In October 2000, the telephone area code is due to change to ☎ 3 from 327, with the digits 27 added to the start of every local number (for example, the number 4-06-93 will become 274-06-93).

Orientation & Information

Rincón de Guayabitos is on the beach, right on highway 200. At the north entrance to town, a high water tower is a distinctive landmark; turn into town here, follow the curve around, and you'll be on Guayabitos' main street, Avenida Sol Nuevo, lined with shops, restaurants, hotels, etc. More restaurants and hotels are along the beach, one block over.

Near the water tower, the Delegación de Turismo (☎/fax 4-06-93) provides information on the local area and the entire state of Nayarit. It's open 9 am to 2 pm and 4 to 6 pm Monday to Saturday, 9 am to 2 pm Sunday.

Guayabitos has basic services including shops and a post office. For more extensive shopping and an Internet café, locals go to La Peñita de Jaltemba, a larger and less touristy town a couple of kilometers north on highway 200.

Places to Stay

Guayabitos has plenty of places to stay, in every budget range. *Bungalows San Miguel* (☎ 4-01-33), on Retorno Laureles half a block from the beach, has a small swimming pool; rooms (without kitchen) are US$22,

bungalows (with kitchen) sleeping four/ eight people are US$27/44. *Posada Jaltemba* (☎ 4-01-65) at the corner of Avenida Sol Nuevo and Laureles, a block from the beach, has rooms without kitchen for US$25 to US$54, bungalows for US$32 to US$71. *Quinta Karla* (☎ 4-09-18, Avenida Sol Nuevo 28) has a swimming pool, parking and 10 air-conditioned studio/one-bedroom bungalows for US$42/53.

The luxurious beachfront *Villas Buena Vida* (☎ 4-02-31) is a great place to splash out; comfortable studio/one-bedroom/two-bedroom apartments, all with private balconies overlooking the sea and the beachfront swimming pool, are US$88/118/147.

Places to Eat

Many restaurants are along Avenida del Sol. *Plaza Sol Nuevo*, beside the pharmacy, serves good ice cream and coffee; try the iced coffee frappé. In the same block are several open-air places for BBQ chicken; a whole chicken served with rice, salad and tortillas, a big meal for two people, costs US$5.50. The *El Dorado Restaurant & Pizzeria Mona Lisa* serves tasty pizza 5 to 11 pm daily, November to April. The *Del Sol Steak House* serves their specialty BBQ ribs (US$6) and steak (US$8 to US$10) 4 to 10 pm daily.

Rincón Mexicano, attached to the beachfront Hotel Estancia San Carlos, has a lunch and dinner menu with imaginative dishes such as shrimp wrapped in coconut with apple and pineapple sauce, or shrimp in mango and red wine sauce, each US$8; other specialties include BBQ ribs and many interesting beef dishes. Open 8 am to 9 pm, daily except Wednesday.

Getting There & Away

Second-class buses coming from Puerto Vallarta (1½ hours, US$5.50) or Tepic (2 hours, US$6) may drop you on the highway at Guayabitos, but sometimes they don't stop here. A couple of kilometers toward Tepic, La Peñita is a sure stop. Colectivo vans operate frequently between La Peñita and Guayabitos (10 minutes, US$0.40), or you can take a taxi (US$2.75).

AROUND RINCÓN DE GUAYABITOS

Other pleasant little beach towns south of Rincón de Guayabitos make good day trips from either Guayabitos or Puerto Vallarta; they all have places to stay and eat, too, if you want to stay over. **Playa Los Ayala**, around the southern point of Guayabitos' beach, is about 2km south of Guayabitos. **Lo del Marco**, 13km south, **San Francisco**, 22km south, and **Sayulita**, 27km south, are other beautiful little beach towns. **Chacala**, about 30km north of Guayabitos, is another lovely little spot (see Chacala, earlier in the chapter).

SAYULITA
* **pop 1000 ☎ changing**

The tiny coastal village of Sayulita is a low-key, relaxed fishing and surfing town on a beautiful sandy beach shaded by a backdrop of coconut trees. Surfers and beachgoers come here from Puerto Vallarta, an hour away by bus, or find a place to stay in this much more relaxed little town.

Surfboard and bicycle rentals, as well as diving, hiking and other excursions, are available at Santa Crucecita Expediciones (santacrucecita@hotmail.com) on the main street. Nomadas Explorer, also on the main street, offers surfing and fishing trips, mountain biking, horseback riding, jungle trekking, diving, snorkeling and kayaking.

Sayulita has several good places to stay and eat. The beachfront *Sayulita Trailer Park & Bungalows* (☎/fax *5-02-02*) is attractive, with lots of shady coconut trees around a well-tended lawn. Tent and trailer spaces with full hookups are US$12, with discounts for longer stays. One-bedroom beachfront bungalows (with kitchen) are US$50 to US$65; two-bedroom garden bun-

galows are US$40 to US$55, cheaper by the week.

Behind the trailer park is the *Diamante International Hotel*; it's cheaper, around US$11 per night, but not very attractive. Much more pleasant is the friendly *Bungalows Las Gaviotas* (☎ *3-616-3402 in Guadalajara*) on Calle Gaviotas, half a block from the plaza and half a block from the beach. Five bungalows (with kitchen) are US$44 November to May, US$33 June to October; three rooms without kitchen are US$22/17 in winter/summer.

Several pleasant restaurants and cafés are near the plaza and along the beach.

To reach Sayulita, take the turnoff from highway 200, about 35km north of Puerto Vallarta and 25km south of Rincón de Guayabitos. Sayulita is 3km from the turnoff.

Ten buses per day operate between Sayulita and the Puerto Vallarta bus terminal (1 hour, US$1.75); otherwise, any 2nd-class bus will drop you at the turnoff.

PUERTO VALLARTA
* **pop 121,800 ☎ 3**

Puerto Vallarta is on the Río Cuale, lying between green, palm-covered mountains and the sparkling blue Bahía de Banderas (Bay of Flags). It's in Jalisco state, one hour ahead of neighboring Nayarit.

Formerly a quaint seaside village, Vallarta has been transformed into a world-famous resort city with 2.5 million visitors annually (one million foreigners, 1.5 million Mexicans). Some of the most beautiful beaches, secluded and romantic just a few years ago, are now dominated by giant luxury mega-resorts. Tourism – Vallarta's only industry – has made it a bilingual city, with English almost as commonly spoken as Spanish. But the cobblestoned streets, lined with old-fashioned white adobe buildings with red tile roofs, still make Vallarta one of Mexico's most picturesque coastal cities.

Vallarta's attractions suit all tastes and pockets, with idyllic white-sand beaches, water sports and cruises, horseback rides and tours, shopping, art galleries, abundant restaurants and active nightlife.

In October 2000, the telephone area code is due to change to ☎ 3 from 327, with the digits 27 added to the start of every local number (for example, the number 5-02-02 will become 275-02-02).

CENTRAL PACIFIC COAST

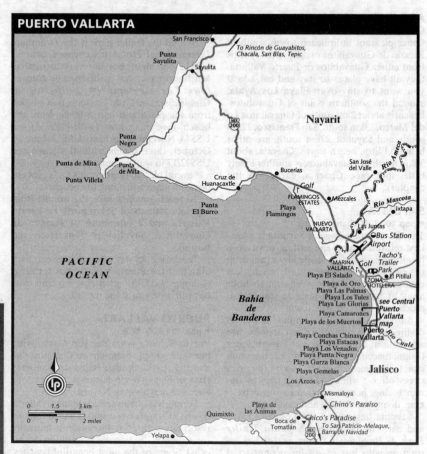

PUERTO VALLARTA

History

Although indigenous peoples probably lived in this area for centuries, as they did elsewhere along the coast, Puerto Vallarta's recorded history is not very long. The first documented settlement here was in 1851, when the Sánchez family came and made their home by the mouth of the Río Cuale, which now divides the city. Farmers and fisherfolk followed. By 1918, enough people lived around the Río Cuale to give the settlement a name on the map. The name Vallarta was chosen in honor of Ignacio Luis Vallarta, a former governor of the state of Jalisco. It was called 'puerto' (port)

because farmers had been shipping their harvests by boat from a small port area north of the Río Cuale.

Tourists began to visit Vallarta in 1954 when Mexicana airlines started a promotional campaign and initiated the first flights here, landing on a dirt airstrip in Emiliano Zapata, an area that is now the center of Vallarta. But it was not until a decade later, when John Huston chose the nearby deserted cove of Mismaloya for the shooting of the film version of Tennessee Williams' *The Night of the Iguana*, that the town was put on the international tourist map.

During that film's shooting, the paparazzi of Hollywood descended to report on every development in the romance between Richard Burton and Elizabeth Taylor. Burton's co-star Ava Gardner also raised more than a few eyebrows, and Puerto Vallarta suddenly became world-famous, with an aura of steamy tropical romance. Tour groups began arriving not long after the film crew left, and they've been coming ever since.

Orientation

The town center is around the Río Cuale, with the small Isla Cuale in the middle of the river and two bridges allowing easy passage between the two sides of town. North of the city are the airport (10km), the bus station (a kilometer or two north of the airport), and two recent developments: Marina Vallarta, a large yachting marina about 1km south of the airport, and Nuevo Vallarta, farther north around the bay, about 25km from the city center. Also north of the city are a host of giant luxury hotels fanning out along the shore, and some fine beaches. To the south of the city are more resorts and some of the most beautiful beaches in the area.

The heart of the city center is Plaza Principal, also called Plaza de Armas, beside the sea between Morelos and Juárez, the city's two principal thoroughfares. The crown-topped cathedral, Templo de Guadalupe, towers a block behind the plaza, while seaside of the plaza is an amphitheater with arches, which have become a symbol of Vallarta. The Malecón, the wide seaside walkway stretching about 10 blocks north from the plaza, is lined with bars, restaurants, nightclubs and boutiques.

South of the river is a district with hotels, restaurants and the only two beaches in the city center: Playa Olas Altas (poorly named, because it doesn't really have 'big waves') and Playa de los Muertos (Beach of the Dead), which takes its strange name from a fierce fight there sometime in the distant past.

City traffic has been reduced dramatically by the opening of a *libramiento* or bypass road on the inland side of the city center, diverting traffic away from the center.

Information

Tourist Offices Vallarta's municipal tourist office (☎ 223-25-00 ext 230, 231, 232, fax 223-25-00 ext 233), in the municipal building on the northeast corner of Plaza Principal, has free maps, multilingual tourist literature and friendly bilingual staff; it's open 8 am to 4 pm Monday to Friday.

The state tourist office, Dirección de Turismo del Estado de Jalisco (☎ 221-26-76 to 221-26-80, fax 221-26-78, dirturpv@pvnet.com.mx), is north of town in Marina Vallarta, at Plaza Marina, Local 144 and 146; open 9 am to 5 pm weekdays.

Club Paco Paco (☎ 222-1899, info@pacopaco.com, www.pacopaco.com), Vallarta 278, acts as an informal center for Vallarta's gay community (see Entertainment); open noon to 6 am daily. Pick up their free *Paco Paco Tourist Info & Map*, with information on gay hotels, cruises, tours, entertainment etc. Another useful resource is www.GayPuertoVallarta.com.

Consulates The US consulate (☎ 222-00-69), upstairs at Zaragoza 160 on Plaza Principal, is open 10 am to 2 pm, Monday to Friday. One floor below is the Canadian consulate (☎ 222-53-98, 223-0858, emergency 01-800-706-2900), open 9 am to 5 pm weekdays.

Money Most businesses in Vallarta accept US dollars as readily as they accept pesos, though the rate of exchange they give is usually less favorable than at banks, which offer the best rate. Several banks are found around Plaza Principal, but they often have long queues. Banamex, on the south side of the plaza, is open 9 am to 5 pm Monday to Friday, 9 am to 2 pm Saturday. Most banks have ATMs.

Vallarta has many casas de cambio; it may pay to shop around, since rates differ. Though their rates are less favorable than the banks', the difference may be slight, and the longer opening hours and faster service may make using them worthwhile. Most are open around 9 am to 7.30 pm daily, sometimes with a 2 to 4 pm lunch break. Look for them on Insurgentes, Vallarta, the Malecón and many other streets.

CENTRAL PUERTO VALLARTA

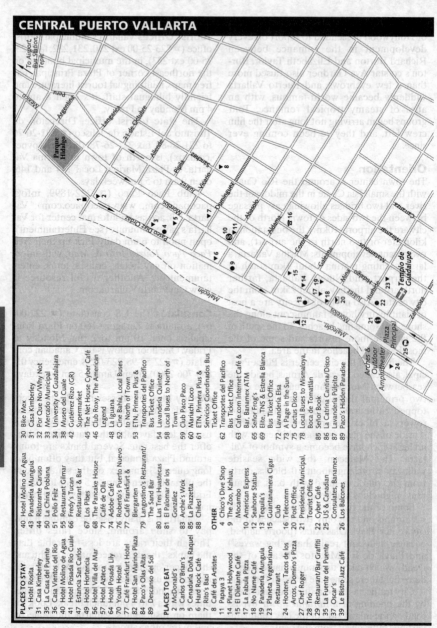

PLACES TO STAY
1 Hotel Rosita
31 Casa Kimberley
35 La Casa del Puente
36 Casa Vientos del Río
40 Hotel Molino de Agua
41 Hotel Posada Río Cuale
47 Estancia San Carlos
49 Hotel Hortencia
56 Hotel Villa del Mar
57 Hotel Azteca
64 Hotel Posada Lily
70 Youth Hostel
77 Café Frankfurt Hotel
82 Hotel San Marino Plaza
84 Paco's Olas Altas
89 Descanso del Sol

PLACES TO EAT
2 McDonald's
3 Carlos O'Brian's
5 Cenaduría Doña Raquel
6 Hard Rock Café
7 Rito's Baci
8 Café des Artistes
11 Papaya 3
14 Planet Hollywood
15 El Diletante Café
18 La Fabula Pizza
19 No Name Café
19 Panadería Munguía
23 Planeta Vegetariano Restaurant
24 Hooters, Tacos de los Arcos, Domino's Pizza
27 Chef Roger
28 Trio
29 Restaurant/Bar Graffiti
35 La Fuente del Puente
37 Oscar's
39 Le Bistro Jazz Café

40 Hotel Molino de Agua
43 Panadería Munguía
44 Ristorante Caruso
50 La China Poblana
51 Pollo Feliz
55 Restaurant Gilmar
66 Fredy's Tucan Restaurant & Bar
67 Los Pibes
68 The Pancake House
71 Café de Olla
74 Adobe Café
76 Roberto's Puerto Nuevo
77 Café Frankfurt & Biergarten
79 Langostino's Restaurant/ The Sand Bar
80 Las Tres Huastecas
81 El Palomar de los González
83 Archie's Wok
85 La Piazzetta
88 Chiles!

OTHER
4 Chico's Dive Shop
9 The Zoo, Kahlua, Mocambo
10 American Express
12 Seahorse Statue
13 Tequila's
15 Guantanamera Cigar Club
16 Telecomm
21 Post Office
21 Presidencia Municipal, Tourist Office
22 Cyber Café
25 US & Canadian Consulates, Banamex
26 Los Balcones

30 Bike Mex
31 Casa Kimberley
32 Por Que No/Why Not
33 Mercado Municipal
34 University of Guadalajara
38 Gutiérrez Rizo (GR) Supermarket
42 Museo del Cuale
45 The Net House Cyber Café
46 Club Roxy, The American Legend
48 La Iguana
52 Cine Bahía, Local Buses to North of Town
53 ETN, Primera Plus & Transportes del Pacífico Bus Ticket Office
54 Lavandería Quinter
58 Local Buses to North of Town
59 Club Paco Paco
60 Mariachi Loco
61 ETN, Primera Plus & Servicios Coordinados Bus Ticket Office
62 Transportes del Pacífico Bus Ticket Office
63 Cafe.com Internet Café & Bar, Banamex ATM
65 Señor Frog's
69 Elite, TNS & Estrella Blanca Bus Ticket Office
72 Lavandería Elsa
73 A Page in the Sun
75 Cactus Disco
78 Local Buses to Mismaloya, Boca de Tomatlán
85 Señor Book
86 La Catrina Cantina/Disco
87 Lavandería Pulpito
89 Paco's Hidden Paradise

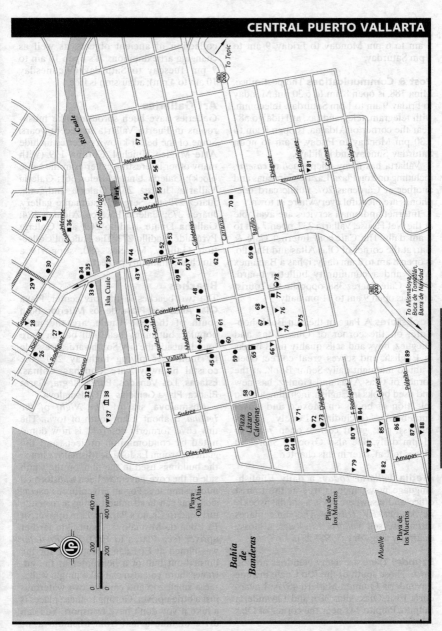

CENTRAL PUERTO VALLARTA

To Tepic

Río Cuale

Footbridge

Park

Jacarandas

Aguacate

Isla Cuale

Insurgentes

Constitución

Aquiles Serdán

Madero

Vallarta

Suárez

Olas Altas

Plaza Lázaro Cárdenas

Cuauhtémoc

Guerrero

Libertad

A. Rodríguez

Encino

Cárdenas

Carranza

Badillo

Díeguez

F. Rodríguez

Gómez

Púlpito

Díeguez

F. Rodríguez

Gómez

Púlpito

Amapas

Bahía de Banderas

Playa Olas Altas

Playa de los Muertos

Playa de los Muertos

Muelle

To Mismaloya, Boca de Tomatlán, Barra de Navidad

CENTRAL PACIFIC COAST

400 m

400 yards

0   200   400

0   200   400

American Express (☎ 223-29-55), at the corner of Morelos and Abasolo, is open 9 am to 6 pm Monday to Friday, 9 am to 1 pm Saturday.

Post & Communications The post office, Mina 188, is open 8 am to 6.30 pm Monday to Friday, 9 am to 1 pm Saturday. Telecomm, with telegram, telex and fax, at Hidalgo 582 near the corner of Aldama, is open 8 am to 7.30 pm Monday to Friday, 9 am to noon Saturday, Sunday and holidays.

Vallarta has many telephone/fax *casetas*, including one on Plaza Lázaro Cárdenas and another at Cárdenas 267. Public card telephones are plentiful everywhere in town.

Internet and email services are available at the Net House, Vallarta 232, open 7 am to 2 am daily. The Cafe.com Internet Café & Bar, at the corner of Olas Altas and Badillo, is open 8 am to 2 am daily; it has a Banamex ATM and a community bulletin board. Cyber Café, Juárez 388, opposite the tourist office, is open 9 am to 11 pm daily.

Bookstores A Page in the Sun Bookshop-Café, on the corner of Olas Altas and Diéguez, buys and sells quality used books in English, and serves great coffee; open 8 am to midnight daily. Señor Book, at the corner of Olas Altas and Gómez, has new and used books in English, including a good selection of books on Mexico and travel guidebooks (including Lonely Planet guides), plus great coffee; open 7 am to 11 pm daily. See also Grocery Stores in Places to Eat, later in this chapter.

Media *Vallarta Today*, a daily English-language newspaper, is free at the tourist office and elsewhere, as is a similar weekly newspaper, *PV Tribune*. The same places often also sell *Vallarta Lifestyles*, a glossy quarterly magazine (US$3.25).

Laundry There are many laundries around town. Those south of the Río Cuale include Lavandería Quinter, Madero 407A; Lavandería Elsa, Olas Altas 385; and Lavandería Púlpito, Púlpito 141 near the corner of Olas Altas.

Museo del Cuale

This tiny museum on Isla Cuale has a small collection of ancient objects, as well as changing art exhibitions. It's open 10 am to 7 pm Tuesday to Saturday (Wednesday 10 am to 4 pm); admission is free.

Art Galleries

Galleries have been sprouting like mushrooms in Puerto Vallarta in recent years. Some of the better-known galleries include Arte Mágico Huichol, Corona 179 (with many other interesting galleries in the same block); Galería Uno, Morelos 561; Galería Vallarta, Juárez 263; Galería Indígena, Juárez 270; the Sergio Bustamante gallery, Juárez 275; Galería Pacífico, Aldama 174; Galleria Dante, Badillo 269; and Galería Pyrámide, Badillo 272. The Huichol Collection Gallery, Morelos 490, supports a Huichol community project.

Beaches

The two beaches in the city center, **Playa Olas Altas** and **Playa de los Muertos**, both south of the Río Cuale, are the most popular, but many beautiful beaches are found outside the city. Southward, accessible by minibuses plying highway 200 (the coastal highway), are **Conchas Chinas**, **Estacas**, **Los Venados**, **Punta Negra**, **Garza Blanca**, **Playa Gemelas** and **Mismaloya**.

Mismaloya, site of *The Night of the Iguana*, is about 12km south of town. The tiny cove, formerly deserted, is now dominated by condominium projects and the giant 303-room La Jolla de Mismaloya hotel; the buildings used in the film, on the south side of the cove, have now been transformed into restaurants. For an adventurous excursion you can head inland along a riverside dirt road to Chino's Paraíso, 2km upriver, or El Edén de Mismaloya, about 5km farther upriver (see Places to Eat). The *Predator* was filmed at El Edén, accounting for the burned-out hull of a helicopter at the entrance; here you also can take jungle walks, see a small zoo and explore two waterfalls just a little upriver. Getting to these places is a hike if you don't have transport. You can drive or take a taxi from Mismaloya, or

Bahía de Banderas

The Bahía de Banderas (Bay of Flags) is the seventh-largest bay in the world, with an area of about 34km by 52km, a 161km shoreline and a probable depth of around 1800m (depth-measuring instruments have never found the bottom). Supposedly the bay was formed by the sunken crater of a giant, extinct volcano. If you fly over the bay you might actually see the perimeter of this crater.

The bay is teeming with life, but has the unusual distinction of being virtually shark-free. This is because dolphins inhabiting the bay bear their young all year round. To protect their colony they mount a patrol at the bay's entrance to keep sharks out.

Whales are also present in the bay. Humpbacks, the bay's most numerous and oft-sighted whales, are here from around November to the end of March, mating and bearing babies conceived the year before. Bride whales are much less numerous, but unlike humpbacks they are not a migratory whale – they remain in tropical waters all year round, so there's a remote chance of seeing one at any time of year. Gray whales, which migrate between Baja California and Alaska, are very rarely seen here, but they have been sighted.

The bay's giant manta rays – with 4m 'wingspans' – mate in April. During that month they often jump above the water's surface, and you can sometimes witness their acrobatics from the shore.

✽ ✽ ✽ ✽ ✽ ✽ ✽ ✽ ✽ ✽ ✽ ✽

come up on horseback along a jungle trail. The walk back is downhill all the way and makes a pleasant stroll.

About 4km past Mismaloya, **Boca de Tomatlán** is a peaceful, less commercialized seaside village in a small cove where the Río de Tomatlán meets the sea – a jungly place with quiet water, a beach and several small restaurants.

Farther around the south side of the bay are the more isolated beaches of Las Ánimas, Quimixto and Yelapa, accessible only by boat. **Playa de las Ánimas** (Beach of the Spirits), a lovely beach with a small fishing village and some *palapa* restaurants offering fresh seafood, is said to be the most beautiful beach on the bay. **Quimixto**, not far from Las Ánimas, has a waterfall accessible by a half-hour hike, or you can hire a pony on the beach to take you up.

Yelapa, farthest from town, is probably Vallarta's most popular cruise destination. This picturesque cove is crowded with tourists, restaurants and parasailing operators during the day, but empties out when the tourist boats leave in late afternoon. The charming village at Yelapa has a sizable colony of foreign residents; you can easily find a place to stay if you ask around. Take a hike upriver to see the waterfalls.

Still more beaches are found around the north side of the bay. Nearest Vallarta are the beaches in the Zona Hotelera: **Camarones**, **Las Glorias**, **Los Tules**, **Las Palmas**, **Playa de Oro** and, past the Marina, **El Salado**. Nuevo Vallarta also has beaches. Farther on around the bay are **Playa Flamingos**, **Bucerías**, **Destiladeras**, **Punta el Burro**, **Paraíso Escondido**, **El Anclote** and **Punta de Mita**, at the northern boundary of the bay.

Water Sports

Snorkeling, scuba diving, deep-sea fishing, water-skiing, windsurfing, sailing, parasailing, riding the 'banana' and just plain swimming are all popular in Vallarta. Most activities can be arranged on the beaches in front of any of the large hotels. The tourist offices can help connect you with operators.

The most spectacular spots for snorkeling and diving are **Los Arcos**, a protected ecological zone on an island rock formation just north of Mismaloya, and the **Islas Marietas** at the entrance to the bay, with impressive reefs, underwater caves, tunnels, walls and opportunities to see dolphins, whales and giant manta rays.

Vallarta has several diving and snorkeling operators. Chico's Dive Shop (☎ 222-18-95, 222-54-39), on the Malecón at Paseo Díaz Ordaz 772, open 8 am to 10 pm daily, is the biggest outfit, offering several good diving

MARK HONAN

Seahorse statue at sunset, on the Malecón

travel agency can tell you which cruises are operating, details of where they go, what they offer (many include meals, open bar, live music and dancing) and current prices. For something different, try the *Marigalante* Pirate Ship – it's been receiving rave reviews – or the *Rainbow Dancer* gay cruise.

If you just want to visit the beaches, a cheaper way to get there is by water taxi (see Getting Around).

Dolphins & Whales
Always wanted to swim with dolphins? You can do it in Vallarta at the dolphin center operated by Vallarta Adventure (see Organized Tours). Dolphins are present in the bay all year round; you're likely to see some if you go out on a boat.

Whale-watching trips operate from December to March, when humpback whales are in the bay mating, bearing young and caring for new calves. Open Air Expeditions is a popular operator; Vallarta Adventure also does whale-watching trips (see Organized Tours).

Horseback Riding
Vallarta has many horseback riding operators in different areas; the tourist offices keep a list of operators. Two larger operators are Rancho El Charro (☎ 224-01-14) and Rancho Ojo de Agua (☎ 224-06-07). At Mismaloya, Rancho Manolo (☎ 228-00-18, 222-36-94) offers three-hour horseback trips from Mismaloya beach up a jungle trail to El Edén, plus longer nine-hour mountain trips. Rancho Palma Real (☎ 221-12-36) and La Huerta Rancho Turístico (☎ 222-03-86), upstream on the Río Cuale at Colonia Paso Ancho 245, near the footbridge, also offer horseback riding. A group of horses is usually available on Olas Altas at the corner of Carranza, offering simple rides safe for children; horse owners also offer beach rides north of the Río Cuale. Expect to pay around US$11 per hour for horseback riding.

Golf & Tennis
These are both popular sports at Vallarta. Golf courses north of the city include the exclusive Marina Vallarta Golf Club (☎ 221-

and snorkeling trips. A two-tank diving trip costs US$76 or US$95, depending on where you go. A three-day PADI open water diver certification course costs US$266 (cash) or US$291 (charge); advanced courses are also available.

Deep-sea fishing is popular all year, with a major international sailfish tournament held every November. Prime catches are sailfish, marlin, tuna, red snapper and sea bass. The tourist office can recommend fishing operators for the type of trip you have in mind.

See the Getting Around section for information on hiring private yachts and lanchas for snorkeling and fishing trips.

Cruises
A host of daytime, sunset and evening cruises are available in Vallarta, some including snorkeling stops at Los Arcos (see Water Sports). The most popular are probably the cruises to Yelapa and Las Ánimas beaches; other cruises go to the Islas Marietas, farther out. The tourist office or any

05-45) and the less exotic Los Flamingos Golf Club (☎ 329-02-80).

A favorite with tennis players is the John Newcombe Tennis Club (☎ 224-43-60 ext 500) in the Zona Hotelera, also north of the city. Most of the large luxury hotels have courts; phone them to reserve a court. Sheraton Buganvilias (☎ 223-04-04), Hotel Krystal (☎ 224-02-02) and the Marriott Hotel (☎ 221-00-04) all have courts available, and there are plenty of others.

Bungee Jumping

You can bungee jump from a platform on a sea cliff between Puerto Vallarta and Mismaloya, about 1km north of the Los Arcos rocks, 10 am to 6 pm daily.

Language Courses

The University of Guadalajara's Foreign Student Study Center (☎ 223-20-82, cipv@cepe.edu.mx, www.cepe.udg.mx), Libertad 105-1 opposite the Mercado Municipal, specializes in teaching Spanish and can arrange lodging with a Mexican family. Beginning, intermediate and advanced courses are offered year-round, plus intensive and super-intensive sessions; they also offer a one-week 'basic skills for tourists' session. Summer courses include Mexican culture, Mexican history, and Spanish summer sessions for children age seven to nine and 10 to 13. University credit can be earned for most courses.

Organized Tours

The tourist offices and travel agents can set you up with city tours, jungle tours, bicycle tours, horseback riding tours and archaeological tours, among others.

Bike Mex (☎ 223-16-80), Guerrero 361, offers hiking and mountain bike tours with experienced bilingual guides, tailored to your level of fitness and experience, plus mountain bike rentals for self-guided tours. B-B-Bobby's Bikes (☎ 223-00-08), at the corner of Iturbide and Miramar, also offers guided and self-guided mountain bike tours.

Mid-November to late April, the International Friendship Club (☎ 222-54-66) offers 2½ hour tours of some of Puerto Vallarta's luxurious private homes. The tours depart at 11 am from Hotel Molino de Agua, Vallarta 130, every Wednesday and Thursday; the US$25 donation benefits local charities.

Or you can take a tour of Casa Kimberley, the house that Richard Burton bought for Elizabeth Taylor back in the 1960s, still with its original furnishings. It's at Zaragoza 445, in 'gringo gulch' (☎ 222-13-36); tours are given 9 am to 6 pm daily (US$6).

Don't miss the amazing natural wonders around Vallarta, on land and sea. Several tour companies specialize in nature and outdoor tours; the tourist offices can recommend reliable operators. Vallarta Adventure (☎ 221-06-57, adventure@acnet.net, www.vallarta-adventures.com), Edificio Marina Golf, Local 13-C, Calle Mastil, Marina Vallarta, operates a variety of land and sea nature tours, as well as their dolphin center (see Dolphins & Whales). Open Air Expeditions (☎ 222-33-10, openair@vivamexico.com, www.vivamexico.com/open, www.vallartawhales.com), Guerrero 339, offers whale-watching, sea kayaking, snorkeling, bird-watching, hiking and customized tours. Nomadas Explorer (☎ 275-00-82, 221-23-55) also offers a variety of nature tours.

Specialty tours include an archaeological tour to the Santuario del Rey (King's Sanctuary) by Carlos Arceo (cellular ☎ 044-329-46761), and guided Harley-Davidson motorcycle tours of the area (you drive); contact the American Legend (☎ 222-24-00), Vallarta 237.

Special Events

Regatta Marina del Rey-Puerto Vallarta, held during February in odd-numbered years, is a boat race beginning at Marina del Rey, near San Diego, California, and ending with festivities here.

Semana Santa (Easter week) is the busiest holiday of the year in Puerto Vallarta. Hotels fill up and hundreds (or thousands) of excess visitors camp out on the beaches and party. It's a wild time.

Fiestas de Mayo, a city-wide fair with cultural and sporting events, music concerts, carnival rides and art exhibits, is held throughout May.

Timeshares

Attending a timeshare presentation is one way to get a greatly discounted (perhaps even free) cruise, dinner, jeep rental or horseback ride. This involves putting up with a 90-minute sales pitch (with a free breakfast) about the benefits of investing in one of Puerto Vallarta's burgeoning timeshare condominium projects, and then touring the project. You'll see many timeshare hawkers along Puerto Vallarta's main streets.

Generally you must be over 25 years old, in possession of a major credit card and employed; many hawkers also require that you be married, and that both husband and wife attend the presentation. They will pay the taxi fare from your hotel to the project. You are under no obligation to buy or sign anything.

Travelers give mixed reports about the presentations. Some say it's a painless enough way to get a cheap jeep, tour or cruise. Others are still angry days later, after fending off the 'hard sell.'

❋❋❋❋❋❋❋❋❋❋❋❋❋❋

A big, international Torneo de Pesca is held each year in November; dates vary according to the phase of the moon, which must be right for fishing. The tourist offices can provide exact dates.

Día de Santa Cecilia (November 22) honors the patron saint of mariachis, with all the city's mariachis forming a musical procession to the Templo de Guadalupe in the early evening. They come playing and singing, enter the church and sing homage to their saint, then go out into the plaza and continue to play. During the entire day one or another group of mariachis stays in the church making music.

All Mexico celebrates December 12 as the day of the country's patron saint, the Virgen de Guadalupe. In Puerto Vallarta the celebrations are more drawn out, with pilgrimages and processions to the cathedral day and night from November 30 until the big bash on December 12.

Places to Stay

Vallarta has a good selection of accommodations in every price range. Most hotel prices are higher during Vallarta's high season, roughly from December to April. For accommodations at the very busiest times – Semana Santa or between Christmas and New Year's – be sure to reserve in advance.

Places to Stay – Budget

Camping Closest in is the *Puerto Vallarta Trailer Park* (☎ 224-28-28, Francia 143), in Colonia Versailles in the Zona Hotelera, a few kilometers north of the city. It has plenty of shady trees and 60 tent/trailer spaces with full hookups for US$16.50, with weekly and monthly discounts. A few kilometers farther north, *Tacho's Trailer Park* (☎ 224-21-63), on Avenida Prisciliano Sánchez opposite Colonia Aramara, has a swimming pool and 120 tent/trailer spaces with full hookups for US$17.50. *KOA* (☎ 298-08-53), on highway 200 at Km 149, about 10km north of town, has tent/trailer spaces with full hookups for US$12/18, 'kamping kabins' for US$25. In town, *Café Frankfurt Hotel* (see Hotels) has three trailer spaces with full hookups for US$16.50 (no tents).

Hostels The clean, pleasant *Youth Hostel* (☎ 222-21-08, Aguacate 302A) has bunks for US$7.75 per day, US$46 per week, US$82 for two weeks or US$131 per month.

Hotels Vallarta's cheapest lodgings are south of the Río Cuale, particularly along Madero. All are basic but clean, with fan and private bath.

Hotel Villa del Mar (☎ 222-07-85, Madero 440) has 49 rooms, many featuring private balconies with chairs and flowering plants; rooftop sitting areas offer a view over town. Singles/doubles are US$17/21; studio apartments with fully equipped kitchens are US$29/30 or US$400/450 a month.

Hotel Azteca (☎ 222-27-50, Madero 473) has clean, pleasant singles/doubles for US$14/18; rooms with kitchenettes and cable TV are US$25.

Several other hotels along Madero charge the same rates, around US$14/18. They are more basic, but perfectly acceptable.

Hotel Hortencia (☎ 222-24-84, *Madero 336*) charges US$24/26; telephone and refrigerator are available for an extra US$2 each, air-con for an extra US$4.50.

The oft-recommended *Hotel Yazmín* (☎ 222-00-87, *Basilio Badillo 168*) has singles/doubles for US$24/28. It's clean and friendly, with courtyard gardens, a good restaurant next door, and it's just a block from Playa de los Muertos, the most popular beach in Vallarta.

Places to Stay – Mid-Range

Café Frankfurt Hotel (☎ 222-34-03, *Badillo 300*) is an older hotel with a friendly family atmosphere, a garden café and enclosed parking. Regular rooms are US$28, cabañas US$38; one- and two-bedroom apartments with kitchen are US$38/55. All prices include accommodation for two children; rates are cheaper monthly.

Hotel Posada Lily (☎ 222-00-32, *Badillo 109*), at the corner of Olas Altas half a block from Playa de los Muertos, has singles/doubles/triples for US$22/33/38 December to March, US$17/28/33 April to November. All rooms come with refrigerators, most with cable TV, and some with air-con.

Estancia San Carlos (☎/fax 222-54-84, *Constitución 210*) is a good deal for mid-range apartments, with a courtyard swimming pool, covered parking and 24 clean, modern apartments with fully-equipped kitchen, air-con, TV and private balcony. One-bedroom/two-bedroom apartments are US$38/60, cheaper monthly.

Hotel Posada Río Cuale (☎/fax 222-04-50, *Serdán 242*), on the corner of Vallarta, is a pleasant hotel with swimming pool, poolside restaurant/bar and air-con singles/doubles for US$44/49 December to April, cheaper May to November.

Casa Corazón (☎/fax 222-63-64, 505-523-4666 in USA, *Amapas 326*) is an attractive B&B guesthouse with beautiful, spacious terraces overlooking Playa de los Muertos (the front gate opens onto the beach). Bed-and-breakfast is US$45 to US$65 mid-December to mid-April, US$25 to US$45 the rest of the year, cheaper for singles. The same family operates the Looney Tunes restaurant/bar, right there on the beach.

Beside the beach at the north end of the Malecón, *Hotel Rosita* (☎/fax 222-10-33, *Paseo Díaz Ordaz 901*) is a popular older hotel with a beachside swimming pool, restaurant and bar. Rates start at US$32 for interior rooms with fan; rooms and suites with sea view or air-con cost more.

One of Vallarta's hidden treasures is the tiny *La Casa del Puente* (☎ 222-07-49, 415-775-1970 in USA), tucked behind the Restaurant La Fuente del Puente beside the Río Cuale, with just a one-bedroom apartment and a two-bedroom apartment; each costs US$87 November to May, US$41 the rest of the year. Molly Muir, the owner, is a wonderful hostess and impromptu tour guide.

Dick Baker at *Casa Vientos del Río* (☎ 222-17-58, *Cuauhtémoc 460*) offers two one-bedroom units and one two-bedroom unit, each with kitchen, for US$55 to US$85 October to April, about half that price June to September. It's very attractive, with a terrace swimming pool and lovely view overlooking the river.

Club Paco Paco, the gay bar/disco (see Entertainment), operates three popular mid-range gay hotels. Most economical is *Paco's Olas Altas* (☎ 223-02-77, *Olas Altas 465*); singles/doubles are US$30/45, breakfast included. *Descanso del Sol* (☎ 223-02-77, *Suárez 583*) has singles/doubles for US$57/68, cheaper in the off-season. *Paco's Hidden Paradise*, on a private, secluded beach near Boca de Tomatlán, is accessible only by boat.

Places to Stay – Top End

Puerto Vallarta has many beautiful places to stay at the upper end of the market. From mid-April to mid-December, low-season discounts bring even some of the finest places down to a more affordable level.

One of Vallarta's best and most centrally located hotels is *Hotel Molino de Agua*

(☎ 222-19-07, *Vallarta 130*), facing the beach on the south side of Río Cuale. Though it's in the city center, it's remarkably quiet and peaceful, with 59 cabins, rooms and suites set among tropical gardens covering two city blocks. Prices are US$67 to US$109 most of the year, US$92 to US$150 mid-December to mid-April.

Casa Kimberley (☎/fax 222-13-36, *Zaragoza 445*), the former villa of Elizabeth Taylor and Richard Burton (see Organized Tours), offers B&B in style.

Top-end hotels line the beach at Playa de los Muertos. Typically they are high-rises with air-con, beachfront swimming pools and restaurants. For example, *Hotel San Marino Plaza* (☎ 222-30-50, *Rodolfo Gómez 111*) charges US$99/160 single/double in winter, US$63/126 the rest of the year, all-inclusive (three meals daily, open bar).

Many giant five-star and Grand Tourism-category hotels, often with hundreds of rooms, line the beaches north and south of town. Some of the most attractive are on the beaches south of town, including the *Camino Real*, *Presidente Inter-Continental* and *La Jolla de Mismaloya*. In the Zona Hotelera are the *Sheraton Buganvilias*, *Qualton*, *Plaza Las Glorias*, *Krystal Vallarta*, *Continental Plaza*, *Fiesta Americana* and *Holiday Inn*. Farther north, in Marina Vallarta, are the *Marriott Casa Magna*, *Paradisus*, *Bel-Air*, *Westin Regina*, *Vidafel* and *Velas Vallarta*. Still farther north in Nuevo Vallarta are the *Sierra Radisson*, *Diamond Resorts* and *Jack Tar Village*. Travel agents can connect you with any of these places; they all do big business in foreign package tours.

Several elegant guesthouses provide a comfortable gay-friendly ambiance, including *Casa de los Arcos* (☎ 222-59-90), a luxurious mountainside villa overlooking the south part of town, and *Casa Panorámica* (☎ 222-36-56), Km 1 on the highway to Mismaloya.

Places to Eat

Restaurants – South of Río Cuale Several small, cheap, family-run restaurants are along Madero. One is *Restaurant Gilmar*

(*Madero 418*), providing good tasty food at low prices; the *comida corrida* (US$2.60) includes three courses and a drink. *La China Poblana (Insurgentes 222)* has typical Mexican food and an upstairs dining terrace. Several nearby places offer broiled chicken, including *Pollo Feliz* on the corner of Madero and Insurgentes, with half/whole chickens for US$2/4 medium and US$3/6 large.

Many other restaurants south of the river are a step up in class; this being the city's main hotel district, most are heavily patronized by tourists.

Two restaurants on Badillo claim to serve the best breakfast in town: *The Pancake House (Badillo 289)* and *Fredy's Tucan Restaurant & Bar*, on the corner of Badillo and Vallarta. Each has been nominated in letters from travelers as winning 'hands down' so you'd best decide for yourself. Both have about 20 varieties of pancakes and waffles, plus treats such as eggs Benedict, cheese blintzes and omelettes, pancakes and waffles, or eggs with hash browns, toast and coffee, for around US$3 at either place. The Pancake House is open 8 am to 2 pm daily; Fredy's Tucan, serving breakfast, lunch and dinner, is open 8 am to 2.30 am.

This block of Badillo also has several other good restaurants. *Los Pibes (No 261)* is an Argentine restaurant serving excellent steaks (US$11 to US$28); open 2 pm to midnight (closed Tuesday). Opposite is the pricey, stylish, air-con *Adobe Café (No 252)*, open 6 to 11 pm (closed Tuesday). The popular *Roberto's Puerto Nuevo (No 284)* offers good seafood and other meals, noon to 11.30 pm daily.

Café de Olla (Badillo 168), beside Hotel Yazmín, is a good find – a small, busy, very pleasant restaurant with good traditional Mexican food (from US$3) and an 'Old Mexico' atmosphere, open 10 am to 11 pm (closed Tuesday). *Las Tres Huastecas*, at the corner of Olas Altas and Rodríguez, serves meals of good, economical Mexican food 7 am to 6 pm.

La Piazzetta, corner Olas Altas and Gómez, a pizzeria and Italian restaurant/bar, is often recommended for Italian food, with pizzas and pastas from US$4.50 to US$7; open 1 pm to midnight (closed Sunday). *Janssen & Johnson (Olas Altas 474)* is a 'Nederlands-International' restaurant and bar open 8 am to 1 am. For German food and drink, try the **Café Frankfurt & Biergarten** in the pleasant garden courtyard of the Café Frankfurt Hotel at the corner of Badillo and Constitución.

Near Olas Altas, *Chiles! (Púlpito 122)* is a favorite, with an enjoyable, friendly atmosphere and simple but delicious food to take away or eat there. Huge grilled burgers or veggie burgers are US$4.25, half/whole roast chickens are US$2.25/4.25, and a selection of salads, roasted potatoes or vegetarian chili-with-beans are US$1/2 small/large. Open November to May, 11 am to 6 pm (closed Sunday).

One of Vallarta's best-known restaurants, *Archie's Wok (Rodríguez 130)*, half a block from the Playa de los Muertos pier, was created by the former personal chef of film director John Huston and is still operated by his family. Archie's features wok specialties from many parts of Asia, with vegetarian or meat selections such as gingery stir-fried vegetables (US$5.25 to US$8.50) or fish sautéed in coconut milk, lemon grass and Thai red chili (US$11). Many readers have written to praise this place; it's open 2 to 11 pm (closed Sunday).

El Palomar de los González (☎ 222-07-95, *Aguacate 425*) is a hillside restaurant with good food, live music and an exceptional view over the city and bay, especially at sunset. Open 6 to 11 pm, it's a great place for a special night out; reservations are recommended. Another elegant, peaceful spot is the garden restaurant of the **Hotel Molino de Agua**, on Vallarta just south of the Río Cuale, open 8 am to 11 pm; though luxurious, its dishes are no more expensive than other restaurants. The attractive **Ristorante Caruso** (*Insurgentes 109*), beside the Río Cuale, has a riverside garden section and an indoor air-con section. Pasta is US$6 to US$7.50, meat and seafood dishes are more expensive; open 10 am to 11 pm.

Playa de los Muertos has plenty of beachside restaurants. A good one is *Langostino's*

Restaurant/The Sand Bar, atmospheric and inexpensive, with good seafood, ribs and breakfasts; open 7 am to 11 pm. On the south end of Playa de los Muertos, *Looney Tunes* is a good restaurant/bar right on the beach. Next door, you can't miss the *Blue Chairs*, with lots of blue chairs out on the beach, a prime fun-and-sun gathering spot for gay visitors.

Restaurants – North of Río Cuale As in most Mexican towns, one of the cheapest places to eat is at the *Mercado Municipal*, and in Vallarta the market is relatively clean and pleasant. It's on the north side of the Río Cuale beside the inland bridge, and the upstairs floor has a number of simple restaurant stalls serving typical Mexican market foods. You can eat well here for US$2; open 7 am to 9 pm daily.

An all-you-can-eat vegetarian buffet is provided by *Planeta Vegetariano Restaurant (Iturbide 270)*, up the steps from Hidalgo. It's a small place, open noon to 6 pm (closed Sunday); the buffet (US$5) is served noon to 6 pm. Another healthy choice is *Papaya 3 (Abasolo 169-173)*, an attractive little '100% natural' restaurant serving fresh juices, salads, soups, pastas, hot cakes, soyburgers and Mexican dishes, with most meals around US$3 to US$4.50; open 8 am to 10 pm (Sunday 9 am to 5 pm).

Cenaduría Doña Raquel (Vicario 131), half a block off the Malecón, serves inexpensive but delicious traditional Mexican food, 6 to 11.30 pm (closed Monday).

Also just off the Malecón, *Rito's Baci* (☎ 222-64-48, *Domínguez 181*) is a tiny Italian restaurant with delicious food, serving excellent pastas (US$7 to US$13.50), pizzas (US$13 to US$18) and salads (US$3 to US$7) in addition to meats and seafood. Open 1 to 11.30 pm daily; reservations suggested. Phone for free delivery within the city.

The immensely popular *Trio (Guerrero 264)* is a European-style restaurant/bar/café created and operated by two European chefs whose motto is 'Mediterranean food cooked with love.' Seafood and meat dishes are US$11 to US$18. Open 6 pm to midnight year-round; November to April it's also open for lunch, noon to 4 pm.

Chef Roger (☎ 222-59-00, *Rodríguez 267*), an expensive but high-quality Swiss restaurant, is also very popular; open 6.30 to 11 pm (closed Sunday). *Café des Artistes* (☎ 222-32-28, *Sánchez 740*) at the corner of Vicario, is very expensive and has a fine ambiance to match its good French cuisine; open 6 to 11.30 pm, reservations necessary.

Much smaller and simpler, *Restaurant/ Bar Graffiti* (*Miramar 271*) is a tiny restaurant and wine bar with a French owner, open 9.30 am to 2 pm and 5 pm to 1 am (closed Sunday).

La Fuente del Puente on Insurgentes just north of the inland bridge over the Río Cuale, is a pleasant open-air restaurant/bar with a traditional Mexican quartet every evening. It serves Mexican dishes; open 8 am to 10.30 pm (closed Sunday).

Hooters, beside the sea on the south side of the arches near the plaza, is a large air-con sports bar and grill, open 11 am to midnight. Downstairs, the popular *Tacos de los Arcos* serves simple, economical Mexican fare.

The Malecón is lined with boutiques, restaurants and bars. Many have upstairs terraces with fine views of the bay. Prices are considerably higher than in other parts of the city. The *Hard Rock Café* and *Carlos O'Brian's* both serve expensive food but are nonetheless popular with visitors for their festive atmosphere in the evening; *Planet Hollywood*, on the corner of Morelos and Galeana, is similar. Various other places along the Malecón also have music and dancing (see Entertainment).

No Name Café (☎ 223-25-08, 222-60-19) at the corner of Morelos and Mina, on the Malecón near the seahorse statue, is a fun restaurant and sports bar serving famous BBQ pork spareribs (1lb/2lb rack US$11/19); their other specialty, deep-dish 2-inch-thick Chicago-style pizzas, start at US$13/16 a medium/large. It's open 8 am to 1 am; phone for free delivery.

Nearby, *La Fabula Pizza* (*Morelos 484*), upstairs overlooking the seahorse statue, has an all-you-can-eat pasta/pizza/salad buffet for US$4, served noon to 5 pm daily; it's open noon to 11 pm.

A few US fast-food chains have made it to Vallarta, including *McDonald's* on the north end of the Malecón and *Domino's Pizza* on the south side of the Malecón, overlooking the arches.

Restaurants – Elsewhere Isla Cuale, the island in the middle of the Río Cuale, has several atmospheric restaurants. The enjoyable *Le Bistro Jazz Café* has good (but pricey) food and great jazz recordings; if the menu is beyond your budget, you can still stop by to enjoy a drink and the exceptionally beautiful tropical scenery. Or there's *Oscar's*, at the sea end of Isla Cuale, with a sea view and romantic music in the evening.

North of town, Marina Vallarta is surrounded by good-quality restaurants. Try *Porto Bello* for Italian, *Los Pibes* for Argentinean and steaks, or *Chang Cheng – La Gran Muralla* for gourmet Chinese.

South of town, Mismaloya has two well-known restaurants: *Chino's Paraíso*, 2km upriver from the beach, and *El Edén de Mismaloya*, about 5km farther upriver. Both are beautiful (but expensive) open-air restaurants with tables under palapas at spots where you can swim and stretch out in the sun on the boulders, and maybe see some meter-long iguanas doing the same. Both are open 11 am to 6 pm daily.

Cafés South of the river, on Olas Altas, *A Page in the Sun* and *Señor Book* (see Bookstores) both serve great coffee, light meals and desserts along with their intellectual fare, as does *Cafe.com Internet Café & Bar*, at the corner of Olas Altas and Badillo. North of the river, the artsy *El Diletante Café* (*Corona 164*), just off the Malecón, has wonderful coffee, homemade chocolate pastries, Häagen-Dazs ice cream, light meals and many other treats, including classical music and art.

Bakeries The *Panadería Munguía* (*Juárez 467*) is a good bakery with everything from sweets to healthy whole-grain baked goods; it's open 7 am to 10 pm daily (9 pm Saturday and Sunday). A smaller branch on the corner of Insurgentes and Serdán, south of the Río Cuale, is open the same hours.

Grocery Stores The giant air-con Gutié-rrez Rizo (GR) supermarket, on the corner of Constitución and Aquiles Serdán on the south side of the Río Cuale, has local merchandise and items imported from the USA, including magazines and paperbacks in English. Open 6.30 am to 11 pm daily.

Entertainment

Dancing and drinking are Vallarta's main forms of nighttime entertainment. At night many people stroll down the Malecón, where they can choose from everything from romantic open-air restaurant/bars to discos with riotous reveling. Entertainment is often presented in the amphitheater by the sea, opposite Plaza Principal. Softly lit Isla Cuale makes a beautiful, quiet, romantic haven for strolling in the evening.

Bars & Discos Along the Malecón, the *Hard Rock Café* has live rock music and dancing nightly from around 10.30 pm to 2 am. Nearby, *Kahlua, Mocambo* and *The Zoo* also have music and dancing. Or there's *Carlos O'Brian's*, a favorite restaurant and drinking haunt for fun-seeking, rabble-rousing gringos, with dancing into the wee hours. *Planet Hollywood*, on the corner of Morelos and Galeana, is similar, with food, dancing and big-screen music videos.

South of the Río Cuale, *Club Roxy (Vallarta 217)* has live music nightly, with rock, blues and reggae. Next door, *The American Legend (Vallarta 237)* also has live music nightly with a similar mix. *Señor Frog's*, at the corner of Vallarta and Carranza, features live rock and disco music.

For jazz fans, the classy *Le Bistro Jazz Café* on Isla Cuale has more than 1000 jazz CDs and a lush, tropical atmosphere. It is open 9 am to midnight (closed Sunday). At the sea end of Isla Cuale, *Oscar's* has a view of the ocean and romantic music in the evening.

Discos in Vallarta appear and disappear with some regularity. Two popular discos south of the Río Cuale are *Cactus (Vallarta 399)*, with different theme nights and con-

tests throughout the week, and *La Catrina Cantina/Disco (Olas Altas 508)*. North of the city, *Christine*, at the Hotel Krystal about 7km north of the city, is another popular disco, as is *Collage* at Marina Vallarta.

Many of the large resort hotels offer evening entertainment. The *Camino Real* south of town gives a free concert, including a free cocktail, starting at 9 pm on the first Thursday of every month.

Gay Venues Puerto Vallarta has a relaxed, congenial gay scene. *Club Paco Paco (Vallarta 278)* is a gay disco and bar where you can get all the latest scoop on gay accommodations and activities; it's open noon to 6 am daily. Paco now operates several other bars in the same area, too, including *Paco's Olas Altas (Olas Altas 465)*, *Paco's Ranch (Carranza 239)* and *Paco's Sunset Bar (Suárez 583)* on the rooftop terrace of the Descanso del Sol hotel. The bar/restaurant at *Paco's Hidden Paradise*, outside the city and reachable by boat, is also enjoyable (see Places to Stay).

Other popular gay nightspots include *Los Balcones (Juárez 182)*, near the corner of Libertad, upstairs with a dance floor and lots of little balconies. *Por Que No/Why Not (Morelos 101)*, on the north side of the Río Cuale beside the seaside bridge, is upstairs and has a disco, video bar and rooftop cantina/grill with a marvelous view; open noon to 4 am. The *Blue Chairs* at the south end of Playa de los Muertos is a popular gay beach hangout.

Mariachis Traditional Mexican mariachi music can be enjoyed at several places around town. On the Malecón near the seahorse statue, the upstairs *Tequila's* restaurant/bar features live mariachi music every night except Monday, starting around 7.30 or 8 pm. The *Mariachi Loco* restaurant and bar on the corner of Cárdenas and Vallarta presents a show of mariachis and other entertainment nightly, 9 pm to 2.30 am, with a special Tuesday mariachi concert featuring more than 20 artists.

Fiestas Mexicanas An old Vallarta favorite, *La Iguana* (☎ 222-01-05, Cárdenas 311) presents a Fiesta Mexicana with traditional Mexican folkloric dances, mariachis, *ranchero* rope tricks, a piñata, bloodless cockfights, a Mexican buffet, an open bar and a dance band for dancing under the stars every Thursday and Sunday evening, 7 to 11 pm. This is said to be the original of what has become a much-copied tourist show; entry is US$29 per person. Other Fiesta Mexicana nights are held at some of the giant luxury hotels, including the ***Sheraton Buganvilias*** *(☎ 226-04-04)*, ***Hotel Krystal*** *(☎ 224-02-02)* and ***Holiday Inn*** *(☎ 226-17-00)*, all north of town.

Cinemas Cinemas include *Cine Bahía*, on Insurgentes near Madero, and *Cine Luz Maria (Avenida México 227)*, a few blocks north of the center. Often the films are shown in English with Spanish subtitles.

Cigar Clubs The *Guantanamera Cigar Club & Bar (Corona 186)* is the pride of the Ojeda family, who make their own cigars here, sell a wide variety of Cuban cigars and provide a fine lounge bar at which to enjoy them; open 10 am to 10 pm (closed Sunday). *La Casa del Habano (Aldama 170)* has an extensive selection of Cuban cigars, plus a cigar lounge and bar.

Spectator Sports
Bullfights are held at 4 pm Wednesday, September to May, in the bullring opposite the marina.

Shopping
Shops and boutiques in Puerto Vallarta sell just about every type of handicraft made in Mexico, but prices are higher here than elsewhere. Try the Mercado Municipal for anything from Taxco silver, *sarapes* and *huaraches* to wool wall-hangings and blown glass. The market has more than 150 shops and stalls; it's open 9 am to 8 pm Monday to Saturday, 9 am to 2 pm Sunday. Many other shops line Agustín Rodríguez, facing the market.

Getting There & Away
Air Puerto Vallarta's international airport, on highway 200 about 10km north of the city, is served by several national and international airlines. Direct flights, all with connections to other places, are offered by:

Aeroméxico
Plaza Genovesa, Locales 2 & 3, Zona Hotelera (☎ 224-27-77, 01-800-021-4000); flies to Aguascalientes, Guadalajara, León, Los Angeles, Mexico City, San Diego (California), Tijuana

Alaska Airlines
Airport (☎ 221-13-50, 001-800-252-7522); flies to Los Angeles, San Francisco, Seattle, Phoenix

America West
Airport (☎ 01-800-235-9292); flies to Phoenix

American Airlines
Airport (☎ 221-12-21); flies to Dallas

Continental
Airport (☎ 221-22-13, 01-800-900-5000); flies to Houston

Mexicana
Centro Comercia l Villas Vallarta, Local G-18 (☎ 224-89-00, 01-800-366-5400); flies to Chicago, Guadalajara, Los Cabos, Mazatlán, Mexico City

Bus Vallarta's long-distance bus station is just off highway 200, about 12km north of the city center and a kilometer or two north of the airport. Local buses marked 'Ixtapa,' 'Juntas' and 'Mojoneras' connect the bus station with the center of town (5 am to 11 pm; US$0.30). A taxi between the center and the bus station costs US$6.50.

Most intercity bus lines also have offices south of the Río Cuale, where you can buy tickets without having to make a trip to the bus station. They include Elite, TNS and Estrella Blanca, on the corner of Badillo and Insurgentes; ETN, Primera Plus and Servicios Coordinados, at Cárdenas 268; Transportes del Pacífico, at Insurgentes 282; and ETN, Primera Plus and Transportes del Pacífico, at Madero 364.

Buses depart from the main bus station. Some buses make an additional stop in town – for example, Autocamiones Cihuatlán's southbound buses make a stop on Carranza at the corner of Aguacate after leaving the main terminal, and will drop off passengers there by request when arriving from the south.

Buses departing from the main terminal include:

Barra de Navidad – 225km, 3½ to 4 hours 1st-class (US$12 to US$14), 5 hours 2nd-class (US$11.50); same buses as to Manzanillo

Guadalajara – 344km, 5 hours; 1st-class hourly, 24 hours, by Futura (US$27), 18 daily by Transportes del Pacífico (US$27), 11 daily by Primera Plus (US$30), 11 daily by ETN (US$37); 2nd-class, 7 daily by Transportes del Pacífico (US$24)

Manzanillo – 285km; 5 hours 1st-class at 7.45 am and 12.30 pm by Primera Plus (US$14), midnight and 1 am by Elite (US$17), 4 pm and 11 pm by Autocamiones Cihuatlán (US$18); 6½ to 7 hours 2nd class, 5 daily by Servicios Coordinados (US$12), 8 daily by Autocamiones Cihuatlán (US$15)

Mazatlán – 459km, 8 hours; 2nd-class at 3 pm, 10 pm and 2.30 am by TNS (US$30), 12.05 pm and 9.15 pm by Transportes del Pacífico (US$26)

Mexico City (Terminal Norte) – 880km, 12 to 13 hours; 1st-class, four daily by Elite (US$61), two daily by Transportes del Pacífico (US$61), one daily by Primera Plus (US$66), two daily by ETN (US$82); executive, one daily by Elite (US$82)

Rincón de Guayabitos – 60km, 1½ hours (US$5.50); same buses as to Tepic

San Blas – 175km, 3 hours; 2nd-class at 12.15 and 2.30 pm by TNS (US$11)

San Patricio-Melaque – 225km; 3½ to 4 hours 1st-class (US$12 to US$14); 5 hours 2nd-class (US$12); same buses as to Manzanillo

Sayulita – 38km, 1 hour; 10 daily 9.15 am to 8 pm by Transportes del Pacífico (US$1.75)

Tepic – 169km, 3½ hours; 2nd-class every half-hour 4 am to 8 pm, and at 10.30 pm, by Transportes del Pacífico (US$12)

Zihuatanejo – 720km, 15 hours; 1st-class at midnight and 1 am by Elite (US$44), continuing to Acapulco (18 hours, US$55)

Car & Motorcycle Rental agencies in Puerto Vallarta include:

Advantage	☎ 221-18-09
Ansa	☎ 222-65-45
Avis	☎ 221-11-12
Budget	☎ 222-29-80
Clover	☎ 224-03-53
De Alba	☎ 222-29-59
Dollar	☎ 222-42-56
Hertz	☎ 221-14-73
Marina	☎ 224-69-69
National	☎ 221-12-26
Quick	☎ 222-00-06

To rent a vehicle you must be at least 25 years old and hold a valid driver's license (a foreign one will do) and major credit card. If you don't have a credit card you'll have to pay a large cash deposit. Rates vary widely; it pays to shop around.

Getting Around

To/From the Airport *Colectivo* vans operate from the airport to town, but not from town to the airport. The cheapest way to get to/from the airport is on a local bus for US$0.30; the 'Aeropuerto,' 'Juntas' and 'Ixtapa' buses all stop right at the airport entrance. A taxi from the city center costs around US$6.50.

Arriving at the airport, beware of inflated taxi prices. You may be quoted a rate of US$13 for a ride into town, when a sign inside the official airport taxi booth says it should cost US$9.25. However, you can walk across the street from the airport and get a regular taxi for US$6.50.

Bus Local buses operate every five minutes, 5 am to 11 pm, on most routes and cost US$0.30. Plaza Lázaro Cárdenas at Playa Olas Altas is a major departure hub. Northbound local bus routes also stop in front of the Cine Bahía, on Insurgentes near the corner of Madero.

Northbound buses marked 'Hoteles,' 'Aeropuerto,' 'Ixtapa,' 'Pitillal' and 'Juntas' pass through the city heading north to the airport, the Zona Hotelera and Marina Vallarta; the 'Hoteles,' 'Pitillal' and 'Ixtapa' routes can take you to any of the large hotels north of the city.

Southbound 'Boca de Tomatlán' buses pass along the southern coastal highway through Mismaloya (20 minutes) to Boca de Tomatlán (30 minutes). They depart from Constitución near the corner of Badillo every 10 minutes, 6 am to 10 pm (US$0.40).

Taxi Cab prices are regulated by zones; the cost for a ride is determined by how many zones you cross. Always determine the price of the ride before you get into the taxi.

Bicycle Bike Mex (☎ 223-1680), Guerrero 361, rents mountain bikes for guided or self-guided tours, as does B-B-Bobby's Bikes (☎ 223-0008) at the corner of Iturbide and Miramar. Rentals cost around US$5.50/27 per hour/day; guided tours start at US$44.

Boat In addition to taxis on land, Vallarta also has water taxis to beautiful beaches on the south side of the bay that are accessible only by boat.

Water taxis departing from the pier at Playa de los Muertos head south around the bay, making stops at Las Ánimas (25 minutes), Quimixto (30 minutes) and Yelapa (45 minutes); fare is US$16.50 round-trip for any destination. Boats depart at 10 am, 11 am and 4 pm, and return in mid-afternoon (the 4 pm boat returns in the morning).

A water taxi also goes to Yelapa from the beach just south of Hotel Rosita, on the north end of the Malecón, departing at 11.30 am, Monday to Saturday (30 minutes, US$7.75 one-way).

Cheaper water taxis to the same places depart from Boca de Tomatlán, south of town, which is easily reachable by local bus. Water taxis to Las Ánimas (15 minutes), Quimixto (20 minutes) and Yelapa (30 minutes) depart here daily at 10.30 and 11.30 am, 1, 2, 4 and 5.30 pm, or more frequently if enough people want to make the trip; one-way fare is US$4.50 to any destination (double for round-trip).

Private yachts and *lanchas* can be hired from the south side of the Playa de los Muertos pier. They'll take you to any secluded beach around the bay; most have gear aboard for snorkeling and fishing. Lanchas can also be hired privately at Mismaloya and Boca de Tomatlán, but they are expensive.

HOTELITO DESCONOCIDO

Ninety kilometers south of Puerto Vallarta, on a spit of land between the Pacific Ocean and El Ermitaño estuary, the rustic yet luxurious Italian designed and operated *Hotelito Desconocido* (☎ 3-222-25-26, hotelito@pvnet .com.mx, www.hotelito.com) has attracted

international attention as a superb ecological resort. Bird-watching is excellent here, and a sea turtle protection project operates June to February. The resort's all-inclusive rates include many enjoyable activities, plus transfers to/from the Puerto Vallarta airport. Singles/doubles start at US$400/500 January to April, US$365/457 May to December. To reach the Hotelito, turn west off highway 200 to La Cruz de Loreto, 90km south of Puerto Vallarta, and follow the road to the Estero El Ermitaño.

COSTALEGRE BEACHES

Many good beaches stretch along the coast south of Puerto Vallarta. Tourism promoters have dubbed part of this stretch of coast, from **Playa Quémaro** northwest of Chamela all the way southeast to Barra de Navidad, as the **Costalegre** ('happy coast').

Notable beaches include **Playa Pérula** (Km 76), **Chamela** (Km 72), **El Negrito** (Km 64), **Careyes** (Km 54), **Careyitos** (Km 52), **Cuitzmala** and **Teopa** (Km 44), **El Pirata** (Km 36), **El Tecuan** (Km 33), **Tenacatita** (Km 30), **Los Ángeles Locos** (Km 26), **Boca de Iguanas** (Km 19), **La Manzanilla** (Km 14) and **Cuastecomates**, which is 3km west of San Patricio-Melaque. All of these distances are measured on highway 200, heading northwest from the junction of highways 200 and 80 at San Patricio-Melaque (the highway to Guadalajara).

Chamela

Chamela, 165km south of Puerto Vallarta, is actually a scattering of small settlements along the 11km shore of the Bahía de Chamela. Much of this shore consists of fine, untouched beaches – perfect escapes, though tourism is slowly creeping in to alter the landscape.

From Chamela's Super Mercado, a kilometer-long road leads to the beachfront *Villa Polinesia & Camping Club* (☎ 3-285-52-47, 3-616-11-45 in Guadalajara), with 12 villas, 35 Polynesian-style huts, and shaded trailer spaces with full hookups (but no tent spaces). The appropriately named *Motel Trailer Park* is just north of the turnoff to Villa Polinesia. Other places to stay include

Hotel Chamela (☎ 3-285-51-27) and *Bungalows Mayor* (☎ 3-643-9318 in Guadalajara).

Tenacatita

Bahía de Tenacatita, 30km northwest of San Patricio-Melaque, is known for its beautiful beaches, good snorkeling in crystal clear waters, and its large mangrove lagoon, which is great for bird-watching. Jungle boat bird-watching tours can be arranged; ask at the Restaurant Fiesta Mexicana on the beach. Jungle boat tours to Tenacatita are also offered by the boat cooperative in Barra de Navidad; since these tours travel farther, they cost more.

Most visitors stay in San Patricio-Melaque or Barra de Navidad and visit Tenacatita just for the day. There's a row of palapa seafood restaurants on the beach and a small village. But there are a couple of places to stay if you're so inclined.

Camping is fine on the beach; trailers park along the spit between the beach and lagoon. *Hotel Paraíso de Tenacatita* (☎ 3-357-69-72), a small, beachfront hotel-restaurant about 2km from the village, has singles/doubles for US$17/22.

More expensive, the large *Blue Bay Resort* (☎ 3-351-50-20), on beautiful Los Ángeles Locos beach, offers all-inclusive packages starting at US$125/196 single/double (promotions sometimes lower the price to around US$75 per person). Non-guests can pay US$33 per day to use all the hotel's facilities, a good value; call ahead for reservations. *Punta Serena* (☎ 3-351-50-13) is a holistic retreat with all-inclusive packages starting at US$150/245 single/double.

SAN PATRICIO-MELAQUE
• pop 6260 ☎ 3

Known to locals as Melaque, the small beach resort town of San Patricio-Melaque on the lovely Bahía de Navidad is 60km southeast of Chamela, just after highway 80 from Guadalajara merges with highway 200. Although it's a little larger than its twin resort town of Barra de Navidad 2km southeast along the beach, it rarely appears on maps.

Two *haciendas* owned by foreigners, San Patricio (on the east side) and Melaque (on the west), used to stand side by side here, with the dividing line between them running where Calle López Mateos is today. Settlements gradually grew around the two haciendas, and eventually merged into one town that preserves the names of both.

Besides being a popular beach resort for Mexican families when school is out, and a low-key, relaxed hangout for norteamericanos (principally Canadians) from December to April, the town is famous for its weeklong St Patrick's Day celebrations (Fiesta de San Patricio) in March.

The crumbling walls of the once proud Casa Grande Hotel & Resort are a reminder of the October 1995 earthquake, which damaged the town.

Orientation

Everything in Melaque is within walking distance. Most of the hotels, restaurants and public services are concentrated on or near Gómez Farías, running beside the beach, and López Mateos, the street coming in from the highway. Building numbers on Gómez Farías and some other streets are not consecutive, so refer to the map for locations. Barra de Navidad is accessible from Melaque via highway 200 (5km) or by walking down the beach (2km).

Information

The tourist office in Barra de Navidad has information available on San Patricio-Melaque.

Money Banamex, on Gómez Farías near the bus terminal, is open 9 am to 3 pm Monday to Friday. Foreign cash (US and Canadian) is changed during these hours; traveler's checks are changed 9 am to noon only. Casa de Cambio Melaque, in the Pasaje Comercial Melaque on Gómez Farías opposite the bus station, changes cash and traveler's checks 9 am to 2 pm and 4 to 7 pm Monday to Saturday, 9 am to 2 pm Sunday.

Post & Communications The post office, on Orozco near the corner of Corona, is open 8 am to 3 pm Monday to Friday, 8 am to noon Saturday. Telecomm, Morelos 53 near the plaza, is open 9 am to 2.30 pm Monday to Friday.

There are several telephone casetas with fax, including one on the north side of the plaza at the corner of Morelos and Hidalgo, another at Corona 60 between Hidalgo and Guzmán, and one on Gómez Farías beside the bus station.

Ciber@Net, in the Pasaje Comercial Melaque on Gómez Farías opposite the bus station, offers Internet services 9.30 am to 2.30 pm and 4 to 8 pm Monday to Saturday.

Laundry Lavandería Costalegre, Juárez 63, is open 8 am to 8 pm Monday to Saturday.

Things to See & Do

This is a peaceful little beach town with not a lot to do – swimming, lazing or walking on the beach, watching the pelicans fish at sunrise and sunset, scaling the hill to the *mirador* (lookout) at the west end of the bay, or walking down the beach to Barra

de Navidad are the main activities here. It's a great place to simply relax and take it easy.

A flea market is held every Wednesday starting around 8 am, on Orozco two blocks east of the plaza.

Fiesta de San Patricio

St Patrick's Day, the day of the town's patron saint, is celebrated in a big way, with weeklong festivities leading up to March 17 – parties all day, rodeos, carnival, music, dances and a fiesta with fireworks every night in the plaza. The 17th begins with a mass and the blessing of the fleet.

Places to Stay

Room rates vary greatly depending on the season; the town fills up with tourists (mostly Mexican families) during the school holidays in July and August, in December and at Semana Santa, when prices are higher and it's best to reserve a room in advance. The

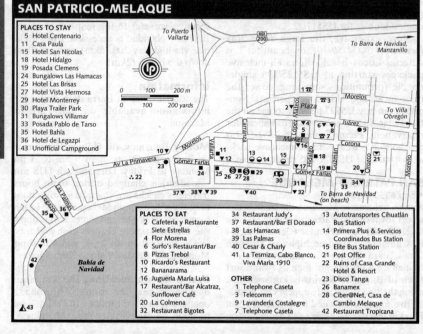

SAN PATRICIO-MELAQUE

PLACES TO STAY
5   Hotel Centenario
11 Casa Paula
15 Hotel San Nicolas
18 Hotel Hidalgo
19 Posada Clemens
24 Bungalows Las Hamacas
25 Hotel Las Brisas
27 Hotel Vista Hermosa
29 Hotel Monterrey
30 Playa Trailer Park
31 Bungalows Villamar
33 Posada Pablo de Tarso
35 Hotel Bahía
36 Hotel de Legazpi
43 Unofficial Campground

To Puerto Vallarta
To Barra de Navidad, Manzanillo
To Villa Obregón
To Barra de Navidad (on beach)
Plaza
Market
Bahía de Navidad
0   100   200 m
0   100   200 yards

PLACES TO EAT
2   Cafetería y Restaurante Siete Estrellas
4   Flor Morena
6   Surfo's Restaurant/Bar
8   Pizzas Trebol
10 Ricardo's Restaurant
12 Bananarama
16 Juguería María Luisa
17 Restaurant/Bar Alcatraz, Sunflower Café
20 La Colmena
32 Restaurant Bigotes

34 Restaurant Judy's
37 Restaurant/Bar El Dorado
38 Las Hamacas
39 Las Palmas
40 Cesar & Charly
41 La Tesmiza, Cabo Blanco, Viva María 1910

OTHER
1   Telephone Caseta
3   Telecomm
9   Lavandería Costalegre
7   Telephone Caseta

13 Autotransportes Cihuatlán Bus Station
14 Primera Plus & Servicios Coordinados Bus Station
15 Elite Bus Station
21 Post Office
22 Ruins of Casa Grande Hotel & Resort
23 Disco Tanga
26 Banamex
28 Ciber@Net, Casa de Cambio Melaque
42 Restaurant Tropicana

rest of the time it's pretty quiet, and many hotels will give discounts. Bungalows – apartments with kitchens – are common here.

Camping The beachfront *Playa Trailer Park* (☎ 355-50-65, *Gómez Farías 250*) has 45 spaces with full hookups for US$5.50/9 single/double in a tent, US$11 for two in a trailer, US$1 for each extra person. An *unofficial campground* is in a flat area by the beach at the west end of town; it has no water or other facilities (you can buy water from a truck that comes by), but the price is right at US$1 per night. Most of the beachside palapa restaurants nearby will let you have a free shower.

Hotels *Casa Paula* (☎ 355-50-93, *Vallarta 6*) is a simple, family-run place with just four courtyard rooms with bath; singles/doubles are US$9/11. *Hotel Centenario* (☎ 355-63-08), in the market street at Corona 38, has nine rooms with bath for US$8/13. *Posada Clemens* (☎ 355-51-79, *Gómez Farías 70*), on the corner of Guzmán, has clean, simple singles/doubles for US$9/11. *Hotel Hidalgo* (☎ 355-50-45, *Hidalgo 7*) has simple rooms for US$14/17 (cheaper if you stay a few days), with a courtyard and communal kitchen area. *Hotel San Nicolas* (☎ 355-50-66, *Gómez Farías 54*), upstairs, has singles/doubles for US$8/17; street-facing rooms have private balconies with a bit of sea view.

At the west end of town, *Hotel Bahía* (*Legazpi 5*), half a block from the beach, is a pleasant little family-run hotel. It's also one of the best deals in town, clean and well-maintained, with an open-air guests' kitchen and sitting areas. Its 20 rooms with bath are US$13/17 a single/double, with cheaper weekly rates; two rooms with kitchen are slightly more expensive. Contact Rafael Gálvez or Evelia Moreno (☎ 355-56-81).

Nearby, *Hotel de Legazpi* (☎ 355-53-97, *Avenida Las Palmas*), on the beach, has a swimming pool and 16 large, bright rooms, some with sea view and balcony; double rooms are US$27 May to September, US$36 October to April, US$3.25 extra with kitchenette (children 10 and under free).

Pelicans abound in Melaque.

Bungalows The *Bungalows Villamar* (☎/fax 355-50-05, *Hidalgo 1*) are pleasant and relaxed, with five spacious garden bungalows, a children's pool and a raised beachfront terrace. Studio bungalows are US$10/12 single/double; two-bedroom bungalows are US$20 for two people, US$5 each extra person, with discounts for stays of a few days or more. It's popular with North Americans (English is spoken). The beachfront *Bungalows Las Hamacas* (☎ 355-51-13, *Gómez Farías 13*) has a small swimming pool, parking, an inexpensive beachfront restaurant and bungalows for US$17/27 single/double, with larger bungalows (up to six beds) available.

The following, all attractive beachfront places with swimming pools, offer both bungalows (with kitchen) and regular rooms. All have rooms and bungalows for one or two people, plus larger rooms and bungalows good for families or groups.

Hotel Monterrey (☎ 355-50-04, *Gómez Farías 27*) has beachfront terraces with trees, tables and chairs and a lovely sea view, plus a large beachfront swimming pool, restaurant and parking. Rooms are US$22/33 a single/double, bungalows US$42 for two. *Hotel Vista Hermosa* (☎ 355-50-02, *Gómez*

Farías 23) has regular rooms for US$22/27 single/double, and a variety of one-, two- and three-bedroom bungalows starting at US$33/40 single/double; free for children 10 years and under.

Hotel Las Brisas *(☎ 355-51-08, Gómez Farías 9)* has regular rooms with fridge and outdoor communal kitchens for US$20/31 single/double; bungalows with private kitchen are US$40 for two. **Posada Pablo de Tarso** *(☎ 355-51-17, Gómez Farías 408)* is attractive, with a large beachfront pool and terrace. Well-appointed air-con rooms are US$20/35; bungalows start at US$48 for one to three persons.

Places to Eat

Melaque has many enjoyable restaurants. A favorite for breakfast is **Bananarama** *(Gómez Farías 14)*; it's popular in the morning with expats and visitors, and is an excellent place to pick up local information. Their special waffle with fruit is just US$2, and the coffee's delicious; open 7 to 11 am daily. **La Colmena**, at the corner of Gómez Farías and Orozco, is another cheerful, inexpensive breakfast place, open 8 to 11.30 am daily.

Several good, cheap eateries are around the plaza. **Flor Morena**, on the south side of the plaza, is inexpensive and immensely popular for typical Mexican food in the evening. The most expensive thing on the menu is the shrimp *pozole* (hominy stew) for US$2; a good meal of four enchiladas or tacos served with salad is just US$1.30. Everything is made fresh daily, and most meals are available vegetarian; it's open 6 to 11 pm (closed Monday). In the evening, from around 6 pm to midnight, lots of little **food carts** set themselves up in the street on Juárez, in the block to the east of the plaza, and serve inexpensive, simple Mexican fare to a happy crowd; a meal of *carne asada* (grilled beef) costs around US$2.75.

On the west side of the plaza, **Cafetería y Restaurant Siete Estrellas** *(☎ 355-64-21)* is another simple family place serving good, inexpensive Mexican dishes. It's open 7 am to midnight daily; phone for free delivery. Also offering free delivery is **Pizzas Trebol** *(☎ 355-63-84)*, at the corner of Juárez and

Guzmán a block east of the plaza, open 10 am to 11 pm daily; pizzas are US$2.50 to US$9.50.

Delicious fresh fruit and vegetable juices, *licuados* and other healthy concoctions, as well as *tortas* (hot roll sandwiches) and burgers, are available 7 am to 11 pm daily at **Juguería María Luisa**, on the corner of López Mateos and Corona. Lots of other little restaurants are along Corona, in the two market alleys on either side of López Mateos.

Restaurant Judy's *(Gómez Farías 56)*, at the corner of Orozco, is popular with North American visitors. It serves Tex-Mex food, 'north of the border' and Mexican foods, with inside or patio dining. It features Sky-Tel, US satellite sports and CNN news, and has live music and dancing nightly. Hours are 8 am to 1 pm and 5 pm to 2 am, Monday to Saturday.

The **Restaurant/Bar Alcatraz**, on López Mateos at Gómez Farías, is a small, cheerful restaurant upstairs under a palapa roof. Lunch and dinner are US$2 to US$6.50, or try Chateaubriand for two for US$15; open 2 to 10.30 pm (closed Thursday). Downstairs, the **Sunflower Café** is another cheerful spot, with good coffee and superb pies and pastries; it's open 8 am to noon and 6 to 9 pm daily.

Ricardo's Restaurant *(Av La Primavera 3)* is lovely in the evening, with tropical atmosphere, soft lighting and candles, a high palapa roof, and live music. It specializes in steaks and seafood (US$4 to US$5.50); try the shrimp served in a hollow pineapple. Saturday night is BBQ night from October to April, a great deal for US$6. It's open noon to midnight daily.

Surfo's Restaurant/Bar *(Juárez 43)*, upstairs near the plaza, has a pool table, and is fun and casual. It has separate bar and restaurant sections, so you can sit under palapa roofs or out under the stars. Pub food and burgers are US$3 to US$4; open 6 to 11 pm daily.

Several good restaurants are right on the beach. **Cesar & Charly**, on the beach near Hotel Monterrey and Hotel Vista Hermosa, is a pleasant restaurant and bar serving a variety of inexpensive dishes including healthy 'light-hearted fare.' A steamed or grilled vegetable plate with chicken, shrimp or fish is US$4, a huge Mexican plate is US$7, or try the Hawaiian-style shrimp for US$6.50, a house specialty. Open 7 am to 10 pm daily.

At the beach end of López Mateos, *Restaurant Bigotes* is a pleasant beachfront restaurant specializing in seafood; house specialties include *huachinango a la naranja* (red snapper a la orange) and *camarones al cilantro* (shrimp with cilantro) for US$5.50 each. The two-for-one happy hour from 2 to 8 pm is very popular; open 8 am to 9 pm daily.

A row of pleasant, palm-thatched palapa restaurants stretches along the beach at the west end of town. *Cabo Blanco* is a favorite with visitors and locals alike; also along here are *Restaurant La Tesmiza* and *Viva María 1910*. A fancier beachside restaurant/bar is the *Restaurant/Bar El Dorado*, with live music on weekend evenings. Nearby are two cheaper places, *Las Palmas* and *Las Hamacas*.

Entertainment
Sunday evening, most everyone in town gathers on the plaza to enjoy socializing, a snack and the balmy night air.

Several of the restaurants are popular for evening entertainment. *Restaurant Judy's* has live music and dancing nightly, the beachfront *Restaurant/Bar El Dorado* has live music on weekend evenings, and *Ricardo's Restaurant* has live music nightly; *Surfo's* is another popular hangout (see Places to Eat).

Disco Tanga on Gómez Farías is the only one in town; it's open 10 pm to 3 am every night in high season, Friday to Sunday night otherwise. *Restaurant Tropicana*, on the beach at the west end of town, has a dance popular with young locals every Sunday afternoon.

Getting There & Away
Air For flight details, see the following Barra de Navidad Getting There & Away section. A travel agent for flight arrangements can be found in that town.

Bus Melaque has three bus stations. The Cihuatlán and Primera Plus/Servicios Coordinados stations are side by side on the corner of Gómez Farías and Carranza. Both have 1st-class Primera Plus and 2nd-class buses and serve similar routes with the same prices, though departure times vary. Buses departing from these stations go to the following destinations:

Barra de Navidad – 5km, 10 minutes; every 15 minutes 6 am to 9 pm (US$0.25), or take any southbound long-distance bus

Guadalajara – 294km; 11 1st-class (5 hours, US$19.50) and 21 2nd-class (6 to 7½ hours, US$16.25)

Manzanillo – 65km; 11 1st-class (1 hour, US$4); at least hourly 2nd-class 3 am to 11.30 pm (1½ hours, US$3.25)

Puerto Vallarta – 220km; 4 1st-class (3½ to 4 hours, US$13.25) and 17 2nd-class (5 hours, US$11.50)

The 1st-class Elite bus station is on Gómez Farías, a block east of the other bus stations. Two buses daily go to Puerto Vallarta (3½ hours, US$12.50) and continue up the coast all the way to Tijuana. Elite's southbound buses depart from Manzanillo.

Taxi Taxis between Barra and San Patricio-Melaque cost US$3.25.

BARRA DE NAVIDAD
● pop 2970 ☎ 3
The beach resort town of Barra de Navidad (often called 'Barra,' locally) is squeezed onto a sandbar between the Bahía de Navidad and the Laguna de Navidad. It's around the bay from San Patricio-Melaque. The waves are bigger here than in Melaque; locals from Melaque often come over here for surfing, especially in January when the waves are best. The Grand Bay Hotel's marina is popular with yachties November to May.

Orientation
Legazpi, the main street, runs beside the beach. Veracruz, the town's other major street and the route to the highway, runs parallel to Legazpi before merging with it at the south end of town, which terminates in a fingerlike sandbar.

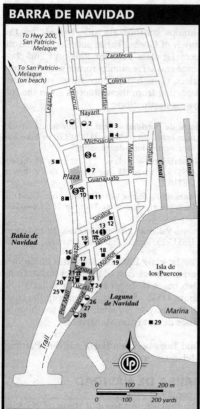

BARRA DE NAVIDAD

To Hwy 200,
San Patricio-
Melaque

To San Patricio-
Melaque
(on beach)

Zacatecas

Colima

Nayarit

Michoacán

Plaza

Guanajuato

Sinaloa

Jalisco

Morelos

Bahía de
Navidad

Isla de
los Puercos

Laguna
de Navidad

Marina

Trail

Veracruz

Legazpi

Mazatlán

Manzanillo

Tampico

Canal

Canal

Sonora

Yucatán

0   100   200 m
0   100   200 yards

Information

Tourist Offices The Delegación Regional de Turismo (☎/fax 355-51-00), Jalisco 67, is open 9 am to 5 pm, Monday to Friday.

Money There are no banks in Barra de Navidad; the nearest bank is in San Patricio-Melaque. You can change money at Vinos y Licores Barra de Navidad on Legazpi near the southwest corner of the plaza, open 8.30 am to 11 pm daily, and at the Casa de Cambio, Veracruz 212, between Michoacán and Guanajuato.

Post & Communications The post office is inconveniently out of the way on Nueva España, six blocks north and four blocks east of the bus stations; it's open 8 am to 3 pm Monday to Friday, 9 am to 1 pm Saturday. Telecomm, on Veracruz at the southeast corner of the plaza, is open 9 am to 2 pm Monday to Friday.

Mini-Market Hawaii, on the corner of Legazpi and Sonora, has a telephone and fax caseta and is open noon to 10 pm daily. Another caseta, at Veracruz 102, is open 9 am to 10.30 pm daily.

At the time of writing, the nearest Internet café was in San Patricio-Melaque, but plans were afoot to establish a branch of Ciber@Net on Veracruz, near the Casa de Cambio.

Travel Agencies The Nayah Haviva travel agency (☎ 355-56-66), Veracruz 204 opposite the plaza, can make flight arrangements. It's open 10 am to 2 pm and 4 to 7 pm, Monday to Saturday.

Laundry Lavandería Jardín, Jalisco 71, is open 9 am to 2 pm and 4 to 7 pm Monday to Friday, 9 am to noon Saturday.

Activities

The beach, of course, is Barra's prime attraction. Boating on the lagoon is also popular. The local boat operators' cooperative, the Sociedad Cooperativa de Servicios Turísticos Miguel López de Legazpi, at Veracruz 40, is open 7 am to 8 pm daily, with a price list posted on the wall. Tours range from half-hour trips around the lagoon (US$16) to all-day jungle trips to Tenacatita (US$130); prices are for up to eight people. They also offer deep-sea fishing, snorkeling and diving trips and rides on the 'banana.'

For serious fishing trips, Brian Wilson at Z Pesca (☎ 355-64-64, zpesca@aol.com, www .Zpesca.com), Legazpi 213, has better boats and equipment; a six-hour trip for four people costs from US$150.

Tours may also be taken to the village of Colimilla across the lagoon (US$11). Or you can go halfway down the block and catch a colectivo boat (water taxi) to Colimilla for US$0.50 round-trip (see Getting There & Away later in this section).

Surfboards, boogie boards, snorkeling gear, kayaks, bicycles and even cars, houses and apartments can be rented from Crazy Cactus (☎ 355-60-99), Jalisco 8, open 9.30 am to 6 pm Monday to Saturday.

The Grand Bay Hotel's 27-hole championship golf course (☎ 355-61-94) welcomes non-guests; cost is US$161 for two people for 18 holes. A water taxi will drop you there for US$1 round-trip.

Fishing Tournaments

National and international fishing tournaments are held annually for marlin, sailfish, tuna and dorado, with prizes that include boats and cars.

The most important, the Torneo Internacional de Pesca de Marlin, Pez Vela y Dorado por Equipos, is held for three days around the third week in January. The second most important is the Torneo Internacional de Marlin Club de Pesca Barra de Navidad, held for two days during late May or early June, with another two-day tournament in mid-August. The final tournament of the year is held before Independence Day on September 15 and 16.

Places to Stay

Budget Cheapest in town, the very basic *Casa de Huéspedes Mama Laya* (no ☎, *Veracruz 69*) has a pleasant rooftop terrace with a view of the sea and lagoon; singles/doubles with communal bath are US$6/11, or pitch a tent on the roof. The popular

'Christ of the Cyclone'

The Christ figure hanging on the cross of the San Antonio church in Barra de Navidad is different than any other you will see in any other part of Mexico; its arms hang at its sides, rather than being outstretched on the cross. The figure originally had arms outstretched, but at dawn on September 1, 1971, when Hurricane Lily hit Barra de Navidad and the surrounding area with full force, the statue's arms came down from the cross without falling to the ground. Locals believe that when the Christ's arms fell, it calmed the hurricane and saved the town. Ever since, they have believed that 'el Cristo del Ciclón' has miraculous powers.

✳✳✳✳✳✳✳✳✳✳✳✳

Hotel Caribe (☎ *355-59-52, Sonora 15*) offers one of the best budget deals in town. It has a rooftop terrace and 18 clean rooms with bath; singles/doubles are US$11.50/17, with some larger rooms. Also good is *Posada Pacífico* (☎ *355-53-59, Mazatlán 136*) on the corner of Michoacán, with 25 large, clean rooms for US$12/14, plus four bungalows (with kitchen) for US$29 for up to four people. If these are full, *Hotel San Lorenzo* (☎/fax *355-51-39, Sinaloa 7*), near the corner of Mazatlán, has singles/doubles for US$13/14 with one bed, US$16.50 with two.

Mid-Range & Top End Barra has several good mid-range hotels. One of the best is *Hotel Delfín* (☎ *355-50-68, Morelos 23*), with 22 large, clean, pleasant rooms looking out onto wide walkways; from most rooms you can view the lagoon and the swimming pool below. Singles/doubles are US$22/26 May to November, US$35 December to April, with a breakfast buffet served in the outdoor restaurant for US$3. Also pleasant, *Hotel Sands* (☎/fax 355-50-18, Morelos 24) has a lagoon-side swimming pool and a poolside restaurant/bar. Singles/doubles are US$32/43, breakfast included; bungalows (with kitchen) start at US$80.

Several good beachfront hotels are on Legazpi, including *Hotel Bogavante* (☎ 355-53-84), with singles/doubles for US$31/37, bungalows with kitchen for US$52. *Hotel Barra de Navidad* (☎ 355-51-22, *Legazpi 250*), with a beachside swimming pool, has 60 attractive rooms with air-con and cable TV for US$49/58.

Polo's Bungalows (☎ 355-64-10, *Veracruz 174*) has one- and two-bedroom bungalows with kitchen and air-con for US$33/55, cheaper monthly. *Bungalows Mar Vida* (☎ 355-59-11, *Mazatlán 168*) is a fine little guesthouse with a swimming pool and five studio apartments, with air-con and cable TV, for US$53; English is spoken.

The super-luxury *Grand Bay Hotel* (☎ 355-50-50), on a peninsula in the lagoon, is very expensive, but magnificent. Off-season rates start at US$322, going up to US$2925 for the presidential suite. Golf, tennis and other packages are available (three-night minimum stay). Take a water taxi to get here (US$1, every 10 minutes).

Places to Eat

Barra has many good restaurants. Several are on terraces over the beach, and have a beautiful sunset view. Several more overlook the lagoon. Many simple, inexpensive little indoor-outdoor restaurants are along Calle Veracruz, in the center of town – stroll along and take your pick.

The beachfront *Mariscos Nacho* on Legazpi near Yucatán has a wide selection of breakfasts and seafood, proudly proclaiming itself *'el rey del pescado asado'* ('the king of BBQ fish'). *Sea Master Café* on Legazpi at Yucatán is another good beachfront restaurant/bar, and there are many others.

Beside the lagoon, *Veleros* on Veracruz is a good restaurant/bar with a fine view. Nearby, also overlooking the lagoon, are *Restaurant Eloy* and *El Manglito*.

Restaurant Ambar, upstairs on the corner of Veracruz and Jalisco under a high palapa roof, is a hidden treasure for evening meals. Verónica, the French owner/cook, provides enjoyable ambiance, high-quality food and a good wine list. Imaginative dinner crepes served with salad are a house specialty (US$4 to US$14). Open 8 am to noon and 5 to 11 pm daily, November to April and July to August.

Entertainment

Hotel Sands has the *El Galeón* disco, and a poolside bar open November to Easter; the two-for-one happy hour from 4 to 6 pm is popular, especially since it includes the use of their lagoonside pool. On Legazpi at Yucatán, *Piper Lover's Bar & Grill* has happy hour 5 to 6 pm and 9 to 10 pm, and sometimes has live music. Next door, the upstairs *La Azotea* bar is popular with young people, with loud music and a pool table. Several beachfront restaurant/bars along Legazpi are good for watching the sunset, with happy hours and evening entertainment.

Getting There & Away

Air Barra de Navidad and Melaque are served by the Playa de Oro international airport, 25km southeast on highway 200, which also serves Manzanillo. To get there, take a taxi (30 minutes; US$20), or a bus 15km to Cihuatlán and a cheaper taxi from there. See the Manzanillo section for flight details.

Bus See San Patricio-Melaque earlier in this chapter; long-distance buses stopping there also stop here (15 minutes before or after). The Cihuatlán bus station is at Veracruz 228; virtually opposite is the Primera Plus bus station.

In addition to the long-distance buses, local buses connect Barra and Melaque (every 15 minutes 6 am to 9 pm; US$0.25), stopping in Barra at the long-distance bus stations (buses stopping on the southbound side of the road loop round Legazpi and back to Melaque).

Taxis between Barra and San Patricio-Melaque cost US$3.25.

Car & Bicycle Crazy Cactus (☎ 355-60-99), Jalisco 8, rents cars and bicycles, in addition to water sports equipment (see Activities).

Boat Water taxis operate 24 hours from the south end of Veracruz, offering service to the

Grand Bay Hotel, the marina, the golf course and Colimilla. Fare is US$1 round-trip.

MANZANILLO
• pop 80,600 ☎ 3

Manzanillo is a major port and industrial city, with shipping piers, train tracks and a bustling central district. Away from the center, out around the Bahía de Manzanillo and Bahía de Santiago, are many fine beaches. There's also deep-sea fishing, and good bird-watching in the lagoons and around the golf course. Manzanillo calls itself the 'World Capital of Sailfish'; in 1957 it was the site of a world record when 336 sailfish were caught during a three-day fishing tournament.

Orientation

Manzanillo extends 16km, northwest to southeast. The resort hotels and finest beaches begin on Playa Azul, across the bay from Playa San Pedrito, the closest beach to the center (about 1km away). Farther around the bay is the Santiago Peninsula, a rocky outcrop occupied by Las Hadas Resort and the beaches of La Audiencia, Santiago, Olas Altas and Miramar. Just west of Miramar is the Laguna de Juluapan.

Central Manzanillo is bound by the Bahía de Manzanillo to the north, the Pacific Ocean to the west, and the Laguna de Cuyutlán to the southeast and south. Avenida Morelos, the principal avenue, runs along the northern edge of the city, beside the sea, west from Avenida Niños Héroes, which leads to highway 200. The city center begins at the zócalo (also known as Jardín Obregón) on Avenida Morelos, and then continues southward with the major street, Avenida México, crossed from west to east by a number of streets, which change names on either side of it.

Information

Tourist Offices The municipal Departamento de Turismo (☎ 332-10-02 ext 247, fax 332-11-17) operates a tourist information desk on the sidewalk of the Presidencia Municipal, out in front of their office. It's staffed 9 am to 7 pm daily, with free maps. The tourist police office is behind the Presidencia Municipal.

The helpful state-run Secretaria de Turismo (☎ 333-22-77/64, fax 333-14-26, sectur@bai.net.mx), around the bay in Playa Azul at Boulevard Miguel de la Madrid 1033,

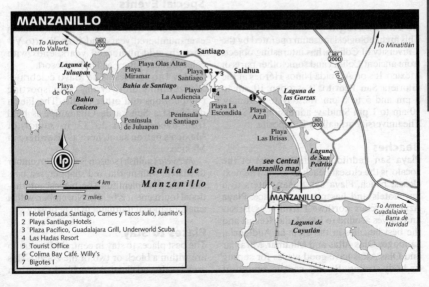

1 Hotel Posada Santiago, Carnes y Tacos Julio, Juanito's
2 Playa Santiago Hotels
3 Plaza Pacífico, Guadalajara Grill, Underworld Scuba
4 Las Hadas Resort
5 Tourist Office
6 Colima Bay Café, Willy's
7 Bigotes I

between the Fiesta Mexicana and Marbella hotels, is open 9 am to 2 pm and 5 to 7.30 pm Monday to Friday, 10 am to 2 pm Saturday.

Money Many banks are scattered around the city center, most with ATMs. Bital, on Avenida México a block south of the zócalo, is open 8 am to 7 pm Monday to Friday, 9 am to 2.30 pm Saturday.

Post & Communications The post office, south of the zócalo at Galindo 30, is open 9 am to 5.30 pm Monday to Friday, 9 am to 1 pm Saturday. Telecomm, with telegram, telex and fax, is in the Presidencia Municipal, on the southeast corner of the zócalo. It's open 8 am to 7.30 pm Monday to Friday, 9 am to 12.30 pm Saturday, Sunday and holidays.

Public telephones are plentiful around the center. Computel, with long-distance telephone and fax, has offices at Avenida Morelos 144 and at Avenida México 302, on the corner of Cuauhtémoc. Both are open 7 am to 10 pm daily.

There's an Internet café in the La Luna silver shop, Avenida México 69, half a block south of the zócalo.

Museo Universitario de Arqueología

This archaeological museum operated by the University of Colima, has interesting objects from ancient Colima and some other parts of Mexico. It's on Avenida Niños Héroes at the Glorieta San Pedrito. It is open 10 am to 2 pm and 5 to 8 pm Tuesday to Saturday, 10 am to 1 pm Sunday; admission US$1.25. The university art gallery is opposite.

Beaches

Playa San Pedrito, about 1km east of the zócalo, is the closest beach to town. The next closest beach, **Playa Las Brisas**, caters to a few hotels and has plenty of space. **Playa Azul** stretches northwest from Las Brisas and curves around to Las Hadas Resort and the best beaches in the area: **La Audiencia, Santiago, Olas Altas** and **Miramar**. Miramar and Olas Altas have good waves for surfing or body-surfing. Boards can be rented at

Miramar. Playa La Audiencia, on a quiet cove at the west side of the Santiago Peninsula, has more tranquil water and is popular for water-skiing.

Getting to these beaches from the town center is easy: take any local bus marked 'Santiago,' 'Las Brisas' or 'Miramar.' The 'Miramar' bus to Playa Miramar takes 40 minutes, stopping en route at Las Brisas, Playa Azul, Santiago, La Audiencia and Olas Altas. The 'Las Hadas' bus takes a scenic, circular route down the Santiago Peninsula – there's a magnificent view of the beaches on either side if you get off 30m up from the Hotel Risco la Audiencia.

Water Sports

Snorkeling, diving, windsurfing, water-skiing, sailing and deep-sea fishing are all popular water sports around the bay. Underworld Scuba (☎/fax 3-06-42), in the Plaza Pacífico on the Santiago Peninsula, charges US$80 for two beach or boat dives including equipment. You can feed eels and octopuses by hand at Playa La Audiencia, or view the cargo ship that sank in 1959 and sits 9m under water near Playa Miramar.

Special Events

In early February a sailing tournament, which comes from San Diego, California, in even-numbered years and from Puerto Vallarta in odd-numbered years, ends with celebrations at the Las Hadas Resort.

May 1 to 10, Fiestas de Mayo celebrates Manzanillo's anniversary with sporting competitions and other events. The Fiesta de Nuestra Señora de Guadalupe is held from December 1 to 12 in honor of Mexico's patron saint, here as elsewhere in Mexico.

Pez vela (sailfish) season is from November to March, with marlin, red snapper, sea bass and tuna also plentiful. The biggest international tournament is held in November, with a smaller national tournament in February.

Places to Stay

The best places to stay in central Manzanillo are within a block or two of the zócalo. This area is safe and clean. A few blocks south in

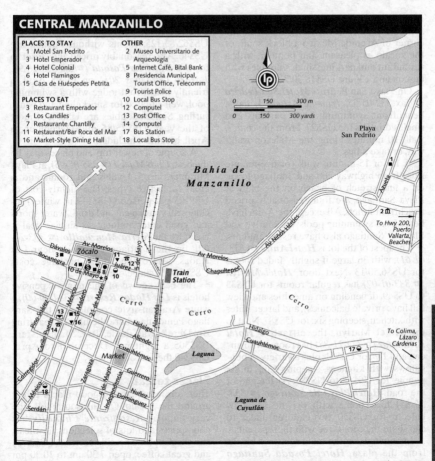

CENTRAL MANZANILLO

PLACES TO STAY
1 Motel San Pedrito
3 Hotel Emperador
4 Hotel Colonial
6 Hotel Flamingos
15 Casa de Huéspedes Petrita

PLACES TO EAT
3 Restaurant Emperador
4 Los Candiles
7 Restaurante Chantilly
11 Restaurant/Bar Roca del Mar
16 Market-Style Dining Hall

OTHER
2 Museo Universitario de
   Arqueología
5 Internet Café, Bital Bank
8 Presidencia Municipal,
   Tourist Office, Telecomm
9 Tourist Police
10 Local Bus Stop
12 Computel
13 Post Office
14 Computel
17 Bus Station
18 Local Bus Stop

Bahía de Manzanillo

Playa San Pedrito

To Hwy 200, Puerto Vallarta, Beaches

Train Station

To Colima, Lázaro Cárdenas

Laguna de Cuyutlán

the city center there are more places to stay, but the area is comparatively dirty and squalid. Around the bay, where the better beaches are, hotels tend to be more expensive; Playa Santiago, half an hour away by bus, is an exception.

Budget The only trailer park is *La Marmota* (☎ 336-62-48) on the road to Minatitlán, but the tourist office has received complaints about it.

Half a block from the southwest corner of the zócalo, the simple but clean *Hotel Emperador* (☎ 332-23-74, Dávalos 69) has

singles/doubles with one bed for US$8.75/11; two-bed doubles are US$13. Top-floor rooms are brighter than the rest. The hotel's restaurant has good food and is one of the cheapest in town.

Hotel Flamingos (☎ 332-10-37, Madero 72), half a block south of the zócalo, is nicely furnished for a budget place; singles/doubles are US$8.75/11.25.

Casa de Huéspedes Petrita (☎ 332-01-87, Allende 24) is very basic, but economical and clean. Singles/doubles with one bed and shared bath are US$6.50/8; rooms with two beds and private bath are US$16.50.

CENTRAL PACIFIC COAST

Mid-Range The *Hotel Colonial* (☎/fax 332-10-80, 332-12-30, Bocanegra 100), on the corner of Avenida México a block south of the zócalo, is pleasant and popular, with a restaurant and parking; singles/doubles with air-con and TV are US$18.50/22.

On Playa San Pedrito, *Motel San Pedrito* (☎/fax 332-05-35, Teniente Azueta 3) has a beachfront swimming pool, parking, and singles/doubles for US$27. From the center, walk 10 minutes along the Malecón walkway, or take a bus.

A 10- or 15-minute walk (or five-minute ride) from highway 200 and Santiago town, on a fine stretch of beach on the bluff at Playa Santiago, are four reasonably priced beachfront hotels. All except the Anita have beachfront swimming pools; the Marlyn and Playa de Santiago also have restaurant/bars.

Cheapest of the lot is *Hotel Anita* (☎ 333-01-61), with 36 large if slightly faded rooms for US$6.50/13. Next door, *Hotel Marlyn* (☎ 333-01-07) has regular rooms for US$33 to US$49, depending on amenities and view (all have private balconies), and larger suites with kitchen, sleeping six, for US$87. Next to the Hotel Marlyn, the attractive *Hotel Brillamar* (☎ 334-11-88) has rooms with air-con and TV for US$31, plus a variety of bungalows with kitchens, sleeping four to six people, for US$65 to US$87. At the end of the road, *Hotel Playa de Santiago* (☎ 333-00-55) has rooms with private sea-view balcony for US$50; two children under 10 can share the room free with their parents.

In Santiago, on the main road two blocks from the plaza, *Hotel Posada Santiago* (☎ 333-00-14), Blvd Miguel de la Madrid Km 13.5, is a simple place with singles/doubles for US$11/20. Good places to eat are nearby.

Top End Most of Manzanillo's top-end hotels are on or near the beaches outside the city center. Many are found along the beach side of the main road along Playa Azul.

Moderately priced, *Hotel Villas La Audiencia* (☎ 333-08-61) on the Santiago Peninsula is a good value in the top-end range, especially for families. All the villas come with kitchen, air-con and satellite TV, and there's a swimming pool and restaurant/bar. One/two/three-bedroom villas rent for US$62/83/125; rooms without kitchen are US$46. Also reasonably priced and closer to town is *Hotel La Posada* (☎/fax 333-18-99, Lázaro Cárdenas 201) on Playa Azul, a friendly beachfront lodge with a swimming pool, well-situated for snorkeling and windsurfing. Singles/doubles are US$59/64 most of the year, US$75/85 mid-December to April, breakfast included.

A couple of newer top-end places may be the best. *Club Maeva* (☎ 335-05-95), at Playa Miramar, has 514 villas and rooms and is great for active types. The nightly cost of US$105 per person (US$119 in winter) includes all you can eat and drink, water sports and good entertainment. A similar deal is given by the *Sierra Manzanillo* (☎ 333-20-00), on the Santiago Peninsula near Las Hadas, where the whole package costs US$176/212 single/double.

The best known of the more expensive hotels is *Las Hadas Resort* (☎ 334-00-00), a white Arabian-style complex on the Santiago Peninsula where the film *10*, featuring Bo Derek, was made. Its 220 rooms are US$305 a night mid-December to April, US$240 the rest of the year.

Places to Eat

There are a number of good places to eat around the zócalo. On the south side, the very popular *Restaurante Chantilly* has good prices and lots of selections for meals and snacks, plus a comida corrida (US$3.75) and great coffee; open 7.30 am to 10.30 pm every day except Saturday. On the east side of the zócalo, *Restaurant/Bar Roca del Mar* has pleasant atmosphere and is good for all meals. Among its specialties is a seafood comida corrida with seafood soup, rice, fish or shrimp, and dessert for US$5.50.

Los Candiles, the restaurant/bar at the Hotel Colonial, a block south of the zócalo, has a pleasant patio section; comida corrida costs US$4.50, breakfast costs US$3.25 to US$4.50.

Restaurant Emperador, on the ground floor of the Hotel Emperador, half a block west of the zócalo, is simple and small but has good food at some of the most economical prices in Manzanillo. Comida corrida meat or seafood meals are US$2.75, breakfast or enchiladas US$1.50; open 8 am to 11.30 pm daily.

A market-style dining hall on the corner of Madero and Cuauhtémoc is open 7 am to 9 pm daily, with a number of stalls to choose from.

Many more restaurants are spread out around the bay. *Bigotes I* on the highway at Las Brisas, Km 1.5, is popular for seafood. *Colima Bay Café* on the highway at Playa Azul, Km 6.5, is a fun place with good music and good food. Also on Playa Azul, *Willy's* is one of the best restaurants in the area for French and international dining. *Guadalajara Grill*, upstairs in Plaza Pacífico, at the beginning of the road to Las Hadas, is another fun restaurant.

In Santiago, on the highway about 300m west of the Jardín, is *Carnes y Tacos Julio*, serving excellent inexpensive meat choices noon to 1 am daily. The similarly named place a few doors down is also good. Across the road 100m to the west is *Juanito's*, popular with gringos.

Entertainment

If you're here on a Sunday evening, stop by the zócalo, where everyone from toddlers to grandparents is out enjoying an ice cream, the company and the balmy night air. This tradition, which has disappeared in many parts of Mexico, is still alive and well in Manzanillo. Sometimes a band plays in the gazebo to entertain the crowd. It's also worth stopping by the zócalo any evening around sunset to hear the cacophony of the exuberant *zanates* (black birds) as they settle into the trees for the night.

Tourist nightlife is mostly spread out around the bay. *Vog*, on the highway at Playa Azul, is a popular disco. Next door, *Bar de Felix* has no cover charge and many people like it better for dancing. *Teto's Bar*, near Hotel Fiesta Mexicana on Playa Azul, is another popular dancing spot with live music. Also on Playa Azul, *Colima Bay Café* (see Places to Eat), in the Carlos Anderson chain, puts on a good time for tourists.

Kitzias Discotheque, Km 10.5 on the highway, is another popular disco. *Ole Ole*, closer in at Km 7.5, has dancing with live salsa and tropical music. Near Las Hadas, *Cantina del Vaquero (Blvd Miguel de la Madrid 5010)* is a cantina with carne asada and music for dancing.

On Playa Miramar, the luxurious *Club Maeva* has *Disco Boom Boom* and the *Tropical Hut*. They present theme entertainment several nights weekly; phone for reservations (☎ 335-05-96 ext 4).

Getting There & Away

Air The Playa de Oro international airport is 35km northwest of Manzanillo on highway 200. Mexicana, Aero California and Aeromar all offer direct flights to/from Mexico City. Aerolitoral (under Aeroméxico) has flights to/from Guadalajara. Aero California and Alaska Air both fly to/from Los Angeles; America West flies to/from Phoenix. All have connections to other places.

Bus The bus terminal is about 1.5km east of the center. Ticket offices, luggage storage, a telephone caseta and small restaurants are in a row of huts along the north side. Destinations include:

Armería – 45km, 45 minutes (US$2); 2nd-class, every 15 minutes 4 am to 10 pm, by Autobuses Nuevo Horizonte; hourly 2 am to 10 pm, by Autotransportes del Sur de Jalisco

Barra de Navidad – 60km, 1 to 1½ at least hourly 1st (US$4) and 2nd-class (US$3.25) 4.30 am to 12.15 am, by Transportes Cihuatlán

Colima – 101km, 1½ to 2 hours; 2nd-class every half hour 2 am to 10 pm, by Autobuses Nuevo Horizonte, Autotransportes del Sur de Jalisco (US$3.75), La Linea Plus (US$4.50) and ETN (US$5.50)

Guadalajara – 325km; 1st-class 4½ hours, US$15 to US$22, 16 by La Linea Plus, 5 by Transportes Cihuatlán, 6 by ETN; 2nd-class 5 to 8 hours, US$13.50 to US$17.25, 12 by Transportes Cihuatlán, 7 by Autotransportes del Sur de Jalisco

Lázaro Cárdenas – 313km, 6 hours; 1st-class at 2 am and 6 am, by Elite (US$19.50); 2nd-class, 6 by Autotransportes del Sur de Jalisco and Galeana (US$13.50)

Mexico City (Terminal Norte) – 843km, 12 hours; *via corta* (short route) or via Morelia; 1st-class at

7.30 pm and 9 pm by Elite (US$49.50), 7.30 pm by ETN (US$32.75)

Puerto Vallarta – 285km; 1st-class, 5 hours at 4 pm, 7.30 pm and 9.30 pm by Elite (US$16.25), 8 am and noon by Transportes Cihuatlán (US$17.50); 2nd-class, 6½ hours, 9 by Transportes Cihuatlán (US$14.50)

San Patricio-Melaque – 65km, 1 to 1½ hours; same as to Barra de Navidad

ETN (☎ 334-10-40) has its own bus terminal near Santiago at Km 13.5 on the highway; its deluxe buses go to Mexico City, Guadalajara and Colima.

Getting Around

To/From the Airport Transportes Turísticos Benito Juárez (☎ 334-15-55) operates a door-to-door van to/from the airport. Fare is US$22 for private service (one or two people), or US$7.75 per person when there are three or more people. A taxi from the center to the airport costs about US$16.50.

Bus Local buses heading around the bay to San Pedrito, Salahua, Santiago, Miramar and all the beaches along the way depart from Avenida México, from the corner of Juárez and 21 de Marzo near the zócalo and from the main bus station, every 10 minutes from around 6 am to 11 pm. Fares are US$0.25 to US$0.55, depending on how far down the line you choose to go.

Taxi Taxis are plentiful around Manzanillo. From the center of town it's US$1.10 to the bus station, US$2.75 to Playa Azul, US$4 to Playa Santiago, US$5 to Playa Miramar and US$16.50 to the airport. Agree with the driver on the price before you get into the cab.

CUYUTLÁN & EL PARAÍSO

Cuyutlán • pop 940 ☎ changing
El Paraíso • pop 210 ☎ changing

The small, black-sand beach resort towns of Cuyutlán and El Paraíso are southeast of Manzanillo. Cuyutlán, the more developed of the two, is near the southeastern end of Laguna de Cuyutlán, about 40km from Manzanillo and 12km from Armería. El Paraíso is 6km farther southeast.

Both towns have a few hotels and restaurants popular with Mexican families and seldom visited by norteamericanos. Consequently, beachfront accommodation costs much less here.

In Cuyutlán most of the hotels and places to eat are clustered near the beach. If you arrive in town by bus you'll be let off on Hidalgo, on one side of the zócalo. Walk four blocks toward the sea on Hidalgo, and you'll be right in the middle of the hotel and restaurant area beside the beach.

Aside from its long stretch of relatively isolated beach, Cuyutlán is known for its 'green wave' in April and May, caused by little green phosphorescent critters. There's also a turtle farm on the beach about 3km toward Paraíso; open daily (US$1).

El Paraíso is a smaller fishing village, with a black-sand beach, several hotels and *enramadas* (simple thatch-roof seafood restaurants) and a good surfing spot about 3km south.

Information

Cuyutlán has a post office (El Paraíso does not), but neither town has a bank; for this you'll have to go into Armería. Both towns do have public telephones and telephone casetas, however. Cuyutlán's caseta is on Hidalgo, in the shop on the corner one block past the zócalo, heading away from the beach. In Paraíso it's in the restaurant opposite the beach and the bus stop.

Places to Stay

At Christmas and Semana Santa, Cuyutlán's hotels fill up with Mexican families on holiday; reserve in advance at these times. Also during these holidays, most hotels require that you take three meals a day; cost for room and meals will be around US$22 per person.

On December 1, 2000, the telephone area code is due to change to ☎ 8 from 86, with the digit 6 added to the start of every local number (for example, the number 33-09-10 will become 633-09-10).

Cuyutlán You can camp on the beach to the right of the hotels. A couple of simple thatch-roof restaurants nearby rent showers.

As you come to the beach on Hidalgo you'll reach the corner of Veracruz, the beachside road. On this corner are two of Cuyutlán's best budget hotels, with other hotels a block or two either side. *Hotel Morelos* (☎ 6-40-13, Hidalgo 185), on the corner of Hidalgo and Veracruz, has a swimming pool and 48 clean, pleasant rooms with bath for US$7.75 per person (room only), or US$18.50 per person including three meals. Opposite, *Hotel Fénix* (☎/fax 6-40-82) is another good place, with 14 rooms for US$6.50 per person downstairs, US$8.75 upstairs; English is spoken.

Also pleasant is *Hotel El Bucanero* (☎ 6-40-05), on the beachfront behind Hotel Fénix; interior/seaview rooms are US$7.75/9.75 per person. Opposite this, also right on the beach, the large *Hotel María Victoria* (☎ 6-40-04, Veracruz 10) is more luxurious, with rooms for US$17.50 per person. To its left, *Hotel San Rafael* (☎ 6-40-15, Veracruz 46) has a swimming pool and beachfront restaurant/bar; singles/doubles are US$13/19.50. The seaview rooms here are especially attractive, with good views and a large shared balcony.

El Paraíso A simple place, *Hotel Valencia* (☎ 2-00-25) has eight rooms with one/two beds for US$9.75/13. A few similar places are nearby. Otherwise you could camp on the beach, or probably string up a hammock under one of the enramadas. Of the hotels, the fancy one is the *Hotel Paraíso* (☎ in Colima ☎ 331-2-10-32, 331-2-47-87), with a swimming pool, pleasant terraces, a seafood restaurant and 60 rooms for US$20 to US$24.50 for up to two adults and two children.

Places to Eat

Cuyutlán Several of the hotels have good seafood restaurants. *El Bucanero* and *Siete Mares*, attached respectively to the Hotel El Bucanero and the Hotel San Rafael, are attractive beachfront restaurant/bars. On the corner of Hidalgo and Veracruz, also in hotels, are two of Cuyutlán's most economical eateries: *Restaurante Morelos* and *Restaurante Fénix*. Both offer good-value meals for about US$3. For a simple snack, stands on the beach sell seafood and cold drinks. Or grab a snack at one of the restaurants near the plaza.

El Paraíso All the beachfront enramadas serve basically the same food at the same price. The classiest restaurant is poolside at the *Hotel Paraíso*.

Getting There & Away

Cuyutlán and Paraíso are connected to the rest of the world through Armería, a dusty town on highway 200 about 46km southeast of Manzanillo and 55km southwest of Colima. From Armería to Cuyutlán it's 12km down a paved road passing through orchards and coconut plantations; a similar road runs 8km southwest from Armería to El Paraíso.

To reach either place by bus involves going first to Armería and changing buses. The Sociedad Cooperativo de Autotransportes Colima Manzanillo and Autotransportes Nuevo Horizonte bus lines both have an office and bus stop on Armería's main street and operate 2nd-class buses to Manzanillo every half-hour, 5 am to 12.30 am (45 minutes, US$2.25) and to Colima every half hour, 5.45 am to 10.30 pm (45 minutes, US$2.25). Buses go every 20 minutes to Tecoman (25 minutes, US$0.50), where you can connect with buses going southeast on highway 200 (to Lázaro Cárdenas, etc). A couple of doors away, Flecha Amarilla has 2nd-class buses to Mexico City and Guadalajara. Across the street, Autotransportes del Sur de Jalisco operates buses with similar services going to Manzanillo and Colima.

Buses to Cuyutlán and El Paraíso depart from Armería's market, one block north and one block east of the long-distance bus offices. To Cuyutlán they depart every half hour, 6 am to 7.30 pm (20 minutes, US$0.50). To El Paraíso they go every 45 minutes, 6 am to 7.30 pm (15 minutes, US$0.50).

Between Cuyutlán and El Paraíso, there are taxis but no buses; to go by bus from one to the other, you must return to Armería and change buses there. By taxi, Armería to Cuyutlán is US$4.50, Armería to El Paraíso is US$3.25, and Cuyutlán to El Paraíso is US$4.

MICHOACÁN COAST

Highway 200 hugs the shoreline most of the way along the beautiful 250km coast of Michoacán, one of Mexico's most beautiful states, passing dozens of beautiful, tranquil beaches – some wide expanses of soft sand, some tucked into rocky little coves and bays, some at river mouths where quiet estuaries are home to multitudes of birds. Some of the beaches have quiet waves and are good for swimming; others have big waves great for surfing. Many of the beaches are uninhabited; some have small communities. Mango plantations are all along here, as are coconut, papaya and banana plantations.

On the northwest part of Michoacán's coast, at the border of Colima state, **Boca de Apiza**, at the mouth of the Río Coahuayana, is a good beach where there are seafood restaurants; turn off the highway at the town of Coahuayana.

Just a bit farther south, after the highway meets the coast, **San Juan de Alima** is an attractive beach community with beachfront restaurants and several modern hotels. Places to stay include the *Villas de San Juan* (☎ 331-4-29-84) and the *Miramar*, *Parador* and *Ocean View*, all of which can be reached through the town's telephone caseta (☎ 332-7-00-02). Also, there's *Bungalows Antony's* (☎ 453-6-00-03).

A short distance down the coast, **Las Brisas** is another beachside community with places to stay. Still farther along, **La Ticla** is a good surfing beach, with beachfront *cabañas* (cabins) offering accommodations.

Next along here, **Faro de Bucerías** is known for its beauty, with clear, pale-blue waters, yellow sand and rocky islands – a good spot for camping, swimming and snorkeling. The Náhuatl community here prepares good fresh seafood.

Farther along, **Bahía de Maruata**, known as one of Michoacán's most beautiful beaches, has clear turquoise waters and

white sands. This is the principal beach where black sea turtles lay their eggs; these and other species of sea turtles are set free here each year by sea turtle conservation programs. Restaurants here serve fresh seafood, accommodations are available in rustic cabañas, and there are camping areas.

Farther south, **Pichilinguillo** is in a small bay, good for swimming. Farther still are beautiful **Nexpa**, popular with surfers, and Caleta de Campos, on a lovely little bay. **La Soledad** ('loneliness') is a very beautiful, tranquil little beach. **Las Peñas**, farther along toward Lázaro Cárdenas, is another good beach for surfing. Playa Azul, 24km from Lázaro Cárdenas, is a laid-back beachfront community, which is easy to visit and has surfable waves (see the Playa Azul section).

CALETA DE CAMPOS
☎ 753

A small village on a cliff overlooking a small, lovely blue bay, Caleta de Campos is a quiet place, but it does have a couple of pleasant hotels. They're very near one another and are both good and clean, with sea views.

Travelers like the *Hotel Yuritzi* (☎ 1-50-10, 1-50-20), with safe parking and a night watchman. Clean rooms are US$13/16.50 a single/double with fan, US$28/33 with aircon and TV. Nearby, *Hotel Los Arcos* (☎ 1-50-38) is also good; singles/doubles are US$11/13 without sea view, US$16.50 with sea view, US$33 with air-con; TV available in any room for US$5.50 extra.

Buses depart Caleta de Campos for Lázaro Cárdenas every 25 minutes, 5 am to 7 pm (1½ hours, US$3). In Lázaro Cárdenas, these buses depart from the Galeana terminal on Avenida Lázaro Cárdenas (see the Lázaro Cárdenas section).

A taxi between Caleta de Campos and Playa Nexpa is US$2.75. In Caleta de Campos the taxi stand is beside the highway.

PLAYA AZUL
• pop 3190 ☎ changing

Playa Azul is a small beach resort town backed by lagoons formed by a tributary of the Río Balsas. It attracts Mexican families during Semana Santa and the Christmas holidays, when all the hotels fill up, prices rise and reservations are necessary; the rest of the time the town is quiet and peaceful, with a trickle of foreign travelers enjoying its beautiful beach and surfable waves. A strong undertow, however, can make swimming in the sea here dangerous; also beware of stingrays lying on the sand. Swimming is better at Barra de Pichi, on the coast a kilometer or two east of Playa Azul, where there's a large estuary with boat trips for seeing the plants, animals and birds.

Orientation & Information

Playa Azul is so small, and everything is so close that there's little need for street names, since everyone knows where everything is. Basically there are four streets in town, all running parallel to the beach. The beachside street, usually referred to as the Malecón, is officially named Zapata. The next street inland is Carranza, the next one is Madero and the fourth is Independencia.

A Pemex station (la gasolinera) on the corner of Independencia marks the beginning of town as you enter from the highway. This is a major landmark, with buses and combis arriving and departing from here. The beach is three blocks straight ahead. A few blocks east (left as you face the sea) is a large plaza. Almost everything you need is somewhere between the plaza and the gasolinera. A long row of beachfront restaurants (enramadas) stretches along the beach.

The post office, on Madero at the northwest corner of the plaza, is open 9 am to 3 pm, Monday to Friday. Telecomm is in the same building (different entrance). The town has several telephone casetas; there's one on Carranza and another can be found near the gasolinera.

In November 2000, the telephone area code for Playa Azul is due to change from 753 to 7, with the digits 53 added to the start of every local number (for example, the number 6-00-11 will become 536-00-11).

Activities

Pools provide a safer alternative to swimming in the sea. **Balneario Playa Azul**, on the Malecón behind the Hotel Playa Azul, has a large swimming pool, a big water slide and a restaurant/bar. It's open 10 am to 6 pm, Saturday and Sunday only; admission US$1.30 per person, but free to guests of the Hotel Playa Azul or its trailer park.

The Hotel Playa Azul and Hotel María Teresa Jericó have courtyard swimming pools with poolside restaurants (see Places to Stay).

There are swimming and boat trips at **Barra de Pichi**, one or two kilometers east down the beach. You can walk there in half an hour, or take a taxi for US$2.75. Lanchas can be hired for lagoon tours; the estuary is good for swimming and bird-watching.

Places to Stay

Camping You can string up a hammock at most of the enramadas along the beach; ask permission from the family running the restaurant, who probably won't mind, especially if you eat there once or twice. If you don't have your own hammock they may let you use one of theirs. A couple of enramadas provide public showers and toilets.

Hotel Playa Azul has a small trailer park with full hookups in the rear; the cost of US$11 per space includes use of the balneario and the hotel's swimming pool.

Hotels & Bungalows The *Hotel Costa de Oro*, on Madero near the plaza, has parking and clean rooms with one/two beds for US$11/16.50.

Bungalows de la Curva (☎ 6-00-58), on Independencia one block toward the beach from the Pemex station at the entrance to town, has parking and a small swimming pool. Small/large bungalows with kitchens, sleeping three/six persons, are US$18/28; rooms without kitchen are US$13. Next door, *Hotel Delfín* (☎ 6-00-07), on Carranza, is pleasant, with clean rooms around a small swimming pool courtyard; singles/doubles are US$12/18.

Bungalows Delfín (☎ 6-00-06), on Madero on the west side of the plaza, has 10 bungalows with kitchens for US$13/20/25 a single/double/triple, US$30 for four or five people.

Hotel María Isabel (☎ *6-00-16*), on Madero on the far side of the plaza, has a swimming pool and 30 spacious, clean rooms. Singles/doubles are US$13/16.50; larger rooms sleeping six people are up to US$33, depending on the number of people. Air-con is available for an extra US$5.50.

The large, 73-room ***Hotel Playa Azul*** (☎ *6-00-24/88*), on Carranza, is the town's most upmarket hotel, with 'económica' rooms for US$22. Rooms around the pool are US$33/49 with fan/air-con.

Another attractive hotel, and a better value, is the ***Hotel María Teresa Jericó*** (☎ *6-00-05, Independencia 626*), on the inland side of the plaza. It has a swimming pool and poolside restaurant/bar, parking, and 42 clean, comfortable rooms, all with air-con and TV; singles/doubles are US$26/30 (10% discount for stays of three days or more).

Places to Eat

Enramadas line the beachfront, all charging basically the same prices and serving pretty much the same selection of fresh seafood. Try the *pescado relleno*, a regional specialty – filet of fish stuffed with shrimp, octopus and other seafood.

Two small family restaurants, ***Restaurant Galdy*** and ***Restaurant Familiar Martita***, both on the market street near Madero, around the corner from the Hotel Playa Azul, are often recommended by locals. Both serve good food at economical prices and are open daily from around 7 am to 11 pm. Galdy has good comida corridas for US$2.25.

The poolside restaurant/bar at the ***Hotel Playa Azul*** is a favorite with travelers; if you come here to eat or drink, you can swim in the pool for free. It's open 7.30 am to 10.30 pm daily. The ***Hotel María Teresa Jericó*** also has a poolside restaurant/bar.

Getting There & Away

Combis run about every 10 minutes, 5 am to 9 pm, between Playa Azul and Lázaro Cárdenas (24km, 30 minutes, US$1.10). They enter Playa Azul and go down Carranza,

dropping you off anywhere along the way. In Playa Azul, catch the combis on Carranza or when they loop back on Independencia.

Intercity buses do not pass through Playa Azul; they will drop you off at the highway junction in La Mira, 7km away. If you want to go from Playa Azul to Caleta de Campos or beyond, you can catch the northbound bus at La Mira without having to go into Lázaro Cárdenas.

A taxi between Lázaro Cárdenas and Playa Azul costs about US$11.

LÁZARO CÁRDENAS
• **pop 63,700 ☎ changing**

Lázaro Cárdenas is the largest city on the coast of Michoacán, one of Mexico's most beautiful states. Originally named Melchor Ocampo, in 1970 its name was changed to honor Lázaro Cárdenas, the reform-minded leader who served as governor of Michoacán from 1928 to 1932, and as president of Mexico from 1934 to 1940.

An industrial city and significant port, where major development has occurred since the 1970s, Lázaro has nothing of real interest to travelers – but since it's the terminus of several bus routes, travelers do pass through. Reasons to stop here include changing buses, stocking up on food and water, and heading for Playa Azul, a beach resort 24km to the west.

Orientation & Information

Avenida Lázaro Cárdenas is the city's main street. Everything you need is on or near this main avenue.

The center of town, around the bus terminals, is a busy area with shops, restaurants, hotels and lots of activity. If you do need to spend the night here, several decent hotels are available.

 In 2000, the telephone area code for Lázaro Cárdenas is due to change from 753 to 7, with the digits 53 added to the start of every local number (for example, the number 2-15-47 will become 532-15-47).

The state-run Delegación Regional de Turismo (☎ 2-15-47), Nicolás Bravo 475, occupies an office at the front of the large, highly regarded Hotel Casablanca, about four blocks northwest of the Galeana bus station and a block over from Avenida Lázaro Cárdenas. Free city and regional maps and information are available; open 9 am to 7 pm Monday to Friday, 10 am to 1 pm Saturday.

Places to Stay & Eat

Several decent hotels are in the area around the bus stations. *Hotel Reyna Pio (☎ 2-06-20, Corregidora 78)*, at the corner of 8 de Mayo one block from Avenida Lázaro Cárdenas, has singles/doubles with air-con and TV for US$11/14. *Hotel Viña del Mar (☎ 2-04-15, Javier Mina 352)*, half a block from Avenida Lázaro Cárdenas, has a small courtyard swimming pool and rooms with air-con, TV and phone for US$18/21. Or there's the large, luxurious *Hotel Casablanca (☎ 7-34-80, Nicolás Bravo 475)*, a block from Avenida Lázaro Cárdenas, with singles/doubles for US$27/39.

Many restaurants are around this area, serving everything from simple snacks to more elaborate fare. For an ample meal at reasonable prices, locals recommend *Restaurant El Tejado*, on Avenida Lázaro Cárdenas between Corregidora and Javier Mina.

Getting There & Away

Air Lázaro Cárdenas has an airport served by a couple of small airlines. Aeromar flies to/from Mexico City; Aero Cuahonte flies to/from Uruapan, Morelia and Guadalajara.

Bus Lázaro has four bus terminals, all within a few blocks of each other. The Galeana (☎ 2-02-62) and Parhikuni (☎ 2-30-06) bus lines, with services northwest to Manzanillo and inland to Uruapan, Morelia and Mexico City, share a terminal at Avenida Lázaro Cárdenas 1810, on the corner of Constitución de 1814. Opposite, at Avenida Lázaro Cárdenas 1791, is the terminal shared by Autobuses de Jalisco, La Linea, Vía 2000 and Sur de Jalisco (☎ 7-18-50); the same destinations are serviced, plus Colima and Guadalajara.

The Estrella Blanca terminal (☎ 2-11-71), used by the Elite and Cuauhtémoc bus lines, is at Francisco Villa 65, two blocks behind the Galeana terminal. It has buses heading southeast to Zihuatanejo and Acapulco; buses heading up the coast to Manzanillo, Mazatlán and Tijuana; inland to Morelia and Uruapan; and to Mexico City. Estrella de Oro (☎ 2-02-75), Corregidora 318, two blocks farther back from Estrella Blanca, has buses to Zihuatanejo, Acapulco and Mexico City. Buses from Lázaro Cárdenas include:

Acapulco – 340km, 6-7 hours; Estrella Blanca, nine 1st-class (US$15), hourly 2nd-class, 4.15 am to 9 pm, and 2.30 am (US$12), Estrella de Oro, 1st-class 6.30 am (US$14), hourly 2nd-class, 4.50 am to 2.50 pm (US$11)

Caleta de Campos – 65km, 1½ hours; Galeana, 2nd-class buses every 25 minutes, 5 am to 8 pm (US$3)

Colima – 320km, 6 to 6½ hours; Autobuses de Jalisco/La Linea, Sur de Jalisco, same buses as to Guadalajara (US$14 and US$17)

Guadalajara – 540km, 9-11 hours; Autobuses de Jalisco/La Linea, 'Plus' 10.30 am, 8.45 and 9.15 pm (US$31), 1st-class 11.15 pm (US$28), Sur de Jalisco, 2nd-class 2.30 and 7 am, 1 pm (US$23)

Manzanillo – 313km, 6-7 hours; Estrella Blanca, 1st-class 12.30 and 2.30 pm (US$19), Galeana, 2nd-class, four buses (US$14), Sur de Jalisco, 2nd-class 2.30 and 5.30 pm (US$14), or take their bus to Tecomán, 5½ hours (US$12), and take a frequent local bus from there

Mexico City (Terminal Sur) – 711km, 10-11 hours; Estrella Blanca, 1st-class 8 am, 8 and 9.45 pm (US$38 and US$43), Estrella de Oro, 1st-class 7 and 8 am, 9 pm (US$38)

Mexico City (Terminal Observatorio) – 711km, 12 hours; Vía 2000, 1st-class, 3 buses (US$35)

Morelia – 406km, 8 hours; Galeana/Parhikuni, 'Plus' 14 buses (US$24), 2nd-class 14 buses (US$20), Estrella Blanca, 1st-class 11.30 pm (US$21), Vía 2000, 1st-class 3 buses (US$22)

Uruapan – 280km, 6 hours; same buses as to Morelia (US$13 to US$17)

Zihuatanejo – 120km, 2-3 hours; same buses as to Acapulco (US$3.50 to US$5)

Combis to Playa Azul, via La Mira, go along Avenida Lázaro Cárdenas every 10 minutes, 5 am to 9 pm (24km, 30 minutes, US$1.10).

CENTRAL PACIFIC COAST

Highway 200: Road Conditions & Warnings

At the time of writing, Highway 200 between Lázaro Cárdenas and Zihuatanejo was not very good, making for slow driving. People said the road was slowly being improved, but no one could guess when (or if) it would become a good road. Some of our readers have written to warn other travelers that driving between Lázaro Cárdenas and Zihuatanejo took them much longer than they would have expected from looking at the map; they ended up driving late at night, which they had wanted to avoid.

A new *autopista* (super highway) connecting Lázaro Cárdenas with Mexico City, via Pátzcuaro and Morelia is scheduled to be built, but no one knows when this highway will be started, let alone finished.

Locals all along the coast repeatedly warned us not to travel the entire stretch of Highway 200 from Tecomán to Acapulco at night – not only because of poor road conditions, but also because of highway bandits. Due to several missed bus connections, we did end up traveling on this highway at night, and were none the worse for the experience. Nevertheless, we received warnings about this so universally that it seems like a good idea to pass the warning along.

They stop outside the Autobuses de Jalisco bus terminal, opposite Galeana. A taxi between Lázaro Cárdenas and Playa Azul costs about US$11.

ZIHUATANEJO & IXTAPA

Zihuatanejo • pop 54,500 ☎ 7
Ixtapa • pop 1240 ☎ 7

Not so long ago, Zihuatanejo ('see-wah-tah-NAY-ho') was a small fishing village, and nearby Ixtapa ('iks-STAP-pah') was a coconut plantation. Then in 1970 Fonatur, the Mexican government tourism development organization that built Cancún, decided that the Pacific coast needed a Cancún-like resort to bring more tourist dollars into Mexico.

Using market studies of American tourists, Fonatur chose Ixtapa, 210km northwest of Acapulco, for its resort complex. Proximity to the USA, an average temperature of 27°C, tropical vegetation and the quality of the beaches were its criteria. Fonatur bought the coconut plantation, laid out streets, built reservoirs, strung electrical lines and invited hotel chains to begin construction.

Today, Ixtapa is a string of impressive resort hotels spread out along the Bahía del Palmar; the Club Méditerranée and some fine beaches are farther west beyond Punta Ixtapa. The luxurious hotels, restaurants and

shops of Ixtapa are expensive, and many travelers cringe at the artificial glitz created for the gringos.

Zihuatanejo, on the other hand, 8km away, though quite touristy, retains an easygoing, coastal town ambiance, and its setting on a small, beautiful bay with several fine beaches makes it a pleasant place to visit. Small-scale fishing is important to the town's economy; if you walk down on the beach near the pier in the early morning you can join the pelicans in greeting the returning fishermen and see the morning's catch. Seafood is great in this town.

Orientation

Though Zihuatanejo's suburbs are growing considerably, spreading around the Bahía de Zihuatanejo and climbing the hills behind the town, in the city's center everything is compressed within a few square blocks. It's difficult to get lost; there are only a few streets and their names are clearly marked. Ixtapa, 8km away, is easily reached by frequent local buses or by taxi.

Information

Tourist Offices In Zihuatanejo the municipal Dirección de Turismo (☎/fax 554-23-55, 554-75-23 ext Turismo; ixtapa-zihuatanejo@

terra.com; www.ixtapa-zihuatanejo.com) is upstairs in the Ayuntamiento (City Hall) building, Zihuatanejo Poniente s/n, Colonia La Deportiva, about 2km from the town center (local buses between Zihuatanejo and Ixtapa stop in front). It's open 8 am to 4 pm, Monday to Friday.

They also operate a small kiosk office in the heart of town, on Álvarez immediately east of the basketball court. It offers free maps and brochures, and the staff can answer most tourists' questions; open 9 am to 8 pm daily.

In Ixtapa, the state-run Sefotur tourist information office (☎/fax 553-19-67), officially called the Sub-Secretaría de Fomento Turístico de la Costa Grande de Guerrero, is at Seco la Puerta 2, near the tourist police station and opposite the Hotel Presidente Inter-Continental. It's open 8 am to 8.30 pm Monday to Friday, 8 am to 3 pm Saturday.

Ixtapa has several sidewalk kiosks and small offices with tourist information. While their real purpose is to promote time-share schemes, they also provide free maps and answer questions.

Money Zihuatanejo and Ixtapa both have many banks and casas de cambio where you can change US dollars and traveler's checks. The banks give the best rate of exchange. Zihuatanejo has Bancomer and Banca Serfín on the corner of Juárez and Bravo, Bancrecer on the corner of Juárez and Ejido, and Banamex on the corner of Ejido and Guerrero. All are open from around 9 am to 5 pm Monday to Friday, 10 am to 2 pm Saturday, and have ATMs.

The casas de cambio give a slightly less favorable rate but they're open longer, more convenient hours. In Zihuatanejo, Casa de Cambio Guiball, Galeana 6, is open 8 am to 9 pm daily.

American Express (☎ 553-08-53), in Ixtapa at the Hotel Krystal Ixtapa, is open 9 am to 6 pm, Monday to Saturday.

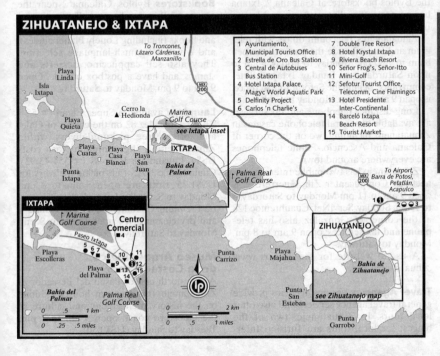

ZIHUATANEJO & IXTAPA

1 Ayuntamiento, Municipal Tourist Office
2 Estrella de Oro Bus Station
3 Central de Autobuses Bus Station
4 Hotel Ixtapa Palace, Magyc World Aquatic Park
5 Delfinity Project
6 Carlos 'n Charlie's
7 Double Tree Resort
8 Hotel Krystal Ixtapa
9 Riviera Beach Resort
10 Señor Frog's, Señor-Itto
11 Mini-Golf
12 Sefotur Tourist Office, Telecomm, Cine Flamingos
13 Hotel Presidente Inter-Continental
14 Barceló Ixtapa Beach Resort
15 Tourist Market

To Troncones, Lázaro Cárdenas, Manzanillo

Playa Linda

Isla Ixtapa

Cerro la Hedionda

Marina Golf Course

Playa Quieta

see Ixtapa inset

IXTAPA

Bahía del Palmar

Palma Real Golf Course

Playa Cuatas
Playa Casa Blanca
Playa San Juan

Punta Ixtapa

To Airport, Barra de Potosí, Petatlán, Acapulco

IXTAPA

Marina Golf Course

Centro Comercial

Paseo Ixtapa

Playa Escolleras

Playa del Palmar

Bahía del Palmar

Palma Real Golf Course

ZIHUATANEJO

Punta Carrizo

Playa Majahua

Bahía de Zihuatanejo

Punta San Esteban

see Zihuatanejo map

Punta Garrobo

0   .5   1 km
0   .25   .5 miles

0   1   2 km
0   .5   1 miles

'Las Gatas' Were Not Cats . . . & Other Tales of Zihuatanejo

Several places around Zihuatanejo and Ixtapa have names rooted in the distant past. The name 'Zihuatanejo' comes from the Náhuatl word 'Zihuatlán,' meaning 'place of women' (it was occupied solely by women); the Spanish added the suffix '-ejo,' meaning 'small.' 'Ixtapa,' also from the Náhuatl dialect, means 'white place.' It was so named not only for its white sands but also for the white guano left by the seabirds on the rocky islands just offshore.

The beaches around the Bahía de Zihuatanejo also have historical names. Playa Madera (Wood Beach) got its name from the timber that was sent from here to various parts of the world; at one time there was also a shipyard here. The name of Playa La Ropa (Beach of the Clothes) commemorates an occasion when a cargo of fine silks washed ashore here from a wrecked Spanish galleon coming from the Philippines. Playa Las Gatas (Beach of the Cats) was not actually named for cats, but for the nurse sharks that inhabited the waters here in ancient times – harmless sharks without teeth, called 'cats' because of their whiskers.

Post & Communications Zihuatanejo's post office, north of the town center, is open 8 am to 3 pm Monday to Friday. Several other places in town, near postboxes serviced daily, also sell stamps. Among them is the Byblos bookstore, at Galeana 2. Ixtapa has no post office, but you can mail letters from any big hotel.

Zihuatanejo's Telecomm office, with telegram and fax, is beside the post office; open 8 am to 7.30 pm Monday to Friday, 9 am to noon Saturday and Sunday. Ixtapa's Telecomm office, behind the Sefotur tourist office, is open 9 am to 3 pm, Monday to Friday.

Long-distance telephone and fax services are available at several telephone casetas in Zihuatanejo, including two on the corner of Galeana and Ascencio. Public telephones are everywhere around town.

Zihuatanejo has two public Internet connections. Compucenter Zih, Guerrero 9, is open 9 am to 11 pm Monday to Saturday, 3 to 11 pm Sunday. ServiNet, Cuauhtemoc 128 at the corner of González, also has telephone and fax services; open 9 am to 8 pm, Monday to Saturday.

A useful website for the area is www .zihua-ixtapa.com.

Travel Agencies Various agencies provide general travel agency services and also offer local tours. In Zihuatanejo, two of the biggest for local tours are Turismo Inter-nacional del Pacífico (TIP) (☎ 554-72-10, 554-75-11), Juárez at Álvarez, Local 2, and América-Ixtamar Viajes (☎ 554-35-90), at the corner of Cuauhtémoc and Bravo.

Bookstores Byblos, Galeana 2 near the corner of Bravo, sells a small selection of English-language newspapers, magazines and books (including Lonely Planet guides), and a wider Spanish-language selection. They also sell cappuccino, desserts and stamps, and have a postbox outside. Open 9 am to 9 pm, Monday to Saturday.

Laundry Lavandería Super Clean (☎ 554-23-47), González 82 on the corner of Galeana, offers free pickup/delivery within Zihuatanejo; a 3kg minimum wash costs US$4. Lavandería Express (☎ 554-43-93), Cuauhtémoc 37A, offers pickup/delivery for US$1.75. Both are open 8 am to 8 pm, Monday to Saturday. Lavandería y Tintorería Premium, Cuauhtémoc 34, does laundry and dry cleaning; it's open 9 am to 8 pm, Monday to Saturday.

Museo Arqueológico de la Costa Grande

At the north end of Paseo del Pescador in Zihuatanejo, this museum houses exhibits on the history, archaeology and culture of the Guerrero coast; open 9 am to 7 pm, Tuesday to Sunday (US$0.50).

Beaches

Waves are gentle at all the Bahía de Zihuatanejo's beaches. If you want big ocean waves, you can go to Ixtapa, only a few minutes away by local bus.

On Bahía de Zihuatanejo, **Playa Municipal**, in front of town, is the least appealing for swimming. Standing on this beach you can see several other beaches spread around the bay, starting with Playa Madera just past the rocky point on your left, then the long, white stretch of Playa La Ropa past that, and finally, directly across the bay, Playa Las Gatas.

Playa Madera was formerly isolated from Playa Municipal by a couple of rocky points, but now a lighted walkway around the rocky sections has made it an easy five-minute walk from town.

Walk over the hill along the coast road for about another 20 minutes from Playa Madera, and you reach the broad, 2km expanse of **Playa La Ropa**, bordered by palm trees and seafood restaurants. It's a pleasant walk, with the road rising up onto cliffs offering a fine view over the water. About the most beautiful beach on the bay, La Ropa is great for swimming, plus parasailing, waterskiing and the 'banana.' You can also hire sailboards or sailboats.

Opposite Zihuatanejo, **Playa Las Gatas** is a protected beach, crowded with sunbeds and restaurants. It's good for snorkeling (there's some coral growth) and as a swimming spot for children, but beware of sea urchins. According to legend, Calzontzin, a Tarascan chief, built a stone barrier here in pre-Hispanic times to keep the waves down and prevent sea creatures from entering, making it a sort of private swimming pool. Beach shacks and restaurants rent snorkeling gear for around US$4 per day.

Boats to Playa Las Gatas depart frequently from the Zihuatanejo pier, 8 am to 5 pm daily. Tickets (US$3.50 round-trip) are sold at the ticket booth at the foot of the pier; one-way tickets can be bought on board. Or you can reach Playa Las Gatas by walking around the bay from Playa La Ropa; a road takes you half the way, then there's 10 minutes of scrambling up and down rocks before you reach Playa Las Gatas.

Between Zihuatanejo and Ixtapa, **Playa Majahua** is accessible via a road serving a new hotel zone there, similar to Ixtapa. The beach, facing the open sea, has large waves and similar conditions to Ixtapa.

Ixtapa's big hotels line **Playa del Palmar**, a long, broad stretch of white sand. Be very careful if you swim here: the large waves crash straight down and there's a powerful undertow. The west end of this beach, just before the entrance to the lagoon, is called **Playa Escolleras** by locals, and is a favorite spot for surfing. Farther west, past the marina, are three small beaches that are among the most beautiful in the area: **Playa San Juan, Playa Casa Blanca** and **Playa Cuatas**.

To the west, past Punta Ixtapa, are **Playa Quieta** and **Playa Linda**. From Playa Linda boats run every half-hour (if there are enough passengers) to **Isla Ixtapa**, which is just offshore and has four beaches, excellent for snorkeling. The round-trip boat ride (5 minutes each way) costs US$3.50; boats operate 8 am to 5 pm daily.

A boat also goes to Isla Ixtapa from the Zihuatanejo pier, but only when there are eight passengers or more. It departs at 11 am, and leaves the island at around 4 pm. The trip (US$11 round-trip) takes an hour each way. The ticket office is at the foot of the pier.

About 10km south of Zihuatanejo, halfway between town and the airport, **Playa Larga** has big waves, beachfront restaurants and horseback riding. Nearby **Playa Manzanillo**, a secluded white-sand beach reachable by boat from Zihuatanejo, is said to offer the best snorkeling in the area. Between these two beaches is **Playa Riscalillo**. To reach Playa Larga, take a 'Coacoyul' combi from Juárez opposite the market, and ask to get off at the turnoff to Playa Larga; another combi will take you from the turnoff to the beach.

Snorkeling & Scuba Diving

Snorkeling is good at Playa Las Gatas and even better on Isla Ixtapa and Playa Manzanillo. There's an abundance of species here due to a convergence of currents, and sometimes great visibility, up to 35m. Migrating humpback whales pass through from December to February; manta rays can be seen all year, but there's greater likelihood of seeing them in summer, when the water is clearest, bluest and warmest.

Snorkel gear can be rented at Playa Las Gatas and Isla Ixtapa for around US$4 per day. The same beaches also have dive operators, who will take you diving for around US$45/65 for one/two tanks, or give you scuba lessons in the quiet water. Carlo Scuba (☎ 554-35-70) on Playa Las Gatas offers a variety of PADI courses.

Zihuatanejo's most professional dive outfit is the NAUI-affiliated Zihuatanejo Scuba Center (☎/fax 554-21-47; divemexico@mail.com; www.divemexico.com), Cuauhtémoc 3, offering daily morning and afternoon dives at more than 30 dive sites. Stop by to look at their underwater photos and pose any questions about diving in the area.

Snorkeling trips are made by boat to Playa Manzanillo, about an hour's ride south from Zihuatanejo. Zihuatanejo Scuba Center takes snorkeling trips there; the *Tristar* trimaran (see Cruises) also goes there, but only allows about 20 minutes for snorkeling. Or you can hire a boat at the foot of the Zihuatanejo pier, stop at Playa Las Gatas to rent snorkeling gear, and off you go.

Sport Fishing

Sport fishing is also popular. Sailfish are caught here year-round; seasonal fish include blue or black marlin (March to May), roosterfish (September-October), wahoo (October), mahi mahi (November-December), and Spanish mackerel (December).

Three fishing cooperatives are based near Zihuatanejo's pier: the Sociedad Cooperativa de Lanchas de Recreo y Pesca Deportiva del Muelle Teniente José Azueta (☎/fax 554-20-56) at the foot of the pier; Servicios Turísticos Acuáticos de Zihuatanejo Ixtapa (☎/fax 554-41-62), Paseo del Pescador 6; and Sociedad Cooperativa Benito Juárez (☎ 554-37-58), next door at Paseo del Pescador 20-2. Any of these can arrange deep-sea fishing trips, from about US$120

PLACES TO STAY	
4	Hotel Lari's
6	Hotel Posada Coral
8	Bungalows Pacíficos
9	Bungalows Sotelo
10	Bungalows Allec, Bungalows Ley
11	Hotel Brisas del Mar
12	Hotel Palacios
14	Hotel Raúl Tres Marias
18	La Casa Que Canta
20	Hotel Sotavento-Catalina
22	Trailer Park Los Cabañas
21	Hotel Villa Mexicana
23	Trailer Park La Ropa
24	Villa del Sol
26	Hotel Paraíso Real
29	Owen's Beach Club Bungalows
32	Casa de Huéspedes Miriam
34	Hotel Imelda
43	Hotel Casa Aurora
46	Hotel Amueblados Valle
50	Hotel Casa Bravo
64	Hotel Ulises
65	Hotel Raúl Tres Marías Centro
70	Hotel Villa del Ángel
71	Hotel Amueblados Isabel
74	Posada Citlali
75	Hotel Susy
84	Hotel Avila, Casa de Huéspedes La Playa

PLACES TO EAT	
13	Casa Puntarenas
15	Restaurant Kau-kan
16	Puesta del Sol
17	El Mirador
25	La Perla
27	Rossy's
28	La Gaviota
31	Restaurante Oliverio, Chez Arnoldo's
38	Los Braceros
39	Tamales y Atoles Any
41	Cafetería Nueva Zelanda
44	Ristorante-Bar-Pizzeria Don Juliano, Il Paccolo
48	Fonda Economica Susy
49	Pollos Locos
62	Paul's
65	Garrobo's
68	Restaurant El Patio
72	JJ's Grill, Panificadora El Buen Gusto
73	Pizzas Locas, Emilio's, La Casa del Burrito
78	La Sirena Gorda

79	Casa Elvira
80	Café Marina
83	Mariscos Los Paisanos
84	Restaurant/Bar Tata's

OTHER	
1	Post Office, Telecomm
2	Local Buses to Ixtapa
3	Cinema Gemelo
5	'La Correa' Route Bus Stop (To Long-distance Bus Stations)
7	Buses to Petatlán, La Unión
15	Paradise Disco & Beach Club
19	Mirador
30	Las Gatas Pier
33	Lavandería Super Clean
35	Mercado Municipal de las Artesanías
36	Lavandería y Tintorería Premium
37	Lavanderia Express, ServiNet
40	'Coacoyul' Route Bus Stop (To Playa Larga)
42	Plata de Taxco
47	Compucenter Zih
47	Banamex
51	Bancrecer
52	Bancomer
53	Banca Serfin
54	Cine Paraíso, América-Ixtamar Viajes
55	Byblos
56	Vinos y Licores Pamela, Renta de Motos
57	Casa de Cambio Guiball
58	Telephone Casetas
59	D'Latino
60	Hertz
61	Mexicana
63	Turismo Internacional del Pacífico (TIP)
66	Aero Cuahonte
67	Aeroméxico
69	Church
70	Zihuatanejo Scuba Center
76	Ticket Office for Boats to Playa Las Gatas, Isla Ixtapa
77	Harbor Master
79	Sport Fishing Operators
80	El Jumil
81	Basketball Court
82	Tourist Office
85	Museo Arqueológico de la Costa Grande
86	Plaza Olof Palme

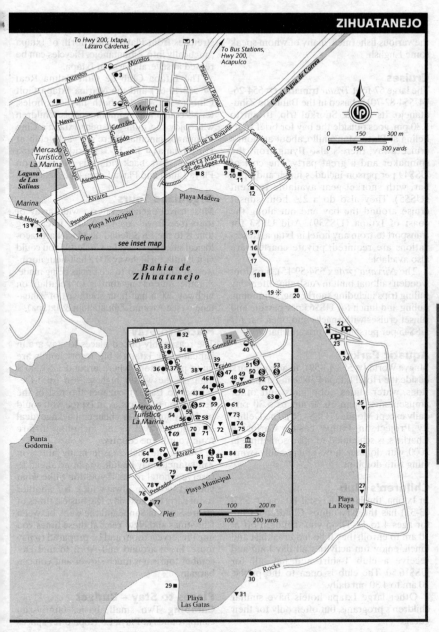

To Hwy 200, Ixtapa,
Lázaro Cárdenas

To Bus Stations,
Hwy 200,
Acapulco

Canal Agua de Correa

Morelos

Morelos

Altamirano

Juárez

Paseo del Palmar

Market

Nava

Cinco de Mayo

Galeana

Cuauhtémoc

González

Guerrero

Ejido

Bravo

Paseo de la Boquita

Mercado
Turístico
La Marina

Cerro La Madera
Ec de López Mateos

Camino a Playa La Ropa

Ascencio

Laguna
de Las
Salinas

Alvarez

Andrita

Marina

La Noria

Pescador

Playa Municipal

Playa Madera

Pier

see inset map

Bahía de
Zihuatanejo

0   150   300 m
0   150   300 yards

Punta
Godornia

Nava

Cinco de Mayo

Galeana

Guerrero

Juárez

González

Ejido

Bravo

Mercado
Turístico
La Marina

Ascencio

Alvarez

Pescador

Playa Municipal

Pier

0   100   200 m
0   100   200 yards

Playa
La Ropa

Playa
Las Gatas

Rocks

CENTRAL PACIFIC COAST

for four people including equipment. You can also walk along the pier and talk with the various fishermen, many of whom speak some English.

Cruises

The large 67-foot *Tristar* trimaran (☎ 554-26-94, 554-82-70) is based in the Bahía de Zihuatanejo. Its Sail & Snorkel trip, 10 am to 2.30 pm, goes outside the bay for brief snorkeling at Playa Manzanillo, about an hour's cruise away; there's also flying from the spinnaker and a great party. The cost of US$49 per person includes lunch and open bar, with snorkel gear available for rent (US$5). They also do a 2½ hour sunset cruise around the bay and out along the coast of Ixtapa (US$39). Add US$3 for transport to/from any hotel in Ixtapa. Reservations are required; private charters are also available.

The *Nirvana* (☎/fax 554-59-15), a 65-foot wooden sailboat built in Australia, offers day sailing trips including snorkeling, swimming, sailing and lunch for US$65 per person, and sunset cruises with snacks and open bar for US$45 per person, plus private charters.

Aquatic Parks

Magyc World (☎ 553-13-59), an aquatic park beside the Hotel Ixtapa Palace in Ixtapa, has rides, water slides, toboggans and other amusements; open 10.30 am to 5.30 pm, daily except Monday (US$4.50). The Delfinity Project, in Ixtapa beside Carlos 'n Charlie's, is scheduled to open sometime in 2000, with dolphin shows and possibly swimming with dolphins.

Children's Club

In Ixtapa, the Hotel Krystal Ixtapa (☎ 553-03-33) has the Krystalitos Children's Club for ages 4 to 12. Drop your children off at 10 am to enroll; they'll be fed breakfast and lunch, enjoy fun activities all day long and receive a club T-shirt and hat, all for US$16.50. The club is open to the public, 10 am to 4.30 pm daily.

Other large Ixtapa hotels have similar children's programs, but often only for their guests.

Other Activities

A new 15km *ciclopista* (bicycle path) stretches from Playa Linda north of Ixtapa practically into Zihuatanejo. Bicycles can be rented at several places in Ixtapa.

The Ixtapa Club de Golf Palma Real (☎ 553-10-62) and the Marina Ixtapa Golf Club (☎ 553-14-10) both have 18 holes, tennis courts and swimming pools. Children will enjoy the mini-golf near Ixtapa's Cine Flamingos cinema. There's a yacht club at Porto Ixtapa (☎ 553-11-31) beside the Ixtapa Marina. Horseback riding is available on Playa Linda and Playa Larga (see Beaches).

Organized Tours

Most travel agencies offer a wide array of tours (see Travel Agencies). One interesting tour is to the La Soledad de Maciel archaeological site, also called La Chole. Or you could visit Pantla, on highway 200 a half-hour northwest of Zihuatanejo, to see bricks being made. Another interesting tour is to Petatlán, on highway 200 a half-hour southeast of Zihuatanejo (see Around Zihuatanejo & Ixtapa).

Places to Stay

The reasonably priced places to stay are in Zihuatanejo; Ixtapa's big resort hotels are quite pricey, somewhere around US$200 a night in the winter high season (mid-December to Easter), cheaper the rest of the year. If you want to stay in Ixtapa, you could probably arrange a cheaper package deal through a travel agent, including airfare from your home country.

During the high season many hotels in Zihuatanejo may be full, so phone ahead to reserve a hotel room; if you don't like what you get, you can always look for another room early the next day. The busiest times of all are Semana Santa and the week between Christmas and New Year; at these times you must reserve a room and be prepared to pay more. From around mid-April to mid-December tourism is much slower and you can bargain.

Places to Stay – Budget

Camping Two small, basic, family-run campgrounds at Playa La Ropa offer spaces for trailers and tents. *Trailer Park La Ropa* (☎ 554-60-30), beside the Mercado de Artesanías, has no sign, but it does have tent spaces for US$3.25 per person, and 10 trailer spaces with full hookups for US$11 per trailer. Across the street, *Trailer Park Los Cabañas* (☎ 554-47-18) has just five spaces up behind the house, with electric (but not water) connections for trailers. Prices are US$3.25 per person for tents, US$11 per trailer. Tents and camping gear are available for rent.

Hotels Facing the beach in Zihuatanejo, beside the larger Hotel Avila, *Casa de Huéspedes La Playa* (☎ 554-22-47, *Álvarez 6*) is an inexpensive guesthouse with just six simple rooms – with bath (no hot water). From December to March it's often full with guests who return every year. English is spoken.

On Armada de México, 50m inland from the pier, the family-run *Hotel Ulises* (☎ 554-37-51) is a good deal for the price. It has 16 simple rooms with bath (hot water) for US$11/16.50 a single/double. Upstairs rooms are brighter.

Casa de Huéspedes Miriam (*Nava 8*) is a simple but clean and quiet guesthouse with rooms with bath for US$6.50 per person. *Hotel Lari's* (☎ 554-37-67, *Altamirano 4*) is similar, with off-street parking and singles/doubles for US$13/19.50. *Hotel Posada Coral*, on Los Mangos at Las Palmas near the market, has clean rooms with tiled bathrooms for US$13/16.50.

Hotel Casa Aurora (☎ 554-30-46, *Bravo 27*) has a 2nd-floor terrace and rooms for US$11 per person (US$33 with air-con); ask for an upstairs room. *Hotel Casa Bravo* (☎ 554-25-48, *Bravo 12*) has clean, pleasant rooms with TV for US$16.50 per person – a good deal for solo travelers, not such a bargain for doubles. Traffic outside can be noisy.

Hotel Villa del Ángel (*Cuauhtémoc 5*) has pleasant singles/doubles with private terraces at the front of the hotel for US$16.50/22. Interior rooms are cheaper, but not very appealing.

Posada Citlali (☎ 554-20-43, *Guerrero 3*) is very pleasant, with terrace sitting areas and rooms around a courtyard filled with trees and plants. The rooms are comfortable and clean and cost US$33/38 December to April, US$22/27 the rest of the year. Next door at the corner of Álvarez, *Hotel Susy* (☎ 554-23-39, *Guerrero 3*) is also clean and enjoyable, with singles/doubles for US$27/33.

Hotel Raúl Tres Marias (☎ 554-21-91, 554-25-91, *La Noria 4, Colonia Lázaro Cárdenas*) is just across the water from town, over a small footbridge. This is many budget travelers' favorite place to stay in Zihuatanejo; many of its 25 rooms open onto large terraces with flowers and views over town and the bay. Rooms with cold-water bath are US$19/27 December to April, US$17/24 the rest of the year.

Places to Stay – Mid-Range

Central Zihuatanejo The *Hotel Imelda* (☎ 554-76-62, *González 70*) has two swimming pools, an elevator, enclosed parking, and a restaurant/bar open in high season. Clean rooms with air-con and cable TV are US$44/55/66 with one/two/three double beds.

Hotel Raúl Tres Marías Centro (☎ 554-67-06, 554-57-29, *Álvarez 52*) has simple but clean singles/doubles with air-con for US$46 (cheaper by week).

Hotel Avila (☎ 554-20-10, *Álvarez 8*), right on the beach, has terraces overlooking the sea, private parking and large, well-equipped rooms with air-con, fan and cable TV. Rooms with/without sea view are US$82/65, December to April. The rest of the year, singles/doubles are US$55/65 with sea view, US$49/55 without, with discounts for longer stays.

Hotel Amueblados Valle (☎ 554-20-84, ☎/fax 4-32-20, *Guerrero 67*) is a good deal, with five large, airy apartments with everything you need, including fully equipped kitchens. One/two bedroom apartments are US$46/80 high season, US$34/54 low season, with three-bedroom apartments also available.

If they're full (which they often are in high season), try *Hotel Amueblados Isabel* (☎ 554-36-61, *Ascencio 11*), with fully equipped two/three-bedroom apartments with air-con, telephone and TV for US$71/82 in low season (high season, add US$5). Or ask Luis Valle at Hotel Amueblados Valle about other apartments in town and on Playa La Ropa, which may be cheaper, especially for longer stays.

Playa Madera Playa Madera, only a five-minute walk from the center of Zihuatanejo, has several good places to stay, most of them bungalows with fully equipped kitchens, all with large terraces offering fine views of the bay.

Closest to town, **Bungalows Pacíficos** (☎/fax *554-21-12*), on Eva S de López Mateos, Cerro de la Madera, has six attractive, moderately priced bungalows with ample sea-view terraces and fully equipped kitchens. Anita Hahner, the Swiss owner, is a gracious and helpful hostess who speaks English, Spanish and German, and can help you find anything from good restaurants to good bird-watching spots.

Also on Eva S de López Mateos, **Bungalows Sotelo** (☎ *554-63-07*) has attractively remodeled one/two/three-bedroom bungalows for US$60/120/160 (half-price in May, June, September, October and November). Next door, **Bungalows Allec** (☎/fax 554-20-02) has one/two-bedroom bungalows with sea view for US$40/85. Next door again, **Bungalows Ley** (☎ 554-45-63, 554-40-87) has air-conditioned one/two-bedroom bungalows starting at US$33/80, and rising to US$76/100 in high season (June to August and November to April).

Hotel Brisas del Mar (☎/fax *554-21-42, Eva S de López Mateos*) is a pleasant hotel with a large swimming pool, terraces, and a beachfront restaurant. Sea-view rooms with kitchen are US$61 with fan, US$87 with air-con from mid-December to mid-May, US$52 with fan, US$76 with air-con the rest of the year. Rooms with street view and no kitchen are US$38/46 in low/high season.

Hotel Palacios (☎ *554-20-55*), on Adelita, a pleasant family hotel with beachfront terrace and swimming pool, has singles/doubles for US$44/60 with air-con, US$42/55 with fan, from December to April, when prices include breakfast. The rest of the year, rooms are cheaper (around US$20 to US$50) but meals are not served.

Playa Las Gatas Playa Las Gatas has just one place to stay, **Owen's Beach Club Bungalows** (☎/fax *554-83-07, owensbungalows@ yahoo.com*), with seven freestanding bungalows around peaceful grounds with only the sound of the surf and the sea breezes rustling through the palms. The bungalows, all made of natural materials, cost US$70 December to May, US$50 the rest of the year; some sleep up to eight people. It's operated by Owen Lee, an ex-New Yorker who has been living on this beach since 1969 'and loving every minute of it.' The first American diver to work with Jacques-Yves Cousteau, and author of a large book about diving and snorkeling, Owen has also written a useful guidebook to Zihuatanejo and Ixtapa.

Places to Stay – Top End

Most of the top-end places to stay are giant resorts in Ixtapa, but Playa La Ropa also has some good luxury hotels. **Hotel Paraíso Real** (☎ *554-38-73*), on Playa La Ropa, offers garden and beachfront rooms for US$94 mid-November to April, US$59 the rest of the year. Operated by Zihuatanejo Scuba Center, they also offer hotel-and-dive packages.

Villa del Sol (☎ *554-22-39, toll-free in USA and Canada* ☎ *888-389-2645*), on Playa La Ropa, is a luxury resort where rates start at US$188 most of the year, US$270 January to March. A breakfast-and-dinner plan for US$60 per person is mandatory in winter, optional the rest of the year. Children under 14 are not allowed in winter. Also on Playa La Ropa, **Hotel Villa Mexicana** (☎ *554-84-72, 554-36-28*) has rooms for US$98 to US$150 December to February, US$64 to US$110 the rest of the year.

An old favorite, **Hotel Sotavento-Catalina** (☎ *554-20-32/34*), on the hill overlooking Playa La Ropa, has one of Zihuatanejo's most beautiful settings; its white terraces are visible from all around the bay. Singles/doubles are US$53/59 to US$140 December to April, depending on size, view and facilities, US$34/38 to US$88 the rest of the year, children under 12 free.

Nearby, the luxury *La Casa Que Canta* (☎ 554-65-29, *toll-free in USA* ☎ *888-523-5050*), whose reddish adobe-style walls and thatched awnings are also visible from all around the bay, is much more expensive, with rooms starting at US$400 January to April, US$345 the rest of the year. The film *When a Man Loves a Woman* with Meg Ryan was filmed here.

Other top-end hotels, all in Ixtapa, include the *Barceló Ixtapa Beach Resort*, *Riviera Beach Resort*, *Pacifica Villas & Hotel Resort*, *Westin Brisas Resort*, *Doubletree Resort*, *Hotel Krystal Ixtapa*, *Stouffer Presidente* and *Continental Plaza*.

Hotels with all-inclusive rates include *Club Méditerranée*, *Hotel Presidente Inter-Continental*, *Qualton Club*, *Melía Azul Ixtapa*, *Fontan Ixtapa Beach Resort* and *Aristos*. Travel agents can arrange packages at any of Ixtapa's big top-end hotels.

Places to Eat

Central Zihuatanejo Seafood in Zihuatanejo is fresh and delicious; many great choices for seafood are in the area near the pier. *Casa Elvira (Paseo del Pescador 8)*, open 8 am to 10 pm daily, specializes in seafood and has some of the best food in town. So does the pricier *Garrobo's*, behind it at Álvarez 52; try the paella, a house specialty, for US$17.

La Sirena Gorda, Paseo del Pescador near the foot of the pier, is a casual open-air place famous for seafood tacos (US$3.50 to US$7), plus delicious burgers, shrimp and other dishes; open 9 am to 11 pm (closed Wednesday). Also on Paseo del Pescador, beside 'El Jumil and just west of the basketball court, the pleasant little *Café Marina* makes good pizza (US$5.50 to US$9) and fabulous chocolate cake (US$3.25); closed Sunday.

On Paseo del Pescador just east of the basketball court, *Mariscos Los Paisanos* and *Restaurant/Bar Tata's* are inexpensive, specialize in seafood, and have tables inside and right out on the beach, with fine views of the bay. Both are open from 8 am until late in the evening, and have popular happy hours.

Around town, just a couple blocks from the waterfront, are many other good eating options.

Fonda Economica Susy (Bravo 24B) serves some of the cheapest food in town, with comida corrida for US$2; open 8 am to 6 pm daily. As in many places in Mexico, inexpensive food is also available in the *Mercado*, on Juárez, around the same hours.

Tamales y Atoles Any (☎ 554-73-73, Ejido 15), on the corner of Guerrero, serves excellent traditional Mexican food. It's attractive and colorful, with a high palapa roof, and reasonably priced; open 8 am to midnight daily. Phone for free delivery.

Casa Puntarenas on La Noria, across the water from town over a small footbridge, is a simple, family-run patio restaurant open for breakfast 8.30 to 11 am, and for dinner from 6 to 9 pm daily. The atmosphere is relaxed and enjoyable, and its reputation for serving large portions of good, inexpensive food draws a steady crowd; open December to March only.

Cafetería Nueva Zelanda (Cuauhtémoc 23), stretching through the block to Galeana, is a clean, popular café open 7 am to 10 pm daily. English and Spanish are spoken, and you can get anything they have 'to go' *(para llevar)*. They make good cappuccino; so does *Byblos*, a block away (see Bookstores).

Los Braceros (Ejido 21) specializes in grilled and skewered meat and veggie combinations, and has a sidewalk grill where you can see the meat being cooked. They have 29 combinations to choose from (most US$4.50), and many other tasty meat dishes, with more than 100 items on the menu; open 8 am to 1 am daily.

Pollos Locos (Bravo 15) is a simple open-air place serving inexpensive wood-grilled chicken and other meats; open 1 to 10.30 pm daily.

For Italian food there's *Ristorante-Bar-Pizzeria Don Juliano* and *Il Paccolo*, side by side at Bravo 19 and 22, near the corner of Guerrero. Il Paccolo serves delicious lasagna (US$5.50) as well as pizza, pasta, meats and seafood; open 4 pm to midnight daily. Don Juliano serves similar fare, for similar prices; open 3 to 11 pm (closed Wednesday).

On Guerrero, between Álvarez and Bravo, are three more pizzerias: *Pizzas Locas, Emilio's* and *La Casa del Burrito*. All boast pizzas baked in wood-fired brick ovens.

Opposite these, *JJ's Grill (Guerrero 6)* is a pleasant and popular restaurant, bar, sports lounge and pool room. Their food is delicious and economical; giant burgers (US$4.50), filet mignon steak sandwiches (US$9), grilled tuna steak (US$10.50), clam chowder (US$2.75), Caesar salad (US$3.25) and many other tempting treats round out the menu; open 11 am to 2 am daily.

On the same block, *Panificadora El Buen Gusto (Guerrero 8A)* is a good bakery, open 7.30 am to 10 pm daily.

A couple of other restaurants are more expensive, but good. On Juárez near Bravo, *Paul's* (☎ 554-65-28), named after its Swiss owner/chef, has a piano bar and serves delicious food, with main dishes US$10 to US$20; open 3 pm on (closed Sunday). *Restaurant El Patio* (☎ 554-30-19, *Cinco de Mayo 3*) is another similarly-priced but pleasant place, serving Italian and Mediterranean cuisine; open 8 am to 11 pm daily, but only in high season.

Along the Bay A couple of restaurant/bars up on the cliffs between Playa Madera and Playa La Ropa offer spectacular bay views. *El Mirador*, with a happy hour from 4 to 6 pm, is open noon to 10 pm daily. The fancier *Puesta del Sol* (☎ 554-83-42) is open 2 pm to midnight daily; reservations recommended. Both are moderately priced, with full dinners for around US$15, and are great spots for watching the sunset. Also along here, the pricier gourmet *Restaurant Kau-Kan* has that same great view.

The gourmet restaurant at the luxurious *La Casa Que Canta* (see Places to Stay) is the most expensive in Zihuatanejo, with dinner easily coming to over US$60, wine and drinks extra. The public is admitted only for dinner, 6.30 to 10.30 pm; reservations required.

Playa La Ropa and Playa Las Gatas both have plenty of beachside restaurants specializing in seafood. On Playa La Ropa, *Rossy's*, *La Perla* and *La Gaviota* are popular and good. On Playa Las Gatas, *Restaurante Oliverio* and *Chez Arnoldo's* prepare good seafood. Also on Playa Las Gatas, *Owen's Beach Club* (see Places to Stay) has a nicely situated restaurant, open 8 am to 5.30 pm, with dinner by arrangement; their water taxi provides transport in the evening.

Ixtapa Ixtapa has plenty of restaurants in addition to those in the big hotels. *Carlos 'n Charlie's, Señor Frog's* and *Señor-Itto* are all popular for a good meal and a good time. The latter two are side by side in the Centro Comercial, opposite the Presidente Inter-Continental; Carlos 'n Charlie's is farther west, by the Hotel Posada Real.

At Ixtapa marina, the indoor-outdoor *Beccofino* (☎ 553-17-70) has a good reputation for delicious Italian cuisine. Many other good restaurants are around the marina.

For a special night out with a great sunset view, try *Villa de la Selva* (☎ 553-03-62), an elegant restaurant in the former home of Mexican president Luis Echeverría, on the cliffside overlooking the ocean, near the Westin; reservations recommended.

Entertainment

Many bars have a happy hour. *Restaurant/Bar Tata's* and *Mariscos Los Paisanos*, side by side on the beach on Zihuatanejo's Playa Municipal, attract a jolly sunset crowd. The lobby bar on the top terrace of the *Hotel Sotavento-Catalina* (see Places to Stay), perched on the cliffs over Playa La Ropa, is a great place to watch the sunset, with a magnificent view over the whole bay (the bar is open 3 to 11 pm; happy hour 6 to 8 pm). The bar/restaurants *El Mirador* (happy hour 4 to 6 pm) and *Puesta del Sol* (see Places to Eat) have similar beautiful views.

Zihuatanejo has a disco, *D'Latino*, on the corner of Bravo and Guerrero. Around the bay, *Paradise Disco & Beach Club* draws a gay crowd.

Otherwise, most area nightlife is in Ixtapa. All the big hotels have bars and nightclubs, and most also have discos. The best disco is *Christine*, at the Hotel Krystal Ixtapa. The *Sanca Bar* at the Barceló Ixtapa Beach Resort is popular for dancing, with Latin music. Be sure to check out the lobby bar at the *Westin*. Also popular in Ixtapa are *Carlos 'n Charlie's* and *Señor Frog's*, lively restaurant/bars with dancing; both are in the Carlos Anderson chain. Behind Señor Frog's is *Los Mandiles*, a restaurant/bar with an upstairs disco. *Millenium*, in the Magyc World aquatic park, is a newer disco. At Marina Ixtapa, *El Faro*, a bar at the top of a 25m-high lighthouse, is great for watching the sunset, and it also has music and dancing.

Several of Ixtapa's big hotels hold Fiestas Mexicanas in the evening, with a Mexican buffet and open bar, and entertainment including traditional Mexican dancing, mariachis, rope and cockfighting demonstrations, as well as door prizes and dancing; total price is around US$40. The *Barceló Ixtapa Beach Resort* holds fiestas all year round; in the high season several other hotels also have fiestas, including the *Dorado Pacífico*. The *Riviera Beach* hotel holds a weekly show with a pre-Hispanic theme; *Club Med* and the *Melía Azul Ixtapa* present a variety of international theme shows. Reservations can be made directly or through travel agents.

Zihuatanejo has two cinemas: *Cine Gemelo* on Juárez at the corner of Morelos, and *Cine Paraíso* on Cuauhtémoc near the corner of Bravo. Ixtapa has a newer, plusher cinema, *Cine Flamingos*, behind the tourist office and opposite the Plaza Ixpamar and mini-golf. All three cinemas show two films nightly, usually in English with Spanish subtitles.

Shopping

Mexican handicrafts, including ceramics, wood carvings, huaraches, shells and shell crafts, silver from Taxco and masks from around the state of Guerrero, are available. In Ixtapa the Tourist Market is opposite the

---

Don't Buy the Coral

In Zihuatanejo, don't buy things like dried seahorses, coral and shells. These things are being wiped out, and it's the tourist industry causing this devastation. Resources are not infinite here, and this commercial trade contributes to the destruction of Zihuatanejo's beautiful natural marine ecology. The purchase of coral, in particular, should be avoided, as the coral forms the basic environment that sustains so much other sea life.

Barceló Ixtapa Beach Resort. In Zihuatanejo the Mercado Turístico La Marina on Cinco de Mayo has the most stalls. A few stalls are in the Mercado Municipal de las Artesanías on González near Juárez. Many artesanías shops are in the block west of the basketball court, such as El Jumil, Paseo del Pescador 9, specializing in authentic Guerrero masks. Guerrero is known for its variety of interesting masks and there are some museum quality ones here, many costing around US$12.

Several shops around Zihuatanejo sell silver from Taxco. Plata de Taxco on the corner of Cuauhtémoc and Bravo has a large selection of quality items. Beach clothing is sold at a great many shops around Zihuatanejo. Large Pacific shells are sold at shops on Zihuatanejo's Playa Municipal (but see 'Don't Buy the Coral').

Getting There & Away

Air The Ixtapa/Zihuatanejo international airport is 19km from Zihuatanejo, about 2km off highway 200 heading toward Acapulco. Airlines serving this airport, and their direct flights, are listed below; all have connections to other centers.

Aero Cuahonte
Álvarez 34 (☎ 554-39-88, 554-70-61); flies to Morelia

Aeroméxico
Álvarez 34, corner Cinco de Mayo, Zihuatanejo (☎ 554-20-18/19); Airport (☎ 554-22-37, 554-26-34); flies to Guadalajara, Mexico City

Alaska
  Airport (☎ 554-84-57, 001-800-252-7522); flies to Los Angeles, San Francisco

America West
  Airport (☎ 001-800-235-9292); flies to Phoenix

Continental
  Airport (☎ 554-42-19, 01-800-900-5000); flies to Houston

Mexicana
  Guerrero 15 near the corner of Bravo, Zihuatanejo (☎ 554-22-08/9); Hotel Dorado Pacífico, Ixtapa (☎ 553-22-08/9); Airport (☎ 554-22-27); flies to Guadalajara, Mexico City

Bus Estrella Blanca (☎ 554-34-77) has a large bus terminal, the Central de Autobuses, on highway 200 about 2km out of Zihuatanejo, heading toward Acapulco. It includes 1st-class Elite, Futura, Plus and Cuauhtémoc buses. Estrella de Oro (☎ 554-21-75) has its own smaller terminal, across a side road from the Central de Autobuses, heading toward town. Buses include:

Acapulco – 239km, 4 hours; Estrella Blanca, hourly 1st-class, 5 am to 9.30 pm (US$11 or US$15), Estrella de Oro, three 1st-class (US$12), hourly 2nd-class, 5.30 am to 5 pm (US$7)

Lázaro Cárdenas – 120km, 2 hours; Estrella Blanca, 11 1st-class, 1 am to 9.30 pm (US$5), hourly 2nd-class, 9 am to 10 pm (US$3.50), Estrella de Oro, 1st-class at 11 am (US$4.25), 2nd-class every hour or two, 5.40 am to 6 pm (US$3.50)

Manzanillo – 433km, 8 hours; Estrella Blanca, 1st-class at 9.40 am, noon and 2.15 pm (US$26). The same buses continue to Puerto Vallarta (718km, 14 hours, US$42) and Mazatlán (1177km, 24 hours, US$70); the noon bus goes all the way to Tijuana.

Mexico City (Terminal Sur) – 640km, 8-9 hours; Estrella Blanca, Ejecutivo at 10.30 pm (US$49), Futura at 6 and 10 am, 12.30, 10 and 11 pm (US$39), Estrella de Oro, 1st-class, 10 daily (US$32), 'Plus,' 1 daily (US$37), deluxe Diamante service, 2 daily (US$49)

Mexico City (Terminal Norte) – 640km, 10 hours; Estrella Blanca, 1st-class at 6.30 pm (US$32)

Petatlán – 32km, 30 minutes, US$1.25; Estrella Blanca every half-hour, 3.45 am to 11.20 pm; Estrella de Oro hourly, 7 am to 6 pm. Most buses to Acapulco stop in Petatlán. Or take a local bus from the bus lot east of the mercado, in Zihuatanejo.

Car & Motorcycle Car-rental companies in Zihuatanejo and Ixtapa include:

Alamo	☎ 553-02-06, 558-84-29
Avis	☎ 554-22-48, 554-22-75
Budget	☎ 554-48-37
Econo Franquicia	☎ 554-78-07
Economovil	☎ 553-05-30
Europcar	☎ 553-10-32, 553-18-58
Galgo	☎ 554-53-66, 554-23-14
Hertz	☎ 554-22-55, 554-25-90
Quick	☎ 553-18-30, 553-03-33
Rent-A-Car	☎ 553-16-30

Motorbikes can be hired in Zihuatanejo at Renta de Motos, based at Vinos y Licores Pamela (☎ 554-31-49), Galeana 25A near Ascencio, for around US$10/38 per hour/day; open 9 am to 2 pm and 5 to 10 pm Monday to Saturday. Ixtapa has about five places renting motorbikes and mountain bikes, including Rent-A-Car (☎ 553-16-30) in the Centro Comercial Patios. Most places require that you have a driver's license and credit card to rent a motorbike; Renta de Motos in Zihuatanejo requires ID only.

Getting Around
To/From the Airport A colectivo van provides transport from the airport to Zihuatanejo or Ixtapa for US$5.50 per person, but not in the other direction. A taxi to the airport costs US$7.75 from Zihuatanejo, US$10 from Ixtapa.

Bus Local buses run frequently between Zihuatanejo and Ixtapa, a 15-minute ride, departing every 15 minutes, 6 am to 11 pm (US$0.50). In Zihuatanejo the buses depart from the corner of Juárez and Morelos. In Ixtapa the bus stops all along the main street, in front of all the large hotels.

Some of these buses, marked 'Zihuatanejo-Ixtapa-Playa Linda,' continue through Ixtapa to Playa Linda (US$0.50), stopping near Playa Quieta on the way. These operate only from around 7 am to 7 pm.

The 'Correa' route goes from Zihuatanejo to the Central de Autobuses. Catch it at a bus stop on Juárez at the corner of Nava, 6 am to 9.30 pm (US$0.30).

'Playa La Ropa' buses head south on Juárez in Zihuatanejo and out to Playa La Ropa every half-hour, 7 am to 8 pm (US$0.50).

'Coacoyul' buses, heading toward Playa Larga, depart Zihuatanejo from a stop on Juárez near the corner of González, every five minutes, 6 am to 10 pm (US$0.50).

Taxi Cabs are plentiful in Ixtapa and Zihuatanejo. Always agree on the price of a ride before climbing into the cab. Prices from Zihuatanejo are around US$3.25 to/from Ixtapa, US$2.25 to/from Playa La Ropa, US$4.50 to/from Playa Larga.

Bicycle Most of the places in Ixtapa that rent motorbikes also rent mountain bikes, for around US$3.25/16.50 per hour/day.

TRONCONES
☎ 7

About a 25-minute drive northwest of Zihuatanejo, Playa Troncones is a beach on the open sea with several beachfront seafood restaurants, a popular outing for Zihuatanejo families. It has just two roads: the road coming in from the highway, and another stretching along the beach for 5km. On the north end is Playa Manzanillo, on a lovely little bay; just around the bay is the village of Majahua, where there's another road out to the highway.

Several world-class beach breaks are right here in Troncones; it's best to get out there in the morning, before 11 am, when the breeze starts to come up. Troncones Point is a good spot, and there are about 20 other surfing spots, good for beginning to advanced surfers, along the coast within about 20km. Saladita, 7km from Troncones, has an awesome half-mile left-hand break.

There's good snorkeling at Manzanillo Point, on the north end of Troncones. Other activities include fishing, sea kayaking, boogie boarding, horseback riding, hiking, bird-watching and sea-turtle-watching (you can observe sea turtles lay their eggs here in the sand on moonlit nights) and plenty more. Relaxing on the beach is another major activity.

Jaak Wassmuth, a friendly, exuberant surfer and outdoorsman who calls Troncones 'the no stress zone,' operates Jungle Tours (☎ 553-28-62; jungletours@cdnet.com.mx; www.mexonline/jungletours.htm) from his place opposite the Casa de la Tortuga (see Places to Stay). Jaak offers surfing trips and surfboard repair, great caving trips (US$15 per person), mountain bike tours (US$30) and 'beach days' (US$15). Jaak's surfing lessons (US$30 for a three-hour lesson and use of the board all day) come with a guarantee that you'll be able to stand up and ride a wave, or your money back! Jaak also rents surfboards (US$12/60 per day/week), boogie boards (US$6/35 per day/week), snorkeling gear (US$6/30 per day/week) and mountain bikes (US$12/60 per day/week), and provides surfers' transport to Saladita. He'll help you book accommodations over his website.

Karolyn and Dewey of the Casa de la Tortuga (see Places to Stay) started a new project in 1999, the Esperanza de la Selva Wildlife Center (☎ 553-28-12, tortuga@cdnet .com.mx), which is dedicated to breeding endangered Mexican wildlife and rehabilitating sick or injured animals.

A useful website for information about Troncones is www.mexonline/troncones.

Orientation
The village of Troncones, about 100m from the beach, is on the road coming in from the highway – but most of what you'll be interested in is along the beachfront road. Where the road coming in from the highway meets the sea, the Burro Borracho is about 1.5km to your left, the Casa de la Tortuga about 1.5km to your right, and Playa Manzanillo is about 2km farther on past that. Majahua, a 10-minute walk past Playa Manzanillo, is a small village with another road out to the highway.

Places to Stay
While still a very sleepy place, Troncones has had a low-key building boom and now boasts 80 hotel rooms in several small hotels spread out along its 5km coastline.

The cheapest places to stay are the two rooms over *Miscelanea Jasmín*, a shop in the village. Rooms are around US$11; talk to Manuel. Asking at the shops might reveal other similarly priced places to stay around the village.

The *Burro Borracho* (☎ 553-28-34) is a popular beachfront restaurant/bar with three attractive duplex bungalows (six units), all with relaxing hammocks on beachfront terraces. Singles/doubles are US$50/60 December to April, half-price the rest of the year, breakfast included (cheaper for longer stays); there's an outdoor guests' kitchen. Or pitch a tent (US$5 includes showers and toilets).

A couple of other accommodations are nearby, including the attractive four-room *Puesta del Sol* (☎ 553-28-18/19, reservations in USA ☎ 323-913-0423, 818-553-3374), with a variety of rooms including a simple surfers' room (US$20/30), a mountain view room (US$40/65), an ocean view room with kitchen (US$65/85) and a super-luxurious penthouse apartment (US$150/185); the higher prices are charged in high season, mid-November to mid-April.

Dewey and Karolyn, a friendly, easy-going American couple from Seattle, operate the *Casa de la Tortuga* (☎ 553-28-12, tortuga@cdnet.com.mx), a pleasant guesthouse with doubles for US$50 (two beds, shared bath) or US$75 (one big bed, private bath), breakfast included (half-price, May to November).

Another beachfront place is the *House of Flowers – Xochicalli* (☎ 556-60-80), operated by Anita Hahner of Bungalows Pacífico on Playa Madera (see Places to Stay in the Zihuatanejo section). Priding itself as 'the cheapest on the beach,' it's a lovely place with four bungalows for US$30 to US$50. There's a communal kitchen, or private kitchen can be arranged.

Casa Ki (☎ 553-28-15) is another attractive beachfront guesthouse, with rooms for US$50 to US$80. Or there's *Casa Delfín Sonriente* (☎ 557-01-22), the 'Smiling Dolphin,' a lovely villa with swimming pool and rooms starting at US$85 (40% cheaper, May to mid-November).

On Playa Manzanillo, on the north end of Troncones, *Hacienda Edén* (☎ 553-28-02; evaandjim@aol.com; www.edenmex.com) is a six-room beachfront guesthouse with beautifully decorated rooms and a gourmet restaurant. Rooms are US$65 and US$75, or sometimes US$50, breakfast included; open November to April only. The friendly proprietors, Eva and Jim, are gracious hosts. They allow camping – just one tent! – for free, if you eat some meals at the restaurant.

If you need a cheaper place to stay around Playa Manzanillo, you could ask Eva and Jim, or just ask around. You could also camp for free on the municipal beach at Playa Manzanillo, or on the beach at Majahua.

Places to Eat

The beachfront *Burro Borracho* (see Places to Stay) is the favorite hangout for visitors and expats, and for plenty of locals, too. The friendly proprietors, Marty and Jeannie, let you use boogie boards and sea kayaks for free; this is also the informal information center for Troncones, with a bulletin board and English-language lending library. It's open Tuesday to Sunday, 10 am to 10 pm.

La Cosina del Sol, the restaurant at Hacienda Edén on Playa Manzanillo (see Places to Stay), is operated by Christian, an international chef who creates magnificent food. Breakfast, lunch and dinner are served Monday to Saturday (dinner one seating only, at 7 pm, reservations recommended). Sundays there's breakfast, and a barbecue from 1 to 5 pm. You can use their boogie boards and sea kayaks for free.

Other good Mexican-owned beachfront restaurants include the *Costa Brava*, a favorite of locals, and *Doña Nica's* nearby. The *Tropic of Cancer*, operated by Anita LaPointe from Quebec, is another popular spot. On Playa Manzanillo there's a vegetarian snack bar at *Las Chozas* (English spoken), and the *Restaurant Playa Manzanillo*, otherwise known as *María's*. In Majahua, *Las Brisas Mexicanas* is a typical Mexican seafood restaurant.

The cheapest dining is in the village of Troncones, 100m back from the beach; there are lots of taco and enchilada stands where you can eat well for around US$1 a meal.

Getting There & Away

To get to Troncones, head northwest from Zihuatanejo on highway 200, as if going to Lázaro Cárdenas. Around Km 30 you'll see the marked turnoff for Troncones; follow this road 3km to the beach.

Second-class buses heading toward Lázaro Cárdenas or La Unión will let you off at the highway turnoff, but there are no buses all the way to Troncones. In Zihuatanejo, buses heading for Lázaro Cárdenas depart from the long-distance bus terminals; the La Unión bus departs from the bus lot a couple of blocks east of the market. Ask to be let off at the Troncones turnoff (30 minutes, US$1).

A truck offers transport from the crossroads into Troncones, and vice versa, about every half-hour in morning and evening, and about every 45 minutes during the day (US$0.30). Locals say it's easy and safe to hitch from the turnoff into Troncones, and also back, but that you'll probably only get a ride (or be able to flag down a bus out on the highway for the return trip to Zihuatanejo) during daylight hours.

A taxi to/from Zihuatanejo costs around US$33/44 one-way/round-trip (negotiable). Jaak of Jungle Tours offers round-trip transport to Troncones from the Hotel Ixtapa Palace in Ixtapa for US$13 per person, with 24-hour advance booking.

BARRA DE POTOSÍ
☎ 7

About a 40-minute drive from Zihuatanejo, Barra de Potosí is a popular area with a long, sandy, open sea beach, beautiful but dangerous for swimming, and another beach on a large (8 sq km) lagoon with good swimming. You can take a boat trip or rent a canoe and paddle around the estuary (good birdwatching); horseback riding and hiking trails are other possibilities.

Most families come out here just for the day; many palapas and seafood restaurants are along the beach. Right on the beach, the good, new *Hotel Barra de Potosí* (☎ 554-82-

90/91) has a swimming pool, parking, and rooms for US$15 and US$25 (US$35 with sea view), plus larger suites with sea view and kitchen (US$60).

Getting There & Away

To get there, drive on highway 200 heading toward Acapulco; turn off at the town of Los Achotes, about 25km from Zihuatanejo, and head for the sea, about another 10km. Any bus heading to Petatlán will drop you at the turnoff; Petatlán buses depart from Zihuatanejo's long-distance bus stations, and from the bus lot a couple of blocks east of the market. Tell the driver you're going to Barra de Potosí, and you'll be let off where you can meet a minibus going the rest of the way. The cost is about US$2 if you go by bus; a taxi from Zihuatanejo costs about US$33/44 one-way/round-trip.

PETATLÁN

A colonial town half an hour from Zihuatanejo, Petatlán is best known for its Santuario Nacional del Padre Jesús de Petatlán, a large, modern sanctuary attracting pilgrims from near and far. Gold is sold cheaply from many little shops beside the church. Petroglyphs and other pre-Hispanic artifacts are displayed in the center of town. During Semana Santa there's a traditional fair with food, music and handicrafts exhibitions. Petatlán's religious festival is held on August 6.

Getting There & Away

Petatlán is on highway 200, 32km from Zihuatanejo, heading toward Acapulco. Buses to Petatlán depart frequently from Zihuatanejo's long-distance bus stations. Or you can catch a local bus from the bus lot a couple of blocks east of the market in Zihuatanejo (32km, 30 minutes, US$1.10).

LA BARRITA

About an hour south of Zihuatanejo, La Barrita is a small town on an attractive beach. Not many tourists stop here; there's one hotel, with double rooms for around US$6.50. Second-class buses heading south from Zihuatanejo or north from Acapulco will drop you at La Barrita.

ACAPULCO
- pop 592,500 ☎ 7

Acapulco is the granddaddy of Mexican coastal resort cities. Tourism is the city's number one industry and has been for decades. The name Acapulco evokes images of white-sand beaches, high-rise hotels, glittery nightlife and the divers at La Quebrada gracefully swan-diving into a narrow chasm with the surf rising and falling below.

Acapulco is a fast-growing city of dual personalities. Around the curve of the Bahía de Acapulco stretches an arc of beautiful beaches, luxury hotels, discos, shopping plazas and restaurants with trilingual menus (many French Canadians come here). Just inland is a none-too-glamorous commercial center with filthy streets, crowded sidewalks, congested traffic and long lines of loud, fuming buses choking passersby.

Throughout the year you can expect average daytime temperatures of 27 to 33°C and nighttime temperatures of 21 to 27°C. Afternoon showers are common from June to September, but quite rare during the rest of the year.

Orientation
Acapulco is on a narrow coastal plain along the 11km shore of the Bahía de Acapulco. Reached by highway 200 from the east and west and by highways 95 and 95D from the north, it is 400km south of Mexico City and 240km southeast of Zihuatanejo and Ixtapa.

For tourism purposes, Acapulco is divided into three parts: 'Acapulco Naútico' (Nautical Acapulco, formerly known as Acapulco Tradiciónal), in the west (old) part of the city; 'Acapulco Dorado' (Golden Acapulco), heading around the bay east from Playa Hornos; and 'Acapulco Diamante' (Diamond Acapulco), a new luxury tourist resort stretching from the peninsula on the southern tip of Puerto Marqués – a bay about 18km southeast of Acapulco proper – and continuing about 10km down Playa Revolcadero to the international airport. In Pie de la Cuesta, a lagoon and beach area about 10km west of Acapulco, tourism is more low-key (see Around Acapulco).

At the west end of Bahía de Acapulco, the Peninsula de las Playas juts south from central Acapulco. South of the peninsula is the popular Isla de la Roqueta, and nearby is the so-called underwater shrine, a submerged bronze statue of the Virgen de Guadalupe. From Playa Caleta on the southern edge of the peninsula, Avenida López Mateos climbs west and then north to Playa La Angosta and La Quebrada before curling east back toward the city center.

Playa Caleta also marks the beginning of Avenida Costera Miguel Alemán. Known alternatively as simply 'La Costera' or as 'Miguel Alemán,' it's Acapulco's principal bayside avenue. From Playa Caleta, La Costera cuts north-northwest across the Peninsula de las Playas and then hugs the shore all the way around the bay to the Icacos naval base at the east end of the city. Most of Acapulco's major hotels, restaurants, discos and other points of interest are along or just off La Costera. After passing the naval base, La Costera becomes La Carretera Escénica (the Scenic Highway) for 9km, at which point it intersects highway 200 on the left and the road to Puerto Marqués on the right. The airport is 2.5km straight ahead.

As in most Spanish colonial cities, the heart of the old central district is the cathedral and the adjacent zócalo.

Information
Tourist Offices The Centro de Atención y Protección del Turista (☎/fax 484-44-16), in the yellow building on the front grounds of the Centro de Convenciones, La Costera 4455, offers tourist information and assistance for all manner of tourist needs, problems or complaints. They offer free medical care for tourists, a money exchange desk and handicrafts for sale. They also sell tickets for local attractions and for bus and air travel – tickets are cheaper here than at travel agencies, since it's a government service and no commissions are charged. The center is open 9 am to 11 pm daily.

The Secretaría de Fomento Turístico del Estado de Guerrero, or Sefotur (☎ 484-24-15, fax 481-11-60), inside the Centro de Convenciones, has information on Acapulco and the state of Guerrero. It's open 9 am to 3 pm and 6 to 8 pm Monday to Friday, 9 am to 3 pm Saturday.

Immigration Migración (☎ 484-90-14), on the corner of La Costera and Elcano, near the CICI water-sports park, is open 8 am to 2 pm, Monday to Friday.

Consulates Many countries have consulates in Acapulco; see 'Embassies & Consulates in Mexico' in the Facts for the Visitor chapter for a partial listing.

The Casa Consular (☎/fax 481-25-33) in the Centro de Convenciones is a helpful agency giving consular assistance to foreign tourists of all nationalities. It's open 9 am to 2 pm and 5 to 7 pm, Monday to Friday.

Money You can change money at many places around Acapulco. The numerous banks give the best rates. The casas de cambio pay a slightly lower rate but are open longer hours and are less crowded than the banks; shop around, as rates vary. There are many banks and casas de cambio near the zócalo and all along La Costera.

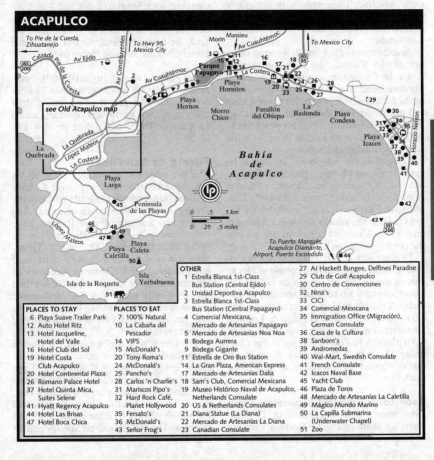

ACAPULCO

PLACES TO STAY
6 Playa Suave Trailer Park
12 Auto Hotel Ritz
13 Hotel Jacqueline,
   Hotel del Valle
16 Hotel Club del Sol
19 Hotel Costa
   Club Acapulco
20 Hotel Continental Plaza
26 Romano Palace Hotel
37 Hotel Quinta Mica,
   Suites Selene
41 Hyatt Regency Acapulco
44 Hotel Las Brisas
47 Hotel Boca Chica

PLACES TO EAT
7 100% Natural
10 La Cabaña del
   Pescador
14 VIPS
15 McDonald's
20 Tony Roma's
24 McDonald's
25 Pancho's
28 Carlos 'n Charlie's
31 Mariscos Pipo's
32 Hard Rock Café,
   Planet Hollywood
35 Fersato's
36 McDonald's
43 Señor Frog's

OTHER
1 Estrella Blanca 1st-Class
   Bus Station (Central Ejido)
2 Unidad Deportiva Acapulco
3 Estrella Blanca 1st-Class
   Bus Station (Central Papagayo)
4 Comercial Mexicana,
   Mercado de Artesanías Papagayo
5 Mercado de Artesanías Noa Noa
8 Bodega Aurrera
9 Bodega Gigante
11 Estrella de Oro Bus Station
14 La Gran Plaza, American Express
17 Mercado de Artesanías Dalia
18 Sam's Club, Comercial Mexicana
19 Museo Histórico Naval de Acapulco,
   Netherlands Consulate
20 US & Netherlands Consulates
21 Diana Statue (La Diana)
22 Mercado de Artesanías La Diana
23 Canadian Consulate
27 AJ Hackett Bungee, Delfines Paradise
29 Club de Golf Acapulco
30 Centro de Convenciones
32 Nina's
33 CICI
34 Comercial Mexicana
35 Immigration Office (Migración),
   German Consulate
36 Casa de la Cultura
38 Sanborn's
39 Andromedas
40 Wal-Mart, Swedish Consulate
41 French Consulate
42 Icacos Naval Base
45 Yacht Club
46 Plaza de Toros
48 Mercado de Artesanías La Caletilla
49 Mágico Mundo Marino
50 La Capilla Submarina
   (Underwater Chapel)
51 Zoo

CENTRAL PACIFIC COAST

Hotels will also change money, but their rates are usually not good.

American Express (☎ 469-11-00) in the Gran Plaza, La Costera 1628, changes American Express traveler's checks at the same rates as the banks, with no crowds and with convenient hours: 10 am to 7 pm, Monday to Saturday.

Post & Communications The main post office, La Costera 125 in the Palacio Federal beside the Sanborn's department store, a couple of blocks east of the zócalo, is open 8 am to 8 pm, Monday to Saturday. In the same building, Telecomm, with telegraph, telegram and fax, is open 8 am to 7 pm Monday to Friday, 9 am to noon Saturday and Sunday.

Another post office and Telecomm office are at the Estrella de Oro bus station, Avenida Cuauhtémoc at the corner of Massieu, upstairs on the outside right corner of the building. This post office is open 8 am to 3 pm Monday to Friday, 9 am to 1 pm Saturday. The Telecomm office is open 8 am to 7.30 pm Monday to Friday, 9 am to noon Saturday, Sunday and holidays.

Long-distance telephone calls can be made from pay phones – plentiful throughout the city – or from telephone casetas (look for signs saying 'larga distancia'). Telephone and fax services are available on the west side of the zócalo at Caseta Alameda on La Paz. Many other casetas are around the center and along La Costera.

Internet services are available at Compusistem, in the old building a couple of blocks east of the zócalo, at Ignacio de la Llave 2, Local 9; open 9 am to 8 pm, Monday to Saturday. A couple of blocks west of the zócalo, Compunet@Milenium, Hidalgo 6, Local 2, also offers Internet services; open 9.30 am to 9 pm Monday to Friday, 9.30 am to 3 pm Saturday, 11 am to 3 pm Sunday. A couple of other Internet service places are along La Costera.

Bookstores Sanborn's department stores have books and magazines in English. There's a Sanborn's on La Costera, a couple of blocks east of the zócalo, and another on La Costera a couple of blocks past the CICI water-sports park. The Comercial Mexicana on La Costera opposite CICI has magazines in English. Wal-Mart, farther along on La Costera, also has English-language books and magazines.

Laundry Lavandería Lavadín (☎ 482-28-90), on the corner of La Paz and Iglesias a couple of blocks west of the zócalo, is open 8 am to 10 pm, Monday to Saturday; pickup and delivery service costs US$2.75. Lavandería y Tintorería Coral, Juárez 12, next door to hotel La Mama Hélène, also does dry cleaning; open 9 am to 2 pm and 4 to 7 pm Monday to Friday, 9 am to 2 pm Saturday. Several more laundries are along La Costera, including Lavandería del Sol at the Hotel Club del Sol (see Places to Stay).

Emergency Locatel (☎ 481-11-00), operated by the state tourist office, is a 24-hour hot line for all types of emergencies; their office is in the Centro de Convenciones, on La Costera. The tourist police are at ☎ 480-02-10.

Fuerte de San Diego

This five-sided fort was built in 1616 atop a hill just east of the zócalo to protect the naos (galleons) that conducted trade between the Philippines and Mexico from marauding Dutch and English pirates. It must have done some good, because this trade route lasted until the early 19th century. Apparently it was also strong enough to forestall independence leader Morelos' takeover of the city in 1812 for four months. The fort had to be rebuilt after a 1776 earthquake damaged most of Acapulco. It remains basically unchanged today, having been restored to top condition.

The fort is now the home of the **Museo Histórico de Acapulco**, a museum with interesting exhibits, open 9.30 am to 6.30 pm Tuesday to Sunday. In 2000, while remodeling is underway, admission is free; after that, no one knows what the admission price will be, but it's always free for children 13 and under, and free to all both on Sunday and on holidays.

OLD ACAPULCO

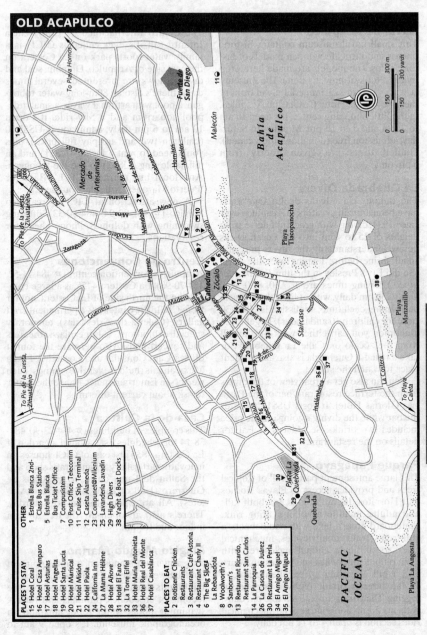

To Playa Hornos

Fuerte de San Diego

Malecón

Bahía de Acapulco

Mercado de Artesanías

To Pie de la Cuesta, Zihuatanejo

HWY 200

Acacias

Aquiles Serdán

Av Cuauhtémoc

Zaragoza

Progreso

Escudero

Paraná

Mina

Mendoza

5 de Mayo

Galeana

Y de León

Morelos

Hornitos

La Costera (Costera Miguel Alemán)

Playa Tlacopanocha

Playa Manzanillo

Playa Caleta

To Playa Caleta

La Costera

Inalámbrica

Staircase

Cathedral

Zócalo

Madero

La Quebrada

Iglesias

Valle

Azueta

La Paz

4 de Enero

Av López Mateos

Guerrero

To Pie de la Cuesta, Zihuatanejo

Plaza La Quebrada

La Quebrada

PACIFIC OCEAN

Playa La Angosta

0   150   300 m
0   150   300 yards

CENTRAL PACIFIC COAST

PLACES TO STAY
15 Hotel Coral
16 Hotel Casa Amparo
17 Hotel Asturias
18 Hotel Angelita
19 Hotel Santa Lucía
20 Hotel Mariscal
21 Hotel Misión
22 Hotel Paola
24 California Inn
27 La Mama Hélène
28 Hotel Añove
31 Hotel El Faro
32 La Torre Eiffel
33 Hotel Maria Antonieta
36 Hotel Real del Monte
37 Hotel Casablanca

PLACES TO EAT
2 Rotisserie Chicken
   Restaurants
3 Restaurant Café Astoria
4 Restaurant Charly II
6 The Big Slice;
   La Rebanadota
8 Woolworth's
9 Sanborn's
13 Restaurant Ricardo;
    Restaurant San Carlos
14 La Parroquia
26 La Casona de Juárez
30 Restaurant La Perla
34 El Amigo Miguel
35 El Amigo Miguel

OTHER
1 Estrella Blanca 2nd-
   Class Bus Station
5 Estrella Blanca
   Bus Ticket Office
7 Compusistem
10 Post Office, Telecomm
11 Cruise Ship Terminal
12 Caseta Alameda
23 Compunet@Milenium
25 Lavanderia Lavadín
29 High Divers
38 Yacht & Boat Docks

Museo Histórico Naval de Acapulco

This small naval museum contains historic photos and intricate wooden models of historic ships. The models are made here; stop by for a look at how it's done. The museum is at La Costera 123, immediately in front of the lobby of the Hotel Costa Club Acapulco, in the little shopping center. It's open 10 am to 2 pm and 5 to 10 pm, Monday to Saturday; admission free (donations appreciated). Guided tours are given hourly from 6 pm on.

La Quebrada Divers

The famous clavadistas de La Quebrada have been amazing visitors to Acapulco ever since 1934, diving with graceful finesse from heights of 25 to 45m into the ocean swells below. Understandably, the divers pray at a small shrine before leaping over the edge. (So did Elvis Presley in the film *Fun in Acapulco*.) Diving times are 1, 7.30, 8.30, 9.30 and 10.30 pm daily, with at least three divers performing each time; admission is US$1.30 (free for children 10 and under). To get to La Quebrada you can either walk up the hill from the zócalo on Calle La Quebrada or take a taxi. La Quebrada is also an excellent place to watch the sunset.

You can also get a great view of the divers from the terrace restaurant/bar of the Plaza Las Glorias Hotel. It costs US$14 to enter the bar while the diving's going on; the price includes two drinks. See Places to Eat for details on the restaurant.

Parque Papagayo

This large amusement park is full of tropical trees and provides access to Playas Hornos and Hornitos. Its attractions, for both kids and adults, include a roller-skating rink, skateboard area, a lake with paddleboats, a children's train, quadricycles, mechanical rides, sports fields, animal enclosures with deer, rabbits, crocodiles and turtles, an aviary and a hill affording an excellent view. A 1150m 'interior circuit' pathway is good for jogging. The park is open 6 am to 8 pm daily, with no admission charge. The mechanical rides section is open 4 to 11 pm daily.

CICI

The Centro Internacional de Convivencia Infantil (all it's ever called is CICI) is a family water-sports park on La Costera on the east side of Acapulco. Dolphin, seal and diving shows are presented several times daily; there's also an 80m-long water toboggan, a pool with artificial waves, a small tidepool aquarium and a Sky ride. It's open 10 am to 6 pm daily; admission is US$5.50 (children two and up pay full price), plus you'll need to rent a locker (US$1) and an inflatable ring (US$2) to use the toboggan. Any local bus marked 'CICI,' 'Base' or 'Puerto Marqués' will take you there.

A new attraction at CICI is Acapulco Mágico (☎ 481-02-94, 484-80-33), offering swimming with dolphins. Phone ahead for reservations.

Centro de Convenciones

Acapulco's convention center (☎ 484-71-52, 484-70-98), La Costera 4455, is a large complex on the north side of La Costera, not far from CICI. The center has a permanent craft gallery (Galería de Artesanías), temporary special exhibitions, a large plaza, theaters and concert halls. Also here are the tourist offices, Casa Consular and Locatel. A Fiesta Mexicana is held several evenings each week (see Entertainment). Phone the center to ask about current offerings.

Casa de la Cultura

This complex of buildings (☎ 484-23-90, 484-38-14 for schedules), set around a garden at La Costera 4834 just east of CICI, houses an innovative art gallery, a handicrafts shop and the Salon de Fama de los Deportistas de Guerrero (Hall of Fame of Guerrero Athletes). All are open Monday to Saturday. There's also an open-air theater and an indoor auditorium.

Mágico Mundo Marino

This aquarium stands on a small point of land between Playas Caleta and Caletilla. Highlights include a sea lion show, the feeding of crocodiles, piranhas and turtles, swimming pools, water toboggans and an oceanographic museum. It's open 9 am to

A Long & Illustrious History

The name 'Acapulco' is derived from ancient Náhuatl words meaning 'where the reeds stood' or 'place of giant reeds.' Archaeological finds show that when the Spaniards arrived, people had been living around the Bahía de Acapulco and the nearby bay of Puerto Marqués for about 2000 years, and had moved from being a hunting and gathering society to being an agricultural one.

Spanish sailors discovered the Bay of Acapulco in 1512. Port and shipbuilding facilities were later established here because of the substantial natural harbor.

In 1523 Hernán Cortés, Juan Rodríguez Villafuerte and merchant Juan de Sala joined forces to finance an overland trade route between Acapulco and Mexico City. This route, known as the 'Camino de Asia,' was the principal trade route between Mexico City and the Pacific; the 'Camino de Europa,' continuing from Mexico City to Veracruz on the Gulf Coast, formed a link between Asia and Spain.

Acapulco became the only port in the New World authorized to receive *naos* (Spanish trading galleons) from the Philippines and China. During the annual Acapulco Fair, lasting three to eight weeks after the galleons arrived from Manila in spring, traders converged on Acapulco from Mexico City, Manila and Peru.

By the 17th century, trade with Asia was flourishing, and Dutch and English pirate ships abounded in the Pacific and along the coastlines of Mexico and Baja California. To ward off the pirates, Fuerte de San Diego was built atop a low hill overlooking the bay. It was not until the end of the 18th century that Spain permitted its American colonies to engage in free trade, ending the monopoly of the naos and the Manila-Acapulco trade route. The naos continued trading until the early 19th century.

Upon gaining independence, Mexico severed most of its trade links with Spain and Spain's colonies, and Acapulco declined as a port city. It became relatively isolated from the rest of the world until a paved road was built in 1927 linking it with Mexico City. As Mexico City grew larger, its citizens began flocking to the Pacific coast for vacations. A new international airport was built, and by the 1950s Acapulco was a booming resort.

✳ ✳

6 pm daily; admission US$3.25 (US$1.75 for children three to 12).

Isla de la Roqueta

In addition to a popular beach and snorkeling and diving possibilities, Isla de la Roqueta has a zoo featuring telescopes and children's games. The zoo is open 10 am to 5 pm daily except Tuesday; admission US$0.50. Snorkeling gear, kayaks and other water gear are available for hire.

From playas Caleta and Caletilla boats make the eight-minute trip about every 20 minutes (US$2.75 return). Or a less direct glass-bottomed boat departs from the same beaches for Isla de la Roqueta via La Capilla Submarina (the Underwater Chapel), a submerged bronze statue of the Virgen de Guadalupe. The roundtrip fare is

US$4.50; the trip takes about an hour, or you can alight on the island and take a later boat back.

Beaches

Visiting Acapulco's beaches tops most visitors' lists of things to do here. The beaches heading east around the bay from the zócalo – playas **Hornos**, **Hornitos**, **Condesa** and **Icacos** – are the most popular. The highrise hotel district begins on Playa Hornitos, at the eastern side of Parque Papagayo, and heads east from there. City buses constantly ply La Costera, the beachside avenue, making it easy to get up and down this long arc of beaches.

Playas **Caleta** and **Caletilla** are two small, protected beaches beside one another in a cove on the south side of the Peninsula de las Playas. They're especially popular among families with small children, as the water is very calm. All buses marked 'Caleta' heading down La Costera go there. The Mágico Mundo Marino aquarium on a tiny point of land separates the two beaches, and regular boats go from there to Isla de la Roqueta.

Playa La Angosta is in a tiny, protected cove on the west side of the peninsula. From the zócalo it takes about 20 minutes to walk there. Or you can take any 'Caleta' bus and get off near the Hotel Avenida, on La Costera, just one short block west of the beach.

Other good beaches are farther afield, including **Puerto Marqués**, **Playa Revolcadero** and **Pie de la Cuesta** (see Around Acapulco, later in this chapter).

Water Sports

Just about everything that can be done on, under or above the water is done in Acapulco. On the Bahía de Acapulco, waterskiing, boating, 'banana-boating' and parasailing are all popular activities. The smaller Playas Caleta and Caletilla have all of these plus sailboats, fishing boats, motorboats, pedal boats, canoes, snorkel gear, inner tubes and water bicycles for rent.

Scuba-diving trips and/or instruction can be arranged through several diving operators, including Aqua Mundo (☎ 482-10-41), Divers de México (☎ 482-13-98, 483-60-20) and Mantarraya (☎/fax 482-41-76).

Deep-sea fishing is another possibility. Aqua Mundo, Divers de México and Mantarraya all offer fishing trips, as does Fish 'R' Us (☎ 487-87-87, 482-82-82). The cost for a six-hour fishing trip is around US$200 or higher, depending on the size of the boat; Fish 'R' Us offers trips for US$70 per person.

For a fast, white-knuckle boat ride on the Río Papagayo, contact Shotover Jet (☎ 484-11-54) at the Hotel Continental Plaza, La Costera 121.

Other Activities

Acapulco has three 18-hole golf courses. Club de Golf Acapulco (☎ 484-65-83) is on La Costera; in Acapulco Diamante (near the airport) there are Tres Vidas (☎ 444-51-26) and another course at the Acapulco Princess Hotel (☎ 469-10-00). The Vidafel Mayan Palace Hotel (☎ 462-00-20) has a nine-hole course.

For tennis, try the Club de Golf Acapulco (☎ 484-12-25, tennis section), Club de Tenis Hyatt (☎ 484-12-25), the Villa Vera Racquet Club (☎ 484-03-33), the Hotel Panoramic (☎ 481-01-32) or the Acapulco Princess Hotel (☎ 469-10-00).

AJ Hackett Paradise Acapulco (☎ 484-75-29), La Costera 107, has a bungee tower right over the Delfines Paradise dolphin pool, opposite the Hotel Romano Palace.

Unidad Deportiva Acapulco (☎ 486-10-33), Calle Chiapas s/n, Colonia Progreso, has an Olympic-size pool, children's pool, gymnasium, stadium, sports courts and fields. The cost is US$1 to swim in the Olympic-size pool, US$0.50 for the children's pool and US$0.25 to jog around the stadium track. It's open noon to 6 pm Tuesday, 9 am to 6 pm Wednesday to Sunday; closed Monday.

You can swim with dolphins at CICI (see above) or at Delfines Paradise (☎ 481-00-61), La Costera 101, under the Hackett bungee tower.

Acapulco also has gymnasiums, squash courts and facilities for other sports. The tourist office has information on sports in Acapulco.

Helicopter & Ultralight Tours

Helicopter Tours (☎ 486-70-88/90) offers tours of Acapulco and the surrounding area for US$60 per person. Sky Flight (☎ 484-85-75) at Playa Revolcadero offers ultralight rides.

Cruises

Various boats and yachts offer cruises, which depart from the Malecón near the zócalo. Cruises are available day and night; they range from multilevel boats with blaring salsa music and open bars to yachts offering quiet sunset cruises around the bay. All take basically the same route – they leave from the Malecón, go around the Peninsula de las Playas to Isla de la Roqueta, pass by to see the cliff divers at La Quebrada, cross over to Puerto Marqués and then come back around the Bahía de Acapulco. The *Hawaiano* (☎ 482-21-99, 482-07-85), the *Fiesta* and *Bonanza* (☎ 483-18-03), and the large *Aca Tiki* catamaran (☎ 484-61-40) are all popular; you can make reservations by calling them directly, or through any travel agency and most hotels. Divers de México (☎ 482-13-98, 483-60-20) also offers cruises.

Special Events

Probably the busiest time of the year for tourism in Acapulco is Semana Santa, when the city fills with tourists and there's lots of action in the discos, on the beaches and all over town.

A Tianguis Turístico, a special, tourist-oriented market, is held the second week in April. The Festivales de Acapulco, held for one week in May, features Mexican and international music at many venues around town.

International film festivals include the Festival de Cine Negro (Black Film Festival) held the second week of June, and the Festival de Cine Francés (French Film Festival) held for a week in late November. The Congreso Mundial Omni (World UFO Congress) is held the second week of December.

The festival for Mexico's patron saint, the Virgen de Guadalupe, is celebrated all night on December 11 and all the following day, with street processions accompanied by small marching bands, fireworks and folk dances, all converging on the cathedral in the zócalo, where children dressed in costumes congregate.

Expo-Acapulco, an industrial and commercial exposition encouraging investment in Acapulco, takes place December 20 to January 7.

Places to Stay

Acapulco has a great number of hotels in all categories and over 30,000 hotel rooms. Tourism is seasonal; high season is from the middle of December until the end of Easter, with another flurry of activity during the July and August school holidays. Most hotels raise their rates during these times, to as much as

double the low-season price, though some do this for only part of the season. At other times of year you can often bargain for a better rate, especially if you plan to stay a while. At Semana Santa or Christmas to New Year's Day, be sure to have hotel reservations or you may do a lot of searching for a room.

Places to Stay – Budget

Camping Closest in is the *Playa Suave Trailer Park* (☎ 485-14-64, La Costera 276), with 38 tent and trailer spaces with full hookups for US$14.50 per space. The entrance is on Vasco Nuñez de Balboa, between Mendoza and Malaespina, a block behind La Costera.

Southeast of town in the Diamante area, *Trailer Park Diamante* (☎ 466-02-00, Copacabana 8, Fraccionamiento Playa Diamante) is 3km from the beach but has two swimming pools; tent and trailer spaces with full hookups are US$14.25. *Trailer Park El Coloso* is at Carretera Pinotepa Nacional, Km 2.5, Colonia La Sábana. Three other trailer parks are at Pie de la Cuesta, half an hour west of town (see Around Acapulco).

Hotels Most of Acapulco's budget hotels are concentrated around the zócalo area and on Calle La Quebrada, the street going up the hill from behind the cathedral to La Quebrada, where the divers do their stuff.

A good place near the zócalo is *Hotel Maria Antonieta* (☎ 482-50-24, Azueta 17), with reasonably quiet rooms for US$9 per person and a kitchen you can use. *California Inn* (☎ 482-28-93, La Paz 12) is another good place; clean, pleasant rooms set around a courtyard full of plants are US$11/20 a single/double, and English is spoken. *Hotel Añove* (☎ 482-32-62, Juárez 17) has simple, clean singles/doubles for US$9/16.50. *Hotel Paola* (☎ 482-62-43, Azueta 16) is another clean place, with rooms for US$10 per person; outside rooms have small private balconies, interior rooms are quieter. *Hotel Santa Lucía* (☎ 482-04-41, López Mateos 33) has clean rooms for US$7.75 per person. *La Mama Hélène* (☎ 482-23-96, Juárez 12) has rooms set around an interior courtyard for US$9/13 a single/double.

On Calle La Quebrada, *Hotel Angelita* (☎ 483-57-34, *La Quebrada 37*) is clean and popular, with singles/doubles for US$11/16.50 and a guests' sitting room out front. Next door, *Hotel Mariscal* (☎ 482-00-15 *La Quebrada 35*) has rooms for US$8.75 per person (cheaper by the week). *Hotel Asturias* (☎ 483-65-48, *La Quebrada 45*) is popular and friendly, very clean and well tended, with pleasant rooms on a courtyard with a small swimming pool; singles/doubles are US$14/19.50. Also with a small swimming pool is *Hotel Coral* (☎ 482-07-56, *La Quebrada 56*), with rooms for US$6.50 per person. *Hotel Casa Amparo* (☎ 482-21-72, *La Quebrada 69*) also has a pool; rooms are US$5.50 per person.

Up the hill at the top of Calle La Quebrada is Plaza La Quebrada, overlooking the sea. The large attended parking lot here is a safe place to park, but it gets very busy and loud in the evening when the cliff divers perform. The hotels here are somewhat cooler than places down the hill in town, since they catch the sea breezes. Perched on a hill above the plaza, *La Torre Eiffel* (☎ 482-16-83, *Inalámbrica 110*) has a small swimming pool and large balconies with sitting areas set up for a view of the sea. Its bright rooms are US$11/16.50 a single/double. Right on the plaza, *Hotel El Faro* (☎ 482-13-65, *La Quebrada 83*) has large rooms with balconies for US$9/16.50 (US$11/22 December to Easter).

Places to Stay – Mid-Range

In the zócalo area, *Hotel Misión* (☎ 482-36-43, *Valle 12*) is a relaxing colonial-style place offering stylish rooms with tiles and heavy Spanish furniture. Rooms are set around a lovely, shady courtyard where breakfast is served for US$2.75 (continental) or US$5.50 (complete); rooms are US$22/33 per person in low/high season.

On the east side of Parque Papagayo, near La Costera and the popular Playa Hornitos, *Hotel Jacqueline* (☎ 485-93-38) has 10 air-conditioned rooms for US$27/33 (higher at busy times) around a pleasant little garden. Next door, *Hotel del Valle* (☎ 485-83-36/88) has a small swimming pool,

kitchens (US$6.50 surcharge per day) and rooms for US$32/42 with fan/air-con. Both are on Espinosa, though the nearest street sign indicates Morín (which actually starts a block north).

Half a block from Playa Hornitos on Avenida Wilfrido Massieu, *Auto Hotel Ritz* (☎ 482-40-78, 485-52-42) is an attractive six-story hotel with indoor parking. Rooms with air-con, cable TV, carpet and private terraces overlooking the swimming pool are US$44.

Near CICI and Playa Icacos are a number of hotels, including two with large apartments, swimming pool, parking, air-con and fully equipped kitchens. *Suites Selene* (☎ 484-36-43, 484-29-77, *Colón 175*), one door from the beach, has rooms for US$41, plus attractive air-conditioned one/two-bedroom apartments with kitchen for US$54/107 December to April (20% cheaper May to November). Ask for a sea view room; they have spacious balconies and cost no more.

Hotel Quinta Mica (☎ 484-01-21/22, *Colón 115*) has simpler apartments for US$38 Monday to Thursday, US$49 Friday to Sunday. The Comercial Mexicana supermarket nearby is convenient for groceries.

The high-rise hotels along La Costera tend to be expensive. One of the more economical ones is *Romano Palace Hotel* (☎ 484-77-30, *La Costera 130*), whose luxurious rooms have private balconies and floor-to-ceiling windows with a great view of Acapulco; ask for an upper-story room for the best view (there are 22 floors). Rooms are US$60 for one to four people most of the year, US$75 during holidays.

Also on La Costera, *Hotel Club del Sol* (☎ 485-66-00, *La Costera at Ascencio*) is a large hotel with four swimming pools (including two for children), a 200-foot water slide, a gym, squash, volleyball, aerobics, sauna, Jacuzzi, game room, disco, restaurant, bar and a 24-hour supermarket. The rooms, all with air-con, cable TV, kitchenette and private balcony, are US$53 to US$111 most of the year, US$218 to US$283 at busy times.

Over on Playa Caletilla, *Hotel Boca Chica* (☎ 483-63-88, *Privada de Caletilla*) is a lovely waterside hotel with a natural swimming pool beside the sea, gardens with a view of Isla de la Roqueta, an open-air sea view restaurant/bar, and air-conditioned rooms with fine vistas. Singles/doubles are US$76/87, with breakfast included, December to April; cheaper the rest of the year.

Also with magnificent views, high on a hill on the Peninsula de las Playas, are the fancy, linked *Hotel Real del Monte* and *Hotel Casablanca* (☎ *482-12-12/13, Cerro de la Pinzona 80*). Rooms are US$38 with fan, US$45 with air-con, and there's a swimming pool.

Places to Stay – Top End

If you want to spend lots of money, there's plenty of opportunity for it in Acapulco, with its numerous deluxe 'grand tourism' and 'special category' hotels. The super-luxury special category hotels include the *Las Brisas*, *Acapulco Princess*, *Pierre Marqués*, *Camino Real* and the *Hyatt Regency Acapulco*. Grand tourism hotels include the *Costa Club Acapulco*, *Radisson Resort*, *Villa Vera*, *Fiesta Americana Condesa* and *Vidafel Mayan Palace*. Many of the luxury hotels are found in the new Acapulco Diamante development, east of Puerto Marqués, and on the beachfront along La Costera; the high-rise hotel zone begins at the east end of Parque Papagayo and runs east around the bay. Travel agents should have literature on all these hotels.

Places to Eat

Old Acapulco On the east side of the zócalo, *The Big Slice/La Rebanadota* is very popular, with tasty, economical food and attractive tables both out on the plaza (great for people-watching) and inside where it's air-conditioned. Specializing in pizza, pasta and salads, their 'big slices' of pizza for US$1.30 are gigantic. Open daily except Tuesday, 10 am to 3 am.

Hidden away at the back of the plaza, east of the cathedral, *Restaurant Café Astoria* has outdoor tables in a pleasant, shady, quietish spot. It's open 8 am to 11 pm daily, with economical prices and a comida corrida (US$2.25) served 1 to 4 pm. Around the corner on the Carranza pedestrian street, with sidewalk tables under a large shady tree, *Restaurant Charly II* is another economical place; comida corrida is US$2.25, or get an order of seven tacos for US$1.65 to US$2.75. Open 7.30 am to 11 pm daily. On the west side of the zócalo, *La Parroquia* specializes in German food.

A couple of blocks east of the zócalo on Avenida Escudero, the *Woolworth's* department store has an air-conditioned restaurant open 7 am to 10 pm daily, offering good-value set breakfasts, lunches and dinners.

Nearby, *Sanborn's* department store also has a restaurant, but it's much more expensive.

Coming out of the zócalo on the west side, Calle Juárez has about a dozen restaurants. *Restaurant Ricardo* (*Juárez 9*) is popular with locals, with economical prices and comida corrida for US$2.50; open 8 am to midnight daily. A couple of doors closer to the zócalo, *Restaurant San Carlos* (*Juárez 5*), with an open-air patio, nicer ambiance and similar prices, is open 8 am to 10.30 pm daily. In the next block west, *La Casona de Juárez* (*Juárez 10*) is an attractive patio restaurant with comida corrida for US$2.75 or the 'special' for US$5.50; open 9 am to 9 pm, Monday to Saturday.

There are more restaurants west of the zócalo, many specializing in seafood. On the corner of Juárez and Azueta, the open-air *El Amigo Miguel* is one of the most patronized, with delicious seafood at economical prices; paella on Sunday is US$6, fish filets US$4. Open 10 am to 9 pm daily. El Amigo Miguel has two restaurants opposite one another, on this same corner. Several other seafood restaurants are nearby.

For rotisserie roasted chicken, eat-in or takeout, go to 5 de Mayo, where there are four places side by side.

La Costera There are dozens of restaurants as you head east down La Costera toward the big high-rise hotels. *Fersato's*, on La Costera opposite the Casa de la Cultura, near CICI, is a long-standing family establishment with delicious Mexican food. Comida corrida is US$4; open 8 am to midnight daily. One block west of CICI, side by side, are the famous (and much more expensive) theme restaurants, *Hard Rock Cafe* and *Planet Hollywood*; both are open daily, noon to 2 am. Another block west, *Mariscos Pipo's* is known for its good seafood; try a combination seafood plate for US$10 (small) or US$13 (large). Open 1 to 9.30 pm daily.

Back along La Costera, the *Hotel Club del Sol* restaurant serves a breakfast buffet Monday to Thursday, 9 am to noon, for US$6 to US$7.75. Their dinner buffet, with something different served every night, costs around US$11, drinks included; it's served Monday to Saturday, 6 to 10 pm.

VIPS in the Gran Plaza, at the corner of La Costera and Massieu, is big, bright and air-conditioned; open 7 am to midnight Sunday to Thursday, 7 am to 2 am Friday and Saturday. *Tony Roma's*, on La Costera near the La Diana traffic circle, boasts 'the best ribs in America.'

Carlos Anderson's *Carlos 'n Charlie's (La Costera 112)* has rowdy music and a quirky bilingual menu. It's not cheap, but it shows the tourists a good time; open 1 pm to 1 am daily. Anderson's *Señor Frog's*, on the Carretera Escénica on the east side of the Bahía de Acapulco, has a great view.

The open-air *Pancho's (La Costera 109)* is reasonably priced and serves tasty Mexican and international food, especially grilled and barbecued meats; open 6 pm to midnight daily. Many other open-air beachfront restaurant/bars are along here near Pancho's, opposite the Romano Palace Hotel. All of them are open in the evening; stroll along and take your pick.

For cheaper fare near La Costera, try the small *La Cabaña del Pescador* on Morín, with good home-style Mexican cooking. Comida corrida costs US$2, seafood meals US$3.25; also ask about daily specials. Open 8.30 am to 7 pm daily.

Restaurants in the *100% Natural* chain are found throughout Acapulco; there are several along La Costera, serving mostly vegetarian fare. *El Fogón* is another chain with several branches along La Costera, serving traditional Mexican dishes. Several US chain restaurants are also found along La Costera,

including *Shakey's Pizza*, *Domino's Pizza*, *Pizza Hut*, *Kentucky Fried Chicken*, *Subway* and several *McDonald's*. *Telepizza* (☎ 484-10-00, 484-03-76) and *Dominós* (☎ 482-89-91, 486-57-27) offer delivery.

Playa Caletilla Many open-air seafood restaurants are under the big trees lining the rear of Playa Caletilla, all with similar inexpensive menus. The attractive open-air restaurant at *Hotel Boca Chica* on the west end of the beach, under a high palapa roof with a view across to Isla de la Roqueta, serves buffet lunch (12.30 to 2.30 pm) and dinner (7.30 to 10 pm) daily for US$11.

La Quebrada You can splurge at the *Restaurant La Perla* (☎ 483-11-55) in the Plaza Las Glorias Hotel on Plaza La Quebrada. The nightly à la carte meal on candlelit terraces under the stars, offered 7 to 11 pm, is overpriced (US$30 per person), but the great view of the divers makes for a special evening.

Grocery Stores The large *Comercial Mexicana*, *Bodega Gigante* and *Bodega Aurrera* combination supermarkets and discount department stores are along La Costera between the zócalo and Parque Papagayo. Another Comercial Mexicana is opposite CICI. *Sam's Club* and yet another Comercial Mexicana are on highway 95, just inland from the La Diana traffic circle. *Wal-Mart*, on the east end of the city, is open 24 hours. *Costco* is farther east.

Entertainment
Discos, Clubs & Bars Acapulco's active nightlife rivals its beaches as the main attraction. Much of it revolves around discos and nightclubs, with new ones continually opening up to challenge the old. Most of the discos open around 10 pm and have a cover charge of US$11 or more, sometimes with an open bar.

Enigma and the *Palladium* are popular places in the Las Brisas area in the southeast part of Acapulco; Palladium attracts the younger crowd. Some locals say these two are Acapulco's best.

A popular disco on La Costera, *Andromedas* is a techno-pop disco with a nautical theme. Nearby on La Costera is *Salon Q*, with Latin rhythms and live music. Also here is *Baby'O*; it has a laser light show and is supposedly one of the best discos in Acapulco, attracting a younger crowd. About 400m south on La Costera, *El Alebrije* disco/concert hall bills itself as 'one of the largest and most spectacular discos in the world.'

Disco Beach, on La Costera in the line of beachfront restaurant/bars opposite the Romano Palace Hotel, is also popular, and right on Playa Condesa. *B&B (Gran Via Tropical 5)* in the Caleta area features hits of the 1950s to 1980s.

Don't forget the *Hard Rock Cafe (La Costera 37)*; the Acapulco branch of the famous chain, just west of CICI, is open noon to 2 am daily, with live music 11 pm to 1.30 am. Its neighbor, *Planet Hollywood*, open the same hours, has dancing from around 11 pm (or movie shows if it's a quiet night). *Nina's*, on the other side of the Hard Rock Cafe, specializes in live Latin music.

Acapulco has an active gay scene and several predominantly gay bars and clubs. Drag shows are one feature of the scene: *Tequila's Le Club (☎ 485-86-23, 483-82-36, Urdaneta 29, Fraccionamiento Hornos)*, three blocks behind the Gigante supermarket, presents a famous transvestite show 11.30 pm to 1 am Monday to Saturday, with an international show at 11.15 pm and a Latin show at 1 am. Chippendale, a male stripper show for ladies only, is presented 8.30 to 10.45 pm Thursday and Saturday. Phone for reservations.

If you don't feel up to a disco, most of the big hotels along La Costera have bars with entertainment, be it quiet piano music or live bands.

Dance, Music & Theater The Centro de Convenciones holds a Fiesta Mexicana every Monday, Wednesday and Friday night, 7 to 10 pm, featuring regional dances from many parts of Mexico, mariachis, the famous Papantla voladores and a rope performer; there's also a sumptuous Mexican buffet.

Cost per person for the buffet, open bar and show is US$44. Or you can skip the buffet and come for the two-hour show at 8 pm; cost is US$25 for the show and open bar. Phone ☎ 484-71-52 for reservations.

Other theaters at the Centro de Convenciones present plays, concerts, dance and other cultural performances, as does the Casa de la Cultura (☎ 484-23-90, 484-38-14); phone or stop by for current schedules. Outdoor entertainment events are also sometimes presented at Parque Papagayo (☎ 485-71-77, 485-96-23).

Cinemas Acapulco has several cinemas – there are at least three on La Costera, and several more around town. Current cinema listings are found in the *Novedades* and *Sol de Acapulco* newspapers.

Spectator Sports

Bullfights are held at the Plaza de Toros southeast of La Quebrada and northwest of Playas Caleta and Caletilla every Sunday at 5.30 pm, December to March; tickets are sold at the bullring from 4.30 pm and at travel agencies. Travel agencies or the bullring ticket office (☎ 482-11-82, 483-95-61) have details. The 'Caleta' bus passes near the bullring.

Shopping

Acapulco's main craft market, the 400-stall Mercado de Artesanías, is a few blocks east of the zócalo between Avenida Cuauhtémoc and Vicente de León. Paved and pleasant, it's a good place to get better deals on everything that you see in the hotel shops – sarapes, hammocks, jewelry, huaraches, clothing and T-shirts. Bargaining is definitely the rule. It's open 9 am to 8 pm daily. Other artesanías markets include the Mercados de Artesanías Papagayo, Noa Noa, El Pueblito, Dalia and La Diana, all on La Costera, and another at Playa Caletilla.

Getting There & Away

Air Acapulco has a busy international airport. Many flights connect through Mexico City or Guadalajara, both short hops from Acapulco. Airlines serving Acapulco and their direct flights, all with connections to other cities, include:

Aeroméxico/Aerolitoral
La Costera 286; also La Costera 91, Local 1, Condominio Nikko (☎ 466-92-96, 800-021-40-00); flies to Mexico City, Guadalajara

Aerolineas Internacionales
La Costera 127, Local 9 (☎ 486-56-30, 486-00-02); flies to Cuernavaca

America West
Airport (☎ 800-235-92-92); flies to Phoenix

American Airlines
La Costera 116, Plaza Condesa, Local 109 (☎ 481-01-61, 800-904-60-00); flies to Dallas

Continental Airlines
Airport (☎ 466-90-46/63, 800-900-50-00); flies to Houston

Mexicana
La Gran Plaza, La Costera 1632, corner Wilfrido Massieu, ground floor, Local G8-9-10 (☎ 486-75-85/86/87/90, 466-91-21, 800-502-20-00); flies to Mexico City

Northwest
Airport (☎ 800-900-08-00); flies to Minneapolis (one Saturday flight, December to April)

Bus Acapulco has two major 1st-class long-distance bus companies: Estrella Blanca and Estrella de Oro. The Estrella de Oro terminal (☎ 485-87-05) is on the corner of Avenidas Cuauhtémoc and Wilfrido Massieu. Estrella Blanca has two first-class terminals: Central Papagayo (☎ 469-20-80), Cuauhtémoc 1605, opposite Parque Papagayo, and Central Ejido (☎ 469-20-28/30), Ejido 47. Estrella Blanca also has a 2nd-class terminal (☎ 482-21-84) at Cuauhtémoc 97, which has small buses going to nearby towns.

Estrella Blanca tickets are sold at several agencies around town, as well as at the bus stations. One agency (☎ 482-53-49) is at Ignacio de la Llave 3-1, a block east of the zócalo. Another is in the Centro de Convenciones (☎ 484-34-41), La Costera 4455. Another (☎ 482-85-66) is at Playa Caleta, on La Costera opposite Hotel Caleta. Another agency (☎ 486-83-60/61) is in the Gran Plaza, La Costera 1616. Yet another is in the Agencia de Viajes Zócalo (☎ 482-49-76), La Costera 207, Local 2, a couple of blocks east of the zócalo.

Both bus companies offer frequent services to Mexico City, with various levels of luxury; journey durations depend on whether they use the new, faster autopista (highway 95D) or the old federal highway 95. Both lines have buses to the Terminal Sur and Terminal Norte in Mexico City. Destinations include:

Chilpancingo – 132km, 1½ to 2 hours; 1st-class or Plus every hour or two, 6.30 am to 9 pm, by Estrella de Oro (US$5.50), 5 2nd-class by Estrella de Oro (US$5.50), 5 Futura (US$5.75), 2 Ejecutivo (US$6.50) by Estrella Blanca, Central Papagayo, 2nd-class from Estrella Blanca's 2nd-class terminal every half-hour, 5 am to 7 pm (3 hours, US$4.50)

Cuernavaca – 315km, 4-5 hours; 2 Primera (US$18.25), 3 Plus (US$20), and 5 2nd-class (US$12) by Estrella de Oro, 7 Primera (US$18.25), 1 Plus (US$20) and 1 Futura (US$22) by Estrella Blanca, Central Ejido, 3 Futura (US$22) by Estrella Blanca, Central Papagayo

Iguala – 231km, 3 hours; 5 Primera (US$11) by Estrella de Oro, Ordinario (2nd-class) hourly, 6 am to 9 pm, by Estrella de Oro (3½ hours, US$8.50), 17 Primera (US$11) by Estrella Blanca, Central Ejido

Mexico City (Terminal Sur) – 400km, 5 hours; 3 Primera (US$23), 17 Plus (US$24), 4 Crucero (US$25) and 5 Diamante (US$36) by Estrella de Oro, Futura hourly, 3 am to 7 pm, plus 9 pm, midnight, 12.30, 1.30 and 1.45 am (US$24), 4 Ejecutivo (US$36) by Estrella Blanca, Central Papagayo, 5 Primera (US$23), 8 Futura (US$24) by Estrella Blanca, Central Ejido

Mexico City (Terminal Norte) – 400km, 6 hours; 1 Plus (US$24) by Estrella de Oro, 9 Futura (US$24), 1 Ejecutivo (US$36) by Estrella Blanca, Central Papagayo, 2 Económico (US$23), 2 Futura (US$24) by Estrella Blanca, Central Ejido

Puerto Escondido – 400km, 7 hours; 3 Primera (US$17.50) by Estrella Blanca, Central Ejido

Taxco – 266km, 4 hours; 5 Primera (US$13) by Estrella de Oro, 4 Primera (US$13) by Estrella Blanca, Central Ejido

Zihuatanejo – 239km, 4 hours; 3 Plus (US$12), 2nd-class hourly, 4.50 am to 5.30 pm, plus 8.15 pm (5 hours, US$7) by Estrella de Oro, 15 Primera (US$10.50), 2 Futura (US$15) by Estrella Blanca, Central Ejido

Car Many car-rental companies hire Jeeps as well as cars; several have offices at the airport as well as in town, and/or offer free delivery to you. As always, it's a good idea to shop around to compare prices. Rental companies include:

Alamo	☎ 484-33-05, 466-94-44
Avis	☎ 466-91-90, 462-00-75
Europcar	☎ 466-02-46, 466-07-00
Galgo	☎ 484-30-66, 484-35-47
Hertz	☎ 485-89-47, 466-91-72
Saad	☎ 484-34-45, 484-53-25

Getting Around

To/From the Airport Acapulco's airport is 23km southeast of the zócalo, beyond the junction for Puerto Marqués. Arriving by air, buy a ticket for transport into town from the colectivo desk before you leave the terminal; it's US$7 per person for a lift directly to your hotel.

Leaving Acapulco, phone Móvil Aca (☎ 462-10-95) 24 hours in advance to reserve your transport back to the airport. They'll pick you up 90 minutes before your flight for domestic flights, two hours before your flight for international flights; the cost is US$7 per person. Shuttle (☎ 462-10-95) offers a similar service. Taxis from the center to the airport cost about US$17 if hailed in the street; 'hotel rates' are higher.

Bus Acapulco has a good city bus system, with buses going every few minutes to most places you'd want to go. They operate 5 am to 11 pm daily and cost US$0.30; fancier, air-conditioned buses cost a bit more, around US$0.45. From the zócalo area, the bus stop opposite Sanborn's department store on La Costera, two blocks east of the zócalo, is a good place to catch buses – it's the beginning of several bus routes so you can usually get a seat. The most useful city routes include:

Base-Caleta – from the Icacos naval base at the southeast end of Acapulco, along La Costera, past the zócalo to Playa Caleta

Base-Cine Río-Caleta – from the Icacos naval base, cuts inland from La Costera on Avenida Wilfrido Massieu to Avenida Cuauhtémoc, heads down Cuauhtémoc through the business district, turning back to La Costera just before reaching the zócalo, continuing west to Caleta

Puerto Marqués-Centro – from opposite Sanborn's, along La Costera to Puerto Marqués

Zócalo-Playa Pie de la Cuesta – from opposite Sanborn's, to Pie de la Cuesta; Buses marked 'Playa' or 'Luces' go all the way down the Pie de la Cuesta beach road; those marked 'San Isidro' or 'Pedregoso' stop at the entrance to Pie de la Cuesta

Taxi Cabs are plentiful in Acapulco and taxi drivers are happy to take gringos for a ride, especially for fares higher than the official rates. Always agree on the fare before you climb into the cab; it never hurts to bargain with taxi drivers.

AROUND ACAPULCO

Just northwest of Acapulco, Pie de la Cuesta has a relaxed beach scene. About 18km southeast of Acapulco, **Puerto Marqués** is a cove much smaller than the Bahía de Acapulco. You get a magnificent view of the Bahía de Acapulco as the Carretera Escénica climbs south out of the city. The calm water at Puerto Marqués is good for waterskiing and sailing. Buses marked 'Puerto Marqués' run along Acapulco's La Costera about every 10 minutes, 5 am to 9 pm (US$0.30).

Past Puerto Marqués and heading out toward the airport, **Playa Revolcadero** is the long, straight beach of the new Acapulco Diamante luxury tourism developments. The waves are large and surfing is popular here, especially in summer, but a strong undertow makes swimming dangerous. Horseback riding on the beach is a popular activity.

During Semana Santa, the Passion of Christ is acted out in the town of **Treinta**, 30km northeast of Acapulco; the Acapulco tourist office can provide details.

PIE DE LA CUESTA
☎ 7

About 10km northwest of Acapulco, Pie de la Cuesta is a narrow 2km strip of land bordered by the beach and ocean on one side and the large, freshwater Laguna de Coyuca on the other. Compared to Acapulco, it's quieter, cleaner, closer to nature and much more peaceful. Swimming in the ocean at

Pie de la Cuesta can be dangerous, however, due to a riptide and the shape of the waves; each year a number of people are killed in the surf. Laguna de Coyuca, three times as large as the Bahía de Acapulco, is better for swimming; in the lagoon are the islands of Montosa, Presido and Pájaros, which is a bird sanctuary.

Pie de la Cuesta has many beachside restaurants specializing in seafood, and it's a great place for watching the sunset. There's no nightlife, so if you're looking for excitement you may be better off staying in Acapulco. Water-skiing is popular on the Laguna de Coyuca; several water-skiing clubs provide the equipment (around US$38 per hour). Boat trips on the lagoon are also an option; you can cross to the place where Sylvester Stallone filmed *Rambo*. Negotiate a price for your own boat any time, or take one of the colectivos (US$4.50 per person), which depart at specific hours. You can also ride a horse on the beach.

Places to Stay

For accommodations, Pie de la Cuesta is a good alternative to Acapulco. Since there's only one road, you can easily check out the 15 or so hotels along the 2km stretch between the beach and the lagoon. Every hotel provides private, safe parking.

Camping Pie de la Cuesta has two clean, pleasant trailer parks at the far end of the road from the highway: *Trailer Park Quinta Dora* (☎ 460-11-38) and the *Acapulco Trailer Park & Mini-Super* (☎ 460-00-10). Both have full hookups and are good for tents and trailers. Take a look at both parks and ask for prices before you choose your spot; they're only about a two-minute walk from each other but most campers have a distinct preference for one or the other. Each place has camping areas on both the beach and lagoon sides of the road. Spaces cost around US$8/10 for tents/trailers.

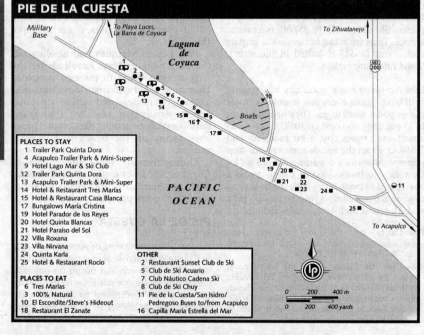

PIE DE LA CUESTA

Military Base

To Playa Luces, La Barra de Coyuca

Laguna de Coyuca

To Zihuatanejo

MEX 200

Boats

PACIFIC OCEAN

To Acapulco

PLACES TO STAY
1   Trailer Park Quinta Dora
4   Acapulco Trailer Park & Mini-Super
9   Hotel Lago Mar & Ski Club
12 Trailer Park Quinta Dora
13 Acapulco Trailer Park & Mini-Super
14 Hotel & Restaurant Tres Marías
15 Hotel & Restaurant Casa Blanca
17 Bungalows María Cristina
19 Hotel Parador de los Reyes
20 Hotel Quinta Blancas
21 Hotel Paraíso del Sol
22 Villa Roxana
23 Villa Nirvana
24 Quinta Karla
25 Hotel & Restaurant Rocio

PLACES TO EAT
6   Tres Marías
3   100% Natural
10 El Escondite/Steve's Hideout
18 Restaurant El Zanate

OTHER
2   Restaurant Sunset Club de Ski
5   Club de Ski Acuario
7   Club Náutico Cadena Ski
8   Club de Ski Chuy
11 Pie de la Cuesta/San Isidro/
    Pedregoso Buses to/from Acapulco
16 Capilla María Estrella del Mar

0   200   400 m
0   200   400 yards

On Playa Luces, about 4km farther past Pie de la Cuesta, **KOA** (☎ 444-40-62) is a large, 100-space landscaped camping park. Trailer spaces with full hookups are US$16, tent spaces US$14, double-size beachfront spaces US$25, with cheaper weekly and monthly rates. Amenities include a large beachfront swimming pool, a restaurant/bar, children's playgrounds and Internet service. They also rent three rooms, at US$33 each. The 'Pie de la Cuesta – Playa Luces' bus stops at the gate.

Hotels & Guesthouses Accommodations are mostly small-scale, friendly, family-run and by the beach. Places are listed in order from east to west.

Hotel & Restaurant Rocío (☎ 460-10-08) has rooms with one/two/three beds for US$25/35/44. Félix López, the resident bartender, chef, guitarist and songster, provides music and good times. Spiffy new beachfront rooms with large balconies cost the same as other doubles – ask for one of these.

Quinta Karla (☎ 460-12-55) has a restaurant, swimming pool and bungalows with kitchenette for US$33 a single, US$44 for up to four people, US$55 in high season. Regular rooms, without kitchen, are US$11/16.50 a single/double, US$33 in high season.

Villa Nirvana (☎ 460-16-31) provides a garden with a beachside swimming pool and a pleasant restaurant serving breakfast; accommodations include regular rooms (US$28), a beach house with kitchen facilities (US$44), and a large apartment sleeping six (US$65). (These prices are December to May; it's cheaper the rest of the year.) To get there, you must go straight through the *Villa Roxana* (☎ 460-32-52), a similarly attractive and spotlessly clean place, which has lovely gardens with plenty of hammocks and shade, a small swimming pool, a restaurant serving breakfast, and attractive rooms with one/two/three beds for US$16/20/25. English and Spanish are spoken at both places.

Hotel Quinta Blancas (☎ 460-03-12) has a big swimming pool and 24 large rooms for US$16.50/19 with one/two beds, all year round.

Hotel Paraíso del Sol (☎ 460-04-12), about 50m from the coast road down a narrow lane, is an excellent choice by the beach, with a lovely shaded garden, swimming pool, tennis court and restaurant/bar. Regular rooms are US$33, large four-bed rooms US$55.

Hotel Parador de los Reyes (☎ 460-01-31) is an economical choice, with singles/doubles for US$11/13. It's right beside the road, with a small courtyard swimming pool.

Bungalows María Cristina (☎ 460-02-62), run by a friendly family that speaks English and Spanish, is a clean, well-tended, relaxing place with a barbecue and hammocks overlooking the beach. Rooms are US$28, or US$66 for large beachfront bungalows with kitchen sleeping up to five people.

Hotel Lago Mar & Ski Club (☎ 460-31-51) is on the lagoon side and has a swimming pool, lovely lagoon view, restaurant/bar and water-skiing club. Its big rooms have a bit of style, with tiled floors and bathrooms; prices are US$28 Monday to Thursday, US$33 Friday to Sunday, US$12 extra with air-con, higher in high season.

Hotel & Restaurant Casa Blanca (☎ 460-03-24) is another clean, well-tended place on the beachfront, with a homey atmosphere; singles/doubles are US$11/22 (US$22/33 in high season). *Hotel & Restaurant Tres Marías* (☎ 460-01-78) has a swimming pool and good doubles for US$49/60 with one king-size/two double beds year round.

At Playa Luces, 5km farther along from Pie de la Cuesta and 1km past KOA, *Quinta Erika* (☎ 444-41-31) is a small, quality lodging with five large rooms and one bungalow on 2 hectares of landscaped grounds beside the lagoon. The price of US$50 per room (for two people) includes breakfast and boat tours, as well as use of the hotel's kayaks, sailboats and speedboats. Quinta Erika takes pride in being private, quiet, restful, attentive, and most of all exclusive. Reservations are required. German, English and Spanish are spoken.

Places to Eat
Restaurants are known for their fresh seafood. There are plenty of open-air places

right beside the beach, though some close early in the evening. Nearly all the hotels and guesthouses have restaurants, as do some of the water-skiing clubs. The *Tres Marías* by the sea is known to have some of the best food in the area; opposite, the *Tres Marías* on the lagoon side, run by the same family, is more expensive. There's also a lagoonside *100% Natural* restaurant.

Restaurant El Zanate beside the road is a small, simple place with meals for just US$1.60. Across the street, *El Escondite/Steve's Hideout*, built on stilts over the water, has a fine view.

Getting There & Away

From Acapulco, take a 'Pie de la Cuesta' bus on La Costera opposite the post office (the one next to Sanborn's, near the zócalo), on the bay side of the street. Buses go every 15 minutes, 6 am until around 8 pm; the 35-minute ride costs US$0.30. Buses marked 'Pie de la Cuesta – San Isidro' or 'Pie de la Cuesta – Pedregoso' stop on the highway, at the arched entrance to Pie de la Cuesta; those marked 'Pie de la Cuesta – Playa Luces' come all the way along Pie de la Cuesta and continue to Playa Luces, about 5km farther.

Be sure to find out what time the last bus leaves Pie de la Cuesta for the return trip. A taxi costs about US$9 one way, or there are colectivo taxis operating 24 hours, for US$1.

COSTA CHICA

The coast of Guerrero is known as the **Costa Grande** ('large coast') from Acapulco northwest to the border of Michoacán, and as the **Costa Chica** ('small coast') from Acapulco southeast to the border of Oaxaca.

On highway 200 60km (about an hour) east of Acapulco, **San Marcos** is an unremarkable town, but it can provide basic services. **Cruz Grande**, another small town, is on highway 200 about 40km farther east.

About 2½ hours southeast of Acapulco, **Playa Aventura** is a pure beach with soft white and gold sand, clear water, a number of simple beachfront fish restaurants and some simple places to stay. From Playa Aventura you can walk about 1km to another good beach, Playa La Piedra.

Horseback riding is available. You won't find Playa Aventura on any map – on maps it's called **Juan Álvarez**. To get there from Acapulco, first take a bus heading southeast on highway 200 from Acapulco to **Copala** (120km, two hours, US$4.25), a small town on highway 200. Buses depart from Estrella Blanca's 2nd-class terminal on Avenida Cuauhtémoc every half hour, 3.30 am to 7 pm. In Copala, microbuses and camionetas depart for Playa Aventura every half hour (13km, 30 minutes, US$1).

Marquelia, 20km farther east of Copala on highway 200, is another town providing basic services, with four inexpensive hotels. From Marquelia you can take a combi (US$0.30) to the nearby **Playa La Bocana**, where the Río Marquelia meets the sea and forms a lagoon. Another beach, **Playa Las Peñitas**, is 5km from La Bocana. There's no public transport from Marquelia to Playa Aventura; this operates from Copala. The same buses that depart Acapulco for Copala also continue to Marquelia (140km, 2½ hours, US$1.50).

Punta Maldonado, also sometimes referred to as **El Faro**, is a more remote beach on the Costa Chica. On a small bay fine for swimming, the tiny town of Punta Maldonado has some fish restaurants on the beach and one small hotel, which unfortunately is none too beautiful. To reach Punta Maldonado, take a camioneta from **Cuajinicuilapa** (people usually call it Cuaji), a small town on highway 200, about 200km southeast of Acapulco. Camionetas depart hourly from Cuaji (45 minutes, US$1.50), or you can take a taxi. Coming from Acapulco, Estrella Blanca 2nd-class buses to Cuaji depart hourly, 3.30 am to 6.30 pm (200km, five hours, US$9.50).

CHILPANCINGO
• pop 123,500 • elev 1360m ☎ 7

Chilpancingo, capital of the state of Guerrero, is a university city and agricultural center. It lies on highways 95 and 95D, about 130km north of Acapulco and 270km south of Mexico City. It's a rather nondescript place between two much more interesting destinations, Acapulco and Taxco.

Murals in the former **Palacio Municipal** showing the 1813 Congress of Chilpancingo are the only remaining signs of the city's important place in Mexico's history. In the spring of 1813, rebel leader José María Morelos y Pavón encircled Mexico City with his guerrilla army and then called for a congress to meet in Chilpancingo. The congress issued a Declaration of Independence and began to lay down the principles of a new constitution. Their achievements, however, were short-lived as Spanish troops broke the circle around Mexico City and recaptured most of Guerrero, including Chilpancingo. Morelos was tried for treason and executed by firing squad.

The state-operated tourist office in Chilpancingo, called the Delegación de Turismo (☎ 472-95-66), Calle Moisés Guevara 8, Colonia Cuauhtémoc Norte, can provide information on the town, the region and the state of Guerrero. It's open 9 am to 3 pm and 6 to 9 pm, Monday to Friday.

Places to Stay
Hotel Laura Elena (☎ 472-48-80, Madero 1 at Abasolo) has singles/doubles for US$17/18. *Hotel El Presidente* (☎ 472-97-31, Calle 30 de Agosto 1), a block from the bus station, has singles/doubles for US$21/25.

Getting There & Away
Chilpancingo is served by two bus companies: Estrella Blanca (☎ 472-06-34) and Estrella de Oro (☎ 471-09-39). Buses operate to/from Acapulco (1½ hours), Mexico City (3½ hours), Taxco (two hours), Iguala (four hours) and Chilapa (45 minutes).

AROUND CHILPANCINGO
Chilapa
The small town of Chilapa, about 45 minutes east of Chilpancingo, holds a traditional market every Sunday, starting in early morning. Market day has almost a pre-Hispanic feel; indigenous people come out of the hills, and all types of handicrafts, foodstuffs, animals and other goods are brought to market. Buses can take you from Chilpancingo.

Grutas de Juxtlahuaca
Near the small town of Juxtlahuaca, southeast of Chilpancingo, the Grutas de Juxtlahuaca is an impressive cave system 1.5km long, with a subterranean river and 19 caverns. Profesor Andrés Ortega Jiménez (☎ 7-474-70-06), known as 'El Chivo,' leads cave tours, as does his brother Enrique Ortega Jiménez.

Olinalá
The small, remote town of Olinalá is famous throughout Mexico for the beautiful lacquered boxes and other lacquered woodcraft made here. Linaloe, the fragrant wood used to make the boxes, grows in this area. Olinalá is very remote, up in the mountains (altitude 1350m), so it's not often visited. If you do make it here, there are simple hotels around the plaza, and places to eat.

A 2nd-class bus heading from Chilpancingo to Tlapa will drop you at the crossroads for Olinalá (4½ hours); from there you must catch another bus (one more hour) to Olinalá.

CENTRAL PACIFIC COAST

Western Central Highlands

West of Mexico City lies an upland area of great geographical and cultural variety, encompassing the inland parts of the states of Jalisco, Michoacán and Colima. (These states' narrow Pacific coastal plains are covered in the Central Pacific Coast chapter.) This region is off the really major tourist routes but has many attractive destinations, among them the country's second largest city, Guadalajara, capital of Jalisco; the fine capital of Michoacán, Morelia, and the brilliant El Rosario monarch butterfly sanctuary to its east; the lovely colonial town of Pátzcuaro in the Michoacán highlands; and the volcano Paricutín, which rose in 1943 from the lush Michoacán country surrounding Uruapan. Beyond these lie hundreds of kilometers of little-visited backcountry, with rugged landscapes, fertile valleys and timeless villages.

History

The western central highlands were remote from Mexico's major pre-Hispanic empires, though a fairly advanced agricultural village society flourished in parts of the region as early as 200 BC. In the 14th to 16th centuries AD, the Tarascos of northern Michoacán developed a major pre-Hispanic civilization with its capital at Tzintzuntzan, near Pátzcuaro. The zenith of the Tarascan empire coincided with the Aztec empire, but the Tarascos always managed to fend off Aztec attacks. West of the Tarascos – and occasionally at war with them – was the Chimalhuacán confederation of four indigenous kingdoms, in parts of what are now Jalisco, Colima and Nayarit states. To the north were Chichimecs, whom the Aztecs regarded as barbarians.

Colima, the leading Chimalhuacán kingdom, was conquered by the Spanish in 1523, but the region as a whole was not brought under Spanish control until the 1529–36 campaigns of Nuño de Guzmán, who tortured, killed and enslaved indigenous people from Michoacán to Sinaloa in his pursuit of riches, territory and glory. Guzmán was appointed governor of most of what he had conquered,

Highlights

- Guadalajara – the country's most Mexican city, birthplace of mariachi music, tequila and *charreadas*
- Morelia – distinguished colonial architecture, fine food, Spanish courses, and a lively student population
- Santuario de Mariposas El Rosario, the winter resort for millions of migratory monarch butterflies
- Pátzcuaro – a handsome little highland town in the homeland of the Purépecha people
- Volcán Paricutín – unforgettable trekking up to the smoldering crater and around a lava flow that engulfed two villages

but eventually his misdeeds caught up with him and in 1538 he was sent back to Spain. These territories came to be called Nueva Galicia and retained some autonomy from the rest of Nueva España until 1786.

A rebellion in Jalisco in 1540 set that area aflame in what is known as the Mixtón War; it was ended the next year by an army led by the Spanish viceroy. Guadalajara was established in its present location in 1542, after three earlier settlements were abandoned in the face of attacks by hostile indigenous groups.

Although the region was slower to develop than mineral-rich areas such as Zacatecas or

Guanajuato, it did develop. Ranching and agriculture grew, and Guadalajara, always one of Mexico's biggest cities, became the 'capital of the west.' The church helped by fostering small industries and handicraft traditions in its effort to ease the poverty of the indigenous people.

In the 1920s Michoacán and Jalisco were hotbeds of the Cristero rebellion by Catholics against government antichurch policies. Lázaro Cárdenas of Michoacán, as state governor from 1928 to 1932 and then as national president from 1934 to 1940, instituted reforms that did much to allay anti-government sentiments.

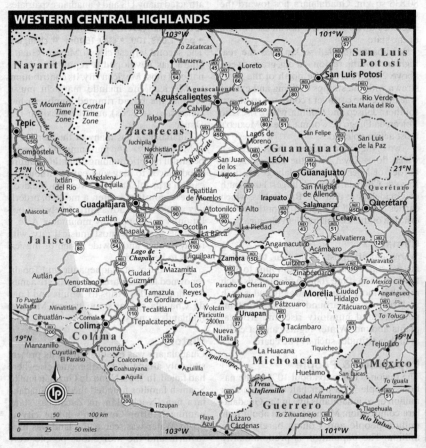

Geography

The western central highlands reach from the southern outliers of the Sierra Madre Occidental, in the north of Jalisco, to the western extremities of the Sierra Madre del Sur, which rise behind the southern Pacific coast. In between, part of the Cordillera Neovolcánica sweeps east-west across the region. Between these ranges lie lesser hills and basins. Among the most rugged, sparsely populated expanses are the remote northern spur of Jalisco and the rather inaccessible ranges backing the Pacific coast.

Jalisco is Mexico's sixth largest state, at 80,836 sq km. Guadalajara lies toward the west end of an agriculturally rich basin that stretches down from the northeast portion of the state.

Michoacán (59,928 sq km) has the real highlands of the region – a big, green sweep above 2000m across the north of the state, strewn with the stumps of living and extinct volcanoes. The cordillera continues west into southern Jalisco and Colima, where rises the Volcán de Fuego de Colima, one of Mexico's most active volcanoes.

Two of the major rivers are the Río Lerma, which flows down from the east along the border of Michoacán and Jalisco and into Lago de Chapala, Mexico's largest lake, south of Guadalajara; and the Río Balsas, which carries almost all the runoff from the southern side of the Cordillera Neovolcánica.

Climate

Warm and dry most of the year, the region has a distinct rainy season from June to September, when some 200mm of rain falls each month in most areas. At lower altitudes, such as Uruapan and around Colima city, temperature and humidity rise and tropical plants abound. Winter nights can get chilly at higher altitudes such as Pátzcuaro.

Population & People

The region is home to about 10% of the nation's people. Well over half of Jalisco's six million or so inhabitants live in the Guadalajara conurbation. Michoacán has about four million people and Colima barely half a million. The population is predominantly *mestizo*, with the 130,000 Purépecha of Michoacán and 60,000 Huichol in northern Jalisco forming the only large indigenous groups.

Guadalajara & Around

The city of Guadalajara itself is the major attraction of inland Jalisco, but Lago de Chapala, 40km south of the city, provides a nice change, with an idyllic climate that has attracted many US and Canadian expatriates.

GUADALAJARA

• pop 1,633,100 • elev 1540m ☎ changing

The second largest city in Mexico, Guadalajara has developed a reputation as the nation's most Mexican city. Its contributions to Mexican life include mariachi music, tequila, the broad-rimmed sombrero hat, *charreadas* (rodeos) and the Mexican Hat Dance.

Guadalajara has many of the attractions of Mexico City – fine museums and galleries, beautiful historic buildings, nightlife, culture, good places to stay and eat – without the capital's problems. It is western Mexico's biggest industrial center, a modern, orderly city where traffic flows fairly freely and pollution is not trapped by mountains. Also, it may be Mexico's most musical city, with many venues and a wide range of musical styles to be heard.

The suburbs of Tlaquepaque and Tonalá, renowned for their arts and crafts, are a must for shoppers. Day trips to Tequila and Lago de Chapala reveal some typical Mexican highlands scenery.

History

Guadalajara was established on its present site only after three settlements elsewhere had failed. In 1532, Nuño de Guzmán and 63 Spanish families founded the first Guadalajara near Nochistlán, in Zacatecas state, naming it after Guzmán's home city in Spain. Water was scarce, the land was hard to farm and the indigenous people were

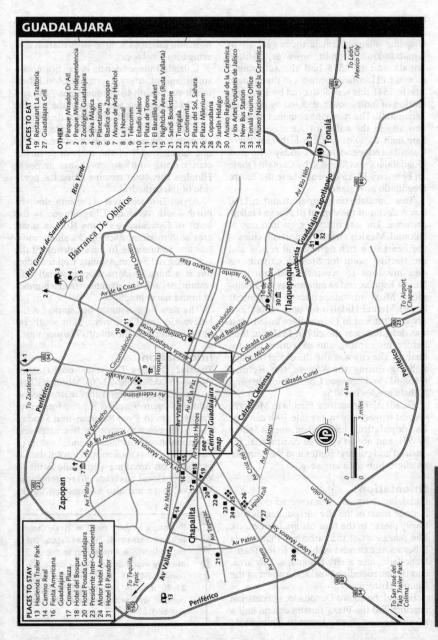

GUADALAJARA

PLACES TO STAY
13 Hacienda Trailer Park
14 Camino Real
16 Fiesta Americana
17 Crowne Plaza
18 Hotel del Bosque
20 Hotel Posada Guadalajara
23 Presidente Inter-Continental
24 Motor Hotel Américas
31 Hotel El Parador

PLACES TO EAT
19 Restaurant La Trattoria
27 Guadalajara Grill

OTHER
1 Parque Mirador Dr Atl
2 Parque Mirador Independencia
3 Zoológica Guadalajara
4 Selva Mágica
5 Planetarium
6 Basílica de Zapopan
7 Museo de Arte Huichol
8 La Normal
9 Telecomm
10 Estadio Jalisco
11 Plaza de Toros
12 El Baratillo Market
15 Nightclub Area (Ruta Vallarta)
21 Sandi Bookstore
22 Tropigala
23 Continental
25 Plaza del Sol, Sahara
26 Plaza Milenium
28 Copacabana
29 Jardín Hidalgo
30 Museo Regional de la Cerámica
   y los Artes Populares de Jalisco
32 New Bus Station
33 Tonalá Tourist Office
34 Museo Nacional de la Cerámica

see Central Guadalajara map

hostile, so in 1533 Captain Juan de Oñate ordered the settlement moved to the pre-Hispanic village of Tonalá, today a suburb of Guadalajara. Guzmán, however, disliked Tonalá and in 1535 had the settlement moved to Tlacotán, northeast of the modern city. In 1541 this was destroyed by a confederation of indigenous tribes led by the chief Tenamaxtli. The surviving colonists picked a new site in the valley of Atemajac beside San Juan de Dios creek, which ran where Calzada Independencia is today. The new Guadalajara was founded by Captain Oñate on February 14, 1542, near where the Teatro Degollado now stands.

This Guadalajara prospered, and in 1560 it was declared the capital of Nueva Galicia province. The city quickly grew into one of colonial Mexico's most important cities – the heart of a rich agricultural region and the starting point for Spanish expeditions and missions to western and northern Nueva España, and as far away as the Philippines. Mexican independence movement leader Miguel Hidalgo set up a revolutionary government in Guadalajara in 1810 but was defeated near the city in 1811, not long before his capture and execution in Chihuahua. The city was also the object of much fighting during the War of the Reform (1858-61) and between Constitutionalist and Villista armies in 1915.

Guadalajara overtook Puebla as Mexico's second biggest city by the late 19th century. Its population has mushroomed since WWII, and now it's a huge commercial, industrial and cultural center and the communications hub for a large region.

Orientation

Guadalajara's giant twin-towered cathedral is at the heart of the city, surrounded by four lovely plazas in the four cardinal directions. The plaza east of the cathedral, Plaza de la Liberación, extends two blocks to the Teatro Degollado, also a city landmark. This area, and the surrounding blocks, is known as the Centro Histórico.

Behind the Teatro Degollado, a pedestrian precinct and the Plaza Tapatía extend half a kilometer east to the Instituto Cultural de Cabañas, another historically significant building. Just south of Plaza Tapatía is Mercado Libertad, a three-story market covering four city blocks.

Calzada Independencia is a major north-south central artery. From Mercado Libertad, it runs south to Parque Agua Azul and the old bus station, and north to the zoo, the Plaza de Toros and the Barranca de Oblatos canyon. Don't confuse Calzada Independencia with Independencia, the east-west street one block north of the cathedral. In the center, north-south streets change names at Hidalgo, the street running along the north side of the cathedral.

About 21 blocks west of the cathedral, the north-south Avenida Chapultepec is the heart of Guadalajara's Zona Rosa, a smart area with modern office blocks, shops and a few fine restaurants. In the southwest of the city, Plaza del Sol on Avenida López Mattes Sur is a huge modern shopping mall with restaurants and entertainment, and a number of brand-name hotels.

The new long-distance bus station is the Nueva Central Camionera, 9km southeast of the center past the suburb Tlaquepaque.

Information

Tourist Offices The state tourist office (☎ 668-16-00, 800-362-22-00), Morelos 102, is in Plaza Tapatía behind the Teatro Degollado. It's open 9 am to 8 pm Monday to Friday, 9 am to 1 pm Saturday and Sunday. This is the place to come for free maps and information on Guadalajara and the state of Jalisco. English is spoken, and information is available on anything you could want to know, from local bus routes to retirement in Mexico. There are also information kiosks

Beginning at some point in 2000, there will be no area code in Guadalajara. The old code ☎ 3 will be added to the start of every local number (for example, the number 845-21-20 will become 3845-21-20; if calling from long distance, the number will be the same as the local number).

scattered around the central area, and an information desk in the Palacio de Gobierno, facing the Plaza de Armas just south of the cathedral, open 9 am to 3 pm and (generally) 4 to 8 pm Monday to Friday, 9 am to 1 pm Saturday.

Consulates More than 30 countries have consular offices in Guadalajara (some of these are listed in 'Embassies & Consulates in Mexico' in the Facts for the Visitor chapter). The tourist office has a complete list, or you can contact the Consular Association (☎ 616-06-29) for information.

Money Banks are plentiful in Guadalajara and are open for currency exchange and other services from about 9 am to 5 pm Monday through Friday and 9 am to 1 pm Saturday. Many have ATMs. *Casas de cambio* on López Cotilla, in the three blocks between Corona and Molina, offer competitive exchange rates, quicker service and sometimes longer hours.

The American Express office (☎ 818-23-19), Avenida Vallarta 2440, is in the small Plaza Los Arcos shopping center. It's open 9 am to 6 pm Monday to Friday and 9 am to 1 pm Saturday, but issues traveler's checks only 9 am to 2 pm and 4 to 4.30 pm. Banamex is one of the few banks that will change traveler's checks issued in Canadian dollars.

Post & Communications The main post office is located on Carranza, between Juan Manuel and Independencia. It's open 8 am to 6 pm Monday through Friday, 9 am to 1 pm Saturday.

The Telecomm office, with telegram, telex and fax services, is nine blocks north of the center, in the Palacio Federal on Alcalde at Calle Hospital, opposite the Santuario church. It's open 9 am to 7 pm Monday to Friday, 9 am to noon Saturday. There's a post office branch there too.

Computel, with long-distance telephone and fax services, has several offices around the city. There's one on Corona, in a shopping center opposite the Hotel Fénix. Another is at 16 de Septiembre 599.

Several places around the central area offer Internet access for around US$2.50 per hour – CCCP Internet, upstairs on Avenida Alcada, at Juan Manuel, is open around 9 am to 9 pm daily; Cybercafe and CMC, both on Parque Revolución, 10 blocks west of the center, are open about 10 am to 10 pm daily.

Bookstores A fair selection of books and magazines in English is available in the gift shops of most major hotels and at many of the larger bookstores. Sandi Bookstore (☎ 121-42-10), Avenida Tepeyac 718, about 1km west of Avenida López Mattes, has a good travel section. Many of the newsstands in central Guadalajara sell English-language periodicals.

Newspapers & Magazines *The Guadalajara Colony Reporter* is a daily English-language newspaper covering Guadalajara and has lots of information about cultural events in the city. The Spanish-language *Público* also covers Guadalajara on a daily basis. *Ocio* is an insert in Friday's edition, containing information on cultural activities in Guadalajara for the coming week – it's *the* place to look for movie listings and information on exhibits and the club scene.

Let's Enjoy, a free monthly bilingual magazine, contains features on Jalisco's people and places and often can be found at the tourist office. *Guadalajara Weekly* is a free, but not very informative, newsletter for visitors, available at the tourist office and some hotels.

If you're thinking of retiring here, get a copy of *Retiring in Guadalajara* (☎ 121-23-48), Aptdo 5-409 7S, Guadalajara.

Laundry There's a laundry at Aldama 125, open 9 am to 8 pm Monday to Saturday. Drop your stuff off and return for it 2 hours later; it'll be waiting, clean and folded, in the same sack you brought it in. They charge about US$3 for a machine load.

Cathedral

Surrounded on all four sides by plazas, Guadalajara's twin-towered *catedral* is the city's most famous symbol and most conspicuous landmark. Begun in 1558 and

CENTRAL GUADALAJARA

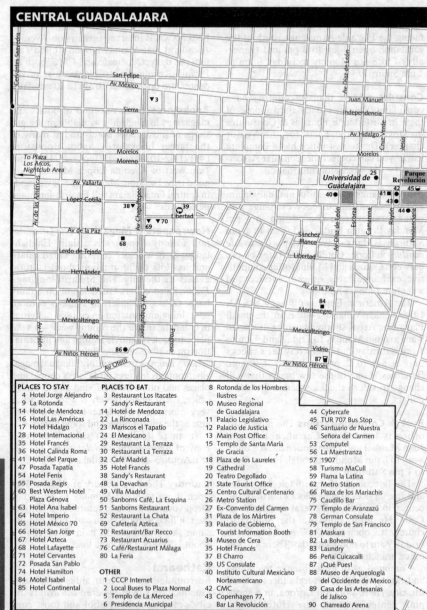

PLACES TO STAY
4 Hotel Jorge Alejandro
9 La Rotonda
14 Hotel de Mendoza
16 Hotel Las Américas
17 Hotel Hidalgo
28 Hotel Internacional
35 Hotel Francés
36 Hotel Calinda Roma
41 Hotel del Parque
47 Posada Tapatía
54 Hotel Fenix
55 Posada Regis
60 Best Western Hotel
   Plaza Génova
63 Hotel Ana Isabel
64 Hotel Imperio
65 Hotel México 70
66 Hotel San Jorge
67 Hotel Azteca
68 Hotel Lafayette
71 Hotel Cervantes
72 Posada San Pablo
74 Hotel Hamilton
84 Motel Isabel
85 Hotel Continental

PLACES TO EAT
3 Restaurant Los Itacates
7 Sandy's Restaurant
14 Hotel de Mendoza
22 La Rinconada
23 Mariscos el Tapatío
24 El Mexicano
29 Restaurant La Terraza
30 Restaurant La Terraza
32 Café Madrid
35 Hotel Francés
38 Sandy's Restaurant
48 La Devachan
49 Villa Madrid
50 Sanborns Café, La Esquina
51 Sanborns Restaurant
52 Restaurant La Chata
69 Cafetería Azteca
70 Restaurant/Bar Recco
73 Restaurant Acuarius
76 Café/Restaurant Málaga
80 La Feria

OTHER
1 CCCP Internet
2 Local Buses to Plaza Normal
5 Templo de La Merced
6 Presidencia Municipal

8 Rotonda de los Hombres
  Ilustres
10 Museo Regional
   de Guadalajara
11 Palacio Legislativo
12 Palacio de Justicia
13 Main Post Office
15 Templo de Santa María
   de Gracia
18 Plaza de los Laureles
19 Cathedral
20 Teatro Degollado
21 State Tourist Office
25 Centro Cultural Centenario
26 Metro Station
27 Ex-Convento del Carmen
31 Plaza de los Mártires
33 Palacio de Gobierno,
   Tourist Information Booth
34 Museo de Cera
35 Hotel Francés
37 El Charro
39 US Consulate
40 Instituto Cultural Mexicano
   Norteamericano
42 CMC
43 Copenhagen 77,
   Bar La Revolución

44 Cybercafe
45 TUR 707 Bus Stop
46 Santuario de Nuestra
   Señora del Carmen
53 Computel
56 La Maestranza
57 1907
58 Turismo MaCull
59 Flama la Latina
62 Metro Station
75 Plaza de los Mariachis
75 Caudillo Bar
77 Templo de Aranzazú
78 German Consulate
79 Templo de San Francisco
81 Maskara
82 La Bohemia
83 Laundry
86 Peña Cuicacalli
87 ¡Qué Pues!
88 Museo de Arqueología
   del Occidente de Mexico
89 Casa de las Artesanías
   de Jalisco
90 Charreado Arena

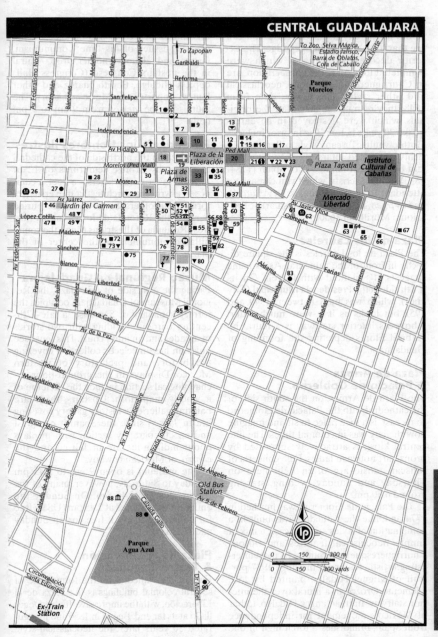

CENTRAL GUADALAJARA

consecrated in 1618, the cathedral is almost as old as the city itself. Up close you can see that it's a stylistic hodgepodge. The exterior decorations, some of which were completed long after the consecration, are in Churrigueresque, baroque, neoclassical and other styles. The towers date from 1848; they're much higher than the originals, which were destroyed in an earthquake 30 years before. The interior includes Gothic vaults, Tuscany-style pillars and 11 richly decorated altars given to Guadalajara by King Fernando VII of Spain (1784-1833). In the sacristy, which you can ask an attendant to open for you, is *La Asunción de la Virgen*, painted by Spanish artist Bartolomé Murillo in 1650.

Plaza de los Laureles

The Plaza de los Laureles is the square directly in front of the cathedral. As its name suggests, it's planted with laurels. On its north side is the **Presidencia Municipal** (City Hall), which was built between 1949 and 1952 but looks as if it were much older. Above its interior stairway is a mural by Gabriel Flores depicting the founding of Guadalajara.

Plaza de Armas & Palacio de Gobierno

The Plaza de Armas, on the south side of the cathedral with the Palacio de Gobierno to its east, is a nice place to sit and imagine how the city was in colonial times. The fine central kiosk is attractively supported by bronze art nouveau ladies. Free concerts of Jaliscan music are often held here on Thursday and Sunday evening, starting around 6.30 pm.

The Palacio de Gobierno was finished in 1774 and, like the cathedral, was built in a combination of styles – in this case, a mix of simple, neoclassical features and riotous Churrigueresque decorations. Its most interesting artistic feature is the huge 1937 portrait of Miguel Hidalgo painted by José Clemente Orozco in a mural over the interior stairway. In it, an angry Hidalgo, father of Mexico's movement for independence from Spain, brandishes a torch high in one

fist while the masses struggle at his feet. In this mural Orozco also comments on the pressing issues of his time: communism, fascism and religion. Another Orozco mural in the upstairs Congreso (Congress Hall) depicts Hidalgo, Benito Juárez and other figures important in Mexican history. The murals can be viewed from 9 am to 9 pm daily.

Rotonda de los Hombres Ilustres

The plaza on the north side of the cathedral is ringed by bronze sculptures of 12 of Jalisco's favorite characters – a poet, a composer, a writer, an architect, a university reformer and others. Six of them are buried beneath the Rotonda de los Hombres Ilustres (Rotunda of Illustrious Men), the round pillared monument in the center of the plaza.

Museo Regional de Guadalajara

Facing the east side of this plaza, the Regional Museum of Guadalajara occupies the former seminary of San José, a late-17th-century baroque building with two stories of arcades and an inner court. This must-see museum has an eclectic collection covering the history and prehistory of western Mexico. Displays in the ground-floor archaeological section include the skeleton of a woolly mammoth. Upstairs, there are painting galleries, a history gallery covering life in Jalisco since the Spanish conquest and an ethnography section with displays about indigenous life in Jalisco and the *charro*, or Mexican cowboy.

The museum is open 9 am to 5.45 pm Tuesday to Saturday; however, many of the rooms close at 2.45 pm. On Sunday the entire museum closes at 2.45 pm (US$2; free for children under 13; free for all Sunday and Tuesday).

Plaza de la Liberación & Teatro Degollado

East of the cathedral on the former site of several colonial buildings is the Plaza de la Liberación, with the impressive Teatro Degollado at its far end. Begun in 1856 and inaugurated 30 years later, the neoclassical-style theater has been reconstructed many times. Over the columns on its front is a frieze depicting Apollo and the Nine Muses. The five-tiered theater's interior is decorated with red velvet and gold and is crowned by a Gerardo Suárez mural based on the fourth canto of Dante's *Divine Comedy*.

Frequent performances are staged in the theater (see Entertainment). It can be visited 10 am to 1 pm Monday to Saturday (free).

On the north side of the Plaza de la Liberación is the **Palacio Legislativo** (State Congress), with massive stone columns in its interior courtyard. On the south side of the Plaza, the new **Museo de Cera** (☎ 825-89-56) is a good place to meet the heroes, leaders and popular figures of Mexico's past and present. They're all here in wax effigy form, along with some international celebrities and the usual chamber of horrors. It opens 11 am to 8.30 pm daily (US$2.20/1.10 for adults/children).

Palacio de Justicia

Across Hidalgo from the Teatro Degollado, the Palacio de Justicia (State Courthouse) was built in 1588 as part of the Convento de Santa María, Guadalajara's first nunnery. A 1965 mural by Guillermo Chávez, depicting Benito Juárez and other legendary Mexican lawmakers, graces the interior stairway.

Also near the theater, at the corner of Hidalgo and Carranza, is the **Templo de Santa María de Gracia**, which served as the city's first cathedral (from 1549 to 1618).

Plaza Tapatía

Just behind the Teatro Degollado, Plaza Tapatía is a modern square and pedestrian mall of shops, restaurants, street performers, fountains and the tourist office. It stretches half a kilometer east to the Instituto Cultural de Cabañas. Calzada Independencia passes underneath it at about its midpoint.

Instituto Cultural de Cabañas

This huge neoclassical gem at the east end of Plaza Tapatía was built between 1805 and 1810 by Spanish architect Manuel Tolsá. Called the Hospicio Cabañas after its founder Bishop Don Juan Cruz Ruiz de Cabañas, it served mainly as an orphanage for over 150 years until 1980, often housing up to 3000 children at a time. It has also served as an insane asylum, a military barracks and a jail.

Between 1936 and 1939 José Clemente Orozco painted murals in the main chapel. They are widely regarded as his finest works. Most notable is *El Hombre de Fuego* (The Man of Fire) in the dome, which has been the subject of widely varying interpretations. Fifty-three other frescoes cover the walls and ceiling of the chapel, which is furnished with benches on which you can lie back and look straight up. A small book in English and Spanish, *The Murals of Orozco in the Cabañas Cultural Institute*, on sale at the main entrance, gives information on the artist and the murals.

The Instituto Cultural de Cabañas is a cultural institute housing a museum, theater and school. All 23 courts and the chapel that Tolsá designed are intact; tours in English and Spanish are available. The museum features a permanent exhibition of more than 100 Orozco drawings and paintings, plus temporary exhibitions of painting, sculpture and engraving. The institute also hosts dance festivals, drama performances and concerts.

The institute is open 10.15 am to 5.45 pm Tuesday to Saturday, 10.15 am to 2.45 pm Sunday (US$1, free on Sunday).

Plaza de los Mariachis

The Plaza de los Mariachis, near the intersection of Avenida Javier Mina and Calzada Independencia Sur, is arguably the birthplace of mariachi music. It's had a facelift recently, and several restaurants have tables out on the plaza, where you can sit, eat and drink while wandering mariachis come and offer music to the customers – for US$5 and up per song. Unfortunately the plaza attracts some unpleasant types after dark, and it's probably unwise to linger after 9 pm.

Mariachis

In many minds no image captures the spirit of Mexico better than that of proud-faced mariachis, in matching garb and broad-rimmed sombreros, belting out traditional Mexican ballads before a festive crowd. But the origin of the word 'mariachi' is something of a mystery.

Some historians contend that 'mariachi' is a corruption of the French word *mariage* (marriage) and that the name stems from the time of the French intervention in 1861-67. Mariachi bands were said to have played at wedding ceremonies during that period, hence the name.

Others say that the word was in use before the French arrived and that it had arisen from festivals honoring the Virgin Mary at which musicians performed. They note that the mariachi is indigenous to the region south of Guadalajara, probably derived from the name María with the Náhuatl diminutive '-chi' tacked on.

Still others point out that in the 1870s a Mexican poet designated as *mariache* the stage upon which dancers and musicians performed *jarabes*. A jarabe consisted of an ensemble that played and sang while a couple – a man attired as a Mexican cowboy in chaps and a wide-rimmed hat and a woman in a handwoven shawl and full, brightly colored skirt – danced beside them.

Today's mariachi bands are of two types. The original version consists of musicians who play only string instruments and who limit their repertoire to traditional Jalisco melodies. The modern, more commercial mariachi band's main instrument is the trumpet, and they have quite a broad repertoire. Both types can be heard in Guadalajara's Plaza de los Mariachis, and at indoor venues devoted to mariachi music.

Colonial Churches

Besides the cathedral and the Templo de Santa María de Gracia, there are 13 other churches in central Guadalajara, some quite impressive. The baroque **Templo de La Merced**, near the cathedral on the corner of Hidalgo and Loza, was built in 1650; inside are several fine large paintings, crystal chandeliers and lots of gold decoration.

The **Santuario de Nuestra Señora del Carmen**, facing the small plaza on the corner of Juárez and 8 de Julio, is another lovely church, with lots of gold decoration, old paintings and murals in the dome.

On the corner of 16 de Septiembre and Blanco, the **Templo de Aranzazú**, built from 1749 to 1752, has three ornate Churrigueresque golden altars. Beside it is the older, less showy **Templo de San Francisco**, built two centuries earlier.

Parque Agua Azul

About 20 blocks south of the center, near the south end of Calzada Independencia Sur, Parque Agua Azul is a large verdant park offering pleasant relief from the city hubbub. It features an orchid house, butterfly house, aviary and children's playground. Orchids are best in October, November, April and May. The park is open 10 am to 6 pm Tuesday to Sunday (US$0.50 for adults, US$0.25 for children). Bus No 60 or 62 heading south on Calzada Independencia will bring you there from the city center.

The **Casa de las Artesanías de Jalisco** is on the north side of the park, but has its own separate entrance on Calzada. It displays handicrafts and arts from all over Jalisco, and everything is for sale. Prices are high, but the quality can't be beaten. It's open 10 am to 6 pm Monday to Friday, 11 am to 3 pm Saturday and 11 am to 2 pm Sunday (free).

The small collection of the **Museo de Arqueología del Occidente de México**, on Calzada Independencia Sur opposite the entrance to the park, includes some pre-Hispanic figurines and artifacts from Jalisco and the states of Nayarit and Colima. It's open 10 am to 2 pm and 4 to 7 pm daily (US$0.40).

Universidad de Guadalajara

West of the center, where Juárez meets Federalismo, is another shady park, **Parque Revolución**. Three blocks farther west at Juárez 975 is one of the main buildings of the University of Guadalajara. Inside, the **Paraninfo** (Theater Hall) contains large, powerful murals by Orozco on the stage backdrop and dome.

Zoológico Guadalajara, Selva Mágica & Planetario

The zoo, the Selva Mágica amusement park and the planetarium are near one another just off Calzada Independencia Norte on the northern outskirts of the city. Bus Nos 60 and 62 (marked 'Zoológico'), heading north on Calzada Independencia, will drop you at the entrance monument. From there, it's a 10-minute walk to the actual entrances to the three sites.

The Zoológico Guadalajara (☎ 674-42-30) is a large, older zoo with two pyramid-shaped aviaries, a snake house, a children's petting zoo and a train that will take you around if you don't feel like walking. From the north end of the site there's a view of Barranca de Oblatos canyon. The zoo is open 10 am to 7 pm Wednesday through Sunday, and on holidays on Monday and Tuesday (US$2.50, US$1.25 for children).

Beside the zoo is Selva Mágica (☎ 674-01-38), a children's amusement park with mechanical rides, a dolphin and seal show, and a trained bird show. It's open 10 am to 8 pm daily (US$3.25 for adults or children; animal shows are US$0.75 extra).

About a five-minute walk from the zoo is the planetarium at the Centro de Ciencia y Tecnología (☎ 674-41-06). It has exhibits on astronomy, space, airplanes, the body and other science-related topics. Planetarium shows are held hourly from 10.30 am. The center is open 9 am to 6 pm Tuesday to Sunday (US$0.25, plus an extra US$0.40 for the planetarium show).

Barranca de Oblatos & Cascada Cola de Caballo

You can see the 670m-deep Barranca de Oblatos canyon from the zoo. Otherwise, take bus No 60 north on Calzada Independencia to Parque Mirador Independencia, a little past the entrance to the zoo. The park is always open.

In the canyon, the Cola de Caballo (Horse Tail) waterfall flows all year but is most impressive during the rainy season. For a view of the falls, take a local bus from the center north on Alcalde about 10 blocks, to Plaza Normal shopping center. From there get an Ixcatan bus, and ask to be let off at Parque Mirador Dr Atl.

Zapopan

About 8km from downtown, on the northwestern edge of Guadalajara, the suburb of Zapopan (population 850,300) was a village before the Spanish arrived, and an important maize-producing village in colonial times. Its main attractions are its basilica and the Huichol museum.

The Zapopan tourist office (☎ 818-22-00) is upstairs in the Casa de la Cultura, a block west of the basilica, at Guerrero 233. Staff give out maps of Zapopan and leaflets, in Spanish, detailing places of interest in and around the suburb. It's open 9 am to 8 pm Monday to Friday, 9 am to 1 pm Saturday.

The large **Basílica de Zapopan**, built in 1730, is home to Nuestra Señora de Zapopan (Virgin of Zapopan), a tiny statue visited by pilgrims from near and far. On October 12, during Guadalajara's Fiestas de Octubre, the statue, which has been visiting other churches in Jalisco before reaching Guadalajara, is taken from Guadalajara's cathedral and returned to its home in Zapopan amid throngs of people and much merrymaking. The statue receives a new car each year for the procession, but the engine is never turned on; instead, the car is hauled along by ropes.

To the right of the basilica entrance, the small **Museo de Arte Huichol** (☎ 636-44-30) exhibits many colorful yarn paintings and other fine examples of Huichol arts and crafts. Most of the items on display are for sale. It's open 10 am to 2 pm and 4 to 6 pm Monday to Friday, 10 am to 2 pm Saturday and Sunday (US$0.60).

Regular buses Nos 275, or TUR bus 706 heading north on 16 de Septiembre or Alcalde stop beside the basilica; the trip takes 20 minutes.

Tlaquepaque

Approximately 7km southeast of downtown Guadalajara, Tlaquepaque ('tlah-keh-PAH-keh'; population 434,700) also used to be a separate village, with an initial population of potters swelled by Guadalajara gentry who built mansions here in the 19th century. More recently Tlaquepaque's many artisans decided to capitalize on their talents by cleaning up the central Jardín Hidalgo, and renaming many of the shops (formerly large country homes) 'galleries' to attract tourists. Fortunately, the throngs of crafts-hungry gringos who have descended on the place have not spoiled the refurbishment of central Tlaquepaque.

Many flowers, small benches and monuments grace the plaza. The shops are full of ceramics, papier-mâché animals, bronze figures, handmade glassware, embroidered clothing and other items from all over Mexico. Many shops are closed on Sunday. The Tlaquepaque tourist office (☎ 635-57-56), Prieto 80, next to the post office, is open 9 am to 9 pm, Monday to Friday.

Visit the **Museo Regional de la Cerámica y los Artes Populares de Jalisco**, at Independencia 237, to get an idea of the best handicrafts available in Tlaquepaque. It's open 10 am to 6 pm Tuesday to Saturday, 10 am to 1 pm Sunday (free). Also visit the **glass factory** opposite the museum. There are some good restaurants, many attached to Tlaquepaque's 'galleries,' serving up tasty Mexican food and offering live music – see Places to Eat.

To get to Tlaquepaque, take local bus Nos 275, 275A or 275B, or TUR bus 706, heading south on 16 de Septiembre. The trip takes about 30 minutes. After turning off Avenida Revolución, watch for a brick pedestrian bridge then a small traffic circle. Get off here and on the left is Independencia, which will take you to the heart of Tlaquepaque.

Tonalá

The suburb of Tonalá (population 272,000), beyond Tlaquepaque, about 13km southeast of the center, is the poorer, less touristic relative of Tlaquepaque. The shops here call themselves factories, not galleries – an accurate description considering that many of them manufacture the glassware and ceramics found in Tlaquepaque and in other parts of Guadalajara. On Thursday and Sunday most of the town becomes a street market that takes hours to explore. The best crafts are to be found in the factories, but you can pick up some bargains at the market. Tonalá has several old churches of interest and holds a charreada after 4 pm Saturday.

The Tonalá tourist office (☎ 683-00-47), at Tonaltecas 140 in the Casa de Artesanos, gives out maps and information in Spanish, from 9 am to 8 pm Monday to Friday, 9 am to 1 pm Saturday.

The **Museo Nacional de la Cerámica** (☎ 635-54-04), Constitución 110, houses an eclectic array of pots from all over Mexico. It's open 10 am to 5 pm Tuesday through Sunday (free).

Local buses No 275, 275A or 275B, or TUR buses 706 or 707, heading south on 16 de Septiembre, will take you to Tonalá, passing through Tlaquepaque on the way. The trip takes 45 minutes. As you enter Tonalá, get off on the corner of Avenidas Tonalá and Tonaltecas, and walk six blocks north on Tonaltecas to the tourist office and about five blocks east to the Plaza Principal.

Courses

A number of language and cultural courses are available, the most established being with the Universidad de Guadalajara, the second largest university in Mexico, with over 180,000 students. Its CEPE (Centro de Estudios para Extranjeros, Foreign Student Studies Center) offers 10 levels of intensive five-week Spanish-language courses. It also offers courses in history, culture, politics, economics, literature and other subjects, all taught in Spanish, which can be taken in addition to, or independently of, the language courses. Workshops in folkloric dance, guitar and singing, Mexican cuisine and so forth are also offered, as are special cultural events and excursions to other parts of Mexico.

Registration is US$95, and tuition fees are US$578 for each five-week session of four hours per day Monday to Friday. Lodging and three meals daily can be arranged with local Mexican families at a cost of US$688 for the session. The workshops and excursions are an optional expense.

For more information and an application, contact CEPE (☎ 616-43-99, fax 616-40-13), Universidad de Guadalajara, Apartado Postal 1-1362, Guadalajara, Jalisco 44100, Mexico. Look for the CEPE website at www.cepe.udg.mx.

The Universidad Autónoma de Guadalajara also has an international program – for information, see www.uag.mx. The University of Arizona (☎ 520-621-4729 in the USA) offers a summer program in Guadalajara. Write to Guadalajara Summer School, University of Arizona, PO Box 40966, Tucson, AZ 85717. Another option is the Vancouver Language Center (☎ 826-09-44, vlc@vec.bc.ca), Avenida Vallarta 1151, which is affiliated with a Canadian university.

Organized Tours

Panoramex (☎ 810-51-09), Federalismo Sur 944, offers numerous tours with English-, French- and Spanish-speaking guides. They also can be booked at the tourist office. Standard offerings include:

Tour No 1 (Monday to Saturday) takes 5 hours and visits some of the main sights of Guadalajara and Tlaquepaque (US$10)

Tour No 2 (Tuesday, Thursday, Saturday and Sunday) is a 6-hour tour visiting Chapala and Ajijic (US$12)

Tour No 3 (Monday, Wednesday, Friday) is a 5-hour trip to the town of Tequila and the agave fields, and includes a visit to a tequila distillery (US$13)

During holiday periods (Easter, mid-July to late August, and the second half of December), the tourist office runs free guided walking tours (mostly in Spanish) of the Centro Histórico. They start at 9.30 am at the Plaza de Armas, and take about three hours; book at the tourist office the day before.

Special Events

Several major festivals are celebrated in Guadalajara and its suburbs. They include:

Feria de Tonalá – annual handicrafts fair in Tonalá, specializing in ceramics; the week before and the week after Semana Santa

Fiestas de Tlaquepaque – Tlaquepaque's annual fiesta and handicrafts fair; mid-June to the first week of July

Fiesta Internacional del Mariachi – mariachis come from everywhere to hear, play and celebrate the latest mariachi sounds; late August

Fiestas de Octubre – beginning with a parade on the first Sunday in October, the October Fiestas, lasting all month, are Guadalajara's principal annual fair. There's free entertainment from noon to 10 pm daily in the fairgrounds at the Benito Juárez auditorium plus, around the city, livestock shows, art and other exhibitions and sporting and cultural events. On October 12 a religious element enters the festivities with a procession from the cathedral to Zapopan carrying the miniature statue of the Virgin of Zapopan (see Zapopan, earlier)

Feria Internacional del Libro – one of the biggest book promotions in Latin America; last week of November and first week of December

Places to Stay – Budget

Camping Guadalajara has two trailer parks, both offering full hookups and spaces for tents, trailers and motor homes.

San José del Tajo trailer park (☎ 686-17-38, Lopez Mattes Sur 45560) is southwest of the city center at Km 15 on highway 54/80, the start of the Colima road. Facilities include pool, tennis court, laundry and 210 sites. Sites with hookups cost US$15 for two (extra persons US$2); tent sites are a little cheaper. English is spoken.

Hacienda Trailer Park (☎ 627-17-24, *Circunvalación Poniente 66, Ciudad Granja*) is 10km west of the city center, between Avenida Vallarta and the Periférico. Facilities include pool, laundry and plenty of trees. The communal 'club house' has a barbecue and pool and ping-pong tables. Sites with hookups cost US$14 for two people – the same for small tents and large motor homes.

Centro Histórico A number of the central hotels were quoting high-season prices at the time of research, but most of the year they should discount their rates back to budget levels.

One place in no danger of mid-range status is the popular *Hotel Hamilton* (☎ 614-67-26, *Madero 381*), which offers simple small rooms, clean and generally quiet, at US$5.50/6.50 single/double, US$7.75 for two people with two beds. All rooms have private bath and 24-hour hot water, and a color TV is available for a couple of dollars more. If you stay five or more nights and pay in advance, the rate is slightly lower.

A block west, the *Posada San Pablo* (☎ 614-28-11, *Madero 429*) is a friendly, family-run hotel. It doesn't look like a hotel and there's no sign – just ring the bell at the front door. Its 10 rooms ring an open courtyard. Hot water is usually available. The cheapest rooms, around US$7/8, have shared bathrooms. Three rooms have private bath and cost from US$10/11, or US$13 with two big beds.

Two blocks east of the Teatro Degollado, *Hotel Hidalgo* (☎ 613-50-67, *Hidalgo 14*) has plain but clean rooms, no mod-cons but cheap prices – from US$5.50 for one or two people in a double bed.

The *Hotel Las Américas* (☎ 613-96-22, *Hidalgo 76*), near Plaza Tapatía, has a central but unattractive location, though facilities are good for the price. The 49 rooms are clean and fairly modern, with TV, phone,

carpeting, 24-hour hot water and large windows. Rates are US$11/12 and US$15.50 for a double with two beds. Rooms on the street side are noisy.

Another good value is *Posada Tapatía* (☎ 614-91-46, *López Cotilla 619*), which has a bright, cheerful decor (though some travelers find the management less than cheerful). The 12 rooms with high ceilings and large bathrooms open onto a covered central courtyard with lots of plants. Rates are US$13/18.

The pleasant, friendly *Posada Regis* (☎ 614-86-33, *Corona 171*) is in the upstairs of a converted 19th-century French-style mansion with high ceilings and ornate details. The 19 original rooms open onto a covered patio and are a great value at US$15/18, with bath, phone and 24-hour hot water.

Near Mercado Libertad A number of budget hotels are along Avenida Javier Mina, east of Mercado Libertad and the Plaza de los Mariachis. This part of town is not quite as pleasant or safe as the center, but you can find a cheap room here when every other place is full.

The best of the cheapies is *Hotel Ana Isabel* (☎ 617-79-20, *Javier Mina 164*), opposite the Mercado Libertad. It has 50 clean rooms lined up along three floors of walkways draped with plants. Rooms have TV, private bath and ceiling fan for US$10/12 single/double. Hot water is always available, and there's off-street parking.

Hotel México 70 (☎ 617-99-78, *Javier Mina 230*) has 80 clean rooms with private bath, at US$10/10.50. The bigger rooms have two or more beds, 24-hour hot water, TV and decent mattresses.

Also along here, *Hotel Imperio* (☎ 617-50-42, *Javier Mina 180*) and *Hotel San Jorge* (☎ 617-97-79), *Javier Mina 284*), both offer rooms at around US$10.

Hotel Azteca (☎ 617-74-65, *Javier Mina 311*) is better and more modern, with 70 clean rooms on five floors around an interior well, all with good plumbing, phone, TV and ceiling fan. There's a restaurant and parking too. If you don't mind the rough neighborhood, it's a great value at US$15 for one or two people.

Places to Stay – Mid-Range

Centro Histórico Seven blocks west of the cathedral, *Hotel Jorge Alejandro* (☎ 613-19-14, Hidalgo 656) is a former convent and, fittingly, has a large blue cross on the wall behind every bed in its 28 clean rooms. There's plenty of hot water, and every room has a TV, fan and private bath. Singles/doubles are US$16.50/21.

About 10 blocks west of the center, and easily reached by bus or trolley, the attractive *Hotel del Parque* (☎ 825-28-00, Juárez 845) is near the Parque Revolución. It has a pleasant restaurant, a lobby bar, and sidewalk café tables. The 81 rooms come in two price categories: US$31/39 for quite good rooms with shower, TV and phone; US$44 for even better rooms which also have bathtub, minibar and alarm clock. If you want to be very comfortable, the better rooms here are a sound choice.

More central but with less style, *Hotel Internacional* (☎ 613-03-30, Moreno 570) has 120 carpeted rooms, with TV, air-con and phone – all at US$33/39. It's OK for the price, but only just. A much more appealing, old-style place is *La Rotonda* (☎ 614-10-17, Liceo 130), at US$38/46.

About seven blocks south of the cathedral, the *Hotel Continental* (☎ 614-11-17, Corona 450) has parking and 124 fairly clean, comfortable, 1960s-style rooms. The carpets are worn, the phones are antique, but the TVs have cable. It's OK for US$18/23.

More expensive but infinitely more elegant is the historic *Hotel Francés* (☎ 613-11-90, Maestranza 35), the oldest hotel in Guadalajara. It was founded in 1610 as an inn, with rooms upstairs and horses kept in the arched stone courtyard, which is now a classy lobby bar. The 52 stylish rooms of varying sizes start at US$38 for a single or double, while the eight suites go for US$41 to US$51. All of the rooms have tiled floors, satellite TV and fan; some have bathtub and shower. The exterior rooms have French doors opening onto small wrought-iron balconies. For more details, check the hotel's website www.hotelfrances.com.

A swish, modern alternative is *Hotel Cervantes* (☎ 613-68-46, Sánchez 442), with five floors, 100 elegant rooms, and all the amenities. There's underground parking, a 2nd-floor pool, and a phone beside every bathtub. Rates are a very agreeable US$41/50.

Near the New Bus Station The *Hotel El Parador* (☎ 600-09-10), just across from *módulo* 1 at the Nueva Central Camionera, has 377 clean, functional rooms with color TV at US$22.50 for singles or doubles. There are two reception areas (head for the one on the right under the 'hotel' sign) and two swimming pools (at least one might be usable). If you come into town late, consider spending the night here and finding a more central place in the morning.

West of the Center Avenida López Mattes is Guadalajara's 'motel row.' A good place is the *Hotel del Bosque* (☎ 621-46-50, López Mattes Sur 265, hbosque@vianet.com.mx). It has an interior garden, swimming pool, restaurant and bar, and all 74 rooms have satellite TV. Singles and doubles are US$43 with one twin bed and one single, and US$50 with two twin beds, more carpet and more space.

In unashamedly US motel style, *Motor Hotel Américas* (☎ 631-44-15, López Mattes Sur 2400), opposite the Plaza del Sol mall, is a four-star motel with swimming pool, air-con and other amenities. Most of the 101 rooms cost US$36/41 for singles/doubles; some have a kitchen and cost a few dollars more. There are plenty of other motels near the Plaza del Sol. Bus No 258 heading west on San Felipe will bring you here from the center.

Another fine motel, cheaper and closer to the center, is the *Motel Isabel* (☎ 826-26-30, Montenegro 1572), one block from Avenida de la Paz and eight blocks nearer the center from Avenida Chapultepec. It has 50 rooms for US$37/40 with phone and firm beds, and a pool, restaurant and parking.

Places to Stay – Top End

The *Hotel de Mendoza* (☎ 613-46-46, Carranza 16), on the north side of the Teatro Degollado, was built as the convent to the church of Santa María de Gracia, which is still standing at one side. The convent has been beautifully refurbished, and today is a classy four-star hotel with 104 modern rooms and all the amenities – satellite TV, air-con, restaurant, bar, pool and parking. Some rooms have bathtubs and private balconies. Singles/doubles cost US$77/90, suites up to US$117.

Very centrally located **Hotel Calinda Roma** (☎ 614-86-50), Juárez 170) has a rooftop pool and 172 rooms at US$64. A few blocks farther south, **Hotel Aranzazú** (☎ 613-32-32, Revolución 110) comprises two high-rise towers housing over 500 very comfortable rooms, with Cinemax TV, phone, minibar and air-con, at US$72 a single or double.

Best Western Hotel Plaza Génova (☎ 613-75-00, Juárez 123) offers air-conditioned rooms with phone, cable TV and minibar for US$73 for a single or double, including American breakfast. Facilities include car parking, a gym and a travel agency in the lobby.

Hotel Fénix (☎ 614-57-14, 800-361-11-00, Corona 160) charges US$78 for big, bright, pleasant rooms for one or two people – exterior ones have balconies. It's well set up for business travelers.

The lovely **Hotel Lafayette** (☎ 615-02-52, fax 630-11-12, Avenida de la Paz 2055) in the Zona Rosa just west of Avenida Chapultepec, has a pool, an attractive café and 181 rooms with carpeting, color TV and air-con at US$74/85.

Hotel Posada Guadalajara (☎ 121-20-22, López Mattes Sur 1280) has a popular bar and restaurant and 170 modern rooms on six floors. In cute Mexican style, all rooms flank an open courtyard, which has a swimming pool in the center. Rates are US$57/63.

Guadalajara has its quota of upscale chain hotels, including the **Fiesta Americana Guadalajara** (☎ 825-34-34, Aceves 225), near the Fuente Minerva, at US$154; the **Crowne Plaza** (☎ 634-10-34, López Mattes Sur 2500, crowngdl@acnet.net), from US$170 per room; and the **Presidente Inter-Continental** (☎ 678-12-34, fax 678-12-12), at López Mattes Sur at Moctezuma, at US$221 per room. A little farther out from the center, the **Camino Real** (☎ 634-24-24, 121-80-00, Vallarta 5005, creal@mpsnet.com.mx) has about the most luxurious ambiance, at US$188/200.

Places to Eat

Centro Histórico The Mercado Libertad, just east of the center, has scores of **food stalls**, serving maybe the cheapest eats you'll find in town. Sensitive stomachs beware: the hygiene here is not ideal.

The pedestrian zone around the tourist office has several good eateries, enjoyed by locals as well as visitors. The classy **La Rinconada** is a tasteful covered courtyard where Mexican and US breakfasts cost about US$3, and at lunchtime well prepared salads (US$3), chicken (US$6) or beef dishes (US$5 to US$9) will do you nicely. A few steps to the east, **Mariscos el Tapatío** is a clean, bright place serving up fresh seafood cocktails (from US$4), prawns (US$5.50), fish dishes (around US$4), and ceviche (seafood cocktail, US$2.50). Fill up on inexpensive Mexican food at nearby **El Mexicano**. The walls of this festive, gym-size eatery are lined with photos of revolutionary figures and murals depicting village life. It's not low-fat cooking, but the food is tasty and the prices are right on: breakfasts US$2 or less, comida corrida US$2.80, meat plates about US$3. Live music plays most nights from 6 to 10 pm.

Sandy's Restaurant is upstairs on the corner of Alcalde and Independencia, beside the Rotonda de los Hombres Ilustres. Its US$2.75 buffet breakfasts and great-value set lunches attract local shoppers and office workers.

Restaurant La Chata (Corona 126) has been cooking quality Mexican food for over 50 years. Their specialty is a platillo jaliscience – a quarter chicken, potatoes, a sope, an enchilada and a flauta, all for US$4.20. Enchiladas and chiles rellenos go for less than US$4. The mole sauce and pozole are excellent. Locals stand in line to eat here, though some readers have been disappointed. Find out for yourself, from 8 am to midnight daily.

Another Guadalajara favorite is the *Café Madrid (Juárez 264)*, near the corner of Corona. The Madrid serves good, mid-priced food (nothing over US$4) and excellent coffee from 8 am to 10 pm daily. Smiling waiters in white coats and black bow ties offer brisk, efficient service. Fifties-style decor looks like a US diner, and a huge window opens onto the street.

Restaurant La Terraza, upstairs at the corner of Morelos and Galeana, just off the Plaza de los Laureles, is another popular spot. It serves economical meals, with meat and chicken around US$3.50, burgers US$2.50. A second *La Terraza (Juárez 442)*, near Ocampo, serves only *antojitos*, snacks and beers, and attracts a festive crowd.

The *Sanborns Café (Juárez 305)*, on the corner of 16 de Septiembre, is pricey but popular with locals, and super clean. Directly above Sanborns Café, *La Esquina* offers a large selection of dishes from the US and Mexico, with antojitos and burgers under US$4, steaks around US$7. The balcony tables are delightful for eating and people-watching. *Sanborns Restaurant*, upstairs on the opposite corner, has the usual high standards of Sanborns quality and service.

The spacious *Café/Restaurant Málaga (16 de Septiembre 210)*, 2½ blocks south, is a reasonably priced place with all main dishes under US$6, various salads and enchiladas around US$3, and breakfasts starting at US$2. It's open 7 am to 10 pm daily – sometimes it's packed, and other times empty.

La Feria (Corona 291) is a huge restaurant-bar-music venue in a former mansion. Three levels are filled with comfortable leather chairs and leather-covered tables. The food is decent (no menu item tops US$10), but the main attraction is the live mariachi music (see Entertainment).

All the fancy hotels have classy restaurants. The ones at Hotel Francés and Hotel de Mendoza are magnificent old dining rooms, beautifully done out.

Vegetarian The *Villa Madrid (López Cotilla 223)* is not an exclusively vegetarian restaurant, but its tasty meals include vegetarian options like soy burgers, salad and

fries (US$3) and salads with cottage cheese or soya (US$4). The chicken burritos with mole and the yogurt with fruit are superb. It's open noon to 9 pm daily.

For a great value vegetarian comida corrida (US$2), try *La Devachan (López Cotilla 570)*. The courtyard eating area is delightful, and the Saturday buffet is very popular (open until 6 pm, closed Sunday).

Friendly *Restaurant Acuarius (Sánchez 416)* is a combined vegetarian restaurant and health food store, popular for its filling comida corrida (US$3). They also serve soy-based meals, fresh vegetable juices and yogurt with fruit; it's open 9.30 am to 6 pm daily except Sunday.

Near Avenida Chapultepec Guadalajara's Zona Rosa is basically the few blocks of Avenida Chapultepec north and south of Avenida Vallarta. It's not exactly a full-on nightlife and entertainment district, but it does have some pleasant restaurants on quiet streets. From the city center, catch the 'Par Vial' bus heading west on Independencia and get off at Chapultepec and Vallarta (about 10 minutes).

A block south of Vallarta there's a *Sandy's Restaurant* on the corner of López Cotilla – like the one in the center, it's a reliable place where shoppers and office workers get breakfast and lunch.

Restaurant/Bar Recco (Libertad 1981), just east of Chapultepec two blocks south of Vallarta, is a classy European-style restaurant serving classic Italian dishes for US$6 to US$10. It's open 1 to 11.45 pm Monday to Saturday, 1 to 10 pm Sunday.

A few doors away, at the corner of Libertad and Chapultepec, *Cafetería Azteca* serves up sandwiches, burgers, tacos and meat dishes for US$5 or less, indoors and outdoors. This is a breezy place that lends itself to long chats and letter writing. It's open 8 am to 11.30 pm daily.

Restaurant Los Itacates (Chapultepec 110), 4½ blocks north of Vallarta, is an unassuming eatery specializing in traditional food at surprisingly low prices. A quarter *pollo adobado* with two cheese enchiladas, potatoes, rice and tortillas is only US$3. There are tacos with 19 fillings to choose from at US$1 each, and meat dishes for around US$4. It's open 8 am to 11 pm Monday to Saturday, 8 am to 7 pm Sunday.

Near Avenida López Mattes About 15 blocks west of Avenida Chapultepec, López Mattes is the *avenida* of upmarket hotels, shopping centers and of course restaurants. Bus No 258 from San Felipe in the center runs along López Mattes to, or near, all these restaurants (a 30-minute trip).

Restaurant La Trattoria (☎ 122-18-17, *Niños Héroes 3051*), a block east of López Mattes Sur, is one of the top Italian restaurants in Guadalajara, and not overly pricey. Superbly prepared main courses include a selection of pastas (around US$4), chicken breast with white wine or *pomodoro* sauce (US$6), and *scaloppini* or *saltimbocca* (US$7). It's open 1 pm to midnight daily.

One of several US-style steak bars in the area is *Guadalajara Grill* (☎ 631-56-22, *López Mattes Sur 3711*), at Conchita about a kilometer south of the Plaza del Sol. It's a large, fun place with a lively atmosphere, good music and dancing in the bar. Steak, shrimp and red snapper are US$7, chicken US$5. It's open 1.30 pm to 1 am Monday to Saturday, 1.30 to 6 pm Sunday.

Tlaquepaque Southeast of Tlaquepaque's main plaza Jardín Hidalgo, *El Parián* is a block of little restaurant-bars around an enclosed courtyard full of chairs and tables. It's best on weekends when it's crowded with people eating inexpensive antojitos, drinking moderately expensive beer, and enjoying mariachi music.

More expensive, less chaotic restaurants around Tlaquepaque's main plaza and the pedestrian streets offer fine food, outdoor dining and mariachis. They include *El Patio* (*Independencia 186*) and *Restaurant Abajeño* (*Juárez 231*). *Restaurant Sin Nombre* (*Madero 80*), the 'Restaurant with No Name,' is a favorite spot for good food, live music and a garden setting with parrots and peacocks. *Mariscos Progreso* (*Progreso 80*) specializes in seafood, served under the trees.

Entertainment

Guadalajara has something going on to fit any taste, from classic films to some of the best music in Mexico. The city is in love with music of all kinds, and live performers can be heard any night of the week.

Stop by the tourist office to view its weekly schedule of events; the bilingual staff will help you find something to suit your fancy. The Spanish-language daily *Público*, available at newsstands, lists nightly events; its Friday edition contains the glossy insert *Ocio*, with a calendar of events for the upcoming week. The *Occidental* and *Informador*, also Spanish-language dailies, have entertainment listings, as does the weekly booklet *Ciento Uno*.

Drama, dance and music are performed at the *Teatro Degollado* (☎ 658-38-12) and the *Instituto Cultural de Cabañas* (☎ 617-42-48), both downtown, and at the *Ex-Convento del Carmen* (☎ 614-71-84, *Juárez 638*). Free concerts of typical Jaliscan music are held in the Plaza de Armas at 6.30 pm on most Thursdays and Sundays, and on other days as well during holiday seasons.

Instituto Cultural de Cabañas

NEIL SETCHFIELD

Mariachis You should pay your respects to the mariachi tradition in its home city. The Plaza de los Mariachis, just east of the historic center, is a good place to get a taste of it, but it's unwise to linger here after around 9 pm. Most tourists now get their mariachi experience in one of the sanitized (but safe) venues provided for the purpose. *La Feria (Corona 291)* is a good example, a restaurant popular with Mexican and foreign visitors, where you can eat and drink in a lofty ex-mansion, then listen to traditional and modern mariachi music, which plays after 9 pm most nights, and also on Saturday and Sunday afternoon. More popular with locals is *Casa Bariachi* (☎ 616-99-00, *Vallarta 2221*), a barn-like space, brightly decorated, with bar, restaurant, big margaritas and lots of mariachis. Diagonally opposite, *Bariachi Bar (Vallarta 2308)* is a smaller space with snacks, drinks and coffee and quieter mariachis. The *El Parián* quadrangle near Tlaquepaque's main plaza is another mariachi magnet.

Ballet Folklórico From 10 am to noon Sunday, the Ballet Folklórico of the Universidad de Guadalajara stages a grand performance at the Teatro Degollado. Tickets range from US$3.25 in the gallery to US$11 in the *lunetas* (stalls); buy them at the theater ticket office, open 10 am to 1 pm and 4 to 7 pm daily. On Wednesday night you might check out the Ballet Folklórico of the Instituto Cultural de Cabañas, performing at 8.30 pm (US$3).

Music *Peña Cuicacalli* (☎ 825-46-90, *Niños Héroes 1988*), near Avenida Chapultepec, has a full *musica folklórica* program focused on Mexican and Latino folk music, contemporary Latin sounds and light entertainment. Cover is around US$4.50.

Classical music concerts and recitals are held at *Instituto Cultural Mexicano Norteamericano de Jalisco* (☎ 825-58-38, *Díaz de León 300*), and *Centro Cultural Centenario* (☎ 658-17-58, *Cruz Verde 272*).

Bars The historic center has a few bars serving snacks, drinks and sometimes live music. *La Maestranza* (☎ 613-20-85, *Maestranza 179*) is a hip cantina that attracts a mostly straight 20s crowd (men and women) with cheap beer, salty snacks and lively music. Also fun is the bar *1907*, on Madero near Maestranza, where every night a DJ spins a good mix of popular American and Mexican music to a usually festive crowd. For a quiet drink try *La Bohemia*, a civilized cantina a little farther south on Maestranza. Nearby on Degollado, *Flama la Latina* is a typical salsa bar.

A more sedate but stylish option is the Hotel Francés lobby *piano bar (Maestranza 35)*, near the Plaza de la Liberación. It's quite popular with gringos, and worth a look for the architecture alone.

If you head west of the center along Juárez for about 800m, you go through the middle of Parque Revolución. Facing the west side of the park, *Copenhagen 77* is a restaurant that serves good *paella* and (after 9.30 pm) 'gourmet jazz' to an older audience, Monday through Saturday. Next door, the small *Bar La Revolución* hosts live rock from local bands (US$4 cover charge).

¡Qué Pues! (*Niños Héroes 1554*) has live rock and roll Tuesday night. The rest of the week it's just a bar showing rock videos from the US.

Discos & Dance Clubs West of the center, Avenida Juárez becomes Avenida Vallarta, which has a concentration of nightspots. These places attract young, affluent locals who dress to impress – no track shoes or jeans please. *Lado B* (☎ 616-83-23, *Vallarta 2451*) features funky decor and goes from around 10 pm to 3 am Wednesday to Saturday. Even fancier are *La Máquina* (☎ 615-23-25, *Vallarta 1920*) and *La Marcha* (☎ 615-89-99, *Vallarta 2648*). They all have cover charges from US$5 to US$10 for men, but usually half price (or free) for women. If you're young, rich and gorgeous, you'll feel right at home on the 'Ruta Vallarta,' a Wednesday evening promotion offering entry and drinks at several clubs for a single fee of about US$12, with horse-drawn carriage rides in between. It's no surprise that the new *Hard Rock Café* is also on this stretch of Vallarta, and is also proving popular. Taxis between the center and the nightclub strip cost around US$2.

There's another cluster of nightlife venues on López Mattes Sur south of Vallarta, around the Plaza del Sol. (Bus No 258 west on San Felipe goes out to Plaza del Sol. Bus No 707 and TUR bus 707 travel west from the city center on Juárez, south on López Mattes Sur to Plaza del Sol, then back to 16 de Septiembre in the center.) *Tropigala* (☎ 122-59-03, *López Mattes Sur 2011*) is a large, very hip, multilevel club with live popular Mexican music until 3 am Wednesday to Saturday (cover charge around US$5). For salsa, try *Copacabana* (☎ 631-45-43, *López Mattes Sur 5290*), near Las Águilas neighborhood. It's open 8 pm to 3 am Wednesday to Saturday, but doesn't really get hopping before 11 pm (cover about US$4).

Gay & Lesbian Venues Central venues include *Maskara* (☎ 614-81-03, *Maestranza 238*), a colorful bar with discount drink specials, and *Caudillo Bar*, on the corner of Sánchez and Ocampo, which also has cheap drinks, as well as loud music and late hours – until 3 am.

Sahara is a glittery gay disco in Plaza del Sol, open 10 pm to 3 am (US$5 cover) – their drag shows are a scream.

Cinemas Several cinemas show international films and classics. Check *Ocio* or the local newspapers. Some of the best places to catch them are:

Alianza Francesa (☎ 825-55-95) López Cotilla 1199
Cine Charles Chaplin (☎ 641-54-07) López Mattes Norte 873
Cine Cinematógrafo
No 1 (☎ 825-05-14) Vallarta 1102
No 2 (☎ 630-12-08) México 2222
No 3 (☎ 629-47-80) Patria 600
Cine-Teatro Cabañas (☎ 617-42-48) Instituto Cultural de Cabañas

For recent movie releases, the big shopping centers like Plaza del Sol and Plaza Milenium have multi-screen facilities, as does *Cinepolis*, on Vallarta opposite Plaza los Arcos.

Spectator Sports
Charreadas, Bullfights & Cockfights
Charreadas are held at noon most Sundays in the ring (☎ 619-03-15) behind Parque Agua Azul. Charros and *charras* come from all over Jalisco and Mexico to show off their skills.

The bullfighting season is October to March, but fights are not held every Sunday. There will be a couple for sure during the October fiestas; the rest of the season they may be sporadic. Check with the Plaza de Toros Nuevo Progreso (☎ 63799-82) or the tourist office. When bullfights are held, they're at 4 pm Sunday in the Plaza de Toros at the northern end of Calzada Independencia; bus No 60 heading north on Independencia will take you there.

Soccer (Football) *Fútbol* is Guadalajara's favorite sport. The city usually has at least three teams playing in the national primera división: Guadalajara (las Chivas), the second most popular team in the country after América of Mexico City; Atlas (los Zorros); and Universidad Autónoma de Guadalajara (los Tecos). The teams play at stadiums around the city, but the main venue is Estadio Jalisco (☎ 637-05-63), which has hosted several World Cup games. Contact the stadium or the tourist office for information about forthcoming matches.

Shopping
Handicrafts from Jalisco, Michoacán and other Mexican states are available in Guadalajara. (See the earlier Tlaquepaque and Tonalá sections for information on these two craft-making suburbs.) The Casa de las Artesanías de Jalisco, 20 blocks south of the center, has a good selection – see Parque Agua Azul, earlier.

The **Casa de las Artesanías de Jalisco** is on the north side of the park, but has its own separate entrance on Calzada. It displays handicrafts and arts from all over Jalisco, and everything is for sale. Prices are high, but the quality can't be beaten. It's open 10 am to 6 pm Monday to Friday, 11 am to 3 pm Saturday and 11 am to 2 pm Sunday (free). To get here, take bus Nos 60 or 62, heading south on Calzada Independencia.

Mercado Libertad, just east of the Centro Histórico, is a general market with three floors of shops covering an area equal to four city blocks. It's open daily. Sunday you can check out the huge El Baratillo market on and around Javier Mina and stretching for blocks in every direction. Take the 'Par Vial' bus east along Hidalgo.

Guadalajara's most prosperous citizens prefer to shop at one of the several big shopping centers around town. About 7km southwest of the center, Plaza del Sol on López Mattes Sur has a huge variety of shops, eating and entertainment, as does the newer Plaza Milenium, a little farther south at López Mattes Sur and Otero. Take bus Nos 258 or 258A west on San Felipe to get to these.

El Charro, on the corner of Juárez and Degollado, is the place to buy the cowboy boots, Mexican hat, and mariachi suit that you've always wanted. Several similar (and cheaper) shops are on Juárez to the east of El Charro.

Getting There & Away

Air Guadalajara's Aeropuerto Internacional Miguel Hidalgo (code GDL; ☎ 688-57-66) is 17km south of downtown, just off the highway to Chapala. It is served by many airlines, with direct flights to and from about a dozen North American cities and over 20 Mexican cities, and one-stop connections to many others. There's a tourist office in the terminal.

Book flights with one of the many travel agencies in Guadalajara – look in the phone directory yellow pages under 'Agencias de Viajes.' A number of airlines and travel agents, as well as American Express, have offices in Plaza Los Arcos, Vallarta 2440. Airline offices in Guadalajara include:

Aero California (☎ 616-993-93) Vallarta 2440

Aeroméxico, Aerolitoral & Aeromar (☎ 669-02-02) Corona 196, at Madero

American Airlines (☎ 616-40-90) Vallarta 2440

Continental (☎ 647-42-51) Hotel Presidente Inter-Continental, Avenida Moctezuma 3415

Delta (☎ 630-31-30) López Cotilla 1701

Mexicana (☎ 112-00-11) Otero 2353

TAESA (☎ 616-89-89) López Cotilla 1531

United Airlines (☎ 616-94-89) Vallarta 2440

Bus Guadalajara has two bus stations. The new long-distance bus station, Nueva Central Camionera, is a huge modern terminal with seven separate buildings, called *módulos* or *salas*, in a V shape on two sides of a large triangular parking lot. It's 9km southeast of the center past Tlaquepaque.

Each módulo is the base for a number of bus lines, with ticket desks, places to eat, pay phones, a telephone *caseta* and a place to leave luggage.

Buses, often frequent, travel to/from just about everywhere in western, central and northern Mexico. The same destination can be served by several companies in several different módulos – the companies suggested below have the most frequent departures. Distances, travel times and typical 1st-class prices include:

Barra de Navidad – 291km, 5 hours (US$16); 11 per day by Autocamiones de Cihuatlan, módulo 3

Colima – 220km, 2½ to 3 hours (US$11); Primera Plus, módulo 1

Guanajuato – 300km, 4 hours (US$17); Primera Plus, módulo 1

Mazatlán – 506km, 8 hours (US$29); Elite or Pacífico, módulo 3

Mexico City (Terminal Norte) – 535km, 7 to 8 hours (US$30 to US$32); Primera Plus, módulo 1; Omnibus de México, módulo 6

Morelia – 278km, 3½ hours (US$15); Primera Plus, módulo 1; La Línea, módulo 2

Puerto Vallarta – 344km, 5 hours (US$24); Pacífico, módulo 3

Querétaro – 350km, 4½ hours (US$19); Primera Plus, módulo 1

San Miguel de Allende – 380km, 6 hours (US$15); direct buses at 1 and 3 pm by Primera Plus, módulo 1

Tepic – 216km, 3½ hours (US$14); Omnibus de México, módulo 6

Uruapan – 305km, 3½ to 5 hours (US$12); Primera Plus, módulo 1

Zacatecas – 320km, 5 hours (US$18); Omnibus de México, módulo 6

For deluxe buses to many of these destinations (at considerably higher fares), try ETN, módulo 2.

Bus tickets can be bought in the center at Turismo MaCull, López Cotilla 163, near the corner of Degollado. It's open 9 am to 7 pm Monday to Friday, 9 am to 1 pm Saturday.

Guadalajara's other bus station is called the Vieja Central Camionera (Old Bus Station) and is about 1.5km south of the cathedral, near Parque Agua Azul. It occupies the block bounded by Avenida 5 de Febrero, Los Ángeles and Dr Michel (which is the southward continuation of Avenida Corona). The Vieja Central Camionera has buses to/from destinations nearer Guadalajara. There are two sides and two sets of ticket booths – Sala A is for destinations to the south and east; Sala B is for destinations north and west.

Primera Plus buses go every half-hour, from 6 am to 9.40 pm, to Chapala (40km, 45 minutes, US$2), Ajijic (47km, 55 minutes, US$2) and Jocotepec (68km, one hour, US$2.25). Rojo de Los Altos buses go every 15 or 20 minutes, from 6 am to 9 pm, to Tequila (50km, 1¾ hours, US$2.75).

Train The only train service to/from Guadalajara is the Tequila Express, providing a tourist excursion to the nearby town of Tequila (see the Tequila section).

Car & Motorcycle Guadalajara is 535km northwest of Mexico City and 345km east of Puerto Vallarta. Highways 15, 15D, 23, 54, 54D, 80, 80D and 90 all converge here, combining temporarily to form the Periférico, a ring road around the city.

Guadalajara has many car rental agencies, which are listed in the telephone yellow pages under 'Automóviles – Renta de.' Several of the large US companies are represented, but you may get a cheaper deal from a local company. Agencies include:

Auto Rent de Guadalajara
(☎ 826-20-13) Federalismo Sur 542A
(☎ 689-04-32) Airport

Budget
(☎ 613-00-27) Niños Héroes 934
(☎ 688-55-31) Airport

Dollar
(☎ 826-79-59) Federalismo Sur 540
(☎ 688-56-59) Airport

Hertz
(☎ 614-61-97) Niños Héroes 9
(☎ 688-54-03) Airport

National
(☎ 825-48-48) Hotel Fiesta Americana,
Aceves 225

Quick Rent A Car
(☎ 614-60-52) Niños Héroes 954

Getting Around

To/From the Airport Bus No 176 travels Corona and passes in front of Hotel Vista Aranzazú as it makes its way toward the airport. The cost is US$0.50. The bus passes every 20 minutes, and you'd want to allow an hour for the trip. Tell the driver you're going to the *aeropuerto*, and he'll drop you two blocks from the airport, which is visible from the bus stop. Buses to Chapala from the old bus station also pass the airport (US$0.70). *Colectivo combis* go between the airport and downtown hotels (40 minutes, US$6). Taxis between the airport and the center cost about US$10.

To/From the Bus Stations To reach the city center from the Nueva Central Camionera, you can take any 'Centro' or No 644 city bus, or the more comfortable TUR 707 bus, from the loop road within the station (immediately outside your módulo). These are not very frequent so it's often quicker to walk out of the station between módulo 1 and the Hotel El Parador and take an orange bus No 275, 275A or 275B going to the right (north) along the road outside. These run every 15 minutes from 5.30 am to 10.30 pm, and bring you into the center along Avenida 16 de Septiembre. There's no taxi ticket system, but fares are supposedly determined by zones – to the center (*zona 3*), it's US$5.50 in daytime and US$6.50 at night, for up to four people.

From the city to the Nueva Central Camionera, you can take bus Nos 275, 275A and 275B southward on 16 de Septiembre, anywhere between the cathedral and Avenida Revolución. They run frequently but tend to be crowded and can take half an hour or more to get there. Bus No 644B heading east from the corner of Corona and Revolución is less frequent but takes a more direct route. A taxi should cost about US$4.50.

Bus Nos 60 and 174 south on Calzada Independencia will take you from the city center to the Vieja Central Camionera.

Bus No 616 and other buses run between the two bus stations.

Bus & Combi Guadalajara has a comprehensive city bus system, but the buses are pretty basic and can be crowded. On the major routes, buses go every five minutes or so from 5.30 am to 10.30 pm daily; they cost US$0.30. A few routes are served by *combis*. Many buses pass through the center of town, so for an inner suburban destination you'll have a few to choose from. The routes diverge as they get farther from the center, and you need to know the bus number for the suburb you want. Some bus route numbers are followed by an additional letter, which indicates which circuitous route they will follow in the outer suburbs.

The TUR buses – painted a distinctive turquoise color – are a more comfortable alternative on some routes – TUR 707 goes from Plaza del Sol along Avenida Vallarta through the city center and southeast to the bus station and Tonalá; TUR 706 goes north-south on Avenida 16 de Septiembre. Fares are US$0.60. The tourist office has a list of the 140 bus routes in Guadalajara, and can help you figure out how to get anywhere you want to go.

Metro Two subway lines cross the city. Stops are marked around town by a red and blue 'T' symbol. It's quick and comfortable enough, but doesn't serve many points of visitor interest. Línea 1 runs north-south for 15km all the way from the Periférico Norte to the Periférico Sur – it runs more or less below Federalismo (seven blocks west of the center) and Avenida Colón. You can catch it at Parque Revolución, on the corner of Avenida Juárez.

Línea 2 runs east-west for 10km below Avenidas Juárez and Mina.

Taxi These are plentiful in the center. Taxis are supposed to charge fixed rates, according to distance. Typical fares from the center are US$1.75 to the Vieja Central Camionera or

Parque Agua Azul; US$4 to Plaza del Sol; US$3.50 to Tlaquepaque, the zoo or to Zapopan; US$4.50 to the Nueva Central Camionera; US$6 to Tonalá; and US$10 to the airport. Clarify the fare before you get into the taxi.

LAGO DE CHAPALA

Mexico's largest natural lake, 40km south of Guadalajara, is quite picturesque and ringed by hills, but the water level has fallen significantly and towns that were once on the lakeside now overlook a swath of green several hundred meters wide. Guadalajara's water needs exceed the flow of water into the lake. The main river feeding the lake, Río Lerma, is diminished because water is pumped out to supply Mexico City. The Lerma water that does reach the lake is often polluted with industrial waste, as well as washed-in fertilizers and soil that nourish water hyacinth, a fast-growing plant that now clogs much of the water surface.

Still, the near-perfect climate and lovely countryside around the small lakeside towns of Chapala, Ajijic and Jocotepec have attracted an estimated 5000 full-time residents from the USA and Canada; many are retirees who enjoy lower living costs and higher temperatures than at home.

Getting There & Around

Chapala, Ajijic and Jocotepec are easy to reach by bus from Guadalajara's Vieja Central Camionera (see Getting There & Away in the Guadalajara section). Small buses go west around the lakeside every 15 minutes from Chapala, detouring through the streets of San Antonio, Ajijic and San Juan Cosalá then returning by the same route. They start at the bus station in Chapala but you can wave them down in the street. Bigger buses go all the way from Chapala to Jocotepec every half hour (50 minutes, US$0.50), from 7 am to 10 pm – they stop on the main road at each village, but they don't detour through the streets.

There's also a 'ciclopista' between Chapala and Ajijic, for cycling, jogging or walking.

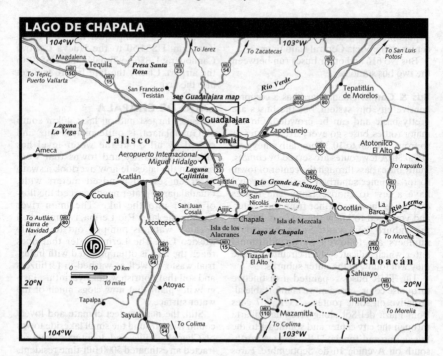

LAGO DE CHAPALA

Around the south shore of the lake, a scenic road makes an attractive alternative route to Michoacán if you're driving. You can catch the scenery and some local color by taking a 2nd-class bus to Zamora from Chapala.

Chapala
• pop 18,000 • elev 1560m ☎ changing

The largest of the settlements toward the western end of the lake, Chapala took off as a resort when president Porfirio Díaz vacationed here every year from 1904 to 1909. DH Lawrence wrote most of *The Plumed Serpent* in the house at Zaragoza 307 – the San Francisco church at the lake end of Avenida Madero, the main street, figures in the book's final pages. Today Chapala might get busy some weekends and holidays, but mostly it's a quiet place catering to older expatriates. A sign outside a *farmacia* summed it up, in English of course – 'Viagra Available Now.'

Orientation & Information From the bus station it's a 10-minute walk down Avenida Madero to the lakeside (or what was the lakeside before the water level fell). Hidalgo heads to the west off Madero 200m before the lake to become the road leading to Ajijic. All services can be found on and around Madero or Hidalgo.

In 2000, the telephone area code is due to change to ☎ 3 from 376, with the digits 76 added to the start of every local number (for example, the number 5-31-41 will become 765-31-41).

The tourist office (☎ 5-31-41), upstairs at Madero 407, is open 9 am to 7 pm Monday to Friday, 9 am to 1 pm Saturday and Sunday.

Libros de Chapala, opposite the plaza three blocks down Madero from the bus station, has many US magazines, plus some newspapers and books. The market is opposite, on the east side of the plaza.

Things to See & Do At the foot of Avenida Madero, where the waterfront used to be, there's a small park and a row of souvenir stalls, some selling attractive, inexpensive weavings from Jocotepec, most selling schlock. There's also a covered crafts market, the **Mercado de Artesanías**, about 400m east along Paseo Corona. Farther east, the expansive **Parque La Cristiania** has a big swimming pool, a playground and nice picnic lawns. It's entered from Avenida Cristiania, off Ramón Corona, the road east round the lake.

At the *embarcadero* (jetty), at the foot of Madero, there's a ticket office for the boats, then a longish walk to the water where the boats actually leave from. **Isla de los Alacranes** (Scorpion Island), 6km south, has some restaurants and more souvenir stalls, but it's mainly an opportunity to get out on the lake. A return trip, with 30 minutes on the island, costs US$18 per boat, for one to eight people.

Isla de Mezcala, also called Isla El Presidio, about 15km east, has ruins of a fort and other buildings. Mexican independence fighters heroically held out there from 1812 to 1816, repulsing several Spanish attempts to dislodge them, and finally won a full pardon from their enemies. A boat there and back, with an hour to look around, will cost around US$76 for up to eight people.

Places to Stay The least expensive accommodation option is *Casa de Huéspedes Las Palmitas* (☎ 5-30-70, *Juárez 531*), just south of the east side of the market. It has 15 clean singles/doubles with private bath, cable TV and 24-hour hot water for a rate of US$11/14.

The long-established *Hotel Nido de Chapala* (☎ 5-21-16, *Madero 202*), near the waterfront, offers a moderately clean pool and fairly pleasant rooms for US$18/22 (US$2 more with TV). The newer rooms behind are smaller but brighter than the old rooms.

The best place in town is the *Villa Montecarlo* (☎ 5-22-16, *Hidalgo 296*), 1km west

of the center. Its peacock-speckled grounds reach the lake and boast a thermal swimming pool. Each room has a private balcony, starting at US$60.

Places to Eat Chapala's specialty is fish of various sorts, but very little now comes from Lago de Chapala, which suffers from overfishing and pollution. The famous *pescado blanco* (whitefish), the same little creature found around Lago de Pátzcuaro, is sold in many places, but it's expensive and probably comes from a fish farm. Another specialty, *charales*, are tiny fish, deep-fried and sold at many stalls near the embarcadero. They're fatty and salty, but not bad with lemon and a beer.

The *Café Paris* and the *Restaurant Superior*, a couple of doors apart on the east side of Madero just north of Hidalgo, both do a good range of decent food at reasonable prices. Both are clean, popular and have sidewalk tables. A four-course comida runs about US$3. The *Gran Hotel Nido* has a slightly more expensive restaurant adorned with photos of old Chapala.

El Arbol de Café, on Hidalgo, keeps sporadic hours but is recommended for its coffee. There are also restaurants in both directions from the embarcadero. East of the souvenir stalls along Ramón Corona, a whole slew of fishy restaurants compete for customers to sit at tables overlooking what used to be the lake. The water view is now somewhat distant, and the seafood is all imported, but these places are still very pleasant and reasonably priced.

Ajijic

• **pop 8500** • **elev 1555m** ☎ **changing**

Ajijic ('ah-hee-HEEK'), about 7km west of Chapala along the lakeside, is a beautiful, friendly little town of cobbled streets and prettily painted houses, and home to a sizable colony of Mexican and US and Canadian artists. Usually Ajijic is fairly sleepy, except during the nine-day Fiesta de San Andrés at the end of November, and over Easter when a reenactment of Christ's trial and crucifixion is staged over three days.

The bigger buses will drop you on the highway at the top of Colón, the main street, which leads six blocks down to the lake. The chapel on the north side of the plaza, two blocks down, dates from at least the 18th century. There are a handful of galleries (look for Colección Moon), and some upmarket crafts shops on and off Colón.

The attractive premises of the Lake Chapala Society, a block or so southeast of the plaza, is a club for expat residents, and provides a library and other good works for local kids.

In 2000, the telephone area code is due to change to ☎ 3 from 376, with the digits 76 added to the start of every local number (for example, the number 5-31-41 will become 765-31-41).

Places to Stay & Eat Actually in San Antonio, 2km east of central Ajijic on the highway toward Chapala, *PAL Trailer Park* (☎ 6-00-40) has a pool, laundry and 110 grassy sites with full hookups. Cost is US$14 a night for one or two people in an RV – tents are not encouraged.

A couple of blocks east of the plaza, *Hotel Mariana* (☎ 6-22-21, Guadalupe Victoria 10) has 30 clean, spacious singles/doubles for US$20/25, including breakfast and cable TV. Visit the rooftop terrace for a nice view of the lake.

Apartments Suite Plaza Ajijic (☎ 6-03-83, Colón 33), on the plaza, is a friendly place with sizable, modern two-room suites with kitchen for US$36/40.

La Nueva Posada (☎ 6-14-44, Donato Guerra 9, nuevaposada@laguna.com.mx), three blocks east of Colón by the lake, is a lovely hotel run by a friendly Canadian family. It has 17 large, tastefully decorated rooms – those with lake views cost US$54/60, those without cost US$52/57. There's also an inviting pool and an excellent restaurant that spills out into a fine lakeside garden. Most meat or fish dishes are US$8 to US$9, but there are cheaper daily specials.

Trattoria di Giovanni, on the highway 1½ blocks east of Colón, is a popular restaurant with some of the best food in town. Chicken and seafood go for US$5 to US$9, pasta US$3 to US$4 and pizzas US$3 to US$4 for a small and US$5 to US$8 for a large. There are happy hours and, often, live music in the evening.

The main cluster of cheaper cafés and restaurants is around the plaza on Colón, and a block or so to the south. Others to look for include *Manix* and *Borsalino*.

San Juan Cosalá

At San Juan Cosalá, 10km west of Ajijic toward Jocotepec, there's a thermal spa in an attractive lakeside setting, with its own natural geyser and several swimming pools. You can stay in the *Motel Balneario San Juan Cosalá* (☎ 3-761-02-22), right on the spot, for US$36/42. Non-residents can use the pools for US$4.50.

Jocotepec
• pop 14,600

Jocotepec ('ho-co-teh-PEC'), 21km west of Chapala and a kilometer from the lake, is far less gringo-influenced than Chapala or Ajijic. It's a pleasant town, but there's nothing special to see or do except look for the handsome blankets, *sarapes* and wall hangings that are woven here and sold along Hidalgo. The main festival is the two-week Fiesta del Señor del Monte in early January.

TEQUILA
• pop 21,600 • elev 1219m ☎ changing

The town of Tequila, 50km northwest of Guadalajara, has been home to the liquor of the same name since the 17th century. Fields of agave, the cactus-like plant from which tequila is distilled, surround the town. You can almost get drunk just breathing the

In 2000, the telephone area code is due to change to ☎ 3 from 374, with the digits 74 added to the start of every local number (for example, the number 5-31-41 will become 745-31-41).

heavily scented air that drifts from the town's distilleries. The tourist office, on the plaza, organizes tours on the hour for US$2.50. The **Museo del Tequila** (Tequila Museum) is near the plaza, as are the two largest distilleries – Sauza and Cuervo – which offer tours on the hour for US$2, including samples.

The **Tequila Express** starts at Guadalajara train station at 10 am, and includes a train ride through the agave fields, a distillery visit, music, a mariachi show, snacks, lunch, and an open bar with *mucho* tequila included. The tour costs US$44 – for information and reservations call ☎ 3-122-79-20 in Guadalajara.

Tequila

In ancient times, the *agave tequilana weber* (blue agave) was used by indigenous Mexicans as a source of food, cloth and paper. The plant even was used in torture. The needlelike tips of its long leaves were customarily thrust into human flesh as penance to the gods. Today, the blue agave is known more widely as the source of Mexico's national drink – tequila.

To ensure quality control, by law the blue agave can be grown only in the state of Jalisco and in parts of Nayarit, Michoacán, Guanajuato and Tamaulipas states. It is here, and nowhere else in Mexico, that conditions are right for the blue agave to produce a good-tasting tequila. At any given moment more than 100 million tequila agaves are in cultivation within this designated territory.

In some ways the production of tequila has changed little since the drink was invented near Guadalajara hundreds of years

Agave farmer goes to town.

ago. The blue agaves are still planted and harvested by hand, and the heavy, pineapple-resembling hearts, from which the alcohol is derived, are still removed from the fields on the backs of mules.

When planted, the agave heart is no bigger than an onion. Its blue-gray, swordlike leaves give the plant the appearance of a cactus, although botanists agree it has more in common genetically with the lily. By the time the agave is ready for harvesting, eight to 12 years after planting, its heart is the size of a beach ball and can weigh 50kg.

The harvested agave heart *(piña)* is chopped to bits, fed into ovens and cooked for up to three days. After cooking, the softened plants are shredded and juiced. The juice, called *aguamiel* (honey water) for its golden, syrupy appearance, is then pumped into vats, where it typically is mixed with sugarcane and yeast before being allowed to ferment. By law, the mixture can contain no less than 51% agave. A bottle of tequila made from 100% agave will bear a label stating so.

There are four varieties of tequila. Which is best is a matter of personal opinion. White (or silver) tequila is not aged, and no colors or flavors are added. The gold variety is unaged but color and flavor, usually caramel, are added. *Tequila reposado* (rested tequila) has been aged at least two months in oak barrels and coloring and flavoring agents usually have been added. *Añejo* (aged) tequila has spent at least one year in oak barrels, also with added coloring and flavoring.

WESTERN CENTRAL

Local buses to Tequila leave every 15 or 20 minutes from the Vieja Central Camionera in Guadalajara (see Getting There & Away in the Guadalajara section).

Inland Michoacán

Michoacán is a beautiful state with a number of fascinating destinations along the Cordillera Neovolcánica, the volcanic range that gives it both fertile soils and a striking mountainous landscape. In a 200km stretch of the cordillera across the northern part of Michoacán are found the spectacular El Rosario monarch butterfly sanctuary; the handsome state capital Morelia; the beautiful colonial town of Pátzcuaro, set near scenic Lago de Pátzcuaro in Purépecha country, with several interesting villages, archaeological sites, islands and other lakes nearby; the town of Uruapan, with a fine miniature tropical national park within city boundaries; and the famous volcano Paricutín a short distance beyond Uruapan.

The name Michoacán is an Aztec word meaning 'Place of the Masters of Fish' – still

an apt description of the Lago de Pátzcuaro area, although nowadays the traditional 'butterfly' nets are used on the lake as much to catch tourists' pesos as fish.

The more tropical coastal areas of Michoacán, reached by spectacular highway 37 down through the hills from Uruapan, are covered in the Central Pacific Coast chapter.

MORELIA
● pop 512,200 ● elev 1920m ☎ changing
Morelia, the capital of Michoacán, lies in the northeastern part of the state, 315km west of Mexico City and 278km southeast of Guadalajara. It's a superbly preserved colonial city, with a university, an active cultural scene and a number of language schools offering Spanish courses – a good place for an extended visit, as many foreigners have discovered.

Morelia was one of the first Spanish cities in Nueva España, officially founded in 1541, although a Franciscan monastery had been in the area since 1537. The first viceroy, Antonio de Mendoza, named it Valladolid after the Spanish city of that name and encouraged families of Spanish nobility to move here. The families remained and main-

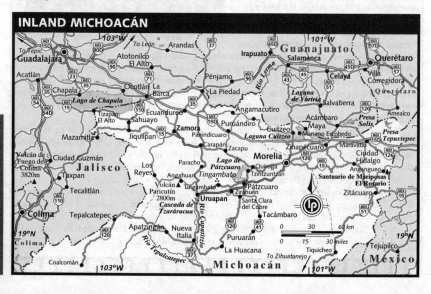

INLAND MICHOACÁN

tained Valladolid as a very Spanish city, at least architecturally, until 1828.

By that time, Nueva España had become the independent republic of Mexico. The state legislature changed the city's name to Morelia to honor one of its native sons, José María Morelos y Pavón, a key figure in Mexico's independence movement.

With its downtown streets lined by colonial buildings, Morelia still looks nearly as Spanish as it did before independence, and city ordinances require that all new construction in the center be done in colonial style with arches, baroque façades and walls of pink stone.

Orientation

Almost everything of interest is within walking distance of the *zócalo*, also called the Plaza Central, Plaza de los Mártires and Plaza de Armas. The imposing, twin-towered cathedral in the middle of the zócalo is a major landmark.

Avenida Madero, along the north side of the zócalo, is the major downtown avenue; to the west of the cathedral it's Madero Poniente, to the east it's Madero Oriente. Other east-west streets change names at the cathedral while north-south streets change names at Madero. On Madero, the elegant row of arched verandas facing the zócalo is commonly called Portal Hidalgo; the arches on Abasolo facing the west side of the plaza are called Portal Matamoros. Nine blocks east of the zócalo on Madero, the Fuente Las Tarascas (Tarascan Fountain) is another main landmark, marking a major intersection; it's here that you will enter Morelia city center if you're driving in from Mexico City.

Information

Tourist Offices The helpful Galería de Turismo (☎ 17-23-71, 800-450-23-00) is a block west of the zócalo on the corner of Madero Poniente and Nigromante, on an outside corner of the Palacio Clavijero. It has free maps and leaflets in Spanish and English about Morelia and Michoacán, plus a monthly calendar of films and cultural events in the city. Hours are 9 am to 8 pm Monday through Friday, 9 am to 6 pm Saturday and Sunday.

In 2000, the telephone area code is due to change to ☎ 4 from 43, with the digit 3 added to the start of every local number (for example, the number 17-23-71 will become 317-23-71).

Money Banks and ATMs are plentiful in the zócalo area, particularly on and around Madero. Most are open all day from Monday to Friday, and until 2 pm Saturday, but some may change currency only until about 1 pm. The numerous casas de cambio have rates only slightly lower, are open longer hours and have faster service. Three convenient ones are marked on the map – Casa de Cambio Majapara, at Suárez 166, is open Sunday.

Post & Communications The main post office is in the Palacio Federal, Madero Oriente 369, open 8 am to 4 pm Monday to Friday, 8 am to 1 pm Saturday. The Telecomm office, in the same building, has telegram, telex and fax services, 9 am to 8 pm Monday to Friday, 9 am to 1 pm Saturday.

Computel has a telephone caseta with fax service at the bus station, advertising 24-hour service.

Internet access is available at Chatroom Cybercafe, on Nigromante ($2 per hour), and at the computer school at López Rayón 190 (US$2.25 per hour). Both are open roughly 8 am to 8 pm Monday to Saturday. Shareware Cybercafe, Madero Oriente 573, is another option, open every day, and with good coffee.

Laundry Lavandería American Klean, at Corregidora 787 on the corner of Bravo, is open 9 am to 7 pm Monday to Saturday, 9 am to 2 pm Sunday.

Cathedral

The catedral dominating the zócalo took more than a century to build, from 1640 to 1744. Architecturally, it is a combination of Herreresque, baroque and neoclassical styles. Its twin 70m-high towers, for instance, have classical Herreresque bases, baroque

MORELIA

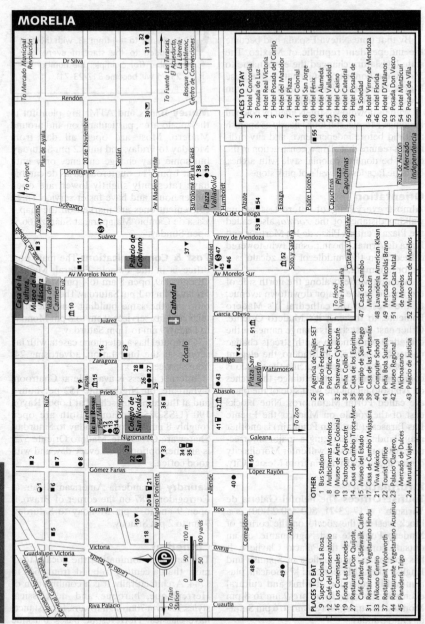

PLACES TO STAY
2   Hotel Concordia
3   Posada de Luz
4   Hotel Real Victoria
5   Hotel Posada del Cortijo
6   Hotel del Matador
7   Hotel Plaza
11 Hotel Colonial
18 Hotel San Jorge
20 Hotel Fénix
25 Hotel Alameda
26 Hotel Valladolid
27 Hotel Casino
28 Hotel Catedral
29 Hotel Posada de
    la Soledad
36 Hotel Virrey de Mendoza
50 Hotel Florida
51 Hotel D'Atilanos
53 Posada Don Vasco
55 Posada de Villa

PLACES TO EAT
9   Super Cocina La Rosa
12 Café del Conservatorio
16 Los Comensales
19 Fonda Las Mercedes
27 Restaurant Don Quijote,
    Café Catedral, Sidewalk Cafés
31 Restaurante Vegetariano Hindu
33 Mikono Centro
37 Restaurant Woolworth
45 Restaurante Vegetariano Acuarius
45 Panadería Trigo

OTHER
1   Bus Station
8   Multicinemas Morelos
10 Museo de Arte Colonial
13 Chatroom Cybercafe
14 Casa de Cambio Troca-Mex
15 Museo del Estado
17 Casa de Cambio Majapara
21 Viva México
22 Tourist Office
23 Palacio Clavijero,
    Mercado de Dulces
24 Maruta Viajes
26 Agencia de Viajes SET
30 Palacio Federal,
    Post Office, Telecomm
32 Shareware Cybercate
34 Chatroom Cybercate
35 Casa de los Espiritus
38 Templo de San Diego
39 Casa de las Artesanias
40 Computer School
41 Peña Bola Suriana
42 Museo Regional
    Michoacán
43 Palacio de Justicia
47 Casa de Cambio
    Michoacán
48 Lavanderia American Klean
49 Mercado Nicolás Bravo
51 Museo Casa Natal
    de Morelos
52 Museo Casa de Morelos

midsections and multicolumned neoclassical tops. Inside, much of the baroque relief work was replaced in the 19th century with more balanced and calculated neoclassical pieces. Fortunately, one of the cathedral's interior highlights was preserved: a sculpture of the Señor de la Sacristía made from dried maize and topped with a gold crown from the 16th century Spanish king, Felipe II. There's also a very large organ with 4600 pipes.

Museo Regional Michoacano

Just off the zócalo, the Michoacán Regional Museum, at Allende 305 and Abasolo, is housed in the late-18th-century baroque palace of Isidro Huarte. The museum displays a great variety of pre-Hispanic artifacts, colonial art and relics, contemporary paintings by local artists and exhibits on the geology and fauna of the region. A highlight is the mural on the stairway by Mexican painter Alfredo Alce. The mural is in halves: The right half portrays people who have had a positive influence on Mexico, and the left half portrays those who have had a negative influence.

The museum is open 9 am to 7 pm Tuesday to Saturday (US$2, free to those under 13 and over 60), and 9 am to 2 pm Sunday (free for everyone!).

The **Palacio de Justicia**, across Abasolo from the museum, was built between 1682 and 1695 to serve as the city hall. Its façade is an eclectic but well-done mix of French and baroque styles, and the stairway in the courtyard has a dramatic mural by Agustín Cárdenas showing Morelos in action.

Museo del Estado

The Michoacán State Museum, at Prieto 176, is a good place to learn about this interesting state. Downstairs is devoted to the history of Michoacán from prehistoric times to the first contact between the Tarascos and the Spanish. Upstairs, the story continues to the present, with exhibits on many aspects of modern life in Michoacán including clothing, handicrafts and agriculture.

The museum is open 9 am to 2 pm and 4 to 8 pm Monday to Friday, to 7 pm on Saturday, Sunday and holidays (free). Ask about the program of free cultural events such as regional music, dance and *artesanías*.

Morelos Sites

José María Morelos y Pavón, one of the most important figures in Mexico's struggle for independence from Spain, was born in the house on the corner of Corregidora and García Obeso on September 30, 1765. Two centuries later, it was declared a national monument and made into the **Museo Casa Natal de Morelos** (Morelos Birthplace Museum). Morelos memorabilia fills two rooms; a public library, auditorium and projection room occupy the rest of the house. An eternal torch burns next to the projection room. Free international films and cultural events are held at the museum (see Entertainment). The museum is open 9 am to 7 pm Monday to Friday, 9 am to 1 pm Saturday (free).

Museo Casa de Morelos

José María Morelos

One of Mexico's greatest heroes, the priest and revolutionary José María Morelos y Pavón (1765-1815), gives his name to streets and plazas all over the country. His home city of Valladolid was renamed Morelia in his honor. Noted for his determination, Morelos came from a humble *mestizo* family, and was well educated at the city's Colegio de San Nicolás, where Miguel Hidalgo was rector. Hidalgo, even then, had come under disfavor for his unorthodox views, and he was later transferred to become a parish priest in rural Dolores, where the church authorities hoped he would be less influential.

Morelos was ordained in 1797, at a time when the Catholic Church was a hotbed of anti-Spanish sentiment. Priests saw first-hand the effects of Spanish policies on the poor of Mexico, and the Spanish crown greatly alienated the church by an 1804 decree confiscating church assets. Along with other priests, Morelos was active in a secret society working toward independence. The group included Hidalgo, who launched the independence war with his famous Grito (Cry for Independence) in September 1810.

Valladolid was among the first towns to fall to the independence movement, and from here Hidalgo's ragtag army began its ill-fated march toward Mexico City. After two major defeats, and the capture, execution and beheading of Hidalgo and three other insurgent leaders in 1811, Morelos became commander of the insurgent forces. For a man trained as a Catholic priest, Morelos had an amazing talent for military leadership, reorganizing and equipping his small army and leading it to a string of victories over well trained royalist forces. From February to May 1812, Morelos and his troops held the town of Cuautla against great odds,

In 1801 Morelos bought the Spanish-style house that stands at Avenida Morelos Sur 323, on the corner of Soto y Saldaña. He added a second story in 1806. This house is now the **Museo Casa de Morelos** (Morelos House Museum), with exhibits on Morelos' life and his role in the independence movement. It's open 9 am to 6 pm daily (US$1.25).

Morelos studied at the **Colegio de San Nicolás**, one block west of the zócalo on the corner of Madero Poniente and Nigromante. The Colegio later became the foundation for the Universidad de Michoacán; it is still in use as a part of the university. Upstairs, the Sala de Melchor Ocampo is a memorial room to another Mexican hero, a reformer and governor of Michoacán. Here are preserved Ocampo's library and a copy of the document he signed to donate his library to the college, just before being shot by firing squad on June 3, 1861. This room and the rest of the college is open 7 am to 8 pm Monday to Friday (free).

Palacio Clavijero & Mercado de Dulces

The Clavijero Palace, in the block west of the Colegio de San Nicolás, between Nigromante and Gómez Farías, was established in 1660 as a Jesuit school. After the Jesuits were expelled from Spanish dominions in 1767, the building served alternately as a warehouse and prison until 1970, when it was renovated as public offices, including the state tourist office and public library.

Be sure to visit the arcade on the western side of the palace to taste some of the

then escaped the siege and went on to defeat the royalist forces at Orizaba and Oaxaca. In his most brilliant tactical encounter, Morelos led the capture of Fuerte de San Diego, and hence the port of Acapulco, in 1812. In all these towns, Morelos established a well organized administration to protect and assist the people.

By spring 1813 Morelos' forces had encircled Mexico City. He now attempted to impose a unity of purpose on the various factions within the independence movement. Convening a congress in Chilpancingo, Morelos proclaimed his Sentimientos de la Nación, a statement of his goals for the new nation. They included independence from Spain, the abolition of slavery, equality before the law, free trade and the protection of private property. After months of debate, the Congress of Chilpancingo incorporated his principles in its Declaration of Independence, and Morelos emerged as a social and political visionary as well as a military genius.

Unfortunately, this time-out for independence politics enabled the royalists to regroup, and led by General Félix Calleja they broke the circle around Mexico City and inflicted a major defeat on Morelos at his home town of Valladolid in late 1813. Forced to fight a running, defensive campaign, and weakened by disputes within the independence movement, Morelos was defeated again and taken prisoner. He was first disgraced and defrocked by the Inquisition, then handed over to the Spanish authorities, who executed him by firing squad on December 22, 1815.

Now the stern face of Morelos frowns from murals, monuments and banknotes all over the country, and the question many may ask is – why does he always have that handkerchief tied around his head? None of the other independence heroes has one, so it couldn't be a military uniform or an early 19th-century fashion statement. Contemporaries of Morelos noted that he suffered badly from headaches, and he apparently tied a cloth tightly around his head to relieve the pain. Looking at portraits of Morelos, it's easy to imagine he was a man under pressure, and one wonders whether his biggest headache was fighting a losing guerrilla war, debating elitist *criollos*, or contemplating the fate of Hidalgo and the other leaders who had lost their heads for the independence cause.

---

goodies on sale in the Mercado de Dulces (Market of Sweets). It's open 9 am to 10 pm daily. Michoacán handicrafts are also sold in the arcade, but you can find better wares at the Casa de las Artesanías.

Museo de Arte Colonial

The Museum of Colonial Art, Juárez 240 at Ruiz, three blocks north of the cathedral, contains 18th-century religious paintings, crucifixes and models of galleons. It's open 10 am to 2 pm and 5 to 7 pm Tuesday to Sunday (free).

A block away, across the Plaza del Carmen, the **Casa de la Cultura**, Avenida Morelos Norte 485, hosts dance and music performances, films and art exhibitions. Stop by for a free monthly brochure describing cultural events in the city.

Also at the Casa de la Cultura, the **Museo de la Máscara** has masks from around Mexico, each labeled with the ethnic group and the particular dance it's associated with. The museum is open 9 am to 1 pm and 3 to 8.30 pm Monday to Friday, 10 am to 6 pm on weekends (free).

Casa de las Artesanías

The House of Handicrafts occupies the Ex-Convento de San Francisco, attached to the Templo de San Francisco, three blocks east of the zócalo. Outside on Plaza de Valladolid, dozens of *tiendas* sell everything from fine handicrafts to shoddy souvenirs. Inside the old convent, arts and handicrafts from all over Michoacán are displayed and sold; they're expensive but some of the best you'll see anywhere in the state. There's also a small selection of cassettes of regional music. Upstairs, small shops represent many of Michoacán's towns, with craftspeople demonstrating how the specialties of their area are made. There are guitars from Paracho, copperware from Santa Clara del Cobre, lacquerware, weaving and much more. It's open 9 am to 2 pm and 6 to 8 pm daily, but the shops keep somewhat individual hours.

Fuente Las Tarascas & El Acueducto

The Fuente Las Tarascas fountain at the end of Madero Oriente, nine blocks east of the zócalo, features a sculpture of three barebreasted Tarasco women supporting a basket of fruits. The original fountain here vanished mysteriously in 1940, and this replacement was installed in the 1960s.

The aqueduct begins at the Fuente Las Tarascas and extends southeast along Avenida Acueducto. Although it looks older, the aqueduct was built between 1785 and 1788 to meet the city's growing water needs. With 253 arches stretching 2km, it is an impressive sight, especially at night when spotlights illuminate the arches and fountain.

The **Bosque Cuauhtémoc**, or Cuauhtémoc Forest, is a large park stretching south from Avenida Acueducto. In the park a couple of blocks from the fountain is the interesting **Museo de Arte Contemporáneo**, at Acueducto 18, with changing exhibitions of modern art. It's open 10 am to 2 pm and 4 to 8 pm Tuesday to Saturday, 10 am to 5 pm Sunday (free).

On Plaza Morelos, about 100m northeast of Bosque Cuauhtémoc, between Avenida Acueducto and the cobbled Calzada Fray Antonio de San Miguel, stands the **Estatua Ecuestre al Patriota Morelos**, a statue of Morelos on horseback trotting to battle. It was sculpted by the Italian artist Giuseppe Ingillieri between 1910 and 1913.

Centro de Convenciones

The Convention Center complex, about 1.5km south of the Bosque Cuauhtémoc on Calzada Ventura Puente, has several places of interest in extensive park-like grounds. You can reach it on the red route ('Ruta Roja') combi heading east on Tapia or 20 de Noviembre.

The **Planetario de Morelia**, with 164 projectors and a cupola 20m in diameter, presents one-hour programs at 5 and 7 pm Friday and Saturday, 6.30 pm Sunday. At 5 pm Sunday there's a separate family program (US$2).

The **Orquidario**, or orchid house, is open 10 am to 6 pm Monday to Friday, 10 am to 3 pm and 4 to 6 pm Saturday and Sunday. Admission is a 'donation' of about US$1; you decide how much. The large, modern **Teatro Morelos** is also in the complex.

Parque Zoológico Benito Juárez

The zoo is 3km south of the zócalo on Calzada Juárez, which is an extension of Nigromante and Galeana. It's a pleasant zoo with many animals, a lake with rowboats for hire, a small train, picnic areas and a playground. It's open 10 am to 6 pm daily.

The pink combi route ('Ruta Guinda'), heading south on Nigromante from the stop on the east side of the Palacio Clavijero, will drop you at the zoo entrance.

Markets

Three markets are within 10 blocks of the zócalo: Mercado Nicolás Bravo on Bravo between Corregidora and Aldama; Mercado Independencia on Ruiz de Alarcón, several blocks southeast of the zócalo; and Mercado Municipal Revolución on the corner of Revolución and Plan de Ayala.

Language Courses

The most central of the several Spanish-language schools is Centro Cultural de Lenguas (☎/fax 12-05-89), Madero Oriente 560. Courses here run from two to four weeks, four hours daily with three hours of classroom work and an hour spent on workshops related to Mexican history, literature and culture. Group lessons (two to six students) cost US$200 per week; one-to-one lessons are US$220 per week. Living with Mexican families is encouraged (US$16 per day, including all meals) and organized by the school.

The Baden-Powell Institute (π/fax 12-40-70), Alzate 565, three blocks south of Madero Oriente, is a small school offering courses in Spanish language and Mexican politics, cooking, culture, guitar playing and folk dancing – mostly on a one-to-one basis, although group classes can be arranged. Most do four hours of instruction per day. One-to-one classes cost US$10 per hour, US$9 after 80 hours. Lodging with a Mexican family is US$15 per day, with three meals. See www.baden-powell.com for more details.

Centro Mexicano Internacional (π 12-45-96, fax 13-98-98), in a large colonial building at Calzada Fray Antonio 173, offers courses in Spanish language, Mexican culture and so forth for US$245 for the first week, US$195 thereafter. Classes run for four hours daily in groups of five students or less. Family living costs US$12 a day double occupancy, US$13 a day single occupancy. Courses can commence any Monday.

Organized Tours

Agencia de Viajes SET (π 13-19-08), on Portal Hidalgo (Madero Poniente) opposite the zócalo, between the Hotel Valladolid and Hotel Casino, arranges guided three-hour city tours, on foot or by van (US$6 to US$8 per person). There are also day tours for US$20 or more to Uruapan; to Los Azufres, a forest reserve in a volcanic area about 100km east of Morelia with pine forests, lakes, geysers and a hot sulfur pool; and, from November to March, to El Rosario monarch butterfly sanctuary (see the Santuario de Mariposas El Rosario section for how to get there independently).

Special Events

Morelia's many annual festivals include:

Feria de Morelia – Morelia's major fair, with exhibits of handicrafts, agriculture and livestock from around Michoacán, plus regional dances, bullfights and fiestas. The anniversary of the founding of Morelia in 1541 is celebrated on May 18 with fireworks, displays of historical photos and more; April 29 to May 20

Feria de Órgano – international organ festival during the Feria de Morelia; first two weeks of May

Festival Internacional de Música – international Music Festival; final week of July and first week of August

Cumpleaños de Morelos – Morelos' birthday is celebrated with a parade, fireworks and more; September 30

Día de la Virgen de Guadalupe – the Day of the Virgen de Guadalupe is celebrated on December 12 at the Templo de San Diego; in the preceding weeks, typical Mexican foods are sold on the pedestrian street Calzada Fray Antonio de San Miguel

Feria Navideña – Christmas Fair, with traditional Christmas items, foods and handicrafts from Michoacán; approximately December 1 to January 6

Places to Stay

Budget The cheapest place to stay in Morelia is *Las Villas* (π 13-31-77), a hostel in the IMJUDE sports complex on the corner of Oaxaca and Chiapas, a 20-minute walk southwest of the zócalo. The hostel is clean, with four beds (two bunks) and a locker in each room, and separate men's and women's areas. Cost is US$5.25 per person, with a discount for HI members. The complex houses a pool, gym and several athletic fields. It's open 7 am to 11 pm.

Two blocks north-east of the zócalo, the *Hotel Colonial* (π 12-18-97, 20 de Noviembre 15) is a colonial-style hotel with 25 rooms at US$11/14.50 singles/doubles, US$22 with two beds, US$5.50 extra for TV. Street-facing rooms are large, with high beamed ceilings and small balconies, but they catch a lot of traffic noise. The interior rooms are quieter. A block farther north, opposite the Casa de la Cultura, *Posada de Luz* (π 17-48-78, Calle del Trabajo 23) offers small, clean, colorful, cheerful rooms for US$10/14.50.

West of the zócalo, the *Hotel Fénix* (π 12-05-12, Madero Poniente 537) offers basic rooms for US$10/13 with splash-everywhere showers (no shower curtains), but the rooms are clean and well maintained and the mattresses are firm. There's no shortage of hot water, and it's a good value for its central location. Parking is available for two vehicles.

A block farther west, *Hotel San Jorge* (π 12-46-10, Victoria 26), at Madero Poniente, has a variety of rooms. Some are bigger, brighter, and better furnished than others, so ask to see a room before registering. Rates start at US$10.

Southeast of the center, **Posada Don Vasco** (☎ 12-14-84, *Vasco de Quiroga 232*) is a colonial-style hotel with rooms ringing a courtyard that has sitting areas and plants. The rooms are varied; some are quite pleasant. All have carpet, phone and private bath (hot water 6.30 am to 2 pm). The price of US$12.50/15 is a real bargain if you get one of the better rooms. The hotel's restaurant is good and cheap.

Opposite the Don Vasco, **Hotel Mintzicuri** (☎ 12-05-90, *Vasco de Quiroga 227*) has 37 small, clean rooms around a courtyard. All have carpet and a phone, and some parking is available. Rooms cost US$12.50/15, and various larger rooms are available at higher prices. Farther southeast, **Posada de Villa** (☎ 12-72-90, *Padre Lloreda 176*) is a comfortable motel-style place, not elegant, but with spacious, comfortable rooms and plenty of parking for US$11/13.50.

Mid-Range Several modern-ish hotels around the bus station have raised their prices, if not their standards, to mid-range levels. The location is convenient for bus travelers, but otherwise unappealing. **Hotel del Matador** (☎ 12-46-49, *Ruiz 531*), right opposite the bus station, has 57 worn rooms with carpet displaying stains in every shape and color. Singles/doubles run US$16/18.50. A little farther west, **Hotel Posada del Cortijo** (☎ 12-96-42, *Ruiz 673*) shares a wall with a porno theater, but its rooms are clean and decent with firm beds, shower curtains and lots of hot water. Rooms run US$14/18.50.

The newer hotels in the bus station area offer better value. **Hotel Concordia** (☎ 12-30-53, *Gómez Farías 328*) asks US$18.50/21 for clean and comfortable rooms. The rooms facing the street have little balconies and big windows, but interior rooms are quieter. **Hotel Plaza** (☎ 12-30-95), at Eduardo Ruiz and Gómez Farías, has comparable rooms and prices. A couple blocks west, **Hotel Real Victoria** (☎ 13-23-00, *Guadalupe Victoria 245*) is a modern, business travelers hotel with 110 clean, pleasant rooms, all with TV and carpet, at around US$40. There's en-

closed parking and a popular restaurant at the center of a covered courtyard.

Closer to the center, some mid-range places offer more character and convenience. On the north side of the zócalo, the Best Western **Hotel Casino** (☎ 13-13-28, *800-450-21-00, Portal Hidalgo 229*) has 48 cozy rooms, all with carpet, phone and color TV. Those facing the street have balconies overlooking the zócalo; the interior rooms open onto a covered courtyard with a popular restaurant on the ground floor. Standard price is around US$50, but ask about the US$38 specials. In the same block, **Hotel Valladolid** (☎ 12-46-63, *Portal Hidalgo 241*), on the corner of Prieto, has a great position, elegant lobby, and OK rooms from US$33.

A couple blocks southwest, **Hotel D'Atilanos** (☎ 12-01-21, *Corregidora 465*) is a well-kept colonial-style hotel with 27 large, comfy rooms, all with color TV and phone, arranged around a lovely covered courtyard. Rooms are US$21/25.

Hotel Florida (☎ 12-18-19, *Morelos Sur 161*), with a conspicuous sign southeast of the zócalo, is clean and comfortable enough, but doesn't offer much charm. Rates are US$22/29.

Top End The entrance is on the side street, but **Hotel Catedral** (☎ 13-07-83, *Zaragoza 37*) has a great location opposite the cathedral. It's another attractive colonial-style hotel with cushy rooms around a covered courtyard. Rates are around US$65, which would be a good price for one of the lovely rooms with a view of the cathedral.

Another attractive colonial option is the **Hotel de la Soledad** (☎ 12-18-88, *Zaragoza 90*), on the corner of Ocampo. Built around 1700, it has been a carriage house, a convent and a private mansion. It has 49 standard rooms at US$58, plus nine suites.

Hotel Alameda (☎ 12-20-23, *Madero Poniente 313*) is well located on the corner of the zócalo. It's an attractive, modern, 116-room hotel, with rooms from US$57 in the older section, US$73 in the newer section. There's a popular restaurant and bar.

For a room with a sweeping view of Morelia, try the **Hotel Villa Montaña**

(☎ 14-02-31, Patzimba 201), 2km from the zócalo. The hotel has 40 courtly rooms with all the modern conveniences and an inviting swimming pool. Rooms go for US$126 to US$225, or US$285 for the presidential suite.

The classiest accommodations in Morelia are undoubtedly at *Hotel Virrey de Mendoza* (☎ 12-49-40, Portal Matamoros 16), on the northwest corner of the zócalo. The former mansion of Antonio de Mendoza, the first viceroy of Mexico, has been converted to a hotel with magnificent public areas and 55 rooms and suites, all different, and all elegantly furnished with antiques and crystal chandeliers. Standard rooms cost US$75, and suites range from US$91 to US$105. It's wonderful.

Places to Eat

Dulces morelianos are a local specialty – delicious sweets made mainly of milk and sugar. Try them at street stalls, markets and *dulcerías*. For more formal meals, Morelia has many fine and reasonably priced restaurants. An excellent choice is *Fonda Las Mercedes* (☎ 12-61-13, Guzmán 47), which occupies a handsome colonial building. Tables are set in a classic covered courtyard with stately potted palms, and in a vast, subtly lit stone hall. The house specialty is *sabana Mercedes* – grilled, thinly sliced fillet of beef lightly covered with fresh parsley, garlic and olive oil (US$8); one delicious serving covers an entire dinner plate (veggies and a baked potato arrive separately). The menu has many creative pastas (US$4), and main courses using chicken (US$6), beef (US$7) or seafood (up to US$9). The fruit crêpe is a divine dessert. Budget on US$15 or so per person, and it will be a highlight of your trip.

Another place with great atmosphere is *Los Comensales*, on Zaragoza 1½ blocks north of the zócalo. The restaurant has tables in several rooms of a lovely colonial building, and under the arches around its central courtyard. There's lots of seafood with that Pátzcuaro favorite, pescado blanco, at US$7.50, or paella, steaks, or chicken mole from US$4 to US$7. Antojitos go for US$1 to US$5. It's open 8 am to 10 pm daily.

Along Portal Hidalgo, on the north side of the zócalo, is a row of restaurants and sidewalk cafés, open from around 8 am to 10 pm daily. The *Café Catedral* is a popular spot, as is the *Restaurant Don Quijote*, the restaurant of the Hotel Casino, with tables both inside and out on the sidewalk. The outside tables are perfect for coffee and people-watching. Breakfasts here run to US$4, the *menú del día* costs US$4, and beers go for US$1.50.

For very inexpensive breakfast or lunch in a friendly family setting without pretension, stop by *Super Cocina La Rosa*, on the corner of Tapia and Prieto, two blocks north of the plaza. It's under US$3 for a filling comida corrida, or select typical Mexican main courses from US$1.50. For something completely different, get your *sashimi* fix at *Mikono Centro*, on Madero Poniente, from US$5 to US$10.

A peaceful place to have coffee is the often-packed *Café del Conservatorio*, facing Jardín de las Rosas with its shade trees and shrubs. Classical music plays as you nibble on a pastry or from a cheese plate and sip wine, coffee or juice. Open 8 am to 10 pm Monday to Friday, noon to 10 pm Saturday and Sunday.

The *Restaurante Woolworth* is a pleasant enough and clean cafeteria in a former church on Virrey de Mendoza, half a block south of Madero. Breakfasts start at US$3, the set lunch is US$3.50 and the set dinner US$3.25 – you won't blow your budget here. It's open daily. Another popular stop for shoppers is *Panadería Trigo (Valladolid 8)*, off the southeast corner of the zócalo. There's a well-stocked deli downstairs, and a café upstairs, doing delicious breakfasts, light lunches and snacks for moderate prices.

For really cheap eats, there are several basic restaurants near the bus station, open 7 am to midnight daily. A comida corrida at one of these costs as little as US$1.50. There's also a row of eating stalls with tables under the covered arches running around three sides of the Plaza San Agustín, one block south of the zócalo; they're open from approximately 3 pm until 1 am daily.

Vegetarian South of the zócalo in an informal covered courtyard, *Restaurante Vegetariano Acuarius (Hidalgo 75)* does healthy breakfasts combining fruit, yogurt and granola for under US$3, and a good comida corrida for US$4. It's open 9 am to 5 pm daily. *Restaurante Vegetariano Hindu (Madero Oriente 549)* serves some vegetable curries, but mainly it's soyburgers, salads, and soups. It stays open until around 7 pm.

Entertainment

Being a university town as well as the capital of one of Mexico's most interesting states, Morelia has a lively cultural life. Stop by the tourist office and the Casa de la Cultura for their free monthly calendars listing films and cultural events around Morelia.

Newspapers like *El Sol de Morelia*, *La Voz de Michoacán* and *El Cambio de Michoacán* have cultural sections with events notices and theater and cinema ads. There are several cinemas around the center.

There are regular band concerts in both the zócalo (Sunday) and the Jardín de las Rosas on the corner of Tapia and Nigromante, and there are frequent organ recitals in the cathedral.

International film series are presented by various cinema clubs, with admission often free. Venues are the *Museo Regional Michoacano*, the *Casa Natal de Morelos* (both several times a week), the *Casa de la Cultura* and *La Librería* (see below for this last).

The Casa Natal de Morelos also presents free talks and other cultural events at its Viernes Culturales, at 7 pm Friday. Regional dances, music, stories and exhibitions from the state of Michoacán are presented at 7.30 pm most Wednesdays at the *Museo del Estado*.

La Librería (Calzada Fray Antonio de San Miguel 284), two blocks east of the Fuente Las Tarascas, is a bookstore and coffeehouse with a pleasant college atmosphere. Its cinema club shows international films at 7.30 pm most Saturdays and live music at 7.30 pm most Sundays. There's rarely a fee – just have a coffee or tea from the café.

One of the many traditional regional dances, the Danza de los Viejitos (Dance of the Old Men), is performed in the bar of the Hotel Alameda at 9 pm most Fridays and Saturdays. The costumed dancers, wearing comical masks of grinning *viejitos* with long gray hair, hooked noses, rosy cheeks and no teeth, enter hobbling on skinny canes. Their dance gets more and more animated, with wooden sandals clacking on the floor, until finally they hobble off again, looking as if they barely can make it to the door. It's a little contrived but great fun for the price of a drink or two.

For recent release movies, check *Multicinemas Morelos* on Tapia.

Two *peña* places near the zócalo host live music on Friday, Saturday and sometimes other nights – *Peña Colibrí* on Galeana, and *Peña Bola Suriana* on Allende. *Casa de los Espíritus*, next to Peña Colibrí, is more of a blues/rock venue. The *Viva México* bar, on Madero Poniente, is another un-fancy place with music, drinks and students. Quite a few dance clubs rock the posh suburbs – for the current hot-spot, ask at the tourist office, dress up, and take a taxi.

Getting There & Away

Air The Francisco J Múgica airport (☎ 12-65-14) is 27km north of Morelia, on the Morelia-Zinapécuaro highway. There are plenty of connections to other Mexican and some North American cities. Maruata Viajes (☎ 17-12-10), in the Hotel Alameda building, is a central agency for air and ETN bus tickets.

Mexicana (☎ 24-38-08), in the lobby of the Gran Hotel at the Centro de Convenciones, has daily flights to/from San Francisco, Chicago, Los Angeles, Guadalajara and Zacatecas. Aeromar (☎ 12-85-45), at Hotel Fiesta Inn, and TAESA (☎ 13-41-05), on Plaza de Rebollones, have daily flights to/from Mexico City. TAESA also serves Tijuana and Zacatecas. Aero Sudpacífico (☎ 13-52-40) flies most days to Uruapan, Lázaro Cárdenas, Mexico City and Guadalajara. Aerolitoral (☎ 13-01-40) has daily direct flights to/from Guadalajara.

Bus Morelia's Central Camionera is conveniently located just a few blocks northwest of the zócalo, on Ruiz between Gómez

Mariachi pants

Balloons for sale, Guadalajara

Cheap eats at Guadalajara's Mercado Libertad

Inside Morelia's cathedral

El Sagrario church, Pátzcuaro

Day of the Dead in Tzintzuntzan, near Pátzcuaro

Farías and Guzmán. In the bus station are a 24-hour Computel telephone caseta with fax service, several cafeterias and places to store your luggage. Daily departures include:

Guadalajara – 278km, 3½ hours by the *autopista*, otherwise 5 hours; by autopista, 8 deluxe ETN (US$22), 5 deluxe Primera Plus (US$16); by the regular road, frequent 1st-class Primera Plus, Autobuses de Jalisco and Servicios Coordinados (US$13), frequent 2nd-class

Guanajuato – 176km, 4 hours; 4 2nd-class Flecha Amarilla (US$9)

Lázaro Cárdenas – 406km, 7 hours; 9 1st-class and 2 express Parhikuni (US$12)

León – 197km, 3½ to 4 hours; 17 deluxe Primera Plus (US$11), 5 1st-class Servicios Coordinados (US$10), 2nd-class Flecha Amarilla every 20 minutes (US$9.50)

Mexico City (Terminal Poniente or Terminal Norte) – 304km, 4 hours; deluxe ETN every 15 minutes (US$22), 9 1st-class Primera Plus (US$17), frequent 2nd-class Herradura de Plata and Autobuses de Occidente (US$16)

Pátzcuaro – 62km, 1 hour; 5 1st-class Parhikuni in the afternoon (US$3), very frequent 2nd-class Galeana and Flecha Amarilla (US$2.50)

Querétaro – 259km, 3 to 4 hours; 7 deluxe and 1st-class Primera Plus, Elite and Servicios Co-ordinados (US$8 to US$10)

Uruapan – 124km, 2 hours; 5 deluxe Primera Plus (US$7), 2 deluxe ETN (US$8), 1st-class Parhikuni every 15 minutes (US$6.50), 11 2nd-class Flecha Amarilla (US$6)

Zitácuaro – 150km, 2½ to 3 hours; 2nd-class Vía 2000 (13 daily), Autobuses de Occidente (every 20 minutes), Transportes Frontera (all US$6)

Getting Around

The 'Zinapécuaro' buses from the Central Camionera will get you to/from the airport; a taxi costs US$16.50. There are several airport taxi services (☎ 15-63-53, 15-06-46, 13-10-43, 12-22-21 or 16-37-78).

Around town, local combis (white VW vans) operate from 6 am to 9 pm (a few operate until 10 pm) and cost US$0.30. Their routes are designated by the color of their stripe: Ruta Roja (red), Ruta Amarilla (yellow), Ruta Guinda (pink), Ruta Azul (blue), Ruta Verde (green) and so on. In the middle of town they mostly follow pretty straight routes – if you need to cross the central area, just hop on a combi that's going your way.

Taxis are plentiful in the center; the average taxi ride costs around US$1.50, or a little more to outer areas like the Centro de Convenciones.

SANTUARIO DE MARIPOSAS EL ROSARIO

In the easternmost part of Michoacán, near the border of México state, is the El Rosario monarch butterfly *(mariposa monarca)* sanctuary. Many millions of monarch butterflies come here every year to breed, arriving from the US and Canada from late October to early November, departing in early March for their long migration back. When they are present, there are so many butterflies in the sanctuary that they cover the trees, turning them a flaming orange; it's a great sight.

The butterflies that arrive in autumn will hibernate for the coolest part of winter, reach sexual maturity and mate in spring, lay their eggs, and die. The eggs hatch as caterpillars, make a cocoon, and then emerge as butterflies, ready to fly north. Environmental threats to the butterflies include damage to these southern breeding grounds by fire and logging.

The sanctuary is open 9 am to 6 pm daily during the butterfly season. The entry fee of US$2 includes a guide who takes you through the sanctuary, explaining the butterflies' life cycle and patterns. You can stay in the sanctuary as long as you like, but it takes only 2 hours to tour it. It's a good idea to get there early – that's when the butterflies are up in the trees. As the day warms up, they begin to flutter around. They end up coming down onto the ground where it's more humid, and there are so many you can't avoid crushing some as you walk.

It's possible to visit the reserve in a day trip from Zitácuaro, a regional commercial center on highway 15 between Mexico City and Morelia, but most people prefer to stay in the small hill town of Angangueo, 25km north of Zitácuaro, for easiest access. Tourist offices in Zitácuaro (☎ 7-153-06-75) or Morelia (☎ 800-450-23-00) may help with information.

Angangueo

• pop 5040 • elev 2980m ☎ changing

Angangueo is an old mining town that still extracts some lead and silver from the rugged hillsides. It's spread out along a single main street (Nacional for most of its length) with the main plaza and two churches at the uphill end. It's enjoyable to stroll around, and there's a miner monument that offers a good view over the town. A regional tourism office, open in the season, is just downhill from the plaza.

In 2000, the telephone area code is due to change to ☎ 7 from 715, with the digits 15 added to the start of every local number (for example, the number 6-01-87 will become 156-01-87).

Places to Stay & Eat Angangueo has several places to stay along its main drag. A few blocks down from the plaza, *Casa Huéspedes El Paso de la Monarca* (☎ 6-01-87) has simple rooms set round a tiered garden with views of the hills. Singles/doubles with private bath cost around US$11/13. *Casa Huéspedes Juárez* has rooms of a similar standard and price, centered on a rose-filled courtyard. Farther down the hill, the very appealing *Albergue Don Bruno* (☎ 6-00-26) is the first place to stay as you come into town, with attractive rooms from US$27/38. Outside the butterfly season, when the town is practically devoid of visitors, all these places might charge a little less (if they're open at all).

The *Restaurant Los Geranios*, at Albergue Don Bruno, has great views and does a fine comida corrida (US$2.75) and other meals. A few places on the plaza are also OK.

Getting There & Away Autobuses de Occidente has infrequent 2nd-class buses direct to Angangueo from Mexico City's Terminal Poniente (around four hours, US$8), but it's probably better to go first to Zitácuaro, then take one of the local buses from there to Angangueo – they leave every 15 minutes (one hour, US$1.25). From Mexico City's Terminal Poniente, bus lines with frequent service

to Zitácuaro include México Toluca Zinacantepec y Ramales, and Autobuses de Occidente (2¾ hours, US$7). From Morelia, the same companies run frequent 2nd-class buses (3 hours, US$6).

Camionetas, or vans, depart from the main road in Angangueo for the rugged 9km, one-hour trip to the monarch sanctuary. It's another 15 minutes on foot from the parking place to the sanctuary. You have to hire the whole van, so the more people sharing the cost, the better. The fee for the 10-person van is about US$21 to US$28 roundtrip (subject to negotiation), including a two-hour wait while you visit the sanctuary. Start early and try to hook up with other travelers at one of the hotels – it's easiest on weekends.

You can walk from Angangueo to the sanctuary, but it's a steep uphill journey that takes around three hours (the near 3000m altitude will make it tougher). The track to the sanctuary is the continuation of Matamoros. After about an hour, you come to a statue of the Virgin of Guadalupe; turn left here then stay on the middle track until you reach the sanctuary's entrance, where there are usually stalls and people milling about. Some people opt for a camioneta going up, then walk down – it's no cheaper but you can spend more time at the reserve.

PÁTZCUARO

• pop 47,100 • elev 2175m ☎ changing

Pátzcuaro is a lovely highland town with some stately colonial architecture in the heart of Purépecha country. The center of town lies 3.5km from the southeast shore of Lago de Pátzcuaro, almost equidistant between Morelia and Uruapan (both are about 60km away on the good highway 14). Mexican tourists come in large numbers over Christmas and New Year, for Semana Santa and for the area's famous Day of the Dead celebrations on November 1 and 2. It can get quite chilly in this mountainous area in winter – bring at least a warm sweater.

History

Pátzcuaro was the capital of the Tarasco people from about 1325 to 1400. Then, on the death of King Tariácuri, the Tarascan state

PÁTZCUARO

PLACES TO STAY
5 Hotel Fiesta Plaza
10 Hotel San Agustín
11 Hotel Posada de la Rosa
12 Hotel de la Concordia
13 Hotel Valmen
14 Posada de la Basílica
18 Gran Hotel
23 Hotel Mansión Iturbe
27 Hotel Posada de la Salud
29 Hotel Los Escudos
37 Hotel Misión San Manuel
38 Hotel Posada de San Rafael
41 Hotel Mesón del Gallo
43 Mandala

PLACES TO EAT
14 Posada de la Basílica
16 Restaurante Don Rafa
23 Restaurant Doña Paca
39 El Patio
40 El Primer Piso
43 Mandala

OTHER
1 Telecomm
2 Post Office
3 Mex Tur
4 Buses & Colectivos to Lake
6 Teatro Emperador Caltzontzin, Computel
7 Biblioteca Gertrudis Bocanegra
8 Colectivos to Bus Station
9 Templo El Santuario
12 Phone Center
15 Basílica de Nuestra Señora de la Salud
16 Meganet
19 Numismática del Lago
20 Bancomer
21 Icser
22 Charandas
24 Banco Bital
25 State Tourist Office
26 Museo de Artes Populares

28 Lavandería San Francisco
30 Municipal Tourist Office
31 La Casa del Gigante
32 Templo El Sagrario
33 Ex-Colegio Jesuita
34 Templo de la Compañía
35 Templo San Francisco
36 Templo San Juan de Dios
42 Casa de los Once Patios
44 CELEP Language School

To Posada de Don Vasco,
Hotel Villa Pátzcuaro,
Hwy 14,
Lago de Pátzcuaro,
Trailer Park El Pozo

became a three-part league comprising Pátzcuaro and, on the east side of the lake, Tzintzuntzan and Ihuatzio. First Pátzcuaro dominated, then Ihuatzio, then Tzintzuntzan. The league repulsed Aztec attacks. The Spanish first came to the area in 1522, when they received a friendly reception. Then they returned in 1529 under Nuño de Guzmán, a conquistador of legendary cruelty.

Guzmán's inhumanity to the indigenous people was so severe that the Catholic Church and the colonial government sent Bishop Vasco de Quiroga, a respected judge and churchman from Mexico City, to clean

up the mess Guzmán left. Quiroga, who arrived in 1536, established a bishopric (based initially at Tzintzuntzan, then, from 1540, at Pátzcuaro) and pioneered village cooperatives based on the humanistic ideas of Sir Thomas More's *Utopia*.

To avoid dependence on Spanish mining lords and landowners, Quiroga successfully encouraged education and agricultural self-sufficiency in the villages around Lago de Pátzcuaro, with all villagers contributing equally to the community. He also helped each village develop its own craft specialty. The Utopian communities declined after his death

WESTERN CENTRAL

in 1565, but the crafts traditions continue to this day. Not surprisingly, Tata Vascu, as the Tarascos called him, is much venerated for his work. Streets, plazas, restaurants and hotels all over Michoacán are named after him.

Orientation

Pátzcuaro has a handsome core of lovely colonial buildings and some less attractive outlying areas stretching as far as the lake. Central Pátzcuaro focuses on the fine Plaza Vasco de Quiroga and the smaller but busier Plaza Gertrudis Bocanegra one block farther north, with the town market on its west side. The center is fairly flat, but some streets climb steeply to the basilica east of the plazas.

Ahumada heads north from Plaza Vasco de Quiroga toward the Morelia-Uruapan highway (highway 14) 2km away, veering west and changing its name first to Avenida Cárdenas then to Avenida de las Américas along the way (these last two names are sometimes used interchangeably). Lago de Pátzcuaro is half a kilometer north of the highway.

The bus station is on a ring road on the southwest side of town, a kilometer from the center.

Information

Tourist Offices The helpful state tourist office (☎ 2-12-14) is to the left of the Palacio

---

The Tarascos, the Purépecha & the Day of the Dead

The territory inhabited by Michoacán's 130,000 Purépecha people extends from around Lago de Pátzcuaro to west of Uruapan. The Purépecha are direct descendants of the Tarascos, who developed western Mexico's most advanced pre-Hispanic civilization, but their early origins are obscure. The Tarascos emerged around Lago de Pátzcuaro about the 14th century, and they may have originated as semi-barbaric Chichimecs from farther north, but neither the modern Purépecha language nor the old Tarasco language has any established links to any other tongue (though connections with languages such as Zuni, from the US southwest, and Quechua, from Peru, have been suggested). The Spanish supposedly began calling them Tarascos because they often used a word that sounded like that.

The old Tarascos were noted potters and metalsmiths, and many Purépecha villages still specialize in some of those crafts. The modern Purépecha also maintain some of the country's most vital and ancient religious traditions. Día de los Muertos (Day of the Dead) remembrances around Lago de Pátzcuaro are particularly famous.

The Día de los Muertos attracts visitors to the Pátzcuaro region from all over Mexico and beyond. The local Purépecha villagers' celebrations have a magical quality and pre-Hispanic undertones. They build special altars of flowers (mainly of marigolds, which have had ceremonial importance since before Spanish times) in graveyards, where women hold candlelit vigils from midnight on the night of November 1-2. Best known – to the point where sightseers almost overwhelm the place – are the events on Isla Janitzio, including traditional dances and a parade of decorated canoes late in the evening on November 1. The tradition arises from a story about Mintzita and Itzihuapa, a pair of royal Purépecha lovers at the heart of a sunken treasure legend. It involves, as so many stories do, the cruelty of the conquistador Nuño de Guzmán. It is said that the royal lovers make their way to the graveyard of the island church on this night.

Picturesque ceremonies also take place in many other villages including Tzintzuntzan, Ihuatzio, Jarácuaro and Tzurumútaro. The state tourist office in Pátzcuaro can provide details. Many more events – including crafts markets, traditional dances, exhibitions and concerts – are held in Pátzcuaro and nearby villages around the Día de los Muertos. In Jarácuaro local dance groups and musicians stage a traditional contest of their skills in the village square on the evening of November 1.

In 2000, the telephone area code is due to change to ☎ 4 from 434, with the digits 34 added to the start of every local number (for example, the number 2-02-15 will become 342-02-15).

de Huitzimengari, on the north side of the Plaza Vasco de Quiroga. Some people here speak English, and they have maps and good information on the state of Michoacán. It's open 9 am to 3 pm and 4 to 7 pm Monday to Saturday, 9 am to 2 pm Sunday.

The municipal tourist office (☎ 2-02-15), at Portal Hidalgo 1 on the west side of Plaza Vasco de Quiroga, is open 10 am to 3 pm Monday to Friday, 10 am to 4 pm Saturday, 10 am to 4 pm Sunday.

Money You can change dollars or traveler's checks at several banks on and around the two main plazas, all of which have ATMs. Some will change money only between 10 am and noon, but Bancomer, at Mendoza 23, and Banco Bital on Iturbide will do so during regular business hours. Numismática del Lago, at Iturbe 30, changes cash and checks from 9 am to 7 pm Monday to Friday, 9 am to 2 pm on Saturday and Sunday, with slightly lower rates and considerably less paperwork.

Post & Communications The post office, at Obregón 13 half a block north of Plaza Gertrudis Bocanegra, is open 8 am to 4 pm Monday to Friday, 9 am to 1 pm Saturday. The Telecomm office, at Títere 15, offers telegram and fax services. Computel, on the north side of Plaza Gertrudis Bocanegra, has long-distance and fax services every day, but the cheapest international calls seem to be from a caseta halfway up the stairs at the Hotel Posada de la Rosa.

Meganet, on Mendoza beside a hamburger shop, has Internet access for US$2.50 per hour, 10 am to 9 pm Monday to Saturday, 10 am to 3 pm Sunday. Icser, on Plaza Vasco de Quiroga, has similar hours and charges US$2 per hour.

Laundry Lavandería San Francisco, on Terán near Templo San Francisco, will wash and dry 3kg for US$3.50, 9 am to 8 pm Monday to Saturday.

Plaza Vasco de Quiroga
Pátzcuaro's wide and well proportioned main plaza is one of the loveliest in Mexico. A tall statue of Vasco de Quiroga gazes benignly down from the central fountain. The plaza is ringed by trees and flanked by arched verandas called *portales*. These form part of the façades of 17th-century buildings, originally grand mansions but now mostly used as hotels, restaurants and shops. The sides of the plaza are named (independently of the street names) Portal Hidalgo (west side), Portal Aldama (south side), and Portal Matamoros (east side). The north side is Portal Allende east of Iturbe and Portal Morelos west of Iturbe.

One of the finest buildings is **La Casa del Gigante** at Portal Matamoros 40 on the east side of the plaza. Built in 1663, it takes its name from a giant statue of a man in the interior courtyard. A sign outside says it's a *galería de artesanías*, but it doesn't seem to be open to the public.

Another old mansion, the **Palacio de Huitzimengari**, on the north side of the plaza, is said to have belonged to the last Tarasco emperor and presently houses a Purépecha cultural organization. It's not open to the public.

Casa de los Once Patios
The House of the 11 Courtyards, a block southeast of Plaza Vasco de Quiroga on the cobbled Calle de la Madrigal de las Altas Torres, is a fine rambling building built as a Dominican convent in the 1740s. Earlier, one of Mexico's first hospitals, founded by Vasco de Quiroga, stood on the site. Today the house is a warren of small artesanías shops, each specializing in a particular regional craft. Copperware from Santa Clara del Cobre, straw goods from Tzintzuntzan, musical instruments from Paracho, as well as gold-leaf-decorated lacquerware, hand-painted ceramics and attractive textiles, can

all be found. It's great for browsing, and artisans can be seen working in some shops. Most are open 10 am to 7 pm daily.

Plaza Gertrudis Bocanegra

Pátzcuaro's second main plaza is named after a local heroine who was shot by firing squad in 1818 for her support of the independence movement. Her statue adorns the center of the plaza, and she looks like a tough woman.

The town's **market** bustles away on the west side of the plaza, especially on Sunday, Monday and Friday. You can find everything from fruit, vegetables and fresh lake fish to herbal medicines, crafts and clothing, including the region's distinctive striped shawls, sarapes and *peruanas* (a kind of sarape-shawl worn by women).

The **Biblioteca Gertrudis Bocanegra** (Gertrudis Bocanegra Library) occupies the 16th-century former San Agustín church on the north side of the plaza. A large, colorful Juan O'Gorman mural covering the rear wall depicts the history of Michoacá from pre-Hispanic times to the 1910 revolution. The library has been under renovation recently.

A small **Mercado de Artesanías** operates in the side street next to the library. Crafts sold here include grotesque Tocuaro masks, carved wooden forks and knives from Zirahuén and pottery. The prices are very favorable.

On the west side of the library, the **Teatro Emperador Caltzontzin** was a convent until it was converted to a theater in 1936. Movies and occasional cultural events are presented here. Murals in the main upstairs hall colorfully remind moviegoers of various epochs in Michoacán's history, including the meeting of Tarasco King Tangahxuan II and the Spanish conquistador Cristóbal de Olid near Pátzcuaro in 1522.

Basílica de Nuestra Señora de la Salud

Two blocks east of the south end of Plaza Gertrudis Bocanegra, the basilica was intended by Vasco de Quiroga to be the centerpiece of his Michoacán community, a cathedral big enough for 30,000 worshipers, but the existing basilica, finished in the 19th century, is only the central nave of the original design. Quiroga's tomb, the Mausoleo de Don Vasco, is just to the left inside the main west doors.

Behind the altar at the east end stands a much revered figure of the Virgin, Nuestra Señora de la Salud (Our Lady of Health). The image was made by Tarascos in the 16th century, on Quiroga's request, from a corncob-and-honey paste called *tatzingue*. Soon people began to experience miraculous healings, and Quiroga had the words 'Salus Infirmorum' (Healer of the Sick) inscribed at the figure's feet. Ever since, pilgrims have come from all over Mexico to ask this Virgin for a miracle. Many make their way on their knees across the plaza, into the church and along its nave. You can walk up the stairs behind the image to see the many small tin representations of hands, feet, legs and so on that pilgrims have offered to the Virgin.

Museo de Artes Populares

One block south of the basilica, this museum of folk arts, at Enseñanza and Alcantarillas, is housed in a rambling building. Quiroga founded the original Colegio de San Nicolás on this site in 1540, arguably the first college in the Americas. The institution was later moved to Valladolid (as Morelia was then called), and much of the present structure dates from the early 18th century. In fact, the whole lot is superimposed on pre-Hispanic stone structures, some of which can be seen behind the museum courtyards.

Exhibits of Michoacán arts and crafts include delicate white lace *rebozos* (shawls) from Aranza, handpainted ceramics from Santa Fe de la Laguna and copperware from Santa Clara del Cobre. One room is set up as a typical Michoacán kitchen with a tremendous brick oven and a full set of ceramic and copper utensils. Also note the tasteful use of cows' knuckle bones as decorations between the flagstones on the floor.

The museum is open 9 am to 7 pm, Tuesday to Saturday, 9 am to 3 pm Sunday (US$1.75, free Sunday).

Templo de la Compañía & Ex-Colegio Jesuita

Built in the 16th century, the Templo de la Compañía and the adjacent plain white building, on the corner of Lerin and Alcantarillas, became a Jesuit training college from the 17th century. The church is still in use and houses some relics from Vasco de Quiroga. The college building fell into ruin after the expulsion of the Jesuits and had various uses. Restored in the early 1990s, it is now used for cultural and community activities.

Other Churches

If you like old churches, Pátzcuaro has several others of interest, including Templos El Sagrario, San Juan de Dios, San Francisco and El Santuario. All are shown on the map.

El Estribo

El Estribo, a lookout point on a hill 4km west of the center, offers a magnificent view of the entire Lago de Pátzcuaro area. It takes up to an hour to walk there but only a few minutes by vehicle. Either way, you take Ponce de León from the southwest corner of Plaza Vasco de Quiroga and follow the signs.

Language Courses

CELEP, the Centro de Leguas y Ecoturismo de Pátzcuaro (☎ 2-47-64, celep@rds2000 .crefal.edu.mx), at Navarrete 47A, offers courses in two-week blocks, starting with an evaluation every Monday. Courses involve four hours of classes every morning for US$250, plus a program of tours and cultural activities every afternoon for an extra US$140. Accommodation and meals can be arranged for local families for US$12 to US$15 per day.

Organized Tours

See the Around Pátzcuaro section for local tour operators.

Special Events

Aside from the famous local events for the Day of the Dead (see the boxed text 'The Tarascos, the Purépecha & the Day of the Dead'), Pátzcuaro stages some interesting events at other times as well.

Pastorelas These dramatizations of the journey of the shepherds to see the infant Jesus are staged in Plaza Vasco de Quiroga on several evenings around Christmas. *Pastorelas indígenas*, on the same theme but including mask dances, enact the struggle of angels against the devils that are trying to hinder the shepherds, and are held in eight villages around Lago de Pátzcuaro on different days between December 26 and February 2. Rodeos and other events accompany them. The tourist offices can provide details.

Semana Santa The week leading up to Easter is full of events in Pátzcuaro and the lakeside villages, including Palm Sunday processions in several places; Viacruci processions, enacting Christ's journey to Calvary and the crucifixion itself, on Good Friday morning; candlelit processions in silence on Good Friday evening; and a ceremonial burning of Judas on Easter Sunday evening in Plaza Vasco de Quiroga. There are many local variations; the tourist offices can provide details.

Nuestra Señora de la Salud On December 8, a colorful procession to the basilica honors the Virgin of Health. Traditional dances are performed, including Los Reboceros, Los Moros, Los Viejitos and Los Panaderos.

Places to Stay – Budget

Camping The *Hotel Villa Pátzcuaro* (☎ 2-07-67, Avenida de las Américas 506), 2km north of the center on the road to the lake, has a small trailer park in pleasant grounds. Two people with a vehicle pay US$9 or US$10 for a space with full hookups, or you can set up a tent on the lawn area for US$4.50 per person. The place has a helpful manager, clean showers, a small kitchen and a swimming pool.

Trailer Park El Pozo (☎ 2-09-37) is on the lakeside, just off highway 14 toward Morelia, 1km east of its junction with Avenida de las Américas. Watch for the sign pointing across the train tracks to the grassy field, which has 20 shaded sites with full hookups for US$4 per person.

Hotels On the west side of the Plaza Gertrudis Bocanegra, *Hotel Posada de la Rosa* (☎ 2-08-11, Portal Juárez 29) is the cheapest decent place in town. Its rooms, along an upstairs patio, all have two beds and lots of hot water. Cost per single/double with shared bath is US$6/7. Next door and upstairs, ***Hotel San Agustín*** (☎ 2-04-42) has small but clean rooms with bath for US$7.75/13. Those on one side of the hall have windows overlooking the market; those on the other side are stuffy, dark and depressing.

A few doors down, atmospheric ***Hotel de la Concordia*** (☎ 2-00-03) has big, old, dark rooms with high ceilings and shared bath for US$7/12, and some nicer rooms with TV and private bath for US$16/24.

Hotel Valmen (☎ 2-11-61, Padre Lloreda 34), a block east of Plaza Gertrudis Bocanegra, is pretty worn but it's OK for the price. The 16 rooms are of various sizes and all have private bath. You pay US$6 per person, but a room for four will cost US$24 even if you're by yourself. Most are around a covered patio and have large windows and plenty of light, but look before registering.

Hotel Posada de la Salud (☎ 2-00-58, Serrato 9), half a block behind the basilica, is a well-kept little place with 15 clean, pleasant rooms looking onto a grassy courtyard. It's a bit away from the center, very quiet (except for noisy plumbing), more for pilgrims than party-goers, but at US$11/16 it's about the best value budget place in town.

Places to Stay – Mid-Range

Several of the 17th-century mansions around Plaza Vasco de Quiroga have been turned into elegant colonial-style hotels, all with restaurants. One of the most attractive is the ***Hotel Los Escudos*** (☎ 2-01-38, Portal Hidalgo 73), on the west side of the plaza. Most of the 30 rooms have colonial paintings on the walls, and all have carpeting, private bath and satellite TV; some have fireplaces. They're set around two patios full of plants and cost US$25 for one or two people and one bed, US$35 for two people and two beds.

On the south side of the plaza, ***Hotel Misión San Manuel*** (☎ 2-13-13, Portal Aldama 12) is a former monastery building with 42 rooms. Some have a fireplace and all have carpeting, tiled bathrooms and beamed ceilings. Cost is US$38 for a single or double, US$49 with two beds. Nearby ***Hotel Posada de San Rafael*** (☎ 2-07-70, Portal Aldama

18) has 103 smaller, more basic rooms, with carpeting and TV, but no fireplaces, at US$21/32 for singles/doubles.

One block south of Plaza Vasco de Quiroga, ***Hotel Mesón del Gallo*** (☎ 2-14-74, Dr Coss 20) is less historic than the hotels on the plaza, but it has a swimming pool, lawn and a pleasant restaurant and bar. The 20 rooms cost US$35/42, including breakfast.

As well as an excellent vegetarian restaurant, ***Mandala*** (☎ 2-41-76, Lerín 14), just east of the Casa de los Once Patios, has a few very comfortable and attractive rooms. The three downstairs share a modern bath and cost only US$12/18, including breakfast. The two upstairs have a fine view, private bath and a higher price tag – they're some of the nicest rooms in town.

Gran Hotel (☎ 2-04-43, Plaza Gertrudis Bocanegra 6) is quite popular at US$24 for one or two people. Rooms are small, clean and nicely furnished.

Hotel Fiesta Plaza (☎ 2-25-15, Plaza Gertrudis Bocanegra 24) is a modern place in colonial style with 60 pleasant, good sized rooms on three floors around two courtyards. It's a well run place, with rooms at US$45/50.

On a hill opposite the basilica, ***Posada de la Basílica*** (☎ 2-11-08, Arciga 6) has cheerful, sizable rooms around an open courtyard that overlooks the red-tile roofs of the town. Rooms are very reasonable at US$33/44, and even better at the special rate of US$22. Wood for the fireplaces is provided. Try for a room with a balcony and a view. Its restaurant is an enjoyable place for breakfast.

The pleasant ***Hotel Villa Pátzcuaro*** (☎ 2-07-67, Avenida de las Américas 506) is set back from the road to the lake, about 2km from the center of town. The 12 cozy rooms – at US$17/22 – all have fireplaces and there's a swimming pool. It's most convenient if you have a vehicle, but local buses to the lake or town pass by every few minutes. The manager here is helpful, knows the area well, and speaks good English.

Places to Stay – Top End

On the north side of Plaza Vasco de Quiroga, ***Mansión Iturbe*** (☎ 2-03-68, Portal Morelos

59) retains all of its colonial elegance, with high ceilings, wood beams and antique furnishings. Each room is different (some have deep bathtubs, others private balconies and so on), so have a look before checking in. Prices start at around US$70, which includes breakfast, newspaper, two hours' bicycle use and coffee at any time. The hotel also has an art gallery and two good restaurants, one with live music.

The Best Western *Posada de Don Vasco* (☎ 2-02-27, *Avenida de las Américas 450*) is about 1.5km north of the center on the way to the lake. It was established as a resort hotel in 1938, in a vague semi-art-deco neocolonial style. Considerably renovated and enlarged, it now has 101 comfortable rooms, plus a tennis court, swimming pool, game room, restaurant and bar. Older rooms have a little character; those in the newer blocks are bigger and brighter. Rates are around US$50/100 for singles/doubles with all mod cons.

Places to Eat

The best-known Pátzcuaro specialty is the tiny pescado blanco (white fish), traditionally caught on Lago de Pátzcuaro using canoes and 'butterfly' nets, but now as likely to come from fish farms. Other specialties include *corundas*, which are *tamales* with a pork, bean and cream filling, and *sopa Tarasca*, a tomato-based soup with cream and bits of crisp tortilla and dried chili.

El Patio (*Plaza Vasco de Quiroga 19*) specializes in regional food at reasonable prices – soups around US$2, chicken US$4, beef US$5, fish US$4 to US$7. Its *sopa Tarasca* is delicious and the rich reddish-brown sauce on the *pollo en mole* will make you drool.

El Primer Piso (*Plaza Vasco de Quiroga 29*) is on the second floor of a very old building and its four balconies are a favorite of romantics and people-watchers. Its menu is eclectic contemporary Mexican, with imaginative dishes like *birria*-stuffed chilis, and chicken breast with mushroom, spinach and cheese sauce, mostly around US$7. Soups run about US$2.50, salads US$4, pastas US$5. If you just want to sit

on the balcony, the café au lait and desserts are excellent.

All the mansions-turned-hotels on Plaza Vasco de Quiroga have restaurants. One of the best is *Restaurant Doña Paca* in the Hotel Mansión Iturbe. It features some excellent, upmarket versions of traditional streetmarket fare like tacos, *gorditas* and enchiladas, all beautifully presented for around US$4. In the evenings you can feast on real market fare at the *food stalls* on the northwest corner of Plaza Gertrudis Bocanegra, where a chicken dinner with vegetables and tortillas will cost less than US$3.

Restaurante Don Rafa (*Mendoza 30*), between the main plazas, is clinically clean and does a popular comida corrida for US$4. For a meal with a view, try the restaurant at the *Posada de la Basílica*, which is open only for breakfast and lunch. Thick tablecloths and heavy Michoacán ceramic plates might inspire some shopping. Breakfasts are US$3 to US$4, lunches about US$5.

Vegetarians and others will enjoy the atmosphere at *Mandala*, just a short walk east of Plaza Vasco de Quiroga. It's bright, friendly and charmingly decorated, and it uses the freshest, most flavorful vegetables for satisfying salads, soups and pastas.

A cheap place to try local fish is beside the main jetty on the lake, where the boats depart for Isla Janitzio. A row of *fish stands* all charge the same – US$5 for pescado blanco, US$3 for *mojarra* (perch) and US$2.50 for a cupful of charales (tiny fish that are eaten whole). You can choose your fish, and they'll fry it up on the spot. Be forewarned: All of Pátzcuaro's wastewater pours untreated into the lake.

Entertainment

Hotel Fiesta Plaza has regular live music on Friday and Saturday evening. Local musicians also perform at the pizza café *Charandas*, just west of the Mansión Iturbe.

The *Teatro Emperador Caltzontzin* is host to occasional performances of theater, music and dance in addition to the usual fare of cinema in small-town Mexico (such as F-grade kung fu movies).

Shopping

The Casa de los Once Patios is the first place to look for Michoacán crafts, and there's also the main market and the Mercado de Artesanías, both next to Plaza Gertrudis Bocanegra (see the earlier entries on these places). On Friday morning a ceramics market, with pottery from different villages, is held in Plaza San Francisco, one block west of Plaza Vasco de Quiroga.

Getting There & Away

Pátzcuaro's Central Camionera is on the southwest edge of town, on the ring road variously called Avenida Circunvalación or El Libramiento. It has a cafeteria, a *guarda equipaje* where you can store your luggage, and a telephone caseta. Buses from Pátzcuaro (2nd-class unless otherwise stated) include:

Erongarícuaro – 18km, 25 minutes; Autobuses de Occidente every 5 minutes, 7 am to 8 pm (US$0.70)

Guadalajara – 347km, 5½ hours; 1st-class Servicios Coordinados at 11.30 pm (US$14), 2nd-class Piedad at 11.50 pm (US$11)

Lázaro Cárdenas – 342km, 6 hours; Galeana, hourly, 6 am to 6.30 pm (US$14)

Mexico City – 366km, 5 hours; 10 1st-class Herradura de Plata to Terminal Poniente, 7 to Terminal Norte (US$19), 2nd-class Flecha Amarilla to Terminal Poniente (US$11)

Morelia – 62km, 1 hour; 5 1st-class Parhikuni in the afternoon (US$3), hourly 2nd-class Galeana and Flecha Amarilla (US$2.50)

Quiroga – 22km, 30 minutes; Galeana every 15 minutes, 5.50 am to 8.45 pm (US$0.60)

Santa Clara del Cobre – 20km, 30 minutes; Galeana every 30 minutes, 5.45 am to 8.25 pm (US$0.50)

Tzintzuntzan – 15km, 20 minutes; same buses as to Quiroga (US$0.40)

Uruapan – 62km, 1 hour; Galeana every 15 minutes (US$2.75)

Minibuses to some nearby towns depart from Plaza Gertrudis Bocanegra (see below).

Getting Around

'Centro' buses and colectivos, from the yard to your right when you walk out of the bus station, will take you to Plaza Gertrudis Bocanegra. Returning to the bus station, catch a 'Central' vehicle from Plaza Gertrudis Bocanegra – colectivos stop on the north side of the plaza, buses on the west side. For the jetty where boats leave for Isla Janitzio, 'Lago' buses and colectivos go to/from the northeast corner of Plaza Gertrudis Bocanegra. Buses cost US$0.30, colectivos slightly more. They run from about 6 am to 10 pm.

AROUND PÁTZCUARO

The most interesting day trips are to villages around Pátzcuaro, all of which can be reached, or nearly reached, by local buses (see Getting There & Away in the Pátzcuaro section). From Pátzcuaro it's possible to circle the lake by bus, stopping at villages along the way – you'll need to change buses at Quiroga and Erongarícuaro in order to get around.

Organized Tours

IPEAC (☎ 434-401-67), based at Erongarícuaro on the west side of the lake, offers guided tours with an emphasis on local ecology and indigenous communities. Led by Francisco Castilleja, the usual tours visit Purépecha villages, learning about medicinal herbs and trying a traditional lunch. Mostly it's done on public buses, but arrangements are very flexible. A typical day trip might cost around US$20, some of which goes to the villagers. Meet Francisco at 10 am in Pátzcuaro at the Hotel Mansión Iturbide, or the tables outside.

MexTur (☎ 434-241-41), Obregón 3, runs small group tours to Isla Janitzio and Santa Clara del Cobre, followed by a guided walk around Pátzcuaro (US$40 per person).

Lago de Pátzcuaro

The lake has one very touristy island and a couple of others that are much less visited. Streams feeding the lake are being depleted, and at the current rate of shrinkage the lake won't exist at all in 50 years. You may find the lake to be prettier from a distance than up close.

Isla Janitzio Janitzio (population 1950), the largest island in Lago de Pátzcuaro, is

LAGO DE PÁTZCUARO

To Zamora

San Jerónimo
Purenchécuaro

Chupicuaro

Santa Fe de
la Laguna

To Morelia

San Andrés
Tziróndaro

Quiroga

*Lago de
Pátzcuaro*

Oponguo

Tzintzuntzan

0   3   6 km
0   1.5   3 miles

Isla
Pacanda

Puacuaro

Isla
Yuñuén

Napizaro

Erongarícuaro

Isla
Tecuéna

San Pedro
Cucuchuchu

San
Francisco
Uricho

*Restaurant
Campestre
Alemán*

Ruins Ihuatzio

Sanabría

Isla
Janitzio

Jarácuaro

*Muelle
General*

Arocutín

Isla
Uranden
Morelos

*Muelle
San Pedrito*

Trailer Park El Pozo

Tzurumútaro

Tocuaro

San Pedro
Pareo

Tzentzénguaro

Huecorio

*Hotel Villa
Pátzcuaro*

To Morelia

Nocutzepo

Santa Ana
Chapítiro

*Posada de
Don Vasco*

San Bartolo
Pareo

Pátzcuaro

To Zirahuén,
Tingambato, Uruapan

Bus
Station

To Santa Clara
del Cobre

heavily devoted to tourism, and on weekends and holidays it is overrun with daytrippers. It has all the hallmarks of a tourist trap, so don't feel bad if you miss it. The 20-minute launch trip to the island offers distant views of villages along the shore, while fishermen occasionally demonstrate the use of their famous butterfly-shaped fishing nets from conveniently placed canoes. They then paddle alongside your launch holding out trays for your coins.

The island itself has plenty of fish restaurants, cheap souvenir shops, and begging kids – you can see everything in an hour. A 40m-high statue of independence hero Jose María Morelos y Pavón stands on its highest point. Inside the statue is a set of murals depicting Morelos' life; for US$0.50 you can go inside and climb all the way up to his raised fist and see the panoramic view.

Isla Yuñuén This smaller island (population 90) has a strong Purépecha community and is developing some small-scale tourism.

Six comfortable *cabins* (☎ 434-2-44-73, 434-2-15-30) on the island cost around US$33 per night, depending on the season and the number of people. Call ahead to arrange a stay.

Getting There & Away For boat trips on the lake, head to the *muelles* (docks), about 3km north of central Pátzcuaro. The Muelle General is well served by local buses and combis marked 'Lago' from Plaza Gertrudis Bocanegra in Pátzcuaro. It has a slew of cheap fish restaurants and souvenir shops, and a ticket office for boat trips. The launches leave when they're full, which is usually about every 30 minutes, from around 7 am to 6 pm (US$2.25 to Isla Janitzio and back, US$2.75 to Isla Yuñuen or Isla Pacanda). Keep your ticket for the return trip.

A short distance round the lake to the west, Muelle San Pedrito is smaller and not as well served by public transport, but the launches are slightly cheaper from here, and it may be a better place to charter a boat – US$11 to Janitzio for up to 10 people, US$33 for a longer trip around Yuñuen and other islands.

Ihuatzio
• pop 3200 • elev 2035m

Ihuatzio, 14km from Pátzcuaro near the eastern shore of the lake, was capital of the Tarascan league after Pátzcuaro but before Tzintzuntzan. Buses run to this village from Plaza Gertrudis Bocanegra. There's a large archaeological site of **Tarascan ruins**, only partly excavated, a short walk from the village. The main feature is an open ceremonial space 200m long with two pyramids at its west end. The unexcavated areas include walled causeways and a round-based building thought to have been an observatory. The site is open 10 am to 3 pm daily (US$0.20). The ruins are more memorable than those at Tzintzuntzan, especially at sunset, mainly because they appear in a more natural setting.

Tzintzuntzan
• pop 3180 • elev 2050m

The interesting little town of Tzintzuntzan ('tseen-TSOON-tsahn') is about 15km from Pátzcuaro near the northeastern corner of Lago de Pátzcuaro. It has impressive buildings from both the pre-Hispanic Tarascan empire and the early Spanish missionary period, and there are modern handicrafts on sale.

Tzintzuntzan is a Purépecha name meaning Place of Hummingbirds. It was the capital of the Tarascan league at the time of invasions by the Aztecs in the late 15th century (which were repulsed) and the Spanish in the 1520s. The Purépecha chief came to peaceable terms with Cristóbal de Olid, leader of the first Spanish expedition in 1522, but this did not satisfy Nuño de Guzmán, who arrived in 1529 and had the chief burned alive in his quest for gold.

Vasco de Quiroga established his first base here when he reached Michoacán in the mid-1530s, and Tzintzuntzan became the headquarters of the Franciscan monks who followed him, although the town declined in importance after he shifted his base to Pátzcuaro in 1540.

Just along the main street from the Ex-Convento de San Francisco, craftspeople sell a variety of straw goods, the local specialty, and other Michoacán artesanías. You can reach the lakeshore by continuing straight down this street for about 1km.

Las Yácatas The centerpiece of pre-Hispanic Tzintzuntzan is an impressive group of five round-based temples, known as *yácatas*, on a large terrace of carefully fitted stone blocks. They stand on the hillside just above the town, on the east side of the road from Pátzcuaro. The site entrance is a 700m walk from the center of the town. There are good views from the higher levels; there are also a few other structures and a small museum. Hours are 9 am to 6 pm daily (US$2).

Ex-Convento de San Francisco On the west side of the main street, Avenida Lázaro Cárdenas, is a complex of religious buildings, constructed partly with stones from Las Yácatas, which the Spanish wrecked. Here Franciscan monks began the Spanish missionary effort in Michoacán in the 16th century. The olive trees in the churchyard are said to have been brought from Spain and planted by Vasco de Quiroga, and are believed to be the oldest olive trees in the Americas.

Straight ahead as you walk into the churchyard is the still-functioning Templo de San Francisco, built for the monks' own use. Inside, halfway along its north side, is the Capilla del Señor del Rescate (Chapel of the Savior), with a much-revered painting of Christ. This painting is the focus of a weeklong festival in February. The cloister of the old monastery adjoining the church contains the parish offices and some old, weathered murals. On the north side of the churchyard stands the church built for the Tarascos, the Templo de Nuestra Señora de la Salud, with a holy image of El Cristo de Goznes (The Christ of Hinges). In the enclosed yard beside this church is an old open chapel, the Capilla Abierta de la Concepción.

Quiroga
• pop 12,900 • elev 2074m
The town of Quiroga, 7km northeast of Tzintzuntzan at the junction of highway 120 with highway 15 between Morelia and Zamora, has existed since pre-Hispanic times. It's named after Vasco de Quiroga, who was responsible for many of its buildings and handicrafts. These days Quiroga has few original old buildings and is not very pretty, but it's a great place to shop for artesanías, especially brightly painted wooden products, leatherwork, wool sweaters and sarapes.

On the first Sunday in July, the Fiesta de la Preciosa Sangre de Cristo (Festival of the Precious Blood of Christ) is celebrated with a long torchlight procession. The procession is led by a group carrying an image of Christ crafted from a paste made of corncobs and honey.

Buses run west out of Quiroga to Erongarícuaro every 90 minutes.

Erongarícuaro
• pop 2510 • elev 2080m
On the southwest edge of Lago de Pátzcuaro, a pretty 18km trip from Pátzcuaro, Erongarícuaro (often just called 'Eronga') is one of the oldest settlements on the lake. It's just a peaceful little town where you can enjoy strolling along streets still lined with old Spanish-style houses. Top attractions are the plaza, the church a block away, and the old seminary attached to the church. The Muebles Finos factory produces unusual furniture – look for the Day of the Dead chair resembling a human skeleton.

On January 6, the Fiesta de los Reyes Magos (Festival of the Magic Kings) is celebrated with music and dance.

Just south of Erongarícuaro, *Restaurant Campestre Alemán* (☎ 434-4-00-06) specializes in German-style smoked trout. It's slightly upmarket, with a lovely outlook, and popular with locals for weekend lunches.

Tocuaro
• pop 630 • elev 2035m
Some of Mexico's finest mask makers live in this sleepy, one-bus-stop town 10km from Pátzcuaro, although you wouldn't know it. Many families in Tocuaro are involved in mask making, but none have shops or even small signs outside their homes indicating as much. And since there are no street signs in Tocuaro, locating the town's mask makers is a bit of an adventure.

To find Tocuaro's most famous mask maker, Juan Orta Castillo, walk up the street that runs from the bus stop and the church; when you're about halfway to the church, knock on a door on the left side of the street and politely repeat his name. If you're at his home, you'll be invited in and shown masks for sale; if not, you'll be pointed the right way. If you're lucky, you will see Orta at work. He has won Mexico's National Mask Maker competition several times.

Tocuaro's other highly regarded mask makers include Gustavo Horta, Felipe Terra and Felipe Anciola. If you're in the market for a mask, knock on doors and ask around for *una máscara*.

Santa Clara del Cobre
• pop 11,800 • elev 2180m
Santa Clara del Cobre (also called Villa Escalante), 20km south of Pátzcuaro, was a

copper-mining center from 1553 onwards. Though the mines are closed, this nice little town still specializes in copperware, with over 50 workshops making copper goods. There's a copper museum too, next to the main plaza.

A weeklong Feria del Cobre (Copper Fair) is held each August; exact dates vary.

Zirahuén
- **pop 2250** - **elev 2240m**

Smaller but much deeper than Lago de Pátzcuaro, the blue lake beside the colonial town of Zirahuén, 20km from Pátzcuaro off the road to Uruapan, makes a peaceful spot for a day trip or for camping. There are some *cabañas*, a few casual lakeside eateries, and launches doing excursions. A few buses go to Zirahuén from the Pátzcuaro bus station; as an option, you could take an Uruapan bus, get off at the Zirahuén turnoff and walk the remaining 5km.

URUAPAN
- **pop 215,400** - **elev 1620m** ☎ 4

When the Spanish monk Fray Juan de San Miguel arrived here in 1533, he was so impressed with the Río Cupatitzio and the lush vegetation surrounding it that he named the area Uruapan ('oo-roo-AH-pahn'), which translates roughly as 'Eternal Spring.' Uruapan is 500m lower in altitude than Pátzcuaro, and much warmer. The vegetation becomes noticeably more tropical on the 62km trip between the two places.

Fray Juan had a large market square, hospital and chapel built, and arranged streets in an orderly checkerboard pattern. Under Spanish rule, Uruapan quickly grew into a productive agricultural center, and today it's renowned for its high-quality *aguacates* (avocados) and fruit. It bills itself as the Capital Mundial del Aguacate, and has an avocado fair in November. Its craftspeople are famed for their hand-painted cedar lacquerware, particularly trays and boxes.

Uruapan is a larger, less tidy place than Pátzcuaro, with far less colonial ambiance, but is still attractive with red-tile roofs and lush hillside setting. A pleasant miniature national park, the Parque Nacional Eduardo Ruiz, lies within the city, only 15 minutes' walk from the center. Uruapan is also the best base for visiting the remarkable volcano Paricutín, 35km west.

Orientation
The city slopes down from north to south, with the Río Cupatitzio running down its west side. Most of the streets are still arranged in the grid pattern laid down in the 1530s. Apart from the bus station in the northeast of town, everything of interest to travelers is within walking distance of the 300m-long main plaza. This is actually three joined plazas named, from east to west, El Jardín Morelos, La Pérgola Municipal and El Jardín de los Mártires de Uruapan. A colonial church stands at each end of the north side of the plaza. The portales, the arched verandas facing the plaza, are individually named, independently of the street names.

Street names change at the plaza, and at other points. The busy street along the south side of the plaza is called Emilio Carranza to the west and Obregón to the east. Farther east, it changes again to Sarabia, which intersects Paseo Lázaro Cárdenas, the main road south to the coast.

Information
Tourist Offices The state Delegación de Turismo (☎ 524-71-99), Juan Ayala 16, is a couple of blocks northwest of the plaza. It stocks brochures (some in English) and a simple map of Uruapan. The office is open 9 am to 2.30 pm and 4 to 7 pm Monday to Saturday, 9 am to 2 pm Sunday.

The municipal Casa de Turista (☎ 524-30-91), in the courtyard at Emilio Carranza 44, may be helpful. It stocks little printed material, but it does have some crafts for sale, and a website, www.uruapan.gob.mx. The office is open 9 am to 6 pm daily.

Money There are a number of banks and ATMs near the central plaza, especially on Cupatitzio in the first two blocks south of the plaza. Most banks are open 9 am to 5.30 pm Monday to Friday and 9 am to 1 pm Saturday, but some have shorter

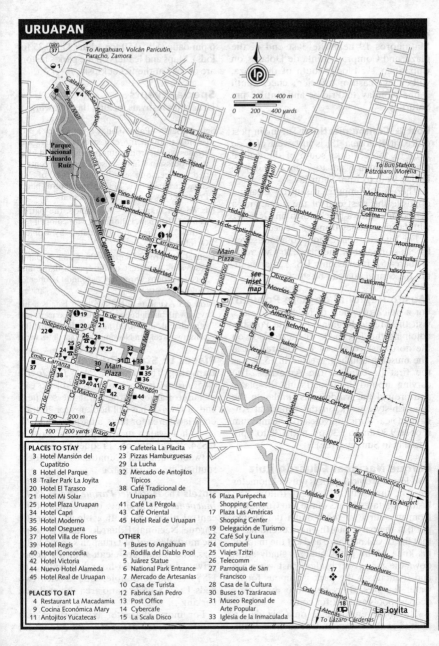

URUAPAN

To Angahuan, Volcán Paricutín,
Paracho, Zamora

To Bus Station,
Pátzcuaro, Morelia

Parque
Nacional
Eduardo
Ruíz

Main
Plaza

see
inset
map

Main
Plaza

La Joyita

To Airport

To Lázaro Cárdenas

PLACES TO STAY
3 Hotel Mansión del
Cupatitzio
8 Hotel del Parque
18 Trailer Park La Joyita
20 Hotel El Tarasco
21 Hotel Mi Solar
25 Hotel Plaza Uruapan
34 Hotel Capri
35 Hotel Moderno
36 Hotel Oseguera
37 Hotel Villa de Flores
39 Hotel Regis
40 Hotel Concordia
42 Hotel Victoria
44 Nuevo Hotel Alameda
45 Hotel Real de Uruapan

PLACES TO EAT
4 Restaurant La Macadamia
9 Cocina Económica Mary
11 Antojitos Yucatecas

19 Cafetería La Placita
23 Pizzas Hamburguesas
29 La Lucha
32 Mercado de Antojitos
Típicos
38 Café Tradicional de
Uruapan
41 Café La Pérgola
43 Café Oriental
45 Hotel Real de Uruapan

OTHER
1 Buses to Angahuan
2 Rodilla del Diablo Pool
5 Juárez Statue
6 National Park Entrance
7 Mercado de Artesanías
10 Casa de Turista
12 Fabrica San Pedro
13 Post Office
14 Cybercafe
15 La Scala Disco

16 Plaza Purépecha
Shopping Center
17 Plaza Las Américas
Shopping Center
18 Delegación de Turismo
22 Café Sol y Luna
24 Computel
25 Viajes Tzitzi
26 Telecomm
27 Parroquia de San
Francisco
28 Casa de la Cultura
30 Buses to Tzaráracua
31 Museo Regional de
Arte Popular
33 Iglesia de la Inmaculada

WESTERN CENTRAL

hours for foreign exchange. Centro Cambiario de Divisas Hispanimex, at Portal Matamoros 19 near the east end of the plaza, and Compra y Venta de Dólares, on Cupatitzio 1½ blocks south of the plaza, will change cash or traveler's checks until 7 pm Monday to Friday, and until 2 pm Saturday.

Post & Communications The main post office, at Reforma 13, is just west of 5 de Febrero, three blocks south of the central plaza. It's open 8 am to 7 pm Monday to Friday, 9 am to 1 pm Saturday.

There's a Computel caseta on Ocampo opposite the west end of the plaza, and a Telecomm office a block north on Ocampo, with fax and money transfer service.

For Internet connection, go about seven blocks southeast of the plaza, to Cybercafe at Juárez 57. It costs only US$2.25 an hour, but the connection can be slow.

Museo Regional de Arte Popular

For a quick overview of Michoacán crafts, visit the Museo Regional de Arte Popular, adjoining the Iglesia de la Inmaculada on the northeast corner of the central plaza. The museum building, erected in 1533, was the first hospital in the Americas. The carving around the door facing the plaza, and around the windows, is similar to the Moorish-style work on the church at Angahuan near Paricutín volcano. The museum is open 9.30 am to 1.30 pm and 3.30 to 6 pm Tuesday to Sunday (free).

Parque Nacional Eduardo Ruiz

This lovely tropical park is only a kilometer west of the central plaza. It follows the lushly vegetated banks of the Río Cupatitzio from its source at the Rodilla del Diablo pool, at the park's north end. Legend has it that the devil knelt here and left the mark of his knee. Many paths guide a shady stroll down the gorge, over bridges, past waterfalls and fountains – the park is famous for its water features. Boys dive into the river's deepest pools and ask for coins.

The main entrance is on Calzada La Quinta at the end of Independencia. Walk, or take a 'Parque' bus up Independencia from Ocampo. The park is open 8 am to 6 pm daily (US$0.50 for adults, US$0.25 for kids). Maps and leaflets on the park's history are on sale at the ticket kiosk.

Special Events

Uruapan's festivals include the following:

Semana Santa – Palm Sunday is marked by a procession through the city streets. Figures and crosses woven from palm fronds are sold after the procession. There's also a ceramics contest, and a weeklong exhibition/market of Michoacán handicrafts fills up the central plaza. Prices get lower as the week goes on

Día de San Francisco – St Francis, the patron saint of Uruapan, is honored with colorful festivities and the Canácuas dance by women; October 4

Festival de Coros y Danzas – the Choir & Dance Festival is a contest of Purépecha dance and musical groups; three days around October 24 (not held every year)

Feria del Aguacate – the Avocado Fair is a big event, with bullfights, cockfights and concerts and agricultural, industrial and handicraft exhibitions; two weeks in November (exact dates vary)

Places to Stay – Budget

Camping The *Trailer Park La Joyita* (☎ 523-03-64, *Estocolmo 22*) is 1½ blocks east of Paseo Lázaro Cárdenas at the southern end of town. It has full hookups for 10 trailers, a lawn area for tents, a barbecue and 24-hour hot water in the showers. Cost is US$4.50 per person. Frequent buses run between here and Cupatitzio, 1½ blocks south of the central plaza.

Hotels The *Hotel del Parque* (☎ 524-38-45, *Independencia 124*), 6½ blocks west of the central plaza and half a block from the Parque Nacional Eduardo Ruiz, is easily the most pleasant of Uruapan's cheap lodgings. The rooms are clean with tile floors, private bath and 24-hour hot water, for US$9/13 single/double, US$16 with two beds. There's a rear patio area and enclosed parking.

For more character but perhaps less comfort, *Hotel Mi Solar* (☎ 524-09-12,

Delgado 10), two blocks north of the plaza, has 20 slightly worn rooms around two open courtyards. They have private bathrooms with uncertain plumbing, and prices of US$6/9.

A trio of cheapies lines up along Portal Santos Degollado at the east end of the plaza. Perhaps the best is the *Hotel Capri (Portal Santos Degollado No 12)*, which has 24-hour hot water and rooms of a habitable size and minimal comfort for US$5, or US$6 with two beds. *Hotel Moderno (☎ 524-02-12)* and *Hotel Oseguera (☎ 523-98-56)* have mostly smaller, darker rooms, though you might get a nicer one overlooking the plaza. All three hotels are very worn, need new beds and have spray-everywhere showers.

Places to Stay – Mid-Range

Hotel Villa de Flores (☎ 524-28-00, Emilio Carranza 15), 1½ blocks west of the central plaza, is a well-kept colonial-style hotel with a colorful pink courtyard surrounded by 27 comfortable rooms. Singles/doubles with private bath, cable TV and fan cost US$17/23.50. The two-bed rooms on the rear courtyard are newer and brighter than other, equally priced rooms.

On the south side of the plaza, *Hotel Regis (☎ 523-58-44, Portal Carrillo 12)* has 40 brightly decorated, mostly well-lit rooms with fans, phones and TV for US$16/22, plus its own restaurant and parking. Next door, the *Hotel Concordia (☎ 523-04-00)* is a comfortable, modern hotel with 63 large, spotless rooms, all with TV and carpeting, for US$23/20. It also has parking, a restaurant, and laundry service.

Half a block south of the central plaza, *Nuevo Hotel Alameda (☎ 523-41-00, 5 de Febrero 11)* is another good mid-range hotel, with clean, comfortable rooms that have TV and phones for US$18.50/22. There's parking as well.

Hotel El Tarasco (☎ 524-15-00, Independencia 2), half a block north of the plaza, is a step up in quality, with 65 large and bright rooms at US$38/48, plus a restaurant and a swimming pool. There are good views from some of the upper floors.

Two other hotels near the plaza are worth considering. *Hotel Real de Uruapan (☎ 523-44-33, Bravo 110)* has 70 rooms in nine stories, some with sweeping views, all very comfortable with carpet, TV and phone. There are junior suites with sitting areas, bathtubs and large TVs. Usual room rates are US$29/33, but they sometimes discount. The four-story, 80-room *Hotel Victoria (☎ 524-25-00, Cupatitzio 11)* has nicer rooms but no views for US$35/40, or US$47/54 for a junior suite.

If you have wheels, you might like the *Motel Pie de la Sierra (☎ 524-25-10)*, 4km north of the center on highway 37 toward Paracho. Located at the foot of the mountains, it has large, well-kept grounds, plus a swimming pool, game room and pleasant restaurant. There are 72 rooms with fireplace, color TV, private terraces and mountain views. Low season rates start at US$20/40.

Places to Stay – Top End

Catering mainly to business travelers, *Hotel Plaza Uruapan (☎ 523-37-00, Ocampo 64)*, at the west end of the main plaza, charges US$50/62 single/double. The exterior rooms have great views through floor-to-ceiling windows.

The hacienda-style *Hotel Mansión del Cupatitzio (☎ 523-21-00, fax 524-67-72)*, at the north end of the Parque Nacional Eduardo Ruiz on Calzada Fray Juan de San Miguel, is the most pleasant hotel in Uruapan. The hotel adjoins the park, and its restaurant overlooks the Rodilla del Diablo pool where the Río Cupatitzio begins. The hotel has a swimming pool, lovely grounds, laundry service and so forth. Rates start at US$51/68 for a standard room, more for a view of the park.

Places to Eat

One of the best places to eat in town is the tiny, cheap *Cocina Económica Mary (Independencia 57)*, 3½ blocks west of the central plaza. Open 8.30 am to 5.30 pm Monday to Saturday, this well-patronized, family-run place serves a delicious US$2 home-style comida corrida of *sopa* followed by a choice of several main courses – which can range from *bístek ranchero* to *pollo con mole* – plus a soda or glass of fresh juice. A breakfast of *huevos Mexicanos* and *café con leche* is US$2.50. One block south, and also recommended, is **Antojitos Yucatecas** *(Emilio Carranza 37)*.

For a slice of junk-food heaven, visit **Pizzas Hamburguesas** *(Emilio Carranza 8)*, a few steps west of the central plaza. The burgers and burritos are particularly good, and it does tasty pizzas with generous toppings – the *chica* size at US$3 is plenty for one person. They dish it up from 8 am to 10.30 pm daily.

The classier **Cafetería La Placita**, beneath the Hotel Plaza Uruapan at the west end of the plaza, does a good breakfast with fruit salad, yogurt and granola (US$2.75) and egg dishes (US$3). Antojitos and snacks are under US$4, but the dinner menu gets more expensive. It's open 7 am to 11 pm daily. All the good hotels have pretty good restaurants – on the 9th floor of **Hotel Real de Uruapan** you can have a US$10 meal with a million-dollar view.

For something special, go to **Restaurant La Macadamia**, beside Hotel Mansión del Cupatitzio overlooking the north end of the national park. The specialty is fresh *trucha* (trout) from the pools in the park.

Several places on the south side of the plaza serve good breakfasts, economical comidas corridas (US$2.50), and adequate à la carte meals for dinner. **Café La Pérgola** *(Portal Carrillo 4)* is very popular, but **Café Oriental** (not a Chinese place!) might be better value.

For those with tight budgets and adventurous eating habits, **Mercado de Antojitos Típicos**, on Corregidora one short block north of the plaza, is a wonderful place to sample local food. Forty stalls serve typical Michoacán dishes every day from around 6 am to midnight. Pick a stall that looks popular.

Cafés Locally grown coffee is a specialty in Uruapan. Enjoy a good, strong cup amid carved wooden furniture at **La Lucha**, half a block north of the central plaza on the small street García Ortiz. Another good spot is **Café Tradicional de Uruapan** *(Emilio Carranza 5B)*, half a block west of the central plaza, with a large selection of coffees. They also serve breakfasts, snacks and cakes.

Entertainment

You might find one or two things to do after dark besides lingering over coffee or going to church. The **Casa de la Cultura** on García Ortiz, half a block north of the plaza, hosts exhibitions, occasional concerts and so on. Check with the tourist office to see what's cooking during your stay in Uruapan.

Café Sol y Luna *(Independencia 15A)* bills itself as an art café and is quite popular with a student crowd. The coffee is good, and some nights it has live jazz, blues or rock.

The Hotel Plaza Uruapan has a bar and disco and live entertainment on weekends. Several of the other better-class hotels near the central plaza also have bars. **La Scala Disco** *(☎ 524-26-09, Madrid 12)* is a favorite dance venue for well-dressed, well-heeled young locals. Cover charge is US$2 to US$3.25, depending on the night and your gender (closed Monday).

Shopping

Traditional Míchoacan costumes, *ropa típica*, are made at Fabrica San Pedro *(☎ 527-21-00)*, near the river a few blocks southwest of the center. You can visit this late-19th-century factory and buy direct.

Local crafts such as lacquered trays and boxes can be bought at the Mercado de Artesanías, opposite the entrance to the Parque Nacional Eduardo Ruiz. A few shops nearby on Independencia sell the same sort of thing. The town market, which stretches more than half a kilometer up Constitución, from the central plaza to Calzada Juárez, is worth a browse too.

Getting There & Away

Air Aeromar *(☎ 523-50-50 at the airport)* has flights daily to/from Mexico City via Morelia. Aerocuahonte flies twice daily, Monday to Saturday, to/from Lázaro Cárdenas, and once or twice per day (except Sunday) to/from Guadalajara. A helpful travel agency for booking flights is Viajes Tzitzi (☎ 523-34-19), beside the entrance to Hotel Plaza Uruapan – they also sell ETN and Primera Plus bus tickets.

Bus The Central Camionera is 3km northeast of central Uruapan on the highway to Pátzcuaro and Morelia. It has a post office, telegraph and fax office, telephone caseta, cafeteria and a *guardería* for leaving luggage. Daily buses run all over central and northern Mexico, including:

Colima – 400km, 6 to 8 hours; 1st-class La Línea at 9.45 pm (US$13, 6 hours), 2nd-class Autobuses de Occidente at 11.15 am (US$12, 8 hours); it may be more convenient to go first to Zamora or even to Guadalajara

Guadalajara – 305km, 3½ to 5 hours, via La Barca; 15 deluxe by ETN (US$17), Primera Plus and La Línea Plus (US$12); 11 1st-class La Línea and Servicios Coordinados (US$11); for the more scenic route around the south side of Lake Chapala, you need to change to local buses at Zamora

Lázaro Cárdenas – 280km, 6 hours; 15 1st-class Parhikuni, La Línea Plus and Vía 2000 (US$12 to US$14), 2nd-class Galeana every 15 minutes (US$10)

Mexico City (Terminal Poniente or Terminal Norte) – 430km, 6 hours; 7 deluxe ETN (US$27), 19 1st-class Primera Plus, Vía 2000 Plus and Vía 2000 (US$19 to US$20), 4 2nd-class Flecha Amarilla (US$18)

Morelia – 124km, 2 hours; 2 deluxe ETN (US$7.50), 7 deluxe Primera Plus (US$6), frequent 1st-class Parhikuni until 11 pm (US$5.50), 2nd-class Galeana Ruta Paraíso every 15 minutes (US$5)

Pátzcuaro – 62km, 1 hour; 2nd-class Galeana Ruta Paraíso every 15 minutes (US$2.50)

Zamora – 115km, 2 to 2½ hours; 3 deluxe ETN (US$7), 5 1st-class Primera Plus (US$5), frequent 2nd-class Flecha Amarilla (US$4)

Getting Around
To/From the Airport The airport is on Avenida Latinoamericana about 8km southeast of the city center, a 15-minute drive. A taxi costs about US$3.50.

Bus Local buses marked 'Centro' run from the door of the bus station to the central plaza. If you want a taxi, buy a ticket from the *taquilla* in the station (US$1.30). On the return trip catch a 'Central Camionera' or 'Central' bus on the south side of the central plaza.

The local buses run from around 6 am to 9 pm every day. They cost US$0.30.

AROUND URUAPAN
Cascada de Tzaráracua
Ten kilometers south of Uruapan just off highway 37, the Río Cupatitzio falls 30m into two pools flanked by lush vegetation. Two kilometers upstream there's another lovely waterfall, the smaller Tzararacuita, which is better for swimming. Tzaráracua buses depart from the middle of the south side of Uruapan's main plaza. They go every half-hour on weekends and holidays (which are when the falls attract crowds). Other days these buses go only every couple of hours, so it's better to take an Autotransportes Galeana bus heading for Nueva Italia from the Uruapan bus station; these depart every 20 minutes and will drop you at Tzaráracua. The buses stop at a car park. From there, it's a steep descent of about 1km to the main falls.

Tingambato
* **pop 6050** • **elev 1980m**
At Tingambato, a village about 30km from Uruapan on the road to Pátzcuaro, are ruins of a ceremonial site that existed from about 450 to 900 AD. They show Teotihuacán influence and date from well before the Tarascan empire. The ruins include a ball court (rare in western Mexico), temple pyramids and an underground tomb where a skeleton and 32 skulls were found. A blue sign with a white pyramid points to the site from the highway, about 1km away.

Paracho
* **pop 15,600** • **elev 2220m**
Paracho, 40km north of Uruapan on highway 37, is a small Purépecha town famous for its handmade guitars. It's worth visiting if you want to buy an instrument or

WESTERN CENTRAL

watch some of the country's best guitar makers at work. The local artisans are also known for their high-quality violins, cellos and other woodcrafts, including furniture. The liveliest time to come is during the annual Feria Nacional de la Guitarra (National Guitar Fair), a big weeklong splurge of music, dance, exhibitions, markets and cockfights in early August.

Many buses from Uruapan to Zamora will stop in Paracho. Autotransportes Galeana has 2nd-class buses leaving Uruapan every 15 minutes for the one-hour trip (US$1.75).

Volcán Paricutín

On the afternoon of February 20, 1943, a Purépecha farmer, Dionisio Pulido, was plowing his cornfield some 35km west of Uruapan when the ground began to shake and swell and to emit steam, sparks and hot ash. The farmer tried at first to cover the moving earth, but when that proved impossible, he fled. A volcano started to rise from the spot. Within a year it had risen 410m above the surrounding land and its lava had engulfed the Purépecha villages of San Salvador Paricutín and San Juan Parangaricutiro. No one was hurt: The villagers had plenty of time to flee as the lava flow was so gradual.

The volcano continued to spit lava and fire, and to increase in size, until 1952. Today its large black cone stands mute, emitting gentle wisps of steam. Near the edge of the 20-sq-km lava field, the top of San Juan's church protrudes eerily from the sea of solidified, black lava. It's the only visible trace of the two buried villages.

Visiting the Area An excursion to Paricutín from Uruapan makes a fine day trip, to see San Juan's church engulfed in a jumble of black boulders and to climb the volcanic cone. The volcano is not particularly high (2800m) – the much bigger Tancítaro towers to its south – but it's certainly memorable and fairly easy to access.

If you want to do it in one day from Uruapan, as most people do, start early. First you have to reach the Purépecha village of Angahuan, 32km from Uruapan on the road to Los Reyes, which branches west off highway 37 about 15km north of Uruapan. Galeana 2nd-class buses leave the Uruapan bus station for Angahuan every 30 minutes from 5 am to 7 pm. Alternatively, flag down a 'Los Reyes' bus near the Calzada de San Miguel traffic circle, just north of the Parque Nacional Eduardo Ruiz in Uruapan. This will save some time getting out to the bus station east of town, then doubling back to the west side, but it won't guarantee you a seat on the bus. The one-hour bus ride to Angahuan (US$0.60) passes the now-forested stumps of a dozen or so older volcanoes.

Buses back to Uruapan will pick up at the Angahuan turn-off (about 1km from the village) until at least 7 pm nightly.

Angahuan
• pop 3970

Angahuan is a typical Purépecha village with wooden houses, dusty streets, little electricity and loudspeakers booming out announcements in the Purépecha language. On the main plaza is the 16th-century Iglesia de Santiago Apostol, with some fine carving around its door done by a Moorish stonemason who accompanied the early Spanish missionaries here.

Festival days in Angahuan are the Fiesta de San Isidro Labrador on May 15, with a weaving contest, and the Fiesta de Santiago Apostol on July 25, with handicrafts displays, music, contests and games.

Apart from the cabins at the 'Las Cabañas' tourist complex, there's a trailer park and campsite. Ask at the municipal tourist office in Uruapan. Guides may be able to offer you lodging in a house at about US$5 per person.

Centro Turístico de Angahuan This low-key tourist complex is commonly called 'Las Cabañas,' and it supposedly costs US$0.90 to enter, though the fee isn't always collected. A small museum here has a good 3-D model of the volcano, but it's often closed. The cabins cost about US$7.75 for a dorm bed, or US$44 for a whole six-bed cabin.

The restaurant here has a minimal menu, and sometimes shows an interesting video about the eruption, which helps fill in the long wait for your order. There's also a small exhibition of photos and press clippings on the volcano and its history. The lookout point here has good views of the lava field, the protruding San Juan church tower and the volcano itself.

To reach Las Cabañas on foot from the bus stop, walk west into the village center, turn right at the main plaza, then left at the fork after 200m, where there's a building with a TV satellite dish. From the fork, the track leads straight to Las Cabañas, about 20 minutes away.

Templo San Juan The ruined church is a 45-minute walk down a path that begins near the entrance to Las Cabañas. The path is wide, gray with volcanic ash, and at times flanked by barbed-wire fences. It's an easy, enjoyable walk, and it costs nothing to visit the church. Getting around the site is surprisingly difficult, as the walls are filled with, and surrounded by, huge boulders of black volcanic rock. The missing tower was not a casualty of the volcano – it was never completed.

Guides & Horses At the Angahuan bus stop, guides with horses will offer to take you 1km to the Centro Turístico de Angahuan (Las Cabañas), the starting point for trips onto the lava field. The guides are mainly interested in taking you on a longer trip – to the church or to the volcano. If you want to go by horse, you can start negotiating at the bus stop. You probably won't get any better choice of guides or horses in town or at the tourist center, and the prices won't be any lower.

A horse and guide just to the church will cost around US$7.75, but you don't really need either. To ride to the base of the volcano and be guided up to the top will cost about US$28 (including the guide, the guide's horse, and your horse). With a guide plus two tourists, it's about US$43. Most of the horses are pretty sedate and the guide

should be able to lead them if necessary, but if you're not accustomed to riding, you might find 4 or 5 hours on a hard Mexican saddle is pretty wearing.

If you'd rather walk up the volcano, you'll still need a guide to show you the way (about US$16.50 per day), but walking guides are harder to find (maybe riding is more macho). One guide who is happy to do walking trips is Jesús Reyes Rodríguez (☎ 4-522-55-74 in Uruapan). He can guide you from Uruapan by public transport.

Some guides are young boys, with very little experience, poor equipment, little Spanish, and zero English. Make sure you deal with the actual person who will be guiding you, and don't agree to go with someone who isn't able to look after himself.

Climbing Paricutín You can ride to the base of the volcano and climb up the last few hundred meters, or you can walk all the way, but either way you should hire a guide. Bring some water and food from Uruapan as there's none on the route, and precious little available in Angahuan. Make sure your guide has something too.

There are two routes to the crater. The more **direct route** begins behind the restaurant at Las Cabañas, to the left of the viewing area. The path is narrow and winds for 500m through a pine forest that can be disorienting. There are a lot of small tracks created by wood gatherers and tree planters, and it's easy to get lost.

A little beyond the pine forest you'll cross a dirt road and pick up the trail on the other side. Within 30m you should pass through a gate and soon afterward the path begins to slope upward considerably. The trail weaves through thickets where wildflowers bloom much of the year. About here, you'll have to leave your horse and continue on foot. (It's not really worth having a horse on this route, but it may be difficult to find a guide willing to walk the whole way.) After about 30 minutes of hiking, there's a campsite (sadly, covered with litter) and then the woods give way to a barren lava field. The path to the crater, over jagged black rock, is marked occasionally with splashes of paint.

About 150m from the summit, the rock gives way to a sandy ash and you'll see steam rising from fumaroles on knolls to the left of the trail. A narrow 40m long trail links the main trail to the knolls, which are worth visiting. They are covered with bright yellow rock that is quite striking amid the surrounding black lava. You can feel steam rising from the crevices around you.

The lip of the crater has two high points. Beneath the northern lip, on the outside of the cone, is a dust slide that is fun to bound down at a fast, high-stepping walk. This brings you down near the flat, dusty horse trail (see below) that returns via the San Juan church. To return across the lava field and through the forest to Las Cabañas, pass on the dust slide and go back the way you came. Most people need 3½ or four hours to reach the summit from Las Cabañas, and another three hours for the return trip using this route.

The **horse trail** to the base of the cone is longer, but not as steep or rugged as the forest and lava field route. This trail starts beside the entrance to Las Cabañas and skirts the southeastern edge of the lava field to San Juan church. From the church, the trail follows a road past some farms, then narrows and passes through brush before reaching an open, sandy area 15 minutes' walk from the foot of the volcano. There the horses are tied up under a shade tree while their riders make the final, 20-minute ascent on foot. The ride takes about two hours each way.

ZAMORA
- pop 121,200 • elev 1560m ☎ 3

Zamora, about 115km northwest of Uruapan and 190km southeast of Guadalajara, is the center of a rich agricultural region known for its strawberries, and a pleasant town to stroll around in. It was founded in 1574 and is home to a curious unfinished cathedral, the **Catedral Inconclusa**. Fifteen kilometers southeast of Zamora, a short distance off

highway 15 at Tangancícuaro, is the clear, spring-fed, tree-shaded **Laguna de Camécuaro**, a lovely spot for drivers to stop and picnic. If you need to spend the night, Zamora has a range of hotels. An acceptable, very inexpensive option is *Hotel Nacional* (☎ 512-42-24, *Corregidora Ote 106*), with rooms from US$8.

The bus station is on the southern outskirts of town. (See Getting There & Away in the Uruapan section for bus details.)

Inland Colima

The tiny (5191 sq km) state of Colima ranges from tall volcanoes on its northern fringes to lagoons near the Pacific coast. The climate is equally diverse – hot along the coast and cool in the highlands. This section deals with the upland area of the state; the narrow coastal plain, with the beach resorts of Manzanillo, Cuyutlán and Paraíso, is covered in the Central Pacific Coast chapter.

Colima, the state capital, is a small, little-visited but pleasant enough semitropical city. Overlooking it from the north are two spectacular volcanoes – the active, constantly steaming Volcán de Fuego de Colima (3820m) and the extinct, snow-capped Volcán Nevado de Colima (4240m). Both can be reached relatively easily if you have a taste for adventure and a not-too-tight budget, though access to the Volcán de Fuego is sometimes barred for safety reasons.

The state's main agricultural products are coconuts, limes, bananas and mangoes. Its biggest industry is mining – one of Mexico's richest iron deposits is near Minatitlán.

History

Pre-Hispanic Colima was remote from the major ancient cultures of Mexico. Seaborne contacts with more distant places may have been more important, and there's even a legend that one king of Colima, Ix, had regular treasure-bearing visitors from China.

Colima produced some remarkable pottery, which has been found in over 250 sites, mainly tombs, dating from about 200 BC to 800 AD. The pottery includes a variety of figures, often quite comical and expressive of emotion and movement. Best known are the rotund figures of hairless dogs, known as Tepezcuintles. In some ancient Mexican cultures, dogs were buried with their owners. It was believed that they were able to carry the dead to paradise. The dogs were also part of the indigenous diet.

Archaeologists believe the makers of the pottery lived in villages spread around the state. The type of grave in which much of the pottery was found, the shaft tomb, occurs not only in the western Mexican states of Colima, Michoacán, Jalisco and Nayarit, but in Panama and South America as well, which suggests seaborne contacts with places much farther south.

When the Spanish reached Mexico, Colima was the leading force in the Chimalhuacán indigenous confederation that dominated Colima and parts of Jalisco and Nayarit. Two Spanish expeditions were defeated by the Colimans before Gonzalo de Sandoval, one of Cortés' lieutenants, conquered them in 1523. That same year he founded the town of Colima – the third Spanish town in Nueva España, after Veracruz and Mexico City. The town was moved to its present site, from its unhealthy original lowland location near Tecomán, in 1527.

COLIMA
• pop 120,700 • elev 550m ☎ changing
Colima lives at the mercy of the forces of nature. Volcán de Fuego de Colima, clearly visible 30km to the north, has had nine major eruptions in the past four centuries. Of even greater concern, the city has been hit by a series of earthquakes over the centuries – the most recent major one was in 1941. Because of these devastating natural events, Colima has few colonial buildings, despite having been the first Spanish city in western Mexico.

Today Colima is a small, pleasant place, graced by palm trees and ringed by mountains. Few tourists come here, but there are a number of interesting things to see and do in town and in the surrounding countryside. Though only 45km from the coast, Colima is at a higher elevation and, consequently, is cooler and less humid. The rainy months are July through September.

Orientation
Central Colima spreads around three plazas, with the Plaza Principal (also known as the Jardín Libertad) at the center of things. The Jardín Quintero lies directly behind the cathedral, and three blocks farther east is the Jardín Núñez. Street names change at the Plaza Principal.

The shiny modern main bus terminal is about 2km east of the center, on the Guadalajara-Manzanillo road.

Information
Tourist Offices The state tourist office (☎ 2-43-60) is in a domed white building at the corner of Hidalgo and Ocampo. It's open 8.30 am to 3 pm and 6 to 8 pm Monday to Friday, 10 am to 2 pm Saturday and Sunday. Friendly, helpful staff (some speak English) give out maps, brochures and information on the city and state of Colima.

Money There are numerous banks around the center where you can change money. Banamex, on Hidalgo a block east of the cathedral, has an ATM and is open 9 am to 5 pm Monday to Friday, 10 am to 2 pm Saturday. Banco Serfin, on Jardín Núñez, has similar hours.

Majapara Casa de Cambio, at the southwest corner of Jardín Núñez, is open 9 am to 2 pm and 4.30 to 7 pm Monday to Saturday. There are other money changers nearby.

On December 1, 2000, the telephone area code is due to change to ☎ 3 from 331, with digits 31 added to the start of every local number (for example, the number 2-43-60 will become 312-43-60).

COLIMA

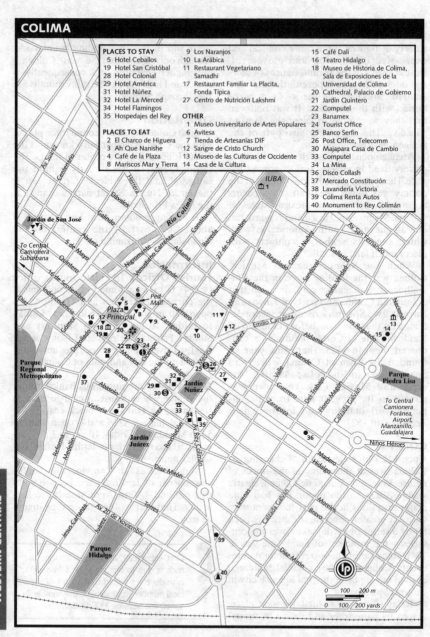

PLACES TO STAY
5 Hotel Ceballos
19 Hotel San Cristóbal
28 Hotel Colonial
29 Hotel América
31 Hotel Núñez
32 Hotel La Merced
34 Hotel Flamingos
35 Hospedajes del Rey

PLACES TO EAT
2 El Charco de Higuera
3 Ah Que Nanishe
4 Café de la Plaza
8 Mariscos Mar y Tierra

9 Los Naranjos
10 La Arábica
11 Restaurant Vegetariano Samadhi
17 Restaurant Familiar La Placita, Fonda Típica
27 Centro de Nutrición Lakshmi

OTHER
1 Museo Universitario de Artes Populares
6 Avitesa
7 Tienda de Artesanías DIF
12 Sangre de Cristo Church
13 Museo de las Culturas de Occidente
14 Casa de la Cultura

15 Café Dali
16 Teatro Hidalgo
18 Museo de Historia de Colima, Sala de Exposiciones de la Universidad de Colima
20 Cathedral, Palacio de Gobierno
21 Jardín Quintero
22 Computel
23 Banamex
24 Tourist Office
25 Banco Serfin
26 Post Office, Telecomm
30 Majapara Casa de Cambio
33 Computel
34 La Mina
36 Disco Collash
37 Mercado Constitución
38 Lavandería Victoria
39 Colima Renta Autos
40 Monument to Rey Colimán

Post & Communications The post office, at Madero 247, is at the northeast corner of Jardín Núñez. It's open from 8 am to 7 pm Monday to Friday, 8 am to noon Saturday. The Telecomm office, with telegram, telex and fax services, is one door to the left of the post office, open 9 am to 8 pm Monday to Friday, 9 am to 1 pm Saturday.

Several coin and card pay phones can be found beside the Plaza Principal and Jardín Núñez. There are also three Computel offices with telephone casetas and fax service: at Morelos 236, facing Jardín Núñez; at Medellín 55, near the corner of Hidalgo; and at the bus station. All are open 7 am to 10 pm daily.

There's an Internet café in the Plaza Country shopping mall, northeast of the center on Felipe Sevilla del Río. A more accessible one may open soon – ask at the tourist office.

Laundry Lavandería Victoria, at Victoria 131 between Ocampo and De la Vega, charges US$2 to wash and dry a 3kg load. It's open 8 am to 2 pm and 3 to 8 pm Monday to Saturday.

Around Plaza Principal

The **cathedral**, or Santa Iglesia, on the east side of the Plaza Principal, has been rebuilt several times since the Spanish first erected a cathedral here in 1527. The most recent reconstruction dates from just after the 1941 earthquake.

Next to the cathedral is the **Palacio de Gobierno**, built between 1884 and 1904. Local artist Jorge Chávez Carrillo painted the murals on the stairway to celebrate the 200th anniversary of the birth of independence hero Miguel Hidalgo, who was once parish priest of Colima. The murals depict Mexican history from the Spanish conquest to independence.

The **Museo de Historia de Colima**, on the south side of the plaza, is worth a visit to see ceramic vessels and figurines (mostly people and Tepezcuintle dogs) unearthed in Colima state. There are also permanent displays of masks, textiles, costumes, basketry and shellwork from the Colima coast, plus temporary exhibits. The museum is open 9 am to 6 pm Tuesday to Saturday, 5 to 8 pm Sunday

(free). Next door is the **Sala de Exposiciones de la Universidad de Colima**, offering changing art exhibitions. It's open the same hours as the museum and is also free.

The **Teatro Hidalgo**, on the corner of Degollado and Independencia, one block south of the Plaza Principal, was built in neoclassical style between 1871 and 1883 on a site originally donated to the city by Miguel Hidalgo. The theater was destroyed by the earthquakes of 1932 and 1941 and reconstruction was undertaken in 1942.

Museo de las Culturas de Occidente

This large, modern cultural center for the state of Colima is at the intersection of Calzada Galván and Ejército Nacional, a little over 1km east of the center.

The chief attraction is the Museo de las Culturas de Occidente (Museum of Western Cultures), fronting Ejército Nacional. Here, in a well-lit building, are exhibited hundreds of pre-Hispanic ceramic vessels, figurines and musical instruments from Colima state, with explanations in Spanish. Most impressive are the human figures and Tepezcuintle dogs, but there's a wide variety of other figures including mammals, reptiles, fish and birds. Some of the species depicted still exist in the area, others have disappeared. Many of the animals are depicted with a cartoon-like expressiveness that Disney would be proud of. The museum is open 9 am to 6.30 pm Tuesday to Sunday (US$1.75).

South of the museum, several architecturally interesting modern buildings comprise the **Casa de la Cultura**. The art gallery has a permanent exhibition of works by the renowned Colima modernist painter Alfonso Michel (1897-1957), and hosts temporary exhibitions. There's also a theater, and the Edificio de Talleres, a workshop complex with a bar/café on the ground floor.

Museo Universitario de Artes Populares

The University Museum of Popular Arts is in the Instituto Universitario de Bellas Artes (IUBA), on the corner of 27 de Septiembre and Gallardo, about 900m northeast of the

Plaza Principal. It displays folk art from Colima and other states, with a particularly good section of costumes and masks used in traditional Colima dances. Other exhibits include textiles, ceramics, models and furniture. Hours are 10 am to 2 pm and 5 to 8 pm, Tuesday to Saturday, 10 am to 3 pm Sunday (free).

Also at IUBA is the interesting **Taller de Reproducciones**, just inside the gate and to your right, where on some mornings you can see the process of reproducing ancient Coliman ceramic figures. Some of these figures may be on sale at the museum shop.

Parks
The **Parque Regional Metropolitano** on Degollado, a few blocks southwest of the center, has a small zoo, a swimming pool, a café and a forest with an artificial lake. You can rent bikes or rowboats to explore the forest paths and lake.

East of the center on Calzada Galván, **Parque Piedra Lisa** is named after its famous Sliding Stone, which is visible from the park entrance (close to the traffic circle where Galván and Aldama meet). Legend says that visitors who slide on this stone will some day return to Colima, either to marry or to die.

Archaeological Sites
Two archaeological sites, **La Campana** and **El Chanal**, are just north of Avenida Tecnológico, which goes east-west past the north side of the city. There's not much to see as the most interesting finds are in museums, but excavations continue.

Special Events
Many masked dances are enacted at fiestas in Colima state. The Museo Universitario de Culturas Populares has a good display of the costumes and plenty of information on the subject. The following festivals take place in or very near Colima city.

Ferias Charro-Taurinas San Felipe de Jesús – this festival, celebrated in honor of the Virgen de la Candelaria (whose day is February 2), takes place in Villa de Álvarez, about 5km north of the city center. Each day of the festival except Tuesday and Friday, a large group rides from

Colima's cathedral to Villa de Álvarez preceded by giant *mojigangos* – figures of the village's mayor and wife, followed by musical groups. When they arrive at Villa de Álvarez the celebrations continue with food, music, rodeos and bullfights; 10 days in late January and early February

Feria de Todos los Santos – also called the Feria de Colima, the Colima state fair includes agricultural and handicraft exhibitions, cultural events and funfairs; late October and early November

Día de la Virgen de Guadalupe – women and children dress in costume to pay homage at the Virgin's altar in the cathedral. In the evenings the Jardín Quintero behind the cathedral fills with busy food stalls; around December 1 to 12

Places to Stay
Budget The *Hotel San Cristóbal* (☎ 2-05-15, *Reforma 98*) is a centrally located, bottom-end option, with 33 basic rooms, 24-hour hot water and firm beds. The cheapest rooms have a shared bathroom, and cost US$6.50. Rooms with private bath cost US$7.75 with one bed, US$10 with two beds.

A more appealing choice is *Hotel Colonial* (☎ 3-08-77, *Medellín 142*), also centrally located, with 46 clean, cool, well-maintained rooms round a courtyard, from around US$8.75/10 for singles/doubles with private bath and TV. Rooms vary in size, quality and features, so ask to see a couple before registering.

Another very good budget place is the *Hotel La Merced* (☎ 2-69-69, *Juárez 82*). All rooms in this small tidy hotel have private bath and fan, and prices start at about US$9. The best rooms are in the older section well back from the street. The two-bed rooms, for around US$13, are a very good size.

A couple of doors down, *Hotel Núñez* (☎ 2-70-30, *Juárez 88*) is basic but tolerable for a night or two. The 32 rooms around two courtyards have no windows, so they tend to be dark and stuffy, but they have fans and TVs and are kept clean, and at US$7 for a single or double, you can't complain about the price.

One of the better budget places is the 1960s-style *Hotel Flamingos* (☎ 2-25-25,

Avenida Rey Colimán 18), with 56 clean, modern rooms with private bath and fan. All rooms have full-wall windows and balconies, and those on the upper floors offer a view over town. There's a restaurant on the ground floor. Rooms are US$14/17, but they sometimes give good discounts. Across the road, the small, friendly *Hospedajes del Rey* (☎ 3-36-83, *Rey Colimán 125*) has just five comfortable rooms at US$15 for one or two people.

Mid-Range The *Hotel Ceballos* (☎ 2-44-44, *Portal Medellín 12)*, on the north side of the Plaza Principal, is a stately building that dates from 1880 and has been the home of three state governors. Many of the 63 clean, pleasant, high-ceilinged, air-conditioned rooms have French windows opening onto small balconies. Singles/doubles are around US$45/48.

More modern is the *Hotel América* (☎ 2-74-88, *Morelos 162)*, half a block west of Jardín Núñez. Its 75 rooms have high wood-beamed ceilings, are air-conditioned, come with color TV and more. Facilities include restaurant, steam baths and a pool. Rates start at US$45.

Places to Eat

The food is good in Colima, with an abundance of fresh fruit and vegetables, seafood, and choice coffee. For a simple meal there are many small restaurants around the Plaza Principal, some just selling cold drinks, ice cream and frozen juices. *Restaurant Familiar La Placita*, in the portales on the south side of the Plaza Principal, is a reasonable all-purpose eatery. It serves breakfasts from US$2, a four-course comida corrida for US$3, antojitos for under US$4 and chicken or beef main dishes for around US$5. It's open 7 am to 10 pm daily.

Above La Placita, *Fonda Típica (Degollado 67)* occupies a breezy, 2nd-story corner location overlooking the Plaza Principal. It's a good place on a hot day, and popular in the evening for a cool drink. The food is pretty good and reasonably priced, with antojitos and sandwiches around US$2, meat dishes about US$3,

and seafood US$6. Musicians play after 9 pm Friday and Saturday.

Café de la Plaza, beside the Hotel Ceballos, is particularly pleasant, with high ceilings and a jukebox full of Mexican and US music. Nothing is priced over US$4, and a large traditional American or Mexican breakfast runs US$2.50. The restaurant is open 8 am to 10 pm Monday to Saturday, 8 am to 5 pm Sunday. Around the corner on the pedestrianized block of Constitución, *Mariscos Mar y Tierra* reminds you that the sea is only 100km away, with fresh fish, seafood cocktails and *sopa de mariscos*.

A clean, pleasant restaurant good for all meals is *Los Naranjos (Barreda 34)*, half a block north of Jardín Quintero. Chicken and meat dishes cost between US$4 and US$8, or you could have three enchiladas for US$3. Overhead fans keep you cool, and sometimes a pianist plays. It's open 8 am to 11.30 pm daily.

Some of the best food in town is served at *Ah Que Nanishe* (☎ 4-21-97, *Calle 5 de Mayo 267)*, west of the center. The name means 'how delicious,' which is apt for the fine Oaxacan specialties here. *Mole* fans will have to choose between *mole negro* (a black mole from Oaxaca made with chocolate and some 50 spices including 10 different chili peppers), *mole verde* (made with a variety of vegetables) and *mole colorado* (sweet red mole made with only one chili). A large chicken breast smothered in mole runs US$4, *chiles rellenos* US$3, tamales US$1 and antojitos US$1 to US$3.

Near Ah Que Nanishe, *El Charco de Higuera* faces the little Jardín de San José. Its menu is more conventional, with grills and the usual Mexican standards, but the outdoor tables are packed with hungry diners enjoying the cool atmosphere. Breakfasts are less than US$5; soups, antojitos and sandwiches are less than US$4; and chicken and beef dishes are around US$5 or US$6.

Vegetarians shouldn't miss the *Restaurant Vegetariano Samadhi (Medina 125)*, three blocks north of Jardín Núñez. It occupies an arched courtyard with a large palm tree and other tropical plants. The menu is large and caters to non-vegetarians too.

Choices include soy burgers with salad, french fries, and mushroom crêpes. The comida corrida is US$3.50, and set breakfasts are around US$3. Samadhi is open 8 am to 10 pm daily, except Thursday when it closes at 5 pm. *Centro de Nutrición Lakshmi (Madero 265)*, near Jardín Núñez, includes a wholegrain bakery, health-products store and a café serving soy burgers, yogurts and more.

La Arábica (Guerrero 162), near the corner of Obregón, is a small coffeehouse where people come to chat at the tables in the front or in the shady patio out back – a cappuccino is US$1.10. It's open 8.30 am to 2 pm and 4 to 8.30 pm Monday to Saturday.

Entertainment

Colima is basically a quiet city, but there are a few things you can do in the evening – hanging out around the plaza, lingering over coffee or beer, is a well practiced pastime here. Students and the young arty-party crowd dance at *Disco Collash (☎ 4-47-00, Zaragoza 521)* until late on Friday, Saturday and Sunday.

Café Dali, near the Casa de la Cultura, is for an older clientele into sedate music and quiet romance. Most nights there's a crooner after 9 pm. *La Mina*, on Avenida Rey Colimán next to Hotel Flamingos, is popular with the middle-aged salsa set.

Concerts, theater and other performing arts are staged at places such as the Teatro Hidalgo, the theater at the Casa de la Cultura and the Museo de Historia de Colima. Stop by these places to see their posted schedules.

Shopping

Tienda de Artesanías DIF, a block north of the Plaza Principal on the corner of Constitución and Zaragoza, has a good range of Colima handicrafts including attractive reproduction Tepezcuintle dogs. The main market is the Mercado Constitución, on Reforma three blocks south of the Plaza Principal.

Getting There & Away

Air Aeromar (☎ 3-55-88) and Aero California (☎ 4-48-50) both fly daily to/from Mexico City, with onward connections. Aero California also has daily flights to/from Tijuana. Avitesa travel agency (☎ 2-19-84), on the corner of Constitución and Zaragoza, a block north of the Plaza Principal, can make flight arrangements, and English is sometimes spoken.

Bus Colima has two bus stations. The main long-distance terminal is the Central Camionera Foránea, 2km east of the center at the meeting of Avenida Niños Héroes and the city's eastern bypass. At this station are pay phones, a telephone caseta, a pharmacy and various restaurants and snack shops. Daily departures from here include:

Guadalajara – 220km, 2½ hours; 6 deluxe ETN (US$17); frequent 1st-class La Línea, Primera Plus, Ómnibus de México, Servicios Coordinados (US$10 to US$12); many 2nd-class Sur de Jalisco (US$9.50)

Manzanillo – 101km, 1½ hours; 6 deluxe ETN (US$5); many 1st-class La Línea, Primera Plus, Servicios Coordinados (US$3.75); frequent 2nd-class Autotransportes del Sur de Jalisco via Tecomán and Armería (2 hours, US$3.50)

Mexico City (Terminal Norte) – 740km, 10 hours; 1 deluxe ETN (US$57); several 1st-class Primera Plus, Servicios Coordinados, and Ómnibus de México (US$42 to US$45); 6 2nd-class Autobuses de Occidente (US$38)

There are also many daily buses to Ciudad Guzmán, Morelia and Uruapan by Autobuses de Occidente.

The second bus station is the Central Camionera Suburbana, also known as the Terminal Suburbana, about 1.5km southwest of the Plaza Principal on the Carretera a Coquimatlán. This is the station for buses to Comala and nearby places, and for 2nd-class Autobuses Colima-Manzanillo, which goes frequently to Manzanillo 1½ hours, US$3), Tecomán (US$2) and Armería (US$2).

Getting Around

To/From the Airport Colima's airport is near Cuauhtémoc, 12km northeast of the city center off the highway to Guadalajara. A taxi to/from the center is about US$12.

Bus & Taxi Local buses (US$0.30) run 6 am to 9 pm daily. Ruta 4A buses from the main bus station (Central Camionera Foránea) will take you to the city center. To return to the bus station you can catch Ruta 4A on 5 de Mayo or Zaragoza. To reach the Central Camionera Suburbana, take a Ruta 2 or Ruta 4 bus west along Morelos.

Taxi fares within town are US$0.75 to US$1.75.

Car Colima's not a bad place to rent a car, and you might want one to explore the volcanoes and the nearby villages. Try Colima Renta Autos (☎ 2-95-84), at the junction of Llerenas and Rey Colmám, which has VW beetles at US$44 for one day, less for longer periods.

AROUND COLIMA
Comala
• pop 7680 • elev 600m

A picturesque town 9km north of Colima, Comala is known for its fine handicrafts, especially its hand-carved wood furniture. It is also a popular weekend outing from Colima. On Sunday there are markets for browsing.

Sociedad Cooperativa Artesanías Pueblo Blanco is famous for colonial-style hand-carved furniture, wood paintings and ironwork. You can visit it, 1km south of town just off the road from Colima, from 9 am to 6 pm Monday to Friday, 9 am to 2 pm Saturday.

The plaza has a fine white gazebo, pretty flowering trees, and a cute little church. Under the arches along one side of the plaza are some inviting *centros botaneros*, which are bars where minors are allowed (but not served alcohol) and where each beverage is accompanied by a free snack. They're open from around noon to 6 pm. Many people come to Comala just to enjoy these restaurants.

Comala buses leave Colima's Central Camionera Suburbana approximately every 10 minutes; the fare is US$0.50 for the 15-minute ride. In Comala, the buses back to Colima depart from the plaza.

Zona Mágica Approximately 6km north of Comala there's a stretch of road that seems to slope downhill, but if you stop your car and let it roll – hey! – it stops then goes backwards. This convincing optical illusion works in both directions – if you're heading south, you can put your car in neutral and it will roll 'uphill.'

Suchitlán
• pop 3240 • elev 1200m

The village of Suchitlán, 8km northeast of Comala and 1km east of the main road, is famous for its animal masks and its witches. The masks are carved in the village and worn by the dancers in the traditional Danza de los Morenos, which takes place here during Semana Santa. The dance commemorates the legend that dancing animals enabled the Marys to rescue Christ's body by distracting the Roman guards. You'll have to ask around for the homes of the mask-makers, who often have masks for sale.

Restaurant Portales de Suchitlán, on the southwest corner of the plaza, is very popular on weekends for a leisurely lunch. Delicious, inexpensive, local dishes are served at the host of indoor-outdoor tables, and the walls are decorated with dozens of animal masks.

Buses to Suchitlán go from the Central Camionera Suburbana in Colima.

San Antonio, La María & Carrizalillos

About 10km north of Suchitlán, on the east side of the road, *El Jacal de San Antonio* is an unusual restaurant where tables under the big *palapas* have an unsurpassed view of Volcán de Fuego de Colima. It's open only on weekends, when it's definitely worth a stop.

The paved road ends at the ex-Hacienda de San Antonio, a 19th-century coffee farm that's been converted into the *Hotel Gran Turismo*, which is booked exclusively through a US travel agent.

A gravel road continues from San Antonio to La María, about a kilometer or so to the east. There's a lovely lake here, the Laguna La María, which is a popular weekend picnic and camping spot. You'll find a few rustic cabins with simple stoves costing

WESTERN CENTRAL

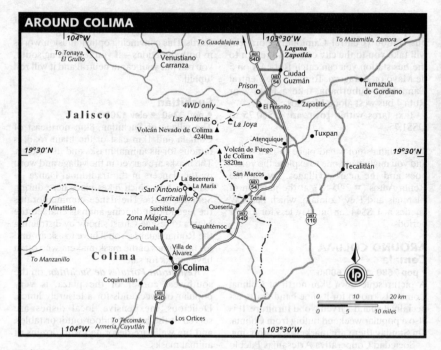

AROUND COLIMA

US$25 to US$30 for four to six people. If you want one at holiday times, call ☎ 331-7-68-02 in Colima to book.

Laguna de Carrizalillos is farther east on the same road, and has picnic tables and accommodations, but it's not as nice as La María.

A few buses run daily from Colima's Central Camionera Suburbana to San Antonio; those saying 'La Becerrera' will go there. From San Antonio you must walk to La María if you don't have a vehicle.

Volcán de Fuego de Colima & Volcán Nevado de Colima

These two dramatic mountains, situated in the Parque Nacional Volcán Neado de Colima, overlook Colima from the north. The nearer one, the steaming Volcán de Fuego de Colima (3820m), is 30km from the city as the crow flies, and still active. Also called Volcán de Fuego (Volcano of Fire) or

Fuego de Colima, it has erupted 30 times in the past four centuries, with a big eruption about every 70 years. A major eruption in 1913 spelled the end of one cycle of activity, and another began in the 1960s and is ongoing. Some 3km of new lava emerged in 1998, and intermittent fireworks persist.

Farther north, Volcán Nevado de Colima (4240m) is bigger, but extinct. 'Nevado' means 'snowy,' and the snow cap will be visible for much of the year.

Most of Fuego, including its crater, and all of Nevado are in Jalisco state, but the city of Colima is the best starting point.

Ascending the Volcanoes Recent eruptions, deadly gases, and the risk of explosions and avalanches make it unwise to approach the crater of **Volcán de Fuego**, and at times of volcanic activity you'll be prohibited from going near it. Information on the current condition of the volcano is posted (in Spanish) on the Internet sites www .cenapred.unam.mx (click 'Boletines' then 'Boletín del Volcán de Colima') and www .ucol.mx/volcan.

If the area is open, and you're driving yourself, the 32km track to Fuego turns west off highway 54 (the free road to Guadalajara), 58km north of Colima and a few kilometers south of the mill town of Atenquique. From Atenquique's parabolic church it's 2.7km up a steep hill to the turnoff, marked 'RMO Cerro Alto.' A faster option is to take the toll road toward Guadalajara and get off at the first exit past Atenquique (the exit is marked 'Tuxpan'), and backtrack through Atenquique to the Fuego turn-off.

On the side road, stay on what seems to be the main route (there are two turnoffs that should not be taken). Expect to brush past bushes and encounter deep potholes. After 18km, there's a large bump in the road to prevent most vehicles from proceeding; at this point you are 14km from the base of the cone. There is little traffic on this road and no water or facilities; if you're fearful your vehicle won't make it, turn around. The track is in poor condition and usually impassable (even for 4WD vehicles) after the July to September/October rains.

For **Volcán de Nevado**, take the free highway 54 almost to Ciudad Guzmán, some 83km from Colima. Or take the toll route 54D as far as the Tuxpan junction, but at the traffic circle take the free road toward Guadalajara ('Guadalajara Libre'). Shortly before Ciudad Guzmán, turn left (west) at the road to 'El Grullo.' Follow this road west past the conspicuous prison, and continue 3.4km to near the village of El Fresnito. On the way you'll pass a small side road to the left with a sign 'Viajes al Nevado . . . .' This directs you to the home of Agustín Ibarra, who provides guide and transport services for those climbing the volcano (see below). At El Fresnito, the road turns sharply right – continue 1km to a side road climbing steeply on your left. On this rough road, by 4WD, it will take almost two hours to cover the 20km to the *refugio* of La Joya, and another

15 minutes to reach Las Antenas (the radio masts; also referred to as *micro-ondas*, the microwave station). From there, it's about a two-hour walk/climb to the summit. You can camp, relax and acclimatize at Las Antenas, though there are no facilities.

For help with transport and organization, as well as guiding services, contact Agustín Ibarra (☎ 3-414-70-03), Montes 85 in El Fresnito. He'll take a group up to Las Antenas, guide them to the top, and take them back after their climb – US$88 for a group of ten; US$44 for a group of two or three. Ibarra speaks a little English, and his son speaks it quite well. People using his guide services usually can stay at his house the night prior to departure. Those planning to walk up the volcano should plan on at least one night up there and take all supplies, including water, with them.

Remnants of a pine forest cover most of Nevado, and alpine desert appears at the highest altitudes. The volcano could have snow on its upper flanks between December and March. The best months to climb Nevado are September through February.

Getting There & Away From Colima's main bus station, Autotransportes del Sur de Jalisco runs frequent 2nd-class buses to/from Ciudad Guzmán (1½ hours, US$3). Once in Ciudad Guzmán you can take a bus to El Fresnito, or Agustín Ibarra can pick you up at the Ciudad Guzmán bus station.

Tampumacchay

There are interesting shaft tombs from about 200 AD on the edge of a ravine at Tampumacchay, near the town of Los Ortices about 15km south of Colima. For a small fee, you can enter the tombs and someone will guide you around. Buses go from Colima's Central Camionera Suburbana to Los Ortices, but you'll have to walk the last 5km unless you happen upon a taxi.

Minatitlán
• pop 4010 • elev 740m

Minatitlán is an iron-ore mining town 55km west of Colima. It's on a scenic route through the mountains from Colima to the coast that drivers might consider as a long alternative to the main toll road or the main free road. About 7km south of Minatitlán, in the direction of Manzanillo, is a lovely waterfall with a natural swimming pool. The last half kilometer to the waterfall is on a steep section of road better traveled on foot.

Querétaro's aqueduct, transporting water for nearly 300 years

San Miguel de Allende's architectural details: an 18th-century doorway and floral motif

Hanging out in Real de Catorce

Iglesia de San Diego, Guanajuato

La Quemada ruins

San Miguel de Allende's Parroquia

Northern Central Highlands

Northwest from Mexico City stretches a fairly dry, temperate upland region comprising the southern part of the Altiplano Central. This was where the Spanish found most of the silver and other precious metals that were so central to their colonial ambitions in Mexico – and where they built some of the country's most magnificent cities from the great fortunes that silver brought them. The most spectacular of these cities are Guanajuato and Zacatecas, which along with Potosí in Bolivia were the major silver-producing centers of the Americas. San Miguel de Allende, Querétaro and San Luis Potosí also have a wealth of colonial architecture. Today most of these cities are of moderate size, and have lively arts and entertainment scenes.

The more fertile land around Guanajuato and Querétaro is known as the Bajío ('ba-HEE-o'), and has long been one of Mexico's major agricultural zones. This is a highly rewarding region to visit. The distances are not huge and the landscape between the cities is always impressive. The Bajío international airport (BJX), 12km southeast of León, has many direct flights to and from the USA that may be more convenient than flying into Mexico City.

The Bajío is known to Mexicans as La Cuna de la Independencia (the Cradle of Independence), for it was here that the movement for independence from Spain began in 1810. The town of Dolores Hidalgo, where the uprising started, and nearby places like San Miguel de Allende, Querétaro and Guanajuato are full of key sites from this historic movement.

Before the Spanish reached Mexico, the northern central highlands were inhabited by fierce seminomadic tribes known to the Aztecs as Chichimecs. They resisted Spanish conquest longer than any other Mexican peoples and were finally pacified in the late 16th century by an offer of food and clothing in return for peace. The wealth subsequently amassed in the region by the Spanish was at

Highlights

- Zacatecas – stylish silver city with a sublime cathedral, plus museums, mountains and a nightclub in a mine tunnel
- Real de Catorce – ghost town of miracles, magic, stark mountains and fine Italian food
- Guanajuato – superb mansions, colorful houses, crooked cobbled alleyways, 21,000 students and a very quixotic festival
- San Miguel de Allende – traditional style meets expat chic; exuberant fiestas, fireworks, food and super shopping
- Sierra Gorda – remote region of archaeological sites, rugged roads and a pyramid of cosmic energy

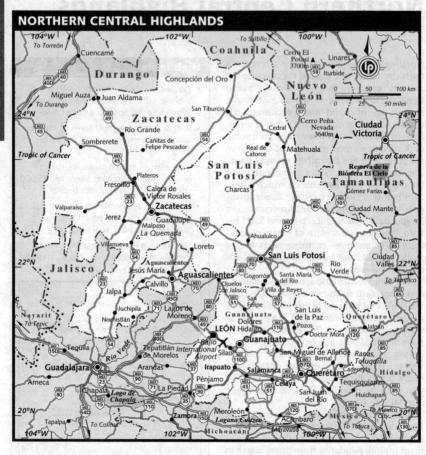

NORTHERN CENTRAL HIGHLANDS

the cost of the lives of many of these people, who were used as virtual slave labor in the mines.

Mining is still important in the region, and there's industry as well – in León, Querétaro, Aguascalientes and elsewhere – but the industry doesn't detract from the region's historical, artistic and scenic attractions.

This chapter encompasses the states of Zacatecas, Aguascalientes, Guanajuato and Querétaro, and most of San Luis Potosí state. Eastern San Luis Potosí state is covered in the Central Gulf Coast chapter.

Zacatecas State

The state of Zacatecas is one of Mexico's largest in area (73,252 sq km) but smallest in population (1.3 million). It's a dry, rugged, cactus-strewn expanse on the fringe of Mexico's northern semideserts, with large tracts almost blank on the map. The fact that it has any significant population at all is largely due to the mineral wealth the Spanish discovered here, mainly around the capital city Zacatecas. Many minerals are still mined in the state, which is currently Mexico's biggest silver producer.

ZACATECAS

• pop 109,100 • elev 2445m ☏ 4

If you've come down from the north, welcome to the first of Mexico's justly fabled silver cities. If you've been visiting more southerly silver cities like Guanajuato, it's worth coming a few hours farther north. Zacatecas is a particularly beautiful and fascinating city.

Some of Mexico's finest colonial buildings, including perhaps its most stunning cathedral, all built from the riches of the local silver mines, cluster along narrow, winding streets at the foot of a spectacular rock-topped hill called Cerro de la Bufa. Set amid dry, arid country, this historic city has much to detain you, from trips into an old silver mine to some excellent museums and the ascent of la Bufa itself by *teleférico* (cable car). A state capital and university city, Zacatecas is sophisticated for its size, and though it's popular with Mexican and European visitors, its off-center location insulates it from hordes of tourists.

History

Before the Spanish arrived, the area was inhabited by the Zacatecos – one of the wilder Chichimec tribes. Indigenous people had mined local mineral deposits for centuries before the Spanish arrived; it's said that the silver rush here was started by a Chichimec giving a piece of the fabled metal to a conquistador. The Spaniards founded a settlement and, in 1548, started mining operations, virtually enslaving many indigenous people in the process. Caravan after caravan of silver was sent off to Mexico City. While some treasure-laden wagons were raided by hostile tribes, enough silver reached its destination to create fabulously wealthy silver barons. Agriculture and ranching developed to serve the rapidly growing town.

In the first quarter of the 18th century, Zacatecas' mines were producing 20% of Nueva España's silver. At this time the city became an important base for missionaries spreading Catholicism as far as what are now the US states of Arizona and New Mexico.

In the 19th century political events diminished the flow of silver as various forces fought to control the city. Although silver production later improved under Porfirio Díaz, the revolution disrupted it. And it was here in 1914 that Pancho Villa, through brilliant tactics, defeated a stronghold of 12,000 soldiers loyal to the unpopular President Victoriano Huerta.

After the revolution, Zacatecas continued to thrive on silver. It remains a mining center to this day, with the 200-year-old El Bote mine still productive.

Orientation

The city center lies in a valley between Cerro de la Bufa, with its strange rocky cap, to the northeast, and the smaller Cerro del Grillo to the northwest. Most facilities and attractions are within walking distance of the center, and this is a wonderful city in which to walk. The two key streets are Avenida Hidalgo, running roughly north-south, with the cathedral toward its north end; and Avenida Juárez, running roughly east-west across the south end of Avenida Hidalgo. If you get lost, just ask the way back to one of these two streets. Avenida Hidalgo becomes Avenida González Ortega south of its intersection with Avenida Juárez.

Information

Tourist Offices The tourist office (☏ 924-40-47) is upstairs in an old colonial building at Hidalgo 403, open 9 am to 8 pm daily. They're very helpful, and have plenty of brochures, in Spanish, on Zacatecas city and state. Some staff members speak English.

Money Plenty of banks around the central area change traveler's checks and cash, from about 9 am to 5 pm Monday to Friday, 10 am to 1 pm Saturday. Nearly all have ATMs.

Post & Communications The post office is at Allende 111, just east of Hidalgo, open

ZACATECAS

PLACES TO EAT
2 Cafetería Rancho Grande
20 Café y Nevería Acropolis
21 La Terraza Café
22 La Cantera Musical
26 El Pueblito
28 Mr Laberinto
31 Viva Pizza
32 Café Zas
35 El Tragadero
40 Mesón La Mina, Restaurant Condesa
43 Restaurant Fonda El Jacalito
47 El Pastor

OTHER
1 Museo Rafael Coronel
3 Fountain
4 Mina El Edén (East Entrance)
5 Lavandería El Indio Triste
6 Mina El Edén (West Entrance), Disco El Malacate
7 Café Arroba
8 CyberNovus
9 Museo Pedro Coronel
10 La Marcha

11 Templo de Santo Domingo
12 Palacio de la Mala Noche
14 Palacio de Gobierno
15 Hospital
16 Casa de Moneda
17 Museo Zacatecano
18 Teatro Calderón
19 El Paraíso

23 El Claustro
24 Ex-Templo de San Agustín
26 Tourist Office
27 Nueva Galicia
29 Rectoría
34 Post Office
34 Málaga
36 Cactus

37 Telecomm
38 Banamex
42 Mercado El Laberinto
45 Mercado Arroyo de la Plata
46 Museo Francisco Goitia
51 Centro Comercial Zacatecas (Old Bus Station)
55 Budget Rent-a-Car

PLACES TO STAY
13 Hotel Continental Plaza
25 Posada de la Moneda
30 Hotel Mesón de Jobito
39 Hostel del Río
41 Hotel Condesa
44 Posada de los Condes
48 Hotel Zamora
49 Hotel del Parque
50 Hotel Quinta Real
52 Hotel María Conchita
53 Hotel Gami
54 Hotel Río Grande de Zacatecas
56 Hotel Colón

To Motel del Bosque

Plazuela de García

To Cerro de la Bufa

Cerro del Grillo Teleférico Station

To Cerro de la Bufa

Plazuela de Santo Domingo

Plaza de Armas

Cathedral

Mercado González Ortega

To Footpath to Cerro de la Bufa

Parque Alameda

Jardín Juárez

Jardín de la Madre

Plazuela Genaro Codina

Jardín Independencia

Parque Enrique Estrada

Acueducto El Cubo

To Biblioteca Central de UAZ, Carretera a la Bufa

To Guadalupe

To Villa Juvenil Hostel, Bus Station

0   100   200 m
0   100   200 yards

8 am to 7 pm Monday to Friday, 9 am to 1 pm Saturday.

There are pay phones at the main entrance to the Mercado González Ortega on Hidalgo, and on Hidalgo near the corner of Callejón San Agustín, just south of the tourist office building. Telephone casetas are in the bus station and on Callejón de las Cuevas, off Hidalgo beside Café Zas. The Telecomm office, on Hidalgo at Juárez, offers public fax service.

Internet access is inexpensive here. Two good places, both charging about US$1.75 per hour, are CyberNovus, upstairs on Calle Lancaster near Villalpando (9 am to 9 pm daily), and Cafe Arroba, Felix Gómez 520 (9 am to 10 pm daily; *arroba* is Spanish for the @ symbol).

Laundry Lavandería El Indio Triste, at Hidalgo 824, opposite the corner of Genaro Codina, does a service wash for US$0.90 per kg. It's open 9 am to 9 pm Monday to Friday, 9 am to 3 pm Saturday.

Cathedral

Zacatecas' pink-stone *catedral* is perhaps the ultimate expression of Mexican baroque. It was built chiefly between 1729 and 1752, just before baroque edged into its final Churrigueresque phase. And in this city of affluent silver barons, no expense was spared.

The highlight is the stupendous main façade, which faces Hidalgo. It is a wall of amazingly detailed yet harmonious carvings. This façade has been interpreted as a giant symbol of the tabernacle, which is the receptacle for the wafer and the wine that confer communion with God, the heart of Catholic worship. A tiny figure of an angel holding a tabernacle can be seen at the heart of the design, the keystone at the top of the round central window. Above this, at the center of the third tier, is Christ, and above Christ is God. The other main statues are the 12 apostles, while a smaller figure of the Virgin stands immediately above the center of the doorway. The whole façade is now shrouded in a fine mesh – it's scarcely visible and a lot less intrusive than a crust of pigeon poop.

The south and north façades, though simpler, are also very fine. The central sculpture on the southern façade is of La Virgen de los Zacatecas, the city's patroness. The north façade shows Christ crucified, attended by the Virgin Mary and St John.

The interior of the cathedral is disarmingly plain, though it was once adorned with elaborate gold and silver ornaments and festooned with tapestries and paintings. This wealth was plundered in the course of Zacatecas' turbulent history.

Plaza de Armas

This is the open space on the north side of the cathedral. The **Palacio de Gobierno** on the plaza's east side was built in the 18th century for a family of colonial gentry. It was acquired by the state in the 19th century. In the turret of its main staircase is a mural of the history of Zacatecas state, painted in 1970 by Antonio Rodríguez.

The lovely, white **Palacio de la Mala Noche** on the west side of the plaza was built in the late 18th century for the owner of the Mala Noche mine near Zacatecas. It houses state government offices.

Mercado González Ortega

South of the cathedral, between Hidalgo and Tacuba, is the impressive, iron-columned building from the 1880s that used to hold Zacatecas' main market. In the 1980s the upper level, entered from Hidalgo, was renovated into an upscale shopping center complete with restaurants.

Teatro Calderón

Dating from the 1890s Porfiriato period, the Teatro Calderón is across Hidalgo from the south end of the Mercado González Ortega. This lovely theater is as busy as ever staging plays, concerts, films and art exhibitions – check the architectural model in the foyer.

Templo de Santo Domingo

Santo Domingo Church dominates the Plazuela de Santo Domingo, reached from the Plaza de Armas by a narrow lane, Callejón de Veyna. Done in a more sober baroque style than the cathedral, it has some fine gilded altars and paintings and a graceful horseshoe staircase. Built by the Jesuits in the 1740s, the church was taken over by Dominican monks when the Jesuits were expelled in 1767.

Museo Pedro Coronel

The Pedro Coronel Museum is housed in a 17th-century former Jesuit college beside Santo Domingo. Pedro Coronel (1923-85) was an affluent Zacatecan artist who bequeathed to his hometown his great collection of art and artifacts from all over the world, as well as much of his own work. The collection includes 20th-century prints, drawings and paintings by Picasso, Roualt, Chagall, Kandinsky and Miró; some entertaining Hogarth lithographs; and many fine ink drawings by Francisco de Goya (1746-1828). The pre-Hispanic Mexican artifacts seem to have been chosen as much for their artistic appeal as their archaeological importance, and there's an amazing collection of masks and other pieces from ancient Egypt, Greece, Rome, Asia, Africa, even New Guinea. It all adds up to one of provincial Mexico's best art museums – open 9.30 am to 5 pm every day except Thursday (US$1.75).

Calle Dr Hierro & Calle Auza

Dr Hierro, leading south from Plazuela de Santo Domingo, and its continuation Auza, are quiet, narrow streets. About 100m from Plazuela de Santo Domingo is the **Casa de Moneda**, which housed the Zacatecas mint (Mexico's second biggest) during the 19th century. A little farther down is the **Museo Zacateno**, largely devoted to Huichol art. It's open 10 am to 5 pm daily except Tuesday (US$1.10).

Another 100m south is the **Ex-Templo de San Agustín**, built as a church for Augustinian monks in the 17th century. During the anticlerical movement of the 19th century, the church was turned into a casino. Then, in 1882, it was purchased by American Presbyterian missionaries who destroyed its 'too Catholic' main façade, replacing it with a blank white wall. In the 20th century the church returned to Catholic use, and its adjoining ex-monastery is now the seat of the Zacatecas

bishopric. The church's finest feature is the plateresque carving of the conversion of St Augustine over the north doorway.

The street ends at **Jardín Juárez**, a tiny rectangle of a park. The Rectoría, or administrative headquarters, of the Universidad Autónoma de Zacatecas is housed in a neoclassical building on its west side.

Mina El Edén

El Edén Mine, once one of Mexico's richest, is a 'must' for visitors to Zacatecas because of the dramatic insight it gives into the source of wealth in this region – and the terrible price paid for it. Digging for fabulous hoards of silver, gold, iron, copper and zinc, the enslaved indigenous people, including many children, worked under horrific conditions. At one time up to five people a day died from accidents or diseases like silicosis and tuberculosis.

El Edén was worked from 1586 until the 1950s. Today the fourth of its seven levels is kept open for visitors. The lower levels are flooded. A miniature road train or an elevator takes you deep inside the Cerro del Grillo, the hill in which the mine is located. Then guides – who may or may not speak a little English – lead you along floodlit walkways past deep shafts and over subterranean pools.

The mine has two entrances. To reach the higher one (the west entrance), walk about 100m around to the southwest from the Cerro de Grillo teleférico station – from this entrance, tours start with an elevator descent. To reach the east entrance, walk west along Juárez and stay on it after its name changes to Torreón at the Alameda park. Turn right immediately after the big hospital above the park. You can take a Ruta 7 bus up Juárez from the corner of Hidalgo past the turnoff to the mine entrance. Mine tours leave every 15 minutes from 11 am to 6 pm daily (US$1.75). For information about Disco El Malacate, the mine's nighttime alter ego, see the Entertainment section.

Teleférico

The most exhilarating ride in Zacatecas, and the easiest way to reach the Cerro de la

Bufa, is the teleférico that crosses high above the city from Cerro del Grillo. Just walk to the left from Mina El Edén (east entrance) and you'll reach the teleférico's Cerro del Grillo station after a couple of minutes. Alternatively, Ruta 7 buses coming from the bus station run up González Ortega, west along Juárez and Torreón and go right by the west entrance on their way to the teleférico.

You could also climb the steps of Callejón de García Rojas, which lead straight up to the teleférico from the north end of Genaro Codina. The Swiss-built teleférico operates every 15 minutes from 10 am to 6 pm daily, except when it's raining or when winds exceed 60km/hour. The trip takes seven minutes and costs US$1.10 each way.

Cerro de la Bufa

Cerro de la Bufa is the rock-topped hill that dominates Zacatecas from the northeast. The most appealing of the many explanations for its name is that *bufa* is an old Spanish word for wineskin, which is certainly what the rocky formation atop the hill looks like. The views from the top are superb and there's an interesting group of monuments, a chapel and a museum up there.

An exciting and convenient way to ascend la Bufa is by the teleférico (see Teleférico). More strenuously, you can walk up it (start by going up Calle del Ángel from the east end of the cathedral). There's also a road, Carretera a la Bufa, which begins at Avenida López Velarde beside the university library. A taxi costs US$2.25. All three routes bring you to the monuments, chapel and museum. Just above the teleférico station is a meteorological observatory.

The **Museo de la Toma de Zacatecas** commemorates the 1914 battle fought on the slopes of la Bufa in which the revolutionary División del Norte, led by Pancho Villa and Felipe Ángeles, defeated the forces of President Victoriano Huerta. This gave the revolutionaries control of Zacatecas, which was the gateway to Mexico City. The museum is open 10 am to 5 pm, Tuesday to Sunday (US$1.10).

La Capilla de la Virgen del Patrocinio, adjacent to the museum, is named after the patron saint of miners. Above the altar of this 18th-century chapel is an image of the Virgin said to be capable of healing the sick. Thousands of pilgrims make their way here each year during the weeks either side of September 8, when the image is carried to the cathedral.

Just east of the museum and chapel stand three imposing equestrian **statues** of the victors of the battle of Zacatecas – Villa, Ángeles, and Pánfilo Natera. A path behind the Villa and Natera statues leads to the rocky **summit** of La Bufa, where there are marvelous views on all sides, stretching over the city and away to mountain ranges far in the distance. The hill is topped by a metal cross that is illuminated at night.

A path along the foot of the rocky hilltop, starting to the right of the statues, leads to the **Mausoleo de los Hombres Ilustres de Zacatecas**, with the tombs of Zacatecan heroes from 1841 to the present day.

You can return to the city by the teleférico or by a footpath leading downhill from the statues.

Museo Rafael Coronel

The Rafael Coronel Museum, imaginatively housed in the ruins of the lovely 16th-century ex-Convento de San Francisco in the north of the city, contains Mexican folk art collected by the Zacatecan artist Rafael Coronel, brother of Pedro Coronel and son-in-law of Diego Rivera. The highlight is the astonishing, colorful display of over 2000 masks used in traditional dances and rituals. This is probably the biggest mask collection in the country. Also to be seen are pottery, puppets, pre-Hispanic objects and drawings and sketches by Rivera. The museum is just off Matamoros, northeast of the center. It's open 10 am to 5 pm every day except Wednesday (US$1.75).

Museo Francisco Goitia

The Francisco Goitia Museum displays work by six major Zacatecan artists of the 20th century. Set in a fine former governor's mansion at Estrada 102, above the pleasant Parque Enrique Estrada south of the city's central area, it's well worth the short walk from the center. Francisco Goitia (1882-1960) himself did some particularly good paintings of indigenous people. There's also a very striking Goitia self-portrait in the museum. Other artists represented include Pedro and Rafael Coronel. It's open 10 am to 5 pm Tuesday to Saturday (US$1.75).

Organized Tours

A couple of companies run tours of city sights and places of interest out of town. A four-hour city tour including the mine and the teleférico costs about US$14; tours including Guadalupe cost about US$20. A five-hour trip to the archaeological site of La Quemada and the town of Jerez is about US$17.

Special Events

La Morisma Usually held on the last Friday, Saturday and Sunday in August, this festival features the most spectacular of the many mock battles staged at Mexican fiestas commemorating the triumph of the Christians over the Muslims (Moors) in old Spain. Rival 'armies' parade through the city streets in the mornings then, accompanied by bands of musicians, enact two battle sequences, one around midday and one in the afternoon, between Lomas de Bracho in the northeast of the city and Cerro de la Bufa. One sequence portrays a conflict between Emperor Charlemagne and Almirante Balam, king of Alexandria. The other deals with a 16th-century Muslim rebellion led by Argel Osmán. The enactments develop over the festival's three days, both culminating in Christian victory on Sunday. Church services and other ceremonies also form part of the celebrations.

Feria de Zacatecas Zacatecas stages its annual feria from about September 5 to 21. Renowned matadors come to fight the famous local bulls; *charreadas* (rodeos), concerts, plays and agricultural and craft shows are staged; and on September 8 the image of La Virgen del Patrocinio is carried to the cathedral from its chapel on the Cerro de la Bufa.

Places to Stay

Budget Zacatecas' cheap lodgings tend to be in extreme contrast to the stately beauty of its colonial architecture. The cheaper places don't have parking, but public lots in the center are only US$1 or so per night.

Hostels The *Villa Deportiva Juvenil* (☎ 922-02-23 ext 7, Paseo la Encantada s/n) is inconveniently located about halfway between the bus station and the center. The hostel is in the far corner of the CREA sports grounds where there is a large swimming pool. From the bus station, take a Ruta 7 or 8 bus and after about seven minutes watch for an overpass before the intersection of Boulevard Nueva Celaya and Avenida 5 Señores. Walk down 5 Señores, turn left onto Calle Ancha, and follow it up the hill to the green hostel. Open till 11 pm, it has 70 or so beds in reasonably spacious, clean dormitories at US$5 per person, and inexpensive meals are available. It's OK as hostels go, but it's too far away from the historic center of town.

Hotels The cheapest place in the center is *Hotel Zamora* (☎ 922-12-00), two blocks south of Jardín Independencia, where basic rooms with bath cost US$6.50/8 for singles/doubles, or US$9 with two beds. The bigger rooms overlook the pretty Plazuela Zamora.

Other cheapies are farther out, on and around Boulevard López Mateos. *Hotel Río Grande de Zacatecas* (☎ 922-98-76, Calzada de la Paz 513) is on a hillside about 1.25km southeast of the cathedral. Calzada de la Paz is a small street almost opposite the old bus station – the hotel is 250m uphill. Small but clean rooms cost US$5.50/7.75; US$10 for a twin. Exterior rooms have great views of la Bufa but also traffic noise.

A better budget option might be *Hotel María Conchita* (☎ 922-14-94, López Mateos 401), where singles/doubles with TV and phone are US$9/11. Farther down the hill, *Hotel Gami* (☎ 922-80-05, López Mateos 309) has a hideous color scheme and small, reasonably clean rooms with TV. They ask US$15 per room, which is too much – ask for a discount.

More conveniently located, between the two busy, noisy streets, is *Hotel Colón* (☎ 922-89-25, *López Mateos 106)*; it has another entrance at López Velarde 508. The medium-size rooms, with bathroom, TV and phone, cost US$11/15 for singles/doubles.

About 1.5km southwest of the cathedral, near Parque Enrique Estrada and opposite the aqueduct, *Hotel del Parque* (☎ 922-04-79, *González Ortega 302-4)* is popular with travelers. The large rooms with private bath cost US$9/11 – they're clean enough but a bit short on natural light.

Mid-Range Mid-range and top-end hotels hike their prices in high season – at other times you may be able to get a discount on the prices given here.

Centrally located *Hotel Condesa* (☎ 922-11-60, *Juárez 5)*, near the corner of Hidalgo, is a good value. Agreeable singles/doubles with private bath are around US$19/23. The best and slightly more expensive rooms are on the renovated top floor. The rooms are around a central well with a plastic roof. Nearly all have exterior windows – those facing northeast have fine views of La Bufa.

Across the street from the Condesa, *Posada de los Condes* (☎ 922-10-93, *Juárez 107)* is a colonial monument over three centuries old, but a recent modernization has removed most evidence of its age from the interior. The rooms, though not big, are pleasant and well kept, with TV, phone and carpet. They cost US$19/22.

Around the corner and back toward the center, *Hostel del Río* (☎ 922-78-33, *Hidalgo 170)* is no hostel, but it has a great location, a bit of character and a small number of spacious, comfortable rooms from US$18/22.

Another fair choice is *Posada de la Moneda* (☎ 922-08-81, *Hidalgo 413)*, a block south of the cathedral. The rooms range along wide corridors. They are pleasant, with TV and bath and Huichol yarn paintings on the walls. Singles/doubles cost US$26/40.

Motel del Bosque (☎ 922-07-45) is on the Periférico (ring road) on the northwest side of town, uphill from the cable car terminal. It's ideal if you have a vehicle but don't want to drive in the congested central area; you can easily walk to the center, but the climb back will be harder! Quiet, comfortable rooms with all modern conveniences cost US$27/33, and some have great views over the city.

Top End The *Hotel Continental Plaza* (☎ 922-61-83, *fax 922-62-45, Hidalgo 703)* is superbly located in a modernized colonial building on the Plaza de Armas. The 115 air-conditioned rooms and suites are attractively furnished and equipped with TV and minibars. There's a good restaurant. Room rates start at US$102, single or double.

Central but peaceful, *Hotel Mesón de Jobito* (☎ 924-17-22, *fax 924-35-00, Jardín Juárez 143)* is another lovely old building with 31 finely decorated rooms and suites from US$120. It has a restaurant and a classy bar.

The top place is the superb and luxurious *Hotel Quinta Real* (☎ 922-91-04, *fax 922-84-40)*, about 1.5km south of the cathedral just off González Ortega. It's spectacularly constructed around Zacatecas' former main bullring, with the arches of the fine old El Cubo aqueduct running across the front of the hotel. Their least expensive rooms are large and very comfortable 'master suites,' at US$172.

Places to Eat
Many restaurants have local specialties using such ingredients as nopal, pumpkin, and pumpkin seeds. Locally produced wine is good. You might also like to try *aguamiel* ('honey water'), a nutritional drink made from a type of cactus. Early in the day, on and around Hidalgo, you'll see burros carrying pottery jugs containing the beverage.

There are two produce markets in the center. Mercado El Laberinto has its main entrance on Juárez. Close by, Mercado Arroyo de la Plata can be entered from the curved street Arroyo de la Plata. There are plenty of budget eateries in this vicinity.

There are lots of mid-range possibilities on Avenida Hidalgo and Avenida Juárez (see the following entries), serving well-prepared Mexican standards, as well as items from the ice cream/hamburger/french fries food group. For expensive top-class meals, make your way to the top hotels like the Continental Plaza or Mesón de Jobito. The restaurant at the **Hotel Quinta Real** (☎ 922-91-04) is especially memorable for its outlook to the bullring and aqueduct, as well as for its elegant ambiance and superb Mexican/international cuisine. With soup and salads to US$6, pasta dishes around US$7, and main courses from US$10 to US$17, it's very reasonably priced for the quality it offers. Restore your budget at some of the less touristy places on the fringe of the historic center, such as the **Cafetería Rancho Grande**, on charming Plazuela de García a few blocks north of the cathedral, where typical dishes like red enchiladas and cheese are around US$2, and a comida corrida is under US$3.

Avenida Hidalgo It's a pleasure to walk this lively street, trying to choose between the many excellent eateries. Most are open daily from around 8 am to 10 pm or even later. **Café y Nevería Acrópolis**, on Hidalgo immediately south of the cathedral, is a popular central meeting place for locals and visitors alike. It's not especially cheap, but there's a wide choice of all sorts of cakes, snacks, meals and drinks. Egg dishes are around US$4, more substantial meals from US$5. A big cappuccino costs US$2.

In Mercado González Ortega, with a balcony overlooking Calle Tacuba, **La Terraza** is a delightful and inexpensive place for a light meal, a drink or a snack. Underneath the market, with its entrance at Tacuba 16, **La Cantera Musical** has classic and truly delicious Mexican food. It's a relaxed place with the kitchen in full view and waiters in ranchero gear. Breakfasts are from US$1.70 to US$2.50, and main courses from US$4.

Farther south on Hidalgo, **Mr Laberinto** has a good reputation but erratic hours. In the same building as the tourist office, **El Pueblito** (Hidalgo 403) offers tasty renditions of most standard Mexican dishes, from US$3 to US$6. It has bright decor, light entertainment and an enjoyable atmosphere.

Popular, clean, friendly **Café Zas** (Hidalgo 201) is toward the south end of Hidalgo and serves decent breakfasts at around US$3, antojitos (appetizers) from US$3 to US$4, and chicken or meat dishes up to US$7.

Avenida Juárez The friendly, family-run **El Pastor** is on the south side of Jardín Independencia, just off the east end of Juárez. It's busy from 8 am to 9 pm serving up charcoal-roasted chicken, tortilla chips and salad for under US$3. Pay a little more for mole and rice.

Several eateries on Juárez between Jardín Independencia and Avenida Hidalgo offer adequate if unspectacular Mexican fare, with antojitos in the US$2.50 to US$4 range, and main courses for US$4 to US$6. These include **Mesón La Mina** (Juárez 15), **Restaurant Condesa** next door and **Restaurant Fonda El Jacalito**, the best of the three, across the street. They all do an economical comida corrida.

El Tragadero, on Juárez a block west of Hidalgo, is a good-value Mexican eatery. To order, you mark your choices on a list. Most items are priced between US$1.25 and US$3.50. Alambre con queso (slices of grilled meat with cheese) is a good choice at US$3.50. There's a tasty platillo vegetariano (US$2.50), and exquisite enchiladas. Nearby is **Viva Pizza**, on the east side of Jardín de la Madre. It has several rooms with folksy decor and serves pretty good pizzas. A small vegetariana (US$4) will fill one person.

Entertainment

At **Disco El Malacate** (☎ 922-30-02) you can get down in a gallery of the Mina El Edén, to a mix of US and Latin dance music with a big crowd of locals, domestic tourists and international visitors. The essential Zacatecas nightlife experience, it opens at 9.30 pm on Thursday, Friday and Saturday, gets going around 11.30 pm and kicks on to about 2.30 am. Cover is US$5.50, and drinks are reasonably priced. Space is limited, so it's a good idea to reserve a table.

In the center, several other dance clubs jump on Thursday, Friday and Saturday nights. *El Claustro* on Aguascalientes, a small street east off the top of Tacuba, has been popular for years. Cover is around US$5, and it keeps going till late. *Málaga*, at the bottom of Tacuba, and *La Marcha (Dr Hierro 409)* are also popular with well-dressed young locals and visitors. *Cactus*, at the Juárez end of Hidalgo, is an enjoyable video-and-billiards bar open till late every night (no cover), with music and dancing on Friday and Saturday (US$3 cover).

El Paraíso is a smart bar in the southwest corner of the Mercado González Ortega on Hidalgo. It has a friendly, varied, mostly 30s clientele, and is open nightly; it's busy on Friday and Saturday. Beers are US$2, cocktails about US$3. The *Nueva Galicia* bar, across the little plaza outside El Paraíso, is similar.

Zacatecas has a tradition of *callejoneadas* – a custom from Spain in which a group of professional musicians in costume leads a crowd of revelers through the city, drinking wine, singing and telling stories along the way. In Zacatecas it's usually horn players leading the parade. There doesn't seem to be a regular schedule but during fiestas and on some weekends callejoneadas set off around 8 pm from the Alameda. You can join in for free. Ask for details at the tourist office.

Teatro Calderón is the top central venue for cultural events.

Shopping

Zacatecas is known for fine leather, silver and colorful sarapes. Try along Arroyo de la Plata and in the indoor market off this street. The Mercado González Ortega is more upmarket with silver jewelry, a shop specializing in local wines and another in *charrería* gear – boots, saddles, chaps, belts, sarapes and more.

Tour companies can take you to visit silversmithing workshops, or ask at the tourist office for details of how to do this independently.

Getting There & Away

Air Mexicana (☎ 922-74-29) flies direct daily to/from Mexico City, Acapulco, Cancún, Monterrey and Tijuana. They also have several direct flights weekly to/from Chicago and Los Angeles, and one to/from Denver.

TAESA (☎ 922-00-50) flies direct most days to/from Chicago, Oakland (California), Mexico City, Ciudad Juárez, Morelia and Tijuana.

Bus The Zacatecas bus station is on the southwest edge of town, about 3km from the center. Many buses from here are *de paso* (en route from another city). The station has a checkroom for baggage (open from 7 am to 10 pm), telephone casetas and a fax office. Daily departures include:

Aguascalientes – 130km, 2 hours; 14 1st-class Futura, Transportes Chihuahuenses or Ómnibus de México (US$6.75), 2nd-class Estrella Blanca every half-hour (US$5.50)

Durango – 290km, 4½ hours; 13 1st-class Ómnibus de México (US$15), 6 2nd-class Estrella Blanca (US$13)

Fresnillo – 60km, 1 to 1½ hours; hourly 1st-class Futura (US$3.50), hourly 2nd-class Estrella Blanca and Camiones de los Altos (US$2.20), 2nd-class every 10 minutes, 6 am to 9.30 pm, from Centro Comercial Zacatecas (old bus station) on Boulevard López Mateos (US$2)

Guadalajara – 318km, 4 hours; frequent 1st-class Ómnibus de México and Transportes Chihuahuenses (US$20), hourly 2nd-class Estrella Blanca/Rojo de los Altos (US$15.50)

Guanajuato – 310km; take a León bus and change there for Guanajuato

León – 257km, 3 hours; 10 1st-class Ómnibus de México (US$12.75)

Mexico City (Terminal Norte) – 602km, 6 to 8 hours; 1 deluxe (US$47), 16 1st-class by Futura, Transportes Chihuahuenses and Ómnibus de México (US$35)

Monterrey – 450km, 5 hours; 5 1st-class Transportes del Norte (US$23), 10 2nd-class Estrella Blanca/Rojo de los Altos (US$20)

San Luis Potosí – 188km, 2 hours; 12 1st-class Futura and Ómnibus de México (US$9), 15 2nd-class Estrella Blanca (US$5.50)

There are also frequent buses to Torreón and several a day to Chihuahua, Ciudad Juárez, Saltillo and Nuevo Laredo.

Car Budget (☎ 922-94-58) has a rental office next to the Hotel Colón on Boulevard

López Mateos. Lloguer (☎ 922-34-07), about a block east at López Mateos 201 offers discounts for guests of several hotels, including Hotel Condesa and Posada de los Condes.

Getting Around

Zacatecas' airport is about 20km north of the city. The cheapest way to/from the center is a combi (☎ 922-59-46, US$3.50). Taxis are about US$13.

Ruta 8 buses from the bus station run directly to the cathedral (US$0.20). Heading back out from the center, they go south on Villalpando. Ruta 7 buses from the bus station run to the intersection of González Ortega and Juárez. Taxis from the bus station to the center cost US$1.50.

GUADALUPE
• pop 65,700 ☎ 4

About 10km east of the Zacatecas city center, Guadalupe has one of Mexico's best collections of colonial art – the **Museo y Templo de Guadalupe**. It's in a historic ex-monastery next to a still-working church, and is worth the trip if you have any interest in colonial history, art or architecture. The art is almost entirely religious – lots of saints, angels and bloody crucifixions.

The monastery Convento de Guadalupe was established by Franciscan monks in the early 18th century as a Colegio Apostólica de Propaganda Fide (Apostolic College for the Propagation of the Faith). It developed a strong academic tradition and a renowned library and was a base for missionary work in northern Nueva España until it closed in the 1850s.

The building now houses the museum, with many works by Miguel Cabrera, Juan Correa, Antonio Torres and Cristóbal Villalpando. Visitors can also see part of its library and step into the choir on the upper floor of the monastery church *(templo)*, with its fine carved and painted chairs. From the choir you can look down into the beautifully decorated 19th-century Capilla de Nápoles on the church's north side. Museum hours are 10 am to 4.30 pm daily (US$2.20, free Sunday).

The exterior of the church next door has some fine baroque carving. Inside, the ground level has a view into the Capilla de Nápoles.

On the other side of the Museo de Guadalupe is the embryonic **Museo Regional de Zacatecas**, with a small collection of old carriages and cars. It's free, and worth the price.

The town holds its annual **feria** from December 3 to 13, focused on the Día de la Virgen de Guadalupe (December 12).

Getting There & Away

From Zacatecas, Transportes de Guadalupe buses run to Guadalupe every few minutes along López Mateos (20 minutes, US$0.25). There's a bus stop just beyond the old bus station, now called the Centro Comercial Zacatecas, on the corner of López Mateos and Callejón del Barro. Get off at a small plaza in the middle of Guadalupe where a 'Museo Convento' sign points to the right, along Madero. Walk about 250m along Madero to a sizable plaza, called Jardín Juárez. The museums are on the left side of the plaza. To return to Zacatecas, you can pick up the bus where you disembarked.

FRESNILLO & PLATEROS
• pop 89,300 ☎ 4

Fresnillo is an unexciting town 60km north of Zacatecas on the road to Torreón and Durango. The village of Plateros, 5km northeast of Fresnillo, is the site of the Santuario de Plateros, one of Mexico's most visited shrines. If you're particularly interested in Mexican Catholicism, you might find the santuario worth visiting. Otherwise, give both Fresnillo and Plateros a miss.

Orientation

Fresnillo's bus station is on Ébano, about 1km northeast of the center of town on local bus Ruta 3. You can get a bus direct to Plateros from the Fresnillo bus station. If you need to go into Fresnillo for a meal or a room, you'll find it's a higgledy-piggledy place with three main plazas. The most pleasant of the three is Jardín Madero with the colonial church of Nuestra Señora de la Purificación on its north side.

Santuario de Plateros

Pilgrims flock to Plateros every day of the year to see El Santo Niño de Atocha – a quaint image of the infant Jesus, holding a staff and basket and wearing a colonial pilgrim's feathered hat. The figure resides on the altar of the 18th-century Santuario de Plateros church. The courtyard in front of the church is regularly packed with pilgrims, and the surrounding streets are lined with stalls selling a vast array of gaudy religious artifacts – Santo Niño souvenirs especially.

A series of rooms to the right of the church entrance are lined with thousands of *retablos*, new and old, giving thanks to the Santo Niño for all manner of miracles. Some older ones go back to WWII, while others recall traffic accidents, muggings and medical operations. More recent ones include copies of school reports and academic records.

Places to Stay & Eat

There are a few hotels in Plateros for pilgrims planning a 6 am mass, but they wouldn't be a very restful option. Right by the Fresnillo bus station, the fairly modern *Hotel Lirmar* (☎ 932-45-98), on the corner of Durango and Ébano, has comfortable singles/doubles with private bath from US$10.50/15.

If you want to stay in central Fresnillo, *Hotel Maya* (☎ 932-03-51, Ensaye 9), one block south of Avenida Juárez and one block west of Avenida Hidalgo, has bright, fairly clean rooms with bathroom and TV for US$12/15. A mid-range option is *Hotel Casa Blanca* (☎ 932-12-88, García Salinas 503), three blocks east of Jardín Hidalgo, with clean and well-furnished rooms for US$21/29.

Facing Jardín Hidalgo, the busy *El Molinito* serves a good-value three-course comida for US$2.75 and à la carte main courses for about the same price.

Getting There & Away

Fresnillo is well served by long-distance buses, though many are de paso. The bus station has a telephone caseta, luggage storage and an impressive mural. Frequent 1st- and 2nd-class buses go to Durango (230km, 3¼ hours, US$12), Torreón (330km, 5 hours, US$18) and Zacatecas (60km, 1 hour, US$2.25), as well as Aguascalientes, Chihuahua, Mexico City, Guadalajara, San Luis Potosí and elsewhere.

Battered buses of the Fresnillo-Plateros line run to Plateros from *andén* (platform) 21 every 15 minutes between 6.50 am and 6.20 pm. Ruta 6 local buses also run to Plateros, from Calle Emiliano Zapata, 2½ blocks east of the Jardín Madero. Fare is US$0.50 on either service.

JEREZ

- **pop 36,600** ☎ 4

A small country town 30km southwest of Zacatecas, Jerez de García Salinas (to use its full name) has some surprisingly fine 18th- and 19th-century buildings that testify to the wealth that silver brought to even the lesser towns of the Zacatecas region. Jerez holds a lively Easter feria with charreadas, cockfights and other activities. It starts on Good Friday and lasts about 10 days.

Orientation & Information

Jardín Páez, the town's main square, has an old-fashioned gazebo and plenty of trees, birds and seats. On its west side, Banco Promex changes traveler's checks and cash weekdays from 8 am to 7 pm and has an ATM. The post office and Telecomm office are on Calle de la Bizarra Capital, off the southwest corner of Jardín Páez. A couple of blocks southwest of Jardín Páez is another attractive plaza, where the small tourist office, next to Teatro Hinojosa, keeps erratic hours.

Things to See & Do

The 18th-century **Parroquia de la Inmaculada Concepción** and the 19th-century **Santuario de la Soledad** have fine stone carvings. To find them go one block south from the southeast corner of Jardín Páez, then one block east for the parroquia, or one block west for the santuario. Just past the santuario, on the north side of Jardín Hidalgo, is a beautiful little 19th-century theater, **Teatro Hinojosa.**

Places to Stay & Eat

Hotel Del Jardín (☎ 945-20-26), on the south side of Jardín Páez, is the cheapest place in town, with adequate singles/doubles for US$8/9. *Hotel Plaza* (☎ 945-20-63), on the west side of the same plaza, has small, bare, clean rooms with bathroom and TV for US$9/11. The hotel's restaurant is OK – a quarter chicken with fries, *frijoles*, greens and tortillas is yours for US$2.25. Several other places around the plaza serve up the standard chicken, *bistec* and beans at very nontourist prices.

Shopping

Fine leatherwork can be found at shops like Zapatería Lo Legalidad on Del Refugio, half a block south of Jardín Páez, or La Palma, which specializes in charrería gear, one block east and half a block north of Jardín Páez.

Getting There & Away

The turnoff to Jerez is near Malpaso, on the Zacatecas-Guadalajara road 29km south of Zacatecas. The Zacatecas-Jerez line runs 2nd-class buses from Zacatecas bus station to Jerez every 30 minutes from 5 am to 9 pm for US$2.25. There are also services by Ómnibus de México and Estrella Blanca/Rojo de los Altos. Jerez's bus station is on the east side of town, about 1km from the center along Calzada Suave Patria. 'Centro-Central' buses, from inside the bus station, run to/from the center for US$0.20. There are also several buses a day to/from Fresnillo (US$2).

LA QUEMADA

The impressive ruins of La Quemada stand on a hill in a broad valley about 45km south of Zacatecas, 2km east of the Zacatecas-Guadalajara road. They're also known as Chicomostoc, because they were once thought to be the place of that name where the Aztecs halted during their legendary wanderings toward the Valle de México. The ruins' remote and scenic setting makes them well worth the trip from Zacatecas. The new museum on the site has fascinating exhibits on the archaeology of the area and is an interesting piece of architecture in itself. Both the museum and the site have explanatory labels in English as well as Spanish.

La Quemada was inhabited between about 300 and 1200 AD and probably peaked between 500 and 900 AD with as many as 15,000 people. From around 400 AD it was part of a regional trade network linked to Teotihuacán, but fortifications at the site suggest that La Quemada later tried to dominate trade in this part of Mexico. Traces of a big fire indicate that its final downfall was violent.

Some of the ruins can be seen up on the hill to the left as you approach from the Zacatecas-Guadalajara road. Of the main structures, the nearest to the site entrance is

---

Crunch, Munch

November must be the high season for crickets in the La Quemada area. The approach road to the site, as I walked along it in that warm, dry month, was carpeted with the creatures – big, fat, juicy ones. Vehicles had inevitably squashed hundreds of them. And the presence of so many fresh corpses had brought thousands more crickets out from the undergrowth for a feast on this source of juicy, immobile nourishment. Many other crickets were in the mood to sate other bodily urges, and were climbing on the backs of the chomping cannibals to procreate. All this produced great heaving mounds of living and dead crickets dotted all the way along the road to the site, and it was impossible to avoid crunching them underfoot if I lifted my eyes from the road to take in the landscape or look for the ruins up on the hill. Happily these crickets were either not of the flying variety or were too sated to do anything but crawl.

For some reason the ruins site itself was cricket-free, and I was able to forget all about them as I climbed up level with the soaring eagles. There I cut red *tuna* – cactus fruit – to munch on while I surveyed the fine views from the top of this thousand-year-old settlement.

John Noble

the Salón de las Columnas (Hall of the Columns), which was probably a ceremonial hall. A bit farther up the hill are a ball court, a steep offerings pyramid and an equally steep staircase leading toward the upper levels of the site. From the upper levels of the main hill a path leads westward to a spur hilltop with the remains of a cluster of buildings called La Ciudadela (the Citadel). A stone wall, thought to have been built for defensive purposes later in La Quemada's history, stretches across the slopes to the north.

The site is open from 10 am to 5 pm daily, but get to the museum before 4 pm (US$2.25 including the museum; free Sunday).

Getting There & Away

From the old bus station in Zacatecas, take a 2nd-class bus (US$2) heading to Villanueva, and ask to be let off at 'las ruinas' – you'll be deposited at the Restaurant Las Siete Cuevas, where you can walk 2km along the paved road going east to the site. When returning to Zacatecas, you may have to wait a while before a bus shows up – don't leave it too late. Ómnibus de México and Rojo de los Altos have regular services from Zacatecas' 1st-class bus station to Villanueva and Guadalajara, and these may also stop at the La Quemada turnoff – they're more comfortable, but less convenient. You can also do an organized tour from Zacatecas from about US$16.

Aguascalientes State

The state of Aguascalientes, bordered on the south by Jalisco and surrounded on its other sides by Zacatecas, is one of Mexico's smallest. It was originally part of Zacatecas; according to tradition, a kiss planted on the lips of dictator Santa Anna by the attractive wife of a prominent local politician brought about the creation of a separate Aguascalientes state.

Aguascalientes is primarily agricultural, with maize, beans, chilies, fruit, grapes and grain grown on its fertile lands. Livestock is also important and the state's ranches produce beef cattle as well as bulls, which are slaughtered at bullfights all over Mexico. Industry is concentrated in and around the capital city, also called Aguascalientes.

AGUASCALIENTES

• **pop 537,500** • **elev 1800m** ☎ **4**

Named for its hot springs, this is a prosperous industrial city, with a few handsome colonial buildings in the well-planned central area. Aguascalientes also has several modern shopping malls, and a brand new bullring. If you're interested in Mexican art, the museums devoted to José Guadalupe Posada and Saturnino Herrán will justify a visit.

History

Some time before the Spanish invasion, a labyrinth of catacombs was built here, so the first Spaniards called it La Ciudad Perforada – the perforated city. Archaeologists have little understanding of the tunnels, which are off-limits to visitors.

Pedro de Alvarado came to subdue this region in 1522 but was driven back by the Chichimecs. A small garrison was founded here in 1575 to protect silver convoys from Zacatecas to Mexico City. Eventually, as the Chichimecs were pacified, the region's hot springs at Ojo Caliente served as the basis for the growth of a town; a large tank beside the springs helped irrigate local farms where fruits, vegetables and grains were cultivated.

Today, more than half of the state's population lives in the city, where industry and textiles and trade from its ranches, vineyards and orchards provide jobs. There's a huge Nissan plant just south of town.

Orientation

Aguascalientes is flat and easy to get around. The center of town is Plaza de la Patria, formerly Plaza de Armas, surrounded by some pleasant pedestrian streets – shops, hotels, restaurants and some fine buildings are within a few blocks. Avenida Chávez/5 de Mayo is the main north-south artery – it passes through a tunnel beneath Plaza de la Patria. Avenida López Mateos, the main

AGUASCALIENTES

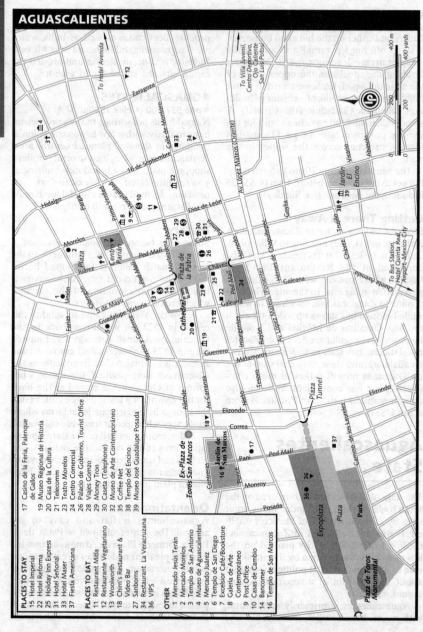

PLACES TO STAY
15 Hotel Imperial
22 Hotel Reforma
25 Holiday Inn Express
31 Hotel Señorial
33 Hotel Maser
37 Fiesta Americana

PLACES TO EAT
11 Restaurant Mitla
12 Restaurante Vegetariano
18 Woolworth
27 Sanborns
34 Restaurant La Veracruzana
36 VIPS

OTHER
1 Mercado Jesús Terán
2 Mercado Morelos
3 Templo de San Antonio
4 Museo de Aguascalientes
5 Mercado Juárez
6 Templo de San Diego
7 Excelsior Café/Bookstore
8 Galería de Arte
    Contemporáneo
9 Post Office
10 Casas de Cambio
14 Bancomer
16 Templo de San Marcos
17 Casino de la Feria, Palenque
    de Gallos
19 Museo Regional de Historia
20 Casa de la Cultura
21 Telecomm
23 Teatro Morelos
24 Centro Comercial
26 Palacio de Gobierno, Tourist Office
28 Viajes Gomzo
29 Money Tron
30 Caseta (Telephone)
32 Museo de Arte Contemporáneo
35 Coffee Net
38 Templo del Encino
39 Museo José Guadalupe Posada

east-west artery across the central part of the city, is a couple of blocks south of the plaza. The bus station is on the south side of town.

Information

Tourist Offices The Delegación de Turismo del Estado de Aguascalientes (☎ 915-11-55) is beside the Palacio de Gobierno on Plaza de la Patria. Open daily (except holidays) from 10 am to 8 pm, it gives out free city maps and information on the city and state of Aguascalientes, mostly in Spanish.

Money There are plenty of banks, with ATMs, around Plaza de la Patria. Hours are generally 9 am to 5 pm Monday to Friday, 9 am to 1 pm Saturday. Casas de cambio include Money Tron, half a block east of the plaza on Montoro, and several on Hospitalidad, near the post office.

Post & Communications The post office is at Hospitalidad 108, a couple of blocks northeast of Plaza de la Patria. It's open Monday to Friday from 8 am to 7 pm, Saturday 9 am to 1 pm. The main Telecomm office, with fax service, is at Galeana 102, a block west of Plaza de la Patria – open Monday to Friday from 8 am to 6 pm, Saturday 9 am to noon.

There are several pay phones on Plaza de la Patria, and a telephone caseta off its southeast corner, open 9 am to 9 pm daily.

Coffee Net in Expo Plaza provides Internet access from 10.30 am to 9 pm daily, for US$2.50 per hour.

Travel Agencies The city has plenty of travel agencies that can book flights – Viajes Gomzo (☎ 916-61-92), at Montoro 114, is especially helpful.

Plaza de la Patria

The well-restored 18th-century baroque **cathedral**, on the west side of the plaza, is more magnificent on the inside than the outside. Over the altar at the east end of the south aisle is a painting of the Virgin of Guadalupe by Miguel Cabrera. There are more Cabrera works in the cathedral's *pinacoteca* (picture gallery) – ask one of the priests to let you in.

Facing the south side of the cathedral is the **Teatro Morelos**, scene of the 1914 Convention of Aguascalientes, in which revolutionary factions led by Pancho Villa, Venustiano Carranza and Emiliano Zapata tried unsuccessfully to patch up their differences. Busts of these three, plus one of Álvaro Obregón, stand in the foyer.

The red and pink stone **Palacio de Gobierno** on the south side of the plaza is Aguascalientes' most noteworthy colonial building. Once the mansion of the Marqués de Guadalupe, a colonial baron, it dates from 1665 and has a striking courtyard of arches and pillars. A mural painted in 1992 by the Chilean artist Osvaldo Barra is on the wall just inside the courtyard. It depicts the 1914 convention, pointing out that some of its ideas were crystallized in Mexico's still-governing 1917 constitution – including the eight-hour workday. Barra, whose mentor was Diego Rivera, also painted the mural on the far (south) wall of the courtyard, a compendium of the historic and economic forces that forged Aguascalientes (look for the depiction of the 1840s Mexican-American War).

Museums & Churches

The fascinating **Museo José Guadalupe Posada** is on the Jardín El Encino (also called Jardín Francisco), on Díaz de León about 450m south of López Mateos Oriente. Posada (1852-1913), a native of Aguascalientes, was in many ways the founder of modern Mexican art. His satirical cartoons and engravings during the Porfiriato dictatorship broadened the audience for art in Mexico, drew attention to social problems and inspired later artists like Diego Rivera. Posada's hallmark was the *calavera* (skull or skeleton), and many of his calavera engravings have been widely reproduced. Less well known are the engravings of current events for periodicals – the series on executions by firing squad conveys some of the violence of the revolutionary period. The museum has a large collection of Posada prints, each displayed alongside the original etched zinc plate so you can appreciate the skill of the printmaker's art. There's also a permanent exhibition of work by Posada's disciple

Manuel Manilla and temporary exhibitions of work by other Mexican artists. The museum is open 10 am to 6 pm Tuesday to Sunday (US$0.60).

The **Templo del Encino**, beside the Posada museum, contains a black statue of Jesus that some believe is growing. When it reaches an adjacent column, a worldwide calamity is anticipated.

The **Museo de Aguascalientes**, at Zaragoza 505 near the corner of Pedro Parga, houses a permanent exhibition of work by Saturnino Herrán (1887-1918), another great Mexican artist born in Aguascalientes. In a graphic style reminiscent of French art nouveau, his portraits and illustrative work depict Mexican people and places with great technical skill and sensitivity. The museum is open 11 am to 6 pm Tuesday to Sunday (US$0.60), and also hosts temporary exhibitions of other artists. Opposite is the **Templo de San Antonio**, a crazy quilt of architectural styles built around 1900 by local, self-taught architect Refugio Reyes. The interior is highly ornate, with huge round paintings and intricate decoration highlighted in gold.

The **Museo Regional de Historia** at Carranza 110, two blocks west of the cathedral, was designed by Refugio Reyes as a family home. It has several rooms of exhibits on Aguascalientes' history from the big bang to the *revolución*, open 10 am to 2 pm and 5 to 8 pm Tuesday to Sunday (US$2, free on Sunday and holidays). The small but interesting **Museo de Arte Contemporáneo**, at Montoro 222, 1½ blocks east of Plaza de la Patria, is open 9 am to 2 pm and 5 to 8 pm Tuesday to Sunday (US$0.60). There's also the **Galería de Arte Contemporáneo** at the corner of Morelos and Primo Verdad, with similar hours.

Expo Plaza & Around

About a kilometer west of Plaza de la Patria, via López Mateos or Nieto, Expo Plaza is a modern, US-style shopping mall with lots of shops, a few cafes, and a multi-screen cinema. On the south side of the mall, a wide and somewhat soulless pedestrian boulevard is dominated by the big new bull-ring at its western end, the **Plaza de Toros Monumental**, notable for its modern-colonial treatment of traditional bullring architecture. Calle Pani, also called Paseo de la Feria, runs two blocks north from the Hotel Fiesta Americana to the 18th-century Templo de San Marcos and the shady Jardín de San Marcos. The Palenque de Gallos, in the Casino de la Feria building on Pani, is the city's cockfighting arena. Near the northeast corner of Jardín de San Marcos, Ex-Plaza de Toros de San Marcos, the old bullring, is now a music and entertainment venue.

Thermal Springs

It's no surprise that a town called Aguascalientes has hot springs. The best-known are at the **Centro Deportivo Ojo Caliente** (☎ 970-06-98), on the eastern edge of the city at the end of López Mateos, about 3.5km from Plaza de la Patria. Bus No 12, which runs along López Mateos, will get you there. Entrance is US$1.75 a day. The large pool, and some other smaller pools, have warmish water; the hot water is in private pools, which cost from US$3 for four people – more for larger pools. In the large park-like grounds are tennis, volleyball and squash courts and a restaurant. Hours are 7 am to 7 pm Wednesday to Friday, 7 am to 8 pm on Saturday, Sunday and holidays. Returning to the city center, bus No 11 will take you along López Mateos to the corner of Chávez just south of Plaza de la Patria.

Feria de San Marcos

This is the biggest annual fair in Mexico, attracting around a million visitors each year for exhibitions, bullfights, cockfights, rodeos, free concerts, and an extravaganza of cultural events, including an international film festival. The big parade takes place on the saint's day, April 25. The fair starts in mid-April and lasts 22 days. Programs of cultural events can be picked up at theaters and museums. Expo Plaza is the hub of things.

Places to Stay

Prices skyrocket during the Feria de San Marcos and places to stay are completely booked for the feria's final weekend – local residents run a lucrative homestay service at this time. Ask around at the feria if you're stuck.

Budget The youth hostel, *Villa Juvenil* (☎ 970-06-78), is about 3km east of the center on the ring road Avenida Circunvalación (also called Avenida Convención at this point), on at the corner of Jaime Nunó. The sign out front says 'Instituto Aguascalentense del Deporte.' The hostel has 72 beds in clean separate-sex rooms holding up to eight people each; the cost is US$3.25. In the park-likeparklike grounds are a cafeteria, swimming pool, gym and various ball courts. Bus No 20 from the bus station, and No 36 from Rivero y Gutiérrez in the city center will take you to the hostel.

The friendly *Hotel Señorial* (☎ 915-16-30, 915-14-73, Colón 1040), just off the southeast corner of Plaza de la Patria, has 32 reasonable rooms with TV and phone. Some of the rooms have balconies. The cheapest single rooms are US$13; bigger rooms with double beds cost US$15, and rooms with two beds are around US$20.

A block west of the plaza on, at the corner of Galeana, *Hotel Reforma* (☎ 915-11-07, Nieto 118) is a wonderful old building where rooms with high ceilings are set around a covered courtyard. It's aging and a bit dilapidated, and the service is not too sharp, but it's decent and it has character. Singles/doubles are US$9/11 with private bath.

For a better value, go a few blocks east of the center to *Hotel Maser* (☎ 915-35-62) is, at Montoro and 16 de Septiembre. It has 47 rooms with private bath around a covered inner courtyard. Very clean singles/doubles cost US$12/13.50, plus US$1.75 for a TV. There's enclosed parking in the rear.

Farther east, *Hotel Avenida* (☎ 915-36-13, Madero 486), about 750m from the plaza, has 48 pleasant, carpeted rooms with cable TV and private bath for US$13/16.50. It also has a small restaurant.

Mid-Range Well- located on the north side of the plaza, *Hotel Imperial* (☎ 915-16-64) looks better from the outside than it does on the inside, but US$19 gets you a good-sized,

modern, clean single or double room with TV and phone.

Top End The *Holiday Inn Express* (☎ 916-16-66, Avenida Chávez 101), on the southwest corner of Plaza de la Patria, is the center's most comfortable option. It has 92 rooms with all modern conveniences from US$87.

The luxury 192-room *Fiesta Americana* (☎ 918-60-10, fax 918-51-18) on Expo Plaza has singles/doubles for US$134/147, nice gardens, a swimming pool, restaurant and other luxury hotel amenities. *Hotel Quinta Real* (☎ 978-58-18, fax 978-56-16, Avenida Aguascalientes Sur 601), on the southeast edge of the city, is a modern place in colonial style, with rooms and suites from US$106.

Places to Eat

Very near the center, on 5 de Mayo just short of Allende, *Woolworth* has good-value breakfasts (from US$3) and other meals (from US$3.25), plus decent coffee. There are several other snack and lunch places in the nearby pedestrian streets, but the most pleasant place to eat is right on the plaza, where a new *Sanborns* restaurant and bar are upstairs in the restored Hotel Francia building, right on the east side of the plaza. Breakfast will run US$2.50 to US$5, Mexican dishes are around US$5, with meat and chicken main courses up to US$7. It's popular with well-to-do locals, and the food is good. *Excelsior* café/bookstore in the Centro Parián is *the* place to read your newspaper, have a sandwich, and sip coffee (a few English books are available here).

A block east of Plaza de la Patria, *Restaurant Mitla* (Madero 220) is large, clean and pleasant, with a varied menu. It's been going since 1938, is popular with local people and welcomes *extranjeros*. The four-course comida corrida is US$4.50, while meat, chicken or seafood dishes range from US$4.50 to US$7. It's open daily from 8 am to 11 pm, and you can linger over coffee or a drink. Also on Madero, just east of Zaragoza, *Restaurante Vegetariano* has a lunch buffet (US$3) Monday through Saturday.

Two blocks east and a block south of Plaza de la Patria, *Restaurant La Veracruzana* on

Hornedo at 16 de Septiembre is a small, simple, family-run restaurant with excellent home-style cooking at a good price: the four-course comida corrida is a bargain at US$2.25, and the frijoles are some of the best in Mexico! It's open 8.30 am to 5 pm Monday through Saturday.

For a night out, head for the Jardín de San Marcos area, where there's a good selection of mid-price eateries on Carranza and on the pedestrian street Pani going south to Expo Plaza. *Chirri's Restaurant & Video Bar*, on Carranza, is a smart place where a big salad costs US$2 and well-prepared meat, poultry and fish are around US$5 to US$7. In the Expo Plaza building itself is a branch of the reliable chain restaurant *VIPS*.

Fresh produce is available in three markets a few blocks north of Plaza de la Patria: *Mercado Juárez*, *Mercado Jesús Terán* and *Mercado Morelos*.

Entertainment
The *Casa de la Cultura*, in a fine 17th-century building on Carranza just west of Galeana, hosts art exhibitions, concerts, theater, dance and other cultural events. Stop in to look at their schedule.

The *Teatro Morelos*, on Plaza de la Patria, and *Teatro de Aguascalientes*, on Chávez at Avenida Aguascalientes in the south of the city, both stage a variety of cultural events. Free concerts, dance and theater are presented some Sunday lunchtimes in the courtyard of the Museo José Guadalupe Posada. Plaza de Toros de San Marcos, the old bullring, is another live music venue.

Two of Aguascalientes' hottest nightspots are *El Cabús* (☎ 973-00-06) in the fancy Hotel Las Trojes, about 15 minutes by taxi north of the center on the highway to Zacatecas, and *IOZ Sushi Bar* (☎ 912-15-15, *Bulevar de la Madrid 1821*).

Getting There & Away
Air Jesús Terán Airport is 22km south from Aguascalientes on the road to Mexico City. Aeroméxico (☎ 916-13-55), at Madero 474, flies direct daily to/from Mexico City and Tijuana, and three times a week to/from

Puerto Vallarta, Los Angeles and Houston. Aerolitoral (same office as Aeroméxico) flies daily to/from Monterrey, San Luis Potosí and San Antonio (Texas). Aero California (☎ 915-24-00), at Montoro 203, and TAESA (☎ 918-26-98), at Madero 447, also have flights.

Bus The bus station (Central Camionera) is about 2km south of the center on Avenida Circunvalación Sur, also called Avenida Convención, at the corner of Quinta Avenida. It has post and fax offices, pay phones, a cafeteria and luggage storage. Daily departures include:

Guadalajara – 250km, 3 to 4 hours; several deluxe ETN (US$19), frequent 1st-class Elite, Futura, Ómnibus de México, Primera Plus (US$14) and Estrella Blanca (US$11)

Guanajuato – 180km, 3 hours; 1 1st-class de paso Ómnibus de México (US$11), 4 2nd-class Flecha Amarilla (US$9), more frequent connections via León

León – 128km, 2 hours; frequent 1st-class Primera Plus (US$8.50)

Mexico City (Terminal Norte) – 521km, 7 hours; 8 deluxe ETN (US$40), frequent 1st-class Futura or Ómnibus de México (US$30), 5 2nd-class Flecha Amarilla (US$25)

San Luis Potosí – 168km, 3 hours; 14 1st-class Futura (US$10.50), hourly 2nd-class Estrella Blanca (US$8.50)

Zacatecas – 130km, 2 hours; 13 1st-class Ómnibus de México, Futura or Transportes Chihuahuenses (US$6.75), 2nd-class Rojo de los Altos every half-hour, 6.30 am to 11 pm (US$5.50)

There's also frequent service to Ciudad Juárez, León, Monterrey, Morelia and Torreón, and two buses daily to San Miguel de Allende.

Getting Around
Most places of interest are within easy walking distance of the center. Regular city buses run from 6 am to 10 pm and cost US$0.30; the red buses are slightly more comfortable, cost US$0.40, and follow the same routes.

Bus Nos 3, 4 and 9 run from the bus station to the city center. Get off at the first stop after the tunnel under Plaza de la Patria: this will be on 5 de Mayo or Rivero y Gutiérrez. From the city center to the bus station, take any 'Central' bus on Moctezuma opposite the north side of the cathedral, or around the corner on Galeana.

Within town and to the bus station, the standard taxi fare is US$1.50; to the airport it's about US$5.50.

San Luis Potosí State

The state of San Luis Potosí ('poh-toh-SEE') has two of the most interesting destinations between Mexico City and the US border: the mountain ghost town of Real de Catorce and the city of San Luis Potosí itself, a major colonial town steeped in history.

The state is high (average altitude around 2000m) and dry, with little rainfall. The exception is its eastern corner, which drops steeply to the tropical valleys of the Gulf Coast (see Tampico & the Huasteca in the Central Gulf Coast chapter for information about this area).

Before the Spanish conquest in 1521, western San Luis Potosí was inhabited by warlike hunters and collectors known as Guachichiles, the Aztec word for sparrows, after their widespread custom of wearing only loincloths and, sometimes, pointed headdresses resembling sparrows' heads.

A couple of Christian missionaries entered the southwest of the state in the 1570s and 1580s, but it was the discovery of silver in the Cerro de San Pedro hills that really awakened Spanish interest in that region. San Luis Potosí city was founded near these deposits in 1592, and Tlaxcalans, Tarascans and Otomíes were brought in to work the mines and cattle ranches.

In the 18th century the area had a reputation for maltreatment of indigenous people. This was partly because a number of parishes were transferred to secular (nonmonk) clergy from the Franciscans, who had done their best to protect indigenous people. In 1767 there was an uprising sparked by the appalling conditions in the mines and the discontent over the expulsion of the Jesuits, who ran the best schools in Mexico and managed their estates relatively well.

Under Spanish reforms in 1786, the city of San Luis Potosí became capital of a huge area covering the modern states of San Luis Potosí, Tamaulipas, Nuevo León, Coahuila and Texas. This lasted only until Mexican independence, and in 1824 the state of San Luis Potosí was formed with its present area.

Today it's a fairly prosperous state. The northern silver mines are some of the richest in the country, and gold, copper, lead and zinc are also extracted. Agriculture (maize, beans, wheat and cotton) and livestock are other major sources of wealth, as is industry, which is mainly concentrated in the capital city.

SAN LUIS POTOSÍ
• pop 586,600 • elev 1860m ☎ 4

The state capital was a major colonial city and has been a mining center, a seat of governments-in-exile and a hotbed of revolutionaries. Today its main importance is as a regional capital and center of industries, including brewing, textiles and metal foundries. Flat and laid out in an orderly grid, San Luis is less spectacular than colonial cities like Zacatecas or Guanajuato, but its historic heart has fine buildings, congenial pedestrian areas, expansive plazas, museums, markets, cafés and a general air of elegance. It's also a university town, with cultural attractions and an active nightlife. Don't be put off by the industrial outskirts – San Luis is lovely in the middle.

History
Founded in 1592, 20km west of the silver deposits in the Cerro de San Pedro hills, San Luis is named Potosí after the immensely rich Bolivian silver town of that name, which the Spanish hoped it would rival.

Yields from the mines started to decline in the 1620s, but the city was well enough established as a ranching center to remain the major city of northeastern Mexico until overtaken by Monterrey at the start of the 20th century.

NORTHERN CENTRAL

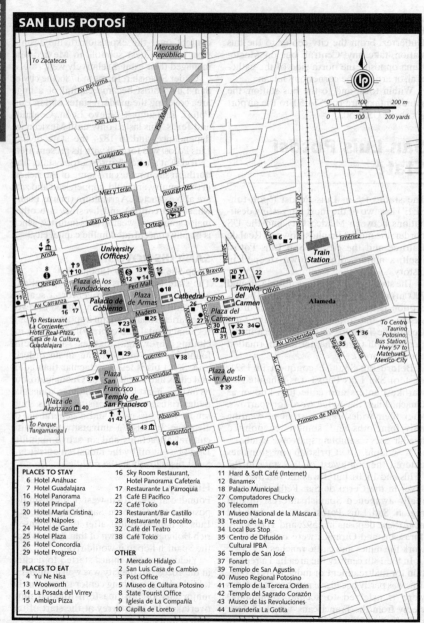

SAN LUIS POTOSÍ

To Zacatecas

Mercado República

Av Reforma

San Luis

Guajardo

Santa Clara ● 1

Mier y Terán

Julián de los Reyes

Zapata

Insurgentes

Salazar ● 2
● 3

Ortega

University (Offices)

Arista

4 5

8 ℹ

Obregón

11

Av Carranza

16 17

To Restaurant La Corriente, Hotel Real Plaza, Casa de la Cultura, Guadalajara

† 9
† 10

Plaza de los Fundadores

12

13
14
15

Ped Mall

Palacio de Gobierno

Plaza de Armas

● 18

Madero

25

● 23
24

5 de Mayo

Iturbide

Cathedral

26

Othón

27

Plaza del Carmen

Templo del Carmen

20
21

19 ●

22

Los Bravos

30
31

32 34
33

Othón

Morelos

Zaragoza

Xóchitl

● 6 7

Jiménez

20 de Noviembre

Train Station

Alameda

To Centro Taurino Potosino, Bus Station, Hwy 57 to Matehuala, Mexico City

28 ■ 29

Guerrero

▼ 38

Av Universidad

Ped Mall

Galeana

Plaza de San Agustín

† 39

37 ●

Plaza San Francisco

Templo de San Francisco

Plaza de Aranzazú 40

To Parque Tangamanga I

Abasolo

41 42

Vallejo

43

Comonfort

● 44

Rayón

Av Constitución

Negrete

Zaragoza

† 36

35

Av Universidad

Primero de Mayor

0   100   200 m
0   100   200 yards

PLACES TO STAY			
6	Hotel Anáhuac	16	Sky Room Restaurant, Hotel Panorama Cafetería
7	Hotel Guadalajara	17	Restaurante La Parroquia
16	Hotel Panorama	21	Café El Pacífico
19	Hotel Principal	22	Café Tokio
20	Hotel María Cristina, Hotel Nápoles	23	Restaurant/Bar Castillo
24	Hotel de Gante	28	Restaurante El Bocolito
25	Hotel Plaza	32	Café del Teatro
26	Hotel Concordia	38	Café Tokio
29	Hotel Progreso		

PLACES TO EAT

4 Yu Ne Nisa
13 Woolworth
14 La Posada del Virrey
15 Ambigu Pizza

OTHER

1 Mercado Hidalgo
2 San Luis Casa de Cambio
3 Post Office
5 Museo de Cultura Potosino
8 State Tourist Office
9 Iglesia de La Compañía
10 Capilla de Loreto

11 Hard & Soft Café (Internet)
12 Banamex
18 Palacio Municipal
27 Computadores Chucky
30 Telecomm
31 Museo Nacional de la Máscara
33 Teatro de la Paz
34 Local Bus Stop
35 Centro de Difusión Cultural IPBA
36 Templo de San José
37 Fonart
39 Templo de San Agustín
40 Museo Regional Potosino
41 Templo de la Tercera Orden
42 Templo del Sagrado Corazón
43 Museo de las Revoluciones
44 Lavandería La Gotita

It was known in the 19th century for its lavish houses and luxury goods imported from the USA and Europe. San Luis was twice the seat of President Benito Juárez's government during the French intervention of the 1860s. In 1910 the dictatorial president Porfirio Díaz jailed Francisco Madero, his liberal opponent in that year's presidential election, in San Luis. Bailed out after the election, Madero hatched his Plan de San Luis Potosí – a strategy to depose Díaz – and announced it in San Antonio, Texas, in October 1910. The plan declared the recent election illegal, named Madero provisional president and designated November 20 as the day for Mexico to rise in revolt.

Orientation

Central San Luis Potosí stretches about 600m from the Alameda park in the east to Plaza de los Fundadores and Plaza San Francisco in the west. Within this triangle lie two more main plazas, Plaza del Carmen and the Plaza de Armas. Hotels and restaurants are mainly in this central area, with most cheaper lodgings close to the Alameda, near the train station.

The bus station is on the eastern edge of the city, about 2.5km from the center. A scattered zona rosa, with upscale restaurants, shops, offices and nightspots, stretches some 3km west from Plaza de los Fundadores along Avenida Carranza.

Information

Tourist Offices The state Dirección General de Turismo (☎ 812-23-57, fax 812-67-69) is at Obregón 520, half a block west of Plaza de los Fundadores. It's open Monday to Friday 8 am to 8 pm, Saturday 9 am to 1 pm. They have tourist maps and brochures with lots of ideas for getting off the beaten track in San Luis Potosí state.

Consulates The new location of the US consular agency (☎ 812-15-28) is at Carranza 2076, Colonia Jacarandas; it's open 8.30 am to 1.30 pm Monday to Friday.

Money Banks and ATMs are scattered around the Plaza de Armas and Plaza de los Fundadores – Banamex, on the corner of Obregón and Allende, changes cash and traveler's checks from 9 am to 2 pm Monday to Friday. Several casas de cambio are on Morelos, toward Mercado Hidalgo north of the center – Casa de Cambio San Luis is at the corner of Salazar.

The American Express agent is Grandes Viajes (☎ 817-60-04), Carranza 1077, a long kilometer west of Plaza de los Fundadores. It's open 9 am to 2 pm and 4 to 6 pm Monday to Friday, 10 am to 1 pm Saturday.

Post & Communications The main post office is at Morelos 235 between Ortega and Salazar, open 8 am to 7 pm Monday to Friday, 9 am to 1 pm Saturday. There are plenty of pay phones in the center. Telecomm, with fax service, is on the south side of Plaza del Carmen, open every day. Access the Internet for only US$1 per hour at Computadores Chucky, on the west side of Plaza del Carmen, from 10 am to 10 pm daily; or at Hard & Soft Café, at Carranza 416 a couple blocks west of Plaza de los Fundadores, which costs twice as much but serves good coffee.

Travel Agencies A handy place for flight arrangements is Solymar (☎ 814-69-63, fax 814-71-87) at Carranza 713, 400m west of Plaza de los Fundadores. Grandes Viajes (see Money) is another big travel agency.

Laundry Lavandería La Gotita, south of the center on 5 de Mayo near Comonfort, does a load for under US$2, from 9 am to 8 pm Monday to Saturday.

Plaza de Armas & Around

Also known as Jardín Hidalgo, the Plaza de Armas is the city's central square, popular for chatting and watching the world go by. It's fairly quiet as traffic is channeled away from it.

The three-nave baroque **cathedral**, built between 1660 and 1730, is on the east side of the plaza. Originally it had just one tower; the northern tower was added in the 20th century. The marble apostles on the façade are replicas of statues in the San Juan de

Letrán Basilica in Rome. The interior, remodeled in the 19th century, has a Gothic feel, with sweeping arches carved in pink stone; the leaf motif on the arches is repeated in blue and gold on the ceiling.

Beside the cathedral, the 19th-century **Palacio Municipal** is a stocky building with powerful stone arches. Finished in 1838, it was the home of Bishop Ignacio Montes de Oca from 1892 to 1915, when it was turned over to the city. In the rear of the building's patio is a stone fountain carved with the heads of three lions. The city's coat of arms in stained glass overlooks a double staircase.

The **Palacio de Gobierno**, built between 1798 and 1816, lines the west side of the plaza. Numerous important Mexicans have lodged here, including Presidents Iturbide and Santa Anna, but its most illustrious occupant was Benito Juárez – first in 1863 when he was fleeing from invading French forces, then in 1867 when he confirmed the death sentence on French puppet emperor Maximilian. In the upstairs rooms that Juárez occupied are various historical artifacts including life-size models of Juárez and, kneeling before him, Princess Inés de Salm-Salm. An American who had married into Maximilian's family, Salm-Salm came to San Luis in June 1867 to make one last plea for his life. The Palacio is open during business hours – go left at the top of the stairs and ask for a custodian to open the Salón de Juárez (free).

Plaza de los Fundadores & Around

The busy Founders' Plaza, also called Plaza Juárez, is where the city started. On the north side is a large building housing the offices of the **Universidad de San Luis Potosí**. It was probably on this site that Diego de la Magdalena, a Franciscan friar, started a small settlement of Guachichiles around 1585. The building, which has a lovely courtyard, was constructed in 1653 as a Jesuit college.

To the west of the offices is the **Iglesia de La Compañía**, also called del Sagrario, built by the Jesuits in 1675 with a baroque façade. A little farther west is the **Capilla de Loreto**, a Jesuit chapel from 1700 with unusual twisted pillars.

One and a half blocks northwest of the plaza, the **Museo de Cultura Potosina**, Arista 340, has models and dioramas explaining the city's history, mainly for children (US$0.25).

Plaza San Francisco & Around

Dominated by the red bulk of the Templo de San Francisco, this quiet square is one of the most beautiful in the city.

The interior of the 17th- and 18th-century **Templo de San Francisco** was remodeled in the 20th century but the sacristy (priest's dressing room), reached by a door to the right of the altar, is original and has a fine dome and carved pink stone. The Sala De Profundis, through the arch at the south end of the sacristy, has more paintings and a stone fountain carved by indigenous artisans. A beautiful crystal ship hangs from the main dome.

The **Museo Regional Potosino** at Galeana 450, along the street to the west of the Templo de San Francisco, was originally part of a Franciscan monastery founded in 1590. The ground floor has exhibits on pre-Hispanic Mexico, especially the indigenous people of the Huasteca. Upstairs is the lavish Capilla de Aranzazú, an elaborate private chapel for the monks constructed in the mid-18th century. It is dedicated to the cult of the Virgin of Aranzazú: according to legend, a Spanish shepherd found a statue of the Virgin in a thornbush and named it Aranzazú, a Basque word meaning 'Among thorns, you.' The museum is open 10 am to 5 pm Tuesday to Sunday (US$1).

The small **Templo de la Tercera Orden** and **Templo del Sagrado Corazón**, both formerly part of the Franciscan monastery, stand together at the south end of the plaza. Tercera Orden, on the right, was finished in 1694 and restored in 1959 and 1960. Sagrado Corazón dates from 1728 to 1731.

A couple of blocks south and west of the plaza at 5 de Mayo 610, the new **Museo de las Revoluciones** covers some of the most dramatic events in Mexican history, with a good account of indigenous resistance to the Spanish conquest. It is open 10 am to 2 pm and 4 to 6 pm Tuesday to Friday, 10 am to 4 pm Saturday, and 10 am to 2 pm Sunday (US$1).

Plaza del Carmen

Plaza del Carmen is dominated by the **Templo del Carmen**, a Churrigueresque church built between 1749 and 1764 and the most spectacular building in San Luis. On the vividly carved stone façade, perching and hovering angels show the touch of indigenous artisans. The Camarín de la Virgen, with a splendid golden altar, is to the left of the main altar inside. The entrance and roof of this chapel are a riot of small plaster figures.

The **Teatro de la Paz**, built between 1889 and 1894, is near the church. It contains a concert hall and exhibition gallery as well as a theater. Posters announce upcoming events; there's usually something on. The art gallery, Sala Germán Gedovius, is open 10 am to 2 pm and 4 to 8 pm Tuesday to Saturday (free). Its entrance is to the right of the main theater entrance.

The **Museo Nacional de la Máscara** (National Mask Museum), in an attractive 19th-century building on the south side of the plaza, has a big collection of ceremonial masks from many regions of Mexico, with explanations of the dances and rituals in which they are used. Look for the papier-mâché *gigantes*. The museum is open 10 am to 2 pm and 4 to 6 pm Tuesday to Friday, 10 am to 2 pm Saturday and Sunday (US$0.30).

Alameda & Around

The Alameda marks the eastern boundary of the downtown area. It used to be the vegetable garden of the monastery attached to the Templo del Carmen. Today it's a large, attractive park with shady paths.

Inside the **Templo de San José**, facing the south side of the Alameda, is the image of El Señor de los Trabajos, a Christ figure attracting pilgrims from near and far. Numerous retablos around the statue testify to prayers answered in finding jobs, regaining health and so on.

The **Centro de Difusión Cultural IPBA** is a cultural center sponsored by the Instituto Potosino de Bellas Artes (Potosino Fine Arts Institute) in a large, modernistic building facing the south side of the Alameda. Inside are art galleries with changing exhibitions and a theater. The galleries are open 10 am to 2 pm and 5 to 8 pm Tuesday to Saturday, 10 am to 2 pm and 6 to 8 pm Sunday (free).

On Universidad, just over the railway bridge east of the Alameda, is the **Centro Taurino Potosino**, with the Plaza de Toros and, just beyond it, a bullfighting museum with intricately decorated matador suits and capes, historical posters and photos, stuffed bulls' heads and more. The museum is only open when there's a bullfight.

Parque Tangamanga I

This large 3.3-sq-km park, about 2km southwest of the center, has a planetarium, outdoor theater, amusement park, two lakes, sports fields and acres of green open spaces. The **Museo de las Culturas Populares** exhibits typical crafts and clothing from all over the state, with some quite good pieces for sale. It's open 9 am to 4 pm, Tuesday to Sunday (free). To get to the park, take a southbound 'Perimetral' bus, or Bus No 25 or 26, from the west end of the Alameda.

Organized Tours

Tranvía city tours (☎ 814-22-26) do a two-hour loop around the historic center in an imitation antique trolley car, starting from the Hotel Panorama (US$2.25). A few of the driver/conductors speak English – ask when you book.

Special Events

Among San Luis' many festivals are the following:

Semana Santa – Holy Week is celebrated with concerts, exhibitions and other activities; on Good Friday morning Christ's passion is reenacted in the barrio of San Juan de Guadalupe, followed by a silent procession through the city.

Festival de Arte Primavera Potosina – The Spring Arts Festival in the last two weeks of May (not held every year) presents concerts, art exhibitions, theater, dance, films and more, with national and international artists; check with the tourist office for dates.

Festival Nacional de Danza – This national festival of contemporary dance is held in the last two weeks of July.

Feria Nacional Potosina – The San Luis Potosí National Fair, normally in the last two weeks of August, includes concerts, bullfights, rodeos, cockfights, sports events and livestock and agriculture shows.

San Luis Rey – On August 25, the Día de San Luis Rey de Francia (St Louis, King of France), the city's patron saint, various events are organized including a large parade with floats and *gigantes*, papier-mâché giants.

Places to Stay

Budget You'll enjoy San Luis Potosí more if you choose a hotel room in the pedestrianized center, away from the traffic and in the midst of the attractive architecture!

Hotel Plaza (☎ 812-46-31, *Jardín Hidalgo 22*) is in an 18th-century building on the south side of the Plaza de Armas. The rooms at the front, overlooking the plaza, are the best, at US$16.50/19 for singles/doubles. The others open onto two upstairs patios, and are darker, dilapidated and somewhat airless, but cheaper at US$14/15.50.

Hotel de Gante (☎ 812-14-92/93, *5 de Mayo 140*), half a block south of the Plaza de Armas, has better rooms but less character. Large, bright, comfortable singles/doubles with sizable bathrooms and color TV cost US$16/18. Nearby, *Hotel Progreso* (☎/fax *812-03-66, Aldama 415*) is another older place, with classic 1920s-looking statues of ladies overlooking the staircase and lobby. In its day it was probably an elegant place. The 51 rooms are larger than many and have high ceilings to add to the spacious feel. Some have been modernized, others haven't, but either way the prices start at US$9/9.75. There are a couple of superior modernized doubles/triples with TV for US$13/14.50.

Out near the train station, *Hotel Anáhuac* (☎ 812-65-04/05, *fax 814-49-04, Xóchitl 140*) has 78 clean, modern rooms for US$12/15, plus US$1 for parking. The rooms vary in size, outlook and price. *Hotel Guadalajara* (☎ 812-46-12, *Jiménez 253*), on the small plaza between the station and the Hotel Anáhuac, has enclosed parking and 33 clean, comfortable rooms with ample

windows, color TV and fan. Cost is US$16.50 single, US$17.50 for a one-bed double, US$22 for two beds.

Hotel Principal (☎ 812-07-84, *Sarabia 145*), three blocks west of the train station, has 18 reasonable rooms with private bath at US$11/16.50 for singles/doubles.

Mid-Range The *Hotel María Cristina* (☎ 812-94-08, *fax 812-88-23, Sarabia 110*), a short block northwest of the Alameda, has parking, a restaurant and modern, comfortable, bright rooms with cable TV, carpet and fan, for US$34/38. Next door, very similar and a little less expensive, is *Hotel Nápoles* (☎ 812-84-18, *fax 812-22-60, Sarabia 120*).

Slightly more central, *Hotel Concordia* (☎ 812-06-66, *fax 812-69-79*), on Othón at Morelos, is an older hotel but in a modern style; its 94 rooms all have TV, carpeting and other amenities. Exterior rooms are nicer than the interior ones, but they all cost US$31/34. There's parking and an inexpensive restaurant.

Near the southwest corner of Plaza de los Fundadores is the very smart 10-story *Hotel Panorama* (☎ 812-17-77, *fax 812-45-91, Carranza 315*). All 126 comfortable rooms have floor-to-ceiling windows and most on the south side have private balconies overlooking the swimming pool. Singles/doubles are US$41/49. The hotel has a good 10th-floor restaurant, a piano bar and a reasonable cafeteria.

Motel Sand's (☎ 818-24-13) is on highway 57 heading out of San Luis toward Mexico City, just beyond the bus station, with rooms at US$31/34. It's OK for the money, but with none of the atmosphere of the downtown lodgings.

Top End More luxurious motels can also be found east of the city on highway 57, including *Hotel María Dolores* (☎ 822-18-82, *fax 822-06-02*), opposite the bus station, with nightclub, bar, restaurant, pool and fully equipped rooms at US$84. Even nicer to look at is *Hotel Real de Minas* (☎ 818-26-16, *fax 818-69-15*), which has landscaped grounds, a big pool, restaurant, bar and 178 rooms at US$90. Both these places offer discounted promotional rates when they need to fill their rooms.

Places to Eat

Center The bright little *Ambigu Pizza*, at the northeast corner of the Plaza de Armas, will do an order of chicken and fries for US$2, and respectable pizzas from US$3.50 to US$6.75. It's quick and clean, with all the ambiance of a fast-food franchise. Just a few doors up Hidalgo and opposite, *Woolworth* has a reliable, inexpensive cafetería with a somewhat more interesting menu.

Much more atmospheric is *La Posada del Virrey*, nearby on Plaza de Armas, in a former home of Spanish viceroys, built in 1736. It has an attractive covered courtyard with live music some lunchtimes. Breakfast specials are available and the comida corrida is US$3.75. Generous meat and seafood meals are US$4 to US$6.50. The menu is mostly quality Mexican cuisine, plus cakes and desserts. It's open daily from 7 am to midnight.

Restaurant/Bar Castillo (Madero 145), half a block west of the Plaza de Armas, is a small, cozy, inexpensive spot for dining or just hanging out over coffee. A big breakfast, with eggs, beans and salad, costs US$2.50; set lunches are around US$4; and main courses for dinner are US$4.50 to US$6. It's open 8 am to 11 pm daily.

The slick and sizable *Café Tokio*, on Guerrero at Zaragoza, two blocks south of the Plaza de Armas, has no trace of Japanese influence, but it serves up the usual Mexican and fast-food standards from 7 am to 11 pm daily. The comida corrida is US$3, and main meals run from US$4 to US$6. (The original Café Tokio is near the Alameda.)

A popular place with *potosinos*, *Restaurante La Parroquia* has big windows looking over the southwest corner of Plaza de los Fundadores. The four-course comida corrida is US$3.50, US$4 on Sundays. Many à la carte main dishes are US$4 to US$6. A huge buffet spread appears at breakfast (US$5) on Saturday and Sunday. It's open 7 am to midnight every day.

Northwest of Plaza de los Fundadores on Arista, *Yu Ne Nisa* is a small vegetarian restaurant in a covered patio behind a health food shop. Healthy snacks include sandwiches, quesadillas, gorditas and soy-burgers from around US$1.75, plus mouth-watering juices and smoothies. The full comida corrida is US$3.25. It's open noon to 6 pm Monday to Saturday.

An interesting option with friendly atmosphere, *Restaurante El Bocolito* has a great location at the northeast corner of charming Plaza San Francisco. It serves up huge platters of food with names like *gringa, sarape* and *mula india*, which are combinations of meats fried up with herbs, onion, chili, tomato and green pepper, often with melted cheese on top (around US$4). Tasty tacos and cheap breakfasts cost US$2.50 to US$3. It's a cooperative venture of the Casas José Martí, benefiting young indigenous students. Open 7.30 am to 10.30 pm daily, it often features live music in the evening.

For a special dinner, the *Sky Room Restaurant* (☎ 812-17-77) on the 10th floor of the Hotel Panorama has floor-to-ceiling windows with a panoramic view of the city. It serves an array of international dishes (US$6 to US$8), and has a dance floor and music (mostly Latin) from 9 pm most nights.

Plaza del Carmen & Alameda The *Café del Teatro*, beside the Teatro de la Paz, is a quirky, inexpensive place, good for a coffee, a meal, a drink or all three. It's also a regular live music venue.

The large, air-conditioned *Café Tokio (Othón 415)*, facing the northwest corner of the Alameda, is the original restaurant of which the central Café Tokio is a branch, with the same food, prices and hours. It's popular for ice cream or coffee after a stroll in the park. *Café El Pacífico*, on Los Bravos at Constitución, is not so slick, but it's open 24 hours, and locally popular for an inexpensive meal, coffee or a snack. The menu has the usual antojitos (US$2 to US$4), *aves* (fowl, US$4) and meats (US$5).

Zona Rosa There's a selection of upscale restaurants along Avenida Carranza ('La Avenida'), west of the center. One of the most attractive is **La Corriente** *(Carranza 700)*, 400m west of Plaza de los Fundadores. This fancy, plant-filled courtyard restaurant specializes in regional ranch-style food. A good US$5 four-course comida corrida is served Monday to Saturday, and in the evenings the à la carte dinner has US$4 antojitos and main dishes from US$5 to US$7.50. It's open daily from 8 am to midnight except Sunday when it closes at 6 pm. Sometimes there's music in the evenings.

Entertainment

San Luis has quite an active entertainment scene. Ask in the tourist office for what's going on and keep your eye out for posters. The Teatro de la Paz has something most nights and Sundays around noon; concerts, theater, exhibitions and other events are also presented at places like the Centro de Difusión Cultural IPBA, the Teatro de la Ciudad in Parque Tangamanga I and the Casa de la Cultura at Carranza 1815, about 2.5km west of Plaza de los Fundadores. *Guiarte* schedules posted at some of these places give full listings of what's happening.

Café del Teatro, beside the Teatro de la Paz, has live blues, jazz or rock from 9 pm on Friday and Saturday, sometimes Thursday too (cover US$0.60).

The more accessible nightclubs are along Avenida Carranza, with one of the most convenient being **Staff** (☎ 814-30-74, *Carranza 423)*, where a mixed crowd gets off on dance and Latin sounds. Other dance spots are in the fancy hotels on the outskirts of town, like *Oasis* (☎ 822-18-82), at the Hotel María Dolores, and *Dulcinea* (☎ 834-41-00) at the Holiday Inn, 5km out on highway 57. All these places are open Thursday to Saturday, and have a cover of about US$4.

Shopping

Fonart, on Plaza San Francisco, has a selection of quality handicrafts from all parts of Mexico. For more local products, try La Casa del Artesano, Carranza 540, a couple of blocks west of Independencia, which stocks potosino pottery, masks, woodwork and

canework; also check the Museo de las Culturas Populares, in Parque Tangamanga I. The main area of shops is between the Plaza de Armas and the Mercado Hidalgo, four blocks north. Just a few blocks farther northeast is the larger, more interesting Mercado República. Milky, sugary sweets are a local specialty, sold in the markets and at shops along Carranza.

Getting There & Away

Air The airport is 23km north of the city on highway 57. Aeromar (☎ 813-05-09, ☎ 817-79-36), Carranza 1030, flies to/from Mexico City several times daily and to San Antonio, Texas. Aerolitoral (☎ 822-22-29), at the airport, flies direct to/from Aguascalientes, Durango, Guadalajara and Monterrey. Aero California (☎ 811-80-50) goes to Mexico City, Tijuana and Bajío international airport (León).

Bus San Luis Potosí is a major bus hub. Its bus station, the Terminal Terrestre Potosina, on highway 57, 2.5km east of the center, has deluxe, 1st-class and some 2nd-class services. Facilities include pay phones, a telephone caseta, luggage storage (open 24 hours) and two cafés. Daily departures include:

Guadalajara – 340km, 5 to 6 hours; 8 deluxe ETN (US$27), 8 1st-class Transportes del Norte and Oriente (US$20), hourly 2nd-class Estrella Blanca (US$17)

Guanajuato – 225km, 4 hours; 4 2nd-class Flecha Amarilla (US$11)

Matehuala – 192km 2½ hours; 9 1st-class Transportes del Norte (US$9), hourly 2nd-class Estrella Blanca (US$8)

Mexico City (Terminal Norte) – 417km, 5 to 6 hours; 16 deluxe ETN (US$30), many 1st-class Primera Plus, Ómnibus de México and others (US$22 to US$25), 10 2nd-class Flecha Amarilla (US$20)

Monterrey – 517km, 6 hours; frequent 1st-class Futura and Altiplano (US$25), 12 2nd-class Estrella Blanca (US$24)

Querétaro – 202km, 2½ to 3½ hours; 3 deluxe ETN (US$14.50), frequent 1st-class Futura, Ómnibus de México (US$11), frequent 2nd-class Flecha Amarilla (US$10)

San Miguel de Allende – 180km, 4½ hours; 6 2nd-class Flecha Amarilla (US$9.50)

Tampico – 410km, 7-8 hours; 5 1st-class Oriente, Ómnibus de México and Futura (US$24), 16 2nd-class Vencedor and Oriente (US$24)

Zacatecas – 190km, 3 hours; 9 1st-class Ómnibus de México (US$9.25)

There are also many buses to Aguascalientes, Ciudad Juárez, Ciudad Valles, Ciudad Victoria, Chihuahua, Dolores Hidalgo, León, Morelia, Nuevo Laredo, Saltillo, Tampico and Torreón, and daily direct Americanos buses to US cities including Laredo, McAllen, Houston and Atlanta.

Car Car rental agencies include Budget (☎ 822-18-12) in the Hotel María Dolores, Dollar (☎ 822-14-11) and Hertz (☎ 812-95-00).

Getting Around

To/From the Airport Taxi Aéreo (☎ 814-38-50) runs a colectivo to/from the airport for US$9 per person, but for two or more people a taxi is cheaper for the half-hour trip.

To/From the Bus Station To reach the center from the bus station, walk out and take any 'Centro' bus; No 10 is the most direct. A convenient place to get off is on the Alameda, outside the train station. Returning from the city to the bus station, take a 'Central' bus southbound on Constitución on the west side of the Alameda. A booth in the bus station sells taxi tickets to the center for US$2.

Buses City buses run from 6.30 am to 10.30 pm and cost US$0.25. For places along Avenida Carranza, catch a 'Morales' or 'Carranza' bus in front of the train station or anywhere on Carranza west of Reforma, 400m west of Plaza de los Fundadores.

SANTA MARÍA DEL RÍO
• pop 10,900 ☎ 4

Forty-seven kilometers south of San Luis Potosí, just off the highway to Mexico City, this small town is known for its excellent handmade rebozos and inlaid woodwork. The rebozos are usually made of synthetic 'silk' thread called *artisela*, in less garish

colors than in many Mexican textile centers. You can see and buy them at the Escuela del Rebozo (Rebozo School) on the central Plaza Hidalgo, and in a few private workshops. A Rebozo Fair is held each year in the first half of August. There's a motel and restaurant, the ***Puesta del Sol*** (☎ 853-00-59), at the entrance to Santa María from the highway. Get there by one of the frequent 2nd-class buses from the old bus station in San Luis Potosí.

GOGORRÓN

The Balneario de Gogorrón is the major hot-springs resort in the San Luis area; its waters reach 42°C and are allegedly beneficial for rheumatism and arthritis. It's 56km south of the city on the Villa de Reyes-San Felipe road, which branches southwest off highway 57. Facilities include four large swimming pools, two children's pools, private Roman baths, large green areas, basketball and volleyball courts and horseback riding. The resort is open daily from 9 am to 6 pm; cost for day use is US$2.75 (children US$1.50).

If you want to stay over, there are comfortable bungalows. Including three meals a day, the cost for two adults is US$84 in a smaller bungalow, US$90 in a large one. The bungalows have private Roman baths.

You can get more information and make reservations at the Balneario de Gogorrón office at Carranza 660 in San Luis Potosí (☎ 4-812-15-50). It's open 9 am to 2 pm and 4 to 7 pm Monday to Friday, 9 am to 1 pm Saturday.

Getting There & Away

Flecha Amarilla buses run every 20 minutes from the San Luis Potosí bus station (1¼ hours, US$2.25) and will drop you right at the gate.

MATEHUALA
• pop 60,700 • elev 1600m ☎ 4

The only town of any size on highway 57 between Saltillo and San Luis Potosí, Matehuala ('ma-te-WAL-a') is an unremarkable but quite pleasant and prosperous place high on the Altiplano Central. It was

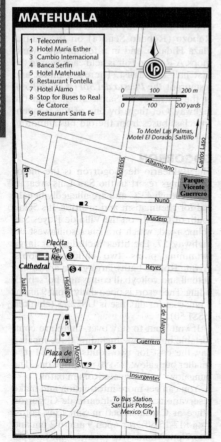

MATEHUALA

1 Telecomm
2 Hotel María Esther
3 Cambio Internacional
4 Banca Serfin
5 Hotel Matehuala
6 Restaurant Fontella
7 Hotel Álamo
8 Stop for Buses to Real de Catorce
9 Restaurant Santa Fe

0   100   200 m
0   100   200 yards

To Motel Las Palmas, Motel El Dorado, Saltillo

Altamirano

Parque Vicente Guerrero

Nuño

Madero

Placita del Rey

Cathedral

Reyes

5 de Mayo

Guerrero

Plaza de Armas

Insurgentes

To Bus Station, San Luis Potosí, Mexico City

founded in the 17th century, but has little left in the way of colonial charm. Most travelers just use it to get to Real de Catorce.

Highway 57 bypasses the town to the east. There is a large parabolic 'arch of welcome' at each end of town – the arches are something of a Matehuala trademark, though they look like they've been recycled from a McDonald's restaurant.

Orientation

Central Matehuala lies between two plazas about 300m apart: the shady Plaza de Armas with a kiosk in the middle, and the bustling Placita del Rey to the north, with its big new concrete cathedral. Cheaper hotels and the town's restaurants are in this area. Between the center and highway 57 is the shady Parque Vicente Guerrero.

The bus station is just west of the highway, about 2km south of the center. To walk to the center, turn left out of the bus station, and go straight along Avenida 5 de Mayo for about 1.5km, then turn left on Insurgentes for a few blocks to reach the Plaza de Armas.

Information

The tourist office at the Motel El Dorado, on the west side of the highway just north of town, has information about attractions in the state of San Luis Potosí.

On Hidalgo, Bancomer and Banco Serfin have ATMs and will change cash or traveler's checks, but you'll get quicker service at the casas de cambio, in the same area. There are pay phones around the plazas, and a Telecomm office, with fax service, on the corner of Jaime Nunó and Juárez.

Places to Stay

In Town The place with the most atmosphere, **Hotel Matehuala** (☎ 882-06-80) on the corner of Bustamante and Hidalgo, has dark rooms with high ceilings, set around a large, covered courtyard. At US$13 for singles/doubles, or US$16 for two beds, it has become somewhat overpriced, but they may give a discount. It's convenient for buses to Real de Catorce.

Hotel Álamo (☎ 882-00-17), on Guerrero, is slightly brighter and also convenient for buses to Real de Catorce. Rooms cost US$8/11, or US$11/14 with TV. Perhaps the best budget place is the family-run **Hotel María Esther** (☎ 882-07-14, Madero 111). Singles/doubles cost US$13.25/15.50, with hot water, TV, parking and a restaurant – the best rooms are off a little plant-filled patio out back.

On the Highway Several very '60s-style motels dot highway 57 as it passes Matehuala. **Las Palmas** (☎ 882-00-02), on the east side of the highway, has very nice rooms around landscaped gardens with a pool from

US$42/51, and also a camping area/trailer park at US$18 per vehicle with full hookups. On the other side of the highway, *El Dorado* (☎ 882-01-74) costs US$27/32 for rooms with air-con and cable TV.

Places to Eat
Restaurant Santa Fe, on the Plaza de Armas, is big, clean and reasonably priced, with generous portions of good plain food for US$2.50 to US$5. The comida corrida is US$3, and the big breakfasts are inexpensive. Just north of the plaza, the relaxed *Restaurant Fontella* (*Morelos 618*) does a solid, four-course comida corrida plus coffee for US$3, and has interesting regional dishes. Their fresh fruit salad makes a healthy breakfast.

Getting There & Away
There are fairly frequent 1st- and 2nd-class buses north and south, but Matehuala is mid-route so they may not have seats available. Daily departures include:

Mexico City (Terminal Norte) – 609km, 7 hours; some 1st-class directo (US$30), many 2nd-class de paso (US$25)

Monterrey – 325km, 4 hours; 8 1st-class (US$16) and 2nd-class (US$14)

Saltillo – 261km, 3 hours; 10 1st-class (US$12) and 2nd-class (US$10)

San Luis Potosí – 192km, 2 hours; hourly 1st-class (US$8.75) and 2nd-class (US$8)

Americanos has daily service to San Antonio (US$35), Houston (US$45) and Dallas (US$50).

Sendor runs 1st-class buses from the Matehuala bus station to Real de Catorce every two hours from 5.45 am to 1.45 pm, and at 5.45 pm (1½ hours, US$3), which can be caught in town about 15 minutes later on Guerrero, a little to the east of and across the street from the Hotel Álamo. During festivals and holidays, buses to Real may be full. When you arrive at the bus station in Matuela, ask if you need to buy a ticket to Real in advance, and whether you can catch the bus in town the next day. If you buy a roundtrip ticket, note the time stated for the return journey – you may have difficulty getting on a bus at a different time!

Getting Around
Beige buses marked 'Centro' run from the bus station to the town center but aren't very frequent; buses marked 'Central' go the other way. It can be quicker to walk.

REAL DE CATORCE
• pop 920 • elev 2756m
This reborn ghost town has a touch of magic. High on the fringes of the Sierra Madre Oriental, Real de Catorce was a wealthy and important silver-mining town of 40,000 people until early in the 20th century. Thirty kilometers west of Matehuala, reached by a road tunnel through former mine passages, the town lies in a high valley with spectacular views westward to the plain below. A few years ago it was almost deserted, its paved streets lined with crumbling stone buildings, its mint a ruin and a few hundred people eking out an existence from old mine workings or from visiting pilgrims.

Pilgrims still come to pay homage to the figure of St Francis of Assisi in the town's church, especially for the festival of San Francisco, on October 4. Between 100,000 and 200,000 people visit the town between September 25 and October 12.

Recently, Real has begun to attract trendier residents – wealthy Mexicans and gringos looking for an unusual retreat. Americans have been restoring old buildings and setting them up as hotels, while a few Europeans have established shops and restaurants. Artists have settled here, and filmmakers use the town and the surrounding hills. One day it may become another Taxco or San Miguel de Allende, but it has a long way to go.

The Huichol people, who live 400km away on the Durango-Nayarit-Jalisco-Zacatecas borders, believe that the deserts around Real are a spiritual homeland called Wirikuta, where their peyote and maize gods live. In May or June every year, the Huichol make a pilgrimage here for rituals involving peyote. This hallucinogenic cactus has great cultural and spiritual significance, and its indiscriminate use by foreigners is regarded as offensive, even sacrilegious.

You can take a day trip to Real de Catorce from Matehuala, but it's worth staying a few days to explore the surrounding hills and soak up the atmosphere.

History

The name Real de Catorce literally means 'Royal of 14': the '14' probably comes from 14 Spanish soldiers killed here by indigenous resisters in about 1700, though this is uncertain. The town was founded in the mid-18th century, and the church built between 1783 and 1817. The original name, Villa Real de Minas de Nuestra Señora de la Limpia Concepción de Guadalupe de los Álamos de Catorce, was shortened for some reason.

The mines had their ups and downs. During the independence war years (1810 to 1821) some of the shafts were flooded and in 1821 and 1822 an Englishman, Robert Phillips, made a yearlong journey from London to Catorce bringing a 'steam machine' for pumping the water out of the mines.

Real de Catorce reached its peak in the late 19th century when it was producing an estimated US$3 million in silver a year. It had a theater and a bullring, and shops that sold imported European goods. A number of large houses from this period of opulence are still standing. The dictator Porfirio Díaz journeyed here from Mexico City in 1895 to inaugurate two mine pumps purchased from California. Díaz had to travel by train, then by mule-carriage and then on horseback to reach Catorce.

Just why Catorce was transformed into a ghost town within three decades is a bit of a mystery. Locals in the town will tell you that during the revolution years (1910 to 1920) *bandidos* took refuge here and scared away the other inhabitants. The official state tourist guidebook explains, perhaps more plausibly, that the price of silver slumped after 1900.

Orientation & Information

The bus from Matehuala drops you at the end of the 2.3km Ogarrio tunnel. If you drive yourself, leave your car in the dusty open space here – local kids will hassle you to watch it all day for a few pesos. Or they'll hassle you to act as a guide, or to take you to a place to stay.

Walk a few steps up from the parking area to Lanzagorta, a stony street heading west through a row of shops, past the church at the center of town. The one telephone in town is on the north side of the plaza near the presidencia Mini-Super San Francisco, one block south of Plaza Hidalgo, may

REAL DE CATORCE

Plaza de Toros

Cemetery

Zaragoza

PLACES TO STAY
1 Quinta La Puesta del Sol
5 Pousada San Francisco
6 El Corral de Conde
7 Hospedaje Familiar
10 Mesón de Abundancia
12 Hotel El Real
15 Casa de Huéspedes La Providencia

PLACES TO EAT
3 Eucalipto
4 El Cactus Café

OTHER
2 Palenque de Gallos
8 Public Telephone
9 Horses for Hire
11 Mini-Super San Francisco
13 Parroquia
14 Museum

Morelos

Juárez

Iturbide

Lefán

Plaza Hidalgo

Zaragoza

Presidencia Municipal

Constitución

Casa de la Moneda

Lanzagorta

Ramón Corona

To Parking Area, Ogarrio Tunnel

Arroyo de la Concepción

0   100   200 m
0   100   200 yards

change cash dollars or traveler's checks if they have plenty of pesos, but don't count on it – bring pesos with you.

Parroquia

The charmingly timeworn parish church is an impressive neoclassical building, the Templo de la Purísima Limpia, always called simply la Parroquia . The attraction for thousands of Mexican pilgrims is the reputedly miraculous image of St Francis of Assisi on one of the side altars. A cult has grown up around the statue, whose help is sought in solving problems. Some believe it can cleanse their sins.

Walk through the door to the left of the altar to find a roomful of retablos. These small pictures usually show some life-threatening situation from which St Francis has rescued the victim, and include a brief description of the incident and some words of prayer and gratitude. Car accidents and medical operations are common themes. Retablos have become much sought after by collectors and are sometimes seen in antique or souvenir shops. Many of those on sale have been stolen from old churches, which must be very bad karma.

Casa de la Moneda

Opposite the façade of the church, the old mint made coins for a few years in the 1860s, but is now used only for occasional art exhibitions. It is in bad repair – restoration is being considered.

Plaza Hidalgo

Farther west along Lanzagorta, past the church and mint, this small plaza is terraced into the hillside. The plaza dates from 1888 and originally had a fountain in the middle, where the small rotunda now stands. It's a beautiful little space, with a sleepy bar/poolroom on the north side that's straight out of a Western movie.

Palenque de Gallos & Plaza de Toros

A block or so northwest of the plaza lies a monument to the town's heyday – a cock-fighting ring built like a Roman amphi-theater. It was restored in the 1970s and sometimes hosts theater or dance performances. Follow Calle Zaragoza north to the edge of the town where the restored Plaza de Toros is used for football practice; the panteón (cemetery) across the street is also worth a look.

Museum

On Lanzagorta, facing one of the sides of the church, is a small museum containing photos, documents and other miscellanea rescued from the crumbling town, including an ancient, rusting car, said to have been the second to reach Catorce. The museum is supposed to be open 9 am to 4 pm Friday and Saturday (US$0.25).

Horseback Riding & Walking

Numerous trails lead out into the stark and stunning countryside around Real. Guided trail rides include a three-hour trip to Montaña Sagrada (Sacred Mountain) for about US$16.50 per person, including a guide. Montaña Sagrada is a big hill and offers wonderful views. Another good trip is to Pueblo Fantasmo (Ghost Town). Horses for rent assemble every morning in a corral south of Plaza Hidalgo, and almost anything can be arranged for a price. Ask at Mini-Super San Francisco about a jeep trip to Estación de Catorce on the edge of the desert west of town (US$2.50 per person). Or you can simply walk out from Real, but be prepared with water, hat and strong footwear – it's unforgiving country.

Places to Stay & Eat

Real de Catorce has assorted cheap casas de huéspedes which cater mainly to pilgrims – kids in the parking area will take you to the more obscure ones. Some excellent mid-range accommodations are in old buildings, newly restored. In Semana Santa, July/August, early October and Christmas/New Year, all the accommodations can fill up. At these times, it's wise to find a room early. There's currently one telephone caseta in Real (☎ 4-882-37-33, fax 4-882-47-33), but that number will take messages for anyone in town.

Huichol Visions

The remote Sierra Madre Occidental, in and around the far north of Jalisco, is the home of the Huichol, one of Mexico's most distinctive and enduring indigenous groups. Even in pre-Hispanic times the Huichol were an independent people, one of the few groups that were not subjugated by the Aztecs, Mixtecs or any of the other dominant kingdoms. Traditionally, they lived by cultivating small, scattered fields of corn in the high valleys and by hunting deer.

The arrival of the Spanish had little immediate effect on the Huichol, and it wasn't until the 17th century that the first Catholic missionaries reached the Huichol homelands. Rather than convert to Christianity, the Huichol incorporated various elements of Christian teachings into their traditional animist belief systems. In Huichol mythology, the elements of nature take a personal form as well as a supernatural form. The gods become personalized as plants, animals and natural objects, while their supernatural form is revealed in religious rituals. For example, rain is personified as a snake, and visions of snakes can indicate when rain might be expected.

Every year the Huichol leave their isolated homeland and make a pilgrimage of about 400km across Mexico's central plateau to what is now northern San Luis Potosí state. In this harsh desert region, they seek out the mescal cactus (*Lophophora williamsii*; often called peyote cactus), a small, well-camouflaged plant that scarcely grows above ground level. The rounded 'buttons' on the top of the cactus contain peyote, a powerful hallucinogenic drug (whose chief element is mescaline) central to the Huichol's rituals and complex spiritual life. Most of the buttons are collected, dried and carried back to the tribal homelands, but a small piece is eaten on the spot, as a gesture to the plant. Small amounts of peyote help to ward off hunger, cold and fatigue, while larger amounts are taken by the Huichol on ritual occasions, such as the return from the annual pilgrimage. In particular, peyote is used by shamans ('medicine men') whose visions inform them about when to plant and harvest corn, where to hunt deer or how to treat illnesses. The cactus is extremely bitter and, when eaten in quantities sufficient to produce hallucinations, causes vomiting.

The closest place to the tunnel is *Casa de Huéspedes La Providencia*, on Lanzagorta. The rooms are very ordinary, and not a great value at US$8.75/11 for singles/doubles with basic bathrooms. A few superior rooms have bathrooms and fine views down the valley, and cost from US$27. The attached restaurant does a comida corrida for US$2.75.

For better values in budget lodgings, walk a few blocks to *Hospedaje Familiar* (Constitución 21), where small, clean rooms with shared bathroom cost US$8.75 for one or two people, US$11 for a twin. Just uphill from Plaza Hidalgo, friendly *Pousada San Francisco*, on Terán , has a few singles/doubles with shared bath from US$5.50/7.75.

A block west of the church, *Mesón de Abundancia* (Lanzagorta 11) is a handsome,

renovated 19th-century bank building, now run as a hotel and restaurant by a Swiss/Mexican couple. The rooms are large, quaint and decorated with local crafts – three have great views. They cost US$16.50/27. The restaurant has a wonderful atmosphere, and the meals are very good and moderately priced.

Another restored building houses *Hotel El Real* (Morelos 20), where the comfortable, well-decorated bedrooms are on three floors around an open courtyard and cost around US$26. Some have views over the town and the hills. The restaurant is open all day, every day, and serves good Italian, vegetarian and Mexican food, but it's quite pricey, with pasta dishes from US$5 to US$8.

Perhaps the most stylish of all is *El Corral del Conde*, on the corner of Morelos

Huichol Visions

The Huichol resisted absorption into the mine and ranch economy of colonial Mexico, and only a few migrated to the growing urban areas in the 19th century. They have not generally intermarried with other indigenous groups or with the mestizo population, most retain the Huichol language, and many still take part in the annual pilgrimages and peyote rituals. Some Huichol do seasonal work on the coastal plantations, and many speak Spanish as well as their own language, but mostly they are on the margins of the modern market economy and materially poor. Development of a unique artistic style has brought new recognition to Huichol culture and provided many Huichol people with a source of income.

Traditionally, the main Huichol art forms were stories of the supernatural (as revealed by peyote hallucinations), and the making of masks, ritual items and colorful, detailed geometric embroidery. In the last few decades, the Huichol have been depicting their myths and visions graphically, using brightly colored beads or yarn pressed into a beeswax-covered substrate. Beadwork generally uses abstract patterns, and is often done on wooden bowls, animal skulls or masks. The 'yarn pictures' are notable for their wealth of symbolism and surreal imagery. The mouth of a deer might be linked by wavy lines to a crescent moon, combining with other shapes to form an eagle, all surrounded by a circular design representing the sun. Weird shapes and brilliant colors interweave in psychedelic style. Snakes, birds and rabbits often appear, along with ritual items like feathers, candles, drums and, of course, peyote cactus.

Huichol artwork is sold in craft markets, shops and galleries in many big cities and tourist resorts. If you buy from a market stall, there's a good chance that the artist, or the artist's family, will be there to explain the various elements of a picture – sometimes the story is written on the back. Prices are usually fixed, and the Huichol don't like to haggle. Huichol art is expensive compared with some souvenirs, but it takes a long time to produce, and each piece is unique. To see the best work, visit one of the specialist museums in Zapopan (near Guadalajara), Tepic or Puerto Vallarta.

✳✳✳✳✳✳✳✳✳✳✳✳✳✳✳✳✳✳✳✳✳✳✳✳✳

and Constitución, where the spacious, stone-walled rooms could be from a medieval castle, though they're tastefully furnished and very comfortable. Doubles cost US$28, and bigger rooms with four beds cost US$44, breakfast included.

On the far side of town, *Quinta La Puesta del Sol*, on Zaragoza, has little old-world charm but a superb view down the valley to the west. Singles or doubles cost US$27; bigger rooms with two beds US$38.

Food stalls along Lanzagorta serve standard Mexican snacks, while several restaurants compete to do the best Italian cuisine in town. As well as Hotel El Real (see above), *El Cactus Café*, on Plaza Hidalgo, and *Eucalipto*, up the small street northwest of the plaza, both do excellent Italian and international dishes, from around US$4. Try to visit both!

Getting There & Away

Bus See Getting There & Away in the Matehuala section.

Car & Motorcycle From highway 57 north of Matehuala, turn off to Cedral, 20km west on a mostly paved road. From Matehuala you can take a back road to Cedral and avoid the highway, then turn south to reach Catorce on what must be one of the world's longest cobblestone streets. It's a slow but spectacular drive, up a steep mountainside, past various abandoned buildings. The Ogarrio tunnel, part of the old mine, is only wide enough for one vehicle; men stationed at each end with telephones control traffic. You may have to wait up to 20 minutes for traffic in the opposite direction to pass. If it's really busy, you may have to leave your car at the tunnel entrance and continue to Catorce on a minibus.

Guanajuato State

The state of Guanajuato has historically been one of Mexico's richest. After silver was found in Zacatecas, Spanish prospectors combed the rugged lands north of Mexico City and were rewarded by discoveries of silver, gold, iron, lead, zinc and tin. For two centuries 30% to 40% of the world's silver was mined in Guanajuato. Silver barons in Guanajuato city lived opulent lives at the expense of indigenous people who worked the mines, first as slave labor and then as wage slaves.

Eventually the well-heeled criollo class of Guanajuato and Querétaro states began to resent the dominance and arrogance of the Spanish-born in the colony. After the occupation of much of Spain by Napoleon Bonaparte's troops in 1808 and subsequent political confusion in Mexico, some provincial criollos began – while meeting as 'literary societies' – to draw up plans for rebellion.

The house of a member of one such group in Querétaro city was raided on September 13, 1810. Three days later a colleague, parish priest Miguel Hidalgo, declared independence in the town of Dolores, Guanajuato (later called Dolores Hidalgo). After Dolores, San Miguel de Allende was the next town to fall to the rebels, Celaya the third, Guanajuato the fourth. Guanajuato state is proud to have given birth to Mexico's most glorious moment and is visited almost as a place of pilgrimage by people from far and wide.

Today Guanajuato state has – in addition to the quaint colonial towns of Guanajuato and San Miguel de Allende, which are its major attractions – some important industrial centers like León (famous for its shoes and leather goods), Salamanca (with a big oil refinery), Celaya and Irapuato. It's also a fertile agricultural state, producing grains, vegetables and fruit – the strawberries grown around Irapuato are famous. And it's still an important source of silver, gold and fluorspar. In the late 1990s the state thrived under its PAN governor, Vicente Fox Quesada, with the lowest unemployment rate in Mexico and an export rate three times the national average, though some critics claim that the poorest people in the state have not benefited from the improved economy. Fox was chosen as the PAN candidate for the 2000 presidential election.

The state government website, www .guanajuato.gob.mx, has information for potential visitors and investors.

GUANAJUATO
- pop 70,000 • elev 2017m ☎ 4

Gorgeous Guanajuato is a city crammed onto the steep slopes of a ravine, with narrow streets that twist around the hillsides and dive underground into a series of tunnels. This impossible topography was settled in 1559 because the silver and gold deposits found here were among the richest in the world. Much of the fine architecture built from this wealth remains intact, making Guanajuato a living monument to a prosperous, turbulent past – it is listed by UNESCO as a World Heritage Site.

But it's not only the past that resounds from Guanajuato's narrow cobbled streets. The University of Guanajuato, known for its arts programs, has over 21,000 students, giving the city a youthfulness, vibrancy and cultural life that are as interesting to the visitor as the colonial architecture and

The boys are back in town.

exotic setting. The city's cultural year peaks in October with the Festival Internacional Cervantino.

History

One of the hemisphere's richest veins of silver was uncovered in 1558 at La Valenciana mine, 5km north of Guanajuato, and for 250 years, the mine produced 20% of the world's silver. Colonial barons benefiting from this mineral treasure were infuriated when King Carlos III of Spain slashed their share of the wealth in 1765. The king's 1767 decree banishing Jesuits from Spanish dominions further alienated both the wealthy barons and the poor miners, who held allegiance to the Jesuits.

This anger found a focus in the War of Independence. In 1810 the priest and rebel leader Miguel Hidalgo set off Mexico's independence movement with his Grito de Independencia (Cry for Independence) in nearby Dolores (see 'Miguel Hidalgo' in the Dolores Hidalgo section). The citizens of Guanajuato joined the independence fighters and defeated Spanish and loyalists, seizing the city in the first military victory of the independence rebellion. When the Spaniards eventually retook the city they retaliated by conducting the infamous 'lottery of death,' in which names of Guanajuato citizens were drawn at random and the 'winners' were tortured and hanged.

Independence was eventually won, freeing the silver barons to amass further wealth. From this wealth arose many of the mansions, churches and theaters that make Guanajuato one of Mexico's most handsome cities.

Orientation

Guanajuato's central area is quite compact, with a few major streets and lots of tiny back alleys (callejones). The main street, running roughly west-east, is called Juárez from the Mercado Hidalgo to the basilica on Plaza de la Paz, then Obregón from the basilica to the Jardín de la Unión, the city's main plaza, then Sopeña as it continues east.

Roughly parallel to Juárez and Obregón is another long street, running from the Al-

hóndiga to the university, and bearing the names 28 de Septiembre, Galarza, Positos and Lascuraín de Retana along the way. Hidalgo, also called Cantarranas, parallels Sopeña and is another important street. Once you know these streets you can't get lost in the center. You can, however, have a great time getting lost among the maze of narrow, crooked callejones winding up the hills from the center.

Another twist on getting around the city is that several of the major roadways are underground. These are for vehicular traffic, but it is possible to access some of the older underground roads by stairs, and a few stretches even have small sidewalks (look around just south of Plaza Baratillo to find one good access point). The main *subterránea* runs under the center of town along the dried-up bed of the Río Guanajuato, which was diverted after it flooded the city in 1905. At least eight other tunnels were constructed in the 1980s and 1990s to cope with increasing traffic without damaging the historic streetscapes.

Surrounding central Guanajuato is the winding Carretera Panorámica, which offers wonderful views of the town and surrounding hills.

Information

Tourist Offices The state tourist office (☎ 732-15-74, 732-82-75, fax 732-42-51) is at Plaza de la Paz 14, almost opposite the basilica – look for the 'Información Turística' sign. The friendly staff, mostly English-speaking, give out free city maps and brochures (in Spanish and English) about the city and state of Guanajuato. The office is open 9 am to 8 pm Monday to Friday, 10 am to 4 pm Saturday and 10 am to 2 pm Sunday.

Money Banks along Avenida Juárez change cash and traveler's checks (some only until 2 pm), and most have ATMs. Bancentro, opposite the state tourist office, is convenient and relatively quick. Divisas, at Juárez 33A, is a casa de cambio with reasonable rates, open 9 am to 3 pm and 4.30 to 7 pm Monday to Friday. The American Express agent is at

GUANAJUATO

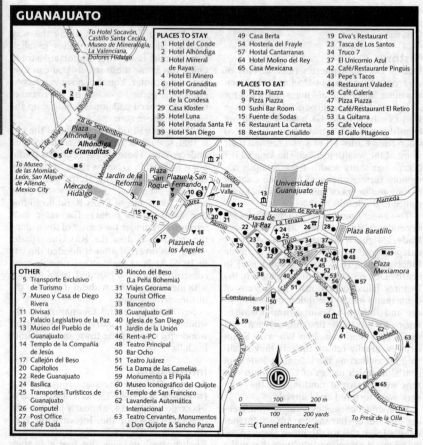

PLACES TO STAY
1 Hotel del Conde
2 Hotel Alhóndiga
3 Hotel Mineral de Rayas
4 Hotel El Minero
6 Hotel Granaditas
21 Hotel Posada de la Condesa
29 Casa Kloster
35 Hotel Luna
36 Hotel Posada Santa Fé
39 Hotel San Diego
49 Casa Berta
54 Hostería del Frayle
57 Hostal Cantarranas
64 Hotel Molino del Rey
65 Casa Mexicana

PLACES TO EAT
8 Pizza Piazza
9 Pizza Piazza
10 Sushi Bar Room
15 Fuente de Sodas
16 Restaurant La Carreta
18 Restaurante Crisalido
19 Diva's Restaurant
23 Tasca de Los Santos
34 Truco 7
37 El Unicornio Azul
42 Café/Restaurante Pinguis
43 Pepe's Tacos
44 Restaurant Valadez
45 Café Galería
47 Pizza Piazza
52 Café/Restaurant El Retiro
53 La Guitarra
55 Cafe Veloce
58 El Gallo Pitagórico

OTHER
5 Transporte Exclusivo de Turismo
7 Museo y Casa de Diego Rivera
11 Divisas
13 Museo del Pueblo de Guanajuato
14 Templo de la Compañia de Jesús
20 Capitolios
22 Rede Guanajuato
24 Basílica
25 Transportes Turísticos de Guanajuato
26 Computel
27 Post Office
28 Café Dada
30 Rincón del Beso (La Peña Bohemia)
31 Viajes Georama
32 Tourist Office
33 Bancentro
38 Guanajuato Grill
40 Iglesia de San Diego
41 Jardín de la Unión
46 Rent-a-PC
48 Teatro Principal
50 Bar Ocho
51 Teatro Juárez
56 La Dama de las Camelias
59 Monumento a El Pípila
60 Museo Iconográfico del Quijote
61 Templo de San Francisco
62 Lavandería Automática Internacional
63 Teatro Cervantes, Monumentos a Don Quijote & Sancho Panza

Viajes Georama (☎ 732-51-01), Plaza de la Paz 34.

Post & Communications The main post office is at the eastern end of Lascuraín de Retana, opposite the Templo de la Compañía, and there's a post office agency in the bus station.

Pasaje de los Arcos, an alley off the south side of Obregón near the tourist office, has pay phones in reasonably quiet surroundings. Computel, opposite the post office, has a telephone caseta and fax service; it's open daily.

The best place for Internet access is Rent-a-PC, upstairs at a kink in the road almost opposite the Teatro Principal, open 10 am to 10 pm Monday to Friday, 10 am to 8 pm Saturday, and noon to 6 pm Sunday (US$3 per hour). Another option is Rede Guanajuato, on Alonso, open 9 am to 8 pm Monday to Friday, 9 am to 2 pm Saturday (US$3.25 per hour).

Travel Agencies You can buy air tickets from agencies like Viajes Frausto (☎ 732-35-80), Obregón 10, between the Jardín de la

Unión and the basilica; Viajes Georama (☎ 732-51-01), Plaza de la Paz 34, in front of the basilica; and SITSA (☎ 732-79-90), in the Aeroméxico office at Hidalgo 6.

Laundry Lavandería Automática Internacional has two branches where you can do your own laundry, or drop it off and they'll do it for about US$3.75 a load. The eastern branch is at Doblado 28, on the corner of Hidalgo, and the western branch at Alhóndiga 35A; both are open Monday to Saturday from 9 am to 2 pm and 4 to 8 pm.

Walking Tour
A slow walk around the main plazas is a good introduction to Guanajuato's historic center. Starting from the east, pretty **Jardín de la Unión**, surrounded by restaurants and shaded by trees, is the social heart of the city. The elegant Teatro Juárez is on its southeastern corner. Walk west on Obregón to **Plaza de la Paz**, the small triangle beside the basilica, surrounded by the former homes of wealthy silver lords.

Wander west and south along the curving Avenida Juárez to **Plazuela de los Ángeles**, where the steps and ice-cream stands are popular gathering spots for students. The Callejón del Beso is just a few meters up from here.

Continue on Juárez to the handsome **Jardín de la Reforma**, behind the row of classical columns. This leads on to **Plaza San Roque**, where *entremeses* (theatrical sketches) are performed during the Cervantino festival. Nearby is the pleasant, shady **Plazuela San Fernando**. These three linked spaces form a superbly picturesque detour northwest of Avenida Juárez.

Farther west on Juárez is the bustling area in front of Mercado Hidalgo, busy with shoppers and souvenir sellers. A block north, **Plaza Alhóndiga** is a usually bare and empty space in front of the Alhóndiga. From there, head back east along 28 de Septiembre (which changes names several times), past museums and the university, and a few twists and turns, to **Plaza del Baratillo** with its Florentine fountain. A right turn and a

short block south from there should bring you back to Jardín de la Unión, where tourists and the local well-to-do congregate in the late afternoon, along with a surfeit of souvenir sellers, street musicians, shoe shiners and snack vendors.

Teatro Juárez & Other Theaters
On Jardín de la Unión, the magnificent Teatro Juárez was built between 1873 and 1903 and inaugurated by the dictator Porfirio Díaz, whose lavish tastes are reflected in the interior. The outside is festooned with columns, lampposts and statues; inside the impression is Moorish, with the bar and lobby gleaming with carved wood, stained glass and precious metals. The steps outside are a popular place to watch the scene on the plaza.

The theater can be visited from 9 am to 1.45 pm and 5 to 7.45 pm Tuesday to Sunday (US$0.60, cameras/videos US$0.20/0.60 extra). Performances are held here during the Cervantino festival as well as other times; check for the current schedule.

The **Teatro Principal**, on Hidalgo near the other end of the Jardín de la Unión, and the **Teatro Cervantes**, at the eastern end of Hidalgo, are not as spectacular as Teatro Juárez. Statues of Don Quijote and Sancho Panza grace the small courtyard of the Teatro Cervantes.

Basilica & Other Churches
The Basílica de Nuestra Señora de Guanajuato, on Plaza de la Paz, one block west of the Jardín de la Unión, contains a jewel-covered image of the Virgin, patron of Guanajuato. The wooden statue was supposedly hidden from the Moors in a cave in Spain for 800 years. Felipe II of Spain gave it to Guanajuato in thanks for riches that accrued to the crown.

Other fine colonial churches include the **Iglesia de San Diego**, opposite the Jardín de la Unión, the **Templo de San Francisco** on Doblado, and the large **Templo de la Compañía de Jesús** on Navarro, which was completed in 1747 for the Jesuit seminary whose buildings are now occupied by the University of Guanajuato.

Universidad de Guanajuato

The University of Guanajuato, whose ramparts are visible above much of the city, is on Lascuraín de Retana one block up the hill from the basilica. It is considered one of Mexico's finest schools for music, theater, mine engineering, industrial relations and law. The buildings originally housed a large Jesuit seminary.

The university includes three art galleries – the Salas de Exposiciones Hermenegildo Bustos and Polivalente on the ground floor of the main building, and the Sala de Exposiciones El Atrio under the front courtyard of La Compañía church next door. On the 4th floor of the university building is the **Museo de Historia Natural Alfredo Dugés**, honoring one of the university's foremost naturalists. The extensive collection of preserved and stuffed animals, birds, reptiles and insects includes some freaks, such as a two-headed goat.

Museo del Pueblo de Guanajuato

Beside the university at Positos 7, this art museum has a collection ranging from colonial to modern times. The museum occupies the former mansion of the Marqueses de San Juan de Rayas, who owned the San Juan de Rayas mine. The private church upstairs in the courtyard contains a powerful mural by José Chávez Morado. The museum is open 10 am to 7.30 pm Tuesday to Saturday, 10 am to 2.30 pm Sunday (US$0.90).

Museo y Casa de Diego Rivera

The birthplace of Diego Rivera, today a museum honoring the painter, is at Positos 46 between the university and the Alhóndiga. Rivera and a twin brother were born in this house in 1886 (his twin died at the age of two). The family moved to Mexico City when he was six years old.

In conservative Guanajuato, where Catholic influence prevails, the Marxist Rivera was persona non grata for years. The city now honors its once blacklisted son with a small collection of his work in this house where he was born. The 1st floor contains the Rivera family's 19th-century antiques and fine furniture. On the 2nd and 3rd floors are some 70 to 80 paintings and sketches by the master, including portraits of peasants and indigenous people, a nude of Frida Kahlo and sketches for some of Rivera's memorable murals. The upper floors also have temporarary exhibitions of work by Mexican and international artists. Hours are 10 am to 6.30 pm Tuesday to Saturday, 10 am to 2.30 pm Sunday (US$0.90).

Alhóndiga de Granaditas

The Alhóndiga de Granaditas, on 28 de Septiembre, site of the first major rebel victory in Mexico's War of Independence, is now a history and art museum.

The Alhóndiga was a massive grain-and-seed storehouse built between 1798 and 1808. In 1810 it became a fortress for Spanish troops and loyalist leaders. They barricaded themselves inside when 20,000 rebels led by Miguel Hidalgo attempted to take Guanajuato. It looked as if the outnumbered Spaniards would be able to hold out. Then, on September 28, 1810, a young miner named Juan José de los Reyes Martínez (better known as El Pípila), under orders from Hidalgo, tied a stone slab to his back and, thus protected from Spanish bullets, was able to set the gates ablaze. While the Spaniards choked on smoke, the rebels moved in and took the Alhóndiga, killing most of those inside. (El Pípila probably perished in the battle, but some versions of the story have it that he survived and lived to a ripe old age.)

The Spaniards later took their revenge: the heads of four leaders of the rebellion – Aldama, Allende, Jiménez and Hidalgo himself, who was executed in Chihuahua – were displayed on the four outside corners of the Alhóndiga from 1811 to 1821. The metal cages in which the heads hung are now exhibited inside. The Alhóndiga was used as a prison for a century, beginning in 1864. It became a museum in 1967. Historical sections of the museum cover Guanajuato's pre-Hispanic past, its great flood of 1905 and modern times. There's also a fine art gallery that houses a permanent collection as well as temporary exhibits. Don't miss Chávez Morado's dramatic murals of Guanajuato's history on the staircases.

The building is open 10 am to 1.30 pm and 4 to 5.30 pm Tuesday to Saturday, 10 am to 2.30 pm Sunday (US$2.25, free on Sunday; US$3.25 extra for a video camera).

Callejón del Beso

The narrowest of the many narrow alleys that climb the hills from Guanajuato's main streets is Callejón del Beso, where the balconies of the houses on either side of the alley practically touch. In a Guanajuato legend, a fine family once lived on this street, and their daughter fell in love with a common miner. They were forbidden to see each other, but the miner rented a room opposite, and the lovers exchanged furtive kisses *(besos)* from these balconies. Of course the romance was discovered and the couple met a tragic end. From the Plazuela de los Ángeles on Juárez, walk about 40m up Callejón del Patrocinio and you'll see Callejón del Beso taking off to your left.

Monumento a El Pípila

The monument to El Pípila honors the hero who torched the Alhóndiga gates on September 28, 1810, enabling Hidalgo's forces to win the first victory of the independence movement. The statue shows El Pípila holding his torch high over the city. On the base is the inscription *'Aún hay otras Alhóndigas por incendiar'* ('There are still other Alhóndigas to burn').

It's worth going up to the statue for the magnificent view over the city; you can climb up inside the statue but the view is just as good from the terraces at its feet. Two routes from the center of town go up steep, picturesque lanes. One goes east on Sopeña from Jardín de la Unión, then turns right on Callejón del Calvario (you'll see the 'Al Pípila' sign). Another ascent, unmarked, goes uphill from the small plaza on Alonso. If the climb is too much for you, the 'Pípila-ISSSTE' bus heading west on Juárez will let you off right by the statue.

Museo Iconográfico del Quijote

This excellent and surprisingly interesting museum is at Doblado 1, on the tiny plaza in front of the Templo de San Francisco. Every exhibit relates to Don Quijote de la Mancha, the famous hero of Spanish literature, and it's fascinating to see the same subject depicted in so many different media by different artists in different styles. There's everything from room-size murals to a tiny picture on an eggshell. Paintings, statues, tapestries, even chess sets, clocks and postage stamps all feature Don Quixote and his companion Sancho Panza. The museum is open 10 am to 6.30 pm Tuesday through Saturday, 10 am to 2.30 pm Sunday (free).

Museo de las Momias

The famous Museum of the Mummies, at the cemetery on the western outskirts of town, is a quintessential example of Mexico's obsession with death. Visitors from far and wide come to see scores of corpses disinterred from the public cemetery – there can be a long queue to enter.

The first remains were dug up in 1865, when it was necessary to remove some bodies from the cemetery to make room for more. What the authorities uncovered were not skeletons but flesh mummified in grotesque forms and facial expressions. The mineral content of the soil and extremely dry atmospheric conditions had combined to preserve the bodies in this unique way.

Today 119 mummies are on display in the museum, including the first mummy to be discovered, the 'smallest mummy in the world,' a pregnant mummy and plenty more. Since space is still tight in the cemetery, bodies whose relatives don't want to pay a fee to keep them there in perpetuity continue to be exhumed – and mummies are still being found. It takes only five or six years for a body to become mummified here, though only 1% or 2% of the bodies exhumed have turned into 'display quality' mummies. The others are cremated.

The museum is open 9 am to 6 pm daily (US$2.25/1.75 for adults/children; US$0.70/1.75 extra for cameras/videos). The price includes entry to the Salón de Culto a la Muerte, a haunted-house-type tourist trap.

Museo de Mineralogía

The Mineralogy Museum at the university's Escuela de Minas campus is among the world's foremost. Over 20,000 specimens from around the world include some extremely rare minerals. The school of mines is a little more than 1km northwest of the center of town, but the trip there on the winding La Valenciana road is more than twice that distance. The museum is open 9 am to 3 pm Monday to Friday (free). Take a 'Presa-San Javier' bus heading west on Juárez and ask to get off at the Escuela de Minas.

Casa de las Leyendas

A new attraction east of town, the 'House of Legends' is pretty hokey, but kind of fun. Dioramas and models depict various legends from Guanajuato's colorful past, from monsters in the mines to treachery in high-ranking families, but you'll need good Spanish to enjoy it. It's open 10 am to 2 pm and 4 to 7 pm daily (US$3.50).

Ex-Hacienda San Gabriel de Barrera

Built at the end of the 17th century, this was the grand hacienda of Captain Gabriel de Barrera, whose family was descended from the first Count of Valenciana of the famous La Valenciana mine. Opened as a museum in 1979, the hacienda has been magnificently restored with period European furniture and art; inside the chapel is an ornate gold-covered altar.

The large grounds, originally devoted to processing ore from La Valenciana, were converted in 1945 to beautiful terraced gardens with pavilions, pools, fountains and footpaths – a lovely and tranquil retreat from the city.

The house and garden, about 2km west of the city center, are open 9 am to 6 pm daily (US$1.25; US$0.60 extra for cameras). Take one of the frequent 'Marfil' buses heading west on Juárez and say you want to get off at Hotel Mission Guanajuato. From where they

drop you, just walk downhill past the hotel and the ex-hacienda will be on your right.

Mina & Templo La Valenciana

For 250 years La Valenciana mine, on a hill overlooking Guanajuato about 5km north of the center, produced 20% of the world's silver, in addition to quantities of gold.

Shut down after the Mexican Revolution, the mine reopened in 1968 and is once again in operation, now cooperatively run. It can be visited any day from around 8 am to 7 pm (US$0.50). It still yields silver, gold, nickel and lead, and you can see the ore being extracted and miners descending an immense main shaft, 9m wide and 500m deep.

Near the mine is the magnificent Templo La Valenciana, also called the Iglesia de San Cayetano. One legend says that the Spaniard who started the mine promised San Cayetano that if it made him rich, he would build a church to honor the saint. Another says that the silver baron of La Valenciana, Conde de Rul, tried to atone for exploiting the miners by building the ultimate in Churrigueresque churches.

Whatever the motive, ground was broken in 1765, and the church was completed in 1788. La Valenciana's façade is spectacular, and its interior is dazzling with ornate golden altars, filigree carvings and giant paintings.

To get to La Valenciana, take a 'Cristo Rey' or 'Valenciana' bus (every 15 minutes) from the bus stop on Alhóndiga just north of 28 de Septiembre. Get off at Templo La Valenciana (be sure to look at the interior) then cross the road to the entrance to the mine area, and follow the dirt track about 300m to the mine itself.

Presa de la Olla

In the hills at the east end of the city are two small reservoirs, Presa de la Olla and Presa de San Renovato, with a green park between them and a lighthouse on the hill above. It's a popular family park on Sunday, when you can bring a picnic and hire small rowboats. The rest of the week it's quiet and peaceful, though not especially scenic. Any eastbound 'Presa' bus, from the underground stop down the steps at the southwest corner of the Jardín de la Unión, will take you there.

Language Courses

Guanajuato is a university town and has an excellent atmosphere for studying Spanish.

The Instituto Falcón (☎/fax 731-07-45, infalcon@redes.int.com.mx), Paseo de la Presa 880, has language courses with two to five students per class, from beginners to advanced level. It offers cultural courses and weekend recreational trips too. Registration (US$75) is every Saturday morning. A course with three 55-minute class lessons per day costs US$75 a week; five lessons per day costs US$100 a week. One-on-one instruction costs US$55 a week for one session per day, US$165 for three sessions per day. The institute can arrange accommodations with Mexican families; average daily cost with three meals is about US$20, or US$16 with shared facilities. For more information, write to Instituto Falcón, Callejón de la Mora 158, 36000 Guanajuato, Gto, Mexico, or check http://institutofalcon.com.

The Universidad de Guanajuato (☎ 732-00-06 ext 8001, fax 732-72-53) offers four-week summer courses in basic, intermediate and advanced Spanish, with classes in Mexican and Latin American culture (US$550); sessions begin in early June and early July with registration in February and May. The university also offers a range of semester-long courses in language and culture, beginning in January and July. Students must register in person and take a placement test (US$4.50) the week before the courses begin. Cost is US$366 per 19-week semester. The university can arrange accommodations with Mexican families for US$13 per day. For more information, write to Centro de Idiomas, Universidad de Guanajuato, Lascuraín de Retana 5, 36000 Guanajuato, Gto, México, or email idioma@quijote.ugto.mx.

The Instituto Calmecac (☎ 732-12-93, calmecac@az-net.com.mx), Callejón de Calixto 2, has courses of three hours per day at US$72 per week, or four hours per day at US$85 per week (registration US$20). Various craft and cultural courses are offered, as well as tours of the town and surrounding area. They can also arrange family accommodations for US$15 per day.

Organized Tours

A few companies offer tours in Spanish of several of Guanajuato's major sights – their deals are identical. You can reach all the same places on local buses, but if your time is limited a tour may be useful.

Transporte Exclusivo de Turismo (☎ 732-59-68), in a kiosk on the corner of Juárez and 5 de Mayo, and Transportes Turísticos de Guanajuato (☎ 732-21-34), below the front courtyard of the basilica, both offer 'Guanajuato Colonial' tours which include the mummies, La Valenciana mine and church, the Pípila monument and the Carretera Panorámica with a view over the town. Trips depart up to three times daily, last 3 to 3½ hours, and cost US$5.50. Longer tours, including ones to Cristo Rey, cost up to US$11. Night tours (5 hours, US$10) take in Guanajuato's views and nightspots and the *callejoneadas* – see Entertainment.

Special Events

Baile de las Flores The 'Flower Dance' takes place on the Thursday before Semana Santa. The next morning many mines are open to the public, with miners erecting altars to Dolores, their patron saint, and hosting 'mine parties' for friends and families.

Fiestas de San Juan y Presa de la Olla The Fiestas de San Juan are celebrated at the Presa de la Olla park from June 15 to 24. The 24th is the big bash for the saint's day itself, with dances, music, fireworks and picnics. On the first Monday in July, everyone comes back to the park for another big party celebrating the opening of the dam's floodgates.

Fiesta de la Virgen de Guanajuato This festival, on August 8, commemorates the date when Felipe II gave the jeweled wooden Virgin now adorning the basilica to the people of Guanajuato.

Festival Internacional Cervantino Guanajuato's arts festival is dedicated to the

Spanish writer Miguel Cervantes, author of *Don Quijote*. In the 1950s the festival was merely *entremeses* (sketches) from Cervantes' work performed by students. It has grown to become one of the foremost arts extravaganzas in Latin America. Music, dance and theater groups converge on Guanajuato from around the world, performing work that nowadays may have nothing whatever to do with Cervantes. (A recent festival brought acts as diverse as traditional Moroccan music, a German silent movie from the 1920s and the Latin beats of the Cuban All-Stars.) The festival lasts two to three weeks and is held in October. If your visit to Mexico coincides with it, don't miss it.

While some events are held in Teatro Juárez and other theaters, the most spectacular *entremeses*, with galloping horses and medieval costumes, are performed in the historic settings of Plazuela San Roque and Plaza Alhóndiga.

Many events, in fact some of the biggest, are free. The festival opens at Plaza Alhóndiga, and you should arrive at any event there a couple hours early if you want to find a seat. On Saturday and Sunday, when Guanajuato's population swells to many times its normal size, there's music – from children's ensembles to rock/hip-hop bands – on practically every corner.

Cervantino events are organized into morning, afternoon and evening sessions, for which tickets range from around US$5.50 to US$20. Tickets and hotels should be booked in advance. Tickets normally go on sale around September 6. In Guanajuato they're sold on the left side of the Teatro Juárez (not in the theater ticket office); in Mexico City they can be bought at the FIC office at Álvaro Obregón 273, Colonia Roma (☎ 5-533-41-21), or from Ticketmaster (☎ 5-325-90-00).

Places to Stay

Prices given here are for the summer season, and may be lower in other months, but may be even higher at Christmas, Semana Santa and during the Festival Internacional Cervantino.

Budget The budget backpackers' choice is *Casa Kloster* (☎ 732-00-88, *Alonso 32*), near the center of town, a short block down an alley from the basilica. Birds and flowers grace the sunny courtyard, and the well-cared-for rooms with shared bath are clean and comfortable. Cost is US$7.75 per person; slightly more in the larger rooms. It's a relaxed, friendly place, but don't leave valuables lying around in your room. Arrive early because the Casa is often booked out.

The friendly *Casa Bertha* (☎ 732-13-16, *Tamboras 9*), a few minutes east of the Jardín de la Unión, is a casa de huéspedes with four doubles at US$10 per person and an apartment suitable for families. It's homey, well-kept and centrally located, with modern bathrooms and a rooftop terrace with views over the town. Walk up the street beside the Teatro Principal to Plaza Meximamora. Head straight uphill, turn first right, then left and follow the path to the door directly ahead.

Another cheapie is *Casa Mexicana* (☎ 732-50-05, *Sostenes Rocha 28*), about 300m southeast of the Jardín de la Unión. Smallish rooms around a central courtyard cost US$5.50 per person with shared bathroom, or US$7.75 per person with private bath. It's a clean, friendly, family-run place.

Rock-bottom lodgings are available at *Hotel Posada de la Condesa* (☎ 732-14-62, *Plaza de la Paz 60*), northwest of the basilica. Rooms have private baths with 24-hour hot water and are passably clean, but they're pretty worn and can be noisy. Some are large and have balconies; others are dark, without windows or ventilation. Prices start at US$10, which is OK for the better rooms but too much for the bad ones.

In the area around Mercado Hidalgo, several cheap hotels line up along the north side of Juárez. The best is *Hotel Granaditas* (☎ 732-10-39, *Juárez 109*), where clean rooms with hot water and TV cost US$16.50 for one or two people.

Mid-Range There are several medium-priced hotels around Plaza Alhóndiga and on Alhóndiga, the street heading north from the plaza. *Hotel Alhóndiga* (☎ 732-05-25, *In-*

surgencia 49), visible from the plaza, has clean, comfortable rooms with color TV. Some have small private balconies; there's also parking. Hot water is sporadic. Single or double rooms are US$32. The nearby *Hotel del Conde* (☎ 732-14-65, *Insurgencia 1*) is better, though its weekend disco is a recipe for lack of sleep. Spacious, bright singles/doubles cost US$25/30.

Around the corner are a couple of economical choices. *Hotel Mineral de Rayas* (☎ 732-19-67, *Alhóndiga 7*) has some nice rooms with balconies, though others are dark and dingy – they all cost US$23. The disco may be noisy on weekends. *Hotel El Minero* (☎ 732-52-51, *Alhóndiga 12A*) is a reasonable place with small, comfortable rooms, all with TV, and many with balconies over the street, at US$22/24 for singles/doubles.

Hotel Socavón (☎ 732-48-85, *Alhóndiga 41A*) is an attractive, well-kept hostelry with rooms around a courtyard. All have copper washbasins, painted tiles in the bathrooms, color TV and plenty of windows; the cost is US$27/31, possibly less at off-peak times. There's a restaurant/bar on the second floor.

On the other side of town, *Hostal Cantarranas* (☎ 732-51-44, *Hidalgo 50*), a short hop southeast of the Jardín, has eight pleasant, bright apartments with two to six beds. Each has an equipped kitchen and a sitting room. Prices start at US$22/33.

A few minutes farther south on Hidalgo, at Calle del Campanero, opposite the Teatro Cervantes, *Hotel Molino del Rey* (☎ 732-22-23) is a good choice for its convenient but quiet location. Set around a pretty patio, the 35 rooms with bath are US$23/31, and it serves inexpensive meals.

If you have a car but wish to avoid driving in the congested center, *Motel de las Embajadoras* (☎ 731-01-05), beside Parque Embajadoras on the corner of Embajadoras and Paseo Madero, has plenty of parking and is only five minutes east of the center on an 'Embajadoras' or 'Presa' bus (you can catch one on Sostenes Rocha). The restaurant/bar is elegant but inexpensive, and the lovely courtyard is full of plants, trees and birds. Clean, comfortable rooms with color TV cost US$36/45.

Top End The classiest address is on Jardín de la Unión, where several venerable hotels charge extra for exterior rooms overlooking the plaza. *Hotel San Diego* (☎ 732-13-00/21, *fax 732-56-26, Jardín de la Unión 1*) has 55 elegant rooms and suites, a large roof terrace and a subterranean bar. Single or double rooms are US$61, or, with a balcony over the plaza, US$88/93. At the other end of the Jardín, *Hotel Posada Santa Fé* (☎ 732-00-84, *fax 732-46-53*) is a sumptuous hotel in an elegant 19th-century mansion. Singles/doubles are US$59/67; rooms with a plaza view are US$88. In between these two, *Hotel Luna* (☎ 732-97-20, *Jardín de la Unión 6*) offers comfortable rooms at US$55, or US$77 for those overlooking the plaza.

A block southeast of the Jardín, *Hostería del Frayle* (☎ 732-11-79, *Sopeña 3*) is a very attractive old building. All the rooms have high wood-beamed ceilings, color TV and other comforts at US$44/55 for singles/doubles. It's right in the center of town, but thick adobe walls keep things quiet.

Other posh places are away from the center of town. West of the city beside the ex-Hacienda San Gabriel de Barrera, *Hotel Mission Guanajuato* (☎/fax 732-39-80), at Km 2.5 on the Camino Antigua a Marfil, has a restaurant, bar, swimming pool, tennis courts and 160 luxury rooms from US$103. For something different, go farther west to the suburb of Marfil, where *La Casa de Espíritus Alegres* (☎/fax 753-10-13), on Real de Marfil, is an attractive B&B with enough artifacts to fill a museum of Mexican folk arts. Individually decorated rooms in the restored hacienda start at around US$90. The sign out front says 'ex-Hacienda La Trinidad,' and buses to/from the center pass every 10 minutes.

Castillo Santa Cecilia (☎ 732-04-77/85, *fax 732-01-53*), on the road to La Valenciana mine at Carretera Valenciana Km 1, is built of stone and resembles a castle. It is known both for its luxurious accommodations and excellent restaurant. Rooms start at US$80. Farther out the same road, *Parador San Javier* (☎ 732-06-26, *Plaza Aldama 92*) offers luxurious accommodations and service in a superbly restored colonial setting, from around US$80.

Places to Eat

Jardín de la Unión & Around The hotels on the west side of the Jardín de la Unión have good but quite expensive restaurants where you can enjoy the atmosphere of the plaza. At the tables outside *Posada Santa Fé*, well prepared *antojitos* will cost US$3 to US$6, and steak dishes around US$7, and you might allow extra for wandering musicians. The adjoining *Hotel Luna* restaurant also has outdoor tables, and a good, if uninspired selection. On the southwest corner of the Jardín, *Hotel San Diego* has an elegant upstairs restaurant with several balcony tables overlooking the plaza – the breakfast specials and the US$4 comida corrida are the best values here.

At the northeast end of the Jardín, unpretentious *Café/Restaurante Pinguis* has no sign out front, but reasonable prices make it one of the most popular places in town. The menu mixes Mexican and fast-food standards, with good coffee, egg dishes (US$1.50), enchiladas (US$2.50), big sandwiches (US$2) and a solid comida corrida (US$2.50). It's open 8.30 am to 9.30 pm daily. On the inexpensive southeast side of the Jardín, *Pepe's Tacos* will fill you up with US$1 burgers and beers, and you can finish up with an ice cream at the nearby stalls. On the corner of the Jardín and Sopeña, opposite Teatro Juárez, the cavernous *Restaurant Valadez* serves economical breakfasts for US$2.50, a comida corrida for US$3.50 and lunch and dinner till 11 pm daily – it's never empty.

Going east along Sopeña takes you past a good selection of places for a snack, a meal or a drink. *Café Galería* is a lively, popular, mid-priced place, with more tables outdoors and across the street, next to the Teatro Juárez. *Café/Restaurant El Retiro*, a few doors down Sopeña, has a similar menu and prices and live music in the evenings. Other options along here include *La Guitarra*, with regular live music, and *Cafe Veloce*, with an excellent pasta selection (around US$3) and a 1950s motorcycle racing theme.

South of the Jardín, up the hill behind Templo San Diego, *El Gallo Pitagórico* is in a bright blue building with a wonderful view over the city. The fine Italian and Mexican meals include assorted antipasti from US$2 to US$4, rich minestrone for US$2.50 and a range of pastas from US$3 to US$5. It's worth the walk.

Pizza Piazza (Hidalgo 14), just off the Jardín de la Unión, has a relaxed student atmosphere and good pizza at good prices. A US$4 *chica* size is enough for one or two, while a US$5.75 *mediana* fills up to four. It's open from 2 to 11 pm daily.

Near the basilica on Calle Truco, *Truco 7* is a small, intimate, artsy café/restaurant/ gallery. It has great atmosphere, delicious food and a mixed crowd of students, teachers and travelers. An à la carte breakfast will cost under US$3, the comida corrida is inexpensive and more imaginative than most, and for dinner it's hard to spend more than US$4 for a main course. Background music includes jazz, blues and classical. It's open daily from 8.30 am to 11.30 pm.

Avenida Juárez & Around Plaza de la Paz is another eating area, where *Tasca de Los Santos* has outdoor tables for tapas and other Spanish specialties (US$5 to US$7). It's a little pricey, but worth it for the great flavors and European ambiance. Farther west on Juárez, and even more upmarket, *Diva's Restaurant* is quietly elegant, with thick tablecloths, unobtrusive service and an original menu of international dishes – if you can afford US$12 or more per person, it's a good splurge. For something different, *Sushi Bar Room*, on Juárez, does reasonable sushi for about US$1 a serving, or teppanyaki from US$5 to US$7.

There's a second *Pizza Piazza* at Juárez 69A, and a third very pleasantly situated nearby on the Plazuela San Fernando. Like the original outlet near the Jardín, these branches have good pizza at good prices in a fun atmosphere.

Farther west, *Restaurant La Carreta*, at Juárez 96, does a good version of the standard Mexican grilled chicken – with large portions of rice and salad it's US$2 for a quarter chicken, US$3.25 for a half. A few doors away at Juárez 120, **Fuente de Sodas** is good for a quick inexpensive juice, licuado, fruit salad or torta. For fresh produce and local sweets, the **Mercado Hidalgo** is not far away.

Vegetarian On Hidalgo near Truco, **El Unicornio Azul** is a health food store with a couple of tables where you can enjoy a yogurt and fruit breakfast (US$0.80) or a soyburger (US$1.25). Just uphill from Plazuela de los Ángeles, **Restaurante Crisalido** (Callejón de Calixto 20) is a peaceful place serving breakfast or a tasty comida corrida (US$3). It's open Tuesday to Sunday from 8 am to 6 pm.

Entertainment

Every evening, the Jardín de la Unión comes alive with students, tourists and others crowding the outdoor tables, strolling, people-watching and listening to the street musicians. The state band and other groups give free concerts in the gazebo some evenings from around 7 to 8 pm and on Sundays from around noon to 2 pm.

On Friday, Saturday and Sunday evenings around 8 or 8.30 pm, *callejoneadas* (or *estudiantinas*) depart from in front of San Diego church on the Jardín de la Unión. The callejoneada tradition is said to come from Spain. A group of professional songsters and musicians, dressed in traditional costumes, starts up in front of the church, a crowd gathers, then the whole mob winds through the ancient alleyways of the city, playing and singing heartily. On special occasions they take along a burro laden with wine – at other times wine is stashed midpoint on the route. Stories and jokes are told between songs, though these are unintelligible unless you understand Spanish well. It's good fun and one of Guanajuato's most enjoyable traditions. There's no cost except a small amount for the wine you drink. Tour companies and others try to sell you tickets for the callejoneadas, but you don't need them!

Bars & Clubs South of the Jardín, behind Templo San Diego, **Bar Ocho** is student hangout with pool tables and drinks specials.

Go west from here along Alonso, to the **Guanajuato Grill** (Alonso 20), a dance and drink spot frequented by more affluent students. It's open most nights till 3 am, but it's really packed after midnight on Friday and Saturday. On quieter nights they try to pull in the punters with drink specials from 9 to 10 pm. A more mature crowd congregates at **Rincón del Beso** (Alonso 21A), also known as La Peña Bohemia since it used to be a rather bohemian club. Often it's deserted but sometimes, after 11 pm, the live music and the booze kick in and it really gets going. There's no cover charge, though the drinks are a bit expensive.

Other clubs include **Capitolios**, at the west end of Plaza de la Paz, which blasts techno and dance to big weekend crowds, and **Chely 'Oh!** disco, at Hotel Mineral de Rayas.

For Latin sounds in an artsy, gay-friendly atmosphere, check out **La Dama de las Camelias** (Sopeña 34), which has a vintage cool clientele and live salsa, flamenco, Andean and so forth until very late. On Plaza Baratillo, **Café Dada** is another artsy place that can be crowded or deserted, according to the caffeine cycle.

Performing Arts Guanajuato has three fine theaters, the **Teatro Juárez**, **Teatro Principal** and **Teatro Cervantes**, none far from the Jardín de la Unión. Check their posters to see what's on. International films are shown in several locations, including the Teatro Principal, Teatro Cervantes and Museo y Casa de Diego Rivera.

The Viva la Magia program runs every weekend from March to September, with Guanajuato's theaters hosting a variety of music, dance and literary events on Thursday, Friday and Saturday evenings. The tourist office has details of what's on each week.

Getting There & Away

Air Guanajuato is served by Bajío international airport (BJX), which is about 40km from Guanajuato, halfway between Léon and Silao. See the León section for specific flight information.

Bus Guanajuato's Central de Autobuses is on the southwest outskirts of town. It has a post office, telephone caseta, restaurant and luggage checkroom. Deluxe and 1st-class bus tickets can be bought in town at Viajes Frausto, Obregón 10. Daily departures include:

Dolores Hidalgo – 54km, 1 hour; 2nd-class Flecha Amarilla every 20 minutes 6 am to 10.30 pm (US$3)

Guadalajara – 300km, 4 hours; 4 deluxe ETN (US$24), 6 1st-class Primera Plus (US$18), 12 2nd-class Flecha Amarilla (US$15.50)

León – 50km, 1 hour; 4 deluxe ETN (US$3.25), 7 1st-class Primera Plus (US$3), 2nd-class Flecha Amarilla or Flecha de Oro every 10 minutes, 5.30 am to 11.30 pm (US$2.25)

Mexico City (Terminal Norte) – 380km, 4½ hours; 8 deluxe ETN (US$27), 10 1st-class Primera Plus (US$22), 7 1st-class Futura and Ómnibus de México (US$20)

San Luis Potosí – 225km, 4 hours; 1 1st-class Ómnibus de México (US$12.50), 4 2nd-class Flecha Amarilla (US$11)

San Miguel de Allende – 82km, 1½ hours; 5 1st-class Primera Plus (US$6), 9 2nd-class Flecha Amarilla (US$4.50)

There are also frequent 2nd-class Flecha Amarilla buses to Celaya and Morelia, plus four to Querétaro and Aguascalientes. For Morelia, it's quicker to take a deluxe bus with ETN to Irapuato (7 daily, US$2.75) and change there.

Getting Around

To/From the Airport For transport to Bajío international airport, call Manuel López (☎ 732-06-74), who charges US$15 for one or two people, US$20 for three or four. Alternatively, take a León-bound bus and ask to be dropped at the airport.

To/From the Bus Station 'Central de Autobuses' buses run frequently between the bus station and city center up to midnight. From the center, you can catch them heading west on Juárez, or on the north side of the basilica. A taxi costs US$2.50.

Bus & Taxi City buses (US$0.20) run from around 5 am to 10 pm. The tourist office is very helpful with bus information. Taxis are plentiful in the center, and charge about US$1.50 for short trips around town.

CRISTO REY

Cristo Rey (Christ the King) is a 20m bronze statue of Jesus erected in 1950 on the summit of the Cerro de Cubilete about 15km west of Guanajuato, said to be the exact geographical center of Mexico. For religious Mexicans there is a significance in having Jesus at the heart of their country, and the statue is a popular attraction for Mexicans visiting Guanajuato.

Tour companies offer 3½-hour trips to the statue (see Organized Tours above), but you can go on your own for only US$1 each way by an Autobuses Vasallo de Cristo bus from the bus station. They depart daily at 6, 7, 9, 10 and 11 am, 12.30, 2, 4 and 6 pm, with additional buses on Saturday, Sunday and holidays. From the bus station it is possible to see the statue up on the hill in the distance.

LEÓN

● **pop 941,600** ● **elev 1854m** ☎ **4**

The industrial city of León, 56km west of Guanajuato, is a big bus interchange point and a likable enough place if you need to stay a few hours or overnight. It's famous for its shoes, saddles and other leather goods; other products include steel, textiles and soap.

In January/February, the Guanajuato State Fair attracts over 5 million visitors with agricultural displays, food and craft stalls, music, dancing, fairground rides, bullfights and cockfights. Some 300 or so shoemakers display their wares in the Centro de Exposiciones (☎ 771-25-00).

Orientation & Information

The heart of the city is the wide main Plaza de la Constitución (also called Plaza Principal), a pleasant pedestrian space with the Palacio Municipal on its west side. The adjoining plaza to the north and several nearby streets are also traffic-free. A board in the Plaza de la Constitución shows a big map of the city center, and an information booth nearby is staffed sporadically. You could also try calling the state tourism department

(☎ 771-17-15, 800-711-10-94) or asking in the Palacio Municipal.

Things to See & Do

Walking around the historic heart of the city is the main attraction – look out for fine buildings like the **Casa de Cultura**, on the smaller, northern plaza. The big, twin-towered, baroque **Catedral Basílica** is a block northeast of the Casa de Cultura on the corner of Obregón and Hidalgo. On Aldama, a block east of the main plaza, the **Teatro Doblado** is a neoclassical 1869 building that still stages concerts, dance and drama. The **Museo de la Ciudad** shows work by local artists.

Take a look at some of the dozens of shoe shops around the center, or the main leather district on Hilario Medina out near the bus station. Plaza del Zapato and Plaza Piel, just south of the bus station, are shopping malls devoted entirely to footwear and leather goods. Ordinary looking shops on Calle La Luz and Hilario Medina can have extraordinary leather bargains.

Places to Stay & Eat

There are many economical hotels near the bus station on Calle La Luz (walk to the right from the station's main exit – La Luz is the first cross-street). In the center, **Hotel Fundadores** (☎ 716-17-27, Ortiz de Domínguez 220), 1½ blocks west of the Plaza de la Constitución, has singles/doubles for US$11/12, or US$2 more with TV. Multistory **Hotel Rex** (☎ 714-24-15, 5 de Febrero 104), one block south and half a block east of the Plaza de la Constitución, has good, sizable rooms at US$20/27, and nicer renovated rooms at US$29/35.

Howard Johnson Hotel Condesa (☎ 713-11-20, Portal Bravo 14) on the east side of the Plaza de la Constitución, offers very comfortable rooms at US$49, and a busy restaurant with outdoor tables – light meals cost US$2.50 to US$6. **Fiesta Americana** (☎ 713-60-40) is the most expensive of the several top-end hotels on Boulevard López Mateos, which runs east of the center and becomes Hwy 45 to the airport. Room rates start at US$110.

Eateries near the center include **Restaurant Cadillac**, where the hours are long, the service is friendly, and the menu is filled with inexpensive and tasty American and Mexican favorites.

For something different, try the **Panteón Taurino** (☎ 713-49-69, Calzado de los Héroes 408), a restaurant/bar/museum where you eat off the gravestones of ex-bullfighters.

Getting There & Away

Air Bajío international airport (often inaccurately called León airport) is about 12km southeast on the Mexico City road. Aerolitoral, Aeroméxico, American, Continental, Mexicana and TAESA provide regular direct connections to Mexico City, Guadalajara, Monterrey, Tijuana, Puerto Vallarta, Zacatecas, Acapulco, Ixtapa, Puebla, Morelia, Cancún, New York, Chicago, Los Angeles, Oakland, Atlanta, San Antonio, Dallas and Houston. Foreign travel agents may not be familiar with this airport – ask for flights to code BJX.

Bus The Central de Autobuses, on Boulevard Hilario Medina, just north of Boulevard López Mateos east of the city center, has a luggage checkroom, money exchange office, cafeteria and pay phones. Regular services go to/from just about everywhere in northern and western Mexico. Over 60 deluxe buses a day go to Mexico City (five hours, US$23) and 29 to Guadalajara (three hours, US$15.50). To Guanajuato, 2nd-class Flecha Amarilla buses run every 10 minutes from 5 am to 10 pm (one hour, US$2.20), and there are regular 1st-class Primera Plus and Servicios Coordinados buses (US$3). Primera Plus runs 1st-class buses to San Miguel de Allende at 2, 4.15 and 6.10 pm (2¼ hours, US$9.50).

Getting Around

Taxis from the city center to the airport cost about US$11.

From the bus station, turn left and walk 150m to López Mateos, where 'Centro' buses go west to the city center (US$0.20). To return to the bus station, catch a 'Central' bus east along López Mateos, two blocks north of the Plaza Principal. A taxi between the center and the bus station costs around US$2.50.

DOLORES HIDALGO
• pop 45,900 • elev 1955m ☎ 4

This is where the Mexican independence movement began in earnest. At 5 am on September 16, 1810, Miguel Hidalgo, the parish priest, rang the bells to summon people to church earlier than usual and issued the Grito de Dolores, whose precise words have been lost to history but which boiled down to 'Long live Our Lady of Guadalupe! Death to bad government and the gachupines!' ('Gachupín' was a derisive term for one of the Spanish-born overlords who ruled Mexico.)

Hidalgo, Ignacio Allende and other conspirators had been alerted to the discovery of their plans for an uprising in Querétaro, so they decided to launch their rebellion immediately from Dolores. After the Grito they went to the lavish Spanish house on the plaza, today the Casa de Visitas, and captured the local representative of the Spanish viceroy and the Spanish tax collector. They freed the prisoners from the town jail and set

off for San Miguel at the head of a growing band of criollos, *mestizos* and *indígenas*.

Today Hidalgo is Mexico's most revered hero, rivaled only by Benito Juárez in the number of streets, plazas and statues dedicated to him throughout the country. Dolores was renamed in his honor in 1824. Visiting Dolores Hidalgo has acquired pilgrimage status for Mexicans, though it's not a very attractive town. If you're interested in the country's history, it's worth a day trip from Guanajuato or San Miguel de Allende, or a stop between them.

Orientation
Everything of interest is within a couple of blocks of the Plaza Principal, which is two or three blocks north of the bus stations.

Information
Tourist Offices The Delegación de Turismo (☎ 182-11-64) is on the north side of the Plaza Principal in the Presidencia Municipal building. The staff can answer, in Spanish, any questions about the town. The office is open 10 am to 3 pm and 5 to 7 pm Monday to Friday, 10 am to 6 pm weekends, but these hours are not totally reliable.

DOLORES HIDALGO

PLACES TO STAY
1 Posada Dolores
5 Hotel El Caudillo
10 Posada Cocomacán
19 Hotel Posada Las Campanas

PLACES TO EAT
7 Fruti y Yoghurt
8 Restaurant Plaza
11 El Patio Restaurant Bar & Grille
12 Restaurant El Delfin

OTHER
2 Museo de la Independencia Nacional
3 Bancomer
4 Presidencia Municipal, Tourist Office
6 Casa de Visitas
9 Casa de Cambio
13 Herradura de Plata Bus Station
14 Museo Casa de Hidalgo
15 Templo de la Tercera Orden
16 Casa de Cambio
17 Post Office, Telecomm
18 Parroquia de la Asunción
20 Primera Plus, Flecha Amarilla
    Bus Station

To San Felipe
To San Miguel de Allende, San Luis de la Paz
Nayarit
Oaxaca
San Luis Potosí
Querétaro
Nuevo León
Chihuahua
Coahuila
Zacatecas
Parroquia de Nuestra Señora de Dolores
Plaza
Market
Plaza Principal
Yucatán
Michoacán
To Guanajuato
Morelos
Hidalgo
Jalisco
Guanajuato
Handicraft Stalls
Veracruz
Guerrero
Sonora
Tamaulipas
Jardín de los Compositores
Chiapas
Puebla
Tabasco
Río Batan

0   100   200 m
0   100   200 yards

Miguel Hidalgo

The balding head of the visionary priest Father Miguel Hidalgo y Costilla is familiar to anyone who's looked at Mexican murals or statues. He was, it seems, a genuine rebel idealist, who had already sacrificed his own career at least once before that fateful day in 1810. And he launched the independence movement clearly aware of the risks to his own life.

Born on May 8, 1753, son of a criollo hacienda manager in Guanajuato, he studied at the Colegio de San Nicolás in Valladolid (now Morelia), earned a bachelor's degree and, in 1778, was ordained a priest. He returned to teach at his old college and eventually became rector. But he was no orthodox cleric: Hidalgo questioned the virgin birth and the infallibility of the pope, read banned books, gambled, danced and had a mistress.

In 1800 he was brought before the Inquisition. Nothing was proved, but a few years later in 1804 he found himself transferred as priest to the hick town of Dolores.

Hidalgo's years in Dolores show that he was interested not only in the religious welfare of the local people but also in their economic and cultural welfare. Somewhat in the tradition of Don Vasco de Quiroga of Michoacán, founder of the Colegio de San Nicolás where Hidalgo had studied, he started new industries in the town. Silk was cultivated, olive groves planted and vineyards established, all in defiance of the Spanish colonial authorities. Earthenware building products such as bricks and roof tiles were the foundation of the ceramics industry which today produces fine glazed tiles and pots.

When Hidalgo met Ignacio Allende from San Miguel, he came to share criollo discontent with the Spanish stranglehold on Mexico. His standing among the mestizos and Indians of his parish was vital in broadening the base of the rebellion that followed.

On October 13, 1810, shortly after his Grito de Independencia, Hidalgo was formally excommunicated for 'heresy, apostasy and sedition.' He answered by proclaiming that he never would have been excommunicated had it not been for his call for the independence of Mexico and furthermore stated that the Spanish were not truly Catholic in any religious sense of the word, but only for political purposes, specifically to rape, pillage and exploit Mexico. A few days later, on October 19, Hidalgo dictated his first edict calling for the abolition of slavery in Mexico.

Hidalgo led his growing forces from Dolores to San Miguel, Celaya and Guanajuato, north to Zacatecas, south almost to Mexico City, and west to Guadalajara. But then, pushed northward, their numbers dwindled and on July 30, 1811, having been captured by the Spanish, Hidalgo was shot by firing squad in Chihuahua. His head was returned to the city of Guanajuato, where his army had won its first major victory. It hung in a cage for 10 years on an outer corner of the Alhóndiga de Granaditas, along with the heads of independence leaders Allende, Aldama and Jiménez. Rather than intimidating the people, this lurid display kept the memory, the goal and the example of the heroic martyrs fresh in everyone's mind. After independence the cages were removed, and the skulls of the heroes are now in the Monumento a la Independencia in Mexico City.

ROBERT REID

Mural at Guanajuato's Alhóndiga de Granaditas

Money Cash and traveler's checks can be changed at several banks around the Plaza Principal, 9 am to 5 pm weekdays, Saturday from 10 am to 1 pm – they all have ATMs. There are some casas de cambio too.

Post & Communications The post office and Telecomm (with fax service) are in the same building at Puebla 22 on the corner of Veracruz. Pay phones are in the post office, outside the tourist office and at the Flecha Amarilla bus station.

Plaza Principal & Around

The **Parroquia de Nuestra Señora de Dolores**, the church where Hidalgo issued the Grito, is on the north side of the plaza. It has a fine 18th-century Churrigueresque façade; inside, it's fairly plain. Some say that Hidalgo uttered his famous words from the pulpit, others that he spoke at the church door to the people gathered outside.

To the left of the church is the **Presidencia Municipal**, which has two colorful murals on the theme of independence. The plaza contains a **statue of Hidalgo** (in Roman garb, on top of a tall column), and a tree that, according to a plaque beneath it, was a sapling of the tree of the Noche Triste (Sad Night), under which Cortés is said to have wept when his men were driven out of Tenochtitlán in 1520.

The **Casa de Visitas** on the west side of the plaza was the residence of Don Nicolás Fernández del Rincón and Don Ignacio Díaz de la Cortina, the two representatives of Spanish rule in Dolores. On September 16, 1810, they became the first two prisoners of the independence movement. Today, this is where Mexican presidents and other dignitaries stay when they come to Dolores for ceremonies. It's open to visitors 9.30 am to 2 pm and 4 to 6 pm daily (free).

Museo de la Independencia Nacional

Half a block west of the Plaza Principal at Zacatecas 6, this museum has few relics but plenty of information on the independence movement and its background. It charts the appalling decline in Nueva España's indige-nous population between 1519 (an estimated 25 million) and 1605 (1 million). It identifies 23 indigenous rebellions before 1800 as well as several criollo conspiracies in the years leading up to 1810. There are vivid paintings, quotations and some details on the heroic last 10 months of Hidalgo's life. The museum is open 10 am to 6 pm Tuesday to Saturday, 10 am to 5 pm Sunday (US$2.25).

Museo Casa de Hidalgo

This is the house where Hidalgo lived and where he, Ignacio Allende and Juan de Aldama decided in the early hours of September 16, 1810, to launch the uprising. It is something of a national shrine. One large room is devoted to a big collection of memorials, wreaths and homages to Hidalgo. Other rooms contain replicas of Hidalgo's furniture and documents of the independence movement, including the order for Hidalgo's excommunication.

The house is on Hidalgo at Morelos, one block south of the Plaza Principal. It's open 10 am to 6 pm Tuesday to Saturday (US$2.25), 10 am to 5 pm Sunday (free).

Special Events

Dolores is the scene of major celebrations on the Día de la Independencia, September 16. (Festivities begin September 15.) The Mexican president often officiates.

Places to Stay

Most visitors stay here just long enough to see the church and museums and eat an ice cream on the plaza. Accommodations can fill up during special events and holiday weekends; at other times you may get a discount on these prices.

The cheapest is *Posada Dolores* (☎ 182-06-42, *Yucatán 8*), one block west of the Plaza Principal. It's a basic, friendly casa de huéspedes, but the very small singles/ doubles are overpriced at US$7/14 with shared bath, US$11/17 with private bath. *Hotel El Caudillo* (☎ 182-01-98, 182-04-65, *Querétaro 8*), opposite the right side of the church, has 32 carpeted rooms that are clean enough, but small and stuffy, for US$17.50/25.

On the east side of the Plaza Principal, **Posada Cocomacán** (☎ 182-00-18) has 50 rooms, all with private bath, good ventilation and parquet floors. They cost US$16.50/25.

The most pleasant place is **Hotel Posada Las Campanas** (☎ 182-04-27, fax 182-24-23, Guerrero 15), 2½ blocks east of the Plaza Principal. It has 40 well-kept rooms, all with private bath, carpet, phone and cable TV, for US$28/32.

Places to Eat

Dolores is famous not only for its historical attractions but also for its ice cream. On the southwest corner of the Plaza Principal you can get cones in a variety of unusual flavors including *mole, chicharrón,* avocado, maize, cheese, honey, shrimp, whiskey, tequila and about 20 tropical fruit flavors. Also look for the delicious, locally made *dulces,* at street stalls and in the markets.

You can grab a torta or a snack at many small eateries on and near the plaza, including **Fruti y Yoghurt** on Hidalgo a little to the southwest. On the south side of the plaza, **Restaurant Plaza** is a good family restaurant with breakfasts, enchiladas and other *antojitos* at US$3 to US$5. The comida corrida and other meals start at US$4.50.

In the same price range, the restaurant/bar at the **Hotel El Caudillo** is cool and pleasant. À la carte breakfasts are inexpensive and there's a good range of antojitos and main dishes. It stays open after 11 pm, when most other eateries have closed, and it makes good coffee. **Posada Cocomacán** has a comida for US$4. Almost next door, **El Patio Restaurant Bar & Grille** has a similar menu – their Sunday buffet comida costs US$5.

For surprisingly good seafood, try **Restaurant El Delfín** at Veracruz 2, a pleasant family place one block east of the Plaza Principal. It's open from 9 am to 7 pm daily. Fare includes fish dishes for around US$4, seafood soup (US$3) and large shrimp servings (US$6.50).

Shopping

Ceramics, especially Talavera ware (including tiles), have been the special handicraft of Dolores ever since Padre Hidalgo founded the town's first ceramics workshop in the early 19th century. A number of shops sell these and other craft items. If you've got wheels, stop by the ceramics workshops along the approach roads to Dolores. Also worth a look are the crafts stall on Guerrero and the central market, at Yucatán and Michoacán. An increasing number of workshops make 'antique,' colonial-style furniture.

Getting There & Away

Nearly all buses to/from Dolores are 2nd class. The station for Flecha Amarilla and Primera Plus is on Hidalgo, 2½ blocks south of the Plaza Principal. Herradura de Plata and Pegasso Plus are in a small station on Chiapas at Yucatán. Daily departures include:

Guanajuato – 54km, 1 hour; 2nd-class Flecha Amarilla every 20 minutes, 5 am to 9 pm (US$3)

Mexico City (Terminal Norte) – 325km, 5 hours; 1st-class Pegasso Plus at noon (US$17), 2nd-class Herradura de Plata or Flecha Amarilla every 40 minutes, 5 am to 7 pm (US$14)

San Miguel de Allende – 43km, 45 minutes; 2nd-class Flecha Amarilla or Herradura de Plata every 30 minutes, 5 am to 8.40 pm (US$2)

There are also regular 2nd-class connections to Querétaro, León and San Luis Potosí.

SAN MIGUEL DE ALLENDE
• pop 53,000 • elev 1840m ☎ 4

A charming colonial town in a beautiful setting, San Miguel is well known for its large expatriate community. The influx started in the 1940s, when artists, writers and other creative types came to San Miguel's Escuela de Bellas Artes, and US citizens came to study at the Instituto Allende. Now several thousand foreigners have retired here permanently, many others come for the winter months, and hundreds more come for crash courses in Spanish. Inevitably, the town has lost much of its bohemian character, real estate offices outnumber art galleries, and English is widely spoken.

For all the foreign influence (partly because of it), San Miguel has preserved its lovely old buildings and quaint cobbled streets, often with unexpected vistas over the

SAN MIGUEL DE ALLENDE

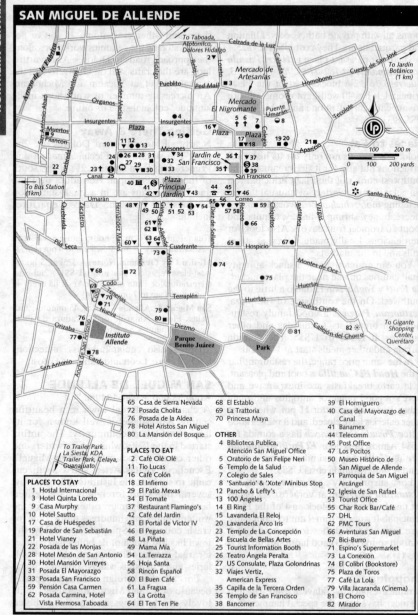

To Taboada,
Atotonilco,
Dolores Hidalgo
Calzada de la Luz

To Jardín
Botánico
(1 km)

Mercado de
Artesanías

Mercado
El Nigromante

Plaza

Jardín de
San Francisco

Plaza
Principal
(Jardín)

To Bus Station
(1km)

Santo Domingo

To Trailer Park
La Siesta, KDA
Trailer Park, Celaya,
Guanajuato

Instituto
Allende

Parque
Benito Juárez

Park

To Gigante
Shopping
Center,
Querétaro

0   100   200 m
0   100   200 yards

PLACES TO STAY
1 Hostal Internacional
3 Hotel Quinta Loreto
9 Casa Murphy
10 Hotel Sautto
17 Casa de Huéspedes
19 Parador de San Sebastián
21 Hotel Vianey
22 Posada de las Monjas
28 Hotel Mesón de San Antonio
30 Hotel Mansión Virreyes
31 Posada El Mayorazgo
33 Posada San Francisco
59 Pensión Casa Carmen
62 Posada Carmina, Hotel
   Vista Hermosa Taboada

65 Casa de Sierra Nevada
72 Posada Cholita
76 Posada de la Aldea
78 Hotel Aristos San Miguel
80 La Mansión del Bosque

PLACES TO EAT
2 Café Olé Olé
11 Tío Lucas
16 Café Colón
18 El Infierno
29 El Patio Mexas
34 El Tomate
37 Restaurant Flamingo's
42 Café del Jardín
43 El Portal de Victor IV
46 El Pegaso
48 La Piñata
54 La Terrazza
58 Hoja Santa
58 Rincón Español
60 El Buen Café
61 La Fragua
63 La Grotta
64 El Ten Ten Pie

68 El Establo
69 La Trattoria
70 Princesa Maya

OTHER
4 Biblioteca Publica,
  Atención San Miguel Office
5 Oratorio de San Felipe Neri
6 Templo de la Salud
7 Colegio de Sales
8 'Santuario' & 'Xote' Minibus Stop
12 Pancho & Lefty's
13 100 Ángeles
14 El Ring
15 Lavandería El Reloj
20 Lavandería Arco Iris
23 Templo de La Concepción
24 Escuela de Bellas Artes
26 Tourist Information Booth
27 US Consulate, Plaza Golondrinas
32 Viajes Vertiz,
   American Express
35 Capilla de la Tercera Orden
36 Templo de San Francisco
38 Bancomer

39 El Hormiguero
40 Casa del Mayorazgo de
   Canal
41 Banamex
44 Telecomm
45 Post Office
47 Los Pocitos
50 Museo Histórico de
   San Miguel de Allende
51 Parroquia de San Miguel
   Arcángel
52 Iglesia de San Rafael
53 Tourist Office
55 Char Rock Bar/Café
57 DHL
62 PMC Tours
66 Aventuras San Miguel
67 Bici-Burro
71 Espino's Supermarket
73 La Conexión
74 El Colibri (Bookstore)
75 Plaza de Toros
77 Café La Lola
79 Villa Jacaranda (Cinema)
81 El Chorro
82 Mirador

plains and distant hills. To protect its charm, the Mexican government has declared the entire town a national monument. The San Miguel locals seem especially fond of festivals, fireworks and parades that make the place even more colorful. It's easy for visitors to feel at home here, the restaurants and bars are many and varied, and every other facility is available, though low-budget lodging can be in short supply.

San Miguel has two peak periods for visitors. The main one is from mid-December to the end of March, when many *norteños* come to escape the northern winter, and there's another influx from June to August. San Miguel has a very agreeable climate and superbly clear light, which is another reason it attracts artists. It's cool and clear in winter; warm and clear in summer, with occasional thunderstorms and heavy rain.

History

The town, so the story goes, owes its founding to a few hot dogs. These hounds were dearly loved by a courageous barefoot Franciscan friar, Fray Juan de San Miguel, who started a mission in 1542 near an often-dry river 5km from the present town. One day the dogs wandered off from the mission, to be found later reclining at the spring called El Chorro in the south of the present town. This site was so much better that the mission was moved.

San Miguel was then the most northern Spanish settlement in central Mexico. Tarascan and Tlaxcalan allies of the Spanish were brought to help pacify the local Otomí and Chichimecs. San Miguel barely survived the fierce Chichimec resistance, and in 1555 a Spanish garrison was established there to protect the new road from Mexico City to the silver center of Zacatecas. Then Spanish ranchers and crop growers settled in the area, and San Miguel grew into a thriving commercial center known for its textiles, knives and horse tackle. It also became home to some of the wealthy Guanajuato silver barons.

San Miguel's favorite son, Ignacio Allende, was born here in 1779. He became a fervent believer in the need for Mexican independence, and a leader of a Querétaro-based conspiracy that set December 8, 1810, as the date for an armed uprising. When the plan was discovered by the authorities in Querétaro on September 13, a messenger rushed to San Miguel and gave the news to Juan de Aldama, another conspirator. Aldama sped north to Dolores where, in the early hours of September 16, he found Allende at the house of the priest Miguel Hidalgo, also one of the coterie.

A few hours later Hidalgo proclaimed rebellion from his church. By the same evening, San Miguel was in rebel hands. Its local regiment had joined forces with the band of insurgents arriving from Dolores. San Miguel's Spanish population was locked up and Allende was only partly able to restrain the rebels from looting the town. After initial successes, Allende, Hidalgo and other rebel leaders were captured in 1811 in Chihuahua. Allende was executed almost immediately, Hidalgo four months later, and when Mexico finally achieved independence in 1821 they were recognized as martyrs to the new nation. In 1826 the town was renamed San Miguel de Allende in honor of the local hero.

The Escuela de Bellas Artes was founded in 1938 and the town started to take on its current character when David Alfaro Siqueiros began mural-painting courses that attracted artists of every persuasion from Mexico and the USA. The Instituto Allende opened in 1951, also attracting foreign students. Many were Americans seeking to escape the conformity of post-WWII USA – Neal Cassady, hero of Jack Kerouac's *On the Road*, died here in February 1968, allegedly walking on the railroad tracks toward Celaya, but another version is that he OD'd at a house in town.

Orientation

The Plaza Principal, called the Jardín, is the focal point of the town. The Gothic-like spires of the parroquia on the south side of the plaza can be seen from far and wide. The town slopes up from west to east.

The central area is small with a straightforward layout, and most places of interest are within easy walking distance of the Jardín. Most streets change names at the Jardín. Canal/San Francisco, on its north side, and Umarán/Correo, on the south side, are the main streets of the central area. The bus station is a little over 1km west of the Jardín on Canal.

Information

Tourist Offices The tourist office (☎ 152-17-47) is on the southeast corner of the Jardín, in a glassed-in office by the Iglesia de San Rafael. They have maps of the town and printed brochures in English and Spanish, and can answer questions in both languages. Hours are 10 am to 5 pm Monday to Friday, 10 am to 2 pm Saturday and Sunday.

The Asociación de Guías de Turistas (☎ 154-51-31) has a tourist information booth on the corner of Canal and Hernández Macías with some printed information; the staff answer questions and sell tours with the local guide association (open 10 am to 5 pm daily).

Consulates The US Consulate (☎ 152-23-57; emergency ☎ 152-00-68 or 152-06-53) is in Plaza Golondrinas near the corner of Canal and Hernández Macías. Hours are 9 am to 1 pm Monday and Friday – other times by appointment.

Money There are several banks with ATMs on and near San Francisco in the couple of blocks east of the Jardín, and Banamex on the west side of the Jardín. Most are open 9 am to 5 pm Monday to Friday (some change traveler's checks only until 2 pm), 10 am to 2 pm Saturday.

Casas de cambio have only slightly less favorable rates than the banks, and are usually less crowded and quicker. Deserve Casa de Moneda, in the Posada San Francisco on the Jardín, is open 9 am to 7 pm Monday to Friday, 9 am to 5 pm Saturday. Deal has branches at Correo 15, Juárez 27 and San Francisco 4, open 9 am to 6 pm Monday to Friday, 9 am to 2 pm Saturday.

American Express (☎ 152-18-56) is at Viajes Vertiz, Hidalgo 1A, half a block north of the Jardín. It's open 9 am to 2 pm and 4 to

6.30 pm Monday to Friday, 10 am to 2 pm Saturday.

Post & Communications The post office is two blocks east of the Jardín, on the corner of Correo and Corregidora, open 8 am to 6 pm Monday to Friday, 9 am to 1 pm Saturday. The Mexpost express mail office is next door on Correo. There's a DHL office opposite, plus FedEx and UPS nearby.

Pay phones are plentiful in the center, and there's a caseta in the bus station. Telecomm, at Correo 16, two doors from the post office, has fax service.

La Conexión (☎ 152-16-87), Aldama 1, is one of several places offering mailboxes, express mail service to the US and 24-hour fax, email and phone message services.

Internet access is generally expensive in San Miguel. The computer center upstairs at the Biblioteca Pública, Insurgentes 25, charges about US$6.50 per hour with a minimum US$1.25 for 10 minutes (the profit is said to subsidize computer classes for local kids). It's open 9 am to 4 pm Monday to Friday, 9 am to 2 pm Saturday (except when classes are on). El Hormiguero, Juárez 7, opposite Jardín San Francisco, is a better value at about US$5 per hour; it's open 9.30 am to 8 pm Monday to Saturday, 10 am to 2 pm Saturday. La Conexión (see above) also has Internet access for about US$6 an hour.

Travel Agencies Viajes Vertiz (☎ 152-18-56), Hidalgo 1A, sells domestic and international air tickets.

Bookstores & Libraries The Biblioteca Pública (Public Library) at Insurgentes 25 also functions as an educational and cultural center with an emphasis on children's activities. It has an excellent collection of books in English and Spanish on Mexico – art, crafts, architecture, history, literature and more. There are English and Spanish sections for general reference books, novels and magazines. Used books in English are for sale at cheap prices. Hours are 10 am to 2 pm and 4 to 7 pm Monday to Friday, 10 am to 2 pm Saturday. The library has a computer center where you can rent PCs and use the Internet (see Post & Communications), a good restaurant and a small souvenir shop.

El Colibrí bookstore, Diez de Sollano 30, 1½ blocks south of the Jardín, has paperbacks, art books and magazines in English and Spanish, plus a few in French and German.

Media The expatriate community puts out a weekly English-language newspaper, *Atención San Miguel* (US$0.60); its office is in the Biblioteca Pública. It's full of local news and events, plus ads for rooms, apartments or houses to sell, rent or exchange, and information about classes in yoga, Spanish, art or dance. You can buy it at the Biblioteca Pública and elsewhere. The same sorts of things are advertised on notice boards in the Biblioteca Pública, language schools and other gringo hangouts like Patio Mexas restaurant, at Canal 15. The Escuela de Bellas Artes has a notice board featuring local cultural events and activities.

A San Miguel home page is at http://unisono.net.mx/sanmiguel/index.html.

Laundry Laundromats charge around US$3.25 to wash and dry a 4kg load. Two good ones are Arco Iris, in an arcade off Mesones, and Lavandería El Reloj, Reloj 34A, both open Monday through Saturday.

La Parroquia de San Miguel Arcángel

The pink 'cotton candy' pointed towers of the parish church dominate the Jardín. These strange soaring pinnacles were designed by indigenous stonemason Zeferino Gutiérrez in the late 19th century. He reputedly based the design on a postcard of a Belgian church, and instructed builders by scratching plans in the sand with a stick. Most of the rest of the church dates from the late 17th century. The crypt contains the remains of a 19th-century Mexican president, Anastasio Bustamante. In the chapel to the left of the main altar is the much-revered image of the Cristo de la Conquista (Christ of the Conquest), made in Pátzcuaro from cornstalks and orchid bulbs, probably in the 16th century. Irish visitors will be pleased to find a statue of St Patrick.

The church to the left of the parroquia, Iglesia San Rafael, was founded in 1742 and has undergone Gothic-type alterations.

Museo Histórico de San Miguel de Allende

Near the parroquia on Cuna de Allende stands the house where Ignacio Allende was born, now a museum. Exhibits relate the interesting history of the San Miguel area, with special exhibits on Allende and the independence movement. An inscription in Latin on the façade says '*Hic natus ubique notus,*', which means 'Here born, everywhere known.' Another plaque points out that the more famous independence hero, Miguel Hidalgo, only joined the movement after being invited by Allende.

The museum is open 10 am to 4 pm Tuesday to Sunday (US$2.25).

Casa del Mayorazgo de Canal

This house of the Canal family is one of the most imposing of San Miguel's old residences. The entrance (study the beautiful carved wooden doors) is at Canal 4, and it stretches above the arcade on the west side of the Jardín. It's a neoclassical structure with some late baroque touches. It now houses Banamex offices.

Templo de San Francisco

This church on the north side of the small Jardín de San Francisco, at San Francisco and Juárez, has an elaborate late-18th-century Churrigueresque façade. An image of St Francis of Assisi is at the top.

Capilla de la Tercera Orden

This chapel on the west side of the same garden was built in the early 18th century and, like the San Francisco church, was part of a Franciscan monastery complex. The main façade shows San Francisco (St Francis) and symbols of the Franciscan order.

Oratorio de San Felipe Neri

This multitowered and domed church, built in the early 18th century, stands near the east end of Insurgentes, on the Plaza Cívica.

The pale pink main façade is baroque with an indigenous influence. A passage to the right of this façade leads to the east wall, where a doorway holds the image of Nuestra Señora de la Soledad (Our Lady of Solitude). You can see into the cloister from this side of the church.

Inside the church are 33 oil paintings showing scenes from the life of San Felipe Neri, the 16th-century Florentine who founded the Oratorio Catholic order. In the east transept is a painting of the Virgin of Guadalupe by Miguel Cabrera. In the west transept is a lavishly decorated chapel, the Santa Casa de Loreto, built in 1735. It's a replica of a chapel in Loreto, Italy, legendary home of the Virgin Mary. If the chapel doors are open you can see tiles from Puebla, Valencia and China on the floor and walls, gilded cloth hangings and the tombs of chapel founder Conde Manuel de la Canal and his wife María de Hervas de Flores. Behind the altar, the camarín has six elaborately gilded baroque altars. In one is a reclining wax figure of San Columbano; it contains the saint's bones.

Iglesia de La Salud

This church, with a blue and yellow tiled dome and a big shell carved above its entrance, is just east of San Felipe Neri. The façade is early Churrigueresque. The church's paintings include one of San Javier by Miguel Cabrera.

Colegio de Sales

This was once a college, founded in the mid-18th century by the San Felipe Neri order. It's next door to the Iglesia de La Salud, which was once part of the same college. Many of the 1810 revolutionaries were educated here. The local Spaniards were locked up here when the rebels took San Miguel.

Templo de La Concepción

A couple of blocks west of the Jardín down Canal is the splendid church of La Concepción, with a fine altar and several magnificent old oil paintings. Painted on the interior doorway are a number of wise sayings to give pause to those entering the sanctuary. The church was begun in the mid-18th century; its dome, added in the late 19th century by the versatile Zeferino Gutiérrez, was possibly inspired by pictures of Les Invalides in Paris.

Escuela de Bellas Artes

This educational and cultural center (☎ 152-02-89), at Hernández Macías 75 near Canal, is housed in the beautiful former monastery of La Concepción church. It was converted into the Escuela de Bellas Artes (School of Fine Arts) in 1938. It's officially named the Centro Cultural Ignacio Ramírez, after a leading 19th-century liberal thinker who lived in San Miguel. His nickname was El Nigromante (The Sorcerer).

One room in the cloister is devoted to an unfinished mural by Siqueiros, done in 1948 as part of a course in mural painting for US war veterans. Its subject – though you wouldn't guess it – is the life and work of Ignacio Allende. (There is a light switch to the right of the door just before you enter!)

Instituto Allende

This large building with several patios and an old chapel at Ancha de San Antonio 4 was built in 1736 as the home of the Conde Manuel de la Canal. Later it was used as a Carmelite convent, eventually becoming an art and language school in 1951. Above the entrance is a carving of the Virgin of Loreto, patroness of the Canal family.

Mirador & Parque Juárez

One of the best views over the town and surrounding country is from the *mirador* (overlook) on Calle Pedro Vargas, also known as the Salida a Querétaro, in the southeast of town. If you take Callejón del Chorro, the track leading directly downhill from here, and turn left at the bottom, you reach El Chorro, the spring where the town was founded. Today it gushes out of a fountain built in 1960 and there are still public washing tubs here. A path called Paseo del Chorro zigzags down the hill to the shady Parque Benito Juárez.

Botanical Gardens

The large Jardín Botánico El Charco del Ingenio, devoted mainly to cacti and other native plants of this semiarid area, is on the hilltop about 1.5km northeast of the town center. It's a lovely place for a walk – particularly in the early morning or late afternoon – though women alone should steer clear of its more secluded parts. Pathways range along the slope above a reservoir and a deep canyon. It's open from sunrise to sunset (US$1). The garden is managed by CANTE, a nonprofit organization that promotes conservation.

The direct approach to the garden is to walk uphill from the Mercado El Nigromante along Homobono and Cuesta de San José, then fork left up Montitlan past the Balcones housing development. Keep walking another few minutes along the track at the top – about 100m after the track levels out, look for a small street sign on the left saying 'Paloma.' If the gate here is shut, follow the fence east to the other entrance.

Alternatively, a 2km vehicle track leads north from the Gigante shopping center, which is 2.5km east of the center on the Querétaro road. Gigante can be reached on 'Gigante' buses from the bus stop on the east side of Jardín de San Francisco. A taxi to the gardens from the center costs about US$1.60.

CANTE also administers **Los Pocitos**, an orchid garden with 2000 plants covering 230 species, at Santo Domingo 38. It's at its best in February, March and April.

Galleries

Galería San Miguel on the north side of the Jardín and Galería Atenea at Cuna de Allende 15 are two of the best and most established commercial art galleries. The Escuela de Bellas Artes and Instituto Allende (see Courses) stage art exhibitions year-round. Many other galleries are advertised in *Atención San Miguel*.

Activities

Rancho La Loma (☎ 152-21-21) rents horses for US$30 per hour, and can arrange instruction and guides. Aventuras San Miguel

(☎ 152-64-06), Recreo 10, conducts morning and afternoon trail rides in the Atotonilco area, from US$30 depending on group size.

Bici-Burro (☎ 152-15-26), Hospicio No 1, conducts mountain bike tours for groups of two or more, including guide, bike, helmet and gloves. Trips include five- or six-hour excursions to Atotonilco (US$38) or Pozos (US$54, including vehicular transport). Good bikes are rented for US$22 per day.

Posada de la Aldea opens its pool to nonguests from Monday to Friday (US$2.25), but it's more enjoyable to visit the balnearios in the surrounding countryside – see the Around San Miguel section.

For a variety of adventure tours, including hiking, biking, camping and horseback riding, as well as small group trips to many destinations in central Mexico, contact Aventuras San Miguel (☎ 152-64-06) at Recreo 10. Prices start at around US$30 per person per day for groups of three or more. The office is open 9 am to 2 pm Monday to Saturday.

Courses

Several institutions offer Spanish courses, with group or private lessons, and optional classes in Mexican culture and history. There are also many courses in painting, sculpture, ceramics, music, dance and so on, at levels from enthusiastic dabbler to experienced professional. Most courses are available year-round, except for a three-week break in December. For classes in meditation, yoga, tai chi and the like, look for notices in *Atención San Miguel*.

Instituto Allende (☎ 152-01-90, fax 152-45-38), in an old mansion on Ancha de San Antonio, offers courses in fine arts, crafts and Spanish. Art and craft courses can be joined at any time and usually entail nine hours of attendance a week. The cost is US$210 a month, plus registration (US$20) and monthly insurance (US$15). Spanish courses begin about every four weeks and range from conversational (50 minutes a day, US$120 for four weeks) to total impact (six hours a day, US$465 for four weeks, maximum six students per class). Write to Instituto Allende, Box 85, San Miguel de

Allende 37700, Gto, Mexico, for details, or check www.instituto-allende.edu.mx.

The Academia Hispano Americana (☎ 152-03-49, fax 152-23-33), Mesones 4, runs courses in Spanish language and Latin American culture at US$250 for two weeks, US$400 for four weeks, US$750 for eight weeks. The cultural courses are taught in elementary Spanish. One-on-one language classes, for any period you like, are also available at US$10 an hour. The school can arrange accommodations with a Mexican family with a private room and three meals per day for US$560 per four-week session. Check http://unisono.net.mx/academia/.

Other organizations offering Spanish courses include:

Centro Mexicana de Lengua y Cultura
(☎ 152-07-63, www.infosma.com/
centromexicano), Orizaba 15 off Ancha
de San Antonio

Inter-Idiomas
(☎ 152-41-15, http://unisono.net.mx/inter/
idiomas.html), 20 de Enero Sur 42

Card Game Spanish
(☎ 152-17-58, http://unisono.net.mx/cardgame),
Pilancón 19

Universidad del Valle de Mexico
(☎ 152-60-49, fax 152-71-91, www.uvmnet.edu),
Zacateros 61.

The Escuela de Bellas Artes (☎ 152-02-89) is at Hernández Macías 75 on the corner of Canal in a beautiful ex-monastery. Courses in art, dance, crafts and music are usually given in Spanish and cost around US$100 a month; each class is nine hours a week. Registration is at the beginning of each month. Some classes are not held in July, and there are none in August.

Organized Tours

Promotion of Mexican Culture (PMC; ☎ 152-16-30, fax 152-01-21), Cuna de Allende 11, conducts two-hour historical walking tours of central San Miguel from US$10 to US$15, plus a variety of day tours by bus for US$60. Stop by for a brochure or check www.pmexc.com. The Asociación de Guías de Turistas (☎ 154-51-31), in the booth at the corner of Canal and Hernández

Macías, also offers a variety of walking and bus tours in town and the surrounding area at similar prices.

A House & Garden tour, visiting some of the lovely houses and gardens in San Miguel that are otherwise closed to the public, sets off by bus about noon every Sunday from the public library. Tickets are on sale from 11 am. Cost is around US$15 for the two-hour tour, with three different houses visited each week.

Special Events

Being so well endowed with churches and patron saints (it has six), San Miguel has a multitude of festivals every month. You'll probably learn of some by word of mouth – or the sound of fireworks – while you're there. Events include:

Blessing of the Animals – This happens in several churches, including the parroquia, on January 17.

Allende's Birthday – On January 21 various official events celebrate this occasion.

Cristo de la Conquista – This image in the parroquia is fêted on the first Friday in March, with scores of dancers in elaborate pre-Hispanic costumes and plumed headdresses in front of the parroquia.

San Patricio – March 17 sees a parade, but celebrations are more saintly than in cities with an Irish tradition.

Semana Santa – Two weekends before Easter pilgrims carry an image of the Señor de la Columna (Lord of the Column) from Atotonilco, 14km north, to the church of San Juan de Dios in San Miguel on Saturday night or Sunday morning. During Semana Santa itself, the many activities include the lavish Procesión del Santo Entierro on Good Friday and the burning or exploding of images of Judas on Easter Day.

Fiesta de la Santa Cruz – This unusual, rather solemn festival has its roots in the 16th century; sensitivity is recommended if you want to observe it. It happens on the last weekend in May at Valle del Maíz, 2km from the center of town. Oxen are dressed in lime necklaces and painted tortillas, and their yokes festooned with flowers and fruit. One beast carries two boxes of 'treasure' (bread and sugar) and is surrounded by characters in bizarre costumes on horses or donkeys. A mock battle between 'Indians' and 'Federales' follows, with a wizard appearing to heal the 'wounded' and raise the 'dead.'

Corpus Christi – This movable feast in June features dances by children in front of the parroquia.

Chamber Music Festival – The Escuela de Bellas Artes sponsors an annual festival of chamber music (*música de cámara*), in the first two weeks of August.

San Miguel Arcángel – Celebrations honoring the town's chief patron saint are held on September 29 (or on the weekend after, if the 29th is a weekday). There are cockfights, bullfights and *pamplonadas* (bull-running) in the streets , but the hub of a general town party is provided by traditional dancers from several states who meet at Cruz del Cuarto, on the road to the train station. Wearing bells, feather headdresses, scarlet cloaks and masks, groups walk in procession to the parroquia carrying flower offerings called *xuchiles*, some playing armadillo-shell lutes. The roots of these events probably go back to pre-Hispanic times. Dances continue over a few days and include the Danza Guerrero in front of the parroquia, which represents the Spanish conquest of the Chichimecs.

San Miguel Music Festival – This largely classical music festival presents an almost daily program with Mexican and international performers throughout the second half of December. Most concerts are at the fine Teatro Ángela Peralta, built in 1910, on the corner of Mesones and Hernández Macías.

Places to Stay

Some of the better-value places are often full; book ahead if you can, especially during the high seasons.

Many hotels give discounts for long-term guests. If you're planning to stay a while in San Miguel, there are houses, apartments and rooms to rent. Check the newspapers, notice boards and real-estate agents. Expect to pay from US$400 a month for a decent two-bedroom house. House-sitting is another possibility.

Budget The *Lago Dorado KDA Trailer Park* (☎ 152-23-01, fax 152-36-86), near the reservoir 5km south of town, has a lounge, laundromat and 80 spaces with full hookups for US$10 per night, less for longer stays. From town, take the Celaya road, then after 3km turn right at the Hotel Misión de los Ángeles and continue another 2km toward the lake, crossing the train tracks.

Trailer Park La Siesta (☎ 152-02-07) is in the grounds of the Motel La Siesta, on the Celaya road 2km south of town. It has 60 spaces with full hookups for US$12 per night.

The friendly *Hostal Internacional* (☎ 152-31-75, hostma@unisono.net.mx, Jaime Nunó 28) is about seven blocks northwest of the center. The building is nothing special, but it has a good kitchen/dining area, and seats outside in the courtyard. Bunk beds in the separate-sex dorms cost US$6.50 (US$5.50 with a student or hostel card), including coffee, tea and continental breakfast. There are also a few private singles/doubles at US$11/13.25. The hostel had to move from its old premises on Órganos, and may move again if a better building becomes available.

Casa de Huéspedes (☎ 152-13-78, Mesones 27) is a clean, pleasant upstairs hostelry and has a rooftop terrace with a good view. All six rooms have private bath. Singles/doubles cost US$13/19.50, slightly more with a kitchenette, but you can probably get a discount for a longer stay or at off-peak times.

Farther up the hill, *Parador de San Sebastián* (☎ 152-70-84, Mesones 7) is quiet, clean and very attractive, but frequently full. It has 24 rooms, all with fireplace and private bath, arranged around an arched courtyard full of plants. Rooms are from US$13.50/15, up to US$27 for bigger rooms.

Continue up the hill to *Hotel Vianey* (☎ 152-45-59, Aparicio 18), where a plant-filled courtyard is surrounded by small, plain rooms that cost US$16.50 for one or two people. Another budget possibility is *Posada Cholita* (☎ 152-28-98, Hernández Macías 114), where smallish, dark singles/doubles start at US$12.50/18. It's a few blocks southwest of the center on a pretty street.

Mid-Range Mid-range options in San Miguel run from adequate but uninspiring accommodations for US$20 to US$30 that would be in the budget price bracket in most other towns, to very attractive places that are quite good values at around US$40. Just off the Jardín, *Hotel Vista Hermosa Taboada* (☎ 152-00-78, Cuna de Allende 11) is in the former category, with 17 rooms with fireplace, carpet and double bed from US$26. In the same block, but considerably more elegant, *Posada Carmina* (☎ 152-04-58, fax 152-01-35, Cuna de Allende 7) is a former colonial mansion with 12 large, attractive rooms with tiled bathrooms and color TV. Singles/doubles cost from US$33/44 to US$62/71. In the leafy courtyard there's a pleasant restaurant/bar.

Half a block from the Jardín, *Hotel Mansión Virreyes* (☎ 152-08-51, fax 152-38-65, Canal 19) is another colonial place with 22 rooms around two courtyards and a restaurant/bar in the rear patio. Rooms are US$34/46. Just as close to the center, but not as picturesque, *Posada El Mayorazgo* (☎ 152-13-09, Hidalgo 8) has comfortable, modern rooms round a sunny courtyard for US$25/32, and an apartment suitable for four adults at US$38.

Just north of the Escuela de Bellas Artes, *Hotel Sautto* (☎ 512-00-52, Hernández Macías 59) is an interesting old building around a big, quiet courtyard, where single/double/triple rooms with high ceilings and bright tiled bathrooms cost US$17.50/22/24. Nearby, *Hotel Mesón de San Antonio* (☎ 152-05-80, fax 152-28-97, Mesones 80) has an attractive courtyard with a lawn, a small swimming pool and rooms at US$49 single or double including breakfast.

The welcoming *Posada de las Monjas* (☎ 152-01-71, Canal 37) is a monastery turned motel, and one of the better values in San Miguel. The 65 rooms are comfortable and nicely decorated, and the bathrooms all have slate floors and handpainted tiles. Rooms in the new section out back are in better condition than those in the old section. Numerous terraces give lovely views over the valley, and there are a restaurant, bar, laundry and parking. Prices start at US$28/30 for singles/doubles; more for larger rooms and those with fireplaces.

Hotel Quinta Loreto (☎ 152-00-42, fax 152-36-16, Loreto 15) is a longtime favorite with visitors from the US. The 38 rooms, simple but pleasant, some with small private patio, are set around large grounds with trees, tennis courts and plenty of parking

space. The restaurant is good. Rooms are US$25/32; US$5 extra with cable TV. Discounts are available for a stay of a week or longer. Reservations are recommended.

Top End The *Posada San Francisco* (☎/fax 152-00-72, ☎ 800-714-68-70, psf@unisono.net .mx, Plaza Principal 2) is a great value for its perfect location, right on the Jardín, and for its classic colonial style. Spacious, comfortable rooms cost US$57 for one or two people.

Opposite the Instituto Allende, *Posada de la Aldea* (☎ 152-10-22, Ancha de San Antonio 15) has wide lawns, a pool, and 66 large rooms at US$64 for a single or double. Behind the Instituto, *Hotel Aristos San Miguel* (☎ 152-03-92, fax 152-16-31, Calzada del Cardo 2) has a large garden with tennis courts and a big pool. Rooms, all with terraces and parking, start at US$70 for one or two people.

San Miguel now has a slew of B&Bs offering comfortable accommodations at quite high prices. One of the nicest is *Casa Murphy* (☎ 152-37-76, casamurphy@cwix .com, San Antonio Abad 22), off Canal, about 400m northwest of the Jardín. Luxurious rooms in this colonial house cost US$70 for two people, and there's a larger casita with kitchen, spa bath and private patio for US$80. More central is *Pensión Casa Carmen* (☎ 152-08-44, ccarmen@unisono.net .com, Correo 31), an old colonial home whose 12 rooms, all with high-beamed ceilings, are set around a pleasant courtyard with a fountain, orange trees and flowers. The singles/doubles price of US$48/70 includes a delicious breakfast.

Another popular place is *La Mansión del Bosque* (☎ 152-02-77, Aldama 65) opposite Parque Benito Juárez. All 23 rooms are different and comfortable with good furniture and original art. Prices start at US$76/79 including breakfast and dinner. Winter and July/August rates are higher. Reserve well in advance. The address is Apartado Postal 206, San Miguel de Allende, Gto 37700.

The most luxurious, elegant and expensive place in town is *Casa de Sierra Nevada* (☎ 152-04-15, fax 152-23 37, sierranevada@

mpsnet.com.mx, Hospicio 35), which was converted from four colonial mansions. It has a swimming pool, fine restaurant, views over the town, and superbly appointed rooms (US$200) and suites (US$270 to US$410).

Places to Eat

San Miguel restaurants serve a wide variety of quality international cuisine, but for cash-strapped budget travelers there are economical options aimed more at local families than trendy expatriates.

Budget For quick cheap eats, there are some excellent bakeries such as *La Colmena Panadería (Reloj 21)*, half a block north of the Jardín. A few food stands on the east side of the Jardín offer cheap, tasty Mexican fare like *elotes* (steamed ears of corn), fried chicken or tamales for around US$2.50.

Northeast of the Jardín, there are a couple of good, basic, family-run chicken restaurants, with chickens turning on spits out front. *Restaurant Flamingo's (Juárez 15)* serves a good-value comida corrida (US$3.50) from 1 to 4 pm. It's open daily from around 9 am to 10 pm. Nearby on Mesones, *El Infierno* will do a full meal of soup, chicken, french fries and vegetables for under US$4. Continue up the hill to a good *taquería* that stays open late.

Round the corner, on a bend on Insurgentes, *Café Colón* is popular with locals for its inexpensive set breakfasts and lunches. *Mercado El Nigromante*, with all the usual Mexican market eateries, is on Colegio only a couple of blocks northeast of here, but light years away from the San Miguel gringo scene.

South of the Jardín are some inexpensive places that attract both locals and visitors. *La Fragua (Cuna de Allende 3)* is a long-popular courtyard restaurant/bar open from noon until at least midnight every day, with live music every night and a happy hour from 6 to 8 pm. The menú del día is only US$3. On the corner of Cuna de Allende and Cuadrante, the little, family-run *El Ten Ten Pie* serves up home-style cooking with

excellent chili sauces. Comida corrida is under US$4, and antojitos, like the tasty cheese-and-mushroom tacos, are under US$2.

A block farther down Cuadrante, *El Buen Café (Jesús 23)* does economical breakfasts and Mexican snacks for around US$3.25. It's open Monday through Saturday from 9 am to 8 pm. North of here at Jesús and Umarán, the convivial *La Piñata* is popular for juices, salads and quesadillas. Downhill toward Instituto Allende, on the corner of Ancha San Antonio and tree-shaded Calle Nueva, two or three food stands assemble in the evenings, selling ice cream, tacos and other snacks. They're very clean, the cost is minimal, the tastes are a treat, and the experience is delightful.

For self-catering, try one of the markets described in Shopping, later in this section.

Mid-Range & Top End There are several lively places around the plaza, open from around 9 am to 10 pm, but you pay a premium for the position. *El Portal de Victor IV*, on the east side, and *Café del Jardín*, on the west side, are both attractively located and OK for ice cream, coffee, cakes and snacks, but not a great value for a full meal. Under the arches next to the tourist office, *La Terrazza* and some other eateries have tables on a balcony at the corner of the Jardín. It's often crowded with people who come to see people, though the food is ordinary and the prices quite high – US$6 for a small pizza, US$2 for a beer.

If you want to blow your budget on some fine food, San Miguel is one of the best places in Mexico to do it. You could start at *El Pegaso*, on Corregidora opposite the post office, for an excellent and not-too-expensive breakfast of fruit, eggs Benedict, fresh bread and coffee for under US$3.50. For a light lunch, try their fancy sandwiches such as smoked turkey or smoked salmon with cream cheese, from US$3 to US$5. For full meals, main dishes start at US$4.75; some are Asian-inspired but there's also Mexican and Italian fare. Closed Sunday.

For a particularly imaginative menu, don't miss *Hoja Santa (Correo 19)*, serving 'nueva Mexicana cocina' – typically Mexican ingredients in new combinations, creatively prepared and beautifully presented. Examples are nopal cactus with cream cheese and shrimp, and pasta sauce made with six different types of chili peppers. The surroundings are comfortable and classy, and the prices very reasonable for food of this quality – starters are around US$3.50, and main courses of steak and seafood are all under US$6.

The long-standing *Rincón Español* (Correo 29) has more traditional Mexican and Spanish dishes, a little on the pricey side at US$6.50 to US$10, but worth it if you come in the evening when flamenco dancers perform. The comida corrida is more affordable at about US$5. It's open noon to 10 or 11 pm daily.

Mama Mía (Umarán 8), just west of the Jardín, is a San Miguel institution – a restaurant, bar, disco and live music venue. The restaurant, in a cool and pleasant courtyard, features the usual range of dishes, with pastas for US$4 to US$6, well-prepared steak and seafood from around US$6.50. Breakfasts (from US$2.50 to US$5) are a much better deal, but Mama Mía is most popular at night – it's open from 8 am till after midnight.

Another place popular for its attractive courtyard setting is the restaurant at *Posada Carmina* (Cuna de Allende 7), just down from the Jardín. The menú del día is around US$5. It's open from 8 am to 9.30 pm daily, and is particularly busy for Sunday lunch. Around the corner, *La Grotta* (Cuadrante 5) is an Italian restaurant said to serve the best pizza in Mexico – a number of places make this claim, but La Grotta supports it with a truly excellent product. Prices start at US$6 for a small one. The pasta here is also good, and the homemade desserts are delicious.

El Patio Mexas (Canal 15) is an enjoyable expats' restaurant/bar that does Tex-Mex favorites in Texas-size portions. Salads are from US$3, burritos and *chimichangas* (tortillas wrapped around a filling and deep-fried) US$4 to US$6, steaks around US$8. It's in a roomy covered courtyard with a pool table and a big-screen TV showing US sports, open from noon to 11 pm daily. *Tío Lucas* (Mesones 103) is another US-style place. It's known for its grills – burgers or chicken cost US$5 to US$7, steaks are US$9 to US$11 – but it also serves a good range of soups (US$3) and salads (US$4). It's open daily from noon, and it often has live blues or jazz at night.

A fun place near the mercado is the friendly, family-run *Café Olé Olé* (Loreto 66), brightly decorated with bullfighting memorabilia. This is one of San Miguel's most popular eateries. The food is mainly char-grilled with prices starting at US$5.50 for chicken and beef. Open from 1 to 8 pm daily.

Some interesting restaurants are sprouting southwest of the center. *El Establo*, near the bottom end of Zacateros, serves tapas and other Spanish fare, but it's quite pricey. *Princesa Maya*, on Codo, is a casual place serving reasonably priced Yucatecan dishes, from US$3.50 to US$4.50. *La Trattoria*, at the junction of Zacateros and Codo, does a good range of medium-priced Italian and vegetarian dishes.

Vegetarian For cocina naturista, eat at *El Tomate* (Mesones 62). Light meals include pasta (US$4.50), whole wheat sandwiches (US$3.25) and salads (US$4), and feature fantastically fresh and tasty ingredients – lettuce you can really taste. Freshly squeezed fruit and vegetable juices cost up to US$2, and the comida corrida is a great value at US$5. It's open 9.30 am to 3.30 pm Monday to Saturday.

Entertainment

Every evening at sunset, the Jardín hosts a free concert of birdsongs as the trees fill with twittering, whistling and preening birds, while the paths below fill with people doing much the same. These days, gray-haired gringos can outnumber flirting teenagers, but it's still a delight to be there, as the air cools and the fragrance of flowers and food stalls floats across the plaza. For more formal entertainment, check *Atención San Miguel* for news about what's on in town. The *Escuela de Bellas Artes* hosts a variety of events including art exhibitions, concerts, readings and theater; check its notice board for the current schedule. Some events are held in English. *Villa Jacaranda (Aldama 53)* shows recent releases of American movies on a big screen at 7.30 pm daily. Entry is US$4 and includes a drink and popcorn.

Several restaurants double as drinking, dancing and entertainment venues. Most of the action is on Thursday, Friday and Saturday nights, but at holiday times some places will have live music and more any night of the week. The perennially popular *Mama Mía (☎ 152-20-63, Umarán 8)* has live South American music nightly from around 8 pm to late. There's a video bar at the front and a sometimes crowded dance floor that usually gets going around 11 pm.

Char Rock Bar/Café (☎ 152-73-73), upstairs at Correo and Diez de Sollano, has bands doing '60s and '70s covers – occasional cheap drinks specials get the students in early, but later on it's mostly an older crowd. *Pancho & Lefty's (☎ 152-19-58, Mesones 99)* is strictly for a young crowd, with live rock music and/or techno/dance on Wednesday, Friday and Saturday from around 10.30 pm to 3 am. Cover charge is about US$2.50 and drinks are inexpensive, especially when they do a special deal. Right next door, *100 Ángeles (☎ 512-59-37)* is a disco/dance club that is San Miguel's premier gay venue. *Café La Lola (☎ 512-40-50, Ancha de San Antonio 31)*, almost opposite Instituto Allende, is a gay-friendly café and bar that occasionally features live music.

The most popular dance club is *El Ring (☎ 152-19-98, Hidalgo 25)*, a flashy place blasting a mix of Latin, US, and European dance music. It opens around 10 pm from Wednesday to Saturday, and from midnight it's usually full (sometimes packed) with young Mexicans and foreigners (cover US$4 to US$6).

Shopping

San Miguel has one of the biggest and best concentrations of craft shops in Mexico, selling folk art and handicrafts from all over the country. Prices are not low, but quality is high and the range of goods is mind-boggling. Casa Maxwell on Canal, a few doors down from the Jardín, is one place with a tremendous array; there are many, many more within a few blocks, especially on Canal, San Francisco and Zacateros. Local crafts include tinware, wrought iron, silver, brass, leather, glassware, pottery and textiles. Most of these crafts are traditions going back to the 18th century. The Mercado de Artesanías is a collection of handicraft stalls in an alleyway between Colegio and Loreto – prices are lower than in San Miguel's smarter shops, but the quality is very variable.

The daily Mercado El Nigromante, on Colegio, sells fruit, vegetables and assorted other goods for the local community. The biggest market takes place on Tuesday out of town beside the Gigante shopping center, 2.5km southeast of the center on the Querétaro road. Take a 'Gigante' or 'Placita' bus (10 minutes) from the east side of the Jardín de San Francisco. Espino's supermarket, at Codo 36, has a large range of necessities for North American expatriates, and fresh fruit and vegetables are sold just outside.

Getting There & Away

Air The nearest airport is Bajío international (BJX), between León and Silao (see the León section for flight information). There are more direct flights to/from Mexico City, and they may be slightly cheaper, but BJX is a lot more convenient for San Miguel.

Bus The small Central de Autobuses has a telephone caseta, snack bar, and not much else. It's on Canal, about 1km west of the center. ETN, Primera Plus and Pegasso Plus tickets can be bought at PMC Tours (☎ 152-16-30), Cuna de Allende 11. Tickets for Primera Plus can also be bought at Transporte Turístico on Diez de Sollano just off Correo. Daily departures include:

Celaya – 52km, 1¼ hours; 2nd-class Flecha Amarilla every 15 minutes, 5 am to 10 pm (US$2.25)

Dolores Hidalgo – 43km, 1 hour; 2nd-class Flecha Amarilla or Herradura de Plata every 30 minutes, 5 am to 10 pm (US$2)

Guadalajara – 380km, 6 hours; 3 1st-class Primera Plus (US$26)

Guanajuato – 82km, 1 to 1½ hours; 4 1st-class Primera Plus (US$6), 1 1st-class Ómnibus de México (US$5), 10 2nd-class Flecha Amarilla, 8 2nd-class Servicios Coordinados (US$4.50)

León – 138km, 2¼ hours; 3 1st-class Primera Plus (US$9.50), 2 2nd-class Servicios Coordinados (US$9)

Mexico City (Terminal Norte) – 280km, 3½ to 4 hours; 4 deluxe ETN (US$22), 2 1st-class Primera Plus, 2 1st-class Herradura de Plata (US$15.50), 2nd-class Herradura de Plata or Flecha Amarilla semi-directo at least every 40 minutes, 5 am to 10 pm (US$14)

Querétaro – 60km, 1 hour; 3 deluxe ETN (US$5.50), frequent 2nd-class Herradura de Plata and Flecha Amarilla, 5 am to 9 pm (US$3)

Other services include seven Flecha Amarilla buses to San Luis Potosí (US$9.50) and two to Aguascalientes (US$9.75), Transportes del Norte buses to Monterrey (US$37) and Americanos buses at 6pm daily to San Antonio (US$57), Houston (US$66), Dallas (US$72) and Chicago (US$123).

Car If you need a car for more than a few days, it may be worth going to Querétaro. San Miguel is an expensive place to rent – to find out how expensive, call Gama (☎ 152-08-15), Hidalgo 3, or Hola (☎ 152-01-98), in the Posada San Francisco. Prices start around US$56 per day for a VW Beetle. You should book at least a week ahead, especially in the winter and summer holiday periods.

Getting Around

To/From the Airports PMC Tours (☎ 152-16-30), Cuna de Allende 11, runs a shuttle to the Bajío international airport at 9.30 am daily (US$15). Asociación de Guías de Turistas (☎ 154-51-31) and Aventuras San Miguel (☎ 152-64-06) also arrange airport transport. Alternatively, take a León-bound bus and ask to be let off at the airport.

Bus Local buses run daily from 7 am to 9 pm and cost US$0.25. 'Central' buses go every few minutes between the bus station and the town center. Coming into town these go up

Insurgentes, wind through the town a bit and terminate on the corner of Mesones and Colegio. Heading out from the center, you can pick one up on Canal.

Taxi A taxi between the center and the bus station costs US$1.75, as do most taxi trips around town.

AROUND SAN MIGUEL DE ALLENDE
Hot Springs

Natural hot springs near San Miguel have been developed as *balnearios* (bathing spots), with swimming pools where you can soak in mineral waters amid pleasant surroundings – it's supposedly good for the skin, and definitely good for relaxation. Entry is about US$4.50 for a whole day. The balnearios are accessed via the highway north of San Miguel – take a Dolores Hidalgo bus from the San Miguel bus station, or a 'Santuario' minibus (half-hourly) from the bus stop on Puente de Umarán, off Colegio and opposite the Mercado El Nigromante. This will stop out front, or within walking distance, of all the main balnearios. Returning to town, hail one of the buses that speed along the highway. Taxis are a good option if you can get a few people together. They cost around US$6 each way, and you can ask the driver to return for you at an appointed time.

The most popular balneario is **Taboada** (☎ 152-08-50), 8km north of San Miguel and then 3km west along a signposted side road. It has a large lawn area and three swimming pools – one Olympic-size with warm water, and two smaller ones that get quite hot. It's open 8 am to 5 pm daily except Tuesday. A small kiosk and a bar provide snacks and drinks. Minibuses to 'Xote,' hourly from the Puente de Umarán bus stop, will get you most of the way to Taboada. Get off where the bus turns off the Taboada side road and walk the remaining 1km to the hot springs.

Other balnearios include **Santa Veronica**, right beside the highway to Dolores Hidalgo, at the Taboada turnoff. Nine kilometers from San Miguel, **Parador del Cortijo** (☎ 152-17-00) is a hotel/restaurant with a thermal pool, sauna, whirlpool bath, and massages. Nearby **Balneario Xote** (☎ 614-58-89) is an inexpensive spa and pool.

Only 100m or so beyond the Parador del Cortijo, on the same side of the highway, **La Gruta** (☎ 152-25-30) has three small pools into which the waters of a thermal spring have been channeled. The hottest is in a cave entered through a tunnel, with hot water gushing from the roof, lit by a single shaft of sunlight. The favorite **Escondido Place** balneario has two warm outdoor pools and three connected indoor pools, each progressively hotter. The picturesque grounds have plenty of space for picnicking, and there's a small kiosk for drinks and snacks.

Santuario de Atotonilco
Turning west off the Dolores Hidalgo highway about 15km north of San Miguel and going about 1km will bring you to the hamlet of Atotonilco, dominated by its sanctuary founded in 1740 as a spiritual retreat. Here Ignacio Allende was married in 1802. Eight years later he returned with Miguel Hidalgo and the band of independence rebels en route from Dolores to San Miguel to take the shrine's banner of the Virgin of Guadalupe as their flag.

Today a journey to Atotonilco is a goal of pilgrims and penitents from all over Mexico, and the starting point of an important and solemn procession two weekends before Easter, in which the image of the Señor de la Columna is carried to the church of San Juan de Dios in San Miguel. Inside, the sanctuary has six chapels and is vibrant with statues, folk murals and other paintings. Extensive restoration has been underway for some time. Traditional dances are held here on the third Sunday in July.

Pozos
● pop 130 ● elev 2305m ☎ 4
Not so long ago Mineral de Pozos was more or less a ghost town. A couple of thousand people lived among abandoned houses and mine workings in what, 90 or so years ago, was a flourishing silver- and copper-mining center of about 50,000. It was targeted for development and there's now a plush place

to stay, the **Hotel Casa Mexicana** (☎ 293-00-17, Ocampo 6), a converted 100-year-old hacienda on the Jardín Principal. Doubles with three meals are US$110. **Hidalgo B&B** (Hidalgo 15) is a low-budget alternative. In Pozos, you can explore the underground tunnels of old mines, check out old ruins and chapels or tour the surrounding area by horseback or mountain bike. There's also an art gallery and a couple of good restaurants. Some of the residents make a living from hand-carved replicas of pre-Hispanic musical instruments, including deerskin drums and rainmakers. These instruments, and pre-Hispanic dances, are featured in fiestas.

Pozos is 14km south of San Luis de la Paz, a detour east of highway 57. To get there by bus from San Miguel, go first to Dolores Hidalgo, then to San Luis de la Paz, and then take a third bus from there to Pozos. By car it's about 35 minutes from San Miguel. Aventuras San Miguel (☎ 152-64-06) runs trips to Pozos, and Bici-Burro (☎ 152-15-26) does it as a bike tour.

La Cañada de la Virgen
A pyramid is being excavated at this recently discovered archaeological site, about 12km northeast of San Miguel. Aventuras San Miguel (☎ 152-64-06) and PMC Tours (☎ 152-16-30) do excursions to the canyon.

Querétaro State

Querétaro is primarily an agricultural and livestock-raising state. Industry has developed around Querétaro city and certain other places, notably San Juan del Río. The state also turns out opals, mercury, zinc and lead. Many visitors never get past Querétaro city, with its fine colonial architecture, active cultural life and rich history, but there are other areas worth visiting, like pretty Tequisquiapan with its thermal springs. In the northeast of the state, the rugged fringe of the Sierra Madre has little-visited archaeological sites, and a dramatic road descending to old mission towns on the fringe of the Huasteca.

QUERÉTARO

• pop 469,500 • elev 1762m ☎ 4

Querétaro's museums, monuments and colonial architecture are less spectacular than those of Guanajuato or Zacatecas, but it's a lively city. It's prettiest at night when many of its handsome buildings are floodlit, and wandering the streets and plazas is a real pleasure. It especially warrants a visit if you're interested in Mexico's history, in which it has played an important role. In 1996 the city officially took back its old name, Santiago de Querétaro, but it's generally known as just Querétaro.

History

The Otomí founded a settlement here in the 15th century that was later absorbed into the Aztec empire, then by Spaniards in 1531. Franciscan monks used it as a base for missions not only to Mexico but also to what is now the southwestern US. In the early 19th century Querétaro became a center of intrigue among disaffected criollos plotting to free Mexico from Spanish rule. Conspirators, including Miguel Hidalgo, met secretly at the house of Doña Josefa Ortiz (La Corregidora), who was the wife of a former *corregidor* (district administrator) of Querétaro.

When the conspiracy was discovered, the story goes, Doña Josefa was locked in a room in her house (now the Palacio de Gobierno) but managed to whisper through a keyhole to a coconspirator, Ignacio Pérez, that their colleagues were in jeopardy. Pérez galloped off to inform another conspirator in San Miguel de Allende, who in turn carried the news to Dolores Hidalgo, where on September 16, 1810, Padre Hidalgo issued his famous Grito, a call to arms initiating the War of Independence.

In 1867 Emperor Maximilian surrendered to Benito Juárez's general Escobedo at Querétaro, after a siege lasting nearly 100 days. It was here that Maximilian was executed by firing squad.

In 1917 the Mexican constitution – still the basis of Mexican law – was drawn up by the Constitutionalist civil-war faction in Querétaro. Mexico's ruling party, the PNR

(which later became the PRI), was organized in Querétaro in 1929.

Orientation

The historic center is fairly compact, with pedestrian streets called *andadores* linking a number of lively plazas – it makes for pleasant strolling. The heart of things is the Plaza Principal, also called Jardín Zenea. Running along its east side, by the Templo de San Francisco, is Corregidora, the main street of the downtown area. The Plaza de Armas (also called Plaza de la Independencia) is two blocks east, and the small Plaza de la Corregidora is a block to the north.

The large and shady Alameda, a few blocks south, is popular for picnics, jogging, roller-skating, strolling and generally just taking it easy.

The bus station is about 5km southeast of the center – local buses link it to the center.

Information

Tourist Offices The Secretaría de Turismo (☎ 212-14-12, 212-10-04), Pasteur Norte 4 off Plaza de Armas, has reasonable maps and brochures of the city. Hours are 8 am to 8 pm daily.

Money There are several banks on and near the Plaza Principal, most with ATMs. The American Express agent is Turismo Beverly (☎ 216-15-11) at Tecnológico 118.

Post & Communications The main post office, at Arteaga 7, is open 8 am to 7 pm Monday to Friday, 9 am to 1 pm Saturday. Telecomm, with fax, *giro* (money order) and Western Union 'Dinero en Minutos,' is at Allende Norte 4. There are pay phones on the Plaza Principal, Plaza de Armas and elsewhere around the center.

The closest Internet place is Ciberspace, northeast of the center at Universidad 297. It charges about US$3.25 per hour.

Templo de San Francisco

This impressive church is on the Plaza Principal, at the corner of Corregidora and 5 de Mayo. Its dome's pretty colored tiles were brought from Spain in 1540, around the time

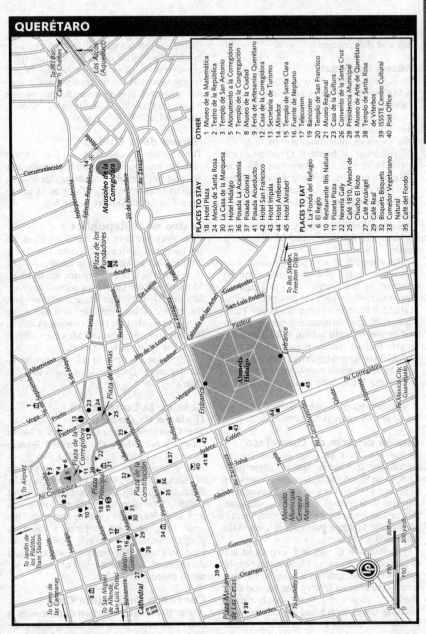

QUERÉTARO

PLACES TO STAY
18 Hotel Plaza
24 Mesón de Santa Rosa
30 La Casa de la Marquesa
31 Hotel Hidalgo
36 Posada La Academia
37 Posada Colonial
41 Posada Acueducto
42 Hotel San Francisco
43 Hotel Impala
44 Hotel Amberes
45 Hotel Mirabel

PLACES TO EAT
4 La Fonda del Refugio
6 El Regio
10 Restaurante Ibis Natura
11 Pizzeti Pizza
22 Nevería Galy
25 Café 1810; Mesón de
   Chucho El Roto
27 Café Arcángel
29 Café Real
32 Bisquets Bisquets
33 Comedor Vegetariano
   Natural
35 Café del Fondo

OTHER
1 Museo de la Matemática
2 Teatro de la República
3 Templo de San Antonio
5 Monumento a la Corregidora
7 Templo de la Congregación
8 Museo de la Ciudad
9 Feria de Artesanías Querétaro
12 Casa de la Corregidora
13 Secretaría de Turismo
14 Mirador
15 Templo de Santa Clara
16 Fuente de Neptuno
17 Telecomm
19 Bancomer
20 Templo de San Francisco
21 Museo Regional
23 Casa de la Cultura
26 Convento de la Santa Cruz
28 Presidencia Municipal
34 Museo de Arte de Querétaro
38 Templo de Santa Rosa
   de Viterbos
39 ISSSTE Centro Cultural
40 Post Office

construction on the church began. Inside are some fine religious paintings from the 17th, 18th and 19th centuries.

Museo Regional

The Regional Museum is beside the Templo de San Francisco. The ground floor holds artifacts and exhibits on pre-Hispanic Mexico, archaeological sites in Querétaro state, the early Spanish occupation of the area and the state's various indigenous groups.

Upstairs are exhibits on Querétaro's role in the independence movement, the post-independence history of Mexico and Querétaro and much religious art. The table at which the Treaty of Guadalupe Hidalgo was signed in 1848, ending the Mexican-American War, is on display, as is the desk of the tribunal that sentenced Maximilian to death.

The museum is housed in part of what was once a huge monastery and seminary, attached to the Templo de San Francisco. Begun in 1540, by 1567 the seminary was the seat of the Franciscan province of San Pedro y San Pablo de Michoacán. Building continued on and off until at least 1727. The tower was the highest vantage point in the city, and in the 1860s the monastery was used as a fort both by imperialists supporting Maximilian and by the forces who finally defeated him in 1867.

The museum is open 10 am to 7 pm Tuesday to Sunday (US$2.20).

Museo de Arte de Querétaro

Querétaro's Art Museum is in a former monastery at Allende Sur 14, adjacent to Templo de San Agustín. It was built between 1731 and 1748 and is a splendid example of baroque architecture. There are angels, gargoyles, statues and other ornamental details all over the building, particularly around the courtyard.

The museum is very well organized and displayed. If you can read Spanish, the explanations with the exhibits add up to an illustrated course in art history. The ground-floor display of 16th- and 17th-century European painting traces interesting influences, from Flemish to Spanish to Mexican art. On the same floor you'll find 19th- and 20th-century Mexican painting, a collection of 20th-century Querétaro artists, and a hall for temporary exhibits. The top floor has a photographic display on the history of the monastery and rooms with more art, from 16th-century mannerism to 18th-century baroque. The museum is open 11 am to 7 pm Tuesday through Sunday (US$1.25, free Tuesday).

Museo de la Ciudad

The 11-room City Museum, on Guerrero at Hidalgo, has some quite good contemporary art, and not terribly interesting displays on the city's recent history. It's open 11 am to 5 pm Tuesday to Sunday (US$0.60).

Teatro de la República

One block north of the Plaza Principal, on the corner of Juárez and Peralta, this lovely old theater was where a tribunal met in 1867 to decide the fate of Emperor Maximilian. Mexico's constitution was signed here on January 31, 1917. The stage backdrop lists the names of its signatories and the states they represented. In 1929, politicians met in the theater to organize Mexico's ruling party, the PNR (now the PRI).

The theater is open to visitors Tuesday to Sunday from 10 am to 3 pm and 5 to 8 pm (free).

Casa de la Corregidora (Palacio de Gobierno)

The Casa de la Corregidora, Doña Josefa Ortiz's home, where she informed Ignacio Pérez of the plans to arrest the independence conspirators, stands on the north side of Plaza de Armas. Today the building is the Palacio de Gobierno, the state government building. The room where Doña Josefa was locked up is upstairs, over the entrance – it's now the governor's conference room. A plaque to one side records Doña Josefa's place in history. The building can be visited during normal office hours, but there's not much to see.

Convento de la Santa Cruz

About 10 minutes' walk east of the center is one of the city's most interesting sights, the

Convento de la Santa Cruz, on Plaza de los Fundadores. This monastery was built between 1654 and about 1815 on the site of a battle in which a miraculous appearance of Santiago (St James) had led the Otomí to surrender to the conquistadors and Christianity. Emperor Maximilian had his headquarters here while under siege in Querétaro from March to May 1867. After his surrender and subsequent death sentence, he was jailed here while awaiting the firing squad. Today the monastery is used as a religious school.

A guide will provide insight into the Convento's history and artifacts, which include an ingenious water system and unique colonial ways of cooking and refrigeration. The guide will also relate several of the Convento's miracles, including the legendary growth of a tree from a walking stick stuck in the earth by a pious friar in 1697. The thorns of the tree form a cross.

The Convento is open 9 am to 2 pm and 4 to 6 pm Monday to Friday, 9 am to 4 pm Saturday and Sunday (free, but your guide will request a donation to the convent at the end of your tour). Tours are given in English or Spanish.

Acueducto & Mirador
Walk east along Independencia past the Convento de la Santa Cruz then fork right along Ejército Republicano, and you come to a mirador with a view of 'Los Arcos,' Querétaro's emblematic 1.28km aqueduct, which was built between 1726 and 1735 with 74 towering arches. The aqueduct runs along the center of Avenida Zaragoza, and still brings water to the city from about 12km away.

Across the street is the **Mausoleo de la Corregidora**, the tomb of Doña Josefa Ortiz (La Corregidora) and her husband, Miguel Domínguez de Alemán. Behind the tomb is a shrine with pictures and documents relating to Doña Josefa's life.

Museo de la Matemática
This one-room museum is upstairs in the university building at 16 de Septiembre 63. It has a fun collection of science models, optical illusions, math puzzles and other educational stuff. It's all in Spanish, but easy enough to enjoy. It's open 10 am to 2 pm and 4 to 6 pm Monday to Friday (US$0.60).

Other Central Sights
Plaza de la Corregidora is dominated by the **Monumento a la Corregidora**, a 1910 statue of Doña Josefa Ortiz bearing the flame of freedom.

One block west of the Plaza Principal along Madero is the **Fuente de Neptuno** (Neptune Fountain), designed by the noted Mexican neoclassical architect Eduardo Tresguerras in 1797. The 17th-century **Templo de Santa Clara**, adjacent, has an ornate baroque interior. On Madero at Ocampo is the rather plain 18th-century **cathedral**. Hidalgo, which runs parallel to Madero two blocks north, is lined with many fine mansions.

At the intersection of Arteaga and Montes stands the 18th-century **Templo de Santa Rosa de Viterbos**, Querétaro's most splendid baroque church, with its pagoda-like bell tower, unusual exterior paintwork and curling buttresses and lavishly gilded and marbled interior. The church also boasts what some say is the earliest four-sided clock in the New World.

Other notable colonial churches include the **Templo de San Antonio** on Peralta at Corregidora Norte, with two large pipe organs, elaborate crystal chandeliers, red wallpaper and several oil paintings; and the **Templo de la Congregación** on Pasteur Norte at 16 de Septiembre, with beautiful stained-glass windows and a splendid pipe organ.

Cerro de las Campanas
In the west of the city, a good 35-minute walk from the center, is the Cerro de las Campanas (Hill of the Bells), the site of Maximilian's execution. The emperor's family constructed a chapel on the spot. Today the area is a park, with a statue of Benito Juárez, a café and the Museo del Sitio (Siege) de Querétaro, open 10 am to 6 pm Tuesday through Sunday. You can get there on a 'Tecnológica' bus going west on Zaragoza at the Alameda Hidalgo. Get off at the Ciudad Universitaria.

Organized Tours

Guided walking tours of the city center, in English or Spanish, leave the tourist office daily at 10.30 am and 6 pm. They cost US$1.75 per person and last around two hours. Queretour (☎ 223-08-33) does city tours for US$11 and longer trips to the highlights of the region.

Special Events

Querétaro's Feria Internacional in the first two weeks of December is one of Mexico's biggest state fairs. While it focuses on livestock, it also covers industry, commerce and artisanry and is the excuse for varied entertainment and fun.

Places to Stay

Budget The *Hotel San Francisco* (☎ 212-08-58, *Corregidora 144 Sur*) is a three-story place with lots of smallish but decent rooms, all with private bath and TV, at US$10/12.50 for singles/doubles. Other cheapies in the same area include *Posada Colonial* (☎ 212-02-39, *Juárez 19 Sur*), where basic room rates start at US$6, but with extras like a TV and a private bath cost US$11, and *Posada La Academia* (*Pino Suárez 52*), with dark, cell-like rooms, B&W TV and shared bath from US$6.50/10 for singles/doubles.

Much more attractive lodgings are at *Posada Acueducto* (☎ 224-12-89, *Juárez 64 Sur*), with well-kept rooms at US$15/17.50, including modern bathroom and color TV.

Hotel Hidalgo (☎ 212-00-81, *Madero 11 Poniente*) is just a few doors off the Plaza Principal. It's an old-style building, and the rooms vary greatly in size and appeal – some upper-floor rooms have small balconies. Singles/doubles cost US$13/15. Rooms with two beds cost more, and the largest rooms can hold up to seven people – they all have private bathrooms. There's parking in the courtyard and an economical restaurant open from 8 am to 10 pm.

Mid-Range The *Hotel Plaza* (☎ 212-11-38, *Juárez 23 Norte*) is a respectable place right on the Plaza Principal. Its 29 tidy, comfortable, charm-free rooms cost US$17.50/22 and up. Some have French doors and small balconies facing the plaza – they offer plenty of light, air and noise.

The modern four-story *Hotel Impala* (☎ 212-25-70, *fax 212-45-15, Colón 1*) is on the corner of Corregidora Sur and Zaragoza, opposite the Alameda Hidalgo. It has underground parking and 108 rooms all with color TV, carpet and phone. Some rooms have a view of the park; interior rooms are quieter and bright enough. Singles/doubles cost US$16.50/21.

Hotel Amberes (☎ 212-86-04, *fax 212-41-51, Corregidora 188 Sur*), also facing the Alameda, is similar but a bit smarter. Rooms are US$31/34, or US$40 with two beds.

Top End Business travelers go for the modern *Hotel Mirabel* (☎ 214-39-29, *fax 214-35-85, Constituyentes 2 Ote*), facing the south side of the Alameda. The comfortable carpeted rooms have color TV, air-con and phone, and some have a view over the park. Prices start at US$46/61.

For something superb, try *La Casa de la Marquesa* (☎ 212-00-92, *fax 212-00-98, Madero 41*). The magnificent 18th-century baroque/Mudéjar mansion was transformed into a hotel full of lavish period furnishings, carved stone, tiles and frescoes (some original). The 25 suites have names such as Alhambra and Maximiliano y Carlota, with style to match – but all with cable TV and air-con. The suites start at US$194, including continental breakfast and welcome cocktail. Less expensive rooms (from US$130) are in a separate building, Casa Azul, a couple of doors west on the corner of Madero and Allende. Children under 12 are not admitted.

Mesón de Santa Rosa (☎ 224-26-23, *fax 212-55-22, starosa@sparc.ciateq.conacyt.mx, Pasteur 17 Sur*), on Plaza de Armas, is another finely restored colonial building. It's built around three patios: one with a heated swimming pool, one with a fountain, one with restaurant tables. There are 21 elegant and comfortable suites, each with a safe and satellite TV, starting at US$89.

Places to Eat

Plaza de la Corregidora is bounded on two sides by restaurants with outdoor tables and a vibrant atmosphere in the evening. Most of them have a menu posted out front, so you can stroll round and take your pick. *La Fonda del Refugio* has a pretty standard menu, with chicken dishes from US$4.50 and steaks around US$7 – it's not cheap, but it's an enjoyable place to eat and the food is well prepared. *El Regio* has a similar setup, with lots of outdoor tables and lower prices. On the south side, *Pizzeta Pizza* is an economical option, with a good range of pizzas from a US$3 small to a US$8 huge.

The surrounding pedestrian streets have plenty of mid-range restaurants and cafés catering to shoppers, workers and snackers. On 5 de Mayo, *Nevería Galy* is a Querétaro institution known for its homemade ice cream. Specialties include *nieve de limón* (lemon sorbet) with mineral water, or cola or red wine.

Plaza de Armas has a handful of more expensive restaurants with indoor and outdoor tables. *Mesón de Chucho El Roto* boasts *'alta cocina mexicana'* (Mexican high cuisine), and offers many interesting Mexican dishes which will appeal to those who appreciate high prices. Next door, *Café 1810* is a little less expensive and has a more standard menu of international and Mexican dishes – try the local specialty *enchiladas Queretanas* (fried enchiladas with chili sauce, cheese and onions).

A couple blocks west, *Bisquets Bisquets* faces Plaza de la Constitución. A small, friendly place with good food at good prices, it does a comida corrida for only US$3. It's open from 7 am to 11 pm daily.

Café del Fondo (Pino Suárez 9) is a relaxed, rambling place with soothing background music from a creaky old sound system. You can get breakfast deals such as eggs, *frijoles*, bread roll, juice and coffee for US$2, or a four-course comida corrida with plenty of choice for US$2.50. It's open 7.30 am to 10 pm daily, and you can linger over a snack or coffee any time.

Café Real, at the corner of Madero and Allende, is part of La Casa de la Marquesa Hotel. It has a gurgling fountain and good food at quite high prices. A block away, *Café*

Arcángel, on the southwest corner of the Jardín Guerrero, is a pleasant, old-fashioned place for a quiet breakfast (US$3.25) or a relaxing lunch. Most main dishes are under US$4.50.

Vegetarians and natural-food fans will like *Restaurante Ibis Natura, (Juárez 47 Norte)*, open daily from 8 am to 9.30 pm. The comida corrida for US$2.50 is an excellent value; so are the soyburgers with mushrooms and cheese at US$1.10. The little *Comedor Vegetariano Natura (Vergara 7)* is a good and inexpensive vegetarian restaurant on a quiet pedestrian street, open Monday through Saturday from 8 am to 9 pm. Main meals and big salads are under US$2.50, and the comida costs about US$3.

La Casa de la Marquesa and the *Mesón de Santa Rosa* (see Places to Stay) both have high-class restaurants.

Entertainment

Querétaro has cultural activities befitting a state capital and university city. You can pick up a calendar of events from the tourist office. Sit in the Plaza Principal any Sunday evening with local families enjoying concerts; the state band performs from around 6.30 to 8.30 pm, sometimes with dancers. On Saturdays in summer, a calle-joneada kicks off from the Plaza de Armas at 8 pm.

The *Casa de la Cultura* at 5 de Mayo 40 sponsors concerts, dance, theater, art exhibitions and other events, as does the ISSSTE Centro Cultural at Arteaga 70. Stop by during office hours to pick up their monthly schedules.

Most of the fashionable bars and nightclubs are outside the historic center, some right out in the suburbs. The tourist office can suggest some current nightspots, and check the entertainment section of Friday's *Diario de Querétaro*. Two reliable standbys are *JBJ Bar* (☎ 213-72-13, *Boulevard Bernardo Quintana 109*), which has live music on weekends, and the local branch of *Carlos 'n Charlies* (☎ 213-90-36, *Boulevard Bernardo Quintana 160*). They're on the city's eastern ring road, south of the aqueduct.

Shopping

Feria de Artesanías Querétaro, at Juárez 49 Norte, is a large crafts shop with a wide range of goods. There are more crafts shops and stalls on Libertad and 16 de Septiembre, east of Corregidora.

Getting There & Away

Air Aeroméxico (☎ 215-64-74) has regular flights to/from Mexico City and Monterrey, while Aerolitoral (☎ 224-27-88) has one or two flights daily to/from Guadalajara with connections to Pacific coast resorts. Turismo Beverly (☎ 216-15-11), Tecnológico 118, can book flights.

Bus Querétaro is a hub for buses in many directions; the big, modern Central Camionera is 5km southeast of the center on the south side of the Mexico City-León highway. There's one building for deluxe and 1st class, another for 2nd class. Both buildings have cafeterías, telephone casetas, coin-operated pay phones, shops and luggage storage. Daily departures include:

Guadalajara – 350km, 4½ to 5½ hours; 7 deluxe ETN (US$27), frequent 1st-class Primera Plus and Ómnibus de México (US$20-21), frequent 2nd-class Flecha Amarilla and Oriente (US$20)

Guanajuato – 165km, 2½ to 3 hours; 2 1st-class Ómnibus de México (US$8), 5 2nd-class Flecha Amarilla (US$7), or take one of the frequent buses to Irapuato, from where buses leave for Guanajuato every few minutes

Mexico City (Terminal Norte) – 215km, 2½ to 3 hours; 30 deluxe ETN (US$16), 1st-class Primera Plus every 20 minutes (US$13), 14 1st-class Ómnibus de México (US$12), 2nd-class Flecha Amarilla every 10 minutes (many directo), 2nd-class Herradura de Plata every 40 minutes (US$11)

Mexico City (Zona Rosa) – 220km, 3 hours; 2 deluxe ETN (US$16)

Mexico City (Terminal Poniente) – 215km, 3 hours; 2nd-class Herradura de Plata every 2 hours (US$10)

Mexico City Airport – 230km, 3 hours; 13 1st-class Aeroplus (US$16)

Morelia – 195km, 3 to 4 hours; 5 1st-class Primera Plus (US$10), 6 2nd-class Flecha Amarilla (US$8.25)

San Luis Potosí – 202km, 2½ hours; 3 deluxe ETN (US$14.50), 20-odd 1st-class Servicios Coordinados, Transportes del Norte or Primera Plus (US$11-12), hourly 2nd-class Flecha Amarilla (US$10)

San Miguel de Allende – 60km, 1 hour; 3 deluxe ETN (US$5.50), 2nd-class Herradura de Plata and Flecha Amarilla every 40 minutes(US$3)

Tequisquiapan – 70km, 1 hour; 2nd-class Flecha Azul every 30 minutes (US$2)

Car If you want a car to explore the Sierra Gorda, Express Rent-a-Car (☎ 216-04-44) has competitive rates.

Getting Around

Once you have reached the city center, you can easily get to most sights on foot. The airport is an 8km taxi ride northeast of the center (US$3).

City buses run from 6 am until 9 or 10 pm and cost US$0.25. They can be infuriatingly slow. From the bus station, they leave from an open lot a few hundred meters away – turn right from the 2nd-class terminal, left from the 1st-class side. Several routes go to the center including Nos 8 and 19, which both go to the Alameda Hidalgo then up Ocampo. For a taxi, get a ticket first from the bus station booth (US$2).

To get out to the bus station from the center, take city bus No 19 or 36 or any other saying 'Terminal de Autobuses' heading south on the east side of the Alameda Hidalgo.

TEQUISQUIAPAN

• pop 24,000 • elev 1880m ☎ 4

This small town ('teh-kees-kee-AP-an') 70km southeast of Querétaro is a quaint, pleasant retreat from Mexico City or Querétaro, popular with city-dwellers on weekends. It used to be known for its thermal spring waters – Mexican presidents came here to ease their aches and tensions. Some local industries now use most of the hot water, but there are still some delightful cool-water pools, some set in pretty gardens at attractive hotels and posadas. It's a pleasure to simply stroll the streets, lined with brilliant purple bougainvillea and colorful colonial buildings. Tequisquiapan's name is sometimes playfully abbreviated to just TX, pronounced 'TEH-kees.'

Orientation & Information

The bus station is a vacant lot on the southwest outskirts of town, a 10-minute walk along Niños Héroes from the center. A local bus (US$0.25) to the Mercado will let you off on Carrizal, a two-minute walk northeast of the central Plaza Principal.

The tourist office (☎ 273-02-95) is on the northeast side of the Plaza Principal, normally open Wednesday to Sunday, with maps, brochures and information on Tequisquiapan and the state of Querétaro. There's a Bancomer branch nearby, with an ATM.

Things to See & Do

The wide and traffic-free **Plaza Principal** is surrounded by *portales* (arcades) glowing in rich orange-pink hues, overlooked by the 19th-century Templo de Santa María de la Asunción on the north side.

The main market, on Ezequiel Montes, and the **Mercado de Artesanías** (Crafts Market) on Carrizal, are just a couple of blocks away through little lanes. The large, verdant **Parque La Pila** is a short distance past the Mercado de Artesanías along Ezequiel Montes.

Balnearios The Hotel El Relox (see Places to Stay) has two excellent spring-fed swimming pools set in large, green, shady gardens. Nonguests can use these for US$12 a day, or take a private pool for US$12 per hour or a hot pool for US$20 per hour.

The large, cool pool at the Hotel Neptuno (see Places to Stay) is not quite so pleasant but a good value at US$2.75 per person. It's open 8 am to 6 pm daily from Easter to October, and just Saturday and Sunday in other months.

Other balnearios are just north of town along highway 120.

Other Activities Look for migratory birds at the **Santuario de Aves Migratorios La Palapa** by the dam at the north end of the lake just south of town – you'll see it on the right if you approach Tequis from San Juan del Río. Other things you can do include horseback riding, tennis and golf (ask at the tourist office or your hotel).

Special Events

The Feria Internacional del Queso y del Vino (International Wine and Cheese Fair), from late May to early June, attracts people from far and wide for tastings, music, charreadas and other events.

Places to Stay

Most places are pretty pricey; the best budget options are the posadas along Moctezuma. *Posada Tequisquiapan* (☎ 273-00-10, Moctezuma 6) has pretty gardens and a splendid grotto-like swimming pool. The spacious rooms have cable TV and start at US$17. Just down the road, *Posada San Francisco* (☎ 273-02-31, Moctezuma 2) also has a large garden and a swimming pool (overlooked by a statue of a ruminating nymph), and rooms at similar prices. There's also *Posada Los Arcos* (☎ 273-05-66, Moctezuma 12), in the same price range.

Hotel/Balneario Neptuno (☎ 273-02-24, Juárez Oriente 5), two blocks east of the Plaza Principal, has a big pool and lots of single/double rooms from US$19/33, as well as larger family rooms. *Posada del Virrey* (☎/fax 273-02-39, Prieto Norte 9) is one block west and two north of the Plaza Principal, at the corner of 16 de Septiembre. It's a pretty building with a pool and 22 rooms around a courtyard for US$42/46, including breakfast.

On the Plaza Principal, *Hotel La Plaza* (☎ 273-00-56, fax 273-02-89, Juárez 10) has a pool, restaurant, bar, parking and 17 varied rooms and suites from US$27 to US$60. On the other side of the plaza, *Hotel Maridelfi* (☎ 273-00-52, fax 273-10-78) is a lovely, comfortable hotel around nice gardens. It's popular with Mexican families. From Monday to Wednesday it costs US$27 per person for a room only; Thursday to Sunday the price is US$50 per person for a room and three meals a day.

Hotel El Relox (☎/fax 273-00-06, 273-00-66) has its entrance on Ezequiel Montes, 1½ blocks north of the Plaza Principal. It's set in extensive gardens with a restaurant, swimming pools, gym, tennis courts and private thermal pools.

Places to Eat

The cheapest place for a meal or snack is the rear of the main market, where many clean little *fondas* (food stalls) have tables under awnings in the patio. They're open daily from around 8 am to 8 pm.

Most places on the plaza are more expensive. *K'puchinos* is a good choice, with indoor and outdoor tables and a standard Mexican menu. Well-prepared main courses are around US$5 to US$7, with pastas and *antojitos* around US$4, and a big choice of coffees. *La Casa de la Arrachera* next door does breakfasts for US$3 and comida for US$4.50.

Getting There & Away

Tequisquiapan is about 20km northeast up highway 120 from the larger town of San Juan del Río, which is on highway 57. Buses to/from Tequis are all 2nd class. Flecha Azul runs every 30 minutes, 5.30 am to 7 pm, to Querétaro (70km, one hour, US$2); Flecha Amarilla goes every 40 minutes, 6 am to 8 pm, to/from Mexico City's Terminal Norte (184km, 2¾ hours, US$8).

NORTHEAST QUERÉTARO STATE
Bernal

• **pop 5200** • **elev 2067**

North of Tequisquiapan, a 10km detour west of highway 120, Bernal is a quaint, cute little town with a thriving weekend tourist trade. The attraction is the rocky peak called Peña de Bernal (2370m), a natural pyramid believed (by some at least) to impart a cosmic energy. It's said that Bernal's residents enjoy extraordinary longevity. You can stay at the plain *Posada Peña* (☎ 4-277-12-77) for US$8, eat at some reasonable restaurants, and browse through numerous craft and souvenir shops.

Highway 120

Those heading to/from northeast Mexico, or with a hankering to get off the beaten track, might consider following highway 120 northeast from Tequisquiapan over the scenic Sierra Gorda to the lush Huasteca area (covered in the Central Gulf Coast chapter). It's possible to get to most places on the way by bus, but it's much better with your own transport.

Heading north from Tequisquiapan, you pass Ezequiel Montes (the turnoff for Bernal) and then the **Freixenet Winery** (☎ 4-277-01-47), where you can see wine being made by '*método champenoise.*'

The next big town is **Cadereyta**, 38km from Tequis. On the eastern edge of town, signs point to the Quinta Fernando Schmoll, a botanical garden with over 4400 varieties of cactus.

After another 38km there's a turnoff going east to San Joaquín. Follow the good but very winding road for about 32km through the rugged sierra; stay on that road straight through San Joaquín, and continue a few kilometers to the little-visited **Ranas** archaeological site, with well-built walls and circular steps incorporated into a steep hillside. There are ball courts and a small hilltop pyramid. Dating from as early as the 8th century, the site is appealing for its rugged forest setting. It's open 9 am to 4 pm daily (US$1.50). San Joaquín has very basic lodgings and some places to eat.

Continuing north, the highway twists and turns up to 2300m at Pinal de Amoles and makes several dramatic descents and climbs before reaching **Jalpan** at 760m. This attractive town centers on the old mission church, constructed by Franciscan monks and their indigenous converts in the 1750s. The Museo de la Sierra Gorda outlines the pre-Hispanic cultures here, and the mission-building period (open daily; US$0.60). *Hotel María del Carmen* (☎ 4-296-03-28), on the plaza opposite the church, has clean, comfortable singles/doubles for US$14.25/20. *Hotel Misión Jalpan* (☎ 4-296-01-64), on the west side of the plaza, is especially attractive, with a good restaurant, big swimming pool, cable TV, carpets, phones and all the comforts of home for US$57. Inexpensive *Restaurant El Mesón*, on the corner of the plaza, serves up solid Mexican fare.

In the mid-18th century, Franciscans established four other beautiful missions in this remote region. Their leader was Fray Junípero Serra, who later went on to found another chain of missions in California. The churches have all been restored and are notable for their colorful façades carved with symbolic figures. Going east from Jalpan on highway 120, there are missions at **Landa de Matamoros** (1760-68); **Tilaco** (1754-62), about 10km south of the highway; and **Tancoyol** (1753-60), about 20km north of the highway. There's another mission north of Jalpan on highway 69, at **Concá** (1754-58).

Central Gulf Coast

The hot coastal plain between the Gulf of Mexico and the Sierra Madre Oriental has long been used as a travel corridor. Cortés and the conquistadors landed on the Gulf Coast and made their way up through the mountains to Tenochtitlán. Later, colonial trade routes crossed the region from the interior settlements to the port of Veracruz, with an important stop in what is now the city of Jalapa. Many modern travelers follow this coast between Mexico's northeast border and the popular regions farther south. The central Gulf Coast has also become a destination in itself; Mexican families flock here for seaside vacations, and in-creasing numbers of outdoor adventurers come to dive the offshore reefs, raft the wild rivers and climb Pico de Orizaba, Mexico's highest mountain.

The city of Veracruz (as opposed to the state) is famous for its tropical port ambiance, festive atmosphere and its riotous Carnaval. Jalapa, the capital of Veracruz state, lies inland. It enjoys a cooler climate, offers many cultural and colonial attractions and is surrounded by pretty towns dotting the Sierra Madre foothills. Other attractive towns include Córdoba, another colonial center, and Tlacotalpan, a once-important river port.

Highlights

- Xilitla's Las Pozas – surreal world of concrete buildings and sculptures, set near swimming holes and waterfalls

- El Tajín – mystical jungle-ringed ruins; extensively reconstructed city of the Classic Veracruz culture

- Voladores – ancient Totonac ceremony, costumed men revolving upside down around a 30m pole

- Jalapa's Museum of Anthropology – seven huge Olmec heads and hundreds of ancient artifacts, superbly exhibited

- Steamy Veracruz – Mexico's historic, heroic port, also a nightlife capital and tropical holiday hot spot

- Gulf Coast Beaches – 500km coastline with everything from secluded coves to Mexican holiday madness

- Wild Water – rivers from the sierra, offering exciting rafting and wonderful waterfalls in the lush rain forests of the Huasteca

- Pico de Orizaba – Mexico's tallest peak, a perfect volcanic cone, challenging for visiting climbers

CENTRAL GULF COAST

This chapter covers the coast and hinterland from Ciudad Madero in the north to Coatzacoalcos in the south – just over 600km as the crow flies but more than 800km by highway 180, which follows the curve of the coast. The region's major archaeological site is El Tajín, near Papantla, which shouldn't be missed; archaeology enthusiasts might also want to see smaller sites like Zempoala and Quiahuiztlán. Southern Veracruz was the Olmec heartland, but little evidence remains of their existence in the area, even at the Olmec headquarters of San Lorenzo. The best collection of the colossal 'Olmec heads' is in Jalapa's excellent Museo de Antropología, which also holds a superb collection of other Olmec artifacts. (Olmec head hunters should also visit Parque-Museo La Venta in Villahermosa; see the Tabasco & Chiapas chapter.)

History

Olmec The Olmec culture, Central America's earliest known civilization, built its first great center beginning around 1200 BC at San Lorenzo, in southern Veracruz state. The Olmecs prospered at San Lorenzo until about 900 BC, when it appears their city was violently destroyed. After it fell, La Venta in neighboring Tabasco became the main Olmec center until around 600 BC, when it too apparently came to a violent end. Olmec culture lingered for several centuries more at Tres Zapotes, in Veracruz, and was gradually subsumed by other cultures.

Classic Veracruz After the Olmec decline, the centers of civilization on the Gulf Coast moved west and north. El Pital, the ruins of which were discovered in the early 1990s, was a large city about 100km northwest of Veracruz port. It existed from about 100 to 600 AD, had links with Teotihuacán and may have held more than 20,000 people.

The Classic period (250 to 900 AD) saw the emergence in central and northern Veracruz of a number of power centers that were politically independent but shared religion and culture. Together they're known as the Classic Veracruz civilization. Their hallmark

is a unique style of carving, with pairs of parallel lines curved and interwoven. The style often appears on three types of mysterious carved stone objects; these objects are probably connected with the civilization's important ritual ball game. They are the U-shaped *yugo*, probably representing a wooden or leather belt worn in the game; the long, paddlelike *palma*; and the flat *hacha*, shaped a little like an ax head. The last two objects, which are often carved in human or animal forms, are thought to represent items attached to the front of the belt. Hachas may also have been court markers.

The most important Classic Veracruz center, El Tajín, was at its height from about 600 to 900 AD and contains at least 11 ball courts. Other main centers were Las Higueras, near Vega de Alatorre, close to the coast south of Nautla; and El Zapotal, near Ignacio de la Llave, south of Veracruz port. Classic Veracruz sites show influences from the Mayan lands and from Teotihuacán; in their turn, Veracruz cultures exported cotton, rubber, cacao and vanilla to central Mexico, influencing developments in Teotihuacán, Cholula and elsewhere.

Totonac, Huastec, Toltec & Aztec By 1200 AD, when El Tajín was abandoned, the Totonacs were establishing themselves from Tuxpan in the north to beyond Veracruz in the south. North of Tuxpan, the Huastec civilization, another web of small, probably independent states, flourished from 800 to 1200. The Huastecs were Mexico's chief cotton producers. They also built many ceremonial sites and developed great skill in stone carving.

During that time, the warlike Toltecs, who dominated much of central Mexico in the early Postclassic age, moved into the Gulf Coast area. They occupied the Huastec center Castillo de Teayo for some time between 900 and 1200. Toltec influence can also be seen at Zempoala, a Totonac site near Veracruz port. In the mid-15th century, the Aztecs subdued most of the Totonac and Huastec areas, exacting tribute of goods and sacrificial victims and maintaining garrisons to control revolts.

Colonial Era When Cortés arrived on the Gulf Coast in April 1519, he was able to make the Totonacs of Zempoala his first allies against the Aztecs – he told them to imprison five Aztec tribute collectors and vowed to protect them against reprisals. Cortés set up his first settlement, Villa Rica de la Vera Cruz (Rich Town of the True Cross), north of modern Veracruz port. Then he established a second settlement at La Antigua, where he scuttled his ships before advancing to Tenochtitlán, the Aztec capital. In May 1520 he returned to Zempoala and defeated the rival Spanish expedition sent to arrest him.

All the Gulf Coast was in Spanish hands by 1523. New diseases, particularly smallpox, decimated the indigenous population. Veracruz harbor became an essential link in trade and communication with Spain and was vital for anyone trying to rule Mexico, but the climate, tropical diseases and threat of pirate attacks inhibited the growth of Spanish settlements along the coast.

19th & 20th Centuries The population of Veracruz city actually shrank in the first half of the 19th century. In the second half, under dictator Porfirio Díaz, Mexico's first railway linked Veracruz to Mexico City in 1872, and some industries began to develop.

In 1901 oil was discovered in the Tampico area, and by the 1920s the region was producing a quarter of the world's oil. That proportion eventually declined, but new oil fields were found in southern Veracruz, and by the 1980s the Gulf Coast held well over half of Mexico's reserves and refining capacity.

Geography & Climate
More than 40 rivers run from the inland mountains to the central Gulf Coast, mostly passing through a well-watered, hilly landscape. Some of these rivers are ideal for white-water rafting, and there are many picturesque waterfalls. The north is primarily an undulating coastal plain, while the flood-prone southeast holds low-lying areas, including marshes and jungles that extend into Tabasco.

The region is warm and humid most of the time: hotter along the coast, wetter in the foothills, hottest and wettest of all in the low-lying southeast. Two-thirds or more of the rain falls between June and September. The city of Veracruz receives about 1650mm of rain a year. From April to October it has temperatures well over 30°C, falling into the teens at night only from December to February. Tuxpan and Tampico, on the north coast, are a bit drier, a little hotter in summer and a fraction cooler in winter. Coatzacoalcos in the southeast gets 3000mm of rain a year.

Population & People
Veracruz, with about 7 million people, is Mexico's third most populous state. Many Africans were shipped as slaves to the Gulf Coast in the 16th century, and their descendants, plus more recent immigrants from Cuba, contribute a visible African element to the population and culture. Of the region's nearly 500,000 indigenous people, the most numerous are the 150,000 Totonacs and 150,000 Huastecs. (See 'The Huastecs,' 'The Totonacs' and 'Voladores' in this chapter for more on these peoples.)

Tampico & the Huasteca

Inland from the port city of Tampico lies the fertile, often beautiful Huasteca ('wass-TEK-a') region, where the coastal plain meets the fringes of the Sierra Madre Oriental. Spread over southern Tamaulipas, eastern San Luis Potosí, northern Veracruz and small corners of Querétaro and Hidalgo, the region is named after the Huastec people who have lived here for about 3000 years.

Heading inland from the Huasteca to the Bajío region or Mexico City, four steep, winding routes cross the Sierra: highway 70, from Ciudad Valles to San Luis Potosí; highway 120, from Xilitla toward Querétaro; highway 85, from Tamazunchale to Ixmiquilpan (near which you can turn off toward

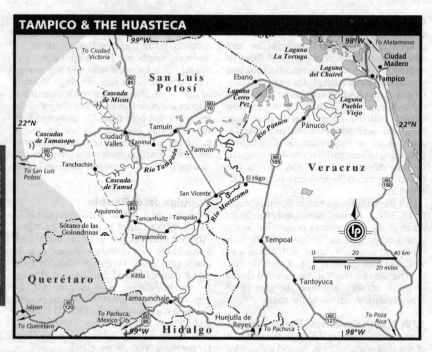

TAMPICO & THE HUASTECA

Quéretaro), Pachuca and Mexico City; and highway 105, from Huejutla to Pachuca and on into Mexico City via highway 85.

TAMPICO & CIUDAD MADERO

Tampico: • pop 279,000 ☎ 1
Ciudad Madero: • pop 171,000 ☎ 1

Sweaty, smelly, seedy but always jolly, Tampico, a few kilometers upstream from the mouth of the Río Pánuco, is at the southeastern tip of the state of Tamaulipas. The nearby beaches are popular with Mexican families on holiday, but few international travelers stop here. Hotel prices are slightly inflated by the oil business, but reasonable-value lodging is available, as is good seafood.

Though somewhat faded since its 1920s heyday, Tampico is still Mexico's busiest port – a tropical place where bars stay open late and sailors search for sleaze in the blocks around the waterfront. In the daytime, the downtown area is surprisingly attractive, particularly the redeveloped Plaza

de la Libertad, surrounded by 19th-century French-style buildings.

Ciudad Madero, between Tampico and the coast, is the processing center for the country's oldest oil fields and has a wide sandy beach.

History

In 1523 Cortés defeated the native Huastecs and founded a colony called San Estéban, now Pánuco, 30km upriver from Tampico. In the next few years he prevailed not only over the rebellious Huastecs but also over Spanish rivals. Nuño de Guzmán was named royal governor of the Pánuco area in 1527, but was pressured by Cortés to move to western and northern regions where he concentrated on pillage, slaughter and slave raids until he was recalled to Spain.

In the 1530s a mission was established in Tampico to convert the Huastecs to Christianity. The town was destroyed by pirates in 1684 but was refounded in 1823 by families from Altamira, to the north. After 1901, when oil was discovered in the area, Tampico suddenly became the world's biggest oil port: rough, tough and booming. The oil and its profits were under foreign control until 1938, when the industry was nationalized by President Lázaro Cárdenas following a strike by Tampico oil workers.

Mexico's 1970s and '80s oil boom took place farther down the coast, but the Tampico-Ciudad Madero area remains important. Pipelines and barge fleets bring oil from fields north and south, onshore and offshore, to the area's refineries and harbor, and

Ciudad Madero is the headquarters of the powerful oil workers' union, the STPRM.

Orientation

Tampico lies in a marshy region near the mouth of the Río Pánuco. The city is ringed by several lakes, including Laguna del Chairel, which is used for recreation, and the unattractive Laguna del Carpintero, which isn't. You'll cross numerous small estuaries as you approach the city from the north or the west. Going south, the spectacular Puente Tampico (Tampico Bridge) crosses the Río Pánuco to Veracruz state.

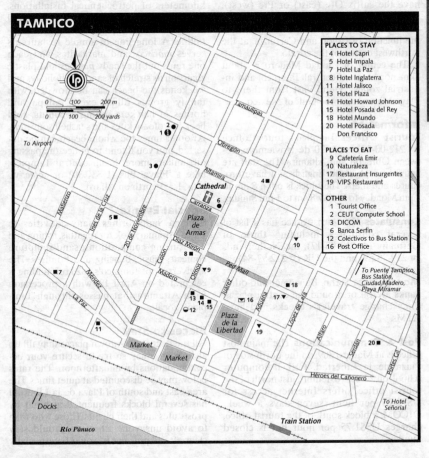

TAMPICO

PLACES TO STAY
4 Hotel Capri
5 Hotel Impala
7 Hotel La Paz
8 Hotel Inglaterra
11 Hotel Jalisco
13 Hotel Plaza
14 Hotel Howard Johnson
15 Hotel Posada del Rey
18 Hotel Mundo
20 Hotel Posada Don Francisco

PLACES TO EAT
9 Cafetería Emir
10 Naturaleza
17 Restaurant Insurgentes
19 VIPS Restaurant

OTHER
1 Tourist Office
2 CEUT Computer School
3 DICOM
6 Banca Serfin
12 Colectivos to Bus Station
16 Post Office

To Airport

Tamaulipas
Obregón
Altamira
Cathedral
Carranza
Plaza de Armas
Díaz Mirón
Colón
Madero
Olmos
Ped Mall
Juárez
Aduana
López de Lara
Altero
Serdán
Pórtes Gil

Matienzo
Inés de la Cruz
20 de Noviembre
Méndez
La Paz

To Puente Tampico, Bus Station, Ciudad Madero, Playa Miramar

Plaza de la Libertad

Market
Market

Docks

Héroes del Cañonero

To Hotel Señorial

Train Station

Río Pánuco

Downtown Tampico centers on two plazas. The *zócalo*, or Plaza de Armas, has a grand rotunda and a 20th-century cathedral on its north side. One block south and one block east is the elegant Plaza de la Libertad, with balconied buildings on three sides. Hotels and restaurants of all grades are within a few blocks of these two plazas. Down a gentle hill south of either plaza you come to a sleazy area containing the market, train station and riverside docks – it isn't very safe at night around here. Tampico's bus station is well north of the downtown area.

Addresses on east-west streets usually have the suffix Ote (east) or Pte (west), while those on north-south streets are Nte (north) or Sur (south). The dividing point is the junction of Colón and Carranza, at the northwest corner of the zócalo.

The center of Ciudad Madero is about 8km northeast of central Tampico, and industrial zones extend east from there to Playa Miramar, on the Gulf of Mexico.

Information

Tourist Offices Tampico's tourist office (☎ 212-00-07) is on 20 de Noviembre, between Obregón and Altamira. The staff are helpful, speak some English and have brochures and maps. The office is open 8 am to 7 pm Monday to Friday, 8 am to 1 pm Sunday.

Consulates The tourist office has a list of several consulates, including those of Germany (☎ 212-98-17), the Netherlands (☎ 219-28-59) and the UK (☎ 212-97-84).

Money Banca Serfin, Bancomer and other banks are on or around the central plazas. They change traveler's checks and have ATMs.

Post & Communications The main post office is at Madero 309, on the north side of Plaza de la Libertad. CEUT computer school, on 20 de Noviembre just north of the tourist office, offers Internet access for US$2.25 per hour, seven days a week. DICOM, a block south of the tourist office, charges US$1.75 per hour but is closed Sunday.

Museo de la Cultura Huasteca

The Museum of Huastec Culture, in Ciudad Madero's Instituto Tecnológico, has a small collection from the pre-Hispanic Huastec culture and a worthwhile bookstore. From central Tampico take a 'Boulevard A López Mateos' bus north on Alfaro and ask for 'Tecnológico Madero.' The museum is open 10 am to 5 pm Monday to Saturday (free).

Playa Miramar

The 10km-long Playa Miramar is about 15km from downtown Tampico; to get there you pass central Ciudad Madero and several kilometers of petrochemical installations. The beach is wide and reasonably clean, and the lukewarm water is clear, if not crystalline. A long line of simple restaurants serves *mariscos* and margaritas, and each one rents out the shady *palapas* and plastic chairs on its stretch of sand. On holidays and weekends the beach can be crowded, with family groups filling every palapa and hordes of hawkers selling coconuts, cold beer, Styrofoam kites and seashell souvenirs. At other times the whole beach can be deserted, and you'll tend to notice the passing oil tankers more. From central Tampico, take a 'Playa' bus (US$0.30) or *colectivo* (US$1.75) north on Alfaro.

Special Events

Semana Santa brings many activities to Playa Miramar; look for regattas, fishing and windsurfing competitions, sand-sculpture contests, music, dancing and bonfires. The anniversary of Tampico's 1823 refounding is celebrated on April 12, with a procession from Altamira that passes through Tampico's zócalo.

Places to Stay

All the decent downtown places may fill up at holiday times, so try to secure your accommodations by midafternoon. The rates below may be discounted at quiet times. The area east and south of Plaza de la Libertad has several blocks frequented at night by prostitutes and their clients. Those who wish to avoid unsavory attention should stay clear after 7 pm, and it would be especially unwise to walk in the dark streets around the market and down toward the waterfront.

Budget The *Hotel Capri* (☎ 212-26-80, *Juárez 202 Nte*) is the best value in town. Small, clean rooms with ceiling fans, private baths and hot water start at US$11 for a single or double, plus a little more with TV. Almost as good is the *Hotel Posada Don Francisco* (☎ 219-25-34, *Díaz Mirón 710 Ote*), a clean, well-kept inn with air-conditioned singles/doubles starting at US$17/22. A cheaper, less convenient option is the *Hotel Señorial* (☎ 212-40-90, *Madero 1006 Ote*), 400m east of the Plaza de la Libertad, with worn beds in tiny rooms for US$9/14 (parking available).

Down among the foul smells, cheap cantinas and air of nocturnal danger near the markets are two inexpensive possibilities: the *Hotel La Paz* (☎ 214-11-19, *La Paz 307 Pte*), with air-conditioned rooms for US$20, fan-cooled rooms at US$16.50; and the *Hotel Jalisco* (☎ 212-27-92, *La Paz 120 Pte*), with small fan-cooled rooms and secure parking for US$17.50.

Mid-Range Most mid-range hotel rooms in Tampico have carpet, cable TV, air-con and phone, for reasonable prices. The *Hotel Posada del Rey* (☎ 214-11-55, *Madero 218 Ote*) is one such place, charging US$30/31 for singles/doubles. It has a good location, with some rooms overlooking the handsome Plaza de la Libertad. *Hotel Plaza* (☎ 214-17-84, *Madero 204 Ote*) has smaller rooms – clean and comfortable enough – for US$22/26 with air-con. Better value can be found three blocks east of Plaza de Armas at *Hotel Mundo* (☎ 212-03-60), on Díaz Mirón between López de Lara and Aduana, where clean, spacious rooms with color TV, air-con, phone and good beds cost US$31/35 for singles/doubles; it also has parking and a popular mid-priced restaurant.

Hotel Impala (☎ 212-09-90, *Díaz Mirón 220 Pte*), 1½ blocks west of the zócalo, has all the mid-range facilities but seems overpriced at US$39/45.

Top End The top downtown place is the Best Western *Hotel Inglaterra* (☎ 219-28-57, *Díaz Mirón Ote 116*), on the zócalo, offering 120 air-conditioned singles or doubles with all the modern conveniences at US$87. It offers its own fancy but reasonably priced restaurant, a small swimming pool and free shuttle service to and from the airport. *Hotel Howard Johnson* (☎ 212-76-76, *Madero 210 Ote*) is also central, with clean, tasteful, modern, air-conditioned singles/doubles for US$60/70.

Out toward the airport, *Hotel Camino Real* (☎ 213-88-11, *Avenida Hidalgo 2000*) is Tampico's most luxurious hotel, with rooms and bungalows facing a tropical garden-courtyard and a large pool. Prices are around US$160 for one or two people.

Out by the beach, *Club Maeva Miramar* (☎ 217-19-94) is a large, imposing and somewhat snooty resort hotel, where a room with all the comforts costs US$194 for two adults in high season, including three meals.

Places to Eat
Tampico is no gourmet paradise, but the seafood can be good. A local specialty is *carne asada tampiqueña*, which is beefsteak marinated in garlic, oil and oregano and usually served with guacamole, strips of chili and corn chips. The smart restaurant at the *Best Western Inglaterra* does a good version of it for about US$9.

Vegetarians (and others) should try *Naturaleza* (*Aduana 107 Nte*), which has a good whole-meal bakery, as well as an excellent vegetarian *comida corrida* for US$3.25. It opens for breakfast but closes at 6 pm.

Cafetería Emir (*Olmos 107 Sur*) is popular with locals despite wobbly tables and loud music. Quesadillas and enchiladas cost about US$2.75, and meat and fish dishes from US$3 to US$6. *Restaurant Insurgentes*, on Díaz Mirón, is a good choice for inexpensive seafood (US$3.50 and up) and meat dishes (US$3).

Popular with prosperous tampiqueños is the *VIPS* on Plaza de la Libertad at the corner of Aduana and Madero. It offers a large selection of salads and American and Mexican dishes, with speedy service and a

CENTRAL GULF COAST

bright and cheery atmosphere. Set meals run US$3.50 to US$4.50, and main dishes are US$4 to US$6.

Getting There & Away

Air Mexicana Airlines (☎ 213-96-00), whose city office is at Universidad 700-1, has flights daily to/from Mexico City. Aerolitoral (☎ 228-08-57) flies to/from Monterrey and Veracruz with connections to Villahermosa.

Bus The new and inconvenient Tampico bus station is 7km from downtown, on Rosalio Bustamente. It has a left-luggage room and a few pay phones, but it lacks a restaurant and has no place to sit down until you have a ticket and are admitted to the departure lounges.

Most of the bus companies don't display their timetables, so you have to ask at each desk to find the next departure time for your destination. Connections are available to most major towns north of Mexico City and down the Gulf Coast. The following daily departure information is for 1st-class and deluxe services – 2nd-class buses also run to most of these destinations.

Matamoros – 570km, 7 hours; 3 Futura, 7 ADO (US$22)

Mexico City (Terminal Norte) – 515km, 9 to 10 hours; 1 UNO deluxe (US$40), 10 ADO, 7 Ómnibus de México (US$25)

Monterrey – 530km, 7½ hours; 10 Futura (US$27)

Nuevo Laredo – 755km, 11 hours; 4 Futura (US$39)

Poza Rica – 250km, 4 to 5 hours; 1 UNO deluxe (US$20), hourly ADO (US$13)

San Luis Potosí – 410km, 7 to 8 hours; 2 Ómnibus de México, 4 Futura (US$24)

Tuxpan – 190km, 3½ hours; hourly ADO (US$10.50)

Veracruz – 490km, 10 hours; 1 UNO deluxe (US$40), 20 ADO (US$24)

Long-distance 1st-class buses also go to Reynosa, Soto la Marina, Villahermosa and Jalapa. Towns in the Huasteca are mostly reached by 2nd-class local buses. The quickest options are probably Vencadora for Ciudad Valles and Tamazunchale, and Autobuses Blancos for Huejutla.

Train For rail buffs only, train No 171 departs for Ciudad Victoria at 7.50 am on Tuesday, Thursday and Saturday (236km, five hours, US$3.75).

Car & Motorcycle Highway 180 north of Tampico is a good four-lane divided highway for about 80km, then it's two-lane northeast to Aldama or northwest to Ciudad Victoria. Heading south from Tampico, highway 180 soars across the Puente Tampico (US$3 toll) and continues down to Tuxpan. It's an adequate two-lane road, but avoid driving it at night.

If you want a car to explore the Huasteca, there are several rental agencies in Tampico, including Dollar (☎ 228-53-81), Fast (☎ 227-25-75), and National (☎ 213-54-34).

Getting Around

Tampico's colectivo taxis are large, old US cars, usually bright yellow, with the destinations painted on the doors. They are inexpensive, but slower than a regular taxi because they stop frequently.

To/From the Airport Tampico airport is 15km north of downtown. Transporte Terrestre (☎ 228-45-88) runs colectivo combis from the airport to anywhere in Tampico-Ciudad Madero for about US$3, depending on distance.

To/From the Bus Station Taxi tickets to the center cost US$2.25. Colectivos wait outside the station and are a little cheaper. From the city center to the bus station, take a 'Perimetral' or 'Perimetral-CC' colectivo from Olmos, a block south of the zócalo (US$0.40).

CIUDAD VALLES
● pop 102,200 ● elev 80m ☎ 1

Ciudad Valles ('VAH-yes') lies at the junction of highway 85 (the Pan-American) and highway 70, which runs east-west from Tampico to San Luis Potosí. If you're heading south on the Pan-American, the city lies just over halfway between Monterrey and Mexico City. It's a convenient overnight stop for motorists and a good base for trips into the

Huasteca region. Cattle and coffee are among its most important commercial products.

The town is pleasant enough, but the real attractions are in the surrounding countryside (see the Around Ciudad Valles section) – they're most conveniently seen by car, but if you have the time you can get to them on local buses.

Orientation & Information

Highway 85, also called Boulevard Mexico-Laredo, curves through town from north to south – for the main plaza, go six blocks west of this road on Avenida Juárez or Avenida Hidalgo. Highway 70 bypasses town on the south side. The main bus station, the Central Camionera, is at the southern edge of town. A small tourist information booth is on the west side of highway 85, just north of the bus station – ask here about getting to nearby attractions by local buses.

Places to Stay

Several budget hotels lie near the bus station. The ordinary looking *Hotel San Carlos* (☎ 381-21-42), straight across the street, has clean, comfy rooms with air-con and TV for US$11/13.

Hotel Piña (☎ 382-01-83, *Juárez 210*), a block east of the plaza, is a good budget hotel, with a choice of clean singles/doubles ranging from US$12/15 with fan to US$19/23 with air-con and TV. *Hotel Rex* (☎ 381-04-11, *Hidalgo 418*), 3½ blocks east of the plaza, is also OK, with moderately sized rooms starting at US$15.50/19. Both have off-street parking.

Stepping up in price, *Hotel San Fernando* (☎ 382-01-84, *Mexico-Laredo 5 Nte*) is a pleasant well-run place, offering spacious, comfortable rooms with air-con, TV, phone and parking for US$23/26.

A few blocks north of the center on the east side of Boulevard Mexico-Laredo, *Hotel Valles* (☎ 382-00-22) is a very stylish motel with a delightful tropical garden and a big swimming pool. The large air-conditioned rooms start at US$44/51, and there's a campground/trailer park where sites with full hookups cost around US$7.50 per person.

Places to Eat

The best places to eat are the hotel restaurants, such as *La Troje*, at Hotel Piña, which does pasta, pizza, and the usual Mexican standards for US$3 to US$4. Hotel Valles has two restaurants – including a good steak house, the *Restaurant Del Bosque* – as well as an open-air bar. The restaurant at *Hotel San Fernando* is open 24 hours.

Getting There & Away

Bus The Central Camionera is in its own little neighborhood, just east of highway 85 on the way to Tamazunchale and Mexico City. It's quite user-friendly, with pay phones and a left-luggage room. A booth sells taxi tickets to the center of town for US$1.60. The principal 1st-class lines are TransPaís, Ómnibus de Oriente, Línea Azul and Transportes Frontera. Flecha Roja and other companies offer 2nd-class service. Many buses are *de paso*. Daily departures include:

Matamoros – 544km, 10 hours; 14 1st-class (US$25), several 2nd-class (US$21)

Mexico City (Terminal Norte) – 495km, 10 hours; 12 1st-class (US$18), hourly 2nd-class (US$15.75)

Monterrey – 514km, 8 hours; 18 1st-class (US$25.50), numerous 2nd-class (US$22)

San Luis Potosí – 262km, 4½ to 5 hours; dozens of 1st-class (US$13), frequent 2nd-class (US$10)

Tampico – 138km, 2½ hours; frequent 1st-class (US$7.50) and 2nd-class (US$6.50)

Regular buses also go to Pachuca, Ciudad Victoria, Tamazunchale and Xilitla.

Car & Motorcycle West to San Luis Potosí (262km), highway 70 is spectacular as it rises across the Sierra Madre to the Altiplano Central. It's a twisting road, and you can get stuck behind slow trucks and buses, so don't count on doing it in a hurry. East to Tampico, highway 70 is in worse condition but is straighter and faster. Going south, highway 85 goes to Tamazunchale and then southwest towards Mexico City. You can also continue east from Tamazunchale to Huejutla, circling the Huasteca back to Tampico.

CENTRAL GULF COAST

The Huastecs

The Huastec language is classified as one of the Mayance family, along with the languages of the Yucatán Maya – possibly stemming from a single tongue once spoken all down the Gulf Coast. The Huastec language may have split from the rest of the family in about 900 BC, when the Olmec culture arose in the intervening area. The central-Mexican feathered serpent god Quetzalcóatl was probably of Huastec origin.

The Huastecs' greatest period was roughly 800 to 1200 AD. Under a number of independent rulers, they built many ceremonial centers, practiced phallic fertility rites and expanded as far west as northeast Querétaro and Hidalgo. They developed great skill in making pottery and in carving stone and shells. The two most interesting Huastec sites to visit are Tamuín (see the Around Ciudad Valles section) and Castillo de Teayo (see the Around Tuxpan section), though neither is spectacular.

After the Spanish conquest, during the second half of the 16th century, slavery and imported diseases cut the Huastec population from an estimated one million to probably under 100,000. Rebellions began and continued into the 19th century. Today, about 150,000 Huastecs live in the Huasteca, mostly between Ciudad Valles and Tamazunchale, and east of Tantoyuca. Many of the women still wear quechquémitls, colorfully embroidered with traditional trees of life, animals, flowers and two-armed crosses. Huastecs still practice land-fertility ceremonies, particularly dances.

AROUND CIUDAD VALLES
Archaeological Sites

The important Huastec ceremonial center of **Tamuín** flourished from about 700 to 1200 AD. Today it's one of the few Huastec sites worth visiting, though don't expect anything spectacular. The only cleared part of the 170,000-sq-meter site is a plaza with platforms made of river stones on all four sides. Look for a low bench, with two conical altars, extending from a small platform in the middle of the plaza – the bench has the remains of some 1000-year-old frescoes that may represent priests of Quetzalcóatl.

Southwest of the Tamuín site are two unrestored pyramids (on private property), and southwest of them is the Puente de Dios (God's Bridge), a notch in a ridgeline on the horizon. At the winter solstice, around December 22, you can stand on the main Tamuín platform and watch the sun set into the Puente de Dios, with the pair of pyramids exactly between them, all aligned with the Río Tampaón.

To get to the Tamuín site, go first to the town of Tamuín, 30km east of Ciudad Valles on highway 70. A kilometer or so east of the town, turn south from the highway down a road marked 'San Vicente.' Follow this road roughly south for 5km to a small 'zona arqueológica' sign; from there it's 800m west to the ruins. Frequent buses between Tampico and Ciudad Valles go through Tamuín. The rest of the way you must walk or take a taxi.

Waterfalls & Swimming Spots

Many rivers flow eastward from the well-watered slopes of the sierra, forming cascades, waterfalls and many shady spots for a cool swim on a hot Huasteca day. One of the nicest areas is around Tamasopo, 5km north of highway 70, about 55km west of Ciudad Valles. **Cascadas de Tamasopo** has good swimming, and there's a beautiful natural arch.

The **Cascadas de Micos** are north of highway 70, just a few kilometers west of Ciudad Valles. They're not so good for swimming, but rental canoes are available on weekends.

Another fun place to get wet is **Coy Parque Acuático** (☎ 1-382-41-59), south of town on highway 85, where a day pass to the water slides and swimming pool costs US$4/3 for adults/children. For detailed information about these and other watery attractions, ask at the tourist information booth in Ciudad Valles.

Taninul

To reach this small village, turn south off highway 70 between Ciudad Valles and Tamuín. The **Museo Lariab**, newly established here, has exhibits on ancient and contemporary Huasteca. It's next to the **Hotel Taninul** (☎ /fax 1-382-00-00), which offers hot mineral springs and moderately expensive accommodations.

Aquismón
• pop 1590

The Huastec village of Aquismón, 5km up a side road west of highway 85, holds its market on Saturday. The Zacamsón dance is a specialty around Aquismón. In its full version it has more than 75 parts, danced at different times of the day and night. At festivals much drinking of sugarcane alcohol accompanies the performances. Traditional dances are also performed for festivals of San Miguel Arcángel and the Virgen de Guadalupe (see Tancanhuitz, below).

About 30km north of Aquismón by rough roads and a walk (allow 1½ hours from Aquismón), **Cascada de Tamul** plunges 105m into the pristine Río Santa María. Alternatively, you can usually reach the falls from Tanchachin, south of highway 70, by a 2½-hour launch trip on the river (this option is unavailable when the river's in flood, at which time the falls can be up to 300m wide).

About 1½ hours west of Aquismón on a rough and roundabout road, **Sótano de las Golondrinas** (Pit of the Swallows) is a 300m-deep hole, home to tens of thousands of swallows and parakeets and a challenge for serious spelunkers. The birds fly out en masse just after sunrise and return in the afternoon around 5 to 5.30 pm.

Tancanhuitz
• pop 2860

The small town of Tancanhuitz, also called Pedro Antonio de los Santos or Ciudad Santos, is in the heart of the area inhabited by modern-day Huastecs. It's in a narrow, tree-covered valley 52km south of Ciudad Valles, 3km east of highway 85. A lively market takes place on Sunday. Pre-Hispanic Huastec remains can be seen near **Tampamolón**, a few kilometers east.

Tancanhuitz and Aquismón are centers for the festivals of San Miguel Arcángel on September 28 and 29 and the Virgen de Guadalupe on December 12. Huastec dances performed then include Las Varitas (The Little Twigs) and Zacamsón (Small Music), which imitate the movements of wild creatures.

XILITLA
• pop 5140 ☎ 1

On the slopes of the sierra at about 1000m, this small town has a 16th-century church and mission, a temperate climate and lots of rain. It's in a rain forest area, with abundant bird life, wild orchids, waterfalls, caves and walking trails. The most notable attraction, however, is **Las Pozas** (the Pools) – a truly bizarre collection of concrete buildings, bridges, pavilions, sculptures and spiral stairways leading nowhere, the surreal fantasy of Sir Edward James (see 'An Eccentric Englishman'). Skillfully cast by local workers in the 1960s and '70s, the concrete and reinforcing rod is already deteriorating in the jungle environment. Swimming holes and waterfalls make this a popular picnic spot on weekends. The site is on a dirt road a few kilometers east of Xilitla – turn left after the bridge about 2km from town. It's usually open 9 am to 6 pm daily (US$1).

In Xilitla, **El Castillo** (☎ 365-00-38, Ocampo 105) was built by Edward James' friend and building foreman, Plutarco Gastelum. It's now a guest house providing comfortable, somewhat unconventional rooms from US$35 to US$75 (advance bookings recommended; check the website at www.junglegossip.com). On the plaza in the middle of town, **Hotel María** (☎ 365-00-49) is an inexpensive family hotel. **El Viejo**, also on the plaza, serves excellent Italian food.

Xilitla can be reached by bus from Ciudad Valles, Tampico or Querétaro. Highway 120, west to Jalpan then southwest towards Querétaro, is an exciting route through the Sierra Gorda (see the Northeast Querétaro section in the Northern Central Highlands chapter).

An Eccentric Englishman

Edward James was born in 1907, descended from the not uncommon union of an American multimillionaire and the lesser English aristocracy. Educated at Eton and Oxford, James was well endowed with money, charm and social connections, and he soon became part of London's lavish social and artistic set. He bankrolled the publication of poems by John Betjeman, supported Dylan Thomas for a short time and sponsored a ballet so his own wife could play the lead. When his marriage broke up, in the early 1930s, he moved to Europe and became absorbed in modern art, especially surrealism. He collected Picassos, was a patron of Magritte and commissioned work by Dalí (he acquired the original Dalí-designed sofa in the shape of Mae West's lips).

As WWII threatened, James moved to the USA – mixing with film people in Hollywood and writers and artists in Taos, NM – and visited Mexico for the first time. Among other projects, he donated money for the bizarre Watts Towers in suburban Los Angeles. In 1945, James discovered Xilitla and was besotted by the exotic plants and birds of the rain forest. Initially he devoted himself to cultivating local orchids, but when a cold snap destroyed his collection in 1962, James turned to a more enduring medium. With the help of his Mexican friend Plutarco Gastelum (who was quite an eccentric in his own right), he hired local workers to make giant, colored, concrete flowers beside his idyllic jungle stream. For the next 17 years, James and Gastelum created ever larger and stranger structures, many of which were never finished and all of which were totally impractical. James died in 1984, making no provision to maintain his creation, which is already decomposing into yet another Mexican ruin. As Salvador Dalí reputedly said: 'Edward James is crazier than all the surrealists put together. They pretend, but he is the real thing.'

❀ ❀ ❀ ❀ ❀ ❀ ❀ ❀ ❀ ❀ ❀

TAMAZUNCHALE
- pop 20,600 • elev 20m ☎ changing

In 2000 the telephone area code is due to change to ☎ 1 from 136, with the digits 36 added to the start of every local number (for example, the number 2-01-43 will become 362-01-43).

Quaint Tamazunchale, 95km south of Ciudad Valles on highway 85, is in a low-lying area of tropical vegetation with exuberant bird life and an attractive river. The Sunday market is colorful but has little in the way of Huastec handicrafts. For the Day of the Dead (November 2), the people spread carpets of confetti and marigold petals on the streets. There's no bus station as such, but buses pull in at various company offices on Avenida 20 de Noviembre (the commercial stretch of highway 85 as it passes through town).

The **Hotel González** (☎ 2-01-36, 20 de Noviembre 301) is the cheapest decent place in town, with basic rooms with fan and TV for US$12/14 for a single/double, US$20 with air-con. Nearby **Hotel Mirador** (☎ 2-01-90) is similar in quality and price. **Hotel Tropical** (☎ 2-00-41, 20 de Noviembre 404) has slightly nicer rooms for US$16/17.50. The best hotel in town is the **Hotel Tamazunchale** (☎ 2-04-96, 20 de Noviembre 122), which offers gorgeous rooms with all the modern conveniences for US$33/52.

Southwest of Tamazunchale, highway 85 climbs steeply to Ixmiquilpan, then continues to Pachuca. This is the most direct route from the Huasteca to Mexico City. It's another steep but scenic route up onto the Sierra Madre. You can encounter mist and fog – start early for the best chance of clear conditions.

HUEJUTLA
- pop 30,300 • elev 30m ☎ changing

On the northern edge of Hidalgo state, but still in the semitropical lowlands, Huejutla (or Huejutla de Reyes) has a fortress-monastery dating from the 16th century, when this area was frontier territory and

In 2000 the telephone area code is due to change to ☎ 7 from 789, with the digits 89 added to the start of every local number (for example, the number 2-01-43 will become 892-01-43).

foreign newcomers were subject to attack by the indigenous population. The big Sunday market in the square attracts many Nahua people from outlying villages. For lodging try the *Hotel Oviedo (☎ 6-05-59, Morelos 12)*. It has bright, clean rooms with air-con and TV for US$11/16.50. Rooms at *Hotel Fayad (☎ 6-00-40)*, on Hidalgo at Morelos, are not quite as nice, and they're slightly more expensive at US$13/17.

SOUTH OF HUEJUTLA
Highway 105 mostly goes through lush, rolling farmland from Tampico, but south of Huejutla it climbs into the lovely Sierra Madre Oriental. It's a tortuous and sometimes foggy road to Pachuca. En route, you'll pass old monasteries at **Molango** and **Zacualtipán**.

The highway then leaves the Sierra Madre and drops several hundred meters to picturesque **Metzquititlán**, in the fertile Río Tulancingo valley. The village of **Metztitlán**, 23km northwest up the valley, has a fairly well preserved monastery. It was the center of an Otomí state that the Aztecs couldn't conquer. Back on highway 105, an 800m climb up from the Tulancingo valley, about 100km by road, brings you to **Atotonilco El Grande**, 34km from Pachuca (see Around Pachuca in the Around Mexico City chapter).

Northern Veracruz

South of Tampico you enter the state of Veracruz, whose northern half is mostly rolling plains lying between the coast and the southern end of the Sierra Madre Oriental. The Laguna de Tamiahua stretches 90km along the coast and is separated from the Gulf of Mexico by a series of sandbars and islands; here you'll find isolated though sometimes polluted beaches, as well as opportunities for fishing and birding. The major archaeological attraction is the site of El Tajín, usually reached from Papantla. Vehicles are stopped and sometimes searched at army checkpoints along this coast – the soldiers are courteous to tourists.

TUXPAN
- **pop 74,700 ☎ 7**

Tuxpan ('TOOKS-pahn,' sometimes spelled Tuxpam) is a fishing town and minor oil port near the mouth of the Río Tuxpan, 300km north of Veracruz and 190km south of Tampico. The city has a wide river and pleasant parks, and it's an agreeable and inexpensive place to break a journey. A nearby beach, 12km away, is popular with vacationing Mexicans, though it doesn't look like an idyllic seaside resort.

Orientation
The downtown area, on the north bank of the Río Tuxpan, spreads six blocks upstream from the high bridge that spans the river. The riverfront road, Boulevard Heroles, passes under the bridge and runs east to the beach at Playa Norte. A block inland from Heroles is Avenida Juárez, with many hotels. Parque Reforma, at the west end of Juárez, functions as a zócalo and is popular in the cool of the evening.

Information
The tourist office (☎ 834-01-77) in the Palacio Municipal is open 9 am to 3 pm and 4 to 6 pm Monday to Friday, but it doesn't offer much. There are pay phones in Parque Reforma, and a Banamex (with ATM) is nearby. Banca Serfin and Bancomer, on Juárez, also have ATMs. The post office is on Mina, a few blocks north of Juárez.

Museums
On the west side of Parque Reforma is a small **Museo Arqueológico** with Totonac and Huastec artifacts. It's generally open 9 am to 1 pm and 4 to 8 pm daily (free).

The **Museo Histórico de la Amistad México-Cuba** (Mexican-Cuban Friendship Museum), on the south side of the river,

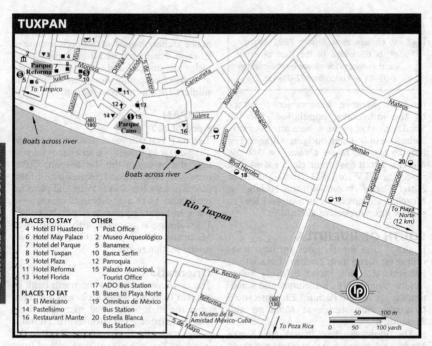

TUXPAN

To Tampico

Boats across river

Boats across river

Río Tuxpan

To Playa Norte (12 km)

To Museo de la Amistad México-Cuba

To Poza Rica

PLACES TO STAY	OTHER
4 Hotel El Huasteco	1 Post Office
6 Hotel May Palace	2 Museo Arqueológico
7 Hotel del Parque	5 Banamex
8 Hotel Tuxpan	10 Banca Serfin
9 Hotel Plaza	12 Parroquia
11 Hotel Reforma	15 Palacio Municipal,
13 Hotel Florida	Tourist Office
	17 ADO Bus Station
PLACES TO EAT	18 Buses to Playa Norte
3 El Mexicano	19 Ómnibus de México
14 Pastelísimo	Bus Station
16 Restaurant Mante	20 Estrella Blanca
	Bus Station

0 50 100 m
0 50 100 yards

commemorates Fidel Castro's 1956 stay in Tuxpan, when he planned and prepared for the Cuban revolution. He sailed from here for Cuba with 82 comrades in a converted private yacht. The museum has a not-very-interesting collection comprising maps, B&W photos and a model of Cuba depicting Castro's campaign. It's open 8 am to 7 pm daily (donation requested). To reach the museum, take one of the small boats across the river (US$0.40), walk several blocks south to Obregón, then turn right. The museum is at the end of Obregón, just before you reach the river again.

Playa Norte

Tuxpan's beach is a wide strip of sand stretching 20km north from the mouth of the Río Tuxpan, 12km east of town. Its beauty is lessened by a power station 2km north of the river mouth, but the water and sand are fairly clean and, apart from holidays and weekends, it's almost empty. Pala-

pas serve seafood and sell souvenirs. Local buses marked 'Playa' leave every 20 minutes from the south side of Heroles and drop you at the south end of the beach (25 minutes; US$0.50). On the way back they do a quick tour of downtown before leaving you on Heroles near the end of Rodríguez.

Diving

Aqua Sports (☎ 837-02-59), a few kilometers from downtown on the road to Playa Norte, is an established scuba-diving operation. A two-day trip to the nearby reefs, with four dives, will cost about US$150 per person with a group of six or seven. Three-day, six-dive trips to Isla de Lobos cost around US$300 per person, all inclusive. Aqua Sports can also arrange fishing trips, water-skiing and windsurfing.

Special Events

A big fishing tournament brings hundreds of visitors to Tuxpan in late June or early July.

Festivities for the Assumption, on August 15, continue for a week with folk-dancing contests, bullfights and fireworks.

Places to Stay

As with many places along the coast, accommodations here can be booked out on holidays and in summer, but discount rates may be available at other times.

Rooms at *Hotel El Huasteco* (☎ 834-18-59, Morelos 41) are somewhat small and dark, but the place is clean, friendly and quite a good value at US$6.50/7 for singles/doubles with fan, US$9/10 with air-con. *Hotel Tuxpan* (☎ 834-41-10), on the corner of Juárez and Mina, has 30 plain rooms (fan only) at US$13. *Hotel del Parque* (☎ 834-08-12), on the east side of bustling Parque Reforma, is somewhat noisy but basically clean, and rates are cheap at US$8.75 for singles or doubles with fan. Some of the beds are better than others.

Stepping up considerably in quality and price, the 77-room *Hotel Florida* (☎ 834-02-22, Juárez 23) offers big clean rooms with good beds, air-con and TV for US$23/28. The upper front rooms have pleasing river views. Equally nice rooms, but without the river view, can be found for US$20/25 at the *Hotel Plaza* (☎ 834-07-38, Juárez 39). Both of these hotels have parking.

Hotel May Palace (☎ 834-88-82), on the south side of Parque Reforma, has a pool and all the modern conveniences at US$36/43 for singles/doubles – more for better rooms with a river view. The next most comfortable place in the town center is the *Hotel Reforma* (☎ 834-02-10, Juárez 25), which has a pleasant covered courtyard and a fountain. Rooms with air-con, phone and TV go for US$36. The fanciest place is 2.5km southeast of downtown, on the other side of the river. It's a *Club Maeva* (☎ 834-24-68) resort hotel where a comfortable room, three meals and an assortment of sporting activities will cost about US$100/160 per day.

Out at Playa Norte, the basic *Hotel Playa Azul* (no phone) is right on the beach and offers fan-cooled rooms for US$16.50. Camping under the coconut palms costs US$4.50 per person. Hot water is available.

Places to Eat

Antonio's in the Hotel Reforma and *El Quijote* at the Hotel Florida serve some of the best fare in town, with a bias toward seafood. Antonio's is the fanciest and priciest place, with the chilliest air-con. El Quijote may be a better value, with its US$4 comida corrida.

Among the other eateries on Juárez is *Restaurant Mante*, toward the east end of the street, a cheap, popular and friendly place offering a range of dishes from *antojitos* (US$1.75) and seafood cocktails (US$3 to US$4.50) to *carne tampiqueña* (US$4). Several bakeries also lie on this end of Juárez.

Pastelísimo, west of Parque Cano, is clean and inviting for cakes and coffee. In the middle of Parque Reforma is a circle of *tiendas* serving fresh fruit, juices and ice cream. On the north side of this plaza, *El Mexicano* is popular from *desayuno* to *cena*, with a bargain buffet in the middle of the day. Out at the beach is a long line of cheap palapa seafood joints, where you typically pay US$3 for fish soup or fresh fish, US$4.50 for a large shrimp cocktail and US$0.75 for a cold beer.

Entertainment

The most popular evening entertainment is hanging out at the Parque Reforma or at the bar or club of the moment – there seems to be a new favorite every year.

Getting There & Away

Book 1st-class buses out of Tuxpan as far ahead as possible, as the buses are en route from elsewhere and only a limited number of seats are reserved for passengers boarding here. You might have to take a 2nd-class bus to Poza Rica and a 1st-class one from there. The modern ADO (1st-class) station, on Rodríguez half a block north of the river, is also used by UNO deluxe buses. Ómnibus de México (ODM) is under the bridge on the north side of the river. Estrella Blanca (EB), on the corner of Constitución and Alemán, two blocks east of the bridge, offers regular 2nd-class service; Turistar, Futura, ABC Blanco, and Coordinados offer a few 1st-class buses from this station.

Daily departures include:

Jalapa – 350km, 5½ hours; 5 ADO (US$13.50)

Matamoros – 760km, 11 hours; 2 each by ADO and Turistar (US$25), several 2nd-class

Mexico City (Terminal Norte) – 355km, 4 hours; 1 UNO (US$23), 13 ADO, 7 ODM (US$14.50)

Papantla – 90km, 1¼ hours; 8 ADO (US$3)

Poza Rica – 60km, 45 minutes; many ADO, ODM (US$2), 2nd-class every 20 minutes

Tampico – 190km, 3½ hours; 23 ADO, 2 ODM (US$10), 2nd-class every 30 minutes

Veracruz – 300km, 5½ hours; 12 ADO (US$13.50)

Villahermosa – 780km, 12 hours; 3 ADO (US$37)

AROUND TUXPAN
Tamiahua
• pop 5370

Tamiahua, 43km north from Tuxpan by paved road, is at the southern end of Laguna de Tamiahua. It has a few seafood-shack restaurants, and you can rent boats for fishing or trips to the lagoon's barrier island. From Tuxpan take a 1st-class ODM bus or a more frequent 2nd-class bus.

Castillo de Teayo
• pop 4160

This small town, 23km up a bumpy road west off highway 180 (the turnoff is 18km from Poza Rica), was from about 800 AD one of the southernmost points of the Huastec civilization. Beside its main plaza is a steep, 13m-high restored pyramid topped by a small temple. It's in Toltec style and was probably built during Toltec rule of the area sometime between 900 and 1200 AD.

Around the base of the pyramid are some stone sculptures that have been found in the surrounding area. Some of these are in Huastec style while others are thought to be the work of Aztecs who controlled the area briefly before the Spanish conquest.

POZA RICA
• pop 153,600 • elev 28m ☎ 7

The oil city of Poza Rica is at the junction of highway 180 and highway 130. It's the main commercial and transport center of the region, and you might find yourself changing buses here. The *Auto Hotel* (☎ 822-16-00),

100m west of the 1st-class bus terminal, has OK rooms with air-con, TV and phone for US$10/18.50 – the condom vending machine near the front desk may be a clue to the clientele. *Hotel Farolino* (☎ 823-24-25), between the bus depot and the Auto Hotel, is more basic but more respectable; rates are US$6.50 for fan-cooled rooms, US$8.50 for air-con and TV. A more central, mid-range option is *Poza Rica Centro* (☎ 822-01-34), on Avenida 2 Nte at Avenida 10 Ote.

Getting There & Away

The main Poza Rica bus station, on Calle Puebla, east off Boulevard Lázaro Cárdenas, has 2nd-class and some 1st-class departures, but most 1st-class buses go from the adjoining ADO building. Daily services include:

Mexico City (Terminal Norte) – 260km, 5 hours; 1 UNO deluxe (US$23), 24 ADO (US$12), regular 2nd-class

Pachuca – 209km, 4 hours; ADO at 1.30 and 2.10 pm (US$8)

Papantla – 25km, 30 minutes; 23 ADO (US$1), frequent Transportes Papantla 2nd-class, directly behind the 1st-class depot (US$0.90)

Tampico – 250km, 4 to 5 hours; 1 UNO deluxe (US$20), 30 ADO (US$12.75)

Tuxpan – 60km, 45 minutes; many ADO, EB and ODM (US$2.50), 2nd-class every 20 minutes

Veracruz – 250km, 5 hours; 1 UNO deluxe (US$19), 18 ADO (US$11)

El Tajín Take one of Transportes Papantla's frequent buses to Coyutla (US$0.60) and ask to get off at 'Desviación El Tajín' (El Tajín turnoff), about 30 minutes from Poza Rica. Autotransportes Coatzintla and other 2nd-class buses to El Chote, Agua Dulce or San Andrés will also go past the El Tajín turnoff.

POZA RICA TO PACHUCA

The 200km Poza Rica-Pachuca road, highway 130, is the direct approach to Mexico City from the northern part of Veracruz state. This very scenic but often misty route climbs up to the Sierra Madre, across the semitropical north of Puebla state and into Hidalgo. The area's population has a high proportion of Nahua and Totonac indigenous people.

Huauchinango, roughly halfway between Poza Rica and Pachuca, is the center of a flower-growing area. You'll also find embroidered textiles in the busy Saturday market. A weeklong flower festival, including traditional dances, reaches its peak on the third Friday in Lent. **Acaxochitlán**, 25km west of Huauchinango, has a Sunday market; specialties include fruit wine and preserved fruit. The Nahua women here often wear richly embroidered blouses.

The traditional Nahua village of **Pahuatlán** is the source of many of the cloths woven with multicolored designs of animals and plants. It is reached by turning north off highway 130, about 10km past Acaxochitlán. A spectacular 27km dirt road winds several hundred meters down to the village, which holds a sizable Sunday market. There's at least one hotel here. About half an hour's drive beyond Pahuatlán is **San Pablito**, an Otomí village where colorfully embroidered blouses abound.

Highway 130 climbs steeply to Tulancingo, in the state of Hidalgo. (See the Around Pachuca section in the Around Mexico City chapter for details on the rest of this route to Pachuca.)

PAPANTLA
- pop 49,900 • elev 198m ☎ changing
Set on a hillside on the edge of the southern Sierra Madre Oriental, Papantla is a convenient base for visiting El Tajín. It's a scruffy town, though the central zócalo is quite pleasant, especially on Sunday evenings when half the town is out and *voladores* perform beside the cathedral. Some Totonacs still wear traditional costume here – men in baggy white shirts and trousers, women in embroidered blouses and *quechquémitls*.

Orientation & Information
Papantla lies just off highway 180, which runs southeast from Poza Rica. The center of town is uphill from the main road. To get to the center from the ADO bus station, turn left as you go out, then follow Avenida Ca-

In 2000 the telephone area code is due to change to ☎ 7 from 784, with the digits 84 added to the start of every local number (for example, the number 2-01-43 will become 842-01-43).

rranza a couple of hundred meters west to Calle 20 de Noviembre. Turn left and go up 20 de Noviembre (it's steep), past the Transportes Papantla bus terminal and the market, to Enríquez, on the downhill edge of the zócalo. The tourist office is hidden away on the ground floor of a government building, opposite the cathedral on 16 de Septiembre a block uphill from the zócalo; it's open 9 am to 3 pm and 6 to 9 pm Monday to Friday.

Zócalo
The zócalo, officially called Parque Téllez, is terraced into the hillside, with the Iglesia de la Asunción above its south side. Beneath the cathedral, a 50m-long mural facing the square depicts Totonac and Veracruz history. A serpent stretches along most of the mural, linking a pre-Hispanic stone carver, El Tajín's Pyramid of the Niches, voladores and an oil rig.

Volador Monument
At the top of the hill, above the cathedral, towers a 1988 statue of a volador musician playing his pipe as preparation for the four fliers to launch themselves into space. A red light adorns one of his fingers to warn off passing aircraft. Take the street heading uphill from the corner of the cathedral yard to reach the statue. Inscriptions around its base give an explanation of the voladores ritual.

Museo de Cultura Totonaca
On the edge of town, on the road to El Chote and El Tajín, this new, small museum has exhibits on Totonac culture from pre-Hispanic times to the present. Spanish-speaking Totonac guides give detailed explanations and can answer questions. It's open 9 am to 6 pm daily (US$1.10).

The Totonacs

Approximately 260,000 Totonacs survive in modern Mexico, mostly living between Teco-lutla on the Veracruz coast and the southern Sierra Madre Oriental in northern Puebla. Roman Catholicism is superimposed on their more ancient beliefs, with traditional customs stronger in the mountain areas. The chief Totonac deities are their ancestors, the sun (which is also the maize god) and St John (also the lord of water and thunder). Venus and the moon are identified with Qotiti, the devil, who rules the kingdom of the dead beneath the earth. Some Totonacs believe that the world is flat, the sky is a dome and the sun travels beneath the earth at night. The Feast of the Holy Cross (May 3) coincides with ceremonies for fertility of the earth and the creation of new seeds.

Special Events

The Corpus Christi festival, in late May and early June, is the big annual event. In Papantla it's a celebration of Totonac culture, and the town is thronged for the parades, dances and other cultural events. The main procession is on the first Sunday, voladores fly two or three times a day, and costumed performers do traditional dances.

Places to Stay

Hotel Pulido (☎ 2-10-79, *Enríquez 205*), 250m east from the downhill side of the zócalo, has small and sometimes grimy rooms around a central parking area for US$8.75/10 single/double, US$12 with two beds. Downhill from the zócalo at the corner of 20 de Noviembre and Olivo, *Hotel Toton-nacapán* (☎ 2-12-16) is a good value at US$12.50/15 for well-equipped, if not elegant, air-conditioned rooms.

The *Hotel Tajín* (☎ 2-06-44, *Núñez 104*), a blue building a few meters uphill from the left end of the zócalo mural, has clean, sizable and well-kept singles/doubles for US$19/27, or US$26/34 with air-con. The rooms in front have balconies overlooking the town.

Best in town is the modern *Hotel Premier* (☎ 2-16-45, *Enríquez 103*), on the north side of the zócalo. Large, comfortable rooms with air-con cost US$30/35 – those in back are much quieter at night. The US$50 suites are nothing special.

Places to Eat

Papantla food is strictly Mexican, with an emphasis on meat in this cattle-raising area – try the beef fillets starting at around US$5 at the restaurant at *Hotel Tajín*. *Restaurant Sorrento* (*Enríquez 105*), on the downhill side of the zócalo, is OK and inexpensive, with standard breakfasts under US$2 and a comida corrida for just over US$2. The most pleasant place is *Plaza Pardo*, upstairs on the same street, with tables on a balcony overlooking the zócalo. Filling main courses cost US$2.50 to US$3, the fried bananas with cream are scrumptious, and the bartender makes a mean margarita.

Shopping

Papantla is Mexico's leading vanilla-growing center, and you can buy vanilla extract, vanilla pods and vanilla *figuras* (pods woven into the shapes of flowers, insects, human figures or crucifixes). Mercado Hidalgo, at the northwest corner of the zócalo, has Totonac costumes (some quite pretty), good baskets and vanilla souvenirs. The Mercado Juárez, at the southwest corner opposite the cathedral, sells mainly food.

Getting There & Away

Few long-distance buses stop here and there's no service at all to or from Tampico (change at Tuxpan or Poza Rica). Most buses are de paso, so book your bus out of Papantla as soon as possible. If desperate, go to Poza Rica and get one of the much more frequent buses from there. ADO is the only 1st-class line serving Papantla. The main 2nd-class alternative is Transportes Papantla (TP), with slow, old vehicles. Daily departures include:

Jalapa – 260km, 4 hours; 8 ADO (US$10), 8 TP (US$8)

Mexico City (Terminal Norte) – 290km, 5 hours; 9 ADO (US$13)

Poza Rica – 25km, 30 minutes; 16 ADO (US$1), TP every 15 minutes (US$0.90)

Tuxpan – 90km, 1 hour; 4 ADO (US$3)

Veracruz – 230km, 4 hours; 6 ADO (US$10), 8 TP (US$8)

El Tajín White microbuses go on the hour to El Tajín from 16 de Septiembre, the street on the uphill side of the cathedral (about 30 minutes; US$0.50). Alternatively, you can do the trip in two stages by getting a bus from the same stop to the village of El Chote, then any of the frequent buses going west (to the right) from El Chote to the El Tajín turnoff (Desviación El Tajín). Other buses from Papantla to El Chote leave from the TP terminal.

EL TAJÍN

Among verdant hills a few kilometers from Papantla is the site of El Tajín ('el ta-HEEN') – Totonac for thunder, lightning or hurricane, all of which can happen here in summer. The ancient Totonacs may have occupied El Tajín in its later stages, but most of it was built before the Totonacs became important. It is the highest achievement of Classic Veracruz civilization, about which little is known.

El Tajín was first occupied about 100 AD, but most of what's visible was built around 600 or 700. It was at its peak from about 600 to 900 – as a town and as a ceremonial center. Around 1200 the site was abandoned, possibly after attacks by

---

Voladores

The *voladores* rite – a sort of slow-motion quadruple bungee jump – starts with five men in colorful costumes climbing to the top of a very tall pole. Four of them sit on the edges of a small, square, wooden frame atop the pole, arrange their ropes and then rotate the square to twist the ropes around the pole. The fifth man dances, bangs a drum and plays a whistle while standing on a tiny platform above them. Suddenly he stops and the others launch themselves backwards into thin air. Upside down, arms outstretched, they revolve gracefully round the pole and descend slowly to the ground as their ropes unwind.

This ancient ceremony is packed with symbolic meanings. One interpretation is that it's a fertility rite and the fliers are macaw-men who make invocations to the four corners of the universe before falling to the ground, bringing with them the sun and rain. It is also noted that each flier circles the pole 13 times, giving a total of 52 revolutions. The number 52 is not only the number of weeks in the modern year but was an important number in pre-Hispanic Mexico, which had two calendars: one corresponding to the 365-day solar year, the other to a ritual year of 260 days. A day in one calendar coincided with a day in the other calendar every 52 solar years.

While it's sad in a way to see a sacred rite turned into a show for tourists (the people who do it say they need the money), the dangerous feat is a spectacular sight.

Totonac voladores rite performed at 30m

RICHARD I'ANSON

Chichimecs, and lay unknown to the Spaniards until about 1785, when an official found it while looking for illegal tobacco plantings.

Among El Tajín's special features are rows of square niches on the sides of buildings, numerous ball courts, and sculptures showing human sacrifice connected with the ball game. The archaeologist who did much of the excavation here, José García Payón, believed that El Tajín's niches and stone mosaics symbolized day and night, light and dark, and life and death in a universe composed of pairs of opposites, though this interpretation has many skeptics. Despite extensive reconstruction in 1991, El Tajín retains an aura of mystery and a mysterious 'lost in the jungle' feel.

Information

The site is open daily 8 am to 7 pm (US$2.75, free on Sunday and for those under 13 or over 60). The whole site covers about 10 sq km, and you need to walk quite a few kilometers to see it all. There's little shade and it can get very hot, especially in the middle of the day – a water bottle and hat are highly recommended.

Outside you'll find a parking lot (about US$0.50) and stalls selling food and handicrafts. The visitor's center has a restaurant, souvenir shops, a place to leave bags, an information desk and an excellent museum with a model of the whole site. The museum exhibits are labeled in English and Spanish, but at the time of research there were no interpretive signs at all on the site itself. Those who want more information should look for the booklet *Tajín: Mystery and Beauty*, by Leonardo Zaleta, which may be available (in English, French, German and Spanish) at some of the souvenir shops.

Totonac Voladores

Totonacs carry out the exciting voladores rite most days from a 30m-high steel pole beside the visitor's center. Performances are usually around 2 and 4 pm; before they start, a Totonac in traditional dress requests donations from the audience (US$1.25).

Around the Site

Two main parts of the site have been cleared and restored: the lower area where the Pirámide de los Nichos (Pyramid of the Niches) stands and, uphill, a group of buildings known as El Tajín Chico (Little El Tajín). Most features of the site are known by the labels used in a 1966 INAH survey, with many called simply 'Estructura' (Structure) followed by a number or letter.

Plaza Menor Inside the site, beyond the unremarkable Plaza del Arroyo, you reach the Plaza Menor (Smaller Plaza), part of El Tajín's main ceremonial center, with a low platform in the middle. A statue on the first level of Estructura 5, a pyramid on the plaza's west side, represents either a thunder-and-rain god who was especially important at El Tajín, or Mictlantecuhtli, a death god. All of the structures around this plaza were probably topped by small temples, and some were decorated with red or blue paint.

Juego de Pelota Sur Some 17 ball courts have been found at El Tajín. The Juego de Pelota Sur (Southern Ball Court), between Estructuras 5 and 6, dates from about 1150 and is the most famous of the courts because its walls bear six relief carvings depicting various aspects of the ball-game ritual.

The panel on the **northeast corner** (on the right as you enter the court from the Lower Plaza) is the easiest to make out. At its center, three ballplayers wearing knee pads are depicted carrying out a ritual postgame sacrifice; one player is about to plunge a knife into the chest of another, whose arms are held by the third. A skeletal death god on the left and a presiding figure on the right look on. Another death god hovers over the victim. The **central north wall** panel depicts the ceremonial drinking of pulque – a figure holding a drinking vessel signals to another leaning on a pulque container. Quetzalcóatl sits cross-legged beside Tláloc, the fanged god of water and lightning. The panel at the **northwest corner** of the same wall is thought to represent a ceremony that preceded the ball game. Two players face each other, one with crossed arms, the other holding a

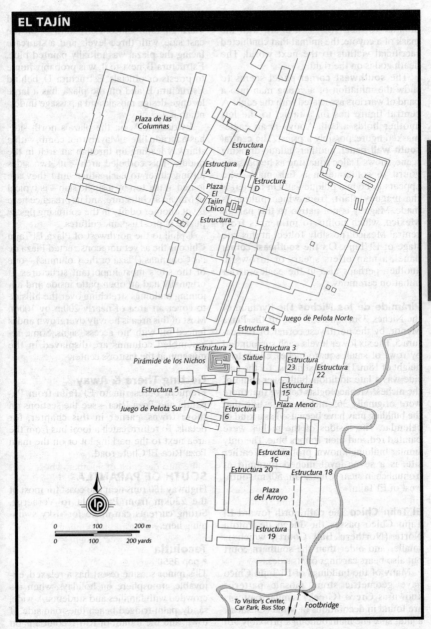

EL TAJÍN

Plaza de las Columnas

Estructura B

Estructura A

Estructura D

Plaza El Tajín Chico

Estructura C

Juego de Pelota Norte

Estructura 4

Estructura 2

Estructura 3

Pirámide de los Nichos

Statue

Estructura 23

Estructura 22

Estructura 5

Estructura 15

Juego de Pelota Sur

Estructura 6

Plaza Menor

Estructura 16

Estructura 20

Estructura 18

Plaza del Arroyo

Estructura 19

0   100   200 m
0   100   200 yards

To Visitor's Center, Car Park, Bus Stop

Footbridge

dagger. Speech symbols emerge from their mouths. To their right is a figure with the mask of a coyote, the animal that conducted sacrificial victims to the next world. The death god is on the right.

The **southwest corner** panel seems to show the initiation of a young man into a band of warriors associated with the eagle. A central figure lies on a table; to the left another holds a bell. Above is an eagle-masked figure, possibly a priest. The **central south wall** panel, another pulque-drinking scene, shows Tláloc squatting as he passes a gourd to someone in a fish mask who appears to be in a pulque vat. On the left is the maguey plant, from which pulque is made. Maguey is not native to this part of Mexico, which points to influences from central Mexico (possibly Toltec) at this late stage of El Tajín. On the **southeast corner** panel, a man offers spears or arrows to another, perhaps also in the eagle-warrior initiation ceremony.

Pirámide de los Nichos The Pyramid of the Niches, 35m square, is just off the Plaza Menor, by the northwest corner of Estructura 5. The six lower levels, each surrounded by rows of small square niches, climb to a height of 18m. The wide staircase on the east side was a late addition, built over some of the niches. Archaeologists believe that there were originally 365 niches, suggesting that the building may have been used as a kind of calendar. The insides of the niches were painted red, and their frames blue. The only similar building known, probably an earlier site, is a seven-level niched pyramid at Yohualichán near Cuetzalán, 50km southwest of El Tajín.

El Tajín Chico The path north toward El Tajín Chico passes the Juego de Pelota Norte (Northern Ball Court), which is smaller and older than the southern court but also bears carvings on its sides.

Many of the buildings of El Tajín Chico have geometric stone mosaic patterns known as Greco (Greek); similar patterns are found in decorations of Mitla (Oaxaca), a later site. The main buildings, probably 9th century, are on the east and north sides of Plaza El Tajín Chico. Estructura C, on the east side, with three levels and a staircase facing the plaza, was initially painted blue. Estructura B, next to it, was probably home to priests or officials. Estructura D, behind Estructura B and off the plaza, has a large lozenge-design mosaic and a passage underneath it.

Estructura A, on the plaza's north side, has a façade like a Mayan roof comb, with a stairway leading up through an arch in the middle. This corbeled arch – its two sides jutting closer to each other until they are joined at the top by a single slab – is typical of Mayan architecture, and its presence here is yet another oddity in the confusing jigsaw puzzle of pre-Hispanic cultures.

Uphill to the northwest of Plaza El Tajín Chico is the as yet unreconstructed Plaza de las Columnas (Plaza of the Columns) – one of the site's most important structures. It originally had an open patio inside and adjoining buildings stretching over the hillside to cover an area of nearly 200m by 100m. Most of this area is heavily overgrown and is fenced off with 'no access' signs. Some re-assembled columns are displayed in the museum at the visitor's center.

Getting There & Away

Frequent buses run to El Tajín from Papantla and Poza Rica – see the sections on those towns, earlier in this chapter, for details. To return, catch a local bus from the area next to the parking lot or on the main Poza Rica-El Chote road.

SOUTH OF PAPANTLA

Highway 180 runs near the coast for most of the 230km from Papantla to Veracruz. Strong currents can make for risky swimming here.

Tecolutla
• pop 3550

This minor seaside resort has a relaxed, enjoyable atmosphere on holidays, when it's crowded with families and students. A wide, sandy, palm-fringed beach lines one side of town, and the mouth of Río Tecolutla is on the other. Launches make trips into the mangroves for fishing and wildlife-watching. *Hotel Ibatros* (☎ *7-846-00-02*), in the middle of town, has clean and comfortable rooms for US$28 in high season, US$21 in low season. Less expensive accommodations are available too, some near the beach, and you'll find a good choice of places to eat and drink. Tecolutla is reached by a side road that branches off highway 180 at Gutiérrez Zamora. ADO and Transportes Papantla buses go to/from Papantla.

Costa Esmeralda

The 20km 'Emerald Coast' has a scattering of hotels, holiday homes and trailer parks along a strip between highway 180 and the dark, sandy, sometimes deserted beach. It's a popular summer and holiday spot but very quiet most of the year. At the north end of the coast, **La Guadalupe** is an OK stop with rooms at *Hotel Catán* for US$22. A more upscale option is *Hotel El Doral* (☎ *2-321-00-04*), farther south, which asks about US$40/46 in high season.

At the mouth of Río Bobos, the small fishing town of **Nautla** dozes on the south side of a toll bridge. Seafood is sold at a couple of simple places near the brown beach.

Laguna Verde

Mexico's controversial first nuclear power station is at Laguna Verde, about 80km north of Veracruz port, on the coastal side of highway 180. The first unit came into operation in 1989, the second in 1996, but government plans for more reactors have been abandoned in the face of public protest. Recent concerns about the safety of this reactor have led to suggestions that it be replaced with natural-gas-powered generators.

Villa Rica

Now just a fishing village, 69km north of Veracruz, Villa Rica is the probable site of the first Spanish settlement in Mexico. Here you can explore traces of a fort and a church on the Cerro de la Cantera or bask on a very nice beach. The nearby Totonac tombs of **Quiahuiztlán** are superbly situated on a hill overlooking the coast.

Central Veracruz

Highway 180 follows the coast past the ruins of Zempoala to Cardel, where a side road leads to the beach at Chachalacas beach and highway 140 branches west to Jalapa, the pleasant state capital. The countryside around Jalapa has some appealing villages, picturesque landscapes and dramatic river gorges that are increasingly popular for rafting trips. The very early colonial ruins at La Antigua are worth a stop on the way to the bustling port city of Veracruz, 35km south of Cardel. From Veracruz, highway 150D heads southwest to Córdoba, Fortín de las Flores and Orizaba, on the edge of the Sierra Madre.

ZEMPOALA

The pre-Hispanic Totonac town of Zempoala holds a key place in the story of the Spanish conquest. Its ruins stand 42km north of Veracruz and 4km west of highway 180 in a modern town called Zempoala. The turnoff is by a Pemex station, 7km north of Cardel. Voladores regularly perform at the ruins, especially on holidays and weekends, around 10 am, noon and 2 pm.

The site is green and lovely, with palm trees and a mountain backdrop. Most of the buildings are faced with smooth, rounded riverbed stones, but many were originally plastered and painted. A typical feature is battlement-like 'teeth' called *almenas*.

History

Zempoala became a major Totonac center after about 1200 AD and may have been the leader of a 'federation' of southern Totonac states. It fell subject to the Aztecs in the mid-15th century, and many of the buildings are in Aztec style. The town had defensive walls, underground water and drainage pipes and, in May 1519 when the Spanish came, about 30,000 people. As Cortés approached the town, one of his scouts reported back that the buildings were made of silver – but it was only white plaster or paint shining in the sun.

Zempoala's portly chief, Chicomacatl, known to history as 'the fat cacique' from a description by Bernal Díaz del Castillo, struck an alliance with Cortés for protection against the Aztecs. But his hospitality didn't stop the Spanish from smashing his gods' statues and lecturing the Zempoalans on the virtues of Christianity. Zempoalan carriers went with the Spaniards when they set off for Tenochtitlán in 1519. The following year, it was at Zempoala that Cortés defeated the Pánfilo de Narváez expedition, which had been sent by the governor of Cuba to arrest Cortés.

By the 17th century Zempoala had virtually ceased to exist. Its population, devastated by diseases, was down to eight families. Eventually the town was abandoned. The present town dates from 1832.

Zempoala Ruins

After you enter Zempoala, take a right where a sign says 'Bienvenidos a Zempoala' – you'll find the main archaeological site at the end of this short road. It's open 9 am to 6 pm daily (US$2, free on Sunday).

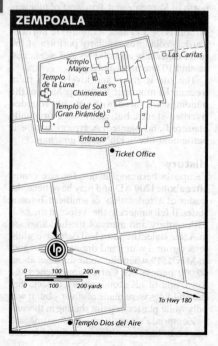

Templo Mayor The Main Temple is an 11m-high, 13-platform pyramid, originally plastered and painted. A wide staircase ascends to the remains of a three-room shrine on top (but you're not allowed to climb it). In 1520 this was probably Pánfilo de Narváez's headquarters, which Cortés' men captured by setting fire to its thatched roof.

Las Chimeneas This is where Cortés and his men lodged on their first visit to Zempoala. The hollow columns in front of the main structure were thought to be chimneys – hence the name. A temple probably topped the seven platforms here.

Other Structures There are two main structures on the west side. One is known as the **Gran Pirámide**, or Templo del Sol, which has two stairways climbing its front side to three platforms on top, in typical Toltec/Aztec style. It faces east and was probably devoted to the sun god. To its north, **Templo de la Luna** has a rectangular platform and ramps in front, and a round structure behind, similar to Aztec temples to the wind god Ehecatl.

East of Las Chimeneas, beyond the irrigation channel, you'll see a building called **Las Caritas** (The Little Heads) on your right. It once held large numbers of small pottery heads in niches. Three other structures formerly stood east of Las Caritas, in line with the rising sun. Another large wind-god temple, known as **Dios del Aire**, is in the town itself – just go back south on the site entrance road, cross the main road in town and then go around the corner to the right. The ancient temple, with its characteristic circular shape, is beside an intersection.

Getting There & Away

Zempoala is most easily reached through Cardel – take a bus marked 'Zempoala' (US$1) from the Cardel bus station, or a taxi (US$4.50).

CENTRAL VERACRUZ COAST
☎ 2
Cardel

The main town in the area, Cardel (or José Cardel) is a stop on the way to the ruins and the beach. It has banks and restaurants, and adequate accommodations are available at **Hotel Cardel** (☎ 962-07-77), on the main plaza. From the Veracruz bus station, regular 1st-class ADO buses to Cardel cost US$2, and frequent 2nd-class AU buses cost US$1.75.

Chachalacas

This unpretentious seaside 'resort' a few kilometers northeast of Cardel has miles of uncrowded beaches and some wild sand dunes north of town. Most of the accommodations are geared to family groups, and at holiday times they ask about US$28 for a large room. More suited to budget travelers is **La Pingüi** (☎ 962-50-01), on the right as you come into town. It has a small pool, and the helpful owners can arrange snorkeling on the reefs and trips to the dunes. Fan-cooled rooms cost about US$18 single/double. The fancy **Chachalacas Hotel-Club** (☎ 962-12-77) is another resort in the Maeva chain. The tariff of US$83/140 includes all meals and many recreational activities. Several restaurants line up along the beach – **Restaurant de Colores** is one of the first you'll see and is a great choice for fresh seafood.

La Antigua

Intriguing La Antigua (population 930) is 2km east of the coastal highway 150, 23km north of Veracruz. A Spanish settlement was established here near the mouth of Río Huitzilapan in 1525, after Villa Rica was abandoned and before Veracruz was founded. The picturesque ruined building, its walls overgrown with tree roots, was the 16th-century customhouse (though it's commonly called the 'Casa de Cortés'). The Ermita del Rosario church, probably dating from 1523, is one of the oldest in the Americas. **Hotel La Malinche** (☎ 971-60-02) is a pleasant hotel near the river, with rooms starting at US$11/19. Small riverside seafood restaurants are popular with daytrippers from Veracruz.

JALAPA
• pop 324,000 • elev 1427m ☎ changing

Cool, clean and civilized, Jalapa (sometimes spelled Xalapa, always pronounced 'ha-LA-pa') is one of Mexico's urban delights. The capital of Veracruz state, this hill-country city has been home to the Universidad Veracruzana since 1944. It enjoys a lively artistic and entertainment scene, a convivial café life and some good restaurants. Its pleasant setting, on the semitropical slope between the coast and the central highlands, offers fine parks and panoramas (though mist and drizzle are common, and the traffic noise and fumes can be vile). Many people come to Jalapa just to see its superb anthropology museum, but most of them leave wishing they had allowed more time to get to know the city.

A pre-Hispanic town on this site became part of the Aztec empire around 1460, and Cortés and his men passed through in 1519. The Spanish town didn't take off until the annual trade fair of Spanish goods was first held here in 1720 (it ran until 1777). Today Jalapa is a commercial hub for the coffee and tobacco grown on the slopes, and the city is also well known for its flowers. The surrounding area has some attractive towns and offers dramatic landscapes with rivers, gorges and waterfalls.

Orientation

The city center is on a hillside, with the plaza, Parque Juárez, more or less in the middle of things. Jalapa's cathedral is on Enríquez, just east of the plaza. Many of the mid-range hotels and restaurants are a little to the east, on Enríquez and Zaragoza. The bus station is 2km east of the center, and the must-see anthropology museum is a few kilometers north.

Information

Tourist Offices The tourist information desk at the bus station is theoretically open 8 am to 9 pm Monday to Saturday, 8 am to noon Sunday, but it actually keeps less regular

In 2000 the telephone area code is due to change to ☎ 2 from 28, with the digit 8 added to the start of every local number (for example, the number 17-01-43 will become 817-01-43).

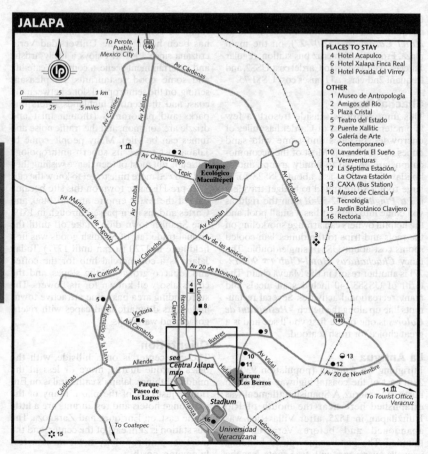

JALAPA

To Perote,
Puebla,
Mexico City

MEX
140

0   .5   1 km
0   .25   .5 miles

Av Cárdenas

Av Xalapa

Av Cortines

1

2

Av Chilpancingo

Tepic

Parque
Ecológico
Macuiltépeti

Av Orizaba

Av Cárdenas

Av Mártires 28 de Agosto

Av Alemán

Av de las Américas

Av Camacho

Av 20 de Noviembre

Av Cortines

Dr Lucio

4

MEX
140

5

Av Ignacio de la Llave

Victoria

6

Revolución

Clavijero

8

7

Av camacho

Ilustres

9

3

Allende

Av Vidal

10

11

Parque
Los Berros

13

12

Av 20 de Noviembre

see
Central Jalapa
map

Hidalgo

14

To Tourist Office,
Veracruz

Parque
Paseo de
los Lagos

Carranza

Stadium

16

Rebsamen

Universidad
Veracruzana

To Coatepec

15

PLACES TO STAY
4 Hotel Acapulco
6 Hotel Xalapa Finca Real
8 Hotel Posada del Virrey

OTHER
1 Museo de Antropología
2 Amigos del Río
3 Plaza Cristal
5 Teatro del Estado
7 Puente Xallitic
9 Galería de Arte
   Contemporaneo
10 Lavandería El Sueño
11 Veraventuras
12 La Séptima Estación,
    La Octava Estación
13 CAXA (Bus Station)
14 Museo de Ciencia y
    Tecnología
15 Jardín Botánico Clavijero
16 Rectoria

hours. The very helpful municipal tourist office (☎ 42-12-00), under the arches at the Palacio Municipal, facing Parque Juárez, is open 8 am to 4 pm Monday to Friday.

Another good tourist resource is the information desk (☎ 15-07-08) on the right as you enter the Museo de Antropología. The state tourist office (☎ 12-85-00) is inconveniently located in the sky-scraping Torre Animas building, 3km east of the center on the highway coming into town.

Money Banca Serfin, Bancomer and Banamex are all on Enríquez, and they all have

ATMs. Casa de Cambio Jalapa, at Gutiérrez Zamora 36, offers quicker exchange services and has slightly longer hours – 9 am to 2 pm and 4 to 6 pm Monday to Friday, 10 am to 2 pm Saturday.

Post & Communications The post office is a few blocks east of the center, at the corner of Zamora and Leño. The Telecomm office, with fax, telex and telegram services, is next door.

You can access the Internet for US$3.25 per hour at Cyberland, in the arcade south off Enríquez, near the corner of Primera

Verdad. It's open 9.30 am to 10 pm Monday to Saturday, 11 am to 9 pm Sunday, and it serves good coffee.

Laundry

Lavandería El Sueño, a block east of the post office, will wash a sizable load for US$2.

City Center

The central Parque Juárez is like a terrace, with its elevated south side overlooking the valley below and (when the weather is clear) the snowcapped mountains in the distance. The arcades of the **Palacio Municipal** are on its north side and the **Palacio de Gobierno**, the seat of the Veracruz state government, is on its east side. The Palacio de Gobierno has a fine **mural** by Mario Orozco Rivera depicting the history of justice; it's above the stairway accessed from the eastern entrance on S Camacho. Facing the Palacio de Gobierno across Enríquez is the cathedral (started in 1772 and still unfinished), from where Revolución and Dr Lucio both lead up to the bustling area above the *mercado*. Farther north, Dr Lucio crosses a deep valley on **Puente Xallitic**, a high arched bridge.

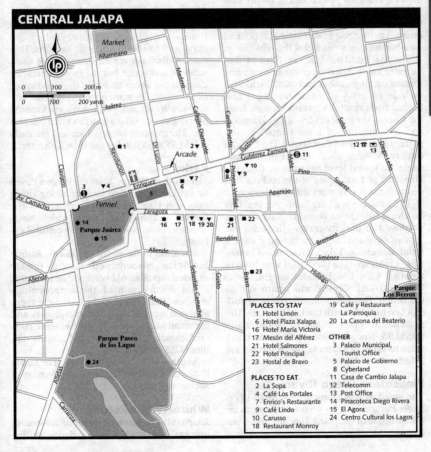

CENTRAL JALAPA

PLACES TO STAY
1 Hotel Limón
6 Hotel Plaza Xalapa
16 Hotel María Victoria
17 Mesón del Alférez
21 Hotel Salmones
22 Hotel Principal
23 Hostal de Bravo

PLACES TO EAT
2 La Sopa
4 Café Los Portales
7 Enrico's Restaurante
9 Café Lindo
10 Carusso
18 Restaurant Monroy

19 Café y Restaurant
   La Parroquia
20 La Casona del Beaterio

OTHER
3 Palacio Municipal,
   Tourist Office
5 Palacio de Gobierno
8 Cyberland
11 Casa de Cambio Jalapa
12 Telecomm
13 Post Office
14 Pinacoteca Diego Rivera
15 El Agora
24 Centro Cultural los Lagos

Museo de Antropología

The Museo de Antropología de la Universidad Veracruzana, devoted to the archaeology of Veracruz state, is one of the best museums in Mexico. Its large collection includes no fewer than seven huge Olmec heads (up to 3000 years old) and 2500 superb artifacts. The spacious layout is a textbook example of museum design. Unfortunately, information explaining the exhibits is available only in Spanish.

The exhibits occupy a series of galleries and courtyards descending a gentle slope, and they're arranged from the oldest to the most recent. First you reach the Olmec material from southern Veracruz – the largest Olmec head here, 2.7m high, is from San Lorenzo. Another San Lorenzo head is pocked with hundreds of small holes, thought to be a deliberate mutilation at the time of San Lorenzo's fall. Apart from many more fine Olmec carvings, other museum highlights include an array of beautiful yugos and hachas from central Veracruz, murals from the Classic Veracruz center of Las Higueras and a collection of huge Classic-period pottery figures from El Zapotal. The El Tajín display includes a fine model of the site, while the lowest level has exhibits from the Huasteca and examples of the codices that describe the first contact with Europeans.

The museum is a long light-gray building on the west side of Avenida Xalapa, 4km northwest of the city center – look for the spacious gardens and the building with a fountain outside. Take a 'Tesorería-Centro-SEP' or 'Museo' bus (US$0.30) west from in front of Cafe Los Portales on Enríquez. Buses marked 'Centro' will return you to the center. Buses can be infrequent or full, so a taxi may be worth the US$1.50 fare. The museum is open 9 am to 5 pm daily (US$1.75, free on Sunday). It costs US$1 extra to bring in a camera, but you can't use a flash.

Pinacoteca Diego Rivera

This small, new art museum (☎ 18-18-19) is *under* Parque Juárez – go down the steps on the west side of the plaza. The 36 works from throughout Rivera's life give an excellent overview of his evolving artistic style, and additional exhibits feature prints and paintings by other Mexican artists. The museum is open 10 am to 6 pm Tuesday to Saturday, 9 am to noon Sunday (free).

Galería de Arte Contemporaneo

This state-run art gallery (☎ 18-04-12) is in a fine renovated colonial building on Xalapeños Ilustres 1km east of the center, just past Arteaga. It houses some excellent temporary exhibitions; contact the gallery to find out what's on. Hours are 10 am to 3 pm and 5 to 8 pm Tuesday to Sunday.

Museo de Ciencia y Tecnología

The eclectic collection here includes old trains, assorted cars, airplanes, ecology displays and hands-on scientific exhibits. Thematic galleries cover the human body, earth sciences and water, but the most interesting displays are about transportation and space exploration. The museum (☎ 12-51-10) is on the southeast side of town on Avenida Murillo Vidal – take a Murillo Vidal bus or a taxi. The museum is open 9 am to 4 pm daily (US$1.75, US$3.50 for the IMAX theater).

Parks

Just south of Parque Juárez is **Parque Paseo de los Lagos**, winding for 1km along either side of a lake. At its northern end is the **Centro Cultural los Lagos**, which hosts courses, concerts and temporary cultural exhibits.

On a hill in the north of the city, **Parque Ecológico Macuiltépetl** is the thickly wooded cap of an old volcano; the turnoff is about 200m south of the anthropology museum. Paths spiral to the top where there are good views. It's popular with joggers, and the small **Museo de la Fauna** has some tethered eagles and regionally indigenous reptiles (US$0.90).

Southwest of town, the attractive **Jardín Botánico Clavijero** has a fine collection of subtropical plants.

White-Water Rafting

Jalapa is the base for a number of 'adventure tourism' operators, several offering rafting trips on nearby rivers. Veraventuras (☎ 18-95-79, 800-712-65-72, veraventuras@yahoo.com) does trips ranging from a half-day outing on the Río Filo-Bobos (US$44) to a three-day expedition on the class 4 rapids of the Barranca Grande, on the upper reaches of Río Pescados (US$196). The company's office is at Santos Degollado 81-8 – go up the driveway and look for the building behind the parking lot. Another established rafting operator is Amigos del Río (☎ 15-88-17, amigosrio@amtave.com), Chilpancingo 205. Rafting trips usually require a minimum of four to eight participants, so it's a good idea to contact the operator ahead of time. Weekend trips offer the best chance of joining up with other people.

Organized Tours

BTT Xalapa (☎ 44-00-23) conducts tours every day, some with English-speaking guides. They include three- and five-hour city tours (US$20 and US$30, respectively), as well as excursions to nearby towns (four hours, US$40) and to archaeological and historical sites (eight hours, US$60).

Places to Stay

Budget An excellent budget choice is the centrally located **Hotel Limón** (☎ 17-22-04, *Revolución 8*). The rooms, which surround a tiled courtyard with a fountain, aren't spacious, but they are clean and come with private bath and hot water. Singles are US$7.75, doubles US$9.50 with one bed or US$11 with two beds. Parking is available nearby.

Another central hotel offering excellent value is the **Hotel Plaza Xalapa** (☎ 17-33-10, *Enríquez 4*). Clean, basic but perfectly adequate single/double rooms cost US$9/10. Avoid the rooms facing the street, or wear earplugs.

Good, clean and slightly larger rooms can be found for US$10 to US$12.50 at **Hotel Principal** (☎ 17-64-00, *Zaragoza 28*). The better rooms have cable TV; the streetside rooms can be noisy. The superclean **Hostal de Bravo** (☎ 18-90-38, *Bravo 11*) is farther down the hill. Prices for the comfortable, well-equipped rooms have climbed to US$13/14.50, or US$16 with two beds, but it's still popular with backpackers.

Hotel Salmones (☎ 17-54-31, *Zaragoza 24*) has a small garden, a big lobby, a restaurant and old-fashioned style. Slightly worn rooms with carpet, phone and TV cost US$15; fine renovated rooms are US$17.50.

A kilometer up the hill from the center, the **Hotel Acapulco** (☎ 18-24-58), on Julian Carrillo between Revolución and Dr Lucio, has bare, basic but clean rooms with private baths for US$8/11.

Mid-Range The **Hotel Posada del Virrey** (☎ 18-61-00, *Dr Lucio 142*), about 300m uphill from the center, is a comfortable, modern hotel with TV, phones, a bar and a restaurant. Moderately sized rooms are not a bad value at US$18, or US$21 with two beds.

The 114-room **Hotel María Victoria** (☎ 18-60-11, *Zaragoza 6*) is close to the center. It has a sparkling white lobby and ultraclean rooms with phone, TV, air-con and heating for US$35/41. Amenities include a restaurant and a bar with entertainment. An interesting place in a central location and with a bit of character is **Mesón del Alférez** (☎ 18-01-13), on the corner of Zaragoza and Sebastián Camacho. It's a renovated old building with a variety of rooms starting at US$30/38, including breakfast.

Top End The top place in town is the modern, 200-room **Hotel Xalapa Finca Real** (☎ 18-22-22), a kilometer west of the center on Victoria, 1½ blocks uphill from Avenida Camacho. The central part is built around a swimming pool, and the complex holds bars, a restaurant and a good cafeteria. Air-conditioned rooms cost US$65 for one or two people.

Places to Eat

Jalapa has plenty of excellent, inexpensive eateries, with one local specialty being *chiles rellenos* (stuffed peppers). A very popular place near the center is **La Sopa**, just up Callejón Diamante, which has a fine comida corrida for US$2 and main courses in the evening for around US$2.50. There's live music on Friday and Saturday nights and a convivial atmosphere at any time.

A good place to soak up the city's ambiance is the *Café Los Portales*, opposite Parque Juárez, where you can eat at sidewalk tables under the arches (inside tables are much quieter). It has a standard Mexican menu, but the service is efficient, and nothing costs more than US$4.75 (for the filling *carne tampiqueña)*.

Other central options include *Enrico's Restaurante*, on Enríquez next door to the Hotel Plaza Xalapa. It's a good place to rest your feet and enjoy a cappuccino (US$1) or a glass of juice (US$1). The set lunch runs about US$3, and à la carte main courses cost from US$2.50 to US$5. Farther east, on Zamora, *Carusso* serves very tasty pizza and pasta – a small, thin-crust pizza fills at least one person for around US$4.

Café Lindo (Primera Verdad 21), just south of Enríquez/Zamora, is one of the trendiest places, with a bright, cheerful atmosphere, cozy chairs, live music and an indoor fountain. Cappuccino or espresso costs about US$1, sandwiches and snacks are US$1 to US$2, and meat or chicken main courses are around US$4. Around the corner on Zaragoza are several reliable restaurants. *Restaurant Monroy* has a wide assortment of antojitos from US$1 to US$3 and a four-course comida corrida for US$3 – it's open 24 hours. Another local institution is *Café y Restaurant La Parroquia (Zaragoza 18)*, where the efficient waitstaff serve up good, solid fare from 7.30 am to 10.30 pm. A set dinner of soup, chicken and chips will cost US$5, a variety of set breakfasts are all US$4 or less, and other snacks and meals range up to US$7.

Next door, *La Casona del Beaterio (Zaragoza 20)* has an even more inviting ambiance in its pretty courtyard or in colorful rooms with photos of old Jalapa. The long menu of reliable choices includes fruit, granola, and yogurt with honey for breakfast (US$3), spaghetti, crêpes, enchiladas (all under US$5), and meat dishes (US$5 to US$8). The five-course comida corrida is a bargain at US$4.

Entertainment

El Agora, an arts center under the Parque Juárez, contains a cinema, theater and gallery, and is the focus of Jalapa's busy arts scene. It's open Tuesday to Sunday 8.30 am to 9 pm and has a bookstore and café. For news of what's happening around town, look here, or on the notice board in the Café La Parroquia on Zaragoza. The *Teatro del Estado Ignacio de la Llave*, the state theater, on the corner of Avenidas Camacho and Ignacio de la Llave, offers performances by the Orquesta Sinfónica de Jalapa and the Ballet Folklórico of the Universidad Veracruzana.

Jalapa's venerable disco twins, *La Séptima Estación (☎ 17-31-55)* and *La Octava Estación (☎ 17-90-15)*, are both at 20 de Noviembre 571, near the bus station. They're open 11 pm to 3 am Wednesday to Saturday (US$2 to US$5 cover, sometimes free for females).

Getting There & Away

Bus Jalapa's gleaming, modern, well-organized bus station, 2km east of the city center, is known as CAXA (Central de Autobuses de Xalapa). Deluxe service is offered by UNO and ADO GL, 1st-class service by ADO, and 2nd-class service by AU (many 2nd-class services are direct, and not much slower, or cheaper, than 1st class). Daily departures include:

Cardel (for Zempoala) – 72km, 1½ hours; 21 ADO (US$2.75), 14 AU (US$2.70)

Mexico City (TAPO) – 315km, 5 hours; 5 UNO (US$24), 7 ADO GL (US$16), 16 ADO (US$14), 17 AU (US$12.50)

Papantla – 260km, 5 hours; 12 ADO (US$11)

Puebla – 185km, 3 hours; 8 ADO (US$8), 15 AU (US$7)

Tampico – 525km, 11 hours; 1 ADO at 10.30 pm (US$24)

Veracruz – 100km, 2 hours; ADO every 20 to 30 minutes, 5 am to 11 pm (US$4.75), 25 AU (US$4)

Villahermosa – 575km, 8 hours; 1 UNO at 11.30 pm (US$40), 4 ADO (US$25)

Other places served by ADO include Acayucan, Campeche, Catemaco, Córdoba,

Fortín de las Flores, Mérida, Orizaba, Poza Rica, San Andrés Tuxtla and Santiago Tuxtla. AU also goes to Salina Cruz.

Car & Motorcycle For car rentals, try Alamo (☎ 17-43-13) or National (☎ 18-22-22). Highway 140 to Puebla is narrow and winding until Perote. The Jalapa-Veracruz road is very good. Going to the northern Gulf Coast, it's quickest to go to Cardel, then turn north on highway 180; the inland road via Tlapacoyan is scenic but slow.

Getting Around
For buses from the bus station to the city center, follow the signs to the taxi stand, then continue downhill to the big road, Avenida 20 de Noviembre. Turn right to the bus stop, from where any microbus or bus marked 'Centro' will take you within a short walk of Parque Juárez for US$0.25. For a taxi to the center, buy a ticket in the bus station (US$1.50), then walk down the ramp and through the tunnel to the taxi stand. To return to the bus station, take a 'CAXA' bus east along Zaragoza.

AROUND JALAPA
The countryside around Jalapa is very scenic, and some appealing old towns lie nearby.

Hacienda El Lencero
About 12km from Jalapa on the Veracruz highway, a signposted road branches right for a few kilometers to the **Museo Ex-Hacienda El Lencero**, on land once granted to a soldier from the army of Cortés. One of the first inns between Mexico City and Veracruz was established here, and the extensive ranch was developed to provide horses and cattle for travelers. Sometime dictator General Antonio López de Santa Anna owned the property from 1842 to the mid-1850s, and the hacienda, chapel and other buildings date mostly from this period. The grand, superbly restored house is beautifully furnished with fine period pieces, and the gardens and lake are delightful – the vast fig tree is said to be 500 years old. The building and grounds are open 10 am to 6 pm Tuesday to Sunday (US$0.90, free Tuesday)

and well worth a visit. From Jalapa, get one of the regular 'Banderia' buses from outside the Plaza Cristal shopping center.

El Carrizal
South of the Veracruz road, 44km from Jalapa, the El Carrizal hot springs feed several sulfurous pools. The site has a restaurant and a spa-hotel.

Coatepec & Xico
Coatepec (population 42,500), a charming colonial town 15km south of Jalapa, is known for its coffee and orchids. The María Cristina orchid garden, on the main square, is open daily. Xico is another pretty colonial village, 8km south of Coatepec. From Xico (population 14,200) it's a pleasant 2km walk to the photogenic, 40m **Texolo waterfall** (a location for several movies).

Buses go about every 15 minutes to Coatepec or Xico from Avenida Allende, about 1km west of central Jalapa.

Parque Nacional Cofre de Perote
The 4274m-high Cofre de Perote volcano is southwest of Jalapa but often obscured by mist. From the town of Perote, 50km west of Jalapa on highway 140, Calle Allende continues southwest to become a dirt road that climbs 1900m in 24km, finishing just below the summit.

Valle Alegre
To reach this 'happy valley' take the highway toward Puebla and turn south after 15km, just west of Las Vigas. Follow the side road through El Llanillo to Tembladeras, where you'll find the **Valle Alegre Hostel** (☎ 2-818-34-84, valle_alegre@correoweb .com), surrounded by an ecological reserve. Dorm beds cost US$6, and amenities include a restaurant and bar. Several buses per week go from Jalapa's bus station to Tembladeras.

VERACRUZ
● pop 381,200 ☎ 2

Often referred to as Puerto Veracruz (to distinguish it from the state, of which it is *not* the capital), this is one of the most festive of

The Heroic City

Veracruz is now officially titled 'Four Times Heroic,' in reference to the final expulsion of the Spanish from San Juan de Ulúa (their last Mexican toehold) in 1825, the triumph over the French in the Pastry War and the resistance to the US in 1847 and 1914.

✳✳✳✳✳✳✳✳✳✳✳✳✳

Mexican cities, with a hedonistic, tropical port atmosphere, a zócalo that becomes a party every evening and one of the biggest Carnavals between Rio de Janeiro and New Orleans. Its people, known as *jarochos*, are good-humored and relaxed. Unfortunately, the seaside here is neither clean nor attractive, though people from Mexico City flood down here. On weekends and at holiday times, and especially around Christmas, Carnaval, and Semana Santa, the city and nearby beaches are jam-packed with visitors.

History

The coast here was occupied by Totonacs, with influences from Toltecs and Aztecs – this mix of pre-Hispanic cultures can be seen at the archaeological site of Zempoala, 42km to the north (see the Zempoala section, earlier in this chapter). After the Spanish conquest, Veracruz was Mexico's main gateway to the outside world for 400 years. Invaders and pirates, incoming and exiled rulers, settlers, silver and slaves – all came and went to make the city a linchpin in Mexico's history.

The Spanish Cortés made his first landing here at an island 2km offshore, which he named Isla Sacrificios because of the remains of human sacrifices he found there. He anchored off another island, San Juan de Ulúa, on Good Friday, April 21, 1519, where he made his first contact with Moctezuma's envoys. Cortés founded the first Spanish settlement at Villa Rica, 69km north, but this was later moved to La Antigua, and finally to the present site of Veracruz in 1598.

Veracruz became the Spaniards' most important anchorage, and until 1760 Veracruz was the only port allowed to handle trade with Spain. Tent cities blossomed for trade fairs when the fleet from Spain made its annual arrival, but because of seaborne raids and tropical diseases – malaria and yellow fever were rampant – Veracruz never became one of Mexico's biggest cities.

In 1567 nine English ships under John Hawkins sailed into Veracruz harbor, with the intention of selling slaves in defiance of the Spanish trade monopoly. They were

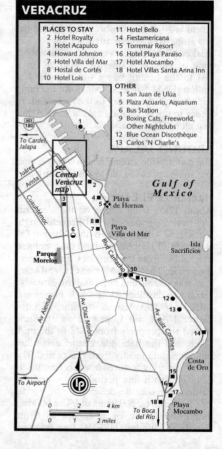

VERACRUZ

PLACES TO STAY
2 Hotel Royalty
3 Hotel Acapulco
4 Howard Johnson
7 Hotel Villa del Mar
8 Hostal de Cortés
10 Hotel Lois
11 Hotel Bello
14 Fiestamericana
15 Torremar Resort
16 Hotel Playa Paraíso
17 Hotel Mocambo
18 Hotel Villas Santa Anna Inn

OTHER
1 San Juan de Ulúa
5 Plaza Acuario, Aquarium
6 Bus Station
9 Boxing Cats, Freeworld, Other Nightclubs
12 Blue Ocean Discothèque
13 Carlos 'N Charlie's

To Cardel, Jalapa

Juárez
Arista
Cuauhtémoc

MEX 180

see Central Veracruz map

Gulf of Mexico

Playa de Hornos

Playa Villa del Mar

Isla Sacrificios

Parque Morelos

Av Alemán
Av Díaz Mirón
Av Ruíz Cortines

To Airport

To Boca del Río

Costa de Oro

Playa Mocambo

0   2   4 km
0   1   2 miles

trapped by a Spanish fleet and only two ships escaped. One of them, however, carried Francis Drake, who went on to harry the Spanish in a long career as a sort of licensed pirate. The most vicious pirate attack of all came in 1683, when the Frenchman Laurent de Gaff, with 600 men, held the 5000 inhabitants of Veracruz captive in the city's church, with little food or water. They killed any who tried to escape, piled the Plaza de Armas with loot, got drunk, raped many of the women and threatened to blow up the church unless the people revealed their secret stashes. They left a few days later, much richer.

19th Century In 1838 General Antonio López de Santa Anna, who had been routed in Texas two years earlier, fled Veracruz in his underwear under bombardment from a French fleet in the 'Pastry War' (the French were pressing various claims against Mexico, including that of a French pastry cook whose restaurant had been wrecked by unruly Mexican officers). But the general replied heroically, driving the invaders out and losing his left leg in the process.

When the 10,000-strong army of Winfield Scott attacked Veracruz in 1847 in the Mexican-American War, over 1000 Mexicans were killed in a weeklong bombardment before the city surrendered.

In 1859, during Mexico's internal Reform War, Benito Juárez's Veracruz-based liberal government promulgated the reform laws that nationalized church property and put education into secular hands. In 1861 when Juárez, having won the war, announced that Mexico couldn't pay its foreign debts, a joint French-Spanish-British force occupied Veracruz. The British and Spanish planned only to take over the customhouse and recover what Mexico owed them, but Napoleon III intended to conquer Mexico. Realizing this, the British and Spanish went home, while the French marched inland to begin their five-year intervention.

Mexico's first railway was built between Veracruz and Mexico City in 1872, and, under the dictatorship of Porfirio Díaz, investment poured into the city.

20th Century In 1914, during the civil war that followed Díaz's departure in the 1910-11 revolution, US troops occupied Veracruz to stop a delivery of German arms to the conservative dictator Victoriano Huerta. The Mexican casualties caused by the intervention alienated even Huerta's opponents. Later in the civil war, Veracruz was for a while the capital of the reformist Constitutionalist faction led by Venustiano Carranza.

Orientation
The center of the city's action is the zócalo, site of the cathedral and the Palacio Municipal. The harbor is 250m east, with the San Juan de Ulúa fort on its far side. Boulevard Camacho follows the coast to the south, past naval and commercial anchorages, to a series of grimy beaches. About 700m south of the zócalo along Independencia is Parque Zamora, a road junction circling a wide green. Near here is Mercado Hidalgo, the main market. The 1st- and 2nd-class bus stations are back-to-back, 2km south of Parque Zamora along Díaz Mirón.

Information
Tourist Offices The city and state tourist office (☎ 932-19-99) is on the ground floor of the Palacio Municipal, on the zócalo. It's open daily 9 am to 9 pm. Staff are well informed and some speak English.

Consulates Several countries have consulates in Veracruz, including France (☎ 935-06-49) and the UK (☎ 931-12-85).

Money Banamex and Bancomer are both on Independencia in the block north of the zócalo – they have ATMs and change traveler's checks. Around the corner at Juárez 112, Casa de Cambio Puebla gives good rates and is open 9 am to 6 pm Monday to Friday.

Post & Communications The main post office is at Plaza de la República 213, a five-minute walk north of the zócalo. It's open 8 am to 4 pm Monday to Friday and 9 am to 1 pm Saturday.

The Telecomm office, next door to the main post office, has public fax, telegram and

CENTRAL GULF COAST

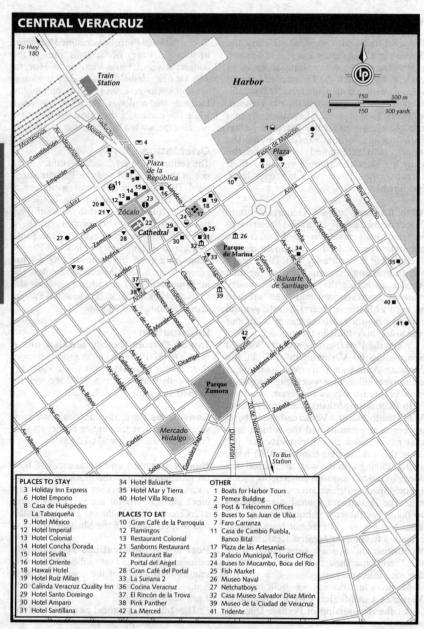

CENTRAL VERACRUZ

To Hwy 180

Train Station

Harbor

0   150   300 m
0   150   300 yards

Montesinos
Av Independencia
Morelos
Viaducto
Constitución
Emparán
Juárez
Lerdo
Zamora
Molina
Serdán
Arista
Av 5 de Mayo
Herrera Nalcozart
Av Independencia
Callejón Reforma
Av Madero
Av Hidalgo
Av Bravo
Av Guerrero
Av Allende
Cortés
González Pagés
Soto
Díaz Mirón
20 de Noviembre
Primero de Mayo
Zapata
Doblado
Mártires del 25 de Junio
Rayón
Ocampo
Canal
Claudio
Av Zaragoza
Gómez Farías
Av 16 de Septiembre
Perla
Av Xicoténcatl
Hernández
Esteban
Blvd Camacho
Paseo de Malecón
Arista
Landero y Coss

Plaza de la República
Zócalo
Cathedral
Parque de Marina
Baluarte de Santiago
Parque Zamora
Mercado Hidalgo

To Bus Station

Plaza

PLACES TO STAY
3 Holiday Inn Express
6 Hotel Emporio
8 Casa de Huéspedes
   La Tabasqueña
9 Hotel México
12 Hotel Imperial
13 Hotel Colonial
14 Hotel Concha Dorada
15 Hotel Sevilla
16 Hotel Oriente
19 Hotel Ruiz Milan
20 Calinda Veracruz Quality Inn
29 Hotel Santo Domingo
30 Hotel Amparo
31 Hotel Santillana

34 Hotel Baluarte
35 Hotel Mar y Tierra
40 Hotel Villa Rica

PLACES TO EAT
10 Gran Café de la Parroquia
12 Flamingos
13 Restaurant Colonial
21 Sanborns Restaurant
22 Restaurant Bar
   Portal del Angel
28 Gran Café del Portal
33 La Suriana 2
36 Cocina Veracruz
37 El Rincón de la Trova
38 Pink Panther
42 La Merced

OTHER
1 Boats for Harbor Tours
2 Pemex Building
4 Post & Telecomm Offices
5 Buses to San Juan de Ulúa
7 Faro Carranza
11 Casa de Cambio Puebla,
   Banco Bital
17 Plaza de las Artesanías
23 Palacio Municipal, Tourist Office
24 Buses to Mocambo, Boca del Río
25 Fish Market
26 Museo Naval
27 Netchatboys
32 Casa Museo Salvador Díaz Mirón
39 Museo de la Ciudad de Veracruz
41 Tridente

telex services and is open 8 am to 7 pm Monday to Friday, 9 am to 5 pm Saturday, 9 am to noon Sunday. There are pay phones on the zócalo.

Netchatboys, at Lerdo 369, has Internet access for only US$1.50 per hour; open 9 am to 9 pm Monday to Friday, noon to 8 pm Saturday and Sunday.

Zócalo

The Veracruz zócalo, also called the Plaza de Armas, Plaza Lerdo and Plaza de la Constitución, is the hub of the city for jarochos and visitors alike. It's a fine-looking place with *portales* (arched arcades), palm trees, a fountain, the 17th-century Palacio Municipal on one side and an 18th-century cathedral on another. The level of activity accelerates as the day progresses, from breakfast and coffee under the arches, to a leisurely lunch to afternoon entertainment on an outdoor stage. In the evening, as the sweat cools off Veracruz bodies, the zócalo becomes a swirling, multifaceted party, with cool drinks and competing street musicians (see Entertainment).

Harbor & Malecón

Veracruz harbor is still busy, though oil ports like Tampico and Coatzacoalcos now handle greater tonnages. The Paseo del Malecón (also called Insurgentes) is a pleasant waterfront walk, starting with the Plaza de las Artesanías; colorful souvenir stalls opposite the plaza sell a mind-boggling selection of seashell knickknacks and tacky T-shirts.

Stroll out along the Malecón and view the ships, cranes and ancient fortress across the water, or take a sight-seeing boat trip for a closer look. At the corner of Boulevard Camacho are monuments to the city's defenders against the Americans in 1914 and to all sailors who gave their lives to the sea. The high-rise building here is an early example of modern Mexican architecture; built in 1940, it now houses Pemex offices and has some interesting murals.

San Juan de Ulúa

This fortress protecting Veracruz harbor was originally an island, but it's now connected to the mainland by a causeway. In 1518 the Spaniard Juan de Grijalva landed here during an exploratory voyage from Cuba. The next year Cortés also landed here, and it became the main entry point for Spanish newcomers to Mexico. The Franciscan chapel is thought to have been built in 1524 and the first fortifications in the 1530s, but most of what can be seen now was built progressively between 1552 and 1779.

The central part of the fortress, Fuerte San José, has also acted as a prison, most notoriously during the Porfirio Díaz regime. Under Díaz, three damp, stinking cells – called El Purgatorio, La Gloria and El Infierno (Purgatory, Heaven and Hell) – were reserved for political prisoners. Many inmates died of yellow fever or tuberculosis.

Today San Juan de Ulúa is an empty ruin of passageways, battlements, bridges and stairways, which you can wander around from 9 am to 4.30 pm Tuesday to Sunday (US$1.75, free on Sunday). Guided tours are available in Spanish and, sometimes, English (US$3.50).

To get there, take a 'San Juan de Ulúa' bus (US$0.30) from the east side of Plaza de la República. The last bus back to town leaves at 6 pm.

Museo Naval

Built as a school for naval officers in the 1890s, this large and handsome building has been beautifully restored, and in 1997 it opened as a museum covering Mexico's maritime heritage and naval history. As well as rooms full of weapons and model ships, the museum holds interesting exhibits on the US attacks on Veracruz in 1847 and 1914, and on revolutionary hero Venustiano Carranza, whose government-in-exile was based in Veracruz for a time. The displays are well laid out in large, air-conditioned rooms, but the information is in Spanish only. The museum entrance is on Arista, two blocks south of the Malecón, though the building occupies a whole block. It's open 10 am to 5 pm Tuesday to Sunday (free).

Faro Carranza

Facing the waterfront on the Malecón, the Faro Carranza is a yellow building that holds a lighthouse and navy offices. The Mexican navy goes through an elaborate parade in front of the building early each morning. Venustiano Carranza lived here during the revolution, in 1914 and 1915, and it was here that the 1917 Mexican constitution was drafted. Exhibits on Carranza and his political struggles are now in the Museo Naval (see above); the Faro Carranza building itself is closed to the public.

Baluarte de Santiago

From the 16th to 19th centuries, central Veracruz was surrounded by a defensive wall that incorporated nine forts. The only fort remaining is the Baluarte (Bastion) de Santiago, built in 1526 beside a canal at what was then the waterfront. Inside the fort is a small exhibit of pre-Hispanic gold jewelry known as Las Joyas del Pescador. The name refers to some fabulous gold artifacts found by a fisherman in Veracruz harbor in 1976, but most pieces on display here, though gorgeous, come from other sources. The fort is at the junction of Canal and 16 de Septiembre, and you can walk around the outside at any time. The interior, including the gold exhibit, is open 9 am to 4.30 pm Tuesday to Sunday (US$1.50, free Sunday).

Museo de la Ciudad de Veracruz

The Veracruz City Museum, on Zaragoza at Morales, has fine displays on the city's early history (particularly slavery); the exhibits on contemporary customs and Carnaval are not as good. It's open 9 am to 8 pm Tuesday to Sunday (free).

Casa Museo Salvador Díaz Mirón

Once the home of celebrated poet Salvador Díaz Mirón (1853-1928), this house, at Zaragoza 322, is now a center for literary and theatrical workshops. Some rooms upstairs are restored and decorated in late-19th-century style. It's open 9 am to 8 pm Monday to Saturday (free).

Acuario de Veracruz

Veracruz's new aquarium is inside the Plaza Acuario shopping mall, near the beach at Playa de Hornos, about 2km south of the city center. The most impressive exhibit is the huge, donut-shaped tank in which sharks, rays and giant turtles swim right around and over the viewers. Numerous smaller tanks and ponds show lots of fish (both freshwater and saltwater species), turtles, coral and so on. The aquarium is open 9 am to 7 pm daily (US$4.50/2.25 for adults/children).

Beaches & Lagoons

Few people venture into the water at Playa de Hornos, just south of the city center, or at Playa Villa del Mar, farther south. Cleaner water and beaches are 5km south of the city at **Costa de Oro** and 7km south at **Mocambo**. For swimming, you're better off paying US$2 to use the seaside pool at the Hotel Mocambo.

Farther south again, the road goes to **Boca del Río**, with popular seafood restaurants. Over the bridge, the coast road continues to **Mandinga**, where you can hire a boat to explore the lagoons, and **Antón Lizardo**.

Diving

The beaches near Veracruz may not be inviting, but there is good diving (including at least one accessible wreck) on the reefs near the offshore islands. Part of the area has been designated an underwater natural park. Tridente (☎ 931-79-34), at Boulevard Camacho 165A, is a PADI dive school and arranges dive trips from Veracruz and Antón Lizardo (45 minutes down the coast). With a group of four people, a day trip with two dives, a guide and equipment will cost around US$55 per person. Other dive-boat operators are based in Boca del Río and Antón Lizardo.

Organized Tours

Boats from the Malecón offer hour-long harbor tours for US$4.50 per person – they leave when they're full, about every 30 minutes from 7 am to 7 pm.

Also leaving from the Malecón, imitation tramcars make a 40-minute circuit of the city's attractions (US$1.50).

Special Events

Carnaval – Veracruz breaks into a nine-day party before Ash Wednesday (February or March; 46 days before Easter Sunday) each year. Starting the previous Tuesday, colorful parades wind through the city daily, beginning with one devoted to the 'burning of bad humor' and ending with the 'funeral of Juan Carnaval.' Other events include fireworks, dances, salsa and samba music, handicrafts, folklore shows and children's parades. See the tourist office for a program of events.

Festival del Caribe – High point of the summer holiday season is the festival of Afro-Caribbean culture in the last two weeks of August. Various Caribbean nations participate in academic forums, trade shows and business conferences, but the main attractions are the dance and music performances (many of them free), film screenings and art expositions.

Places to Stay

The busiest time in Veracruz is Carnaval, when the town is packed and hotels are booked out weeks or months ahead. Other busy periods, when reservations are recommended, are Semana Santa, the summer months from mid-July to mid-September (especially on weekends) and the period from mid-November to mid-January. At other times, plenty of rooms are available, and you should be able to get a substantial discount off the prices listed here.

It's convenient and fun to stay on the zócalo, and there are some budget places nearby. Some of the seafront hotels can offer good value too. The cheapest places are near the bus stations, while the most expensive are the resort hotels in the beach suburb of Mocambo, 7km south of the center.

Places to Stay – Budget

Even the cheapest hotels should have hot water, but check that the room has adequate ventilation and a working fan.

Zócalo Area Just around the corner from the zócalo on Morelos, the basic *Hotel México* (☎ 932-05-60) has lots of brown tiles and quiet, dark rooms with TV and fan for US$11/16 single/double. Farther north on Morelos, hidden behind a photocopy shop,

the even more basic *Casa de Huéspedes La Tabasqueña* (no phone) features airless rooms in cell-block style, also for US$11/16. On the corner of Lerdo, just east of the zócalo but with the entrance on Morelos, the *Hotel Sevilla* (☎ 932-42-46) has big rooms with ceiling fan, TV and private bath for US$19 for a single/double, US$33 with two beds. The rooms are pretty clean but can be noisy, and the management is not exactly friendly.

Other cheapies are grouped a couple of blocks southeast of the zócalo. The *Hotel Santo Domingo* (☎ 931-63-26, Serdán 451) has small, basic rooms with fan and private bath for US$11/22. Across the street, the older *Hotel Amparo* (☎ 932-27-38, Serdán 482) is a simple but clean place with tiled floors and lime-green walls. The small rooms with fan and private bath are US$13.50/17. The slightly bigger, though worn, rooms in the nearby *Hotel Santillana* (☎ 932-31-16, Landero y Cos 209) have the same color scheme and cost US$18 with a double bed, US$33 with two beds. They're cleanish and have TV and fan.

City Seafront For a budget place directly across the street from the ocean, try the *Hotel Villa Rica* (☎ 932-48-54, Boulevard Camacho 7), with small, tidy, fan-cooled rooms at US$13.50/16.

Bus Station Area *Hotel Rosa Mar* (☎ 937-07-47, Lafragua 1100), right opposite the 2nd-class bus station, may be a bit noisy, but it's clean, friendly and respectable. Fan-cooled rooms with private bath cost US$14 single, US$16.50 double with one bed, US$20 with two beds.

A block east from the 2nd-class bus station, *Hotel Azteca* (☎ 937-42-41, 22 de Marzo 218), at Orizaba, is a green building with a small courtyard and helpful management. Air-conditioned singles/doubles with TV and private bath are US$18, or US$23 with two beds, but they start at US$12 in low seasons.

One of the best deals, despite the inconvenient location, is the *Hotel Acapulco* (☎ 932-34-92, Uribe 1327), just west of Díaz

Mirón, nine blocks north of the 1st-class bus station and a similar distance from the city center. Very clean, fairly bright, fan-cooled rooms of a reasonable size and with TV cost US$11/14, including off-street parking.

Places to Stay – Mid-Range

Zócalo Area *Hotel Concha Dorada* (☎ 931-29-96, *Lerdo 77*) is just off the zócalo proper, with clean, small, air-conditioned rooms for US$22 and larger ones with a balcony over the zócalo for US$28, or US$38 with two beds.

Right on the zócalo, the 180-room *Hotel Colonial* (☎ 932-01-93, *Lerdo 117*) has an indoor pool and tiled terraces overlooking the square on the 5th and 6th floors. Prices are US$25/33 for dark, quiet and comfortable interior rooms or lighter rooms at the back. Rooms at the front with balconies over the zócalo are US$34/44 and noisier. All have air-con and TV, but they vary in value, so check out the room before you check in.

A little farther west, *Hotel Imperial* (☎ 931-18-66, *Lerdo 153*) has an elegant lobby, old-fashioned elevator, towering columns and a stained-glass ceiling. A spacious single or double room, with a marble-floored bathroom, costs US$49. For a room with a magnificent king-size bed, expect to pay at least US$80.

Just off the zócalo, *Hotel Oriente* (☎ 931-24-90, *Lerdo 20*) is centrally located and quite a good value. Clean, compact, air-conditioned rooms with TV and phone cost US$17/22. Outside rooms have balconies but also more noise.

Southeast from the zócalo, on a quiet street looking across to the Baluarte de Santiago, the *Hotel Baluarte* (☎ 932-52-22, *Canal 265*), at 16 de Septiembre, is also a good value. Its clean, modern, well-kept rooms go for US$33 with TV and air-con.

Harbor & City Seafront On the Malecón, but a handy six blocks from the city center, *Hotel Ruiz Milan* (☎ 932-27-72) has some economical, fan-cooled rooms for US$32 and better rooms with air-con and harbor views for US$50. Also on the Malecón, a little closer to the center, the modern *Hawaii Hotel* (☎ 931-04-27) is slightly more expensive at US$50/55.

On the corner of Boulevard Camacho and Figueroa, big and busy *Hotel Mar y Tierra* (☎ 931-38-66) has rooms in an older front section for US$27 or in a preferable rear extension for US$33. All rooms have air-con, TV and carpet, but some are better value than others so look first. A little farther from the center, *Hotel Royalty* (☎ 932-39-88), on the corner of Boulevard Camacho and Abasolo, has clean rooms with balconies and air-con for US$27, or US$35 with two beds. They're nothing fancy, but they're good for the money, and the upper floors have good views.

Bus Station Area East of the ADO bus station, *Hotel Impala* (☎ 937-01-69, *Orizaba 650*) has rooms with air-con, TV and phones at US$22/28 for singles/doubles. Half a block north of the bus station, *Hotel Central* (☎ 937-22-22, *Díaz Mirón 1612*) is clean and very busy, with fan-cooled rooms at US$22, air-conditioned rooms for US$28.

Mocambo A short walk from Playa Mocambo, *Hotel Villas Santa Anna Inn* (☎ 922-47-57) is good for families, with a garden, pool, and pleasant, spacious, air-conditioned rooms starting at US$33. Larger bungalows cost US$66. Rates are discounted at least 20% at off-peak times. The hotel faces the inland side of Carretera Veracruz-Boca del Río; enter from the first street on the right a couple of hundred meters south of the traffic circle by the Hotel Mocambo.

Places to Stay – Top End

Zócalo Area & Harbor The most central top-end place is the fully modernized *Calinda Veracruz Quality Inn* (☎ 931-22-33), on the corner of Independencia and Lerdo overlooking the zócalo (the entrance is on Independencia). Well-decorated, air-conditioned rooms, some with balconies, cost US$72 and up – the rooftop pool has a great view.

Around the corner and two blocks from the zócalo, *Holiday Inn Express* (☎ 932-45-

50, Morelos 225) is a new hotel in a stylishly renovated old building. It has a courtyard swimming pool and comfortable rooms with all the modern conveniences for US$94.

On the Malecón at the corner of Xicoténcatl, *Hotel Emporio* (☎ 932-00-20) towers over the harbor, its outside elevator soaring above three swimming pools to a roof garden. Prices start at US$87/96 single/double for a not-very-large 'standard' room.

City Seafront Opposite Playa Villa del Mar, 2.5km south of the zócalo, *Hostal de Cortés* (☎ 932-00-65), on the corner of Boulevard Camacho and Las Casas, is a modern place with a pool and 98 air-conditioned rooms, some with sea-view balconies. Singles and doubles start at US$58, including breakfast. Farther south, *Hotel Villa del Mar* (☎ 931-33-66, *Boulevard Camacho 2707)* is a good value if you can get a room away from the noisy road. It has an outdoor pool, and the rooms, all air-conditioned, are in both a central block and garden bungalows. Few have a sea view, but the location is pleasantly breezy. The rooms start at US$64 for singles or doubles.

More expensive, and a little farther north facing Playa de Hornos, *Howard Johnson* (☎ 931-00-11, *Boulevard Camacho 1263)* has rooms with a sea view for US$77, but interior rooms are almost as nice for US$61.

At the center of the nightlife action, *Hotel Lois* (☎ 937-82-90) is on Avenida Ruiz Cortines near the seafront Boulevard Camacho. It's very new and smart, with modern air-conditioned rooms at US$90 (US$75 in low season). Rooms on the north side have a good view of the Carnaval parade. Also near the nightlife on Ruiz Cortines, *Hotel Bello* (☎ 928-48-28) has some rooms with a sea view and others facing the Carnaval parade route. The high-season rate is US$63 a night for an air-conditioned single or double. The restaurant is good and reasonably priced.

Mocambo The original luxury resort hotel here is the venerable *Hotel Mocambo* (☎ 922-02-05), on Carretera Veracruz-Mocambo 7km south of the city center.

Once the best in Veracruz, it's ever-so-slightly faded but still offers more character and style than most of the more modern places. It has terraced gardens, three sizable pools (two indoors) and more than 100 good-size rooms with air-con, TV and a variety of views. Prices start at about US$80 in high season. Playa Mocambo is a minute's walk from the foot of the gardens.

Other luxury places with pools, gardens and private beaches include the eight-story *Torremar Resort* (☎ 989-21-00, *Ruiz Cortines 4300)*, with scores of rooms starting at US$102, and the smaller *Hotel Playa Paraíso* (☎ 921-86-00, *Ruiz Cortines 3500)*, with rooms and suites starting at US$81. Newest and most luxurious is the imposing *Fiestamericana* (☎ 989-89-89), on Boulevard Camacho, in bright terra-cotta tones with fountains out front, a vast lobby and rates from US$120 to over US$1000 for the presidential suite.

Places to Eat

Veracruzana sauce, found on fish all over Mexico, is made from onions, garlic, tomatoes, olives, green peppers and spices. Uncooked seafood dishes, including ceviche and oysters, disappeared from the menus of most restaurants after a cholera scare a few years ago.

Zócalo Area The cafés under the portales are as much for drinks and atmosphere as for food. Stroll along the line and find one that appeals to you, or stop at any one with a free table. *Flamingos*, outside the Hotel Imperial, is typical, with fish dishes for US$5, seafood cocktails for US$2.50 and inexpensive beer. The classy air-conditioned *Restaurant Colonial*, at the Hotel Colonial, has pretty good food, but expect to spend at least US$10 per person.

On the west corner of the zócalo, a new *Sanborns Restaurant* sits under its own set of portales. It's a tame alternative to the main square, but it offers the usual good-quality Sanborns snacks and meals in a squeaky-clean setting at reasonable prices. On the quieter southeast side of the zócalo, *Restaurant Bar Portal del Angel* offers good value, with main courses for around US$5, including a range of well-prepared seafood dishes.

Gran Café del Portal (Independencia 105), off the south corner of the zócalo, was once a Veracruz institution known as the Gran Café de la Parroquia. It's still a cavernous, convivial café, and customers still request a refill of *café con leche* by clinking spoons on glasses. But the conspicuous coffee-making contraptions are gone, and the large-screen video detracts from the ambiance. On the other hand, the food is better than ever, with typical dishes like fish fillets veracruzana or steak tampiqueño for US$7. Pasta dishes are around US$4.50, and a large cup of the famous milk coffee is US$1.50. A magnet for marimbas and mariachis, it's open 6 am to midnight daily.

Two blocks southwest of the zócalo, on the corner of Zamora and Madero, *Cocina Veracruz* is aimed at locals, not tourists. It serves cheap, basic, wholesome food, including a three-course comida corrida for only US$2.

Two blocks south of the zócalo, look for the quaint Callejón Héroes de Nacozari, between Serdán and Arista. During the day here, popular places like the *Pink Panther* serve set lunches for low prices at quiet outdoor tables. In the evenings, the alley becomes more lively, with the restaurant-bar *El Rincón de la Trova* turning on a large selection of alcoholic drinks and live music Friday and Saturday nights. The menu is limited to simple items (under US$2.50) such as tostadas, empanadas and tamales.

Harbor Inheriting the name, if not the ambiance, of the original institution, *Gran Café de la Parroquia* is a vast restaurant/coffeehouse on the Malecón, facing the harbor. The menu is the same as the Gran Café del Portal, and it gets just as crowded. It's especially popular for breakfast, when the café con leche is in high demand.

The top floor of the municipal fish market, on Landero y Cos, is packed until early evening with *comedores* doing bargain fish fillets or shrimps *al mojo de ajo*. Not for the faint of stomach, the market is heavy on atmosphere and fishy aromas. Nearby, *La Suriana 2*, on the corner of Zaragoza and Arista, has a friendly family feel and excellent seafood at budget prices – *cocteles* and soup at around US$3.50 and the freshest of fish from US$3 to US$6.

Parque Zamora Area *La Merced*, on Rayón between Zaragoza and Clavijero, is Parque Zamora's jolly answer to the Gran Cafés. A filling comida corrida of chicken soup, rice, chicken, sweets and a drink is US$3, meat and fish dishes are US$3.50 to US$6, and antojitos are only US$2.50.

Down the Coast Restaurants at Mocambo beach tend to be pricey and nothing special. The coffee shop at the *Hotel Mocambo* has some atmosphere and does a good breakfast.

Enjoying a seafood meal in the river-mouth village of Boca del Río, 10km south of Veracruz center, is an indispensable part of a visit to Veracruz for many Mexicans – a long Sunday lunch is the favorite way to do it. *Pardiño's (Zamora 40)*, in the center of the village, is the best-known restaurant, but there are several more along the riverside.

Mandinga, about 8km farther down the coast from Boca del Río, is also known for its seafood (especially prawns) and has a clutch of small restaurants.

Entertainment

A café seat under the zócalo portales is a ringside ticket to the best entertainment in town. There you might witness, in two blinks, couples dancing like crazy, families with out-of-control kids, cruising transvestites, and vendors hawking foam-rubber lizards – all to the accompaniment of wandering mariachis, marimbas and guitarists vying to be heard above each other. Some evenings there's scheduled entertainment too, in the form of visiting musicians or dancers on a temporary stage. The level of excitement depends on the crowd – sometimes there are whole groups of revelers going wild, and other times it's all staid tourists sitting at their tables waiting for something to happen.

You can watch the show for nothing from the paths and benches around the zócalo, but it's not too expensive to enjoy a drink in the portales. A beer is only US$1; mixed drinks run to US$3, and they're generous with the booze. Places at the east end of the portales, east of the plaza proper, are cheapest.

Rivaling the portales, especially for the under-25 set, is the nightclub, bar and disco scene along the waterfront Boulevard Camacho near the junction with Avenida Ruiz Cortines. The purple neon tower of *Hotel Lois* is the most conspicuous focus, and its lobby bar attracts a well-dressed crowd. Almost next door are the *Underground* disco and *Ocean*, a long-standing club popular with affluent vacationers and locals. In the same stretch of Ruiz Cortines you'll find a slew of newer nightspots like *Boxing Cats*, *Freeworld* and *Forum*. Most of these places open Thursday through Saturday at around 11 pm and have a cover charge of US$3 to US$8, depending on demand and your gender (it's often less for women). At holiday times, the whole area becomes an outdoor party, with bars and snack stalls along Boulevard Camacho, live, loud music, and dancing in street. Farther south on Camacho, *Blue Ocean Discothéque* and *Carlos 'N Charlie's* are also worth a look.

If you hanker for something more sedate, ask the tourist office for information on concerts and cultural events. Several cinemas, including two on Arista, show recent-release movies.

Getting There & Away

Air Frequent flights between Veracruz and Mexico City are offered by Mexicana (☎ 932-22-42) and Aeroméxico (☎ 935-01-42). Aerolitoral (☎ 931-52-32) flies to and from Tampico and Villahermosa, and Mexicana flies to Tampico and to Cancún via Mérida. Aerocaribe (☎ 922-52-05) has direct flights to Minatitlán, with onward connections to Cancún and other destinations.

Bus Veracruz is a major hub, with good services up and down the coast and inland along the Córdoba-Puebla-Mexico City corridor. Buses to and from Mexico City can be heavily booked at holiday times.

The renovated bus station is about 3km south of the zócalo. The 1st-class/deluxe area

fronts Díaz Mirón on the corner with Xalapa and has mostly ADO (Autobuses de Oriente) 1st-class services, as well as some deluxe UNO and ADO GL buses. It's very modern, but quite inconvenient for users. The waiting area has phones and a snack bar, but you might not be allowed in if you don't have a ticket. The left-luggage room closes at night, and the only alternative is to buy a token for an overpriced locker. Behind the ADO station, the 2nd-class side is entered from Avenida Lafragua and has mostly AU and TRV services. There's a 24-hour luggage room here. Daily departures include:

Acayucan – 250km, 3½ hours; 15 ADO (US$11), frequent AU (US$7.75)

Catemaco – 165km, 3 hours; 11 ADO (US$6.75), 10 AU *directos* (US$6)

Córdoba – 125km, 1½ hours; 25 ADO (US$5.50), hourly AU directos (US$5)

Jalapa – 100km, 2 hours; ADO every 20 to 30 minutes, 5 am to 11 pm (US$4.75), 25 AU (US$4)

Mexico City (TAPO) – 430km, 5 hours; 6 UNO (US$33), 15 ADO GL (US$24), 16 ADO (US$20), 15 AU (US$17)

Oaxaca – 460km, 6½ hours; ADO at 7.15 am and 10.30 pm (US$23), 1 AU directo (US$18.75)

Orizaba – 150km, 2 hours; frequent ADO (US$6.50) and AU directos (US$6.25)

Papantla – 230km, 4 hours; 6 ADO (US$10), hourly AU (US$8)

Poza Rica – 250km, 5 hours; several UNO (US$19) and ADO GL (US$13.50), 21 ADO (US$11)

Puebla – 300km, 4 hours; 7 ADO (US$14), some AU directos (US$12.50)

San Andrés Tuxtla – 155km, 2¾ hours; 12 ADO (US$6), frequent AU (US$4.50)

Santiago Tuxtla – 140km, 2½ hours; 12 ADO (US$5.50), frequent AU (US$4.25)

Tampico – 490km, 10 hours; 2 UNO (US$34), 15 ADO (US$24)

Tuxpan – 300km, 5½ hours; 9 ADO (US$13.50)

Villahermosa – 480km, 8 hours; 2 UNO (US$34), 12 ADO (US$19)

Buses also go to Campeche, Cancún, Chetumal, Matamoros, Mérida and Salina Cruz.

Train The Veracruz station is at the north end of Plaza de la República, a five-minute walk from the zócalo. Ferro Sur runs two trains daily from Veracruz to Mexico City, departing at 8.20 am and 10 pm (464km, 10 to 11 hours or more, US$7).

Trains frequently take longer, sometimes *much* longer, than scheduled times and are recommended only for rail-travel enthusiasts. The information given here may change as Mexico's passenger train services are being privatized and reorganized.

Car Among the many car rental agencies with desks at the Veracruz airport are National (☎ 931-33-12, 931-17-56) and Avis (☎ 932-16-16). Others have offices in big hotels; Hertz (☎ 937-41-00) is at the Howard Johnson, and Powerfull (☎ 932-85-73) is at Hostal de Cortés. Smaller agencies are worth calling if you're shopping around – try Roca Rental (☎ 931-05-04), Fast (☎ 931-83-29), Quick (☎ 937-81-23) or Today's (☎ 935-70-15).

Getting Around
To/From the Airport The Veracruz airport (☎ 934-90-08) is 11km southwest of town near highway 140. There is no bus service to or from town; taxis cost around US$9.

To/From the Bus Stations For the city center, take a bus marked 'Díaz Mirón y Madero' (US$0.30) from in front of the 1st-class bus station. The bus goes to Parque Zamora then up Madero. For the zócalo, get off on the corner of Madero and Lerdo and turn right. Returning to the depots, pick up the same bus going south on 5 de Mayo. At the booth outside the 1st-class depot you can buy a taxi ticket to the zócalo for US$1.75.

Down the Coast A bus marked 'Mocambo – Boca del Río' (US$0.75) leaves every few minutes from the corner of Zaragoza and Serdán near the zócalo; it goes to Parque Zamora then down the seafront Boulevard Camacho to Mocambo (15 minutes; get off at Expover exhibition hall on Calzada Mocambo and walk down the street left of the Hotel Mocambo to the beach) and Boca del Río (25 minutes).

AU buses to Antón Lizardo stop at Boca del Río and Mandinga. They leave from the 2nd-class bus station every 20 minutes till 8.45 pm; the last one back to town leaves around 8 pm.

CÓRDOBA & FORTÍN DE LAS FLORES
Córdoba: • pop 132,000 • elev 924m ☎ 2
Fortín de las Flores: • pop 19,000 • elev 970m ☎ 2

Córdoba ('CORR-do-ba'), 125km from Veracruz, is in the foothills of Mexico's central mountains, surrounded by enticing, verdant countryside. The town has a long colonial history and a pleasant center, and it's worth a stop for the fine food, but there's not a lot to see or do.

In 1618, 30 Spanish families founded Córdoba to stop escaped black slaves from attacking travelers between Mexico City and the coast – the town is consequently known as La Ciudad de los Treinta Caballeros (City of the 30 Knights). Today it's a commercial and processing center for sugarcane, tobacco and coffee from the nearby hillsides and fruit from the lowlands.

Just west of Córdoba, Fortín de las Flores is a center for commercial flower production, though most of the color is confined to the nurseries and to private gardens. Fortín is popular as a weekend retreat for the Mexico City middle class.

Orientation
Córdoba's central Plaza de Armas has fine 18th-century portales on three sides, with a row of busy cafés under the arches on the northeast. The city streets have numbers, not names. Avenidas 2, 4, 6, etc, are northeast of the plaza; Avenidas 3, 5, 7, etc, are southwest of the plaza. The Calles are at right angles to the Avenidas, with Calles 2, 4, 6, etc, northwest of the plaza and the odd-numbered Calles southeast of the plaza.

Fortín's big, open plaza, the Parque Principal, has the Palacio Municipal in the middle and a cathedral on the south side. It's 7km from central Córdoba, but the towns have grown into each other along highway 150.

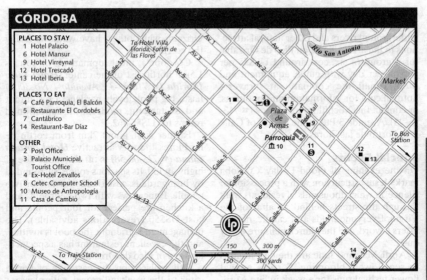

CÓRDOBA

PLACES TO STAY
1 Hotel Palacio
6 Hotel Mansur
9 Hotel Virreynal
12 Hotel Trescadó
13 Hotel Iberia

PLACES TO EAT
4 Café Parroquia, El Balcón
5 Restaurante El Cordobés
7 Cantábrico
14 Restaurant-Bar Díaz

OTHER
2 Post Office
3 Palacio Municipal,
   Tourist Office
4 Ex-Hotel Zevallos
8 Cetec Computer School
10 Museo de Antropología
11 Casa de Cambio

Information

Córdoba's tourist office (☎ 712-25-81) is in the Palacio Municipal, on the northwest side of the plaza, and open 8.30 am to 3 pm and 5 to 8 pm Monday to Saturday. It has some handy maps, brochures and a monthly schedule of activities, all in Spanish.

Córdoba's post office is on Avenida 3, just west of the Plaza de Armas. Banks around the plaza have ATMs and change traveler's checks, and a couple of *casas de cambio* on Avenida 3, southeast of the plaza, also change traveler's checks.

Internet access costs US$1.50 per hour at Cetec, a computer school on the west corner of Córdoba's plaza. It's open 7 am to 9 pm Monday to Friday, 8 am to 6 pm Saturday and Sunday, but sometimes all the machines are being used for computer classes.

Things to See & Do

The **Ex-Hotel Zevallos**, built in 1687, is not a hotel but the former home of the Condes (Counts) of Zevallos. It's on the northeast side of Córdoba's Plaza de Armas, behind

the portales. Plaques in the courtyard record that Juan O'Donojú and Agustín de Iturbide met here after mass on August 24, 1821, and agreed on terms for Mexico's independence. O'Donojú, the new viceroy, had concluded it was useless for Spain to try to cling to its colony; Iturbide, leader of the anti-imperial forces, was a former royalist general who had changed sides. Contrary to the Plan de Iguala, in which Iturbide and Vicente Guerrero had proposed a European monarch as Mexican head of state, O'Donojú and Iturbide agreed that a Mexican could hold that office. Iturbide went on to a brief reign as Emperor Agustín I. The building now houses several restaurants.

At the southeast end of Plaza de Armas, the big, late-18th-century church is **La Parroquia de la Inmaculada Concepción**, famous for its loud bells.

Just off the plaza on Calle 3, the **Museo de Antropología** has a small but well-displayed collection including a Classic Veracruz palma and some beautifully made personal ornaments. It's open 9 am to 2 pm and 4 to 8 pm daily (free).

Organized Tours

Faraventuras runs trips to waterfalls, caves, underground rivers and other natural attractions in the area. Climbs on Pico de Orizaba, for a group of six, cost around US$55 per person per day with guide, equipment and food. Email the company at faraver@ hotmail.com for information and bookings, or contact the Xochítl travel agency (☎ 713-16-95), Avenida 3 Pte at the corner of Calle 2, in Fortín de las Flores.

Special Events

On the evening of Good Friday, Córdoba marks Jesus' crucifixion with a procession of silence, in which thousands of residents walk through the streets behind an altar of the Virgin. Everyone holds a lit candle, no one utters a word, and the church bells are eerily quiet.

April, May and June are the best months to see flowers blooming; Fortín's annual flower festival runs for a week in late April-early May.

Places to Stay

Inexpensive but acceptable accommodations can be found on Avenida 2 in Córdoba, only three blocks downhill from the plaza. *Hotel Trescadó (☎ 712-23-66, Avenida 2 No 909)* is very bare and basic, but single/double rooms cost only US$5/6 (plus US$1 for parking and US$1 for a TV). *Hotel Iberia (☎ 712-13-01, Avenida 2 No 919)* has small, modern rooms with TV and fan for US$8/9, or US$12 with two beds. The rooms are set around a courtyard.

Two places on Córdoba's plaza have some old-style character as well as a great location. *Hotel Virreynal (☎ 712-23-77)*, on the corner of Avenida 1 and Calle 5, is especially good value, with large, clean, fan-cooled rooms for US$17/18. *Hotel Mansur (☎ 712-60-00, Avenida 1 No 301)*, has an elegant lobby and rooms with TV, phone and air-con from US$21/24; try to get an upstairs room overlooking the plaza.

The modern *Hotel Palacio (☎ 712-21-88)*, on the corner of Avenida 3 and Calle 2, is lacking in style, but the rooms are clean and comfortable and have air-con, TV and

phone for US$17/22. Some of the upper rooms have wonderful views of Pico de Orizaba, while others have windows facing the corridor.

Córdoba's most upmarket option is 1.5km northwest of the center. *Hotel Villa Florida (☎ 716-33-33, Avenida 1 No 3002)* has a big pool, lovely gardens, a restaurant and 82 tasteful, modern, air-conditioned rooms for US$54/62.

Farther west, about 2km from Fortín de las Flores, the very attractive *Hotel Posada Loma (☎ 713-06-58)* is off the south side of highway 150. Its spacious rooms, surrounded by lush gardens, cost US$28 for one or two people. Bungalows with two bedrooms and a kitchen are perfect for four people and cost US$50 (reservations advisable). The management is friendly, the pool is inviting, and the excellent restaurant has a spectacular view of Pico de Orizaba.

Other places on the east side of Fortín cater to the weekend crowd, with pleasant gardens and recreational facilities. *Posada El Pueblito (☎ 713-00-33)*, on Avenida 2 Ote between Calles 9 and 11 Nte, has a swimming pool, tennis courts, bulk bougainvillea and sometimes a strong coffee aroma from a nearby factory. Comfortable rooms cost US$22/25.

Places to Eat

Córdoba's Plaza de Armas portales are lined with cafés and restaurants where you can eat well at any hour or just enjoy the local coffee. Prices seem to be highest at the northern end, starting with the *Café Parroquia*, where egg dishes run about US$2.20, antojitos US$3, fish and meat dishes US$6. Farther along, the popular *Restaurante El Cordobés* has some pricey options, but the US$3.50 comida corrida is a good deal. The best location may well be a table overlooking the plaza at *El Balcón*, upstairs in the Ex-Hotel Zevallos building.

For fine seafood try the restaurants on Calle 15 between Avenidas 5 and 7. The local favorite is *Restaurant-Bar Díaz*, where superfresh fish dishes, prepared five different ways, will cost around US$5, depending on the season and the size of the fish – they'll bring a platter to your table and you can take your pick. More unusual offerings include oyster and black pepper casserole, crayfish in chili sauce, and squid wrapped in bacon. If the menu isn't exciting enough, ask about any daily specials.

Another lively place is ***Crepas Y Carnes Los 30's***, on Avenida 9 between Calles 20 and 22. It's a good trek from the zócalo but worth it for the colorful decor, party atmosphere and big selection of mouthwatering crêpes. Also recommended for quality cuisine is the moderately expensive ***Cantábrico***, close to the plaza at Calle 3 No 9.

In Fortín, just north of the plaza on Calle 1 Nte, you could try ***Colorines***, a steak house serving solid main courses for around US$3 to US$5, and ***Lolo***, across the street, with some pretty good seafood dishes for US$3 to US$5. They're both OK, but for a memorable meal, you'd do better in Córdoba.

Getting There & Away

Bus Córdoba's bus station, with deluxe (UNO and ADO GL), 1st-class (ADO and Cristóbal Colón) and 2nd-class (AU) services, is at Avenida Privada 4, 3km southeast of the plaza. To get to the center from the station, take a local bus marked 'Centro' or buy a taxi ticket (US$1.50). To Fortín de las Flores and Orizaba, it's more convenient to take a local bus from Avenida 11 than to go out to the Córdoba bus station. Long-distance buses from Córdoba include:

Jalapa – 260km, 3½ hours; 9 ADO (US$7.75)

Mexico City (TAPO) – 305km, 4½ hours; 2 UNO (US$25), 3 ADO GL (US$18), 24 ADO (US$15.50), 18 AU *locales* (US$11), 17 AU de paso (US$10)

Oaxaca – 317km, 6 hours; 1 Colón at 12.40 am (US$17.50), 1 AU at 12.55 am (US$14)

Puebla – 175km, 3 hours; 14 ADO (US$9.50), 3 AU locales (US$8), 23 AU de paso (US$8)

Veracruz – 125km, 2 hours; 22 ADO (US$5.50), 18 AU (US$5)

In Fortín, local buses arrive and depart from Calle 1 Sur, on the west side of the plaza. A small ADO depot on the corner of Avenida 2 and Calle 6 has mainly de paso services to Mexico City (US$15), Veracruz (US$6),

Puebla (US$9) and Jalapa (US$6.50). UNO has two daily deluxe buses to Mexico City (US$24) and ADO GL has one (US$18).

Train Trains between Mexico City and Veracruz stop at Córdoba and Fortín – they're cheap, slow and unreliable. See the Mexico City and Veracruz Getting There & Away sections for more information.

Car & Motorcycle Córdoba, Fortín de las Flores and Orizaba are linked by the toll road (highway 150D) and the much slower highway 150. A scenic back road goes through the hills from Fortín, via Huatusco, to Jalapa.

ORIZABA
● pop 114,300 ● elev 1219m ☎ 2

Orizaba, 16km west of Córdoba, was founded by the Spanish to guard the Veracruz-Mexico City road. It retains a few colonial buildings and church domes, though much was lost in the 1973 earthquake. An industrial center in the late 19th century, its factories were early centers of the unrest that led to the unseating of dictator Porfirio Díaz. Today it has a big brewery and cement, textile and chemical industries.

Many visitors (especially Europeans) use the city as a base for climbing Pico de Orizaba, one of Mexico's most spectacular volcanoes. The art museum is excellent.

Orientation

The central plaza is Parque del Castillo, with the Parroquia de San Miguel on its north side. Madero, a busy street bordering the west side of the plaza, divides Avenidas into Oriente (Ote; east) and Poniente (Pte; west). Avenida Colón, on the south side of the plaza, is the boundary between the streets called Norte and Sur. All other streets have numbers rather than names – study the map to learn the strange logic of the system. Avenida Pte 7/Avenida Ote 6, three blocks south of the plaza, is the main east-west artery.

Information

The tourist office (☎ 726-22-22 ext 134) is inconveniently located on the 2nd floor of the

Palacio Municipal, on Avenida Colón Pte at Nte 7. It's open 8 am to noon Monday to Saturday. Avenida Ote 2, a block south of the plaza, has two banks with ATMs. Access the Internet in the same block, upstairs at the Rod Pas computer center, for US$2.25 per hour. It's open 8.30 am to 2 pm and 6 to 10 pm Monday to Saturday. The post office is on the corner two blocks farther east.

Things to See & Do

The **Museo de Arte del Estado**, on Avenida Ote 4 between Calles 25 and 27, is a masterpiece. Housed in a splendidly restored colonial building dating from 1776 that has been at times a church, a hospital and a military base, the museum consists of many rooms, each of which adheres to a different theme. In one room, exquisite paintings depict key moments in the history of Veracruz state. Another has contemporary works by regional artists. Some of the works by Diego Rivera may have moved to Jalapa, but there's still a good collection of 20th-century Mexican paintings and drawings.

The **Parroquia de San Miguel**, the big parish church on the north side of Parque del Castillo, is mainly 17th century in style with several towers and some Puebla-type tiles.

The **Centro Educativo Obrero** (Workers' Education Center), on Colón between the Parque del Castillo and the Alameda park, has a 1926 mural by the great muralist José Clemente Orozco.

The **Ex-Palacio Municipal**, off the northwest corner of Parque del Castillo, was the Belgian pavilion at the Paris International Exhibition in the late 19th century. Orizaba bought the prefabricated cast-iron and steel building for US$13,800 and had it dismantled, shipped to Mexico and reassembled as a town hall. The municipal offices have now moved, and the building has been renovated but was empty at the time of writing.

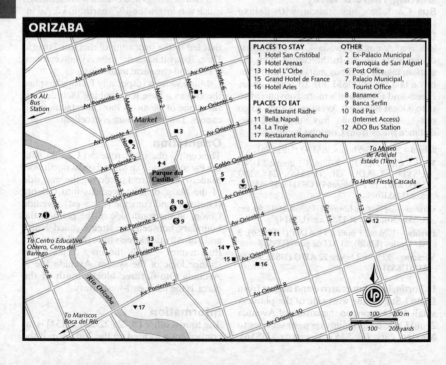

ORIZABA

PLACES TO STAY
1 Hotel San Cristóbal
3 Hotel Arenas
13 Hotel L'Orbe
15 Grand Hotel de France
16 Hotel Aries

PLACES TO EAT
5 Restaurant Radhe
11 Bella Napoli
14 La Troje
17 Restaurant Romanchu

OTHER
2 Ex-Palacio Municipal
4 Parroquia de San Miguel
6 Post Office
7 Palacio Municipal, Tourist Office
8 Banamex
9 Banca Serfin
10 Rod Pas (Internet Access)
12 ADO Bus Station

Hiking

The **canyon** beside the Hotel Fiesta Cascada (see Places to Stay) features a beautiful waterfall emerging from dense forest. A forest-flanked trail begins a few meters west of the hotel and descends to the canyon floor, where it forks. To the left, the trail follows the river for several kilometers. To the right, it crosses a footbridge beside the waterfall and a small power station then reaches a rough road that winds northwest into the mountains, through forest and farmland.

Looming over the Alameda park west of town, **Cerro del Barrego** offers brilliant views if you get to the top very early, before the mist rolls in.

Turismo Aventura Desafío (☎ 725-06-96), Pte 3 No 586, arranges various adventure activities in nearby hills, mountains and canyons, including climbs of Pico de Orizaba (see Around Orizaba).

Places to Stay

Orizaba's best budget value is the friendly, family-run **Hotel Arenas** (☎ 725-23-61, Nte 2 No 169), which has a central location and a courtyard garden. The helpful management has good information about the area. Clean singles/doubles with private bath and cable TV cost US$10/12, or US$12.75 with two beds. Cheaper but less charming is the **Hotel San Cristóbal** (☎ 725-11-40, Nte 4 No 243). It's modern and clean, and the standard rooms are a bargain at US$6.50; larger rooms with fan and TV are US$10. Rooms facing the street can be noisy.

Grand Hotel de France (☎ 725-23-11, Ote 6 No 186) is recently redecorated, with brightly colored rooms around a sunny courtyard. It has off-street parking, and it's a pretty good value at US$13 for a single/double, or US$15.50 with two beds. For more modern conveniences, try **Hotel Aries** (☎ 725-35-20, Ote 6 No 265), a reasonably priced, good-quality hotel with rooms starting at US$17/21. An even better mid-range place is the **Hotel L'Orbe** (☎ 725-50-33, Pte 5 No 3), with new beds and remodeled air-conditioned rooms for US$25/29.

The best hotel in town is the **Hotel Fiesta Cascada** (☎ 724-13-96), at Km 275 on the 150D Puebla-Córdoba road (look for two Pemex stations opposite each other), about 2km east of the center. The Cascada sits above a gorgeous canyon and has a pool, gardens and a private patch of rain forest. Charming, spacious rooms, with minibar, TV and phone, start around US$50.

Places to Eat

Some good taco places lie around the plaza, and the market has cheap eats. Most of the moderately priced restaurants close early – Orizaba is not a party town. **Restaurant Radhe**, on Sur 5, offers very good, moderately priced vegetarian food. Farther south on Sur 5, **La Troje** has lots of atmosphere and an excellent five-course comida corrida for US$3.50. **Bella Napoli**, on Sur 7, makes the best pizza in town. Nonvegetarians should seek out the large and colorful **Restaurant Romanchu**, on Pte 7, which is popular for its beef dishes (US$4 to US$6). A few blocks farther west on Pte 7, **Mariscos Boca del Río** is the best seafood restaurant in town, with large and reasonably priced shrimp cocktails, fish fillets and squid dishes starting at around US$5.

Getting There & Away

Bus The local buses from Fortín or Córdoba stop four blocks north and six blocks east of the center, around Ote 9 and Nte 14. The AU (2nd-class) station is at Zaragoza Pte 425, northwest of the center. To reach the city center from here, turn left outside the depot, cross the bridge, take the first fork right and head for the church domes.

The 1st-class bus station, on Ote 6 at Sur 13, is being rebuilt and modernized; it will handle all ADO, ADO GL and deluxe UNO services (one day it may even replace the inconveniently located 2nd-class station). Daily departures include:

Jalapa – 240km, 4 hours; 10 ADO (US$8.75)

Mexico City (TAPO) – 285km, 4 hours; 2 UNO (US$25), 2 ADO GL (US$23), 17 ADO (US$14.50), frequent AU (US$10.50)

Puebla – 160km, 2½ hours; 12 ADO (US$8.50), frequent AU (US$8)

Veracruz – 150km, 2¼ hours; 21 ADO (US$6.50), frequent directo AU (US$6.25)

There is also 1st-class service to Oaxaca, Tehuacán, Tuxpan and Villahermosa.

Train Orizaba is on the Veracruz-Mexico City line. For information see the Mexico City and Veracruz Getting There & Away sections. The station is south of the city center on the corner of Pte 19 and Sur 10.

Car & Motorcycle Toll highway 150D, which bypasses central Orizaba, goes east to Córdoba and west, via a spectacular ascent, to Puebla (160km). Toll-free highway 150 runs east to Córdoba and Veracruz (150km) and southwest to Tehuacán, 65km away over the hair-raising Cumbres de Acultzingo.

AROUND ORIZABA
Pico de Orizaba (Citlaltépetl)

Mexico's tallest mountain (5611m), called Citlaltépetl in the Nahuatl language, is 25km northwest of the city of Orizaba. The dormant volcano has a small crater and a three-month snowcap. From the summit, in good weather, one can see Popocatépetl, Iztaccíhuatl and La Malinche to the west and the Gulf of Mexico 96km to the east. The only higher peaks in North America are Mt McKinley in Alaska and Mt Logan in Canada.

The most common route up Orizaba is from the northwest, using the small town of **Tlachichuca** as a base. Tlachichuca can be reached by bus via Ciudad Serdán, most readily from Puebla (two hours, US$2.50). *Hotel Panchita* (☎ 2-451-50-35) and *Hotel Gerar* (☎ 2-451-50-75) both have basic accommodations for around US$8/14 single/double, and *La Casa Blanca* is a good, inexpensive place to eat. The Reyes family (☎ 2-451-50-09) offers accommodations, knowledgeable guide service, climbing and camping equipment for rent and 4WD transport farther up the mountain. Hotel Gerar can also help arrange equipment hire and transport. Unless you have navigation skills and a good map, and your group has some experience of snow- and ice-climbing techniques, you should not attempt this climb without a guide.

From Tlachichuca, take a taxi to Villa Hidalgo at 3400m (15km, US$10), then walk 10km farther to the mountain hut (*refugio* or *albergue*) called Piedra Grande, at 4200m. This walk will help with acclimatization, though it's also possible to charter a 4WD all the way to Piedra Grande. The refugio is big but basic, and you'll need to bring a sleeping mat, sleeping bag, stove and cooking gear. Most climbers start at about 4 am for the final climb and try to reach the summit around sunrise or shortly after, before mist and cloud envelops the mountain. The climb is moderately steep over snow that is usually hard – it's not technically difficult, but crampons are strongly recommended (especially for the descent), as are ropes and ice axes for safety. Allow three to five hours for the ascent (depending on the conditions and your abilities) and another two to three hours to return to the refugio. You can arrange to be picked up by 4WD at Piedra Grande after returning from the climb. The whole expedition can be done in two days, without allowing any time at all for acclimatization. This may be OK if you've been trekking around on the altiplano for weeks, but don't try it straight from sea level.

An alternative and less-used route is from the south, via the villages of Atzitzintla and Texmalaquilla and a refugio at 4750m. A guide is recommended for this route.

Experienced climbers doing the northwest route can make all the necessary arrangements in Tlachichuca, but get maps well in advance (the 1:50,000 INEGI map is supposed to be the best, but can be hard to obtain; some specialist books on climbing in Mexico have adequate maps). Agencies in the city of Orizaba or in Fortín de las Flores (see those sections) offer guided trips and can make all the arrangements – they are quite economical if you have a group of about six people. Contact them well ahead of time if you want to join up with some other climbers. Some guides are also based in Tlachichuca. To arrange a climb from Mexico City, contact Mario Andrade (☎ 5-875-01-05), PO Box M-10380, Mexico DF; he charges about US$450 per person, including equipment, guide, food and transport to/from Mexico City (of course, this is more expensive than doing the climb with a local operator). The best climbing period is October to March, with the most popular time being December and January and the clearest weather in October.

Zongolica

A road leads 38km south from Orizaba to this mountain village, where isolated indigenous groups have unique styles of weaving. Buses leave from Ote 3 between Nte 12 and Nte 14 every 15 minutes.

Southern Veracruz & Los Tuxtlas

Southeast of the port of Veracruz is a flat, hot, wet coastal plain crossed by many rivers. Farther south, the towns of Santiago Tuxtla and San Andrés Tuxtla, is a hilly region known as Los Tuxtlas ('TOOKS-lahs'), which is green and fertile, with lakes, waterfalls and an agreeable climate. Mexican vacationers are attracted to Catemaco, a small lakeside resort, while the undeveloped coastline is increasingly popular with foreign visitors.

Los Tuxtlas is the western fringe of the ancient Olmec heartland, and Olmec artifacts can be seen at Santiago Tuxtla, Tres Zapotes and San Lorenzo. The basalt for the huge Olmec heads was quarried from Cerro Cintepec in the east of the Sierra de los Tuxtlas and then moved, probably by roller and raft, to San Lorenzo, 60km to the south.

ALVARADO
• pop 23,800

The busy fishing town of Alvarado, 67km down highway 180 from Veracruz, stands on a spit of land separating the Gulf of Mexico from the Laguna de Alvarado, which is the meeting point of several rivers including the Papaloapan. The channel from the lagoon to the sea is crossed by a long toll bridge east of the town (US$1.50 per car).

Alvarado is a rough-looking place, but it has a few hotels and restaurants and a small bus station where you can change buses for

Tlacotalpan. You may be able to hire boats for trips on the lagoons or up the river to Tlacotalpan (about two hours).

TLACOTALPAN
• pop 8850 • elev 155m ☎ changing

 In 2000 the telephone area code is due to change to ☎ 2 from 288, with the digits 88 added to the start of every local number (for example, the number 2-01-43 will become 882-01-43).

A very quiet old town beside the wide Río Papaloapan, Tlacotalpan was a major port in the 19th century and has preserved its broad plazas, colorful houses and pretty streets. **Museo Salvador Ferrando**, facing Plaza Hidalgo, displays assorted furniture and artifacts recalling Tlacotalpan's glory days. It's open daily except Monday (US$1.50). The **Casa de Cultura**, a few blocks east on Carranza, has memorabilia from Agustín Lara (1900-70), a local musician, composer and pioneering radio personality. Upstairs is a fine collection of modernist paintings by another local, Alberto Fuster.

Tlacotalpan's lively Candelaria festival, in late January and early February, features bull-running in the streets and an image of the Virgin floating down the river followed by a flotilla of small boats.

At **Hotel Reforma** (☎ 4-20-22), beside Plaza Zaragoza, spotless rooms cost US$11/16 single/double with fan, US$20/22 with air-con. **Posada Doña Lala** (☎ 4-25-80) is near the river and has a little more character. Its pleasant rooms go for US$17/19, or US$19/25 with air-con. The restaurant here is good, or you can try one of the breezy eateries along the riverfront.

Highway 175 goes from Tlacotalpan up the Papaloapan valley to Tuxtepec, then twists and turns over the mountains to Oaxaca (320km from Tlacotalpan).

SANTIAGO TUXTLA
• pop 15,500 • elev 285m ☎ changing

Santiago, founded in 1525, is a quiet valley town in the rolling green foothills of the

LOS TUXTLAS

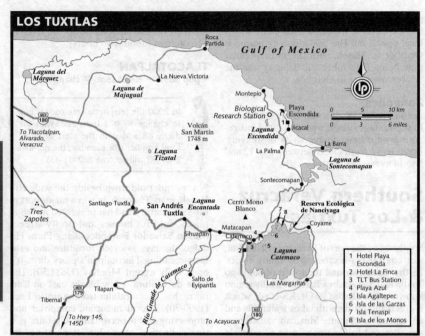

1	Hotel Playa Escondida
2	Hotel La Finca
3	TLT Bus Station
4	Playa Azul
5	Isla Agaltepec
6	Isla de las Garzas
7	Isla Tenaspi
8	Isla de los Monos

volcanic Sierra de los Tuxtlas. It's a pleasant stopover and worth visiting for the Olmec artifacts in the town and at Tres Zapotes, 23km away.

Orientation & Information
ADO and AU buses arriving in Santiago drop you where Calle Morelos runs off the highway. Go south down Morelos a little and the Transportes Los Tuxtlas office will be on your left; turn right (west) here onto Ayuntamiento to reach the Museo Arqueológico, on the south side of the zócalo. The post office is also on the zócalo, as is the Comermex bank, which changes traveler's checks.

In 2000 the telephone area code is due to change to ☎ 2 from 272, with the digits 72 added to the start of every local number (for example, the number 2-01-43 will become 722-01-43).

Things to See & Do
The **Olmec head** in the zócalo is known as the Cobata head, after the estate west of Santiago where it was found. Thought to be a very late or even post-Olmec production, it's the biggest known Olmec head and unique in that its eyes are closed.

The **Museo Arqueológico** exhibits Olmec stone carvings, including another colossal head (this one from Nestepec west of Santiago), a rabbit head from Cerro de Vigía and a copy of Monument F or 'El Negro' from Tres Zapotes, which is an altar or throne with a human form carved into it. The museum is open 9 am to 6 pm Monday to Saturday and 9 am to 3 pm Sunday (US$1.90, free Sunday).

Special Events
Santiago celebrates the festivals of San Juan (June 24) and Santiago Apóstol (St James, July 25) with processions and dances including the Liseres, in which the participants

wear jaguar costumes. The dance costumes also come out in the week before Christmas.

Places to Stay & Eat

The family-run *Hotel Morelos* (☎ 7-04-74, *Morelos 12*) has its entrance on Obregón, which runs off Morelos almost opposite the Transportes Los Tuxtlas bus station. Rooms cost US$6.50/9 single/double, or US$10 with two beds. They aren't very big, and some are brighter than others, but they all have fans and private bath with hot water.

The modern *Hotel Castellanos* (☎ 7-02-00), in a circular building on the north side of the zócalo, is amazingly good for a small-town hotel. It has an inviting swimming pool and 48 clean, air-conditioned rooms of varying sizes, most with fine views. Singles/doubles are US$23/25. The restaurant serves solid main courses for around US$3 and good salads for US$1.75. Cheaper eateries line up on the south side of the zócalo.

Getting There & Away

If no convenient services are available out of Santiago Tuxtla, go first to San Andrés Tuxtla by the frequent but suspension-free buses of Transportes Los Tuxtlas (30 minutes, US$0.60) or less frequent ADO (20 minutes, US$0.70).

ADO and AU both use the same office beside the main road, where buses stop on the way through. Cuenca is a local company using the same office. From Santiago, ADO has 11 de paso buses a day going west to Veracruz (2½ hours, US$5.75) via Alvarado, 10 a day going east to Coatzacoalcos via San Andrés Tuxtla (20 minutes, US$0.70) and Catemaco (US$1.25), and four a day to Acayucan (two hours, US$4). Cuenca has three buses a day to Tlacotalpan (US$3.20). Cheaper but less comfortable Transportes Los Tuxtlas buses depart every 10 minutes for San Andrés Tuxtla, Catemaco and Veracruz, and hourly for Acayucan.

TRES ZAPOTES
• pop 3380

The important late-Olmec center of Tres Zapotes is now just a series of mounds in maize fields, but many interesting finds are displayed at the museum in the village of Tres Zapotes, 23km west of Santiago Tuxtla.

History

Tres Zapotes was probably first occupied while the great Olmec center of La Venta (Tabasco) still flourished. After the destruction of La Venta (about 600 BC), the city carried on in what archaeologists regard as an 'epi-Olmec' phase – a period when the spark had gone out of Olmec culture, and other civilizations, notably Izapa, were adding their marks. Most of the finds are from this later period.

At Tres Zapotes in 1939, Matthew Stirling, the first great Olmec excavator, unearthed part of an interesting chunk of basalt. One side was carved with an epi-Olmec 'were-jaguar,' and the other with a series of bars and dots, apparently part of a date in the Mayan Long Count dating system. Stirling decoded the date as September 3, 32 BC, which meant that the Olmecs preceded the Maya; until then, the Maya were believed to have been Mexico's earliest civilization. Much debate followed, but later finds supported Stirling's discovery. In 1969 a farmer came across the rest of the stone, now called Stela C, which bore the missing part of Stirling's date.

Museum

At the Tres Zapotes museum the objects are arranged on a cross-shaped platform. On the far side is the Tres Zapotes head, dating from about 100 BC, which was the first Olmec head to be discovered in modern times; it was found by a hacienda worker in 1858. Opposite the head is Stela A, the biggest piece, with three human figures in the mouth of a jaguar. This originally stood on its end. To the right of Stela A are two pieces. One is a sculpture of what may have been a captive with hands tied behind his or her back. The other piece has a toad carved on one side and a skull on the other. Beyond Stela A is an altar or throne carved with the upturned face of a woman, and beyond that, in the corner, is the less interesting part of the famous Stela C. (The part with the date is in the Museo Nacional de Antropología,

CENTRAL GULF COAST

but a photo of it is on the wall here.) The museum attendant is happy to answer questions (in Spanish). The museum is open 9 am to 5 pm daily (US$1.50, free on Sunday).

Getting There & Away

The road to Tres Zapotes goes southwest from Santiago Tuxtla (a 'Zona Arqueológica' sign points the way from highway 180). Eight kilometers down this road, you fork right onto a decent dirt track for the last 15km to Tres Zapotes village. It comes out at a T-junction next to the Sitio Olmeca taxi stand. From here you walk to the left, then turn left again to reach the museum.

To get to Tres Zapotes, take a green-and-white taxi from Santiago Tuxtla (for US$1.25 if it's going colectivo, US$5.50 if you have it all to yourself). Taxis leave from the Sitio Puente Real, on the far side of the pedestrian bridge at the foot of Zaragoza, the street going downhill beside the Santiago Tuxtla museum.

SAN ANDRÉS TUXTLA

• pop 54,000 • elev 365m ☎ changing

San Andrés is in the center of the Los Tuxtlas area, surrounded by countryside producing maize, bananas, beans, sugarcane, cattle and tobacco – San Andrés is Mexico's cigar capital. The town itself holds little interest, but several scenic attractions are nearby, including the dormant Volcán San Martín, 1748m high.

Orientation & Information

The main bus station is on Juárez, 1km northwest of the plaza. The cathedral is on the north side of the plaza, the Palacio Municipal is on the west side, and a Banamex is on the south side. When you hit the plaza from Juárez, turn right to go down Madero, which has some mid-range places to stay and

In 2000 the telephone area code is due to change to ☎ 2 from 294, with the digits 94 added to the start of every local number (for example, the number 2-01-43 will become 942-01-43).

eat. The market is three blocks west. The post office is on Lafragua; head down 20 de Noviembre directly across the plaza from the Palacio Municipal and follow it around to the left.

Things to See & Do

At the Santa Lucia cigar factory you can see, and smell, the *puros* being rolled by hand. It's open to visitors 8 am to 5 pm Monday to Saturday (free), and you can buy cigars in assorted shapes and sizes at factory prices.

Twelve kilometers from San Andrés, a 242-step staircase leads down to the 50m-high, 40m-wide Salto de Eyipantla waterfall. Follow highway 180 east for 4km to Sihuapan, then turn right down a dirt road to Eyipantla – frequent Transportes Los Tuxtlas buses make the trip (US$0.80).

The Laguna Encantada (Enchanted Lagoon), a lake that rises in dry weather and falls when it rains, occupies a small volcanic crater 3km northeast of San Andrés. A dirt road goes there but no buses.

At Cerro del Gallo near Matacapan, just east of Sihuapan, is a pyramid in Teotihuacán style, dating from 300 to 600 AD. It may have been on the route to Kaminaljuyú in Guatemala, the farthest Teotihuacán outpost.

Places to Stay

For the cheapest hotels turn left when you hit the plaza from Juárez, then take the second right, Pino Suárez. The best bargain in town is the *Hotel Figueroa* (☎ 2-02-57), at the corner of Pino Suárez and Domínguez. It offers charming, clean singles/doubles with hot water and fans for US$6.50/9; rooms 34 to 42 have vistas. At the same corner, the *Hotel Colonial* (☎ 2-05-52) is the cheapest choice, with single rooms starting at US$3.50 and better rooms with decent beds and hot water for US$6, or US$8 with two beds.

A few doors up Domínguez from the Figueroa is the *Hotel Posada San José* (☎ 2-10-10), which offers 30 perfectly acceptable singles/doubles around a closed courtyard for US$11; better rooms with air-con go for US$17.50.

Hotel Isabel (☎ 2-16-17, Madero 13) offers a variety of decent rooms for US$12/17, or US$16/20 with air-con. *Hotel Del Parque* (☎ 2-01-98, Madero 5) is right on the zócalo and has air-conditioned rooms with phones and color TV for US$20/23. The newer *Hotel De Los Pérez* (☎ 2-07-77, 800-290-3900, Rascón 2) is just down the street beside the Del Parque and offers all the same amenities plus friendlier management. It doesn't have a big lobby, but it's well kept and has sizable air-conditioned rooms for US$17/24.

Places to Eat

An excellent choice is *Cafe Winni's*, just down Madero from the plaza. Soup, egg dishes and antojitos are under US$2.50, and substantial main courses range US$3 to US$4. Try Sabana Winni's, a toothsome steak smothered with ham and melted cheese (US$4). The restaurant at *Hotel Del Parque* has outdoor tables facing the plaza, where regular customers have enjoyed their evening coffee for years. The food is OK, if a little expensive. *Restaurant & Cafetería del Centro*, beneath the Hotel De Los Pérez, is good for American-style breakfasts, snacks and set meals – a good burger is under US$3. It's open 7 am to midnight.

Getting There & Away

Bus San Andrés is the transport center for Los Tuxtlas, with fairly good bus services in every direction – deluxe with UNO, 1st-class with ADO, and good 2nd-class with AU. Transportes Los Tuxtlas (TLT) buses are old and bouncy, but because of their frequent departures they're often the quickest way of getting to local destinations. TLT buses leave from the corner of Cabada and Solana Nte, a block north of the market; they skirt the north side of town on 5 de Febrero (highway 180), and you can get on or off at most intersections. Buses from San Andrés include:

Acayucan – 95km, 1½ hours; 15 ADO (US$3.75), TLT every 10 minutes (US$2.50)

Campeche – 785km, 12½ hours; ADO at 10.30 pm (US$30)

Catemaco – 12km, 20 minutes; 10 ADO de paso (US$0.50), TLT every 10 minutes (US$0.50)

Mérida – 965km, 15 hours; 1 ADO at 10.30 pm (US$39)

Mexico City (TAPO) – 550km, 9 hours; ADO at 9.45, 10.30 and 11 pm (US$27), AU at noon and 9.35 pm (US$23)

Puebla – 420km, 5 hours; ADO at 9.45 and 11.35 pm (US$20), AU at 9.50 pm (US$18)

Santiago Tuxtla – 14km, 20 minutes; 11 ADO de paso (US$0.50), TLT every 10 minutes (US$0.50)

Veracruz – 155km, 2 hours; 20 ADO (US$6), AU at noon and 9.50 pm (US$5), TLT every 10 minutes (US$4)

Villahermosa – 320km, 4 hours; 10 ADO (US$13)

Taxi A taxi to or from Catemaco or Santiago Tuxtla costs about US$5.

CATEMACO

• pop 23,000 • elev 370m ☎ changing

This town on the western shore of beautiful Laguna Catemaco makes most of its living from fishing and from Mexican tourists who flood in during July and August and for Christmas, New Year and Semana Santa. The rest of the year it's a quiet, economical place to visit. The annual convention of *brujos* (witch doctors), held on Cerro Mono Blanco (White Monkey Hill) north of Catemaco on the first Friday in March, has become more a tourist event than a supernatural one.

Orientation & Information

Catemaco slopes gently down to the lake. A tourist information office in the municipal building, on the north side of the zócalo, is open irregular hours and has limited information.

Bancomer, on Aldama, changes cash but not traveler's checks, usually in the mornings only. In a pinch, try the Hotel Los Arcos, which sometimes changes American Express traveler's checks at not-very-good rates. There's an ATM at the Hotel Catemaco.

In 2000 the telephone area code is due to change to ☎ 2 from 294, with the digits 94 added to the start of every local number (for example, the number 2-01-43 will become 942-01-43).

Laguna Catemaco

The lake, ringed by volcanic hills, is roughly oval and 16km long. Streams flowing into it are the source of Catemaco and Coyame mineral water. East of town are a few gray-sand beaches where you can swim in murky water.

The lake has several islands; on the largest, Tenaspi, Olmec sculpture has been found. **Isla de los Monos**, also called Isla de los Changos (Monkey Island), holds about 60 red-cheeked *Macaca arctoides* monkeys, originally from Thailand. They belong to the University of Veracruz, which acquired them for research. Despite pleas from the university for the animals to be left alone, boat operators bring food so tourists can get close-up photos. Boats moored along the lakeside offer trips around the islands and across to the ecological reserve (see below) – the posted price for up to six people is US$26.50, or US$4.50 per person if you go as an individual.

On the north shore of the lake, the **Reserva Ecológica de Nanciyaga** preserves a small piece of rain forest. A guided walk (in Spanish) includes the chance to sample mineral water and to test the cosmetic benefits of smearing black mud on your face. The not-so-wild wildlife includes toucans, monkeys, tortoises, peccaries and raccoons, all in enclosures. It's quite interesting but a bit contrived, like a movie set – *The Last Eden* was filmed here. The reserve is open daily (US$1.10) and can be reached by road or by boat.

Places to Stay

Catemaco has lodging in all price ranges – the rates given here might be discounted at off-peak periods.

Camping *Restaurant Solotepec*, 1km east of town along the road around the lake, has a small camping area/trailer park close to the water. Sites with hookups cost US$6.50. *Hotel Playa Azul* (☎ 3-00-01; see Hotels, below) also has sites with hookups for around US$6. Basic tent sites at the *Reserva Ecológica de Nanciyaga* (☎ 3-01-99) cost US$2.20 per person – ask if any *cabañas* are available.

Hotels The *Hotel Julita* (☎ 3-00-08, *Avenida Playa 10*), near the waterfront just down from the zócalo, is the best budget bargain in

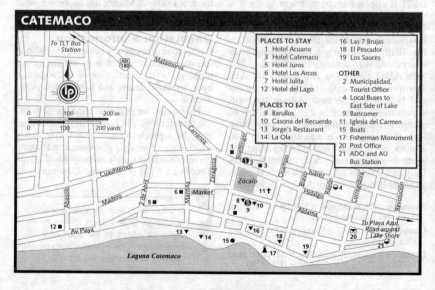

CATEMACO

To TLT Bus Station

MEX 180

Matamoros

0   100   200 m
0   100   200 yards

Carranza

Böettinger

Cuauhtémoc

Abasolo

Madero

de Abril

Mantilla

Zaragoza

Market

Zócalo

Campo

Juarez

Bravo

Hidalgo

Aldama

Rayón

Juárez

Corregidora

Revolución

To Playa Azul,
Road around
Lake Shore

Laguna Catemaco

PLACES TO STAY	
1	Hotel Acuario
3	Hotel Catemaco
5	Hotel Juros
6	Hotel Los Arcos
7	Hotel Julita
12	Hotel del Lago

PLACES TO EAT	
8	Barullos
10	Casona del Recuerdo
13	Jorge's Restaurant
14	La Ola

16	Las 7 Brujas
18	El Pescador
19	Los Sauces

OTHER	
2	Municipalidad, Tourist Office
4	Local Buses to East Side of Lake
9	Bancomer
11	Iglesia del Carmen
15	Boats
17	Fisherman Monument
20	Post Office
21	ADO and AU Bus Station

CENTRAL GULF COAST

town, with basic but adequate singles/ doubles for US$8/11, including fan, hot water and private bath. Right by the zócalo, *Hotel Acuario* (☎ 3-04-18), on the corner of Carranza and Boettinger, is 'a two-star hotel with the service of three.' Comfortable rooms with private bath cost US$6 to US$14, and big rooms for three or four people are US$17. Some rooms are better value than others.

Air-con is standard in all mid-range places. *Hotel Los Arcos* (☎ 3-00-03, *Madero 7*), on the corner of Mantilla, has helpful staff, a swimming pool and clean, bright rooms with balconies for US$27. *Hotel Juros* (☎ 3-00-84) is another good, modern, mid-range place, with well-equipped rooms for US$30 single or double.

Hotel Catemaco (☎ 3-02-03), on the north side of the zócalo, features an inviting pool and rooms with air-con and cable TV starting at US$21/28. The lakefront *Hotel Del Lago* (☎ 3-01-60), on Avenida Playa on the corner of Abasolo, has good, clean, but not very big rooms with TV for US$25. There's a restaurant and small pool.

Hotel Playa Azul (☎ 3-00-01), 2.5km east of town by the lake, adjoins a patch of rain forest and promotes itself as an ecotourism destination, but it looks much like a mass-market American holiday motel. Sterile-looking air-conditioned rooms are surrounded by a garden/parking lot and cost US$56. Facilities include satellite TV, a swimming pool, restaurant and (in high season) a discothèque.

The lakeside, four-star *Hotel La Finca* (☎ 3-03-22) is 2km west of town on the Acayucan road. It's a stylish modern building with 36 comfortable rooms, most with balconies and lake views, for around US$70 single or double.

Places to Eat

The lake provides the specialties here, among them the *tegogolo*, a snail reputed to be an aphrodisiac and best eaten in a sauce of chili, tomato, onion and lime; *chipalchole*, a soup with shrimp or crab claws; *mojarra*, a type of perch; and *anguilas* (eels). *Tachogobi* is a hot sauce sometimes served on mojarra;

eels may come with raisins and hot chilies. Many eating places can be depressingly empty out of season and tend to close early.

Two of the most popular and pleasant of Catemaco's many restaurants are right beside the lake, with breezy garden eating areas. *Jorge's Restaurant* offers decent breakfasts for US$2 to US$3 and local fish dishes for around US$5 (look in the menu under 'Viagra'). Next door, *La Ola* offers food of a similarly high standard for similar prices – it's difficult to choose between these two.

Not far from the lakeside, *Hotel Julita* has a good, budget restaurant with basic filling fare from US$3 to US$5. A little southeast, *Las 7 Brujas* is in an interesting round building and does a good line in local fish. It stays open late and its bar is a popular hangout. The lakeside *El Pescador* and the cheaper *Los Sauces* are also popular spots for eating and drinking in the evening.

Near the zócalo, the restaurant-café-video bar *Barullos* opens at 4 pm and offers plenty of ambiance and fine food. Well-prepared main courses run from US$5 to US$7. A half block east, *Casona del Recuerdo* has delightful balcony tables, friendly service and budget prices. Seafood dishes are all under US$5, and the comida corrida is only US$2.

On the other side of the zócalo, *Restaurant Tanaxpi*, at the Hotel Catemaco, has a more refined atmosphere and is slightly more expensive – chicken and meat dishes are US$5 to US$9, fresh fish is US$5 to US$8.

Getting There & Away

Few long-distance buses reach Catemaco, so you may have to travel via San Andrés Tuxtla (12km west on highway 180) or Acayucan (80km south), taking the more frequent but less comfortable local buses to/ from Catemaco.

ADO has 11 de paso buses a day going west to Veracruz (three hours, US$6.75) via San Andrés Tuxtla (20 minutes, US$0.60), Santiago Tuxtla (40 minutes, US$1) and Alvarado (1¼ hours, US$2), and 10 a day going east to Acayucan (1½ hours, US$3.30) and Coatzacoalcos (3½ hours, US$7). Ten quite good 2nd-class AU buses daily also go to

Veracruz – they're slightly cheaper. Direct buses to Mexico City include ADO at 10 and 11 pm (eight hours, US$26) and AU at 11 am and 9 pm (US$23). An ADO bus goes to Villahermosa at noon (five hours, US$13).

ADO and AU buses operate from a small terminal by the lakeside at the corner of Playa and Revolución. The local Transportes Los Tuxtlas buses pull up at the main road junction on the west side of town.

Getting Around

To explore the villages and country east of the lake, where the mountain Santa Marta stands out, take a local bus going to Las Margaritas. They leave every hour or two from the corner of Juárez and Rayón.

THE COAST NEAR CATEMACO

About 4km northeast of Catemaco there's a fork. The road to the right follows the east side of the lake past the Reserva Ecológica to Coyame and Las Margaritas; the road to the left is sealed and scenic as it goes over the hills toward the coast. At **Sontecomapan**, 15km from Catemaco, you can turn right (east) off the main road and go down to the waterside, where there are a few open-sided restaurants; stroll to the left for 100m to find the idyllic 'Pozo de los Enanos' swimming hole. From this backwater you can rent boats for excursions into the mangroves around Laguna de Sontecomapan (about US$25 for 40 minutes). It's 20 minutes by boat to the mouth of the lagoon, where you may be able to camp on the beach near the fishing village of **La Barra**, but ask first and bring everything you'll need. La Barra can also be reached by a side road from La Palma, 8km north of Sontecomapan.

The road is rough after Sontecomapan, but the countryside is lovely – mainly cattle ranches and rain forest, with green hills rolling down to the shore. About 5km past La Palma, a sign points down another rough side road to Playa Escondida. This takes you past **Jicacal**, a small, poor fishing village with a long gray-sand beach, one restaurant and some basic bungalows. Farther on up a forested headland, *Hotel Playa Escondida* (☎ 294-2-16-14) is about 3km from the main

'road.' This unassuming establishment has basic rooms (shower but no hot water) for US$11/12 single/double, great views and a small restaurant. **Playa Escondida** itself is another 1km down a steep path from the hotel.

Back on the 'road' you pass a biological research station next to one of the few tracts of unspoiled rain forest on the Gulf Coast. A turnoff here leads to pretty Laguna Escondida, hidden in the mountains. The end of the road is at **Montepío**, where you'll find a nice beach at the river mouth, two places to eat and the *Posada San José* (☎ 294-2-10-10), with reasonably comfortable rooms for US$12/15.

Getting There & Away

Public transport to Sontecomapan and beyond is by *camionetas* (pickup trucks with benches in the back), also called *piratas*. They leave Catemaco every half hour or so (when they're full) between 6 am and 3 pm, from the corner of Revolución and the Playa Azul road (from the northeast corner of the plaza, walk five blocks east and six blocks north, and look for vehicles congregating). The 39km trip to Montepío, with numerous stops, takes about 1½ hours and costs US$2.20.

ACAYUCAN

● pop 49,300 ● elev 150m ☎ changing

Acayucan is a road-junction town where highway 180 (between Veracruz and Villahermosa) meets highway 185 (which goes south across the Isthmus of Tehuantepec to the Pacific coast). The new east-west *autopista* (toll road), highway 145D, also passes nearby. You may have to change buses here but try to avoid it – most buses are de paso, the 1st-class bus station is not a great setup (no left-luggage storage), and the 2nd-class buses go from offices scattered in surrounding streets. The town itself has nothing of interest, but archaeology fans might want to seek out the Olmec site of San Lorenzo, 35km to the southeast.

Orientation & Information

The bus stations are on the east side of town – to reach the central plaza, walk uphill

In 2000 the telephone area code is due to change to ☎ 9 from 924, with the digits 24 added to the start of every local number (for example, the number 2-01-43 will become 242-01-43).

through (or past) the market to Avenida Hidalgo, turn left and walk six blocks. The plaza has a modern church on the east side and the town hall on the west. Bancomer and Banamex, both near the plaza, have ATMs and change traveler's checks.

Places to Stay & Eat

The *Hotel Ancira* (☎ 5-00-48), on Bravo a half block southwest of the plaza, offers singles and doubles with fan, phone, private bathroom and hot water for US$6; ask to see a room before checking in. On the south side of the plaza, the *Hotel Joalicia* (☎ 5-08-77) is a better value, with clean, sizable rooms for US$7/9 single/double, or US$12/14.50 with air-con. The Joalicia's restaurant isn't bad either. The top place is the *Hotel Kinaku* (☎ 5-04-10, Ocampo Sur 7), a block east of the plaza, where spacious, comfortable rooms with air-con and TV cost US$32/38.

The Kinaku's restaurant, open 24 hours, is the smartest place in town but is somewhat pricey, with salads around US$3.50 and chicken dishes over US$4. *La Parrilla* restaurant, north of the plaza, does beefy main meals for around US$5. *Los Tucanes Cafetería*, on the pedestrian street a block west of the plaza, is popular, pleasant and open 24 hours. All these eateries have arctic-strength air-con.

Getting There & Away

Bus Most 1st-class buses (ADO and Cristóbal Colón) are de paso, but the computerized reservation systems indicate if seats are available. UNO and ADO GL run a few deluxe services, while AU and Sur provide quite good 2nd-class service. All these companies operate from the same terminal at the lower side of the market. Transportes Los Tuxtlas (TLT) provides very rough and

cheap services to the Tuxtlas area from a terminal on the edge of the market. Travel times given below are by autopista where available, on a directo bus.

Catemaco – 80km, 1½ hours; 8 ADO (US$2.75), frequent TLT (US$2)

Juchitán – 195km, 3 hours; 9 ADO (US$7.50), Sur every 30 minutes (US$5.75)

Mexico City (TAPO) – 650km, 7 hours; UNO at 10 pm (US$53), 2 ADO GL (US$35), 5 ADO (US$31), 4 AU (US$27)

San Andrés Tuxtla – 95km, 2 hours; 7 ADO (US$3.50), 2 AU (US$3.25), frequent TLT (US$2.50)

Santiago Tuxtla – 110km, 2¼ hours; ADO at 1.15 and 2.45 pm (US$3.25), hourly TLT (US$2.75)

Tapachula – 580km, 10 hours; 3 evening Colón (US$13), 2 Sur (US$17)

Tuxtla Gutiérrez – 440km, 8 hours; 3 ADO (US$16.50), 2 Colón (US$16.50)

Veracruz – 250km, 3½ hours; UNO at 2.45 am (US$22), 19 ADO (US$11)

Villahermosa – 225km, 3½ hours; 11 ADO (US$9.50)

Car & Motorcycle The new toll highway, 145D, passes south of town. Heading east, it's signposted to Minatitlán (clear enough); heading west, toward Córdoba or Veracruz, it's marked to 'Isla' (a truly perverse piece of signposting). The tolls are expensive – it costs US$24 to Córdoba.

SAN LORENZO

Near the small town of Tenochtitlán, 35km southeast of Acayucan, San Lorenzo was the first of the two great Olmec ceremonial centers, which flourished from about 1200 to 900 BC.

Ten Olmec heads and numerous smaller artifacts have been found here, but most of the finds are in museums elsewhere. Some heavy stone thrones, with figures of rulers carved in the side, were also found. Tools made from the black volcanic glass obsidian were imported from Guatemala or the Mexican highlands, and basalt for the heads and thrones was transported from the Sierra de los Tuxtlas. Such wide contacts, and the organization involved in building the site,

CENTRAL GULF COAST

JAMES LYON

Ceremonial Olmec head at San Lorenzo

rooms of stone artifacts and a single large head. It's open 8 am to 5 pm daily (free).

Another site, **El Azazul**, is in the countryside about 7km farther south. The hill here seems to have been a large pyramid but is completely overgrown. Halfway up it, under a shelter, are some remarkably well carved stone statues of kneeling figures. They are said to be over 1000 years old, but they're in such good condition that it's hard to believe. Most times there are people in the hut who will show you around in return for a tip.

Getting There & Away
From Acayucan take a bus or colectivo to Texistepec (south of the Minatitlán road), then another to the town of Tenochtitlán (also called San Lorenzo-Tenochtitlán). Then take a local bus or taxi to the 'zona arqueológica' south of town, and look for the cream-colored buildings behind a chain-link fence on the left side of the road.

Infrequent buses go on to the El Azazul site, about 7km from the San Lorenzo museum – look for a road branching left and a hut on the right. Exploring these sites is much more convenient with your own wheels.

MINATITLÁN & COATZACOALCOS
These two towns, 50 and 70km east of Acayucan, respectively, are bypassed by highway 180D, the eastward continuation of 145D. They mushroomed into refining centers during the oil boom of the late 1970s. Minatitlán (population 145,800) is an industrial wilderness, though Coatzacoalcos (population 222,000) retains a pleasant central plaza, and the bridge over the Río Coatzacoalcos is impressive. There are plenty of hotels here for the oil people but nothing to make anyone else want to stay.

show how powerful the rulers of San Lorenzo were. Other features include an elaborate stone-pipe drainage system and evidence of cannibalism. During its dramatic destruction, which occurred around 900 BC, most of the big carvings were mutilated, dragged onto the ridges and covered with earth.

The main structure was a platform about 50m high, 1.25km long and 700m wide, with ridges jutting from its sides, but now the San Lorenzo site looks like nothing more than a low hill. The 'museum' here is just two small

Oaxaca State

The rugged southern state of Oaxaca ('wah-HAH-kah') reaches to within 250km of Mexico City, but in atmosphere it is a world away from central Mexico. Barriers of sparsely populated mountains – crossed by spectacular highway 135D from the north – have always permitted Oaxaca to pursue to a large extent its own destiny.

It enjoys a slower, sunnier existence and a magical quality that has something to do with its dry, rocky landscape, its remoteness, its bright southern light and its large indigenous population. Indigenous people are the driving force behind the state's fine handicrafts and blossoming art scene.

The state capital, Oaxaca city, is a major travel destination, yet remains beautiful and artistic. It's a long-standing handicrafts center. Around the city, in the Valles Centrales (Central Valleys), are thriving village markets and spectacular ruins of pre-Hispanic towns such as Monte Albán and Yagul. On the beautiful Oaxaca coast, Mexico's newest tourist resort is growing up on the lovely Bahías de Huatulco, while Puerto Escondido and the Puerto Ángel area are older beach destinations that remain small-scale and more laid back.

The backcountry of the region is as far from Oaxaca city in culture and traveling time as Oaxaca is from Mexico City. There's enough of it to offer weeks of exploring.

Lying in a region where temperate and tropical climatic zones and several mountain ranges meet, Oaxaca has spectacularly varied landscapes and a biodiversity greater than any other Mexican state. The inland highlands still have cloud forests and big stands of oak and pine, while lower-lying areas and Pacific-facing slopes support deciduous tropical forest.

History
Zapotecs & Mixtecs Pre-Hispanic Oaxaca traded with other parts of Mexico, but its cultures were left largely undisturbed to reach heights rivaling those of central Mexico.

Highlights

- Oaxaca city – a beautiful, lively colonial city with great handicraft shopping
- Monte Albán – ruins of the ancient Zapotec capital on a superb hilltop site
- Puerto Ángel area – great beaches, a laid-back travelers' scene, boat trips, snorkeling, sea turtles, dolphins, crocodiles
- Puerto Escondido – tropical resort-cum-fishing village with great surfing
- Lagunas de Manialtepec & Chacahua – mangrove-fringed lagoons teeming with bird life
- Bahías de Huatulco – a low-key modern resort being built on a set of exquisite bays

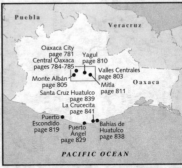

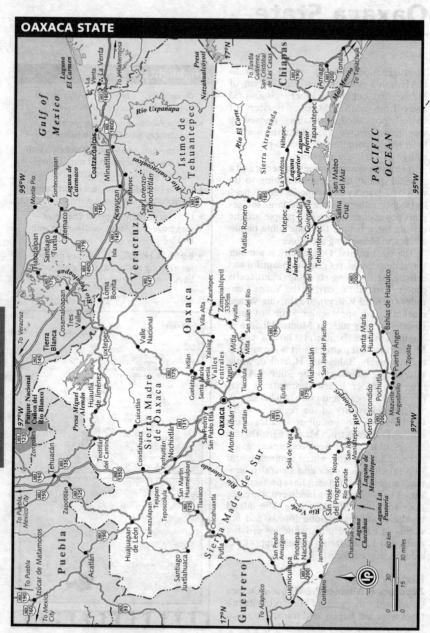

OAXACA STATE

The Valles Centrales have always been the hub of Oaxacan life. The hilltop city of Monte Albán became the center of the Zapotec culture, which extended its control over the Valles Centrales and other parts of Oaxaca by conquest and peaked between 300 and 700 AD. Monte Albán's decline was sudden; by about 750 AD it was deserted, as were many other Zapotec sites in the Valles Centrales. From about 1200, those sites that remained came under growing dominance by the Mixtecs, renowned potters and metalsmiths from Oaxaca's northwest uplands. Mixtec and Zapotec cultures became entangled in the Valles Centrales before the Aztecs conquered them in the 15th and early 16th centuries.

Colonial Era The Spaniards had to send at least four expeditions before they felt safe enough to found the city of Oaxaca in 1529. Cortés donated large parts of the Valles Centrales to himself and was officially named Marqués del Valle de Oaxaca. In colonial times, the indigenous population dropped disastrously. The population of the Mixteca region in the west is thought to have fallen from 700,000 at the Spanish arrival to about 25,000 in 1700. Rebellions continued into the 20th century, but the indigenous peoples rarely formed a serious threat.

Juárez & Díaz Benito Juárez, the great reforming leader of mid-19th-century Mexico, was a Zapotec. He served two terms as Oaxaca state governor before being elected Mexico's president in 1861. (See 'Benito Juárez,' this chapter.)

Juárez appointed Porfirio Díaz, son of a Oaxaca horse trainer, as state governor in 1862. Díaz led Oaxacan resistance to the French intervention in the 1860s but then rebelled against Juárez's presidency in 1871. He went on to control Mexico with an iron fist from 1877 to 1910. While his rule brought the country into the industrial age, it also fostered corruption, repression and, eventually, the revolution. In Valle Nacional in northern Oaxaca, tobacco planters set up virtual slave plantations, most of whose

15,000 workers had to be replaced annually after dying from disease, beating or starvation. Indigenous communal lands were commandeered by foreign and mestizo coffee planters.

Oaxaca Today After the revolution about 300 *ejidos* (peasant land-holding cooperatives) were set up, but land ownership remains a source of conflict today. With little industry, Oaxaca is one of Mexico's poorest states, and many of its residents leave to work in the cities or the USA. The situation is made worse in some areas, notably the Mixteca, by deforestation and erosion. Tourism is thriving in Oaxaca city and nearby villages and in a few places on the coast, but in the backcountry underdevelopment is prevalent.

Geography & Climate

The western two-thirds of the state is rugged and mountainous; the eastern third lies on the hot, low-lying Isthmus of Tehuantepec (Istmo de Tehuantepec). Oaxaca also has a thin plain along the Pacific coast and a low-lying north-central region bordering Veracruz state.

The Sierra Madre del Sur (average height 2000m) enters Oaxaca from the west and stretches along behind the coast. The Sierra Madre de Oaxaca (average height 2500m) runs down from Mexico's central volcanic belt. The two ranges meet roughly in the center of the state. Between them, converging at the city of Oaxaca, lie the three Valles Centrales.

The Valles Centrales are warm and dry, with temperatures in the low teens on winter nights and the low 30s on summer days (both measurements in degrees Celsius). The annual rainfall of 600mm falls mostly from June to September. On the coast and in low-lying areas it's hotter and a bit wetter.

Population & People

Oaxaca's population of 3.3 million includes 15 indigenous groups, which together make up about one-third of the total. Each indigenous group has its own language, but most also speak Spanish. Some indigenous

OAXACA STATE

customs are buckling under the pressure of change – colorful traditional costumes, for instance, are seen less – but you'll still notice a strong indigenous presence in handicrafts, markets and festivals. Indigenous land and housing are usually the poorest in the state. When indigenous organizations have campaigned for land rights, the reaction of the powers-that-be has literally been murderous at times.

Some 400,000 Zapotecs live mainly in and around the Valles Centrales and on the Isthmus of Tehuantepec. You're sure to come into contact with them, though few obvious signs identify them. Most are farmers, but they also make and trade handicrafts, mezcal and other products. Many emigrate temporarily for work.

About 300,000 Mixtecs are spread around the mountainous borders of Oaxaca, Guerrero and Puebla states, with more than two-thirds of them in Oaxaca. The state's other large indigenous groups include the 160,000 or so Mazatecs in the far north, the 100,000 Mixes in the highlands northeast of the Valles Centrales and the 100,000 Chinantecs around Valle Nacional, in the north.

In Oaxaca city you may well see Triquis, from western Oaxaca; the women wear bright red *huipiles* and populate craft markets. The Triquis are only about 15,000 strong and have a long history of violent conflict with mestizos and Mixtecs over land rights.

Internet Resources

Oaxaca's Tourist Guide (http://oaxaca-travel.com) is an excellent photo-filled website with everything from information on beaches and hotels to regional recipes and biographies of famous Oaxacans. Also useful is Oaxaca's Forum (http://bbs.oaxaca.com), a bulletin board where you can look for rented accommodation or shared transport or just ask any old question. Oaxaca's Index (http://index.oaxaca.com) has links to both of the above sites plus listings for language schools and lodgings.

The best mezcal is made in Oaxaca, and the Mezcal de Oaxaca site (http://oaxaca.gob.mx/mezcal) tells you all about it.

Oaxaca Bus Companies

The following abbreviations for 2nd-class bus companies are used in this chapter:

AU	Autobuses Unidos
AVN	Autotransportes Valle del Norte
EB	Estrella Blanca
ERS	Estrella Roja del Sureste
EV/OP	Estrella del Valle/Oaxaca Pacífico
FYPSA	Fletes y Pasajes
TOI	Transportes Oaxaca-Istmo

Dangers & Annoyances

Buses and other vehicles traveling isolated stretches of highway, including the coastal highway 200 and highway 175 from Oaxaca city to Pochutla, occasionally are stopped and robbed. The best way to avoid this risk is not to travel at night.

Oaxaca City

• pop (estimated) 400,000 • elev 1550m ☎ 9

The state's capital and only sizable city has a Spanish-built heart of narrow, straight streets liberally sprinkled with lovely colonial stone buildings. Oaxaca's atmosphere is relaxed but energetic, remote but cosmopolitan. The city's dry mountain heat, manageable scale, old buildings, broad shady plazas and leisurely cafés help slow the pace of life. At the same time, diverse Oaxacan, Mexican and international cultures create a current of excitement.

Head first for the *zócalo* to get a taste of the atmosphere. Then give yourself time to ramble and see what markets, handicrafts, galleries, cafés and festivities you come across. In addition, many fascinating places lie within day-trip distance in the Valles Centrales.

History

The Aztec settlement here was Huaxyacac (meaning 'In the Nose of the Squash'), from which 'Oaxaca' is derived. The Spanish laid

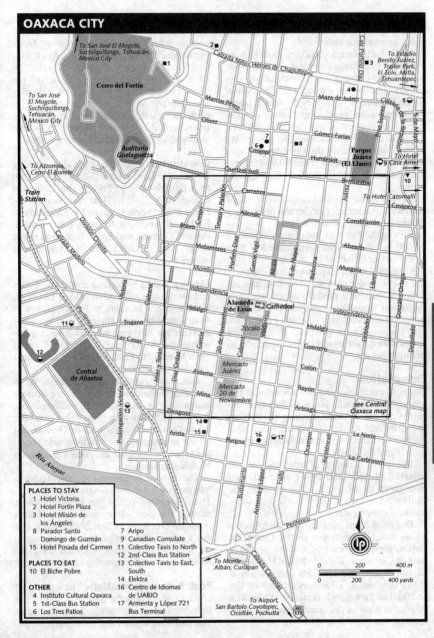

OAXACA CITY

To San José El Mogote,
Suchilquitongo, Tehuacán,
Mexico City

■1

Calzada Niños Héroes de Chapultepec

2■

■3 To Estadio
Benito Juárez,
Trailer Park,
El Túle, Mitla,
Tehuantepec

Cerro del Fortín

4● Maza de Juárez

5● Calzada de la República

To San José
El Mogote,
Suchilquitongo,
Tehuacán,
Mexico City

Marcos Pérez

Oliver

Gómez Farías

7●
6● Cosijopi ■8

To Atzompa,
Cerro El Bonete

Auditorio
Guelaguetza

Quetzalcóatl

Humboldt

Parque
Juárez
(El Llano)

9● To Hotel
Casa Arnel

Train
Station

Berriozábal

Carranza

10●

Crespo

Tinoco y Palacios

Allende

Constitución

To Hotel Cazomalli
Cosijoeza

Bravo

Division Oriente

Matamoros

Porfirio Díaz

García Vigil

Alcalá

5 de Mayo

Reforma

Abasolo

Murguía

Calzada Madero

Morelos

Independencia

Morelos

Hidalgo

Alameda
de León

Cathedral

Independencia

Victoria

Galeana

Trujano

Zócalo

Libres

González Ortega

Deboliedo

11●

Las Casas

García

Mier y Terán

20 de Noviembre

Valdivieso

Cabrera

Hidalgo

Guerrero

Perférica

Central
de Abastos

Díaz Ordaz

Aldama

Mercado
Juárez

Colón

Rayón

12●

13●

Mina

Mercado
20 de
Noviembre

see Central
Oaxaca map

Arteaga

Prolongación Victoria

Zaragoza

14●
15■

Arista

Burgoa

16● ●17

La Noria

Río Atoyac

La Carbonera

PLACES TO STAY
1 Hotel Victoria
2 Hotel Fortín Plaza
3 Hotel Misión de
los Ángeles
8 Parador Santo
Domingo de Guzmán
15 Hotel Posada del Carmen

7 Aripo
9 Canadian Consulate
11 Colectivo Taxis to North
12 2nd-Class Bus Station
13 Colectivo Taxis to East,
South
14 Elektra

PLACES TO EAT
10 El Biche Pobre

OTHER
4 Instituto Cultural Oaxaca
5 1st-Class Bus Station
6 Los Tres Patios

16 Centro de Idiomas
de UABJO
17 Armenta y López 721
Bus Terminal

Bustamante

Armenta y López

Fiallo

Perférico

Ocampo

Xicoténcatl

Calzada Cárdenas

To Monte
Albán, Cuilapan

To Airport,
San Bartolo Coyotepec,
Ocotlán, Pochutla

MEX
175

0   200   400 m
0   200   400 yards

OAXACA STATE

out a new town around the existing zócalo in 1529. It quickly became the most important place in southern Mexico.

Eighteenth-century Oaxaca grew rich on exports of cochineal, a red dye made from tiny insects living on the prickly pear cactus. The boom ended in 1783, when Spain banned debt slavery, by which many of the peasants producing cochineal were bound to traders in the city. But Oaxaca continued to thrive as a textile center: By 1796 it was probably the third-biggest city in Nueva España, with about 20,000 people (including 600 clergy) and 800 cotton looms.

In 1854 an earthquake destroyed much of the city. Decades later, under the presidency of Porfirio Díaz, Oaxaca began to grow again – in the 1890s its population exceeded 30,000. In 1931 another earthquake left 70% of the city uninhabitable.

Oaxaca's major expansion has come in the past two decades, with tourism, new industries and rural poverty all encouraging migration from the countryside. The city's population has roughly doubled in 20 years, and today visitors will find that Oaxaca sprawls well past its old limits, especially to the northwest.

Orientation

Oaxaca centers around the zócalo and the adjoining Alameda plaza in front of the cathedral. Calle Alcalá, running north from the cathedral to the Iglesia de Santo Domingo (a famous Oaxaca landmark), is mostly pedestrian-only.

The blocks north of the zócalo are smarter, cleaner and less traffic-infested than those to the south and, especially, the southwest, where cheap hotels and some markets congregate.

The road from Mexico City and Puebla winds around the slopes of the Cerro del Fortín, then runs east across the northern part of Oaxaca as Calzada Niños Héroes de Chapultepec. The 1st-class bus station is along this street, 1.75km northeast of the zócalo. The 2nd-class bus station is almost a kilometer west of the center, near the main market, the Central de Abastos.

Information

Tourist Offices Oaxaca has two major tourist information offices: one at Independencia 607, facing the Alameda (☎ 516-01-23); the other at 5 de Mayo 200 (☎ 516-48-28). Both are open 8 am to 8 pm Monday to Friday, 9 am to 8 pm Saturday and Sunday. At least one staff member in each can speak English, but the desks are often staffed by student volunteers, whose ability to answer questions is very limited.

Consulates The US consular agency (☎ 514-30-54), at Alcalá 201, is open 10 am to 3 pm Monday to Friday. The Canadian consulate (☎ 513-37-77), at Pino Suárez 700, Local 11B, is open 11 am to 2 pm Monday to Friday. Other consulates, such as the British, French, German and Spanish, tend to move fairly often – check details with tourist offices.

Money Banks with long exchange hours include: Bancomer, at García Vigil 120, open 9 am to 5 pm Monday to Friday, 10 am to 4 pm Saturday; and Banamex, with branches at Hidalgo 821 and on Valdivieso, both within one block of the zócalo, open 9 am to 5 pm Monday to Friday, 9 am to 2 pm Saturday. All three have ATMs.

Casas de cambio save time in bank queues, but their exchange rates are worse – and beware of attempts to shortchange you. Two central ones with reasonable rates for US dollars are Internacional de Divisas, just off the northeast corner of the zócalo (open daily), and Cash Express, Alcalá 201 (open Monday to Saturday).

The American Express representative is Viajes Micsa (☎ 516-27-00), Valdivieso 2. The Telégrafos office, on Independencia next to the post office, and three Elektra shops (at Guerrero 112, on 20 de Noviembre at Zaragoza, and on Colón east of Armenta y López) all offer Western Union's 'Dinero en Minutos' money-transfer service.

Post & Communications The main post office, on the Alameda, is open 8 am to 7 pm Monday to Friday, 9 am to 1 pm Saturday. You can send and receive faxes here.

Viajes Micsa (☎ 516-27-00), Valdivieso 2, runs an American Express client mail service.

Pay phones are available on the zócalo and elsewhere, and many telephone *casetas* are scattered about – the ones on Independencia opposite the Telégrafos office and at Computel on Trujano both offer economical fax service too.

Cafetería Restaurant Gyros Makedonia (☎ 514-07-62), at 20 de Noviembre 225, near the zócalo, is a café-cum-telephone caseta that also has public fax, email and Internet service.

CyberNet, Juárez 101, is a friendly Internet café charging US$0.05 per minute online. It also shows good music videos and serves food and drinks. Hours are 10 am to 10 pm Monday to Saturday.

Other public Internet/email services include Terra Nostra, Morelos 600 (US$0.10 per minute, US$3.50 an hour; open 9.30 am to 7 pm Monday to Friday, 10 am to 6 pm Saturday); Milenium Cybercafe, 5 de Mayo 412, at Plaza Gonzalo Lucero (US$0.08 per minute, open 10 am to 8 pm Monday to Saturday); and Multitel Internet, Alcalá 100A (US$3 for 30 minutes, US$4 an hour, open 7 am to 10 pm daily).

Internet Resources The *Oaxaca Times* newspaper's website (www.oaxacatimes.com) gives you, among other things, access to useful classified ads, where you can look for an apartment or B&B.

Bookstores Corazón El Pueblo, at Alcalá 307 (upstairs in Plaza Alcalá), and Librería Universitaria, Guerrero 108 just off the zócalo, sell books in English about Oaxaca and Mexico. Códice, at Alcalá 403, has books and maps in English, French and German. Proveedora Escolar, Independencia 1001 (at Reforma), has a terrific upstairs Spanish-language section on local history, archaeology and anthropology. Main museums also sell books. Oaxaca's INEGI map sales center is at Independencia 805.

Libraries Oaxaca has some fine reference libraries open to visitors, with material in English and Spanish. The Biblioteca Circu-

lante de Oaxaca (Oaxaca Lending Library), Alcalá 305, has a sizable collection of books and magazines on Oaxaca and Mexico. It's open 10 am to 1 pm and 4 to 7 pm Monday to Friday, 10 am to 1 pm Saturday.

The Instituto Welte de Estudios Oaxaqueños, 5 de Mayo 412, at the back of Plaza Gonzalo Lucero, has an outstanding library with titles on ethnography, archaeology, historical geography and more, including a good section on Oaxacan women. It's open 10 am to 2 pm Monday to Friday. The excellent library of the Instituto de Artes Gráficas de Oaxaca, Alcalá 507, covers art, architecture, literature, botany, ecology and history.

Media A number of free English-language papers and small magazines aimed at tourists are available around town. Most are published monthly. The *Oaxaca Times* and *Oaxaca* have the most useful practical information and small ads. These and the Spanish-language daily *Noticias* have to-let ads for apartments and houses.

Notice boards at Plaza Gonzalo Lucero (5 de Mayo 412), the Biblioteca Circulante (Alcalá 305; see Libraries, just above) and the Instituto Cultural Oaxaca (Juárez 909, at Calzada Niños Héroes de Chapultepec; see Courses, below) are full of ads for accommodations, classes (in everything from Spanish to yoga) and other interesting stuff.

Cultural Centers The Alianza Francesa (☎ 516-39-34), Morelos 306, maintains a small *mediateca* with French books and periodicals. The institute also presents exhibitions and French films.

Laundry Same-day wash-and-dry laundry service is available at Lavandería Azteca, at Hidalgo 404; Superlavandería Hidalgo, at the corner of Hidalgo and JP García; and Clin Lavandería, at 20 de Noviembre 605. All charge US$3.50 for up to 3.5 kg, and all are open 8 am to 8 pm Monday to Saturday.

Medical Services Clínica Hospital Carmen (☎ 516-26-12), Abasolo 215, is open 24 hours daily and has several English-speaking doctors.

OAXACA STATE

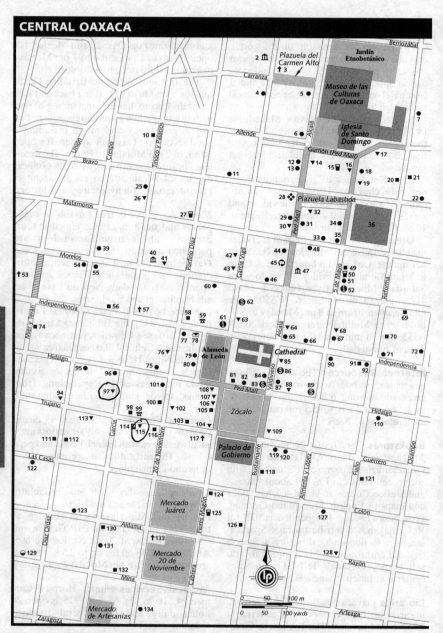

CENTRAL OAXACA

Berriozábal

2 🏛 Plazuela del Carmen Alto Jardín Etnobotánico
† 3

Carranza

4 ● ● 5 Museo de las Culturas de Oaxaca

Alcalá

6 ● Iglesia de Santo Domingo

Allende

10 ■ Gurrión (Ped Mall)

Unión Crespo Tinoco y Palacios

Bravo

▼ 17

12 ● ▼ 14   15 ▤   16 ▼
13 ●   ▼ 18   20 ■   ■ 21

● 11

25 ●   22 ●
26 ▼

Matamoros

28 ❖ Plazuela Labastida

27 ▤

29 ●   ▼ 32
30 ▼ ● 31   34 ●   36

Portirio Díaz García Vigil 5 de Mayo Reforma

Morelos

39 ●   40 🏛   33 ●   35
54 ●   41   42 ▼   44 ●   48 ●
55   43 ▼   45 ↺   ▼ 49
                            🏛 47   ▼ 50
                    60 ●   46 ●   ● 51
                                        ❶ 52

† 53

Independence

■ 56   † 57   58 ●   59 ● $ 62
                    77 ●   61 ●   ▼ 63   69 ■
                    78 ●   ❶
74 ■   ● 64   ▼ 68   ■ 70
                                        ● 65   ● 66   ● 67   72 ■
76 ▼   79 ●   Alameda de León   Cathedral   ● 71   Independence
75 ●   80 ●
Hidalgo
95 ●   96 ●   81 ● 82   84 ●   ▼ 85   90 ●   91 ● ■
94 ■   97 ▼   83 ● $ 86   92
101 ●   Ped Mall 88 ●   89
Trujano   100 ●   108 ▼   87 ● $
98 ● 99   107 ▼
113 ▼ ❶   106 ▼
114 ● ❶ 102 ▼   105 ■   Zócalo   110 ●
       115 ● ●   103 ■   104 ●
111 ■ 116 ●   Hidalgo
112 ■   117 †   ▼ 109
Las Casas
122 ●   Palacio de Gobierno   119 ● 120 ●
                                                118 ●
                          Bustamante Armenta y López   121 ■
                                        Fiallo Ocampo   Guerrero
123 ●   ■ 124   127 ●
              Mercado   Colón
130 ■   Juárez 125 ▤
       Aldama   126 ■
131 ■
○ 129 † 133   128 ▼
       Mercado   Rayón
       20 de
■ 132 Noviembre
       Mina
Mercado de Artesanías   ● 134
Zaragoza   Arteaga

Díaz Ordaz García 20 de Noviembre Cabrera Flores Magón

0   50   100 m
0   50   100 yards

CENTRAL OAXACA

70 Hotel Reforma
74 Hostal Santa Isabel
81 Hotel Marqués Del Valle
91 Casa Nuestra
98 Hotel Mesón del Rey
100 Hotel Francia
103 Hotel Las Rosas
105 Hotel Señorial
111 Hotel Fortín
112 Hotel Vallarta
116 Hostal Santa Rosa
118 Hotel Gala
121 Magic Hostel
124 Hotel Trébol
126 Hotel Aurora
130 Hotel Posada Catarina
132 Hotel Pasaje

PLACES TO EAT

14 Pizzeria Alfredo da Roma
16 Madre Tierra
17 Los Pacos
18 Café Gecko
19 Coffee Beans
21 Café La Olla, Las Bugambilias
26 Restaurant Manantial Vegetariano
28 Hostería de Alcalá
30 Pizza Rústica
32 El Topil
41 Restaurant Flor de Loto
42 Cafetería Bamby
43 Bamby Bakery
63 Tito's
64 Quickly Restaurant
68 Coffee Beans
76 Restaurant Colonial
85 El Sagrario
88 El Mesón
94 Café Alex
97 Restaurante Alameda
102 Cafetería Restaurant
     Gyros Makedonia
104 El Asador Vasco
106 La Cafetería
107 La Primavera
108 La Casa de la Abuela
109 Terranova Café
113 Restaurant Flami
115 Restaurante El Naranjo
128 Restaurant Las Mañanitas

OTHER

1 Advantage Rent-A-Car
2 Museo Casa de Juárez
3 Templo & Ex-Convento
   del Carmen Alto
4 Artesanías Chimalli
5 Instituto de Artes Gráficas de Oaxaca
6 Aviacsa
7 El Sol y La Luna
11 Becari Language School,
    Viajes Xochitlán
12 Códice
13 El Cactus
15 K-Os
18 Plaza Gonzalo Lucero, Milenium
    Cybercafé, Instituto Welte de Estudios
    Oaxaqueños, Cantera Tours
22 Vinigúlaza Language School
24 Clínica Hospital Carmen

25 Museos Comunitarios
   del Estado de Oaxaca
27 La Cucaracha
28 Plaza Alcalá, Corazón El Pueblo,
   Instituto de Comunicación y Cultura
29 Biblioteca Circulante de Oaxaca
31 Centro Cultural Ricardo Flores Magón
33 Fundación Cultural Rodolfo Morales
34 Budget Rent a Car
35 Hecmafer
37 Candela
38 Viajes Jalietza
39 El Infierno
40 Museo Rufino Tamayo
44 La Mano Mágica
45 US Consulate, Cash Express
46 Global Air
47 Museo de Arte Contemporáneo
   de Oaxaca
48 Casa Cantera
50 Café Comala
51 MARO
52 Tourist Office
53 Basílica de la Soledad
54 Alianza Francesa
55 Fonart
57 Templo de San Felipe Neri
59 Telephone Caseta
60 Terra Nostra
61 Tourist Office
62 Bancomer
65 Multitel
66 INEGI
67 La Calenda
71 Proveedora Escolar
72 CyberNet
75 Amigos del Sol Language School
77 Aeroméxico
77 Telégrafos
79 Transportes Aeropuerto
80 Hotel Monte Albán
82 Restaurant El Marqués
83 Internacional de Divisas
84 Hertz Rent a Car
86 Banamex
87 Viajes Micsa (American Express)
89 Banamex
90 Teatro Macedonio Alcalá
92 Mexicana & Aerocaribe
93 Iglesia de La Merced
95 Lavandería Azteca
96 Superlavandería Hidalgo
99 Computel
101 Ticket Bus, Arrendadora Express
110 La Faena
114 Estacionamiento Trujano
117 Iglesia de La Compañía
119 Librería Universitaria
120 Elektra
122 El Rey de los Mezcales
123 Mezcal Perla del Valle
125 La Casa del Mezcal
127 Elektra
129 Autobuses Turísticos (to Monte
    Albán), Viajes Turísticos Mitla,
    Hotel Rivera del Ángel
131 Bicicletas Pedro Martínez
133 Iglesia de San Juan de Dios
134 Clin Lavandería

PLACES TO STAY

8 La Casa de mis Recuerdos
9 Parador del Domínico
10 Hotel Las Golondrinas
20 Hotel Villa de León
21 Las Bugambilias
23 Hostal Guadalupe
36 Camino Real Oaxaca
49 Hotel Principal
56 Hotel Posada del Centro
58 Hotel Antonio's
69 Hotel Santa Clara

Parque Juárez
(El Llano)

Constitución
Abasolo
Murguía
Morelos

OAXACA STATE

Emergency For any emergency service, you can call ☎ 06. The Centro de Protección al Turista (Ceprotur), in the tourist office at Independencia 607, exists to help tourists with legal problems: if you have a complaint, or if you've lost documents or had things stolen, you can report it here.

Zócalo & Alameda

Shady, traffic-free and surrounded by *portales* (arcades) sheltering several cafés and restaurants, the zócalo is the perfect place to relax and watch the city go by. The adjacent Alameda, also traffic-free but without the cafés, is another popular local gathering place.

The south side of the zócalo is occupied by the **Palacio de Gobierno**, whose stairway mural by Arturo García Bustos depicts famous Oaxacans and Oaxacan history. At the top of the mural are revolutionary Ricardo Flores Magón (left), Benito Juárez and his wife Margarita Maza (center) and José María Morelos (right). Porfirio Díaz appears below Juárez, in blue, with a sword. At the bottom, toward the right, Vicente Guerrero's execution at Cuilapan is shown. The left wall shows ancient Mitla. At the center of the right wall is Juana Inés de La Cruz, the 17th-century nun and love poet.

Oaxaca's **cathedral**, begun in 1553 and finished (after several earthquakes) in the 18th century, stands just north of the zócalo. Its main (west) façade, facing the Alameda, features some fine baroque carving.

Buildings near the Zócalo

Fine carved façades also adorn two nearby colonial churches: **La Compañía**, just off the southwest corner of the zócalo; and the popular **San Juan de Dios**, on Aldama at 20 de Noviembre, which dates from 1526 and is the oldest church in Oaxaca. The 17th-century baroque **Templo de San Felipe Neri**, on Independencia at JP García, is where Benito Juárez and Margarita Maza were married in 1843; Maza was the daughter of Don Antonio Maza, who had employed Juárez's sister as a family cook and had been the first to take in young Benito on his arrival in Oaxaca.

The 1903 **Teatro Macedonio Alcalá**, on 5 de Mayo at Independencia, is in the French style that was fashionable under Porfirio Díaz. It has a marble stairway and a five-tier auditorium that holds 1300 people.

Calle Alcalá

Closed to traffic and with its colonial-era stone buildings cleaned up and restored, Alcalá makes a fine pedestrian route from the city center to the Iglesia de Santo Domingo.

The **Museo de Arte Contemporáneo de Oaxaca** (☎ 514-10-55), at Alcalá 202, occupies a lovely colonial house built around 1700 and known erroneously as the Casa de Cortés. The museum's permanent collection – only part of which is usually on display – includes work by leading modern Oaxacan artists, including Rufino Tamayo, Francisco Toledo, Rodolfo Morales, Rodolfo Nieto and Francisco Gutiérrez. Toledo, one of the museum's founders, is a leading campaigner for the cultural life of the city. The museum stages temporary exhibitions and other cultural events and has a pleasant courtyard café. It's open 10.30 am to 8 pm daily except Tuesday (US$1, free Sunday).

Iglesia de Santo Domingo

Santo Domingo, four blocks north of the cathedral, is the most splendid of Oaxaca's churches. It was built mainly between 1570 and 1608, for the city's Dominican monastery. The finest artisans from Puebla and elsewhere helped with its construction. Like other large buildings in this earthquake-prone region, it has immensely thick stone walls. During the 19th-century wars and anticlerical movements it was used as a stable and warehouse.

Amid the fine carving on the baroque façade, the figure holding a church is Santo Domingo de Guzmán (1172-1221), the Spanish monk who founded the Dominican order. The Dominicans observed strict vows of poverty, chastity and obedience, and in Mexico they gave the indigenous people some protection from other colonists' excesses.

The church is usually locked from 1 to 4 pm. The interior, lavishly ornamented in

Iglesia de Santo Domingo

NEIL SETCHFIELD

Emphasis is on the direct lineage between Oaxaca's pre-Hispanic and contemporary indigenous cultures, through exhibits illustrating the continuity of traditions in such areas as crafts, medicine, food, drink and music. An introductory video shows members of each of the state's 15 indigenous peoples speaking their own language. Other exhibits feature plenty of archaeological relics and colonial art. Highlights include the beautiful two-story stone cloister with tinkling fountain, which serves as an antechamber to the museum proper, and, in Sala 3, the Mixtec treasure from Tumba 7 at Monte Albán. This treasure dates from the 14th century, when Mixtecs reused an old Zapotec tomb to bury one of their kings and his sacrificed servants. With the bodies they placed a hoard of beautifully worked silver, turquoise, coral, jade, amber, jet, pearls, finely carved jaguar and eagle bone and, above all, gold. The treasure was discovered in 1932 by Alfonso Caso.

The museum is open 10 am to 8 pm Tuesday to Sunday (US$2, free on Sunday).

Jardín Etnobotánico

This garden of Oaxaca state plants, in the former monastic grounds behind the Museo de las Culturas, has been growing only since the mid-1990s. Guided tours are given at 1 and 5 pm Tuesday to Saturday – ask at the museum ticket desk.

Instituto de Artes Gráficas de Oaxaca

The Graphic Arts Institute (☎ 516-20-45), at Alcalá 507, almost opposite Santo Domingo, is in a beautiful colonial house donated by artist Francisco Toledo. It offers changing exhibitions of graphic art as well as a good library. Hours are 9.30 am to 8 pm daily except Tuesday (donations requested). There's a café in the rear courtyard.

Museo Casa de Juárez

The Juárez House Museum (☎ 516-18-60), at García Vigil 609, opposite the Templo del Carmen Alto, is where Benito Juárez found work as a boy with bookbinder Antonio Salanueva (see 'Benito Juárez,' this

gilded and colored stucco, has a magically warm glow during candlelit evening masses. Just inside the main door, on the ceiling, is an elaborate family tree of Santo Domingo de Guzmán. The 18th-century Capilla de la Virgen del Rosario (Rosary Chapel), on the south side, is a profusion of yet more gilt. The *retablos* behind the main altar and in this chapel date from the mid-20th century – the originals disappeared during the 19th century.

Museo de las Culturas de Oaxaca

The large, excellent and up-to-date Museum of Oaxacan Cultures (☎ 516-29-91) occupies the beautifully restored Ex-Convento de Santo Domingo, adjoining the Iglesia de Santo Domingo. These old monastery buildings were used as military barracks for over 100 years until 1994, when they were handed over to the city of Oaxaca. The museum, opened in 1998, takes you right through the history and cultures of Oaxaca state up to the present day.

chapter). The renovated house shows how the early-19th-century Oaxacan middle class lived. The binding workshop is preserved, along with pictures and a death mask of Juárez, some of his correspondence and other documents. Hours are 10 am to 7 pm Tuesday to Sunday (US$1.50, free on Sunday and holidays).

Fundación Cultural Rodolfo Morales

The building bearing this name at Murguía 105 is actually the Arte de Oaxaca gallery, just one part of the Rodolfo Morales Cultural Foundation. Set up in 1990 by Morales, a native of Ocotlán and one of Oaxaca's leading contemporary artists, the foundation endeavors to foment the arts, education, heritage and social welfare of Oaxaca's Valles Centrales. Its gallery here sells some of the very best Oaxacan art. Prints by Tamayo, Toledo, Rodolfo and Felipe Morales and many younger stars were among the plentiful works on view (and sale) on our last visit. Hours are 11 am to 3 pm and 5 to 8 pm Monday to Friday, 11 am to 3 pm Saturday. Contemporary art lovers should check out the gallery's website (www .artedeoaxaca.com.mx).

Museo Rufino Tamayo

This good museum of Mexican Pre-Hispanic art (☎ 516-47-50), at Morelos 503 in a fine 17th-century house, was donated to Oaxaca by its most famous artist, the Zapotec Rufino Tamayo (1899-1991). The collection

---

Benito Juárez

Benito Juárez (1806-72) was born in the mountain village of Guelatao, 60km northeast of Oaxaca. His Zapotec parents died when he was three. At the age of 12, knowing only a few words of Spanish, he walked to Oaxaca and found work at the house of Antonio Salanueva, a bookbinder. Salanueva became aware of the boy's potential and decided to help pay for an education Juárez otherwise might not have received.

Juárez trained for the priesthood but abandoned it for law and worked as a lawyer for poor villagers. He became a member of the Oaxaca city council and then of the Oaxaca state government. As state governor from 1848 to 1852, he opened schools and cut bureaucracy. The conservative national government exiled him in 1853, but he returned to Mexico in the 1855 Revolution of Ayutla. The revolution ousted General Santa Anna, and Juárez became justice minister in a new liberal national government. His Ley (Law) Juárez transferred the trials of soldiers and priests charged with civil crimes to ordinary civil courts; this was the first of the Reform laws, which sought to break the power of the Catholic Church. These laws provoked the War of the Reform of 1858 to 1861, in which the liberals, after setbacks, defeated the conservatives.

Juárez was elected Mexico's president in 1861 but had only been in office a few months when France, supported by conservatives and clergy, invaded Mexico and forced him into exile again. In 1866-67, with US support, Juárez ousted the French and their puppet emperor, Maximilian.

One of Juárez's main political achievements, was to make primary education free and compulsory. He died in 1872, a year after being elected to his fourth presidential term. Today he is one Mexican hero with an unambiguous reputation. Countless statues, streets, schools and plazas preserve his name and memory, and his maxim *El respeto al derecho ajeno es la paz* (Respect for the rights of others is peace) is widely quoted.

focuses on the aesthetic qualities of pre-Hispanic artifacts and is arranged to trace artistic developments in preconquest times. It's strong on the Preclassic era and lesser-known civilizations such as Veracruz. Hours are 10 am to 2 pm and 4 to 7 pm on Monday and from Wednesday to Saturday, and 10 am to 3 pm Sunday (US$1.50).

Basílica de la Soledad

The image of Oaxaca's patron saint, the Virgen de la Soledad (Virgin of Solitude), resides in this 17th-century church, about 3½ blocks west of the Alameda along Independencia. The church, with a rich carved stone baroque façade, stands where the image is said to have miraculously appeared in a donkey's pack a few centuries ago. In the mid-1990s, the virgin's 2kg gold crown was stolen, along with the huge pearl and many of the 600 diamonds with which she was adorned. The adjoining convent buildings contain a religious museum.

Cerro del Fortín

This wooded hill overlooking the city from the northwest has fine views, but we definitely cannot recommend a visit, as we have heard of several muggings there in recent years.

Courses

Language The number of language schools in Oaxaca is growing, and there's rivalry among them. We have spoken to students from a number of schools, and most seem pleased with their experiences. All schools offer group instruction at a variety of levels, Monday to Friday, and most emphasize the spoken language. Most offer private classes too, and they can usually arrange accommodations for students, either in hotels or with families. Staying with a family costs US$15 to US$20 a day with two meals daily.

Amigos del Sol
(☎ 515-31-04, fax 514-20-49, www.oaxacanews.com/amigosdelsol.htm) Libres 109 (postal address: Apartado Postal 6-09, Oaxaca, Oaxaca 68021); small school with maximum class size of five; students may start any Monday; 3½ hours' daily tuition costs US$72 a week

Becari Language School
(☎/fax 514-60-76, http://antequera.antequera.com/becari) Plaza San Cristóbal, Bravo 210, Oaxaca, Oaxaca 68000; medium-size school with small classes; three hours daily, divided between two teachers; costs US$75 a week; a US$50 registration fee is charged, but discounts are available in some seasons

Centro de Idiomas, Universidad Autónoma Benito Juárez de Oaxaca (UABJO)
(☎/fax 516-59-22) Burgoa s/n at Bustamante (postal address: Apartado Postal 523, Oaxaca, Oaxaca 68000); part of the city's university, offering 12 four-week courses a year, with four hours' classes a day and an average eight students per class; US$90 a week, or US$320 for the full four weeks

Instituto de Comunicación y Cultura
(☎/fax 516-34-43, www.iccoax.com) Alcalá 307-12, Plaza Alcalá, Oaxaca, Oaxaca 68000; three hours' classes daily in groups of three to five, starting any Monday, for US$100 a week; nonrefundable deposit of US$50; school emphasizes its teachers' qualifications and experience

Instituto Cultural Oaxaca
(☎ 515-34-04, fax 515-37-28, http://antequera.com/inscuoax) Juárez 909, at Calzada Niños Héroes de Chapultepec (postal address: Apartado Postal 340, Oaxaca, Oaxaca 68000); 'total-immersion' four-week courses with experienced, qualified teachers, including cultural, arts and crafts workshops and lectures; many classes are held in the school's spacious gardens and terraces; US$400 for four weeks (though it's possible to enroll for less), US$50 registration fee

Vinigúlaza
(☎ 514-64-26) Abasolo 209; classes of three to eight students cost US$35 for two hours a day, US$53 for three hours, US$70 for four hours

Private tutors are not hard to find – check notice boards (see Media, earlier in this chapter). One-on-one instruction costs around US$10 an hour.

Cooking Seasons of My Heart (☎/fax 518-77-26, ☎ 548-31-15) is run by Oaxacan food expert Susana Trilling at her ranch outside Oaxaca (postal address: Rancho Aurora, Apartado Postal 42, Admon 3, Oaxaca 68101). The school offers a variety of English-language classes in Mexican and Oaxacan cooking, from one-day group lessons (usually on Wednesday, for US$75

WELL WORTH THE PRICE!

FANTASTIC!

per person including transportation) to weeklong intensives (US$1595). Classes incorporate market trips to buy ingredients for the feasts to be prepared, and we've heard glowing reports from participants. The company also occasionally offers travel-and-cooking tours through the seven regions of Oaxaca state.

Organized Tours

Several companies offer day trips to places in the Valles Centrales. A typical three- or four-hour trip to Monte Albán, or to El Tule, Teotitlán del Valle and Mitla, costs around US$10. Agencies with a wide choice of itineraries include:

Cantera Tours
(☎ 516-05-12), Plaza Gonzalo Lucero, 5 de Mayo 412

Turismo Marqués Del Valle
(☎ 514-69-62), Hotel Marqués Del Valle, on the zócalo at Portal de Clavería s/n

Viajes Turísticos Mitla
(☎ 514-31-52), Hotel Rivera del Ángel, Mina 518; and (☎ 514-78-00) Hostal Santa Rosa, Trujano 201

Viajes Xochitlán
(☎ 514-32-71), Plaza San Cristóbal, Bravo 210

Bicicletas Pedro Martínez (☎ 514-31-44), JP García 509, offers mountain bike excursions starting at US$18 for three or four hours.

Special Events

All major national festivals are celebrated here. Unique Oaxaca fiestas include:

Virgen del Carmen The streets around the Templo del Carmen Alto, on García Vigil at Carranza, become a fairground for a week or more before the day of the Virgen del Carmen, July 16. The nights are lit by processions and fireworks.

Guelaguetza The Guelaguetza, a brilliant feast of Oaxacan folk dance, takes place in the big open-air Auditorio Guelaguetza on Cerro del Fortín on the first two Mondays after July 16. (The only time the dates vary is when July 18, the anniversary of Benito Juárez's death, falls on a Monday. Guelaguetza is then celebrated on July 25 and August 1.) Thousands of people flock into the city, and a festive atmosphere builds for days beforehand. On the appointed days, known as Los

Lunes del Cerro (Mondays on the Hill), the whole hill comes alive with hawkers, food stalls and picnickers.

From about 10 am to 1 pm, magnificently costumed dancers from the seven regions of Oaxaca (see 'Origins of the Guelaguetza,' this chapter) perform a succession of dignified, lively or

Origins of the Guelaguetza

The people of the Valles Centrales have held festivals about the same time every year on Cerro del Fortín since long before the Spanish conquest. In pre-Hispanic times the rites were in honor of maize and wind gods. After the Spanish conquest the indigenous festivities became fused with Christian celebrations of the feast of the Virgen del Carmen (July 16). In the 18th century a new tradition was established of giants and grotesquely big-headed figures dancing on the hill. Such goings-on were abolished in the 19th century, but people continued to visit the hill on the two Mondays following July 16.

Celebrations in something like their present form began in 1932. In 1957, all seven traditional regions of Oaxaca – the Valles Centrales, the Sierra Juárez (northeast of the city), La Cañada (the Teotitlán del Camino and Huautla de Jiménez area), the Papaloapan area around Tuxtepec, the Mixteca, the Costa Chica (Oaxaca coast) and the Isthmus of Tehuantepec – participated for the first time, and in 1974, the amphitheater built specifically for the celebration was opened. Guelaguetza is a Zapotec word meaning mutual help, cooperation or exchange of gifts, referring to the tradition of people helping each other out at such times as weddings, births and deaths.

Each year on the Saturday before the first Guelaguetza, delegations from the seven regions make a *calenda* (a colorful, musical procession) through the city. On the Sunday evening before each Guelaguetza, *Bani Stui Gulai* – a vibrant show of music, fireworks and dance explaining the evolution of the Guelaguetza – is staged in front of the Basílica de la Soledad.

comical traditional dances to live music, tossing offerings of produce to the crowd as they finish. Excitement climaxes with the incredibly colorful pineapple dance by women of the Papaloapan region, and the stately, prancing Zapotec Danza de las Plumas (Feather Dance), in which men wearing glorious feather headdresses perform a symbolic reenactment of the Spanish conquest.

Seats in the amphitheater (it holds perhaps 10,000) are divided into four *palcos* (areas). For the two palcos nearest the stage, tickets (around US$35 and US$30) go on sale months beforehand from the tourist office on Independencia. Nearer festival time they're also available at other outlets in the city. Tickets guarantee a seat, but you should still arrive before 8 am if you want one of the better ones. The two much bigger rear palcos are free and fill up early – if you get in by 8 am you'll get a seat, but by 10 am you'll be lucky to get even standing room. For all areas take a hat and something to drink, as you'll be sitting under the naked sun for hours.

Blessing of Animals Pets are dressed up and taken to Iglesia de La Merced, on Independencia, about 5 pm on August 31.

Christmas Events December 16 is the first of nine nights of *posadas*, neighborhood processions of children and adults symbolizing Mary and Joseph's journey to Bethlehem. December 18, the Día de la Virgen de la Soledad, sees processions and traditional dances, including the Danza de las Plumas, at the Basílica de la Soledad. On the Noche de los Rábanos (Night of the Radishes), December 23, amazing figures carved from radishes are displayed in the zócalo. You're supposed to eat *buñuelos* (crisp fried pastries), then make a wish while throwing your bowl in the air. On December 24, evening processions called *calendas* leave from churches and converge on the zócalo about 10 pm, bringing music, floats and fireworks.

Places to Stay – Budget

Camping The fairly well-shaded *Oaxaca Trailer Park* (☎ 515-27-96) is on Violetas at Heroica Escuela Naval Militar, 3.5km northeast of the center. The rate for a vehicle and two people is US$7 to US$9, including all hookups. Turn north at the 'Colonia Reforma' sign on Calzada Niños Héroes de Chapultepec, half a kilometer east of the 1st-class bus station, and go about seven blocks.

Hostels The *Magic Hostel* (☎ 516-76-67, magichostel@backpacker.com, Fiallo 305),

two blocks east and half a block south of the zócalo, is a busy hostel owned by a Dane and geared to international backpackers. It has about 56 bunks and beds at US$4 a person (US$9 for one of the few double rooms), 10 hammock spaces (US$3), a kitchen and 24-hour hot water. An economical restaurant here serves Oaxacan food, and tours to villages and Internet access are available too. Drugs are banned in the hostel, control is maintained over who enters, and there's a safe for your valuables.

The British-run *Casa Nuestra* (Independencia 906), two blocks east of the cathedral, upstairs, is a superior sort of hostel with separate-sex bathrooms, a kitchen and Internet access. Spacious rooms cost US$18 or US$20 for one or two people, US$25 for three, and hammock space is US$5. Capacity is just 16. Light breakfast is available.

Other backpacker hostels in Oaxaca come and go. One that looks likely to stay the course is *Hostal Santa Isabel* (☎ 514-28-65, Mier y Terán 103), on a fairly quiet street half a block south of the Basílica de la Soledad. It's basic but friendly, with room for about 40 people in bunk dormitories and varied bedrooms (US$4 per person), plus a kitchen, shared bathrooms and two patios. You can use the Internet for US$2 an hour.

North of the zócalo, *Hostal Guadalupe* (☎ 516-63-65, Juárez 409) offers clean bunk rooms and a small guest kitchen for US$5.

Hotels Most cheap places are in the noisy, crowded streets south and west of the zócalo. Streetside rooms everywhere are likely to be noisy.

South & West of the Zócalo The *Hotel Aurora* (☎ 516-41-45, Bustamante 212), close to the zócalo, has 30 bare but decent new rooms with private bathrooms and hot water at US$10/14 single/double, and a few older rooms around its front courtyard for US$6/8 with shared bathrooms and cold water. Management is friendly.

Calle 20 de Noviembre has several hotels, each typically consisting of a long, narrow courtyard lined by three-story rows of

OAXACA STATE

boxlike rooms. *Hotel Posada del Carmen* (☎ 516-17-79, 20 de Noviembre 712) has spruced-up paint and furnishings and friendly staff. Rooms are clean and cost US$12 for singles or one-bed doubles, US$14 for two-bed doubles.

Hotel Pasaje (☎ 516-42-13, Mina 302) has small but clean rooms with private bath at US$10 single, US$13 to US$15 double.

Another group of cheapies is on Díaz Ordaz, three blocks west of the zócalo. Be prepared for cockroaches and limited hot water. Best is *Hotel Vallarta* (☎ 516-49-67, Díaz Ordaz 309), which has rooms with bath for US$14 single, US$15 or US$17 double, and some parking. *Hotel Fortín* (☎ 516-27-15, Díaz Ordaz 312), across the street, has singles for US$7 and doubles for US$9 or US$10.

North & East of the Zócalo The family-run *Hotel Casa Arnel* (☎ 515-28-56, casa.arnel@spersaoaxaca.com.mx, Callejón Aldama 404), in quiet, cobbled Colonia Jalatlaco, five minutes' walk south from the 1st-class bus station and 20 minutes northeast from the city center, is a long-running travelers' hangout. The clean but smallish rooms mostly surround a big, leafy, bird-inhabited courtyard. Singles/doubles with shared bath are US$7/13; singles/doubles/triples with private bath cost from US$15/18/22 to US$17/22/25; and a few suites holding up to four people are available for US$40 to US$45. In the high seasons (mid-December to mid-January; a week each side of Easter; July and August; and a week each side of the Día de los Muertos) rates go up by 15% to 30% and singles are not available. Casa Arnel also offers laundry facilities, a travel agency (village tours available), breakfast, evening snacks and a roof terrace with bar.

Nearer the center, *Hotel Reforma* (☎ 516-09-39, Reforma 102) is fairly comfortable and has a rooftop sitting area. Rooms vary – those on the top floor have views. Singles/doubles are US$11/13. Little *Hotel Santa Clara* (☎ 516-11-38, Morelos 1004) has fair-sized, clean rooms with bathroom for US$12/14 – not a bad value.

Places to Stay – Mid-Range

Rooms in this range have private bathrooms unless stated otherwise.

Near the Zócalo All these hotels are within 1½ blocks of the zócalo.

Hotel Las Rosas (☎ 514-22-17, Trujano 112) is a good value. The clean, fan-cooled rooms are on two levels around a pleasant courtyard. Singles/doubles are US$21/27, and the hotel has a TV area, a place to wash clothes, free drinking water and, in the lobby, tea and coffee. The entrance is up a flight of stairs.

Hostal Santa Rosa (☎ 514-67-14, Trujano 201) has 17 clean, pleasant rooms with color TV for US$23/28, plus a restaurant. The 27-room *Hotel Mesón del Rey* (☎ 516-00-33, Trujano 212) is also clean and comfy. Rooms are carpeted and have TV and fan for US$22/27. *Hotel Francia* (☎ 516-48-11, 20 de Noviembre 212) is a bit dark, and its rooms a bit poky, but it's clean and amiable (and DH Lawrence stayed here). Rooms with TV, fan and phone are US$18.50/25; smaller ones without TV are US$12/14.

Hotel Antonio's (☎ 516-72-27, Independencia 601) has 15 nice, bright, sizable rooms at US$20 for singles, US$25 or US$30 for doubles. The best are those above the courtyard restaurant.

Hotel Trébol (☎ 516-12-56, Flores Magón 201), almost hidden opposite the Mercado Juárez, has sizable, bright, clean, well-furnished rooms with fan and TV, around a modern courtyard, for US$30/36.

Hotel Gala (☎ 514-22-51, Bustamante 103), just half a block south of the zócalo, has rooms with TV, phone and fan for US$34/40. They vary in size and brightness: those on the street side are biggest. The hotel has a convenient little restaurant.

The two hotels right on the zócalo can get away with marking their prices up because of their incomparable location. *Hotel Marqués Del Valle* (☎ 516-36-77, Portal de Clavería s/n), on the north side, has spacious, comfortable rooms, some with great views, for US$40/50. The 127 rooms at the *Hotel Señorial* (☎ 516-39-33, Portal de Flores 6), on the west side, range from small, dark, interior ones to bigger, airier ones with lots of light. All cost US$47/50 and have TV. The best are on the top floor, with a shared roof terrace.

South & West of the Zócalo The *Hotel Posada Catarina* (☎ 516-42-70, *Aldama 325*) is on a busy street but is large and rambling enough for you to forget the outside world. It has two patios: one covered for sitting, the other bigger with a garden. Rooms are traditional in style but have modern comforts. A single or double with TV, fan and phone is US$25, king-size doubles are US$32, and rooms with two double beds cost US$39 for up to four people.

Hotel Posada del Centro (☎ 516-18-74, *Independencia 403*) is an attractive two-patio building recently converted to a hotel. Rooms (single or double) cost US$19.50 with decent shared bathrooms, or US$24 to US$35 with private bath and TV. Every room has a ceiling fan.

North of the Zócalo The excellent *Hotel Las Golondrinas* (☎ 514-32-98, *Tinoco y Palacios 411*), lovingly tended by friendly owners and staff, has about 18 rooms opening onto a trio of lovely, leafy little courtyards. It's often full, so book ahead. Rooms vary: none is huge but all are tastefully decorated and immaculate. Singles are US$23, doubles US$29 to US$35. Good breakfasts are served from 8 to 10 am.

A long-running travelers' haunt providing good rooms at a reasonable price is the *Hotel Principal* (☎ 516-25-35, *5 de Mayo 208*). Doubles are US$25 (US$30 with two beds). Only a couple of the 16 or so rooms are offered as singles (US$21), but several will function as triples (US$35). Most rooms are large and surround a sunny, peaceful courtyard. The few less attractive rear rooms are smaller.

Hotel Villa de León (☎ 516-19-77, *Reforma 405*) offers adequate singles/doubles with fan, TV and carpets for the fair price of US$15/21.

Hotel Cazomalli (☎ 513-35-13, *Salto 104*), on the corner of Callejón Aldama in quiet Colonia Jalatlaco, is 1.5km northeast

of the zócalo and five minutes' walk from the 1st-class bus station. It's a small, two-story hotel with a pleasant courtyard, tastefully decorated with *artesanías*. Very nice, clean singles/doubles are US$22/30; triples, quads and family rooms are available too.

B&Bs Most so-called B&Bs in Oaxaca are actually attractive guest houses and fall into the middle or top price ranges. One such is the charming and welcoming *La Casa de mis Recuerdos* (☎ 515-56-45, *Pino Suárez 508*). Cost is US$15 to US$25 per person, though only one of the nine attractive rooms is a single. Five rooms have private bath, and the best overlook a central garden. Breakfast is served at a large table in the family dining room.

You'll find more B&Bs advertised in the *Oaxaca Times* and *Oaxaca* newspapers and on the Internet.

Apartments The spacious, clean, well-furnished, modern apartments of *Parador Santo Domingo de Guzmán* (☎ 514-10-19, *Alcalá 804*) are 8½ blocks north of the zócalo. Each has two double beds, a sitting room, bathroom, cable TV and well-equipped kitchen. Other amenities include a pool and hotel-style room service with clean sheets daily. You can rent by the day at US$47/52/55 for singles/doubles/triples or by the week at US$303/324/344 – less during quiet seasons.

La Casa de mis Recuerdos (see B&Bs, above) has two nearby apartments for rent at US$500 a month. Check notice boards and the press (see Media, earlier in this chapter) for more apartments to let.

Places to Stay – Top End
The *Camino Real Oaxaca* (☎ 516-06-11, *oax@caminoreal.com, 5 de Mayo 300*), four blocks northeast of the zócalo, is Oaxaca's ultimate hotel for colonial atmosphere. The entire 16th-century convent of Santa Catalina was converted in the 1970s to create this hotel. The old chapel is a banquet hall, one patio contains an enticing swimming pool, and the bar is lined with books on otherworldly devotion. Thick stone

walls – some still bearing original frescoes – keep the place cool. The 91 varied, well-decorated rooms start at US$197/225 for singles/doubles. If you can, choose one upstairs and away from the street and kitchen noise.

The *Parador del Domínico* (☎ 513-18-12, *dominico@antequera.com, Pino Suárez 410*) is new but in attractive traditional style, with a lovely stone-columned patio housing its restaurant and bar. The 30 or so rooms, with air-con, satellite TV, fax and computer hookups and safe, cost US$61/65.

Most other top hotels are in the north of the city. *Hotel Misión de los Ángeles* (☎ 515-15-00, Calzada Porfirio Díaz 102*), just north of Calzada Niños Héroes de Chapultepec, has more than 150 large rooms in tropical gardens, plus tennis courts and a large pool. Standard rooms, all with two double beds, cost US$81/101, but promotional offers sometimes cut this to around US$70. The six-story *Hotel Fortín Plaza* (☎ 515-77-77, Venus 118*) is immediately above Calzada Niños Héroes de Chapultepec. Its ambiance is low-key and pleasant, with tile and marble decor. The 100 rooms, costing US$66/78, are bright and fairly spacious.

Hotel Victoria (☎ 515-26-33, fax 515-24-11, Lomas del Fortín 1*) stands on the lower slopes of Cerro del Fortín. Many of the 150 large rooms and suites overlook the city, and the hotel has an Olympic-size pool in big gardens. Its restaurant gets good reports too. Standard rooms cost US$95 single or double; villas with two double beds are US$120. The hotel runs a free shuttle to/from the city center.

B&Bs *Las Bugambilias* (☎/fax 516-11-65, Reforma 402*) is a delightful B&B entered through Café La Olla. It's a colonial house with a pretty garden, a library, TV/sitting room and seven individually decorated guest rooms with tiled bathrooms. Some rooms have terraces. In the low season (March to May except for Semana Santa, and August to November except for October 28 to November 3), singles/doubles cost from US$36/48 to US$60/72 depending on the room; at other times rates are from

US$42/54 to US$72/84. One junior suite costs US$95/105/120 for one/two/three people (US$114/126/144 in high season). All these prices include a healthy, traditional breakfast. Las Bugambilias has a website at www.mexonline.com/bugambil.htm.

Places to Eat

Varied new restaurants are opening all the time, and Oaxaca even boasts some good coffeehouses now. Many places offer Oaxacan specialties, but three places that really feature them are La Casa de la Abuela, Restaurante El Naranjo and El Biche Pobre (see the following sections).

For places where you can enjoy music with a meal, see the Entertainment section.

Market Meals Cheap *oaxaqueño* meals can be had in the *Mercado 20 de Noviembre*, south of the zócalo. Most of the many small *comedores* here serve up local specialties such as chicken in *mole negro*. Few post prices, but a typical main dish is about US$1. Pick a comedor that's busy – those are the best. Many stay open until early evening, but their fare is freshest earlier in the day. More comedores can be found in the big *Central de Abastos* (see Shopping, later in this section).

Near the Zócalo All the cafés and restaurants beneath the zócalo arches are great places from which to watch Oaxaca life, but quality and service vary. On the west side, *La Cafetería* concentrates on *especialidades oaxaqueñas (antojitos)* for US$1.50 to US$2.50, though it serves breakfasts too. *La Primavera* is a fairly good restaurant with some vegetarian options, including quesadillas with mushrooms and guacamole (US$2.25).

El Asador Vasco (☎ 514-47-55), upstairs at the southwest corner of the square, serves good Spanish, Mexican and international food. Main dishes are mostly in the US$6 to US$9 range, with steaks and *brochetas* (kebabs) among the best choices. For a table overlooking the zócalo, book early in the day.

La Casa de la Abuela (☎ 516-35-44, Hidalgo 616*), upstairs at the northwest corner, specializes in oaxaqueño food. The *parrillada oaxaqueña*, a sort of Oaxacan mixed grill, gives you six items for US$7.50. The excellent *chiles rellenos de picadillo* (US$5), served with guacamole and frijoles, make a good small meal. It's open 1 to 9.30 pm daily.

Terranova Café, on the east side of the zócalo, is one of the best places on the square, serving breakfasts till 1 pm, pasta or *comida corrida* for around US$3 and pizza, meat or chicken for US$4 to US$6.50.

El Mesón (*Hidalgo 805*), just off the zócalo, prepares tasty, mainly charcoal-grilled Mexican food at ranges in the center of the restaurant. You tick off your order on a printed list – the staff patiently tries to explain what's what. Tacos and quesadillas are the specialties, mostly at US$1.50 to US$2.50 for a serving of two or three. *Tacos rajas con queso* (bean tacos with cheese) are delicious. At lunchtime there's a fairly good buffet for US$3. A selection of mezcals is available from US$0.70 to US$1.50 a shot.

El Sagrario (*Valdivieso 120*), half a block north of the zócalo, is a popular pizzeria/restaurant/bar serving Mexican, Italian and international food. Most main dishes are US$4 to US$8, and there's a US$5 all-you-can-eat buffet, 1 to 5 pm daily.

West of the Zócalo Clean, busy *Café Alex* (*Díaz Ordaz 218*), three blocks west of the zócalo, is well worth hunting out for good-value breakfasts, served from 7 am to noon daily, or an inexpensive lunch or dinner until 9 pm Monday to Saturday. A breakfast of scrambled eggs with potatoes and onion, tortillas, juice or fruit, and coffee or tea is US$2.25. The comida corrida of three courses and coffee or dessert costs US$2.50; individual main dishes (including vegetarian options) are similarly priced. Portions are generous. There's usually a mixed Mexican and gringo crowd here, and service is quick.

A good spot for an inexpensive lunch (from 1.30 pm) is *Restaurant Colonial*, on 20 de Noviembre south of Independencia.

Cocina Oaxaqueña

Good oaxaqueño regional cooking is spicily delicious, and the seven traditional Oaxacan *moles* (sauces) are widely celebrated. Specialties include:

Amarillo (con pollo) – a yellow-orange cumin and chili mole (with chicken)

Chapulines – grasshoppers fried, often with onion and garlic; high in protein and good with a squeeze of lime

Chíchilo – a dark, rich mole made with varied chilies

Colorado – a dark red mole

Coloradito – a brick-red chili-and-tomato mole, usually served over pork or chicken

Manchamanteles – 'tablecloth-stainer': a mole made with pineapple and bananas

Memelitas – small tortillas with varied toppings

Mole negro – the monarch of Oaxacan moles, sometimes called just *mole oaxaqueño*: a dark, spicy, slightly sweet sauce made with many ingredients including chilies, bananas, chocolate, pepper and cinnamon; usually served with chicken

Picadillo – spicy minced or shredded pork, often used for the stuffing in *chiles rellenos*

Tamal oaxaqueño – a tamal with a mole oaxaqueño and (usually) chicken filling

Tasajo – a slice of pounded beef

Tlayuda or *tlalluda* – a big crisp tortilla, traditionally served with salsa and chili but now topped with almost anything, making it into a kind of pizza

Quesillo – Oaxacan stringy cheese

Verde (con espinazo) – a green mole (with pork back) made from beans, chilies, parsley and epazote (goosefoot or wild spinach)

OAXACA STATE

(handwritten annotations: "FABULOUS!!! RESTAURANT MARIA BONITA CALLE MACEDONIO ALCALA 706B", "GOOD LUNCH-VERY LOCAL", "NOT VERY GOOD")

Locals fill the 10 or so tables daily for the US$2 comida, which includes soup, a rice dish, a main course such as *pollo a la naranja* (chicken à l'orange), dessert and *agua de fruta*. **Cafetería Restaurant Gyros Makedonia** *(20 de Noviembre 225)* is run by a Greek-American and doles out good Greek fare such as souvlaki, gyros and pita-bread sandwiches, as well as omelets, hotcakes and more – all around US$1 to US$3.

Restaurante El Naranjo *(Trujano 203)*, 1½ blocks west of the zócalo, is a courtyard restaurant featuring oaxaqueño food with a modern touch. A different Oaxacan mole is served each day of the week with chicken or pork for US$6, and various stuffed chili dishes go for US$4 to US$5. It's open 1 to 10 pm daily.

Calm, clean **Restaurante Alameda** *(JP García 202)*, known by few foreigners, serves good oaxaqueño lunches from 1 to 6 pm daily except Monday. A four-course comida costs US$2.75 to US$4.25 depending on your main course.

Restaurant Flami *(Trujano 301)*, a big, busy place with mainly Mexican customers, does a fair carnivore's comida – soup, rice, choice of three lean meat courses, agua de fruta and dessert – for US$2.50.

North of the Zócalo The following places are listed in approximate south-to-north order.

Tito's *(García Vigil 116)* prepares quite a range of mainly Mexican food, from *tortas* and salads to meat main courses. Varied especialidades oaxaqueñas and *especialidades mexicanas* cost around US$3; breakfasts are US$1.25 to US$3.

The bright, clean **Cafetería Bamby** *(García Vigil 205)* is open 8 am to 10 pm daily except Sunday and serves sizable portions of plain but good Mexican and gringo food – salads, spaghetti, chicken and meats are all US$2 to US$3. The three-course comida is US$2.50.

Quickly Restaurant *(Alcalá 100B)*, 1½ blocks from the zócalo, is a reliable spot for an inexpensive if bland feed. *Parrilladas* – grilled vegetable and rice platters topped with melted cheese and served with tortillas and guacamole – will fill you for US$2.75 to US$3.50. Some have meat too.

Pizza Rústica *(Alcalá 303)*, set in a lovely courtyard with a fountain, serves real, tasty pizzas at US$3.50 to US$6 (medium size) or US$2.50 to US$4.50 (small). The menu also features a wine list, good salads (US$2.50 to US$3.50) and varied pasta dishes with a big choice of sauces (US$3.50 to US$6.50). Some nights you can enjoy jazz or other live music while you dine. It's open 1 to 11 pm (or midnight) daily.

El Topil, on Plazuela Labastida, serves individualistic dishes with the touch of home cooking; *tasajo* with guacamole and frijoles (US$4) is one specialty. The menu also offers a range of soups – the garbanzo soup (US$2.75) is delicious – and some good antojitos.

Hostería de Alcalá, in Plaza Alcalá (on Alcalá facing Plazuela Labastida), is one of Oaxaca's classier restaurants. It's open 8 am to 11 pm daily and is usually busy for lunch. You pay around US$6.25 for a *plato oaxaqueño*, US$3.50 for pasta and US$7 for beef dishes. **Pizzeria Alfredo da Roma** *(Alcalá 400)*, just below the Iglesia de Santo Domingo, has reasonable Italian food. Pastas are mainly in the US$3.50 range; pizzas come in more than 20 combinations and five sizes – those for two people are between US$3.50 and US$6.75. You can rinse it all down with sangria or wine.

The all-you-can-eat breakfast buffet at the **Hotel Camino Real** *(5 de Mayo 300)* costs US$11.50. **Café Gecko** *(Plaza Gonzalo Lucero, 5 de Mayo 412)* serves good hotcakes, croissants and other inexpensive snacks, plus about 20 types of coffee for under US$1.50, in a pleasant leafy patio. **Los Pacos**, nearby on Gurrión, offers good, medium-to-expensive Oaxacan and international food and friendly service. Main dishes cost from US$4 to US$7, and servings are generous. The restaurant occupies a pleasant patio and a roof terrace, which looks across to Santo Domingo.

El Biche Pobre *(Calzada de la República 600)*, 1.5km northeast of the zócalo, specializes in Oaxacan food. Open 1.30 to 9 pm daily, it's an informal place with about a dozen tables, some long enough to stage lunch for a whole extended Mexican family. A big variety of food is available at reasonable prices. For an introduction to Oaxacan fare, you can't do better than the US$3.50 *botana surtida*, a dozen assorted little items that add up to a tasty meal.

East of the Zócalo The *Restaurante Las Mañanitas (Rayón 221A)*, at Fiallo, is an amiable little street-corner *lonchería* serving a three-course *menú del día* for just US$1.50, salads for US$2, and *entomatadas*, *enfrijoladas* or chicken dishes for around US$3. It's open 8.30 am to 10.30 pm daily except Sunday.

Vegetarian Many restaurants have vegetarian options, but the following, all north of the zócalo, have more than most.

Madre Tierra (5 de Mayo 411), a spreading of wings by the long-running Madre Tierra in San Cristóbal de Las Casas, serves a range of tasty, healthy food in a pretty little patio and a couple of rooms that double as art galleries. Salads, vegetarian pasta, soy-burgers, stuffed avocados and whole-wheat tortas with salad cost from US$2 to US$5; steaks and other meat dishes are around US$6.50.

Offerings at *Café La Olla (Reforma 402)* include good whole-grain tortas, salads, pasta and meat dishes and regional specialties, all between US$2 and US$5. *Ensalada sauna* (US$3.25) is steamed vegetables with rice; *ensalada Mitla* (US$2.50) includes cactus and grasshoppers. Good juices cost US$1 to US$1.50, and the comida corrida (US$3.50) is substantial. La Olla is open 9 am to 10.30 pm daily except Sunday.

Restaurant Flor de Loto (Morelos 509) makes a reasonable stab at pleasing a range of palates from vegan to carnivore. The *crepas de espinacas* (spinach pancakes) and *verduras al gratin* (vegetables with melted cheese) are both good, at US$2.50. The US$2.75 comida corrida, with a veggie version available, is a real meal.

Restaurant Manantial Vegetariano (Tinoco y Palacios 303) has a pleasant atmosphere with tables in an open-air court-yard, but the cooking can be amateurish. It's open 9 am to 10 pm daily for breakfast (US$1.50 to US$2.75), menú del día (US$3) and, in the evening, crêpes or spaghetti (US$2 to US$2.50). A buffet (US$3.50) is offered 2 to 5 pm on Sunday.

Cafés & Bakeries The two branches of *Coffee Beans (5 de Mayo 114; 5 de Mayo 400C)* offer a range of real coffee fixes, including local organic varieties. An *americano* or cappuccino is US$1.25, and you can get croissants, pies and baguettes too.

Madre Tierra restaurant *(5 de Mayo 411)* has a bakery section selling whole-grain loaves for about US$1, plus quiches, cakes and other snacks. *Bamby* bakery, on García Vigil at Morelos, is a convenient stop for cakes, *bolillos* and large *pan integral* loaves.

Entertainment

Oaxaca's entertainment and cultural scene gets ever livelier, thanks to its student and tourist populations.

Live Music On the zócalo, *Restaurant El Marqués* has a lively Latin band nightly from 9.30 pm to around midnight. *Terranova Café* has varied live music too. Nearby, there's good Latin music from 9 pm until 2 am in the downstairs bar of *El Sagrario (Valdivieso 120)*. None of these places levies a cover charge. Free concerts in the zócalo generally are given by the state marimba ensemble or state band at 7 pm Monday to Saturday and by the city orchestra at noon on Sunday.

Candela (☎ 514-20-10, Murguía 413) was the jumping place when we were last in town, with locals and foreigners crowding into its patio and surrounding rooms for live salsa from 10.30 pm to 1.30 am Tuesday to Saturday (cover: US$2.50). On Sunday night it has jazz. Candela is open as a restaurant and bar from 9 am.

El Sol y La Luna (☎ 514-80-69, Reforma 502) offers jazz starting at 10 pm Thursday to Saturday (cover: US$2). It's open 8 pm to 12.30 or 1 am Monday to Saturday, with good food: crêpes US$3, pasta US$4, pizza or meat for more.

OAXACA STATE

Los Tres Patios *(Cosijopí 208)*, north of the center, is a relaxed place with jazz, blues or rock starting at 10 pm Wednesday to Saturday (cover: US$1.50). It's got space to dance.

~~***Madre Tierra*** restaurant *(5 de Mayo 411)* has a bar and a music patio~~ at the back where you can hear live salsa or *trova* from 10 pm to 2 am Thursday to Saturday (no cover). At *La Faena* *(Hidalgo 1002A)*, you can drink and/or dance to live salsa till 2 am Tuesday to Saturday nights. Cover is US$2, and beers are two for the price of one.

El Infierno *(Crespo 210)*, a bar/café with a little patio, often presents live music with a small cover charge on Friday or Saturday. The kitchen serves good crêpes, salads and pasta. Hours are 1 pm to 1 am Monday to Saturday, 6 to 11 pm Sunday.

La Calenda music bar on 5 de Mayo, north of Independencia, is the happening place for young Mexicans, with live rock bands Thursday to Saturday (cover: US$1.50).

OVERPRICED

Dance Shows If you're not lucky enough to be in Oaxaca for the Guelaguetza (see Special Events), a substitute is the lively mini-Guelaguetza staged at 8 pm nightly at the ***Casa Cantera*** *(☎ 514-75-85, Murguía 102)*. Various Oaxacan dances are performed in colorful costume with live music. The charge is US$5, with food and drinks available. To book, phone or stop by during the afternoon.

Other Guelaguetza-style shows are offered by local hotels; the ***Hotel Monte Albán*** *(Alameda de León 1)* presents a 1½-hour version nightly (US$4), and the ***Hotel Camino Real*** *(5 de Mayo 300)* stages a similar show on Wednesday and Friday evenings (US$19.50, including buffet dinner).

Bars *Café Comala* *(5 de Mayo 206)* is one of the most *simpático* bars in town. Popular with artsy, studenty Mexicans and foreigners, the Comala is open 8 am to 2 am Monday to Saturday, noon to midnight Sunday. It has a great music collection, and if you go by day you can see some of the quirky art around the place. Breakfasts are served, and from noon onward you can get good snacks *'para el munchies.'*

A cool central music bar, with vaguely psychedelic murals, is *K-Os*, on Gurrión facing Santo Domingo – open 9 pm to 1 am nightly except Monday.

If you feel the need to make the close acquaintance of a few typical Mexican beverages, try *La Cucaracha* *(Porfirio Díaz 301A)*. This specialist bar stocks 50 varieties of mezcal and 60 of tequila. A *degustación* (tasting) of six mezcals and four tequilas costs only US$5. Otherwise they're US$1.25 to US$3 a shot. Everyone's welcome (it's not a cantina), and food is served.

One of Oaxaca's oldest bars, *La Casa del Mezcal*, on Flores Magón 1½ blocks south of the zócalo, also serves good mezcal, for US$0.70 to US$1.50 a shot. It has a sit-down room where food is served, but it's more of a cantina-type place than La Cucaracha; though staff say it's OK for women, most patrons are men.

Other The *Centro Cultural Ricardo Flores Magón* *(Alcalá 302)* puts on varied musical, dance and theater shows most nights. Many events are free; drop by to see the program.

Spectator Sports

The Oaxaca Guerreros baseball team plays March to August at the Estadio Benito Juárez, on Calzada Niños Héroes de Chapultepec, 300m east of the 1st-class bus station. The Guerreros were the 1998 champions of the Béisbol Liga Mexicana. Games are usually at 5 pm Saturday or Sunday or at 7.30 pm other days. Ticket prices range from US$1 to US$5.

Shopping

The state of Oaxaca has probably the richest, most inventive folk art scene in Mexico, and the city is the chief clearinghouse for the products. The best work is generally in shops, but prices are lower in the markets. You may not pay more for crafts in the city than in the villages where most of them are made, but if you buy in the city a lot of your money usually goes to intermediaries. Some artisans have grouped together to market

OAXACA STATE

LOTS OF INTERESTING STALLS

their own products directly: MARO (see Shops, below) is one such enterprise.

Though many traditional techniques remain alive – back-strap and pedal looms, hand-turning of pottery – new product forms frequently appear in response to the big international demand for Oaxaca crafts. The brightly painted wooden animals and monsters known as *alebrijes* were developed only a few years ago from toys that Oaxacans had been carving for their children for centuries.

Special crafts to look out for include the distinctive black pottery from San Bartolo Coyotepec; blankets, rugs and tapestries from Teotitlán del Valle; huipiles and other indigenous clothing from anywhere (those from Yalalag and the Triqui and Amuzgo areas north of Pinotepa Nacional in southwest Oaxaca are among the prettiest); the creative pottery figures made by the Aguilar sisters of Ocotlán; and stamped and colored tin from Oaxaca itself.

Rugs or blankets with muted colors are less likely to have been made with synthetic dyes than some of the more garish offerings. To assess the quality of a woven rug you can:

- gently try to pull the fibers apart to see how tightly it's woven;
- rub your fingers or palm on it for about 15 seconds – if balls appear, the quality is poor;
- crumple it up a bit, then spread it on the floor – the creases will disappear from good rugs.

Jewelry is also sold here, and you'll find pieces using gold, silver or precious stones. The best shops are on Alcalá, but most prices are a bit higher than in Mexico City or Taxco.

Markets The vast main market, the Central de Abastos (Supplies Center), is on the Periférico in the western part of town, next to the 2nd-class bus station. Saturday is the big day, but the place is a hive of activity daily. If you look long enough, you can find almost anything, including handicrafts. Each type of product has a section to itself, so you'll find 20 or so woven-basket sellers here, a couple dozen pottery stalls there, and so on. The care that goes into the displays of food, particularly vegetables, is amazing.

Nearer the city center, the indoor Mercado Juárez, a block southwest of the zócalo, concentrates on food (more expensive than at the Central de Abastos) but also has flowers and some crafts. The Mercado 20 de Noviembre, a block farther south, is mainly taken over by comedores, but you'll find a few inexpensive craft stalls on its west side. The Mercado de Artesanías (Handicrafts Market), a block southwest of the Mercado 20 de Noviembre, gets fewer customers because it's a bit off the beaten track – so you may pick up some bargains. It's strong on pottery, rugs and textiles.

Two smaller craft markets function daily on plazas off Alcalá. On Plazuela Labastida you'll find jewelry, alebrijes, leather belts and artists at work, while Plazuela del Carmen Alto has weavings, embroideries, rugs and other textiles.

RICHARD NEBESKY

Baby saints at the Central de Abastos

Shops The shop beside the Independencia tourist office sells a decent range of reasonably priced Oaxaca crafts. MARO (Mujeres Artesanas de las Regiones de Oaxaca, or Craftswomen of the Regions of Oaxaca), 5 de Mayo 204, is a sprawling store run by a cooperative of artisans dedicated to the preservation of traditional crafts.

The highest-quality crafts are found in the smart stores on and near Alcalá and 5 de Mayo. La Mano Mágica, Alcalá 203, sells particularly good stuff, including weavings by one of its owners, the Teotitlán del Valle master weaver Arnulfo Mendoza. Some of Mendoza's pieces are worth thousands of dollars. The store is also a gallery of contemporary art. El Cactus, Alcalá 401, is good for blankets and rugs. Corazón El Pueblo, Alcalá 307, is just one of several shops in Plaza Alcalá selling beautiful crafts, jewelry or clothes. Hecmafer, 5 de Mayo 301, also stocks a particularly attractive range of goods.

Other good shops in Oaxaca include the government-run Fonart at Crespo 114; Artesanías Chimalli, García Vigil 513 (good for stamped tin and alebrijes); and Aripo, up at García Vigil 809, which is run by the Oaxaca state government.

Most craft shops will mail things home for you if you want. Typical shop hours are 10 am to 2 pm and 4 to 8 pm Monday to Saturday.

Central Oaxaca state is Mexico's leading mezcal-brewing zone, and several shops southwest of the zócalo sell nothing but mezcal, in a variety of strange vessels. Try El Rey de los Mezcales, at Las Casas 509, or Mezcal Perla del Valle, on Aldama west of JP García.

Getting There & Away

Air Direct flights to/from Mexico City (one hour, US$108 and up) are operated by Mexicana four times daily and Aeroméxico once daily. Both these airlines also fly direct to/from Tijuana. Aeroméxico flies to/from Los Angeles.

Aerocaribe flies daily to/from Acapulco and Tuxtla Gutiérrez. Via Tuxtla, without changing planes, you can reach Palenque,

Villahermosa, Mérida, Cancún, or Havana (Cuba) – all daily. The fare to Mérida is about US$170.

TAESA flies daily to/from Acapulco, Tijuana (US$149) and Tapachula (US$85). Aviacsa flies daily to Tuxtla Gutiérrez. Global Air has a couple of flights weekly to/from Acapulco.

Over the years a variety of airlines have offered service over the Sierra Madre del Sur to and from the Oaxaca coast – a spectacular half-hour hop. Currently Aerocaribe flies daily nonstop to/from both Puerto Escondido and Bahías de Huatulco (from US$68 one-way); Aerovega flies a five-seater to/from Puerto Escondido daily (US$57); and Global Air heads to/from Puerto Escondido and Huatulco daily except Thursday and Sunday (each US$58 to US$70).

Airline offices include: Aerocaribe (☎ 516-02-29) and Mexicana (☎ 516-84-14), both at Fiallo 102; Aeroméxico (☎ 511-50-44), Hidalgo 513; Aerovega (☎ 516-27-77), Hotel Monte Albán, Alameda de León 1; Aviacsa (☎ 514-51-87), Alcalá 501A; and Global Air (☎ 516-75-88), Morelos 701. Viajes Jalietza (☎ 516-47-11), at the corner of Murguía and Pino Suárez, also sells Global Air tickets.

Bus Approaching the city from the north, highway 135D takes a spectacular route through sparsely populated mountains in northern Oaxaca state.

The 1st-class bus station is at Calzada Niños Héroes de Chapultepec 1036, 1.5km northeast of the zócalo. It's used by UNO (deluxe service), ADO and Cristóbal Colón (deluxe or 1st-class service), and AU, Sur and Cuenca (2nd-class service). The 2nd-class bus station is about 1km west of the zócalo along Trujano or Las Casas; the main long-distance companies using this station are EV/OP, FYPSA and TOI. Unless otherwise noted, buses mentioned below use one of these two main bus stations.

It's advisable to book a day or two in advance for some of the less frequent services, such as the buses to San Cristóbal de

Las Casas and the better buses to the coast. Ticket Bus, at 20 de Noviembre 204 in the city center, sells tickets for UNO, ADO, Cristóbal Colón, AU and Sur buses from 9 am to 2 pm and 4 to 7 pm Monday to Saturday, 9 am to 3 pm Sunday.

Oaxaca Coast Some buses head down highway 175 through Miahuatlán and Pochutla; some go a longer way round by Salina Cruz then west along the coast; and a few 2nd-class buses take highway 131 (now all paved) direct to Puerto Escondido. To Pochutla (the jumping-off point for Puerto Ángel and nearby beaches), it's 245km and about 6½ hours by highway 175 (a spectacular, winding, downhill ride), or 455km and 8½ hours via Salina Cruz. Puerto Escondido is 65km (1½ hours) west of Pochutla.

Colón (1st-class) runs three times daily to Pochutla and Puerto Escondido (both US$12.50). One of these buses goes overnight by highway 175; the other two go by Salina Cruz and Bahías de Huatulco. Colón also runs one daily 'Plus' service to Bahías de Huatulco for US$16.

EV/OP (2nd-class) runs at least three *directos* and 10 *ordinarios* to Pochutla (US$5.50 to US$6.75) and Puerto Escondido (US$6.50 to US$7.50), and a 10 pm directo to Bahías de Huatulco (7½ hours, US$8). All go by highway 175. You can also catch the directos at a terminal at Armenta y López 721, 500m south of the zócalo.

Services to Puerto Escondido by highway 131, from the 2nd-class bus station, are by ERS (one '1st-class' at 10.45 pm for US$8; three 2nd-class for US$7) and La Solteca (three 2nd-class, US$7).

Other Destinations Other daily buses from Oaxaca include:

Mexico City (most to TAPO; a few to Terminal Sur or Terminal Norte) via highway 135D – 440km, 6½ hours; 6 UNO (US$33), 22 ADO (US$20 to US$23), 15 Colón (US$20 to US$23), 7 AU (US$18)

Mexico City via highway 131 – 450km, 9 hours; 6 AU, 3 Sur (US$16)

Puebla – 340km, 4½ hours; 9 ADO, 8 Colón (both US$15 to US$17.50), 9 FYPSA (US$10)

San Cristóbal de Las Casas – 625km, 12 hours; 2 Colón (US$19.50 to US$23)

Tehuantepec – 245km, 4½ hours; 13 Colón (US$8), many FYPSA, TOI (US$6)

Tuxtla Gutiérrez – 540km, 10 hours; 3 Colón (US$17.50 to US$21), several FYPSA, TOI (US$13.50)

Veracruz – 460km, 7 hours; 1 Colón (US$23), 2 ADO (US$19.50)

Villahermosa – 700km, 12 hours; 3 ADO (US$25)

Train The station (☎ 516-55-62) is at Calzada Madero 511, about 2km west of the zócalo. A train is scheduled to leave for Puebla at 7.20 am, arriving at 6.40 pm. One-way fare is US$7. The railroad takes a scenic backcountry route, winding through the Sierra Madre de Oaxaca.

Car & Motorcycle Car tolls from Mexico City to Oaxaca on highways 150D and 135D total US$24 (from Puebla, US$16); the trip takes about six hours. For some reason, the 135D is also numbered 131D for some stretches. The main toll-free alternative, via Izúcar de Matamoros and Huajuapan de León on highway 190, takes several hours longer.

The Oaxaca region Ángeles Verdes (Green Angels) can be reached at ☎ 516-38-10.

Rental The best deals we found for VW sedans were at Arrendadora Express (US$36 a day with insurance and unlimited kilometers) and Budget (US$45, or US$40 for cash). The airport desks may come up with offers. Arrendadora Express also rents motorcycles. Car rental agencies include the following:

Advantage Rent-A-Car
  (☎ 514-68-17) Berriozábal 309
Arrendadora Express
  (☎ 516-67-76) 20 de Noviembre 204
Budget
  (☎ 516-44-45) 5 de Mayo 315A
  (☎ 511-52-52) Airport
Hertz
  (☎ 516-24-34) Portal de Clavería on Valdivieso, just off the zócalo
  (☎ 516-00-09) Hotel Camino Real, 5 de Mayo 300
  (☎ 511-54-78) Airport

Getting Around

To/From the Airport Oaxaca airport is about 6km south of the city, 500m off highway 175. Transporte Terrestre *combis* from the airport will take you to anywhere in the city center for US$1.50 *colectivo*. A taxi costs about US$5.

You can book a colectivo seat from the city to the airport at Transportes Aeropuerto (☎ 516-27-77), Alameda de León 1G, facing the cathedral. You must pay one day or more ahead. It's open 9 am to 2 pm and 5 to 8 pm daily.

Bus Most points of importance in the city are within walking distance of each other, but you might want to use city buses (US$0.20) to and from the bus stations.

From outside the 1st-class bus station, a westbound 'Juárez' or 'Av Juárez' bus will take you down Juárez and Ocampo, three blocks east of the zócalo; a 'Tinoco y Palacios' bus will take you down Tinoco y Palacios, two blocks west of the zócalo. To return to the bus station from downtown, take an 'ADO' or 'Gigante' bus north up Xicoténcatl or Pino Suárez, four blocks east of the zócalo, or up Crespo three blocks west of the zócalo.

Buses between the 2nd-class bus station and the center pass slowly along congested streets, and it's almost as quick to walk. 'Centro' buses head toward the center along Trujano, then turn north up Díaz Ordaz and Crespo. Going out to the bus station, 'Central' buses head south on Tinoco y Palacios or JP García, then west on Las Casas.

Car & Motorcycle Several guarded parking lots lie around the city center. Estacionamiento Trujano, at Trujano 219, 1½ blocks west of the zócalo, is open 6 am to 11 pm daily. An overnight stay from 7 pm to 7 am is US$2.50.

Taxi A taxi anywhere within the central area, including the bus and train stations, costs US$1.25.

Bicycle You can rent mountain bikes for US$8 a day at Bicicletas Pedro Martínez (☎ 514-31-44), JP García 509. They offer

bike tours too (see Organized Tours, earlier). Arrendadora Express (see Car & Motorcycle) rents bikes in variable condition for US$5 a day.

Valles Centrales

Three valleys radiate from the city of Oaxaca: the Valle de Tlacolula, stretching 50km east; the Valle de Etla, reaching about 40km north; and the Valle de Zimatlán, stretching about 100km south.

In these Valles Centrales (Central Valleys), all within day-trip distance of Oaxaca city, you'll find pre-Hispanic ruins, craft-making villages and thronged country markets. The people are mostly Zapotec. The Oaxaca state tourism department, Sedetur, runs nine small self-catering units called *tourist yú'ùs* in the Valles Centrales. ('Yú'ù,' pronounced 'you,' means 'house' in the Zapotec language.) Most sleep about six people in bunks or on mattresses. Bedding, towels, showers and an equipped kitchen are provided. Cost is US$5 for one person or US$20 for a family of five or six. Some have space for camping at US$2.50 per person. It's advisable to book ahead, either at one of Oaxaca city's two main tourist offices (which can also give you information on the villages where the yú'ùs are) or by calling the individual yú'ù directly.

◗ Market Days

The markets are at their busiest in the morning, and most start to wind down in early afternoon. Here are the main ones:

Sunday – Tlacolula
Wednesday – San Pedro y San Pablo Etla
Thursday – Zaachila and Ejutla
Friday – Ocotlán and Santo Tomás Jalieza

Getting There & Away

Most of the places east of Oaxaca are on or within walking distance of the Oaxaca-Mitla road. TOI's buses to Mitla, every few minutes from Gate 9 of Oaxaca's 2nd-class bus station, will drop you anywhere along this road. South from Oaxaca, highway 175 goes

VALLES CENTRALES

To Santiago Suchilquitongo
MEX 135D
San José el Mogote
Guadalupe Etla
Valle de Etla
To Huajuapan, Tehuacán, Puebla
MEX 190
To Guelatao, Ixtlán, Tuxtepec
MEX 175
La Tuvi
Cuajimoloyas
Benito Juárez
0   5   10 km
0   3   6 miles
San Felipe del Agua
Atzompa
Oaxaca
Cerro El Bonete
Monte Albán
Arrazola
El Tule
Santa Cruz Xoxocatlán
Lachigoló
Teotitlán del Valle
MEX 190
Airport
San Sebastián Abasolo
Santa Ana del Valle
Villa Díaz Ordaz
Cuilapan
Santa Cruz Papalutla
Tlacochahuaya
Dainzú
Valle de Zimatlán
San Bartolo Coyotepec
Valle de Tlacolula
Lambityeco
Yagul
Zaachila
Tlacolula
Mitla
To Ayutla, Zacatepec
MEX 179
San Marcos Tlapazola
San Lucas Quiavini
Mitla
San Lorenzo Albarradas
MEX 131
MEX 135
San Bartolomé Quialana
Xaagá
Zimatlán
San Martín Tilcajete
Santo Tomás Jalieza
Hierve El Agua
San Pablo Huixtepec
MEX 190
To Ejutla, Miahuatlán, San José del Pacífico, Pochutla
To Tehuantepec
Ocotlán

OAXACA STATE

through San Bartolo Coyotepec, Ocotlán, Ejutla and Miahuatlán. Separate roads go to Monte Albán and to Cuilapan and Zaachila. Further details on bus services are given under the individual sites and villages.

An alternative to traveling by bus – though it will cost you twice as much (still cheap!) – is to take a colectivo taxi. These run to places north of Oaxaca (such as Atzompa and San José el Mogote) from the street on the north side of the 2nd-class bus station; and to places east, south and south-west (including El Tule, Teotitlán del Valle, San Bartolo Coyotepec, Ocotlán, Arrazola, Cuilapan and Zaachila) from Prolongación Victoria just east of the Central de Abastos market. They leave when they're full (five or six people).

MONTE ALBÁN
☎ 9

The ancient Zapotec capital Monte Albán ('MONH-teh ahl-BAHN,' meaning White

Mountain) stands on a flattened hilltop, 400m above the valley floor, just a few kilometers west of Oaxaca. The views from here are spectacular.

History
The site was first occupied around 500 BC, probably by Zapotecs from the outset. It probably had early cultural connections with the Olmecs to the northeast.

Archaeologists divide Monte Albán's history into five phases. The years up to about 200 BC (Monte Albán I) saw the leveling of the hilltop, the building of temples and probably palaces, and the growth of a town of 10,000 or more people on the hillsides. Between 200 BC and about 300 AD (Monte Albán II) the city came to dominate more and more of Oaxaca. Buildings were typically made of huge stone blocks and had steep walls.

The city was at its peak from about 300 to 700 AD (Monte Albán III), when the main and surrounding hills were terraced for dwellings, and the population reached about 25,000. Most of what we see now dates from this time. Monte Albán was the center of a highly organized, priest-dominated society. Many buildings were plastered and painted red, and *talud-tablero* architecture indicates influence from Teotihuacán. Nearly 170 underground tombs from this period have been found, some of them elaborate and decorated with frescoes. The Valles Centrales were extensively irrigated and held at least 200 other settlements and ceremonial centers. Monte Albán's people ate tortillas, beans, squashes, chilies, avocados and other vegetarian fare, plus sometimes deer, rabbit and dog.

Between about 700 and 950 AD (Monte Albán IV), the place was abandoned and fell into ruin. Zapotec life centered on other places in the Valles Centrales. Monte Albán V (950 to 1521) saw minimal activity, but Mixtecs arriving in the Valles Centrales reused old tombs they found here to bury their own dignitaries.

Danzantes at Monte Albán

Information

The site (☎ 516-12-15) is open 8 am to 6 pm daily (US$2, free on Sunday). At the entrance are a worthwhile museum (with explanations in Spanish only), a cafeteria and a good bookstore. It's worth asking at the ticket office which tombs are open, since many main ones often aren't. Official guides offer their services outside the ticket office (around US$7 for a small group).

Gran Plaza

The Gran Plaza, about 300m long and 200m wide, was the center of Monte Albán. Its visible structures are mostly from the peak Monte Albán III period. Some were temples, others residential. The following description takes you clockwise around the plaza.

The stone terraces of the deep, I-shaped **Juego de Pelota** (Ball Court) were probably part of the playing area, not stands for spectators. The round stone in the middle may have been used for bouncing the ball at the start of the game.

The **Pirámide** – Edificio P – was topped by a small pillared temple. From the altar in front of the pyramid came a well-known jade bat-god mask, now in the Museo Nacional de Antropología.

The **Palacio** (Palace) has a broad stairway and, on top, a patio surrounded by the remains of typical Monte Albán III residential rooms. Under the patio is a cross-shaped tomb, probably from Monte Albán IV.

The big **Plataforma Sur** (South Platform), with its wide staircase, is good for a panorama of the plaza.

Edificio J, an arrowhead-shaped Monte Albán II building riddled with tunnels and staircases (unfortunately you can't go in), stands at an angle of 45 degrees to the other Gran Plaza structures and is believed to have been an observatory. Figures and hieroglyphs carved on its walls probably record military conquests.

The front of **Sistema M**, dating from Monte Albán III, was added, like the front of Sistema IV, to an earlier structure in an apparent attempt to conceal the plaza's lack of symmetry. (The rock mounds supporting

MONTE ALBÁN

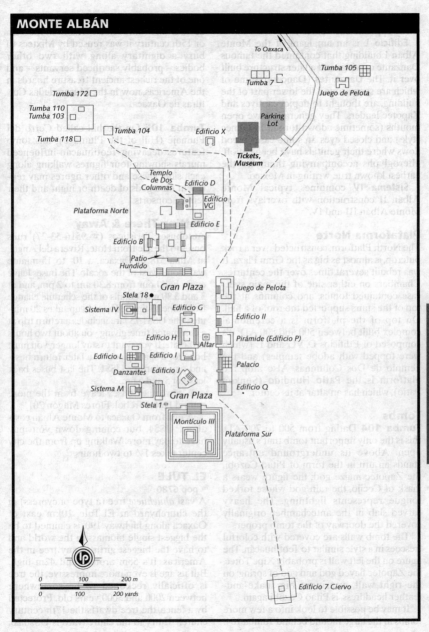

To Oaxaca

Tumba 105

Tumba 7

Juego de Pelota

Tumba 172

Tumba 110
Tumba 103

Tumba 104

Tumba 118

Edificio X

Parking Lot

Tickets, Museum

Templo de Dos Columnas

Edificio D

Edificio VG

Plataforma Norte

Edificio E

Edificio B

Patio Hundido

Gran Plaza

Juego de Pelota

Stela 18

Sistema IV

Edificio G

Edificio II

Edificio H

Pirámide (Edificio P)

Altar

Edificio L

Edificio I

Palacio

Danzantes

Edificio J

Edificio Q

Sistema M

Gran Plaza

Stela 1

Montículo III

Plataforma Sur

Edificio 7 Ciervo

0   100   200 m
0   100   200 yards

the south and north platforms are not directly opposite each other.)

Edificio L is an amalgam of the Monte Albán I building that contained the famous Danzante carvings and a later structure built over it. The **Danzantes** (Dancers), some of which are seen around the lower part of the building, are thought to depict captives and Zapotec leaders. They generally have open mouths (sometimes down-turned in Olmec style) and closed eyes. In some cases blood flows where their genitals have been cut off. Hieroglyphs accompanying them are the earliest known true writing in Mexico.

Sistema IV combines typical Monte Albán II construction with overlays from Monte Albán III and IV.

Plataforma Norte

The North Platform, constructed over a rock outcrop, is almost as big as the Gran Plaza. It was rebuilt several times over the centuries. Chambers on either side of the main staircase contained tombs, and columns at the top of the stairs supported the roof of a hall. On top of the platform is a ceremonial complex built between 500 and 800 AD; it's composed of Edificios D, VG and E (which were topped with adobe temples) and the Templo de Dos Columnas. Also atop the platform is the **Patio Hundido** (Sunken Patio), which has an altar at its center.

Tombs

Tumba 104 Dating from 500 to 700 AD, this is the only important tomb that's usually open. Above its underground entrance stands an urn in the form of Pitao Cozobi, the Zapotec maize god; the figure wears a mask of Cocijo, the rain god whose forked tongue represents lightning. The heavy carved slab in the antechamber originally covered the doorway of the tomb proper.

The tomb walls are covered with colorful frescoes in a style similar to Teotihuacán. The figure on the left wall is probably Xipe Tótec, the Zapotec flayed god and god of spring; on the right wall, wearing a big snake-and-feather headdress, is Pitao Cozobi again.

It may be possible to look into a few more tombs in the large mound behind Tumba 104.

Tumba 7 This tomb, just off the parking lot, dates from Monte Albán III, but in the 14th or 15th century it was reused by Mixtecs to bury a dignitary along with two other bodies – probably sacrificed servants – and one of the richest ancient treasure hoards in the Americas, now in the Museo de las Culturas de Oaxaca.

Tumba 105 On the hill called Cerro del Plumaje (Hill of the Plumage), this tomb features decaying Teotihuacán-influenced murals showing four figures walking along each side. These and other figures may represent nine gods of death or night and their female consorts.

Getting There & Away

Autobuses Turísticos (☎ 9516-53-27) runs buses to the site from Hotel Rivera del Ángel, at Mina 518 in Oaxaca, a 10- to 15-minute walk southwest of the zócalo. The buses leave every half hour from 8.30 am to 2 pm, and at 3 and 3.30 pm (details of the schedule change from time to time). The ride up takes 20 minutes. The US$1.75 fare includes a return trip at a designated time, giving you about two hours at the site. If you want to stay longer, you must hope for a spare place on a later return bus – and pay a further US$1. The last buses back leave at 5 and 6 pm.

A few other buses leave from the more central Hotel Trébol, Flores Magón 201.

A taxi from Oaxaca to Monte Albán costs about US$4, but coming down you may have to pay more. Walking up from the city center takes 1½ to two hours.

EL TULE
• pop 6780

A vast *ahuehuete* tree (a type of cypress) in the churchyard at El Tule, 10km east of Oaxaca along highway 190, is claimed to be the biggest single biomass in the world and to have the biggest girth of any tree in the Americas. It's 58m around and 42m high. But its age is even more impressive; the tree is officially reckoned to be somewhere between 2000 and 3000 years old. Protected by a fence, the tree dwarfs the 17th-century church. Entry to the churchyard is US$0.20.

Long revered by Oaxacans, the mighty Árbol del Tule has come under threat from new industries and housing nearby, which tap the tree's water sources. Campaigners argue that the only long-term solution is full protection of the 110-sq-km basin from which the tree's water is drawn, in combination with a more sustainable level of local development.

AVN buses go to El Tule every 10 minutes (US$0.30) from the 2nd-class bus station in Oaxaca.

DAINZÚ

Twenty-one kilometers from Oaxaca along the Mitla road, a track leads 1km south to the small but interesting ruins of Dainzú, open 8 am to 6 pm daily (US$1, free on Sunday and holidays).

To the left as you approach is the pyramid-like Edificio A, 50m long and 8m high, built about 300 BC. Along its bottom wall are a number of engravings similar to the Monte Albán Danzantes. They nearly all show ballplayers – each with a mask or protective headgear and a ball in the right hand.

Among the ruins below Edificio A are, to the right as you look down, a sunken tomb with its entrance carved in the form of a crouching jaguar and, to the left, a partly restored ball court from about 1000 AD. At the top of the hill behind the site are more rock carvings similar to the ballplayers, but it's a stiff climb, and you'd probably need a guide to find them.

TEOTITLÁN DEL VALLE
• pop 4550

This famous weaving village is 4km north of highway 190, about 25km from Oaxaca. Blankets, rugs and sarapes wave at you from houses and showrooms along the road into the village (which becomes Avenida Juárez as it approaches the center), and signs point to the central **Mercado de Artesanías**, where hundreds more are on sale. The variety of designs is enormous – from Zapotec gods and Mitla-style geometric patterns to imitations of paintings by Rivera, Picasso and Escher.

The weaving tradition here goes back to pre-Hispanic times: Teotitlán had to pay

tributes of cloth to the Aztecs. Quality is still very high in many cases, and traditional dyes made from cochineal, indigo and moss have been revived. Many shops have weavers at work. Teotitlán's most celebrated weaver, Arnulfo Mendoza (born 1954), sells work for thousands of dollars (you can see fine examples in his shop La Mano Mágica in Oaxaca) and now has a large house overlooking the north end of Teotitlán.

Facing the Mercado de Artesanías on the central plaza is the **Museo Comunitario Balaa Xtee Guech Gulal**, open 10 am to 6 pm daily except Monday (US$0.50), with local archaeological finds and material on textile crafts and local traditions. From the plaza, steps rise to a fine broad churchyard with the handsome 17th-century **Templo de la Preciosa Sangre de Cristo** in one corner. The village's regular market, open daily, is behind the top of the churchyard.

Places to Stay & Eat

A *tourist yú'ù* lies on the approach to the village, 500m off the highway – not very convenient to the village, which is 3km farther on. *Restaurante Tlamanalli* (*Avenida Juárez 39*), open daily except Monday for lunch only, serves excellent oaxaqueña food – the chicken in mole negro is about US$6. Exhibits on weaving add to the interest.

Getting There & Away

AVN buses run on the hour daily (except Sunday) to Teotitlán (50 minutes, US$0.40) from Gate 29 at Oaxaca's 2nd-class bus station; the last bus back from the village leaves about 7 pm. Or get any bus to the signposted Teotitlán turnoff on highway 190, then a colectivo taxi (US$0.20) to the village.

BENITO JUÁREZ
• pop 470 • elev 2750m ☎ 9

Up in the refreshing, pine-forested mountains some 20km north of Teotitlán by dirt road, Benito Juárez is one of the most attractive *tourist yú'ù* villages, good for walks and bike rides (US$8 for a three-hour guided ride). In the village center you'll find

OAXACA STATE

Community Museums of Oaxaca

One of the most exciting tourism initiatives in Mexico in recent years is the Museos Comunitarios del Estado de Oaxaca (Community Museums of Oaxaca State) program. About 15 villages, mostly in the Valles Centrales and in the Mixteca in the west of the state, have set up their own community museums, with displays on local crafts, festivals, archaeology and traditions. One of their goals is to help preserve the villages' unique local cultures.

Organized around these museums is a fascinating visitors' program of tours from Oaxaca out to the villages, where villagers act as guides. Each tour typically includes a visit to a community museum, lunch with a village family, local activities (such as horse or bicycle rides, or walks to little-known archaeological sites or natural features) and demonstrations of craft, cooking or agricultural techniques. You might also talk with community leaders or *curanderas* (traditional medicine practitioners), visit schools or participate in local festivals. You'll get inside, firsthand experience of village life through the kind of contact with villagers that can be hard to achieve if you wander in unknown and unannounced or go with an outside tour agency. On a visit to Teotitlán del Valle, for instance, we climbed Cerro de Picacho and found it littered with pieces of pre-Hispanic pottery which, without our local guide, we wouldn't have recognized in a million years; we met and watched an extremely skillful practitioner of the little-known craft of making wax flowers for weddings; and we enjoyed a traditional local lunch in our guide's home, with an aperitif of his extremely smooth mezcal!

You can rest happy in the knowledge that the money you pay for your trip will go directly to the villages, not to intermediaries.

Groups of one to 10 people can usually arrange a tour with one day's notice. Book by 2 pm in Oaxaca city at the Museos Comunitarios office (☎/fax 9-516-57-86, muscoax@antequera.com), Depto (Office) No 12, Calle Tinoco y Palacios 311. Prices on most trips range from US$13 to US$26 per person, depending on how many are in the group. For an English-speaking guide, you may need to ask a few days ahead.

The most commonly visited villages are Teotitlán del Valle and nearby Santa Ana del Valle, both well known for weaving. Other destinations include: San José el Mogote, in the Valle de Etla, with its special archaeological heritage; San Martín Huamelulpan, in the Mixteca, where visits include chats with a curandera; and Santa María Cuquila, also in the Mixteca, where you can join a 1½-hour walk to an attractive *zona arqueológica*.

You can get plenty of additional information by looking at the community museums' website, http://antequera.com/muscoax.

an information office and a good comedor serving home-style fare for all three meals at next-to-nothing prices. The well-run yú'ù, a little downhill from here, has room for 14 people in bunks and double rooms. Comfortable *cabañas* for up to four people, with bathrooms and kitchens, are available at the same price (US$5 per person). Call the village information office (☎ 514-18-71) for reservations (worthwhile on weekends and holidays, as it's a popular spot). A 2.5km walk away is El Mirador, a lookout at 3000m with great views. In the village is the 17th-century Templo de la Asunción (Church of the Assumption), beside which a Sunday market is held.

Benito Juárez is the usual starting point for the mountain bike tours of the sierras to the north offered by Expediciones Sierra Norte de Oaxaca (see the later Northern Oaxaca section).

Getting There & Away

Several daily Flecha de Zempoaltépetl buses from Oaxaca's 2nd-class bus station to various destinations, including Cuajimoloyas, Villa Alta and Yalalag, will drop you at the 'desviación de Benito Juárez' (turnoff for Benito Juárez), 3.5km east of the village and 1¾ hours from Oaxaca. Most buses leave between 6 and 10 am. Service to Benito Juárez itself is offered by Transportes Ya'a-Yana; buses leave from next to the gas station on Calle Niño Perdido, Colonia Ixcotel in Oaxaca, at 4 pm Tuesday, Friday and Saturday. These buses leave Benito Juárez for Oaxaca at 6 am on the same days – check the latest schedule by ringing the village's information office.

LAMBITYECO

This small archaeological site is on the south side of the Mitla road, 29km from Oaxaca. Between 600 and 800 AD, Lambityeco seems to have become a sizable Zapotec center of about 3000 people. Its residents may later have moved to Yagul, a more defensible site.

The interest here lies in two patios. In the first are two carved stone friezes, each showing a bearded man holding a bone (a symbol of hereditary rights) and a woman with Zapotec hairstyle. Both of the couples that are represented, plus a third in stucco on a tomb in the patio, are thought to have occupied the building around the patio and to have ruled Lambityeco in the 7th century.

The second patio has two heads of the rain god Cocijo. On one, a big headdress spreading above Cocijo's stern face forms the face of a jaguar. Lambityeco is open 8 am to 6 pm daily (US$1, free on Sunday and holidays).

TLACOLULA
• pop 10,700

Two kilometers beyond Lambityeco and 31km from Oaxaca, this town holds one of the Valles Centrales' major markets every Sunday, when the area around the church becomes a packed throng. Teotitlán blankets are among the many goods sold.

The church was one of several founded in Oaxaca by Dominican monks. Inside, the domed 16th-century Capilla del Santo Cristo is a riot of golden, indigenous-influenced decoration comparable with the Capilla del Rosario in Santo Domingo,

Oaxaca. Martyrs can be seen carrying their heads under their arms.

Frequent TOI and FYPSA buses run here from Oaxaca's 2nd-class bus station (one hour, US$0.80).

SANTA ANA DEL VALLE
• pop 2150

Four kilometers north of Tlacolula, Santa Ana del Valle is another village whose textile tradition predates the Spanish. Today it produces woolen blankets, sarapes and bags. Natural dyes have been revived, and traditional designs – flowers, birds, geometric patterns – are still in use. Prices in the cooperatively run **Mercado de Artesanías**, on the main plaza, are considerably lower than in Teotitlán del Valle or Oaxaca shops. Also on the plaza are the richly decorated 17th-century **Templo de Santa Ana** and the **Museo Comunitario Shan-Dany**, which has exhibits on local textiles, history and the Zapotec Danza de las Plumas – it's open 10 am to 2 pm and 3 to 6 pm daily. The village also has a few textile shops and workshops open to visitors.

A **tourist yú'ù** is on the approach road about half a kilometer from the village center. You can arrange guided horseback or bicycle rides there. Buses and minibuses run frequently from Tlacolula.

YAGUL

The ruins of Yagul are finely sited on a cactus-covered hill, 1.5km up a paved approach from the Oaxaca-Mitla road. The signposted turnoff is 34km from Oaxaca. The site is open 8 am to 5 pm daily (US$1.50, free Sunday and holidays).

Yagul was a leading Valles Centrales settlement after the decline of Monte Albán. Most of what's visible was built after 750 AD, probably by Zapotecs with Mixtec influence.

Patio 4 was surrounded by four temples. On the east side is a carved-stone animal, probably a jaguar. Next to the central platform is the entrance to one of several underground **Tumbas Triples** (Triple Tombs). Steps go down to a tiny court, with three tombs off of it.

The beautiful **Juego de Pelota** (Ball Court) is the second biggest in Mesoamerica

OAXACA STATE

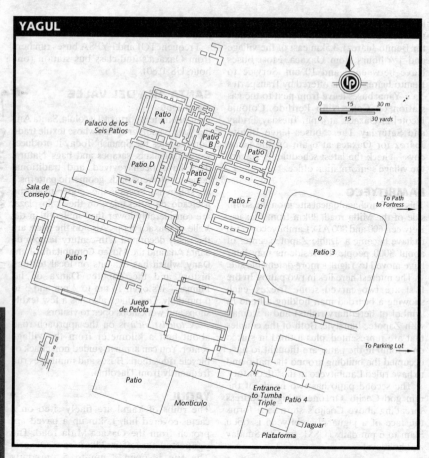

YAGUL

Palacio de los
Seis Patios

Patio
A

Patio
B

Patio
C

Patio D

Patio
E

Patio F

Sala de
Consejo

To Path
to Fortress

Patio 1

Patio 3

Juego
de Pelota

To Parking Lot

Patio

Monticulo

Entrance
to Tumba
Triple   Patio 4

Jaguar

Plataforma

0   15   30 m
0   15   30 yards

(after one at Chichén Itzá). To its west, on the edge of the hill, is **Patio 1**, with the narrow **Sala de Consejo** (Council Hall) along its north side. Behind the hall is a pathway with Mitla-style stone mosaics.

The labyrinthine **Palacio de los Seis Patios** (Palace of the Six Patios) was probably the leader's residence. Its walls were plastered and painted red.

It's well worth climbing the **Fortress**, the huge rock that towers above the ruins. The path passes **Tumba 28**, made of cut stone. From the top of the Fortress the views are great. On the north side is a sheer drop of 100m or more. Several overgrown ruins perch up here.

MITLA
● **pop 7320 ☎ 9**

The pre-Hispanic stone 'mosaics' of Mitla, 46km southeast of Oaxaca, are unique in Mexico. There's little special, however, about the modern Zapotec town in which they stand.

History

The ruins we see today date almost entirely from the last two or three centuries before the Spanish conquest. At that time, Mitla was probably the main Zapotec religious center, dominated by high priests who performed literally heart-wrenching human sacrifices. Evidence points to a short period of Mixtec domination at Mitla in the 14th century, followed by a Zapotec reassertion before the Aztecs arrived in 1494. Somewhere beneath the town may be a great undiscovered tomb of Zapotec kings and heroes; the 17th-century monk Francisco de Burgoa wrote that Spanish priests found it but sealed it up.

It's thought that each group of buildings we see at Mitla was reserved for specific occupants – one for the high priest, one for lesser priests, one for the king and so forth.

Orientation & Information
If you tell the bus conductor from Oaxaca that you're heading for *las ruinas*, you should be dropped at a junction at the entry to the town, where you go left up to the

central plaza. For the ruins, continue through the plaza toward the three-domed Iglesia de San Pablo, 850m farther on. The ticket office is behind this church. The site is open 8 am to 6 pm daily (US$1.50, free on Sunday and holidays).

Grupo de las Columnas
This, the major group of buildings, is just south of the Iglesia de San Pablo. It has two main patios, each lined on three sides by long rooms. Along the north side of the Patio Norte is the **Sala de las Columnas** (Hall of the Columns), 38m long with six thick columns. At one end of this hall, a passage leads to the additional **Patio de Mosaicos** (Patio of the Mosaics), with some of Mitla's best stonework. Each little piece of stone was cut to fit the design, then set in mortar on the walls and painted. The 14 different geometrical designs at Mitla are thought to symbolize the sky, earth, feathered serpent and other important cultural

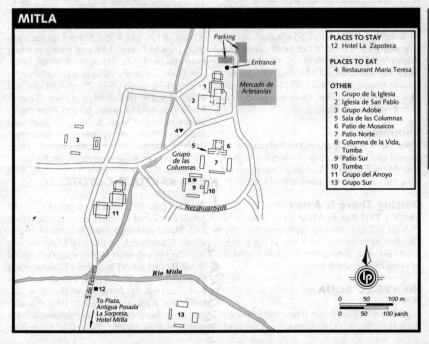

MITLA

PLACES TO STAY
12 Hotel La Zapoteca

PLACES TO EAT
4 Restaurant María Teresa

OTHER
1 Grupo de la Iglesia
2 Iglesia de San Pablo
3 Grupo Adobe
5 Sala de las Columnas
6 Patio de Mosaicos
7 Patio Norte
8 Columna de la Vida, Tumba
9 Patio Sur
10 Tumba
11 Grupo del Arroyo
13 Grupo Sur

Parking
Entrance
Mercado de Artesanías
Grupo de las Columnas
Nezahualcóyotl
Río Mitla
5 de Febrero
To Plaza, Antigua Posada La Sorpresa, Hotel Mitla

0   50   100 m
0   50   100 yards

OAXACA STATE

icons. Many Mitla buildings were also adorned with painted friezes.

In the Patio Sur are two underground tombs. The one on the north side contains the so-called **Columna de la Vida** (Column of Life) – if you put your arms around it, the number of hand widths between your fingertips is supposed (absurdly) to measure how many years' life you have left.

Other Groups

The **Grupo de la Iglesia** is in similar style to the Grupo de las Columnas but less well preserved. The church was built on top of one of the group's patios in 1590. The **Grupo del Arroyo** is the most substantial of the other, unexcavated groups. The remains of forts, tombs and other structures are scattered over the country for many kilometers around.

Places to Stay & Eat

Antigua Posada La Sorpresa, just off the town plaza, serves breakfast and a substantial US$5 comida corrida. Across the street, the very basic but friendly *Hotel Mitla* (☎ 568-01-12) has fanless singles/doubles with lumpy beds for US$6/9 and serves straightforward food at low prices. *Hotel La Zapoteca* (5 de Febrero 8), between the plaza and the ruins, is less friendly, with bare, fanless rooms for US$12.50/15. *Restaurant María Teresa*, near the ruins, has good food at reasonable prices.

Shopping

Mitla's streets are spattered with shops selling mezcal and textiles, many of them made in or near Mitla. The large Mercado de Artesanías near the ruins has the same sort of stuff.

Getting There & Away

Catch a TOI bus to Mitla from Gate 9 of Oaxaca's 2nd-class bus station (US$0.90). The last 4km to the town are along a side road east off highway 190. The last bus back to Oaxaca is about 8 pm.

HIERVE EL AGUA

☎ 9

Highway 179 heads east from Mitla up into the hills. Nineteen kilometers out, a signpost points to the right to San Lorenzo Albarradas, 3km away. Six kilometers past San Lorenzo is Hierve El Agua ('The Water Boils'). Here mineral springs run into icy-cold clifftop bathing pools with expansive panoramas. This cliff and another nearby are encrusted with petrified minerals, giving them the appearance of huge frozen waterfalls – altogether it's one of the most unusual bathing experiences you'll ever have. The waters here were used for irrigation as long ago as 1300 BC.

Hierve El Agua is a popular oaxaqueño weekend excursion. Above the pools and cliffs are a number of comedores, and a good *tourist yú'ù* (☎ 562-09-22) and six similar cottages (some without kitchens) at the same prices.

The area is dotted with maguey fields; San Lorenzo Albarradas, nearby San Juan del Río and the other 'Albarradas' villages produce some of Oaxaca's finest mezcal. There's reportedly a good walk from just south of San Lorenzo Albarradas west over the hills to Xaagá and Mitla – ask about it in town.

Viajes Turísticos Mitla, at the Hotel Rivera del Ángel, Mina 518 in Oaxaca, runs daily trips to Hierve El Agua, giving you two hours there (US$2.50 return). FYPSA buses run from Oaxaca's 2nd-class bus station to Hierve El Agua (US$1.75) at 8.10 am and 1 pm Monday to Saturday, passing through Mitla one to 1¼ hours later. Other buses from Oaxaca or Mitla heading for places up highway 179 such as Ayutla or Zacatepec will drop you at the San Lorenzo turnoff, from which you can walk or perhaps hitchhike.

SAN BARTOLO COYOTEPEC

• pop 2720

All the polished, black, surprisingly light pottery you find around Oaxaca comes from San Bartolo Coyotepec, a small village about 12km south of the city. Look for the signs to the *alfarería* (pottery workshop) of Doña Rosa, east off highway 175, open 9 am to 6.30 pm daily. Several village families make and sell the *barro negro* (black ware), but it was Rosa Real Mateo (1900-80) who invented the method of burnishing it with quartz stones for the distinctive shine. The pieces are hand-molded by an age-old technique in which two saucers are used as a rudimentary potter's wheel. Then they are fired in pit kilns; they turn black because of the iron oxide in the local clay and because smoke is trapped in the kiln.

The village also has a market where black ware is sold. Buses run to San Bartolo (US$0.50) every few minutes from a small terminal at Armenta y López 721, 500m south of the Oaxaca zócalo.

SAN MARTÍN TILCAJETE & SANTO TOMÁS JALIEZA
San Martín: • pop 1650
Santo Tomás: • pop 860
San Martín Tilcajete, just west of highway 175 about 27km south of Oaxaca, is the source of many of the bright copal alebrijes (animal figures) seen in Oaxaca. You can see and buy them in makers' houses.

Santo Tomás Jalieza, just east of highway 175 a couple of kilometers farther south, holds a textiles market on Friday to coincide with the Ocotlán market. Women weave high-quality textiles on back-strap looms here, and their cotton waist sashes have pretty animal or plant designs. Colectivo taxis run from Ocotlán.

OCOTLÁN
• pop 11,500
The big, bustling Friday market at Ocotlán, 32km south of Oaxaca, dates back to pre-Hispanic times. Ocotlán's most renowned artisans are the four Aguilar sisters and their families, who create whimsical, colorful pottery figures of women with all sorts of unusual motifs. The Aguilars' houses are together by the highway before you get into the town center – spot them by the pottery women on the wall. Most renowned are Guillermina Aguilar and her family, at Prolongación de Morelos 430, who turn out, among other things, miniature Frida Kahlos.

Ocotlán is also the hometown of artist Rodolfo Morales (born 1925), who has turned his international success to Ocotlán's benefit by setting up the Fundación Cultural Rodolfo Morales. Aside from providing the town with its first ambulance, establishing a computer center and planting 3500 jacaranda trees between Ocotlán and San Martín Tilcajete, the Morales foundation has renovated Ocotlán's handsome 16th-century Dominican church and is turning the dilapidated neighboring ex-convent, formerly a jail, into a museum of popular and religious art, with a restaurant.

Buses to Ocotlán (45 minutes, US$0.80) leave every few minutes from the terminal at Armenta y López 721 in Oaxaca.

SAN JOSÉ DEL PACÍFICO
San José, about an hour south of Miahuatlán on highway 175 to Pochutla, is not actually in the Valles Centrales but well worth considering for a night or two out of Oaxaca or a stop en route to the coast. It's most famed for its magic mushrooms but is also a good base for walks through the cool mountain pine forests. *Cabañas y Restaurante Puesta del Sol*, by the highway about 500m north of the village, has cabañas and rooms with bath for US$10 to US$15 for two to four people. You can contact it via the village telephone caseta (☎ 9-572-01-11). All buses between Oaxaca and Pochutla stop at San José.

ARRAZOLA
• pop 980
Below the west side of Monte Albán and about 4km off the Cuilapan road, Arrazola produces many of the colorful copal alebrijes that are sold in Oaxaca. You can see and buy them in artisans' homes.

CUILAPAN
• pop 11,200
Cuilapan, 12km southwest of Oaxaca, is one of the few Mixtec enclaves in the Valles Centrales. It's the site of a beautiful, historic Dominican monastery, the **Ex-Convento de Santiago Apóstol** (open 8 am to 6 pm daily, US$1). Construction of the monastery began in about 1555, and its pale stone seems almost to grow out of the land.

In 1831 the Mexican independence hero Vicente Guerrero was executed at the monastery by soldiers supporting the rebel conservative Anastasio Bustamante, who had just deposed the liberal Guerrero from

OAXACA STATE

the Mexican presidency. Guerrero fled by ship from Acapulco, but the ship's captain betrayed him to the rebels at Huatulco. Guerrero was transported to Cuilapan to die.

From the monastery entrance you first reach a long, low, unfinished church that has stood roofless since work on it stopped in 1560. Beyond is the church that succeeded it. Around its right-hand end you reach the two-story Renaissance-style cloister, whose rear rooms have some 16th- and 17th-century murals. A painting of Guerrero hangs in the room where he was held, and outside, a monument stands where he was shot.

The main church is usually closed, but is said to contain the Christian tombs of Juana Donají (daughter of Cocijo-eza, the last Zapotec king of Zaachila) and her Mixtec husband.

Frequent Autobuses de Oaxaca buses from Oaxaca's 2nd-class bus station (US$0.30) stop right by the monastery.

ZAACHILA
• pop 11,800

This part-Mixtec, part-Zapotec village, 6km beyond Cuilapan, has a busy Thursday market. At Carnaval time Zaachila is the scene of a mock battle in which masked priests use crosses and buckets of water to defend themselves from whip-wielding devils. Zaachila was a Zapotec capital from about 1400 until the Spanish conquest, though under Mixtec control for some of that period. Its last Zapotec king, Cocijoeza, became a Christian with the name Juan Cortés and died in 1523. Six pre-Hispanic monoliths and the village church stand on the main plaza.

Tombs

Up the road behind the church, then up a path to the right marked 'Zona Arqueológica,' are mounds containing at least two tombs used by the ancient Mixtecs. In one of them, Tumba 2, was found a Mixtec treasure hoard comparable with that of Tumba 7 at Monte Albán. It's now in the Museo Nacional de Antropología in Mexico City. The famous Mexican archaeologists Alfonso

Caso and Ignacio Bernal were forced to flee by irate Zaacilans when they tried to excavate the tombs in the 1940s and 1950s. Roberto Gallegos excavated them under armed guard in 1962.

The tombs are supposed to be open 8 am to 6 pm daily (US$1, free on Sunday and holidays), but they may not be. Ask in the Palacio Municipal on the village plaza if you can't find anyone to help you. Market day is probably the best day to try.

Getting There & Away

Autobuses de Oaxaca run frequently to Zaachila (US$0.30) from Oaxaca's 2nd-class bus station.

ATZOMPA
• pop 9180

Atzompa, 6km northwest of Oaxaca, is a village with many potters. A lot of their very attractive, often colorful work is sold at excellent prices in the **Mercado de Artesanías**, Avenida Libertad 303, on the main road entering the village from Oaxaca. This market is open daily and has a restaurant.

From the church up in the village center, a 2.5km road (mostly dirt) leads south up **Cerro El Bonete**. The road ends a few minutes' walk from the top of the hill, which is dotted with unrestored pre-Hispanic ruins.

Getting There & Away

Choferes del Sur, at gate 39 of Oaxaca's 2nd-class bus station, runs buses every few minutes to Atzompa. In your own vehicle, follow Calzada Madero northwest out of downtown Oaxaca, turn left along Masseu (signposted 'Monte Albán') at a big intersection on the fringe of town, then go right at traffic signals after 1.5km.

SAN JOSÉ EL MOGOTE

Fourteen kilometers northwest of central Oaxaca on highway 190, a westward turnoff signposted to Guadalupe Etla leads about 2km to San José el Mogote, a tiny village indicated by a 'Museo Comunitario Ex-Hacienda El Cacique' sign. Mogote was the major pre-Hispanic center in the Valle de Etla and the major settlement in Oaxaca before Monte Albán. It peaked between 650 and 500 BC and flourished again between 100 BC and 150 AD. Its main plaza was almost as big as Monte Alban's. The major surviving structures (partly restored) are a ball court and a sizable pyramid-mound on the village periphery. The interesting community museum is in the former landowner's hacienda, in the village center; it's officially open 9 am to 6 pm daily (US$0.80). If it's closed, ask in the little store opposite for someone to find the keeper. A highlight of the museum is 'El Diablo Enchilado' (the Chilied Devil), a red pre-Hispanic brazier in the form of a grimacing face. The museum also has interesting material on the villagers' 20th-century struggle for land ownership.

Buses to Mogote leave from Oaxaca's Periférico ring road, near the 2nd-class bus station. Easier is a colectivo taxi (see the Valles Centrales introductory Getting There & Away section).

Mixteca Alta & Mixteca Baja

The Mixteca (Mixtec region) of western Oaxaca comprises three areas. The Mixteca Baja (Low Mixteca; altitude 1000m to 1700m) spills over from Oaxaca's northwest borderlands, around Huajuapan de León, into Puebla state. The Mixteca Alta (High Mixteca, mostly above 2000m) is the rugged area between the Mixteca Baja and the Valles Centrales. The Mixteca de la Costa (Coastal Mixteca) is a remote zone of southwestern Oaxaca stretching back up into the hills from the coast.

It was from the Mixteca Alta in about the 12th century that Mixtec dominance began to spread to the Valles Centrales. The Mixtecs were famed workers of gold and precious stones, and it's said the Aztec emperor Moctezuma would eat only off their fine Mixteca-Puebla ceramics. The Mixteca Alta and Baja were subjugated by the Aztecs in the 15th century.

Today much of the Mixteca is over-farmed, eroded and deforested, and politics and business are dominated by mestizos. Many Mixtecs have to emigrate for work. Foreign visitors are rather a rarity here. ATMs are available in Tlaxiaco and Putla.

Things to See & Do
The beautiful 16th-century Dominican monasteries in the Mixteca Alta villages of Yanhuitlán, Coixtlahuaca and Teposcolula are among colonial Mexico's finest architecture. Their restrained stonework fuses medieval, plateresque, Renaissance and indigenous styles.

The monastery in **Coixtlahuaca**, 2km off highway 135D and about 115km from Oaxaca, is perhaps the most beautiful of the group. Beside its church stands a graceful, ruined *capilla abierta* (open chapel), used for preaching to crowds of indigenous people. You may need to enlist the caretaker of the cloister museum to open the church itself, which has a lovely rib-vaulted roof.

The weighty monastery at **Yanhuitlán**, designed to withstand earthquakes and serve as a defensive refuge, towers over highway 190, 120km from Oaxaca. It's open 8 am to 6 pm daily (US$1). The cloister has an interesting little museum. The church contains valuable works of art, and a fine Mudéjar timber roof supports the choir.

About 22km southwest of Coixtlahuaca, at **Tejupan** on highway 190, is another giant 16th-century Dominican church.

Thirteen kilometers south of highway 190 on highway 125 lies **Teposcolula**, whose monastery is beside the main plaza. A stately capilla abierta of three open bays stands immediately north of the west end of the monastery church. The cloister is a museum, open 8 am to 6 pm daily (US$1).

About 25km south of Teposcolula, just off highway 125, is **San Martín Huamelulpan**. The Museo Comunitario Hitalulu, on Plaza Cívica, is officially open 9 am to 6 pm daily and focuses on traditional medicine and archaeology. Also worth a visit is the Mixtec archaeological site 500m from the village.

Tlaxiaco, 43km south of Teposcolula on highway 125, was known before the Mexican Revolution as Paris Chiquita (Little Paris), for the quantities of French luxuries such as clothes and wine imported for its few rich families. Today the only signs of that elegance are the arcades around the main plaza and a few large houses with courtyards. The market area is off the southeast corner of the plaza – Saturday is the main day.

South of Tlaxiaco, highway 125, all paved, winds through the Sierra Madre del Sur to Pinotepa Nacional, on coastal highway 200. The major town is **Putla**, 95km from Tlaxiaco. Just before Putla is **San Andrés Chicahuaxtla**, in the small territory of the indigenous Triquis. The Amuzgo people of **San Pedro Amuzgos**, 73km south of Putla, are known for their fine huipiles.

Places to Stay & Eat

You could visit the Mixteca Alta or Baja in a long day trip from Oaxaca, but basic hotels or *casas de huéspedes* are available in Nochixtlán, Coixtlahuaca, Tamazulapan, Teposcolula and Putla, and better ones can be found in Tlaxiaco and Huajuapan de León. San Martín Huamelulpan also has a *tourist yu\ˊù* (see the Valles Centrales introductory section, earlier).

In Tlaxiaco, **Hotel Del Portal** (☎ 9-552-01-54), on the plaza, has big, clean singles/doubles with private bath around a pleasant courtyard from US$12/14.50. **Hotel Colón** (☎ 9-552-00-13), on Colón one block east of the plaza, has rooms with bath for US$11 single or double. **Hotel México** (☎ 9-552-00-86, *Hidalgo 13*) has doubles with shared bath for US$5 or with private bath for US$10. Good food is available at *Cafe Uni-Nuu*, next to the Hotel Del Portal, and at *Restaurant Juanita*, opposite Banamex.

Getting There & Away

Yanhuitlán, Tejupan and Huajuapan, on highway 190, are served by several 1st- and 2nd-class buses daily from Oaxaca. Yanhuitlán is 2½ hours from Oaxaca (US$4.25 in 1st-class). For Coixtlahuaca, take a Puebla- or Mexico City-bound bus and ask to be let off at the turnoff, or take a Huajuapan-bound bus to Tejupan, where colectivo taxis run to Coixtlahuaca.

Teposcolula, Tlaxiaco, Putla and other places on highway 125A are served from

Oaxaca by a couple of 1st-class Cristóbal Colón buses and a dozen or so 2nd-class FYPSA and TOI buses daily. Many of these continue south to Pinotepa Nacional.

Buses run from Mexico City's Terminal Oriente (TAPO) to several Mixteca towns.

Northern Oaxaca

Much of the north is rugged and mountainous. Highway 175, scenic but rough in parts, crosses the sierras to Tuxtepec, the main town in a low-lying region of far northern Oaxaca. In culture and geography, this particular region is akin to Veracruz.

GUELATAO & IXTLÁN
☎ 9

On highway 175, 60km from Oaxaca, Guelatao village was the birthplace of Benito Juárez (see 'Benito Juárez' in this chapter). By the pretty lake at the center of the village is a statue of the boy Benito as a shepherd. Among the adjacent municipal buildings are two statues of Juárez and a small exposition, the Sala Homenaje a Juárez (open 9 am to 4 pm Wednesday to Sunday, free).

In Ixtlán, 3km beyond Guelatao on highway 175, is the baroque Templo de Santo Tomás, where baby Benito was baptized. Note the finely carved west façade.

Ixtlán is the hub of a region of great natural beauty and diversity, and a network of enthusiastic local ecotourism enterprises can help you experience the area's excitements. Within a relatively small region, environments range from cold 3000m mountaintops and large cloud forests to temperate pine and oak woodlands to exuberant tropical forests at altitudes as low as 200m. Five hundred bird species and 6000 plant species have been recorded here. Zapotec, Chinantec and Mixe indigenous villages add to the interest.

There's a Museo de la Biodiversidad (Museum of Biodiversity) on Ixtlán's plaza, and one of its founders, biologist Gustavo Ramírez Santiago (☎ 9-553-61-11 in Ixtlán, grsixt@antequera.com), offers trips into the cloud-forest region known as El Rincón.

Also in Ixtlán is the community ecotourism venture Schia-Rua-Via (☎ 9-553-60-75). Expediciones Sierra Norte de Oaxaca (☎ 9-513-95-18, sierra_norte@infosel.net.mx) offers mountain bike trips in the sierras (superb biking country, by all accounts) for US$65 a day per person, usually starting from Benito Juárez village on the southern edge of the sierras (see the Valles Centrales section).

Another ecotourism venture, Viajes Ecoturísticos Comunitario Shoo Raa (☎ 9-553-60-28, fax 9-553-60-29), is based in the very pretty village of Santa María Yavesía, about 15km southeast of Ixtlán. Varied trips in this area cost about US$15 a day per person, including accommodation and meals. Ingeniero Rodolfo Cruz Hernández (☎/fax 9-512-53-37) at the Hotel Cruz del Ángel, López Mateos 117, in Oaxaca can provide information.

Ixtlán has a couple of basic *hospederías* providing accommodation.

Getting There & Away

The Cuenca and Benito Juárez bus lines serve Guelatao and Ixtlán from Oaxaca. Both are 2nd class, but Cuenca departs from the 1st-class bus station.

HUAUTLA DE JIMÉNEZ

The *hongos* (hallucinogenic mushrooms) used for medical and psychological cures by the Mazatec people of this remote town in the Sierra Mazateca still attract a trickle of foreigners keen to try them. According to legend, such figures as Bob Dylan, the Beatles, Timothy Leary and Albert Hoffman (the inventor of LSD) underwent the experience in the 1950s and '60s. Huautla's fabled *curandera* María Sabina died in 1985, but other curers in the town continue the role. Locals disapprove of mushroom-taking just for thrills.

Fresh mushrooms appear in the rainy season, June to August. Some are preserved in honey for other times, but their efficacy is questionable. When you get off the bus in Huautla, you will likely be greeted by locals who will assume you have come for a mushroom trip. Don't be hurried into selecting a place to stay (there are plenty) or a mushroom-provider. Two good Internet articles are 'Huautla Pilgrims' by Ben Feinberg (at www.planeta.com) and 'High on Huautla' by Derek Peck (at www.salon.com).

Huautla is about 65km east into the hills from Teotitlán del Camino, which is on highway 131. FYPSA buses run there from Oaxaca's 2nd-class bus station.

Oaxaca Coast

A laid-back spell on the beautiful Oaxaca coast is the perfect complement to the inland attractions of Oaxaca city and the Valles Centrales. The trip down highway 175 from Oaxaca is spectacular: South of Miahuatlán you climb into pine forests, then you descend into ever lusher and hotter tropical forest.

In the last 20 years, newly paved roads and scheduled flights to Puerto Escondido and Bahías de Huatulco have brought this once remote area closer to the rest of Mexico. As a result, the fishing villages and former coffee ports of Puerto Escondido and Puerto Ángel have turned into minor resorts. But they remain small and relaxed – Puerto Ángel especially so. Puerto Escondido has famous surf, while Puerto Ángel is at the center of a series of wonderful beaches with plenty of low-cost accommodations – among them that fabled backpackers' hangout, Zipolite. To the east, a big new tourist resort on the Bahías de Huatulco is being developed with respect for the area's lovely surroundings.

West of Puerto Escondido, nature lovers can visit the lagoons of Manialtepec and Chacahua, teeming with bird life.

The coast is hotter and much more humid than the highlands. Most of the year's rain falls between June and September, turning everything green. From October the landscape starts to dry out, and by March many of the trees – which are mostly deciduous – are leafless. May is the hottest month.

Unless otherwise stated, room prices given in this section are for the high seasons, which generally last from Christmas to

Easter and through July and August. At other times prices may come down anywhere between 10% and 40%.

Internet Resources
The website Pacific Coast of Oaxaca (www.eden.com/~tomzap) is a mine of information about the coast.

Dangers & Annoyances
The Oaxaca coast is a rather impoverished region apart from its few tourism honey pots. Be on your guard against theft in Puerto Escondido and the Puerto Ángel-Zipolite area.

PUERTO ESCONDIDO
• pop 30,000 ☎ 9
Known to surfers since before paved roads reached this part of Oaxaca, Puerto Escondido (Hidden Port) remains relatively small, laid-back and inexpensive. Scattered across a hillside above the ocean, it has several beaches, a range of reasonable accommodations, plenty of cafés and restaurants and a spot of nightlife.

In recent years Puerto has achieved cult status among Italians, thanks to Gabriele Salvatores' travel-and-crime movie *Puerto Escondido* which, while very enjoyable, makes the place seem more remote and primitive than it really is.

Any breath of breeze can be at a premium in Puerto, and you're more likely to get one up the hill a little bit than down at sea level. The wettest months are May, June, early July and September.

Orientation
The town rises above the small, south-facing Bahía Principal. Highway 200 runs across the hill halfway up, dividing the upper town where the locals live and work – and buses arrive – from the lower, tourism-dominated part. The heart of the lower town is the pedestrianized section of Avenida Pérez Gasga, known as El Adoquín (*adoquín* is Spanish for paving stone). The west end of Pérez Gasga winds up the slope to meet highway 200 at an intersection known simply as El Crucero.

Bahía Principal curves around, at its east end, to the long surf beach Playa Zicatela, which is backed by loads more places to stay and eat. Other beaches line a series of bays to the west.

Information
Tourist Offices The main tourist office (☎ 582-01-75) is about 2.5km west of Pérez Gasga in Fraccionamiento Bacocho on the road to the airport, at the corner of Boulevard Juárez. Far handier is the tourist information desk at the west end of the Adoquín – at the time of research open 9 am to 4 pm Monday to Friday, 10 am to 1 pm Saturday. Gina Machorro, the energetic English-speaker usually to be found there, can answer most questions you throw at her and has some printed material to give out.

Money Banamex, on the corner of Pérez Gasga and Unión, changes dollars and traveler's checks 9 am to noon Monday to Friday. Bancrecer, on Hidalgo, and Bital, on 1 Norte in the upper part of town, also offers exchange service 10 am to noon Saturday. All these banks have ATMs.

The town's several casas de cambio – all simply called Money Exchange – give worse rates than the banks but are open much longer hours. At least two are on the Adoquín (the one opposite Farmacia Cortés is open 9 am to 9 pm Monday to Saturday, 9 am to 5 pm Sunday); another is on Playa Zicatela in the Bungalows Acuario building.

Post & Communications The post office, on Avenida Oaxaca at 7 Norte, is a 20- or 30-minute uphill walk from the seafront. Postal services operate 9 am to 4 pm Monday to Friday, 9 am to 1 pm Saturday; the fax service (the cheapest in town) stays open till 6 pm Monday to Friday. You can take a 'Mercado' bus or colectivo taxi up Avenida Oaxaca.

A couple of pay phones are on the Adoquín, and a telephone caseta with fax is across the street from the Farmacia Cortés. More pay phones are outside the Money Exchange on Playa Zicatela.

Un Tigre Azul cybercafé and art gallery, above El Son y La Rumba bar on the

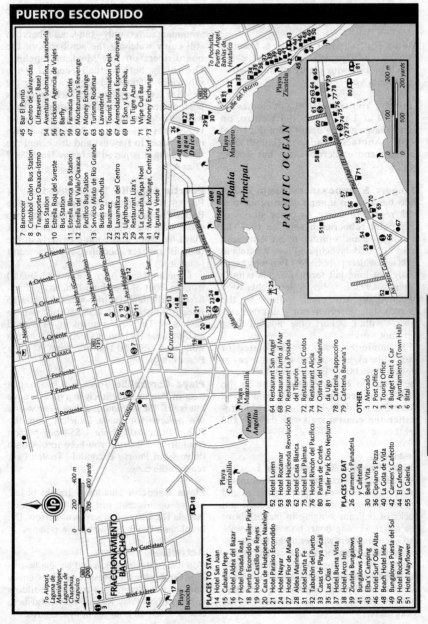

PUERTO ESCONDIDO

7   Bancrecer
9   Cristóbol Colón Bus Station
10 Transportes Oaxaca-Istmo
    Bus Station
11 Estrella Roja del Sureste
    Bus Station
12 Estrella Blanca Bus Station
13 Estrella del Valle/Oaxaca
    Pacífico Bus Station
    Servicio Mixto de Río Grande
    Buses to Pochutla
22 Banamex
23 Lavamática del Centro
25 Lighthouse
29 Restaurant Liza's
34 La Cabaña Papa Noel
41 Money Exchange, Central Surf
42 Iguana Verde

45 Bar El Punto
47 Centro de Salvavidas
    (Lifesavers' Base)
54 Aventura Submarina, Lavandería
56 Erickson Agencia de Viajes
57 Barfly
59 Farmacia Cortés
60 Moctezuma's Revenge
61 Money Exchange
63 Turismo Rodimar
65 Lavandería
66 Tourist Information Desk
67 Arrendadora Express, Aerovega
69 El Son y La Rumba,
    Un Tigre Azul
71 Wipe Out Bar
73 Money Exchange

PLACES TO STAY
14 Hotel San Juan
15 Cabañas Pepe
16 Hotel Aldea del Bazar
17 Hotel Posada Real
18 Puerto Escondido Trailer Park
19 Hotel Castillo de Reyes
20 Casa de Huéspedes Naxhiely
21 Hotel Paraíso Escondido
24 Hotel Nayar
27 Hotel Flor de María
28 Aldea Marinero
31 Hotel Santa Fe
32 Tabachin del Puerto
35 Las Olas
38 Hotel Buena Vista
39 Hotel Arco Iris
41 Zicatela Bungalows
43 Elba's Camping
46 Hotel Surf Olas Altas
48 Beach Hotel Inés
49 Bungalows Puesta del Sol
50 Hotel Rockaway
51 Hotel Mayflower
52 Hotel Loren
53 Hotel Rocamar
58 Hotel Hacienda Revolución
62 Hotel Casa Blanca
75 Hotel Las Palmas
76 Hotel Rincón del Pacífico
80 Palmas de Cortés
81 Trailer Park Dios Neptuno

PLACES TO EAT
26 Carmen's Panadería
    y Cafetería
30 Bella Vita
36 Cipriano's Pizza
40 La Gota de Vida
42 Carmen's Cafecito
44 El Cafecito
55 La Galería
64 Restaurant San Angel
68 Restaurant Junto al Mar
70 Restaurant La Posada
    del Tiburón
72 Restaurant Los Crotos
74 Restaurant Alicia
77 Osteria del Viandante
    da Ugo
78 Cafetería Cappuccino
79 Cafetería Banana's

OTHER
1   Mercado
2   Post Office
3   Tourist Office
4   Budget Rent a Car
5   Ayuntamiento (Town Hall)
6   Bital

Adoquín, charges US$5 an hour for Internet access. It's open 11 am to 11 pm daily.

Media The free paper *El Sol de la Costa*, in English and Spanish, comes out every month or two with plenty of information about what's on.

Laundry You can wash 4kg of clothes for US$1.20 at Lavamática del Centro, on Pérez Gasga a little uphill from the Hotel Nayar. Another *lavandería* (laundry) at the east end of Pérez Gasga has similar prices.

Dangers & Annoyances Puerto Escondido has had an up-and-down reputation with regard to safety. At times, stories of knifepoint robberies have been rife. The brutal rape and murder of an American artist in broad daylight on Playa Zicatela in 1998 was widely publicized. (Two men eventually got long jail terms for this crime.) Later in 1998, new beach floodlights were switched on with much fanfare by the Oaxaca state governor, but – surprise, surprise – within a short time most of them were not working.

To minimize risks, avoid isolated or empty places, and stick to well-lit areas at night (or use taxis). Especially take care on the beach at Playa Zicatela and in the rocks area between Zicatela and Playa Marinero. It's probably best to avoid altogether the coastal walkway passing the lighthouse.

Beaches

Bahía Principal The main town beach is long enough to accommodate restaurants at its west end, sun worshipers at the east end (called Playa Marinero) and occasional flocks of pelicans winging in inches above the waves. Fishing boats bob on the swell, and a few hawkers wander up and down, offering textiles, hammocks and necklaces. The smelly water entering the bay at times from the inaptly named Laguna Agua Dulce will put you off dipping anywhere other than Playa Marinero: don't get too close to the rocks there.

Playa Zicatela The waters of Zicatela have a lethal undertow. They're for strong-swimming surfers only – but landlubbers can still enjoy watching the acrobatics of the board-riders on the 'Mexican Pipeline.' Drownings here virtually ceased when *salvavidas* (lifeguards) began watching the beach a few years ago, but their work has been hampered by a lack of funding. (They welcome donations at their base in front of Hotel Surf Olas Altas.) Zicatela now has many places to stay, eat and drink, and the road along it is paved as far as Hotel Surf Olas Altas.

Puerto Angelito The sheltered bay of Puerto Angelito, about 1km west of the Bahía Principal as the crow flies, has two small beaches separated by a few rocks. Playa Manzanilla, the more easterly of the two, is quieter because vehicles can't reach it.

Lanchas (fast, open, outboard boats) from in front of the Hotel Rincón del Pacífico on Bahía Principal will take you to Puerto Angelito for US$1.50 per person each way. The boat returns at an agreed pick-up time. By land, it's a 20- to 30-minute walk or a US$1.50 taxi ride from Avenida Pérez Gasga.

Playa Carrizalillo This small beach, just west of Puerto Angelito, is in a rockier cove but is OK for swimming. It has a bar with a few *palapas* for shade. Lanchas from the Bahía Principal (about US$4 per person roundtrip) will bring you here too. A path down from Puerto Escondido Trailer Park reaches the cove.

Playa Bacocho This long, straight beach, on the open ocean just west of the Hotel Posada Real, has a dangerous undertow. The hotel has a beach bar with a few palapas.

Activities

You can rent surfboards and boogie boards in several places on Playa Zicatela. Central Surf in the Bungalows Acuario building charges US$8 a day. Kids on Playa Marinero charge US$1 an hour for boogie boards.

Lanchas from the beach in front of the Hotel Rincón del Pacífico will do turtle-viewing trips (and, in winter, dolphin-viewing) for around US$20 an hour. They'll take you sportfishing too.

Apparently the San Andreas Fault begins not far out to sea from Zicatela. Aventura Submarina (☎ 582-23-53), next to Hotel Rocamar, teaches PADI courses and leads dive trips. A three-hour trip with two tanks (about half an hour each) costs US$50 a person.

Rancho La Ilusión (☎ 582-17-10) offers four-hour riverside-and-beach horse rides for US$25.

Organized Tours

Several agencies on the Adoquín offer tours to places out of town (see the Around Puerto Escondido section).

Among trips offered by Iguana Verde (at Carmen's Cafecito), on Zicatela, is a panoramic two-hour inner-tube float down the Río Colotepec, a few kilometers east. The trips run from about mid-October to mid-March and cost US$15 per person.

Special Events

Semana Santa is a big week for local party-ing; the Oaxaca state surf carnival is held at this time. The World Masters Championship surfing contest is normally held here in August. But November is the big month: he Festival Costeña de la Danza, a fiesta of Oaxaca coastal dance, is held over the second weekend of the month; the third weekend sees a sailfish-fishing contest and art exhibitions; and on the last weekend Puerto hosts the national surfing championships. The annual fiesta around February 14 in Bajos de Chila, a few kilometers northwest on highway 200, is one of the biggest in the region.

Places to Stay

In the peak tourist seasons the most popular places may be full. Your best chance of getting into a place you like, if you haven't booked ahead, is to ask early in the day, about 9 or 10 am. Many accommodations lack heated water, but the tap water is usually fairly warm anyway. A lot of rooms on Playa Zicatela have cooking facilities.

Several apartments and houses are available for short and long stays. Ask at the tourist information desk on Pérez Gasga.

Places to Stay – Budget

Camping *Trailer Park Dios Neptuno*, on Bahía Principal, has a dirt camping area with electrical hookups for US$1.50 per person. It also offers some very basic cabañas with bed, light and net for US$5/6 a single/double. The communal showers and toilets are clean. *Palmas de Cortés*, next door, is better (more shade) but much smaller. It charges US$2.50 per person and US$2.50 per vehicle. Amenities include showers, electrical hookups, fireplaces and 24-hour supervision.

Elba's, behind Carmen's Cafecito on Zicatela, is a pleasant coconut palm-shaded spot with electricity, toilets and showers. It charges just US$2 per person (vehicle included) but has only a handful of spaces.

Puerto Escondido Trailer Park occupies a large open area on the cliff above Playa Carrizalillo. It has bathrooms but no electricity. Two people and a vehicle pay US$2.

Playa Marinero & Playa Zicatela The *Aldea Marinero* cabañas, on a small lane going back from Playa Marinero, have canvas beds, mosquito nets, hammocks out front and shared bathrooms, at US$5/7 for singles/doubles.

On Zicatela, *Las Olas* (☎ 582-09-19) has seven good cabañas and bungalows, each with attached bath, fan, screens, fridge and stove. Most cost US$14/16 in high season or US$8/10 low season – good prices for Zicatela. Toward the far end of Zicatela, *Hotel Rockaway* (☎ 582-06-68) has good, solid cabañas with showers, nets and fans, around a pool, at US$10/15/20/25 for singles/doubles/triples/quads.

Avenida Pérez Gasga & Around Friendly *Hotel Mayflower* (☎ 582-03-67), on Andador Libertad (the flight of steps climbing from the west end of the Adoquín), has three fan-cooled dormitories with a total of 15 places.

Rates of US$5.50 per person in high season, US$4.50 low season, include use of a fridge, microwave and filtered water. There's a bar open in the evenings.

Casa de Huéspedes Naxhiely (*Pérez Gasga 301*) has clean, plain, smallish rooms with fans and bathrooms for US$13 double. A little farther up the hill, *Hotel Castillo de Reyes* (☎ 582-04-42) is a good value with 18 sizable and clean rooms, each with two double beds, fans and bathrooms, for US$10/12 single/double.

Cabañas Pepe, on Marklin, east off upper Pérez Gasga, offers fair rooms with fans, nets and private bathrooms for US$8 double.

Places to Stay – Mid-Range

Fan and attached bath are standard issue in this range.

Playa Marinero & Playa Zicatela The
Hotel Flor de María (☎ 582-05-36), on a little lane between Playa Marinero and the highway, is run by a Canadian/Italian couple. Its 24 ample, nicely decorated rooms, each with two double beds, are set around a courtyard. Extras include a small rooftop pool and bar, a TV room and a restaurant. Singles/doubles are US$30/35 in high season.

The American-owned *Tabachín del Puerto* (☎ 582-11-79, http://tabachin.com .mx), at the end of a short lane behind Hotel Santa Fe, offers six studio-rooms of various sizes, all with kitchen, air-con, TV and phone. Most have balcony access; decor and furniture range from folksy Mexican to classical fine-art. High-season prices for up to four people are between US$45 and US$65. Breakfast and lunch are available.

On Zicatela, *Casas de Playa Acali* (☎ 582-07-54) provides eight wooden cabañas – each with one double and one single bed and an outdoor cooking ring – and nine bungalows, each with two double beds and a kitchen. All have mosquito nets. High-season prices are US$15/18/21 for singles/doubles/triples in the cabañas; US$21/21/25/29 for singles/doubles/triples/quads in the bungalows (US$45/45/50/55

with air-con and fridge). Other amenities include a swimming pool and a bar.

On the hillside above Cipriano's Pizza is the plain, well-kept *Hotel Buena Vista* (☎ 582-14-74). The 16 reasonably sized rooms, all with mosquito screens or nets, cost from US$15 to US$25 single or double. The most expensive units have kitchens, and many rooms have breezy balconies with splendid views.

Hotel Arco Iris (☎ 582-04-32) has 26 big, clean rooms with balconies or terraces looking straight out to the surf, plus a large pool and a good upstairs restaurant/bar open to the breeze. A mixed crowd of surfers and others uses this relaxed hotel. All rooms have two double beds: rates with/without kitchen for one or two people are US$30/27 downstairs, US$33/30 upstairs. Mosquito nets are available.

Next door, *Zicatela Bungalows* (☎ 582-07-98) has 12 spacious bungalows, each with three double beds, cooking rings and fridge for US$25 double plus US$5 each extra person. A couple of two-story blocks hold 24 more rooms, each with two double beds, for US$23 double plus US$3 per extra person. All accommodations have mosquito-netted windows and are solidly built, even if they're squeezed a little tightly together. The complex has a restaurant and pool too.

Farther along the strip, *Bungalows Acuario* (☎ 582-10-27) has about 30 rooms and wooden cabañas at US$22 single or double. All have mosquito nets and are set around a nice swimming pool. A little farther along is the new *Hotel Surf Olas Altas* (☎ 582-23-15, Morro 310), the biggest place on Zicatela. Its 60 nice rooms, with TV, cost US$39/47/56 for singles/doubles/triples in high season, US$20/30/40 in low. Most have two double beds, some have one king bed. The hotel has a pool and restaurant out front.

Near the far end of the strip, *Beach Hotel Inés* (☎ 582-07-92) has a range of cabañas and rooms from US$12 to US$32, single or double. The pleasant pool area has a café serving good food. Just east, *Bungalows Puesta del Sol* has a good pool and half a dozen nice, spacious, solidly built bungalows at US$25/29 single/double.

Avenida Pérez Gasga & Around The *Hotel Rincón del Pacífico* (☎ 582-01-93, *Pérez Gasga 900*), on the Adoquín, has 20-odd big-windowed rooms around a palmy courtyard. Rates are US$19/23 single/double (US$28/35 with air-con). Staff are helpful and the hotel has its own beachside café/restaurant. *Hotel Las Palmas* (☎ 582-02-30), next door, has 35 slightly bigger rooms at US$20 single or double, but it's in poorer condition.

A good place on the Adoquín is the friendly *Hotel Casa Blanca* (☎ 582-01-68, *Pérez Gasga 905*), which fills up quickly. It has 21 large rooms; the streetside ones have balconies. Singles/doubles/triples go for US$18/24/28.

Hotel Hacienda Revolución (☎ 582-18-18), on Andador Revolución (the steps leading up beside Farmacia Cortés), has 11 nice, spacious singles/doubles for the good price of US$12/18. All rooms have attractively tiled bathrooms, decent furniture and colorful paintwork, and most have a patio and hammock.

Pleasing double rooms with fan and bath at the *Hotel Mayflower* (☎ 582-03-67), on Andador Libertad (the flight of steps leading up from the west end of the Adoquín), are US$22 in high season, US$16 low; a couple of singles are available for US$18 (US$14 low season). It's a friendly place and has a bar open evenings. *Hotel Rocamar* (☎ 582-03-39), at the west end of the Adoquín, is not a bad value. No-frills but clean rooms of varied size are US$19 single or double. Some have balconies overlooking the street.

A minute uphill from the Adoquín, still on Pérez Gasga, *Hotel Loren* (☎ 582-00-57) charges US$25, single or double, for bare but spacious rooms. All have TV and balcony, but not all catch a sea view. The similar but drabber *Hotel Nayar* (☎ 582-01-13, *Pérez Gasga 407*), just up the street, gets a good breeze in its wide sitting areas/walkways. Its 40 or so rooms have hot water, TV and small balconies. Some have sea views.

Singles/doubles are US$17.50/20 (air-con US$3 extra). Both these hotels have pools.

The friendly *Hotel San Juan* (☎ 582-05-18, Marklin 503), just below El Crucero, has 30 good rooms costing from US$15/17 to US$20/22 in low season, a little more in high season. All have hot water and mosquito screens; the more expensive rooms are bigger, with private terraces and the best views. Most have TV. The hotel has a swimming pool and a rooftop sitting area for catching sun, view or breeze.

Places to Stay – Top End

Top place in the Pérez Gasga vicinity is *Hotel Paraíso Escondido* (☎ 582-04-44, *Unión 10*). Owned and run by a group of architects and designers, it's a rambling whitewash-and-blue place decorated with lots of tile, pottery, stained glass and stone sculpture by well-known Mexican sculptors. It has an attractive restaurant/bar/pool area, and the 20 clean though moderately sized rooms have air-con. Prices are US$85 single or double in high season, US$50 in low.

Beside the rocky outcrop that divides Playa Marinero from Playa Zicatela, *Hotel Santa Fe* (☎ 582-01-70) has 51 rooms attractively set around small terraces and a palm-fringed pool. Rooms vary in size and view, but good design, with tiles cleverly used, makes most of them agreeable. Many have air-con. Singles/doubles are US$70/80. Also available are eight appealing bungalows with kitchens at US$85/95.

Hotel Posada Real (☎ 582-01-33, Boulevard Juárez 11), a Best Western hotel, is about 2.5km west of town in the still-being-developed Fraccionamiento Bacocho. It has big, palm-shaded gardens, a big pool and 100 air-conditioned rooms with balconies. The hotel's three four-story buildings sit on a headland overlooking Playa Bacocho. Rooms are US$100 to US$120 single or double depending on season.

Hotel Aldea del Bazar (☎ 582-05-08, *Boulevard Juárez 7*), also above Playa Bacocho, is a big, plush place in eye-catching modern Moorish style. The 47 spacious, comfortable rooms and suites start at US$105 in

OAXACA STATE

high season, US$75 at other times. Facilities include a fine pool in extensive gardens and a pre-Hispanic spa where you can take a natural-oils massage, a mud bath or a *temazcal* steam bath.

Places to Eat

Thanks to the tide of Italian travelers washed up here by the movie *Puerto Escondido*, a large percentage of Puerto eateries are now pizzerias, *gelaterias* or all-purpose *restaurantes italianos*. At a couple of them, you can even pay in lire.

Most restaurants and cafés are fairly simple, semi-open-air places. Seafood is abundant, and vegetarians are well catered to. The main produce market is in the upper part of town (see map).

Playa Zicatela The airy *Hotel Santa Fe* restaurant, looking down Zicatela, has some tasty seafood and vegetarian fare, but be ready for your choice to be unavailable. It's medium to expensive in price, with fish and seafood dishes from US$4.50 to US$12, and antojitos, pasta, tofu and vegetarian offerings for US$2 to US$7.

Along Zicatela, *Cipriano's Pizza* makes good brick-oven pizzas with a thin, crisp base and lots of good cheese. The only size available is enough for two and costs US$4 to US$8.50. The restaurant also serves breakfasts and meat and seafood main dishes at moderate prices.

The *Hotel Arco Iris* restaurant, with a good upstairs location, serves a tasty mix of Mexican and international fare to satisfy the Zicatela surfers. Most pasta and antojitos go for around US$2; fish and meat courses are US$4 to US$6.50 (to really fill up, you may need to accompany them with, say, a salad). Next door, the *Zicatela Bungalows* restaurant is a good value – try the burgers (meat, soy or fish) at US$1.50 including salad and fries. *La Gota de Vida*, nearby, is an excellent vegetarian restaurant, with salads and crêpes between US$1.50 and US$2.25 and tempeh, tofu or stir-fried main courses for US$3 to US$3.50. Beverages include lots of juices and four varieties of *lassi* (an Indian yogurt-based drink).

Halfway along Zicatela, *Carmen's Cafecito* does a roaring trade – morning, noon and evening. Great pastries, croissants and cakes cost just US$0.50, slices of vegetarian pizza are US$1, and whole-meal tortas go for around US$1.50. At breakfast, French toast and fruit is US$1.50. Homemade lunch and dinner dishes are US$2 to US$4. It's open 6 am to 10 pm daily. There's good food next door too, at *El Cafecito*, which has a breezy upstairs area. Stir-fries, antojitos and burgers are all between US$1.50 and US$2.25; breaded chicken breast with salad, rice, potatoes and sautéed vegetables is US$3.50.

Zicatela has three or four grocery stores, including a 24-hour one at Hotel Rockaway.

Playa Marinero *Carmen's Panadería y Cafetería*, just up from the Hotel Flor de María on the little lane behind Playa Marinero, is a brilliant place for breakfast or lunchtime snacks, with a small fan-cooled palapa-style café and a terrace overlooking plenty of tropical verdure. It's run by the same friendly Mexican/Canadian couple as Carmen's Cafecito. You can get a big serving of fruit salad, yogurt and granola, or whole wheat French toast with butter, honey and lots of fruit, for just US$1.50. The coffee refills are free. A bakery section sells great bread and baked goods. It's all open 7 am to 2 pm daily.

The *Bella Vita* is a popular Italian-inspired beachside restaurant. Spaghetti or risotto is US$3 to US$4.50; chicken and seafood dishes run US$4 or more.

Avenida Pérez Gasga On the Adoquín, *Restaurant Los Crotos*, *Restaurant Junto al Mar* and *Restaurant La Posada del Tiburón*, all with terraces opening onto the beach, serve up fresh seafood at reasonable prices. Most fish dishes – such as a whole juicy snapper with rice or fries and a little salad – go for US$3.50 to US$7.

La Galería, opposite the Junto al Mar, is one of the most popular Italian spots, with art on the walls and good fare on the tables. Pizzas and some interesting and tasty pasta dishes cost US$2.50 to US$5.50.

Around the middle of the Adoquín, little *Restaurant Alicia* is a good value, with spaghetti variations from just US$0.70 to US$2. Seafood cocktails and good fish dishes run US$2 to US$5. It also does cheap breakfasts. Farther east, the good, Italian-run *Osteria del Viandante da Ugo* makes a range of pastas and one-person pizzas from US$3.25 to US$5.50; add a good salad for US$2.50 to US$4. *Cafetería Cappuccino* serves good coffee and other fare ranging from breakfasts, crepas and salads (US$2 to US$4) to steaks and seafood (US$5.50 and up).

At the east end of the Adoquín, *Cafetería Banana's*, also Italian-run, serves decent pizzas from US$3.75, plus pasta and crepas. Popular *Restaurant San Ángel*, almost opposite, does seafood, chicken breast and *filete de res* (steak) for US$4 to US$6.50.

Entertainment
Many Puerto Escondido nights start during happy hour in bars such as *Barfly* (the epicenter, along with *Wipe Out Bar*, of the travelers' social scene), *Cafetería Banana's*, *Moctezuma's Revenge*, *Hotel Las Palmas*, *Restaurant Liza's* or the *Hotel Arco Iris*. Escondido's sunsets are spectacular. Most happy hours run from 5 or 6 to 8 or 9 pm, but at Barfly, on the Adoquín, it was from 8 pm to midnight on our last visit. Another good pub is *La Cabaña Papá Noel*, on Playa Zicatela. Around 2 am the scene migrates to *El Punto*, on the Zicatela sands in front of El Cafecito.

A couple of places usually have live music. On our last visit, *El Son y La Rumba*, on the Adoquín, had a good salsa band.

Shopping
The Adoquín is great for a browse – shops sell fashions from surf designers and from Bali, new-age and silver jewelry, tacky cheap souvenirs and classy crafts that are real works of art.

Getting There & Away
Air See the Oaxaca City section for details on flights to/from Oaxaca. Aerocaribe (airport office: ☎ 582-20-23) flies nonstop to/from Mexico City five days a week (one hour, US$109 and up). Aerovega (☎ 582-01-51) is at Pérez Gasga 502, just off the west end of the Adoquín. Turismo Rodimar (☎ 582-15-51), Pérez Gasga 905B, and Erickson Agencia de Viajes (☎ 582-08-49), also on the Adoquín, sell air tickets.

Bus The terminals of EB (☎ 582-00-86), TOI (☎ 582-03-92), EV/OP (☎ 582-00-50) and ERS (☎ 582-08-75) – all 2nd-class except for a few superior services – are all on Avenida Hidalgo, in the upper part of town: go two blocks uphill from El Crucero and turn right (east). One block farther north, Cristóbal Colón (☎ 582-10-73), on 1 Norte between 1 and 2 Oriente, offers 1st-class service.

It's advisable to book ahead for some of the better and more limited services such as Colón buses and the better services to Oaxaca. Daily departures include:

Acapulco – 400km, 6½ to 7½ hours; 19 EB (US$11.50 to US$15.50)

Bahías de Huatulco – 115km, 2½ hours; 5 Colón (US$3.75), 10 EB (US$3.25 to US$4.50)

Oaxaca via highway 175 – 310km, 8 hours; 3 Colón (US$12.50), 9 EV/OP (US$6.50 to US$7.50)

Oaxaca via highway 131 – 200km, 7 hours; 5 ERS (US$7 to US$8, most overnight), 3 TOI (US$7)

Pochutla – 65km, 1½ hours; 8 Colón (US$2.50), 10 EB (US$2 to US$2.75), Servicio Mixto de Río Grande microbuses from Restaurant Donají by El Crucero every 20 minutes, 5 am to 7 pm (US$1)

Colón offers four daily buses to Tuxtla Gutiérrez (US$19) and two each to San Cristóbal de Las Casas (US$21) and to Mexico City via highway 175 (US$32). Colón and EB go to Salina Cruz (about US$8.50), and Colón runs to Juchitán (US$10).

Car Arrendadora Express (☎ 582-13-55), at Pérez Gasga 502, just off the west end of the Adoquín, rents VW sedans for US$45 a day, with unlimited kilometers. Budget (☎ 582-03-12) has a rental office opposite the tourist office in Fraccionamiento Bacocho.

Getting Around
To/From the Airport The airport is about 4km west of the town center on the north

side of highway 200. For two or three people, a taxi is probably the cheapest way into town, if you can find one (the best place to look is on the main road outside the airport) and agree on a reasonable price (US$2). Otherwise, colectivo combis (US$2.50 per person) will drop you anywhere in town. You should have no problem finding a taxi from town to the airport for about US$2.

Taxi & Lancha Taxis wait at each end of the Adoquín. Taxis and lanchas (see Beaches, earlier in this section) are the only transportation between the central Pérez Gasga/ Bahía Principal area and the outlying beaches if you don't want – or think it's unsafe – to walk. The standard taxi fare to Playa Zicatela or Puerto Angelito is US$1.50.

AROUND PUERTO ESCONDIDO

Highway 200, heading west toward Acapulco, runs along behind a coast studded with lagoons, pristine beaches and prolific bird and plant life. The people here are of mixed ancestry; in addition to those of indigenous Mixtec and/or Spanish bloodlines, the population includes descendants of African slaves who escaped from the Spanish, of itinerant Asians and of Chileans shipwrecked on their way to the California gold rushes.

Laguna de Manialtepec

This lagoon, 6km long, begins about 15km west of Puerto Escondido along highway 200. It's home to ibis, roseate spoonbills, parrots and several species of hawks, falcons, ospreys, egrets, herons, kingfishers and iguanas. The birds are best seen in the early morning, but even at midday in January birders we know logged 40 species. The lagoon is mainly surrounded by mangroves, but tropical flowers and palms accent the ocean side.

Hidden Voyages Ecotours (www.wincom .net/~pelewing/hvecotur.html), run by the knowledgeable Canadian ornithologist Michael Malone, is operated through Turismo Rodimar (☎ 582-15-51), Pérez Gasga 905B in Puerto Escondido. It charges US$32 per person for excellent early-morning or

sunset tours (four or five hours) to Manialtepec, from early December to April 1.

Ana's Ecotours (☎ 582-20-01, 582-12-71), run by Ana Márquez, an excellent, English-speaking local guide leads Manialtepec trips for US$20 per person. Ana's is based at the Internet café Un Tigre Azul.

To do it independently, take an EB bus or drive to either of the small villages of La Alejandría or El Gallo, on the north shore of the lagoon, just off the highway. Both have restaurants with boats for hire. La Alejandría has a shady beach, camping space and some basic cabañas. At El Gallo, *Restaurant Isla de Gallo* serves good grilled fish and has a shaded boat (for up to eight people) with a knowledgeable captain. He charges around US$30 per boatload for a trip of up to 2½ hours, with a stop on the sandbar on the ocean side.

Lagunas de Chacahua

The area around the coastal lagoons of Chacahua and La Pastoría forms the beautiful Parque Nacional Lagunas de Chacahua. Birds from Alaska and Canada migrate here in winter. Mangrove-fringed islands harbor cormorants, wood storks, herons, egrets, ibis and roseate spoonbills, as well as mahogany trees, crocodiles and turtles. El Corral, a mangrove-lined waterway filled with countless birds, connects the two lagoons. From the lagoons you can see huge flocks of birds skidding across the water and soaring in big blue skies, while inland mountains shimmer in the distance.

Zapotalito About 60km from Puerto Escondido, a 5km road leads south from highway 200 to Zapotalito, a small fishing village on the eastern edge of La Pastoría lagoon. A cooperative here runs two-hour lancha tours of the lagoons (around US$55 for a boatload of about six people). Some trips stop for a swim at Cerro Hermoso beach or the beach near Chacahua, a fishing village at the western end of the park. Colectivo boats (about US$5 per person) also link Zapotalito with Chacahua village; they leave when there are seven or eight passengers. The journey is about 25km one-way and takes about 45 minutes. In Zapotalito you'll find the colectivo boats (with canopies for shade) a short walk straight ahead from the lancha tours departure point. A few simple restaurants flank the lagoon.

Chacahua Chacahua village, a five-minute walk from a wonderful ocean beach, is a perfect place to bliss out – for the day, or longer. The good waves here will please surfers, but the currents are strong – ask where it's safe to swim. Several places to stay, such as *Siete Mares*, facing the lagoon, offer basic cabañas for around US$10 double. Cheaper cabañas can be found right on the beach, where there are restaurants with hammocks strung in the shade. The friendly *Restaurant Siete Mares*, on the beach, has big breakfasts for US$1.50 and cooks up *huachinango* or *camarones* for US$5 or so. You can walk round the end of the lagoon to a crocodile-breeding center with a sad-looking collection of creatures kept for protection and reproduction. Chacahua's croc population (not human-eating) has been decimated by hunters.

Getting There & Away Easiest is an all-day guided tour from Puerto Escondido with the same operators as for Manialtepec (US$25 to US$35 per person). But it's an adventure to go independently: from Puerto Escondido take an EB bus to Río Grande (45 minutes, US$1.50 to US$2). They go about hourly. Colectivo taxis (US$0.75) and vans operate between Río Grande and Zapotalito, about 15km west. Complete the independent mode in a colectivo lancha from Zapotalito to Chacahua, and return!

Chacahua village is linked to San José del Progreso, 30km away on highway 200, by a sandy track that is impassable in the wet season and hard going at the best of times.

Pinotepa Nacional
• pop 23,500 ☎ 9

This is the biggest town between Puerto Escondido (145km) and Acapulco (260km). To the southwest there's a fine beach, Playa Corralero, near the mouth of Laguna Corralero (from 'Pino' go about 25km west on

highway 200, then some 15km southeast). You can stay in palapas at Corralero village; two *camionetas* (pickups) run there daily from Pinotepa.

In Pinotepa, *Hotel Carmona* (☎ 543-23-22, *Porfirio Díaz 127*), on the main road through town, has singles/doubles with bath for US$12/14 with fan, US$15/23 with aircon. *Hotel Marissa* (☎ 543-21-01, *Avenida Juárez 134*), half a block from the central plaza, charges US$5.50/10 with fan.

Aside from buses along highway 200, 1st-class Cristóbal Colón buses and 2nd-class FYPSA and TOI buses travel north on highway 125 through the Mixteca Alta, some reaching Oaxaca that way.

Other Destinations
The sulfurous **Aguas Termales de Atotonilco** (Atotonilco Hot Springs) are a 45-minute horseback ride or two-hour walk up the Río Manialtepec from San José Manialtepec, which is just off highway 200, 4km west of Laguna de Manialtepec. You can rent horses for US$5 per person in San José. There's a pool for bathing in, and you can dip in the cool river afterward. The mainly Mixtec town of **Jamiltepec**, 105km west of Puerto Escondido on highway 200, holds a colorful Sunday market with many people in traditional clothing.

The town of **Nopala**, about 35km north-west of Puerto Escondido off highway 131, is set in the foothills of the Sierra Madre del Sur in the indigenous Chatino region. You can visit organic coffee plantations and see ancient steles.

Ana's Ecotours (☎ 582-20-01, 582-12-71), based at the Internet café Un Tigre Azul in Puerto Escondido, can take you to all these destinations. Nopala trips are also offered by Turismo Rodimar (☎ 582-15-51), Pérez Gasga 905B, and the hotel Tabachín del Puerto (☎ 582-11-79, http://tabachin.com.mx), both also in Puerto Escondido.

POCHUTLA
• pop 10,300 ☎ 9

Highway 175 from Oaxaca meets coastal highway 200 about 1.5km south of the market town of Pochutla.

OAXACA STATE

Orientation

Highway 175 passes through Pochutla as Cárdenas, the narrow north-south main street. Hotel Izala marks the approximate midpoint of Cárdenas. Bus stations cluster on Cárdenas 500m to 1km south of the Izala. The main square, Plaza de la Constitución, is a block east of the Izala along Juárez. There are two markets: one on Cárdenas a little north of the bus stations; the other east off Cárdenas two blocks north of the Izala.

Information

Bital bank, on Cárdenas a block north of the Hotel Izala, changes traveler's checks and US dollars 8 am to 5.30 pm Monday through Friday, 8 am to 2 pm Saturday; Bancomer, on Cárdenas a block farther north, offers exchange service 9 am to 2 pm Monday to Friday. Both have ATMs.

The post office, open 8 am to 7 pm Monday to Friday, 9 am to 1 pm Saturday, is on Avenida Progreso behind Plaza de la Constitución. Several pay phones and telephone casetas (some of the latter with fax) are on Cárdenas. The hospital (☎ 584-02-16) is on the east side of the road south of the bus stations.

Places to Stay & Eat

Hotel Izala (☎ 584-01-19, *Cárdenas 59*) has reasonable rooms around an open-air patio at US$13/18 single/double with fan and TV, US$15/25 with air-con and TV. *Hotel Pochutla* (☎ 584-00-33, *Madero 102*), one block north and half a block east of the Izala, has 32 rooms in varying conditions with fan and bath for US$6.50/8. Nicest is *Hotel Costa del Sol* (☎ 584-03-18, *Cárdenas 47*), 1½ blocks north of the Izala, with rooms at US$10/12 with fan, US$13/15 with air-con.

Restaurant Pochutla, on Plaza de la Constitución, is clean and popular. Egg dishes are US$1.25 to US$1.75; meat or chicken US$2 to US$2.50.

Getting There & Away

Bus The three main bus stations, in north-south order down Cárdenas, are EB (2nd-class), on the west side of the street; EV/OP (2nd-class), on the east side; and Cristóbal Colón (1st-class), on the west side. Daily departures include:

Acapulco – 465km, 8 hours; 6 EB (US$13.50 to US$17.50)

Bahías de Huatulco – 50km, 1 hour; 5 Colón (US$1.50), 7 EB (US$1.25), Transportes Rápidos de Pochutla microbuses every 15 minutes, 5.30 am to 7.45 pm, from yard opposite EB (US$0.70)

Mazunte – 22km, 45 minutes; same buses (US$0.60) and camionetas (US$1) as to Puerto Ángel

Oaxaca – 245km, 6½ hours by highway 175; 3 Colón (US$12.50), 17 EV/OP (US$5.50 to US$6.75)

Puerto Ángel – 13km, 20 minutes; some EV/OP (US$0.30), also camionetas (pickups) every 20 minutes, 6 am to 7 pm, from Cárdenas at Allende, one block up from the EB station (US$0.50)

Puerto Escondido – 65km, 1½ hours; 4 Colón (US$2.50), 10 EB (US$2 to US$2.75), Servicio Mixto de Río Grande microbuses from Allende, one block east of Cárdenas, every 20 minutes, 5 am to 7 pm (US$1)

San Cristóbal de Las Casas – 590km, 11 hours; 2 Colón (US$19)

Tuxtla Gutiérrez – 505km, 10 hours; 2 Colón (US$17)

Zipolite – 17km, 30 minutes; same buses (US$0.40) and camionetas (US$0.70) as to Puerto Ángel

Colón and EB go to Salina Cruz. Colón also runs to Tehuantepec and Juchitán and has one bus overnight to Tapachula. All three main companies go to Mexico City.

Taxi Cabs wait on Cárdenas near the EB and EV/OP bus stations. Until about 8 pm they depart fairly often to Puerto Ángel on a colectivo (shared) basis for US$0.60 per person; a whole taxi costs about US$3.

PUERTO ÁNGEL
● pop 2430 ☎ 9

The small fishing town, naval base and travelers' hangout of Puerto Ángel ('PWAIR-toh AHN-hel') straggles around a picturesque bay between two rocky headlands, 13km south of Pochutla. Many travelers prefer to stay out on the beaches a few kilometers west at Zipolite, San Agustinillo or Mazunte, but the marginally more urban Puerto Ángel can be a good base too. It offers its own little beaches, some excellent places to stay and eat, and easy transportation to/from the bigger beaches.

Orientation

The road from Pochutla emerges at the east end of the small Bahía de Puerto Ángel. The road winds around the back of the bay, over an often-dry *arroyo* (creek) and up a hill. It then forks – right to Zipolite and Mazunte, left down to Playa del Panteón.

Information

A sleepy tourist information module on Vasconcelos is open 8 am to noon Monday to Friday. The post office is on Avenida Principal at the east end of town; open 9 am to 3 pm Monday to Friday.

The nearest bank is in Pochutla, but several accommodations and restaurants will

change cash or traveler's checks at their own rates. There's a telephone caseta with fax and expensive Internet service (US$0.40 a minute) in Gambusino's travel agency at Vasconcelos 3, open 7 am to 10 pm daily. Gambusino's can make reservations for flights from Puerto Escondido and Bahías de Huatulco. Caseta Telefónica El Ángel, on Boulevard Uribe just west of the arroyo, has phone and fax service too.

Dr Constancio Aparicio (☎ 584-30-58, 584-30-25) is a doctor recommended by foreign residents. You can ask for him in the pharmacy on Vasconcelos.

Theft and robbery can be a problem, especially on the Zipolite road.

Beaches

Playa del Panteón The beach on the west side of Bahía de Puerto Ángel is shallow and calm, and its waters are cleaner than those near the fishers' pier across the bay.

PUERTO ÁNGEL

OTHER
2 Caseta Telefónica El Ángel
9 Naval Base
10 Bus Stop
14 Tourist Information Module
19 Pharmacy
20 Gambusino's
22 Taxi Stand
23 Post Office

PLACES TO STAY
1 La Buena Vista
3 Casa Arnel
4 Hotel Puesta del Sol
6 Casa de Huéspedes Gundy y Tomás
7 Casa de Huéspedes El Capy
11 Villa Florencia
12 El Almendro
13 Posada Rincón Sabroso

15 Posada Cañon Devata
16 Hotel Cabaña
21 Hotel Soraya

PLACES TO EAT
5 Mercado
8 Rincón del Mar
17 Restaurante Susy, Other Beach Restaurants
18 Restaurant Marisol

OAXACA STATE

To Zipolite, Mazunte, Puerto Escondido

To Playa La Boquilla, Pochutla

To Playa Estacahuite

Arroyo
Palo Bello
Footpath
Blvd Uribe
Vasconcelos
Calle del Tajo
Av Principal

Cemetery

Playa Principal

Playa del Panteón

Beach Restaurants

Bahía de Puerto Ángel

Pier

Islet

0   50   100 m
0   50   100 yards

Estacahuite Half a kilometer up the road toward Pochutla, a sign points right along a path to this beach 700m away. The three tiny, sandy bays here are all good for snorkeling, but watch out for jellyfish. A couple of shack restaurants serve good, reasonably priced seafood or spaghetti, and they may have snorkels to rent.

Playa La Boquilla The coast northeast of Estacahuite is dotted with more good beaches, none of them very busy. A good one is Playa La Boquilla, on a small bay about 5km out, site of the Bahía de la Luna accommodation and restaurant (see Places to Stay). You can get there by a 3.5km road from a turnoff 4km out of Puerto Ángel on the road toward Pochutla. A taxi from Puerto Ángel costs around US$5 each way, but more fun is to go by boat (see Activities, below).

Activities

You can rent snorkeling gear from some of the café-restaurants on Playa del Panteón or get a fisher to take you for a boat trip from Panteón or from the pier on the other side of the bay. A boat to one of the more distant beaches such as Playa La Boquilla or Playa Ventanilla (beyond Mazunte) costs US$20 to US$30, including a return trip at an agreed time. Byron Luna (☎ 584-31-15), who lives across the street from the Hotel Cabaña, offers such trips and also snorkeling and fishing trips with equipment provided, starting at US$8 per person for two hours. He has mountain bikes for rent too.

Places to Stay

Places with an elevated location are more likely to catch any breeze. Mosquito screens are a big plus too. Some places have a water shortage; there's not always enough water to wash clothes. The following accommodations are listed in east-to-west order.

Hotel Soraya (☎ 584-30-09), on Vasconcelos overlooking the pier, is slightly run-down, but its 32 rooms with fan and bath are clean. All have a balcony and many have good views. Singles or doubles are US$15 (US$36 with air-con).

Greenery-shaded *Posada Rincón Sabroso* (☎ 584-30-95) is up a flight of stairs to the right as you start to wind your way around the bay. It has 10 fan-cooled rooms, each with bathroom, terrace and hammock. Singles/doubles are normally US$10/12, but they rise to between US$15 and US$20 in peak periods like Semana Santa. *El Almendro* (☎ 584-30-68), in a shady garden up a little lane a few meters past the Rincón Sabroso steps, has similarly clean rooms. Singles or doubles are US$17.

Villa Florencia (☎ 584-30-44) has 13 pleasant but smallish rooms with private bath, fan and screens. There's a cool sitting area. Singles/doubles/triples cost US$17/23/29 (plus US$3 for air-con).

Casa de Huéspedes Gundy y Tomás (☎ 584-30-68), owned by the same people as El Almendro, has a variety of rooms, all with fans and mosquito nets and/or screens. Singles are US$8 to US$9, doubles US$13 or US$15. The more expensive ones have their own bathrooms. At peak times you can hang or rent a hammock for US$3. Good food is available, including homemade bread and vegetable juices. Other amenities include pleasant sitting areas, an office safe for valuables and exchange service for cash or traveler's checks.

Casa Arnel (☎/fax 584-30-51) is along the lane past the market. Owned by members of the same family as Hotel Casa Arnel in Oaxaca, it has three clean rooms with fan and bath for US$12/16/18/23 singles/doubles/triples/quads. Two more rooms may be ready by the time you go. *Refrescos*, coffee and tea are available, and there's a breezy hammock area.

To reach the excellent *La Buena Vista* (☎/fax 584-31-04), turn right just past the arroyo, then go a short way up the first track on the left. The dozen or so big rooms and couple of excellent mud-brick bungalows here are kept scrupulously clean, and all have private bath, fans, mosquito screens and breezy balconies with hammocks. Prices for two people range from US$25 to US$36. There's a fine restaurant too.

German/Mexican-owned *Hotel Puesta del Sol* (☎/fax 584-30-96, harald_ferber@

hotmail.com) is up to the right just past the arroyo. The 14 rooms are sizable and clean, with fans and screens. Rooms with shared bath cost from US$8/9 single/double to US$11/13 double/triple; doubles with private bath are US$16 to US$22. Some rooms sleep up to six people for US$30. The more expensive rooms have their own terraces. Breakfast is offered, and a small library, satellite TV and videos are available in the sitting room. Hammocks out on the breezy terrace invite relaxation.

On the road descending to Playa del Panteón, *Casa de Huéspedes El Capy* (☎ 584-30-02) has 25 clean, cool but smallish rooms with fan, bath and mostly good views. Singles/doubles start at US$7/10.

Behind Playa del Panteón is the bigger *Hotel Cabaña* (☎ 584-31-05), with 23 comfortable double/triple rooms for US$18/24. Rooms have bath, fan and screens.

Farther along this road and up some steps to the right, the friendly *Posada Cañon Devata* (☎ 584-30-48, *lopezk@spin.com.mx)* has a variety of attractive accommodations scattered among hillside foliage. It's a good place for those seeking a quiet retreat. Rooms range from comfortable singles/doubles with fan and private bath at US$13/16, to a two-room, four-bed unit at US$35 for two plus US$3 for each extra adult. Fine, mainly vegetarian food is available. The posada is closed in May and June.

The European-owned *Bahía de la Luna* (☎ 584-86-38), out at Playa La Boquilla (see Beaches, earlier in this section), has nice adobe bungalows with bath, ranging from US$24/30 single/double to US$55 for five. It also has a good beachside restaurant-café with moderate prices – fish is around US$5, and good salads run US$3 to US$7.50. Some personal development workshops in yoga, astrology and so on are held here. The mailing address is Apartado Postal 90, Pochutla 70900, Oaxaca.

Places to Eat

The excellent restaurant at *La Buena Vista* is open for breakfast and in the evenings only (closed Sunday, except for a light breakfast). On an airy terrace overlooking the bay, it offers very well-prepared Mexican and American fare – from hotcakes (US$2.50) to *tamales* vegetarian or chicken-and-mole fillings for US$3.50 and US$3 respectively. You don't have to be staying at La Buena Vista to eat here.

Nonguests can also eat at the *Posada Cañon Devata*, where a good three-course dinner (US$8) is served at long tables in a lovely palm-roofed, open-sided dining room. Fare is usually vegetarian, with organically grown vegetables. Service starts at 7 pm, and it's best to book early in the day. Until 2 pm you can get items such as yogurt with granola and bananas, enchiladas, muffins and soyburgers on excellent homemade bread.

The *Rincón del Mar* has great views from its cliffside location, reached by steps up from the walkway leading to Playa del Panteón. The food's good too. The fish specialty, *filete a la cazuela* (US$3), is prepared with olives, peas, onions and tomatoes. Octopus and prawns cost around US$5; *verduras al vapor* (steamed vegetables) are just US$1.50.

The Italian *Villa Florencia*, on Boulevard Uribe, usually manages good pasta (try the pesto) from US$2.50 to US$4. It also serves good cappuccino (US$1.50), pizza, seafood, Mexican fare and inexpensive breakfasts.

The restaurants on Playa del Panteón, including *Restaurante Susy*, offer fish and seafood for US$3 to US$5, plus cheaper fare such as entomatadas and eggs. Be careful about the freshness of seafood in the low season. The setting is very pretty after dark.

At the terrace restaurant of *Casa de Huéspedes El Capy* – cool in the evening – fish, shrimp, chicken, meat and salads are mostly around US$3.

You'll find several places to eat on the main town beach and the main street, Boulevard Uribe. They're economical – breakfast around US$1.50, spaghetti and fish US$1.50 to US$2.50 – but none is very well frequented, though *Restaurant Marisol* has good-value food and cheap drinks (beer US$0.60, margarita US$1.25).

OAXACA STATE

Getting There & Away

To reach Puerto Ángel by bus, you first have to get to Pochutla. Frequent buses, camionetas and colectivo taxis run from 6 am to 8 pm between Pochutla, Puerto Ángel, Zipolite, San Agustinillo and Mazunte. After 8 pm you need a taxi. See the Pochutla section for details.

The main bus stop in Puerto Ángel is on the main street near the naval base.

A taxi from Puerto Ángel to Huatulco airport costs around US$20; to Puerto Escondido airport US$30.

ZIPOLITE

• pop 800

The beautiful 2km stretch of pale sand called Zipolite, beginning 3km west of Puerto Ángel, is fabled as southern Mexico's ultimate place to lie back in a hammock and do as little as you like, *in* as little as you like, *for* as little as you like (well, almost).

Once just a small fishing settlement with a few comedores, Zipolite grew fast in the 1990s. Hurricane Pauline in 1997 blew or washed away many of the flimsy budget accommodations, eateries and fisherfolk's homes that had come to line nearly the whole beach. But most establishments got back up on their feet quickly. Within a year Zipolite had probably even more buildings than before. In fact, some new constructions toward the west end of the beach upset some people by going three or even four stories high and using concrete instead of wood.

Zipolite is as great a place as ever to take it easy, its magic stemming from some combination of pounding sea and sun, open-air sleeping, unique scenery and the travelers' scene. The cluster of larger establishments toward the beach's west end is the hub of Zipolite for many, but there's plenty of room elsewhere if you prefer a more private existence. Zipolite is what each person makes of it.

Beware: The Zipolite surf is deadly, literally. It's fraught with rip tides, changing currents and a strong undertow. Locals don't swim here, and going in deeper than your knees can be risking your life. The number of drownings has decreased since local volunteers set up a lifeguard operation a few years ago, and the statistics of their first Semana Santa (Holy Week) of operations are eloquent about the dangers here: in that week the lifeguards rescued 39 people from the Zipolite surf – but couldn't save three people, who drowned. The lifeguards' homes are marked by red crosses and/or signs saying '*Aquí Vive un Salvavidas*' (here lives a lifeguard). They are mostly toward the east end of the beach.

If you do get swept out to sea, your best hope is to swim calmly parallel to the shore to get clear of the current pulling you outward.

Theft can be a problem at Zipolite, and it's inadvisable to walk along the Puerto Ángel-Zipolite road after dark – in fact, while researching this edition we heard of someone robbed at knifepoint on it in broad daylight. If you buy any drugs, be very careful who you buy them from.

Total nudity is more common at the west end of the beach.

Information

A money exchange office on the main road as you enter Zipolite accepts US and Canadian dollars in cash and traveler's checks. Hours are 9 am to 5 pm Monday to Saturday. A little farther west are a laundromat and telephone caseta.

Places to Stay

Palmera Trailer Park is on the road from Puerto Ángel just before you enter Zipolite.

Nearly every building along the beach rents small rooms or cabañas and/or has hammock space for travelers. Wander along and pick one that suits you – it makes sense to choose one where your belongings can be locked up. The following is just a selection of the many options, starting at the low-key east end (nearest Puerto Ángel) and moving west. *Chololo* and *Tomasa*, neighbors at the east end, are both run by friendly Mexican/Italian couples (the two Mexicans are sisters). Each has a few simple rooms for around US$6

Veracruz's 18th-century cathedral

Guitar man of Tamazunchale, in the Huasteca

NEIL SETCHFIELD

Street scene, Oaxaca city

DALE BUCKTON

Zipolite nude beach

JOHN NOBLE

A *motocarro* in Tehuantepec

RICHARD NEBESKY

Mural, Teotitlán de Valle

single or double. You can expect the food to be pretty good. *Lola's*, farther west, is bigger and more expensive, charging US$12/14 for its singles/doubles with fan, mosquito net and private bathroom. *La Palapa del Pescador*, home of the head lifeguard, has rooms for around US$5/6.

At the two-story *Lyoban* you can rent a hammock upstairs for US$2.50 or get rooms for US$3.50/5 to US$5/7. The rooms have no net or fan (the owners swear there are no mosquitoes). Past a few smaller places is *Palapa Katy*, with hammocks for US$2, downstairs rooms for US$4/5 and upstairs rooms for US$8 single or double. *Palapa Aris* has hammocks for US$1.50 downstairs and US$2 upstairs, and cabañas upstairs for US$6/8 facing the sea or US$5/6 not.

After a handful of small places either side of a small lagoon, the larger, more expensive *La Choza* has some rooms with private bath and fan for US$10/12. Sharing bathrooms you pay US$8/10, and there's a third story with hammocks for US$2. The food here gets good reports. A few doors west, *El Eclipse* pizzeria offers a few third-story *cabañitas* with bed, hammock and net for US$5/7. *Tao*, next door, has plenty of simple wood-and-adobe rooms containing a double bed and mosquito net for US$6/7. Past the large, American-owned *Posada Brisa Marina* (cabañas and rooms from US$6 to US$16) is *Restaurant Posada San Cristóbal*, with fan rooms along a leafy garden for US$15 single or double with private bath, US$7 with shared bath.

Past another small lagoon, the varied cabañas of Mexican/Swiss-owned *Lo Cósmico* are built around a tall rock outcrop near the west end of the beach. Each has a double bed, hammock, fan and net, for US$7 or US$8. The food is good here.

The long-established *Shambhala Posada*, also known as *Casa Gloria* after its American owner, climbs the hill at the west end of the beach – with great views back along it. You can camp or sling or rent a hammock here for US$1.50 to US$2 per person. Rooms with mosquito nets go for US$5/6, and the few cabañas here rent for US$10 for

one or two people, US$15 for three. Shambhala has a restaurant, as well as a luggage room to keep your stuff safe. The shared bathrooms are OK.

Places to Eat

Few places at Zipolite have free drinking water. A typical plate of fish, rice and salad in most places costs around US$3 or US$3.50. Some offer spaghetti or other variations for less.

Some places, especially toward the west end of the beach, have greater choices and formal menus – and more customers. One, *El Eclipse*, does good Italian fare, with pasta, pizza, fish and chicken all between US$3 and US$4.50. There's even wine (US$1.50 a glass). *Restaurant Posada San Cristóbal* offers variety from *pan francés* (French toast, US$1.50) or antojitos (US$2 to US$3) to whole fish, prawns or octopus (US$4 to US$5). Popular *El Alquimista* has pizzas, fish or chicken for US$3 to US$4.50, and pasta or salads for US$2 to US$3.

Lo Cósmico, on the rocks near the west end of the beach, has an open-air restaurant with good food prepared in an impeccably clean kitchen. Especially tasty are the delicious crepas (sweet and savory) for US$2 to US$2.50, and the salads.

A couple of blocks back from the beach, roughly behind La Choza, is *Pizzeria 3 de Diciembre*, open 7 pm to 2 am Wednesday to Sunday. As well as excellent pizzas (US$3 to US$4.25), it serves good pastry pies, including vegetarian options such as cauliflower-and-parmesan or baked spinach, for US$1 to US$3.

Entertainment

Down toward the west end of the beach, the beachfront restaurants-cum-bars with happy hours, such as *El Alquimista*, are popular around sunset and after dark. *The Green Hole*, around midbeach just east of the lagoon, has beers for US$0.60. *El Hongo*, behind Restaurant Posada San Cristóbal, often rocks on quite late. For marginally more formal nightlife try *Disco/Bar La Puesta del Sol*, two minutes' walk back from Teponaztli

Mexico's Turtles: Not Saved Yet

Of the world's eight sea turtle species, seven are found in Mexican waters. Turtle nesting sites are scattered all along Mexico's coasts.

Female turtles usually lay their eggs on the beaches where they were born, some swimming huge distances to do so. They come ashore at night, scoop a trough in the sand and lay 50 to 200 eggs in it. Then they cover the eggs and go back to the sea. Six to 10 weeks later, the baby turtles hatch, dig their way out and crawl to the sea at night. Only two or three of every 100 make it to adulthood.

Playa Escobilla, just east of Puerto Escondido, is one of the world's main nesting grounds for the small **olive ridley turtle** (*tortuga golfina* to Mexicans), the only unendangered sea turtle species. Between May and January, about 700,000 olive ridleys come ashore here in about a dozen waves – known as *arribadas* – each lasting two or three nights. Arribadas often (though not always) happen during the waning of the moon. Playa Escobilla's turtles are guarded by armed soldiers, and there is no tourist access to the beach.

The rare **leatherback** (*tortuga Laúd* or *tortuga de altura*) is the largest sea turtle – it grows up to 3m long and can weigh one ton and live 80 years. One nesting beach for the leatherback is Playa Mermejita, between Punta Cometa and Playa Ventanilla, near Mazunte. Another is Barra de la Cruz, east of Bahías de Huatulco.

The smallest and most endangered sea turtle, the **Kemp's ridley**, or parrot turtle (*tortuga lora*), lives only in the Gulf of Mexico. Its nesting beaches are nearly all in the Mexican state of Tamaulipas (see the Northeast Mexico chapter). The approximately 4000 nests recorded there in 1998 were the most since the 1960s, giving hope that joint Mexican-US conservation efforts are bringing the Kemp's ridley back from the brink of extinction.

The **green turtle** (*tortuga verde* or *tortuga prieta*) is a vegetarian that grazes on marine grasses. Most adults are about 1m long. For millennia, the green turtle's meat and eggs have provided

Green turtle

Mexico's Turtles: Not Saved Yet

protein to humans in the tropics. European exploration of the globe marked the beginning of the turtle's decline. By the 19th century, tinned turtle was available in London. In the 1960s, the Empacadora Baja California in Ensenada, Baja California, was canning as many as 100 tons of turtle soup a season. Many green turtle nesting sites are at remote spots in Baja California and Michoacán, though more accessible sites can be found on Mexico's Caribbean coast and in Baja around Bahía Los Frailes and near San José del Cabo.

The **loggerhead turtle** *(tortuga caguama)* is famous for the vast distances it crosses between its feeding grounds and nesting sites. Loggerheads born in Japan and even, it's thought, Australia, cross the Pacific to feed off Baja California. Females later return to their birthplaces – a year-long journey – to lay their eggs.

The **hawksbill turtle** *(tortuga de carey)* nests along both of Mexico's coasts, while the country's seventh species, the **black turtle** *(tortuga negra)*, sticks to the Pacific.

Despite international conservation efforts, turtle flesh and eggs continue to be eaten, and the eggs are still believed to be an aphrodisiac. Turtle skin and shell are used to make clothing and adornments. The world's fishing boats kill many turtles by trapping and drowning them in nets.

In Mexico, hunting and killing sea turtles was officially banned in 1990, but illicit killing and egg-raiding still goes on – hardly surprising, since one clutch of eggs can be sold for more than a typical worker makes in a week. When the soldiers guarding Playa Escobilla temporarily left their posts in 1996 in response to a guerrilla attack at Bahías de Huatulco, poachers descended on the beach, slaughtering turtles and taking an estimated 800,000 to 1 million eggs.

Another major setback to sea turtles in Mexico came in 1997, when Hurricane Pauline destroyed hundreds of thousands of nests on Pacific beaches – especially in Oaxaca state – wiping out a large proportion of that year's eggs.

And greedy politicians and developers continue to pose a threat to turtles without lifting a finger to actually hunt or kill them. Environmentalists were outraged in 1998 when the Caribbean beach of Xcacel was sold to the Spanish hotel group Meliá. Xcacel is a very important nesting beach for loggerhead and green turtles, and it's feared that, despite official claims that the turtles are under protection, disturbance caused by hotel building here will simply scare the creatures away. See the Turtle Happenings Internet site at www.turtles.org for more on the Xcacel shenanigans and further fascinating turtle facts.

Other important Mexican turtle nesting sites include Playa Troncones, near Zihuatanejo, Guerrero; Lechugillas, Veracruz; Celestún, Yucatán; and Pamul, Quintana Roo. Nesting seasons vary, but July to September are peak months in many places.

To help the turtles that use Mexican beaches – and most people who have seen these graceful creatures swimming at sea are likely to want to do that – follow these tips if you find yourself at a nesting beach:

- Try to avoid nesting beaches altogether between sunset and sunrise.
- Don't approach turtles emerging from the sea, or disturb nesting turtles or hatchlings with noise or lights (lights on or even near the beach can cause hatchlings to lose their sense of direction on their journey to the water).
- Keep vehicles, even bicycles, off nesting beaches.
- Don't build sand castles or stick umbrellas into the sand.
- Never handle baby turtles or carry them to the sea – their arduous scramble is vital to their development.
- Boycott shops or stalls selling products made from sea turtles or any other endangered species.

OAXACA STATE

on the beach just east of La Choza. Nothing much happens there before midnight. Nearby *El Chayón* bar also stays open late.

Getting There & Away
The road from Puerto Ángel to Zipolite and Mazunte is paved. Buses, camionetas and colectivo taxis run every few minutes from Pochutla to Puerto Ángel, Zipolite and Mazunte from about 6 am to 8 pm. See Pochutla for details. Puerto Ángel to Zipolite costs US$0.25 in a camioneta, a bit more in a colectivo taxi.

MAZUNTE & AROUND
West from Zipolite, other glorious beaches stretch almost unbroken all the way to Puerto Escondido. The villages of San Agustinillo (4km from Zipolite) and Mazunte (1km farther) have relaxed places to stay and fine safe beaches.

The coast between Zipolite and Puerto Escondido is a major sea turtle nesting site. Until a decade ago some 50,000 turtles were being killed per year at a slaughterhouse at San Agustinillo. Mazunte and San Agustinillo villages grew up around this industry. After killing sea turtles was officially banned in Mexico in 1990, many villagers turned to slash-and-burn agriculture, endangering the nearby forests. In 1991, with the encouragement of a Mexico City-based environmental group, Ecosolar, Mazunte declared itself an ecological reserve, aiming to preserve the local environment while creating a sustainable economy. Projects included printing and natural cosmetics workshops, the building of ecological toilets, and garbage separation. Potential earnings from tourism were a key element, and the government-funded Centro Mexicano de la Tortuga (see below) was also intended to encourage this. Since Hurricane Pauline in 1997, which caused great damage at Mazunte, the influence of Ecosolar has waned, but some ecological projects continue.

Playa Aragón & Playa San Agustinillo
Long, straight Playa Aragón – another beach in the Zipolite mold, but almost empty – stretches west from the headland at the west end of Zipolite. Footpaths cross the headland behind the Shambhala Posada, or you can take the road, which loops inland then comes back down to tiny San Agustinillo village at the west end of Playa Aragón. San Agustinillo's own much shorter beach stretches between two small rocky headlands, and its waves are often good for bodysurfing. It's backed by a line of comedores behind which are the ruins of the turtle abattoir.

There are a few places to stay. Atop the steep slope backing Playa Aragón, *Rancho Cerro Largo* (fax 9-584-30-63) has a handful of superior, fan-cooled cabañas at US$40/50 or US$50/60 for single/doubles, including a good breakfast and dinner. West along the hilltop, *Restaurant El Mirador* has a couple of adobe cabañas with double bed, net and a patio for hammock-hanging, at US$10 single or double. Both these places are reachable by drivable tracks from the road or by paths up from the beach.

Cabañas Sol y Mar, at the west end of Playa Aragón, has rooms on both sides of the road: US$7 on the beach side, US$5 on the land side, or US$1.50 for breezy upstairs hammocks (beach side). *Palapa Olas Altas*, toward the east end of Playa San Agustinillo, has seven or eight breezy upstairs palapas with mosquito nets for US$6, single or double. *Magic Hostel*, a new venture by the hostel of the same name in Oaxaca city, was due to open on San Agustinillo in 2000.

Fish fillet, octopus or prawns at most San Agustinillo comedores costs US$3 to US$4. *Palapa de Evelia* prepares its food well.

Mazunte
• pop 430 ☎ 9
As you enter Mazunte by road from San Agustinillo, the Centro Mexicano de la Tortuga is on the left. A little farther along on the right is the village plaza. Mazunte's fine beach – generally safe, though the waves can be quite big – curves around to Punta Cometa, the headland at its west end.

Centro Mexicano de la Tortuga The Mexican Turtle Center, a government-funded aquarium and research center for Mexico's many turtle species, opened in 1994, was wrecked by Hurricane Pauline in 1997 and reopened in 1999. All seven of Mexico's marine turtle species are on view in fairly large tanks, and it's enthralling to get a close-up view of these creatures, some of which are *big*. The center is open 10 am to 4.30 pm Tuesday to Saturday, 10 am to 2.30 pm Sunday (US$2). Visits are guided (in Spanish) and happen every 10 to 15 minutes.

Cosméticos Naturales Mazunte's Natural Cosmetics workshop and store is by the roadside toward the west end of the village. Set up with help from a range of organizations, including the Body Shop, this small cooperative makes shampoo and cosmetics from things such as maize, coconut, avocado and sesame seeds. It also sells organic coffee and natural soaps and mosquito repellents from elsewhere. The store is open 9 am to 4 pm daily; there are demonstrations at 11 am Monday and Tuesday.

Boat Trips Ask around about the possibility of boat trips out to sea to swim with turtles and/or dolphins. Expect to pay US$20 to US$30 for two hours.

Places to Stay & Eat Most places on the beach have rooms, cabañas or hammock/tent space. Typical prices are US$2 per person to camp or sleep in a hammock, and anywhere from US$5/6 for simple single/double rooms or cabañas to US$40 or so for fancy large cabañas. *Cabañas Ziga*, on a breezy hillock near the turtle center, has four decent little rooms with fan and mosquito net, sharing two bathrooms, for US$10 single or double. In the next couple of places west, double rooms or cabañas range from US$8 to US$20.

On a small, rocky outcrop toward the west end of the beach, *Posada del Arquitecto*, run by an Italian/Mexican couple, has hammocks for US$2.50 and rooms for two at US$10 with a mosquito net and US$15 with private bath. The Italian partner, Guido, is a bioarchitect who works with the

natural features of the land using only natural materials. *El Rinconcito*, at the beach end of the street here, offers simple single/double rooms and palapas for US$6/8. The *Comedor Cruz Marina*, back up the street a little, has two superior cabañas, with double bed, electricity and bath, just above the beach, past El Rinconcito. These cost US$30 and US$40 for two people, and each has a *tapanco* (hanging upper floor) that can be occupied for US$5 and US$6, respectively, per extra person.

Enjoying a lovely, breezy spot up a path from the west end of the beach – and signposted for vehicles from the street nearby – is the *Alta Mira* (☎ 584-31-04), run by the people from La Buena Vista at Puerto Ángel. Prices for this new establishment had not been determined when we visited, but the cool palapa bungalows – four with one bedroom, one with two, and all with nice tiled bathrooms – promised to be great places to stay. The Alta Mira has its own restaurant. Next door is *Las Brisas*, with cabañas for US$8 to US$10.

Typical beach comedor prices are US$3.50 for a fish filet, prawns or octopus; US$1.50 for eggs. *Restaurant El Arbolito*, halfway along the beach, offers more variety and originality than most. Try its prawn-stuffed potato or avocado for US$2.50.

Getting There & Away Buses, camionetas and colectivo taxis shuttle back and forth between Pochutla and Mazunte from about 6 am to 7.30 pm. A camioneta from Mazunte to Puerto Ángel is about US$0.60, to Pochutla US$1. Beyond Mazunte, the paved road continues about 5km to meet highway 200 at San Antonio.

Playa Ventanilla

Some 2.5km along the road west from Mazunte, a sign points left to Playa Ventanilla, 1.2km down a dirt track. A couple of small beachside homes and comedores constitute the settlement here. For about US$5 per person the locals will paddle you around a mangrove-fringed lagoon a little way down the beach, where you'll see crocodiles and a variety of bird life (most prolific during July and August). Horseback rides are also available. Take care if swimming in the sea.

A taxi from Mazunte is US$3.

BAHÍAS DE HUATULCO
• pop 18,000 ☎ 9

Mexico's newest big coastal resort is arising along a series of beautiful sandy bays, the Bahías de Huatulco ('wah-TOOL-koh'), 50km east of Pochutla. Until the 1980s this stretch of coast had just one small fishing village and was known to only a few outsiders as a great place for a quiet swim in translucent waters. Huatulco's developers appear to have learned some lessons from other modern Mexican resorts. Pockets of development are separated by tracts of unspoiled shoreline. The maximum building height is six stories, and no sewage goes into the sea. For now, Huatulco is still an enjoyable, relatively uncrowded resort with a succession of lovely beaches lapped by beautiful water and backed by forest. But it's not a place to stay long on a tight budget.

Orientation
A divided road leads about 5km down from highway 200 to La Crucecita, the service town for the resort. La Crucecita has the bus stations, the market, most of the shops and the only cheap accommodations. One kilometer south, on Bahía de Santa Cruz, is Santa Cruz Huatulco, site of the original village (no trace remains), with some hotels and a harbor. The other main developments so far are at Bahía Chahué, 1km east of Santa Cruz, and Tangolunda, 4km farther east.

The Huatulco bays are strung along the coast about 10km in each direction from Santa Cruz. From west to east, the main ones are: San Agustín, Chachacual, Cacaluta, Maguey, El Órgano, Santa Cruz, Chahué, Tangolunda and Conejos.

Bahías de Huatulco airport is 400m north of highway 200, 12km west of the turnoff to La Crucecita.

Information
Tourist Offices An information booth planned for La Crucecita's Plaza Principal should be operating daily by the time you get there. The Sedetur Oaxaca state tourist office (☎ 587-15-41), on Boulevard Santa Cruz in Santa Cruz, is open 8 am to 5 pm Monday to Friday, 8 am to 2 pm Saturday.

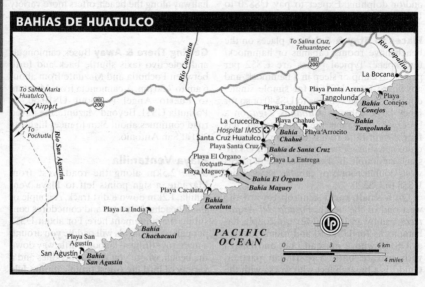

BAHÍAS DE HUATULCO

The Asociación de Hoteles de Huatulco (☎ 587-08-48), next door, also provides tourist information and has similar hours.

Money Bancrecer, at Bugambilias 1104, La Crucecita, changes cash and traveler's checks 9 am to 5 pm Monday to Friday, 10 am to 2 pm Saturday. Banamex and Bancomer on Boulevard Santa Cruz in Santa Cruz also change cash and traveler's checks and have ATMs.

Post & Communications La Crucecita's post office, on Boulevard Chahué, 400m east of the Plaza Principal, is open 8 am to 7 pm Monday to Friday and 9 am to 1 pm Saturday.

Also in La Crucecita, you can use the Internet at Grupo Mare, Guanacastle 203, for US$0.10 a minute. It's open 9 am to 2 pm and 4 to 8.30 pm Monday to Friday, 9 am to 2 pm Saturday.

Laundry Lavandería Estrella, on Flamboyan at Carrizal in La Crucecita, will wash 3kg of laundry for US$2.50 with same-day pick-up. Lavandería Abril, Gardenia 1403, is marginally cheaper.

Medical Services Some doctors speak English at the Hospital IMSS (☎ 587-11-83), on Boulevard Chahué, halfway between La Crucecita and Bahía Chahué. The big hotels have English-speaking doctors on call.

Parque Ecológico Rufino Tamayo

This park on the edge of La Crucecita is composed mainly of natural vegetation, with some paved paths and tile-roofed shelters with benches.

Beaches

Huatulco's beaches are sandy with clear waters (though boats and Jet Skis leave an oily film here and there). As throughout Mexico, all beaches are under federal control, and anyone can use them even when hotels appear to treat them as private property. Some beaches have coral offshore and excellent snorkeling, though visibility can be poor in the rainy season.

Lanchas will whisk you out to most of the beaches from Santa Cruz Huatulco's harbor anytime between 8 am and 4 or 5 pm, and they'll return to collect you by dusk. Taxis can also get you to most beaches for less money, but a boat ride is more fun. Lancha

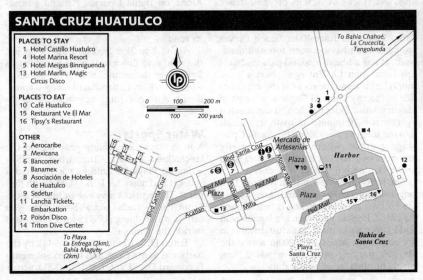

SANTA CRUZ HUATULCO

PLACES TO STAY
1 Hotel Castillo Huatulco
4 Hotel Marina Resort
5 Hotel Meigas Binniguenda
13 Hotel Marlin, Magic
    Circus Disco

PLACES TO EAT
10 Café Huatulco
15 Restaurant Ve El Mar
16 Tipsy's Restaurant

OTHER
2 Aerocaribe
3 Mexicana
6 Bancomer
7 Banamex
8 Asociación de Hoteles
    de Huatulco
9 Sedetur
11 Lancha Tickets,
    Embarkation
12 Poisón Disco
14 Triton Dive Center

To Bahía Chahué,
La Crucecita,
Tangolunda

0   100   200 m
0   100   200 yards

Mercado de
Artesanías

Plaza

Harbor

Bahía de
Santa Cruz

Playa
Santa Cruz

To Playa
La Entrega (2km),
Bahía Maguey
(2km)

OAXACA STATE

tickets are sold at a hut beside the harbor. Roundtrip rates for up to 10 people include: Playa La Entrega, US$10; Bahía Maguey or Bahía El Órgano, US$30. Another possibility for a fun day is a 6½-hour, seven-bay boat cruise with an open bar, leaving daily at 11 am for US$15 per person.

Bahía de Santa Cruz At Santa Cruz Huatulco, the small **Playa Santa Cruz** is kept pretty clean but is inferior to most Huatulco beaches.

Playa La Entrega lies toward the outer edge of Bahía de Santa Cruz, a five-minute lancha trip or 2.5km by paved road from Santa Cruz. This 300m-long beach, backed by a line of seafood palapas, can get crowded, but it has calm water and good snorkeling in a large area from which boats are cordoned off. 'La Entrega' means 'The Delivery': here in 1831, Mexican independence hero Vicente Guerrero was betrayed to his enemies by an Italian sea captain for 50,000 pieces of gold. Guerrero was taken to Cuilapan, near Oaxaca, and shot.

West of Bahía de Santa Cruz Roads to the western bays are, where they exist, unpaved tracks. A 1.5km drivable track leads to **Bahía Maguey** from the road to La Entrega, about half a kilometer out of Santa Cruz. Maguey's fine, 400m beach curves around a calm bay between forested headlands. It has a line of seafood palapas but is less busy than La Entrega. There's good snorkeling around the rocks at the left (east) side of the bay. **Bahía El Órgano**, just east of Maguey, has a 250m beach. You can reach it by a narrow 10-minute footpath that heads into the trees halfway along the Santa Cruz-Maguey track, where that track briefly broadens out. Maguey has calm waters good for snorkeling, but it lacks comedores.

The beach at **Bahía Cacaluta** is about 1km long and protected by an island, though there can be undertow. Snorkeling is best around the island. Behind the beach is a lagoon with bird life. A narrow track that's just drivable in dry conditions heads west 200m above the Maguey parking area and winds 2.5km, mostly through forest, to Cacaluta.

Bahía Chachacual, inaccessible by land, has a headland at each end and two beaches: The easterly Playa La India is one of Huatulco's most beautiful.

Thirteen kilometers down a dirt road from a crossroads on highway 200, 1.7km west of the airport, is **Bahía San Agustín**. After 9km the road fords a river, which can be tricky after rains. The beach is long and sandy, with a long line of palapa comedores, some with hammocks to rent for overnight. It's popular with Mexicans on weekends and holidays, but it's quiet at other times. Usually the waters are calm and the snorkeling is good (some of the comedores rent equipment).

East of Bahía de Santa Cruz A paved road runs to the eastern bays from La Crucecita and Santa Cruz, continuing eventually to highway 200. **Bahía Chahué** has a beach at its west end and a new harbor at its east end. **Bahía Tangolunda** is the site of the major top-end hotel developments to date. The sea is sometimes rough here, and you should beware of currents and heed the colored-flag safety system. Tangolunda has an 18-hole golf course too. Three kilometers farther east is the long sweep of **Playa Punta Arena**, on Bahía Conejos. Around a headland at the east end of Bahía Conejos is the more sheltered **Playa Conejos**, unreachable by road.

About 2 to 3km beyond Bahía Conejos, the road runs down to the coast again at **La Bocana**, at the mouth of the Río Copalita, where you'll find a handful of seafood comedores. Another long beach stretches to the east.

Water Sports

You can rent snorkeling gear beside the lancha kiosk at Santa Cruz harbor for US$4 a day. At Playa La Entrega you can rent a snorkel and mask for US$2 (US$4 with flippers). These prices may rise in high season. From Tipsy's restaurant at Santa Cruz you can go water-skiing (US$15 for 15 minutes) or ride the 'banana.'

Triton Dive Center (☎ 587-08-44), by the harbor at Santa Cruz, and Buceo Sotavento (Leeward Dive Center; ☎ 581-00-51), across

LA CRUCECITA

To Hwy 200,
Pochutla

*Parque Ecológico
Rufino Tamayo*

0   50   100 m
0   50   100 yards

Saball
Cardenia
Pochote
Jazmin
Palo Verde
Palma Real
Ocotillo
Macuil
Macuihtie
Guarumbo
Guanacastle
*Plaza
Principal*
Flamboyan
Canal
Laurel

Av Buganbilia
Blvd Chahué
Camizal

Market
Guamuchil
Flamboyan
Chacah
Colorin
Cocotillo

Av Oaxaca
Blvd Chahué
Blvd Chahué

To Santa
Cruz Huatulco

To Hospital IMSS,
Posada Chahué,
Bahía Chahué,
Tangolunda

PLACES TO STAY
3 Hotel Benimar
5 Posada Michelle
10 Misión de los Arcos
11 Hotel Flamboyant
18 Plaza Conejos Hotel
20 Hotel Busanvi I
22 Hotel Posada Del Parque
25 Hotel Suites Begonias
29 Hotel Arrecife

PLACES TO EAT
14 Comedores
17 Los Portales
23 Cactus Bar & Grill
24 Restaurant-Bar Oasis
26 Restaurant La Crucecita

OTHER
1 Transportes Rápidos de
  Pochutla Bus Stop
2 Park Entrances
4 Lavandería Abril
6 Estrella Blanca/Transportes
  Gacela Bus Station
7 Cristóbal Colón
  Bus Station
8 Budget Rent a Car
9 Bancrecer
12 La Crema
13 Grupo Mare
15 Park Entrances
16 Pemex
19 Colectivo Taxi
  & Microbus Stop
21 Plaza Oaxaca, Sideout,
  Piraguas
27 Lavandería Estrella
28 Post Office

the street from the Sheraton at Tangolunda, will take you diving.

The Copalita and Zimatán Rivers near Huatulco have waters ranging from class 1 to class 4/5 in rafting terms. They're at their biggest in the rainy season, between July and November. Rafting and kayaking trips are offered by Copalita River Tours (☎ 587-05-35) in the Posada Michelle on Gardenia (next to the EB bus station); La Crucecita; Huatulco Outfitters (☎ 581-03-15), Centro Comercial Punta Tangolunda, Local 5, Tangolunda; and Aventuras Piraguas (☎ 587-13-33), Local 19, Plaza Oaxaca, La Crucecita.

With Copalita River Tours, a four-hour beginner/family outing is US$25 per person, and a longer, more challenging trip is US$45. With Huatulco Outfitters, a five-hour trip with some class-4 waters costs US$75 per person; shorter, easier trips are US$35.

Places to Stay

Most Huatulco room rates vary with the seasons. Prices given in this section, unless stated otherwise, are for the season between early January and Easter. Rates typically rise about 30% during the main holiday periods: Semana Santa, mid-July to the end of August, and from about December 20 to January 4. In the remaining periods, they may drop 20%.

Places to Stay – Budget

All these hotels are in La Crucecita. Rates are the same for single or double occupancy.

The varied rooms at the *Hotel Arrecife* (☎ 587-17-07, *Colorín 510*) cost from US$7 to US$20. The best are sizable, with air-con, balcony and TV; the worst are small and open straight onto the street. All have private bath, but in some cases it's outside the room. Decent rooms with fan are US$10 to US$15.

Posada Michelle (☎ 587-05-35) is next to the EB bus station and can be noisy. But it's a friendly place, and the dozen or so rooms are reasonable, ranging from US$12 with fan to US$20 with air-con and TV.

The family-run *Hotel Benimar* (☎ 587-04-47, *Bugambilias 1404*) is clean and adequate. Rooms have fan and bath for US$12.

Places to Stay – Mid-Range

La Crucecita The *Hotel Posada Del Parque* (☎ 587-02-19), on the Plaza Principal, has fairly comfortable and sizable rooms for US$18.50 with fan or US$23 with air-con, single or double. *Hotel Busanvi I* (☎ 587-00-56, *Carrizal 601*) has plain rooms with fan for US$17 or with air-con for US$25, single or double. The *Plaza Conejos Hotel*, on Guamuchil, half a block from the plaza, offers singles/doubles for US$15/20.

The small *Hotel Suites Begonias* (☎ 587-00-18, *Bugambilias 503*) has comfortable rooms with TV and fan, opening on upstairs walkways, for US$22/27.

The pink *Hotel Flamboyant* (☎ 587-01-13), on the Plaza Principal, has a pleasant courtyard, helpful staff, a nice pool, its own restaurant and air-conditioned rooms for US$41 single or double, including breakfast. It runs free transportation to Playa La Entrega.

The *Misión de los Arcos* (☎ 587-01-65, *Gardenia 902*) is a new 13-room hotel embellished by a touch of interior greenery. Its nice, big, bright rooms cost US$30 single or double with fan, or US$35 with air-con.

Elsewhere The *Posada Chahué* (☎ 587-09-45, *Mixe 75*) is about 1km east of La Crucecita and 500m from Playa Chahué. Going down Boulevard Chahué toward Bahía Chahué, take the second turn to the left (east) after the Pemex station. The 12 attractive rooms, each with two double beds, air-con, fans and color TV, cost US$21/28 single/double. The hotel also has a moderately priced restaurant and small pool.

The small *Hotel Plaza Huatulco* (☎ 581-00-35, *Boulevard Juárez 23*) is across the street from the Sheraton in Tangolunda. Standard rooms cost US$35 single or double; suites cost US$40 for one or two people, US$75 for three or four, and US$110 for five or six. All units have air-con and cable TV; the suites also have terraces and kitchenettes.

Places to Stay – Top End

If what you want is a holiday in a top-end Huatulco hotel, a package is very probably your best bet. US and Canadian companies selling Huatulco packages include Apple Vacations, Gogo Tours, MLT, Funjet and Vacances Air Transat. If you're already in Mexico, consider Mexicana airline's VTP (*Viaje Todo Pagado*) packages. Around US$600 could buy two people return flights from Mexico City and three nights in a top hotel.

Santa Cruz Huatulco The *Hotel Marlin* (☎ 587-00-55, *Mitla 28*) has nicely decorated, colorful rooms with TV and air-con for US$55 single or double. It has a restaurant and small pool too.

Hotel Meigas Binniguenda (☎ 587-00-77, *Boulevard Santa Cruz 201*) is Huatulco's oldest hotel, dating from all of 1987. It has a garden, pool, restaurant and 195 air-conditioned rooms with TV at US$59 single or double.

Hotel Castillo Huatulco (☎ 587-01-44), on Boulevard Santa Cruz, has a decent pool, a restaurant and 112 good-size air-conditioned rooms with TV for US$82 single or double. It also has a beach club on Bahía Chahué, with free transportation.

The 40-room *Hotel Marina Resort* (☎ 587-09-63), on the east side of the harbor, charges US$88 single or double and has three pools.

Bahía Chahué The *Hotel Villablanca* (☎ 587-06-06), on Boulevard Juárez about 250m back from Playa Chahué, has a good pool and offers pleasant air-conditioned rooms with satellite TV for US$53 single or double. Main dishes in its restaurant cost from US$4 to US$6.50.

Tangolunda The luxurious *Quinta Real* (☎ 581-04-28, Paseo Juárez 2) has a hilltop position at the west end of Tangolunda, with 27 suites only. They start at US$290 in high season, US$210 in low. All have Jacuzzi and ocean view. The grounds extend down to the beach, with a pool area near the beach.

A little farther east, the *Sheraton Huatulco Resort* (☎ 581-00-55) has more than 300 rooms, all with ocean view, at US$234 single or double. Its big pool sits in a beachside garden, and you'll find all the amenities you'd expect – restaurants, bars, tennis courts, water sports, shops, nightly mariachi entertainment. Next door, and strangely similar in color and architecture, is the *Royal Maeva Huatulco* (☎ 581-00-00), with four pools, a disco and 300 air-conditioned rooms at US$192/320 for singles/doubles in high season, US$138/230 in low. Rates include all meals and drinks, land and water sports, and entertainment. Package visitors rave about this hotel and its friendly staff.

A little farther around the bay, the *Camino Real Zaashila* (☎ 581-04-60, Boulevard Juárez 5) is perhaps the most attractive Tangolunda hotel, with the biggest pool in the nicest gardens. It's also more tranquil than the previous two. Standard rates for the 180 or so rooms are US$200 to US$250 single or double (the more expensive ones have their own small pool), but promotional rates cut that by almost half at times.

Beyond the Zaashila is the elegant *Casa del Mar* (☎ 581-02-03), with 25 air-conditioned suites only, for US$99 single or double.

The 135-room *Crown Pacific Resort* (☎ 581-00-44, Boulevard Juárez 8) climbs the hillside at the back of Tangolunda but has a beach club next to the Sheraton. Rates include meals, drinks and activities and are similar to the Royal Maeva's.

Places to Eat

La Crucecita The very clean *mercado* (market) has several comedores serving up fish or shrimp platters for US$2 to US$3 and enfrijoladas or entomatadas for US$1.50. Market stalls also sell fresh fruit.

Restaurant-Bar Oasis, on the Plaza Principal, has good and moderately priced, if unadventurous, fare, from tortas around US$1.75 to *filete de pescado* at US$5 or steaks around US$6. It takes a stab at Japanese food too. *Los Portales* is also good, with offerings such as an *alambre de pechuga de pollo* (chicken breast kebab) with bell peppers and onions for US$4, or a *farolado de pollo* (two flour tortillas with chicken, bacon and cheese) for US$2.50. Seafood main dishes at *Cactus Bar & Grill*, on the south side of the plaza, run US$7.25 and up. *Restaurant La Crucecita*, Bugambilias at Chacah, a block from the plaza, is open 7 am to 10 pm and serves well-priced breakfasts. Its *sincronizadas a la mexicana* (US$2.50) make a good antojito.

Santa Cruz Huatulco Food at the eateries on Playa Santa Cruz is mostly average, except at *Restaurant Ve El Mar*, at the east end, where the seafood is fine and the margaritas potent. A whole fish or an octopus or shrimp dish costs US$4 to US$6, and lobster is US$8 and up.

Café Huatulco, in the plaza near the harbor, serves good local Pluma coffee in many different ways – the *capuchino frío* (cold cappuccino with a dollop of ice cream) is well worth a splash at US$1.50 – and rich cakes for around US$2.50.

Tangolunda The big hotels offer a choice of expensive bars, coffee shops and restaurants. The *Casa del Mar* hotel has one of the best restaurants, with a great view.

You'll spend US$30 to US$50 for a full dinner with wine.

There are also a few restaurants, medium to expensive in price, along Tangolunda's two streets. The **Argentina Grill**, opposite the Sheraton, serves steaks and other hunks of meat for around US$9. **Restaurant La Pampa Argentina**, at the west end, where the two streets meet, does good steaks for US$12 to US$20.

Beaches The seafood palapas at La Entrega are ordinary (US$5 to US$6 for fish or seafood), but we had a fine meal at Maguey – around US$4 for a whole huachinango. The comedores at La Bocana will cook you up a tasty grilled fish with fries or salad for around US$4.

Entertainment

La Crema bar, overlooking the Plaza Principal in La Crucecita (the entrance is on Gardenia), pulls the coolest crowd. It's open 8 pm to 4 am nightly. A shot of tequila is US$1.50 to US$3, and cocktails and pizzas are available too.

The Santa Cruz 'disco-clubs' – **Magic Circus**, beside Hotel Marlin, and **Poisón**, near the harbor – are open Wednesday or Thursday to Saturday or Sunday, from around 10 pm on. Cover charges are typically US$5 per person, but different nights have different deals.

Noches Oaxaqueñas, by the traffic circle in Tangolunda, presents a Guelaguetza regional dance show Friday, Saturday and Sunday evenings for US$10 (plus drinks and/or dinner).

Getting There & Away

Air Mexicana offers two or more flights daily to/from Mexico City (US$119 and up). Aerocaribe flies to/from Palenque daily and to/from Mérida and Tuxtla Gutiérrez three or four times weekly. For flights to/from Oaxaca, see the Oaxaca Getting There & Away section. Cheap charters from Canada and the US are occasionally available.

Mexicana (☎ 587-02-23, or 581-90-08 at the airport) and Aerocaribe (☎ 587-12-20, or 581-90-30 at the airport) have offices next to the Hotel Castillo Huatulco in Santa Cruz. STS travel agency (☎ 587-12-11), at the Hotel Castillo Huatulco, sells Global Air tickets.

Bus The main bus stations are on Gardenia in La Crucecita. Some buses coming to Huatulco are marked 'Santa Cruz Huatulco,' but they still terminate in La Crucecita. Make sure your bus is *not* headed to Santa María Huatulco, which is a long way inland.

Cristóbal Colón (1st-class, ☎ 587-02-61) is on Gardenia at Ocotillo, four blocks from the plaza. Most of its buses are de paso. EB (☎ 587-01-03), Gardenia at Palma Real, has 'primera' services that are quick and fairly comfortable, though not really 1st-class, and ordinario buses, which are typical ordinario. Daily departures include:

Oaxaca – 405km, 7½ hours, via Salina Cruz; 1 Colón overnight (US$16)
Puerto Escondido – 115km, 2½ hours; 2 Colón (US$3.75), 11 EB (US$3.25 to US$4.50)
Pochutla – 50km, 1 hour; 11 EB (US$1.25 to US$1.75); Transportes Rápidos de Pochutla every 15 minutes up to about 7 pm, from the main road opposite Bugambilias (US$0.70)
Salina Cruz – 145km, 2½ hours; several Colón (US$4.75 to US$5.75), 3 EB (US$5.50)

Colón also runs several buses to Tehuantepec and Juchitán and a few to Tuxtla Gutiérrez, San Cristóbal de Las Casas and Tapachula. EB goes to Acapulco. Colón and EB go to Mexico City.

Car Auto rental agencies include:

Advantage
(☎ 587-13-79) Hotel Castillo Huatulco, Santa Cruz
Budget
(☎ 587-00-34) Ocotillo at Jazmín, La Crucecita
(☎ 587-00-10) Airport
Dollar
(☎ 581-00-55 ext 787) Sheraton Huatulco Resort, Tangolunda
(☎ 581-00-00) Royal Maeva Huatulco, Tangolunda
(☎ 581-90-16) Airport

Fast
(☎ 581-00-02) Boulevard Juárez, Local 6, Tangolunda
(☎ 581-90-31) Airport

Advantage and Fast rent VW Beetles for around US$50 a day with unlimited kilometers as well as other cars starting at around US$60.

Getting Around

To/From the Airport Transportación Terrestre (☎ 581-90-14, 581-90-24) provides colectivo combis for US$5.50 per person from the airport to La Crucecita, Santa Cruz or Bahía Chahué and for US$6.50 to Tangolunda. Get tickets at the company's airport kiosk. For a whole cab at a reasonable price, walk just outside the airport gate, where you can pick one up for about US$8 to La Crucecita, Santa Cruz or Tangolunda – or US$12 to Pochutla. Even cheaper, walk 400m down to highway 200 and catch a microbus for US$0.30 to La Crucecita or US$0.50 to Pochutla. Those heading to La Crucecita may be marked 'Santa Cruz' or 'Bahías Huatulco' or something similar.

Bus & Colectivo Microbuses and colectivo taxis provide transportation between La Crucecita, Santa Cruz Huatulco and Tangolunda. In La Crucecita catch them on Guamuchil at Carrizal, one block from the Plaza Principal. In Santa Cruz they stop by the harbor, and in Tangolunda at the traffic circle outside the Maeva hotel. Fares are the same in either type of vehicle: from La Crucecita to Santa Cruz US$0.20, to Tangolunda US$0.30.

Bicycle Sideout Sport store in Plaza Oaxaca mall, La Crucecita, rents bikes for US$2 an hour or US$10 a day. Eco Discover Tours, Plaza Las Conchas, Tangolunda (opposite the Sheraton), rents mountain bikes for US$2.50 an hour or US$8 a day.

Taxi Taxis are plentiful. From La Crucecita you pay around US$1 to Santa Cruz, US$1.75 to Tangolunda and US$4 to Bahía Maguey.

Isthmus of Tehuantepec

Eastern Oaxaca is the southern half of the 200km-wide Isthmus of Tehuantepec ('tehwahn-teh-PECK'), Mexico's narrowest point. This is sweaty, flat country, but Zapotec culture is strong here. If you spend a night or two here, you'll probably be agreeably surprised by the people's liveliness and friendliness. Government proposals for a new fast road and/or rail transit corridor across the isthmus, as a 21st-century rival to the Panama Canal, along with associated petrochemical and industrial development projects, provoke mixed reactions from *istmeños* wary that the beneficiaries will be outsiders.

Fifteen kilometers northeast of Juchitán, around La Ventosa (where highway 185 to Acayucan diverges from highway 190 to Chiapas), strong winds sweep down from the north and sometimes blow high vehicles off the road.

History & People

In 1496 the isthmus Zapotecs repulsed the Aztecs from the fortress of Guiengola, near Tehuantepec, and the isthmus never became part of the Aztec empire. Later there was strong resistance to the Spanish here.

Isthmus women are noticeably open and confident and take a leading role in business and government. Many older women still wear embroidered huipiles and voluminous printed skirts. For fiestas, Tehuantepec and Juchitán women turn out in velvet or sateen huipiles, gold and silver jewelry (a sign of wealth), skirts embroidered with fantastically colorful silk flowers, and a variety of odd headgear. Many isthmus fiestas feature the *tirada de frutas*, in which women climb on roofs and throw fruit on the men below!

TEHUANTEPEC
● **pop 36,900** ☎ **changing**
Tehuantepec is a friendly town, often with a fiesta going on in one of its *barrios*.

Orientation & Information

The Oaxaca-Tuxtla Gutiérrez highway (190) meets highway 185 from Salina Cruz about 1km west of Tehuantepec. Highway 190 then skirts the north edge of town. All Tehuantepec's bus stations, collectively known as El Terminal, cluster just off highway 190, 1.5km northeast of the town center. Local buses to/from Salina Cruz also stop, more conveniently, where highway 190 passes the end of 5 de Mayo, a minute's walk from the central plaza. To reach the plaza from El Terminal on foot, follow Avenida Héroes until it ends at a T-junction, then go to the right along Guerrero for four blocks to another T-junction, then one block left along Hidalgo.

You can get some tourist information in the Ex-Convento Rey Cosijopí (see below). A couple of banks around the central plaza have ATMs. The dark, almost medieval market is on the west side of the plaza.

> In November 2000, the telephone area code is due to change to ☎ 9 from 971, with the digits 71 added to the start of every local number (for example, the number 7-65-43 will become 717-65-43).

Ex-Convento Rey Cosijopí

This former Dominican monastery on Callejón Rey Cosijopí, a short street off Guerrero, is now Tehuantepec's Casa de la Cultura, holding classes and occasional exhibitions. It's open daily except Saturday afternoon and Sunday. Built in the 16th century, the monastery is named for the local Zapotec leader of the day (who paid for it) and features stout two-story construction around a central courtyard. It served as a prison before being restored in the 1970s.

Guiengola

The hillside Zapotec stronghold of Guiengola, where king Cosijoeza rebuffed the Aztecs, is north of highway 190 from a turnoff about 11km out of Tehuantepec. A sign points to 'Ruinas Guiengola 7' just past the 240 Km marker. You can see the remains of two pyramids, a ball court, a 64-room complex known as El Palacio and a thick defensive wall. There are fine views over the isthmus.

To get there take a bus bound for Jalapa del Marqués from El Terminal. Get off at Puente Las Tejas, from which it's a walk of about 2½ hours. Start early, 6 am or before, to take advantage of the morning coolness. You may be able to find a guide by asking in the Ex-Convento Rey Cosijopí.

Places to Stay

Hotel Donají (☎ 5-00-64, *Juárez 10*), two blocks south of the east side of the central plaza, has clean rooms with private bath on two upper floors with open-air walkways. Singles/doubles are US$7.50/9.50 with fan or US$10/14 with air-con. *Hotel Oasis* (☎ 5-00-08, *Ocampo 8*), one block south of the west side of the plaza, has slightly smaller fan-cooled rooms, bare and basic but with warm-water showers, for US$6.25/7.75 (US$8.75 with two beds). Parking in the courtyard is available.

Places to Eat

Cafe Colonial (*Romero 66*), 1½ blocks south of the plaza, serves generous chicken and meat dishes for US$3 to US$4.50 and antojitos for US$2.50 to US$3.50. *Mariscos Silvia*, on 5 de Mayo facing the market, isn't a bad spot for fish or seafood (US$3 to US$4.50).

Restaurante Scarú (*Leona Vicario 4*), up a side street a block east of the Hotel Donají, occupies an 18th-century house with a courtyard and colorful modern murals of Tehuantepec life. The menu offers varied fish, seafood, meat and chicken dishes, mostly for US$3 to US$4.50. Hours are 7 am to 11 pm daily.

Getting There & Away

The 245km trip from Oaxaca takes 4½ hours in a 1st-class bus. The road winds downhill for the middle 160km.

Cristóbal Colón and ADO (1st-class) and Sur and AU (2nd-class) share one building. Most 1st-class buses are de paso, often in the wee hours. Colón runs 13 daily buses to Oaxaca (US$8 to US$9.50) and a few each to

Tuxtla Gutiérrez, San Cristóbal de Las Casas, Bahías de Huatulco, Pochutla, Puerto Escondido, Mexico City and Tapachula. ADO runs four buses to Villahermosa and a night bus to Palenque. AU has a few buses to Veracruz. Sur runs frequent buses to Arriaga.

TOI (2nd-class), just east of Colón, has hourly buses to Oaxaca (US$6) around the clock, plus a few to Tuxtla Gutiérrez.

Across the street from Colón are local buses to Juchitán (25km, 30 minutes) and Salina Cruz (15km, 30 minutes). They go at least every half hour during daylight hours.

Getting Around

A curious form of local transportation is the *motocarro* – a kind of three-wheel buggy in which the driver sits on a front seat while passengers stand behind on a platform.

SALINA CRUZ
- pop 71,500 ☎ changing

Once an important railway terminus and port, then undermined by the cutting of the Panama Canal, Salina Cruz has revived as an oil pipeline terminal with a refinery. It's a windy city with a rough-and-ready feel.

Orientation

Highway 200 from Puerto Escondido and Pochutla meets the Salina Cruz-Tehuantepec road, highway 185, on the northern edge of Salina Cruz. Avenida Ferrocarril runs 2km south from this junction to the center, with the main bus stations in streets just off it: EB is on Obrero, nearly halfway to the center; Cristóbal Colón, ADO, Sur and AU are together on Laborista, three blocks south of Obrero.

Avenida Ferrocarril becomes Avenida Tampico as it nears the center, passing one block west of the wide, windy plaza.

In November 2000, the telephone area code is due to change to ☎ 9 from 971, with the digits 71 added to the start of every local number (for example, the number 7-65-43 will become 717-65-43).

Places to Stay

Hotel Posada del Jardín (☎ 4-01-62, Camacho 108), 1½ blocks north of the main plaza, has clean little singles/doubles with fan and shower, around a leafy little courtyard, for US$6.50/8.50. The choice central place is the modern *Hotel Costa Real* (☎ 4-02-93, Progreso 22), two blocks north of the plaza. Carpeted, air-conditioned rooms with color TV are US$22/25. It has a decent restaurant and parking, too.

Getting There & Away

Frequent buses to Tehuantepec (30 minutes, US$0.60) and Juchitán (one hour, US$1.25) leave from the corner of Avenida Tampico and Progreso, one block west and two north from the plaza.

Cristóbal Colón and ADO run 1st-class buses, while the other lines are 2nd-class. Five or more Colón and four EB buses run daily to Bahías de Huatulco (2½ hours, US$4.75 to US$5.75), Pochutla (3½ hours, US$6.25 to US$7) and Puerto Escondido (five hours, US$9 to US$9.75). Colón also runs 10 buses to Oaxaca (five hours, US$8.75 to US$10.50) and two to Tuxtla Gutiérrez and San Cristóbal de Las Casas (395km, eight hours, US$13). There's 1st-class service to Tapachula, Veracruz, Villahermosa, Palenque and Mexico City.

Getting Around

Local buses run along Avenida Ferrocarril between the bus stations and town center (US$0.20). Going out to the bus stations, they're marked 'Refinería' or 'Refi.'

JUCHITÁN
- pop 62,100 ☎ changing

Istmeño culture is strong in this friendly town, which is visited by few gringos.

Orientation

Prolongación 16 de Septiembre leads into Juchitán from a busy intersection with traffic signals on highway 190, on the north edge of town. The main bus terminal is about 100m toward town from the intersection. The street curves left, then right, then divides into 5 de Septiembre (the right fork) and 16

In December 2000, the telephone area code is due to change to ☎ 9 from 971, with the digits 71 added to the start of every local number (for example, the number 7-65-43 will become 717-65-43).

de Septiembre (left). These emerge as opposite sides of the central plaza, Jardín Juárez, after seven blocks.

Things to See & Do

Jardín Juárez is a lively central square. A busy **market** on its east side spills into the surrounding streets.

Juchitán's **Lidxi Guendabiaani** (Casa de la Cultura), on José F Gómez a block south of Jardín Juárez, has an interesting archaeological collection and an art collection with works by leading 20th-century Mexican artists, including Rufino Tamayo and *juchiteco* Francisco Toledo. It's housed around a big patio beside the Iglesia de San Vicente Ferrer.

Places to Stay & Eat

Casa de Huéspedes Echazarreta, on Jardín Juárez, has small, clean rooms for US$6 with private bath and fan.

Hotel Santo Domingo del Sur (☎ 1-10-50), by the highway 190 crossroads, has decent air-conditioned singles/doubles at US$17.50/24 and plenty of parking space. *Hotel López Lena Palace* (☎ 1-13-88, 16 de Septiembre 70), about halfway between the bus station and town center, has air-conditioned rooms with multichannel TV and bath for US$14/19. The rooms aren't as

fancy as the hotel's exterior suggests, but they're still fine. Both these hotels have medium-priced restaurants.

The best eatery in town is the *Casagrande Restaurant*, in a pleasant courtyard on the south side of Jardín Juárez. It offers all sorts of goodies, from regional dishes or pasta for US$1.50 to US$3 to seafood around US$8. You'll find several dining options near the bus station.

Getting There & Away

Cristóbal Colón and ADO (1st-class) and Sur and AU (2nd-class) use the main bus terminal on Prolongación 16 de Septiembre. Frequent 2nd-class Autotransportes Istmeños buses to Tehuantepec (30 minutes, US$0.70) and Salina Cruz (one hour) stop at the next corner south on Prolongación 16 de Septiembre during daylight hours. FYPSA (2nd-class) has its own terminal, separated from the main one by a Pemex station.

Many buses are de paso and leave in the middle of the night. To Oaxaca (285km, five hours) there are nine Colón and three ADO buses daily, as well as FYPSA departures about hourly round the clock. Colón runs five daily buses to Bahías de Huatulco and two or three each to Pochutla, Puerto Escondido, San Cristóbal de Las Casas and Tapachula. Colón and FYPSA go several times daily to Tuxtla Gutiérrez. Sur has frequent service to Acayucan. ADO runs four buses to Villahermosa and one at 11 pm to Palenque. Colón and AU go to Mexico City, Veracruz and Puebla.

Getting Around

'Terminal-Centro' buses run between the bus station and Jardín Juárez.

Tabasco & Chiapas

Just east of the Isthmus of Tehuantepec – Mexico's narrow 'waist' – lie the states of Tabasco and Chiapas. Their differences define them: Chiapas is wealthy in natural resources but most of its people are poor, whereas Tabasco is oil-rich. Tabasco, with a long coastline on the Gulf of Mexico, is mostly well-watered lowland, hot and humid, but in its south start to rise the hills that become the cool, pine-clad Altos (Highlands) of Chiapas. Chiapas' indigenous history is Mayan, Tabasco's is chiefly Olmec.

There are river routes into neighboring Guatemala from both states.

Tabasco

Tabasco is kept fertile by huge rivers that meander across it en route to the Gulf of Mexico. It was here, between about 1200 and 600 BC, that the Olmecs developed Mesoamerica's first great civilization. In recent years Tabasco's mineral riches, particularly petroleum, have brought great prosperity.

History

La Venta, the second great Olmec center (after San Lorenzo, Veracruz) was in western Tabasco. Olmec religion, art, astronomy and architecture deeply influenced all Mexico's later pre-Hispanic civilizations. The Chontal Maya who followed the Olmecs built a great ceremonial city called Comalcalco in northwest Tabasco.

Cortés, who disembarked on the Tabasco coast in 1519, initially defeated the Maya and founded a settlement called Santa María de la Victoria. The Maya regrouped and offered stern resistance until they were defeated by Francisco de Montejo, around 1540. Later, pirate attacks forced the original settlement to be moved inland from the coast and it was renamed Villahermosa de San Juan Bautista.

After Mexico won independence from Spain, various local land barons tried to assert their power over the area, causing con-

siderable strife. The economy languished until after the Mexican Revolution, when exports of cacao, bananas and coconuts started to increase.

Highlights

- Jungle-enshrouded Palenque, most romantic of Mayan cities
- The colonial highland town of San Cristóbal de Las Casas and nearby Mayan villages
- The Mayan ruins of Bonampak and Yaxchilán, deep in the Lacandón Jungle
- Villahermosa's Parque-Museo La Venta, a fascinating outdoor Olmec archaeological museum and zoo
- Remote, serene Laguna Miramar, the largest lake in the Lacandón Jungle

TABASCO & CHIAPAS

In the 20th century, US and British petroleum companies discovered oil, and Tabasco's economy began to revolve around the resource. During the 1970s, Villahermosa became an oil boomtown and profits from agricultural exports added to the good times. This prosperity has brought a feeling of sophistication that cuts right through the tropical heat, stamping Tabasco as different from neighboring Chiapas and Campeche.

Geography & Climate

Tabasco's topography changes from flatland near the seaside to undulating hills as you near Chiapas. Due to heavy rainfall of about 1500mm annually (mostly between May and October), there is much swampland, lush tropical foliage and sticky humidity. Outside of Villahermosa, Tabasco can be quite bug-infested (particularly near the rivers), so bring repellent. The state is rather sparsely populated, with 1.8 million people inhabiting 24,475 sq km.

VILLAHERMOSA

● pop 301,200 ☎ changing

Hot, crowded and untidy, downtown Villahermosa is anything but the 'beautiful city'

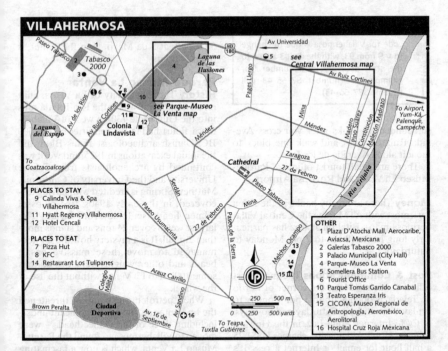

VILLAHERMOSA

PLACES TO STAY
9 Calinda Viva & Spa
   Villahermosa
11 Hyatt Regency Villahermosa
12 Hotel Cencali

PLACES TO EAT
7 Pizza Hut
8 KFC
14 Restaurant Los Tulipanes

OTHER
1 Plaza D'Atocha Mall, Aerocaribe,
   Aviacsa, Mexicana
2 Galerias Tabasco 2000
3 Palacio Municipal (City Hall)
4 Parque-Museo La Venta
5 Somellera Bus Station
6 Tourist Office
10 Parque Tomás Garrido Canabal
13 Teatro Esperanza Iris
15 CICOM, Museo Regional de
   Antropología, Aeroméxico,
   Aerolitoral
16 Hospital Cruz Roja Mexicana

---

that its name implies, despite its situation on
the banks of the Río Grijalva. Courtesy of
the Tabasco oil boom, however, outer areas
of the city enjoy some tree-shaded boulevards, spacious parks, fancy hotels and excellent cultural institutions.

To see everything here, you'll have to stay
at least one night. The chief attractions are
the Parque-Museo La Venta, an excellent
open-air combination of Olmec archaeological museum and Tabasco zoo; the Museo
Regional de Antropología; and Yumká, a
kind of safari park outside the city.

Orientation

In this sprawling city you'll find yourself
walking some distances in the sticky heat,
and occasionally hopping on a minibus
(combi) or taking a taxi.

The older commercial center of the city,
known as the Zona Luz, extends from the
Plaza de Armas in the south to Parque
Juárez in the north, and is roughly bounded

by Calles Zaragoza, Madero and Juárez. It is
a lively area, busy with shoppers.

Villahermosa's main visitor attraction, the
Parque-Museo La Venta, lies 2km northwest
of the Zona Luz, beside Avenida Ruiz
Cortines, the main east-west highway crossing the city. About 1km west of Parque-
Museo La Venta is the Tabasco 2000 district
of modern commercial and government
buildings.

Information

Tourist Offices The main tourist office
(☎ 16-36-33) is inconveniently located at the
corner of Avenida de los Ríos and Calle 13 in
the Tabasco 2000 district in the northwest of
the city. It's open 9 am to 3 pm and 6 to 9 pm
Monday to Friday, 9 am to 1 pm Saturday.
Staff are helpful and have a lot of printed information on Tabasco state. To get there
from the Zona Luz, take a 'Fracc Carrizal'
combi from Madero just north of Parque
Juárez, get off at the big traffic circle

In December 2000 the telephone area code for Villahermosa is due to change to ☎ 9 from 93, with the digit 3 added to the start of every local number (for example, the number 87-65-43 will become 387-65-43).

surrounded by banks after you cross Avenida Ruiz Cortines, and walk one block to the left along Avenida de los Ríos.

There are small tourist offices at Parque-Museo La Venta and Rovirosa Airport.

Money There are many banks in the Zona Luz, most with ATMs (see the Central Villahermosa map). Bital on Juárez has particularly long hours (8 am to 7 pm Monday to Saturday).

Post & Communications The main post office, at Sáenz 131 on the corner of Lerdo de Tejada, is open 8 am to 3 pm Monday to Friday, 9 am to 1 pm Saturday and holidays.

C@fé Internet Zona Luz, in the Howard Johnson Hotel, Aldama 404, charges US$1.25 a half hour for email or Internet access. It's open 9 am to 9 pm daily.

Travel Agencies Viajes Villahermosa (☎ 12-54-56), at 27 de Febrero 207, sells international and domestic tickets; staff speak English and can arrange excursions. Hours are Monday to Friday from 9 am to 8 pm, Saturday 9 am to 7 pm. On our latest visit, the agency was planning to move to Méndez 728, keeping the same phone number.

Turismo Nieves (☎ 14-18-88), Sarlat 202 at Doña Fidencia, is the American Express representative.

Laundry Lavandería Top Klen next to Hotel Madero charges a steep US$2 per kilogram for next-day service. Super Lavandería La Burbuja, north of the Zona Luz at Hermanos Bastar Zozaya 621, is about half that price.

Medical Services The Hospital Cruz Roja Mexicana (☎ 15-55-55) is at Avenida Sandino

716, a short ride southwest of the Zona Luz. Unidad Médica Guerrero Urgencias (☎ 14-56-97/98), at 5 de Mayo 44 in the center, is open 24 hours.

Parque-Museo La Venta

History The Olmec city of La Venta, built on an island near where the Río Tonalá runs into the Gulf some 130km west of Villahermosa, flourished in the centuries before 600 BC. Danish archaeologist Frans Blom did the initial excavations in 1925, and work was continued by archaeologists from Tulane University and the University of California. Matthew Stirling is credited with having discovered, in the early 1940s, five colossal Olmec heads sculpted from basalt. The largest weighs over 24 tons and stands more than 2m tall. It is a mystery how the Olmecs managed to move these massive basalt heads and other weighty religious statues some 100km to La Venta, without the use of the wheel.

When petroleum excavation threatened the La Venta site, the most significant finds – including three of the Olmec heads – were moved to Villahermosa to found the Parque-Museo La Venta, which is now a fascinating combined outdoor museum and tropical zoo.

Admission Parque-Museo La Venta (☎ 14-16-52) is open 8 am to 5 pm daily (US$1.50). The zoo closes Monday. Plan at least two hours for your visit, preferably three. Snack stands provide sustenance.

Zoo Once inside, this is the section you come to first. It's devoted to animals from Tabasco and nearby regions: colorful macaws and toucans, pumas, jaguars, lynxes, ocelots, white-tailed deer, spider monkeys, crocodiles, boa constrictors, peccaries and plenty more. Stop at the informative display in English and Spanish on Olmec history and archaeology as you go through.

Museum A giant ceiba (the sacred tree of the Olmecs and Mayas) marks the starting point of a trail through lush tropical verdure past the 34 Olmec stone sculpture exhibits ranging from the famous heads and other

PARQUE-MUSEO LA VENTA

Museo de Historia Natural

To Central Villahermosa

Aviary

Zoológico

Small Felines

Turtles, Crocodiles

Big Felines

Laguna de las Ilusiones

0 50 100 m
0 50 100 yards

Av Ruiz Cortines

Malecón de las Ilusiones

Plaza de Artesanías

Crafts Shop

Jaguar Compound

Parque Tomás Garrido Canabal

Malecón de las Ilusiones

To Paseo Tabasco

Footbridge

⊙ Toilets
⛺ Shelters

25 Altar Cuadrangular
    (Quadrangular Altar)
26 Personaje con Estandarte
    (Figure with Standard)
27 Cabeza Hendida (Cloven Head)
28 La Silueta (Silhouette)
29 Lápida con Incisiones
    (Stone with Incisions)
30 Altar del Diálogo
    (Dialogue Altar)
31 Altar Erosionado (Eroded Altar)
32 Altar de los Tecolotes
    (Altar of the Owls)
33 Altar Felino (Feline Altar)
34 El Gobernante (Governor)
35 Cabeza Tatuada
    (Tattooed Head)
36 Fragmentos (Fragments)
37 Estela del Rey (Royal Stele)
38 Mosaico-Mascarón
    (Mosaic Mask)
39 Cabeza del Guerrero
    (Warrior's Head)
40 Altar del Jaguar (Jaguar Altar)
41 Basalt Column
    (Columna de Basalto)
42 El Contorsionista (Contortionist)
43 Jaguar Niño (Jaguar Child)
44 El Delfín (Dolphin)
45 Mono Mirando el Cielo
    (Monkey Looking at the Sky)
46 Pond with Crocodiles
47 Mirador de las Águilas

6 Entrance, Tourist Office

ZOOLÓGICO
1 Peccaries
2 Crocodiles, Turtles
3 Snakes
4 Toucans, Parrots
5 Nocturnal Animals
7 Deer
8 Spider Monkeys
9 Los Olmecas de
  La Venta Display

10 Spider Monkeys
11 Cafeteria
20 Giant Ceiba Tree

MUSEUM/NATURE TRAIL
12 El Viejo Guerrero (Old Warrior)
13 El Joven Guerrero (Young Warrior)
14 Estacada de Columnas Naturales
   (Palisade of Natural Basalt Columns)
15 Tumba (Tomb)
16 Mosaico-Mascarón
   (Mask Mosaic)

17 El Hombre Barbado
   (Bearded Man)
18 La Abuela
   (Grandmother)
19 El Trono (Throne)
21 El Caminante (Walker)
22 Diosa Joven
   (Young Goddess)
23 Cabeza Inconclusa
   (Unfinished Head)
24 Altar de los Niños
   (Altar of the Children)

human figures to deities, dolphins and even a stone mosaic mask laid out on the ground. The trail is 1km long and takes at least an hour to walk if you spend a few minutes at each exhibit. Along the way, many trees bear signs giving their names and species. There are also more animal enclosures. Some animals that pose no danger, such as coatis, roam freely.

Getting There & Away Parque-Museo La Venta is 3km from the Zona Luz. A 'Fracc Carrizal' combi (US$0.30) from Madero just north of Parque Juárez in the Zona Luz will

drop you at the corner of Paseo Tabasco and Avenida Ruiz Cortines. Then walk 1km northeast across Parque Tomás Garrido Canabal and along the Malecón de las Ilusiones, a pleasant lakeside path, to the entrance. A taxi from the Zona Luz costs US$1.

CICOM & Museo Regional de Antropología

The Centro de Investigación de las Culturas Olmeca y Maya (CICOM) is a complex of buildings on the bank of the Río Grijalva, 1km south of the Zona Luz. Its centerpiece is the Museo Regional de

TABASCO & CHIAPAS

Antropología Carlos Pellicer Cámara, named for the scholar and poet responsible for the preservation of the Olmec artifacts in the Parque-Museo La Venta. Besides the museum, the complex holds a theater, research center, arts center and other buildings.

The anthropology museum (☎ 12-63-44) is open 9 am to 7 pm daily except Monday (US$1).

Just inside the front door is a massive Olmec head, one of those wonders from La Venta. The best way to tour the museum is to take the elevator to the top floor and work your way down. Although the museum's explanations are all in Spanish, they are accompanied by photos, maps and diagrams.

On the top floor, exhibits outline Mesoamerica's many civilizations, from the oldest Stone Age inhabitants to the relatively recent Aztecs. After you've brushed up on the broad picture, descend to the middle floor, which concentrates on the Olmec and Mayan cultures. Especially intriguing are the displays concerning Comalcalco, the ruined Mayan city not far from Villahermosa.

Finally, the ground floor holds a room of particularly big Olmec and Mayan sculptures, plus temporary exhibits.

CICOM is 1km south of the Zona Luz. You can walk there in about 15 minutes, or catch any 'CICOM' combi or microbus heading south on Madero or the malecón south of Madero.

Museo de Historia

The History Museum, in a blue-tiled building at the corner of 27 de Febrero and Juárez, deals with Tabasco history. It is open daily except Monday (US$0.50).

Tabasco 2000

The Tabasco 2000 complex is a testimony to the prosperity oil has brought to Villahermosa, with its modern government buildings, chic boutiques in the Galerías Tabasco 2000 mall, convention center and pretty fountains. From the Zona Luz, take a 'Fracc Carrizal' combi from Madero just north of Parque Juárez.

Places to Stay

Budget The Zona Luz has plenty of cheap hotels, but few are very inviting. Keep street noise in mind when choosing one – and consider splurging on a pleasant, air-conditioned room.

Posada Brondo (☎ 12-59-61, Pino Suárez 209) is better kept than most cheapies. Bright, clean singles/doubles with fan, TV and bathroom go for US$9.50/11.50 (US$13 for a double bed), or US$15/18 with air-con.

Hotel San Miguel (☎ 12-15-00, Lerdo de Tejada 315) is small and cheap, renting its plain rooms with fan for US$7/8/9 a single/double/triple, or US$15.50/17.50 for singles/doubles with air-con and TV. Neighboring *Hotel Tabasco* (☎ 12-00-77, Lerdo de Tejada 317), charging US$6.75/7.75, is a step worse. *Hotel Oriente* (☎ 12-01-21, Madero 425), around the corner, is marginally better, though the front rooms are noisier. Rates are US$7.25/13.50, or US$8.75/19.50 with TV and air-con.

Hotel San Francisco (☎ 12-31-98, Madero 604) is a considerable improvement. An elevator does away with the sweaty hike upstairs, where you'll find rooms with air-con and TV for US$12.50/14.50. Some have balconies but this street can be *very* noisy. *Hotel Palma de Mallorca* (☎ 12-01-44, Madero 516) charges US$7.75/10.50 for singles/doubles with one bed and fan, US$10.50/13.50 for two-bed rooms with fan, and US$13.50/15.50 for air-conditioned rooms.

Hotel Madero (☎ 12-05-16, Madero 301) is an old building with some rooms remodeled a few years ago. Rooms with one double bed and bath are US$8, or US$17 remodeled with TV and fan. With two double beds the prices are US$12 and US$18 respectively. It all depends on the individual room: some are a lot more pleasant and less stuffy than others.

Mid-Range Most middle-range hotels are in the Zona Luz. The 68-room *Hotel Miraflores* (☎ 12-00-22, Reforma 304), on a pedestrian street just off Madero, offers large, clean air-conditioned rooms with good bathrooms and about 60 TV channels for US$37/44 – if they're not too busy they may

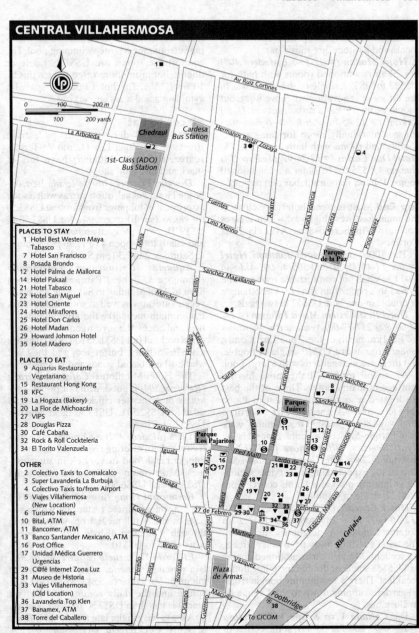

CENTRAL VILLAHERMOSA

0   100   200 m
0   100   200 yards

La Arboleda

Chedraui

Cardesa
Bus Station

1st-Class (ADO)
Bus Station

Av Ruiz Cortines

Hermanos Bastar Zozaya

Fuentes

Lino Merino

Sánchez Magallanes

Méndez

Mina

Castillo

Saenz

Hidalgo

Galeana

Rosales

Zaragoza

5 de Mayo

Iguala

Arteaga

Corregidora

Ayutla

Bravo

Peredo

Acosta

Ocampo

Guerrero

Aldama

Juárez

(Ped Mall)

Lerdo de Tejada

Reforma

Independencia

Martínez

Vázquez

Macuiliz

Alvarez

Doña Fidencia

Carranza

Madero

Pino Suárez

Parque
de la Paz

Constitución

Carmen Sánchez

Sánchez Mármol

Zaragoza

Madero

Pino Suárez

Constitución

Parque
Juárez

Parque
Los Pajaritos

Malecón Madrazo

Río Grijalva

Plaza
de Armas

Footbridge

To CICOM

PLACES TO STAY
- 1 Hotel Best Western Maya Tabasco
- 7 Hotel San Francisco
- 8 Posada Brondo
- 12 Hotel Palma de Mallorca
- 14 Hotel Pakaal
- 21 Hotel Tabasco
- 22 Hotel San Miguel
- 23 Hotel Oriente
- 24 Hotel Miraflores
- 25 Hotel Don Carlos
- 26 Hotel Madan
- Howard Johnson Hotel
- 35 Hotel Madero

PLACES TO EAT
- 9 Aquarius Restaurante Vegetariano
- 15 Restaurant Hong Kong
- 18 KFC
- 19 La Hogaza (Bakery)
- 20 La Flor de Michoacán
- 27 VIPS
- 28 Douglas Pizza
- 30 Café Cabaña
- 32 Rock & Roll Cocktelería
- 34 El Torito Valenzuela

OTHER
- 2 Colectivo Taxis to Comalcalco
- 3 Super Lavandería La Burbuja
- 4 Colectivo Taxis to/from Airport
- 5 Viajes Villahermosa (New Location)
- 6 Turismo Nieves
- 10 Bital, ATM
- 11 Bancomer, ATM
- 13 Banco Santander Mexicano, ATM
- 16 Post Office
- 17 Unidad Médica Guerrero Urgencias
- 29 C@fé Internet Zona Luz
- 31 Museo de Historia
- 33 Viajes Villahermosa (Old Location)
- 36 Lavandería Top Klen
- 37 Banamex, ATM
- 38 Torre del Caballero

TABASCO & CHIAPAS

offer a few dollars' discount. The hotel has a restaurant, a coffeeshop that also serves meals, and a rather dire music bar.

Hotel Madan (☎ *12-16-50, Madero 408*) has 20 air-conditioned rooms with bath for US$27 to US$29, single or double. It was in the throes of renovation when we went, but should be fine. It has a restaurant too. **Hotel Pakaal** (☎ *12-45-01, Lerdo de Tejada 106*) charges marginally more for fair-size air-conditioned rooms with bath and cable TV. **Hotel Don Carlos** (☎ *12-24-99, Madero 418*) charges US$35 for its older air-conditioned rooms. It has a restaurant, bar and parking.

Top End Most top-end hotels are close to the main east-west highway, which crosses northern Villahermosa as Avenida Ruiz Cortines.

The 100-room **Howard Johnson Hotel** (☎/fax *14-46-45*, ☎ *800-505-49-00, Aldama 404*) has small but comfortable rooms in the Zona Luz's pedestrian zone for US$50 single or double in one bed, US$57 in two beds.

Hotel Best Western Maya Tabasco (☎ *14-44-66, 800-237-77-00, Avenida Ruiz Cortines 907*) is 1km north of the Zona Luz. Comfy, modern rooms are US$82 single or double, and there are nice gardens with a large pool.

As an oil town, Villahermosa has no shortage of luxury hotels. Three of the best are located near the intersection of Paseo Tabasco and Avenida Ruiz Cortines (highway 180), a pleasant few minutes' walk from Parque-Museo La Venta. Poshest is the **Hyatt Regency Villahermosa** (☎ *15-12-34, Avenida Juárez 106, Colonia Lindavista*), with all the expected luxury services, including swimming pool and tennis courts, from US$147, single or double.

Hotel Cencali (☎/fax *15-19-99*, ☎ *800-112-50-00*), also on Avenida Juárez in Colonia Lindavista, neighbors the Hyatt. The hotel's setting, away from noisy streets, is excellent. Modern air-conditioned rooms cost US$88 single or double, including buffet breakfast. There's a swimming pool in tropical gardens running down to the Laguna de las Ilusiones.

The **Calinda Viva & Spa Villahermosa** (☎ *15-00-00, 800-711-55-55*), at the corner of Avenidas Juárez and Ruiz Cortines, is a three-story, motel-style, white stucco building surrounding a large swimming pool. The comfortable rooms are US$106, single or double, but promotions often reduce this by 10% or 15%. The hotel boasts a spa with gym, sauna and massage services.

Places to Eat

Zona Luz Madero and the pedestrian streets of the Zona Luz (Lerdo de Tejada, Juárez, Reforma, Aldama) have lots of snack and fast-food shops.

Douglas Pizza (*Lerdo de Tejada 105*), opposite Hotel Pakaal, offers pizzas with a wide assortment of toppings, from around US$3.50 for *chicas* (small) to *grandes* for US$7.50 to US$9. There's a pleasant ambiance, and pasta and salads too – open 4 to 11.30 pm Monday to Saturday, 2 to 9.30 pm Sunday.

Aquarius Restaurante Vegetariano (*Zaragoza 513*), near Parque Juárez, open 8 am to 9 pm Monday to Saturday, has many veggie offerings as well as some menu items that contain meat. Try the granola, yogurt, fruit and honey, the soyburgers, or the mushroom cocktail (all US$1.25 to US$2). There's a US$6.25 lunch buffet too, and they sell whole-wheat baked goods and vitamins.

The Hotel Miraflores' **Cafetería Terraza** (*Reforma 304*) is good, with fair prices – *antojitos* or a quarter chicken with fries and salad for US$2.50 to US$3.50, meats and fish US$5 to US$6.50.

VIPS (*Madero 402*) is a branch of a countrywide chain offering reliable Mexican and international food in very clean surroundings. Most main courses cost between US$3.50 and US$6.50.

Restaurant Hong Kong (*5 de Mayo 433*) is an upstairs Chinese restaurant with a six-page menu. A full meal, from wonton soup through a chicken dish to fortune cookie, costs US$5 to US$10.

El Torito Valenzuela (*27 de Febrero 202*) is a popular *taquería*, open from 8 am to midnight. Varied tacos cost US$0.50 to US$1 apiece and the daily *comida corrida* (set lunch) is less than US$3.50 for four courses.

Always busy in the late afternoon is **Rock & Roll Cockteleria** (*Reforma 307*). A *cocktel* (fish or seafood, tomato sauce, lettuce, onions and a lemon squeeze) with crackers is yours for US$3.50 to US$5.

Eating or drinking on the run? Try *La Hogaza*, a bakery on Juárez, for croissants, doughnuts, Danish pastries, yogurt or boxed juices; *La Flor de Michoacán* just across the street has fresh juices, *licuados*, frozen yogurt and fruit cocktails.

There's excellent coffee at the sidewalk *Café Cabaña* on Juárez.

Elsewhere The luxury hotels near the intersection of Avenida Ruiz Cortines and Paseo Tabasco all have good restaurants – the *Hyatt Regency Villahermosa* has a particularly high reputation. In Tabasco 2000, there are plenty of restaurants in the Galerías Tabasco 2000 mall, including an economical food court.

Overlooking the river near the Museo Regional de Antropología is *Restaurant Los Tulipanes*, open every day from 1 to 11 pm. Seafood and steaks, the specialties, cost between US$5.50 and US$9.

Entertainment
Teatro Esperanza Iris (☎ 14-42-10) just north of CICOM often stages folkloric dance, theater, cinema and music performances.

Live music, usually with dancing, is featured at several hotel bars including the *Calinda Viva, Hyatt Regency, Cencali, Best Western Maya Tabasco* and *Miraflores*.

Getting There & Away
Air Nonstop or one- or two-stop direct flights to/from Villahermosa include:

Cancún – Aerocaribe daily

Guadalajara – Aeroméxico daily

Havana, Cuba – Aerocaribe daily

Houston, Texas – Aeroméxico twice weekly

Mérida – Aerocaribe 3 times daily, Aviacsa daily

Mexico City – Aeroméxico, Mexicana, Aviacsa and Aerocaribe all daily

Monterrey – Aerolitoral 6 days weekly, Aeroméxico 5 days

Oaxaca – Aerocaribe daily

San Antonio, Texas – Aerolitoral 5 days weekly

Tuxtla Gutiérrez – Aerocaribe daily

Veracruz – Aerocaribe twice daily, Aerolitoral 6 days weekly

Mexicana (☎ 16-31-32) is at Locales 5 & 6, Plaza D'Atocha Mall, Tabasco 2000. Aerocaribe (☎ 16-50-46) and Aviacsa (☎ 16-57-33) are on the mall at Locales 9 and 10 respectively. Aeroméxico and Aerolitoral (☎ 800-021-40-00) are in the CICOM complex at Periférico Carlos Pellicer 511-2.

The airport is at ☎ 16-10-80.

Bus The 1st-class (ADO) bus station, Mina 297 (☎ 12-89-00) is three blocks south of Avenida Ruiz Cortines and about 12 blocks north of the city center. It has a luggage room (US$0.20 per hour) and a selection of little eating places. Deluxe and 1st-class buses of UNO, ADO and Cristóbal Colón run from here, as well as a few 2nd-class buses by Colón's Altos service and AU.

Though Villahermosa is an important transportation point, many buses serving it are *de paso,* so buy your onward ticket as early as possible. Daily departures (most in the evening) include:

Campeche – 380km, 6 hours; 13 buses (US$15 to US$18)

Cancún – 875km, 12 hours; 10 buses (US$31 to US$39)

Chetumal – 580km, 8 hours; 11 buses (US$19)

Mérida – 560km, 9 hours; 13 buses (US$22 to US$36)

Mexico City (TAPO) – 780km, 11 hours; 28 buses (US$31 to US$56)

Oaxaca – 700km, 12 hours; 3 buses (US$25)

Palenque – 140km, 2½ hours; 12 buses (US$5)

Playa del Carmen – 850km, 12 hours; 10 buses (US$29)

San Cristóbal de Las Casas – 305km, 7 hours; 1 bus (US$11); or go via Tuxtla Gutiérrez

Tuxtla Gutiérrez – 285km, 6 hours; 10 buses (US$9.50 to US$12)

Veracruz – 590km, 8 hours; 17 buses (US$17 to US$29)

Smaller companies serve destinations within Tabasco from other terminals in Villahermosa.

Car Most rental companies have desks at Rovirosa Airport. Offices in the city include

TABASCO & CHIAPAS

Advantage (☎ 15-50-48), Paseo Tabasco 1203; Budget (☎ 14-37-90), Malecón Madrazo 761; and Dollar (☎ 13-35-84), Paseo Tabasco 600, next to the cathedral. Dollar has another office (☎ 14-44-66) at the Hotel Best Western Maya Tabasco, Avenida Ruiz Cortines 907.

Getting Around
To/From the Airport Villahermosa's Rovirosa Airport is 13km east of the center on highway 186. A taxi between airport and city costs US$8 and takes about 20 minutes. Alternatively go to the road outside the airport parking lot and pick up a colectivo taxi into the city for US$0.70 per person. These terminate on Carranza half a block south of Ruiz Cortines, about 1km north of the Zona Luz. Take a 'Dos Montes' vehicle from there to return to the airport.

Local Transportation To get from the ADO bus station to the Zona Luz, take a 'Centro' combi (US$0.30) or a taxi (US$1), or walk 15 to 20 minutes. To walk, go out of the bus station's side (south) door, turn left onto Lino Merino and walk five blocks to Parque de la Paz, then turn right on Carranza.

From the Zona Luz to the ADO bus station, take a 'Chedraui' bus or combi north on Malecón Madrazo. Chedraui is a big store just north of the bus station.

Any taxi ride within the area between Avenida Ruiz Cortines, the Río Grijalva and Paseo Usumacinta costs US$1. Combi rides within the same area are US$0.30.

YUMKÁ
Yumká (☎ 56-01-07), 18km east of Villahermosa (4km past the airport), is the city's version of a safari park, divided into jungle, savanna and lake areas – representing Tabasco's three main ecosystems. Visits take the form of guided tours of the three areas (30 minutes each). You tour the lake by boat and the savanna – which with its elephants, giraffes and hippos seems more African than Mexican – on a tractor-pulled trolley. In the jungle, on foot, you come across Tabascan species such as howler

monkeys, jaguars, macaws, deer and peccaries (the big cats are enclosed!). Yumká is named for the legendary jungle-protecting spirit of the local indigenous Chontal people.

It's hardly a Kenya game drive, but if you fancy a dose of space, greenery and animals, go. Yumká is open 9 am to 5 pm daily (US$2, US$1 extra for the lake). Drinks and snacks are available. A taxi from the Zona Luz costs US$8.

COMALCALCO
The Chontal Mayan city of Comalcalco flourished during the late Classic period between 500 and 900 AD, when the region's agricultural productivity allowed population expansion. Comalcalcans traded the cacao bean with other Mayan settlements, and it is still the chief local cash crop.

Resembling Palenque in architecture and sculpture, Comalcalco is unique because it is built of bricks made from clay, sand and – ingeniously – oyster shells. Mortar was made with lime from the oyster shells.

As you enter the ruins, the substantial structure to your left may surprise you, as the pyramid's bricks look remarkably like the bricks used in construction today. Look on the right-hand side for remains of the stucco sculptures that once covered the pyramid. In the northern section of the Acrópolis are remains of fine stucco carvings.

Although the west side of the Acrópolis once held a crypt comparable to that of Palenque's Pakal, the tomb was vandalized centuries ago and the sarcophagus stolen. Continue up the hill to the Palacio, and from this elevation enjoy the breeze while you gaze down on unexcavated mounds.

Comalcalco is open 10 am to 5 pm daily (US$1.50, free Sunday and holidays).

Getting There & Away
The 55km journey from Villahermosa to Comalcalco town takes about 1¼ hours. Colectivo taxis leave from the street on the north side of the ADO bus station in Villahermosa, charging US$4 per person. Frequent 2nd-class buses go from the Cardesa terminal on Hermanos Bastar Zozaya and from

the Somellera bus station, northwest of the center on Avenida Ruiz Cortines.

The ruins are about 3km from Comalcalco town. You can cover the distance by taxi, or by a Paraíso-bound combi. Combis may go right to the ruins or they may drop you at the entrance, from which it's about a 1km walk.

AGUA SELVA

If you're hankering to get far off the beaten track, consider a trip to the Agua Selva ecotourism project in the remote, rugged hills of far southwest Tabasco. A series of rustic *cabaña lodgings* have been set up to help visitors enjoy the canyons, waterfalls and caves of the area and the early Classic period Zoque ruins and rock carvings of animals, people and geometric designs at Malpasito. There's transportation into the area from Huimanguillo, 67km southwest of Villahermosa. Villahermosa's main tourist office can provide enough information to set you on your way, and the inexpensive *Hotel del Carmen (Morelos 49)* in Huimanguillo has more details.

TO/FROM GUATEMALA VIA TENOSIQUE

The river route from Tabasco into Guatemala is along the Río San Pedro from La Palma in southeast Tabasco. Compared to the more commonly taken route via Frontera Corozal in Chiapas, the San Pedro gives you a longer river ride but the connecting transportation is less convenient, especially from Palenque.

First you have to get to the town of Tenosique, served by 10 buses a day (3½ hours, US$7) from Villahermosa's ADO bus station. Starting from Palenque you must go first to the town of Emiliano Zapata (one hour by ADO bus or by hourly Transportes Palenque colectivos from 5 am), then get another bus to Tenosique (one hour). A taxi from Palenque to Tenosique is about US$40.

From Tenosique, there are buses to La Palma (one hour) every two hours from 4.30 am to 4.30 pm, from Calle 31. A taxi (45 minutes) costs US$10.

A daily boat leaves La Palma at 8 am for the four-hour trip (US$20) through jungle

and cut-down jungle to the village of El Naranjo, Guatemala. Other boats may leave later in the day. El Naranjo has a few places to stay (basic rooms along the main street for US$2 to US$4, good rooms in *Posada San Pedro* by the river for US$20 to US$30). About five buses daily go to Flores (four hours, US$4). The once-terrible road is being paved now.

Coming from Guatemala, the scheduled boat leaves El Naranjo about 1 pm. If you miss the last bus out of La Palma, there should be trucks.

Tenosique and Emiliano Zapata have economical *hotels*.

Na Chan Kan and Viajes Kukulcan are among the Palenque travel agencies offering packages along this route – around US$75 per person (minimum at least two people) for the roughly 13-hour Palenque-Flores trip (see Organized Tours in the Palenque section).

Chiapas

Mexico's southernmost state has enormous variety, fascinating to anyone with a curiosity about nature, ancient civilizations or modern indigenous peoples. At the center of Chiapas is San Cristóbal de Las Casas, a cool, tranquil hill-country colonial town surrounded by mysterious indigenous Maya villages. Two hours' drive west – and nearly 1600m lower – the surprisingly modern state capital, Tuxtla Gutiérrez, has probably the best zoo in Mexico, devoted entirely to Chiapas' varied fauna. Only a few kilometers from Tuxtla is the 800m-deep Cañón del Sumidero (Sumidero Canyon), through which you can take an awesome boat ride.

About three hours north of San Cristóbal are the Agua Azul and Misol-Ha waterfalls, which are among Mexico's most spectacular. A little farther on are the ruins of Palenque, perhaps the most beautiful of all ancient Mayan sites. In the east of Chiapas is the Selva Lacandona (Lacandón Jungle), one of Mexico's largest areas of tropical rain forest. Within the jungle you can visit beautiful Mayan sites such as Yaxchilán and Bonampak, or lovely Laguna Miramar, a pristine lake. You can cross the jungle-lined Río Usumacinta into Guatemala, en route to Flores and Tikal.

Three hours' travel southeast of San Cristóbal, near the border with Guatemala, is the lovely Lagos (or Lagunas) de Montebello lakes region. A new road along the border links Montebello with the Yaxchilán/Bonampak area. Chiapas also has a steamy Pacific coast where you can explore the beaches and mangrove-fringed lagoons of La Encrucijada Biosphere Reserve or relax at laid-back Puerto Arista.

You'll find a reasonable touristic introduction to Chiapas on the Mundo Maya Internet site (www.mundomaya.com.mx).

Dangers & Annoyances

Since the 1994 Zapatista uprising, the security situation in Chiapas has been volatile. Keep your ear to the ground about where is and is not advisable to go, especially if you are thinking of leaving the main highways. During extensive travels in Chiapas in spring 1999, we encountered lots of military checkpoints but no other outward sign of trouble. A few months later the Mexican army and police launched a campaign of serious intimidation and harassment against pro-Zapatista villages east of Ocosingo, which raised tension throughout the state. At the same time the right-wing state authorities, unhappy about human-rights observers and other foreigners taking an interest in Chiapas politics, seemed to be encouraging a climate of xenophobia.

Make sure your tourist card is valid and keep it and your passport handy: they may be scrutinized at checkpoints. Dozens of foreigners have been expelled from Mexico for supposedly engaging in unauthorized political or journalistic activities or human-rights observation in Chiapas. Some underwent frightening experiences at the hands of Mexican security forces. Since 1998 Mexico has had a special category of FM3 visa for international observers. If the purpose of your visit is anything other than plain tourism, you can ask in advance at a Mexican consulate or embassy about visa requirements.

When traveling by bus, take care of your belongings and don't accept food or drink from other passengers. But traveling by bus is probably safer than driving yourself: we have heard of incidents in which vehicle-loads of foreigners were held up and robbed.

History

Chiapas has always been intimately connected with Guatemala. Pre-Hispanic civilizations straddled what's now the Chiapas-Guatemala border, and for most of the Spanish colonial era Chiapas was governed from Guatemala.

Pre-Hispanic Central and coastal Chiapas came under Olmec influence. Izapa, near Tapachula, peaked between 200 BC to 200 AD and is thought to be a link between the Olmec and the Maya.

During the Classic era (approximately 250 to 900 AD), coastal and central Chiapas were relative backwaters, but lowlying, jungle-covered eastern Chiapas gave rise to splendid Mayan city-states such as Palenque, Yaxchilán, Bonampak and Toniná, which flourished in the 7th and 8th centuries.

After the Classic Mayan collapse, highland Chiapas and Guatemala came to be divided among a number of often-warring kingdoms, many with cultures descended from the Maya but some also claiming central Mexican Toltec ancestry. Coastal Chiapas, a rich source of cacao, was conquered by the Aztecs at the end of the 15th century and became their most distant province, under the name Xoconochco (from which its present name, Soconusco, is derived).

Spanish Era Central Chiapas was brought under Spanish control by the 1528 expedition of Diego de Mazariegos, who defeated the dominant, warlike Chiapa people, many of whom jumped to their death in the Cañón del Sumidero rather than be captured. Outlying areas were subdued in the 1530s and 1540s, though Spain never gained full control over the scattered inhabitants of the Lacandón Jungle. New diseases arrived with the Spaniards and an epidemic in 1544 killed about half the indigenous people of Chiapas.

Administration from Guatemala for most of the Spanish era meant that Chiapas lacked supervision for long periods and there was little check on colonists' excesses against the indigenous people.

The only real light in the darkness was the work of some Spanish church figures. Preeminent was Bartolomé de Las Casas (1474-1566), appointed the first bishop of Chiapas in 1545. Las Casas had come to the Caribbean as a colonist, but in 1510 he entered the Dominican order and spent the rest of his life fighting for indigenous rights in the new colonies. His achievements, including the passing of laws reducing compulsory labor (1542) and banning indigenous (though not black) slavery (1550), earned him the hostility of the colonists but the affection of the native people. (See 'A Different Sort of Liberator,' in the History section of the Facts about the Country chapter).

19th & 20th Centuries In 1821 newly independent Mexico annexed Spain's former Central American provinces (including Chiapas), but when Mexican emperor Agustín de Iturbide was overthrown in 1823, the United Provinces of Central America declared their independence. A small military force under General Vicente Filísola, which Iturbide had sent to the Guatemala/Chiapas region, managed to persuade Chiapas to join the Mexican union, and this was approved by a referendum in Chiapas in 1824.

Since then, a succession of governors appointed in Chiapas by Mexico City, along with local landowners, have maintained an almost feudal control over the state. Periodic uprisings and protests bore witness to bad government, but the world took little notice until January 1, 1994, when a group calling itself the Ejército Zapatista de Liberación Nacional (EZLN, Zapatista National Liberation Army) briefly occupied San Cristóbal de Las Casas and nearby towns by military force. The Zapatistas, fighting for a fairer deal for indigenous peoples, won widespread support around and beyond Mexico, but no real concessions. By 1999, despite a tight Mexican army noose around their areas of strongest support in Chiapas, and other harassment, they were still maintaining a mainly political campaign for democratic change (see 'The Zapatistas').

Geography & Climate

Chiapas' 74,000 sq km fall into five distinct bands, all roughly parallel to the Pacific coast. The heaviest rain in all of them falls from May to October.

The hot, fertile coastal plain, 15km to 35km wide, is called the Soconusco. Rising inland of the Soconusco is the Sierra Madre de Chiapas mountain range, mostly between 1000m and 2500m in height, though Tacaná volcano on the Guatemalan border reaches 4110m. The Sierra Madre continues into Guatemala, throwing up several more volcanoes.

Inland from the Sierra Madre is the wide, warm, fairly dry Río Grijalva valley, also called the Central Depression of Chiapas, 500m to 1000m high.

Next come the Chiapas highlands, Los Altos, mostly 2000m to 3000m high and also extending into Guatemala. San Cristóbal de Las Casas, in the Valle de Jovel in the middle of these uplands, is cool with year-round temperatures between high single figures and the low 20s (°C).

The low-lying northern and eastern parts of the state of Chiapas include some of Mexico's few remaining areas of tropical rain forest. The eastern rain forests, known as the Selva Lacandona (Lacandón Jungle), have shrunk from around 15,000 sq km in 1940 to perhaps only 5000 sq km now, as a result of timber-cutting, colonization by landless peasants from elsewhere and clearing by cattle-ranchers (see 'The Lacandón Jungle & the Lacandones' later in this chapter).

The Zapatistas

On January 1, 1994, an armed left-wing peasant group calling itself the Ejército Zapatista de Liberación Nacional (EZLN, Zapatista National Liberation Army) sacked and occupied government offices in the Chiapas towns of San Cristóbal de Las Casas, Ocosingo, Las Margaritas and Altamirano. The Mexican army evicted the Zapatistas within a few days, with about 150 people killed. The rebels retreated to a remote forest hideout on the fringes of the Lacandón Jungle, having drawn the world's attention to Chiapas.

The EZLN's goal was to overturn a corrupt, wealthy minority's hold on land, resources and power in Chiapas, which had left many indigenous peasants impoverished, marginalized and lacking in education, health care and fundamental civil rights. Some say that the Mexican Revolution of 1910-20 never really happened in Chiapas.

Though the Zapatistas were militarily far outnumbered and outgunned, they attracted broad support and sympathy, and their leader, a masked figure known as Subcomandante Marcos, became a cult figure for many Mexicans.

During 1994, while Marcos waged a propaganda war from his jungle hideout, demanding

Subcomandante Marcos

justice and reform in Mexican politics, peasants took over hundreds of farms and ranches in Chiapas, especially in Las Cañadas (the area between Ocosingo, Comitán and the Montes Azules Biosphere Reserve). Ultimately the government bought some of these properties from their previous owners and handed them over to the peasants. Las Cañadas, settled since the 1960s by thousands of dispossessed and land-hungry campesinos from highland Chiapas, has always been the main hotbed of Zapatista support.

Eventually an agreement on indigenous rights was reached between EZLN and government negotiators at San Andrés Larráinzar, the main center of Zapatista support in the Chiapas highlands, in 1996. The deal was to give limited autonomy to Mexico's indigenous peoples, but by 1997 it was clear that the government did not intend to turn the San Andrés accords into law.

❀❀❀❀❀❀❀❀❀❀❀❀❀❀❀❀❀❀❀❀❀❀❀❀❀❀❀

Economy

Chiapas has little industry but is second only to Veracruz among Mexican states in value of agricultural output, producing more coffee and bananas than any other state – chiefly from the fertile, wealthy Soconusco and adjacent slopes. Tapachula is the commercial hub of the Soconusco.

Chiapas contributes 13% of Mexico's natural gas and 4% of its oil (oil was found in northwest Chiapas in the 1970s), and the Río Grijalva, flowing across the center of the state, generates more electricity than any other river in Mexico at several huge dams. But in this electricity- and water-rich state, half the homes have neither electricity nor running water, and rates of illiteracy and infant mortality are the highest in Mexico. Most *chiapanecos* are in fact very poor, and wealth is concentrated in a small oligarchy.

The Zapatistas

There had been an amnesty since 1995, but the rebels, hemmed in to a remote pocket of jungle territory near the Guatemalan border, remained encircled by government troops. They continued to wage a propaganda war, using the Internet and staging a series of high-profile conventions, including an 'intercontinental encounter against neoliberalism' at the village that is apparently their headquarters, La Realidad, 85km southeast of Ocosingo.

In 1997 and 1998, tension and killings escalated in Chiapas. The Zapatistas set up some 'autonomous municipalities,' ousting officials of the ruling PRI party, whom they said had been elected fraudulently. The Zapatistas' enemies formed paramilitary organizations to drive Zapatista supporters from their villages and oppose the autonomous municipalities. Many of these paramilitaries were aligned with the state government; some were led by prominent local PRI members.

Violence reached its worst point with the Acteal massacre in December 1997 (see 'Indigenous Peoples of Chiapas') and continued in 1998, partly as a result of the seizure of some autonomous municipalities by the army and police.

In 1999 the EZLN organized a nationwide 'consultation' about indigenous rights. It said the 2.85 million respondents overwhelmingly favored the enactment of the San Andrés accords and of special constitutional rights for indigenous people. Subcomandante Marcos appeared in public for the first time in two years at La Realidad in May 1999, at a meeting of some 2000 supporters from around the country. Participants were urged to join students', workers' and farmers' struggles in addition to becoming part of indigenous people's struggles.

The Mexican army had approximately 60,000 troops in Chiapas by 1999, along with lots of imposing new bases and roadblocks all over the place. But a blatant attempt to wipe out the rebels would cause a huge outcry; what the army seemed to be trying to do was grind Zapatista supporters into submission and draw the noose ever tighter around their heartland. In mid-1999 troops, police and paramilitaries launched a major campaign of intimidation, violence and detentions against dozens of pro-Zapatista villages in Las Cañadas and the Lacandón Jungle, from San José La Nueva Esperanza, 10km southeast of La Realidad, to Amador Hernández, 15km north of Laguna Miramar, and as far north as Monte Líbano, 50km east of Ocosingo. Thousands fled their villages and by late 1999 the number of Chiapas indigenous people displaced from their homes was estimated to be as high as 21,000.

Underlying – literally – the whole complicated conflict may be oil, large quantities of which are rumored to be sitting beneath several areas of eastern Chiapas.

To get the Zapatista point of view firsthand, you can visit the EZLN Internet site ¡Ya Basta! (www.ezln.org). You'll get plenty more background on this complicated situation from organizations such as Global Exchange (www.globalexchange.org) and SIPAZ (www.nonviolence.org/sipaz) and on the Mexico Channel site (www.trace-sc.com) under Politics. The Chiapas state government's position can be found on www.chiapas.gob.mx.

✿ ✿

TUXTLA GUTIÉRREZ
• pop 378,100 • elev 532m ☎ 9

Chiapas' lively state capital has several things worth stopping for, among them one of Mexico's best zoos (devoted to the fauna of Chiapas) and easy access to exhilarating boat trips through the 800m-deep Cañón del Sumidero, though both of these trips could also be made in a long day from San Cristóbal de Las Casas.

Tuxtla Gutiérrez is located toward the west end of Chiapas' hot, humid central valley. Its name comes from the Náhuatl word *tuchtlan* (meaning 'where rabbits abound'), and from Joaquín Miguel Gutiérrez, a leading light in Chiapas' early-19th-century campaign to not be part of Guatemala. Tuxla Gutiérrez was not an important city until it became the state capital in 1892.

Orientation

The city center is Plaza Cívica, with the cathedral on its south side. The main east-west street, here called Avenida Central, runs past the north side of the cathedral. As it enters the city from the west this same street is Boulevard Dr Belisario Domínguez; to the east it becomes Boulevard Ángel Albino Corzo.

East-west streets are called Avenidas and they're named Norte or Sur depending whether they're north or south of Avenida Central. North-south streets are Calles and are called Poniente (Pte) or Oriente (Ote) depending whether they're west or east of Calle Central, which runs along the west side of Plaza Cívica. Each street name also has a suffix indicating whether it is east (Oriente, Ote), west (Poniente, Pte), north (Norte) or south (Sur) of the intersection of Avenida Central and Calle Central. So the address 2ª Avenida Norte Pte 425 refers to the western (Pte) half of 2ª Avenida Norte, with 425 being the street number.

Maps INEGI, at 1ª Avenida Norte Ote 220A just east of 2ª Ote Norte, sells 1:25,000 and 1:50,000 maps of many parts of Chiapas and other Mexican states, for US$2.50 each – it's open 8.30 am to 4.30 pm Monday to Friday.

Information

Tourist Offices The Oficina Municipal de Turismo (City Tourism Office, ☎ 612-55-11 ext 214) is at Calle Central Norte and 2ª Norte Ote, in the underpass at the northern end of Plaza Cívica. It's open 9 am to 9 pm Monday to Saturday, 9 am to 2 pm Sunday.

Chiapas' state tourism ministry, Sedetur, has a tourist information office (☎ 800-280-35-00) at Boulevard Domínguez 950, 1.6km west of Plaza Cívica, in the Secretaría de Desarrollo Económico building, which has a big Mayan head statue outside. It's open 9 am to 9.30 pm daily.

Immigration The Instituto Nacional de Migración (☎ 611-42-42), 1ª Calle Ote Norte 323, is open 9 am to 3 pm Monday to Friday.

Money Bancomer, at the corner of Avenida Central Pte and 2ª Avenida Norte Pte, does foreign exchange 8.30 am to 5.30 pm Monday to Friday, 10 am to 2 pm Saturday. Bital, on the west side of Plaza Cívica, exchanges money 8 am to 7 pm Monday to Friday, Saturday 9 am to 7 pm. These and many other city-center banks have ATMs. Hecali, a shop on Calle Central Sur facing the cathedral, does Western Union money transfers.

Post & Communications The post office, on a pedestrian-only block of 1ª Avenida Norte Ote just off Plaza Cívica, is open 8 am to 5 pm Monday to Friday, 9 am to 1 pm Saturday. There are plenty of pay phones around the plaza.

Netcropper, 2ª Avenida Norte Pte 427, is open 9 am to 9 pm daily and charges US$1.50 an hour for computer use, including Internet access.

Laundry Lavandería La Burbuja, 1ª Avenida Norte Pte 369, will wash and dry 3kg for US$2.50 (ready next day). It is open 8.30 am to 8 pm Monday to Saturday, 9 am to 1 pm Sunday.

Plaza Cívica & Cathedral

Tuxtla's broad, lively main plaza occupies two blocks, with the modern Catedral de San Marcos facing it across Avenida Central at the south end. On the hour the cathedral's clock tower bells tinkle out a tune to accompany a revolving parade of apostles' images on one of its upper levels.

Zoológico Miguel Álvarez del Toro (ZOOMAT)

Chiapas, with its huge range of environments, claims the highest concentration of animal species in North America – among them several varieties of big cat, 1200 types of butterfly and over 600 birds. You can see 180 of these species – many of them in danger of extinction – in Tuxtla's zoo, where they're kept in relatively spacious enclosures on a forested hillside just south of the city.

Among the creatures here are ocelots, jaguars, pumas, tapirs, red macaws, toucans,

Saturday night fever in Palenque town

Girl in Chiapas

'Anyone driving this thing?'

Whiz kids, San Cristóbal de Las Casas

Need something to, uh, read?

Templo del Sol, Palenque

Santo Domingo, San Cristóbal de Las Casas

Rush hour at the Chiapa de Corzo *embarcadero*

TUXTLA GUTIÉRREZ

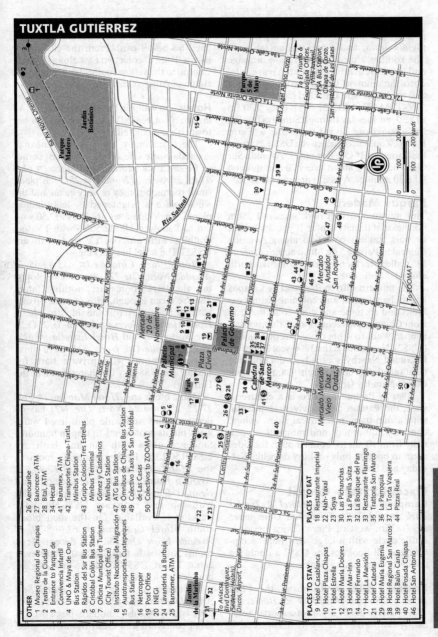

OTHER
1 Museo Regional de Chiapas
2 Teatro de la Ciudad
3 Entrance to Parque de Convivencia Infantil
4 UNO & Maya de Oro Bus Station
5 Rápidos del Sur Bus Station
6 Cristóbal Colón Bus Station
7 Oficina Municipal de Turismo (City Tourist Office)
8 Instituto Nacional de Migración
15 Autotransportes Cuxtepeques Bus Station
16 Netcropper
19 Post Office
20 INEGI
24 Lavandería La Burbuja
25 Bancomer, ATM
26 Aerocaribe
27 Bancrecer, ATM
28 Bital, ATM
34 Hecali
41 Banamex, ATM
42 Transportes Chiapa-Tuxtla Minibus Station
43 Grupo Colosio-Tres Estrellas Minibus Terminal
45 Gómez y Castellanos Minibus Station
47 ATG Bus Station
48 Ómnibus de Chiapas Bus Station
49 Colectivo Taxis to San Cristóbal de Las Casas
50 Colectivos to ZOOMAT

PLACES TO STAY
9 Hotel Casablanca
10 Hotel Plaza Chiapas
11 Hotel Estrella
12 Hotel María Dolores
13 Hotel Mar-Inn
14 Hotel Fernando
17 Hotel La Mansión
21 Hotel Catedral
29 Hotel María Eugenia
37 Hotel Regional San Marcos
38 Hotel Balún Canán
39 Hotel Posada Chiapas
46 Hotel San Antonio

PLACES TO EAT
18 Restaurante Imperial
22 Nah-Yaxal
23 Soya
30 Las Pichanchas
31 La Parrilla Suiza
32 La Boutique del Pan
33 Restaurante Flamingo
35 Trattoria San Marco
36 La Parroquia
37 La Torta Vaquera
44 Pizzas Real

TABASCO & CHIAPAS

a rattlesnake, a boa constrictor, spider monkeys, a monkey-eating harpy eagle *(águila arpia)* and a pair of quetzal birds. The zoo has a clear conservation message and is named after Miguel Álvarez del Toro, the eminent Chiapas conservationist and zoologist who founded it.

ZOOMAT (☎ 612-37-54) is open 9.30 am to 5.30 pm Tuesday through Sunday (free). It has a bookstore. To get there take a 'Cerro Hueco, Zoológico' colectivo (US$0.25) from the corner of 1ª Ote Sur and 7ª Avenida Sur Ote. They leave about every 20 minutes and take 20 minutes. A taxi is around US$1.50.

Parque Madero

This museum-theater-park area is 1.25km northeast of the city center. If you don't want to walk, take a colectivo along Avenida Central to Parque 5 de Mayo at the corner of 11ª Calle Ote, then another colectivo north along 11ª Calle Ote.

The modern **Museo Regional de Chiapas** has archaeological and colonial history exhibits and costume and craft collections, all from Chiapas, plus temporary exhibitions. It is open 9 am to 4 pm daily except Monday (US$2). Next door is the 1200-seat **Teatro de la Ciudad**. Nearby is a shady **Jardín Botánico** (Botanical Garden), open 9 am to 6 pm except Monday (free).

Also in Parque Madero is a children's park, the **Parque de Convivencia Infantil**, with a minitrain, mechanical rides, swings, climbing equipment and minigolf – open daily from 10 am to 9 pm (though the rides seem to operate only on busy days like Saturday and Sunday).

Places to Stay – Budget

Camping *La Hacienda Hotel & Trailer Park* (☎ 612-79-86, *Boulevard Domínguez 1197)*, 3km west of Plaza Cívica beside a traffic circle with a large 'cow horn' sculpture, has all hookups for US$7 a double, a coffeeshop and a tiny pool.

Hostels Tuxtla's youth hostel, the *Villa Juvenil Chiapas* (☎ 613-54-78, *Boulevard Albino Corzo 1800)* is part of a sports center nearly 2km east of Plaza Cívica. For a bed in

a small, clean separate-sex dormitory you pay US$3. Meals cost US$1.50 each. You need no hostel card. From the city center take a 'Ruta 1' colectivo east along Avenida Central to the yellow footbridge just before a statue of Albino Corzo.

Hotels Tap water in the cheaper hotels is *'al tiempo'* (not heated) but, since this is a hot town, it's not cold either.

There are many hotels on and near 2ª Avenida Norte Ote, off the northeast corner of Plaza Cívica. *Hotel Casablanca* (☎ 611-03-05, *2ª Avenida Norte Ote 251)* has plain, small rooms, but they're very clean and the whole place is brightened by leafy indoor plants. Singles/doubles are US$8/12.50 with fan and shower, US$12.50/15 with TV too; doubles with air-con, TV and bath are US$23. The hotel has parking.

Hotel Plaza Chiapas (☎ 613-83-65, *2ª Avenida Norte Ote 229)* has a shiny lobby but the bare rooms are nothing fancy. They're clean enough, with fan and private bath for US$8/9. Across the side street here, *Hotel María Dolores* (☎ 612-36-83, *2ª Calle Ote Norte 304)* and *Hotel Estrella* (☎ 612-38-27, *2ª Calle Ote Norte 322)* have unremarkable rooms with private bath for US$5/7 (or US$4/6 with shared bath, at the Estrella).

Half a block east, *Hotel Mar-Inn* (☎ 612-27-15, *2ª Avenida Norte Ote 347)* has 60 decent rooms and wide plant-lined walkways, but its roof seems to trap in humidity. Singles/doubles with fan and bath are US$10.50/13.50. Farther east again, rooms in the *Hotel Fernando* (☎ 613-17-40, *2ª Avenida Norte Ote 515)* are spacious and clean, if dilapidated. Singles/doubles/triples with fan and bath are US$6.50/7/8.50. Parking is available. On the next block south, *Hotel Catedral* (☎ 613-08-24, *1ª Avenida Norte Ote 367)* has decent, clean rooms with bath, fans, hot water and even cable TV at US$10/12/14/16 for singles/doubles/triples/quads.

Southeast of Plaza Cívica, *Hotel San Antonio* (☎ 612-27-13, *2ª Avenida Sur Ote 540)* is an amicable modern place with a small courtyard and clean rooms for good prices of US$6 with private bath and fan, or US$8 for twin beds.

West of Plaza Cívica, *Hotel La Mansión* (☎ 612-21-51, *1ª Calle Pte Norte 221*) is a good value: decent-sized, air-conditioned singles/doubles with bath cost US$12/15. *Hotel Posada Chiapas* (☎ 612-33-54, *2ª Calle Pte Sur 243*) charges US$7/12.50 for clean but smallish rooms with fan, TV and bath.

Places to Stay – Mid-Range

Hotel Regional San Marcos (☎ 613-19-40, *2ª Calle Ote Sur 176*), a minute's walk from Plaza Cívica, has medium-size rooms with TV and bath for US$15/17.50 a single/double (US$17.50/22 with air-con). Bright, flower-patterned furniture and a recent paint job give the place a tiny sparkle.

East of the center, *Hotel Balún Canán* (☎ 612-30-48, *Avenida Central Ote 944*) has fairly pleasant rooms with air-con, bath and TV for reasonable prices of US$16/19. Get one at the back, not on the noisy street.

La Hacienda Hotel (☎ 612-79-86, *Boulevard Domínguez 1197*), 3km west of Plaza Cívica, has clean doubles with fan for US$24.

Places to Stay – Top End

Most comfortable downtown is *Hotel María Eugenia* (☎ 613-37-67, fax 613-28-60, *Avenida Central Ote 507*). It has a good restaurant, parking, and attractive air-conditioned rooms, all with two double beds, cable TV and bath for US$40/45.

Hotel Bonampak (☎ 613-20-50, fax 612-77-37, *Boulevard Domínguez 180*), 1.6km west of Plaza Cívica almost opposite the state tourist office, has comfortable air-conditioned singles/doubles/triples with cable TV for US$40/45/50. It boasts a pool, travel agency, parking and a copy of one of the famous murals at Bonampak ruins.

Tuxtla's most luxurious hostelry is the modern, 210-room *Hotel Camino Real* (☎ 617-77-77, *Boulevard Domínguez 1195*), which rises like some huge colored-concrete castle of the hospitality industry 1.5km west of Hotel Bonampak. The interior is spectacular, with a pool and water-fall in a large, verdant inner courtyard. Very comfortable air-conditioned singles/

doubles cost US$96/105 and there are plenty of top-end facilities.

Hotel Flamboyant (☎ 615-09-99), on Boulevard Domínguez 1km west of the Camino Real, is in handsome modern Arabic style, with singles/doubles for US$73/86.

Places to Eat

Restaurante Imperial, on Calle Central Norte facing the west side of Plaza Cívica, is a good, clean, busy place, convenient for the 1st-class bus station. A three-course comida corrida with lots of main-course choice is US$2.25; breakfast items (from cornflakes to eggs or hotcakes) are US$0.90 to US$1.50, and there's good chocolate to drink.

A row of popular restaurants with outdoor tables lines up behind the cathedral on Callejón Ote Sur. Most are open from around 7 am to midnight. At *Trattoria San Marco* you can enjoy 20 varieties of pizza (US$1.50 to US$9), baguettes (US$3 to US$3.50), salads, *papas rellenas* (potatoes with filling) or savory *crepas*. *La Parroquia* next door specializes in *a la parrilla* grills, from bacon at US$3.50 to a T-bone for US$6. *La Torta Vaquera* is popular for coffee, tacos (US$0.40) and *quesadillas*.

Restaurante Flamingo (*1ª Calle Pte Sur 17*), down a passage off the street, is a quiet, efficient place with air-con, open 7 am to 10 pm daily. A full hotcakes breakfast, or an order of luncheon tacos or enchiladas, is yours for US$3. Most meat and fish dishes cost US$5 to US$8. For a decent-size meal at a small price, try *Pizzas Real* (*2ª Avenida Sur Ote 557*), opposite Hotel San Antonio, where a comida corrida of rice and two other dishes costs only US$1. One of the best values for comidas corridas in town (US$5) is served in the restaurant of the *Hotel María Eugenia* (*Avenida Central Ote 507*).

A few blocks west of the center on Avenida Central Poniente, *Soya* sells whole wheat breads, fresh yogurt and yogurt ice cream (US$1) for which you can select fruits to be crushed into it and a range of toppings. *Nah-Yaxal* (*6ª Calle Pte Norte 124*), round the corner, is a clean, bright, vegetarian restaurant open 7 am to 9 pm Monday to Saturday, 7 am to 4 pm Sunday. Whole wheat *tortas, antojitos* and an *energética* breakfast salad of fruit, granola, yogurt and honey all go for US$1.25 to US$2.25, and the three-course lunch is US$3.25.

Nearby, *La Boutique del Pan*, on Avenida Central Pte facing the Jardín de la Marimba, is a good bakery with a nice, bright café section where you can sit down for a pastry, sandwich or coffee. *La Parrilla Suiza (Avenida Central Pte 1013)*, nearby, is popular for its *tacos al pastor* at US$0.30 each and grills up to US$3. It stays open till 4 or 5 am.

Farther west, the Hotel Bonampak's *Cafetería Bonampak* is very popular and reasonably priced.

Six blocks east of Plaza Cívica is *Las Pichanchas (Avenida Central Ote 837)*, a courtyard restaurant open noon to midnight daily, with a long menu of local specialties and chiapaneco entertainment. Marimbas play in the afternoon and evening, and there's Chiapas folkloric dance in the evenings too. Try *chipilín*, a cheese-and-cream soup on a maize base; and for dessert *chimbos*, made from egg yolks and cinnamon. In between, have tamales, vegetarian salads (beets and carrots) or *carne asada*. Three courses with drinks cost around US$10.

Entertainment

Popular free marimba concerts are held from 7 to 9 pm nightly in the Jardín de la Marimba, a pleasant park beside Avenida Central Pte eight blocks west of Plaza Cívica.

The city's most popular discos, both attracting a mixed-ages crowd, are *Baby Rock* (☎ 615-14-28) on Calzada Emiliano Zapata, west of the center off Boulevard Domínguez opposite the Camino Real hotel, and *La Uno* (☎ 615-29-57, *Boulevard Las Fuentes 101*), just outside the Camino Real's main door.

Shopping

The Casa de las Artesanías de Chiapas, unhandily located at Boulevard Domínguez 2035, 2km west of Plaza Cívica, sells a good range of Chiapas crafts – it's open 10 am to 8 pm Monday to Saturday, 10 am to 3 pm Sunday.

Getting There & Away

Air Aerocaribe flies daily to/from Mexico City, Oaxaca, Villahermosa, Veracruz, Tapachula, Mérida, Cancún and Havana (Cuba) all at least once daily; and to/from San Cristóbal de Las Casas, Palenque and Comitán each three or four times weekly. Aviacsa flies several times daily to/from Mexico City.

Aerocaribe (☎ 612-00-20, airport ☎ 615-65-76) is at Avenida Central Pte 206, one block from Plaza Cívica. Aviacsa is at Avenida Central Pte 1144 (☎ 611-20-00, airport ☎ 615-10-11), more than 1km farther west.

Bus The Cristóbal Colón terminal (☎ 612-51-22) at 2ª Avenida Norte Pte 268, two blocks west of the main plaza, is the main bus station. Colón's 1st-class and 2nd-class (Altos) services, and ADO's 1st-class buses operate from here. The 2nd-class line Rápidos del Sur is next door, and UNO and Maya de Oro deluxe services are across the street. There's no baggage checkroom, but there are private ones outside on 2ª Norte Pte: look for '*Se guardan maletas*' or '*Se guardan equipaje*' signs.

Most 2nd-class companies' terminals are east of the center:

Autotransportes Cuxtepeques – 10ª Calle Ote Norte at 3ª Norte Ote

Autotransportes Tuxtla Gutiérrez (ATG) – 3ª Avenida Sur Ote 712

Fletes y Pasajes (FYPSA) – 9ª Avenida Sur Ote 1882

Grupo Colosio-Tres Estrellas – 2ª Avenida Sur Ote 521

Ómnibus de Chiapas (OdC) – 3ª Avenida Sur Ote 884

Daily departures include:

Cancún – 1110km, 16 hours; 1 Maya de Oro (US$43), 1 Colón (US$38), 2 ATG (US$30 to US$32)

Ciudad Cuauhtémoc (Guatemalan border) – 255km, 4½ hours; 6 Colón (US$9.50)

Comitán – 175km, 3½ hours; 8 Colón (US$5), 26 Cuxtepeques (US$4)

Mérida – 820km, 13 hours; 1 Maya de Oro (US$32), 1 Colón (US$25), 1 ATG (US$24)

Mexico City (most to TAPO, a few to Norte) – 980km, 17 hours; 1 UNO (US$63), 3 Maya de Oro (US$47), 6 Colón/ADO (US$40)

Oaxaca – 540km, 10 hours; 1 Maya de Oro (US$22), 2 Colón (US$17.50), 8 FYPSA (US$13.50)

Palenque – 275km, 6 hours; 3 Maya de Oro (US$11), 5 Colón (US$9), 8 ATG (US$7.50 to US$9)

Puerto Escondido – 560km, 11½ hours; 2 Colón (US$18.50)

San Cristóbal de Las Casas – 85km, 2 hours; 6 Maya de Oro (US$3.25), 15 Colón (US$2.75), 8 ATG (US$2.50), frequent Colosio-Tres Estrellas minibuses (US$2.25), OdC every half hour 6 am to 7 pm (US$2), frequent colectivo taxis (US$3) from 3ª Avenida Sur Ote 847

Tapachula – 390km, 8 hours; 3 Maya de Oro overnight (US$15.50), 15 Colón (US$13), 20 Rápidos del Sur, 4 am to 2 pm (US$11)

Villahermosa – 285km, 6 hours; 2 Maya de Oro (US$12), 6 Colón (US$9.50 to US$10.50), 5 ATG (US$7.25 to US$11)

Car Rental companies, most also with desks at the airport, include:

Alamo (☎ 612-52-61) 5ª Avenida Norte Pte 2260

Arrendadora Express (☎ 612-26-66) Avenida Central Ote 725

Autos Gabriel (☎ 612-07-57) Boulevard Domínguez 780

Budget (☎ 615-06-83) Boulevard Domínguez 2510

Hertz (☎ 615-53-48) Hotel Camino Real

Getting Around

To/From the Airport Tuxtla's Aeropuerto Francisco Sarabia (☎ 612-29-20), also called Aeropuerto Terán, is 3km south of highway 190 from a signposted turnoff 5km west of Plaza Cívica. Taxi desks in the airport ask US$4.50 to the city center; outside the airport gate you may get one for US$3.

Local Transportation All colectivos (US$0.25) on Boulevard Domínguez-Avenida Central-Boulevard Albino Corzo run at least as far as the Hotel Bonampak and state tourist office in the west, and 11ª Calle Ote in the east. Official stops are marked by 'parada' signs but they'll sometimes stop for you elsewhere. Taxi rides within the city cost US$1.25 to US$1.50.

CHIAPA DE CORZO
● **pop 27,700** ● **elev 450m** ☎ 9

This pleasant colonial town on the Río Grijalva, 12km east of Tuxtla Gutiérrez, is the main starting point for trips into the Cañón del Sumidero.

History

Chiapa de Corzo has been occupied almost continuously since about 1500 BC. Its sequence of pre-Hispanic cultures makes it invaluable to archaeologists, but there's little to see in the way of remains.

In the couple of centuries before the Spaniards arrived, the warlike Chiapa – the dominant people in western Chiapas at the time – had their capital, Nandalumí, a couple of kilometers downstream from present-day Chiapa de Corzo, on the opposite bank of the Grijalva near the canyon mouth. When the Spaniards under Diego de Mazariegos invaded the area in 1528, the Chiapa, realizing defeat was inevitable, apparently hurled themselves by the hundreds to death in the canyon – men, women and children – rather than surrender.

Mazariegos founded a settlement that he called Chiapa de los Indios here, but a month later shifted his base to another new settlement, Villa Real de Chiapa (now San Cristóbal de Las Casas), where the climate and natives were more agreeable.

At Chiapa in 1863, liberal forces, organized by Chiapas state governor Ángel Albino Corzo, defeated conservatives supporting the French invasion of Mexico. The name of Corzo, who was also born in the town and died here, was added to Chiapa's in 1888.

Orientation & Information

Buses and minibuses from and to Tuxtla stop on the north side of Chiapa's spacious plaza, named for Albino Corzo. Chiapa's *embarcadero* for Cañón del Sumidero boat trips is two blocks south of the plaza along 5 de Febrero, the street on the plaza's west side.

There's a tourist information office on the west side of the plaza, where you'll also find Banamex, with an ATM.

The Fiesta de Enero: Cross-Dressing & Blond Conquistadors

Some of Mexico's most colorful and curious fiestas, together known as the Fiesta de Enero, happen in Chiapa de Corzo every January.

From January 9, young men, known as Las Chuntá, dress as women and dance through the streets nightly – a custom said to derive from a distribution of food to the poor by the maids of a rich woman of colonial times, Doña María de Angulo.

Processions and dances of the bizarre Parachicos – men with bright striped sarapes, staring wooden masks and bushes of blond 'hair,' representing Spanish conquistadors – take place in daytime on January 15, 17 and 20.

There's a musical parade on January 19, then on the night of January 21 comes the Combate Naval – an hour-long mock canoe battle on the river, with spectacular fireworks.

The flower-patterned dresses worn by Chiapas women during these festivities are among the most vividly colorful you'll ever see.

✸✸✸✸✸✸✸✸✸✸✸✸✸✸✸✸✸✸✸✸✸✸✸✸✸✸

Things to See & Do

Impressive **arcades** frame three sides of the plaza, a statue of General Corzo rises on the west side, and an elaborate castlelike brick fountain in Mudéjar-Gothic style, said to resemble the Spanish crown and known as **La Pila**, stands toward the southeast corner. The large **Templo de Santo Domingo de Guzmán**, one block south of the plaza, was built in the late 16th century by the Dominican order. Its adjoining convent is now the Centro Cultural, holding an exposition of Mexican prints and the **Museo de la Laca**, which features the local craft specialty, lacquered gourds.

Places to Stay

Casa de Huéspedes Los Ángeles at the southeast corner of the plaza has basic singles/doubles with bath for US$8/10. **Hotel La Ceiba** (☎ 616-07-73, Domingo Ruiz 300), two blocks west of the plaza, has attractive rooms with air-con, fan and folksy decor for US$20/23, and an inviting pool.

Places to Eat

By the embarcadero are eight **restaurants** with almost identical menus and loud music. All are equally overpriced, though the view of the river is nice.

Near the market on Coronel Urbina, across from the Museo de la Laca, are the standard ultracheap market **comedores**.

Restaurant Los Corredores (5 de Febrero at Madero), facing the southwest corner of the plaza, has good cheap breakfasts and plenty of reasonably priced fish plates. One block along Madero from here, and popular with tour groups, is the friendly **Restaurant Jardines de Chiapa** (Madero 395), set around a garden patio, with main dishes for US$3.50 to US$4.50.

Ristorante Italiano Valle d'Aosta, on 5 de Febrero between the plaza and embarcadero, serves cheap pizza and more elaborate, moderately priced Italian-style dishes.

Getting There & Away

Minibuses from Tuxtla Gutiérrez to Chiapa de Corzo are run by Gómez y Castellanos at 3ª Avenida Sur Ote 380 and Transportes Chiapa-Tuxtla on 2ª Avenida Sur Ote at 2ª Ote Sur. Both depart every few minutes for the 20-minute, US$0.50 trip, and will also stop at Cahuaré embarcadero if you wish (see next section).

Buses to/from San Cristóbal de Las Casas don't pass through central Chiapa de Corzo, but most will stop at a gas station on highway 190 on the northeast edge of town. Microbuses (US$0.20) run between the *gasolinera* and the top end of the plaza.

CAÑÓN DEL SUMIDERO

The Cañón del Sumidero (Sumidero Canyon) is a daunting fissure in the earth a few kilometers east of Tuxtla Gutiérrez, with the Río Grijalva flowing northward through it. In 1981 the Chicoasén hydro-electric dam was completed at its northern end, and the canyon became a narrow, 25km-long reservoir.

Fast motorboats carry visitors through the canyon between towering sheer rock walls. The fare per person for a round-trip of about 2¼ hours, in a boat holding around 10 people, is US$6.

Highway 190 crosses the canyon mouth at Cahuaré, between Tuxtla and Chiapa de Corzo. Just east of the bridge and a few hundred meters off the highway is the Cahuaré embarcadero. You can board one of the open, fiberglass motorboats *(lanchas)* here, or at the embarcadero in Chiapa de Corzo a couple of kilometers farther up-stream, between roughly 8 am and 4 pm. You'll rarely have to wait more than half an hour for a boat to fill up. Bring something to drink, something to shield you from the sun

and, if the weather is not hot, a layer or two of warm clothing.

It's about 35km from Chiapa de Corzo to the dam. Soon after you pass under highway 190 the sides of the canyon tower an amazing 800m above you. Along the way you'll see a variety of bird life – herons, egrets, cormorants, vultures, kingfishers – plus probably a crocodile or two. The boat operators will point out a few odd forma-tions of rock or vegetation, including one cliff face covered in thick, hanging moss re-sembling a giant Christmas tree.

At the end of the canyon, the fast, brown river opens out behind the dam. The water beneath you is 260m deep.

SAN CRISTÓBAL DE LAS CASAS
• pop 99,300 • elev 2100m ☎ 9

Highway 190 from Tuxtla Gutiérrez seems to climb endlessly into the clouds before de-scending into the temperate, pine-clad Valle de Jovel, where lies the beautiful colonial town of San Cristóbal (cris-TOH-bal).

San Cristóbal's rewards come from ram-bling its streets, discovering its many fasci-nating and pretty nooks and corners, visiting the unusual nearby indigenous villages (maybe on bicycle or horseback), and ab-sorbing the unique atmosphere. San Cristóbal has a vaguely artsy, bohemian, floating community of Mexicans and for-eigners, a lively bar and music scene and wonderfully clear highland light. Accommo-dations and meals are inexpensive here.

San Cristóbal was catapulted into the limelight on January 1, 1994, when the Zap-atista rebels, fighting for Chiapas' oppressed indigenous people, selected it as one of four towns in which to launch their revolution. San Cristóbal's municipal rulers were (and remain) part of the Chiapas PRI old guard. The Zapatistas seized and sacked govern-ment offices in the town before being driven out within a few days by the Mexican army. They have continued their struggle by mainly political means ever since from vil-lages elsewhere in Chiapas. It is no longer possible to treat the indigenous people of the San Cristóbal area as mere quaint objects of anthropological curiosity. If

CAÑÓN DEL SUMIDERO

SAN CRISTÓBAL DE LAS CASAS

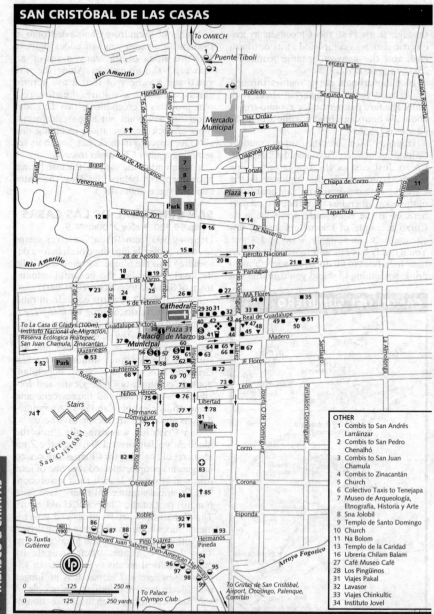

OTHER
1 Combis to San Andrés Larráinzar
2 Combis to San Pedro Chenalhó
3 Combis to San Juan Chamula
4 Combis to Zinacantán
5 Church
6 Colectivo Taxis to Tenejapa
7 Museo de Arqueología, Etnografía, Historia y Arte
8 Sna Jolobil
9 Templo de Santo Domingo
10 Church
11 Na Bolom
13 Templo de la Caridad
16 Librería Chilam Balam
27 Café Museo Café
28 Los Pingüinos
31 Viajes Pakal
32 Lavasor
33 Viajes Chinkultic
34 Instituto Jovel

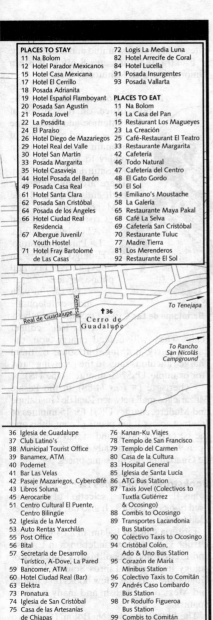

PLACES TO STAY		72	Logis La Media Luna
11	Na Bolom	82	Hotel Arrecife de Coral
12	Hotel Parador Mexicanos	84	Hotel Lucella
15	Hotel Casa Mexicana	91	Posada Insurgentes
17	Hotel El Cerrillo	93	Posada Vallarta
18	Posada Adrianita		
19	Hotel Español Flamboyant	PLACES TO EAT	
20	Posada San Agustín	11	Na Bolom
21	Posada Jovel	14	La Casa del Pan
22	La Posadita	15	Restaurant Los Magueyes
24	El Paraíso	23	La Creación
26	Hotel Diego de Mazariegos	25	Café-Restaurant El Teatro
29	Hotel Real del Valle	33	Restaurante Margarita
30	Hotel San Martín	42	Cafetería
33	Posada Margarita	46	Todo Natural
35	Hotel Casavieja	47	Cafetería del Centro
44	Hotel Posada del Barón	48	El Gato Gordo
49	Posada Casa Real	50	El Sol
61	Hotel Santa Clara	54	Emiliano's Moustache
62	Posada San Cristóbal	58	La Galería
64	Posada de los Ángeles	65	Restaurante Maya Pakal
66	Hotel Ciudad Real	68	Café La Selva
	Residencia	69	Cafetería San Cristóbal
67	Albergue Juvenil/	70	Restaurante Tuluc
	Youth Hostel	77	Madre Tierra
71	Hotel Fray Bartolomé	81	Los Merenderos
	de Las Casas	92	Restaurante El Sol

36	Iglesia de Guadalupe	76	Kanan-Ku Viajes
37	Club Latino's	78	Templo de San Francisco
38	Municipal Tourist Office	79	Templo del Carmen
39	Banamex, ATM	80	Casa de la Cultura
40	Podernet	83	Hospital General
41	Bar Las Velas	85	Iglesia de Santa Lucía
42	Pasaje Mazariegos, Cyberc@fé	86	ATG Bus Station
43	Libros Soluna	87	Taxis Jovel (Colectivos to
45	Aerocaribe		Tuxtla Gutiérrez
51	Centro Cultural El Puente,		& Ocosingo)
	Centro Bilingüe	88	Combis to Ocosingo
52	Iglesia de la Merced	89	Transportes Lacandonia
53	Auto Rentas Yaxchilán		Bus Station
55	Post Office	90	Colectivo Taxis to Ocosingo
56	Bital	94	Cristóbal Colón,
57	Secretaría de Desarrollo		Ado & Uno Bus Station
	Turístico, A-Dove, La Pared	95	Corazón de María
59	Bancomer, ATM		Minibus Station
60	Hotel Ciudad Real (Bar)	96	Colectivo Taxis to Comitán
63	Elektra	97	Andrés Caso Lombardo
73	Pronatura		Bus Station
74	Iglesia de San Cristóbal	98	Dr Rodulfo Figueroa
75	Casa de las Artesanías		Bus Station
	de Chiapas	99	Combis to Comitán

Labels on map: Ketresal · Real de Guadalupe · Cerro de Guadalupe · ✝36 · To Tenejapa · To Rancho San Nicolás Campground

nothing else, the postcards and dolls representing Subcomandante Marcos, the black-balaclava'd Zapatista leader, are enough to make most visitors aware of Chiapas' political and economic struggles.

History

The Maya ancestors of the indigenous Tzotzil and Tzeltal people of the San Cristóbal area moved to these highlands after the collapse of lowland Maya civilization over 1000 years ago. Diego de Mazariegos founded San Cristóbal as the Spanish regional base in 1528.

For most of the colonial era San Cristóbal was a neglected outpost governed ineffectively from Guatemala. Its Spanish citizens made their fortunes from wheat; the indigenous people lost their lands and suffered diseases, taxes and forced labor. The church afforded some protection against colonist excesses. Dominican monks reached Chiapas in 1545 and made San Cristóbal their main base. One of them, Bartolomé de Las Casas (for whom the town is now named), was appointed bishop of Chiapas that year; he and Juan de Zapata y Sandoval, bishop from 1613 to 1621, are both fondly remembered. In modern times Bishop Samuel Ruiz, who retired in late 1999 after a long tenure, followed very much in the Las Casas tradition of support for the oppressed indigenous people – and earned the loathing of the Chiapas establishment for his pains.

San Cristóbal was the state capital from 1824 to 1892 but remained relatively isolated until the 1970s, when tourism began to be an significant factor in its economy. After a hiccup following the Zapatista uprising, tourism has bounced back.

Another change since the 1970s has been an influx of around 20,000 people expelled by their village authorities from Chamula and other indigenous villages for turning Protestant under the influence of foreign evangelical missionaries. These people live in makeshift colonies on the edges of town, especially in the northwest, and many lack employment. Most of the craft sellers around Santo Domingo church are drawn from their numbers.

Orientation

San Cristóbal is easy to walk around, with straight streets rambling up and down several gentle hills. The Pan-American Highway (highway 190) passes through the south side of town. Officially named Boulevard Juan Sabines, it's called 'El Bulevar' by locals.

Nearly all transportation terminals are on or just off the Pan-American. From the Cristóbal Colón bus terminal it's six blocks north up Insurgentes to the central square, Plaza 31 de Marzo, which has the cathedral on its north side.

Places to stay and eat are scattered all around town, but there are concentrations on Real de Guadalupe, Madero and Insurgentes.

Information

Tourist Offices The municipal tourist office (☎ 678-06-65) is in the north end of the Palacio Municipal, on the west side of Plaza 31 de Marzo. It is open 9 am to 2 pm and 5 to 8 pm, Monday to Saturday. Quality of information depends on whether you are attended by an adult staff member or a teenage volunteer.

The tourist information office (☎ 678-65-70) of the Chiapas state tourism department, the Secretaría de Desarrollo Turístico, just off Plaza 31 de Marzo at Hidalgo 2, is open 9 am to 9 pm Monday to Saturday, 9 am to 2 pm Sunday, and has entirely adult, usually English-speaking staff.

Immigration The Instituto Nacional de Migración (☎ 678-02-92), Diagonal El Centenario 30, is open 9 am to 2 pm Monday to Friday.

Money For those who can't use ATMs, Banamex, on the main plaza, is efficient at currency exchange, and Bital bank, half a block west of the plaza on Mazariegos, is open long hours: 8 am to 7 pm Monday to Friday, 9 am to 1.30 pm Saturday. If the banks

are shut, Viajes Chincultik at the Posada Margarita, Real de Guadalupe 34, has better rates than casas de cambio and is open daily.

Elektra at Insurgentes 8 offers Western Union Dinero en Minutos service.

Post & Communications The post office, on the corner of Cuauhtémoc and Rosas, one block west and one south of the main plaza, is open Monday to Friday 8 am to 6 pm, Saturday 9 am to 1 pm.

There are pay phones at both ends of Plaza 31 de Marzo and in the Cristóbal Colón and ATG bus stations. La Pared bookstore, Hidalgo 2, offers an inexpensive fax and phone service.

Be careful with shops or telephone casetas that advertise 'free' collect calls. They will indeed charge you, the calling party, nothing, but some of them charge ridiculous rates to the receiving party (for example, US$24 a minute to the US).

Cyberc@fé (☎ 678-74-88), in the Pasaje Mazariegos mall between Real de Guadalupe and Madero, charges US$1 for 15 minutes of Internet access. It has plenty of computers and the best coffee we found in San Cristóbal – open 9 am to 10 pm daily. Podernet on Real de Guadalupe has the same prices.

Bartolomé de Las Casas

Bookstores & Libraries La Pared, Hidalgo 2, has the town's best selection of new and used books in English. It also buys and trades used books.

Librería Chilam Balam, in a courtyard at Utrilla 33, has a few guidebooks in English and French, and lots of history and anthropology in Spanish. Libros Soluna, Real de Guadalupe 13B, has a few books on Chiapas and Mexico in English, and many more in Spanish.

The 14,000 books at Na Bolom (Guerrero 33, see 'Na Bolom') make up one of the world's biggest collections on the Maya and their lands. Those interested can use the library from 9 am to 4 pm daily.

Laundry Lavasor, Real de Guadalupe 26, charges US$2.50 to wash and dry 2kg, US$3 for 3kg and US$4 for 4kg (same day if you take your clothes in the morning). It is open 8 am to 2.30 pm and 4.30 to 9 pm daily.

Medical Services English-speaking doctors in San Cristóbal include general practitioner Dr Luis José Sevilla (☎ 678-16-26), Calle del Sol 2. There's a general hospital (☎ 678-07-70) on Insurgentes.

Plaza 31 de Marzo

The main plaza was the old Spanish center of town, used for markets until the early 20th century. Today it's a fine place to sit and watch the town life happen around you.

The cathedral, on the north side of the plaza, was begun in 1528 but completely rebuilt in 1693. Its gold-leaf interior has a baroque pulpit and altarpiece, and the detailed stonework on the west façade has recently been attractively picked out in yellow, red and white paint.

The Hotel Santa Clara, on the plaza's southeast corner, was the house of Diego de Mazariegos, the Spanish conqueror of Chiapas. It's one of the few secular examples of plateresque style in Mexico.

Templo & Ex-Convento de Santo Domingo

North of the center on Cárdenas, the Templo de Santo Domingo is the most beautiful of San Cristóbal's many churches – especially when its pink façade is floodlit at night. The church and adjoining monastery were built between 1547 and 1560. The church's baroque façade – on which can be seen the double-headed Hapsburg eagle, symbol of the Spanish monarchy in those days – was added in the 17th century. There's plenty of gold inside, especially on the ornate pulpit.

Chamulan women and bohemian types from elsewhere conduct a daily crafts market around Santo Domingo and the

Traditional Highland Dress

Each indigenous village in the Chiapas highlands has its own distinctive dress. The men of Zinacantán have very distinctive pink tunics embroidered with flower motifs and may wear flat, round, ribboned palm hats. Zinacantán women have pink or purple shawls over white embroidered blouses. In San Juan Chamula, most men wear loose homespun tunics of white wool (sometimes, in cool weather, thicker black wool); cargo-holders – those with important religious and ceremonial duties – wear a sleeveless black tunic and a white scarf on the head. Chamula women wear fairly plain white or blue blouses and/or shawls.

Many of the seemingly abstract designs on these costumes are in fact stylized snakes, frogs, butterflies, pawprints, birds, saints and other beings. Some motifs have religious-magical functions: scorpions, for example, can be a symbolic request for rain, since they are believed to attract lightning.

Some designs have pre-Hispanic origins: the rhombus shape on some huipiles from San Andrés Larraínzar is also found on garments shown on Lintel 24 at the Classic Maya city of Yaxchilán. The shape represents an old Mayan conception of the universe, in which the sky had four corners.

Other costumes are of more recent origin: the typical Chamula men's outfit – tunic, long-sleeved shirt, belt and long trousers – stems from the Spaniards, who felt unhappy about the relative nudity of the loincloth and cloak that Chamulan men once wore.

The sacredness of traditional costume is shown by the dressing of saints' images in old and revered garments at festival times.

❀ ❀ ❀ ❀ ❀ ❀ ❀ ❀ ❀ ❀ ❀

neighboring Templo de La Caridad (built in 1712). You'll find local and Guatemalan textiles, leather bags and belts, homemade toys and dolls, hippie jewelry, *animalitos* from Amatenango del Valle and more.

The Ex-Convento (Ex-Monastery) attached to Santo Domingo contains two interesting exhibits. One is the showroom of

Sna Jolobil, a cooperative of 800 indigenous women weavers from the Chiapas highlands. Here you can see very fine huipiles, hats, blouses, skirts, rugs and other woven items. Prices range from a few dollars for smaller items to over US$700 for the best huipiles and ceremonial garments. Sna Jolobil (the name means 'Weavers' House' in the Tzotzil language) is open 9 am to 2 pm and 4 to 6 pm Monday through Saturday.

The cooperative was founded in the 1970s to foster the important indigenous art of backstrap loom weaving. The weavers have revived forgotten techniques and designs, and developed dyes from plants, soil, bark and other natural sources. For more on indigenous costumes, see 'Traditional Highland Dress' and the Artesanías special section.

The **Museo de Arqueología, Etnografía, Historia y Arte**, also in the ex-convento buildings, deals mainly with the history of San Cristóbal. It's open 10 am to 5 pm Tuesday through Sunday (US$2). Explanatory material is in Spanish.

Mercado Municipal

The flavor of outlying indigenous villages can be sampled at San Cristóbal's busy municipal market, between Utrilla and Belisario Domínguez, eight blocks north of the main plaza, open Monday through Saturday till late afternoon. Many of the traders are villagers for whom buying and selling is the main reason to come to town.

Café Museo Café

This combined café and coffee museum, at MA Flores 10 (☎ 678-78-76), is a venture of Coopcafé, a group of 15,000 small-scale Chiapas coffee growers. In the café you can taste good, organic local coffee. The three-room museum covers the history of coffee and its cultivation in Chiapas, indigenous coffee growing and organic coffee. Coopcafé is part of the international 'fair trade' movement that aims to bring developing nations' commodity producers more of the profits from their products by promoting direct sales to the consumers.

Na Bolom

A visit to the beautiful colonial-style house called Na Bolom at Guerrero 33, six blocks north of Real de Guadalupe, is one of San Cristóbal's most fascinating experiences. For many years this was the home of Swiss anthropologist and photographer Gertrude (Trudy) Duby-Blom (1901-93). Trudy and her Danish archaeologist husband Frans Blom (1893-1963) bought the house in 1950.

The couple shared a passion for Chiapas. While Frans explored, surveyed and dug at ancient Mayan sites including Palenque, Toniná and Chinkultic, Trudy devoted much of her life to studying and protecting the scattered, isolated Lacandón people of eastern Chiapas and the jungle they inhabited, the Selva Lacandona (Lacandón Jungle). See 'The Lacandón Jungle & the Lacandones,' later in this chapter. Na Bolom is now in the hands of trustees who have maintained the thrust of her work by running a tree nursery and providing medical and cultural help to the Lacandones.

The name Na Bolom means 'Jaguar House' in the Tzotzil language, as well as being a play on its former owners' name. The house, visited by around 25,000 people a year, is a treasure-trove for anyone interested in Chiapas, full of photographs, archaeological and anthropological relics and books (see Bookstores & Libraries in the San Cristóbal de Las Casas section).

Visits are by informal guided tour (US$2), in Spanish at 11.30 am daily, and in Spanish and English at 4.30 pm daily. The tours last about 1½ hours including a film on the Lacandones and Trudy Duby-Blom's work.

Na Bolom is also the departure point for interesting tours to local villages and the Selva Lacandona (see Organized Tours), and offers lodging and meals (see Places to Stay). You can find out more about Na Bolom at its website, www.ecosur.mx/nabolom.

Casa de las Artesanías de Chiapas

This has both an exhibition area, displaying the costumes and explaining the crafts of various villages around San Cristóbal, and a sales area with a good range of crafts from around Chiapas. It's on Niños Héroes at Hidalgo – open 10 am to 2 pm and 4 to 8 pm daily (free).

Templo del Carmen & Casa de la Cultura

El Carmen church stands on the corner of Hidalgo and Hermanos Domínguez. Formerly part of a nunnery (built in 1597), it has a distinctive arch-based tower built in 1680 to replace one destroyed by floods. Next door is the Casa de la Cultura, containing an art gallery, library and the Bellas Artes auditorium.

Cerro de San Cristóbal & Cerro de Guadalupe

The most prominent of the small hills over which San Cristóbal undulates are the tree-covered Cerro de San Cristóbal southwest of the center, reached by steps up from Allende, and the Cerro de Guadalupe, seven blocks east of the main plaza. Both are crowned by churches and afford good views, but you may encounter drunks on Cerro de San Cristóbal after about noon.

Organización de Médicos Indígenas del Estado de Chiapas (OMIECH)

This center for traditional Maya medicine in the north of town will interest anyone who's curious about the beliefs and lives of Chiapas' indigenous people. Maya medicine is a matter not of pills and chemical formulae but of prayers, candles, incense, bones and herbs. OMIECH (Organization of Indigenous Doctors of Chiapas) was set up in the 1980s to develop this traditional medicine and has 860 practitioner members. Its Centro de Desarrollo de la Medicina Maya (Maya Medicine Development Center, ☎ 678-54-38) at Avenida Salomón González Blanco 10, on the northward continuation of Utrilla, contains a museum (US$1) explaining how pulse-readers, herbalists, prayer specialists and other traditional practitioners work, a medicinal plant garden and a *casa de curación* where cures are carried out. They sell herbal medicines as well.

The center is open 10 am to 2 pm Tuesday to Friday, 10 am to 4 pm Saturday and Sunday.

Horseback Riding

Almost any place you stay in San Cristóbal can arrange a four- or five-hour guided ride to San Juan Chamula for US$7 or US$8, or to the Grutas de San Cristóbal. You might want to ask about the animals: are they horses or just ponies, fiery or docile, fast or slow?

Language Courses

San Cristóbal has two prominent Spanish-language schools. Competition between them is keen and details of what they offer may change fairly rapidly.

We've heard excellent reports from students at Instituto Jovel (☎/fax 678-40-69, www.mexonline.com/jovel.htm), MA Flores 21. Most classes here are one-to-one, and you get three hours' teaching a day. Five days' tuition and seven days' accommodations with a Mexican family (with a private room and all meals) costs US$150 (US$115 if you take group classes). Individual/group classes without accommodation cost US$6.50/5 an hour.

Centro Bilingüe (☎ 678-37-23, fax 678-41-57, http://mundomaya.com.mx/centrob), at Real de Guadalupe 55 in the Centro Cultural El Puente, charges US$101.25/71.50 a week for 15 hours of private/group instruction and several hours of chat sessions. A week's family stay in a twin room, with meals daily except Saturday, is US$85.

Organized Tours

For tours of **indigenous villages**, see the Around San Cristóbal section. For tours farther afield, agencies in San Cristóbal offer trips. All the destinations can be reached independently but some people may prefer a tour. Typical day tours and prices per person (usually with a minimum of four people) are:

Chiapa de Corzo and Cañón del Sumidero: 7 to 8 hours, US$17

Lagos de Montebello, Chinkultic ruins, Amatenango del Valle: 9 hours, US$18

Palenque ruins, Agua Azul, Misol-Ha: 14 hours, US$23

Toniná: 9 hours, US$18

Agencies offering these kind of tours include:

Kanan-Ku Viajes (☎ 678-61-01) Niños Héroes 2C

Viajes Chinkultic (☎ 678-09-57) Real de Guadalupe 34 in the Posada Margarita

Viajes Pakal – Real de Guadalupe between Plaza 31 de Marzo and Belisario Domínguez

Another option is a three- or four-day trip to Laguna Miramar (see that section for details) or to Bonampak and Yaxchilán. The latter trip – also offered by Na Bolom – usually includes other stops such as Agua Azul, Palenque or Lacanjá in an all-inclusive price around US$135 to US$150 per person.

Special Events
Semana Santa sees much churchgoing on the Thursday evening and Via Crucis processions on Good Friday morning. The Saturday afternoon is the start of the annual town fair, the Feria de la Primavera y de la Paz (Spring & Peace Fair) with parades, bullfights and so on. Sometimes the celebrations of the anniversary of the town's founding (March 31) fall in the midst of it all too!

Also look out for events marking the feast of San Cristóbal (July 17 to 25) and the anniversary of Chiapas joining Mexico in 1824 (September 14), as well as other fiestas celebrated nationwide.

Places to Stay – Budget
Camping The *Rancho San Nicolás* (☎ 678-00-57) camping and trailer park is 2km east of the main plaza, along León. It's a friendly place with a grassy lawn, apple trees, a cafetería, horses grazing and hot showers. Cost is US$2 per person in a tent, or US$2.50 in a cabin or in a camper or trailer with full hookups.

Hostels The *Albergue Juvenil/Youth Hostel* (☎ 678-76-55, Juárez 2) offers bunks in clean four- to eight-person rooms, at $4 in rooms with their own bathroom, US$3.50 sharing bathrooms (10% less with a student card).

Hotels & Casas de Huéspedes There are dozens of budget hostelries in San Cristóbal. The municipal tourist office has lists.

Real de Guadalupe The *Hotel Real del Valle* (☎ 678-06-40, Real de Guadalupe 14) has a nice courtyard and 36 clean rooms costing US$15/18/21 a single/double/triple. *Hotel San Martín* (☎ 678-05-33, Real de Guadalupe 16) has reasonable rooms with private bathroom for US$9/14/18.

Hotel Posada del Barón (☎ 678-08-81, Belisario Domínguez 2) has just a few simple, clean singles/doubles with bath for US$10/12 along a wood-pillared patio.

Posada Margarita (☎ 678-09-57, Real de Guadalupe 34) has long been a popular budget travelers' halt. Decent, clean singles/doubles/triples/quads are US$6/9/12/16. The shared bathrooms are kept very clean and there are plenty of them. There's a wide courtyard and a handy in-house travel agency, and a good restaurant under the same ownership next door.

Friendly *Posada Casa Real* (☎ 678-13-03, Real de Guadalupe 51) has just eight nice, clean rooms, for US$4/8 a single/double. There's a place to wash clothes and a pleasant upstairs sitting area. The door is locked at midnight.

Insurgentes Two blocks below the main plaza at Insurgentes, the attractive, colonial-style *Hotel Fray Bartolomé de Las Casas* (☎ 678-09-32, Niños Héroes 2) has varied rooms around a wide, pillared courtyard with a dribbling fountain. It's an excellent value at US$12/15/17 for singles/doubles/triples.

Friendly *Logis La Media Luna*, on JF Flores off Insurgentes, has just a handful of singles/doubles around a nice yard. Most are US$6/8 but there's one with private bath and TV for US$12/15.

Places at the lower end of Insurgentes, near the bus stations, lack atmosphere. *Hotel*

Lucella (☎ 678-09-56, *Insurgentes 55*), opposite Santa Lucía church, has OK rooms with bath for US$5/10. Rooms at *Posada Insurgentes* (☎ 678-24-35, *Insurgentes 73*) are bare but reasonably modern, with shared baths, for US$5/8. *Posada Vallarta* (☎ 678-04-65, *Hermanos Pineda 10*), half a block off Insurgentes, has bland, modernish rooms with bath and balcony for US$12/14.

North of the Center The *Hotel El Cerrillo* (☎/fax 678-12-83, *Belisario Domínguez 27*) has a beautiful flowery courtyard and big rooms with shower for US$15 single or double. There's a very nice sitting room and guest kitchen. Nearby, family-run *Posada San Agustín* (☎ 678-18-16, *Ejército Nacional 7*) has clean singles/doubles, all with windows, for US$8/10, plenty of hot water, and good views from the roof.

Tidy *Posada Jovel* (☎ 678-17-34, *Paniagua 28*) attracts backpackers with its friendly atmosphere and rates of US$6.75/10 with shared bath, US$8.50/12.50 with private bath. It has four superior new rooms across the street at US$15/17/18 a double/triple/quadruple. *La Posadita* (*Paniagua 30*), next door to the Jovel, has triples for just US$6.

West of the Center Cozy, friendly, relaxed *La Casa di Gladys* (☎ 678-57-75, *Mazariegos 65*), one block west of the edge of the map, has a pleasant patio, a back garden for camping at US$2 per person and rooms for about 20 people at prices from US$3 in a dormitory to US$10 for a double with private bath.

Posada Adrianita (☎ 678-81-39, *1 de Marzo 29*), around a prettily lit courtyard, has doubles and triples for US$9.25 to US$11.50 with shared bath or US$17.50 to US$21 with private bath and TV. Rooms holding four or five people are US$23 to US$29.

Places to Stay – Mid-Range

The following is just a selection from the many choices. New hotels are opening all the time, often in attractive colonial buildings.

Center The pleasant *Posada San Cristóbal* (☎ 678-68-81, *Insurgentes 3*), a block south of the main plaza, has 10 airy, colorful rooms around a pleasant courtyard for US$16/22/28 a single/double/triple.

Posada de los Ángeles (☎ 678-11-73, fax 678-25-81, *Madero 17*) is a colonial-style building with 19 pleasant rooms on three stories around two patios. Singles/doubles with TV and private bath are US$20/25. Indigenous costume prints add an attractive touch, and one patio contains a wood-and-glass-roofed restaurant.

The historic *Hotel Santa Clara* (☎ 678-11-40, fax 678-10-41, *Insurgentes 1*), on the main plaza, has sizable, comfortable rooms, a courtyard with caged red macaws, a restaurant, a bar/lounge and a pool. Singles/doubles/triples/quads are US$29/35/45/55.

Hotel Diego de Mazariegos (☎ 678-06-21, fax 678-08-27, *5 de Febrero 1*) occupies two fine buildings either side of Utrilla one block north of the main plaza. The 77 rooms (US$36/46) are tastefully furnished and 50 have fireplaces. There's a restaurant and a nightclub.

West of the Center *El Paraíso* (☎ 678-00-85, fax 678-51-68, *5 de Febrero 19*) has a cheery flower-filled courtyard and an amiable atmosphere. Comfortable singles/doubles cost US$30/40. The restaurant serves Swiss and Mexican dishes.

Hotel Español Flamboyant (☎ 678-00-45, fax 678-05-14, *1 de Marzo 15*) is an old hotel recently upgraded (Graham Greene stayed here in the 1930s). Rooms are US$35/45 and there's a nice garden.

Hotel Parador Mexicanos (☎ 678-15-15, fax 867-00-55, *5 de Mayo 38*) has big, comfortable rooms with cable TV for US$20/30/38 a single/double/triple, flanking its garden/driveway. A lobby lounge, restaurant, tennis court and verandas add to the appeal.

The modern *Hotel Arrecife de Coral* (☎ 678-21-25, *arrecife@sancristobal.podernet .com.mx, Rosas 29*) has several two-story buildings around grassy lawns. The 50 quiet rooms have baths and TVs and offer good value at US$21/28/33/38.

East of the Center *Hotel Casavieja* (☎ /fax 678-68-68, *MA Flores 27*) is an almost-new

TABASCO & CHIAPAS

hotel in an 18th-century house – very attractive and comfortable. Rooms are arranged around grassy, flowered courtyards, and there's a tidy restaurant. Rates are US$33/45/48.

Hotel Ciudad Real Residencia (☎ 678-10-53, Juárez 1A) is another recently opened colonial-style place, tastefully decorated with pretty bathroom tiling, wooden furniture and upstairs walkways. Rooms, at US$36/45/54, have multichannel TV, and there's a restaurant.

The museum/research institute *Na Bolom* (☎ 678-14-18, fax 678-55-86, nabolom@ sclc.ecosur.mx, Guerrero 33) has good rooms with bath for US$20/35/39 (see 'Na Bolom' for more information).

Places to Stay – Top End

Hotel Casa Mexicana (☎ 678-06-98, fax 678-26-27, 28 de Agosto 1), with its sky-lighted garden, fountains, plants, art and sculpture, exudes colonial charm. Rooms are agreeable, have views of the courtyard and cost US$39/50 a single/double; suites are more.

Places to Eat

San Cristóbal offers a variety of cuisines and plenty of choice for vegetarians. Some eateries try to please everyone with long lists of multinational imitations; those with more focused efforts tend to be better.

Real de Guadalupe This is a good street for economical breakfasts. The pleasant *Cafetería* in Pasaje Mazariegos mall and the *Cafetería del Centro (Real de Guadalupe 15)* will both do eggs, toast, butter, jam, juice and coffee for US$2. *El Sol*, two blocks farther east on Guadalupe, offers the same and other options for US$1.50; later in the day it has comida corrida for US$3 (US$2.25 for the vegetarian variety), or individual main dishes for US$2 to US$3.50.

Restaurante Margarita (Real de Guadalupe 34), adjoining Posada Margarita, offers a broad choice of reliably good food. The family here has been in the business of pleasing travelers' palates for at least two decades. Breakfasts are US$1.75 to US$3.25, salads or spaghetti around US$3, *antojitos*

US$3 to US$4.75 and chicken and meat dishes US$5 to US$6.

Just off Real de Guadalupe on Belisario Domínguez, *Todo Natural* juice bar serves up big plates of fruit, yogurt and granola for US$1.50.

Insurgentes The *Restaurant Tuluc (Insurgentes 5)*, 1½ blocks south of the main plaza, scores with its efficient service, good food and reasonable prices. Most main courses cost US$2.50 to US$4.25, though pasta is less. It's open 7 am to 10 pm daily.

Good coffee and cakes are served in the little *Cafetería San Cristóbal*, on Cuauhtémoc just off Insurgentes. Mexican men bring along chess sets and newspapers to relax.

The long-running *Madre Tierra (Insurgentes 19)* has an eclectic and appetizing vegetarian menu with filling soups, whole-grain sandwiches, pizzas, salads, spinach cannelloni and other pasta. Most items are between US$1.25 and US$3, there are big breakfasts for US$2.25, and the daily set menu costs US$5. Only free-range eggs are used, and excellent whole-grain bread is served with all meals. *Panadería Madre Tierra*, a whole-grain bakery next door, sells breads, muffins, cookies, cakes, quiches, pizzas and frozen yogurt.

The cheapest meals in town are at *Los Merenderos*, a collection of food stalls just south of the Templo de San Francisco. Pick items that look fresh and hot. A full meal can be had for around US$1.50.

Farther down Insurgentes, little *Restaurante El Sol* has just three tables but does good, economical breakfasts and a US$2.25 comida corrida of four courses and coffee.

Madero There are about eight restaurants on Madero within a block of Plaza 31 de Marzo. One of the few that stands out is *Restaurante Maya Pakal (Madero 21A)*, which serves a popular vegetarian comida of three courses and coffee or tea for US$2.50. Salads, pasta, pizza and other main dishes are mostly around US$2, and breakfasts are inexpensive too. It's open 7.30 am to 11 pm daily. A block farther up is the friendly, economical *El Gato Gordo (Madero 28)*, popular with budget travelers. A typical breakfast here costs US$1.75, and there's a veggie comida for US$1.50. Crêpes and pasta are around US$1 to US$1.50, and chicken and meat dishes US$2 to US$2.50. Hours are 8 am to 10 pm except Tuesday.

Hidalgo & Rosas A block south of the main plaza, the upstairs restaurant of artsy *La Galería* (*Hidalgo 3*) serves pizza and pasta for US$3 to US$4.50 and a variety of other stuff.

A block west, carnivores flock into *Emiliano's Moustache* (*Rosas 7*) for tacos starting at US$0.50 each and meat *filetes* (US$3.50 to US$4.25). A specialty is the filling orders of five tacos with combinations of meat, vegetable or cheese for US$2.25 to US$5.50. There are vegetarian possibilities too (including veggie tacos). It's open 9 am to 1 am daily.

Café La Selva (*Rosas 9*) is run by the Unión de Ejidos de la Selva, an association of small-scale Chiapas organic coffee growers. Sit in the courtyard or in either of two clean, bright rooms to enjoy any of 36 types of coffee and/or baguettes, sandwiches or croissants for US$2 to US$3.50. Like Café Museo Café (see earlier in this San Cristóbal section), the Unión de Ejidos de la Selva is a fair-trade venture. Its coffee is exported to the USA, Canada and Europe.

North of the Center *Café-Restaurant El Teatro* (*1 de Marzo 8*) is among the few upscale restaurants in town. The European-based menu includes chateaubriand, crêpes, fresh pasta, pizzas and desserts. Expect to spend US$10 to US$12 for a good full dinner here. The Hotel Casa Mexicana's *Restaurant Los Magueyes* (*28 de Agosto 1*) is another good choice in this sort of price range.

Just opened when we were last in town, but looking like it had staying power, the barnlike *La Creación* (*1 de Marzo 14B*) does good sandwiches, salads, pasta and antojitos for US$2 to US$3. The specialty is *pechuga Creación*, a chicken, ham and mango *creación* served with vegetables for US$5.50.

La Casa del Pan (*Dr Navarro 10*) is an excellent bakery-restaurant with lots of vegetarian fare. A 'high-energy breakfast' of orange juice, fruit, yogurt, granola, organic Chiapas highland coffee and croissant or whole-grain bread is US$2.75. Whole-wheat sandwiches, vegan salads, *hojaldres* (vegetable strudels) and vegetarian antojitos are all between US$1.75 and US$2.75, pasta and pizzas a bit more. Hours are 8 am to 10 pm except Monday.

For unique ambiance, eat at *Na Bolom* (see Places to Stay – Mid-Range). Everyone sits at one long wooden table in the Bloms' old dining room. Dinner is at 7 pm and costs US$6.75 – book an hour or two ahead. Lunch (1.30 pm) is US$6, breakfast (7 to 10 am) US$3.50.

Entertainment

Thanks to San Cristóbal's traveler/student/bohemian scene, you can choose from half a dozen live music spots any night – though the musicianship isn't always the best!

About the funkiest place is *Club Latino's* (*Mazariegos 19*), with nightly live tropical music from 9.30 pm. Moderately priced food is served. *Madre Tierra* restaurant (*Insurgentes 19*) and *La Galería* (*Hidalgo 3*), in its ground-floor patio-bar-gallery, both had live reggae, *son latino* or funk nightly from 10 pm when we were in town. *Bar Las Velas* (*Madero 14*), popular with young locals, had a happy hour from 8 to 10 pm, and a reggae/rock/cumbia band about 11 pm. There's no cover at any of these places.

A-dove (*Hidalgo 2*), popular with a youngish international crowd, features mixed live and DJ music from *rock en español* or dance to salsa or cumbia. It's open from 8 or 9 pm nightly except Monday, often with US$1 cover. There are usually two drinks for the price of one for some part of the night.

Restaurante Margarita (*Real de Guadalupe 34*) has a band nightly – three percussionists and two guitars were in residence on our last visit. You may hear some unusual sounds at *La Creación* (*1 de Marzo 14B*). A bongos-and-chanting Canadian crusty outfit were doing a short season when we dropped in. The bars of the *Hotel Santa Clara* and *Hotel Ciudad Real* (not to be confused with the Hotel Ciudad Real

Residencia) on Plaza 31 de Marzo are two more busy spots with nightly music. Again there's no cover at any of these spots.

San Cristóbal's one high-tech disco is *Palace Olympo Club* (☎ 678-26-00, *Prolongación Rosas 59*), a couple of blocks south of the Pan-American Highway. It is open nightly except Monday.

Centro Cultural El Puente (*Real de Guadalupe 55*) shows a good, well-publicized program of movies. It also has a notice board where you may find out about other interesting goings-on.

There are fairly regular musical and theatrical performances at the *Casa de la Cultura* on Hidalgo.

Shopping

Most San Cristóbal shops are open 9 am to 2 pm and 4 to 8 pm Monday to Saturday. Hosts of them sell Chiapas indigenous crafts. Artistically speaking, the outstanding local *artesanías* are textiles such as huipiles, blouses and blankets, for Tzotzil weavers are some of the most skilled and inventive in Mexico (see 'Traditional Highland Dress'). Another Chiapas specialty is amber jewelry (amber, fossilized tree resin, is mined near Simojovel, north of San Cristóbal). A curiosity is little black-balacalava'd Subcomandante Marcos dolls, effigies of the EZLN leader.

The heaviest concentrations of craft shops are along Real de Guadalupe (prices go down as you move away from Plaza 31 de Marzo) and Utrilla (toward the Templo de Santo Domingo). Also near Santo Domingo are an inexpensive daily crafts market and the showroom of Sna Jolobil, a classy indigenous weavers' cooperative (see Templo & Ex-Convento de Santo Domingo).

The Casa de las Artesanías de Chiapas, at the corner of Niños Héroes and Hidalgo, sells a good range of Chiapas crafts at very good prices.

Food and everyday goods are main stocks-in-trade at the Mercado Municipal, but there are some stalls devoted to crafts too.

In markets, you're expected to bargain unless prices are labeled. The first price quoted is traditionally significantly more than the going rate for the item.

Getting There & Away

Air San Cristóbal airport is about 15km out of town on the Ocosingo road. At the time of writing the only civilian passenger flights were to/from Tuxtla Gutiérrez four times a week by Aerocaribe (US$45 one way). There are onward connections at Tuxtla: San Cristóbal to Mexico City costs US$128. Aerocaribe (☎ 678-65-93) is at the corner of Madero and Juárez. Travel agencies also sell flight tickets. A taxi to/from Tuxtla airport costs around US$30.

Bus, Combi & Taxi A new Central de Autobuses is planned in the south of the town, but for the moment each bus, combi and taxi service has its own terminal. Except for a few serving local villages (see Around San Cristóbal), all are on or just off the Pan-American Highway.

Cristóbal Colón, ADO and UNO (including Colón's Maya de Oro deluxe service and Altos 2nd-class service) share a terminal (☎ 678-02-91) at the junction of Insurgentes and the Pan-American Highway. The baggage checkroom here charges US$0.50 per item for 24 hours.

The 2nd-class line Autotransportes Tuxtla Gutiérrez (ATG) is three blocks west, just north of the highway on Allende. Transportes Lacandonia (TL), also 2nd-class, with old, slow buses, is at Pino Suárez 11A, about halfway between Colón and ATG, just north of the highway.

The 2nd-class bus lines Andrés Caso Lombardo (ACL) and Dr Rodulfo Figueroa have terminals near the others on the Pan-American Highway – as do various combi and colectivo taxi services to Comitán, Ocosingo and Tuxtla Gutiérrez. The combis and colectivos run all day from 6 am or earlier and leave when the vehicle is full. See the map for locations.

Daily departures from San Cristóbal include:

Cancún – 1025km, 14 hours (via Chetumal, Tulum, Playa del Carmen); 3 from Colón terminal

(US$31 to US$40), 1 ATG (US$28), also 1 ATG via Mérida (1045km, US$30)

Chiapa de Corzo – 70km, 1½ hours; take a 2nd-class bus, combi, or colectivo heading for Tuxtla Gutiérrez, but check first that it will let you off in Chiapa de Corzo

Ciudad Cuauhtémoc (Guatemalan border) – 170km, 2½ hours; 6 Altos (US$5), 5 ACL (US$3.50), leave early if you hope to get any distance into Guatemala the same day

Comitán – 90km, 1½ hours; 8 from Colón terminal (US$2.25 to US$3), 5 ACL (US$1.75), combis (US$2) and colectivo taxis (US$2.50) from south side of Pan-American Highway

Mérida – 735km, 11 hours via Campeche; 2 from Colón terminal (US$23 to US$29), 1 ATG (US$22)

Mexico City (TAPO) – 1065km, 19 hours; 6 from Colón terminal (US$37 to US$67), 1 ATG (US$35)

Oaxaca – 625km, 12 hours; 2 from Colón terminal (US$19.50 to US$25)

Ocosingo – 88km, 1½ hours; 4 from Colón terminal (US$2.50 to US$3.50), 6 Figueroa (US$2.75), 6 ATG (US$2.50), 10 TL (US$2.25), combis (US$2.50) and colectivo taxis (US$3) from north side of Pan-American Highway

Palenque – 190km, 4 hours; 5 from Colón terminal (US$6.50 to US$8.25), 6 ATG (US$6.50), 6 Figueroa (US$6.50), 10 TL (US$5.25)

Puerto Escondido – 645km, 13 hours; 2 Colón (US$21)

Tapachula – 335km, 7 hours via Ciudad Cuauhtémoc, Motozintla; 6 from Colón terminal (US$9.75), 5 ACL (US$7)

Tuxtla Gutiérrez – 85km, 2 hours; 5 from Colón terminal (US$2.75 to US$3.25), 9 ATG (US$2.50), Figueroa at least every 40 minutes from 6.20 am (US$2.50), colectivo taxis (US$3) by Taxis Jovel, CM combis 4 am to 9 pm (US$2.25), combis by Altos de Chiapas

Villahermosa – 305km, 7 hours; 3 from Colón terminal (US$12), 4 ATG (US$10)

Car Auto Rentas Yaxchilán (☎ 678-18-71), Mazariegos 36, is a Budget car rental agency.

Getting Around

Combis go up Rosas from the Pan-American Highway to the town center. Taxis are fairly plentiful. One stand is on the north side of the main plaza. A typical trip within the town costs US$1.

Los Pingüinos (☎ 678-02-02), 5 de Mayo 10B, rents bikes for US$5.50 for four or five hours or US$7 for seven to nine hours. It also conducts bicycle tours (see the next section).

AROUND SAN CRISTÓBAL

The indigenous villagers of the beautiful Chiapas highlands are descended from the ancient Maya and maintain some unique customs, costumes and beliefs.

Dangers & Annoyances

A few years ago the danger of armed robberies made it unsafe to walk between villages outside San Cristóbal. The word as we researched this edition was that walking or riding by horse or bicycle between villages was again safe – along the main roads, by day. You should still ask around yourself.

Photography In some villages, particularly those nearest San Cristóbal, cameras are at best tolerated – and sometimes not even that. Some indigenous people apparently believe that appearing in a photograph can put them in danger of losing their souls. Photography is banned in the church and during rituals at San Juan Chamula, and in the church and churchyard at Zinacantán. You may put yourself in physical danger if you take photos without permission. If in any doubt at all, ask before taking a picture.

Markets & Special Events

The villages' weekly markets are nearly always on Sunday. Proceedings start very early, with people arriving from outlying settlements as early as dawn, and wind down by lunchtime.

Festivals often give the most interesting insight into indigenous life, and there are plenty of them. Occasions like Carnaval (for which Chamula is famous), Semana Santa, el Día de los Muertos (Day of the Dead, November 2) and el Día de la Virgen de Guadalupe (December 12) are celebrated almost everywhere. At some of these fiestas a great deal of *posh* – an alcoholic drink made from sugarcane – is drunk, and at Carnaval troops of strolling, posh-sozzled minstrels wander the roads strumming guitars, chanting and wearing sunglasses (even when it's raining) and pointed 'wizard' hats with long, colored tassels.

Organized Tours

A good guide can give you a feel for indigenous village life that you could never gain alone. A few people lead daily small-group tours from San Cristóbal – usually to San Juan Chamula and Zinacantán – that fascinate nearly everyone who joins them. All cost around US$8.

Mercedes Hernández Gómez, a fluent English-speaker who grew up in Zinacantán, has been taking tours for years. You can find Mercedes at 9 am daily near the kiosk in San Cristóbal's main plaza, twirling a colorful umbrella. Her tours generally last five to six hours, traveling by minibus and on foot.

We have also enjoyed the tours led by Alex and Raúl (☎ 678-37-41), whom you can find in front of San Cristóbal cathedral at 9.30 am daily. Their English-language minibus trip to San Juan Chamula and Zinacantán lasts 4½ hours. Other recommended village tours

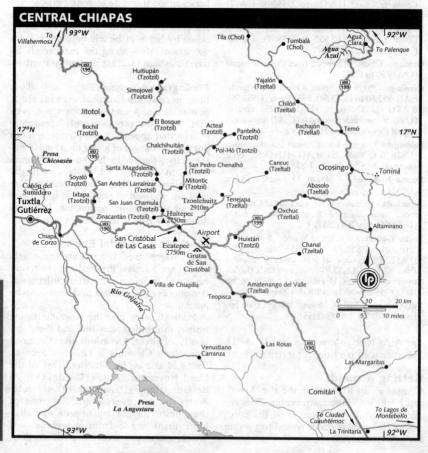

CENTRAL CHIAPAS

leave from Na Bolom at 10 am daily, lasting about six hours. For horseback riding, see the San Cristóbal section.

Bicycle Tours The friendly folk at Los Pingüinos (☎ 678-02-02), 5 de Mayo 10B, lead bicycle tours to little-visited, scenic country areas outside San Cristóbal. The trips (minimum two people) cost from US$16 per person for a three-to-four-hour ride to US$20 for a five- or six-hour trip.

The guides speak English, Spanish and German.

Reserva Ecológica Huitepec

The entrance to the Huitepec Ecological Reserve is about 3.5km from San Cristóbal on the road to San Juan Chamula. A 2km trail mounts 2700m Cerro Huitepec, rising from evergreen oak woods to rare cloud forest. The ascent takes about 45 minutes. The reserve has 60 resident bird species and

---

Indigenous Peoples of Chiapas

Of Chiapas' 3.6 million people, about 900,000 are indigenous (mostly Mayan groups). At least nine languages are spoken. Spanish is the idiom of commerce, most education, and government in the cities. In the countryside in various parts of the state, indigenous peoples speak the Chol, Chuj, Lacandón, Mam, Tojolabal, Tzeltal, Tzotzil and Zoque languages. Although all derived from ancient Mayan, most of these tongues are now mutually unintelligible, so local inhabitants use a second language such as Spanish or the fairly widely understood Tzeltal to communicate with other groups. The indigenous languages also define ethnic groups with common beliefs, traditions and dress customs.

The indigenous people that travelers are most likely to come into contact with are the 310,000 or so Tzotzils who live in a highland area centered on San Cristóbal de Las Casas, about 50km from east to west and 100km from north to south. Tzotzil clothing is among the most varied, colorful and elaborately worked in Mexico. It not only identifies wearers' villages but also marks them as inheritors of ancient Mayan traditions (see 'Traditional Highland Dress'). You may also encounter the Tzeltals, numbering about 340,000, who inhabit the region between San Cristóbal and the Lacandón Jungle. Both of these groups are among Mexico's most traditional indigenous peoples. Their nominally Catholic religious life involves some distinctly pre-Hispanic elements and goes hand in hand with some unusual forms of social organization (see 'Burdens of Honor'). Most of the people live in the hills outside the villages, which are primarily market and ceremonial centers.

Chiapas' indigenous peoples are 2nd-class citizens in economic and political terms, with, on the whole, the least productive land in the state. Some have emigrated to the Lacandón Jungle to clear new land, or to cities in search of work. Their plight was the major reason behind the 1994 Zapatista uprising. But not everyone supports the Zapatistas, and violence between opposing indigenous factions has been an ugly side of the Zapatista upheaval. One series of revenge killings between pro-PRI and pro-Zapatista Tzotzils culminated in the 1997 massacre at the village of Acteal, north of San Cristóbal. Some 45 Zapatista-aligned people, mostly women and children, were gunned down by pro-PRI paramilitaries in a chapel.

Other Chiapas indigenous peoples include about 170,000 Choles, mainly in the north of the state; a few thousand Mexican Mames near the Guatemalan border between Tapachula and Ciudad Cuauhtémoc (around 300,000 other Mames are Guatemalans); and some 40,000 Zoques in the northwest.

Despite their problems, indigenous peoples' identities and self-respect survive with the help of traditional festivals, costumes, crafts and often ancient religious practices. These people remain suspicious of outsiders, and may resent interference – especially in their religious practices. But they also will be friendly and polite if treated with due respect.

over 40 winter visitors. It's open 9 am to 3 pm daily except Monday. The nonprofit conservationist association Pronatura (☎ 678-50-00), Juárez 11B, San Cristóbal, offers tours.

San Juan Chamula
• pop 2060

The Chamulans put up strong resistance to the Spaniards in 1524 and launched a famous rebellion in 1869, attacking San Cristóbal. Today they are one of the largest Tzotzil groups – about 80,000 strong. Their main village, San Juan Chamula, 10km northwest of San Cristóbal, is the center for

some unique religious practices. A big sign at the entrance to the village strictly forbids photography in the village church or anywhere rituals are being performed. Nearby, around the shell of an older church, is the village's graveyard, with black crosses for people who died old, white for the young, and blue for others. Near the old church is a small village museum, Ora Ton, open 9 am to 6 pm (US$0.50).

From dawn on Sunday, people stream into San Juan Chamula from the hills for the weekly market and to visit the church. Busloads of tourists also stream in, so you might prefer to come another day. Everyday necessities are the main goods traded at the Sunday market. Artesanías (mainly textiles) are sold every day for the passing tourist trade.

The main church, white with a colorfully painted door arch, stands beside the main plaza. A sign tells visitors to obtain tickets (US$0.50) at the village tourist office, also on the plaza, before entering the church. Inside, the rows of burning candles, the clouds of incense and the worshipers kneeling with their faces almost touching the pine needle-carpeted floor make a powerful impression. Chanting curanderos may be rubbing patients' bodies with eggs or bones. Saints' images are surrounded with mirrors and dressed in holy garments. Chamulans revere San Juan Bautista (St John the Baptist) above Christ, and his image occupies a more important place in the church. Coca-Cola also occupies an important place in the Chamulan cosmography – it facilitates burping in the church, which is considered to expel evil spirits.

Christian festivals are interwoven with older ones: the important Carnaval celebrations also mark the five 'lost' days of the ancient Mayan Long Count calendar, which divided time into 20-day periods (18 of these make 360 days, leaving five to complete a year). Other festivals include ceremonies for Semana Santa, San Juan Bautista (June 22-25, with up to 20,000 people gathering to dance and drink on the 24th) and the annual change of cargos (December 30 to January 1; see 'Burdens of Honor').

Burdens of Honor

Traditional community leadership positions in Chiapas highland villages are known as cargos (charges or duties) and are held by men. Women focus on domestic work, including weaving, though they also take a leading role in market trading.

Men take turns as cargo-holders. The duties normally last for one year, and include caring for the saints' images in churches and the masks and costumes used in religious ceremonies. Other cargos entail organizing and paying for the ceremonies and celebrations that mark the many saints' days.

Taking on a cargo is both an honor and a burden. Only fairly prosperous villagers can afford the considerable expense involved and their financial success is thus turned to the benefit of all.

Among the Tzotzils, senior cargo-holders called mayordomos are responsible for the care of the saints' images. A mayordomo's expenses in San Juan Chamula can amount to US$5000 a year (and the village's patron saint San Juan Bautista has eight mayordomos). Other cargo-holders, alféreces, organize and pay for fiestas; and capitanes dance and ride horses at fiestas. After having successfully carried out several cargos, members enter the ranks of the principales, or village elders.

Zinacantán
• pop 2850

The road to the orderly village of San Lorenzo Zinacantán, about 11km northwest of San Cristóbal, forks left off the Chamula road before descending into a valley. This is the main village of the Zinancantán municipality (population 40,000). Zinacantán people are Tzotzil and the predominantly pink and purple colors of their costume are very distinctive.

A market is usually held only at fiesta times. The most important celebrations are for the festival of el Virgen de la Candelaria, around August 10.

Zinacantecos are great flower-growers and have a particular love for the geranium, which along with pine branches is offered in rituals to bring a wide range of benefits.

The village has two churches. The central Iglesia de San Lorenzo has been rebuilt following a 1975 fire. Photography is banned in the church and churchyard. There's also a museum, Sna Jsotz'lebetik, with displays on Zinacantán customs, costumes and crafts – open 9 am to 6 pm daily.

Tenejapa
• pop 1440

Tenejapa is a Tzeltal village 28km northeast of San Cristóbal, in a pretty valley with a river running through it. There are over 20,000 *tenejapanecos* in the surrounding area. A busy market fills the village center early on Sunday mornings. On the last Thursday of each month, the village leaders gather at the church in their ceremonial attire of wide, colorfully ribboned hats and long necklaces of silver coins, and there may be a market. Tenejapa women wear brightly brocaded or embroidered huipiles.

There are a few comedores in the main street and one basic posada, *Hotel Molina*, which isn't always open. The main festival is for the village's patron saint, San Ildefonso, on January 23.

Grutas de San Cristóbal

The *grutas* (caves) are in fact a single long cavern 9km southeast of San Cristóbal. The entrance is among pine woods a five-minute walk south of the Pan-American Highway, in the midst of an army encampment.

The first 350m or so of the cave have a wooden walkway and are lit. You can enter from 9 am to 4 pm daily (US$0.30). To get there take a combi heading southeast along the Pan-American Highway from San Cristóbal and ask for 'Las Grutas.'

Amatenango del Valle
• pop 3530

The women of this Tzeltal village by the Pan-American Highway 37km southeast of San Cristóbal are renowned potters. Amatenango pottery is still fired by a pre-Hispanic method, building a wood fire around the pieces rather than putting them in a kiln. In addition to everyday pots and jugs that the village has turned out for generations, young girls now find a ready tourist market with animalitos – little animal figures that are inexpensive but fragile. If you visit the village, expect to be surrounded within minutes by girls selling these.

Amatenango women wear white huipiles with red and yellow embroidery, wide red belts and blue skirts.

From San Cristóbal, take a Comitán-bound bus or combi.

North of Chamula

Villages north of Chamula are in the thick of the Zapatista upheaval and you should inform yourself very well about the security situation before considering venturing up there.

San Andrés Larraínzar is a hilltop Tzotzil and mestizo village 18km north from San Juan Chamula through spectacular mountain scenery. San Andrés is the main center of Zapatista support in the Chiapas highlands, and was the site of the 1996 negotiations between the EZLN and Mexican government representatives that produced the San Andrés accords on indigenous rights (as yet unenacted). A weekly Sunday market is held.

Some 27km northeast of San Juan Chamula – and quite a descent from it – is

TABASCO & CHIAPAS

San Pedro Chenalhó, a Tzotzil village in a valley with a stream running through it. It was in the politically divided Chenalhó municipality that escalating rivalry between pro-PRI and pro-Zapatista Tzotzil groups culminated in the 1997 massacre at Acteal, 20km northeast of San Pedro Chenalhó (see 'Indigenous Peoples of Chiapas'). At the time of writing thousands of pro-Zapatistas driven out of their own villages in the municipality were living as refugees at Pol-Hó near Acteal.

Getting There & Away
Transportation to most villages leaves from points around the Mercado Municipal in San Cristóbal (see the San Cristóbal map for exact locations). Check latest return times before you set out: some services wind down by lunchtime. Combis to San Juan Chamula leave from Calle Honduras fairly frequently up to about 6 pm; for Zinacantán (US$0.60), combis go at least hourly, 6 am to 5 pm, from a yard off Robledo. Colectivo taxis to Tenejapa (US$1.25) leave from Bermudas. For San Andrés Larraínzar and San Pedro Chenalhó, combis leave from yards north and south, respectively, of the Puente Tiboli bridge at the north end of Utrilla.

OCOSINGO
● pop 25,000 ● elev 900m ☎ 9
Around the halfway mark of the 180km journey from San Cristóbal to Palenque – a trip that takes you down from cool, misty highlands to steaming lowland jungle – is the town of Ocosingo, a busy market hub for a large area. En route from San Cristóbal you pass through the Tzotzil town of **Huixtán** and Tzeltal **Oxchuc**, both with large colonial churches.

Ocosingo saw the bloodiest fighting in the 1994 Zapatista rebellion, when rebels who had wrecked and burned the town hall (at the west end of the main plaza) were cornered in the town's market by the Mexican army; about 50 of them were killed.

The market area, three blocks east down Avenida Sur Ote from the main plaza, is the liveliest part of town. Its Tianguis Campesino (Peasants' Market) section is for peasant producers to sell their goods direct: they sit on the bare ground to do so.

Near Ocosingo are the Mayan ruins of Toniná and a beautiful guest ranch that is one of the most enjoyable places to stay in Chiapas. Ocosingo is also the main jumping-off point for beautiful Laguna Miramar.

Orientation & Information
Ocosingo spreads east (downhill) from highway 199, the San Cristóbal-Palenque road. Avenida Central runs down from the main road to the central plaza. Banamex on the plaza has an ATM, but none of the banks in town will change cash or traveler's checks; try Hotel Central.

Places to Stay
Hotel Central (☎ 673-00-24, *Avenida Central 1*), on the north side of the main plaza, has simple, clean rooms with fan, bath and TV for US$10/14/17 a single/double/triple.

Hotel Margarita (☎ 673-02-80) on Calle 1 Pte Norte one block north of Hotel Central, charges US$10/11/12, or US$12/13/15 with TV. Rooms have fan and bath but are rather dilapidated.

At the really cheap end there's **Hospedaje Las Palmas**, on the corner of Calle 2 Pte and Avenida 1 Norte Pte – one block west and one north from the main plaza. It's an adequately clean, family-run place; singles/doubles with shared bathrooms are US$3.50/5. **Hotel San José** (☎ 673-00-39, *Calle 1 Ote 6*), half a block north of the northeast corner of the main plaza, has small, dark but clean rooms with bathroom for US$8/9.

Places to Eat
Ocosingo is known for its *queso amarillo* (yellow cheese), which comes in three-layered 1kg balls. The two outside layers are like chewy Gruyère, the middle is creamy.

You can get a decent comida for US$1.50 at comedores in the **mercado** on Avenida Sur Ote. There are also numerous **comedores** on highway 199 and Avenida 1 Norte, near the bus stations.

Restaurant La Montura (*Avenida Central 1*) has a prime location on the Hotel Central's veranda. It's good for a big breakfast (fruit, eggs, bread and coffee for US$3). Later in the day main dishes are around US$3.50 to US$6.50, and antojitos US$2.50 to US$4. *Restaurant Los Portales* (*Avenida Central 19*), a few doors east, is a homey, old-fashioned place where matronly señoras offer traditional meals for US$2 to US$5. You walk through someone's living room to get to it.

On the opposite side of the plaza, *Restaurant y Pizzas El Desván* has bright orange and blue paintwork and a good upstairs location overlooking the square. Pizzas cost from US$3.50 to US$11 and there are other possibilities including breakfasts. *Restaurant & Pizzería Troje*, a few doors away, does cheap *quesadillas*, and pizzas from US$4 to US$14.

Getting There & Away

Air Servicios Aéreos San Cristóbal (☎ 673-01-88) does small-plane charters from Ocosingo's airstrip behind the Tianguis Campesino (the runway is a narrow strip with houses alarmingly close on each side). Possible destinations include Bonampak and Yaxchilán (around US$120 a person for four or five people) or San Quintín (from which you can reach Laguna Miramar – see that section).

Bus & Combi The main transportation terminals are on highway 199, in the three blocks north (downhill) from the intersection of Avenida Central. First, at Avenida 1 Norte, is the stop for combis and microbuses to San Cristóbal de Las Casas. Half a block farther is the yard of Transportes Lacandonia (TL, 2nd-class buses). Autotransportes Tuxtla Gutiérrez (ATG, 2nd-class buses) and Cristóbal Colón (1st- and 2nd-class buses) straddle the intersection of Avenida 3 Norte, 1½ blocks on down the highway.

Most buses are *de paso*. Departures include:

Palenque – 103km, 2½ hours; 8 Colón (US$3.75 to US$5), 7 ATG (US$3 to US$4), 12 TL (US$3)

San Cristóbal de Las Casas – 88km, 1½ hours; 8 Colón (US$2.50 to US$3.50), 6 ATG (US$2.25 to US$2.50), 10 TL (US$2.25), frequent combis and microbuses (US$2.50)

Tuxtla Gutiérrez – 170km, 3½ hours; 8 Colón (US$5 to US$6.50), 6 ATG (US$4.25 to US$5.25)

Colón and/or ATG also run buses to Campeche, Cancún, Chetumal, Mérida, Mexico City and Villahermosa.

TONINÁ

- **elev 900m** ☎ 9

The Mayan ruins of Toniná, 14km east of Ocosingo, don't match famous Palenque, 95km north, for beauty or extent, but they form a sizable site with large structures on terraces cut from a hillside, and they have a very interesting history.

The site was not excavated until 1979. Since then archaeologists have concluded that it was Toniná that brought about Palenque's downfall. The prelude to Toniná's heyday was a change of dynasty in the late 7th century – from the long-standing Lords of the Lineage of the Underworld to the even unfriendlier-sounding Snake Skull-Jaguar Claw clan. The new rulers demolished their predecessors' palaces and temples and declared war on Palenque about 690 AD. At least three Palenque leaders were held prisoner at Toniná. One, Kan-Xul II, probably had his head chopped off here around 720 AD.

Toniná reached its maximum splendor in the decade following its devastation of Palenque in 730. It became known as the Place of the Celestial Captives, for in some of its chambers were held the captured rulers of Palenque and other Maya cities, destined to be either ransomed for large sums or decapitated. A recurring image in Toniná sculpture is that of captives before decapitation, thrown to the ground with their hands tied.

Around 900 Toniná was rebuilt again, in a simpler, austere style. But Jaguar Serpent, in 903, was the last Toniná ruler of whom any record has been found. Classic Mayan civilization was ending here, as elsewhere.

The Site

The ruins are open 9 am to 4 pm daily (US$2, free on Sunday). There are few explanatory signs, but a new **museum** near the entrance should have opened by the time you get there.

If you have already visited Palenque or Yaxchilán, imagine a similar splendor here. Many of the stone facings and interior walls were covered in paint or frescoes. The path from the ticket office crosses a stream and climbs steps to a **juego de pelota** (ball court), on the edge of the large, flat **Gran Plaza**. The ball court was inaugurated in about the 780s under the rule of the female regent Smoking Mirror. A decapitation altar stands beside it.

At the left (south) end of the Gran Plaza is the **Templo de la Guerra Cósmica** (Temple of Cosmic War), with five altars in front of it.

To the north rises a hillside, terraced into a number of platforms. At the right-hand end of the steps rising from the first to the second platform is the entry to a **ritual labyrinth** of passages (flick the light switch on as you go in). The sarcophagus of Zots-Choj, a ruler of the Snake Skull-Jaguar Claw dynasty who took the throne in 842 AD, lies by the entrance.

Higher up on the right-hand side is the **Palacio de las Grecas y de la Guerra** (Palace of the *Grecas* & War) – a greca being a band of geometrical decoration, in this case a zigzag X-shape in the stone facing of one of the walls. The zigzag may represent Quetzal-cóatl and is also a flight of steps (you're not allowed to climb it!). To the right of the X is a rambling series of chambers, passages and stairways, believed to have been Toniná's administrative center.

Higher again, still toward the right-hand side of the stepped-and-terraced hillside, is Toniná's most remarkable sculpture, the **Mural de las Cuatro Eras** (Mural of the Four Eras). Created sometime between 790 and 840 AD, this stucco relief of four panels (the first, from the left end, has been lost) represents the four suns, or eras of human history in Maya belief. At the center of each panel is the upside-down head of a decapitated prisoner. Blood spurting from the prisoner's neck forms a ring of feathers and, at the same time, a sun. In one panel, a skeleton dances in the underworld and holds a decapitated head with its tongue out. Below is a lord of the underworld who resembles an enormous rodent. This mural was created at a time when a great wave of destruction was running through the Maya world. The people of Toniná at this time believed themselves to be living in the fourth sun, the sun of winter, stillness, mirrors, the direction north and the end of human life.

Near the middle of the same level, a short ladder descends to a tomb with a stone sarcophagus; and toward the left end of the platform, stone steps descend into a narrow opening, the **Tumba de Treinta Metros** (Thirty-Meter Tomb). You'll need a flashlight (torch) to investigate this.

Above this is the acropolis, the abode of Toniná's rulers and site of its eight most important temples – four on each of two levels. The lower level has two smaller temples in the middle and the larger **Templo del Agua** (Temple of Water) on the left and **Templo del Monstruo de la Tierra** (Temple of the Earth Monster) on the right. The latter has Toniná's best-preserved roof comb and was built around 713 AD.

The topmost level has two tall temples behind and two smaller ones in front. The top of the right-hand (eastern), taller one, the **Templo del Espejo Humeante** (Temple of the Smoking Mirror), is 80m above the Gran Plaza. This temple was built, and its neighbor the Templo del Comercio (Temple of Trade) was ruined, by the 9th century ruler Zots-Choj. In that era of the fourth and final sun and the direction north, Zots-Choj needed to raise this, Toniná's northernmost temple, higher than all the others, which necessitated a large artificial northeastward extension of the hill.

Around the left-hand smaller temple on this level, the **Templo de la Guerra** (Temple of War), can be seen stucco figures of prisoners.

Places to Stay

Relaxing, immaculately clean *Rancho Esmeralda* (fax 673-07-11, ranchoes@mundomaya .com.mx) is set amid rolling countryside just a 15-minute walk from Toniná ruins (but a loop of about 6km by road). Its welcoming American owners, Glen Wersch and Ellen Jones, settled here in 1994 because the altitude is right for the macadamia grove they wanted to plant. Their rustic but comfortable guest cabañas, set on grassy lawns, cost from US$22 to US$27 single or double, or US$32 for a family of four. You can camp for US$3 a person (they have a couple of tents to rent for US$5). Excellent meals are served (breakfast US$3.50 to US$4.50, dinner US$7). Three- to four-hour horse rides on the ranch's well-kept animals are popular at US$15 per person; they can also arrange day trips by plane to Yaxchilán and Bonampak.

A taxi from Ocosingo to Rancho Esmeralda is US$4 or US$5. Alternatively, take a Toniná-bound combi from Ocosingo and get off after about 8km at a signed turnoff opposite a military base, from which it's about 1.5km along a dirt road to the *rancho*.

Getting There & Away
Combis to Toniná (US$1) leave from a stop opposite the Tianguis Campesino in Ocosingo. The last one back departs Toniná about 4 pm.

LAGUNA MIRAMAR
• elev 400m

Beautiful, pristine Laguna Miramar, 100km southeast of Ocosingo, is the largest lake in the Lacandón Jungle. It has become known – and accessible – to the outside world thanks to a successful community ecotourism project by the village near its western shore, Ejido Emiliano Zapata.

Surrounded by hills covered in rain forest and echoing with the roars of howler monkeys, the 16-sq-km lake has a beautiful temperature all year and is virtually unpolluted – one of the last expanses of water in Mexico, even the world, of which that can be said. The lake is within the Montes Azules biosphere reserve and the four *ejidos* (communal landholdings) that surround it have agreed to use no motorboats on the lake and to keep a 1km band around it free of settlement, farming and extractive activities. (For more on Montes Azules and the Lacandón Jungle, see 'The Lacandón Jungle & the Lacandones' later in this chapter.)

A visit to Miramar is an unforgettable close encounter with nature. Ejido life in Emiliano Zapata – a poor but well-ordered,

alcohol-free community founded in 1968 by Chol and Tzotzil settlers from northern Chiapas – is fascinating too. It is forbidden to bring alcohol or drugs into the community.

You can visit Miramar in an organized group or on your own. In either case it's advisable to contact in advance Señor Fernando Ochoa, the architect of the ecotourism project, at Calle Dr Navarro 10, Barrio del Cerrillo, San Cristóbal de Las Casas (☎/fax 9-678-04-68, miramar@mundomaya.com.mx). Fernando, who speaks excellent English, takes groups to the lake and will provide other visitors with important information and advice.

Ideally, avoid coming between June and October, when most of the year's 2000mm of rain falls, and roads and paths turn to mud.

When you reach Emiliano Zapata, ask for the Presidente de la Laguna (the villager in charge of lake matters) and/or the Comisariado (equivalent to the mayor). If you have been in touch with Fernando Ochoa, he will probably have told you the names of the people currently occupying these posts. Through them you must arrange details of your visit and pay for the services you need – US$10 a day for a guide to or around the lake (or for animal- or birdspotting), US$5 for a porter to or from the lake, US$10 a day for use of a *cayuco* (canoe), US$3 per person for a night's stay. The village is a spread-out place of huts and a few concrete communal buildings, on a gentle slope running down to the Río Perlas, which is the village's beautiful bathing place.

The 7km walk from village to lake, through milpas and forest, takes 1½ hours. Guides will point out trees like the *caoba* (mahogany) and what they call the *matapalo* (wood-killer), which leans on other trees as it grows and ends up strangling them. Around the lake you hear the incessant growls of howler monkeys *(saraguatos)* and may see these and spider monkeys *(monos arañas)*. Birdlife includes macaws, toucans and prolific butterflies. You may hear jaguars at night. Locals fish for perch *(mojarra)* in the lake, and will assure you that its few crocodiles are not dangerous.

It takes about 45 minutes to canoe across to Isla Lacan-Tun, a 6000-sq-m island covered in overgrown pre-Hispanic remains from the Chol-Lacantún people, who were not conquered by the Spanish until the 1580s. The island was the site of their last stand.

Organized Tours

Fernando Ochoa's trips – for groups of three to eight – last four days (three nights) from San Cristóbal, and cost US$330 a person including flights from Ocosingo to San Quintín and back, equipment, good food, porters and all other fees at the ejido and lake.

Kanan-Ku Viajes (see Organized Tours in the San Cristóbal section) also offers Miramar trips, traveling by road and charging around US$120 per person (minimum four) for three days and two nights.

Places to Stay & Eat

At the lakeshore you can camp or sling a hammock under a *palapa* shelter. There are plans to build a small lodging for tourists in the village: meanwhile they can put people up in the Comisaría, a kind of village hall.

Food supplies in Emiliano Zapata's couple of stores are very basic. You may be able to obtain tortillas in the mornings. There are a few slightly better stocked stores, and a couple of simple comedores, in neighboring San Quintín.

Getting There & Away

To reach Emiliano Zapata you must first get to the neighboring ejido, San Quintín, which has an airstrip and a large Mexican army base (San Quintín supports the PRI; Emiliano Zapata is sympathetic to the Zapatistas). From the bus stop in San Quintín, walk five minutes along the airstrip and turn down a dirt road to the right opposite a complex of military buildings. From here it's a 15- or 20-minute walk to the middle of Ejido Emiliano Zapata.

Air Small planes of Servicios Aéreos San Cristóbal (see Getting There & Away in the Ocosingo section) leave Ocosingo most mornings for San Quintín. If you're at the airstrip by 9.30 am you should get a place. The one-way fare is US$32. Return flight times are less reliable but there's one most days.

Bus & Truck Four or five buses, microbuses or passenger-carrying trucks (*tres toneladas*) run daily to San Quintín from a stop a few meters south of the Tianguis Campesino in Ocosingo. Departure times vary but there's nearly always something at 9 or 9.30 am from Ocosingo (often 10 or 11 am too), and something returning at midnight or 1 am from San Quintín. The five-hour, 130km trip costs US$4.50.

From Ocosingo you start out on the paved Altamirano road, then turn left onto a dirt road after about 7km. The roads across the mountainous territory east of Ocosingo pass along a number of river valleys known as Las Cañadas de Ocosingo. Inhabited mainly by Tzeltal indigenous people, this is one of the main areas of support for the Zapatista rebels. You may pass villages with signs proclaiming '*Territorio Rebelde Zapatista*' (Zapatista Rebel Territory) almost side by side with large military bases, and your documents will be checked at Mexican army checkpoints as you travel through. Keep your passport handy and make sure your tourist card is valid.

There's a shorter dirt road to San Quintín from Las Margaritas, east of Comitán – but it passes through the village of La Realidad, the main Zapatista base, and it's unlikely that foreigners would get through the army checkpoints along this road.

AGUA AZUL, AGUA CLARA & MISOL-HA

Three short detours off the Ocosingo-Palenque road lead to beautiful water attractions: the thundering cascades of Agua Azul, the turquoise Río Shumulha at Agua Clara and the spectacular waterfall of Misol-Ha.

All three can be visited in an organized day tour from Palenque – perhaps best if time is precious – but it's quite possible to go independently, and there are decent accommodations at Agua Clara and Misol-Ha.

The road between Ocosingo and Palenque has in the past been the scene of highway robberies, with bandits stopping vehicles and relieving travelers of their valuables. When we researched this edition there seemed to have been no recent incidents, but it's always wise to ask a few questions, especially if you're driving.

Agua Azul

The turnoff for the superb waterfalls of Agua Azul is about halfway between Ocosingo and Palenque. Scores of dazzling white waterfalls thunder into turquoise pools surrounded by jungle.

On holidays and weekends the site is thronged; at other times you'll have few companions. Admission to the ejido where the falls are located is US$2 per car, US$0.50 for a person on foot. Note that the beautiful blue water color that gives the place its name may be evident only in April and May. Silt can cloud the waters in other months and it turns muddy during the height of the rainy season.

The temptation to swim is great but take extreme care – the current is deceptively fast and there are many submerged hazards like rocks and dead trees. Use your judgment to identify slower, safer areas. Drownings are all too common here.

A paved road leads 4.5km down from highway 199 to a parking lot and the cluster of comedores near the main falls. Most of the comedores have similar menus, charging around US$3 for fish/meat/chicken dishes.

It's well worth walking 1km or so up the riverside path to get away from the crowds: you pass the main falls but the tropical river is just as beautiful – and in places safer for swimming.

About 2km downstream is another set of falls, Cascadas Bolón-Ahau, just before the river from Agua Azul flows into the Río Shumulhá.

Agua Azul is not a good place to stay. There's a camping/hammock-slinging area with a palapa shelter 100m down to the right opposite the parking lot. Cost is US$3 per tent and US$1.50 per hammock. The bathrooms are grotty, and the rooms in the bathroom block are absolutely vile.

Agua Clara

Around 8km toward Palenque from the Agua Azul turnoff, another signed detour leads 2km by paved road to Agua Clara. Here the Río Shumulhá (or Tulijá) is a beautiful, broad, shallow expanse of turquoise water that's a delight to swim in (but test the current before choosing your spot). You can also rent a kayak (US$4 an hour) or take a stroll across a hanging footbridge.

Agua Clara's community-run hotel, *Sna Ajaw* (☎ 934-5-03-56, 934-5-12-10) has eight plain, clean rooms with fan for US$13/18 a single/double, or US$25 for a king-size double. Bathrooms are shared and have hot water. Some rooms have views to the river. There's a reasonably priced restaurant too.

Misol-Ha

About 20km from Palenque, the Río Misol-Ha drops 35m into a wide pool surrounded by lush tropical vegetation. The pool is safe for swimming and a path behind the main fall leads into a cave with some smaller trickles of water.

The waterfall is 1.5km off highway 199 and the turn is signposted. To enter you pay US$0.50 per visitor.

The *Centro Turístico Ejidal Cascada Misol-Ha* at the falls (☎/fax 934-5-12-10 in Palenque) rents good wooden cabins with bathrooms and mosquito netting, at US$15 for one or two people, or US$28 for a family cabin with kitchen. There's also a restaurant open till 6 pm.

Getting There & Away

Many travel agencies in Palenque offer daily trips to Misol-Ha and Agua Azul, with Agua Clara as a possible extra. See the list of agencies under Organized Tours in the Palenque section, then check out a few current deals. Most trips last around seven hours, spending half an hour at Misol-Ha and three hours at Agua Azul. The basic price is about US$7 including admission fees but not food. Add a dollar or two for extras such as breakfast or more comfortable vehicles such as a Chevrolet Suburban. You may also have to pay more if you wish to visit Agua Clara.

To do it independently, take almost any combi heading south at the Maya head statue in Palenque, or any 2nd-class bus along highway 199; they will drop you at any

of the three intersections. The combi fare
from Palenque to the Agua Azul junction
(*crucero*) is US$2.

The distances from the highway to Misol-
Ha and Agua Clara are manageable on foot.
For the 4.5km between the Agua Azul
crucero and Agua Azul itself, there are
passenger-carrying *camionetas* (pickups) for
US$0.50. Check out times of camionetas
going back to the crucero, as it's uphill in
that direction.

A taxi from Palenque to Misol-Ha with a
one-hour wait costs around US$20; to Agua
Azul with a two-hour wait should be US$40.

PALENQUE

● **pop 24,400** ● **elev 80m** ☎ **changing**

The ancient Mayan city of Palenque, with its
superb jungle setting and exquisite architecture and decoration, is one of the marvels of
Mexico. Modern Palenque town, a few kilometers to the east, is a sweaty, humdrum
place with little attraction except as a base
for visiting the ruins.

History

The name Palenque (Palisade) is Spanish
and has no relation to the city's ancient
name, which is uncertain. It could have been

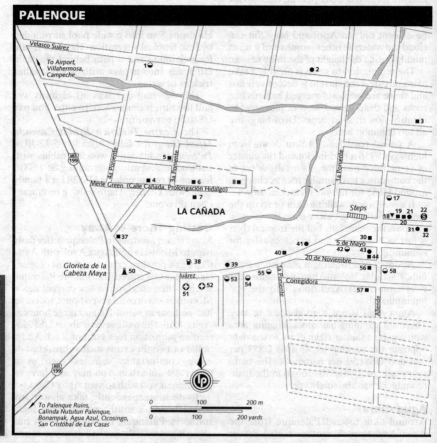

PALENQUE

Velasco Suárez

To Airport,
Villahermosa,
Campeche

La Cañada

MEX 199

Merle Green (Calle Cañada, Prolongación Hidalgo)

Steps

Glorieta de la
Cabeza Maya

Juárez

5 de Mayo

20 de Noviembre

Corregidora

Allende

La Poniente

MEX 199

To Palenque Ruins,
Calinda Nututun Palenque,
Bonampak, Agua Azul, Ocosingo,
San Cristóbal de Las Casas

0   100   200 m

0   100   200 yards

Nachan (City of Snakes), Chocan (Sculptured Snake), Huehuetlapalla, Xhembobel Moyos, Otulum … no one knows for sure.

Palenque was first occupied around 100 BC. It flourished from about 600 to 700 AD, and what a glorious century that was! The city rose to prominence under Pakal, a club-footed king who reigned from 615 to 683 AD. Archaeologists have determined that Pakal is represented by hieroglyphics of sun and shield, and he is also referred to as Sun Shield or White Macaw (in Spanish, Escudo Solar or Guacamaya Blanca). He lived to the age of 80.

During Pakal's reign, many plazas and buildings, including the superlative Templo de las Inscripciones (Pakal's own mausoleum), were constructed in Palenque. The structures were characterized by mansard roofs and very fine stucco bas-reliefs.

Pakal was succeeded by his son Chan-Bahlum II, symbolized in hieroglyphics by the jaguar and the serpent (and also called Jaguar Serpent II or K'inich Kan Balam II). Chan-Bahlum continued Palenque's political and economic expansion and the development of its art and architecture. He completed his father's crypt in the Templo de las

PALENQUE

PLACES TO STAY
3 Posada Bonampak
4 Hotel Maya Tulipanes
5 La Posada
6 Hotel Chablis
7 Hotel Xibalba
8 Hotel La Cañada
9 Hotel Naj K'in
16 Hotel Lacroix
19 Posada Shalom
20 Hotel Nikte-Ha
27 Hotel Casa de Pakal
28 Hotel Chan-Kah
30 Hotel Kashlan
32 Hotel Regional
36 Hotel Vaca Vieja
37 Maya Palenque Hotel
40 Posada Los Ángeles
44 Posada Nacha'n Ka'an
45 Posada Kin
46 Posada Canek
48 Hotel Palenque
56 Posada Santo Domingo
57 Hotel Yun-Kax
59 Posada Charito

PLACES TO EAT
10 Café Te-El
11 Restaurant Virgo's
14 Restaurant Na Chan-Kan
15 Restaurant Artemio's
18 Pizza Palenque
29 Restaurant Maya
34 Mara's
35 Los Faroles, Fuente de Sodas

OTHER
1 Transportes Comitán-Lagos de Montebello
2 Mercado
7 Shivalva Viajes Mayas
12 Post Office
13 Palacio Municipal (Town Hall)
14 Na Chan Kan Travel Agency
17 Colectivos Chambalu
21 Viajes Yax-Ha
22 Banamex, ATM
23 Inter Travel
24 Bancomer, ATM
25 Tourist Office, Shivalva Viajes Mayas
26 Farmacia Central
31 Kim Tours
33 Viajes Misol-Ha
38 Pemex
39 Viajes Mayasol
41 Viajes Kukulcan
42 Autotransportes Río Chancalá
43 Lavandería
47 Cibernet
49 Instituto Nacional de Migración
50 Maya Head Statue
51 Hospital General
52 Centro de Salud
53 Cristóbal Colón/ADO Bus Station
54 Autotransportes Tuxtla Gutiérrez Bus Station
55 Transportes Rodulfo Figueroa & Transportes Lacandonia Bus Station
58 Transportes Palenque

Inscripciones and presided over the construction of the Grupo de la Cruz temples, placing sizable narrative stone stelae within each. One can see the influence of Palenque's architecture in the Mayan city of Tikal in Guatemala and in the pyramids of Comalcalco near Villahermosa.

During Chan-Bahlum II's reign, the rival Maya city of Toniná, 65km to the south, declared war on Palenque. Toniná's hostility was probably the major factor in Palenque's precipitous decline after Chan-Bahlum's death in 702. Chan-Bahlum's brother and successor Kan-Xul II was captured by Toniná and probably executed there. Sources speak of a devastating Toniná attack on Palenque in 730. The last powerful ruler of Palenque was Chaacal III (or K'inich Ahkal Mo'Nab III), who took the throne in 722 and added many substantial buildings.

After the 10th century Palenque was largely abandoned. In an area that receives the heaviest rainfall in Mexico, the ruins were overgrown and lay undiscovered until the 18th century.

Orientation

Highway 199 meets Palenque town's main street, Juárez, at the Glorieta de la Cabeza Maya, an intersection with a large statue of a Maya chieftain's head, at the west end of the town. From here Juárez heads 1km east to the central square, El Parque. The main bus stations are on Juárez just east of the Maya head statue.

A few hundred meters south of the Maya head, the 7.5km road to the Palenque ruins

Rediscovery of Palenque

In 1773, Mayan hunters told a Spanish priest that stone palaces lay in the jungle. Father Ordóñez y Aguilar led an expedition to Palenque and wrote a book claiming that the city was the capital of an Atlantis-like civilization.

An expedition led by Captain Antonio del Río set out in 1787 to explore Palenque. Although his subsequent report was locked away in the Guatemalan archives, a translation of it was done by a British resident of Guatemala who was sufficiently intrigued to have it published in England in 1822. This led a host of adventurers to brave malaria and other dangers in their search for the hidden city.

Among the most colorful of these characters was the eccentric Count de Waldeck who, in his 60s, lived atop one of the pyramids for two years (1831-33). He wrote a book complete with fraudulent drawings that made the city resemble great Mediterranean civilizations, causing all the more interest in Palenque. In Europe, it was mythologized as a lost Atlantis or an extension of ancient Egypt.

In 1837, John L Stephens, an amateur archaeology enthusiast from New York, reached Palenque with artist Frederick Catherwood. Stephens wrote insightfully about the six pyramids he started to excavate and the city's aqueduct system. His was the first scientific investigation and paved the way for research by other serious scholars – over some of whom Palenque has exerted a lifetime's enchantment. Frans Blom, an early-to-mid-20th-century investigator, remarked: 'The first visit to Palenque is immensely impressive. When one has lived there for some time this ruined city becomes an obsession.' It's not hard to understand why.

heads west off highway 199. This road passes the site museum after 6km, then winds on 1.5km to the site's main entrance.

Information

Tourist Offices The helpful tourist office (☎ 5-03-56), on Juárez at Abasolo, has reliable town and transportation information and a few maps. It's open 9 am to 9 pm Monday to Saturday, 9 am to 1 pm Sunday.

Immigration The Instituto Nacional de Migración, on Mina south of 5 de Mayo, is open long hours daily.

Money Bancomer, on Juárez 1½ blocks west of El Parque, changes money from 9 am to 3 pm Monday to Friday. Banamex, a little farther west on Juárez, did not exchange money at the time of writing, but both banks have ATMs. Some travel agencies, hotels and restaurants will change money, at less favorable rates.

Post & Communications The post office, at Independencia and Bravo one block from El Parque, is open 8 am to 3 pm Monday to Friday and 9 am to 1 pm Saturday. There are pay phones around El Parque, along Juárez and elsewhere. Cibernet Internet café (☎ 5-17-10), on Independencia just south of El Parque, is open 9 am to 9 pm Monday to Saturday, 1 to 9 pm Sunday. Cost is US$1 for each 15 minutes or part thereof.

Bookstores A small shop next to the Hotel Regional on Juárez sells a few books in English and Spanish on Mayan and Mexican culture and history.

Laundry The *lavandería* on 5 de Mayo opposite Hotel Kashlan will wash and dry 3kg

for US$3 (same-day service if you drop off in the morning).

Medical Services Palenque's Hospital General (☎ 5-07-33) is at the west end of Juárez, with the Centro de Salud (Health Center, ☎ 5-00-25) next door. There are several pharmacies along Juárez.

Palenque Ruins

Ancient Palenque's 500 buildings are spread over 15 sq km but only a relatively few, in a fairly compact central area, have been excavated. Everything you see here was built without metal tools, pack animals or the wheel. The site stands at the precise point where the first hills rise out of the Gulf Coast plain, and the dense green jungle covering these hills forms a superb backdrop to Palenque's outstanding Maya architecture. The forest is home to toucans, ocelots and monkeys; you may hear the howler monkeys, especially if you stay at a campground near the ruins. As you explore the ruins, try to picture the gray stone edifices as they would have been at the peak of Palenque's power: painted bright red.

The best way to visit is to take a minibus or taxi (see Getting There & Away) to the main (upper) entrance, see the major ruins (the Templo de las Inscripciones, El Palacio and the Grupo de la Cruz), exploring nearby lesser ones as you please, then walk downhill through the jungle visiting minor ruins along and near the Arroyo Otulum, to the museum. From the museum you can catch a minibus back to town.

The archaeological site is open 8 am to 5 pm daily, the museum 7 am to 4 pm daily (US$2.50 for both, free Sunday and holidays); the crypt in the Templo de las Inscripciones, a highlight of Palenque, was closed for maintenance at the time of research but previously was open from 10 am to 4 pm.

A good time to visit is when the site opens, as morning mist wraps the temples in a picturesque haze. The effect is best in winter when the days are shorter. At this time of day it's also cooler and crowds tend to be thinner. Between May and October, bring insect repellent.

In July 2000, the telephone area code for Palenque is due to change to ☎ 9 from 934, with the digits 34 added to the start of every local number (for example, the number 7-65-43 will become 347-65-43).

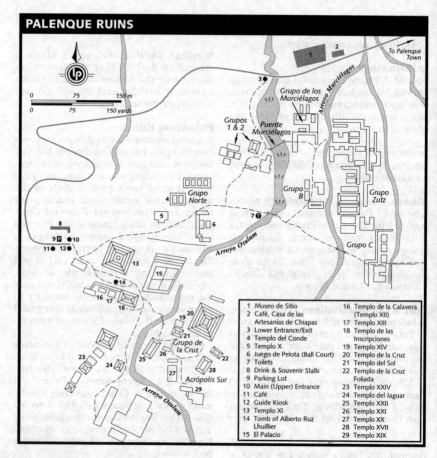

PALENQUE RUINS

0 75 150 m
0 75 150 yards

To Palenque Town

Arroyo Murciélagos

Grupo de los Murciélagos

Grupos 1 & 2

Puente Murciélagos

Grupo Norte

Grupo B

Grupo Zutz

Grupo C

Arroyo Otulum

Grupo de la Cruz

Acrópolis Sur

Arroyo Otulum

1 Museo de Sitio
2 Café, Casa de las Artesanías de Chiapas
3 Lower Entrance/Exit
4 Templo del Conde
5 Templo X
6 Juego de Pelota (Ball Court)
7 Toilets
8 Drink & Souvenir Stalls
9 Parking Lot
10 Main (Upper) Entrance
11 Café
12 Guide Kiosk
13 Templo XI
14 Tomb of Alberto Ruz Lhuillier
15 El Palacio
16 Templo de la Calavera (Templo XII)
17 Templo XIII
18 Templo de las Inscripciones
19 Templo XIV
20 Templo de la Cruz
21 Templo del Sol
22 Templo de la Cruz Foliada
23 Templo XXIV
24 Templo del Jaguar
25 Templo XXII
26 Templo XXI
27 Templo XX
28 Templo XVII
29 Templo XIX

Drinks, snacks, hats and souvenirs (including quivers of arrows sold by Lacandones) are available from stands outside the entrance, and there are cafés here and at the museum. Guide service is available from a kiosk by the entrance (a two-hour tour for up to seven people costs US$26). The ruins are not well labeled, to better support the guides.

Palenque's paths go up and down slopes that are sometimes slippery. Seniors and the disabled may need help, or may have to limit their visit to the main plaza.

An excellent place to read up on Palenque, including news of latest archaeological discoveries, is the official Palenque website, www.mesoweb.com/palenque.

Dangers & Annoyances There have been some muggings of tourists who ventured away from the main frequented parts of the Palenque site. On our last visit the site was patrolled by security guards, a positive sign, but stay alert if you go to outlying ruins such as the Templo del Jaguar or Grupo C.

Templo de las Inscripciones As you climb the slope to the ruins, the grand Temple of the Inscriptions comes into view. Adjoining, to its right, is Templo XIII, in which another royal burial was discovered in 1993; and to the right of that, the Templo de la Calavera (Temple of the Skull). By the path, facing these temples, is the tomb of Alberto Ruz Lhuillier, the tireless archaeologist who revealed many of Palenque's mysteries – including Pakal's secret crypt in 1952.

The magnificent Templo de las Inscripciones is the tallest and most prominent of Palenque's buildings. Constructed on eight levels, it has a central staircase rising 25m (69 steep steps) to a series of small rooms; the tall roof comb that once crowned it is long gone. Between the doorways are stucco panels with reliefs of noble figures. On the temple's interior rear wall are the three panels with a long inscription in Mayan hieroglyphs for which Ruz Lhuillier named the temple. The inscription, dedicated in 692 AD, recounts the history of Palenque and the temple. Also at the top is the access to the slippery stairs down into the tomb of Pakal. An alternative to climbing the steep front steps is the path around the east end of the temple, emerging high up at its rear.

Pakal's jewel-bedecked skeleton and jade mosaic death mask were taken to Mexico City, and the tomb was re-created in the Museo Nacional de Antropología (from where the priceless death mask was stolen in 1985), but the stone sarcophagus lid remains here. This carved stone slab includes the image of Pakal encircled by serpents, mythical monsters, the sun god and glyphs recounting Pakal's reign. Carved on the wall are the nine lords of the underworld. Between the crypt and the staircase, a snakelike hollow ventilation tube connected Pakal to the realm of the living.

El Palacio Diagonally opposite the Templo de las Inscripciones is the Palace, an unusual structure harboring a maze of courtyards, corridors and rooms. Its tower, restored in 1955, has fine stucco reliefs on its walls, but is not open to visitors.

Archaeologists and astronomers believe that the tower was constructed so that Mayan royalty and the priest class could observe the sun falling directly into the Templo de las Inscripciones during the winter solstice.

Templo del Jaguar On the east side of the Templo de las Inscripciones, an uphill path leads south into the jungle to the small, ruined Temple of the Jaguar, clinging to a steep hillside next to a great ceiba tree. The façade of this small temple has fallen downhill toward the Arroyo Otulum stream, exposing the interior that still bears mold-covered traces of colored murals. The large pyramid behind is still a hill of rubble engulfed in jungle.

Grupo de la Cruz Although Pakal had only one building, the Templo de las Inscripciones, dedicated to him during his 68-year reign, his son Chan-Bahlum had four, known today as the Grupo de la Cruz (Group of the Cross), around a plaza southeast of the Templo de las Inscripciones.

The beautiful **Templo del Sol** (Temple of the Sun) on the west side of the plaza has the best-preserved roof comb at Palenque. Carvings inside, commemorating Chan-Bahlum's birth in 635 AD and accession in 684, show him facing his father.

The smaller, less well preserved **Templo XIV** also has tablets showing ritual offerings – a common scene at Palenque.

JON DAVISON

Templo de las Inscripciones

The **Templo de la Cruz** is the largest in this group. Carvings in the central sanctuary show the God L smoking tobacco, and Chan-Bahlum. Behind is a reproduction of a panel depicting Chan-Bahlum's accession.

On the **Templo de la Cruz Foliada** (Temple of the Foliated Cross), the arches are fully exposed, revealing how Palenque's architects designed these buildings. A well-preserved inscribed tablet shows a king (most likely Pakal) with a sun-shield emblazoned on his chest, corn growing from his shoulder blades and the sacred quetzal bird atop his head.

Acrópolis Sur In the jungle south of the Grupo de la Cruz is the group of ruins where archaeologists have focused their recent excavations. You may find the area roped off. In Templo XIX in 1999 diggers made the most important Palenque find for several decades – a large 8th-century limestone throne or bench with beautiful carvings of seated figures and hieroglyphic texts. One of the figures is the ruler to whom the temple was dedicated, K'inich Ahkal Mo'Nab III (Chaacal III), the last powerful lord of Palenque, who ascended the throne in 722 and may have ruled for several decades. The throne will eventually be displayed in the Palenque site museum. Interpretation of its carvings will fill big gaps in Palenque's history.

Grupo Norte North of El Palacio are a **ball court** and the handsome buildings of the Northern Group. Crazy Count de Waldeck (see 'Rediscovery of Palenque') lived in the so-called Templo del Conde (Temple of the Count), constructed in 647 AD under Pakal.

Northeastern Groups East of the Grupo Norte the path crosses the Arroyo Otulum. Some 70m beyond the stream, a right fork in the path will take you to **Grupo C**, a set of buildings and plazas on different levels, thought to have been lived in from about 750 to 800 AD. Large trees now grow from some of these buildings.

The main path descends fairly steep steps to **Grupo B**, with several elongated buildings rising from terraces. Also residential, these buildings were thought to have been occu-

pied around 770 to 850 AD; tombs were found beneath them.

The path continues to another residential quarter, the **Grupo de los Murciélagos** (Bat Group), then turns left down to the **Puente Murciélagos** (Bat Bridge), a suspension footbridge across the Arroyo Otulum. The stream here is a series of inviting falls and pools where people sometimes take a dip. If you've brought your bathers this is where to use them, but be discreet, as swimming is discouraged.

Across the bridge and a bit farther downstream, a path goes west to **Grupos 1 & 2**, a short walk uphill. These ruins, only partly uncovered, are in a beautiful jungle setting. The main path continues downriver to the road, which you can follow to the right across a bridge to the museum.

Museo de Sitio Palenque's Site Museum does a fine job of displaying finds from the site and interpreting Palenque's history. Next door is a branch of Casa de las Artesanías de Chiapas, selling some of Chiapas' best handicrafts, and a pleasant but rather overpriced café.

Getting There & Away A paved footpath, some parts shaded, runs beside the road from the Maya head statue all the way to the museum, about 6km.

Colectivos Chambalu, on Allende at Hidalgo, and Transportes Palenque, Allende at 20 de Noviembre, operate combis to the ruins about every 15 minutes from around 6 am to 7 pm daily. The vehicles will pick you up anywhere along the town-to-ruins road, which helps campers and other staying along that road. Fare is US$0.70.

A taxi from town to ruins costs US$4.

Rafting

Viajes Mayasol (see Organized Tours) offers rafting trips of varied difficulty on Chiapas rivers such as the Río Chacamax, a few kilometers south of Palenque, and the Río Usumacinta on the Guatemalan border. The Usumacinta trip includes a visit to the Piedras Negras archaeological site in Guatemala. Prices range from US$20 to US$75.

Organized Tours

Several agencies in Palenque offer transportation packages to Agua Azul, Agua Clara and Misol-Ha, to Bonampak and Yaxchilán and to Flores (Guatemala), for Tikal. See the sections 'To/From Guatemala via Tenosique,' 'Agua Azul, Agua Clara & Misol-Ha' and 'Bonampak, Yaxchilán & the Carretera Fronteriza' for more information. Agencies include:

Colectivos Chambalu (☎ 5-08-67) Hidalgo at Allende

Inter Travel (☎ 5-15-66) Juárez 48

Kim Tours Juárez 27

Na Chan Kan (☎ 5-02-63) Hidalgo at Jiménez

Transportes Palenque Allende at 20 de Noviembre

Shivalva Viajes Mayas (☎ 5-04-11, 800-232-24-00) Juárez at Abasolo, and Merle Green 9, La Cañada

Viajes Kukulcan (☎ 5-15-06) Juárez s/n

Viajes Mayasol (☎ 5-10-06) Juárez 191

Viajes Misol-Ha (☎ 5-04-88) Juárez 103

Viajes Yax-Ha (☎ 5-07-98) Juárez 123

Places to Stay

Many places to stay are in Palenque town but there are others (including campgrounds) along the road to the ruins. Combis will stop anywhere on this road (see the Palenque Ruinas section). Yet other accommodations are on highway 199, south and north of the Maya head.

Places to Stay – Budget

Camping About half a dozen places to camp are strung along the 7.5km road from highway 199 to Palenque Ruinas. One of the first you reach, 3km off highway 199, is the pleasant *La Aldea del Halach-Uinic* (see Posadas & Hotels), where you can camp for US$2 a tent.

Another 1.5km along is *El Panchán*, a group of basic places to stay and eat in a beautiful rain forest setting. At friendly *Restaurant Michol* you can camp for US$1 per person, sling a hammock under a palapa for US$1.50, or rent a hammock for US$2.50. At *Beto's Café* the prices are respectively US$1, US$1 and US$1.50. Beto's has inexpensive food too. At *Margarita & Ed Cabañas*, single/double cabañas with bathroom and mosquito netting cost US$7.50/10. There are more cabañas at *Rakshita's*, which is also an exotically painted meditation center and an inexpensive vegetarian restaurant, serving curries, other Indian fare and sizable breakfasts for US$1.50 to US$2.

It's 700m farther to *Chaac Camping*, which charges US$1.50 per person, or US$2.50 in a rented hammock. There are a few shabby cabañas here for around US$6, and a restaurant-bar advertising a salsa-and-reggae happy hour from 7 to 8 pm.

Probably the best place to camp – certainly the most convenient for the ruins, with the growls of howler monkeys echoing through the jungle – is *Mayabell Hotel Trayler Park*, just 400m from the site museum. The site has no phone but you can book a few days ahead on ☎ 5-05-97 or fax 5-07-67. For US$2 per person you get clean toilet and shower blocks and some shade. There are palapas for slinging hammocks, and hammocks to rent for US$1 (plus a deposit of US$10 or your passport). The extra charge for a vehicle ranges from US$1 to around US$4, depending on size, but you may have to pay extra for electricity. There are also single/double/triple rooms with private bathroom at US$9.50/12.50/15.50 with fan, or US$20/25/30 with air-con. In the pleasant restaurant nothing costs more than US$2.50. Lockers for guests' use cost US$0.50 a day. A taxi from town is US$3.

Posadas & Hotels Best of the rock-bottom cheapies is *Posada Bonampak* (☎ 5-09-25, Domínguez 33), four blocks north of Juárez. No frills here, but rooms are well kept and of decent size, bathrooms are tiled, and prices are only US$4.50 for a single or double with *cama matrimonial*, US$5.50 with twin beds.

Posada Canek (☎ 5-01-50, 20 de Noviembre 43), southwest of El Parque, has largish rooms, some with a few dorm beds for US$4 a person, others functioning as singles/doubles for US$8/10. Most have private toilet but showers are shared. Reception has safes for your valuables.

Posada Charito (☎ 5-01-21, *20 de Noviembre 15*) and *Posada Santo Domingo* (☎ 5-01-46, *20 de Noviembre 119*) have gloomy rooms with fan and shower for around US$6 a double.

You can get a much better room for three or four dollars more. *Hotel Yun-Kax* (☎ 5-07-25, *Corregidora 87*), handily placed between the bus stations and town center, has clean rooms with shower, around a little patio, for US$7/9 with fan or US$15 with air-con. Friendly *Posada Nacha'n Ka'an* (*20 de Noviembre 25*), a block north, offers clean, good-size, new rooms with ample bathrooms for US$8/10, and a café for breakfast. Nearby, *Hotel Kashlan* (☎ 5-02-97, *5 de Mayo 117*) has drab but clean rooms with fan and bath for US$13/15, and nicer air-conditioned rooms for US$20 single or double. There's a handy restaurant too.

Posada Los Ángeles (☎ 5-17-38), on Juárez almost opposite the bus stations, has bare but newish rooms with fan and bathroom for US$7/8, or with air-con for US$18.

Nearer the town center, *Posada Shalom* (☎ 5-09-44, *Juárez 156*) has clean, modern rooms with fan and bathroom for US$8/10. A couple of doors east, *Hotel Nikte-Ha* (☎ 5-09-24, *Juárez 133*) offers small, clean modern rooms with bath, air-con and TV for US$17 single or double. *Hotel Regional* (☎ 5-01-83, *Juárez 119*) has adequate rooms with shower and fan around a small plant-filled courtyard for US$8/10/12.50/15 a single/double/triple/quad.

The relatively new *Posada Kin* (☎ 5-17-14, *Abasolo 1*), south of Juárez, has clean, decent-size rooms with bathroom and fan, on four floors around a small patio, for US$8/10 including light breakfast. At *Hotel Vaca Vieja* (☎ 5-03-88, *5 de Mayo 42*), east of El Parque, clean, spacious doubles with bathroom and fan go for US$10. There's a restaurant too.

Hotel Lacroix (☎ 5-00-14, *Hidalgo 10*), opposite the church near El Parque, has a courtyard with potted tropical plants, and adequate rooms with fan and shower for US$10/12. The murals in the porch are worth a pause – spot the word '*Bienvenidos*'.

North of Juárez, *Hotel Naj K'in* (☎ 5-11-26, *Hidalgo 72*) is a nice, family-run place where rooms with good bathrooms, hot water and fans cost US$8/13. Doubles with air-con are US$18.

La Posada (☎ 5-04-37, *2ª Norte s/n*), in the leafy La Cañada area, north of the Maya head intersection, is a quiet hangout with a grassy courtyard. Posted prices for the clean rooms with fan and bathroom are US$12/20/24 a single/double/triple, but they'll come down several dollars. There's a pizza restaurant here too.

Out on the road to the ruins, some 4km from town and 4.5km from the ruins entrance, is *La Aldea del Halach-Uinic* (☎ 8-91-54, 5-03-09) with simple palapa-roofed cabañas amid green gardens, each containing two rooms costing US$8 single or double. Each room has two beds and two hammocks on a little porch. There's a small, clean pool, clean shared toilets and showers and a restaurant.

Places to Stay – Mid-Range

On Juárez near El Parque, *Hotel Casa de Pakal* (☎ 5-03-93) has small doubles with air-con and private bath for US$18.50. *Hotel Chan-Kah* (☎ 5-03-18, *Juárez 2*), overlooking El Parque, offers three rooms on each floor with a balcony. All rooms have bathroom, fan, air-con and TV and cost US$33 single or double. There's an elevator.

Hotel Palenque (☎ 5-02-58, *5 de Mayo 15*), just east of El Parque, is the town's oldest hotel. It has been spruced up and offers rooms with bathroom and fan for US$15 single or double, or with air-con for US$35 (US$36/37 triple/quadruple). They're set around a pretty garden courtyard.

Several mid-range hotels cluster in the leafy La Cañada area west of the center. *Hotel Maya Tulipanes* (☎ 5-02-01, *800-714-47-10, Cañada 6*) is the most comfortable. Air-conditioned rooms with TV and phone go for US$48 single or double, US$54 triple. There's a small pool and a nice restaurant. On the same street (which has at least three names) is *Hotel Chablis* (☎ 5-08-70, *Merle Green 7*), where large rooms with air-con and fan cost US$20 single or double. There's a video bar for nighttime amusement.

Opposite the Chablis is *Hotel Xibalba* (☎ *5-04-11, Merle Green 9*), with attractive air-conditioned rooms at US$22/24 above Shivalva travel agency and in another building whose entrance is in concrete imitation of a Maya corbel vault.

Hotel La Cañada (☎ *5-01-02, Prolongación Hidalgo 12*), a collection of cottages at the eastern end of the same street, was once a favorite with archaeologists working at the ruins. The large, fan-cooled rooms, many with huge ceramic bathtubs, cost US$17/18. There's a restaurant with set lunch or dinner for US$4.

The *Maya Palenque Hotel* (☎ *5-07-80*), right by the Maya head intersection, has good air-conditioned rooms with two double beds and cable TV for US$48 single or double. There's a pool and a restaurant.

On the road to the ruins, 4km from town, *Hotel Villa Kin-Ha* (☎ *5-05-33*) has palaparoofed duplex concrete cabañas. The rooms aren't big but are pleasant enough, with fan and bathroom for US$40 single or double, US$45 triple. Add US$5 for air-con. The gardens hold a good-size pool and open-sided palapa restaurant.

Places to Stay – Top End

On highway 199, 3.5km south of town, the *Calinda Nututun Palenque* (☎ *5-01-00*) has modern motel-style buildings set in spacious jungle gardens shaded by palm trees. Large air-conditioned rooms with bath cost US$70 single or double. Naturally there's an enticing pool.

Chan-Kah Resort Village (☎ *5-11-00, fax 5-08-20*) on the road to the ruins, 4.5km from town and 4km from the ruins entrance, is among the most attractive lodgings in Palenque. An enormous stone-bound swimming pool, lush jungle gardens, open-sided restaurant and other accoutrements all enhance the handsome wood-and-stone cottages that have generous bathrooms, ceiling fans and air-conditioning, for US$64 single or double.

Places to Eat

Cheapest fare in Palenque is at the taquerías along the eastern side of the park, in front of the church. Try *Los Faroles* or neighboring *Fuente de Sodas* for a plate of tacos at US$2 to US$3.

Mara's has a prime location at Juárez and Independencia facing El Parque, with a handful of sidewalk tables and an abundance of whirring fans inside. Several set lunch and dinner menús – of one or two courses with a drink or dessert – go for US$3 to US$4. Set breakfasts are similarly priced. There's medium-priced à la carte fare too.

Restaurant Maya, at Independencia and Hidalgo on the northwest corner of El Parque, has been going since 1958. The food is standard and the hours long (7 am to 11 pm), with most main dishes costing US$3 to US$5. Breakfasts are sizable.

Restaurant Na Chan-Kan, facing the northeast corner of El Parque, is popular for its excellent pizzas (US$3 to US$5.50) and other fare including two-course set meals with a drink for US$2.50 to US$3.50. Next door, family-run *Restaurant Artemio's* serves antojitos for US$1.50 to US$3, and chicken and meat *filetes* for US$3.

Restaurant Virgo's (*Hidalgo 5*) offers 2nd-story open-air dining half a block west of the park. White pillars, a red-tile roof and plants set the scene. Try the *burritas al aguacate* (US$2), or one of their pasta plates for US$1.50 to US$2. Meat dishes cost around US$3 to US$4. They serve wine too.

Pizza Palenque (*Juárez 168*) has surprisingly good pizzas from US$2.50 to US$7.50.

The organic coffee at little *Café Te-El* (*Hidalgo 68A*) is the best brew in town – just US$0.40 for *americano*, US$0.70 for espresso, US$1.20 for cappuccino.

Getting There & Away

Air Palenque's airport terminal is little more than a shack, but Aerocaribe (☎ *5-06-18*) flies to/from Oaxaca (US$76) and Bahías de Huatulco daily, and Mérida (US$135), Tuxtla Gutiérrez (US$68), Cancún (US$200) and Flores, Guatemala (US$99) three or four days a week.

Bus Buses serving Palenque – especially night buses to/from Mérida – have a bad record for theft. Take special care of your valuables on these buses and don't accept drinks from strangers. Don't leave anything of value in the overhead rack or under seats, and stay alert. Your gear is probably safest in the luggage compartment under the bus, but watch as it is stowed and removed.

Westernmost of the main bus terminals on Juárez is the joint terminal (☎ 5-13-44) of Cristóbal Colón (deluxe, 1st-class and 2nd-class buses) and ADO (1st-class). A block east is Autotransportes Tuxtla Gutiérrez (ATG, 2nd-class), and together half a block farther east are Transportes Rodulfo Figueroa (1st-class) and Transportes Lacandonia (TL, 2nd-class).

It's a good idea to buy your outward ticket a day in advance. Daily departures include:

Campeche – 365km, 5 hours; 4 Colón/ADO (US$10.50 to US$14), 1 ATG (US$11)

Cancún – 870km, 13 hours; 4 Colón/ADO (US$24 to US$34), 2 ATG (US$23)

Chetumal – 495km, 7 hours; 4 Colón/ADO (US$14 to US$19.50), 1 ATG (US$12.50)

Mérida – 545km, 8 hours; 4 Colón/ADO (US$15.50 to US$21), 1 ATG (US$15)

Mexico City (TAPO) – 1010km, 16 hours; 2 ADO (US$39)

Oaxaca – 815km, 15 hours; 1 ADO (US$28)

Ocosingo – 103km, 2½ hours; 10 Colón/ADO (US$3.75 to US$5), 7 Figueroa, 7 ATG and 10 TL (all US$3 to US$4)

Playa del Carmen – 805km, 12 hours; 4 Colón/ADO (US$23 to US$31), 1 ATG (US$21)

San Cristóbal de Las Casas – 190km, 4 hours; 10 Colón/ADO (US$6 to US$8.25), 7 Figueroa (US$6.50), 7 ATG (US$5.50 to US$6.50), 10 TL (US$5)

Tulum – 745km, 11 hours; 4 Colón/ADO (US$21 to US$28), 1 ATG (US$19)

Tuxtla Gutiérrez – 275km, 6 hours; 9 Colón/ADO (US$8.50 to US$11), 7 ATG (US$7.50 to US$9), 7 Figueroa (US$9)

Villahermosa – 140km, 2½ hours; 11 ADO (US$5), 4 ATG (US$4.25)

To/From Guatemala See this chapter's sections 'To/From Guatemala via Tenosique'

(earlier) and Bonampak, Yaxchilán & the Carretera Fronteriza (later).

Getting Around

The airport is a couple of kilometers north of the Maya head statue along highway 199. Yellow Transportación Terrestre cabs from airport to town cost US$3. In town, taxis wait at the northeast corner of El Parque and at the Colón/ADO bus station. They charge US$2 to the airport. You can call a taxi at ☎ 5-01-12.

BONAMPAK, YAXCHILÁN & THE CARRETERA FRONTERIZA

The ancient Maya cities of Bonampak and Yaxchilán, southeast of Palenque, have become much more accessible in the last few years because of a new paved road, the Carretera Fronteriza, which has been built parallel to the Mexico-Guatemala border all the way from Palenque to the Lagos de Montebello.

Both Bonampak, famous for its frescoes, and bigger Yaxchilán, with a peerless setting above the broad Río Usumacinta, are set amid thick tropical rain forest. Bonampak is 148km by road from Palenque; Yaxchilán is 173km by road then about 22km by boat along the Río Usumacinta.

Visiting this area independently is easier than some travel agencies would have you think. Doing so doesn't necessarily work out cheaper than taking a tour, but it allows you time to explore this intriguing region and visit places such as the Lacandón village of Lacanjá Chansayab. You can cross into Guatemala at several points including Frontera Corozal and Benemérito de las Américas.

It's always worth bringing insect repellent.

Organized Tours

See Organized Tours in the Palenque and San Cristóbal de Las Casas for details of agencies.

Bonampak & Yaxchilán Several Palenque travel agencies offer day tours to Bonampak and Yaxchilán for around US$35 per person, transportation only (you pay for entry fees, food and drink). The trip, usually by air-conditioned van or minibus, lasts about 14 hours. Na Chan Kan agency offers a two-day trip for US$65 per person (minimum six) including camping at Lacanjá Chansayab and meals. There are also tours from San Cristóbal de Las Casas.

Guatemala Palenque agencies offer transportation packages to Flores (near Tikal) for US$30 to US$35. The deal usually includes an air-conditioned van or minibus to Frontera Corozal, river launch to Bethel, Guatemala, and public 2nd-class bus from Bethel to Flores – 10 or 11 hours altogether. Some agencies throw in a visit to Bonampak. A few offer Yaxchilán too at an extra cost of around US$25.

Getting There & Away

Autotransportes Río Chancalá at 5 de Mayo 120 in Palenque runs combis to Frontera Corozal four times daily between 6 am and 2.30 pm (three hours, US$4.50), to Benemérito 14 times between 4.30 am to 4.15 pm and to Chajul once (US$8.50). Transportes Comitán-Lagos de Montebello (☎ 934-5-12-60), on Velasco Suárez two blocks west of Palenque market, runs slower big buses to Frontera Corozal at noon (four hours), Benemérito nine times between 4 am and 3.45 pm and to Chajul five times daily. Fares are similar to the combis. The bus company, like many of the destinations it served but unlike the rest of Palenque, was ignoring daylight saving time in summer – meaning that by Palenque time, buses left one hour after posted times.

All the above-mentioned services stop at San Javier (US$3.50), 140km from Palenque, where a side road branches to Bonampak and Lacanjá Chansayab. They also stop at Crucero Corozal, the intersection for Frontera Corozal. There are *comedores* at both intersections.

There are several military checkpoints along the Carretera Fronteriza. The road has been built, among other reasons, to stem the flow of drugs and illegal immigrants into Mexico, to tighten the noose on the Zapatista rebels and to increase tourism.

Bonampak

Bonampak's setting in dense jungle hid it from the outside world until 1946. Stories of how it was revealed are full of mystery, but it seems that Charles (or Carlos or Karl) Frey, apparently a young WWII conscientious objector from the US, and John Bourne, heir to the Singer sewing machine fortune, were the first outsiders to visit the site when Chan Bor, a Lacandón, took them there in February 1946.

Later in 1946 an American photographer, Giles Healey – who had apparently fallen out with Frey and Bourne during a 1945 expedition to film the Lacandones – was also led to the site by Chan Bor and found the Templo de las Pinturas with its famous murals. Frey drowned when his canoe capsized on another expedition to Bonampak in 1949.

The Bonampak site spreads over 2.4 sq km but all the main ruins stand around the rectangular Gran Plaza. At different periods Bonampak was an enemy and an ally of more powerful Yaxchilán. The major surviving monuments were built under Bonampak's greatest ruler, Chan Muan II, who took the throne in 776 AD at a time of alliance with Yaxchilán. He was a nephew of

BONAMPAK

To Site Entrance

0 25 50 m
0 25 50 yards

Edificio 15

Gran Plaza

Stele 1

Edificio 1 (Templo de las Pinturas)

Stele 3   Stele 2   Edificio 17

Edificio 3

Edificio 2

the Yaxchilán ruler Escudo Jaguar II and was married to Yaxchilán royalty. The 6m-high Stele 1 in the Gran Plaza represents Chan Muan at the height of his reign. He also features in Stelae 2 and 3 on the Acrópolis, which rises from the south end of the plaza. Eight small temples near the top of the Acrópolis are Bonampak's most intriguing architectural feature seen from outside.

But the masterly frescoes painted for Chan Muan *inside* the Templo de las Pinturas (Edificio 1) on the Acrópolis steps are

what give Bonampak its fame (and its name: Bonampak means 'Painted Walls' in Yucatecan Maya and was coined by the 20th-century Mayanist Sylvanus Morley).

Diagrams outside the temple help interpret these murals, which despite restoration in the 1990s would otherwise be hard to understand. Room 1, on the left as you face the temple, shows the consecration of an infant heir – probably Chan Muan II's son – who is seen held in arms toward the top of the right end of the room's south wall, which faces you as you enter. Lavish celebrations for this

The Lacandón Jungle & the Lacandones

Mexico harbors 10% of the earth's living species, on 1.4% of the earth's land. The Selva Lacandona (Lacandón Jungle) in eastern Chiapas occupies just 0.25% (a quarter of one per cent) of Mexico. Yet it contains more than 4300 plant species, about 17% of the Mexican total; 800 types of butterfly, 44% of the national total; at least 345 birds, 33% of the total; and at least 114 land mammals, 27% of the Mexican total. Among these are such emblematic creatures as the jaguar, red macaw, toucan, howler monkey, spider monkey, ocelot, tapir and harpy eagle.

This great fund of natural resources, genetic diversity and protection against global warming is the southwestern end of a 30,000-sq-km corridor of tropical rain forest stretching into northern Guatemala, Belize and the south of the Yucatán Peninsula. But the Selva Lacandona is going, fast. In the 1950s it spread over 15,000 sq km from the edge of the Chiapas highlands to the Río Usumacinta. Today perhaps just 5000 sq km remains (some estimates are as low as 3000 sq km). Most of that is in protected areas such as the Reserva de la Biósfera Montes Azules (3300 sq km).

Those 10,000 vanished square kilometers of jungle have mostly been turned into *milpas* (cornfields) and cattle pasture by some 150,000 land-hungry settlers from Chiapas and Mexico. A more recent threat has been the Zapatista conflict as Mexican army soldiers have built camps and roads in and around Montes Azules and have been accused of illegal logging, hunting and trapping.

The ancient Maya developed major cities such as Yaxchilán and Bonampak in the Selva Lacandona. When the Spanish came, the jungle was probably inhabited by Chol people, some of whom managed to survive unconquered in their forest hideaway until the late 17th century. In the face of conquest and new diseases, the Lacandón Choles then vanished from history. (The modern-day Choles, around 170,000 strong, live mainly in northern Chiapas.)

In the late 19th century, loggers started moving up the Río Usumacinta in search of mahogany and cedar. (The logging camps were infamous for the cruel treatment of their indigenous workers that took place within, a horror described by B Traven in his 'Jungle' novels – see Books in Facts for the Visitor). Loggers and explorers reported encounters with small, scattered groups of people in the jungle. These were the people known today as the Lacandón. They are thought to have reached the Selva Lacandona in the 18th century, fleeing the Spanish in the Yucatán or Guatemala or the British in Belize. They avoided permanent contact with the outside world until the 1950s. Their language is related to Yucatán Maya and they call themselves Hach Winik, the True People.

event are depicted elsewhere in the room. The central Room 2 shows a battle on the south wall and, on the north wall, the torture (by fingernail removal) and sacrifice of prisoners – a scene presided over by Chan-Muan II in jaguar-skin battle dress. A severed head lies on one of the steps below him, beside the foot of a sprawling captive. Room 3 shows a celebratory dance on the Acrópolis steps by lords wearing huge headdresses – and on its east wall three white-robed women puncture their tongues in a ritual bloodletting. By one interpretation, the prisoner sacrifices, the bloodletting and the dance may all have been part of the ceremonies surrounding the new heir – and the wars of Room 2 may have been conducted to gain the necessary captives.

The infant prince probably never came to rule Bonampak; the place was abandoned before the murals were finished, as Classic Maya civilization imploded.

The site is open 8 am to 4.45 pm daily (US$2, free Sunday and holidays). Refrescos and snacks are sold at a house by the entrance.

The Lacandón Jungle & the Lacandones

You may have encountered Lacandones if you have visited Na Bolom in San Cristóbal, where they are regular visitors, or the ruins at Palenque, where they sell quivers of arrows and are readily recognizable in their traditional long white tunics and with their long black hair cut in a straight fringe.

There are about 700 Lacandones. Most now live in the village of Lacanjá Chansayab near Bonampak, just outside the Montes Azules Biosphere Reserve. They congregated here in 1979 after the reserve was declared. At the same time many Chol and Tzeltal settlers gathered in two other new towns near the reserve's eastern fringe – the Choles in Frontera Corozal and the Tzeltals in Nueva Palestina (also called Velasco Suárez). These three groups jointly administer an area of over 6000 sq km called the Comunidad Lacandona, which has a big overlap with the Montes Azules and Lacantún biosphere reserves.

The first waves of settlers deforested the northern third of the Selva Lacandona by about 1960. Another badly deforested zone is the far eastern area called Marqués de Comillas, where settlers from all over Mexico have streamed in since the 1970s. Also badly deforested is the selva's western portion, Las Cañadas, between Ocosingo and the Montes Azules reserve. This zone, one of the main destinations of chiapaneco settlers in the 1950s, '60s and '70s, is the main center of support for the Zapatistas. Many settlers here, as elsewhere in the Lacandón, found that their new land deteriorated fast. Cleared jungle makes a fertile milpa for a couple of years but then yields rapidly drop. The response of many was to sow grass and put cattle on it. Within a few years the grass would turn to weeds and the former jungle was useless, leaving the settlers little better off than before.

Traditional Lacandón agriculture, by contrast, makes it possible to live almost indefinitely off small areas of land. Leaving some plots fallow allows land to regenerate, and many varied crops are planted under a canopy of big trees that are not felled. But like other traditional Lacandón ways, these methods are threatened by the onslaught of modernity. The past four decades have wrought more changes in Lacandón life than the previous several centuries. Few Lacandones now wear their traditional tunics; few stick to the Mayan religion or social customs that were common until recently. Selling crafts to tourists has become the major source of income for many Lacandones.

There seems little to stop the Selva Lacandona from continuing to be cut down. Sometimes logging has been banned, and attempts have been made to slow immigration to the area. But steady erosion of the jungle continues.

Places to Stay The nearest place to stay is *Camping Margarito*, 9km from Bonampak at the Lacanjá Chansayab turnoff. It costs US$1 to pitch your tent in their grassy camping area or US$4 to rent one, and US$2 to hang your hammock under their palapa or US$3 to rent one. Meals are only sometimes available.

Getting There & Away Bonampak is 12km from San Javier on the Carretera Fronteriza. The first 3km, to the Lacanjá Chansayab turnoff, is paved; the rest is good gravel/dirt road through the forest. On foot, you can opt for a jungle path from the Lacanjá Chansayab turnoff onward (about three hours). Camping Margarito at the turnoff should be able to supply a guide for about US$6. A taxi from San Javier to Bonampak and back, with time to visit the ruins, will cost around US$8. You may have to wait a while at San Javier before one turns up, however. Hitching is possible.

Lacanjá Chansayab
• pop 500 • elev 320m

Just 12km from Bonampak is the largest village of the indigenous Lacandón people, Lacanjá Chansayab. This scattered settlement, with an inviting river pool for bathing, was founded around 1980 when the majority of Lacandones, who had previously lived scattered around the Lacandón Jungle, settled here. At least four villagers have set up simple *'campings'* where you can pitch a tent and/or rent a hammock – ask for Carlos Cham Bor Kin near the entrance to the village, or Kin Bor, Vicente or Manuel. Vicente, for one, has a wooden building with hammocks already slung. You pay around US$1 to pitch a tent or US$2 to rent a hammock. The campings should be able to provide a meal or two for a small number of visitors but bring food supplies if you plan to stay more than a night. Your hosts will probably be able to cook for you. Camping Margarito (see Bonampak) is also nearby.

Villagers can guide you to Bonampak (around US$10) and to other places of interest in the nearby forests such as the little-explored Maya ruins of Lacanjá, the 2.5km-long lake Laguna Lacanjá or the Cascadas Lacanjá waterfalls.

Several villagers make and sell rustic but attractive pottery, wood carvings, seed necklaces, arrows and drums.

Getting There & Away Lacanjá Chansayab is 6.5km by paved road from San Javier on the Carretera Fronteriza. A taxi is US$4 (US$1 if you can get it on a colectivo basis) but you might have to walk or hitch.

Frontera Corozal
• pop 5000 • elev 200m

This spread-out, edgy frontier town (also called Frontera Echeverría) stretches back from the southwest bank of the Río Usumacinta, 15km by paved road from Crucero Corozal junction on the Carretera Fronteriza. The broad Usumacinta, flowing swiftly between jungle-covered banks, forms the Mexico-Guatemala border here, and Frontera Corozal is an essential stepping-stone both for the ruins of Yaxchilán and for the village of Bethel on the Guatemalan bank. Bethel is a departure point for buses to Flores, near Tikal.

Corozal's townspeople are mainly indigenous Choles who moved from northern Chiapas to the Lacandón Jungle in the 1950s, '60s and '70s. After the Montes Azules Biosphere Reserve was declared in 1978, the Chol settlers agreed to congregate outside the reserve in Frontera Corozal.

Long, outboard-powered launches come and go from the river embarcadero, below a cluster of wooden buildings that includes several inexpensive *comedores*. Almost everything you'll need is on the paved street leading inland from here – including the immigration office, a couple of hundred meters along, where you should hand in/ obtain a tourist card if you're leaving for/ arriving from Guatemala. There's a telephone caseta in the restaurant of Escudo Jaguar (see Places to Stay).

Places to Stay A short distance along the road back from the river is easily the most comfortable accommodation, *Escudo Jaguar*

(☎ 5-201-64-40, 5-201-64-41 – *precede these satellite phone numbers with the regular long-distance code, 01).* Sizable, spotless rooms in pink palapa-roofed huts, with fans, bathrooms, mosquito nets and screens cost US$15/30, and there's a good restaurant (main dishes US$4 to US$6), which can close as early as 7.30 pm. You may also be able to camp here.

A couple of hundred meters farther inland along the road, *Posada Yhany* has primitive rooms for US$2/4, with fan and shared toilet. About three blocks farther back, then one block east, the *Yax Lum* community association and neighboring *Posada Tumbalá* have better posada rooms, at US$2 or US$3 with fan.

Getting There & Away Buses and combis stop two blocks east of Yax Lum at a small park beside the Auditorio Comunal. Ask directions from there to the accommodations or embarcadero.

If you can't get a bus or combi to Frontera Corozal, try getting one to Crucero Corozal, 20 minutes from San Javier, where you should be able to find a ride – maybe in the back of a *camioneta* (pickup) for US$1.

The last combi from Frontera Corozal to Palenque leaves at 3 pm.

To/From Guatemala Fast river launches *(lanchas)* go from Frontera Corozal to the village of Bethel, on the Guatemalan bank of the Usumacinta 40 minutes upstream.

Ask at the Contratación de Lanchas office in Escudo Jaguar (see Places to Stay), open 8 am to 2 pm daily, or try going directly to the boat people at the riverside. The regular cost for up to four people in a boat is US$37.50; for five to 10 people it's US$50. It's possible to get bicycles, even motorcycles, on the launches.

Second-class Guatemalan buses leave Bethel for Flores at 12.30 and 2.30 pm (subject to change). The trip is a bumpy 4½ hours for around US$7.

Yaxchilán

Yaxchilán is special because of its marvelous jungle setting above a loop of the Usumacinta. Archaeologically, it's famed for its ornamented building façades and roof combs, and stone lintels carved with conquest and ceremonial scenes. Don't forget to look at the undersides of the lintels, which often bear the most important carvings.

Conquests and alliances made Yaxchilán one of the most important cities in the Usumacinta region by the 7th century AD. It peaked in power and splendor between 681 and 800 under the rulers Escudo Jaguar I (Shield Jaguar I, 681-742), Pájaro Jaguar IV (Bird Jaguar IV, 752-768) and Escudo Jaguar II (772-800). Yaxchilán's inscriptions tell more about this 'Jaguar' dynasty than is known of almost any other Mayan ruling clan – but many of the important carvings are now in the Museo Nacional de Antropología in Mexico City and the British Museum in London. The names by which the rulers are known come from the hieroglyphs representing them: the shield-and-jaguar symbol appears on many Yaxchilán buildings and stelae. Pájaro Jaguar IV's hieroglyph is a small jungle cat with feathers on the back and a bird superimposed on the head. Yaxchilán was abandoned around 810 AD.

The site is open 8 am to 4.45 pm daily (US$2, free Sunday and holidays). Refrescos are sold at a shack near the river landing.

As you walk toward the ruins, a signed path to the right leads up to the Pequeña Acrópolis, a group of ruins on a small hilltop. You can visit this later at the end of a circuit of the site. Continuing, you soon reach the labyrinthine passages of El Laberinto (Edificio 19), built between 742 and 752 during the interregnum between Escudo Jaguar I and Pájaro Jaguar IV. A flashlight (torch) is a big help in finding your way through this complicated two-level building. You emerge at the northwest end of the Gran Plaza. Signs in three languages including English explain what most of Yaxchilán's buildings were. Though it's hard to imagine anyone here ever wanting to be any hotter than they already were, Edificio 17 was apparently a sweathouse. About halfway along the plaza, Stele 1, flanked by weathered sculptures of a crocodile and a jaguar, shows Pájaro Jaguar IV in a ceremony that took

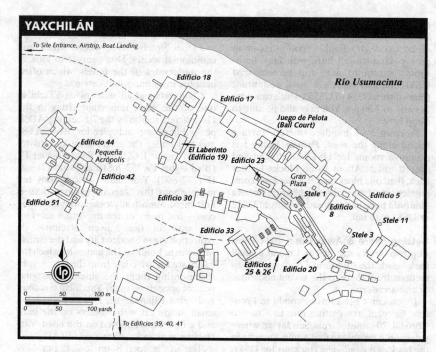

YAXCHILÁN

To Site Entrance, Airstrip, Boat Landing

Edificio 18

Edificio 17

Río Usumacinta

Juego de Pelota
(Ball Court)

Edificio 44

Pequeña
Acrópolis

El Laberinto
(Edificio 19) Edificio 23

Gran
Plaza

Edificio 42

Edificio 30

Stele 1

Edificio 5

Edificio
8

Edificio 51

Stele 11

Edificio 33

Stele 3

Edificios
25 & 26 Edificio 20

0   50   100 m
0   50   100 yards

To Edificios 39, 40, 41

place in 761. Edificio 20, from the time of
Escudo Jaguar II, was the last significant
structure built at Yaxchilán. Stele 11, now at
the northeast corner of the Gran Plaza, was
originally found in front of Edificio 40. The
bigger of the two figures visible on it is
Pájaro Jaguar IV.

A grand stairway climbs from Stele 1 to
Edificio 33, the best-preserved building at
Yaxchilán, with about half its roof comb remaining. The final step in front of the building is carved with many ball-game scenes.
There are fine relief carvings on the lintels'
undersides. Inside is a decapitated statue of
Pájaro Jaguar IV; he lost his head to treasure-
seeking 19th-century timber-cutters.

At the right-hand end of the clearing
behind Edificio 33, a path leads into the
trees. A short distance along this, a sign 'Edificios 39, 40, 41' points up to the left. Follow
this, going left at a fork after about 100m,
and in 10 minutes – mostly uphill – you
reach the three buildings, on a hilltop. You

can climb to the top of Edificio 41 for great
views across the top of the jungle, through
which howler monkey roars will probably
be echoing.

Getting There & Away You can reach
Yaxchilán by chartered plane from places
such as Palenque and Ocosingo, or by boat
from Frontera Corozal.

River launches take 40 minutes for the
downstream trip from Frontera Corozal, and
one hour returning upstream. Ask at the
Contratación de Lanchas office at Escudo
Jaguar (see Places to Stay under Frontera
Corozal). The roundtrip price for a whole
boat, holding 10 people, is US$62.50 includ-
ing two or three hours at Yaxchilán. If there
are only one or two of you, you might
manage to reduce this to US$50, but it's
better to try to join with a tour group. These
come most days, sometimes several of them,
arriving at Frontera Corozal as early as
8.30 am. You can try asking at Contratación

de Lanchas, or talking to the boat people by the river in the morning; in either case they may insist you obtain the group guide's agreement first. Expect to pay US$10 to US$15 per person this way.

Carry your passport and tourist card with you. Although you won't be leaving Mexico, your papers will probably be checked as you leave Frontera Corozal.

Benemérito de las Américas
• pop 6000 • elev 200m

South of Frontera Corozal you soon enter the area in Chiapas' far eastern corner known as Marqués de Comillas (for its Spanish former landowner). After oil explorers opened tracks into this jungle region in the 1970s, land-hungry settlers poured in from all around Mexico. Now it's one of the most deforested parts of the Lacandón Jungle. Cattle and logging have made many of the settlers richer than they could have hoped to be back home. Marqués de Comillas is also a route for drugs entering Mexico. You may receive warnings about violence associated with this.

The main town is Benemérito de las Américas, on the bank of the Río Salinas, an Usumacinta tributary that forms the Mexico-Guatemala border here. It has traces of 'Wild West' atmosphere but no attractions except as a staging post.

The main street is a 1.5km-long stretch of the highway. A side street beside the Farmacia Arco Iris, toward the north end of town, leads 1.25km to the river. About 400m down this street is the Clínica/Hospital de Campo IMSS, with an Urgencias (Emergencies) department. There's a telephone caseta in Minisuper Marisol on the highway. Benemérito has no immigration post; pick up or hand in Mexican tourist cards at Frontera Corozal.

Places to Stay The *Hotel de Las Américas* (☎ 800-029-40-60), by the highway at the south end of town, already looks dilapidated although they haven't finished building it. But the rooms, with bathroom and fan, are all right, costing US$10/12 a single/double. We found the bathroom window couldn't be

closed securely, so we blocked the bathroom door with the (heavy) bed.

The alternative is one of the very basic posadas by the highway around the middle of town. *Hospedaje Siempre Viva* beside the Autotransportes Río Chancalá combi terminal has rooms with fan at US$4 (single or double) or US$5 (double).

Getting There & Away Autotransportes Río Chancalá has its combi terminal on the highway toward the north end of town. Combis run to Palenque about 14 times daily (the last at 4 pm) and Chajul once. There's a taxi stand (☎ 800-029-41-23) next door. The Transportes Comitán-Lagos de Montebello bus stop is about 350m south. Buses leave for Palenque nine times between 5 am and 2 pm and for Chajul five times between 6.30 am and 3 pm.

To/From Guatemala You can hire a lancha for around US$100 to US$150 to take you up the Río Salinas and its tributary the Río de la Pasión to Sayaxché (Guatemala) in three to four hours. On the way, there's Guatemalan immigration at Pipiles. Infrequent cargo boats are cheaper (around US$6 to US$8 per person) and take all day.

An alternative is to take a lancha a short distance downriver to Laureles on the Guatemalan side, for about US$10. From Laureles a bus reportedly leaves at 2 am for the five-hour ride to Sayaxché.

Sayaxché has lodgings and buses to Flores.

Benemérito de las Américas to Lagos de Montebello

South of Benemérito the Carretera Fronteriza heads 60km south before turning due west for the 150km stretch to Tziscao in the Lagos de Montebello.

At the time of research, about 30km of the road, from about 5km west of the Chajul turnoff to the Flor de Café turnoff, remained unpaved (but was being worked on). Public transportation from the east ran as far as the Chajul turnoff, and from the west as far as Ixcán, about 15km east of the Flor de Café turnoff. It's not too difficult to get lifts along the in-between bit. A bus from Benemérito to the Chajul turnoff (Crucero Chajul) takes 2½ hours for US\$4. Combis or buses between Ixcán and Comitán (the Línea Comitán-Montebello bus station) run about hourly: the last departure from Ixcán can be as early as 2 pm. From Ixcán it takes 2½ hours (US\$3.50) as far as Tziscao, 3½ hours (US\$4) to Comitán.

By the time you travel, the whole Carretera Fronteriza may be paved, with public transportation going right through between Palenque and Comitán. On the other hand bridges may be down or fords unpassable. The only sure way to find out if it's passable is to travel it!

East of roughly Ixcán you're passing through jungle or semicleared jungle, crossing several tropical rivers. West of Ixcán starts the climb of over 1000m up to the much cooler, pine-clad highlands around the Lagos de Montebello. There are quite a lot of villages along the way, nearly all founded since the 1960s.

COMITÁN
• pop 62,300 • elev 1635m ☎ 9

Comitán, a pleasant, orderly town with what must be the cleanest streets in Mexico, is the jumping-off point for the Lagos de Montebello and the last place of any size as you travel highway 190 south to the Guatemalan border.

The first Spanish settlement in the area, San Cristóbal de los Llanos, was set up in 1527. Today the town is officially called Comitán de Domínguez, after Belisario Domínguez, a local doctor who was a national senator during the presidency of Victoriano Huerta. Domínguez had the cheek to speak out in 1913 against Huerta's record of political murders and was himself murdered for his pains.

Orientation
Comitán is set on hilly terrain, with a wide, attractive central plaza. North-south streets are Avenidas and east-west ones are Calles.

Information
Tourist Offices The municipal tourist office (☎ 632-19-31), upstairs in the Palacio Munic-

ipal on the north side of the main plaza, is open 9 am to 3 pm and 6 to 8 pm, Monday to Friday. The Delegación (Chiapas state) tourist office is a few doors east.

Consulates The Guatemalan consulate (☎ 632-04-91), at 1ª Calle Sur Pte 26, is open 8 am to 4.30 pm Monday to Friday.

Money There's a branch of Banamex, with an ATM, at the Colón bus station. See the Comitán map for other banks and ATMs.

Post & Communications The post office, at 3ª Avenida Pte Norte 5, is open 8 am to 3 pm Monday to Friday, 9 am to 1 pm Saturday. Pay phones and telephone casetas are dotted around the central area. Café Inter Net, at Local 12, Pasaje Morales, offers email and Internet access for US\$1.25 a half hour or US\$2 an hour. It is open 9 am to 2 pm and 4 to 8 pm, Monday to Saturday.

Things to See & Do
The **Casa de la Cultura**, on the southeast corner of the plaza, includes an exhibition gallery and auditorium. You can walk through from it to the small **Museo Arqueológico de Comitán**, with local artifacts going back to 700 BC – open 10 am to 5 pm Tuesday to Sunday (free). The misshapen pre-Hispanic skulls on display – deliberately deformed (or beautified, in the ancients' eyes) by squeezing infants' heads between two boards – make you wonder what kind of thoughts could have taken shape in such distorted brains.

Casa Museo Dr Belisario Domínguez, the martyr-hero's family home, is now a museum providing fascinating insights into medical practices and the life of the professional classes in early-20th-century Comitán. It's at Avenida Central Sur 35, half a block from the main plaza – open 10 am to 6.45 pm Tuesday to Saturday, 9 am to 12.45 pm Sunday (US\$0.50).

Places to Stay
Comitán has several cheap posadas with small, often dingy and severely plain rooms. One of the better ones is *Posada Primavera*

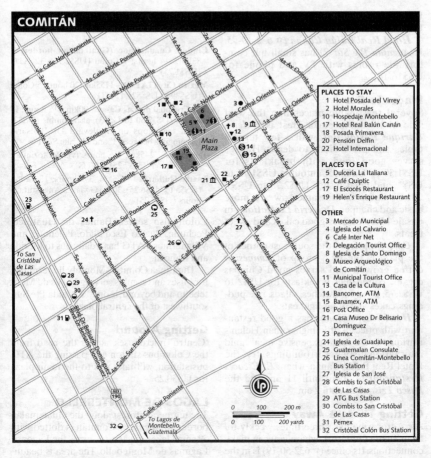

COMITÁN

To San Cristóbal de Las Casas

Main Plaza

To Lagos de Montebello, Guatemala

PLACES TO STAY
1 Hotel Posada del Virrey
2 Hotel Morales
10 Hospedaje Montebello
17 Hotel Real Balún Canán
18 Posada Primavera
20 Pensión Delfín
22 Hotel Internacional

PLACES TO EAT
5 Dulcería La Italiana
12 Café Quiptic
17 El Escocés Restaurant
19 Helen's Enrique Restaurant

OTHER
3 Mercado Municipal
4 Iglesia del Calvario
6 Café Inter Net
7 Delegación Tourist Office
8 Iglesia de Santo Domingo
9 Museo Arqueológico de Comitán
11 Municipal Tourist Office
13 Casa de la Cultura
14 Bancomer, ATM
15 Banamex, ATM
16 Post Office
21 Casa Museo Dr Belisario Domínguez
23 Pemex
24 Iglesia de Guadalupe
25 Guatemalan Consulate
26 Línea Comitán-Montebello Bus Station
27 Iglesia de San José
28 Combis to San Cristóbal de Las Casas
29 ATG Bus Station
30 Combis to San Cristóbal de Las Casas
31 Pemex
32 Cristóbal Colón Bus Station

0 100 200 m
0 100 200 yards

(☎ *632-01-79, Calle Central Pte 4*), a few steps west of the main plaza. It charges US$4/6 for dark singles/doubles with shared bathrooms, and US$10/12 for one room with private bathroom. ***Hospedaje Montebello*** (☎ *632-35-72, 1ª Calle Norte Pte 10*) has clean rooms around a courtyard for US$5, with bathroom.

Hotel Morales (☎ *632-04-36, Avenida Central Norte 8*) resembles an aircraft hangar, with small rooms perched round an upstairs walkway, but it's clean and rooms with bath cost US$9/10. There are renovated rooms with color TV, too, for US$16.

Pensión Delfín (☎ *632-00-13*), on the west side of the main plaza, has nice renovated rooms with TV and bath for US$12/15/20 a single/double/triple, and unrenovated but still spacious rooms for US$8/12/15, plus a pleasant rear courtyard.

Hotel Internacional (☎ *632-01-10, Avenida Central Sur 16*), a block from the plaza, has comfy singles/doubles/triples for US$17/19/23. Also pleasant is ***Hotel Posada del Virrey*** (☎ *632-18-11, Avenida Central Norte 13*), which has small rooms surrounding a courtyard painted purple and white, with a fountain. Rooms, with TV, cost

TABASCO & CHIAPAS

US$15.50/18.50 for singles/doubles, or US$24 with two double beds.

Hotel Real Balún Canán (☎ 632-10-95, *1ª Avenida Pte Sur 7)* has small but comfortable rooms with TV and phone for US$16/18/22.

Places to Eat

Several reasonable places line the west side of the main plaza. Best is *Helen's Enrique Restaurant*, with a few terrace tables and pretensions to decor. Helen's serves good food, with breakfasts for US$1.50 to US$2.75, antojitos US$1.75 to US$3, and meat dishes US$2.75 to US$5. Other places in the same row are more basic and cheaper. *Dulcería La Italiana* in Pasaje Morales does good cakes and sweet treats.

Café Quiptic on the southeast corner of the plaza is run by a group of *campesino* coffee growers and serves good Chiapas organic coffee, plus breakfasts for US$2 to US$2.75, good sandwiches, salads, rice puddings, cakes and other light eats.

Hotel Internacional has a good restaurant with prices a little higher than Helen's Enrique. For a more expensive meal amid international-style surroundings try the Hotel Real Balún Canán, where *El Escocés Restaurant* is open until 11 pm and the *Disco Tzisquirin* until 2 am.

Getting There & Away

Air Aerocaribe flies three times weekly to/from Tuxtla Gutiérrez, where you can make connections. Its office (☎ 632-50-19) is in the Hotel Internacional.

Bus Comitán is 90km southeast down the Pan-American Highway from San Cristóbal, and 83km north of Ciudad Cuauhtémoc. The bus stations of Colón (deluxe, 1st class and 2nd class, ☎ 632-09-80) and Autotransportes Tuxtla Gutiérrez (ATG, 2nd class, ☎ 632-10-44) are on the Pan-American Highway, which passes north-south through the western part of town, about a 20-minute walk from the main plaza. The highway here is named Boulevard Dr Belisario Domínguez and

called simply 'El Bulevar.' Daily departures include:

Ciudad Cuauhtémoc (Guatemalan border) – 83km, 1¼ hours; 7 Colón (US$2.75), 12 ATG (US$1.75)

Mexico City (TAPO) – 1155km, 20 hours; 5 Colón (US$39 to US$52), 1 ATG

San Cristóbal de Las Casas – 90km, 1½ hours; 18 Colón (US$2.50 to US$3), also combis (US$2) from two stops on Boulevard Dr Belisario Domínguez between 1ª and 2ª Calle Sur Pte

Tapachula – 245km, 5½ hours (via Motozintla); seven Colón (US$7.25), 2 ATG

Tuxtla Gutiérrez – 175km, 3½ hours; 18 Colón (US$5 to US$6.25), 30 ATG via La Angostura, 3 hours (US$3.25)

Colón also serves Bahías de Huatulco, Pochutla, Puerto Escondido, Palenque and Villahermosa; ATG has a daily bus to Mérida and Cancún.

The Línea Comitán-Montebello terminal, for buses and combis serving Lagos de Montebello and beyond, is on 2ª Avenida Pte Sur, southwest of the central plaza.

Getting Around

'Centro' microbuses, across the road from the Colón bus station and passing the ATG bus station, will take you to the main plaza for US$0.25.

LAGOS DE MONTEBELLO

The temperate forest along the Guatemalan border southeast of Comitán is dotted with 59 small lakes of varied colors – the Lagos or Lagunas de Montebello. The area is beautiful, refreshing, quiet and not hard to reach. Little-used vehicle tracks through the forest provide some good walks. Some Mexican weekenders come down here in their cars, but the rest of the time you'll probably see only resident villagers and a handful of visitors. At one edge of the lake district are the Mayan ruins of Chinkultic.

Orientation

The paved road to Montebello turns east off highway 190 16km south of Comitán, just before the town of La Trinitaria. It passes

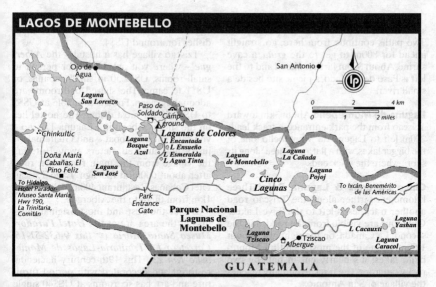

LAGOS DE MONTEBELLO

Chinkultic after 30km, and enters the forest and the Parque Nacional Lagunas de Montebello 5km beyond. At the park entrance (no fee) the road splits. One road continues 3km north between lakes to end at Laguna Bosque Azul. The other heads east, passing turnoffs for several more lakes and the village of Tziscao (9km). Beyond Tziscao it becomes the Carretera Fronteriza, continuing east to Ixcán and ultimately Palenque (see the Benemérito de las Américas to Lagos de Montebello section, earlier in this chapter).

Chinkultic

These dramatically sited ruins lie 2km north of La Trinitaria-Montebello road. The access road is paved.

Chinkultic was on the far western edge of the ancient Mayan area. Dates carved here extend from 591 to 897 AD – the last of which is nearly a century after the latest dates at Palenque or Yaxchilán. Those years span Chinkultic's peak period. Of the 200 mounds scattered over a wide area, only a few have been cleared, but they're worth the effort.

The track brings you first to a gate. Here, take the path to the left, which curves around to the right. On the hill to the right of this path stands one of Chinkultic's major structures, E23. The path reaches a long ball court where several stelae – some carved with human figures – lie on their sides, some under thatch shelters.

Follow the track back to the gate and turn left until you can spot a few stone mounds to the right. On the hillside that soon comes into view is the partly restored temple, El Mirador. The path goes over a stream and steeply up to El Mirador, where there are fine views over the surrounding lakes and down into a big 50m-deep *cenote*.

The Lakes

Lagunas de Colores The road straight on from the park entrance leads through the Lagunas de Colores, whose hues range from turquoise to deep green. The first of these lakes, on the right after about 2km, is Laguna Agua Tinta. Then on the left come Laguna Esmeralda and Laguna Encantada, with Laguna Ensueño on the right opposite Encantada. The fifth and biggest is Laguna Bosque Azul, on the left where the paved road ends.

TABASCO & CHIAPAS

Boys will probably offer you a ride on small horses from the end of the paved road. Two paths continue from here; go straight ahead for 800m to get to the *gruta*, a cave shrine. About 300m farther ahead and to the left is Paso de Soldado, a picnic site beside a small river.

Laguna de Montebello About 3km toward Tziscao from the park entrance, a track leads 200m left to Laguna de Montebello, one of the bigger lakes, with a flat, open area along its shore where the track ends.

Cinco Lagunas & Laguna Pojoj Three kilometers farther along the Tziscao road another track leads left to the 'Five Lakes.' Only four are visible from the road, and the second, La Cañada, on the right after about 1.5km, is one of the most beautiful Montebello lakes; it's nearly cut in half by two rocky outcrops. The track eventually reaches the village of San Antonio.

One kilometer farther along the Tziscao road from the Cinco Lagunas turnoff, a track leads 1km north to clear, deep blue Laguna Pojoj, with an island in the middle.

Laguna Tziscao This lake comes into view on the right 1km farther along the main road. The junction for Tziscao village, a pleasant, spread-out place, is a little farther, again on the right.

Places to Stay & Eat

A few hundred meters past the Chinkultic turnoff, you can rent a rustic cabin and eat good, inexpensive food at *Doña María Cabañas*, also called *La Orquidea*, beside the road. The elderly owner, Señora María Domínguez Figueroa, has been looking after travelers since the 1930s. She has also given a lot of help to Guatemalan refugees in the area. For the cabins, which have electric light but no running water, you pay US$1.50 per person; dinner is US$2.50, breakfast US$2. Next door is *El Pino Feliz*, a newer, rival set of cabañas charging US$2.50 per person.

Inside the national park, you can camp for free at *Laguna Bosque Azul*. There are cabañas here too, costing around US$2.50,

and toilets. *Bosque Azul Restaurant* serves eggs for US$2 and *chiles rellenos* or meat dishes for around US$4.

Tziscao village has a hostel – the *Albergue* – where you pay US$3 per person in small rooms, US$2.50 in small cabañas, or US$1 to camp. The shared bathrooms are adequately clean. Food is available at US$2 to US$2.50 for most dishes. The hostel lies on the shore of beautiful Laguna Tziscao – you can rent a rowboat – and Guatemala is just a few hundred meters away. Entering the village from the main road, turn right after about 600m at the sign 'Lago Tziscao Otel Cabañas Restaurant 400m.' It's actually 1km from there to the Albergue.

By far the best and most original lodgings in the area are at the *Hotel Parador-Museo Santa María* (☎ /fax 9-632-51-16, *Carretera La Trinitaria-Lagos de Montebello Km 22*). This 19th-century hacienda, restored and decorated with period furniture and art, has six rooms at US$40 single or double. Its chapel has been turned into a religious art museum. There's a restaurant serving chiapaneco and international cuisine, and billiards in the bar. A sign points to 'Museo de Santa María' 22km from La Trinitaria on the Montebello road. It's 1.5km from highway to hotel.

Getting There & Away

If you wish, it's possible to make a quick day trip to Chinkultic and the lakes from San Cristóbal de Las Casas, either by public transportation or tour.

Buses and combis to the Lagos de Montebello go from the yard of Línea Comitán-Montebello (☎ 9-632-08-75) on 2ª Avenida Pte Sur in Comitán. There are a number of different destinations, so make sure you get one that's going your way. Combis to Laguna Bosque Azul (US$1.50) run every few minutes until about 6.30 pm; to Tziscao (US$1.50) they go every 30 minutes, 5 am to 5 pm. Combis and buses bound for Ixcán or Flor de Café also pass Tziscao. All these will let you off at the turnoffs for Hotel Parador-Museo Santa María or Chinkultic, or at Doña María Cabañas (US$1.25).

The last vehicles back to Comitán from Tziscao leave at around 5 pm, and from Laguna Bosque Azul around 6 pm.

CIUDAD CUAUHTÉMOC

• pop 1790

This 'city' amounts to little more than a few houses, a hotel and a comedor or two, but it's the last/first place in Mexico on the Pan-American Highway (highway 190). Comitán is 83km north. Ciudad Cuauhtémoc is the Mexican border post; the Guatemalan one is 4km south at La Mesilla. Colectivo taxis (US$1) ferry people between the two sides. There's a bank on the Guatemalan side of the border, and money changers on both sides. Expect to be charged small 'fees' of a couple of dollars by Guatemalan officials as you enter or leave their country.

Hotel Camino Real, above the Cristóbal Colón bus station in Ciudad Cuauhtémoc, has plain, dingy doubles with shared bath for US$10. There are better-looking hotels in La Mesilla.

Getting There & Away

Fairly frequent buses and combis run between Ciudad Cuauhtémoc, Comitán and San Cristóbal. See those two cities' sections for details. The Cristóbal Colón line also runs to Tuxtla Gutiérrez (US$7.25) six times daily, Mexico City (US$43 to US$52) three times, and a few other destinations once each.

Guatemalan buses depart La Mesilla every half hour from 8 am to at least 4 pm for main points inside Guatemala, such as Huehuetenango (84km, 1½ to 2 hours, US$1), Quetzaltenango (also called Xela, 170km, 3½ hours, US$3.50) and Guatemala City (380km, 7 hours, US$4.50). Lago de Atitlán (245km, 5 hours) and Chichicastenango (244km, 5 hours) both lie a few kilometers off the Pan-American Highway. If there's no bus to your destination, take one to Huehuetenango where you may be able to get an onward bus. Before boarding at La Mesilla, try to find out when the bus is leaving. This could save you hours of sitting in a stationary vehicle. Also watch out for overcharging.

RESERVA DE LA BIÓSFERA EL TRIUNFO

The luxuriant cloud forests high in the remote El Triunfo Biosphere Reserve in the Sierra Madre de Chiapas are both a bird-lovers' paradise and a bizarre world of trees and shrubs festooned with epiphytes, ferns, bromeliads, mosses, lichens and vines. The cool, damp cloud forest is formed by moist air rising from the hot, humid lowlands to form clouds and rain on the uplands.

The Sierra Madre de Chiapas is home to over 30 bird species that are nonexistent or rare elsewhere in Mexico. El Triunfo is the one place in the country where it's fairly easy to see the resplendent quetzal. Other birds here include the extremely rare horned guan (big as a turkey, but dwelling high in trees), the azure-rumped tanager, the black guan, the blue-tailed and wine-throated hummingbirds and the blue-throated motmot.

Visits are controlled fairly strictly. Avoid the May-to-October wet season. For a permit and arrangements, contact – at least one month in advance – Claudia Virgen, Ecoturismo (☎ 9-614-03-78, eltriunfo@infosel.net .mx), Reserva de la Biósfera El Triunfo, Calle Argentina 389, Colonia El Retiro, CP 29040, Tuxtla Gutiérrez, Chiapas. There's a minimum group size of six, and a minimum cost of about US$100 per person. For that you get one or two nights at Campamento El Triunfo, 1850m high in the heart of the reserve, guides who are expert bird-spotters and some help with transportation to/from Jaltenango (also called Ángel Albino Corzo), the nearest town, 130km south of Tuxtla Gutiérrez. Jaltenango is served by Autotranportes Cuxtepeques buses from Tuxtla Gutiérrez.

EL SOCONUSCO

The Soconusco is Chiapas' hot, fertile coastal plain, 15 to 35km wide. Its climate is hot and sweaty year-round, with plenty of rain from mid-May to mid-October. The steep-sided Sierra Madre de Chiapas, sweeping up from the plain, provides an excellent climate for coffee, bananas and other crops.

Floods on this side of Chiapas in 1998 killed at least 400 people (possibly more than 1000) and left highway 200 in a dreadful state. About 20 bridges on the road were still down in mid-1999 and it was taking about 4½ hours, instead of three, to travel the 220km Tonalá-Tapachula stretch. Travel times given here assume the same slow progress.

Tonalá
• **pop 29,600** • **elev 45m** ☎ 9

Tonalá, on highway 200, is the jumping-off point for Puerto Arista. There's a tourist office (☎ 663-27-87) on the main street, Hidalgo, at 5 de Mayo, two blocks southeast of the main plaza, Parque Esperanza. *Hotel Tonalá (☎ 663-04-80, Hidalgo 172)*, between Parque Esperanza and the Colón bus station, is a reasonable, moderately priced choice if you have to stay here.

Getting There & Away Cristóbal Colón (deluxe and 1st-class) and Transportes Rápidos del Sur (TRS, 2nd-class) share a bus station toward the northwest end of town on Hidalgo, six blocks from Parque Esperanza. There are frequent buses to Tuxtla Gutiérrez (3½ hours, US$4.75 to US$6.75), Escuintla (three hours, US$4 to US$6) and Tapachula (4½ hours, US$6 to US$8.75) from 5 or 6 am until at least midafternoon. Colón also runs three buses to Mexico City (US$36 to US$42) and one to Oaxaca (US$14.50). For Puerto Arista, combis and microbuses (US$0.70) leave from Juárez and 5 de Mayo, one block southeast of the market, until 6 pm. Colectivo taxis run as late as 8 pm from Matamoros and 5 de Mayo, one block uphill from the combi stop. A taxi is around US$7: you can call a 24-hour radio cab at ☎ 663-06-20.

Puerto Arista
• **pop 760** ☎ 9

Puerto Arista, 18km southwest of Tonalá, stretches lazily for about 2km along part of a 30km gray beach. Though the past few years have seen several substantial concrete buildings join its collection of palm shacks, it remains a sleepy place – most of the time.

On weekends a few hundred chiapanecos cruise in from the towns, and at Semana Santa and Christmas they come by the thousands, while the few permanent residents make their money for the year. The rest of the time, the most action you'll see is when a piglet breaks into a trot because a dog has gathered the energy to bark at it. The temperature's usually sweltering if you stray more than a few meters from the shore, and you get through a lot of *refrescos* while you listen to the crashing of the Pacific waves.

The ocean is clean here but take care: we've heard tales of riptides that can sweep you a long way out in a short time.

Puerto Arista's only real street, interchangeably called Boulevard Matamoros or Boulevard Zapotal, runs along the back of the beach. The road from Tonalá meets it at a T-junction by a lighthouse, the midpoint of town.

Places to Stay & Eat There are plenty of places in both directions from the lighthouse. The following is just a selection.

Head about 850m southeast from the lighthouse, then turn left (inland) near Hotel Lucerito to reach *José's Camping Cabañas* (☎ 664-99-82). Run by a friendly Canadian, this has camping space and five cute cabañas in a coconut and citrus grove. The cabañas have mosquito screens, fan and electric light, and cost US$5/8/11 for single/double/triple occupancy. You can camp for US$1.50 a person, and good food (including vegetarian) is available – about US$4 for a typical fish meal. The nearby, Mexican-run *Maya Bell* has a similar setup. Lots of birds inhabit a canal at the back of these two places.

Hotel Lucerito (☎ 663-01-82 ext 152, 613-00-08) is one of the best hotels at this end of town, with air-con and TV in rooms for US$20 to US$25 a single or double, and a pool. It doesn't front the beach, though. Just 150m southeast of the lighthouse, *Restaurant Playa Escondido* is typical of several beachfront comedores with a few basic little rooms. The bare abodes here are US$4 single or double, or US$5 with private bath. *Restaurant Ocmar*, a block southeast, does some of the best food in town and is not over-expensive.

Almost opposite the lighthouse, the three-story **Hotel Lizeth** has singles or doubles with fan for US$15 or with air-con and TV for US$20. Add US$5 for triple or quadruple occupancy. Fronting the beach one block farther northwest, *Restaurant Hospedaje Brisas del Mar* has bare, medium-size rooms with fan and bath for US$15 single, double or triple.

The top hotel is *Hotel Arista Bugambilias* (☎ 663-01-82 ext 116, 663-06-75), almost 1km northwest of the lighthouse, with a pool, restaurant and bar in gardens fronting the beach, and air-conditioned rooms with TV for US$40 single or double.

Getting There & Away See the Tonalá section. The best place to pick up a Tonalá-bound combi, microbus, colectivo taxi or regular taxi is the T-junction by the lighthouse.

Reserva de la Biósfera La Encrucijada

This large biosphere reserve protects a 1448-sq-km strip of coastal lagoons, sandbars, wetlands, forest and Mexico's tallest mangroves (some above 30m). It's a vital wintering and breeding ground for migratory birds and a well-preserved, important ecosystem. Inhabitants include one of Mexico's biggest populations of jaguars, plus ocelots, spider monkeys, white-tailed deer, four species each of sea and river turtle, river crocodiles, caimans, boa constrictors, green iguanas, fishing bats, anteaters, buzzards, fishing eagles, pelicans and lots of waterfowl. Many of these species are in danger of extinction. There are also about 27,000 people in scattered settlements.

A ride in a lancha through almost any part of the reserve will take you through towering mangroves and past palm-thatched lagoonside villages. You'll see plenty of birds any time of year.

The biosphere reserve has an office (☎ 9-647-00-84, closed Saturday and Sunday) at Avenida Central 4 in the small town of Acapetahua, 6km southwest of Escuintla. It

has another office (☎ 9-614-17-31) at Boulevard Ángel Albino Corzo 856, Tuxtla Gutiérrez. Ask at either office about visits to the reserve's study, protection and vigilance center, Campamento La Concepción, which has guides available. La Concepción is a 25km lancha ride southeast from Embarcadero Las Garzas, which is 16km southwest of Acapetahua. Another *campamento* is being built at Las Garzas, where there are comedores.

Nearer to Embarcadero Las Garzas is Barra de Zacapulco, a small settlement on a sandbar between the ocean and a lagoon. Barra de Zacapulco has a handful of palapa comedores where a big plate of fresh prawns with salad and tortillas costs around US$3, or a coconut to drink is about US$0.50. There's a sea turtle breeding center nearby.

Places to Stay You can camp or sling a hammock at Barra de Zacapulco for a minimal fee. *Campamento La Concepción* (see above) has accommodations for up to 30 people. Southeast of La Concepción, in San José El Hueyate, 24km by a good dirt road from Mazatán, is the beachside *Centro Turístico San José El Hueyate* (☎ 9-625-39-40). This has 10 rustic cabañas holding five people each, and a restaurant. Lancha rides are available here too.

Hotel El Carmen on Acapetahua's main street, Avenida Central, has adequate rooms with bath for US$8 single or double. There are also hotels in Escuintla.

Getting There & Away To reach Embarcadero Las Garzas, first take a bus along highway 200 to Escuintla. Then get a colectivo taxi to Acapetahua (6km, US$0.40). Beside the railway in Acapetahua, get a combi or bus to Embarcadero Las Garzas (16km, US$1). These run about every 30 minutes.

From Embarcadero Las Garzas, a colectivo lancha to Barra de Zacapulco takes 25 minutes for US$2. The last lancha back to Embarcadero Las Garzas may leave Barra de Zacapulco as early as 3.30 pm, and the last combi from Embarcadero Las Garzas to

Acapetahua about 4.30 pm, but double-check these times.

A three-hour personal lancha tour from Embarcadero Las Garzas costs around US$100 to US$150.

TAPACHULA
• pop 163,300 ☎ 9

Mexico's southernmost city is an important gateway to Guatemala and a busy commercial center, overlooked from the northeast by 4110m Tacaná, the first of a chain of volcanoes stretching southeast into Guatemala.

Orientation
The central plaza, Parque Hidalgo, is the site of the tourist office, banks, cathedral and museum. Bus stations and places to stay are scattered around the central area.

Information
Tourist Offices The tourist office (☎ 626-55-25 ext 140), on 8ª Norte facing Parque Hidalgo, is open 9 am to 4 pm and 7 to 10 pm daily.

Immigration The Instituto Nacional de Migración (☎ 626-91-22) is at Carretera del Antiguo Aeropuerto Km 1.5, about 2.5km south of the center.

Consulates The Guatemalan Consulate (☎ 626-12-52), at 2ª Oriente 33, is open 9 am to 3 pm Monday to Friday.

Money There are banks with ATMs around Parque Hidalgo (see the Tapachula map). Elektra on 4ªNorte at 3ª Poniente offers Western Union 'Dinero en Minutos' service.

Post & Communications The post office, east of the center on 1ª Oriente, is open 8 am to 6 pm Monday to Friday, 9 am to 1 pm Sunday and holidays.

Globali@ cybercafé, Calle Central Oriente 16B, charges US$1.25 a half-hour and is open 9 am to 9 pm daily.

Travel Agencies AeroPromociones y Viajes del Centro (☎ 626-88-18) at 4ª Norte 18B is a handy air ticket agency.

Medical Services The Cruz Roja Mexicana (Mexican Red Cross, ☎ 626-76-44, 626-19-49) at the corner of 1ª Oriente and 9ª Norte has ambulances and an *urgencias* (emergencies) section. Sanatorio Soconusco (☎ 626-50-74, 4ª Norte 68) handles urgencias too.

Museo Arqueológico del Soconusco
The Soconusco Archaeological Museum facing the west side of Parque Hidalgo displays some of the best finds from the nearby Izapa ruins, including stone sculptures and a gold-and-turquoise-encrusted skull. It's open 11 am to 6 pm daily except Monday (US$2).

Places to Stay
Budget The *Hospedaje Las Américas* (☎ 626-27-57, 10ª Nte 47), four blocks from Parque Hidalgo, has a leafy patio and clean singles/doubles with fan and curtained-off bathroom for US$5/6 (US$8 for two-bed doubles).

Hotel La Amistad (☎ 626-22-93, 7ª Pte 34), a bit nearer Parque Hidalgo, has clean rooms with bath and fan, around a nice leafy patio, for US$5.50/8 a single/double, but is often full.

Posada del Parque (☎ 626-51-18, 8ª Sur 3) has rooms that are clean, but muggy despite fans. Singles/doubles with small curtained-off bathrooms cost US$9/10.50 (US$13.50 for twin beds, US$16 with air-con).

Around the corner from the Cristóbal Colón bus station is *Hospedaje Chelito* (☎ 626-24-28, 1ª Norte 107). Clean, good-size doubles/triples with TV, fan and bathroom cost US$10.50/13; doubles/triples with air-con and cable TV are US$15.50/18. Attached is a small café.

Mid-Range The *Hotel Santa Julia* (☎ 626-31-40, 17ª Oriente 5), next door to the Cristóbal Colón bus station, has clean air-conditioned singles/doubles with TV, phone and bath for US$25/28.

Hotel Fénix (☎ 625-07-55, 4ª Norte 19), a block from Parque Hidalgo, has good remodeled rooms at US$32/40 a single/double, with air-con and cable TV, but the unremodeled rooms (US$14.50/18 with fan, US$25/31 with air-con) can be poky.

TAPACHULA

To Escuintla,
Tonalá

Market

Palacio
Municipal

Cathedral

Parque
Hidalgo

Río Coatancito

To Instituto Nacional
de Migración, Airport

To Izapa, Talismán,
Ciudad Hidalgo

OTHER
1 Rápidos del Sur Bus Station
3 Cristóbal Colón Bus Station
6 Unión y Progreso Combi
  & Microbus Station
9 Bancrecer, ATM
10 Sanatorio Soconusco
11 Monumento a Benito Juárez
12 Tourist Office
13 Museo Arqueológico del
   Soconusco
17 Inverlat, ATM
19 Elektra
20 Ómnibus de Tapachula
   Bus Station
22 AeroPromociones y Viajes
   del Centro
23 TAESA
26 Aeroméxico
27 Aviacsa
28 Aerocaribe
29 Globali@
30 Post Office
31 Cruz Roja Mexicana
32 Guatemalan Consulate

PLACES TO STAY
2 Hospedaje Las Américas
3 Hospedaje Chelito
4 Hotel Santa Julia
7 Hotel La Amistad
18 Hotel Michell
21 Hotel Don Miguel
24 Hotel Fénix
25 Posada del Parque

PLACES TO EAT
8 El Mestizo
14 La Parrilla
16 Los Comales Grill
16 Taquería
21 Restaurante Los Jarrones
24 Hostal del Rey

The modern ***Hotel Don Miguel*** (☎ 626-11-43, 1ª Pte 18), nearby, is the best city center hotel, and sometimes is full. Rooms are clean and bright with air-con and TV for US$32/39. There's a good restaurant here too.

Just half a block off Parque Hidalgo, ***Hotel Michell*** (☎ 625-26-40, 5ª Pte 23) has reasonable rooms with air-con, TV and desks for US$23/29/37 single/double/triple.

Places to Eat
Several restaurants line the south side of Parque Hidalgo. ***Los Comales Grill*** stays

open late and serves a bit of everything: egg dishes (US$1 to US$2), main dishes (US$4.50 to US$7), tacos and tortas. Tacos are cheaper two doors along at the ***Taquería. La Parrilla***, across the street, does tasty *tortas a la parrilla* for US$1.50, good plates of fruit salad for US$2.50, thirst-quenching fruit drinks such as *agua de maracuyá* (passion fruit juice) and reasonably priced tacos, meat and chicken dishes.

Breakfast at the Hotel Fénix's air-conditioned ***Hostal Del Rey*** (4ª Norte 17), with its pretty decor and bow-tied waiters, is a nice way to begin the day. An early meal of

TABASCO & CHIAPAS

hotcakes or eggs, fruit or juice, and coffee is US$3. Later in the day you may want soup, salad or antojitos (each around US$3), or *aves* or carne for US$4 to US$6.

The Hotel Don Miguel's air-conditioned *Restaurante Los Jarrones* is another of the best and most popular places in town, similarly priced.

El Mestizo on 7ª Pte near Parque Hidalgo is a cleanish, economical place open to the street, serving a range of Chinese and Mexican dishes for US$1.50 to US$2.25. The Chinese dishes come with rice.

Getting There & Away
Air Aviacsa (☎ 626-14-39), Central Norte 18, flies daily nonstop to/from Tuxtla Gutiérrez and Mexico City.

Aeroméxico (☎ 800-021-40-00), 2ª Norte 6, and TAESA (☎ 626-37-02), 1ª Pte 11B, also fly daily nonstop to/from Mexico City.

Aerocaribe (☎ 626-98-72), 2ª Oriente 4, flies daily to/from Mérida via Tuxtla Gutiérrez and Veracruz.

Bus Cristóbal Colón (☎ 626-28-81), on 17ª Oriente 1km northeast of Parque Hidalgo, operates deluxe, 1st-class and 2nd-class buses. The main 2nd-class bus stations are Rápidos del Sur (RS, ☎ 626-11-61), at 9ª Pte 62, and Ómnibus de Tapachula (OT) at 7ª Pte 5.

Transportation to/from the Guatemalan border is covered in the Talismán & Ciudad Hidalgo section. Other departures include:

Comitán – 245km, 6 hours (via Motozintla); 5 Colón (US$7.25)

Escuintla – 85km, 1½ hours; 10 Colón (US$2.50), 37 RS (US$1.50), 52 OT (US$1.50)

Guatemala City – 300km, 7 hours; 2 Colón (US$22)

Mexico City (TAPO) – 1110km, 19 hours; 7 Colón (US$44 to US$51)

Oaxaca – 670km, 13 hours; 2 Colón (US$22 to US$27)

San Cristóbal de Las Casas – 335km, 7½ hours; 6 Colón (US$9.75)

Tonalá – 220km, 4½ hours; 16 Colón (US$7.25 to US$8.50), 37 RS (US$6), 14 OT (US$5.50)

Tuxtla Gutiérrez – 390km, 8 hours; 18 Colón (US$13 to US$15.50), 37 RS (US$11)

Colón also runs one or two daily buses to Palenque, Bahías de Huatulco, Pochutla, Puerto Escondido, Tijuana (via the Pacific coast) and even Brownsville, Texas.

Getting Around
Tapachula's airport is 20km southwest of the city off the Puerto Madero road. Transporte Terrestre (☎ 625-12-87), 2ª Sur 68, charges US$3.75 per person from the airport to any hotel in the city, or vice-versa. A taxi is US$7 or so.

AROUND TAPACHULA
Izapa
The Izapa ruins are important to archaeologists as a link between the Olmecs and the Maya (see History in the Facts about Mexico chapter), but of limited interest to the nonenthusiast. Pre-Hispanic Izapa flourished from approximately 200 BC to 200 AD. The Izapa carving style – typically seen on stelae with altars placed in front – shows descendants of Olmec deities, with their upper lips unnaturally lengthened. Early Mayan monuments from north Guatemala are similar.

At each of the three groups of remains, the caretaking family will get you to sign a visitor's book and ask you for US$0.50.

Izapa is 11km east of Tapachula on the Talismán road. The sign indicating the northern part of the site, on the left of the road coming from Tapachula, is invisible from that direction: watch instead for the small pyramids. Some restoration has been carried out at this part of the site, which has a few low pyramids, a ball court, and several carved stelae and altars. The warden, whose residence, piglets and chicks are all part of the site, has a basic information sheet in Spanish.

From the northern area, go 700m back toward Tapachula and take a signposted dirt road to the left. After 800m, past houses with 2000-year-old sculptures lying in their gardens, you reach a fork with signs to Izapa Grupo A and Izapa Grupo B, each about 250m farther. Grupo A is a set of weathered stela-and-altar pairings around a small field. Grupo B is a couple of grass-covered mounds and more stone sculpture, including three curious ball-on-pillar affairs.

Getting There & Away Take a Unión y Progreso combi (US$0.60) from 5ª Pte 53 in Tapachula.

Talismán & Ciudad Hidalgo

The road from Tapachula heads 9km northeast past Izapa to the international border at Talismán bridge, opposite El Carmen, Guatemala. A branch south off the Talismán road leads to another cross-border bridge at Ciudad Hidalgo (37km from Tapachula), opposite Ciudad Tecún Umán. There are hotels and places to change money at both borders. Both crossings are open 24 hours.

The Guatemalan border posts may make various small charges as you go through, and they may insist on being paid in either dollars or quetzals – so get some before you leave Tapachula. The Ciudad Tecún Umán crossing has a better reputation and more frequent onward buses.

Getting There & Away Combis of Unión y Progreso leave for Talismán from 5ª Pte 53 in Tapachula every few minutes, 5 am to 10.30 pm (US$0.60). They pass the Cristóbal Colón bus station as they leave town. A taxi from Tapachula to Talismán takes 20 minutes and costs around US$5.

Ómnibus de Tapachula buses from 7ª Pte 5 in Tapachula make the 45-minute journey to Ciudad Hidalgo about every 15 minutes from 4 am to 7.30 pm, and at 8.15, 9.15 and 10.15 pm, for US$1. Cristóbal Colón runs a daily bus to/from Mexico City (20 hours, US$44).

Many of the longer-distance buses leaving the Guatemalan side of the border head for Guatemala City (about five hours away) by the coastal slope route through Retalhuleu and Escuintla. If you're heading for Lake Atitlán or Chichicastenango, you need to get to Quetzaltenango (Xela) first, for which you may have to change buses at Retalhuleu or Malacatán on the Talismán-San Marcos-Quetzaltenango road.

The Yucatán Peninsula

The Yucatán Peninsula is the realm of the Maya. Inheritors of a glorious and often violent history, the Maya live today where their ancestors lived a millennium ago. They are proud to be Mexican, but even prouder to be Maya, and it is the Mayab – the lands of the Maya, which also include Guatemala, parts of Belize and much of Chiapas – that they consider their true country.

When the Spanish conquered the Mayan city of Tihó in 1542, they founded Mérida, now the capital of Yucatán state, in its place. For centuries, Mérida answered directly to Spain, rather than Mexico City. Consequently, the peninsula has always looked upon itself as distinct from the rest of Mexico.

The flat and hot Yucatán Peninsula has surprising diversity. Comprising three

Highlights

- Mérida – the 'White City,' traditional capital of the Yucatecan Maya
- Chichén Itzá – the great Maya-Toltec ceremonial center
- Uxmal – the graceful chief city of the Puuc region, birthplace of unique architectural patterns
- Caribbean beaches – coral reefs, 'air-conditioned' sand and a laid-back lifestyle

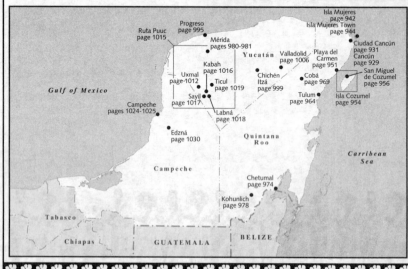

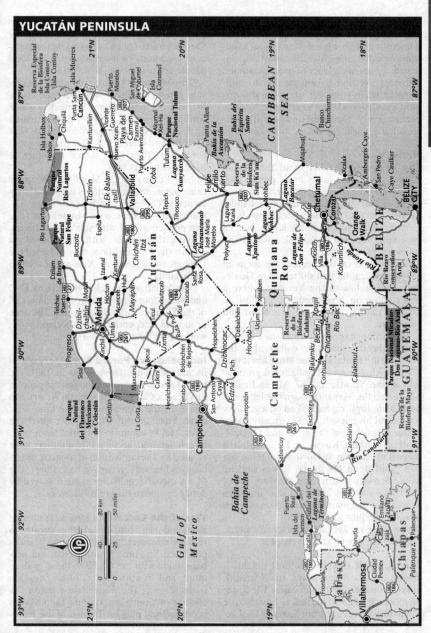

YUCATÁN PENINSULA

Mexican states – Quintana Roo, Yucatán and Campeche – the peninsula is home to numerous archaeological sites, several handsome colonial cities, Mexico's most popular seaside resort and plenty of quiet coastlines. The rainy season is mid-August to mid-October, when you'll get afternoon showers most days. A good time to visit is in November or early December, when it's less crowded and less expensive.

History

The Maya At the height of the Mayan culture, during the late Classic period (600 to 900 AD), the Mayan lands were ruled not as an empire but as a collection of independent but also interdependent city-states. Each city-state had its noble house, headed by a king who was the social, political and religious focus of the city's life.

By the end of the period, the focus of Mayan civilization had shifted from Guatemala and Belize to the Yucatán, where a new civilization developed at Chichén Itzá, Uxmal, Labná, Kabah, Edzná, Sayil and elsewhere.

Prevailing expert opinion has it that classic Mayan civilization collapsed in the 9th and 10th centuries. One story has it that a Toltec king named Topiltzin led an invasion of the Yucatán in 987 AD and easily conquered the Maya. Through battles previously won, Topiltzin had taken on legendary status, and his name became virtually inseparable from that of the great god Quetzalcóatl or, in Maya, Kukulcán. He established himself in Yucatán at Uucil-abnal (Chichén Itzá), and upon his death, it was said he would one day return from the direction of the rising sun and initiate a new era. This legend haunted many Mesoamericans when Spanish conquistadors arrived.

For more on Mayan history and culture, see the Facts about Mexico chapter.

The Spanish Despite political infighting among the Yucatecan Maya, the Spaniards did not conquer the region easily. The Spanish monarch assigned the task to Francisco de Montejo, who set out from Spain in 1527 accompanied by his son, also named Francisco de Montejo. Landing first at Cozumel off the Caribbean coast, then at Xel-ha on the mainland, the Montejos discovered that the local people wanted nothing to do with them.

The Montejos sailed around the peninsula, conquered Tabasco in 1530, and established their base near Campeche, which could be supplied easily with necessities, arms and new troops from central Mexico. They pushed inland, but after four long, difficult years they were forced to return to Mexico City in defeat.

In 1540, the younger Montejo took up the cause again, with his father's support. He returned to Campeche with a cousin named – you got it – Francisco de Montejo, and the two pressed inland with speed and success. Allying themselves with the Xiú Maya against the Cocom Maya, they defeated the Cocoms and gained the Xiús as converts to Christianity.

The Montejos founded Mérida in 1542 and within four years had brought almost all of the Yucatán under Spanish rule. The once proud and independent Maya became peons working for Spanish masters.

Independence Period When Mexico won its independence from Spain in 1821, the new Mexican government urged the peoples of Yucatán, Chiapas and Central America to join it in the formation of one large new state. Yucatán and Chiapas accepted the offer. Mayan claims to ancestral lands were largely ignored, and huge plantations were created for the cultivation of tobacco, sugarcane and henequen (agave rope fiber). The Maya, though legally free, were enslaved by debt peonage to the great landowners.

War of the Castes Not long after gaining independence from Spain, the Yucatecan ruling classes were again dreaming of independence, this time from Mexico, and perhaps union with the US. With these goals in mind, and in anticipation of an invasion from Mexico, the *hacendados* made the mistake of arming and training their Mayan peons as local militias. Trained to use European weaponry, the Maya envisioned a release from their own misery and boldly rebelled against their Yucatecan masters.

The War of the Castes began in 1847 in Valladolid, a city known for its oppressive laws against the Maya. The Mayan rebels quickly gained control of the city in an orgy of vengeful killing and looting. Supplied with arms and ammunition by the British through Belize, they spread across the peninsula.

In little more than a year, the Mayan revolutionaries had driven their oppressors from every part of Yucatán except Mérida and the walled city of Campeche. Just as Yucatán's governor was about to abandon Mérida, the rebels saw the annual appearance of the winged ant. In Mayan mythology, corn (the staff of life) must be planted at the first sighting of the winged ant. If the sowing is delayed, Chac, the rain god, will be affronted and respond with a drought. Thus, the rebels abandoned the attack and went home to plant the corn. This gave the ruling class time to regroup and receive aid from its erstwhile adversary, the government in Mexico City.

The counterrevolution against the Maya was vicious in the extreme. Between 1848 and 1855, the indigenous population of Yucatán was halved. Some Mayan combatants sought refuge in the jungles of southern Quintana Roo, and they continued to fight until 1866.

Yucatán Today Beginning with the development of Cancún during the late 1960s, the peninsula has been undergoing a radical transformation from an agriculture-based economy to one driven by tourism, largely from foreign visitors. A construction boom has taken hold especially in Quintana Roo, where the government has sold off every kilometer of public beach along the Caribbean coast to developers, and many *cenotes* (freshwater pools that once sustained Mayan life) are being privatized and promoted as exotic swimming holes.

Meanwhile, the countryside is emptying of indigenous people seeking to leave behind the hardship of farming in a land with poor soil and few rivers. Descendants of the people who built the great Mayan pyramids are now building the seaside resorts, but the wages they earn are bad even by Mexican standards. As their incomes are outpaced by the rapidly escalating price of land and services on the peninsula, the Maya will probably be forced to leave the region.

Geography & Geology

The Yucatán Peninsula is one vast, flat limestone shelf rising only a dozen meters above sea level. The shelf extends outward below sea level from the shoreline for several kilometers. If you approach the peninsula by air, you should have no trouble seeing the barrier reef that marks the limit of the shelf. On the landward side of the reef, the water is usually no more than 5m to 10m deep. On the seaward side of the reef, the water plunges to a depth of several thousand meters only 10km out.

The underwater shelf makes Yucatán's coastline wonderful for aquatic sports, keeping the waters warm and the marine life (fish, crabs, lobsters, tourists) abundant, but it makes life difficult for traders, who cannot bring their oceangoing vessels near shore to dock.

Anomalies on the otherwise flat peninsula include rolling hills rising to several hundred meters in the Puuc region of Yucatán state, near Uxmal, and the hills in the heavily forested southern section of the peninsula along the Mexico-Guatemala border.

The peninsula has few lakes and exposed rivers, but thanks to the porous limestone it does have underground rivers and pools. Yucatecans have traditionally drawn their freshwater from *cenotes* (limestone caverns with collapsed roofs), which serve as natural cisterns. And south of the Puuc region, in the Chenes region, the inhabitants get water from the *chenes* (limestone pools) that gave the region its name; the pools are more than a hundred meters below ground.

Quintana Roo

The enticing state of Quintana Roo, home to the country's Caribbean beaches, holds hundreds of impressive Mayan ruins and sizzles with the Yucatán's steamiest nightlife. It also boasts some of the finest diving and snorkeling sites in the world – not only offshore, but in underground rivers and subterranean caves that offer incredible journeys for qualified divers. Best of these is Nohoch Nah Chich ('Giant Birdhouse' in Mayan), the world's longest underwater cave system, which consists of colossal connecting hallways filled with speleological wonders.

Quintana Roo was little more than a forgotten backwater for most of the 19th century. So insignificant was this jungly, sparsely inhabited region in the minds of Mexican authorities that it didn't even have an official name until 1902. In that year, when it was given territory status, it was named after army general Andrés Quintana Roo, although he'd never served in the territory. Remarkably, Quintana Roo didn't become a state until 1974. And it likely wouldn't have received statehood even then, except that the government and influential developers had ambitious plans for Cancún, and it was agreed that Cancún would be difficult to promote if it were situated in a region apparently unworthy of statehood.

CANCÚN
- pop 57,200 ☎ 9

In the late 1960s Isla Cancún was a sliver of sand 17km long visited only by local fisherfolk and a few gringo adventurers. Shaped like a wobbly Lucky 7, it was separated from the coast by two narrow channels. When the Mexican government around that time decided to develop a resort on the island, the channels were bridged. Next, a town sprang up (where Ciudad Cancún now stands) to house Isla Cancún's construction workers and their families.

A well-paved street bordered by wide sidewalks was run down the center of the island. Many hectares of mangroves and scrub brush were ripped out, scores of gardens were planted, and 'a very towered land,' as one 16th-century Spanish historian described this Mayan-temple-strewn coast, acquired even more towers as multistory resorts went up.

When Cancún opened in 1974, the carefully developed island – commonly referred to as Cancún, Isla Cancún or the Zona Hotelera – was promoted as a tropical paradise. In short order it began attracting snowbirds from Canada and wealthy beach bums from the US, Europe and elsewhere. Today, more than 2 million visitors descend on Cancún each year, with the number increasing 3% annually.

Tourists often comment that Ciudad Cancún is much more 'authentic' than Isla Cancún. It might seem that way, but the city owes its existence to developers and tourism authorities the same as the resort island. Contrary to some reports, it is not the offspring of a fishing or farming community.

Orientation

Familiarizing yourself with Isla Cancún is easy. It contains fewer than 10 roads in all, only one of which – Boulevard Kukulcán – is more than a few kilometers long. The four-lane boulevard starts on the eastern edge of Ciudad Cancún and heads east out onto the island for 9km to Punta Cancún (Cancún Point), past condominium developments, a youth hostel, some moderately priced hotels and several shopping complexes. It then turns southwest and runs 14km to Punta Nizuc (Nizuc Point), along the way flanked on both sides by mammoth hotels, shopping centers, dance clubs, restaurants and bars. At Punta Nizuc it turns west, rejoins the mainland and continues west through light tropical forest several more kilometers to its southern terminus at Cancún International Airport.

Few of the buildings on Isla Cancún have numbered addresses. Instead, because the vast majority of them are on Boulevard Kukulcán, their location is described in relation to their distance from Km 0, the boulevard's northern terminus in Ciudad Cancún, identified with a roadside 'Km 0' marker.

Tulum: Mayan ruins meet the Caribbean

Chichén Itzá's group of 1,000 columns

Chichén Itzá's El Castillo - 365 steps to the top

JON DAVISON

'For those about to rock...'

JOHN NEUBAUER

Monastery at Izamal

JON DAVISON

Quintana Roo bus in maximum overdrive

SCOTT DOGGETT

Cancún's Zona Hotelera

CANCÚN

PLACES TO STAY
2 Club Las Perlas
3 Atención a la Juventud
4 Costa Real
5 Laguna Inn
9 Cancún Marina Club
11 Gran Caribe Real
12 Sierra Cancún
14 Hyatt Cancún Caribe
16 Piramides Cancún
17 Sheraton Cancún
18 Tucan Cun Beach
27 Crown Paradise Club
30 Kin-Ha
35 Blue Lagoon
36 Sina Suites
37 Imperial Laguna
38 Laguna Real
47 Aristos Cancún

PLACES TO EAT
8 Carlos 'n Charlie's
21 La Dolce Vita
22 Crab House
26 Il Paparazzi
28 Restaurant Río Nizuc
46 Señor Frog's

OTHER
1 Ferry Service Office
7 Playa Linda Marine
   Terminal
7 La Boom
10 Taxi Zone
13 Marina Punta del Este
15 Plaza Flamingo
18 Taxi Stand
20 Plaza Kukulcán
23 AquaWorld
24 Executive Car Rental
25 Zona Arqueológica El Rey
29 Playa Tortugas Dock
31 Turimaz Rent a Car
32 Plaza Terramar
33 Xcaret Bus Station
34 Club Náutico Watertaxi
39 No Name Laundry
40 Plaza Quetzal
41 Dady'O, Dady Rock
42 Centro de Convenciones,
   Museo de Antropología
   e Historia
43 The Forum
44 Christine
45 Happy Wash Laundry

Ferry to Isla Mujeres
To Punta Sam
Puerto Juárez
Av López Portillo
Av Bonampak
MEX 180
Av Uxmal
Av Coba
Av Tulum
Blvd Kukulcán
CIUDAD CANCÚN
see Ciudad Cancún map
MEX 307
Av Amigo

Playa Las Perlas
Bahía de Mujeres
Ferry to Isla Mujeres
Ferry to Isla Mujeres
Water Taxi to Isla Mujeres

Playa Caracol
Punta Cancún
Playa Tortugas
31 33
32
34
29 30
39
38 40
35 36
37
Calle Quetzal
42 44
41
43
45
46 47
Playa Gaviota Azul
0   400   800 m
0   400   800 yards

2 Playa Juventud
3 Playa Linda
5 4
6 Playa Langosta
8 9
10 11
Playa Tortugas
see inset map

Laguna Bojórquez
13 12
14
15
Playa Chac-Mool

Playa Marlin
16
17
18
20 19

Laguna del Amor
Laguna de Nichupté
Isla Cancún

21 Playa Ballenas
22
23
24

25
Playa San Miguelito

Laguna Cabra

CARIBBEAN SEA

26 Playa Delfines
27

Aeropuerto Internacional de Cancún
Laguna Río Inglés
To Hwy 180
MEX 307 (toll)
To Puerto Morelos, Tulum

Blvd Kukulcán

28

Punta Nizuc

0   1   2 km
0   .5   1 mile

Parque Nacional Submarino Punta Nizuc

Each kilometer is similarly marked, all the way to the airport, some 30 or so markers away. The Km 22 marker is near the bridge linking the island's southern tip with the mainland.

In Ciudad Cancún, Boulevard Kukulcán turns into Avenida Cobá. Most of the city's major streets cross Avenida Cobá, starting with Avenida Bonampak. The next major street as you proceed west is Avenida Nader; two short blocks farther is touristy Avenida Tulum. The bus station is at the intersection of avenidas Tulum and Uxmal. The next (and last) major street crossing Avenida Cobá is Avenida Yaxchilán, which is also a tourist haven.

Information

Tourist Offices Remarkably, there are no tourist offices on Isla Cancún. A tourist counter at the Cancún airport, near Immigration, is staffed with friendly, helpful and bilingual receptionists. In Ciudad Cancún, the Quintana Roo Tourism Office (☎ 884-80-73), Avenida Tulum 26, is in front of City Hall in an office beside the Banco Inverlat; it's open 9 am to 9 pm daily and usually has English speakers on staff.

Immigration For visa and tourist-card extensions, visit the Instituto Nacional de Migración (☎ 854-14-04), Avenida Nader 1 in Ciudad Cancún. The office handles extension requests 9 am to noon Monday to Friday.

Money There are no banks on the island, but ATMs and *casas de cambio* are inside all the malls and at Punta Cancún. The casas de cambio are usually open daily from sunrise until well after midnight. Virtually all the resorts on the island will change money, but they offer poor exchange rates and sometimes will change money only for guests. Exchange rates on the island are generally less favorable than those found in Ciudad Cancún, but not so different as to warrant a special trip.

In Ciudad Cancún, several banks, including a Bancomer and a Banamex, lie along Avenida Tulum between Avenidas Cobá and Uxmal. The banks are open 9 am to 5.30 pm Monday to Friday, but they sometimes limit foreign exchange transactions to between 10 am and noon. For better exchange rates use one of the currency exchange booths on the east side of Avenida Tulum between Avenidas Cobá and Uxmal; most are open 8 am to 8 pm daily. ATMs are common in Ciudad Cancún.

Post & Communications Isla Cancún has no post office, but all but the few moderately priced hotels sell stamps at their reception desks and will accept outgoing mail. The main post office is in Ciudad Cancún at the west end of Avenida Sunyaxchén. Its hours for buying stamps and picking up general delivery mail (Oficina de Correos, Cancún, Quintana Roo 77500) are 8 am to 7 pm Monday to Friday, 9 am to 1 pm Saturday and holidays; for international money orders and registered mail, hours are 8 am to 6 pm Monday to Friday, 9 am to noon Saturday and holidays.

Telmex pay phones are on practically every street corner in Cancún, and numerous other pay phones are springing up all the time.

Isla Cancún has two Internet service booths: one at the entryway of the Forum mall in Punta Cancún, the other on the second floor of Plaza Kukulcán mall. Both have had problems with bad telephone connections. Ciudad Cancún has two public Internet facilities. At La Taberna (☎ 887-73-00), Avenida Yaxchilán 23, a popular neighborhood bar that is managed by friendly, English-speaking people, a room off the tavern houses a half dozen computers (US$4 an hour, open 10 am to 5 am daily). The impersonal Sybcom Internet Café (☎ 885-00-55), Avenida Nader 42, offers a handful of computers under garish fluorescent lighting (US$1 for 15 minutes or less, US$2 for 15 to 30 minutes, US$3 for 30 to 60 minutes, with a discount for those with student identification; open 10 am to 10 pm daily).

Fax service is available at both of the Ciudad Cancún Internet facilities and at many businesses in town – look for 'Fax'

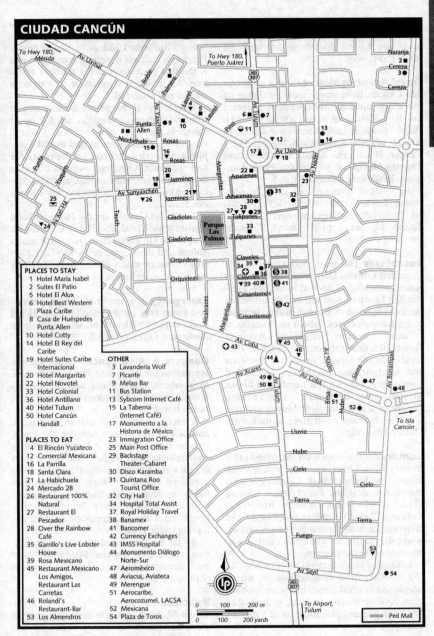

CIUDAD CANCÚN

PLACES TO STAY
1 Hotel María Isabel
2 Suites El Patio
3 Hotel El Alux
6 Hotel Best Western Plaza Caribe
8 Casa de Huéspedes Punta Allen
10 Hotel Cotty
14 Hotel El Rey del Caribe
19 Hotel Suites Caribe Internacional
20 Hotel Margaritas
22 Hotel Novotel
33 Hotel Colonial
36 Hotel Antillano
40 Hotel Tulum
50 Hotel Cancún Handall

PLACES TO EAT
4 El Rincón Yucateco
12 Comercial Mexicana
16 La Parrilla
18 Santa Clara
21 La Habichuela
24 Mercado 28
26 Restaurant 100% Natural
27 Restaurant El Pescador
28 Over the Rainbow Café
35 Garrillo's Live Lobster House
39 Rosa Mexicano
45 Restaurant Mexicano Los Amigos, Restaurant Las Carretas
46 Rolandi's Restaurant-Bar
53 Los Almendros

OTHER
3 Lavandería Wolf
7 Picante
9 Melao Bar
11 Bus Station
13 Sybcom Internet Café
15 La Taberna (Internet Café)
17 Monumento a la Historia de México
23 Immigration Office
25 Main Post Office
29 Backstage Theater-Cabaret
30 Disco Karamba
31 Quintana Roo Tourist Office
32 City Hall
34 Hospital Total Assist
37 Royal Holiday Travel
38 Banamex
41 Bancomer
42 Currency Exchanges
43 IMSS Hospital
44 Monumento Diálogo Norte-Sur
47 Aeroméxico
48 Aviacsa, Aviateca
49 Merengue
51 Aerocaribe, Aerocozumel, LACSA
52 Mexicana
54 Plaza de Toros

signs in the windows along Tulum, Cobá and Yaxchilán. Most hotels will also oblige if you insist you have a document that must be faxed right away.

Travel Agencies Most of the big hotels on Isla Cancún have travel agencies. Three of the most reputable independent agencies are Royal Holiday Travel (☎ 885-14-67), Plaza Flamingo mall, Boulevard Kukulcán Km 11; Mayaland (☎ 883-06-79), 225 Party Center, Boulevard Kukulcán Km 9; and Thomas Moore (☎ 883-49-38), Playa Langosta, Boulevard Kukulcán Km 5.

In Ciudad Cancún, centrally located Royal Holiday Travel (☎ 887-34-00, fax 884-58-92, royalh@telmex.com.mx), Avenida Tulum 33, has a professional, English-speaking staff.

Bookstores The main bookstore on Isla Cancún is Librería Dalí (☎ 885-14-04), Plaza Kukulcán mall, 2nd floor, Boulevard Kukulcán Km 13, where you will find thousands of books in Spanish or English and an impressive selection of books about the Yucatán.

Fama Cancún Bookstore, Avenida Tulum 105, near the southern end of Tulipanes, has the largest variety of domestic and international magazines in Ciudad Cancún and offers a fair number of books as well, most on Cancún, the Yucatán Peninsula and the ancient Mayan civilization. This is also a good place to look for a Mexico road atlas.

Laundry All the resorts on the island offer laundry service, but if you want to save some money try Happy Wash Laundry, Paseo Pok-ta-Pok near the Hotel Suites Laguna Verde. At No Name Laundry, Boulevard Kukulcán Km 7.5, laundry costs US$1 per kilogram for bulk service. Same-day service is usually available when the clothes are dropped off in the morning.

In the city is Lavandería Wolf (☎ 880-77-23), Avenida Bonampak at Cereza, where laundry costs US$1.50 per kilogram for bulk service. Generally, if you leave your clothes by 11 am, you can pick them up at 5 pm the same day.

Medical Services The American Medical Care Center (☎ 883-10-01, 883-01-13 after hours), Boulevard Kukulcán Km 8, beside Plaza Quetzal, has a sterling reputation and is the first place to turn for medical attention. As its name suggests, it is American owned and operated.

Hotels on the island are accustomed to tourists requesting medical aid for upset stomachs, sunburns and the like. If you're staying at a Cancún resort and would like a physician to visit you, contact the concierge and request a house call. Several bilingual doctors perform this service, and the concierges know who they are and will contact one for you.

In Ciudad Cancún are the Hospital Total Assist (☎ 884-10-92, 884-81-16), Claveles 22, next to the Hotel Antillano, just off Avenida Tulum, and the Centro de IMSS (Social Security Center; ☎ 884-23-42), Avenida Cobá west of Avenida Tulum.

Emergency The two most helpful emergency numbers on the island are the Hotel Zone Police (☎ 885-05-69) and the Tourist Assistance Office (☎ 884-80-73).

Dangers & Annoyances Cancún has a reputation for being safe, but as is the case everywhere, don't leave valuables unattended in your hotel room or beside your beach towel.

Vehicular traffic on Boulevard Kukulcán, particularly as it passes between the malls, bars and discotheques at Punta Cancún, is an overlooked but serious concern. At least once a week a drunken visitor stumbles into a moving vehicle. To keep the number of these accidents down, traffic cops are stationed seemingly every 20m down the boulevard. They do a superlative job of enforcing traffic laws.

By far the greatest danger in Cancún is overexposure to the sun. Play it safe and apply sunscreen *liberally*. If you don't, you'll wish you did.

Beaches
Under Mexican law you have the right to walk and swim on every beach in the

country except those within military compounds. In practice, it is difficult to approach many stretches of beach without walking through the lobby of a hotel, particularly on Isla Cancún. However, unless you look suspicious or unless you look like a local (the hotels tend to discriminate against locals, particularly Mayans), you'll usually be permitted to cross the lobby and proceed to the beach.

As you head down Boulevard Kukulcán from Ciudad Cancún to the southern tip of the island, you'll pass (in order) Playa Las Perlas, Playa Juventud, Playa Linda, Playa Langosta, Playa Tortugas, Playa Caracol, Playa Gaviota Azul, Playa Chac-Mool, Playa Marlin, Playa Ballenas, Playa San Miguelito and Playa Delfines. All of the beaches will be to the left side of the road, while beachless Laguna de Nichupté will appear on the right.

The sand varies little from one beach to another, but the personalities of the crowds on them vary greatly. If you want a party atmosphere, head to the north end of Playa Gaviota Azul, directly behind the Forum mall on Punta Cancún. If you're looking for a 'local scene,' head to Playa San Miguelito and neighboring Playa Delfines, both bordered by public parking lots. Because locals don't need to pass through hotels to use these beaches, they tend to congregate here.

Beach Safety

Cancún's Rescate 911 ambulance crews respond to as many as a dozen near-drownings each week. Though Isla Cancún's surf is usually gentle, undertow is possible, and storms can arrive with little warning. Local authorities have devised a system of colored pennants to alert beachgoers of potential dangers. Look for them on the beaches where you swim.

- **Blue**   Normal, safe conditions
- **Yellow** Use caution, changeable conditions
- **Red**   Unsafe conditions; swim in a pool instead

Mayan Ruins

Two sets of Mayan ruins lie on Isla Cancún, and though neither is particularly impressive, both are worth a look if time permits. In the **Zona Arqueológica El Rey**, on the west side of Boulevard Kukulcán between Km 17 and Km 18, are a small temple and several ceremonial platforms, open 8 am to 5 pm daily; admission is US$2, and visitors are occasionally required to be accompanied by a guide. The much smaller **Yamil Lu'um** is atop a beachside knoll on the parklike grounds separating the Sheraton Cancún and Piramides Cancún towers. Only the outward-sloping remains of the weathered temple's walls still stand, but the ruin makes for a pleasant venture, as much for its lovely setting as anything else. Admission is free; to reach the site visitors must pass through either of the hotels flanking it or approach it from the beach; there is no direct access from the boulevard.

Most hotels and travel agencies work with companies that offer tours to various Mayan ruins sites outside Cancún. Sample destinations (and approximate fares, including site admission) are: Chichén Itzá (US$60), Tulum and Xel-ha (US$60), and Xcaret (US$90). Budget-conscious travelers can go to the bus station in Ciudad Cancún and join a tour for a lot less money. Samples (including transportation on an air-conditioned bus and site admission) are: Chichén Itzá (US$40, also including a buffet lunch; departs 9 am, returns 5 pm); Xcaret (US$50, also including maps and an information sheet; departs 9 and 10 am, returns 6 pm); Tulum and Xel-ha (US$38; departs 9 and 10 am, returns 6 pm).

Museo de Antropología e Historia

Cancún's Museum of Anthropology and History is on the south side of the Centro de Convenciones in the Zona Hotelera. Most of the items – including jewelry, masks and intentionally deformed skulls – are from the Postclassic period (1200-1500 AD). Other exhibits include a Classic-period hieroglyphic staircase inscribed with dates from the 6th century, and the stucco head that gave the local archaeological zone its name of El Rey. Most of the informative signs are in Spanish only, but at the ticket counter you can get an English information sheet, which describes in detail the museum's 47 showcases. Open 9 am to 8 pm daily (US$2, free on Sunday and holidays).

Activities

For **diving** and **snorkeling**, the area's premier operator is AquaWorld (☎ 885-22-88, fax 885-22-99, www.aquaworld.com.mx), Boulevard Kukulcán Km 15.2, a PADI-certified outfit that offers a number of dives, tours and courses. Aqua Tours (☎ 883-04-00, fax 883-04-03, info@aquatours.net, www.aquatours.net), Boulevard Kukulcán Km 6.25, and Scuba Cancún (☎ 883-58-46, 883-10-11, fax 884-23-36, scuba@cancun.com.mx, www.scubacancun.com.mx), Boulevard Kukulcán Km 5, are also PADI-certified and offer a wide range of dive options at reasonable prices.

The resort hotels, travel agencies and various tour operators in the area can book you on day-cruise boats that take snorkelers to the barrier reef, as well as to other dive sites within 100km of Cancún. If you're satisfied seeing the sparser aquatic life off Cancún's beaches, you can rent snorkeling equipment for about US$10 a day from most luxury hotels.

Deep-sea **fishing** excursions also can be booked through a travel agent or one of the large hotels and are available from Aqua Tours for US$70 to US$100. A less expensive way to go is to head over to the Puerto Juárez ferry dock just north of Ciudad Cancún in the morning and negotiate a deal with a fishing-boat captain (prospective clients are expected to bargain over the price).

Most of the major resorts rent **kayaks**; a few make them available to guests free. AquaWorld rents **boogie boards**, **inflatables** and snorkel gear (US$11 a day for each). For **water-skiing**, Aqua Tours will provide you with a speedboat, an instructor and water skis for US$1 per minute with a 15-minute minimum.

Places to Stay

With the exception of one inexpensive hostel and a handful of moderately priced hotels, all of the accommodations in the Zona Hotelera are pricey compared to other Mexican vacation retreats. Rates vary seasonally, sometimes doubling during the period from mid-December through March. You can check with a travel agency or the Internet or both to find the best hotel deals available. What you will find is that all the budget accommodations are in Ciudad Cancún.

On Isla Cancún and at other popular Yucatán destinations, seasons influence hotel rates. Rooms can cost twice as much per night from mid-December through March. If you're traveling on a shoestring, your best bet is to stay in Ciudad Cancún; it's just a brief and inexpensive bus ride from the island and the hotel rates are much lower.

Places to Stay – Budget

Four kilometers from the bus station, the area's one hostel is *Atención a la Juventud* (☎ 883-13-37, fax 883-04-84, Boulevard Kukulcán Km 3.2), on the left side of the road just past the Km 3 marker as you come from Ciudad Cancún. Built decades ago as a modern 600-bed complex in honor of youth, it is now dilapidated, with 300 beds still in use. The staff is friendly and the prices are reasonable. A single-sex dorm bed costs US$8 (plus a US$6 deposit for a sheet and pillow). Camping on the lawn out back costs US$4 per person, including a locker and use of shower and bathroom facilities. The hostel is open to all ages, and space is usually available.

All the area's budget hotels are in Ciudad Cancún. *Hotel El Alux* (☎ 884-66-13, fax 884-05-56, Avenida Uxmal 21) is a block from the bus station. The 35 air-conditioned rooms with hot-water shower, phone and TV go for US$22 to US$25 single, US$26 to US$30 double. An *alux*, by the way, is the Mayan version of a leprechaun.

Across Avenida Uxmal is the somewhat quiet, 38-room *Hotel Cotty* (☎ 884-13-19, fax 884-05-50, Avenida Uxmal 44). Rooms with shower, air-con, cable TV and two double beds cost US$25/27/30 single/double/triple. Off-street parking is available.

A few steps farther along Avenida Uxmal is Calle Palmera, where **Hotel María Isabel** (☎ 884-90-15, *Palmera 59*) offers rooms with private shower, air-con and cable TV for US$23/27 single/double. This clean, quiet, nine-room place is perhaps the best value close to the bus station.

From Avenida Uxmal, walk south along Avenida Yaxchilán and turn right after one block at Calle Punta Allen to find quiet **Casa de Huéspedes Punta Allen** (☎ 884-02-25, 884-10-01, *Punta Allen 8*). This family-run guest house has several double rooms with bath and air-con for US$23 to US$27, light breakfast included. **Hotel Colonial** (☎/fax 884-15-35, *Tulipanes 22*) has 50 rooms facing a courtyard and offers very good value at US$26 per room without air-con, US$31 with. This hotel is a favorite with Mexico City-based businesspeople who frequent Cancún.

Around the corner from the bus station is **Hotel Novotel** (☎ 884-29-99, fax 884-31-62, *Avenida Tulum 75*). Rooms in the main building have air-con and cost US$38 single/double; front rooms can be noisy. Behind the main building, rooms in *cabañas* around the pool have fans only and no TV, but they're quiet and cost just US$27 to US$32. Triple and quad rooms are available as well.

Another fine hotel is **Suites El Patio** (☎ 884-35-00, fax 884-35-40, http://cancun-suites.com, *Avenida Bonampak 51*), at the northern end of Cereza, with 13 charming rooms ranging from US$35 to US$55 depending on size, air-con and other amenities. It has a communal refrigerator, TV room and restaurant on the premises and a laundry across the street. The friendly owner speaks English, French and Spanish.

Hotel Cancún Handall (☎ 884-11-22, fax 884-19-76), on Avenida Tulum 50m south of Avenida Cobá, offers air-conditioned rooms with cable TV for US$38 most of the year. Noise can be a problem, but the hotel is comfortable and clean.

Hotel Tulum (☎ 884-1890), at the corner of Avenida Tulum and Claveles, offers 22 rooms with two twin beds, air-con, cable TV, telephone and minibar for US$39 per room. Not as centrally situated but a better value is **Hotel El Rey del Caribe** (☎ 884-20-28, fax 884-98-57, reycarib@cancun.rce.com.mx), at the corner of Avenida Uxmal and Avenida Nader. All 23 units are air-conditioned suites with fully equipped kitchenettes, and the grounds hold a pool, jacuzzi and private parking. Room rates are US$39 single/double most of the year.

Places to Stay – Mid-Range

Isla Cancún In choosing a moderately priced hotel on Isla Cancún (that is, one that's under US$100 for two people most of the year), it's good to keep in mind that the closer you are to Boulevard Kukulcán, the closer you are to cheap and convenient transportation.

The **Laguna Real** (☎ 883-28-99, fax 883-00-03, *Quetzal 8*), 100m off Boulevard Kukulcán Km 7.7, is an excellent find. Each of its 36 air-conditioned rooms has two double beds and cable TV. A pool is on the premises, and guests have use of all facilities at the seaside Gran Caribe Real and Costa Real resorts. Rates range from US$65 to US$95.

A stone's throw from the Laguna Real is the **Imperial Laguna** (☎ 883-00-70, 407-331-7355 in the USA, fax 883-01-06, 407-834-3337 in the USA, *Quetzal 13*), which offers 30 standard rooms, 10 one-bedroom suites, 10 two-bedroom suites and two three-bedroom suites. All of the suites contain at least two double beds and a sofa bed, a kitchenette (with utensils), satellite TV and a balcony. It's a super value at only US$65 a room.

Just down the street is **Sina Suites** (☎ 883-10-17, 883-10-18, 877-666-9837 in the USA, fax 883-24-58, *Quetzal 33*), where each of the 33 spacious suites has a bedroom with two double beds, a separate living room with sofa bed, a kitchen, 1½ baths and satellite TV. Other amenities include a pool, bar and restaurant. The room rate is US$70 except in December, when it's US$106 or US$117. Add US$20 for a master suite that's perfect for two couples (there's a separate bedroom and bathroom for each).

The **Blue Lagoon** (☎/fax 883-12-15, Quetzal 39) offers 24 one-bedroom suites with private balcony, air-con and cable TV. There's a pool, and each suite is roomy and comfortable – a great find for US$60 per room most of the year.

In the vicinity of Playa Linda but facing the lagoon is **Laguna Inn** (☎ 883-20-55, 407-331-7355 in the USA, fax 883-20-61, 407-834-3337 in the USA; Calle del Pescador, Lote D-8-3), with 90 air-conditioned rooms, each containing either two double beds or one queen-size bed. It has a pool, a tree-shaded courtyard and an inviting palapa bar-restaurant. Rooms typically rent for US$70 a night single/double.

The popular **Cancún Marina Club** (☎ 883-15-61, 883-14-09, 800-448-8355 in the USA, Boulevard Kukulcán Km 5.5) has one of the most inviting pools in Cancún and a very pleasant restaurant-bar overlooking the lagoon. The premises hold a travel agency and a water-sports center. Among the 75 rooms are 10 penthouses with Jacuzzis. Expect to pay US$85 per room most of the time.

Considering its location and amenities, the **Aristos Cancún Hotel** (☎ 883-00-11, 800-527-4786 in the USA, fax 883-00-78, intl.sales@aristoshotels.com, www.aristoshotels.com, Boulevard Kukulcán Km 9.6) offers the best value of Cancún's moderately priced digs. Its 250 balconied rooms come with satellite TV, air-con and either two double beds or one king-size bed. All rooms face the sea or the lagoon. Facilities include two pools (one for kids), two tennis courts, pool tables, two restaurants and three bars. Rates generally range from US$80 to US$100.

Ciudad Cancún Directly across from the bus station is the **Hotel Best Western Plaza Caribe** (☎ 884-13-77, 800-528-1234 in the USA, fax 884-63-52), www.bestwestern.com, Avenida Tulum 13), by the intersection with Avenida Uxmal, offering 140 comfortable air-conditioned rooms and all the amenities for US$60 double. A pool and restaurant are on the premises.

The very pleasant **Hotel Antillano** (☎ 884-15-32, fax 884-18-78), on Claveles at Avenida Tulum, has a pool and 48 rooms with air-con and cable TV for US$45/52/58 single/double/triple.

Certainly the nicest place to stay along popular Avenida Yaxchilán is the cheerful **Hotel Margaritas** (☎ 884-93-33, fax 884-13-24, Avenida Yaxchilán 41). Its 100 rooms have air-con, cable TV and bath, and other amenities include a pool, restaurant and bar. Rates are a bargain at US$60 per room.

The **Hotel Suites Caribe Internacional** (☎ 884-39-99, fax 884-19-93, Avenida Sunyaxchén 36) has 80 standard rooms with air-con and cable TV for US$70, as well as numerous junior suites with two beds, sofa, kitchenette and living room for US$85.

Places to Stay – Top End

All of the luxury resorts in this price category border the Caribbean and have rooms with air-con, satellite TV and, in many cases, balconies with sea views. Room rates range from US$100 to US$500; to obtain the best rate, shop around. Often the best rates available are contained in hotel-and-airfare packages. Because the rates offered by each resort vary greatly, depending on when and where guests book reservations, and because all of the resorts are conveniently located along Boulevard Kukulcán, the hotels listed below are arranged by their location along the boulevard rather than by cost.

Club Las Perlas (☎ 883-20-22, fax 883-08-30, clperlas@cancun.rce.com.mx), at Km 2.5, boasts 194 rooms in a close grouping of three- and four-story buildings. The resort's location, at the end of the Hotel Zone, means its beach is considerably quieter than those farther east and to the south. Rates typically start at US$100 double.

Costa Real (☎ 881-73-00, 800-543-7556 in the USA, fax 881-73-99, real@bestday.com, www.real.com.mx), at Km 4, is a large, all-inclusive resort with attractive grounds and a shared-facilities agreement with the much more spectacular Gran Caribe Real to the east. With rates as low as US$100 per person double occupancy, including food, this place offers great value most of the year.

Gran Caribe Real (☎ 881-73-00, 800-543-7556 in the USA, fax 881-73-99, real@

bestday.com), at Km 5.7, has 466 deluxe rooms (all with ocean views), 32 junior suites and two three-story, three-bedroom penthouse suites. All come with private terraces that overlook a dazzling swimming pool and 200m of beach. Room rates start at US$275. An all-inclusive plan runs US$150 per person, double occupancy.

An often-overlooked bargain is the **Kin-Ha** (☎ 883-23-77, fax 883-21-47, *kinha3@ mail.caribe.net.mx)*, at Km 8.1, which consists of 166 suites in four buildings. The property was entirely renovated in 1993. All rooms feature a balcony and two double beds or one king-size bed. A travel agency, car rental agency, mini-market, bars and a gym are on the premises. Room rates start at US$140 much of the year.

Sierra Cancún (☎ 883-24-44, 800-448-5028 in the USA, fax 883-34-86), at Km 10, features 123 standard rooms (mostly lagoon view), 124 mini-suites (all ocean view), and a variety of larger suites. This Mexican-owned and operated resort offers all the usual amenities for a reasonable price of US$90 and up per person, meals included.

Hyatt Cancún Caribe (☎ 883-00-44, 800-233-1234 in the USA, fax 883-15-14, *www .hyatt.com)*, at Km 10.3, has a terrific variety of accommodations and amenities among its 198 lovely rooms and suites. Rooms start around US$180 and villas around US$230.

Piramides Cancún (☎ 885-13-33, fax 885-01-13), at Km 11.75, has 286 charming and balconied rooms and suites. The grounds are idyllic and the beach particularly deep. The resort 'shares' a real Mayan ruin with its neighbor to the south, the Sheraton Cancún. Room rates often start at a very reasonable US$140; add US$60 for high season.

The elegant **Sheraton Cancún** (☎ 883-19-88, 800-325-3535 in the USA, fax 885-02-04, *www.sheraton.com)*, at Km 12, has tremendous appeal, from the lobby to the immaculate gardens to the gorgeous tiled art in the restaurant. At US$130 a room, it's an excellent value.

Tucan Cun Beach (☎ 885-08-14, fax 885-18-50, *ventasj@cancun.com.mx)*, at Km 12.9, is a fun, budget-minded all-inclusive resort with 260 rooms, decent food and an inviting pool with swim-up bar. Per person rates most of the year hover around US$130.

Crown Paradise Club (☎ 885-10-22, 800-544-3005 in the USA, fax 885-17-07, *www .crownparadise.com.mx)*, at Km 18.3, is an all-inclusive resort featuring four restaurants, four bars, four pools and the only water park for children available at a Cancún resort. The curving tower holds 364 rooms, each with a balcony, marble floors, and soothing sea views. Rack rates typically start at US$155 per person.

Places to Eat

Budget Arguably the island's top budget restaurant is **Checándole**, inside Plaza Flamingo, which specializes in good Yucatecan food. No items cost more than US$5. At the west end of Plaza Kukulcán, on the 2nd floor, are **Las Fajitas**, which serves a variety of combination Yucatecan plates for around US$6, and **El Chimichurri**, which specializes in grilled meats prepared Mexican style. Most dishes at El Chimichurri feature top sirloin yet are under US$7.

Facing Boulevard Kukulcán near Km 8.5, and part of the Plaza Terramar, is **La Ruina**, specializing in undeniably unhealthy and delicious Mexican traditionals, best when consumed with one of the restaurant's potent margaritas.

Nothing is priced over US$7 at **Restaurant Río Nizuc**, at the end of a short, nameless road near Boulevard Kukulcán Km 22. It's a nice place to settle in a chair under a palapa and watch caravans of snorkelers in sporty little boats pass by.

Ciudad Cancún's market, near the post office, is a building set back from the street and emblazoned with the name 'Mercado Municipal Artículo 115 Constitucional' – it's called simply **Mercado 28** (that's 'mercado veintiocho') by the locals. In the second courtyard in from the street are the eateries: **Restaurant Margely**, **Cocina Familiar Económica Chulum**, **Cocina La Chaya** and others. Most are open for breakfast, lunch and dinner, and all offer *comidas corridas* for as little as US$3, and sandwiches for less.

Over the Rainbow Café (*Tulipanes 30)* is a charming, air-conditioned café that specializes in crêpes, none of which is more than US$3. The menu also offers a fine variety of sandwiches, salads and pastries (most under US$4) and a good selection of coffee drinks. This is a pleasant and civilized place to start your day.

El Rincón Yucateco (*Avenida Uxmal 24*), across from Hotel Cotty, serves excellent yet inexpensive Yucatecan food. Often overlooked but a good bargain is **Restaurant Pop**, Avenida Tulum near Avenida Uxmal, with outdoor and air-conditioned indoor seating. On the menu are salads, soups and pastas, as well as fish, chicken and beef dishes; few items are over US$6.

Restaurant Mexicano Los Amigos (*Avenida Tulum 10*) is a fairly open-air restaurant that serves decent Mexican and American food for US$4 to US$9. Next door and very similar is the **Restaurant Las Carretas**.

Santa Clara, Avenida Tulum at Avenida Uxmal, specializes in ice cream. The supermarket with the freshest produce and the best selection of meats and cheeses is the **Comercial Mexicana**, also at the intersection of Avenidas Tulum and Uxmal.

Mid-Range One of the island's most popular bar-restaurant-discos is **Pat O'Brien's**, at the north end of Plaza Flamingo. This is the kind of place where cute barmaids pour blue liquor down customers' throats, bar dudes carry drinks on their heads, and the music is always rock 'n' roll. The munchies menu includes burgers, nachos and sandwiches; prices range from US$8 to US$18.

Rainforest Café, in the Forum mall, 2nd floor, is a popular American chain. As its name suggests, the café features walls lined with fanciful faux rain-forest scenes, accompanied by faux lightning, faux thunder and faux rain. Dishes hover around US$8.

Hard Rock Café, also in the Forum mall, is a big hit despite its outrageous prices: burgers for US$9.50, sandwiches for US$10 – even some salads are around US$10. For the same kind of upscale American fast food with some Mexican options but at lower cost, try **Señor Frog's** (*Boulevard Kukulcán Km 9.8*) or **Carlos 'n Charlie's** (*Boulevard Kukulcán Km 5.25*).

Restaurant '100% Natural' (*Boulevard Kukulcán Km 8.65*), on the north side of Plaza Terramar, is one of a chain of 24-hour restaurants specializing in healthy food, including low-fat sandwiches, burgers and pasta dishes, numerous chicken and fish dishes and a wide selection of yogurt-fruit-vegetable combinations. Few items are over US$9. You'll find another branch in Ciudad Cancún at Avenida Sunyaxchén near Avenida Yaxchilán.

Most of the moderately priced restaurants in Ciudad Cancún are in the city center. If you're willing to spend between US$12 and US$20 for dinner, you can eat very well here.

Restaurant El Pescador (*Tulipanes 28*) has been serving dependably good meals since the early days of the two Cancúns. As its name suggests, El Pescador specializes in seafood. Most of the specialties cost US$14 or more.

Rolandi's Restaurant-Bar (*Avenida Cobá 12*), between Avenidas Tulum and Nader just off the southern roundabout, is an attractive Italian eatery serving elaborate one-person pizzas (US$7 to US$11), spaghetti plates and more substantial dishes of veal and chicken.

Los Almendros, on Avenida Bonampak near Avenida Sayil, is the local incarnation of Yucatán's most famous restaurant. Started in Ticul in 1962, it set out to serve country food for the bourgeoisie and claims to have invented *poc-chuc*, a dish of succulent pork cooked with onion and served in a tomato sauce made tangy with bitter oranges. A full meal costs around US$15.

La Parrilla (*Avenida Yaxchilán 51*) is a traditional Mexican restaurant, popular with the city's wealthier residents. The air is fan-cooled, large Spanish tiles cover the floor and pillars, an orange-brown paint coats the walls, and wrought iron abounds. Mariachis make their rounds between the tables, as does the waitstaff, carrying plates of grilled steak wrapped in cactus leaves (US$8), sautéed grouper (US$8) and *mole* enchiladas (US$5).

Top End On Isla Cancún, the **Crab House** (*Boulevard Kukulcán Km 14.8*) is a draw as much for its lovely view of the lagoon as for its seafood. The long menu includes a hearty selection of appetizers (US$6 to US$10), pasta (US$13), many shrimp and fillet-of-fish dishes (around US$15) and a variety of other seafood specials (US$12 to US$23). Crab is priced by the pound (US$20 to US$30 for a full meal).

About 25m north of the Crab House, facing the lagoon, is *La Dolce Vita*, one of Cancún's two fancy Italian restaurants; the other is *Il Paparazzi (Boulevard Kukulcán Km 18)*, overlooking Playa Delfines. Expect to pay around US$20 with beverage at either.

For steak, head to *Ruth's Chris Steak House*, in Plaza Kukulcán, or *Outback Steakhouse*, in Plaza Flamingo. Ruth's Chris is known internationally for its fresh, corn-fed, expensive beef (none of the meat dishes is under US$20 and most are substantially more). Outback is known as a fun Aussie-theme restaurant, and prices are considerably lower.

In Ciudad Cancún, a long-standing favorite is *Rosa Mexicano (Claveles 4)*, the place to go for unusual Mexican dishes and a pleasant hacienda decor. The menu offers some concessions to Cancún, such as tortilla soup and *filete tampiqueña*, but also holds adventurous selections such as squid sautéed with three chilies, garlic and scallions, and shrimp in a sauce made of ground pumpkin seeds and spices. Dinner prices range from US$10 to US$30 (for lobster).

Another favorite is elegant *La Habichuela (Margaritas 25)*, just off Parque Las Palmas in a residential neighborhood. The menu tends toward elegant, easily comprehended dishes such as shish kebab flambé, lobster in champagne sauce and beef tampiqueña. Dinner costs US$20 to US$25.

At the somewhat formal *Carrillo's Live Lobster House (Claveles 35)*, lobster dishes cost around US$30. Also available are numerous shrimp and fish dishes for around US$10.

Entertainment
Most of Cancún's nightlife is loud and booze oriented, and the dance clubs are as wild as you'll find anywhere. Most charge US$10

admission. Some don't open their doors before 10 pm, and none is hopping much before midnight.

Dady'O, opposite the Forum mall (Boulevard Kukulcán Km 9), is one of Cancún's hottest dance clubs. The beat is pure disco, and the setting is a five-level black-walled faux cave with a two-level dance floor and zillions of laser beams and strobes. Next door is *Dady Rock*, a steamy rock 'n' roll club with live music.

Christine (Boulevard Kukulcán Km 8.85) features a synchronized light, sound and video system and English rock from the 1970s and '80s; it attracts a fair number of thirtysomethings. *La Boom (Boulevard Kukulcán Km 3.8)* features Top 40 tunes played at high decibels. *Cat's*, on the south side of Plaza La Parrilla (Boulevard Kukulcán Km 8.75), is the one true reggae club in Cancún, with live music each evening; a hip-hop band usually plays on nights the house band is off.

For live Cuban music, head to *Melao Bar*, Avenida Yaxchilán at Calle Punta Allen, an intimate upstairs club where the atmosphere can be magical. There's no cover, but the performances often don't begin until after 11 pm. Another Cuban venue, with very few tourists, is *Merengue*, on Avenida Tulum near Avenida Cobá, next to the Hotel Cancún Handall. The club presents three shows nightly, at 9.30 pm, 11 pm and 1 am; no cover, but don't come casually dressed.

An excellent alternative to the party scene is the *Folkloric Ballet of Cancún (☎ 881-04-00 ext 193, fax 881-04-02, Boulevard Kukulcán Km 8.8)*, which performs inside the Centro de Convenciones. The first-rate show includes dances from various Mexican regions, including one with ancient Mayan ceremonial themes. Performances take place nightly at 8 pm (arrive no later than 7.15 for good seats) and cost US$28 for the show and a drink, US$46 for the show, a drink and a buffet dinner (the food is delicious).

Gay Clubs Ciudad Cancún has a significant gay scene, but it's not apparent until well after sunset. The *Backstage Theater-Cabaret (☎ 887-91-06, Tulipanes 30)* features drag shows, strippers (male and female), fashion shows and musicals. This is a very cool place, with terrific ambiance and a joyful crowd. Admission is usually US$3.

Disco Karamba, above Ristorante Casa Italiana on the corner of Azucenas and Avenida Tulum, is famous for its frequent drink specials. *Picante*, on Avenida Tulum 100m north of Avenida Uxmal, is mainly for talkers, not dancers.

Getting There & Away

Air Cancún is served by many direct international flights (see the Getting There & Away chapter). The general information number at the airport is ☎ 886-00-49.

From Cancún, between Aerocaribe and Aerocozumel (both owned by Mexicana) there is one flight daily to Campeche (US$85), Ciudad del Carmen (US$85), Mexico City (US$130), Oaxaca (US$115), Tuxtla Gutiérrez (US$115) and Veracruz (US$145). The airlines have a total of two flights daily to Chetumal (US$70), Chichén Itzá (US$50) and Palenque (US$115), three flights daily to Villahermosa (US$115), and four flights daily to Mérida (US$70). They also provide 15 flights daily to Cozumel (US$50), one flight daily to Belize City (US$115), one flight daily (except Thursday and Saturday) to Flores, Guatemala (US$115), and two flights daily to Havana, Cuba (US$115).

Aviacsa, a regional carrier based in Tuxtla Gutiérrez, has flights from Cancún to Mérida, Mexico City, Oaxaca, Tapachula, Tuxtla Gutiérrez, Villahermosa and points in Guatemala. Aviateca runs flights from Cancún to Flores, Guatemala, and on to Guatemala City several times a week. Several major international carriers and the Mexican carrier TAESA also offer domestic flights from Cancún.

If you intend to fly from Cancún to other parts of Mexico, you are well advised to reserve your airline seat ahead of time to avoid any unpleasant surprises. Airline contact information is:

Aerocaribe/Aerocozumel (☎ 884-20-00, 886-01-62 at the airport), Avenida Cobá 5, Ciudad Cancún, www.aerocaribe.com

Aeroméxico (☎ 884-10-97, 886-00-03 at the airport), Avenida Cobá 80, between Avenidas Tulum and Bonampak, Ciudad Cancún, www.aeromexico.com

American Airlines (☎ 884-10-57, 886-00-55 at the airport), Avenida Yaxchilán at Jazmines, Ciudad Cancún, www.aa.com

Aviacsa (☎ 887-42-14, fax 884-65-99), Avenida Cobá 37, Ciudad Cancún, www.aviacsa.com

Aviateca (☎ 884-39-38, fax 884-33-28), Avenida Cobá 37, Ciudad Cancún, www.grupotaca.com

Continental (☎ 886-00-06, fax 886-00-07), Avenida Yaxchilán at Jazmines, Ciudad Cancún, www.continental.com

LACSA (☎ 887-31-01, 887-41-01 at the airport), Avenida Cobá 5, Ciudad Cancún, www.grupotaca.com

Mexicana (☎ 887-44-44, 883-48-81 in the Centro de Convenciones, Zona Hotelera), Avenida Cobá 39, Ciudad Cancún, www.mexicana.com

Northwest (☎ 886-00-46, 886-00-44), at Cancún airport, www.nwa.com

TAESA (☎ 887-43-14, 886-02-07 at the airport), Avenida Yaxchilán 31, Ciudad Cancún, http://taesa.com.mx

Bus The bus station on Avenida Uxmal just west of Avenida Tulum has two separate parts under the same roof; look in both. Companies include Autobuses de Oriente (ADO), Autotransportes de Oriente (Oriente), Transportes de Lujo Línea Dorada (Línea Dorada, a 2nd-class line), Autotransportes del Sur (ATS), Autobuses del Noroeste and Autobuses del Centro. Services are 2nd-class, 1st-class or any of several luxury flavors.

Across from the bus station entrance is the ticket office of Playa Express, which runs shuttle buses down the Caribbean coast to Tulum and Felipe Carrillo Puerto at least every 30 minutes all day, stopping at major towns and points of interest along the way.

Here are some major routes (daily):

Chetumal – 382km, 6 hours; 12 buses (US$10 to US$14)

Chichén Itzá – 205km, 2 to 3½ hours; 10 buses (US$5 to US$9)

Mérida – 320km, 3 to 5 hours; buses at least every half hour, Super Expresso buses make the run in under 3 hours (US$7 to US$12)

Mexico City – 1772km, 20 hours; 6 buses (US$63)

Playa del Carmen – 65km, 40 minutes; Playa Express buses every 30 minutes, others 12 times daily (US$2.50)

Puerto Morelos – 36km, 40 minutes; Playa Express buses every 30 minutes, others 12 times daily (US$2)

Ticul – 395km, 4 to 6 hours; 5 Línea Dorada (US$12)

Tizimín – 212km, 3 hours; 6 buses via Valladolid (US$5)

Tulum – 132km, 1½ to 2 hours, Playa Express buses every 30 minutes, other buses about every 2 hours (US$3.50 to US$5)

Valladolid – 160km, 1½ to 2 hours; buses at least every half hour (US$8)

Villahermosa – 915km, 9 hours; 3 ADO (US$38)

Car & Motorcycle Alamo (☎ 883-06-66), Avis (☎ 886-01-47), Dollar (☎ 886-01-79), Executive (☎ 846-13-87), Hertz (☎ 886-01-50) and Mónaco (☎ 886-02-39) have counters at the airport. Bear in mind that you can receive better rates and have a better selection of vehicles if you reserve ahead of time.

Executive Car Rental (☎ 885-03-72, 885-03-73, fax 884-26-99, www.executive.com.mx), Boulevard Kukulcán Km 15.5, occasionally has vehicles long after the airport offices have rented out all of theirs. Weekly rates are available.

Turimaz Rent a Car (☎ 841-34-70), Boulevard Kukulcán Km 8.25, rents Honda Elite scooters for US$10 an hour, 18-speed bikes for US$2 an hour and electric bikes for US$6 an hour. Marina Punta del Este (☎ 883-12-10), Boulevard Kukulcán Km 10.3, rents Yamaha BWS 100cc scooters for US$10 an hour or US$50 a day.

Getting Around
To/From the Airport Orange-and-beige airport vans (Transporte Terrestre, US$7.50) monopolize the trade, charging taxi fare for a van ride with other travelers. Traditional taxi service will cost you an outrageous US$41. The route into town is invariably via Punta Nizuc and north up Isla Cancún along Boulevard Kukulcán, passing all the luxury hotels before reaching the youth hostel and Ciudad Cancún. If your hotel is in Ciudad Cancún, the ride there may take as long as 45 minutes.

If you walk out of the airport and follow the access road, you can often flag down a taxi that will take you for less because the driver is no longer subject to the expensive regulated airport fares. If you're willing to walk the 2km to the highway, you can flag down a passing bus, which is very cheap (US$0.45).

To return to the airport, you must take a taxi or hop off a southbound bus at the airport junction and walk the 2km to the terminal.

Bus To reach the island from Ciudad Cancún, catch any bus with 'Hoteles' or 'Zona Hotelera' on the windshield as it travels south along Avenida Tulum or east along Avenida Cobá. The fare each way is US$0.45. To get back to town, go to one of the bus stops along Boulevard Kukulcán and board any of the buses headed toward Ciudad Cancún (or, away from the airport). If a bus stop isn't near you, a wave at the driver of an approaching bus often is enough to catch a ride.

To reach Puerto Juárez and the Isla Mujeres ferries, take a Ruta 13 ('Pto Juárez' or 'Punta Sam') bus.

Taxi Cancún's taxis do not have meters, so you must haggle over fares. The fare between Ciudad Cancún and Punta Cancún is US$4 or US$5. To the airport costs US$10 (from Ciudad Cancún) to US$12 (from Punta Cancún). To Puerto Juárez from Punta Cancún you'll pay about US$13.

ISLA MUJERES
● pop 8320 ☎ 9

Isla Mujeres (Island of Women) has a reputation as a backpackers' Cancún – a quieter island where many of the same amenities and attractions cost a lot less. That's not as true today – Cancún makes itself felt each morning as boatload after boatload of package tourists arrives for a day's excursion. But Isla Mujeres continues to offer excellent value, a popular sunbathing beach and plenty of dive and snorkel sites. Though its

YUCATÁN PENINSULA

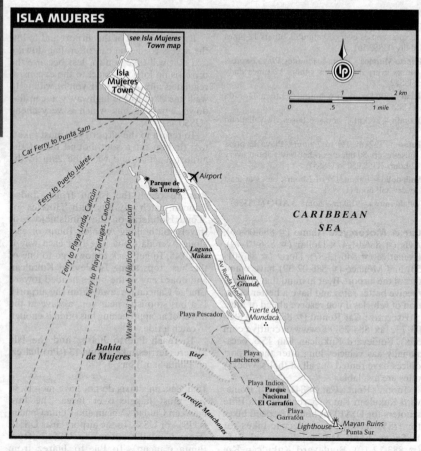

ISLA MUJERES

see Isla Mujeres Town map

Isla Mujeres Town

Car Ferry to Punta Sam

Ferry to Puerto Juárez

Ferry to Playa Linda, Cancún

Ferry to Playa Tortugas, Cancún

Water Taxi to Club Náutico Dock, Cancún

✈ Airport

♣ Parque de las Tortugas

Laguna Makax

Salina Grande

Av. Rueda Medina

Playa Pescador

Fuerte de Mundaca ∴

Bahía de Mujeres

Reef

Playa Lancheros

Playa Indios

Parque Nacional El Garrafón

Playa Garrafón

Arrecife Manchones

Lighthouse ⛯ *Mayan Ruins* Punta Sur

CARIBBEAN SEA

0   1   2 km
0   .5   1 mile

---

character is changing, the island's chief attribute is still its relaxed tropical social life and waters that are turquoise blue and bathtub warm. Fishing remains a big way of life here, just as it has been for years.

History

Although many locals believe Isla Mujeres got its name because Spanish buccaneers kept their lovers on the island while they were out plundering galleons and pillaging ports, a less romantic but still intriguing explanation is probably more accurate. According to the writings of Friar Diego de

Landa, in 1517 Francisco Hernández de Córdoba sailed from Cuba with three ships to procure slaves for the Cuban mines. The expedition came upon Isla Mujeres, where the conquistadors found a stone temple containing clay figurines of Mayan goddesses. Córdoba named the island after the icons.

Orientation

The island is 8km long, 300 to 800m wide and 11km off the coast. The town of Isla Mujeres is at the northern tip of the island, and the ruins of the Mayan temple are at the southern tip. The two are linked by Avenida Rueda Medina, a loop road that hugs the coast. Between them are a handful of small fishing villages, several saltwater lakes, a string of west-facing beaches, a large lagoon and a small airport.

The best snorkeling sites and some of the best swimming beaches are on the southern part of the island along the western shore; the eastern shore is washed by the open sea, and the surf there is dangerous. The ferry docks, the town and the most popular sand beach (Playa Norte) are at the island's northern tip.

Information

Tourist Offices An island-sponsored tourist information office (☎ 877-07-67, ☎/fax 877-03-07, infoisla@qroo1.telmex.net.mex) is on Avenida Rueda Medina between Madero and Morelos. One member of its friendly staff speaks English, but the rest speak Spanish only. It's open 8 am to 9 pm Monday to Friday, 9 am to 2 pm Saturday and Sunday. For information, you also can try the Café Internet (☎/fax 877-04-61), on Hidalgo near Abasolo, whose English- and Spanish-speaking owner knows the island well and is receptive to inquiries from friendly visitors.

Money Several banks lie within a couple of blocks of the ferry docks. All exchange currency, have ATMs and are open 8.30 am to 5 pm Monday to Friday, 9 am to 2 pm Saturday.

Post & Communications The post office, on Guerrero at López Mateos, is open from 8 am to 7 pm Monday to Friday, from 9 am to 1 pm Saturday and Sunday. Telmex pay phones are abundant, and operated least expensively by using a Ladatel phone card.

Internet Resources The Café Internet, on Hidalgo near Abasolo, offers Internet access and email services; as the name suggests, food and beverages are available. Open 10 am to 2 pm and 5 to 8 pm Monday to Friday, 10 am to 7 pm Saturday, 10 am to noon and 6 to 8 pm Sunday. La Casita Bakery, on Madero between Hidalgo and Guerrero, is a great place to nibble on pastries while sending emails. Open 7.30 am to 9.30 pm daily. CompuIsla, on Abasolo just south of Juárez, provides Internet and email services 8 am to 10 pm daily. All three charge US$0.10 per minute and have 15-minute minimums.

Bookstores Cosmic Cosas (Matamoros 82), just north of Hidalgo, is a nifty store that buys, sells and trades English-language books and magazines and carries literature in a number of languages, plus titles on ancient Mayan life, contemporary local cooking and regional history. The store has a comfortable living room where visitors are welcome to relax, and the owner enjoys offering tourist information. Open 9 am to 2 pm and 4 to 9 pm daily.

Laundry Laundries are plentiful on Isla Mujeres. All are in town and will wash, dry and fold 4kg of clothes for US$3.50. They're all open 7 am to 9 pm Monday to Friday, 9 am to 1 pm Saturday and Sunday. Lavandería Automática Tim Phó is on Juárez at Abasolo. Lavandería JR is on Abasolo between Avenida Rueda Medina and Juárez.

Playa Garrafón

Playa Garrafón is part of Parque Nacional Isla Mujeres, Punta Cancún y Punta Nizuc. Although the waters here are translucent and the fish abundant, Garrafón, at the southern end of the island, is a bit overrated. Hordes of day-trippers from Cancún crowd the waters, and the reef has been heavily damaged by hurricanes and careless visitors, which makes it less likely to inflict cuts but also reduces its color and the intricacy of its formations. Average visibility is 10m.

The water can be very choppy, sweeping you into jagged areas. When the water is running fast, snorkeling is a hassle and can be dangerous. Although much of the park contains shallow reef, the bottom falls off steeply close to shore, so those without strong swimming skills should not venture too far.

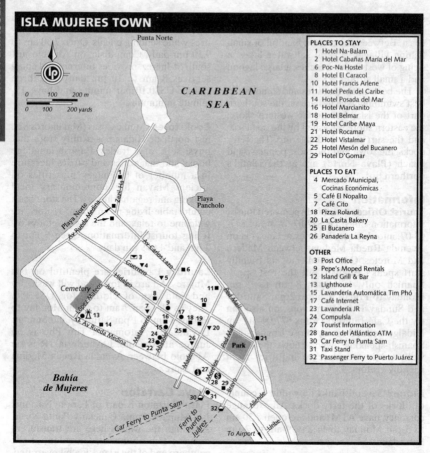

ISLA MUJERES TOWN

PLACES TO STAY
1 Hotel Na-Balam
2 Hotel Cabañas María del Mar
6 Poc-Na Hostel
8 Hotel El Caracol
10 Hotel Francis Arlene
11 Hotel Perla del Caribe
14 Hotel Posada del Mar
16 Hotel Marcianito
18 Hotel Belmar
19 Hotel Caribe Maya
21 Hotel Rocamar
22 Hotel Vistalmar
25 Hotel Mesón del Bucanero
29 Hotel D'Gomar

PLACES TO EAT
4 Mercado Municipal,
   Cocinas Económicas
5 Café El Nopalito
7 Café Cito
18 Pizza Rolandi
20 La Casita Bakery
25 El Bucanero
26 Panadería La Reyna

OTHER
3 Post Office
9 Pepe's Moped Rentals
12 Island Grill & Bar
13 Lighthouse
15 Lavandería Automática Tim Phó
17 Café Internet
23 Lavandería JR
24 CompuIsla
27 Tourist Information
28 Banco del Atlántico ATM
30 Car Ferry to Punta Sam
31 Taxi Stand
32 Passenger Ferry to Puerto Juárez

The park is open 8 am to 5 pm daily (US$4); get there early to avoid the mobs. You can rent lockers and snorkeling equipment (US$8). Garrafón also has a small aquarium and museum. A taxi ride from town costs about US$4. If you elect to walk, take some water with you – it's a hot two-hour trek.

Playa Norte
Walk west along Hidalgo or Guerrero to reach the town's principal beach, sometimes called Playa Los Cocos or Cocoteros. The slope of the beach is gradual, and the transparent and calm waters are only chest-high

even far from shore. But Playa Norte is relatively small for the number of sunseekers who flock to it.

Playa Lancheros
Five kilometers south of town and 1.5km north of Garrafón is Playa Lancheros, the southernmost point served by local buses. The beach is less attractive than Playa Norte, but it has free musical festivities on Sunday.

Isla Mujeres Turtle Farm
Six species of sea turtle lay eggs in the sand along the island's calm western shore. Al-

though they are endangered, sea turtles are still killed throughout Latin America for their eggs and meat, which are considered a delicacy. In the 1980s, efforts by Gonzáalez Cahle Maldonado, a local fisherman, led to the founding of the Centro de Investigaciones and the Isla Mujeres Turtle Farm (☎ 877-05-95, Carretera Sac Bajo Km 5), which protects the turtles' breeding grounds and places their eggs in incubators, out of harm's way. Hatchlings live in three large pools for up to a year, at which time they are tagged for monitoring and released. Because most turtles in the wild die within their first few months, the practice of guarding them until they are a year old greatly increases their chances of survival. Moreover, the turtles that leave this protected beach have the uncanny ability to return here a year later, which means their offspring will receive the same protection. The Turtle Farm is a scientific facility, not an amusement center. But if you'd like to see several hundred sea turtles, ranging in weight from 150g to more than 300kg, this is a place for you. Admission US$2, tours available. The facility is best reached by taxi (about US$2).

Mayan Ruins
Just past Playa Garrafón are the severely worn remains of a temple built to honor Ixchel, Mayan goddess of the moon and fertility, and possibly lesser goddesses. (The conquistadors found clay idols of several women at the site; whether they were all likenesses of Ixchel or represented several goddesses is unclear.) In 1988 Hurricane Gilbert nearly finished the ruins off. Except for a still-distinguishable stairway and scattered remnants of stone buildings, there's little left to see other than a fine sea view and, in the distance, Cancún. You can walk to the ruins, beyond the lighthouse at the south end of the island, from Garrafón. From downtown, a taxi costs US$4.

Fuerte de Mundaca
The ruins of a two-story house, its gardens and a fortress are all that remain of the testament of love built by Fermin Antonio Mundaca de Marechaja, a slave trader and

reputed pirate, for 'La Trigueña' (the Brunette), an island woman who had won his devotion. Unfortunately, she left him for another man while the buildings were still under construction, and Mundaca died brokenhearted. All you'll see today are a stone gate and some walls, but if you look closely, you can make out the name La Trigueña etched into the impressive stone archway. The ruins are east of the main road near Playa Lancheros, about 5km south of town. A taxi ride there costs about US$3.

Diving & Snorkeling
In addition to the good snorkeling at Playa Garrafón (described earlier this section), a handful of lovely reef dives – Arrecife Barracuda, La Bandera, Manchones Xico, El Jigueo and Arrecife Manchones, among others – lie within a short boat ride of the island. A popular nonreef dive destination is El Frío (the Deep Freeze), named for the unusually cool water found there. The site, 90 minutes by boat northeast of Isla Mujeres, contains the intact hull of a 60m-long cargo ship, resting in 30m of water. The ship is thought to have been deliberately sunk.

At all reputable dive centers you'll need to show your certification card and will be expected to have your own gear, though scuba equipment is usually available for rent. The Coral Scuba Diver Center (☎ 877-07-63, fax 877-03-71, www.coralscubadivecenter.com, coral@coralscubadivecenter.com) Matamoros at Avenida Rueda Medina, offers dives for US$39 to US$98; snorkel trips are US$14. Sea Hawk Divers (☎/fax 877-02-96), on Zazil-Ha behind the Hotel Na-Balam, offers dives for US$40 to US$50 and snorkeling tours beginning at US$20.

Places to Stay
The prices shown here reflect those you can expect to find in the off-season. From mid-December to March and during Easter week, many island hotels are booked solid by midday and prices can double.

Budget *Poc-Na Hostel* (☎ 877-00-90, fax 877-00-59), on Matamoros at Avenida Carlos Lazo, is a privately run youth hostel with campsites (US$2.50 per person). The fan-cooled dormitories accommodate men and women together. A bunk and bedding cost US$4; you must put down a deposit for the bedding. Lockers are provided free.

Hotel Marcianito (☎ 877-01-11), on Abasolo between Juárez and Hidalgo, offers excellent value with eight clean, fan-cooled rooms, each containing two beds and a hammock, for US$14. *Hotel Vistalmar* (☎ 877-02-09, fax 877-00-96), on Avenida Rueda Medina between Matamoros and Abasolo, offers 30 very acceptable rooms for US$14/20 single/double with fan, US$18/24 with air-con.

The friendly *Hotel Caribe Maya* (☎ 877-06-84), on Madero between Guerrero and Hidalgo, charges US$17 double with fan, US$21 with air-con. *Hotel Las Palmas* (☎ 877-04-16, Guerrero 20), across from the Mercado Municipal, offers basic but clean rooms with fan and bath for US$13 single/double.

Hotel El Caracol (☎ 877-01-50), on Matamoros between Hidalgo and Guerrero, offers 19 rooms with insect screens, ceiling fans and clean tiled bathrooms; many have two double beds. You pay US$15 double with fan, US$24 with air-con.

Hotel D'Gomar (☎ 877-05-41), on Avenida Rueda Medina between Morelos and Bravo, above a boutique and facing the ferry dock, has four floors of clean air-conditioned rooms with double beds for US$25 double.

Mid-Range The *Hotel Francis Arlene* (☎/fax 877-03-10), on Guerrero between Abasolo and Madero, offers comfortable rooms (many with balconies and sea views) for US$35 with fan, US$40 with air-con.

Hotel Mesón del Bucanero (☎ 877-01-26, fax 877-02-10), on Hidalgo between Abasolo and Madero, is above the restaurant of the same name. Its charming air-conditioned rooms come with two double beds or one queen-size bed for US$36/41 single/double.

Hotel Belmar (☎ 877-04-30, fax 877-04-29), also on Hidalgo between Abasolo and Madero, is above the Pizza Rolandi restaurant and is run by the same friendly family. The comfy, well-kept rooms are a bargain at

US$40 double with air-con. There's also a suite with jacuzzi for US$85.

Hotel Rocamar (☎/fax 877-01-01), at the eastern end of Guerrero, was the town's first real hotel, built decades ago. The 24-room, one-suite hotel has been updated and charges US$40/50/60 single/double/triple. Most of the fan-only rooms have fine sea views and balconies. A pool is on the premises.

Top End The *Hotel Perla del Caribe* (☎ 877-04-44, 800-258-6454 in the USA, fax 877-00-11), on Madero a block north of Guerrero right on the eastern beach, has 91 nice rooms on three floors. All rooms have balconies and air-con, and most have wonderful sea views; US$67 to US$79 double, depending on view. There's a pool on the premises.

Hotel Posada del Mar (☎ 877-00-44, 800-544-3005 in the USA, fax 877-02-66, www .mexhotels.com), on Avenida Rueda Medina between López Mateos and Matamoros, is a lovely newer place with 30 rooms (most with sea views) in a three-story building and 12 bungalows ringing a swimming pool. All units have air-con. Bungalows usually cost US$40, rooms US$50.

Hotel Cabañas María del Mar (☎ 877-01-79, 800-223-5695 in the USA, fax 877-02-13), on both sides of Avenida Carlos Lazo near Playa Norte, offers 29 cabañas and 44 hotel rooms for US$50 to US$80 double. A light breakfast is included, and all rooms have air-con. Other amenities include a restaurant and pool.

Hotel Na-Balam (☎ 877-02-79, fax 877-04-46, www.nabalam.com), on Zazil-Ha, faces Playa Norte on the island's northern tip. Most of the 31 spacious, air-conditioned junior suites have fabulous sea views and numerous nice touches, such as colorful travertine bathroom vanities. Rooms cost US$120 to US$170, and there's a pool.

Places to Eat

By the market are several *cocinas económicas* (economical kitchens) serving simple but tasty and filling meals at the best prices on the island. Breakfasts are rarely more than US$3, and few lunch and dinner items are more than US$4.

La Casita Bakery, on Madero between Guerrero and Hidalgo, has good pastries and sandwiches. *Super Betino*, the food store on the plaza, has a little cafeteria serving tacos and fruit plates for US$1 and change, and sometimes cheap breakfasts. *Panadería La Reyna*, on Madero at Juárez, is *the* place for breakfast buns and snacks.

Café Cito, a small place on Juárez at Matamoros, has a New-Age menu (printed in English and German) offering croissants, fruit, 10 varieties of crêpes and good coffee. Come for breakfast (about US$5) or supper (about US$10). Closed Thursday night.

Café El Nopalito, on Guerrero near Matamoros, specializes in healthful but fancy food, including delicious breakfasts and daily special plates for US$5 to US$7.

El Bucanero, in the Hotel Méson del Bucanero on Hidalgo between Abasolo and Madero, is a fan-cooled restaurant with a pleasing ambiance and a variety of nonalcoholic tropical shakes and drinks. Entrees (most around US$7) include Mexican-style beef tips, fish fillet prepared as you wish and bell peppers stuffed with meat, cheese or tuna. All entrees arrive with soup, beans, rice and coffee.

Across the street, *Pizza Rolandi* serves pizzas and calzones cooked in a wood-fired oven, as well as pasta dishes, fresh salads, fish and some Italian specialties. Expect to pay US$6 to US$10.

Entertainment
The nightlife of Isla Mujeres is fairly nonexistent Sunday through Thursday. On Friday and Saturday nights, the beach bar at *Hotel Na-Balam* draws a crowd with live music and somewhat sedate dancing. Or try *Las Palapas Chimbo's*, on Playa Norte behind the cemetery, where a band uses the restaurant for a public jam session and the foreign youth of the island dance with abandon. The *Island Grill & Bar*, beside the lighthouse on Avenida Rueda Medina at López Mateos, actually has no grill or food service. But it occasionally hosts a rock band, and even without one it's a fine place to have a drink and kick back.

Getting There & Away
Ferries to Isla Mujeres leave from five main points of embarkation on the mainland and Isla Cancún. Starting from the northernmost port and working southeast (see Cancún map), they are:

Punta Sam Car ferries, which also take bicycles, motorcycles and foot passengers, depart from Punta Sam, about 5km north of the city center and 3.5km north of Puerto Juárez. They take at least an hour to reach the island. Departure times are 8 and 11 am and 2.45, 5.30 and 8.15 pm from Punta Sam; 6.30 and 9.30 am and 12.45, 4.15 and 7.15 pm from Isla Mujeres. Passengers pay US$1.50; a car costs US$11, a van US$13, and a bike or motorcycle US$4. If you're taking a car, be sure to buy your ticket and get in line an hour or so before departure time.

Puerto Juárez About 3km north of the city center is Puerto Juárez, where Transportes Marítimos Magaña operates boats every 30 minutes from 6.30 am to 8.30 pm for US$2.25 one-way. It's a 20-minute ride to the island. In addition, the boats *Sultana del Mar* and *Blanca Beatriz* run about every hour from 7 am to 5.30 pm, taking 45 minutes to reach Isla. The fare is US$1 one-way.

Playa Linda Terminal *The Shuttle* departs from Playa Linda on Isla Cancún at 9 and 11.15 am and 4 and 7 pm; return voyages depart Isla Mujeres at 10 am and 12.30, 5 and 8 pm. Round-trip fare is US$14, including free beer and soft drinks on board. Show up at the Playa Linda Marine Terminal (Boulevard Kukulcán Km 5, between the Aquamarina Beach and Calinda Cancún Hotels) at least 20 minutes before departure so you'll have time to buy your ticket and get a good seat on the boat.

Playa Tortugas *Isla Mujeres Shuttle* departs Isla Cancún from the dock near Fat Tuesday's on Playa Tortugas beach at 9.15 and 11.30 am and 1.45 and 3.45 pm, returning from Isla Mujeres at 10 am and 12.30, 2.30 and 5 pm. Fare is US$10 one-way.

Club Náutico Dock Sharing a parking lot with the Xcaret bus terminal and located next to the Fiesta Americana Coral Beach is this new dock, from which a water taxi whisks people to Isla Mujeres at 9 and 11 am and 1 and 3 pm, and back to Isla Cancún at 10 am, noon and 2 and 5 pm. Fare is US$10 one-way.

Getting Around

Bus & Taxi By local (and infrequent) bus from the market or dock, you can get within 1.5km of Playa Garrafón; the terminus is Playa Lancheros. The personnel at the Poc-Na youth hostel can give you an idea of the bus's erratic schedule. Locals in league with taxi drivers may tell you the bus doesn't exist. Unless you're pinching pennies, you'd be better off taking a taxi anyway – the most expensive one-way trip on the island is US$5. Taxi rates are set by the municipal government and are posted at the ferry dock, though the sign is frequently defaced by taxi drivers.

Bicycle & Moped You can rent bicycles from a number of shops on the island, including Sport Bike, on the corner of Juárez and Morelos, a block from the ferry docks. Before you rent, check out a few shops to compare prices and the condition of the bikes, then arrive early in the day to get one of the better bikes. Cost is about US$5 for four hours, a bit more for a full day; you'll be asked for a deposit of about US$10.

If you rent a moped, shop around, compare prices and look for new or newer machines in good condition, full gas tanks and reasonable deposits. Cost per hour is usually US$5 or US$6 with a two-hour minimum, US$25 all day, cheaper by the week. Shops away from the busiest streets tend to have better prices, but not necessarily better equipment. Pepe's Moped Rentals, on Hidalgo between Matamoros and Abasolo, offers mopeds for US$16 a day.

ISLA CONTOY

From Isla Mujeres it's possible to take an excursion by boat to tiny, uninhabited Isla Contoy, a national park and bird sanctuary 25km north of Isla Mujeres. The island's dense foliage is home to more than 100 bird species, including brown pelicans, olive cormorants, turkey birds, brown boobies and red-pouched frigates. In addition, red flamingoes, snowy egrets and white herons make frequent visits.

Bring mosquito repellent, and keep young children clear of the island's brackish ponds; boa constrictors and small crocodiles live in the ponds, and although neither critter would attack an adult, they might take interest in a baby. The snorkeling is good both en route to and just off Contoy, which sees about 1500 visitors a month.

Getting There & Away

Coral Scuba Dive Center (☎ 877-07-63, fax 877-03-71), on Isla Mujeres (Calle Matamoros at Avenida Rueda Medina), offers a day trip for US$35 that includes lunch and opportunities for snorkeling and birdwatching.

At the dock that extends from the western end of Calle Madero in Isla Mujeres are several boats owned and operated by Captain Ricardo Gaitan, who makes daily trips to Isla Contoy for US$38 per person. Gaitan's tour includes a hearty lunch, scientific information on the island, free use of snorkeling gear, fishing en route and your choice of purified water or soft drinks.

ISLA HOLBOX

Isla Holbox is inhabited by friendly fishing families and virtually devoid of gringos; if you're up for roughing it, this place will please. The peninsula (it's not really an island, despite the name) is 25km long and 3km wide, with seemingly endless beaches, tranquil waters and a galaxy of shells in various shapes and colors. Birders will spot red flamingoes and the occasional roseate spoonbill. But the island also has its drawbacks. The water is not the translucent turquoise common to Quintana Roo beaches (here Caribbean waters mingle with those of the darker Gulf of Mexico); seaweed can create silty waters near shore; and mosquitoes are abundant during the rainy season (the entire western end of the peninsula isn't called Punta Mosquito for nothing).

Places to Stay & Eat

Big plans are afoot to develop Isla Holbox, but so far you'll find only three modest hotels: *Hotel Flamingo*, *Hotel Holbox* and *Posada Amapola*. All charge US$15 a night. The few simple restaurants specialize in fish.

Getting There & Away

To reach Isla Holbox, take the ferry (US$2.50) from the port village of Chiquilá. You can catch a direct bus there from Puerto Juárez or Cancún. Try to get to Chiquilá as early as possible; the ferry is supposed to depart for the island at 8 am and 3 pm, and it may not wait for a delayed bus (it may even leave early, should the captain feel so inclined). There are also three buses a day from Valladolid to Chiquilá (155km, two hours, US$6), and in theory the ferry is supposed to wait for them. Ferries return to Chiquilá at 2 and 5 pm. The trip takes about an hour.

PUERTO MORELOS
• pop 830 ☎ 9

Puerto Morelos, 33km south of Cancún, is a quiet fishing village known principally for its car ferry to Cozumel. The town has several good hotels, and travelers who have reason to spend the night here find it refreshingly free of tourists. A handful of scuba divers come to explore the splendid reef 600m offshore, reachable by boat. The reef is threatened by planned resort development in the mangroves nearby, but so far, residents have successfully fought off the developers.

Two kilometers south of the turnoff for Puerto Morelos is the **Jardín Botánico Dr Alfredo Barrera**, with 3km of trails through several native habitats. The orchids, bromeliads and other flora are identified in English, Spanish and Latin. You may catch sight of an iguana or two as well. Open 9 am to 5 pm daily (US$2). Buses may be hailed directly in front of the garden.

Places to Stay & Eat

The *Posada Amor* (☎ 871-00-33, fax 871-01-78, Apartado Postal 806, 77580 Cancún), 100m southwest of the plaza, is the longtime lodging here. Rooms with fan, shared bathroom and a double bed are on the high side at US$22, or US$28 with two beds, single or double. Meals are available.

Hotel Hacienda Morelos (☎/fax 871-00-15), 150m south of the plaza on the waterfront, has appealing, breezy rooms with sea views for US$62 single/double and a decent restaurant called El Mesón.

Farther south, beyond the ferry terminal, is the best place in town, the *Rancho Libertad* (☎ 871-01-81, 888-305-5225 in the USA, fax 719-685-2332 in the USA, www .rancholibertad.com), with 15 charming rooms in one- and two-story thatched bungalows. All rooms have private bath and good ventilation; some have air-con. There's a pleasing beach, and room rates include breakfast for two and use of bikes and snorkel gear. Upstairs rooms are US$55 a double, April to December (add US$20 during the high season). Downstairs rooms are US$45/65 during low/high season. The hotel is managed by a friendly and informative American woman.

Next to Hacienda Morelos is *Las Palmeras*, a good restaurant, though the best is *Los Pelícanos*, just off the southeast corner of the plaza.

Getting There & Away

Playa Express buses running between Ciudad Cancún and Playa del Carmen drop you on the highway. All 2nd-class and many 1st-class buses heading to or from Ciudad Cancún stop at Puerto Morelos. The plaza is 2km from the highway. Taxis are usually waiting by the turnoff to shuttle people into town, and there's usually a taxi or two near the square to shuttle them back to the highway (US$2 each way).

The *transbordador* (car ferry) to Cozumel (☎ 9-872-09-50 in Cozumel) leaves Puerto Morelos at 5 am, 10 am and noon daily. Departure times are subject to change according to season and weather; during high seas, the ferry won't leave at all. Unless you plan to stay awhile on Cozumel, it's hardly worth shipping your vehicle. You must get in line at least 30 minutes before departure and hope there's enough space. The voyage takes 2½ to four hours and costs US$55 per car, US$4.50 per person. Departure from Cozumel is from the dock in front of the Hotel Sol Caribe, south of town along the shore road.

PLAYA DEL CARMEN
• pop 17,600 ☎ 9

For decades Playa was a simple fishing village that foreigners passed through on their way to a ferry that would take them to Cozumel. But with the construction of Cancún, the number of travelers roaming this part of Yucatán exploded, as did the number of hotels and restaurants built to serve them. Playa has overtaken Cozumel as the area's preferred resort town; its beaches are better and nightlife groovier than Cozumel's, and the reef diving is just as good. Most of the town's accommodations are stylish European-owned and -managed inns, and several of its restaurants serve delicious French and Italian cuisine.

What's to do in Playa? Hang out. Swim. Dive. Shop. Eat. Drink. Stroll the beach. Get some sun. Listen to beach bands. Dance in clubs. In the evening, Playa's pedestrian mall, on Avenida Quinta, is a popular place to stroll or have a meal or a drink. If you're looking for some beach reading, try the bookstore La Librería, on Calle 8 between Avenida Quinta and Avenida 10.

Though nudity is allowed on the beach about a kilometer north of the town center, it is not recommended; with the construction boom in Playa has come a nefarious element, and rapes, robberies, and thefts have become common in town and especially on remote patches of beach. Beware the sorry shantytown north of town, where most of the construction workers live, and don't walk alone on the streets late at night.

Activities

Scuba Tarraya (☎ 873-20-40, fax 873-20-60, g_millet@hotmail.com, gmillet@yuc1.telmex.net.mx), at the eastern end of Calle 2, offers several options for **diving**, **snorkeling** and

fishing, and it rents **kayaks**. Other dive centers are Aqua Venturas (☎/fax 873-09-69), Avenida Quinta between Calles 2 and 4; Abyss (☎ 873-21-64, abyss@playadelcarmen.com), at the Blue Parrot Inn, east end of Calle 12; and Phocea Caribe (☎/fax 873-10-24), on Avenida Quinta between Calles 12 and 14.

At Tierra Maya Tours (☎ 873-13-85, fax 873-13-86, tmt@expo-yucatan.com), Avenida Quinta at Calle 6, you can book a tour to nearby **Mayan ruins**; English, German, French and Spanish are spoken.

Places to Stay

Playa del Carmen is developing and changing rapidly. Expect many new hotels and many changes in the existing ones by the time you arrive. The prices here are for the off-season, mid-April through mid-December; the rest of the year they are at least 25% higher.

Budget The youth hostel, or *Villa Deportiva Juvenil* (no phone), on Calle 8 at Avenida 35, offers the cheapest clean lodging (US$4 per bunk), but it's a trek to the beach, and the single-sex dorm bunks are worn. A better bet is *Camping-Cabañas La Ruina* (☎ 873-04-05, fax 872-15-98), on Calle 2 just off the beach, where you can pitch your own tent for US$3 per person, hang your hammock beneath a palapa for US$5, rent a hammock, or rent a simple cabaña with two cots and ceiling fan for US$8 to US$11. A more comfortable cabaña with private bath is US$25 to US$35. To secure your stuff from roaming thieves, rent a locker, but bring your own sturdy lock.

Hotel Casa Tucan (☎/fax 873-02-82), on Calle 4 between Avenidas 10 and 15, features 20 rooms on two levels (the upstairs rooms catch a welcome breeze), a swimming pool and a lovely tropical garden. All rooms are fan-only, with mosquito nets, and an excellent value at US$20.

Hotel Barrio Latino (☎/fax 873-23-84, posadabarriolatino@yahoo.com), also on Calle 4 between Avenidas 10 and 15, offers 14 clean rooms with tiled floors, ceiling fans and hammocks. The enormously friendly Italian owners speak English and Spanish

PLAYA DEL CARMEN

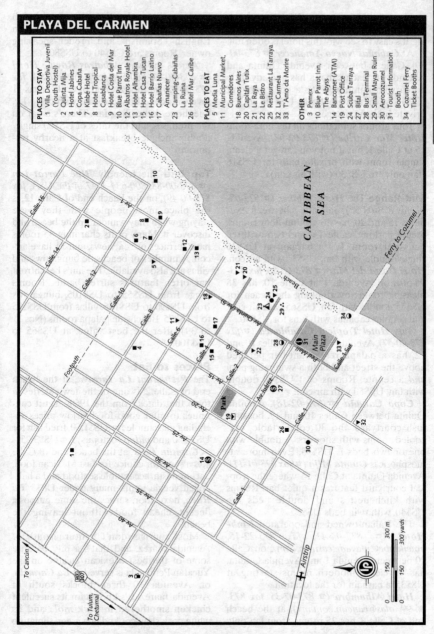

PLACES TO STAY
1 Villa Deportiva Juvenil (Youth Hostel)
2 Quinta Mija
4 Copa Cabaña
6 Hotel Jabines
7 Kimbé Hotel
8 Hotel Tropical Casablanca
9 Hotel Costa del Mar
10 Blue Parrot Inn
12 Albatros Royale Hotel
13 Hotel Alhambra
15 Hotel Casa Tucán
16 Hotel Barrio Latino
17 Cabañas Nuevo Amanecer
23 Camping-Cabañas La Ruina
26 Hotel Mar Caribe

PLACES TO EAT
5 Media Luna
11 Municipal Market, Comedores
18 Buenos Aires
20 Capitán Tutix
21 La Raya
22 Le Bistro
25 Restaurant La Tarraya
32 La Carmela
33 T'Amo da Morire

OTHER
3 Pemex
10 Blue Parrot Inn, The Abyss
14 Bancomer (ATM)
19 Post Office
24 Scuba Tarraya
27 Bital
28 Bus Terminal
29 Small Mayan Ruin
30 Aerocozumel
31 Tourist Information Booth
34 Cozumel Ferry Ticket Booths

CARIBBEAN SEA

Ferry to Cozumel

To Cancún

MEX 307

To Tulum, Chetumal

Airstrip

Footpath

Park

Main Plaza

Beach

Pedestrian Mall

and maintain strict security. With low-season rates of US$20 a room and off-street parking, it's easy to see why this hotel is often full.

At *Cabañas Nuevo Amanecer* (☎ 873-00-30), Calle 4 between Avenida Quinta and Avenida 10, each cabaña has a shady little porch with hammock. It's a good value at US$15 with private bath, US$20 with a private bath and fridge.

Tour groups sometimes fill the nine-room *Hotel Mar Caribe* (☎ 873-02-07), Avenida 15 at Calle 1, but if not you can get a clean, simple room with private bath for US$16 (fan only) to US$30 (with air-con).

Mid-Range The *Hotel Jabines* (☎ 873-08-61, fax 873-03-52), on Calle 8 between Avenidas 15 and 20, has 16 ground-floor rooms, secure parking, cable TV and two or three beds per room. It's a bargain at US$26 single/double with fan, US$31 with air-con. *Hotel Costa del Mar* (☎ 873-00-58, fax 873-08-50), on Avenida 1 at Calle 10, has 38 pleasing rooms overlooking the beach for US$55 double with fan, US$65 with air-con, and simpler cabañas with fans for US$40.

Tidy *Hotel Tropical Casablanca* (☎/fax 873-00-57), Avenida 1 between Calles 10 and 12, has a palapa restaurant-bar perched above the street and both a swimming pool *and* a cenote. Rooms cost US$40 double with fan, US$50 with air-con.

Copa Cabaña (☎ 873-02-18), Avenida Quinta between Calles 10 and 12, boasts a lush courtyard and 30 comfortable, fan-cooled rooms with showers. A double with one or two beds is US$35. Even more atmospheric is *Quinta Mija* (☎/fax 873-01-11), Avenida Quinta at Calle 14, where the tropical courtyard features a quiet bar. Rooms with kitchenettes and double beds are US$40, with twin beds US$50.

The Italian-owned and operated *Kinbé Hotel* (☎ 873-04-41, fax 873-22-15, hotelkinbe@playadelcarmen.com), on Calle 10 between Avenida 1 and Avenida Quinta, has 19 clean, modern rooms starting at US$35, a bargain for the location.

Hotel Alhambra (☎ 873-07-35, fax 873-06-99, olas@cancun.com.mx), at the beach end of Calle 8, has 25 rooms, from fan-only to air-conditioned with balcony and beach view. It has a private rooftop deck and an English-, Spanish- and French-speaking owner. Rooms are US$40 to US$80.

Across the way, *Albatros Royale Hotel* (☎ 873-00-01, 800-538-6802 in the USA, fax 873-00-02), at the east end of Calle 8, has 31 lovely air-conditioned rooms with cable TV, telephone and ceiling fan. There's a bar on the premises, and the rates of US$60 single/double include breakfast at a nearby restaurant.

Top End The friendly *Blue Parrot Inn* (☎ 873-00-83, 800-634-3547 in the USA, fax 873-00-49), on the beach end of Calle 12, is the place most people wish they were staying when they wander up the beach and discover it. Many of its charming 45 rooms have terraces or sea views, and 31 have air-con. A number of beachside bungalows and villas are also available. The inn's beachfront bar often features surfer bands. Rooms range from US$55 to US$105, bungalows from US$90 to US$135, villas from US$135 to US$275. Beachside palapa rooms (Nos 31 to 39) offer the best value, at US$65 to US$100.

Places to Eat

The *Restaurant La Tarraya*, at the beach end of Calle 2, is one of the few eateries in town that dates from the 1960s. Yet it continues to offer good food at low prices, including guacamole for US$1.50, fried fish for US$2.50 and *pulpo* (octopus) for US$3.25.

Capitán Tutix, at the beach end of Calle 4, is a superior choice for fast Mexican food, decent pasta, acceptable seafood and a half-dozen veggie items, many under US$5. *La Raya*, next door, serves the same purpose: decent, cheap food without leaving the beach.

Most tourists don't venture south of Avenida Juárez, and that's a pity because some of the best Mexican cuisine on the Yucatán Peninsula is served at *La Carmela*, on Avenida 10 three blocks south of Avenida Juárez. It's known for its succulent chicken smothered in dark *mole* and its white pork slow-cooked in a green tomatillo sauce, among other dishes. Most specialties are under US$10. Dress nicely.

The best Italian food in town is served at *T'Amo da Morire*, which overlooks the main plaza. Entrees cost US$5 to US$7.

Le Bistro, on Calle 2 between Avenida Quinta and Avenida 10, is a simple, open-sided restaurant with 10 little wooden tables and excellent service. It specializes in savory French home cooking – the meals here are simply divine. Appetizers cost about US$5, entrees about US$7.

If you *love* beef, head to *Buenos Aires*, on Avenida Quinta between Calles 4 and 6, tucked away behind two mediocre restaurants. It's famous in Quintana Roo for its steaks, ribs, burgers and other meaty items (US$6 to US$13), made only with Angus beef.

Media Luna, on Avenida Quinta between Calles 8 and 10, takes top honors in the veggie category, serving a wide variety of good dishes for breakfast, lunch and dinner, all priced for the budget-minded. The same owners run *¡Zas!*, on Avenida Quinta at Calle 12, where the international cuisine is interesting and delicious. A typical entree costs US$8.

Entertainment

The party's hearty at the Blue Parrot Inn's *Dragon Bar*, where Calle 12 meets the sand. Surfer bands play at the open-sided palapa bar during the day; at night there's usually a reggae band. Most nights at *Capitán Tutix*, at the beach end of Calle 4, a band starts up about 10 pm, playing reggae, rock, calypso or salsa. If your one-liners don't go over well there, try *La Raya*, next door, which offers occasional live music (usually salsa) starting after 8 pm. None of these places charges a cover. Secondary music scenes – but not necessarily secondary party scenes – can be found along Avenida Quinta most nights.

Getting There & Away

Air Playa's little airstrip handles mostly small charter, tour and air taxi flights. Aerocozumel (☎ 873-03-50) has an office next to the airstrip, as does Aerosaab (☎ 873-08-04). Flights from Playa to Cozumel are

US$26; round-trip to Chichén Itzá is US$139.

Bus Several bus companies serve Playa's bus terminal, at the corner of Avenida Juárez and Avenida Quinta. Playa Express buses run up and down the coast every 20 minutes, charging US$1.75 from Playa to either Tulum or Cancún.

Chetumal – 315km, 5 hours; 1 Mayab (US$12), 1 ADO GL (US$12), 1 Cristóbal Colón (US$11), 8 ADO (US$10), 1 Altos (US$8)

Chichén Itzá – 272km, 3 hours; 1 TRP (US$7); it's best to take an early bus to Ciudad Cancún, then transfer

Ciudad Cancún – 65km, 40 minutes; frequent ADO, Playa Express, Oriente (US$2.50)

Cobá – 113km, 1½ hours; 1 Premier (US$3.50)

Mérida – 385km, 5 hours; 1 ADO GL (US$15), 1 ADO (US$12.50), 12 Premier (US$12.50), 4 TRP (US$11)

Palenque – 800km, 10 hours; 1 Cristóbal Colón (US$26), 1 Altos (US$23)

San Cristóbal de Las Casas – 990km, 16 hours; 1 Maya de Oro (US$36), 1 Cristóbal Colón (US$32), 1 Altos (US$30)

Tulum – 63km, 1 hour; Playa Express every 20 minutes (US$2.50), 5 ADO (US$2), 3 TRP (US$1.70)

Valladolid – 213km, 3 hours; 2 TRP (US$6); many buses going to Mérida via Cancún stop at Valladolid, but it's faster to go on the *ruta corta* (short route) via Tulum and Cobá (see Cobá)

Boats to Cozumel Ferries to Cozumel run every hour on the hour from 5 am to 10 pm. The ride takes 45 minutes to an hour and costs US$7 one-way.

COZUMEL
● **pop 47,800** ☎ 9

Cozumel, 71km south of Cancún, is a teardrop-shaped coral island ringed by crystalline waters. It is Mexico's only Caribbean island and, measuring 53km by 14km, it is also one of the country's largest. Called Ah-Cuzamil-Peten (Island of Swallows) by its earliest inhabitants, Cozumel has been a favorite destination for divers since 1961, when a Jacques Cousteau documentary on its glorious reefs appeared on TV. Today, no

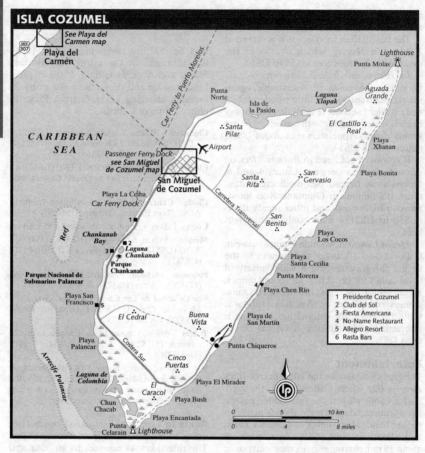

ISLA COZUMEL

fewer than 100 world-class dive sites have been identified within 5km of Cozumel, and no less than a dozen of them are shallow enough for snorkeling. But except for the diving and snorkeling, there's little reason to visit Cozumel.

History

Mayan settlement here dates from 300 AD. During the Postclassic period, Cozumel flourished as a trade center and, more importantly, a ceremonial site. At San Gervasio, near the center of the island, the Mayans erected a temple honoring Ixchel, the god-

dess of fertility and the moon; every Mayan woman on the Yucatán Peninsula and beyond was expected to make at least one pilgrimage to the temple.

At the time of the first Spanish contact with Cozumel (in 1518, by Juan de Grijalva and his men), at least 32 Mayan building sites dotted the island. According to Spanish chronicler Diego de Landa, Cortés a year later sacked one of the Mayan centers but left the others intact, apparently satisfied with converting the island's Maya to Christianity. Smallpox carried over in 1520 wiped out half the 8000 Maya, and of the survivors, only about 200 escaped genocidal attacks by conquistadors in the late 1540s.

The island remained virtually deserted into the late 17th century, its coves providing sanctuary for notorious pirates, including Jean Lafitte and Henry Morgan. In 1848, Maya and other indigenous people fleeing the War of the Castes began to resettle Cozumel.

By the beginning of the 20th century, the island's population was mostly mestizo and was growing, thanks to the craze for chewing gum. Cozumel was a port of call on the chicle export route, and locals worked at harvesting chicle on the island. After the demise of the chicle industry, Cozumel's economy remained strong with the construction of a US air base here during WWII.

When the US military departed, the island fell into an economic slump and many of its people moved away. Those who stayed fished for a livelihood until 1961, when Cousteau's documentary broadcast Cozumel's glorious sea life to the world. The tourists began arriving almost overnight.

Orientation

It's easy to make your way on foot around the island's only town, San Miguel de Cozumel. The waterfront boulevard is Avenida Melgar; along Melgar south of the main ferry dock (the 'Muelle Fiscal') is a narrow sand beach. The main plaza is just opposite the ferry dock. Lockers are available for rent (US$2 per day) at the landward end of the Muelle Fiscal, but they're not big enough for a full backpack. The airport is 2km north of town.

Information

Tourist Offices The tourist office (☎ 872-09-72) is a short distance from the main docks and faces the main plaza, on the corner of Avenida Benito Juárez and Avenida 5 Nte. It's open 8 am to 5 pm Monday to Friday.

Money For currency exchange, try any of the banks near the main plaza shown on the map. All are open 8 am to 4.30 pm Monday to Friday and in the morning on Saturday. Banamex and Banca Serfin have ATMs.

The casas de cambio around town may charge as much as 3.5% commission (versus the bank rate of 1%) to cash a traveler's check, but they keep longer hours. Most of the major hotels, restaurants and stores will also change money.

Post & Communications The post office (☎ 872-01-06) is just past Calle 7 Sur heading away from the ferry dock on Avenida Melgar; open 9 am to 1 pm and 3 to 6 pm Monday to Friday, 9 am to noon Saturday. Telmex pay phones abound and represent the least expensive way to place long-distance calls.

Internet Cozumel, on Calle 1 Sur at Avenida 10 Nte, offers eight computers in an air-conditioned environment for US$0.10 a minute; open 9 am to 10.30 pm daily. The Coffee Net, on Avenida Melgar at Calle 11 Sur, is an Internet café serving coffee and other libations and providing Internet access for US$9 an hour with a US$5 minimum; open 9 am to 10 pm daily.

Bookstores The Gracia Agencia de Publicaciones, on the southeast side of the plaza, is open seven days a week and sells English, French, German and Spanish books, as well as English and Spanish periodicals. Fama Bookstore, one block north along Avenida 5 Nte, carries books and periodicals in English and Spanish.

Laundry Margarita Laundromat, on Avenida 20 Sur near Calle 3 Sur, is open 7 am to 9 pm Monday to Saturday, 9 am to 5 pm Sunday. It charges US$1.50 to wash a load (US$0.40 extra if you don't bring your own detergent), US$0.70 for 10 minutes in the dryer. Express Lavandería, on Avenida 15 Sur just south of Calle 3 Sur, is open 8 am to 9 pm daily.

Museo de la Isla de Cozumel

Exhibits at this fine museum, on Avenida Melgar between Calles 4 and 6 Nte, present a clear and detailed picture of the island's flora, fauna, geography, geology and ancient Maya heritage. Thoughtful and detailed signage in English and Spanish accompanies

YUCATÁN PENINSULA

SAN MIGUEL DE COZUMEL

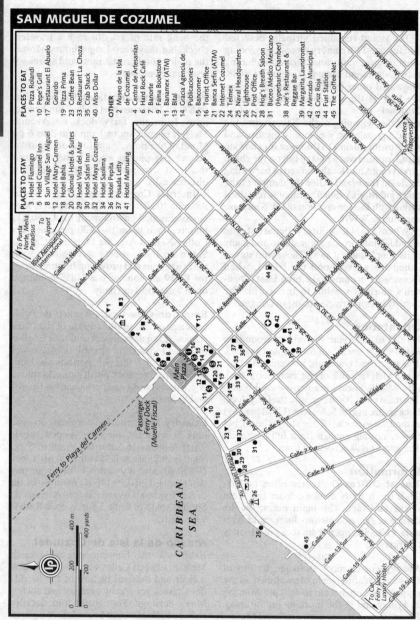

PLACES TO EAT
1   Pizza Rolandi
10   Pepe's Grill
17   Restaurant El Abuelo Gerardo
19   Pizza Prima
23   Coffee Bean
33   Restaurant La Choza
35   Crab Shack
40   Miss Dollar

PLACES TO STAY
3   Hotel Flamingo
5   Hotel Cozumel Inn
8   Sun Village San Miguel
12   Hotel Mary-Carmen
18   Hotel Bahia
20   Colonial Hotel & Suites
29   Hotel Vista del Mar
30   Hotel Safari Inn
32   Hotel Maya Cozumel
34   Hotel Saolima
36   Hotel Pepita
37   Posada Letty
41   Hotel Marruang

OTHER
2   Museo de la Isla de Cozumel
4   Central de Artesanías
6   Hard Rock Café
7   Banorte
9   Fama Bookstore
11   Banamex (ATM)
13   Bital
14   Gracia Agencia de Publicaciones
15   Bancomer
16   Tourist Office
21   Banca Serfin (ATM)
22   Internet Cozumel
24   Telmex
25   Naval Headquarters
26   Lighthouse
27   Post Office
28   Hog's Breath Saloon
31   Buceo Médico Mexicano (Hyperbaric Chamber)
38   Joe's Restaurant & Reggae Bar
39   Margarita Laundromat
42   Mercado Municipal
43   Cruz Roja
44   Fuel Station
45   The Coffee Net

them. It's a good place to learn about coral before hitting the water, and one not to miss before you leave the island. Open 9 am to 8 pm daily (US$3).

Diving & Snorkeling

In a recent reader survey, *Scuba Diving* magazine found Cozumel to be the most popular diving destination in the world. The diving here is unsurpassed for many reasons, chief among them being the incredible year-round visibility of 50m or more. And the scope and variety of resident marine life is jaw-droppingly awesome.

The island has no fewer than 100 dive centers, and Playa del Carmen is home to dozens more. Because of the stiff competition, prices and services are generally comparable. Expect to pay US$60 for a two-tank dive (less if you bring your own BCD and regulator), US$75 for an introductory 'resort' course and US$350 for PADI open-water-diver certification.

Some of the reputable dive shops follow:

Blue Bubble Divers (☎ 872-44-83, 800-878-8853 in the USA, ☎/fax 872-18-65, www.cozumel-diving .net/blue_bubble) Avenida 5 Sur at Calle 3 Sur

Caribbean Divers (☎ 872-10-80, 872-11-45, www .cozumel-diving.net/caribbean_divers) Calle 3 Sur between Avenida Melgar and Avenida 5 Sur

Diving Adventures (☎ 872-30-09, 888-338-0388 in the USA, www.cozumel.net/diving_adventures) Calle 5 Sur near Avenida Melgar

Scuba Du (☎/fax 872-19-94, www.cozumel-diving .net/scubadu) Calle 3 Sur between Avenida Melgar and Avenida 5 Sur

Yucatech Expeditions (☎ 872-56-59, fax 872-14-17, www.cozumel-diving.net/yucatech) Avenida 15 Nte between Salas and Calle 1 Sur; this outfit specializes in diving caves and caverns

Hyperbaric chambers are available in San Miguel at Buceo Médico Mexicano (☎ 872-23-87, 872-14-30, fax 872-18-48), on Calle 5 Sur between Avenida Melgar and Avenida 5 Sur; and at Cozumel Hyperbaric Research (☎ 872-30-70, CHF Radio Channel 65), in the Médico San Miguel clinic on Calle 6 Nte between Avenidas 5 and 10 Nte.

Snorkelers: All of the best sites are reached by boat. A half-day tour costs US$20 to US$35, but you'll do some world-class snorkeling. If you want to be penny-wise and pound-foolish, you can save on the boat fare and walk into the gentle surf at Playa La Ceiba, Chankanab Bay, Playa San Francisco or elsewhere.

Glass-Bottom Boat Rides

The Palapa Marina (☎ 872-05-39), on Calle 1 Sur between Avenidas 5 and 10, offers glass-bottom boat excursions (US$15), departing the Sol Caribe pier, south of San Miguel near the car ferry dock, at 9 am and 1 pm daily.

Places to Stay

Budget To camp anywhere on the island you need a permit from the island's naval authorities. The permits are free and available 24 hours a day from the naval headquarters, beyond the post office on Avenida Melgar. The best camping places are along the island's relatively unpopulated eastern shore.

All rooms at the budget hotels listed below come with private bath and fan, unless otherwise noted.

Hotel Cozumel Inn (☎ 872-03-14, fax 872-31-56), on Calle 4 Nte between Avenida Melgar and Avenida 5 Nte, has 20 rooms for only US$20 double in summer, US$25 with air-con. There's a pool on the premises.

Hotel Saolima (☎ 872-08-86), on Salas between Avenidas 10 and 15 Sur, has clean, pleasant rooms in a quiet locale for US$21, US$23 with air-con.

Hotel Marruang (☎ 872-16-78), on Salas between Avenidas 20 and 25 Sur, is entered from a passageway across from the municipal market. A clean room with one double and one single bed costs US$18 to US$24. Add US$5 for air-con.

Posada Letty (☎ 872-02-57), on Avenida 15 Sur near Calle 1 Sur, offers no-frills rooms for US$20/22 summer/winter.

Hotel Pepita (☎ 872-00-98, fax 872-02-01), also on Avenida 15 Sur near Calle 1 Sur, has well-maintained rooms around a delightful garden for US$25/30 summer/winter. All have two double beds, insect screens, refrigerators and air-con, and there's free morning coffee. A very good deal!

Mid-Range Most of these offer air-con and swimming pools. All have private baths.

After remodeling and the addition of air-con in each room, the island's best budget hotel, *Hotel Flamingo* (☎ 872-12-64), on Calle 6 Nte between Avenida 5 Nte and Avenida Melgar, jumped in price. The 22 rooms cost US$35 to US$50 double, depending on the season.

Hotel Vista del Mar (☎ 872-05-45, fax 872-04-45), Avenida Melgar between Calles 5 and 7 Sur, has 26 air-conditioned rooms (some with balconies and sea views), a pool, restaurant and rental car and travel agencies. Rooms are US$40/45 double summer/winter.

Tried and true, clean and comfortable, the *Hotel Mary-Carmen* (☎ 872-05-81), Avenida 5 Sur half a block south of the plaza, has 27 tidy air-conditioned rooms for US$28/40 double summer/winter. *Hotel Safari Inn* (☎ 872-01-01, fax 872-06-61, div@aquasafari.com), on Avenida Melgar at Calle 5 Sur, offers 12 rooms with air-con and fans for US$40 double. Rooms 1 and 7 face the beach.

Colonial Hotel & Suites (☎ 872-40-34, fax 872-13-87), on Avenida 5 Sur near Salas, has studios and one-bedroom suites (some can sleep four people) with kitchenette and air-con for US$45/55 studio/suite in summer. The similar *Hotel Bahía* (☎ 872-02-09, fax 872-13-87), facing the sea on Avenida Melgar at Calle 3 Sur, is under the same management and charges slightly more.

Hotel Maya Cozumel (☎ 872-00-11, fax 872-07-81), on Calle 5 Sur between Avenida Melgar and Avenida 5 Sur, has rooms with air-con and TV, as well as a very inviting pool surrounded by lawn and bougainvillea. Rates are US$40/45/50 single/double/triple in winter, about US$5 less in summer. A very good value.

Sun Village San Miguel (☎ 872-03-23, 800-221-5833 in the USA, fax 872-18-20), on Avenida Juárez between Avenida Melgar and Avenida 5 Nte, has a pool, air-con, a restaurant and 100 rooms with balconies. A

separate beach club for guests, on the water seven blocks from the hotel, has water-sports facilities. Rates are US$35/75 double summer/winter.

Top End North of town along the western shore are some modest resort hotels that cater mostly to package tour groups.

A string of big luxury resort hotels begins several kilometers south of town. The *Presidente Cozumel* (☎ 872-03-22, fax 872-13-60, cozumel@interconti.com, http://cozumel.interconti.com), Carretera a Chankanab Km 6.5, is hard to miss with its 253 rooms, many with sea views, set amid tropical gardens and swimming pools. Rates start at around $170 double and go to over twice that, depending on room and season.

Club del Sol (☎ 872-37-77, fax 872-58-77, clubdelsol@cozunet.finred.com.mx), Carretera a Chankanab Km 6.8, has 41 air-conditioned rooms, some with kitchenettes, for a very reasonable US$60 single/double.

One of the island's finest hotels is the *Fiesta Americana Cozumel Reef* (☎ 872-26-22, 800-343-7821 in the USA, fax 872-26-66, fiesta@gate.net), Carretera a Chankanab Km 7.5, with 182 oceanfront balconied rooms and 56 suites, plenty of gardens and a spectacular swimming pool. Rates start at US$95.

Allegro Resort (☎ 872-34-43, fax 872-45-08), Carretera a Chankanab Km 16.5, has 300 rooms in two-story, Polynesian-style thatched-roof villas. On the grounds are three restaurants, and a pool with a swim-up bar. Rates start at around $110.

Places to Eat

Budget Cheapest of all eating places, with tasty food, are the little market *loncherías* next to the Mercado Municipal on Salas between Avenidas 20 and 25 Sur. All offer soup and a main course for less than US$3, with a large selection of dishes available.

Restaurant Costa Brava, on Avenida Melgar just south of the post office, is among the more funky places to dine, serving cheap breakfasts (US$2 to US$3) and such filling dishes as chicken tacos, grilled steak and fried fish for US$4 to US$7.

Cocina Económica Mi Chabelita, on Avenida 10 Sur between Calles 1 Sur and Salas, is a tiny, inexpensive eatery run by a señora who serves decent portions of decent food for US$3 or less.

The forthrightly named *Miss Dollar*, on Avenida 20 Sur near Salas, earns its money by providing inexpensive meals to take out. The *Coffee Bean*, on Calle 3 Sur just off Avenida Melgar, serves the latest trendy java recipes. For pastries, try the *Pastelería y Panadería Zermatt*, Avenida 5 Nte at Calle 4 Nte.

Mid-Range The American owners at *Pizza Prima*, on Salas between Avenidas 5 and 10 Sur, produce homemade pasta and fresh pizza (US$6 to US$12) and excellent Italian specialties (US$8 to US$15). Closed Wednesday. *Pizza Rolandi*, on Avenida Melgar between Calles 6 and 8 Nte, serves good one-person pizzas cooked in a wood-fired oven for US$8 to US$10. Homemade pasta is also available. Closed Sunday.

The *Crab Shack*, on Avenida 10 Sur at Salas, is a casual corner joint that whips up some excellent seafood. Dishes cost US$6 to US$10; snow crab clusters, a specialty, cost US$25 per kilo. If you appreciate crab, you'll love this place.

The menu at *Restaurant El Abuelo Gerardo*, on Avenida 10 Nte at Avenida Juárez, is extensive and the prices reasonable. Beef or chicken fajitas (US$7) and fried fish (US$8) are popular. Guacamole and chips are on the house.

Restaurant La Choza, on Salas at Avenida 10 Sur, is an excellent and popular restaurant specializing in authentic regional cuisine. Entrees cost US$7 to US$10, and all include soup.

Top End Cozumel's traditional place for fine dining is *Pepe's Grill*, Avenida Melgar at Salas. Entrees include New York steak, pepper steak or prime rib (US$19) and charcoal-broiled lobster with garlic (market price, typically around US$35).

Entertainment

Most of the year, Cozumel can't keep up with Playa del Carmen as a nightlife desti-

nation. But the *Hard Rock Café*, on Avenida Melgar near the main ferry dock, has live rock most nights of the week, as does the *Hog's Breath Saloon*, on Avenida Melgar four blocks south of the main plaza. For reggae, head to *Joe's Restaurant & Reggae Bar*, on Avenida 15 Sur between Calle Salas and Calle 3 Sur. For disco, the only name in town is *Neptuno's*, Avenida Melgar at Calle 7 Sur, open Thursday, Friday and Saturday nights.

Getting There & Away

Air Cozumel has a surprisingly busy international airport, with numerous direct flights from other parts of Mexico and the US. Flights from Europe are usually routed via the US or Mexico City. From the US, Continental (☎ 872-02-51, 800-525-0280 in the US) and American (☎ 872-08-99, 800-433-7300 in the US) have direct flights to/from Dallas, Houston, and Raleigh-Durham, North Carolina. Mexicana (☎ 872-02-63, 800-354-2562 in the US) offers nonstops to/from Miami, Mérida and Mexico City.

Aerocozumel (☎ 872-09-28, 872-05-03), with offices at Cozumel airport, operates daily flights between Cancún and Cozumel for US$50 one-way and between Cozumel and Belize City for US$165 one-way. Reserve in advance.

Boat Passenger ferries run from Playa del Carmen, and car ferries run from Puerto Morelos. See those sections for details.

Getting Around

To/From the Airport The airport is about 2km north of town. You can take a minibus from the airport into town for less than US$2 (slightly more to the hotels south of town), but you'll have to take a taxi (US$4) to return to the airport.

Taxi Fares in and around town are US$4 per ride. From town to Laguna Chankanab is US$10. There is no bus service.

Car & Motorcycle Rates for rental cars run US$40 to US$55 per day (more during late December and January), all inclusive. At those prices, you could probably haggle with a taxi driver to take you on a tour of the island, drop you at a beach and come back and pick you up, and still save money. If you do rent, observe the law on vehicle occupancy. Usually only five people are allowed in a vehicle. If you carry more, the police will fine you. Gas is available on Avenida Juárez five blocks east of the main square.

Mopeds represent the best way to tour the island on your own, and rental opportunities abound. Prices generally run as little as US$10 to US$15 per day, including gas, insurance and tax. Remember, prices are negotiable; if someone approaches you as you're getting off the ferry offering mopeds for US$25 a day, reply 'US$10 a day.' Often the response is quick acquiescence.

To rent, you must have a valid driver's license, and you must either pay with a credit card or put down a deposit (usually US$100). There is a helmet law and it is enforced (US$25 fine for not wearing one), although most moped rental people won't mention it. Before you sign a rental agreement, be sure to request a helmet.

The best time to rent is first thing in the morning, when all the machines are there. Choose one with a working horn, brakes, lights, starter, rearview mirrors and a full tank of fuel; remember that the price asked will be the same whether you rent the newest machine or the oldest rattletrap.

Don't plan to circumnavigate the island with two people on one moped. A well-used and ill-maintained machine may well break down under the load, stranding you a long way from civilization with no way to get help.

When riding, keep in mind that you will be as exposed to sunshine as you would be on a beach. Slather yourself with sunblock (especially the backs of your hands, feet and neck, and your face), or cover up. Bring a towel to toss on the moped's seat when parked – the black plastic can get blisteringly hot in the sun. Finally, of all motor vehicle operators, the inexperienced moped driver on unfamiliar roads in a foreign country has the highest statistical chance of having an accident. Drive carefully.

AROUND ISLA COZUMEL

In order to see most of the island (except Chankanab Bay) you will have to take a taxi or rent a bicycle, moped or car. The following route will take you south from San Miguel, then counterclockwise around the island.

Bahía Chankanab

Part of a national park, Chankanab Bay is famous for its clear water and fabulously colored fish. Lots of people come here to soak up the sun and to snorkel – so many people, in fact, that the snorkelers often reduce underwater visibility to just 15m with the sediment they kick up. That said, most people are very pleased with the marine life here.

The beach is a beauty, and it's lined with palapas and fiberglass lounge chairs. Topless sunbathing is permitted. Snorkel and dive equipment is available for rent. About 50m behind the beach you'll see a lovely lagoon. You're not allowed to swim or snorkel there, but it's picturesque nevertheless.

A small archaeological park on the grounds contains Olmec heads and Mayan artifacts, a small museum with objects imported from Chichén Itzá, and a botanical garden with 400 species of tropical plants. Also here are dressing rooms, lockers and showers (included in the admission fee), a restaurant, bar and several snack shops. Open 9 am to 5 pm daily (US$7).

Playa San Francisco & Playa Palancar

These two beaches are the loveliest on the island. San Francisco's white sands run for more than 3km; rather expensive food is served at its restaurant. If you want to scuba dive or snorkel at nearby Arrecife Palancar, you will have to sign on for a day cruise or charter a boat.

El Cedral

To see this Mayan ruin the size of a small house – the oldest on the island – go 3.5km down a paved road a short distance south of Playa San Francisco (there's a sign for the turnoff). No signs mark the much-littered ruin, which perhaps is most impressive these

Playa Norte, Isla Mujeres

Cobá ruins

Looking out Chichén Itzá's back door

days for the massive roots that grip the building, remnants of a tree that once grew on the roof. Entry is free.

Punta Celarain

The southern tip of the island has a picturesque lighthouse, accessible via a dirt track, 4km from the highway. To enjoy truly isolated beaches en route, climb over the sand dunes. There's a fine view of the island from the top of the lighthouse.

East Coast Drive

The eastern shoreline is the wildest part of the island and highly recommended for beautiful seascapes. Unfortunately, except for Punta Chiqueros, Playa Chen Río and Punta Morena, swimming is dangerous on Cozumel's east coast because of riptides and undertows. Playa Chen Río has few tourists and, even better, a simple, nameless restaurant where you can get one of the best fresh seafood feasts imaginable, in the company of local families. Lobster, conch, octopus, snapper, grouper – it's all served here, accompanied by large slices of avocado, heaps of rice and chunks of tomato. It costs US$8 to US$13 if you spruce up the meal with one of the restaurant's enormous and delicious margaritas.

Before reaching the nameless but unforgettable restaurant at Playa Chen Río, you'll pass two rasta/reggae bar-restaurants at Punta Chiqueros. Unlike the nameless restaurant, which is authentic Caribbean Mexico, these places are built for gringos and it's gringos who patronize them. That's not a put-down; they are surfside fun centers with beautiful Caribbean views, no question about it.

San Gervasio & Punta Molas

Surveys and excavations undertaken during the past three decades indicate that there were at least 32 Mayan centers on Cozumel at the time of the conquistadors' arrival. The largest appears to have been San Gervasio, the site of a shrine at which women – particularly prospective mothers – worshiped the goddess Ixchel. This site contains Cozumel's only preserved ruins, but there's very little to

them. Some visitors find the jungle en route more interesting.

Beyond where the east coast highway meets the Carretera Transversal, intrepid travelers may take a poorly maintained, infrequently traveled road toward Punta Molas, the island's northeast point, accessible only by 4WD or on foot. About 17km down the road are the Mayan ruins known as El Castillo Real, and a few kilometers farther is Aguada Grande. Both sites are quite far gone, their significance lost to time. In the vicinity of Punta Molas are some fairly good beaches and a few more minor ruins. If you head down this road be aware of the risk: if your vehicle breaks down, you can't count on flagging down another motorist for help.

The best camping spot along the road is Playa Bonita. Playa Xhanan isn't nearly as pretty, and there are no sandy beaches north of it.

XCARET

Once a communal turkey farm, Xcaret ('SHKA-ret'; ☎ 9-883-31-43, fax 9-883-33-24), 10km south of Playa del Carmen, is a heavily Disneyfied ecopark. The beautiful inlet is ringed by minor Mayan ruins and has a cenote for swimming, a restaurant, an evening show of 'ancient Mayan ceremonies' worthy of Las Vegas, a butterfly pavilion, a botanical garden and nursery, and a wild-bird breeding area.

Package tourists from Cancún fill the place every day, happily paying the US$39 admission fee, plus additional fees for attractions such as swimming with dolphins (US$30 to US$80). Open 8.30 am to 10 pm Monday to Saturday, 8.30 am to 6 pm Sunday from April to October; and 8.30 am to 9 pm Monday to Saturday, 8.30 am to 5 pm Sunday from November to March.

PAAMUL

Paamul, 87km south of Ciudad Cancún and 5km north of Puerto Aventuras, is a lovely beach fringed with palms. But there are lots of small rocks, shells and spiked sea urchins in the shallows offshore, so appropriate footwear is necessary. About 2km north of Paamul is an alabaster sand beach.

Giant sea turtles come ashore here at night in July and August to lay their eggs. If you run across one during an evening stroll along the beach, keep a good distance and don't shine a flashlight at it, as that will scare it off. If you let your eyes adjust to the darkness you'll be able to see well enough.

Scuba-Mex (☎ 9-874-17-29, fax 9-873-06-67, www.scubamex.com or http://scubamex .com), run by a couple of friendly Texans, leads **diving** trips to any of 30 superb sites for a reasonable price and offers dive packages and certification courses. Snorkel gear and booties in a limited number of sizes are available, but you're best off bringing your own.

The beachfront **Paamul Hotel** (☎/fax 9-876-26-91) has spacious, if worn, duplex cabañas facing a protected bay with fine coral heads. Each cabaña has a private bathroom with hot water, a ceiling fan and two beds and costs US$41 single/double, US$45 for a triple. Camping costs US$8 for two people per site. There are two communal telephones.

If you intend to reach Paamul by bus, you'll have a 400m walk from the highway to the hotel and beach.

PUERTO AVENTURAS
• pop 900 ☎ 9

This resort community 92km south of Ciudad Cancún and 40km north of Tulum was, like Cancún, a planned development from the start. It was never a fishing village or seaside farming community. Prior to 1990 there were mangroves teeming with wildlife, and sea turtles had returned to the beaches year after year for millennia to lay eggs. Today the area has a golf course, several thousand rooms for rent and a large marina. Though some turtles continue to nest on the beaches here, their numbers diminish yearly, and the untreated waste from the marina, the hotels and the condos is destroying the reef out front.

From highway 307, the road into town winds several hundred meters. Turn right at the first opportunity and you'll reach the beachfront **Papaya Republic** (☎ 873-51-70,

873-51-91), locally famous for its delicious food (US$7 to US$16). It has 10 cabañas, each US$90 a night, and a nice pool.

XPU-HA

Xpu-ha ('shpoo-HA'; ☎ 9-843-33-06, fax 9-887-28-70, xpuhavta@cancun.com.mx), a private ecopark 95km south of Ciudad Cancún, offers most or all of the things the other three ecoparks on the coast offer, but the US$29 entry fee is all-inclusive. Once in, visitors can kayak the park's cenotes, ride a catamaran or a bicycle, boogie board in the surf and visit the crocodiles, turtles and other animals housed here without shelling out any additional fees. Open 9 am to 5 pm daily.

AKUMAL

Famous for its beautiful beach, Akumal (Place of the Turtles) does indeed see some sea turtles come ashore to lay their eggs in the summer, although fewer and fewer each year thanks to resort development. Akumal is one of the Yucatán's oldest resort areas and consists primarily of pricey hotels and condominiums situated on nearly 5km of wide beach bordering four consecutive bays.

Because of its length, Akumal is often referred to by the names given to stretches of the coast or features of the coast within its boundaries. The northernmost area of Akumal is called the Yal-Ku Lagoon, after the name of a beautiful lagoon there that can be accessed for US$5 a day. Heading south are Half Moon Bay, Akumal, South Akumal and Aventuras Akumal. If you are traveling south on highway 307, you will see signs for most of these turnoffs (there is none for Half Moon Bay) starting 105km south of Ciudad Cancún.

Activities
Although population is taking a heavy toll on the reefs that parallel Akumal, **diving** remains the area's primary attraction. Akumal Dive Shop (☎ 9-872-24-53, 800-777-8294 in the USA), Akumal Dive Center (☎ 800-351-1622 or 915-584-3552 in the USA, ☎ 800-343-1440 in Canada) and CEDAM Dive Center (☎ 9-873-51-47, fax 9-873-51-29, www.cedamdive.com) all run dive

trips and deep-sea fishing excursions. A particularly popular dive is the wreck of the Spanish galleon *Mantancero*, which went down in 1741.

Places to Stay & Eat

For the lowdown on most of the lodgings available in Akumal and to make a reservation, call ☎ 800-448-7137 in the US. Few rooms in Akumal are under US$100 a day.

Modern ***Villa Las Brisas*** *(☎ 9-876-21-10, fax 9-876-22-45)*, on the beach in Aventuras Akumal, has two one-bedroom condos, two two-bedroom condos and a studio apartment – all under one roof. Rates run from US$55 to US$125 during the low season; add US$25 during the high season. The owners speak English, Spanish, German, Italian and some Portuguese.

Hotel Club Akumal Caribe/Hotel Villas Maya *(☎ 9-875-90-12, 800-351-1622 in the USA, fax 915-581-6709 in the USA, www .hotelakumalcaribe.com)* offers bungalows starting at US$80 and villas starting at US$120 most of the year. All have air-con, and amenities include tennis and basketball courts.

Las Casitas Akumal *(☎ 9-875-90-71, fax 9-875-90-72)* has cabañas, each one containing a kitchen, living room, two bedrooms and two bathrooms. Rates run US$140 to US$160.

Just outside the walled entrance of Akumal is a grocery store patronized largely by the resort workers; this is your sole inexpensive source of food.

XCACEL

Xcacel ('shkah-CELL') is a beach on a somewhat turbulent bay. Its only structure is a beat-up building occasionally used by biologists studying the sea turtles that lay eggs in the sand here. Because of the turtles, no camping is permitted; indeed, only the biologists are allowed into Xcacel after sunset. A guard is posted at the end of the long dirt road that links Xcacel to highway 307, and during the day this sentry sometimes charges visitors US$2 to enter the area.

In addition to the beach, which is rockier and trashier than most along the coast,

there's an inviting cenote nestled in the scrub brush about 150m away from the surf. To reach it, walk south about 100m on the dirt trail that leaves the dirt parking area and borders the edge of the beach. When you come to a trail that runs away from the beach into the brush, take it. After another 75m or so you'll come to the cenote. It isn't nearly as nice as the cenotes you'd see at the ecoparks along the coast, but then access to it doesn't cost US$25, either.

XEL-HA

Once a pristine natural lagoon brimming with iridescent tropical fish and ringed on three sides by untouched mangroves, Xel-ha ('SHELL-hah') is now a private park with landscaped grounds, a dolphin enclosure (yes, you can frolic with them for a price), numerous restaurant-bars and a gift shop. The fish are regularly driven off by the busloads of sunscreen-slathered day-trippers who come to enjoy the beautiful site and swim in the pretty lagoon. A visit to Xel-ha is worth it only in the off-season (summer) or very early or very late in the day in winter. Open 8.30 am to 5.30 pm daily (US$39). Snorkeling-gear rental is US$8.

Ruins

A small archaeological site lies on the west side of the highway 500m south of the park's turnoff; open 8 am to 5 pm daily (US$2.50). The ruins, which are not all that impressive, date from Classic and Postclassic periods and include El Palacio and the Templo de los Pájaros.

TULUM
• pop 3600 ☎ 9

There are actually several Tulums: Tulum Crucero is the junction of highway 307 and the old access road to the ruins (the new entrance is 400m south of Tulum Crucero); Tulum Ruinas are the ruins, 800m southeast of Tulum Crucero; Tulum Pueblo is the modern settlement 3.5km south of Tulum Crucero; Tulum Zona Hotelera is the assortment of waterfront cabañas 1 to 7km south of the ruins. The Zona Hotelera is reached by an access road 2km south of Tulum

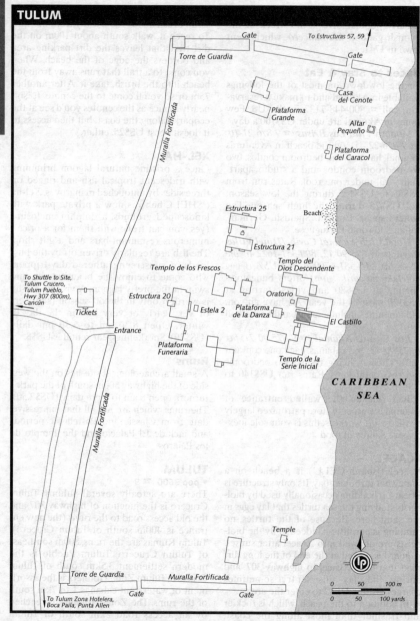

TULUM

To Estructuras 57, 59

Gate

Torre de Guardia

Gate

Casa del Cenote

Plataforma Grande

Altar Pequeño

Muralla Fortificada

Plataforma del Caracol

Estructura 25

Beach

Estructura 21

Templo de los Frescos

Templo del Dios Descendente

Estructura 20

Oratorio

To Shuttle to Site,
Tulum Crucero,
Tulum Pueblo,
Hwy 307 (800m),
Cancún

Estela 2

Plataforma de la Danza

El Castillo

Tickets

Entrance

Plataforma Funeraria

Templo de la Serie Inicial

CARIBBEAN SEA

Muralla Fortificada

Temple

Torre de Guardia

Muralla Fortificada

Gate

Gate

To Tulum Zona Hotelera,
Boca Paila, Punta Allen

0   50   100 m
0   50   100 yards

Crucero (1.5km north of Tulum Pueblo), opposite the Cobá road.

South of the Zona Hotelera, the road enters the Reserva de la Biósfera Sian Ka'an and continues for some 50km past Boca Paila to Punta Allen.

There are Telmex pay phones in town, but few along the coastal road, although there was talk of installing more pay phones along the road in 2000.

You'll find numerous currency-exchange booths in town, but no banks. The booths with the best exchange rates are opposite the bus station.

Ruins

The ruins of Tulum (Mayan for 'Wall'), though very well preserved, would hardly merit rave reviews if it weren't for their setting. The grayish-tan buildings dominate a palm-fringed beach lapped by turquoise waters. Even on dark, stormy days, the majestic cliff-top ruins overlooking vast stretches of pristine beach look fit for the cover of a magazine. But don't come to Tulum expecting anything comparable to Chichén Itzá or Uxmal. The buildings here, decidedly Toltec in influence, were the product of a Mayan civilization in decline.

Tulum is a prime destination for tour buses. To best enjoy the ruins, visit them either early in the morning or late in the afternoon, when the tour groups aren't there. Open 8 am to 5 pm daily; admission US$3, parking US$1.50, shuttle to the site US$1.30.

History Most archaeologists believe that Tulum was occupied during the late Postclassic period (1200-1521) and that it was an important port town during its heyday. When Juan de Grijalva sailed past in 1518, he was amazed by the sight of this walled city, its buildings painted a gleaming red, blue and yellow, with a ceremonial fire flaming atop its seaside watchtower.

The ramparts that surround three sides of Tulum (the fourth side being the sea) leave little question as to its strategic function as a fortress. Averaging nearly 7m thick and standing 3 to 5m high, the walls protected the city during a period of considerable strife between Mayan city-states. Not all of Tulum was situated within the walls. The vast majority of the city's residents lived outside them; the civic-ceremonial buildings and palaces likely housed Tulum's ruling class.

The city was abandoned about 75 years after the Spanish conquest. It was one of the last ancient cities to be abandoned; most had been given back to nature long before the arrival of the Spanish. Mayan pilgrims continued to visit over the years, and refugees from the War of the Castes took shelter here from time to time.

The name 'Tulum,' though Mayan, was not how its residents knew it. They called it Zama, or 'Dawn.' 'Tulum' was apparently applied by explorers in the early 20th century.

El Castillo Tulum's tallest building, appropriately named El Castillo (the Castle) by the Spaniards, is a watchtower fortress overlooking the Caribbean. Note the Toltec-style serpent columns at the temple's entrance, echoing those at Chichén Itzá.

Templo del Dios Descendente The Temple of the Descending God is named for the relief figure above the door – a diving figure, partly human, which may be related to the Mayas' reverence for bees. This figure appears at several other east coast sites and at Cobá.

Templo de la Serie Inicial The restored Temple of the Initial Series is named for Stela 1, now in the British Museum, which was inscribed with the Mayan date corresponding to 564 AD (the 'initial series' of Mayan hieroglyphs in an inscription gives its date). At first this confused archaeologists, who believed Tulum had been settled several hundred years later than this date. It's now believed that Stela 1 was brought to Tulum from Tankah, 4km to the north, a settlement dating from the Classic period.

Templo de los Frescos This two-story building was constructed in several stages around 1400 to 1450. Its decoration was among the most elaborate at Tulum, and

YUCATÁN PENINSULA

included the diving god, relief masks and colored murals on an inner wall. The murals, painted in three levels, show the three realms of the Mayan universe: the dark underworld of the deceased, the middle order of the living and the heavenly home of the creator and rain gods. This monument might have been the last built by the Maya before the Spanish conquest.

Estructura 25 This largely deteriorated site, known as the Great Palace, contains a fine stucco carving of a diving god.

Estructuras 57 & 59 These two small temples are north of the city wall. Estructura 57, about 500m north of the wall, is a one-room shrine in good condition. Estructura 59, another 500m to the north, is another one-room temple with the remains of a roof comb, the only one found at Tulum.

Places to Stay & Eat
Along Highway 307 Right at the junction of highway 307 and the old Tulum ruins access road are several hotels and restaurants. The hotels here have nowhere near the character or charm of the coastal lodgings, but they offer the convenience of not having to take a taxi or make a long hike to the ruins. The well used *Motel El Crucero*, expensive at US$10 to US$15 double with shower and fan, has a restaurant (about US$6 an entree) and shop selling ice, meals, drinks and souvenirs. Across the access road are the *Hotel Acuario* (☎ 871-21-95, fax 871-21-94, http://hotelacuario.com), with air-conditioned rooms for US$35 to US$50 double, and its *Restaurant El Faisán y El Venado*.

Boca Paila-Punta Allen Rd South of the archaeological zone along this coastal road, starting less than 1km from the ruins, is a string of cabaña hotels that cater primarily to budget travelers. Most have simple restaurants but do not have telephones or electricity, or they have electricity only till 9 or 10 pm.

The cheapest way to sleep here is to have your own hammock and a tubelike mosquito net to cover it; if you don't, several of

the cheaper places will rent you what you need. In the cheapest places you'll have to supply your own towel and soap. See 'Tips for Tulum's Cabañas', below.

The following places are listed in the order you'll find them as you travel south on the coastal road from the ruins.

Closest to the ruins, *Cabañas El Mirador* has 28 on-the-sand cabins with beds, but no fans or anything else. Cost is US$10 per room. There's a beach out front and a decent restaurant (meals US$2 to US$4) nearby.

Tips for Tulum's Cabañas

The waterfront *cabañas* south of the Tulum ruins are world famous among backpackers. The first four sit side by side within 1km of the ruins. Thereafter, they are mixed in with more expensive places and spread out over the next 9km. Here are a few tips to keep in mind if you intend to stay at one of them:

- Cabañas closest to the ruins are usually fully occupied by 10 or 11 am every day from mid-December through March and in July and August. Arrive early, or make a reservation the night before.

- Taxis are recommended to cover the 2 to 3km between the cabañas and the bus station or the bus stops at Tulum Crucero and the Zona Arqueológica.

- The cheapest cabañas are made of sticks and built on sand (some have concrete floors). Bring a mosquito net to hang over yourself at night.

- Few of the flimsy, primitive cabañas can be reliably secured. Thieves lift the poles in the walls to gain entrance, or burrow beneath through the sand, or jimmy the locks. Never leave valuables unattended in a cabaña.

- Bring a pair of sandals or flip-flops. Most of the cabañas, even at the pricier places, have shared bathrooms. Shoes help you keep sand out of your bed and reduce the chance of catching athlete's foot.

Next door is **Cabañas Santa Fe**, which has 45 mostly thatch-roofed cabins with sandy floors and sides made of wooden poles. A few of the newer cabañas are cinder block with concrete floors. Prices range from US$11 to US$25. The fancier cabañas have electricity, beds and private bathrooms. Camping is permitted for US$2.

The **Cabañas Don Armando**, just south of Santa Fe and a 10-minute walk from the ruins, have concrete slabs (instead of sand) for US$14 to US$18 single/double. The poles have been filled in with concrete, which makes them more secure but prevents ventilation. Features include lockable doors, hammocks and beds (you pay a deposit for sheets and pillows), and mosquito netting. Lighting is by candles.

Cabañas Playa Conjesa, 500m farther south, has 15 comfortable cabañas, each with a bed suspended by rope from the ceiling, mosquito netting, a concrete floor and slat-pole siding with good ventilation. Guests can use the restaurant at the Hotel Diamante K, two doors to the south. Rates are US$12 to US$15.

Hotel Diamante K (☎ 871-23-76, fax 871-22-83) offers rooms with wooden pole or bamboo siding, suspended beds and a table for a candle (the lights go off at 10 pm). Rates start at US$30 with communal bath, US$70 with private bath. Two communal rooms have beds for US$10 each, a much better deal than the comparably priced places already mentioned. The Diamante K has a small beach and a fine restaurant-bar, and it fills up even in the low season.

About 700m south, just south of the road that links the coastal road and Tulum town, is the popular 15-room **Papaya Playa** (☎ 871-20-91, fax 871-20-92). Four rooms have private bath, furniture and beds; the rest have sandy floors but are otherwise fine. All have screened windows and ocean views. Amenities include a beach and a cozy bar and restaurant. Rooms range from US$40 to US$60; reservations recommended. Teepees and hammocks are available for US$5 each.

Next to the south is **Cabañas Copal**, consisting of three comfortable cabañas with concrete floors, private bath and ocean view for US$50, along with 12 budget cabañas with sandy floors, mosquito nets, firm mattresses and good ventilation.

Continuing south, and by now 4 to 5km south of the ruins, you'll come to the family-run **Cabañas La Conchita** (fax 871-20-92; put 'attn La Conchita'), which has eight rooms that are a major step up from those described thus far. Most have cool, concrete walls, standard windows with some degree of sea view, and lockable doors. The beach here is lovely. Rates are a reasonable US$60 for most rooms, breakfast included.

Restaurant y Cabañas Nohoch Tunich (☎ 876-94-07, fax 871-20-92, www.secom.net/nohochtunich) offers thatch-and-board cabañas as well as appealing hotel rooms with porches and electricity (until 11 pm). Rooms are US$60; most cabañas run US$20 (two have private bath for US$35). Breakfast is included.

Next door is the **Piedra Escondida Hotel y Restaurant** (☎/fax 871-22-17, www.secom.net/piedraescondida), which offers eight well-ventilated hotel rooms each with private bath and a balcony or porch. Rates are US$65 much of the year but up to US$85 in high season.

Cabañas La Perla, the next place to the south, offers six rooms and two cabañas. The rooms have private bath, and they rent for US$40 (one bed) or US$50 (two beds). The rustic cabañas have shared bath for US$20. La Perla shares a small beach with Nohoch Tunich and Punta Piedra.

About 500m to the south is the **Maya Tulum** (☎ 888-515-4580 in the USA, www.mayatulum.com), which is in a different league from all the other places mentioned. It offers 34 deluxe cabañas and two houses, a gorgeous beach nearby, a yoga room, a vegetarian restaurant and massage. Rates run US$60 to US$70 for a shared-bath cabaña, US$70 to US$80 for a cabaña with private bath, and US$120 to US$140 for a house.

Getting There & Away

You can walk from Tulum Crucero to the ruins (800m) or take the shuttle for a fee. Reaching the cabañas is more difficult. The closest are 600m south of the ruins, but to get to them by taxi you have to take a circuitous route because the road to the ruins is closed to private vehicles when the ruins are open. No buses serve the cabañas. The good news is that taxis in Tulum are cheap and the fares fixed. At the center of small, roadside Tulum town you'll see the large sign of the Sindicato de Taxistas, on which the rates are posted. To the ruins it's US$1.60, to most of the cabañas US$2.60 to US$3.

The bus station is at the southern end of Tulum town (look for the two-story building with 'ADO' painted on it in huge letters). When leaving Tulum, you can also wait at Tulum Crucero for a Playa Express or regular intercity bus. Here are some distances and travel times for buses leaving Tulum:

Cancún – 132km, 1½ to 2 hours, US$3 to US$4

Chetumal – 251km, 3½hours; US$5 to US$7

Chichén Itzá – 402km, 5 hours; US$5

Cobá – 45km, 30 minutes; US$1.20

Felipe Carrillo Puerto – 98km, 1¾ hours; US$3.50

Mérida – 320km, 5 hours via Cobá or 6 hours via Cancún; US$10

Playa del Carmen – 63km, 45 minutes; US$2

Punta Allen – 57km, 1 hour; US$1.60

COBÁ

Perhaps the largest of all Mayan cities, Cobá, 50km northwest of Tulum, offers the chance to explore mostly unrestored antiquities set deep in tropical jungle.

History

Cobá was settled earlier than Chichén or Tulum, its heyday dating from 600 AD until the site was mysteriously abandoned about 900 AD. Archaeologists believe that this city once covered 50 sq km and held 40,000 Maya.

Cobá's architecture is a mystery; its towering pyramids and stelae resemble the architecture of Tikal, several hundred kilometers away, rather than the much nearer sites of Chichén Itzá and the northern Yucatán Peninsula.

Some archaeologists theorize that an alliance with Tikal was made through marriage

to facilitate trade between the Guatemalan and Yucatecan Maya. Stelae appear to depict female rulers from Tikal holding ceremonial bars and flaunting their power by standing on captives. These Tikal royal females, when married to Cobá's royalty, may have brought architects and artisans with them.

Archaeologists are also baffled by the extensive network of *sacbeob* (stone-paved avenues) in this region, with Cobá as the hub. The longest runs nearly 100km from the base of Cobá's great pyramid Nohoch Mul to the Mayan settlement of Yaxuna. In all, some 40 sacbeob passed through Cobá, parts of the huge astronomical 'time machine' that was evident in every Mayan city.

The first excavation was by the Austrian archaeologist Teobert Maler in 1891. Little subsequent investigation took place until 1926, when the Carnegie Institute financed the first of two expeditions led by J Eric S Thompson and Harry Pollock. After their 1930 expedition not much happened until 1973, when the Mexican government began to finance excavation. Archaeologists now estimate that Cobá contains some 6500 structures, of which just a few have been excavated and restored.

Orientation

The small village of Cobá, 2.5km west of the Tulum-Nuevo Xcan road, has several small, simple, cheap hotels and restaurants. At the lake, turn left for the ruins, right for the upscale Villa Arqueológica Cobá hotel.

Cobá archaeological site is open 8 am to 5 pm daily (US$3, free on Sunday). Be prepared to walk at least 5 to 7km on paths. Dress for heat and humidity, and bring insect repellent and water; it's hot, and the only drink stands are at the entrance (where you can also buy bug spray). Avoid the midday heat if possible. Most people spend two hours at the site.

Grupo Cobá

Walking just under 100m along the main path from the entrance brings you to the Templo de las Iglesias (Temple of the Churches), on your right, the most prominent structure in the Cobá Group. It's an enormous pyramid, and from the top you can get a fine view of the Nohoch Mul pyramid to the north and shimmering lakes to the east and southwest.

Back on the main path, you pass through the Juego de Pelota (Ball Court) 30m farther along. It's now badly ruined.

Grupo Macanxoc
About 500m beyond the Juego de Pelota, turn right for the Grupo Macanxoc, a group of stelae that bore reliefs of royal women thought to have come from Tikal.

Grupo de las Pinturas
Another 100m beyond the Macanxoc turn-off, a sign points right toward the Conjunto de las Pinturas (Temple of Paintings). It bears easily recognizable traces of glyphs and frescoes above the door and traces of richly colored plaster inside.

You approached the Temple of Paintings from the southwest. Leave by the trail at the northwest (opposite the temple steps) to see several stelae. The first of these is 20m along beneath a palapa. A regal figure stands over two others, one of them kneeling with his hands bound behind him. At the base, sacrificial captives lie beneath the feet of a ruler. Continue along the path past another badly weathered stela to the Nohoch Mul path and turn right.

Nohoch Mul
A further walk of 800m brings you to Nohoch Mul, the Great Pyramid. Along the way, just before the trail bends sharply to the left, a narrow path on the right leads to a group of badly weathered stelae. Farther along, the trail winds between piles of stones – a ruined temple – before passing Templo 10 and Stela 20. The exquisitely carved stela bears a picture of a ruler standing imperiously over two captives. Eighty meters beyond stands the Great Pyramid.

At 42m high, the Great Pyramid is the tallest of all Mayan structures on the Yucatán Peninsula. Climb the 120 steps, observing that the Maya carved shell-like forms where you put your feet. At the top,

two diving gods (similar to the sculptures at Tulum) are carved over the temple doorway. The view from up here is spectacular.

From atop Nohoch Mul, it's a 1.4km, 30-minute walk back to the site entrance. Be advised that at least one person a year loses footing on the pyramid, falls, and dies somewhere on the way down. Wear snug shoes with traction. Most sandals are not recommended.

Places to Stay & Eat
Several small restaurants are by the parking lot. Buy your drinks at either **Restaurant El**

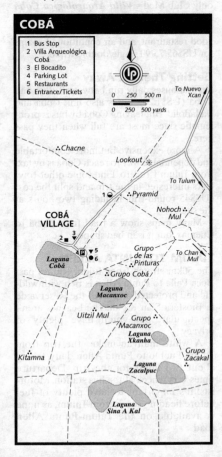

COBÁ

1 Bus Stop
2 Villa Arqueológica Cobá
3 El Bocadito
4 Parking Lot
5 Restaurants
6 Entrance/Tickets

0   250   500 m
0   250   500 yards

To Nuevo Xcan

Chacne

Lookout

To Tulum

Pyramid

Nohoch Mul

COBÁ VILLAGE

Grupo de las Pinturas

To Chan Mul

Grupo Cobá

Laguna Cobá

Laguna Macanxoc

Uitzil Mul

Grupo Macanxoc

Laguna Xkanha

Grupo Zacakal

Kitamna

Laguna Zacalpuc

Laguna Sina A Kal

Faisán or *Restaurant El Caracol*, both of which serve inexpensive meals.

In the village of Cobá, *Restaurant Lagoon* is nearest the lake and has good views and friendly service. *Restaurant Isabel* and *El Bocadito* are also popular. El Bocadito rents rooms with fan and bath for US$10.

No developed campsites are available, but you can try finding a place along the lakeshore. No one is likely to bother you there. Before you go swimming, consider the crocodiles living in the lake.

For upscale lodging and dining there's only Club Med's *Villa Arqueológica Cobá* (☎ 9-884-25-74 *in Cancún*, ☎ 800-528-3100 *in the USA*), which has a swimming pool, a good restaurant, and air-conditioned rooms for US$65/75/90 single/double/triple.

Getting There & Away

Several buses daily run between Tulum and Cobá (US$1.20); buses also link Cobá and Valladolid. But leaving Cobá by bus is problematic since most are full when they pass here.

A more expensive but more comfortable and dependable way to reach Cobá is by taxi from Tulum Crucero. Find some other travelers interested in the trip and split the cost (US$45 round-trip, including two hours at the site).

Many maps show a road from Cobá to Chemax, but it is in bad shape.

TULUM TO PUNTA ALLEN

The 50km stretch from Tulum Ruinas past Boca Paila to Punta Allen is rich with wildlife and protected as part of the Reserva de la Biósfera Sian Ka'an. The beaches aren't spectacular, but you'll have plenty of privacy.

A white minivan makes the trip from Tulum Pueblo to Punta Allen daily, taking about two hours for the trip. Departure times vary; check at the bus station. Motorists: it's important to have plenty of fuel before heading south from Tulum, as none is available on the Tulum-Punta Allen road.

Reserva de la Biósfera Sian Ka'an

More than 5000 sq km of tropical jungle, marsh, mangroves and islands on Quintana Roo's coast have been set aside by the Mexican government as a large biosphere reserve. In 1987 the United Nations appointed it a World Heritage Site – an irreplaceable natural treasure. But there are no hiking trails through Sian Ka'an (Where the Sky Begins) and only two ways to get much out of the reserve. The first is to drive down one of the few roads that intersect the Tulum-Punta Allen road, pull to the side at a promising stretch and walk along the road for a while. Don't enter the forest – there's a good chance you'll become lost.

The other way is to enter the reserve with a professional guide. Aventuras Tropicales de Sian Ka'an (☎ 9-871-20-92 November to April, ☎/fax 218-388-9455 in the USA April to November, ☎ 800-649-4166 in the USA, www.boreal.org/yucatan), based in Punta Allen, runs outings combining sea kayaking, mountain biking, snorkeling, luxury camping, gourmet dining, quality hammock time and total immersion in a truly remote tropical wilderness. Most trips last four to eight days. Birding and ecosystem-study trips are also offered.

Punta Allen

Punta Allen suffered considerable damage from the ferocious winds of Hurricane Gilbert in 1988, but it still has a laid-back ambiance reminiscent of the Belizean cayes. The area is known primarily for its bonefishing, and for that many people come a long way. In addition, a healthy reef 400m from shore offers snorkelers and divers wonderful sights. Though a turnoff to many people, abundant sea grass between the reef and the beach provides food and shelter to lots of critters and is one of the reasons the snorkeling and diving is so good.

The *Cruzan Inn* (☎ 9-834-03-83, fax 9-834-02-92, fishcruzan@aol.com) has eight cabañas on stilts, each with private bath, two beds, mosquito netting and 24-hour lighting; rates are US$50/75 a double in low/high season. Meals are available, and the managers offer snorkeling trips (US$25, gear included) and arrange fishing and birding expeditions.

The ***Ascension Bay Bonefish Club*** (*www .joefish.com*) specializes in guided fishing expeditions, offering packages with six full days of guided fishing, pickup from Cancún, lodge accommodations and meals, all for US$2000 to US$2300.

Let It Be Inn (*www.letitbeinn.com*) has several thatched cabañas with tiled floors, private hot-water baths and sea-view porches with hammocks. The rate of US$55 double includes a hearty breakfast.

FELIPE CARRILLO PUERTO
• pop 16,400   ☎ 9

Now named for a progressive governor of Yucatán, this town 95km south of Tulum was once known as Chan Santa Cruz, the dreaded rebel headquarters during the War of the Castes. It offers the visitor little in the way of attractions, but it does have a gas station and some inexpensive air-conditioned accommodations.

History
In 1849, when the War of the Castes turned against them, the Maya of the northern Yucatán Peninsula made their way to this town seeking refuge. Regrouping, they were ready to sally forth again in 1850 when a 'miracle' occurred. A wooden cross erected at a cenote on the western edge of the town began to 'talk,' telling the Maya they were the chosen people, exhorting them to continue the struggle against the whites, and promising victory. The talking was actually done by a ventriloquist who used sound chambers, but the people looked upon it as the authentic voice of their aspirations.

The oracular cross guided the Maya in battle for more than eight years, until their great victory conquering the fortress at Bacalar. For the latter part of the 19th century, the Maya in and around Chan Santa Cruz were virtually independent of governments in Mexico City and Mérida. In the 1920s a boom in the chicle market brought

prosperity to the region, and the Maya decided to come to terms with Mexico City, which they did in 1929.

Some of the Maya, unwilling to give up the cult of the talking cross, left Chan Santa Cruz to take up residence at small villages deep in the jungle, where they still revere the talking cross to this day. You may see

Time among the Maya

The history of the Talking Cross is not over. Every year on May 3, the Feast of the Holy Cross, Mayas gather in Felipe Carrillo Puerto – known to them as Noh Cah Santa Cruz Balam Na – to celebrate ancient Mayan traditions and specifically the Talking Cross, the last great symbol of Mayan independence.

Just a short drive inland from this city, Mayan villagers observe many aspects of traditional life, including use of the ancient Mayan calendar.

In the mid-1980s, English writer Ronald Wright came here in search of Mayas who still understood the Long Count and lived by the dictates of the *tzolkin*, the ancient Mayan almanac. Wright wrote about his experiences in a fascinating book, *Time among the Maya*, in 1989.

Wright found what he was seeking in X-Cacal Guardia and nearby villages, where descendants of the survivors of the 19th-century War of the Castes settled. Enveloped in the Yucatecan jungle, away from the wealth and centers of power, they guard their ancient crosses and religious beliefs while accepting innovations such as electric light, automobiles and Coca-Cola.

The 25m-long church at X-Cacal Guardia is guarded by men with rifles, its inner sanctum to be entered only by the Nohoch Tata (Great Father of the Holy Cross) himself. It may be that Chan Santa Cruz's famous Talking Cross, spirited away from the doomed city by the Mayas retreating from the last battle of the War of the Castes, has come to rest here. That is Ronald Wright's guess.

some of them visiting the site where the cross spoke, especially on May 3, the day of the Holy Cross.

You can visit the **Sanctuario del Cruz Parlante** (Sanctuary of the Talking Cross), five blocks west of the Pemex fuel station on highway 307 in the commercial center of town, though the cenote is dry now and the stone shelter isn't much to look at. Town residents do not like strangers in the sanctuary, and if they see you using your camera there they will try to take it.

Places to Stay & Eat

El Faisán y El Venado (☎ 834-07-02, *Avenida Juárez 781*) has 13 air-conditioned rooms with private showers, firm mattresses and ceiling fans for US$15 double, and a good, inexpensive restaurant. A few dozen meters south is the *Restaurant 24 Horas*, which is a bit cheaper.

South of the 24 Horas is the *Hotel San Ignacio*, with 12 air-conditioned rooms for US$16 single/double, and an air-conditioned restaurant called *Danburguer Maya*.

Restaurant Familiar La Cozumeleño is a tidy, family-run place, cheaper than the others, in front of the bus station. For breads and pastries, try the *Panadería Mar y Sol*.

Getting There & Away

Numerous buses running to Cancún (230km, 3½ hours, US$8) and Chetumal (155km, 2½ hours, US$4 to US$6) stop here, as do buses traveling from Chetumal to Valladolid (160km, three hours, US$5) and Mérida (310km, five hours, US$9.50). A few buses run between here and Ticul (200km, four hours, US$8); change at Ticul or Muna for Uxmal. Two buses daily run to Tizimín. Bus fare to Tulum is US$3.30.

Note that there are very few services such as hotels, restaurants or fuel stations between Felipe Carrillo Puerto and Ticul.

XCALAK & COSTA MAYA

The coast from south of the Reserva de la Biósfera Sian Ka'an to the small fishing village of Xcalak ('shka-LAK') is often referred to as the Costa Maya. Unknown and difficult to access until 1981, it is now drawing increasing numbers of adventurous travelers in search of that fast-disappearing natural asset – undeveloped coastline.

Today, despite the recent paving of the road linking the town with highway 307, Xcalak remains a relatively primitive part of Mexico. Most residents have electricity only six hours a day.

Xcalak's appeal lies in its quiet atmosphere – older Caribbean-style wooden homes, swaying palms and pretty beaches. Little-explored (and thus unspoiled) Banco Chinchorro, the largest coral atoll in the Northern Hemisphere, is 40km away. Aventuras Chinchorro (☎ 9-838-78-24, 941-488-4505 in the USA or 800-480-4505 in the USA, www.xcalak.com) offers dive and snorkel trips to the atoll and rents equipment.

Places to Stay & Eat

The six-room *Hotel Caracol* (no phone) is the town's only cheap place to stay, offering decent rooms with fan and cold-water private bath for US$9. Electricity is available from 7 to 11 pm. Look for the owner next door to the hotel.

Costa de Cocos (☎ 888-968-6181 in the USA, www.costadecocos.com), 1.5km north of Xcalak, has 14 appealing thatched cabañas with private bath, solar hot water, screened windows and 24-hour electricity. Rooms are US$65 to US$75, including breakfast and dinner.

Hotel Tierra Maya (☎ 800-480-4505 or 941-627-3888 in the USA, fax 941-627-0089, www.xcalak.com) is a modern beachfront hotel featuring six rooms (three quite large), each tastefully appointed and boasting lots of architectural details. All of the rooms have sea-view balconies, hot-water private bathrooms and mahogany furniture; the bigger rooms even have small refrigerators. Electricity is available 24 hours. Rates are a bargain at US$55 double for the smaller rooms, US$65 for the larger rooms. Add US$5 from December 21 to April 14.

Villa Caracol (☎ 9-838-18-72) features two 2nd-floor doubles plus four individual beach cabañas, all with two queen-size beds, purified water, private bath, air-con and 24-hour electricity. A bargain at US$83 double, including breakfast, dinner and unlimited use of the villa's snorkeling equipment, bicycles, paddleboats and fishing tackle.

Small restaurants near the center of town include **Capitán Caribe**, **Brisas del Mar** and **Lonchería Silvia** (the best of the three).

Getting There & Away

It's possible to get to Xcalak by bus, but it's tricky. From Chetumal or Felipe Carrillo Puerto, take a bus that would pass through Limones, which is near the highway 307 turnoff for Xcalak. In Limones, there are somewhat regular but infrequent buses to Xcalak. The other option is to hire a taxi, but it's expensive and taxis aren't always available in Limones. With some negotiating, it should be possible to take a cab to Xcalak for US$90 now that the road's in good shape. The vast majority of tourists who reach Xcalak do so in a rental car.

LAGUNA BACALAR

A large, clear, turquoise freshwater lake with a bottom of gleaming white sand, Laguna Bacalar comes as a surprise in this region of tortured limestone and scrubby jungle.

The small, sleepy town of Bacalar, just east of the highway 125km south of Felipe Carrillo Puerto, is the only settlement of any size on the lake. It's noted mostly for its old Spanish fortress and its swimming facilities. The fortress was built over the lagoon to protect citizens from raids by pirates and indigenous aggressors, and it served as an important outpost for the whites in the War of the Castes. In 1859 it was seized by Mayan rebels, who held the fort until Quintana Roo was finally conquered by Mexican troops in 1901. Today, with formidable cannons still on its ramparts, the fortress remains an imposing sight. It houses a museum exhibiting colonial armaments and uniforms from the 17th and 18th centuries. Open 8 am to 1 pm daily (US$1).

A divided avenue runs between the fortress and the lakeshore northward a few hundred meters to the *balneario*. Small restaurants line the avenue and surround the balneario, which is very busy on Saturday and Sunday.

Costera Bacalar & Cenote Azul

The road that winds south along the lakeshore from Bacalar town to highway 307 at Cenote Azul is called the Costera Bacalar. It passes a few lodging and camping places along the way. The Cenote Azul is a 90m-deep natural pool on the southwestern shore of Laguna Bacalar, 200m east of highway 307. (If you're approaching from the north by bus, get the driver to let you off here.) Meals at the nearby restaurant cost US$8 to US$12. A small sign purveys Mayan wisdom: 'Don't go in the cenote if you can't swim.'

Hotel Laguna (☎ 9-834-22-06, ☎/fax 9-832-35-17 in Chetumal), 3.3km south of Bacalar town along the Costera, is only 150m east of highway 307. Clean, cool and hospitable, it boasts a swimming pool, restaurant and bar. Unfortunately, their mattresses are in need of replacing. Rooms cost US$27 single/double.

Only 700m south of Hotel Laguna along the Costera is **Los Coquitos**, a very nice lakeshore camping area that charges US$5 per couple. Bring your own food and water, as the nearest supplier is the restaurant at Hotel Laguna.

Getting There & Away

Coming from the north, have the bus drop you in Bacalar town, at the Hotel Laguna, or at Cenote Azul, as you wish; check before you buy your ticket to see if the driver will stop.

Departures to the town of Bacalar from Chetumal's minibus terminal on Primo de Verdad at Hidalgo are about every 20 minutes from 5 am to 7 pm (39km, 40 minutes, US$2); some northbound buses (US$1.25) departing from the bus terminal will also drop you near the town of Bacalar.

Heading west out of Chetumal, take highway 307 north 15.5km to the turn on the right marked for the Cenote Azul and Costera Bacalar.

CHETUMAL
• pop 115,200 ☎ 9

Before the Spanish conquest, Chetumal was a Mayan port for shipping gold, feathers, cacao and copper to the northern Yucatán Peninsula. After the conquest, the town was

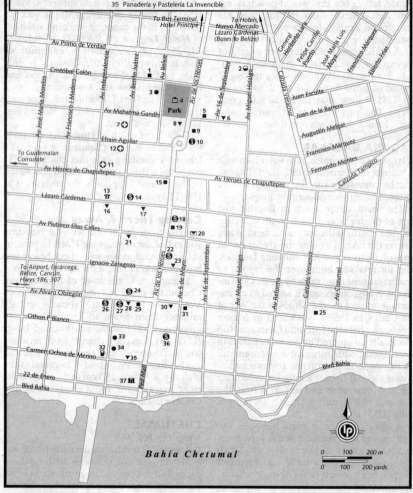

CHETUMAL

PLACES TO STAY
1 Hotel Cristal
5 Hotel Ucum
9 Holiday Inn Chetumal Puerta Maya
15 Hotel Los Cocos
19 Hotel El Cedro
25 Instituto Quintanarroense de la Juventud y El Deporte (Youth Hostel)
29 Hotel María Dolores
31 Hotel Caribe Princess

PLACES TO EAT
6 Restaurant Pantoja
8 Mercado Ignacio Manuel Altamirano
16 Restaurant Vegetariano La Fuente
17 Hawaiian Paradise
21 Restaurant Típico El Taquito
23 Café-Restaurant Los Milagros
28 Pollo Brujo
29 Restaurant Sosilmar, Panadería La Muralla
30 Sergio's Pizzas, Maria's
35 Panadería y Pastelería La Invencible

OTHER
2 Minibus Terminal
3 ADO Bus Ticket Office
4 Museo de la Cultura Maya
7 Clínica de Chetumal
10 Tourist Information Kiosk
11 Cruz Roja
12 Hospital Morelos
13 Telmex
14 Banco Santander Mexicano
18 Banorte, BanCrecer (ATMs)
20 Post Office
22 Chetumal Express Casa de Cambio
24 Banca Serfin (ATM)
26 Bancomer (ATM)
27 Banamex
32 Pemex Station
33 Scorpion's
34 El Palomar
36 Bital
37 Palacio de Gobierno

To Bus Terminal, Hotel Principe

To Hotels, Nuevo Mercado Lázaro Cárdenas (Buses to Belize)

Av Primo de Verdad

Cristóbal Colón

Av José María Morelos
Av Francisco I Madero
Av Independencia
Av Benito Juárez
Av Belice
Av de los Héroes
Av 16 de Septiembre
Av Miguel Hidalgo
Calzada Veracruz
General Hermilo Lara
Felipe Carrillo Puerto
José María Luis Mora
Francisco Márquez
Alberto Frías

Juan Escuita
Juan de la Barrera
Augustin Melgar
Francisco Márquez
Fernando Montes
Calzada Tampico

Av Mahatma Gandhi
Park
Efrain Aguilar

To Guatemalan Consulate

Av Héroes de Chapultepec
Av Héroes de Chapultepec

Lázaro Cárdenas

Av Plutarco Elías Calles

To Airport, Escárcega, Belize, Cancún, Hwys 186, 307

Ignacio Zaragoza

Av de los Héroes
Av 5 de Mayo
Av 16 de Septiembre
Av Miguel Hidalgo
Av Reforma
Calzada Veracruz
Av Cozumel

Av Álvaro Obregón

Othon P Blanco

Carmen Ochoa de Merino

22 de Enero
Blvd Bahía

Red Mall

Blvd Bahía

Bahía Chetumal

0   100   200 m
0   100   200 yards

not actually settled until 1898, when it was founded to put a stop to the illegal trade in arms and lumber carried on by descendants of the War of the Castes rebels. First dubbed Payo Obispo, it was renamed Chetumal in 1936.

In 1955, Hurricane Janet virtually obliterated the town. During the rebuilding, the city planners laid out the new town on a grand plan with a grid of wide boulevards. In times BC (Before Cancún), the sparsely populated territory of Quintana Roo could not support such a grand city. But the boom at Cancún brought prosperity to all, and Chetumal is finally fulfilling its destiny as the important capital city of Quintana Roo. Chetumal is also the gateway to Belize. With the peso so low and Belize so expensive, Belize nearly empties out on Saturday and Sunday with shoppers coming to Chetumal's markets.

Orientation

Despite Chetumal's sprawling layout, the city center is easily manageable on foot. Once you find the all-important intersection of Avenida de los Héroes and Avenida Álvaro Obregón, you're within 50m of several inexpensive hotels and restaurants. The best hotels are only four or five blocks from this intersection.

Information

A tourist information kiosk (☎ 832-36-63), on Avenida de los Héroes at the eastern end of Aguilar, is open 8 am to 1 pm and 5 to 8 pm daily.

The Guatemalan consulate (☎ 832-30-45), is at Retorno Numero 4, Casa 8, Fraccionamiento Bahía. Take Héroes de Chapultepec east to where it ends at the water, The consulate is one block northwest on a street that doesn't quite connect to Bulevar Bahia. It's open 9 am to 4 pm Monday to Friday. People will try to tell you it's at the other end of Chapultepec, but it's moved, trust us. Avenida Héroes de Chapultepec 354, is nine blocks west of Avenida de los Héroes. Look for the blue-and-white flag on the south side of the street. It's open 9 am to 2 pm Monday to Friday and offers quick visa service.

The post office (☎ 832-00-57) is at Avenida Plutarco Elías Calles 2A.

Museo de la Cultura Maya

This superb museum, on Avenida de los Héroes between Colón and Avenida Gandhi, is the city's claim to cultural fame, a bold block-long air-conditioned showpiece designed to draw visitors from as far away as Cancún. Indeed, it is the only significant attraction in the capital city.

The exhibits cover all of the Mayab (lands of the Maya), not just Quintana Roo or Mexico, and seek to explain the Mayan way of life, thought and belief. Among them are beautiful scale models showing the great Mayan buildings as they may have appeared; replicas of stelae from Copán, Honduras; reproductions of the murals found in Room 1 at Bonampak; and artifacts from sites around Quintana Roo.

The museum is organized into three levels, as was the universe in Mayan cosmogony. The main floor represents this world, the upper floor the heavens, and the lower floor the underworld. All exhibits are labeled in Spanish and English. Open 9 am to 7 pm Tuesday to Thursday, 9 am to 8 pm Friday and Saturday (US$2.50/1.25 adults/children).

Places to Stay

Budget The youth hostel, *Instituto Quintanarroense de la Juventud y El Deporte* (☎ 832-05-25), on Calzada Veracruz near the corner of Avenida Obregón, is the cheapest place in town. It has single-sex dorms, an 11 pm curfew and is five blocks east of the intersection of Avenida de los Héroes and Avenida Obregón. Cost is US$4 for a bunk in a room with four or six beds and shared bath. Meals are not available.

Hotel María Dolores (☎ 832-05-08, Avenida Obregón 206), west of Avenida de los Héroes above the Restaurant Sosilmar, is the best for the price. It has tiny, stuffy rooms with fans and private bath for US$9/11/13/15 single/double/triple/quad.

Hotel Ucum (☎ 832-07-11, 832-61-86, Avenida Gandhi 167) has lots of plain rooms around a bare central courtyard. Rooms with fan, TV and shower cost US$12 single/double, with air-con US$22 double. The hotel has a good, cheap restaurant.

Hotel Cristal (☎ 832-38-78, *Colón 207*), between Avenidas Juárez and Belice, has clean rooms for US$9/11/14 single/double/triple with fan, US$23 double with air-con and TV.

Hotel El Cedro (☎ 832-68-78), on Avenida de los Héroes between Avenida Plutarco Elías Calles and Cárdenas, has slightly worn but OK rooms for US$22 double with air-con, TV and private bath.

The quiet *Hotel Caribe Princess* (☎/fax 832-09-00, *Avenida Obregón 168*) has lots of marble and good air-conditioned rooms for US$21/26/30.

One kilometre north of the Museo Maya on the way to the bus terminal, *Hotel Príncipe* (☎ 832-47-99, fax 832-51-91, *Avenida de los Héroes 326*) has decent rooms, a restaurant and even a small swimming pool for US$27 double with air-con.

Mid-Range & Top End The *Hotel Los Cocos* (☎ 832-05-44, fax 832-09-20), Avenida de los Héroes at Avenida Héroes de Chapultepec, has a nice swimming pool, a guarded parking lot and a popular sidewalk restaurant. Air-conditioned rooms with TV cost US$40 to US$50 single/double.

Two blocks north of Los Cocos along Avenida de los Héroes, near the tourist information kiosk, is the *Holiday Inn Chetumal Puerta Maya* (☎ 832-11-00, 832-10-80, 800-465-4329 in the USA, fax 832-16-76, *Avenida de los Héroes 171*). Its comfortable rooms overlook a small courtyard with a swimming pool set amid tropical gardens; there's a restaurant and bar. Rates are US$95 single/double. This is the best place in town.

Places to Eat

Across from the Holiday Inn and the tourist information kiosk is the Mercado Ignacio Manuel Altamirano, where several small, simple market eateries all offer full meals for US$2 or US$3.

Restaurant Sosilmar, on Avenida Obregón below the Hotel María Dolores, is bright and simple. Filling platters of fish or meat go for US$5 to US$7. Next door is the *Panadería La Muralla*, selling fresh baked goods. An even grander pastry shop is the *Panadería y Pastelería La Invencible*, on Carmen Ochoa de Merino west of Avenida de los Héroes.

West of the Sosilmar is *Pollo Brujo*, where a roasted half chicken costs US$3.50. Take it with you or dine in the air-conditioned salon. Be sure to sample the secret sauce.

Restaurant Vegetariano La Fuente (*Cárdenas 222*), between Avenidas Independencia and Juárez, is a tidy, meatless restaurant next to a homeopathic pharmacy. Healthy meals cost US$6 or less.

Café-Restaurant Los Milagros, on Zaragoza between Avenida de los Héroes and Avenida 5 de Mayo, serves meals for US$4 to US$7, indoors or outdoors, and has a book exchange with numerous English titles. It's a favorite for Chetumal's student and intellectual set.

Family-owned *Restaurant Pantoja*, Avenida Gandhi at Avenida 16 de Septiembre, is a neighborhood favorite that opens early for breakfast. Later in the day it offers a comida corrida for US$2.50 and enchiladas and other entrees for US$2 to US$3.

To sample the typical traditional food of Quintana Roo, head for the *Restaurant Típico El Taquito* (*Avenida Plutarco Elías Calles 220*), at Avenida Juárez. In the airy, simple dining room, tacos cost US$1 each, slightly more with cheese, and the daily comida corrida costs US$2.75. This is a good place to go with a jolly group of friends.

Maria's and *Sergio's Pizzas* (*Avenida Obregón 182*), a block east of Avenida de los Héroes, are actually the same full-service restaurant with two wood-paneled, air-conditioned dining rooms. Look for the stained-glass windows, then enter to low lights and soft classical music. In Maria's order one of the many wines offered, then a Mexican or continental dish (around US$7). In Sergio's, order a cold beer in a frosted mug and a pizza (US$4 to US$16).

Hawaiian Paradise, on Lázaro Cárdenas a half block west of Avenida de los Héroes, is a modern juice bar serving iced beverages in many natural and artificial flavors. The *concentrados* (slushies) consist of crushed ice and sweet fruit syrup. The *leches* (milk-based drinks) contain real fruit. The *naturales* contain juice only. A small costs US$0.60, medium US$0.80, large US$1.

Entertainment
The two major clubs in town are next door to one another near the south end of Avenida Benito Juárez. At *El Palomar*, vocalists belt out Mexican traditional songs from 1.30 to 10 pm daily. It's often packed, with attendees ranging in age from 18 to 60. *Scorpion's*, a black-walled club with a heavy disco beat, is popular with Chetumal's 18 to 25 crowd. Few tourists ever enter.

Getting There & Away
If you plan to cross into Belize from Mexico by land, visas to enter Belize can be obtained from the Belizean Consulate in Chetumal (☎ 832-28-71, 882-21-00) Avenida Álvaro Obregon 226A.

Air Chetumal's small airport is less than 2km northwest of the city center along Avenida Obregón and Revolución.

Mexicana's regional carrier Aerocaribe (☎/fax 832-66-75), Avenida Héroes 125, Plaza Baroudi Local 13, flies between Chetumal and Cancún, Cozumel, Flores (Petén, Guatemala) and Palenque.

Aviacsa (☎ 832-76-76, 832-77-87 at the airport, fax 832-76-54, 832-76-98 at the airport) flies nonstop to Villahermosa and Mexico City.

For flights to Belize City (and on to Tikal) or to Belize's cayes, cross the border into Belize and fly from Corozal.

Bus The Terminal de Autobuses de Chetumal is 3km north of the center at the intersection of Avenida de los Insurgentes and Avenida Belice. ADO, Autotransportes del Sur, Cristóbal Colón, Omnitur del Caribe, Línea Dorada and Unimaya provide service. (You can also buy ADO tickets in the city center on Avenida Belice just west of the Museo de la Cultura Maya.) The terminal has lockers, a tourist information kiosk, post

office, bookstore, newsstand, other shops and international phone and fax services. Next to the terminal is a huge San Francisco de Asis department store.

Many local buses, and those bound for Belize, depart from the Nuevo Mercado Lázaro Cárdenas, on Calzada Veracruz at Regundo; go 10 blocks (1.5km) north of the Museo Maya along Avenida de los Héroes, then turn at the Jeep dealership and go three blocks east.

The Minibus Terminal, at the corner of Avenidas Primo de Verdad and Hidalgo, has minibuses to Bacalar and other nearby destinations.

Unless otherwise specified, buses listed below leave from the main Terminal de Autobuses de Chetumal.

Bacalar – 39km, 45 minutes; hourly 2nd-class (US$2.50), minibuses from the Minibus Terminal (US$2)

Belize City – 160km, 3 to 4 hours; 6 Batty's to/from Chetumal's Nuevo Mercado via Orange Walk and Corozal, southbound departing between 10.30 am and 6.30 pm, northbound departing between 5.30 am and 6 pm; Venus Bus Lines hourly (on the hour) to/from, southbound between 4 and 10 am, northbound between noon and 7 pm (US$5 regular, US$7 express)

Campeche – 422km, 7 hours; 3 buses (US$11 to US$14)

Cancún – 382km, 5 hours; 28 buses (US$10 to US$14)

Corozal (Belize) – 30km, 1 hour with border formalities; see Belize City schedule (US$1.75)

Felipe Carrillo Puerto – 155km, 3 hours; 28 buses (US$4 to US$6)

Flores/Tikal (Guatemala) – 350km, 9 hours; 1 Servicio San Juan at 2.30 pm (US$35)

Kohunlich – 67km, 1 hour; take a bus heading west to Xpujil or Escárcega, get off just before the village of Francisco Villa and walk 5km to a hotel, then take a taxi to the site

Mérida – 456km, 8 hours; 12 buses (US$9 to US$13)

Orange Walk (Belize) – 91km, 2¼ hours; 1 Urbina's (US$4), 1 Chell's (US$4), both departing Chetumal's Nuevo Mercado around lunchtime (also see Belize City schedule above)

Playa del Carmen – 315km, 5 hours; 7 ADO (US$10 to US$12), 1 Colón (US$10), 3 Mayab (US$6.50)

Ticul – 352km, 6 hours; 9 buses (US$9)

Tulum – 251km, 4 hours; many buses (US$5 to US$7)

Xcalak – 200km, 4½ hours; Sociedad Cooperativa del Caribe at 6 am and 3.30 pm from the Minibus Terminal (US$3)

Xpujil – 120km, 1½ hours; 8 buses (US$3 to US$4)

Getting Around

Official taxis from the bus terminal to the center overcharge. Walk out of the terminal to the main road, turn left, walk to the traffic circle and catch a regular cab.

KOHUNLICH

The archaeological site of Kohunlich is being aggressively excavated, though most of its nearly 200 mounds are still covered with vegetation. The surrounding jungle is thick, but the archaeological site itself has been cleared selectively and is now a delightful forest park open 8 am to 5 pm daily (US$2.50). Drinks are sometimes sold at the

KOHUNLICH

site. The toilets are usually locked and 'under repair.'

These ruins date from the late Preclassic (100-200 AD) and early Classic (250-600 AD) periods. The site's famous **Pirámide de los Mascarones** (Pyramid of the Masks) features a central stairway flanked by huge, 3m-high stucco masks of the sun god. The thick lips and prominent features are reminiscent of Olmec sculpture. Though there were once eight masks, only two remain after the ravages of archaeology looters.

The masks themselves are impressive, but the large thatch coverings that have been erected to protect them from further weathering also obscure the view; you can see the masks only from close up. Try to imagine what the pyramid must have looked like in the old days as the Maya approached it across the sunken courtyard at the front.

The hydraulic engineering used at the site was a great achievement; a massive system of channels funneled rainwater into Kohunlich's once-enormous reservoir.

Getting There & Away

Currently no public transport runs directly to Kohunlich. To visit the ruins without your own vehicle, you need to start early. Take a bus to the village of Francisco Villa, near the turnoff to the ruins, and from there either walk 5km to the Villas Ecológicas hotel and take a taxi the remaining 4km, or walk the entire 9km.

Better still, take a taxi from Chetumal to the ruins, have the driver wait for you, and then return. Round-trip taxi fare, with the wait, will cost about US$60 per party.

To return by bus to Chetumal or head west to Xpujil or Escárcega you must hope to flag down a bus on the highway; not all buses will stop.

SOUTH TO BELIZE & GUATEMALA

Corozal, 18km south of the Mexico-Belize border, is a pleasant, sleepy, laid-back farming and fishing town, and an appropriate introduction to Belize. It has several hotels catering to a full range of budgets, and restaurants to match.

Buses run directly from Chetumal's market to Belize City via Corozal and Orange Walk. From Belize City you can catch westward buses to Belmopan, San Ignacio and the Guatemalan border at Benque Viejo, then onward to Flores, Tikal and other points in Guatemala.

A special 1st-class bus service operated by Servicio San Juan goes directly between Chetumal's bus terminal and Flores (near Tikal in Guatemala) once daily (350km, nine hours, US$35).

Yucatán

The state of Yucatán is a pie slice at the top of the Yucatán Peninsula. Until the development of Cancún in neighboring Quintana Roo, it was the peninsula's economic engine. While Quintana Roo's tourist-driven economy has surpassed Yucatán's in recent years, historically and culturally Yucatán remains paramount. Here you'll find the peninsula's most impressive Mayan ruins (Chichén Itzá, Uxmal), its finest colonial cities (Mérida and Valladolid) and two coastal communities nationally famous for their wild red flamingoes.

As a tourist destination, traditional Yucatán complements commercial Quintana Roo extremely well, and travel between the two states is convenient and affordable. A high-speed highway served by numerous 1st-class buses links Cancún and Mérida, and the trip to one of Mexico's oldest cities following a visit to one of its most modern resorts is highly recommended.

MÉRIDA
● pop 612,300 ☎ 9
The capital of the state of Yucatán is a prosperous, charming city of narrow streets, colonial buildings and shady parks. Known throughout Mexico as the 'White City' because of the preponderance of quarried limestone and white paint, Mérida has been a center of Mayan culture in Yucatán since before the conquistadors arrived.

Today it is also the peninsula's center of commerce – a bustling city that has bene-

fited greatly from the *maquiladoras* that opened in the 1980s and '90s and from tourism, which also picked up during those decades. The city offers hotels and restaurants of every class and price range, as well as good transportation services to any part of the peninsula and the country.

History
Francisco de Montejo the Younger founded a Spanish colony at Campeche, about 160km to the south, in 1540. From this base he was able to take advantage of political dissension among the Maya, conquering Tihó (now Mérida) in 1542. By the end of the decade, Yucatán was mostly under Spanish colonial rule.

When Montejo's conquistadors entered defeated Tihó, they found a major Mayan settlement of lime-mortared stone that reminded them of Roman architectural legacies in Mérida, Spain. They promptly renamed the city and proceeded to build it into the colonial capital, dismantling the Mayan structures and using the materials to construct a cathedral and other stately buildings. Mérida took its colonial orders directly from Spain, not from Mexico City, and Yucatán has had a distinct cultural and political identity ever since.

During the War of the Castes, only Mérida and Campeche were able to hold out against the rebel forces. On the brink of surrender, the ruling class in Mérida was saved by reinforcements sent from central Mexico in exchange for Mérida's agreement to take orders from Mexico City. Although Yucatán is certainly part of Mexico, there is still a strong feeling in Mérida and other parts of the state that the local people stand a breed apart.

Orientation
The Plaza Mayor has been the center of Mérida since Mayan times. Most of the services visitors want are within five blocks of the square; the rest are on the broad, tree-lined boulevard Paseo de Montejo.

Be advised that house numbers may progress unevenly from street to street; you cannot know whether Calle 57 No 481 and

YUCATÁN PENINSULA

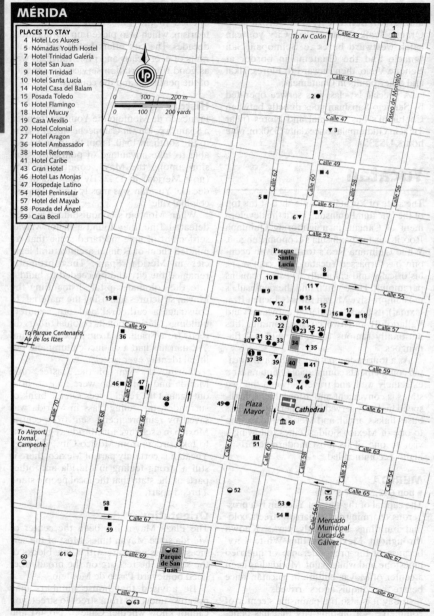

MÉRIDA

PLACES TO STAY
4 Hotel Los Aluxes
5 Nómadas Youth Hostel
7 Hotel Trinidad Galería
8 Hotel San Juan
9 Hotel Trinidad
10 Hotel Santa Lucía
14 Hotel Casa del Balam
15 Posada Toledo
16 Hotel Flamingo
18 Hotel Mucuy
19 Casa Mexilio
20 Hotel Colonial
27 Hotel Aragon
36 Hotel Ambassador
38 Hotel Reforma
41 Hotel Caribe
43 Gran Hotel
46 Hotel Las Monjas
47 Hospedaje Latino
54 Hotel Peninsular
57 Hotel del Mayab
58 Posada del Ángel
59 Casa Becil

PLACES TO EAT
3 La Casona
6 Restaurant-Bar Tiano's
11 Café Pizza Club
12 Pop Cafetería, Restaurante
    Portico del Peregrino
22 La Bella Época
23 Café Peón Contreras
25 Café y Restaurante WAO
28 Los Almendros
30 Café La Habana
31 Pancho's
39 Café-Restaurant Express
41 Cafetería El Rincón
44 Giorgio's Pizza & Pasta

OTHER
1 Museo Regional de
    Antropología (Palacio
    Cantón)
2 Tourist Car Rental
13 Car Rental Offices
17 Lavandería Flamingo
21 Universidad de Yucatán
23 Tourist Information Center
24 Teatro Peón Contreras
26 Cybernet
29 Centro Cultural de los
    Pueblos Mayas
32 Miniaturas Arte Popular
    Mexicano
33 Popol-Na
34 Parque de la Madre
35 Iglesia de Jesús
37 City Tourist Office
40 Parque Hidalgo
42 Palacio de Gobierno
45 Cine Fantasio
48 Casa de las Artesanías
49 Palacio Municipal
50 MACAY (Contemporary
    Art Museum)
51 Casa de Montejo (Banamex)
52 Progreso Bus Station
53 Multi Servicios Rada
55 Main Post Office
56 Autobuses del Noreste en
    Yucatán Bus Station
60 Terminal CAME
61 Old Terminal de Autobuses
62 Minibus to Dzibilchaltún
63 ATS Buses to Celestún

Calle 56 No 544 are one block or 10 blocks apart. Perhaps for this reason, addresses are usually given in this form: Calle 57 No 481 X 56 y 58 (between Calles 56 and 58).

Information

Tourist Offices The tourist information booths at the airport and the bus station (Terminal CAME) are almost useless, but there are two very helpful tourist offices downtown.

Reliable information is available at the Tourist Information Center (☎ 924-92-90, 924-93-89), at the corner of Calles 60 and 57A in the southwest corner of the huge Teatro Peón Contreras, less than two blocks north of the Plaza Mayor. The office is managed by José Acosta Varquez, who is quite knowledgeable about Mérida and speaks English and Spanish.

The City Tourist Office (☎ 923-08-83), at the corner of Calles 59 and 62, is generally staffed with helpful, bilingual people.

Both tourist offices are open 8 am to 8 pm daily; they provide brochures and maps and can offer the most current information on the city's Internet cafés, hotels and restaurants.

Consulates A number of countries have consulates in Mérida:

Belgium
(☎ 925-29-39, 925-29-96) Calle 25 No 159,
between Calles 28 and 30

Denmark
(☎ 925-44-88, 925-45-99) Calle 32 No 198, at
Calle 17, Colonia García Ginerés

France
(☎ 925-22-91, fax 925-70-09) Calle 33B No 528,
between Calles 62 and 64

Germany
(☎ 981-29-76) Calle 7 No 217, between Calles 20
and 20A, Colonia Chuburna de Hidalgo

Honduras
(☎ 944-82-06) Calle 54 No 280, Fraccionamiento
del Norte

Netherlands
(☎ 924-31-22, 924-41-47, 946-11-55) Calle 64 No
418, between Calles 47 and 49

Spain
(☎ 927-15-20, fax 923-00-55) Calle 3 No 237,
Fraccionamiento Campestre

UK
(☎ 928-61-52, fax 928-39-62) Calle 53 No 489, at Calle 58, Fraccionamiento del Norte; information about travel in Belize available here 9.30 am to noon Monday to Friday

USA
(☎ 925-54-09, fax 925-62-19) Paseo de Montejo 453, at Avenida Colón; open 7.30 am to 3.30 pm Monday to Friday

Money Casas de cambio offer faster, better service than banks, but may charge a fee. Try the Money Marketing Centro Cambiario, to the left of the Gran Hotel on Parque Hidalgo; Finex, Calle 59 No 498K, to the left of the Hotel Caribe; or Cambio La Peninsular, on the east side of Calle 60 between Calles 55 and 57.

Lots of banks line Calle 65 between Calles 60 and 62, one block south of the Plaza Mayor. They're open 9 am to 5 pm Monday to Friday, 9 am to 1 pm Saturday.

Post & Communications The main post office (☎ 921-25-61) is in the market area on Calle 65 between Calles 56 and 56A; open 8 am to 7 pm Monday to Friday, 9 am to 1 pm Saturday. Postal service booths at the airport and bus station are open Monday to Friday.

Pay phones are found on the Plaza Mayor, Parque Hidalgo, and at the airport, the bus station, the corner of Calles 59 and 62, the corner of Calles 64 and 57, and on Calle 60 between Calles 53 and 55.

Internet Resources Centrally located Cybernet, on Calle 57A between Calles 58 and 60, has six or so computers in an air-conditioned environment; open 10 am to 8 pm Monday to Saturday. Computer time costs US$0.10 per minute with a 15-minute (US$1.50) minimum. The employees tend to take their lunch together, shutting down the Cybernet from 2 to 4 pm or thereabouts.

Near the Mercado Municipal is the Multi Servicios Rada, on Calle 58 between Calles 65 and 67, charging US$1.50 a half-hour and US$2.50 an hour. The Rada catches a lot of street noise and the owner keeps the radio loud, but it's the only Net service open on Sunday. Hours are 9 am to 8 pm Monday to Saturday, 9 am to 7 pm Sunday.

Internet access is also available at the Instituto Tecnológico de Hotelería, on Calle 57 between Calles 56 and 58, and at the 2nd-floor ICM Internet Club on Calle 59 at Calle 58.

Bookstores Librería Dante Peón, in the Teatro Peón Contreras on the corner of Calles 60 and 57, has books in English, French, German and Spanish. It's open seven days a week. Several other bookstores are on Calle 62 between Calles 57 and 59.

Laundry Lavandería La Fe, Calle 61 No 520, at Calle 64, charges US$1 per kilo to wash and dry your clothing; no other laundry in town is as inexpensive. La Fe offers same-day service, provided you drop your clothes off in the morning. Open 8 am to 7 pm Monday to Friday, 8 am to 5 pm Saturday.

You also can drop off your clothing at the Lavandería Flamingo, on Calle 57 between Calles 56 and 58, and pick it up in the late afternoon. It charges US$0.20 per shirt, pants or shorts, US$0.05 for each undergarment (yes, it's US$0.10 for a pair of socks). Open 9 am to 6 pm daily.

Most of the better hotels, including the Gran Hotel, offer overnight laundry service.

Medical Services The best hospital in Mérida is Hospital O'Horan (☎ 924-41-00), near the Parque Zoológico Centenario on Avenida de los Itzes. For the Cruz Roja (Red Cross), call ☎ 924-98-13.

Dangers & Annoyances Guard against pickpockets, bag-snatchers and bag-slashers in the market district and in any crowd, such as at a performance. They see you, but you won't see them.

Plaza Mayor
The most logical place to start a tour of Mérida is in the Plaza Mayor, a large yet lovely and at times surprisingly intimate square. Also frequently called 'El Centro' (as in the center of town), the Plaza Mayor was the religious and social center of ancient Tihó; under the Spanish it was the Plaza de Armas, or parade ground, laid out by Fran-

cisco de Montejo the Younger. The plaza is surrounded by some of the city's most impressive and harmonious colonial buildings, and its carefully pruned laurel trees provide welcome shade. On Sunday the adjoining roadways are off-limits to vehicular traffic.

Cathedral On the east side of the plaza, on the site of a Mayan temple, is Mérida's hulking, severe cathedral, begun in 1561 and completed in 1598. Some of the stone from the Mayan temple was used in the cathedral's construction.

Walk through one of the three doors in the baroque façade and into the sanctuary. The great crucifix at the east end of the nave is **Cristo de la Unidad** (Christ of Unity), a symbol of reconciliation between those of Spanish and Mayan stock. To your right over the south door is a **painting of Tutul Xiú**, cacique of the town of Maní, paying his respects to his ally Francisco de Montejo at Tihó. (Montejo and Xiú jointly defeated the Cocoms; Xiú converted to Christianity, and his descendants still live in Mérida.)

Look in the small chapel to the left of the principal altar for Mérida's most famous religious artifact, a statue called *Cristo de las Ampollas* (Christ of the Blisters). Local legend has it that this statue was carved from a tree in the town of Ichmul after the tree was hit by lightning and burned for an entire night without charring. The statue was originally placed in the local church, where it is said to have survived the fiery destruction of the church some years later, though it was blackened and blistered from the heat. It was moved to the Mérida cathedral in 1645.

The rest of the church's interior is plain, its rich decoration having been stripped away by angry peasants at the height of anticlerical feeling during the Mexican Revolution. You won't find any stained-glass windows here and only a modest display of religious art and artifacts. Sections of the cathedral's marble floor bear the names of the formerly influential people buried beneath it.

MACAY On the south side of the cathedral, housed in the former archbishop's palace, is the Museo de Arte Contemporáneo Ateneo de Yucatán (Yucatán Contemporary Art Museum and Atheneum or, more commonly, MACAY; ☎ 928-32-58), at Pasaje de la Revolución 1907. The attractive museum holds permanent exhibits of Yucatán's most famous painters and sculptors, as well as changing exhibits of local arts and crafts. Open 10 am to 6 pm daily except Tuesday (US$2.50; free for students, teachers, workers, campesinos and seniors, and free to all on Sunday). There's a cafeteria inside.

Palacio de Gobierno On the north side of the plaza, the Palacio de Gobierno houses the state of Yucatán's executive government offices. It was built in 1892 on the site of the palace of the colonial governors. Inside are murals painted by local artist Fernando Castro Pacheco. Completed in 1978, the murals were 25 years in the making and portray a symbolic history of the Maya and their interaction with the Spaniards. The largest depicts corn, which the Maya held as sacred – the 'ray of sun from the gods.' Open 8 am to 8 pm daily (free). On Sunday at 11 am, there's usually a concert (jazz, classical, pop, Yucatecan) in the Salón de la Historia.

Palacio Municipal Facing the cathedral across the square, the Palacio Municipal is topped by a clock tower. Originally built in 1542, the Palacio was refurbished in the 1730s and again in the 1850s. It continues to serve as Mérida's city hall, and it also serves as a venue for traditional Yucatecan dances. These free performances take place in the street in front of the building on Monday starting around 9 pm (arrive early to get a good seat). The dances and accompanying music, which reflect a mixture of Spanish and Mayan cultures, date from the earliest days of the Vaquería Regional, a local festival that celebrated the branding of the cattle on neighboring haciendas.

Every Sunday at 1 and 6 pm, the city also sponsors a reenactment of a colorful mestizo wedding. The earlier show features child performers, the 6 pm show professional entertainers. Both are highly recommended, and both are free.

Casa de Montejo This building, sometimes called the Palacio de Montejo, is on the south side of the Plaza Mayor and dates from 1549. It originally housed soldiers but soon was converted into a mansion that served members of the Montejo family until 1970. These days it shelters a bank, and you can enter it and look around whenever the bank is open (9 am to 5 pm Monday to Friday, 9 am to 1 pm Saturday).

If the bank is closed, content yourself with a close look at the façade, where triumphant conquistadors with halberds hold their feet on the necks of generic barbarians (who are not Maya, but the association is inescapable). Also gazing across the plaza from the façade are busts of Montejo the Elder, his wife and his daughter. The armorial shields are those of the Montejo family.

Walking up Calle 60

A block north of the Plaza Mayor is the shady refuge of **Parque Hidalgo**. At the far end of the park, several restaurants offer alfresco dining. The city sponsors free marimba concerts here Sunday at noon.

Just to the north of the park rises the 17th-century **Iglesia de Jesús**, also called the Iglesia La Tercer Orden. Built by the Jesuits in 1618, it is the sole surviving edifice in a complex of buildings that once filled the entire city block. Always interested in education, the Jesuits founded schools that later gave birth to the nearby Universidad de Yucatán. The 19th-century general Cepeda Peraza amassed a library of 15,000 volumes, which is housed in a building behind the church.

Directly in front of the church is **Parque de la Madre**, sometimes called Parque Morelos. The modern Madonna-and-child statue is a copy of one that stands in the Jardin du Luxembourg in Paris.

Just north of Parque de la Madre you confront the enormous bulk of the great **Teatro Peón Contreras**, built from 1900 to 1908 during Mérida's henequen heyday. Designed by Italian architect Luis Roncoroni, it boasts a main staircase of Carrara marble and a dome with imported frescoes by Italian artists. The main entrance to the theater is on the corner of Calles 60 and 57. A gallery inside the entrance often features exhibits by local painters and photographers; usual hours are 9 am to 2 pm and 5 to 9 pm Monday to Friday, 9 am to 2 pm Saturday and Sunday. To see the grand theater itself, you'll have to attend a performance.

Across Calle 60 from the theater is the entrance to the main building of the **Universidad de Yucatán**. Though the Jesuits provided education to Yucatán's youth for centuries, the modern university was established in the 19th century by Governor Felipe Carrillo Puerto and General Manuel Cepeda Peraza. The story of the university's founding is rendered in a 1961 mural by Manuel Lizama. Ask for directions to the mural.

The central courtyard of the university building is the scene of concerts and folk performances every Friday at 9 pm (check with the Tourist Information Center for possible schedule changes).

A block north of the university, at the intersection of Calles 60 and 55, is the pretty little **Parque Santa Lucía**, with arcades on the north and west sides. When Mérida was a lot smaller, this was where travelers would get into or out of the stagecoaches that linked towns and villages with the provincial capital. Today the park is the venue for orchestral performances of Yucatecan music on Thursday at 9 pm and Sunday at 11 am. Also here on Sunday at 11 am is the **Bazar de Artesanías**, the local handicrafts market.

To reach the Paseo de Montejo (discussed below), walk 3½ blocks north along Calle 60 from Parque Santa Lucía to Calle 47. Turn right on Calle 47 and walk two blocks; Paseo de Montejo is on your left.

Paseo de Montejo

The Paseo de Montejo was an attempt by Mérida's 19th-century city planners to create a wide boulevard similar to Mexico City's Paseo de la Reforma or Paris' Champs Elysées. Though more modest than either of those, the Paseo de Montejo is still a beautiful swath of green, open space in an urban conglomeration of stone and concrete.

The powerful hacendados and commercial barons of the Yucatán Peninsula, who maintained good business and social contacts with Europe, also derived architectural and social inspiration from Europe, which is evident along the paseo in the surviving mansions, built around the turn of the 20th century. Many have since been torn down to make way for banks, hotels and other establishments. Most of those remaining are north of Calle 37, which is three blocks north of the Museo Regional de Antropología, and on the first block of Avenida Colón west of Paseo de Montejo

Every Saturday from 9 pm to midnight, at the southern end of Paseo de Montejo (where it meets Calle 47), the city celebrates 'Mexican Night' with mariachis and other traditional Mexican musicians. The festivities are well worth catching.

Museo Regional de Antropología The great white Palacio Cantón, on the corner of Paseo de Montejo and Calle 43, houses the Regional Anthropology Museum of Yucatán. The mansion was designed by Enrico Deserti. Construction took place from 1909 to 1911. The mansion's owner, General Francisco Cantón Rosado (1833-1917), lived here for only six years before his death. No building in Mérida exceeds it in splendor or pretension. It's a fitting symbol of the grand aspirations of Mérida's elite during the last years of the Porfiriato.

The museum covers the peninsula's history since the age of mastodons. Exhibits on Mayan culture include explanations (in Spanish only) of forehead-flattening, which was done to beautify babies, and other practices such as sharpening their teeth and implanting them with tiny jewels. If you plan to visit archaeological sites near Mérida, you can study the many exhibits here – lavishly illustrated with plans and photographs – which cover the great Mayan cities of Mayapán, Uxmal and Chichén Itzá, as well as lesser sites. Open 9 am to 8 pm Monday and Wednesday to Saturday, 9 am to 2 pm Sunday (US$2, free on Sunday). The museum shop is open 9 am to 3 pm (till 2 pm Sunday).

Parque Centenario
About 12 blocks west of the Plaza Mayor lies the large, verdant Parque Centenario, bordered by Avenida de los Itzaes, the highway to the airport and Campeche. A zoo in the park specializes in the fauna of Yucatán. To get there, take a bus west along Calle 61 or 65. The park is open 6 am to 6 pm Tuesday to Sunday (the zoo is open 8 am to 5 pm, free).

Museo Nacional de Arte Popular
This Art Museum, on Calle 59 between Calles 48 and 50, behind the ancient ex-Convento de la Mejorada, holds fine displays of indigenous arts and crafts. It will satisfy your curiosity about the weaving of colorful *huipiles*, the carving of ceremonial masks, the weaving of hammocks and hats and the turning of pottery. Open 8 am to 8 pm Tuesday to Saturday, 9 am to 2 pm Sunday (US$1).

Organized Tours
You can choose from many group tours going to sights around Mérida. Ask at your hotel reception desk for brochures, or consult any of the various travel agencies along Calle 60. Here are typical destinations and prices: Chichén Itzá (US$17), Chichén Itzá with drop-off in Cancún (US$29), Uxmal and Kabah (US$17), Uxmal light-and-sound show (US$17), Ruta Puuc (US$32), Izamal (US$23). All prices include transportation, guided tour and lunch.

One of the city's top travel agencies is Turismo Bolontikú (☎/fax 924-72-85), Calle 60 No 486, between Calles 55 and 57, offering guided tours to: Celestún, leaving 9 am and returning 5 pm, Tuesday to Sunday; Ruta Puuc and Loltún Caves, leaving 9 am and returning 7 pm, on demand; Uxmal light-and-sound show, leaving 5 pm and returning 10.30 pm, daily; Uxmal light-and-sound show and dinner, leaving 1 pm and returning 10 pm, daily; Uxmal-Kabah, leaving 9 am and returning 5 pm, daily; Chichén Itzá, leaving 9 am and returning 5 pm, daily.

Paseo Turístico (☎ 927-61-19) offers guided two-hour bus tours of Mérida for US$7 (narration is in English), departing from the Parque Santa Lucía, Calle 55 at Calle 60, at 10 am and 1, 4 and 7 pm Monday to Saturday, and at 10 am and 1 pm Sunday. Seating capacity is 30 people. You can buy your tickets ahead of time at nearby Hotel Santa Lucía.

Special Events

Prior to Lent, in February or March, Carnaval features colorful costumes and nonstop festivities. It is celebrated with greater vigor in Mérida than anywhere else in Yucatán. Also during the last days of February or the beginning of March (the dates vary) is Kihuic, a market that fills the Plaza Mayor with handicraft artisans from all over Mexico.

From September 15 to October 15, the *Cristo de las Ampollas* (Christ of the Blisters) statue in the cathedral is venerated with processions.

Another big religious tradition is the Exposicíon de Altares, held the night of November 1, when the Maya welcome the spirits of their ancestors with elaborate dinners outside their homes. Although this custom is more apparent in the countryside, Mérida observes it with elaborate festivities in the center of town from 11 am November 1 to 11 am the next day.

Places to Stay

Mérida's high season is from mid-December through March and in July and August. You'd be wise to reserve a hotel room ahead if you intend to visit the city during these times, and expect the hotel rates to be 20% or more higher than the low-season rates quoted here.

Budget Prices for inexpensive lodgings a short walk from the plaza range from US$7 to US$20 for a small but clean double with fan and private shower a short walk from the plaza. All hotels should provide purified drinking water, usually at no extra charge. (Sometimes the water bottles are not readily evident, so ask for *agua purificada*.)

Cozy **Hotel Las Monjas** (*☎/fax 928-66-32, Calle 66A No 509*), off Calle 63, is the best deal in town. All 31 rooms have ceiling fans and sinks or private baths with hot and cold water. Doubles with one bed cost US$10, with two beds US$12. One room has air-con for US$12. You will find most rooms are tiny and dark, but they're clean. Room Nos 30 and 12 are best for their superior ventilation.

The **Hospedaje Latino** (*☎ 923-50-87, Calle 66 No 505*), between Calles 61 and 63, offers 29 fan-cooled rooms with good mattresses and private hot-water baths for US$6/7 single/double, and three air-conditioned rooms for US$11. It's a bit noisy, though.

The **Nómadas Youth Hostel** (*☎ 924-52-23, ☎/fax 928-16-97, nomadashostel@hotmail .com, www.hostels.com.mx, Calle 62 No 433*) smack at the end of Calle 51, is HI affiliated. There are 14 beds in two co-ed dorms, for $7 each, and a room with private bath and two double beds for $17/21/25 double/ triple/quad. Guests are entitled to use the full kitchen with fridge and purified water, 24-hour hot showers and hand-laundry facilities, and good Internet access is available.

Hotel Mucuy (*☎ 928-51-93, fax 923-78-01, Calle 57 No 481*), between Calles 56 and 58, is a family-run place with 22 tidy rooms facing a long, narrow garden courtyard. Señora Ofelia Comin and her daughter Ofelia speak English. Singles/doubles/triples with ceiling fan and private shower cost US$14/16/19.

Casa Becil (*☎ 924-67-64, Calle 67 No 550C*), between Calles 66 and 68 near the bus station, is a 13-room house offering small, sometimes hot rooms with private shower and fan for US$13 to US$16 double. The lobby has a high ceiling and doubles as a sitting room.

The **Hotel Flamingo** (*☎ 924-77-55, fax 924-70-70, Calle 57 No 485*), near Calle 58, offers 39 worn rooms with air-con, TV, telephone and private hot-water bath for US$15. You'll be glad to discover that there's a laundry service, restaurant, pool and a travel agency.

If you don't mind walking a few extra blocks and you really want to save money, try the **Hotel del Mayab** (*☎ 928-51-74, fax*

928-60-47, Calle 50 No 536A), between Calles 65 and 67, near the bus stations. Streetside rooms can be noisy, but interior rooms with shower are quiet, and there's a swimming pool. Rates are, all for US$11 a double with fan, US$17 with air-con.

Clean, secure and very popular, the *Hotel Santa Lucía* (☎ 928-26-62, ☎/fax 928-26-72, Calle 55 No 508), between Calles 60 and 62 facing the Parque Santa Lucíia, has a pool and 51 decent doubles with air-con, TV and telephone for US$19/22 single/double.

The colonial *Hotel Trinidad* (☎ 923-20-33, fax 924-11-22, ohm@sureste.com, Calle 62 No 464), between Calles 55 and 57, is run by artists. The 19 fan-cooled guestrooms, unfortunately, exhibit both artistic charm and squalor. Rates, starting at US$13 a double with shared bath, and US$19 a double with private bath, include a continental breakfast. Guests can use the pool at the Trinidad's sister hotel, the *Hotel Trinidad Galería* (☎ 923-24-63, fax 924-23-19, Calle 60 No 456), at Calle 51, which has presentable rooms with fan and private shower for US$20/25 single/double.

The 45-room *Hotel Peninsular* (☎ 923-69-96, fax 923-69-02, Calle 58 No 519), between Calles 65 and 67, is in the heart of the market district. You pass through a long corridor to find a neat restaurant and a maze of rooms, most with windows opening onto the interior spaces. It has a pool and costs US$12 single/double with private bath and fan; US$16 with air-con. There's a pool.

The neo-colonial 30-room *Posada del Ángel* (☎ 923-27-54, Calle 67 No 535), between Calles 66 and 68, is three blocks northeast of Terminal CAME and is quieter than most other hotels in this neighborhood. It's convenient, and priced at US$13 to US$18 a double, US$18 to US$/22 with air-con.

The *Hotel Reforma* (☎ 924-79-22, fax 928-32-78, hreforma@yuc1.telmextelmex.net.mx, Calle 59 No 508), between Calles 60 and 62, has 50 rooms ringing a courtyard with a swimming pool. Each room contains a TV, telephone and ceiling fan. Laundry service is available. Rooms with fan run US$16/20 single/double with fan, with air-con US$18/22 with air-con.

The *Hotel San Juan* (☎/fax 924-17-42, Calle 55 No 497), near Calle 58, offers a pool and 60 air-conditioned rooms with phone, TV and private hot-water bath for US$20/24 single/double. This and the Hotel Santa Lucía are the best in this price category.

The *Hotel Aragon* (☎ 924-02-42, fax 924-11-22, www.hotelaragon.com, Calle 57 No 474), between Calles 52 and 54, offers 17 clean air-conditioned rooms for US$24 per room. Free purified water, tea and coffee are available 24 hours.

Mid-Range Mérida's mid-range places provide surprising levels of comfort for what you pay. Most charge between US$35 and US$60 double with air-con, ceiling fan and private shower, and most have restaurants, bars and little swimming pools.

Gran Hotel (☎ 924-77-30, fax 924-76-22, granh@sureste.com, Calle 60 No 496), between Calles 59 and 61, is on the southern side of the Parque Hidalgo. All 28 rooms have air-con and cost a very reasonable US$35/40 single/double most of the year.

Hotel Colonial (☎ 923-64-44, 888-886-2982 in the USA, fax 928-39-61, hcolonial@finred.com.mx, Calle 62 No 476), corner of Calle 57, features 73 comfortable air-conditioned rooms in a building with lots of pleasing arches and a pool. Rates are a reasonable US$35 single or double.

Hotel Caribe (☎ 924-90-22, 800-712-00-03, 888-822-6431 in the USA, fax 924-87-33, Calle 59 No 500), near the Parque Hidalgo, is a favorite with visiting foreigners because of its central location, rooftop pool and two restaurants. Most rooms have air-con. Rates range from US$30 for a small single with fan to US$42 for a large double with air-con.

The romantic *Casa Mexilio* (☎/fax 928-25-05, ☎ 800-538-6802 in the USA, info@turqreef.com, Calle 68 No 495), between Calles 59 and 57, is Mérida's most charming pension, a well-preserved and -decorated house with a pool and 10 quiet rooms for US$40 to US$58 double, breakfast included. Some of the rooms have air-con.

Posada Toledo (☎ 923-16-90, 923-57-35, ☎/fax 923-22-56, Calle 58 No 487), at Calle

57, three blocks northeast of the main plaza, is a colonial mansion with a classic courtyard and a dining room straight out of the 19th century. Small, modernized doubles with air-con go for US$30. The newer, upstairs rooms are larger than the ground-floor rooms.

Hotel Ambassador (☎ 924-21-00, fax 924-27-01, www.ambassadormerida.com, Calle 59 No 546), between Calle 66 and 68, offers 100 comfortable, modern rooms with TV for US$62 per room. It has a pool, a travel agency, a car-rental outfit and laundry service.

Top End Top-end hotels charge between US$70 and US$150 for a double with air-con. Every hotel in this category has a restaurant, bar, swimming pool and probably other services such as a newsstand, hair salon, travel agency and nightclub. If you reserve your top-end room through your travel agent at home, you're likely to pay international-class rates. But if you walk in and ask about *promociones* (promotional rates), or – even better – look through local newspapers and handouts for special rates aimed at a local clientele, you can lower your lodging bill substantially.

Mérida's most luxurious hotel is the 17-story, 300-room *Hyatt Regency Mérida* (☎ 942-12-34, fax 925-70-02), Avenida Colón at Calle 60, 100m west of Paseo de Montejo and about 2km north of the Plaza Mayor. Rooms with all the comforts cost US$95 to US$135.

Holiday Inn Mérida (☎ 925-68-77, 800-465-4329 in the USA, fax 925-77-55, Avenida Colón 498), at Calle 60, half a block off the Paseo de Montejo, is one of Mérida's most luxurious establishments, with 213 air-conditioned rooms for US$75 to US$95.

Across Avenida Colón from the Hyatt and Holiday Inn is the *Fiesta Americana Mérida* (☎ 942-11-11, 800-343-7821 in the USA, fax 942-11-12), charging US$115 to US$140 for its comfortable rooms and junior suites.

Centrally located *Hotel Casa del Balam* (☎ 924-21-50, 800-624-8451 in the USA, fax 924-50-11, www.yucatanadventure.com.mx, Calle 60 No 488), at Calle 57, charges US$85 per room, with discounts offered when it's not busy.

For all-around quality, convenience and price, try the 109-room *Hotel Los Aluxes* (☎ 924-21-99, 800-782-8395 in the USA, fax 923-38-58, Calle 60 No 444), at Calle 49. Popular with tour groups, it charges US$70 single/double.

Places to Eat

Budget Mérida's least expensive eateries are on Calle 67 near the Mercado Municipal. Here you'll find family-run *El Chimecito*, *La Temaxeña*, *Saby*, *Mimi*, *Saby y El Palon*, *La Socorrito*, *Reina Beatriz* and others. Comidas corridas here start at US$1.50. Main-course platters of beef, fish or chicken with vegetables and rice or potatoes cost as little as US$2.50.

The best cheap breakfasts consist of a selection of *pan dulces* (sweet rolls and breads) from one of Mérida's several *panificadoras*, such as *Panificadora Montejo* at the corner of Calles 62 and 63, at the southwest corner of the main plaza, where a full bag of breads usually costs US$2 or so.

The air-conditioned *Café y Restaurante WAO*, on Calle 57A near Calle 58, offers lots of delicious food at reasonable prices: around US$4 for *poc chuc*, chicken *mole* or chicken *pibil*, around US$2 for breakfast items.

Mid-Range Those willing to spend a bit more money can enjoy the pleasant restaurants of the Parque Hidalgo at the corner of Calles 59 and 60. The least expensive, yet one of the most pleasant, is the *Cafetería El Rincón* (the stained-glass sign above the door reads El Mesón), in the Hotel Caribe. Meat, fish and chicken dishes cost US$4 to US$7, but sandwiches and burgers are less.

The 24-hour, air-conditioned *Café La Habana*, corner of Calles 59 and 62, is one of the most popular restaurants in town, but tourists tend to overlook it. Too bad, because it offers good food at low prices: breakfast items and soups cost US$1 to US$3, sandwiches US$2 to US$4, chicken US$3 to US$4 and seafood US$5 to US$6. There's a full bar as well.

Restaurant-Bar Tiano's, on Calle 60 between Calles 51 and 53, is often recommended by locals guessing what tourists like, but the food is mediocre. It's best avoided.

Café-Restaurant Express, on Calle 60 near Calle 59, is a popular, noisy meeting place, with prices a little on the high side for OK food. It's one of the few places in town where you can get a cappuccino. Also available are juices and shakes that go down easily in the heat of the day.

A few steps north along Calle 60 from the Parque Hidalgo is *Cafe Peón Contreras*, with a long, varied menu including breakfasts for US$2.50 to US$4, pizzas for around US$6 and a combination plate of Yucatecan specialties for around US$10.

Pop Cafetería, on Calle 57 between Calles 60 and 62, is plain, modern and cool. The menu includes hamburgers and spaghetti, but smart diners will choose the chicken *mole* (US$4) and some delicious guacamole. Breakfast is offered as well.

The best pizza in town is served at *Giorgio's Pizza & Pasta*, next to the Gran Hotel and facing the Parque Hidalgo. The pizzas cost US$3 to US$7, the portions are generous, and the outdoor tables present prime people-watching opportunities. Pizza aficionados might want to try *Café Pizza Club*, on Calle 55 between Calles 58 and 60, for comparison purposes; pies cost US$2 to US$6.

Pancho's, on Calle 59 between Calles 60 and 62, tends to bring out the party animal in people. Its three spacious dining areas and two full bars are served by the bandolier-toting, sombrero-wearing waitstaff. There's live music most nights starting about 11 pm, and the happy hour (6 to 8 pm) is always festive. The food is only fair (pasta, fish, burgers, local specialties for US$6 to US$15), but the atmosphere makes up for it.

Yucatecan Cuisine: Food of the Maya

Called by its Maya inhabitants 'the Land of the Pheasant and the Deer,' Yucatán has always had a distinctive cuisine. Here are some of the Yucatecan dishes you might want to try:

Frijol con puerco – Yucatecan-style pork and beans, topped with a sauce made with grilled tomatoes and decorated with bits of radish, slices of onion and leaves of fresh cilantro; served with rice

Huevos Motuleños – 'Eggs in the style of Motul': fried eggs atop a tortilla, garnished with beans, peas, chopped ham, sausage, grated cheese and spicy chile; high in cholesterol, fat and flavor

Papadzules – Tortillas stuffed with chopped hard-boiled eggs and topped with a sauce of marrow squash or cucumber seeds

Pavo relleno – Slabs of turkey layered with chopped, spiced beef and pork and served in a rich, dark sauce; the Yucatecan *faisán* (pheasant) is actually the *pavo* (ocellated turkey)

Pibil – Meat wrapped in banana leaves, flavored with *achiote*, garlic, sour orange, salt and pepper, and baked in a barbecue pit called a *pib*; the two main varieties are *cochinita pibil* (suckling pig) and *pollo pibil* (chicken)

Poc-chuc – Tender pork strips marinated in sour orange juice, then grilled and topped with a spicy onion relish

Puchero – A stew of pork, chicken, carrots, marrow squash, potatoes, plantains and *chayote* (vegetable pear), spiced with radish, fresh cilantro and sour orange

Salbutes – Yucatán's favorite snack: a hand-made tortilla, fried, then topped with shredded turkey, onion and slices of avocado

Sopa de lima – 'Lime soup'; chicken broth with bits of shredded chicken, tortilla strips, lime juice and chopped lime

Venado – Venison, a popular traditional dish, might be served as a *pipián*, flavored with a sauce of ground marrow squash seeds, wrapped in banana leaves and steamed

Top End The secret to enjoying a meal at *La Bella Época*, on Calle 60 between 57 and 59, opposite the Parque de la Madre, is to get there early enough to get one of the five little tables on the 2nd-floor balconies. An appetizer, *pollo pibil*, dessert and a beer will cost around US$12. Open for dinner only.

Restaurante Portico del Peregrino, on Calle 57 between Calles 60 and 62, has several pleasant, traditional dining rooms (some air-conditioned) around a small courtyard. Yucatecan dishes are the restaurant's forte, but you'll find many continental dishes as well. A full meal costs US$12 to US$20.

La Casona, on Calle 60 between Calles 47 and 49, occupies a fine old city house. Tables are set out on a portico next to a small but lush garden; dim lighting lends an air of romance. Italian dishes and a few Yucatecan choices cost US$10 to US$20. Open for dinner only.

Los Almendros, on Calle 50A between Calles 57 and 59, specializes in authentic Yucatecan country cuisine and is famous for its rendition of the zingy onion-and-tomato pork dish *poc-chuc*. Full meals cost US$9 to US$15.

Entertainment

The city of Mérida sponsors nightly *folkloric events* by local performers of considerable skill. Admission is free. Check with the tourist office for the schedule and venues.

Many English-language films, some of fairly recent release, are screened in Mérida with Spanish subtitles. Buy your tickets (usually about US$2) before show time and well in advance on Saturday and Sunday. Popular cinemas include *Cine Fantasio*, Calle 59 at Calle 60, between the Gran Hotel and Hotel Caribe; *Cinema 59*, Calle 59 between Calles 68 and 70; and *Plaza Cine Internacional*, Calle 58 between Calles 57 and 59.

For dancing to live salsa, head to *Pancho's*, on Calle 59 between Calles 60 and 62.

Shopping

Mérida is *the* place on the peninsula to shop. Purchases you might want to consider: a wonderfully comfortable Yucatecan hammock and traditional Mayan clothing, such as a colorful embroidered huipil or a Panama hat woven from palm fibers.

Mérida's main market, the Mercado Municipal Lucas de Gálvez, is bounded by Calles 56 and 56A and Calle 67, southeast of the Plaza Mayor. The surrounding streets, all part of the large market district, are lined with shops selling everything one might need; the Bazar de Artesanías, Calle 67 at Calle 56A, is set up to attract tourists. You should have a look at the stuff here, then compare the goods and prices with independent shops outside.

Guard your valuables extra carefully in the market area. Watch for pickpockets, purse-snatchers and slash-and-grab thieves.

Handicrafts The Casa de las Artesanías, on Calle 63 between Calles 64 and 66, is a government-supported market for local artisans selling just about everything you can think of: earthenware, textiles, wicker baskets, sandals, wind chimes, ceramic dolls, vases, purses, and pouches, figurines of Mayan deities and bottles of locally made liquor. Open 8 am to 8 pm Monday to Saturday, 9 am to 1.30 pm Sunday.

Popol-Na, on Calle 59 between Calles 60 and 62, sells high-quality hammocks and guayaberas (they are the same quality as those found at Jack's, a Yucatecan-clothing store adjacent to the Gran Hotel, only much cheaper), as well as carved Mayan calendars, masks of Mayan gods, quilts, tablecloths, clothing, jewelry, panama hats, bags and earthenware.

At Miniaturas Arte Popular Mexicano, also on Calle 59 between Calles 60 and 62, are *lots* of miniature figurines of varying quality. Open 10 am to 2 pm and 4 to 8 pm, 'más o menos,' according to the sign.

Panama Hats Locally made panama hats are woven from palmlike jipijapa leaves in caves, where humid conditions keep the fibers pliable when the hat is being made. Once exposed to the relatively dry air outside, the panama hat is surprisingly resilient and resistant to crushing. The Campeche town of Becal is the center of the

Yucatecan Hammocks: The Only Way to Sleep

The fine strings of Yucatecan hammocks make them supremely comfortable. In the sticky heat of a Yucatán summer, most locals prefer sleeping in a hammock, where the air can circulate around them, rather than in a bed.

Yucatecan hammocks are normally woven from strong nylon or cotton string and dyed in various colors; there are also natural, undyed versions. In the old days, the finest, strongest, most expensive hammocks were woven from silk.

Hammocks come in several widths. From smallest to largest, the names generally used are: *sencillo* (about 50 pairs of end strings, US$8 to US$10), *doble* (100 pairs, US$10 to US$15), *matrimonial* (150 pairs, US$12 to US$20) and *matrimonial especial* or *cuatro cajas* (175 pairs or more, US$18 to US$30).

Because hammocks fold up small and the larger hammocks are more comfortable, consider the bigger sizes, but check to be sure that you're really getting the width you're paying for.

On the streets of Mérida you often will be approached by hammock peddlers. They may quote very low prices, but street-sold hammocks are mediocre at best. Check the hammock very carefully.

You can save yourself a lot of trouble by shopping at a hammock store with a good reputation. La Poblana, at Calle 65 No 492, between Calles 58 and 60, is one. Some travelers report slightly cheaper prices for good quality at El Aguacate, Calle 58 No 604, at the corner of Calle 73.

It's interesting to venture out to the nearby village of Tixcocob to watch the hammocks being woven. A bus runs regularly from the Progreso bus station, south of the main plaza at Calle 62 No 524, between Calles 65 and 67.

---

hat-weaving trade, but you can buy good examples of the hatmaker's art in Mérida.

The best quality hats have a fine, close weave of slender fibers. The coarser the weave, the lower the price should be. Prices range from a few dollars for a hat of basic quality to US$50 or more for top quality. They can be found at the Casa de las Artesanías and Popol-Na.

Getting There & Away

Air Mérida's modern airport is a 10km, 20-minute ride southwest of the Plaza Mayor off highway 180 (Avenida de los Itzaes). It has car rental desks and a tourist office that can help with hotel reservations but not much else.

Most international flights to Mérida are connections through Mexico City or Cancún. The only nonstop international services are Aeroméxico's daily flights from Miami and Aviateca's flights to Guatemala City. Domestic flights are operated mostly by smaller regional airlines, with a few flights by Aeroméxico and Mexicana.

Aerocaribe (☎ 924-95-00, 923-00-02), Paseo de Montejo 476A, flies between Mérida and Cancún, Havana (Cuba), Chetumal, Ciudad del Carmen, Mexico City, Oaxaca, Tuxtla Gutiérrez (for San Cristóbal de Las Casas), Veracruz and Villahermosa

Aerolíneas Bonanza (☎ 926-06-09, fax 927-79-99), Calle 56A No 579, between Calles 67 and 69, flies round-trips daily from Mérida to Cancún, Chetumal and Palenque

Aeroméxico (☎ 927-95-66, 927-92-77), Paseo de Montejo 460, has a few flights

Aviacsa (☎ 926-32-53, 926-39-54, fax 926-90-87), at the airport, flies nonstop to Cancún, Villahermosa and Mexico City

Aviateca (☎ 924-43-54), at the airport, flies to Tikal and Guatemala City several times a week

Aerolitoral (☎ 800-021-4000 from Mexico, 800-237-6639 from the US) flies to Ciudad del Carmen, Veracruz and Monterrey

Mexicana (☎ 924-66-33), Calle 58 No 500, has nonstop flights to/from Cancún and Mexico City

Bus Mérida is the bus transport hub of the Yucatán Peninsula. If you take an all-night bus, don't put anything valuable in the overhead racks – gear being stolen at night has been a problem.

Bus Stations Mérida has several bus stations. Here's a rundown of stations and companies that serve them.

Terminal CAME – Mérida's main bus terminal, seven blocks southwest of the Plaza Mayor at Calle 70 No 555, between Calles 69 and 71, is known as Terminal CAME ('KAH-meh'). It handles ticketing and departures for ADO. Come here if you're headed for Campeche, Palenque, Villahermosa, Tuxtla Gutiérrez, San Cristóbal de Las Casas or major cities elsewhere in Mexico. Buses run by Línea Dorada and UNO depart from CAME, but their ticket counters are in the old Terminal de Autobuses. CAME has pay phones and a hotel desk.

Terminal de Autobuses – The old bus terminal, around the corner from CAME on Calle 69, has ticket counters for Línea Dorada, UNO, Autotransportes de Oriente, Autotransportes del Sur, Omnitur del Caribe and Transportes Mayab. Come here for buses to points in the state and elsewhere on the Yucatán Peninsula, and some beyond.

Parque de San Juan – This terminal, on Calle 69 between Calles 62 and 64, is the terminus for Volkswagen minibuses going to Dzibilchaltún Ruinas, Muna, Oxkutzcab, Peto, Sacalum, Tekax and Ticul. Fares from here generally don't exceed US$2.

Oriente & Noroeste – Autotransportes de Oriente and Autotransportes del Noroeste en Yucatán share a terminal at Calle 50 No 527A, between Calles 65 and 67.

Autotransportes del Sur (ATS) – Though most ATS buses depart from the old Terminal de Autobuses, the company also runs buses to Celestún from its new terminal at Calle 71 between Calles 64 and 66.

Progreso – The separate bus terminal for Progreso is at Calle 62 No 524, between Calles 65 and 67.

Bus Companies Here's a list of bus companies and the destinations they serve.

Autobuses de Oriente (ADO) – long-haul 1st-class routes to Campeche, Palenque, Villahermosa, Veracruz, Mexico City and beyond

Autotransportes de Oriente (Oriente) – frequent buses between Mérida and Cancún stopping at Chichén Itzá and Valladolid; other buses between Mérida and Cobá, Izamal, Playa del Carmen and Tulum

Autotransportes del Sur (ATS) – hourly buses to Cancún and buses every 20 to 40 minutes to Campeche; other buses to Bolonchén de Rejón, Cancún, Celestún, Chiquilá, Ciudad del Carmen, Emiliano Zapata, Hecelchakan, Hopelchén, Izamal, Ocosingo, Palenque, Playa del Carmen, San Cristóbal de Las Casas, Tizimín, Tulum and Valladolid. Special buses serve the Ruta Puuc and Uxmal (for the evening light-and-sound show; see Uxmal for details).

Expresso – 16 deluxe nonstop buses to Cancún and 8 deluxe buses to Valladolid

Línea Dorada – a deluxe line serving Felipe Carrillo Puerto and Chetumal

Noreste – service to many small towns in the northeastern part of the peninsula, including Río Lagartos and Tizimín

Omnitur del Caribe (Caribe) – deluxe service between Mérida and Chetumal via Felipe Carrillo Puerto; ticket counter in the old Terminal de Autobuses

Super Expresso – 8 deluxe buses to Cancún, 4 to Chetumal, 1 to Ticul

Transportes Mayab (Mayab) – buses to Cancún, Chetumal, Felipe Carrillo Puerto, Peto and Ticul; ticket counters and departures in the old Terminal de Autobuses

Transportes de Lujo Línea Dorada (LD) – deluxe service to Felipe Carrillo Puerto and Chetumal; ticket counter in the old Terminal de Autobuses, departures from Terminal CAME

UNO – super-deluxe service on major routes, such as Mérida to Cancún and Mérida to Villahermosa and Mexico City

Bus Routes Here's information on daily trips to and from Mérida.

Campeche – 195km (short route via Becal), 2½ to 3 hours, or 250km (long route via Uxmal), 4 hours; 13 ADO (US$6.50), ATS every 20 to 30 minutes (US$3 to US$3.50)

Cancún – 320km, 4 hours; UNO morning and evening super-deluxe (US$11), 8 Super Expresso (US$11), 16 Expresso deluxe (US$11), Oriente every 30 minutes (US$9), 21 ADO deluxe (US$8.75), hourly ATS (US$7)

Celestún – 95km, 1½ to 2 hours; 12 buses, departing the Unión de Camioneros de Yucatán terminal on Calle 71, between Calles 62 and 64 (US$2.30)

Chetumal – 456km, 8 hours; several Caribe deluxe (US$13), 4 Super Expresso deluxe (US$11), other LD and Mayab for less

Chichén Itzá – 116km, 2 hours; 10 buses, most in the morning (US$2.75 to US$3.50); Oriente stops right at the Chichén ruins

Dzibilchaltún – 15km, 30 minutes; minibuses and *colectivo* taxis depart when full from the Parque de San Juan and go within 1km of the ruins (US$0.55); the alternative is a bus from the Progreso terminal, which drops you on the highway at the Dzibilchaltún access road, 5km west of the ruins

Felipe Carrillo Puerto – 310km, 5 hours; assorted Caribe, LD and Mayab (US$6.50 to US$8); see Chetumal

Izamal – 72km, 1½ hours; 20 Oriente (US$1) from its terminal on Calle 50, between Calles 65 and 67

Kabah – 101km, 2 hours; buses on the 'chenes' or inland route between Mérida and Campeche may stop at Kabah on request (US$2)

Mexico City (TAPO) – 1550km, 20 hours; 5 ADO (US$52)

Palenque – 556km, 9 hours; 2 each (1 morning and 1 evening) by ADO (US$17) and ATS (US$15) direct to Palenque; many others stopping at Catazajá, the main highway junction 27km north of Palenque Town, from where you can hitchhike or catch a bus or colectivo to Palenque

Playa del Carmen – 385km, 7 hours; 9 ADO (US$10 to US$12), several others by Mayab (US$10) and ATS (US$8)

Progreso – 33km, 45 minutes; Autoprogreso every 6 minutes 5 am to 9.45 pm from the Progreso bus terminal (US$0.70)

Ticul – 85km, 1½ hours (US$3); 1 deluxe Super Expresso bus from CAME (7.30 am), frequent Mayab (US$2), plus minibuses from the Parque de San Juan terminal

Tizimín – 210km, 4 hours; a few Noreste, Oriente and ATS (US$3.75), or take a bus to Valladolid and change there for Tizimín

Tulum – 320km, 4 hours (via Cobá), or 450km, 5 hours (via Cancún); a few ADO (US$8.25) and Oriente (US$7)

Tuxtla Gutiérrez – 995km, 14 hours; 3 Colón (US$25), or change at Palenque or Villahermosa

Uxmal – 80km, 1½ hours; 6 ATS, including two special excursions: the Ruta Puuc excursion (US$4.50), departs Mérida's old Terminal de Autobuses at 8 am, goes to Uxmal, Kabah and several other sites, departing Uxmal on the return journey to Mérida at 2.30 pm; the light-and-sound excursion (US$3.75) departs Mérida at 6 pm and Uxmal at 10 pm

Valladolid – 160km, 3 hours; 8 Expresso deluxe (US$6), many ADO, Oriente, ATS and others (US$5); see Cancún

Villahermosa – 700km, 9 hours; 1 UNO (US$32), 10 ADO (US$20), several ATS (US$16)

Car Rental car is the optimal way to tour the many archaeological sites south of Mérida, especially if you have two or more people to share costs. Assume you will pay a total of US$40 to US$60 per day (tax, insurance and gas included) for the cheapest car offered, usually a bottom-of-the-line Volkswagen or Nissan.

Tourist Car Rental (☎ 924-94-71, 924-62-55, harrycaam@hotmail.com), Calle 60 between Calles 45 and 47, offers rates the big-name agencies often can't touch – especially if you offer to pay in cash. It's occasionally possible to get a VW for as little as US$25 a day. It all depends on demand, form of payment and length of rental (weekly rates, for example, are available).

Other car rental agencies in Mérida include Dollar (☎ 928-67-59, fax 925-01-55), Hertz (☎ 924-28-34, fax 984-01-14) and National (☎ 923-24-93), all with offices on Calle 60 between Calles 55 and 57.

Getting Around

To/From the Airport Bus 79 ('Aviación') travels infrequently between the airport and the city center for US$0.50. Most arriving travelers use the Transporte Terrestre minibuses (US$10) to go from the airport to the center; to return to the airport you must take a taxi (US$8.50).

To/From CAME Bus Station To walk from CAME to the Plaza Mayor, exit the terminal, turn left, then right onto Calle 69; the old Terminal de Autobuses will be on your right. Walk straight along Calle 69 for four blocks, through Parque de San Juan, to Calle 62. Turn left on Calle 62 and walk the remaining three blocks to the plaza.

Bus Most parts of Mérida that you'll want to visit are within five or six blocks of the Plaza Mayor and are thus accessible on foot. Given the slow speed of city traffic, particularly in the market areas, travel on foot is also the fastest way to get around.

City buses are cheap at US$0.20 per ride (US$0.30 in a minibus), but routes are confusing. Most start in suburban neighborhoods, meander through the city center and terminate in another distant suburban neighborhood.

To travel between the Plaza Mayor and the upscale neighborhoods to the north along Paseo de Montejo, catch a 'Tecnológico' bus or minibus on Calle 60 and get out at Avenida Colón; to return to the city center, catch almost any bus – López Mateos, Chedraui, and others – along Paseo de Montejo.

The bus system is supplemented by colectivo minibuses, which are easier to use, as they run shorter and more comprehensible routes. Most useful is the Ruta 10, which departs the corner of Calles 58 and 59, half a block east of the Parque Hidalgo, and travels along the Paseo de Montejo to Itzamná.

Taxi Taxis in Mérida are not metered, but Mérida's taxi drivers' union has set rates to various destinations. A broad sampling of those rates is posted beside the taxi stand at the corner of Calles 60 and 57A (across from the Tourist Information Center). Currently, no ride within the city limits exceeds US$3.50. To call a taxi, dial ☎ 928-53-22 or 923-12-21; service is available 24 hours.

DZIBILCHALTÚN

Dzibilchaltún (Place of Inscribed Flat Stones) was the longest continuously used Mayan administrative and ceremonial city, serving the Maya from 1500 BC or earlier until the European conquest in the 1540s. At the height of its greatness, Dzibilchaltún covered 80 sq km. Archaeological research in the 1960s mapped 31 sq km of the city, revealing some 8500 structures.

You enter the site along a nature trail, which terminates at the modern, air-conditioned **Museo del Pueblo Maya**, featuring artifacts from throughout Mexico's Mayan region. Exhibits explaining Mayan daily life and beliefs from ancient times

through the present are in Spanish and English. Beyond the museum, a path leads to the central plaza, which has an open chapel dating from early Spanish times (1590-1600).

The **Templo de las Siete Muñecas** (Temple of the Seven Dolls), which got its name from seven grotesque dolls discovered here during excavations, is a 1km walk from the central plaza. It is most impressive for its precise astronomical orientation and its function in the Great Mayan Time Machine. While you are still a good distance away from the temple, note that you can see right through the building's doors and windows on the east-west axis. But when you approach, this view is lost. The temple's construction is such that you can't see through from north to south at all. The rising and setting sun of the equinoxes 'lit up' the temple's windows and doors, making them blaze like beacons and signaling this important turning point in the year.

The **Cenote Xlacah**, now a public swimming pool, is more than 40m deep. In 1958 an expedition sponsored by the US National Geographic Society sent divers down and recovered 30,000 Mayan artifacts, many of ritual significance. The most interesting of these are now on display in the site's museum.

Dzibilchaltún is open 8 am to 5 pm Tuesday to Sunday (US$2.50, free on Sunday). Parking costs US$0.50, and there's a US$4 fee for use of a video camera.

Getting There & Away

Minibuses and colectivo taxis depart frequently from Mérida's Parque de San Juan, on Calle 69 between Calles 62 and 64, for the village of Dzibilchaltún Ruinas (15km, 30 minutes, US$0.55), only a little over 1km from the museum.

PROGRESO
• pop 40,000 ☎ 9

This is a seafarers' town, the port for Mérida and northwestern Yucatán. The Yucatecan limestone shelf declines so gradually into the sea here that a *muelle* (pier) 6.5km long had to be built to reach the deep water. It is Mexico's longest pier, and when seen from the popular beach immediately to the east, it seems endless.

This same gradual slope affects Progreso's long beach; the waters are shallow, warm and safe from such dangers as riptide and undertow, though they're usually murky with seaweed and swirling sand. But the beach is nearly shadeless, having lost its palm trees to hurricanes, and the few small shelters are inadequate for the crowds. The beach at Yucalpeten, a 10-minute bus ride west, is much better.

Progreso is normally a sleepy little town, but on Saturday and Sunday, especially in summer, it seems as if all of Mérida is here. Don't expect to find a Cancún-like beach here. The beach faces the Gulf of Mexico, not the Caribbean, so you won't find any spectacular coral heads, and water visibility even on calm days rarely exceeds 5m.

Orientation

Progreso is long and narrow, stretched out along the seashore. Though it has an apparently logical street grid, it is illogically subject to two numbering systems 50 numbers apart. One has the city center's streets numbered in the 60s, 70s and 80s, another has them in the 10s, 20s and 30s. Thus you might see a street sign on Calle 30 calling it Calle 80, or find a map referring to Calle 10 as Calle 60. Both numbering systems are indicated on this book's map.

The bus stations are near the main plaza. It's six short blocks from the plaza to the Malecón and the muelle.

Places to Stay

Progreso is looked upon as a resort, if a modest one, so rooms here tend to be a bit more expensive than in other Yucatecan towns. On Sundays in July and August, the cheapest hotels fill up.

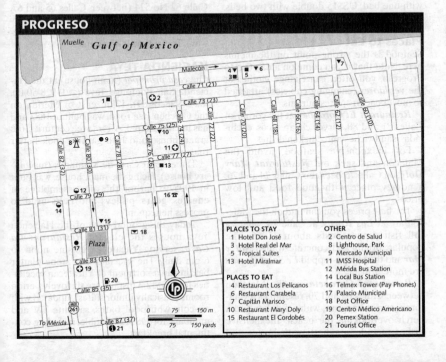

PROGRESO

Muelle   **Gulf of Mexico**

Malecón

Calle 71 (21)
Calle 73 (23)
Calle 75 (25)
Calle 77 (27)
Calle 79 (29)
Calle 81 (31)
Plaza
Calle 83 (33)
Calle 85 (35)

To Mérida   MEX 261   Calle 87 (37)

0   75   150 m
0   75   150 yards

PLACES TO STAY	OTHER
1 Hotel Don José	2 Centro de Salud
3 Hotel Real del Mar	8 Lighthouse, Park
5 Tropical Suites	9 Mercado Municipal
13 Hotel Miramar	11 IMSS Hospital
	12 Mérida Bus Station
PLACES TO EAT	14 Local Bus Station
4 Restaurant Los Pelicanos	16 Telmex Tower (Pay Phones)
6 Restaurant Carabela	17 Palacio Municipal
7 Capitán Marisco	18 Post Office
10 Restaurant Mary Doly	19 Centro Médico Americano
15 Restaurant El Cordobés	20 Pemex Station
	21 Tourist Office

Hotel Don José (no phone), on the corner of Calles 78 and 71, offers 17 rooms: 12 with fan only for US$13, five with air-con for US$15. It has a pool.

Hotel Miralmar (☎ 935-05-52, Calle 77 No 124), at Calle 76, offers rooms with private shower, fan and one double bed for US$11, two beds for US$14. Rooms on the upper floor are not as dungeonlike as the ground-floor rooms. The three bubble-shaped rooms may look a tad bizarre, but they offer the best ventilation.

At the corner of the Malecón and Calle 70 is seaside **Tropical Suites** (☎ 935-12-63, fax 935-30-93), with 21 tidy rooms with shower and fan for US$28 double with fan, US$30 with air-con. Be sure to request a room with a sea view.

Hotel Real del Mar (☎ 935-07-98), on Calle 70 at Calle 71, behind the Restaurant Los Pelícanos, is an older hostelry, but it's still a good deal. The 15 rooms with shower and fan cost US$11 single, US$14 double with one bed, US$15 double with two beds, US$24 double with sea view.

Places to Eat

Seafood is the strong point on the menus here. Note that if you come on a day trip to Progreso, you often can change clothes at the *vestidores* (changing cubicles) attached to most beachfront restaurants.

Restaurant El Cordobés, at the corner of Calles 81 and 80, serves cheap tacos, enchiladas, sandwiches and chicken dishes.

For inexpensive seafood, avoid the Malecón and seek out **Restaurant Mary Doly**, on Calle 75 between Calles 74 and 76, a homey place with good food and low prices.

The best prices you can find on the Malecón are at **Las Rocas**, at Calle 78, where a full fish dinner costs about US$5. The popular, bright and concrete-walled **Sol y Mar** and the palapa-topped **Le Saint Bonnet** are more upscale.

Restaurant Carabela, on the Malecón between Calles 68 and 70, resembles a California surfer hangout, with a full bar and a perch overlooking the beach. Inexpensive dishes include spaghetti with butter and

cheese (US$2), lime soup (US$2) and fillet of grouper (US$4).

Restaurant Los Pelícanos, on the Malecón at Calle 70, by the Hotel Real del Mar, has a shady terrace, sea views, a good menu and moderate prices.

At the eastern end of the Malecón between Calles 62 and 60, almost 1km from the muelle, stands **Capitán Marisco**, perhaps Progreso's fanciest seafood restaurant. Very few items on the wide-ranging menu are priced over US$7.

Getting There & Away

Both Dzibilchaltún and Progreso are due north of Mérida along a fast four-lane highway that's basically a continuation of the Paseo de Montejo. If you're driving from Mérida, head north on the Paseo and follow signs for Progreso.

Progreso is 18km (20 minutes) beyond the Dzibilchaltún turnoff. In Mérida, Autoprogreso buses depart the Progreso bus terminal, Calle 62 No 524 (between Calles 65 and 67, 1½ blocks south of the Plaza Mayor), every 12 minutes from 5 am to 9 pm (US$0.90 one-way). Travel time is 45 minutes.

HACIENDA TEYA

The *casa principal* (main house) at the Hacienda San Ildefonso Teya (☎ 9-928-50-00, fax 9-928-18-89), 13km east of Mérida on the Chichén Itzá road, was built in 1683 and has its own chapel. After three centuries, the grand house and lush gardens look better than ever.

The elegant Casa de Maquinas (machinery house), facing the main house, was built in 1905 to harbor the oily assemblage of engines, gears, pulleys and belts used to process henequen.

Today the ground floor of the Hacienda Teya houses the elegant **Restaurant La Cava**, serving Yucatecan cuisine noon to 6 pm daily. The specialty is a stone platter bearing an assortment of Yucatecan specialties for US$12. Upstairs are six lovely period rooms (basically junior suites), updated with air-con, whirlpool baths, satellite TV and minibars, for US$120 double, including continental breakfast.

IZAMAL

• pop 14,500 ☎ 9

Izamal, a colonial gem easily explored on foot, is a great day trip from Mérida. The quiet provincial town retains the atmosphere of life from generations past; many people still rely on horse-drawn carriages to get around.

In ancient times Izamal was a center for the worship of the supreme Mayan god, Itzamná, and the sun god, Kinich-Kakmó. A dozen temple pyramids here were devoted to these or other gods. Perhaps these bold expressions of Mayan religiosity were why the Spanish colonists chose Izamal as the site for an enormous and impressive Franciscan monastery, the Convento de San Antonio de Padua, which today stands at the heart of this small city.

Shadowed by the gargantuan bulk of the monastery lie Izamal's two principal squares, surrounded by arcades painted in the town's signature yellow – Izamal is known throughout the peninsula as the Ciudad Amarilla (Yellow City). Three blocks directly north of the monastery and visible from it is Kinich-Kakmó, the only pyramid among the original 12 to have been restored. Some 207m long and 190m wide, it was rebuilt in the early 1990s. There's no cost to climb it.

Convento de San Antonio de Padua

When the Spaniards conquered Izamal, they destroyed the major Mayan temple, the Popul-Chac pyramid, and in 1533 began to build from its stones one of the first monasteries in the Western Hemisphere. The work was finished in 1561. Under the monastery's arcades, look for building stones with an unmistakable mazelike design; these were clearly taken from the earlier Mayan temple.

The monastery's principal church is the Santuario de la Virgen de Izamal, approached by a ramp from the main square. Walk up the ramp and through an arcaded gallery to the Atrium, a spacious arcaded courtyard in which the fiesta of the Virgin of Izamal takes place each August 15. It is the largest enclosed atrium in Mexico.

At some point, the 16th-century frescoes beside the entrance of the sanctuary were completely painted over. For years – no one knows how many – they lay concealed under a thin layer of whitewash. A few years ago they were discovered by a maintenance worker who was cleaning the walls.

In a courtyard beside the church you'll see a carved-stone sundial. It is not original, despite what most of the local guides believe. However, if while you're in the courtyard you look up toward the sky you will see the original sundial, at the roof's edge. Likewise, most local guides tell visitors the church's altar is original. It is not. A fire, believed to have been started by a fallen candle, consumed the original altar. The one you see now was built in the 1940s.

Entry to the church is free. The best time to visit is in the morning, as it is occasionally closed during the afternoon siesta.

Places to Stay & Eat

In front of the monastery are numerous inexpensive eateries and two budget hotels: *Hotel Kabul* and *Hotel Canto*. Kabul is the more attractive of the two, offering worn but clean rooms for US$4 with shared bath, US$8 with one bed and private bath, US$9 with two beds and private bath.

About eight blocks southwest, in a residential neighborhood only 10 minutes' walk from the center of town, is the much nicer *Hotel Green River* (☎/fax 954-03-37, Avenida Zamna 342), between Calles 39 and 41. It has 14 air-conditioned rooms with cable TV, minibar, purified water, telephone and private parking. Rates are typically about US$20 per room.

Restaurant Kinich-Kakmó, on Calle 27 between Calles 28 and 30, is casual and cozy, offering fan-cooled patio dining beside a garden. It specializes in traditional Yucatecan food, and you can have an absolute feast for less than US$10.

Getting There & Away

Oriente runs frequent buses between Mérida and Izamal from its terminal in Mérida on Calle 50 between Calles 65 and 67; there are buses from Valladolid as well.

Coming from Chichén Itzá you must change buses at Hóctun. If you're driving from the east, turn north at Kantunil. Izamal's bus station is one block west of the monastery.

From Izamal it's possible to take buses to Cancún, Valladolid and Dzitas (the same bus goes to all three, leaving at 5, 6.30 and 9 am, and 1 and 5 pm). Auto Centro has medium-class buses to Mérida, Cancún, Dzitas and elsewhere.

CHICHÉN ITZÁ
☎ 990

The most famous and best restored of the Yucatán Peninsula's Mayan sites, Chichén Itzá will awe even the most jaded visitor. Many mysteries of the Mayan astronomical calendar are made clear when one understands the design of the 'time temples' here.

But one astronomical mystery remains: why do most people come here from Mérida and Cancún on day trips, arriving at 11 am when the blazing sun is getting to its hottest point, and depart around 3 pm, when the heat finally begins to abate? You'd do better to stay the night nearby and do your exploration of the site either early in the morning or late in the afternoon.

Should you have the good fortune to visit Chichén Itzá on the vernal equinox (March 20 to 21) or autumnal equinox (September 21 to 22), you can witness the light-and-shadow illusion of the serpent ascending or descending the side of the staircase of El Castillo.

History

Most archaeologists agree that Chichén Itzá's first major settlement, during the late Classic period, was pure Mayan. In about the 9th century, the city was largely abandoned for unknown reasons.

The city was resettled around the late 10th century, and shortly thereafter, Chichén appears to have been invaded by Toltecs who had moved down from their central highlands capital of Tula, north of Mexico City. Toltec culture was fused with that of the Maya, incorporating the cult of Quetzalcóatl (Kukulcán, in Maya). You will see images of both Chac, the Mayan rain god, and Quetzalcóatl, the plumed serpent, throughout the city.

The substantial fusion of highland central Mexican and Puuc architectural styles makes Chichén unique among the Yucatán Peninsula's ruins. The fabulous El Castillo and the Plataforma de Venus are among several outstanding architectural works built during the height of Toltec cultural input.

After a Mayan leader moved his political capital to Mayapán while keeping Chichén as his religious capital, Chichén Itzá fell into decline. Why it was subsequently abandoned in the 14th century is a mystery, but the once-great city remained the site of Mayan pilgrimages for many years.

Orientation & Information

Most of Chichén's lodgings, restaurants and services lie along 1km of highway in the village of Piste ('PEES-teh'), to the western (Mérida) side of the ruins. It's 1.5km from the ruins' main (west) entrance to the first hotel (Pirámide Inn) in Piste, or 2.5km from the ruins to Piste village plaza, which is shaded by a huge tree. Buses generally stop at the plaza; you can make the hot walk to and from the ruins in 20 to 30 minutes.

On the eastern (Cancún) side, it's 1.5km from the highway to the eastern entrance to the ruins, along the access road.

Chichén's little airstrip is north of the ruins, on the north side of the highway, 3km from Piste's main plaza.

You can change money in the Unidad de Servicios, at the western entrance to the ruins, or at your hotel. There are several telephone *casetas* in Piste; look for the signs.

Zona Arqueológica

Chichén Itzá is open 8 am to 6 pm daily; the interior passageway in El Castillo is open only 11 am to 1 pm and 4 to 5 pm. Admission costs US$7.50 (free on Sunday and holidays and for children under 12), US$10 extra for your video camera and US$5 extra if you use a tripod with your camera. Parking costs US$1. Explanatory plaques are in Spanish and English.

The main entrance is the western one, which has a large parking lot and a big,

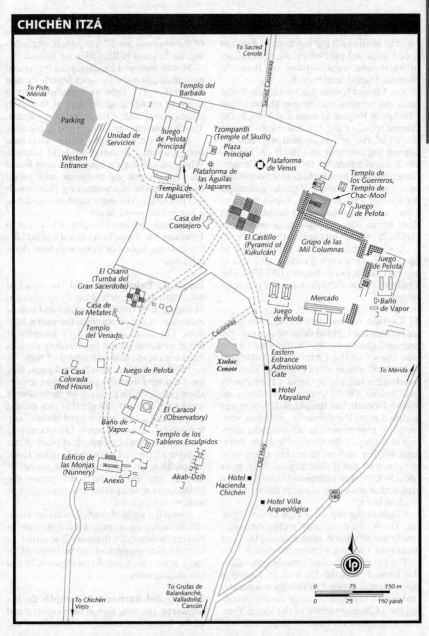

CHICHÉN ITZÁ

To Piste, Mérida

To Sacred Cenote

Parking

Templo del Barbado

Western Entrance

Unidad de Servicios

Juego de Pelota Principal

Tzompantli (Temple of Skulls)

Plaza Principal

Plataforma de Venus

Templo de los Jaguares

Plataforma de las Águilas y Jaguares

Casa del Consejero

El Castillo (Pyramid of Kukulcán)

Templo de los Guerreros, Templo de Chac-Mool

Juego de Pelota

Grupo de las Mil Columnas

Juego de Pelota

El Osario (Tumba del Gran Sacerdote)

Casa de los Metates

Templo del Venado

Mercado

Baño de Vapor

Juego de Pelota

La Casa Colorada (Red House)

Juego de Pelota

Xtoloc Cenote

Eastern Entrance Admissions Gate

To Mérida

El Caracol (Observatory)

Templo de los Tableros Esculpidos

Hotel Mayaland

Baño de Vapor

Edificio de las Monjas (Nunnery)

Anexo

Akab-Dzib

Hotel Hacienda Chichén

Hotel Villa Arqueológica

Old Hwy

MEX 180

To Chichén Viejo

To Grutas de Balankanché, Valladolid, Cancún

0   75   150 m
0   75   150 yards

modern entrance building called the Unidad de Servicios, open 8 am to 10 pm. The Unidad has a small but worthwhile museum (open 8 am to 5 pm) with sculptures, reliefs, artifacts and explanations of these in Spanish, English and French.

The Chilam Balam Auditorio, next to the museum, screens audiovisual shows about Chichén in English at noon and 4 pm. In the central space of the Unidad stands a scale model of the archaeological site, and off toward the toilets is an exhibit on Thompson's excavations of the Sacred Cenote. Other facilities here include two bookstores with a good assortment of guides and maps, a currency exchange desk (open 9 am to 1 pm) and a *guardarropa* at the main ticket desk where you can leave your belongings (US$0.35) while you explore the site.

A 45-minute light-and-sound show in Spanish begins each evening at 7 pm in summer and 8 pm in winter (US$3.75). The English version (US$5) starts at 9 pm year-round.

El Castillo As you pass through the turnstiles from the Unidad de Servicios into the archaeological zone, El Castillo (the Castle, also known as the Pirámide de Kukulcán) rises before you in all its grandeur. Standing nearly 25m tall, the pyramid was originally built before 800 AD, prior to the Toltec invasion. Nonetheless, the plumed serpent was sculpted along the stairways and Toltec warriors are represented in the doorway carvings at the top of the temple. No doubt this is grist for the mill of those historians who believe that the Toltec capital Tula, near Mexico City, was influenced from Chichén Itzá, rather than vice-versa, as conventional wisdom has it.

Climb to the top for a view of the entire site. This is best done early in the morning or late in the afternoon, both to avoid the heat and to see Chichén without the crowds.

The pyramid is actually the Mayan calendar formed in stone. Each of El Castillo's nine levels is divided in two by a staircase, making 18 separate terraces commemorating the 18 20-day months of the Vague Year. The four stairways have 91 steps each; add the top platform and the total is 365, the number of days in the year. On each façade of the pyramid are 52 flat panels, symbolizing the 52 years in the Calendar Round.

Most amazing of all, during the spring and autumn equinoxes (around March 21 and September 21), light and shadow form a series of triangles on the side of the north staircase that mimic the creep of a serpent. The illusion lasts three hours and 22 minutes.

This pyramid holds more surprises: there's another pyramid *inside* El Castillo. When archaeologists opened it, they found the brilliant red jaguar throne with inlaid eyes and spots of shimmering jade, which still lies within. The inner sanctum also holds a Toltec *chac-mool* figure.

The inner pyramid is open only 11 am to 1 pm and 4 to 5 pm. Entry is not a good idea for claustrophobes or those who hate close, fetid air.

Juego de Pelota Principal The principal ball court, the largest and most impressive in Mexico, is only one of the city's eight courts, indicative of the importance the games held here. The court is flanked by temples at either end and bound by towering parallel walls with stone rings cemented up high.

There is evidence that the ball game may have changed over the years. Some carvings show players with padding on their elbows and knees, and it is thought that they played a soccerlike game with a hard rubber ball, forbidding the use of hands. Other carvings show players wielding bats; it appears that if a player hit the ball through one of the stone hoops, his team was declared the winner. It may be that during the Toltec period the losing captain, and perhaps his teammates as well, were sacrificed.

Along the walls of the ball court are stone reliefs, including scenes of decapitations of players. Acoustically the court is amazing – a conversation at one end can be heard 135m away at the other, and if you clap, you hear a resounding echo.

Templo del Barbado & Templo de los Jaguares The structure at the northern end of the ball court, called the Temple of the

Bearded Man after a carving inside it, has some finely sculpted pillars and reliefs of flowers, birds and trees. The Temple of the Jaguars, to the southeast, has some columns with carved rattlesnakes and tablets with etched jaguars. Inside are faded mural fragments depicting a battle.

Tzompantli The *tzompantli*, a Toltec term for 'temple of skulls,' is between the Templo de los Jaguares and El Castillo. You can't mistake it, because the T-shaped platform is festooned with carved skulls and eagles tearing open the chests of men to eat their hearts. In ancient days this platform held the heads of sacrificial victims.

Plataforma de las Águilas y Jaguares Adjacent to the tzompantli, the carvings on the Platform of the Eagles and Jaguars depict those animals gruesomely grabbing human hearts in their claws. It is thought that this platform was part of a temple dedicated to the military legions responsible for capturing sacrificial victims.

Plataforma de Venus The Toltec symbol for the planet Venus is a feathered serpent bearing a human head between its jaws, and you can see many examples of this image on the Platform of Venus, just north of El Castillo.

Sacred Cenote A 300m-long rough stone road runs north (a five-minute walk) to the huge sunken well that gave this city its name (Chichén Itzá means 'mouth of the well of the Itzá people' in Mayan). The Sacred Cenote is an awesome natural well some 60m in diameter and 35m deep that was used by the Mayans in their religious ceremonies (see 'Chichén's Sacred Cenote').

The walls between the rim and the water's surface are ensnared in tangled vines and other vegetation. Next to the cenote are the ruins of a small steam bath, as well as toilets and a modern drinks stand.

Grupo de las Mil Columnas Comprising the Templo de los Guerreros (Temple of the Warriors), Templo de Chac-Mool (Temple

---

Chichén's Sacred Cenote

Around 1900, Edward Thompson, a Harvard professor and US Consul to Yucatán, bought the hacienda that included Chichén Itzá for US$75. No doubt intrigued by local stories of female virgins being sacrificed to the Mayan deities by being thrown into the cenote, Thompson resolved to have the cenote dredged.

He imported dredging equipment and set to work. Gold and jade jewelry from all parts of Mexico and as far away as Colombia was recovered, along with other artifacts and a variety of human bones. Many of the artifacts were shipped to Harvard's Peabody Museum, but many have since been returned to Mexico.

Subsequent diving expeditions in the 1920s and again in the '60s turned up hundreds more valuable artifacts. It appears that all sorts of people, including children and old people, the diseased and the injured, and the young and the vigorous, were forcibly obliged to take an eternal swim in Chichén's Sacred Cenote.

❋ ❋ ❋ ❋ ❋ ❋ ❋ ❋ ❋ ❋ ❋ ❋

---

of Chac-Mool), and Baño deal Vapor (Sweat House or Steam Bath), this group behind El Castillo takes its name (Group of the Thousand Columns) from the forest of pillars in front.

The platformed Temple of the Warriors greets you with a statue of the reclining god, Chac, as well as stucco and stone-carved animal deities. The temple's roof, once supported by columns entwined with serpents, disappeared long ago.

Archaeological work in 1926 revealed the Temple of Chac-Mool beneath the Temple of the Warriors. You may enter via a stairway on the north side. The walls inside bear badly deteriorated murals, which are thought to portray the Toltecs' defeat of the Maya.

Just southeast of the Temple of the Warriors lies the rubble of a Mayan sweat house, with an underground oven and drains for the water. The sweat houses were regularly used for ritual purification.

El Osario The Ossuary, otherwise known as the Bone House or High Priest's Grave (Tumba del Gran Sacerdote), is a ruined pyramid southwest of El Castillo. As with most of the buildings in this southern section, the architecture is more Puuc than Toltec.

La Casa Colorada Spaniards named this building La Casa Colorada (the Red House) for the red paint of the mural on its doorway. The building has little Toltec influence, and its design shows largely a pure Puuc Maya style. Referring to the stone latticework at the roof façade, the Maya named this building Chichán-Chob, or House of Small Holes.

El Caracol Called El Caracol (the Snail Shell) by the Spaniards for its interior spiral staircase configured like the inside of a giant snail or conch shell, this observatory is one of the most fascinating and important of all the Chichén Itzá buildings. Its circular design resembles some central highlands structures, although, surprisingly, not those of Toltec Tula. In a fusion of architectural styles and religious imagery, Mayan Chac rain god masks preside over four external doors facing the cardinal directions.

The windows in the observatory's dome are aligned with the appearance of certain stars at specific dates. From the dome the priests decreed the times for rituals, celebrations, corn-planting and harvests.

Edificio de las Monjas & El Anexo Thought by archaeologists to have been a palace for Mayan royalty, the Edificio de las Monjas (the Nunnery), with its myriad rooms, resembled a European convent to the conquistadors, hence their name for the building. The building's dimensions are imposing: its base is 60m long, 30m wide and 20m high. The construction is Mayan rather than Toltec, although a Toltec sacrificial stone stands in front. A small building added to the southeast is known as El Anexo (the

Annex). These buildings are in the Puuc-Chenes style, particularly evident in the lower jaw of the Chac mask at the opening of the Annex.

Akab Dzib On the path east of the Nunnery, the Akab Dzib is thought by some archaeologists to be the most ancient structure excavated here. The central chambers date from the 2nd century. 'Akab Dzib' means 'Obscure Writing' in Maya and refers to the south-side annex door, whose lintel depicts a priest with a vase etched with hieroglyphics. The writing has never been translated, hence the name. Note the red fingerprints on the ceiling, thought to symbolize the supreme deity Itzamná, from whom the Maya sought wisdom.

Chichén Viejo Chichén Viejo (Old Chichén) comprises largely unrestored ruins, scattered about and hidden in the bush south of the Nunnery. The predominant architecture is Mayan, with Toltec additions and modifications. Though trails lead to the most prominent buildings, you may want to hire a guide.

Grutas de Balankanché

In 1959 a guide to the Chichén ruins was exploring a cave on his day off when he came upon a narrow passageway. The guide, whose name history records only as Gómez, then explored the passageway for 300m, meandering through a series of caverns. In each, perched on mounds amid scores of glistening stalactites, were hundreds of ceremonial treasures the Maya had placed there 800 years earlier. In the years following the discovery, the ancient ceremonial objects were removed and studied. Eventually most of them were returned to the caves, placed exactly where they were found.

The Grutas de Balankanché are 6km east of the ruins of Chichén Itzá and 2km east of the Hotel Dolores Alba on the highway to Cancún. Second-class buses heading east from Piste toward Valladolid and Cancún will drop you at the Balankanché road. You'll find the entrance to the caves 350m north of the highway.

As you approach the caves, you'll enter a botanical garden displaying native Yucatecan flora. The entrance building holds a ticket booth, a little museum and a shop selling cold drinks and souvenirs. The museum features large photographs taken during the exploration of the caves and descriptions (in English, Spanish and French) of the Mayan religion and of the offerings found in the caves.

Also on display are photographs of modern-day Mayan ceremonies called Ch'a Chac, which are held in all the villages in the Yucatán during times of drought and consist mostly of praying and making offerings of food to Chac.

Plan your visit for an hour when the compulsory tour and light show will be given in a language you can understand: the 40-minute show (minimum six people, maximum 30) is given in the cave at 11 am, 1 and 3 pm in English; at 9 am, noon, 2 and 4 pm in Spanish; and at 10 am in French. Tickets are available daily between 9 am and 4 pm (last show). Admission costs US$3.75.

Places to Stay

Most of the lodgings convenient to Chichén and the caves are in the mid-range and top-end price brackets, but some budget options are available. No matter what you plan to spend on a bed, don't hesitate to haggle in the off-season (May, June, September and October), when prices should be lower.

Budget Campers are welcome at the agreeable *Pirámide Inn*, in Piste. For US$4 per person you can pitch a tent or hang a hammock under a palapa, enjoy the inn's pool and watch satellite TV in the lobby. Other amenities include hot showers and clean, shared toilet facilities.

Posada Olalde, two blocks south of the highway by Artesanías Guayacan, is the best of Piste's several small pensions, offering seven clean, quiet and attractive rooms for US$13/17 double/triple. Four bungalows on the premises are even cheaper.

Posada Chac-Mool, just east of the Hotel Misión Chichén on the opposite (south) side

of the highway in Piste, charges US$17 for a basic double with shower and fan. *Posada Novelo*, on the west side of the Pirámide Inn, charges the same for similar accommodations, but you can use the Pirámide's pool.

Hotel Posada Maya (☎ 851-02-11), a few dozen meters north of the highway (look for the sign), charges US$14 double for clean rooms with shower, fan and good beds. You can also hang a hammock here for US$4 a night. *Posada Poxil*, at the western end of town, charges the same for relatively clean, quiet rooms.

Mid-Range The *Hotel Dolores Alba* (☎ 9-928-56-50 in Mérida, fax 9-928-31-63, www.doloresalba.com), on highway 180 (the free highway to Cancún) at Km 122, is just over 3km east of the eastern entrance to the ruins and 2km west of the road to Balankanché. It has an air-conditioned restaurant and 40 modern, air-conditioned rooms facing two inviting swimming pools. The hotel will transport you to and from the ruins. Singles/doubles cost US$25/39.

The *Pirámide Inn* (☎ 851-01-15, fax 851-01-14, www.piramide.inn.com), in Piste less than 2km from Chichén, was entirely renovated in 1999. It offers 42 air-conditioned rooms, a pool and a Mayan-style sauna, as well as a restaurant serving international and vegetarian cuisine. Here, you're as close as you can stay to the archaeological zone's western entrance. Rooms cost US$44.

Stardust Inn (☎/fax 851-01-22), next to the Pirámide Inn, is an attractive place with two tiers of rooms surrounding a shaded swimming pool and restaurant. The 57 rooms, all with air-con and TV, cost US$48 single/double.

Top End All of these hotels have swimming pools, restaurants, bars, well-kept tropical gardens, comfortable rooms and tour groups coming and going. Several are very close to the ruins.

The *Hotel Mayaland* (☎ 851-01-28, 800-235-4079 in the USA, fax 851-00-77, www.mayaland.com), a mere 200m from the eastern entrance to the archaeological zone, was built around 1923 and is the most gracious hotel in Chichén's vicinity. Rooms cost US$114/126 single/double.

The elegant **Hotel Hacienda Chichén** (☎ 9-924-21-50 in Mérida, 800-624-8451 in the USA, fax 9-924-50-11 in Mérida, www .yucatanadventures.com.mx), a few hundred meters farther away from the entrance, is a converted colonial estate that dates from the 16th century. The archaeologists who excavated Chichén during the 1920s lived here. Their bungalows have been refurbished, new ones have been built, and a swimming pool has been added. Bungalows cost US$70 single/double, US$80 triple, and have ceiling fans, air-con and private baths but no TVs or phones.

Club Med's **Hotel Villa Arqueológica** (☎ 851-00-18, 800-258-2633 in the USA, ☎ 801-802-803 in France, fax 851-00-34), is a few hundred meters farther still. The 40 air-conditioned rooms are small but comfortable and cost about US$65 most of the year.

On the western side of Chichén, in the village of Piste, **Hotel Misión Chichén-Itzá** (☎ 851-00-22; fax 851-00-23, misionchichen@ finred.com.mx) is comfortable without being distinguished. Its 42 rooms with air-con and cable-TV cost US$75 single/double. It would be a good value if it slashed its rates in half.

Places to Eat

The cafeteria in the **Unidad de Servicios**, at the western entrance to the archaeological zone, serves mediocre food at high prices in pleasant surroundings. Although there's a restaurant at the site, you'd be wise to plan your midday meal elsewhere.

The highway through Piste is lined with more than 20 small restaurants. The cheapest are the market eateries on the main plaza opposite the huge tree. The others, ranged along the highway from the town square to the Pirámide Inn, are fairly well tarted up in a Mayan villager's conception of what foreign tourists expect to see. **Los Pajaros** and **Cocina Económica Chichén Itzá** are among the cheapest ones, serving sandwiches, omelets, enchiladas and quesadillas for around US$3. **Restaurant Sayil**, facing the Hotel Misión Chichén, offers good value: bistec, cochinita or pollo pibil for US$2.50.

Restaurant Ruinas serves big plates of fruit for US$2, and hamburgers, sandwiches, fried chicken, and spaghetti plates for around US$4.

The restaurant at Hotel Dolores Alba specializes in Yucatecan food. Good pollo pibil costs US$4.50, boneless red snapper US$6.50. Across the street is the **Ik Kil Parque Ecoarqueológico**, an 'eco/archaeological park.' Basically, it's a wooded area with a cenote in the middle and a restaurant a short walk away. The cenote offers an absolutely divine plunge after a day of ruins roaming (US$3/1.50 adults/kids). Buffet breakfast is served 9 am till noon (US$4), and a buffet lunch is offered from noon till 5 pm (US$9). The food is very good.

The big **Restaurant Xaybe**, opposite the Hotel Misión Chichén, has decent food for about US$10 per person. Customers of the restaurant get to use its swimming pool free, but even if you don't eat here, you can still swim for about US$2.

Getting There & Away

Air Aerocaribe runs same-day round-trip excursions by air from Cancún to Chichén Itzá, charging US$109 for the flight. Aerocozumel runs a similar service from Cozumel for US$118.

Bus The fastest buses between Mérida, Valladolid and Cancún travel by the Cuota (toll highway) and do not stop at Chichén Itzá. Autotransportes de Oriente has a ticket desk right in the souvenir shop in Chichén's Unidad de Servicios. Oriente's 2nd-class buses from the ruins leave for Mérida at 9 and 10 am, noon, and 2, 2.30 and 5 pm (US$3.50). Buses leave Cancún and Valladolid at 9.30, 10.30 and 11.30 am, and 12.30, 2.30, 3.30 and 4.30 pm (US$5.40 and US$1.50, respectively). Buses leave at 8.30 am and 1.30 pm from Playa del Carmen (US$7.20), Tulum (US$5.40) and Cobá (US$4.30).

Additionally, 1st-class buses leave the ruins for Mérida at 1 and 5 pm (US$3.90); Playa del Carmen at 2.45 pm (US$9.20);

Cobá at 8 am (US$3.20); Tulum at 8 am (US$4.70); Valladolid at 11.15 am and 2.45 pm (US$1.30); and Cancún at 3.30 pm (US$5.70).

Getting Around

Be prepared to walk at Chichén: from your hotel to the ruins, around the ruins, and back to your hotel, all under a broiling sun. For the Grutas de Balankanché, you can set out to walk early in the morning when it's cooler (it's 8km from Piste, less if you're staying on the eastern side of the ruins) and then hope to hitch a ride or catch a bus for the return.

A few taxis are available in Piste and sometimes at the Unidad de Servicios car park at Chichén Itzá, but you cannot depend on finding one unless you've made arrangements in advance. Despite a demand for them, taxis are fairly uncommon in these parts.

VALLADOLID

• pop 34,900 ☎ 9

Valladolid is only 40km east of Chichén Itzá and 160km west of Cancún, but as it has no sights of stop-the-car immediacy, few tourists spend time here. It's just as well, for that preserves Valladolid for the rest of us.

In addition to glossing over the city's historic sites, most visitors to Valladolid miss an evening ritual many local residents enjoy: at sunset they fill the benches of the Parque Francisco Cantón Rosado to socialize and catch an evening breeze under the trees, which fill with happily cackling birds.

History

Valladolid was once the Mayan ceremonial center of Zací. The initial attempt at conquest in 1543 by Francisco de Montejo, nephew of Montejo the Elder, was thwarted by fierce Mayan resistance, but the Elder's son Montejo the Younger ultimately conquered the town. The Spanish laid out a new city on the classic colonial plan.

During much of the colonial era, Valladolid's distance from Mérida, its humidity and the surrounding forests kept it isolated from royal rule and thus relatively autonomous. Banned from entering this town of pure-blooded Spaniards, the Maya rebelled,

and in the War of the Castes of 1847 they made Valladolid their first point of attack. Besieged for two months, Valladolid's defenders were finally overcome. Many fled to the safety of Mérida, but the rest were slaughtered.

Orientation & Information

The old highway goes right through the center of town, though all signs direct motorists to the toll highway north of town. To follow the old highway eastbound, take Calle 41; westbound, take Calle 39 or 35.

Recommended hotels are on the main plaza, called Parque Francisco Cantón Rosado, or just a block or two away from it. Facing the park is the Ayuntamiento (City Hall), on the 1st floor of which is a tourist office (☎ 856-25-29), open 8 am to 9 pm daily except during siesta. The staff speaks English and has maps of the city.

Also on the east side of the plaza is the main post office, open 8 am to 5 pm Monday to Friday, 9 am to 1 pm Saturday. Several banks are near the center of town and generally are open 9 am to 5 pm Monday to Friday, 9 am to 1 pm Saturday.

Templo de San Bernardino & Convento de Sisal

The Church of San Bernardino and the Convent of Sisal, 1.5km southwest of the plaza, are said to be the oldest Christian structures in Yucatán. Constructed in 1552, they were designed to serve a dual function as fortress and church.

If the convent is open, you can go inside. Apart from the likeness of the Virgin of Guadalupe on the altar, the church is relatively bare, having been stripped of its decorations during the uprisings of 1847 and 1910.

To get to the church from the main plaza, walk west on Calle 41 to Calle 41A and turn left; Calle 41A leads to the church.

Cenotes

The **Cenote Zací**, on Calle 36 between Calles 39 and 37, is Valladolid's most famous cenote. Set in a pretty park that also holds the town's museum, an open-air amphitheater and traditional stone-walled thatched

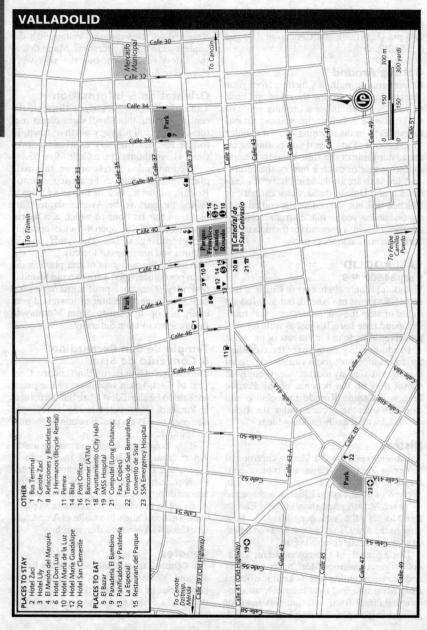

VALLADOLID

PLACES TO STAY
2 Hotel Zací
3 Hotel Lily
4 El Mesón del Marqués
10 Hotel Don Luis
12 Hotel María de la Luz
12 Hotel María Guadalupe
20 Hotel San Clemente

PLACES TO EAT
5 El Bazar
13 Panadería El Bambino
13 Panificadora y Pastelería
   La Especial
15 Restaurant del Parque

OTHER
1 Bus Terminal
7 Cenote Zací
8 Refacciones y Bicicletas Los
   3 Hermanos (Bicycle Rental)
11 Pemex
14 Bital
16 Post Office
17 Bancomer (ATM)
18 Ayuntamiento (City Hall)
19 IMSS Hospital
21 Computel (Long Distance,
   Fax, Copies)
22 Templo de San Bernardino,
   Convento de Sisal
23 SSA Emergency Hospital

houses, it is vast, dark, impressive and covered with a layer of algae and bat guano. Open 8 am to 7 pm daily (US$0.50/0.25 adults/children). There is a small zoo on the premises.

Much more enticing, but less accessible, is the **Cenote Dzitnup** (also sometimes called Xkakah), 7km west of Valladolid's main plaza. To reach it from the center of town, follow the old highway west toward Mérida for 5km. Turn left (south) at the sign for Dzitnup and follow the road for just under 2km; the site will be on the left. As you approach, a horde of village children will likely surround you, each wanting to be your 'guide' to the cenote, 10m away. Even if you don't appoint one, they often will accompany you down into the cave. Be sure to look for the blind fish that inhabit the cenote. Bring a bathing suit and towel and go for a swim – if you don't, you'll wish you had.

A taxi from Valladolid's main plaza charges US$14 for the excursion there and back, with a half hour's wait. To pedal to the site, rent a bicycle (US$2 per hour) from the Refacciones y Bicicletas Los 3 Hermanos, on Calle 44 between Calles 39 and 41. Check out your bike carefully before putting money down – they rent some clunkers, and you don't want your bike to break down. The first 5km are not particularly pleasant because of the traffic, but the last 2km are on a quiet country road. It should take you only 20 minutes to pedal to the cenote.

You also can hop aboard a westbound bus, ask the driver to let you off at the Dzitnup turnoff, then walk the final 2km (20 minutes) to the site, which is open 7 am to 6 pm daily (US$1.50). A restaurant and drinks stand are at the cave entrance.

Places to Stay
Budget The *Hotel María Guadalupe* (☎ 856-20-68, Calle 44 No 188), between Calles 39 and 41, is a study in modernity in this colonial town. The eight simple rooms cost US$9 single/double with private shower and fan.

Hotel Lily (☎ 856-21-63, Calle 44 No 190) is cheap and basic but reasonably priced with 20 rooms at US$7/11 single/double with private bath and fan. The one air-conditioned room has three beds and costs US$18.

Hotel Don Luis (☎ 856-20-08, Calle 39 No 191), at the corner of Calles 39 and 38, is a motel-style structure with a palm-shaded patio, murky swimming pool and acceptable rooms for US$10 single/double with fan, US$12 with air-con.

Mid-Range & Top End Most of Valladolid's better hotels have swimming pools, restaurants and secure parking facilities. The best is *El Mesón del Marqués* (☎ 856-20-73, fax 856-22-80, h_marques@chichen.com.mx, Calle 39 No 203), on the north side of the main plaza. It has two beautiful colonial courtyards, a pool and modernized rooms with air-con and ceiling fans. Rates are US$45 a suite most of the year.

Next best is the *Hotel María de la Luz* (☎ 856-20-71, fax 856-11-81, maria_luz@chichen.com.mx), on Calle 42 near Calle 39, at the northwest corner of the plaza. It offers serviceable air-conditioned rooms around a pool for US$21 single/double.

At the agreeable *Hotel San Clemente* (☎/fax 856-22-08, Calle 42 No 206), at the southwest corner of the main plaza, colonial decor abounds. The 64 doubles with private bath and fan cost US$22, US$24 with air-con. There's a swimming pool as well.

The well-kept *Hotel Zací* (☎ 856-21-67, Calle 44 No 191), between Calles 37 and 39, has 50 rooms built around a quiet courtyard with a swimming pool. Rooms with fan cost US$15/18 single/double and cost US$17/22 with air-con.

Places to Eat
El Bazar is a collection of open-air, market-style cookshops at the corner of Calles 39 and 40 (the northeast corner of the plaza). They're popular for big, cheap breakfasts, and at lunch and dinner, comidas corridas cost less than US$5 – if you ask for prices before you order. Try Doña Mary, El Amigo Panfilo, Sergio's Pizza, La Rancherita or El Amigo Casiano.

The restaurant at *Hotel María de la Luz* has breezy tables overlooking the plaza. The breakfast buffet costs US$4, a luncheon comida corrida the same or a little more. The old-fashioned, high-ceilinged **Restaurant del Parque**, on the plaza's southwest corner, offers an even cheaper comida corrida, along with many natural juices.

Valladolid has several good bakeries, including **Panificadora y Pastelería La Especial**, on Calle 41 less than a block west of the plaza, and **Panadería El Bambino**, on Calle 39 a half block west of the plaza.

The best restaurant in the area is the **Hostería del Marqués**, the dining room of the Hotel El Mesón del Marqués, on the north side of the main plaza. A three-course meal costs about US$10.

Getting There & Away

Bus The bus terminal is on Calle 39 at Calle 46. The main companies are Autotransportes de Oriente Mérida-Puerto Juárez (1st- and 2nd-class) and Expresso de Oriente.

Buses run from Valladolid to:

Cancún – 9 1st-class, first departure at 7.30 am, last at 10 pm (US$5.50); 24 2nd-class (US$4.30)

Chetumal – 2 2nd-class, at 5.30 am and 2.30 pm (US$8.10)

Chiquilá – 1 2nd-class, at 2.30 pm (US$4.10)

Cobá – 2 1st-class, at 9.15 am and 3.50 pm (US$2); 3 2nd-class (US$3.20); buses continue on to Tulum

Espita – 2 2nd-class, at 10.30 am and 3 pm (US$1.30)

Izamal – 2 2nd-class, at 1.10 am and 7.30 pm (US$2.40)

Mérida – 11 1st-class, first departures at 6.45 am, last at 9.45 pm (US$5.50); no fewer than 22 2nd-class (US$4.30), all passing the turnoff for Chichén Itzá along the way (be sure to tell the driver to let you out along there if you're on your way to the ruins; fare to Chichén Itzá is US$1.20)

Playa del Carmen – 8 1st-class, first departure at 7.45 am, last at 7.15 pm (US$7.50); 5 2nd-class (US$6.10)

Tizimín – 14 2nd-class (US$1.40)

Tulum – 2 1st-class (US$3.50); 3 2nd-class (US$4.30)

The 2nd-class ride to Tulum and Cobá costs more than the 1st-class because of the different routes taken.

Taxi A quicker, more comfortable way to get to Cancún, Mérida or elsewhere is to take one of the shared taxis that park outside the bus station and leave as soon as all seats are filled. The trip costs at least twice the bus fare, but if you're sick of buses, splurge and enjoy.

TIZIMÍN
• pop 38,300 ☎ 9

Many travelers bound for Río Lagartos change buses in Tizimín (Place of Many Horses), the third-largest city in the state of Yucatán (behind Mérida and Progreso). There is little to warrant an overnight stay, but the tree-filled central plaza is pleasant, particularly at sundown.

Two great colonial structures – the Convento de los Tres Reyes Magos (Monastery of the Three Wise Kings) and the Convento de San Francisco de Asis (Monastery of Saint Francis of Assisi) – are worth a look. Five lengthy blocks from the plaza, northwest on Calle 51, is a modest zoo, the Parque Zoológico de la Reina.

The Banco del Atlántico, next to the Hotel San Jorge on the southwest side of the plaza, changes money between 10 am and noon Monday to Friday. Banco Internacional is open 9 am to 1.30 pm Monday to Friday.

Places to Stay & Eat

The **Posada María Antonia** (☎ 863-23-84, Calle 50 No 408), on the east side of the Parque de la Madre, has 11 air-conditioned rooms for US$15 single/double. You can place international calls at the reception desk.

Hotel San Jorge (☎ 863-20-37, Calle 53 No 411) has basic rooms with air-con and private bath for US$18 single/double. Avoid Room 3, which is noisy and has a bad bed. **Hotel San Carlos** (☎ 863-20-94, Calle 54 No 407) also charges US$18 single/double for 25 somewhat worn rooms.

The **market**, a block northwest of the bus station, has the usual cheap eateries. The bakery **Panificadora La Especial** is on Calle 55, down a pedestrian lane from the plaza.

The festive **Restaurant Tres Reyes**, on the corner of Calles 52 and 53, opens early for breakfast and is a favorite with town notables, who show up around 9 am. Lunch or dinner costs US$4 to US$7.

Facing the plaza are several simple places good for a quick, cheap bite; try *Los Portales*. The popular *Pizzería Cesar's*, at the corner of Calles 50 and 53, serves pizza, pasta, sandwiches and burgers. Few items are over US$5.

Getting There & Away
Autotransportes de Oriente (see Valladolid map) runs a number of intermediate-class buses to Cancún (seven daily, US$5); to Cobá at noon (US$4.60); to Playa del Carmen at 8.30 am and noon (US$7.10); to Tulum at noon (US$5.70); to Mérida at 6 and 11.20 am (US$5); to Izamal at 11.20 am (US$3.80); and to Valladolid (14 daily, the first departing at 4.30 am and the last at 7 pm, US$1.40).

Autobuses del Norte en Yucatán (see Valladolid map) runs 1st-class buses to Mérida (seven daily, US$5.50) and Río Lagartos (11 daily, US$1.40).

A taxi to Río Lagartos or San Felipe costs US$15.

about developing the area for tourism, this has not happened yet.

Flamingoes
When you see a flock of hundreds of these brilliant orange-red birds take flight, the sight of the suddenly fiery horizon will make you forget all about the long hours on the bus to get here. Depending on your luck, you'll see hundreds of flamingoes or thousands of them.

Fishing boats hired from town take visitors out to the four primary flamingo haunts: Punta Garga, Yoluk, Necopal and Nahochin. The names refer to the patches of mangrove near the flamingo colonies. The greatest number of flamingoes can usually be found at Nahochin, the farthest from town. In the interests of the flamingoes' well-being, ask your boat captain not to frighten the birds into flight. You can generally get to within 100m of flamingoes before they walk or fly away.

To hire a boat, head to the kiosk at water's edge. The captains don't speak English, but the man at the kiosk does and

RÍO LAGARTOS
• pop 1910 ☎ 9

It is worth going out of your way to this little fishing village, 103km north of Valladolid and 52km north of Tizimín, to see the most spectacular flamingo colony in Mexico. The estuaries are also home to snowy egrets, red egrets, great white herons and snowy white ibis. Although Río Lagartos was named after the once substantial alligator population, don't expect to see any alligators these days , as hunting has decimated the local population. Were it not for the flamingoes, you would have little reason to come here. Although the state government has been making noise

will hook you up with a captain and negotiate the destination and price (typically US$30 to US$35). Or you can visit the Restaurant Isla Contoy and hire friendly Diego Nuñez Martínez, who speaks English and charges US$20 to US$40 for flamingo tours. If you'll be staying in town a night, consider hiring him to take you on a night ride looking for crocodiles and, from May through September, sea turtles (US$40 per boat).

Places to Stay
The *Posada Leyli* (☎ 862-01-06), on Calle 14 at Calle 11, has six pleasing, fan-cooled rooms: two singles with shared bath for US$9,

two singles with private bath for US$10, two doubles with private bath for US$15.

Two blocks north, where Calle 14 meets the lagoon, is *Hotel Villas de Pescadores* (☎ 862-00-48), which offers three suites with air-con, TV, sofa and minibar for US$35 single/double and nine rooms with two beds and fan for US$20 single/double. All rooms have good cross-ventilation.

If all went as planned, the *Hotel Hol Koben* (www.riolagartos.com.mx), on Calle 14 at Calle 17, should now be completed. The manager swore the rooms would boast air-con, two double beds, a bathtub, a library with large-screen TV, a living room and an artists' room where paint, clay and musical instruments would be provided at nominal cost. Also planned were a swimming pool and a rooftop café with live music. The expected rate was US$60 single/double, including continental breakfast.

Places to Eat
The popular *Restaurante-Bar Isla Contoy*, on Calle 19 at water's edge, serves seafood for US$4 to US$5. It's a good place to meet other travelers.

At *Restaurant Los Negritos*, on Calle 10 near the town entrance, the *filete de camarones* (grouper stuffed with shrimp and lots of mayonnaise) is the house specialty. The *pescado frito* and *ceviche de pulpo* (octopus ceviche) both cost US$5.

Getting There & Away
From Río Lagartos, Autobuses del Noreste en Yucatán offers direct buses to Mérida (5.30 and 11 am and 12.30 and 4 pm, US$7.40), Tizimín (same hours as Mérida, US$1.70) and Cancún (11 am and 4 and 5 pm, daily except Wednesday, US$7.20). Noreste also offers semidirect buses to Tizimín (hourly from 5.30 am to 5.30 pm, US$1.40) and San Felipe (seven daily, US$1).

SAN FELIPE
● pop 1520 ☎ 9
This tiny, seldom-visited fishing village of painted wooden houses on narrow streets makes a nice day trip from Río Lagartos –

it's 12km to the west. Bird-watching is the main attraction, just across the estuary at Punta Holohit.

At the very nice *Hotel San Felipe de Jesús* (☎ 863-37-38, fax 862-20-36), on Calle 9 between Calles 14 and 16, six of the 18 rooms are large and have private balconies. All rooms have good cross-ventilation and are a super bargain at US$22 single/double. Smaller rooms go for US$16. The restaurant offers tasty seafood at low prices.

Some buses from Tizimín to Río Lagartos continue to San Felipe. The 12km ride takes about 20 minutes. To save time, take a taxi from Tizimín. From San Felipe, six buses daily travel to Tizimín (US$1.50) and continue to Valladolid (US$2.50). There are no taxis in Río Lagartos or San Felipe.

CELESTÚN
● pop 5200 ☎ 9
Famed as a bird sanctuary, Celestún makes a good day trip from Mérida. Although this region abounds in anhingas and egrets, most bird-watchers come here to see the flamingoes.

The town sits on a spit between the Río Esperanza and the Gulf of Mexico. The white-sand beach is appealing, but on some afternoons fierce winds swirl clouds of choking dust through the town, making the sea silty and unpleasant for swimming. Row upon row of fishing boats outfitted with twin long poles line the shore. Given the winds, the best time to see birds is in the morning.

The best place to hire a boat for bird-watching is at Restaurant Celestún, at the corner of Calle 12 and Calle 11. The people here seem a little more with it than elsewhere. The guide with the best reputation in town is Alberto Rodríguez, who can often be found at the restaurant. The typical bird-watching tour arranged here lasts about 2½ hours and puts you in view of egrets, herons, cormorants, sandpipers and – the big attraction – flamingoes. Depending on the tide, you may see hundreds or up to 7000 of the colorful birds. After that the boat winds through mangroves to a freshwater cenote, where you can take a swim. The cost for this tour is around US$55 for two persons, US$60 for three or four.

You can also hire a boat at the bridge on the highway into town (about 1.5km from the beach); tours from here generally last about an hour and involve simply getting into a boat and heading over to the flamingoes. The cost is US$30 for the boat *and* US$2 per person, up to six persons per boat.

Be advised that there is no bank in town, and the tours are cash only.

Places to Stay
Celestún has numerous hotels, all of which are on Calle 12 within a short walk of each other. The better places are mentioned here.

Hotel María del Carmen (☎/fax 936-20-51) offers 40 clean, pleasant beachfront rooms with balcony. Four have air-con for US$20/23 single/double; the rest are fan-cooled for US$18/20.

The next-best hotel in town is *Hospedaje Sol y Mar (☎ 9-944-97-87 in Mérida)*, which offers 16 rooms, half with air-con (US$25 single/double) and half without (US$15 single/double).

The new *Hospedaje Sofía* (no phone) offers seven fan-cooled rooms for US$10/12. It's *the* place to stay if you're low on funds.

Places to Eat
Celestún's specialties are crab claws and fresh fish. To keep from pricing themselves out of business, the restaurants have agreed on prices for main items. Service and decor vary from restaurant to restaurant, but the menu for the most part does not. Expect to pay US$4 for the catch of the day, US$6 for ceviche, US$3 for a conch cocktail.

Restaurant Celestún offers good service, pleasing decor and good food, but several other beachside restaurants are just as good.

Getting There & Away
Buses from Mérida head for Celestún 12 times daily beginning at 5 am. They leave from the Unión de Camioneros de Yucatán terminal on Calle 71 between Calles 62 and 64. The last bus leaves at 8 pm. The 95km trip takes about 1½ hours and costs US$2.30.

UXMAL
☎ 9
Set in the Puuc Hills, which lent their name to the architectural patterns in this region, Uxmal ('oosh-MAL') was an important city during the late Classic period (600-900 AD) in a region that encompassed the satellite towns of Sayil, Kabah, Xlapak and Labná. Although Uxmal means 'thrice built' in Maya, it was actually reconstructed five times.

How a sizable population ever flourished in this area is a mystery, as there is precious little water in the region. The Mayan *chultunes* (cisterns) must have been adequate.

History
First occupied around 600 AD, the town was architecturally influenced by highland Mexico and features the well-proportioned Puuc style, which is unique to this region.

Given the scarcity of water in the Puuc Hills, Chac, the rain god, was of great significance. His image is ubiquitous here in monsterlike stucco masks protruding from façades and cornices.

Scholars speculate as to why Uxmal was abandoned around 900 AD. Drought conditions may have reached such proportions that the inhabitants had to relocate. One widely held theory suggests that the rise to greatness of Chichén Itzá drew people away from the Puuc Hills.

Rediscovered by archaeologists in the 19th century, Uxmal was first excavated in 1929 by Frans Blom. Although much has been restored, there is still a good deal to discover.

Orientation & Information
As you come into the site from the highway, the big new Lodge at Uxmal hotel is on the left, with the Hotel Villa Arqueológica beyond it; the site parking lot is to the right (US$1 per car).

You enter the site through the modern Unidad Uxmal building, which holds the air-conditioned restaurant Yax-Beh, a small museum, shops selling souvenirs and crafts, an auditorium and toilets. The Librería Dante has a good, if expensive, selection of travel and archaeological guides in English, Spanish, German and French.

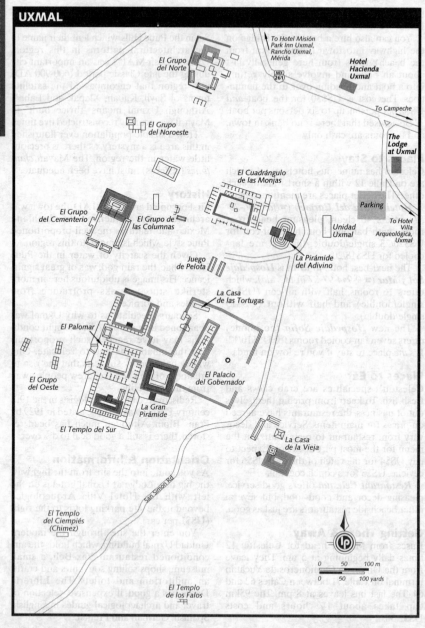

UXMAL

El Grupo del Norte

To Hotel Misión
Park Inn Uxmal,
Rancho Uxmal,
Mérida

MEX 261

Hotel
Hacienda
Uxmal

To Campeche

El Grupo
del Noroeste

The
Lodge
at Uxmal

El Cuadrángulo
de las Monjas

Parking

El Grupo
del Cementerio

El Grupo de
las Columnas

Unidad
Uxmal

To Hotel Villa
Arqueológica,
Uxmal

La Pirámide
del Adivino

Juego
de Pelota

La Casa
de las Tortugas

El Palomar

El Grupo
del Oeste

El Palacio
del Gobernador

La Gran
Pirámide

La Casa
de la Vieja

El Templo del Sur

San Simón Rd

El Templo
del Ciempiés
(Chimez)

0   50   100 m
0   50   100 yards

El Templo
de los Falos

The archaeological site at Uxmal is open 8 am to 5 pm daily (US$7.50, free on Sunday). The Unidad Uxmal building stays open till 10 pm because of the 45-minute Luz y Sonido (Light and Sound) show, held each evening in Spanish (US$4) at 8 pm and English (US$5.50) at 9 pm.

If you come for the day and want to stay for the evening light-and-sound show, plan to have dinner and a swim at one of the restaurants; most hotels allow restaurant patrons to use their pools.

As you pass through the turnstile and climb the slope to the ruins, the rear of the Pirámide del Adivino comes into view.

Pirámide del Adivino

The Pyramid of the Magician, 39m high, was built on an oval base. The smoothly sloping sides have been restored and date from the temple's fifth incarnation. The four earlier temples were almost completely covered in the rebuilding; only the high doorway on the west side was retained from the fourth temple. Decorated in elaborate Chenes style, the doorway proper forms the mouth of a gigantic Chac mask.

The ascent to the doorway and the top is best done from the west side. Heavy chains serve as handrails to help you climb up the steep steps.

From the top of the pyramid, you can survey the rest of the archaeological site. Directly west is the Cuadrángulo de las Monjas; on its south side, down a short slope, is a ruined ball court. Farther south stands the great artificial terrace holding the Palacio del Gobernador; between the palace and the ball court is the small Casa de las Tortugas. Beyond the Palacio del Gobernador are the remains of the Gran Pirámide, and next to it are El Palomar and the Templo del Sur. There once were many other structures at Uxmal, but most have been recaptured by the jungle and are now just verdant mounds.

Cuadrángulo de las Monjas

Archaeologists guess that the 74-room Nunnery Quadrangle might actually have been a military academy, royal school or palace complex. The long-nosed face of Chac appears everywhere on the façades of the four separate temples that form the quadrangle. The northern temple, grandest of the four, was built first, followed by the south, east and west temples.

Several decorative elements on the façades show signs of Mexican, perhaps Totonac, influence. The feathered-serpent (Quetzalcóatl) motif along the top of the west temple's façade is one of these. Note also the stylized depictions of the *na*, or Mayan thatched hut, over some of the doorways in the northern and southern buildings.

Juego de Pelota

Pass through the corbeled arch in the middle of the south building of the quadrangle and continue down the slope to the ball court, which is much less impressive than the one at Chichén Itzá.

Casa de las Tortugas

Climb the steep slope up to the artificial terrace on which stands the Palacio del Gobernador. At the top on the right is the House of the Turtles, which takes its name from the turtles carved on the cornice. The frieze of short columns or 'rolled mats' that runs around the top of the temple is characteristic of the Puuc style. The Maya associated turtles with Chac. According to Mayan myth, when the people suffered from drought so did the turtles, and both prayed to Chac to send rain.

Palacio del Gobernador

The magnificent façade of the Governor's Palace, nearly 100m long, has been called 'the finest structure at Uxmal and the culmination of the Puuc style' by Mayanist Michael D Coe. Buildings in Puuc style have walls filled with rubble, faced with cement and then covered in a thin veneer of limestone squares; the lower part of the façade is plain, the upper part festooned with stylized Chac faces and geometric designs, often latticelike or fretted. Other elements of Puuc style are decorated cornices, rows of half-columns and round columns in doorways.

The stones forming the corbeled vaults in Puuc style are shaped like boots.

Gran Pirámide

Adjacent to the Governor's Palace, the 32m-high Great Pyramid has been restored only on the northern side. Archaeologists theorize the quadrangle at the top was largely destroyed in order to construct another pyramid above it. This work, for reasons unknown, was never completed. At the top are some stucco carvings of Chac, birds and flowers.

El Palomar

West of the Great Pyramid sits a structure whose roof comb is latticed with a pigeon-hole pattern – hence the building is called House of the Pigeons. The nine honey-combed triangular belfries sit atop a building that was once part of a quadrangle. The base is so eroded that it is difficult for archaeologists to guess its function.

Places to Stay & Eat

Budget As there is no town at Uxmal, you cannot depend on finding cheap food or lodging.

Campers can pitch their tents at *Rancho Uxmal* (☎ 950-11-18), 5km north of the ruins on highway 261 (the road to Mérida), for US$2.50 per person. The ranch also offers 28 basic rooms with shower and fan for US$25 double, expensive for what you get. It has a restaurant and a pool (which is usually bone dry for reasons that aren't clear).

Parador Turístico Cana Nah, next door, has a 'trailer park' camping lot as well. Other than these two, there's no cheap lodging in the area. If you don't want to return to Mérida for the night, make your way to Ticul.

Salon Nicté-Ha, just across the highway from the road to the ruins, on the grounds of the Hotel Hacienda Uxmal, is an informal air-conditioned restaurant open 1 to 8 pm daily. It offers sandwiches, fruit salads and similar fare at prices slightly higher than those at the Yax-Beh. There's a swimming pool for restaurant patrons.

Top End Mayaland Resorts' *Hotel Hacienda Uxmal* (☎ 926-20-12, 800-235-4079 in

the USA, fax 926-20-11), 500m from the ruins and across the highway, originally housed the archaeologists who explored and restored Uxmal. An exceptionally comfortable place to stay, the hotel features high ceilings (with fans), tiled verandas, good cross-ventilation and a beautiful swimming pool. Simple rooms in the annex cost US$50 single/double; nicer rooms in the main building cost US$70. Unremarkable meals are moderately priced.

The Lodge at Uxmal (☎ 923-22-02, 800-235-4079 in the USA, fax 925-00-87), another Mayaland Resort property, is just opposite the entrance to the archaeological site and is Uxmal's newest, most luxurious hotel. Rooms with all the comforts cost US$90 single/double with fan, US$120 with air-con. Amenities include a pool and a restaurant-bar.

Hotel Villa Arqueológica Uxmal (☎/fax 928-06-44, ☎ 800-258-2633 in the USA, ☎ 801-802-803 in France), run by Club Med, is an attractive modern hotel with a swimming pool, tennis courts, a French-inspired restaurant and air-conditioned rooms for US$60 single/double.

The hilltop *Hotel Misión Park Inn Uxmal* (☎ 924-73-08, 800-448-8355 in the USA, fax 924-25-16) is 2km north of the turnoff to the ruins. Many rooms have balcony views of Uxmal, but they are a bit overpriced at US$80 single/double. There's a lovely pool.

Getting There & Away

From Mérida's Terminal de Autobuses, it's 80km (1½ hours) to Uxmal. The inland route between Mérida and Campeche passes Uxmal, and most buses coming from the cities will drop you there. But when you want to leave, buses may be full and may not stop.

The daily Ruta Puuc excursion (US$4.50) run by Autotransportes del Sur departs Mérida's old Terminal de Autobuses at 8 am, goes to Uxmal, Kabah and several other sites and leaves the parking lot of Uxmal for the return trip at 2.30 pm, reaching Mérida by 4 pm. If you're going to Ticul, take a northbound bus, get off at Muna and take another bus east to Ticul.

For buses to Kabah, the Puuc Route turnoff and points on the road to Campeche, flag down a bus at the turnoff to the ruins.

RUTA PUUC

Uxmal is undoubtedly the finest Mayan city in the Puuc Hills, but visiting the ruins at Kabah, Sayil, Xlapak and Labná, as well as the impressive Grutas de Loltún (Loltún Caves), will provide you a deeper acquaintance with the Puuc Maya civilization. Kabah's Codz Poop (Palace of Masks) and Sayil's El Palacio are especially worth seeing.

The best way to see these sites is via rental car or guided tour. Many tours of the region can be booked out of Mérida and Cancún. It is also possible to move from one site to another via local bus, but these buses are infrequent.

An excellent option is to make your way to Muna in time to catch a tour bus (US$4) departing for Labná, Xlapak, Sayil, Kabah and Uxmal at 9 am and returning at 2.45 pm. There are no hotels in Muna, but you can stay in Ticul, only 22km away. For more information see the Ticul section later in this chapter.

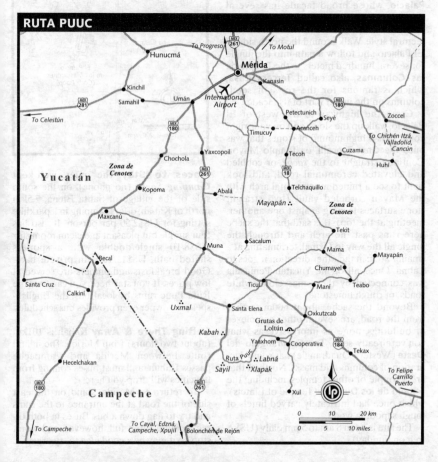

RUTA PUUC

Kabah

The ruins of Kabah, just over 18km southeast of Uxmal, are right astride highway 261. The sign says 'Zona Arqueológica Puuc.' The guard shack and a souvenir shop selling snacks and cold drinks are on the east side of the highway as you approach.

Undoubtedly the most impressive building here is the **Codz Poop** (Palace of Masks), set on its own high terrace on the east side of the highway. It's an amazing sight, with its façade covered in nearly 300 masks of Chac, the rain god or sky serpent.

To the north, past a small pyramid, is **El Palacio**, whose broad façade has several doorways; in the center of each doorway is a column, a characteristic of the Puuc architectural style. Walk around the north side of El Palacio and follow a path into the jungle for several hundred meters to the **Templo de las Columnas**, also called **Tercera Casa**, which is famous for the rows of semi-columns on the upper part of its façade.

Cross the highway to the west of El Palacio, walk up the slope, and on your right you'll pass a high mound of stones that was once the **Gran Teocalli**, or Templo Mayor. Continue straight to the *sacbe*, or cobbled and elevated ceremonial road, and look right to see a ruined monumental arch with the Mayan corbeled vault (two straight stone surfaces leaning against one another, meeting at the top). It is said that the sacbe here runs past the arch and through the jungle all the way to Uxmal, terminating at a smaller arch; in the other direction it goes to Labná. Once, all of the Yucatán Peninsula was connected by these marvelous 'white roads' of rough limestone.

Beyond the sacbe, about 600m farther from the road, are several other complexes of buildings, none as impressive as what you've already seen. The **Cuadrángulo del Oeste** (Western Quadrangle) has some decoration of columns and masks. North of that are a couple of other temples, including the **Templo de los Dinteles** (Temple of Lintels), which once had intricately carved lintels of tough sapodilla wood.

The site is open 8 am to 5 pm daily (US$2, free on Sunday).

KABAH

To Santa Elena, Uxmal, Mérida · MEX 261 · Las Tumbas · Templo Mayor · El Arco · To El Cuadrángulo del Oeste · Office · El Palacio · Templo de las Columnas · La Pirámide de los Mascarones · La Casa de las Brujas · El Palacio de los Mascarones (Codz Poop) · To Sayil, Campeche · MEX 261 · 0 100 200 m · 0 100 200 yards

Places to Stay The quiet, well-kept *Camping Sacbé* (no phone), on the south side of the village of Santa Elena, 7.5km north of Kabah, offers camping in a parklike setting for US$2.50 per person. It also has four simple but pleasant and clean rooms for US$8/10 single/double with a spotless shared bath, US$11/13 with private bath. Good breakfasts and dinners are served at low prices. If you stay here, you can tour the Ruta Puuc ruins by local bus; the English-speaking owner even provides bus schedules.

Getting There & Away Kabah is 101km (about two hours) from Mérida. The inland route between Mérida and Campeche passes Kabah, and most buses coming from the cities will drop you here.

To return to Mérida, stand on the east side of the road at the entrance to the ruins and try to flag down a bus. Buses in both directions are often full, however, and won't stop, so it may be a good idea to try organize a lift back with some other travelers at the site itself. Many visitors come to Kabah by private car and may be willing to give you a lift, either back to Mérida, or southward on the Puuc Route. If you're trying to get a bus to the Puuc Route turnoff, 5km south of Kabah, or to other sites along highway 261 farther south, stand on the west side of the highway.

Sayil

Five kilometers south of Kabah a road turns east off highway 261; this is the Puuc Route. Despite the interesting archaeological sites along the route, there is not much traffic, and hitchhiking can be difficult. The ruins of Sayil are 4.5km east of the junction with highway 261, on the south side of the road. Sayil is open 8 am to 5 pm daily (US$2, free on Sunday).

El Palacio Sayil is best known for El Palacio, the huge three-tiered building with a façade some 85m long reminiscent of the Minoan palaces on Crete. The distinctive columns of Puuc architecture are used here over and over, as supports for the lintels, as decoration between doorways and as a frieze

above the doorways, alternating with huge stylized Chac masks and 'descending gods.'

Climb to the top level and look to the north to see several *chultunes*, stone-lined cisterns in which precious rainwater was collected and stored for use during the dry season. Some of them can hold more than 30,000 liters.

El Mirador If you take the path south from the palace for about 800m you come to the temple named El Mirador, with its interesting roosterlike roof comb once painted bright red. About 100m beyond it by the path to the left is a stela beneath a protective palapa. It bears a relief of a phallic god, now badly weathered.

Xlapak

From the entrance gate at Sayil, it's 6km east to the entrance gate at Xlapak ('shla-PAK'). The name means 'Old Walls' in Maya and was a general term among local people for ancient ruins, about which they knew little. The site is open 8 am to 5 pm daily (US$2, free on Sunday).

The ornate palace at Xlapak is smaller than those at Kabah and Sayil, measuring only about 20m in length. It's decorated with the inevitable Chac masks, columns, colonnades and fretted geometric latticework of the Puuc style. To the right is the rubble of what were once two smaller buildings.

Labná

Archaeologists believe that at one point in the 9th century, some 3000 Maya lived at Labná. To support such numbers in these arid hills, water was collected in chultunes. At Labná's peak there were some 60 chultunes in and around the city; several are still visible. From the entrance gate at Xlapak, it's 3.5km east to the gate at Labná. The site is open 8 am to 5 pm daily (US$2).

El Arco Labná is best known for its magnificent arch, once part of a building that separated two quadrangular courtyards. It now appears to be a gate joining two small plazas. The corbeled structure, 3m wide and 6m

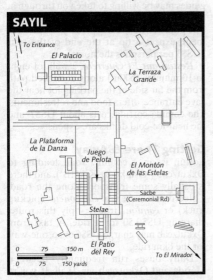

SAYIL

To Entrance
El Palacio
La Terraza Grande
La Plataforma de la Danza
Juego de Pelota
El Montón de las Estelas
Sacbe (Ceremonial Rd)
Stelae
El Patio del Rey
To El Mirador

0   75   150 m
0   75   150 yards

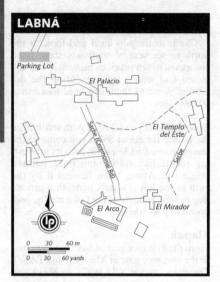

LABNÁ

Parking Lot

El Palacio

El Templo del Este

Sacbe (Ceremonial Rd)

Sacbe

El Arco

El Mirador

0   30   60 m
0   30   60 yards

high, is well preserved and stands close to the site's entrance. The mosaic reliefs decorating the upper façade are exuberantly Puuc in style.

If you look at the ornate work on the northeastern side of the arch, you will make out mosaics of Mayan huts. At the base of either side of the arch are rooms of the adjoining building, now ruined, including upper lattice patterns constructed atop a serpentine design.

El Mirador On the opposite side of the arch and separated from it by the limestone-paved sacbe is a pyramid topped by a temple called El Mirador. The pyramid itself is largely stone rubble. The temple, with its 5m-high roof comb, looks like a watchtower, true to its name.

El Palacio The palace, the first edifice you come to at Labná, is one of the longest buildings in the Puuc region and is connected by a sacbe to El Mirador and the arch. Its design is not as impressive as that of the palace at Sayil. A ghoulish sculpture at the eastern corner of the upper level depicts a serpent gripping a human head in its jaws.

Close to this carving is a well preserved Chac mask.

GRUTAS DE LOLTÚN

From Labná it is 15km east to the village of Yaaxhom, which is surrounded by lush orchards and palm groves – a surprise in this dry region. From Yaaxhom a road goes another 4km northeast to Loltún.

The Loltún Caves, the most interesting and largest cave system in Yucatán, provided a treasure trove of data for archaeologists studying the Maya. Carbon dating of artifacts found here reveals that the caves were first used by humans 2500 years ago. Chest-high murals of hands, faces, animals and geometric motifs were apparent as recently as 20 years ago, but so many people have touched them that scarcely a trace of them remains. Today, visitors to the illuminated caves mostly see natural limestone formations, some of which are quite lovely.

Loltún is open 9 am to 5 pm daily (US$4). To explore the labyrinth you must take a guided tour. The hour-long tours are scheduled at 9.30 and 11 am, and at 12.30, 2, 3 and 4 pm, but they may depart early if enough people are waiting. The English-speaking guides may be willing to take you through at other hours if you offer a few dollars' tip. The guides, who are not paid by the government, expect a tip at the end of the tour (US$3 per person is the norm).

Restaurant El Guerrero, a walk of eight to 10 minutes (600m) along a marked path from the far side of the parking lot near the cave entrance, offers food and refreshments. The comida corrida costs about US$7, and the near-ice-cold drinks are expensive.

Getting There & Away

Loltún is on a country road leading to Oxkutzcab ('Osh-kootz-KAHB'), and there is usually some transport along the road. Colectivos – often a *camioneta* (pickup truck) or *camión* (truck) – ply this route, charging US$0.50 for a ride. A taxi from Oxkutzcab may charge US$6 or so, one-way, for the 8km ride.

Daily buses run frequently between Mérida and Oxkutzcab via Ticul. If you're driving from Loltún to Labná, drive out of the Loltún parking lot, turn right and take the next road on the right, which passes the access road to the restaurant. Do not take the road marked for Xul. After 4km you'll come to the village of Yaaxhom, where you turn right to join the Puuc Route west.

TICUL
• **pop 26,900   ☎ 9**

Ticul, 30km east of Uxmal, is the largest town south of Mérida in this ruin-rich region and has several agreeable hotels and restaurants. It's a center for fine huipil weaving, and ceramics made here from the local red clay are renowned throughout the Yucatán.

Because of the number of Mayan ruins in the vicinity from which to steal building blocks and the number of Mayans in the area needing conversion to Christianity, Franciscan friars built many churches in the region. Among them is the one at Ticul, construction of which dates from the late 16th century. Although looted on several occasions, the church is remarkable for its original touches, among them the choir window, dated 1625 (most likely the year the church

was consecrated); doorway-flanking stone statues of friars in primitive style; and a Black Christ altarpiece ringed by crude medallions.

Saturday mornings here are particularly memorable, as Calle 23 in the vicinity of the public market is closed to motorized traffic and the street fills with rickshas transporting shoppers.

Orientation & Information
Ticul's main street is Calle 23, sometimes called the Calle Principal. It runs from the highway northeast, and goes past the market and the town's best restaurants to Plaza Mayor, the main plaza. A post office and bank face the plaza, and the bus station is less than 100m away.

Places to Stay
The **Hotel Plaza** (☎ 970-19-97, fax 972-00-26), on Calle 23 at Calle 26, is the best hotel in town, offering 17 rooms with air-con, telephone and cable TV for US$22. It also offers five rooms with fan for US$18.

Hotel Sierra Sosa (☎ 972-00-08, fax 972-02-82, Calle 26 No 199A), half a block northwest of the plaza, has basic rooms for US$12

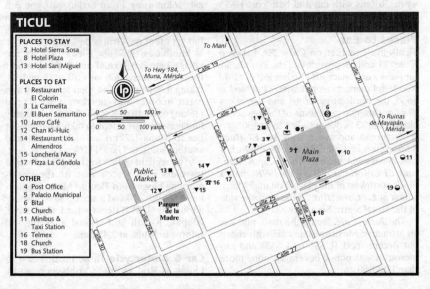

TICUL

PLACES TO STAY
2 Hotel Sierra Sosa
8 Hotel Plaza
13 Hotel San Miguel

PLACES TO EAT
1 Restaurant
     El Colorin
3 La Carmelita
7 El Buen Samaritano
10 Jarro Café
12 Chan Ki-Huic
14 Restaurant Los
     Almendros
15 Lonchería Mary
17 Pizza La Góndola

OTHER
4 Post Office
5 Palacio Municipal
6 Bital
9 Church
11 Minibus &
     Taxi Station
16 Telmex
18 Church
19 Bus Station

To Maní

To Hwy 184,
Muna, Mérida

To Ruinas
de Mayapán,
Mérida

Public
Market

Parque
de la
Madre

Main
Plaza

Statue of Mayan warrior, Ticul

with fan, US$18 with air-con. A few rooms at the back have windows, but most are dark.

Hotel San Miguel (☎ 972-03-82, *Calle 28 No 195*), near Calle 23 and the market, used to be a good deal but its rooms are now worn. Rooms with fan and bath cost US$5 single, US$6 to US$7 double.

Places to Eat

Ticul's lively market, on Calle 28A between Calles 21 and 23, provides all the ingredients for picnics and snacks. It also has lots of those wonderful market eateries where the food is good, the portions generous and the prices low. For variety, try out some of the loncherías along Calle 23 between Calles 26 and 30.

For bread and sweet rolls, try *El Buen Samaritano*, on Calle 23 west of Calle 26. For a sit-down meal, head for the cheap *Restaurant El Colorín* (*Calle 26 No 199B*), half a block northwest of the plaza. You might have a look at *La Carmelita*, on the opposite side of the Hotel Sierra Sosa, as well.

The *Jarro Café*, facing the main plaza, is an attractive Mexican-style café with cheap but decent food (US$1 to US$3) and numerous nonalcoholic beverages, none more than US$1.50.

Pizza La Góndola, Calle 23 at Calle 26A, serves the best pizza in Ticul (US$4 to US$6), but it isn't really all that good. A half-dozen pastas are also available here. *Chan Ki-Huic*, on Calle 23 west of Calle 28, is bright and clean. The *Lonchería Mary*, on Calle 23 east of Calle 28, is a clean, family-run place.

Restaurant Los Almendros (*Calle 23 No 207*), between Calles 26A and 28, specializes in Yucatecan food. The *combinado yucateco* (Yucatecan combination plate), with a soft drink or beer, costs less than US$7. This is the best restaurant in town.

Getting There & Away

Bus Ticul's bus station is behind the massive church off the main square. Autotransportes Mayab makes the 85km, 1½-hour run between Mérida and Ticul every 40 minutes during daylight hours (US$3). There are five buses daily to Felipe Carrillo Puerto (US$7), frequent ones to Oxkutzcab (US$1), nine a day to Chetumal (US$9.50) and eight to Cancún (US$13).

Catch a *combi* (minibus) from the intersection of Calles 20 and 25 in Ticul to Mérida's Parque de San Juan or to Oxkutzcab, 16km away. From Oxkutzcab, you can get a minibus or pickup truck to Loltún (8km); ask for the 'camión to Xul' ('shool'), but get off at the Grutas de Loltún.

Minibuses to Santa Elena (15km), the village between Uxmal and Kabah, depart from the intersection of Calles 23 and 28, taking a back road and then leaving you to catch another bus northwest to Uxmal (15km) or south to Kabah (3.5km). You may find it more convenient to take a minibus or bus to Muna (22km) on highway 261 and another south to Uxmal (16km).

An excellent option for Ruta Puuc-bound travelers is to catch one of the early-morning buses from Ticul to Muna (departing at 6, 6.30, 7.10 and 8 am; US$0.60), where a tour bus (US$4) departs for Labná, Sayil, Xlapak, Kabah and Uxmal at 9 am and returns to Muna at 2.45 pm.

Car & Motorcycle Those headed east to Quintana Roo and the Caribbean coast by car can take highway 184 from Muna and Ticul via Oxkutzcab to Tekax, Tzucacab and Peto. At Polguc, 130km from Ticul, a road turns left (east), ending after 80km in Felipe Carrillo Puerto, 210km from Ticul, where there are hotels, restaurants, fuel stations, banks and other services. The right fork of the road goes south to the region of Bacalar.

From Oxkutzcab to Felipe Carrillo Puerto or Bacalar there are very few places to eat (those that exist are rock-bottom basic), no hotels and few fuel stations. Mostly you see small, typical Yucatecan villages, with their traditional Mayan na (thatched houses), *topes* (speed bumps) and agricultural activity.

Getting Around
The local method of getting around is to hire a three-wheeled cycle, Ticul's answer to the ricksha. You'll see them on Calle 23 just up from the market, and the fare is less than US$0.50 for a short trip.

TICUL TO MÉRIDA
Via Muna & Yaxcopoil
From Ticul to Mérida you have a choice of routes. The western route, to Muna and then north on highway 261, is fastest, with the best bus services.

Muna, an old town 22km northwest of Ticul, has several interesting colonial churches, including the former Convento de la Asunción and the churches of Santa María, San Mateo and San Andrés. It's worth a brief visit, but it has no hotels.

Muna is a major transportation hub for the area. From Muna, it's possible to take Mayab buses to: Mérida (18 buses daily, US$1.70); Felipe Carrillo Puerto (six buses daily, US$6.40); Cancún (at 7 and 10.35 am, US$12.50); Playa del Carmen (at 9 and 11 pm, US$10.60); Uxmal (five buses daily, US$0.50); Ticul and Oxkutzcab (hourly from 5 am to 10 pm, US$0.40 and US$1.10, respectively); Campeche (four buses daily, US$4).

The hacienda of Yaxcopoil, 29km north of Muna on the west side of highway 261, has numerous French Renaissance-style buildings that have been restored and turned collectively into a museum of the 17th century;

open 8 am to 5 pm Tuesday to Saturday, 9 am to 1 pm Sunday (US$2.50). This vast estate specialized in the growing and processing of henequen.

From Yaxcopoil it's 16km north to Umán, then another 17km to the center of Mérida.

Via Ruinas de Mayapán
The eastern route north follows Yucatán state highway 18 from Ticul via the ruins of Mayapán to Tecoh, Acanceh and Mérida. Transport on this route is difficult without a car. Buses and colectivos run sporadically, so you should plan the better part of a day, with stops in Ruinas de Mayapán and Acanceh, to travel the route by public transport.

Those taking this route should be careful to distinguish between Ruinas de Mayapán, the ruins of the ancient city, and Mayapán, a Mayan village some 40km southeast of the ruins past the town of Teabo. If you're driving to the ruins, follow the signs from Ticul northeast via Chapab to Mama (25km), which has a peculiarly fortresslike church, then farther northeast to Tekit (7km). At Tekit, turn left (northwest) on Yucatán state highway 18 toward Tecoh, Acanceh and Kanasin. The Ruinas de Mayapán are 8km northwest of Tekit on the west side of the road.

RUINAS DE MAYAPÁN
The major Mayan capital of Mayapán was huge, with a population estimated at around 12,000. Its ruins cover several square kilometers, all surrounded by a great defensive wall. More than 3500 buildings, 20 cenotes and traces of the city wall were mapped by archaeologists working in the 1950s and early '60s.

However, the city's workmanship was inferior to the great age of Mayan art; though the Cocom rulers of Mayapán tried to revive the past glories of Mayan civilization, they succeeded only in part. A visit to these partially restored ruins after seeing Uxmal or Chichén Itzá will likely disappoint.

History
Mayapán was supposedly founded by Kukulcán (Quetzalcóatl) in 1007, shortly after the former ruler of Tula arrived in

Yucatán. His dynasty, the Cocom, organized a confederation of city-states, including Uxmal and Chichén Itzá. Despite their alliance, animosity between the Cocoms and the Itzaes during the late 1100s led to the storming of Chichén Itzá by the Cocoms, which forced the Itzá rulers into exile. The Cocom dynasty under Hunac Ceel Canuch emerged supreme in all of the northern Yucatán Peninsula and obliged the other rulers to pay tribute.

Cocom supremacy lasted for almost 2½ centuries, until the ruler of Uxmal, Ah Xupán Xiú, led a rebellion of the oppressed city-states and overthrew Cocom hegemony. The great capital of Mayapán was utterly destroyed and remained uninhabited ever after.

But there was no peace in Yucatán after the Xiú victory. The Cocom dynasty recovered, and frequent struggles for power erupted until 1542, when Francisco de Montejo the Younger founded Mérida. The ruler of the Xiú people, Ah Kukum Xiú, submitted his forces to Montejo's control in exchange for a military alliance against the Cocoms. The Cocoms were defeated and – too late – the Xiú rulers realized that they had willingly signed the death warrant of Mayan independence.

The Site

Jungle has returned to cover many of the buildings, but several of the larger ones have been restored, and you can visit several cenotes (including Itzmal Chen, a main Mayan religious sanctuary). Though the ruins today are far less impressive than those at other sites, Mayapán has a stillness and a loneliness (usually undisturbed by other tourists) that seems to fit its sorrowful later history. The site is open 8 am to 5 pm daily (US$2).

RUINAS DE MAYAPÁN TO MÉRIDA

About 2km north of the Ruinas de Mayapán is **Telchaquillo**. Beneath the village plaza is a vast cenote filled with rainwater, which is still used as a water source during the dry months.

From Telchaquillo it's 11km north to **Tecoh**, with its church and well-kept Palacio Municipal separated by a green soccer field. From Tecoh it's only 35km to Mérida, but you should plan a short stop in Acanceh.

The road enters **Acanceh** and goes to the main plaza, which is flanked by a shady park and the church. To the left of the church is a partially restored pyramid (admission US$1.50), and to the right are market loncherías where you can get a snack. In the park, note the statue of the smiling deer; the name 'Acanceh' means 'Pond of the Deer.' Another local sight of interest is the cantina Aqui Me Queda (I'm Staying Here), a ready-made answer for husbands whose wives come to urge them homeward.

Continuing northwest you pass through Petectunich, Tepich, San Antonio and Kanasin before coming to Mérida's *periférico* (ring road).

Campeche State

Of the Yucatán Peninsula's three states, Campeche is the least visited. But it has a lot to offer, including the uncrowded Mayan archaeological sites of Edzná, Calakmul and Chicanná; the impressive walled city of Campeche, with its ancient fortresses and colonial architecture; and the Reserva de la Biósfera Calakmul, Mexico's largest biosphere reserve.

The state is flat, like other parts of the peninsula, but instead of light forest and brush, 30% of Campeche's 56,000 sq km is covered with jungle. Marshlands, ponds and inlets are common along the state's coastline, which faces the dark and generally uninviting waters of the Gulf of Mexico.

CAMPECHE
● pop 178,200 ☎ 9

During its heyday in the 16th and 17th centuries, the wealthy city of Campeche was a favorite target of raids by pirates. To protect against further attack, the city erected a protective wall and *baluartes* (bastions) around the city in the late 17th century. Today these fortifications, along with some still-standing mansions of upper-class Spanish families and other colonial constructions, are the city's chief attractions. Of the eight bastions, seven survive in their original state and one has been restored. Large segments of Campeche's famous wall have survived as well.

History

Campeche was once a Mayan trading village called Ah Kim Pech (Lord Sun Sheep-Tick). The Spanish first arrived in 1517, but, faced with strong Mayan resistance, were unable to fully conquer the region for nearly 25 years. Colonial Campeche was founded in 1531 and later abandoned because of Mayan hostility. By 1540 the conquistadors had gained sufficient control, under the leadership of Francisco de Montejo the Younger, to found a settlement that survived. They named it Villa de San Francisco de Campeche, and under the careful planning of Viceroy Hernández de Córdoba, the settlement soon flourished as the major port of the Yucatán Peninsula. Locally grown timber, chicle and dyewoods were major exports to Europe, as were gold and silver mined from other regions and shipped out of Campeche.

Such wealth did not escape the notice of pirates. For two centuries they terrorized Campeche, attacking ships, invading the port, robbing and raping its citizens and burning its buildings. In their most gruesome assault, in early 1663, the various pirate hordes set aside their jealousies to converge as a single flotilla upon the city and massacre many of its residents.

It took this tragedy to make the Spanish monarchy take preventive action, but not for five years. Starting in 1668, 3.5m-thick ramparts were built. After 18 years of construction, a 2.5km hexagon incorporating eight strategically placed baluartes surrounded the city. A segment of the ramparts extended out to sea so that ships literally had to sail into a fortress, easily defended, to gain access to the city.

Orientation

Though the baluartes still stand, the city walls themselves have been mostly razed and replaced by Avenida Circuito Baluartes, which rings the city center just as the walls once did.

Many of the city's downtown streets are paved with cut stone taken from the segments of the wall that were brought down.

Besides the modern Plaza Moch-Cuouh, Campeche has its Parque Principal, also called the Plaza de la Independencia. This standard Spanish colonial park has a cathedral on one side and the former Palacio de Gobierno on another.

According to the compass, Campeche is oriented with its waterfront to the northwest, but tradition and convenience hold that the water is to the west and inland is to the east; this book observes that rule. The street grid is numbered so that streets running north-south have even numbers and east-west streets have odd numbers; street numbers ascend toward the south and east.

Information

Tourist Offices A state-run General de Turismo (☎ 816-60-68, 816-67-67) is on Calle 57, opposite the Parque Principal. The staff is very friendly and available 9 am to 1 pm and 5 to 8 pm daily.

The city runs a Coordinación Municipal de Turismo, on Calle 55 at Calle 8, just west of the cathedral facing the Parque Principal. It does not maintain regular hours.

Money Banks are open 9 am to 4 pm Monday to Friday, 9 am to 1 pm Saturday. Most have ATMs.

Post & Communications The central post office is at the corner of Avenida 16 de Septiembre and Calle 53, in the Edificio Federal. Hours are 8 am to 7 pm Monday to Friday, 8 am to 1 pm Saturday, 8 am to 2 pm Sunday.

The air-conditioned En Red Cibercafé, at the corner of Calle 12 and Avenida Circuito Baluartes Sur, is open 9.30 am to 11.30 pm Monday to Friday and 11.30 am to 9.30 pm Saturday and Sunday. Cost is US$1 for 30 minutes; coffee and sodas are available.

Walking Tour

To see the baluartes, follow Avenida Circuito Baluartes around the city (it's a 2km walk). Because of traffic, you might want to limit your excursion to the first three or four

CAMPECHE

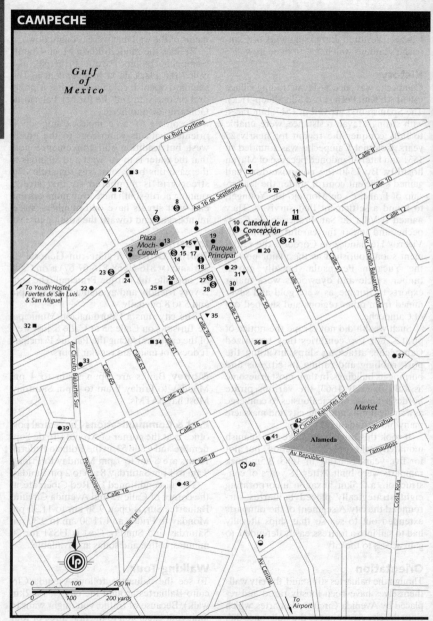

Gulf of Mexico

Av Ruiz Cortines

Calle 8

Calle 10

Calle 12

Av 16 de Septiembre

Plaza Moch-Cuouh

Catedral de la Concepción

Parque Principal

Av Circuito Baluartes Norte

Calle 51

Calle 53

Calle 55

To Youth Hostel
Fuertes de San Luis
& San Miguel

Calle 57

Calle 59

Calle 61

Calle 63

Av Circuito Baluartes Sur

Calle 14

Calle 16

Calle 18

Pedro Moreno

Calle 16

Calle 18

Av Circuito Baluartes Este

Market

Alameda

Chihuahua

Tamaulipas

Costa Rica

Av República

Av Central

To Airport

0   100   200 m
0   100   200 yards

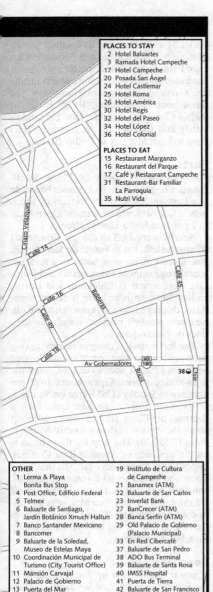

PLACES TO STAY
2 Hotel Baluartes
3 Ramada Hotel Campeche
17 Hotel Campeche
20 Posada San Ángel
24 Hotel Castlemar
25 Hotel Roma
26 Hotel América
30 Hotel Regis
32 Hotel del Paseo
34 Hotel López
36 Hotel Colonial

PLACES TO EAT
15 Restaurant Marganzo
16 Restaurant del Parque
17 Café y Restaurant Campeche
31 Restaurant-Bar Familiar
   La Parroquia
35 Nutri Vida

OTHER
1 Lerma & Playa
   Bonita Bus Stop
4 Post Office, Edificio Federal
5 Telmex
6 Baluarte de Santiago,
   Jardín Botánico Xmuch Haltun
7 Banco Santander Mexicano
8 Bancomer
9 Baluarte de la Soledad,
   Museo de Estelas Maya
10 Coordinación Municipal de
   Turismo (City Tourist Office)
11 Mansión Carvajal
12 Palacio de Gobierno
13 Puerta del Mar
14 Inverlat Bank
18 Coordinación General
   de Turismo
19 Instituto de Cultura
   de Campeche
21 Banamex (ATM)
22 Baluarte de San Carlos
23 Inverlat Bank
27 BanCrecer (ATM)
28 Banca Serfin (ATM)
29 Old Palacio de Gobierno
   (Palacio Municipal)
33 En Red Cibercafé
37 Baluarte de San Pedro
38 ADO Bus Terminal
39 Baluarte de Santa Rosa
40 IMSS Hospital
41 Puerta de Tierra
42 Baluarte de San Francisco
43 Baluarte de San Juan
44 Sindicato del Campesino
   (Bus to Edzná)

baluartes described, which house museums and gardens. If you'd rather have a guided tour, sign up for a city tour (US$20) at the Ramada Inn.

Start at the southwestern end of the Plaza Moch-Cuouh. Half a block from the modern Palacio de Gobierno, at the intersection of Calles 8 and 63, near a ziggurat fountain, is **Baluarte de San Carlos**. The interior is now arranged as the Sala de las Fortificaciones (Chamber of Fortifications), with some scale models of the city's fortifications in the 18th century. You can also visit the dungeon and the roof. Baluarte de San Carlos is open 9 am to 1 pm and 5 to 7.30 pm daily (free).

Head back north along Calle 8. At the intersection with Calle 59, notice the **Puerta del Mar** (Sea Gate), which provided access to the city from the sea before the area to the northwest was filled in. The gate was demolished in 1893 but rebuilt in 1957 when its historical value was realized.

Baluarte de la Soledad, on the north side of the Plaza Moch-Cuouh near the intersection of Calles 8 and 57, is the setting for the **Museo de Estelas Maya**. Many of the Mayan stelae are badly weathered, but the precise line drawing next to each stone shows you what the designs once looked like. The museum also has an exhibit on colonial Campeche. Among the antiquities displayed are 17th- and 18th-century seafaring equipment, and armaments used to battle pirates. The museum is open 9 am to 2 pm and 3 to 8 pm Tuesday to Saturday, 9 am to 1 pm Sunday (US$1).

Just across the street from Baluarte de la Soledad is **Parque Principal**, Campeche's favorite park. Whereas the sterile, modernistic, shadeless Plaza Moch-Cuouh was built to glorify its government builders, Parque Principal is where locals spend their time.

On the north side of the park is the **Catedral de la Concepción**, where latecomers to Sunday mass can often be seen huddled around the buildings' entrances. Construction of the cathedral began in the mid-16th century, shortly after the conquistadors established the town, but wasn't completed until 1705.

Continue north along Calle 8 several blocks to **Baluarte de Santiago**, at the intersection of Calles 8 and 51. It houses the minuscule yet lovely **Jardín Botánico Xmuch Haltun**, with 250 species of tropical plants set around a courtyard of fountains. The garden is open 8 am to 7 pm Tuesday to Sunday (free); tours are given between 5 and 6 pm Tuesday to Friday.

From Baluarte de Santiago, walk inland along Calle 51 to Calle 18, where you'll come to **Baluarte de San Pedro**, in the middle of a complex traffic intersection that marks the beginning of Avenida Gobernadores. Within the baluarte is the Exposición Permanente de Artesanías, a regional crafts sales center; open 9 am to 2 pm and 5 to 8 pm Monday to Friday (free).

To make the entire circuit, head south from Baluarte de San Pedro along Avenida Circuito Baluartes to **Baluarte de San Francisco**, at Calle 57, and, a block farther at Calle 59, the **Puerta de Tierra** (Land Gate). **Baluarte de San Juan**, at Calles 18 and 65, marks the southernmost point of the old city walls. Bear right from here along Calle 67 (Avenida Circuito Baluartes) to the intersection of Calles 14 and 67 and **Baluarte de Santa Rosa**. From here Avenida Circuito Baluartes leads back to Calle 8 and the Plaza Moch-Cuouh.

Evening Stroll

To see some beautiful houses, many painted in cheerful pastels with white trim, walk through Campeche's streets – especially Calles 55, 57 and 59 – in the evening, when the sun is not blazing, and interior lighting illuminates courtyards, salons and alleys.

Centro Cultura

Housed in an 18th-century building beside Parque Principal, the Cultural Center displays furniture from the 18th and 19th centuries and gives a good idea of how the city's high society lived back then. It also contains several interactive exhibits on the main tourist attractions in the city and state of Campeche. Open 9 am to 9 pm daily (free).

Mansión Carvajal

The Mansión Carvajal, on Calle 10 between Calles 51 and 53, started its eventful history as the city residence of Don Fernando Carvajal Estrada, one of Campeche's richest hacendados, and his wife, Señora María Iavalle de Carvajal. The monogram you see throughout the building, 'RCY,' is that of Rafael Carvajal Ytorralde, Don Fernando's father and founder of the fortune. Open 8 am to 2 pm Monday to Friday (free).

Forts

Four kilometers south of Plaza Moch-Cuouh along the coast road stands **Fuerte de San Luis**, an 18th-century fortress of which only a few battlements remain. Open 8 am to 7 pm Tuesday to Sunday (free).

Nearby, a road off to the left (southeast) climbs the hill 1km to **Fuerte de San Miguel**, a restored fortress now home to a museum containing exquisite vases, masks and plates that were found at Calakmul and Edzná, and at Jaina, an island site north of town. Also displayed are Mayan arrowheads, weapons, seashell necklaces and clay figurines of various gods.

The fort is itself a thing of beauty, having been restored to mint condition and topped with more than a dozen cannons. Even the drawbridge works. Open 8 am to 7 pm Tuesday to Sunday (US$1, free on Sunday).

To reach Fuerte de San Luis, take a 'Lerma' or 'Playa Bonita' bus southwest along the coastal highway toward Villahermosa (US$0.20). The stop for these buses is on the west side of Avenida Ruiz Cortines, opposite the Puerta del Mar. Tell the driver when you board to take you to Fuerte de San Luis. You will be let out at the turnoff for the fort, Avenida Escenica, which is opposite Fuerte de San Miguel. The walk from the coastal road up the hill to the fort is only 1km, but it's arduous.

Beaches

If you're really hard up for a swim, head southwest to the town of Seybaplaya, 33km from Plaza Moch-Cuouh. The highway skirts narrow, pure-white beaches dotted with fishing shacks. The best beach is called

Payucan. The beaches don't overlook turquoise waters like those on the eastern coast of the peninsula, but they are pleasant all the same.

Organized Tours

City tours are offered from the Puerta de Tierra at 10 am and 4 pm daily (US$8). Tours to Edzná also depart from the Puerta de Tierra, at 9 am and 2 pm (US$15).

Places to Stay

Budget Campeche's hostel, *Albergue de la Juventud* (☎ 816-18-02), is in the Centro Cultural y Deportivo Universitario, on Avenida Agustín Melgar, 3.5km southwest of the Plaza Moch-Cuouh off the shore road. Dormitory beds cost US$4 per night, and a cafeteria serves inexpensive meals. The shore road is Avenida Ruiz Cortines in town, but becomes Avenida Resurgimiento as it heads toward Villahermosa. Buses marked 'Avenida Universidad' will take you there. Ask the driver to let you off at the Albergue de la Juventud. Avenida Melgar heads inland between a Volkswagen dealership and a Pemex gasoline station. The hostel is 150m up on the right.

Of the cheapest hotels, only *Hotel Castlemar*, on Calle 8 at Calle 61, and *Hotel Roma*, on Calle 10 between Calles 59 and 61, are worth trying. They're dumpy (expect peeling paint and missing patches of plaster), but they usually charge only US$5 per room. Centrally located *Hotel Campeche* (☎ 816-51-83, Calle 57 No 2), above Café y Restaurant Campeche facing Parque Principal, charges US$10 for rooms with cold water, US$12 with hot water.

Readers report it's noisy, but *Hotel Colonial* (☎ 816-22-22, Calle 14 No 122) is popular with budget travelers. Housed in what was once the mansion of Doña Gertrudis Eulalia Torostieta y Zagasti, former Spanish governor of Tabasco and Yucatán, the rooms have good showers with hot water. Rates are US$11/13 single/double with fan, US$16/18 with air-con.

Posada San Ángel (☎ 816-77-18, Calle 10 No 307) has 14 modern, clean, spartan rooms with private bath; US$13/16 with fan,

US$18/21 with air-con. Some sheets need replacing, so ask to see several rooms before registering.

Mid-Range The *Hotel América* (☎ 816-45-88, fax 816-45-76, www.campeche.com.mx/hamerica, Calle 10 No 252) is a converted colonial house with 49 spacious, spartan rooms ringing an interior court. Singles with fan cost US$17. Doubles with fan cost US$24, with air-con US$29.

Hotel López (☎ 816-33-44, fax 816-24-88, Calle 12 No 189) offers slightly less appealing rooms and charges US$17 single/double with fan, US$29 with air-con. *Hotel Regis* (☎ 816-31-75, Calle 12 No 148) is conveniently located and has adequate air-conditioned rooms for US$24/28.

Top End The best value is *Hotel del Paseo* (☎ 811-01-00, 811-00-77, fax 811-00-97, cslavall@etzna.uacam.mx, Calle 8 No 215), with 42 air-conditioned rooms for US$35/40 single/double and six suites for US$60. It has a restaurant and bar but no pool.

The well-used rooms at *Hotel Baluartes* (☎ 816-39-11, fax 816-24-10, baluarte@campeche.sureste.com), on Ruiz Cortines, have air-con, and half of them have sea views. Rates are US$35/40, and there's a pool.

The 119-room *Ramada Hotel Campeche* (☎ 816-22-33, fax 811-16-18, Avenida Ruiz Cortines 51) charges US$90 single/double, US$150 for a master suite. It has a restaurant, bar, pool and disco.

Places to Eat

Among the best eateries in town is the air-conditioned *Restaurant Marganzo*, on Calle 8 between Calles 57 and 59, facing the sea and Baluarte de la Soledad. Breakfast costs US$3 to US$4, lunch and dinner US$3 to US$8; the menu includes lots of regional dishes and shrimp.

Café y Restaurant Campeche, on Calle 57 opposite Parque Principal, is simple, bright with fluorescent lights and loud with a blaring TV set. Few dishes cost more than US$3.

In the same block facing the plaza is *Restaurant del Parque*, a cheerful little place serving fish, meat and shrimp for around US$4 a platter.

Every now and then a brave entrepreneur opens a natural foods restaurant in Campeche, only to close soon after. Hopefully the *Nutri Vida*, Calle 12 No 167, will still be in business when you visit.

Perhaps the best known restaurant in town is *Restaurant-Bar Familiar La Parroquía*, on Calle 55 between Calles 10 and 12. This complete restaurant-café-hangout serves breakfasts Monday to Friday for US$2.50 to US$4, as well as substantial regional lunches and dinners for under US$10.

Entertainment

Every Sunday at 7 pm in Parque Principal you can hear popular Campeche music free, performed by the Banda del Estado (the State Band). Every Saturday from 7 to 11 pm at the Plaza Moch-Cuouh, near the Puerta del Mar, you can enjoy performances of the traditional folkloric music and dancing of Campeche; also free and very popular.

Getting There & Away

Air The airport is at the end of Avenida López Portillo (Avenida Central), 3.5km from Plaza Moch-Cuouh. You must take a taxi (US$5) to the city center.

Bus Campeche's 1st-class ADO bus terminal is on Avenida Gobernadores, 1.7km from Plaza Moch-Cuouh and about 1.5km from most hotels. The 2nd-class terminal is directly behind it.

Here's information on daily buses from Campeche:

Cancún – 512km, 9 hours; 2 buses, at 10 pm and 11.30 pm only (US$12 to US$15); better to catch any bus to Mérida, then catch a Cancún-bound bus

Chetumal – 422km, 7 hours; 1 bus, at noon (US$11 to US$14)

Edzná – 66km, 1½ hours; catch bus to Pich or Hool from the Sindicato del Campesino on Avenida Central, or take a faster bus to San Antonio Cayal (45km) and hitch south from there

Hopelchén – 86km, 2 hours; 8 Autobuses del Sur 2nd-class (US$2)

Mérida – 195km (short route via Becal), 2½ to 3 hours, or 250km (long route via Uxmal), 4 hours; 10 ADO (US$7), ATS every 30 minutes (US$6)

Mexico City (TAPO) – 1360km, 20 hours; 2 ADO, at 3.30 and 4 pm (US$57)

Palenque – 362km, 6 hours; 1 ADO (US$13), 2 Colón (US$13), 2 ATS (US$10); many other buses drop you at Catazajá (Palenque turnoff), 27km north of Palenque town

San Cristóbal de Las Casas – 820km, 14 hours; 2 Colón, at 10.10 pm (US$15 to US$18), 1 Maya de Oro (US$24)

Villahermosa – 450km, 6 hours; 15 buses (US$14 to US$17); they'll drop you at Catazajá (Palenque junction) if you like

Xpujil – 306km, 6 hours; one ADO, at noon (US$8), 4 ATS (US$8)

CAMPECHE TO MÉRIDA – SHORT ROUTE (HWY 180)

This is the fastest way to get between the two cities, and if you buy a bus ticket from Campeche to Mérida this is the route your bus will likely follow. If you'd prefer to go the long way via Edzná, Kabah and Uxmal, ask for a seat on one of the less frequent long-route buses. If you'd like to stop at one of the towns along the short route, catch a 2nd-class bus.

Hecelchakan, Calkini & Becal

At Hecelchakan, 77km northeast of Campeche, is the impressive **Museo de Hecelchakan**, housing burial artifacts from Jaina and ceramics and jewelry from other sites. The museum also exhibits many artists' renditions of ancient Maya going about their daily lives. It's in a restored colonial building facing the main plaza; open 9 am to 6 pm Tuesday to Saturday (US$2).

The **Iglesia de San Francisco** is said to be built on the foundation of a Mayan temple. The mission dates from the 16th century, but its dramatic features – a massive octagonal dome and a pair of monumental bell towers – are 18th-century additions. The church is the center of festivities on October 4, the day the townsfolk celebrate their patron saint. From August 9 to 18 (give or take a day or two), a popular festival called the Novenario is held, with bullfights, dancing and refreshments.

From Hecelchakan it's 24km to Calkini, site of the 17th-century **Iglesia de San Luis de Tolosa**, with a plateresque portal and lots of baroque decoration. The Festival of San Luis is celebrated here August 19.

Becal, 8km from Calkini near the border with the state of Yucatán, is a center of the Yucatán Peninsula's panama-hat trade. The soft, pliable hats, called *jipijapas* by locals, have been woven by townsfolk from the fibers of the huano palm tree in small, humid limestone caves since the mid-19th century. There's at least one cave on every block, generally reached by a hole in the ground in someone's backyard. They provide just the right atmosphere for shaping the fibers, keeping them pliable and minimizing breakage. About 1000 of the town's 3000 adult residents make their living making hats, which cost US$10 to US$50. From Becal it's 85km to Mérida.

CAMPECHE TO MÉRIDA – LONG ROUTE (HWY 261)

Most travelers take the long route from Campeche to Mérida in order to visit the various ruin sites on the way.

Edzná

The closest ruins to Campeche are 61km southeast, at Edzná, which means both 'House of Grimaces' and 'House of Echoes.' The site was settled from approximately 600 BC to 1500 AD. Most of the carvings visible at the site date from between 550 and 810 AD.

Though a long way from such Puuc Hill sites as Uxmal and Kabah, Edzná's architecture is similar to Puuc style. Archaeologists believe Edzná was an independent kingdom. What led to its decline and gradual abandonment remains a mystery.

Although the archaeological zone covers 2 sq km, the best part is the **Plaza Principal**, which is 160m long, 100m wide and surrounded by temples. Every Mayan site has huge masses of stone, but at Edzná there are cascades of it – terrace upon terrace of bleached limestone.

The major temple, the 30m-high **Edificio de los Cinco Pisos** (Temple of Five Levels), is to the left as you enter the plaza from the ticket kiosk. Built on a vast platform, it rises five levels from base to roof comb, with vaulted rooms and some weathered decoration of masks, serpents and jaguars' heads on each level. A great central staircase of 65 steps rises to the top. The temple was erected over five different construction periods. The one that's visible today, a hybrid of a pyramid and a palace, belongs primarily to the Puuc architectural style. The impressive roof comb atop the temple is a clear reference to the sacred buildings at Tikal, in Guatemala.

In the **Templo de los Mascarones** (Temple of the Masks) are portrayals of the sun god. The central motif is that of a head of a Mayan man whose face has the appearance of a jaguar.

The **Plataforma de los Cuchillos** (Platform of the Knives), near the entrance of the site, takes its name from the offerings of flint knives found within it. On top it's still possible to see several walls that once formed rooms, which archaeologists suspect were used by high-ranking figures.

The **Nohochná** (Big House), on the main plaza, was topped by four long halls that likely served administrative tasks. The built-in benches facing the main plaza clearly were designed to serve spectators of special events.

On the opposite (right) side of the plaza as you enter is a monumental staircase 100m wide, which once led up to the **Casa de la Luna** (House of the Moon), one of the site's numerous temples. At the far end of the plaza is a ruined temple that may have been the priests' quarters.

Edzná is open 8 am to 5 pm daily (US$4, free on Sunday).

Getting There & Away Picazh Servicios Turísticos (☎ 816-44-26, fax 816-27-60, Calle 16 No 348), between Calles 57 and 59 in Campeche, runs excursions to Edzná (US$15, not including admission; US$5 extra for a guided tour in Spanish or English). The trips require two or more people and depart daily from the plaza next to the Puerta de Tierra at 9 am and 2 pm.

You also can catch a 2nd-class village bus early in the morning headed for Edzná from near the Sindicato del Campesino, in Campeche on Avenida Central east of the Circuito Baluartes; it may be a bus going to Pich, 15km southeast of Edzná, or to Hool, 25km southwest. Either will drop you at the access road to the site.

Coming from the north or the east, get off at San Antonio Cayal and catch a bus 20km south to Edzná.

A sign just north of the Edzná turnoff on highway 261 says 'Edzná 2km,' but the ruins are just 500m beyond the sign, only about 400m off the highway.

When you leave you'll have to depend on flagging down a bus to get you to San Antonio Cayal, where you can catch a bus west back to Campeche or east and north to Hopelchén, Bolonchén and ultimately Uxmal.

Bolonchén de Rejón & Xtacumbilxunaan

Forty kilometers east of San Antonio Cayal is Hopelchén, where highway 261 turns north. The next town to appear out of the flat, dry jungle is Bolonchén de Rejón, after

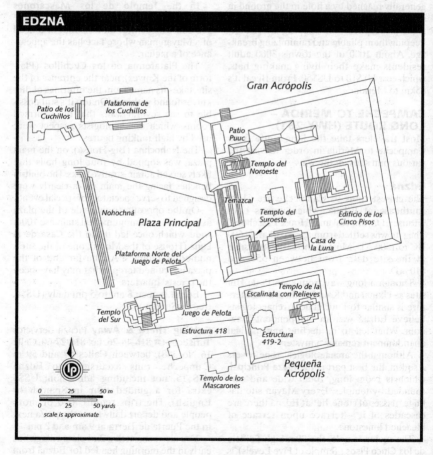

EDZNÁ

Gran Acrópolis

Patio de los Cuchillos

Plataforma de los Cuchillos

Patio Puuc

Templo del Noroeste

Temazcal

Templo del Suroeste

Edificio de los Cinco Pisos

Nohochná

Plaza Principal

Casa de la Luna

Plataforma Norte del Juego de Pelota

Templo de la Escalinata con Relieves

Templo del Sur

Juego de Pelota

Estructura 418

Estructura 419-2

Pequeña Acrópolis

Templo de los Mascarones

0   25   50 m
0   25   50 yards
scale is approximate

34km. Its local festival of Santa Cruz is held each year on May 3.

Bolonchén is near the Grutas de Xtacumbilxunaan ('SHTAA-koom-beel-shoo-NAHN'), about 3km south of town. You can visit the cavern by taking a 30- to 45-minute tour with the guide-caretaker for the price of a tip. The wet, slippery cave holds no art or other objects and has few stalactites and stalagmites. Off a trail that winds through it, there appears to be a bottomless pit; the guide will tell you there's a cenote at the bottom, and there may well be, but it's inaccessible. The cave is 'open' whenever the caretaker is around, usually during daylight hours.

Highway 261 continues into Yucatán state to Uxmal, with a side road leading to the ruins along the Ruta Puuc. See the Uxmal and Ruta Puuc sections earlier in this chapter for more information.

ESCÁRCEGA
• pop 25,200   ☎ 9

Most buses between Villahermosa, in Tabasco, and the Yucatán Peninsula stop in Escárcega to give passengers a refreshment break. But there is no other reason to stop in this town at the junction of highways 186 and 261, 150km south of Campeche and 301km from Villahermosa. Indeed, as most buses arrive in town full and depart in the same condition, you may find it difficult to get out of Escárcega if you break your trip here.

The town is spread along 2km of highway 186 toward Chetumal. It's 1.7km between the ADO and Autobuses del Sur bus stations. The ADO station is at the junction of the highways, whereas the 2nd-class bus station is on highway 186 on the west side of intersection. Most hotels are nearer to the Autobuses del Sur station; most of the good restaurants are near the ADO station.

ESCÁRCEGA TO XPUJIL

Highway 186 heads due east from Escárcega through the scrubby jungle to Chetumal, in Quintana Roo, a 261km, three-hour ride.

The largest town between Escárcega and Chetumal – and the only one with accommodations – is Xpujil ('shpu-HEEL'), on highway 186 about 20km west of the Campeche-Quintana Roo border. The only gasoline station between Escárcega and Chetumal is about 5km east of Xpujil.

Between Escárcega and Xpujil are numerous archaeological sites, all of which are being restored. The most significant historically is Calakmul, which also is the most difficult to reach; from the highway to the ruins it's a 60km trip in each direction on a paved road, which winds through some light rain forest. It is not reachable by bus, but it's possible to hire a taxi in Xpujil.

Balamku

Discovered only in 1990, Balamku is famous for the exquisite façade of one building. It's decorated with a well-preserved stylized bas relief figure of a jaguar flanked by two large mask designs, and it's topped with designs of other animals and humans. This elaborate, unusual design bears little resemblance to any of the known decorative elements in the area's characteristic Chenes and Río Bec styles and has mystified archaeologists.

Balamku is 60km west of Xpujil junction (less than 3km west of the town of Conhuas), then just under 3km north of the highway along a paved road. Admission costs US$1. A round-trip taxi ride from Xpujil with a one-hour visit costs US$30.

Calakmul

Most Mayanists agree that Calakmul (Adjacent Mounds) is an important site – it's larger than Tikal, in Guatemala – but so far only a fraction of its 100-sq-km expanse has been cleared, and few of its 6500 buildings have been consolidated, let alone restored.

The ruins, at the heart of the vast, untrammeled Reserva de la Biósfera Calakmul, were discovered in 1931 by American botanist Cyrus Lundell. Like Tikal, they are surrounded by rain forest, which is best viewed from the top of one of the several pyramids. A visit to these ruins represents the best opportunity to explore the biosphere reserve without risk of getting lost in the jungle.

From about 250 to 750 AD, Calakmul was the leading city in a vast region known as the Kingdom of the Serpent's Head. Its perpetual rival was Tikal, and its decline began with the power struggles and internal conflicts that followed the defeat by Tikal of Calakmul's king Garra de Jaguar (Jaguar Claw).

As at Tikal, there are indications that construction occurred over a period of more than a millennium. Beneath Edificio VII, archaeologists discovered a burial crypt with some 2000 pieces of jade. Other jade offerings were found beneath other structures. The site boasts at least 120 carved stelae, though many are eroded.

Calakmul is open 8 am to 5 pm daily (US$2.50). There's a 500m walk from the parking lot to the ruins. A round-trip taxi ride from Xpujil with a two-hour visit costs US$50.

Chicanná

Almost 12km west of the Xpujil junction and 800m south of the highway, Chicanná (House of the Snake's Jaws) is a mixture of Chenes and Río Bec architectural styles buried in the jungle. The city flourished from about 660 to 680 AD.

Enter through the modern palapa admission building, then follow the rock paths through the jungle to Grupo D and Edificio XX (750-830 AD), which boasts two monster-mouth doorways, one above the other, topped by a roof comb.

A five-minute walk along the jungle path brings you to Grupo C, with two low buildings (Edificios X and XI) on a raised platform.

The buildings in Grupo B have some intact decoration, and there's a good roof comb on Edificio VI.

At the end of the path is Chicanná's most famous building, Edificio II (750-770 AD) in Grupo A, with its gigantic Chenes-style monster-mouth doorway, believed to depict the jaws of the god Itzamná, lord of the heavens, creator of all things.

Chicanná is open 8 am to 5 pm (US$1.50). A round-trip taxi ride from Xpujil with a one-hour visit costs US$10.

Becán

Becán ('Path of the Snake' in Mayan) sits atop a rock outcrop. It is well named, as a 2km moat snakes its way around the entire city to protect it from attack. Seven causeways once crossed the now-dry moat, providing access to the city. Becán was occupied from 550 BC until 1000 AD.

This is among the largest and most elaborate sites in the area. The first building you reach, Edificio I on the Plaza Sureste (Southeast Plaza), has two towers typical of Río Bec style. Climb a stairway on the east side of the building to get to the plaza, which is surrounded by four large temples and has a circular altar (Edificio III-A) on the east side.

Arrows direct you to a path that leaves the plaza's northeast corner and descends a flight of stairs, then turns left (west) and passes along a rock-walled walkway and beneath a corbeled arch. At the end of the path is a huge twin-towered temple with cylindrical columns at the top of a flight of stairs. This is Edificio VIII, dating from about 600 to 730 AD. The view from the top is good in all directions.

Northwest of Edificio VIII is the Plaza Central, surrounded by the 30m-high Edificio IX, tallest building at the site, and the better-looking Edificio X.

More ruins await in the jungle. The West Plaza, west of Edificio X, is surrounded by low buildings, one of which is a ball court.

Becán is 400m north of the highway; open 8 am to 5 pm (US$1.50). A round-trip taxi ride from Xpujil with a one-hour visit costs US$10.

XPUJIL

The hamlet of Xpujil (Place of the Cattails, in Mayan), at the junction of the east-west and northern highways, is growing into a village and is a great base from which to visit the area's archaeological sites, but services are still few and basic. There is no bank or laundry, and the nearest gasoline station is 5km east of town. Several restaurants, three hotels and a taxi stand are near the bus depot.

From the junction, the Xpujil ruins are 1.5km west, Becán is 8km west, Chicanná is 11.5km west, and Balamku is 60km west.

Places to Stay & Eat

About 1km west of the bus station is **Mirador Maya** (☎ 9-871-6028, fax 9-871-6005), with nine bungalows and two new rooms. The rooms include, fan and private bath with hot water for US$30. Two of the bungalows look rustic from the outside but they're OK, with fan, private bath and two beds in each for US$20. The seven other bungalows are definitely rustic and have a shared bath for US$15.

About 300m west of the bus station, **Hotel Calakmul** (☎ 9-871-60-29) has four comfy new rooms with air-con, private bath and TV for US$25. The hotel also has nine cabins with four shared baths for US$12.

Each hotel has a restaurant, and those are the best eateries along the highway.

Ramada Chicanná Ecovillage Resort (☎/fax 9-876-22-33), highway 186 at Km 144, 12km west of Xpujil junction, then 500m north of the highway, has large, airy rooms with private bath and ceiling fan for US$75 to US$95. The rooms are grouped four to a bungalow and set amid lawns. The small dining room and bar serve decent but expensive meals.

Getting There & Around

Xpujil is 220km south of Hopelchén, 153km east of Escárcega and 120km west of Chetumal. There are seven buses between Xpujil and Campeche every day, and four between Xpujil and Chetumal. No buses originate in Xpujil, so you must hope to find a vacant seat on one passing through. The bus station is 100m east of the highway junction in Xpujil, on the north side of the highway.

The Xpujil ruins are within walking distance of Xpujil junction. You may be able to hitch a ride to the access roads for Becán and Chicanná, but for other sites you will need to join a tour. Your own wheels will get you to the sites along the highway, but you may want to abandon them and join a

tour to Calakmul or Hormiguero, relying on the guide's 4WD vehicle to get you there and back.

Ruins

The Mayan city of Xpujil flourished from 400 to 900 AD, though a settlement existed here much earlier.

Built about 760 AD, Edificio I in Grupo I, with its lofty towers, is a fine example of the Río Bec architectural style. The three towers (rather than the usual two) have traces of impractically steep ornamental stairways and several fierce jaguar masks (go around to the back of the tower to see the best one). See the Río Bec section for a fuller description of this architectural style. About 60m to the east is Edificio II, an elite residence.

Xpujil is a far larger site than may be imagined from these two buildings. Three other structure groups have been identified, but it may be decades before they are restored. The site, 200m north of the highway, is open 8 am to 5 pm (US$1.50). A round-trip taxi ride with a one-hour wait costs US$5.

Hormiguero

Hormiguero (Anthill, in Spanish) prospered during the late Classic period, but it is an old site, with some buildings dating from 50 to 250 AD. Here you'll see one of the most impressive buildings in the region. The 50m-long Edificio II has a huge Chenes-style monster-mouth doorway, with much of its decoration in good condition. Though similar to the huge monster-mouths at Hochob and Chicanná, Hormiguero's is even bigger and bolder. You'll also want to see Edificio V, 60m to the north, and Edificio E-1 in the Grupo Oriente (East Group).

The site is 22km southwest of Xpujil junction (6km beyond the village of Carrizal). Admission is US$1.50. If you're driving you will have no trouble with the road, which is in good shape, or you can opt for a round-trip taxicab ride with a one-hour wait for about US$20.

Río Bec

'Río Bec' is the designation for an agglomeration of small sites, 17 at last count, in a 50-sq-km area southeast of Xpujil. Of these, the most interesting is certainly Grupo B, followed by Grupos I and N.

Río Bec gave its name to the region's prevalent architectural style, characterized by long, low buildings that look as though they're divided into sections, each with a huge serpent-mouth for a door. The façades are decorated with smaller masks, geometric designs and columns. At the corners of the buildings are tall, solid towers with small, steep, nonfunctional steps, topped by small temples. Many of these towers have roof combs as well.

The best example of Río Bec architecture is Edificio I at Grupo B, a late Classic building dating from around 700 AD. Though not restored, it has been consolidated and allows appreciation of its former glory.

At Grupo I, look for Edificios XVII and XI. At Grupo N, Edificio I is similar to the grand one at Grupo B.

The entrance to the ruins can be found at the east edge of town.

El Ramonal

These impressive ruins (US$1.50) are all within walking distance of the Ejido 20 de Noviembre collective farm, reached by a road 10km east of Xpujil junction. Look for signs, turn south and follow the unpaved *ejido* road for 5km to the farm and its U'lu'um Chac Yuk Nature Reserve. As you come into the village, with its free-roaming livestock and thatched huts, look for the 'museum,' the fourth building on the right side of the road. Ask there for guides to show you the sights of El Ramonal. (Guides from the ejido can also show you the various sites of Río Bec, about 13km away.) A round-trip taxi ride with a one-hour wait costs US$20.

Language

Pronunciation

Pronunciation of Spanish is not difficult, given that many Spanish sounds are similar to their English counterparts, and there is a clear and consistent relationship between pronunciation and spelling. Unless otherwise indicated, the English words used below to approximate Spanish sounds take standard American pronunciation.

Vowels Spanish has five vowels: **a**, **e**, **i**, **o** and **u**. They are pronounced something like the highlighted letters of the following English words:

a as in 'father'
e as in 'met'
i as in 'feet'
o as in the British 'hot'
u as in 'put'

Diphthongs A diphthong is one syllable made up of two vowels, each of which conserves its own sound. Here are some diphthongs in Spanish, and their approximate pronunciations:

ai as in 'hide'
au as in 'how'
ei as in 'hay'
ia as in 'yard'
ie as in 'yes'
oi as in 'boy'
ua as in 'wash'
ue as in 'well'

Consonants Many consonants are pronounced in much the same way as in English, but there are some exceptions:

c is pronounced like 's' in 'sit' when before 'e' or 'i'; elsewhere it is like 'k'
ch as in 'choose'
g as the 'g' in 'gate' before 'a,' 'o' and 'u'; before 'e' or 'i' it is a harsh, breathy sound like the 'h' in 'hit.' Note that when 'g' is followed by 'ue' or 'ui' the 'u' is silent, unless it has a dieresis (ü), in which case it functions much like the English 'w':
guerra 'GEH-rra'
güero 'GWEH-ro'
h always silent
j a harsh, guttural sound similar to the 'ch' in the Scottish 'loch'

ll as the 'y' in 'yellow'
ñ nasal sound like the 'ny' in 'canyon'
q as the 'k' in 'kick'; always followed by a silent 'u'
r a very short rolled 'r'
rr a longer rolled 'r'
x like the English 'h' when it comes after 'e' or 'i,' otherwise it is like English 'x' as in 'taxi'; in many Indian words (particularly Mayan ones) 'x' is pronounced like English 'sh'
z the same as the English 's'; under no circumstances should 's' or 'z' be pronounced like English 'z' – that sound does not exist in Spanish

There are a few other minor pronunciation differences, but the longer you stay in Mexico, the easier they will become. The letter **ñ** is considered a separate letter of the alphabet and follows 'n' in alphabetically organized lists and books, such as dictionaries and phone books.

Stress There are three general rules regarding stress:

- For words ending in a vowel, 'n' or 's,' the stress goes on the penultimate (next-to-the-last) syllable:

  naranja na-RAHN-ha *joven* HO-ven *zapatos* sa-PA-tos

- For words ending in a consonant other than 'n' or 's,' the stress is on the final syllable:

  estoy es-TOY *ciudad* syoo-DAHD *catedral* ka-teh-DRAL

- Any deviation from these rules is indicated by an accent:

  México MEH-hee-ko *mudéjar* moo-DEH-har *Cortés* cor-TESS

Gender

Nouns in Spanish are either masculine or feminine. Nouns ending in 'o,' 'e' or 'ma' are usually masculine. Nouns ending in 'a,' 'ión' or 'dad' are usually feminine. Some nouns take either a masculine or feminine form, depending on the ending; for example, *viajero* is a male traveler, *viajera* is a female traveler. An adjective usually comes after the noun it describes and must take the same gender as the noun.

Greetings & Civilities

Hello/Hi.	*Hola.*
Good morning/Good day.	*Buenos días.*
Good afternoon.	*Buenas tardes.*
Good evening/Good night.	*Buenas noches.*
See you.	*Hasta luego.*
Good-bye.	*Adiós.*
Pleased to meet you.	*Mucho gusto.*
How are you? (to one person)	*¿Como está?*
How are you? (to more than one person)	*¿Como están?*
I am fine.	*Estoy bien.*
Please.	*Por favor.*
Thank you.	*Gracias.*
You're welcome.	*De nada.*
Excuse me.	*Perdóneme.*

People

I	*yo*	they (f)	*ellas*
you (familiar)	*tú*	my wife	*mi esposa*
you (formal)	*usted*	my husband	*mi esposo, mi marido*
you (pl, formal)	*ustedes*	my sister	*mi hermana*
he/it	*el*	my brother	*mi hermano*
she/it	*ella*	Sir/Mr	*Señor*
we	*nosotros*	Madam/Mrs	*Señora*
they (m)	*ellos*	Miss	*Señorita*

Useful Words & Phrases

For words pertaining to food and restaurants, see the Food and Drinks sections of the Facts for the Visitor chapter.

Yes.	*Sí.*	I am ...	*Estoy ...*
No.	*No.*	(location or temporary condition)	
What did you say?	*¿Mande?* (colloq)	here	*aquí*
	¿Cómo?	tired (m/f)	*cansado/a*
good/OK	*bueno*	sick/ill (m/f)	*enfermo/a*
bad	*malo*		
better	*mejor*	I am ...	*Soy ...*
best	*lo mejor*	(permanent state)	
more	*más*	a worker	*trabajador*
less	*menos*	married	*casado*
very little	*poco* or *poquito*		

Buying

		## Nationalities	
How much?	*¿Cuánto?*	American (m/f)	*(norte)americano/a*
How much does it cost?	*¿Cuánto cuesta?*	Australian (m/f)	*australiano/a*
	or *¿Cuánto se cobra?*	British (m/f)	*británico/a*
		Canadian (m & f)	*canadiense*
How much is it worth?	*¿Cuánto vale?*	English (m/f)	*inglés/inglesa*
I want ...	*Quiero ...*	French (m/f)	*francés/francesa*
I do not want ...	*No quiero ...*	German (m/f)	*alemán/alemana*
I would like ...	*Quisiera ...*		
Give me ...	*Deme ...*		
What do you want?	*¿Qué quiere?*		
Do you have ...?	*¿Tiene ...?*		
Is/are there ...?	*¿Hay ...?*		

Languages

I speak ...	*Yo hablo ...*	I understand.	*Entiendo.*
I do not speak ...	*No hablo ...*	I do not understand.	*No entiendo.*
Do you speak ...?	*¿Habla usted ...?*	Do you understand?	*¿Entiende usted?*
Spanish	*español*	Please speak slowly.	*Por favor hable*
English	*inglés*		*despacio.*
German	*alemán*		
French	*francés*		

Crossing the Border

birth certificate	*certificado de nacimiento*	immigration	*inmigración*
		insurance	*seguro*
border (frontier)	*la frontera*	passport	*pasaporte*
car-owner's title	*título de propiedad*	temporary vehicle	*permiso de*
car registration	*registración*	import permit	*importación temporal de vehículo*
customs	*aduana*		
driver's license	*licencia de manejar*	tourist card	*tarjeta de turista*
identification	*identificación*	visa	*visado*

Getting Around

street	*calle*	forward, ahead	*adelante*
boulevard	*bulevar, boulevard*	straight ahead	*todo recto* or *derecho*
avenue	*avenida*	this way	*por aquí*
road	*camino*	that way	*por allí*
highway	*carretera*	north	*norte (Nte)*
corner (of)	*esquina (de)*	south	*sur*
corner/bend	*vuelta*	east	*este*
block	*cuadra*	east (in an address)	*oriente (Ote)*
to the left	*a la izquierda*	west	*oeste*
to the right	*a la derecha*	west (in an address)	*poniente (Pte)*

Where is . . . ?	*¿Dónde está . . . ?*
the bus station	*el terminal de autobuses/central camionera*
the train station	*la estación del ferrocarril*
the airport	*el aeropuerto*
the post office	*el correo*
a long-distance phone	*un teléfono de larga distancia*
bus	*camión* or *autobús*
minibus	*colectivo*, *combi* or (in Mexico City) *pesero*
train	*tren*
taxi	*taxi*
ticket sales counter	*taquilla*
waiting room	*sala de espera*
baggage check-in	*(recibo de) equipaje*
toilet	*sanitario*
departure	*salida*
arrival	*llegada*
platform	*andén*
left-luggage room/checkroom	*guardería* (or *guarda*) *de equipaje*
How far is . . . ?	*¿A qué distancia está . . . ?*
How long? (How much time?)	*¿Cuánto tiempo?*
short route (usually a toll highway)	*vía corta*

Driving

gasoline	*gasolina*	full	*lleno* or '*ful*'
fuel station	*gasolinera*	oil	*aceite*
unleaded	*sin plomo*	tire	*llanta*
fill the tank	*llene el tanque; llenarlo*	puncture	*agujero*

How much is a liter of gasoline?	*¿Cuánto cuesta el litro de gasolina?*
My car has broken down.	*Se me ha descompuesto el carro.*
I need a tow truck.	*Necesito un remolque.*
Is there a garage near here?	*¿Hay un garaje cerca de aquí?*

Highway Signs

Though Mexico mostly uses the familiar international road signs, you should be prepared to encounter these other signs as well:

road repairs	*camino en reparación*
keep to the right	*conserve su derecha*
do not overtake	*no rebase*
dangerous curve	*curva peligrosa*
landslides or subsidence	*derrumbes*
slow	*despacio*
detour	*desviación*
slow down	*disminuya su velocidad*
school (zone)	*escuela (zona escolar)*
men working	*hombres trabajando*
road closed	*no hay paso*
danger	*peligro*
continuous white line	*raya continua*
speed bumps	*topes* or *vibradores*
road under repair	*tramo en reparación*
narrow bridge	*puente angosto*
toll highway	*vía cuota*
short route (often a toll road)	*vía corta*
have toll ready	*prepare su cuota*
one-lane road 100 meters ahead	*un solo carril a 100 m*

Accommodations

hotel	*hotel*	shower	*ducha* or *regadera*
guesthouse	*casa de huéspedes*	hot water	*agua caliente*
inn	*posada*	air-conditioning	*aire acondicionado*
room	*cuarto, habitación*	blanket	*manta, cobija*
room with one bed	*cuarto sencillo*	towel	*toalla*
room with two beds	*cuarto doble*	soap	*jabón*
room for one person	*cuarto para una persona*	toilet paper	*papel higiénico*
		the check (bill)	*la cuenta*
room for two people	*cuarto para dos personas*	What is the price?	*¿Cuál es el precio?*
		Does that include taxes?	
double bed	*cama matrimonial*	*¿Están incluidos los impuestos?*	
twin beds	*camas gemelas*	Does that include service?	
with bath	*con baño*	*¿Está incluido el servicio?*	

Money

money	*dinero*
traveler's checks	*cheques de viajero*
bank	*banco*
exchange bureau	*casa de cambio*
credit card	*tarjeta de crédito*
exchange rate	*tipo de cambio*
ATM	*caja permanente* or *cajero automático*
I want/would like to change some money.	*Quiero/quisiera cambiar dinero.*
What is the exchange rate?	*¿Cuál es el tipo de cambio?*
Is there a commission?	*¿Hay comisión?*

Telephones

telephone	*teléfono*
telephone call	*llamada*
telephone number	*número telefónico*
telephone card	*tarjeta telefónica*
area or city code	*clave*
prefix for long-distance call	*prefijo*
local call	*llamada local*
long-distance call	*llamada de larga distancia*
long-distance telephone	*teléfono de larga distancia*
coin-operated telephone	*teléfono de monedas*
card-operated telephone	*teléfono de tarjetas telefónicas*
long-distance telephone office	*caseta de larga distancia*
tone	*tono*
operator	*operador(a)*
person to person	*persona a persona*
collect (reverse charges)	*por cobrar*
dial the number	*marque el número*
please wait	*favor de esperar*
busy	*ocupado*
toll/cost (of call)	*cuota/costo*
time & charges	*tiempo y costo*
don't hang up	*no cuelgue*

Times & Dates

Monday	*lunes*	Saturday	*sábado*
Tuesday	*martes*	Sunday	*domingo*
Wednesday	*miércoles*	yesterday	*ayer*
Thursday	*jueves*	today	*hoy*
Friday	*viernes*		

tomorrow (also at some point, or maybe)	*mañana*
right now (meaning in a few minutes)	*horita, ahorita*
already	*ya*
morning	*mañana*
tomorrow morning	*mañana por la mañana*
afternoon	*tarde*
night	*noche*
What time is it?	*¿Qué hora es?*

Numbers

0	*cero*	9	*nueve*	18	*dieciocho*
1	*un, uno* (m), *una* (f)	10	*diez*	19	*diecinueve*
2	*dos*	11	*once*	20	*veinte*
3	*tres*	12	*doce*	21	*veintiuno*
4	*cuatro*	13	*trece*	22	*veintidós*
5	*cinco*	14	*catorce*	30	*treinta*
6	*seis*	15	*quince*	31	*treinta y uno*
7	*siete*	16	*dieciséis*	32	*treinta y dos*
8	*ocho*	17	*diecisiete*	40	*cuarenta*

50	cincuenta	100	cien	700	setecientos
60	sesenta	101	ciento uno	900	novecientos
70	setenta	143	ciento cuarenta y tres	1000	mil
80	ochenta	200	doscientos	2000	dos mil
90	noventa	500	quinientos		

Mexican Slang

Pepper your conversations with a few slang expressions! You'll hear many of these slang words and phrases all around Mexico, but others are particular to Mexico City.

¡Quiúbole!	Hello!
¿Qué onda?	What's up?, What's happening?
¿Qué pex?	What's up?
¿Qué pasión? (Mexico City only)	What's up?, What's going on?
¡Qué padre!	How cool!
fregón	really good at something, way cool, awesome
Este club está fregón.	This club is way cool.
El cantante es un fregón.	The singer is really awesome.
ser muy buena onda	to be really cool, nice
Mi novio es muy buena onda.	My boyfriend is really cool.
Eres muy buena onda.	You are really cool (nice).
estar de pelos	to be super, awesome
La música está de pelos.	The music is awesome.
unas serpientes bien elodias	some ice-cold beers (sounds like *unas cervezas bien heladas*)
pomo (in the south)	booze
pisto (in the north)	booze
alipús	booze
echarse un alipús, echarse un trago	to go get a drink
Echamos un alipús/trago.	Let's go have a drink.
dar un voltión	go cruising, drive around
tirar la onda	try to pick someone up, flirt
ligar	to flirt
irse de reventón	go partying
¡Vámonos de reventón!	Let's go party!
reven	a 'rave' – huge party, lots of loud music and wild atmosphere
un toquín	an informal party with live music
un desmadre	a mess
Simón.	Yes.
Nel.	No.
Naranjas Dulces.	No.
No hay tos.	No problem. (literally 'there's no cough.')
¡Órale! – positive	Sounds great! (responding to an invitation)
¡Órale! – negative	What the *#*!? (taunting exclamation)
¡Caray!	Shit!
¿Te cae?	Are you serious?
Me late.	Sounds really good to me.
Me vale.	I don't care, 'Whatever.'

Sale y vale.	I agree, Sounds good.
¡Paso sin ver!	I can't stand it!, No thank you!
¡Guácatelas! ¡Guácala!	How gross! That's disgusting!
¡Bájale!	Don't exaggerate!, Come on!
¡¿Chale?! (Mexico City only)	Really?! No way!
¡Te sales! ¡Te pasas!	That's it! You've gone too far!
¿Le agarraste?	Did you understand?, Do you get it?
un resto	a lot
lana	money, dough
carnal	brother
cuate, cuaderno	buddy
chavo	guy, dude
chava	girl, gal
jefe	father
jefa	mother
la tira, la julia	the police
chapusero	a cheater (at cards, for example)

Glossary

For food and drink terms, see the Food and Drinks sections in the Facts for the Visitor chapter; for bus and train terms, see the Getting Around chapter; for general terms, see the Language chapter.

AC – *antes de Cristo* (before Christ); equivalent to BC

adobe – sun-dried mud brick used for building

aduana – customs

agave – family of plants including the *maguey*

aguardiente – literally 'burning water'; strong liquor usually made from sugarcane

Alameda – name of formal parks in several Mexican cities

albergue de juventud – youth hostel

alfarería – potter's workshop

alfiz – rectangular frame around a curved arch; an Arabic influence on Spanish and Mexican buildings

Altiplano Central – dry plateau stretching across north central Mexico between the two Sierra Madre ranges

amate – paper made from tree bark

Ángeles Verdes – Green Angels; government-funded mechanics who patrol Mexico's major highways in green vehicles; they help stranded motorists with fuel and spare parts

antro – bar with (often loud) recorded music and usually some space to dance

Apdo – abbreviation for Apartado (Box) in addresses; hence Apdo Postal means Post Office Box

arroyo – brook, stream

artesanías – handicrafts, folk arts

atlas (s), **atlantes** (pl) – sculpted male figure(s) used instead of a pillar to support a roof or frieze; a *telamon*

atrium – churchyard, usually a big one

autopista – expressway, dual carriageway

azulejo – painted ceramic tile

bahía – bay

balneario – bathing-place, often a natural hot spring

baluarte – bulwark, defensive wall

barrio – neighborhood of a town or city, often a poor neighborhood

billete – bank note

boleto – ticket

brujo, -a – witch doctor, shaman; similar to *curandero, -a*

burro – donkey

caballeros – literally 'horsemen,' but corresponds to 'gentlemen' in English; look for it on toilet doors

cabaña – cabin, simple shelter

cabina – Baja Californian term for a telephone *caseta*

cacique – regional warlord or political strongman

cafetería – a snack bar or coffeehouse

calle – street

callejón – alley

callejoneada – originally an Spanish tradition, still enjoyed in cities such as Guanajuato and Zacatecas, in which musicians lead a crowd of revellers through the streets, singing and telling stories as they go

calzada – grand boulevard or avenue

calzones – long baggy shorts worn by indigenous men

camarín – chapel beside the main altar in a church; contains ceremonial clothing for images of saints or the Virgin

camión – truck or bus

camioneta – pickup truck

campesino, -a – country person, peasant

capilla abierta – open chapel; used in early Mexican monasteries for preaching to large crowds of indigenous people

casa de cambio – exchange house; place where currency is exchanged, faster to use than a bank

caseta de larga distancia, caseta de teléfono, caseta telefónica – public telephone call station, often in a shop

cazuela – clay cooking pot; usually sold in a nested set

cenote – a limestone sinkhole filled with rainwater, used in Yucatán as a reservoir

1043

central camionera – bus terminal

cerro – hill

Chac – Mayan rain god

chac-mool – pre-Hispanic stone sculpture of a hunched, belly-up figure; the stomach may have been used as a sacrificial altar

charreada – Mexican rodeo

charro – Mexican cowboy

chilango, -a – citizen of Mexico City

chinampas – Aztec gardens built from lake mud and vegetation; versions still exist at Xochimilco, Mexico City

chingar – literally 'to fuck'; it has a wide range of colloquial usages in Mexican Spanish equivalent to those in English

chultún – cement-lined brick cistern found in the *chenes* (wells) region in the Puuc hills south of Mérida

Churrigueresque – Spanish late-baroque architectural style; found on many Mexican churches

cigarro – cigarette

clavadistas – the cliff divers of Acapulco and Mazatlán

Coatlicue – mother of the Aztec gods

colectivo – minibus or car that picks up and drops off passengers along a predetermined route; can also refer to other types of transport, such as boats, where passengers share the total fare

coleto, -a – citizen of San Cristóbal de Las Casas

colonia – neighborhood of a city, often a wealthy residential area

comedor – literally 'eating place,' usually a sit-down stall in a market or a small, cheap restaurant

comida corrida – set lunch or dinner special

completo – no vacancy, literally 'full up'; a sign you may see at hotel desks

conasupo – government-owned store that sells many everyday basics at subsidized prices

conde – count (nobleman)

conquistador – early Spanish explorer-conqueror

cordillera – mountain range

correos – post office

coyote – person who smuggles Mexican immigrants into the USA

criollo – Mexican-born person of Spanish parentage; in colonial times considered inferior by peninsular Spaniards (see *gachupines, peninsulares*)

Cristeros – Roman Catholic rebels of the late 1920s

cuota – toll; a *vía cuota* is a toll road

curandero, -a – literally 'curer'; a medicine man or woman who uses herbal and/or magical methods and often emphasizes spiritual aspects of disease

damas – ladies; the sign on toilet doors

danzantes – literally 'dancers'; stone carvings at Monte Albán

DC – *después de Cristo* (after Christ); equivalent to AD

de lujo – deluxe; often used with some license

delegación – a large urban governmental subdivision in Mexico City comprising numerous *colonias*

de paso – a bus that began its route somewhere else, but stops to let passenger on or off at various points – often arriving late; a *local* bus is preferable

descompuesto – broken, out of order

DF – Distrito Federal (Federal District); about half of Mexico City lies in the DF

edificio – building

ejido – communal landholding

embarcadero – jetty, boat landing

encomienda – a grant made to a *conquistador* of labor by or tribute from a group of indigenous people; the conquistador was supposed to protect and convert them, but usually treated them as little more than slaves

enramada – literally a bower, but often refers to a thatch-covered, open-air restaurant

enredo – wraparound skirt

entremeses – hors d'oeuvres; also theatrical sketches, such as those performed during the Cervantino festival in Guanajuato

escuela – school

esq – abbreviation of *esquina* (corner) in addresses

estación de ferrocarril – train station

estípite – long, narrow, pyramid-shaped, upside-down pilaster; the hallmark of Churrigueresque architecture

ex-convento – former convent or monastery

excusado – toilet

faja – waist sash used in traditional indigenous costume

feria – fair or carnival, typically occurring during a religious holiday

ferrocarril – railway

ficha – locker token available at bus terminals

fonda – eating stall in market; small restaurant

fraccionamiento – subdivision, housing development; similar to a *colonia*, often modern

frontera – border between political entities

gachupines – derogatory term for the colonial *peninsulares*

giro – money order

gringo, -a – US or Canadian (and sometimes European, Australasian, etc) visitor to Latin America; can be used derogatorily

grito – literally 'shout'; the Grito de Dolores was the 1810 call to independence by parish priest Miguel Hidalgo, which sparked the struggle for independence from Spain

gruta – cave, grotto

guarache – also *huarache*; woven leather sandal, often with tire tread as the sole

guardería de equipaje – room for storing luggage, eg, in a bus station

guayabera – also *guayabarra*; man's shirt with pockets and appliquéd designs up the front, over the shoulders and down the back; worn in place of a jacket and tie in hot regions

güero, -a – fair-haired, fair-complexioned person; a more polite alternative to *gringo*

hacha – flat carved-stone object from the Classic Veracruz civilization; connected with the ritual ball game

hacendado – *hacienda* owner

hacienda – estate; Hacienda (capitalized) is the Treasury Department

hay – there is, there are; you're equally likely to hear *no hay* (there isn't, there aren't)

henequén – agave fiber used to make sisal rope; grown particularly around Mérida

hombres – men; sign on toilet doors

huarache – see *guarache*

huevos – eggs; also slang for testicles

huipil, -es – indigenous woman's sleeveless tunic, usually highly decorated; can be thigh-length or reach the ankles

Huizilopochtli – Aztec tribal god

iglesia – church

INAH – Instituto Nacional de Antropología e Historia; the body in charge of most ancient sites and some museums

indígena – indigenous, pertaining to the original inhabitants of Latin America; can also refer to the people themselves

INI – Instituto Nacional Indigenista; set up in 1948 to improve the lot of indigenous Mexicans and to integrate them into society; sometimes accused of paternalism and trying to stifle protest

ISH – *impuesto sobre hospedaje*; lodging tax on the price of hotel rooms

isla – island

IVA – *impuesto de valor agregado*, or 'eebah'; a 15% sales tax added to the price of many items

ixtle – *maguey* fiber

jaguar – jaguar, a panther native to southern Mexico and Central America; principal symbol of the Olmec civilization

jai alai – the Basque game *pelota*, brought to Mexico by the Spanish; a bit like squash, played on a long court with curved baskets attached to the arm

jarocho, -a – citizen of Veracruz

jefe – boss or leader, especially a political one

jipijapa – Yucatán name for a Panama hat

jorongo – small poncho worn by men

Kukulcán – Mayan name for the plumed serpent god Quetzalcóatl

lada – short for *larga distancia*

Ladatel – the long-distance telephone system operated by the former monopoly Telmex

ladino – more or less the same as *mestizo*

lancha – fast, open, outboard boat

larga distancia – long-distance; usually refers to telephones

latifundio – large landholding; these sprang up after Mexico's independence from Spain

latifundista – powerful landowner who usurped communally owned land to form a *latifundio*

libramiento – road, highway

licenciado – university graduate, abbreviated as Lic and used as an honorific before a person's name; a status claimed by many who don't actually possess a degree

licuado – drink made from fruit juice, water or milk, and sugar

lista de correos – literally 'mail list,' a list displayed at a post office of people for whom letters are waiting; similar to General Delivery or Poste Restante

lleno – full, as with a car's fuel tank

local – can mean premises, such as a numbered shop or office in a mall or block, or can mean local; a *local* bus is one whose route starts at the bus station you are in

machismo – Mexican masculine bravura

madre – literally 'mother,' but the term can be used colloquially with an astonishing array of meanings

maguey – a type of agave, with thick pointed leaves growing straight out of the ground; *tequila* and *mezcal* are made from its sap

malecón – waterfront street, boulevard or promenade

mañana – literally 'tomorrow' or 'morning'; in some contexts it may just mean 'some time in the future'

maquiladora – assembly-plant operation usually in northern Mexico and owned, at least in part, by foreigners; allowed to import equipment, raw materials and parts duty-free for finishing or assembly by Mexican labor

mariachi – small ensemble of street musicians playing traditional ballads on guitars and trumpets

marimba – wooden xylophone-type instrument, popular in Veracruz and the south

Mayab – the lands of the Maya

mercado – market; often a building near the center of a town, with shops and open-air stalls in the surrounding streets

Mesoamerica – the region inhabited by the ancient Mexican and Mayan cultures

mestizaje – 'mixedness,' Mexico's mixed-blood heritage; officially an object of pride

mestizo – person of mixed (usually indigenous and Spanish) ancestry, ie, most Mexicans

metate – shallow stone bowl with legs, for grinding maize and other foods

Mexican Hat Dance – a courtship dance in which a girl and boy dance around the boy's hat

mezcal – strong alcoholic drink produced from *maguey* sap

milpa – peasant's small cornfield, often cultivated by the slash-and-burn method

mirador, -es – lookout point(s)

mole – a spicy sauce usually made with chilies and usually chocolate and served with meat

Montezuma's revenge – Mexican version of Delhi-belly or travelers' diarrhea

mordida – literally 'little bite,' a small bribe to keep the wheels of bureaucracy turning

mota – marijuana

Mudéjar – Moorish architectural style, imported to Mexico by the Spanish

mujeres – women; seen on toilet doors

municipio – small local-government area; Mexico is divided into 2394 of them

na – Mayan thatched hut

NAFTA – North American Free Trade Agreement TLC

Nahuatl – language of the Nahua people, descendants of the Aztecs

naos – Spanish trading galleons

norteamericanos – North Americans, people from north of the US-Mexican border

Nte – abbreviation for *norte* (north), used in street names

Ote – abbreviation for *oriente* (east), used in street names

paceño, -a – person from La Paz, Baja California Sur

palacio de gobierno – state capitol, state government headquarters

palacio municipal – town or city hall, headquarters of the municipal corporation

palapa – thatched-roof shelter, usually on a beach

palma – long, paddle-like, carved-stone object from the Classic Veracruz civilization; connected with the ritual ball game

panadería – bakery, pastry shop

panga – fiberglass skiff for fishing or whale-watching in Baja California

parada – bus stop, usually for city buses

parado – standing up, as you often are on 2nd-class buses

parque nacional – national park; an environmentally protected area in which human exploitation is supposedly banned or restricted

parroquia – parish church

paseo – boulevard, walkway or pedestrian street; also the tradition of strolling in a circle around the plaza in the evening, men and women moving in opposite directions

Pemex – government-owned petroleum extraction, refining and retailing monopoly

peña – evening of Latin-American folk songs, often with a political protest theme

peninsulares – those born in Spain and sent by the Spanish government to rule the colony in Mexico (see *criollo, gachupines*)

periférico – ring road

pesero – Mexico City's word for *colectivo*

petate – mat, usually made of palm or reed

peyote – a hallucinogenic cactus

pinacoteca – art gallery

piñata – clay pot or papier-mâché mold decorated to resemble an animal, pineapple, star, etc; filled with sweets and gifts and smashed open at fiestas

playa – beach

plaza de toros – bullring

plazuela – small plaza

poblano, -a – person from Puebla, or something in the style of Puebla

pollero – same as a *coyote*

Porfiriato – Porfirio Díaz's reign as president-dictator of Mexico for 30 years, until the 1910 revolution

portales – arcades

potosino – from the city or state of San Luis Potosí

presidio – fort or fort's garrison

PRI – Partido Revolucionario Institucional (Institutional Revolutionary Party); the political party which ruled Mexico for most of the 20th century

propina – tip; different from a *mordida*, which is closer to a bribe

Pte – abbreviation for *poniente* (west), used in street names

puerto – port

pulque – thick, milky, alcoholic drink of fermented *maguey* juice

quechquémitl – indigenous woman's shoulder cape with an opening for the head; usually colorfully embroidered, often diamond-shaped

quetzal – crested bird with brilliant green, red and white plumage, native to southern Mexico, Central America and northern South America; quetzal feathers were highly prized in pre-Hispanic Mexico

Quetzalcóatl – plumed serpent god of pre-Hispanic Mexico

rebozo – long woolen or linen shawl covering the head or shoulders

refugio – a very basic cabin for shelter in the mountains – usually free, and available on a first come basis

regiomontano, -a – person from Monterrey

reja – wrought-iron window grille

reserva de la biósfera – biosphere reserve; an environmentally protected area where human exploitation is steered towards ecologically unharmful activities

retablo – altarpiece; or small painting on wood, tin, cardboard, glass, etc, placed in a church to give thanks for miracles, answered prayers, etc

río – river

s/n – *sin número* (without number); used in street addresses

sacbe (s), **sacbeob** (pl) – ceremonial avenue(s) between great Mayan cities

sanatorio – hospital, particularly a small private one

sanitario(s) – toilet(s), literally 'sanitary place'

sarape – blanket with opening for the head, worn as a cloak

Semana Santa – Holy Week, the week from Palm Sunday to Easter Sunday; Mexico's major holiday period, when accommodations and transport get very busy

servicios – toilets

sierra – mountain range

sitio – taxi stand

stele (s), **-es** or **stelae** (pl) – standing stone monument(s), usually carved

supermercado – supermarket; anything from a small corner store to a large, US-style supermarket

Sur – south; often seen in street names

taller – shop or workshop; a *taller mecánico* is a mechanic's shop, usually for cars; a *taller de llantas* is a tire-repair shop

talud-tablero – stepped building style typical of Teotihuacán, with alternating vertical (*tablero*) and sloping (*talud*) sections

tapatío, -a – person born in the state of Jalisco

taquería – place where you buy tacos

taquilla – ticket window

telamon – statue of a male figure, used instead of a pillar to hold up the roof of a temple; see also *atlas*

telar de cintura – backstrap loom; the warp (lengthwise) threads are stretched between two horizontal bars, one of which is attached to a post or tree and the other to a strap around the weaver's lower back, and the weft (crosswise) threads are then woven in

teleférico – cable car

templo – church; anything from a wayside chapel to a cathedral

teocalli – Aztec sacred precinct

tequila – vaguely vodka-like liquor produced, like *pulque* and *mezcal*, from the *maguey* plant

Tex-Mex – Americanized version of Mexican food

Tezcatlipoca – multifaceted pre-Hispanic god, lord of life and death and protector of warriors; as a smoking mirror he could see into hearts, as the sun god he needed the blood of sacrificed warriors to ensure he would rise again

tezontle – light-red, porous volcanic rock used for buildings by the Aztecs and *conquistadors*

tianguis – indigenous people's market

tienda – store

típico, -a – characteristic of a region; particularly used to describe food

Tláloc – pre-Hispanic rain and water god

TLC – Tratado de Libre Comercio, the North American Free Trade Agreement (NAFTA)

topes – speed bumps; found on the outskirts of many towns and villages, they are only sometimes marked by signs

trapiche – mill; in Baja California usually a sugar mill

tzompantli – rack for the skulls of Aztec sacrificial victims

UNAM – Universidad Nacional Autónoma de México (National Autonomous University of Mexico)

universidad – university

viajero, -a – traveler

villa juvenil – youth sports center, often the location of an *albergue de juventud*

voladores – literally 'fliers,' the Totonac ritual in which men, suspended by their ankles, whirl around a tall pole

War of the Castes – bloody 19th-century Mayan uprising in the Yucatán peninsula

were-jaguar – half-human, half-jaguar being, portrayed in Olmec art

yácata – ceremonial stone structure of the Tarascan civilization

yugo – U-shaped carved-stone object from the Classic Veracruz civilization; connected with the ritual ball game

zaguán – vestibule or foyer, sometimes a porch

zócalo – main plaza or square; a term used in some (but by no means all) Mexican towns

Zona Rosa – literally 'Pink Zone'; an area of expensive shops, hotels and restaurants in Mexico City frequented by the wealthy and tourists; by extension, a similar area in another city

Artesanías

ARTESANÍAS

Mexico is so richly endowed with appealing *artesanías* (handicrafts) that even the most hardened non-hunter of souvenirs finds it hard to get home without at least one pair of earrings or a little model animal. There's a huge and colorful range of arts and crafts, much of which is sold at reasonable prices, so that virtually everyone is irresistibly attracted to something, somewhere along the way.

Selling folk art to tourists and collectors art has been a growing money-earner for Mexican artisans since before WWII. But bringing in foreign tourist dollars is only one of the roles handicrafts play in Mexican life. For one thing, Mexicans themselves are eager buyers and collectors of such handicrafts. More fundamentally, Mexicans have been producing artesanías for millennia. The colorful, highly decorative crafts that catch the eye in shops and markets today are, in a way, counterparts to the splendid costumes, beautiful ceramics and elaborate jewelry used by the nobility of Aztec, Mayan and other pre-Hispanic cultures. On a more mundane level, contemporary Mexican artisans still turn out countless handmade objects – pots, hats, baskets, toys, clothes, sandals, to name but a few – for every-day use just as they did centuries before the Spanish came.

Many modern Mexican crafts are easily traced to their pre-Hispanic origins, and some techniques, designs and materials have remained unchanged since long before Europeans' arrival. The Spanish brought their own artistic methods, styles and products, and, although these mingled to some extent with older traditions, indigenous crafts were generally regarded as inferior during the colonial period. But with the search for a national identity after the Mexican Revolution in the early 20th century, a new interest – inspired partly by artists such as Frida Kahlo and Diego Rivera – arose in older, specifically Mexican, craft traditions. A lot of handicrafts today show a clear fusion of pre-Hispanic and Spanish inspirations, and sometimes eclectic modern influences, too. Because many of Mexico's indigenous peoples maintain age-old skills and traditions, it's no surprise that the areas producing the most exciting artesanías are often those with prominent indigenous populations, in states such as Chiapas, Guerrero, México, Michoacán, Nayarit, Oaxaca, Puebla and Sonora.

Buying Handicrafts

You can buy artesanías in the villages where they are produced, or in shops and markets in urban centers. In towns and cities you'll generally find a wider range of wares, usually of good quality. But traveling to the

Above: Talavera pottery from Dolores Hidalgo, Guanajuato

villages gives you more of a chance to observe artisans at work, and if you buy there you'll have the satisfaction of knowing that more of your money is likely to go to the artisans themselves, and less to entrepreneurs.

Prices are not necessarily lower in the villages. For example, in Oaxaca city, which is the major clearinghouse for handicrafts from all over the state of Oaxaca, the number of stores and markets selling crafts helps keep prices competitive. What's more, goods from Oaxaca become more expensive when they're transported to Mexico City or elsewhere.

City shops devoted to artesanías will give you a good overview of what's available. Some towns and cities – such as Mexico City, Guadalajara, San Miguel de Allende, Puerto Vallarta and Oaxaca and others with large numbers of long-staying foreigners or craft-aware tourists – have stores offering handicrafts from all over the country. In shops in other cities, you'll find wares from around the local region. Even if you don't buy in these stores, they'll show you good-quality crafts and give you a basis for price comparisons.

Museums can also be good sources of information and examples of handicrafts. Many towns have artesanías museums showing local crafts and techniques, sometimes with items for sale. The upper floor of the Museo Nacional de Antropología, in Mexico City, is devoted to the modern lifestyles of many of Mexico's indigenous peoples, and it's interesting to compare these displays with the artifacts of their pre-Hispanic ancestors in the ground-floor archaeological sections of the museum.

Markets, of course, are a major source of handicrafts. A few cities have special markets devoted to crafts, but ordinary daily or weekly markets always sell some handicrafts – often regional specialties that attract buyers from farther afield, as well as everyday objects, such as pots and baskets, used by local people. The quality of market goods may not be as high as in stores, but you'll usually pay less; bargaining is expected in markets, whereas shops generally have fixed prices.

Below: Colorful blankets at a Tijuana market

Specific shops, markets, villages and museums with notable handicrafts are listed in this book's regional sections.

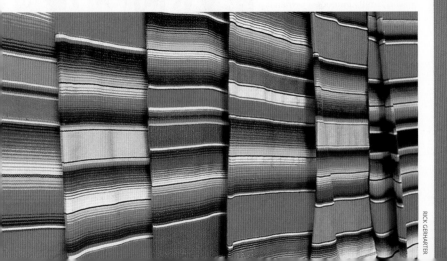

RICK GERHARTER

Textiles

Traditional Costume

Although traditional indigenous clothing is rarely worn in towns nowadays, if you get out to some of Mexico's villages you'll be intrigued by the variety of colorful everyday attire, differing from area to area and often from village to village. In general, the more remote an area is, the more intact its costume traditions tend to be. One town where you will come across indigenous people in traditional dress is San Cristóbal de Las Casas, in Chiapas, which is visited every day by numerous people from nearby villages. Traditional costume – more widely worn by women than men – serves as a mark of the community to which a person belongs and may also have meanings related to a person's status in the community, or to religious or spiritual beliefs.

Much laborious, highly skilled work goes into creating such clothing. Many of the garments and the methods by which they are made – and even some of the designs worked into them – are little changed since before the Spanish reached Mexico, and indigenous clothing is a reminder of the continued identity of these peoples.

The following four types of women's garment have been in use since long before the Spanish conquest:

Huipil – a sleeveless tunic, often reaching as low as the thighs or ankles, though some are shorter and may be tucked into a skirt. The huipil is found mainly in the southern half of the country.

Quechquémitl – a shoulder cape with an opening for the head, now worn mainly in the center and north of the country.

Enredo – a wraparound skirt, almost invisible if worn beneath a long huipil.

Faja – a waist sash that holds the enredo in place.

Blouses, introduced by Spanish missionaries who thought the quechquémitl immodest when worn without a huipil, are now often embroidered with just as much care and detail as the more traditional garments. They have caused quechquémitls to shrink in size and have replaced huipiles in some places.

The *rebozo*, which probably appeared in the Spanish era, is a long shawl that may cover the shoulders or head or be used for carrying.

Indigenous men's garments are less traditional than women's. In Spanish times the church encouraged modesty, so loose shirts and *calzones* (long baggy shorts) were introduced. Indigenous men may carry shoulder bags because their clothes lack pockets, though many of them have adopted ordinary modern clothing. The male equivalent of the rebozo, also dating from the Spanish era, is the *sarape*, a blanket with an opening for the head.

Above: Traditional Huichol dress

DAVE G HOUSER

Most eye-catching about indigenous clothing – especially women's – are the colorful, intricate designs woven or embroidered into them. Some garments are covered with a multicolored web of stylized animal, human, plant and mythical shapes, the production of which can take months to complete.

The basic materials of indigenous weaving are cotton and wool, which were once home-produced and homespun. Today, labor-saving factory yarn, including synthetic fibers, is common.

Colors, too, are often synthetic – Mexicans use bright modern shades in some highly original combinations – but some natural dyes are still in use or are being revived. Among the colors produced by natural dyes are deep blues from the indigo plant; reds and browns from various woods; reds, pinks and purples from the cochineal insect (chiefly used in Oaxaca state); and purples and mauves from a secretion of the *caracol púrpura* (purple sea snail), found on rocks along the southwestern coast of Oaxaca. Cloth with natural dyes is highly valued, but it's tough for the untrained eye to tell the difference between natural and artificial colors. Thread dyed from the caracol púrpura, however, is said to always retain the smell of the sea.

The basic indigenous weaver's tool – invented before the Spanish conquest and, now as then, used only by women – is the *telar de cintura* (back-strap loom). In simple terms, the warp (long) threads are stretched between two horizontal bars, one of which is fixed to a post or tree, while the other is attached to a strap that goes around the weaver's lower back; the weft (cross) threads are then woven in. The length of a cloth woven on a back-strap loom is almost unlimited, but the width is restricted to the weaver's arm span.

Above: *Sarapes* for sale in a Cancún market

A variety of sophisticated weaving techniques, including tapestry and brocading, are used to create amazing patterns in the cloth. Embroidery is another widespread decorative technique. The intricacy of some final products has to be seen to be believed. Huipiles, skirts, blouses, sashes, quechquémitls and other garments and cloth are decorated in these ways.

The huipiles of indigenous women in the south and southeast of the country are among Mexico's most intricate and eye-catching garments. In the state of Oaxaca, the Mazatecs, Chinantecs, Triquis, the coastal Mixtecs and some Zapotecs, in villages such as Yalalag, create some of the finest, most colorful designs. The Amuzgos, whose communities straddle the southern part of the Oaxaca-Guerrero border, are superb textile artisans as well. In Chiapas, the most skilled weavers are the highland Tzotzils, and the Maya of the Yucatán Peninsula also create some attractive huipiles.

The variety of color and pattern in the clothing of different indigenous peoples is immense. In some areas there are even big differences between the styles of neighboring villages. That is especially noticeable around San Cristóbal de Las Casas, in Chiapas, where each of the dozen or so indigenous villages within about 30km of the town has an entirely distinct clothing design. Differences also exist between everyday huipiles and special ceremonial huipiles, and each individual huipil is likely to have its own unique features.

Some especially beautiful embroidered blouses and quechquémitls are created by Nahua women in Puebla state, the Mazahua in the western part of México state, and by the Huichol people who live in a remote region on the borders of Nayarit, Jalisco and Durango states.

An exception to the generally less elaborate design of indigenous men's clothing occurs in southwestern Oaxaca; the garb of the Tacuate people is embroidered with hundreds of tiny, colorful birds, animals and insects – an idea now widely copied on clothing commercially produced elsewhere.

Indigenous clothing is not embellished simply for the joy of decoration. Costume and its patterning may have a magical or religious role, usually of pre-Hispanic origin. In some cases, the exact significance has been forgotten, but among the Huichol, for instance, waist sashes are identified with snakes, which are themselves symbols of rain and fertility, so the wearing of a waist sash is a symbolic prayer for rain. Diamond shapes on some huipiles from San Andrés Larrainzar, in Chiapas, represent the universe of the ancient Maya, ancestors of these villagers, who believed that the earth was a cube and the

NANCY KELLER

Left: Detail of an embroidered dress

sky had four corners. Wearing a garment with a saint's figure on it is also a form of prayer, and the sacred nature of traditional costume in general is shown by the widespread practice of dressing saints' images in old, revered garments at festival times.

Indigenous costume is not something you're likely to buy for practical use, but collectors purchase many items as works of art, which the finest examples certainly are. Outstanding work doesn't come cheap: several hundreds of dollars are asked for the finest huipiles in shops in Oaxaca and San Cristóbal de Las Casas. A less expensive representation of Mexican costume comes in the form of the cloth dolls found in several parts of the country; some are quite detailed in their reproduction of indigenous dress.

Above: Rug from Teotitlán del Valle, Oaxaca, with pre-Hispanic motif

Below left: Oaxacan rug colored with natural dyes

Below right: Oaxacan rug colored with bright synthetic dyes

Other Textiles

One textile art that's practiced by men is weaving on a treadle loom, a machine introduced to Mexico by the Spanish and operated by foot pedals. The treadle loom can weave wider cloth than the back-strap loom

MARK HONAN

and tends to be used for blankets, rugs and wall hangings, as well as rebozos, sarapes and skirt material. It allows for great intricacy in design. Mexico's most famous blanket- and rug-weaving village is Teotitlán del Valle, Oaxaca, which produces, among other things, fine textile copies of pre-Hispanic and modern art, including versions of works by Picasso, Escher, Rivera and Miró, as well as pre-Hispanic-influenced geometric patterns. Some appealing wall hangings, depicting simple village and other scenes, are woven in Jocotepec, near Lago de Chapala, Jalisco, and sold in local towns.

Also suitable as a wall hanging is the cloth embroidered with multitudes of highly colorful birds, animals and insects by the Otomí people of San Pablito, a remote, traditional village in northern Puebla state. This cloth is found in many shops and markets around central Mexico.

The 'yarn paintings' of the Huichol people – created by pressing strands of wool or acrylic yarn onto a wax-covered board – make for colorful and unique decorations. The scenes resemble visions experienced under the influence of the hallucinatory drug peyote, which is central to Huichol culture and believed to put people in contact with the gods. Huichol crafts are found mainly in the states of Nayarit and Jalisco, on whose remote borders the Huichol live. There's a museum in Zapopan, Guadalajara,

Above: Huichol yarn painting

where you can buy Huichol crafts, and Huichol artisans can be found at work most of the year at the Centro Huichol, in Santiago Ixcuintla, Nayarit. Some galleries in Puerto Vallarta sell Huichol work too.

Not to be forgotten beside the more authentic textile products is the wide range of commercially produced clothing based to varying degrees on traditional designs and widely available in shops and markets throughout Mexico. Some of these clothes are very attractive and of obvious practical use.

Also useful and decorative are the many tablecloths and shoulder bags found around the country. Commercially woven tablecloths can be a good buy, as they're often reasonably priced and can serve a variety of purposes. Lovely ones are found in Oaxaca and Michoacán. Bags come in all shapes and sizes, many incorporating pre-Hispanic or indigenous-style designs. Those produced and used by the Huichol are among the most authentic and original.

Right: Cow figurine from Oaxaca

JOHN NOBLE

Ceramics

Mexicans have been making ceramics of both simple and sophisticated designs for several millennia. Owing to its preservability, pottery has told us a great deal of what we know about Mexico's ancient cultures. Wonderful human, animal and mythical ceramic figures can be seen in almost any archaeological museum.

SCOTT DOGGETT

Today the country has many small-scale potters' workshops, turning out anything from the plain, everyday cooking or storage pots that you'll see in markets to elaborate decorative pieces that are true works of art.

A number of village potters work without a wheel: molds are employed by some, while others use a board resting on a stone or two upturned dishes, one on top of the other, as devices for turning their pots. Two villages producing attractive, inexpensive, and unique styles of unglazed pottery by these methods are Amatenango del Valle, Chiapas, and San Bartolo Coyotepec, Oaxaca. Amatenango women make jars and plates turned on boards, but the village is best known for its *animalitos* (tiny animal figures), many of which are made by children. Amatenango pottery is fired by the pre-Hispanic method of burning a mound of wood around a pile of pots, and painted with colors made from local earth.

San Bartolo is the source of all the shiny, black, surprisingly lightweight pottery you'll see in Oaxaca and farther afield. It comes in hundreds of shapes and forms – candlesticks, jugs and vases, decorative animal and bird figures, you name it. Turning is by the two-dish method. The distinctive black color is achieved by firing pottery in pit-kilns in the ground; this method minimizes oxygen intake and turns the iron oxide in the local clay black. Burnishing and polishing give the shine.

A more sophisticated and highly attractive type of Mexican pottery is Talavera, named after a town in Spain whose pottery it resembles. Talavera

Above: Juan Quezada, a potter from Mata Ortiz, Chihuahua, poses with his work.

Below: *Animalitos* from Amatenango del Valle, Chiapas

JOHN NOBLE

has been made in the city of Puebla since colonial times; Dolores Hidalgo is another Talavera production center. Talavera comes in two main forms – tableware and tiles. Bright colors (blue and yellow are often prominent) and floral designs are typical, but tiles may bear any kind of design. In Puebla, Talavera tiles, some painted with people or animals, adorn the exteriors of many colonial-era buildings. The basic Talavera method involves two firings, with a tin and lead glaze and the painted design applied between the two.

Another of Mexico's distinctive ceramic forms is the *árbol de la vida* (tree of life). These highly elaborate candelabra-like objects, often a meter or more high, are molded by hand and decorated with numerous tiny figures of people, animals, plants and so on. Trees of life may be brightly or soberly colored. The most common themes are Christian, with the Garden of Eden a frequent subject, but trees of life may be devoted to any theme the potter wishes. Some of the best are made in Acatlán de Osorio and Izúcar de Matamoros, Puebla, and Metepec, in the state of México. Artesanías shops in several major centers sell trees of life, as well as the striking clay suns from Metepec.

The Guadalajara suburbs of Tonalá and Tlaquepaque are also renowned pottery centers. Tonalá is the source of most of the better work, and its products are sold in both places, as well as farther afield. The towns produce a wide variety of ceramics; among the most outstanding work is Jorge Wilmot's heavy 'stoneware' – mostly tableware in delicate blue colors, fired at very high temperatures.

Below: Distinctive black pottery from San Bartolo Coyotepec, Oaxaca

DAVE G HOUSER

One truly eye-catching method of decoration, employed by the Huicholes (practitioners of so many unusual techniques), is to cover the ceramics in dramatic, bright patterns of glass beads pressed into a wax coating. The Huicholes also use this technique on masks and gourds and even to create pictures. A walk around almost any Mexican market or craft shop will reveal interesting ceramics. All kinds of decorative animal and human figurines, often with strong pre-Hispanic influence, are sold around the country. Copies of pre-Hispanic pottery can be attractive as well, one notable example being figures of the pudgy, playful, hairless Tepezcuintle dogs that formed part of the diet of ancient western Mexicans.

Many pottery Tepezcuintles have been unearthed around the city of Colima, and skillful reproductions of them are sold in several places in the city.

Before you go overboard buying pottery, remember that it needs very careful packing to get it home unbroken.

Opposite: Tiles adorn the Casa de Azulejos in Mexico City.

Right: Talavera pottery from Puebla

Below left and right: Tiles from Dolores Hidalgo, Guanajuato

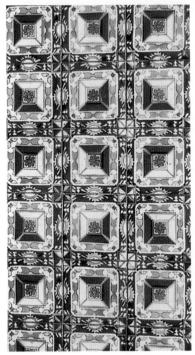

SUSAN KAYE

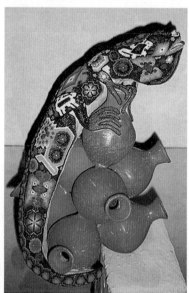

NANCY KELLER

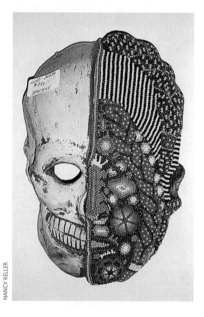

NANCY KELLER

Masks & Headdresses

Like so many other Mexican crafts, mask-making dates back to pre-Hispanic times. In authentic use, masks were and are worn for magical and religious purposes in dances, ceremonies and shamanistic rites: the wearer temporarily becomes the creature, person or deity depicted by the mask. The exact meanings of some masked dances performed in indigenous festivals today may be forgotten, but often the dances enact a mythical story intended to bring fertility or scare away enemies or other evil forces. These dances often have a curious mixture of pre-Hispanic and Christian or Spanish themes. In some cities, traditional dances, some with masks, are regularly performed in *folklórico* shows.

A huge range of masks is employed, differing from region to region and dance to dance. Though masks obviously have much more life when in use, you can still admire their variety and artistry at museums in cities such as San Luis Potosí, Zacatecas, Morelia and Colima, and at artesanías shops and markets around the country. The southern state of Guerrero has produced probably the most varied range of fine masks.

Wood is the basic material of most masks, but papier-mâché, clay, wax and leather are also used. A mask will often be painted or embellished with real teeth, hair, feathers or other adornments. 'Tigers' – often looking more like leopards or jaguars – are fairly common, as are other animals and birds, actual and mythical. Also numerous are masks depicting Christ, devils and Europeans, whose pale, wide-eyed, mustachioed features obviously looked pretty comical to the native Mexicans.

Opposite top: Bright ceramic suns

Opposite bottom left: Huichol beadwork iguana, Galería Pyrámide, Puerto Vallarta, Jalisco

Opposite bottom right: Huichol beadwork mask, Galería Pyrámide, Puerto Vallarta, Jalisco

Top right: Miniature wooden 'tiger' mask

Bottom right: European-faced mask

Today, masks are also made for hanging on walls. While these may not have the mystique that surrounds genuine ceremonial masks, some of which are of considerable age, they're often brighter and in better condition. Even miniature masks can be attractive. Distinguishing genuine dance masks from imitations can be nearly impossible for the uninitiated. Some new masks are even treated so that they will appear old.

Unless you know something about masks or have expert guidance, the best policy when buying them is simply to go for what you like – if the price seems right.

Another spectacular element of some dance costumes is the brilliant feathered headdress, recalling the famous ones that adorned the Aztec emperor Moctezuma and other ancient Mexican nobles. Unless you're lucky enough to be present at a festival in Puebla state where the Danza de los Quetzales (Quetzal Dance) is being performed, or in Oaxaca state for the Zapotec's stately Danza de las Plumas (Feather Dance), the best chance you'll have of seeing these magnificent creations is at folklórico dance shows. The *conchero* dance, frequently staged by informal groups in the Mexico City Zócalo to the accompaniment of loud, upbeat drumming, features feathered headdresses that are almost as superb. Huicholes also adorn some of their hats with impressive feather arrays.

LEE FOSTER

Above: Ceramic mask from Zihuatanejo

Below: Brilliant Totonac headdress

JAMES LYON

Lacquerware & Woodwork

Gourds, the hard shells of certain squash-type fruits, have been used in Mexico since antiquity as bowls, cups and small storage vessels. Today they serve many other uses, including children's rattles, maracas and even hats. Since pre-Hispanic times, too, gourds have been decorated. The most eye-catching technique is the lacquer process, in which the outside of the gourd is coated with layers of paste or paint, each left to harden before the next is applied. The final layer is painted with the artisan's chosen design, then coated with oil varnish to seal the lacquer. All this makes the gourd nonporous and, to some extent, heat resistant. The painted designs often show birds, plants or animals, but the possibilities are infinite.

Wood, too, can be lacquered, and today the majority of lacquerware you'll see in Mexico – sold all over the central and southern portions of the country – is pine or a sweetly scented wood from the remote village of Olinalá, in the northeastern part of Guerrero state. Characteristic of Olinalá crafts are boxes, trays, chests and furniture lacquered by the *rayado*

Above: Eye-catching gourds from Chiapa de Corzo, Chiapas

Right: Detail of a lacquered wooden tray from Olinalá, Guerrero

NANCY KELLER

DAVE G HOUSER

method, in which designs are created by scraping off part of the top coat of paint to expose a different-colored layer below. Other lacquering centers are Chiapa de Corzo, in Chiapas, and Uruapan and Pátzcuaro, in Michoacán. Some lacquer artists in Uruapan practice the *embutido* method, in which they scrape a design in the top layer of lacquer and fill in the resulting depressions with different colors, sometimes with beautiful results.

Among the finest wooden crafts made in Mexico are the polished *palo fierro* (ironwood) carvings done by the Seri people of the northwestern state of Sonora. The hard wood is worked into a variety of dramatic human, animal and sea-creature shapes. Seris sell their work in Hermosillo, Kino Viejo and Kino Nuevo.

Other attractive woodcrafts are the brightly painted copal animals and dragons and other imaginary beasts produced by villagers in San Martín Tilcajete, Arrazola and La Unión Tejalapan, near Oaxaca city. Multitudes of these creatures, called *alebrijes*, are arrayed in shops and markets in Oaxaca. The craft emerged as a form of souvenir only in the late 1980s, from toys the local people had been carving for their children for generations. It has brought relative wealth to many families in the villages involved.

The Tarahumara people of the Barranca del Cobre (Copper Canyon) area in northwest Mexico produce dolls, toys and animals. Quiroga, near Pátzcuaro in Michoacán, is well known for its brightly painted wooden furniture.

San Miguel de Allende and Cuernavaca are other wooden furniture centers.

Top left: Wood carver plying his trade in Mazatlán, Sinaloa

Top right: Marionettes on display in a handicrafts market, Cancún, Quintana Roo

Musical Instruments

Mexico's finest guitars are produced in Paracho, near Uruapan in Michoacán, which also turns out violins, cellos and other instruments. There are many shops and workshops in the town, which holds a guitar festival every August. The Tarahumara also make violins.

Elsewhere you'll come across maracas, tambourines, whistles, scrape boards and a variety of drums in markets and shops. Interesting to look out for, though not particularly common, are 'tongue drums' – hollowed-out pieces of wood, often cylindrical in shape and attractively carved or decorated, with two central tongues of wood, each giving a different note when struck.

Bark Paintings

Colorful paintings on *amate*, paper made from tree bark, are sold in countless souvenir shops. While many are cheap, humdrum productions for an indiscriminating tourist market, others certainly qualify as art, showing village life in skillful detail.

Bark paper has been made in Mexico since pre-Hispanic times, when some codices – pictorial manuscripts – were painted on it. It has always been held sacred. The skills for making amate survive only in one small, remote area of central Mexico where the states of Hidalgo, Puebla and Veracruz converge. A chief source of the paper is the Otomí village of San Pablito. The paper is made by women, who boil the bark, then lay out the fibers and beat them until they blend together. The resulting paper is dried in the sun. Most of it is then bought by Nahua villagers from the state of Guerrero, who have been creating bark paintings since the 1960s. More recently, San Pablito villagers have taken up bark painting, some producing unorthodox designs representing San Pablito's traditional deities.

Shamans in San Pablito still use bark paper cutouts portraying the deities for fertility and medicinal rites, and some of these highly unusual works are also sold.

Right: *Amate* painting

NANCY KELLER

Leather

Leather belts, bags, *huaraches* (sandals), shoes, boots and clothes are often of good quality in Mexico and usually much cheaper than at home. They're widely available in shops and markets all over the country, but towns and cities in the northern and central ranching regions – such as Zacatecas, Jerez, Hermosillo, Monterrey, Saltillo, León and Guadalajara – have some especially well crafted gear. These towns are also the places to look if you want to make a present of a Mexican cowboy saddle or pair of spurs to your steed back home.

León is renowned as Mexico's shoe capital and has dozens of shoe stores, but in fact every other sizable city has plenty of good ones, too. Check quality and fit carefully before you buy. Mexicans use metric footwear sizes.

DAVE G HOUSER

Jewelry & Metalwork

Some ancient Mexicans were expert metal smiths and jewelers, as museum exhibits show. The Spanish fever for Mexico's gold and silver led to indigenous people being banned from working those metals for a time during the colonial period, during which European styles of jewelry predominated. Indigenous artisanship was revived in the 20th century, however – most famously in the central Mexican town of Taxco by the American William Spratling, who initiated a silver-craft industry that now boasts more than 300 shops in Taxco. Silver is much more widely available than gold in Mexico, and is fashioned in all manner of styles and designs and with artistry ranging from the dully imitative to the superb. Earrings are particularly popular. It's quite possible to buy good pieces at sensible prices – see Shopping in the Taxco section of the Around Mexico City chapter for hints on buying silver jewelry. For gold, including some delicate

Above: Leather sandals on display at a Oaxaca market

Opposite top : Beaten copper basins from the Bajío area, in Mexico's Northern Central Highlands

Opposite bottom: Earrings fashioned from silver, Puerto Vallarta

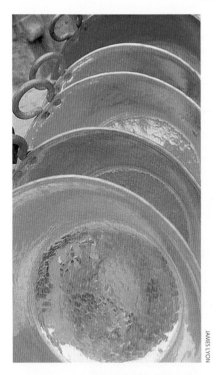

filigree work, Guanajuato and Oaxaca cities are two good places to look.

Necklaces of a wide variety of materials, including glass or stone beads, wood, seeds and coral, are worn by many Mexican women and are quite easy to come by. Many original jewelry creations, mostly from inexpensive materials, are also sold at the weekend market in the Mexico City suburb of Coyoacán and by vendors in travelers' haunts such as Oaxaca and San Cristóbal de Las Casas.

Precious stones are much less common than precious metals. True jade, beloved of ancient Mexicans, is a rarity; most 'jade' jewelry is actually jadeite, serpentine or calcite. One abundant stone is the opal, which is mined in Querétaro state, where the town of San Juan del Río, near Tequisquiapan, has become quite a gem and jewelry center.

Santa Clara del Cobre, Michoacán, is a center for copperware, turning out shining plates, pots, candlesticks, lamps and more from dozens of workshops. Oaxaca city is the center of a thriving craft of tin plates, stamped into low relief and painted with hundreds of attractive, colorful, small shapes.

JAMES LYON

LEE FOSTER

Retablos

An engaging Mexican custom is to adorn the sanctuaries of specially revered saints or holy images with *retablos*, small paintings giving thanks to the saint in question for answered prayers. Typically done on small sheets of tin, but sometimes on glass, wood, cardboard or other materials, the retablos depict these miracles in touchingly literal images painted by their beneficiaries. They may show a cyclist's hair's-breadth escape from a hurtling bus, a sailor's survival of a shipwreck, or an invalid rising from a sickbed, beside a representation of the saint and a brief message along the lines of, 'Thanks to San Milagro for curing my rheumatism – María Suárez González, 6 June 1999.' The Basílica de Guadalupe in Mexico City, the Santuario de Plateros near Fresnillo in Zacatecas and the church at Real de Catorce in San Luis Potosí state all have fascinating collections of retablos. Diego Rivera was among the first to treat these works as real folk art, and the Museo Frida Kahlo in Coyoacán, Mexico City, the former home of his artist wife, displays some of his collection.

JAMES LYON

DAVE G HOUSER

Baskets, Hats & Hammocks

Handmade baskets of multifarious shapes and sizes are common in Mexican markets. If you take a fancy to one, at least you can use it to carry other souvenirs home. Materials used to make baskets include cane, bamboo, and rush or palm-leaf strips. The latter may be wound around a filling of grasses. The more pliable materials enable a coiled construction, but weaving is most common. Many baskets are attractively patterned or colored.

The classic wide-brimmed, high-crowned Mexican *sombrero* is now largely a thing of the past, except on a few mariachi musicians and in a few souvenir shops. Contemporary everyday men's hats are smaller but still often woven from palm strips, either in factories or by hand. The best are considered to be the *jipijapas* (Panama hats) made in caves at Becal, Campeche, where the humidity prevents the fibers from becoming too brittle during the production process. Mérida is a good place to buy a jipijapa.

Another product of practical use to many travelers is the hammock. A hammock is the most comfortable and economical place to sleep in many hot, southern areas. Generally made of cotton or nylon, hammocks come in a variety of widths and an infinite number of color patterns. Notable places where they're made or sold include Mérida, in Yucatán state; Palenque, in Chiapas; and Mitla and Juchitán, in Oaxaca. You can watch them being made in Tixcocob, near Mérida. (Also see 'Yucatecan Hammocks: The Only Way to Sleep' in the Yucatán Peninsula chapter).

Left top and bottom: Colorful straw baskets

DAVE G HOUSER

Festival Crafts

Some Mexican crafts are produced for specific events. The national obsession with skull and skeleton motifs, by which Mexicans continually remind themselves of their own mortality, reaches a crescendo in the weeks before Día de los Muertos (Day of the Dead, which is celebrated on November 2), when the souls of the dead are believed to revisit the earth and people gather in graveyards with gifts for them. As the Day of the Dead approaches, families build altars in their homes, and shops and markets fill with countless toy coffins and skeletons made of paper, cardboard or clay, many of them engaged in very un-skeletonlike activities such as riding a bicycle, playing music or getting married. Most amazing are the rows of chocolate and candy skulls, skeletons and coffins that appear in market stalls – proof of the almost joyful nature of the festival, which reunites the living with their dead.

Most Mexican children's birthdays would be incomplete without a *piñata*, a large, brightly decorated papier-mâché star, animal, fruit or other figure, constructed around a clay pot or papier-mâché mold. At party time, the piñata is stuffed with small toys, sweets and fruit and suspended on a rope. Blindfolded children take turns bashing it with a stick until it breaks open and showers everyone with the gifts inside. Piñatas are also broken after the traditional pre-Christmas processions called *posadas*, which are still held in some towns.

JOHN NOBLE

Top: Panama hats on display in Cozumel, Quintana Roo

Right: Candy skulls for the Day of the Dead

NADA EN ESTE MUNDO DURA
FENECEN BIENES Y MALES
UNA TRISTE SEPULTURA
A TODOS NOS HACE IGUALES

JOHN NOBLE

Another Christmas craft is the creation of *nacimientos*, nativity scenes, in homes or town plazas. Clay or wood figures of the personages in these scenes may be reused year after year. Some larger-scale nacimientos even feature live sheep and goats.

Above: Day of the Dead altar at the Templo Mayor, Mexico City

Acknowledgments

THANKS
Many readers wrote with helpful information and suggestions, including:

Audria Abel & Jimmy Davies, Edward Abse, Campamento Adame, Mike Agnew, Carlos Aguilera, Carlos Escudero Albarran, Heidi Albert & Gareth Lowndes, Karen Alexopoulos, Curtis Allan, Wim Allegaert, Anne Allen, Emily Allen, Kaia Ambrose, Jeff Ames, De Coen An, Veronica Anderson, Fabian Andersson, Rachel Andrews, William Apt, Caroline & Joelle Apter, Deborah Arambula, Jan E Arctander, Robert Armstrong & Suzanne Aubry, Nicholas Aster, Judith & Marvin Atchley, Jacqueline Atkinson, Jörg Ausfelt, John Ayre, Christina Baez, Elaine Bainard, Lisa Baird, Danielle Baker, John Baker, Katia & André Balty, Kevin Banker, Bass Bannick, Norberto Barba, James Barbato, Paul Barber, Bob & Debbie Barker, John & Liz Barlow, Anne Barnett & Kieran Larkin, Carlos Barragan, Nallely Barragan, Sue Barreau, John Barreiro, Lynne Bateman, Dorothy Batz, Sarah Bayly, Jack Beard, P Beauchamp, Sallie G Beck, Buster Becker, Eric Beecroft, Graham Beedie, Theo Beekman, Georgina Behrens, Mike Beier, Beverly Bell, James Bell, Rob Bell, Alessia Bello, Gary Benedyk, Charles Bennett, Janine Bentley, Caryl & Brian Bergeron, Mauricio Bergstein, Marianna Berkley, Lee Bernstein & Alicia Park, Joel Berry, Steffen Berthold, Kimberly & Felipe Berzunza, Alan JF Betrancourt, Jan Betts, Steve Bey, Guido de Bie, Joanna Biggs, Sarah Billyack, Trista Bilmer, Roderick Binns, Scott Bishopp, John Black, Theresa Black, Jenny Blaker & Neil Hancock, Mookie Blaylock, KV Blunt, Steve Boanas, Gunnar Bohne, Richmond Bollinger & F Wagner, Andre Bookelmann, David Boniface, K Boom!, Tjeerd Boonman, Bridget Booth, Kim Borchard, Art Borkent, Kris Borring, Taffy Bos, Robert Bosch, Erik Botsford, Phillip Boulton, David Bowen, J Bradbrook, Alison Brandsma, Gordon E Brauninger, Connie Breedlove, Paul de Brem, Sarah Kate Bridgewater & Vicky Scrivens, Elizabeth Briggs, Tracey Brignole, Daniel Brill, George Broché, Hugh R Brodie, Iden Bromfield, James Brooks, Tom Brosnahan, Joanna Brown, Nigel Brown, Joe Bruckner, Tanja de Bruin & Yvonne Buijink, Jake Bryant, Silke Buchholz, Becky Buck, Michael Buechler, A Bullock, Jan Bulman, April Burge, Anke Burger, Jeannine Burk, Andrew Burns, Russell Burrows, Dana Gay Burton, Christine Busby, Delores Bushong, Eric Calder, Murray Cambie, Claude Camirand, Frank Campbell, Keith Campbell, KW Campbell, Lila Campbell & Fred Hart, Jeff Cardille, Ingeman Carlsson, Ricardo Robledo Carmona, C Carol, Sandy Cartwright, Chuck Cassity, Annick Ceuppens, June Challoner, J & E Chanecka, Linda Chapel, Bob Chase, Simon Cheatham & Bindi Edmonds, Sally Childs, Thomas Chladek, Lars Bruun Christensen & Krista Vanggaard, Dianne Christy, Michael Clark, Wayne Clarke, Steve Clift, Stacey Clinesmith, Joann Clirftn, Amy Coates & Becca Critchley, FS Cockburn, Robert Cocovinis, Seth Cohen, Valerie P Cohen, Margaret Collins, Kevin Connor, Tom Connor & Jane Challoner, Geoff Cook, Steve Cook & Esmé-Jane Lippiatt, Pamela Cooper, William Corrin, Nicholas Couis, Marie-Lou Coulombe, Roy Couwenberg & Frederike ven Riel, Rob Craig, David Croome, Jorge Penagos Cruz, George N Cull, Patty & Rosario D'Alessandro, Rachael Daniel & Rafael Ramirez Raad German, Victoria & Christopher Darke, Graham Darling, Pamela Darling, Maria Darlington, Amanda Dates, Rob & Georgie Davidson, J Davies, Richard Davies, Brenda Davis, Lisa Davis, Simon Davis, Kristin Dawley & Jack Bell, Peter Day & Wendy Lawton, Koen De Boeck, David Delaney, Luis Delgado, Bill Denny, Paul De Zardain, Paul Dickerson, Al & Amy Dieste, Cisco Craig Dietz, Martin Dillig, Joanne Dinsmore de López, Carsten Dittmann, Clement Djossen & Lotta Andersson, Anna Doddridge, Michaela & Martin Dohnalkova, Scott Donahue, Annick Donkers, Anka de Dood, William Doris, Julia K Dotson, K Douglas, Norma Douglas, Sally Drake, Erika Drucker, Eddie Dry, Alex Dunne, Jim Dutkiewycz, Mr & Mrs J Dutton, Wim Dykstra & Gon Bloemendal, Tom Earle, Paul Eastman, Sven Eberlein, Zsolt Edelenyi, Joyce Edling, Libby Edwards, Andrea Eggenstein & Manuela Sartory, Eve Eidelson, Donald Eischen, Naomi Eisenstein, Anna Elfors, Mei-Ling Ellerman, Kate Elliott, Sue Elliott, David Ellis, Bijan Elmdust, Kari Eloranta, Julie & Steve Elver, Diane England, Chris Englund, Peter

Epanchin, Louisa Ersanilli, John Evans, Sherry Evoy, Craig Faanes, Annabel Falk, Thomas Farrell, Megan Faunce, Renée Feather, Evgeni Fedotov, Grace Felfe, Brian Fenn, Maurice Ficheroux, Lee Fields, Frances Figart & Barry Brolley, Brian Fillmore, Bill Finch, Daniel Finke, Nick Fischer, Andrea Fitzsimmons, Tom Fletcher Jr, M Fonteyn, Lisa Foresee, Rudi Forster, John Foster, Helen Fowler & Gus Sevier, Bill & Caroll Fraser, Astrid Frey, Beth Fridinger, Flair Friesen, Thomas Fritzsche, Franco Fubini, Dave Fuller, Geraldine Fuller, Erik Futtrup, Dick Gabriel, Michael Gacquin, Rikke Gadegaard, Paulo Gaeta, Simona Gaggiani, Granluca Ambrosini & Cristina Lazzaroni, Kate Gale, Helene Gallis, Bobby K Galveston, David Gannon, Delphine Garcia, Hans & Yonalkis Durrer Garcia, Mathilde Garnier, Micheline Garrity, Joe & Alma Gaskill, Eniko Gasko & George Balator, RWJ Gates, Pat Gaudry, Damon Gautama, Gary Geating, Kristof Geldmeyer, Mneesha Gellman, Daniela Giannini, Massimo Giannini, Iain Gibbs, Dave Gibson, Eric W Gilliam, David W Gillio, Pamela Ginder, Werner Ginzky, Leo Girard, Paolo Giubellino, Morten Gjerrild & Anne Bondo Hune, Christian Glossner, Warren Glover, Robert Goad, Charles P Goff, Adam Goldstein, Peter Goltermann, Gerardo Gonzalez, Saul Goodwin, Donna Gottardi, Emanuel Graef, Albert Graf, Andy Graham, Brian Graham, Marko Grahl, Catherine Grange, Rachel Grant, Carrol Greenbaum, Helena Greenwood, Line Gregoire, Mark Gregory, Caroline Greig, Ben Griffin, Sylvia Grisez & Sherry Griffiths, Leen Groffils & Bart Weekers, Christel Grosse, Ayala & Yosi Grosskop, Sasha Gubser, Alejandro Guerra, Manuel Bernal Guerra, Olivier Guidet, Alex Gunz, Camilla Gustafsson, Mattias Gustavsson & Rasmus Hemph, Arturo Gutierrez, Noah Guy, Monika Hachiya, Gad Hachlili, Daniel Haenni & Andrea Gautschi, Malreen Haentjens, Oliver Hagemann, Michael Hahne, Steve & Em Hahoney, Mirén Haines, Marc Hale, Ian Halling, Ann & Brian Halpin, Ladislav R Hanka, Katja Hanke, Rhonda Hankins, Lene Hansen, James Hardy, Megan Harker, Dylan Harris, Sarah Harris, Heiko Hartmann, Faye Haskins, Mr & Mrs Hasson, Mary Hatch, Lewis Haupt, Shirley Hawatt, Michelle Hawk, Gay Haworth, Doug & Cheryl Hayden, Micheline Healy & Bernard Lamarche, C Heard, Robert J Heerekip & Simone de Haan Pavel Heimlich, Mike Hellemn, R Hellier, Stefan Henz, Philip Herold, Miguel Herrera-Martinez, Art & Bob Hess, R Hethey, NG Hetterley, Kate Heuisler, Marcel Heutmekers, Patricia Hicks, Michael Hill, Graeme Hind, Rachel Hirschi & Heidi Tschanz, Thomas Hirt, Esther & Winston Ho, David Hobson, Richard Hoch, John Hoffman, Katrina Hoffman, Rick Hogan, Bruce Hogg, David C Holcomb, Ralf Hollmann, Victoria Holtelies, David Holyrod, Els 't Hooft, Nic Hopkins, Tanya Bianca Hoppe, Olaf Horn & Aira Teras, Edward Horne, Rachel Horsley, Alistair How, Ron Hruby, Teri Hruska, Grace Hucul, Graham Hughes & Marcia Marini, Errol Hunt, Shabnam Hussain, Steve Immel, Philip M Isaacson, Christian Iyer, David Iza, Erik Jacobsen, Francisco Jaimes, Michael James, Alex Jantzen, Berit Johns, Kay Johnson, Tim Johnson, Julie Johnston, Ryan Johnston, Don & Lynne Jones, Ken Jones, Natalie Jones, Werner Joos, Arnold Joost & Annemieke Wevers, Mark Jordan, Wiley Jordan, Claudius Jstier, Faisal Juma, Nancy Jusari, Rachel Kahn, Vladimir Kalista, B Kane, Stephan Karkowsky, Nik Katsourides, Volker Katz, Ufuk Kayserilioglu, Ron & Sara Keen, Pascal Kellenberg, Angie Kelly, Cyndi Kelly, John Kelly, Susan Kelly, Debbie Lee Keltz, Micah Kemelman, Jim Kentch, Dietmar Kenzle, Ian Kerr, Monique Kettelarij, Herb Kieklak, Tuomas Kiiski, Jacqueline Kijkema, Mark Kiker, Russell Kilday-Hicks, Erik King, Jeff King, Kimberly King, Jeanine Kitchel, Russel Kivell, Michael Kleinheinz & Rachéle Lamontagne, Andrea Knaf, Manuela Knight, David Knox, Lindsay S Koehler, Steven Koenig, Ulli Koester, Susie Koestner, Simone Koliwyer, Charles & Betty Konopa, Joseph Kortsch, Kenneth D Kostel & Anne-Marie Runfola, Naama Kostiner, Nuamo Kostiner, Lisa Kralovic, Robert Kramps, Robert Krauser, Raghu Krishnan, Sandra Küenzi, Jim Labelle, Mieke Lagae, Amadej Lah & Natasa Platise, Elco Lakwijk, Kerry Lamont, Louise Lander, Cull Frank Landers, Leslie Lane, Anouchka Langford, Chris Larkin, Leah Larkin, Anne Larsen, Dean Larsen, Lynn Larson, Sunny Larson, Robert M Larson, Sallie Latch, Michal Lavi & Aviv Fried, Wendy Lawton, Andrew Lay, Brian Leach, Steve Leavitt, Daniel Lebidois, Denis Le Cam, Jeroen de Leeuw den Bouter, Guido Lehnen, Katja Schüller & Corinna Schüller, Adam Leibowitz, Stephan Leinert, AH Lenz, Scott Leonard, Thibaut Lespagnol, Irving Levinson, Robin LeWinter, Danny Lewis, Marina Lewis, Michael Lewis, Steve Lidgey, Frederico Lifsichtz, Nino Lind, Matthew Linnell, Amanda Lireg,

Dana Lissy, Vicki Littlefield, Elisa Llamas, David Lloyd, Bill Locascio, Jos & Ellen Lommerse, Mirco Lomuth, Giovanni Longo, Christy Loop, Gaute Losnegard, Anthony Lott, Markus Low, Susanne Knauer Lucile, Carey Luff, Jane Luis, Daniel Lund, Guate Lund, Karl Lundberg, Lene & Peter Lykke-Olsen, Susan Lynch, Freya Maberly, Elspeth Macdonald, Matt Mahlau, Clara Mai, Olivier de la Maisonneuve, Mary Makena, Erika Malitzky, Thyra Mangan, Rebecca Maple, Alessandro Marcolin, Joe & Joan Margel, Dina Marshall, Zeus Marofo & Roberto Alcalar, Jan Martens & Karin Van Hout, Jacques Martin, Neil Martin, Paolo Marzitta, Paolo Marzuttini, Julian Mason, Larry Matheson, Stefano Mattana, Mia Matusow, Evelyn Mau, Eduardo Maubert, Chris S Maun, Cheryl Maxwell-Buckeridge, Ted & Mary Lou Mayer, Leonard G Mazzone, Chris McCauley, Keely McCauley, Mike McConnell, Brian McCumber, Bruce McGrew, MA McIntosh, Chris McKenna, Edith McLaren, Margaret McLean, Grant McMillan, Tawnie McNeil, Cameron McPherson, Ramon Medina, Kathleen Meehan, Lorna Meek & Anne Fleming, Annalise Mellor, M Michael Menzel, Marie Meyer, D Meyers, Stuart Michael, Ty Milford, Angela Millar, Belinda Miller, Larry & Phyllis Miller, Suzanne Miller, Jason Milligan, Ricardo Briseo Milln, Stéphanie Mills, Carolina A Miranda, Max Miranda, Jordan Mitchell, Lester H Moffatt, Rubina Mohamed, Duane & Liz Mohling, Jock, Janice & Rachel Moilliet, Hans Molenaar, Peter Møller, Sebastian Mollers, Andrew G Moncrieff, A Montondo, Paul Montore, Frank Moore, Alexis Morgan, N Moristsugu & A Currier, Dan Morris, Lenie Mosaic, Alex Moss, Pauline Mourits, Thorsten Mueller, W Mueller, Ashish Mukharji, Shayo Mukhopadhyay, Barbara Müller, Mark Mulligan, Todd Munro, Paolo A Muraro, Jean & Geoff Murphy, Pat & Mary Murray, Andreas Musolff, Eli Nadel, Marian Nadler, Leila Nafissi, Nancy Nancarrow, Daniel Nardin, Lou Neal, Nicoletta Negri, KAJ Nengerman & HME Lier, Jan Nesnidal, Kirk & Susan Nevin, Mark Nicklas, Jo Niemann, Maggie Niemkiewicz, Adrian Nordenborg, B Norman, Justin Norman & Helen Hagan, Larry Norris, James Nouvet, John Oakes, Peter & Joan O'Brien, Andrew O'Connor, Betty Odell, Josefin Ohlsson, Karyn Okazaki, Kevin Okell, Marian Oker, Peter Ormand, Carmelo Orosz, Lawrence Oswald, Valentina Otaoio, Mike Otoole, Alisa Ouellette, Patty Owen, Chris Oxley, Aydin Ozkaya, Axel B Pajunk, Josuld Palen, Esa Palmborg, Paul Palmera, Lucie Parker, Patrik Paulis, John Payne, Brendan Peace & Andrea Fitzsimmons, Nigel Peacock, Ben Pelle, Chuck & Laurie Pence, Deborah Pencharz, Angélica Pérez, Len & Geri Perkins, Roberta Merighi Perosa, Nisse Perry, Iris Persak, Maurits Pesch, Oliver Peter, Cameron Phillips, Stefano Piazzardi, Lisa Pidruchney, Fabrizio Piemontese & Alessia Bello, Darlene S Pinch, Julie Pingue, Catherine Pizani, Bartek Pogoda, Daniel Pöhlke, Françoise Pohm, O Pollux, Alison & Simon Porges, Hans Possin, Lucille Poulin & Chris Osterbauer, Jim Power, Ellen Powers, Harald Praschinger, Jacqueline Pratt, Marilena Preda, Nicole Prefontaine, Kerry Preibisch & Gustavo Lopez, Georgina Prendiville, Philip Preston, Jose Cabrara Priego, Andreas Prolingheuer & Maren Müller, Neil Pyatt, Hugh E Quetton, Kenyatta Quinones-Street, Paic Diego Quiroz, Talya & Rick Rabern, Ann Rabin, Caroline Raingeard, Nigel Rains, Katherine Ramos, Mandy Rampling, Prasada Rao, Shelley Rapson, Henrik Rasmussen & Vikki Vermod, Thomas Rau & Andrea Rogge, Cristiano Ravalli, Dev Ray, George Redman, Jay Collier Reed, Brian Reid & Sonja Golinsky, Julian Remnant, R Rensing, David Mestres Ridge, Shaun Ridwell, Angelika Rieck, John & Bridget Roberts, Paul Robinson, Richard Robinson, Elizabeth Roche, Juan Kdiaz-Roche, Pinhas Rodan, Karen Rogers, Andrica Rogge, Steve Rogowski, Pilar Rojas-Wong, Rossie Lugo Roman, Patrick Römer, Sherry Ronick, Hans de Roo, Margaret de Roo, Ana Roque, Eric Rose, Paul Rotheroe, John Rowe, Linnéa Rowlatt, Andy Rowles, Deborah Rubio, Julian Rubio, Bob Russel, J Russell, Stefan Ruthner, Jono Ryan, Magda & Piotr Rybka, Fleming Rysholm, Ed Sacchette, Martes Saha, Carme Sala & Xavi Juanico, Pekka Salo, Kevin Samarasingha, Marietta Sander, Kirsti Sarheim, Nathan Sato, Wendy Saunt, Alexandra Savage, Diana Sayers, Tarisa Scarlet, Michael Schaich, Louse Schlein, Susanna Schlette & Dirk Bremecke, Emery Schmel, Ralph Schmens, Richard Schmitt, Joerg Schnabel, Kerstin Schneiderkotter, Marius Schoenberg, Wim Schramms, Teresa L Schriever, John Schultz, Lee & Brenda Schussman, Gunter Schwarz, Thomas Schwarz, Sandra Scofield, Claire Scott, Steve Scott, Thijs Vancay Seele, Kim Segal, Jacob Seligmann, Shelly Selin, Johanna Sell, Erin Sellers, Joanna Settle, Gus Sevier, Bridgid Seymour-East, Katie Shannon, Justine Shapiro,

1076   Acknowledgments

Amisa Sharma, Joli Sharp, Florence & Peter Shaw, Ken Shaw, P Shenkin, Nicole Silverman, Mark Simkin, David & Linda Simmonds, Richard Simpkins, Deborah Simpson, Marco Sims, Marit Sivertsen, S Skerritt, Dan Skog, Mitsy Sleurs, William Sleurs, Mary Slusser, Lisa Smailes, Ana Smallwood, Dan Smith, Ellen Smith, Gary Smith, Iain Smith, Ali Smookler, Goran Soderberg, Kjell Solli, Kurt Sollinger, Janne Solpark, Montse Sors & Martí Gríera, Alfredo Sosa, Leopold Soucy, Patrick Spanjaard, Rich & Julie Spear, Kathrin Speidel, Hermine Spitz, Gabi Spitzer, Detlef Spötter, Imelda Stack, Christian Staeubli, Marco Stambul, Jochen Stange, Paul Stark, Susi Stead, Susan Steed, Hugo Steeds, Fiona Steggles, Jack Stein, David Steinberg, David Stephens, Edel Stephenson, Bruce Stern, Louisa Stevens, Simon A Still, Richard Stockwell, GM Stoffel, Stefan Stoffels, Rob Stokes, Michael Strah, Carrie Strashok, Helene Strauss, Bruce Stroud, Mitja Strukelj, Koen Stuyck, Lisa Suett, Anne & Roman Suttner-Streuselberger, Thomas Singh Suzuki, Miha Svalj, Christian Svane, Helen K Svane, Karen Svanholm, John Tanner, Arthur Tauck, Krysta Taylor, Linnet Taylor, Dan Thatcher, Frédéric Thébaud, Raphaël Thiry, Aled Thomas, Ross Thomasson, Jackie Thompson, Keith & Birgid Thompson, Rod Thompson, Trish Thompson, Michael Thomsen, George Thorsen, Mary Tiesen, Paul Tilley, Miquel Tintore, Mark Tipping, Selviana Tjiong, R Tokgoz, Maarten Tol, Bob & Jackie Tomlinson, Ellen Torp, Werner Toutzschler, Rachel Toyen, Darren Trentepohl, Beatrix Trojer, John Trotter, E Tsitrone, John Tuffrey, Salome Twinberger, Evelyne Udry, J Ulmanis, Anna Utéch, Anne Van Acker, Sebastian van de Beek, Bob van der Mark, Sandra van der Pas & Erik Agterhuis, Andre van der Plas, Peter van der Terp & Diane Hofstetter, Susan van der Welt, Michel Vande Veegaete & Carine Paques, Dreas van Donselaar, Sandra & Hester van Hees & Ubbink, Berit Van Laneshem, Marc & Mirjan van Maastricht, Gerda Van Pee, Marleen Van Daele & Rita Geysens, Marieke van Putten, Wim Van Rompay, M van Wallenburg, Michael Van Wyk, Esther Veenendaal & Auke van Stralen, Iliana la Vega Arnaud, Torben Vejloe, Martin Velazquez, David M Vella, Jos ven der Palen, Steven Verdekel, Sabine Verhelst, R Vermaire, Vikki Vermod & Henrik Rasmussen, Matt Vesce, Michael Vestergaard & Helle Bjerre, Philippe Veyrat, Isabelle Vial, Javier Perez Vicente, Erica Visser, Eirik Krogh Visted, Peter de Vocht, Jacob von Domarus, Johan & Marie Von Matern, Peter von Zezschwitz, A de Vries, Aron Wahl, Laura K Wahmann, Shahar Waks, Ben Walker, Jamie Walker, Richard Walker, Fred Wallace, Dyimpna Walsh, Daniel Ware, Tom Waring, Stephen Warren, Kim Watkins, Thomas Watrous, Nicola Watson, Paul Watson, Bonita Wauls, Mariette Waverijn, K Weatherell, Guido Weber, Bart Weekers, Marilyn Welch, NS Welch, A Went, Dorothy C Wertz, Abraham Westermann, A White, Mishi Whiteley, Beth Whitman, Barbara Whyte, Anneke Wieling & Jan Gulden, Sharen Wiggins, John Wight, Anne Wijns, Eleanore Wilde, John D Wildi, Scott Wilhelm, Patrick William-Powlett, Dave & Ann Williams, Michael Williams, Stuart Williams, Brian Wilson, Nick Wilson, Victor Wishalla, Pip Witheridge, Paul Witkover, William Wolf, Julia Wood, Sara Wood, Judy & Chris Woods, Ken Woods, Tim Woods, Barrie Wraith, CA Wright, Pat Wright, Stamatios Xanthoulis, Sharon Yarwood, Anna Young, Rebecca Young, Sally Young, Aiko Yokozuka, Victoria Zafra, Susan Zakin, RA Zambardino, Fred Zanger, Dave Zapanta, Judy Zavos, Carmen Zeisler, Lars Zimmermann, Sabine Zimmermann, Dario Zito, Jolee Zola, Andrea & Agar Zuin, Magda Zupancic.

LONELY PLANET

You already know that Lonely Planet produces more than this one guidebook, but you might not be aware of the other products we have on this region. Here is a selection of titles which you may want to check out as well:

Yucatán
ISBN 1 86450 103 0
US$17.99 • UK£11.99

Diving & Snorkeling Cozumel
ISBN 0 86442 574 0
US$14.95 • UK£8.99

Healthy Travel Central & South America
ISBN 1 86450 053 0
US$5.95 • UK£3.99

World Food Mexico
ISBN 1 86450 023 9
US$11.95 • UK£6.99

Baja California
ISBN 0 86442 445 0
US$16.95 • UK£10.99

Latin American Spanish phrasebook
ISBN 0 86442 558 9
US$6.95 • UK£4.50

Available wherever books are sold.

LONELY PLANET

Guides by Region

Lonely Planet is known worldwide for publishing practical, reliable and no-nonsense travel information in our guides and on our Web site. The Lonely Planet list covers just about every accessible part of the world. Currently there are 16 series: Travel guides, Shoestring guides, Condensed guides, Phrasebooks, Read This First, Healthy Travel, Walking guides, Cycling guides, Watching Wildlife guides, Pisces Diving & Snorkeling guides, City Maps, Road Atlases, Out to Eat, World Food, Journeys travel literature and Pictorials.

AFRICA Africa on a shoestring • Cairo • Cairo City Map • Cape Town • Cape Town City Map • East Africa • Egypt • Egyptian Arabic phrasebook • Ethiopia, Eritrea & Djibouti • Ethiopian (Amharic) phrasebook • The Gambia & Senegal • Healthy Travel Africa • Kenya • Malawi • Morocco • Moroccan Arabic phrasebook • Mozambique • Read This First: Africa • South Africa, Lesotho & Swaziland • Southern Africa • Southern Africa Road Atlas • Swahili phrasebook • Tanzania, Zanzibar & Pemba • Trekking in East Africa • Tunisia • Watching Wildlife East Africa • Watching Wildlife Southern Africa • West Africa • World Food Morocco • Zimbabwe, Botswana & Namibia
Travel Literature: Mali Blues: Traveling to an African Beat • The Rainbird: A Central African Journey • Songs to an African Sunset: A Zimbabwean Story

AUSTRALIA & THE PACIFIC Auckland • Australia • Australian phrasebook • Australia Road Atlas • Bushwalking in Australia • Cycling Australia • Cycling New Zealand • Fiji • Fijian phrasebook • Healthy Travel Australia, NZ and the Pacific • Islands of Australia's Great Barrier Reef • Melbourne • Melbourne City Map • Micronesia • New Caledonia • New South Wales & the ACT • New Zealand • Northern Territory • Outback Australia • Out to Eat – Melbourne • Out to Eat – Sydney • Papua New Guinea • Pidgin phrasebook • Queensland • Rarotonga & the Cook Islands • Samoa • Solomon Islands • South Australia • South Pacific • South Pacific phrasebook • Sydney • Sydney City Map • Sydney Condensed • Tahiti & French Polynesia • Tasmania • Tonga • Tramping in New Zealand • Vanuatu • Victoria • Walking in Australia • Watching Wildlife Australia • Western Australia
Travel Literature: Islands in the Clouds: Travels in the Highlands of New Guinea • Kiwi Tracks: A New Zealand Journey • Sean & David's Long Drive

CENTRAL AMERICA & THE CARIBBEAN Bahamas, Turks & Caicos • Baja California • Bermuda • Central America on a shoestring • Costa Rica • Costa Rica Spanish phrasebook • Cuba • Dominican Republic & Haiti • Eastern Caribbean • Guatemala • Guatemala, Belize & Yucatán: La Ruta Maya • Havana • Healthy Travel Central & South America • Jamaica • Mexico • Mexico City • Panama • Puerto Rico • Read This First: Central & South America • World Food Mexico • Yucatán
Travel Literature: Green Dreams: Travels in Central America

EUROPE Amsterdam • Amsterdam City Map • Amsterdam Condensed • Andalucía • Austria • Baltic States phrasebook • Barcelona • Barcelona City Map • Belgium & Luxembourg • Berlin • Berlin City Map • Britain • British phrasebook • Brussels, Bruges & Antwerp • Brussels City Map • Budapest • Budapest City Map • Canary Islands • Central Europe • Central Europe phrasebook • Corfu & the Ionians • Corsica • Crete • Crete Condensed • Croatia • Cycling Britain • Cycling France • Cyprus • Czech & Slovak Republics • Denmark • Dublin • Dublin City Map • Eastern Europe • Eastern Europe phrasebook • Edinburgh • Estonia, Latvia & Lithuania • Europe on a shoestring • Finland • Florence • France • Frankfurt Condensed • French phrasebook • Georgia, Armenia & Azerbaijan • Germany • German phrasebook • Greece • Greek Islands • Greek phrasebook • Hungary • Iceland, Greenland & the Faroe Islands • Ireland • Istanbul • Italian phrasebook • Italy • Krakow • Lisbon • The Loire • London • London City Map • London Condensed • Madrid • Malta • Mediterranean Europe • Mediterranean Europe phrasebook • Moscow • Mozambique • Munich • the Netherlands • Norway • Out to Eat – London • Paris • Paris City Map • Paris Condensed • Poland • Portugal • Portuguese phrasebook • Prague • Prague City Map • Provence & the Côte d'Azur • Read This First: Europe • Romania & Moldova • Rome • Rome City Map • Russia, Ukraine & Belarus • Russian phrasebook • Scandinavian & Baltic Europe • Scandinavian Europe phrasebook • Scotland • Sicily • Slovenia • South-West France • Spain • Spanish phrasebook • St Petersburg • St Petersburg City Map • Sweden • Switzerland • Trekking in Spain • Tuscany • Ukrainian phrasebook • Venice • Vienna • Walking in Britain • Walking in France • Walking in Ireland • Walking in Italy • Walking in Spain • Walking in Switzerland • Western Europe • Western Europe phrasebook • World Food France • World Food Ireland • World Food Italy • World Food Spain
Travel Literature: A Small Place in Italy • After Yugoslavia • Love and War in the Apennines • On the Shores of the Mediterranean The Olive Grove: Travels in Greece • Round Ireland in Low Gear

INDIAN SUBCONTINENT Bangladesh • Bengali phrasebook • Bhutan • Delhi • Goa • Hindi/Urdu phrasebook • India • India & Bangladesh travel atlas • Indian Himalaya • Karakoram Highway • Kerala • Mumbai • Nepal • Nepali phrasebook • Pakistan • Rajasthan • Read This First: Asia & India • South India • Sri Lanka • Sri Lanka phrasebook • Trekking in the Indian Himalaya • Trekking in the Karakoram & Hindukush • Trekking in the Nepal Himalaya
Travel Literature: In Rajasthan • Shopping for Buddhas • The Age of Kali

ISLANDS OF THE INDIAN OCEAN Madagascar & Comoros • Maldives • Mauritius, Réunion & Seychelles

MIDDLE EAST & CENTRAL ASIA Bahrain, Kuwait & Qatar • Central Asia • Central Asia phrasebook • Dubai • Hebrew phrasebook • Iran • Israel & the Palestinian Territories • Israel & the Palestinian Territories travel atlas • Istanbul • Istanbul city map • Istanbul to Cairo on a shoestring • Jerusalem • Jerusalem city map • Jordan • Jordan, Syria & Lebanon travel atlas • Lebanon • Middle East • Oman & the United Arab Emirates • Syria • Turkey • Turkey travel atlas • Turkish phrasebook •Yemen
Travel Literature: The Gates of Damascus • Kingdom of the Film Stars: Journey into Jordan • Black on Black: Iran Revisited

NORTH AMERICA Alaska • Backpacking in Alaska • Baja California • Boston • California & Nevada • California condensed • Canada • Chicago • Chicago city map • Deep South • Florida • Hawaii • Las Vegas • Los Angeles • Miami • New England • New Orleans • New York City • New York city map • New York condensed • New York, New Jersey & Pennsylvania • Oahu • Pacific Northwest USA • Puerto Rico • Rocky Mountain States • San Francisco • San Francisco city map • Seattle • Southwest USA • Texas • USA • USA phrasebook • Vancouver • Washington, DC & the Capital Region • Washington, DC city map
Travel Literature: Drive Thru America

NORTH-EAST ASIA Beijing • Cantonese phrasebook • China • Hong Kong • Hong Kong city map • Hong Kong, Macau & Guangzhou • Japan • Japanese phrasebook • Japanese audio pack • Korea • Korean phrasebook • Kyoto • Mandarin phrasebook • Mongolia • Mongolian phrasebook • North-East Asia on a shoestring • Seoul • South-West China • Taiwan • Tibet • Tibetan phrasebook • Tokyo
Travel Literature: Lost Japan • In Xanadu

SOUTH AMERICA Argentina, Uruguay & Paraguay • Bolivia • Brazil • Brazilian phrasebook • Buenos Aires • Chile & Easter Island • Chile & Easter Island travel atlas • Colombia • Ecuador & the Galapagos Islands • Healthy Travel Central & South America • Latin American Spanish phrasebook • Peru • Quechua phrasebook • Rio de Janeiro • Rio de Janeiro city map • South America on a shoestring • Trekking in the Patagonian Andes • Venezuela
Travel Literature: Full Circle: A South American Journey

SOUTH-EAST ASIA Bali & Lombok • Bangkok • Bangkok city map • Burmese phrasebook • Cambodia • Hanoi • Healthy Travel Asia & India • Hill Tribes phrasebook • Ho Chi Minh City • Indonesia • Indonesia's Eastern Islands • Indonesian phrasebook • Indonesian audio pack • Jakarta • Java • Laos • Lao phrasebook • Laos travel atlas • Malay phrasebook • Malaysia, Singapore & Brunei • Myanmar (Burma) • Philippines • Pilipino (Tagalog) phrasebook • Read This First Asia & India • Singapore • South-East Asia on a shoestring • South-East Asia phrasebook • Thailand • Thailand's Islands & Beaches • Thailand travel atlas • Thai phrasebook • Thai audio pack • Vietnam • Vietnamese phrasebook • Vietnam travel atlas • World Food Thailand • World Food Vietnam

ALSO AVAILABLE: Antarctica • The Arctic • Brief Encounters: Stories of Love, Sex & Travel • Chasing Rickshaws • Lonely Planet Unpacked • Not the Only Planet: Travel Stories from Science Fiction • Sacred India • Travel with Children • Traveller's Tales

LONELY PLANET

ON THE ROAD

Travel Guides explore cities, regions and countries and supply information on transport, restaurants and accommodations, regardless of your budget. They come with reliable, easy-to-use maps, practical advice, cultural and historical facts and a run down on attractions both on and off the beaten track. There are over 200 titles in this classic series, covering nearly every country in the world.

 Lonely Planet Upgrades extend the shelf lives of existing travel guides by detailing any changes that may affect travel in a region since the book has been published. Upgrades can be downloaded for free on **www.lonelyplanet.com/upgrades**.

For travelers with more time than money, **Shoestring** guides offer dependable, firsthand information with hundreds of detailed maps, plus insider tips for stretching money as far as possible. Covering entire continents in most cases, the six-volume shoestring guides have been known as 'backpackers' bibles' for over 25 years.

For the discerning short-term visitor, **Condensed** guides highlight the best a destination has to offer in a full-color, pocket-sized format designed for quick access. From top sights and walking tours to opinionated reviews of where to eat, stay, shop and have fun.

CitySync lets travelers use their Palm™ or Visor™ handheld computers to guide them through a city's highlights with quick tips on transport, history, cultural life, major sights and shopping and entertainment options. It can also quickly search and sort hundreds of reviews of hotels, restaurants and attractions and pinpoint the place on scrollable street maps. CitySync can be downloaded from **www.citysync.com**.

MAPS & ATLASES

Lonely Planet's **City Maps** feature downtown and metropolitan maps as well as transit routes and walking tours. The maps come complete with an index of streets, a listing of sights and a plastic coat for extra durability.

Road Atlases are an essential navigation tool for serious travelers. Cross-referenced with the guidebooks, they also feature distance and climate charts and a complete site index.

LONELY PLANET

ESSENTIALS

Read This First books help new travelers to hit the road with confidence. These invaluable predeparture guides give step-by-step advice on preparing for a trip, budgeting, arranging a visa, planning an itinerary and staying safe while still getting off the beaten track.

Healthy Travel pocket guides offer a regional run down on disease hot spots and practical advice on predeparture health measures, staying well on the road and what to do in emergency situations. The guides come with a user-friendly design and helpful diagrams and tables.

Lonely Planet's **Phrasebooks** cover the essential words and phrases travelers may need when they're strangers in a strange land. It comes in a pocket-sized format with color tabs for quick reference, extensive vocabulary lists, easy-to-follow pronunciation keys and two-way dictionaries.

Lonely Planet's **Travel Journal** is a lightweight but sturdy travel diary for jotting down all those on the road observations and significant travel moments. It comes with a handy time zone wheel, world maps and useful travel information.

Lonely Planet's eKno is an all-in-one communication service developed especially for travelers, with low-cost international calls, free email and voicemail so that you can keep in touch while on the road. Check it out on **www.ekno.lonelyplanet.com**.

FOOD & RESTAURANT GUIDES

Lonely Planet's **Out to Eat** guides recommend the brightest and best places to eat and drink in the top international cities. These gourmet companions are arranged by neighborhood, packed with dependable maps, garnished with scene-setting photos and served with quirky features.

For people who live to eat, drink and travel, **World Food** guides are full of lavish photos good enough to eat. They come packed with details on regional cuisine, guides to local markets and produce, sumptuous recipes, useful phrases for shopping and dining, and a comprehensive culinary dictionary.

Index

Bold indicates maps.

Bold indicates maps.

Bold indicates maps.

Bold indicates maps.

Boxed Text

MAP LEGEND

BOUNDARIES

·–·–·–·–	International
············	Province

HYDROGRAPHY

	Water
	Coastline
	Beach
	River, Waterfall
	Swamp, Spring

○	NATIONAL CAPITAL
◉	State, Provincial Capital
●	LARGE CITY
●	Medium City
●	Small City
●	Town, Village
○	Point of Interest

■	Place to Stay
▲	Campground
⛟	RV Park
⛺	Refugio (Shelter)

▼	Place to Eat
♒	Bar (Place to Drink)

ROUTES & TRANSPORT

	Freeway
	Toll Freeway
	Primary Road
	Secondary Road
	Tertiary Road
=====	Unpaved Road
	Pedestrian Mall
– – – –	Trail, Track
············	Walking Tour
– – – –	Ferry Route
+++++	Railway, Train Station
—Ⓜ—	Mass Transit Line & Station

MAP SYMBOLS

✚	Airfield
✈	Airport
∴	Archaeological Site, Ruins
⑤	Bank
◇	Baseball Diamond
⌇	Beach
✦	Border Crossing
☻	Bus Depot, Bus or Colectivo Stop
⛪	Cathedral
⌂	Cave
†	Church
⬛	Dive Site
⊖	Embassy, Consulate
⊱⊰	Footbridge
⚓	Fish Hatchery
⚘	Garden
⛽	Gas Station
⊕	Hospital, Clinic
ⓘ	Information
⚊	Lighthouse
☀	Lookout

ROUTE SHIELDS

Ⓜ15	Mexico Highway	🔟	Interstate Freeway
Ⓜ15D	Mexico Toll Highway	54	US Highway
16	State Highway		

AREA FEATURES

	Building
	Cemetery
	Ecological Reserve
┌	Golf Course
	Park
	Plaza

♛	Mine
♟	Monument
▲	Mountain
🏛	Museum
⌂	Observatory
←	One-Way Street
♠	Park
Ⓟ	Parking
)(	Pass
⋔	Picnic Area
★	Police Station
⌷	Pool
✉	Post Office
❖	Shopping Mall
🏛	Stately Home
✡	Synagogue
☏	Telephone
▣	Tomb, Mausoleum
衣	Trailhead
⚶	Winery
🐾	Zoo

Note: Not all symbols displayed above appear in this book.

LONELY PLANET OFFICES

Australia
Locked Bag 1, Footscray, Victoria 3011
☎ 03 8379 8000 fax 03 8379 8111
email talk2us@lonelyplanet.com.au

USA
150 Linden Street, Oakland, California 94607
☎ 510 893 8555, TOLL FREE 800 275 8555
fax 510 893 8572
email info@lonelyplanet.com

UK
10A Spring Place, London NW5 3BH
☎ 020 7428 4800 fax 020 7428 4828
email go@lonelyplanet.co.uk

France
1 rue du Dahomey, 75011 Paris
☎ 01 55 25 33 00 fax 01 55 25 33 01
www.lonelyplanet.fr

World Wide Web: www.lonelyplanet.com *or* AOL keyword: lp
Lonely Planet Images: lpi@lonelyplanet.com.au